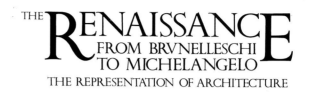

THE RENAISSANCE
FROM BRVNELLESCHI TO MICHELANGELO
THE REPRESENTATION OF ARCHITECTURE

THE RENAISSANCE
FROM BRVNELLESCHI TO MICHELANGELO
THE REPRESENTATION OF ARCHITECTURE

Edited by

Henry A. Millon and Vittorio Magnago Lampugnani

RIZZOLI
NEW YORK

First published in the United States of America in 1994 by
RIZZOLI INTERNATIONAL PUBLICATIONS, INC.
300 Park Avenue South, New York, NY 10010

Copyright © 1994 RCS Libri & Grandi Opere S.p.A.
Via Mecenate 91, Milan, Italy

ISBN 0-8478-1828-4
LC 94-65749

Printed and bound in Italy

Among the exhibitions of the figurative arts, those on architecture are perhaps the most overlooked, for obvious reasons.

Palazzo Grassi has found a way to overcome the impossibility of physically moving the subject matter—the buildings themselves—by assembling an exhibition of the original scale models built by the Renaissance architects to illustrate their projects.

The retrieval of these models was not easy; in many cases their poor physical condition necessitated careful restoration and repair.

Their original significance and splendor reinstated, these artifacts now escort the visitor on a fascinating journey—albeit largely ideal—through space and history.

The sight of Antonio da Sangallo's colossal model for St. Peter's is a thrilling experience that takes one back to the sixteenth century. Despite the distance in time, the visitor is made to feel like a participant in the very act of creation.

The title "Renaissance: from Brunelleschi to Michelangelo" intimates the "ideal" content of the exhibition itinerary, in which the history of ideas, styles and tastes are interwoven with the vicissitudes of a society which perceived these masterpieces as expressions of its very being, its way of thinking.

This townscape of scale models is complemented by abundant illustrative material, paintings, inlaid work, manuscripts, illuminated codices and books, architectural surveys, sculptures, foundation medals, drawings, and antique prints.

An ideal itinerary of such a vast scope cannot but prompt a great deal of reflection and speculation. The intention here is not merely to lead the visitor through an adventure of the spirit. Nor is it merely a reiteration of architecture's role as an expression of the civilization it represents (and what greater expression than our Renaissance). It is also to offer scholars an opportunity for further analysis and study, a forum for the confrontation of ideas and for continued research.

The exhibition presented by Palazzo Grassi is therefore, as always, not merely a gift to its visitors, but a prompt to scholars and historians to carry their personal enquiries a stage further, and thereby raise awareness of our cultural and scientific legacy.

Feliciano Benvenuti

Elsewhere in this catalog other contributors eloquently illustrate the fruits of the profound and often tortuous research carried out into both works and authors, the real legacy of this extraordinary exhibition which, owing to the very complexity of its contents, has prompted the organizers to set up a special seminar for further discussion.

For my part, I wish to limit myself to a somewhat reduced outline of the lead-up or proto-history of this cultural event, with the aim (or ambition) of shedding light on the underlying motives that generated it, and the ideas that have kindled it.

In October 1988, Paolo Viti and I were in the National Gallery of Washington in the company of Carter Brown, Henry Millon, and many other Michelangelo scholars of renown who had gathered for the special exhibition devoted to the Master and his works.

My personal task had been to present the day's study program, organized for the occasion by the museum. The said event seemed to both Viti and myself as undeniably important, but somehow ephemeral. On that almost Ecumenical morning of 9 October 1988, a broader panorama of the architecture of the Renaissance suddenly appeared to be an utmost necessity, an imperative undertaking of our age.

While the atrocities that have since become our daily fare had not yet begun to work their evil, the ensuing upheaval of moral values and ideals inevitably ushered in a period of utter confusion, misdemeanor, silence and apprehension, disregard and omission.

Why architecture as the choice of theme?

And why Renaissance architecture?

The resulting debate sparked questions of an esthetic nature, but also raised many moral issues and convinced us of an obligation to pursue our enquiry and analysis and, above all, to communicate the fruits of this heartfelt research to the overwhelming number of people who are distracted and bogged down in the daily mire of consumer demands and materialism.

It would not, however, have been up to us to decide: the final say in the matter lay ostensibly with the works and authors themselves, with the protagonists of the arts, civilization and culture of the Renaissance.

A discussion followed and we agreed that, just as the history of philosophy could be equated in the Hegelian sense to philosophy itself, so the history of art inevitably becomes a phenomenon only through artworks themselves, with their freight of topical relevance: the present contains the fruit of the past and also the seeds of the future. Indeed, the secret of every artist lies in his ability to fashion a synthesis of space and time, and yet sever their intrinsic links—in short, to be an expression of the historical and environmental context in which he lives, and at the same time foster renewal. Hence the "topicality" and "universality" that characterizes all art, which lives on the verge of contemporary mores, for the express purpose of forging beyond them.

We also recollected our friendship with men of the caliber of Giulio Carlo Argan, whom many of us held in great esteem as an art historian because he was by all accounts a philosopher of the subject. We felt that the speculative approach (which is not merely a mental process but, as the French philosopher Maritain would have said, a quality of the "Integral Man") favors a means of access to a far more critical (albeit problematic, and hence human) reading of our subject matter.

Which of the arts could confirm this approach if not architecture?

And which era could express it if not the Renaissance?

Perhaps it is symbolic that the last major scholarly task undertaken by Argan was his study of Michelangelo the architect.

What is architecture if not the merger of art and science? the Platonic idea of beauty and the Aristotelian dialectic of power-action, and the Vichian gamble of verum et factum converuntur?

And what is the Renaissance if not the assertion of Vitruvius' importance in the universe of humankind, of his ideals, his more enduring values, the tradition of progress, his humanae litterae *and his "new science"?*

Given that the architecture of the Renaissance is an amalgam of the theoresis *and* praxis *of organic being in space and time, in which, as Spinoza observed, form and substance are equated with each other.*

This brings us to the fruit of our lengthy deliberations, which have involved scholars from Italy and abroad, from divers schools of thought, all deeply committed "priests" of culture, a phenomenon that admits neither bias nor faction.

This exhibition begins with Brunelleschi and closes with Michelangelo, while affording a key role to Bramante. The period covered is therefore not particularly long—less than two centuries all told, and yet it constitutes a veritable era.

It all began in Florence. In 1414 Poggio Bracciolini came across the Latin manuscript of Vitruvius' De architectura. The codex of ten books dealt with every possible aspect of ars aedificandi or the art of building (fragments of it had passed through the hands of scholars in previous centuries, including Petrarch, who shared them with Boccaccio). But Bracciolini's discovery sparked an authentic revolution in architecture, and in a certain sense heralded the dawn of Humanism, which in turn generated the Renaissance. The start of the new era saw the emergence of two figures of particular consequence, Filippo Brunelleschi and Leon Battista Alberti.

The itinerary of the exhibition begins with Brunelleschi, the architect who so closely observed antiquity, assimilating the traditions of the classical world. Recording his observations of the Roman monuments with a clinical eye, he essayed to decipher the grammar of their structure, and hence obtain the key to the human creativity at their core. Filippo Brunelleschi was a man of mature, rational, and historical vision whose humanist approach prompted him to supersede abstract spatial values and study the world without denial or contrast; his was a philosophy of transcendence. Alberti dedicated his own architectural thesis De re aedificatoria to Brunelleschi; Vasari hailed him as the harbinger of the new art. In our own day such scholars as De Angelis d'Ossat, Argan, Garin, Gioseffi, Sampaolesi and others have reflected on ideological impact of the new theories of perspective and on that resurgence of rationalism which, despite itself, believed so firmly in the immortal destiny of man.

Brunelleschi, therefore, ushers in our theme, Renaissance architecture. To keep apace with the chosen itinerary of the exhibition, it is worth at this point noting the succession of fundamental theoretical writings that epitomize the reasoning underlying the exhibition's theme: Vitruvius, Alberti, Francesco di Giorgio Martini, Serlio, Vignola, and Palladio. Without wishing to subordinate the philological reading of the produced works themselves and their relative contexts, the theoretical texts are the summae behind our constantly renewed questioning and queries.

The period under study spans from classicism, with its lingering freight of Gothic self-questioning, to the exuberance of Mannerism, a genre that some see as a forerunner of the more recent movements of Expressionism and Subjectivism.

As the "Brunelleschian revolution" drew to a close in Florence, the epicenter shifted to Milan and the Sforza duchy of Lodovico il Moro, dominated by Leonardo and Bramante, and enhanced by the presence of Francesco di Giorgio, Giuliano da Sangallo, and the mathematician Luca Pacioli. At this point the exhibition itinerary brings us to the codices of Leonardo (and I am reminded of my long and warm connections with Salmi and the Commissione Vinciana), and to the fabulous legacy of Bramante's period in Milan: S. Maria delle Grazie, S. Ambrogio, and S. Maria presso S. Satiro. At the close of the century, however, Bramante was to move to Rome, where an utterly different cultural setting awaited him. Notwithstanding its population of 40,000 (against the 300,000 of the Lombard capital), in 1503 Rome boasted the patronage of Julius II, the pope who launched a sweeping program of renewal that affected both city and religious structures. And it was to the Urbino-born architect Bramante that the pontiff entrusted his ambitious urban improvement scheme. Under Bramante's influence came a host of other artists and architects, among whom Baldassarre Peruzzi, Antonio da Sangallo the Younger (together with his uncles Giuliano and Antonio the Elder), and both Andrea and Jacopo Sansovino.

Here in Rome Bramante drafted his project for New St. Peter's, the Cancelleria, the Palazzo dei Tribunali, the Palazzo Caprini, and the Tempietto of S. Pietro in Montorio, the Belvedere and part of the Cortile di S. Damaso; among the improvement schemes he piloted were Via Giulia and Via della Lungara. In 1508 Bramante enrolled his fellow townsman Raphael, perhaps as a means of guaranteeing the continuity and coherence of his program of work.

Raphael indeed took over the tenure of St. Peter's, appointed by the newly elected Medici pope, Leo X, to supervise the work on the holy site, and carry through his mentor's project, which he, however, proceeded to remodel to his own ideas. The impassioned and industrious school of the two Urbino-born masters was shattered by the Sack of Rome in 1527.

Seven years later, having already earned recognition as a sculptor and painter of supreme ability, Michelangelo turned his hand to architecture, remodeled the Campidoglio with the Palazzo dei Conservatori and Palazzo del Senatore, designed a dome for St. Peter's (which was further elaborated *by Giacomo della Porta and Domenico Fontana), fashioned a memorial chapel for the Sforza family in S. Maria Maggiore, built the Porta Pia, and created the church of S. Maria degli Angeli out of the central hall of the Baths of Diocletian.*

Besides the architects already mentioned, Rome also witnessed the work of Vignola, who left posterity an important treatise Regola delli Cinque Ordini d'Architettura, *Bartolomeo Ammannati, Pirro Ligorio, and Giorgio Vasari, who published his famous* Lives of the Artists *in Florence.*

By this time, architecture was practiced as an art in its own right. Bologna opened its doors to the Renaissance with Pagno di Capo Portignani, while Naples, the city of the viceroy proclaimed itself with the works of Luciano Laurana and Mormando. Across the Veneto the genius of Palladio reigned supreme, while Venice enriched itself with the work of Jacopo Sansovino, Michele Sanmicheli, and Bartolomeo Ammannati. In Mantua the genius of Giulio Romano dominated, in Genoa that of Galeazzo Alessi, while Ferrara grew in dimension and stature with the new language of Biagio Rossetti.

At this point our itinerary nears its end: after the death of Michelangelo a certain Andrea di Pietro della Gondola, once a poor scalpellino, *was raised to fame and fortune by his tutor, the philosopher Giangiorgio Trissino, and took the name Palladio. And while his palazzi and villas, churches and theaters impressed the new "Palladian" vocabulary and style on the world's architecture, his* Quattro Libri dell'Architettura, *published in 1570, marked the zenith of organic theoretical writing in the Vitruvian mold, embracing all forms of architecture: the acropolis, the citadel, the city, the countryside, idealizing the art of architecture as the prime mover in the creation of a new Paradise on earth.*

The entire era in question was one of momentous consequences, fraught with contradictions and blessed with moments of sublime achievement, steered by patrons such as Lorenzo de' Medici, il Magnifico—an era dazzled by the navigational feats of Columbus, an era that saw the monk Savonarola burn at the stake in the central square in Florence, an age that doted on the words of Machiavelli, and shrunk from the censure of the Dutch humanist Erasmus, from the wave of Reformation initiated by Luther's 95 theses and the austere doctrines of Calvin, an era which reeled under the ignominious Sack of Rome, and sought to retrieve the doctrine of faith with the Council of Trent (during which the question of architecture was dealt with in the Instrutiones fabricae et suppellectis ecclesiasticae) *and the Catholic Reformation, an era which witnessed many an enlightened and unbiased ruler, many a pontiff concerned with art and architecture, but which also suffered untold nepotism and brutality. The Spanish churchman and founder of the Jesuits, Ignatius of Loyola, who ushered in an authentic* renovatio *of architecture, even advocating a grandiose, emphatic style, albeit "for the greater glory of God."*

The history of the entire period discussed here is duly inscribed in stone, in its architecture. It was a period in which, as Vitruvius would have it, architecture was put at the service of humankind.

But the forward momentum of the Renaissance spirit takes us straight to the triumphs of the Baroque, and we take our leave of the exhibition's itinerarium mentis et cordis *with a final forward glimpse of the* città ideale, *the ideal city—an image, or simply a metaphor, which proposes to today's "medieval" man, heir to the coming millennium, the utopian splendors and harmony of what could be, pointing the way to a culture of hope, a path of deliverance, of integral humanism, a much yearned-for and long-awaited, second Renaissance.*

First and foremost, while wishing the visitor a stimulating and thought-provoking experience at the present exhibition, I take the opportunity to express my thanks to all those who have made this experience possible, particularly to Palazzo Grassi for their customary diligence in curating such a significant expression of the country's cultural heritage.

An exhibition becomes a cultural triumph when it is the culmination of long research and the devoted retrieval of the works on exhibit.

The seminar, catalog, and the scrupulous restoration carried out on a great many architectural models present at the exhibition (of which the "colossus" of Sangallo's project for St. Peter's is a superb example), together with the vast selection of drawings, paintings and other documents, all amply testify to the efforts and devotion of the researchers, and make the present exhibition an event to remember, a true cultural happening.

Francesco Sisinni
Direttore generale
del Ministero per i Beni Culturali e Ambientali

Acknowledgments

Cardinal Angelo Sodano
Cardinal Virgilio Noè
Archbishop Giovanni Battista Re
Archbishop Francesco Marchisano

Minister Alberto Ronchey
Francesco Sisinni
Francesco Sicilia
Salvatore Mistruzzi

Cristina Acidini Luchinat
Giancarlo Ambrosetti
Germana Aprato
Ermanno Arslan
Alessandro Bagnoli
Nino Baldeschi
Dante Benazzi
Maria Grazia Benini
Monica Bietti
Henning Bock
Evelina Borea
Leonard Boyle
Senio Bruschelli
Roberto Buonanno
Mariagiulia Burresi
Luigi Cacciabue
Omar Calabrese
Enzo Carli
Lanfredo Castelletti
Adolfo Cattin
Adele Chatfield-Taylor
Alessandra Chiappini
Pierre Cockshaw
Giorgio Comez
Michele Cordaro
Marzio Dall'Acqua
Antonio De Bonis
Philippe de Montebello
Anne d'Harnoncourt
Wolf-Dieter Dube
Alexander Dueckers
David Ebitz
Gianmaria Erbesato
Bernd Evers
Giovanna Gaeta Bertelà
Paolo Galluzzi
Vittoria Garibaldi
Jean Claude Garreta
Giovanna Giacobello Bernard
Olle Granath
Anna Maria Guiducci
Carla Guiducci Bonanni
Alan Irvine
Simon Jervis

Bernd Kluge
Olgierd Kokocinski
James Lees-Milne
Pierluigi Leone de Castris
Anna Lenzuni
Emanuel Leroy Ladurie
Bernard Leskien
Jill Lever
Francis R. Maddison
Fabrizio Mancinelli
Rosalia Manno Tolu
Michael Mezzatesta
Ernesto Milano
Rosetta Mosco
Fausta Navarro
Giovanna Nepi Sciré
Konrad Oberhuber
Beatrice Paolozzi Strozzi Pellegrini
Hans Albert Peters
Pietro Petraroia
Cristina Piacenti
Carlo Pietrangeli
Carlo Pirovano
Earl A. Powell III
Paul Quarrie
Pina Ragionieri
Isabella Ricci Massabò
Jane Roberts
Cosimo Rucellai
Claudio Salsi
Bruno Santi
Uwe Schneede
Magnolia Scudieri
Ettore Spalletti
Urano Tafani
Manfredo Tafuri
Oswald Mathias Ungers
Françoise Viatte
Donata Vicini
Christopher White
Uwe Wieczorek
Carla Zarilli
Marino Zorzi

Contents

Exhibitions of architecture are always something of a challenge. The simple, fundamental reason for this is that the subject matter itself is never actually present. While an exhibition of paintings, sculptures, drawings or photographs generally entails the display of the original items themselves, this is not the case with an architectural exhibition. The architecture itself can only be represented via surrogates—by sketches, drawings, models, paintings, and photographs. Although these surrogates are in every respect completely authentic, the buildings to which they refer remain in their respective locations and consequently, for the visitor to the exhibition, they are absent.

Despite these limitations, as a product of human ingegno *architecture seems destined* a priori *for display: its cogent visual impact, its three-dimensionality (with the incumbent drawbacks for reproduction in book form), its invariable presence in our daily lives, and not least its inherent complexity, which therefore requires explanation. The explanatory material (which we have rather irreverently dismissed as "surrogates") is fascinating in its own right, and very often equally beautiful. Consequently, the basic obstacle [posed by the physical immovability of the exhibition's original subject—the buildings—] merely kindles our sense of the adventure. An architectural exhibition is indeed an adventure, as much for those who invent, assemble and realize it, as for the people who come to enjoy it. If the curators succeed in their intentions, a visit to such an exhibition becomes a kind of imaginary journey through territories foreign or familiar, along a route lined with monuments unknown or celebrated, whose individual and absorbing stories are duly narrated. The visitor discovers that architecture is not just a question of projects, construction sites and finished buildings, but is primarily concerned with ideas—visions and dreams, quotations and plagiarism, instances of self-questioning and of confidence, contradiction and emotion.*

There are three reasons for our conceiving and organizing the exhibition and collating the extensive documentary material contained in the catalog. First, the desire to initiate a vast, non-specialist public in the complexities and contradictions of Renaissance architecture, a phenomenon of uncertain origin with myriad paths of development and a somewhat elusive conclusion. Second, the desire to provide a means for delving deep into the discipline of architecture and revealing the design process—from its beginnings in the quick sketch, the technical drawing and the explanatory or illustrative model, to the building site itself and the glory of the finished achievement. Third, we were spurred to turn a spotlight on the architecture of the Quattrocento which, despite the disciplinary clarity of which it is informed, was often influenced and sometimes even instrumentalized by theoretical and philosophical argument, constrained by political and economic strategy, conditioned by technical and scientific innovations, by esthetic and cultural implications.

These three objectives fell on remarkably fertile ground. We found an astonishing quantity of largely unknown, original material available, including manuscripts, sketches, drawings, paintings, medals, inlaid panels, work tools and—the most spectacular of all—an extraordinary array of wooden models dating more or less to the time of the buildings (or unrealized projects) which they represent. Thanks to their historical significance, their marked illustrative nature and evocative potential, these wooden models were chosen as the main poles of attraction for an exhibition designed to illuminate the discoveries rather than the course of its history. The dilemma of this choice is obvious, and continues to cause misgivings [for the organizers]. On the one hand, there is the vast history of the Renaissance, overflowing with events, deeds and coups de théâtre, *and torn by unfathomable inner conflicts. On the other hand, there is the material tiself, which tells another, different story, cruelly limited and conditioned by chance survival or destruction. The conviction that setting up an exhibition is quite different from writing a book, and that the presentation of original drawings, paintings and objects is an imperative, led us to decide on the second course. This choice is to some extent arbitrary, however—more arbitrary than the choice normally faced by the historian when he extrapolates his personalized version of history from the facts of the past.*

We are aware of this and we are also a little overawed. Here and there we have inserted quotes from Renaissance historians, theoreticians and architects to fill the more evident gaps (while leaving unfilled more than we would care to admit). This, however, is the price one has to pay in the creation of an exhibition in the original and full sense of the term.

The collaboration of the lenders was both valuable and fundamental. Institutions as well as private owners of the artifacts we hoped to exhibit duly entrusted their treasures to us, setting aside jealousies and overcoming the red tape. These lenders were won over perhaps by the sheer breadth of scope of our project and the capabilities of the organizing body.

Thanks to the generosity of the Gruppo Fiat and Palazzo Grassi we were able to sponsor some important restoration campaigns. The most complicated and spectacular operation, lasting three years, was the complete restoration of the colossal model of Antonio da Sangallo the Younger's design for New St. Peter's. The restoration campaigns made it possible to move some works which would otherwise have been in a too precarious state; we were also able to save others from certain ruin.

The seriousness and soundness of the project was decisive in winning the support of the world's most renowned historians of Italian Renaissance architecture. We appealed to all those who possess a profound knowledge of the many branches of Renaissance history, and others who have a special acquaintance with a particular work or group of works. Nearly all the scholars we approached accepted the invitation to contribute, and their collaboration has been most generous. The essays and other contributions to the catalog are evidence of this collaboration, and are the product of intense and important discussions.

Our warmest thanks go to all those who helped us in this undertaking. Their names appear in the colophon, index, and list of acknowledgments. Without this large and illustrious team the exhibition and catalog would not have been possible. If the merit is collective, the errors and shortcomings are only ours.

V.M.L.
H.A.M.
Milan and Washington, D.C., February 1994

Part One

The Renaissance
from Brunelleschi to Michelangelo

Francesco Salviati (attrib.)
Portrait of Giovanni and
Paolo Rucellai
Private collection
Cat. no. 39

Models in Renaissance Architecture

Anonymous
Casket in Imitation of
Alberti's Holy
Sepulcher for the Cappella
Rucellai, S. Pancrazio
*Monselice, Ca' Marcello,
Regione Veneto*
Cat. no. 44

[1] Models that might well have been included in this exhibition comprise those for the cathedral of Milan (Museo della Fabbrica del Duomo), for the *ballatoio* of the cathedral of Florence (four models that have yet to be restored after being damaged in the flood in 1966), for the drum and dome of the cathedral at Orvieto (Museo dell'Opera del Duomo, Orvieto), for the drum and dome of S. Maria degli Angeli, Assisi (Museo del Convento di S. Maria degli Angeli), for the Logge Vasariane at Arezzo (Casa Vasari, Arezzo), for the drum and dome and sanctuary extension of the Santuario di Caravaggio (Santuario di Caravaggio), the town model of Reggio Emilia (Musei Civici Gallerie d'Arte, Reggio Emilia), and the models of fortifications and towns such as Orzinuovi (Istituto Storico e di Cultura dell'Arma del Genio, Rome, inv. no. 2002), Peschiera (Istituto Storico e di Cultura dell'Arma del Genio, Rome, inv. no. 1995), and Ostende (Museo di S. Marco, Florence, inv. no. 713).
[2] For studies of the architectural model in the Renaissance, see Goldthwaite 1980: 372-375; Pacciani 1987; Puppi 1987b; Scolari 1988; Contardi 1991.
[3] See Berti 1990: 70-71.
[4] See for example Schattner 1990, pls. 4, 21, 24-26.
[5] For examples of Egyptian house models, see *Egypt's Golden Age...* 1982: 34-35. For examples of Etruscan house models and cinerary urns in the form of a house, see Camporeale 1992: 73, and the temple shown in Briguet 1986, IV-48.
[6] The plan of the tomb of Rameses IV and the drawing of the shrine from Ghorâb are both illustrated in Clarke and Engelbach 1990, figs. 48-49.
[7] Bücher, on the other hand, sees reliquiaries, censers, coffrets, and shrines from the eleventh century onward as experimental fields for architects (Bücher 1974: 73).

Hundreds, if not thousands, of models for buildings and portions of buildings constructed in the Renaissance in Italy have been lost. Only a small fraction have been preserved, most of these for ecclesiastical structures. The thirty-odd models in this exhibition are virtually all the known extant models from the fifteenth and sixteenth centuries.[1] The recent study of many of these models by historians of architecture has underscored their historical importance and the artistic value of this heritage dating from the Renaissance.[2]

This exhibition, which draws attention to architectural models and their use in the Renaissance, may serve as a stimulus to further the study of models and related materials as well as the craftsmanship that the models themselves exhibit.

While the architects of the Renaissance did not invent the use of architectural models, they appear to have built models more consistently than any of their predecessors. A scholar has recently suggested that in the Renaissance in Italy a model was customary in the consideration of a design by both architect and client (Goldthwaite 1980: 373-375). Documents confirm this assessment.

Excavations of ancient Roman sites have revealed small models of houses and temples, some perhaps prepared as votive offerings.[3] House models also existed in ancient Greece.[4] Still others have been found in tombs as dispersed as Egypt (New Kingdom) and Etruria.[5] Such models from the ancient Mediterranean do not appear to have been intended to be used for realizing full-scale structures but rather as a representation of architecture.

Plan drawings of architecture are also known from antiquity (MacDonald 1977: 31-32). They perhaps parallel the use of models. From the ancient Near East, a sculpture of Gudea with a tablet in his lap, now in the Louvre, shows a plan of a temple enclosure or city wall (Tallon 1992, figs. 12, 12a). In the Egyptian Museum in Turin, a drawn plan shows the tomb of Rameses IV.

Another Egyptian drawing on papyrus, from Ghorâb, now at University College in London, depicts a shrine in both front and side elevation on a modular grid.[6] This drawing may be one of the earliest preserved for the making of a structure rather than the representation of an existing or imagined shrine.

During the Middle Ages, documents indicate the frequent use of models in Italy, but there is less evidence for the remainder of Europe (Kostof 1977: 74). Often mentioned in the literature is a document first published by Schlosser for a model in wax, preparatory to the construction of the Abbey of St. Germain d'Auxerre (Schlosser 1891: 36). The paucity of documentation for the use of models in the Middle Ages north of the Alps has led Bischoff to conclude that models for structures were little used before the sixteenth century (Bischoff 1989: 288).[7] The extant papier-maché model of the church of St. Maclou in Rouen dates most likely to the sixteenth century (Bischoff 1989: 286-287), when construction of the church was nearly completed[8], and the gilded city model of Soissons is dated 1560.[9]

North of the Alps there are, however, over a hundred plans, elevations, perspective elevations, and sections, many to scale, drawn primarily on parchment. A number of the elevations of facades and towers are two to four meters high, larger than any extant medieval drawings in Italy (Recht, ed. 1989: 381-420).

Ample documentation exists for the use of models in the fourteenth century for cathedrals in Milan, Florence, and Bologna, as well as for more modest structures.[10] A number of drawings from Italian *cantieri* also survive. Some of them are included in the introductory section of the exhibition.

Filippo Brunelleschi (1377-1446), as his predecessors at the cathedral of Florence, relied on models. In his life of Brunelleschi, written in the late 1480s, Antonio Manetti mentions the existence of a fourteenth-century model for the dome (probably the brick model of 1367 embodying the design of the master masons and painters, as cited by Saalman 1964: 487-491, and Saalman, ed. 1970: 135), when Brunelleschi and others made models of projects for completion of the drum and dome in 1419. Brunelleschi won the commission for construction of a dome without centering by building what must have been a large model in brick (and wood) of the dome "sanza alchuna armadura" (Guasti 1857, doc. 18).

Front prospect and flank of a temple drawn on papyrus Ghorâb, 18th dynasty London, University College

Ancient project for the tomb of Rameses IV Turin, Museo Egizio

[8] The date of the model of St. Maclou has been much discussed. See Lafond 1974: 65-75 and Bischoff 1989: 287 and notes 6-7. The model is reproduced in Bischoff 1989: 286.

[9] The sixteenth-century model of the town of Soissons (Trésor de la cathédrale SS. Gervais et Protais) includes within the town walls an assembly of the religious structures of the town. In according prominence to the major monuments, the model continues a tradition for the representation of cities through models in portable form, known from the literature of ancient Rome. Models that represented captured cities were carried in Roman triumphal processions. A fifteenth-century representation of the use of models for this purpose may be seen, for example, in the series of paintings (now in the Royal Collections at Hampton Court) of an ancient Roman triumphal procession painted by Andrea Mantegna. An extant model of Reggio Emilia from the sixteenth century (Musei Civici e Gallerie d'Arte, Reggio Emilia) also emphasizes the major public monuments of the town. For the model of Soissons, see *Les trèsors des eglises de France* 1965, no. 98. For the model of Reggio Emilia, see Baricchi et al. 1978, pl. xii. 17.

[10] For Milan, see *Annali* 1877-1880, I: 200; for Florence, see Pietramellara 1984: 132-139; Saalman 1980: 58-69; for a chapel of S. Maria delle Grazie by Jacopo di Caroccio degli Alberti at a bridgehead in Florence, see Paatz and Paatz 1952: 3-5 (a wooden model of the chapel was made at a scale of 1:8); for Bologna, see Lorenzoni 1983: 53-56 (a model of 1390 was built in brick at a scale of 1:12).

[11] Vasari's fresco of 1565 in the Palazzo Vecchio in Florence shows Brunelleschi presenting a model for S. Lorenzo to Cosimo de' Medici. Although Manetti does not mention a model for S. Lorenzo, Vasari cites it specifically and shows it in his painting, even though there is no supporting evidence that a model was shown to Cosimo de' Medici for approval. On the other hand, Vasari reports that Cosimo rejected Brunelleschi's design for the Palazzo Medici, suggesting that a model was indeed presented for approval.

[12] Though models of fortifications are known from documents throughout the later fifteenth and sixteenth centuries, those preserved in Italy all date from the late sixteenth century and early seventeenth century. See for example the model of the fortifications at Ostende made for Giovanni de' Medici (1597-1621), and the models of Orzinuovi and Peschiera reproduced in Fara 1989, pls. xx and xxi.

During construction he certainly employed drawings and also made models of details. As reported by Manetti (Saalman, ed. 1970: 93; Tanturli and De Robertis 1976: 97), Brunelleschi's carved details for the workmen were made of clay, wax, wood, and even large winter turnips. In 1436 Brunelleschi, Lorenzo Ghiberti (1378?-1455) and several others submitted models for the lantern of the cupola (Saalman, ed. 1970: 149, no. 153). Brunelleschi's design was chosen, but he died before the lantern was completed.

Documents confirm a wooden model for S. Spirito by Brunelleschi, and he may also have prepared models for S. Maria degli Angeli, the Cappella Pazzi at S. Croce (Vasari, ed. Milanesi 1878-85, II: 366), S. Lorenzo, and the Medici Palace (a design rejected by Cosimo de' Medici, see Vasari, ed. Milanesi 1878-85, II: 371).[11]

Models of fortifications became common in the sixteenth century[12], but according to Manetti (Saalman, ed. 1970: 119; Tanturli and De Robertis 1976: 119; Vasari, ed. Milanesi 1878-85, II: 368), Brunelleschi had earlier been called upon for models in clay and wood of the fortresses at Vicopisano, Pisa, and Pesaro.

With the exception of the model for the lantern of the dome of the cathedral of Florence

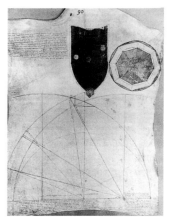

Filippo Brunelleschi
Modern Model of the Lantern of Florence Cathedral
Florence, Museo dell'Opera di S. Maria del Fiore
Cat. no. 262

Giovanni di Gherardo Gherardi
Drawing with Critical Observations on the Dome of S. Maria del Fiore
Florence, Archivio di Stato
Cat. no. 263

Federico Zuccari
Self-Portrait with Vincenzo Borghini
Rome, Biblioteca Hertziana

that was detailed with abundant ornamentation (Saalman, ed. 1970: 116; Tanturli and De Robertis 1976: 117) (cat. no. 262), Brunelleschi's models were intentionally incomplete, showing without ornament only the relationships of members of the principal walls. Perhaps to insure that Brunelleschi retained control, Manetti reports, "It seemed that [he] was concerned that whoever would make the model should not discover his every secret, expecting to make all things precisely and well as they followed bit by bit in the actual building" (Saalman, ed. 1970: 116; Tanturli and De Robertis 1976: 117).

Leon Battista Alberti (1404–72) too argues for models that exclude decoration, that show plainly and simply the parts to be considered, that focus attention on certain calculated standards of architecture rather than on the ingenuity of the fabricator of the model (Orlandi and Portoghesi, eds. 1966, I: 98)[13]. In Book II of *De re aedificatoria*, Alberti also recommends the use of models for practical purposes such as the "relationship between the site and the surrounding district ... the parts of a building ... and furthermore, a model will provide a surer indication of the likely costs ... by allowing one to calculate the width and height of individual elements, their thickness, number, extent, form, appearance, and quality" (Orlandi and Portoghesi, eds. 1966, I: 96–98).

But for Alberti models have another important function. An idea, or *disegno*, in architecture could only be realized through a model. The idea, as formed in the mind, was imperfect and could only be given its consequent form through examination, exercise of judgment, and modification of the idea through drawings. Further, the drawings were to be studied, assessed, and improved through models, thereby ultimately approaching an embodiment of the idea. In Book IX, in a section which proposes that the architect possess

[13] The simple bare surfaces of the drum and dome model of the cathedral of Florence and those of the model of S. Giuseppe in Florence (though this model may merely be unfinished), provide, perhaps, the best indication of what Brunelleschi and Alberti meant by advocating models that showed only the principal walls, without indications of the finished decoration.

Filippo Brunelleschi
Wooden Model of the Dome
and Apse Sections of Florence
Cathedral
*Florence, Museo dell'Opera
di S. Maria del Fiore*
Cat. no. 261

knowledge of painting and mathematics, Alberti says, "Per quanto mi riguarda, debbo dire che molto frequentemente mi è venuto fatto di concepire delle opere in forme che a tutta prima mi parevano lodevolissime, mentre invece, una volta disegnate, rivelavano errori, e gravissimi, proprio in quella parte che più mi era piaciuta; tornando poi di nuovo con la meditazione su quanto avevo disegnato, e misurandone le proporzioni, riconoscevo e deploravo la mia incuria; infine avendo fabbricato i modelli, spesso, esaminandone partitamente gli elementi, mi accorgevo di essermi sbagliato anche sul numero" (Orlandi and Portoghesi, eds. 1966, II: 860–862). The model, then, for Alberti, was not a vehicle to

present an idea to a client, but a means to study and realize an idea. For Brunelleschi and later for Michelangelo (1475-1564), on the contrary, the model was apparently the representation of an idea already formed in the mind to serve as a guide for workmen in construction. In Alberti's treatise, the model was necessary to study the design, to improve its proportions, to arrive at the final project, but as we have seen, the model was then able to serve a useful and practical purpose (as discussed in Book II) in enabling the architect to determine quantities of the various materials required for construction. Alberti apparently neither considered the model as a vehicle to obtain approval by a patron nor as a guide for the builder to follow in construction. The model was seen as part of the design process, related to developmental drawings, rather than integral to the construction of the edifice. Given Alberti's use of models to study a design, when he says, "Il disegno sarà un tracciato preciso e uniforme, concepito nella mente, eseguito per mezzo di linee ed angoli" (Orlandi and Portoghesi, eds. 1966, I: 20), by implication he includes the model as one of the means to realize the intellectual conception or idea.

In contrast to the stages in a design process explicitly discussed by Alberti, Vasari, in his preface to the *Vite*, writes of *disegno* as "producendo dall'intelleto," as a "certo concetto ... che si forma nella mente," which is "una apparente espressione e dichiarazione del concetto che si dia nell'animo, e di quello che altri si è nella mente immaginato e fabbricato nell'idea." It may be that both a narrow reading of Alberti's definition of *disegno*, which overlooked his understanding of the development of a design, and a similarly limited interpretation of Vasari's discussion of design or drawing, have contributed to the greater attention paid to architectural drawings than to architectural models.

Bernardo Buontalenti
Model of the Facade
of Florence Cathedral
Florence, Museo dell'Opera
di S. Maria del Fiore
Cat. no. 246

Bernardo Buontalenti
Model of the Facade of
Florence Cathedral, detail
*Florence, Museo dell'Opera
di S. Maria del Fiore*
Cat. no. 246

Giovanni Antonio Dosio
Model for the Facade of
Florence Cathedral
*Florence, Museo dell'Opera
di S. Maria del Fiore*
Cat. no. 248

*Giovanni de' Medici
with Alessandro Pieroni
Model for the Facade of
Florence Cathedral
Florence, Museo dell'Opera
di S. Maria del Fiore
Cat. no. 250*

29

Giambologna (Giovanni Bologna)
Model for the Facade
of Florence Cathedral
*Florence, Museo dell'Opera
di S. Maria del Fiore*
Cat. no. 254

FERDINANDVS M.   M.DVX.ETR.V

31

*Anonymous
(formerly attributed to
Michelangelo)
Model of the Drum
and Ballatoio of Florence
Cathedral
Florence, Museo dell'Opera
di S. Maria del Fiore
Cat. no. 271*

Antonio Averlino, called il Filarete (ca. 1400–after 1465), in his treatise written as a dialogue in 1460–65, advocates making a model in wood to show to the patron, presumably for approval: (Grassi, ed. 1972, I: 40).

He is explicit about the need to make drawings (and models) to scale, using square modules of varying size. In Book VII, his description of drawing a foundation suggests that a wooden model at the same scale should be constructed on top of the drawing, confirming a direct relationship between scale drawings and scale models (Grassi, ed. 1972, I: 207, and LXVII).

Francesco di Giorgio Martini (1439–1501), also author of a treatise on architecture, began his career in Siena as a sculptor and painter. His treatise (Maltese, ed. 1967) exists in a number of versions (and copies), corrected, modified, and expanded over his lifetime, but always with copious illustrations. These stand in contrast to Alberti's treatise, which was unillustrated, and Filarete's, which had but few. Though Francesco di Giorgio is known to have had models made for buildings (for example S. Maria del Calcinaio in 1485 [Fiore and Tafuri 1993: 251]), his treatise, though it discusses drawings, does not mention models.

Documents that record payments to architects, *falegnami*, *tornitori*, and *intagliatori* for wood models are commonly found from the late 1400s and early 1500s in both north and central Italy. Payments to *falegnami* and *intagliatori* are recorded, for example, for wooden models of designs for the *tiburio*, or crossing tower, of the cathedral of Milan, following designs by Francesco di Giorgio, Bramante (1444–1514), Leonardo (1452–1519), and others (*Annali* 1877–85, III: 38, and Beltrami 1903: 73–76). Similar documents attest to models constructed for the cathedrals of Pavia (Bruschi 1969a: 765–767) (cat. no. 54) and Bologna (Fanti 1970: 34–35) (cat. nos. 151–152), for S. Maria delle Carceri in Prato by Giuliano da Sangallo (ca. 1443–1516) (Morselli and Corti 1982, Doc. 6: 87–89), for the

Antonio Manetti Ciaccheri
(attrib.)
Model of the Drum
and Ballatoio of Florence
Cathedral
Florence, Museo dell'Opera
di S. Maria del Fiore
Cat. no. 268

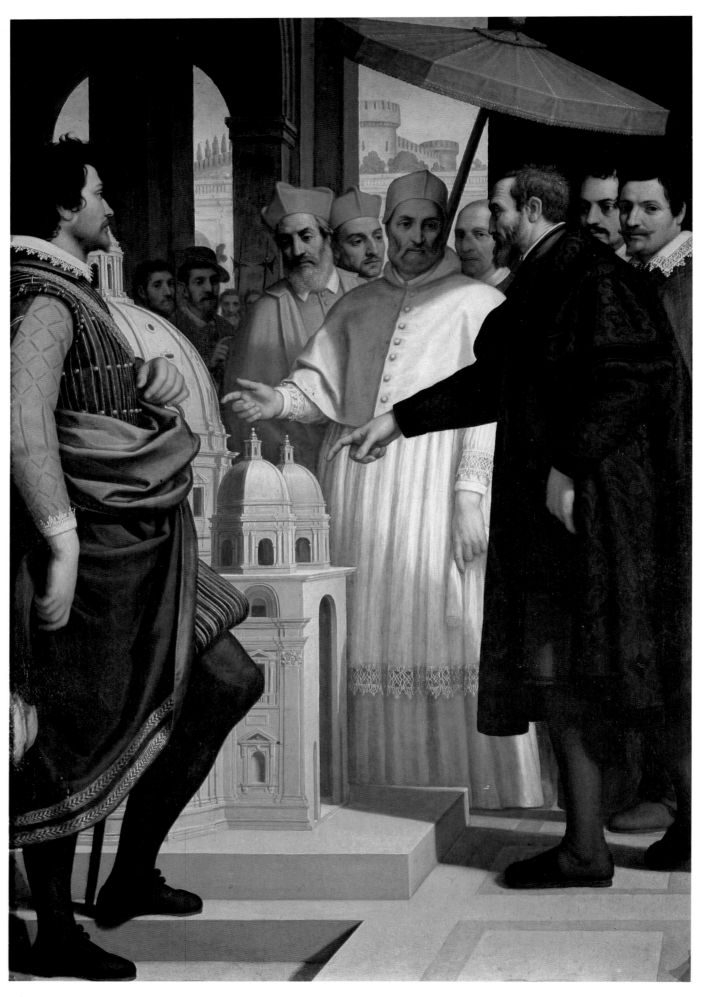

34

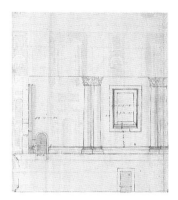

Anonymous
Elevation of an Apse
at St. Peter's
Florence, Uffizi, Gabinetto
Disegni e Stampe, Uff. 95Av.
Cat. no. 374

Antonio da Sangallo
the Younger
Wooden Model of the Project
for St. Peter's
facade
Vatican, Fabbrica di S. Pietro
Cat. no. 346

opposite
Domenico Cresti da Passignano
Michelangelo Presenting his
Model to Pope Paul IV
Florence, Casa Buonarroti
Cat. no. 399

on the following pages
Antonio da Sangallo the
Younger
Wooden Model of the Project
for St. Peter's
apse
Vatican, Fabbrica di S. Pietro
Cat. no. 346

Palazzo Strozzi in Florence (Pampaloni 1982: 53–85) (cat. nos. 143–145), made by Giuliano da Sangallo (Goldthwaite 1980: 378–379), for the facade of S. Lorenzo in Florence (Millon 1988: 69–73) (cat. no. 235), S. Maria di Loreto and the Santa Casa, both by Bramante (Bruschi 1969a: 964–965), S. Maria della Consolazione in Todi (Bruschi 1991: 134) (cat. no. 142) and for S. Biagio in Montepulciano by Antonio da Sangallo the Elder (ca. 1453–1534) (Cozzi 1992: 73).

St. Peter's in Rome alone provides a hundred-year history of models by Bramante,[14] Raphael (1483–1520),[15] Peruzzi (1481–1536),[16] Antonio da Sangallo the Younger (1484–1546),[17] Michelangelo,[18] Giacomo della Porta (1532/33?–1602),[19] and Maderno (ca. 1556–1629).[20] Of all these models, only one by Sangallo (cat. no. 346) and two by Michelangelo survive, and one of Michelangelo's contains alterations by della Porta (cat. no. 396). The wooden model of Sangallo's project for St. Peter's, built by Antonio Labacco, was preserved at St. Peter's and is today the largest extant model of the Renaissance in Italy. It was constructed over a seven-year period, from 1539 to 1546, to record Sangallo's final design for the basilica and to be used as a guide for workmen. Construction of the basilica, according to the design of the model, continued throughout the period.

Non yet complete at the death of Sangallo, the model today bears traces of a hurried completion; documents indicate it was built partially by candlelight in the early morning hours (K. Frey 1913: 29, no. 317.41).

The model was large and costly. Payments for it, transcribed from documents in the Archivio della Reverenda Fabbrica di San Pietro (hereafter AFP) have been published in: K. Frey (1909: 167–170, nos. 1–34 and, in a modified form, in K. Frey 1913: 21–29). Vasari said that the carpentry and wood alone for the model amounted to 4184 *scudi* (Vasari, ed. Milanesi 1878–85, V: 18, 467; K. Frey 1913: 21–29, nos. 317.1–39; note on 23 records expenditures for a total of between 5500 and 6000 *scudi*).

The model, large enough to walk into, was built to show both the exterior and interior in some detail. The barrel vaults of the transepts and nave, for example, include the coffering of the vault, drawn in ink on sheets of paper attached to the curved wood surface of the vault. The interior of the model was painted yellow for architectural memebering and gray for the remainder, presumably to simulate travertine and stucco sheathing. Though now of exposed wood, the exterior originally was also painted in two colors although the exterior surfaces of the basilica under construction were most likely all to be travertine.[21] Traces of the exterior paint remain in places difficult to reach. Sculptured reliefs in paste were inserted in the metopes of the Doric order. A few are still extant on the model. Figures, in terracotta, were situated at strategic locations on the model (K. Frey 1913: 28–29, no. 317.18).

The Sangallo model was probably originally intended to rest on a base similar to its present one (113 cm high). The base, repainted if not replaced in the eighteenth century, contains an inscription dated 1704, commemorating the restoration of the model during the reign of Pope Clement XI. A base of this height allowed access to the interior of the model through the hinged halves of the apse wall of the north transept, most likely part of the original project for the model.

Built at a scale of 1:30 (or 2 *minuti* to 1 *palmo*, or 7.44 mm to 223 mm) the width of the transept on the interior of the model is about 80 centimeters, as wide as, or wider than, the corridor on a train. The height of the barrel vault above the level of the pavement (omitted in the model), or from the base of the pilasters of the main arches, is about 155 centimeters. The model maker, perhaps aware that a viewer would enter the model with an eye level considerably above that of a scale figure at pavement level, built the barrel vault of the transept, the nave and the choir without the stilting, or the raising of the base of the vaults as they already existed in the basilica. (The stilting of the vaults follows a traditional and recommended practice: it compensates for the fact that a portion of the vault is hidden from a viewer standing at pavement level by the projecting cornice of the main entablature.)[22]

[14] Though there are no recorded payments for a model of St. Peter's by Bramante, Serlio (1600, Book III, 64v., "...il modello rimase imperfetto in alcune parti...") and O. Panvinio ("*De rebus antiquis... Basilicae Sancti Petri...*" [cited in Murray 1967: 8] "*... exemplari quoque ligneo imperfecto relicto ...*") specifically mention incomplete models. According to Murray, Panvinio probably wrote the passage during the pontificate of Pope Pius V (1566-72).

[15] In addition to recorded payments to both Raphael and Fra Giocondo for separate models of St. Peter's (AFP, Armadi, I, 93v., and K. Frey 1911: 66, no. 103), in an undated letter to Baldassarre Castiglione (Bottari 1754, I: 116), Raphael mentions the model he made ("...e tanto più, quanto il modello, che io ne ho fatto, piace a Sua Santità ...").

[16] Two payments for a model by Peruzzi are recorded on 27.IV.1520 (15 ducats, AFP, Armadi, II, 114. [Francia 1977: 37]) and on 15.VI.1521 (30 ducats, AFP, Armadi, II: 110 [K. Frey 1911: 68, no. 117 and Francia 1977: 37]).

[17] Payments for a model by Sangallo in 1521 are recorded in AFP, Armadi, II: 106, 107r., and 108 (K. Frey 1911: 67-68, nos. 110, 112, 113). Another, more complete and extant, model by Antonio da Sangallo was constructed from 1539-46 (K. Frey 1913: 21-33). See below.

[18] There were four major models for St.

Giovanni Antonio Dosio
View of the Crossing of
St. Peter's from the South Arm
Florence, Uffizi, Gabinetto
Disegni e Stampe, Uff. 91A
Cat. no. 401

Peter's by Michelangelo. Model I, a small model for the entire basilica, was cited by Vasari (Milanesi, ed. 1878-85, VII: 219) but questioned by Saalman (1975: 381) who later modified his view when the Arberino correspondence confirmed its existence (Bardeschi Ciulich 1977: 235-275; Saalman 1978: 483). Model II, for a major portion of the basilica, was constructed in wood from 3 December 1546 to 2 September 1547 (AFP, I: 50, 316 [Millon and Smyth 1976: 202-205 and Saalman 1975: 381-386]). Model III is known through a payment to an individual for having made and baked a clay model for the main dome (K. Frey 1916: 81, no. 668.1). Model IV, built of wood in 1558-61, was constructed at a scale of 1:15 and, with modifications by della Porta, is still extant (AFP I, Mazzi 27-29; K. Frey 1909: 171-180; Millon and Smyth 1988a: 119-128).

[19] Though no documents have yet been found that record alterations made by della Porta to Michelangelo's model of the drum and dome, the extant evidence indicates the modifications were made shortly before completion of the drum and construction of the dome in 1588-90 (Millon and Smyth 1988a: 98-100, 123-128; Wittkower 1964a: 74-77; Orbaan 1917: 189-207).

[20] For the model of 1607 for the completion of St. Peter's by Carlo Maderno (now lost), see Hibbard 1971: 159, 169-170.

[21] For a recent discussion of the surface coloration of the Sangallo model, see Zänder 1986: 175-186, with an appendix by conservator Nazareno Gabrielli from the Gabinetto di Ricerche Scientifiche dei Musei Vaticani.

opposite
Anonymous
View of the Nave of
St. Peter's
James Lees-Milne Collection
Cat. no. 384

above
Antonio da Sangallo
the Younger
Wooden Model of the Project
for St. Peter's
interior of apse
Vatican, Fabbrica di S. Pietro
Cat. no. 346

on the following pages
Antonio da Sangallo
the Younger
Wooden Model of the Project
for St. Peter's
interior of the dome
Vatican, Fabbrica di S. Pietro
Cat. no. 346

41

*Michelangelo, Giacomo
della Porta, Luigi Vanvitelli*
Model of Half of the Drum
and Dome of St. Peter's
Vatican, Fabbrica di S. Pietro
Cat. no. 396

44

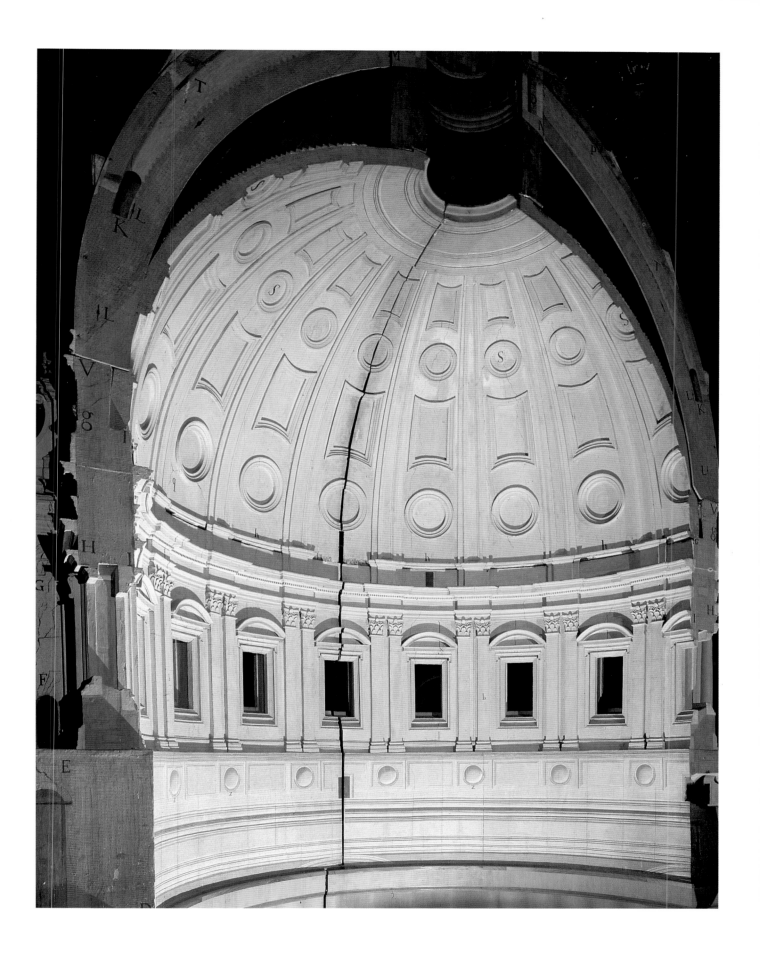

opposite
Michelangelo
Wooden Model for
the Facade of S. Lorenzo
Florence, Casa Buonarroti
Cat. no. 235

Jacopo Chimenti da Empoli
Michelangelo Presenting
Pope Leo X and Cardinal
Giulio de' Medici (the
future Clement VII) his
Models for the Facade of

S. Lorenzo, and the Cappella
Medicea, and his Project
Drawing for the Biblioteca
Laurenziana
Florence, Casa Buonarroti
Cat. no. 234

Michelangelo
Project for a Niche and Pair
of Columns for the First
Story of the Facade of
S. Lorenzo
Florence, Casa Buonarroti
CB 100A
Cat. no. 229

²² For a discussion of the stilting of the
barrel vault of the Sangallo model, see
Millon and Smyth 1976: 162-168.

That either the model maker or Antonio da Sangallo made this subtle but important "adjustment" is, perhaps, confirmed by the way the coffers of one of the vaults are drawn on the surface of the vault. On the building, the coffering consists, in part, of rectangular and square coffers. Some of the square coffers contain an octagon with a central rosette. In a portion of the drawn coffering, the octagons are regular toward the crown of the vault, but become increasingly distorted toward the spring point and cornice, as though seen at a changing angle from the pavement below.

If these anomalies are taken to be calculated adjustments by the model maker, they not only attest to the care taken to provide visual veracity, but also to the expectation that viewers would inspect the interior of the model. Those who entered the model would, of course, not be aware of these "subtle adjustments" (indeed, the lack of stilting of the vault was noticed only recently), but would be expected to experience a simulation of the projected basilica as completed.

Michelangelo did not like the Sangallo model. He felt that Sangallo had departed from Bramante's design and "chiunche s'è discostato da decto ordine di Bramante, come à facto il Sangallo, s'è discostato della [verità ...]." He was dismayed by the ambulatory surrounding the apses that blocked light, and by the many hiding places that would encourage "scoundrels" to hide and would require twenty-five men to search them out at closing time (*Carteggio* 1965–83, IV, MLXXI).

Although most of the models for St. Peter's were made of wood, documents indicate that Michelangelo's first and third models were of clay. (Michelangelo made a model in clay for the facade of S. Lorenzo in Florence,²³ for the stairs leading to the reading room of the Biblioteca Laurenziana,²⁴ and, according to Vasari, Michelangelo had Calcagni build a clay model for S. Giovanni dei Fiorentini in Rome [Vasari, ed. Milanesi 1878–85, VII: 263].) Michelangelo's second model for St. Peter's (Model II) was made in 1547 of wood and included a large portion of the structure (Millon and Smyth 1976: 202–205).

Model for S. Maria
della Consolazione in Todi
total and detail
Todi, Museo Comunale
Cat. no. 142

49

A painting by Domenico Passignano in the Casa Buonarroti, showing Michelangelo presenting a model of St. Peter's to a pope (cat. no. 399), may represent Model II. Michelangelo's fourth model for St. Peter's (Model IV) is the large wooden model of half of the drum and dome constructed in 1558-61 and now preserved in the Vatican (cat. no. 396).

In addition to models of large portions of St. Peter's, Michelangelo had models of smaller sections made in wood for the cornice on the interior of the main crossing in 1549 (AFP, I: 57, 22ff.; K. Frey 1916: 67, no. 597), which included 5 *rosoni* (AFP, I: 57, 79); for an otherwise unidentified model of a tabernacle in December 1548 (AFP, I: 44, 811; II: 57, 87, 92 and 118); for a model for the vault of the south hemicycle (Millon and Smyth 1976: 162-184), and full-scale models in stone in 1560 by a group of *scarpellini* for the cornice of the north hemicycle, the Cappella dell'Imperatore (AFP, I: 28, 711ff.); and for what was most likely also a full-scale model in stone for the salient entablature and capitals of the buttresses of the drum, which is mentioned in contracts dated 1561 and 1562 with each of the *scarpellini* (K. Frey 1916: 121-125, nos. 698a-699t).

Baccio d'Agnolo
Model for S. Giuseppe
or S. Marco in Florence
Florence, Museo di S. Marco
(deposited with the Church
of S. Giuseppe)
Cat. no. 47

It seems likely there were many more models made during Michelangelo's tenure, since he said that he made a model of everything he did in a letter to Vasari concerning the apse vault of the south transept at St. Peter's (*Carteggio* 1965-83, V, MCCLXI). The statement implies that models of portions of the structure were final models, which were to be followed in construction. Of the models cited, it is most likely that seven of Michelangelo's models for St. Peter's were intended to serve as construction models: Model II, the cornice models in wood and stone, the tabernacle model, the wooden drum and dome model (Model IV), the probable model for the entablature and capitals of the drum and—if we are to believe Michelangelo's letter to Vasari—a final model for the apse vault of the south hemicycle. The splendid wooden model for the facade of S. Lorenzo in Florence is the larger of two final models made by Michelangelo following a succession of preliminary models, one of which was made of clay. The smaller of the two final models, now lost, but recorded by Giovan Battista Nelli in the seventeenth century, when it still retained some of its sculptural decoration (Millon 1988: 63-65), was most likely constructed as a presentation model used to secure the approval of Pope Leo X. The larger extant model seems to have been made thereafter as a guide for construction (Millon 1988: 69-73). At the inception of Medici plans to complete the renovation of S. Lorenzo, there were a number of architects who submitted proposals for the project.

[23] A model in clay by Michelangelo for the facade of S. Lorenzo is mentioned in his letter of 2 May 1517 from Carrara to Domenico Buoninsegni in Rome (*Carteggio* 1965-83, I, CCXXI).
[24] The clay model for the stair is mentioned in a letter of Michelangelo from Rome on 16 December 1558 to his nephew Leonardo in Florence (*Carteggio* 1965-83, V, MCCLXXX).

Giovanni de' Medici with Alessandro Pieroni
Model for the Facade of
S. Stefano dei Cavalieri in Pisa
Pisa, Museo Nazionale di S. Matteo
Cat. no. 62

Cristoforo Solari
Model of the Apse of Como
Cathedral
exterior
Como, Musei Civici
(deposited with the Cathedral)
Cat. no. 56

Cristoforo Solari
Model of the Apse of Como
Cathedral
interior
Como, Musei Civici
(deposited with the Cathedral)
Cat. no. 56

Selection of a design in a competition through the comparison of projects, usually models, was a traditional procedure among those responsible for major civic and religious projects. The histories of the cathedrals of Como, Milan, Bologna, and Florence include many competitions decided through the comparison of models submitted by architects or teams of architects, painters, and sculptors.

Though there are records of occasional competition models for an entire structure,[25] most often competitions were held for portions of a structure, a facade,[26] a choir, the extension of a nave, or a lantern above a dome. Several models are preserved that resulted from two competitions for the facade of the cathedral of Florence in the late sixteenth century (cat. nos. 246, 248, 250, 254). Likewise preserved are models for two alternatives for the choir of the cathedral of Como (cat. no. 56),[27] and models of two competing proposals for the nave of S. Petronio in Bologna.[28]

At the cathedral in Florence, in addition to the competition for the design of the facade, and for the construction of the dome over the crossing, won by Brunelleschi, as mentioned earlier, there were competitions for the design of the lantern atop the dome (also won by Brunelleschi).[29]

53

Cristoforo Solari
Model of the Apse of Como Cathedral
interior
Como, Musei Civici (deposited with the Cathedral)
Cat. no. 56

Cristoforo Solari
Model of the Apse of Como Cathedral
exterior
Como, Musei Civici (deposited with the Cathedral)
Cat. no. 56

*Prospero Sogari (called
Il Clemente)*
Model for the Facade
of Reggio Emilia Cathedral
total and detail
Reggio Emilia, Musei Civici
Cat. no. 60

60

Cristoforo Rocchi and Giovanni Pietro Fugazza
Wooden Model of Pavia Cathedral
facade, and detail
Pavia, Fabbriceria della Cattedrale (deposited with the Musei Civici)
Cat. no. 54

on the following pages
Cristoforo Rocchi and Giovan Pietro Fugazza
Wooden Model of Pavia Cathedral
Pavia, Fabbriceria della Cattedrale (deposited with the Musei Civici)
Cat. no. 54

[25] At least two models were made for S. Maria delle Carceri in Prato, one by Giuliano da Maiano, probably octagonal in plan, and the Greek-cross design chosen by Lorenzo de' Medici by Giuliano da Sangallo after seeing a model for Alberti's S. Sebastiano in Mantua, sent to Florence at the request of Lorenzo de' Medici (Morselli and Corti 1982: 16, 24).

[26] Competitions for the design of a facade for an existing church were not uncommon. Examples include the completion for the facade of the cathedrals of Milan, Florence, and Bologna, and S. Lorenzo, Florence, S. Stefano dei Cavalieri, Pisa, Reggio Emilia, Chiesa Nuova, Rome.

[27] Competing models for the choir of the cathedral of Como by Tommaso Rodari and Cristoforo Solari are still preserved in the Museo Civico, Como (Binaghi Olivari 1981: 118-119).

[28] One example is the discussion about the nave of S. Petronio in Bologna where the two competing models of 1592 are still extant and recorded in an engraving by F. Ambrosini (D'Amico 1990: 72, nos. 201-202).

[29] Manetti, in his life of Brunelleschi, states that a number of models for the lantern of the cathedral of Florence were prepared for judgment (Saalman, ed. 1970: 113; Tanturli and De Robertis 1976, 113). In addition to the model by Brunelleschi, other models in the competition included those by Lorenzo Ghiberti, Antonio Manetti Ciaccheri, Bruno di ser Lapo Mazei, and an otherwise unidentified tinsmith named Domenico (Guasti 1857, docs. 269-273, cited in Saalman, ed. 1970: 149).

[30] Modifications made to the model for the church and sanctuary at Caravaggio (most likely in the seventeenth century) have been studied by T. Barton Thurber and will appear in a forthcoming publication.

There were also two competitions for a solution to the incomplete junction between the base of the dome and the upper level of the drum (the *ballatoio*) (cat. nos. 268, 269, 270, 271, 274). Those in charge of a construction which extended over a considerable period often found a model previously approved and used as a guide for construction, to be useful at a later date. An existing model could be altered when, for example, the construction of a nave had been completed up to the facade, or when the crossing had been built and the construction of the drum and dome were being contemplated. New ideas, reflecting new awareness through building experience or new attitudes, often prompted a revision of the earlier design. A new design for a facade or dome could conveniently be added to an existing model for assessment. A new addition could be retained and followed in construction. The model for S. Maria della Consolazione in Todi is a case in point (cat. no. 142). The model of the church, probably built to be used as a guide for construction, includes a drum and dome that were added later, perhaps replacing an earlier version, when the construction of the building reached that stage. Another example, the model for the sanctuary of Caravaggio, includes modifications made when the construction of the sanctuary extension was being contemplated. There, one half of the model was retained in its original state while the other half was lengthened to match with a new project.[30]

The transition to higher levels of craftsmanship, the inclusion of sculptural detail, the precise rendering of architectural members in miniature, and the simulation of materials in some sixteenth-century models suggest a significant change in the notion of models from the fifteenth to the sixteenth centuries.

*Cristoforo Rocchi, and Giovan
Pietro Fugazza*
Wooden Model of Pavia
Cathedral
*details of exterior
Pavia, Fabbriceria
della Cattedrale
(deposited with the Musei
Civici)
Cat. no. 54*

*Cristoforo Rocchi and Giovan
Pietro Fugazza*
Wooden Model of Pavia
Cathedral
*interior of apse
Pavia, Fabbriceria
della Cattedrale
(deposited with the Musei
Civici)
Cat. no. 54*

Antonio da Lonate (?)
Wooden Model of Vigevano
Cathedral
Vigevano Cathedral
Cat. no. 55

Brunelleschi, perhaps to maintain control, and Alberti, to insure that the eye was not seduced by color and decorative detail, both advocated architectural models that were bare, showing only the disposition of the larger elements. On the other hand, the Sangallo model of St. Peter's, the models for the *ballatoio*, and the facade models for the cathedral of Florence all depend on the appreciation of the relation between the minute sculptural detail and the presentation of the whole, a consistent attention from the design of the whole to the smallest part. Less is left to be decided as work progresses, less is left to be studied and modeled at full-scale (here Michelangelo seems to be an exception among his contemporaries). Consequently, in the sixteenth century, there is less left undecided, less that the architect needs to or can alter during construction (though differences between a construction model and a structure as built often occur and are usually revealing). Fully detailed models also provide greater control for the client who is better able to assess and understand both the whole and the detail, and, therefore, in a better position to intervene at a stage when still possible.

Several different categories of models have been discussed. Models used to study a design were best described by Alberti. Michelangelo used the model of the apse vault of the south hemicycle of St. Peter's to study the design of the vault. Filarete advocated presentation models. Brunelleschi's model of the Palazzo Medici was, most likely, a presentation model if Cosimo de' Medici was able to reject the design upon his examination of the model. Among the many other presentation models, Michelangelo's first model of St. Peter's was also made to gain the pope's approval. Models prepared for competition abound. They are, perhaps, a special category of presentation models.

In addition to these categories—study, presentation, and competition models—there are also final models, or models that are used as guides to construction. (Both presentation and competition models may become final models once approved by a patron or a client group.) Further, models of details, either to scale or full-size, form a discreet category much used in construction. *Modani*, or full-scale profiles in wood, cardboard, or metal, are a special

Antonio da Lonate (?)
Wooden Model of Vigevano
Cathedral
detail
Vigevano Cathedral
Cat. no. 55

class of detail models. Within this general category of detail models is the copy model, that is, a portion of an existing structure, an admired capital, cornice, or pediment that may be cited as an element to be copied either at the same size or modified to fit a new project. Architectural models continued to be used throughout the seventeenth and eighteenth centuries in Italy and the rest of Europe. Many or most of the models have been lost. Among those preserved in Rome are the several models for the sacristy of St. Peter's and for the facade of S. Giovanni in Laterano. In Piedmont, models still exist for the projects of Filippo Juvarra (1678–1736), for the castle at Rivoli, and the Superga basilica. In Britain, the magnificent large model of Christopher Wren's design for St. Paul's was recently the focus of an exhibition at the Royal Academy in London.[31]

It seems that the Ecole des Beaux-Arts may have discouraged model making in its curriculum, and the tradition languished during the nineteenth century. It was revived in the early twentieth century when models were used in a variety of ways by Antoni Gaudí, Mies van der Rohe, Le Corbusier, and Frank Lloyd Wright, among others.[32] A history of architectural models as an integral part of the design process has yet to be written.

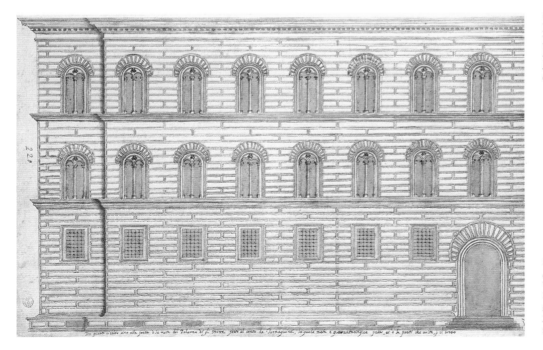

[31] The exhibition included some of the drawings for St. Paul's by Christopher Wren and his contemporaries.
[32] For architectural models in Britain, see Wilton-Ely 1967: 26-32, and 1968: 250-259. For models in France, mostly modern, see "Enquête..." 1983.

74

Kathleen Weil-Garris Brandt The Relation of Sculpture and Architecture in the Renaissance

Unknown French Illuminator
Vitruvius Presents his Book
to Augustus
and Vitruvius Teaching his
Disciples
illuminated page from De
architectura by *Vitruvius*
15th cent.
*Florence, Biblioteca Medicea
Laurenziana*
Cod. Plut. XXX.10, c. 1r.
Cat. no. 88

An impressive number of the architectural drawings in this exhibition, from the earliest examples on, show that figurative sculpture was planned as an integral part of the design of building exteriors as well as in their interior decoration. Designs for the New St. Peter's and for S. Petronio in Bologna, for instance, remind us that Renaissance architectural projects for facades in particular, so often left unfinished on Italian churches, envisaged an abundant sculptural apparatus.

Architectural models like that of the facade of S. Lorenzo or Sangallo's model for New St. Peter's were also originally decorated with figures and reliefs in wax or stucco. Paintings like those by the Barberini Master , depict a Renaissance architecture, alive with sculpture. Surviving Renaissance buildings are not, however, remarkable for their freight of sculpture. Twentieth-century scholars and critics, raised in the traditions of architectural modernism, also saw powerful evidence in Renaissance writers that proportion, ideal geometric forms, pure surfaces and the language of the antique columnar orders, were the prime concerns of Renaissance architects. All together, it is easy to understand why today the copious indications for sculpture by Renaissance designers are usually ignored in discussions about architecture. By the same token, building designs by architects have not been seen as fruitful sources for students of Renaissance sculpture.

Precisely because this exhibition focuses on the methods of planning and visualization used by Renaissance architects, it also gathers together a unique body of information about the significance of sculpture in their creative thinking. If we reexamine these images together with Renaissance writing about architecture, however, it quickly becomes apparent that the relationship between the architecture and sculpture was highly unstable, that the stakes involved in the issue were high and that the matter was fraught with intertwined problems. To cut that Gordian knot, we shall restrict this discussion primarily to facades, which were the prime focus for monumental figural decoration. To get an inkling of the assumptions that patrons and practitioners brought to the subject, we need to return to canonical texts for Renaissance architecture: the late first century B.C. treatise by the Roman architect Vitruvius, and Leon Battista Alberti's *De re aedificatoria*, completed by 1450.

Finally, we shall examine a painting depicting architecture, in this exhibition, the panel attributed to Piero di Cosimo (cat. no. 86), for the clues it may provide for the reception and dissemination of Albertian ideas about architectural sculpture and their implications for Renaissance theory and practice.

Vitruvius traced the invention of architecture to the imitation of nature. Seeking shelter from the elements, our earliest ancestors had learned lessons from the skill with which swallows and bees built their habitations. Then, humans had themselves learned to construct dwellings from the materials of nature and, when they intended the classical architectural orders: the Doric, Ionic and Corinthian; their shapes were based on the forms and proportions of nature's greatest architecture, the human body. Indeed, Vitruvius affirmed that the figure of a man could be inscribed both in the circle and the square; the fundamental geometrical forms on which the universe was ordered.

Vitruvian manuscripts were copied in the Middle Ages, but it was only in the fifteenth century that Italian humanists and artists turned to the ancient author as a guide to how the rule and magnificence of ancient architecture could be given a modern rebirth. At the same time, the Vitruvian equation of the human body with the fundamental geometrical, proportional order of being and with the architectural orders, validated the humanist vision of "man as the measure of all things." Leonardo da Vinci's famous depiction of the "Vitruvian Man" gave these ideas their best-known expression (Krinsky 1969: 17–18; Zollner 1987; Long 1980: 54–56). Thus the only architectural treatise surviving from antiquity had implications for Renaissance thinking about all three of the visual arts.

If architecture was grounded in the imitation of nature and of the human body on the basis of their shared reflection of a cosmic order of geometrical proportionality, Vitruvian architecture could be linked to the representational arts in order to fortify Renaissance arguments affirming the underlying unity of painting, sculpture and architecture. By emphasizing the theoretical unity, consistency and rational order of the three media, on the basis of a common goal (imitation of nature and its underlying principles) writers sought to

Donatello
Annunciation
*(the "Cavalcanti
Annunciation")*
1435
pietra serena with gilding
Florence, S. Croce

75

Master of the Barberini Panel
Presentation of the Virgin
15th cent.
Boston, Museum of Fine Arts

Francesco di Giorgio Martini
Flagellation
detail
second half 15th cent.
Perugia, Galleria Nazionale
dell'Umbria
cat. no. 38

[1] These observations are gleaned from Alberti's three treatises on the visual arts. See Alberti 1972 for *De pictura* and *De statua* and, for *De re aedificatoria*, Alberti 1966a and Alberti 1988. Vernacular translations of the treatises on painting and on architecture were published in 1847 and 1546 respectively. Citations are made to Ryckwert's English translation of *De re* followed by the page numbers of Orlandi's Latin text in parentheses. For Ghiberti's *Commentari*, see Ghiberti 1947.
[2] Colossi are appropriate for heroes and gods, but Gauricus also privileges the equestrian monument and is less hierarchical in this respect than the Tuscan writers.

demonstrate that the visual arts possessed the intellectual criteria required for inclusion in the canon of the traditional *artes liberales*.

The rational analysis, individuation and exposition of each of the visual arts and their relationships was, however, part of the same intellectual and rhetorical project (Farago 1991: 23-34). Practicing artists rather than the humanists initiated this task but they too turned to antique literature for significant models. In his *Natural History*, Pliny the Elder had treated the history of painting, of sculpture and of architecture, separately according to the materials they utilized. From their different perspectives, the first Renaissance writers on sculpture, Alberti and Lorenzo Ghiberti, prescribe that the sculptor must be versed in the other arts, but both authors define sculpture as a fully autonomous art, governed by theory and practice.[1] Both artists recognize the worth of relief sculpture but, they follow Pliny's assumption that the statue, the *statua virile*, is the prime task of sculpture and that the colossus is its highest challenge. Pomponius Gauricus, not a sculptor but a humanist trained in the Paduan milieu, takes a similar view in his *De sculptura* of 1503 (Gauricus 1969).[2] In other words, the paradigmatic work of Renaissance sculpture was, in theory, understood as the freestanding monumental nude, independent of an architectural setting (Seymour 1967: 1-27; Keutner 1969: 11-24; for useful introductions to the tasks of Renaissance sculpture). In practice, the situation was quite different. During the Middle Ages as well as in succeeding centuries, freestanding single figures could indeed decorate fountains or be elevated on columns as monuments to saints and heroes, and equestrian monuments could stand in piazzas. Such freestanding works, like Donatello's bronze *David*, his *Judith and Holofernes* or his *Gattamelata* in Padua were, however, very much the exception. Michelangelo's *David* is often taken as the symbol of the expressive eloquence and artistic autonomy of sculpture in the Renaissance. It is telling, though, that the marble colossus was carved from a block originally designated for one of the finial figures planned for the buttresses of Florence Cathedral (Tolnay 1943: 151-152; Seymour 1967: 21-41). The fact is that the overwhelming preponderance of commissions for monumental figural sculpture, both in the Middle Ages and during the Renaissance, were destined for architectural settings.

This had been taken for granted in earlier centuries as cathedral facades like those of Orvieto and Siena remind us. An elaborate sculptural apparatus was often anticipated in the planning of the building or could enrich pre-existing buildings. Where tradition, decorum or function did not decree otherwise; where patronage, materials and skills were available, decorative carving, relief and figural sculpture sprang up in abundance. The relatively simple articulation and large wall fields of these facades, could be subdivided or united with considerable flexibility to accommodate a rich complement of sculpture. Decorative moldings, often exploiting natural forms, enframed scenes in mosaic or panels of colored marble. Figural relief scenes could fill out the wall fields or reach beyond them to unify architectural elements. Statues filled a multitude of tabernacles or, as finials, crowned pediments and pinnacles. Sculptural decoration could be expanded almost indefinitely.

A primary function of Gothic church facades was to bear significant images and to negotiate relations between them and the spectator. Sharing in the plasticity of the architecture and in the figural language of mosaic or painted scenes, sculpture acted as the essential mediating ornament of facades and imbued the architecture with semiotic specificity and richness.

As Renaissance architects began to adopt the abstract vocabulary and proportions of the antique architectural orders, however, this familiar symbiosis with sculpture was thrown into doubt. Indeed, the system of ancient architecture transmitted by Vitruvius was based on a restrictive code, focused on the orders and their disposition and their canonical non-figurative repertoire of ornaments.

Throughout the Renaissance, fidelity to Vitruvius could imply that the proportional rule and the pure vocabulary of the classical architectural orders constituted a self-sufficient formal and symbolic discourse to which sculpture was essentially unnecessary or indeed a contaminant (see Thoenes 1972; Günther and Thoenes 1985; Günther 1988d). All meaning was arrogated to the language of the orders. The price of such architectonic purity was high: a loss of the specific semiotic dimension that only figurative sculpture could give. Even before the full rigor of the Vitruvian canon was enforced in modern architecture, it implied a new discipline for the placement and role of sculpture. The facade of Brunelleschi's Ospedale degli Innocenti is an interesting case in point. For all the abstract purity and laconic conciseness of the architectural membering, the traditional identifying and communicative role of figuration could not be dispensed with. Perhaps architectural forms alone could not, after all, adequately convey the identity and social function of the foundling hospital. A monumental inscription might have done so, but was the clientele of the Innocenti predominately literate? Some painted image of the *innocenti* might have

Andrea della Robbia
glazed terracotta tondo
ca. 1487
Florence, Ospedale degli
Innocenti, portico

Filippo Brunelleschi
Interior of the dome and
cupoletta
1419–28
Florence, S. Lorenzo, Old
Sacristy

sufficed, but Brunelleschi chose to represent the swaddled figures of foundling infants in glazed terra-cotta roundels. The disciplined polychromy of this technique gave the images unique powers of visual signage while evoking the dignity of ancient cameos. Apparently Brunelleschi thought the three-dimensional materiality, preciousness and durability of sculpture could be more easily reconciled than painting with the decorum of architecture. The figural reliefs are framed off from the architectural articulation in geometrical surrounds. Their representational task is considered so important that the tondi fill out the entire spandrel even though this will create problems of architectural design at the lateral terminations of the arcade. Roundels do not belong to the strict canon of the orders but could be assimilated to it from antique triumphal arches and other oculi[3]. Here, however, Brunelleschi uses the enframements to clarify the "otherness," in respect to the architecture of sculpture, and to define its precise communicative identity and function.

We do not know whether Brunelleschi intended to exclude sculpture from his other buildings, but he apparently objected to the sumptuous sculptural decoration Donatello installed in the Old Sacristy of S. Lorenzo (Manetti 1970: 105, 109). The enthusiasm with which the Sacristy and other Quattrocento buildings, particularly interiors, were embellished with sculpture reminds us, however, of the enduring value assigned to the semiotic and decorative functions of architectural sculpture for modernly antique buildings.

Fortunately, the surviving ruins of Rome provided a visible alternative to the austere and exclusive image of antiquity implied by the Vitruvian text. Despite the depredations of centuries, temples, theaters and above all triumphal arches were alive with reliefs and statues. Tuscan architects and sculptors like Michelozzo, Donatello and Leon Battista Alberti saw in these examples a mandate and a means to recover the resources of sculptural figuration for modern buildings. Thus, for instance, the *all'antica* architectural enframements for Donatello's sculpture (as in the *Cavalcanti Annunciation*) took on unparalleled licence and expressive force and Alberti's facade projected for the Tempio Malatestiano in

[3] In *De re*, VII, xv, 238 (619), Alberti suggests in a similar way that roundels for ceilings be framed off by moldings derived from elements of the cornice.

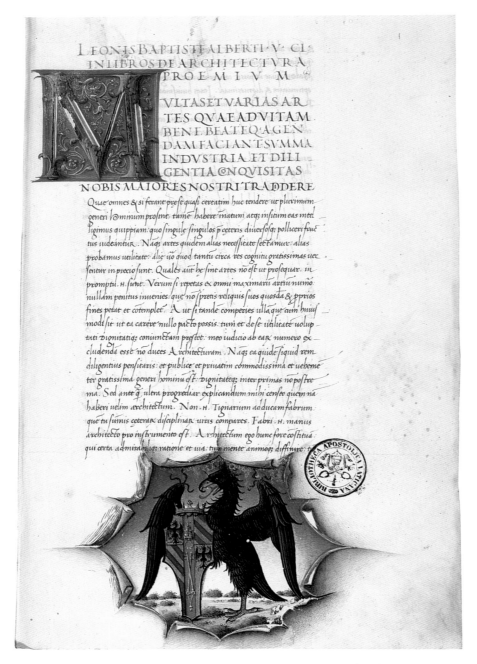

Leon Battista Alberti
De re aedificatoria
1483
Vatican, Biblioteca Apostolica
Vaticana, Cod. Urb. Lat. 264
Cat. no. 46c

Leon Battista Alberti
Self-Portrait
Paris, Bibliothèque Nationale
inv. 2508
Cat. no. 40

Rimini would have been bedecked with figures, reliefs and garlands of gigantic size. In *De pictura* (Alberti 1972, 65) Alberti had already reveled in the limitless abundance of sculptors in ancient Rome and throughout *De re aedificatoria* his descriptions of the sculpture on ancient buildings reflect his own experience of Rome. He exhorts modern architects to revive antique standards and decorative magnificence, and calls on sculptors to take surviving antique sculpture as their model.

Alberti's *De re aedificatoria*

Alberti's seminal treatise on architecture was undertaken as a rationalization and explication of Vitruvius so that the antique rules of architecture could again become available to architects of Alberti's own day. In fact, however, Alberti's treatise departs strongly from his Vitruvian model, rethinks and expands its range in highly original ways (Krautheimer 1969c: 265; 1969a: 323–332). His attempts to harmonize Vitruvian tenets with his own ideas, however, forced Alberti into a number of contradictions which created problems for his readers and for practicing artists.

The clash between old and new was of the most profound significance for the relation of sculpture and architecture in the Renaissance. Vitruvius had made a few passing references to sculptural monuments and occasionally to architectural carving, but, *ex silentio*, he seemed to exclude sculpture from the matter of architecture. Alberti, on the contrary, de-

Giovanni Bettini da Fano
Tempio Malatestiano under
Construction
1457–68
Paris, Bibliothèque de l'Arsenal
Cod. 630, c. 126r.
Cat. no. 98

votes extraordinarily great attention to sculpture in the architectural context. Rome had been so rich in statues, he says, that it appeared to be inhabited by a second population of marbles—such remarks were already familiar from ancient authors such as Pliny (1976: 29 [XXXIV, 16, 36]). Sculpture was desired by all as a sign of virtue, wealth and fortune (VII, xvi, 239-240 [649-655]). The very presence of copious antique sculpture on a building defines it as dignified and magnificent for Alberti and he assumes that all types of modern architecture should also be enriched with figural sculpture (VII, iii, 194 [547]; xvi, 240-241 [655-657]; IX, viii, 312 [843]).

At the same time, however, Alberti fully espoused the fundamental Vitruvian principle that architecture should adhere to a single, consistent (*certa et constans*) proportional rule in all its parts (II, ii, 34 [99]; IV, ii, 156 [448]) and this discipline applied as well to sculpture in an architectural setting.

In *De statua*, Alberti had elevated the status and autonomy of sculpture as an art requiring intellectual understanding and skill. Ironically, however, when Alberti wrote as an architect, his very enthusiasm for architectural sculpture could serve to denigrate it in relation to the other visual arts. In *De re aedificatoria*, figurative sculpture is subordinate to architecture, obedient to its proportions and decorum. Sculpture loses its autonomy as an art to become an ornament.

Alberti's famous distinction between beauty and ornament is fundamental to this issue. "Beauty is that reasoned congruity (*concinnitas*) of all the parts within a body, so that nothing may be added, taken away, or altered but for the worse." Beauty depends on a "consistent standard" of proportion. Whereas beauty is inherent and pervasive, "ornament (is) a form of auxiliary light (*lux*). It is a further embellishment to beauty and obeys the same proportions and consistent rules, but ornament "has the character of something attached or additional" (VI, ii, 156 [447-449]; Alberti 1988: 367-368, 420).

This division determines the structure of the treatise as a whole. If beauty is a mental general ideal, ornament is the working out of this ideal in the physical world of individual phenomena and tasks. Thus ornament is ultimately considered as the conceptual equivalent of practice itself. This bipartite concept leads to a doubling in Alberti's exposition (Krautheimer 1969a: 327, 330-331). The first five books are devoted to the matters belonging integrally to the lineaments and body of architecture. This discussion progresses from the general conditions and materials of building, through the proportions and construction of buildings, walls, columns and the Vitruvian orders, to end with the finishing of roofs and interiors.

In the second half of the treatise, all these topics are rehearsed once more, but now in relation to ornament. Plan, elevation, and construction return. It is striking, for instance, that Alberti consigns all discussion of construction machines to the rubric of ornament (VI, vii-ix). The rationale seems to be that such engines hoist statues and other ornamental elements into place. On the model of Cicero (*De oratore*, III, 83) and Quintilian (*Institutio oratoria*, VIII, iii, 49, 61-67; XII, x, 66; Baxandall 1972: 131-132, 169)[4] Alberti defines ornament as the domain of the particular. In architecture as in oratory, ornament is the great instrument of differentiation among types and the formal and symbolic detail which identify them (VII, i, 189 [529]; Krautheimer 1969c: 265).

In Books VII-IX, therefore, Alberti reconsiders the different building types (temple, basilica, palace, etc.) and the Vitruvian orders and ornament proper to each. In the first half of the treatise he had defined the column as a residuum of the wall; that is, an element of structure (I, x, 25 [7]). Now, instead, he defined the column as the chief ornament of buildings—something added on (VI, xiii, 183 [521]). The architectural orders depend on their ornaments as much as on their proportions for their identity, and buildings are defined as dignified and magnificent when they are embellished by reliefs and statues (e.g., 180, 194, 241, 244, 292-293, 312 [520, 545, 655, 665, 783-787, 845]).

In the introduction to the next book (VII, i, 189 [529]), devoted to the ornament of sacred buildings, Alberti explains the plan of his exposition using the metaphor of a statue, and the subject of sculpture winds throughout the following chapters. The history and function of statues marks the culmination of Alberti's discussion of commemorative monuments of all kinds (VII, xvi, 238-240 [649-655]). Here Alberti's text has led to different interpretations. The sequence and immediate context of his ideas suggests that statues are the best kind of commemorative monument because they are suitable ornaments to every type of architecture, sacred and private, and make excellent memorials both to men and deeds (VII, xvi, 240 [655]).[5] In the ensuing chapter of Book VII and in the broader context of all Alberti's references to sculpture in *De re*, however, it seems that he perceives statuary and all sculpture as the culminating and most elegant ornament for all types of architecture (e.g., IX, viii, 311-312 [845]).[6] It gives the most specific form of signification to architecture, defining it as truly splendid and completely realized.

Alberti prefers sculpture to painting as architectural decoration (VII, xv, 238 [649])[7] and is much concerned with the decorum of sculptural ornament. He opposes the argument that sacred buildings require a pure austerity devoid of statues (VII, xvii, 241-242 [657]). He believes, on the contrary, that sculpture, which originated in religious images, induces piety and awe. Temples should, therefore, be as magnificent in sculpture as skill and money allow. Since there can never be too much, the decoration of temples can go on without end (VII, iii, 194 [545]; VII, x, 220 [609]; VIII, i, 244 [655]). In theory, he then establishes a descending hierarchy of ornament and figurative sculpture appropriate to the many kinds of other public and private buildings, such as law courts, palaces and private residences (VII, xvi, 241 [657]). He disapproves of excess and warns lest ostentation excite envy (IX, i, 292; viii, 312 [781-783, 845]). In the end, however, Alberti confesses "I feel that those who spend so much on the bulk of their buildings that they cannot afford to adorn them deserve even greater censure than those who overspend slightly in ornament" (IX, i, 292 [783]).

The purpose of ornament is to confer a "graceful and pleasing appearance" on all forms of building or, as Alberti reiterates, endow them with "*dignitas ac venustas*" (VI, ii, 155, 156 [447-449]). This effect depends, however, on the rigorous application to ornament of the same standards of proportion and correctness that also define the fundamental nature of beauty (VI, ii, 156-157 [449]).

There was also a powerful developmental argument against variability in architectural ornament. "The ignorant" (Gothic sculptors and architects?) maintain that the criteria for beau-

[4] In this important passage, Quintilian equates *ornamenta* with *imago* with "living truth [displayed] to the eyes of the mind." Cicero's definition of ornament as the highest distinction of eloquence is also relevant.

[5] Riess 1979: 1-17 gives an excellent account of the civic dimension of Alberti's concept of sculpture.

[6] "*Sed omnium [monumentarum?], ni fallor, egregius fuit usus statuarum. Ornamentum enim veniunt et sacris et prophanis et publicis et privatis aedificiis, mirificamque praestant memoriam cum hominum tum et rerum.*" Rykwert (1988: 240), however, translates Alberti to say "But, unless I am mistaken, the greatest ornament of all is the statue." In any event, it is clear from the Latin text that Alberti speaks of statues in the plural.

[7] In *De pictura* (Alberti 1972, 67), on the contrary, Alberti had defined painting as the finest ornament of all things.

Leon Battista Alberti
Tempio Malatestiano, exterior
and detail of entrance
1450

ty and ornament in architecture are relative and variable according to individual taste and must not be bound by any rules. Alberti will "correct this error" by demonstrating how the history of the arts progressed to the stage of "knowledge and reason" and thus to the mature insight that "consistent theory is the mark of true art" (VI, ii, 156–157 [449]). The implications for these prescriptions for sculpture become explicit in Alberti's discussion of triumphal arches. The rich sculptural ornament to be seen on surviving antique buildings exemplified magnificence and dignity of ornament and its correct architectural disposition. Furthermore, Alberti's design for the facade of the Tempio Malatestiano shows that he thought triumphal arches offered an appropriate antique model that could be applied with greater ease than a temple front to the exterior and interior facades of modern churches (see also VIII, iv, 257, [699]).

Alberti's triumphal arch is crowned with monumental chariots, large figures, and finial statues, whereas the walls are to be decorated with inscriptions and narrative reliefs (*historiae*) in circular or square enframements. The architectural articulation of the arch determines the placement and number of all the sculptural elements, and Alberti expresses their sizes as fractions of the height of the wall, attic or columns they adorn (VII, vi, 265–268 [723]; see also VIII, iii, 254 [691] and IX, ix, 314 [851] for similar formulas). In other words, Alberti's "calculated standard" and "consistent theory" apply to the proportions of architecture and sculpture alike.

In part, these prescriptions for the relation of sculpture to architecture could be gleaned from observation of antique monuments; but they also had a theoretical dimension. Alberti was inspired by the Vitruvian equivalence between the column and the human body (IX, vii, 309 [835]). The antique author treated the three columnar orders as the basic units of construction and of architectural language. Alberti, however, who considered the

column primarily as an ornament to walls and who defines ornament as the realm of specific differentiation, logically postponed his exposition of the several orders to his discussion of ornament in the second half of *De re*.[8] If the proportions of men, women and maidens determined the proportions of the Doric, Ionic and Corinthian orders (IX, vii, 309 [835]), it follows that the proportions of statues will obey the orders of the architecture they adorn. Alberti's other treatises testify that he associated Vitruvius with a single standard for both architectural and human proportions.[9] Since the goal of sculpture is likeness, *similitudo* (Alberti 1972, 4: 123) to nature, the proportions of statues, even colossi, implicitly obey an architectural canon.[10] This preference for a single standard was also driven by the need to demonstrate the fundamental unity of all the visual arts for only such underlying consistency of theory would validate their claim to be considered as branches of rational knowledge (Baxandall 1971: 104, 117–120, 130).

If statues are in essential ways architectural ornaments like columns, individual sculptures adorning similar architectural elements should be as much alike as possible. Alberti consistently speaks of "statues" in the plural, and he is quite frank in his admiration for the "custom of the ancients" which requires that all sculptural elements, even reliefs, "must be arranged so that they appear to be in their natural and fitting place, as though twinned"; the ancients took care that statues "on one side differed not a whit, either in their lineaments or in their materials, from those opposite." For Alberti, this consistency is a sign of "outstanding skill," surpassing the work of nature which never makes "so much as one nose identical to the other" (IX, vii, 310 [839]).

If the uniformity required in carving sequences of architectural elements predisposed to a similar standard for statuary, and if the latter was an amplification of architecture, it followed that the style of sculpture should, ideally, also approach the decorum of the Vitruvian canon. This reinforced the desirability of a neo-antique mode of sculpture but further restricted its models to a classicizing figure style and compositional scansion found only in the most restrained normative aspect of Roman sculpture. All these factors threatened modern sculpture with monotony and a devaluation of individual creative effort as well as a heavy dependence on workshop participation (Brandt 1984).[11]

Alberti realizes this and is entirely sanguine about it. He is concerned about the practical difficulties in finishing a building's ornament and thus advises that its sculpture (but also frescoes) "be, for the most part, the work of many hands of moderate skill" (IX, viii, 312 [845]). Alberti is willing to admit that there is such a thing as "unusual" sculpture of great quality, and he allows statues a degree of variety since he suggests a number of decorous poses and gestures for them (VII, xvii, 247 [663]). Nonetheless, this variety resides in the gamut of appropriate types, not in the individual image. Rhetorical theory, so fundamental for the shape and content of Alberti's treatise, also provided a rationale for Alberti's attitude toward sculpture. As in oratory, the different types of ornaments (sculpture) differentiate and color the argument (architecture). They lend elegance and eloquence (magnificence) through their appropriateness and artifice, not their content (see Baxandall 1972: 131–132; Farago 1991: 23–34). This, then, is the role of sculpture as well. In the context of architecture, its contribution is typological and symbolic, not discursive and iconographic, and depends primarily on its appropriate presence (IX, ix, 313–314 [851]).

[8] The theme of the proportions of the three orders and their relationships to humans occurs in several places implicitly as well as explicitly. Rykwert (1988: 368 n. 12) traces the notion to Cicero *De oratore*, III: 45, 179.

[9] In *De pictura*, Alberti specifically disagrees with Vitruvius who derives the height of a man from the length of his foot (Alberti 1972, II, 36, 75). Yet, in *De statua*, the height of the figure is given as six times the foot: the proportions Vitruvius assigns to the Doric order (Alberti, 1972, 6: 175).

[10] *De re*, VII, xii, 228 [627]; VIII, iii, 250–256 [683–695], gives complex and explicit proportions for historiated and other triumphal columns up to 100 feet high and their crowning statues.

[11] This situation can be compared with the problem that confronted Renaissance Latinists who espoused strict Ciceronianism in the early Cinquecento. See D'Amico 1983: 76–77.

In public, decorum rules. In the private sphere, the greatest modesty should prevail. Having made this apodictic pronouncement, Alberti reverses himself with insouciant charm. In the ornament of houses, villas and gardens, it may be permitted, for the sake of variety, to "stray a little from the dignity and calculated rule of lineaments." In hiding, so to speak, variety may be tolerated. In fact, both architect and sculptor may release their individual fantasy, inventiveness, wit and even trickery, to take "a degree of licence ... according to taste" (IX, i, 293-294 [787]).

From the sensational examples of licence that flood from Alberti's pen, it becomes clear that his attachment to decorum comes not from a dry or naturally orderly temperament but from an urgent personal sense of the need to maintain control over a burgeoning imagination that threatens chaos and dissolution if given free play.[12] Suddenly capitals startle us with gorgon heads or writhe with bundles of snakes, columns swell or diminish, bulge with rustication, sprout branches or fruit or transform themselves into huge caryatids in the shape of slaves. No wonder that three-dimensional, representational sculpture poses special dangers to decorum.

Alberti's treatise also contained, however, arguments which could give special privilege to sculpture. His exposition embodies two kinds of progression which are seen as inherent in each other although they move in opposite directions. On the one hand, he charts a progress from theory to practice; on the other, from the analysis of individual insights or inventions to their unification. The elements of architecture are discussed first in general and then in respect to particular types. He narrates the process of actual building from design through execution and thus from lineaments to ornament. He parallels this with a conceptual hierarchy of utility, soundness and beauty in which the last is "the noblest and most necessary of all" (VI, i, 155 [445]).

These developments are also reflected in the general historical progress of architecture from nature to artifice, from ancient to modern times, and are recapitulated in the history of architecture in Italy. Ornament is privileged in all these progressions. Alberti even faults architecture that does not allow embellishment with columns and statues (IX, viii, 312 [843]). Ornament corresponds to the highest category of building, beauty (VI, i, 155 [445]; VI, iii, 159 [457]; VII, 189 [529]) and, because it is an artificial invention, ornament outdoes nature (IX, vii, 310 [839]). Thus sculpture, in its privileged role in architectural ornament, could derive status and value from it.

Alberti's definition of sculpture as ornament brought interlocking contradictions in its wake which were to have grave consequence for both sculptors and architects. If sculpture was merely the handmaiden of architecture, something added on, it could also be omitted from the building. If, on the contrary, architecture could achieve the antique standard of dignity and magnificence only through sculpture, buildings lacking it would remain "naked" (IX, viii, 312 [845]) and imperfect.[13]

As architects increasingly valued the linguistic correctness of the Vitruvian canon, the Albertian mandate to integrate it with figural ornament could imply theoretical tensions. As architects and patrons envisaged ever larger and more imposing buidings, the practical obstacles to completing their ornament became overwhelming. Both figures and ornaments like garlands would perforce become colossal when scaled up consistently with the buildings they were to adorn. (The problems inherent in this colossality can be seen in the sculpture projected for the Raphael and Antonio da Sangallo designs for the St. Peter's facade). For sculptors, Vitruvian rigor imposed burdensome formal and expressive constraints and the production required for a huge architectural project could compromise the quality of individual works. Worse still, the investment of money, will, and time involved often meant that the sculptural decoration was simply not undertaken.

In his first great architectural commission, for the facade of S. Lorenzo, even Michelangelo still found himself in an Albertian dilemma. He announced that the facade would be "the mirror of architecture and sculpture for all Italy," but, in part for just this reason, the project was abandoned.[14] The other great Cinquecento facade projects, like the facade of S. Petronio in Bologna and Florence, all suffered a similar fate.

It is surely no coincidence that only drawings, models and paintings survive to remind us of Albertian dicta on the relation of sculpture and architecture.[15]

The *spalliera* panels in this exhibition, which depict ideal architecture and cityscapes, can be read as recapitulating the different options available to architects in respect to sculpture in the later Quattrocento. The Urbino panel (cat. no. 178a) represents an essentially Vitruvian position where the types of architecture "speak for themselves." The painter has provided sumptuous, plastically carved ornament *all'antica*, but it pertains exclusively to the architectural orders. Figuration is completely avoided.

In the Baltimore panel (cat. no. 178b), by contrast, sculpture takes back its full Albertian semiotic role as ornament. It dignifies, identifies and differentiates civic functions and

[12] Alberti had already warned against the artist's too *"fervens ingenium"* (Alberti, 1972, 44, 84). For a parallel interpretation of Alberti's rhetorical strategies, see Baxandall 1990-91: 39-43. For the dangers of *"dissolutus"* style, see Baxandall 1971: 136-139.

[13] This theme becomes explicit in the famous Raphael letter to Leo X, on which see Thoenes 1986.

[14] The unfinished facades of Florence have been discussed by Isabelle Hyman in various lectures beginning in 1988; a publication is planned.

[15] The historiated, illusionistic facade of the Scuola di S. Marco in Venice is an important exception.

space. In the foreground, large, neo-antique figures of civic Virtues define the privileged public core of the city, centered on the fountain which nourishes the citizens (Kemp 1991e: 251).[16] Further away, in the transition from urban center to periphery, a tower is framed by a triumphal arch in the antique mode, bedecked with equestrian battle scenes in relief. Alberti thought triumphal arches especially suitable for the piazza or the forum (VII, vi, 265 [717]). He approved relief decorations for public architecture (VII, v, 164; VII, x, 220; VIII, iv, 256–257 [473, 609, 699]) and, in *De pictura*, he had defined narrative, *historia*, as the highest and most complex task of painting. The carved *historiae* of the Baltimore arch appear to glorify the city and reassure its inhabitants but, although they communicate more discursively than the foreground statues, they are subsumed in the architecture which supports them, and they remain less important than statuary in the Albertian hierarchy. Only the *spalliera* panel in Sarasota (cat. no. 86) displays the copiousness and magnificence of monumental architectural statuary which Alberti associated with ancient Rome. The attribution to Piero di Cosimo remains problematic[17] but, whoever the painter may have been, the picture reflects a critical phase in the developing interaction between the two arts and suggests, through its fiction, why Alberti's definition of statuary as architectural ornament began to pose practical problems around the turn of the sixteenth century.

The Sarasota Spalliera Panel

The painting depicts a splendid modern edifice *all'antica* surrounded by ornate porticoes crowned with a throng of statues and set in a landscape whose foreground is crowded with workmen engaged in the varied tasks and crafts of architectural construction. It seems to

Piero di Cosimo
The Building of a Double Palace
ca. 1515–20
Sarasota, The John and Mable Ringling Museum of Art
Cat. no. 86

[16] If the background figures of more prestigious citizens are original, it would appear that the picture intends a more specific civic iconography than we now suppose. The Verrocchio-like *Cupid* standing on a sphere atop the wellhead may bespeak charity and fecundity.
[17] It would be most convenient for my argument if the painting were unquestionably by Piero and if it could be dated, ideally to 1503-04 when Piero sought matriculation in the Medici e Speziali, the guild to which painters belonged. Still, I cannot suppress doubts about the attribution when looking at the curiously weak and disjunctive figures, the relatively conventional landscape and the curiously uncomprehending rendering of the architecture. A glance at Piero's portraits of Giuliano da Sangallo and Francesco Giamberti in Amsterdam (Bacci 1976, pls. XXII, XXXIII) shows how convincingly he

could depict buildings and their construction. Zeri's (1973a) attribution of the Sarasota panel to the Serumido Master (Bacci 1966: 104–105) would bring the Sarasota painter even closer to the Albertian milieu, since the scholar identified him as Aristotile da Sangallo; but this attribution also remains problematic. See Barriault 1985: 161, 205 n. 38. Perhaps a follower of Francesco di Giorgio in the neighborhood of Pietro di Francesco Oriolo should also be considered. Cf. Bellosi 1993: 332–337; 448, 456–461 et passim.

[18] In conversation, Caroline Elam has stressed the importance of this fact for the identification of the building type and the picture's iconography. Kemp (1991e: 252) suggests parallels with ancient fora as described by Vitruvius. Alberti's descriptions of Greek fora with double porticoes and "stone beams" (Alberti 1988, VII, vi, 264 [715]) are also suggestive. Unfortunately, the scant space between the Sarasota buildings and other details speak against this interpretation. Bacci (1966: 105), proposed the Temple of Solomon on analogy with the *Judgment of Solomon* in the Galleria Borghese in Rome which Zeri had also given to Aristotile da Sangallo (see above, note 17). Alberti refers several times to the Temple (Alberti

belong to the genre of "storie piccole" for which Piero della Francesca was famous; filled, Vasari says, with "buildings and animals, diverse costumes and instruments" and which were thought to be mythologies (Vasari 1962–87, IV: 66–67).

The Sarasota panel has been related to other idealizing architectural depictions on *spalliera* panels like those in Berlin, Baltimore and Urbino.

Richard Krautheimer and Martin Kemp (Krautheimer, essay; Kemp 1991e) have proposed that all these pictures, like Alberti's *De re*, have a rhetorical purpose. They identify architecture as a social enterprise, they exalt the patronage of building as civic virtue, and they advocate the language of modern architecture *all'antica* as the privileged instrument in the creation of a more perfect society.

The Sarasota painting is unlike the other architectural *spalliere* in several troublesome respects. Does the rigidly symmetrical secular building belong to ancient or modern times? What is its function? Is it part of a narrative or mythological subject? On the one hand, the Sarasota painting is not a townscape like the other panels.

The artfully designed building stands alone in the countryside,[18] neither is it unambiguously the protagonist of the composition. In a sense, the building serves as the background for the laborers, craftsmen and the technologies needed for its production. Furthermore, the linear perspective lacks the "remorseless consistency of the ideal cities" (Martin Kemp, written communication). On the other hand, it is not what it is usually thought to be, a scene of construction. Unlike other Renaissance depictions of architectural *cantieri*,[19] the artisans shown in the Sarasota panel offer no rational exposition of building technique. They work on architectural elements that have no place in the building and, what is more, there seems to be no motive for their labors since the edifice has no scaffolding and appears to be fully finished.[20]

No wonder it has seemed that the figures were intended merely for pictorial effect. Such disjunctive vignettes are common, however, in *spalliere* as a genre. Even when these scenes lack sequence or integration with the perspective they nevertheless contribute to the *historia* (Barriault 1985: 87–89, 90–91, 98–100, 123–165, especially 138). This is true of Piero's other *spalliere* and perhaps the capricious and arbitrary effect of the activities depicted in the Sarasota painting is also simply an indication that they belong to a conceptual rather than a narrative visual order.

As a type of domestic decoration, the *spalliere* have been convincingly linked to Alberti's precepts in *Della Famiglia* and to his concepts of *historia* in *De pictura* (Barriault 1985: 163–168 and passim). Panofsky thought that Vitruvius was the source for Piero's "piccole storie" of mythic times, when divine artificers and human ingenuity fostered the progress of civilization (Panofsky 1937–38: 16–19). Skillful depictions of buildings in perspective were already familiar picturial types to Lorenzo il Magnifico (Barriault 1985: 161). Thus it would not be surprising if the Sarasota picture reflected similar concerns.

If Piero was conversant with the specifically textual culture of Albertian theory, he was also closely associated with the practicing artists steeped in Albertian thought and its Vitruvian foundation.[21] He was linked, in particular, with Giuliano da Sangallo[22] and even more with Leonardo. Whoever the Sarasota painter may be, the dashing troop of cavalry in the background of the Sarasota picture certainly betokens his debt to the latter. Giuliano and Leonardo, like others in Piero's generation, were versed in the theory and practice of architecture and the figurative arts, and in the arguments about their relative hierarchy codified in Leonardo's *Paragone* (Kemp 1989: 20–46 and Baxandall 1971: passim, for the prehistory of these debates).

The Sarasota painting may well have been based on an iconographical conceit, in the usual sense. If so, it remains to be deciphered. Nonetheless, someone conversant with Alberti's treatise on architecture could have recognized much that was familiar, precisely in the combination of ideal edifice and scenes of labor. It may well be doubted that the painting was planned as an illustration of Alberti's ideas, but it seems to offer evidence of their profound and disseminated impact.

Regardless of the painting's authorship or iconography, it reflects an Albertian vision of the ideal relation between practice and theory, patron and practitioner, and of the visual arts to society. In this conceptual structure, the relation of sculpture to architecture plays a special role which can tell us something of how Albertian ideas were perceived and of the dilemmas they were to pose in the real world of practice.

At the beginning of his treatise Alberti defines the architect in this way: "Him I consider

Piero di Cosimo
The Building of a Double Palace
detail of carpenters at work
ca. 1515–20
Sarasota, The John and Mable Ringling Museum of Art
Cat. no. 86

1988, II, iii, 38; VI, iv, 161; VI, xi, 180; VII, x, 221 [109, 463, 513, 615]), mentioning its portico, and the preparation, speed and foreign architects involved in its construction—all elements which could be relevant to the painting, particularly as an allegory of architecture. The Sarasota building looks, however, less like a temple than a palace, but what sort of a palace would be isolated in the countryside? (see below, note 25). The perfect symmetry of the double building suggests a palace for two inhabitants of equal status. For two golden temples to Jove, see Alberti 1988, VI, v, 163 [469–470].

[19] See Appendix, below.

[20] Alberti says that scaffolding is not always necessary (Alberti 1988, III, x, 76, 219), but Piero depicts it in his portrait of Giuliano da Sangallo (Bacci 1976, pl. XXXII). A rope of the hoist, belayed at the window of the *piano nobile*, shows that no floor divides the upper stories on that side of the structure. The door frames are empty and the windows lack mullions. No roof is visible, although Alberti thinks of roofs as prime elements of noble architecture and forbids that they be flat (Alberti 1988, I, i, 26–27; III, xii, 79; VI, v, 163 [75, 77, 223, 473]). See also the Urbino and Baltimore panels (cat. nos. 178a, 178b). The planks, bricks and reeds in the painting could be intended for

an architect, who by sure and wonderful reason and method, knows both how to devise through his own mind and energy, and to realize by construction, whatever can be most beautifully fitted out for the noble needs of man, by the movement of weights and the joining and massing of bodies. To do this he must have an understanding and knowledge of all the highest and most noble disciplines" (Prologue, 3 [2]).

Alberti will expand this definition in later parts of the book to enumerate the many skills which the architect must understand. But throughout, he returns to the theme that theory is inseparable from practice and is, indeed, ultimately dependent on it (Prologue, 5 [15]). The perspectival structure of the Sarasota painting and the size and placement of its pictorial elements make the same point. Linear perspective defines the central axis of the symmetrical, paired buildings, and passes through the intervening piazza into a garden *allee* that disappears on the horizon. The building's centrality in the pictorial field and its consistent perspective are the visual indications of its conceptual importance. Perspective is the intellectual and visual expression of the "single consistent theory" of proportion which, for Alberti, determines all the parts of architecture and their relation to the whole and which constitutes its essential beauty.

The high placement of horizon and vanishing point assure that the building will remain visible in the composition, but dictates that the architecture be relegated to the middle ground and decrease in size. The figures which occupy the immediate foreground are depicted from a lower viewpoint or are excused from the discipline of foreshortening and scale which the architecture imposes.[23] These figures become large and are brought close to the spectator but they and their activities are placed lower than the architecture.

These arrangements may seem visually naive but they correspond to what Alberti says about the conceptual status of architectural practice in relation to theory. On the one hand, the ideal architectural vision pre-exists above the realm of practice. On the other hand, the work of building occurs in the material and contingent world of craftsman and patron, but it is the essential condition to the realization of the ideal. Thus the edifice in the Sarasota panel is already finished because it represents the goal of building rather than its process. In turn, the absence of narrative sequence in the foreground groups suggests that they are conceptually simultaneous exempla of the many skills and tasks which the architect must understand.[24]

Despite the perspectival inconsistencies of the largest foreground figures, their materials, tools, and activities clearly refer visually back toward the building, and its perspective regime increasingly controls the actions of the figures as they approach it. Ultimately, the scattered and diverse construction materials and the activities required for their transformation into architecture are gathered together and focused on the building by perspective. It can function as a metaphor of the architect himself. His organizing vision includes intellectual forethought and practical experience.

Again and again Alberti warns that the architect must know exactly what to do before construction can begin. The building must already be fully complete in his mind. He must have made drawings and scale models complete in every detail, including the sculptural decoration, so that he can estimate costs, prepare his materials and work force and bring them to the building site.

Only thus can he avoid errors of design and execution, and prevent cost overruns; only thus can the building be erected with sufficient speed and economy within the lifetime of a single patron and architect (Prologue, 5; II, i, 33; iii, 37-38; IX, vi, 318 [15, 95-97; 107, 109; 865-867]). Failure in forethought spells failure for the outcome. Organization and dispatch display the ingenuity of the architect (IX, ix, 314-315 [853]).

The painting depicts the three agents which Alberti's architect must bring together in the creation of perfect architecture. Nature determines the qualities, availability and suitability of materials. The architect's intellect decides proportion, choice and arrangement of the building, while the hand of the artisan is responsible for realizing this idea by cutting, trimming and shaping the materials of nature to the archict's purpose.[25] Labor and *ingegno* transform *materia* into an artificial human order: the *lineamenta*, *structura* and *ornamentum* of architecture as exemplified in the noble fictive edifice (VI, iv, 159 [457]; Alberti 1988: 422-430).

The architect must understand the quality and uses of all his materials. In the painting, workers bring timber from the forests, stone from the mountain quarries and perhaps sand from the distant lake. Cut stone (or perhaps unfired brick or tufa blocks, cf. II, ix, 49 [139], and Alberti 1988: 375 n. 101) have been stacked in orderly fashion. Carpenters and masons are the architect's "instruments," but he must understand their crafts and the technology that facilitates them (Prologue, 3, 5, II [15]; iv-xiii). Even the carpenters in the painting use a large vise to hold a plank, an awkward arrangement whose function nonetheless depends on geometry and physics.

roof construction (Alberti 1988, III, xii, 79; III, xv, 88, 89 [223, 225]). The figures on the balcony near the hoist seem to be there only to watch and discuss. The building does not appear to be ready for use or habitation, just as the garden is not yet fully decorated. Is at least some of the work underway concerned with the finishing of the interior? In Albertian terms this seems unlikely, since he strongly advocates that sculpture be installed only at the end of the building campaign (Alberti 1988, IX, viii, 312 [845]). Does he show a construction pause (Alberti 1988, III, x, 76 [219])? Does the continuing work tell us that in a temple, for instance, the work of ornament is never finished, or does Piero portray only the first building of what will be a great city?

[21] Piero was closely associated with Cosimo Rosselli, Botticelli, Filippino Lippi, Giuliano da Sangallo and Bertoldo, all of whom depicted or planned buildings copiously enriched with classicizing sculpture.

[22] Kemp (1991e) sees Sangallesque elements in the Sarasota palace, but this is difficult to demonstrate. For the close stylistic ties between Piero di Cosimo and the Sangallo, see Degenhart 1955: 172, 178, 248, 254.

[23] I am grateful to Martin Kemp for his acute observations on the picture's perspectival discrepancies.

[24] See Barriault 1985: 173-174 et passim for examples of the relationship of spatial placement and narrative order.

[25] Like Vitruvius, Alberti had begun with a general discussion of locality, site and materials for building. Piero does not insist upon his landscape but perhaps its forests, mountains, a plain (and perhaps a lake?) minimally fulfill Alberti's requirements for a locality that is salubrious as well as rich in materials needed for architecture. The building is set on a sandy building site: leveled terrain already set off from nature. It is already an Albertian *area* in the sense of building site.

A special mark of the architect's ingenuity is his ability to design a hoist for a stone or a statue (III, vi, 70; VI, vi, 164; vii, 168-169, 172-173; IX, x, 316 [199, 473, 481, 487, 491, 857]). As a bronze statue is lifted into place, a party of cavalry watch as their captain and his troops approach from the right. The architect can also construct "ballistic engines and machines of war ... the skill and ability of the architect have been responsible for more victories than have the command and foresight of any general ... And what is more important, the architect achieves his victory with but a handful of men and without loss of life" (Prologue, 4 [11]).

Like a general, the architect must also marshal his artisan troops. Leon Battista Alberti knows that the success of an architectural campaign ultimately depends on the quality of the artisans (Prologue, 5 [15]; I, iv, 38 [109].[26] Indeed, the emphasis on engineering and production may also suggest the widespread, ultimately Vitruvian idea (Vitruvius 1970: 21, I, i, 15) that the success of the building depends on technical competence as much as on design or precious materials.

Most of all, the architect depends on the *adstitores*, literally assistants, or foremen who direct the artisan troops and see that the architect's orders are properly carried out. At the center of the Sarasota composition, a horse and rider gallop straight at us near the central perspectival axis.

His important placement, his sense of urgent mission and the perspectival brio with which he is depicted suggest that he comes on an errand from one of these invaluable foremen (perhaps the mounted figures pointing to the palace) "zealous, circumspect and strict ... [who] supervise the necessary work with diligence, application, and their constant presence" (IX, xi, 318 [865]) to bring order and dispatch to the work.

Vasari thought it significant that Piero di Cosimo loved to paint horses (Vasari 1962-87, IV: 62), and the latter play a variety of roles in the Sarasota picture. They have great utility as on-site transport, but they may also indicate rank, and the background cavalcade suggests that the painter shared Leonardo's passion for the horse as the fusion of proportional beauty and dynamic vital energy.[27] The gem-like antique profile view and mettlesome gait of the steed on the right[28] suggest that he and his riders have some special status.[29] Alberti recommends that architects and many craftsmen from other places be brought together for their various skills (II, iii, 38 [109]). The horseman brings a boy, wearing the distinctive turban of an apprentice. Through experience, the greatest teacher of architects (IX, x, 316 [857]), the *garzone* will learn the elements of his master's craft. The larger rider wears a hat customary for architects and sculptors,[30] but his tunic is unique in the picture both for its brilliant green and its arrangement *all'antica* with one shoulder bared. There is an aura here of the mythic craftsman as a presiding and teaching deity—and he may hold the key to the identity of the building.[31]

Alberti repeatedly cites nature's construction of animals as the model for building. Giordano Ruffo's Quattrocento treatise on the horse (Baxandall 1972: 37, 156)[32] defines it as a living architecture whose beauty and utility reside in the perfect relation of its parts to the whole. Horses also had this special meaning for Alberti in his history of world architecture. In Asia, great wealth produced huge buildings. Greek ingenuity added proportion and symmetry; in a word, beauty. But it was the special genius of the Italians to unite beauty with utility as in the horse. "[The Romans] realized that where the shape of each member looked suitable for a particular use, so the whole animal itself would work well in that use. Thus they found that grace of form could never be separated or divorced from suitability of use" (VI, iii, 158 [453]).

Thus the horse is Leon Battista Alberti's image of *partitione*: the appropriateness and correspondence of all the parts (I, ix, 23 [65]), as well as of the symbolic historical evolution toward perfection to which modern Italian architects are heir. It is not clear that the horses in the Sarasota painting deliberately symbolize such ideas but they are generally congruent with them.

In the middle ground of the painting, on the right, a huge column lies on the ground. Alberti had considered the column both as an element of structure and as the prime architectural ornament. Is the column in the picture unfinished or an antique spoil from which the secrets of proportions can be learned (VI, iv, 160 [461-463])? It is certainly much too large for the palace.[33] Its size seems to reflect its conceptual importance.

A dignified figure in a long black robe and cap points to the column with a pair of compasses, in consultation with a man dressed in a short coat and red hose and hat who wields a set square. At his feet is a box with instruments. The mallet near his foot suggests they may be chisels. Since a similarly clothed man nearby hauls a barrow, the red-hatted figure is perhaps a mason or a *mensuratore*? Who is his interlocutor? Would the architect himself be compositionally so insignificant?[34] Does his long robe suggest that he is an intellectual consultant of some type? Does his set-square suggest that he is a geometer? In any event,

Piero di Cosimo
The Building of a Double Palace
detail of center of scene
ca. 1515-20
Sarasota, The John and Mable Ringling Museum of Art
Cat. no. 86

[26] Alberti refers both to "*periti artificii manu*" and the "*fabri.*"
[27] For Leonardo's interest in horses, Kemp 1981: 204-205.
[28] Leonardo (Kemp 1981: 63) depicted horses from several viewpoints, and this practice is also used by Uccello and other earlier painters of horses like Pisanello. The profile horse is contrasted with the rider seen head-on at the middle of the picture.
[29] Like the messenger, they ride bareback and barefoot, while the more dignified horsemen in the left appear to use stirrups.
[30] Piero's portrait in the Rijksmuseum of Giuliano da Sangallo (Bacci 1976, pl. XXXII) shows him wearing a similar hat. The Sarasota *scarpellini*, however, sport similar headgear.
[31] The garment resembles the Greek *exomis*, but, since it leaves the right arm bare, it can be appropriate for a worker both in antique and Renaissance contexts. The hat could also be appropriate for an antique traveler or foreigner. Could they be Daedalus and Icarus, builders of the palace of Minos? The lame Vulcan rides, sometimes with Dionysus but on a donkey or mule. Cheiron as the teaching centaur would presumably need no headgear. But the sculptor on the left wears similar headgear. It also fits into a Medicean context. Mercury, Albertian protector of fora and of the arts, does not ride.
[32] My thanks to Richard Krautheimer for reminding me of Alberti's *De equo animante*.
[33] The building recalls Alberti's constant warning to avoid grandiosity and to attempt only the possible and fitting (Alberti 1988, IX, viii, 312 [845]; II, ii, 35 [101]; IX, i, 292 [783]).

the two men exemplify the complementary relation of theory to practice (or mind and hand?). For both, measurement, proportion and understanding of the Vitruvian orders are of prime concern.

This pair of consultants, or others like them, can also be glimpsed in the background. Alberti constantly reiterates the crucial importance of asking the advice of experts at every phase of the project, to avoid blame, harvest the fruit of learned opinion as a writer does and, above all, to gain reputation and fame (II, i, 34, 35; iii, 37; iv, 38, 39; VI, iii, 49; IX, vii, 313; x, 317; xi, 319 [99, 101, 107, 111, 165, 847, 859–863, 867]). The architect must understand many matters but cannot and should not try to be a specialist in all of them (IX, x, 317 [859]; Krautheimer 1969a: 323, 326). This is a decisive departure from Vitruvius, who makes the architect expert in all things. For Alberti, in fact, the surest path to failure and opprobrium is for the architect to take responsibility for every aspect and detail of the work. Delegation is difficult and frustrating, but the architect should let the specialists do their work unimpeded (IX, xi, 318 [865]). Dignity and prudence dictate that the architect remain a controlling spectator, above and outside the building site like the stage manager of a spectacle (Jarzombek 1989: 154–155, sees this as a problem). Perhaps this problematic distancing explains why he is not a real protagonist in the Sarasota painting.

In contrast, stonecutters bulk large in the painting's visual hierarchy. They are more raggedly dressed than the pair discussing the column, as befits a less intellectual, more

Piero di Cosimo
The Building of a Double Palace
detail of work under way in middle ground
ca. 1515-20
Sarasota, The John and Mable Ringling Museum of Art
Cat. no. 86

34 Filarete depicts himself as a sculptor in such a short coat but carries dividers (Seymour 1966, pl. 55b). Alberti himself wears such clothes in the portrait drawing in the Biblioteca Nazionale, Rome (Jarzombek 1989: 116, fig. 6). For the short tunic, see Filarete's frieze of the sculptor and his assistants on the doors of St. Peter's. For the set-square as the symbol of the architect, see the tomb of Hughes Libergier, in Panofsky 1964, fig. 205 (my thanks to Jonathan Alexander for this reference).

[35] Vasari's fresco in the Palazzo Vecchio depicting the construction of S. Lorenzo also shows such a capital near the stonemason (Micheletti 1979, fig. on page 8).

[36] For Alberti's belief that trabeated construction and porticoes also belong to the highest ornaments of buildings, see below, note 49.

[37] Rykwert 1988: 393 n. 75 notes Alberti's use of the Composite order on the Tempio Malatestiano facade. For the Composite order in the Renaissance, see Onians 1981; Günther and Thoenes 1985.

[38] Portoghesi 1966, II: 586 n. 1 (VII, viii) mentions the Arch of Titus as an example of the antique Composite; but sketchbooks like those of Giuliano da Sangallo are full of them, even including the order of the Florence Baptistery.

[39] Francesco Colonna 1964, I: 46, 91; II: 83, n. 1; uses the term "composto" as the equivalent of *concinnitas*, the term which Alberti had used to define the basis of beauty. For Colonna, in

physical task (*vide* Leonardo's *Paragone*, Kemp 1989: 38-39). In Albertian terms, however, the work of sculptors is ornament. It is subsequent to the tasks of construction and brings the building to ultimate perfection.

In the left foreground, two carvers (a master and his assistant?) work on a large block of quarried stone. To the right lies a finished Composite capital. It refers, conceptually, to the ornaments of Vitruvian architecture and also to one side of the *scarpellino*'s craft.[35] Two youths further back carve out a cornice, which is less demanding work of the same type. Is the capital a model from which others will be made? Its square neck destines it for a pier like those of the loggia behind,[36] though it is not clear that the capitals are of the same order. Vitruvius does not specifically mention Composite capitals, but Alberti is the first author to theorize what he must have seen on Roman, medieval and Brunelleschian buildings.[37] He picks it out as the culminating achievement in the history of the architectural orders. He sees a progress in ornament from the Doric to the Ionic, leading to the most elegant, the Corinthian. This progression leads up to the invention of the native "Italic" capital, which exceeds all others because it combines "all the ornament of the other three" (VII, vi, 201; viii, 209 [565, 567, 585]).[38]

In more general Albertian terms, the Italic (Composite) capital is also superior because it unifies the greatest number of elements; thus it is an example of *compositio*; the highest and most synthetic activity of architect or painter (Baxandall 1971: 130, 136-137).[39]

The block beside the capital seems dark for marble, but its rectangular format, repeated

Piero di Cosimo
The Building of a Double
Palace
*detail of figures in foreground
ca. 1515–20
Sarasota, The John and Mable
Ringling Museum of Art
Cat. no. 86*

in the stone just arriving by oxcart, suggests that both are meant for statues. To the left, between the two blocks, a white, marble (?) [40] nude lies on the ground. Here is the noblest task for the carver: as sculptor of figures. We cannot see much of the figure except that it is a monumental, white marble standing nude: the characteristics necessary to identify it as sculpture in the antique manner.

The idea that Roman statuary was a guide to nature and, in its ideality, surpassed it in beauty had already been voiced in the Trecento and had become an accepted humanist fact by Alberti's time (Krautheimer and Krautheimer-Hess 1969: 297), but the predeliction for neo-antique proportions and form became a requirement in a Vitruvian context where the human body and the column were reciprocal expressions of a common proportional order. In the painting, however, *figura* and *colonna* are each other's equivalents, also in the specifically Albertian context: both are *ornamenti* of architecture.

In Book VII (i, 189 [529]), Alberti allows the sculptor responsibility for the *lineamenta* of the statue. In his own realm, the sculptor is like the architect, even though ultimately subordinate to him. Indeed, wherever Alberti specifies that statues belong on a building type, he states as a matter of course that the size of figures is determined by the proportions of the building to which they belong. In the painted palace, however, there is no place for marble statues. Yet, the foreground statue is strongly foreshortened [41] and, on an orthogonal near the center of the composition, the figure (or a second one) in the same foreshortened pose, is being carried toward the building.[42] If we follow out this sight line, it arrives at a flash of white, deep in the garden.[43] This seems to be the destination of the other figures still being carved or transported. The other rectangular block being brought to the sculptors in the foreground seems to confirm that they are carving a series of statues and that the painter depicts several of them rather than the same figure in successive moments.

The statue is not a discrete, unique creation but a process of production closely related to the carving of architectural decoration: a normative, standardized image designed to be repeated at will.

Leon Battista Alberti cannot decide whether marble or bronze is the nobler material for sculpture but seems to opt for the latter (VII, xvii, 243 [663]). All things being equal, however, he sanctions the use of precious materials (IX, xi, 318 [865]). In his history of sculpture, the use of bronze was a later technological and artistic development, like the Composite capital.

In the painting, do the marble sculptors look up, figuratively as well as literally to the last gilded bronze figures being hoisted into place on the balcony above the loggia? All watch

turn, "concinnitura" is equivalent to "ornamento" (I: 91) used in respect to an encrustation of gems. Interestingly, Baxandall 1971: 88, cites Guarino Guarini's reference to carving a statue as a metaphor of *compositio*.
[40] Alberti says stone gets dark when wet and suggests wetting marble before carving (Alberti 1988, II, vii, 48 [139]; III, x, 76 [219]). The statue could perhaps also be the hard white calcareous tufa useful for statues and all other purposes because of its durability and color (II, ix, 49 [137–139]). Perhaps this stone would be dark or darken when wet. Alberti concurs with Vitruvius that the architect must make the best use of available materials even when the best ones are not available (II, xii, 58 [165]; Long 1980: 157).
[41] Since viewpoint determines how we see the statue, the sculptor must be aware of perspective and optics, not just of carving techniques. The foreshortening of three-dimensional objects in space is a basic subject for all writers on perspective, and the work of Alberti's friends Ghiberti and Donatello show that sculptors realized the need to adjust their figures in respect to the spectator's viewpoint. This is mooted by Pomponius Gauricus and is taken for granted by Vasari. Strangely enough, however, Alberti says nothing concrete on this topic in any of his treatises. In *De sculptura* and in *De re*, the proportions of figural sculpture are treated in a purely objective fashion.
Depictions of such supine figures appear in Renaissance painting, as demonstrations of perspectival skill; but they are unusual, if only for reasons of decorum. They occur in *Resurrections* or battle scenes to denote death or unconsciousness (Alexander 1983: 133-134). Does Piero di Cosimo's sculpture take on life only once it is associated with the architecture for which it was made? Both carvers look away from their work and up at the building as though they knew that the destination of their work on the architecture will determine the proportions of the sculpture.
[42] The departing statue is identical with the foreground figure, so they cannot be plaster models. Since yet another rectangular block is being brought to

94

Piero di Cosimo
The Building of a Double Palace
detail of stonecutters at work
ca. 1515–20
Sarasota, The John and Mable Ringling Museum of Art
Cat. no. 86

the sculptors in the foreground, it is likely that the figures are part of a series carved of this marble or stone.

[43] Alberti describes such gardens with high hedges, (e.g., IX, iv, 300 [809]) and advocates the use of garden statues. He will even tolerate dwarves and grotesques (Alberti 1988, IX, iv, 300 [809]), provided they are not obscene. Such statues inhabit a conceptual limbo; they are freestanding but, as multiples, are staffage figures.

[44] The frieze cornucopias belong to the vocabulary of antique grotesque as recorded in Giuliano da Sangallo's sketchbooks, but were also familiar emblems of Ceres, Virtue, Abundance and related concepts. For that matter, the cornucopia can refer to the Augustan zodiacal sign of Capricorn. Depending on the date of the Sarasota panel, the cornucopia may signal Medici connections. See Cox-Rearick 1984: 214.

There are even consonances between details of the painting and Albertian views of ornament if one wishes to see them. Messer Battista approved statues on roofs and delighted in temples whose cornices were crowned with lights (Alberti 1988, VII, xii, 229 [631]). His exemplum of magnificent ornament teetering on the brink of excess is the golden torch-bearing statues described by Lucretius (IX, i, 292 [781]). Francesco Colonna had coined the word "splendifera" for torch-bearing statues in the *Hypnerotomachia Poliphili* (Colonna 1964: 336). Piero's statues do show forth the splendor of the patron, and the light of the architect's *ingegno*. If the figures in the Sarasota panel do bear torches, they could make an apt if fortuitous embodiment of Albertian ornament as the bringer of *lux* to architecture.

[45] Alanus de Insulis 1855, col. 453.

[46] Alberti places this ekphrasis in the discussion of ornament for temples, but it is difficult to know how the scenes mention relate to them.

[47] Daniele Barbaro was to praise Vitruvius for demonstrating all stages of the progress of an individual building from construction to completion (Long 1980: 188). The Sarasota painter, of course, fails to do this but may have had such ideas in mind.

as the architect's ingenuity puts in place the ultimate element of magnificence that makes the building complete and perfect.

The bronze figures are draped elegantly *all'antica* and are very similar one to another. They are remarkable not as individual works but in the aggregate. The statues are made of precious materials, and their number makes their putative cost immense. They hold what may be cornucopias, a motif explicit in the loggia frieze.

These familiar ancient attributes of abundance and *virtù* may have specific iconographical meaning[44] but, more broadly, they reiterate the abundance of the patron's wealth and the Albertian requirement for *copia* of ornament.

Conclusions

It now becomes possible to see Piero's painting as a celebration of ornament and as a metaphor of architecture and of all the visual arts in Albertian terms.

Writing in the twelfth century, Alanus de Insulis described the work of the Creator "like the skillful architect of a stupendous production, like the industrious workman, of a wonderful work, fashioning the form of this earthly palace."[45] By the fifteenth century, the Divine Architect had become an argument for the worth of human architecture and architects and the venerable topos has devolved in the Sarasota picture to a genre scene of artisan labor. Nonetheless, the definition of Creation specifically as the realization of the Ideal through work in the world of matter and practice, still resonates both in Alberti's treatise and in the painting.

Leon Battista Alberti's equation of practice with ornament allows us to see the Sarasota painting in these terms. The square-piered porticos and throngs of statues pertain to ornament but so do the cutting of planks and hauling of stone, since all are images of practice for a particular site. In fact, Alberti's broad definition included even the human uses to which a building is put: he adduces a wealth of examples such as "a plain thick with troops and their triumphal banners; a forum crowded with elders wearing civic dress and other such scenes" (VII, xiii, 229 [629]) which recall the richness of visual incident in the Sarasota painting.[46]

Like *spalliera* paintings by Piero, the Sarasota panel seems to allude to the historical progress of the arts as well as their progress, in conceptual terms, from structure to ornament. In our picture, however, all these dimensions are presented, simultaneously, in terms of the relation of the parts to the whole.[47] At the same time, the Sarasota painter depicts

Foundry of Alessio Beccaguto
Bernardino Arrigoni (attrib.)
Model for bricks
1554
Mantua, Museo Civico di
Palazzo Te
Collezione Gonzaghesca
Cat. no. 108

the conceptual qualities and functions of ornament. Decorum and variety, partition and symmetry, composition and magnificence, are embodied in the double building, its elements and its copious sculpture. The diversity of types, ages and activities themselves provides Albertian *varietà*. The importance given to sculpture signals its importance as ornament. Perhaps Alberti's commitment to statues as the premier mode of sculpture explains why only statuary and not reliefs appear in the Sarasota panel. Actually, Alberti praises the use of reliefs on ancient buildings and he prefers them to painting as a decoration for modern architecture. Reliefs, like other sculpture, can teach the painter *rilievo* (Alberti 1972, 101) but nonetheless they lack the powers of imitation and fiction reserved for paintings and remain, in his theoretical construction, a lesser category.[48] In turn, the work scenes with their diversity of types, ages and actions develop the ideal of *varietà* into the domain of *historia*.[49]

The picture thus mobilizes the powers special to the art of painting on behalf of architecture. Pictorial perspective is the master principle that rationalizes the depiction of the building but it also determines the relation of image to spectator when the picture is installed in the actual room for which it was painted. Whether or not the perspectival split between building and foreground figures was intended to do so, it brings the dimension of practice to the viewer's immediate attention.[50]

As Alberti explains, the only human concern more urgent than building is virtue (I, vi, 18 [51]); but evidently the patron can have both. The construction of lavishly ornate buildings increases the patron's status and reputation. It can make him seem more politically and socially powerful than he is, while he provides the greatest good for the greatest number (Prologue, 2, 3 [5]; see Rykwert et al. 1988: 367 n. 12). The Sarasota painter is careful to show women and children and food as well as men of different social classes. Since the patron gives moral and economic support to the many artisans and crafts which architecture requires, he encourages their development and the progress of civilization. Indeed, Alberti does not hesitate to say that only a rich patron can afford the investment in materials, skill and organization to turn their castles in the air into buildings of requisite dignity and magnificence (IX, xi, 318 [865-867]).

Equally important, the patron must have enough understanding of architecture to chose a good architect and to appreciate the range of his skills, if only because professional dignity forbids that the latter make the first move (IX, xi, 318 [863]).

Like Alberti's *De pictura* (Baxandall 1971: 124-127), however, the Sarasota *storia* also seems to have a broader audience in mind.[51] The allusive and symbolic mode of visual discourse suggests the painter was addressing himself to the learned, but it is well to remember that Florentines in general were given to allegories and puzzles. A knowledge of the theory and practice of architecture is valuable even for others than patrons of buildings. (Baxandall 1971: 126-129 and passim for the authoritative account of the humanist audience. See also Krautheimer 1969a: 321; Jarzombek 1989: 152-155, 178.) Architecture is of interest to cultivated persons "in ciascuna aetate," in particular to

[48] A degree of *varietà*, an extension of ornament (Rykwert 1988: 426), is a quality desirable in buildings; but its power to confer eloquence on visual rhetoric make it essential to *historia*, the privileged domain of painting. In contrast, Alberti defines the highest task of sculpture as the statue, not the narrative relief as consistency might have prescribed. Thus, *compositione*, the harmonization of many figures, the highest quality of history painting, is vouchsafed only in lesser degree to the sculptor whose paradigmatic task is defined as the single figure. Statues may acquire a higher level of *compositione* when multiplied and symmetrically ordered in an architectural context. Then, conversely, they confer the ultimate degree both of *varietà* and *compositione* by perfecting the building. We have come full circle. *Varietà* has a limited place in sculpture.

[49] The figural scenes allow reprises and variations of these themes. Alberti had picked out the horse as the metaphor of compartition, which he describes as the domain of ornament as a whole (Alberti 1988, VII, i, 189 [529]). The Italic capital marks the culminating development of ornament. Its combination of the other orders makes it to ornament what *compositione* is to architecture as a whole: the highest unity. If the capitals being carved correspond to those of the loggia, the same can be said for the building. For the value assigned to trabeated porticoes and frame piers, see I, x, 25 [73]; VII, vi, 200 [563].

[50] Barriault 1985: 59 n. 22, 89, 154 on such effects in other *spalliere*.

[51] On the audiences intended for *De pictura*, Baxandall 1971: 122-129; Wright 1984: 52-86.

Andrea Pisano
The Art of Building
and Architecture
14th cent.
Florence, Museo dell'Opera di
S. Maria del Fiore

⁵² My thanks to Caroline Elam for discussing the interaction of patron and architect in these commissions and for adducing Giuliano da Maiano and Baccio Pontelli as examples of architects who designed *intarsie*. For the artistic and patronage context from which perspective *intarsie* arose, see Haines 1983.

⁵³ See note 55 below for the unity of the arts; also notes 17, 18. Zeri (1973a) attributes the Borghese *Solomon* panel and ours to the architect Aristotile da Sangallo; however Degenhart 1955: 178, 248, 254 closely associated Piero di Cosimo with sketchbooks and drawings by Giuliano da Sangallo. In theory, an architect could have set up the perspective of the palace for the painter, but this seems too complicated for such a small commission.

⁵⁴ Thus Lorenzo de' Medici's reference to the pleasures to be had from paintings of "... buildings and foreshortenings and proportions of perspective ..." quoted and discussed by Barriault 1985: 69.

⁵⁵ As usual this agenda is most blatant and reiterated in Filarete, who continually harangues his Sforza patron in this sense. The Florentine artist writes that the patron should treat the architect like a wife (Alberti 1972, 43), and he repeatedly adduces the story of Alexander and Dinocrates toward the same point (45-46, 52, 378-379). Baxandall 1971: 60, 104, 118, 130-131, traces Alberti's theme of the unity of the arts under *disegno* to Horace and Petrarch. Cennini and Ghiberti make the same point.

friends and practitioners of the arts (Long 1980: 117-122, 202, citing Cesariano). Altogether, the Sarasota painting emerges as, literally and figuratively, a work of edification: a visual lesson, made agreable through its variety of exempla, on architecture and the role of the architect.

The paintings of perspectival cityscapes offered patrons a compelling new model of the power of theory to create an ideal society, but the element of practical realization was only implied. In contrast, depictions of crafts in the fourteenth and early fifteenth centuries, or even of building construction, were primarily images of practice in which the existence of theory was only hinted at by the presence of instruments like the compass and square. Ultimately, the oddities and awkwardnesses of the Sarasota panel result from the combination of these two largely separate visual traditions. By doing so, however, the painter communicated the central message of Alberti's treatise, that realization of theory depends on skillful practice. The painter, in turn, enriched the ideal architectural depiction with a new rhetorical and persuasive dimension. He transformed the genre into an active invitation to the patronage of real buildings.

Some caution may nonetheless be warranted before we interpret the surviving architectural *spalliere* too narrowly as the architect's exhortation to patrons of architecture. It is possible that the painters of the Baltimore and Urbino panels were also architects by profession or worked from their designs. The best *intarsiatori* often practiced as architects.⁵² It need not be assumed, however, that all *intarsie* or other perspectival architectural depictions were designed in this way.⁵³ It might also be asked whether the patron or learned friends of patron or architect did not provide the impetus for these depictions.⁵⁴ In any event, as ideal cityscapes entered the artisan repertoire and were produced in a variety of materials and with differing levels of competence, they may sometimes have signified little more than fashionable modern ornament.

By their rigorous perspective, rational lighting and meticulous rendering, these images nonetheless proclaim to patrons, practitioners and cultivated amateurs the scientific basis of all the visual arts. This was, of course, a fundamental enterprise of Renaissance writing on the arts as well as the leitmotif for Vitruvius and Alberti.⁵⁵ Both the painter and the architect, and the sculptor as well, are broadly educated intellectual creators with insight into the order of divine creation. At the same time they are skilled professionals whose practical skills make possible the realization of their own ideals and those of the patron, in the realm of the senses.

In *De re aedificatoria*, Alberti championed the essential unity of the arts and emphasized that the architect be deeply versed in painting (IX, x, 317-318 [859-863]), yet he also insisted on the differences between architecture and painting. As an architect Alberti expects to show his patrons "fine drawings"—and drawing is, for him, an essential preliminary tool of design. But the painter draws to study light, shadow and the illusion of relief (qualities best learned from sculpture). The architect's working drawings, on the contrary, shun all illusion and are concerned with lineaments and the "calculated standards" derived from the ground plan (II, i, 34 [99]).

Therefore, the architect's essential instrument is the three-dimensional scale model. Alberti says that models should be used both to establish the design and to aid throughout construction of a building. They may be "plain and simple," although they evolve in size and detail to include sculpture. Under no circumstances, however, should presentation models be "colored and lewdly dressed with the allurement of painting" (34), for this is seductive fiction; a mark both of conceit and deceit (II, i, 34, 35 [99]; 316-318 [859-863]).

The powers of illusion that disqualify painting for the architect, however, recommended it to Alberti as the author of *De pictura*. Alberti's God is not an architect but a painter. "Is it not true that painting is the mistress of all the arts or their principal ornament? If I am not mistaken, the architect took from the painter architraves, capitals, bases, columns and pediments and all the other fine features of building. The stonemason, the sculptor and all the workshops and crafts of artificers are guided by the rule and art of the painter" (Alberti 1972, II: 61-63).

This concern with the *paragone*, or the theoretical hierarchy of the arts, may also be reflected in the Sarasota painting. The hegemony of painting is based on its universality. Painting can imitate nature more fully than architecture and sculpture and can even imitate these other arts through its superior powers of illusion. In these terms, a perspectival depiction of architecture can be a statement about the primacy of painting.

The mastery of perspective required to represent the architecture is itself a demonstration of the painter's art. The emphasis on sculpture in the Sarasota panel would also fit into the context of the *paragone* and the Albertian conceptual milieu. Sculptural ornament, we remember, was the culminating element of architecture and corresponded to its highest category, delight or beauty. Alberti recommends his discussion of ornament specially to painters, for they are the most "exacting seekers of delight" (VII, i, 189 [529]). Indeed, ornament transcends the imitation of nature by means of its artificial inventions (IX, vii, 310 [839]). By implication, at least, ornament can be considered a metaphor of art itself. The Sarasota painting thus focuses on the highest concerns of architecture and can even counterfeit the full sculptural decoration it requires but all too often is denied. Through perspective, illusion and color the painter can claim to convey the complete vision of the architect's ideas to the patron even more fully than a three-dimensional model.[56] Perhaps the curious reduction or even absence of the figure of the architect in the picture accords with such ideas.

Alberti had recommended sculpture to train the painter's eye in representing *rilievo*, and Leonardo had advised the painter to study architecture.[57] Ultimately, however, they agree that only painting can supply what architecture and even sculpture lack; the full eloquence of *historia*. Thus the painting, just because it is one, can imply that it is the painter who best pleads the architect's case to patrons and to society at large.

Perhaps then, we might interpret the Sarasota scene, more generally, despite its pictorial awkwardness, as an attempt to gain for visual language something of the conceptual and rhetorical power of text.[58] Many of the *spalliera* painter's images have parallels with literary texts about architecture, whose authors—and others equally well known—also wrote about the place of architecture, as well as painting, in the theoretical hierarchy of the visual arts. Thus it seems significant that the tropes of ancient and modern rhetoric on the universality of painting recall so many elements and juxtapositions in the Sarasota picure and, indeed, its basic scenario.

As in so many other ways, Leonardo's praise of painting incorporated and summed up the discourse of the preceding centuries. For him, painting surpasses all the works of man because it is concerned with the noblest sense, vision. "Now do you not see that the eye embraces the beauty of all the world?" It has "generated architecture, perspective and divine painting. Oh excellent above all other things created by God!" (Kemp 1989: 20–21). Leonardo addresses the same call to consider the wonderful works of nature and of man, specifically to the painter: "Do you not see how many different animals and trees ... there are, the diversity of mountainous regions and plains ... cities, public and private buildings, machines designed to benefit mankind, various costumes, decorations (ornament) and arts? All these things have a claim to be of equal use and value to him whom you would call a good painter" (Kemp 1989: 201).[59]

In its modest way, the "piccola storia," in Sarasota, takes up this great challenge.

Acting on Alberti's advice that one should consult experts and friends at all phases of the work, I have incurred formidable debts of gratitude to Richard Krautheimer, Caroline Elam, Juergen Schulz, Jonathan Alexander, and Henry Millon, who read the manuscript and made invaluable comments, as well as to Eve Harrison, Martin Kemp, Gunter Kopcke, Marvin Trachenberg, and Mrs. Paul E. Geier. My warmest thanks go to James Ackerman and to the graduate students in our joint seminar on Renaissance Criticism at the Institute of Fine Arts in 1992. I also know the value of Alberti's insight on the crucial importance of worthy *adstitores*. I am much obliged to my assistant, Louis Waldman, for his research skills as well as for the "zeal and constant presence" which he and Matthew Horner brought to the enterprise.

Bernardo Butinone (?)
A Palace under Construction, *illumination from* Trattato d'Architettura, *by Filarete 1488–89*
Venice, Biblioteca Nazionale Marciana
MS. Lat. cl. VIII, 2 (-2796) c. 5r., incipit
Cat. no. 87

[56] In Book II, i, 33 [97] Alberti says the architect should make "*modus et pictura.*" While translators render this as "drawings and sketches," is it possible that "*pictura*" could have been understood as "painting"?

[57] (To avoid errors in your own work), "first see to it that you are an accomplished perspectivist. Then acquire a thorough knowledge of the proportions of men and other animals and, additionally, become a good architect ..." (Through draftsmanship, painting) "teaches the architect how to make his buildings convey pleasure to the eye" (Kemp 1989: 45, 203).

[58] For the equivalence of verbal and painted *historia*, VII, x, 220 [609]. See also Farago 1991, particularly 33-34.

[59] Bacci 1976: 5 cites this passage in another context. Alberti had already evoked a very similar image of variety and abundance in the painting of *historia* (Alberti 1972, 40, 79).

Appendix: Toward a Checklist of Construction Scenes in Renaissance Art

Spinello Aretino, *Foundation of Alessandria della Paglia by Pope Alexander III*, 1317. Goldthwaite 1980: 137.
Florentine, *Sant'Umilita Building a Church*, 1341. Goldthwaite: 134.
Benozzo Gozzoli, *Tower of Babel*, 1470-71. Camposanto, Pisa. Lagaisse 1934, pl. XLV.
Ghirlandaio, *St. Clement Condemned to Work in a Quarry*. Goldthwaite 1980: 226.
Antoniazzo Romano (attrib.), *Construction of the Hospital under Sixtus IV*, Rome, S. Spirito in Sassia.
Piero di Cosimo, *Building of a Double Palace* (cat. no. 86).
Apollonio di Giovanni, *Meeting of Aeneas and Dido*. Florence, Bib. Riccardiana, MS. 492. For a cassone panel variant, see Callman 1974, pl. 44.
Pesellino, *Construction of the Temple of Jerusalem*. Goldthwaite 1980: 149.
Francesco del Cossa, *Extinguishing of a Fire*, Vatican, Pinacoteca.
Alvise Vivarini, *St. Peter Martyr Healing the Leg of a Young Man*, New York, Metropolitan Museum of Art. Zeri 1973a, pl. 100.
Andrea Mantegna, *Landscape* (detail of Camera degli Sposi), 1472-74. Palazzo Ducale, Mantua.
Sodoma, *St. Benedict Appearing to Two Monks*, 1505-08. Goldthwaite 1980: 153.
Memorial to Mule Who Collaborated in the Building Works of the Pitti Courtyard. Palazzo Pitti, Florence. Vodoz 1942: 57.
Andrea Pisano, *Architecture*, Museo dell'Opera, Florence.
Apollonino di Giovanni, *The Walls of Carthage*, Yale University, New Haven.
Mantegna, *Christ as Man of Sorrows*, 1489, Copenhagen.
Mantegna, *Madonna delle Cave*, Uffizi, Florence.
Raphael, *Disputa*, Stanze, Vatican.
Italian School, sixteenth century, pen and wash, *St. Francis Rebuilds the Church of St. Damian*, in *Drawings by Taddeo and Federico Zuccari and Other Artist, from the Collection of the British Rail Pension Fund*, 1990, Sotheby's, N.Y., 80.
Giovanni da Fano, *The Construction of the Tempio Malatestiano in Rimini*, two illustrations for Basino's *Epos Hesperis*, cf. most recently, F. Borsi, *Leon Battista Alberti*, Electa/Rizzoli, New York, 1989, figs. 108, 109.

ANTONII AVERVLINI ARCHITECTI AD
MAGNV ANTONIO ASCVLANO E MATER-
NA LINGVA IN LATINV COVERSA

Vm te prestanti animo pre-
ditum excellentissimo quo-
q; virtutum artiumq; gener
noverim mirifice delectari:
qd preclara ingenia fidelitat:
q; hiis maxime reb; intenta
sunt: quib; nom; imortali-
tatis comparetur, hec me
cum reputas, Mag.ce Petre i
unicum medicorum dec
haud ingratum t futuru
ee existimavi si edificandi roem edificiorum q, om
nium mos & mensuras hiis t lucubrationib; aperire
Id.n. prestantes viros qtum deceat, hinc facile iudica
ri pot. Nam edificando ditissimorum bona mul
tis ipartiuntur: q aut medicare cogentur, aut fame
pirent. Accedit liberalitatis, & Magnificetie nom: qd
diuite prestat imortale. Hec no laus t familieq; tue
no imerito deb& ascribi: &q maxime pri: q profu
sa Mag.ti ceteris iure deb& an poni: qd no assentato
ris nome dictum e. Mirabilia ac excelsa extat, edi
ficia: q tuam & pietissimi pris Mag.ta plane testatu
ac tuum Cosmi q, nom nunq interire patiuntur.
Nam cum prina semper pfuisissima liberalitate ce
tasti. Quid edificia in floretina Vrbe a pre tuo erec
ta comemore: quid ornatissima annuntiate diue
Virginis ediculam: quid alia no mo domi sed fo
ris erecta: Mediolani clarissima sunt Cosimianç o
Mag.ce monumta: Ide q, apd Barbaras natioes lic&
itueri. Vbi nam tepestate nra i priuato uiro tantum
liberalitatis & Mag.te inueneris: Vbi tantu laudis

99

Bernardo Prevedari
Temple Interior
1481
Engraving
Milan, Civica Raccolta Stampe
Achille Bertarelli
Cat. no. 121

1. Villard de Honnecourt
Plan of Cambrai Cathedral
detail

2. Villard de Honnecourt
Interior and Exterior
Elevations of Reims
Chatedral

Christoph Luitpold Frommel Reflections on the Early Architectural Drawings

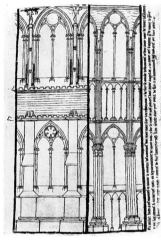

[1] W. Lotz, "Das Raumbild in der italienischen Architekturzeichnung der Renaissance," in *Mitteilungen des Kunsthistorischen Institutes in Florenz* 7 (1956): 193-226; English edition in J. S. Ackerman, H. A. Milllon, W. Chandler Kirwin, eds., *Studies in Renaissance Architecture*, Cambridge (MA) and London 1977: 1-65; R. Schofield, "Leonardo's Milanese Architecture: Career, sources and graphic techniques," in *Achademia Leonardi Vinci* 4 (1991): 111-157.

[2] "Les batisseurs des cathédrales gotiques," ed. R. Recht, Strasbourg 1989: 227ff.; W. Müller, *Grundlagen gotischer Bautechnik*, Munich 1990: 21-34.

[3] H.R. Hahnloser, *Villard de Honnecourt*, Vienna 1935: 65ff., 162ff.

[4] D. Kimpel, R. Suckale, *Die gotische Architektur in Frankreich* 1130-1270, Munich 1985: 227ff.

[5] op. cit.

[6] D. Gioseffi, *Giotto architetto*, Milan 1963.

[7] J. White, *Art and Architecture in Italy 1250 to 1400*, Harmondsworth 1966: 336ff.; Schofield, op. cit.

[8] Müller 1990: 29-34.

[9] B. Degenhardt, A. Schmitt, *Corpus der italienischen Zeichnungen 1300-1450*, Berlin 1968ff., vol. I, cat. 38, 54; Schofield 1991: 128.

Present-day methods of representing architectural projects were for the most part already in use by the start of the sixteenth century. The masters of the Renaissance made use of the triad—plan, elevation and section—as well as various kinds of perspectives, with a degree of virtuosity and precision that has rarely been equaled since.[1] In spite of all the changes in style and technique, this continuity in the methods of design links the architecture of our time to that of the Renaissance; likewise, in ecclesiastical and secular building this tradition has never really come to an end. The study of architectural drawing now reveals that there had never been such continuity between antiquity and the Renaissance, that methods of architectural design had in fact been partially forgotten in the Middle Ages and were developed anew with Gothic architecture.[2]

This process was strictly tied to the general development of architecture. The greatest impetus came from two artistic circles: the High Gothic in northern France, and the Tuscan pre-Renaissance and early Renaissance starting with Giotto. If fairly simple design procedures were sufficient for the architects of Roman buildings, the Gothic style, completely centered on transparency, on structural logic and filigree ornamentation, required an increasingly masterly and precise project. The most beautiful example comes from the cathedrals, recorded by Villard de Honnecourt in about 1230 in his famous sketchbook covering various building sites (figs. 1-3).[3] He not only drew plans, but compared the elevations of the inner and outer wall of Reims Cathedral. No one had ever tried before to find the correspondence between the outer and the inner construction and to bring into close relations all the single elements of the body of the building by means of visual axes and cornices. The horizontal and vertical coordinates appear even more clearly in the few surviving projects of the early Gothic style, such as the superimpositions of Reims, where, in fact, it appears that these coordinates were used by the draftsman as his starting point (fig. 4).[4]

Everything could be represented through an orthogonal projection, but sections and elevations were sufficient for workshop projects and drawings of details. Difficulties arose only when draftsmen tried to represent buildings in three dimensions, as in the illustration of the choir of Reims Cathedral. Perspective techniques were not sufficiently developed for distinguishing at a glance the parts of the building which should have projected toward the observer and those which should have remained in the distance. And where the graphic techniques failed, the architects' creative energy must have reached its limits.

Only through this kind of formation and an improvement of the strictly graphic methods of design could the figure of an architect in the modern sense evolve during the first half of the thirteenth century, where projects to be transmitted to the builder-craftsmen existed independently of the finished building.[5] This growing autonomy of the architect-designer with respect to the craftsmen made it possible, at the end of the fourteenth century, for a painter such as Giotto (1266-1337) to become an eminent architect.[6]

It is significant that Gothic architecture and Gothic design techniques gained a footing only in Milan, the most northern city where northern European architects were always being called in for new tasks (fig. 5).[7] The first creative impetus developed in Tuscany since Florence was by tradition too strongly influenced by late antiquity (to be seen in Florence Baptistery or the church of S. Miniato) to adapt itself unconditionally to the new northern European style. Moreover, Giotto and his contemporaries succeeded, thanks to their new knowledge of the Gothic style, in rediscovering the pictorial space that had been lost at the end of antiquity, by means of a form of classification that was unimaginable before the Gothic style and with rapid strides led to Brunelleschi's central perspective.

These new abilities allowed painters to arrive at more accurate and penetrating images of the plasticity of a building and its inner spaces. In this way, they opened up the road for new kinds of architectural projects, while the *cantieri* in the north remained prisoners of their strictly orthogonal tradition.[8] In his projects for the campanile in Florence, Giotto himself must have gone beyond the strictly linear drawing of the elevation, and have used colors, chiaroscuro, and perhaps even some form of perspective similar to the project for the campanile in Siena of 1350, which followed on directly from the Florentine prototype in stylistic terms as well.[9] The graphic technique corresponded to the character of the project here as it had done with the Gothic style: instead of a filigree skeleton there was a stereometric body; in the place of abstract lines, there was the precious materiality of a consistent surface. Probably these first illusionistic projects preceded even the first architectural models still unknown during the period of High French Gothic, which was then making its triumphal entry in Tuscany.[10] The architectural model must have evolved because of the same need for material and spatial clarity and could have even been the response of the master builders to the illusionism of the painter-architects.[11] Not only did the builder-craftsmen benefit from this new form of illustration, but it also laid the premises for the more active participation of patrons.

This new three-dimensional way of thinking soon spread beyond the Tuscan border. When Antonio di Vincenzo was commissioned to build S. Petronio in Bologna in 1389 he borrowed clearly from the filigree project for Milan Cathedral, whose section was consistent with the plan,[12] (fig. 5) but he also tried to give body to the abstract schema in the area of the base and the capital and in a detail of the external construction to be seen on the verso. However it is not surprising that he turned toward the more simple, more plastic and spacious forms of Florence Cathedral in the final project.

A similar interest in spatial clarity can be observed as early as 1310 in the area of the portal drawn on the elevations for Orvieto Cathedral.[13]

The *cantiere* of Florence Cathedral soon became the hub of research into new design techniques. There was such a confusion of projects and models there in about 1365 that it was decided to destroy all of them, except for the final project.[14] Generally the success of an architectural project was tied exclusively to its feasibility. After a building was completed the drawings of the final project were destroyed; as a result, today there is much written information about the Florence building site dating back to the fourteenth century, but not one drawing.

The drawing dated 1425 by Giovanni di Gherardo da Prato, Brunelleschi's rival and a learned humanist, certainly derives from this tradition—architecture at that time was the province both of scholars and of artists (fig. 6).[15] In order to represent the problem of the curve of the dome—which was first and foremost a structural problem—he used a strictly orthogonal section. He then added a plan, on a smaller scale, with its auxiliary geometrical lines and the whole area of the dome, together with the connecting section and perspective view introduced in the early Trecento. Only by utilizing perspectives and equally pictorial chiaroscuro did he succeed in demonstrating the problems of directing the illumination, which had in the meantime become an equally central component of architectural calculation.

By the start of the fifteenth century, therefore, illusionistic design had not replaced but had been integrated with Gothic orthogonal sections; there was no reason to believe that Brunelleschi and his successors would have given up the orthogonal triad of plan, elevation and section.[16]

Like Giotto, Brunelleschi (1377-1446) had begun his career as a figurative artist interested in the perspective illustration of pictorial space before designing his first buildings.[17] He was the first to achieve a "correct" central perspective of Florence Baptistery and the Piazza della Signoria, and drew illusionistic architectural illustration toward more objective grounds. He brought architecture and painting continually closer, until pictorial space had an architectural structure and architecture became increasingly pictorial, conceived as a subject visible from a fixed viewpoint. This step inaugurated a new phase in architectural drawing. Brunelleschi too—as well as Leonardo—had to analyze the effect and the structural premises of his projects with the help of various plans, sections and perspectives.

According to his biographer, Manetti, during his long sojourn in Rome Brunelleschi utilized new and more precise procedures of representation so as to study and reconstruct together with Donatello various kinds of buildings of antiquity, as well as the methods and techniques used by the ancients for the curvature of vaults, the Vitruvian orders, or musical proportions—pioneering achievements which his pupil Alberti was to take advantage of later on.[18] It is clear that Brunelleschi was proceeding from a classification similar to the one Alberti was to advise artists to use for investigating the human body in his treatise of 1435 on painting.

In the practice of architecture Brunelleschi appears not to have gone beyond strictly orthogonal projects and models, as suggested by the fact that before he departed for a long journey he simply left his master builder on the Loggia degli Innocenti building site an elevation drawn according to the scale and unit of measurement used in Florence at the time, the *braccio piccolo*.[19] In his ensuing projects and models he only prepared the plain body of the building, explaining details by word of mouth—as Manetti says—so that the workers very often had insufficient information. It is quite likely that later on he proceeded in the same way as Michelangelo did, and designed a detail only when the stage of construction made it necessary. There is no doubt that when doing this he used a combination of executive drawings, models of details, and molds because the stonemasons had not yet learnt to master the vocabulary of the ancients.

The strict orthogonality of Brunelleschi's detail projects distinguished them first and foremost from the architecture of Masaccio's *Trinity* (1401-28); that architecture is so stylistically akin

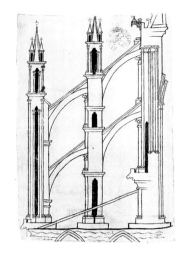

3. *Villard de Honnecourt*
Elevation of Reims Cathedral

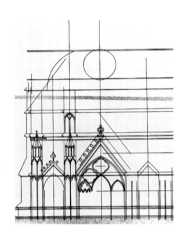

4. *Reims Cathedral*
superimpositions and project

[10] see pp. 318-347.
[11] see pp. 18-73.
[12] Lotz 1956: 194, fig.1.
[13] White 1966: 21ff.
[14] Schofield 1991: 120-131.
[15] H. Saalman, "Giovanni di Gherardo da Prato's Design concerning the Cupola of Santa Maria del Fiore in Florence," in *Journal of the Society of Architectural Historians* 18 (1959): 11-20.
[16] cf. Lotz 1956: 193ff.; P. Tigler, *Die Architekturtheorie des Filarete*, Berlin 1963: 141ff.
[17] A. Manetti, *Vita di Filippo di Ser Brunellesco*, ed. H. Saalman, Pennsylvania State University Press 1970: 43ff.
[18] op. cit.: 51ff.
[19] op. cit.: 97.

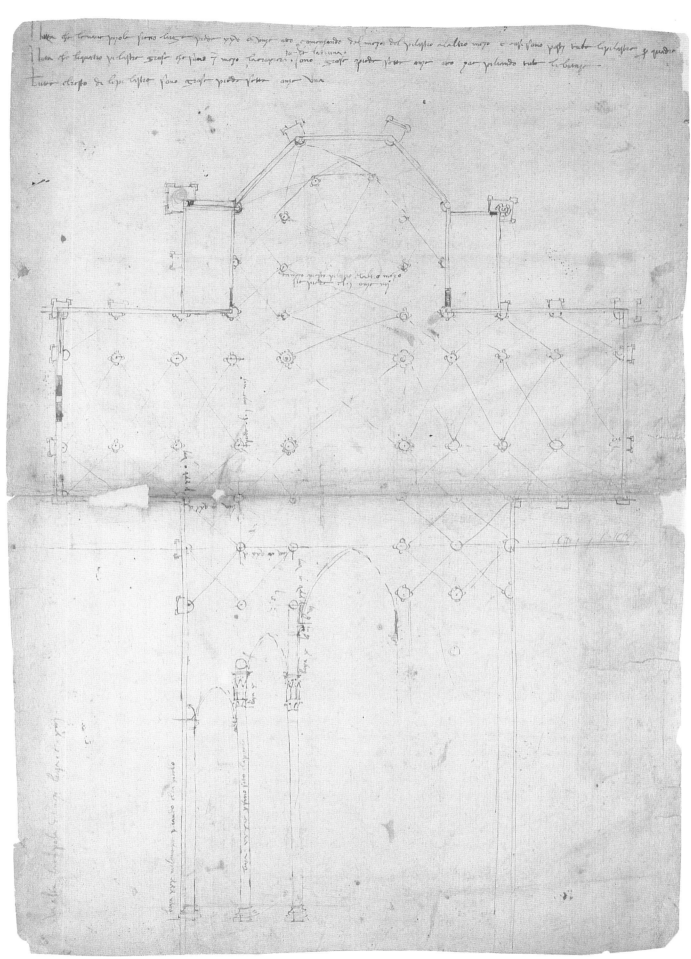

5. Antonio di Vincenzo, Surveys of Milan Cathedral
Bologna, Museo di S. Petronio, cartella 389, no. 1, Cat. no. 6

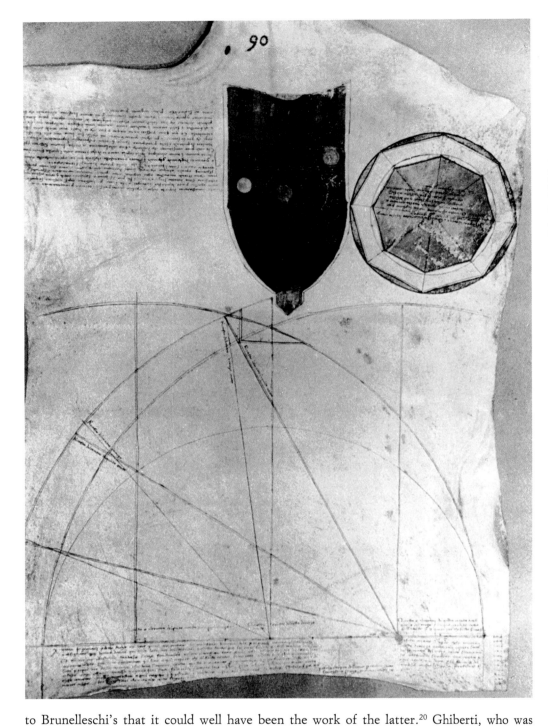

6. *Giovanni di Gherardo Gherardi*
Project of the Illumination of the Dome of Florence Cathedral
Florence, Archivio di Stato Cat. no. 263

to Brunelleschi's that it could well have been the work of the latter.[20] Ghiberti, who was much more active as a sculptor and, all in all, more closely tied to the tradition of the Trecento, is very different, for example, in his project—drawn likewise before 1428—for the Stephanus of Orsanmichele, where he stuck to the principle of the perspective elevation (fig. 7).[21]

In fact it was the painter-architects and sculptor-architects who developed new techniques of representation and established more direct links with the traditions of antiquity. It was no coincidence that Leon Battista Alberti dedicated his treatise on painting in about 1436 to his friend and teacher, Brunelleschi: it described the ancient orders of columns as inventions of painters.[22] If *firmitas* and *utilitas* were the concerns of real master builders, only the painter-architect and the sculptor-architect with their draftsmanship could meet Vitruvius' third prerequisite of *venustas*, beauty, and design the ornament.

The fundamental contrasts between Brunelleschi's and Alberti's buildings must not mask the fact that Alberti (1404–74) was probably the only contemporary to fully understand Brunelleschi's methods of representation and design and to develop them. In his *De re aedificatoria* he advised architects learning the trade to study and carefully analyze all the most important buildings, and to keep them in mind always as models: "*diligentissime spectabit, mandabit lineis, notabit numeris, volet se deducta esse modulis atque exemplaribus; conoscet repetet ordinem locos genera numerosque rerum singularum.*"[23]

[20] E. Battisti, *Filippo Brunelleschi*, Milan 1976: 106ff.
[21] B. Degenhardt, A. Schmitt 1968, vol. I: 293ff., cat. 192.
[22] L. B. Alberti, *On painting and on Sculpture*, ed. C. Grayson, London 1972: 60.
[23] L. B. Alberti, *L'architettura (De re aedificatoria)*, ed. P. Portoghesi, translated G. Orlandi, Milan 1966, IX, 10: 856ff.

7. *Lorenzo Ghiberti*
Project for the Stephanus
Niche at Orsanmichele, Florence
Paris, Musée du Louvre
Cabinet des Dessins, inv. 1231

8. *Agostino di Duccio*
(after Leon Battista Alberti?)
Rimini, S. Francesco
Detail of the Temple
of Minerva
Ark of the Ancestors and
Descendants

[24] op. cit., II, 1: 98ff.
[25] op. cit., II, 1: 96ff.
[26] R. Wittkower, *Architectural Principles in the Age of Humanism*, London 1949: 3ff.; C. L. Frommel, "Kirche und Tempel: Giuliano della Roveres Kathedrale Sant'Aurea in Ostia," in U. Cain, H. Gabelmann, D. Salzmann, eds., *Festschrift für Nikolaus Himmelmann*, Mainz 1989: 491.

Alberti's new classification of antiquity prepared the way for a method of designing architecture that was no less fundamental. With almost polemical rigor, he made a distinction between the orthogonal design procedures which an architect was to follow, and the architectural perspective representation of the painter—certainly because it was increasingly tempting to take patrons by surprise with enticing views of a project.[24] A wooden model again offered the architect greater guarantees that a project would be carried out completely: "*non perscriptione modo et pictura, verum etiam modulis exemplariisque factis asserula*"[25]; only the model could supply the definitive information about site and arrangement, about the thickness of walls and vaults, or about the costs of the construction. Such an exact model however presupposed the triad plan, elevation and section which is why for Alberti the model and the drawings were not alternatives, but complements necessary for the elaboration of the complete project. In utterly separating the elaborated project from its realization, in giving greater importance to the *lineamenta*, or artistic design, Alberti completed the last passage in the process that had been developing since the Gothic style.

Thanks to his profound humanist education and his long sojourn in Rome, Alberti was able to carry the study of antiquity even further than Brunelleschi, and amply denied the difference between antique buildings and contemporary ones in his *De re aedificatoria*.[26] Since he began working as a painter and decorated his first buildings with excellent ornament, he must have been an able draftsman, even though the only drawing known as his so far offers merely a faint idea of his capabilities.[27] In this drawing he placed the various functions of an ancient *thermae* in a square area. It was first and foremost a theoretical exercise, and was perhaps even destined for publication and therefore had little to do with his final projects. He must have prepared later complex works such as S. Andrea in Mantua through careful orthogonal studies which then provided a basis for a model.[28] His "pictorial" drawings of antiquity could have appeared as the backgrounds to the two reliefs by Agostino di Duccio for Sigismondo and Isotta Malatesta's funerary chapels in 1454 (fig. 8).[29]

The seeds of Alberti's teaching germinated only after the turn of the century. However, even if we knew nothing about Brunelleschi's or Alberti's methods of representation, the effects they had are perceivable in the changes in Tuscan art from 1430 onward. The most direct offshoot can be found perhaps in the work of the Florentine sculptor Filarete (ca. 1400-69).[30] As early as 1433-45 Filarete reconstructed Roman monuments and imperial baldachins in the reliefs for the great bronze doors of S. Peter's with a classicizing splendor that cannot be found in either Donatello or Ghiberti, and which returned to the fore only in Alberti's Tempio Malatestiano.[31] Even though Filarete still had some difficulty in fully mastering pictorial space and perspective, his work already showed the influence of Alberti, who was in the service of the pope at that time.

Alberti's ideas are even more in evidence in Filarete's description of the ideal city of Sforzinda, which comprised his own real experiences as the architect of the Duke of Milan.[32] It is significant that Filarete praised most of all Alberti's "disegno, il quale è fondamento e via d'ogni arte che di mano si faccia, e questo lui intende ottimamente, e in geometria e d'altre scienze è intendentissimo" ("design, which is the basis and path to all manual art, and he is very expert at it, and in geometry and other sciences is excellent").[33] With the expression "disegno" Filarete intended the same concept as Alberti's *lineamenta*, meaning development of ideas and not its graphic expression: the graphic technique defined by Alberti with the word *pictura*. Filarete discussed this at another point where he distinguished between a drawing out of scale, "disegno in di grosso" (a rough sketch), and one based on a grid measured in *braccia*, a "disegno proporzionato" (proportioned drawing)[34]—as Alberti did himself in a letter to Lodovico Gonzaga in 1470.[35] He also sent a sketch of an idea for S. Andrea with this letter, adding: "Se ve piasera daro modo de rectarlo in proportione" ("if you like it I will have it drawn correctly in proportion"). From a scale plan Filarete then built a wooden model, the "disegno rilevato" (relief design). Filarete knew the designs for the Palazzo Medici and the Palazzo Rucellai and so also he could have been inspired by Brunelleschi's and Alberti's projects in the way he chose to represent the plan of the palace on fol. 66 recto.[36] In the majority of the remaining plans he included an elevation of the arcades in the medieval manner. While he still had occasional problems with perspective, he drew most walls to be built in perspective, or as a perspective elevation, enhanced with wash, to help his princely patron understand the strictly orthogonal sections. That he was familiar with elevations can be seen, for example, in his proposals for various types of windows.[37]

Alberti's influence, if not his way of representation, can be noted lastly in Filarete's reproductions of ancient kinds of buildings, such as the circus, amphitheater and theater, and of exceptional monuments such as the Colosseum, or of ancient themes such as the system of Castel Sant'Angelo, or the then little-used theater motif.[38]

Although a dilettante, Filarete's contemporary Ciriaco d'Ancona used similar methods of illustration in a virtually orthogonal drawing of the Parthenon, an elevation and perspective elevation of the Temple of Hadrian in Kyzicus; he likewise drew the Basilica of S. Sofia at Constantinople in a bird's-eye view and perspective section.[39] His view of Castel Sant'Angelo gives the impression that he might have discussed it with Filarete.[40]

Francesco di Giorgio (1439-1502)—a generation younger—began his career as a painter and sculptor and only in later life became one of the most sought-after architects and engineers in Italy.[41] He studied and made surveys of ancient monuments as far as Campania and was well-known as a translator of Vitruvius and author of treatises on architecture.[42] In spite of all his scholarship and range of knowledge, of the brilliance of his designs and architectural ingeniousness, he did not live up to Alberti's expectations in his studies of antiquity (fig. 10). None of his surveys could have been transformed into a model that would have stood up to Alberti's criteria.[43] His reproduction of the Colosseum in plan, perspective section and view corresponds to a manner of representation already common before Alberti and it is, in its schematic simplicity, hardly more precise than Filarete's view drawn about thirty years previously (fig. 9).[44]

This limitation can be explained in terms of the backwardness of Siena, Francesco di Giorgio's native town, at the time, and does not occur in the almost contemporary drawings of Il Cronaca and Giuliano da Sangallo, who had absorbed the spirit of Brunelleschi and Alberti in Florence. Il Cronaca (ca. 1458-1508) had probably studied and drawn to scale the most important monuments in Rome and Florence as a youth.[45] According to Vasari, he worked in Antonio del

27 H. Burns, "Un disegno architettonico di Alberti e la questione del rapporto fra Brunelleschi ed Alberti," in *Filippo Brunelleschi. La sua opera e il suo tempo. Proceedings of the International Congress Florence 1977*, Florence 1980: 105ff.; H. Günther, *Das Studium der antiken Architektur in den Zeichnungen der Hochrenaissance*, Tübingen 1988: 105.

28 E.J. Johnson, "S. Andrea in Mantua," thesis, University of New York 1970.

29 J. Poeschke, *Die Skulptur der Renaissance in Italien*, vol. I: *Donatello und seine Zeit*, Munich 1990: 133, pl. 181, with bibliography. Agostino never created another work with such a masterly use of perspective, and no other pictorial background in those decades came so close to the conception of triumphal architecture.

30 W. Lotz 1956: 197ff; P. Tigler 1963.

31 J. Poeschke 1990: 130ff., pl. 176, 177.

32 P. Tigler 1963; *Antonio Averlino detto il Filarete, Trattato di architettura*, ed. A. M. Finoli, L. Grassi, Milan 1972.

33 P. Tigler 1963: 146.

34 P. Tigler 1963: 154ff.

35 L. Fancelli, *Architetto epistolario gonzaghesco*, ed. C. Vasic Vatovic, Florence 1979: 119ff.

36 Filarete, *Trattato*: 227, 255, 695ff., pl. 42.

37 Filarete, *Trattato*: 266, pl. 44.

38 Filarete, *Trattato*: 247ff., 290ff., 33ff., pl. 41, 52, 65, 66.

39 H. Günther 1988: 17ff.

40 I would like to thank U. Nilgen, who is studying Filarete's doors, for mentioning this.

41 H. Günther 1988: 29ff.; P. Fiore, M. Tafuri, eds., catalog of the exhibition (Siena 1993) "Francesco di Giorgio Martini, architetto," Milan 1993.

42 H. Günther, loc. cit.; H. Burns, in ed. P. Fiore, M. Tafuri 1993: 330-357.

43 P. Fiore, "Gli ordini nell'architettura di Francesco di Giorgio," in J. Guillaume, ed., *L'emploi des ordres dans l'architecture de la renaissance. Actes du colloque Tours 1966*, Paris 1992.

44 H. Günther 1988, 33 fig. 22.

45 op. cit.: 66-103, 331ff.

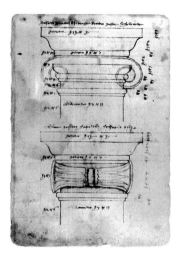

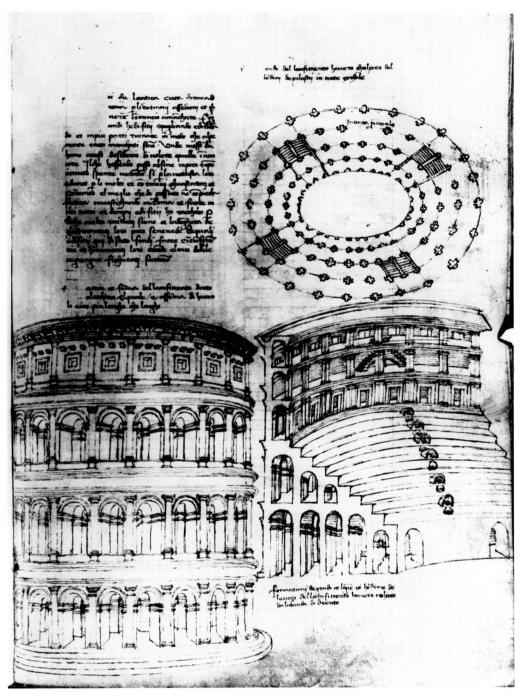

Pollaiuolo's workshop at the time and therefore he gained direct experience in the figurative arts as well. Later on, however, Il Cronaca worked exclusively as an architect and only used the orthogonal method of representation. Like Brunelleschi before him, his first drawings were schematic outlines, and his designs probably corresponded.[46] He measured bases, capitals and cornices with an accuracy worthy of Alberti, and reproduced, for example, capitals in plan, elevation and side view (fig. 10).[47] His most mature designs, in which he made use of pictorial media such as watercolor, precise concessions to perspective and the insertion of figurative ornament, compared well to the drawings of antiquity of Giuliano da Sangallo, with whom he had worked in 1493 on the sacristy of S. Spirito and had evidently also exchanged drawings of antiquity.[48] It is quite likely that he had also occasionally drawn perspective views.

Giuliano da Sangallo (ca. 1445-1516) also started his professional life as a woodworker and sculptor. His figurative drawing was inspired first and foremost by Ghirlandaio (1449-94).[49] Figurative decoration of the kind he admired in the ancient triumphal arches in fact played an even greater role in his designs than in those of his contemporaries. Giuliano himself wrote that he had started his studies of antiquity in Rome in around 1465 when he might have met Alberti.[50] It seems however that he retouched his sketchbooks (kept in Siena and the Vatican) much later on so that the surviving images are at most partially corrected copies from these early studies.[51]

[46] op. cit.: ann. I, pl. 1-7.
[47] op. cit.: ann. I, pl. 5a, 12a.
[48] op. cit.: pl. 8-11.
[49] S. Borsi, *Giuliano da Sangallo. I disegni di architettura e dell'antico*, Rome 1985; H. Günther 1988: 104-138.
[50] H. Günther 1988: 111.
[51] C. L. Frommel, in C. L. Frommel, N. Adams, eds., *The Architectural Drawings of Antonio da Sangallo the Younger and his Circle*, New York 1993: 7ff.

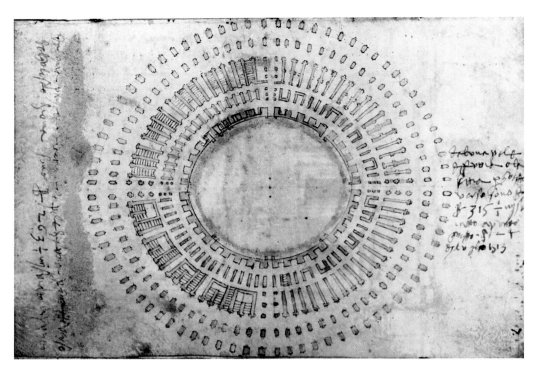

11. Giuliano da Sangallo
Plan of the Colosseum, Rome
Siena, Biblioteca Comunale
Taccuino Senese IV 8, *fol. 7r.*

12. Giuliano da Sangallo
Perspective Section of the
Colosseum, Rome
Siena, Biblioteca Comunale
Taccuino Senese IV 8, *fol. 5v.*

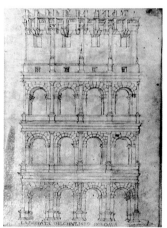

13. Giuliano da Sangallo
Elevation of the Colosseum
Rome
Siena, Biblioteca Comunale
Taccuino Senese IV 8, *fol. 6r.*

His first sketchbook, the *Taccuino Senese*, only contains drawings of the period before 1500 and its undatable projects and surveys perhaps correspond to his years in the service of Lorenzo il Magnifico (ca. 1483-92), and Cardinal Giuliano della Rovere (ca. 1494-97).[52] Sangallo was even more sparing with the pictorial devices of chiaroscuro and perspective in this sketchbook than in the one in the Vatican, where he approached the mature style of Il Cronaca.

Of the few buildings not belonging to antiquity included in his sketchbooks, such as his own more classicizing achievements, only the Cappella Piccolomini in Siena and the Torre degli Asinelli in Bologna were shown in perspective elevation; all the others were illustrated in plan only.[53] His favorite ancient monuments were those with rather flat facades, and only occasionally did he add a side view and a schematic plan. These reproductions may be more accurate from the archaeological point of view than the views of the ancient monuments painted by Botticelli or Perugino in the Cappella Sistina as from 1481, but they never achieve the same vividness and classicizing splendor.[54]

Only the Colosseum was given a full analysis in the *Taccuino Senese*. Giuliano drew it in plan, elevation, perspective section and perspective view.[55] While in the section, elevation and plan of the pier system he worked with much more precision than Francesco di Giorgio, on the plan he drew a nearly circular shape—a perhaps deliberate correction that is even more surprising considering that Alberti and Manetti had already discussed oval plans, and that both Filarete and Francesco di Giorgio had got much more closer to its real oval shape. As for the section, Giuliano offered such scant information that Alberti would never have given his approval. His studies of antiquity also suffered from his apparent lack of familiarity with Alberti's writings, and he must have doggedly worked out the vocabulary of the ancients, step by step.[56] Even in his last project, which can be attributed to the period after the death of Bramante, the Doric entablature seemed surprisingly out of date.[57]

The pages of the *Taccuino Senese* reveal little more of Giuliano's early design methods than that he had mastered the current techniques of orthogonal and perspective representation and that, all in all, he worked with less precision than he did later, in his old age. The projects he presented to his patrons must have been like the plan for S. Maria delle Carceri of about 1485 (fig. 14).[58] His sketches might have already been like those post-1503: quick and precise proposals for the solution of concrete architectural problems, much as Brunelleschi and Alberti must have done.[59]

A good understanding of the variety of perspective possibilities in such pre-1500 creative drawings can be obtained from the architectural drawings of Leonardo da Vinci (fig. 26).[60] During his years in Milan Leonardo studied only a few aspects of the Lombard tradition, and surprisingly little of Alberti's late works or his friend Bramante's early ones. He looked instead to Florentine prototypes—to the dome of the cathedral, the neighboring baptistery, and S. Maria degli Angeli—in a much more authoritative and creative way than Giuliano. As a typical Florentine, he cared more about the clear contours of the crystalline form than the expansion of the interior space, and preferred the organism expanding cell by cell, to the antique monumentality.

[52] R. Falb, *Il Taccuino di Giuliano da Sangallo*, Siena 1902; S. Borsi 1985: 250-314; H. Günther 1988: 112ff.; C. L. Frommel, in: C. L. Frommel, N. Adams 1993.
[53] R. Falb 1902: 38, 50, pl. 20, 44.
[54] H. Günther 1988: 37ff.
[55] C. L. Frommel, in C. L. Frommel, N. Adams 1993.
[56] H. Biermann, "Palast und Villa. Theorie und Praxis in Giuliano da Sangallos Codex Barberini und im Taccuino Senese," in *Les Traités d'Architecture de la Renaissance. Actes du colloque Tours 1981*: 138; H. Günther, "Die Anfänge der modernen Dorica," in J. Guillaume, ed., *L'emploi des ordres dans l'architecture de la Renaissance: Actes du colloque Tours 1966*, Paris 1992: 103ff.
[57] S. Borsi 1985: 481-489.
[58] S. Borsi 1985: 417ff.
[59] S. Borsi 1985: 453ff.
[60] R. Schofield 1991: 131ff.

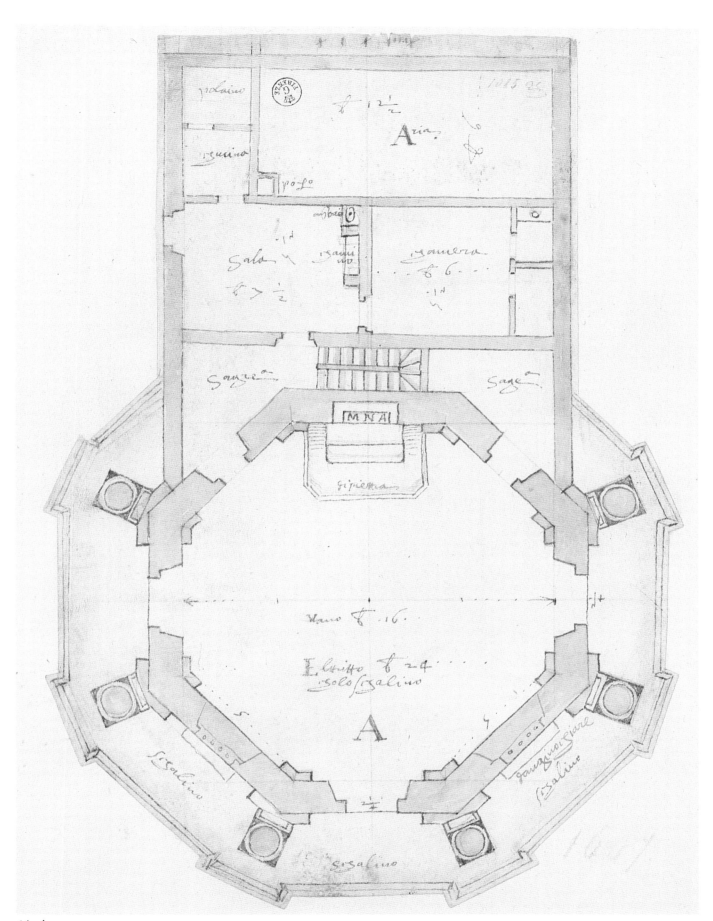

14. Anonymous
Plan of S. Maria delle
Carceri
Florence, Uffizi, Gabinetto
Disegni e Stampe
Uff. 1607Ar.

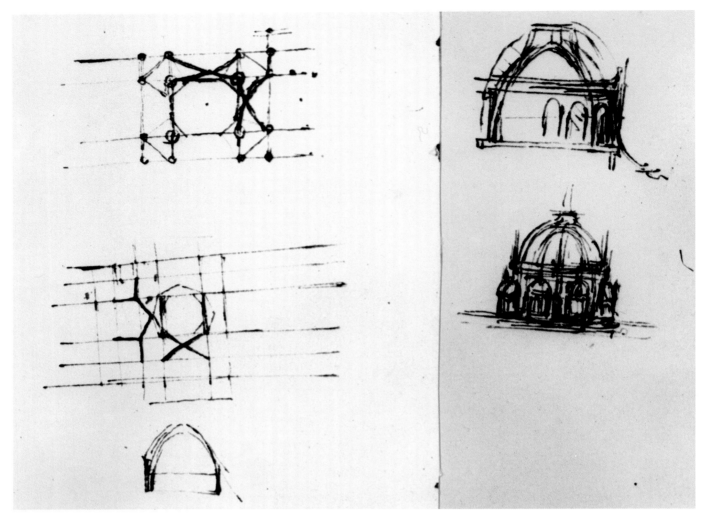

The impatient dynamism of Donato Bramante's only surviving sketch belonging to his years in Milan contrasts sharply with the scientific precision of Leonardo's drawings (fig. 16).[61] His way of pressing round in circles and circumscribing the question was characteristic of his Roman sketches as well. Bramante (1444–1514) was a contemporary of Giuliano, and his formative influences were the circles of Piero della Francesca, Melozzo da Forlì, and Mantegna; he therefore became acquainted with his most important master, Alberti, in a completely different way from his Florentine associates.[62] Like the three founding fathers of Renaissance architecture, Giotto, Brunelleschi and Alberti, Bramante approached the art of construction in a roundabout way through the perspective illustration of space. In ca. 1481 Piero della Francesca (perhaps Bramante's teacher) wrote a treatise, *De prospectiva pingendi*, inspired by Alberti, giving precise instructions on how to draw architectural perspectives from various viewpoints; he also indicated new methods of achieving natural lighting in pictorial spaces (fig. 17).[63] He placed the figures in his *Flagellation* in such an organic arrangement of the space as only Giovanni Bellini, the Venetian painger, knew how—offering important premises for Bramante's Prevedari engraving of 1481, the only graphic evidence of his Milanese beginnings.[64]

Even though Bramante was already about thirty-seven years old, the *aurea latinitas* of architectural language seemed not to have stimulated him greatly. He had probably not yet visited Rome to study the ancient monuments.[65] At this time he was much more interested in the representation of an expansive space, which is why he appealed to the viewer's imagination to extend the ruined fragment in all directions, to step into the picture, to join the groups of people and peep into the darkest corner of the quincunx. He might have learnt about this imaginative involvement of the observer in the pictorial space from his friend Leonardo, but certainly not from Piero, Mantegna or Melozzo. This is why Bramante was destined to translate to architecture the fruits of two hundred years' research into pictorial space.

Like Brunelleschi and Alberti, Bramante must have made a clear distinction during the almost twenty years he spent in Milan, between "pictorial" representation (as employed in the Prevedari engraving and his frescoes) and architectural projects based on the orthogonal triad of plan, elevation and section. This has in fact been corroborated by his sketch for the gallery in S. Maria presso S. Satiro,[66] and by the surprising correspondence between the inside and

[61] R. Schofield, "A Drawing for Santa Maria presso San Satiro," in *Journal of the Warburg and Courtauld Institutes 39* (1976): 246-253.

[62] A. Bruschi, *Bramante*, Bari 1969; F. Graf Wolff Metternich, "Der Kupferstich Bernardos de Prevedari aus Mailand von 1481," in *Bramante und St. Peter*, Munich 1975: 111ff.; F. Borsi, *Bramante*, Milano 1989: 143ff.

[63] Piero della Francesca, *De prospectiva pingendi*, ed. G. Nicco Fasola, Florence 1984.

[64] F. Graf Wolff Metternich 1975: 98-178; see Ferino Pagden above.

[65] A. Bruschi, "Bramante," in *Dizionario Biografico degli Italiani*, vol. 13, Rome 1971: 712-725; F. Graf Wolff Metternich, "Bramante, Skizze eines Lebensbildes," in Wolff Metternich 1975: 179-221.

[66] see note 60.

the outside of this church—a correspondence that is not found in any earlier building in the Italian Renaissance, and which was obviously influenced by the Gothic manner.[67]

Even before his appointment as consultant to the Milan Cathedral site, and before becoming one of the architects of Pavia Cathedral, Bramante had had firsthand experience of the structural principles of Gothic construction. Moreover, since he always considered each building as an organic whole—more so than his contemporaries—he must have been particularly fascinated by the transparency of the load-bearing structure. While the domes of late antiquity, such as that of S. Lorenzo in Milan, which had inspired Bramante's conceptions of space,[68] revealed their splendor principally in the interior, the Gothic style drew closer links between interior and exterior, making the internal structure legible from the outside, and vice versa (figs. 2, 3). It took an architect of Bramante's ingeniousness to merge in a single style the extraordinary light-flooded spaciousness of the centrally planned buildings of late antiquity with the soaring skeletal transparency of Milan Cathedral and the imperial monumentality of Alberti's last works.

The only drawing that can give an idea of Bramante's methods of design when he was in Milan is the great facade project conserved in the Louvre, even though it appears to have been drafted by his pupil Cristoforo Solari toward 1505 (cat. no. 58). In an entirely Gothic interpretation, the giant order reflects the load-bearing structure of the three aisles, the arches mirror the

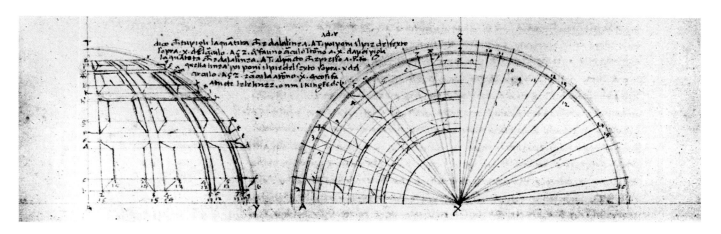

vaults and the colonnades probably support extensive galleries. The traces of perspective in the round window and great cornice detract nothing from the orthogonal accuracy of this project—probably the earliest surviving detailed project of an elevation in the Renaissance. Likewise, the deep shading of the wall openings reveals his efforts to make it easier for his patron to understand the plain orthogonal drawing he presented.

Only a few drawings of his Roman years—from 1499 to 1514—have been left to posterity.[69] According to Vasari, once in Rome Bramante spent his time studying the ancient monuments which, like his friend Leonardo, he had so far ignored.[70] The speed with which he assimilated not only the ancient orders and the formal language of the past, but also the systems and types as well as the teachings of Vitruvius and Alberti, can be seen in his earliest projects for the Tempietto, the Palazzo Caprini, and the Belvedere Court.[70a] Just the calculation of the concentric Doric friezes of the Tempietto—four on the same round construction and perhaps another three in the surrounding circular courtyard—presuppose extraordinarily detailed calculations and precise methods of representation; it was, in short, the most elaborate method so far required in a Renaissance building.[71] In the division of the perimeter of the various circles into metopes and triglyphs Bramante must have made mathematical calculations in the same way that his pupil Antonio da Sangallo did for the entablature of the Palazzo Farnese,[72] probably calling in mathematicians to help. In any case, he must have studied the final project very carefully by means of the model.

The only surviving drawing of antiquity probably executed by Bramante himself, however, dates to as late as 1505 (cat. no. 281). At the time Bramante had just begun to take in hand the designing of St. Peter's, and was therefore forced to deepen his knowledge not only of the various kinds of antique buildings and the classical vocabulary but also of the early methods of construction. Using a scale of measurement of Roman *palmi* he sketched the Baths of Diocletian in sanguine—evidently on-site—and then added particular significant details in ink, marking their approximate measurements. Perhaps, as the first master post-antiquity, he understood the complex alternation of space and wall masses and did not hesitate to use the same means of expression shortly afterward in his great parchment plan for St. Peter's (cat. no. 282). The closed body of the building, with the arms of the cross projecting beyond it, together with the octagonal corner spaces and their dimensions, were themselves inspired by the Baths of Diocle-

[67] C. L. Frommel, "Il complesso di S. Maria presso S. Satiro e l'ordine architettonico del Bramante lombardo", in: "La scultura decorativa del Primo Rinascimento," *Atti del I convegno internazionale di studi di Pavia 1980*, Pavia 1983: 153ff.

[68] C. Thoenes, "S. Lorenzo a Milano, S. Pietro a Roma: ipotesi sul 'piano di pergamena'," in *Arte Lombarda* 86/87 (1988): 94-100.

[69] C. L. Frommel, in C. L. Frommel, N. Adams 1993: 8ff.

[70] G. Vasari, *Le vite...*, ed. G. Milanesi, vol. IV, Florence 1879: 154.

[70a] C.L. Frommel, "Living *all'antica*," in this catalog: 182-203.

[71] H. Günther, "Bramantes Hofprojekt um den Tempietto und seine Darstellung in Serlios drittem Buch", in *Studi Bramanteschi, Atti del congresso internazionale* 1970, Rome 1974: 483-501.

[72] C. L. Frommel, "Sangallo et Michel-Ange (1513-1550)," in A. Chastel, ed., *Le Palais Farnèse*, Rome 1981, vol. I, 1: 135, fig. 21.

tian. But Bramante was following fundamentally other formal principles when he made the building irradiate outward from the dome dominating the Greek cross. This is why he had already sketched on the verso of the sheet (Uff. 104A) a drawing preliminary to the parchment plan, showing the basilica surrounded with a huge concentric peristyle—close in form to the ancient bath complex—spreading out into exedrae and concluded with corner towers.

The surviving projects for St. Peter's covering the period 1505–09 (see construction history elsewhere in this catalog[73]) allow us for the first time to examine in detail the evolution of a given architectural project during the Renaissance. The first stage consisted undoubtedly of a freehand sketch; one such example is the sketch on Uff. 8A verso (cat. no. 280), which in this case gave the pope a preliminary idea of the architect's proposal. After agreeing on a quincunx system, on the site of Peter's tomb and the high altar, and on the reutilization of Nicholas V's choir, Bramante ordered his assistant to draw the first scale drawing, or "disegno proporzionato," to use Filarete's term. As he later did for his project for the Palazzo dei Tribunali, in the case of St. Peter's Antonio da Sangallo drew up a set of local conditioning factors, simplified building forms, accompanied by approximate dimensions. These measurements were deduced—following the method described by Filarete—from a simple square grid based on half the width of the central aisle of Nicholas V's choir, i.e., 20 *braccia*.[73a] The central quincuncial system took absolute priority in the elaboration, and at first there was no precise definition of the limits of the external construction or of the arrangement of the longitudinal body. Numerous intermediate projects that have been lost must have prepared the way for the next surviving project, which, since it was drawn using an unusually large scale on precious parchment and carefully watercolored, was executed to present the project to the pope (cat. no. 282).

If Bramante only drew half the (presumably) centrally planned building, he was simply applying the same method he had used on Uff. 3A recto and for the numerous other projects of that period (cat. nos. 280, 283, 288, 296), because the continuation of its form was so evident there was no need to go on. Even though a scale in Roman *palmi* may once have been inserted in the lower margin of the parchment (which is slightly torn all round), the approximate extension of the project is already discernible from the constant size of the dome arch. As in the plan of Uff. 3A recto the half width of the nave served now as a module for a grid of 60 × 60 *palmi*. Moreover, Bramante chose a scale of exactly 1:150 so that two and a half modules equaled one *palmo*. As with the two projects that followed closely (cat. nos. 283, 288), he was able to construct a measurement grid with squares 2-*minuti* wide (ca. 7.4 mm) based on the 60-*minuti* subdivision of the *palmo*; each 2-*minuti* represented five *palmi* in the project. Proceeding in this way, Bramante had likely already prepared a similar study in sanguine (before the parchment project), from which he could determine the individual measurements without difficulty. The auxiliary lines necessary for the more or less mechanical transcription could have been marked in sanguine and then erased. A final project ready for presentation to the pope, however, such as the one on Uff. 1A, presupposed detailed studies concerning the elevation, and in fact sketches of plans were combined with elevations on three of his later preparatory studies (cat. nos. 280, 283, 288).

The parchment plan can be distinguished from a real executive project by its "ideal" character. Bramante in fact studied its detailed elaboration only after he had convinced the pope of the project. He then reinforced the piers and the pier arches and verified every detail according to static, functional and esthetic criteria (cat. no. 283) before having the famous foundation medal coined (cat. no. 284).[73b] When, in spite of everything, the pope rejected his project, Bramante was forced to start all over again. Second thoughts about the pre-existing building, an even more radical reinforcement of the load-bearing structures and the elimination of the superfluous secondary spaces led him, step by step, toward the final project of April 1506. The surviving intermediate project drawings illustrate how, in this second phase, he still started his designs from sketches (cat. nos. 283, 287, 288), and how he elaborated their tiniest details by means of projects using grids for the measurement, while explaining the individual parts with the help of repeated sketches of elevations. No other project of Renaissance architecture has provided such an ample example of the gradual genesis of a complex organism such as the plan drawn in sanguine on Uff. 20A. Here Bramante kept the plan of the old basilica in front of him, and with it the identity of the venerable original building on which the pope was placing an ever-increasing emphasis. Bramante's superb skill as a draftsman allowed him to draw numerous phases, one upon the other, on a single sheet, with such methodical frugality as to make their distinction clearly possible today. At first he used a compass and straightedge and then drew freehand more and more often, using the grid as a guide and at times uniting here and there two of his 5-*palmi* squares with a mark.

In a similar plan he must have then drafted the final executive project, and only afterward was he ready to prepare the exact elevations and the wooden model in the spring of 1506 (cat. nos. 293, 292). The model was however already outmoded the time work began on it. However,

[73] C. L. Frommel, "St. Peter's," in this catalog, pp. 398–423.
[73a] op. cit., fig. 2.
[73b] op. cit.

112

18 - *Baldassarre Peruzzi*
Interior of S. Stefano
Rotondo, Rome
Florence, Uffizi
Gabinetto Disegni e Stampe
Sant. 161r.

it was only after having finally settled the fundamental dimensions that the long and complicated process of elaborating the mostly orthogonal projects for the constructive details—from the capitals to the pendentives and centering—could go ahead (cat. nos. 295, 296, 297). This continual series of projects demonstrates how Bramante in the lengthy process from the simple ideal schema to the project for presentation to the patron and to the final executive project departed continually from the simple forms, from the precise module and the grid, and how the measurements were already complicated on the plan drawn in sanguine; and, lastly, how he reintroduced the original 60-*palmi* module only in the arcades.[73c] In his opinion the grid and model were first and foremost professional aids and not an end in themselves, and therefore all attempts to discover ideal proportions in the executive project similar to those of the early projects are destined to fail.

Neither the architect nor the patron denied the possibility of introducing alterations, even during the building process itself. Since the details were elaborated only when the building process reached a stage that made them necessary, the modifications of the forms also reflected the architect's own maturity—the most obvious example is perhaps the Cappella Medici of 1519 onward, in which Michelangelo even sacrificed the harmony of the form to the novelty of the detail.[74] This is why Bramante left the exact shape of the dome undecided right to the end, perhaps after reflecting on static problems as well.

After the death of Julius II, when the pier arches and the vault of the choir were already built, Leo X—like many of his successors—gave orders that the architects were to elaborate a new and larger project immediately. The basilica was to become bigger, more magnificent and more

[73c] C. L. Frommel, "St. Peter's," in this catalog, fig. 23.
[74] C. L. Frommel, "S. Eligio und die Kuppel der Cappella Medici," in *Akten des 21. Internationalen Kongresses für Kunstgeschichte Bonn 1964*, Berlin 1967, vol. 2: 53ff.

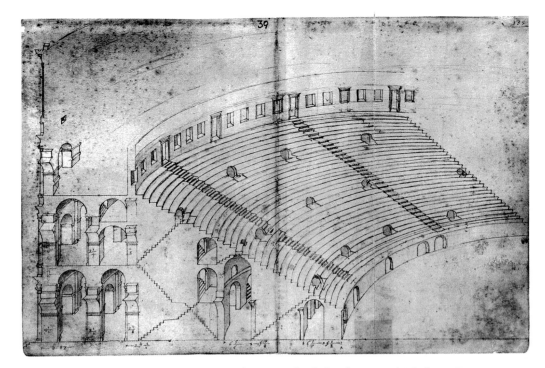

19. Bernardo della Volpaia
Perspective Section of the
Colosseum, Rome
*London, Sir John Soane's
Museum*
Codex Coner, *fol. 39A*

antique looking (cat. nos. 306, 307). This period of the design, which kept Bramante engaged for the rest of his life, was the time when he elaborated his monumental project for the dome that Serlio perhaps copied from the original (cat. no. 303). This project deserves particular attention for the way it was represented. It is the very first surviving project in which the plan is correlated directly with its complementary elevation and section, and in the same scale. This close linking of the orthogonal triad was probably established by Bramante himself, who had been particularly impressed by the structural transparency of the Gothic style, and who had already placed plan and section in a complementary relationship in his projects for the pendentives (cat. no. 296). When he drew the lantern in plan, he illustrated—as in the project for the Tempietto saved for posterity by Serlio—the radial relations between the parts bearing and discharging the load of the dome and lantern. This axial system, which also stems from Gothic architecture, is one of the fundamental differences from the Pantheon, the most important prototype for the dome of St. Peter's. Therefore, once again there is an intimate relationship between the project and its method of representation.

20. Raphael
Project for a Stage Design
*Florence, Uffizi
Gabinetto Disegni e Stampe*
Uff. 560Ar. and Uff. 242Ar.

If Bramante's structural research led to the perfection of the orthogonal procedure of architectural design, the eminently visual quality of his buildings and the fundamental role played by light required right from the start projects drawn in one-point perspective with strong chiaroscuro, a technique of representation such as the one used in the Prevedari engraving (cat. no. 121). Bramante used this kind of central perspective not just for his project of the choir in his first Milanese building, the church of S. Maria presso S. Satiro, but also for his Roman buildings such as the Belvedere Court.[75] He conceived both of these buildings as a spatial and visual unit and overcame the conditioning factors of the site with pictorial devices. While in the Milanese church he added to the regular longitudinal body the scenographic make-believe of a choir arm denied to the clergy, in the Cortile della Pigna he carried out the shortening of the pilasters so imperceptibly that it was noticed only recently, thus weaving pictorial space and architecture in an as yet quite unknown form.

The spatial effect from an ideal position—in the case of the Belvedere Court from the pope's rooms in the Borgia apartment—was examined by Bramante however in other projects where he was not forced to introduce perspective devices such as the great plan drawn in sanguine for St. Peter's (cat. no. 288). In his sketches on the verso he drew the vault of the crossing and a coved vault from a low viewpoint and the drum and exterior construction from a high viewpoint. Similar changes in position can be noticed in his images for medals. He showed the exterior of St. Peter's rising up in a hierarchical manner, in a front view from a low viewpoint while the Belvedere Court, which was difficult to represent from the front, was illustrated in bird's-eye view from the side. In both cases Bramante deviated from the strict rules of central perspective for love of effect.

Like in the Prevedari engraving these perspective projects acquired their greatest illusionistic potential by a play of light. Bramante succeeded in illustrating the alternation of light areas and dark corners so typical of his Roman architectures, such as the last project he elaborated for St. Peter's or the two colonnades of the Tempietto, only by using chiaroscuro. The young Peruzzi could have been inspired by the project for the Tempietto or by the concentric court-

[75] A. Bruschi 1969: 295ff.

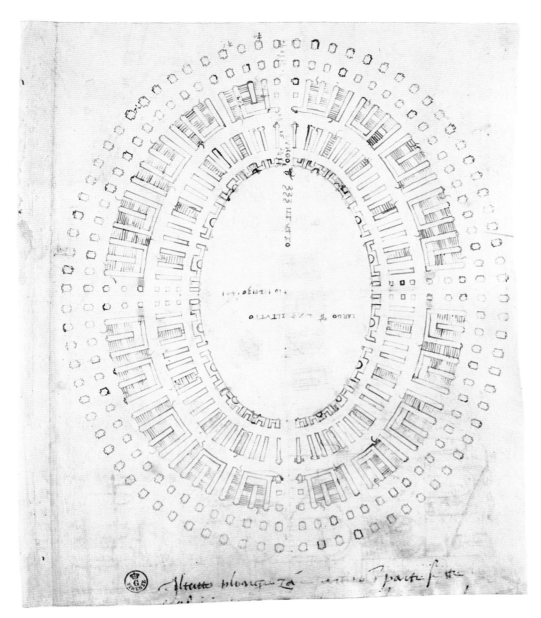

21. *Antonio da Sangallo
the Younger*
Plan of the Colosseum, Rome
*Florence, Uffizi
Gabinetto Disegni e Stampe
Uff. 1555Ar.*

yard when he designed the interior of S. Stefano Rotondo in about 1503–04 (fig. 18).[76]
Whatever the case, this representation, with its unusually wide viewpoint and artistic distribution of light and darkness, is much more like the Prevedari engraving (cat. no. 121) or Bramante's sketches on the plan drawn in sanguine than either Giuliano da Sangallo's drawings or even those of Francesco di Giorgio. It would be difficult to imagine the perspective views of the so-called Pseudo-Sansovino master[77] (cat. nos. 293, 292) without Bramante's illusionistic projects or especially those conserved in the *Codex Coner* since their author, Bernardo della Volpaia, next to monuments of antiquity drew almost exclusively buildings by Bramante (fig. 19).[78]

The real heir, however, to the masterly methods of architectural design and representation was Raphael, whom the pope had summoned to Rome in 1508,[79] probably on Bramante's own suggestion. As early as 1509 Raphael adopted Bramante's new style and his illusionistic method of representation for the architecture in the background of the *School of Athens*. With an awareness of how he himself had developed, Bramante must have seen Raphael, in his steady progress from the pictorial spaces of the Stanze to his first building for Agostino Chigi, as his rightful heir. This is why he advised the pope to nominate Raphael as his successor instead of Antonio da Sangallo, his more technically expert assistant. The sketches in sanguine for the Chigi stables or the disorderly outlines of the square plan projects for the Chigi funerary chapel place Raphael much nearer his teacher's methods of architectural design than Sangallo. In 1514 Raphael also verified the spatial effects of his first projects for St. Peter's with the help of perspective drawings (cat. no. 309), in the same way as Bramante had done on the back of his plan in sanguine. Toward 1515 he borrowed not only the idea of groups of pilasters from the Belvedere Court but the same perspective devices for the Palazzo Jacopo da Brescia.[80] The shape of the dome and the whole method of representation of his second project for St. Peter's copied Bramante's project for the dome of five year's earlier (cat. no. 311). Lastly, Bramante's

[76] C. L. Frommel, "Peruzzis römische Anfänge von der 'Pseudo-Cronaca-Gruppe' zu Bramante," in *Römisches Jahrbuch der Bibliotheca Hertziana* 27/28 (1991-92): 173 fig. 36.
[77] C. L. Frommel, in C. L. Frommel, N. Adams 1993: 32.
[78] op. cit.: 27.
[79] op. cit.: 29ff.
[80] C. L. Frommel, in C. L. Frommel, S. Ray, M. Tafuri, *Raffaello architetto*, Milan 1984: 157-162.

22. *Antonio da Sangallo the Younger*
Perspective Section of the Colosseum, Rome
Florence, Uffizi Gabinetto Disegni e Stampe Uff. 1555Av.

23. *Antonio da Sangallo the Younger*
Survey of the Mausoleum of Theodoric, Ravenna
Florence, Uffizi Gabinetto Disegni e Stampe Uff. 1563Ar.

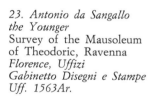

artistically illuminated perspectives came to life in a project for theatrical scenery created by Raphael in his last years (fig. 20).[81]

It would however be too simple to consider Raphael as the heir of Bramante alone. Raphael had never worked in Milan, an experience which Bramante adhered to almost programmatically in one of his first sketches for St. Peter's (cat. no. 287). Skeletal structures such as Milan Cathedral and post-Constantinian interiors such as S. Lorenzo had less influence on Raphael than the Pantheon or the imperial baths, which he had learnt to comprehend under the watchful eye of Bramante.

Raphael's response to these monuments was the sweeping project for a complete reconstruction of ancient Rome, which he described precisely to his patron (presumed to be Leo X) in the *Memorandum*, a dedicatory letter of 1519-20. The procedures for the survey and representation proposed followed the methods introduced by Bramante, whether they were the orthogonal triad, the use of the compass or perspective views. The understanding of the monuments and the relative sources, the tendency toward a rigid scientific methodology increased at an even more surprising rate in the years immediately after the death of Bramante. Even though there are no proven links between the many known surveys of ancient monuments and Raphael's project to reconstruct imperial Rome, the drawings of his most advanced contemporaries from 1518 onward evince a concerted effort to achieve scientific accuracy and objectivity.[82]

Antonio da Sangallo (1485-1546) was Raphael's closest ally in this effort to arrive at a more extensive and deeper knowledge of antiquity.[83] Antonio was educated in the spirit of his uncle Giuliano. As early as 1504-05 he had made a much more accurate and analytic survey of the Colosseum, proving himself to be an authentic architect more interested in the three-dimensional structures than in the facades (figs. 21, 22). In about 1506-07 Giuliano moved into Bramante's circle and drew an orthogonal elevation of the Mausoleum of Theodoric, probably on the basis of a survey made by Bramante himself during the military campaign at Bologna in about 1506 (fig. 23). The pictorial shading in this elevation recalls Bramante's later project of the dome. As soon as Giuliano returned to Florence in the spring of 1509, Bramante summoned Antonio to work as his chief assistant, and when gout made drawing increasingly difficult, Antonio appears to have drafted Bramante's last projects following the master's instructions.

Even though Sangallo was proficient in the use of perspective and employed it in his sketches and occasional theatrical scenery, he concentrated much more than his contemporaries on a strictly orthogonal method of representation, both in his projects and in his drawings of antiquity. Since he proceeded from well-defined volumes rather than from the expansion of space, the greater part of his projects are based not on the neutral square grid but on incised axial coor-

[81] C. L. Frommel, in C. L. Frommel, S. Ray, M. Tafuri 1984: 225-228.
[82] C. L. Frommel, in C. L. Frommel, N. Adams 1993: 30-34.
[83] op. cit.: 10ff.

25. *Baldassarre Peruzzi*
Project for the Completion
of S. Petronio, Bologna
Bologna, Museo di S. Petronio

dinates in the same way that Antonio da Pellegrino, his fellow townsman, had used them, and which were common practice from the time of the Reims superimpositions. This strictly orthogonal method corresponded to a continuity of all the horizontal and vertical components—as in his early works such as the Palazzo Farnese (1513 and later)—in such a consistent manner not even to be found in Bramante. In his second and completely independent survey of the Mausoleum of Theodoric in 1526, and in his later projects for St. Peter's (cat. nos. 347–372), he achieved a methodical accuracy that Bramante had never been capable of, and would never be bettered in the centuries to come.

Baldassarre Peruzzi (1481–1536) was quite the reverse. He worked alongside Antonio for many years on the St. Peter's building site, but he never denied his artistic origins.[84] His fanciful interpretations of ancient monuments and bird's-eye view presentations of his first designs were the fruit of Francesco di Giorgio's influence over him.[85] Only after considerable time did he arrive at a capacity to observe objectively more like Giuliano da Sangallo or Il Cronaca, and in the surprising view of the interior of S. Stefano Rotondo he could have imitated the superbly illuminated wide-angle perspectives of Bramante's Roman years (fig. 18). As from about 1506, more or less at the same time as Sangallo, he started adopting Bramante's orthogonal methods of representation and drew details of decaying ancient monuments with a precision and beauty never seen before (fig. 24).

He continued to use orthogonal drawings for the projects of his later years too. But it is hardly a coincidence that not one orthogonal triad can be found in all the vast legacy of his drawings, nor even a single complementary use of elevation and section. Similarly, symmetry, continual axes or cornices played a minor role in his later projects compared to Sangallo. For this reason he was among the few capable of designing extraordinary buildings like the Palazzo Massimo on uneven ground, assimilating ancient walls, and even taking advantage of the irregularities to achieve spectacular innovations and scenographic effects.

This highly scenographic relationship with architecture gained recognition in his projects for the presentation to the pope drawn in perspective, the only ones to continue Bramante's tradition of perspective projects. Surviving perspective projects, with masterly illumination, dating back to the first years of Leo X's papacy,[86] demonstrate how much Peruzzi owed to Bramante, his esteemed mentor. It is quite likely that he followed Bramante's example if he subjected his own more complex projects only partially to the rules of central perspective: like the Tuscan masters of the Trecento and Quattrocento or the draftsman of the Codex Coner, he foreshortened the lines leading to the background while representing every picture plane parallel to the first as an orthogonal elevation—a compromise which guaranteed a certain degree of objectiveness without diminishing the illusion. In his drawing of the project for S. Petronio of 1522–23 he

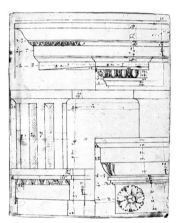

24. *Baldassarre Peruzzi*
Survey of the Entablature of
the Basilica Iulia, Rome
Florence, Biblioteca Nazionale
Codex Magliabechiano
II.I.429, fol. 16r.

[84] H. W. Wurm, *Baldassarre Peruzzi. Architekturzeichnungen*, Tübingen 1984.
[85] C. L. Frommel 1991-92: 159ff.
[86] C. L. Frommel, "Baldassarre Peruzzi als Maler und Zeichner," in *Beiheft des Römischen Jahrbuches für Kunstgeschichte* 11 (1967-68): 32ff., pl. 22c, d, 92c.

26. *Leonardo da Vinci*
Project of a Church
*Windsor, Royal Library
RL 12609v.*

eliminated a large part of the outer wall in order to illustrate on an inner plane the orthogonal section through the longitudinal body and the area of the dome, and the view into the adjacent secondary spaces (fig. 25).[87] Even though it was not in scale, he represented the thickness of the wall and the vault in this way as well, as Alberti had said it should be for a good model; in the open area he even showed the foreshortened plan. By uniting plan, elevation, section and perspective view in a single drawing, he replaced the orthogonal triad and the complementary relation between elevation and section introduced from the time of Bramante's project for the dome, with a method of representation whose variety of information was much greater, though it was slightly less objective.

Early traces of this masterly procedure can be found in Leonardo's Milanese sketches, in which the front half of a building can be seen in a foreshortened plan and the back half in perspective section (fig. 26).[88] The same type of representation returned in the reconstructions of the Baths of Diocletian based clearly on surveys carried out by Bramante and Antonio da Sangallo in 1504–06, but the exaggerated bird's-eye view and elongated proportions seem to have more in common with Peruzzi's early drawings (fig. 27).[89] Peruzzi might therefore have learnt the technique during his first years in Rome working alongside Bramante. In his late project for St. Peter's he returned to the bird's-eye view to present the building from a slightly oblique position where the entrance portal can be seen only in the foreshortened plan, the front half of the interior is as high as the top of the niches and only the last half, at the back, illustrates the vault. Here too, all elements parallel to the picture plane were drawn in approximately orthogonal elevation (cat. no. 331). While the project for S. Petronio, with its low viewpoint, gave the observer an idea of the monumental spaciousness of the building, he seems to have cared more about the exemplary transparency of Bramante's quincunx system in the bird's-eye view of St. Peter's.

Any description, however brief, of early architectural drawing in Italy cannot leave out Michelangelo. From the time of his arrival in Rome and the commission for Julius II's mausoleum in the spring of 1505, he was intensely involved in architectural activities.[90] In the first two projects for the mausoleum of March 1505 (cat. nos. 278, 279) his classicizing approach was similar to Giuliano's. The volutes, pedestals and entablatures in the numerous surviving perspectives recall the style of Giuliano at that time.[91] Bramante's influence is already undeniable in the dominant *piano nobile* and its niche opening into space, and especially in themes such as the rhythmical arrangement of the orders (the *travata ritmica*) or the energetic use of projecting elements. Michelangelo adopted Bramante's strictly orthogonal method of representation, with its pictorial chiaroscuro, in the spring of 1513—perhaps even before Giuliano, and more or less at the same time as Raphael's and Antonio's first projects. In the projects for the

[87] H. W. Wurm 1984: 132.
[88] C. Pedretti, *Leonardo architetto*, Milan 1978: 23ff.
[89] A. Nesselrath, "Monumenta antiqua romana. Ein illustrierter Romtraktat des Quattrocento," in R. Harpath, H. Wrede, eds., *Antikenzeichnung und Antikenstudium in Renaissance und Frühbarock. Akten des internationalen Symposions 8.-10. September 1986 Coburg*, Mainz 1989: 33ff.
[90] J. S. Ackerman, *The Architecture of Michelangelo*, London 1961; C. G. Argan, *Michelangelo architetto*, Milan 1990.
[91] S. Borsi 1985, figs. pp. 424, 469, 473, 477.

facade of S. Lorenzo he therefore treated the plan, elevation and section in no less a sovereign way than Raphael or Sangallo, and avoided concessions to perspective in an even more thoroughgoing manner (cat. nos. 223-235). Only in particularly voluminous structures, such as the staircase in the Biblioteca Laurenziana, did he illustrate the project by means of perspective sketches. In these early projects he took pains first of all to obtain a plastic relief and an accurate articulation of the detail, emphasizing their effects with the help of strongly contrasting wash. He modeled the elevation for S. Lorenzo, dating to the years 1516–17, in this way, bringing the light in directly from the south in a much more realistic and spatialistic way than Giuliano's slightly earlier rival projects. Moreover, since Raphael and Peruzzi were aiming at a similar richly contrasting form of model in their contemporary projects (figs. 20, 25) it is clear that Bramante was their common source of inspiration. Michelangelo maintained these methods of representation all his life, and in fact, the orthogonal section enhanced with highly imaginative shading was to make its way triumphantly throughout Europe in the centuries to come.[92]

The development of the new architectural drawing was condensed ultimately into a few stages that were decisive for architectural construction as well: the early Gothic style in France which had discovered or—more probably—re-discovered the orthogonal triad; Giotto's era, in which perspective elevations and models afforded substance, concreteness, spatiality, and chiaroscuro; and, lastly, the early Renaissance in Florence, during which Brunelleschi, Alberti and Leonardo probed all the perspective possibilities of representation. The experience of three centuries flowed together into the project of the new St. Peter's under Bramante, bringing a detailed method of design within reach for the first time whose roots went a long way back, but had hardly ever before been amalgamated with such consequence, complexity and precision. Bramante's followers perfected each of these methodological possibilities: in particular, Antonio da Sangallo the orthogonal procedure and Peruzzi, the perspective representation. The most illustrious designers of the years to come, from Vignola and Palladio to Borromini and Juvarra, inherited a highly developed patrimony which needed no fundamental improvement. In the same way in which every step forward in the development of graphic representation was linked to transformations in the history of architecture, so the retention of these methods of designing also implied a continuity of the architectural forms.

27. Anonymous
Survey of the Baths of
Diocletian, Rome
early 16th cent.
Florence, Uffizi
Gabinetto Disegni e Stampe
Uff. 1863Ar.

[92] W. Nordinger, in W. Nordinger, F. Zimmermann, eds., *Die Architekturzeichnung vom barocken Idealplan zur Axonometrie*, Munich 1986: 8ff.

122

Arnaldo Bruschi

Religious Architecture in Renaissance Italy
from Brunelleschi to Michelangelo

In the humanistic, Renaissance and Counter-Reformation cultures, as previously in the sphere of medieval Christianity, the place of worship represented the pinnacle of architectural values. More than any other type of architecture, church construction demanded the highest commitment from the architect, the builders and their patrons. The theoretical writings are explicit in this respect, and, despite the emergence of other building types, such as the palazzo and the villa, the church's primacy is confirmed by the sheer number and quality of the works produced. "In all architecture," writes Leon Battista Alberti in his *De re aedificatoria* (1966, Book VII, chap. 3)—which in the early 1450s established the foundations and the most lucid exposition of Renaissance ideas on the art of building—"there does not exist any work which requires greater talent, care, skill and diligence than that needed for building and decorating the temple. Needless to say, a well-tended and ornate temple is without doubt the foremost and primary ornament of the city." It is dedicated to divinity, he affirms, and religious worship is of great importance to the community. "For these reasons," he continues, "I would like the temple to be of such beauty that it would be impossible to imagine a more beautiful appearance for it; and I wish every detail be carefully studied in such a way that visitors, upon entering, are struck with wonder and astonishment at the sight of things so worthy of admiration and can barely refrain from exclaiming: what we are witnessing is truly a place of God." Again in the late sixteenth century, once the crisis of the Reformation was past, these ideas returned, for example, in Cataneo (1554, Book III) and in Palladio (1570, Book IV). The preeminence of the temple over all other forms of architecture seemed to find support among the ancients as well. Vitruvius himself had devoted more attention to the subject of temples than to other building types, and many antique (or putatively antique) structures consisted in temples (or were commonly believed to be temples). Compared to other building types, the temple permitted the most thorough-going implementation of the architectural principles of humanism (Wittkower 1962) in relation to the site and to its overall configuration and that of its *ornamenti* (ornaments) as a distinguishing element of the city or territory.

It is a well-known fact that innovation, especially in religious architecture, started with Brunelleschi (Heydenreich and Lotz 1974; Battisti 1976; *Filippo Brunelleschi...* 1980). However, not only did he receive support from his patrons and the humanistic circles of the city, but the groundwork for it had been laid by the previous generation of Florentine artists. For some time the Florentines had proudly believed that their cathedral baptistery was a work which, as Coluccio Salutati observed, was "neither Greek nor Etruscan, but certainly Roman," and that several of their churches, such as SS. Apostoli and S. Miniato al Monte, possessed at least some features of the "correct" architecture of the ancients. And as early as the close of the thirteenth century, signs of renewal had begun to appear throughout Florence, a rebirth which found its most complete expression in the art of Brunelleschi. In particular, S. Maria del Fiore (which Alberti also greatly admired) embodies the most authoritative implementation of what Francesco di Giorgio Martini later called "composto" (composite) church design, involving the fusion of a longitudinal body with a centralized plan capped by a dome: it was a design laden with symbolic value and ideally evocative of the great structures of antiquity. Thus, this "Gothic" building was to stand as a conceptual prototype of a church design that was to be, as we shall see, characteristic of the Renaissance world. Furthermore, this occurred at a time of growing interest in the visual aspects of architecture, when sculptors such as Arnolfo da Cambio and painters such as Giotto were *capomaestri* of the cathedrals, when sculptors and, especially in the Trecento, Florentine and Sienese painters played an essential role: from Arnolfo da Cambio to Giotto, the Lorenzetti and Taddeo Gaddi (Burns 1971; Bruschi 1978a; 1979). Filippo Brunelleschi took his cue from them, but in a way that was no longer intuitive and empirical; rather he was "scientific," "rational," and systematic. The orientation of these artists was at the base of his experiments, especially in the field of religious architecture.

The Old Sacristy of S. Lorenzo was practically a manifesto of the new humanistic architecture. Started around 1420, it was to be the funerary chapel of Giovanni de' Medici (father of Cosimo the Elder) and his wife. The strikingly new design of the chapel seems to have taken some suggestions from the Padua Cathedral baptistery, and was almost certainly inspired by the symbolism underlying the resurrection and spiritual glorification of the dead, who, from the earthly sphere—represented by the cubic base—are transported heavenward in a crescendo of light, epitomized by the dome illuminated by twelve windows (representing the Apostles?) and by a lantern borne on columns culminating in a spiral-form roof. But this design and its symbolism were achieved in an

Andrea da Firenze (Andrea
Bonaiuti)
Triumph of the Church
detail of fresco in the
Cappellone degli Spagnuoli
14th cent.
Florence, S. Maria Novella

123

Filippo Brunelleschi
Apse and dome of Florence
Cathedral
1423–38

exceedingly simple and clear whole: a cubic space—with four corner pilasters (Pliny's "*columnae quadrangulae*") surmounted by arches supporting a hemispherical umbrella dome with spherical pendentives—opens with an arch opposite the entrance onto a smaller space, the *scarsella* (altar chapel), also cubic, marked at each corner by a slender pilaster, with shallow concave niches and a small hemispherical dome raised on pendentives. Herein lay the fundamental points of Brunelleschi's reworking of the architectural code, as adopted throughout the Renaissance. The Old Sacristy, completed in 1428, became, at least for the rest of the century, a fundamental prototype, many times copied and redesigned in different interpretations and dimensions.

It is possible to reconstruct, albeit tentatively, the original project chosen by Giovanni de' Medici (between 1421 and 1425, approximately) from among the "many alternatives" proposed to him by Brunelleschi for the reconstruction of the church of S. Lorenzo (which had been begun with another project in 1419). Work on the building continued through the 1420s, but was interrupted upon Giovanni's death in 1429. It was resumed in 1442, shortly before Brunelleschi's death, by Cosimo the Elder, with substantial modifications by Antonio Manetti Ciaccheri. While the building that has come down to us may correspond only in part to Brunelleschi's original intentions, it nonetheless

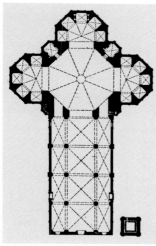

Interior and plan of Florence Cathedral

evinces the application of Brunelleschi's scheme for rationalizing the medieval Cistercian design with which the church was begun, a formula that was later taken up by the mendicant orders (S. Trinita, the Carmine, S. Maria Novella). At any event, in Brunelleschi's project the cruciform plan with spaces of varying heights demonstrated in elevation the rigorous syntactical merger of two systems—namely, architectural order plus arch—used in different scales to form three-dimensional square bays. This approach, which Brunelleschi also applied for S. Spirito, provided later architecture (and religious architecture in particular) with a fundamental tool for solving the problem of coordinating spaces of different sizes—such as the nave, aisles and chapels.

The church plan in which the traditional longitudinal space with columns (whose relationship to the world of antiquity had been demonstrated by the monumental Christian buildings erected by Constantine in Rome) terminates in a centralized, domed core was reapplied for the design of S. Spirito with extraordinary maturity. The building, designed it seems in 1434, when a model of it was made, appears not to have been started until 1444. The first column was brought to the construction site just a few days before Brunelleschi's death in April 1446, and the end of the church toward the facade was not completed according to the master's plan. However, it is the most complete expression of Brunelleschi's ideas. Everybody knows that Giuliano da Sangallo copied Filippo Brunelleschi's original plan (counseling Lorenzo il Magnifico to maintain the author's ideas) as contained in fol. 14r. of the *Codex Barberini*, Lat. 4424, in the Biblioteca Vaticana. It has been suggested that cues for the idea may have been provided by schemes present in Florentine Gothic architecture and by certain features of the cathedrals of Pisa and Siena or by the extradosed semicircular chapels of Orvieto Cathedral. But it was essentially a new invention which, perhaps stemming from a critical revision of S. Lorenzo, is the direct and cogent result of the designing methods and principles that guided him. The fundamental solution is that of making the basic three-dimensional module of the aisle-bays continue all around the building's perimeter, even in the transept, the choir and—audaciously—in the facade itself, introducing the bipartition of the ends of the main cruciform space, with a column set on each of the geometrical and visual axes. At the same time, the Gothic counterpoint between the structural membering and the planes of masonry is practically eliminated by replacing the flat surfaces with semicircular niche chapels the same height as the nave arches. The structure of S. Spirito—an almost "ideal" church—must have seemed too theoretical and abstract, too liturgically unwieldy, to be understood and to serve as a model for others, or even to be completed according to the master's ideas with four doors on the facade (that is, with two doors instead of one in correspondence with the nave). However, it surely impressed the most discriminat-

Filippo Brunelleschi
Detail of the Old Sacristy
of S. Lorenzo, Florence
1419–28

ing artistic elite: Giuliano da Sangallo, probably Francesco di Giorgio and certainly Leonardo (who sketched its plan on fol. 11 of Manuscript B in Paris) and Bramante in Milan, who drew inspiration from it.

Brunelleschi had adopted the centralized scheme since his design for the Old Sacristy, though it was not strictly based on a central plan; in fact the axis toward the *scarsella* with its ample "Serliana" arrangement visually dominates the others. In the case of S. Spirito, the centralized nucleus was reconciled with the longitudinal one in forceful, undifferentiated modular units. In 1429, when the Old Sacristy was nearing completion, Brunelleschi started work on the Cappella Pazzi, the chapter house for the Franciscan order based at S. Croce (Guillaume 1990), on a site that was heavily conditioned by existing structures. The layout is similar to that of the Old Sacristy with its *scarsella*, but the central space with a dome supported by pendentives is flanked on the transverse axis by two coffered barrel vaults. Thus, here again, the plan was not centralized. However, it was an easy step (to an architect like Giuliano da Sangallo, for example, in the church of S. Maria delle Carceri in Prato) from the extensions on the sides with the barrel vaults to a similar extension following the entrance-to-altar axis, giving rise to a centralized cross-plan layout; likewise it may have provided the cue for structuring the transept of a church, as Bramante was to do in S. Maria presso S. Satiro in Milan. Or—as Luca Fancelli was to do in the Cappella della Incoronata in Mantua Cathedral, or Bramante in the choir of S. Maria del Popolo—its spatial and structural layout could be rotated, placing the entrance and altar along the main axis, to turn it into a chapel, a small church, or a choir. The conviction that antique temples typically had a domed centralized plan must have been widespread in the humanistic culture of Florence in Brunelleschi's time. In the first place, it seems to be attested by the baptistery, which was believed to have been the temple of Mars in the Roman city, and the circular one of the Pantheon, the most prestigious and best-conserved edifice of antiquity, as well as a number of ancient buildings believed to be pagan temples, such as the so-called temples of Minerva Medica and Bacchus (S. Costanza), in Rome and elsewhere. Early Christian or medieval churches with central plans—such as S. Lorenzo or S. Satiro in Milan—were conceived as temples in the manner of the ancients. That their layout was compatible with Christian worship—despite opinions to the contrary related to liturgical exigencies and "pagan" connotations—is confirmed by their frequent, easy transformation into churches, and by the use of the octagonal plan for baptisteries—which had even been suggested by such church fathers as St. Ambrose and St. Augustine; another decisive factor was Constantine's use of the centralized form in the most venerated sanctuary of Christendom, the Holy Sepulcher in Jerusalem. Moreover, as often pointed out, in

*Filippo Brunelleschi
Interior of the Cappella dei
Pazzi in S. Croce, Florence
ca. 1430*

humanistic culture and religious practice, the forms of the central plan offered a more cogent set of symbols for the complex cosmic, philosophical and theological notions than did the traditional longitudinal church (Wittkower 1962; Larsen 1965; Lotz 1977b).

The opportunity to design a church with a central plan—the first of the Renaissance—was afforded Brunelleschi in around 1434, when it was decided to use the inheritance of Filippo Scolari (Pippo Spano, d. 1426), administrated by the Arte di Calimala, or bankers' guild, for the church of S. Maria degli Angeli in the convent of the Camaldolite Order, one of the most important centers of Florentine humanism, directed by Ambrogio Traversari, a man who was exceptionally fluent in Greek and Hebrew and a renowned scholar of patrology. The extraordinarily avant-garde approach may have been his suggestion. The octagonal plan—which had already appeared, perhaps for symbolic purposes, in earlier churches dedicated to the Virgin Mary, such as S. Maria Maggiore in Lanciano (thirteenth century) and S. Maria del Fiore, and later in a great many Marian sanctuaries—must have seemed the most suited form to celebrate (returning, as well, to the symbology of the baptisteries, as recommended by the Fathers of the Church) the figure of the Madonna as a privileged divine instrument in the mystery of the Incarnation and as a key figure in the cosmic process of Redemption. The money for the construction of the church (begun around 1435) was soon diverted to finance the war, and building work on the site, interrupted in the spring of 1437, was never resumed. In any case, the part that was built and a few antique drawings (such as the one on fol. 15v. in the Giuliano da Sangallo codex in the Vatican, with plan and interior elevation; a perspective sketch, perhaps of the model, copied by Francesco di Giorgio, and a succinct view of the exterior in the *Codex Rustici* in the Biblioteca del Seminario, Florence) afford a reasonably clear idea of Brunelleschi's project. The overall layout makes reference only in a remote way to specific ancient Roman buildings such as the Minerva Medica temple, but it closely copies (even more than the baptistery type) that of the massive Gothic tribunes of S. Maria del Fiore. As in these, the central octagon is ringed by eight square spaces making chapels delimited by triangular-plan partitions; but these partitions (this time in direct reference to antique Roman structures) are cut into by niches forming the chapels inside, and conch niches on the exterior, forming the more complex, sixteen-sided perimeter. The chapels inside, all inter-communicating, have vaulted ceilings (barrel or groin?) and are delineated at the corners by an order of pilasters (*columnae quadrangulae*). They opened onto the octagonal space with eight arches tangent to a continuous entablature surmounted by the drum arches inset with oculi. The octagonal cloister vault, like that of S. Maria del Fiore, was probably buttressed externally by volutes and capped by a small lantern. The exterior with sixteen sides framed by mold-

FVORA DIRM I MIGLO

STVNO IMANCHO VARONE ALA GERMANO
IVTO LEGODATO DIFVCHO
ALTO &· VI· EPOI CHOMINCIA LABOTE

FVORA DIROMA INVERSOMARINO·III·A·

·ALE·III·PERGHOLE·EDEVI·AV1· LVPAI NELAVOLTA

LAGHVGLIA
MISV

QVESTA E VNA SEPOLTVRA A·MPOVA
VECHIA

DIROMA
RATA

Giuliano da Sangallo
Five Plans of Centralized
Buildings, and the Vatican
Obelisk
Vatican, Biblioteca Apostolica
Vaticana
fol. 8

ings, and niches possibly alternated with shell-capped windows with equilateral triangular pediments, must have evoked—translated into the terms of Brunelleschi's new architectural idiom—the image of S. Maria del Fiore or its large polygonal tribunes, as it was represented in frescoes of the Cappellone degli Spagnuoli at S. Maria Novella, and call to mind its significance of the glorification of the Madonna, Regina Coeli.

Despite the premature interruption of its construction, the structure of S. Maria degli Angeli, sometimes mediated with the lantern of the cathedral dome, made a strong impression on the Renaissance world. Echoes of its model may be seen in Florentine paintings of the period, and continued to appear in various interpretations throughout the sixteenth century and longer. Its layout offered Leonardo in particular—who made a sketch of it on fol. 12r. of Manuscript B in Paris—many ideas for reinterpretation and development in his Milanese studies for centrally planned religious buildings (Guillaume 1987).

The so-called *tribune morte*, hemispherical in plan with pairs of half-columns positioned along the axes of the decagon and framing shell-capped niches—a device which Brunelleschi placed around the dome of S. Maria del Fiore—also hark back to classical antiquity, and were many times copied afterward. The great lantern, as well, with its radial, volute buttresses—the Renaissance's first—of the Florentine dome (designed by Brunelleschi in 1436, represented in a wooden model, and realized with a few modifications after the master's death) was a frequent source of inspiration for later architects. Nearly all the places of worship designed by Brunelleschi established organic schemes that were later directly imitated. But, above all, they offered implicit possibilities for re-elaboration and development.

Working alongside Filippo Brunelleschi were Ghiberti, Donatello, Masaccio, Luca della Robbia, and Michelozzo—outstanding sculptors and painters with a quick grasp of ideas, albeit far less methodical, and leading contributors to the sweeping artistic renewal under way in Florence. These artists brought morphological innovations especially to the fixed furnishings of churches: altars,

Leonardo da Vinci
Centrally Planned Churches,
with Annotations
Manuscript B, fol. 17v.
ca. 1490
Paris, Institut de France

128

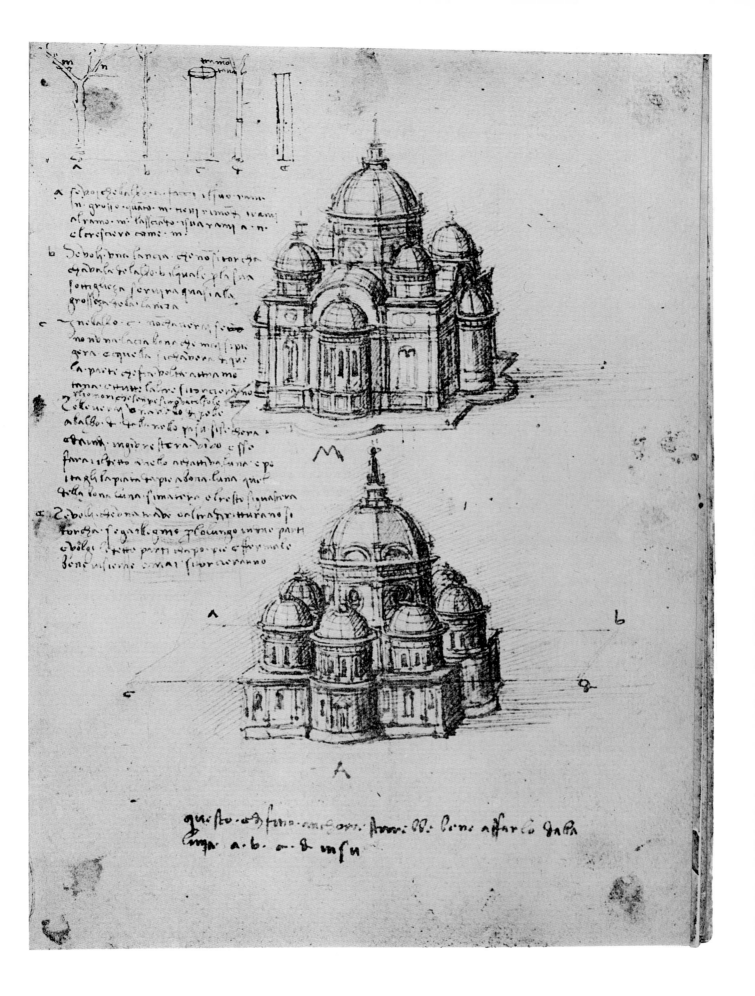

tombs, pulpits, *cantorie*, presbytery enclosures, tabernacles, and so on. Furthermore, at times they gave representations of *all'antica* architecture in their figurations, often following paths that diverged from the master's. The closest in spirit to Brunelleschi seems to have been Masaccio; especially in the famous perspective fresco of the *Trinity* in S. Maria Novella (ca. 1425-26), with the representation of a chapel (according to many, designed by Filippo himself), the plan of which was copied (before 1440?) by Brunelleschi's adoptive son Andrea Cavalcanti, called Buggiano, in the Cappella Cardini at S. Francesco di Pescia. Note should also be taken of the representations of classicized buildings in Ghiberti's panels of the second door (ca. 1430-35) of Florence Baptistery (Krautheimer and Krautheimer Hess 1956); for example, the great round "temple," with arches framed by orders and a low, windowed "attic," and the *Solomon's Temple* in which—despite the pointed arches—a longitudinal structure appears with a vaulted masonry framework, foreshadowing Alberti's church of S. Andrea in Mantua; and the facade of a church against a symmetrical backdrop with a cityscape on the front of the *Reliquary Urn of St. Zanobius* in S. Maria del Fiore, which is a prototype of the most typical scheme, with two orders, of Renaissance facades. Also worth mentioning are Donatello's fantastic architectural figurations in the antique manner in Florence, Siena and Padua.

Unlike Brunelleschi, the sculptors in particular—Ghiberti, Donatello, Michelozzo—offered ideas for the solution of the problem of the church's new facade. Early on (at the close of the 1430s? or around 1460?), in fact, Michelozzo (Ferrara and Quinterio 1984) began to build the facade of the church of S. Agostino in Montepulciano, with its articulation of pilasters.

After working as Ghiberti's assistant and Donatello's partner, Michelozzo subsequently became the architect of Cosimo the Elder. He started out by timidly revising traditional schemes, working on existing structures, such as the church of S. Francesco al Bosco (between ca. 1420 and 1430) and other churches of monasteries, including the Dominican church of S. Marco. In a rather late work (1445), the Cappella del Noviziato or Sacristy at S. Croce, he mingled traditional features with Brunelleschian ideas, turning the simple, vaulted rectangular hall end into a *scarsella* of the type found in the Old Sacristy; this became a widely used device in chapels and churches, large and small, and not just in Tuscany. But in the remodeling of the Servite church of SS. Annunziata (Roselli 1971; Brown Beverly 1989; Ferrara and Quinterio 1984), Michelozzo—who was closely acquainted with Rome and its ancient monuments—added, at the end of a simple longitudinal body with a single

nave flanked by chapels, a large, round tribune with seven large, semicircular niches on the perimeter arranged on ten radial axes, as found in the Temple of Minerva Medica. Work on Michelozzo's project (which dates to the autumn of 1444, when Brunelleschi was still active) was begun with various sources of funding, including a bequest by Giovan Francesco Gonzaga, Marquis of Mantua. Michelozzo's project seems to have called for an ambulatory with piers (or columns) supporting a lower ceiling than the present one, with allusions to the tomb of S. Costanza and to the Holy Sepulcher in Jerusalem, perhaps intended as a tomb (?) for the Gonzaga. A change of plans, with the demolition of the pillars and the removal of the ambulatory, seems to have taken place, following an interruption of the work, in around 1453, in a phase supervised by Antonio Manetti Ciaccheri (who had in his workshop the wooden model of a "round temple," very probably SS. Annunziata's tribune) and financed by Lodovico Gonzaga. Once again interrupted in 1460, work was resumed in 1470, with the consultancy of Leon Battista Alberti (who had been Gonzaga's architect), amid fierce debate as to how to proceed: radically different alternatives were proposed, but discarded under Alberti's direction.

Instead of a unitary synthesis between the centralized and longitudinal plans found in the project for S. Spirito by Brunelleschi (who, it appears, did not spare his criticism of Michelozzo's project), in SS. Annunziata there must have been a juxtaposition of the two elements. Before later transformations, the round chapels of the tribune which Michelozzo had worked on faced the interior with a series of arches on pilasters that recalled Brunelleschi's motif in the chapels of S. Maria degli Angeli, though less refined in their application here. The hemispherical dome resting on a drum with windows and deep arches on the exterior in the "Roman" manner (Mausoleum of S. Elena) seems to be the result of work undertaken after 1470; it is not known what kind of roof was originally intended, nor exactly how the tribune and the nave were to be linked.

It is interesting to note that at the start of the 1470s public feeling still ran high against the central plan that was being realized according to Alberti's project. The criticism, as expressed by a certain Giovanni Aldobrandini, a merchant, mainly regarded the problem of the structure's liturgical functionality: the chapels were too small, forcing the congregation to encroach on the adjacent tribune; the singing of the sixty friars in the choir (itself too small) beneath the vaulted ceiling (acoustically unsuitable) would have been a disturbance to the congregation attending mass in the chapels, whose presence would in turn have upset the friars, especially the presence of "secular women"; temples similar in form to Roman ones were "made to decorate the tombs of those emperors" and, in any case, could be "officiated by four or six chaplains" at the most, and not by a monastery of many monks; and, furthermore, in order for it not to seem "a poor and unadorned thing" it would have been necessary, following the example of those that are "decorated by mosaics, and other things of enormous expense," that the part above the chapels not be left "all white." In short, in the words of architect Giovanni da Gaiuoli, who proposed an alternative model, and called on Brunelleschi's assessment to substantiate his arguments, "the said work is entirely doomed," because "there is no room for either an altar or a choir, nor room to use the chapels."

When Alberti (1404-72) took over at SS. Annunziata toward the end of his life he had already made contributions of extraordinary importance to the renewal of religious building types. Having entered the architectural profession rather late, perhaps sometime after 1445, after decisive formative experiences and with a vast background in philosophical and scientific humanism, he seems to have been alone among the architects of his time to have grasped Vitruvius' *De architectura*, and having lived more or less steadily in Rome (1432-34, then from 1444 on) had made an in-depth study of the city's legacy of ancient monuments. Alberti's *De re aedificatoria* (nearly complete in 1452) includes his fundamental treatise on "temple" construction, according to the new humanistic principles (Book VII, ii) which continued to be a point of reference at least until the Counter-Reformation.

According to Alberti, the temple, which should be situated in a raised and privileged position in the city, could assume a variety of shapes—round, polygonal, square—depending on its assigned function. The preferable form was, however, the centralized plan—a "perfect" form preferred by nature in many of its manifestations. Such a structure was to be completed by apses or chapels (*tribunalia*), of which the largest should house the altar, and by a portico, either encircling the full perimeter, or just at the entrance. In the temple especially, all the building's parts must be in close correspondence, as in a living organism (*animal, animans*) such that a single part discloses all the dimensions of the others. Furthermore, the temple in particular must include the use of "ornament," in the sense of *columnationes* or established architectural orders of antiquity. Frivolities and gratuitous ornament were to be avoided—anything that might distract the faithful from their religious thoughts—and, instead, emphasis must be given to purity of form and simplicity of color. Inside, the altar (preferably only one, as in primitive Christianity) must occupy the most eminent position. Instead of frescoes, the walls should be decorated with paintings on panels or—better still—reliefs (*signa*). At any event, all decoration of the walls (and likewise of the floor) must be conducive to lofty and philosophical thoughts; this could involve employing inscriptions, symbols or geometrical figures. The roof must be vaulted, to ensure its perpetuity and safety, variously decorated with ornamental elements, geometrical or structural, and even with the representation of the heavenly sphere. The temple should be illuminated by windows of average size—affording a certain obscurity, particularly around the altar so as to enhance the sense of veneration and to accentuate the light of the sacred candles, the most important ornament in the place—and be set up high in the wall, so that only the sky can be seen.

Earlier in his work (VII, iv), among the types of religious buildings described—interpreting Vitruvius in his own manner—is a temple designed according to the *vetusto Etruscorum more*: with three *cellae* (chapels) on each side of a nave ending in a *tribunal* (apse) and preceded by a porticoed entrance functioning as a vestibule; it resembled the Basilica of Maxentius, then believed to be the ancient Templum Pacis. Alberti himself, as we shall see, designed the church of S. Andrea in Mantua, and with this interpretation of the Etruscan temple, he opened the way to the reinstatement of the presumed principles of the classical architects, fostering a widespread use of the traditional scheme of nave and lateral chapels.

After discussing temple construction, Alberti describes the *basilica* (VII, xiv, xv), the site of the administration of justice; this was similar in nature, but less dignified, to the temple. In fact, it was often used as a church (VII, iv), only because it corresponded typologically to liturgical requirements and was acoustically suited to preaching, despite its static defects (I, x). Although he interprets Vitruvius in part, Alberti seems to have in mind the Early Christian and medieval basilican types in Rome and Florence, rather than the forum basilicas of classical antiquity—in addition to (though perhaps with an underlying vein of criticism) the examples wrought by Filippo Brunelleschi.

More or less around the time when he was drafting *De re aedificatoria*, it is possible (Magnuson 1958; Gadol 1969; Westfall 1974; Tafuri 1992) that Alberti was acting as advisor to his former study-companion Tommaso Parentucelli di Sarzana, then Pope Nicholas V (1447-55), and his architects for the restoration of early Roman churches. In fact, S. Stefano Rotondo was remodeled under the supervision of Bernardo Rossellino (1453), following to some extent the new principles. The church of S. Teodoro, with its circular plan combined with pre-existing structures and dome (the first to be built in Rome in the 1400s), recalls the Florentine manner, especially in the "crest and sail" dome resting on heavy corbels.

At this time, Rossellino (or someone on his behalf) drafted for Nicholas V a grandiose project for

Matteo De' Pasti
Medal showing the facade of the
Tempio Malatestiano, Rimini
1450
Berlin, Staatliche Museen
Preussischer Kulturbesitz
Münzkabinett
Cat. no. 49

Masaccio
Trinity
1426-28
Florence, S. Maria Novella

133

remodeling Old St. Peter's (Urban 1963). Culminating in a large apsidal choir (the construction of which was started behind the original apse, and completed by Bramante during the papacy of Julius II, between 1506 and 1514), it seems to have required the consolidation of the nave and aisles and the reconstruction and enlargement of the projecting transept with vaults and a dome in the center. With its references to antique symbology, the new plan, according to Giannozzo Manetti (Battisti 1960a), in a humanistic way took after the image of a human figure with outstretched arms, like Christ on the Cross, with the head of the body represented by the new tribune (because "the form of the human figure is superior, is more noble, than any other thing ... and, in fact, it was believed ... to have been made in the likeness of the entire world"). It also must have recalled Noah's Ark, an image of the church as the ark of salvation. And the tribune's crown of circular windows, recalling antique symbologies of light, was intended "to give the devout a idea of divine glory." Architecturally, the project mingled generically "antique" styles, echoes of Florentine architecture and medieval nuances, Roman ones too (such as the Gothic transept of S. Francesco a Ripa, with cross vaults supported by columns set against the wall). Alberti seems to have been against this project, and, according to Mattia Palmieri, recommended the pope to halt the work and to limit the operation—as illustrated in *De re aedificatoria* (I, xi; X, xvii)—to the consolidation of the old structures. In any case, Nicholas V's project, in a political and cultural world quite different from that of Florence, is the first attempt after Brunelleschi to remodel a major church, and represents a milestone in the process of renewal of religious architecture in the Rome area.

At this time (ca. 1450), Leon Battista Alberti was engaged by Sigismondo Malatesta, Lord of Rimini, to transform the church of S. Francesco into a dynastic sepulchral temple (work was abandoned in 1468). The original structure comprised a single nave and chapels, renovated inside by various artists, including Matteo de' Pasti and Agostino di Duccio. The new scheme involved incorporating this structure within a new, Roman-style shell whose design was directly borrowed from ancient monuments in the Rimini and Ravenna area. The temple was to include a domed rotunda (perhaps suggested by the Pantheon and something like the "composite" structure of SS. Annunziata) with the ribbing of the vault exposed on the exterior, though it was never realized. In the lower part of the facade, the motif of the Arch of Augustus in Rimini was reworked, and set with half-columns framing arches. But the proposed central section of the facade (as seen in Matteo de' Pasti's medal) was to join with the lower part at the sides (according to an autograph sketch in a letter from Alberti to Matteo de' Pasti) by means of a double volute on a half-tympanum, with a large arch at the center, flanked with pilasters. This upper part was never completed. The arched front and roofing of the nave (probably timber barrel-vaulting, as in medieval churches of the Veneto, with accentuated ribbing) would have offered a solution (presumably illustrated by a wooden model) that was particularly widespread in the Veneto area.

The typically Albertian motif adopted for the church facade—foreshadowed by the Florentine architects, and by Ghiberti in particular—reemerged, this time in an "antique" though patently Florentine idiom—in the completion of the existing fourteenth-century facade of S. Maria Novella. The resulting design (which has links with the facade of S. Miniato al Monte) became a widely used model. The lower portion was reworked with half-columns of the Corinthian order, the outer ones braced by bold corner pilasters (of antique inspiration) and the inner two framing the central arched entrance portal. Rising above a continuous band, the upper story is articulated by four pilasters (like the front of an ancient temple translated into stonework), crowned by a triangular pediment, and joined either side to the lower portion by large scroll volutes. Again in Florence, the sacellum—which may have been coeval (ca. 1455–67) with the S. Sepolcro chapel—inserted in the center of the rectangular Cappella Rucellai in S. Pancrazio once again proposes the design of an ideal small temple in masonry with an apse and the external walls articulated by an order of pilasters, translated into terms of "Florentine" antiquity. This motif was later repeated frequently in Renaissance chapels and churches. Moreover, it is possible that in around 1450 or earlier, Alberti had given his advice for the campanile of Ferrara Cathedral (completed as far as the third upper story in 1464), for the first time enhanced with superimposed classical orders.

As early as the decade of 1450-60 Alberti's ideas seem to have penetrated the artistic culture of humanistic Italy, especially in the central and northern regions. Presumably, this occurred by way of his personal contacts with artists, with men of learning and the nobility, in addition to his on-site work and the circulation of his treatise, which was still in manuscript form at the time. Thus, Fra Angelico shows an early acquaintance with Alberti's style, depicted in his frescoes of the Cappella Niccolina in the Vatican (ca. 1447–50). Nor is it possible to overlook Mantegna's paintings in the Cappella Ovetari at the Eremitani in Padua, and the architectural forms depicted by Piero della Francesca, from the early fresco *Sigismondo Malatesta and his Patron Saint* (1451) in the Tempio Malatestiano in Rimini, to later works in Arezzo (the church facade featured in the True Cross choir frescoes), and in Urbino. Such images contributed to the spread of the new ideas in religious architecture.

Various Florentine architects—often those engaged in the completion of Brunelleschi's works (Borsi et al. 1979)—also manifested a shift toward Alberti's outlook. This appears already in the church

Leon Battista Alberti
Facade of S. Maria Novella
Florence

Leon Battista Alberti
Sacellum of S. Sepolcro
Florence, S. Pancrazio
Cappella Rucellai

YHESVM QVERITIS N

IOHANNES RVCELLARIVS
PAVLI·F·VT·INDE·SALVTEM·SVAM
PRECARETVR·VNDE·OMNIVM·CVM
CHRISTO·FACTA·EST·RESVRRECTIO
SACELLVM·HOC
AD·INSTAR·IHEROSOLIMITANI·SEPVL
CHRI·FACIVNDVM·CVRAVIT
M·CCCC·LXVII

Andrea Mantegna
Martyrdom of St. Christopher
*detail of fresco in the Cappella
Ovetari*
1456–57
Padua, Chiesa degli Eremitani

of the Badia at Fiesole, a complex begun in 1456 under the personal supervision of Cosimo de' Medici and built to plans drawn up by his friend Timoteo Maffei. The foundation stone of the church was laid in 1461, but its design dates as early as 1456. The identity of the architect is still unknown, and although Vasari pointed to Brunelleschi, the master had died ten years earlier. Other suggested names include Michelozzo, Bernardo Rossellino and Cosimo himself (a skilled architect, according to Vespasiano da Bisticci), and even Alberti. In fact, the architect must have moved in Alberti's sphere of influence, and was not without knowledge of Brunelleschi's heritage, but lacked the latter's rigorous methodical approach. In any case, the simple Latin cross plan, with barrel-vaulted nave and a groin vault over the crossing, emphasized by a continuous architrave-cornice resting on corner pilasters, represented a decisive step toward a new Renaissance style in the design of the aisle-less monastic church with square chapels, deep choir and short transept; the Badia stood as a prototype for later elaborations.

Echoes of Alberti's approach as expressed in his *De re aedificatoria* may also be discerned in the cathedral of Pienza (Mack 1987; Faldi and Guglielmi 1990), dedicated to the Madonna, built between 1459 and 1462 by Bernardo Rossellino (in Rome during the papacies of Eugenius IV and Nicholas V, and in contact with Alberti) under the patronage of Pope Pius II Piccolomini. The plan, which did not exclude certain Gothic elements, skillfully links a nave and two aisles ending in a polygonal structure based on three sides of an octagon opening on to rectangular chapels (perhaps suggested, if only in part, by S. Maria degli Angeli?). The nave is separated from the aisles not by columns, but instead by square piers set with half-columns on each face, freely interpreted from the antique, with "Doric" capitals and simple torus bases. Their low and "incorrect" tripartite entablature is surmounted by another, high *membratura*—as already experimented in Siena and then in later churches—over which the arches and the cross vaults rise, to the same height and with the same diagonal ribbing of the roof. The design offered a sort of *Hallenkirche*, with the nave and aisles of approximately equal height, divided by piers. This kind of church, not unknown in Italian Gothic architecture, was especially widespread in southern Germany, where Piccolomini had had occasion to admire it during his diplomatic assignments. The device turned up again in later Renaissance churches.

Despite its faltering, hybrid style, Pienza Cathedral met Alberti's guidelines—as intended by the patron and the architect—by translating the basilican plan into masonry and utilizing elements borrowed from antiquity. The accurate description which Piccolomini himself gives of the cathedral in his *Commentari* (Book IX) reflects his agreement with Alberti's ideas on religious architecture. Of particular interest in this respect is the text of a famous bull which he issued as Pope Pius II to safeguard—on penalty of excommunication—the integrity and the "commendable candor" of the church, with which he was so highly satisfied. The bull forbade anyone to clutter the space with tombs, to deface the cleanness of the walls and the columns, to paint them or hang pictures, to erect chapels or altars in greater number than those planned; to change, in general, the form of the temple. The facade, too, in some respects interprets Alberti's principles, projecting the vertical structures and the arches of equal height to the nave, and culminating, as in ancient temples, with a large triangular tympanum.

In this period (1459–60) Alberti was commissioned by Lodovico Gonzaga of Mantua to design the

Fra Angelico
St. Sixtus Ordaining
St. Lawrence
fresco
1450
Vatican City
Cappella Niccolina

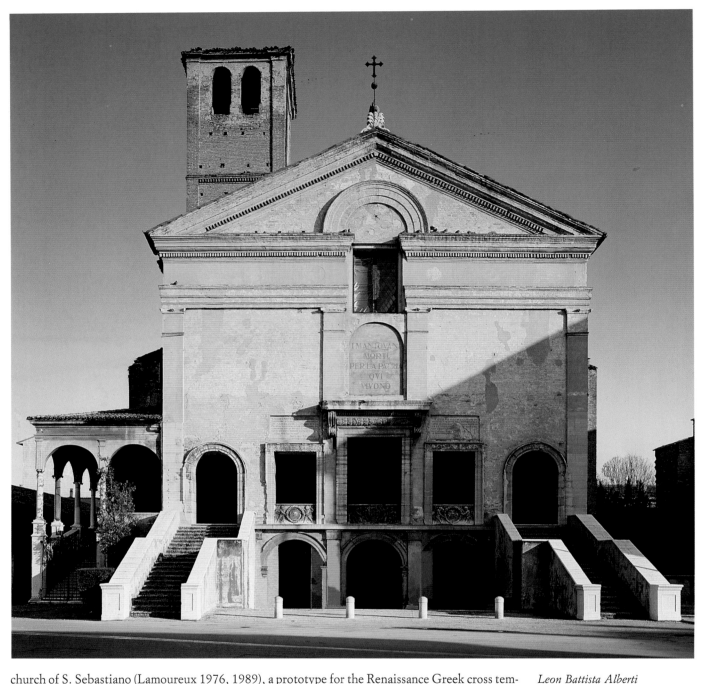

church of S. Sebastiano (Lamoureux 1976, 1989), a prototype for the Renaissance Greek cross temple. After a speedy start, its construction progressed slowly and it was not completed until toward the end of the century, long after Alberti's death and possibly with modifications to his plan (perpetuated in the modern restoration of the church). Moreover, Alberti himself had proposed alterations in the autumn of 1470 ("to reduce the pillars"—the pilasters, that is—"of the portico"). Thus, there is uncertainty in the reconstruction of Alberti's aims: uncertainty about the front prospect of the temple, raised on a vast crypt of piers and cross vaults; about the number and placement of the pilasters across the temple front; about the roof of the nave, with a large cross vault, as it appears now, or with a spherical dome (as indicated in a rough sketch by Antonio Labacco, assistant to Antonio da Sangallo the Younger, which may be taken from a drawing of the church which Lorenzo il Magnifico had commissioned from Luca Fancelli in 1485, in preparation for the construction of the church of S. Maria delle Carceri in Prato by Giuliano da Sangallo).

Despite such uncertainties, the historical importance of S. Sebastiano is evident, and even in the form in which it has reached us, it embodies a full and mature expression of Alberti's ideas on the temple as set forth in his treatise. With its subtle echoes of early Christian models, the square centralized space expands into a cross with three rectangular apsidal chapels (*tribunalia*), with the fourth arm forming a vestibule (according to Labacco's sketch, flanked by two small campaniles, foreshadowing sixteenth-century solutions), preceded by the entrance portico in a massive block of masonry pierced with doorways, the whole raised on steps in the manner of a classical temple front. One year after Alberti's death in 1472, cardinal Francesco Gonzaga, the son of Lodovico, expressed

Leon Battista Alberti
Facade of S. Sebastiano
Mantua
ca. 1460

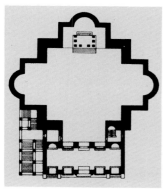

*Interior and plan of
S. Sebastiano, Mantua*

his perplexity about S. Sebastiano, wondering "if we have indeed built a church, mosque, or synagogue." In any case, even with the occasional inclusion of medieval features, the idea spread that the centralized plan rather than the longitudinal plan was best suited to inspiring a sense of celebration and glorification—be it of a saint, hero or martyr of the faith, of the Virgin Mary, or even of an illustrious corpse. Hence it was particularly appropriate to votive churches, sanctuaries, chapels, or burial sacella and the like.

The design of Brunelleschi's Old Sacristy spread to assorted chapels and churches from central Italy to the north, often undergoing variations and local interpretations. Worthy of mention is the Cappella Portinari at the church of S. Eustorgio in Milan, which appears to have been started in 1462 to designs by a Tuscan architect (perhaps Filarete or Michelozzo), but subsequently took a local, Lombard slant. Amadeo adapted its plan in the first years of the 1470s for the Cappella Colleoni in Bergamo. But, meanwhile, in June 1460—almost contemporary with S. Sebastiano—Antonio Manetti Ciaccheri (who died the following November), already at work on SS. Annunziata, provided a model for the important chapel known as the Cappella del Cardinale di Portogallo (Chapel of the Cardinal of Portugal) at S. Miniato al Monte, Florence, later decorated by Luca della Robbia and Antonio Rossellino: the chapel is square with a sail-vault ceiling and an order of corner pilasters framing the arches of rectangular chapels with barrel vaults situated on the four sides to form a centralized cross plan. This is the most direct antecedent to the Prato church by Giuliano da Sangallo. This same period may have seen the start of work on the church of S. Maria di Bressanoro in Castelleone (Cremona, Lombardy). The building develops the layout of Brunelleschi's Old Sacristy, placing four *scarselle* on the sides of a square, resulting once again in a Greek cross plan. The Florentine architect Filarete (Antonio Averlino) had proposed a similar solution in a chapel for Francesco Sforza, Duke of Milan (his design is known through a medal by Sperandio). Of great importance to the elaboration and diffusion throughout northern Italy of new plans for churches, was Filarete's activity in Milan from the early 1450s to the mid-1460s as architect of the Sforza family (this followed a lengthy stay in Rome, starting in 1433, as sculptor of the doors of St. Peter's). Of mixed and sketchy learning, but a friend of Francesco Filelfo and other humanists, he combined his experiences in Florence in the sphere of Brunelleschi and Florentine sculptors with a fair acquaintance with the antique monuments of Rome and early Christian and early medieval structures in Milan. His *Trattato d'Architettura* (written between ca. 1460 and 1464, and dedicated first to Sforza and then to Piero de' Medici) provides descriptions and drawings of many churches.

Antonio Manetti Ciaccheri
Cappella del Cardinale di
Portogallo
ca. 1460
Florence, S. Miniato al Monte

140

These concern, primarily, centralized plans and cross plans inscribed within a square (or quincunx), inspired by S. Lorenzo and the sacellum of S. Satiro in Milan: the cathedral of the imaginary city of Sforzinda (Book VII, fol. 49v.), the church in the center of the market square (Book X, fol. 76v.), that of the S. Benedetto monastery (Book XI, fol. 78v.), that of the Ospedale Maggiore (Book XI, fol. 81v.) and even a "hermit's church" (Book XV, fol. 117v.), in addition to the temples of the imaginary city of Plusiapolis (Book XIV, fols. 107v., 108r.; Book XV, fol. 119v.). These church designs—especially the ones based on the Greek cross inscribed in a square with a dome at the center and smaller units at the corners, at times with four corner campaniles—with their complex articulation of volumes and space, offer a spectacular and fanciful overall effect, rich in symbolic potential. Filarete's schemes provided models for later elaborations not only by Lombard architects of the late fifteenth century, but also by Leonardo and, in particular, Bramante, before his activity in Rome. It is interesting that most of Filarete's church proposals are for centrally planned buildings—freely interpreted from presumed temples of antiquity. The designs themselves vary considerably, with little distinction between cathedrals, city churches, monastic churches, and so forth, and scant concern for addressing the liturgical needs dictating the customary schemes adopted for church design.

The established church plan, however, tended to be preferred in spheres that were less affected by the new culture inspired by antiquity, or where, as in Lombardy and the Po Valley in general, the medieval building tradition was still strong. Here, new plans were sometimes proposed in which the new concept of the religious building could play a role, despite the "Gothic" vocabulary. At the close of the fourteenth century Antonio di Vincenzo took the lesson of S. Maria del Fiore to heart: his unrealized scheme for S. Petronio in Bologna envisaged a large octagonal crossing dome over an aisled nave, complete with choir and transept, divided into three by rows of piers. Later, between 1440 and the close of the century, the church of S. Giovanni in Monte was built in the same city following Antonio's example. This theme seemed particularly adapted not only to large churches and cathedrals but also to the liturgical requirements of a large sanctuary, with the opportunity to place the object of veneration in the octagon, permitting the circulation of a large number of pilgrims. This scheme was adopted in the church built in L'Aquila, begun in 1454, to house the tomb of St. Bernardino of Siena. But the "composite" plan suggested by S. Maria del Fiore must have seemed particularly appropriate to the great sanctuary of Loreto (Grimaldi 1986), begun at the close of the 1460s, also with the involvement of Pope Paul II, to house the highly venerated "little house of the Madonna" not only for practical and liturgical reasons, but also for symbolic ones. With the central part, it could evince complex cosmic and theological concepts which in the culture of the period were linked to the idea of temple and sanctuary, echoes of famous Palestinian churches and symbolic relationships between the octagon of the central space and the figure of the Madonna, conserving—with the longitudinal part with aisled nave and vaults of equal height (as in Pienza)—the memory of the *ecclesia* of medieval Christian tradition. Although neither the identity of the author nor the provenance of the project (the execution of which was begun by Marino di Marco Cedrino, and in successive phases continued by Giuliano da Maiano, Baccio Pontelli and Giuliano da Sangallo until 1500) is certain, it represented a rationalized version of the "composite" scheme, quite similar to the S. Petronio project with a few innovations brought on by the Renaissance climate, such as the four octagonal sacristies in the corners and the originally semicircular chapels (as in S. Spirito) in the longitudinal body. In this respect, as we shall see, it stands as the model most similar to Bramante's design for the cathedral at Pavia.

Another attempt at a synthesis between the main centrally planned section and the longitudinal section, with transept and choir terminating in a triconch arranged around an octagonal crossing tower grafted onto a longitudinal body with a nave and two aisles and square chapels, is the Certosa at Pavia (1429–73), built in Gothic style to designs by the Solari. For other religious buildings in the city—such as the Dominican church of S. Maria delle Grazie (begun in 1463, while Filarete was in Milan, later completed with a tribune designed by Bramante), or S. Pietro in Gessate (slightly later)—Guiniforte Solari (1429–81), while still using schemes of the late fourteenth century (such as that of S. Maria del Carmine in Pavia), adopted vaulted Latin cross plans with transept and deep choir. Here, the nave and aisles, flanked by square or polygonal perimeter chapels, are now divided, following Brunelleschi's example, not by masonry pillars but by columns.

In this context—still in some respects uncertain, especially as far as the new typologies of longitudinal churches were concerned—Alberti's design for S. Andrea in Mantua (Johnson 1975) is strikingly innovative. It was linked to a sweeping renewal scheme carried out on the city center around 1470, a project to which Alberti contributed. What was needed was a large church in which "many people could see the blood of Christ," wrote Alberti, in a letter to Marquis Lodovico Gonzaga, in October 1470, referring to the Mantuan relic of the "preziosissimo sangue." Perhaps Antonio di Tuccio Manetti (the future biographer of Brunelleschi, with whom Gonzaga and Alberti were in contact for SS. Annunziata) had put forward a "model" to Alberti for his opinion. Though he gave his approval, Alberti submitted a project of his own, a larger building that he considered "more eternal, worthy and charming," as well as more economical, whose form was "*se nomina apud veteres Etruscum sacrum*" (Krautheimer 1961).

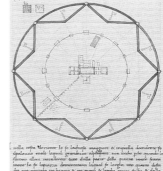

Filarete (Antonio Averlino)
Plan of the Ideal City of Sforzinda
1462-64
Florence, Biblioteca Nazionale Centrale, Codice Magliabechiano *II, 1, 140, fol. 43r.*
Cat. no. 181

Leon Battista Alberti
Facade and plan of S. Andrea
Mantua
ca. 1470

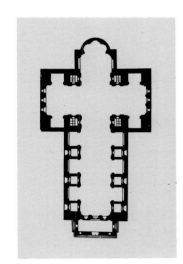

For a city believed to be of Etruscan origin, it seemed more appropriate to take inspiration from the typology of the *Etruscorum more* temple described by Vitruvius and interpreted by Alberti in *De re aedificatoria*, represented among antique monuments by the plan of the Templum Pacis (Basilica of Maxentius) and in the one in the central area of the imperial baths (Book VIII, x): an *"atrium amplissimum et dignissimum cum cellis"*; that is, a large, vaulted hall flanked by three chapels on the sides, the whole in plan in a 6:5 proportion.

The foundation stone was not laid until 12 June 1472 (following Alberti's death in Rome at the beginning of April) and we do not know if Alberti's model, conditioned by existing structures and interruptions in the work, was faithfully carried out, especially since by the turn of the century, only the nave with its large coffered barrel vault had been completed. Thus, in the present stage of research, it is not possible to know how freely the idea of the "Etruscan temple" was followed, and, especially, if the church's late completion with the transept and the dome reflect Alberti's conception. Nevertheless, at least as far as the structure of the nave—with three barrel-vaulted chapels per side, open, between large nuclei concealing smaller sail-vaulted chapels, with arches framed by pilasters on pedestals placed at different intervals in rhythmic succession ("travata ritmica")—it is certain that S. Andrea takes shape as a spatial-structural organism, three-dimensional and completely in masonry. As such, it fully corresponds to Alberti's principles and the results are strikingly innovative and mature. It was to stand as a fundamental prototype for later religious architecture, though not simply because of its formula of the single, aisle-less nave and chapels.

143

Leon Battista Alberti
Interior of St. Andrea, Mantua
ca. 1470

The entrance area—limited to the central part of the temple because of an existing campanile—is conceived, as hypothesized in *De re aedificatoria* (Book VII, v) and carried out in a different form in S. Sebastiano, as a large masonry portico open at the center with a large barrel vault perpendicular to the facade, flanked by two smaller transverse vaults. The facade, which mirrors the nave structure, ingeniously combines (Wittkower 1962) the triumphal arch (as in Rimini) and the classical temple-front (as in S. Sebastiano), both vehicles of humanistic intents. Like the interior, this facade provided fundamental cues to later religious architecture, starting with the work of Bramante.

In Rome, Alberti's conception of architecture appeared with a direct copy of ancient Roman models in the Benediction Loggia at St. Peter's, begun in 1461 by Pius II, utilizing ancient columns, and continued in 1463 and 1464 (when in Florence a mysterious wooden model of the work was paid for), and later resumed by Paul II and his successors. Originally built with four bays composed of three registers of arches framed by architectural orders (later destroyed), the revised loggia was to comprise a new porticoed front with eleven bays spanning the entire facade of the basilica. Under Paul II, the idea, with an analogous situation of three bays and two orders of arches, comprising elements taken directly from such monuments as the Colosseum, was copied (1465 and later) in the porticoed facade with loggia in the church of S. Marco, in turn remodeled according to the new principles in the Palazzo Venezia complex (Frommel 1983b). Scholars are almost unanimous about the influence of Alberti's ideas in these works, though in this writer's opinion, no one has produced truly convincing arguments about their authorship. At any event, the portico-and-loggia type of church facade returns in other fifteenth-century Roman churches such as that of the SS. Apostoli—with forms that are different, but still related to those of the S. Marco complex—which was also remodeled in the "modern style."

For a century already Rome had been a meeting ground of disparate architectural cultures. Many master craftsmen (masons, carpenters, carvers, etc.) worked for patrons of all kinds and origin. Sometimes referred to as "architects," these craftsmen were of various provenance and background (Tomei 1942; Magnuson 1958; Urban 1961-1962; Golzio and Zander 1968), but prevalently Florentine and Tuscan (S. Borsi et al. 1989), though there were Lombards as well and craftsmen from the Po Valley in general. Their work was well-accepted in a local climate which was open to different stimuli and which, by tradition and also thanks to the initiatives of humanistic popes, learned men of the Curia and especially apostolic scribes and functionaries—like Alberti himself or Francesco del Borgo—who were interested in architecture, was precociously receptive to the suggestions of antiquity. However, in building yards which by and large retained medieval working methods, it is difficult to attach single works to individual personalities or to distinguish the true architects from those who merely executed their designs, or even from the administrators. In any case, the papacy of Sixtus IV saw the construction of several churches of major importance which, while not introducing crucial typological innovations, contributed to changing the panorama of religious architecture in the last thirty years of the century, giving new "Roman-style" interpretations of traditional schemes, copying the brickwork and travertine, especially for exteriors. Furthermore, the use of vaulted roofing became widespread, with a preference for continuous cross-vaulting, as used in antiquity; semicircular chapels and apses were also widespread, while windows continued to be of the "medieval" type.

Perhaps at the suggestion of the patrons, the plan for the church of S. Maria del Popolo (ca. 1472–80) of the Augustinian Order of the Province of Lombardy (Bentivoglio and Valtieri 1976) may be likened to the Milanese type exemplified by S. Pietro in Gessate, from which it copied the floor plan and the polygonal chapels. But surrounding an octagonal "Tuscan" cloister dome set over a high, windowed drum, the great, continuous cross vaults of the nave and the square vaults of the jutting transept and of the choir—in turn, ending in semicircular apses—rest directly on, as in antiquity, the entablature of an order of half-columns, suggesting originally, in a cruciform plan with nave and chapels, the Late Roman grandiosity of the Basilica of Maxentius and other thermal complexes. The facade (probably finished in 1477), entirely in travertine, offers a terse interpretation of the temple-front composed of a superimposed order of pilasters enhanced with refined details of classical extraction, with the higher central part capped with a triangular pediment.

Soon afterward, on 1 November 1479, the great church of S. Agostino was refounded by Guillaume d'Estouteville, camerlengo to Sixtus IV; built by Jacopo da Pietrasanta, it was finished, including the facade, in 1483. It shows a completely vaulted, Latin cross plan with a spherical dome at the crossing of transept and choir, both with apses, perhaps vaguely echoing Nicholas V's project for St. Peter's. The succession of semicircular chapels to the sides may have been inspired by Brunelleschi's S. Spirito. But, while the cross vaults of the nave and the aisles are continuous as in other Roman churches, following the example of antiquity, for the nave (which is exceptionally tall, probably in accordance with the tastes of the French patron), square piers alternate with pillars set with half-columns, in a rhythm characteristic of the Middle Ages, especially in the Po Valley. The facade rises above a high ramp of stairs, similar to the type used for S. Maria del Popolo and later adapted for S. Giacomo degli Spagnoli—perhaps, as in the latter case, reworking ideas that had originated in Florence. The superimposed orders are separated by a horizontal frieze bordered at either

Giovanni Pinadelli
Sixtus IV Surrounded by his
Building Works
1589
Milan, Civica Raccolta Stampe
Achille Bertarelli

TEMPLA·DOMVM·EXPOSITIS·VICOS·FORA·MOENIA·PONTES·
VIRGINEAM·TRIVII·QVOD·REPARARIS·AQVAM·
PRISCA·LICET·NAVTIS·STATVAS·DARE·COMMODA·PORTVS·
ET·VATICANVM·CINGERE·SIXTE·IVGVM·
PLVS·TAMEN·VRBS·DEBET·NAM·QVAE·SQVALORE·LATEBAT·
CERNITVR·IN·CELEBRI·BIBLIOTHECA·LOCO·

Melozzo da Forlì
Sixtus IV Appoints Platina
Prefect of the Biblioteca
Vaticana
ca. 1490
fresco transferred to canvas
Vatican, Pinacoteca Vaticana

side by a half-pediment surmounted by an enormous volute, a more sculptural interpretation of those used by Alberti for S. Maria Novella.

Slightly earlier (ca. 1474), Florentine architect Giuliano da Maiano created a structure similar to the nave of S. Agostino for the cathedral of Faenza. Here, however, the structure comprised a Latin cross plan rigorously proportioned according to Brunelleschi's method, with basic square units distinguished by sail vaults. An important model in the Po Valley and Adriatic area, the cathedral in Faenza has pillars supporting large, sail-vaulted bays decorated by a taller order of pilasters, alternating with a lower order of columns supporting the arches.

A few religious buildings of central Italy in particular (S. Maria Maggiore in Città di Castello, S. Agostino in Ascoli, etc.), but also in the north (Turin Cathedral, 1491–98) are similar in plan to the monastic church type that appeared in Rome around Sixtus IV's time. Most of them were built by Tuscan masters in the second half of the fifteenth century. Probably in preparation for the 1475 Jubilee, the basilican plan of the ancient church of SS. Nereo e Achilleo in Rome was remodeled, replacing the columns with octagonal piers. Elsewhere, the basilican division by columns was re-

tained throughout northern Lazio, as in the church of S. Maria della Quercia near Viterbo, which boasts a domed centralized plan.

The formula of semicircular side chapels flanking an aisle-less nave—very similar in form to one of the schemes in Francesco di Giorgio's treatise—crops up again in Rome in the church of S. Pietro in Montorio (after 1472; ca. 1480–1500), begun in the polygonal choir and the cross-plan presbytery by the Franciscan order of Blessed Amadeo Menez da Silva, and continued, probably with modification to the original project, especially in the 1480s and 1490s. Once again, similar to what happened in S. Agostino, the pilasters of the order framing the niches alternately jut out more and are crowned, something like in Pienza, with capitals supporting the corbels of the cross vaults. However, the rectangular facade in particular, entirely in travertine, rising up to a pediment and marked at the corners by superimposed pilaster strips, is of a higher architectural refinement than the interior, and may be compared to the schemes of Francesco di Giorgio Martini. The church of S. Maria della Pace (after 1478; ca. 1482–92) also had a simple rectangular facade with a portal and rose window, and at the ends pilasters supporting a pediment. Its clear-cut structure, suited to a votive temple dedicated to the Madonna, combines a large domed octagon with chapels on the sides with a short, two-bay

Federico Barocci
Study for a Flight of Aeneas,
Showing Bramante's
Tempietto
ca. 1588
Florence, Uffizi, Gabinetto
Disegni e Stampe, Uff. 135A
Cat. no. 141

148

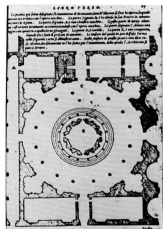

cross-vaulted nave, with two semicircular chapels framed by a single order of pilasters. A free interpretation of the scheme of the exterior of the ancient tetrastyle temple-front translated into masonry in the manner of Alberti (as in the sacellum of S. Sepolcro) by means of walls and pilasters on pedestals (also taking cues from Roman temples and tombs) with lively references to architectural developments in Urbino, is represented by the new, small but important, cathedral of S. Aurea in the town of Ostia. It was built as a simple hall with a barrel-vaulted rectangular choir on commission by Giuliano della Rovere, the future Pope Julius II, bishop of the diocese from 1483 (Danesi Squarzina 1981).

These last-mentioned works—the facade of S. Pietro in Montorio, S. Maria della Pace, and S. Aurea, all datable to after 1482—introduce innovative elements to the earlier, composite Roman architecture. These breakthroughs have often been seen in relation to the presence in Rome after 1482 of the Florentine architect Baccio Pontelli, a pupil—like Giuliano da Sangallo—of Francione, who, following a period of activity in Tuscany as a carpenter (1471–79), worked alongside Francesco di Giorgio Martini in Urbino (1479–81) until the death of Duke Federico da Montefeltro (1482). His name appears beneath that of his patron, Giuliano della Rovere, with the qualification of "architect" on the entrance door to the Ostia fortress and archive documents portray him primarily as a military architect, with no mention of these Roman churches. However—also in light of his later work in the church of S. Maria delle Grazie in Senigallia (1491) and S. Maria Maggiore in Orciano (1492), for Giovanni della Rovere—Pontelli's experience in Urbino may explain the features of this group of Roman churches.

In fact, in the composite world of Urbino, under Federico da Montelfeltro, Battista Sforza (d. 1472) and Ottaviano Ubaldini, with its direct links to Alberti, Piero della Francesca and the Florentine and northern Italian humanistic culture, architecture, including religious structures, made great strides into maturity, not so much with Luciano Laurana (1467–72) as with the arrival of Francesco di Giorgio Martini (1475–76, or earlier?), until the death of Federico (1482). Perhaps some time before or around 1474, in the palazzo, beneath the famous Studiolo which celebrates together the heroes of antique and Christian wisdom, two small adjoining sacella with coffered barrel vaults were architecturally defined: one with an apse framed by an order of columns, dedicated to the Holy Ghost; the other is dedicated to the Muses, with Apollo and Pallas, and they are separated only by a "*parvo discrimine,*" to stress the humanistic convergence of classical antiquity and Christianity (Rotondi 1950).

The famous *Brera Altarpiece* by Piero della Francesca, dating to around the same time (ca. 1472), shows the interior of a temple that adopts and develops—with Albertian accents, echoes of Florentine architecture and its repercussions in Urbino—the idea of the central area, possibly domed, expanding into a cross with simple barrel-vaulted arms ending in an apse. A Latin cross plan—with a deep apsidal choir, as in the *Brera Altarpiece*, a dome resting on an octagonal drum with windows at the crossing of arms with large barrel vaults and simple, square piers in the nave and a succession of semicircular niches in the aisles—distinguished the new cathedral at Urbino (Tafuri 1993c), perhaps designed before 1474 and begun by Francesco di Giorgio before the death of the duke, and nearly completed in 1499. Completely remodeled at the close of the eighteenth century and known only through drawings, it was a work of great importance, described (1717): "unadorned … without gold, without paintings and adorned in the antique manner in the secondary cornices and the main cornice." The facade, never finished, seems to have been tripartite with orders of pilasters framing lateral arches and a large central arch, probably taking its inspiration from Pienza Cathedral and perhaps even from S. Andrea in Mantua. Francesco di Giorgio Martini must have endowed the interior and the facade with a distinguishing personal touch. But before 1477, when he settled permanently in Urbino, other architects—or painter-architects, like him, such as Fra Carnevale Corradini or the young Bramante, and sculptor-architects, such as the Lombard Ambrogio Barocci—as well as Piero della Francesca and Duke Federico himself, renowned as a talented dilettante of architecture, must have been active, perhaps often in collaboration with one another. In one of the panels

of the St. Bernardino series (dated 1473, now in the Galleria Nazionale, Perugia), a perspective painter and architect trained in the Urbino school and influenced by Piero della Francesca, Alberti and Mantegna—who in the present writer's opinion can only be Bramante—depicted a part of a church facade that reflects, one year after the master's death, motifs that Alberti used in Rimini and Mantua (where work on S. Andrea was starting and Mantegna was finishing his Camera degli Sposi). Another of these panels shows on the far side of a small, square courtyard a small, round, peripteral temple with a dome. And, as everybody knows, Montefeltro had envisioned, perhaps before 1474–75, in the courtyard known as the Pasquino of his palazzo, a round, dynastic funerary temple (of which a model existed at the end of the sixteenth century). Later, the duke discarded the idea. However, according to his biographer Vespasiano da Bisticci, he left instructions in his will to build a new church—later dedicated to St. Bernadino—for the monastery of the Observant Franciscans, where he wished to be buried. This church was built (ca. 1482–95) after his death, under the supervision of Ottaviano Ubaldini to designs by Francesco di Giorgio Martini (Tafuri 1993b; Burns 1993b). One of his drawings (Florence, Biblioteca Laurenziana, *Codex Ashburnham* 1828, App., fols. 63v.–64r.) has been identified as a project for the church. Another drawing from the same codex, perhaps copied from an original by Martini, shows the interior in perspective. Both drawings, published and studied by Howard Burns (1974; 1993b), concern a design phase that, once the mausoleum in the palace courtyard had been abandoned, may have started even before the duke's death, and before Bramante (?) left for Lombardy, where he had settled by 1477. It is a "composite" plan, with clear sepulchral and symbolical content, that Bramante was to show a good grasp of: a triconch—with four corner columns, as in the Roman sacella (and, for example, as in S. Salvatore in Spoleto), supporting the arches of the spherical dome on pendentives—preceded by a longitudinal, barrel-vaulted space.

From the mid-1460s to the 1480s Urbino served as a focus for the assimilation and synthesis of the emerging ideas of the Renaissance. As in Florence, interest in Vitruvius was lively in the court of Federico. Giovanni Sulpicio da Verulano was a native of Urbino; in the second half of the 1480s, he dedicated to Cardinal Raffaele Riario the first printed edition of Vitruvius' *De architectura* (Pagliara 1986). In the 1480s (or shortly thereafter?), Francesco di Giorgio wrote (Maltese 1967; Mussini 1993) the first draft of his treatise (*Codex Saluzziano* 148, Turin) in which he offers a thorough survey of temple typologies (Fehring 1956; Fiore and Tafuri 1993a): longitudinal, hall-church style, with nave and aisles, with or without transepts; central plan, round, octagonal, pentagonal, decagonal, etc. with or without interior ambulatories or exterior porticoes, with or without chapels or satellite spaces; composed of the two types. In the appendix of the same codex (fols. 71–100), a group of drawings showing antique monuments of Rome and Hadrian's Villa, of Gubbio, Minturno, Spoleto and so forth, though fancifully rendered, offers insight to the knowledge the preferences and the tastes at that time.

Although the various drafts of Francesco di Giorgio Martini's *Trattato* and his drawings were not published until more recent times, they were widely known by the likes of Leonardo and probably by Bramante, Raphael and his pupil and main disciple Peruzzi, Antonio da Sangallo the Younger, Serlio, Cataneo, Scamozzi and others; Martini's work contributed significantly to the spread of new typologies, especially those based on the central plan. After 1482, he himself built a round church in the convent of S. Chiara in Urbino (Fiore and Tafuri 1993b), perhaps designed in a previous version with an octagonal center and cross arms and round chapels in the corners (*Codex Ashburnham* 1828, App., fol. 159). In Siena, toward the end of his life (1493–94), he began work on the church of S. Sebastiano in Valle Piatta (Tafuri 1993a), based on a Greek cross plan. The extent of his architectural skills, now that the cathedral of Urbino has been lost, may be seen in the exemplary votive church of S. Maria del Calcinaio near Cortona (begun 1484 on commission from the city and, it seems, at the initiative of Luca Signorelli; Matracchi 1992; Gori Sassoli 1993). The church comprises a simple Latin cross with barrel-vaulted arms and a high octagonal dome over the crossing, with bare walls articulated by pilasters and semicircular chapels carved out of the thick walls, illuminated by aedicular windows with pilasters and triangular pediments.

Meanwhile, the precocious introduction, direct or indirect, of Tuscan Renaissance styles in the Adriatic area (the Marche, Emilia-Romagna, Veneto and Dalmatia) had led to linguistic innovations and typological influences (McAndrew 1980; Lieberman 1982; Wolters 1986). By the end of the 1460s, Mauro Codussi (d. 1504; Olivato and Puppi 1977) had already introduced to the Veneto tradition styles that were linked with Alberti's ideas. He started work on the church of S. Michele in Isola at the end of 1468, while Alberti was still alive and Luciano Laurana was working in Urbino, and completed it in 1476; it had a basilican layout with columns and apsidal choir with a dome on a circular base. The facade is a variation on the Rimini temple-front with pilasters and "Vitruvian" isodomum stonework; he may even have obtained some suggestions from his study of ancient monuments in the Veneto. Variations on this scheme, which Codussi reutilized elsewhere (the facade of S. Zaccaria in Venice, already started with the nave and its pedestals in around 1460 by Antonio Gambello), became very widespread, examples of it extending as far as the Dalmatian coast (the cathedral at Sibenik, Croatia, after 1477). Echoes of Tuscan and Albertian ideas appear in a unique Lombard and Veneto variant: the church of S. Maria dei Miracoli, built by Pietro Lombardo in 1481 to a model of 1480 as a shrine for a sacred icon. The simple rectangular timber-vaulted hall terminates (1485) in a square, domed choir which, thanks to Ambrogio Barocci, who had also worked on the Palazzo Ducale in Urbino, evinces refined Urbino influences. Subsequently (1491–92 and later), Codussi interpreted the cruciform basilican scheme with nave and transept with cross vaulting, apsidal choir and dome on a circular base in S. Maria Formosa, replacing the traditional columns with simple square piers and placing small domes in the aisles. Again Codussi proposed in 1497 for S. Giovanni Crisostomo a cross layout inscribed in a square (a quincunx, as in St. Peter's, later) on piers, according to a scheme which had attracted the interest of Bramante and Leonardo in the early 1480s while in Milan, and was widely used in northern Italy toward the end of the century.

This scheme, of Byzantine origin, appeared in Milan in the sacellum of S. Satiro, a ninth-century building believed at the time to date from antiquity. It was proposed by Filarete early in his career and reappears in Bramante's drawing (reproduced in a large copperplate engraving by Bernardo Prevedari) of a Christianized classical temple in ruins (Bruschi 1969a, 1985b; Metternich 1967–68). The image redounds with references (Urbino, Alberti, Piero della Francesca, Mantegna, and even "Romanesque" and Lombard ones), as well as in symbolic messages and content. In its hierarchical and constructively logical three-dimensional organization of structures and spaces syntactically coordinated among one another, a new synthesis of Brunelleschi's and Alberti's principles takes place. At around the same time, or slightly earlier, Bramante (Bruschi 1969a, 1985b) was at work on the church of S. Maria presso S. Satiro in Milan (with certainty, starting in 1482). Begun as a "chapel" in the area of the present transept, before 1478, it was then enlarged into a church around 1480. The cruciform plan with vaulted nave was heavily conditioned by pre-existing structures, with its ingenious *trompe l'œil* perspective device for the choir, recalls the form of Brunelleschi's S. Spirito. The organization of the transept with the dome at the center is reminiscent of the Cappella Pazzi, also as far as the handling of the details is concerned. But instead of orders of columns, the architect chose the Roman-style arch framed orders, as seen earlier in S. Andrea, Mantua, and later in many other churches. Everything is translated into Albertian planes of masonry, and suggestions from Piero della Francesca and Mantegna (indicated by the sources written as Bramante's teachers), as well as from Urbino and Po Valley styles, are not lacking. All these elements converge here in an

Miracles of St. Bernardino

Healing the Ulcer of the Daughter of Giovanni Antonio Petrazio of Rieti
inv. no. 223
Cat. no. 36a

Healing of a Boy
inv. no. 229
Cat. no. 36b

Posthumous Healing of a Blind Man
inv. no. 226
Cat. no. 36c

Raising of the Stillborn Child through Prayer
inv. no. 222
Cat. no. 36d

Posthumous Healing of a Youth Wounded by a Pike
inv. no. 227
Cat. no. 36e
Perugia, Galleria Nazionale dell'Umbria

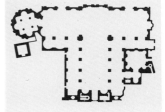

Donato Bramante
External View and Plan of
S. Maria presso S. Satiro, Milan
ca. 1480

image believed to be *all'antica* with a lively use of colors and decoration and a compelling distribution (later modified) of many different sources of light. The monumental octagonal sacristy (as in Loreto), conceived as an independent centralized temple directly inspired by the sacella added to S. Lorenzo and perhaps by the study of Lombard baptisteries, was the model for later churches, sacristies and small temples. The ancient sacellum of S. Satiro was also remodeled (before 1482–83), with the construction of a new circular perimeter with niches framed by pilasters, which may have borrowed some notions from Brunelleschi's S. Maria degli Angeli.

In the very first years of the 1480s—after Urbino Cathedral but before or contemporary to the construction of the church of S. Bernardino of the Observant Franciscans and before S. Maria del Calcinaio at Cortona—the so-called Prevedari engraving and the S. Satiro complex were early signs of a renewal of religious architecture.

In the year following the start of work on the Cortona church (1484–85), the votive church of S. Maria delle Carceri in Prato was begun (October 1485; Bardazzi et al. 1978; Morselli and Corti 1982). It, too, was built in celebration of a miraculous event (July 1484). In May of 1485, the citizens chose a project by Giuliano da Maiano (active from 1483 in Loreto) with an octagonal layout (usually identified with Uff. 1606r. and 1607A). Once a model was paid for, the first stone was laid on 25 May of the next year. Worship of the Virgin had intensified in the wake of Sixtus IV's proclamation of the Immaculate Conception in 1476, and as a consequence, there was an upsurge in the number of churches dedicated to her in this period. The octagonal form—already used in S. Maria del Fiore and S. Maria degli Angeli, and in 1482 or 1483 chosen by Sixtus IV himself for S. Maria della Pace in Rome—seemed particularly suited to celebrating the Madonna. Furthermore, the form lent itself

Donato Bramante
Apse of S. Maria presso
S. Satiro, Milan
ca. 1480

Giuliano da Sangallo (?)
S. Maria delle Carceri, Prato
1485–95

to the conservation of the miraculous object of veneration, forming a sort of tabernacle; the formula often included three separate entrance doors (perhaps alluding to the Trinity) in order to permit the orderly circulation of the worshippers. But for the church of Prato, Lorenzo il Magnifico—who had asked Luca Fancelli, civil and military architect to the Gonzaga in Mantua, for a drawing of S. Sebastiano—personally selected in October 1485 a project for a church of medium size based on a Greek cross plan designed by Giuliano da Sangallo. This kind of layout, after the example of Mantua and various other attempts in the second half of the 1400s, must have seemed to the Neoplatonic society of Florence (where Alberti's much-discussed *De re aedificatoria* was published in 1485) more suited than the octagon to represent the idea and complex significances of the Christian temple (Wittkower 1962). In the clear layout of the plain interior based on the simple relationships between the parts, in the clean distribution of the external volumes and in the free but direct and learned references to the classical language of architecture, the church of the Carceri, with its centralized plan, isolated unto itself, stands as a paradigm of the "ideal church" of Florentine humanism in the time of Lorenzo il Magnifico.

In the same period, a layout that had already been used, especially by Michelozzo (S. Marco, SS. Annunziata), received new treatment in Florence: a new type of large monastic church with single nave, flat roof, flanked by a series of vaulted chapels, without transept but with a square choir. The Cistercian church of S. Maria di Cestello (later dedicated to S. Maria Maddalena dei Pazzi) in Borgo Pinti (1484? and later), was preceded, like SS. Annunziata, by a cloister designed by Giuliano da Sangallo (1491 and later). On commission from Lorenzo, the same architect also designed (1486 and later) the Augustinian monastery and church at the Porta S. Gallo, also single-naved, with chapels and a square, domed choir behind which stood a rectangular choir for the monks (Uff. 1573A and

Interior of S. Maria delle Carceri, Prato

1574A). This scheme, but with barrel-vaulted chapels framed by an order of pilasters, was used in an exemplary way by Il Cronaca (Simone del Pollaiuolo) for the church of S. Francesco (S. Salvatore) al Monte (under construction in 1493), itself a model for later designs. Using this kind of structure, the traditional liturgical requirements were made more rational, by freeing the nave of the choir screen and distinguishing it from the presbytery (as earlier in S. Giobbe, Venice, 1471; Ackerman 1980). Thus, this kind of layout was frequently reproposed and elaborated further in the ensuing years.

In any case, the octagonal model of temple with chapels or niches to the sides—more or less directly linked to antique structures or to the baptistery in Florence—was anything but foreign to the Florentine culture of this period and, in general, to the humanistic culture of central and northern Italy (also demonstrated by the many representations by painters). The sacristy designed by Giuliano da Sangallo (several years after S. Satiro) for Brunelleschi's S. Spirito, a project which was approved in August 1489, was octagonal with niches, preceded by a rectangular vestibule. But Giuliano also proposed a similar scheme for the votive church of S. Maria dell'Umiltà in Pistoia (started 1495; Belluzzi 1993). The domed octagon, with niches or chapels of different origins and dimensions seemed appropriate not only for sacristies, but also for sanctuaries, which were often dedicated to the Virgin, especially from the 1480s on (among the many examples are the Incoronata in Lodi and the church of S. Maria della Sughera in Tolfa, erected for Agostino Chigi at the beginning of the sixteenth century); it was also considered suitable for funerary monuments (such as the one for Trivulzio in Milan by Bramantino) or small, isolated votive temples (such as S. Maria della Peste in Viterbo, 1494; S. Giovanni in Oleo in Rome, 1508; and the Cappella del Quo Vadis, etc.). After S. Maria del Fiore and Loreto, the grafting of a domed octagonal nucleus onto a naved longitu-

155

Pavia Cathedral

dinal structure must have seemed particularly suited to cathedrals dedicated to the Virgin. This scheme was the basis for a project of the new cathedral at Pavia, commissioned by Ascanio Sforza, brother of Lodovico il Moro; it is very likely that Bramante played a decisive role in the new cathedral's design (August–December 1488). In June 1490, Francesco di Giorgio Martini and Leonardo visited the site to offer advice on problems that had arisen during its construction. After 1495 the project, started in the crypt and the apsidal part, was partially modified by Giovanni Antonio Amadeo, Gian Giacomo Dolcebuono and Giovan Pietro Fugazza. Fugazza prepared the model that has come down to us on the basis of what had already been started.

Though never finished, Pavia Cathedral (Bruschi 1969a: 85) is the most important example of Renaissance cathedral design before St. Peter's itself. The building draws from a wide variety of sources—early Christian, Gothic, fifteenth-century. In this case, the scheme of the Loreto sanctuary (with which Bramante was almost certainly familiar), comprising a central octagonal nucleus extending into the arms of the cross and with four octagonal sacristies at the corners, is recomposed into a hierarchical sequence of organically coordinated spaces, in conformance with Alberti's principles and Brunelleschi's S. Spirito.

Schemes of large churches that come close to this extraordinary idea of a modern cathedral had already appeared in the first draft (*Codex Saluzziano* 148, Turin; after 1486?) of Francesco di Giorgio's *Trattato*, a copy of which (*Codex Ashburnham* 361, Florence, Biblioteca Laurenziana) Leonardo owned. This artist, who developed an interest in architecture in the late 1480s and was a close friend of Bramante, also studied scheme of religious buildings similar to the one in Pavia. But during these years, he mainly focused on central-plan temples—often based on the octagon with radial chapels of various shapes, but also using a cross inscribed in a square and quadrilobate structures. In these studies of temples, different sources of inspiration—ranging from the baptistery of S. Maria del Fiore to S. Maria degli Angeli, S. Spirito, SS. Annunziata in Florence and early Christian and medieval structures in Lombardy, Bramante's own sources of reference—gave rise to a wide repertory of buildings in which spaces and volumes of various size and shape were combined in three-dimensional structural patterns that sometimes foreshadowed typologies to come (Pedretti 1978; Guillaume 1987).

The meeting of Bramante, Leonardo and Francesco di Giorgio Martini in 1490 in Milan, where they came into contact with the Lombard tradition and local architects such as Amadeo, seems to have been decisive to later developments. On the same occasion, Martini worked with Amadeo on the definitive project for the Gothic crossing tower of Milan Cathedral (Guillaume 1987; Schofield 1989), for which Leonardo had devised an ingenious project and Bramante had drafted a written report. At the start of the 1490s Bramante, Leonardo and Amadeo were once again united among the "highly expert architects" engaged by Ludovico il Moro to transform the Dominican church of S. Maria delle Grazie (Bruschi 1983a) into a mausoleum for the Sforza family. It seems that the church, having been completed just a few years earlier, was to have been remodeled according to a project that called for the addition of a longitudinal hall with side-chapels to a large central-plan tribune with a dome. This tribune was built (the foundation stone was laid on 29 March 1492) to designs which Bramante seems to have influenced in no small measure; departing from Brunelleschi's scheme for the Old Sacristy in S. Lorenzo (used in Lombardy in the Cappella Portinari at S. Eustorgio in Milan and in the Cappella Colleoni in Bergamo designed by Amadeo in the early 1470s), it was enhanced (as for S. Bernardino degli Osservanti in Urbino) by two large lateral apses. The *scarsella* was transformed into a square apsidal choir housing the tombs of the dukes. Not without references to the "imperial" style of late antiquity, the idea of the funerary temple-cum-mausoleum was expressed not only by the domed central plan with extensions to the sides and in depth, but also by the distribution of the light, the symbol of divine grace as an instrument of victory over death, of resurrection and eternal glorification of the illustrious deceased. Again in the 1490s in Milan, the triconch layout appeared in various pictorial representations as well as in the small Cappella Pozzobonella, very probably another work of Bramante's. At the same time and in the early years of the following century, in the Po Valley and elsewhere in central Italy, many sacred buildings were erected with centralized layouts more or less directly inspired by the work of Leonardo and above all Bramante (S. Maria della Croce in Crema, S. Magno in Legnano, S. Maria di Canepanova in Pavia, S. Maria di Piazza in Busto Arsizio, the cathedral of Tirano, the sanctuaries of Finale Ligure, Mongiovino and many others, such as the Cappella del SS. Sacramento in the parish church of Caravaggio). Often they were the work of Lombard master-builders. In the church of S. Maria Nuova in Abbiategrasso, the lower order (1497) of the facade with its triumphal arch and twin columns, may perhaps be traced to a project by Bramante, to whom it has been attributed (in absence of any documented alternative). The upper order was in fact rebuilt toward the end of the sixteenth century. It does not lack in cues from Alberti's works in Mantua, and perhaps from Venetian circles. A few drawings of churches from the Biblioteca Ambrosiana and one of a facade (now at the Louvre) also recall Bramante's ideas.

Bramante's arrival in Rome (in the summer of 1499?) is often seen as the start of a new phase of the Renaissance. Despite some continuity with his Lombard work, his direct study of the monu-

Elevation of Facade of Model for Pavia Cathedral
from Memorie storiche della Fabbrica della Cattedrale di Pavia, *pl. IV*
Pavia, Museo Civico del Castello Visconteo

ments of Rome and a clearer grasp of Vitruvius' text, especially as far as the architectural orders were concerned, as well as stimulating exchanges with men of the Curia interested in antiquity and with learned architects of the Medici court, such as Antonio da Sangallo the Elder and later Giuliano da Sangallo, produced an extraordinary renewal of his ideas on religious architecture. The famous round peripteral Tempietto of S. Pietro in Montorio (after 1502; Bruschi 1969a: 85; Günther 1974), one of the classical typologies illustrated by Vitruvius, represents a turning point in the concept of the votive temple type. It was built on the traditional site of the crucifixion of the Apostle Peter, commissioned by Cardinal Bernardino de Carvajal "on behalf of the Spanish royal family" (author of the reworking in 1499–1500 of S. Giacomo degli Spagnoli, for which, according to Vasari, Bramante was consulted). With its classically-inspired Doric colonnade with triglyphs ("rediscovered" by Bramante), it is an impressive synthesis of antiquarian and Christian motifs, reminiscent more of Roman monuments than of Vitruvius, and perhaps of the unrealized round mausoleum in Urbino and the small temples designed by Francesco di Giorgio (*Codex Saluzziano*, Turin, fol. 84). Upsetting traditional styles, the tiny, round cella capped with a dome raised on a windowed drum articulated with niches of alternating size framed by Doric pilasters set at different distances from one another, following an utterly new rhythmic arrangement ("travata ritmica") that soon became a model for later interiors of chapels or centrally planned churches. This idea is linked to the brilliant solution for the crossing of New St. Peter's where, more than anywhere else, there is an innovative and mature concept of the relationships between spatial plasticity and structural mass, a concept that took firm root in the centuries to follow.

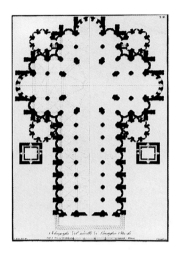

Pavia Cathedral plan and interior

For the renovation (*instauratio*) of the old basilica, Bramante, in competition with Giuliano da Sangallo, examined many solutions which showed different detailing though they all envisaged the quincunx type of layout (Metternich 1972; Metternich and Thoenes 1987).

His initial ideas (Uff. 1A) may have been oriented toward a central-plan temple, a mausoleum for the apostle and at the same time a glorification of Pope Julius II, whose tomb was to be designed by Michelangelo and installed in the choir begun by Nicholas V. Later, it seems at the pope's wish, Bramante's design calls for a "composite" temple, with a central, quincunx portion and a longitudinal one with nave, probably similar in parts to the one which Raphael later proposed (Serlio, Book III: 37), in which the problem of the smooth transition between the two parts was skilfully solved by the coincidence of the twin orders with the arches. The basilica's outstanding size—which was originally intended to surpass anything built in antiquity, by "raising the Pantheon over the Basilica of Maxentius," and therefore a round temple over an Etruscan one—and the calculated intention to imitate the monumental force of Roman constructions resulted in an exceptional enlargement and new articulation of the masonry structures, together with a heightening of the spatial complexity of the original quincunx scheme. In order to consolidate the structural support of the pendentives for the enormous dome, the angles of the square central cell were filled in, forming an octagon of unequal sides, and hence making the four crossing piers obtuse on the inside. After St. Peter's, such obtuse-angled crossing piers were widely used to support domes. When the wooden model was made and the first stone laid (18 April 1506), Bramante built the choir and the central nucleus with the four main piers and the adjoining buttressing for the dome; this was largely derived from the Pantheon type, but raised on a colonnaded drum crowned by a lofty lantern (Serlio, Book III: 35). Bramante got as far as the imposts of the drum, the beginnings of the four great arches, the pendentives and the giant interior order of Corinthian pilasters. These structures accountably conditioned the later projects, all of which aimed to define the peripheral parts of the building, which Bramante himself perhaps never completely defined.

Fra Giocondo was a learned architect and humanist who in 1511 published the first edition of Vitruvius to be accompanied by drawings; in 1492 he had all of 126 drawings from Francesco di Giorgio's *Trattato* copied for the king of Naples. For St. Peter's, he too submitted a project to the pope (Uff. 6A), sometime before April 1506. It was based on the scheme of St. Mark's in Venice, with a "neo-Byzantine" plan comprising seven domes linked by barrel vaults in a cruciform nave and ending in an ambulatory with radial chapels. Although this project was discarded (some of its ideas reappear in the studies of Bramante and his disciples), Leo X appointed Fra Giocondo as co-architect to Bramante and Giuliano da Sangallo, and subsequently to Raphael. It is surprising that in Venice, during or slightly after work started on the new basilica, before August 1506 Giorgio Spavento built a model for the reconstruction of the church of S. Salvatore (Tafuri 1985b), which proposed a plan (to which Tullio Lombardo contributed from 1507 onward) characterized by the rigorously structured repetition (typical of Bramante's works in Milan) of two orders of different dimensions—betraying subtle classical references—of three quincunx units cleverly linked in a longitudinal sequence. The overall effect was spectacular but also of outstanding unity. This church made a highly original contribution to the reappraisal of longitudinal religious spaces, reworking the stock "Byzantine" elements—already a focus of Bramante's and Leonardo's work in Milan—in light of the emerging principles of humanism. Shortly afterward in 1507 work began on the church of S. Fantino in Venice to designs by Sebastiano da Lugano; the new church adopted the same scheme but with large cross vaults.

*Pavia Cathedral,
interior*

A similar layout, with cross vault and more accentuated references to Bramante's work in Lombardy, was given to the church of S. Sepolcro in Piacenza, the construction of which began around 1513 under the direction of Alessio Tramello. The domes and juxtaposed sail vaults returned in the great S. Giustina church of the Montecassino Benedictines in Padua (begun 1532, Matteo da Valle and Andrea Moroni)—where, however, the formula was combined with those of the cathedral of Faenza and S. Nicolò in Carpi—as well as in the church of SS. Flora e Lucilla in Arezzo, built later to a design by Giorgio Vasari.

Meanwhile, in Rome, Bramante transformed the choir of S. Maria del Popolo into a burial chapel for cardinals Ascanio Sforza and Girolamo Basso della Rovere, powerfully lit by an unprecedented Serlian window, appearing here for the first time, with a central sail vault flanked by two coffered barrel vaults and ending in a semicircular apse. In the church of S. Biagio at the Palazzo dei Tribunali in Via Giulia (1508 and later), never finished, he had composed a centralized nucleus with short apsidal arms and a short hall with niches. Both in the destroyed church of S. Celso in Banchi (1509 and later) and in the coeval church of Roccaverano (Morresi 1991) in the Piedmont (designed for Cardinal Enrico Bruno, but incorrectly executed), Bramante returned to the central quincunx scheme of St. Peter's, though here smaller and simpler. The church of S. Celso, inserted in the urban fabric and preceded by a row of shops, was to open onto the street with a simple portal flanked by columns (Uff. 1859A, by Antonio da Sangallo the Younger). Instead, in Roccaverano, the temple front and triumphal arch were blended in a novel way, with the central part bearing an arch framed by a giant order capped by a pediment with a smaller order to the sides, in turn framing a smaller arch. A new scheme for the facade is used here for the first time; it was later used by Peruzzi (1514–15) in his design for S. Maria in Castello, Carpi (known as the Sagra) and, later in studies by Sangallo that were never realized, and it turned up again in Palladio's churches. For the church of Loreto, he instead proposed a simple facade with a pediment set between two campaniles (1509). Bramante himself (after 1508) was probably the author of the project for the isolated, centrally planned sanctuary of S. Maria della Consolazione at Todi (Bruschi 1991), commissioned by the city as a tabernacle for a holy relic. Though the original project of a domed, quadriconch structure was modified during its lengthy construction (1508–1607), it stands as a typical example of the "ideal" Renaissance temple. From this time on, Rome was the epicenter of the most avant-garde architecture and Bramante's models were taken as exempla (Serlio and Palladio, among others, referred to them in their treatises)

Raphael
School of Athens
1509-10
Vatican, Stanza della Segnatura

Raphael
Expulsion of Heliodorus
1511-12
Vatican, Stanza d'Eliodoro

and reworked and personalized by his successors, while the impact of his contributions both in and outside Rome is visible everywhere, especially in central and northern Italy.

While Bramante was still alive (d. April 1514), Raphael adorned his Stanze frescoes (Frommel et al. 1984a) with architectural models directly derived from the master's ideas, as can be seen in the *School of Athens* (1509–10) and the *Expulsion of Heliodorus* (1511–12). Around the same time, Antonio da Sangallo the Younger used the scheme of S. Biagio dei Tribunali for Cardinal Farnese in the isolated central-plan temple of S. Egidio di Cellere (1513–14; Frommel 1986c), the facades of which may be associated with the Roccaverano type. Not long afterward Raphael offered his own, refined interpretation of Bramante's application of square space with diagonal corners (at St. Peter's), by adding niches on the diagonals, together with statues and pictures, for the funerary chapel of Agostino Chigi at S. Maria del Popolo (after 1507; in 1516 the mosaics of the originally extradosed chapel had already been started; Bentivoglio 1984). The device marks a high point in his use of symbolic language and his mastery of imagery. Soon afterward he used the simple scheme of the Greek cross with dome, now resting on short, angled piers, for S. Eligio degli Orefici (begun around 1515; Valtieri 1984), later finished by Peruzzi, woven into the urban fabric, but distinguished by a simple Doric facade surmounted by an "attic" illuminated by a Serliana.

Elsewhere in Italy there are several slightly later central-plan temples which, despite their differences and the presence of extraneous components, all betray the influence of Bramante, and these are: S. Biagio in Montepulciano (begun 1518; Satzinger 1991), a powerfully rustic but rejuvenated version of S. Maria delle Carceri in Prato, by Antonio da Sangallo the Elder, brother of Giuliano; and the church of S. Maria della Steccata in Parma (begun 1521, by Giovanfrancesco and Bernardino Zaccagni; Adorni 1982b), with a quadriconch cross plan and four corner cellae, for which Alessio Tramello, Correggio, and Antonio da Sangallo the Younger were consulted between 1525 and 1526. Almost at the same time (1522), Tramello started the Madonna di Campagna in Piacenza, based on the quincunx with the arms of the cross emerging from the square, with strong Lombard accents; while echoes of Bramante's Roman works may be seen in Milan in the work of Cristoforo Lombardino, as in the octagonal drum of S. Maria della Passione, begun by Battagio in 1489 and finished before mid-century.

The death in Rome of Julius II on 22 February 1513, and of Bramante not long after in April the following year, heralded the start of a new phase in religious architecture under the papacy of

163

Leo X (March 1513-December 1521). The son of Lorenzo il Magnifico, Pope Leo X was a restorer of peace and patron of the arts, though most of the projects he sponsored remained unrealized (Tafuri 1992). The new papacy brought a phase of experimentation and of the development of Bramante's ideas; Raphael's study of Roman monuments had important consequences, as did the work of Peruzzi and Jacopo Sansovino, but the period was marked above all by the rise of Sangallo the Younger. Raphael (Frommel et al. 1984a), the "first architect" of St. Peter's after Bramante, proposed (1514) alone and later in competition with Sangallo (ca. 1516-18) a model for its completion (Serlio, Book III: 37; *Codex Mellon*, New York, Pierpont Morgan Library, fols. 71v. and 72r.-v.). Antonio da Sangallo's ideas were quite different (Bruschi 1992b). As "second architect" from 1516 Sangallo devised projects characterized—like Fra Giocondo's (Uff. 6A)—by a sequence of domes over the central nave and in the transept (Uff. 254A, 252A left half, and 35Ar.). After tormented studies, he arrived at a highly effective layout (Uff. 255Ar.), quite different from Raphael's, that envisioned a single large dome over the nave in addition to one over the crossing, but he accepted some ideas of his rival for other parts. The two architects in collaboration (ca. 1519-20) drew up the definitive version of the ambulatories and the Doric solution for the perimeter of the exterior. Both architects later tackled the problem of the disproportionately large facade, and settled on a portico. After Raphael's initial idea (1514) of a colonnaded portico, at Sangallo's suggestion perhaps, both chose (ca. 1518-20) a solution with a wall with Colossal orders offset by smaller orders. But the former (*Codex Mellon*, fol. 72r.) referred to the front of the temple, as in Alberti's S. Andrea, framed by two enormous bell towers; the latter primarily evoked the idea of the triumphal arch (Uff. 70A, 72A, 73Ar.). Both have clear symbolic references.

S. Biagio, Montepulciano

Earlier, the theme of the facade of a large church had been tackled in Florence as well as in Pavia. There, Lorenzo il Magnifico had announced a competition (1490) for the facade of S. Maria del Fiore (Foster 1981)—echoes of which it is believed may be present in the facade of S. Cristina in Bolsena (1493-95), commissioned by the future Pope Leo X when he was still a cardinal (and, perhaps, in Uffizi drawing 2170A tentatively attributed to Giuliano da Sangallo, and in a project, *Codex Wicar*, Lille, fol. 752; Munich, Staatl. Graph. Sammlung, inv. 33257, for the church at Loreto). The usual scheme must have been accentuated by paired pilasters, an "attic" beneath the upper order and above all the profuse ornament and narrative relief in a style typical of the tastes of Lorenzo and Leo X (Bruschi 1983c). Following the Medici's expulsion (1494) from Florence and their later reinstatement, when Leo X made his triumphal entrance into the city (November 1515), the provisional facade of S. Maria del Fiore, with paired orders and reliefs simulating sculptures by the young Jacopo Sansovino and Andrea del Sarto (as Vasari describes it), seemed to conjure up the splendor of Lorenzo's time.

These same "triumphal" themes appear again in certain other designs for the facade (Uff. 277 and 278A) submitted by Giuliano da Sangallo (d. October 1516) to the "competition" (Ackerman 1961; S. Borsi 1985; Tafuri 1992) held by Leo X (late 1515-early 1516) for the facade of the Medici's church of S. Lorenzo. These designs had been prepared earlier (before 1515?) for a church dedicated to the Virgin, and were submitted together with others (such as Uff. 280 and Uff. 276 and 21A, dated 1516) prepared for the occasion. Similar themes, again for S. Lorenzo, appear in Uff. 2048A, probably a copy of Raphael's project, and in an eighteenth-century engraving that seems to be a reproduction of Jacopo Sansovino's project (Tafuri 1992). Some of these projects by Giuliano (Uff. 280A, which has two large campaniles, foreshadowing Raphael's facade for St. Peter's in the *Codex Mellon* and Uff. 281A) and by Raphael (Uff. 2048A) called for, with a feature reminiscent of Alberti, a narthex or interior portico in the facade. Similar themes, suggested by the projects submitted to the competition, were to be reproposed by Michelangelo as well, for the same facade (Lille 722; Uff. 1923; CB 45, 47, 44, 91) in his studies of the second half of 1516. He returned to them again, in a version with a three-dimensional structure of a facade with narthex, in his projects of 1517-18 (CB 43; Uff. 790A by Antonio da Sangallo, etc.), through to the definitive wooden model (Ackerman 1961; Millon and Smyth 1988b; Argan and Contardi 1990).

These proposals for S. Lorenzo are linked to Giuliano da Sangallo's background under his Medici patrons, but they are also unimaginable without the work of Bramante, who between 1509 and 1513 designed a similar solution, with his "travata ritmica" of Corinthian half-columns for the facing of the Santa Casa of Loreto, later carried out under Andrea Sansovino. In any case, especially the idea of the "travata ritmica" with pairs of columns or pilasters framing niches or the like, had far-reaching consequences in the years to come: in addition to the Sangallo studies for St. Peter's, it appears in such projects as the one in fols. 789 and 790r.-v. in the Albertina, Vienna, perhaps for S. Giovanni dei Fiorentini and in projects by Antonio da Sangallo the Younger, such as the one (1521) actually implemented for the same church (Uff. 176A) and those for S. Marco in Florence (Uff. 1363 and 1365A). The scheme reappears in the work of Cola dell'Amatrice on S. Bernardino in L'Aquila (before 1527) and in that of Jacopo Sansovino in Venice (project for the Scuola Grande della Misericordia, rejected in 1532, reworked by Palladio in a drawing now in Vicenza; the facade of S. Antonio di Castello—early 1548—and of S. Giminiano). Later, it turned up again in the two facades of "Corinthian temples" in fols. 53v., 54r., 57v., and 58r., of Serlio's Book IV, and became increas-

ingly widespread, spawning several variants. For example, this solution in various combinations with others can be seen in the drawing by Leonardo (ca. 1515) of a church facade (Venice, Accademia) and in a number of Sangallo's designs for St. Peter's. In other cases, as already in fifteenth-century projects (e.g., the model for Pavia Cathedral; the above-mentioned facade for Loreto, etc.) the scheme is simplified through the adoption of simple paired orders (e.g., S. Maria di Loreto in Rome by Antonio da Sangallo, etc.).

At the explicit request of the patron, Bramante's studies for St. Peter's form the basis for Peruzzi's important project (Garuti 1987; Tafuri 1992) for the new cathedral in Carpi on invitation by Alberto Pio (lord of the town until 1525, and later a highly cultured exponent of the "magnificence" of religious buildings, running counter to the Reformation currents and to Erasmus in particular). The request dates to early February 1514 and the model was made before 1515. A quincunx nucleus with apsidal arms extends toward the entrance with three further bays of equal width to the corner cells, the small domes of which continue into the aisles, while the lunetted barrel vaults of the crossing arms follow through into the nave in an organically homogeneous whole. But the pillars of the longitudinal body are double, as in the Basilica of Maxentius and some of Bramante's studies for St. Peter's. The deep choir, taking an idea that was dear to Peruzzi, is flanked by octagonal sacristies. Bramante's diagonal piers supporting the dome become convex toward the interior (as in some of Hadrian's constructions and in the Oratorio del Crocifisso) and from their convexity emerges a giant order of pilasters directly supporting the massive entablature on which the dome rests; according to an idea for a giant order of columns formulated by Bramante in his preliminary studies (1505–06) for St. Peter's (Uff. 7945Ar.-v. and 20Ar.), which Raphael copied in his *Expulsion of Heliodorus* (1511–12) and later, around 1520, Sangallo used (in the above-mentioned Uff. 1365A for S. Marco in Florence; Tafuri 1992).

Alessandro Cesati (called Il Grechetto)
Medal of Pope Paul III
obverse showing Antonio da Sangallo's model for St. Peter's
1546
Florence, Museo Nazionale del Bargello
inv. I 6266 P.I. 405
Cat. no. 369

For the same patron, in early 1518 to 1519, Peruzzi—in addition to the Bramantesque facade of the Sagra (S. Maria in Castello, Carpi) with its giant order of columns—completed the Franciscan church of S. Nicolò (Frommel 1961: 153–154), already started with a quincunx plan (1493 and later) with central dome and smaller domes in the corners. He made the spectacular addition of a basilican structure with three large sail-vaulted bays extended at the sides by transverse barrel vaults. Later (starting 1532), Andrea Moroni finished in a similar way the great church of S. Giustina in Padua (Bresciani and Alvarez 1970), also begun with a quincunx plan.

Between 1518 and 1521, in Rome the start of work on S. Giovanni dei Fiorentini (Tafuri 1992: 159ff.), a church which occupied a strategic position in the urban fabric between the Tiber and the Via Giulia, offered an occasion for highly innovative proposals. Following a project (not known) by Bramante (before December 1508), Giuliano da Sangallo may have examined (Bentivoglio 1975) two solutions between 1513 and 1515 (*Codex Barberini*, Lat., Vatican, 4424, fols. 59v. + 74 and fol. 61). In accordance with Leo X's "twin cities" program linking Rome and Florence, the first solution blended the idea of the Pantheon with echoes of the Florence Baptistery, resulting in a round, domed temple with four chapels inside, a *scarsella* at one end and three vestibules. The exterior, articulated by an order of Corinthian half-columns between outward jutting prothyra on columns, rising to a low attic beneath the dome with conical extrados and small lantern, must have been similar to the image (typical of Sangallo's work) of the round temple in the celebrated picture of a town in elaborate perspective at Urbino. The other project, known only in plan, was octagonal on the exterior and circular in the interior. It closely copied the plan of the temple believed dedicated to the Cumaean Sibyl at Baia, Naples, a drawing of which appears in the same codex on fol. 8v., replete with references to the Pantheon and the "forceps" atrium of S. Costanza in the entrance atria and in the choir. The use of the octagon (as in the baptistery), the circle (as in the Pantheon) and the cross, probably had symbolic connotations, but it is the references to antique models which are much more explicit and literal here than in any other fifteenth-century precedent. The exact details of Jacopo Sansovino's winning project in Leo X's competition (1518-19) for the new church are not known. Vasari reports that it had domes at the four corners and a larger dome at the center. Thus, it must have been in some way an interpretation of Bramante's quincunx scheme. Another project, which an annotation links to the church (Munich, Staatsmuseum, 36/1928b), has been attributed to Raphael (Schütz 1984) or, more credibly, considered (Tafuri 1992) an interpretation by Giulio Romano of one of the master's ideas; it shows a central cell with radial chapels framed by Doric columns, extending into an independent cruciform choir, similar to the type represented by Raphael's S. Eligio, and preceded by an octastyle pronaos with pediment, flanked by campaniles. There are clear references to the Pantheon, to Raphael's ideas and, in the drum pierced by window niches, to the Mausoleum of S. Elena in Via Labicana. Baldassarre Peruzzi seems to have devised other central-plan proposals for the same occasion. In Uff. 510Ar. the reference to the Pantheon, in the cylindrical perimeter and in the way the facade is grafted onto the rest of the structure, is canceled by the hexagonal interior which—as shown in two alternatives—governs the opening of the chapels, framed by half-columns placed at rhythmically alternated intervals, aligned along twelve axes. In both alternatives—as in other of Peruzzi's projects—the chapels corresponding to the narrower bays come in different forms, mostly derived from antique models. But two have an unusual hexagonal matrix and one, for the first time,

Lorenzo Fragni
Medal of Gregory XIII
1572–85
Vatican, Biblioteca Apostolica Vaticana, Medagliere XXVIII 1173
Cat. no. 398

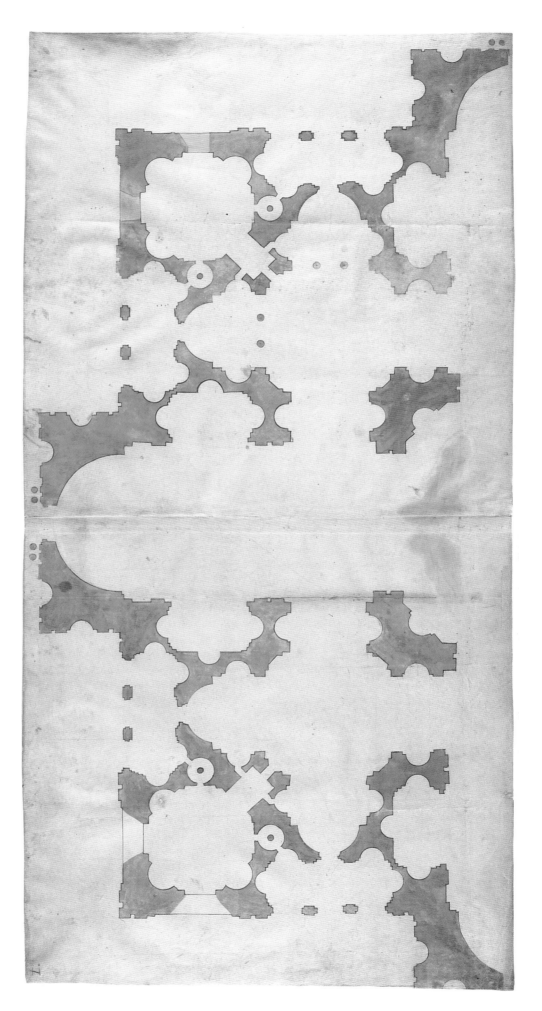

Donato Bramante
Plan
parchment, 1505
Florence, Uffizi, Gabinetto
Disegni e Stampe, Uff. 1A
Cat. no. 282

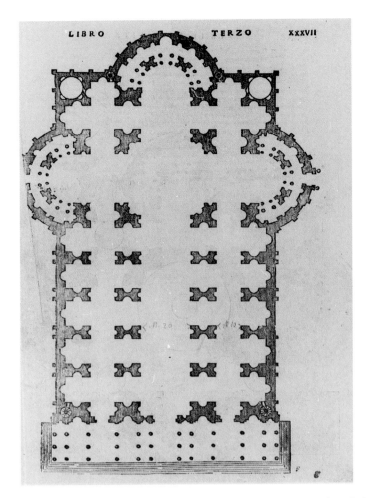

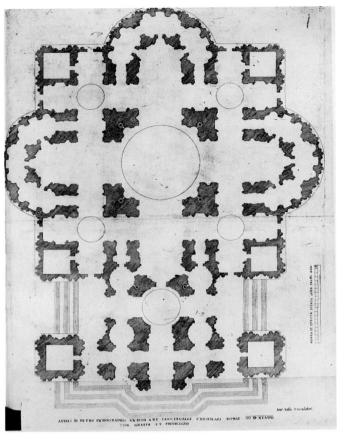

Raphael
Plan of St. Peter's
from Sebastiano Serlio's
L'Architettura
Book III, fol. 65
Venice, Biblioteca Marciana
Cat. n. 308

Antonio da Sangallo
Plan of model of St. Peter's in
an engraving by Antonio
Salamanca
Milano, Civica Raccolta Stampe
Achille Bertarelli
Cat. no. 370e

proposes an oval layout with niches, a form that Peruzzi employed elsewhere, becoming very popular later in the sixteenth century and Baroque ages. On the verso of the same Uffizi drawing 510A is another study, unfinished, probably for the same church; the perimeter could be circular, but the central area is hexagonal (like one of the churches in Serlio's treatise), preceded by a "forceps" atrium screened by columns and terminating in an apse with a colonnaded ambulatory. In Uff. 505Ar. (perhaps also linked to the competition) a triconch chapel plan is arranged around an octagonal area, in alignment with the main axes. Along the diagonal axes are aligned unique hexagonal chapels with alternated rectangular and semicircular niches arranged according to the intersection of two triangles, a plan similar to Peruzzi's studies in the famous sketch in Uff. 553Av., which boldly anticipates Borromini's scheme for S. Ivo. Thus, even before 1520 (if these studies are, as they seem to be, for the Church of the Fiorentini), Peruzzi was combining the ideas of Francesco di Giorgio, antiquity, Bramante, Giuliano da Sangallo and Raphael, and setting them within the context of a rigorously organic whole, fostering a previously unknown imaginativeness and geometrical variety in the conformation of space.

Antonio da Sangallo in turn studied various solutions with both central and basilican plans and with three or five bays, eventually opting for the round and longitudinal plans (see Uff. 1292A). The round plan (Uff. 199A, 200Ar.) once again borrows from the Pantheon, but in this case the domed space is ringed by sixteen radial cells, one of which serves as the vestibule and another as a round choir (Uff. 1292A, in hexagonal form). The elevation, published by Antonio Labacco (1552), shows a rigorous structural and syntactic logic insuring the building's unity, with a striking crown of statues and radial buttresses (as in S. Maria degli Angeli, drawings by Francesco di Giorgio, and the temple of Physizoa Venus in Colonna's *Hypnerotomachia Poliphili*). The basilican solution (Uff. 862Ar.), inscribed in a rectangle with the sides in a 6:5 ratio, as in Vitruvius' and Alberti's "Etruscan temple" (Tafuri 1992), shows piers with a giant order of half-columns in the nave and five chapels per side. Sansovino's project was chosen and work on the foundations—made difficult because of the proximity of the Tiber—began in 1520. But at the start of 1521 Sansovino left the worksite, and immediately afterward Antonio da Sangallo, having been paid for a model he did, worked alone as the construction supervisor. The idea of laying a piazza before the facade was abandoned, and he proposed (Uff. 864Ar.) two alternative basilican solutions. Of these, the design on the right-hand side sheet was selected (repeated in section in Uff. 1364A), terminating in ambulatories and radial chapels, as in Fra Giocondo's Uff. 6A. Work on the definitive project (Uff. 175A)—with an aisled nave and chapels, terminating in the centralizing structures of the choir and apsidal transepts—was started

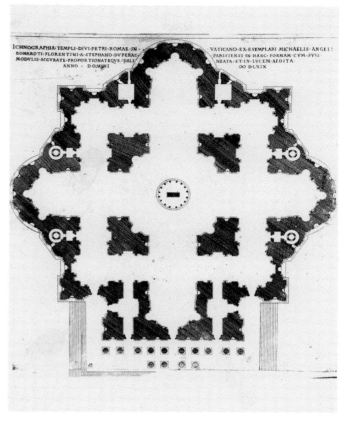

Baldassarre Peruzzi
Plan for St. Peter's, Rome
New York, American Academy
of Rome, inv. no. 23
Cat. no. 330

Michelangelo
Plan for St. Peter's
in an engraving by Dupérac
1569
Milan, Civica Raccolta Stampe
Achille Bertarelli
Cat. no. 395

immediately, over massive substructures. This provided a standard model for the late sixteenth-century and baroque longitudinal type of church. Giacomo della Porta, who took over as chief architect in 1583, strayed very little from the original plan. The splendid facade (Uff. 176A), the lower part of which was begun by Sangallo in 1521, creatively elaborated ideas taken from the solutions for S. Lorenzo in Florence and themes from Sangallo's studies for St. Peter's.

In Leo X's time, and especially around 1520, the idea of the "antique" central-plan temple was often proposed by architects, though the patrons did not seem to like it. For this reason, Sangallo frequently provided an alternative. For S. Maria di Monserrato (begun 1518), he devised an aisle-less nave solution with three chapels per side and one with a single octagon with unequal sides (the short sides were rounded, as later in the Cappella Medici at Montecassino, Uff. 172A). Both alternatives ended in a rectangular, apsidal choir (developed respectively in Uff. 171 and 168A). The longitudinal plan—inspired by late fifteenth-century Florentine monastic schemes along with the "Etruscan" type of the Basilica of Maxentius—offers a structurally organic prototype that successfully addresses the most common practical liturgical requirements. This design therefore enjoyed widespread application in the second half of the sixteenth century and throughout the Baroque age. A more directly "Florentine" plan, with a flat-roofed hall and lateral chapels was chosen by Jacopo Sansovino for the reconstruction (1519–20 and later) of the fire-damaged church of S. Marcello al Corso (Tafuri 1986), entrusted to the Florentine order of the Servites. Sangallo submitted a counterproposal, based on a similar scheme but with three chapels on each side (as in the Basilica of Maxentius) framed by paired pilasters and ending in a domed space of the Cappella Chigi type; or, as an alternative, ending in a majestic semicircular choir for the monks, with a semidome, almost like the *cavea* of a theater. With the latter solution, as in other churches that he designed for religious communities, Sangallo shows his concern to meet the emerging functional requirements with new forms, though he still borrows from antique models. His solution for the abbey of Montecassino (Uff. 181A) was similar to that of S. Marcello; but later, with the aim of transforming the Gothic choir of S. Maria sopra Minerva into a mausoleum for the Medici popes, Leo X and Clement VII, he proposed extending it with a splendid domed cella occupying seven sides of a decagon (De Angelis d'Ossat 1987; Valtieri 1986).

The alternative between central-plan and longitudinal solutions also returned (ca. 1520, according to Tafuri 1992; not 1525–30, as proposed by Giovannoni) in the unrealized projects for the Dominican church of S. Marco in Florence, with the comparison on the same sheet (Uff. 1254A) of a single-nave plan with five chapels and rectangular choir (sketched in Uff. 1649A) and an octagonal central

259

plan expanding into a cross. A second central-plan alternative (Uff. 1363, 1365A), with rectangular cruciform chapels and domed chapels, like the Cappella Chigi, on the diagonal axes, is completed by a large, reversed semicircular choir. Studies for the elevation show original attempts to resolve the facade through the intersection of a giant order (as in S. Marcello, as well) with a lesser order (Uff. 1363v.), or with the insertion of an attic (Uff. 1365A), again combining the idea of the temple with that of the triumphal arch; and to fuse into an imaginative image the base, the drum and the octagonal dome (Tafuri 1992). Similar ideas were initially studied by Antonio da Sangallo (Uff. 1786A) for the exterior of the church of S. Maria di Loreto in Rome, an octagon inscribed in a square (built, except for the dome, to a design by Sangallo dating to 1522; Benedetti 1967; Jobst 1986). Antonio da Sangallo frequently adopted this kind of regular octagonal plan, often with semicircular chapels on the diagonal axes—derived from the Roman baths and proposed by Giuliano da Sangallo as early as 1488 for the chapel of the King of Naples' palace; examples range from the designs for S. Giacomo in Augusta and for S. Maria Porta Paradisi (1519 and later; built with a triumphal arch facade set between pairs of pilasters and topped by a pedimented attic), to those for the small Isola Bisentino (Lake Bolsena) temples and for the church of S. Maria di Montemore (early 1520s),

Antonio da Sangallo the Younger
Project for Longitudinal Plan for St. Peter's
South Prospect
1538
Florence, Uffizi, Gabinetto Disegni e Stampe, Uff. 259A
Cat. no. 349

170

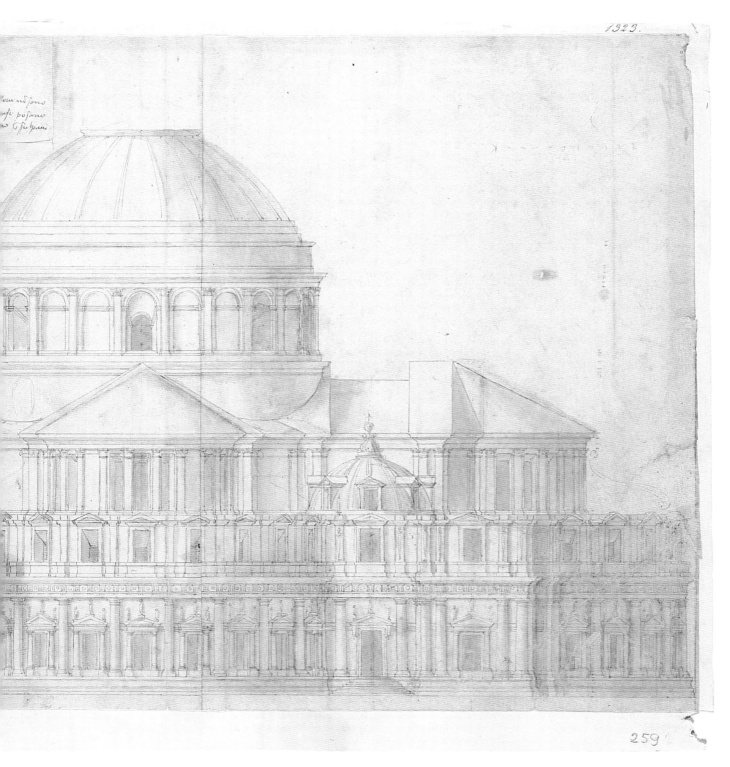

where the octagon is juxtaposed with a circular, domed choir (Giovannoni 1959). The interest in the octagonal model also characterizes the early work in Lazio of the Veronese architect Michele Sanmicheli (the Cappella Petrucci at S. Domenico, Orvieto, ca. 1516; cathedral of Montefiascone, ca. 1520; Puppi 1986a), who during this period was in contact with Sangallo. The octagonal plan again appears (Uff. 305, 1349A) as an alternative to a longitudinal one in Sangallo's studies for S. Giacomo a Scossacavalli (1520–21, now Via della Conciliazione). For the longitudinal alternative, realized and later demolished, two solutions (Uff. 1374, 908, 1350A) were examined because the site stood at the intersection of a street and a square, both of which were main thoroughfares. They show a single, rectangular space with three chapels on each side; that is, a rectangular one flanked by two semicircular ones, thus introducing a transverse axis according to a scheme, suggested by ancient tombs, that became important for later developments.

During the same years (1519–20), once the idea for the facade of S. Lorenzo in Florence had been discarded, Leo X and Cardinal Giulio de' Medici (the future Pope Clement VII) commissioned Michelangelo to erect the New Sacristy to house the Medici mausoleum in the same church (Ackerman 1961; Argan and Contardi 1990). Following a characteristic symbolic program of death, resurrection and glorification, the scheme of the Old Sacristy was transformed and enlivened, both through the placement of the marble tombs of Lorenzo and Piero de' Medici on either side of a simple square space, and by raising the imposts of the coffered dome by inserting a second, minor order of pilasters below the pendentives. Instead of the complex, three-dimensional articulation of spaces and structures and the clever manipulation of antique models typical of the work of Bramante and his disciples, Michelangelo chose to characterize this substantially elementary space (fifteenth century) through the idiosyncratic definition of the structural *membratura* and a sculptural treatment of the walls.

When Raphael died (6 April 1520), both Antonio and Peruzzi (Bruschi 1992a, 1992b) presented, in competition, their models for the completion of parts of St. Peter's that had not yet been defined, such as the area near the entrance. Antonio worked on a variant (Munich, Bayerische Staatsbibliothek, *Codex Iconographicus Monacensis* 195) of the alternative shown to the left in parchment drawing U 255A, proposing a second dome or sail vault between two barrel vaults with lunettes, at the center of the short entrance nave. Peruzzi, instead (Serlio, Book III: 38), brought the end ambulatory around to the entrance side, perhaps preceding it with a facade with masonry portico on three sides (Uff. 31A), thus, it seems, proposing a quincunx central plan. Sangallo's idea—while construction practically ground to a halt following Leo X's death (1 December 1521) and his succession by the staid Adrian VI (9 January 1522–14 September 1523)—seems to have prevailed, especially when Clement VII confirmed Antonio as "first architect" of St. Peter's (1524). Peruzzi, "second architect," complied with it to a certain extent in a splendid solution (Uff. 14A) which, while accepting the large sail vault or dome at the center of the nave, organized the space in a complex basilican form, reutilizing the columns of the ancient basilica, the image of which he wished to elicit in his own way.

The religious, economic and political crisis of the years leading up to 1527 and then, in May, the traumatic Sack of Rome (Chastel 1983) triggered a process of change (Calì 1980; Benedetti 1984) that, in an apparently smooth transition, particularly affected religious architecture. A general climate of uncertainty and the germination, crystallization and explosion of reformist ferments in the Catholic camp soon rendered obsolete the humanistic idea of the convergence of antiquity and Christianity—which had made possible, for example, the Tempietto at S. Pietro in Montorio, and Raphael's *School of Athens* fresco. The ideals of purity and evangelical austerity, sustained by a fundamentally rigorist ethic, meant limiting sacred construction to initiatives that were strictly necessary for worship, and had nothing to do with the ambition and magnificence of patrons. At the same time, distance was taken from the stimulating plurality of the antique models that had fueled the experiments of Bramante's disciples. Perceived as futile "vanity" and at odds with the demands for religious renewal, this relationship tended to become conventional, pared down to a few typologies and abstract, stilted canons, though it produced some functionally adequate results, satisfactory for a few cultured and refined patrons but also for a broad public. And what was demanded of the architect—who was an increasingly docile interpreter of the widespread needs of a growing group of patrons—was not so much personal creative abilities as specialized technical and professional skills.

In any case, research and experimentation with new plans, even in conformity with the new religious aims, still characterized Peruzzi's later work. Before the Sack of 1527, he designed a church to be sited on the Pincio in Rome (Uff. 452A) for rigorist Giovan Piero Carafa—Bishop of Chieti and the future Pope Paul IV, founder and protector of the new order of Theatines; the church had a simple rectangular area with corners, probably covered with a sail vault or an oval dome; the area extended along the longitudinal axis with apsidal terminal bays (De Angelis d'Ossat 1987). This scheme—of which Peruzzi developed a number of variants (Uff. 493, 567A) for other projects as well (Uff. 492, 503, 4127A)—was in part inspired by Roman bath complexes, but was substantially innovative, and Serlio adopted it for a church in his treatise (Book V). Vignola used it for the church of S. Maria del Piano in Capranica di Sutri, and in some ways it anticipates Borromini's S. Carlo alle Quattro Fontane. It must have corresponded to ideals of evangelical simplicity held by the new order of the Theatines. It was no coincidence that the agent for the purchase of the land (1525) was the datary Giovan Matteo Giberti. Already a prominent figure as the agent for Giulio de' Medici (future Pope Clement VII) during the final years of Leo X's papacy, and one of the first members of the Congregation of the Oratory, Giberti was a leading exponent of reformist evangelism and a friend of Ochino, Valdés, and Gasparo Contarini. Then, as Bishop of Verona (1528), he commissioned Sanmicheli to do the choir for the city's cathedral, and Giulio Romano to carry out its decoration. He was also the author of a number of tracts on religious constructions and, in particular, initiated the shift of emphasis to the main altar and the tabernacle in the presbytery, foreshadowing the standards set by the Council of Trent and even Borromeo's *Instructiones* (after 1572, published 1576). In around 1535 Peruzzi drew up a restructuring scheme (perhaps again for the Theatines) for the ancient church of S. Maria della Strada "in Via di Campidoglio," giving it an octagonal plan (De Angelis d'Ossat 1987), in the area later occupied by the Jesuits for their mother church. But even before then, as we have seen, Peruzzi had already begun exploring unorthodox plans based on geo-

Anonymous
View of St. Peter's from the
Southeast
1580–81
Frankfurt, Städelsches
Kunstinstitut
814
Cat. no. 377

metric forms, such as the hexagon and the oval. The latter shape (Lotz 1955) is also featured in a project for S. Giacomo in Augusta, Rome (Uff. 577Ar.), and in other drawings, such as Uff. 4137Ar., an extraordinary redesign of S. Costanza, with a short annular nave, colonnaded choir and oval dome over the nuclei created by four freestanding, load-bearing columns, perhaps conceived for his unpublished treatise (along with other drawings, including imaginative reworkings of ideas for St. Peter's, such as the highly elaborate Uff. 581Ar.). Especially during his stay in Siena (after 1527 to the early 1530s), Peruzzi (Wurm 1984) examined new religious typologies even for real buildings, such as Siena Cathedral (Uff. 497Ar.–v., 457Av.); and returned to a theme he had already explored for S. Nicolò in Carpi, and S. Agostino at Monte S. Savino, with its impressive succession of groin or domical vaults along an aisle-less nave characterized by the articulation of the walls and the distribution of the light (Uff. 504Ar.) and in the many, extraordinary studies (after 1531) for the church of S. Domenico in Siena; or the impressive prospective section at the Ashmolean Museum (N.R. 40, BL. 51), Oxford.

Though without concrete results, like the above examples, Peruzzi's activity in St. Peter's (Bruschi 1992a) had important consequences. After the Sack he greatly scaled down his previous project (Uff. 14Ar.) in successive variants (starting with some drawn directly on the same sheet), developing increasingly simple and economic solutions (Uff. 15, 16, 17, 18A) by eliminating the quincunx terminals and ambulatories and the multiple naves with columns. The schemes at this point now closely resemble that of the stark brickwork of the Basilica of Maxentius. The attention to economy, and perhaps religious scruples, is evident. But in Paul III's time (ca. 1534–35), in the last known studies (Uff. 16v., 19Av.), the central plan makes a comeback, once again in a quincunx arrangement with ambulatories. Preceded by a facade with colonnaded porch, it crystallizes in the last solution (known through a drawing formerly held by the American Academy in Rome, probably a copy). Although when Peruzzi died the project was not pursued, the central plan, ingeniously combined with a great masonry facade, returned in Antonio da Sangallo's final project, known through Labacco's huge model (1539-46), the realization of which was under way when Michelangelo stepped in.

As noted above, in Rome after 1527, under Clement VII and Paul II, the construction of new churches practically came to a halt: perhaps more due to the general mood of uncertainty and religious upheaval than because of the lingering economic and demographic crisis brought on by the Sack. When Peruzzi died, Antonio da Sangallo, unrivaled and protected by his "sect" of assistants, dominated the profession. He was responsible for the reconstruction (1538-45 ca.) of the church of S. Spirito in Sassia, along the artery leading into Via della Lungara in the Borgo Vaticano; he gave it a simple rectangular plan with a flat roof, apsidal choir and five semicircular chapels framed by pilasters on each side. Its facade, with superimposed orders of Composite pilasters joined by volutes, abstains from any reference to the idea of the triumphal arch or of the ancient temple, and stood (Giovannoni 1935a) as the prototype for a long series of facades typical of the second half of the sixteenth century and all of the seventeenth (S. Caterina dei Funari, 1564, by Guidetto Guidetti; S. Maria in Traspontina, 1565 and later, begun by Sallustio Peruzzi; the Gesù, 1569, 1571, etc.)

It is interesting that the spatial and structural layout and the facade hark back to simple schemes of the second half of the fifteenth century, with restrained but linguistically mature forms, that show a generic and conventional relationship with antiquity. Also quite typical of Sangallo's and Paul III's approach at this time is the Cappella Paolina in the Vatican (1539-40; Frommel 1964): a simple rectangular hall, covered by a unifying cloister vault with lunettes; the walls (later frescoed by Michelangelo) sported a series of pilasters to suggest a transverse axis, and there was a square choir. As in Peruzzi's project for the Theatines on the Pincio, the quest for spatial reduction is obvious; it had already appeared in Sangallo's earlier project, but here is more austere, rigid and largely free of the former links with antiquity.

In particular cases, however, as in the designs for S. Tolomeo at Nepi (ca. 1538-39; Uff. 957, 865, 866, 551A), built primarily for the veneration of relics pertaining to local martyrs, Sangallo returns to the theme of the link between an octagonal central-plan nucleus, here with a crypt, and a longitudinal vessel with aisled nave and chapels. For S. Giovanni Evangelista at Pesaro (1543 and later), Girolamo Genga (d. 1551) invented a unique plan (Pinelli and Rossi 1971; Groblewski 1976), not lacking in references to Francesco di Giorgio Martini and Bramante, in which an octagonal cloister-domed nucleus with unequal sides opens into a rectangular choir, linking up with an aisle-less nave with three apsidal chapels per side.

The longitudinal type now appeared frequently everywhere, in variants that reflected his preceding schemes to a greater or lesser degree. Sansovino proposed the type with aisled nave and chapels in Venice for the church of S. Francesco della Vigna. Antonio reproposed it for the Franciscan church in Pitigliano (Uff. 811Av.). In Rome, the aisled nave type with chapels was used in S. Luigi dei Francesi (Frommel 1987b); the aisle-less single nave type, as in S. Spirito in Sassia with three semicircular chapels per side was proposed again for in S. Caterina dei Funari. Other, more idiosyncratic solutions enjoyed lesser diffusion, such as the ones that Giulio Romano put forward respectively for the remodeling of the church of Polirone Abbey at S. Benedetto Po (1539-44; Tafuri 1989a) with vaulted nave and aisles articulated with Serliana windows and an imposing, porticoed facade; or for Mantua Cathedral, austerely organized into a nave flanked by two aisles per side, aiming to evoke, particularly with the architraved columns of the nave, windows and flat ceiling, an early Christian look. The longitudinal schemes now seemed "more in conformity with common conventions" (Serlio, Book V, Paris 1547) and with the requirements of churchmen and urban communities. However, even in some reformed spheres (such as the Theatines and often the Barnabites), the idea of the central-plan "temple" with biblical and Christian connotations, and not just humanistic and "pagan," was still alive. Perhaps prompted by religious convictions as well, Peruzzi opted for a centralized plan for St. Peter's in 1534-35, and, once Paul III had accepted this plan (not long before the convocation of the Council of Trent for the reform of the Church), Sangallo reformulated it in the executive version. Michelangelo's affirmation of the centralized plan for St. Peter's after Sangallo's death (1546) was even more decisive, and he reduced the peripheral spaces and articulation, guided by a need for economy and by his personal religious commitment (Ackerman 1961; Argan and Contardi 1990).

Of extraordinary historical importance at this time was Serlio's treatise, especially Book V (1547) dedicated (Bruschi 1989a) to "temples" or churches. In the prefatory dedication to Margherita di Navarra, Serlio's ideas evince a shift toward the Reformation position (Tafuri, in *Sebastiano Serlio* 1989). The treatise illustrates a series of seven examples of temples "of a single body only" (two round temples, one oval, one pentagonal, one hexagonal and two octagonal), two composed "of several members" and, lastly, just two "oblongs" (longitudinal single-nave structures with chapels or of the basilican type) and one single space with two apses (as in Peruzzi's plan for the church of the Theatines on the Pincio). It may not be a coincidence (seen in relation to some reformist positions?) that of the twelve examples given, nine have central plans. Significantly, the oval—basically unknown to the antique and medieval worlds—is included among these; it must have seemed to com-

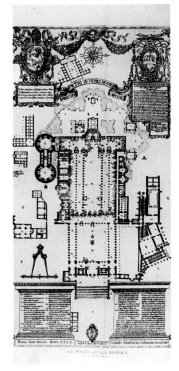

Alfaranus
Plan of the Ancient Basilica of St. Peter
1589-90
Vatican City, Fabbrica di S. Pietro, Archivio Capitolare
Cat. no. 277

174

bine the advantages of the central plan and the longitudinal one in a sort of ambiguous synthesis of an ideal, liturgically appropriate "temple." It is also worth noting that in these examples their formal austerity is accentuated, and the use of orders is conventional and standardized, while the proportions and ratios are elementary.

By this time, especially toward the mid-1540s, a new phase was starting up in which the cultural expansiveness enjoyed before the Sack seem to be effectively irretrievable. Although, as we have seen, starting in the 1520s with Peruzzi and continuing with Serlio, oval churches had been designed (Lotz 1955), none had ever been built. It fell to Giacomo da Vignola (Walcher Casotti 1960; Lotz 1974)—like Serlio, a native of the Emilia region with ties to Peruzzi—to build the first oval dome covering the votive chapel erected by Julius III in S. Andrea (1550-53) on the Via Flaminia in Rome, and later (ca. 1568-72), after other unrealized projects, the first oval church, S. Anna dei Palafrenieri, on the new street of Borgo Pio leading into the Vatican (opened by Pius IV Medici, 1559-65). The interior of S. Andrea—a rectangular unit with a dome rising on pendentives, and terminating in a rectangular *scarsella*—if compared with Sangallo's projects for S. Giacomo a Scossacavalli, with Peruzzi's for the Theatines on the Pincio, or even with the Cappella Paolina, shows further simplification and more autonomy from antiquity (despite the allusion to Roman sepulchers in the layout and to the Pantheon in the dome). The interior of S. Anna dei Palafrenieri—the prototype for many later oval churches—is structured by eight half-columns set at rhythmically unequal intervals (like the pilasters in the cella of Bramante's Tempietto), in a way that highlights the axes marked by the arches of the entrance area and the arch over the altar, and by two shallow chapels set on the transverse axes. Even compared with Serlio's oval church, the tendency to spatial reduction is noticeable.

Sanmicheli's religious buildings in Verona (Puppi 1986a) also had widespread influence. Not long after his return to the city (1526), he started work on the large Cappella Pellegrini (1529 and later) in S. Bernardino, circular and preceded by a barrel-vaulted atrium. With links to the Pantheon, the organization of the space, with eight half-columns set at different intervals (as in Bramante's Tempietto and in the extraordinary Cappella Caracciolo in S. Giovanni a Carbonara, Naples, 1516, perhaps to a design by Giuliano da Sangallo), large, trapezoidal niches and pedimented tabernacles, shows direct knowledge of the work of Bramante and his disciples as well as in-depth study of Roman and Veronese antiquity (Arch of the Gavi, Arch of Jupiter Ammonium) which it recalls and fuses in an elegant whole, enlivened by sumptuous sculptural decoration. But about thirty years later, in a city seething with reformist ferment and marked by the pastoral activities of Giovanni Matteo Giberti, the sanctuary of the Madonna di Campagna (Puppi 1986a; Davies 1990), which Sanmicheli designed in 1559 the custody of a miraculous image, reveals a different climate. The centralized structure, octagonal inside and circular outside, with an extradosed dome resting on a galleried drum, extends into a square *sacellum* with angled corners creating a cruciform plan, where the miraculous image itself is housed. As a whole, it develops ideas that emerged in Rome in the 1520s, especially in the work of Antonio da Sangallo (S. Giacomo in Augusta, the sanctuary church di Montemoro, etc.). But the bare spaces of the interior are rigid with an unmistakable hierarchy. The Composite order, no longer of half-columns, but of pilasters, frames arches and shallow niches. The square, almost abstract structural members (as in the dome of S. Giorgio in Brayda, which he began in ca. 1536 within the context of Giberti's general revision of church liturgy) accentuate the effect of austere monumentality. This jibes with the purism of the exterior, in a conceptual, ambiguous link to Bramante's diminutive Tempietto, with the high domed cylinder emerging from a peripteral Tuscan-Doric colonnade (constructed after the architect's death, and possibly not as high as he had intended) and visible from a great distance in the surrounding countryside.

Slightly earlier, in the treatise of Siena-born Pietro Cataneo (1554, Book III) there had appeared an illustration of an "ideal" round temple, an enlargement of Bramante's Tempietto, also encircled by a colonnade, and of a volume comparable to that of the Madonna di Campagna. Cataneo's temple is shown alongside another round one with sixteen perimetral cells, as in the project that Sangallo (Uff. 199, 200A) submitted for S. Giovanni dei Fiorentini. Interestingly, two years earlier (Rome, 1552) Antonio Labacco had published the Sangallo project, claiming it to be his own—a single modern, unrealized building among the "antiquities" of Rome in his *Libro Appartenente all'Architettura*. Cataneo presented two other central-plan temples: one octagonal, with twenty-four chapels, and one based on a simple Greek cross plan. But, although "the antiques had given to the city's main temple a circular [as in the Pantheon], oval, quadrangular, octangular form, and with more or fewer corners or sides," in a Christian city it was more suitable—he advocated—to adopt, for the main temple, the longitudinal cross form, in memory of the Redemption and of Christ crucified, "and from his holiest figure"—the ideal human figure—"take the measures of the temple" (as in Nicholas V's St. Peter's, and following the example of Francesco di Giorgio). Before the four central-plan temples, Cataneo therefore shows six examples, basilican or single-nave with chapels, of cruciform churches (that is, churches with transepts) of different sizes, depending on the functional requirements and the size of the city; these designs were also useful for "parish churches, monasteries and for other pious places."

Giulio Romano, after Raphael
Old St. Peter's in the fresco
Constantine's Donation
1523–24
Vatican, Sala di Costantino

177

While or slightly before Sanmicheli was designing the Madonna di Campagna, eighty-four-year-old Michelangelo in Rome was exploring a central-plan solution (1559–60) for the Florentine "nation" for S. Giovanni dei Fiorentini, work upon which had been interrupted after Sangallo's start. We do not know for what reasons—practical and economical or ideal and in memory of early Christian churches (S. Stefano Rotondo, S. Costanza) and baptisteries (Ackerman 1961)—Michelangelo and his patrons and backers, who included Duke Cosimo I Medici, decided to abandon Sangallo's longitudinal plan in favor of a centrally planned church. Significantly, the design springs from a circular scheme rather similar to those of Sangallo's studies (Uff. 199, 200A) with radial chapels, published shortly beforehand (1552, then 1557 and 1559) by Labacco. Michelangelo's initial idea (CB 124; see Ackerman 1961, and successive editions), is far from the geometrical and constructive logic of Antonio da Sangallo. Successive solutions get even further away from it (CB 121, 120); all are based on the axial tension of spaces arranged on the cross (+) and diagonal (x) axes. The final project (Uff. 3185)—of which Tiberio Calcagni, after making a rough model in clay, seems to have prepared two wooden models—had a circular space with two orders of columns set at different intervals in such a way as to frame arches leading into narrow rectangular areas along the cross-axes and into oval chapels along the diagonal axes. On the exterior, from the complex but austere complex perimeter—something like Michelangelo's St. Peter's—emerged the extradosed semicircular dome on a plain cylindrical drum.

Detail of the apse of St. Peter's showing Michelangelo's dome

Shortly afterward, once again with the help of Tiberio Calcagni, Michelangelo redesigned a space in S. Maria Maggiore heavily conditioned by pre-existing structures to hold the burial chapel of Cardinal Ascanio Sforza (begun 1564, after Michelangelo's death). Four columns arranged diagonally at the corners of a square space (as Peruzzi had already done in the Cappella Ghisilardi in the church of S. Domenico, Bologna) bear up a sail vault, the arches of which open on the sides into large, deeply recessed apses, circular in section, flanked by columns, and on the longitudinal axis, into the narrow entrance area and the square one of the altar. The Renaissance scheme of the triconch (the subject of a preliminary study, CB 104) is completely overturned in a dramatic association of central-plan and axial tensions that provided creative stimuli to Baroque architects, and to Borromini in particular (S. Carlo alle Quattro Fontane, etc.).

In 1561 Michelangelo submitted to Pius IV Medici (Ackerman 1961; Argan and Contardi 1990) a proposal for the reconstruction of the central part of the Baths of Diocletian as a church dedicated to S. Maria degli Angeli. The design was sponsored by Carlo Borromeo, and involved a plan that is neither centralized nor longitudinal. Michelangelo's contribution is conspicuously limited to addressing the religious needs and economic and functional concerns related to the passage of the church to the monastic order of the Carthusians, and his formal intervention was minimal. He created three entrance portals, of which the main one crossed the ancient round *caldarium* along the original axis of the baths, and defined by means of a few partitions the spaces of two side vestibules and a deep rectangular choir on the side toward the Carthusian monastery, screened from the church by two original columns. The whole plan unfolds along two axes of nearly the same length, as in a Greek cross. The scheme with three entrances and a choir beyond the altar was typical of the Renaissance. But the overall layout of the space—bare wall structures and great cross vaults resting on columns and flanked by the barrel-vaulted spaces of the ancient baths—was utterly new, with its transverse emphasis with respect to the entrance-to-choir axis (practically a large, isolated transept without nave). In fact, far from representing "unfinished architecture" (Zevi 1964) or a real "repudiation of architecture" (Argan 1990), it was the Christian appropriation of a "temple of idols and demons" (Ackerman 1961) entailing the physical reutilization of its structures by patrons whose main motivations were devotional. For his part, the architect was motivated by his personal religious feeling, humbly addressing the liturgical requirements and unselfishly applying his superb gifts of creativity to the greater glory of God. Such lack of ambition and personal gain was not unique to Michelangelo during this period.

The great upheaval that had afflicted the Church ever since the late fifteenth century, culminating in the Council of Trent, had led to the spread of doctrinal barriers and liturgical considerations that had to be urgently addressed (Ackerman 1977 and 1980). For example, since the end of the fifteenth century, there had been growing acceptance of freeing the nave of the obstruction of the choir by moving it to the back of the church, into a separate space. In this way the attention of the worshippers could focus on the main altar (which Alberti had already made the only one in the church), highlighted by its position and the luminosity of the presbytery. The growing insistence on liturgical functionality (Benedetti 1984)—demanded by reformed religious orders and bishops such as Giberti, and, later, Carlo Borromeo and others—gave rise to revised solutions for existing and new church structures in which reciprocal disturbance between the celebrants in the main hall of worship and the side chapels of the nobility, brotherhoods, or special orders, was avoided by means of passageways from the sacristy to the communicating chapels. The burgeoning congregations, the practice of delivering sermons, and even the diffusion of polyphonic music, meant that the church layout had to take visibility and acoustics into account. In general, a more precise and analytical identification of the various functions led to a more rational distribution, greater specialization and hierarchy

St. Peter's, Rome
interior of Michelangelo's dome

of spaces and circulation. Furthermore, especially after the Sack, a general criterion of austerity and simplicity made itself widely felt—without sacrificing ornament—especially in the interiors; it became a function of the exterior, especially the facade, to proclaim to the city that it was the place of worship, so much the better if it had a dome that was visible from a distance. In this aim, the humanistic ideal of the organic integrity of the building conceived as "similar" to the human figure was abandoned and the rigorous correspondence to the interior it required (Ackerman 1977) gave way to hyperbolic forms.

Carlo Borromeo, Archbishop of Milan from 1565, is well known for his translation into practical and organizational terms of the principles of the recent Council of Trent (1563) in his famous *Instructiones fabricae et suppellectiles ecclesiasticae* (Milan 1577), which he disseminated with repeated pastoral visits and direct intervention on bishops of various cities, especially in northern Italy. As far as the typologies were concerned, he only shows a preference for the "form of the cross, as it appears in the sacred Roman basilicas" and a mistrust of the circular-plan temple which, he deemed, was "little used among Christian peoples and customary in idolatrous temples."

In general, during these years, functionality, rational spatial simplicity and solidity tend to come to the fore. Beauty and ornament also tend to become a tool of liturgical expression. But in fact, each of the types developed in the Renaissance (longitudinal, basilican or hall-type with chapels, centralized or "composite") by now well established with many variations and organized according to visual

Bibliographical note

Given the vast scope of the theme dealt with here, it is practically impossible (and perhaps even pointless) listing the countless bibliographical references. Consequently, for an in-depth bibliography, the reader is advised to consult L.H. Heydenreich and W. Lotz, *Architecture in Italy, 1400-1600*, Penguin Books Ltd, Harmondsworth-Baltimore, 1974, p. 397ff., which continues to be the most exhaustive overall guide to the complex sphere of Renaissance architecture. Nonetheless, the following is a helpful shortlist of titles that cover the architecture in question and other pertinent aspects of the period (though occasionally "out of date"), while providing a partial update of Heydenreich and Lotz's 1974 bibliography:

P. Laspeyers, *Die Kirchen der Renaissance in Mittelitalien*, Berlin-Stuttgart, 1882

H. Strack, *Zentral und Kuppelkirchen der Renaissance in Italien*, Berlin, 1892

R. Wittkower, *Architectural Principles in the Age of Humanism*, London, 1962 and later editions

A. Chastel, *Art et humanisme à Florence au temps de Laurent le Magnifique*, Paris, 1959

S. Sinding Larsen, "Some Functional and Iconographical Aspects of the Centralized Church in the Italian Renaissance," in *Acta ad archeologiam et artium historiam pertinentia* II, 1965, p. 203ff.

W. Lotz, "Die ovalen Kirchenräume des Cinquecento," in *Römisches Jahrbuch für Kunstgeschichte* VII, 1955, p. 7ff.

W. Lotz, "Notizen zum kirchlichen Zentralbau der Renaissance," in *Studien zur toskanischen Kunst* (Festschrift L.H. Heydenreich), Munich, 1964, p. 157ff.; republished in W. Lotz, *Studies in Italian Renaissance Architecture*, M.I.T. Press, 1977

Various, "Palladio e l'architettura sacra del Cinquecento in Italia," in *Bolletino Centro Internazionale Storia Archit.*, Vicenza XIX, 1977

M. Fagiolo, *Chiese e cattedrali*, Milan, 1978

J. Ackerman, "Observations on Renaissance Church Planning in Venice and Florence, 1470-1570," in *Florence and Venice: Comparisons and Relations* (Villa I Tatti, 1976-77), Florence, 1980, II, p. 287ff.

M. Licht, *L'edificio a pianta centrale. Lo sviluppo del disegno architettonico nel Rinascimento*, exhibition catalog, Florence, 1984 (with debatable contributions)

L. Patetta, *Storia e tipologia*, Milan, 1989

L'église dans l'architecture de la Renaissance, Proceedings of the International Seminar of the Centre d'études supérieure de la Renaissance, Tours, 1990 (in preparation).

Given the decision to forgo detailed references according to regions, cities, or architects, the reader is invited to follow the bibliographical references in the text notes, which cite only a few of the great many texts available, and were chosen for various reasons as valuable material for consultation.

principles, customary constructive and linguistic methods, could be compatible or adaptable to the new programs and contents, especially if stripped of over-explicit references to the pagan world, and freighted with Christian symbology. Therefore, at least from the mid-century to the 1570s, no type in particular seemed to prevail, and the preferences of the different patrons and religious orders widely varied.

The basilican type still seemed suited to large city churches and to monasteries (e.g., the abbey of the Cassinese Benedictines in Arezzo by G. Vasari, 1565; S. Giorgio Maggiore, also occupied by Benedictines, in Venice, by A. Palladio, 1566; Vignola's designs for S. Maria in Traspontina, ca. 1565, and perhaps those for the Gesù, 1568; S. Maria degli Angeli in Assisi, by G. Alessi, 1569; S. Vittore al Corpo by V. Seregni and others, 1560 and later; etc.). The single-hall type with chapels, with or without transept, presbytery (sometimes domed) and separate choir—functionally very satisfactory—enjoyed the favor of such reformist orders as the Jesuits (e.g., the early designs for the Gesù in Rome, by Nanni di Baccio Bigio and later possibly Michelangelo, between 1550 and 1555) and to some extent the Barnabites. The latter religious order, after having used the central plan in S. Maria di Canepanova in Pavia (1557) with success, and without discarding later centralized schemes (cross-plan in Casale Monferrato, 1584; quincunx in S. Alessandro, Milan, by the Barnabite L. Binago; in Rome's S. Carlo ai Catinari, designed 1652 by the Barnabite Mazenta, etc.), modified, with G. Alessi's contribution, an existing church, obtaining an exemplary barrel-vaulted hall-type with communicating chapels, raised presbytery and large apsidal choir, as in the important church of SS. Barnaba e Paolo in Milan (1561-67). The type received original treatment from P. Pellegrini, Borromeo's architect, in the Jesuit church of S. Fedele in Milan (plans dating from 1567, begun 1569). Showing echoes of Roman baths and of Peruzzi's studies, this church has two bays with sail vaults resting on corner columns and a domed, apsidal presbytery. The hall-type with chapels, triconch presbytery and large, separate choir was also chosen by the Venetian senate (1577) for the votive Redentore church, designed by Palladio after the plague of 1576, which has strong references to St. Peter's in particular. Consideration had also been given to a round form for this church, preferred by Daniele Barbaro and Palladio (Book IV, 6; R.I.B.A. no. IXV, 13) who instead chose it for the parish church (or "tempietto") of S. Paolo in Maser. After the same plague of 1576, in Milan a round plan by Pellegrini was chosen for the municipal church of S. Sebastiano, a liberal reduction of the Pantheon, perhaps justified by its dedication to an early Christian martyr. A few reformed religious orders, such as the Barnabites and especially the Theatines, now seemed actually to prefer centralized forms. For the latter order, Scamozzi started (1582) the church of Padua, octagonal with unequal sides with presbytery and separated choir. Furthermore, the "composite" type—from which Palladio's churches and even S. Fedele in Milan basically derive—had not disappeared; it was also used in the layout of the Gesù in Rome, agreed upon (1568-69) by Cardinal Alessandro Farnese, the Jesuits and Vignola (Pecchiai 1952; Schwager 1977). Similarly, at the close of the century, oval plans were still in use (S. Giacomo degli Incurabili, Rome, by Francesco da Volterra, 1590-92; the sanctuary of Vicoforte, Mondovì, by Ascanio Vitozzi, 1596).

Nearly all of these types of church made up the development of the schemes that emerged between the 1420s and the 1520s: a century of intense creativity that radically changed the panorama of religious architecture.

Christoph Luitpold Frommel

Living *all'antica*: Palaces and Villas from Brunelleschi to Bramante

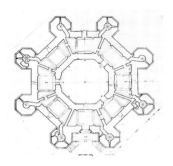

1. Castel del Monte plan

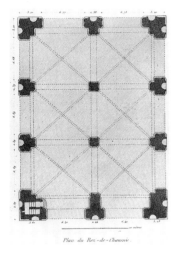

2. Florence, Orsanmichele plan

Richard Wilson
Rome from the Villa Madama
(detail)
1753
*New Haven, Yale Center
for British Art
Paul Mellon Collection
Cat. no. 219*

[1] K. M. Swoboda, *Römische und romanishes Paläste*, Vienna 1919; J. S. Ackerman, *The villa. Form and ideology of country houses*, London 1990.
[2] H. Götze, *Castel del Monte. Gestalt und Symbol der Architektur Friedrichs II.*, Munich 1991.
[3] E. Arslan, *Venezia gotica. L'architettura civile gotica veneziana*, Milan 1970, 1-76.
[4] J. Paul, *Der Palazzo Vecchio in Florenz. Ursprung und Bedeutung einer Form*, Florence 1969; H. Klotz, "Der Florentiner Stadtpalast." Zum Verständnis einer Repräsentationsform," in F. Möbius and E. Schubert, *Architektur des Mittelalters. Function und Gestalt*, Weimar 1984, pp. 307-343.
[5] J. White, *Art and architecture in Italy 1250 to 1400*, Harmondsworth 1966, 173.

The Early History

Ecclesiastical and secular buildings followed two different paths of development until the start of the fifteenth century.[1] While sacred buildings had come to represent the highest duty of architecture and had been studied to achieve the greatest perfection possible—whether they were the Parthenon, the Pantheon, the Basilica of S. Sofia or a cathedral—secular buildings, and in particular homes to live in, were destined to undergo much greater oscillations. If, moreover, after places of worship, other new kinds of buildings such as theaters, basilicas, triumphal arches or thermal complexes adopted equally pregnant forms, this was only possible because they were destined exclusively for public use. The more private they were, the more indefinite their architectural form.

Even well into late antiquity there were few residences that could claim to compete as seats of equal dignity with ecclesiastical or public buildings. This tradition still existed in the Middle Ages with the homes of emperors, kings and popes. In the pope's palace at Avignon in the late Gothic age, residential towers, halls, chapels, staircases, courtyards and gardens, were still grouped together without any rigid order. Only the need for protection was a unifying force, which could be noticed in the homes of late antiquity, such as Diocletian's palace at Split, the porticoed villa between corner avant-corps of late antiquity, or medieval castles. The nucleus of a new type of development can already be observed in Frederick II's Castel del Monte, in which both the external construction and the courtyard not only have completely centralized and symmetrical forms, but are also subject to the principles of an octagon[2] (fig. 1). Secular building began also to be a task of high architecture, as a result, not surprisingly, of a commission from a prince for whom religion no longer had absolute priority. At the same time, interest in a kind of symmetrically organized residence with artistic proportions developed in Venice[3]. With the protection of the ambitious Venetian Republic and the lagoon, fortification was no longer necessary. The opening into arches not just of the wall of the hall on the upper story but also the entrance area and both sides went beyond the imperial palace on the waterfront at Split or other villas of late antiquity. The more the facades were opened up, the more the precious marble facing was decorated with gold, ornament and sculptures. But only toward the end of the fifteenth century were princely builders in central Italy such as Federico da Montefeltro or Raffaele Riario to decorate their homes with similar luxuries, so that for centuries the Venetian palaces remained an exception admired by all.

The real first impetus for Renaissance residences did not come from Venice but from Florence. In the earliest period of the Renaissance buildings were already constructed in Tuscany more *all'antica* than elsewhere, but the designs were exclusively for ecclesiastical architecture such as the Florentine Baptistery or Pisa Cathedral. In the elaboration of the design there was an interest—quite the opposite of Venice—in articulating the whole body of the building, and in this sense, centrally planned buildings like the Baptistery were particularly suitable. This strong feeling for a freestanding building and for its relative plastic articulation was a characteristic of Florentine architecture during the Duecento and Trecento, and one of its best early examples was the external construction of Florence Cathedral, with its continuous marble facing. At more or less the same time, secular architecture became the subject of artistic creation. Attempts were made to eliminate the numerous irregularities in the Palazzo Vecchio that had been built about fifty years earlier, and to group into a single building the large hall, courtyard, tower, chapel and rooms used as offices, and even to give the entrance facade a symmetrical design.[4] The stereometric compactness of this body was further and astonishingly emphasized when its freestanding fronts were given an antique-style rusticated facing, perhaps inspired by the Hohenstaufen castles, enlivened by an almost continual row of marble two-light windows linked together by cornices and crenelation all round. About forty years later, another secular building, the now Orsanmichele, was built freestanding, without elements of fortification, and with a completely symmetrical arrangement decorated with ornament right up to the final cornice[5] (figs. 2, 3). However, the difference between these and the material and artistic splendor of sacred buildings—long since outshone by the refined facades of Venetian palaces—still remained considerable.

3. Florence, Orsanmichele facade

4. Florence Palazzo di Parte Guelfa

From Brunelleschi to Giuliano da Sangallo

When, in the early years of the Quattrocento, antiquity first began to acquire an incontrovertible role as a model, Brunelleschi, in particular, tried to transfer the ancient principles of construction to secular buildings as well, without making fundamental distinctions between the two kinds of building. As early as 1419 he designed the facade of the Ospedale degli Innocenti with the same system of arcades flanked by a great order of pilasters that he gave the interior of S. Lorenzo or of S. Spirito, using even the same materials and details.[6] Toward 1435 he embellished the three exposed corners of the Palazzo di Parte Guelfa, a building with a large hall, comparable to Orsanmichele, with a giant order that embraced a large and a small row of windows[7] (fig. 4).

According to contemporary sources, just before Brunelleschi died he presented a model for the Palazzo Medici, a commission that gave him greater pleasure than any that had preceded it[8] (fig. 5). The palace portal was in front of that of S. Lorenzo—in the same way that the portals of the baptistery and the cathedral (to whose construction Brunelleschi had contributed so much) faced each other. The palace, which was also freestanding, would have flanked a second square by the side of the subsequent Palazzo Medici so that its appearance would have had an effect that only the Palazzo Vecchio had achieved so far. Lastly, it would have been so large and expensive that Cosimo would have feared the envy of his fellow citizens; it was consequently rejected (to his later regret) in favor of Michelozzo's more modest scheme. It is quite probable, therefore, that Brunelleschi wanted to cultivate here the ideas that had been sown in his first town-planning projects, that is, the construction of a regular square with *all'antica* buildings. Like all his other buildings, he would have embellished not

[6] H. Saalman, *Filippo Brunelleschi. The Buildings*, London 1993, p. 32ff., 106ff., 338ff.

[7] op. cit.: 286ff.

[8] C. Elam, in G. Cherubini and G. Finelli, *Il Palazzo Medici-Riccardi di Firenze*, Florence 1990, pp. 44-57; B. Prayer, in op. cit.: 58-75; H. Saalman 1993: 152-156. Manetti could have omitted Brunelleschi's project out of deference to the Medici family. Although Gelli described it for the first time, it corresponds to Brunelleschi's tendencies much more closely than anything else built in Florence in the early sixteenth century, including a project of another kind by Leonardo which could hardly be a posthumous invention.

5. *Florence, Palazzo Medici*
Brunelleschi's project
alternative to the reconstruction
by C. Elam

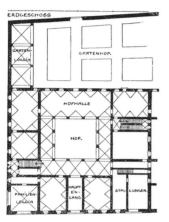

6. *Florence, Palazzo Medici*
plan and garden

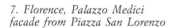

7. *Florence, Palazzo Medici*
facade from Piazza San Lorenzo

[9] Filarete (Antonio Averlino), *Trattato di architettura*, ed. A. M. Finoli and L. Grassi, Milan 1972, pls. 20, 33, 42, 60, 65, 67, 77, 85, 90, 93, 94, 103, 121, 122, 124, 125; C. L. Frommel, "Reflections on the Early Architectural Drawings," essay in the present catalog.
[10] *Il Palazzo Medici Riccardi...* 1990; A. Tönnesmann, "Zwischen Bürgerhaus und Residenz. Zur sozialen Typik des Palazzo Medici," in A. Beyer and B. Boucher, eds., *Piero de' Medici "Il Gottoso" (1416-1469)*, Berlin 1993, pp. 71-88.

only the facade of S. Lorenzo with orders, but also the palace opposite—and not just one or two of its facades, but the whole building which in all probability was considerably symmetrical with respect to the axes. This solution would not only have merged Florentine solidity with Venetian splendor but it would have inserted a patrician residence in an urban context in a more symmetrical and exemplary manner than in any other setting of antiquity or the Middle Ages. The classification and archaizing of the secular buildings, starting with the Loggia degli Innocenti and the Palazzo di Parte Guelfa, would now have included the residences—an enormous challenge to Brunelleschi's powers of creativity, inasmuch as he now had to adapt the height of the stories and the bays to the rules of the ancient order of columns, and also bring together rooms of different sizes, staircases, baths, toilets and kitchens into one completely symmetrical body. That these ideas found an immediate response in his contemporaries can be seen first of all in the works of Alberti and Filarete. Toward 1460 Filarete furnished a surprising number of architectural works with orders in his ideal city, Sforzinda, and tried to insert their freestanding and completely symmetrical shapes into an equally organized context.[9] The version of the palace actually built by Cosimo as from 1445 derived directly from the merchant traditions of his home town[10] (figs. 6, 7). The outer construction followed the example of the Palazzo Vecchio in the number of its stories, the ashlar on the ground floor and the two-light windows. Since it was protected by the city walls of Florence and was part of a stable state, Cosimo did not need to build towers and battlements. He had the corners opened up to create a domestic loggia and crowned the building with a cornice *all'antica*. There is a trace of the fortification spirit still in the rustication at the base, a feature that had long been eliminated from Venetian palaces. Michelozzo also tried to unite the various rooms into a single body. The facade system, however, was

185

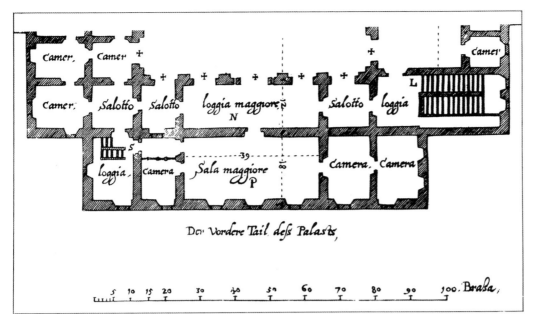

8. Florence, Palazzo Pitti
plan

interrupted, strangely enough, right on the back of the building facing Piazza S. Lorenzo—probably because this was where it gave on to the garden, and hence its loggia, and the inner courtyard, set behind a wing of the same height, would have been too dark. The slightly off-center placement of the portal, the irregular features of the southern facade, the lack of an axial relationship between the openings of the ground story and those of the upper two, or the plan itself reveal Michelozzo's difficulties in bringing the multiple functions and limitations of a residence built on a pre-existing site into a harmonious context. Probably perfect symmetry did not as yet have the same significance for Cosimo and Michelozzo that it had for Brunelleschi.

The square courtyard also had a more traditional effect than can be imagined in Brunelleschi's project, and only has a complete order on the upper story. The symmetrical peristyle with its arcades *all'antica*, sgraffiti, reliefs and statuary, could have represented Cosimo's intention to create an "antique" house.

The inner layout could have been arranged according to the ceremonials of the great palaces belonging to popes and cardinals. Visitors came through the central passage of the lower loggia and up the double flight of barrel-vaulted stairs to the left to the *piano nobile*, then along a corridor that brought them directly before a large hall positioned on the privileged corner site.[11] This continued into the wing of the facade on Via Larga divided into a series of increasingly smaller rooms kept for the owner, ending with the chapel, as in the papal palaces. As with Nicholas V's palace or Pius II's palace at Pienza, it appears that there were various apartments for the changing seasons, such as the summer apartment in the southern wing on the ground story leading directly in to the garden. During the next fifteen years Alberti and Bernardo Rossellino attempted to render the palace even more regular and *all'antica*. Perhaps before 1460 Alberti succeeded in amalgamating all three stories of the Palazzo Rucellai by combining Florentine rustication with complete orders of pilasters, thus transferring Brunelleschi's principles the residential palace—at least for the entrance facade. It is probable that Alberti was also behind the design of almost contemporary Palazzo Pitti (1458)[12] (fig. 8). In around 1453 Alberti had defined suburban palaces for the first time in his treatise: *"est et genus quoddam aedificii privati, quod una aedium urbanarum dignitatem et villae iucunditates exigat. Hi sunt orti suburbani."*[13] The enormous block of the Palazzo Pitti also corresponded to his idea of *all'antica* monumentality. It had no internal courtyard but spread out sideways and the ample arcades protected by balustrades opened onto a square in front. While it had no orders whatsoever, the entrance facade with its rustication was much more classicizing than the Palazzo Medici, and likewise the inner layout was substantially closer to the ideal of perfect symmetry. In his Palazzo Piccolomini in Pienza (1461), Rossellino exploited all these new achievements and designed a palace with three symmetrical sides involving windows, false doors, and hiding the loggias on the southern side behind the side fronts[14] (figs. 9, 10). Only the kitchens remained in a separate building. Since he opened the back of the palace to the view of the surrounding countryside it was difficult to connect the palace symmetrically with the cathedral facade. Unlike Brunelleschi, Pius II and his architect also maintained the hierarchical tradition, characterizing the facade with only pale limestone and freestanding columns. The papal palace was built with simple materials and flat pilasters, while the other buildings in the square were simply plastered.

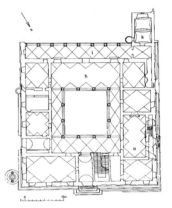

9. Pienza, Palazzo Piccolomini
plan of the piano nobile

[11] W. Bulst, in *Il Palazzo Medici Riccardi...* 1990: 98-120.
[12] K. H. Busse, "Der Pitti-Palast...," in *Jahrbuch der preussischen Kunstsammlungen* 51 (1930), pp. 110-132; A. Tönnesmann 1983b: 77ff.; L. H. Heydenreich and W. Lotz, *Architecture in Italy 1400 to 1600*, Harmondsworth 1974, p. 40, 337ff.; A. Tönnesmann, *Der Palazzo Gondi in Florenz*, Worms 1983, p. 68ff.
[13] L. B. Alberti, *L'architettura (De re aedificatoria)*, ed. P. Portoghesi, trans. G. Orlandi, Milan 1966, IX, 2, p. 791.
[14] C. R. Mack, *Pienza. The creation of a Renaissance City*, Ithaca-London 1987; A. Tönnesmann, *Pienza. Städtebau und Humanismus*, Munich 1990.

10. *Pienza, Palazzo Piccolomini*
flank and corner of the cathedral

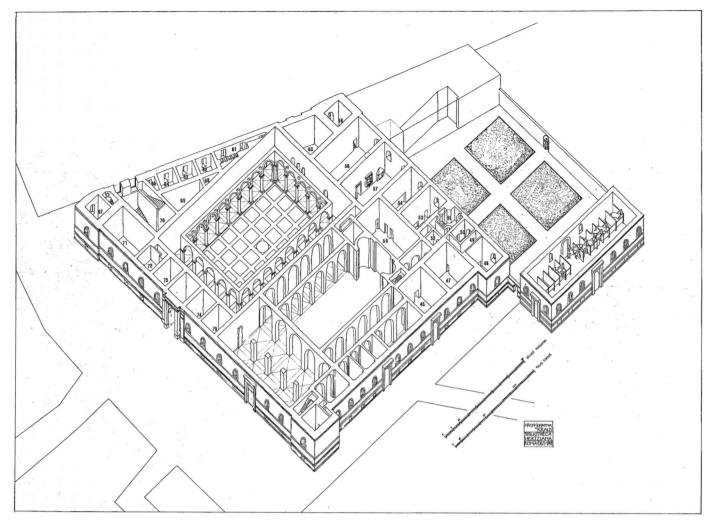

Even though he was designing a papal palace, Rossellino was more influenced by Florentine patrician palaces in his choice of dimensions and plan. It was much more difficult to introduce these fundamental innovations in the extensive regal palaces in Rome and Urbino. The papal ceremonials required not only a church and a private garden in the immediate neighborhood, but also a benediction loggia and a sequence of great halls. If, in Paul II's Palazzo Venezia (begun 1465) the wing of the hall, the residential tower, court, church and garden courtyard are placed loosely one next to the other, this is due most of all to the objective difficulties of its architect, Francesco del Borgo, who came from Borgo S. Sepolcro and learnt his profession in Rome: he could only follow at a distance the developments of the last twenty years.[15] His adhesion to the ideas of Alberti and interest in ancient monuments can be seen in particular in the barrel vaulted entryway and in the theater motif of the benediction loggia. Like many aspects of the project, the two adjacent rectangular squares in front of the palace and the church, could have been inspired by the Piazza della Signoria rather than by Brunelleschi's project for Piazza S. Lorenzo. Luciano Laurana, the first architect of the Palazzo Ducale in Urbino, was not a Florentine either; likewise he did not unite the individual wings into a homogeneous whole with decorative orders all round.[16] On the contrary, the crenelation and irregular wall openings reveal that the external construction followed even more traditional ideas. All the more significant were the developments introduced by Laurana and his successor Francesco di Giorgio in the area of the courtyard, in the furnishings and in the whole organization of the palace: the colonnade of the courtyard was wider and more *all'antica*, the staircase broader, lighter and accessible, rising up almost directly from the entrance loggia. Numerous large windows create an extraordinary amount of illumination. The private apartment is connected to the Studiolo, the chapel, bathroom, *giardino segreto* and loggia with a view of the surrounding hills, and this arrangement made the palace more beautiful and comfortable than any other princely palace since antiquity. The priorities of the court environment were quite different from those of patrician Florence. Even greater efforts were made in Florence to recreate the antique-style house and to make the body of the building symmetrical. Giuliano da Sangallo provided a good example of this in his first work, the Palazzo di Bartolomeo Scala (begun ca. 1473)[17] (fig. 11). Like many ancient villas and Alberti's *suburbanum*, it was sited on the edge of the city. The residential

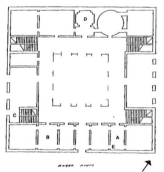

11. Florence, Palazzo della Scala plan

*13. top
Rome, Palazzo della Cancelleria axonometric projection of the ground floor
(drawing J. Kraus)*

[15] C. L. Frommel, "Francesco del Borgo: Architekt Pius' II. und Pauls II.: 2: Palazzo Venezia, Palazzetto Venezia und San Marco," in *Römisches Jahrbuch für Kunstgeschichte* 21 (1984), p. 138ff.
[16] P. Rotondi, *Il Palazzo Ducale di Urbino*, Urbino 1951.
[17] A. Tönnesmann 1983b: 93ff.; L. Pellecchia, "The patrons' role in the production of architecture: Bartolomeo Scala and the Scala Palace," in *Renaissance Quarterly* 42 (1989) pp. 258-291.

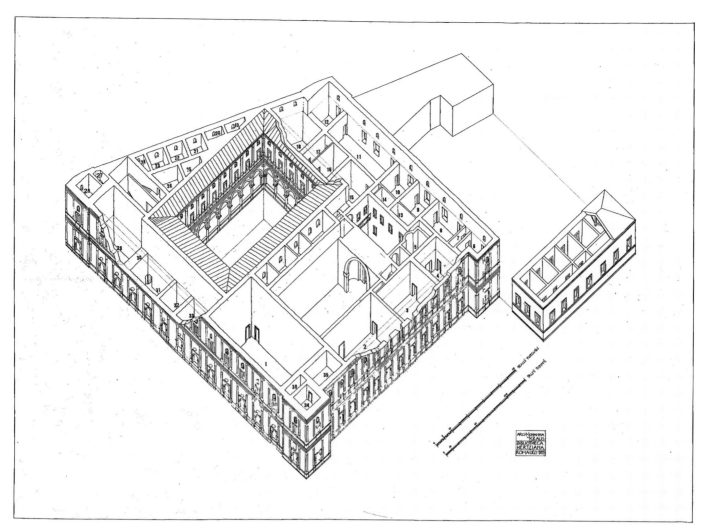

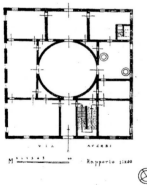

12. Mantua, Casa del Mantegna outline

14. top
Rome, Palazzo della Cancelleria axonometric projection of the piano nobile
(drawing J. Kraus)

[18] E. E. Rosenthal, "The House of Andrea Mantegna," in *Gazette des Beaux-Arts* 60 (1962) pp. 327-348; M. Harder, *Entstehung von Rundhof und Rundsaal im Palastbau der Renaissance in Italien,* Freiburg 1991, p. 30ff.
[19] C. L. Frommel, "Il Palazzo della Cancelleria," in *Il Palazzo dal Rinasciento a oggi. Atti del Convegno Internazionale Reggio Calabria 1988,* Rome 1989, pp. 29-54.

part was on the ground floor, as in ancient villas, and gave on to gardens at the back. It was decorated mostly on the inside, while the exterior did not have any real facade. The four residential wings were grouped almost concentrically round the square courtyard, and were connected by means of square corner rooms. With this palazzo, Giuliano came much closer to the ideal centrally-planned secular building, surpassing the Palazzo Medici and the Palazzo Piccolomini. The arrangement of the lower loggias in the courtyard and the relief on the upper story reveal his deep understanding of Roman monuments, while the corner solution and richly stuccoed vaults appear to have been derived already from the palace at Urbino. On the other hand, Urbino must have been an example for Lorenzo de' Medici as well, given that in 1480 he had the exact plans sent to him by Baccio Pontelli.

Similar ideas characterized the house of Mantegna, built three years later, which also had a symmetrical design and, being sited in the outskirts of the city, gave on to a garden[18] (fig. 12). The small cylindrical courtyard has an order, while the windows of the stairs give an asymmetrical appearance to the simple entrance facade. Similar plans can be found in the works of Francesco di Giorgio, and therefore it is likely that their common denominator was once again Alberti. To what extent patrons and architects took advantage of each other, even from a distance, and how quickly their respective innovations spread abroad, can be observed in the Palazzo della Cancelleria, built by Cardinal Raffaele Riario (1489 and after)[19] (figs. 13, 14). Its first architect was perhaps Baccio Pontelli, who exploited his Florentine schooling and long experience in Urbino and Rome. From the Palazzo Venezia he borrowed the ceremonial itinerary arranged on the inside with the series of rhythmically decreasing rooms, and the connection with a church or residential tower next to the garden at the back of the building. His ample inner court with as many as five arches by eight on two stories, and convenient staircase and apartment vied with the Palazzo Ducale in Urbino. The synthesis of the enormous residential palace, and even of the church in one homogeneous body with an order of pilasters running all round it is, however, typical of the Florentine tradition. For the first time the immediate influence of ancient monuments and the Roman humanists brought about the substitution of the medieval remains with the help of a vocabulary, an *aurea latinitas*, taken directly from the ancients.

Lastly, the hierarchical principle was introduced for the first time in the external construction of the Cancelleria which, thanks first of all to Bramante's palaces, was to achieve centuries of recognition: the ground floor was subordinated to the two upper stories, especially to the dominating *piano nobile* where the owner lived. Only the entrance facade was completely faced in travertine and characterized by the triumphal arch motif of the araeosystyle pilasters. The *piano nobile* was embellished with a golden heraldic rose motif and with richly decorated marble aedicules. From the typological point of view the Cancelleria did not derive from the block-shaped patrician palaces in Florence, but rather from fortified city castles with corner towers. Like Luca Fancelli in Federico Gonzaga's Domus Nova of 1480, the builders of the Cancelleria also followed Alberti's advice about eliminating all threatening fortification elements from the city residence, transforming it into a pacific *regia*.

Few Renaissance palaces have conserved as much of their internal layout as the Cancelleria, which provides an excellent example of the individual functions, in a sequence similar to that of the Palazzo Medici and most other palaces in Central Italy: the barrel-vaulted entranceway led into the enormous inner courtyard where all activity was centered. The pope and all the noble visitors had to walk through the loggia to the staircase on the left. During carnival time or on other holidays, the courtyard provided the ideal setting for theatrical entertainments, with the stage mounted next to the ground-floor loggia opposite the entrance and the other loggias on the upper two stories for the public. Wood, wine and oil as well as all the other necessities passed through the court on their way to the cellars and kitchens of all the *familiari* situated on the ground floor of the back wing (fig. 13, no. 60). Most of the three hundred plus familiars serving Cardinal Riario lived on the upper or mezzanine stories, and ate their meals in the two large dining halls near the kitchen (fig. 13, nos. 57–58). The court must have been a hive of activity, because, apart from the nobility, members of the household and tradesmen, there must have been a never-ending stream of visitors, assistants, negotiators, bidders and petitioners calling on the camerlengo, who was responsible for revenues, law, public safety, town planning, tariffs and trade. Those visiting the camerlengo went up to the first floor, or *piano nobile*. Riario certainly must have gone to fetch the pope personally when he visited him, but other guests of high standing would have been met on the threshold or led up the first flight of stairs (fig. 14, no. 78). According to ceremonial these guests were conducted up the large staircase and through the upper loggia in the great hall (fig. 14, no. 1), the most important closed space in the building, where all the principal ceremonies, the official banquets took place, and, when the weather was bad, the theatrical entertainment as well. As in the papal palaces, the succession of increasingly smaller rooms (fig. 14, no. 2, 3) served to receive less important visitors, and, as in the Palazzo Medici, this ceremonial sequence of rooms terminated in a large audience room (fig. 14, no. 4) with the cardinal's private chapel next to it (fig. 14, no. 5) and beyond this, his private apartment. It is significant that his bedroom was situated in the northwest tower, one of the safest rooms in the palace with a view toward Castel Sant'Angelo and the Basilica of St. Peter (fig. 14, no. 6). This secret room was connected via a secret staircase (fig. 13, no. 49; fig. 14, no. 7) to the enormous garden and neighboring stables. In the upper mezzanine of the tower was a *studiolo*, in the lower one a bath with a domical vault decorated with grotesques (fig. 13, nos. 51, 52). On the ground floor was a cool room for the summer, close to the garden (fig. 13, no. 48). His private kitchen and larder (fig. 13, no. 53) was in a small, low court (fig. 13, no. 69) next to his dining room, while the wine cellar was probably below it. The cardinal's dining room, with its grotesque work (fig. 13, no. 47) could also be reached by privileged guests through its own entrance in the northern wing. Riario's bedroom in the northwest tower was also the last room at the end of a series of private rooms in another wing (fig. 14, nos. 8–18) that could be accessed through the central vestibule of the *piano nobile* of the rear wing (fig. 14, no. 17), and was directly comparable to the Borgia apartment or the Stanze in the Vatican, the pope's private apartment during the Renaissance. Visitors on business probably did not use the ceremonial route to reach the cardinal, but passed through the private suite, and petitioners used the long rectangular room as an antechamber (fig. 14, no. 11). On the other hand, only the little rooms on the *piano nobile* of the entrance wing have similar precious ceilings. And since Riario doubtless used the balcony in the southeast tower to watch the processions along Via dei Pellegrini and to bless the crowds, there must have been another private apartment there as well (fig. 14, no. 28). He probably used this apartment on certain occasions or during certain seasons, and perhaps his more important guests used the reception rooms on the front wing which were more formal and less comfortable than those near the northwest tower (fig. 14, nos. 27–33). On one occasion he assigned a room to a bishop (a relation) on the piano nobile in the northeast tower and the one next to it, separated from the rest of the palace by large halls, but which had its own staircase (fig. 14, 34–36). He must have distributed the other numerous rooms on the upper and mezzanine floors according to his whims or to hierarchical criteria, while the attic was certainly only inhabited by the lower ranks. Not only the *piano nobile* was organized on a hierarchical basis

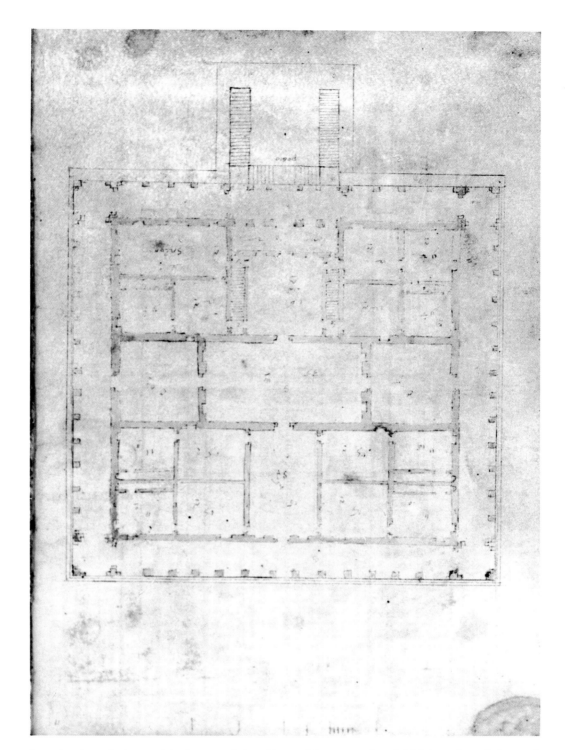

*15. Giuliano da Sangallo
Poggio a Caiano
Villa Medici, plan
Siena, Biblioteca Comunale
Taccuino, fol. 19v.*

but also its relations with the remaining floors. Moreover the rigid hierarchy of the real exterior seems to suggest the kind of activity going on inside the building.

The derivation from the four-towered castle scheme was still noticeable in shape of country houses; this became one of the tasks of high architecture during the fifteenth century. If symmetry and axiality dominated at Belriguardo, the Delizia degli Este near Ferrara as early as 1435, it is totally ascribable to the influence of Venice, as evidenced by the enormous hall and late Gothic vocabulary.[20] It appears rather as if, here too, an attempt was being made to approach the Vitruvian house with its *atrium, vestibulum, peristylum* and numerous *hospitalia*. But such a trend was also a consequence of seeking a "conventual" kind of solution which, in the opinion of the humanists, was the direct descendant of the idea of the antique house prototype. Similar tendencies could be seen in Florence only just before 1460. In the Villa Medici at Fiesole Michelozzo eliminated all signs of fortification from the building which had instead dominated the earlier designs of the Trebbio a Cafaggiolo and the Villa Medici a Careggi, but the symmetry and decoration due its status were still on a smaller scale compared to urban palaces.[21] The pleasant climate of the site above Florence, the loggia-vestibule to the east leading into the ground floor hall, with its in-

[20] C. L. Frommel, "La villa Médicis et la typologie de la villa italienne à la Renaissance," in A. Chastel, ed., *La Villa Médicis*, Rome 1991, p. 324 fig. 11; P. Kehl is preparing a detailed study of this *delizia*.
[21] C. L. Frommel, *Die Farnesina und Peruzzis architektonisches Frühwerk*, Berlin 1961, pp. 86-89; D. Coffin, *The Villa in the Life of Renaissance Rome*, Princeton 1979, p. 87ff.; J. S. Ackerman 1990b: 63-88.

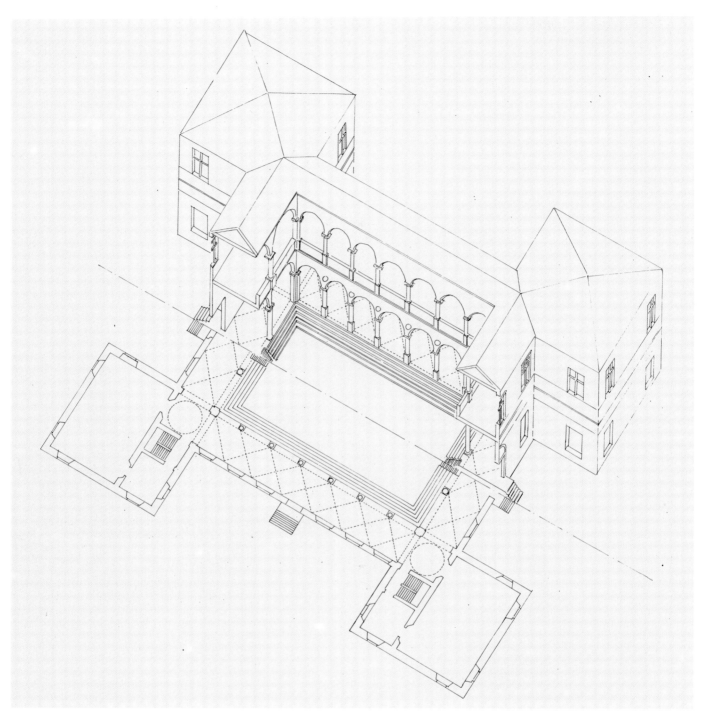

*16. Naples, Poggio Reale
axonometric reconstruction
(drawing J. Kraus)*

direct lighting, or the loggia-belvedere looking west, all corresponded already to Alberti's ideas (IX, ii).

The Medici Villa of Poggio a Caiano by Giuliano da Sangallo (1485 and after) was designed, unlike the Villa Medici at Fiesole, to host a large court for a greater length of time[22] (fig. 15). It is quite likely that Lorenzo de' Medici himself took part in the design of the symmetrical building. Several of its characteristics recall Giuliano's earlier Palazzo di Bartolomeo Scala: instead of a courtyard there is a decorated hall, while four apartments replace the square corner rooms, revealing their derivation from corner towers. The *piano nobile* lies on an arched base, a classicizing *podium villae*, and by designing the entrance through a temple portico, or pedimented *vestibulum*, Giuliano was adopting the outer construction and entrance typical of the antique *villa*. The exterior, with its simple articulation and numerous irregularities, is fundamentally different from another urban palace designed at that time by Giuliano, the Palazzo Gondi. Residential tower, hall wing and courtyard were the most important elements of Giuliano projects for a royal palace (1488), or Giuliano da Maiano's for the Villa di Poggioreale in Naples (1489), by which Lorenzo de' Medici was able to strengthen his influence on the ruling dynasty in Naples.[23] (fig. 16) Whether the residential towers stood outside the main body of the building, such as in Giuliano's Neapolitan project, and in the

[22] P. E. Foster, *A Study of Lorenzo de' Medici's villa at Poggio a Caiano*, New York 1978; A. Tönnesmann 1983b: 103ff.

[23] H. Biermann, "Das Palastmodell Giuliano da Sangallos für Ferdinand I., König von Neapel," in *Wiener Jahrbuch für Kunstgeschichte 23* (1970) pp. 154-195; C.L. Frommel, "Poggio Reale: Problemi di ricostruzione e di tipologia," in *Atti del Convegno Giuliano da Maiano, Fiesole 1992* (forthcoming).

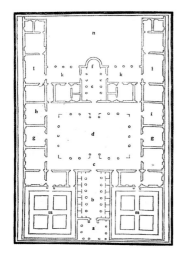

17. *Antonio di Pellegrino (for Bramante) Rome, Palazzo dei Tribunali project Florence, Uffizi Gabinetto Disegni e Stampe Uff. 136A*

18. *Fra Giocondo Reconstruction ot the Plan of the* casa antica *(from Vitruvius 1511, fol. 65r.)*

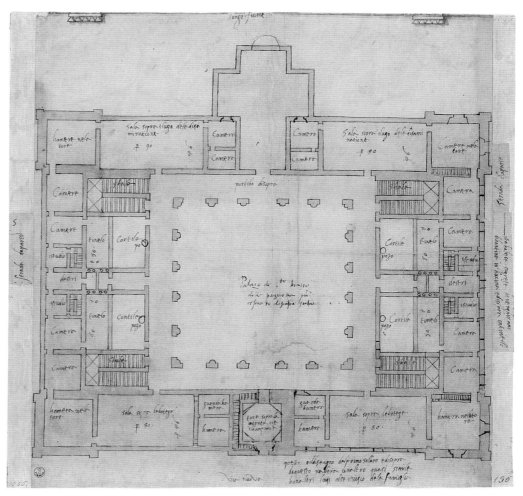

Villa di Poggioreale, or when they disappeared completely inside the building, such as in the villa at Poggio a Caiano, or when the center of the building was designed as a hall or a courtyard, the fundamental elements were always the same and were combined and redesigned according to the varying requirements and circumstances. Gardens close by and the surrounding countryside began to acquire greater importance in the design of urban palaces, which began to include loggias providing the transitional feature from inside to outside, and offering a refuge in inclement weather. Sangallo's great project for Naples and his later one for the Medici family both included characteristics of the *villa*, even though they were designed as urban residences.[24]

Bramante and the High Renaissance in Rome

All these experiences were utilized by Donato Bramante when he was commissioned by Julius II in about 1503–04 to renovate the Palazzo Vaticano.[25] In order to place the temporal authority of the church and its imperial pretensions in the correct light, Julius tried to outshine all the European royalty and go back directly to the tradition of the ancient imperial palaces. The Belvedere Court designed by Bramante was a new *domus transitoria* whose 300-meter-long wings enclosed a gigantic courtyard for ceremonials, tournaments and theatrical entertainments. As in the Temple of Fortune at Palestrina—the presumed palace of Julius Caesar—staircases and terraces led up toward the Belvedere exedra with a statue garden and a plan for baths. Bramante also designed the Palazzo dei Tribunali for Julius II in about 1508, which was supposed to substitute the functions and role of the medieval Palazzo Comunale on the Campidoglio[26] (fig. 17). Bramante urbanized the four-towered castle, just as Baccio Pontelli had done twenty years earlier, and only emphasized the podium story with rough rustication and, like Brunelleschi in the Palazzo di Parte Guelfa, he embellished the upper stories of the four corner avant-corps with a giant order symbolizing the patron's sense of his own importance more than ever. This giant order towering up from the ground story was later not surprisingly perfected by Raphael, Michelangelo, Palladio and Bernini, and became one of the leading motifs of courtly architecture. Bramante's design for the arcades of the square inner courtyard approached the dimensions and form of those of the Colosseum. The

[24] L. Pellecchia, "Reconstructing the Greek House: Giuliano da Sangallo's Villa for the Medici in Florence," in *Journal of the Society of Architectural Historians* 52 (1993) pp. 323-338.
[25] J. S. Ackerman, *The Cortile del Belvedere*, Vatican City 1954; A. Bruschi, *Bramante*, Bari 1969, p. 290ff.; C. L. Frommel, "Il Palazzo Vaticano sotto Giulio II e Leone X," in *Raffaello in Vaticano* (exhibition catalog, Vatican 1984), Milan 1984, p. 122ff.; C. L. Frommel, "Bramante e la progettazione del Cortile del Belvedere," in *Atti del Convegno "Il Cortile delle Statue nel Belvedere"* Rome 1992 (forthcoming).
[26] C. L. Frommel, *Der römische Palastbau der Hochrenaissance*, Tübingen 1973, vol. I, pp. 96, 143, vol. II, pp. 327-335.

longitudinal axis led into a church, like Fra Giocondo's reconstruction of an ancient house in 1511 (fig. 18).[27] The dome would have been broader than the single nave, and the church entrenched on the shore of the Tiber. The main building, well-proportioned on all sides, would have been a landmark not only from the neighboring square and the other side of the river, but also from afar. Its enormous travertine blocks, tall campanile and dome with the four crenelated corner towers would have left the unmistakable stamp of Julius II's imperial authority on the city. The Palazzo Farnese developed (1513-14 and after) as a direct descendent of the Palazzo dei Tribunali. It was a true princely residence whose architect, Antonio da Sangallo the Younger, had worked as Bramante's assistant from 1509 to 1513 (figs. 19-20).[28]

Once again it is clear how there was no precise distinction between the various types and functions of the palaces and villas. Alessandro Farnese, the future Pope Paul III, expressed his modest ambitions in the reduced size, the elimination of the avant-corps and an external order, or in the simple materials of the first project. Rather, by limiting the rustication to the corners and the portal, and by simply plastering the facade, the exterior of the building in 1513-14 appeared to be more unassuming than the Palazzo Gondi or the Palazzo Strozzi and other Florentine patrician palaces. In spite of this, it is not surprising that the Palazzo Farnese became the prototype of Roman palaces. Under the influence of the Palazzo dei Tribunali, Sangallo succeeded in designing a residence in the city center with a symmetrical structure on all four sides.

This is all the more admirable considering that originally even the great staircase was illuminated by the windows of the front looking on to the square, and Sangallo had to assimilate parts of various earlier buildings into his project. Where Rossellino and Baccio Pontelli, had achieved symmetry only by means of false windows and doors, and had connected the facade and courtyard in only a loose kind of way, with the help of bays and running cornices Sangallo created an astonishing correspondence between the inner and outer construction, so that from the windows of one of the side fronts it was possible to see the windows on the opposite front by looking across the courtyard. The constant effort to achieve a design ever closer to the Vitruvian house can be seen here first of all in the three aisle atrium, whose reconstruction had been studied by Antonio's uncle, Giuliano, and Fra Giocondo, and which also served as the load-bearing structure for the central hall. The direct influence of Bramante's Palazzo dei Tribunali can also be seen in the rectangular

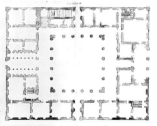

19. Antonio da Sangallo the Younger
Rome, Palazzo Farnese project
Florence, Uffizi Gabinetto Disegni e Stampe Uff. 298A

20. top
Anonymous
Rome, Palazzo Farnese project for its completion ca. 1546
Modena, Archivio di Stato Fabbriche 77

[27] Vitruvius, *De architectura libri decem*, ed. Fra Giocondo, Venezia 1511, fol. 64v.
[28] C. L. Frommel, "Sangallo et Michel-Ange (1513-1550)," in A. Chastel, ed., *Le Palais Farnèse*, Rome 1981, vol. I, 1, pp. 127-224.

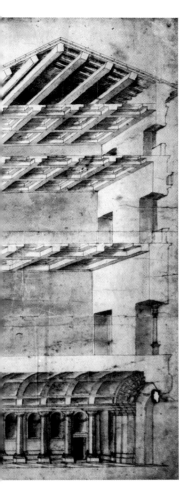

shape, and the three-story courtyard, whose arched piers were inspired by the Theater of Marcellus, where the orders complied closer with the Vitruvian canons.

It is significant that during the papacies of two Medici popes, Leo X (1513–21) and Clement VII (1521–34), the plain exterior of the three-story Palazzo Farnese with its defense-like corner rustication, was hardly imitated at all at first, and that Sangallo and his patron decided before 1527 to make both the upper floors appear even more classicizing by means of a giant order, thus adopting another characteristic of the Palazzo dei Tribunali.[29]

Already by 1501 Bramante had shown with the Palazzo Caprini that, at a low cost, it was possible to build houses much closer to the ideal of architecture *all'antica* than the Cancelleria

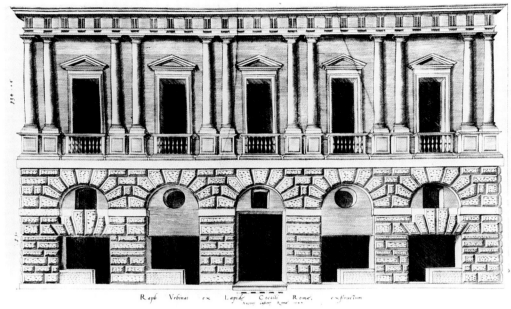

itself[30] (fig. 21). Later on there was more success in furnishing the homes of the middle-ranking clergy, merchants, lawyers, doctors or artists with an archaizing splendor and with all the dignity of a real palace, and therefore in renewing the image of the city much more quickly than the few monumental palaces built previously had ever done. Bramante designed a rusticated podium story in the Palazzo Caprini and built the Doric columns on the *piano nobile* with stuccoed brickwork, giving new life to an old technique. This reduced the costs of construction considerably and made the possibilities of a direct imitation of the ancients very inviting to patrons with reduced financial means. Without this economical technique, Bramante's direct successors—not just Raphael, Peruzzi, and Giulio Romano, but also Jacopo Sansovino, Sanmicheli and Palladio—would never have been able to achieve some of their most important works.

The completely organized palazzetto, articulated on both the inside and the outside, included a small inner courtyard and five or seven, or even occasionally only three window bays. In spite of this, its internal arrangement and spatial sequences followed the same schema of the great patrician, cardinalate and papal palaces. Here too, access was through an entryway into a loggia, courtyard and staircase leading into a hall and from there into the owner's apartments containing a *studiolo* and often a bathhouse and private chapel.

The Palazzo Baldassini by Sangallo (1513),[31] the Palazzo Branconio dell'Aquila by Raphael (1519)[32] and the Palazzo Massimo alle Colonne by Peruzzi (1532)[33] can well be considered as the most successful examples. They illustrate how the members of the upper class in the space of a few decades had become the most avant-garde patrons in Rome, and how, with the adoption of the *piano nobile*, they symbolized their efforts to elevate themselves above the populace and climb the social ladder. They no longer accepted gloomy light shafts, narrow staircases, low ceilings, and irregular rooms; nor had they any intention of following the spartan life styles of their ancestors. Instead they began to enjoy a life of comfort comparable to that which, thirty years earlier, had been the privilege of the Duke of Urbino alone. The knowledgeable architects now created well-proportioned, luminous, richly furnished rooms with sometimes surprisingly stylish dimensions, chimneys that drew well, a heated bathhouse, and kitchens inside the palace building. Even though these upper class patrons rarely succeeded in making their palaces stand out in the urban context their high standard of living went hand in hand with an increasingly courtly lifestyle, in which the familiar form of address "tu" was replaced by the more formal "voi" after 1520. Someone who could afford to built

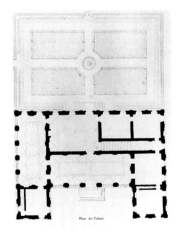

22. Rome, Villa Farnesina plan with garden

*21. top
Antonio Lafreryi
Palazzo Caprini
(House of Raphael)*

[29] C. L. Frommel, in C. L. Frommel and N. Adams 1993: 38.
[30] C. L. Frommel 1973, vol. I, pp. 93, 80-87; A. Bruschi, "Edifici privati di Bramante a Roma: Palazzo Castellesi e Palazzo Caprini," in *Palladio* n.s. 2 (1989), no. 4, pp. 5-44.
[31] C. L. Frommel 1973, vol. I, p. 122ff., 151ff., vol. II, pp. 23-29.

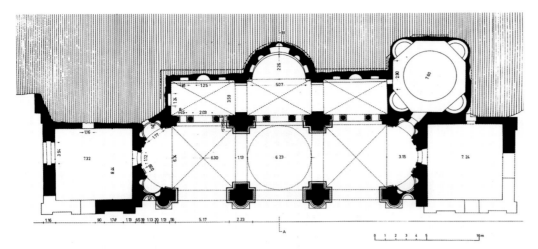

23. *Genazzano, Nymphaeum plan*

himself a palace the size of the Cancelleria or of the Palazzo Farnese, however, was the wealthy Agostino Chigi (fig. 22).[34] And yet he preferred to build a palazzetto the shape of a villa, like a Plinian *tusci*, in the vineyards on the outskirts of Rome between the Tiber and Via della Lungara; it is quite likely that his choices were influenced by the Palazzo di Bartolomeo Scala. The corner towers (as for the Cancelleria) were transformed into urban avant-corps and linked (Villa Medici at Poggio a Caiano) by a central loggia-vestibule. There was also a second loggia (like in the Villa Medici at Fiesole) on the side of the river, while the hall was situated on the upper floor in the style of urban palaces.

The continuous sequence of pilasters all round the building makes the Farnesina more like an urban palace than the other villas built in the previous decades. Rooms of different sizes and even a comfortable staircase are arranged in the symmetrical freestanding building in an even more skillful way than in the Cancelleria. Palazzo and villa therefore almost became true works of art which, through their proportions and similarity to the models of antiquity, certified the mastery of the architect.

In spite of the loggias and projections, behind this increasingly rigid formalization there was a danger of losing the direct relationship with the physical setting, a feature that had so far characterized the much more flexible structures of the ancient villas. The Farnesina was, in the final analysis, still an "urbanized castle" that did not bring the owner into contact with his surroundings so much as place him over and above them. In this sense it is significant that neither of the two loggias formed a direct link between palace and gardens. The entrance loggia gave on to an open courtyard, and the arches of the loggia looking over the Tiber were balustraded. Where once it had been the fortified building that separated the owner from the outside world, now it was the increasingly rigorous regulation of the immediate surroundings into symmetrical terraces and walks—a tendency that would reach its first climax with the Villa d'Este in 1560.

In spite of this, even in its relations with nature, the Farnesina took a definite step forward beyond the Palazzo di Bartolomeo Scala, which had been the most important *suburbanum* of the Quattrocento in Florence. To the disappointment of Julius II it did not contribute to embellishing the new thoroughfare Via della Lungara, but was hidden from view. Chigi also eliminated all the fortification-type features, together with the travertine facing, and opted for more humble materials perhaps for the same preoccupations that Cosimo de' Medici had once had, or for chiefly esthetic reasons. However, he made up for this outward modesty in his choice of materials by decorating the exterior and interior with scenes of antiquity painted by the leading artists of the time, the same who were employed by Julius II.

In the ensuing decades, both the suburban palazzo and suburban villa in their various shapes and plans were to become one of the most fruitful themes of Roman architecture. The liberty architects enjoyed can already be seen just in the distance between the nymphaea built at Genazzano and the Villa Madama.

In the Nymphaeum at Genazzano (ca. 1508–09) Bramante substituted the bricks used in the Palazzo Caprini with even cheaper tufa stonework, and with the help of a few travertine and marble columns and cornices he succeeded in achieving spatial forms like the imperial *thermae* for the first time ever (fig. 23).[35] Given that in the loggia in front of square rooms he followed the same arrangement of the space used in the porticoed villa with corner avant-corps, like Peruzzi at the Farnesina slightly earlier, it is probable that Bramante, too, considered this kind of villa *all'antica*. But it is the formal facade of the villa that reveals his fundamental distance from the ancient villa model. He achieved a more classicizing effect when he returned to the one-story building, as advised by Alberti, to the shell-capped exedrae of

[32] op. cit., vol. I, p. 105ff., 152ff., vol. II, pp. 13-22; P. N. Pagliara, in *Raffaello architetto* 1984: 197-216; C. L. Frommel, "Raffaels Paläste: Wohnen und Leben im Rom der Hochrenaissance," in *Gewerblicher Rechtsschutz und Urheberrecht* 1986, pp. 101-110.
[33] H. W. Wurm, *Der Palazzo Massimo alle Colonne*, Berlin 1965; C. L. Frommel 1973, vol. I, p. 133ff., 164ff., vol. II, pp. 233-250; C.L. Frommel, in *Baldassarre Peruzzi pittura scena e architettura nel Cinquecento*, Rome 1987, pp. 241-262.
[34] C. L. Frommel 1961; C. L. Frommel 1973, vol. I, p. 101ff., vol. II, pp. 149-174; C. L. Frommel, "Peruzzis römische Anfänge. Von der 'Pseudo-Cronaca-Gruppe' zu Bramante," in *Römisches Jahrbuch der Biblioteca Hertziana* 27-28 (1991-1992) pp. 177-180.
[35] C. L. Frommel, "Bramantes 'Nymphaeum' in Genazzano," in *Römisches Jahrbuch für Kunstgeschichte* 12 (1969) pp. 137-160; D. Coffin 1979: 243ff.
[36] C. L. Frommel, in *Raffaello architetto* 1984: 311-356; D. Coffin 1979: 245ff.; G. Dewez, *Villa Madama. A memoir relating to Raphael's project*, London 1993.

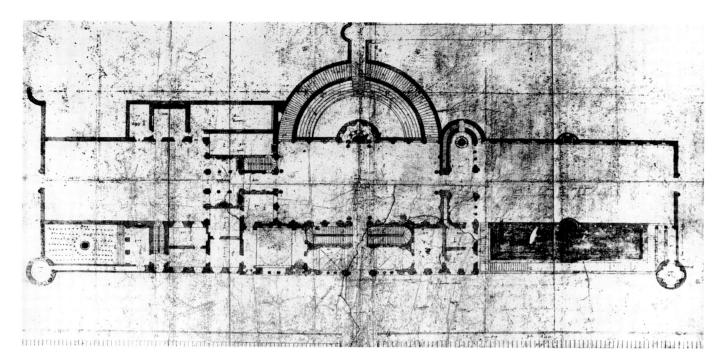

the loggias, to the opening of the back wall for a real nymphaeum and the addition of an open octagonal pool. Even in the dam designed to flood the valley below the loggia, probably for *naumachiae*, Bramante and his presumed patron, Cardinal Prospero Colonna, created an ideal setting for living *all'antica*.

Raphael and Cardinal Giulio de' Medici followed similar objectives ten years later in their design for the Villa Madama (figs. 24, 25).[36]

Raphael also started from a similar nucleus. He enlarged the rooms flanking the loggia, and arranged them (as in the Villa Medici at Poggio a Caiano) for palace life, so that the cardinal's court could stay there for long periods at a time. It seems that the cardinal preferred to spend his longer sojourns in the suburban area beyond the Ponte Milvio (Milvian Bridge) rather than live in the crush of the city center. Here his mania for building was unrestricted, and only here could he achieve in total liberty his ideal of a suburban villa in the antique style with loggias, a hippodrome, theater, nymphaeum, baths, *peschiere* and ample terraced gardens—all elements that Alberti had envisaged and whose prototype was the villa of Giulio de' Medici's ancestors at Fiesole. When illustrating his project, Raphael paid less attention to the antique forms and more to the life-styles *all'antica*. The cardinal and his friends would have been able to take the baths in real *thermae*, perform dramatic works in the Vitruvian theater, organize horse races in the hippodrome, and entertain in real *cenationes*. Here too, the increasing need for outward show in the Renaissance led to the monumental facade overlooking the valley, whose giant order and complex articulation are comparable only with the contemporary projects for St. Peter's.

The Late Renaissance in Northern Italy: Giulio Romano, Sanmicheli, Sansovino

The Golden Age, the peak of the high Renaissance, came to an end with the death of Pope Leo X (1513–21). When Federico Gonzaga commissioned Raphael's favorite pupil, Giulio

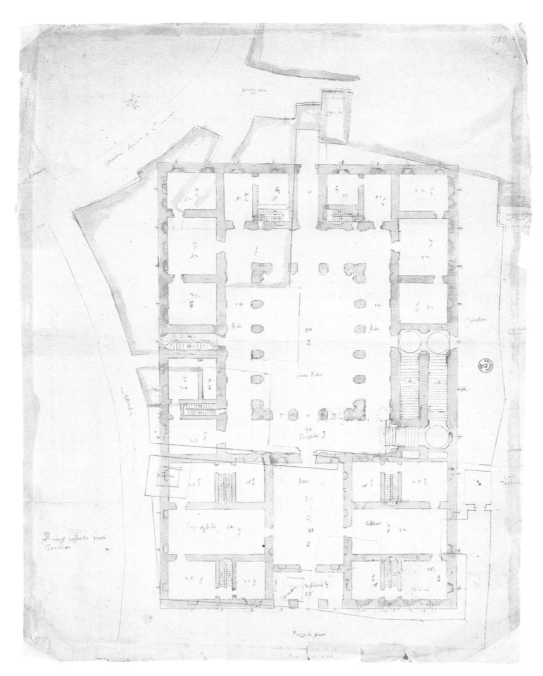

26. Antonio da Sangallo
the Younger
Orvieto, Palazzo Pucci
project
Florence, Uffizi
Gabinetto Disegni e Stampe
Uff. 969A

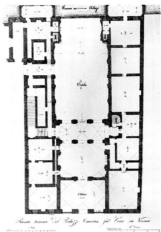

27. Verona, Palazzo Canossa
plan

Romano, to refurbish his residences, he asked him to create, first and foremost, a setting *all'antica* for the court.[37] In spite of the space and the remarkable size of the Palazzo del Te (ca. 1525 and after), this one-story building had no theater, no *diaetae*, and no *peschiera*. By contrast, there were numerous halls for entertainment, and numerous apartments for guests. Where the principal aim of Bramante and Raphael had been to superseded ancient architecture on its own terms, in the Palazzo del Te the main intention was apparently to provide the Gonzaga with a setting for their amusement.

In other respects the palazzo was another example of the countless and rather unclassifiable variety of types built in that period. Was it a suburban palace, a suburban villa or a *delizia*? As was often the case, it appears to have been a mixture of many of these types without sparking any new trends.

When Giulio Romano (the only one of the most sought-after architects to have been born in Rome) left his native city for ever, this was the first sign of a future trend. After Leo X's death, Rome lost its magical attraction for artists. Even before the Sack of Rome in 1527 and the subsequent impoverishment of the city, some of the most brilliant architects— Baldassarre Peruzzi, Jacopo Sansovino, Michele Sanmicheli—were tempted away to Northern Italy. Proud city-states such as Venice and Bologna, ambitious princes like Federico Gonzaga in Mantua, and Giovanni Maria della Rovere in Urbino, or local patriots like Lodovico Canossa in Verona, made efforts to imitate the splendor of the architecture of Bramante's Roman circle.

[37] A. Belluzzi and K. Forster, in *Giulio Romano* (exhibition catalog), Mantua 1989, pp. 317-335.

While Antonio da Sangallo the Younger began to dominate the scene in Rome—falling into an increasingly prosaic run in his reconstruction of Vitruvian types and orders—the epicenter of innovation in palace and villa design shifted further and further north. With their love of decoration, the northern Italians were particularly receptive to the Raphael's *ultima maniera* and to the splendid style of his circle.

Two years after Giulio Romano had found fertile ground in the Gonzaga court for his endless inventiveness, Sanmicheli found a perfect outlet for his boundless talent in nearby Verona. Like Giulio in the Palazzo del Te, Sanmicheli in the Palazzo Canossa for Bishop Lodovico Canossa (1526 and after) took the *casa antica* as his starting point, with its *vestibulum, cavaedium and peristylium* akin to those developed by Sangallo after the death of Raphael (figs. 26, 27).[38] Not only did he open up the entrance wing with a *vestibulum* like those of the Villa Medici at Poggio a Caiano, the Farnesina, the Palazzo del Te and, later, of the Palazzo Massimo, but he added an atrium leading off into the loggia of the *peristylium* and the *cavaedium* of the courtyard. And while the facade and courtyard reflected the dry language characteristic of mature Sangallo, for his Palazzo Bevilacqua (slightly later) Sanmicheli revived the variety of structural possibilities rediscovered by Bramante, Raphael and Giulio Romano, and by Falconetto in Padua.[39] Such new insights provided him with a key for imitating the ancient monuments of Verona—the Arena, the Porta dei Borsari, and the triumphal Gavi Arch.

In the meantime, in Venice Jacopo Sansovino drew on Sanmicheli's reconstruction of the *casa antica* and the magnificent wealth of his contemporary's classical language when in 1536–37 he designed the three magnificent buildings around St. Mark's Square, and for the Palazzo Corner (Ca' Grande, 1545) on the Canal Grande.[40]

Sansovino had to adapt, more than Giulio Romano in Mantua or Sanmicheli in Verona, to the special traditions and conditions of Venice. Land available for building was even more precious here, and the position, on the Canal Grande, a rare privilege. For more than three hundred years the central part of the palace opened with great arches on to a deep entrance

28. Villa La Soranza plan

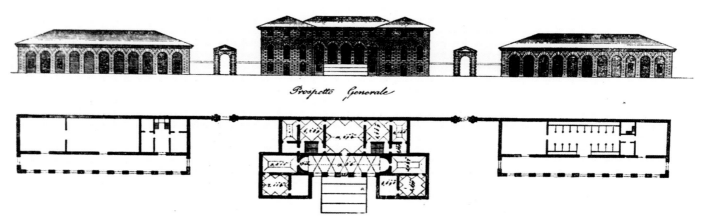

Prospetto Generale

atrium on the ground floor, and had consequently conserved the ancient *vestibulum* throughout the Middle Ages. For the Zecca (Mint) and the Palazzo Corner, Sansovino resumed Sangallo's and Sanmicheli's reconstructions of the Roman house, and he must have been well aware of this exceptional coincidence.

A similarly convincing synthesis between Venetian tradition and Roman High Renaissance can be found in Sansovino's treatment of elevations. While neither he nor Sanmicheli were capable of elaborating a homogeneous pattern for a whole building, Sansovino did at all events include a side bay in the articulation, giving at least the illusion of having superseded the flat facade. The *piano nobile* with its half-columns rose up over the rusticated podium story in a totally Bramantesque way. The Venetian character is conserved in the narrower sequence of arches illuminating the central hall. Sansovino succeeded therefore in shaping a model for post-medieval Venetian palaces in a more fertile and clearer way than his fifteenth-century predecessors.

Sansovino was less successful in his attempts to father a similar tradition in villa building. Like many Venetian villas, his Villa Garzoni at Pontecasale (begun ca. 1540) was flanked by agricultural *barchesse* or long arcaded barns. Its facade opens up with a *vestibulum* and develops along three wings, which in reality formed a *peristylium* with loggias giving on to an inner courtyard in the manner of Roman palaces.

The Villa La Soranza by Sanmicheli (before 1540?) came even closer to the Roman model (fig. 28).[41] With its lateral *barchesse*, it was immediately recognizable as a Venetian country

[38] P. Gazzola and M. Kahnemann, *Michele Sanmicheli*, Venice 1960, pp. 118-121; L. Puppi, *Michele Sanmicheli, architetto di Verona*, Padua 1971, p. 46ff.; C. L. Frommel, "Roma e l'opera giovanile di Sanmicheli. Atti del seminario internazionale di Storia dell'Architettura 'Michele Sanmicheli', Vicenza 1992," in *Annali di Architettura* 1994 (forthcoming).
[39] P. Gazzola and M. Kahnemann 1960: 121-124; L. Puppi 1971: 62ff.
[40] M. Tafuri, *Jacopo Sansovino e l'architettura del '500 a Venezia*, Padua 1969, p. 28ff.; D. Howard, *Jacopo Sansovino architecture and patronage in Renaissance Venice*, New Haven-London 1975, pp. 847, 132-146.
[41] B. Rupprecht, "Sanmichelis Villa Soranza," in *Festschrift Ulrich Middeldorf*, Berlin 1968, pp. 324-332.

199

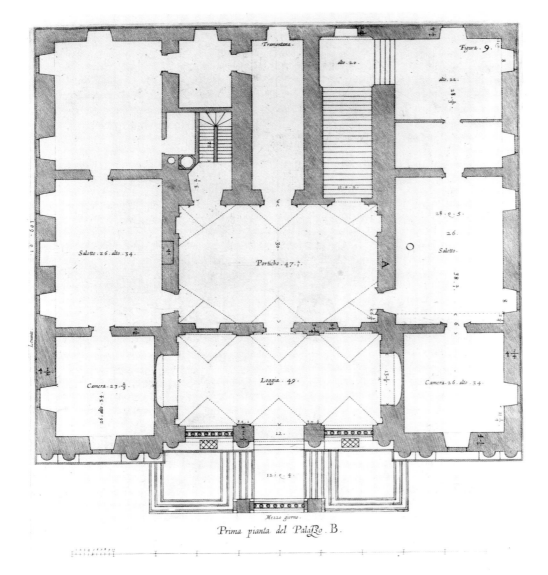

Tramontana

Figura. 9.

alto. 20.

alto. 22.

28. e. 5.

26.

Salotto.

Salotto. 26. alto. 34.

O

A

Portiche. 47.½.

Camera. 23.½.

26. alto. 34.

Loggia. 49.

Camera. 26. alto. 34.

12.

12. e. 4.

Mezzo giorno

Prima pianta del Palazzo. B.

29. Genoa, Villa Cambiaso plan

house, even though the loggia of the vestibule, inserted between the avant-corps on the front facade, the one-story plan and the exedrae of the loggia are unmistakable offspring of Bramante's Nymphaeum at Genazzano (fig. 23). The Villa La Soranza with these characteristics and the (fake?) ashlar reminiscent of Giulio Romano, seems to have paved the way for Palladio's first villas.

Rome after the Death of Sangallo

After Sangallo's death in 1546, the developments in Roman architecture followed a new course. The first impetus came from Michelangelo and his projects for the Campidoglio (1539 and after), for the Palazzo Farnese (1546 and after) and for St. Peter's (1546–47 and after).[42] Michelangelo moved his own anti-dogmatic, joyous and sometimes even dissonant language toward Bramantesque prototypes and away from Sangallo's dry Vitruvianism— perhaps deliberately and certainly more than he had ever done in his Florentine works. In the Palazzo del Senatore he was inspired by the design for the Palazzo dei Tribunali, and in the two side palaces of the Campidoglio, by the arms of the transept in Bramante's last project for St. Peter's, whereas the third story of the Palazzo Farnese was inspired by the Ionic order of the Belvedere Court. Lastly, in the design of St. Peter's he returned essentially to Bramante's original 1506 project. Antique orders acquired new imposing significance in all these projects. He even adopted Bramante's giant order in the Campidoglio and in St. Peter's, which the aging Sangallo had abandoned in his projects for the exterior of St. Peter's and the Palazzo Farnese. Under Michelangelo's direction the columns of the Palazzo dei Conservatori and the drum of St. Peter's relived the physical intensity that had been slowly lost under Sangallo. Michelangelo's reflections on Bramante's High Renaissance, on the giant order, the columns and rich decoration could have contributed to convincing Cardinal

[42] J. S. Ackerman, *The Architecture of Michelangelo*, London 1961, p. 54ff.; G. C. Argan and B. Contardi, *Michelangelo architetto*, Milan 1990, p. 211ff.; C. L. Frommel, "Roma e la formazione architettonica di Palladio," in A. Chastel and R. Cevese, eds., *Andrea Palladio: nuovi contributi. Atti del Settimo Seminario Internazionale di Storia dell'architettura*, Milan 1990, p. 154ff.

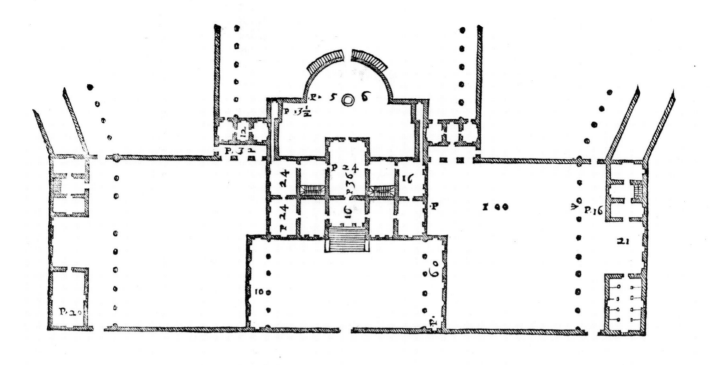

30. Andrea Palladio
Lonedo, Villa Godi
plan, elevation
(from Palladio, Quattro Libri...
fol. 65r.)

Girolamo Capodiferro in 1548–49 to have his palace decorated with opulent stuccowork in imitation of the Palazzo Branconio and of Francis I's gallery at Fontainebleau.[43] However, the choice of a small gallery in the entrance wing and the siting of the main hall toward the rear gardens reveal the first influences of French residential models. Michelangelo even took part in the design of the Villa Giulia (1551 and after), the most significant villa of those years.[44] The theater-shaped courtyard, the nymphaeum, and the emphatic longitudinal section extending into the large gardens, enter into the great tradition of the Belvedere Court, and note least the Villa Madama, which Julius III visited many times while the project was under way. Nevertheless, after the Sack of Rome the attitude toward antiquity changed fundamentally. In the same way that Michelangelo himself, as from about 1540, under the influence of Vittoria Colonna, had moved away from neo-Platonism toward a Pauline Catholicism,[45] so the admiration for the ancients lost its existential premise. Consequently a master of the caliber of Pirro Ligorio remained even further aloof from the ancients than did the artists of Julius II and Leo X.[46] Closeness to antiquity became more of a learned attitude, a cultural medium, around which the spirit of absolutism and Counter-Reformation began to take hold. The progressive detachment from the Renaissance's real objectives was expressed in a quite unmistakable way in the less obvious field of ornament. This was also true of the first independent buildings designed by masters such as Alessi, Vignola, Vasari or Ammannati. Galeazzo Alessi, Sangallo's favorite pupil, had his first chance of building a monumental residence in 1548 with the Villa Cambiaso at Genoa (figs. 34, 35).[47] Significantly, the choice fell on a suburban villa, in which Alessi, with his preference for freestanding and symmetrically designed buildings, revealed himself heir to Bramante and Sangallo. He followed the prototypes of the mature Sangallo in the rational organization of the interior as well, employing both vestibule and atrium. The introduction, however, of the rich stuccowork decoration inside and out marked a breach with Sangallo's grammar, while the details and ornament derived from his own particular non-conformist approach.

[43] C. L. Frommel 1973, vol. I, p. 139ff., 169ff., vol. II, pp. 62-79; L. Neppi, *Palazzo Spada*, Roma 1975.
[44] T. Falk, "Studien zur Topographie und Geschichte der Villa Giulia in Rom," in *Römisches Jahrbuch für Kuntsgeschichte* 13 (1971) p. 101ff.; D. Coffin 1979: 150ff.
[45] R. De Maio, *Michelangelo e la Controriforma*, Bari 1978, p. 422ff.; C. L. Frommel, *Michelangelo e Tommaso de Cavalieri*, Amsterdam 1979, p. 91ff.
[46] D. Coffin 1979: 267ff., 311ff.
[47] E. Poleggi, "Genova e l'architettura di villa del secolo XVI," 1969, pp. 231-242; C. L. Frommel 1991: 335, see note 21.

The only architect of the mid-sixteenth century who successfully opposed these counter-tendencies was Andrea Palladio, discovered by one of the greatest poets and humanists of the Renaissance who taught him to understand Vitruvius and ancient architecture.[48] The persistent influence of Giangiorgio Trissino (1478–1551) over Palladio was one of the reasons why the latter remained faithful all his life to the examples of the ancients. Trissino himself had studied the question of the reconstruction of the *casa antica*, and perhaps with the help of Palladio he had begun in 1537 to redesign his Villa Trissino at Cricoli, while conserving the Venetian tradition of a villa on two stories with corner towers and central entrance loggia. Palladio developed avant-garde prototypes in one of his first independent designs, the Villa Godi at Lonedo of about 1540 (fig. 30).[49] Even though he placed the real residential story on a *podium villae* and gave the house a central staircase, and similarly, only gave the upper story small windows and limited the articulation of the facades to applying fake rustication, it appears that he must have been acquainted with Sanmicheli's design for the Villa La Soranza (fig. 28). In any case, he was near the ideal one-story building as Alberti had advised for an *all'antica* house and Bramante had built for the first time with his Nymphaeum at Genazzano. In 1541 Palladio accompanied Trissino to Rome, where he probably met Sangallo and witnessed the latter's most recent reconstructions of ancient houses. At any event, Palladio's projects for palaces and villas dating back to the period before 1547 are clearly influenced by his first visit to Rome, not only in the rational organization of the plan and in the Vitruvian-style design for country houses comprised of peristyle, vestibule and atrium, but also in the few elements comprising the articulation of the facades such as the serlian window, the rusticated surrounds borrowed from Giulio Romano's Roman house, the thermal windows,[50] and thermal–type roofs (fig. 31). Palladio and his learned mentor could have already perceived in country houses the original seed of all human constructions,[51] and from then on Palladio began to dedicate more attention to the villa, giving it a priority in his various activities that no other Renaissance architect had ever conceded. Taking antiquity as a model and learning from the experience of the last decades, within a few years Palladio had become a virtuoso of the interior arrangement as regards the harmonious sequence of the rooms, the transparency of the axes, the variety of shapes used for the vaulting, and the generous illumination. The projects emanate his deep knowledge of the palaces and villas designed by Bramante, Raphael, Giulio Romano, Peruzzi, Sangallo and Sanmicheli.

While his predecessors only rarely had the chance of expressing their creativity in the unconstrained field of villa design, Palladio always succeeded in convincing his Vicentine patrons of his projects: they combined modest dimensions, simplified articulation and economical materials, with the pretensions of a residence *all'antica*. These works signaled the maturity of villa design, a maturity that Bramante had achieved in 1501 with urban palaces.

In the design of palaces for insertion in the urban fabric, the ideal reconstruction of the *casa antica* had been forced to accept site compromises, inasmuch as the urban context required at least two main stories. However, from about 1542 Palladio came much closer to achieving the plan of a Vitruvian house in his first masterpiece—the Palazzo Thiene—than Sangallo had managed with the Palazzo Farnese, Giulio Romano with the Palazzo del Te, or Sanmicheli with the Palazzo Canossa (fig. 32).[52] The temple-front vestibule now projected beyond the plane of the facade—a theme repeated in his later villas—strongly characterizing the entire front of an otherwise completely symmetrical building.

It seems however that Palladio fully appreciated the beauty of ancient columns and the techniques for creating them in stuccoed brickwork only on his successive visits to Rome in the years 1545–47.[53] Only after 1547 did he abandon the dry abstraction of the mature Sangallo, which was perhaps due to his already being influenced by Michelangelo's projects. In any case, as from 1549, he borrowed from the final project for St. Peter's and from the Palazzo Iseppo da Porto the idea of the salient column surmounted by a statue, a characteristic of the triumphal arch theme that Michelangelo had recently proposed for the drum of St. Peter's. In his increasing efforts, building by building, to achieve not only archaic types of architecture, an ancient vocabulary and syntax as well as classicizing details, Palladio can be considered as the last pupil of Bramante, whom he described in his *Quattro Libri* as "the first to bring to light the good and beautiful architecture which had been hidden from antiquity to that day."[54] Palladio's adhesion to the beliefs of the high Renaissance is even more remarkable when considering how his first teachers, Giulio Romano, Sangallo, Sanmicheli and Sansovino, had deviated from Bramante's heritage during the 1540s. What Alberti had longed for and what Bramante and his pupils had achieved only in part, that is to say, the completely *all'antica* style development of a town and its surroundings, only Palladio actually succeeded in doing. It is probable, however, that the greater part of his patrons had given birth to and developed their own opinions already under different conditions. Renaissance

*31. Andrea Palladio
Vigardolo, Villa Valmarana
project
London, Royal Institute
of British Architects
Palladio XVII/2*

[48] R. Wittkower, *Principles of Architecture in the Age of Humanism*, London 1949, p. 51ff.; L. Puppi, "Un letterato in villa: Giangiorgio Trissino a Cricoli," in *Arte Veneta* 25 (1971) p. 72ff.; C. L. Frommel 1990: 146ff.

[49] op. cit.: 149ff.

[50] op. cit.: 149ff.

[51] A. Palladio, *I quattro libri dell'architettura*, Venice 1570, p. 6: "... essendo molto verisimile, che innanzi, l'huomo da per se habitasse, et dopo ... la compagnia de gli altri huomini naturalmente desiderasse ...".

[52] L. Magagnato, *Palazzo Thiene*, Vicenza 1966; L. Puppi, *Andrea Palladio*, Milan 1981-82, p. 251ff.; C. L. Frommel 1990: 154.

[53] op. cit.: 154ff.

[54] A. Palladio 1570: 64.

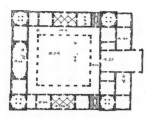

32. *Andrea Palladio*
Vicenza, Palazzo Thiene
plan, elevation
(from Palladio, p. 13)

architecture was thus fulfilled exactly when the ground was slipping from under its feet. What trend lay behind the multitude of phenomena that could be observed more or less between 1420 and 1550? The first thing that springs to mind is that perhaps for the first time in western history, secular dwellings succeeded in rising to the level of ecclesiastical buildings. The evident hierarchical distance that separates places of worship such as S. Lorenzo and S. Maria Novella in Florence, the cathedral in Pienza, the benediction loggia of S. Marco in Rome, from the palaces built for the same patrons, slowly diminished. If, in Urbino the cathedral was furbished more modestly compared to the neighboring Palazzo Ducale, and if, in the Cancelleria in Rome, the church was hidden behind the facade of the palace, it was probably the patron who had elaborated this decision. But if, on the other hand, Palladio characterized his design for the Villa Rotonda, a *suburbanum* built in the hills outside Vicenza for a middle-ranking prelate, with symbols of dignity from the Pantheon in Rome, this certainly also reflected his own desires to arrive at the great prototypes wherever he had the chance to. He probably justified the fact he designed a villa like a temple by appealing to the common origins of all kinds of houses. It is clear, however, that the local climate was such that no one was scandalized by this evident effacement of the hierarchical distinctions. This change in priorities was valid both for patrons and for architects. At a time when nepotism was rampant, it was not surprising that patrons thought more about their worldly fame, posterity and their dynastic establishment in impressive town or country seats. Cardinal Raffaele Riario's motto was *Hoc opus sic perpetuum*, which revealed his intimate intentions that the Cancelleria should bring him and his descendants eternal fame. There is no evidence that he made similar efforts to save his soul. Similarly, the future Pope Paul II built the Palazzo Farnese from the outset for his two sons, some time before he undertook the construction of equally ponderous ecclesiastical buildings or charitable institutions.

Naturally the increasing importance attributed to residential buildings cannot be separated from the closer identification with the ancients which was easier to express in secular palaces, especially in villas, than in churches. Lastly, the unrivaled authority of ancient writers justified every attempt of the great patrons to imitate the ancients and to surround themselves with all kinds of luxuries and every comfort. It is significant however that the need to impress, the desire for luxury and comfort accelerated—just when the admiration for the ancients was beginning to fade and religion became once again an uncompromising commitment—and resulted in increasingly elaborate designs for entrances, carriage ways, staircases and furnishings, in the perfection of windows, bathrooms, toilets, fireplaces and household management.

Patrons enjoyed not only the social and civilizing improvements deriving from increasingly perfect residential building, they were also enthusiastic clients who took part impatiently, stimulating the design and construction right through to the end. Moreover, it appears that it was extraordinary patrons like Lorenzo de' Medici and Julius II, who spurred their architects on to achieve their finest accomplishments.

On the other hand, the architects were products of the same epoch and were roused by similar motives, even anticipating their patrons. Moreover, surprisingly often their ideas and dreams were music to the ears of the mighty. Just the extension of their creative powers to the field of villa and palace design must have been vitally important for them. If, during the first half of the Quattrocento their artistic potential had been limited to the design of mostly ecclesiastical buildings, in the sixteenth century nearly every palace and villa was the opportunity for competing with the most beautiful buildings of the ancients. As a result in particular of the methodological vigor, of the admiration for the ancients and the continual drive of a few Florentine masters such as Brunelleschi, Alberti, Michelozzo or Giuliano da Sangallo, residences gradually became real works of art, and not only as far as their construction and articulation was concerned, but also in the individual component parts: the vestibule, courtyard, staircase, halls and adjoining garden.

At first, all energies were poured into residential palaces, but more than fifty years went by before its symmetrical and structural design was within the grasp of everyone. Villa design was somewhat behind so that Raphael could still avoid symmetry and the order in certain areas of his 1518 project for the Villa Madama (fig. 23). Palladio was the first to take the ultimate step toward the formalization of the villa—in actual fact it came to the fore in an urban palace—and in projects like the Villa Rotonda, he amalgamated the Pantheon with the primeval ideal of the far-reaching centrally planned building. Similar ideas were at the root of Baroque castles and only after a return to a natural garden did the architects of the late eighteenth century begin again to slowly free themselves from the rigid principles that had dominated Italian residential architecture from Brunelleschi onward.

Nicholas Adams
Laurie Nussdorfer

The Italian City, 1400-1600

The city is the invisible and silent presence in an exhibition devoted to architectural models. Though they appear to be objects complete in themselves, with their richly grained surfaces and elegant proportions, the models are generally part of the preparation for the construction of a building to be inserted into an urban fabric. In this essay we try to recover that fabric, a context that is not just an inert background for the still models on exhibition but a muscular partner in the changing life of city people between 1400 and 1600. The history of urbanism in this period reflects the social, political, intellectual, and military transformations that swept cities and citizens along in their wake.

1400-1500

In contrast with both the preceding and the following centuries, the scale of the physical changes to the city in the one hundred years between 1400 and 1500 is relatively small. From the mid-thirteenth until the mid-fourteenth century, the face of the Italian city was radically transformed by the most dramatic changes since antiquity. Massive town halls, vast cathedrals with their giant cupolas, palaces of justice, were planned, constructed or reconstructed to provide new services and a new architectural definition for civil and ecclesiastical protection and the rule of law in the Italian commune. Most remarkable of all, perhaps, was the expansion of the city's walls for populations that optimistic governments must have thought would be in continual growth. Even today the great walls created in the thirteenth and fourteenth centuries in cities like Siena have left extensive green spaces for urban agriculture.

Likewise, the period from 1500 to the early years of the seventeenth century was witness to a further set of large-scale changes to the city. New piazzas, wall systems and fortresses were built, more massive and more elaborate than before; and the results of increasingly centralized authority can be seen in new campaigns of church construction and reconstruction, and new administrative palaces. So although the overall scale of urbanistic intervention in the fifteenth century does not match that of the centuries before and after, there is a transformation in the way cities were conceptualized in this period. And there are subtle rhetorical shifts in the relation of building to street that ultimately change forever the way that cities look.

For the urban elite one of the most far-reaching developments set in motion in the fifteenth century was the rediscovery of classical antiquity. While the ancient world was always a presence on the Italian peninsula (for how could it be otherwise?), cultivation of its architectural forms and its literary remains was something new. Though its streets and monumental buildings had decayed as a result of successive contractions in population after the fifth century, the Italian city around 1400 was still heir to a powerful tradition of political thought about urbanity reaching back to the ancient world, a tradition it now looked toward longingly. One result of this new interest in antiquity was that the city and its architecture (not just its inhabitants) were seen as the direct descendants of ancient traditions. In the fifteenth century, the Baptistery of Florence, that quintessentially Romanesque structure, was mistaken for the ancient Temple of Mars. And Leonardo Bruni (1369–1444) could write a *Panegyric to the City of Florence* (1403–04) modeled on Aelius Aristides' panegyric to the city of Athens, the *Panathenaicus*, the first such work dedicated to a city since antiquity. What citizens did and built received new validation from these links to the classical past. "Indeed", wrote Bruni in his *Panegyric*, "this city is of such admirable excellence that no one can match his eloquence with it" (Kohl and Witt 1978: 135). With its pedigree of antiquity, whether justified (as in the city of Florence) or not (as in the Baptistery), the city took on new resonance as the bearer of traditions so rich and so profound, that it is safe to say that no aspect of city life was left untouched, from the laying of drains to symbolizing authority.

A second important influence on the style of fifteenth-century urbanism comes from changes in government. Over the period 1300–1700 we see a progressive concentration of power in fewer hands. Communal government by a broadly based cross-section of the upper-middle and upper classes declines, and we see the development of one-family or one-person seignorial rule culminating in the rise of the absolutist state.

This transformation, whose beginnings can be found in the fourteenth century, comes slowly

Domenico di Michelino
Dante and the Three
Kingdoms *(detail)*
1465, oil on canvas
Florence Cathedral

and irregularly to the peninsula. Though it passes through many forms in different Italian centers, it leaves a characteristic imprint on the city (Martines 1979). As governments change, so the way they represent themselves and project their image changes. In the fifteenth century, architecture and city planning were given important symbolic political roles to play. The humanist pope, Nicholas V (1447–55), is one of the earliest rulers to elaborate this role and his example resonates beyond papal circles. This pope turns to architecture as a kind of *Biblia pauperum* to provide an image of the Church's authority to its subjects (Tafuri 1992: 37). City building, as we shall discover, has novel tasks and meanings for the new lords, whether they are former bankers, mercenaries, or papal princes.

Finally, for urbanites in general there was a shift from civic collectivities to the individual family was a vehicle for social ascent and as the locus of political energies, a return to the pre-communal principles of family power in a new guise (Brucker 1977). The elite family displaced the communal republican institutions, contesting or eviscerating their authority. In this redefinition of the old *consorteria* or clan, members of the patriciate continued to gather power through traditional means (wealth accumulation, church and political office, dynastic marriage, the funding of ecclesiastical activities), but they began the practice of expressing that power through architecture in the city. Thus, in the major cities on the peninsula, elite families built large-scale private palaces to house their leading members. As the Florentine Giovanni Rucellai confided to his commonplace book, "Due cose principali sono quelle che gl'uomini fanno in questo mondo: la prima lo 'ngienerare: la seconda l'edifichare" (Kent et al. 1981: 13). In Florence, Cosimo de' Medici was one of the first to build a palace of this sort (begun 1444), and many other families soon followed suit. This change in the social significance of architecture produced what the economic historian Richard Goldthwaite has called a "building boom" in the city of Florence (Goldthwaite 1980). And we register a similar, though smaller, expansion of private urban construction elsewhere. In Siena, for example, the Piccolomini family built two palaces (delle Papesse, begun 1460; Piccolomini, begun 1459) during the rule of the Piccolomini pope, Pius II (1458–64) and other Sienese families, such as the Spannocchi (begun 1470) soon followed suit. Justification for the conspicuous ostentation of architecture by individuals and families comes through what comes to be called, rather grandly, the "theory of magnificence," a self-serving dogma that allowed private individuals to justify conspicuous architectural consumption in the name of civic improvement (Jenkins 1970).[1] Even so, though these hefty new palaces proliferate throughout peninsular cities, overall they make less impact on the urban environment than did the great civic palaces of the thirteenth century.

Despite these important cultural, political, and social changes in the fifteenth century, there is no immediately identifiable style of Quattrocento urbanism. City development took place on foundations that had, literally speaking, already been built over many times. Though its population was much depleted, Rome's skeletal frame remained the major roads leading out of the city through openings in the Aurelian walls—the Appia, Nomentana, Flaminia (Ackerman 1982: 5). This urban palimpsest was notably respected in those cities whose major early growth came during their flowering as Roman outpost towns (Florence, Padua, Milan, Pavia). Moreover, much civic improvement was based on earlier practices of urban amelioration. The Roman *maestri di strada*, who in the fifteenth and later in the sixteenth centuries laid out streets and direct the destruction of buildings to open new thoroughfares, have a history that goes well back into the thirteenth century when street cleaning, the control of overhanging balconies and street paving were their only responsibilities (Re 1920; Ceen 1986: 89–103). Such groups (they are called *Viari* in Siena, the *Six in Charge of the Recuperation of the Rights, Jurisdiction, and Property of the Commune* in Florence, the *Balivi Viarum* in Volterra, *Ufficio dei Padri del Comune* in Genoa) had responsibility for ensuring that proper street widths were maintained and that benches in the front of shops, used for the display of merchandise, did not project into the streets. Throughout the peninsula, even into Spanish Sicily (Aricò 1981) these urban improvements rested on earlier practices.

Yet the case of street paving illustrates that, despite continuities, the fifteenth century gave a distinctive spin to changes in the city's appearance. Paving, already under way by the beginning of our period, was a major activity during the fifteenth century. In Siena, for example, most of the streets were already paved by 1400 (Balestracci and Piccini 1977: 59); but other towns, such as Viterbo, made efforts only after mid-century to pave the main squares (Madonna 1983: 54). One reason why is suggested by a conversation between two diplomats after the Congress of Mantua in early 1460. The agent of the marquis Ludovico Gonzaga reported to his employer that the papal ambassador had "greatly praised Your Lordship and Mantua ... saying that apart from the mud there was no city in the world more adapted or convenient for the Papal court ... I replied to him that Your Excellency had begun paving the piazzas and wanted [to] go on to do the rest of the city" (Burns 1981: 28–29). Mud did not fit well with an image of seignorial dignity in the Quattrocento.

Michelozzo Michelozzi Florence, Palazzo Medici-Riccardi facade on Via Cavour

The authors wish to acknowledge the help of Isabelle Frank, David Friedman, Paula Spilner, and Richard J. Tuttle.

[1] An ancient precedent for this could be found in the gifts made by patricians to the cities of the classical world (Veyne 1976).

206

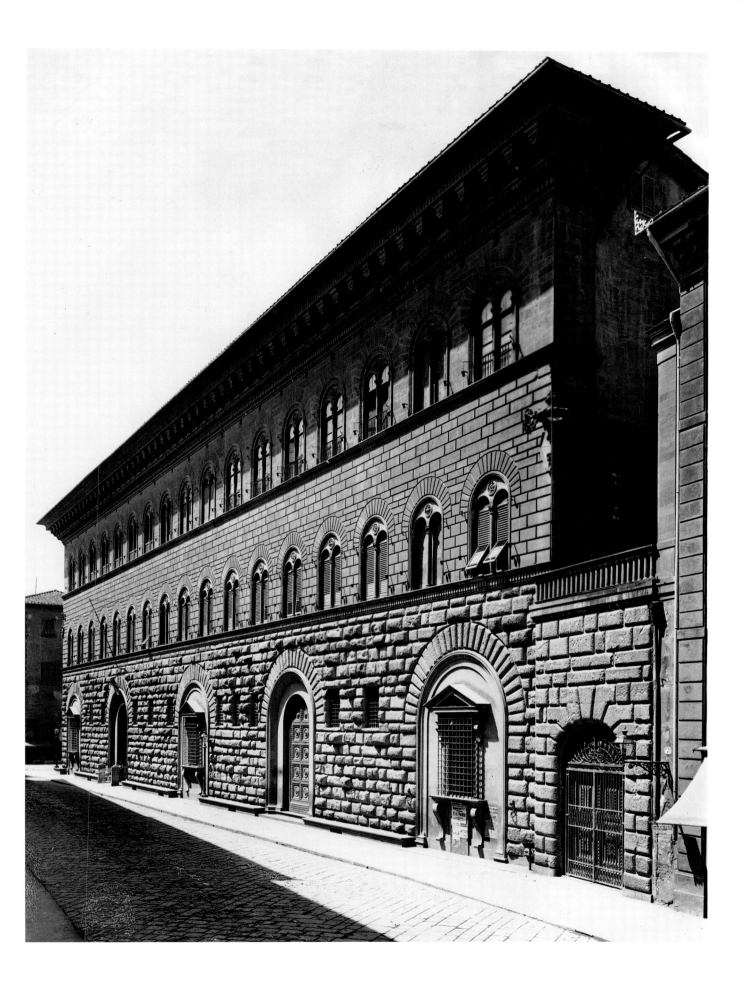

Bernardo Rossellino
Pienza, Palazzo Piccolomini
and the cathedral

208

It is interesting that when Pius II rebuilt his native village of Corsignano (1459–64) he paved only the piazza before the new cathedral and the new Palazzo Piccolomini, perhaps to distinguish this zone of high civic and seignorial importance from the town streets (Mack 1987: 99–104). In short, the kinds of improvement begun in the Middle Ages continue through the fifteenth century. But something has altered about these improvements.

What changes, more than anything, is the style of thinking about the city. In a sense the shift is rhetorical, suggesting a new inflection of pride in traditional needs and practices. This shift is marked by the revival of an ancient literary genre praising cities, to be sure, and it is also denoted by the appearance of a new generation of writers and architects whose exploration of the past helped draw tight the link between the values and principles of the ancient past and the needs (broadly defined) of contemporary patrons of architecture and civic improvement. Leon Battista Alberti's (1404–72) *De re aedificatoria* was, in large measure, an attempt to provide an up-dated revision of Vitruvius. An early version was given to Pope Nicholas V and the first printed edition (1486) was dedicated to Lorenzo de' Medici by Angelo Poliziano, and delivered to him gather by gather as he relaxed in the baths at S. Filippo. The treatises of Antonio Filarete (1400–69) and Francesco di Giorgio Martini (1439–1502) from the second half of the fifteenth century, though certainly less learned than that of Alberti, attempted to provide similar insights for specific wealthy clients into the ways of the ancients; Filarete's treatise was dedicated to Francesco Sforza, duke of Milan (1401–66); Francesco di Giorgio's treatises were dedicated to Federico da Montefeltro, duke of Urbino (1422–82) (Filarete 1972; Francesco di Giorgio 1967). These treatises were received by a new group of humanistically educated rulers and wealthy citizens anxious to be informed about practices of the ancient world and passionate about embellishing their own towns to honor family and city; here, then, was that symbiosis of wealth and ancient culture on which depends the new urbanistic rhetoric that powered the changes of the Italian fifteenth century.

The clearest evidence of the synthesis of the influence of the classical world, enhanced family prestige, and new seignorial power can be seen in the family palace. In the medieval city, clan strength was expressed through a nucleated series of dwellings grouped around a tower (or towers) to form a stronghold. In Siena, for example, where such an agglomeration was called a *castellare*, it is still possible to see its remains. The Corte del *castellare* degli Urgurieri, with the stump of a medieval stone tower on one side of an irregularly shaped central courtyard, is a remarkable survival. Located near the Campo, the *castellare* is sited strategically on a knoll so that the family could control nearby ground from its tower. The courtyard, effectively the space left over at the center of the block, is guarded along its two entrances by small barrel-vaulted passageways. From the street, along Via Cecco Angiolieri and Via S. Vigilio there is no architectural device to unify the parts of the *Castellare*. The structures that surround the courtyard appear as distinct units, possibly from different periods or built by different patrons. Varied brick and stone patterns are knit together erratically by an irregularly applied intonaco. Buildings such as these, in the Late Middle Ages, may have been further camouflaged with temporary projections, jetties (*sporti*) supporting small rooms, or awnings—the awnings often associated with shops or workshops (Friedman 1992). Here the clan turns its back on the city, and addresses the urban audience directly only in its tower. In short, the street is not a place for self-presentation.

Yet the Middle Ages also saw the beginnings in civil architecture of what we would think of as a unified face or facade for a single structure that could be used to deliver a message to passers-by. Though the word facade in Italian (*facciata*) seems to enter the language only in the mid-Trecento (Toker 1985) it was first given architectural form in monumental public buildings of the Middle Ages. Communal palaces, such as the Palazzo della Signoria in Florence (begun 1294), demonstrate its form: a clear, well-defined, rusticated wall, almost cliff-like in character. The Palazzo della Signoria is also distinguished by a tower, and a crenelated crown. Rich in references to imperial, ancient, and military power, a building such as the Palazzo della Signoria demonstrates how sculptural relief decoration attached to (or integral with) the face of a secular building could be used to represent complex messages of a political and historical sort. Stone rustication recalled Roman sources (the Forum of Augustus, Rome) as well as the Hohenstaufen castles in the imperial South (Paul 1969). Towers, an ancient prerogative of the nobility, were now appropriated by the organs that had replaced them (indeed, subjugated them and their values) in order to symbolize communal power. In Siena the tower of the Palazzo Pubblico, the new city hall (begun 1297; largely complete 1342) combined a clock, a preeminent product of the new bourgeois mercantile culture, with a tower: thus communal officials could use the face of public buildings to represent the symbols of past and present authority (Balestracci and Piccini 1977: 105).

The facade as the expressive emblem of political power takes on new significance in the hands of private patrons in the fifteenth century. Borrowing the concept of facade and its rhetorical

Palazzo Rucellai, Florence

ability to address the populace, wealthy merchants and seigniorial rulers began the construction of bulky palaces that reflected the transfer of power from the commune to seigniory and family. These palaces now employ their face to speak first of private rather than public magnificence.[2] While the stone facade of a building like the Palazzo Medici on Via Larga (now Via Cavour) still may recall medieval Florentine family palaces where low relief rustication was used (Preyer 1983), the aggressive undercutting and sheer massiveness of the wall (its natural *fortezza*) refers to the Palazzo della Signoria where such rustication was best known (Hyman 1977; Ackerman 1983). Indeed the rustication practically invades the street. The facade of the private urban palace is given even more elaborate form in buildings like the Palazzo Rucellai (begun 1453) or the Palazzo Gondi (begun 1490) in Florence, where the rhetorical messages are more overtly classical (Preyer 1981; Tönnesmann 1984). Examples of the incorporation of a classical message can be found on buildings in many other cities throughout the peninsula, where the adoption of a classical vocabulary results in a new complicated architectural language. In Venice, for example, the Ca' del Duca (1462–66) uses diamond-

[2] One form of self presentation long practiced in Italy was the placement of one's sculpted coat of arms on a facade. These become quite elaborate in the later sixteenth century when the architecture of the facade becomes rather more plain.

shaped rustication in stone to distinguish the house of its patron, Duke Francesco Sforza, from those of the other nobles along the Grand Canal (McAndrew 1980: 12–14). In Siena the Palazzo Piccolomini with its round-headed arches and classicizing capitals not only employs a classical language, but stands out on the streets of Siena: rusticated stone architecture vividly calls to mind Roman and imperial themes within a city made almost exclusively of brick.[3]

New attention was paid to facades of all kinds of buildings. The Palazzo Diamante in Ferrara (begun 1493), for example, one of the most extravagantly decorated of late fifteenth-century facades, is covered entirely with carved stone diamond points, the symbol of the Este family, its patrons. Elsewhere structures that had been left without a facade by a previous generation of builders were completed or projected. At S. Maria Novella in Florence (begun 1470), Alberti made a remarkable adoption of the Roman temple to the typical profile of the Christian church with a nave and two aisles, and sprayed emblems of the Rucellai family across the

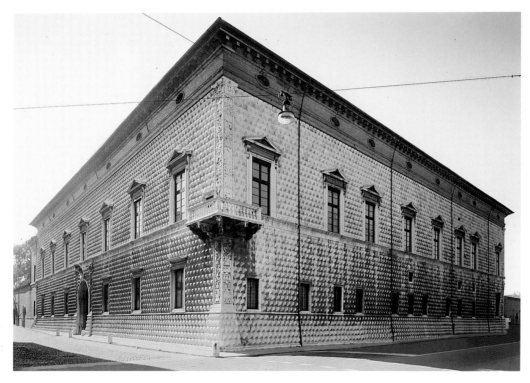

Biagio Rossetti
Ferrara, Palazzo dei Diamanti
view of facade and flank

frieze. Filippo Brunelleschi's plans for the reorganization of Florence's church of S. Spirito, had they been executed, would have reoriented the facade to front a long piazza leading down to the Arno and thus given it a position of enormous urbanistic importance (Manetti 1970, 125). In some cases facades of buildings were updated or modernized, as Pius II did along the main street of Pienza (Mack 1987: 148–150) or as Ludovico Gonzaga did with his program for painting shop fronts in Mantua (Burns 1981: 29).

But, beyond that, the building was placed in a new relation to the urban fabric, one that now emphasized the building's distinctiveness from the street or defined the relation between building and viewer in ways that were more precise. Alberti noted that Roman temples were raised up from the street, "free of any profane contamination ... and perfectly visible from every direction" and he advocated this practice for Christian temples (Alberti 1988, Book VII, iii, 195); it can be seen in a church like Giuliano da Sangallo's S. Maria delle Carceri in Prato (1484–95) (Wittkower 1952: 1–28). In private palaces, too, the buildings are set up on a base (Ca' del Duca, Venice), a bench (Palazzo Ammanati, Pienza), or both (Palazzo Rucellai, Florence; Palazzo Piccolomini, Siena; Palazzo Ducale, Urbino). Here again, however, the shift from earlier practice is rhetorical in nature. After all, buildings were often made of different materials from their surroundings or set on a foundation or base; now the transition becomes a significant architectural feature in its own right employing, in many instances, the rich language of classical forms.

Locating or aligning buildings to take advantage of a point of view was another strategy that underwent a subtle rhetorical development in the fifteenth century with the application of principles of linear perspective to the streetscape. In Pienza, for example, the facade of the duomo stands across an optical plane, parallel with the edge of the main piazza as seen from the head of the piazza. The grid lines across the piazza help mark the spatial recession (Heydenreich 1937). The ideal viewing point of the Palazzo Bandini in Siena, probably built in

[3] The effect of these stone buildings would have been increased by the use of brick as the fifteenth-century paving material of choice; in a red city of brick those few works of gray or white stone would have stood out prominently.

Baldassarre Lanci
Perspective Scene with
Florentine Buildings
Florence, Uffizi, Gabinetto
Disegni e Stampe, Uff. 404P
Cat. no. 170

the 1470s by Antonio Federighi, is along the street in front of the church of S. Vigilio. This location allows the viewer to see the unbalanced five bays of the palace as a three-bay facade, symmetrical around the central door; the main approach allows the creation of what is, in effect, an ideal viewing point. The facade of the Scuola di S. Marco in Venice (begun 1489) uses the perspective recession of the two barrel vaults to define an ideal point from which the viewer may admire the facade (McAndrew 1980: 182–183). Thus, in all these examples, point of view is not just an agreeable location from which to see a building but something more. As in a painted perspective, where the viewer's eye is drawn along the orthogonals to the heart of the painting, so too in this relationship of building to street a focus on the building and by extension on its owner is produced.

An interesting example of the tensions at play in such urbanistic strategies, unrealized as it happens, concerns the Palazzo Piccolomini in Siena, built by Piero Paolo Porrina. In a document of 1469 the nephews of Pius II, Andrea and Jacomo Piccolomini, request permission from the Sienese authorities to occupy ten *braccia* of the Campo, the great medieval communal piazza, so that their palace ("opera meravigliosa, et ne la città vostra dignissimo ornamento") may be seen "in quadro" (i.e., square) (Milanesi 1854, II: 337–339). New design appetites neatly further family ambitions at the expense of communal resources. (The Palazzo Piccolomini, like the Palazzo Medici in Florence, would have had three facades had it been completed to plan; see below.) Such wishes reveal the intersection of the new esthetic, civic politics, and family power in the urban transformations of the fifteenth century.

Family power is also expressed in the creation by private individuals of new kinds of spaces before the palaces. At times, as in Pienza, where a quasi-feudal ruler could have his way in a relatively small area, it was possible to create perspectival effects, but in most instances what we find is an *ad hoc* cutting open of space near the family palace. Open space in the heart of the city, once the prerogative of the communal government or the Church, is now

an instrument by which patrician families display their status, sometimes by setting the palace back from the street to make it visible (see below, the Palazzo Pitti) or by creating a zone in which familiars could gather. An early proposal for the Palazzo Medici in Florence would have given it three facades: one toward Via Larga, another toward S. Lorenzo, and a third, to the north facing a newly opened piazza (Elam 1990: 46–48). The Rucellai family created a piazza and a loggia intended both to show off the facade of their new palace and serve as a gathering place (Preyer 1977). The Piccolomini did much the same in Siena with the creation of palace, piazza, and loggia (the Logge del Papa). And the "great and magnificent edifice" constructed by Filippo Strozzi included a private square, as documents published by F. W. Kent state: "per honore della nostra famiglia, per aoperarla per le letitie et per le tristitie" (Kent 1972: 42; 1977). It is a space that the Strozzi guarded jealously well into the nineteenth century (Elam 1985). Somewhat larger still was the piazza Pitti, in front of the original seven-bay palace built by Luca Pitti (begun before 1457) along Via Romana on a hillock hard against what later became the Boboli Gardens. These initiatives ultimately lead to the creation in the sixteenth century of large-scale family piazzas such as the Piazza

Farnese in Rome where a corridor was planned from Piazza Navona to the facade of the Palazzo Farnese (Spezzaferro and Tuttle 1981). As Howard Saalman has put it: "the longer the perspective view of the house, the further the extension of the personality of the owner!" (Saalman 1990: 81), although it must be said that none of these fifteenth-century piazzas have the grand scale of the open spaces created in the fourteenth or sixteenth centuries; at best they are more like outdoor rooms.[4] It is interesting to note, too, that these urban contexts are never revealed in the architectural models, although it is not hard to imagine patrons looking at a model of their palace and longing to replicate the same quality of view within their own city.

The elaboration of seignorial regimes produced a new kind of planned urban residential quarter in the city. Lorenzo de' Medici's plan to create a *zona medicea* along Via Laura and his plans for a *forum all'antica* in the area in front of the church of SS. Annunziata, though realized in part only by his descendants, is a clear expression of that wish (Elam 1978). And in Ferrara, Duke Ercole d'Este, with the help of his architect Biagio Rossetti (1447–1516), opened a new zone of broad right-angled streets, the largest of which (Strada degli Angeli,

Florence, Palazzo Pitti main facade and piazza

today called Corso Ercole I d'Este) was sixteen meters wide with four meters dedicated solely to pedestrians, a division in traffic largely unknown in the Middle Ages. Here is another way of distinguishing street and fabric to force a new view of the city (Zevi 1960; Gamrath 1990). Tax incentives were offered to new residents to build and live in the newly laid out district. Along this and other streets elegant palaces were built and urban piazzas laid out. The entire project thus virtually doubled the size of the previous city and created a zone of elite dwellings uninhibited by the spatial constraints of the old city.

Did these innovative neighborhoods partake of ancient thinking about the advantages of social segregation in cities? It is difficult to know for sure, but Renaissance theorists were certainly familiar with such notions. In his *De re aedificatoria*, Alberti, echoing ancient sources, had written that some might prefer "residential quarters of the gentry to be quite free of any contamination from the common people"[5] (Alberti 1988, Book VII, i, 192). Leonardo da Vinci's proposals for the reorganization of the city of Milan also seem to reflect those kinds of distinctions with the separation of residential areas and service functions.

Finally, the impact of seignorial regimes on urbanism expresses itself most clearly during the fifteenth century in the production of new treatises that incorporate important discussions on city building. Stimulated by the fantasy of attaching unlimited political power to the lessons of ancient building, these treatises, like the wooden models and drawings, helped open a world of imaginative possibilities to architects and their patrons. Perhaps the most seductive description of seignorial participation in urban design can be found in Antonio Filarete's *Trattato d'architettura* written between 1451 and 1464 (Filarete 1972). Though not the product of a humanist, Filarete's text is the most brilliant demonstration of the role of adviser and patron in fifteenth-century urbanism. Written in the form of a novella, the treatise shows how a prince (Lodovico Sforza) might create a new city (coincidentally named "Sforzinda") and a port (Plusiapolis) for himself and his subjects.

Federico Barocci and Assistants detail of the Crucifixion *showing the Palazzo Ducale of Urbino 16th cent. Urbino Cathedral*

on the following pages Rome, Piazza Colonna at the time of Sixtus V 16th cent. Vatican, Biblioteca Apostolica Vaticana

[4] The harmonic analogy between city and palace is stressed by Alberti: "The city is like some large house, and the house is in turn like some small city" (Alberti 1988, Book I, ix, 23).

[5] These early examples of elite neighborhoods spawn later examples, such as the Strada Nuova in Genoa (Polleggi and Caraceni 1983), the piazzas of Palladio in Vicenza and the squares of seventeenth- and eighteenth-century London. This urban typology is, of course, alive and well in twentieth-century America, see, for example, Leisure World in Laguna Hills, California. On this phenomenon, see the *Economist*, July 25-31, 1992: 25-26.

*Rome, Piazza Navona
detail of the perspective plan
by G. B. Maggi, 1625
Milan, Civica Raccolta Stampe
Achille Bertarelli*

Rich in specific details about the practice of laying out cities, the treatise is a sustained meditation on the nature of ideal planning. In this urbanistic dream, the architect becomes the mediator between the wealth of the patron and a vision of ancient architecture.[6]

In the end, after the development of these new styles of thinking, does the city actually look any different after the hundred years 1400–1500? The medieval city had been characterized by relatively small, irregular, multi-use buildings (Saalman 1990). While there were zones for specialized trades (glassmakers, tanners, metalworkers and so on), commercial and residential zones were not distinguished; this produced a relatively high population density at all times of day and night. This situation is as true for Genoa, say, as it is for Florence or Rome. Streets tend to be relatively narrow (three or four meters wide), and at times unpaved. Open areas are generally associated with ecclesiastical or civic authorities. During the fifteenth century a new relation emerges between the single building and the urban fabric (Goldthwaite 1972). Some buildings are now set up from the brick-paved street, either on an architectural base or through the use of refined materials, such as marble. Efforts are made, in some instances, to make them stand out from their neighbors (Saalman 1990: 78–79). The creation of the family's piazza attempted to give the family's palace the status that only the old monumental civic structures of the Middle Ages had had (Fanelli 1973: 202). And the large-scale private palace creates a wall or screen along the street (Saalman 1990: 76–77). No longer is the street a varied mixture of structures with different functions, forms and colors; rather it is more uniform, and the palace, a bulky, looming mass shading the street with its cornice, is at times out of scale with its surroundings. (This was certainly the case for the Palazzo Strozzi, Florence.) In visual terms, the street may also be less busy, for many of the new palaces eliminated the stores and workshops at the lowest levels of their main facade. Where commercial ventures were maintained, as at the Palazzo della Cancelleria in Rome (begun 1485) or the Palazzo Piccolomini in Siena, they were confined to a minor, less prominent facade, in Rome along Via del Pellegrino, in Siena along Via Rinaldini.

*Piazza Navona in Rome
in an anonymous painting
La giostra del Saracino
17th cent.
Rome, Museo di Roma*

1500–1600

With relatively few exceptions, up until ca. 1500 changes to the Italian city were relatively small-scale: alterations to a section of the city, quilt-like adjustments that need to be followed with a microscope across the city's seams. As a result of the invasion of the French king

[6] It is remarkable that among the models to have survived from this period none seem to have been exclusively theoretical or fantastic in nature. Alberti speaks of the model as a functional aid and nothing more. The model, he notes solemnly, should not be "colored and lewdly dressed with the allurement of painting" (Alberti 1988, Book II, i, 34). On the use of the model in architecture, see Scolari 1988.

221

Charles VIII in 1494–95 and the successive Hapsburg-Valois Wars that brought the armies
of Charles V onto the peninsula, seignorial regimes in Italy consolidated into fewer and larger
political blocs. The rise of the territorial state presumes the need to extend authority over
a wider area and a larger population; the great towers of the communal palaces can only be
seen so far. Florence under the Medici dukes became the capital of the expansionist Grand
Duchy of Tuscany (proclaimed 1569) that conquered all of its surrounding towns. In each
of its subjugated cities and towns (Arezzo, Pisa, Livorno, Pistoia, Prato, Grosseto, Siena and
so on) the Grand Duchy built fortresses and administrative outposts to implement its policies
and represent its power (Spini 1983). The papacy, notably under Paul III, brought greater
control over recalcitrant subjects in the Papal States through an extensive policy of fortress
building and rebuilding (Rome, Perugia, Ancona, Castro). Venice, too, sought to assert its
authority through a plan for the imposition of secure military control over its territory. The
notion of Venetian territory as a kind of articulated organism, "a consolidated machine composed of elements with specialized functions" (Tafuri 1989c: 109) has its origins in the 1520s
in the circle of military experts led by Francesco Maria della Rovere (Concina 1983). Over
the century, an extensive campaign of fortress construction (Legnano, Palmanova, Candia,
Spalato, Zara, Orzinuovi, Brescia, Peschiera) was undertaken.

The rise of territorial states upon the foundations of the seignorial regimes of the fourteenth
and fifteenth centuries has two critical effects on the city. First, new large-scale bureaucracies
needed new structures to house their functions and represent their authority both in their
new capitals and in their subjugated provinces; large, new, secular buildings are thus laid over

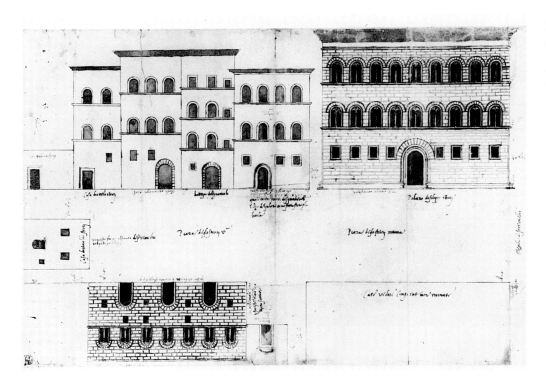

Palazzo Strozzi, Florence

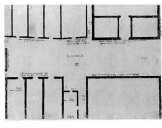

Baccio d'Agnolo
Ground Plan of Piazza Strozzi
16th cent.
Florence, Uffizi, Gabinetto
Disegni e Stampe, Uff. 1561A
Cat. no. 148

older neighborhoods (Litchfield 1986). Second, the incessant nature and expanded scale of sixteenth-century warfare combined with the improved technology of modern cannon, brings radical transformations to the shape and image of the city (De La Croix 1972).

Larger states with their capitals presume the creation of subject towns; in both, the ruler needed representation for the assertion of control through bureaucratic means (Litchfield 1986). Thus in the capital of the future Grand Duchy of Tuscany, Cosimo I de' Medici destroyed the neighborhood between the Palazzo Vecchio and the river in order to create a huge office complex, the Uffizi (begun 1560), next door to the old fourteenth-century Palazzo della Signoria (Forster 1971; Spini 1983). He moved (in 1540) from the (private) Palazzo Medici, to the Palazzo della Signoria, and then moved again to the Palazzo Pitti (after 1549), which was now linked to the Palazzo della Signoria and the Uffizi by a flying corridor that passed over the Ponte Vecchio. The palace that was once the residence of the priors ("Palazzo dei Priori") was now neither the seat of government of the community ("Palazzo del Popolo") nor the seat of an oligarchic government ("Palazzo della Signoria"), but rather the Palazzo Ducale, or princely residence (Fanelli 1981: 96). At the Palazzo Pitti the duke and his court imitated the spectacles of Madrid and Paris. Indeed the urbanistic changes in the city of Florence are, at root, about providing a setting for the absolutist ruler (Spini 1983: 168–175). A new business center, the Loggia di Mercato Nuovo, was built (1547–51) in the heart of the old city. And new bridges were built (S. Trinita, begun 1567) to facilitate communications across the Arno to the duke's new residence at the Palazzo Pitti, and pleasure gardens

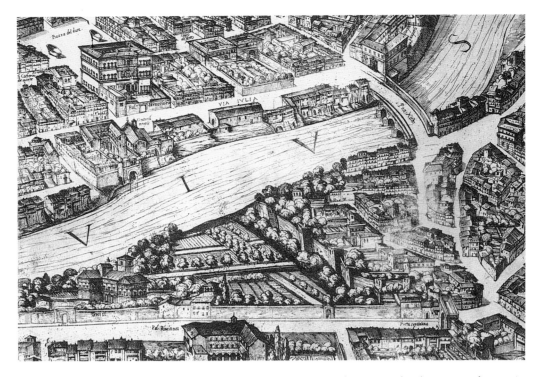

Antonio Tempesta
Map of Rome, *detail*
showing Via Giulia and Ponte
Sisto
engraving, 1593
Milan, Civica Raccolta Stampe
Achille Bertarelli

(the Boboli) and streets were renovated to create Medicean paths between the main bureaucratic and defensive nodes: Palazzo Vecchio, Palazzo Pitti, Fortezza da Basso (Via dei Servi, Via Tornabuoni, Borgo degli Albizi, Via Maggio). Statues and columns (piazzas S. Marco, S. Trinita, S. Felice) were erected along them to commemorate the regime's achievements in symbolic fashion and to provide a visual focus that would not allow subjects to forget the duke or his rule. Cosimo I's son, Ferdinando I (1587–1609), made an even more powerful use of the statue when he placed an effigy of himself on horseback at the center of the great square of the SS. Annunziata.

It is significant, too, that in these years new facades were proposed for Florence Cathedral. The Florentine church hierarchy was of great interest to the Medici dukes and bishops were, effectively, appointed by Florence not by Rome; thus the provision of an appropriate home for its ministers was one of their great concerns (Litchfield 1986: 95–96), as the many models for the facade prove. In short, a new urbanistic order was provided, one that represented the duke and his interests, that reflected his view of rule, and that responded decisively to the practical needs of his regime and person.[7]

Absolutist rule in the capitals was brought to the periphery in a number of ways. Cosimo I embarked on a master plan for the refortification of the smaller towns in the duchy (Pistoia, Portoferraio, Livorno, Pisa, Arezzo, Cortona, Borgo S. Sepolcro) about which we will hear more later on. And in the towns and cities of Tuscany important new large-scale government palaces and churches were built to represent his rule. In Siena, for example, a massive, square, stone palace, the Palazzo Reale, was built during the 1590s alongside the cathedral in the oldest area of the city (Morviducci 1980). Cosimo I wisely left the Palazzo Pubblico and the Campo alone; new officers stripped the old of their duties, but left the existing palaces and ritual spaces intact. Elsewhere within the Grand Duchy public palaces, churches and markets were built. In Montepulciano, for example, the Palazzo Del Monte was taken over as ducal residence; next door a new cathedral (begun 1592) and a new market loggia were built (Spini 1983: 189). The construction of the Palazzo delle Logge in Arezzo (begun 1573), for which a model of two bays survives, is part of the same plan to bring Medicean political and administrative order to Tuscany (begun 1573). The loggias provided rental space on the ground floor for workshop and stores; the upper level contained the offices of the Monte di Pietà, the customs officials, and the chancellery. More than one hundred meters in length, both its scale and purpose exemplify the urbanistic impact of statebuilding (Satkowski 1979: 98–135). Elsewhere in Italy princely rulers also reinforced control over the towns through ambitious building programs: new ducal residences were built in Parma and Piacenza (from 1558) for the Farnese (Adorni 1974; 1982a) and in Perugia the upper section of the Rocca Paolina looking down into the town across the Piazza Rivarola became a residence-fortress for the papal governor on the model of the Roman residence-fortress of the pope, the Vatican Palace-Castel Sant'Angelo (Grohmann 1981: 91–94).

Along with a new bureaucracy, designed to create symmetries of action throughout the state, went a new emphasis on efficiency of function through the city. While dreams of the trans-

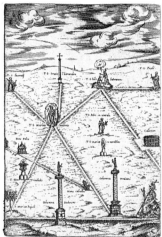

Sixtus V's new street scheme
in an engraving by F. Bordino
1588
Milan, Civica Raccolta Stampe
Achille Bertarelli

[7] Although there is little indication of the plans which Bramante (or Antonio da Sangallo the Younger) might have had for the urban setting of a renovated St. Peter's, it may be useful to situate their conception of a mammoth building here, in the context of absolutist rule. A design for the representation of the temple of the prince of the apostles and his heir, the Supreme Pontiff, chosen by God as His representative on earth, required a building of appropriate scale.

[8] Although Julius II's plans for Rome are better known, it should be pointed out that, probably aided by Bramante, he planned a similar kind of street in his subject city of Bologna, the "strada Giulia," a fortress at the Porta Galliera, and a renovation of the Palazzo Comunale for the official residence of the pope or his legate (Tuttle 1982).

Giorgio Vasari
Model of Two Bays of the
Logge, Arezzo
1572
Arezzo, Casa Vasari

Giorgio Vasari
Cosimo De' Medici among
His Artists
Florence, Palazzo Vecchio
Sala di Cosimo I

formation of cities during the fifteenth century had remained largely at the level proposal and hypothesis, as we remember from the fate of Lorenzo de' Medici's plans for a *zona medicea*, in the sixteenth century such efforts were actually brought to fruition. Pope Julius II (1503–13), for example, opened up Via della Lungara which gave new access for visitors to the administrative heart of the Church.[8] This long straight street traveling through the rural countryside along the Tiber linked the Borgo directly to Trastevere and the main business centers. Via Giulia was constructed to provide both a new residential street and a direct link from St. Peter's to the heart of the commercial district and the Palazzo della Cancelleria. Along its path Julius planned a monumental palace of justice with its own piazza (Frommel 1973, II: 327–335). Later, Leo X (1513–21) opened Via Leonina (present-day Via della Scrofa and Via di Ripetta) to connect the commercial and market center with the developing area of the Campo Marzio and the Porta del Popolo. In this period the *trivium*, that characteristically Roman urban device for moving from one main street into three or vice versa, is developed (Günther 1984b). It too helps create a more open, more easily traveled city. Later, Paul III (1534–49) and Sixtus V (1585–90) ploughed new streets through old neighborhoods to provide links between the major section of the city. For Paul III the major effort was an attempt to open streets between the Palazzo Farnese and Piazza Navona along the newly created Via Baullari (Spezzaferro and Tuttle 1981: 115–123). The most radical work was undertaken late in the century by Sixtus V. Radiating from key nodal points, marked by ancient obelisks, the straight wide streets laid out by Domenico Fontana for the pope unite a modern sense of rational efficiency with respect for the ancients. They were intended, at one level, to facilitate the movement of pilgrims between the major religious sites and to accommodate the new fashion of traveling by coach (Lotz 1973). Beyond that, however, Sixtus may have wanted to use the streets to help redistribute the population across the lightly populated hills,

Etienne Dupérac
Piazza del Campidoglio,
according to Michelangelo's
Scheme
*Milan, Civica Raccolta Stampe
Achille Bertarelli*

as well as providing for freer movements of all goods and services through the city (Spezzaferro 1983: 374-381).

Rulers may have promoted urbanistic improvements for needs of state, but they could not contain the meanings that their subjects imposed on changes in street facades. Straight streets speak about the decorum and dignity to which they point. Francesco De Marchi, who was present at the demolitions that cut a corridor to the Palazzo Farnese, was in no doubt about the purpose of this fashion: "quando si vuol favore alla casa d'un'amico in laudarla si dice ella è in una bella strada longa, e larga e dritta, con un'alta, e larga, e dritta, e bella facciata..." Despite their cachet and antique origin, De Marchi was skeptical about the value of straight streets. He argued that when Nero had straightened the streets of Rome, he had only made them more dangerous and less healthy (Spezzaferro and Tuttle 1981: 117). Despite De Marchi's doubts, the prestige of an address on a "bella strada longa" was here to stay, as Genoa's Strada Nuova (1558-87) forcefully demonstrated (Poleggi and Caraceni 1983).

The concept of facade was also reinterpreted. Modeled on the form of the portico of the ancient street or forum, the facade was now stretched along an entire street or around an entire piazza. The message of this elongated unified facade in the sixteenth century was antiquity, regularity, dignity, and authority. Already at the beginning of the sixteenth century there were proposals to ring the walls of the medieval Campo of Siena with regularizing portico arcades. In Piazza Ducale in Vigevano (1492-94), and Piazza SS. Annunziata in Florence we see the development of antique fora (Lotz 1977b: 117-139). At Loreto, too, the architect Donato Bramante, who had so important a role in the refoundation of St. Peter's, proposed to turn the old medieval open space into a *piazza grande* modeled on the Forum of Julius Caesar in Rome (Bruschi 1973: 118-119; Posner 1973). In Venice we see the construction of the Procuratorie Vecchie with its extensive three-story colonnade screen around Piazza S. Marco beginning in 1513. (According to documentary sources there was a model for work there by a little-known Tuscan architect, "il Celestro".) The renovation of the Capitoline Hill in Rome (begun 1536), designed by Michelangelo with identical opposing facades, is, in some measure, part of this trend. Although these examples, and the Uffizi in Florence, had ancient references, this form of monumental facade did not require ancient allusions. The commercial "strada maggiore" in Brescia was built with rigorous zoning regulations; the three-story buildings with workshops form a unified architectural facade (Guidoni and Marino 1982: 486-497).

The role that military defense plays in conditioning urban planning in the sixteenth century

Antonio Tempesta
Map of Rome,
*detail showing the Campidoglio
engraving, 1593*
*Milan, Civica Raccolta Stampe
Achille Bertarelli*

Vigevano, perspective view of main square

can hardly be overestimated. The siting of cities and the paths taken by their wall boundaries is, of course, an obvious matter. But fortifications froze paths through the city and created grand entry markers at the major portals. While the city's development as a whole is subject to many cultural and political influences, the impact upon it of military architecture is a product of important advances in technology.

While the city of the Middle Ages had developed wall systems to a degree unknown to the ancient world, the fact of the matter is that they were really little more than thin curtains; they could be moved or changed over time with relative ease (Braunfels 1953: 45–85). Florence, for example, was witness to three significant alterations to her circuit from Roman times to the fourteenth century (Fanelli 1973; Sznura 1975). The walls of Siena underwent a similar series of transformations through the Middle Ages as did many other cities (Balestracci and Piccini 1977: 17–40). But with the development of relatively accurate longer range cannon fire it was agreed that the only effective defense would involve sheathing the city in thick, escarped, angled walls that could not only provide gun positions for defensive fire out into the countryside, but complementary coverage along the face. These walls were not only costly to build, but largely indestructible. Furthermore, such bastioned wall defenses were often surrounded by a free fire zone outside their limits. Thus the spatial extent of the city was effectively frozen; the era of organic city development, slowed for demographic and economic reasons, was now brought to an end for military reasons.

The angle bastion proved so successful that by the middle years of the sixteenth century this technique of defense was applied almost universally. Fortresses were cut into or flanked the old medieval walls. With their heavy weapons, they overlooked the city, rendering the old wall circuit virtually obsolete. Beginning as theoretical sketches in treatises and in architectural drawings, fortresses such as the Fortezza da Basso in Florence (begun 1531) built for Cosimo de' Medici by Antonio da Sangallo the Younger, were virtually unassailable (Hale 1970). In Siena, Baldassarre Lanci built the Fortezza di S. Barbara for the Medici following the Wars of Siena around mid-century (Coppi 1980). One could duplicate this pattern of construction throughout Italy (Piacenza, Parma, Ancona, Arezzo, Cesena, Venice). In Perugia, Antonio da Sangallo built the Rocca Paolina for Pope Paul III (begun 1540), composed of two separate fortresses linked by a flying corridor. Built over the Colle Landone, the district inhabited by the pope's major antagonists in Perugia, the Baglione, the fortress wiped out their power base in the city. Absolutist papal power needed to make clear the subordinate status of local families (Chiacchella 1987). The fortress building

Palmanova, aerial view

Filarete (Antonio Averlino)
page from Trattato
d'Architettura
showing sketch of fortified
building 1460–65
Florence, Biblioteca Nazionale
MS. II.I.140, fol. 42v.

campaigns of the Venetian follow a similar pattern (see the models of Orzinuovi and Peschiera).

The effectiveness of these political and defensive strategies encouraged many military leaders to imagine the possibility of ringing cities entirely with such bastioned walls. Large-scale cities on a radial plan had been considered by Filarete and Francesco di Giorgio in the fifteenth century, but in the sixteenth century military specialists such as Pietro Cataneo, Girolamo Maggi, and Francesco De Marchi outlined large-scale radial plans adapted for military defense (De La Croix 1960). The radial plan, with its regular geometry, a fantasy of humanistic cosmology, was transformed into a military machine. At Palmanova in the Friuli region (begun 1593), for example, Giulio Savorgnan and Bonaiuto Lorini laid out an ideal military city on a radial plan with a large open *piazza d'armi* at the center, with wide, straight streets, and bastions around the outside.

Proposals were also made during the sixteenth century to ring the old walls with modern bastions. But there were many difficulties with such plans, as we see in Rome, where efforts foundered in the face of construction costs and the opposition of important landowners (Pepper 1976). Only in a few locations was it possible to encircle the old walls of a city completely with new bastions. The sheathing of the walls of Lucca with eleven modern bastions corresponding to the eleven urban administrative areas, for example, allowed the city to maintain its anomalous status as an independent republic in the face of a hostile Tuscan neighbor; at the same time, it choked further development, leaving the city emarginated in the larger political world of the sixteenth century. Indeed, a remarkable concession for the sake of safety, the construction required the demolition of lucrative suburban gardens and vineyards around the city (Barsali 1980). In an absolutist state of the seventeenth century, such as Turin, the dreams of safety and military might came closer to realization (Pollak 1991).

It is in military architecture that the architectural model acquires new forms and new uses. In the model of Peschiera (Rome, Museo dell'Istituto Storico e di Cultura dell'Arma del Genio) we begin to get, in a limited way, a topographic context, something conspicuously absent in the models for civil and ecclesiastical buildings.

Topography in military affairs was, in these instances, a matter of life or death and model-making was an essential part of the military architect's work hitherto. The architect's conception was aided by the three-dimensional character of the model and the general too could plan his strategy using a model.

In 1550 a certain Giambattista Romano was commissioned to make a model of the city of Siena and its fortifications to be carried to Charles V for his opinion on the placement of a new fortress (Pepper and Adams 1986: 60). And Giorgio Vasari depicted Cosimo de' Medici hunched over a plan with a model of the city of Siena in the background. It was, perhaps, following study of a model such as this located in Florence that Cosimo gave orders to the field forces attacking the city of Siena in his successful campaign to conquer the independent republic.[9]

[9] The model is, of course, more easily legible to the uninitiated—graphic conventions can present tricky problems—but for the study of the battlefield it continues to remain important. Martin Middlebrook, *First Day on the Somme 1 July 1916* (New York, 1972: 67, 106) documents the importance of the model for the first wave of attackers on that fateful day. Evidently sent home for rest prior to the battle a young officer amused himself with a model he had made of his section of the battlefield. To his horror he discovered that the point at which he was "to go over the top" was overlooked by a German machine-gun nest. On his return, over maps and charts, he attempted to explain this to his officers who refused to believe him. When the time came to attack, he and many others left the trench and were killed by the enemy machine guns just as the model had predicted.

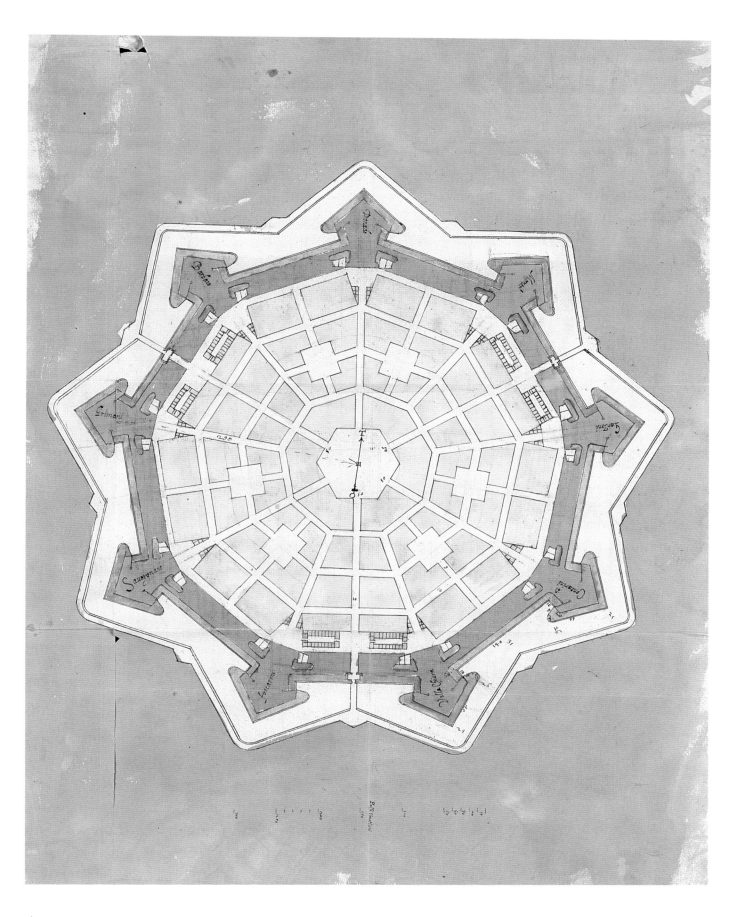

Anonymous
Plan of Palmanova
17th cent.
Torino, Archivio di Stato
Architettura Militare
vol. V c. 43r.
cat. no. 187

Conclusion

This outline of Italian urban development between 1400 and 1600 has stressed three sources of change: the recovery of the ancient world and its architectural and urbanistic vocabulary; the elaboration of new concepts of family dignity; and the growth of seignorial rule and the consolidation of larger political units on the Italian peninsula. We have traced the effects of these processes in the key of urbanistic innovations of the period: the facade; new kinds of open spaces and streets that alter ways of looking at and moving through the city; and novel kinds of administrative and military building types. Isolated from the city's heart, military architecture is, at first glance, the odd man out in this story, a product of technological as well as social, political, and administrative changes. Yet in its scale and in its purpose the fortress speaks most clearly about the city in the sixteenth century. No visual representation of the city in this period could be considered complete without its walls or the star-shaped plan formed by the bastions. Indeed, one might even say that it was military architecture with its devastating power to destroy the city that shaped more completely than anything else the image of the city for the next century and a half. Thus the fortress and the new urban walls, silent vigilant monitors, define the city's boundaries and ensure its survival.

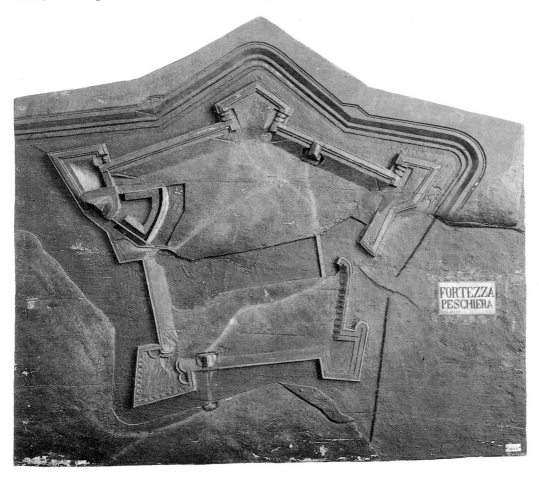

Anonymous
Model of the Fortezza of
Peschiera
17th cent.
Rome, Istituto Storico e di
Cultura dell'Arma del Genio
inv. 1995

Giorgio Vasari
Cosimo I Studies the Plans to
Conquer Siena
Florence, Palazzo Vecchio
Salone dei Cinquecento

230

BELLVM COGITANTES
PRAEVENIT

The Panels in Urbino, Baltimore and Berlin Reconsidered

[1] Whether or not a slice was cut off the bottom of the Urbino panel (Morolli 1992) had best be left suspended until further evidence is provided.
[2] For the summary descriptions of the technical evidence of the panels I have been able to base myself:
a. For the Urbino panel on the careful report on the findings obtained in 1978 (*Il Restauro della Città Ideale* 1978); on the photographs taken at that time showing the preparatory incisions and under infrared the dark underdrawing, kindly provided by the Istituto Centrale di Restauro through the director, Professor Evelina Borea; finally, on the diagnostic report by Maurizio Seraceni 1992b: 469ff.). My warm thanks go to Dottoressa Vastano of the Soprintendenza alle Gallerie in Urbino for supplying me with the catalog and with photographs.
b. For the Baltimore panel on an inspection under infrared light on 4 May 1992, carried out by the Senior Conservator for Paintings of the Walters Art Gallery, Mr. Eric Gordon (which I was fortunate enough to attend), and on an ensuing correspondence with Mr. Gordon; finally, the report "Technical Notes on the Walters' Ideal City" to be published by Mr. Gordon in the *Journal of the Walters Art Gallery*, 52 (1993). I am greatly indebted to Mr. Gordon for having answered patiently my numerous questions and for providing me with infrared slides, a color transparency of the panel, and other material. I also want to thank Mr. Robert Bergman, then director of the Walters Art Gallery, for his support.
c. For the Berlin panel Dr. Wilhelm H. Köhler was good enough to investigate it under infrared light, to inform me of the results and to provide detailed photographs; I am most obliged to him.
[3] Seraceni (1992b) briefly sums up the evidence for that underdrawing. An extensive description by D. and M.G. Bernini is found in *Il restauro della Città Ideale* 1978. Underdrawing on or incision into the grounding are techniques widely used in Italian Quattrocento painting to prepare a linear framework for architecture and the perspective grid. It should be noted however, that Piero della Francesca uses no incisions in the preparatory underdrawing for the *Pala di Montefeltro*, nor for the *Flagellation*, but only black chalk.
[4] As kindly pointed out to me by Professor Christof Thoenes.

I might as well start with a *confiteor*. Forty-odd years ago I placed the "Ideal City" panels in Urbino and Baltimore into the context of Renaissance stage design as codified by Serlio; not so much projects for stage sets—granted that my terminology was deplorably vague—but experiments *ante litteram*: painted commentaries to Vitruvius' chapter on the Tragic and Comic Scene (Krautheimer 1948; critically Ploder 1984; and Riegel 1988). That old paper of mine has engendered a good deal of discussion, much of it critical, in particular in recent years. Rightly so. Nobody today could be harder on it than myself. This, my self-condemnation, concerns not so much the thesis at its core. To be sure, even that cannot stand in its original form. However, I feel deeply ashamed in retrospect on account of the method by which I built toward that thesis, or better, the lack of method. I started with what I thought was a bright notion before exploring the hard facts: the physical as well as the visual evidence provided by the three panels. True, I had had a close look at the Baltimore panel in 1946-47. But the Urbino panel I fear I had not seen since the late 1920s, nor the one in Berlin. Thus for Urbino I relied on an old Alinari photograph; the one in Berlin I simply disregarded. That first capital crime was compounded by another. Enamored with my original bright notion I was led to select from and misinterpret the evidence. Having overlooked the cross atop the Urbino rotunda—old Alinaris are often dark—and misreading as windows the porphyry plaques on its walls, it became instead of a *templum* a *macellum*; the basilica turned into a church, a city gate into a regia. Everything seemed to fit neatly my *scena comica* and *tragica*; too neatly. No beginning student should fall into such a trap. If a mature scholar fell into it, he can only confess to it, apologize and warn: bright notions are dangerous.

For my sins of yore I have taken it upon myself to have a second look at the panels—all three of them: to reconsider their original physical function; the archaeological evidence—material, underpainting, construction of the composition; their subject matter; finally their purport.

All three panels, of poplar wood and each composed of two or three horizontal boards, seem to have served as *spalliere*—sections of woodwork rising from the back of a piece of furniture; or as inserts into the wainscoting of a room (cat. no. 178 a, b, c). In the Berlin panel the bottom part, which is slanted, imitates in painting wainscoting. The other two, in Urbino and Baltimore, show traces of having been ripped from such *spalliere* or paneling.[1] Since the level of the vanishing point in the three panels is placed 15 to 29 centimeters from the lower edge, the panels presumably would have been mounted roughly 1.20–1.30 meters from floor level. The differences in length are minor; but the proportions of the painted surface vary considerably ranging as they do from 1:2.3 to 1:3.5.[2]

In all three panels the perspective grid as well as the outlines of the buildings have been prepared in minute detail on the grounding. In the Urbino panel the orthogonals of the grid were incised into that layer. So were the outlines of a first project for the right hand palace providing for six lower groundfloor arcades on the main facade. Only in the final version did the painter change them to their present number of five, and give them their slender proportions; concomitantly he shifted the building slightly to the right. That early project also envisaged, sketched on the grounding in dark lines, visible to the right and behind the rotunda and hence probably in its place, a monumental structure, pedimented and colonnaded (Seraceni 1992b). Skeleton and detailing of the palaces right and left likewise were outlined on the grounding. The preparatory design for the majority of the architecture was drawn in fine black chalk lines. Ruler and compasses were employed for both incision and underdrawing; the compass holes are visible all over the panel.[3]

In the Baltimore panel, too, the perspective grid as well as the architecture were prepared on the grounding by a network of verticals, horizontals and orthogonals incised and/or drawn with some dry material, possibly black chalk. Contrary to the Urbino panel, however, it is the skeleton of the buildings which is outlined by incision, except the smallest details such as capitals, whereas the perspective grid, except a few lines incised, is drawn on the grounding. Moreover as a base for the grid the lower edge of the panel has been divided in thirty units, numbered, and each 73 millimeters long, equaling one Vitruvian *passus minor*.[4] One of the divisions, no. 14, left of center, carries in the underdrawing a square in perspective, outlined doubly and crossed by two diagonals, leading, it appears, to the dis-

tance points of a bifocal construction placed on the lateral edges of the panel (Kemp 1985). Further numbering and lettering visible in the underpaint along a wide horizontal and midway across the panel was still to be explained. Neither the numbered partitioning of the base line nor the numbering across the panel have been observed in either of the other two panels. On the other hand, pinholes all over the surface reveal the use of string or compasses in all three panels.

Likewise in the Berlin panel the composition has been prepared by incising into the grounding the skeletons and details of the architecture, a few of the orthogonals, the horizontals of the grid in the pavement, as well as the outlines of the scenery in the background. Also, as in the Baltimore panel, two lines crossing diagonally have been observed on the center plaque of the pavement in the foreground. No traces are left of an underdrawing, if ever there was, in black chalk or another dry material.

The small squares of the grid, both in Urbino and Baltimore, served only as a base to carry the widely different patterns of the pavements in large octagons, squares and diamonds. Both the underdrawing and the incisions on the preparation, in fact, in all three panels were disregarded and changed in the painting whenever corrections in composition, architectural design, scenery or perspective were deemed desirable: the right-hand palace in the Urbino panel and the left-hand one in the Baltimore panel were shifted somewhat toward the center and correspondingly expanded. Likewise in the Baltimore panel the underdrawing reveals numerous earlier experiments in positioning the structures both left and right of the octagon to the right—it recalls the Florentine Baptistery, in the flights of stairs ascending from the sunken piazza and elsewhere. The pavement pattern in the Urbino panel, planned as octagons, each divided into eight sections, was in the finishing turned into the present design. Corrections of minor errors in preparing the perspective or the structures are frequent in both the Urbino and Baltimore panels.

Nor are the three paintings the same in composition, coloring and tonality. The Urbino panel is built up firmly and clearly stresses the volume and solidity of the structures. It is dominated center stage by the cylindrical volume of the rotunda, placed on the gray and white grid of the pavement and its pattern in diamonds and octagons. The cream-colored engaged colonnades of the structure, upper and lower, are solid and contrast with the purplish porphyry plaques of the inserts. Right and left, the long rows of palaces and houses vary in design, height and color as they recede into depth and offset each other, gray-blue against cream, red on white, or white on gray membering. Colonnades stand against solid facades, the skyline of the structures moves, broken by a garden wall, a low building, a tall palace between smallish houses, all this under a deep blue sky. Altogether the rendering breathes vitality. In the Balti-

Unknown Central Italian Artist
Ideal City
end 15th cent.
Urbino, Galleria Nazionale
delle Marche
Cat. no. 178a

more panel, on the contrary, a sense of stately solemnity prevails. Space rather than volume is the constituent element. The center is taken up by the expanse of a square, set on two planes, the lower sunken and inlaid with a design of inscribed and circumscribed octagons, diamonds and squares. That pavement is kept in strong colors—cream, green, white, gray— while the upper piazza is paved plain white. Set on it, and thus raised above the sunken piazza on twin podiums, two palaces face one another, richly articulated but monotonous in color, gray and cream respectively. Backstage, the monuments of antiquity are lined up: the amphitheater a dark, the triumphal arch a light gray; that reticent coloring is broken only by the green and purple of the right-hand octagon and by the burnt red slivers of minor housing and of the city wall far back. Altogether volume and coloring of the structures seem subordinate to the space that envelops them, much in contrast to its subordinate role in the Urbino panel. The subdued tonality is completed by a grayish-blue sky, set with a few clouds, gilded by a dim sun. It has been proposed to view the Baltimore panel as representing ancient Rome, the one in Urbino modern Florence (Saalman 1968); I am unconviced. Again the Berlin panel offers one or more variants. A loggia, behind the slimmest strip of a pavement front stage, leads into the painting. Its walls, pilasters and columns seem substantial; but their volume is held down by the coloring in subdued browns, yellows and grays. The layout of the pavement too, is simple, enlivened only by a design of squares with diamonds inscribed in the foreground. The diamond shaping of the coffers in the ceiling presented to the draftsman a welcome experiment in perspective rendering. Space flows through the loggia onto the harbor square paved in a simple grayish and rust-brown grid, continuous rather than on two planes as at Baltimore. The square is bordered by houses and palaces, their membering set off against the walls, the windows round-headed or gabled, the capitals of the loggia a free variant of the composite order, the column shafts fluted. Between such samples of an advanced Renaissance design rise a crenelated palace and a version of Castel Sant'Angelo in its medieval garb. The panel altogether lacks the liveliness in composition and coloring of its counterpart in Urbino as well as the stately spaciousness of the one in Baltimore.

Notwithstanding such differences in size, preparation and finishing, the three paintings have always been seen as a group. Both in subject matter and in rendering they are intimately related to one another; and in subject matter anyhow they altogether stand apart in fifteenth-century Italian painting.

The panels depict visions of an urban setting: a square, bordered by and set with noble structures and monuments: stately palaces; a church, *templum* in fifteenth-century parlance; a loggia; a line-up of buildings from Roman antiquity; honorific columns, a fountain, wellads.

on the following pages
Unknown Central Italian Artist
Ideal City
detail
end 15th cent.
Urbino, Galleria Nazionale
delle Marche
Cat. no. 178a

Central Italian Artist
Ideal City with a Fountain
and Statues of the Virtues
end 15th cent.
Baltimore, Walters Art Gallery
Cat. no. 178b

The three versions differ, but all seem to be variations on the same theme: a grand architectural setting representative of a city, whether as its prestigious center or as an impressive forecourt abutting the harbor.

The city proper, ordinary housing along narrow streets, is barely sketched beyond the borders of the square; and the urban is set off against the non-urban ambient: the countryside, green hills far outside the walls, or the expanse of the sea with its islands beyond the masts of ships at anchor.

There are no human figures in either the Urbino or the Berlin panel. Those scattered over the Baltimore panel have been suspected regarding their authenticity, painted as they are lightly over the finishing layer of the architectural setting. In any case they are lost in the vastness of the spatial composition.

Nor does the matrix where the structures envisioned in the panels are rooted need any lenghty discussion. The squares and the buildings in their variations were all conceived in the spirit and are represented in the idiom of the architecture of fifteenth-century humanism. There are the monuments of antiquity, as classified by humanist scholars at the time, Flavio Biondo for one, in three or four main categories: theaters, triumphal arches, temples—this latter represented by the Tempio di Marte, the Florentine Baptistery; honorific columns, city walls. There are, too, the public buildings, ecclesiastical and secular, as demanded by fifteenth-century architectural theory: a main church, the cathedral—the monumental colonnaded rotunda that dominates the Urbino panel; next to it the facade of a basilica, the court of law; grand palaces to house in style the heads of the civic administration and their offices; a square surrounding the cathedral, another fronting the basilica. Or else, in the Baltimore panel, a large forum entered through a triumphal arch and set with honorific columns, presumably—so Alberti—for the *patres togati* to meet. Buildings and squares, as brought out long ago (Kimball 1927; recently Morolli 1992a), are clad in the vocabulary of humanism as perfected by Alberti and developed in his wake in ever new combinations through the latter third of the fifteenth and the early years of the sixteenth century. The facades of palaces and churches are articulated in double and triple superimposed

orders: of pilasters, single or paired or marking alternating narrow and wider bays; or of engaged columns; or of half-columns combined with blind arches mounted on half-piers. Porticoes open on the ground floors of the palaces, carried by trabeated colonnades or by arcades resting on piers; or by rows of piers carrying trabeations. A loggia, colonnaded and trabeated, surrounds the top floor of a palace. Windows, rectangular or round-headed, are set off by profiled frames, those rectangular surmounted at times by a fleuron. Low pediments rise from the top cornice, flanked by squarish pedestals, Alberti's *arulae*, and intended to carry statues (Brandt, in this catalog). The squares are paved with colorful marble *opus sectile* laid out in large-scale geometric patterns. The palaces in all three panels look almost like sample cards of the possible permutations of an Albertian and post-Albertian architectural vocabulary (Morolli, 1992a).

Hunting for comparisons of architecture designed and built in brick and stone at the time nonetheless turns out to be a futile exercise (Riegel 1988). Certainly it will not help in establishing either the date or local origin of the panels. After all, what is here depicted is not an architect's project; rather it is a vision of an urban ambient, a utopia, a higher world ruled by the principles of humanism. Unattainable within the limitations—financial, technical and organizational—set by fifteenth-century conditions and urban realities, that higher world could be built easily with ruler, T-square, compasses and paint on the surface of a panel. But it remains a vision, a never and nowhere realm: this, notwithstanding the concreteness of the designer's architectural imagination, the clarity of spatial relations and of the interaction of space and volumes, the precision in working out proportions and the minute detailing of orders, capitals and profiles. However, architectural visions by their very nature anticipate, often by decades, the appearance in "real," built architecture of buildings or details envisioned: the palace facades, articulated by orders of pilasters, envisaged in the 1420s in Masaccio's Theophilus fresco in the Cappella Brancacci, do not occur in built architecture before the 1450s and 1460s. Moreover, the architectural vision, more often than not foreshadows elements or combinations thereof that remain abortive: as witness the grand structures dreamed up in Donatello's tondi in the Sagrestia Vecchia.

on the following pages
Unknown Central Italian Artist
Ideal City with a Fountain
and Statues of the Virtues
end 15th cent.
Baltimore, Walters Art Gallery

239

242

Unknown Central Italian Artist
Architectural Perspective
detail
end 15th cent.
Berlin, Staatliche Museen
Preussischer Kulturbesitz
Gemäldegalerie

244

Piero della Francesca
Flagellation
1450–60
Urbino, Galleria Nazionale
delle Marche

Or to stay with our panels, a loggia like that in the Berlin panel; a cathedral on the plan of the rotunda in the Urbino panel; or palaces opening in deep ground-floor porticoes onto a public square; or rows of stout piers surmounted by an entablature carrying the full weight of a tall palace wall. The panels, then, depict for their own sake visions of urban settings. The buildings by themselves are the subject matter. Such autonomy of an architectural setting is in Quattrocento painting not an ordinary phenomenon. To be sure, very early in the century Brunelleschi had evolved a system of scientific linear perspective by which to envisage true to proportion a structure or a space bordered by buildings, parallel or at an angle to the picture plane—the Baptistery, Piazza della Signoria.

Such an image would have been to him, one supposes, purely an architect's tool. Whether or not based on horizon line, vanishing and distance point and the resulting grid of orthogonals and horizontals, the procedure was transferred and applied for use in the figurative arts.

Starting with Masaccio, presumably in concert with Brunelleschi, in the Cappella Brancacci, a grid pavement in linear perspective and framed by buildings became the constituent means for painters and sculptors to tell convincingly a *storia*; speaking in technical terms to create on a two-dimensional surface a credible three-dimensional space within which to place figures proportionate to the dimensions of the grid. By relating, as codified by Alberti in 1435, the dimensions of the grid proportionate to the height of the figures, the *storia* and its ambient became measurable. The mathematical foundations for the procedure were finally provided by Piero della Francesca (Kemp 1985).

In the Cappella Brancacci the framing buildings are either of a type which the painter and his public passed daily, or they are clad in the new *all'antica* vocabulary which Brunelleschi was just beginning to explore. However, they are insubstantial and out of proportion in both size and volume to the figures. The *storia*, the figures interacting are the dominant element, crowded into a shallow foreground. The framing structures are mere stage props. So is the terminating backdrop; its architectural or landscape elements suggest a space, deep but unconvincingly linked to that of the *storia*.

This construction of the picture space continues in general unchanged into the 1470s and 1480s. Furthermore, in general the architectural setting of the *storia* is increasingly upstaged by the burgeoning overabundance of ornamentation. Demoted to the role of "showcases"

Masaccio
Resurrection of the Son
of Theophilus
detail of the frescoes
in the Cappella Brancacci
1424–27
Florence, S. Maria
del Carmine

[5] The *prospettiva* on that *sovraporta*, given its measurements, probably does refer to an urban vista. However, the term as a rule simply means a *trompe-l'oeil*, offering the view of a cupboard, its shutters open and inside a clutter of books, a lute, a piece of armor, an armilla sphere, a flower vase.

of archaeological learning, as in Botticelli's *Calumny of Apelles* or in the Barberini panels, these "props" attract attention without gaining substance and volume or creating a space which convincingly conveys a sense of depth. The great exception is Piero della Francesca's oeuvre; the *Pala di Montefeltro* and the *Flagellation*, both prior to 1473 (see *Piero e Urbino* 1992). The panels in Urbino, Berlin and Baltimore run counter to this declassification of the architectural setting. The foreground, rather than being given over to the *storia*, is empty save for a strip of pavement, which, in the Urbino panel, is set with two well-heads. From there however, the space expands convincingly and acquires depth articulated by the patterns of the pavement. The buildings, placed at the borders or rising into the expanse of the picture space, characterized by their successive orders, provide the rhythm necessary to create a third dimension. No action is needed. The setting itself is the *storia*. It is told by the convincing expanse of space, by the substantial volumes of the structures, by the credibility of the interweaving of mass and void. Here, the rendering of architecture, of the urban environment, has gained autonomy, freeing itself, as it were, from the narrative. The architectural setting, which for Brunelleschi was an architect's device, had been turned by the painters into a tool to provide a stage for the *storia*. In the three panels it has become a text in its own right, worthy to be told.

It has been suggested that the panels in Urbino, Baltimore, and Berlin are isolated vestiges of the once common practice of painting landscapes on furniture, *spalliere*, and wainscot panels (Kemp 1991e)—a plausible suggestion given that such articles, being household objects subject to daily wear and tear, were invariably fragile, expendable, and very often discarded once they went out of fashion.

History, however, is not always on the side of plausibility. The fact is that there are exceedingly few examples of isolated urban *vedute* of this kind executed in fifteenth-century Italy. Inventories of household furniture have rarely been published (Shearman 1975; Sangiorgi 1976; Lydecker 1987a), and seldom include works such as the *sovraporta* in the Palazzo Ducale at Urbino, "un quadro lungo con prospettiva," or as a *spalliera*.[5] Among hundreds of painted *cassoni*, the one category of furniture that has survived in large numbers, only a handful show urban vistas and of these none is comparable with our panels. The execution is poor; the perspective, while wide-angled, lacks conviction; the buildings represented are old-fashioned—basically medieval with an occasional Renaissance structure in between. The

247

*Cristoforo and Lorenzo
da Lendinara*
Townscape
*wood inlay of choir stall
Modena Cathedral*

entire setting, furthermore, is that of a down-to-earth *veduta*, rather than an urban "vision" (in the manner of Alberti), as found here in the panels at Urbino, Baltimore and Berlin. Forty years ago André Chastel called attention to the abundance from the 1460s on of urban vistas executed in wood intarsia (Chastel 1953; repr. 1978; also 1987). The core of his thesis was that the tradition of the *intarsiatori* and its fusion *ab ovo* with the rise of linear perspective provided the source for the panels in question. Apart from the recent over interpretations of Chastel's clear proposal (Ferretti 1982; 1986), I cannot agree with that proposal either. The urban views done in intarsia which concern us, that is those dating from the last third of the Quattrocento, presented the architectural reality which the craftsmen as well as their clients daily saw or could have seen: the Piazza del Duomo in Cremona, the baptistery in Parma, the Santo in Padua; or a vignette that was or could have been a familiar view seen through an archway or from a window, its shutters open—houses crowding in on the upper walls and the roof of an eight-sided structure, presumably a baptistery (see wood inlay of the door of Modena Cathedral); the slope of a steep street bordered by narrow-breasted tall houses; the towered silhouette of a hill-town; a bridge, high-shouldered, crossing a creek in the midst of town (see the wood inlay from Lucca): medieval reality inherited (Ferretti 1982; 1986). Vocabulary and concept of the Renaissance reach the workshops of the *intarsiatori* but rarely in the framing architectural setting of a *storia*, designed by a major artist such as Giuliano da Maiano (Haines 1983). In autonomous renderings of grand visionary urban settings, the new style in intarsia work did not gain acceptance until the second decade of the Cinquecento.

Generally speaking, that is. Because the examples of intarsia representing urban settings done between 1474 and 1482 for the doors in the ducal apartments in the palace at Urbino stand apart from the realistic and conservative urban views customary in their time among the general run of *intarsiatori* (Trionfi Honorati 1992). The drawings from which the craftsmen at Urbino worked, whether or not their own *invenzioni*, had been touched by the concepts of the architecture of humanism which pervades our three panels. They borrow freely from the new vocabulary, if at times awkwardly and not without misunderstandings. The inlays on the two wings of a door join to expand into the view of a square, wide-angled though slightly forced (see the door to the Appartamento della Duchessa). Bordered by impressive structures it presents a vision rather than a *veduta*. A grand palace in the new style is raised on a podium above the level of a piazza; its ground floor opens in an arcade on piers, the *piano nobile* articulated by an order of pilasters, though strangely slender; the windows are gabled, the top floor is enveloped by a loggia, trabeated and on piers. Or else two *palazzine*, opposite one another (see the doorway of the Sala del Trono), each but three bays wide, are marked by classical cornices, entablatures, friezes and corner pilasters; the pavement, a white grid with black border, guides the eye toward a rusticated triple arch that opens onto a harbor. However, such humanist visions and borrowings are mingled with structures of a very different kind, that of the real fifteenth-century world: old-fashioned houses, a medieval church and tower, prominently the turreted and crenelated facade of what may be the prince's *regia* opposite the grand palace. Crenelations are placed antithetically atop a palace facade articulated by a classical order of arcades, pilasters and architraves.

*opposite
Cristoforo da Lendinara*
Townscape
*wood inlay
Lucca, Museo Nazionale
di Villa Guinigi*

*on the following pages
Door to the Appartamento
della Duchessa*
Townscape
*wood inlay
Urbino, Palazzo Ducale*

.DOMINICI.BERTINI.ÆDILITAE
.CONSVMATVM.

251

*A perspective view
of a Palazzo
Doorway of the Sala del Trono
wood inlay
Urbino, Palazzo Ducale*

It has been claimed that our panels imitate the tradition of the *intarsie* (Ferretti 1986). The shoe, it seems to me, is on the other foot. To be sure, the designers of both the panels and the inlays at Urbino drew on the same source, namely, the envisioned architecture of humanism, and were presumably members of Alberti's circle. The panels are solidly rooted in the concepts of that sphere. The inlays on the doors of the ducal apartments pick out elements of the vocabulary and employ them inconsistently, and are frequently misapplied.[6] Even so the *intarsiatori* active in Urbino in the 1470s and 1480s, or whoever designed for them, broke away in their architectural vistas from the usages of the craft. They stand by themselves among their contemporaries, as do the artist or artists who designed and painted our panels.

Granted, then, that the three panels were parts of furniture or of the wainscoting of a room, they still stand by themselves within that category. Unique in the fifteenth century, such autonomous perspectives of architectures clad in the vocabulary of humanism do not reappear among examples of intarsia before the end of the first decade of the Cinquecento

[6] The proposed attribution to Bramante of the *intarsie* with architectural perspectives at Urbino is unconvincing (Bruschi 1969b; Trionfi Honorati 1992).

A perspective view
of a Palazzo
Doorway of the Sala del Trono
wood inlay
Urbino, Palazzo Ducale

(Trionfi Honorati 1992). And the question of whether or not such renderings of humanist urban settings once were widespread in the fifteenth century had best be left open. So far I see no existing, conclusive proof either way.

Attribution and dating of the panels have been widely contended, but none of the names proffered so far has convinced the experts (Conti 1976). Nor has agreement been reached as to whether one artist did the three panels (Clark 1951; Zeri 1976) or at least the two in Urbino and Baltimore (Kimball 1927; *Il restauro della città ideale* 1978) or whether all three show different hands (Chastel 1978; Shearman 1975; Kemp 1991e, if hesitantly). It has also been suggested that an architect as designer, and a painter (and not necessarily the same team) collaborated on each of the panels (Sanpaolesi 1949).

I have never had the eye nor the training of a connoisseur of painting, and it would therefore be foolhardy to venture into the jungle of attributions and attributionists. Nor dare I conjecture as to whether the panels should be assigned to one and the same author, or to two or three different hands. However, I am willing to take a stand on three points: a date in

253

Piero della Francesca
Sacra Conversazione
1472–74
Milan, Pinacoteca di Brera

the 1490s (Sanpaolesi 1949) or around 1500 (Kemp 1991e) for any of the panels seems precluded by the intarsia inscriptions on the doors of the ducal appartments, 1474–82; they do, after all, draw on and at times misapply the vocabulary of the architectural matrix in which the panels are firmly rooted. The panels, therefore, are either contemporary with the intarsia work, or antedate it. Second, nothing comparable to the subject matter of the panels, the autonomous rendering of an urban setting in the idiom of humanism, exists elsewhere in Italian Quattrocento painting. To assign the panels to Florence (as has often been done) seems therefore mistaken. Finally, collaboration between an architect responsible for designing the preparatory underdrawing and a painter responsible for the execution seems out of the question: the painter so freely discards the preparatory design—the grand building in place of the rotunda in the Urbino panel; shifting site and design of both the right-hand and the left-hand palaces in the Baltimore panel—that he must have been the designer of both the earlier projects and the author of the final changes. Notwithstanding interpretations of the data to the contrary (*Il restauro della città ideale* 1978; Saraceni 1992b) this seems the logical conclusion to be drawn from the evidence. In attempting to establish the place of these panels in fifteenth-century art it is altogether advisable not to think primarily of painters, nor of the general run of builders or architects. We are dealing after all with utopian visions of urban settings. Hence one might as well (and perhaps preferably) turn to those who put their utopian visions of architecture and urbanism in writing, and to those to whom these writings were addressed: Alberti, and in his wake Filarete and Francesco di Giorgio; and their patrons, actual and prospective, who, it was hoped, might in some distant future turn their dreams of urban renewal into reality. Alberti, one should remember, never saw himself as an architect, nor indeed was he. He considered himself a "counsellor-at-humanism," and from that lofty peak he inquired into the principles and the techniques of a wide range of human activities, advising his readers (and not least his listeners) on matters of philosophy, on religion, on husbandry, on horsebreeding and on politics, on painting and sculpture. As a humanist adviser he also laid down his thoughts on architecture in *De re aedificatoria*. "Concerning all matters linked to building" renders adequately, if awkwardly, the meaning of the title chosen by Alberti in place of Vitruvius' Graecising and moreover vague *De architectura*. From building practice and design he leads up to the categories of buildings needed in and representative of an ideal urban layout of the Quattrocento: a *templum*, that is, the principal church or cathedral; a *basilica*, meaning a law court; palaces for those in authority, serving as both the seat of administration and as the living quarters for their large households; spacious squares for commercial needs and for meetings of the *patres togati*; and housing for the lower classes, though this is mentioned only in passing—they have to arrange themselves as best possible. Alberti's building categories then corresponds to the needs and activities of a utopian political and social community, composed of a hierarchy of classes and peaking in an oligarchy of both ecclesiastical and secular nature; a utopia, however, adapted to the realities of fifteenth-century Italy and thus envisioned under different forms of government—a republic; a prince ruling in accord with his subjects; or one imposing his will, a *tyrannus*. Architecture then interlocks with social needs and obligations, with politics and with statecraft. It had perhaps best be left open whether and, if so, to what extent such meshing of urbanism and statecraft in the Ideal City is linked to the resurgence of Platonic ideas (Garin 1965) and whether the "myth of the Ideal City" applies to the rule of Federico da Montefeltro in Urbino (Castelli 1992).

In fact the Ten Books of Alberti's *De re aedificatoria* (composed in Latin, let us keep in mind) were not written for the benefit of builders, nor for that matter, of architects. After all, whom among his contemporaries would Messer Battista at the time of writing have called an architect, except for Brunelleschi, who had died in 1446? As I see it, *De re* is addressed to patrons; and since among older rulers humanist patrons were rare, Alberti aimed to educate a new generation of patrons, able to understand and willing to promote an architecture of humanism.

These new patrons Alberti saw in the young rulers of Ferrara, Mantua, Urbino—Lionello and Meledusio d'Este, Lodovico Gonzaga and his brother Carlo, Federico da Montefeltro—all come to power in the 1440s, all aged twenty or so, and all tutored by humanists, such as Guarino da Verona and Vittorino da Feltre; hence expected to be versed in and conversant with the language of humanism, Latin, and with its spirit. Attuned to the new ideas they might listen to his "visione fantastica." So might an elderly humanist, recently risen to the papal throne, Nicholas V. Messer Battista may even have toyed with the idea of such a patron collaborating with him, as Filarete ten years later imagined working in concert with his prince on the design for his utopian Sforzinda.[7]

One of the new patrons to be educated might even build a *templum* or a palace in the idiom of the new dispensation—or at least start building one, as decades passed before they were completed, if ever. Fragmentation was imposed by the hard facts of finance and the existing urban reality.

However, such restraints did not prevent architects, painters, humanist princes and courtiers from dreaming up the new architecture on a vast scale and keeping the dream alive by turning it into a quasi-reality, an *ekphrasis*, such as Giannozzo Manetti's account of the projects fancifully attributed to Nicholas V for the Vatican Palace, the remodeling of St. Peter's, of the Borgo (Dehio 1880; Westfall 1974; see however Tafuri 1992, who reassesses the humanist encomium of Manetti and its claims in light of the real situation). Alternatively, that dream was translated into a fresco, such as Fra Angelico's rendering of St. Peter's, rebuilt in the language of humanism, as proposed—or so I believe—by Alberti (Krautheimer 1977b); or painted on a wooden panel, showing an entire city square, arranged with buildings and structures of varying type, function and design, but all conjugating that new language in all its possible variations.

Should one then see in panels as those preserved in Urbino, Baltimore and Berlin mementos, visual rather than literary reminders, designed to keep such visions of an architecture of humanism lastingly before the eyes of concerned contemporaries, namely, princely patrons and their humanist retinue? They would probably have been aware that such urban settings were

Piero della Francesca
Federico da Montefeltro
Duke of Urbino
*Florence, Galleria
degli Uffizi*

[7] I am indebted to Christof Thoenes for having called my attention to the pertinent passages in Filarete, Book VII.

not feasible, at least not yet. But they would be reminded forever that the new architecture and the new society it was to serve, must be striven for, whether or not they could be realized. The ultimate purport of the three panels is I think hortatory.

That raises new questions as to their origin and the commissioning patron or patrons. In terms of their subject matter and function, they form a close-knit group. However, they differ from each other in technical preparation and finishing. If so, were they then commissioned by three different patrons, each with his eye on furthering the novel architecture of humanism? Humanist patrons were still rare in Italy in the latter half of the Quattrocento. Is it possible, then, that the three panels were commissioned by just one patron? Given the variances between the panels, perhaps this patron commissioned three different artists to design separate versions of the humanist urban setting—suggested either by a humanist thinker in the prince's retinue, or by the prince himself with the former's assistance. Alternatively, the prince may have commissioned only one artist, who "experimented with three different approaches" (Kemp 1991e). The identification of that conjectural patron or patrons is bound to remain guesswork, and has little data to go by. Similarly, the provenance of the panels and their place of origin have yet to be determined.

Only the provenance of the Urbino panel can be established with any certainty. It comes from S. Chiara in Urbino, a church attached to the convent founded by Elisabetta, daughter of Duke Federico da Montefeltro. It can be left open, whether the painting reached the convent through her or at a later time and, in that latter case, whether or not it should be identified with a "sovraporta con una prospettiva" listed as in the ducal chambers of Federico's palace from 1582 to 1631. Either way, the provenance of the panel from Urbino is doubtful. No provenance has been plausibly established for either the Baltimore or the Berlin panel.[8]

The place of origin of a work of art does not coincide necessarily with its provenance. Nonetheless the Urbino panel would seem to have been designed and painted for the Palazzo Ducale, as it was built and decorated since the 1460s or before under Federico da Montefeltro. As summed up earlier, the architecture of humanism and its vocabulary formed the matrix from which between 1474 and 1482 the *intarsiatori* working on the doors of the ducal chambers derived piecemeal the idiom of their architectural depictions.

Given the closeness in subject matter of the panels in Baltimore and Berlin to that in Urbino and their uniqueness in fifteenth-century painting in Italy, it is not impossible that they too were executed in Urbino.

The patron who most likely commissioned the Urbino panel (and possibly all three) would therefore have been Federico da Montefeltro. From what we know of him, the duke fills the part to perfection: listening, according to Vespasiano de' Bisticci, to the opinions of architects in his retinue, but then following his own judgment; discoursing on building "as if it were the primary craft he had ever pursued"; reasoning on and carrying out construction of his own counsel. De' Bisticci's is obviously an encomium, but Federico was, after all, closely associated with Alberti. Not only is there in the long speech praising Federico's temperate lifestyle, placed by Landino in Alberti's mouth, the casual and therefore probably trustworthy remark on his having annually visited the prince for the sake of his health and repose to escape the Roman autumns and the extravagance of the Curia. There are also Federico's own words in his note of thanks to Landino for the dedication to him of the *Disputationes Camaldulenses* (see Lohr 1980, IX): "nothing was more intimate and more cherished [by us] than the friendship by which we were bound," meaning himself and Alberti.

One might therefore attribute to Alberti the design and execution of the Urbino panel (Morolli 1992), or ideed, of all three panels, assuming he experimented with different approaches (Kemp 1991a). A good deal seems to favor such a hypothesis: the vision of an urban setting conceived in the spirit and consistently worked out in the concrete concepts and the vocabulary of an architecture of humanism; the emphatic use of a scientific linear perspective as the very foundation for the rendering of that setting in accordance with Alberti's codification in *De pictura* of the procedure in the Baltimore panel: the partitioning of the ground line into equal parts and tracing of one square crossed by diagonals as a basis for the grid and its distance points; the use for that partition of Vitruvius' *passus minor* and therefore a thorough acquaintance with his work. Notwithstanding the evidence, I am unwilling to sanction such an attribution. No painting of Alberti's has emerged so far; by 1470 his writing and ideas, however, were as widely known as Vitruvius' *De architectura*. Nonetheless, Morolli's is a bright notion.

And now a last look back to that early paper of mine, in which the panels in Urbino and Baltimore were discussed as experiments *ante litteram* in stage design. Identifying them respectively as the Comic and Tragic Scene of Serlio's was clearly a major blunder, admittedly based on a number of misreadings. Nor can the panels, dating as in my opinion they do from the 1470s, be linked directly to Serlio's *scene* or for that matter to earlier stage

8 The *sovraporta* is listed 1582 as "lungo tre braccia o poco più et alto un braccio e mezzo incirca" (Sangiorgi 1976, *Documenti*, no. 233) that is + 1.80 × 0.88 m. Given the measurements of the panel 2.20 × 0.67 m, its identification with the *sovraporta* has been rejected. However, assuming a transcription error in the original entry "tre braccia e mezzo o poco più et alto un braccio incirca", that is 2.10 × 0,59 m, roughly the measurements of the panel and the *sovraporta*, would approximate one another.

Urbino has also been proposed as the provenance of the Baltimore panel (*Il restauro della Città Ideale* 1978; *Piero e Urbino* 1992). That claim was founded on the painting's having been acquired from the (19th century?) collection which Massarenti housed in the Palazzo Accoramboni-Rusticucci in Rome, the residence in the seventeenth century of an archbishop of Urbino. Notwithstanding the reference to "quadri riguardevoli" in the palace (Titi, *Descrizione*, 1763: 432) the evidence seems too weak to be acceptable.

The Berlin panel was bought late in the nineteenth century from a dealer in Florence. It reportedly came from a villa nearby.

Sebastiano Serlio
Tragic Scene
engraving, 17th cent.
Milan, Museo Teatrale
alla Scala

sets around 1510. Nonetheless, a bond does exist between the panels and Renaissance stage design, despite the gap of forty years or more. To build of laths, canvas and paint on a stage a never-and-nowhere grand architectural setting is not so different from designing and painting it on a panel. Both, whether in the fifteenth or in the sixteenth century, draw on the same legacy of humanist architecture. Both are intimately linked to the consistent use of perspective. Both conjure up an artificial world into which the spectator is forcefully drawn, a world beyond the reality of everyday life. They are related to one another; though far more distantly than I thought half a century ago.

EN TOYTΩI NIKA

258

Hubertus Günther

The Renaissance of Antiquity

In the retrospective observation of antiquity during the Middle Ages, Priscian's optimistic declaration about progress—*Quanto juniores, tanto perspicaciores,* in other words, "the younger, the wiser"—was transformed into the image of modern spirits akin to dwarfs on the shoulders of giants. Faith in the progressive expansion of man's knowledge and understanding was strong, but antiquity overshadowed the results. It seemed that the only wise way to display one's work was atop the commanding pedestal of the antique heritage. In many spheres of civilization, antiquity continued to show the right way: it set parameters in various sectors of technology, science, philosophy, historiography and law; it determined the language; it lived on in the institution of the Church. The awareness of this link was expressed in the pretence of the continuation of the Roman Empire in the Holy Roman Empire or in the many analogies with antiquity created by rhetoric, such as in the names of such cities as New Rome. The awareness of the link was clearly expressed in the persistence of both antique customs in ceremonies and in symbols of power, and antique forms and motifs in the figurative arts and in the architecture.

In Italy—and particularly in Rome—the awareness of antiquity as part of native heritage and tradition was more acute than elsewhere in Europe. Attesting to this are the many foundation legends involving heroic figures of antiquity, by means of which a city could claim its pedigree and noble origins. In both figurative arts and architecture, the forms and motifs of antiquity were used more frequently and more explicitly here than in the rest of Europe. The classical orders of columns continued to be applied everywhere. Single elements from antiquity were also cited as the tokens of particular requirements, such as the fragments of triumphal arches on the city gates. The great works of the so-called Florentine proto-Renaissance, with their characteristic combination of classical decorative elements and marble facings, to some extent offered a sometimes more realistic idea of the original impact of imperial-age monuments than that produced by the ruins in their present state of conservation. Furthermore, in Rome, it was possible to reutilize the remains of antique buildings not only for the realization of important monuments but also for insertion in more commonplace building fabric: workshops of a certain caliber were frequently graced with pillars integrated with fragments of ancient columns, often topped by modern imitations of Ionic capitals.

Antique statues, and even obelisks, were erected as symbols of power. The interiors of many buildings were remodeled to suit new purposes: the Pantheon and other temples, the Curia or Basilica of Junius Bassus were utilized as churches; mausoleums and triumphal arches were conserved as strongholds, and porticoes housed workshops. Certain antique public-utility structures such as the Aurelianic wall and several bridges and aqueducts continued to serve their original purposes. The exile of the papal court to Avignon and the devastating consequences of the great plague of 1348 made the Italians painfully aware of the enormous disparity between the miserable conditions of their own age and the enormous stature of the Roman Empire. At the same time, study of the rediscovered rhetoric of antiquity intensified, fueled by a growing conviction that such rediscovery was necessary. Dante, Petrarch and Boccaccio were the leading exponents of this attitude. People greatly revered their forebears for their omnipotence, their civilization, their culture and their ethical standards. This rediscovery of antiquity gave rise to "nationalist" sentiments that had barely existed before—witness Petrarch's contempt for the barbarians north of the Alps, Guido da Siena's homage to Italy as the most noble country of all, or the representation of specifically Roman heroes in place of the universal heroes of former days. Cola di Rienzo expressed this nationalist sentiment in a surprisingly direct way, advocating Rome's reinstatement to its ancient status as the center of the world and proclaiming himself tribune, conjuring up the ethical aura of the republican *condottiere* and along with it the splendor of the imperial might.

This trend continued steadily in the fifteenth century, at times gaining intensity. The Florentine chancellors Coluccio Salutati and Leonardo Bruni are an example of it. National sentiment played as much a role in the antique revival now as ever. Even political ideologies were inspired by antiquity: in Rome the link between antique revival and political ideology reach its height of expression. Conspicuous examples are the Porta Argentea, with its representations of Roman history and the imperial portraits, or several different pilgrims' guidebooks that proclaimed Rome's supremacy in their introductions, evoking the antique tradition, to

Draftsman of Giovanni Marcanova
Thriumph of a General
from Collectio Antiquitatum
by Giovanni Mascanova
1465
Modena, Biblioteca Estense
Cod. Lat. L. 5, 15 - fol. 33r.

opposite
Raphael and Giulio Romano
Apparition of the Cross
details of monuments
of ancient Rome
ca. 1520
Vatican, Sala di Costantino

strengthen the position of the papacy. And yet, such sentiments, never affected the heart of the antique revival. In the 1400s it made such a leap in magnitude that it can hardly be described as a mere intensification of the earlier phenomenon. Instead, it had reached a turning point. The movement originated in Florence, probably under Cosimo de' Medici. Then it extended to the papal court, in the period in which Eugenius IV was visiting Florence. Though the movement came to Rome from the outside, it was there where it yielded the most decisive fruits in the field of ancient studies, thanks to the proximity of the antique ruins and the extraordinarily favorable climate established there by the humanists.

Respect for the intellectual and ethical authority of the ancients was no longer enough; the hymns of admiration for its splendors were suddenly inadequate. The new generation of classical scholars cast doubt upon the cultural heritage handed down to them; they rejected it as spurious when it was not corroborated by the written sources; the new literature on Rome dismissed the legends that had grown up around the monuments. Lorenzo Valla went so far as to declare Constantine's donation a fake. Even the authenticity of established holy places began to be doubted; heated debate arose regarding the site of St. Peter's crucifixion. This subversive skepticism cast almost everything into doubt and lent itself well to the new interest in satirical expressions. Leon Battista Alberti, one of the leaders of the new classicism, played a leading role in this field as well. Antiquity itself no longer offered any certainty. Alberti boldly lashed out against the entire world of antique divinities with a sharpness of wit that (if the reader will indulge the comparison, which vividly illustrates how radical the

Agnolo Bronzino
Cosimo I Grand Duke
of Tuscany
16th cent.
Florence, Palazzo Vecchio
Studiolo of Francesco I

intellectual revolution was) to some extent rivals Jacques Offenbach's *Orphée aux enfers*. Instead of seeking to penetrate the essence and the heritage of antiquity, instead of evaluating and esteeming the value and the quality of its achievements, which had long been the established scholarly approach to the subject, students of antiquity now stressed certain fairly simple questions about the nature of antique objects and their contexts. "A mind capable of distinguishing things comes closer to the truth than a mind that aspires to the pinnacle of science"; these words, attributed to Ptolemy and inscribed on the tomb of Pope Sixtus IV, clearly define the new attitude, which is reflected above all the collections of inscriptions and the remains of antique literature, in the formidable job of collation, study of antique styles and ancient forms of writing and the study of rules of grammar and rhetoric. From the writings, the positivists culled and assembled all the information that could be derived therefrom to reconstruct ancient history and culture. They systematically compiled this vast material, as if a *traditio studii* did not exist, even though, as Guarino Guarini protested at the time, it only served to confirm what was already known.

Initially, the ancient literary sources were the main focus of attention, but interest soon broadened to include all the accomplishments of the ancient world, not only in terms of valuable artistic works, but also items of everyday use, simple objects such as measuring sticks and weights. Architecture was of particular interest; its properties and functions were closely analyzed and compared against the accounts in the written sources.

The inductive method, which was used in the new analyses, did not merely determine a new way of observing antiquity; it sparked a revolution in the sciences and broke the circle of deduction, of the logical inference of thought within a closed intellectual system. The new researchers sought to arrive at knowledge based on experiences derived from the analysis of objects, from objective experiments. The analysis of Cestius' pyramid, at the time one of the most famous monuments of antiquity, reveals the attitude of the avant-garde scholars. Cestius' pyramid had been conserved, as Flavio Biondo writes, "nearly intact," and with it the inscription on the tomb that bears the dedication to Caius Cestius in not one, but two places. However, it was barely legible because the pyramid was overgrown with plants, the roots of which had penetrated between the stones. In the fourteenth century, many—including Petrarch—generally believed the pyramid to be the tomb of Remus and, along with the other pyramid in the Vatican on the opposite side of the city, identified as Romulus' tomb, it stood as a monument commemorating the Eternal City's foundation. In around 1400, Pier Paolo Vergerio, a pupil of Petrarch, referred to the inscription as proof of the true dedication, pointing out how the vegetation made it difficult to read. Giovanni Francesco Poggio Bracciolini and many others seconded him. Poggio, who played a leading role in a systematic study of epigraphs, specifically stated his astonishment that an individual as learned as Petrarch could believe in the ancient legend, in spite of the clear testimony of the inscription. On the same occasion, made a statement of the principles behind his working method: the search for inscriptions hidden beneath the vegetation and their interpretation reveal greater prudence despite the lesser theoretical superstructure (*minore cum doctrina majorem diligentiam praebuerunt*). The words that Petrarch himself wrote in his *De sui ipsius et multorum ignorantia* find partial confirmation here: the access to truth about ancient Rome had been hindered by vegetation and brambles. In the sixteenth century, Poggio's commentary in the guidebooks to Rome was once again revised. Prompted by this error, Andrea Fulvio warned that he did not agree with the widely held opinion, but, rather, preferred the historical tradition, which had always proved to be truer. In some respects, during the Renaissance Cestius' pyramid became a monument to the foundation of the inductive method.

Since induction today forms the basis of the modern sciences, it is easy to appreciate the innovative achievements of the new studies of antiquity. Above and beyond our admiration, however, we must not lose sight of what was lost: with scientific experimentation, the set of questions concerning the higher meaning, the true substance, faded into background. The new line of research could thus seem, and in part, rightly, fragmentary, formalistic, limited and senseless, This is what Guarini criticized about Niccolò Niccoli's studies, though the latter had attracted the support of many leading figures of the new intellectual stance. Leonardo Bruni considered the new positivist studies "useless in life," as he failed to see an ethic component in them. Thus, they were sometimes overlooked, to preserve the traditional context. Studies based on the inductive method demanded a new brand of scientist, one who stepped down from his podium to gain practical experience, through work. Petrarch and Giovanni Colonna continued to meditate on the virtues of antiquity seated on the roof of the Baths of Diocletian, enjoying a broad panorama of the Roman ruins. Poggio, or in the same way Alberti, as Pius II reveals, penetrated the weeds and brambles to find the scattered remains of antiquity. Guarini mocked Niccoli for "rolling up his shirt sleeves" and clambering up crumbled arches to see what was there. But they were not content with just seeing. The new researchers counted and measured what they found. Gradually, taking measures became a

Hermannus Posthumus
Fantastic Landscape with Ruins
1538
Liechtenstein, Vaduz, The Princely Collections
Cat. no. 11

TEMPVS EDAX RE-
RVM TVQVE INVI-
DIOSA VETVSTAS
OĨA DESTRVITIS

Vincenzo Foppa
Boyhood of Cicero
ca. 1464
detached fresco
London, Wallace Collection

veritable passion. During the Renaissance, the analysis of antique measures and weights developed into a branch of study in its own right, in which little by little most European scholars of a certain rank took an interest. Nicola Cusano considered measuring equal to knowledge. For Cusano a field of knowledge became science only after the transition from a qualitative point of view to a quantitative one, after the transformation of the questions of substance into ones of appearance and function, by way of measurement. For scientists of a traditional stamp, such as John of Salisbury and once again decidedly Petrarch, the written sources established the image of antiquity. In the course of the fourteenth and fifteenth centuries, instead, the emphasis was increasingly placed on remains of ancient sculptures and buildings as historical evidence. The scientific method of formulating objective questions was not entirely unknown in the Middle Ages. The guidebooks to antique Rome and a few visitors to the city—for example, Magister Gregorius—made use of it. Before then, this way of formulating questions was not held in as much consideration as in the Renaissance. The method was not followed systematically and, since researchers were not as intensely concerned with it, it did not reach the same levels as it was to during the Renaissance. Obviously, antique inscriptions had been discovered and studied before the Renaissance, especially and increasingly in the fourteenth century; Petrarch's writings bear witness to this. A striking example is the rediscovery of the Lex Regia, the fragment of the Roman senate's decision to hand the empire over to Vespasian, and its subsequent use by Cola di Rienzo as a political document. However, it is worth repeating that during the period in question, events of this kind remained from the academic point of view at best isolated phenomena.

Nor was the concept of the inductive method completely new. It had already been developed

Jacopo de' Barbari
Portrait of Fra Luca Pacioli
with a Young Man
1495
Naples, Museo e Gallerie
Nazionali di Capodimonte
Cat. no. 67

in the early Midlle Ages, but was not practiced in university spheres. This discrepancy arose from the accepted role of the academician: his work was an intellectual expression. Work in the field was the prerogative of craftsmen, whose sphere of activity included practical experiments, even if they were not guided by scientific theory. There are examples in arms technology; surely there are others in other fields, such as the textile and dyeing industries, which were vital sectors in many towns of Tuscany, or in figurative art and architecture. The extravagant debates over the *tiburio* of Milan Cathedral illustrate the limits of practical theory as it was back then, even in the sphere of craftsmanship. However, it is not entirely a coincidence that the architecture of the Renaissance was ushered in with the solution of the technical problem posed by the Florence Cathedral dome, which Filippo Brunelleschi solved (1417), in part by taking some cues from antiquity.

In any case, most of the innovators did not occupy academic posts, but worked in more practical trades. This applies to Niccoli, Ciriaco da Ancona and Cristoforo Buondelmonte. Skilled craftsmen, artists such as Lorenzo Ghiberti, Leonardo da Vinci and many others took an interest in the sciences. Brunelleschi and Piero della Francesca made important contributions to the advancement of applied geometry and algebra. In the same context, such craftsmen now perceived the need to adopt a more scientific approach within their own professions. And even the role attributed to such professions underwent a corresponding transformation: the intellectual aspects and theoretical bases of the figurative arts and architecture were now the main focus. For the architects, the rediscovery of antiquity shifted from the imitation of antique forms in pursuit of formal rules to the analysis of structures in archaeology, which became more like the traditional sciences. Architects even turned to literary studies in order to try to understand Vitruvius' treatise on architecture, written during the Augustan age. This treatise was known throughout the Middle Ages; it was copied and sometimes approximately cited. Poggio found a new manuscript of it, the quality of which led him to believe that it was the antique original.

Architects found in Vitruvius and other writers of antiquity the grounds for raising their discipline to the rank of science. Artists with scientific proclivities and scholars of the new stamp entered into contact with one another and even struck up friendships. However, a certain distance was often maintained between scholars and the unlettered. Leonardo complained of this problem. Most of the artists pointed it out. Artists took the trouble to introduce their theoretical writings with a double-edged note stating that their ambition as artists unschooled in the field of literature was not to entertain the reader but to share objective knowledge for the use of all. This declaration, modest at first sight, within the context of scientific advancement instead proves to be pride in a new way of thinking.

The new model of science cannot be explained merely as a development in the academic sphere but rather, as a modification in the concept of what science represented, a modification that took place for the most part outside of the universities. It seems that the new inductive method, with its orientation toward such criteria as real efficacy, verifiability and interest in practical activities corresponded with the pragmatism of successful merchants, bankers and *condottieri*. The new scientists and artists interested in science received from these categories the support for realizing their ideas. Cosimo de' Medici, in this period the most powerful banker in the West, financed Niccoli and the activities undertaken in his sphere; he hired progressive artists and even saw to the education of their offspring. Federico da Montefeltro, the must successful *condottiere* of the time, left to posterity a document in which he explicitly expressed his desire to find a learned architect. Many potentates of the fifteenth century seem to have attached great importance to assembling in their courts avant-garde artists and scholars. Alfonso di Calabria had Francesco di Giorgio Martini translate Vitruvius. Pope Leo X sponsored a great collective project in which artists and scholars alike participated, aimed at stimulating the study of antiquity.

The first architectural studies of the Renaissance were undertaken by Niccoli, Brunelleschi, Alberti, and in the field of ancient Greek culture, Ciriaco da Ancona and Buondelmonte. Ciriaco and Niccoli concentrated on the analysis, measuring and graphic reproduction of existing structures. Brunelleschi seems to have sought from the very outset, both here and in painting, a set of natural rules. This is a remarkable reversal in orientation, where Niccoli had become quite the scholar and Brunelleschi a simple craftsman. Practically nothing of these early studies has survived. Just a few decades after their start, Flavio Biondo's and Alberti's studies of antique architecture reached their climax, which was determining for the entire Renaissance and, in some respects, through to the Enlightenment. Biondo wrote guidebooks to the antiquities of Rome and Italy, largely based on his own intense analyses (*Roma instaurata* and *Italia illustrata*). His working method may be described briefly as follows: Biondo gathered from all the literary sources available (essentially the same ones that are available today) information about antique structures. Then he sought to set this information in relation to the ruins that were still standing. For the most important structures, such as the Pantheon, the Colosseum and the *thermae*, he could go by the medieval tradition or at least

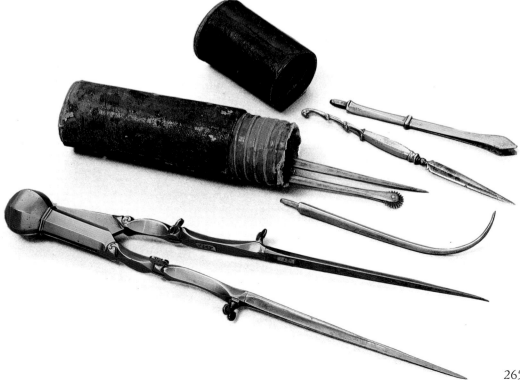

Dividing Compass
16th cent.
Florence, Istituto e Museo
della Scienza
Cat. no. 85

though he could. Where the inscriptions were known, he analyzed written accounts of them. In other cases, he went in search of clues. Not always did his experiments lead him to develop the opinions upheld by modern archaeologists, but his way of furnishing proof remained a fundamental principle in archaeology up to our own times, and often his motivations were so well chosen that they remained in currency for centuries. In the same period as Biondo, using a similar method, Poggio, too, wrote a guidebook to Rome. Biondo's work, however, is much more complete, because he sought, wherever possible, to project an image of the life that went on in the structures he examined. This aspect is crucial in his late epochal work describing Roman culture (*De Roma triumphante*).

Alberti wrote an encyclopedia of architecture, *De re aedificatoria* that appeared as a new version of Vitruvius' treatise. He carried out an analysis as in-depth as Biondo's of all antique literature as well as a study of the ruins. Vitruvius had barely lived in the imperial age; and

L'Architettura, by Leon Battista Alberti 1550 Florence edition, frontispiece Milan, Archivio Storico e Biblioteca Trivulziana

it was precisely in this period that the great monuments that aroused widespread admiration had been built. Alberti now wished to include all of antiquity. Instead of Vitruvius' crude linguistic style, he wanted to improve the literary quality following Cicero's model of rhetoric. He wish to incorporate the most disparate rules of craftsmanship into a cogent theory. He used the antique ruins to justify his correction of Vitruvius.

In the same period, when Biondo, Alberti and Poggio were at work, Giovanni Tortelli, Pope Nicholas V's librarian, wrote his encyclopedia *De orthographia*, which may be concisely described, in a certain sense, a new edition of Aulus Gellius' *Noctes atticae*. Here again, antique architecture is the topic and again the examination of it is founded on in-depth study, but this time it is more literary. This approach to architecture in the broad context of an encyclopedia fashioned after antique documents, particularly Pliny the Elder's *Natural History*, was to find wide consensus; to name just a few of the best-known authors, Ermolao Barbaro, Niccolo Perotti, Francesco Grapaldi, Raffaele Maffei and Luigi Ricchieri. Until now the researchers in this field have shown too little interest in this entire sector of literature. With Hippodamus of Miletus, the architect's status was raised to that of state theoretician. Evidence of the political importance ascribed to the architecture of antiquity may be found in a few Renaissance treatises, starting with Alberti's satirical work *Momus*; and Francesco Patrizi made particularly precise references to ancient architecture according to the literary sources in his book *De institutione reipublicae*. Giovanni Pontano and the younger Poggio Bracciolini cited it as an example in their praise of *magnificentia* as a princely virtue.

Drawing Instruments ca. 1540 Oxford, Museum of the History of Science Cat. no. 84

Nothing that could really compete with Biondo's guidebook to Rome appeared until the close of the fifteenth century, when new information about the ancient list of the "regions" of Rome was discovered. This list, at the time attributed to Publius Victor, was a decisive aid in the identification of the antique structures of Rome. Pomponius Laetus published a new edition of the list. Bernardo Rucellai, one of the sons of Alberti's Florentine patron Giovanni Rucellai, drafted a lengthy commentary to the list. Though Bernardo, as he himself states several times, had learned from Alberti about analyzing the ancient structures, he resolutely stuck to the literary sphere. His commentary was not published during the Renaissance. In 1527, Andrea Fulvio published a guide to Rome in the same style as Biondo, but updated to include all the new archaeological knowledge acquired in the meantime. In 1534, Bartolomeo Marliano continued the series of learned guidebooks to Rome, enriching it this time not only with the new knowledge, but also with definitely innovative concepts. On the whole, he respected the antique measurements. In 1542–43, Lucio Fauno and Paolo dal Rosso translated Biondo's and Fulvio's guidebooks into the vernacular. Bernardo Gamucci brought the genre down from its lofty position to the level of popular literature, often referring to Biondo. Biondo's attempt to establish links between the ruins and the literary sources continued to be the most lucid representation of ancient Rome and he was hailed as the new Romulus and Remus for having refounded lost Rome, delivering it from obscurity.

The Italian humanists made no further attempts to rework Alberti's treatise. Their successive theoretical studies of architecture focused on Vitruvius' treatise, which Giovanni Sulpicio published and distributed for the first time around the year 1486. In 1511, after many decades of preliminary study, Fra Giocondo published it with a discriminating edited text and carefully selected illustrations. The illustrations, quite unusual in humanistic literature, were intended as a reconstruction of the original form of the treatise, since Vitruvius repeatedly refers to illustrations that explain or integrate the text. It seems that Lorenzo Valla had already illustrated Vitruvius' work (1492), which, in the meantime, had also been translated. Cesare Cesariano published in 1521 in Como a translation with printed illustrations. Comparison between this work and those of Biondo, Alberti and Fra Giocondo truly sets the latter three in a positive light. In Cesariano, the accumulation of knowledge at times seems to be more for the purpose of demonstrating the author's erudition than for a good understanding of Vitruvius. Cesariano's translation fails to interpret the problematic words or passages, like most of the early translations of Vitruvius during the Renaissance, except that by Fabio Calvo, who, it seems with the help of Raphael, systematically included illustrations of antique ruins, supplemented by comments on architecture as an aid to understanding the text.

More and more architects turned out new treatises. Antonio Averlino, known as Filarete, Francesco Sforza's court architect, drafted, probably with the help of Hellenist Francesco Filelfo, a novel about the construction of an architecturally ideal city. While departing from the existing social setting, Filarete oriented himself toward Plato's *Atlantis* and attributed to the architect in the narrow sense of the word an importance similar to that of Hippodamus of Miletus, seeing in him the role of princely tutor. Filarete introduced in his description of ideal architecture fantastic medieval expressions and rules derived, from a Renaissance perspective, from the ruins and antique writings, especially from Vitruvius. Francesco di Giorgio, who, as architect of the Republic of Siena, was obliged to teach courses in architecture,

sought to realize a contemporary version of Vitruvius, similar in method—at least in the second draft—to Alberti's work, but with a greater focus on the architects and on procedure, and written in the vulgar with illustrations. Francesco di Giorgio's writings are based on indepth study of antiquity, though he was not up to the task since he lacked the necessary theoretical preparation. Baldassarre Peruzzi, a pupil of Francesco di Giorgio, envisioned writing a similar treatise though of broader scope; Sebastiano Serlio, a pupil of Peruzzi, continued in the realization of this project, but in a greatly simplified form. Already at the time, however, such pragmatic thinkers as Alvise Cornaro criticized the genre of treatises which sought to treat the entire field of architecture, since this would limit their practical effect. Serlio, himself, realizing that the most interesting parts of his project were the books on the orders of columns and on ancient structures, published them first.

Initially, there was a wide gap between the need to analyze the antique written sources and the fulfillment of this need; the architects who were concerned with such questions often lacked the theoretical background necessary for understanding the texts. The humanists, instead, were often not familiar enough with the ruins to construct an image based on the complicated information provided by Vitruvius. Alberti was an exception, as he qualified in both areas of expertise, thanks to which he was able to complete a comprehensive work on the new principles of architecture. This treatise, however, had the same flaw as Vitruvius', namely, the use of the Latin language and the lack of illustrations, which precluded its understanding by the unlettered, a limitation that Francesco di Giorgio harshly criticized. What was

left
Giuliano da Sangallo
Studies of Architectural
Elements from Ancient
Monuments
Vatican, Biblioteca Apostolica Vaticana

center
Giuliano da Sangallo
Studies of Architectural
Details and Putto
Vatican, Biblioteca Apostolica Vaticana

M ATQ3 LATINORVM MORE PERFIGVRATVM ·

Cesare Cesariano
Greek Forum and Roman
Forum
studies after Vitruvius
1521
Milan, Archivio Storico
e Biblioteca Trivulziana
Book V, LXXIIv.

needed was an artist who could combine a knowledge of the antique ruins with scholarly instruction and who was at the same time willing to convey his knowledge to all, writing in the vulgar and supplementing the text with illustrations. In this respect, Giancristoforo Romano made an important contribution in charting out the rules about orders in architectural theory. In the course of the sixteenth century many manuals on the Orders were published which progressively tended to reduce the space devoted to text and replace it with more explicit illustrations and guidelines to proportions.

However, the architects' main contribution to the study of antiquity was in the practical field: in the analysis, measurement and illustration of the architectural remains.

Of the studies from the period ending around 1470, little has come down to us; moreover, this material is quite assorted, with drawings of decorative architectural details, such as capitals or entablatures, and depictions of ruins or free reconstructions of famous monuments, such as Filarete's representations of Hadrian's Mausoleum or of stadiums and arenas, or the plans of the buildings on the Roman hills that Francesco di Giorgio drew during the papacy of Paul II. These reconstructions are largely based on the imagination, though they do not stray quite as boldly into the field of fantastic visions as some other representations of antiquity in the medieval tradition; here and there, they already take their inspiration from reality.

From about 1470 a deep change can be noted in the style of studies of antiquity. Artists of different regions made their contribution: Il Cronaca (Simone del Pollaiuolo) and Giuliano da Sangallo of Florence, Giancristoforo Romano of Rome, all three still quite young and in their learning stage, and with them the expert, Francesco di Giorgio. Pope Sixtus IV and Lorenzo il Magnifico must also have contributed to this change. The publication of Alberti's treatise on architecture, which seems to date precisely to this period, may also have provided some impetus. The new studies were characterized by fastidious measurements, precision and accuracy, down to the smallest details. Il Cronaca earned his nickname "the chronicler" for his meticulous illustrations of antique structures. Free reconstructions were no longer in tune with the positivist style of these reproductions. Francesco di Giorgio preserved a record of what was brought to light during excavations in the Basilica of Constantine. Most of these drawings are quite lacking in charm, but at the time they aroused great admiration. They represented the grounds for an objective analysis of antique architecture. They demonstrate the new "saper vedere" advocated by Leonardo. Giancristoforo's studies instead show the transition to the formulation of theories based on a comparison of the structures with the information contained in the writings of Vitruvius and Alberti.

With Bramante, such precise studies became standard in architectural procedure. His approach brought him renown as the renovator of antique architecture, an ability of which his Tempietto of S. Pietro in Montorio is an outstanding example. Strangely enough, however, no studies that may be reliably attributed to Bramante have come down to us, nor even copies, while a half-dozen separate sets of copies after Giancristoforo Romano's drawings have survived. A possible explanation for this paradox could lie in the fact that Bramante studied antiquity not so much as an end in itself, but directly in relation to his building projects. The well-known testimonies to his work would support this argument and, furthermore, it corresponds with the approach adopted during Julius II's papacy. This pope placed practical activity above intellectual study and under his aegis, humanistic literature on antiquity suffered a decline. Such important works as Raffaele Maffei's *Commentaria urbana* (1506) and Fra Giocondo's edition of Vitruvius were produced without his patronage. The guidebook to Rome dedicated to the pontiff by Francesco Albertini is further illustration of the situation: it describes modern contributions to the city's architecture, while the references to antiquity afford scant new information. When Leo X, the son of Lorenzo il Magnifico, was elected pope, the cultural climate of Rome underwent a deep change. The promotion of study was one of this pope's key objectives. He systematically continued the legendary patronage of the Medici family and intensified it in keeping with the rank and means offered by his position in the Curia. Immediately after Leo X was proclaimed pope, Andrea Fulvio dedicated a guide to antiquity to him. Giuliano da Sangallo, Lorenzo's architect, promptly presented some reproductions of antique structures, executed with unprecedented diligence. It seems that he saw these works as part of a project to reproduce with the same precision all of the ancient monuments. In any case, during this period in Rome there was intense activity, under the direction of Giuliano da Sangallo and his nephew Antonio, aimed at realizing such a collection. The results were drawn by Bernardino della Volpaia in a codex that was much larger than Serlio's book on antiquity (*Codex Coner*). The codex is ordered in a systematic way, and the drawings are uniform in style. Bernardo developed a particularly concise expressive style that came close to isometric drawing. The drawings themselves are distinguished by great precision in the representation and in the indications of measurements as well as their high artistic quality. In the decorative details, the artist shows his awareness of the theories about column orders, and in fact, it seems that in preparation for these drawings, Sangallo's circle made special studies of them. However, this collection is not limited to a retrospective look at antiquity but, like Serlio's book on antiquity, also illustrates its links with contemporary architecture. Such famous modern buildings as the Tempietto or the project for the reconstruction of St. Peter's basilica are included in the work and occasionally contemporary ideas about architectural uniformity are introduced into the representations of antiquity. When Giuliano left Rome in 1515 work on the project was interrupted. Leo X, however, had not completely lost interest in the initiative. To the contrary, it seems that his expectations had grown, and that the old conception of the work was no longer sufficient. Now thoughts turned to a new project aiming at a full-blown map of ancient Rome, reproducing all its monuments; the survey work undertaken for the project signaled remarkable advances in the field of archaeology. Such progress was made possible by the collaboration of humanists and architect in the service of the pope. In his role as *capomaestro* at St. Peter's, Raphael took note of the suggestions of the humanists Fabio Calvo and Andrea Fulvio and undertook the supervision of the new project, while Antonio da Sangallo as usual oversaw the more specifically practical tasks. During his lengthy work with the ruins, he developed such a deep knowledge of the theoretical aspects as well that even some humanists referred to his assessments. The new project strayed further from the modern construction procedures than Giuliano's and the interest in antiquity took on even greater importance. The ambition was to create a full plan of antique Rome, following Ptolemy's model. The ancient buildings were therefore to be reproduced in context, and not as architects had always shown them until then, that is,

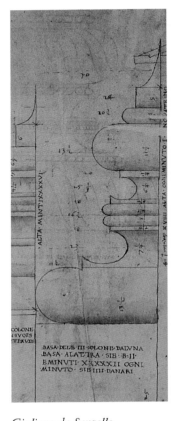

Giuliano da Sangallo
Profile of a Column Base
detail of fol. 71
Vatican, Biblioteca Apostolica Vaticana

Opus imitabile? tempus minuit destruere? prohibet aut nostram per curam.
Sed o rex excelse aperi nobis domum quam tempus non tangit.

KYMO ΔOBHI
NHФIA ωN NΥΒaωN
ΠIΣTω ΤHI ΘEAΣI

Alme sophie sapientie ue sacru in byfantio a iustiniano cesare templum maximum & emi porfireis
Serpentinis ac marmoreis columnis diuerforeq nobilui & cospicuum lapidum in figne antemio tramio
& isidoro milesio nobilibus architectore principis.

Ab eterna templi & occidua parte figura a qua primu uestibulum aeq ingressum habuisse uidetur cuius
amplitudo per latu cubit .q. 81. aleff uo cubit cxx. metita est.

CIVITASATHENA

Eadem bones
ciues cora de
coran di fino
cosuetudine
introducere a
nexis ramiliu
claug pericles
accuendo ea
pue pbabile
inftituitu fere
fu persona
intueri uelis
naglititutu
uberrima ali
menti ehonas
agericles dad
fet aq raues
inexecis dada
pereheas experit

ΔIONY
ΣIOΣ
AMM
ΩNIOY
ANAФ
ΛΥΤI
O
Σ

Giuliano da Sangallo, after
Ciriaco d'Ancona
Survey of S. Sofia in
Constantinople
Vatican, Biblioteca Apostolica
Vaticana

isolated and examined in terms of form alone. Here, the intention was to elaborate the reconstruction of the buildings; many new technical means were developed to achieve this. The methods introduced in this period remained fundamental in archaeology. Thereafter systematic excavation assumed a new priority: new measuring techniques (with the aid of the *bussola* or surveyor's graphometer for the more complex situations), new kinds of graphic expression (orthogonal projection), systematic surveying of each monument's the state of conservation, all integrated with the combined information from on-site surveys of the structures, and correlated with the ancient written sources, especially the works of Vitruvius. Systematic cross-referencing with the literary sources had a remarkable effect in enriching architectural theory, to a greater extent in sectors concerned with archaeology and less so in the area of construction work itself.

Work on the map of Rome was interrupted with the deaths of Raphael (1520) and Leo X (1521). It may have been resumed again under the second pope in the Medici line, Clement VII, who continued the work of his predecessors in such a programmatic way that the two

ROMA

Taddeo di Bartolo
Map of Rome
1406-14
Siena, Palazzo Pubblico,
Anticappella

terms of the Medici popes appear in some respects to be merged into one. The new *capimaestri* under Clement VII—Antonio da Sangallo and Baldassarre Peruzzi—made sure that the studies would be handed down to posterity by having copies made, but the plan of Rome was such a vast undertaking that it was practically impossible to complete in that period. A synergy between practice and the theory as fruitful as was created under Leo X did not occur again until Andrea Palladio, Giangiorgio Trissino and Daniele Barbaro appeared on the scene. Meanwhile, the Roman humanists, who met at the Accademia delle Virtù, drew up a sweeping program for the study of antiquity (1542), though it was of the literary conception. The analysis of the structures—to be carried out by an assistant with practical training (the young Vignola)—was only of minor interest. Pirro Ligorio, as a self-taught artist, sought to obtain a broad historical and cultural perspective of which architecture represented just one of many facets. His vision embraced sectors that until then had been the exclusive domain of academics, such as the calculation of antique scales of measurement and weight. Ligorio assembled an astonishing array of materials that continue to be a valuable source for archaeologists even today. The men of letters, however, privately criticized him because this material had been gathered indiscriminately. For them, Pirro was merely a "man of manual abilities, and no scholar." Notwithstanding the sweeping renewal under way in the Renaissance, the boundaries between theory and practice remained tightly sealed.

In a letter of 1411 sent from Rome to the Byzantine emperor, Manuel Chrysolaras describes how the city's monuments stimulated his imagination of antiquity: "In the remains of these statues and columns, of these funerary monuments and buildings, you could recognize [all the main traits of this city]: their wealth of gold and creative power, their artistic sense, as well as their greatness and majesty, their sensibility for lofty things and their love of beauty, their lavishness and their luxury. Beyond this is added their fear of God, their generosity, their love of opulence, their political insight and their victories, all their wealth and their dominion over peoples, the esteem they enjoy and their military exploits." Brunelleschi, too, must have developed through his studies a personal image of the city during the period before its decline. The images that had been made in that period corresponded only minimally to the picture presented by the new archaeologists; they were closer to those paintings or scenic views typical of the Renaissance that sought to reproduce the ancient atmosphere by inserting imposing monuments—imaginary or real (such as the Colosseum, Pantheon, or Trajan's Column)—among residential buildings more or less representative of the period, set around spacious piazzas infused with an aura of hushed dignity, without signs of human life; as early as the fourteenth century, the visual representations of townscapes were a far cry from the "smoky, rich, noisy Rome" (Horace) described by many ancient writers. During the Renaissance there was little interest in the urban fabric of ancient Rome. The maps of ancient Rome by Fabio Calvo (1527 and 1553) and Pirro Ligorio (1561) are little more than "compendiums" of monuments. In Ligorio's map, the open space between monuments often simply follow the medieval streets flanked by houses. When by way of exception consideration was given to antique roads, reference was made to Hippodamus' model of a regular grid-plan. This is

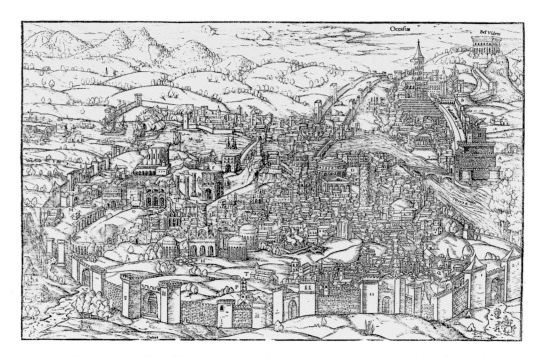

Sebastiano Münster
Rome at the End of the
15th Century
engraving from the
Cosmographiae universalis
1550
Milan, Civica Raccolta Stampe
Achille Bertarelli

what Andrea Fulvio did within the context of a tribute to the renewal of the district between Via di Ripetta and Via del Corso started by the Medici popes. Ancient accounts that mention the narrow alleyways of Rome, the frequent fires, the constant danger of collapsing buildings, etc. were already available in that period, but they were not given consideration as they did not correspond to the majestic vision of the ancient empire which was the main focus of interest in the rediscovery of antiquity. Only by way of exception did some streets attract interest, such as the major arteries leading out of the city, the Via Sacra or the route along which triumphal processions passed. However, the route imagined for the Via Trionfale was slightly different from the idea that modern archaeologists now have; it was assumed to be similar to the route that the popes followed during the "Possesso" procession that traveled from the Vatican to the Lateran palace after the coronation. The squares were also rarely taken into consideration. Few had survived and they were little known. Pirro Ligorio, Sallustio Peruzzi and Etienne Dupérac were the first to present differentiated reconstructions of the Roman Forum, but this only served to confirm in general the ideas about ancient Rome, imagined as an incoherent complex of monumental structures.

It was probably no accident that Manuel Chrysolaras began his treatise on ancient Rome with a discussion on the funerary monuments. The triumphal arches, the commemorative columns and the mausoleums had just a minor practical purpose, but nevertheless they fulfilled, as Alberti states, a key function as a stimulus to imitation of the great models. The memorial monuments were often easy to identify thanks to their inscriptions. The reliefs on the trium-

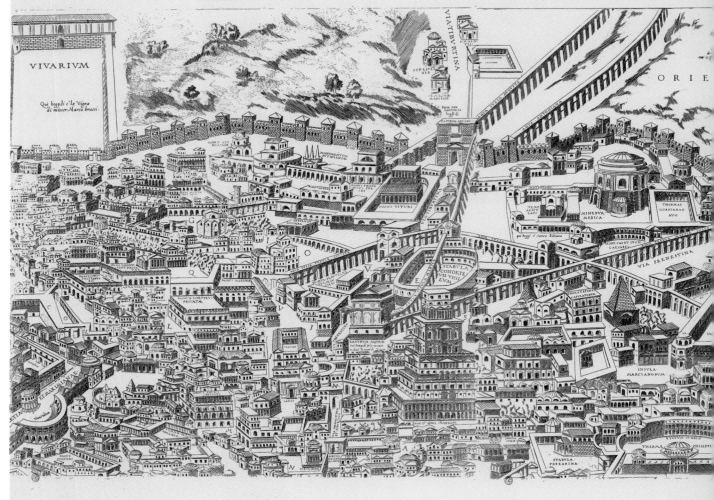

VIVARIVM

Qui beggli è la Vigna
di misser Marco brace.

VIATIBVRTINA

ORIE

Pirro Ligorio
Map of Rome
details
1552
Milan, Civica Raccolta Stampe
Achille Bertarelli

phal arches and the commemorative columns had already given Cola di Rienzo a clear idea of life in antiquity. Manuel Chrysolaras found them even more instructive than the literary sources. Thanks to such sculptures and the written information, knowledge about the ancient military organization was particularly well-developed. This provided motivation—and not only to the *condottieri*—for fostering the study of antiquity. Triumphal processions were imitated for public displays of all kinds, even those held for peaceful reasons, such as the Possesso. The staging of "triumphs" of this kind was one of the tasks of Renaissance architects. The most imposing and opulent structures of antiquity known in the Renaissance were those serving the amusement of the people: theaters, amphitheaters, arenas, stadiums, baths. Their size exceeded that of any building erected during the Renaissance. Accounts of the facilities and the running costs of these structures seem fabulous even today. What was farthest-removed from the Renaissance reality was the fact that all these structures were merely for amusement, while the greatest buildings of the Renaissance, like those of the Middle Ages— the churches, the noble residences and city government structures—represented the driving social forces. This difference had already been pointed out in the fifteenth century.

Information about classical theater handed down through to the Middle Ages appears to have been rather vague and distorted, almost abstruse. The monk St. Gall believed that the public watched the performances of the tragedies or comedies seated in a dark place in the middle of the theater. The illustrations of theaters in late medieval manuscripts of the Roman playwright Terence's work correspond to this vision. Renaissance men of letters were particularly interested in theater from the very outset. Thus, it was already possible for Biondo and Alberti to develop precise ideas about the exteriors of theaters and other spaces for performances or gladiatorial contests, about the function of their constituent parts and how the shows were carried out, taking their reference from Vitruvius, historical accounts and from the ruins themselves. Since the theaters of Rome were heavily damaged or destroyed, the Colosseum was often taken as a prototype for the entire genre of structures for performances

274

or gladiatorial contests. Francesco di Giorgio later reproduced the Ferento theater; Giuliano da Sangallo saw the well-conserved theater in Orange, France; Giancristoforo Romano must have visited the Roman amphitheater on Mt. Zaro in Pula, which remained almost intact until the seventeenth century, though none of his studies of it have come down to us. During work preparatory to making the plan of Rome for Leo X, Antonio da Sangallo and Baldassarre Peruzzi made a very precise analysis the Theater of Marcellus.

The *thermae* or baths were a slightly different matter. The building structures of the two main thermal complexes (of Caracalla and Diocletian) were in large part conserved and the written sources, especially the *Historia augusta*, already had provided Biondi with many clues about their public functioning. However, the function of the many individual parts of the vast bath structure remained a distinctly open question. The ideas proposed, starting with Alberti stemmed from the ethical standards of the Renaissance: Biondo and his numerous followers criticized the fact that structures as imposing as the baths could have served a function as trivial as that of bathing. From the Renaissance point of view, this was in stark contrast with the decoration. On the other hand, it was precisely these structures, with their extraordinary amplitude and opulence, that showed all of the splendor of ancient Rome. This gave rise to an important contradiction in the eyes of the intellectuals. Alberti and his many disciples solved the dilemma with the theory that using the bath complexes was actually tied to loftier activities from the ethical point of view; curative therapies and gymnastics ensured physical well-being, while for mental well-being, there were philosophical conversations, libraries, museums, places of worship. Even considering this purpose, the large main spaces of the baths seemed rather wasted; thus, it was believed that they were used as public performance sites. For the reconstruction of these functions, the evidence found was more or less indirect. This reasoning seems far-fetched if seen within the context of the debate in that period, but it led the assessment of the baths in such a positive direction that it is still valid today in archaeology. Obviously, today their origin is barely discussed any more.

Many temples were known during the Renaissance, but the ideas then held about the usual appearance of an ancient Roman temple were far from present-day ones. Vitruvius describes in detail various types of temples. He discusses different kinds of plan, mainly rectangular. Overall, he defines temples as structures with a cell, usually surrounded on all sides by porticoes. His focus is on these porticoes. Starting with Palladio, archaeologists assumed that Roman temples were usually rectangular in plan with a porticoed entrance.

Until the High Renaissance, however, no temple of this sort had been found in Rome. It was hard to recognize remains of temples in the groups of columns in the Forum or in the Theater of Marcellus. The Forum column groups were also believed to be the remains of the bridge that Caligula was said to have built between the Campidoglio and the Palatine. The three republican temples at the Forum Holitorium, reconstructed during the preliminary studies for Pope Leo X's map of Rome, had been successively built over beyond recognition. The surviving Imperial Fora were also considered to be palaces, like what is known as Caracalla's Temple of Serapis at the Quirinal, the imposing ruins of which were still standing. Well-conserved temples like that of Minerva in Nerva's Forum and of Antoninus Pius were dismissed as "loggias," while loggias like the Portico of Octavia were often considered temples from the Middle Ages through the entire sixteenth century. Only a few rectangular-plan temples were known, and most of them lacked a peristyle. Only two great examples of this kind of temple were known during the Renaissance: the present-day Temple of Venus and Rome behind S. Francesca Romana, often identified back then as the Temple of Sol and Luna, or in any case as a temple dedicated to two divinities. Impressive remains of the double cella of this temple were still standing, while not even a trace of its antique peristyle was still recognizable. The other temple of this type known was the present-day Basilica of Constantine, until well into the nineteenth century usually identified as the Templum Pacis or Temple of Peace, which Vespasian had erected after the conquest of Jerusalem, according to Pliny the "most beautiful work the world has ever seen." Reconstructions of both, up to and including Palladio's, lacked the peristyle and at most had the portico before the entrance.

Most of the structures believed to be temples had circular plans, such as the Pantheon, which during the Renaissance was better-known than any other antique construction, S. Costanza ("Temple of Bacchus"), the imperial mausoleums in old St. Peter's ("Temple of Apollo") and other mausoleums (the "Tempio della Dea Tosse," the "Temple of Fortune," in Ostia, etc.), S. Stefano Rotondo ("Temple of the Faun"), the late antique Pavilion in the Licinian garden (see below), and other circular-plan structures that in the meantime had been set in relation to the baths and the parks; outside Rome, the baptistery of Florence Cathedral in particular was long often considered to be the Temple of Mars.

Il Cronaca
Circular Temple and
Reconstruction of the Baths
of Diocletian
*Florence, Uffizi, Gabinetto
Disegni e Stampe*

Francesco di Giorgio Martini
Plan and Elevation of the
Basilica of Constantine
Turin, Biblioteca Reale
Codex Saluzziano 148, fol. 76

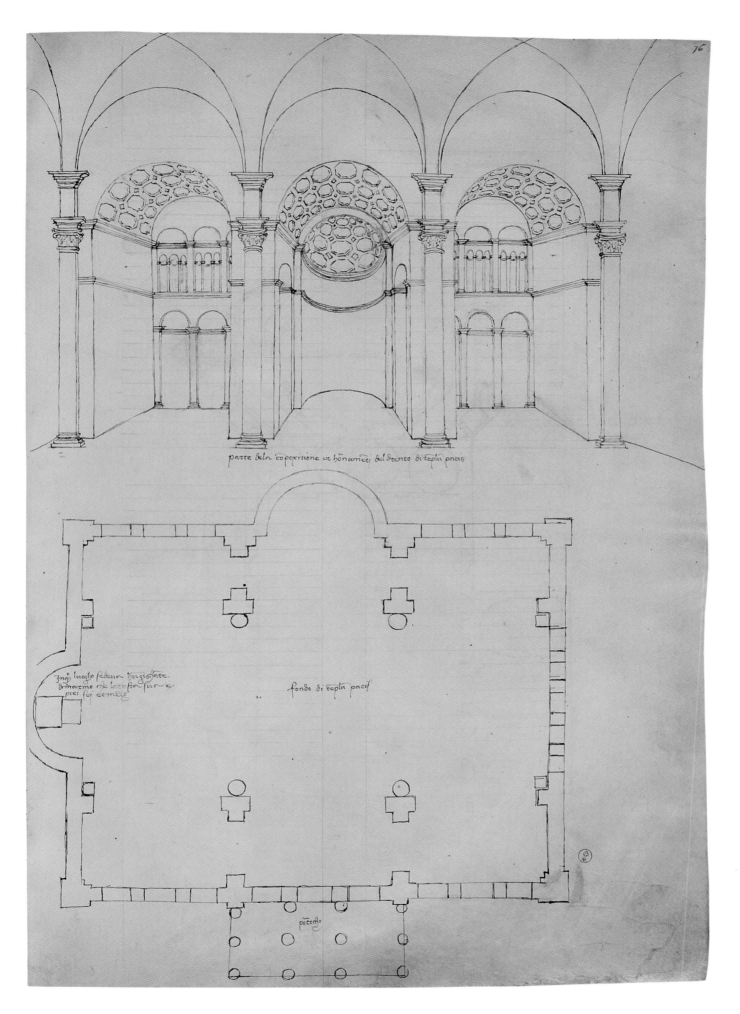

parte dela copoxitione et hõnameti del dento di teplu pacis

Jngni luogho federno Jngioflate
dimoreno iñfa latefta fuo e
piei foi dembig

fondo di teplu pacis

poterno

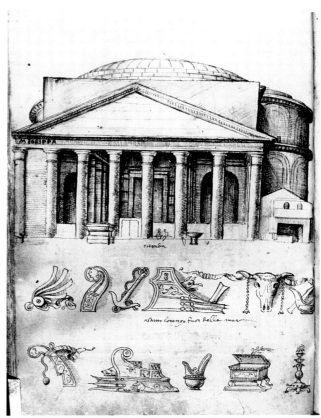

Domenico Ghirlandaio
Drawing of the Pantheon
with Decorative Details
*El Escorial (Madrid),
Real Monasterio*

The Pantheon, Rome

Until the High Renaissance, Roman temples were often associated with central-plan structures. This may be seen in the representations of antique scenes in paintings, descriptions of fantastic buildings and in other forms used to express the ideal of the time. Of this, evidence may be found in work in the archaeological field. The *Codex Coner* shows many antique central-plan structures, which Giuliano da Sangallo believed to be temples, but there are no rectangular-plan temples with peristyle; in their place, the so-called Templum Pacis and Temple of Sol and Luna are shown, both without peristyle, the main facade of what is today known as the Temple of Serapis at the Quirinal (believed to be the Palace of Maecenas),

just the rear wall of the Forum of Augustus (believed the Palace of Nerva); two of the groups of columns mentioned above—known somewhat vaguely as the "three columns"—were included in the section about single columns and obelisks. A similar array may be found in other drawings of the same period, for example those by Raniero Nerucci. In the manuscripts of Buondelmonte's description of the island of Delos and in the map of ancient Nola, published by Ambrogio Leoni in 1514, all the temples are depicted with a circular plan. In 1536, Johann Fichard summed up archaeological knowledge about antique temples with these words: "Throughout the city there are countless temples and holy places. Those that have survived since antiquity have a single basic form. In fact, they are usually round (although some were square)..."

Two small temples with galleries all round the exterior attracted particular notice: the round peripteral temples on the Roman side of the Tiber and in Tivoli, often believed to be holy sites dedicated to the goddess Vesta. The presumed Templum Pacis and many other examples (such as the temples presumed to be of Sol and Luna and of Bacchus) instead seemed to demonstrate that the Romans preferred to keep the decoration of the exteriors of their structures to a minimum, reserving the rich ornamentation to the interiors, as with large monuments such as the Basilica of Constantine. Even the outside of the Pantheon is essentially undecorated; only the entrance has a portico. The rich decoration of the interior corresponded to the idea that the ancient religious rituals were performed inside. Vitruvius barely touches on the subject of the interior space; whoever wished to formulate ideas about it had to make his own enquiry. It is likely that Alberti did this to confirm his notions on temple interiors: for the round temples, he probably referred to the Pantheon and the mausoleums believed to be temples, and for the rectangular-plan temples, to the two famous models, from them deducing that: antique holy buildings did not have, despite the Church of Constantine, the form of basilicas. They were topped by a vault, as all the examples mentioned show. For the rest, two general possibilities for the layout of the interior emerged: either only niches or exedra were contiguous with the main space (as in the mausoleums believed to be temples and in the double temple behind S. Francesca Romana), or separate secondary spaces and/or chapels adjoined the main space (as in the Pantheon and the presumed Temple of Peace). In the rectangular-plan temples, Vitruvius distinguished two kinds of interiors: the first is the one typical of the classical temple, which evolved, according to Vitruvius, in Greece.

The Pantheon, Rome
interior

About this type, Vitruvius says no more. It was not subdivided into rooms and had at most, as in the double temple behind S. Francesca Romana, niches along the walls. The other type is that of the Etruscan temple. Here, according to Vitruvius, there were separate rooms to the sides which, in the interpretation given to Vitruvius' texts during that period, were essentially like those of the presumed Templum Pacis. From this point of view, Alberti could perfectly match his findings with Vitruvius' affirmations.

It was probably not until the preparatory work for Leo X's plan of Rome was undertaken that ideas about ancient temples began to change, culminating with Palladio's vision.

During the Renaissance it was only possible to get very vague ideas about the exteriors of antique houses. Houses lined up in rows, like those still present in Ostia or Pompeii, were not at all known. The ruins known with certainty at the time to be the ruins of palaces did not suggest an image of everyday life. The oversized, spacious, intricate remains of the Palatine are still unclear, even after excavation. They were never analyzed really in depth until the High Renaissance. The same thing happened with the ruins on the Pincio, which back then were still extensive and were believed to be part of the Palace of Augustus. The form of the Sessorian Palace, in which the church of S. Croce was erected, is still today very difficult to make out. Francesco di Giorgio's theoretical reconstruction of it merely goes to

show that it took a free imagination to arrive at an idea of the buildings, without drawing conclusions from study of the existing ruins. Only a few studies of the ancient villas outside Rome have come down to us, and not even a building as famous as Hadrian's Villa in Tivoli was held in much consideration; what little has come down to us from the period before Ligorio was hardly fit to evoke an overall image of a villa. Three well-conserved Roman ruins of impressive size were often considered palaces; as mentioned earlier, until the High Renaissance, the so-called Forum of Augustus was at times considered an emperor's palace and the so-called Temple of Serapis at the Quirinal, which in the meantime had deteriorated considerably, was seen as the Palace of Maecenas or another great patron. Prominent humanists considered the so-called Baths of Constantine, which back then were well-conserved, a house of the *gens* Cornelii. As different as these three structures are from one another, they share their formidable size and rich exterior decoration. They show how the Renaissance imagined the luxurious homes of important Roman personalities.

In ancient literature, there is frequent mention of homes and villas, parts of them and sometimes even entire complexes. From this, it may be inferred once again that the ancient Romans could afford a luxury that far exceeded Renaissance means. Some houses, such as Nero's Domus Aurea, stretched over vast territories. Martial and Horace literally praised to the skies the palaces of Augustus and Maecenas, describing them as reaching the clouds. In these texts, reference is made to ample porticoes and tympanums, spacious halls, baths with every comfort and an extraordinary opulence in the furnishing and fixtures. There is also information about household functions, and one may discover that all this luxury did not serve for private enjoyment but found justification in public representation since high-ranking officials tended to

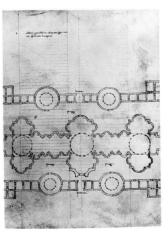

some of their business in their homes, and this fact heightened Renaissance society's esteem of their forbears. But not even the literature gives us even a somewhat coherent idea of the typical layout of the houses. It hardly tells us anything about the external appearance. As far as private homes are concerned, Vitruvius' detailed treatise must have represented during the Renaissance an impenetrable jungle of technical expressions that were ambiguous or difficult to grasp, especially in light of all the different interpretations that were made of it in this period. Biondo offered a brief but credible description of the ancient home in his treatise on Roman society, according to which, the home was a cubic unit with a central courtyard surrounded by columned arcades. He reached this conclusion starting from the idea that the classical layout of the house was handed down from antiquity to the Renaissance, through the Middle Ages, like most types of functional constructions, city walls, bridges, etc. To tell the truth, this kind of house was also discovered in the so-called Palace of Maecenas. In his treatise on architecture, Alberti offers a detailed description of the ancient home and its functions. He seeks to take into consideration as many variants as possible. But he must have had in mind just two basic types: one with a central courtyard already described by Biondo and a second type with an axial layout, clearly similar to the imperial baths. It seems that he referred to the house presumed to be of the Cornelii family, today known as the Baths of Constantine.

A school of thought crystallized around Biondo's reconstruction, whose followers included Antonio da Sangallo and his circle. A similar interpretation of Vitruvius' concepts, as Antonio's studies show, in any case did not bar a completely different reconstruction of the layout, for example, similar to that of a Venetian palace. Fra Giocondo, in his edition on Vitruvius of 1511, presented two variations of the plan of the antique home. One essentially follows

Hadrian's Villa, Tivoli

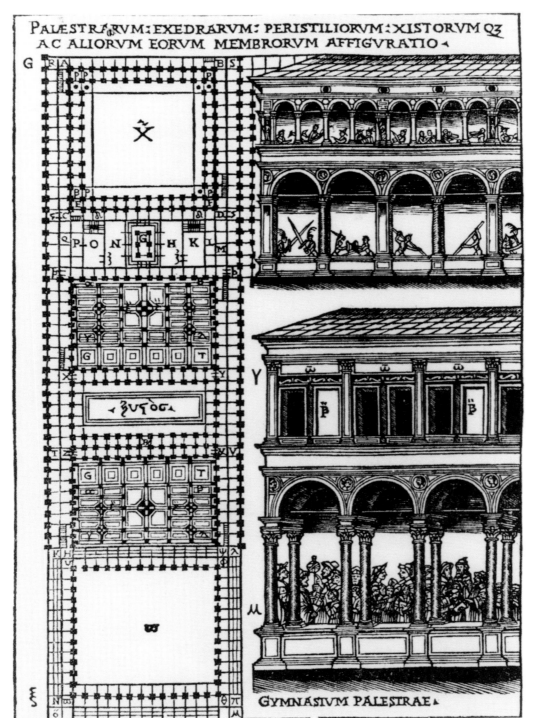

GYMNÁSIVM PÁLESTRAE·

Francesco di Giorgio Martini
"chasa sichondo el modo
grecho"
Turin, Biblioteca Reale
Codex Saluzziano 148, *fol.*
24r.

Cesare Cesariano
Reconstruction of Ancient
Buildings
after Vitruvius
1521
Milan, Archivio Storico
e Biblioteca Trivulziana
Book V, LXXIIv.

the model offered by Biondo. The other has the main rooms succeeding each other along an axis. The basic lines of the second variation are still followed by modern archaeology and with little modification seem to be in conformity with the findings of excavations. Vitruvius was not Fra Giocondo's only reference. It can be demonstrated that all things considered, he merely transposed to a graphic representation the old literary scheme that called for a succession of rooms one in back of the other. He based himself concretely on the description of the ancient home developed by Niccolò Perotti, linking Vitruvius' confused indications with Pliny the Younger's clear description of the Villa Laurentina. The particular merit of this reconstruction, and the one that determined its success, lay in the fact that it could be supported even with a completely contrary interpretation of Vitruvius' concepts. This may already be seen in Cesariano's edition of Vitruvius of 1521. Thus, rhetorical *topoi* could at times be useful to fill the gaps in knowledge of antique architecture, when there were no physical remains and the written sources did not provide clear information.

Shortly after the mid-sixteenth century Pirro Ligorio introduced the findings of excavations into the debate about the form of ancient housing. What he later presented as a reconstruction, however, seems instead the result of an architectural notion of his own time.

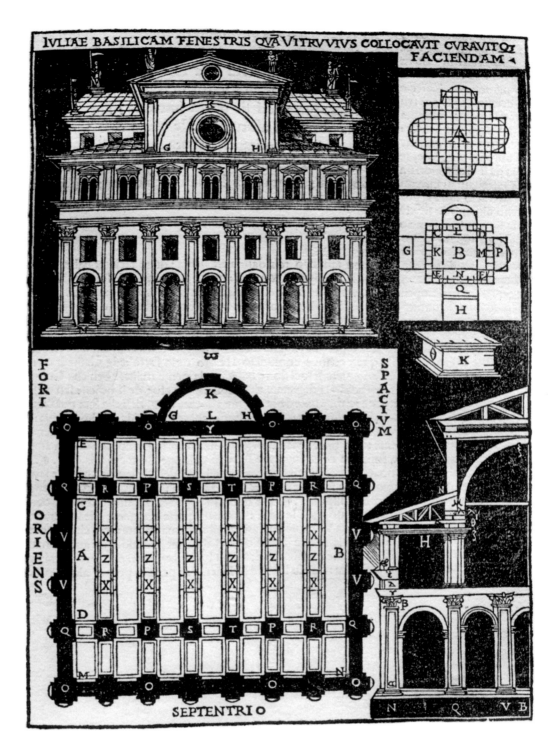

Cesare Cesariano
Prospect and Plan of
a Basilica after Vitruvius
1521
Milan, Archivio Storico
e Biblioteca Trivulziana

The Renaissance did not produce a history of ancient architecture. However, there were certain ideas about how construction methods evolved. In Alberti's opinion, architecture first appeared in the East. There, the rich and enormously powerful princes vied with one another, erecting buildings of vast dimensions. The Greeks had lesser means at hand and could therefore afford only more modest works. However, their intellectual capacity helped them to offset their lack of means. They were the ones who developed the artistic canons. Later, the ancient Romans were the only ones able to combine great means with artistic skill. Not even this crude line of development should be interpreted as a coherent historical scheme; it served above all to establish the peak of architectural accomplishment in Rome. In light of this, Alberti hastened to defend Roman imperial-age architecture against Biondo's and other historian's criticisms of its excessive opulence: "Under these circumstances they successfully combined the princely wealth with the ancient parsimony in such a way as not to sacrifice either parsimony to utility or function to richness." Obviously, this is more an ethical postulate than the result of an historical analysis. In his treatise on the thermal complexes, Alberti shows how far back in history he intended to project his postulate; after all, even he could hardly have failed to notice the inconsistencies of his evolutionary scheme.

287

It was known that the ancient Greeks had constructed colossal wonders such as the Temple of Diana at Ephesus and other such works.

Starting with Alberti, the pyramids at Giza were held up as an example of the early architecture of the Orient. They had remained famous throughout time. In the Middle Ages they were believed to be the grain deposits that Joseph had built as a precaution against years of poor harvests. During the fifteenth century, the idea that they had instead been conceived as commemorative monuments rapidly took hold. Initially, it was believed that they served no other function. It was not until the sixteenth century that the funerary chambers inside them were discovered. Pliny felt that the Egyptian pyramids were a "useless and foolish display of wealth," a view often repeated during the Renaissance. Alberti refers to the pyramids

Cesare Cesariano
Reconstruction of the Port and Mausoleum of Halicarnassus, with the "Fons Salmacidis"
1521
Milan, Archivio Storico e Biblioteca Trivulziana
Book III, fol. XLVIII

as an extreme example of megalomania and hunger for glory. Serlio describes them as useless, deleterious, a waste, however magnificent.

During the Renaissance, knowledge of Greek architecture was nearly exclusively based on the written sources, once again Vitruvius in particular. Vitruvius also taught that it was the Greeks who developed the artistic canons of architecture. Where the written sources provided detailed enough descriptions, reconstructions were attempted, following the indications, such as the Mausoleum of Halicarnassus and the Temple of Diana at Ephesus. It was not possible to identify the work of Greek architects in Rome mentioned by the sources; nor did they offer a complete picture of Greek architecture. Starting with the antique *gymnasium*, which seems to have been recreated in the University of Bologna, in 1563 Pompilio Amaseo sought to produce a compendium of Greek architecture. Here again, the Greeks figure as the inventors of fine architecture, but what they accomplished is not diminished by comparisons with Roman monuments. Instead, Amaseo found a Greek setting for what was known about types of Roman buildings. The information regarding the remains of Greek architecture still standing continued to be, despite the fundamental historical importance attributed them, incredibly vague, even if these remains were sited in Italy. Not even Paestum was taken into consideration. The Greek works in Rome were still not identified as Greek; indeed, Greece itself was increasingly overlooked.

At the start of the Renaissance, Cristoforo Buondelmonte and Ciriaco da Ancona copied Greek works and some artists, such as Michelozzo, Filarete and Giancristoforo Romano traveled to the East. Urbano Bolzanio, tutor of the young Giovanni de' Medici, the future Pope Leo X, also visited Greece. His account of the ancient structures of Athens bears witness to a loss, rather than an enrichment, of knowledge; he considered the Parthenon an "antique temple of the Romans," even though Ciriaco had linked it to the Athenian sculptor Phidias. In Book III of his treatise, devoted to works of antiquity, Sebastiano Serlio refers

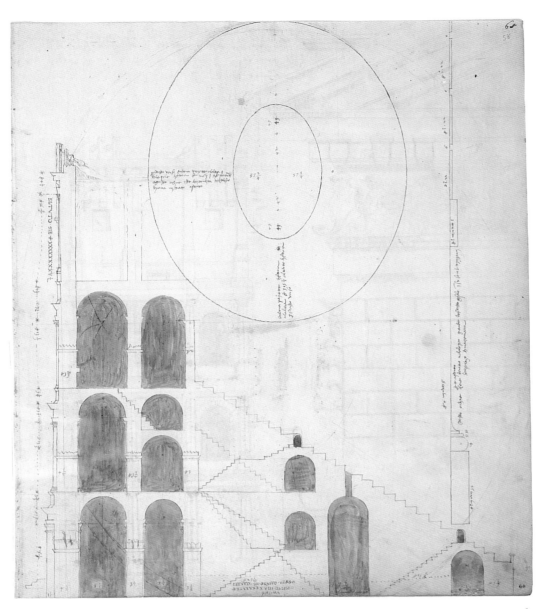

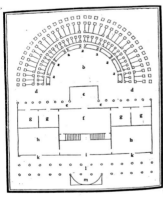

to only two works that he does not link to the Roman cultural setting: the Great Pyramid of Cheops and a building in Athens—not the Parthenon or the Theseion Ephaisteion, which has come down to us today more intact than most Roman temples, but the ruins of a structure reportedly having 100 columns inscribed on a square base, about which he had no direct knowledge, but only hearsay. He comments that the ancient Greeks had, according to Vitruvius, invented fine architecture, but that almost all of it had been destroyed. The reader thus must settle, Serlio continues, for the fantastic reconstructions of an incomprehensible forest of columns. While it is not clear from Serlio's woodcuts, they represent, as the present writer has determined from a number of studies, the Olympieion (the Temple of Zeus), founded by the tyrant Pisistratus, a poor example of the classical architecture of the Greeks. Pisistratus imitated, as can be read in the guide to Greece by Kirsten-Kraiker, the megalomania of the princes of the ancient Orient. But he did not succeed in constructing more than the foundations of the temple, because, Kirsten-Kraiker continue, the small city-states of Greece lacked the means for such costly monuments. Most of the Olympieion, they state, was realized under Emperor Hadrian.

On the other hand and despite the scarcity of evidence, the Etruscans, as the progenitors of the Tuscans, received such attention that some scholars of local history, such as Annio da Viterbo, resorted to invention and falsification in order to fill the gaps left by the tradition lore about this people's culture. The Etruscans were attributed with the birth of the first autonomous Italian culture. In what span of time this culture developed was a controversial issue; however, it must have been in a very remote time, and some actually believed it preceded Greek civilization. Notwithstanding the particular interest, not much was learned about Etruscan architecture. It seems to have remained quite simple, like everything about the life of the Etruscans. According to the information provided by Vitruvius, the Etruscans knew only one type of temple: it was still characterized by the use of wood externally. Alberti could not find any trace of the crude decorations of the Etruscans described by Vitruvius, but he believed he had recognized some of their fortifications; their walls were distinguished by the use of enormous, unhewn masses. Later scholars attributed to the Etruscans works that met this description, built with economical materials and having simple forms. The only truly famous Etruscan work that had survived was the tomb of Porsenna, made, according to Vitruvius, of massive slabs and pyramidal blocks arranged one on top of the other in a primitive way, similar to the early architecture of the Orient, also considered primitive at the time. Pliny's opinion of Porsenna's tomb was no better than the one he had pronounced on the Egyptian pyramids: the tomb bore witness to the wild insanity (*vesana dementia*) of squandering the state finances for such a huge work of no utility. Nevertheless, during the Renaissance Porsenna's tomb was more popular than the pyramids, as it belonged to the national heritage. It seems that the Romans were oriented, at first, toward Etruscan architecture; the Temple of Jupiter on the Capitoline must have copied elements of the Etruscan temple. Besides, until the high Renaissance, there was little information available about the Roman architecture of the late imperial period that was more explicit than the knowledge of Etruscan architecture. Scholars might have imagined that it was simple, matched to the austere and simple lifestyle that many writers of antiquity celebrated after the decline, comparing it with the opulence of the late period in terms of the architecture as well. An example are the descriptions of the baths of the republican period, which suggest, among other things, that marble did not become fashionable as a building material until the late republican age. Biondo points out with great accuracy the individual elements adopted in Roman architecture according to the ancient sources when prosperity became widespread.

When the Romans became a world power, starting with the great rulers of the late republican age, architecture flourished; proof of this may be found in the accounts of the enormous theater with park, porticoes and annex buildings that Pompey had built, or in the incredible magnificence shown by Marcus Scaurus in a theatrical performance. The Romans now flaunted their much-admired opulence. At the same time, they mastered the artistic skills of the Greeks. The fact that the forms of the Roman constructions derived for the most part from the Greeks was deduced mainly from Vitruvius' writings and later from other sources: Plutarch, for example, reports that Pompey had a sketch made of the theater in Mytilene in order to copy it, in grander scale, however.

Suetonius reports, as quoted in Biondo, that Augustus splendidly renewed the city using marble, while until then it was made only of brick. Many great writers, such as Horace, Virgil and Ovid demonstrated the high level reached by Roman civilization under Augustus. The peak of architectural achievement in this period seemed to be expressed by the Pantheon, commonly believed the work of Agrippa, Augustus' son-in-law, because of the inscription on the porch cornice and literary testimony. Otherwise, it was difficult to get a concrete idea of the period of the maximum splendor. Petrarch complained, "Where is the Theater of Marcellus? Where are the many buildings realized by such famous artists under that emperor [Augustus] in many places of Rome, after such great effort and at such great expense? Look in the books and you will find their names. But if you look for them today in Rome, you will find none of this, or you will find scant remains of such imposing buildings." Poggio and Biondo set out immediately in search of these buildings. Poggio perceived in the ruins over which rose the Savelli residence—in Biondo's eyes, strangely still an *atrium regium*—a theater that he identified as the one Augustus had dedicated to his nephew Marcellus. This idea met with widespread agreement. Biondo identified the basilica founded by Augustus for his nephews Gaius and Lucius, as the magnificent Decagon in the Licinian gardens, greatly admired during the Renaissance as the finest monument in Rome after the Pantheon. This identification, despite the difference in the type of building, was considered very convincing. Later a basilica was reconstructed adjacent to the central-plan building. With the aim of demonstrating the splendor of Augustus' age through its buildings, Biondo associated the palace of the great patron of Augustinian poets, Maecenas, with the ruins at the Quirinal, presently known as Caracalla's Temple of Serapis, which back then must have appeared monumental like few other ancient buildings. This identification clearly conflicted with Publius Victor's list of "regions" and therefore met with other scholars' criticism. But it satisfied so fully the desire to have an image of the period of Roman splendor that it held sway in tradition as long as the ruins at the Quirinal remained standing. Only Ligorio and Palladio identified Augustus' forum as we do today; scholars had learned from the written sources that it was adjoining the Roman Forum and no remains could be seen there any longer. Furthermore, the search for it does not seem to have roused much interest, as in consideration of the ancient residential district, Augustus must have settled for a smaller construction than planned.

The evolution of architecture during the Imperial Age could have already been seen during the Middle Ages, in particular starting in the mid-fifteenth century: there were the examples of Nero's Domus Aurea, Vespasian's Templum Pacis, the Colosseum, the Arch of Titus,

Nerva's and Trajan's Fora, Hadrian's Mausoleum (then much better conserved than it is today), the Temple of Antoninus Pius and his commemorative column (the latter is today attributed to Marcus Aurelius), Septimius Severus' Triumphal Arch, the Baths of Caracalla and of Diocletian, the Aurelianic wall, the Arch of Constantine, the Christian basilicas of Constantine and the Lateran baptistery, and so forth. A list of this sort was not compiled during that period. To the contrary, opinions about the history of architecture in the imperial age varied widely; in fact, there were two opposite views.

One position was characterized by the common idea that with the decline of the republic, morals gradually became corrupted and indeed the entire civilization progressively degenerated. This decadence was already criticized by many writers of antiquity. It seemed in the end to be the cause of the decline of Rome and its conquest by the Barbarians. Serlio and Palladio thus wished to establish a decadence in the artistic quality of the architecture in spite of the great magnificence of the imperial age.

On the other hand, Rome did not reach the peak of its power and splendor until the period in which the great moral ideals gave way to the appetite for opulence. Nero represented a bad example of the dichotomy of this evolution. Even Alberti criticized his buildings, describing them as "hypertrophic." Platina quotes Tacitus, that is, that the emperor set the torch to Rome in order to renew it, conferring greater splendor on the city, and he associates the notorious vices of this era with its exaggerated opulence, including its magnificent architecture. The theory of decadence was subject to various opinions: some felt that the flourishing of culture lasted until power reached its peak, that is, up until the adoptive emperors. Decadence set in only at that point. The subsequent decline of the figurative arts had to be proved by comparing the sculpture of Trajan's or Antoninus Pius' time with similar works of Diocletian's or Constantine's, which were ridiculous. However, the architecture did not suffer the decline of the figurative arts, as the Baths of Diocletian or the Arch of Constantine show. To the eyes of Raphael or Antonio da Sangallo, Roman architecture maintained its old qualities and followed the classical canons, that is those expressed by Vitruvius, through to the period of the very last, powerful emperors.

The theory of the constancy of ancient architecture's quality was not suited to a stylistic history similar to today's. As long as the Pantheon, Caracalla's Temple of Serapis and the late antique pavilion in the Licinian gardens were all considered works of the Augustan age while Augustus' Forum was instead attributed to Nerva or Trajan, it was impossible to perceive a stylistic evolution in architecture. In the endeavors to classify the ruins, questions of style played a very minor role. Given that the so-called Templum Pacis or the imperial *thermae* had been governed by the classical canons, even though their layout corresponds only margi-

nally if at all to Vitruvius' description, then this could only mean that the classical orders had been conserved over time. The orders were the key element that seemed to link the ancient structures both to one another, independently of their period, and to the architectural theories, when only a few other parallels could be drawn between them and Vitruvius. Proof of the fundamental role attributed to them may be found in Antonio Manetti's account of primitive architecture, where he says that such structures "must have appeared very disorderly, because the orders were not yet in use."

Many Renaissance paintings show just how little the idea of evolution had influenced the common image of ancient architecture: they show the heroic exploits of the early history of Rome, against sumptuous architectural backdrops, sometimes with famous monuments of the imperial age, such as the Colosseum or Trajan's Column. Thus were shown the two faces of ancient Rome, so admired in the Renaissance: the moral virtues and the high level of civilization. Even in negative contexts, such as when pagan holy places were shown as a sign for unbelievers, the artists interested in antiquity used Roman buildings of the imperial age, independently of the period depicted, even in scenes taken from the Old Testament. Benozzo Gozzoli, for example, in a picture of Babylon around the time of the tower's construction,

Andrea Mantegna
Marchese Gonzaga Welcoming his Son Cardinal Francesco *detail of the landscape with ancient buildings*
1470
Mantua, Palazzo Ducale, Camera degli Sposi

put together a pyramid and the Pantheon along with Florence Cathedral and the Palazzo Medici. The lasting image of ancient architecture that reached the paintings of the Renaissance passed through the entirety of antiquity, showing, for example, Hercules and other heroes of Greek mythology before a scene of the Pantheon and other Roman monuments or one of Bramante's Tempietto that is transformed into the main temple of Troy, into the Temple of Baal, destroyed by the devout, into a Roman temple or a Christian shrine, if not into a symbol of the Christian church. As has already been demonstrated several times, even evaluations were part of Renaissance studies of antiquity. Even though they were not always clear and univocal, a few criteria may be discerned.

As in the evaluation of contemporary buildings, most of the time the accent was placed on the admiration of size. Both scholarly writings and architects' drawings are proof. In his discussion of Greek architecture, Serlio presented, despite the Greeks' legendary lack of means, the largest building that could be found in Athens. This admiration probably expressed a naive wonder. However, it could be justified from a theoretical point of view, thanks to the overriding principle of *decorum* in architecture. The concept of *decorum* called for the appropriateness of function and use. Furthermore, as was already argued in antiquity, the buildings had to correspond to the social position of whoever had them built, and, the inverse of this, that the buildings provided evidence of the social status of whoever had them built, was often also asserted. Large buildings thus were evidence of the greatness of whoever had them built. This applied in individual cases and in general: the greatness of Roman architecture offered proof during the Renaissance and Middle Ages of the greatness of ancient Rome. An expression of this idea may be found in the famous words of Hildebert von Lavardin, often repeated during the Renaissance: *Roma quanta fuit, ipsa ruina docet.*

However, the principle of *decorum* gave rise to some problems. Architectural *decorum* still had to be based on ethical standards. Greatness and opulence therefore had to correspond to the ethical level of the function. However, many of the great Roman structures served only a trivial, dissolute and brutish amusement. The reactions to this problem have already been discussed in relation to the baths and the pyramids, but the triumphal arches, the *naumachiae*, arenas, theaters and other like structures were also subject to criticism. Thus, in 1477 English humanist Robert Flemmyng denounced them for serving exaggerated ambition (*insana voluptas ambitione*) and ostentation rather than utility (*necessitas*) or devoutness (*pietas*). Biondo felt that the emperors had ordered the construction of such oversized structures for the end purpose of keeping peace and order among the citizens, satisfying them with diversions, games and luxury. Alberti and others sought to salvage the honor of such monuments, attributing them with ethical functions, even if only that of stimulating, through the memory of important men, the imitation of the great feats that had made them famous. Justification for the theaters, despite all the excesses starting in the imperial age that had given rise to the ill repute of the performances staged in them, may be found in Augustus' declaration that they "were not introduced to Rome by the vices of men, but by order of the gods" (Ricchieri 1513). While the ethical evaluations were the task of scholars, the architects were busy with evaluations based on the canons of their discipline. The partiality for the plastic qualities of the individual architectonic structures is revealed by the number of studies, and it was occasionally explicitly stated. Thus the capitals of what is today known as the Temple of Castor and Pollux were often considered "the finest and best crafted work in Rome."

In the evaluation of structures in general, the architects referred primarily to the classical canons. These were found in the ancient ideals, such as the conception of the circle and the sphere as perfect forms, and in Vitruvius' treatise. Vitruvius was usually considered canonical, at least on paper. In practice, the effects of this attitude were limited until the architects were able to acquire a proper understanding of the text, and even then, the effects continued to be limited as the idea began to emerge that Vitruvius could only be fully understood by referring his work to the extant structures of antiquity. A few, such as Serlio, actually reached the conclusion that the ancient buildings stood in contrast with some of Vitruvius' rules. However the relevance of Vitruvius' works was formulated, the consequence was a limitation of his authority, making way for new standards.

The ancient structures were sometimes criticized. Not even the most famous ones, such as the Pantheon, the Templum Pacis or the thermal complexes, were exempt. The criticism was expressed not only directly but also indirectly, for example, by modifying single parts in representations of buildings. Only exceptionally did such criticism arise from an awareness of departures from Vitruvian canon. It usually conformed with principles that the Renaissance had instead inherited from the early Middle Ages; the parts of a structure and its decorations had to be set in relation to one another according to simple geometric schemes. Thus, a scheme could seem wrong when non-matching or dissimilar elements were arranged in axis, as in the atrium of the Pantheon or in the ambulatory of the Temple of Bacchus (S. Costanza); or when matching or similar structures were not aligned, such as inside the Pantheon or in the decorations of the Temple of Bacchus; or when the structure was broken down into individual elements without continuity, such as the parts of the entablature beneath the impost of the vault in the so-called Templum Pacis, in the Baths of Diocletian, and in many other ancient structures. Finally, tradition played a leading role in the evaluations. The Pantheon, the Colosseum and the Templum Pacis—which in the books on antiquity by Serlio, Giuliano da Sangallo, Bernardino della Volpaia (*Codex Coner*) and Palladio are presented as clearly distinct from the other monuments—already in antiquity and the Middle Ages aroused more admiration than the other monuments in Rome.

Evaluation, like placement in an historical context, can also give rise to various objective archaeological theories. The reconstruction of the functions of the baths was, as already mentioned, largely influenced by moral preconceptions. Opinions about the formal quality of the Pantheon led to the reconstruction of a particular building history: the conflict between the high appraisal of the structure as a whole and the objection to the arrangement of its details was solved by a thesis inspired by accounts of construction initiatives implemented after Agrippa. The presumed discrepancies were supposed to have stemmed from the fact that the Pantheon was later modified. On the assumption that Vitruvius practiced good architecture,

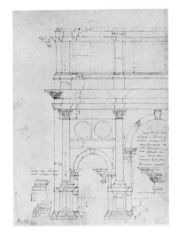

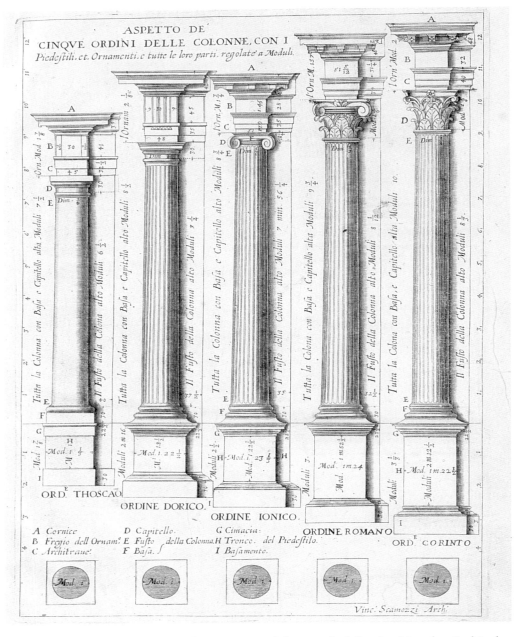

Cesare Cesariano
The Five Orders
Studies from De architectura
libri decem *by Lucius*
Vitruvius Pollione (Vitruvius)
Como, Gotardo da Ponte, 1521
Cologne, Ungers Archiv für
Architekturwissenschaft

Palladio reconstructed the original appearance of the temple following his rules. In his theories about the columns, he referred to the ruins reconstructed according to those rules. The ideas that the typical ancient temple had a centralized plan and that the interior was sumptuously decorated arose as a consequence of the archaeological knowledge that had developed earlier during the Renaissance. Of course, this archaeological knowledge could be interpreted in the inverse sense, that is, as the consequence of the ideal images that had become widespread in the Middle Ages and lived on in Alberti's treatise on architecture. In any case, the two deductive routes were closely linked to one another. The inductive method did not exclude the formulation of hypotheses, which were initially based on existing ideas. Many of the archaeological theories that emerged during the Renaissance were long-lived, despite their ideological bias; some, like the reconstruction of the bath facilities, are still current today. However, at times their true origins are often overlooked, from the elevated vantage point, "on the shoulders of giants."

Throughout the Renaissance, people often remonstrated that the great achievements of antiquity were beyond the reach of their own era, and at the same time, others could exalt their own era as being superior to antiquity. The same thing occurred in architecture. Both attitudes were in their own way justified by the age-old image of "dwarves on the shoulders of giants" and, appropriately, they were to be toppled. This is what Serlio did, for example, to the credit of his book on the classical orders: with a little effort it would be possible to rise above the Romans, if not in size, then in esthetic sense. In fact, it was easier to complete inventions than to create them, as the ancients did, but first a number of new discoveries had to be made.

The doubts about the attainability of the achievements of antiquity, and the exaltation of the superiority of the present age had the same, if not greater tradition as the image of dwarves on giants' shoulders. During the Renaissance, however, this rhetorical *topos* acquired a new ingredient. What had been a vague, generalized thought during the Middle Ages now became concrete: the aspiration to supersede antiquity spurred architects to select and borrow whatever they could from the past.

At least until Palladio, very ancient buildings were rarely imitated. Bramante's adoption of the round peripteral temple as it appeared from the interpretation of Vitruvius' description at the time, for his Tempietto was an exception. It may have stemmed from the attempt, under unusual circumstances, to reconstruct to some degree the ancient memory of the crucifixion of St. Peter and perhaps even from the remoteness of the patrons, the royal family of Spain, from the Italian tradition. Buildings with much feebler echoes of antiquity had already met with incomprehension where they departed from the usual in their general layout. Proof is the harsh criticism of SS. Annunziata in Florence or the church of S. Sebastiano in Mantua. Michelangelo's idea of setting a portico of columns before St. Peter's, as if it were a temple, was not carried out. The principle of *decorum* usually curtailed revisitations of antiquity. Just as the town councilors of Renaissance Florence could not suddenly appear dressed in togas in imitation of republican heroes, it would not have been appropriate to build the new basilica according to Vitruvian canons in the square before the Palazzo Vecchio. If Cosimo de' Medici, often hailed as the new Maecenas, had come up with the idea of building his new residence in the likeness of the so-called Palace of Maecenas, he would have shown that he had enormous financial means and a good knowledge of archaeology at

297

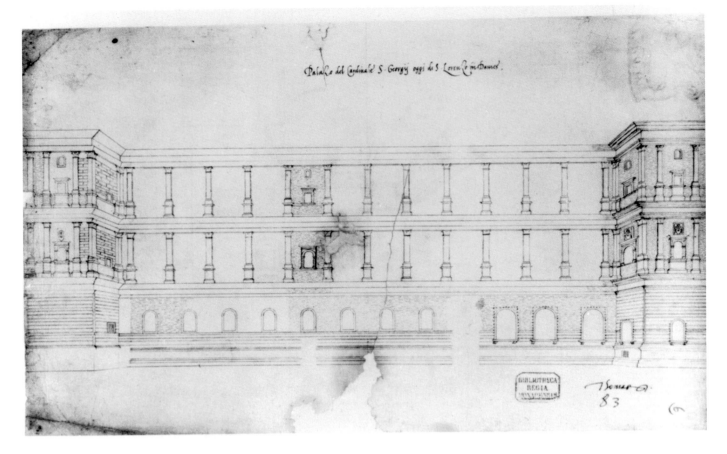

his disposal, but he would have also revealed that he did not know what was proper. He could not afford such a political blunder. Thus, he rejected Brunelleschi's costly model, "più per fuggire l'invidia che la spesa." Nor was the traditional distribution of household functions changed; hardly any patron of the Renaissance wished to move the reception rooms from the *piano nobile* of his palace to the ground floor (where is was situated in antiquity), which until then had been used as the storeroom or to conduct business.

In their approach to antiquity, Renaissance architects and, perhaps even more so, their patrons were mainly interested in reviving the artistic canons and single formal elements of classicism. The orders of columns—which in that period, it seems, were considered the key element of ancient architecture and in Manetti's opinion, mentioned above, the constituent element of order in architecture—were the model for reviving antiquity. Especially in Rome, even complex motifs were borrowed from antiquity, initially following the model offered by the ruins (the structure of half-columns interposed among the arches, of the type found in the Colosseum, the Palazzo Venezia, or the structure of the entrance to the Cappella Chigi in S. Maria del Popolo, as in the Pantheon), then following the model given in the source literature (inspired by Vitruvius, the three-aisled vestibule in the Palazzo Farnese, in projects for the Villa Madama, in the Palazzo del Te and in the Villa Imperiale, or inspired by Pliny the Younger's description of the Villa Laurentina, the circular courtyard of the Villa Madama). Function played an important role in the form of decoration as well: in Florence, ancient motifs that had remained in use during the Middle Ages, such as marble facing to decorate churches or ashlar work for palaces, continued to be utilized, but now they were restored to their true forms, following the ancient models, or what were supposed to be such. In Rome, the architecture came closer than elsewhere to the ancient models, not only thanks to the presence of the ruins, but also because here the artistic tradition had been arrested in the fourteenth century with the exile of the papal court to Avignon.

The literature of the Renaissance rarely highlighted the contrast between the return to the formal canons of antiquity and the ongoing use of the traditional layout. To the contrary, it often generalized the revival of antiquity and this generalization went so far that during the Renaissance the concept of *decorum*—a concept that had developed during antiquity as a fundamental principle of architecture and art and was handed down through the Middle Ages—disappeared from the vocabulary of architectural theory. It was not until the seventeenth century that it was reinstated to its fixed position in art theory, after an absence of two hundred years. Medieval architects were able to refer to custom, of which this principle was part, and those of the Baroque era on did the same. But the change that took place during

Palazzo della Cancelleria (Chancellery) drawing of side prospect Munich, Bayerische Staatsbibliothek Cod. Icon. 195, fol. 6

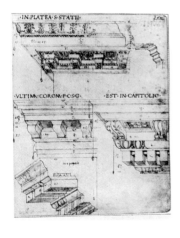

Sketches of Architectural
Details
Crowning Cornice for the
Palazzo della Cancelleria,
and Other Cornices
*London, Sir John Soane's
Museum*
Codex Coner, *fol. 64*

top
*Palazzo della Cancelleria
project for the courtyard
Munich, Bayerische
Staatsbibliothek*

on the following pages
Pirro Ligorio
Map of Rome
1552
*Milan, Civica Raccolta Stampe
Achille Bertarelli*

the Renaissance forced theorists to make an adjustment in their thinking: Alberti was the first to substitute the concept of *decorum* with that of *utilitas*, more suited to function and the antique model.

During the Renaissance, the revival of antiquity may have had a greater impact than reckoned by modern archaeology, because the great gaps in knowledge of antiquity were often filled, consciously or not, by traditional images. In short, where an antique structure could be imagined on the basis of custom, the modern building could also appear antique, if it followed the custom. In this respect, the Ponte Sisto, for example, may be compared "with any ancient bridge" (Aurelius Lippus Brandolinus). The retrieval of antiquity was in a certain sense over, although individual forms still made reference to it. For example, the Palazzo Farnese: the overall layout is contemporary, but ancient ornamental forms were added, especially the three-aisled vestibule, considered the "Vitruvian atrium." Thus, the gaze was focused on the return to antiquity, and this permitted Giovanni Battista da Sangallo to consider the central courtyard the perfect reflection of the courtyards of ancient houses—just as Vitruvius had described it—even though he had faithfully complied with contemporary style. Biondo compared the Palazzo Medici with the private homes of the high-ranking families of ancient Rome. This analogy is, in its way, compelling, as Biondo imagined such homes to be directly comparable. Furthermore, every part of the Palazzo Medici revives antique architectural forms or adapts traditional elements according to antique models (for example, ashlar work, as Paolo Cortese pointed out in 1510, following the model of Trajan's Forum, today known as Augustus' Forum, to Biondo's mind Nerva's Forum, and to others the imperial palace). Or, in Giuliano da Sangallo's project for the construction of a university at Pisa commissioned by Lorenzo il Magnifico: as was frequently the case with universities or other similar scholastic institutions at the time, all the rooms were grouped around a central courtyard with arcades on all sides. However, Giuliano doubled the entrance portico. With this small modification, the structure was transformed into a supposedly antique building type. Overall, it only resembles in plan the *palaestra* described by Vitruvius. From Alberti on, this description was applied to academic institutions and was given the name *gymnasium*, and the same concept of *gymnasium* was used to refer to universities and similar scholastic structures.

In the place of worship, it was possible to attribute falsely the traditions to antiquity, especially since Vitruvius mentions very little about temple interiors. The Etruscan temple, later reconstructed by Alberti, corresponds on the whole, if you will, to the typical structure with large hall of late medieval Tuscan houses of prayer where lateral chapels were added in a regular pattern over the years, and the main space is covered by a vault, as in the Badia of Fiesole,

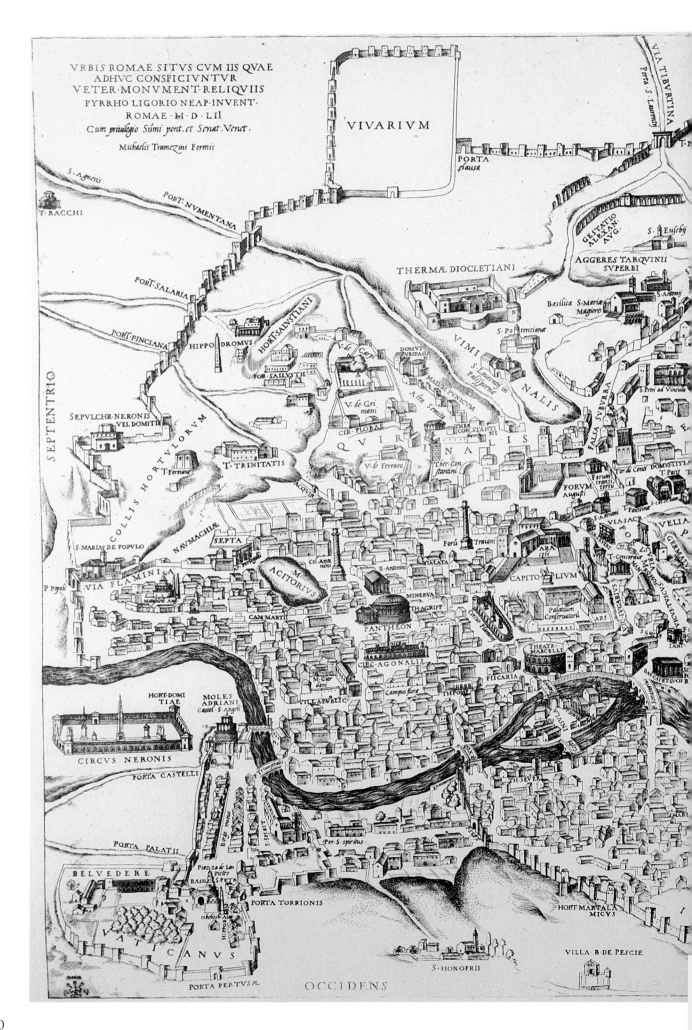

URBIS ROMAE SITUS CUM IIS QUAE
ADHUC CONSPICIUNTUR
VETER·MONUMENT·RELIQUIIS
PYRRHO LIGORIO NEAP·INVENT·
ROMAE·M·D·LII
Cum priuilegio Sũmi pont. et Senat. Venet.
Michaelis Tramezini Formis

VIVARIUM

ORIENS

HIPPODROMVS

VIA LABICANA

VIA PRENESTINA

Porta Maior

MEDICÆ

Amphi theatr.
Castrense

T. Veneris

S. Crucis in
Hierusalem

Lymphæum
A Ioanni Aug.

Porta San Giouan

NOV.VIA VALERIA

AQVA MARTIAE

Aqua cerulia et Curtia

AQVÆ DVCTVS AQ

Domus Laterani

Basilica Lateranen

Philippi Aug.

S. Pietro marcellino

CLAVDIÆ

Hospitale S. Ioha
tonis

AQVA CRABRA

Matei

FABERNOLIÆ

Clementis

S. Quattuor

CARINÆ

COELIOLVS

S. Giouanni

PORT.LATINA

THEATR.

S. Ioannis et Pauli

AQVA CLAVDIA

T. FAVNI

S. Stephani Rotond.

CVR.HOSTILI

TEM.CLAVDII

COELIVS

S. Maria
Nauicella

S. Sixti

VIA LATINA

PORT.S.
SEBASTIANI

SVBVRA

S. Gregorj

S. Thomæ
Hospitali

VIA APPIA

MERIDIES

SEPTIZONIVM

PISCINA PVBLICA

Aqua Crabra

S. Prisca

AVENTINVS

THERMÆ ANTONIANÆ

MVR

MAXIMVS

VICVS ARM.LVSTRI

S. Sabina

S. Alexij

S. Maria

S. Balbina

PVBLICVS

CLIVVS PVBLICVS

T. Bonæ Deæ

VIA HOSTIENSIS

PORT.S.PAVLI

EMPORIVM

HORT.ID
CON.SAGA

SALINA

HORREA DOMITIANI

S. Cat
Castij

NAVALI

TESTACEVS
siue Doliolum

AGR.CINCENNATI

HORT. C. CAESARI

PORTA PORTVENSIS

ICVLVM

PANCRATII

301

near Florence. Compatibly with this, Alberti called his project for S. Andrea in Mantua an "Etruscan" temple, perhaps in to commemorate Mantua's supposed foundation by the Etruscans.

Even fewer analogies would be sufficient to compare antiquity with modern architecture, at times so few that a real *tertium camparationis* would practically be lacking.

The decoration of the square that opens up before SS. Apostoli in honor of Eleonora of Aragon's visit to Rome (1473) was likened either to Marcus Scaurus' and Pompey's theaters or to the Olympic games arena. Paolo Palliolo admired the facade of the Capitoline theater, built in 1513 for the conferment of Roman citizenship on the nephews of Pope Leo X, erected as a simple wall with a wooden framework and an order of columns: "To the gaze of those who climbed Campidoglio, it appeared so superb and magnificent that it seemed a real image of the antique palaces that were built with great artistic sensibility and at inestimable cost for the emperors and the leading citizens of Rome when the city was still flourishing, and before which, we, in our times, show wonder, observing what little has remained, in ruins and rubble." The modern homes were compared in the same way to the ancient palaces of the emperors, with particular rigor in Rome: Pius II and Antonino Ponte (1524) espied in the new residences of Cardinal Rodrigo Borgia (Palazzo Sforza-Cesarini) and Raffaele Riario (Cancelleria) Nero's Domus Aurea, which is almost like saying they rivaled the dwellings of the gods or paradise. Similarly, Raffaele Maffei compared the urban renewal measures taken by Sixtus IV in Rome with Augustus' urbanization programs and Julius II boasted that his urban improvement measures were worthy of the "Majesty of the Empire"; Andrea Fulvio compared the new district to the south of Piazza del Popolo created by the Medici popes to the ancient street plan, just because the boundaries of the housing blocks and the streets

Perin del Vaga
Naumachia in the Belvedere Court
detached fresco
Rome, Castel Sant'Angelo,
appartamento del castellano

302

had been set in strict alignment "with the aid of a plumb-line." The appeal of such comparisons eclipsed even the most patent contradictions: Biondo, praising the *magnificentia* of Cosimo de' Medici, went so far as to claim that he, as author of the guidebook to Rome (*Roma instaurata*), could guarantee that none of the still-standing private houses of the high-ranking citizens of ancient Rome could surpass the Palazzo Medici in the cost of its construction. And yet, in his guide to Rome he had identified the monumental ruins at the Quirinal with the Palace of Maecenas, which had been much more costly than the Palazzo Medici. In other parts of the book, where it was not a question of praising Cosimo, but merely of presenting an objective comparison, Biondo reaches the conclusion that the houses of the ancient Romans were much larger than modern ones. The comparisons made during the Renaissance between contemporary and antique architecture may therefore be taken at face value only within certain limits. Only rarely may a deeper sense be discerned behind the analogies between antiquity and modernity sought with the enthusiasm of hymns of praise. They often have a purely rhetorical significance. The transposition to antiquity of the period's own ideas on order was understood in some respects in a similar way: it could be proposed if it was a question of citing an authority in order to justify an opinion, and it could easily be retracted when it was a question of celebrating the superiority of the period compared to antiquity.

Even apparently objective descriptions of modern buildings were meant literally and subject to reservations during the Renaissance, as they contained antique rhetorical elements. Leonardo Bruni in his *Laudatio* to Florence (1403–04), for example, describes the palaces as Vitruvius described ancient dwellings, with all the specific technical terms, even though these were only understood in part, and he included particular arrangements such as the

303

separation between summer and winter homes, even if this was no longer in use. In this way, Florence must have come closer to being a new Athens, instead of a new Rome, as the *Laudatio* assiduously imitates Aristides' praise of Athens. Antonino Ponte describes the pope's palace as if it practically touched the sky, not because it really seemed to be a skyscraper, but because Martial celebrates in this way the imperial palace on the Palatine. Or again: the Belvedere Court had already been described in the foundation medal and then frequently in Renaissance literature on Rome as a triple portico (*triplices porticus*), not simply because it consists of three successive terraces, but also because Suetonius described the Domus Aurea in this way. Giovanni Pontano explained, referring in this case to Virgil, what such epithets meant: they simply intended to say that the buildings aroused awe and admiration. Here a medieval tradition was being kept alive, this time inspired by antiquity, namely, the custom of ranking buildings with the achievements of imperial Rome, or attributing to them every imaginable precious material.

In his *Laudatio* to Giulio Romano, Pietro Aretino articulated, using appropriate rhetorical expressions, the importance that a comparison between modernity and antiquity had assumed during the Renaissance. Giulio's artistic ideas seemed to him at once "anciently modern, and modernly ancient" ("anticamente moderni and modernamente antichi"). He claimed that Apelles and Vitruvius would also have admired Giulio's buildings and paintings, had they been able to see them.

While the new historians and archaeologists were aware of the remoteness of their age from antiquity, in their eulogies Renaissance rhetoricians could transfer their own ideas to antiquity, just as some novel-writers did during the same period, in such a way as to merge antiquity and modernity into a single utopian whole.

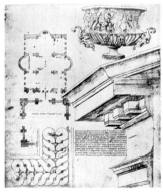

From Petrarch's time on, whoever studied antiquity complained of the constant deterioration of the monuments. Popes who had an interest in antiquity took measures to protect the ruins.

In his famous bull of 1462, Pius II explains the need for such conservation, citing esthetic, historical and even, expressed with greater precision, moral reasons: the monuments represented for the city a remarkable ornament; they proved the skill and the virtue of the ancient Romans; they also inspired imitation and they served as a reminder of the evanescence of earthly fortunes. Archaeological considerations had secondary importance from this point of view.

The protection sought mainly concerned parts of buildings that were still standing and still fairly well conserved, while the less important remains and rubble could be recycled freely as usual as building material. Yet despite the moderacy of the appeal, the warnings and efforts had a limited effect.

Not even the most famous works were safe. Some, such as the Basilica of Aemilia, continued to be used as stone quarries. Others, such as the so-called pyramid of Romulus, were sacrificed, notwithstanding the formidable job of excavation, if they stood in the way of urban renewal measures. Some monuments were modified to suit new uses, for example Baths of Diocletian, the central rooms of which Michelangelo transformed into the church of S. Maria degli Angeli. The monuments that still served a practical purpose, such as the Pantheon, or public utility works, such as the aqueduct, were restored. It seems that Leo X sought, not only with words, but also concretely, to reconcile the renewal of Rome with the protection of antiquity. But otherwise, the old had to make way for the new, as usual when progress demands it.

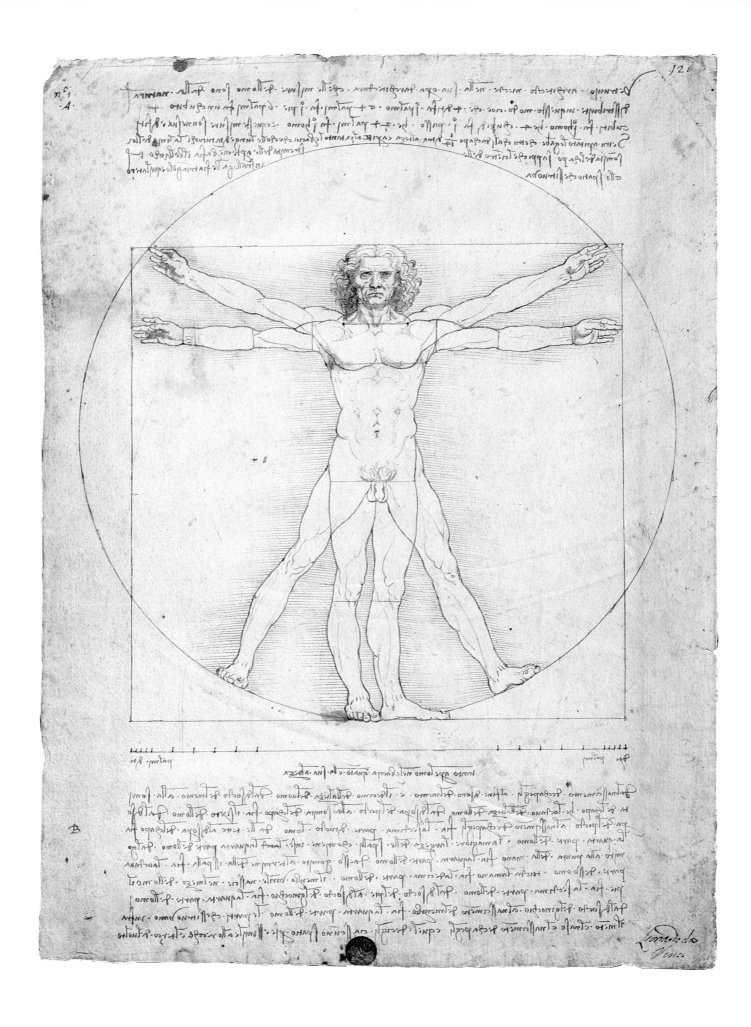

Cesare Cesariano
Vitruvian Man, *1521*

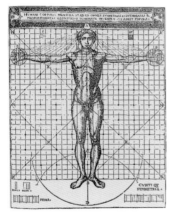

Cesare Cesariano
Vitruvian Man, *1521*

Oswald Mathias Ungers

Ordo, fondo et mensura: the Criteria of Architecture

When in 1399 the *capomaestro* Jean Mignos, a native of southern France, was called in as a consultant for the construction of Milan Cathedral (begun 1386), he coined a maxim that neatly encapsulates the spirit of the Renaissance sensibility: *Ars sine sciencia nihil est*—Art without science is naught. He was in fact echoing a saying that originated long before him in ancient Rome: *Artem sine scientia esse non posse.*

Throughout antiquity, and notably in the architectural works of Phidias and Polyclitus, mathematical rigor and geometrical severity were deemed to be the basis of all artistic expression. Things were not beautiful because they were outwardly pleasing to behold, but because they were the expression of a system of precise harmonic rules and relationships. This conception of beauty was summarized by Plato: "If one were to separate from the arts the doctrine of numbers, measure, and harmony, little would be left but miserable remains. By beauty of form, I do not refer to what most people consider beauty, such as the beauty of humans or certain paintings. By beauty I mean, rather, something square or circular, or surfaces and solids formed with the aid of a compass, straightedge and set-square: such things are always beautiful in themselves, and embody artistic feelings of a very special nature" (*Philebus*, 51c).

The Pythagoreans also maintained that the purpose of humanity was to fulfill the universal divine order (an order of a strictly mathematical nature); they reasoned that harmony depended on numerical relationships, and that numbers were the essence of all things.

With this in mind, St. Augustine, philosopher of Early Christianity and great teacher of the Church, borrowed from one of King Solomon's sayings, namely, "You have given order to all things according to size, number, and weight" (*ordo, fondo et mensura*). Augustine developed the notion of the harmony of the spheres, a characteristic of the Middle Ages. For him, God was the origin of all beauty, and beauty was expressed through measurements, number and harmony. By this transcendental system, music and architecture were seen as an outward reflection of eternal beauty. Hence Augustine interpreted architecture as a science based on the application of geometrical laws.

A key figure in hastening the transition from the Middle Ages to the Renaissance was the German artist Albrecht Dürer. Guided by his disposition for empirical method, Dürer attempted to prove that art was founded on a set of rules. He wrote three essays on the subject, in which he summarized his theories on art, and supplied evidence that the "foundations of art" are based on an exact science. These writings, which were conceived as a program, and published in Nuremburg, comprise: *Underweysung der Messung mit der Zirkel und richscheyt, in Linien Ebnen unn ganen Corporen / durch Albrecht Dürer zusammen gezogen...* (1525), a text on the application of geometry; *Etliche underricht, zu befestigung der Stett, Schloss und Flecken* (1527), a treatise on fortification; and *Vier bücher von menschlicher Proportion* (1528), on the proportions of the human body. Dürer's doctrine on human proportions is the essence of his life's work. The artistic theory it embodies is wider in scope than the theories of his Italian contemporaries Piero della Francesca, Leon Battista Alberti, and even Luca Pacioli. Notwithstanding his superlative theoretical contribution to the Renaissance, Dürer's writings are still undeservingly neglected. The doctrine unfolds in a logical program quite unprecedented for the period and, proceeding through to the metamorphoses and morphological shifts contained in the fourth volume on proportions, it far outshines all other theories that have so far come to our notice. A close friend of the Nuremburg humanist Wilibald Pirckheimer, Dürer had access to the latter's magnificent library and consequently made his acquaintance with the fundamental writings of antiquity, such as Euclid's *Elements* and Vitruvius' *De architectura libri decem*, to which Dürer pays explicit homage in his own work: "As regards any discussion on building, or of its elements, I believe none among our eminent *capimaestri* or artisans have overlooked how the ancient Roman author Vitruvius wrote so splendidly in his books regarding the decoration of architecture: his example is a lesson to all."

During his travels through Italy Dürer doubtless came across the early Italian writings on the arts, such as Piero della Francesca's *De prospectiva pingendi* (ca. 1465), the

opposite
Leonardo da Vinci
Study of Proportions
(Vitruvian Man)
Venice, Gallerie dell'Accademia

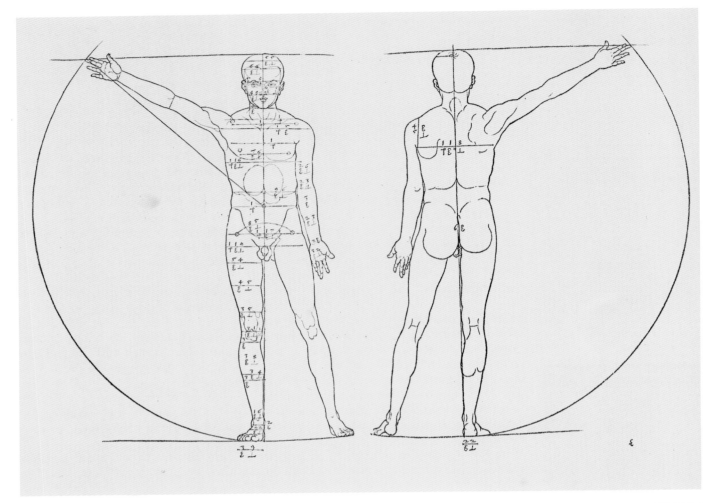

mathematician Luca Pacioli's *De divina proportione* (1509), and Leon Battista Alberti's *De pictura* (1540). Here too he came into contact with both Pacioli and Leonardo da Vinci, who executed the illustrations for the former's mathematical treatise.

Leonardo may even have provided the illustrations for the important 1521 edition of Vitruvius, edited by Cesare Cesariano. The *De architectura* was the point of departure for a crescendo of interest in art theory throughout the western world, beginning with the writings and technical treatises of the humanists of Northern Italy in the Quattrocento and Cinquecento: Piero della Francesca, Luca Pacioli, Fra Giocondo, Andrea Palladio, Daniele Barbaro, Giacomo da Vignola, Sebastiano Serlio, Filarete, Vincenzo Scamozzi, Leon Battista Alberti, Francesco di Giorgio Martini. (Indeed, the influence of Vitruvius has endured even in more recent studies on the theory of proportions.) Vitruvius was the fountainhead of all Renaissance thought on art and the techniques of representation. The theoreticians of the period all drew on his fundamental writings in the *De architectura libri decem*, which have become to art historians what the Sacred Scriptures are to the theologians: Vitruvius' work is the "bible" of artistic doctrine. The *De architectura* was written during the reign of Augustus, to whom it was in fact dedicated. Although the original Roman manuscript has long been lost to us, no less than fifty-five copies of it have survived, the earliest of which dates to the beginning of the ninth century. It was not until 1486, however, that the work appeared for the first time in movable type, an incunabula version, devotedly compiled by the Veronese scholar Sulpicius da Veroli, archaeologist to the Accademia Romana during the reign of Pope Innocent VIII.

Vitruvius' texts were already the subject of discussion in the days of Charlemagne and his court. The Frankish regent's historian, Bishop Einhard, is known to have asked the English churchman Alcuin, who was a guest of Charlemagne's court, for explanations of some of Vitruvius' more awkward technical terms. Some three centuries later, there is evidence that the Holy Roman Emperor Frederick II was acquainted with the *De architectura*, as the buildings he commissioned bear the signs of great mathematical rigor. The first illustrated edition dates to the Renaissance. Assembled by the architect Fra Giocondo in Venice in 1511, the new publication of Vitruvius' text marked the start of a long series of constantly amended and revised editions—a tradition

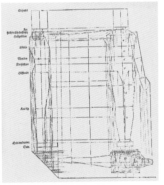

Albrecht Dürer
Human Proportions, *1528*

Pietro di Giacomo Cataneo
Human Proportions, *1554*

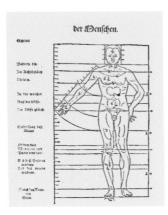

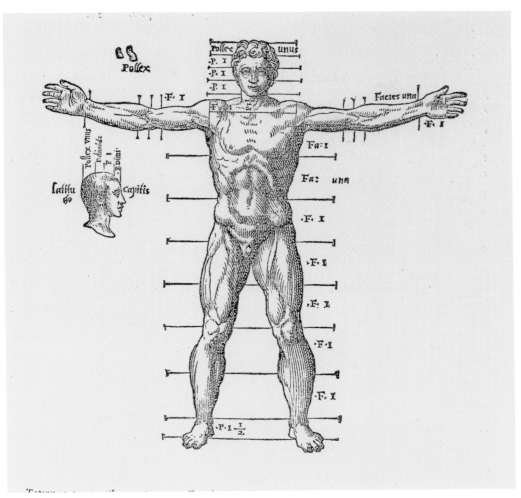

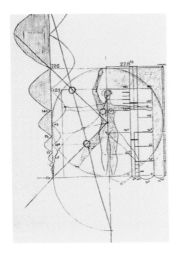

that has continued to the present day, unfolding in the course of five centuries like a chronological table of cultural history. In all this time, Vitruvius' *De architectura* has been translated into all the languages of the western world, sometimes accompanied by ample explanatory texts, and each time with new, stimulating illustrative matter. Taking their cue from the ancient conception of the Sophists—as summarized by Prothagoras of Abdera's famous saying: "Man is the measure of all things, of existence of all things that are and the nonexistence of all things that are not"—[for the Renaissance theoreticians?] the human figure became the fulcrum of thought and of the world, not only an object of man's enquiry into proportion, but the yardstick itself of proportion. Basing himself on the teachings of Vitruvius, whose writings also cover questions of art and the human body, Leonardo da Vinci devised an ideal form of beauty for the human body, the proportions of which were based on the circle and the square. In the famous Como edition of Vitruvius, published in 1521, Cesariano reproduced Leonardo's set of illustrations.

Dürer too, in his manuscript *Speis der Maler*, on the chapter dealing with the human arts, illustrates the canons of beauty outlined by Vitruvius, and comments thus: "That master of the ancient world Vitruvius, architect of grandiose buildings in Rome, states that he who intends to build should conform to human beauty, because the body conceals the arcane secrets of proportion. Hence, before discussing buildings, I intend to explain the form of a well-built man, and then a woman, a child, and a horse. In this way you will acquire an approximate measure of all the things about you. Heed first, therefore, what Vitruvius has written on human body learned from great masters, painters and sculptors who earned great renown.

"They stated that the human body must be such that the face, from the chin to the hairline is one tenth of the human form; the open hand is of the same length; the head itself is an eighth, and the breast to the hairline is one sixth. Likewise the face, from the hair to the chin, is divided into three parts, the first being the forehead, then comes the nose, and lastly the mouth and chin. The foot is one sixth of the human form, the arm a quarter, the chest another quarter. In this way the body's members are subdivided. If a man is laid down on the ground, spread-eagle, his hands and feet will lie on the circle described by a compass with its point fixed at his navel.

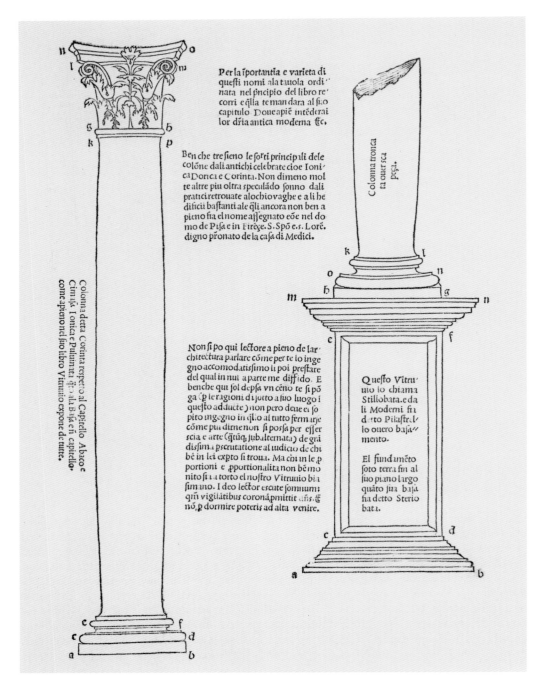

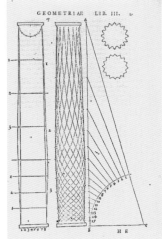

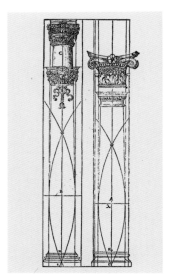

In this way he shows the structure in quarters. And thus he has gathered the human limbs in a structurally perfect number, ordering them in such a precise way as to avoid contradiction with either the ancient texts or with posterity. Anyone who so wishes may read how he enunciates the finest prerequisites of structure."

In Renaissance architectural theory, the proportions of the human body assumed a crucial role in the formulation of the architectural orders. Ever since Vitruvius, architecture had established an anthropomorphic matrix both for the building as a whole, and for its separate elements, or "ornament." In his treatise *De re aedificatoria*, Alberti goes back as far as the idea of the building as an organism, constituted of lines and matter, in which the lines stem from the spirit of man, and the matter from nature. "Beauty," retained Alberti, "is a form of sympathy and consonance of the parts within a body, according to definite number, outline and position, as dictated by *concinnitas*, the absolute and fundamental rule of nature." Alberti's concept of *concinnitas* regulates nature, and is one of the rules of Creation, standing above the laws of nature. Architecture is not simply accorded a status equal to that of nature, but is proposed as one of the principles of natural order, whose multiplicity of manifestations are reflected in the architectural orders: "Following the example of nature, they consequently idealized the structures of decoration for buildings, giving them names that derived from those who had served the same function. One of these orders was com-

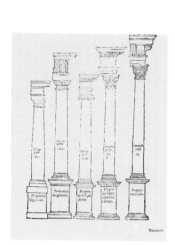

Giacomo da Vignola
The Orders, *1640*

Sebastiano Serlio
The Orders
from De Architectura libri
quinque, *1569*

Georg Caspar Erasmus
The Tuscan and Doric
Orders, *1667*

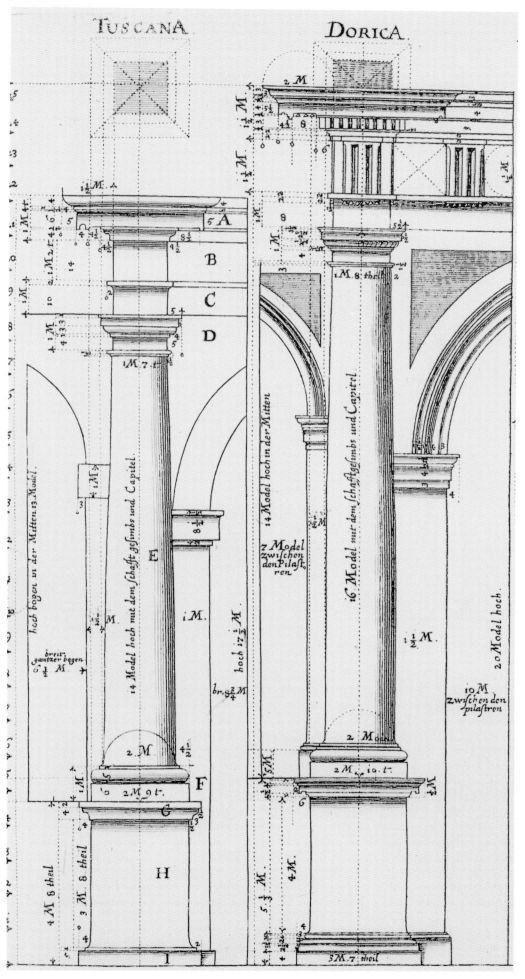

plete, suitable for work and endurance, and they called it Doric. The second was lighter, more cheerful, and they called it Corinthian. The central one, however, became to some extent an amalgam of the other two, and was called Ionic. In this way they devised similar names for the entire body." As yet, however, Alberti was not acquainted with the architectural orders in the true sense. Nor had he systematically compared their relative ratios and proportions—a task that was undertaken in some detail later by Vignola, Serlio, Scamozzi and other architects.

Vitruvius himself had opened the door to the personalization of the columns. The Doric column, he noted in Book VI, exemplified the "proportion, strength and grace of a man's body"; the Ionic was characterized by "feminine slenderness," harmonious and pleasant to look at; and the Corinthian column alluded to the "slight figure of a girl." He then went a step further, and ascribed each of the different columns to a deity: Doric was equated with the masculine nature of Minerva, Mars, and Hercules; the harmonious Ionic column was associated with Juno, Diana, and Bacchus; while the decorative Corinthian column was identified with Venus, Flora, and Persephone.

For his part, Luca Pacioli extended this association of the orders to embrace certain Christian saints. In his *Theatrum vitae humanae* (1577), the Flemish painter and drafts-

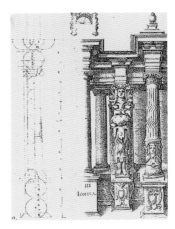

Wendel Dietterlin
The Ionic Order
1593-98

Gabriel Krammer
The Tuscan Order, *1606*

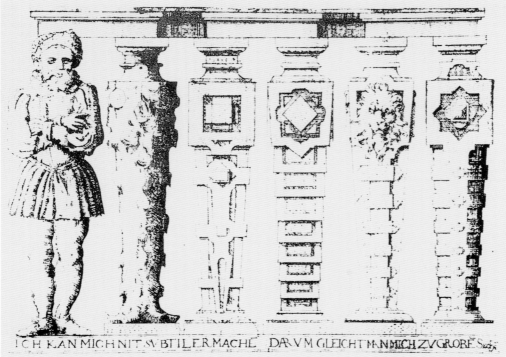

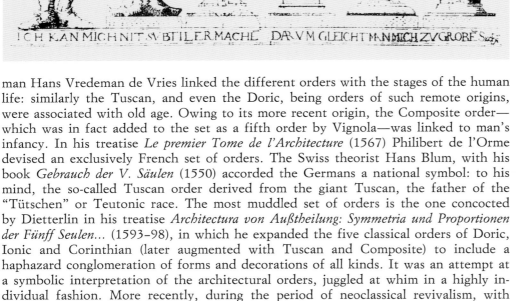

ICH KAN MICH NIT SVBTILER MACHE DARVM GLEICHT MAN MICH ZV GROBES

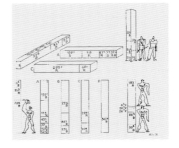

Le Corbusier
The Stele of Proportions,
1947

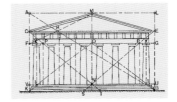

André Lurcat
Study of Proportions of the
Parthenon, *1944*

man Hans Vredeman de Vries linked the different orders with the stages of the human life: similarly the Tuscan, and even the Doric, being orders of such remote origins, were associated with old age. Owing to its more recent origin, the Composite order—which was in fact added to the set as a fifth order by Vignola—was linked to man's infancy. In his treatise *Le premier Tome de l'Architecture* (1567) Philibert de l'Orme devised an exclusively French set of orders. The Swiss theorist Hans Blum, with his book *Gebrauch der V. Säulen* (1550) accorded the Germans a national symbol: to his mind, the so-called Tuscan order derived from the giant Tuscan, the father of the "Tütschen" or Teutonic race. The most muddled set of orders is the one concocted by Dietterlin in his treatise *Architectura von Außtheilung: Symmetria und Proportionen der Fünff Seulen...* (1593–98), in which he expanded the five classical orders of Doric, Ionic and Corinthian (later augmented with Tuscan and Composite) to include a haphazard conglomeration of forms and decorations of all kinds. It was an attempt at a symbolic interpretation of the architectural orders, juggled at whim in a highly individual fashion. More recently, during the period of neoclassical revivalism, with Schinkel, Klenze and Stühler, the order of columns, pillars, and entablatures had an important role in the structure of buildings.

Even Le Corbusier, in his *Le Modulor* (1950 and 1955), made a detailed survey of the arrangement of pedestals, establishing a set of different orders. The orders were not simply categorized by taking a random height, according to proportional relationships

opposite
Neralco
The Pantheon, *1763*

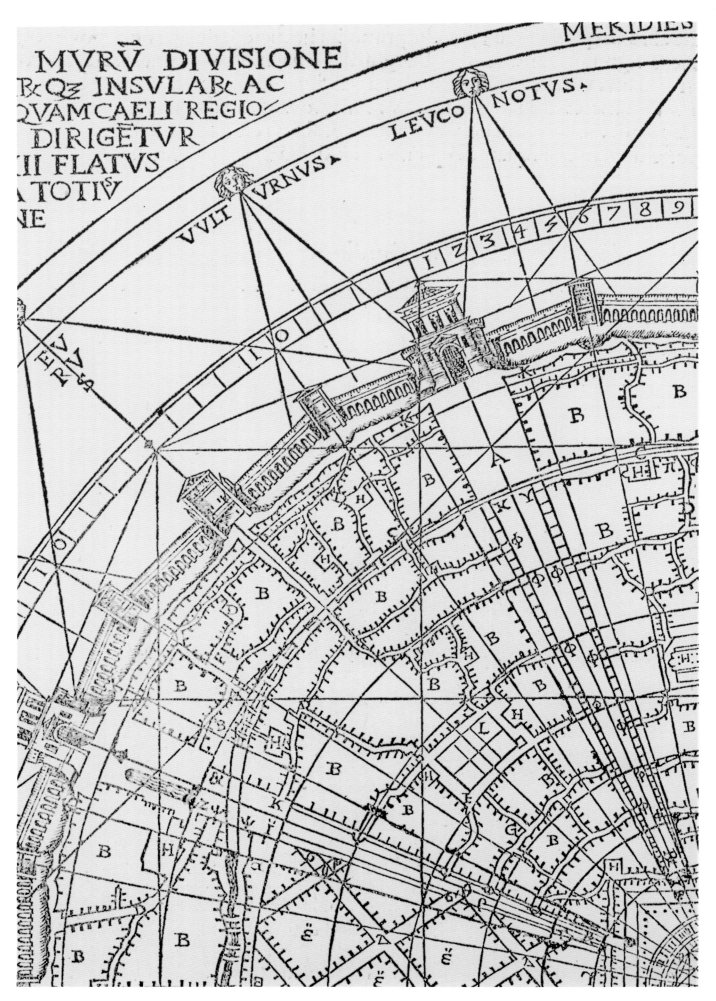

MVRŪ DIVISIONE
RₑQₑ INSVLARₑ AC
QVAM CAELI REGIO
DIRIGĒTVR
ẸII FLATVS
Ạ TOTIVˢ
ẸNE

MERIDIES

LEVCO NOTVS

VVLT VRNVS

EV R V S

1 2 3 4 5 6 7 8 9

1 2 3

I O

II O

B
B
A
B
H
B
B
B
K Y
φ
B
Φ Φ
Φ
B
B
B
H
B
B
L H
B
B
B
B
H
H
B
K
B
B
B
H
B
B
Ẹ
ẹ

314

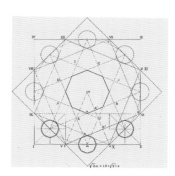

Heinz Götze
Castel del Monte
geometric scheme of the plan
1984

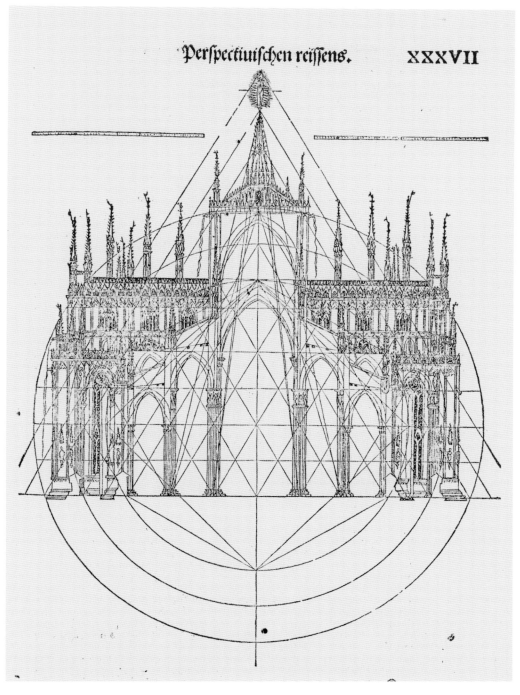

Walther Rivius
Ortographic Projection
of Milan Cathedral
1558

with the human body, between height and girth (Doric 1:7, Ionic 1:9, and Corinthian 1:9½) and their relative applications in building design—they expressed a stylistic conception directly referring to modern architecture. The Doric order, with its limpid, rational design, devoid of arabesque features, corresponded to the current of Rationalist architecture, with its accent on geometrical forms and elementary bodies. The Ionic order was equated with a more elegant architectural expression, of the Constructivist kind. The Corinthian or Composite orders—particularly as regards the free interpretations of Dietterling and Gabriel Krammer—were seen to represent an emphatic, unrestrained architectural language in which system and order are ruled out, and structure depends solely on experience and whim.

Evidently, the debate on the architectural orders has not yet run its course, but continues to be discussed in the context of modern architecture.

Not only Vitruvius, but also Francesco di Giorgio and most of those who theorized on architecture turned to nature's own forms—and particularly the human body—to deduce the elements of proportion as much for the architectural orders as for buildings as a whole. The essential geometrical figures remained the circle and the square, as representations and synonyms for the cosmos. Just as the human body was a clearly defined organism, with head and limbs, so were buildings.

opposite
Cesare Cesariano
Vitruvian Plan, 1521

315

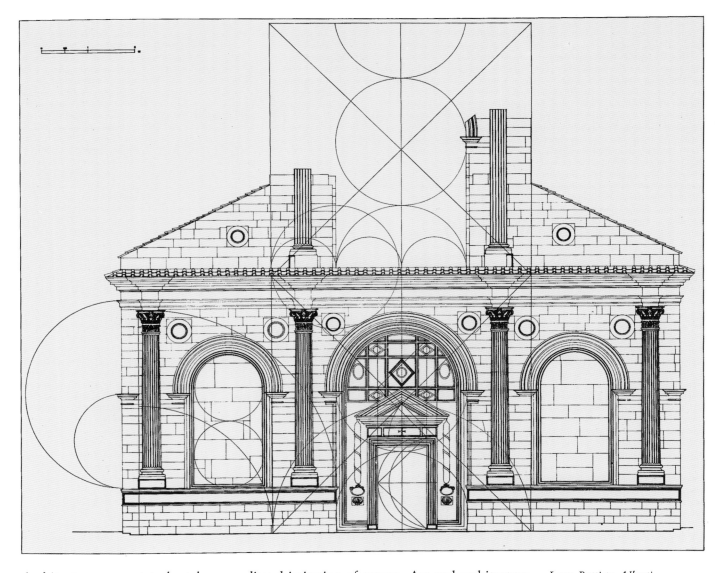

Leon Battista Alberti
Study of Proportions of
the Facade
Tempio Malatestiano

Architecture was not to be taken as a literal imitation of nature. Art and architecture were determined by *ratio*: they were sciences manifested through the relationships of proportion. For this reason, the rigid geometry underpinning Renaissance architecture was also the root of all the architectural rules. Form was not a random occurrence but the outcome of applied logic, and hence comparable with the result of applying proportional relationships. Seen in this light, architecture was a question of giving order to matter, physical data, and reality through the application of reason, and was explained in its underlying proportionality. By this means, matter was subjected to the rigors of form. Such a logic excluded any concept of an ideal of matter or functionality. Architecture was comparable to a science that had lost sight of the absolute, the Platonic concept of reality, truth and beauty.

As a consequence, buildings came to be clad in smooth, unembellished surfaces, because what counted was the clear form of the whole, and its geometrically determinable proportions. With its rigid artistic modeling, the work of art achieved its maturity and dignity—that magnificence and completeness which had been sought for so long. The original geometric forms of the circle, rectangle and sphere, the cone, ellipse and so forth, supplied the necessary structure for transforming natural objects into symbols of the spirit and soul of man. The finest, most noble form, the most harmonious and true form of all was an expression of the ideal proportions, an affirmation of the cosmic link with nature, which only art and science could offer. The essence of art was seen to be number, dimension, proportion. Pursuing this line of thought, in our own century the sculptor Hildebrand developed the basics for which "the question of forms is the absolute issue of art." In the days of the great humanist theoreticians on art, creative and artistic activity was held in far greater esteem than it is today. Scholarship, knowledge, cognition, evidence and demonstration—science in its broadest sense—were both prerequisites and constituents of art. Shapes necessitated explanation, demanded to be proved by theory. Methods and procedures had to guarantee results—results that could be taught and handed down as proper methods. Value judgments and chance were ruled out from the field of infinite possibilities.

Alberti's outline of the practicing architect is a demanding one: the true architect must be a scientist of the utmost moral correctness, a representative of a spiritual elite. "A great thing is architecture, and not all men are so equipped to try their hand at it. He who claims to be an architect must possess a lofty spirit, inexhaustible diligence, considerable learning, and above all a profound capacity for judgment and great wisdom. In architecture the greatest virtue is being able to exactly judge what is necessary; building is a matter of necessity; having constructed in a suitable fashion depends on need and utility: but to construct in such a way, to earn the assent of the wise without being scorned by the common people, is the undertaking of a proficient, well-informed and judicious artist."

right
Andrea Palladio
Villa Rotonda
Study of Proportions
from I Quattro Libri
dell'Architettura
Venice, 1570

Le Corbusier and Pierre
Jeanneret
Maison Ozenfant
Study of Proportions
1923

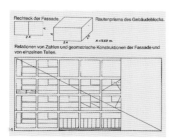

Giuseppe Terragni
Proportional Relations of the
Facade of the Casa del Fascio
Como

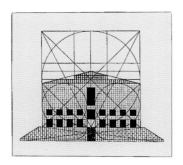

Oswald Mathias Ungers
Study of Proportions
Facade of the Kunsthalle
Hamburg, 1986

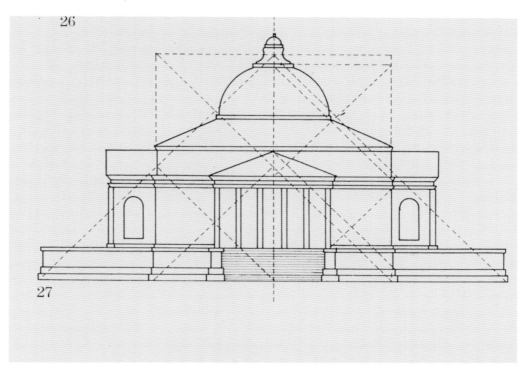

ACKNOWLEDGMENTS:
Albrecht Dürer, *Hierin sind begriffen view bücher von menschlicher Proportion.* Norimberga 1528; Cesare Cesariano, *De Architectura Libri Decem di Lucio Vitruvio Pollione.* Como, Gotardo da Ponte, 1521; Cesare Cesariano, *De Architectura Libri Decem di Lucio Vitruvio Pollione.* Como, Gotardo da Ponte, 1521; Albrecht Dürer, Hierin sind begriffen vier bücher von menschlicher Proportion. Norimberga 1528; Albrecht Dürer, *Hierin sind begriffen vier bücher von menschlicher Proportion.* Norimberga 1528; Pietro di Giacomo Cataneo, *I Quattro Primi Libri di Architettura...* Venezia, Aldus, 1554; Daniele Barbaro, *M. Vitruvii Pollionis De Architectura Libri Decem.* Venezia, F. Senensis & J. Criegher, 1567; Heinrich Lautensack, *Deß Circkelß und Richtscheyts / auch der Perspectiua / und Proportion der Menschen und Rosse ... Underweisung deß rechten gebrauchs ...* Francoforte, S. Schambercers, 1618; Le Corbusier. Le Modulor 1. Boulogne: Editions de l'Architecture d'Aujourd'hui, 1950. Le Modulor 2 – dto, 1955; Le Corbusier *Le Modulor 1.* Boulogne: Editions de l'Architecture d'Aujourd'hui, 1950. Le Modulor 2 dto. 1955; Luca Pacioli, *Divina proportione, opera a tutti glingegni perspicaci e curiosi...* Venezia, P. de Paganinis, 1509; Albrecht Dürer, *Underweysung der Messung, mit dem Zirckel und richtscheyt, in Linien, Ebnen unn ganßen Corporen ...* Norimberga 1525; Walther Rivius, *Der Architektur fürnembsten ... Mathematischen und Mechanischen Künst ... in drei fürneme Bücher abgetheilet.* Norimberga Gabriel Heyn, 1558; Giacomo Barozzi da Vignola, *Buonaroti, Michel Angelo. Regola delli cinque ordini d'architectura...* Amsterdam: I. & C. Blaev, 1640; Sebastiano Serlio, *De Architectura Libri Quinque.* Venezia, F. Senensis & J. Criegher, 1569; Aviler, Augustin Charles d'. Les Cinq Ordres d'Architecture de Vincent Scamozzi ... Paris: J.B. Coignard, 1685; Georg Caspar Erasmus, *Seülen-Buch Oder Gründlicher Bericht von den Fünf Ordnungen der Architekture-Kunst ... Norimberga, Chr. Gerhard, 1667; Oswald Mathias Ungers, Die Thematisierung de Architecktur.* Stoccarda DVA, 1983; Wendel Dietterlin, *Architectura und Austheilung der V Seüln.* Stoccarda 1593-98; André Lurcat, *Formes, Composition et Lois d'Harmonie. Eléments d'une science de l'esthétique architecturale,* V. Paris, Editions Vincent Fréal (1944); Neralco (d.i. Gius. Ercolani). *Descrizione del Colosseo Romano del Panteon e del Tempio Vaticano.* Ancona, Stamperia di Niccola Belelli, 1763; Cesare Cesariano, *Architectura Libri Decem Di Lucio Vitruvio Pollione De Como,* Gotardo da Ponte, 1521; Heinz Götze, *Castel del Monte. Gestalt und Symbol der Architektur Friedrichs II.* Monaco Prestel, 1984; Walther Rivius, *Der Architektur fürnembsten ... Mathematischen und Mechanischen Künst ... in drei fürneme Bücher aggetheilet.* Norimberga Gabriel Heyn, 1558; Franco Borsi, *Leon Battista Alberti. l'Opera Completa.* Milano, Electa Editrice, 1980; Michele Furnari, *Atlante del Rinascimento. Il disegno dell'architettura da Brunelleschi a Palladio.* Napoli, Electa Napoli, 1993; Le Corbusier, *Kommende Baukunst.* Stoccarda u.a.O.: DVA, 1926; Bruno Zevi, *Giuseppe Terragni.* Zurigo, Artemis, 1989; Fritz Neumeyer, *Oswald Mathias Ungers. Architektur 1951-1990.* Stoccarda, DVA, 1991.

Quotations from: Cologne, Ungers Archiv für Architekturwisenschaft

Giovanni di Agostino (?)
Project for the Facade
of the Palazzo Sansedoni
1340
*Siena, Collezione Monte
dei Paschi*
Cat. no. 4

The Italian peninsula during the Renaissance was divided into many states of different size and character; there was no common purpose that would generate a national consciousness. Naples and Sicily constituted a kingdom; the Papal States reached from south of Rome to as far north as Bologna, Parma and Piacenza, and were governed autocratically from the Vatican; there were *signorie*—mostly duchies, active in the patronage of architecture: the Este in Ferrara, the Montefeltro and della Rovere in Urbino, the Gonzaga in Mantua, the Sforza in Milan. Florence, Venice and Genoa, city-states that controlled large territories in central and northern Italy, had republican constitutions but were, in fact, ruled by a restricted group of patricians. While each state posessed extensive lands, its regional culture developed primarily in, and radiated from, its central city.

Because Renaissance architects were intent on reviving the vocabulary, the technical command, and the gravity of classical monuments, they assiduously examined and recorded the Roman ruins and studied Vitruvius' *De architectura*, of the first century B.C., the only surviving ancient architectural treatise. (Greek architecture did not figure in the classical revival primarily because Greece was in Ottoman control, and hostile to westerners.) In many of the regions of the peninsula there were few or no ancient remains, and almost every architect traveled to Rome, where they were most plentiful. This helps to account for the preeminence of Rome as an architectural center by the early years of the sixteenth century. The climate of the peninsular is temperate and because the topography of the areas where most new building went on is roughly similar, with plains, hills and rivers, there was not a compelling environmental need for marked differences in design from north to south. Yet the expression, materials and tecnhique of each region of the peninsula were distinctive, especially in the fifteenth century. The character of local stone strongly influenced the conception and appearance of buildings. In Florence, the dense gray-green *pietra serena* employed for the orders and combined with the off-white stucco used for the wall surfaces accentuated the articulation and also gave buildings a particular sobriety. In Rome, travertine, a warm creamy pitted volcanic stone, gave a rich and vigorous texture particularly suited to large-scale structures; the *pietra d'Istria* employed in Venice became brilliant white where exposed to the elements, and collected dark residues beneath projections, which further accentuated the major lines and imparted a unique brilliance.

Local economic, political and social structures imposed divergent objectives on architects, though most of the many books of theory by practitioners, from Leon Battista Alberti's *De re aedificatoria* (ca. 1450, published 1485) sought to establish a universal *all'antica* approach to design. The following essay briefly characterizes the particular architectural character of the principal regions (Tafuri 1992).

Tuscany

Tuscany, and Florence in particular, was the cradle of Renaissance architecture. Architects elsewhere during the fifteenth century were all in some degree dependent on the innovations of Tuscan architecture and on the architectural treatise of Leon Battista Alberti and, to a lesser extent, those of Filarete and Francesco di Giorgio Martini. There were few ancient buildings in Tuscany: though Florence and Lucca retained the plan of a Roman military town. But a vigorous revival of antiquity had already occurred in the Romanesque period of the eleventh and twelfth centuries (Florence Baptistery, which was believed to be an ancient temple of Mars, S. Miniato al Monte, the facade of the Badia di Fiesole). The great period of urban and architectural development in Florence and Siena started in the thirteenth century. In Florence during the 1290s the defensive walls were extended for the third time, the cathedral, the Palazzo de' Signori (Palazzo Vecchio), the Loggia dei Priori, the churches of S. Croce and S. Maria Novella were being constructed, and the Palazzo del Podestà rebuilt, leaving almost no public building to be done in the Renaissance. Florence and Siena still give the appearance of being late medieval towns (the Sienese Palazzo Sansedoni represented in the drawing of 1339 is of a type repeated throughout the city) in spite of the destruction by republican regimes of the medieval family towers and the brilliance of their early

opposite
Florence Baptistery
detail of the exterior
11th–12th cent.

319

Palazzo Medici
Florence

Filippo Brunelleschi
Ospedale degli Innocenti
(Foundling Hospital), Florence
detail of the portico
1419-24

Renaissance architecture. What gave Florence in particular its early lead in the arts and letters was first, its particularly strong economic position based on industry—especially the manufacture of cloth and silk goods, banking and trade; second, the early (1250) and violent establishment of a republican government committed to consolidating economic strength (representative, yet controlled by the Guelph *magnati*) and repression of the Ghibellines; and third, the early (mid-fourteenth-century) development of a humanist culture kindled by Petrarch and Boccaccio. Humanism prompted an ardent interest in everything surviving from classical antiquity; its manifestation in architecture led to intense study and the emulation of ancient remains, especially in Rome, and the resurrection and adoration of Vitruvius' treatise.

The Florentine oligarchs were enthusiastic patrons of the arts, and competed for distinction in the building of palaces and sponsorship of churches and monasteries (Gombrich 1960; Kent 1987; Lydeche 1987b). They did so both as individuals and in consort through the guilds (*arti*), which were dominated by those referred to today as "management." The construction and maintenance of Florence Cathedral and the Baptistery, for example, were supervised by committees of the guilds known as the Arte della Lana (wool manufacturers) and Arte dei Mercanti di Calimala (merchants, bankers) (Brucker 1983). Returning from exile in 1434 the Medici quickly gained control of the government from behind the scenes—it was basic to their policy that they should not wield their power overtly—and launched a vigorous architectural program involving, for example, the building (by the family architect Michelozzo Michelozzi) of the family palace from 1444 on, which became a model for later palace design, of S. Lorenzo, the Library of S. Marco, the Badia di

Fiesole and five family villas (Elam 1978; Gobbi 1980; Goldthwaite 1972; Gombrich 1960). Lorenzo il Magnifico, the last powerful Medici before the expulsion of the family, in 1494, built the most imposing of these starting in 1485 at Poggio a Caiano, designed by Giuliano da Sangallo, the first to incorporate a temple portico into the entrance facade, an element suggested in Alberti's treatise, which was published in the same year (Ackerman 1990a; Bierman 1969). Lorenzo, a discriminating amateur of architecture, also launched major planning schemes for Florence that were left unrealized at his death in 1492. Competing families, notably the Rucellai and the Strozzi, soon built imposing three-story palaces to advertise their wealth and position: "magnificence" was considered a virtue in this culture. Florentines favored rustication, which suggested strong defense and also referred to ancient Etruscan (Tuscan, and therefore regional) practice.

Quattrocento architecture did not imitate antiquity in the sixteenth-century sense; designers felt free to allude to ancient practice while freely inventing new forms that often, as in the work of the first great Renaissance architect, Filippo Brunelleschi (1377–1446), made opportune use of local Gothic practice. Indeed, Filippo's dome of Florence Cathedral is grounded in the ribbed technique of Gothic vaults, and the employment of a facade portico for the Ospedale degli Innocenti (Foundling Hospital) is derived from the fourteenth-century Ospedale di S. Matteo. The machines invented by Brunelleschi to lift building materials to the great heights of the cathedral dome sparked progress in construction, and were often copied by other artists into the sixteenth century.

Leon Battista Alberti, a gentleman-architect as well as a writer on an imposing range of subjects, came closer than did Brunelleschi to the spirit of ancient architecture, as may be seen in his facade for the church of S. Francesco in Rimini, which is based on a Roman arch

Filippo Brunelleschi
Loggia of the Ospedale degli Innocenti (Foundling Hospital), Florence
1419–24

in the walls of that town. While serving as a papal secretary he surveyed ancient and modern Rome. As a theorist, Leon Battista Alberti also best exemplified a non-antique passion of the early Renaissance for numerical proportion systems and geometrical constructions; among these, artificial perspective, an innovation of the Renaissance, exerted a powerful influence on architecture.

The Sienese architect and theorist Francesco di Giorgio Martini executed a group of fortresses for Federico da Montefeltro of Urbino, which, realizing his theoretical writings and drawings, revolutionized fortification design, particularly with respect to the invention of the low-profile bastion as a more effective defense against the newly developed mobile artillery (von Moos 1974). With his predecessor Francesco Laurana, Francesco di Giorgio also executed the exceptionally harmonious court and interiors of the ducal palace in Urbino, perhaps the most genial princely dwelling of the Renaissance.

His churches, S. Maria del Calcinaio in Cortona, and S. Bernardino in Urbino, exemplify his system of proportion based on the human body, and make only a nod to antique precedent (see *Francesco di Giorgio architetto* 1993).

The Florentine Bernardo Rossellino was called upon in 1460 by the Sienese Pope Pius II Piccolomini to develop the town plan for Pienza, the centerpiece of which was an innovative and influential trapezoidal piazza ringed by newly designed palaces: the one for the pope is close to being a replica of Alberti's Palazzo Rucellai in Florence (Tönnesmann 1990). Tuscan architects also exported the new style to Milan (Filarete's Ospedale Maggiore and the destroyed Banco Mediceo, possibly by the same architect) and Naples (Villa Poggioreale by Giuliano da Maiano, 1487 on).

Giusto Utens
The Medici Villa at Pratolino
ca. 1599
Florence, Museo Storico
Topografico
"Firenze com'era"

In the elegant S. Maria delle Carceri (begun 1484–85) in Prato, Giuliano da Sangallo produced a homage to Brunelleschi in a central-plan church that anticipates the noble scale of early sixteenth-century buildings. As in Venice, political problems caused a break in the architectural tradition in the early sixteenth century.

The Medici were replaced by a republican government which was in turn toppled on the return of the Medici, who were able to exercise still more power after the election of Lorenzo's nephew to the papacy as Leo X, in 1514. Leo revived the family commitment to the church of S. Lorenzo, and in 1516 asked the major architects of Rome and Florence to submit designs for the facade.

Michelangelo was given the commission and devised a church facade distinguished by being entirely of Carrara marble and by the richness of its sculptural program. The fine wooden model (1518) does not reveal this, but does show the originality of the artist's resolution

322

RATOLINO

of the problem faced by all Renaissance designers of church facades, of adjusting the ancient orders, scaled after the human body, to the great height of the nave. Michelangelo was later given the commission for the Cappella Medici and then the library, the Biblioteca Laurenziana, both of which preserved elements of fifteenth-century Florentine style within the most unclassical and fantastic design of the Renaissance.

The duchy of Tuscany lost the architectural preeminence that characterized the work of the fifteenth century; architects became courtiers, which raised their social status but helped to give their work the coolness and tightness revealed in the competition models for the facade of S. Maria del Fiore, Florence Cathedral (1587), and in Giorgio Vasari's project for the loggia on the main square of Arezzo (1573).

The landscape architecture of the ducal villas that ringed Florence was the greatest achievement of late Renaissance Tuscan designers (Gobbi 1980).

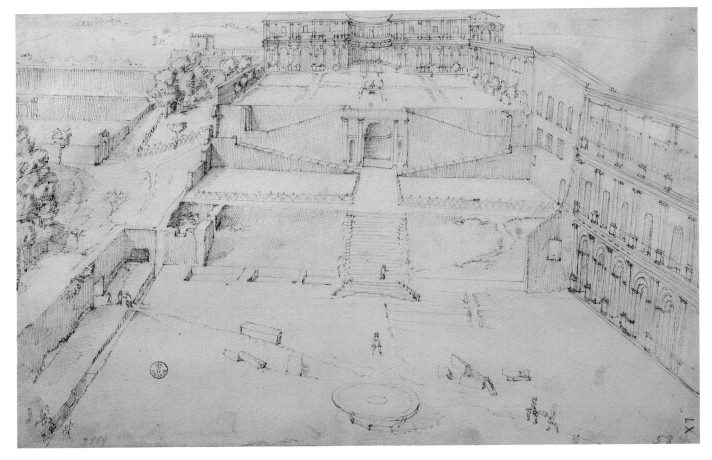

The most spectacular garden was that of Bernardo Buontalenti at Pratolino (1569), where the imitation of nature—as in the waterfall—broke down the formality that had characterized gardens of the period.

Giovanni Antonio Dosio
View of the Belvedere Court
Rome
*Florence, Uffizi, Gabinetto
Disegni e Stampe, Uff. 2559A*
Cat. no. 131

Rome

The fact that Rome was the locus of the capital of the ancient Roman Empire and that the remains of its walls, its buildings and its roads were everywhere apparent had an overwhelming impact on the formation of its Renaissance architecture. Its site was also a powerful constituent influence; the Tiber flowed in a great bend that enclosed a flat area of modest extent at the foot of seven low hills; this was the extent of the small late medieval settlement of some 17,000 people, a population depleted in the fourteenth century by the loss of its economic support consequent to the departure of the papacy and its court to France. This "Babylonian Captivity" came to an end in 1420 with the return of Martin V and the Curia to Rome, but it was some time before the economy could support major building enterprises (Rome, which never did develop adequate manufacture and trade, depended primarily on service functions and on the wealth of the Church). Gradually, in the later years of the century, increasing numbers of churches and papal and cardinals' palaces were built, but, while papal projects were ambitious, achievements remained modest, and expression particularly reserved; the available architects were not of the first rank (Bruschi 1985a; Burroughs 1990; Westfall 1974).

A radical change occurred in the first years of the sixteenth century due first to the emergence of the papacy as a major power with pretensions of equality with the emerging nation states and the Holy Roman Empire, and second to the diversion of the wealth of ecclesiastical property and the contributions of believers throughout Christendom to support the lavish life of popes, cardinals and bishops in Rome. This fortuitously coincided with the fall of the Medici government in Florence in 1494 and of the Sforza dukedom in Milan in 1499, which forced artists in those states to migrate to the more favorable milieu of patronage in Rome, among them Leonardo da Vinci, Bramante, Michelangelo, Raphael, and the Sangallo family. These exceptional talents were inspired to great achievements both by the proximity of the monuments of ancient Rome, and by association and rivalry with one another.

The iron will and limitless ambition of Pope Julius II della Rovere (1503–13) set grandiose goals for the newly arrived artists that spurred them to extraordinary achievements—the

Caradosso (Cristoforo Foppa) (?)
Foundation Medal for New
St. Peter's
1505
Milan, Civiche Raccolte
Archeologiche e Numismatiche
Cat. no. 284

Donato Bramante
Tempietto of S. Pietro
in Montorio, Rome
1508

Basilica of St. Peter, the Belvedere Court and the Palazzo dei Tribunali of Bramante, the Vatican Stanze of Raphael, the Cappella Sistina ceiling and Julian tomb of Michelangelo; of these, only the ceiling could be completed during the patron's lifetime. Julius II's example set a high standard for succeeding popes and spurred contemporary Roman patrons, who employed the same artists, to apply their inventiveness to smaller-scale projects such as the memorial Tempietto of S. Pietro in Montorio of ca. 1502, where Bramante demonstrated how antique elements could be reconstituted in a modern context and how grandeur of scale could be achieved in a small building. Bramante and Raphael also developed for patrons of more modest means a new urban house type of two stories with ground-floor shops (Frommel 1973, II; Valtieri 1988).

The new Basilica of St. Peter (1506), Julius II's greatest enterprise, was to be the grandest church in Christendom, and took over a century to build. The evolution of the design and construction of St. Peter's illustrates the uniqueness of Roman patronage: each succeeding pope immediately took up the task on the death of his predecessor, often selecting new architects and altering the design. Julius II's conception was a daring undertaking that seemed pagan to some contemporaries: it required the razing of the revered fourth-century basilica of the Emperor Constantine and it was modeled on the great ancient baths of Rome in technique and form, and Bramante's design was to be crowned by a saucer dome modeled on that of the Pantheon. Bramante's initial project, which had roots in the church studies of Leonardo da Vinci, proposed a central plan, either as an alternative to a longitudinal one, which he put forward in later proposals (Uff. 20A) or as his preferred solution. It was powerfully influenced by the ruins: the masonry work adapted ancient concrete techniques to brick-and-mortar in the great arches, and the dome and the Colossal order was copied from the Pantheon. The workshop was the training-ground of the major architects of the succeeding generation: Raphael, Antonio da Sangallo the Younger, Baldassarre Peruzzi, who became in turn the architects-in-chief. The further history of the Basilica is discussed elsewhere in this volume.

*Gianfrancesco da Sangallo
for Raphael*
Plan Project for the Villa
Madama
*Florence, Uffizi, Gabinetto
Disegni e Stampe, 273Ar.
Cat. no. 212*

Hendrick Frans Van Lint
Villa Madama
1748
*Cambridge, Fitzwilliam Museum
Cat. no. 218*

326

Enrico van lint
delta studio F. Roma 1748

The majesty goals of Julius II were taken up by his successor Leo X Medici, who turned to Raphael as Bramante's heir. Raphael's most ambitious project was the Villa Madama, designed for the pope's cousin, later Clement VII, a huge complex outside the walls on the slopes of Monte Mario at the entrance to the city (Belli Barsali 1970).

Raphael's letter describing his project was closely modeled on a similar letter of Pliny the Younger (ca. A.D. 100). Leo X's keen interest in the preservation and restoration of ancient monuments encouraged widerspread surveying and drawing of the remains which Raphael had urged upon him. Raphael was also the initiator of the influential plan for the Piazza del Popolo at the northern gate to the city with its three radiating streets, the westernmost of which, then called Via Leonina, extended to the Medicean Palazzo Madama by Piazza Navona.

Urban design was a major concern of sixteenth-century pontiffs; Paul III Farnese completed Leo X's *trivium* at Piazza del Popolo and was the sponsor of Rome's civic center, the Campidoglio, which Michelangelo designed on a trapezoidal plan as an enclosed outdoor room around the ancient equestrian statue of Marcus Aurelius.

The most ambitious urban scheme of the Renaissance was Sixtus V's project to bind all parts of the city and to develop the southeastern quarter by bringing water onto the Esquiline Hill. Broad avenues marked by terminal obelisks joined major pilgrimage churches and set the style for much Baroque planning (Portoghesi 1971).

Cardinals as well as popes contributed major buildings to the urban context. Many, like the Medici and the Este, brought great private wealth to Rome from other cities; others, like the Farnese, whose palace was the grandest of its time, built up wealth and dynasties out of their ecclesiastical privileges (Keller 1980).

Villas like that of the Este in Tivoli outside Rome were lavish retreats for the princes of the Church to spend summers or times of plague in *villeggiatura*. As clerics, they pursued more sedentary diversions than secular villa-builders; almost none of the Roman villas, for example, were related to agricultural enterprise, as were those of Tuscany and the Veneto (Belli Barsali 1975; Coffin 1979; Lazzaro 1985).

Antonio da Sangallo the Younger and Michelangelo Palazzo Farnese, Rome

328

*Giacomo della Porta
The Gesù, Rome
detail of the facade
1565*

*Giacomo da Vignola
The Gesù, Rome
detail of the nave
1568 and after*

Churchbuilding in sixteenth-century Rome proceeded at an unprecedented rate, and the typical longitudinal plan of the Renaissance developed there. Prior to the era of the Counter-Reformation, the typical church had a boxlike form, like Antonio da Sangallo the Younger's S. Spirito in Sassia, the facade of which exercized a strong impact on subsequent work. The first Jesus church, the Gesù, begun in 1551 by Giacomo Barozzi da Vignola (facade by Giacomo della Porta, 1565 and later), became paradigmatic for late Renaissance design—barrel-vaulted to improve acoustics, the broad nave flanked by rows of cupola-topped chapels, heavily constructed to sustain the thrust of the vault. The influence of the Gesù on later design is evident in the Chiesa Nuova model.

When Rome was sacked in 1527 by the unpaid and undisciplined forces of Emperor Charles V, its architects fled and brought their experience at the core of ancient and modern achievement to princes and states throughout Italy and beyond.

Venice and the Veneto

Venice, the only surviving metropolis built in the water, was created from the sixth to the eighth century by mainland people fleeing invaders from northern Europe. It is largely an artifact formed by expanding the circumference of scattered islands with piles and landfill to borders that could be joined by bridges across the intervening canals. To some extent the islands retained their identity in having a core *campo* (piazza), with a church, rimmed by palaces and more modest houses, all tightly compacted because of the fixed perimeter of the city.

The Grand Canal, a natural "river" within the lagoon, winds sinuously through the city, providing the setting for a brilliant array of patrician palaces that contrasts markedly with the dispersed siting of palaces in other cities.

The typical palace plan, reflecting Byzantine forerunners, differs radically from those elsewhere, being divided in depth into three tracts of which the center, open from front to rear, is used on the ground floor for storage, loading and unloading of goods, and access to the main stairway, and for public dining and reception halls above. Facades, from the earliest surviving buildings, reflect this plan in a tripartite vertical division the center segment of which is the more open, often with loggias on the ground floor and rows of windows above (Diruf 1990; Howard 1981).

The Venetian lagoon, shielded from the Adriatic by a narrow archipelago with a few passages wide enough to admit shipping, formed the finest port in the Mediterranean basin and helped to make Venice the major mercantile power of the early Renaissance. Her exceptionally large fleet traded with Byzantium and the Levant, carrying the prized spices and wares of Asia to the Rialto markets that attracted merchants from all of Europe. Venetian architecture reflects these bonds with the East: the oldest palaces are Byzantine in style, as

are the domed churches, many with the Byzantine quincunx plan, from the eleventh-century St. Mark's into the sixteenth century.

The watery setting was also a major factor in the protection of the Republic and the stability of its government.

Because the lagoon provided better protection than the thickest city walls (no foreign power managed successfully to besiege or enter Venice prior to Napoleon), patrons and architects could disregard the kind of defensive considerations that affected design elsewhere (Florence, Palazzo Strozzi). The Piazza S. Marco opens hospitably toward the sea, and many palace facades have a lacy transparency.

The city was governed by patrician families (the number of which was strictly limited), who elected a doge from their midst.

Venice remained politically stable for a millennium, avoiding the violent revolutionary disruptions of Florence and many other mainland cities, and this permitted an unbroken evolution of local architectural styles (Tafuri 1985b).

A Gothic style, sustained in part by economic ties to northern Europe, survived in Venice well into the fifteenth century, gradually assimilating aspects of Renaissance taste. The first importation of a fully Renaissance vocabulary occurred toward the end of the century, when architects from outside Venice fused elements of the Florentine Renaissance of Brunelleschi and Alberti with further echoes of Byzantine style, as in the unique church of S. Maria dei Miracoli by Pietro Lombardo (begun 1481). The churches, palaces and *scuole* of Mauro Codussi were among the most innovative of the late fifteenth century anywhere in Italy (Palazzo Vendramin-Callergi, ca. 1502). Yet the architecture of Venice, in contrast to that of Florence, had little influence outside the territorial borders.

By the end of the fifteenth century, the expansion of the Venetian city-state across northern Italy aroused the apprehension of other nations, and in 1509 the allied forces of the papacy and major European states brought enemy soldiers to the shores of the lagoon. The threat continued seven years, so depleting public and private resources that building virtually ceased between 1510 and 1530.

The state dwellings/offices on the Piazza S. Marco (*Procuratie*, begun 1513) were virtually the only secular structures initiated in this period.

When construction finally resumed, most architects remaining from the prewar era were out of touch with the major architectural innovations of the early sixteenth century, and were no longer capable of giving Venice a forward-looking image. This situation coincided fortuitously with the Sack of Rome in 1527; artists who had been beneficiaries of papal patronage escaped to other cities, and Venice harbored the Florentine Jacopo Sansovino and the

Jacopo de' Barbari
Perspective Map of Venice
Venice, Museo Correr

Mauro Codussi
Palazzo Vendramin-Calergi
Venice
ca. 1502

Pietro Lombardo
S. Maria dei Miracoli, Venice
ca. 1481–89

Veronese Michele Sanmicheli. Sansovino, a sculptor-architect who had worked in Rome alongside the major artists of the Roman Renaissance, became *proto* (chief designer) of the administrators of the central area, in 1527, and was assigned the Loggetta, the Zecca (mint) and the Biblioteca Marciana (begun 1527), structures facing the Doge's Palace in the Piazzetta di S. Marco and contiguous wharf, the most conspicuous sites in the city. These brought to Venice the mass and grandeur of ancient as well as modern Rome in an ambience where earlier architecture had emphasized the surface plane; but the architect also imparted to his buildings a peculiarly Venetian sensitivity to light, shadow and color. The library, for all its basilica-like monumentality, models light and dark with a painter's sensibility, intensifying the festive quality of the square.

These buildings also incorporate an ambitious symbolism of Venetian power and a proud evocation of a glorious and largely invented Roman past: they were in a sense the stone equivalents of the state histories being commissioned by the senate in the early sixteenth century. Concurrently, Sansovino and other contemporaries designed for more conservative, anti-Roman and anti-papal clients in an indigenous, even anonymous style with minimal or no classical detail (Lewis 1981b).

On the Venetian terra firma, the cities of Verona and Vicenza and the country estates around them were enriched by the architecture of Michele Sanmicheli and Andrea Palladio. In both communities a feudal nobility with allegiance to the Holy Roman Empire adopted humanist and antiquarian interests which they charged their architects to advertise (Kubelik 1977; Muraro 1986). Verona, moreover, possessed remains of major ancient monuments which exerted a powerful influence on Sanmicheli, a Veronese who had apprenticed in Rome.

Jacopo Sansovino
Biblioteca Marciana, Venice
ca. 1534

on the following pages
Vittore Carpaccio
Healing of Someone Possessed
detail from the Miracle of the
Relic of the True Cross
ca. 1494
Venice, Gallerie dell'Accademia

333

Paris Bordone
Fisherman Presenting
St. Mark's Ring to the Doge
1534–35
Venice, Gallerie dell'Accademia

336

Andrea Palladio was a unique phenomenon who rose out of obscurity as a Paduan stone carver with the help of his Vicentine and Venetian patrons to become the most celebrated architect of modern times. Essential to his development was his contact with ancient and early sixteenth-century buildings, primarily through trips to Rome, acquaintance with drawings of ancient monuments elsewhere made by other architects, and with Vitruvius and other Roman writers. The Roman cast of his palaces and villas appealed to the local nobility and to Venetians who built country houses on the mainland, but the distinction of his work resided not primarily in porticoes and pediments, but in his command of proportion and scale, in the geometrical clarity of his masses and voids, and in his ability to assimilate in-

Andrea Palladio
Villa Emo
Fanzolo
16th cent.

digenous traditions such as the characteristic Venetan barns (*barchesse*) that he adapted as porticoed wings to his villas.

Commissions in Venice, which came to him late in his career, transformed Venetian ecclesiastical architecture by combining grandeur with a great scenographic flair particularly adapted to the beauties of the Venetian light and ambience (Lieberman 1977). The same quality may be seen in his unexecuted project for the Rialto Bridge. Comparing this project to its modest early Renaissance predecessor is a telling measure of the expansion of Venetian architectural ambition in the course of the sixteenth century.

Lombardy

From early medieval times through the Baroque, Lombardy was the training ground for the finest masons of Italy, and one finds there buildings of a particular richness of color and texture.

The Lombard architecture of the fifteenth century was less influenced by Tuscan precedent than that of other centers; a characteristic brick construction with stone accents and rich molded terra-cotta ornament was employed in religious structures that retained late Gothic plan schemes or elements such as the handsome tower of Chiaravalle or S. Gottardo in

Milan. The earliest Quattrocento building of international stature is the Certosa or monastery near Pavia, a project initiated by the Visconti rulers and completed by the Sforza (final construction begun 1473).

The basically monastic-Gothic plan of the church is extended by apses on the crossing arms and choir modeled on regional twelfth-century Romanesque antecedents, perhaps conceived as a stepping-stone to ancient Rome; the sculptural richness of the marble facade by Amadeo (1473–after 1501), who had already built the jewel-like Cappella Colleoni in Bergamo in the 1470s, exemplifies the Lombard taste for richness of ornament, already evident in the late Trecento cathedral of Milan (see *Giovanni Antonio Amadeo* 1989).

Lodovico Sforza, known as "il Moro" (1477–99), an enterprising patron of architecture and urban design, brought Donato Bramante from Urbino to Milan in about 1480, when he was still primarily a painter, and commissioned a number of major projects. The main piazza at Vigevano, carved invasively out of the center of the town (1493; see the cathedral model), realized Renaissance urban ideals in surrounding the entire space with uniform arcades and in seeking to revive the ancient forum; the Lombard taste for surface ornament is here realized by frescoes on all the facades, some representing triumphal arches. Bramante's first architectural essays picked up on Lombard regionalism, as can be seen in the print that he designed for Previderi in 1481.

Regional influence is most apparent in the design for the tribune and choir of S. Maria delle Grazie in Milan (Guiniforte Solari's nave of a few years earlier is still an example of Gothic survival), which Lodovico intended to serve as the Sforza mausoleum. On the exterior Bramante employed characteristically rich terra-cotta detailing, and its grand dome is hidden behind an arcaded screen, while the interior in its simple amplitude of spatial volume

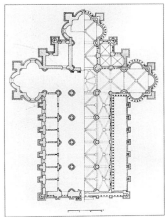

Certosa of Pavia
plan

Certosa of Pavia
the small cloister and
tiburio
ca. 1473

Donato Bramante
S. Maria delle Grazie, Milan
exterior of choir apse

Donato Bramante
S. Maria delle Grazie
detail of the nave
toward the main altar
1466–90

on the following pages
Galeazzo Alessi
Palazzo Marino, Milan
detail of the courtyard
ca. 1558

anticipates the monumentality of the early sixteenth century in Rome, which in effect stemmed from Bramante (see *Bramante a Milano* 1986). Leonardo da Vinci, who had come to Milan in 1492, exerted a powerful influence even without designing actual buildings. His many drawings, and particularly his projects and sketches for central-plan churches, also preserve the local traditions on the exterior, but propose plans and a disposition of interior space without which Bramante's projects for St. Peter's in the Vatican could not have been conceivable.

The model for Pavia Cathedral, ca. 1485–1526, in which the two artists both played a part, represents a transition in which regional aspects are displaced by the new interest in interior spatial volumes, but the articulation of its walls and cupola are far from the simplicity of the first design for St. Peter's of only a few years later (Bruschi 1986).

With the expulsion of Lodovico il Moro by the French, the artists of his court dispersed, and Milanese architecture lay virtually dormant until the arrival of Galeazzo Alessi in Milan in 1557. Alessi, who had been trained in Rome in the circle of Antonio da Sangallo the Younger, brought a distinctive style firmly grounded in a personal interpretation of ancient ornament, enriched by an idiosyncratic fantasy derived from decorative painting and stucco-work, most impressively deployed in the huge Palazzo Marino (begun 1558; see also *Galeazzo Alessi* 1975).

The earlier tradition did not exert an impact on him (unless we see it as the source of the ornamental lavishness, which is quite different from his contemporary work in Genoa), though his adaptation of human herms to pilaster shafts became an element of later Lombard style.

341

Giulio Romano
Palazzo Te, Mantua
detail of the entrance portal
ca. 1525-35

In the design of SS. Paolo e Barnaba (1561–67), the church of the newly-recognized Barnabite Order, he applied many features reflecting the concerns of the Counter-Reformation. Later in the century, when Cardinal Carlo Borromeo came to Milan as archbishop and undertook to realize the spirit of the Council of Trent by establishing firm control of the churches and institutions of the archdiocese, he called the painter Pellegrino Tibaldi to realize the principles later expounded by Carlo Borromeo in his small tract, *Instructionum fabricae et suppellectilis ecclesiasticae*, 1577.

The collaboration led to notable innovations in design, as at the Collegio Borromeo in Pavia and the sanctuary basilicas at Rho and Caravaggio (1575–79).

Tibaldi's best-known work in Milan, S. Fedele, for the Jesuits, alongside Palazzo Marino, is innovative in providing a single vessel without side aisles, which made for a simplified facade design.

The cardinal's nephew and successor Federico Borromeo (1564–1631) pursued a vigorous building campaign in the early years of the seventeenth century, following his uncle's spirit more than his word.

Other Centers

In Naples, the only southern city affected by the Renaissance, the Spanish prince, Alfonso of Aragon, after taking possession from the Angevins in 1443, started to build a magnificent palace, which remained incomplete at his death fifteen years later; a record of his patronage survives in the triumphal arch of the gatehouse to the palace, placed between two plain round defensive towers, of 1453 (Hersey 1973); his successors commissioned the Porta

Giulio Romano
Palazzo Te, Mantua
detail of the loggia
ca. 1525-35

Anonymous
The French Fleet
Besieges Genoa
in 1684
17th cent.
Genoa, Museo Navale

Capuana, a simpler and more harmonious structure similarly framed by towers, by the Florentine Giuliano da Maiano, in 1485, as an element in an ambitious urban plan. Aspirations to develop an indigenous Renaissance architecture were frustrated by political instability, which continued to limit building through the sixteenth century.

Mantua, a town of modest size and population, was consistently enriched in the period by virtue of the patronage of the ruling Gonzaga family. In the fifteenth century Lodovico invited Alberti to design the central-plan church of S. Sebastiano and the large basilica of S. Andrea (1470 and later), which were executed by an able local architect, Luca Fancelli, but these were not examples of regional architecture.

The old brick *castello* or castle, with four rectangular corner towers, overlooking the bridge that connected the lakebound city to the plains of the Po Valley, was at once representative of local character, and in harmony with a widespread Western European tradition of seignorial fortress-palaces.

In the following century, Federico Gonzaga attracted, in 1524, a major Roman architect, Giulio Romano, to the north, even before the Diaspora after the Sack of Rome. Giulio's work at the palace and at the suburban villa, the Palazzo del Te (begun 1525), may have picked up some of its fantasy from the local fifteenth-century vernacular, but was primarily based on the sophisticated decorative vocabulary of the school of Raphael in Rome (*Giulio Romano* 1989). Giulio built himself a small palace (ca. 1540) which reflects the type invented by Bramante for the Casa Caprini in 1508.

Genoa's great period of Renaissance architecture came late, due to the conservatism of its ruling families, who had traditionally inhabited private complexes, called *alberghi*, in the tightly-packed center.

The city circles theater-like around a fine harbor, rising steeply to embracing hills, providing, at least in the uppermost portions, panoramic views. The first indigenous Genoese Renaissance building is the Villa of Andrea Doria, 1521–29 with later additions, which was pieced together from older dwellings; its grand terraced garden by the Florentine Montorsoli (1540s) was widely celebrated.

346

Galeazzo Alessi
Villa Cambiaso, Genoa
ca. 1548–50

But the golden age began with the arrival in 1548 of Galeazzo Alessi, who had worked in Rome and in his native Perugia, where he did not yet exhibit the genius that later ranked him with his contemporaries Vignola and Palladio; his designs for a group of suburban villa-palaces in cubic form such as the Villa Cambiaso, of 1548, created a new genre, more formal and urban than the villas of other centers, and his reinterpretation of the central-plan scheme of St. Peter's in the Vatican for S. Maria di Carignano (1549), was unique for its prominent high drum and dome and tall corner towers, both of which capitalized on its prominent hilltop site on what was at the time the edge of the city (*Galeazzo Alessi* 1975). In developing the Strada Nuova (project 1551, construction beginning 1558), a broad street lined entirely with grand palaces and gardens that on the up-hill side climbed the slopes in terraces linked by imposing staircases, Alessi's fertile imagination (the actual builder was apparently the city architect Cantone) combined with the readiness of the leading families to abandon the center for ampler dwellings on the hillside above, led to the development of one of the most innovative speculative planning schemes of the Renaissance (Poleggi 1972). Economic constraints and the indifference of the Genoese patriciate may explain why Genoa's Renaissance did not radiate into the rest of Liguria.

Regional disparities, marked in the early Renaissance, lessened after the early years of the sixteenth century, when most of the major architects had apprenticed in the Roman workshops and moved out to other cities, carrying with them a similar approach to form and technique.

347

The Angevin Capital and the Aragonese Capital

Naples was one of medieval Europe's dominant cities. Considered in the long term, however, it was the Angevin sovereigns who turned the city into a capital. They were responsible for the administrative restructuring of the city into *Sedili* or constituencies in 1268, and for the promulgation of the *Capitoli di Regno* in 1289. These new legislative measures were the means by which the Angevins effected their sweeping program of urban renewal, thereby transforming Naples into one of the very first capitals of medieval Europe. On this point, Yves Renouard advocates that the new scheme of norms and town planning owed a great deal to the legacy of Frederick II, but was largely modeled on Paris.[1] This soon became a factor distinguishing the Aragonese from their precursors. Through the discerning mind of Alfonso I of Aragon (known as the "The Magnanimous") the source of inspiration was not Paris, but the cities of classical antiquity, such as those proposed by the Roman architect and theorist Vitruvius, as seen through the eyes of Leon Battista Alberti and enriched by the burgeoning humanistic spirit.

Although it in fact contested none of the strategic choices of the Angevins, the normative and ideological model pursued by Alfonso was of a distinctly different nature, and hence the title of this essay, in which the term "utopia" refers to that sweeping albeit unrealized program outlined by Alfonso and his successors.

During this same historical period, the learned elite of other cities such as Venice, Florence and even Siena vied for the position of second capital after Rome. For internal reasons of an institutional nature, the Neapolitan humanists disdained this rivalry, which was intimately bound to the republican ideal. Be that as it may, the drive for *renatio* is manifest in certain planning and architectural schemes that influenced the city's structure.

The close of the 1200s witnessed the insitution of one of the most imposing urban planning schemes ever applied to the city: the removal of the manufacturing activities from the old core had a vast impact on the city's makeup, such that even today Piazza Mercato and its neighborhood have a persistently marked functional layout. At the same time Charles turns his sights on the fortress of the Castel Nuovo. The complex answered the dual need for a strategic stronghold and a keystone for the urban planning scheme. The fortress made the port impregnable and catalyzed the creation of the Corregge quarter, which quickly became the most attractive and elegant residential neighborhood of the city. From hereon the Castel Nuovo offered a strategic link in the city's defense, and the adjacent area became the fulcrum of administrative activities, a busy "enterprise zone." The upper magistrates and the high court were installed in the new palazzo-fortress. By contrast, most of the many (and in some cases, sizable) monastic complexes founded under the Anjou dynasty were clustered in the old city above—with the exception of the Belforte and the S. Martino charterhouse, marking the first stages of expansion up the hill. The Angevin vision of the city was therefore directed toward the south and east, and toward the northwest slopes of the surrounding hillside.

The city into which the triumphant Alfonso marched in 1442 was radically different from the one the Angevins had witnessed upon their arrival. It was far more extensive, more open to the new needs of the burgeoning manufacturing activities and trade, and boasted a splendid castle and opulent residential quarter. While the Angevins shelled out enormous sums for the construction of churches—not only in Naples but all across the kingdom, their successors took a quite different course. After the subtle policy of Alfonso V, they decided to subordinate the needs of the church to those of the crown. Consequently far fewer churches or convents were founded under the Aragonese and, after the earthquake of 1450, work on religious buildings came to a halt.

Another major factor distinguishing the two dynasties is the different relations entertained with the Papal States and hence with Rome.

A more detailed exposition of building and planning policies can be found in my volume on Naples;[2] suffice it to say here that the Aragonese development program was spread over sixty years, and although they made no alterations to the original organism of the city, they completed the scheme initiated by the Angevin dynasty, and added numerous new features of their own. These enhancements were so fundamental, however, that they affected the func-

[1] Y. Renouard, *Les villes d'Italie de la fin du Xe siècle au debut du XIXe siècle*, Paris 1969 (It. trans. Milan, 1976).
[2] Cf. C. de Seta, *La città nella storia d'Italia*. Napoli, Rome-Bari, 1981, especially pp. 35-93.

Ferraiolo
Expulsion of the French from
Naples in July 1495
detail from Cronaca della
Napoli aragonese
15th cent.
New York, Pierpont Morgan
Library, MS. 801

Duchy of Ferdinand I of Aragon
Naples, Museo Archeologico
Nazionale

tional and social patterns of certain areas of the city. Crucial innovations include the dynamic restructuring of the Castel Nuovo (bar the Palatine chapel), the Castel dell'Ovo and the Belforte to the west, and the Castel Capuano and the Carmine bastions to the east. The alterations to the Castel Nuovo, which included rebuilding and extending the citadel, required the demolition of many neighboring buildings, mostly severely damaged during the siege of 1442. Excluding the residence of Conte d'Alife, most of the former wealthy quarter of Corregge was cleared to make way for the fortified wall around the new fortress and the so-called "emperor's kitchen garden" as handsomely captured in the sixteenth-century view by Jan van Stinemolen (1582). This slice of the city therefore lost the residential status it had enjoyed under the Angevins, though not its preeminently representative role. Other crucial schemes include the redevelopment of the area corresponding to the Selleria quarter, the opening of Via dell'Olmo, and the extension of Via dei Lanzeri, which became an internal thoroughfare (in alternative to the coast road) linking the port district with the east end of the market. The alterations to the Castel dell'Ovo after the earthquake also saw the opening of Via del Chiatamone, which runs along the seafront beneath the Pizzofalcone promontory, to the Castel Nuovo citadel. During the long reign of Ferdinand from 1458 to 1494, the city became the focus of the most imposing of all development schemes undertaken by the Aragonese dynasty, namely the enlargement of the defense walls on the east side of the city, a project carried through to completion by Ferdinand's successor, Alfonso II. Under the direction of Giuliano da Maiano (1432–90) the new walls enclosed the Castel Capuano—one of the outposts of the earlier defense system—and the Villa della Duchesca, also the work of the Tuscan architect Maiano.

In accord with his colleague Sepe, the scholar George Hersey has drawn attention to the

Francisco de Holanda
View of Castelnuovo
from Desenhos das Antigualhas
que vio Francisco D'Ollanda
1539–40
El Escorial (Madrid),
Real Monasterio
28.1.20, fol. 53v.

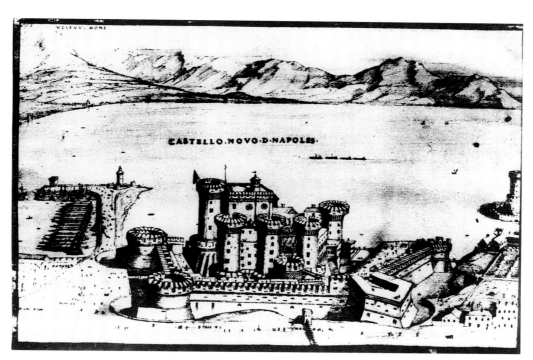

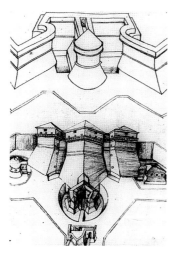

After Francesco di Giorgio
Martini
Sketches of Bastions
Florence, Biblioteca Nazionale
Codex Magliabechiano
II.1.141, fol. 241r.

entity of forces channeled into the defense works; the scheme also entailed a complete overhaul of the city's water mains and drainage systems.[3] Such were the principal features of the urban developments effected by the house of Aragon.

Renovatio urbis: *the Humanistic Project for the Ideal City*

In this essay I aim to show to what extent utopia merged with reality: Alfonso styled himself a humanist, and his concept of the city is incomplete without due attention to this factor in his design. The cultural phase through which the city was passing is illustrated by the fact that the Studio located in the Castel Nuovo fortress became an eminent focus for a revival of Vitruvian thought, and had a powerful influence on Naples' development in general. Alfonso I's interests in Vitruvius are documented in various sources: Panormita reports that the undertaking on the Castel Nuovo was done with consultation of Vitruvius' texts. Lorenzo Valla, a leading humanist thinker of his generation, was lector and secretary to Alfonso for eleven years from 1436 to 1447. Indeed, the city boasted a brilliant circle of artists and humanists, as amply documented.[4] What has been largely overlooked, however, is the

Antonio Lafrery
Map of Naples
detail
1566
Milan, Civica Raccolta Stampe
Achille Bertarelli

[3] Cf. G. H. L. Hersey, *Alfonso II and the Artistic Renewal of Naples 1485-1495*, New Haven-London, 1969; G. Sepe, *La murazione aragonese di Napoli, studio di restituzione, Napoli 1942*; and the more recent volume by L. Santoro, *Le mura di Napoli*, Rome, 1984.

[4] See M. Sanudo, *La spedizion di Carlo VIII in Italia*, ed. R. Fulin, Archivio Veneto, Venice 1873: 240. For the many questions of humanis culture, see G. Toscano, "Il 'bel sito di Napoli': fonti letterarie e iconografiche dal regno aragonese al viceregno spagnolo," in the reprint of B. Di Falco, *Descrittione dei luoghi antichi di Napoli e del suo amenissimo distretto*, ed. T. R. Toscano, Naples, 1992.

presence in the city of the Siena-born friend of Enea Silvio Piccolomini, Francesco Patrizi, later Bishop of Gaeta from 1462 until his death in 1492. Patrizi is considered one of the most accomplished Vitruvians of his time. In his work *De institutione rei publicae* the author dips liberally into Vitruvius' *De architectura*, and evinces an authoritative knowledge of the works of Alberti. Patrizi's *De institutione* pivots on Alberti's idea of the city as a lofty focus of civilian life: the whole of Book IV is devoted to fortifications, earthworks and gates, to streets and galleries, to types of private and public building. Vitruvius' hallmark is everywhere in evidence, as are Books IV and especially VIII of Alberti's celebrated treatise. Reference to Patrizi's work, which was begun in 1463, is offered by the author's request to the Bishop of Ferrara a few years earlier of a copy of Vitruvius; it is likely that he already had a manuscript copy of Alberti's work *De re aedificatoria*, which was first published in 1485, fifteen years after the author's death.

The *De institutione rei publicae* is dedicated to Sixtus IV della Rovere, the humanist pope whom Ferdinand of Aragon visited in Rome in January 1475. Recently Pier Nicola Pagliara[5] has suggested that some sections of Book VIII are not so much utopian proposals as for an existing city, perhaps Naples. This idea is based on a passage which recommends (and here the reference to Alberti is also evident) the regularity and uniformity of private building: "*Secundum vias privatae aedes longo ordines ad pares (si fieri potest) dimensiones constituendae sunt ut speciem urbis ornent. Nec quippiam exporrectum habeant, quod viis impedimento esse possit.*" We can say with some certainty that the *virtus* of architecture is part of that *nova ratio* that geared to exalting and endorsing the Ragion di Stato. This humanistic outlook was shared by popes Nicholas V, Pius II Piccolomini and Sixtus IV della Rovere, and by Lorenzo il Magnifico and Alfonso II of Aragon—who saw the regular layout to the city and the *ars aedificatoria* as the physical manifestation of a political will embodied in the *auctoritas* of the sovereign.

Giuliano da Maiano
Porta Capuana, Naples

Alfonso II's Urban Scheme, and the Vitruvian Tradition

We therefore have to consider the plan of Alfonso II, though not exactly from scratch but on the restructuring of the exist urban fabric, as a scheme for the ideal city, in line with the architectural treatises and culture of the second half of the Quattrocento. By virtue of its adherence to the urban reality and to the image of the state it represented, an elaborate plan for an ideal city along the lines of Filarete's "Sforzinda" for Milan.

The ideal city discussed in the treatises was an expression of political and cultural ideals, a perfect urban organism" capable of addressing all the problems of the large town—and particularly those relative to defense, hygiene and ceremonial status. It therefore took from the ideal city of Alfonso II, described by the Neapolitan humanist Pietro Summonte in a famous letter to Marcantonio Michiel, dated 20 March 1524. Having acknowledged Florence's supremacy in such matters, and the importance of Leon Battista Alberti's theoretical contribution, Summonte drew up an urban plan in honor of the humanist sovereign Alfonso II and his desire to beautify his city on the model of those of antiquity. "Extendere ad linea recta tucte le strade maestre," writes Alberti, "from city wall to city wall; remove the porticoes, corners and uneven sections; extend likewise the transverse roads from end to end, so that the straightness of the streets and alleys and the natural slope of the land from north to south, render this the cleanest and finest city ... in Europe, which even a light shower will wash clean like a plate of polished silver."

As it happens, a scheme of urban renewal, albeit only affecting the area of the Castel Nuovo, was already under way under Ferdinand, as discussed by Sixtus IV on the occasion of his visit to Rome on 6 January 1475. But Alfonso's plan extended the project to encompass the entire city, influenced (it would seem, from the contents of Summonte's letter) by the counsel of Francesco di Giorgio Martini, who is referred to as "Francesco da Siena."

The other prominent Vitruvian present in the court of Aragon was the Dominican friar, Giovanni Giocondo. His edition of Vitruvius' *De architectura* (1511), with its thorough philological approach and superb illustrative material, was a landmark in the studies into the Roman architect's ideas. Fra Giocondo was in contact with both Patrizi and Francesco di Giorgio, with whom (according to written sources) he discussed the Vitruvian treatise.

According to Maltese, and endorsed by Fontana,[6] in 1491 and 1492 he many have translated Vitruvius' treatise for Francesco di Giorgio. "In 1492, Francesco was in the employ of the Duke of Calabria, and Fra Giocondo was paid for the execution of 126 drawings from which 'Francesco da Siena' made into two books of papyrus, handwritten, one on architecture and the other on artillery and other defense machinery. These volumes may well be copies of the original set of drawings used by Francesco to illustrate, we think, the *Codex Magliabechiano.*"[7]

Naples, Castel Nuovo
Triumphal Arch, detail

[5] P. N. Pagliara, "Vitruvio da testo a canone," in *Biblioteca di Storia dell'Arte*, vol. III, Turin, 1986.
[6] V. Fontana, *Fra' Giovanni Giocondo architetto 1432-1515*, Vicenza, 1988 pp. 21-26.
[7] F. Di Giorgio Martini, *Trattati di Architettura Ingegneria e Arte Militare*, ed. C. Maltese, Milan, 1967, with introduction by Corrado Maltese.

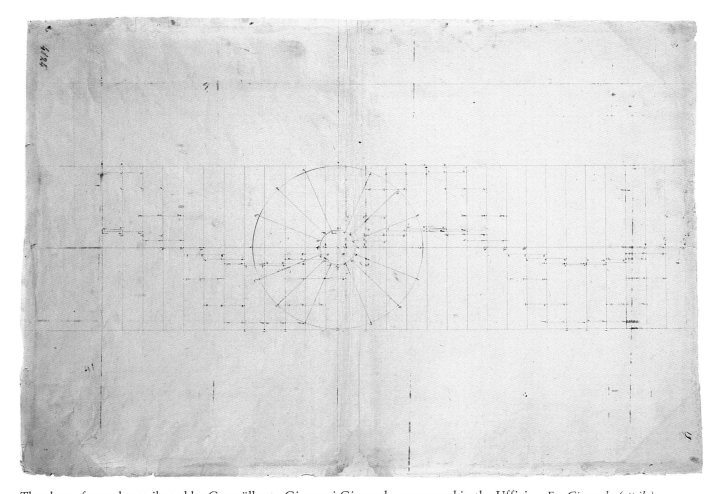

The sheet, formerly attributed by Geymüller to Giovanni Giocondo, conserved in the Uffizi (Uff. 4124Ar.-v.) has been related to the plan of the city as described by Summonte: the verso represents the compass-card divided into 16 segments in accordance with Vitruvius' treatise; the recto represents the three *decumani* stretching into infinity. In 1965 the Danish archaeologist Gustav Hamberg[8] suggested this possibility after mapping the drawing onto the ancient layout of Neapolis which, albeit skewed 22,5°, corresponds to Naples' system of *decumani*. In his study of the drawing, Hamberg noted certain links between Veronese's illustrations (1511) for Vitruvius and the Greco-Roman layout of the city of Neapolis: the *plates* "distinguish the street—*platea*—from the *angiportus* or *vicus*, in the same way as the Latin author does, eschewing the Roman custom of ascribing the same status to both *decumani* and *cardines*. Veronese," notes Fontana in his recent monograph on Fra Giocondo, "had therefore fully grasped the obscure Vitruvian passage, thanks to his firsthand experience of Naples. Here in fact the upper *platea* in Naples (corresponding to Via Sapienza, Via Anticaglia, and Via SS. Apostoli), the lower *platea* (now Via S. Biagio dei Librai and Vicaria Vecchia) and the central *platea* (Via Tribunali), cut the city from west to east on an east-northeast axis, barely 185 meters apart; ... the *vici* cut through from north to south (oriented southsoutheast) 37 meters apart, creating a proportion of 5:1." These observations, in the wake of Hamberg's studies, confirm that the layout of Naples "was drawn up according to plans (now lost) with which Vitruvius was well acquainted, and Fra Giocondo's studies of Vitruvius demonstrate his ability to trace out a median using the gnomon, and consequently also the compass-card; from this he was able to map out the city in such a way that the *plateae* and *vici* eluded the prevailing winds." It is also worth noting that the layout of the *plateae* corresponds to the description of Vitruvius' urban system of *decumani*, and is hence distinct from the ancient plans of Turin, Lucca, and Timgad. The insulae of Neapolis in the Uffizi drawing are an idealized version "corresponding proportionally to the Neapolitan street layout, with a circle drawn in its midst, divided into sixteen segments according to the astronomical and meteorological tenets reported from Greek sources by Vitruvius in his *De architectura*, I, chap. 6."[9] Given the depth of this reading, one can see why Fontana rejected his own analysis, and suggested that the drawing shows a screw stair represented in both plan and elevation, in which the steps become *cardines*, and the risers, with their symmetrical axes, become *decumani*. The coincidences are many and the sheet in question is peculiarly ambivalent; it would not be the first time a drawing served two distinctly different functions.

In his description of Alfonso II of Aragon's plan for the city of Naples, Summonte makes

Fra Giocondo (attrib.)
Representation of the three decumani
Florence, Uffizi, Gabinetto Disegni e Stampe, Uff. 4124r.

[8] G. Hamberg, "Vitruvius, Fra' Giocondo and the City of Naples" in *Acta Archaeologica*, XXXVI, 1965: 105-125.
[9] V. Fontana, op. cit.: 27-28.

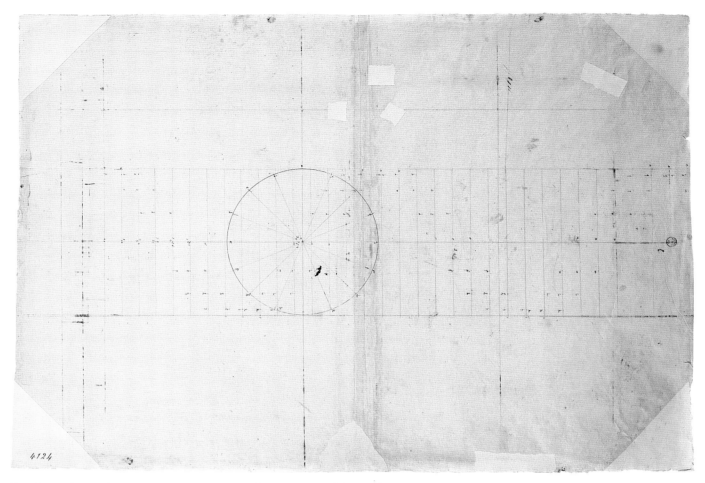

4124

Fra Giocondo (attrib.)
Compass card
Florence, Uffizi, Gabinetto
Disegni e Stampe, Uff. 4124v.

on the following pages
Georg Braun
Map of Naples
from Civitas orbis terrarum
16th cent.
Genoa, Museo Navale

a statement that is essential for understanding the sovereign's intentions: "extendere ad linea recta tucte le strade maestre, da muro a muro della città."[10]

The enlargement scheme toward the west, obtained by extending the *decumani* (or "main streets" as noted by Summonte), met the demand for increasing the number of noble mansions. Among the more important buildings in this corner of the city were the residence (1406) of Antonio Penna (secretary to King Ladislau) on the edge of the original ancient nucleus of the city; the residence (1470) of Antonello Petrucci (secretary to Ferdinand I of Aragon) in the Piazza S. Domenico Maggiore; the residence (1466) of Diomede Carafa (first Count of Maddaloni) on the lower *decumano*; the Palazzo de Scortratis (end 1400s) alongside S. Paolo Maggiore; the Palazzo Sanseverino (1470) built by the princes of Salerno at the western end of the lower *decumano*, near the Porta Reale; the Palazzo Marigliano (1513) in Via S. Biagio dei Librai, the work of Giovanni Mormando, who was also responsible for Palazzo Vietri Corigliano and the Palazzo Carafa di Montorio; the original Palazzo Pignatelli in Largo Trinità Maggiore; and the Palazzo Orsini di Gravina.[11] This concentration of patrician buildings between the *decumani* and *cardines* was a token of the crown's emphasis on the oldest nucleus of the city, a quite different choice from that of the Angevin dynasty, which chose to concentrate the nobility and the royal court itself on Largo delle Corregge, which lay outside the classic core of the city, adjacent to the Castel Nuovo.

That the Veronese friar Giocondo's ideal took its cue from the exemplary urban structure outlined by Vitruvius is evidenced in his project drawings. When he was called to present a plan for the new market in the Rialto borough in Venice, he drew up a square forum, enclosed by two concentric arcaded buildings with a central thoroughfare. The scheme would have thereby taken up the entire Rialto *isola*, requiring the extensive reorganization of the canal linkage. The workshops were designed to give onto the surrounding canal, whereas the shops opened onto the central square, crowned in its center by a temple for the use of the tradesfolk.

The now-lost project dates to July 1514, and fulfilled the ideal scheme of a public forum. In his report of the description, Sanuda was quite right in adding rather bluntly that "fra Ziocondo quale non è qui locho non capisse": that the friar basically did not know what he was doing.[12]

In truth, this keen advocate of Vitruvius and passionate documenter of monuments from classical antiquity had the extraordinary experience of dealing directly with an ideal city, patterned on the model outlined by Vitruvius. At any event, the idea of Naples as a perfectly

[10] Cf. F. Nicolini, *L'arte napoletana del Rinascimento e la lettera di P. Summonte a M. A. Michiel*, Naples, 1925; and C. De Seta, *Napoli...*, op. cit.: 92-93.
[11] For more on these buildings, compare R. Pane, *Il Rinascimento nell'Italia meridionale*, Milan, 1975-77, 2 vols.
[12] Cf. V. Fontana, op. cit.

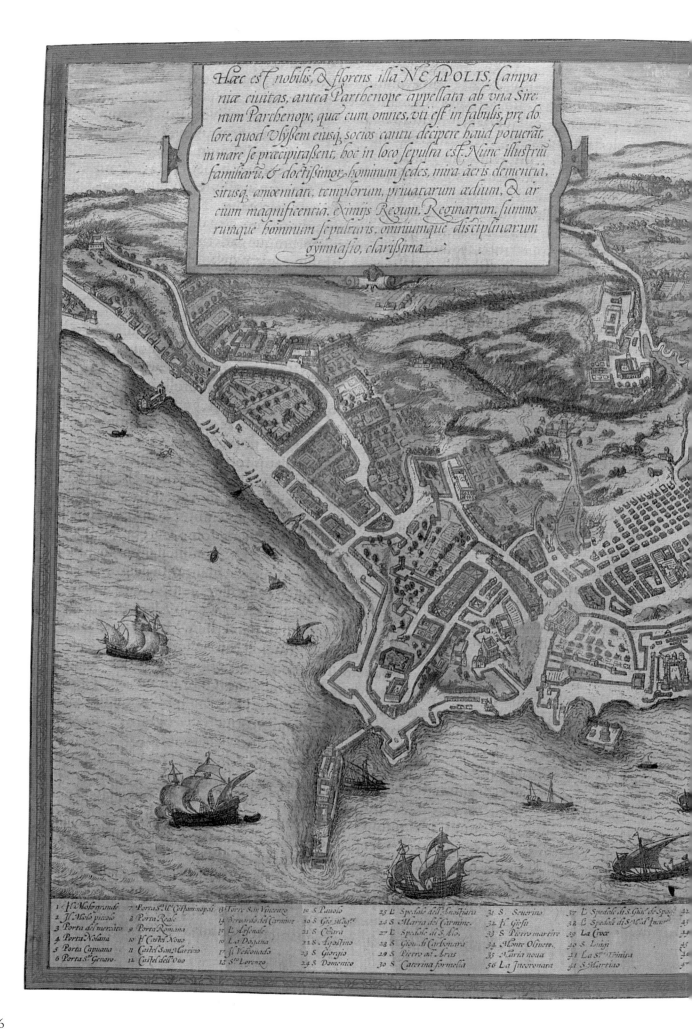

Hæc est nobilis, & florens illa NEAPOLIS, Campa
niæ ciuitas, anteà Parthenope appellata ab vna Sire:
num Parthenope, quæ cum omnes, vti est in fabulis, præ do
lore, quod Vlyssem eiusq, socios cantu decipere haud potuerãt,
in mare se præcipitassent, hoc in loco sepulta est. Nunc illustriũ
familiarũ, & doctissimor. hominum sedes, mira aeris clementiã,
situsq, amœnitate, templorum, priuatarum ædium, & ar
cium magnificentia, Eximijs Regum, Reginarum, summo:
rumquè hominum sepulturis, omniumque disciplinarum
gymnasio, clarissima

1 Il Molo grande	7 Porta S.t'e' Costantinopoli	13 Torre San Vincenzo	19 S Pauolo	25 L Spedale dell'Inostiare	31 S. Seuerino	37 L Spedale di S.Giu' de Spagn.
2 Il Molo piccolo	8 Porta Reale	14 Bernardo del Carmine	20 S Gio: Mag.re	26 S Maria del Carmine.	32 Il Giesu	38 L Spedale di S.M. al Incur.
3 Porta del mercato	9 Porta Romana	15 L Arsenale	21 S Chiara	27 L Spedale di S. Aso.	33 S Pietro martire	39 La Croce
4 Porta Nolana	10 La Dogana	16 Il Vescouado	22 L Agostino	28 S Gioua: Carbonara	34 Monte Osiuero	40 S Luigi
5 Porta Capuana	11 Castel S.to Martino	17 Il Vescouado	23 S Giorgio	29 S Pietro ad Aras	35 Maria noua	41 La S.ta Trinita
6 Porta S.to Genaro	12 Castel dell'Ouo	18 S.to Lorenzo	24 S Domenico	30 S Caterina formella	36 La Incoronata	42 S Martino

356

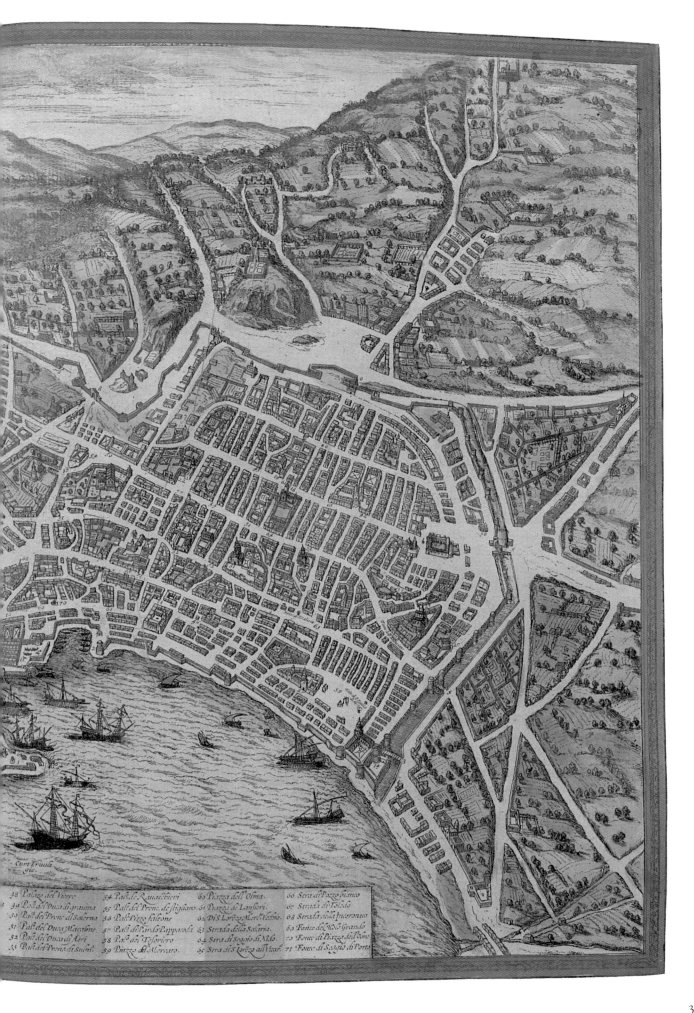

48 Palazo del Vicere
49 Palo del Duca di gratuna
50 Palo del Prenc di Salerna
51 Palo del Duca Macedone
52 Palo del Duca di Arri
53 Palo del Prenc di Suini

54 Palo de Ramaccieri
55 Palo del Prenc de stigliano
56 Palo Pizzo falcone
57 Palo di Paolo Pappaoia
58 Palo del Tesoriero
59 Piazzo del Mercato

60 Piazza dell Olma
61 Piazza di Lanfieri
62 Di S Lorezo Mere Vecchio
63 Strada della Salaria
64 Stra di Seggio di Nido
65 Stra di S Lorezo all Vicar

66 Stra di Pazzo sianco
67 Strada di Toledo
68 Strada ficola fuora mano
69 Fonte del Chiaio Grande
70 Fonte di Piazzo del Cione
71 Fonte di Seggio di Porta

laid out city crops up outside the local hagiographical writings. In his *Doctor Faustus* (III, i), Christopher Marlowe has his hero soar, like some Icarus, over Naples and "rich Campania," and notes:

> Buildings fair, and gorgeous to the eye
> Whose streets straight, and paved with finest brick,
> Quarter the town in four equivalents;
> There saw we laerned Maro's golden tomb,
> The way he cut an English mile in lenght
> Throught a rock of stone in one night's space.

Fra Giocondo, Francesco di Giorgio, and Giuliano da Maiano in the Court of Alfonso of Aragon

The plan to which Summonte referred was perfectly in line with the culture and projects of the Veronese friar, and he seems to be the most likely author. In fact, Summonte underlines that among the architects in the retinue of Alfonso, he had above all the "singulare fra' Iucundu da Verona" (the outstanding friar Giocondo of Verona). The Renaissance utopia of the ideal city must have been foremost in Alfonso's mind. The king styled himself on his enlightened Florentine precursor Lorenzo il Magnifico, surrounding himself with eminent humanists such as Jacopo Sannazzaro and Giovanni Pontano, and even attended the seminars of the Accademia Pontaniana. Similarly, he heeded the lesson of his predecessor Alfonso V of Aragon, whose court harbored prominent thinkers such as Panormita (Antonio Beccadelli), Bartolomeo Facio, and Lorenzo Valla.

The research into classical antiquity, whose model was to be emulated and surpassed in the construction of the new city, focused on the study of the Campi Flegrei, which Giovanni Pompei considered to be a great challenge for anyone attempting to advance the art of architecture. This part of the city, with its strikingly scenic array of ancient monuments, was visited by Giocondo in the company of Jacopo Sannazzaro, and likewise by Giuliano da Sangallo and Francesco di Giorgio Martini, who diligently surveyed the ancient remains and transcribed the epigraphs they bore. According to Vasari, the Campi Flegrei were later studied by Raphael, and by Bramante. The presence of the latter—who (according to R. Pane [13]) was summoned by his client Cardinal Oliviero Carafa to work on the cloister of S. Maria della Pace and for the upper section of the cathedral in Naples—apparently induced Baldassarre Peruzzi also to transfer himself to Rome in the early 1500s. Pane argues that the mind behind Alfonso II's plan, as outlined by Summonte, was the Sienese architect and sculptor Francesco di Giorgio Martini. We should not forget that Martini was still in Naples in February 1494, and collaborated during the battles of December 1495, when the Aragonese defeated the French using war machinery designed by Martini himself.

The Sienese architect is documented as having been in Naples on at least three occasions [14]: in 1491, for a few months, in 1495 for approximately a year, during which on 27 November he detonated a mine beneath the Castel Nuovo during a battle against the surviving troops of Charles VIII, who were cornered in the castle; and, finally, a brief sojourn in 1497 to survey the defense works that had been gradually built in the course of the years. His most important task was perhaps begun in 1484 and culminated in his fundamental treatise of 1490, and concerned the eastern tract of the city walls from the Porta del Carmine to the Porta Capuana as far as S. Giovanni a Carbonara, and the proceeding northern section of new wall, in which nine new city gates were opened, and twenty-one or twenty-two new towers were erected. Other building campaigns undertaken by Francesco di Giorgio regard the Castel Nuovo itself, the citadel, and sections of the western walls. Although Francesco di Giorgio's treatise is the closest in the fifteenth century to Vitruvian theory, whose translation into the vernacular reveals close links with the writings of the former,[15] it should be noted that Francesco's intentions were to reinterpret the ancient treatise, adapting it to the new requirements of engineering and architectural design, while departing from the Albertian captioned format. As a consequence, his use of Vitruvius was unbiased, quite independent from the Latin text, and instead veined with medieval allegorical references in its set of drawings analyzed by Paolo Marconi, prepared by Francesco as expressions of urban form.[16]

Giuliano da Sangallo's Project for the Law Courts, and the Splendor of Poggio Reale

The large-scale project by Giuliano da Sangallo belongs to this same context. The model for the scheme was taken to Naples in 1488, and a well-known drawing exists in the Vatican. In a close analysis carried out later, Pane interprets this building as Palazzo dei Tribunali,

[13] Cf. R. Pane, op. cit, II (1977): 101 ff.
[14] See N. Adams, "L'architettura militare di Francesco di Giorgio," and "Castel Nuovo a Napoli," in *Francesco di Giorgio architetto*, ed. F. P. Fiore and M. Tafuri, Milan, 1993, II: 139-144, 228-295. These writings are for the most disappointing, with oversights and certain serious omissions, indicating an insufficient knowledge of Francesco di Giorgio and his history, and of relative critical writings.
[15] Cf. P. N. Pagliara, "Vitruvio...," op. cit, p. 26.
[16] Op. cit.: 27.

Carlo Coppola
Piazza della Vicaria, with
Palazzo dei Tribunali
*Naples, Museo Nazionale
di S. Martino*

the central courthouse. This suggestion means that Sangallo's work and the ideas of Lorenzo il Magnifico had made their way to Naples. The utopian connotations of the project can be seen in the attempt to cluster several functions in a single, large building, to be sited near the Castel Nuovo, namely, the courthouse and the marketplace. As Summonte notes, the scheme envisaged "a large building near the Castel Nuovo in Piazza della Coronata, in which several rooms would contain all the courts of law, thereby enabling the merchants to visit without having to trail back and forth." The sites centrality also influenced the adoption of multiple uses for the Incoronata complex, which comprised the church itself, the *ospedale* or hospital, and lodgings for the attorneys and medical staff. Sangallo's project, contemporary to the Palazzo di Poggio Reale, has typological links with the Medici villa in Via Laura, Florence, designed by Antonio da Sangallo the Elder to ideas of Giuliano da Sangallo and Lorenzo il Magnifico, particularly as regards the perimeter wall enclosing the palazzo, for the symmetrical layout and above all for the stepped central *invaso* or entrenchment. The project for

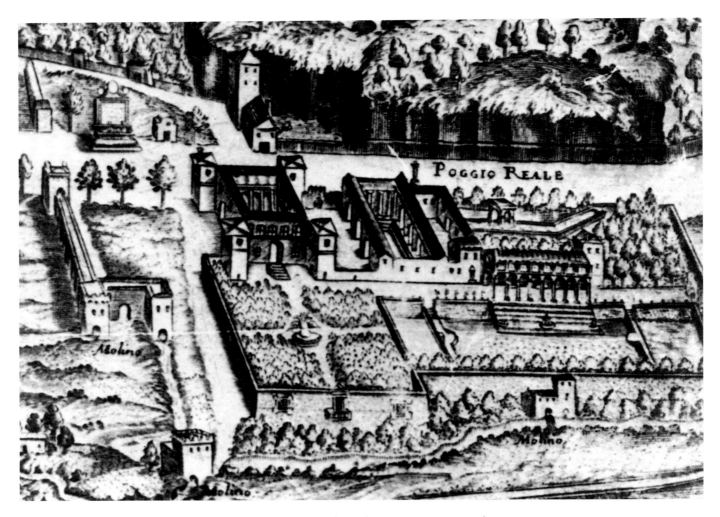

POGGIO REALE

*Palazzo di Poggio Reale, Naples
engraving by A. Baratta
1670
Milan, Civica Raccolta Stampe
Achille Bertarelli*

the courts, formerly interpreted as a royal palace for Ferdinand I, was commissioned to Sangallo through Lorenzo il Magnifico, and matches with the one mentioned by Summonte. Vasari reports that the king was suitably impressed by the scale model and that building work (of which no trace remains) was in fact undertaken. For certain, Giuliano da Sangallo was paid by Ferdinand I on 28 February 1489 to carry out detailed survey work on the ancient temples of Baia, Capua and Cassino.

The magnificent Palazzo di Poggio Reale, whose construction was begun in 1487 (one year after the first printed edition of Vitruvius' *De architectura*) to plans by Giuliano da Maiano, was already nearing completion by 1490. Maiano, who was stationed at several occasions in Naples between 1484 and 1490, was also responsible for part of the Aragonese defense works—the southeast tract of the walls—whose construction was supervised by Alfonso, Duke of Calabria; other projects include designs for the Porta Capua (realized in tandem with is brother Benedetto), the Villa della Duchesca (1487) cradled between the Castel Capuano and the church of S. Caterina a Formello, and the alterations to the Castel Capuano itself. The Palazzo di Poggio Reale, which Summonte hailed as worthy of comparison with the marvels of ancient Rome, became very widely known due to a drawing of it executed by Sebastiano Serlio; in his treatise, where, altered with a forced centrality, it is presented in the form of a fortified palace. It was built during the period in which Giuliano da Sangallo and Antonio da Sangallo the Elder, who came to Naples in 1488 to present the model of the court house to King Ferdinand: Fra Giocondo and Francesco di Giorgio Martini.[17]

There is no proof that Fra Giocondo did actually take part in the realization of the palace at Poggio Reale or the palace gardens (as put forward by Fontana), even though the project's completion is generally attributed to him. Evidence of Giocondo's presence as architect to the court of Aragon is found in a set of payment slips dated 1489 concerning studies on archaeological sites, an activity he had pursued in Rome; on the basis of this it has been suggested that he took over from Giuliano da Maiano on the latter's death in 1490, as related by Summonte: "the construction of Poggio Reale attracted some of the most acclaimed architects of the time: Giuliano da Maiano, Francesco da Siena, master Antonio [da Sangallo the Elder], though the latter was more concerned with weaponry and defense machinery; and above all came the outstanding friar Giocondo da Verona." Also attributable to Fra Giocondo are the drawings of bastioned villas by Baldassarre Peruzzi, but the most painstaking

[17] On the Palazzo di Poggio Reale, see the terse debate between G. Harsey and A. Blunt in the pages of the *Burlington Magazine*, and *Architectura*; see also critical reconstruction of events in C. de Seta, *Napoli...*, op. cit.: 85-88.

Præfenti quidem figura tum exteriores, tum interiores quoque ædificij partes demonftrare contendi-
mus. A, partem exteriorem primùm proponit: B, interiores ambulationes porticus'ue deinde defignat:
C, interiora conclauia demum oftendit. In fubfcripta autem defignatione contecti ædificij fpeciem ne-
quaquam exhibuimus: ipfum nanque, ob agrorum amœnitates liberius oculis perluftrandas contemplan-
dafque, fub dio potius conftitutum uellemus.

REGALIS PODII NEAPOLITANI ICHNOGRAPHIA.

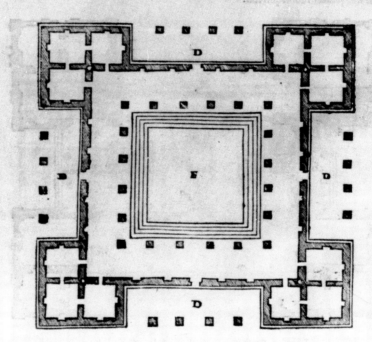

T   Nobis

Sebastiano Serlio
Prospect and Plan
of Palazzo di Poggio Reale
from Trattato di Architettura,
Book III

graphic documentation, which includes details on the architectural orders of the building, is
the Antonio Baratta *veduta* of 1629, which offers the definition of building volumes, the articulation of the various sections and their links with the surrounding gardens. The canvas
by Viaviani Codazzi, showing one side of the central *invaso*, helps to evidence the Florentine
flavor of the layout in the galleries and ornamental motifs.[18]

There is one particular type of building that offers a sufficiently coherent model for coordinating building developments on the scale of the Palazzo di Poggio Reale, the court house and
the Medici villa in Via Laura, Florence. This unique and very precise model to which all three
projects refer is the Roman thermal bath. The Roman bath layout as a type crops up in
Giuliano's drawings for establishing the symmetry of the plan, delimiting the perimeter and
rationalizing the internal linkage, and not least for siting the church at the far end of the mirror
axis, the position allocated for the *caldarium*. If we take into account the stepped central
entrenchment—the *piscina* so to speak—the echoes of the ancient baths becomes even more
explicit, as in the plan of the baths of Diocletian (*Codex Saluzziano*, fol. 73, pl. 133) published

[18] On the painting by Codazzi, compare
D. Marshall, "A View of Poggioreale by
Viviano Codazzi and Domenico Gargiu-
lo," in *Journal of the Society of Architectural Historians*, 1986, XVL, 1: 32-46.

*Antonio Rossellino and
Benedetto da Maiano
Cappella Piccolomini
1475–90
Naples, S. Anna dei Lombardi*

by Francesco di Giorgio Martini, and his sketches of the tradesmen's dwellings (*Codex Magliabechiano*, fol. 17, pl. 193). The central *invaso* (which can be flooded) at Poggio Reale is a foretaste of Sangallo's two solutions for the general layout, and his choice of prototype. One project that particularly epitomizes the cultural environment of the time is the Cappella Pontano (1492), formerly attributed by Roberto Pane to Giovanni Giocondo, and later ascribed to Francesco di Giorgio Martini[19] owing to its stylistic links with the church of S. Maria del Calcinaio at Cortona; Vincenzo Fontana, however, prefers the attribution to Fra Giocondo, who was engaged in 1492 to design fortresses and defense works for the house of Aragon.[20] More recently Manfredo Tafuri has ascribed the work to the circle of Francesco di Giorgio. But despite these borrowings, the chapel is a work of superb simplicity and classicizing elegance. Its analogies with Roman sepulchers are probably due to an alliance between the architect and the humanist poet Giovanni Pontano (1426–1503), who is most likely advocated the choice of epigraphic motifs and antiquities for the interiors. The church's main feature is its position on the end of the *decumano*, Via Tribunali, and therefore in the center of the ancient nucleus—a choice that alludes to the urban renewal operations under way and offers a philosophical link with classical antiquity. But it was also a sign of the privileged status of the humanist, who two years before had published his *De principe*

[19] R. Pane, op. cit.
[20] V. Fontana, op. cit.

362

bearing the dedication: "*Ad Alfonsum Calabriae ducem*," a text[21] that pivots on the teachings of the classical authors destined to transmit the virtues necessary for upright government to the young duke. Like Rome, the city of Naples, with its stratification and suburbs (Baia, Cuma, Pozzuoli), afforded immediate comparisons with antiquity and with Vitruvius' treaty. Visiting Naples became a compulsory stage for architects who intended to venture beyond the terrain opened by Masaccio, Donatello and Brunelleschi and the treatise of Alberti, and continue the renewal of architectural language. The upshot was a rapid diffusion of Vitruvianism throughout the Aragonese kingdom and the presence of Florentines, and Fra Giocondo, not to mention the documentation they supplied through their drawings.

Summonte provides generous coverage of our archaeological heritage: "In Baia, Cuma and Pezòlo we have many ancient ruins which amaze the world. Where, besides the baths, villas and sepulchers, fine amphitheaters, circuses, vast freshwater lakes and reservoirs, created for the use of Roman armies on their way to Africa, from which aqueducts carry water to the same, such that all Mt. Miseno is empty below and supported on pillars of the roots themselves of the mount: things of great wonder and imagination indeed. I omit many reservoirs in the sea, not only in Baia and Pezòlo but also in Paisylippo, around the Castello dell'Ovo and the Castelnovo, even unto the port of Naples. They are therefore all antique buildings, and now resemble hillocks or are overgrown, and are in far greater number than there are in Rome."[22] The determination to supersede the monuments of the classical world with a vigorous new architecture, and restore the city of Naples to its role as an ideal city emerges in the Albertian formula of architecture-city, a formula that included works of a more complex nature, such as the Palazzo di Poggio Reale and the Palazzo dei Tribunali. Other factors that cannot be overlooked, however are Filarete's Sforzinda, and the continuing exchange of ideas that took place within the Aragonese court between Alfonso II, Francesco di Giorgio Martini and Fra Giocondo. The full impact of Vitruvius on the development of design and planning in Naples is yet to be assessed. In this essay I have attempted to piece together some of the tesserae, while showing the new global vision that began to take root in the Quattrocento, thanks to the tenaciousness of such sovereigns as Alfonso the Magnanimous, and Alfonso, Duke of Calabria.

The Tavola Strozzi and Francesco Rosselli

The first and most fascinating "portrait" of the city of Naples is the so-called Tavola Strozzi, a tempera painting on panel of unusual dimensions (82×245 cm) depicting the city in all its splendor in the mid-fifteenth century. The event narrated in the immediate foreground is the arrival of the Spanish fleet after its victorious battle off the coast of Ischia in July 1465 against the pretender John of Anjou. The Renaissance scholar Corrado Ricci came across the panel in Filippo Strozzi's palace in Florence in 1901. The discovery marked the start of scholarly inquiry into the panel, which is among the most superb painted townscapes of the Renaissance to have survived. The renowned Italian historian and philosopher Benedetto Croce published a preliminary study of the panel in the magazine *Napoli Nobilissima* in March 1904, which included a large-format reproduction of the painting accompanied by a running caption explaining its contents; a further, more lengthy study came fifteen years later, in 1919.[23] In the course of this century, no scholar of Neapolitan art and culture has omitted to delve into the panel in some way or other. The reasons are self-evident: the panoramic image is of the utmost pictorial quality, and provides a fabulous source for the history of the city. The discovery of the Tavola Strozzi immediately aroused a number of important questions. What is the historical episode represented? Who commissioned the work? When was it executed? Who are its author or authors? How reliable is the topographical detail it contains? Opinions have varied greatly, sometimes drastically, but there is one point on which scholars seem to be generally agreed—that the episode represents the triumphant return of the Aragonese fleet. As for the other questions, there is much debate over who commissioned the work, and who executed it; the accuracy of representation is also questioned. The somewhat scant bibliography on the Tavola shows that, after Riccardo Filangieri's paper of 1938,[24] there is a long silence of some thirty years. Renewed interest came in 1969 when I used the panel as a source of iconographic material[25] to describe the city's transformations under the Aragonese. Since then the bibliography has grown considerably. Raffaello Causa returned to the theme in 1973, underlining the panel's great "documentary fidelity," together with its outstanding pictorial quality, particularly as regards the left half; he concluded that the panel was the work of Colantonio,[26] and dated it to "around 1480." He was therefore responsible for separating the date of execution from the event represented. Causa's suggestion was refuted by Roberto Pane (1975), who favored a previous attribution by the scholar Mario Salmi to an artist in the Florentine milieu, "more likely executed

[21] Cf. *Prosatori latini del Quattrocento*, E. Garin, ed., Turin 1977: 1024-1063.
[22] F. Nicolini, op. cit.
[23] See the long caption of the reproduction by B. Croce, "Veduta della città di Napoli del 1479 col trionfo navale per l'arrivo di Lorenzo de' Medici," in *Napoli Nobilissima*, vol. XII, fasc. IV, 1904, pp. 56-57, and B. Croce, "Vedute della città nel Quattrocento," in *Aneddoti di varia letteratura*, vol. I, Bari, Laterza, 1953, pp. 267-271.
[24] Cf. R. Filangieri, *Rassegna critica delle fonti per la storia di Castelnuovo*, vol. II, Naples, 1938, p. 31, and bibliography.
[25] Cf. C. de Seta, *Cartografia della città di Napoli. Lineamenti dell'evoluzione urbana*, Naples 1969 and 1975 (2), vol. I, pp. 82-85; C. de Seta, *Napoli. Le città nelle storia d'Italia*, Rome-Bari 1986 (2), pp. 69-74.
[26] R. Causa, *L'arte nella Certosa di S. Martino*, Naples 1973, p. 20 n. 17.
[27] M. Salmi, "Introduzione," in G. Pampolini, *Palazzo Strozzi*, Rome 1963, p. 12.
[28] Essential literature includes the essay by V. Spinazzola, "Di Napoli antica e della sua topografia in una tavola del XV secolo," in *Bollettino d'arte del Ministero della Pubblica Istruzione* IV, 1910, pp. 1-19. Besides Filangieri, all more recent essays and articles overlook this text, which the present author had noted and borrowed from in 1969.
[29] R. Pane, *Il Rinascimento nell'Italia meridionale*, Milan 1975, vol. I, pp. 143-144; disputing R. Causa, Pane writes: "If the left-hand section of the panel is of greater descriptive interest, it is only because it contains the more important Aragonese; the suggestion of a minor

by a manuscript illuminator than by an artist."[27] This observation had also been made by Vittorio Spinazzola much earlier in 1910 in an excellent essay that draws on a wealth of arguments[28] and has been unjustly overlooked in all the more recent enquiries.

Pane affirms that the panel depicts the "return from the victorious battle off Ischia, waged against the Angevin forces in 1462[sic]," and its contents should be considered as part real, and part imaginary, indicating the "scarce veracity of the painting of the compact mass of urban fabric in the historical center," given that the cityscape "has always been largely defined by terraced roofs (indeed, in ancient times they were called 'lastrici a cielo') the painting—which was probably commissioned by Filippo Strozzi—contains a great deal of red Tuscan-style roofing." Pane consequently considers it questionable to accept any section of the painting as direct documentary data, since the panel was not painted from life, but was designed to serve as a model.[29] In this last respect, Pane's assertion differs from that of Salmi.

In a volume devoted to the figurative culture during the period of Aragon rule, Ferdinando Bologna suggested that the panel was commissioned by Duke Alfonso of Calabria between 1486 and 1487 to commemorate the dynasty's victory over the newly insurgent feudal lords; the panel, he proposed, was a gift to Filippo Strozzi for his constancy toward the Aragonese crown. The date of execution is determined by a visual clue, namely, the absence of the lantern on the wharf, built in 1487. The scholar Bologna concluded by attributing the work to the Neapolitan painter Francesco Pagano,[30] endorsing his argument on the basis of stylistic analogies with known works executed by Pagano upon his return from Valencia. The analogies in question, however, are somewhat vague and uncorroborated. Upon closer analysis it is clear that the detail showing Castel Sant'Angelo that appears in a section of the *Legend of St. Michael* is wholly insufficient to substantiate the attribution; furthermore, Pagano was hardly capable of creating a painting of the dimensions and topographical precision of the Tavola Strozzi, whose system of perspective is highly consistent. Moreover, the landscape background in the *Crucifixion* from the *Trittico dei Sarti* is very conventional in manner; as a background it is unremarkable and devoid of any characteristic to link it with the Tavola; nor does it evince much topographical aptitude. These arguments apply, albeit in a different manner, to Causa's attribution to Colantonio.

In his reply to Ferdinando Bologna, Pane sustained that "the theme illustrated is actually the glorification of the Aragon dynasty in a symbolic representation." In order to endorse his supposition that the panel was not painted in Naples but in Florence, Pane cited the want of fidelity in the representation. "The Torre dell'Oro," he wrote, "[is] colored yellow, as if faced in tufa instead of gray trachyte; more significantly still, the houses are all roofed in red tiles."[31] This argument had already been aired in the preceding volume. In truth, the "clues" arrogated as proof of the scant veracity of the Tavola (which is supposed at this point to have been painted outside Naples, after a drawing), are not altogether convincing. As it happens, the Torre dell'Oro—one of the five towers of the castle—was made of tufa (and still is), and therefore has a yellowish hue, just as the anonymous panel painter represented it. Moreover, our artist was so attentive a witness (and most likely worked on-site) that he distinguished the tone of the trachyte of the other four towers from that of the Torre dell'Oro. This kind of passion for detail is a peculiarity of manuscript illuminators. On the question of the Torre di S. Vincenzo, Pane himself had already noted that "it appears so minutely described that even the different materials of the structure are defined through different tones of color. The cylindrical part of the tower is brick-red, and likewise the two octagonal sections terminating the tower; the artist used gray for the base of the building, the crenelated wall over the water, and the upper walkways resting on corbels. With its alternating brick and trachyte, this strikingly singular civic building became a model for many subsequent constructions."[32] Actually the gray trachyte is used only for the lookout walkway; the cylindrical base with its small jutting tower is not trachyte, but is a faithful representation in illuminator's style of lead sheeting—documented by Aragonese bookkeeping records[33]—applied to the base of the tower around 1450, distinct from the gray trachyte owing to its sheen. For Pane, the decisive evidence of the "scarce veracity" of the painting was the fact that "nearly all the houses of the city had roof terraces." In actual fact a great many of the houses are terraced: many more than appear at first glance in the sweeping townscape: the red of the single or double sloping roofs tends to outweigh the other colors of the *veduta*—evidently more than the light grays, whites, and pinks of the terraces. Besides, many large buildings of Angevin manufacture—churches, convents, hospitals—are also unmistakably fitted out with red roofs. The invaluable radiographic study effected by Professor Dino Catalano, which has offered detailed insights into each stage of the painting's execution including the pentimenti and the alterations to the painted surface, has confirmed that the right-hand section of the painting has undergone a great many modifications; "by contrast ... for the whole of the left part the two images match each other,"[34] that is, the image visible to the naked

a

d

Fra Giovanni da Verona
Architectural Perspectives
Naples, S. Anna dei Lombardi
Cat. nos. 162 a, b, c, d

draftsman for the execution of the right half, containing the urban panorama, is refuted by the absolute formal uniformity of the painting" (p. 77). That uniformity was in turn disproved by Dino Catalano's X-ray studies of the panel (see below, note 34). In his own note 13 on p. 93, Pane writes "the painting was executed to commemorate the above event shortly after 1465, and not 'toward 1480'."
[30] F. Bologna, *Napoli e le rotte mediterranee della pittura. Da Alfonso il Magnanimo a Ferdinando il Cattolico*, Naples 1977, pp. 195-201.
[31] R. Pane, "La Tavola Strozzi tra Firenze e Napoli," in *Napoli Nobilissima*, vol. XVIII; fasc. I, Jan.-Feb. 1979, pp.

b

c

4-5. The author forgot he had already written: "One could object that the anonymous painter also painted the Torre dell'Oro red, visible above the loggias, unlike the others, which are in trachyte," (*Il Rinascimento...*, op. cit., p. 143). There is in fact no doubt that the Torre dell'Oro was and still is made of tufa, but it is not painted red, but golden yellow.

[32] Ibid.

[33] Cf. R. Filangieri, *Castelnuovo regia angioina e aragonese di Napoli*, Naples 1934, p. 54.

[34] D. Catalano, "Riparliamo della Tavola Strozzi," in *Napoli Nobilissima*, vol. XXI, fasc. I-II, Jan.-Apr. 1982 (with foreword by R. Pane, op. cit.), p. 64. This sweeping analysis of the X-ray studies on the panels is preceded by a summary·report: cf. Catalano, "Indagine radiologica della Tavola Strozzi," which appeared in the same issue of *Napoli Nobilissima*, following R. Pane's article "La Tavola Strozzi...," op. cit.; and idem, "Ancora sulla Tavola Strozzi," *Napoli Nobilissima*, vol. XXIV, fasc. III-IV, May-Aug. 1985, pp. 81-83, which offers a reply to the important essay

eye, and that revealed under X-ray. It can be noticed that many roof terraces were later altered to sloping roofs once the painting was finished. This is further confirmation, to my mind, of the faithfulness of representation, which was begun, drafted, and then minutely completed in the left section in all its details by a painter who must perforce have had the city before him—how else could he have distinguished the materials? How else could it have admitted an analysis of such philological precision as that carried out by Spinazzola, of by Filangieri for the Castel Nuovo and its surrounding fabric? Causa seemed to have intuited this in his observation of the quality of the left half and its consequent attribution to Colantonio; whereas the right half, he considered, was executed by someone of lesser expertise. The radiographs seem to confirm this possibility. The panel may have been finished off by a workshop assistant who did not have the city before him, and made the modifications that show up under X-ray. Nonetheless, the fact that the intrinsic painterly qualities of the panel vary from side to side—plus the later modifications, additional pentimenti, over-painting and inexpert retouching—does not necessarily mean that the right-hand part is topographically unsound. The authenticity and realism accorded by most scholars to the left half of the panel, is to some degree reflected in the right half, as I will now try to substantiate.

In recent years I have attempted to demonstrate—with concrete examples—that this type of landscape or urban panorama painting, with its accent on topographical detail, is drafted on the basis of land survey material and proper documentary data on the town depicted. In certain cases, it is the painter himself who proves to be in the possession of certain technical skills that can rarely be attributed to other artists, whatever their gifts. To paint a *veduta* or townscape of the size of the Tavola Strozzi requires considerable firsthand knowledge of the town in question, together with proficiency in topographical and architectural surveying, and expertise in the use of perspective—not only the basics, but as a manifold tool for the correct representation of the city in all its complexity. In the second half of the Quattrocento there were few specialized artists who could claim such skills; fewer still are the extant coeval paintings or engravings showing an entire town that can rival the Tavola Strozzi for quality or size. In my overview of the production of this period, I came across a fragment at the Società Colombaria in Florence of another large-format *veduta* of Florence engraved on metal and datable to the ca. 1472, the work of a Florentine, Francesco Rosselli. This engraving was copied to six woodcut panels (known as the "Catena" panels, Berlin, Staatliche Museen) whose execution is attributed to Lucantonio degli Uberti; the engraving is considered the most lifelike portrait of Florence at the close of the Quattrocento. The woodcut (measuring 58.5 × 131.5 cm) has been studied in detail, and served as a prototype for a large-format vertical painting executed some twenty years later (now in a private British collection). Published by Fanelli,[35] who dated it 1489–95 after careful scrutiny, the panel (92.5 × 143.5 cm) is painted in tempera—the same technique used for the Tavola Strozzi. The author of the engraved fragment, and perhaps of the painted panel, is Francesco Rosselli, son of Lorenzo and younger brother of the more famed Cosimo. Francesco Rosselli, born in Florence in 1447 or 1448 (d. before 1513?), debuted as a manuscript illuminator in the circle of Liberale da Verona with an *antiphonarium* for Siena Cathedral in around 1470. As a cartographer and illuminator he was active at Buda in the employ of the celebrated library of the King Matthias Corvinus of Hungary from 1476 to 1480. In 1482 he returned to Florence (records note the purchase of a farmstead at Ripoli); in 1505 and 1508 he is recorded as active in Venice. It is also known that, in addition to the Florence townscape, Rosselli also painted panoramic views of Pisa, Rome and Constantinople.[36] Rosselli was therefore clearly an able and versatile technician who moved wherever his commissions took him. His cosmography, conserved in London and realized in Venice in 1506, is signed "*Francisci Rossellj florentini fecit*," and is the first known cosmography completed on a single sheet, in a "manageable and practical format[37] (just over a meter in width). Francesco was an accomplished book illuminator and cosmographer, and as a consequence of these talents he also painted *vedute*, given that he possessed the technical and cognitive means to draft plans and elevations of towns, and define them with the painstaking accuracy of an illuminator.

The inventory of his workshop (regrettably incomplete) reveals that Rosselli had also completed a large-format *veduta* of Rome on "12 fogli reali,[38] datable to between 1478 and 1490. This *veduta* was the source for Jacopo Foresti's woodcut of the Supplementum Chronicarum (Venice, 1490), and later for Münster's *Cosmographia* (Basel, 1550),[39] confirming the fact that Rosselli's work became the model for the representation of the holy city. This engraved prototype served for the tempera on canvas (118 x 223 cm), datable to 1538, originally with the friars at the Convento dei Carmelitani and now in the Palazzo Ducale, Mantua.[40] There are no other *vedute* dating from this period that in any way match the work of Rosselli. The engraved view of Ferrara of 1499[41] has neither its topographic precision nor its size. One possible contender is the view of Genoa of 1481 reproduced in 1597 by Cristoforo De Grassi.[42] The surviving specimens of Rosselli's work show him to be fully

versed in the most advanced rules of geometry and topography of his day, and Ragghianti[43] suggests, with reason, that the artist or his collaborators used the same geodetic tool for their survey work that Leon Battista Alberti adopted (and described) for his map of Rome.[44] It was not before October 1500, with Jacopo de' Barbari's outstanding *veduta* of the city of Venice,[45] that anything of comparable excellence was seen.

Two of Rosselli's city views, therefore, are known to us, both constructed with the same methodical rules of perspective and, in each case, the earliest and most complete views of Florence and Rome respectively.[46] One of their chief characteristics is an accentuated horizontal extension, with a ratio of 1:2. To judge from the composition of the "Catena" woodcut, Rosselli's painting of Florence has quite probably been cropped along either side. But while there are scant grounds for comparing the "Catena" woodcut with the later replica representing Rome, comparisons can nonetheless be made between the strictly topographical criteria adopted for documenting the two cities in question. Both are viewed from an elevated vantage point to show the city in its entirety, including the perimeter walls.[47] For Florence, Rosselli chose the summit of the Monte Oliveto, which is in line with the dome of S. Maria del Fiore; the cone of the perspective projection has a 60° angle. Within this angle the city's features all comply with the rules of perspective, which Rosselli is, however, obliged to enhance by liberally adopting a set of successive vanishing points. By contrast, the section comprising the Oltrarno, the Palazzo Pitti and the Porta Romana, is strongly compressed because it lies outside his chosen optical cone and much closer to the Monte Oliveto. A similar though far less noticeable contraction has been applied to the left section beyond the Torre della Serpe. Here, however, the artist is helped because we are in the town's outskirts, with the hillside behind neatly attenuating the optical distortion.

The *veduta* of Rome is constructed in much the same way. The chosen viewpoint, however, is not the traditional one adopted by illustrators—the Piazza del Popolo—but an imaginary point suspended above the Porta Pia. This enables us to admire the city from above, in a line with St Peter's, just as Florence was viewed in line with S. Maria del Fiore. Using the same criterion for the perspective cone (here wider thatn the usual 60° and taking in the entire residential quarter of the Tiber,[48] situated ideally alongside the Palazzo del Belvedere on the Vatican Hill, the other side borders with the Basilica of Maxentius, behind which the countryside recedes with scattered *mirabilia*. Here again we find the same topographic distortion noted in the hillside beyond the Arno, a necessary expedient for this type of representa-

Francesco Rosselli (attrib.)
Fleet of Ferdinand I in the
Bay of Naples after the Battle
of Ischia, July 1465
*Naples, Museo e Gallerie
Nazionali di Capodimonte*

by M. Del Treppo, "Il re e il banchiere," in *Spazio, società e potere nell'Italia dei Comuni*, Naples 1986.
[35] Cf. G. Fanelli, *Firenze. Le città nella storia d'Italia*, Rome-Bari 1981, pp. 76-86, with illustrative graphics and extensive bibliography.
[36] For the information summarized here on Rosselli, see J. Schulz, "The printed plans and panoramic views of Venice," in *Saggi e memorie di Storie dell'arte*, no. 7, 1970, p. 19-29, together with the valuable bio-bibliographical notes; the only detail that escaped the author is that the important inventory of the Rosselli workshop was published before A. M. Hind's *Early Italian Engraving* (London-New York 1938-48, I, p. 304ff.), with an commentary by I. Del Badia, "La Bottega di Alessandro di Franceso Rosselli merciaio e stampatore. 1525," in *Miscellanea fiorentina di erudizione e storia*, 1894, pp. 24-30. Having consulted this printed source, I discovered that the inventory was not in fact complete. For an up-to-date account of the activities of Francesco, see K. Oberhuber, "Francesco Rosselli," in *Early Italian Drawings from the National Gallery of Art*, Washington, 1973, pp. 47-62 (with a complete bibliography). On Rosselli and the urban panoramas of the fifteenth and sixteenth centuries, see also the recent Italian edition of essays by Jürgen Schulz compiled in J. Schulz, *La cartografia tra scienza e arte. Carte e cartografi nel Rinascimento italiano*, Modena 1990.

[37] E. Borea, "Stampa figurativa e pubblica dalle origini all'affermazione del Cinquecento," in *Storia dell'Arte Italiana*, vol. I, ed. G. Previtali, *L'artista e il pubblico*, II, Turin 1979, p. 339.

[38] J. Schulz, "The printed plans...," op. cit., p. 20.

[39] See C. de Seta, "Significati e simboli della rappresentazione topografica negli Atlanti dal XVI al XVIII secolo," in de Seta, *Le città capitali*, Rome-Bari 1985, pp. 17-66, with extensive bibliography.

[40] See the catalog for the exhibition "Palazzo Venezia. Paolo II e le fabbriche di San Marco," Rome 1980, cat. no. 51, pp. 93-94, ed. M. L. Casanova Uccella.

[41] For the panoramic view in the Archivio di Stato di Modena, see G. Agnelli, "I monumenti di Niccolò III e Borso d'Este," in *Atti e memoria della deputazione ferrarese di storia patria*, XXIII, 1919. More recently it was reproduced by B. Zevi in *Biagio Rossetti architetto ferrarese*, Turin 1960, fig. 188.

[42] For this veduta, see E. Poleggi, *Iconografia di Genova e della Riviera*, Genoa 1977 (2); and E. Poleggi and P. Cevini, *Le città nella storia d'Italia*. Genova, Rome-Bari 1981, pp. 76-80, figs. 29-34, cat. no. 2, pp. 251-252.

[43] See C. L. Ragghianti, *Filippo Brunelleschi un uomo un universo*, Florence 1977, p. 440.

[44] L. Vagnetti, "La 'Descriptio Urbis Romae' uno scritto poco noto di Leon Battista Alberti," in *Quaderni dell'Istituto di elementi di architettura e rilievo dei monumenti*, no. 1, 1968.

[45] In addition to J. Schulz's "The printed plans...," op. cit. and passim, further up-to-date reading can be found in L. Puppi, "Venezia tra Quattrocento e Cinquecento. Da 'Nuova Costantinopoli' ad 'Roma altera' nel segno di Gerusalem," in *Le città capitali...*, op. cit., pp. 55-66.

tion, in which the artist is obliged to toe the line between the canons of perspective and the demand for providing topographic and morphological detail. In this view of Rome, for example, the Palazzo del Belvedere seen from the Porta Pia should really lie to the right of the Castel Sant'Angelo. But this would have meant an even broader perspective range and hence greater distortion of the left quadrant: hence the string of vanishing points for the areas lying outside the more dense focus, which is documented from the artist's vantage point. All the alignments (of the right-center) travel in fact to a single point, or near as may be.

The *vedute* of Florence and of Rome both reveal fairly clearly the process by which the disposition of the entire city is reached, and that is by adopting an identical approach for both topography and perspective—with a book illuminator's handling of the definition of the details of each of the more important buildings; the urban fabric itself is simply conveyed with blocks, foreshortened prisms, and roofing.

The same method of construction can be identified in the Tavola Strozzi, but in the case of Naples, the anonymous artist has no raised vantage point to help him and has consequently chosen the jetty, and thence the waterfront. The somewhat convoluted makeup of the city has prompted a host of ingenious devices for the *veduta*. The focus of the Tavola—though not geometrical—is undoubtedly the Castel Nuovo, the citadel, and the neighboring port area. To embrace the entire city, the author has gathered several accurate partial views into a single perspective pattern that simulated a single viewpoint, with his vanishing points receding to infinity. If we therefore follow the silhouette of the roofs that terrace the hillside down toward the sea, they are evidently all oriented in one direction, along an axis running from top right to bottom left, endorsing the gradient of the land between the cardines and *decumani* of the urban layout. Monumental buildings thrust out of the urban fabric—with an ultra-precise rendering of the Castel Nuovo and the band of buildings hugging it. But there are many other less salient details worth identifying: on the left of the Torre dell'Oro and above the residence of the Taranto princes lies a small patch of green with enclosure wall; this is most likely S. Croce di Palazzo and SS. Trinità di Palazzo,[49] both founded under Angevin rule. Moving to the right past the Castel Nuovo, one notes the hulking outline of the customs building and arsenal, portrayed with two bays as attested on an Aragonese bank bill.[50] Behind this, further up, lies the convent of Monte Oliveto, with the Cappella Tolosa, then S. Maria La Nova with its campanile, and nearby S. Giovanni Maggiore. Above rises the church of S. Chiara with its apsidal facade and three round windows; the roof of the cloister is also discernible. Further up comes S. Domenico Maggiore with its apse. Toward the east rises S. Lorenzo with its facade and soaring campanile; then the cathedral proper, with its transept, and a glimpse of S. Giovanni a Carbonara above and to the far right. An imaginary dividing line runs vertically between the cathedral and S. Giovanni, and in fact the roofs begin to flow in another direction. To convey this east section of the city, the painter shifts his viewpoint along the shoreline to beyond the Carmine bastions: the vanishing lines, still leading to infinity, are rotated 90° to those for the western section, or left of the picture. Through this shrewd bending of the topographical representation and rules of perspective, the artist manages to include this whole section of the urban panorama as well. It is as if he had rotated the entire section along the imaginary vertical hinge identified above, affording us this extra panorama. If he had continued with other viewpoints—all on the west side—the east side would not have appeared at all, or would have been too distorted. As it happens we can make out S. Agostino alla Zecca with its campanile, and in the background the high gray towers of the Porta Capuana, with the turreted square of the Castel Capuano. The old castle looks onto the sweeping profile of S. Eligio, with its tower and transept. A direct comparison of this detail with the equivalent in the Baratta panel confirms this identification: in the first decades of the seventeenth century, the arch of S. Eligio still jutted out conspicuously from the fabric of the city. Isolated on the right stands S. Pietro ad Aram, with its campanile.

The complex topographical realiability of the painting is confirmed by the fact that the main buildings are aligned along the horizontal succession of the *decumani*, and their distances respect the orthogonal grid of the cardines. Consequently, the alignments and distances between the buildings are not conventional as such, but imply the prior construction of a street plan, however approximate, to which the two deliberately opposite perspective viewpoints were then applied. It is equally evident that the artist was forced to accentuate the morphology of the plain on which the city is spread in order to give due relief to the more important urban monuments.

Along the waterfront one can clearly see the city walls and gates: "They are called," writes Spinazzola, "Porta S. Martire, Porta della Carille or 'dei Barillari,' Porta S. Andrea, Porta della Marina Grande (in the clearing before the Castelnuovo two others are marked, evidently those formerly known as Porta della Ficha, and Porta della Marina di Porto)."[51]

To sum up, all three of these magnificent *vedute* are contemporary: the view of Florence is datable to 1489–95, the original engraved in Rome (from which the Mantua copy was taken) dates to 1478–90, and the Tavola Strozzi to before 1487 (all dates proposed long ago by Spinazzola, and analyzed in depth by Bologna). Moreover, all three are executed with the same type of technical drawing apparatus, the kind used by a cosmographer and certainly not by a painter—be he as talented as Colantonio or as versatile as Francesco Pagano—who would not be versed in the already precise codified rules governing the use of geodetic instruments, indispensable for trigonometry and for constructing reliable ground plans capable of furnishing the kind of data needed for making reliable perspective *vedute* of this complexity. The artist is also a manuscript illuminator, as attested by the many minute details pointed out by Spinazzola, who wound up his precise and acute reading of the panel thus: "One fact can be inferred directly from the painting: that the artist had the city before him as he painted, and reproduced it with the utmost fidelity. There is no rhetoric, no poetical adulation. ... Everything is caught truthfully, albeit drafted in compliance with traditional norms of representation. Accordingly, in order to make them stand out against the uppermost border of the city, the painter has raised the level of the sacred buildings, and has foreshortened some distances and increased others in order to be able to fit into the panel those features he deemed appropriate, or to improve the overall image, or to afford a more enclosed and artistic view: attributes of similar panoramic vedute, which, while not miracles of perspective in the modern sense, overcome obstacles of representation with appropriate devices which we would not be able accomplish."[52] This is a view that I share completely, having personally tried to fathom just those "opportuni adattamenti" or devices which the scholar so aptly intuited.

Another attribution to Francesco Rosselli and his workshop is the panorama depicting the *Burning of Savonarola* in Piazza della Signoria (Florence, Museo di S. Marco); its similarities with the Florentine veduta only confirms the attribution (L. D. Ettlinger, in *The Burlington Magazine* XCIV, no. 591, June 1952, p. 160ff., fig. 12) for the precision with which the Palazzo Vecchio is represented, and the meticulous glimpse (left) of the dome of the cathedral: the relative dimensions of the buildings are perfectly harmonized thanks to the painstaking use of perspective, and can be verified with the slabs of the piazza, which serves as a visual guide to the spatial logic of the picture. This same technique was used in the renowned, almost contemporary, *Ideal City* (Urbino, Palazzo Ducale, Galleria Nazionale della Marche). But the most telling feature linking the Florentine *veduta* with the Tavola Strozzi

is, once again, the perspective devices used for the building fabric, with sloping roofs and crenelated walls that recede to the limits of the city walls, beyond which can be seen the gentle slopes of the Arno hillside. To some extent Rosselli manipulates the topography of the place represented to give greater weight to the scene of the victim burning at the stake in the middle of the piazza, and allow for the placement of clusters of figures that seem quite indifferent to the grim execution taking place. The picture is curiously suspended in time, despite the figures animating the scene; the same can be said of the Naples *veduta*, in which the galleys populated by minute figures seem quite incidental to the temporal fixity of the image.

Further and definitive proof of my attribution has come in the form of new documentary finds made by Mario del Treppo, to whom I am most grateful for having provided me with advance information. Among the papers of the Strozzi archives in Florence the scholar came across a document (soon to be published) proving that the Tavola was part of a sumptuous gift from Filippo Strozzi to Ferrante of Aragon. The panel was painted in late 1472 early 1473, as the *spalliera* of a *lettuccio* or small bed, and is described as being the work of an artist with special accomplishments in the art of perspective. The painting was sent from Florence on 15 April 1473 together with other gifts from the Florentine banker to Ferdinand. Strozzi paid a conspicuous fee to the architect Benedetto da Maiano, the "artefice del lettuccio," to commission the view of Naples from a painter in the Florentine milieu. The date indicated in the document coincides with that of Francesco Rosselli's engraving of Florence; the document also explains the fact that the foredecks of four of the galleys pictured in the panel bear a round shield with a red band adorned with three silver crescent moons: the emblem of the Strozzi family, who may well have financed the launching of these ships. The newly found document clears up a century-old problem: while there is still no clear proof of the artist's name (nor perhaps will there ever be), there are many clues to suggest Francesco Rosselli, or someone with his qualities and specialization in this kind of pictorial undertaking. Come what may, it is no longer tenable to consider the author of the panel of Neapolitan descent, as advanced by Riccardo Filangieri in the 1930s, and repeated by Raffaello Causa in the 1970s with his attribution to Colantonio, and finally reproposed with ample arguments by Ferdinando Bologna with his attribution to Francesco Pagano, with the corollary that the Tavola was part of an allegorical cycle painted to glorify the Aragon line. Ferrante received the painting from Filippo Strozzi and not the other way round. What remains to explain is how the panel found its way back to Florence, where it was discovered at the start of the present century in the Palazzo Strozzi.

Tommaso Manzuoli (called Maso da S. Friano)
Double Male Portrait
Naples, Museo e Gallerie Nazionali di Capodimonte
Cat. no. 410

Cosimo de' Medici's Arrival
in Siena (detail)
"tavoletta di biccherna," 1561
Siena, Archivio di Stato

Carlo Bertelli

A Tale of Two Cities: Siena and Venice

Siena's bishop, Gabriele Condulmer— the future Pope Eugene IV—was not actually a local man but a Venetian, and as bishop he remained in the city from 1407 to 1431, some twenty-four years. Despite this link, there had never really been much interchange between the artists of Siena and Venice, although the lagoon capital had proved to be entirely receptive to "outsiders," especially to artists from Florence and Lombardy. Even the presence of the Sienese artist Andrea di Bartolo in and around Venice is tied to special circumstances, and a network of ongoing exchanges.[1] Nevertheless, this absence of a more concrete exchange of ideas did not impede the emergence of certain affinities. As it was, both republics promoted painting of a historic and didactic character as a stimulus to patriotism. The history of Venice was narrated to citizens and visitors through large pictorial programs. Each year on Ascension day—the feast of the "Sensa" in the Venetian calendar—the doors to the Sala Maggiore of the Doges' Palace were thrown wide to the public. Writing in 1446, Michele Savonarola recalled the throngs of believers, people of every nationality, who from early morning flocked to admire the joyous scenes and grandiose battle frescoes of Guariento. The crowds would remain in stunned contemplation, and no one was in a hurry to leave.[2]

In Siena, too, the Palazzo Pubblico was not without its share of frescoes of a political nature,[3] and by a remarkable coincidence, these repeated the theme of Guariento's frescoes of 1366, namely Barbarossa's invasion of Italy. The Sienese cycle is attributed to Spinello Aretino and has been dated to 1407, the year in which the Bishop Condulmer took his appointment in Venice. Spinello's frescoes, dedicated to the Sienese pope, Alexander III (Bandinelli), concludes with the image of *The Victory of the Venetians at Punta Salvatore against the Fleet of Barbarossa* and almost at the beginning, like a second episode, presents *Pope Alexander III Entrusting his Sword to the Doge Ziani*. Some decades later, Guariento's frescoes were destroyed by fire and Vittore Carpaccio was commissioned to punctiliously depict the scene of the pope handing over the insignia to the doge in the presence of Barbarossa.[4]

In Siena, paintings of a political nature were an established tradition, and followed a coherent program spanning several decades. Simone Martini heralded this development around 1316 with his *Maestà* fresco in the Sala Maggiore, the same subject that Duccio had painted for the altarpiece of the cathedral. The insignia of the commune, which includes the image of the city's patron, the Virgin Mary, is arranged at the base of Martini's superb composition, lending the work an unmistakable civic stamp. In 1321 Martini repainted the fresco in part; nine years later (2 May 1331) he was commissioned to include the castles of Montemassi and Sassoforte, both newly captured by the Sienese forces. Other conquests must have found their way into the frescoes in the course of time, as the room was described in an early document as the place where *sunt picta alia castra acquistata per Comune Senarum.*[5]

In this way the city's victories were gratefully offered up to the Virgin, just as other castles and towns had formerly been portrayed on the shutters of the doors of S. Clemente at Causauria, and full battle scenes and maps along the arcade of the Cistercian church of the Tre Fontane at Rome, punctuated by plaques recording the possessions of the abbey in the Maremma, in a sort of revival of *pictura triumphalis*. Siena's identification with its patron gave a sacred justification to the state's appropriation of new land, and the eleventh-century image in Montecassino showing the presentation of the abbey's lands to its patron may have influenced this exceptional survey of castles portrayed on the walls around Martini's *Maestà*.[6]

Duccio di Buoninsegna's panel for the great altarpiece in the cathedral shows a forced shift in iconography and style: the scene shows the devil tempting Jesus with a kingdom that has been rendered identifiable by detailing its towns, each one pictured in true perspective as in a scale model, with all its urban features neatly defined.[7]

In 1338–40 in the Sala della Pace of the Palazzo Pubblico, Siena, next door to the *Maestà*, Ambrogio Lorenzetti completed his renowned frieze depicting the effects of good and bad government. The life of the city and the surrounding countryside was featured in a more concrete form, entrusted to the virtues linking the wise rulers to the public cause: an Aristotelian and Thomist world which replaced the simplistic imagery of prayer or fortune with an analysis of causes and effects.[8]

In 1344 Ambrogio Lorenzetti was commissioned to create an enormous mobile map, the *Mappamondo* (hence the name of the room), depicting the castles ruled by Siena, seen in their

[1] G. Freuler, "Andrea di Bartolo, Fra Tommaso d'Antonio Caffarini, and Sienese Dominicans in Venice," in *Art Bulletin* LXIV, no. 4, 1978, pp. 570-586. Other links between Venice and Tuscan artists and patrons, apart from those of Florence which are often the subject of study, concern patrons from Lucca and involve one of the principal masters of the Quattrocento, Gentile da Fabriano: M. Ceriana and E. Draffa, "Il polittico di Valle Romita, la sua storia nel museo," in *Gentile da Fabriano, il polittico di Valle Romita*, Milan, 1993, pp. 25-35, especially pp. 27-30.

[2] *Rerum Italicarum Scriptores*, XXIV, XV, new ed., 1902, Michele Savonarola, *Libellus de magnificis ornamentis regie civitatis Padue*, ed. A. Segarizzi; A Segarizzi, *Della vita e delle opere di Michele Savonarola*, Padua, 1990; J. Schlosser Magnino, *La letteratura artistica, Manuale delle fonti della storia dell'arte moderna*, Florence, 1977, pp. 109 and 118: "*cuius intuitus* [Guariento's] *tanta cum aviditate expectatur, ut cum adest Ascensionis dies, quo omnibus ingressus licet, nulla supersit diei hora, qua locus innumerabili diversarum patriarum hominum copia non repleatur, tantusque est earum admirandarum figurarum iucundus aspectus, et tanti depicti conflictus admiranda res, ut nemo exitum querat.*"

[3] N. Rubinstein, "Political Ideas in Sienese Art: the frescoes by Ambrogio Lorenzetti and Taddeo di Bartolo in the Palazzo Pubblico," in *Journal of the Warburg and Courtauld Institutes* XXI, 1858, pp. 179-207; E.C. Southard, "The Frescoes in Siena's Palazzo Pubblico, 1289-1539," Phil. Diss. (1978), London-New York, 1979.

[4] One of Carpaccio's drawings for *Pope Alexander III Handing over the Insignia to the Doge Zani at Ancona in the Presence of Barbarossa* has been conserved. Cf. *Die Zeit der Staufer*, exhibition catalog, Stuttgart, 1977, no. 1045.

[5] M. Seidal, "*Castrum pingatur in palatio*. I. Ricerche storiche e iconografiche sui castelli dipinti nel palazzo Pubblico di Siena," in *Prospettiva* 28, 1982, pp. 17ff. A payment from 2 May 1330 of 16 lire was made to Simone Martini for his painting of Montemassi and Sassoforte in the Palazzo Pubblico. Recently there has been some discussion as to whether this payment actually refers to the Guidoriccio fresco on the wall opposite the *Maestà*; G. Moran, "An Investigation Regarding the Equestrian Portrait of Guidoriccio da Fogliano in Siena Palazzo

geographical context. The massive pivot on the wall and the grooves scored into the lower frame of the Guidoriccio fresco[9] give an idea of the sheer size of Lorenzetti's invention. In 1424 a new map of the Sienese state was drawn up.[10] The landscapist tradition of the frescoes of Ambrogio Lorenzetti was far from waning—on the contrary, it remained an unmistakable, enduring feature of Sienese painting. And so, in 1438, more or less at the time when Michele Savonarola wrote about his contemporaries' admiration for the Venetians masters of the Trecento, the Republic of Siena embarked on a project that betrayed the same backward-looking esthetic: a master weaver of Brussels, Rinaldo Wauters (known as Boteram), was commissioned to make a tapestry of the frescoes of the Sala della Pace to cover the rostrum erected in Piazza del Campo for civic ceremonies.[11] In Siena the revival of the fourteenth-century tradition rekindled that period's potential for research. In this respect it is significant that two famous fragments showing views of castles (both conserved in the Pinacoteca in Siena), were for a long time unanimously attributed to Ambrogio Lorenzetti until they were identified as the remains of an altarpiece that Sassetta painted for the woolcarders guild in 1423–26.[12] The tapestries thus displayed before the public in the Piazza del Campo offered a fabulous marriage between the cream of fourteenth-century Sienese painting and one of the most advanced and typical techniques of northern Europe. The influence was reciprocal, however. The Dutch tapestry master, who around 1400 illuminated the superb manuscript copy of the *Revelations* in the Bibliothèque Nationale, Paris (Néerl. 3), seems to have been acquainted with the cluster of castles and towns at the feet of Christ in Duccio's *Maestà*.[13] Meanwhile, the itinerary from the Sala del Mappamondo to the Sala della Pace, and thence to the antechapel with the frescoes of Taddeo di Bartolo created in 1407 showing an imaginary vision of ancient Rome, soon became famous. When Jean Pucelle adopted a typically Sienese architectural style and perspective to depict the siege of Orléans in his illustration of a codex (lost in the battle of Poitiers in 1356, but later retrieved), he was not simply reproducing his memories of the landscape but one of the images in the Sala del Mappamondo which, until about ten years ago, were hidden beneath the Guidoriccio fresco.[14] An unmistakable reference to this fresco is also found in a French codex, now tentatively attributed to Jacques Coène, in which a horseman with flapping cape is pictured before an open landscape.

Pubblico," in *Paragone* 333, 1977, pp. 81-88, has raised further questions on this point, promoting archive research, the restoration of the fresco, and in particular the discovery of another fresco, on the same wall, showing a horseman and a magistrate (?) in front of a castle. Ed. L. Bellosi, *Simone Martini*, Convention proceedings, Siena, 1985, Florence, 1985; the balanced review of S. Gardner, in *Burlington Magazine*, 1989; and also M. Mallory and G. Moran, *Burlington Magazine* CXXVIII, April 1986, and A. Martindale, "The Problem of Guidoriccio," ibid., pp. 259-273; Idem, *Simone Martini*, Oxford, 1988; P. Leone De Castris, *Simone Martini*, Florence, 1989, pp. 104-108, 138, with bibliography. Also, C.B. Strehlke, "Niccolò di Giovanni di Francesco Ventura e il Guidoriccio," in *Prospettiva* 49, 1987, pp. 45-48 and L. Bellosi, "Ancora sul Guidoriccio," ibid., pp. 49-55.

[6] H. Bloch, *Monte Cassino in the Middle Ages*, I, Rome, 1986, pp. 138-627 (*The Bronze Doors of Monte Cassino*). According to legend Charlemagne donated twelve castles to the Tre Fontane abbey as an *ex voto* for the miraculous fall of Ansedonia. The episode was related in the frescoes of the portico, and again represented in the image of twelve castles in enamel on the frame of the icon of S. Anastasio, dated 1283, but now lost. Through its properties in the Maremma, the Roman abbey of the Tre Fontane was closely linked with Sienese Cistercian houses, in particular with S. Galgano. See C. Bertelli, "Caput Sancti Anastasii," in *Paragone* 247, September 1970, pp. 12-25.

[7] F. Deuchler, *Duccio*, Milan, 1983, pls. 147-150, q.v.

[8] N. Rubinstein, op. cit. in note 3.

[9] L. Bellosi, 1987, op. cit. in note 7, notes the presence of another hole beside that of the definitive pivot for the *Mappamondo* and suggests that the installer was trying to find the best way of fixing the huge device onto the wall. G. Moran, 1986, proposes that the grooves scored on the top of the Guidoriccio painting are due to the map of 1425.

[10] G. Moran, 1986, op. cit. in note 5.

[11] W. Braghirolli, *Sulle manifatture di arazzi in Mantova*, Mantua, 1875; G. Campori, *L'arazzeria estense*, Modena, 1876.

[12] F. Zeri, "Richerche sul Sassetta. La pala dell'arte della Lana (1423-1426)," in *Quaderni di Emblema 2*, Bergamo, 1973, pp. 22-34.

[13] M.H. Dubreuil, *Valencia y el gótico internacional*, pp. 132-133, pls. 369-370.

[14] This is the *Miracles de la Vierge* by Gautier de Coincy, Paris, Bibliothèque Nationale, Nouv. Acq. fr. 24541: K. Morand, *Jean Pucelle*, Oxford, 1962, n. 8, pp. 42-43.

[15] The author (*Corriere della Sera*, 26 July 1988, p. 3) noted the relationship between the Guidoriccio fresco and the miniature on fol. 3r. in the codex in the Bibliothèque Municipale, Châteauroux, MS. 21, which C. Sterling tentatively attributes to the Maître du Maréchal de Boucicaut (Jacques Coène?); and recorded by C. B. Strehlke, "Niccolò di Giovanni di Francesco Ventura e il Guidoriccio," in *Prospettiva* 49, April 1987, pp. 45-48. Strehlke also correctly points to links with the view of the sup-

top
Simone Martini
Guidoriccio da Fogliano
fresco, 1330
Siena, Palazzo Pubblico
Sala del Mappamondo

above
Unknown
Giuncarico Castle
fresco, 14th cent.
Siena, Palazzo Pubblico
Sala del Mappamondo

on the following pages
Ambrogio Lorenzetti
Allegory of Good
Government (*detail*)
fresco, 1338
Siena, Palazzo Pubblico

375

COSTEI VOCHE REGGIETE CHE QVI FIGVRATA 7 PSVE CIELLEGA CORONATA LAQVAL SEPRA CIASCVN S

Another French text illuminator, Jacquemart de Hesdin, also borrowed from the same fresco, reproducing the massive fortress in all its detail (identified as the castle of Montemassi).[15] Yet another manuscript illuminator, Pol de Limbourg, during his visit to Siena between 1407 and 1416, had occasion to admire the castle scene and maybe even turn Lorenzetti's *Mappamondo*; he must have remembered this when he decided to insert a realistic view of a castle for each month in his sumptuous manuscript *Les Très Riches Heures* for the duc de Berri.[16]

Siena was not the only Tuscan town that fostered this form of urban "portrait." Although it is not known whether that "Comune rubato da molti" cited by Vasari among the works of Giotto also included a representation of Florence, it is certain that the "portraits of infamy" in the Bargello depicting those guilty of crimes against the state, also included the towns accused of treachery. Similarly, the illustrations of the so-called *Biadaiolo* attest to the degree of subtlety which Florentine artists had attained in urban portraiture.[17]

This genre, therefore, also seems to foreshadow the art of the *veduta*. But the vogue for fourteenth-century-style landscape painting was swept aside by a new spirit epitomized by the frescoes by Paolo Uccello and Andrea del Verrocchio on the walls of the cathedral, respectively portraying the famous *condottieri* Giovanni Acuto (alias Sir John Hawkwood) and Niccolò da Tolentino—not as real people but as heroic figures in bronze or marble, riding in a kind of triumphal limbo, with no visual clues as to time or place.[18]

In the meantime, Paolo Uccello's fresco of 1436 (coeval with the publication of Alberti's treatise on painting) showed the difficulties of applying the new rules of perspective to painting. The different viewpoints adopted—one for the horse and one for the base—confirm his studies into foreshortening on single objects, but without a central unifying point.

Undeniably, it was technically difficult to translate to monumental painting the optical experiments proposed by Filippo Brunelleschi, with his peepshows in which the painted image was shown against the virtual mirrored image, observed through a small hole in the model.[19]

posed Montemassi, over which I had hesitated, as this part of the fresco is evidently a later addition. Admittedly, the "restorer" could have seen the deteriorated part of the old fresco before replacing it with as faithful a replica as possible.

[16] H. Boder, "The Zodiacal Miniatures of the 'Très Riches Heures' of the Duke of Berry," in *Journal of the Warburg and Courtauld Institutes* XI, 1948, pp. 1-34. Paul de Limbourg's visit to Siena is confirmed by the insertion of Taddeo Bartolo's plan of Rome, from the Palazzo Pubblico, into the *Très Riches Heures*, discussed later. On the interest of the Limbourgs for the representation of the city: E. Morand, "La ville de Riom et la fête de Mai dans les 'Très Riches Heures' du duc de Berry," in *Bulletin de l'Académie des Sciences, Belles-Lettres et Arts de Clermont-Ferrand*, 1954, pp. 1-5.

[17] G. Pinto, *Il libro del Biadaiolo. Carestia e annona a Firenze dalla metà del '200 al 1348*, Florence, 1978. In particular on the representation of cities: C. Bertelli, preface by D. Lenzi, *Il Biadaiolo*, Milan, 1981.

[18] It is remarkable that in the late sixteenth century the Guidoriccio fresco was considered to be like a statue: "having ... been ... honored by an equestrian statue painted in the Sala delle Balestre, now the Council Chamber, by the hand of Simone Martini, master painter of his time ... still visible today above the globe with the emblem of Montemassi," quoted by A. Martindale, 1986, op. cit. in note 5, p. 261.

Vecchietta (Lorenzo di Pietro)
Landscapes with Castles
(detail) fresco
Castiglione Olona, Palazzo
Branda Castiglioni

Paul and Jean de Limbourg
The Month of March
illumination from the Très
Riches Heures
1412–15
Chantilly, Musée Condé
MS. 65

For this reason it is only natural that the first to properly apply perspective to narrative scenes was not a painter, but the sculptor Donatello.[20]

Heedless of these problems, the artists of the Po Valley continued to subscribe to the fourteenth-century style of representing the townscape proposed by the Florentine artist Giusto de' Menabuoi.

In the history of St. James in the church of S. Antonio, Padua, the painter Giusto de' Menabuoi shows a keen interest in architecture, adopting the form of the basilica of S. Lorenzo (which he had so admired during his sojourn in Milan) for his depiction of the temple of Solomon.

The building appears twice: once frontally and once obliquely; though only approximate, the latter representation is quite advanced for its time (ca. 1382). These frescoes by Giusto testify to how far Florentine artists had come in their study of perspective – a field of inquiry which Brunelleschi would take even further, using scientific method; it also shows what stage such research had reached in Padua.

This explains Savonarola's great admiration for the perspective skills of the Paduan painters of the Trecento, whose work offers practical examples of what the science of perspective was later to deduce.[21]

In his *Crucifixion of St. Philip* Giusto's portrayal of the city of Hierapolis follows the Paduan prototype to the letter, whereas in the *Vision of the Blessed Luca* his representation of Padua is remarkably objective.[22]

Siena's proximity to Florence made it impossible for there not to be an immediate examination of the new principles in relation with the longstanding tradition of site surveying. While older painters such as Sassetta employed an intuitive approach, the arrival in Siena of Donatello's two "manifestos" of the new science of perspective—the *Banquet of Herod* for the baptismal font, and the tomb of Bishop Giovanni Pecci[23]—forced the younger generation of artists such as Vecchietta (Lorenzo di Pietro) to take account of the principles that had been established.

Vecchietta in Lombardy

Given the long, parallel paths of development of art in Venice and Siena, one can imagine the welcome Vecchietta received on his arrival in the lagoon capital.

The young Sienese master gave the first proof of his abilities outside his native region in the Lombard town of Castiglione Olona, where he worked in collaboration with Masolino in the service of Cardinal Branda Castiglioni. Masolino had already executed frescoes in the chapel of the basilica of S. Clemente in Rome for this same cardinal.[24]

Their first commission at Castiglione probably involved the decoration of a small room in the cardinal's residence: a rather narrow fascia situated high on the walls (as in the Guidoriccio *paesaggio*), running the full perimeter of the room. The Castiglione frieze, however, shows an unadorned view of mountains and towns, with no narrative or figures. The old master and his young assistant divided the job in half, with Vecchietta responsible for the part seen on the left of the viewer. Vecchietta's hand is identifiable in the tight pattern of castles and towns over the mountainsides, neatly arranged within the tectonic framework. The light source is set low to accentuate the relief, and shines from the left, coinciding with one of the windows of the room. The established canons for conveying a sense of distance are inverted, as the mountains appear fainter the further away they are, foreshadowing the technique later known as "aerial" perspective.[25]

The logic Vecchietta's rendering of the landscape was grasped with remarkable speed by the Venetian master Jacopo Bellini, and promptly employed for the background of the *Madonna* painted for Lionello d'Este, now in the Louvre;[26] this is an indication of how alert the contemporary modern Venetian painters were regarding the advances of Sienese artists.

Here too the mountains become fainter as they recede in the distance, and the somewhat accelerated perspective of the town on the left, or the towns and castles clinging to the slopes,

Vecchietta (Lorenzo di Pietro)
Prophet
fresco
Castiglione Olona
Palazzo Branda Castiglioni
chapel

above
Vecchietta (Lorenzo di Pietro)
Saints of the Religious Orders
before an Ideal Villa
fresco
Castiglione Olona, Palazzo
Branda Castiglioni

Vecchietta (Lorenzo di Pietro)
View of an Ideal Basilica
fresco
Castiglione Olona, Collegiata

Recent research for precursors of the Guidoriccio fresco continues to overlook the only ancient equestrian statue still in existence, that of Oldrado da Tresseno in the Palazzo della Ragione, Milan. As Italian communes were obliged to choose the *podestà* from outside the citizenry, these personages must have had an enormous effect on the spread of iconography from one commune to the next.

[19] M. Kemp, *The Science of Art*, London-New Haven, 1990.

[20] A. Rosenauer, *Donatello, l'opera completa*, Milan, 1993, pp. 24-25.

[21] G. Bresciani Alvarez et al., *La cappella del Beato Luca e Giusto de' Menabuoi nella Basilica di Sant'Antonio*, Padua, 1988, pl. on pp. 76 and 102. The full passage from Savonarola runs (ed. quoted in note 2, p. 44): "*Postremo ad mechanicos gloriosos et sua arte illustres viros me converto, quorum scire a philosophia non est longiquum, et mathematicarum artium practica est. Hi sunt pictores, quibus lineamenta figurarum et radiorum proiectiones nosse datum est, ut quibus prospectiva scientia gloriatut per eos practicos demostretur.*" Among the said famous figures were Guariento and Giusto. It was Giotto, however, who initiated the Paduan school of painting: "*de geometria sic aliquid a nobis actum, cum perspectiva picture mater habeatur, et pars ea digniora, cum de stupenda radiorum proiectione peractet.*"

[22] C.B. Semenzato, ed., *La Cappella del Beato Luca e Giusto de' Menabuoi nella Basilica di S. Antonio*, Padua 1988, pp. 50, 54-55, 72-76, 102.

[23] A. Rosenauer, op. cit. in note 20, pp. 77-82; pp. 62, 69 and passim.

[24] Vecchietta's collaboration with Masolino at Castiglione was determined for the first time by R. Longhi, "Fatti di Masaccio e Masolino," in *La Critica d'arte* XXV-XXVI, 1940, pp. 145-191, republished in *Fatti di Masolino e Masaccio e altri studi sul Quattrocento, Opere complete*, VIII/1, Florence, 1975, pp. 3-65. For a more extensive study of Vecchietta's activities in the Lombard town and the attribution of the landscape of the Palazzo dei Castiglioni, see C. Bertelli, "Masolino e il Vecchietta a Castiglione Olona," in *Paragone* XXXVIII, n.s., 5 (451), 1987, pp. 25-47.

[25] See E.H. Gombrich, "The Lustre of Apelles," Pilkington Lecture at the Whitworth Gallery of Art, Manchester, May 1972, in *The Heritage of Apelles. Studies in the Art of the Renaissance*, Oxford, 1976.

[26] C. Eisler, *The Genius of Jacopo Bellini, The Complete Paintings and Drawings*, New York, 1988, p. 46, illus. at p. 47.

[27] Over Masolino's fresco of *The Sermon of the Baptist*, some time later another master, close to Pisanello and even more to Domenico Veneziano, painted a new figure (see C. Bertelli, op. cit. in note 17). However, this is certainly not the same painter of the Palazzo dei Castiglione di Monteruzzo, as we can see now that restoration has almost entirely revealed these frescoes. The Greek style of headdress worn by the figure furthermore suggests it dates after the Council of Florence of

seem so faithful to the world of Vecchietta that we can presume that the Venetian painter was acquainted with similar works of his young Sienese contemporary: such ideas could have come from his master Gentile da Fabriano.

However, Jacopo Bellini's knowledge of the landscapes of Vecchietta does not imply that the Venetian painter traveled to Castiglione Olona, even though the small town was the destination of many artists of northern Italy.[27] He more probably saw Vecchietta's works in Venice itself; consequently, Bellini's *Madonna*, which C. Eisler calculates was executed a little after 1429, may in fact date to around four or five years earlier.[28]

Again in the Collegiata at Castiglione Olona, the hand of Vecchietta is discernible in the upper sections of the vault – limited but demanding tracts of the decoration. Here he realized the landscapes and, in particular, defined the perspective arrangement of the buildings on the spandrels. Roberto Longhi, a historian with little interest for the theories of perspective, revealed the presence of Vecchietta here, on account of the "perspective acuteness" present in the central spandrel.[29] After this, Vecchietta was given more space in which to work in the baptistery. His interventions in Masolino's compositions regard in particular the background landscapes, but he realized an entire scene himself, namely, the *Imposition of the Name of the Baptist*, in which he again demonstrates great skill in defining the perspective of the barrel vault on the lunettes.

And finally in the depiction of the Baptism—again in collaboration with Masolino—

Vecchietta (Lorenzo di Pietro)
Arliquiera, *two internal panels*
Siena, Pinacoteca Nazionale

on the opposite page
Vecchietta and Michele
Giambono *(attrib.)*
Presentation of the Virgin
(detail) mosaic
Venice, St. Mark's
Cappella dei Mascoli

1439, when exotic clothing of this kind became very popular in Italian painting. M. Natale notes the significance of the small busts set in niches in the frescoes of the palace's chapel, as the beginnings of a theme quite widespread in the decoration of Lombard wooden ceilings.

[28] C. Eisler, op. cit. in note 26.

[29] R. Longhi, op. cit. in note 24.

[30] M. Tafuri, in *Francesco di Giorgio*, ed. F.P. Fiore and M. Tafuri, Milan, 1993, p. 32.

[31] See "Paolo Schiavo," in *La pittura in Italia, Il Quattrocento*, ed. F. Zeri, II, Milan, 1987, pp. 725-726.

[32] H.W. van Os, *Vecchietta and the Sacristy of the Siena Hospital Church*, The Hague, 1974. According to van Os, the frescoes were completed at a later date. Nevertheless, the tomb for the cardinal, who died at a great age in 1443 and whose arcosolium conditioned Vecchietta's frescoes, must have been ready for some time seeing as it forms part of the same set of statuary documented as existing in 1431 (T. Foffano, "La costruzione di Castiglione Olona in un'opera inedita di Francesco Pizzolpasso," in *Italia medievale e umanistica* II, 1960, pp. 153-187. On the sculptures, see W. Wolters, *La scultura veneziana gotica, 1300-1460*, Venice, 1976, pp. 107-111). Moreover, in 1444 Branda's nephew Baldassarre Castiglioni bequeathed 100 florins for the decoration of the Chiesa di Villa, without mentioning the Collegiata, which must have been already completed.

[33] T. Foffano, op. cit. in the preceding note. A. Natali, "La Chiesa di Villa a Castiglione Olona e gli inizi del Vecchietta," in *Paragone* 407, 1984, pp. 3-14, notes the Venetian character of the arch in the upper part of the *Dance of Salome* in the baptistery, formerly attributed by R. Longhi to Vecchietta. Prior to the conclusion of the work with Masolino, Vecchietta was already acquainted with Venetian works. A. Natali quoted the author's text—published later in *Paragone*—presuming it was the same as the one published in the Convention proceedings from Milan and Florence of 1982.

[34] For an accurate description, an almost complete bibliography and a critique of former texts on the chapel and its mosaics, see G. Rossi Scarpa, "I mosaici della cappella dei Mascoli," in R. Polacco et al., *San Marco, la basilica d'oro*, Milan, 1991, pp. 287-304. For the attempt on the life of Francesco Foscari, see A. Da Mosto, *I dogi di Venezia nella vita pubblica e privata*, Milan, 1960, p. 166.

[35] W. Wolters, ibid., cat. 235. There is no proof, according to Wolters, that the altar had been installed before the inscription (but: Thieme and Becker XXXVII, 1950, p. 225).

[36] R. Pallucchini suggested repair work resulting from the infiltration of water, *La pittura veneziana del Quattrocento, il gotico internazionale e gli inizi del rinascimento*, Bologna, 1956, pp. 192ff.; E. Merkel, "Un problema di metodo: la

Vecchietta conceived the perspective structure of the building using as his model the internal octagonal of the Lateran baptistery; in this case, instead of columns, he included octagonal pillars, which are better suited to showing off perspective skills.

On close examination, the mountains painted on the background of the *veduta* of Rome, in the fresco immediately adjacent to this above the door, prove that this section was by the same person working alongside Masolino at the cardinal's residence. The young Sienese artist was therefore responsible for the first truly "realistic" *veduta* of Rome. Here again, the realism lies in making the city's monuments recognizable, but instead of isolating them (as in the celebrated maps of Taddeo de Bartolo in the Palazzo Pubblico of Siena), they rise out of the urban fabric. It is as if there were a mental link between the realism achieved in this view and the work which Vecchietta had so admired in Siena.

This *veduta*, together with an evident knowledge of the interior of the Lateran baptistery, suggests that Vecchietta had witnessed it firsthand, and must therefore have visited Rome. Manfredo Tafuri has associated the tripartition of Vecchietta's fresco in the Pellegrinaio of Siena—dated to 1441, and therefore executed some years after the work at Castiglione Olona—with some knowledge of Roman arches with three barrel vaults.[30] Perhaps Vecchietta had visited Masolino's workshop in Rome while he was busy on the frescoes of S. Clemente, completing what Masaccio had left unfinished. It is tempting to attribute Vecchietta with the modification in the sinopia of the *Crucifixion* which brought about a radical revision of the original arrangement of the landscape.

In Rome, among his many encounters, Vecchietta may also have met Leon Battista Alberti. But in the case of the subject treated here, it is sufficient to note that the tripartition, which in Siena is rather loaded with antique motifs, appears in a more contemporary form in the mosaic of the *Visitation* in the Cappella Mascoli in Venice.

Vecchietta's industrious phase at Castiglione Olona was interrupted by the departure—or death—of Masolino. He was replaced by the Florentine Paolo Schiavo, who executed further frescoes in the Collegiata below the vaults painted by Masolino and Vecchietta; the dates of this intervention emerge from the fact that Schiavo was still in Florence in 1436, as proven by his fresco in S. Miniato dated to that year; in fact he returned by 1440, the date of another of his frescoes in S. Apollonia.[31]

Meanwhile, work at Castiglione Olona was suspended until Vecchietta himself concluded it soon after.[32]

Paolo Schiavo's involvement suggests that in the meantime Vecchietta had left Castiglione. Another group of frescoes by Vecchietta in the chapel of the cardinal's residence in the same town, although still charged with references to Masolino and Sassetta, testifies to his interest in the rules of foreshortening, a technique that occupied many Florentine painters at that time; but it also suggests he made a visit to Venice and its hinterland. This group contains a detail that was specific to Venetian architectural ornament, namely, the sphere-in-disc motif which Paolo Uccello imported to Florence in 1436.

Michael conhono generis

Andrea del Castagno and
Jacopo Bellini
Dormitio Virginis
mosaic
Venice, St. Mark's
Cappella dei Mascoli

384

Throughout Vecchietta's later work this became a recurring motif, from the fresco of the Pellegrinaio to the reliquary cabinet in the Ospedale, known as the *arliquiera*. As for the frescoes in the Collegiata, executed in the second phase of his period in Lombardy, Vecchietta added the complex motif of a centrally planned church, demonstrating an authentic interest in the architecture of the Veneto, and manifesting the profound impression he had received from Giusto's architecture in his frescoes at Padua. Although Padua was yet to see the arrival of Donatello, it was already possible to admire significant works by Paolo Uccello and Filippo Lippi. For a young emigrant in Lombardy, a visit to Venice was entirely natural; the works of Venetian sculptors had already reached Castiglione Olona, and from Venice Cardinal Branda awaited the bells for the Collegiata which were being shipped from England.[33] Vecchietta was therefore in a position to unite the presentation of his bishop with that of his patron, the cardinal.

The Cappella Nova: Paolo Uccello and Vecchietta

"MCCCCXXX DVCANTE INCLITO DOMINO FRANCESCO FOSCARI..." begins the memorial tablet high on the altar wall in the chapel of St. Mark's, Venice (known since the seventeenth century as the Cappella della Madonna dei Mascoli). The tablet therefore provides the date and name of the governing doge during Venice's transition into the Renaissance.[34] It is not certain whether the transformation of one of the basilica's entrance halls into a chapel dedicated to the Virgin was the result of an *ex voto* following the unsuccessful coup of 11 March 1430, the same year that the Sienese ambassador to Venice had saved Francesco Foscari's life; the date on the tablet also seems to be borne out stylistically by the sculptures of the altar.[35] The chapel itself is half as wide as it is long, with barrel vaults rising half the total height. But rather than the architecture, the most intriguing features are the reliefs of the marble polyptych, bordered by the concentric curves of the veins of red jasper, and particularly the mosaics, so close that they seem to project from the wall.

A report made after an attempted theft in the basilica reveals that in 1448-49 the work was not complete, perhaps due to repairs.[36]

Assuming work on the mosaics started in 1430, this coincides with Paolo Uccello's definitive departure from Venice after five years' steady work on the mosaics in the main basilica (in January of the following year he was in Florence). A record of his work is conserved in the great figure of *St. Peter*, situated in a spire on the facade of St. Mark's.[37]

A signature in the left section of the vault (the only one in the chapel, albeit reworked) reads clearly *Michael Cambono venetus fecit.*; of the other signature only the word *fecit* remains. Giambono (documented 1420-62) was therefore thought to be the only author of the mosaics, a hypothesis which has now been untenable for some time for two reasons: first, the disparity in styles suggests more than one author and, second, it is hardly likely that the Republic would have needed to look for mosaicists if its official painter, Michele Giambono, was so skilled in this art.

Instead, owing to internal regulations governing the corporations, being a Venetian citizen, Giambono was placed at the head of a team of artists mostly of foreign origins,[38] as testified by part of the design for the sumptuous fascia running the length of the top of the vault. Three tondi interrupt the frieze; the central one features a Madonna and Child – a muscular, semi-nude Infant, draped in the style of the Tuscan Trecento. Despite the decorative character of the fascia, with its interweaving Gothic fretwork similar to other Venetian and Lombard decorations,[39] the tondo is interpreted as a real aperture in the vault: a great window behind the figure of the Madonna, enclosing a glimpse of the starry sky.

With a decisive gesture, which has no relation to the canonical iconography of Hodighitria, the Infant twists in his Mother's arms toward the faithful gathered in the chapel below. The left hand of the Virgin extends from the folds of drapery to touch the edge of the mantle. The translation into mosaic has in no way impaired the energy of this invention, which was wholly unprecedented in Venice.

The same problem of attribution re-emerges for the set of plaques depicting the prophets. The gesture of Daniel pointing to his chest echoes the pose of *St. Matthew* in Ghiberti's statue in Orsanmichele; other details, such as the folds of the tunic and mantle, also refer to Ghiberti's work, which Giambono is unlikely to have been acquainted with. The headdress of *Isaiah* corresponds to those of the prophets on Ghiberti's first doors. Perhaps this is an echo of the lost "half figure of a prophet" of Orsanmichele executed by Ghiberti before his journey to Venice in 1425.[40]

It therefore seems that in many cases Giambono may have only prepared the cartoons for the mosaicists, tracing these from drawings by masters from other regions. In the figures of the vault and in the conception of the central *opaion*, the debt to Paolo Uccello is evident.

Paolo Uccello and Michele Giambono
Prophet
mosaic
Venice, St. Mark's
Cappella dei Mascoli

Andrea del Castagno and Jacopo Bellini
Dormitio Virginis
(detail) mosaic
Venice, St. Mark's
Cappella dei Mascoli

'Dormitio Virginis' dei Mascoli," in *Arte veneta* XXVII, 1973, pp. 65-80 suggests that the work continued until 1451. G. Rossi Scarpa, op. cit. in note 34, p. 288, correctly observes that no date is evident on the mosaics. It is surprising that the decoration of such a small space took some thirty years, but as we see later, the adoption of Masaccian style for the *Dormitio* triggered lengthy discussions.

[37] G. Fiocco, "Il rinnovamento toscano dell'arte del mosaico a Venezia," in *Dedalo* VI, 1925, pp. 109ff.; A. Chastel, "La mosaïque à Venise et à Florence au XVe siècle," in *Arte veneta* VIII, 1954, pp. 119-130 (republished in A. Chastel, *Favole, forme, figure*, Turin, 1988, pp. 69-91); M. Muraro, "L'esperienza di Paolo Uccello," in *Atti del XVIII Congresso Internazionale di Storia dell'Arte*, Venice, 1956, p. 197. M. Salmi, *Commentari*, 1950, identified the image of St. Peter executed in mosaic by Paolo Uccello, and confirmed by sources, in a detail of the painting by Gentile Bellini, *The Procession of the Relics of the Cross*, today in the Accademia. R. Longhi, in *Vita artistica*, I, 1926, p. 129, in

*Vecchietta and Michele
Giambono (attrib.)*
Visitation
mosaic
Venice, St. Mark's
Cappella dei Mascoli

on the following page
*Vecchietta and Michele
Giambono (attrib.)*
Birth of the Virgin
mosaic
Venice, St. Mark's
Cappella dei Mascoli

Viatico a cinque secoli di pittura veneziana, Florence, 1946, pp. 8, 59, and also in *Disegno della pittura veneziana*, Florence, 1979, p. 188, attributed all the architecture to Paolo Uccello, excluding that of the *Dormitio* which he considers the work of Andrea da Murano. G. Rossi Scarpa, p. 294, suggests that Zanino di Pietro had "conceived the first Gothic decoration of the Cappella Nova" and compares the *Annunciation* in the lunette of the Mascoli to the same scene painted by Zanino (ca. 1437) around the tomb of the Beato Pacifico in the church of the Frari. However, the *Annunciation* in the Cappella Mascoli involved two cartoons by different hands as evinced in the diverse spatial perception.

[38] M. Muraro, "The Statues of the Venetian Arti and the Mosaics of the Mascoli Chapel," in *Art Bulletin* LXII, 1961, pp. 263-274.

[39] At Treviso, in the *Stories of S. Eligio* in S. Caterina (see the recent publication of *Il ritorno di Sant'Orsola, affreschi restaurati nella chiesa di Santa Caterina in Treviso*, ed. G. Delfini Filippi and E. Manzato, Treviso, 1992, p. 26) or in the Palazzo dei Castiglioni di Madruzzo at Castiglione Olona (undocumented frescoes).

[40] R. Krautheimer, *Lorenzo Ghiberti*, Princeton, 1970, pp. 73, 74-75, n. 18.

[41] F. von Thode, "Andrea del Castagno in Venedig," in *Festschrift Otto Benndorf*, Vienna, 1898, pp. 307-317. Cf. F. Hartt, "The Earliest Works of Andrea del Castagno," in *Art Bulletin* LXI, 1959, pp. 151 and 225-236.

[42] Mantegna's name was proposed by A. Venturi, *Storia dell'arte italiana*, VII; *La pittura del Quattrocento*, part III, Milan, 1914, p. 99; and G. Fiocco, "Michele Giambono" in *Studi di arte e di storia*, Venice, 1920, p. 207 and id., *L'arte di Andrea Mantegna*, Venice, 1959, p. 103. On Jacopo Bellini see the recent work of C. Eisler, op. cit. in note 26, pp. 66-67.

[43] J. Crowe and G.B. Cavalcaselle, *A History of Painting in Northern Italy*, London, 1871, p. 14. Cf. C. Bertelli, "Il rinascimento del mosaico," in *Il mosaico*, ed. C. Bertelli, Milan, 1988, pp. 225-232.

[44] L. Martini, *Pienza e la val d'Orcia*, Genoa, 1984, pp. 42-50.

[45] G. Rossi Scarpa, op. cit. in note 34, attempts an iconographical interpretation on p. 302, though unfortunately with incorrect identifications.

[46] P. Toesca, *Il Trecento*, Florence, 1950, pp. 566-567.

[47] *La pittura in Italia*, op. cit. in note 25, II, p. 325.

[48] G. Rossi Scarpa proposes that this is the same type of base found in the iconostasis by the Dalle Masegne family in St. Mark's; excluding the proportions, however, the polychromy of the base in the mosaic is definitely Tuscan.

[49] D. Gioseffi, *Perspectiva artificialis, spigolature e appunti*, Trieste, 1951, correctly confirms that the two sections of the vault of the Mascoli borrow from two of Brunelleschi's experiments in perspective: the frontal view of the baptistery and the corner view of the Palazzo Vecchio.

[50] Supposing that the architectural types in the mosaics, excluding the *Dormitio*, are Venetian, G. Rossi Scarpa (op. cit. in note 34) supports the theory that the intention was to represent the Venetian chapel as the "New Jerusalem." M. Muraro (op. cit. in note 38, p. 272) is perhaps stretching the point when he says that the lantern of the cupola in the *Presentation in the Temple* was in the style of Brunelleschi. O. Demus, *The Mosaics of Saint Mark's*, Washington, D.C., 1986, pp. 1-15, has revealed penetrating obser-

The presence of Andrea del Castagno, who in 1442 left his signature in the chapel of S. Tarasio at S. Zaccaria, Venice, was recognized by F. Thode in the conception and in part of the execution of the scene of the *Dormitio Virginis*;[41] it has also been suggested that Andrea del Castagno worked with the young Andrea Mantegna. However, regarding the "more advanced" architecture, current opinion unanimously attributes it to Jacopo Bellini and the mid-fifteenth century.[42]

Until recently, G. B. Cavalcaselle's identification of Vecchietta's hand in the scene of the *Visitation*, has been overlooked.[43] And yet the collaboration of the Sienese artist seems indisputable if we compare the heads of the putti in the frieze running under the three pediments in the architecture of the *Visitation* with those painted in the fresco of the Pellegrinaio at Siena. These represent a type which Vecchietta conserved throughout his career; twenty years later the same full face of the Infant is repeated in the triptych conserved in the cathedral of Pienza.[44]

Several sketches made on the walls of the workshop of the mosaicists in St. Mark's indicate that the artist's principal concern was to give an architectural arrangement to the scene: three pediments in the antique style, each with a central patera enclosing a shell, with every element relating to a central vanishing point, as in Masaccio's fresco of the *Trinity* in the church of S. Maria Novella.

The architecture conceived by Vecchietta, however, is not an inactive setting but is inhabited by domestic objects which probably relate to the figure of a young woman at the window. Vecchietta has thereby created an "ambience" that contributes to the narrative. Those everyday episodes relegated to the background in Masolino's *Resurrection of Tabitha* in the Cappella Brancacci have suddenly acquired the right to occupy the foreground.

From the outset, even in the sketch on the wall of the workshop, Vecchietta clearly intended the architecture to play an active part, as proved by the perspective study of the vase. And in the mosaic, the woman at the window is the recurring "witness" from the *Visitation* iconography, endorsing the framework as an active part of the scene.

The attribution of this work to Vecchietta is confirmed by other references: the closed ampullae on the shelf above is like a quote from the *natura morta* which the young master saw in the cardinal's palace in Castiglione; the ape busily cleaning itself is borrowed from one of Masolino's frescoes in the Cappella Brancacci. At Castiglione Olona, too, Vecchietta reused ideas of Masolino for the vault of the palace's chapel. His personal contribution to the motifs here are the dove, the cage and the oriental, brass carafe.[45]

Vecchietta undoubtedly did not portray the historical figures—that was the job of his Venetian colleague Michele Giambono. Instead he created the picture space for them to inhabit: in the narrow blind alley, Mary and Elisabeth are observed through two doorways; not unlike the triptych by the Master of Flémalle in the Cloisters Museum, New York, from the half-open door, the donor watches the angel make his announcement in Mary's room.

The small bridge linking the two houses is a typical feature of Venetian architecture, and in many cases is used to indicate that the two buildings belong to the same family or proprietor. Here the symbol is ingeniously employed to represent the family ties between Mary and Elisabeth.

This device is a demonstration of the significance of civic symbology, and belongs to the same terrain as Ambrogio Lorenzetti's *Good and Bad Government* fresco, in which the correspondence of urban types to specific functions gives the impression of a real city.

The attribution of the *Birth of Mary* is made easier by the fact that it betrays a precise Sienese model, created by Pietro Lorenzetti in 1342,[46] and reintroduced and updated by Paolo di Giovanni Fei at the beginning of the fifteenth century.[47] With respect to the model the scene has been turned through forty-five degrees; the side wall of the prototype, where the bed is positioned, is now viewed frontally.

Given this genealogy, the initial design can only be Vecchietta's, though he may not have translated it into mosaic. The mosaicist in fact has misinterpreted the gesture of the woman, who is testing the temperature of the water with her hand.

Although the architecture reflects none of the classical rigor of the *Visitation*, and despite the presence of acute arches and Gothic fretwork, even in its nomenclature it is neither Gothic nor Venetian. The polychrome bases with scattered diamond shapes are in fact Florentine or at least Tuscan,[48] as are the door lintels and corbels. The two buttresses which end in approximately Corinthian capitals—an innovation in Venetian sculpture—support a running cornice which unifies the whole building. The link between inside and outside is resolved elegantly by extending the interior toward the exterior with a loggia, in which we observe a woman spinning wool. The loggia also presents a clearly fifteenth-century Tuscan style.

Structurally, the house is formed by walls and right angles which presumably continue on each floor. The jamb illuminated by the low sunlight reveals a passageway to a room out of view.

The plans of the buildings visibly relate to a logical distribution based on function. In the *Visitation* even the tie rods of the arches endorse the perspective and at the same time perform a structural function.

The two constructions of the *Visitation* and of the *Birth of the Virgin*, positioned on opposite sections of the vault, offer the painter and Venetian connoisseur two perfect illustrations of angle perspective and central perspective, in conformance with Brunelleschi's research, and at the same time the display of architecture framing the narrative is an updated revival of the tradition of Giusto de' Menabuoi and Altichiero.

One might argue that only a Sienese master could reconcile tradition with the new, in a spirit amenable to the characteristic discretion of the Venetians. In fact Vecchietta's architectural inventions have been regularly mistaken for a typically Venetian style.[50]

The three triangular pediments of the *Visitation* are not in the Venetian style at all, nor those concluding the parallelepiped from which the drum of the dome extends in the *Presentation in the Temple*.

The gap between the *Birth of the Virgin* and the *Presentation in the Temple* narrows toward the horizon, the vanishing lines running to a central point positioned at the top of an imaginary triangle. The empirical system of the workshops of the early fifteenth century has been applied: on a horizontal line a point is fixed equidistant from two extreme points and the regular arrangement of the base lines joins, with three radii, to the set points. On the left wall of the Branda Castiglioni chapel in Rome, Masolino had already experimented with this method, linking two adjacent scenes using a similar invisible grill.[51]

It is not improbable that the designer of the *Birth of the Virgin* scene (namely, Vecchietta) left instructions also for the other; however, Guariento, the artist responsible for the realization of the work and who inserted a small notice with his signature in the gap between the two constructions, did not have the same knowledge of perspective.

A *terra verde* composition, formerly of the Cini collection at Monselice, attributed to an artist of northern Italy of the second half of the fifteenth century, shows clearly that the composition of the two episodes within a single system as a type, was reinvestigated with the new understanding of perspective, in which an attempt is made to make all the vanishing lines converge on a point located on the line equidistant from the plane.[52]

To some extent the Cini composition successfully achieves what is only hinted at in the mosaic. It not only resumes the cupola motif with its curious lantern, but also repeats the great peacock—for centuries a typical motif of mosaics—in the upper section, outside the architecture of the *Birth of the Virgin*.

The Cini master then supplemented these visual quotes with a set of warrior statues mounted on the pilasters, reminiscent perhaps of the giant figures on the exterior of Milan cathedral, as well as on the carved capitals inside. In particular, however, these figures refer to one of the more "modern" motifs found on the tomb of Doge Foscari in the Frari church. Furthermore, the frieze on the architrave of this tomb, decorated with putti heads and foliage, is an evident homage to those of Vecchietta in the *Visitation*.[53]

Opposite the section with the *Birth* and the *Presentation in the Temple*, in the scenes of the *Visitation* and the *Dormitio*, the artist has not bothered to create a unitary composition; the two scenes stand one beside the other, each locked in its own perspective arrangement.

While for the *Visitation* it is relatively simple to discern the operative process—from a drawing of Vecchietta, executed under his direction in the upper area, the execution was passed to Giambono, who worked in complete autonomy—the *Dormitio* involved a succession of contributions. Some of these are the handiwork of Andrea del Castagno in Venice and hence date from around 1442; others are later and have been dated hypothetically to 1450, a year which was once legible in the mosaics, apparently, although it is known that in 1449 the chapel mosaics were already under way.[54]

Certainly the figure of the Virgin belongs to Castagno as does the almond shape with Christ, and perhaps the medallions in the frieze which have also been attributed to the young Mantegna. The realistic quality of the clothing of the first two apostles on the left, where the weight of the material causes the vertical arrangements of folds and the oblique lines caused by the movement of the leg also belong to Castagno's manner; while the sharp profile of the young apostle anticipates the work of Niccolò Acciaiolo in the series of *Famous Men*, 1448-49.

But considering the broadness of the haloes in these first two figures, their perspective variation, and the fact that the left hand of the younger figure is raised in a way that seems anatomically incorrect, it is likely that this was composite work.

Perhaps a drawing left by Paolo Uccello in which the great haloes dominating the figures, as in the frescoes of the *Creation* in the Chiostro Verde, had become so popular with Venetian commissioners that Castagno was asked to conserve the motif. The suggestion of an initial cartoon by Uccello becomes more convincing if we move to the right to the apostle at the edge of the composition seen from the back: his raised shoulder partly covering his beard,

vations on the conservative spirit dominating Venice, especially in the programme of mosaics executed for St. Mark's.

[51] R. Klein, in "Etudes sur la perspective à la renaissance, 1956-63," in *Bibliothèque d'Humanisme et Renaissance* XXV, 1970, pp. 577-587; reprinted in R. Klein, *La forme et l'intelligible*, Paris, 1970, pp. 278-293.

[52] C. Eisler, op. cit. in note 26, pp. 197, 207, 343.

[53] J. McAndrew, *Venetian Architecture of the Early Renaissance*, Cambridge, Mass.-London, 1980, (pp. 24-27, It. ed., *L'architettura veneziana del primo rinascimento*, Venice, 1983).

[54] G. Rossi Scarpa, op. cit. in note 34, pp. 287-288.

[55] W. Wolters, op. cit. in note 34, cat. 89, p. 95, fig. 324.

[56] F. Saccardo, "Mosaici e loro iscrizioni," in *La Basilica di San Marco...*, ed. F. Ongania, Venice, 1888, p. 308.

[57] Recently K. Christiansen, "La pittura a Venezia e in Veneto nel primo Quattrocento," in *La pittura in Italia*, op. cit. in note 31, pp. 119-146, especially pp. 144-145, admits the presence of Jacopo Bellini, though with reservations. In the Louvre drawing no. 76 (Eisler, pl. 130) the standing figures squeeze under the arch like the apostles behind the Virgin's catafalque in the mosaic. At the same time, the figures arranged on ground level in the same drawing and various other drawings by Jacopo, suggest how the artist might have composed the scene if he had been free from restrictions.

[58] E. Battisti and G. Saccaro Battisti, *Le macchine cifrate di Giovanni Fontana*, Milan, 1984. In my view the studies of D. Gioseffi have shown that there could have only have been one course in the study of perspective. On the other hand the words of Savonarola (op. cit. in note 2) attest to derivations from Vitruvius and link the studies on perspective to the humanist milieu of Padua.

[59] Louvre 53; cf. C. Eisler, op. cit. in note 2, p. 209, pl. 92.

[60] P.W. Lehmann, *Cyriacus of Ancona's Egyptian Visit and its Reflections in Gentile Bellini and Jeronimus Bosch*, Locust Valley, N.Y., 1977.

[61] C. Bertelli, op. cit. in note 24.

[62] A. Natali, op. cit. in note 33.

[63] J. McAndrew, op. cit. in note 53, p. 20.

[64] C. Bertelli, op. cit. in note 17. This is the typology which K. Swoboda, quoted by C. Frommel (*Die Farnesina und Peruzzis architektonisches Frühwerk*, Berlin, 1961, pp. 100-101) defines *Portikusvilla mit Eckrisaliten*. The evolution of this type has been studied by C. Frommel, "La villa Madama e la tipologia della villa romana nel Rinascimento," in *Bollettino dell'Istituto di Studi Andrea Palladio* XI, 1969, pp. 47-64. On the link between the Belvedere and the convent of S. Chiara at Urbino, see M. Tafuri, op. cit. in note 23, p. 72, n. XII.2.3.

[65] M. Tafuri, op. cit. in note 30.

[66] The significance of this loggia, which is designed to give proper status to the "back" of the church, is explained by E. Maneri Elia in the report accompanying the proposed plan for the transformation of the Ospedale di S. Maria della Scala. It is hoped that this important study will soon be published. Other recent studies on Francesco di Giorgio Martini seem to overlook the influence of the main structures of the S. Maria della Scala in his design of the enlargement of the palazzo at Urbino.

Jacopo Bellini
Herod's Feast
from the Libro dei Disegni
R.F. 1484. fols. 15v.–16
Paris, Musée du Louvre

the perspective game of the broad halo, the constructive logic of the clothing, still gothic in style and even his severe face with the hooked nose, framed by the thick head of hair and the flowing beard all resemble the sinopia and fresco of the *Creation of Man* in the Chiostro Verde. If Paolo Uccello was responsible for the drawing of the *Dormitio*, the other eight apostles situated beyond the sarcophagus must have been conceived after the first two couples seen at the head and at the foot of the bier. The dimensions and poses of the apostles arranged at the extremities make this fairly definite.

The composition reflects the traditional iconography of Venice in around 1360, as can be observed in the reliefs of the tomb of the Doge Giovanni Dolfin in SS. Giovanni e Paolo; and at Treviso in around 1430, in the chapel of the Innocenti in S. Caterina.[55] In both cases the scene is dominated by the almond shape containing Christ, who waits to welcome his Mother, as in the mosaic.

Here, however, the triumphal architecture revives the commemorative function experimented in Masaccio's *Trinity*, with the addition of Venetian motifs, which Paolo Uccello took with him to Tuscany: the marble balustrade (as in the frescoes of Prato), and the patera with the small sphere at the centre, described above.

Unlike Masaccio's model, here the arch is not a frame to the scene, but a background. The positioning of the architecture in the middle ground would have been more evident if the group of apostles had been placed beyond the coffin. Instead here we perceive an aperture onto the long, deserted street and an innovative arrangement of the apostles, who seem to cluster to one side, allowing an unobstructed view of the scene beyond.

The confirmation of Paolo Uccello's intervention in the medallions of the vault and in the initial conception of the *Dormitio* presents conflicting halves of the decoration.

After the execution of the drawings for the *Virgin and Child with Prophets*, Paolo Uccello must have designed the arch of the *Dormitio* and offered a preliminary idea for at least three of the apostles.

But the insertion of an element like the arch, so strongly in Masaccio's style, must have been very disconcerting. It is surely a sign of keen intuition and typical of the Venetian esthetic, that in 1888 Francesco Saccardo attributed the drawing of that triumphal arch to the sculptor and architect Michelozzo.[56]

Perhaps it was the boldness of such an idea which brought Paolo Uccello's collaboration at St. Mark's to an abrupt halt.

Vecchietta found a means of attenuation through the graceful architecture of the *Visitation*,

[67] F. Fumi Cambi Ggado, in L. Bellosi, *Francesco di Giorgio e il Rinascimento a Siena*, Milan, 1993. It is remarkable that in the Frari monument (attributed to the brothers Antonio and Paolo Bregno) of Doge Francesco Foscari (d. 1457), the lintel echoes certain motifs used by Vecchietta for the Cappella Mascoli, such as the grooved patera and the putti peeping out from the foliage. The statues situated on the columns, also recall the Cini panel discussed earlier. Cf. J. McAndrews, op. cit. in note 53, pp. 24-27, pl. 2.1, 2.2.

391

and while mindful of the experiments of Masolino in giving compositional and perspective unity to the narrative in the chapel in S. Clemente, he single-handedly designed (but did not realize) the entire western half of the vault, inserting compositions of Sienese origins within architecture of new invention.

The problem now arose of how to continue the work started by Paolo Uccello. The arrival of Andrea del Castagno was a determining factor in the decision to proceed with Uccello's project; but not even Castagno finished the work begun by the older Florentine master.

Jacopo Bellini

The group of apostles who crowd together under the vault, forming a hinge between the foreground and background, has been correctly attributed to Jacopo Bellini.[57] Indeed, the contribution of Bellini to the conclusion of the mosaic would have involved more than the simple execution of a preparatory cartoon.

In the scene of the *Dormitio Virginis* and in the dais of the *Annunciation* in Brescia, Jacopo Bellini abandoned the traditional iconographic arrangement, allowing the viewer to perceive

Gentile Bellini
Procession in Piazza
San Marco
1496
Venice, Gallerie dell'Accademia

the architecture beyond the sarcophagus. The apostles form wings at either sides, arranged with attention to the perspective.

St. Peter moves toward the feet of the Virgin on the left to sprinkle the sacred water on her body, while St. John kneels beside the Madonna's face for a last farewell.

As in the St. Mark's version, the almond shape with the figure of Christ waiting to welcome his Holy Mother divides the balustrade completing the architecture above; beyond the body of the Madonna we glimpse a portico with two bays and two windows at the back. The contrast of the inert horizontal element in the foreground with the perspective drive to the back, applied here for the first time, later became a favorite theme of Jacopo Bellini. It was not an invention of Andrea del Castagno, who, enchanted with the reflecting Byzantine marble surfaces of Venice, now endeavored to contrast the sculptural relief of the foreground with the abstract design of the marble surfaces.

The architecture seen beyond the triumphal arch betrays nothing of the Florentine style. On the right we see a passage below a house; in the background a construction, the upper story of which opens with a loggia; on the left a house facing the street with two receding facades and finally a church. This last building is of particular interest.

The facade is broken by five deep round arches typical of the Paduan style (witness the churches of S. Antonio and the Carmini) prior to the classical reworking of the Tempio Malatestiano, which was begun after 1450.

The drawing of a putto with the signature "Jacopo" on a wall of the mosaicists' workshop in the basilica bears the date 1451, and is attributed with good reason to Jacopo Bellini, suggesting that he was still working on the mosaics in that year; however, it seems that this particular drawing was not used in the Cappella Mascoli. None of Jacopo Bellini's drawings include architecture of the Alberti style like that described; his sketchbooks document a keen interest in the details of the architecture of the Veneto and display an intention to interpret this in a Renaissance style, or all'antica; this was part of a tireless quest for the "ideal city" in which to set the historic narrative, thereby endowing it with an element of grandeur. Many of his drawings show a glimpse of a townscape beyond a triumphal arch.

The road seen beyond the apostles, its slight curve complying with Alberti's doctrine on urban form, is neither inhabited nor identifiable. Its purpose is not to offer some comment to the narrative. It is the product of a transformation of the indistinct situation conceived by Vecchietta in the adjacent panel, into a monumental, urban space in its own right. The perspective suggests only a part of the architecture, leaving the rest to the imagination: a section of a door and an arch, for example, or the entrance to the church, clearly indicated by the gap in the base of the structure.

Vecchietta (Lorenzo di Pietro)
History of the Blessed Sorore
(detail) fresco
Siena, Spedale di S. Maria
della Scala
Sala del Pellegrinaio

The fact that the Paduan engineer and natural philosopher Giovanni Fontana dedicated a treaty on perspective (no longer extant) to Jacopo Bellini suggests that the science of perspective was being investigated in northern Italy—and especially at Padua—following a different research itinerary from Brunelleschi's.[58] Although the orthogonal lines of the scene do not converge on a single point, in my view these errors of construction are not sufficient proof that Jacopo Bellini had his own theory of perspective, different from Alberti's.

Bellini actually spent a great deal of time exploring perspective; in his representations of the city he combined ideas he had received with the result of his own experiments, and formulated new hypotheses.

His investigations are testified by a page from the Louvre section of his celebrated silverpoint sketchbook: a building inspired by the temple in the *Presentation of the Virgin* in the Cappella Mascoli is set alongside the aqueduct built by Valens in Constantinople.[59]

When Jacopo Bellini's son Gentile painted the grand processional canvas of *St. Mark Preaching at Alexandria*, he expressly followed the method of his father: the basilica of Alexandria is conceived like that of St. Mark's (albeit reworked in classical style) flanked by an obelisk; the beacon has been interpreted as a column with Corinthian capital surmounted by a lantern and surrounded by a square of buildings with porticoes in the Lombard style. The square is populated by a range of racial types, attesting to the burgeoning interest in anthropology.[60]

The work was concluded by his brother Giovanni, who replaced some of the figures portrayed and added new ones—including the *condottiere* Bartolomeo Colleoni. Giovanni also completed his brother's anthropological coverage, adding some Portuguese figures with leather hats. But above all he transformed the architecture. In place of the buildings with the Venetian and Lombard arcades, he introduced closed units, typical of the architecture of Cairo.

In this way there was a distinct shift from a portrayal of an imaginary setting, based on ornamental criteria, to a realistic reconstruction of an existing place, recognizable despite its exotic slant. Thus the development of Venetian painting toward a realistic representation of the city and city life continued in its long and involved path, a path of development to which the young Sienese painter Vecchietta had made a crucial contribution very early on.

Vecchietta after Venice

Vecchietta's sojourn in the Veneto region was decisive for his personal development. The source of that solemn framing of the Pellegrinaio fresco lies in Paolo Uccello's *Dormitio* in the Cappella Mascoli. Likewise, the patera that Uccello positioned on the sides of the arch reappears in the Pellegrinaio, and the tripartition magnificently recaptures the disposition of the *Visitation* in the chapel mosaics. Above all, Filippo Lippi's frescoes in the basilica of S. Antonio and those of Paolo Uccello in Padua may have prompted Vecchietta to work around a plan initiated by Uccello, while striving to curb the heroic afflatus. New ideas of grandness came to him, together with that sense of disquiet, as he tried to reconcile the desire for innovation with a sentimental attachment to the past. Vecchietta's frescoes in the Collegiata at Castiglione Olona was formerly dated to around the same period as the decoration of the Cappella Manto in the Ospedale at Siena (ca. 1460); this date was questioned when other works of Vecchietta turned up unexpectedly at Castiglione Olona: a fresco of the *Corpus Domini*, on the facade of the Villa church, and a fully frescoed chapel in the house of Cardinal Branda. Other additions to the catalogue of Vecchietta's works include the painted and sculpted deco-

Vecchietta (Lorenzo di Pietro)
Dream of the Blessed Sorore
fresco
Siena, Spedale di S. Maria
della Scala
Sala del Pellegrinaio

ration of the facade of the Scolastica, an institution for which the cardinal had obtained a papal bull from Eugene IV in 1439.[61]

An interesting new study[62] attributes the Villa church itself to Vecchietta as his first architectural project, a building that evinces rigorous conformance with the canons of Brunelleschi. Only a Sienese master could have reworked the dance of putti with garlands on the lintels of the church, repeating the same motif conceived by Jacopo della Quercia for the tomb of Ilaria del Carretto. Vecchietta had already used the motif in a false relief among the frescoes of the baptistery. Vecchietta actually left two other architectural schemes at Castiglione Olona, two prototypes that were followed up much later.

The basilica depicted in the *Story of St. Lawrence* in the Collegiata is a building of extraordinary complexity, in which contemporary Florentine architecture is blended with the layout of Roman thermal baths, and the wooden structure of Venetian cupolas: a large square enclosure with an apse set into each of its sides; this enclosure itself is divided by another square form, the angles of which meet the first square at the middle of its axes. The equilateral triangles formed between the two squares are occupied by circular chapels surmounted by cupolas. And the internal square is covered by a central drum with four cupolas around it. There are four great apertures in the drum and the cupola has a wooden structure.

This complex plan with its adjacent rooms within a square grid immediately brings to mind the ideas presented by Filarete in his treaty some thirty years later. The model gives the impression of a Roman thermal bath or, to a greater extent, articulated buildings like S. Lorenzo in Milan. The cupolas of the minor chapels beside the central one recall the relation between the minor cupolas and the central block in the *Presentation in the Temple*.

The link between these two buildings and Milan's S. Lorenzo, represented by Giusto de' Menabuoi in the frescoes at S. Antonio in Padua, becomes evident.

The drum of the central dome, however, has links with S. Maria del Fiore, while the niches of the windows on the external enclosure refer to Florence's Baptistery. The loggias below the dome, which follow the external wall are not of Florentine origins, but echo Venetian architecture such as S. Fosca at Torcello. Furthermore, the great monument rising beyond the city wall in the same fresco comprises an arch derived from the raised sepulcher type protected by a roof, a type that was fairly widespread between Bologna and Padua. These features are further confirmation of Vecchietta's ability to gather and elaborate the architectural types that he encountered on his travels. The frescoes in the private chapel also show the strong Venetian slant to Vecchietta's original Sienese training. On the wall at the entrance, the crenelated building behind the religious group commands a prominent position; the central block is wedged between two towers with an arcade running the full length of the building, including the bases of the towers, whose apertures indicate they have no defense function. Apart from the crenelation, the building is a notable example of Tuscan reworking of a Venetian building type exemplified by the Fondaco dei Turchi and the Ca' Morolin on Rio S. Polo, which are more or less contemporary with these frescoes.[63]

The building, conceived by Vecchietta as a backcloth to the saints who represent the church militant—pontiffs and hermits alike—stands opposite the *Crucifixion* on the fresco of the back wall, and hence may have symbolic significance. As an architectural proposal, comparisons with the Belvedere castle, attributed to Baccio Pontelli, are inevitable.[64]

Recently, Manfredo Tafuri has linked the Belvedere to the design (attributed to Francesco di Giorgio Martini) of the convent of S. Chiara at Urbino: a portico between two wings facing the valley, as in the elevated "open" castle depicted by Vecchietta. The facade, with its loggias overlooking a valley, turns up again in the Palazzo Piccolomini at Pienza.[65] Consequently, the building conceived by Vecchietta seems to have had a long and remarkable path of origin. Vecchietta's intuition during his Lombard experience—an extremely fertile period of his life—may have had practical consequences in Siena also. The Ospedale di S. Maria della Scala, with its long loggia distinguishing it from the city wall below, is an open, peaceful structure. Constructed during Vecchietta's lifetime, the Ospedale is basically an exact translation into travertine and brick of that first construction conceived in the fresco.[66] The cultural exchange initiated by Vecchietta between Venice and Siena was to last many years to come. Indeed, when the Foscari were looking for an artist to realize a *gisant* for the tomb of Gerolamo Foscari in S. Maria del Popolo in Rome (in around 1489), Lorenzo di Pietro, "il Vecchietta," was already dead but the family evidently remembered his outstanding skills as a bronzeworker, and chose another Sienese master, Giovanni di Stefano, to carry out the work.[67]

Domenico di Bartolo
Bishop Giving Alms
fresco
1440
Siena, Spedale di S. Maria della Scala
Sala del Pellegrinaio

queste e ntrono di Sta pietro dalla porta della chiesa
a calar incisa all organo mezzo la testa della croce di bramante

1-III

St. Peter's: The Early History

Battista Naldini (?)
View of the crossing of
St. Peter's from the west side
of the nave
Hamburg, Kunsthalle, 21311
Cat. no. 400

The precedents

During the Middle Ages the Basilica of St. Peter had come to represent the heart of the western world.[1] Originally built as the funerary church of the Prince of the Apostles, and as the burial ground of the local Roman parish, St. Peter's became the place of pilgrimage *par excellence* for Europeans and, from the thirteenth century, the most important setting for all the great papal ceremonials. The nave of the old Constantinian basilica, with its unusual breadth of more than 231 meters and its thin walls, began to show signs of being unable to support the weight of the great wooden roof (cat. no. 277). With an ever-growing court, the 18-meter-wide apse containing the throne of the pope and where the papal Masses were celebrated, became an ever-tighter fit, and the high altar was also partially hidden by a kind of rood screen. The Chapter of St. Peter's had grown to 92 members during the course of the fifteenth century, and up until 1478 the chapter house occupied the last part of the nave, creating another barrier between the celebrants and the ceremonies held in the presbytery.[2] The aisles were occupied by chapels and oratories, while parts of the nave arcades were filled with altars, therefore it became increasingly difficult for the popes and other dignitaries to find satisfactory space for their mausoleums. The funerary Masses read by the canons regular before the altars were one of their greatest sources of income. The canons also had dozens of other tasks to fulfill daily—from Masses for the innumerable saints, to baptisms, funerals and confessions. The basilica, overladen with chapels, with only one entrance wall and a relatively narrow transept, could barely cope with the crowds of pilgrims surging forward to touch the altar over the tomb of St. Peter. The Benediction Loggia built in front of the atrium from where the pope blessed the faithful on feast days, remained a wooden structure until 1460.[3]

These were the reasons why Pope Nicholas V, the first pope to reign permanently in Rome after the period of exile in Avignon, began to contemplate the large-scale renovation of the old basilica.[4] In order to transform Rome into a modern seat of the papacy, alterations had to be made not only to the basilica and its atrium, but also to the neighboring papal palace, and the staircase connecting the palace and the church; while for the city, a new defensive system and road network was necessary. On his deathbed, Nicholas reconfirmed the concept that the authority of the Holy Roman Church could only be manifested to the faithful through the grandeur of its buildings.[5] His biographer, Manetti, acclaimed him as the true architect of the Church, the new Solomon, who would have surpassed not only the ancient Wonders of the World but also the works of the Old Testament. Nicholas planned to keep the old longitudinal body and to reinforce only the outer aisles by inserting chapels, and to destroy the greater part of the ancient constructions attached to it, together with all the funerary monuments from the sacred area. On the other side of the crossing, a 46-meter-long tribune would have continued the longitudinal body and housed the choir stalls serving not only the Chapter but the cardinals and papal court (fig. 1). The pope's throne was to be raised in order to be visible from afar and sited in the semicircular apse, while the high altar was to lie underneath the triumphal arch at the beginning of the tribune, as shown in the "Tribuna S. Petri" medal of 1470[6] and in the reconstruction by Grimaldi and Ferrabosco.[7] With its well-illuminated lantern, the primary function of the dome—perhaps without a drum—would have been to mark St. Peter's burial ground.[8] This would have been just slightly to the west of the center of the dome as it is today,[9] and it would have been identified by a pavement slab with a *fenestrella*, similar to the one in Cosimo de' Medici's tomb in S. Lorenzo.[10]

In every respect, this grandiose project was heavily influenced by Brunelleschi's Florentine churches. All the same, here the choir arm rather than the area under the dome would have assumed the functions of the old apse, serving as a *capella magna* for the papal Masses. Cross vaults would have improved the building both statically and esthetically and the large transept would have eased the flow of pilgrims. The transept would have been even better illuminated than the tribune and would have represented the two arms of an anthropomorphic organism. A vestibule with two campaniles was to be placed in front of the atrium, while the Benediction Loggia, in the project, should have been sited near or even on Nicholas V's tower, at a certain distance from the atrium.

In 1452, when the walls of the choir arm were already 1.75 meters high and 7 meters thick, Nicholas V suddenly brought building work to a halt.[11] Evidently Alberti had convinced him that Rossellino's sober and somewhat archaic project did not correspond to the extraordinary task required of it. Perhaps equally influenced by Alberti, Pius II (1458–64) revealed a similar opinion when

[1] R. Krautheimer, S. Corbett, A. K. Frazer, *Corpus Basilicarum christianarum Romae*, Vatican 1980: 176ff.

[2] Tiberius Alpharanus, *De basilicae vaticanae antiquissima et nova structura*, ed. D. M. Cerrati, Rome 1914: 59ff., n. 39.

[3] C. L. Frommel, "Francesco del Borgo: Arkitekt Pius'II. und Pauls III., 1. Der Petersplatz und weitere römische Bauten Pius' II," in *Römisches Jahrbuch für Kunstgeschichte* 21 (1984): 144ff.

[4] L. von Pastor, *Geschichte der Päpste seit des Ausgang des Mittelalters*, vol. 1, Freiburg 1924-25: 514ff.; T. Magnuson, "Studies in Roman Quattrocento architecture," in *Figura* 9 (1958): 55ff.; G. Urban, "Zum Neubau von St. Peter unter Papst Nikolaus V.," in *Festschrift für Harald Keller*, Darmstadt 1963: 131-173; M. Tafuri, *Ricerca del Rinascimento*, Turin 1992: 33ff.

[5] Tafuri 1992: 38.

[6] F. G. Hill, *The medals of Paul II*, London 1910: 8ff.

[7] Urban 1963: 146, 148, no. 66, fig. 6.

[8] Urban 1963: 142; see the reconstruction of the section, to be revised in the details, in H. Saalman 1989, fig. 120.

[9] G. Poggi, *Il duomo di Firenze*, Berlin 1990, vol. 1: cxx and ff., 234ff. Brunelleschi's proposal to place the choir in the area of the dome and to move the altar from the center toward the apse, was approved in 1435.

[10] I. Lavin, *Past-Present Essays on Historicism, in Art from Donatello to Picasso*, Berkley-Los Angeles-Oxford,: 6ff.

[11] Pastor 1924-25, I: 523ff.

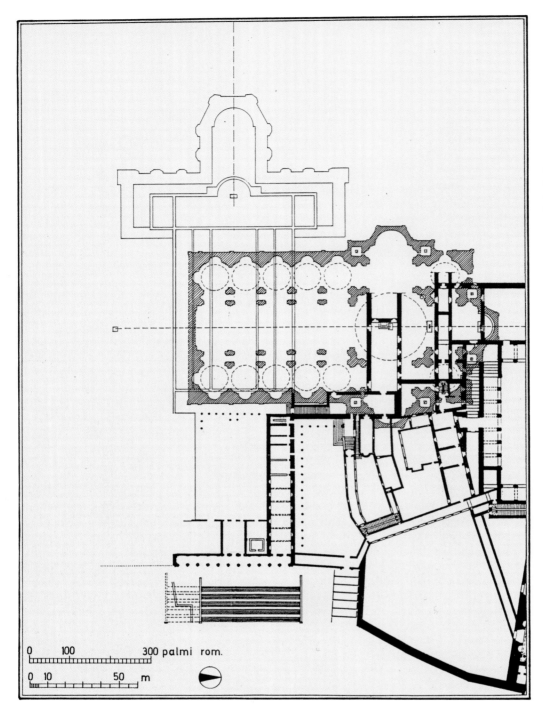

1. Hypothetical reconstruction
of the project described
by Egidio da Viterbo showing
Nicholas V's choir
and the Vatican buildings
(drawing P. Foellbach)

0   100   300 palmi rom.

0 10   50   m

he began building the Benediction Loggia to a style strongly reminiscent of antiquity.[12] One of the few popes in those years who escaped the Albertian sway was Paul II (1464–71), who planned to complete Rossellino's tribune in time for the Holy Year in 1475, and to bring the piazza back to new splendor, which involved transfering the Obelisk to its center. These two objectives had also been a part of Nicholas V's project, but Paul II died before he was able to achieve them.[13]

If his successor, Sixtus IV della Rovere (1471–84) decided to hold up the work again, with only three years separating him from the Holy Year, it was possibly due to the interference of his nephew Giuliano. Sixtus instead united the Chapter choir with his own funerary chapel, dedicated to the Immaculate Conception and attached to the outer aisle, thereby resolving one of the more serious functional defects in a totally egocentric way:[14] the intercession of the Mother of God, the prayers of the members of the chapter house, and the chanting of chorus formed during his papacy were supposed to accompany his soul to the life hereafter. No other project was suggested for the basilica during his lifetime—even though he was one of the most active patrons of the Quattrocento, and in Rome alone built four new churches dedicated to the Virgin Mary. After his death an explanation for this curious behavior was given by a General of the Augustinians, Father Egidio da Viterbo (1469–1523), a confidential friend of Sixtus IV's nephew, the future Julius II. A divine voice had convinced Sixtus that the new temple would be built by one of his nephews,

[12] Frommel 1984: 118ff.
[13] Pastor 1924-25, II: 351.
[14] Frommel 1977: 3ff.

and that was why Sixtus had raised three of his nephews to the purple.[15] Giuliano and his nephew Raffaele Riario believed fervently in this mysterious prophesy and each tried in every possible way to get himself elected pope. Independently of Egidio's explanation, Julius II himself confessed in a bull in February 1507 concerning the construction of New St. Peter's, that ever since he had become a cardinal he had thought about renovating and enlarging the basilica[16]—a project whose footing depended in any case on his election to the papacy.

The Project During the Reign of Julius II

When Giuliano della Rovere finally crowned his ambition on 1 November 1503, he had been settled in Rome for only a few months. Ever since his flight in 1494, he had maintained close ties with the French royal family, and had aimed at the downfall of Alexander VI.[17] He traveled throughout France and must have admired its castles and cathedrals. At that time his architect was Giuliano da Sangallo (ca. 1445-1516), who had begun to build his palace at Savona in 1494, and subsequently followed him to France for two years.[18] The Cardinal may have visited with him the ancient monuments in southern France and discussed possible projects on the chance he might be elected.

The future papal architect, however, was to be Donato Bramante, whom Cardinal Giuliano perhaps met only in the late summer of 1503 in Rome. The buildings that Bramante had already built by then in Rome included, first and foremost, the cloister of S. Maria della Pace, the Tempietto, and the Palazzo Caprini. An unusual convergence of their architectural ideas must have brought the newly elected pope's choice to fall on Bramante. In fact Giuliano da Sangallo did not arrive until spring of 1504, when Bramante had already started work on the first of Pope Julius II's great projects for the Vatican, the Belvedere Court.[19]

This was an ambitious attempt to merge imperial Roman tradition with new trends from the courts in Europe, and to make the Vatican the most magnificent residence in Christendom. It is unlikely that in the early months of his papacy Julius and his architect were only planning to create new gardens and courtyards, but rather that they had also in mind the renovation of the medieval papal palace, the basilica and the whole Vatican complex—exactly as Nicholas V had done. If, in fact, the longitudinal axis of the Belvedere Court is extended south, it arrives, intentionally, directly before the atrium of the Old Basilica (fig. 1). When Vasari wrote that Bramante had drawn up a project "to restore and straighten the pope's palace" he probably meant that he wanted to regularize the medieval palace.[20]

That the very papal palace was not inviolable is also evident from an examination of the projects for new St. Peter's. Egidio da Viterbo wrote of a previous project that had perhaps been the subject of debate during the winter of 1503/04, before Bramante started on the Belvedere Court, but unlikely after the winter of 1504/05, when the project for St. Peter's had reached a more concrete stage. In this project, according to Egidio, Bramante had tried to convince the pope to transfer the main entrance of the new basilica from east to south, to the side of the Obelisk, placing the tomb of St. Peter along this new longitudinal axis.[21] The pope, however, refused to disturb this holy ground (fig. 1).

Bramante's buildings were characterized right from the start by their extraordinary spaciousness, their hierarchical development, their masterly illumination and, from the time Bramante was in Rome, by a new and quite unique cohesion with antiquity. The commission for the new "Temple of Solomon" (and Julius II felt he was his legitimate successor) must have fulfilled Bramante's boldest dreams. The recent awakening to the extent of his power gave Julius II the strength to unite the essence of the Christian religion with the monumentality of the imperial age.

Julius, however, was also parsimonious and—as the nephew of Sixtus IV and a longstanding cardinal—an expert on the institutions, ceremonials and multiple functions of the Church. Evidently he insisted in the first place that the fragmentary walls of Rossellino's choir should be included in the new building. Moreover the project was to be based on the same Latin cross, to maintain the dimensions of Constantine's original basilica and to keep in mind the numerous functions and traditions not only of the basilica but of the atrium, the benediction loggia and the passages connecting it to the neighboring papal palace. Julius must have also planned right from the beginning to move the funeral chapel of his uncle Sixtus IV into the new choir arm, where he would place his own mausoleum.

Julius had begun his ecclesiastical career as a Franciscan monk, and even when he was cardinal he continued to maintain close contacts with the Franciscan communities living at S. Pietro in Vincoli and at the SS. Apostoli.[22] He had widened the choir area in both these churches to create more space for the monks and to provide a more solemn liturgy.[23] His source of inspiration, as for all popes from Nicholas V onward, was Florence Cathedral, for which reason he also opened the presbytery toward the longitudinal body, so the faithful could follow Mass. S. Maria del Fiore in Florence must have seemed to him to represent the prototype of magnificence and functionality. Such a wide crossing under the dome provided an ideal setting for the spectacular papal ceremonials. Be-

[15] loc. cit.

[16] loc. cit.

[17] Pastor 1924-25, II: 564; III: 384ff.; for Giuliano della Rovere's travels in the years 1496-1503, see M. Sanudo, *Diarii*, Venice 1886-1903, vols. 1-3.

[18] For Giuliano's itineraries see, C. von Fabriczy, "Giuliano da Sangallo," in *Jahrbuch der königlichen preussischen Kunstsammlungen* 23 (1902), supplement, p. 7.

[19] For the date of the Belvedere Court, see also, C. L. Frommel, in *Raffaello in Vaticano*, exhibition catalog, Vatican 1984: 122ff.

[20] Vasari, ed. Milanesi 1878-85, IV: 160.

[21] Wolff Metternich and Thoenes 1987: 45ff., fig. 48. Since the project in Uff. 3A (cat. no. 280), elaborated after the project described by Egidio but before the one of Uff. 1A, is noticeably smaller than the project on the medal and evidently concerns a longitudinal body, it is perhaps nearer these first ideas. Panvinio too, in about 1560 (Frommel 1976: 90ff.), emphasized Bramante's influence over the pope. His eloquence succeeded in convincing the pope about the feasibility of his project, in spite of the opposition of a majority and effectively of most of the cardinals, and he built a wooden model of it. There are also references to Panvinio and his very detailed account in F. M. Mignanti, *Istoria della sacrosanta patriarcale basilica vaticana*, Rome-Turin, 1987, I: 21; II: 11ff.

[22] Pastor 1924-25, II: 481ff. It is significant that in the palaces next to S. Pietro in Vincoli and next to SS. Apostoli, where he lived as a cardinal from 1471-94, there was no distinct separation between the cardinal's reception rooms and the dormitories of the monks (Magnuson 1958: 312ff.).

[23] G. Urban, "Die Kirchenbaukunst des Quattrocento in Rom," in *Römisches Jahrbuch für Kunstgeschichte* 9/10 (1961-62): 269.

sides, thanks to its dome the cathedral dominated the city skyline more than any other church had done before it. It is quite possible that at first Julius considered simply modifying Nicholas V's project, enlarging the area of the dome and maintaining the old longitudinal body, as the writings of both Condivi and Vasari suggest.[24]

Bramante had already faced a similar project in the choir arm of S. Maria delle Grazie in Milan, and therefore must have appeared to be the most competent architect for this case. Here too Bramante was anxious to better even Brunelleschi's highly praised prototypes, and to create a round dome, full of light, using the language of antiquity and an articulated network connecting the various component parts.[25]

A first idea of this early phase of the project can be gleaned from the drawing in Uff. 3A, a hitherto little known workshop sketch (cat. no. 280, figs. 2, 23). There Bramante clearly started from Nicholas V's project. Therefore he utilized Florentine *braccia* (0.586 m) for measurements and gave the three arms of the cross a width of 40 *braccia*. He also moved the high altar from Peter's tomb and placed it under the triumphal arch so that the papal ceremonies could occupy the whole area under the dome. Being free to use the area between the three arms of the cross, he opened Rossellino's uniform walls to create four secondary areas, necessary for both functional and iconographic reasons. He transformed the quincuncial plan, that is, an axially symmetric block forming an inscribed Greek cross. This highly symbolic and multifarious model descended from the vaulted architectures of the Roman and Byzantine empire. It was a direct emanation of Bramante's vision of space, which he had avouched in his early architectural "manifesto," the Prevedari engraving of 1481 (cat. no. 121).[26]

In order to give the area of the dome dimensions similar to Florence Cathedral, Bramante cut diagonal faces into Rossellino's squared piers; and to achieve a round dome like that of the Pantheon he made these diagonal faces develop upward into pendentives. He thus combined the ample octagonal base of the Florentine dome with Nicholas V's dome and its system of pendentives, creating a perfect "chorum seu ciborium," as Paris de Grassis defined the area of the dome as early as April 1506.[27] Quite naturally this distribution of the area about the altar providing the utmost space and excellent lighting was soon copied by everyone. While in Florence Cathedral the longitudinal body and the area of the dome stood next to each other quite independently, in Bramante's St. Peter's the one grew out of the other, both vertically and horizontally. He drew on his experiences in Pavia, buttressing the piers by means of secondary domes and reducing the quantity of piers and pier arches compared to Florence Cathedral. This statically hazardous reduction of the piers of the dome made it possible for Bramante to create a harmonious passage between the area of the dome, the arms of the cross and the secondary domes, creating a sense of spatial hierarchy. Bramante amalgamated this highly ramified arrangement of space with homogeneous illumination and a monumental order. The barrel vaults would have intersected to form cross vaults with lunettes probably designed with Serlian windows, like those in the choir in S. Maria del Popolo (fig. 3).[28]

This last example can provide an idea of the elevation of the choir arm drawn in Uff. 3A. There too the high altar is under the choir arch, followed originally by a bay with a cross vault and in front of the narrower apse there was a shorter bay with a barrel vault. The choir of S. Maria del Popolo had been designed in the summer of 1505 by Julius II and Bramante also as the choir of a mausoleum. Thus it is significant that in his first projects for the tomb of Julius II in March 1505, Michelangelo was also working on a wall tomb scheme, to be sited inside the arch in front of the apse in the drawing in Uff. 3A; this would hardly have been possible in Bramante's successive projects (fig. 2). Michelangelo's subsequent project for a freestanding mausoleum, decided in April 1505, required a change in the choir arm too (cat. nos. 278, 279, Paris and New York projects, figs. 4-7).

The functions of the Capella Papalis were probably similar to those of the church of the papal palace, the Cappella Sistina renovated by Julius' uncle, Sixtus IV.[29] During Mass the pope used to sit either behind the altar, as in Old St. Peter's or, if there was no apse, to the left of the high altar, as portrayed in the Cappella Sistina and in numerous representations of the sixteenth century. The pope's throne would have been to the left in front of the high altar, probably in front of the diagonal face of the southwest pier of the dome, investing it with special importance. The stalls for the cardinals and for the large papal retinue would have been placed either side of the pontiff. The Chapter would have been able to use the apse with the altar dedicated to the Virgin Mary. Perhaps a grid as before in the floor of the area of the dome would have given a view of the tomb of St. Peter. The sketches on the verso of Uff. 3A, perhaps in Bramante's own hand, show the area of the dome leading into a longitudinal body whose five arcades probably reached as far as the old pronaos. In these sketches Bramante did not limit himself simply to extending the arms of the cross, but attempted to widen the nave, referring directly to the plan of the ancient Basilica of Maxentius. If the saying that, for St. Peter's, Bramante intended to "pile the Pantheon on top of the Basilica of Maxentius" was of his own invention, then no other drawing of his projects can bear greater confirmation of it than this one in Uff. 3A.[30]

In April 1505 Julius II approved Michelangelo's project for a freestanding mausoleum, probably

[24] Frommel 1976: 88.
[25] R. Schofield, "Bramante and Amadeo at Santa Maria delle Grazie in Milan," in *Arte Lombarda* 78 (1986), 3: 41ff.
[26] C. Thoenes, "S. Lorenzo a Milano, S. Pietro a Roma: ipotesi sul 'piano di pergamena,'" in *Arte Lombarda* 86/87 (1988): 94ff.
[27] Frommel 1976: 94.
[28] Frommel 1977b: 49ff.; E. Bentivoglio, S. Valtieri, *Santa Maria del Popolo*, Rome 1976: 35ff.
[29] For the order of seating during Mass see, Frommel 1977b: 45.
[30] Wolff Metternich and Thoenes 1987: 85, n. 135.

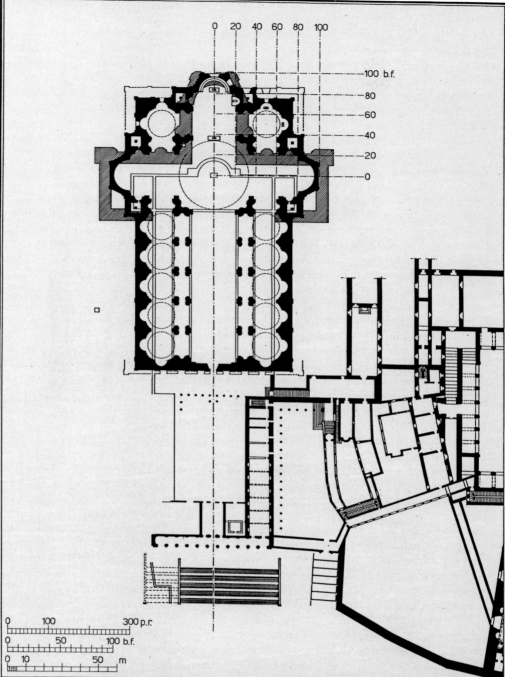

2. Hypothetical reconstruction of the Uff. 3A project with a grid showing the Vatican buildings and Julius II's wall tomb (drawing P. Foellbach)

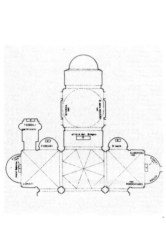

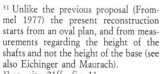

3. Rome, S. Maria del Popolo reconstruction of the choir with mausoleums and apse

[31] Unlike the previous proposal (Frommel 1977) the present reconstruction starts from an oval plan, and from measurements regarding the height of the shafts and not the height of the base (see also Eichinger and Maurach).
[32] op. cit.: 21ff., fig. 11.
[33] Urban 1963: 137ff.
[34] Wolff Metternich and Thoenes 1987: 108ff.

stimulating a new phase in the design process as a result.[31] Bramante too followed the pope's desire for greater monumentality. At the same time he exploited the pope's receptiveness to convince him of the advantages of a strictly centrally planned building, such as not even the sketch on the verso of Uff. 3A had yet elaborated. In the great parchment plan (cat. no. 282) which he developed the next few months, St. Peter's tomb and the high altar were probably placed together once again to the west of the center of the dome, and the crossing is still concentric compared to Rossellino's scheme (figs. 6-8, 23). With its diameter of ca. 185 *palmi* the dome was so similar to Brunelleschi's dome for Florence Cathedral (diam. 187.6 *palmi*) that it could hardly be considered a coincidence. Michelangelo's freestanding mausoleum could now have a whole bay to itself, with chapels to the side; furthermore, not only the area of the secondary domes, but also the corner towers and sacristies, as well as the vestibules could be sited in a much more satisfactory way in the areas between the longer arms than on the alternative project illustrated in Uff. 3A (cat. no. 280). The complete plan of the centralized building would have already extended over a greater area than Nicholas V's project. The addition of a longitudinal body has to be ruled out because of the difficulties in connecting the secondary areas with the aisles. The junction between the eastern arm of the cross and a fragment of the old basilica was equally problematic.[32]

In Nicholas V's project[33] and in the final project of 1506,[34] unity was reached by the repetition of the ratio of 1 : 2 on an increasingly larger scale from the arcades to the transverse section of

4. *Reconstruction of
Michelangelo's project of 1505
for the mausoleum of Julius II
plan and elevation
(drawing P. Foellbach)*

the arms of the cross and the area of the dome. The same ratio of 1:2 is likely for the reconstruction
of the projects in Uff. 3A and Uff. 1A. The pilaster shafts were in Uff. 1A still more or less the
same width as those in Uff. 3A, but now they were doubled so that the four pier arches measured
22.5 *palmi* (almost the size of those in Florence Cathedral) but they were still not sturdy enough
to bear the thrust of the drum and dome. Bramante also took up again the question of widening
the arms of the cross, as in Uff. 3A verso, and their consequent detachment from the Capella Papalis. The enlarging of the drum and the lantern and the supposed doubling of the lunettes in the arms
of the cross would have increased the amount of light considerably, creating an ingenious contrast
with the shadows in the chapels, exedrae and niches.

If the altar of St. Peter and the pontiff's throne—which may once again have been placed in the
niche of the dome's southwest pier—were to be the focal points of the area of the dome, the western
arm was a possible site for the choir and the Capella Iulia.[35] As in Uff. 3A, the altar dedicated to

[35] Frommel 1977b: 43ff.

404

5. Reconstruction of
Michelangelo's project of 1505
for the mausoleum of Julius II
longitudinal section and
elevation (drawing P. Foellbach)

the Virgin Mary was most likely to be in the center of the apse with the choir stalls hugging the walls, while the new bay in front of it could have been calculated for Michelangelo's freestanding tomb. Both the lunettes, the oculus on top of the semidome and at least three windows in the wall of the apse, would have illuminated Michelangelo's sculptures. The pope's choristers would have occupied one of the two chapels to the sides of the bay.

This hierarchy, which develops from the secondary spaces toward the dome, would have been highlighted even more on the exterior of the new building. The image on the medal (cat. no. 284) fixed a more mature stage of the project that had been prepared on detail in Uff. 7945A recto (cat. no. 283, figs. 9, 23). On that drawing Bramante reinforced the pier arches, enlarged the secondary domes and placed the towers beyond the main body of the building. First of all, however, he was concerned about laying an even more conspicuous accent on the Capella Magna. He sketched in fact the papal throne in the niche of the southwest pier and framed all the

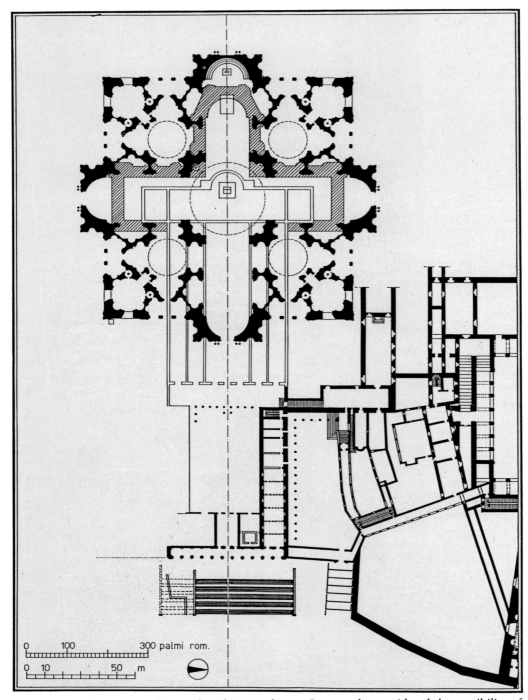

6. Reconstruction of the Uff. 1A project with the Vatican buildings (drawing P. Foellbach)

niches of the four piers with an order of giant columns. Later on he considered the possibility of extending these giant columns and forming a circle, isolating the Capella Papalis from the rest of the church, almost as it had been in Old St. Peter's.

Perhaps it was already his intention in the drawing in Uff. 1A to make the exterior design of the apses of the four arms of the cross similar to the main dome with its drum, dome and lantern. This served to emphasize the analogous functions of the Capella Iulia and the Capella Petri, Julius II's mausoleum and that of the first Vicar of Christ, without effacing their hierarchical disparities.

The flow of pilgrims was improved not only by portals in three of the four arms, but also by the eight *all'antica* vestibules. These would have led into the arms of the secondary areas, where two columns would have separated them from the real area of the secondary domes in the style of the ancient *thermae*. The altars which were perhaps even placed in the center, could have been destined for the veneration of the four Evangelists or for the more sacred relics such as the Volto Santo of St. Veronica, the head of St. Andrew, the holy spear and the Nail of the Cross.[36] The corner octagons were connected to these areas and were probably designed for sacristies or for the baptistery, as indicated in Uff. 8A recto (cat. no. 287). A staircase could have connected the northeastern octagon with the papal palace.

Visitors to the basilica would have been drawn immediately toward the center of this hierarchical universe bathed in light, and from there, they would have felt the radiating force of the monumen-

[36] Alpharanus, ed. Cerrati 1914: 177ff.

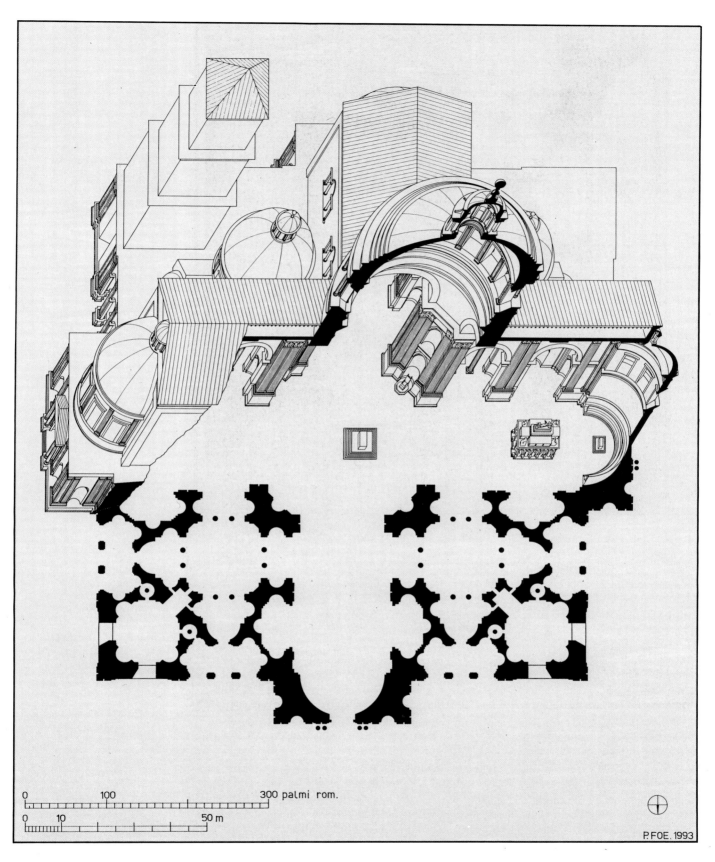

tal area of the dome, and passing between the vestibules, they would have admired the gradual crescendo of light inside the highly articulated organism. Although Bramante had gone way beyond Nicholas V's plans and had abandoned the highly respectable tradition of a basilica with a nave and four aisles, he must have succeeded in persuading the pope to accept his project. Otherwise Julius would never have had several foundation medals coined of such an unconventional centrally planned building, presenting it to the Christian world.

After having decided up until then not to build any kind of construction in the area of the basilica, Julius now must have had such clear ideas about the future shape of the palace and the basilica that

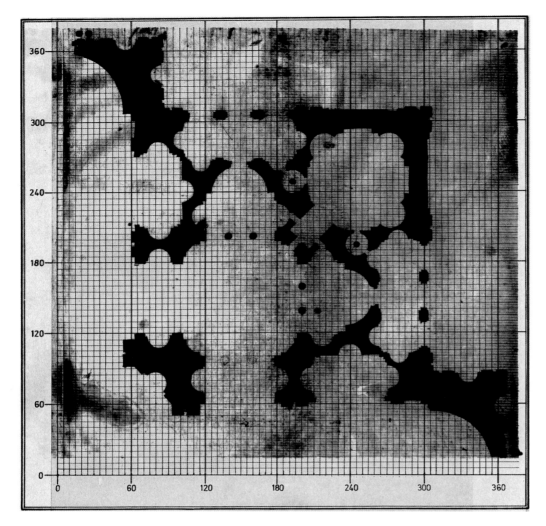

8. The Uff. 1A project inserted in a 5-palmi grid (drawing P. Foellbach)

he could commission Bramante at the beginning of September 1505 to continue Pius II's Benediction Loggia along the western side of St. Peter's Square, with a total lenght of ca. 700 *palmi* (156.38 meters).[37] The southern half of the palace with the Sala Regia would have had to be demolished for a new, considerably larger and deeper atrium from where it would have been possible to get a full view of the whole facade and its two towers (figs. 7, 23). The completely centralized building itself could only have been appreciated from the surrounding hills. Julius was therefore planning a partial renewal of the papal palace, but without introducing the classicizing radicalism, which characterizes Bramante's sketch in Uff. 104A verso (cat. no. 281).

At the latest, in the autumn of 1505, when the pope was raising the funds for the imminent project, second thoughts of a religious, functional and perhaps economic nature as well must have induced him to introduce a fundamental change in the project. The pope's quick mind and radical approach can already be seen on the verso of Uff. 7945A (cat. no. 283), in which Bramante referred not only to the shape of the Basilica of Constantine but also to its material elements. He again placed St. Peter's tomb at the center of the area of the dome, as he had done in the plan in Uff. 3A, and tried to conserve the ancient colonnades in a longitudinal project, perhaps even without arcades, but with ambulatories and galleries running all round. He kept the crown of columns in the area of the dome and even considered bringing the columns in front of the piers to a site under the base of the drum, while increasing them to a height of about 50 meters so as to create a colossal Capella Papalis.

Almost at the same time Giuliano da Sangallo must have submitted his rival project to the pope (Uff. 8Ar., cat. no. 287). The type and spatial elaboration of his project reflected the one shown on the foundation medal. However he emphasized not so much the articulation of the various areas and their hierarchical development as the massive structure of the piers and the solidity of the four arches supporting the dome. This aspect brought his project much closer in concept to Florence Cathedral compared to Bramante's. Giuliano's evocation of the most successful construction of a dome so far, and perhaps the skepticism of the other experts, must have convinced the pope of the fragility of Bramante's constructive system. In truth, during an audience with his patron Bramante must have sensed that his project was at risk, and hastily sketched another proposal on the back of Giuliano's drawing. Here he returned to the Latin cross and colonnades of the project in Uff. 7945A verso, but he connected them both to Giuliano's more solid pier system with its series of niches and to the spacious quincunx system of his own foundation medal project. This ingenious

[37] Frommel 1984: 224.

408

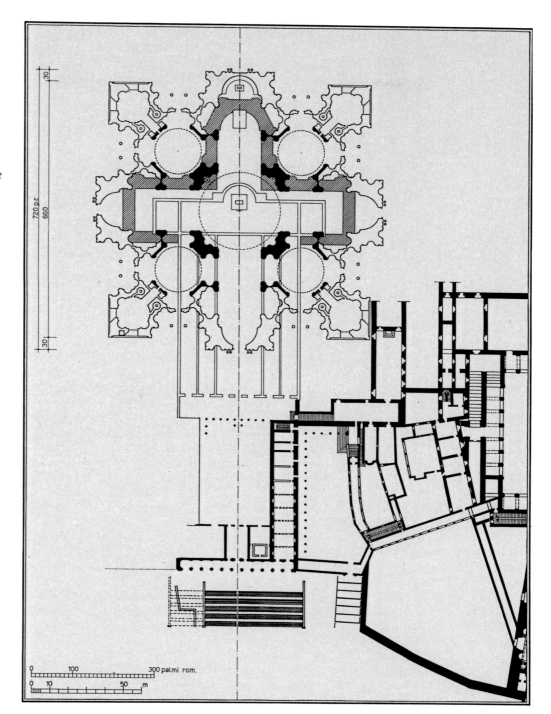

9. Hypothetical reconstruction of the Uff. 7945A recto project plan (drawing P. Foellbach)

step forward was inspired by certain Milanese prototypes, such as the cathedral and S. Lorenzo, whose plans he illustrated on the same sheet, the Milanese projects of Leonardo (fig. 10),[38] and perhaps also by the *Opinione* that Fra Giocondo had presented to the pope in the same period that autumn (cat. no. 286, figs. 11, 23). The enormous vessel of this latter project—measuring nearly 350 meters in length and equipped with seven domes, side towers, a narthex (undoubtedly designed to incorporate a benediction loggia), a choir ambulatory along the lines of French cathedrals, a set of galleries—had been so carefully studied from the static and functional point of view, that it must have increased the pope's doubts about the corresponding features of the medal project.

All these ideas and afterthoughts merged into the project in Uff. 20A (cat. no. 288), the most instructive of Bramante's surviving drawings. Similar plans, drafted on a precise grid, with the plan of the ancient basilica and Nicholas V's choir must have led the way to the projects in Uff. 3A and Uff. 1A (figs. 2, 8). In the plan sketched on the bottom right of the sheet Bramante returned once again directly to the drawing in Uff. 7945A verso, while keeping in mind the measurements of Nicholas V's project. But before arriving at a further reworking of this version, he must have come to an agreement with the pope over the innovations introduced in Uff. 8A verso, which he developed in more detail in the remaining part of the plan.

In this scheme he sacrificed the additional bays inserted in Uff. 1A in front of the apses to the

[38] Wolff Metternich 1975: 85, fig. 24, in which there is also an altar of the choir under the dome and a second altar in the apse.

409

ambulatories, and reduced the areas of the secondary domes considerably. Michelangelo's funerary monument would therefore have had to be placed either between the arches of the choir or in one of the secondary centers, and the altar dedicated to the Virgin Mary could have been sited in the center of an apse which is supported by a series of piers or columns. There is no evidence as to where he wanted to place the choir stalls and the *cantoria*. The functions of the Capella Iulia seem to have been neglected to the wings, which was reason enough to irritate the pope. It is interesting to note that Bramante was again centering all his attention on the area of the dome with the papal throne, the giant order of columns and the three arms of the cross, while he did not elaborate a complete solution for the longitudinal body in either static or formal terms. Bramante's decision not to touch the Obelisk and the Cappella Sistina reveals his intention to create a sound project that really could be built (figs. 12, 23).

The enlargement of the piers, the arcades and the order had a considerable effect on the elevation. Since Bramante only slightly increased the diameter of the dome, maintained the same length of the nave, and certainly kept the same system of proportions, these modifications would have affected first and foremost the walls of the central nave, the penetration of light and the shape of the drum and dome. The final decision to adopt an order with a shaft width of 12 *palmi* (as he had already considered in a detail in Uff. 7945A recto) became feasible also in the light of the 60-*palmi* wide arcades, and made it possible to give the pilasters proportions that were nearer the classical canons. By placing niches between the pilasters on the sides of piers of the dome Bramante doubled to nearly 45 *palmi* the depth of the pier arches, creating the premises for a much more solid dome. The sketch in Uff. 20A verso shows a drum with eight windows without the ring of columns belonging to his final project for the dome (cat. no. 288), and can be explained in terms of Bramante still paying more attention here to questions of construction rather than to the final design. Light would have penetrated indirectly through the ambulatories and directly only from on high—another aspect inspired by antiquity, hardly to the benefit of Michelangelo's mausoleum. Lastly, thanks to the challenge raised by Giuliano's solid project, Bramante acquired greater knowledge of massive wall structures, whose construction techniques had been forgotten since late antiquity. Whereas spatial expansion had dominated the parchment plan and the reduction of the already fragile wall masses brought the structural aspect to a dangerous minimum, now solid piers embraced the space of their ample niches and created a new reciprocal harmony. Even though the pope was not totally against Bramante's new proposals at first, he must have expressed objections regarding the functional problems, and doubts about the repeated increase of volumes and consequently the rise in costs. In his counter-proposal in the *Codex Coner* (cat. no. 289) Giuliano certainly took up the last variation drawn in Uff. 20A as regards the shape of the piers, the design of the ambulatories and the longitudinal body with its nave and four aisles, and even extended the latter far beyond the old atrium; but he gave up the quincunx system for the time being and reduced the arcades of the longitudinal body, the diameter and piers of the dome, and the side chapels (figs. 13, 23).

It is difficult to imagine Bramante himself producing a similar project for the reduction of St. Peter's. Without the quincunx system he would probably never have kept the ambulatories and he would hardly have gone back to a longitudinal body with such narrow aisles and the supposed galleries. Giuliano's unconvincing plan could however have contributed in any case to making him move the center of gravity of his project from the quincunx system to a longitudinal, axially structured basilica, and to accept the elimination not only of the ambulatories and the secondary domes, but also of the vestibules and corner sacristies. He hinted at a similar reduction in the plan in Uff. 20A, in which he shortened the south arm to the length of Nicholas V's choir arm and eliminated not only the quincunx system but the ambulatory as well, while hastily filling the arcade going toward the adjoining area of the secondary dome with a triconch-like solution.[39]

These reflections probably matured toward the end of 1505 and therefore the disappointing reactions to his November missives could have prompted Julius to make a more precise calculation of the costs. It is clear that at this point the pope must have insisted even more blatantly than a few weeks earlier on the significance and traditions of Old St. Peter's, forcing Bramante moreover to return to one of his first ideas, which placed the Capella Iulia in a completely isolated choir raised on the foundations of Rossellino's choir project, as Michelangelo had originally suggested. At this time Michelangelo had just returned to Rome from Carrara and was in fact beginning to work on the great project for the freestanding mausoleum; this brought him again in close contact with the pope (cf. Michelangelo's letters of 1523 and 1546-47) and thus he may have had a direct influence on the project during this period.

Bramante's Final Project for Julius II

Bramante prepared the final project no later than the beginning of 1506, and the foundation stone was laid by the pope on 18 April 1506.[40] Bramante reduced the piers of the dome compared to the later versions drawn in Uff. 20A, and returned to a dome with a diameter of 185 *palmi* while aban-

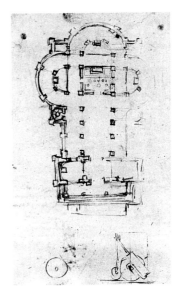

10. Leonardo da Vinci Project for S. Sepolcro, Milan ca. 1487-90 (?) Paris, Bibliothèque Nationale MS. B, fol. 35r.

[39] Clodt has made similar observations of his own (1992).

[40] Frommel 1976: 94ff. A little known description of the ceremony can be found in the writings of the Florentine Bonsignori: "In Rome [Julius II] began to build great walls. He had St. Peter's demolished and started to build it again. I was present when his Holiness laid the foundation stone which was a great cross. It was immediately covered by foundations, under which, the abovementioned Pope placed many gold, silver and bronze medals. This was the first foundation of the column or pier behind the altar of St. Peter's toward the cemetery beyond the chapel dedicated to S. Petronilla to the glory of God. All the most reverend cardinals and other prelates took part in a solemn procession in the ceremony of placing the said cross." See E. Borsook, "Michelozzo and Bonsignori in the Levant," in *Journal of the Warburg and Courtauld Institutes* 36 (1978): 176ff.

doning the diagonal faces in the area of the aisles. The total isolation of the choir arm (figs. 14–16, 23) made it possible to create intense light inside it, which would have been to the advantage of the rite and of Michelangelo's funerary monument, but the scheme also modified the spatial effect of the entire interior. The thickness of Rossellino's walls enabled Bramante to open colossal windows measuring nearly 6.70 meters in the side walls, a width that he had designated also for the three windows in the apse of the wooden model (cat. nos. 293, 292). Two pairs of rows of columns coming from the aisles of Old St. Peter's would have been repositioned in the arches of these windows. So that Bramante transformed the ambulatories drawn in Uff. 8A verso and Uff. 20A into a kind of monumental openwork typical of Gothic cathedrals. He then added the great basket-arch windows in the barrel vaults, through whose diagonal shafts the light poured into the area of the funerary monument (cat. no. 301). Static problems were perhaps the reason why he reduced the three windows in the apse by 10 *palmi* before he was building them. The windows drawn in Uff. 3A and Uff. 1A were much smaller, so it is possible that Bramante calculated this intense illumination not only in consideration of Julius II's funerary monument but also with regard to the decidedly longitudinal development of the new project, to create an ever-increasing brilliance from the entrance through to the apse which, not without reason, he marked with double pilasters in the version actually built. For the same reason, it is also highly unlikely that he already wanted to eliminate direct illumination from the transept arms by means of costly and hardly justifiable ambulatories; these would have completely upset the equilibrium of both the inner and outer constructions.[41] The longitudinal principle forced Bramante to replace the cross vaults (which in the previous projects would have visualized the interpenetration of the main and secondary arms of the quincunx system) with barrel vaults whose classicizing coffering in the version actually built produced an even greater axial accent than the model (cat. nos. 293, 292). The continuity of the longitudinal axis was emphasized even more by setting the piers of the nave in line with the dome piers, and by increasing their similarity by adopting pilasters separated by niches. Bramante calculated this design so that three bays covered almost exactly the distance to the old entrance wall (figs. 14, 23). In this move he must also have been inspired by Alberti's S. Andrea in Mantua, an analogy that is lacking in all the earlier projects, and which therefore cannot be dissociated from the longitudinal emphasis of the entire basilica. The connection with the papal palace was in itself a good reason for not exceeding the old longitudinal body (fig. 14). The three triumphal arches along the longitudinal body transformed it into an authentic *via triumphalis*, the ceremonial route the popes followed since late antiquity to reach the presbytery.

The narrow disk-like piers of the longitudinal body were arranged as in the majority of the earlier longitudinal projects, so that the former division into a nave and four aisles of Old St. Peter's could still be maintained. In about 1509, when the western piers of the longitudinal body were already rising up, Raphael in his *Disputa* reproduced with astonishing precision the southern pier as the symbol of Julius II's renovation of the Christian Church (fig. 17).[42] All the same, Raphael inserted pedestals, which would have hardly been compatible with the niches starting at floor level (cat. no. 341). Each of these ca. 10-*palmi* wide niches could have held an altar, and that is why Sangallo raised the problem in his *Memoriale* of 1520–21 (cat. no. 320) whether the pilasters of the inner order should have pedestals, "per li inconvenienti che fanno nelle chapelle." The pilasters of the giant order would have had therefore a ratio of 1:10.6, thereby accentuating the verticality of the inner space. Since Bramante in no way had preferred a reduced vertical upthrust in all of his Roman works, he may have returned here to the Gothic cathedral as his model for Christian devotion. For the rest, the disk-shaped piers were still under discussion in Giuliano's projects of 1514 (cat. no. 307) and in Peruzzi's and Sangallo's projects of the years 1531–35 (cat. nos. 326, 339).

If Maerten van Heemskerck drew plastered perimetral arches on the north and east faces of the eastern pier of the dome, and right-angled corners on the piers toward the aisles confirming the plan conserved in the *Codex Coner* of 1515 (cat. no. 310), then Bramante must have planned groined or coved vaults for the inner and outer aisles. It is likely that given the giant external order, there would have been ulterior spaces for the clergy above the four aisles. The outer aisles would have been illuminated in all probability by natural light from the arched 30-*palmi* wide windows, like the choir arm and the chapels in the transept. Since these windows were sited at a height of 45–50 *palmi*, the area of 10 × 60 *palmi* underneath could be used for side chapels with aedicular altars. These windows would have been reduced internally to a width of 20 *palmi* in the apses of the transept as in the choir arm. With a total of nineteen windows of this size, perhaps fitted with stained glass, and twelve windows in the vaults, the interior would have achieved an astonishing luminosity for the Renaissance, and would have again continued the tradition of Gothic cathedrals.

The well-documented choir arm (cat. nos. 298, 337) offers important points of reference for the reconstruction of the exterior of the building.[43] The external articulation of Bramante's choir arm opened up completely new roads in architecture, by developing the strictly paratactic rhythm of Rossellino's choir and perhaps of his own wooden model of 1506 into unprecedented heights of dynamism and plasticity. In the bay with the large arched windows bearing a minor load he was satisfied with a 5.36 meter thick wall and simple corner pilasters. In the passage toward the real apse

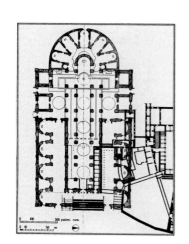

11. Hypothetical position of Fra Giocondo's project in relation to the Vatican buildings (drawing P. Foellbach)

[41] Cf. the reconstruction of Bramante's 1506 project in Wolff Metternich and Thoenes 1987: 105ff.

[42] I would like to thank Wolfgang Jung for the correct representation of this pier (fig. 17).

[43] For the reconstruction of Bramante's choir, see also Wolff Metternich and Thoenes 1987: 112ff.; A. Bruschi 1987b, fig. 22, 23.

he intensified the plasticity of the order much more energetically than on the inside, placing the pilasters one after another, uniting them in groups and making them protrude beyond the intermediate elements. This dynamism culminates and is extinguished in both piers at the head of the apse where the pilasters are separated by niches. It is difficult to establish whether Bramante gave the four piers of the apse the entire 10.30-meter thickness of Rossellino's wall for static reasons, when in his early projects he had often reduced the load-bearing wall to a minimum, whether, that is, he was elaborating the bracing of the apse, or simply complying with the pope's desires to maintain the exact dimensions of Nicholas V's choir, or lastly, decisions of a formal character had the upper hand. The five niches between the pilasters of the head were also an example of Bramante's dynamic conception as they become smaller toward the top. Below they descend considerably beyond the window sills so that proper pedestals on the pilasters would have been out of the question. The pilasters would have therefore really had the ratio of more than twelve widths of the shaft that Sangallo criticized in his *Memoriale* of 1520 (cat. no. 320) and they would have stimulated the sense of sweeping verticality. This dynamism would have been intensified by the emphatic jutting and it would only have terminated in the highly protruding cornice. The angled corner pilaster proves that Bramante wanted to continue the giant order along the rest of the outer construction. He may have tried doing for the rest of the building what he had achieved in the choir, creating an ample correspondence between the inner and outer orders. The walls of the longitudinal body consequently follow a sequence similar to that of the head of the apse, i.e., alternating pilasters and niches with broad arched windows (figs. 14, 15). For formal reasons the arms of the transept could have been designed like the choir arm even though, unlike the latter, there was no need to build them on pre-existing foundations. Their external articulation would certainly have been a continuation of the choir and the walls of the longitudinal body. It is not clear however what shape Bramante planned to give the western walls of both arms of the transept. Sangallo's plan of before 1513 hints at a more simple design than that of the adjacent choir.[44] In order to guarantee the uniformity of the exterior Bramante would have had to flood the chapels of the transept with light using 30-*palmi* arched windows as well, and push the walls of the windows further out to create a salience. In the 1506 project, the sacristies could therefore have been placed only on top of the chapels in the transept and access to them would have been up the great staircases inside the piers of the dome.

A clue to the facade of the definitive project, while not being totally reliable, is given in the sketch in Uff. 5A recto (cat. no. 292). In spite of all the distortions, this view could not correspond to any other project except the model of 1506. The slender proportions of the order—without any pedestals—and the dynamic intensification toward the center block in the facade at that time were already plainly nearer the version of the choir arm actually built. In fact, the simple Doric order of the tower develops into the Corinthian aedicules with groups of pilasters and freestanding columns projecting in front of the broken pediment, creating a sense of contemporary momentum and conclusion in the extensive center block. Bramante succeeded here in integrating characteristics of the imperial *thermae* into a highly complex system in a much more convincing way than Giuliano had managed with his recently submitted alternative (cat. no. 289). The idea of setting towers on the sides, however, had already been superseded in May 1506 when the Scala Regia was built. The towers would have also been incompatible with a planned road that was to open up the view from St. Peter's Square to the Obelisk. This prospect had been decided on by Julius II in March 1507[45] but, like several other solutions, it was never realized. The project for this road utterly contradicts all the hypotheses for the reconstruction of a basilica over 550 *palmi* in length (123 meters) in Julius II's final project. Moreover the fact that the pope still wanted to complete Pius II's Benediction Loggia in May 1507 and that Bramante instead wanted to demolish even the parts already built "according to the new design for the church of St. Peter's,[46] demonstrates once more how the ideas of the architect and his patron were not always coordinated. Whatever the case, Bramante must have felt he was capable of gradually bringing the pope round to accepting an open facade with a portico, its own benediction loggia, and the extension of St. Peter's square right up to the facade. The longitudinal body of this project would certainly have been one bay shorter, but it would have been considerably wider than the present one, and would have exceeded Florence cathedral in length, breadth and the size of the dome. If Bramante gave the blind arcades of the choir arm the same dimensions as the other arcades, this does not necessarily mean that he was including the possibility of a later integration of the choir arm in a quincuncial system or had even considered as only provisional a choir that by itself had already cost tens of thousands of ducats.[47] Not one of the numerous attempts of Bramante's successors to solve this problem can be considered satisfactory (cat. nos. 311, 316, 317). The shape of the choir arm was entirely calculated as a part of the longitudinal system, and the thickness of its walls must have competed with those of the *thermae*, as if Julius II wanted to ensure a similar life span for his funerary chapel.

Like the facade, the dome of the presumed wooden model seems incomplete; the question was therefore probably not yet decided between the pope and his architect as to whether they would settle for a drum with arched windows (cat. no. 292) or much more likely a colonnade on the outside—perhaps the old columns from the central nave, which otherwise would not have found any comparable reutilization.

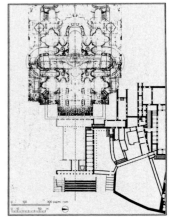

12. *Position of the Uff. 20A project in relation to the Vatican buildings (drawing P. Foellbach)*

[44] The half-built pier which in Sangallo's plan in Uff. 44A (cat. no. 337) turns again northwest in front of the southwestern chapel, dates back to the years 1511-13, to the period immediately after Sangallo's survey drawn in Uff. 43A, or—much more likely—to the years 1513-15, when Bramante and Fra Giocondo continued to build in this area. The southern corner pilaster could then have led toward the inner articulation of a western ambulatory.

[45] Frommel 1984: 256.

[46] loc. cit.

[47] Wolff Metternich and Thoenes 1987: 143.

The same financial problems which forced Julius II to reduce the dimensions of Bramante's first projects, conditioned him over the choice of materials. The walls were mostly built of *breccia*, probably that cheap crushed tufa typical of the surrounding countryside;[48] the vaults were at least partly cast, and bricks were used especially for the thin walls and to obtain particular shapes, jutting, or, as in the case of the southwestern pendentive, complex curves.[49] Travertine was only used for the bases, the capitals and the cornices of the orders. A lack of funds was certainly not the last of the reasons for deciding to eliminate the secondary domes, the pedestals and continual cornices of the impost or to reutilize the columns of the old aisles in the windows. It is therefore likely that Bramante had planned to used a fake travertine finish on the walls as he had already done so masterfully for the Palazzo Caprini.[50]

Toward the end of his life Julius II wanted to give the area of the choir a more magnificent appearance. In a papal bull of February 1513 he wrote about marble walls and everlasting (*diuturnos*) sculptural and pictorial works. Next to Michelangelo's freestanding mausoleum with its marble statues and gilded bronze reliefs, he perhaps planned to introduce sculptures in the numerous niches, mosaics and stained glass, as he had already done in the choir of S. Maria del Popolo, in the Sala Regia and in the Stanze.[51] He also mentioned a mosaic floor, which would certainly have been similar to the Cosmato work floor in the Cappella Sistina, and, as in that case, would have indicated the course of the pope's procession. A marble inscription by Julius had already been inserted in the frieze of the giant order instead of the hieroglyphics originally planned by Bramante. All these elements would have certainly been tuned by Bramante into perfect harmony. When his pupil Raphael designed the Cappella Chigi in the last years of Julius II's reign, he drew not only on the architectural shape of the area of the dome, but also on the polychrome splendor of the planned interior.[52]

The organization of the building site must also have been "clear and simple," the very expression Michelangelo had used for Bramante's project.[53] Bramante was responsible for the technical and artistic elaboration, while Giuliano Leno was in charge of construction activity. The accounts were kept by some of the pope's closest familiars, such as Cardinal Fabio Santoro, Archbishop Enrico Bruni and two canons, Mario Maffei and Bartolomeo Ferratino. From 1506 to 1511 Julius II spent a total of just over 80,000 ducats for the new basilica, most of which came from the sale of indulgences.[54]

Work began first on the choir arm and on both the western piers of the dome where the partial insertion of the walls of Nicholas V's choir created problems of subsidence, resulting in dangerous cracks. The substance of the old basilica was not touched yet. Only in April of 1507 when the impatient pope ordered the construction of the two eastern piers, parts of the old choir had to be demolished (cat. no. 294).[55] In May 1507 the area surrounding Nicholas V's choir was leveled for the choir arm. This included a part of the early Christian cemetery.[56] A huge crack appeared at the end of May, perhaps because the western piers were being built over Nicholas V's foundations.[57] The four arches of the dome were completed in 1511.[58] After a fruitless military campaign in northern Italy, the pope's once frenetic building activity stopped and only resumed in the summer of 1511. Here the records in the *Liber Mandatorum* (accounts registers) come to an abrupt halt.[59] During the last years of his life Julius II focused his efforts on getting the choir completed, together with the tribune containing his funerary monument. He furnished magnificently the newly founded chapel of the choristers, who were to accompany the liturgies in the Capella Iulia, and ordered marble for the interior of the choir.[60] Under Julius work also began on the technical preparation for constructing the dome proper, and the vaulting began in the Capella Iulia, which was just completed in April 1514, when Bramante died (cat. nos. 299, 300).

During the seven years of building activity under Julius II, Bramante prepared the various stages of construction, first in concert with Antonio di Pellegrino, then, from 1510, with Antonio da Sangallo the Younger as well. The studies for the Corinthian capital of the inner order, perhaps executed by Bramante himself (cat. no. 295), and for the centering of the arches of the dome (cat. no. 296), together with Antonio di Pellegrino's drawings of the curve of the pendentives (cat. no. 297), and Sangallo's studies of the dome (cat. no. 299) and for the vaulting of the apse (cat. no. 300) all illustrate the methodical precision of the design process. The building site was suddenly brought to a halt by Julius' death in February 1513 and by the election of Leo X, a pope of a different character altogether.

Bramante's Project for Leo X

In March 1513 the thirty-seven year old Leo X, son of Lorenzo il Magnifico, succeeded Julius II. From his childhood he had been familiar with the principles of *all'antica* architecture, and he was sufficiently young and optimistic to want to outdo Julius II's monumental projects (cat. no. 294). For the first eight months Bramante was the sole architect at work on St. Peter's, and when Leo X appointed two prominent counsellors to flank him, he did it perhaps for both personal and technical reasons. First and foremost, Bramante's energy was beginning to fail him.[61] Fra Giovanni

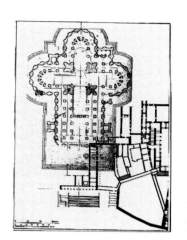

13. *Hypothetical position of the* Codex Coner *project, fol. 17 in relation to the Vatican buildings (drawing P. Foellbach)*

48 Frommel 1976: 93.
49 op. cit.: 93, 128.
50 See cat. no. 123.
51 Frommel 1976: 126ff.; Frommel 1977: 43-46.
52 Frommel 1984c: 21ff.
53 Frommel 1976: 74ff.
54 Op. cit.: 64, fig. 5.
55 Frommel 1984c: 256
56 Frommel 1976: 100.
57 "The wall of St. Peter's of Julius II, built over the old [church] has already begun to produce a crack from the lowest to the highest part. The opinion is that these modern architects cannot find the way of the ancients" See Borsook 1973, n. 37.
58 Frommel 1976: 67ff. Grossino sent the following missive to Mantua on 27 May 1511: "Once they [the Bishop of Ivrea and Federico Gonzaga] went to the top of the vault of the chapel of St. Peter's which are all four vaulted ... which are very beautiful and there you can see all Rome"; and on 12 July 1511 he wrote: "All four arches of the great chapel [of St. Peter's] are vaulted which is a lovely thing and admirably fine to see." A. Luzio, "Isabella d'Este di fronte a Giulio II," in *Archivio Storico Lombardo* 39 (1912): 326; kindly pointed out to me by John Shearman.
59 Frommel 1976: 71.
60 Pastor 1924-25, IV, 1: 542ff.
61 Frommel 1984c: 42ff., 241ff.

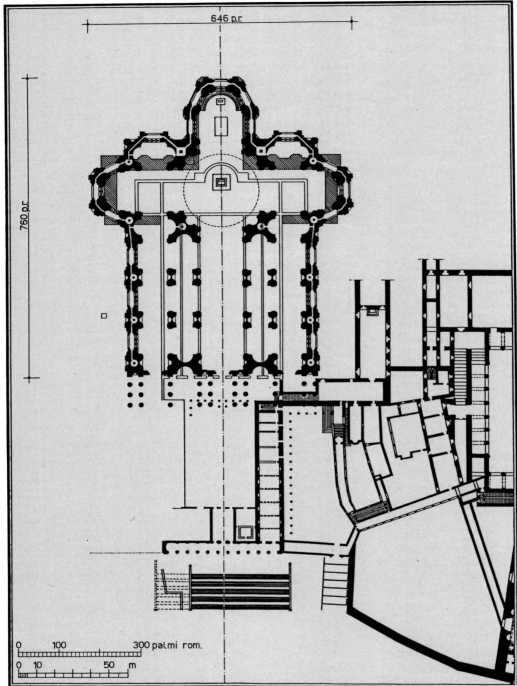

646 p.r.

760 p.r.

0   100   300 palmi rom.

0 10   50   m

14. Hypothetical reconstruction of Bramante's project of April 1506, plan in relation to the Vatican buildings (drawing P. Foellbach)

Giocondo was appointed on 1 November 1513. He was already eighty, but was famous as a theorist and a connoisseur of antiquity thanks to the edition of Vitruvius he had edited and in 1513 dedicated to Giuliano de' Medici, the pope's brother. He was also considered one of the best engineers in Europe and was therefore indispensable for the imminent problem of vaulting the dome. Giuliano da Sangallo instead was nominated only on 1 January 1514, when Bramante was close to death. This was significant because he was a fellow countryman of the Medici family, someone who had served them for years. Giuliano had in fact rushed off to Rome immediately after the election of Leo X, obviously hoping the pope would make amends for what he had had to go through during the previous papacy. Neither of them it seems acquired any significant influence over the design process while Bramante was still alive. Bramante's new project could date back to the period immediately after Leo's election, so that the work on hand could have been started again in 1513. At the latest in October 1513 the pope ordered Bramante to protect the old presbytery, which had been left exposed to the elements since 1507—evidently because he forecast a much more lengthy period of construction than his predecessor (cat. no. 305). In reality, from the outset Leo X paid greater attention to the enlarging of the project and to the building of the external construction with expensive travertine. He told Raphael that he would spend more than a million gold ducats, 60.000 a year, thus at least tripling the costs. The project of the dome which Serlio attributed to the end of Bramante's life (cat. no. 303), the variations of the plan by Giuliano da Sangallo and Raphael

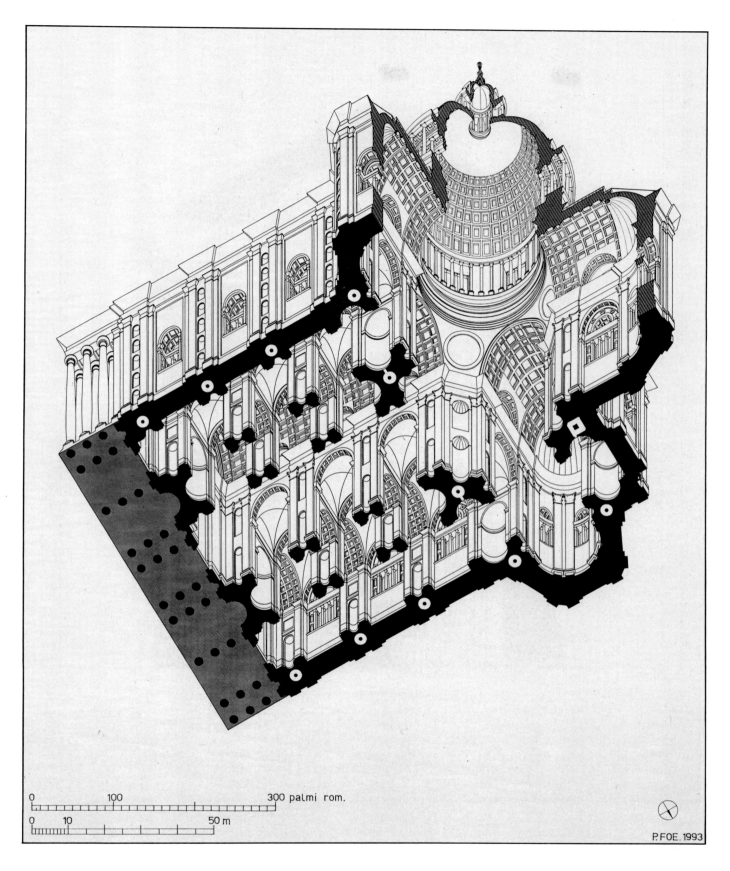

15. *Hypothetical reconstruction of Bramante's project of April 1506 (drawing P. Foellbach)*

(cat. nos. 306, 307), the surveys conserved in the *Codex Coner* (cat. no. 310), and Scorel's and Heemskerck's views of St. Peter's (cat. nos. 341-344), all contribute to forming an idea of Bramante's last project. The project of 1506 had suffered in particular from a lack of large chapels and easily accessible secondary spaces. By enlarging the longitudinal body to five bays, closing the narrow inner aisles with semicircular chapels, and making the outer aisles extend into centrally planned chapels, Bramante reduced the longitudinal body to a nave and two aisles (figs. 18, 19, 23) but, at the same time, he widened it to ca. 137.40 meters—a size that would have meant the demolition of the Scala Regia and the removal of the Obelisk. Only the Cappella Sistina would have been safe. The new

415

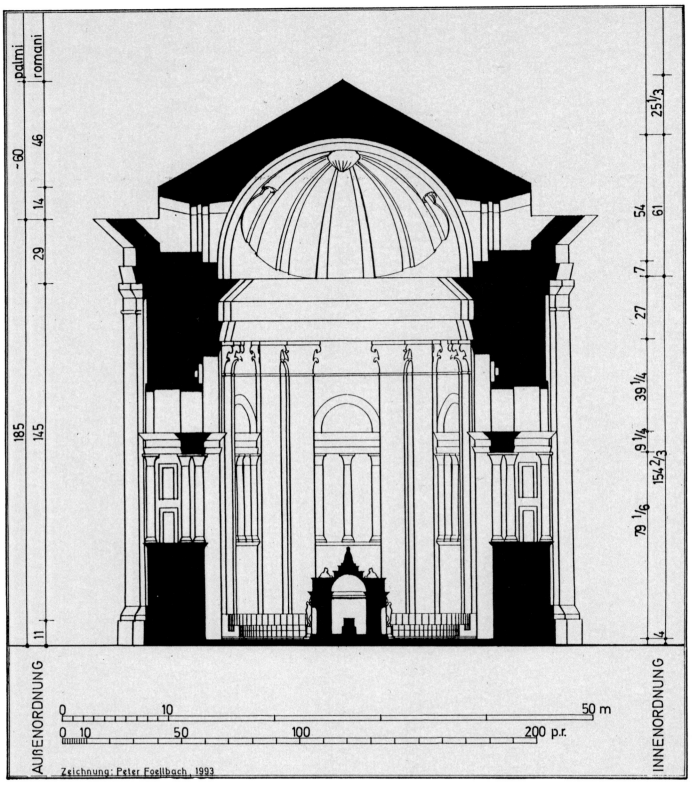

vestibule would have stopped short of the eastern inner wall of the old atrium, making a connection possible with a new south wing of the papal palace. He placed ambulatories around the arms of the transept of the 1506 project, which probably formed semicircular segments beyond the perimeter of the building, as drawn in Uff. 20A (cat. no. 288).[62] However, while the ambulatories in the plan in Uff. 20A made the choir end seem top-heavy, they were now continued by the new chapels and allowed the clergy to reach the sacristies in the side aisles without passing through the main arm of the transept. Considerable obstacles stood in the way of these alterations to the choir arm that had just been completed. Leo X was hardly interested in the overpowering funerary chapel of his predecessor, and by May 1513 Michelangelo had to convert his freestanding monument back into a wall sepulcher, which would perhaps have been placed in front of the piers of the transept (cat. no. 304, fig. 18). If Leo X had excluded the total or partial demolition of the choir, his architects would not have continually tried to bring him round to it. The plans of Giuliano

16. Reconstruction of the choir from Bramante's project of April 1506 (drawing P. Foelbach)

[62] This has already been suggested by Wolff Metternich and Thoenes 1987: 159, and Bruschi 1984: 285.

416

and Bernardino della Volpaia (cat. nos. 307, 310) show that Bramante had gone as far as contemplating the surrounding Julius' choir with an ambulatory. Perhaps even the so-called "nicchia di Fra Giocondo," the niche built after his death, and the two sacristies next to it belong to his project. In support of the possible facing is the equilibrium of the three arms of the choir—so evidently upset for example in Giuliano's drawing in Uff. 7A (cat. no. 307)—and also the system of illumination of the new ambulatories and chapels. This was no longer compatible with the 30-*palmi* windows of Bramante's 1506 project, which is why he might have designed the windows resting on a cornice—as Sangallo emphasized them in 1518-19 in his facade project in Uff. 257A. These would have started at a height of 115 *palmi* from the floor and would therefore have risen up to just under the entablature of Bramante's giant order on the outside. Light would have penetrated the building obliquely, as in the vault (cat. no. 301). This kind of window could have illuminated not only the chapels in the longitudinal body and the tall ambulatories, but also (indirectly) the windows of the arcades of Julius II's choir.

Bramante was already borrowing from the Pantheon when he designed the colonnades of the ambulatories. Perhaps he even wanted to make them similar to the windows of the choir with arcades. He used the Pantheon not only as a model for the ambulatories, but also for the drum, with all its measurements (cat. no. 303). While organizing the horizontal and vertical axes in perfect equilibrium and surrounding his cylinder with a *tholos* comprising narrow intercolumniation according to the principles of Vitruvius, Bramante in fact used the dome for his ideal reconstruction of Pantheon.[63] The lower ambulatories would have prepared visitors to the miracle of the dome—a Christianized Pantheon, whose canonical severity, airiness and luminosity would have given body to the most intimate ambition of the Renaissance as no other building could have done. Not surprisingly this was Bramante's last word in architecture, the synthesis of his immense creative capacities and perhaps the part of the church where he was least subject to compromise.

The portico of giant columns that Bramante had perhaps already contemplated introducing in 1506-07 to the facade must have seemed like the embodiment of antiquity to Pope Leo X as well. The prototype was once again evidently the Pantheon, even though the portico was more or less twice the height and four times the length. Bramante probably wanted to increase the somewhat slender columns to 14 *palmi*, as Raphael and Sangallo were in fact to propose in 1518-19 (cat. nos. 311, 313, 318). The job of facing the choir would perhaps have induced Bramante himself to accept an order that respected the canons better. It is likely that he would have surmounted the large central colonnade as well as the lateral ones with alternating pediments, as Peruzzi did some years later in his projects for Paul III (cat. no. 334).

Raphael and Antonio da Sangallo the Younger

Knowledge of the background history so far discussed is vital for understanding Raphael's first project. It was drafted in the summer of 1514, just before the pope appointed him papal architect and successor to Bramante. In the project that Serlio published in his treatise (cat. no. 308), Raphael first returned to the quincuncial system of Bramante's first set of projects, linking it in a more harmonious way to the larger longitudinal body and to Bramante's ambulatories (perhaps already segment-shaped); such a scheme meant demolishing a large part of Julius II's choir. Even the sacristies in both the western corner towers borrow ideas directly from the plan in Uff. 20A. The care Raphael took in harmonizing the secondary visual axes in the longitudinal body can be seen in his only surviving sketch for St. Peter's (cat. no. 309). In this drawing he also considered the possibility of substituting the overly vertical order of the exterior of Bramante's choir with a system that corresponded better to the inner organism.

Fra Giocondo finally arrived in Rome toward the end of May 1514, before Raphael had been awarded tenure at St. Peter's, and soon played a leading role in the project. According to Vasari, he designed the connection of the foundations of the piers of the dome with those of the buttressing piers started by Bramante in around 1513. In July 1514 it appears that Fra Giocondo was already working on the foundations of the niche that took his name, i.e., on the closure of the southwestern chapels of the transept, perhaps still following a project by Bramante, by which the quincunx system had been eliminated.

If neither this niche nor the adjoining sacristies went beyond the initial phase of construction, Raphael must have imposed his ideas early on, perhaps even before Fra Giocondo died on 1 July 1515. Whatever the case, it is unclear what project was valid and what was built in the years 1515-17—possibly large parts of the cornice of impost and the projecting cornice of the 40-*palmi* niches criticized by Sangallo in his *Memoriale* of 1520-21 (cat. no. 320). Both still corresponded wholly to Bramante's ideas. The supplies of marble in 1517-18 could have been ordered for the projecting cornices of the 40-*palmi* niches, which Leo X had decided to build in marble.[64] On 1 December 1516 Antonio was nominated successor to his uncle Giuliano, who had died a few weeks earlier. So far, however, it has not been possible to ascribe any project to Anto-

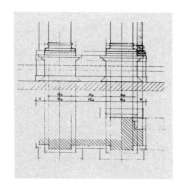

17. *Pilaster of the Basilica of St. Peter: reconstruction from the* Disputa, *plan and elevation (drawing W. Jung)*

[63] For Sangallo's ideal reconstruction of the Pantheon in about 1535 inspired by Bramante's dome, see Frommel, in Frommel and Adams 1994, I: 34.
[64] Frommel 1984c: 245; *Il carteggio di Michelangelo*, ed. P. Barocchi and R. Ristori, Florence, 1965-83, I: 244ff.

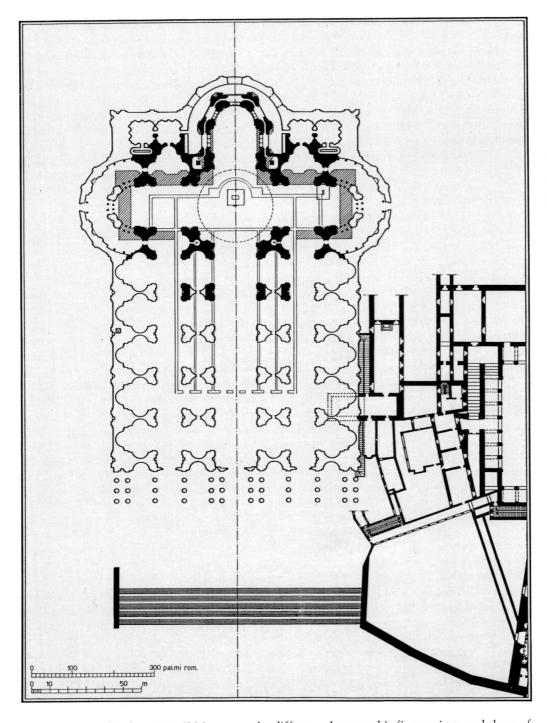

18. Hypothetical reconstruction of Bramante's project of 1513–14 with the project for Julius II's mausoleum of 1513 (drawing P. Foellbach)

nio in the period before 1518.[65] Moreover, the difference between his first projects and those of Giuliano is so striking; and yet the affinities with Raphael's projects for the Villa Madama are so evident that it is unlikely that they were elaborated before the summer of 1518 (cat. nos. 312, 313, 314, 316).

After the death of Fra Giocondo and Giuliano's departure just a few weeks later, Raphael finally had become the undisputed head of the building site. His ca. 1518 project (cat. no. 311) reveals that he concentrated first of all on the remodeling of the exterior (fig. 19). As Sangallo's projects of 1518–19 illustrate (cat. nos. 312, 316), until then the project had still kept Bramante's great Doric order created for Julius II's much more modest project, an order which now was to be extended way above the height of the new chapels in the longitudinal body and the aisle domes and which would moreover have made the narrow ambulatories exceptionally high. In his 1518 project Raphael reutilized the precious columns from Old St. Peter's not just in the ambulatories but in the facade as well, continuing the 5-palmi order also along the rest of the exterior. Having established this, he was free to introduce a second order in the area of the chapel windows and to move these inward. While the new articulation of the secondary prospects as conserved in the *Codex Mellon* are not very convincing, the effect of the facade on the square (where Raphael varied once more the design of Bramante's ambulatories) is magnificent. As in the 1506 model, Raphael made the central section of the portico

[65] Frommel 1984c: 266ff.; A. Bruschi, "I primi progetti di Antonio da Sangallo il Giovane per S. Pietro," in *Architektur und Kunst im Abendland. Festschrift zur Vollendung des 65.Lebenjahres von Günther Urban*, Rome 1992: 63-81.

as wide as the whole area of the dome, and inserted a benediction loggia in the upper story in a organic way. But the result could not have been more different. The closely knit arrangement of the towers and the bays of the side porticoes lacks Bramante's monumental spaciousness and dynamism. Splitting the facade in single autonomous blocks Raphael probably followed once more prototypes of Imperial Rome which had used only tridimensional volumes, while the flat facade had been introduced during the Middle Ages.

Antonio da Sangallo pursued completely different objectives. His first projects, such as the alternative on the left of the plan in Uff. 252A (cat. no. 316), or the plan in Uff. 34A[66], which preserve Bramante's choir, the polygonal sacristies and semicircular ambulatories, and the isolated towers, bring to mind Giuliano's plan in Uff. 7A. In his project for the facade in Uff. 257A (cat. no. 312) he continued to preserve Bramante's giant external order. Nevertheless, when he reduced the bays and the piers of the ambulatories, walled the atrium, made the rhythm of the order more elaborate and enriched it with 5-*palmi* columns, he must have already known Raphael's project of 1518 (cat. no. 311). Sangallo's personal contribution was above all the widening of the nave through the addition of *cappelle maggiori*, large chapels which he intended to furnish with their own cupolas and altars, in a project which could have had three such chapels as in the plans in Uff. 252A, Uff. 254A and Uff. 36A,[67] or just one as in the plan in Uff. 37A. The central nave with its succession of equal bays as Bramante and Raphael had designed them, seemed to him to be "as long, narrow and tall as an alleyway."[68] If he tried to find a remedy for this "malformation" with more crossing-like centers of gravity, it was perhaps because he remembered the nave in Bramante's Uff. 8A verso, but first of all because he was inspired by Venetian Byzantine prototypes such as St. Mark's in Venice, or S. Antonio in Padua, which had also been the main source of Fra Giocondo's project in Uff. 6A.

Raphael succeeded avoiding the inclusion of such domes in the longitudinal body and, as the right-hand alternative of the plan in Uff. 252A shows, he won the tug of war with his rival over the majority of the other disputes. It is true that Sangallo conserved the domes of the longitudinal body in that plan, but he borrowed from Raphael the quincunx system, the segmental arms of the cross as well as the integration of the towers and the sacristies into a single unit. At the same time he used 9-*palmi* diameter half-columns, an order mediating between Bramante's giant order and Raphael's 5-*palmi* pilasters. It appears to have been Sangallo himself who took the initiative to introduce the 9-*palmi* order, and he later developed it with Raphael during the summer of 1519 to make it ready for the construction stage. The 9-*palmi* order arrived nearly to the height of the main floor of the papal palace and thus facilitated its connection with the basilica. It conformed to the pilaster strips or the aisles and their chapels and respected the principle of correspondence between the inside and the outside. This solution made it possible to move the area of the windows back as before and resulted in a much more monumental system than Raphael's 5-*palmi* one. Even the highly plastic detail—*all'antica* through and through—has close affinities with that of the courtyard of the Palazzo Farnese, and is fundamentally different from the flat and abstract detail of Raphael's previous buildings. The project to which Leo X gave his blessing in the autumn of 1519, was therefore in reality a synthesis of the ideas of all three, Bramante, Raphael and Antonio da Sangallo—a synthesis, however, that complicated Bramante's original ideas and led the even more logically consistent Sangallo on a paper chase (fig. 20).

If Leo X spent the last two years of his life urging the completion of the southern arm of the transept, there were probably several explanations for his decision. The Cappella S. Petronilla (known also as the King of France's Chapel since Innocent VIII had conceded his patronage)[69] had been sacrificed as early as 1513 to the southern arm of the transept. No later than 1514 Leo X extended the name of this chapel to the whole southern arm of the transept,[70] whose southeastern buttressing pier had already caused the partial demolition of the ancient round building (cat. no. 277). As a member of the Medici family, the pope was linked by tradition to the French crown. Not without reason, Raphael gave his Charlemagne the face of François I when he painted the *Coronation* in 1516-17.[71] Leo X, like Paul III,[72] must have hoped for contributions from the ruling families of Europe by conceding them the patronage of important spaces inside St. Peter's. Moreover, in his letter of November 1519 to Isabella d'Este there is mention of "the chapel that the King of France is having built."[73] But first of all it must have been his predilection for the ambulatories which he owed to Bramante and in which he must have seen the essence of classicizing architecture—notwithstanding Sangallo's harsh critics.

When work was going on in the late autumn of 1519 on the foundations of the southern ambulatory, the plan of the transept arms had probably been already settled and perhaps the time-consuming process of cutting the stone for the outer construction had started—now using only travertine. When Raphael died in April 1520 the walls of the southern apse were just beginning to rise above the floor. As from 1519, when both his princely nephews were dead and the war in Urbino that had been a drain on his resources had come to an end, Leo X redoubled his efforts to finance the new building: since Bramante's death in fact the work on the basilica had been far from constant.[74] Antonio da Sangallo must have written his *Memoriale* for the pope soon after Raphael's

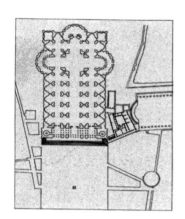

19. *Raphael
project of ca. 1518, plan
in relation to the Vatican
buildings (drawing G. Kohlmaier)*

[66] Wolff Metternich 1972: 42, fig.40, 42; A.B.

[67] op. cit.: 44, fig. 37.

[68] Frommel 1984c: 296.

[69] K. Weil-Garris Brandt, "Michelangelo's Pietà for the Cappella del Re di Francia," in *Il se rendit en Italie. Etudes offertes à A. Chastel*, Rome 1987: 79ff., 87.

[70] op. cit.

[71] F. Mancinelli, "L'incoronazione di Francesco I," in C. L. Frommel and M. Winner, eds., *Raffaello a Roma. Il convegno del 1983*, Rome 1986.

[72] Pastor 1924-25, V; under Paul III the northern arm of the transept was known as the "Cappella dell'Imperatore," perhaps after Charles V's visit to Rome in 1536 (Frey 1913: 87 n. 431).

[73] Weil-Garris Brandt 1987: 107.

[74] Frommel 1984c: 251ff.

20. Raphael
project of 1519, section of
the longitudinal body
(drawing E. von Branca
and G. Kohlmaier)

death. At long last he gave vent to all his bottled-up criticisms, and listed all the serious "errors" in the standing project (cat. no. 320). He complained about the lack of large chapels, the inconsistencies of Bramante's choir which was by no means destined to be demolished, the static problems of the dome, the exaggerated verticality of the central nave, the feeble lighting, the erroneous detail of the orders and even about the ambulatories with their new order which had obviously been started in spite of his unfavorable opinion. The enormous sums of money which such a project would have swallowed up, would have been "thrown away"—drastic words, just like those Michelangelo was to adopt in similar circumstances twenty-six years later. Sangallo, who was appointed architect-in-chief to the papacy in 1520, presented a new wooden model illustrating his proposals for changes in all the features that the pope appeared to agree upon as early as the spring of 1521 (cat. no. 321). As in some of his previous projects, he shortened the longitudinal body to three bays and enlarged the central one to create a second *cappella grande*. He also simplified the side chapels and made the newly polygonal sacristies extend beyond the building perimeter. In an even more economical alternative he proposed keeping Bramante's choir and abandoning both the quincuncial system and the choir ambulatory. This rash of changes was the result of the new pragmatic spirit that characterized Sangallo's early period of tenure.

The tendency toward reducing the volume that had been dilated in the first years of Leo X's reign—a direct reflection of the critical state of the papal coffers—was continued by Baldassarre Peruzzi, who took over Sangallo's former role as the second architect of St. Peter's in 1520. By transforming the quincunx system with ambulatories of the 1519 project into a strictly centralized scheme (cat. no. 322), and by thus uniting Raphael's last ideas with Bramante's first, Peruzzi reconsidered a line of thought that Sangallo had sketched in about 1519 in the margin of the plan in Uff. 252A. Together with the version published by Serlio, Peruzzi probably presented an alternative which included an atrium and a passage to the papal palace. The view attributed to Jan van Scorel (cat. no. 323) illustrates the state of the building site at the start of Clement VII's reign (1523–34) while those drawn by Maerten van Heemskerck about eleven years later (cat. nos. 341, 342, 343, 344) record the situation at the time of the Sack of Rome. From a comparison of these drawings it is clear that under Clement VII the emphasis moved from the building of the apse of the southern arm of the transept to its main bay,[75] which was completed by Peruzzi. After 1523 both the additional spaces of the southern arm of the transept were duly vaulted; furthermore, the walls themselves were also raised to the height of the entablature of the giant order. In some places Sangallo had Bramante's lower niches walled in (cat. no. 343). He reduced the cornice of the impost (cat. no. 341) and inserted the pedestals and bases agreed upon in 1519, together with the cabling and fluting. It is quite likely that Pope Clement VII, who was quite an expert himself on construction, shared Sangallo's doubts about the suitability of the costly ambulatories. By 1542 both the longitudinal body and the northern arm of the transept had hardly changed from how they were in 1514.

21. Draftsman after Peruzzi project for the interior of ca. 1531–34 Siena, Biblioteca Comunale, Taccuino S, IV, 7, fol. 37r

Peruzzi and Sangallo: the Reduction Projects for Pope Clement VII

The Sack of Rome by the imperial army in May 1527 and the following long crisis of the Curia Romana brought this fourth stage of the building of the basilica to a sudden standstill. In 1531, after having returned to Rome, Clement gave orders to his two architects to reduce the project drastically, and to retain only the most important elements from the functional point of view. In the most radical version of his only surviving reduction project, Sangallo restricted himself to a single nave longitudinal body without a central dome. He also gave up the quincunx system, the ambulatories (cat. no. 336) and a real facade. In an equally drastic scheme of reduction, Peruzzi calculated total expenses at 420,000 ducats (cat. no. 329). These projects are particularly interesting for the fact that even without the quincunx system their volume is only slightly smaller than the present building. In other projects the two architects tried to salvage at least the aisles, the chapels and the vestibule (cat. nos. 326, 336).

During these critical years, during which most of Peruzzi's time was spent on projects for fortifications, for S. Domenico or for Siena Cathedral, his work shows an unprecedented inventiveness.[76] If he started out from a longitudinal body with a nave and two aisles and a central dome, this does not mean that he had accepted unconditionally Sangallo's ideas, but rather that it was a form of respect for the Medicean pope who had given his general approval to Sangallo's 1521 project (cat. no. 321). In spite of this, Peruzzi undertook a completely new approach, considering, for example, the possibility of raising the floor level ca. 30 *palmi* (6.67 meters), thereby reducing the vertical proportions and making the orders more faithful to the vitruvian canons. The change effectively modified the entire architectural system of the building (cat. no. 326). He substituted the arcades with insertions of colonnades—like Bramante in some of his early projects (cat. nos. 287, 283)— thus continuing the ambulatory system in the transept and nave. By calculating the aisles and secondary areas as lower, he transformed Bramante's highly ramified and hierarchically graded organism into a homogeneous space without any dynamic oscillations. These unifying and anti-dynamic principles went hand in hand with a new approach to antiquity. Peruzzi tried therefore to imitate examples of antiquity to the letter, and brought columns to play leading roles in his projects: a step closer to Palladio and to classicism, compared to Bramante or Raphael. However, even in the majority of his reduction projects, as well as in the 1520 one, Peruzzi lacked that sense of concreteness and functionality with which Sangallo was so well endowed. All the same, not one of Sangallo's reduction proposals was adopted before Clement VII died.

22. Anonymous draftsman after Peruzzi, project for the facade of ca. 1535 Siena, Biblioteca Comunale, Taccuino S, IV, 7, fol. 36v

The First Projects for Paul III

The first builder to have the same energy and perspicacity as Julius II was Paul III Farnese (1534–49).[77] Totally optimistic about the prospect of having the Curia's finances within his grasp, he must have decided from the moment of his election to revive the beauty of Julius II's projects, as he in fact hinted in his first missives.[78] It is quite likely that Sangallo had kept him well-informed about all the vicissitudes of the projects for St. Peter's from as early as 1513, when he was Paul's personal architect,[79] and therefore that the pope knew exactly why Julius II had rejected the medal project in favor of the 1506 project with the longitudinal body. On the other hand, not only

[75] Pastor 1924-25, IV, 2: 559ff.
[76] A. Bruschi, "Le idee del Peruzzi per il Nuovo S. Pietro," in *Quaderni dell'Istituto di Storia dell'Architettura* 15-20 (1990-92), pp. 447-484.
[77] Pastor 1924-25, V: 798ff.
[78] op. cit.: 799ff., n. 1ff.
[79] Frommel 1981: 129ff.

Michelangelo, whom the pope recognized as the greatest living authority on art, but Peruzzi too, must have strengthened his preference for a centralized scheme. Only seven weeks after his election, Paul III doubled Peruzzi's pay, bringing it to the same level as Sangallo's. Vasari too, emphasized that the pope expected great things of Peruzzi.[80]

In his famous bird's-eye view of the project (cat. nos. 331, 332, 330) Peruzzi took a decisive step back toward Bramante's centralized project in Uff. 1A (cat. no. 282), giving diagonal faces and niches to the piers of the secondary areas, and therefore reasserting a direct analogy between the center and the secondary spaces of the quincunx. Moreover, he designed an enormous pronaos comprising exclusively of an order of 9-*palmi* columns set in a U that all but encircled the eastern arm of the cross, and whose three sections, surmounted by an attic and pediments, would have led into the nave areas of the main and secondary cupolas.

Perhaps it was difficulty of connecting these colonnades to the palace, perhaps the consent of the pope over raising the floor moderately, which induced Peruzzi in yet another project to maintain the tripartite pronaos, but to return to a 12-*palmi* order and to 5-*palmi* engaged columns (cat. no. 334), ideas introduced by Raphael in his project in the *Codes Mellon* (cat. no. 311). The facade thus certainly reacquired its original monumentality, but not the hierarchical dynamism.

This is the reason why Peruzzi's facade, perhaps the most harmonious of all the known projects, is animated by the same classicizing *genius loci* as his reduction projects for transforming the interior (cat. no. 326).

Sangallo himself was certainly not against a return to the central plan. However, his first surviving project from the time of the new papacy (cat. no. 338) illustrates all the disadvantages of this type compared the longitudinal body connected to the palace. At first, like Peruzzi, Sangallo maintained the quincunx system, with ambulatories opened with pairs of columns and the 40-*palmi* niches which would still have been compatible with the scheme for sglightly raising the floor by ca. 13.5 *palmi*. Soon afterward, however, Sangallo eliminated both the ambulatories, the quincunx system and the dome of the longitudinal body. He opened the piers of the longitudinal body to create inner aisles, and even went as far as reconsidering once again the conservation of Bramante's choir. Evidently he wanted to make an impression on the pope with his radical reflections on Bramante's

23. Summary of the main dimensions of the projects from 1505 to 1514

[80] Vasari, ed. Milanesi, IV: 160.
[81] C. L. Frommel, "Antonio da Sangallos Cappella Paolina: Ein Beitrag zur Baugeschichte des vatikanischen Palastes," in *Zeitschrift für Kunstgeschichte* 27 (1964) pp. 1-42. In contrast with the suppositions expressed there, everything supports the hypothesis that the project for the Cappella paolina and for the renovation of the Sala Regia must have been closely connected to the final project for the basilica. In the projects immediately prior to the project of the model, the Cappella Paolina was not taken into consideration, and only after the late decision to enlarge the atrium to the east was it possible to connect the centrally planned building with the palace. It is unlikely that the poperwould have embellished the chapel with pre-

PROIECTS	Exterior Length (without pronao)	Exterior Width longitudinal body	Exterior Width transept	Span of the crossing arches	Dome: diameter of the springing line	Diagonal of the crossing	Diameter of the secondary domes
Old St. Peter's [1]	547,45	297,35	407	107,6	—	—	—
Nicolas' V project	ca. 760	ca. 330	ca. 550	40 b. (104,4)	40 b. (104,4)	148	—
Uff. 3A v. 1	—	—	—	40 b. (104,4)	ca. 56 b. (146,16)	ca. 72 b (188)	—
Uff. 3A r.	ca. 760 (?)	160-170 b. (417,6-443,7)	200 b. (522)	40 b. (104,4)	66 b. (172,26)	ca. 79 b. (206)	ca. 23¹/₃ b. (61)
Uff. 3A v. 2	ca. 760	ca. 192 b. (500)	—	36 b. (93,96)	66 b. (172,26)	ca. 79 b. (206)	ca. 32 b. (83,5)
Uff. 1A	ca. 600	ca. 600	ca. 720	ca. 105	ca. 185	ca. 216	ca. 92,25
Uff. 104A v.	—	—	—	ca. 105	ca. 185 (?)	—	—
Uff. 7945A r.	ca. 640	ca. 600	ca. 640	105	ca. 195	ca. 220	116,5
Fondation medal	ca. 628	ca. 628	ca. 720 (?)	105 (?)	ca. 195 (?)	ca. 220 (?)	116,5 (?)
Uff. 7945A v.	ca. 685-720	ca. 580	—	ca. 105	185 (?)	ca. 216	—
Uff. 8A r.	700	—	700	100	200	ca. 210	ca. 70
Uff. 8A v.	ca. 900	ca. 575	ca. 800	100	200	ca. 210	—
Uff. 6A	1550 (?)	800 (?)	—	100 (?)	110 (?)	—	—
Uff. 20A r. 1	ca. 760	ca. 380	ca. 775	105	ca. 185	ca. 216	ca. 90
Uff. 20A r. 2	ca. 900	ca. 500	ca. 800	105	ca. 205	ca. 230	ca. 90
Codex Coner, fol. 17	ca. 970	ca. 400	ca. 800	ca. 105	ca. 160	ca. 195	ca. 50
Uff. 124A r.	—	—	—	104	184,5	216¹/₆	—
Uff. 44A	—	—	—	104	184,5	216¹/₆	ca. 66
Final project of 1506	ca. 760	ca. 470	ca. 646	104	184,5	216¹/₆	—
Bramante's project for Leo X	ca. 980	ca. 750	ca. 780 (?)	104	184,5	216¹/₆	—
Uff. 9A	1280-1300	ca. 750	332b. (866,52)	104	184,5	216¹/₆	—
Uff. 7A	ca. 980	ca. 615	ca. 910	104	184,5	216¹/₆	—

[1] According to Krautheimer, *Corpus*

first project—not the problematic scheme featured on the medal (preferred by Peruzzi) but the one actually approved by Julius II.

Anyhow, he did not succeed to distract the pope from the centralized scheme—neither with Uff. 256A nor with his following more expansive longitudinal projects. Already in spring of 1538 when Sangallo started the Cappella Paolina,[81] he presented Paul III with a compromise that could have been accepted by everyone involved. He extended the centralized inner building through the atrium, bringing it more or less to the limit of the old atrium so that he could connect the papal palace with the atrium by means of a staircase, and link the Sala Regia to the Benediction Loggia through the Cappella Paolina. Only in June of 1539 the Congregation of St. Peter's obliged him to build the wooden model in the unusually monumental scale of 1:30—not because the general project had not been yet ready, but because one hoped to assure its faithfull realization.[82]

In conclusion, if this model was merely utopian, as has often been charged, then whoever controlled the purse strings would never have contemplated commissioning such an unusually large and extraordinarily expensive model. Moreover, after the death of Sangallo the congregation of St. Peter's would hardly have insisted on the completion the model.[83] After thirty-four years of irresolution and a series of smaller models, most of them perhaps even incomplete, there was a desperate need for clarity about the project, and Sangallo drew on all his experience to meet the requirements not only of the papal ceremonials and to solve the static problems, but also to unite the various fragments into a single, coherent whole.

Only Michelangelo succeeded in convincing the pope of the need to demolish the fragmentary ambulatory and to accept many other alterations already suggested by Sangallo in his *Memoriale*. Like his predecessor, Michelangelo planned to introduce more regular proportions in the giant orders both inside and out. He also abandoned the nave and four-aisle longitudinal body, created new sources of light, walled up the 40-*palmi* niches and modified the entablatures. It is however unclear what Michelangelo's intentions were with regard to the linkage with the papal palace to which Sangallo had dedicated so much of his time. When Paul V obliged Maderno to return to a reduced longitudinal vessel with inner aisles and an atrium directly connected to the papal palace, he was simply proceeding from considerations similar to Sangallo's in the years 1531–39.

cious stonework and have commissioned Michelangelo to decorate it, if he already considered it as only provisional. The The chapel would have been ca. 100 *palmi* above the level of Old St. Peter's, more or less as high as the mezzanine of the tower. The area of the windows and the vaults of the Cappella Paolina would have arrived at the Ionic story of the tower, so that Sangallo could have used its arched windows for the illumination of the thermal windows of both the chapel and the Sala Regia.

[82] E. Francia, *1506-1606, Storia della costruzione del nuovo San Pietro*, Rome 1977: 49. In June 1539, the Congregation of St. Peter's with the pope at its head, decided the following: "*Quad architectos salaria mandarunt non satisfieri nisi incepto modello.*" Sangallo had probably taken such a long time over starting the model that his patrons had lost their patience.

[83] H. Saalman, "Michelangelo at St. Peter's: The Arberino Correspondence," in *Art Bulletin* 60 (1987): 489.

Width of the dome pier	Span of the arcade	Giant inner order	Depth of the crossing arches	Recession of the diagonal faces	External order	Distance between the central axis and the axis of the aisles	Scale	Date
—	—	5	—	—	—	—	—	ca. 320
—	—	—	—	—	—	—	—	1451
ca. 14 b. (36,54)	20 b. (?) (52,2)	ca. 4 b. (10,44)	ca. 4 b. (10,44)	ca. 8 b. (20,9)	—	ca. 44 b. (114,8)	ca. 1:470	March 1505 (?)
20 b. (52,2)	20 b. (52,2)	ca. 4 b. (10,44)	ca. 4 b. (10,44)	ca. 13, 3 b. (34,7)	ca. 4 b. (10,44)	ca. 50 b. (130,5)	ca. 1:470	March 1505 (?)
20 b. (52,2)	20 b. (52,2)	ca. 4 b. (10,44)	ca. 4 b. (10,44)	ca. 13, 3 b. (34,7)	ca. 4 b. (10,44)	ca. 64 b. (167)	ca. 1:470	March 1505 (?)
ca. 67,5	ca. 57,5	ca. 10	ca. 22,5	40	ca. 8	150	ca. 1:150	spring 1505
—	57,5 (?)	10 (?)	—	—	—	—	1:116²	spring 1505
72,5	57,5	10-12	ca. 22,5	40	8 (?)	153,75	—	summer 1505
72,5 (?)	57,5 (?)	10	ca. 22,5 (?)	—	8 (?)	153,75 (?)	—	summer 1505
72,5 (?)	40-45	10-16	ca. 22,5	40	—	153,75	1:470²	autumn 1505
ca. 115	55	27 (?)	ca. 32	50	8 (?)	185	1:470²	autumn 1505
ca. 115	55	—	ca. 32	—	—	185	—	autumn 1505
ca. 30 (?)	40/100 (?)	ca. 22 (?)	ca. 22 (?)	—	ca. 22 (?)	100 (?)	—	autumn 1505
ca. 70	40	10 (?)	ca. 20	40	—	ca. 145	1:300²	autumn 1505
105-115	57,5	12-15	ca. 45-50	40	ca. 20	ca. 190	1:300²	autumn 1505
ca. 80	40	ca. 15	ca. 50	ca. 30	ca. 15	ca. 152	—	winter 1505-06
—	—	—	—	—	—	—	1:106²	1508-09
85	60	12	39	40,25	12	167	—	ca.1535
85	60	12	39	40,25	12	167	1:137²	before April 1506
85	60	12	39	40,25	12	167	—	after February 1513
85	60	12	39	40,25	12	167	1:524²	spring 1514
85	60	12	39	40,25	12	167	1:522²	spring 1514

According to Thoenes 1990: 39

423

Part Two

THE WORKS

S.B.	Sandro Benedetti
	Arnaldo Bruschi
	Ferruccio Canali
	Alessandro Cecchi
	Christine Challingsworth
T.E.C.	Tracy E. Cooper
H.D.	Hubert Damisch
S.E.	Sabine Eiche
	Isabelle Frank
C.L.F.	Christoph Luitpold Frommel
	Vittoria Garibaldi
	Luisa Giordano
C.G.	Carla Ghisalberti
H.G.	Hubertus Günther
	Willem D. Hackmann
C.J.	Christoph Jobst
	Ursula Kleefisch-Jobst
D.L.	Daniela Lamberini
M.A.L.	Marilyn Aronberg Lavin
	Pierluigi Leone de Castris
A.L.	Amanda Lillie
P.C.M.	Pietro C. Marani
H.A.M.	Henry A. Millon
	Mara Miniati
	Giovanni Morello
A.M.	Andrew Morrogh
	Fausta Navarro
A.N.	Alessandro Nova
	Riccardo Pacciani
S.F.P.	Sylvia Ferino Pagden
L.P.	Linda Pellechia
L.P.	Luciano Patetta
	Leon Satkowski
	Giovanna Nepi Sciré
M.S.	Massimo Scolari
	Simone Soldini
C.S.	Christine Smith
C.H.S.	Craig Hugh Smyth
	Claudio Strinati
	Giusi Testa
C.T.	Christof Thoenes
A.P.T.	Annamaria Petrioli Tofani
R.J.T.	Richard J. Tuttle
	Mariella Utili
	Donata Vicini
	Monica Visioli
A.E.W.	Anna Elisabeth Werdehausen

For section curators, names are written in full after the relative section, and are abbreviated to initials at the foot of their individual catalog entries; the names of contributing authors are written in full at the foot of their respective entries.

Glossary of foreign terms used in essays:
capomaestro, capimaestri = architect-in-chief, site supervisor
fabbrica = fabric, i.e., building under construction
legnaiuolo = carpenter, wood-turner
scarpellino, scalpellino = stonemason

Abbreviations for the most commonly cited drawings:
CB = Casa Buonarroti (Florence)
RL = Royal Library (Windsor Castle)
Uff. = Galleria degli Uffizi, Gabinetto Disegni e Stampe (Florence)

Late Italian Gothic
Carla Ghisalberti

In order to outline the specific characteristics of architectural drawing during the Late Middle Ages, it is worthwhile to identify some of the key issues presented, on the one hand, by the relationships between the drawing and the finished architecture and, on the other, by the theoretical basis underlying each drawing.

First of all, the place in which drawings were collected, used and frequently even produced was the builder's workshop of Gothic times. The specimens of written documentation that have survived, in some cases in great quantity (as for Milan Cathedral), make it very clear that such workshops were in continuous evolution, and witnessed a rapid turnover of both ideas and people. The working methods themselves were constantly in flux, altering to accommodate shifts in taste or approach, and to put new technical solutions to the test. Within this perpetually evolving world, architectural drawing played a vital role. It was both a tool and a point of reference for the countless modifications and transformations applied to the design under way. The problem of providing a definitive and, in many respects, more comprehensible picture of the building under construction was solved by producing a scale model. For the construction of S. Petronio in Bologna, for instance, an extraordinary walk-through model on a scale of 1:12 was built, using real building materials.

Drawings, both in plan and elevation, were better suited to the analytical presentation of individual technical solutions, the result of precise choices. On the building site itself, drawings could serve a dual function. There is an important distinction between descriptive drawings intended for demonstration purposes, and drawings made specifically for the project. This distinction is often difficult to make in the case of early workshop drawings, as for the Sienese parchment featuring a campanile (cat. no. 1), in which there are elements that qualify it as a project to be executed, though certain vital constructive elements are omitted. Generally speaking, working drawings tend to contain all the necessary instructions for the practical task of realizing the building: structural details, measurements and specifications for the choice of materials to be used. Such is the case with the Sienese projects for the Palazzo Sansedoni, or the Cappella di Piazza (cat. nos. 4, 3). The informative drawing on the other hand was a means of providing a "view" of the finished product, and often a way of presenting a range of solutions side by side, to enable the patron or client to make his choices. The drawing for the facade of the baptistery of Siena is a case in point (cat. no. 2).

The application of a scale to a drawing does not necessarily qualify it as a "technical" drawing. However, working drawings were often accompanied by indications of measurement, making them full-fledged tools for site use.

What was the process by which a drawing was created, a two-dimensional blueprint, from which a three-dimensional construction could be built? The masters of the Gothic period proceeded using geometric modules. Once they had chosen a module—usually the square, but occasionally a triangle or other two-dimensional figures—it was mapped, rotated, extruded or multiplied to mark out the main structure, and used again in reduced size to design the details. Drawings conceived with this method did not need to include an elevation. It was considered sufficient to apply the same modular progression. The distinguishing feature of this *modus operandi* is the lack of any arithmetical calculation. In reality, as evidenced by a great many of the drawings in question, some

degree of cross-checking for the measurements was made possible, however, by the application of a preset scale to the drawing—usually 1:24, 1:36 and 1:48. These were all based on twelfths, owing to the most diffuse system of weights and measurements in the Middle Ages, of *braccia* and *piedi*.

This standard geometrical procedure seems to have fallen into disuse in the late Gothic period, as architects and artisans began to recognize the need for a more reliable and scientific criterion with which to work. The transition is clearly seen in the drawings of Antonio di Vincenzo for Milan Cathedral, which were undoubtedly based on projects drafted in the site workshop (cat. no. 6), and the Bianconi copy of the project by Stornaloco, exemplary proof of this evolution of working methods. The drawings of Antonio di Vincenzo, and later those of the mathematician Stornaloco, mark an important departure from the *ad quadratum* system on which such work had been based until then. The new drawings were based on an arithmetic and not mathematical system of calculation.

The same distinction between mere visual exemplification and technical drawing proper can be extended to include townscapes, of which the *veduta* attributed to Ambrogio Lorenzetti and the plan for the town of Talamone are highly representative examples (cat. nos. 5, 7). In the former, the architecture portrayed is lifted from real prototypes (houses, towers and city walls) and reassembled to create a representation of the ideal city. In the second, the schematic and even crude rendering of details is not in fact for demonstration purposes, but a proper town plan, an a priori definition of the urban fabric, with its focuses of public life (the castle and churches, etc.), its building plots ready to be assigned to individual citizens for the construction of houses, and the designated areas for craft activities and land for farming.

Among the many texts for further reference (with relative bibliographies), the most up-to-date, authoritative works include: Recht 1989; Conrad 1990; Mecca and Sernicola 1990; Cadei 1991a: 83-103.

1
<small>UNKNOWN SIENESE</small>
Project for a Campanile
ca. 1339

Siena, Museo dell'Opera del Duomo, 154
Drawing in brown and colored inks, on parchment; sfumato gray-brown for the horizontal inserts, light red for the squared frames of the windows; gray-blue for the inserts between the tympanums of the three two-light windows on the sixth floor; dark brown for the shading of the windows and the background to the campanile; dense hatching for the gable over the window in the octagonal termination to indicate the parts to be decorated with mosaic (Degenhart and Schmitt 1968).
222 × 32 cm

BIBLIOGRAPHY: Milanesi 1854; Nardini Despotti Mospignotti 1885a; K. Frey 1892; Von Schlosser 1896; Lusini 1911; Lanyi 1933; Crispolti 1937; Paatz 1937; Salvini 1937; Toesca 1941; Carli 1946b; Toesca 1951; Braunfels 1953; Gioseffi 1963; Braunfels 1964; Romanini 1965; Degenhart and Schmitt 1968; Trachtenberg 1971; Kreytenberg 1978; Carli 1979; Brandi 1983; Mandelli 1983; Middeldorf Kosegarten 1984; Toker 1985; Ascani 1989.

The document was found in the Opera del Duomo di Siena by Nardini Despotti Mospignotti (1885a), who published it that year, noting a formal likeness between the campanile it depicted and the one alongside Florence Cathedral, and inferring that the drawing might be a copy of Giotto's design for the campanile of S. Maria del Fiore. K. Frey (1892) disagreed with Nardini's supposition, and considered the document to be the work of a master active in the second half of the Trecento. Lusini (1911) disputed that the drawing referred to a scheme by Giotto for the campanile in Florence: certain stylistic features, such as the accentuated verticality of the whole, and the handling of the sculptural features seemed rather to indicate a Sienese workshop, and hence Lusini suggested the design was of the new campanile for Siena, probably designed by Lando di Pietro, who in 1339 was the *capomaestro* at the cathedral site in Siena. However, Lusini proposed that Lando di Pietro did in fact go to Florence in 1337 (though in fact the document quoted by Lusini and others does not appear to refer to Lando di Pietro; the artist's only recorded visit to Florence was in 1322: Milanesi 1854, I: 231). For Lusini, that meant a likely acquaintance with the bell tower while it was under construction (work began in 1334), and hence may have prompted Lando's design, at least for the lower fascias. From this moment on, scholarly opinion on the authorship of the Sienese drawing was split between those who considered it of Florentine origin, and expressed fairly conclusive ideas on the issue of Giotto's authorship, and those who consider it from Siena, though acknowledging a fairly definite link with Giotto's masterpiece.

Von Schlosser (1896) reckoned the parchment to be by Giotto's hand. Paatz (1937), however, drew far less definite conclusions about Giotto's authorship; he felt that Giotto's contribution to the parchment was indirect, albeit undeniable, particularly when compared against his painted works, and especially as regards the decorative fascias and hexagons on the vault and the plinth in the Cappella dell'Arena in Padua, or the frieze of the throne in the Stefaneschi polyptych. Salvini (1937), Braunfels (1953, 1964) and Toesca (1941, who later changed his mind) agreed with Paatz that the document was a copy of sorts, or a derivation from a prototype by Giotto. Gioseffi (1963) decided to analyze the parchment again, and concluded it was a full-fledged project after carefully matching the dimensions recorded in the drawing with those of the campanile in Florence. On the basis of the affinities outlined by Paatz between the architecture in Giotto's pictorial works and certain details of the parchment, Gioseffi was forced to recognize Giotto's influence, though he hesitated to declare it autograph. By comparing the dimensions and internal proportions of the drawing's campanile against those of the building in Florence, Gioseffi was able to deduce the measurements of the campanile, had it actually been built: 23.5 *braccia* (Florentine) wide at the base and an overall height of 175 *braccia*. These measurements were mooted by Toker (1985) and later also by Ascani (1990), who pointed out that the drawing conforms to a scale of 1:48, with a ratio between width and height of 1:8. Gioseffi looked for a plausible explanation for the discrepancies between the base fascia of the campanile and that of the Siena drawing, and noted that certain details on the parchment (such as the metal bars jutting from the *occhiello* of the side ogives of the cuspidate fascia, and set obliquely in the direction of the spire to anchor the reinforcement structure of the flèche to the cylindrical mass) are ample evidence of the artist's knowledge of structural design. Those taking Gioseffi's line more recently are Trachtenberg (1971), who also suggests links with more northern workshops in Europe; and Kreytenberg (1978), who stressed the similarities between the typically Giottesque pictorial decorative elements and those visible in the parchment. Taking his cue

427

from Gioseffi's stylistic analysis, Mandelli (1983) proposed a three-dimensional reconstruction of the parchment campanile, from which emerges a distinct modular rhythm lending proportion to the entire construction, with references to the square and octagon throughout. Without making any definitive statement on the drawing in terms of its design content, copy or elaboration, Middeldorf Kosegarten (1984) considers the parchment to be undeniably linked to Giotto's campanile in Florence, and dates the drawing to shortly after 1334. The "Sienese" hypothesis developed by Lusini was initially followed up by Lanyi (1933) and Crispolti (1937), and was later accepted by Carli (1946b) and Toesca (1951). On the basis of stylistic analysis, Romanini (1965) also concluded that the parchment was by a Sienese hand; she also thought that it could have been styled on a design by Giotto, given the similarities between the lower fascia of the campanile and that of the building in the parchment. Degenhart and Schmitt (1968) were the first to link the parchment drawing with another two drawings made in the workshop of the new cathedral in Siena, and reaffirm their conviction that it was a design for a new campanile. According to these two authors, the link with the Sienese manner is particularly evident when compared with the goldwork of Ugolino di Vieri, and Viva di Lando (as in the reliquary of S. Savino at Orvieto). Like Lusini, they surmised it to be by Lando di Pietro, dating it to around 1339. Brandi (1983) also reckoned the parchment to be of Sienese production, and estimated a similar date. Working from data assembled by Toker on the dissimilarities between the real scale of the Florentine campanile and the hypothetical ones in the drawing, Ascani (1989) upheld that there is no connection whatever between the Sienese parchment and Giotto's campanile in Florence. Today, the most credible hypothesis is that the drawing represents a proper building project, perhaps a final plan, given the definition of scale and the geometrical proportions linking the separate features. Furthermore, the author of the drawing shows a keen understanding of architecture, and his style is more discernibly Sienese than Florentine in manner, as attested by the formal and compositional ideas, especially in the tendency of the building to taper upward, which is achieved through the multiplication of the voids created by the windows against the masses of the lower fascias. The most probable date is the one proposed by Degenhart and Schmitt, around 1339.

C.G.

2
ANONYMOUS
Project for the Facade of the Baptistery, Siena
1320-40

Siena, Museo dell'Opera del Duomo, 20
Drawing in pen on parchment, in dark brown and red ink for the decorations of the lower fascia; the white ground behind the scene of the Coronation of the Virgin on the tympanum has been interpreted as a superimposition of mosaic for the group on a gold ground (Degenhart and Schmitt 1968).
126.5 × 58.5 cm

BIBLIOGRAPHY: Lusini 1901; Justi 1903; Lusini 1911; Ciaranfi 1932b; Bacci 1932; Keller 1937; Carli 1946b; Valentiner 1947; Toesca 1951; Burckhardt 1958; Degenhart and Schmitt 1968; Carli 1979; Middeldorf Kosegarten 1984; van Os 1985; Ascani 1989.

The drawing was published by Lusini (1901-11), who attributed it to Giacomo di Mino del Peliciaio (endorsed by Burckhardt in 1958) on the basis of a document of 1382 which reads: "A maestro Jachomo del Peliciaio a dì 14 d'ottobre per uno disegniamento che die' all'Uopara della facciata di S. Giovanni" ("To master Giacomo del Peliciaio on the day of 14 October for a drawing made for the Opera of the facade of S. Giovanni," Archivio dell'Opera del Duomo, *Libro del Camerlingo* ad an., c. 39v.). The critical problem posed by this particular drawing lies in the fact that, bar certain details, its lower section corresponds substantially with the present facade of the Siena Baptistery, whereas the upper part is conspicuously different. This variance has triggered a wide range of suggestions on the origin, function and not least the date of the drawing. It is widely considered to be a final plan that was only partially drafted and was abandoned while building work was in progress. Others, however, believe it was made in two stages, the first of which is therefore a straightforward view of the lower section of the extant facade. If this is so, then the drawing was not part of the design phase of the monument.
Justi (1903) was the first to refute Lusini's chronology—which Ciaranfi (1932b) continued to uphold—and he supported his argument with documents published by Milanesi, and with the chronicles of Bisdomini, stating that work on the facade in fact began in 1317 and finished in 1370. By his reckoning the drawing dates from around 1339.
Bacci (1932) and Keller (1937) were the first to later suggest two stages of drawing on the parchment. According to Bacci, the drawing was made in the fourth decade of the fourteenth century by Giovanni di Duccio, whose contribution to the work on the facade is documented elsewhere. On the basis of stylistic analysis, Keller contested both Lusini's later dating and Justi's earlier one, hypothesizing a date around the 1350s or 1360s, a phase of building which saw the participation of Domenico di Agostino. Keller also pointed out that certain architectural features in the drawing—particularly the windows along the southern side of the main nave and transept, and those along the side of the choir—recurred in various parts of the extant cathedral. As further confirmation of the suggested date he noted that these very parts were completed shortly after 1350. Keller's attribution of the drawing to Domenico di Agostino was subsequently followed through by Carli (1946b) and Toesca (1951).
Later, Valentiner (1947) preferred the earlier date on the basis of studies on the sculptural works of Tino di Camaino (especially the funeral monument to Cardinal Petroni in Siena Cathedral) and set the date of the statuary in the drawing to the 1320s.
Degenhart and Schmitt (1968) retain that certain technical details, and the overall consistency of style, rule out the possibility of more than one author for the drawing; they also reject the idea of the upper section as a drawing of the extant building and the bottom section a project. According to the authors, the existence of divergences between otherwise symmetrical parts suggests rather an alternative scheme for construction, and the numerous discrepancies between the upper fascia of the drawing and the one on the baptistery are the result of new decisions while work was under way. As for the drawing's date, Degenhart and Schmitt propose 1339 or thereabouts on the basis of comparisons between sections of the cathedral completed that year and certain sculpted features in the campanile design. Although they do not suggest a precise attribution, the authors reject all those previously formulated: Domenico di Agostino worked on the upper part of the baptistery only, without taking account of the drawing; the sculptures of Giovanni di Agostino for the cathedral's facade are too modern (though some links may

be drawn between several specimens made by the same sculptor in 1336 for the S. Bernardino oratory at Siena) and, lastly, the archive regarding Giacomo di Mino del Peliciaio (1382) may be just a reference to his possessing a drawing of an earlier date.
Agreeing with the position taken by Degenhart and Schmitt, Carli (1979) suggested the possible contribution of a goldsmith (perhaps Ugolino di Vieri), especially for the upper part of the drawing with the rose window and the five high, slender spires. Van Os (1985) assigned the drawing an even earlier date (1310s), arguing that it was executed before 1316, the year in which the decision was taken to enlarge the choir. Van Os observed, however, the stylistic and compositional affinities with the graphic manner of the polyptychs of the second half of the Trecento. Middeldorf Kosegarten (1984) agrees on this date, and considers the drawing to be not a reworking of an existing project drafted prior to 1317, but a project in its own right realized before that date, and subsequently modified while work was under way in response to the survey carried out by Lorenzo Maitani and the commission of architects regarding the enlargements to the old cathedral (1322). Ascani (1989) states the need for an in-depth study that goes beyond the strictly stylistic analysis and defines the possible technical links between the enlargement scheme and the Sienese drawing (links already discerned by Degenhart and Schmitt), and with other drawings made in Siena closely tied to Giovanni di Agostino, so as to have a clearer idea of the artist's activities as architect.

C.G.

3
ANONYMOUS
Elevation of the Cappella di Piazza, Siena
ca. 1370

Siena, Museo dell'Opera del Duomo, 16
Drawing on parchment in pen and brush, with bistre and red-brown ink for the marble inserts; notations of measurements and, in one case, also the materials.
83 × 39.3 cm

BIBLIOGRAPHY: Lusini 1911; Keller 1937; Degenhart 1937; Carli 1946b; Toesca 1951; Paatz 1952; Degenhart 1965; Degenhart and Schmitt 1968; Ascani 1989.

The drawing, first published by Lusini (1911), was attributed by him to Giacomo di Mino del Peliciaio and linked to the Cappella di Piazza, Siena. Keller (1937) studied it alongside certain illustrations from the *Ovide moralisé* in Gotha, Germany, and drew unequivocal parallels between the two works. He also stressed links with Andrea Orcagna's reliefs for the tabernacle in Orsanmichele, which contains a similar design for the crowning cupola. Keller set the date to 1365-70. As for the drawing's authorship, Keller (1937) suggests the hand of a Florentine artist (perhaps from Orcagna's circle), or a Sienese artist trained in Florence. Keller remains largely alone in his attribution to Florence. Degenhart (1937), who had previously suggested mid-fourteenth century, preferred the Sienese attribution, which was later backed up by Carli (1946b), Toesca (1951) and Paatz (1952). At first Keller (and also Toesca) had suggested a date between 1359 and 1377.

In a second phase of analysis, Degenhart (1965), and again later in conjunction with Schmitt (1968), pointed out that the drawing includes several measurements, and in the case of the two rose windows, the word "vetro" (glass) is used repeatedly. He also remarked on the weakness of links between the drawing and the actual Cappella del Campo, while stressing the affinities with certain Florentine works, such as the arches of the ground floor of the Orsanmichele loggia with their trefoil windows designed by Francesco Talenti (1367-80), distinctly echoing the rhythm of the drawing's three-light window and little columns creating a triple bay, with the central bay extending to the ground, and the two side ones terminating in a balustrade. Likewise, the statuary inserted into niches in the pilasters are similar to those of Orsanmichele, and the same applies to the openwork motif in the upper fascia. The Sienese drawing also includes the cupola and angels carved into the tabernacle by Orcagna (1359), again at Orsanmichele; while the characteristic lobed tympanum motif of the Strozzi chapel altarpiece (1357, again by Orcagna) crops up in the drawing in the fascia over the three-light window. Despite the evident links with the Florentine milieu, Degenhart upholds the Sienese provenance of the drawing's author, which is reinforced by the strong sumptuary slant, and the handling of the sculpted figures, which are reminiscent of certain illustrations in the *Meditationes Vitae Christi* codex in Paris (Bibliothèque Nationale, Ital. MSS. 115) and dated to around 1370. On the basis of these correlations, Degenhart proposed a new date of 1370, attributing the work to the circle of the Agostino family, particularly to Giovanni di Agostino due to parallels between the sculptures of the Madonna di Gavorrano (attributed to him), with the figures on the tympanum in the drawing. The circumstance under which Giovanni's brother Domenico was appointed in 1350 head of works at the duomo site (and of the construction of the Cappella di Piazza) seems to bear out this attribution. On this score, Ascani (1989) appeals for a more detailed analysis of the handwritten measurements, which could then be matched with those on other project drafts for the cathedral workshop, some of which are attributable to Giovanni di Agostino.   *C.G.*

BIBLIOGRAPHY: Milanesi 1854, I: 232-240, no. 51; Braunfels 1953; Garzelli 1973: 36-41; Toker 1973; 1985; Ascani 1989.

The drawing is among the documents attached to a contract which Gontiero di Goro Sansedoni stipulated in February 1340 with Agostino di Giovanni, Giovanni di Agostino and the two assistants Agostino del Rosso and Cecco di Casino for the construction of the palazzo (Milanesi 1854, I, 232-240, no. 51). The drawing, which features the facade from the side of the Banchi di Sotto, was mentioned by Braunfels (1953) and Toker (1973), after which it became the object of a close study of formal details, carried out by Garzelli (1973: 36-41). Garzelli noted how this drawing, which is mostly executed freehand, is rather clumsy in some parts, and confident in others (such as the upper windows). The correlation with the actual building is limited to the portals, of which only the central one remains, with its small window above and order of larger window bays. Garzelli notes the measurements in Sienese *braccia* and a series of other explanatory notes (contained also in the contract), and concludes that the document is an executive project; the scholar proposes a hypothetical reconstruction of the geometrical procedures applied by the drawing's author for realizing the scheme. As for the attribution, Garzelli affirms that the similarities of the handwriting in the contract to those of the measurements in the drawing indicate them both to be by Giovanni di Agostino. Toker (1985) limits the role played by Agostino di Giovanni and his team of assistants to mere supervision. This in no way refutes the paternity of the project itself, which Toker identifies in stylistic traits—such as the windows with full or segmental arches—that belong to the repertoire of Agostino di Giovanni and his son Giovanni. Toker also noted that the drawing is on a scale of 1:48, taking the Tuscan *braccio* as the unit of measurement. By means of a diagram he illustrated the possible geometrical basis to the drawing, Toker identified a composition of *ad triangulum* and *ad quadratum* figures in the upper and lower parts of the building. The scholar suggested that the general clumsiness of the drawing was due to its being a preliminary sketch, probably a copy of the original project, no longer extant. Ascani (1989) complemented Toker's analysis with a close study of the many measurements on both drawing and contract, compared the graphics, proportions, and measurements of the drawing with those found in other Sienese projects, many of which have already been attributed to the Agostini family's workshop.   *C.G.*

an analysis of style and particular chromatic details. Several scholars hold it to be one of the first examples of "true" landscape painting and—together with a second *tavola* picturing a castle overlooking the water (Pinacoteca Nazionale, Siena, no. 71)—is thought to be part of a composite work, perhaps a decorated *armadio* or wardrobe. The back of both panels bear evident signs of a wooden strut for holding the various components of the wardrobe door together. Ragghianti (1961) suggested a slightly different arrangement; the panel may be part of the lost *Mappamundus Volubilis* painted by Ambrogio for the main hall of the Palazzo Pubblico, Siena, a room which continues to be called the Sala del Mappamondo ("globe" room). Two factors seem to controvert this, however. The *mappamondo* may well have been painted on parchment and, given that it was built to rotate, it would not have comprised panels arranged lengthwise in a row. According to Ronen (1963), the panel is a section of a larger work, an altarpiece, and is rather the work of Giovanni di Paolo, and not Ambrogio Lorenzetti.

A similar conclusion was reached by Zeri (1973b), who considers the painting to be part of an altarpiece made for the Arte della Lana, or wool merchants' guild, by Sassetta somewhere between 1423 and 1426.

Borsook (1966) claims that there are definite signs of the panel having been reduced in size by cutting; the gaps in the paint along the upper and left edges, exposing traces of gold and bolus ground suggest it was made smaller at a later date. Torriti argues against this, stating that the paint on the edges came away when the panel was removed from its original frame, which was an integral part of the painting. In several places in fact patches of stucco are still visible, slightly more prominent than the painted surface, where the panel was fixed to the frame. Torriti (1977) also remarks on the cut made along the left border, noting that the hole for the dowel is 8.5 cm less deep on this side as it is on the right. As to the town featured in the painting, Carli (1962) suggests the fortified port of Talamone; Testi (1961) identifies the place as San Miniato al Tedesco. Torriti (1977) subscribes to the Talamone theory, and notes the odd figure of a woman on the shoreline (right), which could be meant to represent the toponym "il bagno delle donne" (women's bathing place), which actually exists at Talamone.   *C.G.*

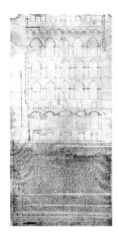

4
GIOVANNI DI AGOSTINO (?)
Project for the Facade of the Palazzo Sansedoni, Siena
1340

Siena, Collezione Monte dei Paschi
Brown ink on paper, with inscriptions; traces of erasure.
(Garzelli 1973: 36-41); 122 × 58 cm

5
SASSETTA (?)
Sea Port
ca. 1420

Siena, Pinacoteca Nazionale, 70
Paint, on poplar panel.
22.8 × 33 cm (above) and 33.5 cm (below)

BIBLIOGRAPHY: Brandi 1933; 1935; Carli 1946a; Cristiani Testi 1961; Ragghianti 1961; Carli 1962; Ronen 1963; Borsook 1966; Carli 1970; Zeri 1973b; Torriti 1977; 1982.

This painting shows a view of a towered town enclosed in a defense wall, situated on the sea front or lakeside. The work is attributed to Ambrogio Lorenzetti on the basis of

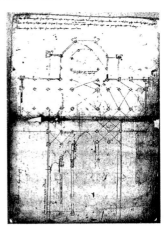

6
ANTONIO DI VINCENZO
Plan and Transverse Section of Milan Cathedral
ca. 1390

Bologna, Archivio della Fabbriceria di San Petronio, cartella 389, no. 1
Drawing in brown ink on paper, with inscriptions; the verso bears a drawing of the elevation of the eastern external wall of the north sacristy of Milan Cathedral, also the work of Antonio di Vincenzo.
47 × 33 cm

BIBLIOGRAPHY: Beltrami 1887; 1888b (Cassi Ramelli 1964); Boito

1889; Siebenhüner 1944; Frankl 1945; Ackerman 1949; Ghidiglia Quintavalle 1961; Romanini 1964; 1973; Ascani 1989; Cadei 1991a; Ascani 1991.

Beltrami (1887, 1888b) tied the drawing to the possibility that the Bolognese architect Antonio di Vincenzo may have worked at the building site of the Milan Cathedral in 1390, or shortly after; he considered it an interesting record of the stage the construction had reached at that point. Beltrami's study, essentially based on a close comparison of the dates noted on the drawing and the effective state of the cathedral, provided the cue for the subsequent analysis of Boito (1889), who in turn noted the measurements transcribed in Bolognese *piedi* and Milanese *braccia*. This combination suggested that the drawing of the plan was realized on site, whereas for the section Antonio di Vincenzo referred to previous surveys of the building work which used Milanese *piedi*. Most scholars are agreed on this point; in particular, Siebenhüner (1944) regarding the sectional drawing reckons it was copied directly from the original project (1387), contemporary with the lead model built by Anechino de Alemania, though the latter is not necessarily the author of the project plan from which Antonio di Vincenzo made his copy. Siebenhüner also attempted to include the section drawing into an *ad quadratum* scheme, though this was generally rejected by his colleagues on the basis of actual studies on the drawing's proportions. Frankl (1945) sustained that the drawing does not appear to be based on an *ad figuram* scheme; he therefore excludes the existence of geometrical patterns governing the composition, suggesting rather a mathematical basis. This idea was accepted at first by Ackerman (1949), who also noted the differences between the pillars at the crossing of the transept and the others, saying that the drawing represents a brief intermediate phase in the design, prior to the decision to make all the pillars the same size as those supporting the lantern. In agreement with Ackerman's proposal, Romanini (1964, 1973) referred to documents from the building site and fixed the date of this drawing to a period spanning July 1390 to May 1392, stressing that the drawing by Antonio di Vincenzo is based on mathematical not geometrical ratios (namely, 5:8 and 5:6), and was therefore an innovation. As regards the elevation, Romanini reckons that the architect either had a wood model of the cathedral, or a previous drawing. The fact that in the drawing by Antonio di Vincenzo, the transept has an extra second bay and hence differs from the design actually carried out was interpreted by Romanini as an indication of a possible unrealized project, perhaps inspired by the cathedral of Cologne. Affinities with the Gothic cathedrals beyond the Alps, however, are countered by the semi-hexagonal layout of the choir, flanked by closed chapels (used as sacristies), an arrangement more equitable with Lombard style than that of beyond the Alps; the detail in question is more of a local interpretation of Parlerian projects. Another discrepancy between the drawing and the actual duomo lies in the *ad quadratum* system applied by Antonio di Vincenzo to his sectional drawing; later he opted for the *ad triangulum* system, and abandoned the idea of an accentuated difference in height between the nave and the side aisles, which would have required a passageway or a triforium. This factor seems to give further weight to Romanini's theory that this was an early phase of the design that was abandoned in favor of other solutions.

Cadei (1991a) focused on verifying the type of module that Antonio di Vincenzo used for the design, and concluded that the plan in the drawing was constructed on a grid of 16 Milanese *braccia*; the elevation, however, follows a grid of 10 *braccia*, and the vaults of 9 *braccia*. The innovation lies in the fact that the building's rectangular form is free of any geometrical pattern, which meant that work proceeded with a numerical and not geometrical system. Cadei also noted that by increasing the main vault by a single unit (9 *braccia*), the entire elevation would fit in a square, not unlike Cologne Cathedral's design. However, this correlation is superficial, as in the German

Cathedral the rectangular module has its sides compatible with the ratio between base and height of an equilateral triangle. The substantial difference with respect to the *ad quadratum* scheme of Cologne Cathedral lies in the fact that for the duomo in Milan the square never becomes the "effective system of dimension." In conclusion, Cadei pointed out that—taking the Milanese *braccia* as the standard unit—the drawing seems to follow a scale of 1:96, when compared against the actual building. That scale becomes 1:48 (one of the most frequent during the neo-Gothic period) taking the standard as 2 Milanese *braccia*. Cadei's proposal regarding the elevation was then directly verified against the drawing of the plan by Ascani (1989, 1991), from which it was noted that not only the section but also the plan drawing had certain sections measured out in *braccia* (except for the longitudinal portion above the elevation drawing, showing the openings of the nave and aisles). This would seem to endorse the idea that Antonio di Vincenzo referred to a preceding model available among the various drawings of the site workshop (as already suggested by others), and did not in fact take measurements. The attribution of the drawings to Antonio di Vincenzo is further corroborated, in Ascani's opinion, by the fact that both the structure and module of the basilica of S. Petronio (by the same architect) are very similar to those for the cathedral in Milan.   *C.G.*

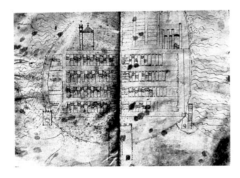

7
ANONYMOUS
Plan Project for the Town of Talamone
1306

Siena, Archivio di Stato, Capitoli, 3, fols. 25v.-26r.
Drawing on parchment in brown ink, with inscriptions.
442 × 596 mm (on two sheets)

BIBLIOGRAPHY: Braunfels 1953; Bowsky 1970; 1981; Guidoni 1983; Friedman 1988: 50-53; Ugolini 1990: 77-82.

The drawing bears the date 4 April 1306, and is considered by Braunfels (1953) to be the earliest extant example of a town plan. The document was drafted for a specific purpose: the town of Talamone which had been sold to Siena by the abbot of Monte Amiata in 1303, was scheduled to be rebuilt and repopulated. According to Braunfels the plan is the work of an inexpert hand, whose rather heedlessly traced perimeter wall, towers, town gates, churches and other urban features are contrasted by a set of overly detailed building lots lining the main thoroughfare. Each plot of land is marked with the future owner's name. For this reason, notes Braunfels, the drawing is more of a settlement scheme than a town plan as such. The repopulation was never actually carried through (about which Dante wrote: "Seek them among those harebrains who will lose More hopes in Talamone than they lost Digging to set the alleged Diana lose; Though there the admirals stand to lose the most." *Purgatory*, XIII, 151-154); for a long time the Statuti carried a regulation by which the town council had to meet every two months to discuss the completion of the port and the town of Talamone.
The queries surrounding the document of 4 April 1306 are further discussed by Bowsky (1970, 1981) regarding Siena's purchase of the abbey of Monte Amiata, and of the

abbey's claims on Talamone Castiglione Valdorcia, and other small possessions. As soon as the purchase was made, Siena began to pour investments into Talamone in a bid to make it the most important port of central Italy. The writ immediately preceding this drawing is dated 19 March 1306, and states that the administration had to see to the construction of churches, an adequate water main and drainage system, and assign 100 allotments to those who intended to settle there and build their homes. The document of 4 April seems to suggest that the lots were already allocated by that date. Besides the names of the individual townsfolk, the notary has marked the site for a church, the town walls, a citadel and several towers; however, notes Bowsky, many plots of land were apparently still untaken. Each assignee was provided with a site for the house, kitchen garden, vineyard and a patch of land of one, eight or thirty *staia* (1 *staio* = literally, a bushel, meaning the area for sowing 1 bushel of grain = a third of an acre).
The drawing was also briefly discussed by Guidoni (1983) who stressed that the architectural details are not given in plan but in elevation. In this sense, the drawing offers a blend of technical and geometrical detail as applied to the individual properties, while the figurative-landscape detailing is conferred only to the main architectural features, namely, the church and the fort.
Although the buildings represented are not linked by any proportional relationship, the overall image of the city is conveyed with precision. According to Friedman (1988) the chief reason for this clarity stems primarily from the nature of the street grid: Talamone's layout was planned on an orthogonal grid based on the three fundamental geometric concepts of the straight line, the parallel, and the perpendicular.
According to a more recent study completed by Ugolini (1990), careful comparisons with the current cadastral maps have shown that the fourteenth-century drawing is an authoritative master plan that was adhered to through into the modern age. Although the drawing has only a few features in common with the current town plan (city gates and towers) a tentative planimetric reconstruction has been made, which has revealed notable congruencies between the layout of the medieval port and the axis that crosses Talamone today in a north-south direction. In addition to this reconstruction a full metrological study has revealed a standard module of P = 30 cm. A second basic measurement is 19 P (the length of the main thoroughfare), which is very close to the 10 *braccia* standard used in the *Caleffo nero*.   *C.G.*

Stained Glass
Giusi Testa

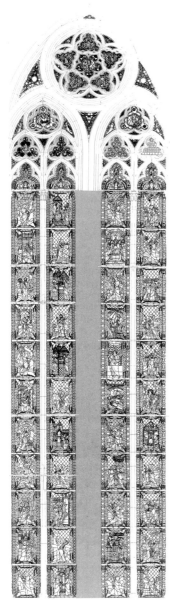

8
GIOVANNI DI BONINO D'ASSISI (?)
Christ among the Doctors

Orvieto Cathedral (tribune windows, fifth panel from bottom of the fourth window from the left)
Lead, glass, and grisaille, fired at high temperature.
103.75 × 82 cm

PROVENANCE: Orvieto, Opera del Duomo.

Besides being one of the most signal narrative stained glass works of the Gothic period, the stained glass of Orvieto Cathedral affords one of the most complex iconographic and figurative structures in existence. Bellosi in fact notes that "the wealth of the iconography is matched by the exquisite craftsmanship, and enhanced by a mysterious undertone of French figurative sensibility" (Bellosi 1992). The window measures 16.3 meters high and 4.55 wide, and follows the pattern of the *quadrifora* or four-light opening crowned with a rose window picturing a Benedictory Christ at its center, and the Symbols of the Evangelists and Cherub around it. Each one-light window culminates in a small trefoiled arch containing an Angel, and is subdivided into eleven rectangular panels in which the Prophets alternate with episodes of the *Life of the Virgin*, from the *Christ and the Money Changers* to the *Crucifixion*. The design and execution of this masterpiece of stained glass have been attributed to Giovanni di Bonino d'Assisi, whose is documented as active in Orvieto from 1325 to 1334, *ad facendum finestras*.
The records cite him as "Johanne dal vetro" or as "Maestro Johanni pictori." While the first name speaks of his evident fame as a master glassworker, the second refers explicitly to his skill as painter. The presence of someone of Giovanni's ability was necessary to Lorenzo Maitani, *capomaestro* until his death in 1330, in order to guarantee adhesion to the spirit intended for the tribune apse. The close interaction between the window design and the architecture of the building is self-evident, and would not have been feasible without a deliberate collaboration between the master painter-glassworker and the Siena-born architect Maitani. As noted earlier by Testa (1992a, 1992b), the Orvieto window is the only work of this artist so far documented in the archives. On the basis of this chronological datum, and in light of stylistic comparisons, other windows have been consequently attributed to Bonino, such as those of the chapels dedicated to St. Ludovico and St. Anthony in the Lower Church of S. Francesco at Assisi. In the case of the windows of two other chapels, St. Martin's and St. Catherine's, however, although Bonino has been ascribed the material execution, the cartoons are not considered autograph. Despite the uncertainties regarding the effective *corpus* of works by this artist, the windows of Orvieto Cathedral offer an unequivocal basis for the stylistic analysis of his output. At first sight one can discern a background training of mixed Giottesque and Assisian origin, supplemented by a highly personal perception of models from beyond the Alps, as attested by the pillars of the cathedral facade. Since the second half of the fourteenth century the work

in question has undergone many alterations, repairs, and bouts of retouching—from Giovanni di Buccio Leonardelli to the more recent intervention of Francesco Moretti (1885-1905), and not least the current renovation program (Andreani 1992). For the past few years the Soprintendenza di Umbria (the regional heritage department), whose duties include the safeguarding and conservation of the region's monuments and art works, has been carrying out a focused campaign on Orvieto Cathedral. The restoration program under way on the stained glass is just part of a wider conservation operation being applied to the building as a whole.
Following a careful examination in 1988, conservation experts became aware of the deteriorated state of what Castelnuovo declared to be "the most signal and original work in the entire history of Italian stained glass" (Castelnuovo 1958). Further investigations were promptly initiated by the technicians of the I.C.R. chemical laboratory, and the Murano-based Stazione Sperimentale, to establish a conservation program. Subsequently three panels were restored—the *The Virgin in the Temple*, the *Flight to Egypt*, and the *Christ among the Doctors*—chosen because they offered the widest range of conservation problems, from which a full range of intervention procedures could be determined.
The type of damage found in the panels was typical, and included general decay on both faces, as indicated by the restorers (Funaro and Rivelli 1992), such as "the deformation of the panels, constricted by the sealant around the edges, and weighed down by inadequate reinforcement strips in iron; fractures in the glass sections, dust and foreign matter on both faces; opacification and corrosion of the tesserae on the outer face due to exposure to sharp fluctuations in temperature; broken leading that weakens the panel; loss of putty, detachment and alteration of the grisaille due to previous cleaning, and thermal and mechanical stress, or due to poor adhesion through insufficient firing of the painted material in the first place, and loss of elasticity of the leading."
The panels were taken down and laid flat in order to fix the severely weakened grisaille that was liable to come away. After cleaning the panels were easier to read, and the substituted pieces more easy to identify, together with the retouched areas and fractures previously concealed by the leading. After a full structural and technical overhaul, the painted sections of the panels could be properly treated, and the missing parts replaced. Because of the transparency of the glass, the verso offered a means of repairing the panels without the new painted details altering the original grisaille in any way.
So far the upper section of the panels have been successfully restored as far as the springing line of the arch. The current program comprises 31 of the existing 44 panels; other sections have yet to be worked on before the operation is complete, and hence the results given here are only partial. It may seem premature to present a small part of the work before the entire operation is complete, but the importance of the research and the results achieved prompted us to write the present contribution.
The panel depicting *Christ among the Doctors* is the fifth from the bottom, in the fourth window from the left.
The architectural subject occupies most of the picture space, and presents a polygonal building supported by slender columns resting on a balustrade decorated with geometrical pattern. Jesus is seated at the center, in discussion with six or seven doctors arranged about him. The background is blue, as in all the *storie*, whereas the background for the Prophet sections is red. The entire scene is enframed by an elaborate border.
As pointed out above, the Gothic building dominates the scene, gathering the figures and the commotion of the moment, conveyed by the gesticulating foreground figures and by Jesus' pose. Carli (1965) held that this was "one of the scenes most likely to have reached us in its original form; it is almost kaleidoscopic in its use of vivid, simple colors, without intermediate tones, and densely interlocking pieces." Once it was restored, however, it was soon noticed that its design differed from other pieces consi-

As with all the other preparatory studies for the restoration campaign under way on Orvieto Cathedral, the apse windows were first of all examined in great detail to determine their state of repair. For this purpose, a system of close-up photogrammetric surveys were made, with an envisaged scale of reproduction of 1:5. This data could then be replotted life-size on a scale of 1:1, thereby ensuring the maximum precision of detail through the entire procedure. A special scaffold was set up at a fixed distance from the glass, in order to guarantee the consistency of the distance and orthogonal stability. Steps were taken to minimize certain technical difficulties: the daylight filtering through the glass was neutralized by strong counterillumination from the interior. To maximize the readability of the reproductions, the glass was photographed in black and white as well as color, facilitating a two-phase analysis—an accurate chromatic evaluation, accompanied by a graded grayscale quantification. The resulting readings were then collated in a table of two columns for each separate section of the windows. The first columns provides data on the lead, iron, and support structure in genera; the second on the stained glass section themselves, and on the designs they bear. This arrangement afforded a clear representation of all the collected data for each of the three constituent parts: lead, drawing, iron, and structure.

dered autograph: the cartoon may be by Bonino, but the choice of glass and the way the grisaille has been applied testify to another hand. It was therefore suggested that either Bonino was assisted by Giovanni di Buccio Leonardelli, or that the latter executed the panels during his intervention fifteen years later.

The restoration has brought out the polychromy: the relationship between the violet of the floor and the red, green and ocher of the transenna, the green of the figure in the right foreground, and the red of Jesus' cape and of that worn by the doctor on the left. A fundamental change took place with the replacement of two dark blue pieces of glass for a lighter blue, resulting from a misguided attempt at restoration at some previous date; these were chosen to inserted to match two other pieces that had actually become pale over time. The result is greater comprehensibility, with an airy building whose pine-cone ornaments at the cusps can be more readily appreciated, together with the grisaille, which underscores the loggia and elaborate vegetal ornament of the gable frames. Marchini (1973a) noted that the compositional links with the cathedral's facade becomes evident by comparing the same scene pictured high in the third pillar: the figure types, hair, and beards are fashioned with the same nervous, calligraphic *ductus*.   G.T.

9
GIOVANNI DI BONINO D'ASSISI
The Virgin in the Temple

Orvieto Cathedral (tribune windows, fifth panel from bottom of second window from left)
Lead, glass, and grisaille, fired at high temperature.
107 × 82 cm

PROVENANCE: Orvieto, Opera del Duomo.

The panel features a two-roomed building with the Virgin Mary seated in one, busy reading with an *educanda* behind a partition. This scene, as noted by Marchini (1973a) is singular indeed, and probably stems from ch. 6 of the Apocryphal Gospel of pseudo-Matthew, which narrates the days Mary passed in prayer during her stay at the temple. Carli (1965) mistakenly identifies the main figure as St. Anne, and the *educanda* as the Virgin Mary; he also believed it to be heavily restored. As in other *storie* panels, in this one the buildings are no longer symbolic background sets, but virtually feasible works of architecture completely integrated with the narrative. In this case, the architecture confers greater intimacy on the scene, creating atmosphere. The one-point foreshortening for such a complex construction shows considerable ability. The restoration has revived much of the brilliance and transparency of the background, and the removal of lead mending has made the narrative fully legible once more. Note the accuracy of the architectural details: the two-light windows, the rose, the decorative molding of the entrance.   G.T.

10
GIOVANNI DI BONINO D'ASSISI
The Blossoming of Joseph's Staff

Orvieto Cathedral (tribune windows ninth panel from bottom of second section from left)
Lead, glass, and grisaille fired at high temperature.
107 × 82 cm

PROVENANCE: Orvieto, Opera del Duomo

The panel depicts the blossoming of Joseph's betrothal staff in the temple, in the presence of the High Priest Abiathar. This scene is also taken from the Apocryphal Gospel, chapter seven, which narrates how Abiathar had declared that the fourteen-year-old Mary would be given in marriage to a pretender from the House of David, and more specifically, to the one whose ritual staff would miraculously burst into flower, as prophesied by Isaiah. The scene depicted is identical to the seventh panel featuring *The Pretenders Deliver their Staffs*, the only variant being Joseph's haloed face instead of the face of the first pretender to the girl's hand.

It is likely that the repetition of the design was not merely for economic reasons, but to show that the two scenes take place virtually at the same time in the same place. Carli (1965) considered the panel to be largely reworked; Marchini (1973a) pointed out (as indeed Carli had done) the similarities with the Pretenders panel and its good state of conservation. The restoration work under way has made it possible to ascertain the panel's authorship; the fine and elegant *ductus* of the portraiture, the folds and drapery, and Joseph's footwear, is the same used to depict the symbols of the Evangelists panel in the upper section of the window. It is also worth noting that the figure on Joseph's right seems to be dressed according to the period of execution; this may be the *soprastante*. In this panel too it is possible to discern direct links with the relief work on the cathedral facade executed by the so-called Maestro Sottile; furthermore, the architecture in the panel is not merely a scenic backdrop but a structural feature of the narrative.   G.T.

The Study of Antiquity
Christoph Jobst

The material presented in this section provides an idea, albeit limited, of the significance of ancient architecture for the architects and draftsmen of the Italian Renaissance. The selection of material has been deliberately reduced to drawings and documents which offer a fundamentally objective and realistic image of ancient monuments while allowing a scientifically based approach to ancient architecture. One equally fascinating aspect of the study of antiquity is, however, not dealt with here, namely, the pictorial representation of imaginary ancient buildings, a widespread practice in the fifteenth century that may seem bizarre to our modern way of thinking. Such imagery was transmitted to us by Francesco di Giorgio Martini in the Appendix of the *Codex Saluzziano* 148 in Turin. This section will examine first and foremost the question of the motives and criteria which in the fifteenth and sixteenth centuries led to a rational and systematic procedure for analyzing the cultural heritage of antiquity.

The Interpretation of Vitruvius and the Study of Ancient Buildings

Throughout the fifteenth and sixteenth centuries architects and theoreticians were incentivated to study the *De architectura libri decem*, written by the ancient theorist of architecture Vitruvius, and analyze its contents in direct relation to extant Roman buildings. Though many of these were no more than ruins, some continued to withstand the ravages of time. The drive to deduce a comprehensive idea of ancient architecture from this comparative analysis is exemplified by the works of Leon Battista Alberti. In a letter to Lodovico Gonzaga of October 1470 Alberti drew a direct correlation between the Etruscan temple described by Vitruvius and his project for S. Andrea in Mantua. Alberti's reconstruction of the Etruscan temple, however, differs from that expressed by Vitruvius; he based his idea on the form of the Basilica of Constantine in Rome, which was already largely destroyed. In the case of Alberti's church, the correlation of Vitruvius' ideas and the study of ancient monuments (in this case, the Basilica of Constantine) proved very rewarding for the design of a contemporary place of worship. The same applies to the numerous other attempts in the fifteenth and sixteenth centuries to reconstruct the original form of the Basilica of Constantine (see cat. nos. 12-16), which betrayed the influence of Alberti's idea of a *templum etruscum* with three hemicycle apses on the short and on the long sides (cat. no. 16). At the same time, Francesco di Giorgio's reconstruction of the plan of the Basilica of Constantine in the Appendix to the *Codex Saluzziano* 148 includes the southern atrium, discovered during excavations in 1484. This reconstruction effectively contrasts with the theoretical interpretation of the Basilica of Constantine as a *templum etruscum* with three great apses (cat. no. 13).

One curiosity of the studies of Vitruvius is the reconstruction of plans and sections of ancient temples on a Greek cruciform plan, such as those in Cesare Cesariano's commentary on the *De architectura*, in which he adopts a Byzantine building type (which he presumes to be antique) to illustrate Vitruvius' text.

The hypothetical reconstruction of Roman theaters based on Vitruvius' descriptions—and in particular the reconstruction of the Theater of Marcellus—are evidence of the burgeoning links in the early sixteenth century between Vitruvian critique and the study of ancient buildings and ruins in the "archaeological" sense. The results of these investigations were subsequently applied in the design and construction of new buildings. Between 1518 and 1520 numerous architects surveyed the Theater of Marcellus, taking detailed measurements, and drafted hypothetical reconstructions (cat. nos. 25-27). Antonio da Sangallo the Younger in particular drew great profit from his comparative studies of ancient theaters and Vitruvius' theories. Working as Raphael's assistant in 1519, Sangallo designed a theater for the Villa Madama based on ancient Roman models (cat. nos. 34-35). The term "archaeology" in reference to the research on ancient buildings carried out in the fifteenth and sixteenth centuries does not imply the sophisticated methods and procedures applied by today's archaeologists. However, those architects and scholars of the Renaissance who studied antiquity—Il Cronaca (Simone del Pollaiuolo), Giuliano da Sangallo and his nephew Antonio da Sangallo the Younger, and above all Raphael—adopted methods of measurement and analysis which to some extent foreshadow modern archaeological method. The fundamental difference in procedure between then and now is that, in many cases, the architects of the Renaissance did not unquestioningly accept the heritage left by the ancients, but tended to apply the theoretical and esthetic principles of their epoch as a means of comprehending the ancient monuments.

The Archaeological Inventory

The urge to delve into antiquity, and the thoroughness of the studies carried out in the Renaissance—especially after the turn of the sixteenth century—was prompted by several factors. First, the survey of ancient buildings became more accurate and stimulated analytic studies of the architectural details; second, new technical aids borrowed from geodesy and navigation made it possible to study and reconstruct buildings which until then had seemed obscure and dauntingly complex, or were mostly ruined or largely obliterated by later constructions; and last, there was a greater effort to achieve objectivity in research and in the reconstruction of ancient buildings; at the same time, drawings became working instruments for the faithful reproduction of buildings, enabling their dimensions and proportions to be deduced with accuracy. One such architect who performed a major role in fostering objective, realistic reproductions and surveys of ancient buildings in the late fifteenth and early sixteenth centuries was Il Cronaca. This Florentine scholar used his observations and surveys to reintroduce an antique repertory of forms in his own projects and constructions, achieving some highly unorthodox solutions (cat. nos. 17, 18).

A new campaign of archaeological fieldwork on the Colosseum in Rome, carried out by Giuliano da Sangallo in 1513, heralded a new phase in the survey of ancient buildings. The results of this research can be seen in a set of drawings in the *Codex Coner* in London, executed by Bernardino della Volpaia (cat. no. 19). Volpaia's unit of measurement, the *braccio fiorentino*, was subdivided into 60 *minuti*, a smaller, less common unit of reference. The detailed survey of the entablature of the Temple of Castor and Pollux (the Dioscuri) was carried out jointly by Bernardino della Volpaia, Antonio da Sangallo, and Giovanni Battista da Sangallo (cat. no. 19). The reproductions of the entablature in Uff. 1181A and in the *Codex Coner* set are striking documents of the meticulous method of recording and comparing the ornamental details of the buildings; the discrepancies arising from the different readings are dutifully registered in *minuti*.

An even more ambitious undertaking than the *Codex Coner* was the commission Raphael received from Pope Leo X to design a map of ancient Rome, placing the ancient monuments in their exact positions. It was also the pope's intention to promote projects for the reconstruction of the buildings. Assisted by Baldassarre Castiglione, Raphael wrote a kind of preface to the map of Rome, the *Memorandum*, which has survived in three versions. The Munich version illustrated in this catalog was written in about 1519-20 (cat. no. 22). Raphael's *Memorandum* allows an important view of the state of scholarship and ar-

chaeological research toward the end of Pope Leo X's reign. It includes fundamental information about measuring techniques, the different perspectives and orthogonal projections used in the drawings and the critical appraisal of ancient architecture.

For the first time in history Raphael explained in detail the utility of the magnetic compass as an instrument for obtaining exact measurements of a building, even those with an irregular or complex shape (cat. no. 23). With the use of a compass, Antonio da Sangallo successfully measured (and subsequently drafted a reconstruction of) the entire site of the Theater of Marcellus, which was largely destroyed and built over by later structures (cat. no. 25). Hubertus Günther recently wrote a compelling essay examining the link between the methods described by Raphael in the *Memorandum* of 1519-20 and the numerous drawings of the Theater of Marcellus, the Imperial Fora, and the Forum Holitorium executed by Peruzzi and Sangallo between 1518 and 1520. These illustrations were part of the fieldwork that was preparatory to the map of Rome; the campaign came to a halt with the deaths of Raphael (1520) and his patron, Pope Leo X (1523).

Raphael's *Memorandum* reveals the theoretical motivation behind the graphic procedure which he called "the architect's way of drawing" ("el modo del disegnar che più appartiene allo architetto") and which modern terminology defines as "orthogonal projection." Unlike a drawing in one-point perspective, which creates an illusion of space, the lines and the views deriving from an orthogonal projection do not have a common vanishing point. The walls of a building and the individual structures are reproduced in the elevation and section as they really are, "senza errore," as Raphael put it. The horizontals (cornices, entablatures) and the vertical elements (columns, pilasters, openings, etc.) are all represented at right-angles to each other. The precise measurements and the lack of perspective distortion enable accurate readings of the dimensions and proportions of the building, while excluding its spatial and plastic aspects. A perception of the latter, notes Raphael, can only be achieved with the introduction of central perspective. Architects who anticipated the application of orthogonal projection were Il Cronaca (cat. no. 24), Giuliano da Sangallo (cat. no. 20), and Antonio da Sangallo the Younger. Many of their works clearly show the benefits and limits of orthogonal projection with respect to perspective drawings (cat. nos. 24, 33).

Antiquity as a "Model" and the Growing Critique of Antiquity

The enterprising project for the map of Rome, documented in Raphael's *Memorandum* to Pope Leo X, laid the foundations for the scholarly study of antiquity. Raphael's comments about the qualitative difference between Bramante's "modern" architecture and ancient architecture affirm that around 1520 the increasingly intense study of antiquity was by no means sterile, but served to provide standards for the quality and possibilities of modern architecture. Antiquity was to be used as a "model" for new architecture, but not unquestioningly: Raphael noted what he reputed to be "signs of decadence" in the Arch of Constantine (cat. no. 22), though it must be said that he was referring to the sculptural elements and not the architecture as such. The sheer variety of expression is what makes the architecture of antiquity important. A careful distinction is to be made between buildings and their ornamentation, between the "better" and "minor" qualities of the decorative elements. Antonio da Sangallo's exemplary critique of the Pantheon (ca. 1535) evinces a further improvement in the methodology used to represent and establish distinctions between contents and ideas: the survey of extant buildings, their reconstruction through drawings, and their subsequent criticism (cat. no. 31). The new critical approach to antiquity was developed from around 1520 onward, in a period during which the extant monuments were being studied in utmost detail. And it was this new awareness of the past that makes the Renaissance analysis of antiquity so important.

11
Hermannus Posthumus (Herman Postma)
Fantastic Landscape with Ruins
1538

Oil on canvas; signed and dated.
98 × 114.5 cm
Inscribed: *Herman[nus] posthum[us] pingeb[at] 1536.*

Provenance: Liechtenstein, The Princely Collections, Vaduz.

Bibliography: Olitsky Rubistein 1985; Dacos 1985; *Liechtenstein... 1985-86*; Baunan 1986; Klock 1986; Günther 1988c; Dacos 1989; Boon 1991.

There is nothing in the entire legacy of Renaissance painting to compare with this extraordinary canvas, discovered a mere decade ago and published for the first time in 1985 by R. Olitsky Rubistein. The painting affords a "programmatic" glimpse into the world of classical antiquity, a guided tour of the vestiges of ancient Rome, [such as that] which G. F. Poggio Bracciolini cited at the beginning of the Renaissance in his treatise *De varietate fortunae*.

The painting presents a hillside landscape dotted with ruins of a building of undeniable classical inspiration, whose original form it is no longer possible to determine. In the right foreground stands a rotunda, evidently inspired by the church of S. Costanza, once known as the Temple of Bacchus. This kind of "ideal" ruin is a frequent subject of sixteenth-century art. Further in the background, on the left, rise imposing structures reminiscent of the Palatine or Tivoli. Spreading along the horizon is an unfinished metropolis, dotted with pyramids. In the foreground are several openings of grotto-like vaults leading underground, similar to the openings that gave access to Nero's Domus Aurea. Among the ruins—some fallen, others still standing—can be seen the scattered remains of antique statuary, precious tableware, and architectural elements, concentrated mainly in the immediate foreground. Nearly everything pictured is damaged in some way, even some of the fragments of retrieved architecture walled into other buildings. In the middle ground stand two monuments—non-existent but faithful imitations of antiquity; on the right, a monument dedicated to Jupiter, as indicated by the little statue with eagle and thunderbolt; opposite this, on the left, a banquet scene laid out in undisguised imitation of the so-called Trophies of Marius (now on the Campidoglio), with ornate pedestals and border, bearing a male bust in its center—an emperor, evidently—sporting a laurel crown and hence a homage to the prototypes of the glorious statesman of imperial Rome. In the midst of all this are two fine statues representing the reclining river gods, in imitation of the Nile and Tiber statues on the Campidoglio. According to the iconography of antiquity, these figures represent the prosperity that was enjoyed under the dominion of Jupiter and the illustrious leader of the Roman state.

But in front of these tokens of ancient splendor, below the personification of the rivers, one can make out a famous sarcophagus, built in antiquity and used during the Renaissance to house the remains of two former Roman emperors, Vespasian and Titus. Resting on the tomb is a huge slab bearing an inscription that serves as a caption to the entire painting: *TEMPVS EDAX RERVM TVQVE INVIDIOSA VETVSTAS O[MN]NIA DESTRVITIS*. The words are taken directly from Ovid's *Metamorphosis* (XV, 234f.), and tie in with Pythagoras' reflections on the nature of time. The passage from Ovid opens with some general comments on how all things must surely pass, and how all images are evanescent ("*cuncta fluunt omnisque vagans formatur imago*"). Endorsing this notion are several examples, which are purposely arranged in a crescendo: the different aspects of sky and earth in the course of the day, the changes in the vegetation through the seasons, the evolution of the human body with the onset of age (that is, growth followed by decay), and the phases of fortune and disgrace in the history of man (such as the decline of Troy, the collapse of the great Greek cities, and the emerging splendor of the Eastern Roman Empire). The "cells" referred to in the plaque inscription are those of the human body.

The concept of the inexorable flow of time is underlined in two other features. In the middle ground, left, before the monument to the emperor, one can clearly discern a sundial; this was the ancient sundial known as the *Menologium rusticum Vallense* because it was once in the collection of a certain Bernardino della Valle (no longer extant, but reproduced accurately in numerous Renaissance illustrations). The various units of time and relative inscriptions are reproduced with the utmost accuracy: the cylindrical surface with its curved symbols marking the various phases of the day, and the vertical surfaces arranged either side of the first indicating the winter solstice, the equinox, and the summer solstice. Just below this lies a calendar marked with signs of the zodiac, complete with months and individual days. The statue atop the monument to Zeus stands out on a blue sphere bearing the signs of the zodiac. Ruins and fragments reveal that Ovid's words about the evanescence of things refer to culture and civilization, and both monuments testify that the painting was intended as an illustration of the unpredictability of fortune in the history of mankind. The examples supplied by Ovid in this regard are premonitory: the fall of what was once florid Rome is an outspoken example of the capricious nature of fate.

In spite of everything, the painting also presages rebirth. This is represented by a group of figures gathered around the plaque that bears the inscription (the "caption" explaining the meaning of the painting); the figures are engaged in studying the past, taking notes, and making drawings. Armed with torches, they descend into the underground passages, and marvel at the river gods. Several other, closer figures at the center, near the plaque on the sarcophagus, can be observed as they measure and draw copies of the pedestal of a column. Gestures and actions of a constructive nature surround the plaque's carved motto, with its prediction of destruction.

Considered from three different viewpoints, the action of these figures signifies rebirth, *renaissance*. The breach with the legacy of the past means that civilization can evolve, as expressed in words attributed to John of Salisbury, who declared that, in comparison to our forebears we are like dwarves on giants' shoulders—desperately small, and yet always in a position outdo them because we are able to build something new upon them. In his book on the ruins of antiquity (published 1540) Serlio also refers to this passage from Ovid. Similarly, John of Salisbury's words are dramatically echoed by the way in which the ruins utterly dwarf the men busy exploring and studying them. Secondly, they also link to the start of the Renaissance, which, by definition, means the resuscitation of the classical world through systematic and objective research. The human figures immortalized by Postma in this painting are the incarnation of the Renaissance spirit of enquiry, captured as they record the measurements of a statue (the right shoulder of the left river god). This type of enquiry also epitomizes the kind of rebirth intended by Francesco Maria Molza in his funeral eulogy for Raphael: bemoaning the fall of ancient Rome, Molza praised the deceased artist because the buildings he represented in his paintings were a faithful evocation of the splendors of antiquity. The ruins were thus reborn in another medium (painting) that salvaged them from the vicissitudes of time and fate ("hor salda et immortale Si vedea riuscire et post fuore D'ogni ingiuria di tempo et di fortuna") (Günther 1988c: 319 n. 317e).

Formerly little was known about the painting's author. Only recently in fact N. Dacos and others began to look into his life and work. The artist was in the habit of signing himself "Hermannus Posthumus," a Latinized version of his real name, Herman Postma. Born in the Low Countries in 1513 or 1514, he died before 1588. Postma most likely learned his trade in the workshop of Jan van Scorel in the town of Utrecht. In 1534, Duke Ludwig X of Bavaria sent him to study under Giulio Romano (Förster 1989: 512). Despite a few interruptions, Postma seems to have sojourned in Mantua until the end of the 1530s, and, as Giulio Romano's assistant, was in a position to take an active part in the decoration of the Palazzo del Te and the Palazzo Ducale. Between 1540 and 1542 he was put in charge of the decoration of the palace at Landshut, whose foundation stone was laid by Duke Ludwig himself in 1537. In around 1536 Postma moved to Rome to study the ancient monuments—witness the inscription inserted into the painting's representation of the Domus Aurea; in Rome he may have come into contact with Maerten van Heemskerck. This would explain certain similarities in their work, such as their common fascination for imaginary ancient ruins. In 1535-36 Heemskerck painted a *Rape of Helen* set in a large-format fantastic landscape with ruins (Grosshans 1980, no. 199); however, he never produced a programmatic canvas comparable to Postma's painting in Liechtenstein.

Dacos' studies included a tentative inventory of the works of Postma. This task was greatly helped by a series of annotations that have been proved autograph (Günther 1988c: 10; Boon 1991). One particularly interesting proposal is Dacos' association of Postma with the so-called "Anonymous A," whose drawings are bound with those of Heemskerck in the Berlin collection; this *corpus* is largely comprised of views of Rome drawn by the said "Anonymous A." One such drawing contains the words of Hildebert of Lavardin, "*ROMA QUANTA FUIT IPSA RUINA DOCET*," which Sebastiano Serlio included in the preface to his volume on ancient ruins. Attributed to "Anonymous A" are many detailed studies of antique architectural monuments; these drawings are now in the Staatliche Kunstsammlung in Kassel (Günther 1988f: 364; 1988c). There is a fairly close link between these "photographic" portraits of ancient buildings, and Serlio's text on ruins. The former also have affinities with a copy executed by "Anonymous A" of a treatise on the classical orders, which follows the sequence established by Diego de Sagredo. The passion for architectural theory communicated by the drawings in the Kassel collection are comparable to the spirit of the Liechtenstein painting which—witness the title invented in 1550 by Vasari for Alberti's *De re aedificatoria*—offers a most fitting title for a treatise on architecture.

Hubertus Günther

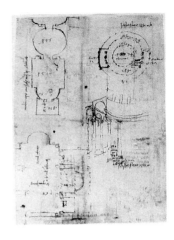

12

FRANCESCO DI GIORGIO MARTINI
The Basilica of Constantine, Rome
before mid-1486 (perhaps between 1464 and perhaps between 1464 and 1475)

Florence, Galleria degli Uffizi, Gabinetto Disegni e Stampe, Uff. 330Av.
Pen and ink, on paper.
286 × 201 mm
INSCRIBED: *Tenp[l]u[m] pacis/tenpiu[m] pacis/longo p[iedi] 240/vestibulo.*

BIBLIOGRAPHY: Bartoli 1914-22, pl. VII, fig. 16; Weller 1943: 264, no. 330; Buddensieg 1962: 37-48; Ericsson 1980: 127-130; Scaglia 1980: 9; Günther 1988f: 32-33.

On the bottom left of Uff. 330A verso is a sketch of a plan of the Basilica of Maxentius and Constantine drawn by Francesco di Giorgio. It illustrates the west and north apses. Along the central axis of the north apse Francesco has drawn an entrance, while in front of and inside the apse he has drawn a series of columns. This entrance, defined as a "vestibulo" does not derive from any of the reproductions of the Basilica of Constantine (cat. nos. 13-16). The plan and the elevation in the *Codex Coner* and the view of the interior of the basilica in the *Codex Destailleur* (OZ 109, fol. 16r., Kunstbibliothek SMPK) in Berlin shows a series of columns in the apse. Francesco seems to have preferred a portico entrance on the basis of this internal colonnade. He evidently knew nothing about the entrance on the south side of the basilica, which was discovered in 1486 (cat. no. 13). He probably misunderstood the significance of the still visible remains of the eastern portico, as he drew a continuous wall to the east with a small side opening. Comparing these sketches, probably drawn on-site, with the highly detailed plan in the *Codex Saluzziano* 148 (cat. no. 13) brings us to the conclusion that Uff. 330A must have been drawn before the excavations in 1486. The archaeological research brought to light the southern portico and the remains of the huge marble statue of Constantine in the western apse. The results of the excavations are clearly illustrated in the *Codex Saluzziano* 148. The differences between the two drawings make it clear that the Turin sheet cannot simply be a literal reproduction of the Uffizi sketch. Hubertus Günther (1988f: 34 n. 155) recently suggested that there was yet another, intermediate drawing. The sketch in the Uffizi was drawn by Francesco di Giorgio himself and is presumably one of the earliest drawings of the Basilica of Constantine. It could have been executed during his first sojourn in Rome, during the reign of Pope Paul II (1464-75).

Ursula Kleefisch-Jobst

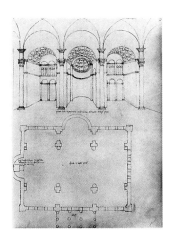

13

FRANCESCO DI GIORGIO MARTINI (and/or? GUIDOCCIO COZZARELLI)
The Basilica of Constantine, Rome
after mid-1486

Turin, Biblioteca Reale, *Codex Saluzziano* 148, fol. 76r.
Pen and brown ink, on parchment.
383 × 265 mm
INSCRIBED: *parte dela co[m]positione et ho[r]name[n]ti del drento di te[m]plu[m] pacis; Inqu[est]o luogho sedeva hu[n] gighante / di marmo ch[e] la testa sua e / piei suj; etmezo; fondo di te[m]plu[m] pacis; po[r]ticho.*

BIBLIOGRAPHY: Buddensieg 1963: 37-48; Francesco di Giorgio Martini 1967; Buddensieg 1971: 259-267; Scaglia 1980: 7-25; Günther 1988f: 32-33.

The *Codex Saluzziano* 148 is composed of two parts: a treatise on architecture, drafted by Francesco di Giorgio probably sometime after 1477 at the court of the Duke of Urbino, and a series of reproductions of ancient buildings, drawn by the same author mostly between 1485 and 1486, including fol. 76 discussed here. The original edition of the treatise has not survived: the *Codex Saluzziano* 148 is one of the two remaining copies probably commissioned from Francesco di Giorgio at Siena (Scaglia) or at Urbino (Maltese 1967). According to Scaglia, the text of the treatise was copied in a Sienese *scriptorium* in about 1486, and the drawings were executed by the painter Guidoccio di Giovanni di Marco Cozzarelli. The Appendix, containing illustrations of ancient buildings, is only to be found in the Turin copy. Francesco di Giorgio's preliminary studies for this work can be seen in the so-called *Taccuino dei Viaggi* in the Uffizi (cat. no. 12). Fol. 76 shows a view of the interior and the plan of the Basilica of Maxentius and Constantine, known as the Templum Pacis until the nineteenth century due to its position near the Forum Pacis, built by Vespasian.
The series of drawings shown here, reproducing the Basilica of Constantine, makes it quite clear that the archaeological discoveries had considerable direct influence on the illustrations of the buildings. Inside the plan of the west apse Francesco di Giorgio drew a double base for a statue and wrote next to it: "In this place, a marble giant sat; his head and feet six and a half," meaning that the colossal statue was of Constantine sitting down (the remains of this are kept today in the Palazzo dei Conservatori). The fragments of the statue were taken away from the Templum Pacis in 1486, as an inscription on the Campidoglio informs us. How reliable is Francesco's drawing? A tiny sketch by Peruzzi (Uff. 539Av.) also illustrates the place where the statue was standing at the west apse of the basilica.
There is a south portico in Francesco di Giorgio's drawing placed opposite the north apse, added at a later date by Constantine. All the other reproductions of the Basilica of Constantine, excepting the paper conserved in Vienna (cat. no. 14), put another apse in its place. The portico colonnade was discovered during nineteenth-century excavations, though this had a smaller number of columns

compared to those drawn by Francesco. This all confirms the statement made by Buddensieg: "The Turin drawing of the Basilica of Constantine made by Francesco is the result, if not the direct demonstration of the excavations in mid-1486 which brought to light the colossus, and perhaps fragments of a porphyry column" (Buddensieg 1962: 40). We may presume that the remains of the portico were covered over again immediately after their discovery, because, with only one exception (cat. no. 14), the portico is never drawn again in any other successive reproductions of the building. The fact that many authors of later drawings reconstructed a third apse in place of the portico is connected to the idea that the Basilica of Constantine was a temple, and was general thought to be a *templum etruscum* because of its two visible apses, of the kind described by Alberti (1966a) in Books VII, iv, and VIII, x. The reason why Francesco di Giorgio did not draw the east portico, whose remains are still visible today, in spite of all the precision in his plan, can be explained only by considering that he imagined the south atrium to be the main entrance and that he wanted to place an emphasis on the north-south axis with a mind to Constantine's rebuilding of it.
The view of the interior of the Basilica of Constantine, as Francesco di Giorgio drew it, does not correspond in many aspects with the information we have deduced from the monument's remains. It contrasts with his highly reliable plan that was based on the archaeological discoveries. The most evident contradiction is the elongated proportions which alter the original rather shortened and wide character of the interior, similar in shape to the huge *frigidaria* of Roman bath complexes, resulting in a more reduced, church-like scheme. The elevation of the wall also recalls a church. Instead of the huge arched windows on two floors, Francesco has drawn narrow arches in front of the niches on the lower story (or so it seems in the elevation) and above them he has drawn a sort of triple window. The majestic dome is constructed with great precision from the ruins: the barrel vaults of the side niches, decorated with octagonal lacunars, which he has placed higher up because of the more elongated structure in the interior, and the impressive thermal vault. Francesco reproposed an emphasis on the supposed north-south axis, in the elevation as well, reconstructing the columns in front of the walls only along this axis and placing pilasters in front of the other walls.
Francesco's drawing of the interior of the Pantheon, one of the set of reproductions of ancient buildings in the *Codex Saluzziano* 148 (fol. 80r.), repeats the same characteristics that modify the elevation in the view of the interior of the Basilica of Constantine: more elongated proportions and a more lightweight structure. Buddensieg (1971) first drew attention to the fact that this was not a case of a poor reproduction or an error of interpretation, but rather a deliberate alteration to the design—a form of criticism—an utterly "anti-antique" modification.

Ursula Kleefisch-Jobst

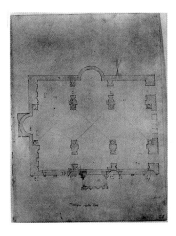

14

ITALIAN MASTER A
The Basilica of Constantine, Rome
1480-1500 (perhaps before 1486, Buddensieg)

Vienna, Graphische Sammlung Albertina, *Skizzenbuch des Italieners A*, Egger no. 54r.
Pen and brown ink, on paper; measurements in *piedi, once*.
415 × 283 mm
INSCRIBED: *Tempio della Pace.*

BIBLIOGRAPHY: Egger 1903, no. 54; Buddensieg 1962: 37-48; Valori 1985a: 19-21, no. IV.

Egger attributed a series of papers in the Albertina to a so-called "Unknown Italian Master A." He dated these drawings to the last two decades of the fifteenth century and asserts that only a small part of the buildings illustrated were actually drawn from life by the so-called Master A. In Egger's opinion, he copied other reproductions and sometimes checked their exactness by personal observation. The present sheet is an interesting example of this supposition. It shows the plan of the Basilica of Constantine with the west and north apses, an entrance on the east side and an atrium on the south. Egger noticed that the latter was added to the drawing at a later date, but probably by the same artist. The southern portico was discovered during excavations in mid-1486, as confirmed by Francesco di Giorgio's drawing in the *Codex Saluzziano* 148 (cat. no. 13). This entrance must have been demolished shortly afterward, since all the authors of later drawings, excepting Master A, give no portico in this position. The Vienna sheet probably belongs to the period before the excavations of 1486 and was then completed on the basis of the finds. Master A's knowledge of the southern entrance was probably from written documents and hearsay rather than from personal observation, or from an acquaintance with Francesco di Giorgio's drawing. This reconstruction, in fact, has little in common with the archaeological discoveries and offers a rather free interpretation of the basilica, as in the case of the external niches on the south wall.

Ursula Kleefisch-Jobst

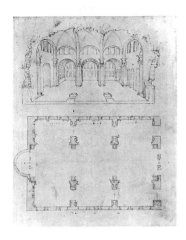

15
ITALIAN MASTER C
The Basilica of Constantine, Rome
1519

Vienna, Graphische Sammlung Albertina, *Skizzenbuch des Italieners C*, Egger no. 9r.
Pen and brown ink, on paper; measurements in *piede antico*, *once*; scale of 100 *piedi* in lower margin.
279 × 208 mm

BIBLIOGRAPHY: Egger 1903, no. 9; Buddensieg 1962: 37-48; Valori 1985b: 102-105, no. XVII; Günther 1988f: 341, no. 9.

This sheet contained in the sketchbook compiled by the so-called "Unknown Italian Master C," dated 1519, presents a view of the interior and a plan of the Basilica of Maxentius and Constantine (cat. nos. 12-14 e 16). Only the west apse and the east apse are showed in the plan. Master C did not draw the north apse added by Constantine, though this still stands today. It seems that he knew nothing (in 1519) of the south portico excavated in 1486. For the draftsman, an apse on the north side may have been incomprehensible without a corresponding projection on the south side. He decided to accentuate the east-west axis and—consciously or unconsciously—reconstructed the original plan of the basilica, as built by Maxentius.

The view of the interior is proof of the intense studies of the building, especially when compared to Francesco di Giorgio's view in the *Codex Saluzziano* 148 (fol. 76r.; cat. no. 13). The Vienna drawing offers a fine rendering of the vast space; it was presumably for this purpose that the section was made level with the side rooms to the south. The main hall is illuminated by the thermal windows and the heavy cross vaults are divided into several parts by string courses. Master C has drawn two rows of arched windows in the barrel-vaulted side rooms. There are niches along the sides of the passages connecting the various adjacent rooms.

When comparing Francesco di Giorgio's "anti-antique" reconstruction of the interior of the Basilica of Constantine with this archaeologically more precise view by Master C, we should not forget the interior view of 1513-15 in the *Codex Coner* (Ashby 1904, no. 59).

Ursula Kleefisch-Jobst

16
GIOVANNI BATTISTA MONTANO
The Basilica of Constantine, Rome
early 17th cent. (ca. 1610-11)

London, Sir John Soane's Museum, Giovanni Battista Montano, vol. II, fol. 30

BIBLIOGRAPHY: Zander 1958: 1-21; 1962, IL/L: 1-32; Buddensieg 1962: 37-48; Bedon 1983: 111-126.

This sheet by Giovanni Battista Montano was originally planned as an engraving for his treatise on architecture, and hence the image is inverted. There is a longitudinal section of the basilica, an east view associated to a cross-section and a plan. The longitudinal section shows the colossal statue of Constantine placed inside the west apse. This had been discovered in 1486, as confirmed by Francesco di Giorgio's drawing in the *Codex Saluzziano* 148 (fol. 76r.; cat. no. 13). Montano's drawing proves that up until the seventeenth century the statue was traditionally positioned in the west apse of the basilica. He has drawn a third apse instead of the south portico, which had also been discovered in 1486. The author probably believed that the Basilica of Constantine was the *templum etruscum* described by Alberti. Montano's reconstruction of the elevation favors this notion: he has set tympanums above the east portico to give the facade a temple front.

Ursula Kleefisch-Jobst

17
IL CRONACA (SIMONE DEL POLLAIUOLO)
Fragment of Wall Base, Hadrian's Mausoleum (Castel Sant'Angelo), Rome
before 1504

Berlin, Staatliche Museen, Preussischer Kulturbesitz, Kupferstichkabinett, KdZ 5714r.
Pen and brown ink, on paper, with shading; indications of measurements.

20.5 × 14.5 cm
VERSO: details of the Piccolomini altar in Siena Cathedral.

BIBLIOGRAPHY: Nesselrath 1986a: 87-147; Günther 1988f: 71-73, 332, pls 9a, 10.

Simone del Pollaiuolo (1457-1508), the Florentine master stonemason, was already known as "Il Cronaca" (the Chronicler) in the sixteenth century owing to his surveys and reproductions of the ancient ruins of Rome. His ability was much praised by Giorgio Vasari in his *Lives* (Vasari 1878-85, IV: 442ff). Though only a few autograph drawings have survived (now in museums in Berlin, Montreal, New York and Florence), Günther has nonetheless convincingly shown that many drawings of other sixteenth-century artists reflect elements of Il Cronaca's studies of antiquity (see cat. nos. 18 and 24). The frequency of these copies is evidence of the esteem Il Cronaca enjoyed among his contemporaries.

Il Cronaca lived in Rome for about ten years (from 1475 to 1483 or 1486; Günther 1988f: 68), working in Antonio del Pollaiuolo's workshop. When he returned to Florence he worked on several important building projects, and was awarded the tenure of the cathedral site in 1495.

Il Cronaca utilized his profound knowledge of ancient monuments for his own architectural constructions. He imitated the so-called "spogliacristi" entablature of Trajan's Forum for his heavy cornice crowning the Palazzo Strozzi (partly finished in 1500), while modifying the proportions of the individual profiles of the original. Il Cronaca's method of drawing parts of ancient buildings has its physical correlation in the way he liberally transplanted such elements to new buildings. In the drawings the parts are isolated from their original context and shown as single elements, enabling them to be applied to new architectural settings. The part of the wall base of Hadrian's Mausoleum (now Castel Sant'Angelo) drawn by Il Cronaca on this sheet, was copied in the architectural framework of a fireplace in Palazzo Strozzi. This fireplace of which we show a photograph was built in 1504, while Il Cronaca was *capomaestro* at the Palazzo Strozzi. The attribution of the idea and the project for this sumptuous fireplace in the Palazzo Strozzi to Il Cronaca is logical, considering its obvious correspondence with the Berlin drawing of Hadrian's Mausoleum, which was identified as autograph by Matthias Winner.

The sheet offers an unpretentious but very precise illustration of the structure and the details of the wall base of Hadrian's Mausoleum. Some dimensions are given. The hallmarks of Simone del Pollaiuolo's "chronicle" style are very evident; he eschews all embellishments and invents nothing. A model for the abovementioned fireplace was perhaps derived from this very sheet or from one of Il Cronaca's preliminary studies for the drawing. The illustration is particularly important because only rarely during the Renaissance were copies of ancient monuments faithful to the originals. The cornice of the fireplace reproduces the structure and details of the base of Castel Sant'Angelo as illustrated in Il Cronaca's drawing in Berlin. All the same, slight departures from the original model betray an attempt to simplify and to render the shape of the fireplace more severe. The strict, square forms, the corner pilasters with characteristic wide capitals and the profiles of the entablature, all derive from the wall base of Castel Sant'Angelo, even though the pilaster bases are more simple than those in the drawing of Hadrian's Mausoleum. The parts inserted in the panels of the fireplace pilasters emphasize the vertical upthrust of the pilaster structure against the horizontal emphasis of the severe squared stones and entablature. The ovolo molding concluding the two bands of the architrave has not been copied in the fireplace with a pearl-like fusarole but rests on a thin smooth profile. Instead of the frieze of just garlands and bucrania, Il Cronaca has included Filippo Strozzi's emblems—lambs and eagles.

The drawing of a twined grapevine on KdZ 5713 recto (Berlin, Kupferstichkabinett) must have served as a model for the foliage ornaments framing the Strozzi coat of arms on the upper edge of the fireplace.   *C.J.*

18

UNKNOWN ITALIAN
(AFTER SIMONE DEL POLLAIUOLO, IL CRONACA)
Plan of Centralized Building
early 16th cent.

Florence, Galleria degli Uffizi, Gabinetto Disegni e Stampe,
Uff. 4378A
Pen and ink on paper; preliminary incised lines for reference.
32 × 22 cm
INSCRIBED: (recto) *Dalluno vivo allo altro di questi / due anguli b[raccia] XX appunto* (in the hexagon); *Ilvano b[raccia] XXvII ¾* (in portico); *(in lower half of sheet) Questo tempio ha di dentro faccia 6 e faccie XII di fora ogni faccia fora / e dentro [è] br[accia] X daterra alregolo della p[rim]a cornice è br[accia] 13 son br[acci]a 13 s.1 d. 9 dalla p[rim]a cornice al regolo della seconda dove pose lavolta b[raccia] 10 ¼ lavolta leva sopra lacornice / b[raccia] 10 e nel colmo della volta è meza tonda cioe testevale senza spigole / o anguli p[er]che li anguli alzano ¼ della volta e poi diventa tonda Ipilastri dentro / e le colone delportico b[racci]a 1⅛ grosse e larghe e alti 9 teste e mezo lentrate delle capele / longhe b[raccia] 6 i[n]boccha drento b[raccia] 8 Il nicchio b[raccia] 5 imboccha alto b[raccia] 8⅓ chenne [?] / Il voto alto b[raccia] 13⅓ Labocccha larga 6 alta b[raccia] 10 lostipito ha di piano dalle entrate / delle cappelle ⅝ e dalato dallo angolo ¼ di emicicli di fora larghi i[n] bocca / b[raccia] 4¼ alti b[raccia] 7½ il simile q[ue]lli delportico lentrate delportico p[er] fianco larghe / b[raccia] 6 alte b[raccia] 10 tucti i capitelli alla dorica ogni cosa di matone / excerpte le colonne che son del travertino*; further indications of measurements in Florentine *braccia*.

BIBLIOGRAPHY: Günther 1988f: 92-97 n. 94, ill. II.49; Jobst 1992: 71 n. 165.

This drawing, the work of an unknown Italian artist active at the beginning of the sixteenth century, shows a centrally planned building, complete with measurements. A copy of this same building with measurements in *braccia fiorentine* is contained in the Michelangelo Sketchbook in the Musée Wicar in Lille (*Pluchart* 809). The project was probably drafted for a religious building in Florence. It is highly unlikely that the punctilious caption that appears on the lower half of the sheet, together with detailed measurements, elevation, and other details, refer to a merely theoretical scheme. According to Günther, the drawing, copied again in the seventeenth century derives from an original project by Simone del Pollaiuolo, called Il Cronaca (cat. no. 17); the project may be connected to Luca Landucci's plans for a church dedicated to St. John Evangelist, to be erected in the enlarged sacristy of S. Lorenzo, Florence. An entry in Landucci's diary for 20 December 1505 speaks of a sketch for the church of S. Giovanni, which he himself had entrusted to Il Cronaca. The way in which the project is presented in this copy after Il Cronaca's original reflects a practice diffuse among architects in the fifteenth century, namely, to represent the building in plan, and to personally explain to the patron the details of the elevations.
The text in the bottom half of the sheet would enable an experienced reader to form a clear idea of how the centrally planned building would look in elevation. The plan ex-

poses certain links between the references to models from antiquity and the architecture current in Florence in the fifteenth century. The Florentine accents suggest a modern project rather than a reproduction of some antique prototype. The centrally planned building is hexagonal externally, with a corona of chapels and semicircular exedrae around the perimeter; the model is clearly S. Maria degli Angeli in Florence, one of Brunelleschi's masterpieces, which in turn derives from an antique model. Internally S. Maria degli Angeli is octagonal, with sixteen sides externally; hence, here the plan has undergone modification. The spacious atrium with its colonnade terminating at the corners of the facade with angled piers draws directly on antique structures, such as the Portico of Octavia and the pronaos of the Pantheon. As in the Pantheon, the columns of the atrium are in fact in line with the main axes and semicircular niches. In this way the architect deliberately employed a feature of the Pantheon that was still much debated in the sixteenth century by both treatise-writers and architects (cat. no. 30). The draftsman's knowledge of antiquity, and his regard for certain uncanonical features of ancient architecture, are noticeable in other aspects of the design as well. The text on the lower half of the sheet, describing the elevation of the building's interior, talks of a particular type of vaulted ceiling. Taking his distance from the Florentine tradition, which favored a polygonal plan with composite groin vaults, or domical vaults reinforced with ribbing (see Brunelleschi's ceilings for the Old Sacristy and the Cappella de' Pazzi), the architect in this case opted for a hemispherical dome rising from a hexagonal base. At all events, the vaulting here has a hexagonal plan, becoming spherical toward the crown ("li anguli alzano ¼ della volta e poi diventa tonda"), as shown in the reconstruction by Hubertus Günther. Although this marks a break with Renaissance tradition, the solution could be studied directly from examples of antiquity (the so-called Tor de' Schiavi in Rome, and the octagonal halls of the Baths of Caracalla), and was a forerunner of the dome raised on pendentives. Similarly, the inscription on lines eleven and twelve on this drawing regarding brick and travertine as building material ("ogni cosa di matone, excerpte le colonne che son del travertino") is a further direct reference to ancient Roman building technology. These choices suggest an author with an incomparable ability to blend Florentine tradition with ancient Roman architecture. Given this, it is reasonable to affirm the original scheme from which this copy derives, as being the work of Il Cronaca. *C.J.*

19

BERNARDINO DELLA VOLPAIA and ANTONIO DA SANGALLO THE YOUNGER (recto) GIOVANNI BATTISTA DA SANGALLO and ANTONIO DA SANGALLO THE YOUNGER (verso)
Entablature of the Temple of Castor and Pollux (the Dioscuri)
ca. 1513

Florence, Galleria degli Uffizi, Gabinetto Disegni e Stampe,
Uff. 1181Ar.-v.
RECTO: pen and light sepia ink (Bernardino della Volpaia), pen and dark sepia ink (Antonio da Sangallo), on thick paper, incised lines.
VERSO: pen and ink; scale in Florentine *braccia, minuti*.
322 × 299 mm
INSCRIBED: (recto) *bernardo; le tre cholonne; Damezei cholonna ameza / cholonna sie b[raccia] 6 e 27 e dieci; me[n]sole 3 i[n]terni e dua meze / e dentilli 11 i[n]teri e dua mezi* (this caption together with the measurements and calculations in dark brown ink are in the hand of Antonio da Sangallo; the measurements in light brown ink are by Bernardino della Volpaia); (verso) *battista; Tre cholonne; Queste o prese 10 la cholonna / chrosa da pie b[raccia] 2 mi[nuti] 31. / La basa adochietto 29 / Da cholonna a cholonna b[raccia] 3; 55 ½; dachapo b[raccia] 2 minuti 10 la diminutione / e partita i[n] 14 dapie e 12 dachapo b[raccia] 2; 31½ / I[n] fondo la cholonna e grosa b[raccia] 2; 31½ / la base ad ochietto e grosa meta cholonna (?) b[raccia] 3; 30; di castello s[ant] anchillo* (this caption, measurements, and calculations are by Antonio).

BIBLIOGRAPHY: Bartoli 1914-22, pl. CCXXIII, figs. 380r., 381v.; Buddensieg 1975: 89-103; Günther 1988f: 165, 200, 252.

This drawing from the Uffizi collection presents an axonometric section, drawn with the help of a straightedge, showing the entablature of the Temple of Castor and Pollux (the Dioscuri), which was known during the Renaissance period as, simply, the "tre colonne" (three columns). The author of this particular section of the drawing is Bernardino della Volpaia, as indicated by a note by Antonio da Sangallo ("bernardo") penned in the frieze area. On the basis of this annotation, and on careful comparisons of this drawing with that of the Dioscuri entablature in the *Codex Coner* (fol. 69r.), Buddensieg (1975) concluded that the latter codex was the work of Bernardino della Volpaia. Alongside Volpaia's work Antonio made a second sketch of the profile of the entablature, and drew an orthogonal projection of the dentils, which he subsequently crossed out (on the question of orthogonal projections, see cat. no. 24). Antonio's main preoccupation was to note two flaws in Bernardino's drawing. Each console of the entablature rests on its own slab, giving marked emphasis to its autonomy (in Antonio's profile drawing, he marks the slab with a bold line). In the gaps between the dentils are inserted half blocks. Antonio corrected this mistake directly in Volpaia's drawing. Above Bernardo's measurements in light ink Antonio added some more in the area of the dentils and the consoles. These calculations are purely mathematical, as testified by the orthogonal projection of the dentils on the right, the caption, and the calculations on the sheet (these were studied for the first time by C.

Dittscheid in his contribution to forthcoming volume *Corpus der Sangallo Zeichnungen*). Antonio had observed the rigorous axial alignment of the individual components of the entablature. This feature of the Dioscuri entablature is still much admired by archaeologists today. Antonio tried to provide a mathematical explanation for this axiality, starting from the axes of the columns themselves (see caption) (cf. Dittscheid in *Corpus der Sangallo Zeichnungen*).

On the verso of the Uffizi drawing, Giovanni Battista da Sangallo ("battista") made a further sectional sketch of the Dioscuri entablature, this time correcting Volpaia's two mistakes. He then added detailed measurements, which he himself probably took on-site. Unlike Volpaia, Battista obtained many detailed readings for the dentils and consoles.

It seems that Bernardino della Volpaia first took the measurements directly from the Dioscuri temple, and Antonio subsequently made the adjustments according to his observations, while offering a mathematical explanation for the entablature's singularity, namely, its severe axiality. Later, Battista was sent out with Volpaia's drawing to take additional measurements. He may have been instructed to verify to what extent Antonio's calculations differed from those on the monument itself; this might explain why Antonio crossed out the sketch of the dentils. The representation of the Dioscuri entablature by Volpaia in the *Codex Coner* is in fact based on Battista's on-site measurements, and not on Antonio's set of mathematical calculations.

On the verso of the sheet, alongside the sectional study of the entablature, Battista drew a profile of the architrave, with a rough sketch of the column, capital, and first fascia, indicating the more important measurements. The lower portion of the sheet shows a profile of the plinth of Castel Sant'Angelo, as indicated by the inscription ("castel s[ant] anchillo").

The Uffizi drawing is a rare demonstration of the great pains taken to record the exact measurements of the architectural elements, so as to have a definite idea based not only on observation but also on proper measurements and the proportions of the parts. In the case of the Dioscuri temple, it is unthinkable that the measurements were not taken directly from the monument, as they correspond almost exactly with the real thing (see measurements by C. Jobst). The first methodical campaign of study on the dimensions of the ancient monuments of Rome began with the detailed site survey of the Colosseum on 24 July 1513 under the supervision of Giuliano da Sangallo. Again Günther has made an in-depth examination of the role played by Bernardino della Volpaia as draftsman and *misuratore* in Giuliano's assiduous study program of antiquity over the period 1513-15 (Günther 1988f: 199ff.).

Volpaia was born into a renowned family of engineers and constructors of machinery. It is likely that he too built mechanical devices, in addition to working as an *agrimensore* or landsurveyor. Such tasks presuppose solid training as a draftsman (Günther 1988f: 167), as superbly exemplified in the *Codex Coner*. The ultimate responsibility for surveying the monuments of antiquity doubtless lay with Antonio da Sangallo, as evidenced by this drawing from the Uffizi (Günther 1988f: 200, 252); as such, besides the keen attention to measurements and sculptural rendering, Antonio's interest in the theoretical aspects of his work is self-evident.

Ursula Kleefisch-Jobst

20
GIULIANO DA SANGALLO
Greek Temple

Florence, Galleria degli Uffizi, Gabinetto Disegni e Stampe, Uff. 131Ar.
Pen and ink, with wash, on paper.
443 × 745 mm
INSCRIBED: (verso) *Tempio grecho*.

BIBLIOGRAPHY: von Fabriczy 1902b: 96, 131; Bartoli 1914-22, pl. LXI, fig. 95; Lotz 1953-56: 210-211; Günther 1988f: 121.

This drawing executed by Giuliano da Sangallo with the aid of a straightedge and compass, shows the section of a building with a vaulted ceiling. Von Fabriczy identified the drawing as a reconstruction and conversion into a church of the central hall of the Baths of Diocletian. Lotz, however, linked the drawing to Giuliano's last projects for St. Peter's at the end of his life. The relation between the subject of the drawing and the inscription "Tempio grecho" penned on the verso has not been yet clarified. In this respect, the form of representation is of particular interest. It involves an amalgam of perspective and orthogonal projection (cat. no. 24). The central section of the building (the vaults of the *thermae*, the upper cornice of the clerestory, and the barrel-vaulted niche at the center) has been drawn in perspective, and enhanced with heavy shading. The individual elements of the elevation of the wall plane are instead drawn orthogonally, each detail with its own vanishing point. In this way the separate profiles and proportions can be clearly apprehended. The sheet bears no indications of measurement, but a scale key is provided in the bottom margin (cat. no. 33). This mixed technique affords both a generalized view of the space in question, and a detailed representation of each of the architectural features. The spatial effect, however, is provided exclusively by the vaulting. The drawing is in fact less clear toward the extremities, where the rules of orthogonal projection are more rigidly applied. It is consequently not possible to deduce a proper plan of the building shown. The "multiple perspective" (Lotz 1953-56: 211) crops up in Giuliano da Sangallo's later works and in those of Baldassarre Peruzzi (Uff. 161A). Lotz saw this mixed technique as the last stage before the use of proper orthogonal projection, as explained by Raphael in his *Memorandum* to Pope Leo X (cat. no. 22). However, "multiple perspective" is essentially another form of projection, alongside one-point perspective and orthogonal projection. The artists of the Renaissance were well aware of the limitations of both perspective and orthogonal projection (cat. nos. 24, 30).

Ursula Kleefisch-Jobst

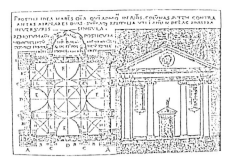

21
CESARE CESARIANO
Ancient Temples
1521

Woodcut print, on paper; from Cesariano's edition of *De architectura libri decem*, by Vitruvius.

BIBLIOGRAPHY: Soergel 1958: 82-84; Cesariano, ed. Krinsky 1969; Huse and Wolters 1975: 140-141.

In Book III of the *De architectura libri decem*, Vitruvius describes the seven basic forms of the Greco-Roman temple: *templum in antis*, prostyle, amphiprostyle, peripteral, pseudo-peripteral, dypteral, and hypaethral. In his commentary to the Como edition of 1521, Cesariano (cat. no. 28) explains the Greek concepts reported by Vitruvius and illustrated in the accompanying woodcuts, with only partial success. The plans and elevations of the *templum in antis*, the *prostylos*, and the *amphiprostylos* on fol. 52 recto and verso, are not considered by the author to represent different types of classical temple, with different relationships between the inner cella and the surrounding colonnade. Instead, Cesariano gives each of the three types a similar ground plan and arrangement, according to what in modern terms would be called a "building on a Greek cross plan surmounted by a dome"—i.e., the quincunx. This type of sacred building was borrowed for Byzantine architecture, starting in the Middle Ages in Venice (S. Giacomo di Rialto), and the Marche (S. Vittore delle Chiuse, S. Croce a Sassoferrato), and spreading to other regions of the peninsula. The characteristics of the quincunx is the square plan with four attached exedra or apses, and four piers (the so-called *baldacchino*) supporting the central dome; each of the four arms is barrel-vaulted, starting from the center and radiating outward along the main axes of the building; finally, the last feature is the set of square *baldacchini* at each junction of the arms, capped by complementary minor domes.

In the course of the fifteenth and sixteenth centuries Mauro Codussi reintroduced the domed Greek-cross plan to Venice (for example, S. Giovanni Crisostomo). The new churches signaled a revival of local tradition (Odenthal 1985: 79ff.). It is still a question of debate whether Bramante's projects for Greek-plan churches (e.g., SS. Celso e Giuliano, Rome) were *all'antica* reworkings of this basic type. The interpretation of the Greek-cross plan as an antique temple plan is only documented in the commentary on Vitruvius supplied by Cesariano, who was a pupil of Bramante.

The drawings of the plans and elevations of *templii in antis* (fol. 52r., top) and *templum prostylo* (fol. 52r., bottom), and the *amphiprostylo* (fol. 52v.), present few differences. In the case of the latter two, the diameters of the main domes, and spans of the archivolts (L), are defined by squares and concentric circles. In the case of the *templum in antis*, the concentric circles continue to the crown of the main dome. In the case of the amphiprostyle (not shown), the diameter and perimeter wall of the exedra, together with the position and breadth of the facade pillars, are mapped out in a series of squares and concentric circles emanating from the center of the plan. The *templum in antis*, and the prostyle and amphiprostyle temples are distinguishable by their general structure, and for the articulation of their facades. Instead of framing the main facade of the *templum in antis* (fol. 52r., top) with elements set slightly away from the wall plane (ante), Cesariano only slightly accentuates the *antae* or corner pillars (A) with respect to the other (B) facade orders. For the prostyle (fol. 52r., bottom), instead of a colonnaded atrium, Cesariano offers two-story projecting sections either side (elevation) and/or half-columns (plan).   *C.J.*

22

RAPHAEL, BALDASSARRE CASTIGLIONE
and UNKNOWN SCRIBE
Memorandum from Raphael to Pope Leo X
("Manuscript B")
1519-20

Munich, Bayerische Staatsbibliothek, Cod. It. 37b,
fols. 1r.-11v.
Pen and ink, on paper.

BIBLIOGRAPHY: Golzio 1936: 78-92; Castiglione 1942: 70; Shearman 1977: 137; Bonelli 1978: 461-483; Burns and Nesselrath 1984: 437, cat. 3.5.1.; Thoenes 1986: 373-381; Morolli 1984: 51 n. 70, 80 n. 93, 135 n. 143; Günther 1988f: 60ff. and 318ff.

This document, dating 1519-20, which is generally defined as a memorandum or letter, from Raphael to Pope Leo X regarding the map of ancient Rome, has survived in several versions; it describes the objectives, needs, and *modus operandi* of one of the most ambitious cognitive schemes of the entire Renaissance—the creation of a complete chart of ancient Rome, complete with texts and drawings of all its monuments.

Giovanni de' Medici, who ruled the papacy as Pope Leo X from 1513 to 1521, launched a sweeping scheme for recording the measurements of ancient Rome, and reconstructing its appearance by means of drawings. The man deemed worthy of the task was Raphael, who combined supreme artistic talent and firsthand experience of archaeology, with excellent organizational skills and a methodical work style. Raphael drew up the scheme for the map, and marshaled a group of noted scholars and architects to work alongside him.

According to contemporary sources, the map was intended to be read like a book—along the lines of Ptolemy's *Geography*—and to present a list of buildings, zone by zone. As a guide, they used a list of areas purportedly compiled by Publius Victor. Together with this general map of ancient Rome they were to include representations of individual buildings—each one shown in its topographical context—and a set of drawings showing the ancient monuments as they once stood.

These reconstructions were the main focus of interest for the historians of architecture (cat. no. 25), and were to be accompanied by theoretical writings on architecture, and historical sources. The text of Raphael's *Memorandum* has received various attributions: to Donato Bramante and Baldassarre Peruzzi, to the humanists Andrea Fulvio and Fabio Calvo. The name of Baldassarre Castiglione (1478-1529) was first suggested in the sixteenth and seventeenth centuries (by Marliani and Negrini). A version of the text

(Version A) was published by the Volpi brothers in 1733 as being by Castiglione. The printed edition was based on a manuscript in the possession of Scipione Maffei. The first to suggest Raphael was D. Francesconi. In the third volume (1858) of his monographic series on Raphael, Johann David Passavant, inspector of the Städelsches Kunstinstitut of Frankfurt and author of books on art, published a second version of the letter (known as Manuscript B), which had surfaced in Munich in 1834. A third version of the letter subsequently came to light in Mantua; it was discovered among the posthumous papers of Baldassarre Castiglione by Vittorio Cian, who recognized it to be by the hand of the former (Cian 1942: 70ff.). The Mantua manuscript is identifiable as a preliminary project for the map of Rome. The published edition (A) and the Manuscript B of Munich differ greatly. Consequently, the paternity and chronology of the different versions, and the extent of Raphael's contribution and that of Castiglione to each, has sparked much debate among scholars. Both Shearman and Thoenes drew attention to the fact that the Munich manuscript was written later than Version A, as published in 1733, and that Manuscript B is incomplete because it is a reworking of Version A. While positive identification has been made of Castiglione's contribution to the Mantua manuscript and the printed edition, it was Raphael who had the major share in the Munich version.

In recent years there has been agreement over the date of the Munich version—between summer/autumn 1519 and 6 April 1520 (the day of Raphael's death). Version A appears to date between summer/autumn 1518 and summer/autumn of the following year. In 1977, however, Shearman proposed a new date for Version A: between spring 1513 and spring 1514; Manuscript B dated to one year later. Both proposals depend on a different date for Raphael's sojourn in Rome. In 1986 Thoenes summarized the discussion and convincingly upheld the traditional date for the Munich manuscript of 1519-20. The date 1517-18 proposed by Burns and Nesselrath in 1984 for Manuscript B has so far received little consensus.

The letter to Leo X was conceived as a sort of preface to the map of ancient Rome. The best coverage of the project itself is afforded by the Mantua version discovered by Cian. References to the map of Rome appear in various sources of the time (Günther 1988f: 318ff. n. 317).

The Munich version includes two thematic features of fundamental interest: a general section on the history of architecture, and an extensive debate on technical particulars.

It opens with a tirade against the destruction of ancient buildings; this section comprises a heartfelt appeal by Leo X to safeguard the miserable remains of ancient Rome as a testament of the city's glorious past. Subsequently, Raphael discusses the task the pope had entrusted to him: "Avendimi Vostra Santità comandato che io possessi in disegno Roma antica, quando cognoscier si può per quello che oggidì si vede." By this he meant that those engaged on the project intended to inform themselves on the original form of Rome through a close study of the actual state of the city and its buildings. This is a prelude to the detailed discussion of scientific procedure that ensues in the second part of the text.

The methodical study of ancient architecture was, however, linked directly to esthetic discrimination, and as such the memorandum is a deliberate synthesis of scientific and artistic judgment. The architects of the period saw antiquity as a "model," an example ("ché avegna che a' dì nostri l'architettura sia molto svegliata, e venuta assai proxima alla maniera delli antichi, come si vede per molte belle opere di Bramante. ...").

The comparison between antiquity and the works of Bramante critically clarifies the distance between the antique model and Bramante's architecture, of which it was said, "niente di meno li ornamenti non sono di materia tanto preziosa come li antichi, che non infinita spesa par che mettessero ad effetto ciò imaginarno e che solo el volere rompesse ogni difficultate" (Bonelli 1978: 473; previous excerpts also taken from Bonelli's transcrip-

tion). While the chief requirement of Raphael and his contemporaries was for greater artistic quality—in this case with regard to decoration and materials—his personal veneration for things antique was not unreserved. The architects of antiquity, in Raphael's opinion, were also prone to the laws of excellence and decline described by Pliny the Elder, as exemplified by the Arch of Constantine: "Il componimento del quale dell'Arco di Costantino è bello e ben fatto in tutto quel che appartiene all'architettura, ma le sculture del medesimo arco sono schiocchissime, senza arte o disegno alcuno buono" (Bonelli 1978: 474). In truth, Raphael was limiting his exceptions to the reliefs and statuary added to the Arch of Constantine during the Trajan period and early second century. This differentiation between the levels of quality in architecture and sculpture offers another clue about the map of Rome: the predisposition and ability of its drafters to take a discerning view of antiquity. The critique is quite dynamic, even in the drawings of Antonio da Sangallo the Younger (cat. no. 31), and particularly noticeable in Alberti's letter to Lodovico Gonzaga. They denote a resolute departure from the idea of antiquity as the paradigm for contemporary works.

The second part of the letter in the Munich version exhibited here, which dates to 1519-20, contains a disquisition on the technique of taking measurements, the visual representation of buildings, and the various standard drafting techniques (in perspective, or in orthogonal projection).

These different issues are dealt with in other catalog entries (cat. nos. 23, 24, 30, 33, and Uff. 1602). Given the broad range of subjects discussed, one might say that Raphael's memorandum-letter to Pope Leo X embodies the artistic and scientific efforts of the architects of the Renaissance to resuscitate and restore the art and architecture of the classical world.   *C.J.*

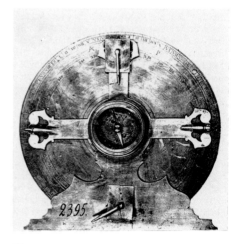

23

UNKNOWN MASTER
Graphometer
17th cent.

Rome, Osservatorio Astronomico, 136
Brass.
diam. 16.5 cm

BIBLIOGRAPHY: Calisi 1984: 446, cat. no. 3.5.16.

The "bussola della calamità" was defined by Raphael in his *Memorandum* to Pope Leo X in 1519-20 (cat. no. 22) as a scientific apparatus for measuring buildings of all kinds. Precise descriptions are given for the forms and usages of the graphometer, of which the one shown here represents a somewhat complex version; the device was a precursor of the modern surveyor's theodolite. Raphael's use of the term "bussola" (magnetic compass) is slightly misleading, as the compass itself is only one element of the graphometer which, though originally invented for navigation purposes, assumed an increasingly important role in landsurveying and cartography. Leonardo da Vinci used a "bussola" in fact when drawing up his map of Imola in 1502.

The *Memorandum* to Pope Leo X, written by Raphael in concert with Baldassarre Castiglione, underlines (cat. no. 22) the fact that the "bussola" served for measuring buildings of all types (and plans in particular), even those of irregular shape. The measuring device could even be used to study and accurately represent manifold buildings such as the Roman thermal complexes. In order to carry out the project for the map of Rome, in his *Memorandum* Raphael notes the absolute necessity of obtaining the type of measurements that could be provided by the graphometer. The adoption of geodetic methods and map-making procedures for measuring buildings signaled an important step toward creating an archaeological inventory of all the ancient monuments of Rome.

Raphael was the first to describe such methods in detail, but both Baldassarre Peruzzi and Antonio da Sangallo the Younger adopted such procedures for their building survey work (cat. no. 25). The seventeenth-century instrument shown here—very similar to the one Raphael describes in his memorandum to the pope—is composed of a circular, palm-size disk of brass in the center of which is inserted a magnetic compass. Two wing-like markers (known as "alidade") rotate around the central pivot; at the end of these are small swiveling clips for marking points in the distance and reading off the resulting angles.

One of the rotating markers widens with a concave and convex pattern toward the base, forming a stand 16 cm wide. The border of the disk is marked with a scale of 360 degrees, subdivided into 8 by 9 segments. Each of these divisions corresponds to 5 degrees. Consequently, 9 units (each marked with a Roman numeral from I to VIIII) correspond to a 45-degree segment. In turn, each segment of 45 degrees corresponds to one of the 8 prevailing winds, whose symbols (or abbreviated name) is inscribed in the second of the two concentric scales. The innermost scale repeats the 360-degree division, this time in Arabic numbers. For the survey of land or floor plans the disk is held flat; using the built-in compass, the operator first finds the north-south axis (i.e., the direction of the "tramontana" or northerly wind). The marker with the stand is aligned so that the edge of the sights is pointing toward the user and can be oriented in the required direction. The second marker is used to fix the position of a preset point of the area or building being measured.

The resulting angle between the north-south line and the axis created by the second marker can be read off on the scale. In this way the direction and extension of a wall can be accurately established. The section of the wall or object that lies between the angle is then measured. At the end, the procedure is repeated from the start, taking another fixed point on the building or area to be measured. Section by section, the complete form of the building is established, with all its dimensions and wall configurations. Raphael's *Memorandum* (cat. no. 22) describes the procedure in the following way: "Si indirizzi el traguardo [the rotating marker] con una regola di legno, o di ottone, giusto a file di quella parete, o strada, o altra cosa che si voglia misurare, lassando lo strumento fermo, acioché la calamità [i.e., the compass needle] servi el suo diritto verso tramontana. Di poi guardarsi al qual vento e a quanti gradi volta per dritta linea quella parete, la quale misurerassi con la canna o cubito o palmo, fina a quel termine che 'l traguardo porta per diritta linea e questo numero si noti: cioè tanti cubiti, a tanti gradi di ostro, o syraco [names for the south and southwest winds] o qual sia. Dippoi che 'l traguardo non serve più, per diritta linea devesi alor svolgerlo, cominciando l'altra linea, che si ha da misurare, dove termina la misurata; e così indirizandolo a quella, medeimamente notar li gradi del vento e 'l numer delle misure, fin tanto si circuisca tutto lo edificio" (Bonelli 1978: 480-479). As noted above, the "bussola" in Raphael's text resembles the device shown here, which is composed of a disk ("instrumento tondo e piano"),

showing the compass card and a built-in magnetic compass ("bussola di calamità"). Unlike the object shown here, however, Raphael's graphometer had only one rotating marker ("traguardo"), and the north-south line was determined simply by the compass needle ("calamità"). *C.J.*

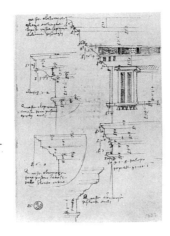

24

UNKNOWN DRAFTSMAN
(after originals by Bernardino della Volpaia and Il Cronaca)
Sketches of the Theater of Marcellus
after 1513

Florence, Galleria degli Uffizi, Gabinetto Disegni e Stampe
Uff. 1602Ar
Pen and ink on paper
214 × 145 mm

INSCRIBED: *choloseo desauegi; queste misure sono / leuate di mano di berna[r]do / della golpaia e quelle delle chornjce auemo da simo[n]e del polaiuolo; questa e la chornjce/ e frego architraue / che posa insue le prime/ cholonne de sauegli; Questa e la prima / cimasa doue posano / e primi archi; Questa e la cimasa / doue posano le base / dello sichondo ordine; Questa e la cimasa / de sichondi archi* many measurements in Florentine *braccia, soldi,* and *denari.*

BIBLIOGRAPHY: Bartoli 1914-22, pl. LXXIV, figs. 129, 130; Günther 1988f: 73-74, 82.

This drawing was originally part of the *Codex Strozzi* which passed from the Strozzi family in the eighteenth century and entered the Uffizi collections, where it is conserved in individual folios.

The drawing shows details of the Theater of Marcellus in elevation ("choloseo desauegi"), with the particulars of both orders. Of special interest is the caption penned in the left margin of the sheet; it states that the artist copied the elevations of Bernardino della Volpaia, the principal author of the *Codex Coner*, while the details are by Il Cronaca (Simone del Pollaiuolo). The verso of the sheet presents further details of the Ionic order, confirming these indications: "questa e la sichonda chornice de sauegli auuto da simone" ("this is the second cornice of the Sauegli, received from Simone"). Günther has shown that the elevation of the Theater of Marcellus must indeed be by Volpaia, as the measurements recorded tally with those in the *Codex Coner*. The subdivision of the measurements, typical of the London album, into one Florentine *braccio* and 60 *minuti*, has been converted by the Florentine author of the Uffizi sheet into Il Cronaca's customary system of 20 *soldi* of 12 *denari* each. The *Codex Coner* also contains details of the Theater of Marcellus; however, the measurements indicated do not match those of the *Codex Strozzi*. This discrepancy confirms that the second source of the sheet's author was Il Cronaca.

Of particular interest here is the type of representation adopted: the elevation is shown as a "development" (Lotz

1953-56: 220), that is, the curved main wall of the theater is represented as a flat plane. In this way all the architectural elements are represented with proper right-angles, with no perspective foreshortening whatsoever. In this drawing the artist has applied what Raphael later described in his missive to Pope Leo X as one of the three most important types of representation for understanding ancient architecture: "Di poi tra queste due linee extreme, che fanno l'altezza, si pigli la misura delle colonne, delli pilastri, delle finestre e degli altri ornamenti dissegnati nella metà dinante della pianta dello edificio; e faciasi el tutto sempre tirando, da ciascun punto delle extremitate delle colonne, pilastri, vani, o ciò che si siano, linee parallele da quelle due extreme" (Bonelli 1978: 461-483, cat. no. 22). Today this type of projection is known as "orthogonal." Unlike one-point perspective, an orthogonal projection involves a separate vanishing point for each detail represented. Lotz (1953-56: 193) described it clearly as follows: "The orthogonal view means that the parts of the building outside the sectional plane but parallel to it are drawn without foreshortening, while curved or sloping walls and vaults are drawn with the relative foreshortening on the section plane, as if the observer was in front of the part of the building at the same level as the section." In the *Codex Coner* the elevation is drawn in perspective, showing the "volume" of the building. Plasticity is one of the characteristics of the drawings in the London album. The *Codex Strozzi* is more decisively objective and realistic in its portrayal of the Theater of Marcellus. The fundamental feature is the relationship between the single architectural elements and the exact reproduction of the individual profiles of the orders, each one complemented with its various measurements—a requirement amply borne out by the extensive captions provided here. The representation of the cyma of the first order (left half of sheet) presents the limits to the clarity of orthogonal projection. The frieze on the lower part of the cornice slab would not be visible in a true orthogonal projection. In order to show this detail as well, the draftsman has tilted it upward. By means of shading he has also indicated the lower face of the slab resting on the triglyphs. Günther has gathered a series of drawings that he considers copies of lost originals by Il Cronaca. Each of these sheets are characteristic for their objective, "scientific" representation of the object. Vasari praised Il Cronaca's keen understanding of antiquity, and notes the accuracy with which the latter took the measurements of the ancient monuments, and the objectivity and exacting standards of his reproductions (Günther 1988f: 69, cat. no. 17).
Ursula Kleefisch-Jobst

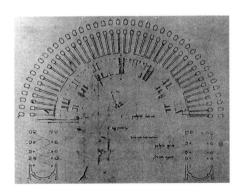

25

ANTONIO DA SANGALLO THE YOUNGER
and GIOVANNI BATTISTA DA SANGALLO
Plan and Section of the Theater of Marcellus
ca. 1518-20

Florence, Galleria degli Uffizi, Gabinetto Disegni e Stampe
Uff. 1270Av
Pen and ink, on paper; on recto, other drawings of Roman monuments
430 × 580 mm

INSCRIBED: (on right half of sheet, by Antonio da Sangallo the Younger) *Sauelli; pulpito latino; sciena latina; pulpito greco; scena greca.*

BIBLIOGRAPHY: Bartoli 1914-22, fig. 437; Frommel 1974b: 180 and ill. 93; Günther 1982-83: 12-15; 1988f: 61, 266 and ill. VII.28; 305 and ill. VII.73, 74; 377; Pochat 1990: 258.

This plan of the Theater of Marcellus in Rome, executed by Antonio da Sangallo the Younger in ca. 1518-20, combines a record of the actual state of the ruins of the building (despite their pitiful condition), with a reconstruction of the destroyed sections based on what remains together with the indication supplied by Vitruvius on the structure of theaters in Books VII and VIII of his *De architectura*. The Theater of Marcellus, constructed over the period 31-11 B.C., was used during the Middle Ages as a fort. In around 1519 Baldassarre Peruzzi built the Palazzo dei Savelli on its ruins (Frommel 1973, I: 45 n. 65); this is why the theater is labeled with the abbreviation "Sauelli" (upside-down at center of sheet).

According to Sebastiano Serlio (1540 Book III, *Libro delle antiquità di Roma*), during the construction of the new palazzo, Peruzzi took detailed measurements of the partially destroyed building, which had been built upon several times in the past.

Antonio and Giovanni Battista da Sangallo also made attentive studies of the theater ruins, despite the practical impediments to examining a building in such utter disrepair. Even in more recent archaeological studies, the indications of the stage structures are anything but certain. Hubertus Günther has convincingly identified the drawings executed by Peruzzi and the Sangallo shop representing the Theater of Marcellus, the Forum of Augustus, and the Forum Holitorium as preparatory to the map of Rome commissioned by Pope Leo X. Raphael, who in the period 1519-20 was the director and coordinator of this grandiose archaeological undertaking, was assisted by a pool of scholars and architects (cat. no. 22). The latter group included above all Antonio da Sangallo and Baldassarre Peruzzi. Their drawings of the Theater of Marcellus, completed in the main around 1518-20, correspond most evidently with the goals set out by Raphael in his *Memorandum* on the map of Rome.

One of the cardinal features of the enterprise outlined in the *Memorandum* was the reconstruction of the original buildings on the basis of their remains. This objective was met in the present plan of the Theater of Marcellus on Uff. 1270 verso. The outer face of the theater, and the radial walls around the *orchestra* supporting the *cavea* (stepped seating) have been drawn in a semicircle, though little in fact remains of the part in question. The position and the direction of the parts could be completed and hence reconstructed, even though most of the building lay in ruins, and had in many places been covered by other buildings added at a later date; the field measurements were taken with the aid of the *bussola* or graphometer (cat. no. 23) described by Raphael in the *Memorandum*. Thanks to this device it was also possible to reconstruct the two colonnaded *basilicae* with their terminating apses, situated either side of the stage. The parts of the building fanning around the *orchestra* are so destroyed that their shape is only sketched in places.

As for the stage section, time has obliterated it completely. Sangallo's decision to mark out at least the position and extension of the original *pulpitum* (forestage) and *scaena* (stage proper) according to Vitruvius' indications was not prompted by a concrete requirement alone; he clearly wanted to show how closely Vitruvian theory tied in with the actual building practices applied in ancient Rome, and stated as much in his foreword (1531) to a proposed 1539 edition of Vitruvius (Giovannoni 1959: 395-397).

Instead of taking the "circle" of Vitruvius' theater as the outer limit of the *cavea* and of the entire monument (see cat. no. 27)—as intended by Fra Giocondo, Cesare Cesariano (cat. no. 28) and by most contemporary architects and theoreticians—Antonio drew links exclusively between the "circle" and the perimeter of the semi-

circular *orchestra* in the theater's midst. This is endorsed by the circle that has been inscribed around the *orchestra* on the original sheet, and clarified by the drawings exhibited here, on which I have traced out the structure of the Greek and Roman theaters as described by Vitruvius. In his drawing of the building's plan, Sangallo's captions indicate the alternative design of the two types of stage, Greek and Roman. The different position, and the limit between *pulpitum* and *scaena* in Greek and Roman (marked "latino") derives from the fact that, according to Vitruvius (Book V, vii) the circle of the Greek theater contained three squares, each with a separate orientation; the lower side of one of these determined the position and alignment of the "pulpito greco," while the limit of the "scena greca" is always tangent to the circle drawn around the center of the *orchestra*. In the Roman theater, however (Vitruvius, Book V, viii), the "pulpito latino" and the "scena latina" lie further toward the semicircular auditorium; the *orchestra* at the foot of the stepped seating is considerably reduced in size.

Although for this reconstruction of the Theater of Marcellus Sangallo took his cue from Vitruvius—witness the circle inscribing only the *orchestra*, and the scattered annotations on the plan—it must be noted that the lines inscribed inside the circle of the *orchestra* do not demarcate the triangular constructions described by Vitruvius for the theater; consequently, Sangallo's inscribed line represents in effect a modification of the Vitruvian scheme.

Below the drawing of the plan is a small section of the tunnels of the Theater of Marcellus; here a third floor has been added over the existing two, and a small scale key, albeit with no indication of the units used.   *C.J.*

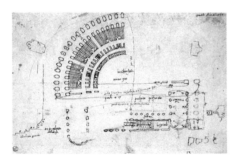

26

GIOVANNI BATTISTA DA SANGALLO
and ANTONIO DA SANGALLO THE YOUNGER
The Theater of Marcellus

Florence, Galleria degli Uffizi, Gabinetto Disegni e Stampe
Uff, 626Ar
Pen and ink, on paper
250 × 390 mm
INSCRIBED: (recto, G. B. da Sangallo) *delcuiseo grande; p[iedi] 4¹/9 altutto / dallabasa* (Colosseum); *teatro di marcello; lorchestra; vano 194; dalla finestra delpol... [?] aldifuora pie 307; piedi 417; pulpito proscenio; piedi trecentosesantaquattro; aula regia / sala regia hospitali* (Theater of Marcellus); (verso) *lultima misura; dalla finestra del gallinaro [?] al difuora* (G.B. da Sangallo); *sauellj* columns of figures in Antonio's hand; other measurements

BIBLIOGRAPHY: Bartoli 1914-22, fig. 529; Frommel 1974b: 181 (mistakenly marked as Uff. 626v.); Günther 1988f: 260 and ill. 19, 305, 377 (as Uff. 626v.); Pochat 1990: 258 and ill. 182, 271 (as 626v.)

The drawing of the plan of the Theater of Marcellus in Uff. 626A recto has been attributed to Giovanni Battista, brother of Antonio da Sangallo the Younger. The drawing was executed over preparatory incised lines made with a straightedge and compass, but only the left half of the plan—gone over with sepia ink—follows the incised underdrawing; whereas the drawing of the stage section

(only partly rendered) with its *basilicae* or foyers either side of the stage, and the scattered architectural details, are all sketched freehand. The indications of length in *piedi (antichi?)* stem from fieldwork in which Antonio da Sangallo probably took part; his hand is recognizable in the sketch of a temple front, and the columns of figures on the verso of the sheet.

While the stage has been drawn freehand, and the plan rendered somewhat inaccurately, there is an evident correlation with the plan (cat. no. 27) reproduced in Sebastiano Serlio's Book III, *Libro delle antiquità di Roma* (1540). As in Serlio, the *scaena* is placed at the same level as the beginning of the exedra of the *basilicae* (plan, at right). At either side of the stage stand the *hospitalia*, though only the right half of the stage is in fact drawn (for more on the *hospitalia*, see cat. no. 28). In the center lies the area defined as *aula regia* or *sala regia*, with a staircase either side (also not completed symmetrically in the drawing). This sequence of rooms matches those in Serlio's woodcut. From all these parallels one may reasonably surmise that Giovanni Battista's drawing (and other sheets too) served as models for Serlio.

If this was the case for Serlio's interpretation of Vitruvius' Roman theater, then also the drawing of the building's plan in Uff. 626A recto was aimed at determining the location and extension of the destroyed stage section of the Theater of Marcellus, in compliance with the Vitruvian guidelines for Roman stage construction, with a large base circle encompassing the *cavea*, and containing large equilateral triangles (as in Serlio's interpretation). This arrangement entails a greater distance between the rows of seating and the front edge of the stage; in Antonio da Sangallo's version (cat. no. 25) that distance was inferior, as he had chosen a smaller circle, encompassing the *orchestra*. It is also worth noting here that, in his reconstruction of a Roman theater in Sulpicio's edition of Vitruvius (Rome, Biblioteca Corsiniana, Inc. 50, f. 1, fol. 57r.) Giovanni Battista da Sangallo opted for a large base circle, encompassing the *cavea*, and therefore taking a distance from the ideas of his brother Antonio.   *C.J.*

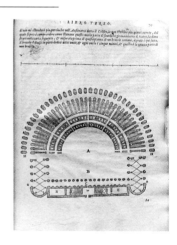

27

SEBASTIANO SERLIO
Plan of the Theater of Marcellus
1540

Venice, Biblioteca Marciana, 43.D.16.2
Woodcut print on paper, from Book III, *Libro delle antiquità di Roma*

BIBLIOGRAPHY: Günther 1988f: 305-308 and ill. VII.75 and VII. 76, 377; Pochat 1990: 270-274

The previous catalog entry (cat. no. 26) noted the links between the plan of the Theater of Marcellus drawn by Giovanni Battista da Sangallo (Uff. 626Ar.), and the woodcut in Book III of Serlio's treatise on architecture. From the woodcut, and from the accompanying drawing of the structural principles of the theater, one can see Serlio's concept of the construction of the Roman theater as indicated in Book V of Vitruvius' *De architectura*, an idea that may perhaps be traced back to Giovanni Battista. In Serlio's plan, the base circle, described by Vitruvius (Book V, vii) as the starting point for reconstructing the whole complex, encompasses the entire surface area of the building, including the *cavea* with its semicircular facade and the stage section; a subsequent increase in size is also noted for the three inscribed triangles prescribed by Vitruvius for the construction of the Roman theater, a feature that also delimits the edges of the stage. On this question, Serlio and Giovanni Battista da Sangallo (cat. no. 26) agree with most sixteenth-century architectural theorists. For his part, however, Antonio da Sangallo the Younger (cat. no. 25) reached different conclusions for the construction of the theaters of antiquity. In his complementary text, Serlio attributes the fieldwork on the area exclusively to Peruzzi, who took the measurements when he was commissioned to build the Palazzo Savelli (Serlio actually misnames the building "casa Massimi"). Serlio, however, took part in the survey work. Peruzzi's role in the undertaking was considerable; indeed, the bulk of information upon which the reconstruction of the Theater of Marcellus is based was in fact Peruzzi's doing. Serlio evidently received his data from Sangallo's circle. In his description of the plan, Serlio only occasionally uses Vitruvius' Latin terminology (which at times stems from Greek) relative to the components of the Roman theater. He replaces *orchestra* with "piazza del teatro," and the *proscaenium* before the *scaena* (letter B) becomes "piazza della scena." *C.J.*

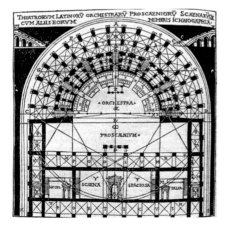

28
CESARE CESARIANO
Plan of "Latin" Theater
1521

Woodcut, print on paper, from Cesariano's edition of *De architectura libri decem*, by Vitruvius, fols. 81v. and 82r

BIBLIOGRAPHY: Cesariano, ed. Krinsky 1969; Günther 1988f: 303-304, and fig. VII.70; Pochat 1990: 260-266, and fig. 186-187.

Cesare Cesariano (1483-1543) trained under the painter-architects Leonardo da Vinci and Donato Bramante, and earned widespread·fame with his vernacular edition of Vitruvius' famous treatise *De architectura*, which he worked on from 1513 and finally had published in 1521 by Gottardo da Ponte in Como. For his new edition, augmented with a set of explanatory texts and relative woodcut illustrations, Cesariano drew on earlier sources, such as Fra Giocondo's own edition of Vitruvius, first printed in 1511 in Venice (though Cesariano may have only been in possession of the economic edition published in Florence by Filippo Giunta). There is no documentary evidence to back up Vasari's comment that Cesariano sojourned in Rome (Vasari 1878-85 IV: 149; VII: 490); it seems fairly likely that Cesariano never actually saw Rome's monuments firsthand.

Theater structures are first discussed by Cesariano on fol. 75 of his commentary. The plan of the Greco-Roman theater is presented in two versions. Fol. 75 verso affords a line drawing detailing Vitruvius' description of the structure of the Roman theater, complete with its typical location, arrangement of rooms and facilities; letters in Roman and Greek index the various features to their relative sections in the commentary. Fol. 8 verso shown here contains a high-contrast woodcut reproduction of the theater plan. The wedges of the *cavea* with its stepped seating fanning around the *orchestra*, and the walls of the stage, are all cut heavily into the wooden matrix. Over this, in finer lines, Cesariano has etched in the structure described by Vitruvius, consisting of a base circle and four equilateral triangles. Cesariano follows the same reasoning as most sixteenth-century architectural theorists and commentators on Vitruvius: the base circle indicated by Vitruvius (V, vii) for mapping out the plan of the Latin (i.e., Roman) theater applies to the outer perimeter of the entire theater—namely, the curved external wall encircling the *cavea* (see also cat. no. 27) and not, as Antonio da Sangallo perceived it, as delimiting the circumference of the *orchestra* (cf. cat. no. 25). The increase in size of the base circle means increasing the four equilateral triangles also, and a greater distance between the points of intersection. As a consequence, the *proscaenium* is likewise enlarged and in the present illustration covers barely more than half of the plan. In this respect Cesariano's reconstruction concurs with that of Fra Giocondo.
Some of the individual parts of the building are defined by captions ("orchestra," "podium," "proscenium," etc.); others are marked with Greek or Latin letters that correspond with sections of the commentary on fols. 81-82. For example, the small elevation of a tabernacle doorway marked "B" in the plan of the "scena spaciosa" is defined in the finely printed commentary on fol. 82 as "valva seu porta Regie," i.e., the royal palace gate; the orators' tribune (labeled "pulpito") in the semicircle of the *orchestra*, marked with a "Z," is an addition of Cesariano's. Vitruvius assigns the term *pulpitum proscaenii* to the central part of the stage only. As in Vitruvius (V, vii), the senatorial seats ("sedia de li Senatori"), marked "x" and "y," are situated in the orchestra (see also cat. no. 34). One of the main features of Cesariano's edition of Vitruvius is the appeal and clarity of the page layout: the vernacular translation of Vitruvius' Latin text is printed in large characters, with titles and drop capitals to open each section, whereas the commentary itself is printed in small, dense type; the woodcuts themselves, while simplified, are of outstanding quality. *C.J.*

29
RAPHAEL
Interior of the Pantheon
ca. 1506-07

Florence, Galleria degli Uffizi, Gabinetto Disegni e Stampe
Uff. 164Ar
Pencil and mixed sepia inks, on white paper
278 × 404 mm
INSCRIBED: *panteon*

BIBLIOGRAPHY: Geymüller 1870: 80, 84; Bartoli 1914-22, pl. LXIV, fol. 99; Lotz 1953-56: 218-220; Buddensieg 1968: 68-69;

Sherman 1977: 109-117; Frommel 1984d, nos. 3, 2, 4; Ferino Pagden 1984b: 323-327, cat. no. 23; Nesselrath 1986b: 358.

Ever since its first publication by H. V. Geymüller in 1870, this Uffizi sheet showing the interior of the Pantheon on the recto, and the pronaos on the verso, has been generally considered the work of Raphael.
This view of the Pantheon's interior must have soon become known by Raphael's contemporaries, as copies of the drawing exist in abundance. One such copy is contained in the *Codex Escurialensis*. The codex was purchased in Rome between 1506 and 1508 by Rodrigo de Mendoza, and by early 1509 was already circulating in Spain. Raphael's drawing must therefore have been executed before this. Shearman, who analyzed the Uffizi drawing in depth, suggested that Raphael drew the Pantheon between 1506 and 1507. It has yet to be established whether the Uffizi sheet is a copy Raphael made from another drawing, which in turn served as the model for the later copies (Oberhuber, in Ferino Pagden).
Shearman maintained that Raphael was not the only author of the present sheet, but that it was finished off by another artist, whose *ductus* is quite distinct from that of the former, and who used a different ink. For Ferino Pagden, the difference originates in two phases of execution. Shearman has ventured an explanation for the particular manner of representation: it stems from the diversity of style between the two artists. The drawing adopts perspective technique for the elevation of the wall between the main niche and the entrance, and hence attempts to portray a full half of the building. However, the artist has chosen a viewpoint from which it is technically impossible to see everything that is represented. Hence he has left out a quarter of the wall structure: a second columned recess is missing, together with an aedicule with segmental pediment. Shearman is convinced that Raphael drew the interior on-site. The drawing includes a stretch of the wall of the exedra as far as the second colonnaded curved niche, in some places simplifying the details. A second artist must, in Shearman's view, have completed this drawing, using another drawing by Raphael (now lost), showing the other quarter of the wall plane, including the entrance section. It was, therefore, the second artist who adopted the unorthodox viewpoint, making the elevation similar to a view. Alternatively, as Lotz tried to prove (Lotz 1953-56: 219), the artist deliberately wanted to create a partially "distorted" view—partly to represent the building as it would look to an observer standing inside the building, and partly to provide an accurate record of the elevation from an unusually close viewpoint. For the first time, after a century of attempts by Raphael's predecessors, the architectural space of a historical building was drawn in such a way that the observer seems to be inside it (Buddensieg 1968: 68). The two interior views of the Pantheon in the *Codex Coner* (Ashby nos. 35, 36), clearly show that half of the building can be reproduced in full if the hypothetical observation point is higher and outside the building. In this way, however, it is no longer possible to convey the sense of space, nor a precise image of the architectural elements, owing to the accentuated foreshortening. Raphael's drawing is a kind of watershed between two techniques: one-point perspective (as in the two views in the *Codex Coner*) and orthogonal section, as described by Raphael in his *Memorandum* to Leo X (Lotz 1953-56: 219, cat. no. 22). No draftsman before Raphael—nor for that matter long after him—managed to convey such spatial illusion. The many copies made during this period, some of which imitating the *ductus* of the original, are an outspoken testimony of the widespread admiration for the effect created by the drawing, and of the many attempts to fathom how such an effect was achieved.

Ursula Kleefisch-Jobst

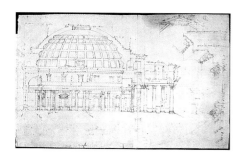

30
**BALDASSARRE PERUZZI**
The Pantheon
1531-1535

Ferrara, Biblioteca Comunale Ariostea, MS. Classe I, no. 217
Pencil and sepia ink, on paper; measurements used include
Florentine *braccia* and *minuti*.
279 × 427 mm

INSCRIBED, on Pantheon section: *74 m. 20 el tucto* (in frieze of
upper order); *clausa* (in window of upper order); *tucto el vano /
alto b. 73 m. 12* (between two windows of upper order); *di
porfido* (in frieze of lower order and on panels between capitals
of lower order); *serpe[n]tino* (in segmental pediment of left
aedicule); *strie 24 / strie 9* (number of flutes in columns and
pillars); *m. 20 / alza el pavimento* (on pavement); *questa no[n] ve*
(on pillar added by Peruzzi to the entrance portal pier)
antepagm[en]to (on inner pillar near entrance portal); *porta* (on
inner pillar near door); *vacuo* (in space above entrance portal);
fastigio piu / antiquo de op[er]a / lateritia (in vestibule pier
cornice); *misurata p[er] br[accia] fiorent[n]jno* (over portico); *era
volta a bocte alcunj credono che fusse di metallo* (over architrave
of vestibule); *ornata di figure di metallo* (alongside portico
tympanum); on sketch of roof truss: *Incanalatura di bro[n]za /
doppie tavole di metallo*; on pronaos entablature: *misurata con
palmo romano p[ar]tito in 12 e ogni...?*; *cornjce dela porta di
pantheon*; on sketch of entrance portal: *porta*

BIBLIOGRAPHY: Burns 1966: 251; Günther 1988f: 243, 257

This sheet, which shows a section and various details of
the Pantheon on the recto, and a plan of the Arena of Verona on the verso, is part of the Ferrara municipal library
collections. In 1965-66 the drawing was convincingly attributed by Burns to Peruzzi. Originally, the drawing may
have been part of a set of studies of antiquity carried out
by Peruzzi over the period 1531-35. The other sheets of
this set are currently in the Uffizi. Alongside the section
of the Pantheon are several studies of architectural details: an elevation of the entrance portal, a cutaway view
of the entablature of the portal, and at the top a sketch of
the roof trusses of the pronaos with its beams decorated
with bronze. In the lower margin Peruzzi sketched a
garland of fruit copied from the panels flanking the entrance, and also a section of the columns to show the fluting. Alongside this sketch, Peruzzi made a written note
that the columns had 24 grooves and the pillars 9.
For the section, Peruzzi chose the central axis (running
from the entrance to the main exedra), as used in many
previous drawings; in this way he could cover both the interior and the pronaos, and thereby demonstrate the relationship between the two parts.
Peruzzi traced the main contours of the building with the
aid of a straightedge and compass, adding the details freehand. The section is an orthogonal projection (cat. no.
24), thus avoiding the use of foreshortening and perspective. However, this approach is not entirely possible with
centrally planned buildings (as the drawing here demonstrates). In this case, one of the projecting columns of the
central niche obscures part of the neighboring aedicule,
thereby conveying the sense of the building's curvature.
Similarly, the coffering along the central axis and at the
entrance is foreshortened to emphasize the curvature of
the vault. Everywhere else the representation is rigorously orthogonal, enabling a precise reading of measurements
and the proportions of the parts—particularly the

heights. The measurements are given in Florentine *braccia*, subdivided into *minuti*, a unit used throughout the
Codex Coner and by the Sangallo circle (Günther 1988f:
174-175). Peruzzi nonetheless indicated the dimensions
of the entablature in Roman *palmi*, and the height of the
frieze in *braccia*. This difference in units suggest that
Peruzzi's indications are not based only on his own measurements, but that he used those recorded by others as
well, or took them from other drawings.
Peruzzi's section of the Pantheon is purely analytical.
Owing to its orthogonal projection, the drawing is devoid
of the sculptural and spatial elements that so distinguish
the work of Raphael and the two interior views of the Pantheon of the *Codex Coner* (cat. no. 29). The "scientific" intent pursued by Peruzzi in his drawing is endorsed by the
comprehensive use of captions based on assiduous observation *in situ*. For example, Peruzzi noted that the floor
level rose toward the center of the building ("m 20 alza il
pavimento"). Like some of his contemporaries, he believed the Pantheon to have been erected in phases. He
considered the block linking the main body with the pronaos the oldest part in brick ("fastigio più antiquo de
op[er]a lateritia").
In this drawing Peruzzi has "corrected" a structural detail
to conform with his own canons: in the vestibule linking
the entrance to the interior, he has added a pillar in the
corner nearest the entrance in correspondence with the corner pier in the passageway toward the rotunda. He marked
the innovation with the words "questo no[n] ve" ("this is
not there"). Like Volpaia in the *Codex Coner*, Peruzzi did
not draw in the order of pilasters of the upper story, and
chose to align the windows exactly with the frames of the
coffering. It is doubtful whether this is a deliberate critique of this particular feature of the building, as there are
no comments to the effect.
If Peruzzi's view is compared with that of Raphael, the
importance of orthogonal projection to the artists of the
Renaissance is plain to see. It made possible an exacting,
analytical representation on which all the building's features could be precisely measured, together with their
relative proportions. This was how Raphael described it
in his *Memorandum* to Leo X (cat. no. 22). In the second
version ("Manuscript B" in Munich), Raphael put perspective and orthogonal projection on the same level,
making them equal. The reason for this can be understood
from the two drawings in question. Only the perspective
drawing communicates any real sense of space. However,
Raphael claimed that both techniques were important for
comprehending an ancient building, and that these should
be combined with a floor plan.

Ursula Kleefisch-Jobst

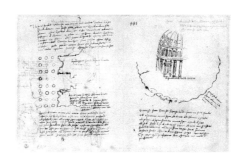

31
**ANTONIO DA SANGALLO THE YOUNGER**
Critical Studies of the Pantheon
ca. 1535

Florence, Galleria degli Uffizi, Gabinetto Disegni e Stampe
Uff. 874Ar
Pen and ink, on paper
29 × 43 cm
INSCRIBED: (recto, Antonio da Sangallo) *i[n] lo portico della
rito[n]da sie uno erore quale avoluto imitare lo te[m]pio / pseudo

*dittero cioe falso alato e levare via lo secondo ordine delle / colonne
e fare loportico di largeza di due i[n]- tercolunnij e di una / grosseza
di colonna e affatto una nichia dovera lecolone / levate ela colonna
della faccia delporticho ascontro alle levate / e restata batte i[n]
mezo lanichia come quisotto apare cosa p[er] / nitiosa quale poteva
evitare come qui si dimostrera / luno elaltro eprima come sta
alpreze[n]te i[n]opera sta come qui sotto; le pu[n]tteggiate sono le
colonne levate; Le pu[n]tteggiate sono le colonne levate / poteva
stare come qui / elopilastro segnate B poteva stare / cosi e no[n]
i[n]pediva lo i[n]tercolunnio / e risaltare qua[n]to e la diminui /
tione della colonna cioe lar / chitrave; Apresso di dentro cie uno
altro erore chene partorisce molti/ e questo sie che li pilastrie
ecolonne no[n]so espartiti parime[n]ti / e li pilastri disopra no[n]
ve[n]go[n]o sopra aquelli disotto ni le... (?) li spa/rtire parime[n]ti e
cosi quelli pettorali dellavolta delle sfo[n]dati / no[n] correspondono
sopra alli pilastri e posano sopra livani delle / finestre cosa
p[er]nitiosissima che selli avessi partito le colonne e pi/lastri
parime[n]ti no[n] lisaria venuti questi i[n]co[n]venie[n]ti ma tutti /
p[er]fettame[n]te sariano collocati come qui si dimo[n]strera; Se
avesse fatto come sta, i[n] questa ba[n]da sarieno stati quadri / 48 e
sarieno venuti sopra alli diritti delle colonne o pilastri / eli pilastri
di sopra sarieno venuti sopra aquelli di sotto / elli sodi sopra li sodi
eli vani sopra livani una p[er] rispetto / chelli i[n]tercolunnij no[n]
venissino troppo stretti saria ne/cesario farla alqua[n]to di maggiore
corpo ma averia/ i[n] se una gra[n] perfetione dove alprexente vi e
molti i[n] / perfetione; (on the plan and elevation, right-hand
section) pettorali; Li quadri della rito[n]da sono 28; questo sodo
viene / sopra al vano delle / finestre e i[n]tercolu/nnio.*
VERSO: Pantheon niches, and a project for the Corpus Domini
chapel for S. Maria sopra Minerva.

INSCRIBED: *Riformatione della ritonda / p[er] correggiere li falsi sono
/ i[n] ditto edifitio; Errori nella ritonda da / corregersi prima nelle /
capele quelle di dentro / Li mezi pilastri segnati A / sono falsi
p[er]che entrono / i[n] lo intercolunnio si possono / coregere come
li sotto scritti; questo e falso; poteua fare cosi e dire perfetto come B
e C; poteua fare cosi e dire ancora perfetto; (in the chapel plan)
p[er] lo corpus domini / della minerua.*

BIBLIOGRAPHY: Bartoli 1914-22, fig. 414; Buddensieg 1971: 265
and ill. 3a; 1973

Antonio da Sangallo the Younger made several detailed
drawings of the Pantheon, a building that was held in the
utmost esteem in the Middle Ages for its sheer size, its architectural conception, its use of elements, and not least
for its remarkable state of conservation. Despite all this,
the building was considered "imperfect" relative to the esthetic canons of the Renaissance. The obscure, transgressive characteristics which Renaissance observers perceived in the Pantheon aroused a great deal of thought. It
was considered that the building was the work of several
architects at work in ancient Rome; this was the only way
to account for the lack of adherence to the classical canons
(cat. no. 30).
Sangallo, however, took an altogether different approach.
In Uff. 874A he tried above all to capture the state of the
building and what he felt to be its underlying architectural
conception, by means of drawings and comments; this
done, he hazarded some "adjustments" to both plan and
elevation. Sangallo had already made similar "corrections" to other buildings, antique and contemporary. The
detachment with which he went about his critique of ancient architecture—often with the aid of the architectural
theories of Vitruvius—can be witnessed in many of his
drawings, which have much in common with similar
studies effected by Raphael on the architecture and decoration of the Arch of Constantine (cat. no. 22). The critique of architecture, often coupled with a critique of antiquity in general, did not actually begin with Raphael or
Antonio da Sangallo (cf. studies by Tilmann Buddensieg),
but some time later, in around 1520, by means of drawings and commentaries of considerably clarity. Fine examples of such documentary work are Raphael's
Memorandum and the present drawing from the Uffizi.
This sheet is an important document to this effect, and
contains a clear itemization of all the extant parts of the
building, with an overview of the architectural concept,
and an accompanying critique.

The left half of the recto shows the plan of the Pantheon; to the right, laid alongside each other in a circle, three horizontal sections illustrating the different levels of the building, together with an elevation of the inside and dome, showing five segments of the coffering. The drawings are executed freehand, with lengthy explanatory texts.

The verso of the sheet contains three drawings in plan of the Pantheon's rectangular recesses; these are also accompanied by extensive commentaries. The other drawings on the verso—a plan and elevation of the inside of the Cappella Corpus Domini for S. Maria sopra Minerva, as indicated by the captions—enables us to date the sheet to ca. 1535, when Sangallo is known to have designed such a chapel (according to Ursula Kleefisch-Jobst; for the date, see also Buddensieg 1971: 226 n. 1).

The plan of the Pantheon's entrance shows the precise position of the columns of the pronaos, the back walls of the same, and the area of the entrance chamber. The columns supporting the gabled roof of the pronaos are associated by Sangallo with the pseudodipteral temple, as noted in the caption ("pseudo dittero cioe falso a lato"). According to Vitruvius (III, ii), the dipteral temple has two rows of the columns on all sides of the cella. The pseudodipteral temple, while having the double row of columns on the pronaos, has only one row of freestanding columns flanking the cella either side, and another row of half-columns engaged to the cella walls themselves. Here, Sangallo equates the three-deep colonnade with those of the dipteral and pseudodipteral temples; in this he has misinterpreted Vitruvius.

The "missing" columns of the second and third rows of the pronaos are marked by a dotted line in his plan; he sustains, moreover, that one of the architects removed them to flesh out the pronaos. With this Sangallo is making a clear distinction between the building as it stood in his day, and what he considered to be the original design (a pseudodipteral temple); this opinion is reflected in both commentary and technical drawings, by which he distinguishes the actual columns from those he considered would be necessary to complete the building as planned.

In Sangallo's own words, it is a "pernicious mistake" ("cosa p[er]niciosa") that the two pronaos columns alongside the corner columns are aligned with the semicircular niches flanking the entrance. In the upper part of the plan Sangallo has documented the pronaos niche as it is; in the lower part, however, the niche has been walled up, with a central pilaster in line with the corresponding column at the front of the pronaos. Meanwhile, the corresponding inner corner element alongside what used to be the niche has been crossed out, "corrected" from an L-shaped pier to a simple cantoned pillar. This detail is marked B in the drawing, and commented in full, saying that these corner pillars must taper upward, like columns, and that the architrave over the pillars should be correspondingly set back. In this way, the pronaos plan offers two contrasting versions of the design, in juxtaposition, a system used regularly by Sangallo to underline the difference of contents and intentions of his drawings.

The remaining drawings and comments on the recto of the sheet concern the interior of the Pantheon. One of the features of the Pantheon that aroused admiration and criticism among Renaissance architects was the fact that the columns and pilasters of the ground story are not vertically aligned with the pilasters of the attic story and the buttresses ("pettorali") between the coffering ("sfondati"). None of the Renaissance critics managed to equal the rigorous reworking of the interior elevation accomplished by Antonio da Sangallo the Younger in this sheet. Here, the columns and pilasters of the lower story are locked in a system of unrelenting symmetry with the buttresses and coffers, right to the crown of the dome. Small recesses have been inserted between the load-bearing elements (columns, pillars and rib buttressing) and the aedicules of both stories, continuing up through the coffered vault to the crown. In these studies of the Pantheon's plan, as in his comments on the verso of the sheet, Sangallo discusses

the volumetric ratios and the axial relationships of the orders across the front of the recesses, together with the pilasters at the back of them. Buddensieg's careful comparison of this "corrected" version of the Pantheon (and the interior elevation in particular) and the typically Gothic alignment of the bays and elements, has shown how Sangallo's "obsession for alignment" (Buddensieg 1973) is resoundingly uninspired.

Sangallo eschews any thought of merging old and new, as his critique of the Pantheon shows. Inasmuch as he sharpens his critical acumen of the building, he forfeits his artistic input: he has misguidedly abandoned the original "model" of antiquity, with its virtually inexhaustible repertory of forms and idea, in favor of a patently scholastic, doctrinaire outlook.   *C.J.*

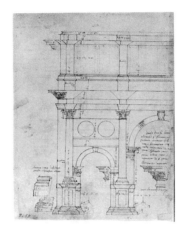

32

Antonio da Sangallo the Younger
(after Giancristoforo Romano)
The Arch of Constantine

Florence, Galleria degli Uffizi, Gabinetto Disegni e Stampe, Uff. 2055Av.
Pen and ink, on paper; measurements in Florentine *braccia, once, minuti.*
280 × 205 mm
Inscribed: *Larcho d[i] trasi fum / isurato p[er] Giouani cri / stofano romano chollo b / racco fiorentino elq / ale e ripartito in 20 / parte chiamate once / euna di dete once e / ripartita in 8 parte / chiamate minuti; el vano intra la cholona / tonda al pilastro on[ce] 14.*

Bibliography: Bartoli 1914-22, pl. ccxcviii, fig. 488; Günther 1988f: 142-143.

The sheet offers a drawing in elevation of the Arch of Constantine, with details of the cornices and column bases and pedestals. The author, Antonio da Sangallo, has noted in the margin that it was a copy of a drawing by Giancristoforo Romano. The inscriptions give detailed indications of the basic unit of measurement (Florentine *braccio*) and its subdivisions. Günther considers the division of the *oncia* into 8 *minuti* unorthodox (Günther 1988f: 145); the system is in fact a peculiarity of the drawings of Giancristoforo Romano, none of whose autograph works has survived. Günther has assembled a set of drawings, some from the Biblioteca Nazionale Centrale in Florence (codices II-I-429) and some from the so-called *Codex Kassel*, all of which he retains to be the work of Giancristoforo Romano.

Reputedly born ca. 1460, Romano's main works included the sarcophagus of Gian Galeazzo Visconti in the Certosa of Pavia, and the funeral monument (destroyed) of S. Osanna Andreasi in Mantua. Romano was a man of some learning, versed in Latin, and an artist of divers interests who frequented the courts of the most important princes on the peninsula. His advice was widely considered essen-

tial for the purchase of antique sculpture. He was among the first to be able to examine the *Laocoön*, which was unearthed in 1506. It is not clear why Pope Julius II summoned him to Rome. Romano died in May 1512 at Loreto, where he had been working as an architect since 1510 (Günther 1988f: 142-143).

In this context, what most interests us is the representation of the Arch of Constantine. The technique of the representation is orthogonal (cat. no. 24), except for two small details: the bases of both pedestals continue back into the arch, lending a sense of depth to the entire construction. In contrast with the sheet by Giuliano da Sangallo (cat. no. 20), here the orthogonal projection predominates. It is not a drawing of an interior space, but an elevation of a building with rigorously defined facades. The use of orthogonal projection for this elevation of the Arch of Constantine offers a precise rendering of the architectural and sculptural detail, forgoing vanishing lines and perspective; it also makes it possible to correlate the different proportions of the various profiles. "E perché el modo del dissegnar," wrote Raphael in his *Memorandum* to Leo X, "che più si appartiene allo architecto è differente da quel del pictore, dirò qual mi pare conveniente per intendere tutte le misure e sapere trovare tutti li membri delli edifici senza errore" (Bonelli 1978: 461, 483, 480). Raphael goes on to explain in detail the procedure involved in orthogonal projection, and ranks it alongside perspective technique as the most important system for comprehending the monuments of antiquity (cat. no. 22). Lotz attributed the development of orthogonal projection to Antonio da Sangallo (Lotz 1953-56: 216). The technique, however, can be found in the drawings of Giuliano da Sangallo before him (cat. no. 20), together with those of Il Cronaca (cat. no. 24), and—as this sheet amply demonstrates—in the work of Giancristoforo Romano. In the drawings attributed to Unknown Italian Master C of 1519, the technique of orthogonal projection is coherently used throughout in the manner explained by Raphael in his *Memorandum* to Pope Leo X (cat. no. 33).

Ursula Kleefisch-Jobst

33

Master C
The Arch of Constantine
1519

Vienna, Graphische Sammlung Albertina, *Skizzenbuch des Italieners C*, Egger 1r
Pen and sepia ink, on paper; measurements in *piede antico, once* scale key of *25 piedi* in lower margin of sheet
270 × 197 mm
Inscribed: *1519* (upper margin, trimmed)

Bibliography: Egger 1903: 13; Buddensieg 1962: 44, cat. 11; 1968: 68 n. 82; Valori 1985a: 76-78; Nesselrath 1984: 439-440, cat. nos. 3, 5, 7; Günther 1988f, VI: 340

The sheet is the first of an album of drawings in the Albertina, Vienna, cataloged by H. Egger in 1903, and denominated the *Sketchbook of Italian Master C.* The top margin of the sheet has been trimmed, regrettably obliterating half of a date written in the center; Egger interpreted this as 1513 or 1514. Buddensieg's reading of 1519 is perhaps more defensible; he attributed the drawing to the circle of Raphael, whereas Günther has identified Master C as Riniero Neruccio da Pisa.

The album of drawings, comprising 19 sheets, contains highly precise drawings of secular buildings of ancient Rome, executed with straightedge and compass. The most striking drawings are those showing five triumphal arches, notably those of Constantine, Titus, and Septimius Severus in Rome, the Arch of Trajan at Ancona, and the Triumphal Arch at Pula. The techniques of representation are always the same: on the first sheet, a plan and elevation in the same scale, followed by details of the architectural features. The measurements are all given in Roman *piedi*, with 32 subdivisions. The scale key supplied on each of the drawings is of particular interest; on the sheet with the Arch of Constantine it is along the bottom, center. The scale varies from sheet to sheet, according to the dimensions of the paper itself. The author established a length for the scale at whim; then, on the basis of this, he recorded the results of his readings with a compass. It will be noted that the Master C used the same scale for the Constantine and Septimius Severus arches for the Vienna album and for the autograph drawings in the Chatsworth collection. "The Italian Master C," writes Günther, "seems to have noted the correlation between the main proportions of the two arches, and thereby brought this correspondence to our notice" (Günther 1988f: 233). The use of a scale key as an aid for the measurements of a drawing presupposes a certain type of representation, without foreshortening or linear distortion. The Master C in fact opted for an orthogonal projection. In both albums (Vienna and Chatsworth), this technique is employed with unprecedented precision in both the elevation and the representation of architectural detail. In an orthogonal projection every element lying parallel to the picture plane has its own vanishing point; this is quite otherwise with one-point perspective, which, as its name suggests, requires a single vanishing point (cat nos. 24, 30). There is therefore no perspective rendering or linear distortion. In his *Memorandum* to Pope Leo X (cat. no. 22), Raphael offers a precise explanation of the characteristics of orthogonal projection, explaining in particular how this type of representation enables architects to render the exact measurements of every point of the drawing.

Raphael maintained that every building should be represented in plan, in elevation, and in section: "El dissegno adunque delli edifici pertenente al architecto si divide in tre parti, delle quali la prima si è la pianta, o—vogliamo dire—el dissegno piano; la seconda si è la parete di fuora, con li suoi ornamenti; la terza è la parte di dentro, pur con li suoi ornamenti" (Bonelli 1978: 480). This is exactly the method with which the Master C proceeded for the drawings in this album.

Ursula Kleefisch-Jobst

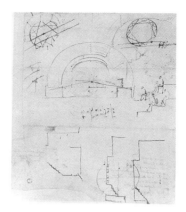

34
ANTONIO DA SANGALLO THE YOUNGER
Villa Madama, Rome; Theater Plans
1519

Florence, Galleria degli Uffizi, Gabinetto Disegni e Stampe
Uff. 1267Ar
Pen and sepia ink, on paper; verso contains further sketches of Villa Madama
34.1/34.3 × 28.8/29.2 cm
INSCRIBED: *frons sciene*

BIBLIOGRAPHY: Frommel 1974b: 179-180 and ill. 91; 1975: 77-78 and ill. 16, 17, 84, 85, 8; 1984d: 312, 336, cat. no. 2.16.10; Günther 1988f: 307-308, no. 248, 256

Building projects of the Renaissance period in Italy present such a dense overlapping of Vitruvian exegesis, monument study, and archaeological knowledge, as the Villa Madama on the Monte Mario in Rome, a superb design begun by Raphael during the reign of Pope Leo X. In this drawing the artist explores a feature of theater construction, and in particular the design of ancient Roman theaters. Together with Uff. 1228A (cat. no. 35), this sheet of drawing was executed by Sangallo for Raphael in the spring of 1519; the drawings shed light on the extent to which his careful reconstruction of the plan of the Theater of Marcellus (cat. no. 25) affected Sangallo's work as an architect.

The recto of Uff. 1267A contains several sketches in both plan and section of the theater for the Villa Madama. In the upper margin he has sketched the two schemes indicated by Vitruvius (V, vii and viii) for the layout of Roman (left) and Greek (right) theaters; the floor plan of the Roman theater shows the base circle encompassing the *orchestra* and three equilateral triangles, instead of the four prescribed by Vitruvius. The three triangles nonetheless adequately delimit the *scaena*, denoted by the lower of the two parallel lines, and the *pulpitum*, whose border with the *orchestra* is marked by the other parallel. Fanning round the *orchestra* is the *cavea* or auditorium.

Similarly, the little sketch of a Greek theater plan at the top right, labeled "frons [sciene]," presents an unusual feature: the three squares inscribed in the circle encompassing the *orchestra* are in turn framed by a large arc describing half an oval. By this Sangallo was hypothesizing that the Greek theater was based on the amphiteater, cut in half lengthwise. He also toyed with this idea in his tentative reconstruction of the Theater of Marcellus. The rough diagram of the Greek theater on this sheet ties in with a similar theater layout rendered in a finished draft in Uff. 1240 verso. The sketches on either side of the present sheet show different stages of the construction in both plan and section. The large floor plan in the center of the recto clarifies the position of the *pulpitum*, which here extends into the *orchestra* at the center of the stage. To the right of this diagram is a sketch of the tiered seating of the *cavea*. In the lower half of the sheet (rotated 90° anticlockwise, and reversed with respect to the plans) are three sectional diagrams showing the tiered *cavea*, the *orchestra*, and the slightly raised *pulpitum*, together with the

four rows of seating for the senators, as prescribed by Vitruvius and duly indicated by Cesariano (1969, ed. Krinsky, fol. 81v., cat. no. 28). Superimposed on the sectional diagram is a circle divided into 8 segments, which may represent the compass card.
C.J.

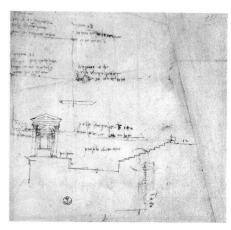

35
ANTONIO DA SANGALLO THE YOUNGER
Villa Madama, Rome; Section of Roman Theater (recto)
Sketches for the Villa (verso)
1519

Florence, Galleria degli Uffizi, Gabinetto Disegni e Stampe
Uff. 1228Ar
Pen and ink, on paper
21.1 × 21.9/20.9 cm
INSCRIBED: *pulpito; profilo di teatro.*

BIBLIOGRAPHY: Frommel 1974b: 180 and ill. 89; 1975: 77-78 and ill. 14, 15, 84, n. 7; 1984: 312, 335, cat. no. 2.16.9.

This sheet is complementary to Uff. 1267A (cat. no. 34) and also dates to the spring of 1519. On the recto Antonio da Sangallo the Younger has sketched a section of the theater ("profilo del teatro") for the Villa Madama on the Monte Mario, Rome. The diagram clearly shows the difference of level between the stage (left) and the adjacent *pulpitum* (marked "pulpito"), extending into the *orchestra*. Right of the *orchestra*, and slightly lower, are the first of ten tiers of the *cavea*. The units of measurement on the drawing are unknown. The verso contains annotations by Antonio and several sketches relating to the garden of the Villa Madama.
C.J.

445

Painted Architecture
Sylvia Ferino Pagden

"If I am not mistaken, the architect took from the painter architraves, capitals, bases, columns and pediments, and all the other fine features of buildings." (Alberti, *De pictura*, II, 26)

Alberti undoubtedly wrote this passage in his treatise *De pictura* in order to praise and to stimulate the imagination of painters. Architecture, or the architectural setting, has always played a highly important role in *historie* or narrative paintings. The majority of *historie* were given a cultural setting usually symbolized by the urban environment, that is, an architectural context. Giotto had already introduced architectural elements as an effective compositional device in his painted works. With space becoming "measurable" thanks to the system of centralized perspective, architecture—which, by necessity is based on scientific principles—took on a leading role in Quattrocento painting. The first experiments in painting devised to highlight the principles of the newly discovered centralized perspective were Brunelleschi's representations of architecture.

In the second half of the fifteenth century painters learnt to exploit expressively the possibilities of central perspectives. These could be used to emphasize dramatic and poetic sensations through the use of vanishing points placed far away in the architectural setting. Sometimes the architectural scene constructed on a centralized perspective was deliberately distorted in order to achieve even greater expressive force (Kemp 1977: 181f.). Real architecture, that is to say, existing or possible buildings, became the protagonists of painted works. This measurable space in painting could also be used to fix the moment in time occupied by the *historia*, and to offer new structural possibilities in which buildings were fundamental.

In the period in question, ca. 1470-85, architecture assumed a prominent role in painting—and by analogy in prints and drawings, reliefs, and *intarsia*, which all followed the rules of centralized perspective to give an illusion of space on a more or less two-dimensional surface; the representation of buildings became central to narrative works, providing the setting and becoming an instrument of composition, and even at times the general framework determining the *historia*. Paradoxically a kind of competition between art and architecture emerged. While painters could have indulged in flights of fancy with veritable "castles in the air," they chose instead to represent the real, to depict what could effectively be built, as can be seen in the St. Bernardino panels. These paintings portray buildings that were architecturally possible, as if complying with some unwritten rules, forgoing the license that painting alone could enjoy. This becomes evident through a comparison between the architecture painted on the St. Bernardino panels, and the essentially more ambitious buildings represented on the Boston and New York panels, which can be attributed to the painter-architect Fra Carnevale (Christiansen 1979: 198f.). Bramante's vision of architecture in 1481, which was engraved by Prevedari, went beyond even the painter's imagination. Even if we accept that the action in this scene is to be identified with "The Departure of the Apostle Barnabus after the Conversion of Milan to Christendom" (Mulazzani 1978: 67ff.), we have to admit that the *historia* has become a pretext for an architectural "manifesto." At all events, it was an outspoken invocation to model the new Christian temples on the architectural culture of antiquity, which, despite its defeat, still provided mankind with a paradigm of infinite grandeur (Metter-

nich 1967-68: 9ff.). The architectural settings portrayed in the St. Bernardino panels have prompted art historians for the past eighty years to consider them the work of an architect or a theoretician of architecture. This is not only inferred from the dominance that the settings assume in these "miracle stories," in which the characters playing out the stories are virtually reduced to the role of extras, but also from the painter's evidently expert knowledge of contemporary architecture. While not offering manifestos as such, many examples of *intarsia* work have also been noted by art historians to prefigure certain architectural designs that were not actually built until later. Perhaps the inclination to attribute to actual architects and theoreticians of architecture all these manifestations in the two-dimensional arts corresponds to modern art historical divisional thinking in different media rather than to the artistic practices of the time.

Real architecture had become an intense ambition within communes and courts alike, and it was soon to involve all artists, whatever their field. It was part of the projected image of Self of the new, self-aware individual, and one of the desires of every artist, be he active in the real or imaginary three-dimensional sphere, as painter, draftsman, or *intarsiatore*.

In its role as "the window on the real world," painting was in a position to depict both contemporary architecture and utopian visions. For painter-architects such as Francesco di Giorgio or Donato Bramante, painting, relief work, and copperplate engraving offered a chance to portray real projects or utopias at will. The images of towns in Francesco di Giorgio's reliefs are ideal visions of antique, unrealizable cities.

The art of *intarsia*, however, was faced with an additional problem. The *intarsiatori* essayed to imitate painting using a technically more difficult means of expression. The decision to make architecture the subject of their work offered advantages from the purely technical point of view: it was easier to cut out geometrical forms from the veneers. The problems involved here were not of a specifically architectural nature, but of "prospectiva seu casamenti" (Ferretti 1986: 73ff.), that is to say, of *viste*, *vedute* of architecture or townscapes. The images of buildings in the narrative scenes of the period have also been compared to stage scenery designs. The architecture illustrated on the inlaid doors of the Palazzo Ducale, Urbino, is indeed reminiscent of the oldest surviving projects for stage scenery (Trionfi Honorati 1983: 49). While architecture as the principal subject matter continued to flourish in inlaid work, in painting the portrayal of townscapes as a promotion for existing or realizable architecture lost ground. With Leonardo's advances in the organization of the picture space, which saw man at its center and space as a device for creating ambience and atmosphere, the architectural setting in the painting of *historie* resumed its subordinate role as a support, as an aid to the narrative.

BIBLIOGRAPHY: Alberti 1975; Christiansen 1979: 198-201; Kemp 1977: 184ff.

36
WORKSHOP OF 1473
The Miracles of St. Bernardino of Siena

Perugia, Galleria Nazionale dell'Umbria, formerly Sagrestia di S. Francesco al Prato
Tempera on panel

A) Pietro Perugino: Healing of Rosa, the six-year old girl who fell into a well, inv. 223
79 × 57 cm

B) Pietro di Galeotto (?): Healing of a boy, son of Nicola di Lorenzo da Prato, wounded by a bull, inv. 229
78.5 × 56.5 cm

C) Pietro Perugino: Posthumous healing of a blind man, inv. 226
76 × 56.7 cm

A

D

D) Pietro di Galeotto (?): Resurrection of a stillborn child through prayer, inv. 222
76.3 × 56.3 cm

Panels E, F and G are not on exhibit.

H) Assistant of Bonfigli and pupil (?): Posthumous healing of a youth, wounded by a pike, inv. 227
76.5 × 56.5 cm

PROVENANCE: Perugia, Oratorio di S. Bernardino

BIBLIOGRAPHY: Orsini 1784 (1973): 313; Vasco 1974: 64-67; Mariotti 1788: 115; Siepi 1822: 793-797, 807-808; Vermiglioli 1839: 262; Rosini 1842, pl. XLIX; Bombe 1912: 130-139; Venturi 1913: 470-482, 574-576; Kimball 1927: 149; Van Marle 1933: 15-171; Richter 1943: 5; Longhi 1946a: 112; Rotondi 1951: 119-120; Zeri 1961: 25, 33, 34, 36, 38, 39; Santi 1963; Santi 1977: 49-53; Santi 1985: 86-90, with a complete bibliography; Damiani 1992; Garibaldi 1992: 316-317.

These five panels, which belong to a group of eight paintings illustrating the miracles of St. Bernardino of Siena, are among the most problematic paintings from the Quattrocento. Nothing is known about their purpose, nor who they were commissioned by, nor are the authors unanimously identified. Very different opinions have been ex-

B

C

H

pressed regarding the authorship of these outstanding architectural scenes. If not an architect, the artist must have been a theoretician of architecture. Or perhaps the facades are the as yet unidentified juvenile works of one of the major architects who preluded or even ushered in the High Renaissance.

Considering the importance given to the setting in these *historie*, the question can hardly come as a surprise. The relationship between man and context has been turned upside down. While the representation of architecture in Quattrocento narrative painting is limited or highly fragmentary, leaving ample room for the human figures, here the scenery—the architecture—steals the show. In panel A, a set of finely decorated columns leads toward a triumphal arch. In panel C, the sumptuous facade is composed of a series of arches resting on massive columns and an upper story of rich pedimented windows. Panel B shows the facade of a palazzo with three bays and a highly decorative portal. Panel D presents a three-story palace and courtyard with open arcades that lead the eye beyond to the surrounding countryside. Panel H shows a square courtyard before a circular building with dome resting on columns. In each of these tall panels, the human figures acting out the *historia* have been relegated to the lower

third of the picture. Not all the miracles are easily identifiable; many are in fact posthumous incidents, diligently assembled to hasten the saint's canonization.

The majority describe an urban situation which required an architectural setting. Only the three panels not included here presented a rural environment.

The individual miracle scenes were originally arranged in two groups of four on a large wooden panel, which was later sawn into several sections. The elaborately simulated frames simulated encrusted with pearls and precious stones were reduced by half at the top and bottom when the main panel was divided into separate sections. The only perfectly conserved part is the bottom frame of the first two scenes that were painted in the lower section of the original large panel (panels A and B).

Panels A, C, E, and G were set in the left side of a niche housing St. Bernardino's gonfalon, and panels B, D, F, and H, were set in the right. According to the restorers, the side borders of the panels, which are set at a wide angle to the picture planes, are original, together with the gold decorations on red ground set into them. This suggests that the sides of the niche formed a wide angle toward the observer, and that the niche narrowed to a trapezoidal shape toward the middle. Orsini described it in 1784 in the following passage: "They were sawn from a niche which contained the statue of St. Bernardino. Above, ribbons formed an elaborate Chi-Rho and this piece has still not yet found a home, but is lodged with the PP, together with the painting by Benedetto Bonfigli, which was at the back of the said niche, and is mentioned by Vasari. The painting, however, is on canvas, not a panel." The wooden panel with the Chi-Rho, and Bonfigli's gonfalon are also conserved in the Galleria Nazionale, Perugia. Only the statue has disappeared without trace. Panel A is the only one of the set that bears an inscription, and therefore plays a leading role: to judge from the presence of the imposing well in the center, the scene purportedly represents, as Weber suggested in 1904 (p. 60) the posthumous "resuscitation of Rosa, the six-year-old daughter of Battista da Perugia, who fell into a well" (AA. SS. 304) and not, as Kaftel suggested (1959: 205), "the healing of the little daughter of Giovanni Petrazio da Rieti," which took place during Bernardino's life. Perugia would be the more appropriate setting for a panel of this importance, and the date and inscription ("*S.P.Q.R. DIVO . TITO . DIVI . VESPASIANI . FILIO . VESPASIANO . AUGUSTO . AA.D.M.C. C.C.C.L.XXIII. FINIS.*") would make more sense here. Together with the date of completion, the inscription could indicate (as Orsini suggested in 1784) that the panel was commissioned by Tito Vespasiano Strozzi, the humanist at the court of Borso d'Este in Ferrara. During the

festive journey to Rome, where Borso d'Este was to be invested with the dukedom, the party stopped in Perugia, where Borso's ambassador Strozzi had prepared for the sojourn of his patron and retinue. The representation of the ancient triumphal arch might almost be considered an *impresa* or personal emblem of Strozzi. The black eagle on a gold background on panel D (the symbol of the Este family) or the fake medallion in relief showing a head bearing a lion skin on panel C (an allusion to Ercole d'Este), support Vasco's assertion of a commission originating in the Ferrara court. The panels have a decisively courtly air about them, evident in the Grecized clothing of the characters and their gestures (especially the grayhound in panel G, not on exhibit) and likewise in the architecture of the magnificent palaces and the triumphal arch.

The courtly tone of the panels caused them at one point to be attributed to Pisanello, until a more differentiated analysis located them to Umbria or central Italy. Bombe's close examination of the architecture represented in the paintings led him to suggest that the painter-architect Francesco di Giorgio Martini was responsible for them, and may even have had a hand in painting them. Venturi considered Perugino more likely as the artist responsible for the whole cycle, aided by three other artists: Pinturicchio, Caporali, and Fiorenzo di Lorenzo. According to Van Marle the composer of the panel was the "Unknown Master of 1473" who, as a follower of Fiorentine art, personally painted panels A, B, C, and D, and was assisted by unknown collaborators for panels F and H; panels E and G were the work of Pinturicchio.

The close connection between the architecture in the panels and that of the Urbino school was first highlighted by Kimball in 1927. Richter in the following therefore proposed that panels A, B, C, and D might have been the work of the young Bramante.

Furthermore, not without noting a strong Ferrarese influence in the panels, Rotondi insisted on Perugino, suggesting that he received his artistic training in Urbino under Piero della Francesca. Longhi and Zeri also considered Perugino to be the artist chiefly responsible for the panels. In the opinion of Santi (1963, 1977) these architectural scenes are the work of a theoretician of architecture, and have much in common with Alberti's built works and those invented or described in his treatise; the artist was a native of Urbino, and painted panels B and D himself; Perugino was entirely responsible for panel A, whereas panel C was painted in concert with Pinturicchio; the latter was the sole author of panels E and G; while Bonfigli painted panels F and H.

Two further discoveries are important for identifying this "Urbino artist of 1473": Bellosi's presentation of the gonfalon in the Oratorio dei Disciplinati di S. Francesco in Perugia, which he attributed to the young Bramante; and Mancini's publication of documents of great importance for this gonfalon, confirming Pietro di Galeotto as the author and a completion date of 1480. Until then, Galeotto was only known through written documents, which profile an excellent and highly appreciated painter. The stylistic link between this gonfalon and panels B and D of the St. Bernardino legends is now clear enough to safely attribute the execution of at least these two to Pietro di Galeotto, as already suggested by Mancini and Scarpellini. A close look at the types of people portrayed in the panels, with their expressive gestures and the strong light on their faces, the superficial metallic character and the undulating folds of the fabrics and clothing, betray the style of the Ferrara school; as Richter already noted, the manner is reminiscent of Francesco del Cossa, especially of his Griffoni *predella*. It is therefore reasonable to suppose that the panel artist had stayed for a certain period in Ferrara. From his only secure work, the gonfalon we cannot with certainty identify Pietro di Galeotto as the same person as Santi's "Urbino artist of 1473," the presumed *spiritus rector* of the architectural scenes in the panels. Undoubtedly, there must have been a sort of master plan by which four different artists painted the eight miracle scenes—Perugino (panels A and B), his assistant Pinturicchio (panels E and G), the presumed Pietro di Galeotto (panels B and D), and his assistant, a pupil of Bonfigli (panels F and H).

Santi justifiably asserts that the architecture depicted in the panels was based on buildings described or actually built by Alberti, and on the Palazzo Ducale, Urbino.

Santi associates the five columns and central triumphal arch in panel A with the *porta regia* of Alberti's stage design (Book VIII, vii), and with his senatorial *basilica* (Book VIII, ix); moreover, the model for the three-arched facade with tondi in the spandrels in panel B was probably the facade of the Tempio Malatestiano. The S-shaped consoles were copied directly from Alberti's S. Sebastiano in Mantua. The lower structure of the wall with its deep arches and massive columns in panel C recall the flanks of the Tempio Malatestiano. The courtyard and the adjacent, centrally planned building in panel H (in which the dome seems to rest on a cylinder that rises into a cone) can be compared to Alberti's description of an atrium for a patrician villa (Book V, xvii) giving onto a *sacrarium* identifiable with the circular building depicted here.

Santi and Bruschi believe the large courtyard in panel D to be strongly reminiscent of the architecture of the palaces in Urbino. The scansion of the windows and columns reflect the ratios of the "sezione aurea" (golden section), endorsing the supposition that the inventor of these scenes was an architectural theoretician. The rich and luxurious decorations would also have their origins in Urbino, in the Sala degli Angeli, the Sala delle Veglie, in the great fireplaces and the duchess' bedroom, etc. Even the well in panel A derives from the one in the courtyard at Urbino. The windows in panel C anticipate Francesco di Giorgio's solutions for S. Maria del Calcinaio; however these too, especially their fluted pilasters, would have found models in Urbino. The buckle and ribbon motifs and other ornamental devices recall the stucco work on the vaults of the church's vestibules.

In her recent profound analysis of all the problems involved with the St. Bernardino panels (in print 1994), Laura Teza takes up once again the relationship with Francesco di Giorgio, postulated by Bombe as early as 1912. On the basis of a drawing by this master with the inscription "a santo Agniolo in Perugia" in the Uffizi (Uff. 335r.) showing a capital of this very church, she can prove that the Sienese Master really was at Perugia. This same capital can be found among those in the first row in panel A. Despite Francesco Santi's and Laura Teza's indubitably correct observations of the details, and their conclusions, the question remains whether the buildings portrayed really were conceived by an architect or by a theoretician of architecture.

The settings are all drawn with a centralized perspective, and therefore comply with Alberti's indications in *De pictura*, with facades placed parallel to the picture plane, and geometrically designed pavements. The buildings appear to delimit a shallow "stage" on which the action takes place. The difference in the way architects depict buildings in a painting can be seen by comparing these panels with those by Fra Carnevale conserved in Boston and New York, in which the artist conveys a striking, complex, and almost intricate experience of an architecturally structured space, which develops into infinity. Furthermore, comparisons with the famous *vedute* of "ideal cities" clearly shows that the buildings in these panels were conceived by a pictorial mind. This is supported by the evident pleasure the artist derived in his portrayal of differently colored materials such as brick, stone, marble, variegated stuccowork, and metallic ornaments, weathercocks, etc. Furthermore, observations such as the differently opened windows in panels C and D, which recall nothern genre-painting, support the idea that we are dealing with painters' minds. These windows also provide information on the use of membranes instead of glass during this period. Furthermore, certain incongruities in panel E, such as the pilasters with their functionless capitals, or the purely ornamental consoles, would be unsatisfactory for an "architect." Similar inconsistency can be noted in the building in panel B, whose upper level does not correspond whatsoever to the lower one; not even a linking part, as in the Palazzo Ducale in Pesaro, which Bruschi quotes as an example. If these architectural scenes are indeed attributable to a painter, the most viable candidates are Perugino and/or Pietro di Galeotto. Nothing is known about Pietro di Galeotto's developments in this field. Perugino's buildings in his latter paintings are more rigid and stylistically more spare, with a decidedly Florentine touch about them; on the other hand, they nonetheless evince a sound knowledge and surprisingly wide comprehension of architecture.

The fascination of the buildings portrayed in these panels lies in the fusion between an apparently deep knowledge of the new advances in architecture, and their utilization and application in painting.

The panels are not an illustrated record of existing architecture. Nor are they theoretical "manifestos" or designs for future projects. They are instead architectural fantasies expressed in painting, belonging to a period in which "modern" architecture promised a new image of the world through Alberti's discoveries and the ambitions of patrons such as Federico da Montefeltro.

For a certain period, new, rich buildings exemplifying the emerging architectural order succeeded in dominating even narrative painting, particularly in the case of the panels depicting the miracles of St. Bernardino.   *S.F.P.*

37
WORKSHOP OF 1473
Miracles of St. Bernardino of Siena
1473
Perugia, Galleria Nazionale dell'Umbria
(formerly Sacristy of S. Francesco al Prato)
Tempera on panel.
Healing of the Little Girl, no. 223 80 × 56 × 5 cm

Healing of a Boy, no. 229
78.5 × 56.5 × 5 cm

Posthumous Healing of the Blind Man, no. 226
76 × 56.7 × 5 cm

Posthumous Raising of a Stillborn Child through Prayer, no. 222
76.3 × 56.3 × 5 cm

Posthumous Healing of a Youth Wounded by a Pike, no. 227
76.5 × 56.2 × 5 cm

The two main unsolved enigmas regarding these tavolette, which narrate eight miracles worked by St. Ber-

Execution technique
Preparatory Drawing

── *Transfer of the drawing by means of incised lines made freehand*

- - - *Transfer of the drawing by means of incised lines made with straightedge or compass*

⬤ *Reference points*

◯ *Compass holes*

nardino, are their provenance and their original arrangement, especially since the studies effected by the Italian scholar Bombe, who was the first to tackle the specific issue of their function.

All those who have studied the panels have linked them to a processional gonfalon or standard depicting St. Bernardino, painted by Benedetto Bonfigli in 1465 (Galleria Nazionale dell'Umbria, cfr. Santi 1985, no. 164), and to a panel bearing the St. Bernardino Trigram inscribed on a garland of fruit and flowers (Galleria Nazionale dell'Umbria, no. 273); these two religious artifacts traditionally constitute what is known as the "Nicchia di S. Bernardino."

Very little is in fact known about that niche. The scattered

pieces of information that have emerged are all of relatively recent date. Orsini, the first scholar (1784) to report the presence of the panels in the sacristy of S. Francesco al Prato, commented that "eight small panels are positioned around the sacristy, [depicting] the deeds of St. Bernardino of Siena, painted in tempera with utmost diligence. They were cut from a niche that housed a statue of St. Bernardino. Above stood a Lord Jesus, with a *bello scherzo di fettuccia*; this piece had not yet been installed anywhere, but was lodged with the PP, together with the painting by Benedetto Bonfigli, which stands at the rear of the niche and was mentioned by Vasari; the piece in question is, however, painted on canvas, not on panel" (Orsini 1784: 313). After Orsini, there is a very brief mention by Mariotti: "We have some beautiful paintings by him [Pisanello, then thought to be the author of the panels] in S. Francesco" (Mariotti 1788: 115); the next mention is by Siepi (1822), who noted: "They formed the framework of a niche that housed the statue of the said saint, at the rear of which was the picture by Benedetto Bonfigli, which can now be seen in the main altar of the St. Bernardino church," and that the panel with "the name of Jesus," i.e., the St. Bernardino Trigram, at the time serving as plinth to Perugino's panel of St. John the Baptist amid four saints

(Galleria Nazionale dell'Umbria, no. 280) and now at the first altar to the right, on entering the church of S. Francesco al Prato, was the "frontispiece" of the niche itself (Siepi 1822: 793).

The accounts reported by Orsini, Mariotti and Siepi clearly derive from oral tradition, as indicated by certain evident inaccuracies and discrepancies. Vasari, who was in Perugia in 1566 for the decoration of the Refectory of S. Pietro, mentions only the Gonfalon (standard) by Bonfigli in the Oratorio of St. Bernardino, attached to S. Francesco al Prato, in the 1568 edition of his *Lives*, and it is described only in general terms: "In the church of St. Bernardino, he painted Christ in the air, accompanied by St. Bernardino, and a crowd below" (Vasari 1906: 506). Curiously, he makes no mention of the tavolette which, if they were present, would have been hard to ignore. Consequently, if the tavolette, Gonfalon and Trigram formed a single composition, this must have been disassembled less than one hundred years after its construction. Vasari would never have overlooked paintings of such superb quality while noting Bonfigli's Gonfalon; he therefore cannot have seen the tavolette, which had presumably already been dismembered and transferred elsewhere, separately from the Gonfalon. The dismantling of the niche and the relocation of the tavolette in the important sacristy of S. Francesco could, perhaps, date back to 1537, when the Oratory of S. Andrea was built next to the Oratory of St. Bernardino. The two buildings were connected by means of two doors at the sides of the high altar of the Oratory of St. Bernardino on the end wall, the only one whose size and importance could do justice to such a complex structure as the niche. The Gonfalon remained in the Oratory, where it was seen by Vasari.

The tavolette, together with the Trigram and the Gonfalon, could have been painted specifically for the same room, but could have formed two separate compositions whose common origins and the cult of St. Bernardino subsequently brought together. The Gonfalon also went through its own critical vicissitudes according to local historiography. After Vasari, it was Morelli who, in 1683, specified its location within the Oratory: "inside the church, to the right, there is still another old panel depicting the Lord Jesus, St. Bernardino and the angels in the air, with a large crowd below" (Morello 1683:117).

When Orsini was writing, the Gonfalon was not sited anywhere in particular, but was conserved together with the Trigram "by the Parish Priests" (Orsini 1784: 313). Modestini saw it in 1787 "over the high altar" (Modestini 1787: 35), and likewise Siepi said it was "now to be admired over the high altar" (Siepi 1822: 793). He was echoed by Cavalcaselle and Morelli in 1861 (1896: 296). Then in 1863, following new legislation on state property, it passed to the Pinacoteca Vannucci. While in the Pinacoteca it was not reassembled with the tavolette. In 1878 (according to the Inventario Carattoli) it was exhibited on the right side of the university church, while the tavolette were in the Jewelry Room, placed over the entrance; the Trigram was set over the door of the first room. Frizzoni does not mention it, Lupatelli (1885) cites it as on exhibit in the Bernardino di Mariotto Room, while the tavolette and the Trigram are located in the Gabinetto di Fiorenzo di Lorenzo (Lupatelli 1885: 22, 23). It was in the same place in 1887 (Lupatelli 1887: 5) but as from 1907 it was exhibited in the Bartolomeo Caporali Room (Lupatelli 1909: 8) until 1945 when, on the occasion of the exhibition celebrating the 500th anniversary of the birth of Pietro Perugino, Bertini Calosso reconstructed the niche on the basis of the descriptions of Orsini and Siepi.

In effect, these scholars fail to provide secure and incontrovertible indications as to the original composition of the tavolette. Indeed Orsini described them as being in the sacristy of S. Francesco al Prato: "Among the aforementioned cabinets eight tavolette are to be seen, excellently painted in tempera," and he went on to describe their exact whereabouts in the sacristy. He did not, however, note the original location of the niche "from which they had been sawn"; the reference to the picture by Bonfigli "painted on canvas, not on a panel" may also

be imprecise. During that period two Gonfalons in fact had been painted for the Oratory, both with the image of the saint; these two works were repeatedly confused by authors until Ricci (Ricci 1913: 14). Both Santi (1963: 5, 6; 1985: 41, 42) and, more circumstantially, Mancini (1992: 110) have refuted such a hypothesis. In fact, the first, depicting only the image of St. Bernardino, was commissioned in 1450. This had already been restored by Ottavio di Lorenzo and Bartolomeo Caporali in 1463, and the damage it suffered during processions must have been considerable if, by 1496, another one was already on the books. In the meantime, in 1465 Bonfigli painted another gonfalon with a much more complex iconography, for celebratory rather than devotional purposes, which still shows the signs of wear and tear from processions. There was a second gonfalon at S. Francesco al Prato painted jointly by Bonfigli and Mariano d'Antonio in 1453-54 for the chapel of S. Maria della Pace, depicting a *Madonna della Misericordia* with St. Bernardino of Siena and other saints. Teza (forthcoming) quite rightly observes that art historians after Orsini and Siepi "completely abandoned all reference to the statue contained in the niche. In all probability the gonfalon theory took precedence insofar as it seemed to be connected to the only element still *in situ*, while the allusion to the statue was even more vague... now no longer traceable."

None of the hypotheses of reconstruction of the niche proposed to date are entirely convincing, but each one contains useful elements which, together with the information gathered from the recent restoration, seem to shed some light on the one of the most complex and problematic artistic events of the second half of the Quattrocento.

In 1912 Bombe was the first to propose a complex graphic and photographic reconstruction of an articulated structure comprising various elements "present in the eighteenth century in the Sacristy of S. Francesco al Prato or other, unknown location" (Bombe 1912: 130-134, figs. 8, 9). In the scholar's opinion the rear of the niche was occupied by the Bonfigli Gonfalon of 1465, surmounted by a panel depicting the Holy Spirit (Galleria Nazionale dell'Umbria, no. 173) and completed at the sides by four panels with angels and baskets of roses (Galleria Nazionale dell'Umbria, nos. 165, 167, 171, 172) by Bonfigli, arranged in pairs on the splays of the niche (recently retraced by Mancini, 1992: 114-115, to the Gonfalon with the Madonna delle Grazie of S. Francesco, where they were used as lids for a reliquary chest. The eight tavolette of St. Bernardino would have been mounted on the doors of this niche, four on the outside (on the left, from top to bottom nos. 222 and 229; and on the right, from top to bottom nos. 226 and 223) and four on the inside (on the left, from top to bottom, nos. 228 and 227; on the right, from top to bottom, nos. 225 and 224).

This great wooden structure, with its precious frames, would have been completed by a double cymatium at the top formed by the panel with the St. Bernardino Trigram (which was then in a state prior to the damage caused by Bertini Calosso's reconstruction, but already somewhat remodeled with respect to the state in which it had been found) and by a lunetta with the Holy Father and two angels by a follower of Bartolomeo Caporali (Galleria Nazionale dell'Umbria, no. 159). Recognition should certainly be given to Bombe for having understood that the niche of St. Bernardino must have been a most complex and articulated structure.

It is impossible, however, to accept his composition of the elements, which neither refer to the sources nor correspond to the dimensions or to other indications that could in some way support his theory. The four panels with the Angels must in fact have been doors themselves: they are lightly built and have a keyhole. The thin tavolette, in turn, could neither have borne panels, nor have been inserted in panels, since they are all framed on all four sides. On the occasion of the exhibition "Quattro secoli di pittura in Umbria" in 1945 Bertini Calosso presented a reconstruction of the niche showing the eight tavolette arranged in two sets of four, on the lateral splays of the niche, the Trigram of St. Bernardino on the underside of the "lintel" and the Gonfalon by Bonfigli at the back. According to Santi, given the lack of documentary evidence in the archives of the Galleria Nazionale, this reconstruction was based on the discovery of "decorations on the sides of the tavolette, which seem to indicate their being positioned in two groups, like two overlapping pilasters; this supposition seems to be confirmed by the state of the painted frames on the short sides of the little paintings" (Santi 1965: 87). According to this reconstruction, the following miracles appeared on the left side of the niche, from the base upward: 1) *Healing of a Little Girl*, no. 223; 2) *Posthumous Healing of a Blind Man*, no. 226; 3) *Posthumous Liberation of a Prisoner*, no. 225; 4) *Resurrection of a Murdered Man under a Tree on the Road to Verona*, no. 224; on the right side, from the base: 1) *Healing of a Man Crushed by a Bull*, no. 229; 2) *Resurrection of a Stillborn Child through Prayer*, no. 222; 3) *Nocturnal Apparition and Healing of a Man Wounded in an Ambush*, no. 228; 4) *Posthumous Healing of a Youth Wounded by a Pike*, no. 227. Bertini Calosso's reconstruction involved the modification of the fragment (that is, the removal parts of both the short sides and the full length of one of the long sides) of the Trigram panel, in all probability, from the dimensions to which it had been reduced when it was remodeled as a predella to the painting (no. 280)—176.5 × 51 × 5 cm, see.

On this occasion the restorer added two inserts of wood with the grain positioned orthogonally, and variously inclined on the short sides. Some fillets were added to the upper side, of the same width as the decorative strip of the lower face. A jeweled frame was painted on these exactly like the one surrounding the tavolette. Wooden staves were added to the short sides which followed the trapezoid profile of the extension whose function (according to Bertini Calosso) was to allow the Trigram to rest on the tavolette, and to finish the incomplete decorative strip of those positioned higher up. The fillets that completed the frame on the short sides, thereby giving the paintings a certain self-sufficiency (visible in the Alinari photographs of 1909), were removed from the tavolette, while the decorative part of the outer frame, involving one of their long sides, was enlarged and terminated with a gilt band. This solution was also adopted for one of the long sides of the Trigram, so that the niche was completely enclosed by the cornice. The Gonfalon was also reduced in size, thereby concealing the decorative strip with a white foliage motif.

The archives of the Soprintendenza provide documentary evidence of the restoration program performed on the eight tavolette in 1953. The work comprised the "cleaning, integration, and complete restoration" of the small paintings, and was carried out by Francesco and Augusto Cecconi.

Bertini Calosso's recomposition was dismantled in 1958 by Santi, the new director of the Galleria Nazionale dell'Umbria. Santi held that the vertical and oblique arrangement of the paintings was unacceptable: their interpretation had been seriously compromised, and the inconvenient positioning of the Gonfalon at the rear of the niche would, moreover, certainly have damaged the tavolette during processions. In 1963, while excluding the theory of doors because of the lack of circumstantial evidence (such as hinges or the like), Santi proposed that the eight tavolette could have formed "two high frontal pilaster strips to the sides of the niche, something like a frame, in which the Trigram formed a part of the entablature." The "vertical connection" of the tavolette, he advocated, is confirmed by the remains of the gilt and painted decoration on the sides of the tavolette; the original arrangement of the tavolette "placed the two with the most complex architecture at the base of the pilaster strips" (no. 229, 223) since "they have a painted frame which goes all round at the base"; two other tavolette must have once been present at the top, "since no such tavolette with frames all round at the top exist" (Santi 1963: 7).

Santi therefore proposed to compose the paintings in a way that would somehow reconcile both the scientific requirements and their interpretation, and subsequently arranged them in Room XIV, thus: on the far wall the Gonfalon was surmounted by the Trigram, while the tavolette were arranged horizontally, in two groups of four, along the walls to the sides; on the left wall, starting from the entrance, were nos. 223, 226, 225, 224; on the right wall, nos. 229, 222, 228, 227.

The complex history of the tavolette and the paintings associated with them, as well as the circumstances leading up to the decision to remove them so as to redesign the framework of their setting, led the Soprintendenza ai Beni A.A.A.S. of Perugia to embark upon the reconstruction of the whole group in 1991, as part of a broad program of restoration. The restoration of the Gonfalon by Bonfigli and of the eight tavolette was entrusted to Sergio Fusetti and Paolo Virilli; the Trigram to the C.B.C. company, under the supervision of the present author. The practical work of restoration was preceded by detailed and specific research aimed at shedding light on certain problems that the documentary sources had failed to solve. As far as the Trigram is concerned, restoration has revealed the close ties with the tavolette: identical characteristics have been found regarding the wood (poplar), the thickness of the panels (5 cm), the techniques of realization and the jeweled frame. It was not possible, however, to establish the original dimensions of the painting, given its fragmentary state.

Two iron rings were discovered at the top of one of the two pieces of wood which form the Trigram; the question of their belonging to the original painting or not is proved by the presence of two iron elements, inserted during the construction of the wood panel, which lie under the painted and varnished surface. These inserted parts appear to confirm the use of the picture as a "celetto" or scenographic ceiling panel. Evidence for an original horizontal position is provided by the rendering of light and shadow; the light travels from top to bottom, or rather, from the outside toward the inside, and from left to right. If it had been set upright as a kind of entablature (Santi 1963: 7) above the tavolette, the light would have had to come from a lateral source, or from below, traveling upward. The same cannot be said of the Gonfalon. While being clearly different from the tavolette from the stylistic point of view—since it was not only painted eight years earlier, but was also the fruit of a decidedly less advanced cultural context—it does not offer iconographic or technical links or references to connect it to the little paintings.

Its dimensions, which can be interpreted in various ways, do not offer any definite indications. Bertini Calosso's reconstruction failed to take into consideration the decorative strip with the white foliage motif and another, red border strip, which was probably originally flanked by a fairly elaborate frame that covered the canvas used for keeping the Gonfalon in place, anchored to the frame on which it was mounted for devotional processions (at least for a certain period). This hypothesis is substantiated by the numerous lacerations, missing parts and other damage caused by dynamic stress; by the repairs and numerous restoration attempts; and not least by the pictorial technique adopted.

Consequently the measurements can be interpreted as follows: 3.19 × 192.4 cm (comprising only the little palm tree strip visible after Bertini Calosso's reconstruction); 334 × 206.5 cm (including the white foliage strip); 337.5 × 213 cm (with the red strip); and at least 3.50 × 2.25 cm (considering the whole wooden frame).

The restoration work carried out on the tavolette (which were in fair condition) has confirmed some of the earlier conjectures while providing other new facts; but many queries remain regarding their original composition.

The original support of the eight tavolette comprised two pieces of poplar wood ca. 5 cm thick; four scenes were painted on each one. The two panels were completed with two molded and gilt frames (one on the right and the other to the left) which are now fragmentary. Subsequently, a ground of red color was applied to the gilt base of the cornices and then partially scraped away, with the help of a stencil, to obtain a foliage motif and reveal the brilliance of the metal. This decoration was broken off vertically

and its original dimensions cannot be established, but it seems to imply a certain continuation sideways. The somewhat quick and careless process applied to the already gilded frame, was revealed by some chance scratch marks (not ascribable to any specific purpose) detected in the gilt finish; these were painted over at some unknown date, perhaps on the occasion of the mounting of the wooden structure. The connections between the pieces of wood forming the support (the main piece is ca. 54 cm and a small one 2 cm, including the molding of the side section of frame) are covered with a strip of canvas to provide a kind of lagging. The inclination of the beveled edges on the long sides of the original panel determined the angle between the tavolette and a backing panel, which must have been an oblique angle of approximately 100°, enabling the position of the painted panels of the altarpiece to be established with precision.

As Santi had already noted, the tavolette reveal no trace of having once been fitted with either hinges or locks, or of other types of joints to substantiate their use as doors to a cabinet. There are however fairly consistent traces of the reconstruction carried out by Bertini Calosso, the reversal of which caused just as much damage.

On the back the two panels were prepared traditionally with a succession of layers of plaster and glue. The plaster had become impregnated with impurities such as granules, which became dislodged during polishing, leaving tiny pockets on the surface.

A detailed study of the incised guide lines for transferring the preparatory drawing to the prepared surface has confirmed the existence of a global project linking the eight paintings, and has provided precious information about the various phases of its realization. First, the transposition of the design of the outer jeweled frame separating each scene from the next was performed by freehand incisions directly onto the wooden surface; subsequently the incised lines circumscribing the scenes and delineating the architecture were made with a straightedge and compasses. Five of the tavolette have a vertical incision, generally covering the full length of the painting, that cuts the scene exactly in half (nos. 228, 222, 227, 229, 223). Traces of compass holes are evident in tavolette nos. 226, 227 and 229, while reference points are evident in 226 and 227. The architectural composition is defined in minute detail and is completely independent from the figurative scene, which was painted on later. Only in a few cases was the superimposed figurative part roughly set out by means of incisions. The original drawing, evidently executed in paint or ink and later covered by the layers of paint, is not visible to the eye and does not show up with reflectography, as it probably consisted of painted outlines. The systematic analysis of these incised lines—first manually and then electronically, combined with an analysis of the pictorial technique—has provided further interesting information. The tavoletta no. 223, which must certainly have stood at the bottom because of its complete decorative strip, and to the left, because it ended with the gilt frame on this side, exhibits a substantial anomaly with regard to the other paintings. In fact, the decorative strip

was painted on directly, without the assistance of the freehand incisions to be found only on the upper part. It was almost like the starting point for a second artist who felt the need to incise all the ornamental details before executing them in color on the next tavoletta up, no. 226. The buildings on this tavoletta too, defined here by direct incisions using a straightedge or compasses in an extremely detailed manner, are the only ones to be embellished by the presence of gold. This was designed to highlight decorative motifs executed with great fluidity and plasticity that glitter in the light coming from left to right and top to bottom on the decorative strip and from left to right, but from the bottom upward in the picture. The pictorial composition is also very precise, as it is in almost all of the other tavolette, but here it stands out for its particular creative freedom. Figures, landscape and decorative motifs, including the jeweled strip, are executed in pure colors, with no black or white, and without the need for contours to define the shapes. The gestures are never excessive, but composed and essential. They radiate a sense of silence, of equilibrium, a calm message, which only a painter of the highest caliber could have conceived and accomplished. Not surprisingly, this particular tavoletta has always been attributed to Perugino, who later developed his ethereal painting—a precursor of future chromatic sensitivity—in vibrations of color.

The correspondence of the incised lines on the decorative strip of the upper edge with those of the same decoration on the lower edge of no. 226, as well as that of the grain of the wood, visible on the back of the paintings, are conclusive proof that the latter lay over the first.

The author of this second scene, greatly aided by both freehand and straightedge incisions, felt the need to build up the images with the help of contours, defining the color in an essentially decorative division of the space. While still maintaining the same high quality, the identical ornamental motifs are less finely wrought, less plastic; the technique is heavier and more mechanical. The ribbon fastened to the garlands is very similar to the one depicted in the panel with the St. Bernardino monogram. The clothing, hair and ornamental details of the characters are a masterly composition of folds, light and shadow and metallic reflections. These fully correspond with the jeweled setting executed (as for all the tavolette), by the same author of the figurative scene, unanimously held to be Pinturicchio.

The heads and hair of some of the characters, and perhaps the robes of the blind man, however, seem to be attributable to the painter of tavoletta no. 223 (and therefore to Perugino), owing to the evident technical and pictorial analogies with the characters of the scene positioned immediately below. As elsewhere, in this tavoletta the light source of the frame (from left to right and from top to bottom) does not correspond with that of the scene (left to right, but from the bottom upward). The other two *historie* that decorated the original panel are ascribable to Pinturicchio, and were executed in the following order: *Posthumous Liberation of a Prisoner*, no. 225; and *Resurrection of a Murdered Man under a Tree on the Road to Verona*,

no. 224. This last picture provides very interesting information about the original structure of the wooden framework. The painted surface and the preparatory layer of the jeweled frame of the short top side reveal a slightly upturned rim, exactly where the decorative motif is interrupted half way up, indicating a different conclusion to the panel from that reconstructed by Bertini Calosso. This could presumably be the continuation of the jeweled strip on the Trigram panel. In actual fact the scene seems to have been surmounted by some kind of protruding decorative motif, whose other characteristics remain a mystery. It has not been possible to confirm this suggestion by an examination of the last part of the right panel because the end of the tavoletta is fragmentary.

The completely conserved jeweled strip of tavoletta no. 229 indicates its original position at the bottom of the right panel. Executed using a series of detailed incisions to delineate and construct the buildings before the scene was painted, this picture differs in its execution from the previous subjects, in particular for its more expressive figures and the apparent impression of movement. The painter has utilized many characters, arranged in an almost casual way, in order to build up a miraculous event whose content and effect is then weakened, at the same time, by their presence. The distribution of light in the scene is also confused: there are two sources, one for the architecture and one for the story in the foreground.

The elaboration and technique of the following scene (no. 222) is very different. The accent on expressiveness turns into an attention to outward appearances, and everything becomes a subtle play of equilibrium. A great painter, and a great architect, was the author of this picture, one who simply required guidelines, not outlines. The architecture is impalpable. The jutting fragments of the upper story are superbly silhouetted against the sky. The shadows are evanescent, but strangely solid. The entire composition is a play of geometric forms, from the clouds to the circular trees and the folds of the clothing, which evoke solid fluted columns. Even the layout of the medium responds to the same exercise of calculated equilibrium.

The third story, in which St. Bernardino appears by night at the bedside of Giovan Antonio Tornano (wounded in an ambush) to cure him (no. 228), betrays links with the painter of tavolette nos. 224 and 225, though it shows a certain rigidity and simplification of movement and some coarseness in the details, which do not measure up to the quality of Pinturicchio.

The right panel was concluded by the scene in no. 227, certainly the weakest of the whole group, both for the way in which the buildings are represented and for the elaboration of the figures, which are little more than caricatures. In this case too, the decoration and the frame surrounding the scene were first laid out with direct and freehand incisions, then the vertical incision was made, dividing the scene down the center, and lastly, the architecture was drawn. The dimensions of the lantern were determined by two circumferences. The figurative part was inserted later, when the mantles of some figures and the two dogs present in the scene were drawn with freehand incisions. One incised line, later modified when it was actually painted in, directed the ray of light from the saint to the man wounded by a pike.

It is not possible to establish from technical evidence when the two panels were subdivided into eight parts, or to confirm or refute the documentary information. The dismantling seems to have been carried out when the panels were already worm-eaten, but this does not exclude that it could have been done some ten years after the construction of the composition. It was sawn along the middle of the jeweled decoration separating each scene from the next. Bits of decoration can also be seen on the remaining perimeter.

Calosso's reconstruction of the "niche" involved joining the tavolette with wooden pins inserted into each panel, fixed to the rear with wooden cross pieces, fixed with casein and nails for the full length of the vertical sides. This configuration was undone by G. Mancini in 1958, with the probable loss of part of the outer frame.

On the back, approximately 6 cm from the outer edge and 4.3 cm on the inside of the tavolette, are traces of a scratchy incision that runs along their full length. This circumscribed the plaster and glue preparation that also protected the unseen surfaces. Presumably, therefore, there were originally two lateral supporting structures (larger than those used by Bertini Calosso), which strengthened the entire composition and perhaps served to support some extra piece that completed the structure at the top (not forgetting that the molded frames, which certainly had quite different dimensions then, added to the thickness of the tavolette). Even today an exact idea of the original structure is not feasible. While we can safely discard various earlier hypotheses on the basis of information provided by written records, together with the careful examination of the paintings, however fragmentary, and the comparative analysis of the techniques adopted, the research discussed here is effectively only a starting point for a further, more in-depth study.

At present we can confirm with certainty that the eight paintings of the *Miracles of St. Bernardino* and the Trigram panel formed part of a single unit, but it is quite impossible to establish in what way the various elements were composed. The same difficulties apply to ascertaining whether the Trigram was indeed the "ceiling" piece; the evidence so far is unconvincing. Not even the presence of the original rings on the rear is easy to explain; they were useless if the Trigram panel was the ceiling piece of a niche, there being insufficient space for the two tie-rods (unless these were part of a projecting devotional altar combination, high enough on the wall to conceal the rods from view). Perhaps they had a practical function in a system of cords for opening an altar or niche arrangement containing the statue of St. Bernardino—a common practice for relics on processional litters; in that case the Trigram would have served as a type of *antependium*. The top-down source of light in the painting could be explained either by the panel's lying face down inside the niche, or upright, and therefore below the historiated tavolette. At any event, the information is insufficient to allow for any secure conclusions.

The inclined position and the sequence of the two larger historiated panels is now a certainty, however. Their provenance from a single workshop has been established, and the existence of a global project for both, as evidenced by the keen depiction of space and the imaginative painted buildings, which must have been directly influenced by the "architecture" of the wooden composition itself. The entire artifact was to be a "monument within a monument," a major devotional feature of the St. Bernardino Oratory. Apart from its traditional references to the architecture of Urbino (and to Bramante), the facade of the oratory seems to quote and evoke the buildings in the painted panels; similarly, the position of the tavolette mirrors the lateral splays of the entrance portal—a detail that Bombe may have already noted when he envisaged the four paintings with the angels and baskets of roses.

There were certainly at least five or even six painters at work on the execution of the scenes, each one working within an explicitly defined framework, though free to express himself as he felt. The distribution of the work, however, was not even; there seems to be no correlation between competence or mastery of the craftsmen and the physical hierarchy of the scenes in either of the panels, be they organized horizontally or vertically. The impression is almost one of a competition of skill among young or established painters engaged in a task of the utmost cultural and religious significance.

Vittoria Garibaldi

451

38
Francesco di Giorgio Martini
Flagellation

Perugia, Galleria Nazionale dell'Umbria, 746
Bronze, black patina
55.5 × 40.5 cm

Provenance: the bronze was donated, according to Santi (1985), between 1872 and 1875 by Count Demetrius Boutorlinn to the Musei Civici, Perugia.

Bibliography: Schubring 1907: 186; Weller 1943: 151-154; Toledano 1987: 132 n. 52; Santi 1985 (1989): 236-238, with a complete bibliography; Giannatiempo Lopez 1992: 124-125; Fumi Cambi Gado 1993: 360-361.

It is not known who commissioned this extraordinary bronze relief, what its function and intended destination were, or when it was made. Nor is it certain whether it really was one of the bronze works created by Francesco di Giorgio Martini for Duke Federico da Montefeltro, as Santi has suggested. However, there does seem to be a clear connection between this work and a bronze basrelief, the *Deposition*, realized for Federico da Montefeltro in ca. 1475 (conserved in S. Maria del Carmine, Venice).
The same types of figures appear in the two bronze reliefs, together with the same expressiveness, ranging from strong, articulate gestures to a lifeless, empty passivity. But the masterful way in which Francesco makes space and architecture penetrate actively in the structure of the drama shows a certain improvement since the *Deposition*. According to Fumi (1993, no. 12), the relief does not belong to the 1470s, as held by the majority of art historians, but to the period 1480-85.
The real drama is taking place on a central podium bordered on either side by a balustrade—a sort of stage in an imaginary space. With respect to the crowd of figures, the figure of Christ at the column is in sharp relief, and slightly off-center, with an angry scourger to the left, and the enthroned judge to the right, placed higher. The range of relief used for the various figures is striking. Steps lead down from the "stage" to the highly detailed foreground where five figures, either bent or seated, create a link between the observer and the dramatic scene. The outstretched hand of the Virgin Mary is particularly compelling, and, as Alberti conceived it, was intended to lead the gaze into the circle of the drama. Apart from the raised arm, the young man on the right leaning on his spear and shield is in the same pose as the antique statue of Kithara Apollo, with a shield instead of a lyre.
The buildings of the architectural setting are also inspired by antiquity. They are expressed with a ghostly transparency, and without any signs of life. This background alone links the groups of figures, emerging with differing degrees of emphasis, to the bronze surface within the imaginary space. Only the backdrop offers a solution to the difference of imagery between the foreground and the podium, creating a more consistent impression of space.

The center of the composition is dominated by a magnificent prostyle with a flat roof and Ionic columns decorated with fluted necking. The three portals are crowned with triangular pediments. Is it a pagan temple, a high court? On either side the buildings diminish according to the rules of centralized perspective—palaces, theaters, circular towers—all of which are frequently found in Francesco di Giorgio Martini's reliefs and drawings (for round buildings, see Maltese 1967, I, s. 14, 21, 71 recto and verso, 72, 84, and passim). A building similar to the two-story architecture with arches supported by pilasters (a theater) on the right, inspired by the Colosseum or the Theater of Marcellus, recurs in another of Martini's reliefs, which has only survived in two plaster copies, known as the *Discordia* and conserved in London and Siena (Toledano 1987, nos. 50-51); further analogies are noticeable in the design of other buildings depicted in the two reliefs.
The flattening of the architectural backdrop was a device that Martini learned from Donatello. In the cogent but *sfumato* portrayal of mood, and in the violence of the gestures, the manner comes close to that of Leonardo; this is why, but not without reason, Del Bravo (1970: 100) dated the relief to 1490, when Francesco di Giorgio was in Milan.   *S.F.P.*

The Winged Eye: Leon Battista Alberti and the Visualization of the Past, Present, and Future
Christine Smith

One of the most pervasive features of fifteenth-century culture is the belief that nothing is truly known unless it is seen. Intellectuals often appealed to the authority of Aristotle in affirming this view. Thus Nicholas Cusanus wrote (in 1458): "I consider that Aristotle rightly said in the beginning of the *Metaphysics* how all men by nature desired to know, and he declared this [desire] to be in the sense of sight." At the turn of the century, Luca Pacioli would remark in his *De Divina proportione* that Aristotle held that knowledge begins with seeing, and that nothing is in the intellect that is not first experienced by sensation. For many, intellectuals and not, the eyes of the mind were as powerful instruments for acquiring knowledge as the eyes of the body. Leonardo Bruni explained that he had written a commentary on the First Punic War because "those outstanding men ... since I cannot see them with my eyes, as the next best thing I willingly embrace in my mind and imagination." This passionate desire to visualize led Antonio di Tuccio Manetti to ask about the exact location, shape, and measurements of Dante's hell. In devising new methods for visualizing the past, the present and the future, Leon Battista Alberti (1404-72) was a central figure.
Alberti's contributions to the visualization of the present were varied in character. Especially striking is his decision to represent himself in one, and perhaps two, bronze self-portrait plaques (cat. no. 40), the earlier of which, of about 1435, anticipates, and may have been a catalyst for, Pisanello's prolific activity as portrait medalist begun in 1438. Alberti's notion of a portrait was not confined to the presentation of physical appearance; it also included the representation of character through the choice of a device and motto. Alberti chose the winged eye and motto "*QUID TUM*" (cat. nos. 40, 41 and 42). A self-portrait drawing in a manuscript containing one of his dialogues (in which he is one of the speakers) has also been attributed to him. If the autobiography attributed to him is indeed authentically his, then he also provided a word-picture of his appearance and character. As Alberti presented himself, so he was represented by others, as in Matteo de' Pasti's portrait medal (cat. no. 42).
Alberti was no less concerned with the visualization of the world around him. He was the first to devise a system of coordinates within which the relative locations of the major monuments of Rome could be represented, thus fostering the visualization of the city as a unified whole of related parts.
The desire to understand topography as an ordered and measurable spatial continuum which underlies Alberti's *Descriptio urbis Romae* also accounts for the popularity of Ptolemy's *Geography*, available in Latin for the first time in the early fifteenth-century (cat. no. 43). While the nine views of cities which began to accompany the text in the 1450s are less stringently mathematical than Alberti's depiction of Rome, they derive from drawings in the same circle of antiquarian investigation.
Yet another aspect of the visualization of the present involved making copies of existing buildings: some of the works are examples of how structures designed by Alberti were used by other artists. Changes in function, medium, and scale in the wooden copy of Alberti's Holy Sepulcher for the Rucellai family (cat. no. 44); in essential form in Antonio Labacco's drawing of S. Sebastiano in Mantua (cat. no. 45); or in selected design features, as in Antonio da Sangallo the Younger's drawing of the Tempio Malatestiano show how the process of knowing is inseparable from the act of interpretation. These works not

452

only record the present—that is, the act of seeing—but comment on that experience. The artists' responses to Alberti's works correspond to the architect's own advice about how to learn from sense experience.

Alberti's role in fostering the visualization of what does not yet exist—the future, that is—is no less remarkable. He was the first, in his treatise on architecture *De re aedificatoria* (cat. no. 46), to urge architects to prepare drawings and models of works they proposed to build. Although none of Alberti's own models survives, the wooden model for a Florentine church, attributed to Baccio d'Agnolo, illustrates the kind of visualization Alberti recommended (cat. no. 47). A drawing for a bath complex attributed to Alberti shows the relation between mental and graphic image which he discusses in the treatise (cat. no. 48). The way in which verbal and graphic description combine to project the desired image is demonstrated by Alberti's autograph letter to Matteo de' Pasti. Visualizations of projected buildings could also serve to enhance the image of patrons, as Matteo de' Pasti's depiction of the Tempio Malatestiano and Sperandio's of the Sforza mausoleum attest (cat. nos. 49 and 50). These are images not only of the future, but also for the future.

Of special fascination to fifteenth-century men was the attempt to visualize the past, about which they knew primarily from literary sources. The longing to know through sight applied to biblical events no less than to Roman history. Until the very end of the century, an inability to conceive of the past as fundamentally different from the present, together with the need to understand the unknown in terms of the known, produced images in which past and present are curiously intertwined (cat. nos. 51, 53). In some cases as when, in the 1420s, a Florentine painter depicted Brunelleschi's as-yet-unbuilt dome atop a structure like Florence Cathedral as the setting for one of Christ's miracles, past, present and future were conflated (cat. no. 51). Faced with almost no visual evidence for the original settings of biblical events, artists relied on their imaginations, or adapted settings whose associations at least seemed appropriate.

The visualization of Roman antiquity, by contrast, was aided by the study of Roman ruins. Alberti's involvement in the process of recuperating the original appearance of ancient buildings developed over time. In his treatise on architecture, he tells us that he "never stopped exploring, considering, and measuring everything, and comparing the information through line drawings" in addition to reading, but that "to collate material from sources so varied, heterogeneous, and dispersed ... required an ability and learning greater than I would profess to have" (Alberti 1988, VI.1: 155). The Marcanova manuscript (*Quaedam antiquitatum fragmenta*) (cat. no. 52), in which painstakingly accurate transcriptions of ancient Roman inscriptions and fantastic pictorial evocations of Roman life serve as complementary approaches to the task of the recuperation of the past, illustrates an early moment in this process. Later, the measurement of classical structures, a closer study of ancient descriptions of buildings, and the completion of these in plan and elevation with the aid of imagination, enabled artists to propose verbal and graphic visualizations of their original appearance. At the end of Alberti's life, in 1472, when he escorted Bernardo Rucellai, Lorenzo il Magnifico and Donato Acciaioli around Rome, Alberti was able to reconstruct the original appearance of the ancient structures in plan, elevation and surface treatment (Rucellai). Poliziano, in his preface to the first edition of *De re aedificatoria*, attributes even more to the old Alberti, claiming that "so thorough had been his examination of the remains of antiquity that he was able to grasp every principle of ancient architecture, and renew it by example" (Alberti 1988): in other words, he could design new structures using the principles of the ancients. Alberti was not alone in this endeavor: Francesco di Giorgio attempted reconstructions of the fora of Augustus and Nerva, the Capitoline, the Imperial Palace on the Palatine, and the Serapeum on the Quirinal (among others) in the 1470s (*Codex Saluzzianus*, 148, Bib. Reale, Turin). Although he admitted that he had to make most

of it up, because one could understand so little from the ruins (Francesco di Giorgio 1967: 9), and that he therefore relied on his "debile ingenio" (*Ibid*: 275), he won praise from Giovanni Santi as "restaurator delle ruine antiche e delle spente un supremo inventore." Francesco di Giorgio explicitly related the need for drawings to Aristotle's theory of knowledge in the *Posterior Analytics* and *On the Soul*, explaining that images appeal more to the imagination than words, and are more easily fixed in the memory; besides, not everything can be described in words. A drawing of Roman imperial palaces which some scholars place in the circle of Francesco di Giorgio and the *Hypnerotomachia Poliphili* (cat. no. 53), illustrate how archaeology and imagination contributed to the visualization of antiquity between 1465-1500.

Past, present and future: each a reality which fifteenth-century men longed to know through sight. Beginning with the self and extending forward to the reality which was to be made, as well as back to the reality that established the traditions and much of the identity of the present, visualization served as an instrument of knowledge. Leon Battista Alberti was deeply engaged in each aspect of this enterprise as inventor, spokesman, and advisor.

39
FRANCESCO DE' ROSSI (called Salviati) (attrib.)
Portrait of Giovanni di Paolo Rucellai

Private Collection
Tempera on panel.
119 × 96 cm

BIBLIOGRAPHY: Gregori 1960; Perosa 1981; Zaccaria 1992; Cecchi 1993b.

This painting owes its fame to the fact that it is the only accurate portrait of the celebrated banker and patron (Florence 1403-81) who was the author of the *Zibaldone Quaresimale* (Lent commonplace book), an important collection of reminiscences and teachings intended for members of his family. This relates to 1457-81, the period in which, thanks to his political prowess, Giovanni was able to regain the favor of the Medici after he had been "rejected by the state and suspected by it" for twenty-seven long years, from 1434 to 1461, as a result of his marriage to Jacopa, the daughter of Palla Strozzi, one of those responsible for the exile of Cosimo il Vecchio. After he had won back the favor of Piero il Gottoso in 1461, when his eldest son Bernardo was betrothed to Nannina, sister of Lorenzo il Magnifico, and, with the considerable resources he had available, he was able to finance the major building projects which had been commissioned from Leon Battista Alberti, "a very close friend" according to Vasari. Illustrated in the view which extends behind the eminent sitter and built between 1464 and 1470, they included the family palace and loggia in Via della Vigna, the completion of the Gothic facade of the Dominican church of

S. Maria Novella and the shrine of the Holy Sepulcher in the church of S. Pancrazio.

In 1960 Gregori considered this painting to have been inspired by Giorgio Vasari and, more recently in 1981 and 1992, it has been attributed to Jacopo Coppi, a lesser painter of the "Studiolo." However, the portrait, which was probably derived from an unknown fifteenth-century painting, may be ascribed to a Florentine artist of the first half of the sixteenth century who was clearly influenced by Venetian art as regards the brilliant colors of the rustling satin and the sumptuous damask of the sitter's clothes, shot through with an iridescence that evokes Titian's finest works.

Among the artists of Vasari's generation the one who seems to have taken the greatest interest in things Venetian was the restless, perceptive Salviati, Vasari's childhood friend, who stayed in Venice in 1539-40; he executed the poignant *Pietà*, formerly in the church of Corpus Domini in Venice, now at Viggiù in Lombardy, and the *Virgin and Child with Saints* in the church of S. Cristina in Bologna. These works have close affinities with the portrait of Giovanni di Paolo Rucellai, whose long delicate hands with their tapering fingers are also evidence of Salviati's admiration for the Parmigianinesque paintings he had seen in Bologna and elsewhere in Emilia.

It is probable that the artist was commissioned to paint the most famous member of the Rucellai family by Palla di Bernardo (Florence 1473-1543), a descendant of the branch of the family that had received the cultural and political legacy of Giovanni; this was perhaps through the good offices of Pietro Aretino, who was accustomed to playing the role of intermediary and was in touch with the Rucellai, since as early as May 1539 he had made the acquaintance of Piero, Palla's son, who had been sent to him by Varchi and Ugolino Martelli.

The book lying on the table in the right background, which is open at the page headed "Delle Antichità," is almost certainly *De Urbe Roma*; written by Bernardo, Giovanni's son and Palla's father, the volume contained a detailed account of a visit to the Roman antiquities which took place in 1471. The erudite guide was Leon Battista Alberti, who is quoted with great admiration a number of times in the text.

Alessandro Cecchi

40
LEON BATTISTA ALBERTI
Self-Portrait

Paris, Bibliothèque Nationale, 2508
Bronze
19.7 × 13.3 cm
Obverse, portrait of Leon Battista Alberti with legend . L . Bap. at right and a winged eye at left; reverse blank.

PROVENANCE: unknown.

BIBLIOGRAPHY: Lewis 1994: 41-43.

This previously unpublished self-portrait relief is evidence of the new importance placed on visualization in fifteenth-century culture. In *Della pittura*, Alberti lauds the "truly divine power" of painting to make the absent present and to represent the dead to the living in future centuries. That portraits serve both the present and the future has been underscored by recent observations about the uses of portrait medals: not only were they sent as gifts to various people (both friends and political connections), thus serving in the present to celebrate the sitter and affirm his role in the world; but they were also placed in the foundations of buildings and in tombs because, as Filarete explained in his treatise on architecture (ca. 1462), all things come to an end, and when the end [of a building] comes future men will remember us as we remember them when we find things in ruins which tell us of the men who made them (Trenti Antonelli 1991: p. 30).

The Paris relief has been identified as an aftercast of the well-known plaquette by Alberti in the National Gallery in Washington by Douglas Lewis (Department of Sculpture, National Gallery, Washington). The date of the Washington version usually been thought to be in the mid-1430s (Pope Hennessy 1966) or 1438 (Watkins 1960); the most recent opinion would advance that to 1432-33. Not only the date, but also the place—and therefore the cultural milieu—where it was produced has been the subject of debate: arguments for Venice, Florence, Ferrara and Rome have been made.

Watkins' dating of 1438 for the Washington relief rested in part on a passage in the *Vita anonyma*, believed to be an authentic work of Alberti of about 1437, in which we read that "in Venice he portrayed the countenances of his friends, whom he had not seen for a year and months on end ... He copied his own expression and likeness so that from this painted and modelled semblance he would be more easily known to strangers approaching him" (Watkins 1960: 256; Fubini and Gallorini 1972: 30; Alberti 1953: 488). Since Alberti left Florence in 1436 in the suite of Eugene IV and again in 1443, if the medal were made in Venice after more than a year's absence from Florence it would have to date either ca. 1438 (which Watkins prefers on account of Alberti's youthful appearance on the relief) or 1445.

Pope Hennessy, instead, connected Alberti's interest in self-portraiture to the Florentine milieu, on the basis of Vasari's report of a self-portrait by him in the Palazzo Rucellai; the drawing attributed to him in a manuscript of *Della Tranquillità dell'Animo*, written in Florence ca. 1442; and the interest shown in portraiture in Alberti's treatise on painting of 1435, also composed in Florence (Pope Hennessy 1966: 66; Grayson, ed. 1972: 8).

For Lewis, instead, the relief is the product of Alberti's first period in Rome (1432-34) and specifically from the earliest part of that stay when Donatello was also working for the Curia. The immediate inspiration for it would have been the collections of coins and sculpture being formed by members of the papal court.

These different datings are of some importance, since if Alberti's self-portrait medal dates from 1432-33 or 1435, it precedes Pisanello's earliest bronze medal (of Emperor John Palaeologus) by some years and may thus be seen as a catalyst for the development of what became a popular Quattrocento genre; whereas the later date, although it could be pushed back to 1437 (since Alberti says he had been away from Florence for "a year and months"), would suggest that his interest in portraiture and Pisanello's were nearly simultaneous. Further, since Pisanello's medal of the Byzantine emperor was made at the time of the Ferrara/Florence Council, at which Alberti was also present, the 1438 date raises the possibility that both portraits were made in Ferrara on that occasion. However, since Pisanello was painting at the Lateran Basilica in 1431-32, he could have seen Alberti's portrait relief in Rome, if Lewis' early dating for it is accepted. Thus the date of the Washington relief is essential for determining Alberti's role in the development of Renaissance portraiture.

The Renaissance self-portrait medal or plaque differs from contemporaneous painted profile portraits in its clear antique inspiration, especially from ancient coins and gems (a cameo portrait of Augustus has been related to our plaque) but also from ancient pottery lamps and mirror backs (Lewis 1994, Spencer 1984). However, the addition of the emblem of the winged eye in the Washington and Paris reliefs—an idealized, paradigmatic, or cryptic representation of the subject's character—also shows affinities with courtly and chivalric culture. Such a confluence of classicizing and chivalric trends may be more typical of the courts of Ferrara and Mantua—where the presence of humanist educators like Guarino Veronese did not lessen their students' interest in French romances—than of Florence or Rome. And the fact that virtually all of the early portrait medals come from court ambiances, and none from Florence, might suggest that the Washington relief was made while Alberti had closer contact with the northern courtly culture, hence in 1438. On the other hand, the emblem, which is a kind of hieroglyph, could be considered evidence of Alberti's encounter with the obelisks in Rome. Curiosity about their inscriptions could have led him to Horapollo's *Hieroglyphics*, a work discovered in 1419, and to experimentation with this kind of imagery in our relief. *C.S.*

41

Leon Battista Alberti
Winged Eye with Motto "Quid Tum"

Florence, Biblioteca Nazionale, cod. II.IV.38, formerly Magl. XXI. 119, fol. 92r
Pen and ink
29.6 × 22

Provenance: Strozzi

Bibliography: Alberti 1987: 216, 261 nn. 4, 14; 1988, xvi; *Da Pisanello* ... 1988: 46-47; Jarzombek 1989: 50, 64; *Le muse e il principe*... 1991: 166.

Found in a collection of Alberti's vernacular works, the drawing occurs at the end of *Della famiglia* (*Da Pisanello* 1988; *Le Muse* 1991) and not before the dedicatory letter to Brunelleschi which precedes *Della pittura* in the same codex (Watkins 1960). The last book (IV), of *Della famiglia* was probably written in 1437-38 (Grayson 1966), although an earlier date cannot be ruled out (Watkins 1957). This suggests a *terminus ante quem* of 1438 for the drawing, which is believed to be autograph on the basis of its epigraphy, and because it is executed in the same ink with which Alberti made corrections in the margins of *Della famiglia (Da Pisanello)*. A manuscript of *Philodoxeos*, which Alberti sent to Leonello d'Este in 1436 *Le muse* 1991; Watkins 1957) or 1438 (Watkins 1960) also has the emblem of the winged eye (*Codex Estense*, Lat. 52. VI.A.12), confirmation that Alberti had adopted this device by 1436-38. While it would be important for the history of portraiture to determine whether the Washington self-portrait (text figure 1), emblem, and motto were all conceived together and at the same moment as mutually reinforcing and complementary modes of self-representation, or separately, this question must remain open until the problems of their respective dates are resolved.

Uncertainty exists regarding the cultural context within which Alberti first adopted the emblem and motto. If its first use is in the copy of *Philodoxeos* which Alberti sent to Leonello d'Este in 1436 or 1438, then its message might be interpreted in terms of the interests of the court at Ferrara, classicizing but also strongly chivalric. On the other hand, it has been suggested that Alberti adopted the device either during his first Roman Sojoven of 1432-34 (Lewis) or when he joined the Roman "Academy" founded by Pomponio Leto: and in either of this cases its meaning would more likely be related to classical literature or antiquarian concerns such as hieroglyphics (Alberti 1988, xvi). That Alberti was interested in emblems at an earlier date is suggested by *Anuli*—one of the *Intercoenales* probably written in 1432, and the main subject of which is the explication of such devices—and by the two occurrences of the emblem before Alberti's involvement with the Roman "Academy."

Opinion on the significance of the winged eye varies, although many scholars believe its meaning to be related to a passage in *Rings* (*Anuli*) (Alberti 1987: 260 n. 1), where Alberti interprets the meaning of a ring depicting a winged eye in the center of a crown (Parronchi 1962a; Gadol 1969; Watkins 1960; Jarzombek 1989: 50; Alberti 1987: 261, n. 14; Alberti 1988, xvi; *Da Pisanello* 1988): "There is nothing more powerful, swift, or worthy than the eye. In short, it is the foremost of the body's members, a sort of king or god. Didn't the ancients regard God as similar to the eye, since he surveys all things and reckons them singly? On the one hand, we are enjoined to give glory for all things to God, to rejoice in him, to embrace him with all our mind and vigorous virtue, and to consider him as an ever-present witness to all our thoughts and deeds. On the other hand, we are enjoined to be as vigilant and circumspect as we can, seeking everything which leads to the glory of virtue, and rejoicing whenever by our labor and industry we acheive something noble or divine" (Alberti 1987: 213-21).

Jarzombek, interpreting this passage as referring to the reason and omnipotence of divine intelligence, suggested that the meaning of Alberti's device is better explained by a different passage from *Anuli*, in which the image of Pegasus flying over the ocean represents the power of human intellect (Jarzombek 1989: 64): "As we hasten toward the havens of a better life, we must use wings to avoid sinking into the waves. These wings are the powers of our human intellect and the gifts of our minds which help us attain even the heavens in our study of nature, and which join us to the gods in piety and virtue" (Alberti 1987: 216).

For other scholars, the winged eye refers to Alberti's exaltation of the faculty of sight (Chastel 1975: 110); "the quasi-divine act of 'rational seeing'" (Gadol 1969); or Alberti's inventions in optical science (Hill 1930: 39). Others still have seen it as referring to the vigilant all-powerful gaze of the artist (Lewis 1994: 42); representing the eye of God which metes out judgment (Wind 1958: 187; Watkins 1960); or derived from Egyptian hieroglyphics, in which the eye represents divinity and the wings omnipresence (Wind 1958: 186; Cieri Via 1986: 63). Another line of interpretation, focusing on animal lore, relates the emblem to Aristotle's discussion of the eye of the eagle, who looks into the sun without being blinded (Badt: 1957-59: 81); to Aelian's discussion of eagles, who test the legitimacy of their children by making them look directly at the sun without blinking, and of lions, who are said to be born with their eyes open and never sleep (Schneider: 1990: 266); to Philo and Statius' claim that the lion's eye had the power of retaining his majesty after his body died (Alberti 1988, xvi); or to Lucian's association of the power of the eye and the eagle's wing in *Icaromenippus* (Alberti 1987: 261 n. 4).

To these, I would add the evidence of a literary source

which I believe is consonant with, and therefore supportive of, the text describing the winged eye from *Anuli*. In Eunapius' *Lives of the Philosophers*, he describes the fourth-century philosopher Maximus thus: "the very pupils of his eyes were, so to speak, winged ... his glance revealed the agile impulses of his soul" and in conversation, "one could hardly endure the swift movements of his eyes or his rapid flow of words."

Similar diversity of opinion exists over the meaning of the motto "*quid tum*," which means, "what then?" or "what next?" or even "so what?" Classical literary sources have been suggested in Cicero (*Tusculan Disputations*, II. xi.26); Virgil (*Aeneid*, IV.543 or *Eclogues*, X.38); Horace (*Satires*, II, III.230); and Terence (*Eunachius*, II.iii.47) (Wind 1958: 187; *Da Pisanello* 1988: *Le muse* 1991). Two of these citations (Terence and Vergil, *Eclogues*) occur in a humorous and erotic context; in Horace the context is a story of a young man throwing away his inheritance; in the *Aeneid*, it is Dido's debate about whether to kill herself; in Cicero, it prefaces his explanation of why he is able to quote poetry. To this writer, none of these sources elucidates the problem. Alternatively, the motto has been said to refer to the "*quid tunc*" of the *dies irae* service (Watkins 1960). In short, there is no agreement either on its exact literal meaning or literary source, and therefore none on its significance.   *C.S.*

42
MATTEO DE' PASTI
Portrait of Leon Battista Alberti with Winged Eye and "Quid Tum" on the Reverse

Washington, National Gallery of Art, formerly A 792.56A, now 1957.14.648
Bronze
diam 9.3 cm
Obverse, portrait of Leon Battista Alberti with inscription *LEO BAPTISTA ALBERTUS*; reverse, winged eye with motto *QUID TUM* and inscription *MATTHIAEI PASTII VERONENSIS OPUS*.

PROVENANCE: Samuel Kress Collection.

BIBLIOGRAPHY: See no. 1 and, in addition, Tonini 1904; Ricci 1924: 46; Hill 1930: no. 161; De Baranano 1980; Pasini 1987: 143-159; *Le muse e il principe* 1991: 166.

Matteo de' Pasti, the son of a doctor, was born into a propertied family of some social standing in Verona ca. 1420. He began his artistic career as a miniature painter for Piero de' Medici and then Leonello d'Este. Although his first documented presence in Rimini dates 30 June 1449, he is believed to have come there in 1446, at which time he is thought to have begun his activity as a medalist. Matteo was an educated man, active in contemporary literary society: he owned a copy of Ciriaco d'Ancona's *Commentaries* (Ciriaco was in Rimini in 1449); Alberti sent him a book (Ricci 1924: 49) and referred to him as "amico dulcissimo" (Grayson 1957); his epigraphy shows familiarity with the most recent advances in that field (Mardersteig 1959). He was in contact with Giovanni Marcanova. He also served as a diplomat, entrusted with a mission to Turkey for Sigismondo Malatesta in 1461 (Panvini Rosati 1968: 22), and as superintendant at the

Tempio Malatestiano (see, cat. no. 49). He died in 1467/68 or about 1490.

His portrait medal of Alberti, combining the portrait on the obverse with the emblem and motto on the reverse, probably dates from the time of their association on the rebuilding of the Tempio Malatestiano, and therefore from the 1450s, although an earlier date and an association with the court of Ferrara (where Matteo made a medal of Guarino Veronese) cannot be excluded. That it was made in Rimini 1446-50 (Hill 1930; Watkins 1960), seems unlikely since Alberti's involvement there seems to have begun at a later date. In any case, since the medal was made after Alberti invented his emblem and chose his motto, it suggests that the subject of the medal, not the artist, determined the image. The medal is therefore not Matteo's interpretation of Alberti, but a representation of Alberti's chosen self-definition. Pasini's suggestion that the medal dates 1454, the year in which there was an exchange of letters between Matteo and Alberti and in which Matteo seems to have visited the architect in Rome, seems likely.   *C.S.*

43
PTOLEMY
Geography
(with illustrations by Pietro del Massaio)

Vatican, Biblioteca Apostolica Vaticana, *Codex Vat. Urb.* Lat. 5699
Parchment, bound in red leather
59.5 × 44 cm, 130 folios, fol. 127r.

PROVENANCE: the manuscript was made for Nicolò Perotti, head of Cardinal Bessarion's household in 1455 and translator from Greek to Latin for Nicholas V.

BIBLIOGRAPHY: De Rossi 1879; Ratti 1911; Zippel 1910; Mercati 1925; Boffito 1925-26: 286-292; Omont 1926; Fischer 1932; Almagia 1944-45; Ehrle and Egger 1956; Frutaz 1962, vol. 1: 137; Scaglia 1964; Vagnetti 1967; Gadol 1969: 183; Edgerton 1974: 278; Westfall 1974: 85-90; Schulz 1978: 435-436, and 456-458; Maddalo 1988: 71; Jacks 1990: 457.

Ptolemy's *Geography* (written ca. A.D. 150) was rediscovered by the Byzantine scholar Planudes in the late thirteenth century, at which time, since the original twenty-seven maps of the regions of the world were lost, Planudes ordered new ones to be made. Manuel Chrysolaras brought a copy of the *Geography* to Italy, and under this influence the work was translated into Latin by Jacopo d'Angelo da Scarperia in 1405.

Although Ptolemy seems to have left space for abbreviated representations of cities on his regional maps, the idea of adding separate views of famous cities belongs to the fifteenth century. The most recent opinion suggests that the archetypal manuscript of this new type was probably a now-lost work by the French scribe Niccolò de Comminellis di Mezières, reflected in three copies by Pietro del Massaio, of which the earliest (Paris, Bib. Nat. lat. 4802) dates before 1456 (Jacks 1990). The latest, *Codex Vat. Urb.* lat. 277, dates 1472; and the remaining copy, here exhibited, bearing the date 28 November 1469, was copied by Hugo de Comminellis and illustrated by the

Florentine Pietro del Massaio (1424-before 1496).

Our manuscript has views of nine cities: Milan, Venice, Florence, Rome, Constantinople, Damascus, Jerusalem, Cairo, and Alexandria. The cities are shown in bird's-eye view, characterized by the shape of their walls and by the major monuments distributed in approximately accurate relationships to each other and to the walls. No streets, piazzas, or vernacular buildings are shown.

The original designer, or designers, of the views is unknown. The view of Constantinople may copy that of Cristoforo Buondelmonte, made during his visit to that city in the 1420s; since the view of Florence identifies the cathedral as S. Reparata instead of S. Maria del Fiore, Boffito suggested that it derives from a prototype of 1404-20, when that designation was still in use. The view of Rome is more problematic. Whereas Gadol believed it to be within the same tradition as Taddeo di Bartolo's fresco of 1414 in the Palazzo Pubblico in Siena, Schulz saw it as copying a lost drawing made for Biondo Flavio's *Roma instaurata* (1444-46). A fuller version of this same lost drawing can be recognized, in the so-called Strozzi plan (Bib. Laur., MS. Redi 77) (Schulz 1978; Scaglia 1964). Whereas the Strozzi plan reveals new ideas about representation in its emphasis on topographical relations, and the inclusion of some streets and aqueducts, the Ptolemy map omits these in favor of a presentation of the city as a historical, rather than topographical, reality (Westfall 1974; Schulz 1978).

Connections between the Ptolemy illustration, the lost map for Biondo's antiquarian work, and Alberti's *Descriptio urbis Romae*—the latter two works both ca. 1445—are not lacking. Both Biondo and Alberti sought new ways to visualize the city in which they were living and working; both views contributed to a more complete and systematized image of Rome. Alberti's view was stimulated by the rediscovery of Ptolemy; Biondo's served as a model for the illustration of his work. The function of Ptolemy's coordinate tables of world geography was to establish the exact position of particular places, and the relations between those places (*Geography*, I.1.19). This is precisely what Alberti's *Descriptio* did for the city of Rome, imposing on a map of the city a system of coordinates giving the exact location of its buildings (Vagnetti 1967; Schulz 1978). Alberti's map and graph linked the geography of the city (for example, the course of the Tiber) to its major monuments within a consistent system of measurement. This system, if only "distantly related to the latitude method of Ptolemy" (Schulz 1978: 436) may, nonetheless, be seen as inspired by that work (Edgerton 1974; Gadol 1969). Common to both approaches is the desire to visualize the world not only with the instruments of empirical observation, but with the use of a mathematical system which makes its order apparent.   *C.S.*

44
ANONYMOUS
Box Imitating Alberti's Holy Sepulcher in the Cappella Rucellai, S. Pancrazio, Florence

Monselice, Ca' Marcello, 844 (inside the box is the number 966)
Wood, painted and gilded.
38.5 × 47.8 cm (at projecting cornice) 45.5 cm (across body) × 33 cm (at cornice), 28 cm (across body)

PROVENANCE: bought for the Castello di Monselice in Florence in the 1930s by Giorgio Cini; earlier, Palazzo Davanzati, Florence.

BIBLIOGRAPHY: Barbatini 1940; no pagination.

The box is a close copy of Alberti's version of the Holy Sepulcher in the Cappella Rucellai of S. Pancrazio, Florence. Not only do these share the rectangular shape, the decoration in square panels divided by pilasters with geometric motifs in the center of each panel, and a cornice of carved fleurs-de-lis, but there is also a rough proportional correspondence between the works. The height of Alberti's Sepulcher, up to the cornice, is 3.40 m, that of the box, 38.5 cm; the length of the Sepulcher is 4.10 m, of the box, 45.6 cm; the width of the Sepulcher is 2.25 m, that of the box 29. Since the length and width of the Holy Sepulcher are approximately half those of the Holy Sepulcher in Jerusalem, the box also has a rough proportional relationship to the tomb of Christ. Although the box might be a model for Alberti's Sepulcher, the fact that it is entirely finished in terms of painting and gilding, and equipped with a small door in the front which originally opened with a key, suggest that it served an independent purpose and therefore that it is a copy after the Albertian work. Moreover, the appearance of the box contradicts Alberti's recommendations about models. Alberti condemned "models that have been colored and lewdly dressed with the allurement of painting" as "the mark of no architect intent on conveying the facts; rather of a conceited one, striving to attract and seduce the eye of the beholder". Thus the date of 1467 inscribed on the Rucellai Holy Sepulcher provides the *terminus post quem* for the box. The top of the box has been damaged: most of the frieze is lost and it is now opened by a lid which is painted dark brown, unlike the rest of the box. The false door on the left side, imitating the entrance into Alberti's Sepulcher, seems to have been cut into the box at a later date; the opening is filled with a block of wood added from the inside and decorated with balustrades in a Baroque style. Originally, then, the door on the front of the box was its only opening; the lid and false door seem to represent later modifications.

Although the original purpose and location of the box are unknown, it may be supposed that it contained relics. Indeed, the practice of housing relics in boxes placed either on or under an altar, common in the Early Christian period, was revived in fifteenth-century Florence with urns such as Ghiberti's for the bones of St. Zenobius (1439). Most likely the wooden box held a relic associated with the Passion, perhaps a piece of the True Cross. While it is tempting to connect its original location with the chapel of the Holy Sepulcher which once existed on the Ponte Vecchio, this must remain speculation.   C.S.

45
ANTONIO LABACCO
Drawing of S. Sebastiano, Mantua

Florence, Galleria degli Uffizi, Gabinetto Disegni e Stampe, Uff. 1779A
Pen with traces of brown chalk on paper.
24.1/24.7 × 17.3/17.9 cm

BIBLIOGRAPHY: Ackerman 1954a; Saalman 1959: 101; Bassani et al. 1974: 243; Lamoureux 1979: 5-23; Licht 1984: 74-75; Günther 1988f: 25.

The only Renaissance drawings after Alberti's buildings are three copies of the same drawing of S. Sebastiano, and a drawing of the Tempio Malatestiano attributed to Antonio da Sangallo the Younger. Those representing S. Sebastiano are the Antonio Labacco drawing here exhibited, a drawing in a sketchbook attributed to Aristotile and Giovanni Battista Sangallo of 1535-40 (Lille, Palais des Beaux-Arts, Fonds Wicar, fol. 840) and a copy of the Sangallo version in Oreste Vannocci's sketchbook of ca. 1580 (Bib. Comunale, Siena, S.IV,1, fol. 140). The date of the Labacco drawing is unknown. Also in question is whether it represents S. Sebastiano as actually built or records Alberti's original project for that structure. Since the measurements on the drawing are given in the Mantuan *ell* of ca. 46.5 cm, Labacco, who never visited that city, must be copying a drawing made there. There are numerous discrepancies between the drawing and the church (Bassani et al. 1974). The real depth of the arms is about one *braccio* less; the height of the portico is also less; the height of the dome in the drawing suggests that it should be hemispherical on the interior; and the drawing shows pinnacles at the corners of the facade. Günther, following Lamoureux, argued that the drawing, its inscriptions, and the measurements preserve the essential features of an Albertian original. Most problematic with this solution, in my view, is that the Labacco drawing ignores the spatial complexity of S. Sebastiano, eliminating the lower, or crypt, level entirely, omitting the two small domed rooms which flank the entrance arm, and ignoring the subdivision of the portico into two levels on the interior. In reducing Alberti's building to a single-story centralized building, Labacco has represented something perhaps more useful as a model for imitation in other contexts, but lacking what was most particular and original in Alberti's design. Ironically, precisely those problems which, according to Saalman, stimulated the development of measured architectural drawings after 1460—that is, the impossibility of representing the multi-unit, multi-form spaces of the new architecture in terms of a plan and some modular elements of membering—are not addressed in the Labacco drawing. While it remains possible that the drawing does reproduce an Albertian original, and even that Alberti himself was unable to capture the complexity of his spatial vision in drawings, another explanation seems possible. We know that, in 1480, Lorenzo il Magnifico asked for drawings of S. Sebastiano, perhaps in connection with the project for S. Maria delle Carceri in Prato, and that he himself was in Mantua in 1483. Might Labacco have co-

pied drawings prepared in Mantua for Lorenzo rather than an Albertian original? Such an hypothesis would account for the omissions of crypt, side rooms, and upper story in the portico, elements unnecessary for the small oratory planned for Prato; while explaining the use of the Mantuan unit of measurement. What we know of Labacco's professional activity may further support this suggestion. Active in Rome between 1528-67, Labacco worked closely with Antonio da Sangallo, executing the wooden model of his project for St. Peter's. Lamoureux's observation that the other two drawings of S. Sebastiano are connected with the Sangallo family as well and that all three might therefore be drawn from material in the Sangallo workshop collection might suggest that the prototype was owned by Giuliano da Sangallo, architect of S. Maria delle Carceri and noted collector of architectural drawings. Regardless of the precise relation of Labacco's drawing to Alberti's building, it follows Alberti's precepts on how the architect should record the buildings he sees. These instructions reveal yet another facet of Alberti's insistence on the necessity of visualization as a means to understanding our experiences.   C.S.

46
LEON BATTISTA ALBERTI
De re aedificatoria

Windsor, Eton College Library; cod. MSS. 128
Paper, in quires of ten leaves, bound in red leather
33.02 × 20.93 cm, 244 ff.

PROVENANCE: this is probably the manuscript originally owned by Bernardo Bembo (Venetian ambassador to Florence) which passed to his son Pietro and then to Sir Henry Wotton (English ambassador to Venice), who donated it in 1639 to Eton College, of which he was provost.

LEON BATTISTA ALBERTI
De re aedificatoria

Modena, Biblioteca Estense, Alpha 0.3.8 (Lat. 419)

PROVENANCE: the manuscript was made for Matthias Corvinus, King of Hungary.

C

LEON BATTISTA ALBERTI
De re aedificatoria

Vatican, Biblioteca Apostolica Vaticana, *Codex Vat. Urb.* Lat.
264
Ink on parchment.
33.3 × 21.1 cm; 197 fols.

PROVENANCE: library of Federico da Montefeltro; CRITICAL
EDITION: Alberti 1966a; English trans. Alberti 1988.

BIBLIOGRAPHY: Mancini 1911: 353; Grayson 1960; Borsi 1980a:
387; *Da Pisanello...* 1988: 35; Morolli et al. 1992: 130-131.

There are ten known manuscripts of Alberti's treatise on
architecture earlier than the *editio princeps* of 1486, not all
of which are extant or complete (Alberti 1988: xviii). Interestingly, except for the fragment owned by Alberti's
cousin Bernardo Alberti (which may be the archetype), all
the known manuscript copies of Alberti's treatise date after his death in 1472. The earliest of these, made for Bernardo Bembo and now in Eton College Library (Codex
MSS 128), dates 1478-80; the others, in Modena, Rome,
Florence, Olomouk (Czechoslavakia), Venice, and Chicago, all seem to date in the 1480s—just prior to the first
printing. While the importance of the work is great, it
does not seem to have been widely read during Alberti's
lifetime. Most scholars accept that the treatise was essentially composed between 1443-44 and 1452 (in which
year it was presented to Pope Nicholas V); some hold that
only some of the ten books were complete by then and
that the others were composed between 1455 and Alberti's death in 1472; the most recent opinion is that the work
was substantially complete in 1452, but that additions
and changes were made later.
Alberti's treatise, written in Latin and without illustrations, was intended for an educated public; patrons, that
is, not architects. It set out, as did its model, Vitruvius *Ten
Books on Architecture*, to inform patrons about the materials, processes and criteria (both practical and esthetic) of
design and building. It is not surprising, therefore, that
copies were sought by great patrons such as Nicholas V,
Federico da Montefeltro and Lorenzo il Magnifico. The
work combines a great deal of technical or, one might say,
"professional" information and advice with abundant examples of architectural projects, and notions about architecture, derived from Alberti's reading of antique
authors and his own observations. The temporal framework of the discussion is ambiguous: some passages are
clearly aimed at guiding modern practice, while others—
for example on how to design a theater or a bath—clarify
the usages of the ancients without any apparent direct
relevance for contemporary building.
The passages of interest for this exhibit belong to the
former of these categories: Alberti has a good deal to say
about the use of architectural models. Condemning poorly thought-out constructions, and the consequent errors
in finished buildings, he writes: "For this reason I will always commend the time-honored custom, practiced by
the best builders, of preparing not only drawings and
sketches, but also models of wood or any other material.

These will enable us to weigh up repeatedly and examine
with the advice of experts, the work as a whole and the
individual dimensions of all the parts, and, before continuing any farther, to estimate the likely trouble and expense" (*De re aedificatoria*, II.1, Alberti 1988: 33).
He returns to this argument in Book IX: "I must urge you
again and again, before embarking on the work, to weigh
up the whole matter on your own and discuss it with experienced advisors. Using scale models, reexamine every
part of your proposal two, three, four, seven—up to ten
times, taking breaks in between, until from the very roots
to the uppermost tile there is nothing, concealed or open,
large or small, for which you have not thought out,
resolved, and determined, thoroughly and at length, the
most handsome and effective position, order, and number." (*Ibid.*, IX. 8: 313).
Alberti's insistence on the use of models is evidence of the
great importance he placed on visualization in regard to
that which does not yet exist—that is, the future. In a certain sense, through models the future edifice becomes a
present reality, the merits of which can be assessed as if
it were already built. Battisti's careful analysis of Alberti's design process suggested to him that one of the characteristics of Renaissance design, as opposed to medieval design, is precisely the exploration of various possible solutions over an extended period (Battisti 1974). Whereas
the medieval architect was thought to hold the total idea
of the building in his mind and then manipulate matter to
match it, the Renaissance practitioner arrived at the idea
as the final result in a series of judgments involving
sketches, measured drawings and, finally, the model.
C.S.

47
BACCIO D'AGNOLO
Model for S. Giuseppe or S. Marco, Florence

Florence, Museo di San Marco, inv. P.n. no. 58
Wood.
58 × 129 × 171 cm

PROVENANCE: the model was discovered in the oratory
of S. Giuseppe in Florence in 1913.

BIBLIOGRAPHY: Chiappelli 1921-22; 1925; Tosi 1928-29; Borgo
and Saalman 1978; Vasari 1982; Sframeli, ed. 1989: 510.

The wooden model discovered in S. Giuseppe and now in
S. Marco presents a puzzle. On the one hand, Baccio
d'Agnolo's only documented work is S. Giuseppe in Florence. Vasari tells us that the architect made a wooden
model for that project, and the model was found in that
church in 1913. On the other hand, the model in question
doesn't bear much formal relation to the small oratory of
S. Giuseppe, and would seem, instead, to be related to the
1512 project to rebuild S. Marco, a project for which we
have documentary evidence of a model made by Baccio
d'Agnolo. Nothing came of this project until the 1520s,
at which time the commission involved different architects. If for S. Marco, how did the model come to be
in S. Giuseppe? And if for S. Giuseppe, why is there so
little relation between the model and the church?
Whatever its original purpose, the wooden model is of the
kind recommended by Alberti in his treatise (see cat. nos.
44 and 46). It is not painted; incisions and markings in red
chalk suggest the various features not actually built in
wood. The model shows, above all, the disposition and relation of the parts of the building, their proportions, and
the scheme of lighting. There is no hint of surface treat-
ments or other ornamentation. As Alberti said, "the work

ought to be constructed naked, and clothed later; let the
ornament come last" (*De re aedificatoria*, IX, viii, Alberti
1988: 312). We know that Alberti himself made models
for his buildings from his treatise (see cat. no. 46) and
from contemporary references to a model for the Tempio
Malastiano.
C.S.

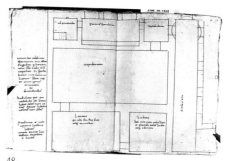

48
LEON BATTISTA ALBERTI (attrib.)
Plan of a Bath Complex

Florence, Biblioteca Medicea-Laurenziana, *Codex Ashb.* 1828,
(App.) cc. fol. 56v. 57r.
Pen and ink on paper, cut down on the bottom and right edges.
27.3 × 38.5 cm

PROVENANCE: the drawing was discovered in a collection of 15th-
and 16th-century drawings gathered by the 17th-century Urbinate
architect Muzio Oddi.

EXHIBITION: Rome, Museo Capitolino, 1988.

BIBLIOGRAPHY: Burns 1979a; 1980; Scaglia 1988b; *Da Pisanello...*
1988: 49.

Burns, who discovered the drawing and first presented it
as an autograph by Alberti at a congress in 1977, believed
it to represent a project for a bath which Alberti might
have made for himself, for Nicholas V or for Federico da
Montefeltro (Burns 1979a, 1980). His attribution, resting largely on the epigraphy, was rejected by Scaglia precisely on this criterion in 1988 (1988b: 85), and re-
affirmed on this and other grounds in the same year (*Da
Pisanello* 1988). Burns observed that the drawing, which
would be the only autograph we have by Alberti, was
drawn to scale with a ruler, and that although it is difficult
to determine what unit of measurement is being used, the
plan shows a concern for proportional relationships between the parts (Burns 1979a: 49). The inscriptions on the
drawing identify various parts of a bath complex (*tepidarium*, *lavatio*, *sudarium*, etc.); the notation at left claims that
the building "will be seen with the greatest pleasure," and
"will be very bright, uncluttered, and elegant." Thus the
drawing is not a record of an existing ancient bath, but a
project for a building.
The most recent opinion suggests that the project, dating
ca. 1454, was based on literary sources such as Vitruvius,
Pliny the Younger, Seneca, and Martial (sources which,
in my view, describe nothing related to this drawing) and
on the remains of small ancient baths like those at Viterbo
(*Da Pisanello* 1988). The same source affirms, further, a
relation between Alberti's discussion of baths in Book
VIII, x of his treatise and the drawing. This relation, between works purportedly close, moreover, in date, is tenuous at best. Among other differences, the treatise calls for
an atrium in the center of the bath structure, the place occupied by the *tepidarium* in the drawing; the drawing
omits the passageway leading from vestibule to atrium
described in the treatise, as well as the large open space
opening off the north side of the atrium, its portico and
cold bath, the three resting rooms for men and women,
and the large open space surrounding the building complex. Nor can it be maintained that the drawing reveals
Alberti's belief in the healthfulness of baths, following
Galen and Celsus (ibid.); the treatise takes no such stand,
but observes that "some have despised baths, claiming

that they weaken the body; others have so approved of them that they bathed several times a day" (Alberti 1988: 287). As so often, Alberti records quite opposite opinions, leaving the reader to choose between them. Finally, since Alberti makes it quite clear that to him, all bath structures are very large, and "almost always measure over one hundred thousand square feet" (Ibid.: p. 290), the treatise does not provide support for the Albertian attribution of the drawing. This is not to say that the drawing cannot be by Alberti, but only that the attribution is not supported by evidence in his treatise. The only reliable criterion in this case, since there can be no comparison with other Albertian drawings, is the epigraphy, a matter outside my competence, and at the moment contested.

Whether or not the drawing is by Alberti, it illustrates his view that the desire to design is a natural instinct in all human beings and one which he himself felt: "It often happens that we ourselves, although busy with completely different things, cannot prevent our minds and imagination from projecting some building or other" (ibid.: p. 4). Such had already been his practice in the early 1440s, as he tells us in *Della Tranquillità dell'Animo* (Book III): alone at night, to distract himself from bitter cares and worries, he designed buildings in his mind. The drawing of the thermal establishment seems just this kind of drawing; that is, neither an antiquarian attempt to reconstruct the plan of an ancient bath, nor a project for a structure to be built, but a solitary musing about problems of design and function loosely related to a classical theme. The mental idea of something lovely and pleasure-giving is recorded partly by visualization of the spatial disposition and partly through the verbal gloss identifying functional areas and expressing the visual effect of the whole.   *C.S.*

49

Matteo de' Pasti
Representation of the Tempio Malatestiano (S. Francesco), Rimini

Berlin, Staatliche Museen Preussischer Kulturbesitz, Münzkabinett
Bronze; diam. 40 mm.
Obverse, portrait of Sigismondo Malatesta with inscription: *SIGISMUNDUSPANDULFUS MALATESTA PAN F*; reverse, facade of the Tempio Malatestiano with inscription: *PRAECL ARIMINI TEMPLVM AN GRATIAE VF MCCCL.*

BIBLIOGRAPHY: Ricci 1924: 216; Hill 1930: no. 183; Salmi 1960; Ragghianti 1965; Panvini Rosati 1968: 23; *Sigismondo Pandolfo Malatesta...* 1970: 118; Middeldorf and Stiebral 1983: no. xxv; Graham Pollard 1984: 87; Scapecchi 1986: 155-164; Pasini 1987: 149; *Le muse e il principe...*, eds. 1991: 110; Hope 1992: 51-154.

Matteo de' Pasti's medal of the Tempio Malatestiano, showing the building as it was intended to be built, presumably copies Alberti's project and perhaps his model; in fact, the great dome at the rear of the basilica was never carried out and the upper parts of the facade are incomplete. The date of 1450 on the medal has been the subject of much scholarly discussion, for if the medal was indeed made in that year we would have to assume that the project, and Alberti's involvement in it, date from the late 1440s—an assumption not supported by the surviv-

ing documents. Most scholars agree that the date on the medal refers, not to the year in which it was struck, but to the time of Sigismondo's decision to rebuild the church. This decision has been related to the Jubilee year of 1450 and to Sigismondo's meeting with Nicholas V in Fabriano in August, at which time the pope, who granted Sigismondo large territories, might have suggested his secretary and advisor Alberti as architect (Ricci 1924: 216). The medal would refer, in this hypothesis, to the principles of *justitia* and *religio* (*Le Muse* 1991). The new project has also been related to a vow made by Sigismondo in connection with his victory over Ferdinand of Aragon at Vado in 1452-53 (*Sigismondo* 1970: 139; Pasini), recorded by the court poet Basinio da Parma: "*Hinc ad Arimineam fertur laetissimus urbem / Victor ubi superis votum dum solvit, honorem, / Ipse Deo reddens summo mirabile templum / Marmore de pario construxit, et urbe locavit in medio*" (*Hesperidos*, XIII: 343-347).
In this case, the medal would celebrate "the glory of the victor and the founding of the Temple" (Pasini). Since, as Middeldorf and Stiebral observed, the vow is recorded in the inscription on the reverse (*VF* = "*votum fecit*") and Sigismondo is shown laureate, this connection seems firm. Less clear is the connection between the vow and the chronology of the building project. Renovation was already under way in the church before 1450 and Piero della Francesca's frescoed portrait of Sigismondo in the building, of 1451, makes no reference to the vow. Yet, since the medal bears the commemorative date 1450, it seems likely that the vow was made in that year. The medal would seem to date in or before 1454, because Matteo's letter to Sigismondo of 17 December 1454 reports that he has sent 20 medals to Senigallia and is making a mold in order to cast other small silver versions (*Sigismondo* 1970: 139, 143). It therefore seems possible that while the vow might have been made in 1450 when work was already in progress at S. Francesco, its fulfillment, presumably with a marked change in the nature, scope or funding of the project, dates 1453-54 and is commemorated by the medal. Whether the beginning of the Albertian phase of the project dates 1450 or 1453-54, by this last date the design was considered sufficiently established for a visualization of its completed form to be disseminated. The medal not only served to advertise Sigismondo's person, his prestige, and his vow, to allies, friends, and political acquaintances; six were found in his tomb, arranged in the shape of a cross beneath his body (*Sigismondo* 1970: 139). By visualizing the future, Sigismondo gained prestige in the present, established his fame as patron for posterity, and—who knows?—perhaps hoped this concrete token of his piety might, as a record of his past, recommend him to Divine Mercy at the Last Judgment.   *C.S.*

50

Sperandio (Bartolomeo di Savelli)
Representation of a Domed Centralized Church

Washington, National Gallery of Art, 1957.14.708
Copper alloy.
diam. 8.6 cm
Obverse: portrait of Francesco Sforza with inscription *FRANCISCUS SFORTIA VICECOMES DUX MEDIOLANI QUARTUS*;

reverse, domed centralized church with inscription *OPUS SPERANDEI.*

BIBLIOGRAPHY: Hill 1930: no. 361. Lang 1968: 220; Panvini Rosati 1968: 27.; Scaglia 1970b: 19-20; Pedretti 1973: 32; 1978: 95; Graham Pollard 1984: 203-204; Lloyd 1987: 102-103; Eiche and Lubkin 1988: 547.

Sperandio (ca. 1425-1504) is first documented as active in Ferrara in 1445, a city in which he worked intermittently between 1463-77, and again in 1490/91-1494. He is known to have been in Faenza (1477), Bologna (1478), Padua (1494) and Venice (1496).
The medal here exhibited depicts Francesco Sforza (1401-66), Duke of Milan, on the obverse, and a reflection of Filarete's project for his mausoleum on the reverse. Panvini Rosati and Lang believed the medal to date 1466, shortly after the death of Francesco. If so, it transmits to the future the mausoleum that the duke wished to build, associating him as patron with a project whose real existence is limited to the medal itself, and at the same time celebrating his importance, expressed in the grandiose image of his tomb.
The Sforza's desire for a central-plan mausoleum continued under Francesco's successor Galeazzo Maria who, in a document of 1471, left money for a church with chapels to be built of marble and "in modo del" ("after the manner of") Florence Baptistery or that of Pisa (Eiche and Lubkin 1988). The project was revived again under Lodovico il Moro in a series of drawings by Leonardo of ca. 1478-90 (Pedretti 1973) and finally initiated in Bramante's rebuilding of the east end of S. Maria delle Grazie.
Typological similarities seem to connect the centralized, five-domed, structure shown on the medal with the illustrations in Filarete's treatise on architecture (ca. 1462) and, to a lesser extent, the centralized structure shown in the Louvre Plaquette, a work also attributed to Filarete (Hyman 1981). In Scaglia's view, however, the image belongs to "the fabulous world of antiquity" as imagined in Lombard-Venetian circles, and is to be associated with the Santarelli drawings and the Marcanova manuscript. A distant relation to Alberti's S. Sebastiano in Mantua, conceived in 1459 but not executed as planned, may also be suggested (see cat. no. 45).
That Sperandio knew of Alberti's plans is suggested by the reverse of his medal of Giovanni d'Orsinio de' Lanfredini (ca. 1476-77) (Lloyd 1987). The medal attempts to capture some of the complexity of a strongly compartmentalized Greek-cross space, a problem not addressed in Labacco's drawing, while offering an idealized version of how the facade of such a structure might be completed.   *C.S.*

51

Andrea di Giusto, or Francesco d'Antonio (attrib.)
Christ Healing a Possessed Boy, and Judas Recovering the Blood Money

Philadelphia, Philadelphia Museum of Art, Johnson Collection, JC 17
Tempera on canvas, transferred from panel.
115 × 106 cm, cut down

PROVENANCE: First known in the W.B. Spence collection, Fiesole, the work was sold through Somzée in Brussels to the Lanz collection, from which Johnson acquired it in 1911.

BIBLIOGRAPHY: Berti 1988: 208 (with summary of the earlier scholarship); Berti and Paolucci, eds. 1990: 200; Johannides 1991b: 32.

The painting has been connected with a lost work by Masaccio showing Christ liberating the possessed boy; Vasari, who saw Masaccio's painting in the house of Ridolfo Ghirlandaio, praised its combined interior and exterior views of "casamenti" as an example of the painter's skill in perspective. Differences between the style of the Johnson painting and that of Masaccio's autograph works have led many scholars to accept a relationship between the two works but to attribute the former to Andrea di Giusto (Berenson 1963; Salmi 1947; Longhi 1940; Berti 1988; Berti and Paolucci 1990). The exact nature of the relationship of the Johnson picture to Masaccio has been a matter of debate: Longhi believed both the lost Masaccio and the Johnson picture to belong, conceptually at least, to Brunelleschi, to whom he also attributed another scene of Christ healing in an elaborate architectural setting, the Louvre Plaquette. Berti, instead, while accepting influence from Brunelleschi in the use of two-point perspective (as in Brunelleschi's view of Piazza della Signoria) and the Louvre Plaquette (for which he accepted Brunelleschi's authorship), considered the Johnson painting to have been designed by Masaccio himself, ca. 1423-24, and executed by a member of the shop, perhaps Andrea di Giusto. A different explanation, proposed by Shell, has been re-affirmed in the most recent discussion of the problem. In this view, the painting does indeed owe something to Masaccio, especially in the relation between the main group of figures and the *Tribute Money* in the Cappella Brancacci, but nothing to Brunelleschi, since it uses an empirical perspective like Trecento painting and not a true two-point perspective. Further, the style as a whole and especially the architectural vocabulary (e.g., the wooden piers), show a closer relationship to Masolino than Masaccio. Shell suggested that the Johnson picture, or a painting by Masolino, was the work seen by Vasari (who was therefore mistaken in his attribution) and that the painter was Francesco d'Antonio (documented 1393-1433). The work would date ca. 1429. Johannides, noting affinities both with Masolino and Masaccio, as well as with the Louvre Plaquette (which he believed to be by Donatello) argued for this attribution to Francesco d'Antonio and a date of ca. 1426.
Of particular interest here is the representation of the dome, clearly a visualization (although not an accurate one) of how Brunelleschi's dome for Florence Cathedral, begun in 1420, would appear when completed. The painter must have been guided, as were the men at work on the dome, by Brunelleschi's large brick model which stood next to the cathedral itself. Indeed, there is an interesting divergence between the architecture of the main body of the church which, I agree with Shell, relies on traditional formulae and which not only has little relation to the structure of the cathedral but is hardly buildable, and that of the dome, based on Brunelleschi's model. Shell explained the juxtaposition of the scene of Christ healing the possessed boy with that of Judas accepting the blood money as following the textual sequence in Matthew 17, where the cure is described in verses 14-18, and in 22-23 Jesus foretells his betrayal. But Shell omitted the significance of the intervening verses, 19-21 which, I submit, explains the significance of the dome for the painting. When the disciples asked Jesus why they had been unable to cast out the boy's demon, Jesus replied that "if your faith were the size of a mustard seed you could say to this mountain, 'Move from here to there,' and it would move; nothing would be impossible for you." In the 1420s

when the success of Brunelleschi's proposal to erect the dome was uncertain, these lines would have had special resonance since, as is clear from all the epitaphs composed at Brunelleschi's death, the achievement of the dome was seen exclusively as a problem in engineering—the lifting and moving of weights.
The painting belongs to a group of Florentine works in which scenes of healing are placed in complex architectural settings. Vasari records, in his life of Stefano Fiorentino, a lunette in the cloister of S. Spirito showing Christ healing the possessed boy: the painting's complex staircase was said to have inspired Lorenzo il Magnifico's design for the stairs at Poggio a Caiano. Three other versions of the same subject also use elaborate settings: Masaccio's lost representation, the Johnson painting and the Louvre Plaquette. The formula was also used for scenes of St. Zenobius (patron saint and first bishop of Florence): both Ghiberti's urn for his relics (1437-39) and Botticelli's scenes of the bishop's life show him healing in a recognizably Florentine architectural setting.
The painting also needs to be understood within the context of a new demand for portraits of famous buildings by patrons, and a new enthusiasm for this type of representation on the part of artists. Works of art depicting miracles or biblical scenes as occurring in contemporary Florence are evidence of this taste. Filarete asserted that Piero de' Medici loved looking at architecture and enjoyed looking at architectural drawings, "sì che lui ha voluto da bonissimi maestri gli sieno stati ritratti gli edifici di Roma e d'altri luoghi, e in questi disegni molte volte si diletta in essi" ("so much that he had the best masters make portraits of the buildings in Rome and elsewhere, and often he delights in these") (Filarete, XXV: 688). Alberti himself participated in this development if it is true, as Vasari records, that he painted a view of Venice showing St. Mark's.
C.S.

52
GIOVANNI MARCANOVA (compiler)
FELICE FELICIANO (scribe)
ANONYMOUS (illustrator)
Marcanova Manuscript

Modena, Biblioteca Estense, Alpha L.5, 15 (lat. 992)
Parchment.
34.1 × 24 cm, 233 fols.
On fol. 10v. the inscription: *Ioannes Marchanova ar[tium] et med[icinae] doct[or] Pat[avinus] s[ua] p[ecunia] fac[iendum] c[uravit] anno gratiae MCCCCLXV B[ononiae].*

PROVENANCE: although made as a gift for Malatesta Novello, his death in 1465 resulted in the manuscript remaining in the home of Giovanni Marcanova. At Marcanova's death in July 1467, it passed to the Paduan convent of S. Giovanni in Verdara. In the early 18th century in was in the collection of Lorenzo Patarol, from which it passed to Obizzi del Cataio. It came to the Estense Library in 1817.

BIBLIOGRAPHY: Dorez 1892; Hülsen 1907; Lawrence 1927; Dennis 1927; Pratilli 1939-40; Weiss 1959: 172; Meiss 1960: 108; Mitchell 1960: 479; Bruschi 1967: 43; Fiorio 1981: 66; Vitali 1983; Chiarlo 1984: 286; Brilliant 1984: 225; King 1986: 392-393; Günther 1988f: 16; *Da Pisanello...* 1988: 29-30, 38-42; Martineau, ed. 1992: 18.

This collection of materials (entitled *Quaedam antiquitatum fragmenta*, or *Collectio antiquitatum*) was gathered by Giovanni Marcanova between 1457-60, the date of the earliest version of the work (Bern, Burgerbibliothek B 42). The Modena version, bearing the date 1 October 1465, has more epigraphical material and eighteen illustrations of ancient Rome (fols. 25-44). The Garrett manuscript in Princeton, dates from the same year but has only fifteen views of Rome which are not in the same order as those in the Modena manuscript. Other copies are in Paris (Bib. Nat. lat. 5825) and Genoa (Bib. Civica Berio, 11.6.32) (without illustrations).
Giovanni Marcanova (ca. 1410/18-1467) was a doctor of medicine who taught medicine in Padua until 1452 and then taught philosophy in Bologna until 1467. He enjoyed a reputation as an orator: perhaps he is that "Ioannes de Mercatonovo" who delivered the inaugural orations at the beginning of the academic years 1443 and 1444 at Padua University (Bernardinello 1982-83: 369); he certainly spoke before Fantin Dandalo, later Bishop of Padua, in 1447) (Martineau 1992: 10). As an author, we known that he composed the inscription for the base of Donatello's Gattamelata monument and a now-lost treatise *De dignitatibus romanorum triumpho et rebus bellicis*, in addition to the introduction and some epitaphs in our manuscript (Martineau 1992: 10). The inventory of his library shows that he was trained in Scholastic philosophy, and was an Aristotelian. He owned all the major humanist writings on ancient Rome, including Poggio Bracciolini's *De varietate fortunae*, Flavio Biondo's *Italia illustrata*, *Roma instaurata*, *Roma triumphantes* and *Decades*, Petrarch's *Africa*, Giovanni Tortelli's *De orthographia* and Leonardo Bruni's *Historia rerum in Italia gestarum*; as well as an epitome of Livy, a translation of Suetonius, Poggio's translation of Diodorus Siculus, and Josephus' *Jewish Antiquities*

(Vitali 1983: 147-161, Sighinolfi 1921: 206-221). His was an unusual collection, rare in combining Aristotelian and Scholastic philosophy with the new humanist interest in ancient history. It reveals a mind as interested in knowledge derived from logical definition as in that drawn from historical example.

His culture is best understood within the context of Paduan humanism, the specific nature of which is glimpsed in the city's enthusiastic reception of the supposed bones of Livy, found at the Paduan monastery of S. Giustina in 1413. Although plans for a mausoleum to house them were not carried out, Sicco Polenton, chancellor of Padua (d. 1448) had an inscription and bust erected at the Palazzo della Regione in 1426. The invention of Livy's relics, like those of a saint, the plan to build a martyrium for them, and the commemoration of the great authority on Roman history in the governmental center of the city, all reveal an attitude to antiquity which was not fettered by a sense of distance between past and present. And it is this refusal to acknowledge any essential disjunction between past and present which informs the illustrations of Marcanova's manuscript.

Among the Paduan humanists was Pietro Donato, bishop since 1428 (d. 1448), who collected books, among them one of the first illustrated copies of the *Notitia dignitatum* (1436, now Oxford, Bodleian Lib. Can. Misc. 378); Ciriaco d'Ancona copied out inscriptions for him in 1443. Another member of the circle, Felice Feliciano (1433-80), wrote the first treatise on the design and proportion of capital letters based on the measurement of antique inscriptions, was a friend of Ciriaco (he may have owned one of Ciriaco's manuscripts, the *Codex Trotti*, Bib. Ambrosiana 373, Fiorio: 65) and was employed as a scribe by Marcanova. Another friend of Ciriaco and collector of antique medals and gems was Cardinal Ludovico Trivisan (ca. 1401-65); while in Padua in 1459 he bought the Roman arena, including the Cappella Arena with Giotto's frescoes (Martineau 1992: 16). Many of these patrons worked closely with artists. Feliciano recorded an outing on Lake Garda of 1464 during which, dressed in togas and crowned with ivy leaves, Andrea Mantegna, Samuele da Tradate, Giovanni Marcanova and Feliciano plucked the cythera as they boated about in search of antiquities (for the *Jubilatio ad viridarios paradiseos*, see Mitchell 1960: 477; *Da Pisanello* 1988: 29). It may be that Marcanova and Feliciano were consultants on classical antiquity for Mantegna and Marco Zoppo (Fiorio 1981: 70). Certainly Padua was the center for a new epigraphy, reviving the Roman Imperial majuscule, used in humanist books like the 1457 Ptolemy (see cat. no. 43), the 1458-59 Stabo and the 1457 Solinus; as it was the center for the illustration of these, especially in the circle of Squarcione and Marco Zoppo (Meiss 1960: 108; Fiorio 1981: 68). It was also a center for luxury book production: the Strabo has the earliest tooled gold bookbinding; the next earliest is our Marcanova manuscript (Hobsen 1958).

This is the culture reflected in the Marcanova manuscript, partly copied by Feliciano himself in the new epigraphy, and illlustrated.

Who did the illustrations? Hülsen, who first published them, believed them to be by Cyriacus himself, whom we know to have made drawings of Rome and some of whose drawings we know were full-page. But Weiss denied the attribution on the grounds that the reconstruction of ancient Rome in the manuscript is not based on observation of ruins, but of small-scale objects like cinerary urns. Fiorio, agreeing with this assessment, attributed the views to Marco Zoppo (a friend of Feliciano) and two assistants. Other scholars have preferred an attribution to Feliciano himself (Mitchell 1961; Günther 1988f); to the circle of Mantegna (Lawrence 1927: *Da Pisanello* 1988); or to the the circle of Maso Finiguerra (Chiarlo 1984).

Saxl observed, regarding the new trend of illustrating the works of ancient authors, that "the reader wishes to see pictures of what he enjoys in the text and the pictures in turn help him to read the text with the right understanding." The effect of such illustrations, he concluded, was not to create historical distance but to destroy it utterly.

This is precisely what the views of Rome in the Marcanova manuscript attempt. They follow immediately after the description of Rome known as the *Anonimo Magliabechiano* (ca. 1411), which is little more than a version of the twelfth-century *Mirabilia urbis Romae*. The text does not describe the visual effect of Rome; rather, it defines the city through naming and enumeration. The views, therefore, complement the text by contributing what it lacks. They represent: 1) the city gate; 2) the rione of Monte dei Cocci (Monte Testaccio); 3) the palace of Caesar; 4) the Capitol; 5) a market (the Roman Forum); 6) a historiated column; 7) the equestrian statue of Marcus Aurelius; 8) a city street with the palaces of Cicero and Crassus; 9) a view of the Roman countryside outside the walls; 10) a triumphal arch; 11) the Vatican obelisk; 12) the Baths of Diocletian; 13) sacrifice in front of a temple; 14) Castel Sant'Angelo (Hadrian's tomb) and Ponte Sant'Angelo; 15) a "vivarium" (place to keep wild animals); 16) a Roman cemetery; 17) the "Tarpea" (mint below the Capitoline?); and 18) an amphiteater.

Strangely, the series has never been analyzed in relation to the text which precedes it, although almost every illustration corresponds to it. The *Anonimo* opens with a discussion of the walls and gates of Rome, the subject of the first illustration. The second topic, streets, is ill. 8; the fourth, triumphal arches, is ill. 10. Then comes a discussion of the hills of Rome, followed by a discussion of the regions (ill. 2). The baths are next (ill. 12), then palaces, including the palace of Caesar on the Via Sacra (ill. 3). The next topic is bridges, including "*Pons Hadrianus, idest pons Sancti Petri vel castelli Sancti Angeli*" (ill. 14). The obelisks follow (ill. 11) and the columns of Trajan and Antoninus (ill. 6); this section ends with the Colosseum, identified both as a round amphitheater and as a temple to the Sun (ill. 18). Equestrian statues are listed next, without, however, specific mention of the Marcus Aurelius (ill. 7). The next topic is temples, beginning with the round temple of Apollo next to St. Peter's (actually a late antique mausoleum consecrated to St. Andrew). Since the author explains that the world Vatican comes from the word *vates* meaning priest this may correspond to the scene of sacrifice (ill. 13). The text takes up Hadrian's tomb, then that of Augustus. Here it recounts a story of how Augustus set aside this area as the burial place for all Roman emperors and filled it with tombs (ill. 16). Next are mentions of various temples, including the templum Asili beneath the Capitoline, now called "the old mint," which used to be the meeting place of the senators (perhaps ill. 17). After other temples comes the Campidoglio (ill. 4), and the temple of Mercury where the merchants gathered. This is said to be near Trajan's Column and may correspond to ill. 5. Only the view of the Roman countryside (ill. 9) and the *vivarium* (ill. 15) are unaccounted for in the text.

The views are not merely illustrations of the written text, although their subjects in most cases seem to depend on it. The order of illustrations does not follow that of the verbal description; moreover, many of the drawings depict more than one monument and therefore can be related to multiple passages in the text. They reveal, as Mitchell so well put it, "the shift of an interest in antiquity on the site to antiquity in the mind, from a world of fact to a world of imagination" (Mitchell 1960); and in Brilliant's formulation, they show the desire to "actualize what once existed materially" (and to reposess the historical reality behind the present ruins. But it was difficult for artists in the third quarter of the fifteenth century to represent ancient scenes in a historically correct way. Frequently, as in the Marcanova manuscript, figures in modern dress pretended to be ancient Romans.

While this was condemned by Filarete, few painters were able to envision antiquity as a cultural whole including dress and bearing as well as topography and setting. Despite occasional attempts at historical reconstrucion—Piero della Francesca's Roman armor in the Arezzo frescoes, for example—most artists sought to understand the unknown in terms of the known.

C.S.

53
FRANCESCO COLONNA
Hypnerotomachia Poliphili

Florence, Biblioteca Mediceo-Laurenziana, D'Elci 15
Paper, bound in brown leather; 234 unnumbered pages.
322 × 203 mm

PROVENANCE: first published in Venice by Aldo Manuzio, 1499; critical edition, Pozzi and Ciapponi, 1964, repr., 1980; partly transcribed into Italian in Bruschi et al. 1978b; English trans. Fierz-David 1950.

BIBLIOGRAPHY: Hülsen 1910a; Argan 1934; Khomentovskaia 1935; Stein 1944: 27-30; Summerson 1948: 50; Weis 1959: 194; Casella and Pozzi 1959; Mitchell 1960: 463; Menegazzo 1962; Pozzi and Ciapponi 1963; Calvesi 1965; Kahr 1966; Kretzulesco Quaranta 1967; Donati 1968; Burke 1969: 623; Kretzulesco Quaranta 1970; Goebel 1971: 47, 67; Wilk 1972-73: 78, 81 n. 64; Chastel 1975: 148; Donati 1975; Schmidt 1978; Calvesi 1983; Pelosi 1986; Kruft 1986: 66; Danesi Squarzina 1987; Calvesi 1987; Onians 1988: 207-216.

Although the attribution of the romance dated 1467 and entitled *Hypnerotomachia Poliphili* to Francesco Colonna, a monk at SS. Giovanni e Paolo in Venice, goes back to 1723, since 1965 much of the scholarly attention to this work has focused on the defense of the traditional identification against a growing body of evidence that identifies Francesco as a Roman prince of the Colonna family, Lord of Palestrina. The chief defenders of the traditional view have been G. Pozzi and L. Ciapponi, editors of the critical edition of the work; M. Calvesi had led the dissenting thesis. The question is crucial for the interpretation of the author's culture. The traditional view placed Colonna in the circle of Felice Feliciano and Marcanova, that is, the humanism of Padua and the Veneto; the alternative would connect him with the Roman circle of Niccolò Perotti and Pomponio Leto's academy.

Further dispute centers on the date. Although the work bears the date of 1467, the marked Albertian influence suggests that the final form (published in 1499) must date after the first edition of Alberti's treatise in 1485. Thus many believe that the *Hypnerotomachia* may have been begun in 1467, or as early as 1465, but that it was reworked until 1475, into the 1480s, or even the 1490s (Schmidt 1978: 145; Kruft 1986; Pozzi and Ciapponi 1963: 8).

The author of the woodcuts is unknown; nor is there agreement about whether the text was always illustrated, or whether these were prepared for the 1499 printing.

The cultural importance of this "antiquarian novel" (Burke), which recounts (Book 1) Poliphilus' dream-pursuit of his love, Polia, their adventures and (Book 2) the story of Polia, and which is written in a bizarre hybrid of Italian and Latin, has been hotly debated. For Weiss, "antiquarian humanism induced even Fra Francesco Colonna to apply his mediocre archaeological knowledge in a series of fantastic reconstructions in his fantastic love story," whereas for Mitchell, "this fantastic romance was in many respects the perfect flower and consummation of fifteenth-century antiquarian scholarship" (Mitchell

1960). Some have sought to explain the work by opposing Alberti's objective, scientific and intellectual approach to antiquity to Colonna's romantic, emotional and intuitive approach: "Alberti, the man of rules, insistent on the concrete, the absolute, the present. Colonna, the dreamer, never formulating, but only discovering and recording the Golden Past, refracted in his own imagination" (Summerson). Others used the work to characterize the difference between a fanciful Venetian attitude toward antiquity (characterizing also Jacopo Bellini and the Marcanova manuscript) "quite different from the sober Florentine reaction" (Wilk).

I believe the objects gathered here show that such oppositions are untenable. All exercises in visualization involve the subjective faculty of imagination, and this is true for Alberti as it is for Colonna. Moreover, the culture of few, if any, of the objects can be defined as purely Paduan-Venetian or Roman-Florentine. For example, the descriptions in the *Hypnerotomachia* (and Goebel has characterized the work as nothing else than a succession of descriptions, hardly linked to each other by narrative, time or space) show a "Venetian" love of rich materials together with an Albertian/Vitruvian appreciation for proportion. The author, who had studied Pliny, Herodotus and Lucretius, used their descriptions for his inventions. Thus the pyramid, labyrinth and forecourt, draw from Herodotus II. 148-150 and Pliny, xxxvi. 30-31, 91-93 (Goebel 1971: 47; Hülsen 1910a: 171). The Temple of Venus Physizoa, in part inspired by Lucretius, *De rerum natura*, I. 1ff, also shows firsthand knowledge of 5. Costanza in Rome and an awareness of Alberti's architectural criteria. The very structure of the work as a dream cannot be adequately explained as continuing the conventions of medieval romances popular in the northern Italian courts, since it is also influenced by the poetic hermeticism of the Platonic Academy in Florence and in particular by Ficino's *De Vita coelitus comparanda* (Mitchell 1960; Chastel 1975: 148; Pelosi 1986; Onians 1988). The uncertainty about whether the author of Santarelli 163 is northern Italian, Florentine, Sienese or Urbinate; the difficulty in untangling the Florentine, Albertian, Urbinate and Mantegnesque influences on the Master of the Barberini Panels; and the fact that the unknown, but probably Paduan, artists of the Marcanova manuscripts were adding illustrations to an account of ancient Rome written in Rome, for a patron who possessed all the recent antiquarian works by authors in the Roman circle, warn against clear-cut distinctions between the various centers interested in antiquity. Certainly the cultural influences and emphases in these differ, but the amount of exchange and travel between them also favored cross-fertilization. In this process, Alberti, familiar in Venice, Ferrara, Padua, Rimini and Urbino as he was in Florence and Rome, was a pivotal figure.   C.S.

Wooden Architectural Models in Lombardy
Luisa Giordano

Renaissance treatises on architecture stress the importance of the construction and use of models as aids to the successful design of buildings. It was Leon Battista Alberti who dealt with this subject most thoroughly and clearly in his *De re aedificatoria* (1966a II, i): for the architect, models are complementary to sketches and drawings because they provide the opportunity to reassess the project and carefully evaluate the way the various parts are disposed, thus allowing changes to be made, even radical ones if necessary. The function which the models have to perform requires them to be as simple as possible, without any superfluous ornament; thus the models are to be "*nudos et simplices, in quibus inventoris ingenium, non fabri manus probes*" ("plain and simple, in which, rather than the manual skill of the maker, the capacity of the architect is evident"). Lastly, the models are to be objects on which the architect can mediate, allowing informed discussion about the project and an exchange of views between him and the other experts; these may be identified as other architects and builders and those who had commissioned the building: "*et eos tecum ipso et una cum pluribus examinasse et iterum alque iterum recognovisse*" ("and you yourself can examine them alone and in the company of others and learn to recognize them"). Filarete (cfr. 1972) also refers to models in a very significant passage describing the relationship between client and architect (*Trattato*, II): the former is the father of the building while the latter is the mother who concludes her gestation of the work with "a small wooden model, made to scale, of the building as it will be, to show the father."

Despite the different language and expository criteria, the two writers are in agreement with regard to the features that are typical of models and allow them to be useful: they are three-dimensional objects that are easier to understand than drawings; thus they facilitate debate among the experts, as well as between architects and their clients. They are for immediate use, so that there is no need for them to be either large or elegantly finished.

The interpretation that appears in these treatises reflects accepted building practice, which is known to us thanks to the testimony of contemporary documents and because a few artifacts have survived over the centuries. The history of architecture in late medieval and early Renaissance Lombardy was similar to that of the other regions of Italy: models were frequently prepared here to assist with the design of buildings, but after the latter had been completed the former were invariably dismantled, while more intricate and refined artifacts have survived and are still admired today. The collation of the information provided by the documents, the interpretation of the treatises, and the comparison with the few surviving objects afford an overview of the principal events in Lombardy in a convincing historical perspective.

The custom of preparing models for use by the architect was a very common one, but only rarely was it documented. They were used in the workshops and were prepared by those working there; normally they were dismantled when the architect or his assistants believed that they had outlived their usefulness as a working tool or item of historical importance.

Interesting evidence of the widespread use of this type of model is provided by a sixteenth-century document which, unusually, established that they should be restored and preserved. On 23 April 1535 the Fabbrica del Duomo di Milano (the Board of Works of Milan Cathedral) ordered that the material relative to the cathedral's construction—drawings, models and molds

—contained in the bequest of the deceased architect Gerolamo della Porta should be purchased, restored and displayed in a room belonging to the *fabbriceria*. This decision was consistent with the policy of this Milanese institution which, from its earliest days, had favored the conservation of all material that served to tell the story of the design of the cathedral. It was, however, an unusual extension of the normal instructions, since these generally referred to particularly well-made drawings and wooden models, not those for everyday use. The resolution states: "*Ordinatum fuit quod aperiatur capsa in qua sunt modelli parvi et designationes nunc quondam magistri Hieronymi de la Porta, olim ingeniarii prefatae fabricae. Et quod de praesenti fiat inventarium seu repertorium per cancellarium praefatae fabricae de ipsis modellis et designationibus, nec non de omnibus aliis modellis et designationibus ad fabricam facientibus; et consignetur in manibus magistri Christofori de Lombardis ingeniarii praefatae fabricae. Et hinc ad diem dominicam, quae erit dies nona mensis maji proxime futuri, extendantur supra telaribus et fortificentur, ut possint appendi parietibus salae praefatae fabricae, sitae in camposancto ipsius fabricae, ubi alias solebat legere, quam salam ex nunc preafati domini praefecti eligunt ad effectum ut ibi conserventur, et pateant oculis omnium super eis studere volentium*" ("It was decided to open the chest containing the small models and drawings belonging to the deceased Master Gerolamo della Porta, former architect of the aforementioned *fabbrica*. Furthermore, the chancellor of the aforesaid *fabbrica* should make an inventory of these models and drawings forthwith, as well as of all the other models and drawings relating to the *fabbrica*; this inventory should then be entrusted to Master Cristoforo Lombardi, architect of the said *fabbrica*. Moreover, from this day until Sunday 9 May next [the drawings] should be placed on stretchers and reinforced so that they may be hung on the walls of a room belonging to the said *fabbrica*, situated by the cathedral cemetery, where he [Gerolamo della Porta] would read in the past; this room has now been selected by the superintendents as the most suitable place for the conservation of the models and drawings, where they may be displayed for the benefit of all those who may wish to study them"; *Annali*: 1877-80 III: 259).

The models built for use during the construction of the building also served to illustrate the project to the workers and to help guide them in their tasks; evidence of this is provided by a resolution of the *fabbriceria* of S. Maria presso S. Celso, which decreed in 1514 that a new model should be made for use by the building workers: "*Quod de novo fiat modellus ecclesie sancte Marie pro maiori instructione magistrorum laborantium in prefata eccelsia*" ("[*The fabbrica*] orders that a new model of the church of S. Maria should be constructed so that those working in the aforementioned church may be given clearer instructions regarding their tasks"; Baroni: I, 1940: 253).

Apart from wood, which was the most important, the materials used for the architect's models included cardboard, clay and stucco: for example, a model in "chieso" or "gieso," in other words stucco, was made in 1593 during the construction of the campanile in the municipal tower of Pavia (Visioli 1991: 139-140).

Striking confirmation of the use that Alberti had foreseen for models as valuable tools for explaining the project and stimulating the discussion that preceded the making of the final choice was provided by the debate relating to the building of the *tiburio* or crossing tower of Milan Cathedral. The earliest information we have in this regard dates from 1487, when Luca Fancelli was asked to express his opinion concerning the models of the crossing tower: "*Modellos constructos ad similitudinem tiburii prefate eccelesiae majoris, factos per nonnullos ingeniarios*" ("The models of the crossing tower of the aforementioned cathedral, made by a number of architects"; *Annali*, III: 39-40.) In January the following year Leonardo da Vinci was paid for the work which he had financed for the execution of a model of the crossing tower (*Annali*, III: 41); other payments for the construction of models were made in May 1488 to one of the makers, Master Pietro da Gorgonzola (*Annali*, III: 42) and to Giovanni Maineri in April of the following year (*Annali*, III: 47); lastly, in May 1490 an advance was given for another model that was to be constructed (*Annali*, III: 57).

The debate about the works which got through the intermediate stages of the selection process took place on 27 June 1490 in the castle of Porta Giovia in the presence of Lodovico Sforza: on that occasion models of projects by Francesco di Giorgio, Giovanni Antonio Amadeo and Gian Giacomo Dolcebuono (in collaboration), the priest Simone da Sartori and Giovanni Battaggio (*Annali*, III: 60). For each stage of the discussion regarding the choices to be made a model showing a simplified version of the crossing tower was made, but these were soon dismantled or simply abandoned. On occasion the decisions of the *fabbrica* make references, either casual ones or for financial reasons, to the precarious nature of this short-lived patrimony. The model built by Pietro da Gorgonzola had already been dismantled before the maker had been paid in order to re-use the materials: "*Qui modelus destructus fuit in ejus absentia, pro faciendo unum alium modelum de materia dicti modeli*" ("This model was destroyed in his absence in order to make another model with the materials of the aforesaid model"; *Annali*, III: 42). Moreover, when Luca Fancelli returned to the building site in 1490 he asked to be given the model of the crossing tower because he wanted to repair the abutments which had been broken and detached. The models of the crossing tower gave three-dimensional form to the projects which were intended to complete this part of the building and allowed discussion between architects in the presence of the clients, who were able to participate actively. Similarly, in 1536 wooden models were made for the door known as the "porta verso il Compito" in Milan Cathedral (*Annali*, III: 262) and, in 1498, for the church of S. Maria presso S. Celso a "model of lantern for the crossing/tower" (*modellum lanterne tiburii*) was commissioned (Baroni 1940, I: 238); the same approach was taken with regard to the arrangement of the choir in Como Cathedral. Models of parts or details of the building under construction were also made when the work had already started in order to ensure that it was carried out correctly by the laborers. According to an account by the Abbot Matteo Valerio, in 1496 Giovanni Antonio Amadeo made a model of at least one part of the facade of the Certosa at Pavia: "He made a clay model so that the work on the facade could be carried out in the best possible manner" (*Memorie* 1879: 138).

Models of parts were also made to illustrate details which might cause problems: this was the case with Bramante, who made a model of the corner pillar in the cloisters at S. Ambrogio: "This has been made in order to demonstrate how the piers, which will be placed in the cloisters instead of columns, will be constructed" (Baroni 1940, I: 58). The debate that took place in 1490 with regard to Milan Cathedral is a good example of the kind of relationship that architects were able to establish with their clients thanks to the use of models. The particular suitability of the model, inasmuch as it provides a three-dimensional scale representation of the planned building and may be viewed from various angles, is the feature that makes the model exceptionally valuable for the client, since he sees it as complementary to the drawings and finds it easier to understand.

With regard to the Certosa at Pavia, the documents inform us that the architects only presented Gian Galeazzo Visconti with the final version of the drawings on parchment: in fact, Giacomo da Campione was paid for "*certorum designamentorum per eum factorum in Mediolano pro soprascriptis laboreriis ostentis per eum prefato domino nostro*" ("certain drawings he had executed in Milan for the aforementioned works he had shown to the aforesaid lord of ours"; Beltrami 1896: 188). For other clients, high-ranking ones included, three-dimensional models were made to give a more adequate explanation of the project than that provided by the drawing; in 1498, for instance, Lodovico Sforza wrote to his brother, Cardinal Ascanio, to inform him that he would be sending him "a model and a drawing" of the project for the cloisters of S. Ambrogio

(Baroni 1940, I: 57). Moreover, Giovanni Battaggio, who had been commissioned by the community at Crema to prepare a project for the planned shrine of S. Maria della Croce, on 16 July 1490, a few months after he had received the commission, sent the model illustrating the project to Crema (Giordano 1990: 85). In these cases, too, it is likely that models were very simple ones in which the finer details were lacking—as suggested by the fact that the model was completed so soon after the commission had been received.

On important occasions or for the construction of major buildings such as cathedrals, the patrons, sometimes acting on their own initiative, decided to have wooden models made displaying those features which Alberti had censured: they were noteworthy for their magnificence and the finishing touches that resembled those of full-scale buildings.

The model of Milan Cathedral to which reference was made in documents of 1392 was probably one of this type: the person responsible was Simone Cavagnera, one of the citizens who had been on the payroll of the *fabbrica* since 1387. As was recorded in a document of 1392, the model had been properly finished off and painted (*Annali*, I: 70). The paradigmatic nature of these artifacts, the function, which they acquired from the moment it was decided to construct them, as a statement of the underlying ideology and intentions of the patrons that was also addressed to posterity is also proclaimed by contemporary documents. For example, in 1399 the Milanese *fabbriceria* ordained that the "church made of wood" by Giovannino di Grassi should be completed "*ut in exemplum remaneat semper ad evidentiam cujuslibet personae, pro avisamento operum ipsius fabricae*" ("so that it may remain forever as a splendid example for all to admire of the project for the work undertaken by this *fabbrica*"; *Annali*, I: 200). The next wooden model, which was commissioned in 1519 from Bernardino Zenale, who was assisted by Cristoforo Solari, was also intended to be testimony to the work of the *fabbrica* and, for the benefit of the experts in their disputation about the errors which it was feared might lead to serious faults in the design, a scale representation of the building that had caused this controversy (*Annali*, III: 208). As was stated above, the models, the function of which was essentially a prestige one, were generally large, carefully made with a wealth of detail and were kept, isolated so that they could be seen to the best effect, in rooms adjacent to the *fabbricerie*. The most magnificent prestige artifact of the Lombard Renaissance was the wooden model of Pavia Cathedral: its sheer size and the care taken over its carving cannot fail to arouse the admiration of the observer. The relationship of this cathedral of wood with the real building is complex and still not entirely clear, as is explained elsewhere in this catalog. This model may also be seen as a part of an architectural fantasy, since it is evident that it represents an imposing building of considerable length, the construction of which would have had a devastating effect on the centuries-old network of streets and squares which to this day is the focal point of the daily lives of the citizenry.

54

CRISTOFORO ROCCHI and GIOVAN PIETRO FUGAZZA
Wooden Model of Pavia Cathedral

Pavia, Musei Civici del Castello Visconteo
5.05 × 3.64 × 3.64 m

PROVENANCE: Fabbriceria della Cattedrale.

BIBLIOGRAPHY: Malaspina 1816: 5-12, 20-23; Maiocchi 1903, 1: 201-233; Malaguzzi Valeri 1915b, II: 87-112; Gianani 1930; Gianani and Modesti 1932; Maiocchi 1937, I, passim; 1949, II: passim; Maiocchi, MS. II 34 E, 2611; Arslan 1956: 642-650; Bruschi 1969a: 765-773, or 1990: 61-66; Brizio 1974: 1-26; Struffolino Krüger 1971: 292; Cadei 1972: 35-60; 1975: 137-141; Comincini 1988: 53-85; Weege 1988: 137-140; Ippolito 1988: 141-145; Borsi 1989: 178-185; Tafuri 1993b: 54-55.

The monumental wooden model, an extraordinary iconographic document of the complex history of the design of the centuries-old cathedral of Pavia, was originally kept in a storeroom near the Fabbriceria della Cattedrale. In 1942 it was removed to the bishop's palace and is now conserved in the Visconti castle museum. Over a hundred years ago it was attributed by art historians to Cristoforo Rocchi from Pavia, as can be seen in the plates engraved by Amati in Malaspina's book (plates nos. II, III, and IV). Rocchi, a *magistro a lignamine* (master carpenter) and *ingeniario* (inventor), was mentioned for the first time, together with Amadeo, in connection with the cathedral in a document dated March 1488 as having presented a project and models for the new cathedral to Cardinal Ascanio Sforza. This was a year after the first "*designa a perito architectore confecta*" (drawings by an expert architect) had been dispatched to Cardinal Sforza in Rome, together with the request to demolish the old cathedral and neighboring baptistery in order to build a new duomo.

After the laying of the foundation stone on 29 June 1488, Rocchi's name appears in a document dated 22 August of the same year, next to those of Bramante and Amadeo, as engaged on "*certum designum seu planum de ecclesia maiori Papie construenda*," illustrated by "*certa memorialia*," with precise measurements and instructions about the structure of the building "*fiendi supra terra tantum*." The document establishes that the memorial had to refer to a "*modelum fiendum iuxta ipsum designum*," to be assigned to Rocchi. This was the model which the nobleman Cristoforo Bottigella, the cathedral *fabbriciere*, complained had not yet been built when the foundations of the building were already under way, and he insisted that it should be finished "*cum partecipatione alliorum inzigneriorum*" within the brief space of fifteen days. The chronological reference could raise doubts about the type of model required if the document had not made it clear that the model was to be a simple structure without any ornamentation. What Bottigella wanted was therefore a three-dimensional representation of the design they were agreed on, a simple model carried out using cheap materials, even cardboard, as imaginatively suggested by Malaspina (1816: 9). In December that year Rocchi was paid 12 lire "*pro parte solutioni modelli per ipsum fiendi*." Models and drawings are mentioned again on 23 December 1488 in connection with Bramante and Dolcebuono's arrival in Pavia. When Francesco di Giorgio visited Pavia in June 1490 in the company of Leonardo da Vinci, he was asked to express his opinion on the *fabbrica* and the model (Tafuri 1993b: 55).

By 1492 the crypt had been completed. In November 1493 Rocchi paid the rent for a room *"causa gubernandi et fabricandi modellum magnum ipsius fabrice ligneum."* This was the first reference to a wooden model which, despite the brevity of the description, appears to correspond to the actual model built. How far Rocchi was involved in the construction we cannot tell. A document dated 1496, cited by Malaspina, shows that the *fabbricieri* assigned a larger space in the bishop's palace in order to make work on the model easier, and to hasten its completion (Malaspina 1816: 14). In 1497 Cristoforo Rocchi died; tenure of the building site was assigned to Amadeo, Dolcebuono, and Giovan Pietro Fugazza, a *"magistro ab intalio, intersega et lignamine"* (master engraver, carpenter, and joiner) from Pavia, who was immediately commissioned to build a model for the new project developed by Amadeo and Dolcebuono, *"juxta principium ipsius ecclesie factum,"* a clear reference to the raised part of the building that was actually visible (*"jam apparens super terram"*). Fugazza received his first payment in July 1497. The new model, built *"ut semper sit speculum ipsius fabrice et edificii quibuscumque personis laborare debentibus in dicta ecclesia,"* a concern which seemed to foresee the century-long struggle to build the cathedral, was placed alongside the cathedral chancellery, next to the prison, in a place called the Camussoni, where it was still to be found in 1501 when the *fabbricieri* called in two wood-engravers from Pavia, Giacomo del Maino and Agostino Bigarelli, to put in an estimate. The resulting report revealed that Fugazza had so far only defined the structure of the base of the model, the apsidal area and a part of the presbytery. The estimate listed the frame of the wooden structure as made of willow ("lo telaro del fondamento fato de salexo"); the part of the base toward Piazza Cavagneria was in walnut: ("lo basamento de noxe ... verso la marzaria"). Then there was half of the base toward the big square, a part of the apse, the "second order where it starts over the light of the confessional," four corner buttresses, six tall columns, four piers of the crossing tower, four small niches, two large niches, and other assorted members and elements. It seems therefore that by 1501 Fugazza, who was also *capomaestro* of the yard itself, had built as much of the model as was necessary for the work in progress. In Maiocchi's opinion the wooden model and the building of the cathedral proceeded hand in hand, with the model slightly in advance of the other, as suggested by records of 1503 and 1504 relating to the services of stonemasons and stonecutters at work on the apse and presbytery areas of the cathedral. There is no reference in the 1501 estimate to wooden models of the two sacristies, whose foundations were laid in early 1505. These and the apse are characterized by the outstanding workmanship of the wooden elements and details—a likely indication of Rocchi's authorship, which is also justified by a "more marked and convincing Bramantesque influence" than that of the overall model (Cadei 1975: 138).

After an interval of about four years, the *fabbricieri* drew up a new contract with Fugazza in July 1505. He was awarded tenure of the building site and charged with the completion of the wooden model. Its execution now involved the participation of other master woodworkers. Fugazza's name disappears from the site records after 1507. New names are registered as *"intaliatores et magistri a lignamine"*: Francesco Formenti, Battista Boni de Villanova (called Guastamessa), and Agostino Bigarelli, author of the 1501 estimate for the model. Agostino's name, together with that of his brother Baldassarre, appears regularly in the documents until 1524; the name of another woodcarver, Francesco de Cerviis, continues to be registered until 1526. None of the documents in our possession refer to further work on the model, and consequently the exact date of its completion has never been established. The model was attributed by nineteenth-century historians to Rocchi, while Giovan Pietro Fugazza's contribution, in their opinion, was limited to building the last four bays and the facade according to a project sketched out in rough as early as 1488 (Malaspina 1816; Chierici 1942). Later on, it was more accountably

ascribed to Fugazza alone. According to Gianani, Cristoforo Rocchi built a simple model before 1497, as a means of offering a three-dimensional version of the design, as mentioned above (Gianani and Modesti 1932: 20-22). Alternatively, Maiocchi asserted, on the basis of certain documents, that Rocchi had already started the great wooden model which was abandoned and substituted by Fugazza's because it no longer corresponded to the changes introduced in the actual building (Maiocchi 1903; Malaguzzi Valeri 1915b; Borsi 1989: 181). The historians who put forward the hypothesis of Rocchi's having built (or partially built) a wooden model, as the documents seem to imply, then hypothesized a new sixteenth-century model that reintroduced parts of Rocchi's model, especially the parts already built or under way, as well as Amadeo's modifications to the original. This new model would have retained Bramante's original ideas (Brizio 1970: 17; Arslan 1956: 650; Bruschi 1969a: 766; 1990: 62). There is an even more interesting suggestion, however, that some of the original parts made by Rocchi may have been conserved and integrated with the new model (Cadei 1975; Weege 1988; Ippolito 1988). The hypothesis already advanced by Cadei concerning the sacristies built in all probability before 1497 and then combined with the new model, has been confirmed by a direct examination carried out on the model when it was dismantled prior to restoration in 1981 (Ippolito 1988: 144). Weege believes that the apse also originates from Rocchi's model, but there is no proof of this in the 1501 estimate, which lists supplies of wood for the second order necessary for realizing the crypt ("sechondo hordine dove se piglia sopra la luze del confesore"), which Cadei takes to mean that Fugazza began the construction of the new model from the base, and from the "first parts of the apse."
The 1497 model therefore embraces part of Bramante's

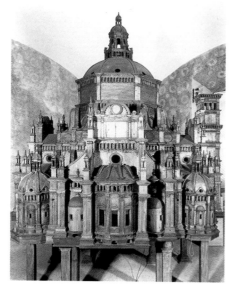

project—the sections already built—and integrates it with the new *"designum plani"* elaborated by Amadeo and Dolcebuono. It comprises different stylistic and architectural solutions, as can be noted when comparing the apse to the facade—the latter having much in common with the model of the nearby Certosa. Fugazza's model obviously left out the crypt with its more marked Bramantesque features completed by 1492, the year when the structure of the foundations of the east side was being busily discussed (Cadei 1972: 42-45). Supplies of marble and the names of *"magistri a marmoribus"* or stonecutters were listed in the registers between 1493 and 1494. The sacristies were built to the designs of Rocchi's earlier models. A deed was drawn up in October 1496 in the northern sacristy, while the other one was only founded in 1505 (Gianani 1930: 29). Cadei holds that, at the time of Rocchi's death in 1497, work on the external base of the eastern side had come to a standstill. This was clear

evidence that progress on the two areas was out of phase, as confirmed by the dilated proportions of the main section compared to those of the crypt and the other underground support structures (Cadei 1972: 48-53). Site activity recorded from 1501 to 1507 illustrates the close connection with the part of the model already completed. In 1504 work was still being carried out on the "Capella Magna" or main apse while in 1507 the builders were erecting the presbytery area and the arm of the transept *"versus nullam horam,"* i.e., to the north (Maiocchi, MS. II 34 E, 2611; Gianani and Modesti 1965; Cadei 1972: 50). At the same time one pier of the *tiburio* or crossing tower was being positioned (one of the four piers listed in the 1501 estimate).
The building site was run by other master craftsmen after Fugazza's death for an indeterminate period. The longitudinal development of the naves, which does not correspond to the actual building, has elicited various explanations: Cadei attributed to Fugazza's assistants and successors the responsibility for the longitudinal section of the model, attested on the inside by the different arrangement of the wooden diaphragms between the nave and aisles from the fifth bay onward. The interruption is justified by Chierici in terms of it being Fugazza's hurried completion of the original project, which was already settled as being a longitudinal plan and prepared almost entirely by Rocchi. Bruschi also favors the original longitudinal plan and refers to a drawing conserved in the De Pagave collection, copied by Amati as well (pl. I), showing a longitudinal section of the cathedral that is believed to be the copy of Bramante's original design. Taking an opposite view, Gianani suggests that the extension of the wooden model—originally based on a Greek cross plan—was due to Amadeo's reconsidering the design at an advanced stage of the construction. The most convincing thesis is the one which attributes the actual form of the model to the 1497 project, whose base and therefore whose main measurements were already fixed by Fugazza before 1501 (Weege 1988: 138; Ippolito 1988).
The evident conflict between the monumental length of the nave of the model and the urban fabric in which it was to be inserted, have raised many doubts, especially if one considers that while the new building was being inaugurated, the bishop's palace was moved to the west side of Piazza del Regisole in order to leave more space for the foundations of the apse and presbytery of the growing cathedral. In a missive dispatched on 15 July 1494 to Lodovico il Moro concerning his intention to demolish certain buildings around Piazza del Regisole in order to generally improve the look of the city, the commissioner of Pavia wrote that the project for the new cathedral did not, in 1494, require any enlargement of Piazza del Regisole: "Se siamo transferiti sopra el loco ... et anche parlando con lo inzignero de la fabrica quale ce ha facto intendere che per el desegno facto del Domo, la Piaza de Regisole non va più agrandita de quello chel è al presente" ("We went to visit the site, and spoke to the site engineer who gave us to believe that according to the designs of the cathedral, Piazza de Regisole does not need to be any larger than it is at present"). This seems to be incontestable evidence that the cathedral was originally designed with a centralized plan. The church was therefore to be inserted in the urban context as it was, without any need for drastic demolitions. The letter continued, however, by asserting that even if the square needed to be enlarged, this would not be necessary for at least another two hundred years because work on the cathedral was progressing so slowly and would require at least another three hundred years before its conclusion ("quando pur col tempo paresse a chi li sarà, che se dovesse tore via et agrandire dicta piaza, anderà a un'altra età che sarà forse da qui a duecento anni. Per che non lavorandose più gagliardamente de quello se fa non se fornirà che da qui a trecento anni"; Comincini 1988: 82, no. 8). The words of the Pavian commissioner, written before Amadeo and Dolcebuono had drafted their monumental project, offer, five hundred years later, an almost premonitory statement about the running of the cathedral building site and its

later developments. The acute comment about the length of time required to do anything and the mentality of those responsible for the site, suggests a possible justification of the contrast—still unresolved—between the colossal project and the reality of the urban space where it was to be built.

Monica Visioli

Note on the Cognitive Study Program on the Wooden Model of Pavia Cathedral

On the occasion of the exhibition, updated in 1981, the Musei Civici initiated a program of study into the metric and structural characteristics of the model of Pavia Cathedral, and made use of the occasion to carry out a systematic enquiry into the model and its history.
For the first time in its recent history, the model was examined with criteria appropriate to its current condition —given that it was necessary to remedy the errors of the previous restoration campaign and the model's subsequent reassembly (1952, after its transfer from the Vescovado to the Musei Civici); the same criteria were also directed toward effecting an objective historical and critical assessment.
The study campaign, directed by Adriano Peroni, involved a restoration program and a full photogrammetric survey, conducted respectively by Eugenio Gritti and Lamberto Ippoliti (University of Florence).
The photogrammetric survey was subsequently extended to include the apse of the cathedral, in order to carry out necessary comparative metrical studies with the Renaissance-built parts of the monument itself.
The studies focused on the intrinsic significance of the model as a tool for representing architectural projects, and shed light on the textual importance of scale models—and the Pavia model in particular—and on the extremely intricate processes of graphical and representational mediation between the architectural design as conceived, and its subsequent development in the actual construction.
The limited span of the doorways of the model's new location (the fourteenth-century Visconti castle) provided an opportunity to completely disassemble the model (comprised of over 500 constituent elements), and hence solve outstanding queries and provide complementary historical and documentary information resulting from the direct observation of the disassembled model.
The photogrammetric survey gave precedence to the parts that are not normally visible or accessible for inspection in the assembled model. The documentation produced up to now consists of graphic representations and thematic diagrams, based on interpretative and selective parameters inferred from the survey data. Now that all the data have been transcribed and the results of the research carried out by the museum have been made available to the public, it is possible to obtain a reliable, objective picture of the model; in the meantime, parallel studies into its integrity and origins have been made, in light of modern restoration operations and of those of the past, for which a previously undefined itinerary of interventions now exists (e.g., the restoration carried out in 1633 by the carpenter Giulio Sarchà according to the specifications of Richino; a model for the campanile, built by Tibaldi, who was paid 25 *lire imperiali* on 21 January 1568; the presence of "two great lateral towers of the church", confirmed by the "visual inspection and observation" of the model in 1729; the Veneroni-Ramis engraving of 1775).
Further crucial insights are offered by an unpublished record documenting the Fabbriceria's request to the city council (discussed in the Convocato di Provvisione of 13 December 1494), for a place either below the prison and in the prison tower (*intus camussone*). The *fabbricieri* plead their need of the unused (*vacuus*) chamber adjacent to the cathedral chancellery to transfer the large wooden model of the church (*modellum magnum ligneum*), and for other needs of the *fabbrica* (Archivio Storico Civico, archiv.

com. cart. 3, fol. 214). This information confirms the existence of Rocchi's model, at a date in which the proposal for the centralized plan for the church was established. Despite doubts regarding the extent of work already carried out (in the sense of the overall model itself, and of the job of scaling up of the individual parts), the document in question necessitates further inspection to verify and correlate the so-called "ripensamenti" or design revisions evinced by the model in the junctions of the parts, and in the constructional modifications affecting the base and the corresponding internal elevations of the fifth longitudinal bay.

Donata Vicini

55
Antonio da Lonate (?)
Wooden Model of Vigevano Cathedral

Vigevano, Duomo
1.92 × 1.04 × 1.025 m

Provenance: Tesoreria del Duomo.

Bibliography: ACaV, SC2 R5 N1 F1 (13); ACaV, SC2 R5 N1 F2; ACaV, SC2 R4 N30; ASM, Culto, p.a., 1422, doc; 1549; ASCV, art. 179, Simone del Pozzo 1552: cc. 534v., 537v., 538; ASCV, art. 64, 4, 1, doc: 1541; ASCV, Antico Catasto, 49, Simone del Pozzo 1571, cc.11v., 12; Nubilonio 1584: 103; Brambilla 1669: 12-13, 15; Biffignandi Buccella 1810: 85; Gianiolo 1844; Chierici 1880: 142-145; Malaguzzi Valeri 1915b: 174, fig. 202; Barni 1919: 35-38; Aschieri 1939: 123-128; Giacinto Marino 1975-76; Cattaneo Cattorini no. 86-87: 160-166; Morresi 1991: 135 (141). (Key: ASCV: Archivio Storico Civico di Vigevano, ACaV: Archivio Capitolar di Vigevano, ASM: Archivio di Stato di Milano.)

The wooden model of Vigevano Cathedral, attributed to Antonio da Lonate, the royal engineer accountable for the site between 1534 and 1535, is now conserved in the first chapel on the left, inside the cathedral. The model has undergone various restorations since the 1930s. Except for a few parts in firwood, the model is almost entirely built of poplar, and corresponds to the plan of the actual church, whose erection on the site of the ancient church of S. Ambrogio took place in the early 1540s. At the time of the rise to power of Lodovico il Moro, the little church of S. Ambrogio was charged to perform liturgies previously carried out by the churches within the castle; these had been demolished to make way for new kitchens. The church was repeatedly "reformed" and enlarged until Francesco II Sforza ascended the throne (Simone Del Pozzo 1552: c. 534 verso). After the duke had conferred the status of "city" upon Vigevano, and it was made a bishopric by a papal bull issued by Clement VII on 16 March 1530, Francesco had a large chapel built in S. Ambrogio in 1532 to compensate for the inadequate choir, and to create a larger space for the clergy ("[per] loccare magior numero de preti"; Simone Del Pozzo 1552: c. 538 recto). Later on, probably between 1533—the date inscribed on the stone placed in the altar of the cathedral—

and the beginning of 1534, he decided to rebuild the entire cathedral. The architect responsible for the project suggested demolishing the entire choir so that the facade of the church would be perfectly perpendicular to the square ("Dopo fatta la capella [il Duca] stabilì di fare una chiesa di bella architectura onde lo Architectore consiliò Sua Signoria che tal chiesa non si gitava a terra quella capella qual era fatta senza considerazione dilla nova chiesa e tenendo quella in piede non si poteva poner pianta justa al dritto della piaza"; Simone Del Pozzo 1552: c. 538 verso). The large chapel was not, however, demolished, either because the duke wanted to see the work finished before he died ("di ciò sia causa fusse il desiderio [del Duca] di videre il fine dubitandose per la infermità in la qual era di non viver tanto, come fu in effetto che tal chiesa si finisse"), or because the engineer running the building site succeeded in changing Francesco II's mind about demolishing the choir (Simone Del Pozzo 1552: c. 538 verso, and Simone Del Pozzo 1571: c. 11 verso). In the 1571 *Registro*, Simone Del Pozzo records one Antonio de Lonate as the chief engineer and *capomaestro*, as borne out by the uninterrupted payments entered in the register and by documents of the cathedral archives (Giacinto Marino 1975-76). Lonate worked at the site from 1534 to 1535 when, upon the death of Francesco II, the building—at this point composed of the choir, two side chapels, the four piers of the crossing tower and another two chapels—came to a standstill. None of the payments entered in the registers and documents about the work done between 1534 and 1535 refer to a wooden model, either existing or under construction.
In 1541 the Marquis Del Vasto contributed 300 *scudi* to the cathedral fund for the new building. The decree recalls the "desegno" or memorial drawn up for Francesco II in 1534, a surviving copy of which was sent from Milan to Vigevano. The decree and the design of the cathedral are mentioned again in another missive sent in October 1549 to the governor of Milan, Ferrante Gonzaga. The site remained unfinished for years, as Carlo Borromeo complained in 1578 during his pastoral visit to Vigevano. The items entered in the registers in May 1600 when work started again on the construction of the last six chapels and the facade of the church, repeatedly indicate the existence of a model to which the suppliers must refer. In 1603, the *fabbricieri* were paying master stonecutter Giovan Giacomo for the execution of a new facade design, evidence that there had been a change of plan while work was in progress. While the base of the facade was in fact built, as observed in a *Nota della misura de fondamenti della fazzada verso piaza* conserved in the Chapter archives, the rest of it was never completed before Caramuel's revolutionary intervention; this is testified by the clearly unfinished section of stonework on the right side of the front, behind the curved, late eighteenth-century facade, and confirmed by contemporary historical sources (Gianiolo 1844: 78 no. 16). The attribution of the whole project of the cathedral to Antonio de Lonate dates back to the second half of the nineteenth century, when historians asserted that Francesco II had part of the church rebuilt in the years 1532 onward to the Doric designs of "Maestro Antonio de Lonate." The wooden model, which still lacks the little pilasters of the loggetta of the crossing tower, the cusp of the campanile and several basic details, was first brought to public notice by Malaguzzi-Valeri in 1915, and later examined by Barni, who ascribed its authorship to Antonio da Lonate, a proposal which has so far been accepted by the critics (Barni 1919). Eugenio Gritti led the team responsible for the recent restoration of the model. After close examination it was noted that part of the roof of the model, made of firwood, most likely stemmed from a later, perhaps eighteenth-century, intervention. Fir was also used for the external structure of the choir and the two chapels at the sides of the apse. The discovery of these and successive interventions, and the general examination of the model, its craftsmanship and state of conservation have raised several doubts about the correct dating of the entire work.

Monica Visioli

56
CRISTOFORO SOLARI
Model of the Apse of Como Cathedral
1519

Como, Musei Civici
Poplar wood, stained black.
133.5 × 99 × 45 cm

PROVENANCE: Fabbrica del Duomo.

BIBLIOGRAPHY: Ciceri 1811; Calvi 1865: 219-234; Fossati 1887; Monti 1896; Meyer 1897: 214-215; Frigerio 1950; Arslan 1957: 541-544; Bernasconi 1970: 33-104; Gatti 1976: 21-30; Zecchinelli 1981: 117-118; Werdehausen 1985: 400-403; Agosti 1986: 57-65; Frommel 1990a: 52-63.

The first references in the records of the Fabbrica del Duomo in Como to a model for the construction of the choir go back as far as 19 and 22 December 1487, a few months after Tommaso Rodari's appointment as head architect of the Como Cathedral building site. Small sums were paid on those dates for the construction of a model "*pro capella magna*" (Arch. Stor. Diocesi Como, *Liber appelatus Contraliber...* [1485-89], fols. 102 and 275v.). Twenty years passed before the long and laborious question of the cathedral choir was taken up again, when on 5 march 1510 Bishop Scaramuzza Trivulzio obtained permission from Charles d'Amboise, the governor of the Duchy of Milan, to erect the apse of the church "*cum tiberio et aliis circumstantiis*" (Arch. Stor. Diocesi Como, *Repertorium Ordinationem et Instrumentorum Fabrice* [1444-1598], 15.5.1510). Both the commemorative slab set into the wall outside the central apse and precise information left us by Benedetto Giovio (Fossati 1887: 209) fix the laying of the foundation stone at 22 December 1513. Nevertheless, the chosen design was questioned yet again and changed in 1519. On 3 January that year Cristoforo Solari was called in and built an alternative to the previous model designed by Rodari. These two models were examined by Giovanni da Molteno, Bernardino da Legnano and Ambrogio dei Ghisolfi ("*in architectura peritissimos*"). Their preference for Solari's project was endorsed by the *fabbricieri* (Arch. Stor. Diocesi Como, idem., 3.1.1519). Both Solari and Rodari were summoned a few months later by the *fabbricieri* and the city authorities to present their designs for the alterations to the choir. After much debate the choice fell on Solari's project. He was then asked to build a new wooden or cardboard model with the lantern, apse and dome (Arch. Stor. Diocesi Como, idem., 2.5.1519). After he had delivered the model Cristoforo Solari is no longer recorded at the cathedral site in Como, and work went ahead most probably under the direction of Tommaso Rodari, who is mentioned in the books of the Fabbrica until 1526. He was assisted and later succeeded by Franchino della Torre. The latter was paid *255 lire per annum* by the Fabbrica, starting from 1523.
On the basis of information contained in the Fabbrica records, the two wooden models—which were discovered by C. F. Ciceri at the beginning of the nineteenth century in a storeroom inside the Fabbrica (Ciceri 1811: 90) and

later transported to the Musei Civici in Como—were ascribed to various architects. The majority (Ciceri 1811: 15, 90; Monti 1896: 85; Frigerio 1950: 128; Bernasconi 1970: 60, 64; Zecchinelli 1981: 118-119) attributed the single-apse model to Rodari and the three-apse design to Solari (perhaps in concert with Rodari). Others (Meyer 1897: 215; Arslan 1957: 542-543) were of the opinion that both models were the products of a much more mature architectural language than that expressed by Rodari. In the light of new research on Cristoforo Solari (Gatti 1976; Werdehausen 1985) Frommel made a further study of the models and endorsed the attribution of the single-apse model to Solari, but not the three-apse, which he considered "less consistent, more archaic in style, and unworthy of his craftsmanship" (Frommel 1990a: 61). While the model's precarious state of conservation hinders analysis, Frommel's doubts over the three-apse model seem justified for a series of reasons. First, the fragmentary application of architectural elements in this model contrasts strongly with the unity of the single-apse model. The height and frailty of the bases and the half-columns of the two orders find no confirmation in any of Solari's definite or attributed works. The approximate execution of the details, in particular the Corinthian capitals and the little columns of the triple windows of the upper order, clashes with the precision of the single-apse model. Lastly, there is the utilization of an uncharacteristic decoration designed on the base between the half-columns of the lower order. The shifting of the triple windows to the upper story—a solution which links the three-apse model for Como to the one actually built for the Duomo in Pavia (Meyer 1897: 214)—and the addition of the niches under the large windows, with a consequent tendency to articulate the wall surfaces in sets of bands, suggests that it was an attempt to adjust the Solari project to a more local conception of architecture, less inspired by examples from Rome. However, given the analogies between the two, it may also be that the three-apse model—which closely resembles the one actually built—derived from the single-apse project. As such, Solari may also have been responsible for the design for the three-apse choir.
The first striking aspect of the single-apse model is the contrast between the inside and the outside, which leads us to believe that the architect must have given only very general instructions about the outside, without entering into details. The inside, which has been executed very carefully, is divided into two levels with five bays. The lower order is comprised of Doric half-columns with entasis, fluting and cabling, supporting an entablature that breaks forward only in correspondence with the columns. The walls have square paneling and the lower part appears to be slightly projecting. There is a passage behind the blind triple windows. The moldings that conclude the lower part repeat the Attic base of the half-columns and that of the bases.
The upper story is characterized by a neutral order of pilasters with entasis, surmounted by an entablature composed of consoles in the frieze supporting the markedly projecting cornice. Inside the arches, the windows and oculi are separated by emphatic moldings and placed to the back in order to leave room for a passage. The apse is capped by a coffered dome, and geometrical decorations provide unity to the walls at both levels. The bare external walls do not repeat the superimposed arrangement used for the interior, but are simply articulated by six buttressing piers; the narrow cornices of the openings lend unity to the upper and lower windows.
Comparisons with other projects by Solari confirm the validity of attributing the single-apse model to him. There are no grounds, however, for ascribing it to Tommaso Rodari, considering the difference in his type of architectural language—with its decidedly local influence (the project of S. Maria in Piazza at Busto Arsizio should date to about 1515)—and that of the wooden model, which has evident references to examples from antiquity and the Renaissance in Rome. References to Roman prototypes, discovered by E. Werdehausen in the cloister of S. Pietro al Po in Cremona, corroborate those historical sources

Interior of the Apse of Como Cathedral

(Calvi 1865: 219) which assert that Solari stayed in Rome not just once, in 1514, but also for a certain period immediately after the fall of Lodovico il Moro, in around 1499 (Agosti 1986: 59, 62).
The Como model betrays precise references to Roman Renaissance architecture: from the Doric half-columns with the projecting entablature in the loggia of the courtyard of the Palazzo Venezia, to the frieze consoles in the cloister of S. Maria della Pace.
The type of Doric column with the Attic base and fluting and cabling was probably borrowed from an ancient monument in Rome; as such it was a surprising innovation, the only one of its kind in Lombardy in the early sixteenth century. All Solari's documented or attributable projects (the cloister of S. Pietro al Po in Cremona; the forecourt of S. Maria presso S. Celso; Palazzo Rabia and Palazzo Salvatico in Milan; S. Maria delle Grazie at Castelnovo Fogliani) are characterized by elements or details found in the model for the choir of Como Cathedral: half-columns or pilasters on solid bases; the three gradually projecting strips of the architraves and arches; heavily projecting cornices; Doric capitals of the lower order similar to the cloister in Cremona, and to the Palazzo Rabia and, especially, when considering the short necking of the columns, to the Palazzo Salvatico; lastly, the superimposition of plain pilasters over Doric half-columns (as in the cloister of S. Pietro al Po and the Palazzo Rabia).

Simone Soldini

57
LEONARDO
Perspective View of a Church (verso)
Drawings and Notes on Mechanics (recto)

Venice, Gallerie dell'Accademia, inv. 238
Pen and ink, on paper.
21.3 × 15.2 cm
INSCRIBED: *(on the recto) a-b-d-c; Tratta prima de' pesi e poi de' sua*

465

sostentaculi e poi della sua confregazione e poi del moto suo e, in ultimo, della sua percussione. Il grave pesa per tutte quelle linie donde esso è in potenzia di discendere. Quanto il grave si moverà per linia più vicina alla centrale, tanto si dimostrà di maggiore gravezza, cioè per linia meno obliqua. Tanto si dimostrà il grave esser minore, quanto la linea del suo moto fia remota dalla linia centrale, cioè quanto il moto è più obliquo; (center, drawing of balance pole with letters and weights) *c a b-n-p-4 1;* (left, beam and support, marked *n a b m-c) Il trave m n essendo congiunto col sostenaculo c a nel punto a, si fermerà in equilibra sopra del punto c, e fia come se esso sostenaculo a fussi situato per la linia b c;* (beam and *sostenaculo,* marked *m-ab-fqpcn.) Il trave m n è in potenzia di discendere per tanto peso quanto è la metà della sua gravezza. e 'l sostegno a c, il quale è fermo in a, non ha alcuna potenzia contro al discenso del trave come ha la linia a f, e nella linia c b non è valido il sostegno perché è basso;* (right) *f-a-b-d-e-g; Per la linia a c non è sostenuto, perché al mon tocca e non ha sostenta[culo], e per la linia a c non è sostenuto infra angoli equali e perciò non vale, e per la linia c b è sostenuta, perché termina in b infra angoli equali, ma è fori del centro a;* (drawing marked a-b) *a b è vero sostegno;* (drawing of a rod and *sostentaculo,* marked *n-a-c-b-m) a b, sostentaculo, non è soffiziente a sostenere l'aste n m nel suo dato sito, perché ell'è nella medesima potenzia del sostentaculo b c, il quale [...] sostiene la predetta aste molto più in basso che 'l suo vero mezzo a; e però la parte c m, non potendo resistere alla parte c n, è necessitata a dare loco al discenso della maggiore parte dell'aste c n;* (drawing of rod and *sostentaculo,* marked a-c-b) *Quando il pié del sostentaculo della gravità fia premanente e stabile, il peso che sopra la sua cima si posò fia premanente e sia piantato per qualunche linia si voglia, ché sempre farà uffizio tale che parrà terminare nell'aste infra angoli equali, come se a b fussi fermo in b. E se 'l predetto piedi del sostentaculo non fussi né fermo né premanente, purché sia in contatto d'angoli equali coll'aste da lui sostenuta, esso si dimonsterrà di premanente e stabile fermamente come b c;* (upper right corner, in Leonardo's hand) *132;* (by another) *143 C* (i.e., 143 sheets) (Marani 1932)

BIBLIOGRAPHY: Heydenreich 1949, pl. XIX; Maltese 1954: 358; Firpo 1963: 62; Brizio 1964: 402; Cogliati Arano 1966: 23-25; Pedretti 1977, I: 373; Pedretti 1978, ed. 1988: 254-255; Cogliati Arano 1980: 45-47 (with further bibliography); Marani 1992a: 236-241; Spezzani 1992: 184-185.

The verso of the sheet depicts a view of the facade and flank of a church.

The studies and annotations on the recto relate to the mechanics of equilibrium, centres of gravity of masses, to the movement of structural members, the *sostentaculi* (supports), and shows geometric methods of restraint for the points of equilibrium.

Heydenreich sensed that the folio might be a page from a *quaderno* (as suggested by the recto of fol. 132), a compendium of studies on mechanics perhaps; however, as Marani has shown, the size and type of the paper are very similar to those of pages of Manuscript 8937 in the Biblioteca Nacional, Madrid, which is datable to between 1493 and 1497. Sixteen pages are missing from that manuscript, one of which could be the drawing in question, originally somewhere near the verso of fol. 133, which contains notes accompanying a drawing of a wheel whose radius is "loaded with two different weights"; the drawing includes a commentary on the scientist Biagio Pelacani.

The notes of fol. 133 verso seem to be a further stage of those on the present sheet, making this the earlier of the two, with an execution date of ca. 1493-95.

The church on the verso—one of Leonardo's rare loose folios dedicated to architecture—must belong to the same period in which the notes on mechanics were executed. The chronology of the work has nevertheless given rise to a crucial problem for Leonardo scholars, who have propounded dates as early as 1490, and (unconvincingly) linked the drawing with a project for Pavia Cathedral (A. Venturi 1938; and Heydenreich 1949, who in 1933 dated the sheet to before 1500, but revised his opinion in 1954 to after 1500); subsequently it was assigned various dates: from 1490 to a period "much later than 1500" (Arslan 1956); to 1504 (Maltese 1954) on the basis of comparison with the palace on the recto of the Windsor drawing RL

12591; to 1513-15 by Pedretti (1978), who linked it to the facade of S. Lorenzo in Florence.

Marani (1992a) affirmed that connections with the facade of the unrealized Certosa church could not be ruled out, and suggested it might be a study for S. Maria delle Grazie in Milan.

The building sketched into the background of the unfinished *St. Jerome* in the Pinacoteca Vaticana affords a specular version of the church in the Venetian drawing, with few variations. As far as the latter is concerned, infrared reflectographs (Spezzani 1992) have revealed how Leonardo's quick metalpoint sketch included only the facade of the church—in an updated interpretation of an Alberti-style church on the lines of S. Maria Novella in Florence—and though the right-hand part was unfinished, the sketch was perfectly harmonious and correct in terms of the perspective. Only at a later stage did Leonardo continue the building, in ink, completing the facade and adding a flank, thereby turning the simple elevation into an axonometric view. This hurried crystallization of the ideas resulted in imbalance and architectural incongruity.

Giovanna Nepi Sciré

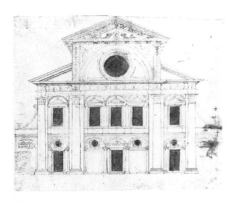

58

CRISTOFORO SOLARI (?)
Project for the Facade of S. Maria delle Grazie, Castelnovo Fogliani

Paris, Musée du Louvre, Cabinet des Dessins, inv. MI 1105
Pen and ink with watercolor; straightedge and freehand; on paper.
INSCRIBED: (on left-hand plate) *ludovicuh fo;* (on right-hand plate) *ludovisa foliana.*

BIBLIOGRAPHY: Beltrami 1901a: 33ff.; Biscaro 1910: 172ff.; Malaguzzi-Valeri 1915b, II: 48ff.; Baroni: 106; Forster: 98ff.; Wittkower 1949: 82; Bruschi 1969a: 210ff., 758ff.; Borsi 1989: 220ff.; Frommel 1990b: 52ff.

This project is particularly interesting if only for the fact that it represents the most important link between the facade of S. Andrea in Mantua by Alberti and the facade of the church of Roccaverano (1509) by Bramante.

Beltrami assigned the drawing to Bramante's Milan years, and referred convincingly to the two plates with the inscriptions of the Marchese Lodovico Fogliani, a relative of the Sforza family, and his wife, Lodovica Pallavicini, whom he married in 1479. Bramante is supposed to have designed the facade of S. Maria presso S. Satiro for this event.

This project cannot however be connected either to the cross-section and the limited space available at S. Maria presso S. Satiro, or to Bramante's style of ca. 1480. This is confirmed by a comparison of the detail with that of the substantially more Quattrocentesque facade of the choir of S. Maria presso S. Satiro. The two Fogliani, who never appear in the books of this church (Biscaro 1910), did in fact found a convent in 1504, with a church dedicated to the Madonna delle Grazie, on their

family estate at Castelnovo Fogliani near Fidenza. Julius II signed a papal bull on 4 November 1504 approving the request of Fogliani to "found a monastery for the health of his soul and that of his wife, Lodovica Pallavicini" (Bertuzzi 1931).

The church that was actually built creates a certainly more modest impression compared to the project conserved in the Louvre (Frommel 1990b, figs. 19, 20; I would like to thank B. Adorno for the invaluable information he provided about this building).

The project appears to have an interior comprising a central nave and two aisles with galleries, barrel vaults and side chapels.

According to deductions deriving from the steps in front of the portal, the giant order would have had a 2-*braccia* wide shaft, the central nave would have been 15-*braccia* wide and the whole facade a height of at least 36 *braccia*. Like the project for S. Maria Novella, the project is based on three squares (Bruschi 1969a, fig. 142), which do not however coincide exactly with the order.

If the project did in fact date back to the period around or after 1504, Bramante should be automatically excluded as the architect.

The arcade and the decorated area of the tympanum conform much more to his Milanese style. On the other hand, the complex system goes much further than his known works before the turn of the century. It is more likely that Cristoforo Solari (before 1470-1527) was responsible; Solari became an architect during Bramante's Milanese sojourn and kept in close touch with him even after the latter left for Rome (Frommel 1990b).

In the few buildings that can be safely ascribed to him, and which all date after 1504, Solari used the classical theater motif which Bramante had only used sporadically in Milan but had adopted with enthusiasm in Rome. In the cloister of S. Pietro al Po in Cremona (ca. 1505) he combined it even with lower arcades, alternating between a Doric and a Corinthian order. He gave his columns a marked entasis, something which Bramante did for the first time in the Tempietto.

It is not possible therefore to establish even if the giant order of the project conserved in Paris included half-columns or pilasters.

In the atrium of S. Maria presso S. Celso (1505) he placed an even greater emphasis on the differences between the Vitruvian orders, a question which Bramante had not given primary importance to when he was in Milan. He also used pedimented aedicules similar to those in the Paris sheet, while similar projections and a similar play of layers of wall emerge for the first time in his presumed model of 1519 for Como Cathedral (Frommel 1990b: 61). The interior articulation of the church in Castelnovo Fogliani is nonetheless comparable to the deep blind arcades of this model, and the three polygonal arms of the cross recall Como Cathedral.

The project for a centrally planned building conserved in the Biblioteca Ambrosiana—which has always been linked to the drawing in the Louvre ever since Beltrami first analyzed it—is much nearer Solari's first constructions (Bruschi 1969a: 159 n. 9, fig. 102, 103). In fact the elevation is likewise composed of an area dominated by tall tapering columns and by a completely ornamental upper level with blind arches surmounted by pediments. The Paris project however is striking not just for its orthogonal projection compared to the Quattrocento perspective of the sheet conserved in the Biblioteca Ambrosiana, but also for its much more complex system.

It appears that this system presupposes precise knowledge of the projects elaborated in Bramante's Roman circle, such as, for example, the Sforza tomb in S. Maria del Popolo, probably designed by Andrea Sansovino before October 1505 and heavily influenced by Bramante. In both cases the central arch with the oculus is flanked by smaller secondary bays.

Then in both cases a Corinthian-like order is superimposed on the pilasters of the arcade. This order projects and proceeds vertically in the markedly ornamental panels on the upper level. Lastly, in both cases the ornamental detail of the entablature is comparable. Solari had therefore consciously adopted a system strictly inspired by funerary culture from the time of the Cappella Piccolomini in Siena Cathedral. The orthogonal representation and the highly specific solution that the Paris project gave to the problem of the basilican facade, can be explained only in terms of firsthand knowledge of Bramante's Roman projects. Toward 1509 Bramante developed the facade of the church of Roccaverano, starting from an analogous basilican design with a blind central arch, a giant order and pediments over all three bays (the nave and the two aisles). Perhaps he was even attempting here to reconstruct the Vitruvian basilica at Fano (Wittkower 1949: 82). Moreover, Solari's pupil Cesariano was certainly aware of the project now conserved in the Louvre when he made his reconstruction of the same basilica. Bramante's projects for St. Peter's could have prompted the double-colonnade motif running across the pilasters of the Paris project, making the system close in type to the Justinian churches. Numerous unclear points such as the projecting parts next to the aisles reveal that the draftsman still had problems with the various layers of the wall. How he imagined the relations of the upper story to the arcades is also not evident. Since these support the main entablature on which the oculus rests, a loggia behind the arches and windows must be excluded (cf. Frommel 1990a, fig. 3). There are many reasons for supporting the hypothesis that Solari elaborated the design around 1505-10 for the convent church of Castelnovo Fogliani.

Christoph Luitpold Frommel

The Instruments of Design: the Facade

59
BERNARDINO BRUGNOLI (?)
Project for the Facade of the Cathedral, Reggio Emilia
1570-73

Reggio Emilia, Musei Civici, Disegni 159d
Pen and ink, edges of lower left corner damaged.
210 × 94 cm
a) facade elevation
b) plan of first order of facade (below elevation)
c) plan of second order of facade (bottom)
INSCRIBED: *sec. xvi / variante al progetto / della facciata del duomo / di Prospero Spani* (on a cartouche glued to the sheet).

PROVENANCE: Capitolo della Cattedrale, Reggio Emilia.

BIBLIOGRAPHY: Monducci and Nironi 1984: 137.

The drawing shows the facade of a church comprised of two stories and surmounted by an octagonal tower crowned by a dome with lantern. The first story enframes the central, barrel-vaulted arch, set with a keystone, with angels in the spandrels; the facade. It is characterized by pairs of free-standing Corinthian columns on plinths with joined bases, supporting the main entablature; these paired columns enframe narrow niches, which alternate with pedimented tabernacles aligned over the side portals, creating a giant order in ratio to the smaller columns, which rise on simple plinths either side of the entrances and support the intermediate entablature. The small columns flanking the central portal are without capitals. The side portals are tapered according to the canons of the Doric order. In the upper story, the central pairs of trabeated pilaster strips and half-columns support a triangular pediment, while the wings either side are crowned with a balustrade. The central barrel-vaulted bay contains a Serliana window with small columns and coupled pilasters. The pilaster pairs enclose panels and concave niches, alternated with tabernacle windows with segmental pediments. The first story of the tower, articulated by an order of pilasters, comprises a tabernacle niche containing a Virgin and Child with young St. John in the central bay. Aligned with this on the second story a trabeated triple window with a balustrade occupies the entire central face, while the others contain niches and panels. The niche motif is repeated in the lantern.
Given the drawing's provenance, together with certain other features—such as the tower with the statue of the Virgin, the organization of the lower order of the facade

(which on the whole matches that of the actual building)—it can plausibly be identified as a project for the new facade of the cathedral in Reggio Emilia, as stated on the nineteenth-century cartouche.
Recently it was attributed to Bernardino Brugnoli (Monducci and Nironi 1984: 136-138); this Veronese architect, the great nephew and builder of the works of Michele Sanmicheli (Puppi), is known to have received and accepted the commission on 15 July 1570, after the Cathedral Chapter had proposed the same, evidently without success, to Terribilia; the project was approved on 6 August 1573. There is evidence that Brugnoli was present in Reggio Emilia for a few days in June 1578. The version of the project to which this drawing belongs was perhaps developed in another city, probably Verona, from where the marble for the new facade was sent via canal as from 1544. The new project was conditioned by elements that had been introduced to the facade since that first shipment date, under the technical supervision of Prospero Sogari (until 1558), though the origin of the project he was executing is unknown (Manenti Valli 1981). When work was interrupted in about 1557-58, the main portal, the two side portals, and part of the central pilasters had been completed and a start made on the side pilasters (Monducci and Nironi 1984: 142). The fact that the upper section of the central portal was not completed as drawn in this project could be due to the architect's having received insufficient information on what had already been realized.
The project appears to be conditioned by the need to conform to the existing layout of the facade's lower story. However, it attempts to find equilibrium with the vertical upthrust imposed on the facade by the thirteenth-to-fifteenth-century tower; this was to be raised even higher and crowned with a cupola. The second level therefore has the task of confirming the horizontal arrangement of the first story while anticipating the upthrust of the tower and its succession of superimposed orders. The facade's second story involves a complex arrangement of three types of order that delineate a temple-front based on a giant order of pilasters on the central axis.
The organization of this second story betrays the influence of other motifs. The author shows an awareness of the terms for using the "Palladian" facade articulated with a giant order, and the "Roman" aedicular arrangement (Whitman 1970), whose most famous example was Vignola's project for the Gesù, dated between 1568 and 1571 (Ackerman and Lotz 1964: 18-19). Other contacts with the architectural culture of Rome can be seen, for example, in the Serlian motif of the window crowned by trapezoid paneling, which could have been prompted by memories of Antonio da Sangallo the Younger's project for the facade of St. Peter's (Uff. 73A).
The lack of other graphic material by Brugnoli with which to make comparisons (Barbieri) and the uncertainty regarding built works ascribable to him (Puppi), cast doubt on the paternity of the drawing in question, which could even be the only drawing by Brugnoli so far identified. By way of further confirmation, Brugnoli's contact with Sanmicheli would have been the means by which the mixture of Roman stylistic features and Palladian ideas and methods (such as the rigorous orthogonal projection of the elevation) found their way into the project.

Riccardo Pacciani

60
PROSPERO SOGARI (called IL CLEMENTE)
Model for the Facade of the Cathedral, Reggio Emilia
1583

Reggio Emilia, Musei Civici, Arti Industriali 196
Pear wood with integrations; scale: 1 : 14.
190.5 × 191.4 × 45.2 cm

PROVENANCE: Capitolo della Cattedrale, Reggio Emilia, 1911.

BIBLIOGRAPHY: Monducci and Nironi 1984: 143-144.

The commission for the construction of the model was awarded to Sogari by the Cathedral Chapter in 1538, after the death of Bernardino Brugnoli in Mantua the same year. Brugnoli was the author of the project for the facade approved ten years earlier. The design of the facing of the cathedral differs from his project in several ways, and it was probably Sogari himself who introduced the changes. There is a tendency toward simplifying the articulation of the second story, which still had to be built. The mixture of the three classical orders devised by Brugnoli has been reduced here to the coordination of a minor order of pilasters strips and columns with a major order of pilasters supporting the pediment. Only the facing for the lower order of the first story of the new facade was actually completed; the details of the ornamentation are closer to those of the wooden model rather than those of Brugnoli's project.

Riccardo Pacciani

marmo di Caldana, al farli legati in marmo bianco come è questo, o farli in fondo di pardiglio come è l'altro disegno a canto, et il simile attorno alle due finestre, et all'arme di mezo, che pare più ricca quella dove è il pardiglio, che questa che è legata in marmo bianco che apparisce povera, perché in una piazza grande li duoi bozzi di Caldana rimangano spogliati. Però a S.A.Ser.ma sta il risolvere come a lei piace.
BIBLIOGRAPHY: Ferri 1885: 112; Daddi-Giovannozzi 1937-40: 65; Paliaga in *Livorno* and *Pisa...* 1980, no. B.II.14; Morrogh 1985a: 128; Codini 1989: 217.

Daddi-Giovannozzi attributed this drawing to an unknown assistant of Don Giovanni, and the handwriting tentatively to Don Giovanni himself. The writing on our sheet is that of Pieroni, known from many documents (see the inscriptions on Uff. 4505A, ibid., fig. 76). The relatively free pen-work of the drawing may be compared with that of Louvre 11083, by Pieroni (ibid., fig. 77). The drawing should be dated not long after the model of 1593. Pieroni asks for the grand duke's decision as to the colored marbles for the facade. The left elevation shows the original scheme, that of the model: there were to be large panels of pink marble from Caldana in the lower story, and very little anywhere else. On the right, Pieroni has introduced large areas of grey marble ("pardiglio," i.e., *bardiglio*), which will, he says, produce a richer effect in the large piazza on which the church stands. The grand duke chose the second alternative. Later the panels of pink marble were framed by slender strips of white marble; and the grey marble was substituted by black marble from Portovenere, which was also introduced around the door (Codini 1989: 218, 256-257). No doubt these changes too were approved by the grand duke. The facade project presents striking parallels with that for the Cappella de' Principi, Ferdinand's chapel attached to S. Lorenzo in Florence (Cresti 1990: 77-93). There the atmosphere was one of constant experimentation with the display of colored stones. Decisions as to what stones should go where were taken at the highest level, by the grand duke himself; who must have based them, to a considerable extent, on colored drawings representing the various alternatives (e.g., Cresti 1990: 92, ills.). There too, in the final design, the colored stones were to be set off against a background of black marble. As the present drawing so interestingly demonstrates, the need perceived at S. Stefano was for a display that would work from a distance, at once rich and clear.

Andrew Morrogh

BIBLIOGRAPHY: Paliaga 1980, no. B.II.11; Codini 1989: 218.

S. Stefano dei Cavalieri was the chief church of a crusading order, the Cavalieri di S. Stefano, founded by Duke Cosimo de' Medici in 1562. The following year Vasari designed the church. A simple structure with a single large nave, it was dedicated in 1569. Vasari intended to erect a facade of colored marbles from the quarries at Seravezza and from a quarry that had just been just discovered near Pisa (Codini 1989: 197-220). The facade catered both to the growing interest in colored marbles and to Cosimo's extraordinary enthusiasm for *breccia* from Seravezza, which he had himself discovered. The project was revived by Grand Duke Ferdinand I, who gave the commission to his half-brother Don Giovanni de' Medici. In 1593 Orazio Migliorini and Andrea Ferrucci reproduced Don Giovanni's design in the present model, for which they recieved 35 *scudi* each (Paliaga). The facade, showing slight variations from the model, was completed in 1596. It is, so far as I know, the only colored-marble facade erected in sixteenth-century Italy. The facade represents a variant of Buontalenti's first project for the facade of Florence Cathedral, at least in the lower order (Daddi-Giovannozzi 1937-40: 88-90). The detail is probably due partly to Don Giovanni himself and partly to his assistant Pieroni. Pieroni designed the door of the interior facade (Uff. 3035A: Morrogh 1985a, no. 64), and, as the more competent draftsman, would have been responsible for the details of the order. The most interesting feature of the design is the way it allows for the display of large slabs of colored marble, which were much appreciated by contemporary taste. Lacking facades that might serve as models, Don Giovanni and Pieroni seem to have turned to contemporary colored-marble chapels for the idea of setting the slabs in white marble frames in the lower story; initially they were to be surrounded by two such frames. The panels were given the same breadth as the windows above, and almost the same height; the frames were taken over into the upper story. The result is a perhaps excessive uniformity, but serves to integrate the panels of colored marble into the overall design.

Andrew Morrogh

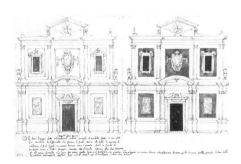

61
ALESSANDRO PIERONI
Project for the Facade of S. Stefano dei Cavalieri, Pisa

Florence, Galleria degli Uffizi, Gabinetto Disegni e Stampe, Uff. 2926A

Pen and gray-brown ink over balck chalk, colored washes; 280/283 × 424/421 mm
Scale: not given, but ca. 5.84 mm = 1 *braccio*, i.e., 1:100.
INSCRIBED: (in Pieroni's hand:) *Ser.mo Gran Duca. Li duoi disegni fatti col medesimo ordine secondo il modello fatto, si son fatti per mostrare le differenza che fanno li fondi attorno alli bozzi di*

62
GIOVANNI DE' MEDICI with ALESSANDRO PIERONI
Model for the Facade of S. Stefano dei Cavalieri, Pisa

Pisa, Museo Nazionale Civico di S. Matteo, 4602
Lime wood; ca. 1340 × 1344 × 170 mm
Scale: not given, but approx. 34.15 mm = 1 *braccio*.

PROVENANCE: S. Stefano dei Cavalieri, Pisa.

63
GIACOMO LAURO
Engraving of a Design by Martino Longhi il Vecchio for the facade of the Chiesa Nuova (S. Maria in Vallicella), Rome
1586-88

Milan, Raccolta delle stampe Achille Bertarelli, Castello Sforzesco
480 × 350 mm
INSCRIBED: (in a cartouche below the coat of arms of a cardinal of the Cesi family in the upper left) *Ill.mo et R.mo P.D. Angelo / Cesio Epo Tudert. et Cam: Apost. / Clerico. Martinus longus Mediol. / oriund. ex oppido Viglue et Civis Rom. / Archit.: Dic.;* (in an elaborate cartouche in the upper right) *Defuncti ut*

sponsam accipet lex iusserat
olim / Frater. et ex illa susciperet sobolem. / Legerat hanc tuus, Antistes meri.me sponsam / Frater et in coeli Templa receptus obit. / Haec tibi debetur fratri ne reiice maestam / Hinc surget proles haud moritura tibi; (in the frieze of the second story) *DEIPARÆ VIRGINI SACRVM*; (in the panels below the statues in the niches of the upper story, on the left) *S. Io. BAPT.* (on the right) *S. Io. EVAN* (in the panels below the statues in the niches on the first story, from left to right) *S. IACOB, S. PETRVS, S. PAVLVS, S. ANDRE*; (below the facade) *ANTERIOR FACIES ECCLESIÆ SANCTÆ MARIÆ VIRGINIS IN VALLICELLA DE VRBE / Martinus Longus Architectus inventor Rome* (below the scale) *Palmi romani 22.34*; (in the lower right) *Nico. VanAelst fer.; Iacobus Laurus sculp.*

BIBLIOGRAPHY: Baglione 1642: 68; Arrigoni and Bertarelli 1939: no. 1246; Hess 1963: 215, 226, 228-229, fig. 9; 1967, I: 353, 359-361, fig. 9; Bonadonna Russo 1968: 114 n. 29, 115, 117, 121, n. 46; Pinelli 1969: 356; Patetta 1980: 46, 47, fig.; Fagiolo 1982: 46, 64, fig. 19.1; Kummer 1987: 127; Nova 1988: 387, 390, 392, fig. 2.

The engraving is of a church facade of two levels. Broad Ionic pilasters demarcate the five bays of the first story. The four outer bays contain niches with statues. Ornate panels below the niches bear the names of the saints. Empty panels are set above the niches. The portal is framed by thin moldings and crowned by a severe pediment carrying two winged figures. The second story repeats the three central bays of the first level, with the exception of a window for the door. The coat of arms of the Cesi is set at the top of the triangular pediment over the window. Obelisks mark the outer bays of the second story. A triangular pediment containing a medallion with the Virgin and Child covers the three central bays. A cross on the Cesi mountains is set on top of the pediment. The Cesi mountains and oaks mark the outer edges of the main pediment. The coat of arms of a Cesi cardinal with an inscription tablet below is set at the upper left. At the upper right is an ornate cartouche containing an inscription. The engraving was published by Nicolaus van Aelst between 1586 and 1588, and most likely in the first months of 1587. It was first reproduced by Jacob Hess. This must be the "modello di facciata, che hora nelle stampe è rimasto" mentioned by Baglione in his life of Martino Longhi il Vecchio. Nova states that Longhi commissioned Lauro to make the engraving. The print documents Longhi's project for the facade of the Chiesa Nuova before it was expanded to a nave and two side aisles. There are few differences between Longhi's drawing that served as the model for the engraving and the print. Inscriptions are included only in the print. The wall of the facade is indicated in a dark shade in the print. Also added in the engraving is a flight of stairs before the portal, two winged figures on the pediment over the door, and the substitution of a medallion of the Virgin and Child for the standing figure of the Virgin. Interest has been attracted to the inscriptions. On the left is a dedication to Bishop Angelo Cesi of Todi and his brother, Cardinal Pier Donato, the recently deceased patron of the church. The inscription on the right is a passage from the Old Testament, Deuteronomy XXV, verses 5-10. It relates the levirate law, according to which a widow would marry her husband's brother. The Chiesa Nuova is thus presented as the widow to be cared for by Angelo Cesi after the death of Pier Donato. Bonadonna Russo believes that the inscription is not Longhi's, but rather the work of an Oratorian. She notes that the print was an attempt to draw Bishop Cesi's attention to the church, then under construction and lacking a facade.

After the Chiesa Nuova was enlarged beginning in 1586, Longhi's design was no longer appropriate. While the expansion was underway, Longhi received the commission from Sixtus V to build a facade for S. Giovanni degli Schiavoni. The facade, which was built from 1588 to 1590, is a direct application of Longhi's then obsolete design for the Chiesa Nuova (Hess 1963: 229; Hess 1967, I: 361; Nova 1988: 392).

Christine Challingsworth

64
FAUSTO RUGHESI
Model for the Facade of the Chiesa Nuova (S. Maria in Vallicella), Rome
1593-94

Rome, Congregazione dell'Oratorio di S. Filippo Neri, S. Maria in Vallicella
Wood.
190 × 134 cm (approx.)

BIBLIOGRAPHY: Baglione 1642: 68; Strong 1923: 71 and fig. VI; Ponnelle and Bordet 1932: 415, n. 10; Bonadonna Russo 1961: 423, 424, n. 41; Hess 1963: 215, 226; 1967, I: 353, 359; Bonadonna Russo 1968: 121-122; Pinelli 1969: 356; Hibbard 1971: 137; Patetta 1980: 46-48, fig. p. 47; Pericoli Ridolfini 1980: 16; Fagiolo 1982: 46, 64, fig. 19.4; Nova 1988: 387, n. 2, 392, n. 18.

The model is for a church facade of two levels of equal height with an attic and pediment set over the central bay. The width of the first story is extended by narrow recessed bays. The main portal is larger than the two lateral doors. The outer bays on both levels are articulated by pilasters, Corinthian below and Composite above, supporting plain entablatures. The side entrances were originally covered by segmental pediments. Above the lateral doors are relief panels decorated with scrolls, swags and shells. Empty niches crowned with triangular pediments and ornate relief panels are set in the lateral bays of the upper level. Attention is focused on the central bay by the doubled columns of the first level that support the broad segmental pediment, the large window on the second level marked by colonettes and a segmental pediment, and the crowning attic and triangular pediment. A relief panel is set above the main entrance. A medallion of the Virgin and Child, flanked by garlands, occupies the segmental pediment over the door. Garlands decorate the low attic. The coat of arms of the Cesi family is placed in the triangular pediment, set with dentils. The isolated sculptural forms contrast with the flatness of the architectural elements.

Compared with a related project drawing (cat. no. 65) and the facade as built, the model has suffered only minor losses. They include the small columns framing the main portal and the broken triangular pediment they supported, the shell and swag at the bottom of the panel over the left door, the balustrade of the window, the brackets connecting the upper story with the first level, and the capital of the second pilaster from the left in the upper story. Also missing are the cross on the mountains of the Cesi family coat of arms at the crest of the main pediment, one of the finials on the outer edge of the pediment, and the decorative elements (statues, finials or urns) set on the outer bays of both levels. The Cesi mountains atop the pediment are still visible in the photograph in Strong (1923: fig. VI). A model for the facade of the Chiesa Nuova is mentioned in 1642 by Giovanni Baglione in his biography of Martino Longhi il Vecchio: "Nella Chiesa nuova edificò il di dentro di detta fabrica, e vi fece un modello di facciata, che hora nelle stampe è rimasto; se bene poi la facciata fu fatta da Fausto Rughesi da Montepulciano, e con suo disegno,

e modello nobilmente compita" (Baglione 1642: 68). The model was first discussed and reproduced by Eugénie Strong in 1923 (71 and fig. VI). She, however, attributed it to Martino Longhi il Vecchio, a better known artist than Rughesi and architect of the Chiesa Nuova from 1586 until his death in 1591. Ponnelle and Bordet (1932: 415, n. 10) argue that the model must be by Rughesi since the documents show that Rughesi's project was selected in 1593 and already in 1595 a print of the awarded design, which closely resembles the model, appeared in a guidebook to Rome. The printmaker must have had the recently chosen design before him. In 1961 Maria Teresa Bonadonna Russo (1961: 423, 424, n. 41) maintained the attribution to Longhi. The model was securely attributed to Fausto Rughesi by Jacob Hess (Hess 1963: 226; 1967, I: 359). Following Hess' study, Bonadonna Russo (1968: 121-122) accepted the model as the work of Rughesi. The model was included in the catalogs of two exhibitions on the Longhi family held in Rome in 1980 and 1982 (Patetta 1980: 46-48; Fagiolo 1982: 46, 64-65).

In June 1586 the Oratorians appointed Martino Longhi il Vecchio architect of the Chiesa Nuova (Hess 1963: 219; Hess 1967, I: 355-356). The patron, Cardinal Pier Donato Cesi, stipulated that the church and monastery carry the Cesi arms (Ponnelle and Bordet 1932: 407; Connors 1980: 9). Cardinal Cesi died in September 1586. Shortly thereafter it was decided to expand the church from a single nave to a central nave and two side aisles (Hess 1963: 219-220; Hess, 1967, I: 356). Connors (1980: 9) suggests that Filippo Neri himself was behind the change. Hess (1963: 222; Hess, 1967, I: 357) dates the enlargement of the nave to 1586-88. Ponnelle and Bordet (1932: 411-412) state that the expansion was not finished until 1590. Kummer (1987: 129-130) notes that the rebuilding of the chapels continued after 1591 and that the nave was vaulted only in 1592-93.

Before the expansion of the nave, Longhi had prepared a design with a single portal for the facade of the church. Once the decision had been made to enlarge the church to a nave and two side aisles, however, Longhi's design for a facade of a single central opening was no longer suitable. It is not known if Longhi prepared additional elevations for the facade of the Chiesa Nuova with three openings. He died in June 1591.

Angelo Cesi, bishop of Todi and brother of Pier Donato, succeeded the cardinal as patron of the church and promised 7,300 *scudi* to pay for the facade (Bonadonna Russo 1961: 422). He organized a competition late in 1593 for a design for the facade. The participants were Giacomo della Porta, Giovanni Antonio Dosio, both architects selected by the Oratorians, Fausto Rughesi, an architect and cartographer from Montepulciano, and a certain "Leonardo" (Ponnelle and Bordet 1932: 414-415; Hess 1963: 226; Hess, 1967, I: 359; Bonadonna Russo 1968: 118-120). Hess (1963: 226; I, 1967: 359) identifies "Leonardo" with Leonardo Sormani, a sculptor who had worked for the Cesi family, but Bonadonna Russo (1968: 119, n. 43) doubts this and concludes only that an unknown architect from Todi participated in the competition. Bishop Cesi seems to have favored the little-known Rughesi from the beginning.

The facade of the Chiesa Nuova as it appeared at the time of the competition is presented in the plan of Rome by Antonio Tempesta published in 1593. The temporary facade is barely discernible. A square or rectangular window is shown in the upper half of the facade, but no door is indicated. Two or three curved steps are shown before the church.

The architects participating in the competition of 1593 apparently submitted to Angelo Cesi drawings with their designs for the facade. A sheet attributed to Giovanni Antonio Dosio (cat. no. 66) is preserved in the archive of the Oratorio. Rughesi's proposal is presented in Uff. 3179A (cat. no. 65). The drawings by della Porta and the fourth competitor are lost or yet to be identified. After Bishop Cesi selected Rughesi's design, the sheet must have served as the basis for the construction of the wooden model. The model agrees in all major details with Uff. 3179A.

The principal source for Rughesi's design for the facade of the Chiesa Nuova is easily identified in the facade of the Gesù, as proposed by Vignola and as built by Giacomo della Porta. The connection with the Gesù was not casual. Cardinal Pier Donato Cesi had seen himself in direct competition with the Farnese patrons of the Jesuit mother church (Bonadonna Russo 1961: 423, n. 34; Nova 1988: 390-391). The earlier church provided the general articulation of the two stories and the specific motif of the broad segmental pediment over the central bay of the lower level. Nathan Whitman (1970: 110-111), however, justly faults Rughesi's facade in comparison with its prototype for its "stunted outer panels, the overbearing size and projection of the segmental pediment, and the lumpy ornament."

The facade as built agrees with Rughesi's model up to the level of the cornice of the second story. At some point during the construction, the attic and small pediment over the central bay in Rughesi's model were set aside in favor of a triangular pediment over the width of the facade. In addition, narrow volutes were substituted for the brackets on the outer bays of the lower level. The change from the attic and small pediment, a Florentine motif found, for example, in the models of the 1580s and 1590s for the facade of Florence Cathedral (see relevant section), created a work more consistent with the early Baroque style of architecture in Rome.

Christine Challingsworth

65
FAUSTO RUGHESI
Project Elevation for the Facade of the Chiesa Nuova (S. Maria in Vallicella), Rome
1593

Florence, Galleria degli Uffizi, Gabinetto Disegni e Stampe, Uff. 3179A
Pen and brown ink, brown wash.
468 × 353 mm
INSCRIBED: (in the panel over the left portal) *TOTA PVLCRA / ES / AMICA MEA*; (in the panel over the main portal) *DEIPARAE VIR / GINI / SACRVM*; (in the panel over the right portal) *ET MACVLA / NON / EST IN TE.*

BIBLIOGRAPHY: Felini 1610: 115, fig.; Ferri 1885: 25; *Mostra di Roma secentesca* 1930: no. 167; Hess 1963: 227, n. 50; 1967, I: 359, n. 7; Bonadonna Russo 1968: 114, n. 29, 121, n. 46, 122; Borsi et al. 1976: 268-269, fig. 311; Fagiolo 1982: 46, fig. 19.2; Nova 1988: 387, n. 2, 392, n. 18.

The drawing presents a church facade of two levels, almost equal in height, crowned by an attic and pediment over the central bay. The narrow outer bays of the lower story are set back from the three middle bays. Single pilasters mark the outer edges. Doubled Corinthian pilasters are set at the juncture of the bays containing the side portals. Doubled columns, supporting a broad seg-

mental pediment, frame the larger central portal. Inscribed panels are set above each of the doors. The panels are decorated with brackets, shells, and swags. The coat of arms of the Cesi family is set on a field of swags in the center of the segmental pediment. The second story repeats the divisioning of the first level. The outer bays consist of narrow sloping walls anchored at the ends by tall finials. Doubled Composite pilasters demarcate each bay. Niches containing statues and blank panels surrounded by cartouches are set in the side bays. A large window decorated with colonettes, a balustrade, and a segmental pediment occupies the larger central bay. The facade is crowned with a low attic supporting a triangular pediment. Two blank panels and a central one containing a mask and swags fill the attic. The triangular pediment contains a medallion of the Madonna and Child. Statues mark the outer edges of the superstructure. The mountains of the Cesi family coat of arms supporting a cross are set at the crest of the pediment.

The facade design as presented in the drawing was first published in 1595 in a Roman guidebook, *Stationi delle chiese di Roma* (Strong 1923: 64, 71). The same woodcut was used for Felini's *Trattato nuovo delle cose maravigliose dell'alma città di Roma*, first published in 1610, with later editions (Felini 1610: 115). The woodcut summarily indicates the inscriptions in the panels over the doors and suggests the presence of the medallion of the Virgin and Child in the main pediment. The inscriptions are not included in the model (cat. no. 64), where the medallion of the Virgin and Child is set in the pediment over the main portal.

Ferri (1885: 25) identified the drawing only in a general manner as one of several elevations of various types for churches. He also identified it as a work of "Antonio Dosio" with a question mark. In the catalog of an exhibition held in Rome in 1930, the drawing is identified as by Fausto Rughesi and as a design for the facade of the Chiesa Nuova (*Mostra di Roma...* 1930: no. 167). Hess (1963: 227, n. 50; 1967, I: 359, n. 7) mentions that the drawing is close to Rughesi's model for the Chiesa Nuova. Bonadonna Russo (1968: 121, n. 46) identifies the drawing as by Rughesi. Gabriele Morolli (Borsi et al. 1976: 268), however, maintains the attribution to Dosio and connects the sheet with the facade of the Basilica of Loreto, constructed during the 1570s. He sees a close correspondence between the design in the drawing and the facade of the Basilica in the short flight of stairs, the divisioning into three bays, the Ionic colonettes flanking the main portal, and the pediments over the portals. The similarities, however, are of a generic nature and the connection of the design with the facade of the Basilica of Loreto is not convincing. Although Morolli (Borsi et al. 1976: 269) notes the Marian character of the inscriptions, he does not identify and discuss the coat of arms of a Cesi cardinal in the pediment over the main portal.

Rughesi submitted the drawing to Bishop Cesi in his competition organized in late 1593 for a facade for the Chiesa Nuova (Bonadonna Russo 1968: 121, n. 46; Fagiolo 1982: 46). The drawing then served as the basis for construction of the model (cat. no. 64).

There are few differences between the drawing and Rughesi's model for the facade. Losses in the model, such as pediments and sculptural elements (statues, finials, etc.), account for some of these minor discrepancies. One interesting change is the switch between the Cesi coat of arms, placed in the pediment over the door in the drawing and in the main pediment in the model, and the medallion of the Virgin and Child, set in the main pediment in the drawing and in the pediment over the door in the model. The placement of the medallion in the pediment over the main portal, where it is today, gives it better visibility and underscores for the visitor the dedication of the church to the Virgin.

Christine Challingsworth

66
GIOVANNI ANTONIO DOSIO (attr.)
Project Elevation for the Facade of the Chiesa Nuova (S. Maria in Vallicella), Rome
1593-94

Rome, Congregazione dell'Oratorio di San Filippo Neri, S. Maria in Vallicella, C.II.8, 36
Pen, ink and wash; 483/532 × 420 mm

BIBLIOGRAPHY: Ponnelle and Bordet 1932: 414, n. 8; Hess 1963: 227, fig. 11; 1967, I: 359, fig. 7; Bonadonna Russo 1968: 118, n. 39, 121; Blunt 1980: 66, 77, n. 27; Fagiolo 1982: 46; Kummer 1987: 131.

The sheet presents a design for a church facade of two nearly equal stories covered by a triangular pediment. The first level contains three portals separated by paired Corinthian pilasters. The doors are crowned by segmental pediments; a triangular pediment supported by colonettes is set within the arched pediment over the main entrance. Large relief panels are placed over the portals. The panels are devoid of inscriptions or reliefs, but are surrounded by moldings of distinctive geometric forms. The upper level contains two niches and a central window, each set over a narrow panel, separated by doubled Composite pilasters. The pediment contains a medallion of the Virgin and Child on a field of rays surrounded by unusual moldings and bracketed by hexagonal panels containing busts of the warrior saints Maurus and Papias (Blunt 1980: 77, n. 27). The Cesi coat of arms is placed above the relief panel over the central portal and the Cesi mountains appear again at the ends of the arch over the window of the second level and at the crest of the main pediment.

Hess (1963: 227; 1967, I: 359) first connected the drawing with the competition of 1593 for the design of the facade of the Chiesa Nuova. Ponnelle and Bordet (1932: 414, n. 8) cite three letters that mention that three designs by Dosio were submitted, two in 1593 and a third in 1594 after Rughesi's project had already been accepted. Bonadonna Russo (1968: 121) mentions a letter of December 1593 which indicates that Dosio's design was the first to be rejected. It is not clear which of Dosio's three proposals is presented in this drawing.

Dosio had worked for the Oratorians on earlier occasions. Documents of 1580 and 1581 indicate that he advised the congregation on the decoration of several of the chapels of the church before the rebuilding begun in 1586 (Bonadonna Russo 1968: 118, n. 39). In 1593 he was in Naples building the church of the Oratorians there (Ponnelle and Bordet 1932: 414, 417).

Blunt (1980: 66) identifies Dosio's design as belonging to the tradition of church facades of two equal stories, such as Michelangelo's projects for S. Lorenzo, Florence, Giacomo della Porta's S. Luigi dei Francesi, Rome, and Tibaldi's S. Fedele in Milan. Leaving aside decorative elements, the major distinction between Dosio's design and the facade as constructed is the addition of the recessed bays on the outer edges of the built work.

Christine Challingsworth

The Instruments of Design: the Drawing

67
JACOPO DE' BARBARI
Portrait of Fra Luca Pacioli with a Young Man

Naples, Museo e Gallerie Nazionali di Capodimonte, Q.58.
Oil on panel.
99 × 120 cm

The panel was acquired by the State in 1903 for the collection of the Museo Nazionale of Naples through the regional Exportation Department, where the picture had been presented a little earlier by Charles Fairfax Murray who, in his turn, had bought it from Eustachio Rogadeo di Torrequadra, Count of Bitonto; the count, who resided in Naples, had come into possession of it through his wife, a Vargas-Machuca and heir on her mother's side to the estate of the Medici di Ottaviano family; the picture in question in fact was originally part of this estate (De Rinaldis 1928: 13).

The painting's subject is the Franciscan monk Luca Pacioli—born in Borgo S. Sepolcro ca. 1440, teacher of mathematics and theory, and scholar on the science of proportions—standing at a table decked with the instruments of his profession: chalk and erasing sponge, goniometric contact gauge, a pair of dividers, a copy of Euclid's *Elements* open alongside a small drawing slate on which one of the problems described in Book XII of Euclid's treatise has been traced out. To the right there is a heavy tome, bound in red, whose inscription "LI. R. LVC. BVR." (*Liber Reverendi Luca Burgensis*) reveals it to be none other than Pacioli's own *Summa de Arithmetica, Geometria, Proportione et Proportionalità*, published in Venice in 1494. Perched on this tome is a dodecahedron model made from wood. To the left, another polyhedron fashioned in clear glass hangs suspended in midair. Both models were solid representations used in the study of geometry, which Pacioli (according to documents of 1496 and 1508) utilized and produced in person. Finally, to the right, on the green surface of the table is a *cartellino* or card bearing the inscription "IACO. BAR. VIGEN/NIS.P.1495," on which sits a fly.

Ever since it was first exhibited in public, the painting, the objects and figures portrayed, and in particular the inscription on the *cartellino* with its clue as to the author of the work, have been the subject of interminable debate. First, on the basis of the inscription, Ricci (1903b) and Venturi (1903) put forward the name of the Venetian painter Jacopo de' Barbari, known primarily as an engraver and for his work in Germany and the Low Countries; the word "vigennis" could be interpreted as the adjective "vicentino" (from Vicenza) or, better still, "ventenne" (twenty-year-old). Nevertheless, soon afterward Ricci (1903a) and Venturi (1913) changed their opinion

and revoked their attribution to Jacopo de' Barbari: convincing analogies to his known works were lacking, and it was hardly likely—as immediately pointed out by Bode (1903) and Gronau (1905)—that an artist twenty years of age in 1495 would receive a pension in 1512 from the Arch Duchess Margherita, Queen of the Low Countries, "considérant sa débilitation et vieillesse" (i.e., in consideration of his debility and old age). Subsequently, studies focused on a more liberal examination of the formal characteristics of the painting. The figures of the monk and the youth, the typical Urbinate references, the links with Piero della Francesca, Pedro Berruguete, Melozzo da Forlì, Palmezzano—even with Bramante—were underlined by the Italian critics (Bode 1903; Venturi 1913; Briganti 1938; Forlì 1938; Longhi 1963; Causa 1982); other scholars indicated links with Venice and the circle of Giovanni Bellini and Alvise Vivarini (Berenson 1916; De Rinaldis 1928; Heinemann 1962; Levenson 1978). The latter tendency has in the last thirty years induced various scholars (Gilbert 1956; 1957; 1967; Battisti 1971; Rusk Shapley 1979; Ciardi Dupré in *Urbino e le Marche...* 1983; Kemp 1991d) to re-evaluate the attribution to Jacopo de' Barbari, whose youthful activities are so far undocumented and who may have frequented the studio of Alvise Vivarini in Venice, or have been a frequent visitor. The meaning of "vigennis" could therefore be "Vicentine," or "nei vent'anni" (i.e., in the 1520s), tallying with Jacopo's forty-five years at that date, and hence of pensionable age in 1512.

The ongoing debate over authorship is inextricably bound up with the question of the place of origin and of the identity of the young man behind the monk. In 1905 Gronau stressed how the sixteenth-century *Vite dei Matematici* by Baldi cites "ne la Guardaroba de' nostri serenissimi Principi in Urbino il ritratto al naturale d'esso frato Luca col suo libro avanti de la *Somma dj aritmetica* et alcuni corpi regolari finti di cristallo appesi in alto" ("in the *Guardaroba* of the Highnesses the Princes of Urbino the portrait of Fra Luca with his book *Somma dj aritmetica* before him and some false crystal geometric figures suspended from above"), reportedly by the hand of "Pietro de' Franceschi, suo compatriota" and friend. Gronau also pointed out how the same painting was later cited in an even more circumstantial way—with its dimensions—in the 1631 inventory of the Palazzo Ducale; the packing crates belonging to the della Rovere estate transferred from Urbino to Florence ca. 1648-50; furthermore, the panel crops up in the inventory of the estate of the last heir, Vittoria della Rovere, in 1654: "Un ritratto di un frate di S. Bernardino con un giovane appresso vestito di pelliccia all'antica segnato al basso: Divo Principi Guido in Tavola"; other mentions follow: "A Monk, said to be the portrait of Fra Luca dal Borgo, by an unknown hand, teaching Euclid to Duke Guido, of the Guardaroba of Urbino"; "Un quadro in tavola inalto braccia 1 ²/₃, largo 2 di un Frate che insegna matematica. Del Ghirlandaio ò di Luca Signorelli." Despite some misgivings regarding the first mention quoted above (Servolini 1944; Thornton 1973), which some think may refer to an earlier prototype for the painting being discussed here (possibly by Piero della Francesca), the correspondence of both location and description of contents, and the earliest possible date ascribable to the *Summa* (published 1494), substantiate without doubt the identification of the picture in Naples with the one described in Urbino, which was subsequently transferred to Florence (*Raffaello e Brera* 1984: 50). The stamp on the rear of the panel, recently deciphered by Fiorillo (1983) as a miter with dappled cross and the letters—in Late Gothic script—"a" and "e" (*austriae dux*), provides added confirmation of origin. In fact, the widow of Federico della Rovere (the last Duke of Urbino), Claudia de' Medici—mother to Vittoria della Rovere—remarried after 1631 to Leopold V of Hapsburg, Archduke of Austria and Count of the Tyrol; formerly Bishop of Passau (1605-07), Leopold had received the pope's assent to relinquish his obligations to the Church. Thus, in 1632-33 (at all events, before 1648), independently of whether the painting was taken to the Tyrol or left in Urbino, it would have

entered the estate of the new couple, and would have therefore been marked with their emblem. What remains to be discovered, however, is how the work passed from the Florentine Medici collection to the collection of the Medici of Ottaviano in Southern Italy—two branches of the same family that had long been separated and apparently without contact, even with regard to their interests as collectors of art (De Rinaldis 1928).

The della Rovere inventories of Urbino and Florence, which refer to a dedication written at one time "in basso" of the frame (no longer extant), strongly support the identification of Pacioli's young "pupil" as Guidobaldo da Montefeltro, born in 1472 and therefore twenty-three in 1495. Such an identification is preferable to other proposals (such as Jacopo de' Barbari himself), given the painting's origins in the Palazzo Ducale of Urbino, given also the authority of the sources, the nobility of the figure represented, and the fact that Pacioli—perhaps Guidobaldo's teacher in Urbino between 1493 and 1494—dedicated his finished *Summa* to the young man in 1494 thus: "*grecis latinisque litteris ornatissimus et mathematicae disciplinae cultor ferventissimus.*"

On the other hand, there is a *Portrait* in the National Gallery of Washington whose subject closely resembles the "Guidobaldo" of our panel; once again, the painting is believed to be a self-portrait of Jacopo de' Barbari (Rusk Shapley 1979), painted perhaps slightly later than the one in Naples, and therefore much more acceptable as a work (though not as a self-portrait) by the Venetian painter because of its emphatic use of the visual language of Dürer and Alvise Vivarini. This would endorse the interpretation of the much-discussed inscription as reading "1495," and the attribution to Jacopo de' Barbari, refuting the other fruitless attributions to the elusive "Giacomo Barucco" of Venice, and "Jacopo Barocci" of Urbino.

The question is liable to remain unresolved. Even the authenticity of the *cartellino* inscription has been repeatedly challenged—by Heinemann (1962), Causa (1982), and Fiorillo (1983)—on the basis of radiographic studies, which have revealed that all the main inscriptions (on the book, the drawing slate, and *cartellino*) do not show up. This was probably due (Kemp 1991d) to the fact that the *biacca* (white lead) does not let the X-rays pass. The date 1495 certainly corresponds to the apparent age of the Pacioli figure in the painting, and to the publication date of the *Summa* in Venice; the dedication of the treatise tallies with the dedication to Guidobaldo mentioned in the written sources. The entire episode therefore took place in the period 1494-95, and the contingencies with the Urbino-Venice milieu are historically hard to deny—a milieu, furthermore, which the young Jacopo de' Barbari, advocate of the need for liberal and "modern" artists to study geometry, arithmetic and the laws of proportion too (Servolini 1944: 105-106), may well have frequented.

Yet to be explained are the pervasive Urbino accents—a presence that is endorsed by the images of the Palazzo Ducale reflected in the crystal polyhedron, and further accentuated by the references to Piero della Francesca and Berruguete, especially with regard to the figure of the monk; this is so marked as to suggest two distinct interventions by separate artists. In the absence of data on Barbari's early period (which Ciardi Dupré in *Urbino e le Marche...* 1983 assumes to have been mostly spent in Urbino), the earlier hypothesis (albeit of a somewhat roundabout nature) of the existence of a prototype for this portrait of the monk—however partial—executed by Piero della Francesca in person, cannot be entirely ruled out. In the course of the 1470s, and even as late as 1482, when Piero drafted his *De prospectiva pingendi*, the destinies of the Master and his "pupil" Pacioli were closely intertwined as they commuted between the Urbino milieu under the Montefeltro and their common birthplace of Borgo S. Sepolcro—and so close is this correlation that some scholars have identified the monk's likeness in the face of the St. Peter Martyr figure in Piero's celebrated *Brera Altarpiece* (Ricci 1903b). Nor is it spurious or misteading in this respect to note the Pierfrancescan tone of the supposed "true" portrait of Pacioli, engraved for the Venice edition of the *Summa*, predating and independent from the Naples portrait, in which Pacioli appears younger.

Pierluigi Leone de Castris

68

GIOVANNI ANTONIO DOSIO (?)
Sectional Elevation of S. Giovanni dei Fiorentini

Florence, Galleria degli Uffizi, Gabinetto Disegni e Stampe, Uff. 233A

BIBLIOGRAPHY: D. Frey 1920; Nava 1935-36; Venturi 1939; Wachler 1940; Giovannoni 1959; Ackerman and Lotz 1964; Schwager 1975; Dosio 1976.

While most scholars have ascribed this drawing to Giovanni Antonio Dosio, some have favored attributions to Antonio da Sangallo, Labacco, or even Tiberio Calcagni (including Frey 1920: 57ff.; Wachler 1940: 220; Ackerman and Lotz 1964: 13; Dosio 1976: 371ff.; Schwager 1975; Giovannoni 1959: 217, 219; Nava 1935-36: 107; Venturi 1939, XI/2: 192). The elevation shown represents a variant to Vignola's project for S. Giovanni dei Fiorentini (cat. no. 208). These two sketches greatly resemble each other, even in the detailing (as in the representation of the section of outside wall of the *ballatoio*, and the double staircase, or the arrangement of the vestibule, etc.). Unlike Vignola's elevation, however, here the building is conceived on a round plan, and the construction seems to be divided into sixteen bays, as envisaged by Sangallo in an earlier scheme. However, this arrangement has not been properly thought out, and as a result the central nave arcading is in the proportion of 1:3.5, unthinkable in the Renaissance. This same variant reappears in a drawing, drawn in a characteristic hurried style, from the album of sketches by Oreste Vannocci Biringucci (fol. 42v.), together with Vignola's tabernacle for S. Antonio Martire in Fara in Sabina (Ackerman and Lotz 1964: 13). Upon comparison with Vignola's elevation (cat. no. 208), the differences and analogies of this drawing of S. Giovanni dei Fiorentini become evident—the fleur-de-lis pinnacle crowning the dome on Uff. 233A. There is no documentary evidence of Dosio and Biringucci having worked together on S. Giovanni.

Hubertus Günther

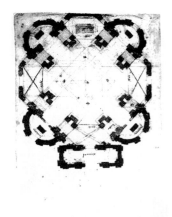

69

MICHELANGELO BUONARROTI
Project for S. Giovanni dei Fiorentini (octagonal plan)

Florence, Casa Buonarroti, CB 120r.
Pen and ink, wash, black pencil.
292 × 422 mm
INSCRIBED: *archi; in bocte; sacrestia; portico; a travi; fiume* (Michelangelo).

PROVENANCE: Tolnay 1980, no. 610.

Michelangelo reached a high point in his experiments in form with this project. The plan appears more of a geometrical exercise than the elaboration of traditional architectural shapes. However, Michelangelo felt under obligation here, unlike in his other projects for S. Giovanni dei Fiorentini, to add a few explanations about the architectural shapes and the functions. In spite of this, it appears the Florentines had some difficulty in understanding the project. The collocation of this project among those for S. Giovanni dei Fiorentini is based on its similarity to CB 124 recto, and on the fact that the foundations end on the shores of the Tiber (the line flanking the choir is marked "fiume"). This regular octagon with four short and four long sides has apses inserted in the long sides, while the entrances and main altar are on the short sides. The entrances to the inner arcades are flanked by pairs of enormous pilasters, matched by another pair further inside. This creates an octagonal central area surrounded by double pilasters next to secondary polygonal areas lying on the main axes and serving as vestibules and the choir, while, on the secondary axes, long passages lead to the apsidal sacristies. The secondary polygonal areas have cross vaults, whereas the areas between the double pilasters have barrel vaults parallel to the walls. The passages between them also have barrel vaults, perpendicular to the wall; consequently the central area would have opened up with alternating small and large arches, surmounted presumably by a clerestory. It was not planned to roof the central area with a traditional dome, but with a ribbed vault rising from the double pilasters. Alongside this drawing is a sketch of the underlying geometric schema; the octagon has equal sides, but this would have made the apses too small to serve as sacristies. The verso of CB 120 reveals another two geometrical sketches whose design is similar to the one behind the project on the recto. Both are regular octagons with four long and four short sides. In one of them the apses extend the full length of the long sides in a layout that recalls S. Lorenzo in Milan and the early projects for St. Peter's. On the other plan, three-quarter circular sacristies are attached to the short sides, while the polygonal arms extend from the long sides. The result is a plan similar to Michelangelo's coeval experiments for the Cappella Sforza in S. Maria Maggiore. The projects on CB 120 recto and verso indicate particularly clearly that Michelangelo's technique of elaborating a design was based fundamentally on Leonardo's more theoretical projects for centrally planned buildings.

Hubertus Günther

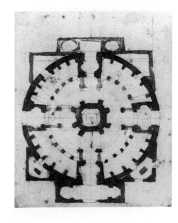

70

MICHELANGELO BUONARROTI
Project for S. Giovanni dei Fiorentini (rotunda plan)

Florence, Casa Buonarroti, CB 121r.
Pen and ink, wash, black pencil.
210 × 282 mm

PROVENANCE: Tolnay 1980, no. 609.

While Michelangelo had drawn a variant on CB 124 recto of Jacopo Sansovino's winning project for S. Giovanni dei Fiorentini, in this design he started from a building similar in layout to Antonio da Sangallo's design published by Labacco. Michelangelo's rotunda with columned ambulatories is reminiscent of the design of S. Costanza, though characterized in particular by the inclusion of vestibules in the ambulatories on four sides, in front of the entrances and the space designated for the altar. In the central space before the vestibules are small atriums, also with oval vaults. The pairs of columns separating them correspond with columns in front of the corners of the central octagonal "enclosure." The project could easily be for a baptistery, and it is difficult to imagine how it could have functioned as a parish church for the Florentine community in Rome. The insertion of this project among the S. Giovanni dei Fiorentini group is based on its general stylistic affinity with CB 124 and 120 (nos. 71, 69). The patent lack of functionality is a characteristic of his other projects for the building (though less so). Michelangelo was probably more interested in exploring shapes, paying little attention to practical questions. At least four of the five projects elaborated were in fact rejected; furthermore, the Florentine community still had the option to suggest changes to meet their functional requirements.

Hubertus Günther

71

MICHELANGELO BUONARROTI
Project for S. Giovanni dei Fiorentini (central plan with corner apses)

Florence, Casa Buonarroti, CB 124r.
Pen and ink, wash, sanguine and black pencil.
292 × 422 mm

PROVENANCE: Tolnay 1980, no. 612.

BIBLIOGRAPHY: Gaye 1840; Thode 1908-13; Frey 1920; Nava 1936; Ackerman 1961; Gioseffi 1964a: 653-669; *Carteggio* 1966-83; Schwager 1973: 33-96; Tolnay 1980; Hirst 1988b; 1989; Argan and Contardi 1990.

The preliminary drawing shows that Michelangelo developed his design from a scheme of intersecting geometrical figures (for his drawing techniques, see Hirst 1988b: 35ff.; 1989, no. 62). In this case, the scheme is composed of a circle superimposed on a square, with eight pairs of regularly intersecting parallel lines. The square with rounded corners delineates the building perimeter; the circle defines the central area; the pairs of parallel lines establish the position of the four apses in the corners of the square, and the four rectangular spaces attached to the square, which form the choir and vestibules. A thin wall connecting paired columns and creating niches between them separates the circular ambulatory from the rest of the central area, as indicated in the little drawing at top left. Michelangelo explored a similar solution in detail on CB 36 recto (Tolnay 1980, no. 611r.), adding a rough sketch of the elevation. The central area is surrounded by rhythmically spaced pilasters: while the wall planes with paired columns terminated in an entablature; the accesses to the secondary areas between them opened onto ample arches rising from the entablature. These passages probably had barrel vaults, while the areas between the partition walls of the central area and the outer walls would have been roofed with cross vaults. Michelangelo drew a square in the center of the church which probably indicated the altar rail. On the verso is a carefully drawn design for a window similar to those inserted between the side chapels under the dome in the model for S. Giovanni dei Fiorentini.
Michelangelo became involved in the building of S. Giovanni dei Fiorentini in 1550. When Giovanni Maria del Monte, a Florentine, became Pope Julius III, the Florentine community decided to resume work on the church, which had not advanced since the death of Antonio da Sangallo. They persuaded the pope to have his funerary monument erected in their national church. Michelangelo was consulted and supported the Julius III's suggestions (as confirmed in a letter to Vasari), but recommended they first complete the half-built church ("e io ne lo confortai assai, stimando, che per questo mezza decta chiesa s'abbi a finire"; *Carteggio*, 1965-83, no. 1148). His irony produced the desired effect, and Julius III kept his distance from the project. He told Vasari two months later that it would be better to forget all about the church ("Basta, che nella chiesa de Fiorentini non mi par s'abbi più a pensare"; *Carteggio*, 1965-83, no. 1155). In 1559, however, Michelangelo took the project for S. Giovanni dei Fiorentini in hand, as described thoroughly by Vasari, and detailed in the exchange of letters (between the Duke, the Florentine community, and Michelangelo), and reported in the *cantiere* records (Vasari 1878-85 VII: 261ff.; Gaye 1840: 20ff., 23ff., 40; *Carteggio*, nos. 1303-05, 1312, 1319, 1326ff., 1330, 1332; Nava 1936: 354ff. Besides the general bibliography on the construction of S. Giovanni dei Fiorentini, see also Thode 1908-13, II: 178-183; Frey 1920: 77-88; Ackerman 1961: 103-109, 117-121; Gioseffi 1964a; Tolnay 1980: 104-107; Argan and Contardi 1990: 297ff., 342-337). Together these documents provide a minutely detailed account of Michelangelo's development of the project, allowing for a margin of bias and misrepresentation of the events.
After much debate the Florentines agreed to resume the construction of the church: "Then, after they had argued whether they should follow the original plans or try to do something better, it was decided to raise a new edifice on the old foundations" (Vasari). At the comunity's request, Duke Cosimo de' Medici commissioned Michelangelo to draft a new project for the building, to be approved by the

community by duly addressing its needs (",proportionato a tutte quelle considerazioni che vi sono" *Carteggio*, no. 1303). Michelangelo therefore presented the Florentines with a choice of five different church designs (three projects have survived: cat. nos. 74, 209, 210, 211; CB 123 may not be part of this group as it represents a plan for a small chapel, as denoted by the dimensions of the door and columns). At first the Florentines preferred to leave the choice to Michelangelo, but it appears they subsequently chose CB 124 recto, prompted by Michelangelo himself. The community then submitted the project to Cosimo for approbation, at which the design would become decisive: after this official approval the project could be elaborated in detail, including the relative elevations. As Michelangelo discreetly informed the duke, the Florentines had "elected" Tiberio Calcagni to lighten his load. Calcagni, who had been the aging master's close assistant for some time (Schwager 1973: 40-43), built a wooden model and made a final draft of the project, which was submitted for Cosimo's opinion. The marked differences between the model and Michelangelo's original project can be explained by the fact that the Florentines asked for modifications in the meantime. Noting the changes to the project in the drawings that Calcagni had presented him, the duke, referring to Alberti, pointed out that "volendovi cresciere, non si può, et levando si guasterieno" ("to add something would be too much, to take something away would be to ruin it"; Calcagni to Michelangelo, *Carteggio*, no. 1327). Cosimo requested Calcagni to repeat the quote to Michelangelo, and warned the Florentines personally that nothing was to be added or detracted from Michelangelo's project ("non vi si potendo aggiungere cosa alcuna, né diminuire"; Gaye, no. 40).
The site was once more set in motion, under the direction of Calcagni's direction; two years later, however, with only the foundations fully completed, work again came to a halt: funds had reportedly run dry. Michelangelo's model was put on show in the Oratorio.
In truth, Michelangelo's project was not suited to the foundations that had been laid, which had the shape of Antonio da Sangallo's basilica scheme (the Florentine community's first choice, before Michelangelo was invited to continue the church). Michelangelo's proposals were all for central-plan churches. As for his work on St. Peter's, Michelangelo showed his refusal to pick up from where the loathed Sangallo "sect" had left off, and obviously preferred to start afresh. His project for S. Giovanni dei Fiorentini was similar to Jacopo Sansovino's winning proposal for S. Giovanni dei Fiorentini, and had the same dimensions.
It seems that Michelangelo did not respect the obligation to meet all the Florentine community's requirements. He disregarded the foundations completed by Antonio da Sangallo, and did not take into account that S. Giovanni was to be the parish church of the entire Florentine community in Rome. Consequently, there was barely sufficient space for a large congregation. Sensing perhaps from the outset that the community's approval would not have been enough to guarantee the execution of the project, Michelangelo took to exhorting them: with this church, he claimed, the modern Etruscans (i.e., Tuscans) would have "produced a work superior to anything done by either the Greeks or the Romans." Such rhetoric, says Vasari, was not at all typical of Michelangelo, who "was a very modest man."

Hubertus Günther

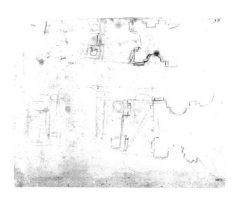

72
MICHELANGELO BUONARROTI
Sketches of Plan and Elevation of the Nave of S. Giovanni dei Fiorentini

Florence, Casa Buonarroti, CB 36A
Black pencil.
141/146 × 171/172 mm

BIBLIOGRAPHY: Tolnay 1980, no. 611r.

This sheet contains preliminary sketches for the plan project in CB 124Ar. (cat. no. 71), even though the concepts expressed here differ considerably from those of the final scheme. It is more akin with the project sketches on the verso of CB 120A (cat. no. 69) which, like CB 124Ar., attests its debt to the polygonal plan of S. Giovanni dei Fiorentini on the recto of CB 120A, with its even more marked geometrical arrangement.
The plan sketches here make more sense when compared with the pentimenti in CB 124. Michelangelo's first scheme involved semicircular rather than oval corner chapels. In the sketches (near bottom and top edges) the side chapels open wide onto the nave of the church; in the pentimenti on CB 124, however, their entrances are reduced by the addition of enclosure walling either side. Michelangelo made the remaining section of wall between the corner chapel openings and the entrances to the church the same breadth as the wall segment opposite each one. From the elevation, drawn on the left, it can be seen that he calculated the wall sections delimiting the nave to be much broader than it actually is on CB 124 recto; at all events, he made these sections equal in breadth to the openings themselves. The way in which these different solutions merged becomes clearer in CB 120A and in CB 124 itself. The chapels sketched out in CB 124A, with the wall segments enclosing the entrances are clearly based on CB 120A. The entrances spaces, which were altered to the sketch design, are based on the scheme presented in CB 120A, though they are narrower, and have rounded-corners. The lower sketch of the floor plan (upper margin) indicates the structure of the passageway to one of the entrance antechambers. It was not until later that Michelangelo applied two fundamental changes: he replaced the original octagonal scheme divided into two pairs of parallels, with a rotunda scheme, in which the entire arrangement of elements is determined from the central point. His second innovation was to greatly enlarge the antechambers to the church.

Hubertus Günther

73
<small>ANONYMOUS</small>
*Elevation and Section of Michelangelo's Model for
S. Giovanni dei Fiorentini*

Berlin, Staatliche Museen, Preussischer Kulturbesitz,
Kupferstichkabinett, KdZ 20.976

<small>BIBLIOGRAPHY:</small> Noehles 1969; Tolnay 1980.

This drawing, first published by K. Noehles (1969, pl. 56)
coincides in all its particulars with one of the two copperplate engravings printed by Valérian Régnard in *Praecipua
urbis templa* (Rome, 1650). It even shows greater precision
in certain details. It may, as suggested by Tolnay (1980:
106ff.), be the original drawing on which the engraving
was modeled. For the details of the representation, see the
entry on Régnard's copperplate print (cat. no. 209).

Hubertus Günther

74
<small>JACQUES LE MERCIER</small>
*S. Giovanni dei Fiorentini
(model of final scheme)*

Paris, Bibliothèque Nationale
Copperplate engraving.
135 × 192 mm (plate dimensions)
<small>INSCRIBED:</small> *Disegno d'un Modello non messe in opera fatto per San
Gioani dei Fiorentini in roma la redduttione del quale è di doi
palmi per oncie la longhezza et larghezza è di pal. 9 ¼ et l'altezza
pal. 7. Michel Angelo Bonarota Inventore Jacobus
Mercier Gallus fecit Romae Ano. 1607.*

<small>BIBLIOGRAPHY:</small> Totti 1638; Titi 1686; Vasari, ed. Pagliarini 1759-
60; Titi 1763; Robert-Dumesnil 1835-71; Gaye 1840; Thode 1908-
-13; D. Frey 1920; Panofsky 1920-21: 35-45; Tolnay 1932: 231-
253; Nava 1936: 337-362; *Carteggio* 1965-83; Schwager 1973:
33-96.

(Note: Le Mercier's engraving, already included in the 1835-71
edition of the Robert-Dumesnil encyclopedia [VI, 152, no. 1], was
quoted for the first time in Panofsky's studies of Michelangelo in
1920-21, and published by Tolnay in 1930)

Le Mercier was less interested in illustrating Michelangelo's project for S. Giovanni dei Fiorentini, than in showing Tiberio Calcagni's model of Michelangelo's project

looked like. This is clear from both the inscription of the
engraving and the particularly lively representation. The
model is shown in perspective, as it would be seen by an
observer; even the trestle table on which it stands has
been drawn in detail. A comparison with the other pictures of Michelangelo's model reveals that Le Mercier's
is the most accurate. Moreover, he is the only artist to include the dimensions (207 × 207 × h 156 cm); the scale is
reported to have been 1:24, which means that
Michelangelo's church that would have been 222 *palmi*
long and 168 *palmi* high. According to Biringucci's copy
of the project plan (cat. no. 210), the length and height
would have been 220 *palmi*. Vasari writes that Tiberio
Calcagni was commissioned to draw a final copy of
Michelangelo's project for S. Giovanni dei Fiorentini,
and was appointed tenure of the building site (Vasari;
Nava 1936: 343, doc. 11-12; Gaye 1840, III, no. 40;
Michelangelo, *Carteggio*, 1965-83, nos. 1304, 1319,
1327). Old age obliged Michelangelo to employ assistants, and Calcagni was one of his favorites (Schwager
1973: 40-43). Vasari notes that Calcagni was contracted
to build a model of Michelangelo's project. He first built
a clay model to Michelangelo's instructions that was only
"8 *palmi* long" and which took him ten days. After the approval of the clay model Calcagni was ordered to build
another, this time in wood. The result was described by
Vasari as "a building as rare in its ornate variety as any
church ever seen." He states, furthermore, that the said
model was lodged in the Florentine consolate.
In the seventeenth century the model was considered one
of the obligatory sights for visitors to Rome (Thode 1908-
13, II: 180; Frey 1920: 83). In 1638 Pompilio Totti (Totti
1638: 245) wrote that the model was in the Florentine oratory, and was a sight "well worth seeing," and such recommendations were repeated by later guides to Rome (Titi
1686: 393). Much earlier even, in 1583, when it became
clear that Michelangelo's church would never be realized,
Diomede Leoni petitioned the Grand Duke of Tuscany to
have it brought to Florence to ensure its conservation
(Gaye 1840, III, no. 383); regrettably, Leoni's advice was
ignored. Filippo Titi's guide to Rome (Titi 1763: 422)
notes that the model was kept in the Florentine oratory
until 1720, but was later destroyed. Bottari confirmed
that the model "was kept in a room in S. Giovanni dei
Fiorentini until my own time, but was in a bad state. It
is now no longer there, and it is believed to have been
burnt by the priests" (Vasari 1759-60, III: 300).

Hubertus Günther

75
<small>ANONYMOUS</small>
*Plan of Michelangelo's Model for
S. Giovanni dei Fiorentini*
(from *Praecipua urbis templa*, by Valérian
Régnard)
1650

Florence, Galleria degli Uffizi, Gabinetto Disegni e Stampe,
Uff. 3185A

<small>BIBLIOGRAPHY:</small> Ferri 1885; Venturi 1939; Schwager 1973: 33-96;
Collobi Ragghianti 1974; Tolnay 1980; Argan and Contardi 1990.

This drawing coincided perfectly with one of the two engravings reproduced by Valérian Régnard in *Praecipua urbis templa* (Rome, 1650); Tolnay in fact considers it to be
the original drawing for the engraving. Even the peculiar
altar arrangement is identical. However, the engraving is
less precise in certain particulars, such as the subdivision
of the walls of the lantern. This suggests a sketch rather
than a copy based on the engraving. The practice of drawing perfect copies of engravings was, moreover, common
in this period. A. Venturi published the drawing in *Storia
dell'arte italiana* (1939, XI: 189, pl. 2), ascribing it to
Tiberio Calcagni, who was in charge of making scale
models for Michelangelo. The attribution to Calcagni was
repeated over the years (latterly by Argan and Contardi
1990). To judge from the stylistic traits of Calcagni's
drawing bearing the caption "Di Tiberio Calcagni è sua inventione" (Uff. 225r.), there is no question of this drawing being the work of the same author (see Ferri 1885:
xxii; see also the critical comparison of Calcagni's graphic
works in Schwager 1973, n. 144; see also the numerous illustrations attributed to Calcagni in Collobi Ragghianti
1974: 149f., pls. 269-270). For the peculiarities of this
horizontal projection, see observations on Régnard, cat.
no. 209.

Hubertus Günther

Michelangelo and the Porta Pia
Henry A. Millon

A new gate in the Aurelian wall became necessary when Pius IV developed plans to cut a straight new avenue from the Quirinale to S. Agnese, more than a kilometer beyond the wall. The avenue required the straightening and leveling a new roadway, the displacement of the old Via Nomentana, and the closing of the Porta Nomentana a short distance to the southeast along the Aurelian wall. Within the walls, from the Quirinale to the new gate, to line the north of the Baths of Diocletian, the avenue was laid through vineyards and orchards, demolishing houses and structures in its path. New walls and gates leading to vineyards and villas came to line the avenue named for Pius IV. Descriptions of the project at the time of its initiation, 18 January 1561, and six months later on 18 June 1561, when the cornerstone was laid by the pope (with at least twelve medals coined to commemorate the event [K. Frey 1909b: 166]), are recorded in letters written by the Mantuan ambassador to the duke (Pastor 1928, XVI: 463, no. 5, 465, no. 11). Work on altering Via Nomentana was already under way in January 1561 and a contract for construction of the Porta Pia itself was signed on 2 July, two weeks after the cornerstone ceremony. Medals for the ceremony were ordered from Giovanni Federigo da Parma, called Bonsagni, before 1 April (Bertolotti 1875: 77), which confirms that Michelangelo prepared designs for the gate before that date. Extant drawings indicate most of his attention concentrated on the portal itself. In May 1561 preparatory work for laying the foundations was begun under the direction of Pier Luigi Gaeta as *sottoarchitetto* (Gotti 1875, II: 162). A payment of 20 August 1563 cites Gaeta as the "agent" for Michelangelo. (In November 1561 Michelangelo attempted unsuccessfully to have Gaeta added to the supervisory staff at St. Peter's [*Carteggio* 1965-83, V, MCCCLXVII].) The sculptors Jacopo del Duca and Luca (not otherwise identified) were paid in 1562 for the Medici escutcheon (Gotti 1875, II: 162) and in 1565 Nardo de' Rossi completed the angels flanking the escutcheon (Bertolotti 1875: 77). Schwager (1973: 54ff) suggests the angels by Nardo de' Rossi were substituted for the standing nudes that appear in the engraving of 1568 by Bartolomeo Faleti. The original figures were, according to Schwager, placed in the pediment of S. Luigi dei Francesi in Rome. Payments for construction cease in July 1565 (Bertolotti 1875: 77).

Even though scholars and critics think the third level of the Porta Pia (as depicted in the engraving by Faleti) exhibits little that is Michelangelesque, it seems likely to have been completed in the summer of 1565. Engraved "plans" of Rome by Mario Cartaro (1576) and Etienne Dupérac (1577) show the third level complete with triangular pediment. The upper portion of the third level appears to have collapsed, if we are to believe the representation of the Via Pia and Porta Pia in a fresco in the Lateran Palace (Sala del Concistoro), executed ca. 1590, as wel l as in the Tempesta map of Rome (1593), the Falda plan of 1676, etc., all of which agree in showing an incomplete third level. The third level was rebuilt by Virginio Vespignani in 1853 (Zanghieri 1953: 42). Although it is known that Michelangelo worked on designs for the exterior gate (letter of August 1561 to Lionardo Buonarroti from Tiberio Calcagni, an assistant of Michelangelo's [(Papini 1949: 603]), work was never undertaken. The exterior gate was built to Vespignani's designs in 1861-68 (Zanghieri 1953: 42ff.; Schiavo 1953: 265ff.).

The Porta Pia design was one of a number for gateways requested of Michelangelo by Pius IV (Vasari, ed. Milanesi 1875, VII: 260). Vasari also notes that Michelangelo

made three designs for the Porta Pia and that the pope selected the least expensive to execute (ibid.). If these three were presentation drawings, they have not survived. Nor, apparently, are there any extant drawings by Michelangelo for the additional gates.

76
MICHELANGELO BUONARROTI
Study for the Porta Pia

Florence, Casa Buonarroti, CB 106Ar.
Black chalk, pen and brown ink, brush and bistre wash, white lead body color.
442 × 281 mm; irregularly cut; the sheet consists of five pieces of paper pasted together.

PROVENANCE: Casa Buonarroti.

BIBLIOGRAPHY: Thode 1913, III, no. 70; Tolnay 1930: 41 and 45; Düssler 1959, no. 134; MacDougall 1960: 97ff.; Ackerman 1961, II: 128ff.; Barocchi 1962a, I: no. 169; Ackerman 1964, II: 132; Portoghesi and Zevi 1964: 965ff.; Hartt 1971, no. 529; Hedberg 1972: 63-66; Tolnay 1975b: 123; Joannides 1978: 176; Tolnay 1980, IV, no. 619r.; Hirst 1988a: 155-157; Hirst 1988b: 88ff.; Argan and Contardi 1990: 301ff., 351, fig. 414; Marani 1992b: 465, 500.

Recent scholarship has accepted CB 106Ar. as from the hand of Michelangelo (Hartt 1971: 366; Tolnay 1975b: 123; Tolnay 1980, IV, 112-113; Hirst 1988a: 155-156; Argan and Contardi 1990: 351; and Marani 1992b: 500). Other scholars have thougth it was either drawn by or finished by assistants (Düssler 1959: 86; MacDougall 1960: 100; Barocchi 1962a, I: 210; Ackerman 1961, I: 116; Ackerman 1964, II: 132). The decisive transformation of undivided elements, dramatic rendering with body color, and bold juxtapositions of curvilinear and blocklike forms argue for the direct involvement of Michelangelo. The initial underdrawing may have sketched the outline of a "simple" window or doorway flanked by freestanding columns and crowned by a segmental pediment. Hedberg (1972: 63-66) has shown how Michelangelo began a study of the windows of the third level of the Palazzo Farnese in Rome, using a sheet with a rudimentary drawing of a window with flanking columns, much like that of the straightforward robust windows of the second level of the Palazzo dei Conservatori on the Capitoline. The underdrawing underwent a series of transformations that ended in the compressed and disjunctive window of the Palazzo Farnese. The initial drawing on CB 106Ar. seems to have defined a tall and narrow entry (with a keystone) flanked by banded rustic columns or half columns. The column capitals, just above the level of the lintel of the opening, seem originally to have supported a tall salient entablature (treated as a ressaut), crowned by a simple segmental pediment (or possibly a broken, scrolled pediment). When the entry was widened and heightened, the opening was spanned by a flat arch with haunches, pronounced voussoirs, and a much enlarged keystone. A successive large, broken triangular pediment

(also scrolled?), in black chalk, seems to have preceded the generation of a "C" scroll, fluted segmental pediment framing, in the center, a flattened shell-like shape. Between the shell and the keystone is a rectangular tablet with a salient central section. Above, yet another broken segmented pediment, drawn in brown wash, suggests, perhaps, an element that appears later in the triangular pediment enclosing the entry portal on the structure as built. Because of elements that recall the design of the portal found on the Bonsagni medal, CB 106Ar. is thought to reflect an early stage in Michelangelo's study of the design. The flanking columns, scrolled segmental pediment with a shell in the center, and a salient keystone in the lintel of the opening are found on both the medal and drawing. The layered drawing provides evidence of Michelangelo's drawing method and habits in his middle eighties. It appears he did not have a piece of paper large enough for his purpose, and five sheets, some already drawn upon, were glued together. One of the horizontal joints became, in the end, useful in marking the junction between frieze and cornice, the other lies somewhere within the area of the architrave and divides the keystone of the flat arch. The drawing is among the most notable of Michelangelo's career in that the representation of the portal with chalk, wash, and body color on paper approaches the three-dimensionality of a sculptural object.

H.A.M.

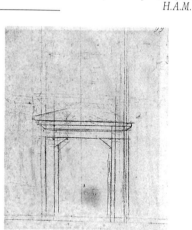

77
MICHELANGELO BUONARROTI
Study for the Porta Pia

Florence, Casa Buonarroti, CB 99Ar.
Black chalk, pen and brown ink; 166 × 124 mm.

PROVENANCE: Casa Buonarroti.

BIBLIOGRAPHY: Thode 1913, III, no. 154; Tolnay 1930: 43ff; Düssler 1959, no. 129; MacDougall 1960: 101ff.; Ackerman 1961, II: 128ff.; Barocchi 1962a, I, no. 165; Portoghesi and Zevi 1964: 966; Hartt 1971, no. 525; Tolnay 1980, IV, no. 617r.; Argan and Contardi 1990: 301ff., 350-351, fig. 486.

CB. 99Ar. appears to have been drawn rapidly using a straightedge, then reinforced with pen and ink. Verticals extend upward into a second level. The flat arch with haunches spans an opening wider than that in CB 106Ar. and is flanked by pilasters or columns. The unbroken entablature is topped by an incompletely drawn (or perhaps a broken) triangular pediment that may enclose an oval. Beneath the triangular pediment at left is the suggestion of a segmental pediment. Above the portal in the second level are faint indications of openings and a segmental pediment. The width of the opening of the portal suggests an early moment in the development of the design for the Porta Pia, close to the design on the medal of Bonsagni. The authenticity of the drawing has not been questioned.

H.A.M.

78
MICHELANGELO BUONARROTI
Study for the Porta Pia

Florence, Casa Buonarroti, CB 84Ar.
Black chalk.
110/111 × 80 mm

PROVENANCE: Casa Buonarroti.

BIBLIOGRAPHY: Thode 1913, III, no. 146; Tolnay 1930: 43ff.; Düssler 1959, no. 118; MacDougall 1960: 101; Ackerman 1961, II: 130; Barocchi 1962a, I: no. 166; Portoghesi and Zevi 1964: 968; Hartt 1971, no. 523; Tolnay 1975b, no. 190; Tolnay 1980, IV, no. 614r.; Argan and Contardi 1990: 301ff., 351, fig. 490; Marani 1992b: 465, fig. 196.

CB 84Ar., drawn in at least two phases, encloses an arched opening with keystone surmounted by a triangular pediment within a larger aedicule topped by a segmental pediment. The entablature of the arched opening may be supported on consoles or brackets. To gain sufficient height for the architrave of the larger aedicule, the flanking columns (or pilasters) are placed on pedestals. The entablature between the columns recedes to the plane of the wall behind the pediment. A large tablet is placed in the center of the segmental pediment, extending down through the cornice and frieze. To either side of the flanking columns, further pilasters or columns (as on CB 111Ar. [Tolnay 1980, no. 555]) suggest a lateral extension or direction. In the final version the flanking verticals are pilasters on plinths, the arch becomes a flat arch with haunches. The recessed area of the architrave and frieze above the opening contains a relieving arch and the lower triangular pediment rises and enlarges to enclose the segmental pediment, now scrolled and enclosing a tablet. Pilaster bunches topped by volutes at left and right return the portal to the lateral walls. CB 84Ar. marks a significant advance in the definition of the separate areas and their relationships.
Most scholars have associated the drawing with designs for the Porta Pia. Ackerman, due to the section of the dome of St. Peter's that pre-existed on the sheet (upper right, now cut) suggests it may have been related to the studies for the basilica (Ackerman 1961, II: 130).
H.A.M.

79
MICHELANGELO BUONARROTI
Study for the Porta Pia

Florence, Casa Buonarroti, CB 102Ar.
Black chalk, brush and bistre wash, white lead body color.
470/468 × 280 mm; the upper portion of the sheet shows traces of once having been covered by an additional piece of paper.

PROVENANCE: Casa Buonarroti.

BIBLIOGRAPHY: Geymüller 1904: 40; K. Frey 1909-11, no. 237; Thode 1913, III, no. 157; Tolnay 1930: 43ff.; Düssler 1959, no. 476; MacDougall 1960: 101; Ackerman 1961, II: 128; Barocchi 1962a, I, no. 168; Portoghesi and Zevi 1964: 967; Hartt 1971, no. 527; Tolnay 1975b, no. 194; Tolnay 1980, IV, no. 618r.; Hirst 1988b: 88-90; Argan and Contardi 1990: 301ff., 351, fig. 487.

CB 102Ar. combines elements from CB 106Ar. and CB 84Ar. It retains the flat arch with haunches and voussoirs, the banded columns and tall entablature with undifferentiated architrave and frieze, a tablet with a raised central section, segmental pediment, and enclosed shell form, all from CB 106Ar. From CB 84Ar. come the more clearly defined column, entablature, and pediment areas, and the decisive layering with its accompanying acknowledgment of the lateral direction to either side.
As in the constructed Porta Pia, CB 102Ar. includes a relieving arch below the cornice and a segmental pediment within a triangular pediment. The tablet below and shell above are held in defined spaces. Subsequently the shell was eliminated and the tablet migrated to the pediment. At the second level (probably among the portions drawn initially), the string course is intersected by the triangular pediment. The sheet size and effort expended in transforming and developing the idea suggest it was a major study for the portal.
H.A.M.

80
MICHELANGELO BUONARROTI
Studies for the Porta Pia (?) Doorways and Windows

Florence, Casa Buonarroti, CB 97Ar.
Black chalk, pen and brown ink.
283/282 × 255/254 mm

PROVENANCE: Casa Buonarroti.

BIBLIOGRAPHY: Thode 1913, III, no. 152; Tolnay 1930: 42ff; Düssler 1959, no. 128; MacDougall 1960: 104; Ackerman 1961, II: 130; Barocchi 1962a, I, no. 167; Portoghesi and Zevi 1964: 967; Hartt 1971, no. 526; Schwager 1973: 33ff.; Tolnay 1975b, no. 192; Tolnay 1980, IV, no. 616r.; Hirst 1988b: 88; Argan and Contardi 1990: 301ff., 351, fig. 489.

If this drawing (bottom right) is for the Porta Pia, which is doubted by some (MacDougall 1960: 104; Ackerman 1961, II: 130), it represents a phase before the area of the entablature became a field for experimentation. Barbieri and Puppi think the triangular shaped arch with heavy keystone became fundamental to the later development of the design.
The thinness of the entablature separates the lower level (opening with flanking columns or pilasters) from the attic with its elaborate central section.
The drawing at top left (oriented to the left edge of the sheet), with its guttae and undifferentiated architrave and frieze, is perhaps an early study for the entablature above the pilaster to the left of the opening of the Porta Pia. Other drawings on the sheet have been associated by Tolnay (1980, IV: 110) with windows of the Biblioteca Laurenziana and the attic of St. Peter's.
H.A.M.

81
TIBERIO CALCAGNI (?) (after Michelangelo)
Study for the Porta Pia

Florence, Galleria degli Uffizi Gabinetto Disegni e Stampe, Uff. 2148A
Pen and brown ink.

BIBLIOGRAPHY: Ferri 1885: 189; Wachler 1940: 241; MacDougall 1960: 103, fig. 13; Ackerman 1961, I: 119; Ackerman 1964, II: 133; Schwager 1973: 48ff.; Borsi et al. 1976, no. 345; Ackerman 1986: 331; Argan and Contardi 1990: 350-351.

Uff. 2148A was assigned to Giovanni Antonio Dosio until Schwager (1973: 48ff.) suggested Tiberio Calcagni as the draftsman.
Calcagni was one of Michelangelo's assistants during the last years of his life. Though noted by both Ferri (1885: 189) and Wachler (1940: 241), it was MacDougall who first discussed the drawing in relation to Michelangelo's design, indicating it was drawn from working drawings for the portal seen in the Michelangelo studio. The draftsman noted differences in the cornice between the drawing and what he may have been copying or between a drawing being copied and the building.
Among the discrepancies between the drawing and the Porta Pia are the proportions of the members of the cornice. On the building the fascia is taller. There is an additional return above the volute against the wall. The open-

ing is flanked by smooth columns, not fluted pilasters, and at the sides of the opening drafted masonry is not indicated. There are six, not seven, guttae above the columns capitals, and, as originally drawn, the pediment volute begins as a raking cornice. When this drawing was made, either a final working drawing or model did not yet exist, or the draftsman did not have access to it. It seems more likely the design was still fluid. *H.A.M.*

82
BARTOLOMEO FALETI
Elevation of the Porta Pia
1568

Engraving.

INSCRIBED: (upper right) *PORTAM PIAM A MICHAELIS ANGELI / BONAROTI EXEMPLARI ACCVRATISSIME / DELINEATAM ROMAE MDLXVIII*; (lower right) *ex typii Bart. faleti.*
Scale: 10 *palmi* (?)

BIBLIOGRAPHY: Tolnay 1930: 45, fig. 35; Zanghieri 1953: 24-32; Schiavo 1953: 266; MacDougall 1960: 100; Ackerman 1961, II: 130; Ackerman 1964, II: 131-132; Schwager 1973: 43ff.; Ackerman 1986: 330; Argan and Contardi 1990: 350-351.

The engraving by Faleti of the Porta Pia in 1568 was first discussed by Tolnay (1930: 45), who noted differences in addition to the obelisks between the engraving and the Porta Pia as built, such as the absence in the print of the pronounced keystone of the arch above the mask, the smaller tablet in the print than on the structure, and fewer guttae on the pilasters and at the bottom of the draped moldings over the tondi in the attic. The moldings also hang further down than on the gate. In other respects Tolnay (1930: 45) and Schwager (1973: 43-45, 47-48) feel the design of the frontispiece at the third level may reflect an earlier design by Michelangelo. MacDougall (1960: 100) and Ackerman (1964, II: 131-132) believe the third level to be a later design by a member of the studio. The third level appears complete in the engraved plans of Rome by Cartaro (1576) and Dupérac (1577), but lacking its upper portion in all engravings of the Porta Pia from Tempesta (1593) to Nibby (1826). Ackerman (1961, II: 130), following a suggestion of Zanghieri (1953: 24-32), supposes the third level was completed by 1565, when payments ceased, but partially collapsed late in the century. Therefore, the third level may have been completed as depicted in the engraving by Faleti, but if so, the muteness of the design in comparison with the design of the portal below indicates it is not likely to have received Michelangelo's attention nor to reflect an early, abandoned design. *H.A.M.*

83
FEDERICO BONSAGNI
Medal with a View of the Porta Pia
1561

Vatican, Biblioteca Apostolica Vaticana, Medagliere
Bronze.
31 mm ∅

PROVENANCE: unknown.

BIBLIOGRAPHY: K. Frey 1909b: 166; Tolnay 1930: 44 n. 1; Papini 1949: 603; Schiavo 1949, fig. 164; Schiavo 1953: 267; MacDougall 1960: 99-100; Ackerman 1961, II: 131; Ackerman 1964, II: 131; Pollard 1967, no. 372; Schwager 1973: 44 and n. 92; Millon and Smyth 1975: 165 n. 5; Whitman 1981, no. 8; Ackerman 1986: 330; Schiavo 1990: 551-569; Argan and Contardi 1990: 350-351.

Documents recording payments to Giovanni Federico da Parma in June and July 1561 for striking a total of either 72 (Gioseffi 1964b: 728) or 155 medals of Pio IV and the Porta Pia, in gold, silver, bronze, and gilded (bronze?) are cited in Frey (1909b: 166). Tolnay (1930: 42, fig. 32) first reproduced the medal and associated it with the drawing of the portal on CB 106Ar. (44 n. 1). The medal was thought to depict the exterior gate by MacDougall (1960: 100), Ackerman (1961, II: 131), and Millon and Smyth (1975: 165 n. 5). Papini (1949: 603) published a letter by Tiberio Calcagni, Michelangelo's assistant, written to Leonardo Buonarroti in August 1561 (Schiavo 1953: 267; Ackerman 1961, II: 131) saying that Michelangelo was now at work on the design of the exterior gate which he had not done. This statement was interpreted by Schwager (1973: 43-45, 47-48) to mean that Michelangelo had not done any drawings at all for the exterior at that date. Ackerman (1986: 330) and Argan and Contardi (1990: 350) agree.
The foundation ceremony for the gate was held on 18 June 1561 and the construction contract signed on 2 July (Ackerman 1961, II: 125). When these dates are considered together with the date in August of the Calcagni letter, the design shown on the medal must depict the interior or city side of the gateway. Further, the drawings by Michelangelo that have been associated with the Porta Pia all seem to be related in some respects to the design of the medal. If these associations can be sustained for the drawings, they, too, must date from the spring of 1561. The Porta Pia as shown on the medal has only two levels—that of the portal and an attic. The attic is held to the width of the portal. Octagonal turrets of three stories, taller than the second level, flank the attic and mark the extremities of the gate. These turrets may be reflected later in the obelisks found in that position on the engraving by Faleti. In the event, the base of the second level was lowered to coincide with the cornice of the portal and above a tall third level, the width of the portal, replaced the two turrets. Though only representing an initial idea, elements that appear on the gate as constructed are indicated on the medal. The portal is capped by a double pediment, with a salient panel above the width of the second level. The attic level contains an escutcheon and is topped by Medici *palle*. On the Porta Pia today the attic is capped by Medici *palle*, while the escutcheon has been elevated to the third level.
The design on the medal, characterized by Whitman (1981: 27) as "pleasantly awkward," together with the

group of drawings by Michelangelo associated with the Porta Pia, seem to record an initial phase of the design, before the extent of the attic was determined and before the third level was conceived. The final design probably entailed a further series of studies, now lost, which may have included an initial consideration of the third level, if not a final design for it. *H.A.M.*

84
ANONYMOUS
Set of Italian Drawing Instruments
ca. 1540

Oxford, Museum of the History of Science, 2170

PROVENANCE: Stowe Collection; Drake Collection; Arnold Collection; Lewis Evans Collection.

BIBLIOGRAPHY: Robinson 1862: 546 cat. no 6593; Burns et al. 1975: 85-86 cat. no 155; Hambly 1988; Turner 1987: 82-85.

Unsigned, but probably Milanese. The drawing instruments are of steel damascened with gold and silver inlay; their inner surfaces are of gilt. The casket, which has similar gold and silver decoration, contains three ink-wells and a pounce-box. On the top of the lid of the casket, the damascening has been obliterated and a thin slab of green marble added. The set consists of two pairs of dividers of the type known as *maître de danse*; a graduated folding rule; a combined dividers and graduated folding rule; proportional dividers (ratio 1:1 and 1:4); a pair of compasses for use with ink; a pencil or charcoal holder; a pair of compasses for use with pencil or charcoal; and a grip, probably for holding vellum or paper when writing. Note that the leather-covered case is nineteenth century.
The decorative technique of damascening was known in Europe but appears during the Middle Ages only to have been practiced in the East. It was reintroduced in the West by the 1540s when Milan was a very important center for this type of work. The technique, especially popular for decorating armor and arms, consisted of first heating the steel until it changed to a violet or blue color. Then it was hatched criss-cross all over with a sharp tool, after which the design was drawn on this hatching with a fine point. Finally, thin gold or silver wire was carefully chased into the design with a copper tool. It has been noted (see the Palladio catalog) that this set resembles a casket in the Museo dell'Età Cristiana in Brescia, and an inkwell in the Victoria and Albert Museum in London. The crescents in the decoration of the box may indicate that this set belonged to Diane de Poitiers (according to private communication from B. Wolpe). The exquisite nature of the set certainly indicates that it was made for a very wealthy person. The set was exhibited at the Special Exhibition of Works of Art, South Kensington, June 1862 (entry 6593), when the then owner, W. R. Drake, described it as: "Both box and instruments are exquisitely damascened with the most minute and beautiful arabesques in gold and silver of the usual most beautiful Milanese type." There is no reference of the leather-covered case in which the instruments are displayed.
Willem D. Hackmann

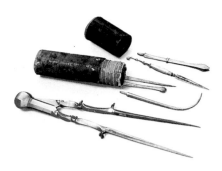

85
Dividers
16th cent.

Florence, Istituto e Museo di Storia della Scienza, 1357
Brass and steel.
length 300 mm

BIBLIOGRAPHY: *Catalogo degli strumenti del Museo di Storia della Scienza*, 1954: 132; Miniati 1991: 16.

The draftsman's dividers are among the more common and frequently used drawing instruments of the Renaissance period. As a work-tool its origins seem to hark back to the distant realm of mythology and the art of Daedalus. In its most simple form, the device consists of two arms with pointed terminations; these may be fitted with a range of accessories according to need, thereby changing the function and purpose of the tool. The drafting compass exhibited here is made of two brass arms, hinged on a slightly polygonal, spherical head. The arms are retractable and can be fixed in the required position by two steel screws. At the ends of the arms themselves two steel extension points are held in place by steel screws. The dividers (disassembled) are housed in a cylindrical, black cardboard case, which also holds the various standard accessories for compasses of this type: a drawing pen, a pencil attachment, a toothed wheel, a knife, and two curved points, all made of steel with brass finish. This compass is said to be that of Michelangelo Buonarroti, since it was found among the objects belonging to the great artist.

Mara Miniati

Machines for Use on Building Sites
Daniela Lamberini

"The machine is the perpetual, controlled joining of materials that gives great power to the movement of weights." Vitruvius, *I dieci libri di architettura tradotti e commentati da Daniele Barbaro*, 1567, (Book X, 1: 442).

Architecture, which according to Vitruvius was engendered by practice and theory (*ex fabrica et ratiocinatione*), inevitably means that the architect has to deal with the question of the use of machines on the building site. In fact, the etymology of the Italian word for building site (*cantiere*) suggests that the main problem of the latter is that of the transport and setting in position of building materials. The Italian word derives from the *Greek canterios*, the donkey used as a beast of burden, which in Latin became *cantherius*, a gelded horse; this was used to refer to the trestle or rafter and the term was then extended to the whole area in which these structures were used. With regard to the building site, the place where the art of building is practiced and there is ample opportunity to learn and train, the architect is not only responsible for the construction of the building that his project has generated, but at the same time he must determine its forms and parts through the organization of the work, while the machine allows him to establish the extent to which he can intervene in the natural world.

The ability to organize space and people and a rational approach to the machine seen from a humanistic standpoint are inherent in the architectural theory of Leon Battista Alberti, who in his *De re aedificatoria* wrote: "I shall call an architect whosoever can, with sound methodology, design in a rational manner and give physical form to works that are wholly suitable for the most pressing needs of man by means of the movement of weights and the joining of bodies" (Alberti 1966a: Prologue). He continues: "Machines are comparable to animate bodies which are endowed with exceptionally strong hands and behave exactly like each of us in order to move weights. Thus, in machines it is necessary to imitate the dimensions and joints of our own limbs, which, thanks to the muscles, allow us to stand up, push, pull and carry objects" (VI, VIII). The Renaissance building site was intended to emulate the ancients through the metaphorical reconquest of equilibrium, in contrast with the corrupt and cursed site of the Tower of Babel, where the machines did not function and the workmen carried out their customary tasks backward, because in order to humble the pride of the people: "... the Lord did there confound the language of all the earth: and from thence did the Lord scatter them abroad upon the face of all the earth" (*Genesis 11: 1-9*; cf. Vandekerchove 1989a: 67-70; Stabile 1990; Minkowski 1991).

The Renaissance building site rediscovered the centrality of the machine and with this the basic principle of its movement, which according to Vitruvius was contained in the lever, the simple device studied by Hero of Alexandria from which all the others derived. This is what Vitruvius states in the *Machinatio*, the tenth book of *De architectura* (the source here is the version which Daniele Barbaro translated into Italian and commented): "Everything originated from the lever; the lever derived from the steelyard, the steelyard from the balance and, lastly, the balance from the properties of the circle. [... And] the continuous rotation of the world which Vitruvius says is like a machine and thus is also called the machine of the world" (Vitruvius 1987, X, Proem: 440-441; Fontana 1985: 59-60; Tafuri 1986: 185-212; Fleury 1993: 88 ff.; cat. no. 86). Organization and solidity, given concrete form by

the renewed centrality of the machine, are the most outstanding features of the building site that were described by all leading Renaissance writers. Of these, the account by the military engineer Francesco De Marchi (1504-76) is particularly interesting; an emulator of Vitruvius and Leon Battista Alberti, he was a witness to the colossal work carried out on the Roman building sites under Pope Paul III. In his treatise he wrote: "The ancients lifted very heavy weights with devices made like tongs; these had rings through which ropes passed and when the winches were turned and the stays drew the ropes toward them, causing the lower part to be raised, these pincers closed together so tightly that nothing could be freed from them unless they broke or the heavy weight collided with something causing the rope to go backward. In this manner I have seen heavy columns lifted in Rome at the site of St. Peter's. There is also another method, involving the use of metal hooks called *impuglioli*, which are turned outward: a hole is made in the stone which is larger inside than at its mouth; these hooks, which consist of two parts, are put inside this hole and another piece of metal is driven into it. These two hooks thrust outward so strongly that they can lift heavy stones. In this way I have seen heavy objects raised. This system is used on building sites in Rome where, with the use of a number of stays and winches, I have seen columns and similar objects lifted. However, the greatest possible care must be taken when lifting weights because there is no task on the building site that is trickier or more hazardous than lifting heavy weights. For this reason it is of vital importance that the whole operation should be properly coordinated from start to finish" (Florence, Biblioteca Nazionale Centrale, Fondo nazionale, II.I.277, Book II, XVI, fols. 85-86; Lamberini 1990a).

It is significant that Vasari credited Brunelleschi with the rediscovery and putting into operation of the lewis, which was known to the ancients, in order to lift huge blocks of stone during the construction of the dome of Florence Cathedral (Vasari 1878-85, II: 361). This was despite the well-known technological continuity which, in the field of machines for use on building sites, took the form of the long term described by the French historian Fernand Braudel; this traditionalism only died out in the early part of this century as an inevitable consequence of the Industrial Revolution. Thus, it should be not be a cause for surprise if, for example, manually operated winches similar to the ones drawn by Mariano di Jacopo, called Taccola (see cat. no. 89) were still used in major ports in Northern Europe well into the nineteenth century; a sixteenth century example was discovered in Great Britain in 1923 (Drachman 1962; Ferguson 1976: 570), or if the classical trestle described by Vitruvius was still being used all over Italy in 1942 to help protect works of art sited on historical buildings and in the streets and squares from bombing raids (*La protezione* 1942), or if ancient windlasses are still in operation in the lofts of a number of churches in Alsace (Czarnowsky 1949).

The building of Brunelleschi's dome, the "great machine" as Michelangelo very fittingly described it, took on a formative function for later generations of architects and its construction involved total immersion in the art of building, which even at that time was the blanket term applied to the whole operation, including the complex organization of the building site, the design of the machines and the construction techniques employed. The machinery used by Brunelleschi is known to us thanks to the drawings by Taccola, Bonaccorso Ghiberti, Francesco di Giorgio Martini and Giuliano and Antonio da Sangallo and had a continuous echo in the graphic output of the following generations (cf. cat. nos. 89-94, 99, 106). Supported by the machines for everyday use and the extraordinary winches designed by Francesco di Giorgio with which the architects aspired to transport the great monoliths inherited from antiquity and set them upright (cf. cat. nos. 94, 102), it inaugurated the era of antiquarian scientism, which, from the time when Francesco wrote his treatises, increasingly assumed the form of a parallel elaboration of Vitruvius' theories (Fiore 1979: 42-43). As time passed they became the products of the mechanical arts with the essential contribution of the mathematical sciences, so that it was evident that machines were essentially the concern of engineers and other specialists. This product was pre-eminently a cerebral one, since, according to Barbaro's interpretation, it originated from what was inherently a mental process. Thus, at the close of the Renaissance, having become "a wonderful artifice" and an object for admiration and spectacle, it was transformed into the focus of interest for court collections and, as a consequence of this, played a leading role in the Baroque "mechanical theaters" (cf. cat. nos. 101-102).

86
PIERO DI COSIMO
The Building of a Double Palace
ca. 1515-20

Sarasota, John and Mable Ringling Museum of Art
Oil on panel; strip 51 mm wide added to upper edge.
77.5 × 196.9 cm (original dimensions)
82.6 × 196.9 cm (with addition)

PROVENANCE: Collections Mussin Pouschkine; Meazza, Milan; Emile Gavet, Paris; William K. Vanderbilt, Newport, Rhode Island (USA); Mrs. Oliver H. P. Belmont, Newport, Rhode Island (USA).

BIBLIOGRAPHY: Langton Douglas 1946: 117-118, pl. LXXI; Suida 1949: 21, no. 22; Morselli 1957: 149, fig. 24; Morselli 1958: 84; Zeri 1959: 44; Berenson 1963, I: 175-176; Fahy 1965: 206; Bacci 1966: 104-105, pl. 54; Bacci 1976: 96-97, pls. LII-LIII; Tomoroy 1976: 14-15, fig. 8; Barriault 1985: 268-269 and passim; Kemp 1991e: 251-252; Fermor 1993, pl. 38: 102-103.

The painted *spalliere* are panels decorated with mythological and allegorical scenes which adorned the wooden furniture in the rooms of patrician homes in Renaissance Florence. This large-format example, one of the best-known of the genre, first came onto the market in 1884, when it was put up for sale in Milan with the attribution to Luca Signorelli. The painting was taken to Paris, during which time Bernard Berenson ascribed it to Giuliano Bugiardini; subsequently the work found its way to the United States, to the Vanderbildt and Belmont collections, and was finally purchased by the Ringling Museum in 1928-29 (Bacci 1966; Tomoroy 1976).

The panel, which is both undated and unsigned, is now unanimously attributed to the Florentine painter Piero di Cosimo (ca. 1426-1521), a pupil of Cosimo Rosselli; its style suggests it was executed in the latter years of activity of this intriguing, eccentric painter (Langton Douglas 1946; Morselli 1958; Bacci 1966; Fermor 1993), whose best-known works include a set of allegorical cycles depicting the history of mankind. Several of these panels, commissioned by Piero del Pugliese for his house in Via de' Serragli in Florence, now in Oxford and New York, have been associated with the *Building of a Double Palace* panel, though no correspondences have been established in terms either of style or of dimensions (Zeri 1959; Fahy 1965; Bacci 1966: 104; Barriault 1985: 268-269). Likewise, no proper connections have been established with the *spalliere* produced by Piero di Cosimo in concert with the architect Baccio d'Agnolo for the construction of *cas-*

soni con spalliere commissioned from them by Filippo Strozzi in 1510 (Kemp 1991e: 251).

The difficulty in reconstructing the original *spalliere* made for Florentine houses in the Quattrocento lies in the fact that most have been dismembered (Cieri Via 1977: 6). In the absence of any proven documentation relative to the commission, or evidence of the architectural context for which they were designed, the subject of the Sarasota panel is particularly difficult to unravel or interpret; while the scene depicted is undoubtedly allegorical, it has nonetheless sparked considerable debate and controversy. Among the suggested interpretations are an Old Testament scene, or a setting from the world of classical antiquity; it has been said to represent the "Triumph of Architecture," or a posthumous homage to Giuliano and Antonio da Sangallo (reputedly the figures on horseback riding toward the construction at the center); Piero di Cosimo was in fact a close friend of the Sangallo brothers, and worked for them as a *legnaiuolo* (carpenter) for the construction of triumphal arches; he was also responsible for two portraits—one of Giuliano, from whose design for a double palace this painting seems inspired, and the other of their father Francesco—now in the museums of Amsterdam and The Hague (Tomoroy 1976: 14). Recently a comparative examination with the perspective panels of Urbino, Baltimore, and Berlin has been suggested (cat. no. 178), regarding the spatial order accorded to the architecture, which can be traced to Vitruvius and Leon Battista Alberti (Kemp 1992). In the present catalog, furthermore, the content of this painted *spalliera* is offered with a compendium of the different options open to architects with regard to ornament and statuary in the late fifteenth century (see contribution by K. Weil-Garris Brandt in the present catalog, pp. 75-99).

The most important feature in this construction scene is undoubtedly the majestic symmetrical palazzo, with its twin buildings, shown in central perspective in the very middle of the picture, in a harmonious landscape setting. Presumably clad in marble, the palazzo is encircled by a peripteral porch of pillars with Corinthian capitals; the entablature is crowned with statues over each column, the last of which is being set in place before our eyes, on the right center, above the elaborate frieze of swags and cornucopias. The building is idealized and highly modern in design, and doubtless purports to be modeled on an antique building, whose function—symbolic, and worthy of the Renaissance notion of the Ideal City—remains for the time being unrevealed. The site around the double palace swarms with people engaged in construction activity, reproducing metaphorically the various phases of construction in a logical sequence, from left to right, of the Vitruvian building cycle: the supply of materials (wood, stone, marble, sand), their transportation from the quarries with carts, donkeys, mules and braces of oxen; the shaping of the stone by the *maestranze* under the watchful eye of their superiors and the architects; the employment of the materials in the actual construction; and, finally, the enjoyment of the finished building. The entire scene is informed with a strong sense of symmetry, and unfolds in an orderly manner, with a clear demarcation of roles and phases, leaving nothing to chance, in what has been described as a "striving for perfect equilibrium" (Bacci 1966: 104). That balance is not merely formal, or typical

of the classical composition of early sixteenth-century Florence. Here, as one of the chief characteristics of a well-run *cantiere*, it is added to the recondite significance of sophisticated humanistic thought and the pacific dominion of the world for which the *spalliera* was elected to portray, while affording one of the most explicit and lively accounts of building technology in the Renaissance. Care has also been taken to convey the hierarchy of the various figures at work in the *cantiere*, each portrayed with his relative work tools—from the architect on the far right, dividers in hand, teaching a youth with a set-square how to construct the shaft of a column, down to the humblest of the site's *garzoni*: carpenters with their axes and set-squares, dividers, gimlets, drills and augers; the sculptors and *scarpellini* or stonemasons in the center foreground with their mallets and bushhammers, gouges and chisels, all engaged in sculpting statues and fashioning decorative elements such as capitals and entablatures; the humble but fundamental barrow on which four laborers are carrying lime to the mixing pit for slaking. In the middle ground two men are drawing a small cart toward the building, while a third keeps his eye on their precious cargo of finished statuary, ready to be mounted in place. At center right is an attentive representation of a large framesaw, worked by two carpenters, with a *garzone* assigned to gather up the sawdust; this type, of saw has very distant origins indeed, and figures in identical form in a twelfth-century mosaic in Monreale Cathedral depicting Noah's Arc (Thompson 1962, fig. 357). Similar care in faithful documentation can be witnessed in the portrayal of the painting's only machine—the device for hoisting the statues into place on the colonnade entablature. The machine is a classic Vitruvian crane, known as a *stella* (star), consisting of a cantilevered, T-shaped derrick of two braced jibs, with a winch driven by a man-powered treadwheel, exploiting the momentum of the wheel; the machine is described by Leonardo da Vinci in the *Codex Atlanticus* (fol. 138r., see cat. nos. 89, 97, 98). The artist's illustration of the four stay ropes of the hoist shows considerable technical insight: the two anchored to the ground are taut, while the other two are slack because the derrick has been tilted over the entablature to enable the workmen to maneuver the statue onto its pedestal.

The precision in technical observation, the accuracy in defining the working methods, and the artist's evident knowledge of the practicalities of role division, illustrate one of the principal components of the Renaissance building site, namely, that the *cantiere* was a veritable arena for instruction and apprenticeship in the Vitruvian and Albertian sense. All this is not only portrayed through the rank of the *maestranze*, by the presence of two figures on horseback in the right foreground, dressed *all'antica*, or by the mother bringing her children to the site—not so much to amuse them as to show them what work is all about. The significance of the *cantiere* is also communicated by the spirit of playfulness—so far ignored by those who have studied the panel—discernible almost everywhere in the painting: the children on their improvised seesaw of a beam, ready-cut for use; the boys shinning up a rope tied to the statues on the left of the portico are being harassed by another two boys armed with branches; other youthful figures are at play in the central court between the two buildings; while in the background on the far right two groups of horsemen blow their trumpets to announce an imminent tournament to be held in the vast plain adjacent to the new building; they have been momentarily distracted by a spectacle of a different kind altogether: the virtuoso display of technical skill on the part of the workmen raising the last statue onto the portico. This admirable mechanical feat is a perfect foil for the pageant being celebrated by the horsemen, creating "a delicate and subtle interplay of symbolism" (Ricciardi 1992: 78).

The element of recreation and diversion in the Sarasota panel—communicating a newly found balance between physical and mental activities, and the ludic implications of instruction in the science of architecture, a discipline that merges the aptitudes of the mind with those of the body—is entirely congenial to the art of a painter-carpenter of Piero di Cosimo's caliber. Piero's passion for engineering technology and his notoriety as a *festaiolo fiorentino* or local reveler are attested by Vasari, who describes Piero's bizarre and fantastic mechanical inventions for the allegorical parades, meant that he was "much consulted for the masques for carnival pageants" (Vasari 1878-85, IV: 134). The double palazzo is, furthermore, sited in the middle of the countryside, in compliance with Alberti's maxim: *sapiat solitudinem*, i.e., relish solitude (*De re aedificatoria*, V, viii); the spacious portico encircling the buildings, making in possible to practice physical activities outdoors, and spiritual activities inside, the way the majestic building extends into the neighboring woodland by means of the *ragnaia*, or net for catching fowl built at the back, where lines of trees continue the central perspective effect of the building, where figures on horseback are perhaps setting off on a hunt, the seigniorial activity *par excellence*. All these visual clues suggest that the double building is intended as a kind of *gymnásion*, in the Greek style, as described by Vitruvius in *De architectura* (V, xi: 2), and taken up by Leon Battista Alberti in *De re aedificatoria* (V, 8; VIII, 8) in reference to gymnasiums and *ambulationes* (public thoroughfares).

The Sarasota panel—so perfectly in keeping with the "Vitruvian vocabulary" that typified Raphael's ardent years of *instauratio urbis* (urban renewal) in Rome—stands as a symbol of the sophisticated elites of the Florentine humanist milieu during the reign of the Medici pope, Leo X. In Vitruvian terms, the metaphor embodied by this image of the Renaissance *cantiere* is leverage—from the simplest lever, which, since the days of Aristotelian mechanics has been the underlying principle of equilibrium and movement in all mechanical devices, as illustrated by Vitruvius in Book X of *De architectura*. Equipoise—in all its manifestations, whether material or moral—and movement are the basis to all the action unfolding in the Sarasota panel: the children's see-saw, with its application of the mechanical balance; the four figures in the center, carrying a heavy beam, its weight wisely distributed between them; the crane, with its adroit application of Aristotelian mechanics. With its absorbing fusion of recreational spirit and virtuoso mechanical ability, the *cantiere* becomes a spectacle unto itself.   *D.L.*

87
<small>Bernardo Butinone (?)</small>
Construction of a Palace
(from Averulinus, Antonius seu Filareti, *De architectura, libri XXV.Ex italico traducti et Mathiae regi dicati ab Antonio Bonfinis*)
ca. 1488-89

Venice, Biblioteca Nazionale Marciana, MS. Lat. cl. VIII, 2 (= 2796), fol. 5r., *incipit*
Illuminated parchment codex Latin, in quarto format containing fols. 1 + 174 + 2; *rotunda* humanistic script, with many ornaments and 214 figs.; arms of Matthias I Corvinus,

dedication to Piero de' Medici.
308 × 490 mm

<small>PROVENANCE:</small> Library of King Matthias Corvinus, Budapest; Biblioteca del Convento dei SS. Giovanni e Paolo, Venice.

<small>BIBLIOGRAPHY:</small> Morelli 1802: 405-409; Valentinelli 1877: 183; Oettingen 1896: 20-32; Lazzaroni and Munoz 1908: 240; de Hevesy 1911: 115-116; de Hevesy 1923: 34-35, 76-77, pl. XLVIII; *Mostra* 1954: 416; Salmi 1954: 71, pl. LXXb; Romanini 1962: 663-664; Tigler 1963: 9-10, 13; Filarete 1965, I: XVIII; *Bibliotheca Corviniana* 1969: 67-68, pl. XC, [129]; Grassi 1972, I: CXII-CXIII; Filarete 1972, I, fig. on verso of frontispiece; Daneu Lattanzi 1972: 248-250, fig. 29 (p. 250); Dal Canton 1973: 103; Puppi 1973b: 75; Klanickzay 1974: 19; Cogliati Arano 1979: 60ff.; Concina 1988: fig. 57, 66ff.; Caniato and Dal Borgo 1990: 152, 168, passim; Galluzzi 1991b: 185, Cogliati Arano 1992: 55.

This magnificent codex in the Biblioteca Marciana contains one of the six translations into Latin of the treatise on architecture by Antonio di Francesco Averlino (ca. 1400-1469/70), the Florentine who adopted the Greek name of Filarete, "lover of virtue." Written in the vernacular ca. 1465 for Francesco Sforza, Duke of Milan and dedicated to Piero di Cosimo de' Medici, it is divided into twenty-five books and narrates in dialogue form the construction of Sforzinda, an ideal city that became the apotheosis of the Renaissance town planning scheme. The court historian Antonio Bonfini (he came from Ascoli Piceno) was commissioned to translate the text by Matthias I Corvinus, King of Hungary; the latter was a humanist and bibliophile (in the *incipit* his arms are depicted at top center with the initials M[atthias] R[ex] and in the festoon at the bottom). The work was completed in only three months in 1488-89 (de Hevesy 1923: 34; Klanickzay 1974: 19; Cogliati Arano 1979: 53). Rather than a faithful translation it is a free adaptation by Bonfini, who abridged the last book, in which Filarete describes buildings constructed by the Medici; he also omitted parts he considered superfluous or obscure and added a conclusion (Lazzaroni and Munoz 1908: 240, Grassi 1972, I: CXII). The codex, one of the finest in the splendid Corvina Library, was sumptuously illuminated by artists of an exceptionally high calibre who were then working at court. It was originally attributed to the Parisian artist Master Cassiano, or a hypothetical Flemish pupil of his (de Hevesy 1911: 112ff.; ibid. 1923: 77). However, Salmi observed in the illuminator not only a Late Gothic imprint reflecting the influence of Belbello di Pavia, but also a link with the Renaissance milieu in Lombardy (Salmi 1954: 72; *Mostra* [1954]: 416). Thus, more recent writers, accepting these suggestions, have put forward the name of Francesco da Castello, a Lombard painter who worked at the court of Buda (Daneu Lattanzi 1972) and subsequently, although dubitatively, that of the Bergamasque Bernardino Butinone (Cogliati Arano 1979: 58-60; ibid. 1992: 55), who combined the Northern Italian spirit of Mantegna with the style of the Flemings. In the *incipit* the illumination surrounds the text with a very rich ornamental border, dotted with putti, allusive trophies and mythological animals; this is dominated by bright colors: red, lapis lazuli and gold used profusely to simulate pearls and precious stones. The lower margin of the page is occupied by an architectural scene: the construction of a palace, with the portico and coupled columns already set upright, the polychromy of which suggests the use of precious stone and marble, materials about which Filarete writes at length in his third book. The figures are depicted with great precision: they include stonemasons, bricklayers, hodmen and boys at ground level or on the scaffolding (on the left it is of the leaning type) busy at their various tasks; in particular, note the one in the right foreground, who is mixing mortar in a basin with a long-handled implement, or the two workers operating the simple cranes. This demonstrates Filarete's great familiarity with the building site—he devotes the fourth book to the management of this—and his technical and engineering skills (his capacity as a hydraulic engineer is particularly well known, see Spencer 1956: 58; ibid. 1963; Pigozzi 1973). This is

confirmed in the text by the frequent enthusiastic praise of his Bolognese friend Aristotele Fioravanti (his name was anagrammatized as Letistoria), whose extraordinary ability to move towers and straighten campaniles had made him a legend in his own time. Besides the technical aspect, this representation of the building site sums up the predominant theme of the "praise of patronage" (Grassi 1972: XIV) which Filarete's treatise constituted; this involved the concept of the rigidly hierarchized training inherent to the traditions of the building site. In the first place this concerned the skilled workers: note, for example, the trio on the right consisting of the master mason and an elderly bricklayer wearing an apron who are giving directions to a youth perched on the lintel while he checks the perpendicularity of the columns with a plumb-line. But even more it referred to the higher orders. Who would fail to recognize the elegant couple taken from life in the foreground, engaged in an erudite conversation about architecture, as being Filarete himself in the company of his "young lord"; maybe this was the son of his patron, Francesco Sforza, Galeazzo, whose taste and culture the architect aimed to mold?   *D.L.*

88
<small>Unknown French Illuminator</small>
Vitruvius Presenting his Book to Augustus (left)
and *Vitruvius Teaching his Pupils* (right)
(in Vitruvii, *De architectura*, Book X)
ca. 1400-05

Florence, Biblioteca Medicea Laurenziana, Cod. Plut. XXX. 10, fol. 1r.
Illuminations; parchment codex, Latin, manuscript with two columns, in f°, with decorated gold initial letters; annotated in Greek and Italian; consisting of fols. 1 + 116, of which fols. 1r.-60v.: Vitruvius, *De architectura*, fols. 61-78r.: Cato, *De re rustica*, fols. 78v.-116r.: Varro, *Rerum rusticarum et architectura*, decorated with initial letters.
290 × 400 mm

<small>INSCRIBED:</small> (on fol. 116r., explicit) *Mitia fata mihi Francisci Sassetti Thomae filii civis Florentini.*

<small>PROVENANCE:</small> Francesco Sassetti, Florence; Biblioteca Medicea Privata, Florence.

<small>BIBLIOGRAPHY:</small> Bandini 1775: 74; Piccolomini 1875: 87; Sabbadini 1914: 165; Fontana 1933: 311, fig. 1, 320-321; *Mostra* 1949: 41; Ciaranfi 1949: 187, fig. 2; *Mostra* 1953: 454; Billanovich 1964: 345-350; Krinsky 1967: 54-55; Meiss 1974: 409, 473, fig. 58; De La Mare 1976: 178; Juren 1978: 289; Morolli 1992c: 192.

This elegant codex, which contains transcriptions of the Latin texts by Vitruvius, Cato and Varro, was produced, with a lavishness worthy of a great patron (perhaps Jean de Montreuil; Meiss 1974: 409) by a French Gothic copyist at the beginning of the fifteenth century and exquisitely illuminated by an anonymous French illuminator of the school of Paris in the circle of Jacques Coen, according to Mario Salmi (*Mostra* 1949: 41; Ciaranfi 1949: 187; *Mostra* 1953: 454), or by the Master of Virgil, according to

Millard Meiss (1979: 20, 245); Fontana (1933: 320-321) believed it was by an artist of the Florentine school.
It was subsequently purchased by the Florentine banker Francesco di Tommaso Sassetti, the Geneva agent of the Medicean bank (see de Roover 1966: 361 and passim), who indicated his possession on the last folio and took it with him to Florence in 1459 together with other antiquities which this famous banker and humanist, a relative of the Medici and a close friend of Lorenzo il Magnifico and the intellectuals at his court, had acquired north of the Alps. After his death in 1491, his heirs lent 67 codices belonging to him to the Medici, including this one, which, after the events following the expulsion of Piero de' Medici, remained in the Biblioteca Laurenziana (Piccolomini 1874, no. 511, 115, 124).
The presence in Florence of various copies of Vitruvius' treatise and the interest taken in this by Lorenzo and other members of the Medici family are evidence of the great cultural significance which the refined Renaissance princes, the rich patrons of great architectural projects, and the intellectuals associated with them, attached to the only complete text on architecture to survive from antiquity. This treatise, written ca. A.D. 27 by Marcus Vitruvius Pollio—*architectus litteris imbutus* (an architect who dabbles in literature), as he described himself when addressing Emperor Augustus—to thank his imperial patron, was a text that had a lot of shortcomings and was often misunderstood because the surviving edition was unillustrated, it had been corrupted in many parts by the medieval copyists and it contained obscure prose (Pellati 1932; Ciapponi 1960). In fact, in the Renaissance the ten books of *De architectura* were of vital importance if the rules of classical architecture were to be interpreted and its forms and functions recreated. Consequently it came to be regarded as a vade mecum for architects, to the extent that, together with the Bible, it was among the first incunabula (the first printed edition by Giovanni Sulpicio da Veroli and Pomponio Leto was published in Rome ca. 1486; Ciapponi 1984: 72 ff.). Before the first illustrated edition was published in 1511 by the cultured Veronese engineer and antiquarian Fra' Giovanni Giocondo, in other words before the long task of philological restoration of the text had begun and before it had been completely understood (this was a joint effort by philologists and architects in the sixteenth century, who added illustrations to the treatise [Ciapponi 1960: 99; ibid. 1984; Pagliara 1977; Fontana 1988]), Vitruvius was represented, independently of the text, in the illuminations of the fourteenth and fifteenth centuries as the very personification of architecture (Pagliara 1986, esp. figs. 1-2), and his treatise as the bible for the learning of this art, in the medieval sense of the term.
This is also how the splendid illustration should be interpreted, with its delicate colors and fine drawings on a checkered background; in fact, in a very distinctive way it summarizes the contents of the codex brought from France by Sassetti. Surrounded by a border in which geometrical patterns and small leaves are interlaced, the illumination is divided into two square compartments. In the first, Vitruvius, depicted as a venerable old man with a flowing white beard, is kneeling before the emperor (who, seated on his throne, is surrounded by elegant courtiers and dignitaries) humbly offering him his book, which is held by a young page. In the right-hand compartment Vitruvius is represented as the architect who, seated in the professorial chair like a philosopher of antiquity, is teaching the lesser masters the art of building by reading *De architectura* to them. The four attentive pupils (who are certainly *compagnonnes du travail*, given the French origin of the codex), may be recognized by their tools: the trowel and mortarboard of the bricklayer, the adze of the carpenter, the pick and dressing ax of the stonemason and the hammers, anvil and long pincers of the blacksmith. Truly a fitting prelude to the building site!   *D.L.*

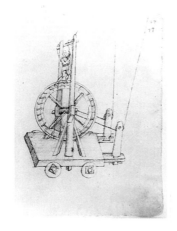

89
MARIANO DI JACOPO (called TACCOLA)
Mobile Windlass with Two Pulleys Operated by a Treadwheel (in *De ingeneis*, Books I-II)
1427-38

Munich, Bayerische Staatsbibliothek, MS. Lat., CLM 197.ii, fol. 27r.
Drawing; pen and ink on paper; Latin manuscript, paper, of fols. 1-136, modern numbering, of which: fols. 1-75, *Liber leonis* (Book I *De ingeneis*); fols. 76-98, *Liber draconis* (Book II *De ingeneis*); fols. 99-136, addenda to Books I and II.
298 × 220 mm

PROVENANCE: Francesco di Giorgio Martini; Johann Albrecht von Widmanstetter; Palatine Library of Duke Albert V of Bavaria.

BIBLIOGRAPHY: Venturi 1815: 12, 14, Jaehns 1889, I, 278ff.; Berthelot 1891: 472-521; Halm 1892: 41ff.; Beck 1899: 270-290; de Laborde 1924: 500; Fontana 1936: 103; Thorndike 1955: 15-22; Michelini Tocci 1962; Beck 1968; Prager 1968; Rose 1968: 338, 346; Taccola 1969: 25; Scaglia 1971, I: 10-28 and passim; Gille 1972: 78-87; Prager and Scaglia 1972: 10, 96-99; Degenhart and Schmitt 1982: 1-20, 24, pl. 35ab; Taccola 1984a; Taccola 1984b: 12-13, 28-29; Galluzzi 1991c: 19 ff., 192; Scaglia 1992: 56-57 and index.

The majority of the machines used on the building sites of the early Renaissance derived directly from classical antiquity without undergoing substantial modifications during the Middle Ages. A typical case is that of devices for lifting, such as this large windlass with two pulleys, placed on a mobile platform, which was used for raising heavy loads. Working on the elementary principle of the lever, it utilized both the force of gravity and the weight of a man. The treader, balancing precariously on the wheel (this gave rise to the name of "flying man"), operated the windlass by pushing with his feet against the external rungs of a large wheel, which Vitruvius called the drum; this is fixed to the horizontal winch, which winds two ropes—one attached to the counterweight, the other to the load—round the central beam, thus allowing the materials to be hoisted and lowered. This extremely vivid drawing was executed by the Sienese Mariano di Jacopo Vanni, called Taccola (1381-1453/58).
With this first autograph treatise, to which should be added the third and the fourth books of the *Codex Palatino* 766 in the Biblioteca Nazionale in Florence (cat. nos. 91 and 92) and the next ten books of *De machinis*, in the libraries of Münich, New York and Paris (see Galluzzi 1991d: 192-198), the Sienese Archimedes, as he described himself, offered a wide audience of experts and cultured Renaissance patrons, rather than his own original inventions, the sum total of the technology of his day. This paved the way for the engineering treatises of the Renaissance and meant that his work would continue to be seminal for an exceptionally long period (Galluzzi 1991c; Lamberini 1991c).
Together with Brunelleschi, a friend of his whose ingenious technical innovations had a great influence on him (see cat. nos. 91 and 92), Taccola should be numbered among the most outstanding engineers of the Renaissance

and considered the precursor of the great age of Tuscan engineer-artists which culminated in the late fifteenth century in Francesco di Giorgio Martini and Leonardo da Vinci and continued to bear fruit for the whole of the sixteenth century, until the time of Galileo.
This spectacular windlass probably derives from the famous *rota magna* (large wheel) used by Brunelleschi during the construction of the dome of Florence Cathedral before the arrival of the revolutionary *colla* or *cholla*, a windlass with three speeds and a reverse mechanism. In the Latin text describing the drawing Taccola rightly insists on the improvement resulting from the fact that the operator treads on the outside of the wheel. This is in contrast with the traditional windlasses in which one or more treaders pushed with their feet on the inside of the huge wheel, a system used to operate giant cranes on building sites and in ports and shipyards from antiquity (the treadwheel crane depicted on the Roman Tomb of the Haterii of the first century A.D. is a famous example) right up to the last century (regarding the long life of these machines see Drachmann 1962 and Ferguson 1976: 570). In reality, the position of the nimble treader, shown here posing like a manikin, is incorrect because his weight is directly above the axis of the wheel. For the machine to function properly the force should be exerted laterally rather than vertically (this is the concept of moment), an effect which the operator could obtain by keeping as far as possible to one side of the wheel, however precarious this might be!
There is an accurate copy of this treadwheel windlass in the Vatican *Codicetto* (fol. 93v.) belonging to Francesco di Giorgio Martini, who evidently studied the treatise written by his townsman and reputed mentor (cat. no. 93).   *D.L.*

90
MARIANO DI JACOPO (called TACCOLA)
Mobile Windlass with Counterweight (in *De ingeneis*, Books I-II)
1427-38

Munich, Bayerische Staatsbibliothek, MS. Lat., CLM 197.ii, fol. 22v. [formerly 32v.]
Drawing, pen and ink on paper; Latin manuscript, paper, of fols. I-136, modern numbering, of which: fols. 1-75, *Liber leonis* (Book I *De ingeneis*); fols. 76-98, *Liber draconis* (Book II *De ingeneis*); fols. 99-136, addenda to Books I and II.
298 × 220 mm

PROVENANCE: Francesco di Giorgio Martini; Johann Albrecht von Widmanstetter; Palatine Library of Duke Albert V of Bavaria.

BIBLIOGRAPHY: Venturi 1815: 12, 14, Jaehns 1889, I: 278ff.; Berthelot 1891: 472-521; Halm 1892: 41ff.; Beck 1899: 270-290; de Laborde 1924: 500; Fontana 1936: 103; Czarnowsky 1949: 17, fig. 13; Thorndike 1955: 15-22; Michelini Tocci 1962; Beck 1968; Prager 1968; Rose 1968: 338, 346; Taccola 1969: 25; Scaglia 1971, I: 10-28 and passim; Gille 1972: 78-87; Prager and Scaglia 1972: 10, 96-99; Degenhart and Schmitt 1982: 1-20, 13, fig. 16; Taccola 1984a; Taccola 1984b: 12-13, 28-29; Galluzzi 1991c: 19ff., 192; Scaglia 1992: 56-57 and index.

This delightful drawing by the Sienese Mariano di Jacopo, called Taccola, included in the *Liber leonis*, the first book of his treatise *De ingeneis* which may be dated to the second or third decade of the fifteenth century, depicts a windlass for raising and lowering small loads at the same time.

The continuous movement of the windlass, which is placed on a mobile platform, lifts a full bucket and lowers an empty one using a single rope, which passes through the two pulleys, and just one man, with a considerable saving in time and effort.

This is despite the fact that the delicate Sienese Gothic curve which Taccola has given the worker's back suggests his task is indeed an arduous one. A drawing of another windlass of this type, but with the pulleys fixed to the ground and not to the mobile platform, which is mounted on four wheels only, was also executed by Taccola in the Addenda to the first two books of *De ingeneis* on fol. 102r. The machines in *De ingeneis* were annotated and studied by Taccola's pupil, the Sienese Francesco di Giorgio Martini, who owned the codex; in fact, many of these contrivances may be found in Francesco's treatises, including this windlass, drawn without an operator, together with many others on fol. 93v. of the Vatican *Codicetto* (cat. no. 93). *D.L.*

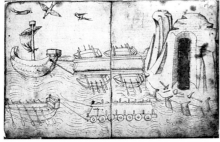

91
MARIANO DI JACOPO (called TACCOLA)
A System for Extracting a Column from the Living Rock and Transporting it by Sea
(from *Liber tertius de ingeneis ac edifitiis non usitatis*, Books III-IV)
1431-33

Florence, Biblioteca Nazionale Centrale, *Palatino* 766, [366.-21, 2], fols. 14v.-15r. [formerly 40v.-41r.].
Drawing; pen and ink on paper; Latin codex, manuscript, paper, in notarial cursive, of fols. 48 with modern numbering.
299 × 238 mm
INSCRIBED: (fol. 1) *In dei nomine amen. Anno MCCCCXXXII tempore adventus principis Sicismundi regis Buem[orum et] Romanorum semper agusti*; (fols. 2-30) *Incipit liber tertius de ingeneis ac edifitiis non usitatis*; (fols. 31-45) *Incipit quartus liber de edifitiis cotidianis*; (colophon) *In domo Sapientiae civitatis Senarum in anno domini millesimo CCCCXXXIJ (st. com. 1433) die mensis XIII° Januarij.*

PROVENANCE: Florence, Biblioteca di Carlo di Tommaso Strozzi (?)

BIBLIOGRAPHY: Gentile 1891; Thorndike 1955: 24ff.; Mitchell 1962; Beck 1968: 313-318; Prager 1968: 132, 135; Rose 1968: 338, 345; Scaglia 1968: 428-432; Taccola 1969: 155; Prager and Scaglia 1970a: 72ff., 121ff., 130-131; Scaglia 1971, II: 15; Prager and Scaglia 1972: 95, fig., Galluzzi 1980: 154; Degenhart and Schmitt 1982: 21-69; *Laboratorio su Leonardo* 1983: 80, 98, 139; Galluzzi 1991c: 19ff., 193-194; Scaglia 1992: 56, passim.

Unlike the first two books in Münich (CLM 197xx, cf. cat. nos. 89 and 90), which are fragmentary and incoherent, this autograph codex (it probably came to the Palatine estate through Senator Carlo Strozzi's library), contained in the third and fourth books of *De ingeneis*, is written in a homogeneous manner without alterations and is carefully paginated. It was written by Taccola between 1431 and 1433 and dedicated to Emperor Sigismund, who was briefly in Siena at that time, in the hope of enter-

ing his service and moving to Hungary, although this wish was not fulfilled (Galluzzi 1991d: 193; Beck 1968; 1969). In the Palatine codex the drawings of machines and buildings, whether they are extraordinary or everyday ones, are not numbered, but are differentiated by delightful animals, ranging from the most common domestic ones to exotic and mythical ones, taken from the medieval bestiary by Ciriaco d'Ancona (Mitchell 1962; Beck 1969: 17-18).

Many of the machines illustrated by Taccola echo the famous, though controversial, inventions of his illustrious friend and contemporary Filippo Brunelleschi. In fact, Taccola reports the great architect's celebrated affirmation of the need to forbear from divulging workshop secrets and details of inventions—*noli cum multis partecipare inventionis tuas* (you should keep your inventions to yourself)—in order to avoid the attacks of one's adversaries and widespread plagiarism (in CLM 197xx: fol. 107v. [formerly 228v.], cf. Reti 1965: 6; Prager 1968, Beck 1969: 15; Galluzzi 1991).

In the drawing on fols. 14v.-15r. Taccola deals with a much debated problem of his day: how to transport large monoliths from the quarry to a distant building site by sea (see Klapisch-Zuber 1973: 101 fols. regarding transport from the quarries at Carrara). According to Taccola the solution was to apply the concept of intermodal transportation; this is explained by the drawing, where the technical precision is such that tools used in a quarry—chisels, a stonemason's hammer and a dressing ax—are shown in detail, and by the Latin annotation on fol. 15v., where particular importance is given to the amphibious vehicle with 14 wheels, seven on each side, used for carrying the huge column on both land and sea. A copy of this drawing was also made in a sixteenth-century Venetian codex (Lamberini 1991c: 218) after it had been included in the Vatican *Codicetto* belonging to Francesco di Giorgio (f. 143v). In it there are reminders, especially in the large wheeled raft in the foreground, of the unsuccessful *badalone*, an invention patented by Brunelleschi in 1421 (possibly the first patent in the modern sense of the word) for the transport of marble from Carrara to Florence. The contrivance, which unfortunately proved to be a failure, exploited the principal of intermodal transportation and could be converted from land vehicle to boat and vice versa (Galluzzi 1991b: 187). *D.L.*

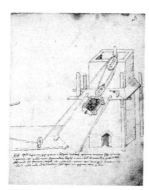

92
MARIANO DI JACOPO (called TACCOLA)
Windlass with a Trolley for Hoisting Material onto the Scaffolding during the Construction of a Tower (from *Liber tertius de ingeneis ac edifitiis non usitatis*, Books III-IV)
1431-33

Florence, Biblioteca Nazionale Centrale, *Palatino* 766, [366.-21, 2], fols. 13v.-14r. [formerly 39v.-40r.]
Drawing; pen and ink on paper; Latin codex, manuscript, paper, in notarial cursive, of fols. 48 with modern numbering.

299 × 238 mm
INSCRIBED: (fol. 1) *In dei nomine amen. Anno MCCCCXXXII tempore adventus principis Sicismundi regis Buem[orum et] Romanorum semper agusti*; (fols. 2-30) *Incipit liber tertius de ingeneis ac edifitiis non usitatis*; (fols. 31-45) *Incipit quartus liber de edifitiis cotidianis*; (colophon) *In domo Sapientiae civitatis Senarum in anno domini millesimo CCCCXXXIJ (st. com. 1433) die mensis XIII° Januarij.*

PROVENANCE: Florence, Biblioteca di Carlo di Tommaso Strozzi (?)

BIBLIOGRAPHY: Gentile 1891; Thorndike 1955: 24ff.; Mitchell 1962; Beck 1968: 313-318; Prager 1968: 132, 135; Rose 1968: 338, 345; Scaglia 1968: 428-432; Taccola 1969: 143, 155; Prager and Scaglia 1970: 72ff., 121ff., 130-131; Scaglia 1971, II: 15; Prager and Scaglia 1972: 96, fig.; Carpiceci 1978: 218-219, fig. 1; Galluzzi 1980: 154; Degenhart and Schmitt 1982: 24; *Laboratorio su Leonardo* 1983: 80, 98, 139; Galluzzi 1991c: 19ff., 193-194; Scaglia 1992: 56, passim.

Distinguished by a vivid *ad leprarium canem*, one of the famous animals drawn by Taccola on the folios of the third book of *De ingeneis*, the drawing shows a tower under construction; this is surrounded by scaffolding onto which building materials are being hoisted. The operation is being carried out with the assistance of a windlass and single tackle with indirect traction, consisting of two blocks, the upper one fixed, a pulley on the ground and the rope, known as the *menale*, hauling a laden trolley, which Francesco di Giorgio called a *carrozzo* (carriage), up an inclined plane (cat. no. 93).

The mechanism, as the author himself explains in the Latin annotation under the drawing, is easily comprehensible and Taccola emphasizes that the machine saves a great deal of time and effort: "*Quamquam istud arganum per se pateat in designo trahens parvum currum super planum pontem, est multo utile ad portandum lapides et omne aliud ad murandum illud quod faciunt sex fartores. / Et sola illa curricula perta una vice .X. fartores. Et ideo est valde utile ad fulciendum ill[l]ud opus / ne operari tempus perdant*" (fol. 14r.).
The inclined plane is treated as if it were one of Hero of Alexandria's simple mechanical devices, the sixth after the windlass, the lever, the pulley, the wedge and the screw (see Hero of Alexandria, *Mechanica*, Book III). In reality, in this machine the benefit derives first and foremost from the ratios of the windlass, then from the inclination of the plane and, finally, from the transmission of the blocks, in this case with either single or double tackle, with a ratio of one to three (Beck, in Taccola 1969: 143). Of greater interest for us is the fact that this system of hoisting material by means of a trolley on an inclined plane, the utility of which is questionable, may have been derived from the system used by Brunelleschi to haul trolleys laden with materials up the extrados of the dome of Florence Cathedral while it was being built (Carpiceci 1978: 218). A modern reconstruction of a trolley used for this purpose is kept in the Museo dell'Opera in Florence (cat. no. 110). *D.L.*

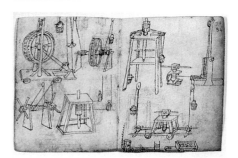

93
FRANCESCO DI GIORGIO MARTINI
Various Types of Windlass for Building Sites
(from *Taccuino di disegni e annotazioni*, called the *Codicetto*)
ca. 1472-77

Vatican, Biblioteca Apostolica Vaticana, Cod. Urb. Lat. 1757, fols. 91v.-92r.

Drawing; parchment manuscript, untitled, *adespota*, of fols. 1 + 191, with over a thousand drawings, many autograph annotations.

81 × 59 mm

PROVENANCE: Biblioteca Feltresca di Castel Durante.

BIBLIOGRAPHY: Venturi 1914: 415, 451-452; Vasari 1917: 55-56; Stornajolo 1921, III: 678; Fontana 1936: 103; Papini 1946: figs. 301-302; Salmi 1947: 27-29, 32, 47; Michelini Tocci 1962; Parronchi 1966a: 167; Francesco di Giorgio, ed. Maltese 1967, I: XXVIII-XXX, XLI-XLII; Prager and Scaglia 1970: 65, 163, 191-194; Scaglia 1970a; Betts 1971: 18, 158-159 nn. 24-25, 219 n. 17; Parronchi 1971: 170; Prager and Scaglia 1972: 191-194, Scaglia 1976: 133; Fiore 1978: 27-28, 38; Scaglia 1980: 7-15; Moranti and Moranti 1981: 369-450; Degenhart and Schmitt 1982: 27, 33-64; Dechert 1984: 109-112; *Raffaello* 1985-86: 29-30; Scaglia 1988a: 177; Michelini Tocci 1989; Galluzzi 1991c: 29-30, 32-33, 37, 202; Mussini 1991: 86-88, 90, 108; Scaglia 1991a: 60-61; Scaglia 1992: 25, 51-52; Mussini 1993: 359-360.

The most representative of the numerous codices and treatises on engineering and architecture by the Sienese Francesco di Giorgio Martini (1439-1501) is the small notebook in the Biblioteca Apostolica Vaticana, known as the *Codicetto*. In fact, it testifies to the working methods, based on study, research and the continuous elaboration of the sources, of this important artist—an engineer who, thanks also to the exhibitions recently held in Siena (1991, 1993), may be numbered among the leading figures of the Renaissance. The *Codicetto* is one of the series of personal notebooks that artists and architects always had on their person in order to make on-the-spot notes and sketches which they would amplify subsequently. It may be dated to the early 1470s; this was the period when Francesco was training to be an engineer. After this he was called to the court of Urbino as architect to Duke Federico da Montefeltro, where he wrote the fair copy of the *Opusculum de architectura* (London, British Museum, MS. 197, b, 21), which included many drawings from the *Codicetto*. Dedicated to the duke in 1477, this work was the first of a long series of treatises on architecture and machines (for the dating of Francesco's treatises see Mussini 1993). This pattern book is typical of workshop books of medieval origin: it contains 1,200 drawings in pen and ink that are small but neatly executed and are accompanied by texts. Dealing with subjects that range from a wide variety of applications of hydraulic engineering to the most diverse types of machines for military or building purposes, it combines traditional sources, antiquarian research and bold innovation with typically Renaissance verve. In fact, Francesco drew on a variety of sources, including Vegetius' *Epitome rei militaris*, Vitruvius' *De architectura*, the 1477 edition of *De re militari* by Roberto Valturio, which he had discovered at the court of Urbino, Julius Frontinus and Marco Greco as well as ideas derived from Brunelleschi (Fiore 1978; Michelini Tocci 1989; Galluzzi 1991: 202; Mussini 1993); but his main inspiration was his fellow townsman and reputed mentor Mariano di Jacopo, called Taccola, the Sienese Archimedes. In the *Codicetto* Francesco translated Taccola into the vernacular and paraphrased his work; he reproduced the majority of the drawings from *De ingeneis*, introducing audacious innovations in both the first and second versions, which were later codified in the official treatises on engineering and architecture written in the 1480s and early 1490s (Maltese, in Francesco di Giorgio 1967; Mussini 1993). These drawings on fols. 93v.-94r. are examples of windlasses, the source of which is clearly Taccola. The first machine depicted is a treadwheel windlass, driven by a man pushing with his feet on the outside of the wheel; this derives from the *De ingeneis* in Münich (see cat. no. 89). Only the bearings of the pulleys attached to the mobile platform have been modified; the advantage over wheels where the treaders are placed inside (the weight of the treader is added to his movement) is again confirmed by Francesco in the second version of the treatise (Flor-

ence, Biblioteca Nazionale Centrale, *Codex Magliabechiano*, II.I.141, fol. 97v.).

Then follow, from left to right, a treadwheel windlass, a windlass driven by two sets of rotating levers and a windlass with counterweights, which has a large vertical drum that Francesco called the *curba*. On fol. 94r. there are drawings of three windlasses with counterweights, suitable for lifting heavy loads, all having only a single drive; the second, which has a long shaft (*arbore* according to Taccola), is reminiscent of Vitruvius' *polispastos*. At the bottom is depicted a small trolley loaded with material which Francesco often used; he called this a *carrozzo*.   D.L.

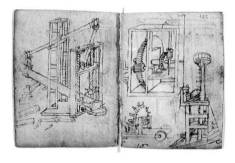

94

FRANCESCO DI GIORGIO MARTINI
Device for Raising Columns, Mill and Self-propelled Vehicle (from *Taccuino di disegni e annotazioni*, called the *Codicetto*)
ca. 1472-77

Vatican, Biblioteca Apostolica Vaticana, Cod. Urb. Lat. 1757, fols. 119v.-120r.

Drawing; parchment manuscript, untitled, *adespota*, of fols. 1 + 191, with over a thousand drawings, many autograph annotations.

81 × 59 mm

PROVENANCE: Biblioteca Feltresca di Castel Durante.

BIBLIOGRAPHY: Venturi 1914: 415, 451-452; Vasari 1917: 55-56; Stornajolo 1921, III: 678; Fontana 1936: 103; Papini 1946: figs. 301-302; Salmi 1947: 27-29, 32, 47; Michelini Tocci 1962; Parronchi 1966a: 167; Francesco di Giorgio, ed. Maltese 1967, I: XXVIII-XXX, XLI-XLII; Prager and Scaglia 1972: 191-194; Scaglia 1970a; Betts 1971: 18, 158-159 nn. 24-25, 219 n. 17; Parronchi 1971: 170; Scaglia 1976: 133; Fiore 1978: 27-28, 38; Scaglia 1980: 7-15; Moranti and Moranti 1981: 369-450; Degenhart and Schmitt 1982: 27, 33-64; Dechert 1984: 109-112; *Raffaello* 1985-86: 29-30; Scaglia 1988a: 177; Michelini Tocci 1989; Galluzzi 1991c: 29-30, 32-33, 37, 202; Mussini 1991: 86-88, 90, 108; Scaglia 1991a: 60-61; Scaglia 1992: 25, 51-52; Mussini 1993: 359-360.

Among the bold innovations which Francesco di Giorgio Martini introduced in the Vatican *Codicetto* and repeated in the two versions of his treatise on architecture and engineering, may be numbered the remarkable machines included in the category of "lifting and pulling." These include self-propelled vehicles, mostly used for celebrations and theatrical performances, and devices for raising columns and moving obelisks. Similarly to mills, *pestrini* (hand-driven mills) and hydraulic pumps, these do not appear in the works by Taccola that Francesco studied and elaborated. One of Francesco's notable technical innovations for the transmission of movement and the gearing down of power, in contrast with the traditional cogwheel combined with the sprocket wheel or lantern pinion employed by Taccola, was the extensive use of the worm-gear and rack and the use of the connecting-rod and crank system together with the flywheel.

A clear example of the innovations introduced by Francesco is provided by the machines drawn on fols. 119-120r. The principle of the lever forms the basis of the huge device for raising columns on fol. 119v., which is comprised of a long beam pivoted between vertical supports

five or six meters in height, although it works in a simple manner. It is operated by two people who turn the two worms at the same time; these are correctly shown as being left-handed in one case and right-handed in the other. The base of the column is placed on a mobile trolley, called a *carrozzo* by Francesco, which allows it to move during the raising operation. As the beam with the articulated metal arms is raised, the column is wedged up with stacks of planks and sections are removed from the arms in order to shorten them. A pulley fixed to the top of the supporting structure serves to raise or lower the main beam. Francesco, who has as usual depicted the technical details (such as the articulated arm in the foreground and the wooden wedges), with great precision, only shows this device for raising columns again in the *Opusculum de architectura* (London, British Museum, MS. 197, b, 21, fol. 56v.), substituting the two sources of power by a single windlass, while in the two versions of the treatise he draws more complex devices for raising columns, with a vertical worm and a rack. On fol. 120r. there is a hand-powered mill with a sprocket and cogwheel transmission. This is one of Francesco's renowned *pestrini*, waterless mills drawn in the characteristic "perspective box," an invention of his that, by means of a graphic convention, allowed the arrangement of the parts to be shown in an easily comprehensible manner (Kemp 1991a). This convention was very successful (cat. nos. 101, 103) and was clear evidence that the Sienese artist and engineer was greatly superior to his contemporaries in terms of draftsmanship (Galluzzi 1991c: 39). This pre-eminence was only challenged by the unparalleled heights reached by Leonardo da Vinci, who was familiar with Francesco's work and in 1504-05 added annotations in his own hand to *Codex L* of Francesco's first version of the treatise (Florence, Biblioteca Medicea Laurenziana, *Codex Ashburnham* 361; cf. Marani 1979; Mussini 1993: 360-361). Next to the mill are depicted a self-propelled vehicle and a war machine; the latter is a mobile fort fitted with a wooden mantelet at the base to protect the assailants, who were able to approach the enemy walls with this siege engine. Of very ancient origin, it was still in use long after the introduction of firearms. The promiscuous presence on this and many other folios of the *Codicetto* of designs for hydraulic, building and military machines is testimony to Francesco's total command of engineering techniques in a pluridisciplinary sense; this was a typical feature both of him and all the other artist-engineers of the Renaissance, who, with regard to architecture, thought and acted like the classical Vitruvian universal man.   D.L.

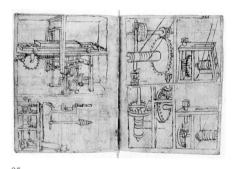

95

FRANCESCO DI GIORGIO MARTINI
Hydraulic Saw, Device for Raising Columns, Drills and Various Types of Windlasses for Building Sites (from *Taccuino di disegni e annotazioni*, called the *Codicetto*)
ca. 1472-77

Vatican, Biblioteca Apostolica Vaticana, Cod. Urb. Lat. 1757, fols. 165v.-166r.

Drawing; parchment manuscript, untitled, *adespota*, of fols. 1 + 191, with over a thousand drawings, many autograph annotations.

81 × 59 mm

PROVENANCE: Biblioteca Feltresca di Castel Durante.

BIBLIOGRAPHY: Venturi 1914: 415, 451-452; Vasari 1917: 55-56;
Stornajolo 1921, III: 678; Fontana 1936: 103; Papini 1946: figs.
301-302; Salmi 1947: 27-29, 32, 47; Michelini Tocci 1962; Parronchi 1966a: 167; Francesco di Giorgio, ed. Maltese 1967, I:
XXVIII-XXX, XLI-XLII; Scaglia 1970a; Prager and Scaglia
1970: 65, 163, 191-194; Betts 1971: 18, 158-159 nn. 24-25, 219
n. 17; Parronchi 1971: 170; Prager and Scaglia 1972: 191-194;
Scaglia 1976: 133; Fiore 1978: 27-28, 38; Scaglia 1980: 7-15;
Moranti and Moranti 1981: 369-450; Degenhart and Schmitt
1982: 27, 33-64; Dechert 1984: 109-112; Raffaello 1985-86: 29-
30; Scaglia 1988a: 177; Michelini Tocci 1989; Galluzzi 1991c: 29-
30, 32-33, 37, 202; Mussini 1991: 86-88, 90, 108; Scaglia 1991a:
60-61; Scaglia 1992: 25, 51-52; Mussini 1993: 359-360.

The machines drawn by Francesco di Giorgio on fol.
165v. of the Vatican *Codicetto* include a device for raising
columns with a vertical rack linked to a mobile carriage,
placed in his "perspective box" and never depicted again
in any other work, and a gimlet and a hand drill, which
transform circular into linear motion, acting along the
axis of rotation; the latter are humble building tools to the
design of which Francesco devoted a great deal of attention in his treatises. Of particular interest is the first
drawing, which shows a hydraulic saw.
The machine functions automatically. The toothed blade
of the saw, which in the drawing is shown cutting a large
block of wood into planks, is powered by the flow of the
water turning the waterwheel underneath; attached to
this is a connecting-rod which transforms the rotary motion into linear motion, thereby raising and lowering the
blade as the frame on which the block is placed moves forward; the frame is fitted with rollers and the feed is regulated by a ratchet-wheel.
The origins of this saw are lost in the mists of time (a simplified saw of the same type is depicted in the famous
medieval notebook of Villard de Honnecourt; Paris, Bibliothèque Nationale, MS. fr. 19093, fol. 44) and it appears
to have been a very successful design; in fact, traces of its
existence have been found in the Cistercian monastery of
Abbadia S. Salvatore on Monte Amiata in Tuscany (Galluzzi 1991: 433-435). It was repeated by Francesco both
in the *Opusculum* (fol. 72v.) and in the first and second
editions of the treatise (*Codex Saluzziano* 148, fol. 48v.
and *Codex Ashburnham* 361, fol. 43v.). Subsequently we
find it reproduced and variously interpreted in numerous
sixteenth-century codices, notebooks and treatises such
as Leonardo da Vinci's *Codex Atlanticus* (fol. 389r.), Benvenuto della Volpaia's notebook (Venice, Biblioteca
Nazionale Marciana, MS. It. cl. IV, 41, [= 5363], fol.
90v) the codices of Cosimo Bartoli and Bernardo Puccini
(Florence, Biblioteca Nazionale Centrale, E.B.16.5.xx,
fol. 124v. and *Codex Palatino* 1077, fol. 63r., cf. cat. no.
101) and the printed treatises of Agostino Ramelli (1588),
Jacopo Strada (1617-18) and Giovanni Branca (1629) (cf.
Scaglia 1981: 16-32, figs. 11-20; Lamberini 1991c:
235-236).
The four windlasses and counterweights depicted on fol.
166r. are fairly elementary machines, with the drive shaft
based on the sprocket and cogwheel system (Francesco
calls this *ribecco*). Although they are operated by just one
person, they are very powerful thanks to the very high ratio of the gears. A distinguishing feature of the first windlass, with the balanced drive shaft, is the trapezoid roll
sprocket, an innovation which Francesco preferred to the
traditional cylindrical sprocket. In fact, it could be a very
simplified version of the *colla centrale*, the spectacular
hoisting machine invented by Brunelleschi to lift heavy
weights during the construction of the dome of Florence
Cathedral.   D.L.

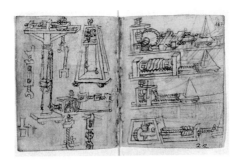

96
FRANCESCO DI GIORGIO MARTINI
Hoisting Machine and Building Crane,
Divaricators and Obelisk Transporter
(from *Taccuino di disegni e annotazioni*,
called the *Codicetto*)
ca. 1472-77

Vatican, Biblioteca Apostolica Vaticana, Cod. Urb. Lat. 1757,
fols. 166v.-167r.
Drawing; parchment manuscript, untitled, *adespota*, of fols.
1 + 191, with over a thousand drawings, many autograph
annotations; 81 × 59 mm.

PROVENANCE: Biblioteca Feltresca di Castel Durante.

BIBLIOGRAPHY: Venturi 1914: 415, 451-452; Vasari 1917: 55-56;
Stornajolo 1921, III: 678; Fontana 1936: 103; Papini 1946: figs.
301-302; Salmi 1947: 27-29, 32, 47; Michelini Tocci 1962; Parronchi 1966a: 167; Francesco di Giorgio, ed. Maltese 1967, I:
XXVIII-XXX, XLI-XLII; Scaglia 1970a; Prager and Scaglia
1970: 65, 163, 191-194; Betts 1971: 18, 158-159 nn.
24-25, 219 n. 17; Parronchi 1971: 170; Prager and Scaglia 1972:
191-194; Scaglia 1976: 133; Fiore 1978: 27-28, 38; Scaglia 1980:
7-15; Moranti and Moranti 1981: 369-450; Degenhart and
Schmitt 1982: 27, 33-64; Dechert 1984: 109-112; Raffaello 1985-
86: 29-30; Scaglia 1988a: 177; Michelini Tocci 1989; Galluzzi
1991c: 29-30, 32-33, 37, 202; Mussini 1991: 86-88, 90, 108;
Scaglia 1991a: 60-61; Scaglia 1992: 25, 51-52; Mussini 1993:
359-360.

During the Renaissance Francesco di Giorgio was one of
the first to translate, interpret and illustrate Vitruvius'
obscure Latin text. He paid particular attention to the
renewal of the Vitruvian machines (Francesco di Giorgio
1841; 1967; Fiore 1978; Scaglia 1985; Mussini 1993). He
embodied, also from the engineering point of view, the
traditional figure of the Renaissance architect-archaeologist, and he was a theoretician, renewer and popularizer
of building practice. This had to be freed from the restraints of the techniques used on the medieval building
sites, which were fettered by the secrecy of the guilds, so
that the "harmonious forms" of the new architecture
could be imposed and the new technologies that had been
developed from those of the ancients applied. In fact,
many of the innovations introduced by Francesco to Taccola's repertory of machines went in this direction. For instance, there were the models for the *tirari*, devices which
were intended to move large monoliths, obelisks or
columns horizontally; involving the combined use of
worms (the Vitruvian version of the Archimedean screw
or Francesco's *lumaca* [snail]) and the cogwheel and rack,
these were associated with the Sienese artist's stay in
Rome in the 1460s and 1470s (Galluzzi 1991). A desire
to outdo the ancients, together with continuous progress
and updating are evident in the *Codicetto*, for instance on
this folio where four *tirari* are depicted; these are also
shown in the *Opusculum de architectura* (fols. 10, 26). The
enormous machines, which, on paper at least, appear to
function, are a reflection of the stimulating cultural climate of the day, when memories of the amazing feats of
the Bolognese Aristotele Fioravanti were still fresh. According to his friend Filarete he was "very skilled in making devices to move heavy weights"; thus, with the aid of
no more than an Archimedean screw he was able to move
whole towers and buildings. Moreover, the lively debate
regarding the moving of the Vatican obelisk was still un-

derway; this problem, which had been raised first by Pope
Nicholas V and then by Paul II, had yet to be solved.
On fol. 122v., together with some of Taccola's divaricators, jacks consisting of a worm coupled to metal hooks
known as *rampi*, which served to force apart the bars in
gratings, there is a mobile hoisting machine for lifting
weights and, in the center of the folio, a dual-purpose mobile revolving crane which could be used for the horizontal
movement of weights of medium size. This crane, which
Francesco described and illustrated with some variations
in his subsequent writings, from the *Opusculum* (fols.
11v.-12r.) to the two editions of the treatise (*Codex Saluzziano* 148, fol. 52r. and *Codex Magliabechiano* II.I.141, c.
92v.), is a combination of two machines. In fact, the windlass raises the load from the ground with the double pulley
fixed to the central post; when it reaches the top, the load
is attached to the hooks moved by the horizontal screws
and positioned by rotating the jib of the crane. Francesco,
who always paid heed to the problems deriving from friction, was particularly careful in his choice of the cylindrical components, certainly made of metal, placed in the
bearings of the crane, which do not seem to reduce the
complexity of the rotation of the jib, just as the lack of a
counterweight only allows a very limited range for the
moving of heavier loads (Galluzzi 1991: 392-393).
The drawing certainly shows one of the machines used
by Brunelleschi for the construction of the dome of Florence Cathedral. In fact, a crane that was similar, but
correctly counterweighted and shown with the minutest
details, may be found among the many drawings of
machines by Antonio da Sangallo the Younger in the
Uffizi (Uff. 1449Av.; Galluzzi 1991: 257). Antonio,
who was acquainted with Francesco's machines through
the drawings of his uncle Giuliano da Sangallo, in the
autograph annotations which accompany the drawing of
the crane, stresses the need to use counterweights. This
shows that, compared with his illustrious predecessor,
the Florentine architect was more familiar with
Brunelleschi's technical innovations, which he had assimilated on the spot, in the city itself and also thanks
to the works of Giuliano and his contemporaries of the
"first Italian generation," such as the Florentine Bonaccorso Ghiberti (cat. no. 99).   D.L.

97
GIOVANNI BETTINI DA FANO
The Tempio Malatestiano in Rimini under
Construction
(in Basini Parmensis, *Hesperis*, Book XIII)

Oxford, Bodleian Library, Canon. class. lat. 81, fol. 137r.
Miniature; parchment manuscript, of fols. 137 r.-v.; humanistic
script; with 19 miniatures on the following folios: Book I, 2r.,
16r.; Book II, 16v.; Book III, 27r.; Book IV, 37v., 49v.; Book
V, 50r., 60v.; Book VI, 61r., 70r.; Book VII, 70v., 82v.; Book
VIII, 83r.; Book IX, 91r.; Book X, 100v.; Book XI, 112r.,
112v.; Book XII, 123r.; Book XIII, 137r.
335 × 222 mm

PROVENANCE: Biblioteca dei Minori Conventuali, Bologna; Collezione Matteo Canonici, Venezia.

BIBLIOGRAPHY: Affò 1794; Coxe 1854; *Italian Illuminated Manuscripts* 1948: 38, pl. XIII; Pächt 1951: 92, Saxl and Meier 1953: 323, pl. 33; Campana 1965: 95; Pächt and Alexander 1970: 85, no. 830; Pasini 1970: no. 76, 148-149; Borsi 1973: 105, figs. 106, 109, no. 35; Battisti 1976: 130; Ugolini 1991: 82.

The signature of Giovanni di Bartolo Bettini da Fano does not appear in this illuminated copy of the *Hesperis* of Basinio da Parma, believed to have been lost, but in fact sold by the Venetian heirs of Matteo and in Oxford since 1817 (Pächt 1951: 92). By stylistic analogy with the two signed examples in the Vatican and Paris (cat. no. 98), the miniatures in the codex, which may be considered the finest of the three and the prototype of the series (Pasini 1970: 148), may be attributed to the same miniaturist who, under the supervision of Roberto Valturio, illuminated various copies of Basinio's epic poem at the court of Rimini, in order to celebrate the glorious feats of Sigismondo Pandolfo Malatesta.

This animated scene of the building operations is an accurate record of the construction of the Tempio Malatestiano in Rimini, depicted here with a few interesting differences from the Paris copy (cat. no. 98). In fact, the attention of the observer is focused on the left flank of the church, where Alberti's marble shell is being constructed, on the facade it has been completed up to the entablature. On this corner, as in the Paris version, an imposing mobile crane is mounted; this is a machine with ancient origins frequently referred to by Vitruvius and known as the *stella* ("star") or *falcone* ("falcon") in the Renaissance. The "star" was comprised of a long post (the *arbore* or *tignum* [beam] in Vitruvius) which resembled the mast of a ship; provided with rungs to allow it to be climbed, it was fixed at the bottom to a mobile trolley and braced at the top by four strong ropes (*reticula quadrifarium*) that gave it its star shape. The length of these could be adjusted by tackle consisting of two fiddle blocks, as is clearly shown in the miniature. The ends of the ropes (these were referred to as *menali* by Francesco di Giorgio) were attached to the base of the post and could be adjusted as necessary from this point. The load was hoisted by an ordinary vertical windlass; this was equipped with self-locking hoisting tongs (Vitruvius' "scissors") or with lewises, and was operated with long bars by two men.

The "star" was one of the most widely used machines on Renaissance building sites. In the documents relating to the construction of Brunelleschi's dome on Florence Cathedral there are frequent references to the *stella della cupola* ("star of the dome"). Illustrations depicting very similar cranes to the one used for the building of the Tempio Malatestiano are to be found in Bonaccorso Ghiberti's *Zibaldone* and in Leonardo da Vinci's studies; a very effective description is provided by Vincenzo Scamozzi in his Venetian treatise (1615: VIII, xxx, 368; cf. Reti 1965a: 24). The other windlass which can be seen in the drawing is also of considerable interest; it was used to hoist building materials up to the scaffolding on the left flank. It is a horizontal fixed windlass with a counterweight, consisting of a cogwheel, possibly provided with *palei* (pegs), fixed to the driving shaft around which the rope winds. An identical windlass is illustrated and described by Francesco di Giorgio Martini in his first treatise (*Codex Saluzziano* 148, fol. 51r).   D.L.

98
GIOVANNI BETTINI DA FANO
The Tempio Malatestiano in Rimini under Construction
(in Basini Parmensis, *Hesperis*, Book XIII)

Paris, Bibliothèque de l'Arsenal, Cod. 630, fol. 126r.
Miniature; parchment manuscript, of fols. 126 r.-v.; humanistic script; with 17 miniatures on the following folios: Book I, 1r., 15r; Book II, 15v.; Book III, 26r.; Book IV, 45v.; book VI, 61r.; Book VII, 61v., 73v.; book VIII, 74v., 82r; Book IX, 82v., 90v.; Book XI, 102r., 112r.; Book XII, 112v., 113r.; Book XIII, 126r.
148 × 145 mm

PROVENANCE: Library of the Baron of Heiss.

BIBLIOGRAPHY: Affò, in Basini 1794, I: 32ff.; Martin 1885, I: 475ff.; De' Ricci 1927: 156, 158; Ricci 1928. 20-22; C[ampana] 1928, [Michelini Tocci] 1950: 43, no. 64; Campana 1951: 104, Pächt 1951: 92-93; Campana 1965: 95; Pasini 1970: 148-149; 1978: 120-125, fig. 3; 1983: 147-152; Ugolini, 1991: 81; Hope 1992: 101 n. 201, 116, pl. 19a.

The most outstanding artists and humanists who surrounded Sigismondo Pandolfo Malatesta, *signore* of Rimini, *condottiere*, politician and enlightened patron of the arts, included Leon Battista Alberti, Piero della Francesca, Agostino di Duccio, Matteo de' Pasti, Roberto Valturio, and Basinio da Parma. The latter, a refined poet, went to the court of Rimini in 1449, attracted by the munificence of Sigismondo, to celebrate the glories of the Malatesta dynasty in verse (Campana 1965). He attained a position of great prestige in the *pandulphiades patria* (the Malatesta state) and his literary output increased in the 1450s. This was the period when the magnificence of his patron had reached its peak: the Tempio Malatestiano was under construction in Rimini, Roberto Valturio was exalting the military prowess of Sigismondo in *De re militari* and humanists from Rimini and elsewhere were vying with one another to sing the praises of the famous Malatesta and his beloved Isotta degli Atti. This was, therefore, at the height of the Renaissance prince's political, military and economic power, which was destined to fall into an inexorable decline in the following decade.
The Latin poem *Hesperis* or *Hesperidos* (the title means "land of the west," that is, Italy), which in thirteen books gives an account of the recent wars waged in Italy by Sigismondo, the champion of Italian national identity who fought against the barbarians, was the last of Basinio's writings and an outstanding example of fifteenth century humanistic plan literature. Basinio, who had not managed to put the finishing touches to his work when he died, entrusted it to Sigismondo, laying down in his will that it should not be altered in any way and that he should be buried in one of the large sarcophagi of the Roman type that had been built in the side walls of the Tempio Malatestiano. In fact, with the burial of Basinio in the first sarcophagus on the side of the temple (the fourth was assigned to Valturio), Sigismondo initiated his humanistic plan for the allocation of these tombs to poets and cholars,

so that his own tomb and that of Isotta should be surrounded in accordance with a commemorative scheme that was unique in his day (Campana 1965: 94).
In his will Basinio linked his poem in humanistic terms to the equally incomplete *Aeneid*, in an attempt to create a parallel between himself and Virgil and Augustus and Sigismondo. He confided the autograph of his work to his friend Valturio, but it did not circulate widely (only seven copies are known to exist, of which three are illustrated), nor was there a printed edition until the end of the eighteenth century (Basini 1794, edited by Affò with engravings by Francesco Rosaspina, cf. Ricci [1925]). However, Sigismondo commissioned an edition of the *Hesperis* illustrated with miniatures, the text of which was faithful to the last version left by the poet; various copies were made of this work under the supervision of Valturio in the court scriptorium between 1457, the year the poet died, and 1468, the year when Sigismondo and Matteo de' Pasti died; previously it was believed that the latter was responsible for the miniatures (Ricci [1925]; Pasini 1974; 1978). In reality, for at least two of the three surviving illuminated copies of the *Hesperis* (these copies are now in Paris, Oxford, and Vatican City) the authorship was attributed with certainty (De' Ricci 1927: 158; Ricci 1928; Pächt 1951: 93) to the miniaturist Giovanni di Bartolo Bettini da Fano, who had also illuminated some codices of the *De re militari* by Valturio for Sigismondo in 1460 (C[ampana] 1928).
The author's signature, OP.[US] IOANNIS PICTORIS PHANESTRIS, appears at the bottom of the miniature, which depicts the construction of the Tempio Malatestiano and illustrates the thirteenth and final book of the *Hesperis*, both in this codex, now in Paris (fol. 126r.), which the Bibliothèque de l'Arsenal acquired in 1781 after it had been purchased by the Marquis d'Argenson, the founder of the library (Ricci 1928: 44), and in the copy in the Biblioteca Apostolica Vaticana (Vat. Lat. 6043, fol. 133v.). Believed to have been lost, the latter was rediscovered by Michelini Tocci on the occasion of the Vatican exhibition held in 1950.
The representation of the Tempio Malatestiano under construction, which concludes this supremely celebratory and propagandistic work, thanks to the narrative accuracy and the technical skill of the miniaturist is a reliable record of both the organization of the building operations, which were competently supervised by Matteo de' Pasti, and the condition of the thirteenth century church of S. Francesco at that time. In fact, Sigismondo had commissioned Leon Battista Alberti to rebuild this completely as a classical temple, to the greater glory of his dynasty (Pasini 1970; Borsi 1973: 91-131; Hope 1992).
In the 1460s, about ten years after the construction of the Tempio Malatestiano had begun, work was interrupted because Sigismondo had fallen into disgrace. At this point the facade had been completed up to the level of the entablature, on which the inscription in elegant Roman lettering had already been engraved, and work was under way on the left flank. Evidently wishing to make his illustration as complete as possible, Bettini depicts the men at work in detail with machines and tools; in fact, this degree of accuracy is not surprising, since he is the artist who illustrated Valturio's book of military machines. In the foreground, in front of the building, masons are hard at work putting the finishing touches to blocks of stone, cornices and capitals. Particularly worthy of note are the capitals of the Composite order, described as "bellissimi" by Matteo de' Pasti, adorned by cherub heads, which had already been placed in position on the facade (Pasini 1970: 146-147; Burns 1980: 115). The tools used have left clear traces on the surfaces of the blocks of Istrian stone and marble, many of which were reused; in fact, in 1991 the latter were the subject of a study by Andrea Ugolini, who also cataloged the numerous mason's marks. The tools are probably of two types: the hack hammer with two toothed blades, used to eliminate the irregularities left on the stone by the chisels and picks after it had been roughhewed, and the "polka" with toothed edges. Among the chisels may be noted the tooth chisel, used above all for

dressing work; each block, which was perfectly squared and worked with chisels, possibly of the toothed variety, was provided with a lug made with a chisel or mason's hammer to allow it to be positioned easily, which explains why the masons' tools always included squares.

In front of the portal, next to the grating protecting the tomb of Blessed Galeotto Roberto (Sigismondo's brother), stands an elegantly dressed figure; perhaps he is the architect himself, who did not shun the building site as many writers would have us believe (Canali 1992-93), or he may be the works supervisor, Alberti's assistant. His attention is focused on the point where the most important and most difficult activity is taking place: the operation of the large braced crane, known as the *stella* ("star"), mounted on the corner of the temple for the hoisting of heavy blocks of stone; it is powered from the ground by a windlass turned by two men. Beyond this another horizontal fixed windlass, also operated by two men, supplies the workers on the scaffolding on the side wall with materials. In the background may be seen part of the monastery of San Francesco with the arch that still linked it to the church. The windlasses, the monastery and the nearby houses, which are clearly shown the miniatures in the Paris and Oxford codices (cat. no. 97), are not present in the Vatican copy. While the miniatures in the first two codices are surrounded by simple architectural frames simulating red marble, which resembles those in Verona marble used in many of the panels in the temple, the Vatican *Codex Bettini* restricts the field of vision to the facade and frames the scene with a varied border consisting of intertwined ribbons, in the longstanding tradition of the *bianchi girari* (Pasini 1983: 152-153).   D.L.

99

Giovanni Battista da Sangallo (il Gobbo) and
Antonio da Sangallo the Younger
Crane on Swiveling Platform for Constructing the Lantern of the Dome of Florence Cathedral (left)
Hook Systems and Brunelleschi Screw Coupling (right)
first half 16th cent.

Florence, Galleria degli Uffizi, Gabinetto Disegni e Stampe, Uff. 1665Ar.

Pen and ink, on white paper; fold down center; annotations in pen in top left and bottom right.
400 × 273 mm

Provenance: Fondo Mediceo-Lorenese.

Bibliography: Ferri 1885: 47; Geymüller 1885: 48 n. 3; Fabriczy 1892: 102 n. 1; Falb 1902: 34; Niccoli 1938: 285 n. 3; Paatz and Paatz 1952: 463 n. 106; Giovannoni [1959], I: 96, 447; Scaglia 1960-61; Prager and Scaglia 1970: 76; Reti 1974, fig. 20; Marchini 1977: 22-24, fig. 6; Carpiceci 1978: 216; Galluzzi 1980: 154; Scaglia 1981: 13-14, fig. 17; Borsi 1985: 328; *Léonard de Vinci* 1987: 346, 350; Galluzzi 1991b: 190.

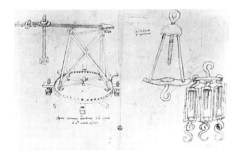

Faithful to his opening tenet: *Noli cum multis partecipare inventiones tuas* (i.e., you should keep your inventions to yourself), Filippo Brunelleschi shrouded in utter silence the extraordinary machinery he invented for the construction of the dome of Florence Cathedral (see cat. no. 91). But for his contemporaries and subsequent generations—particularly Florentines—the fame and

lively curiosity for these exceptional *ingegni* long outlasted their creator and, once the medieval lore of workshop secrecy was superseded, Brunelleschi's inventions were freely interpreted and copied, generation after generation, becoming part of the technical and cultural heritage of the architects and engineers of the Renaissance (see cat. no. 106). Among the many documents testifying to this legacy is the present drawing executed by two Florentine architects, Giovanni Battista Cordini, called Il Gobbo (1496-1548), and his elder brother Antonio the Younger (1483-1546), both of whom are more commonly known by the place-name "da Sangallo," which was ascribed to their maternal uncle Giuliano Giamberti by Lorenzo de' Medici, and remained the patronym of the uncles, cousins and nephews of what was to be known as the Sangallo "sect" (Bruschi 1983; Pagliara 1983, and bibliog.).

The fold in the paper indicates that the sheet was part of the brothers' *taccuino* of notes and on-site studies of architecture and machinery. The left-hand drawing, executed with a straightedge, together with its neatly penned caption below ("chome simuro lalanterna della cupola di sa[n]ta maria delfiore"), are by Battista; the other drawing, on the right, together with the annotation alongside ("Dallibretto di giuliano"), was executed by Antonio the Younger in what the scholar Marchini (1977c: 23) has called his "typical vibrating stroke."

The sheet provides confirmation of the close collaboration between the Sangallo brothers, in which Battista, subordinate to Antonio, carried out and supervised the execution of the numerous tasks assigned to his more prestigious brother. Their partnership is confirmed by Vasari's outline of il Gobbo: "A discerning person who spent all his time in his buildings," meaning those of his brother Antonio (Vasari 1878-85, V: 471), and was virtually a replica of the bond that had linked their maternal uncles Giuliano (the undisputed leader of the family) and Antonio (generally known as Antonio the Elder to distinguish him from his nephew). Younger by ten years, Antonio similarly played the role of faithful executor and indispensable assistant to his elder brother Giuliano, in accordance with a custom widely practiced in family-run *botteghe* in Florence during the fifteenth and sixteenth centuries.

The Uffizi sheet also bears witness to the mechanisms by which technical knowledge and skills were handed down to subsequent generations; moreover, it indicates the survival through to the Cinquecento of the legacy of mechanical devices invented by Filippo Brunelleschi. The drawings show the rotating platform crane Brunelleschi devised for constructing the dome lantern as far as the drum (at which point it was replaced with a circular platform for raising the cone, see Reti 1965b: 22), together with relative hooks, screw coupling, and a triple hook—the so-called "Hero" crab hook (see Hero of Alexandria, *Mechanica*, Book III), which were fixed to the jib of the crane to hoist loads to heights of almost one hundred meters from the ground; such loads consisted of massive hewn slabs of Carrara marble for the lantern—an authentic *tempietto* on a central plan (Carpiceci 1976: 230)—standing 20 meters tall over the great oculus of what Michelangelo praised as the "gran macchina," the cathedral's superb dome.

Brunelleschi favored strictly empirical working methods, without the aid of modern theories of virtual work, preferring to apply technical know-how acquired from other fields of activity such as horology (see Manetti 1992: 65), and successfully exploited the mechanical properties of the worm screw, in this case devised to move in all directions in order to hoist the load level with the top of the substructure. Brunelleschi's apprenticeship as a goldsmith and founder gave him firsthand knowledge of the friction coefficients of the various metals. The screw coupling and hook mechanism consists of an iron screw turning inside a bronze die; the interaction of one metal with another of different composition reduces the incidence of friction. This also applies to the extant examples of hooks and screw coupling (identified by Sanpaolesi as being by Brunelleschi) discovered in association with other mechanical devices in the apses of the dome and transferred to the museum of the Opera di S. Maria del

Fiori (cat. no. 110; Sanpaolesi 1977: 39-43; idem 1980: 145; Battisti 1976: 134-135; Marchini 1977c: 23). The crane and its corresponding hooks were first copied by Bonaccorso Ghiberti, nephew of the sculptor Lorenzo Ghiberti, in his famous *Zibaldone* (Florence, Biblioteca Nazionale Centrale, B.R. 228, fols. 104r. and 117r.; Scaglia 1960-61; Prager and Scaglia 1970: 74ff.; Galluzzi 1980: 154), without fully understanding the lifting mechanisms of the device, which is composed of four elmwood screws applied beneath the rotating platform; Ghiberti in fact omitted them. The machine is more correctly reproduced, upside-down, by Leonardo da Vinci in the *Codex Atlanticus* (fols. 295v.-b, and 389v.-b ganci), with an annotation explaining how it works (Reti 1965b: 22ff.; Carpiceci 1978: 216-217; Scaglia 1981: 6-7). The crane (supplied with only two of the four screws) and the hooks, perfectly delineated, are both accompanied by notes by Giuliano da Sangallo in the Sienese *taccuino* (Siena, Biblioteca Comunale, S. IV. 8, fols. 12r. and 48v.-49r. ganci), prior to their being copied in final draft to the *Codex Barberini* in the Vatican (Cod. Vat. Lat. 4424, fol. 13r.). It was from the Sienese *taccuino* that Antonio the Younger correctly copied the hooks, and Battista the crane (albeit misconstruing its mechanism). The rig supporting the jib is not in fact properly connected to the profiled rollers of the base (drawn in detail by Leonardo, *Codex Atlanticus*, fol. 295v.-b), nor to the ring of *palei* (pegs) arranged around the circular platform, which act as bearings; as shown, the crane could not rotate and would hence be unusable (Marchini 1977c: 22).

Antonio da Sangallo the Younger's interest in building machinery (documented by a substantial body of drawings in the Uffizi; Galluzzi 1991a: 246-247), is connected to important commissions in Rome in the early 1500s; Sangallo in fact worked on the site of New St. Peter's, first as Raphael's assistant, then as *capomaestro*, and subsequently (from 1536) as the chief architect on all papal building projects; his brother Battista worked alongside him as *mensuratore*, surveyor, and supervisor. Confirmation of the Sangallo brothers' ability in erecting scaffolding and setting up site machinery (Carpiceci 1975) is offered by the firsthand accounts of the treatise-writer and military architect Francesco De Marchi, who witnessed the Farnese pope's building works in Rome, and shared Battista's devotion to Vitruvius' *De architectura* (Pagliara 1983; Lamberini 1990a).   D.L.

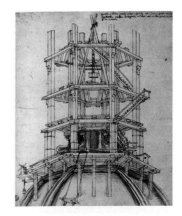

100

Anonymous
Scaffolding for the Restoration Work on the Lantern of Florence Cathedral
ca. 1601

Florence, Galleria degli Uffizi, Gabinetto Disegni e Stampe, Uff. 248Ar.

Pen and ink, on white paper; traces of pencil, sepia, and wash in ink and red; sanguine; inscription at top right.
360 × 459 mm

Provenance: Fondo Mediceo-Lorenese.

BIBLIOGRAPHY: Guasti 1857: 154-164, 208; Ferri 1885: 47; Müntz 1889, I: 447; Fabriczy 1892: 102; *Disegni* 1904, pl. LXXVI; Niccoli 1938: 286; Sanpaolesi 1941, fig. 14; Parker 1956, II: 408, no. 770; Rossi 1956: 128, fig. 1; Prager and Scaglia 1970: 95, fig. 27; Collobi Ragghianti 1973a: 33-34, 114, no. 10, 117, no. 15, 47, fig. 19; Collobi Ragghianti 1973b: 47; Fanelli 1973, II, fig. 244; Collobi Ragghianti 1974: 53; Battisti 1976: 262, fig. 291; Marchini 1977d: 9-13, fig. 1; Marchini 1977c: 23-24; Saalman 1980: 213, fig. 105; Scaglia 1981: 9-10, 13-14, fig. 17; Salvagnini 1983: 105-107, fig. 8; *Léonard de Vinci* 1987: 49, 346, fig. 26.

On the night of 27 January 1601 a bolt of lightning struck the dome of S. Maria del Fiore, severely damaging most of the lantern. Vasari noted that "it seems the heavens are envious, as they continue to hurl fiery arrows upon it all day long" (Marchini 1977c: 24).

It was not the first time that the forces of nature had unleashed their destructiveness on the work of Brunelleschi, who is reported as having said of his dome: "I have defended you from earthquakes, may God guard you from thunderbolts" (Guasti 1857: 212); nor would it be the last time it was struck—at least until 1885, when it was equipped with a more efficient lightning rod (Del Lungo 1990; Rossi 1956).

The damage wrought that January, however, was severe—worse than during the disastrous storm of 1492, which had dislodged the gilded bronze orb set in place on the dome's crown a mere twenty years earlier; that incident had been an omen for the Florentines, foretelling the death of Lorenzo il Magnifico, and ushering in the gruesome era of Savonarola.

In the wake of the new spate of damage, Grand Duke Ferdinando I de' Medici, who was in Livorno at the time, ordered the ageing Bernardo Buontalenti (1523-1608), the painter Alessandro Allori (1535-1607), the then chief of works, and Gherardo Mechini (ca. 1550-1621), a curious technician-cum-bureaucrat employed as architect for the Medici's building works (Salvagnini 1983; Lecchini Giovannoni 1991: 311-312), to ensure that the "desolate" lantern was duly restored "in compliance with its former shape and architecture, without changing anything in the slightest way" (Guasti 1857: 150). Ferdinando instructed the three technicians to draft a joint project on paper and submit it for his approval; in the meantime, the Grand Duke kept in close contact with Buontalenti, who was infirm and confined to his bed, in order to secure his advice and approval.

In order to rebuild the lantern, and make it identical to Brunelleschi's original masterpiece which, in the late mannerist Florence of Buontalenti's day, could not be altered in any way whatsoever, it was necessary to have a visual record of the "old design" and, given the lack of survey drawings or precise scale models, they were obliged to procure them from "among all the draftsmen in Florence" (Guasti 1857: 151). Without doubt, it was this dramatic occurrence that prompted the construction of the official wooden model of the dome, formerly in the Museo dell'Opera, which got damaged in the floods of 1966 (Saalman 1980: 146) and was afterward restored. (see cat. no. 261).

The three technicians duly carried out the Grand Duke's orders to the letter, though the complicated restoration workshop had very little time to complete its task. The new lantern, identical to the one destroyed though somewhat patched up and laden with chains and iron rods (Rossi 1956: 132), was inaugurated on 1 November 1601, "to the great satisfaction and praise of His Highness and of the Florentine populace" (C. Tinghi, manuscript *Diario*, in Florence, Biblioteca Nazionale Centrale, *Capponi* 261, fols. 38r.-v.; op. cit. in Salvagnini 1983: 106-107); the new crowning orb, slightly larger and removable for inspection (as recommended by Buontalenti), was set in place in October 1602.

Credit for this accomplishment is due above all to the younger of the three architects, the industrious Mechini, "ignegnere valentissimo," who acted as works supervisor. According to his contemporary Tinghi, Mechini made "a wooden scaffold 70 *braccia* [ca. 40 m] tall from the lantern

base, right to the crown of the cross; the said scaffold comprised five circular platforms of theretofore unseen beauty and stability, designed with great skill and application" (ibid.).

One of the many representations of Mechini's "ponte stabile e gagliardo" ("daring and stable scaffolding"; Guasti 1857: 154) is this large-format drawing in ink and watercolor, diligently traced out with a straightedge by a confident, expert hand, despite the somewhat approximate perspective and poverty of detail; the drawing was clearly intended for presentation to the demanding patron, as confirmed by the note: "Questo ultimo ponte viene appunto alla palla siche avoler condur la palla bisognia alzare uno altro ponte alto b[raccia] 12 incirca" ("This last scaffolding is for mounting the orb, which, in order to be complete should be raised about 12 *braccia* farther"); this note enables us to date the drawing to the first months of 1601.

Apart from the impressive appearance of the scaffold, which comprised a great many cantilevers, with unbraced uprights (as was the practice), lodged in the outer shell of the dome; three for each segment (Battisti 1973: 257), the building site was of the utmost simplicity, especially when compared with Brunelleschi's. The system in fact required only two elementary hoists, a windlass on the left for raising a bucket, and a Vitruvian trestle (cf. Rusconi 1590: 129).

This was a highly simple, adaptable device that was easy to dismantle and reassemble; here it is mounted on the third level. By means of two pulley blocks and a lewis, a heavy block of stone could be lifted directly to the top (Drachmann 1962). The other details featured in the drawing are a small cabin, lower, right, for stowing tools; a staircase complete with handrail linking the different platform levels (incorrectly drawn); and a sled device for lowering or raising material over the curved dome.

From the early 1800s the drawing was believed to be a record of the scaffolding built by Brunelleschi for building the original lantern. The first to link the drawing with the structural damage of 1601 were Guasti and Karl Parker in 1956 (II: 408, no. 770), though their suggestion was not taken up by later scholars.

On the occasion of the Brunelleschi celebrations of 1977, Giuseppe Marchini—independently and for stylistic reasons, such as the "heavy manneristic handling of the volutes, an aspect inadmissible before mid-sixteenth century" (Marchini 1977a: 10; 1977b)—reached the same conclusions as his British colleague. After examining Guasti's fundamental documentation, he affirmed the drawing to be by the architect Gherardo Mechini, the author of the restoration itself; this attribution was sanctioned by later scholars, with the exception of Scaglia (1981: 13-14) and Saalman (1980: 145, 213), who preferred not to hazard any paternity.

Their research was ignored by the author of the monograph on Mechini (Salvagnini 1983), who uncritically accepted Marchini's excellent thesis, even though he added sufficient documentary data to permit the identification of autograph works by this underrated "architect of His Excellency."

After further in-depth enquiry, it is fair to assert that the circumvoluted, unsure and contorted *ductus* typical of many writings and drawings of Gherardo Mechini do not match the more geometrical hand evinced by this drawing—particularly the annotations, which are quite alien to the penmanship of the Medici technician (in terms of content also), who shows a degree of scholarship superior to the modest levels achieved by Mechini; such training, witness Buontalenti, was no impediment to fine workmanship; nor would it disqualify a person from being appointed architect to the grand duchy.

In absence of any final confirmation of the author of the drawing, it is prudent to limit the attribution of the Uffizi sheet simply to one of the many "huomini da disegno" (draftsmen) of the Florentine milieu known to have commuted between the Medici court and the renowned construction site in the course of 1601.

D.L.

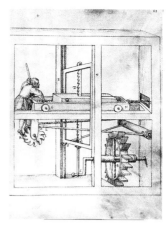

101
UNKNOWN PALATINE ARTIST
Hydraulic Saw
(from Bernardo Puccini, *Disegni e Descrizioni di Mulini, Macchine ecc.*)
ca. 1570-75

Florence, Biblioteca Nazionale Centrale, *Palatino* 1077, [1005.-21,3], fol. 63r.
Pen and ink on parchment, bound in mixed paper and parchment manuscript, unbound into fascicles of fols. 1 + 208 + 3, numbered later, with 222 illustrated plates on parchment, and 21 on paper.
220 × 302 mm

PROVENANCE: Museo di Fisica e Storia Naturale, Florence; Biblioteca Mediceo-Palatina, Florence.

BIBLIOGRAPHY: Rambaldi and Saitta Revignas 1950: 83-85; Klapisch-Zuber 1968, fig. p. 1810; Klapisch-Zuber 1973: 107-108, no. 68; Galluzzi 1980a: 160; Scaglia 1981: 19-20, no. 43, fig. 13; *Laboratorio su Leonardo* 1983: 141, 61; *Léonard de Vinci* 1987: 339, fig. p. 342; Lamberini 1990b: 15, 49-58, figs. 4, 8, 13, 17; Scaglia 1991b, XVII-XIX, no. 4, XX, no. 27, XXII; Lamberini 1992: 144-163; Scaglia 1992: 73-78, 92, 123, 137, 249, 262.

Of all the numerous versions of the hydraulic saw copied in the fifteenth, sixteenth and seventeenth centuries from the original prototype by Francesco di Giorgio (cf. cat. no. 95), this drawing, contained in a Florentine manuscript dating to the early 1570s, is undoubtedly the finest.

In this particular version, the saw, which is driven by a horizontally mounted paddle-wheel, i.e., the archetypal Vitruvian hydraulic wheel (Ferguson 1991, LX), connected to the saw-blade and the trolley on which the block of wood rests to be cut by means of a rod-crank—automatic in all the earlier and later drawings and variants (Scaglia 1981)—is distinguished by the somewhat spectacular inclusion of a treader who, while offering little advantage from the point of view of the mechanics, acts as a kind of human ratchet gear on the cog with curved teeth (left). "Uno che galca in piede sopra i denti della ruota K" (person turning the cog K with his feet) runs the author's caption for this illustration from the manuscript codex on machinery; "Quando la vuol fermare che la non seghi, è mette l'asta LM sopra il rocchetto NM" (when he wants to stop the machine sawing, he shifts the bar LM onto the sprocket NM) (*Codex Palatino*, fol. 62r.).

The author of the manuscript, which was broken up at some date and lacks several parts, is Bernardo Puccini (1521-75), "gentiluomo fiorentino," mathematician, military architect, treatise-writer, and above all a man of the court and a functionary of considerable weight in the Medici administration of public works; Puccini devoted the last five years of his life to this work, left incomplete upon his sudden death in October 1575 (Lamberini 1990b; 1991a: 234, and passim; 1992: 144-163; very debatable dating and attribution in Scaglia 1992: 72-78).

Like his treatises, Puccini's codex—an illustrated catalog of *exempla* complemented by thoughtful explanatory texts—was dedicated to the young sovereign Francesco I de' Medici, the pensive "Principe dello Studiolo," whose multiple interests in scientific matters and experimentation are well documented. The over 200 drawings of mills and other mechanical devices derive mainly from Francesco di Giorgio's prototypes, though he turned also to other sources, some unpublished, especially the manuscript codex of Cosimo Bartoli (Florence, Biblioteca Nazionale Centrale, E.B.16.5.ii); translator of Alberti, though a Florentine, Bartoli resided many years in Venice, and Puccini had used his work on several earlier occasions to great advantage (Lamberini 1990b: 163ff.; 1991a: 223; 1992; Scaglia 1992: 78-82). Puccini's collection, which foreshadows the grand period of interest in machinery of the sixteenth, seventeenth, and eighteenth centuries, and exalts, as with all the devices built expressly for courtly collections, the quantity and spectacularity, rarity and beauty of the subject, stands out from all other coeval examples owing to the superb quality of the drawings, which are executed in pen and ink on parchment by the hand of an artist of great caliber, who was equally skilled with both pen and engraver's tool; under the direction of Puccini, this artist most likely prepared the drawings ready to be engraved and printed, thereby creating a luxurious collector's item, in which the mechanisms and scientific veracity of the objects were unabashedly eclipsed by the theatrical *maraviglia* of appearances.

The anonymous author of the drawings in the Puccini codex, called Unknown Palatine owing to his preoccupation with production for the court, undoubtedly stems from the variegated milieu of Flemish engravers working in Florence under Grand Duke Cosimo I de' Medici and his son Francesco, either at the palazzo itself or in the many *botteghe* set up expressly in the Galleria degli Uffizi (Lamberini 1992: 149-150). Among these Flemish artists, following the valuable indications afforded me by Alessandro Cecchi, to whom I am indebted, the possible candidates are Cornelis Cort (*The Illustrated Bartsch* 1986) and Philips Galle (*The Illustrated Bartsch* 1987), whose assured hand, at once pliant and incisive, and choice of subject matter (human figures, animals, dramatic studies, lively and picturesque scenes, in true Nordic fashion), seems to be behind the marvelous draftsmanship of the machines, with his outstanding Florentine mannerist style (cf. cat. nos. 102-104).   *D.L.*

102
UNKNOWN PALATINE ARTIST
Foundation Pile-Driver
(from Bernardo Puccini, *Disegni e Descrizioni di Mulini, Macchine ecc.*)
ca. 1570-75

Florence, Biblioteca Nazionale Centrale, *Palatino* 1077, [1005.-21.3], fol. 4r.
Pen and ink on parchment; bound in mixed paper and parchment manuscript, in unbound fols. of 1 + 1 208 + 3, numbered later, with 222 plates on parchment and 21 on paper.
220 × 302 mm

PROVENANCE: Museo di Fisica e Storia Naturale, Florence; Biblioteca Mediceo-Palatina, Florence.

BIBLIOGRAPHY: Rambaldi and Saitta Revignas 1950: 83-85; Klapisch-Zuber 1968: 1810; Klapisch-Zuber 1973: 107-108, no. 68; Galluzzi 1980a: 160; Scaglia 1981: 19-20, no. 43; *Laboratorio su Leonardo* 1983: 141; *Léonard de Vinci* 1987; 339; Lamberini 1990b: 15, 49-58, figs. 11-18; Lamberini 1991b: 234, 264-271, 138-146, figs. 4, 8, 13, 17; Scaglia 1991b, XVII-XIX, no. 4, XX, no. 27, XXII; Lamberini 1992: 144-163; Scaglia 1992: 73-78, 92, 123, 137, 249, 262.

When the foundation shafts (usually cut from oak trunks) were particularly large—as was often the case with foundations laid in shallow-water sites such as Venice, or in the construction of bridges and port structures (Binaghi 1993: 130-132)—it became necessary to use pile-drivers mounted on tall strong wooden scaffolds. The efficacy of these devices, as detailed in Alberti's *De re aedificatoria*, lay not so much in their being equipped with hammers, mallets, or rams, as in the ability to strike the pile "with great frequency, because the heavier rams tend to split the wood when they are brought down with violence; whereas the ground inevitably gives way under the frequency of blows" Alberti 1966a, III, iii, 184).

Francesco di Giorgio had also clearly grasped the concept of raining repeated blows, this "constant battery," with regard to the weight of the mallet, and he designed the prototype for this rotary pile-driver, to work "in mare come in terra" (in water and on land); the drawing occurs in both versions of his *Treatise* (*Codex Saluzziano* 148, fols. 48v. and 49r.; and *Codex Ashburnham* 361, fol. 44r.); it is repeated in a boat-mounted version (in which the runged wheel is replaced by a rack system) in the *Opusculum de architectura* (London, British Museum, MS. 197.b.21 [1 and 2], fol. 48v.); this version in fact served as a model for the panel adorning the frieze at the Palazzo Ducale, Urbino.

Francesco di Giorgio's pile-driving device was copied by Cosimo Bartoli and included among the mechanical apparatus in the Palatine codex in the Galleria National Centrale, Florence (E.B.16.5.ii, fol. 71r.); no explanatory caption is provided, but the mechanics of the device are reasonably clear, albeit crudely drafted and with one of its essential features completely misconstrued. Bartoli's design, the main source for Puccini's unfinished treatise on machinery (cf. cat. nos. 101-104), was reproduced with a caption, beginning thus: "La ruota A è girata da uno che sta dentro e con i suoi denti fa girare il rocchetto B, et lo porta seco" (Wheel A is turned by a person from within, and turns a sprocket-wheel B, taking it with it). The sprocket-wheel in turn interacts with the sprockets of the vertical rack C, taking it to the end position; when the wheel A, fitted with teeth for only half its circumference, reaches the smooth section the sprocket-wheel releases the rack, which takes the mallet block crashing downward onto the pile. The faster the operator, the machine's "engine," works the treadwheel, the more frequently the rack and hammer strike the pile.

In copying Bartoli's machine, the anonymous Palatine engraver has misrepresented his master Puccini (though he was not the only one). The treadwheel, it can be seen, is actually without any sprockets at all, and being smooth, could never possibly turn the sprocket-wheel and hence the hammer-rack. Furthermore, the treadwheel would require two upright supports, not one, and hence the entire machine could not function.

While these may have been oversights, the same cannot be said for the "engine," whose direction in the treadwheel is not the correct one for raising the hammer-rack. This misrepresentation stems from Bartoli, who drew the figure in the same position; in his case, however, the treader is a kind of ragamuffin who seems to be working the treadwheel for fun. Here, a splendid bearded figure is bent on this thankless task, earning his daily bread by the sweat of his brow. The picture has gained a dramatic undertone, typical of a Nordic and mannerist outlook, drawn with a highly precise line using what seems more

like a burin than a pen. This only confirms the hypothesis regarding the origins and specialization of this refined anonymous craftsman, who was most likely a Flemish artist working in the Medici court as an engraver (cat. no. 101).   *D.L.*

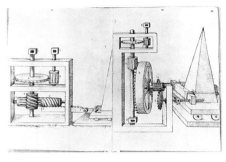

103
UNKNOWN PALATINE
Obelisk-Mover (after designs by Francesco di Giorgio Martini)
(from Bernardo Puccini, *Disegni e Descrizioni di Mulini, Macchine ecc.*)
ca. 1570-75

Florence, Biblioteca Nazionale Central, *Palatino* 1077, [1005.-21,3], fols. 27v.-28r.
Pen and ink on parchment, with traces of pencil; bound down center; from mixed paper and parchment manuscript, in loose fols. of 1 + 208 + 3, numbered later, with 222 prints on parchment and 21 on paper.

PROVENANCE: Museo di Fisica e Storia Naturale, Florence; Biblioteca Mediceo-Palatina, Florence.

BIBLIOGRAPHY: Rambaldi and Saitta Revignas 1950: 83-85; Klapisch-Zuber 1968: 1810; Klapisch-Zuber 1973: 107-108, no. 68; Galluzzi 1980a: 160; Scaglia 1981: 19-20, no. 43; *Laboratorio su Leonardo* 1983: 141; *Léonard de Vinci* 1987: 339; Lamberini 1990b: 15, 49-58, figs. 11-18; Lamberini 1991b: 235, 264-271, 138-146, 4, 8, 13, 17; Scaglia 1991b, XVII-XIX, no. 4, XX, no. 27, XXII; Lamberini 1992: 144-163; Scaglia 1992: 73-78, 92, 123, 137, 249, 262.

In his introduction to the section of the Palatine manuscript on the "traction of heavy loads on a plane" (fol. 24r.), while utilizing virtually the entire body of *tirari* or traction mechanisms described and drawn within the notebooks and treatises of Francesco di Giorgio Martini, as usual mediated through the codex of Cosimo Bartoli (cf. cat. nos. 101-104), Bernardo Puccini opted to refer directly to Vitruvius' *tractorie*, drawing inspiration from the eminent antique source, and supplying the reader with an introductory essay, which, regrettably, has not survived (Lamberini 1992).

The texts that illustrate the working mechanisms of these two *tirari* invented by Martini—as always, expounded in an elemental and pragmatic style rather than going into practical details of use—a certain emphasis is given to the virtual potential of the device, and the desire to derive general rules from specific cases. This attitude is evident from the passage that closes the description of the *tirare* in fol. 28r.: "Quanto più si accresce ruota, rocchetti e vite, tanto più si ha facile il tirare, sebben si fa più tardo" (The greater the number of wheels, sprockets and screws, the easier it is to haul, though it will take longer) (*Disesgni ...*, fol. 24v.), and provides clear proof of the fact that Puccini, with his training as a mathematician, took account of the question of friction.

Leaving aside the observations expressed in the texts, one notices that, as represented in the drawings themselves, the *tirari* could never have been made to work. The first (fol. 27v.) with a worm screw and rack, is an enhanced version of Martini's prototype in his first treatise (*Codex Saluzziano* 148, fol. 51r.); the other device (fol. 28r.), composed of screws, cogs and sprockets, is derived from the *Opusculum de architectura* (London, British Museum, MS. 197.b.21, fol. 22r.). The two drawings are presented alongside each other, devoid of explanatory texts, in Cosimo Bartoli's treatise (Florence, Biblioteca Nazionale Centrale, E.B.16.5.ii, fols. 120r.-v.), from which, under Puccini's direction, our anonymous Palatine artist dutifully duplicated in a fine copy, but without correcting the flagrant defects present in Francesco di Giorgio's original: the incorrect representation of the thread of the kinematic pairs, which in order to work would have to be helical (as first correctly drawn by Ramelli for his treatise on mechanics in 1588). To make matters worse, the artist added errors of his own: in the *tirare* in fol. 28r., he misconstrued the transmission mechanism (and was not the only one to do so, see Lamberini 1991b: 266); he arranges the sprocket and cogwheel system I and H on different planes to the sprocket G, and fails to show (as Bartoli did, albeit in rough and erroneously), the rear of the screws connected to the horizontal jib, which, in order to work would have to have a left-hand thread, and the other a right-hand thread.

What we have, then, are spectacular but "impossible" machines, destined exclusively for the court's amusement. However, as these appealing machines were repeatedly proposed, a decade later, in 1585, Domenico Fontana, capitalizing on the engineering experience of his predecessors and contemporaries, successfully carried out the utopian undertaking coveted by the popes for 130 years, namely, to transport and erect the colossal obelisk of Julius Caesar in the square before St. Peter's (Fontana 1978; D'Onofrio 1965).

The pencil lines noticeable at the critical point of the parchment illustration suggest that someone examined the machine and noted the mechanical error—and though there is no proof, it would be nice to think that it was Puccini himself. *D.L.*

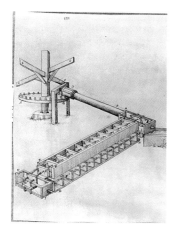

104
Unknown Palatine Artist
Device for Extracting Water from Foundations, known as the "Macchina di Treviso"
(from Bernardo Puccini, *Disegni e Descrizioni di Mulini, Macchine ecc.*)
ca. 1570-75

Pen and ink on parchment; from mixed parchment and paper manuscript, in loose fols. of 1 + 208 + 3, numbered at later date, comprising 222 illustrations on parchment and 21 on paper.

Provenance: Museo di Fisica e Storia Naturale, Florence; Biblioteca Mediceo-Palatina, Florence.

Bibliography: Rambaldi and Saitta Revignas 1950: 83-85; Klapisch-Zuber 1968: 1810; Klapisch-Zuber 1973: 107-108, no. 68; Galluzzi 1980a: 160; Scaglia 1981: 19-20, no. 43; *Laboratorio su Leonardo* 1983: 141; *Léonard de Vinci* 1987: 339; Lamberini 1990b: 15, 49-58, figs. 11-18; Lamberini 1991b: 223, 234-235, 264-271, 138-146, figs. 4, 8, 13, 17; Scaglia 1991b: XVII-XIX, no. 4, XX, no. 27, XXII; Lamberini 1992: 144-163; Scaglia 1992: 73-78, fig. 25.

"This device is for removing water from foundations or ditches in quantity and at great speed; the wheel AB is turned by four horses tethered to the beams C." Thus Bernardo Puccini begins his description of the machine in question (fol. 133v.), the drawing of which, entrusted to the elegant hand of our "Anonimo Palatino" working under his direction, is as usual taken from the codex of Cosimo Bartoli in the Biblioteca Nazionale Centrale, Florence (E.B.16.5.ii, fol. 23v.; cf. Lamberini 1991b: 223; Scaglia 1992, fig. 25).

The mechanism of this particular continuous pumping device, derived from Vitruvius' bucket waterwheel is fairly simple and is made evident in the illustration. The cog-and-sprocket wheel pair turns the drive shaft, winding round a second sprocket wheel (hidden from view), the paternoster, made up of small wooden boards held together by an iron chain that runs in a conduit, so that: "as these boards pass through the conduit," writes Puccini, "they carry off the water, and when they reach the top of the sprocket-wheel they turn over and pass below the conduit and over the board LM, whence they return" (*Disegni ...*, fol. 133v.).

Puccini's bland, technical description of the mechanics is nicely offset by Bartoli's lively illustration, which offers historical data and measurements, completely disregarded by Puccini. "This machine was made not long ago by the Venetians to fortify Treviso—though of Florentine origin, Bartoli was resident in Venice; in order to construct a bastion they laid the foundations in water, which, despite using a great many pumps, they were unable to get the better of" (E.B.16.5.ii, fol. 23v.). Here Bartoli is referring to the radical works on the city's enceinte, designed and undertaken at the start of the century by Fra Giovanni Giocondo, an illustrious military architect in the employ of the Venetian Republic (Fontana 1988: 72-73). The diameter of the wheel, continues Bartoli, was around 6 *braccia* (3 1/2 meters), and to each of the four crank handles, 6 *braccia* long, was tethered a horse.

This dry and intellectual approach—typical of the climate of the Florentine court, shot though with an experimental and theoretical vein—characterizes the entire treatise. Conceived in the 1570s and interrupted by the death of its author Puccini, the treatise was carried to completion by the thirst for technical *cognoscenza* of his sovereign, Francesco I de' Medici (see cat. no. 101). That dry tone, while not exactly a contradiction, contrasts with the effective professional aspirations and building experience acquired by this Florentine gentleman in his years as military architect and superintendent of the Uffizi.

In the course of his tenure as overseer at the Uffizi building site, Puccini was also involved in the construction of the S. Trinita bridge, which was being built in Florence in the mid-1560s to designs by Bartolomeo Ammannati (Lamberini 1990b: 264-265). In September 1565 Cosimo Bartoli sent Francesco de' Medici a scale model from Venice of the Treviso water pump so that it could be constructed on-site to serve for the excavation of the foundations for the bridge, a task that was proving highly difficult for the architect and other site technicians, among whose ranks was Alfonso Parigi the Older, brother-in-law of Ammannati and conscientious executant of his projects (*Taccuino* 1975: 11-16).

With his incomplete treatise, in which the Martinian and Venetian machines derived from Bartoli were complemented by the Vitruvian devices recently published by Daniele Barbaro in his erudite translation of *De architectura* (Lamberini 1991b: 240; 1992: 153-154), Puccini helped foster that distinctive channel of exchange between Venetian and Florentine technical circles. This legacy was soon to be taken up by another *gentiluomo* and military engineer of Florentine descent, Bonaiuto Lorini, also in Venetian employ, who in the first edition of his treatise on defense works presented a "device for pumping out water in quantity, and draining off swamplands"; this was the updated version of the much earlier "macchina di Treviso" (Lorini 1596, V, 10: 197). Lorini, who worked in open opposition to his fellow citizens and mentors (Lamberini 1990b: 130-140), supplied a detailed

operations guide to this pumping device, expressing his personal disapproval (in anticipation of Galileo) of the continued practice of representing celebratory objects that were unable to function whatsoever. *D.L.*

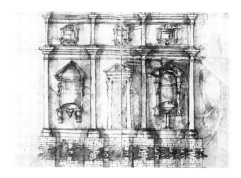

105
Unknown Florentine Draftsman
Jacks for Raising the Facade of a Building
(from Anonymous, *Disegni di Macchine Diverse*)
second half 16th cent.

Florence, Biblioteca Nazionale Centrale, *Codex Magliabechiano*, cl. XVIII, cod. 3, fols 35v.-36r.
Ink on paper with touches of pen, in paper codex of 46 recto and verso quarto folios, comprising only drawings.
179 × 270 mm

Provenance: Libreria di Antonio Magliabechi, Florence.

Bibliography: Klapisch-Zuber 1973: 108, no. 68; Galluzzi 1980a: 161, fig. 4.30, 162; Lamberini 1991c: 233; Lamberini 1992: 153, no. 27; Scaglia 1992: 122-124, 249.

The nameless Florentine author of this interesting codex of drawings, datable to the second half of the sixteenth century (the watermark on several sheets, close to Briquet 6273 [II, 361], implies late 1560s, cf. also Scaglia 1992: 123), was familiar with building construction and also with the carving of semiprecious stones (an occupation that began in Florence under Cosimo I de' Medici, and burgeoned in the grand duchy of his sons Francesco and Ferdinando). This is demonstrated by the designs of machinery in watercolor, drawn in confident, masterly strokes that owe much to the prototypes of Brunelleschi (cat. no. 106) and Francesco di Giorgio Martini, which had filtered down to this generation via copies made by fifteenth- and sixteenth-century followers. These pictured appliances for shaping and cutting semiprecious stones; numerous machines employed on building sites, such as cranes and winches, traction and lifting machines, and hydraulic devices such as water-scoops, garden pumps, and watermills.

While some of these machines are evident copies of widely circulated prototypes that were well-known to sixteenth-century architects and technicians, and had become stereotyped (cf. cat. no. 106), other machines testify to the anonymous engineer's personal interest in building site activities, and this drawing is a case in point. It shows a highly original method for raising the facade of a building by means of jacks; the operation is seemingly improbable, but was in fact successfully put in practice by engineers of caliber from the fifteenth to seventeenth century: the legendary Bolognese engineer Aristotele Fioravanti, who in 1455 shifted the Torre Magione in his hometown, and transferred an entire building in Rome, while elsewhere up and down the peninsula he was responsible for setting walls upright and moving buildings (*Arte Lombarda* 1976, nos. 44-45); Francesco di Giorgio Martini, who in 1482 devised the system for raising the roof of the church of S. Francesco in Siena; Buontalenti; Ammannati; and later, in the seventeenth century, Alfonso Parigi il Giovane, an underrated figure in Galileo's circle who, in 1638-40 restored equilibrium to the entire structure of Brunelleschi's Palazzo Pitti, which had suffered fire damage, by cutting away part of the "muraglia antica" and straightening the facade by means of metal tie-beams, deftly concealed in the masonry of the mezzanine stories (Baldinucci 1975: 54-55).

The jacks that were employed in this drawing are, correctly, of two different kinds and fully workable. The first three on the left are screw-jacks on a *puntazza* or pile shoe, and presumably made from metal. The other three are of the *doppia stampa* or die-and-housing variety, as illustrated in Francesco di Giorgio's *Codicetto* in the Vatican (fol. 167v.); the dies of both types house the levers used for turning them. This part of the operation was particularly delicate: under the punctilious supervision of the chief architect-engineer, each jack turned with the perfect timing and orchestration essential for the correct running of a construction site.   *D.L.*

106
UNKNOWN FLORENTINE DRAFTSMAN
Building Winch (left)
Mobile Brunelleschian Winch (right)
(from Anonymous, *Disegni di Macchine Diverse*)
second half 16th cent.

Florence, Biblioteca Nazionale Centrale, *Codex Magliabechiano*, cl. XVIII, cod. 3, fols. 41v.-42r.
Ink on paper, with touches of pen; quarto format sheets in paper codex, comprising drawings only, of 46 recto and verso sheets.
179 × 270 mm

PROVENANCE: Libreria di Antonio Magliabechi, Florence.

BIBLIOGRAPHY: Klapisch-Zuber 1973: 108, no. 68; Galluzzi 1980a: 161, fig. 4.30, 162; Lamberini 1991c: 233; Lamberini 1992: 153, no. 27; Scaglia 1992: 122-124, fig. 60, 249.

The machinery invented by Filippo Brunelleschi for the building site for the dome of Florence Cathedral enjoyed unbounded success throughout the Renaissance; on the contrary, in the course of the sixteenth century, when Florence finally ceded its technological primacy to Rome, in an upsurge of "nationalistic" pride, the memory of Brunelleschi's signal achievements experienced a revival through the didactic work of such figures as Giorgio Vasari the Younger (Lamberini 1991c: 238), and was put into historical context. There was an increase in the appreciation and reproposal of Brunelleschi's inventions, perhaps filtered through the studies of the Sienese architect Francesco di Giorgio and the engineers of the "first Italian generation" (Galluzzi 1991b: 184-190).

The examples are many, and can be easily identified in the drawings, notebooks, and codices of the Sangallo and Volpaia families, and in those of Bartoli, Alberti, Saminiati, Strada, Puccini, Vasari the Younger, as well as many other authors who remain nameless (Lamberini 1991c: 229-238 and passim).

That set of anonymous artists includes the unknown Florentine author of this Magliabechi codex, who on fols. 41v.-42r. drew two windlasses that are strongly imitative of Brunelleschi's machines. The first, pictured in the process of raising a hewn boulder derives from Brunelleschi's three-speed horizontal windlass with built-in

reverse gear, which in the records for the dome construction was called "cholla centrale."

The other device featured here is a reworking of Brunelleschi's second windlass, the "secret" windlass, referred to as "edificio II" (Scaglia 1992: 123). In either case here the mechanism has been misinterpreted: in the first, consisting of a simple sprocket and cogwheel system (in bronze or wood?) where cogs set at 90° replace the pegs of Brunelleschi's original, composed of bearings or rollers mounted on a drive-wheel and rotating on their own axis, clearly represented here by the light winching device with roller-cogs that appears in Bonaccorso Ghiberti's *Zibaldone* (fols. 95r., 98v.), and in the wheel of the second winch on fol. 42v. [recto?], which however is missing the hole for the rope to pass through. As presented here, the two winches would not work. In the first, the two ropes lifting the block wind round two separate cylinders, making the mechanics unfeasible, as the ropes would therefore move at different speeds. Similarly, the mechanics of the second hoist are hardly practical, even though the artist has drawn a fine ratchet wheel in the foreground with traditional Tuscan-style curved cogs to ensure proper meshing, comparable to Leonardo's impeccable ratchet brake mechanisms, proving the fact that his technical know-how owed more to the miniature systems peculiar to the making of timepieces and luxury objects (Lamberini 1991: 233), than to the construction of the kind of heavy-duty *alzari* invented in the Quattrocento, copied and recopied until, by the last decades of the sixteenth century, they had become purely symbolic, mythical machines of a glorious past.   *D.L.*

107
FOUNDRY OF ALESSIO BECCAGUTO
BERNARDINO ARRIGONI (attrib.)
Model for Tiles
1554

Mantua, Museo Civico di Palazzo Te, Collezione Gonzaghesca, old inv. no. 11483, Palazzo Ducale
Bronze.
57.9 × 28.9 × 2.1 cm

BIBLIOGRAPHY: Ozzola 1950: 72; Mozzarelli 1987: 62-65; Negrini 1984: 183; *Mantova. La Sezione Gonzaghesca...* 1987: 234; Bertani: *Missiva...* 19.09.1565.

Among the standard bronze models commissioned in 1554 by Guglielmo Gonzaga of Mantua, probably from the foundry of Alessio Beccaguto, there is this example for roof tiles consisting of an isosceles trapezoid with four rods having a rectangular section. This model bears a double inscription: "*imbricum moduli legitimum exemplar 1554*" and "il modello da coppi MDXXXXXIIII."

With this standardization operation, the legal value of which is attested by the Latin inscription (*moduli legitimum*) and which had its roots in the overall reorganization of the Gonzaga state fostered by Margherita Paleologo, the government sought to have direct control over the brick industry. At that time this was located near Mantua in "four brick-kilns on the Mincio," as Giovan Battista Bertani, prefect of the ducal buildings, reported.

This regulation, which was obtained by means of this simple bronze trapezial model and pertained to the dimensions of *coppi* (curved over-tiles) in the Italian inscription, and more generally to those of *imbrices* (flat under-tiles) in the Latin one, allowed state officials to immediately

recognize foreign products so that customs duty could be charged. Moreover, it was a guarantee of the quality of the products of the local brickworks; these were carefully stamped in accordance with a practice introduced to Northern Italy in Roman times and continued during the Middle Ages. In addition, this standardization of the tiles ensured a certain degree of uniformity in the distribution of weight on the roof, avoiding the danger that excessive loading might occur where tiles of larger dimensions were concentrated.   *Ferruccio Canali*

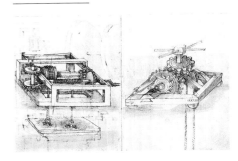

108
FOUNDRY OF ALESSIO BECCAGUTO
BERNARDINO ARRIGONI (attrib.)
Model for Bricks
1554

Mantua, Museo Civico di Palazzo Te, Collezione Gonzaghesca, old inv. no. 11479, Palazzo Ducale
Bronze.
39.3 × 17.4 cm

BIBLIOGRAPHY: Vitruvius, Amati ed. 1829-30: 41-42; Alberti 1966a: 144-150; Francesco di Giorgio Martini 1985: 83; Cesariano 1969: XXXIIII; Bertani: *Missiva...* 30.09.1556; Ozzola 1950: 72; Bertani 1558; Vignola 1562; Palladio 1570; Scamozzi 1615; Negrini 1984: 183; *Mantova. La Sezione Gonzaghesca...* 1987: 235; Adam 1984: 64; *Giulio Romano* 1989: 223, 370-374; Cairoli Giuliani 1990: 152-160.

Consisting of a parallelepiped with four sides, this bronze mold, which is kept in the Museo del Palazzo Ducale in Mantua, is evidence of the particular importance that various Renaissance governments attached to the standardization and classification according to size of the bricks produced in the different states. The importance that must have been given in Mantua to these special dimensions is demonstrated by the fact that the end of this standard mold is decorated with small semicircles, chains and festoons linking a series of heraldic devices including the coats of arms of the Paleologo, in homage to the regency of Margherita, Cardinal Ercole, who was responsible for the rationalization of the Gonzaga civil sector, and the city of Mantua. On one end, in the largest panel surrounded by a frame comprised of three thin strips, among rich decoration, is the inscription "il modello da mattoni MDXXXXIIII"; on the other end is the Latin equivalent: "*laterum moduli legitimum exemplar 1554.*"

In this case, and in that of the model for roof tiles from Mantua, a custom dating from the second century B.C. in the Po Valley, according to which standard measures were provided for bricks and tiles, was perpetuated in the Gonzaga state; at the brickworks these consisted of wooden molds (copied from the official model) divided into a number of compartments, or, as in this sixteenth century exemplar, having just one.

Already in Roman times both Pliny (35, 170-175) and Vitruvius (II, viii), proposed that the dimensions of bricks should be based principally on three types of Greek origin: the Lydian brick, one *piede* in length and half a *piede* in width (29.6 × 14.8 cm), and having a ratio of approximately 1:2 between the ends and the sides (as in the case of the bronze model from Mantua), even though in Roman brick production preference was usually given to the square form which was then divided into smaller rectangular and triangular bricks; the *tetradoron* or *pedale*, four *palmi* in length, forming a square *piede* (29.6 × 29.6 cm); lastly the *pentadoron* of five *palmi* (37 × 37 cm).

But even in antiquity production was much more varied than the above classification, with *bessali* (20 × 20 cm), *sesquipedali* (45 × 45 cm) and *bipedali* (60 × 60 cm), while the *manubriato* (literally "with handles") brick (30 × 45 cm) was common in the Po Valley. Thus, there was a wide range of sizes that was considerably extended by political particularism in the Middle Ages, so that almost every town had its own type of brick, the only size limit being that of manageability, and this diversity still existed in the Renaissance.

Even though these were not respected in practice, Vitruvius' guidelines continued to be of fundamental importance for theory and exegesis in architecture during the Renaissance. This included, for example, Leon Battista Alberti's *De re aedificatoria* (II, x), the combined translation and treatise by Francesco di Giorgio Martini of the *Codex [Vitruvius] Magliabechiano* and, above all, the perceptive commentary by Cesare Cesariano that was intended to supplement the rules laid down in *De architectura*. "From the cubic quadrilateral form likewise [the bricks] will be produced and cut out; as models for the manufacture of different types they are well known, not only to architects ... but also to brickmakers, who know how to mold them. ... [The] *didoron* is a *piede* in length ... but, even though Vitruvius did not specify it, I believe the width of this brick should be one *palmo*" (II, iii).

Thus, in the Renaissance, both at the theoretical and legislative levels, there was standardization of the sizes of bricks. Where this was imposed by law, the dimensions of the bricks were inevitably established within the state by an approved measure, as may be inferred from a letter written by Giovan Battista Bertani in Mantua a few years after the casting of the bronze model in 1554: "In the side of the wall containing this doorframe I have seen Master Copino start to make a hollow in order to construct a joint with this wall ... this joint will be made of 4 ends [of bricks]"; according to the dimensions of the bronze model, this must have been approximately 17.4 × 4 cm (= 69.6 cm).

Thus, the standardization of building materials such as bricks (these played a major role in the city's architecture, even though they were usually plastered over) that seems to have taken place in Mantua around the middle of the sixteenth century could not only have been the result of political and administrative requirements. However, this standardization of materials and sizes, which was a sort of legislative forerunner of what was to take place a few years later thanks to Vignola, Palladio, and Scamozzi, with greater regulation of all building materials and procedures, ranging from the exposition of the precepts in the exemplary atlas of the *Regola delli cinque ordini* to the wide-ranging treatment of the *Idea dell'architettura universale*. Commissioned by the Gonzaga, the latter operation found in Giovan Battista Bertani—himself a standardizer, on a theoretical level with his *Oscuri e difficili passi* and, on a practical level, with the facade of his own house—an illustrious source of inspiration who played an active role in the cultural developments of the mid-sixteenth century.

Besides, Mantuan artistic circles must have taken an interest in the techniques and structure of building around 1550, that is after various types of brickwork had been analyzed by Giulio Romano and his assistants in the Sala dei Giganti in the Palazzo del Te, in an esthetic study of bricks, creating a balance between architectural forms and building techniques.

Ferruccio Canali

109

FOUNDRY OF ALESSIO BECCAGUTO
BERNARDINO ARRIGONI (attrib.)
Measure of Length Corresponding to a Mantuan "braccio"
1554

Mantua, Museo Civico di Palazzo Te, Collezione Gonzaghesca, old inv. no. 11488, Palazzo Ducale
Bronze, 58.7 × 1.8 cm

BIBLIOGRAPHY: Vitruvius, Amati ed. 1829-30: 78, 85; Filarete 1972: 21-23; Francesco di Giorgio Martini 1967; 1985: 83; Serlio 1559; Bertani: *Missiva...* 19.09.1565; *Missiva...* 14.07.1566; Palladio 1980; Serlio 1978; Martini 1883, see entries for *Firenze, Mantova, Milano*; Bertolotti 1890: 51; Ozzola 1950: 71; *Mantova. La Sezione Gonzaghesca...* 1987: 233; Gelardi 1993: 94.

This bronze unit of linear measure, corresponding to a *braccio* of 58.7 cm, consists of a rod having a rectangular section with two brackets and a ring at the ends; two sides bear relief decorations of rings and a bilingual inscription which evidently specified standard dimensions for the local intendants of architecture and building workers: "*mensurae qua muros agros et lignea / quaecumque metiaris legis exemplar*"; "*Il braccio da oncie per misurar / terra muri et legni 1554*" (The *braccia* divided into *oncie* for measuring / land, walls and wood 1554). Besides, the Latin inscription was intended to stress that the measure—*metiaris legis exemplar*—had legal validity for the whole of the Gonzaga state, which was thus characterized by a system of measurements distinct from those of the neighboring states, as well as the typical roof-tiles and bricks.

Moreover, this bronze Mantuan *braccio* can be viewed as but one example of a procedure that must, in fact, have been widespread and was based on architectural theory and design, the construction of buildings which then became influential models and building practice itself.

In fact, Vitruvius, having proposed the design of the buildings and their ornaments through modular proportions, thus avoiding the need to give precise measurements, stipulated that, in the event of unusual spatial dimensions or heights, the criterion of design *per partes* should be applied. This involved the subdivision of the specific dimensions, which could be expressed quantitatively in parts and then distributed among the various moldings or members. Vitruvius, whose example was followed by Alberti with the same twofold design procedure based on modules and measurements, expressed these dimensions in *piedi* (*pedes*), as in the case of the different division of columns measuring between fifteen and over sixty *piedi* in height. Also in relation to this method of designing buildings, both according to measured parts and unmeasured modules, Francesco di Giorgio Martini asserted that in his treatise he wanted to show the reader "measurements and *perfetioni* [modules] [of buildings]," using, in the manner of Vitruvius, for the measurements, the usual *piè*. Already in ca. 1460 Filarete had predicted what was to become a central feature of architectural theory and practice in the sixteenth century: the abandonment of the old *piede* or *pes* and its replacement with units of measurement that, while they varied from town to town, were based on the Renaissance *braccio*. This is what Filarete affirmed in his treatise, postulating a close link between the old *piede* and the new *braccio*: "they [the ancients] multiplied [the size of] the head by three. ... Man has no other member which is closer in length to this

[found] unit of measurement, and if you measure your arm [It. *braccio*] in the way I have suggested, clenching your fist, you will find three of these heads, yet this unit of measurement was called *braccio*. This *braccio* includes six types of measurement and rather like the *libra* it is divided into twelve parts which are called *oncie* and in some places are called *polisi* [*pollici*, i.e., inches]. It is also divided into eight parts ... [and then in six, four, three and two parts]. ... Thus in each country there are units of measurement that vary according to the place and what is being measured. ... Yet another unit of measurement is called *piè*, which is little used, although it survives in some places, and this *piè* measures two clenched fists, in other words four fingers placed together and the fifth outstretched" (I, 21-23).

Thus there was a variety of uses for the units of measurement referred to by Sebastiano Serlio, who in the fourth book of *L'Architettura* (1537) aligned himself with Vitruvius' tenets of proportion linked to the size of the module ("the measurement of the size [of the column] at the base": p. 127v.); on the other hand in the third book of 1540, which regarded the antiquities of Rome, he asserts that for the measurement of the Temple of Peace he used the *braccio*, half of which is represented (23.2 × 2 = 46.4 cm in the 1559 edition, a copy of which also belonged to Palladio, p. 21). In the third book Serlio also affirmed that he had used, as a unit of measurement for the palace on Monte Camillo, a *braccio*, a quarter of which was reproduced (1584 ed., p. 86v., 14.4 × 4 = 57.6 cm); for the Antonine Baths he used a "modern *braccio*, a third of which will be here next to the building" (1584 ed., p. 91, 18.1 × 3 = 54.3 cm). Lastly, for the Baths of Diocletian he stated that the "line below is a third of the old *piede*" (1584 ed., p. 96, 10.9 × 3 = 32.7 cm), in other words a third of the *piede* which in the seventh book, a pattern-book for villas, palaces and other buildings, is the basis of all the new designs produced by Serlio himself. But such diversity of units of measurement, which was found not only in the treatises but also according to the place and what was being measured (for example: in Florence the *braccio* for land was 55.12 cm in length, the one for cloth and buildings 58.3 cm; in Milan the mercantile *braccio* measured 59.49 cm; in Mantua the mercantile *braccio* was 63.79 cm in length, the *piede* for land 46.68 cm), could not fail to cause enormous problems at both practical and theoretical levels, especially with regard to the comprehension of the instructions provided and the use of correct procedures on building sites.

Andrea Palladio must have been well aware of these problems when he wrote in 1570: "It should be known that when dividing and measuring the orders I have avoided using fixed units of measurement that are characteristic of certain cities, such as the *braccio*, *piede*, or *palmo*, knowing that there are as many units of measurement as there are cities ... but following Vitruvius' example ... I will use as a module the diameter of the column at its base" (I: 16).

However, the specific unit of measurement could not remain wholly unrelated to the measurement of ancient buildings carried out by Palladio himself, even in the light of the uniqueness of the units of measurement which was unknown to Serlio and was applied systematically.

So it was that in this variegated technical and theoretical panorama, the introduction in 1554 of the sample *braccio* to Mantua must have permitted a greater degree of certainty in architectural design in the Gonzaga state, especially with regard to the measurements. Thus, Giovan Battista Bertani, the leading ducal architect at the time, must have been able to benefit from this development, avoiding all ambiguity or misunderstanding regarding his buildings, purchases and measurement of buildings on behalf of the state administrators: "There is no lack of solicitude regarding the requirements of the building, which is now two *braccia* higher than the church" (Bertani, 19.09.1565); "three *capimaestri* have asked me, as their last price, five lire and eight *soldi* for a *braccio* of this [marble] cornice" (Bertani, 14.07.1566).

Ferruccio Canali

Instruments
Florence, Museo dell'Opera
di S. Maria del Fiore

I *Modani*: Template Drawings
Tracy E. Cooper

View of the fabbrica *dell'Opera del Duomo di Firenze,* modani.

In speaking of *disegno*, Vasari notes that it is most crucial for the art of architecture, since architecture's designs are created only of lines—*profili*—"the beginning and the end of that art" (Bettarini and Barocchi 1966, *Vite*, I-I: 112, ch. XV, "il principio e la fine di quell'arte"). Everything else follows from these lines, Vasari maintains, such as the models of wood that were derived to serve as a guide to the stonecutters and masons. The category of models, however, with which this essay is concerned, *i modani*, or template drawings, seem eligible to be considered as *disegno*, expressing the idea formed in the mind of the artist through line. Yet this is the only type of model to be regarded universally throughout the history of architecture as an indispensable construction guide. The examina-

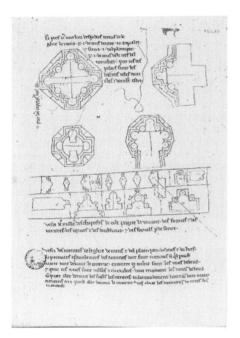

Drawings of moldings for Reims Cathedral Paris, Bibliothèque National, ms. fr. 19093, fol. 32r.

tion of a type of object at once so utilitarian as rarely to be preserved, much less exhibited, may provide the link between theory and practice and may also represent the most direct means of transmission from the mind of the architect to those executing the work.

Modani most often are thought of as being drawn to provide a cut-out template for stonecutters to follow in carving ornamental details. Yet this definition does not capture the range of drawings and functions possible within this category of model (and which can be seen in this section of the exhibition). Terminology in the Renaissance reflects some of this variety. They were referred to in Central Italy as *modani*, and in North Italy as *sagome*; they may loosely be called *profili*, but this could refer equally to drawings of profiles not cut out; they were sometimes generically called *modelli*, although these usually would be three-dimensional detail models.

Terminology of architectural drawing employed by the ancient Greeks was influential to the categories of theorists from Vitruvius to Vasari. Three of these terms can be associated with the execution of architectural details;

anagrapheus and *hypographe* with two-dimensional drawing practices, and *paradeigma* with a three-dimensional form, or model. (The latter term is found in reference to full-size detail models, of capitals, for instance, and eventually to models of buildings, thus referring to other categories of models represented in the exhibition.) Evidence seems to suggest that in pre-Hellenistic Greece various graphic means were possible in the creation and communication of architectural ornament, with *anagrapheus* most closely approximating our notion of a template design furnished by the architect, most often applied to a complex stone molding, and *hypographe* perhaps referring to the rendering of a full-size profile on a surface at the work site, such as a wall or floor (still visible at Didyma, Priene, Pergamon, etc.). Echoes of both of these methods can be found in medieval practice, even given its new vocabulary of ornament, and into the Renaissance as well. J.J. Coulton has argued that the Greek architect required only the rules of proportion, written specifications, and full-size renderings of architectural details which were created only during the execution of a building (1977: 51-73; and 1985: 103-122). These renderings were "not just a mason's drawing which repeats a design worked out elsewhere, for the visible modifications to the initial profile show sucessive stages of design," and thus a part of the architect's creative process (Coulton 1985: 105, after Loren Haselberger).

In the Renaissance, a vital component of an architect's education lay in drawing after the remains of classical architecture, generally plans and details, as few elevations survived intact (Ackerman 1964: 9). Accustomed to the syntax of classical vocabulary, the architect could turn the skills of recording into those of invention. The Vitruvian concepts of ornament and proportion as governing the beauty of architecture ensured the attention to detail that is accorded to the Renaissance architect. The harmony of a building and its proportions as a whole would be summarized in the parts of architectural ornament. It was held, from Filarete to Michelangelo, that the true architect could only be one who had mastered the human figure, the anatomy of the orders. *Modani* remained not only "the *only* drawings *required* for the construction phase," but also fertile fields for displaying the erudition and invention of the architect (Saalman 1959: 103, my italics; many examples are given in Goldthwaite 1980: 377). Filippo Brunelleschi jealously guarded his, making his models "without the ornaments—capital types, architraves, friezes, entablatures, and so on... as he was concerned that whoever would make the model should not discover his every secret" (Saalman 1970: 116-177, "sanza or-

namenti o modi di capitelli o d'architravi, fregi et cornici etc... che lo avessi caro, perche chi facieva nel modello none intendessi ogni suo segreto"). Such a value placed on the individual association of the master with his template designs represented a long tradition of craft secrecy. In the medieval period, the high regard the template assumed in the building process for its association with the hand of the master—as a product of his creation, and not simply belonging to the working materials—is illustrated by the fact that it was considered his property and not that of the project (unlike plans, for instance; see Harvey 1975: 120). Creating and communicating architectural ornament through full-scale profiles drawn or incised on a surface at the site and cut templates distributed to stonemasons continued into the Renaissance in Italy. The materials for cut templates were expanded to include paper, which superceded parchment and became the primary support for the architect's rendering, as evidenced by the examples included in this exhibition. The cartoon or cut-out paper template would be transferred (see cat. no. 117 for transfer marks) or traced onto a firmer support, usually wood planks or thin sheets of metal such as tin ("fogli stagniati," see cat. no. 114). Brunelleschi even praises the turnip (*rape grande*, Saalman 1970: 93) as a material for models! Alberti provides a prescription that combines the site profile and wood template when he describes columns and their ornaments (Book VI, xiii): "on the Pavement, or upon the flat Side of a Wall which is proper for the Drawing [of] your Design, draw a strait Line, of the Length which you intend to give the Column, which is perhaps as yet in the Quarry ... this will make in your Design what we called the Outline of the Column, and by this Line you may make a Model of Wood by which your Masons may shape and finish the Column itself" (Rykwert 1955: 131; Orlandi and Portoghesi 1966: 526, "si taglierà una sottile tavola, da servir di modello ai tagliapietre," 527, "tabula gracilis deformabitur, qua fabri lapicidae"). It may be that the most significant changes came not in the development of new technology in producing architectural details, but rather in elevating the role of the architect in the design process through graphic invention. Michelangelo's drawing style stands as a paradigm for a type of *modano* designated here as a study profile (see cat. no. 111, CB 92A), in which the delineation of classical ornament is transformed in the creative process, bases and pedestals traced out across the sheet, one finally being cut out for further consideration. Admiring, yet somewhat perplexed by Michelangelo's departure from classical models, Vasari termed the beautiful profiles of moldings designed for S. Lorenzo in Florence, and in Rome at the Palazzo Farnese and St. Peter's, the new Composite order—"Perche niuno può negare che questo nuovo ordine composto, avendo da Michelangelo tanta perfezione ricevuto, non possa andar al paragone degli altri" (Bettarini and Barocchi 1966, *Vite*, I-I: 65, chap. III). In addition to the study profile, there are examples of the control that Michelangelo exercised over all phases of the design process of his ornament: from original profiles, consisting of the cut-out paper template (see cat. no. 113), to the copy profiles, that were needed in the workshop to maintain an accurate record of the templates given to the stonecutters (see cat. no. 112), and even site profiles, such as the *disegni murali* at S. Lorenzo. Similar practices can be seen in the organization of the Sangallo workshop in Rome under Antonio the Younger; his training as an architect included employment at St. Peter's, one of the largest *fabbriche*. His *modano* for Raphael of the monumental interior pilasters demonstrates both study after the antique (the Pantheon) and prowess in executing a large-scale original profile (see cat. no. 116). The efforts of his workshop were recorded in copy profiles which are extant for a number of projects. The architect's control over the execution of architectural ornament grew with greater adherence to the classical vocabulary. In northern Italy, master stonecutters continued to play a large role well into the sixteenth century, in the strong tradition of Lombard sculptor-carvers. Andrea Palladio broke with this division in his building projects and provided *sagome* to be followed (see cat. no. 118). Howard Burns has remarked on the absence of detail drawings from Palladio's own projects in *I Quattro Libri*, where only the ancient orders are represented (1973: 179-180). In the treatise planned by Bartolomeo Ammannati, on the other hand, it seems that *modani* were to be included among subjects that ranged from the social role of architecture to its practical application (see cat. no. 115). The perfection—or imperfection—of architecture was seen to reside in its various parts. According to Vincenzo Scamozzi, the signature of the architect could be found in the details (R.I.B.A. 1964, Pt. II: 141).

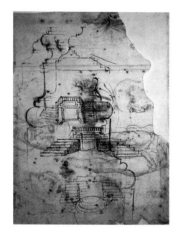

111
MICHELANGELO BUONARROTI
Modani for Profiles of Bases, Drawings of Stairways and Figures (Laurentian Library, S. Lorenzo, Florence)

Florence, Casa Buonarroti, CB 92Ar.-v.
Red chalk, black chalk, pen and ink and wash, cut out along profile on verso; large patch at upper right corner replacing area cut out for profile, repairs along horizontal join of 2 sheets, somewhat worn with discolorations and small tears repaired.
386 × 280 mm (maximum dimensions, without repair)
RECTO: a)-d) 4 profiles of bases and plinths (all pen and ink; left profiles: [a] top far left, [b] left center, [c] center; right profile: [d] center to bottom right); e)-h) 4 studies of stairs (all pen and ink; profile of 2 flights, center top; elevation with double flight, center, second from top; elevation with double flight, third from top; elevation with tripartite stair with concave and

convex center, bottom); i)-n) studies of figures and drapery (seated torso and legs, lower right, rotated 90°, black chalk; feet, left margin above center, rotated 180°, pen and ink; 4 studies of heads in red chalk, right center, and right bottom, both rotated 270°, and left center, and left bottom, both rotated 90°; drapery, upper right, red chalk)
VERSO: a)-b) 2 left profiles bases and plinths ([a] cut out, top left, pen and ink over red chalk; [b] center to bottom, pen and ink and wash over red chalk); c)-f) 4 studies of stairs (all pen and ink; all rotated 180°; elevation of tripartite stair, top center; detail of tripartite stair juncture of central and side flights, right, above center; elevation of stair with concave center, right, center; plan of tripartite stair, left, center); g) study of tabernacle or window frame (pen and ink, bottom right); h)-i) 2 figure studies (red chalk; rotated 270°; seated torso and legs, lower left; head, upper center).

PROVENANCE: Casa Buonarroti.

BIBLIOGRAPHY: Cavallucci 1875: 176; Gotti 1875, II: 180; Berenson 1903b, II: 79, cat. no. 1444 (r. as v.); Thode 1908-13, II: 126, no. xxi, 127, no. xxiv, 129, no. xxx, III: 61-62, cat. no. 138 (r. as v.); K. Frey 1911, II, pls. 164-165, and III, 79-81 (r. as v.); Panofsky 1922, pl. 48, 270-271, 273; Popp 1925: 19, cat. no. 4; Tolnay 1928: 404-405, pl. 21-22, 406-407, 409; Wittkower 1934: 152, figs. 24-25, 155, 157-158, 161; Berenson 1935: 275, 277, fig. 27, 279; Tolnay 1935, II: 102 and 104 n. 1; Berenson 1938, II: 172, cat. no. 1444, III, fig. 804; Marchini 1942: 42; Tolnay 1951 (Florence ed.): 174, and (Paris ed.): 173; Wilde 1953: 72 (describes r. as v., after Frey); Düssler 1959: 82, cat. no. 124 (r. as v.); Ackerman 1961, I: 47, figs. 22-23, II: 41, cat. nos. 11-12; Berenson 1961, no. 1444; Barocchi 1962a, I: 112-114, cat. no. 89; II, pls. CXXXVIII-CXLII (r. as v.); 1962c: 29-30, cat. no. 62 (r. as v.); 1962d, III: 882 n. 493 (r. as v.); 1964b: 43, cat. no. 90, fig. LXII (r. as v.); Zevi 1964: 16; Portoghesi and Zevi 1964: 200, 221, 232, 240, 256-257, figs. 213-214, 859, 1006 (r. as v.); De Angelis d'Ossat 1967: 302-305, figs. 63 and 67, 306 (both sides as recto); Hartt 1971: 199, cat. nos. 283-284, 207-208, figs. 283-284 (r. as v.); Hibbard 1975: 217-218, fig. 147; Tolnay 1975b: 101, cat. no. 148; 1975c, fig. 337; Hibbard 1978: 135; Wittkower 1978: 26-30, 32, figs. 20-21, 237-238 nn. 45, 54, 57, and 58; Tolnay 1980, IV: 53-54, cat. nos. 525r. and 525v., 128 (note concordance follows Hartt 1971, r. as v.); Tolnay and Squellati Brizio 1980: 66, fig. 101r. and

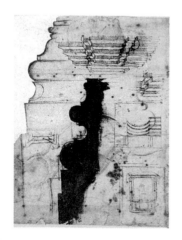

v., 94, cat. no. 101; Murray 1984: 146; Berti 1985: 21, 140-141; Caronia 1985, fig. 117; Ackerman 1986: 113, 116-117, figs. 48-49, cat. nos. 11-12; Nova 1984, figs. 70-71; Hirst 1988a: 76, cat. no. 31, pl. 77 (recto; notes Hartt confusion r. as v.); Hirst 1989: 76, cat. no. 31; Argan and Contardi 1990, cover illus., 189, 192, fig. 260; Marani 1992b: 456, fig. 187; Porn and Wallace 1992: 476, cat. no. 146, pl. 477.

Vasari assuaged his doubts about Michelangelo's unorthodox use of the classical orders by praising his "novelty and variety in the creation of such beautiful cornices, capitals and bases, doors, tabernacles, and tombs." ("...nelle novità di sì belli cornici, capitegli e basi, porte, tabernacoli, e sepolture fece assai diverso ...," Barocchi 1962d, I: 58.) In particular, Vasari was speaking of Michelangelo's work at S. Lorenzo, in the New Sacristy and the Biblioteca Laurenziana. Nowhere is this power of invention more

in evidence than in CB 92A, a sheet long admired for its studies of the stairway of the library vestibule, here highlighted for its profile drawings of the basement order. CB 92A is unusual in this section of the present exhibition as it records the creative phase of template production. Michelangelo's mastery of the vocabulary of the classical orders was linked to his study of ancient architecture; like other Renaissance artists, he learned by copying classical details, examples of which are to be seen amongst his drawings. The profiles on CB 92A show variations on the theme of the double-torus Attic base and plinth. On the recto, the profiles were drawn in fluid pen and ink; while on the verso, the profiles were drawn in red chalk, gone over in pen and ink, and finally studied for their effect in relation to negative space through the application of a brown wash. One of these, which has since been patched, was then cut out for a template, although a final version would likely have been cut from a fresh sheet of paper. This sheet served several different purposes. Scholars agree that its first use was for the red and black chalk figure and drapery studies, thought by most to be the hand of a pupil or someone in the workshop of Michelangelo, possibly Antonio Mini (following the suggestion of Bernhard Berenson 1903b: 79; in 1938: 172, he also proposed Pietro Urbano). (Tolnay 1975b, 101, made a guarded attribution to Gherardo Perini; since taken up only by Porn and Wallace, in Marani 1992b: 476.) Excepting Jacopo Cavallucci (1875: 176), only Johannes Wilde (1953: 73) had attributed the drapery and seated figures to Michelangelo, which he considered to precede the other figure studies, until recently, when Michael Hirst (1988a: 76) supported Michelangelo's authorship of the drapery (K. Frey 1911, III: 80, too had allowed this possibility). The drapery and figure studies show the sheet was then cut down. The order of the sequence between the drawing of the stairs and of the profiles is less clear, but can be connected to the development of the vestibule project. Karl Frey (1911, III: 80) associated the development in the sketches from a double-flight to a unified stairway with a letter of 12 April 1525 expressing Clement VII's wishes for the latter (Poggi 1965-83, *Carteggio*, III: 141); this has been argued as the *terminus ante quem* for the drawings of the stairs (Porn and Wallace, in Marani 1992b: 476). (Berenson 1935: 279, is alone in thinking the stairs might be by a lesser hand, which may explain why he thought them the last to be executed.) Although it is reasonable to suppose that Michelangelo was contemporaneously working on his designs for the stairway and for the interior elevation of the vestibule, and hence the profiles (as does Barocchi 1962a, I: 113; Porn and Wallace, in Marani 1992b: 476), there is some evidence to support a later phase of execution for the profiles. The drawings for the stairway and those of the profiles are oriented on the sheet in the same direction as on the recto; however, on the verso, those for the stairway are rotated 180° to those on the recto, whereas the profiles are consistent in direction on both sides. (Note here in the catalog entry bibliography the longstanding and unremarked confusion over which side constitutes the recto and which the verso of CB 92A.) Furthermore, the profiles can be matched to those of a drawing in the British Museum (Wilde 36r.-v.), that represent a stage in the development of the basement level of the elevation that has been dated to the last quarter of 1525 (Wilde 1953: 72, inv. 1859-6-25-550). Henry Thode was the first to connect Wilde 36r. with CB 92Av. (g), but for the study of the tabernacle (1908-13, II: 126). The similarity of the profiles on CB 92A to the state of the vestibule elevation on Wilde 36 was perceived by Rudolf Wittkower (1934: 155). Close to the basement level as actually built (the niches below the tabernacles were eliminated), Wittkower thought it dated to 23 February 1526, when Clement VII approved the final form of the vestibule ("Circha al ricetto, disse: 'Ringratiato sia Dio che la cosa debe essere in modo aviata che Michelagnolo non v'arà più a perdere tenpo' " [Poggi 1965-83, *Carteggio*, III: 210]), after a controversy over the fenestration of the upper story and the height of the walls had been settled.

That only the upper stories were affected by this controversy was argued by Johannes Wilde in his study of the British Museum drawing; he believed the articulation of the lower story was already finalized by 29 November 1525 when the pope disagreed with the solution for the top story, by then already roofed (Nostro Signiore à preso grande piacere quando lesse a fare il ricetto [Poggi 1965-83, *Carteggio*, III: 186, see also 194, from 23 December 1525]). It has been observed subsequently, that while the profile of the basement in Wilde 36r. is substantially like the built elevation, there have been changes in the proportional relations between the parts, thus supporting Wilde's earlier dating of the design, only modified to accommodate the heightening of the upper stories (Portoghesi and Zevi 1964: 224-225). Hence the profiles of CB 92A would have been realized contemporary to Wilde 36, by November 1525.

In addition to the basement elevation on Wilde 36r., on the verso there are a number of profile studies of column bases and plinths, drawn in pen and ink over chalk studies of heads (the latter not by Michelangelo; Barocchi 1962a, I: 113, attributes the heads to the same hand as those in CB 92A). The presence of the profile heads on the sheet seems to have tempted Michelangelo into a witty *concorrenza* with the "physiognomies" of his column and plinth profiles, lending an often-noted anthropomorphic character to his architectural ornament. The profiles on CB 92A are quite closely comparable: on the recto, particularly the plinth facing to the right on CB 92Ar. (d), which matches the basement elevation on Wilde 36r., a torus above a cavetto, then fillet, astragal, torus, plinth; two of those facing to the left, (a) and (c), are analogous to Wilde 36v. (second from bottom right, his "U"), a fillet, torus, fillet, cyma recta, preceding a cavetto, fillet, astragal, torus, plinth; whereas there is a variation on the profile in (b) and Wilde 36v. (bottom right, his "V"), substituting a scotia for the cyma recta of the previous moldings; on the verso, the cut-out profile (a) is similar to one on Wilde 36r. (below upper right, his "P"), a cyma reversa (rather than the cyma recta of "P"), fillet, torus, fillet, scotia, fillet fol-

lowed by the plinth; the column base (b) shares characteristics with several on Wilde 36v. (bottom middle, his "R" and "S"), with an astragal, scotia, fillet, torus, fillet, then repeated on a larger scale, a scotia, fillet, torus, plinth. Michelangelo employed drawing as a tool for invention, with variations on the themes of the classical orders, repeated motifs, diminuendos and crescendos, embellishments that lend a distinctively personal signature to the composition. It was from such parts as these, generated with such graphic freedom, that Michelangelo produced a commensurate whole, the "grazia più risoluta nel tutto e nelle parti," claimed by Vasari for the library vestibule (Barocchi 1962d, I: 58). *T.E.C.*

112

MICHELANGELO BUONARROTI
Modani for Doorways between Vestibule and Reading Room, Cloister and Vestibule Step (Laurentian Library, S. Lorenzo, Florence)

Florence, Casa Buonarroti, CB 53Ar.-v.
Pen and brown ink, some red chalk on recto; folded, major repairs along vertical join of 2 sheets, large patch lower left corner, and horizontal tears; watermark: cardinal's hat (Roberts 1988, 22, 'Hat C: large,' reproduced; as Briquet 3387. Barocchi 1962, 117; Tolnay 1980, 59; as Briquet 3394).
250/360 × 552/430 mm (without corner repair)
RECTO: a) profile of cornice of door (left); b) profile of doorjamb (center); c) profile of doorstep (right); d) 5 faint red chalk profiles of plinths, bases, cornices (rotated 90°, upper half).
INSCRIBED: 1) *de modani / lacopia della cornice delle porte della libreria date accechone* (a); 2) *elmodano dato a ccechone / degli sti[pi]lti delle decte porte della lib[re]ria* (b); 3) *e modani degli scaglioni dati / accechone* (c).
VERSO: (rotated 90°); a) profile of pediment of door (above); b) profile of pediment of door (below);
c) 5 faint red chalk profiles.
INSCRIBED: 1) *modano della decte porte del fro[n]tone to[n]do dirieto* (a); 2) *frontespitio/ elmodano del Fro[n]tone [tonodo* (canceled)] *delle decte porte cioè de dinanzi* (b).

PROVENANCE: Casa Buonarroti.

BIBLIOGRAPHY: Cavallucci 1875, 176; Gotti 1875, II: 178-179; Geymüller 1904: 44, pl. 4, fig. 4; Thode 1908-13, II: 130, no. xxxiv, 135, III: 53, cat. no. 108; Frey 1909-11, I, pls. 49-50, III: 28-29 (not Michelangelo, suggests Stefano di Tommaso Lunetti); Stegmann and Geymüller 1924, II: 33, fig. 4; Wittkower 1934: 186-189; Wilde 1953: 74; Düssler 1959: 75, cat. no. 94; Ackerman 1961, II: 39, cat. no. 20; Barocchi 1962a, I: 116-118, cat. no. 93, II, pl. CXLV; Barocchi 1964a, III: 86, 89, 91, 141; 1964b: 45, cat. no. 94; Portoghesi and Zevi 1964: 240, 274, figs. 236–237, 859, 1006; De Angelis d'Ossat 1967: 304, figs. 80-81; Hartt 1971: 198, cat. nos. 277-278, 205, figs. 277-278; Wittkower 1978: 46, 240 n. 117; Tolnay 1980, IV: 59, 60, cat. nos. 534r. and 534v., 127-128; Berti 1985: 152; Ackerman 1986: 303, cat. no. 20; Roberts 1988: 22; Argan and Contardi 1990: 195, 197, fig. 274.

Clement VII's judgment of the designs Michelangelo had sent him for the Biblioteca Laurenziana doorways was

"that he had never seen one more beautiful, neither ancient nor modern" ("Della porta disse che e' nonnaveva veduta mai la più bella, né antica né moderna" [Poggi 1965-83, *Carteggio*, III: 221]). Michelangelo's readiness to begin designing the doorways had already been indicated on 3 April 1526, when Giovanfrancesco Fattucci advised him not to worry about the resolution of the rare book room, as the interior facade of the reading room should be matched to the vestibule (Poggi 1965-83, *Carteggio*, III: 217).

Fattucci reported the pope's approval of the designs and his comment, as given above, on 18 April, and returned the drawings to Michelangelo on 6 June with further instructions about the inscription (Poggi 1965-83, *Carteggio*, III: 224). The inscription was to go in the triangular pediment over the door leading from the vestibule to the reading room; the papal arms in the segmental pediment over the door from the reading room to the vestibule.

The *pietra serena* membering of the vestibule was well under way (5 columns of the main story were in place by 17 June 1526; Poggi 1965-83, *Carteggio*, III: 227), including the interior doorway to the cloister. However, building activity here, as elsewhere at S. Lorenzo, was interrupted by outside events from late 1526 until the 1530s, when a contract ordering the construction of the doorways and stairs was finally drawn up in 1533 (Milanesi 1875a, *Lettere*: 707). Even then only the doorways between the vestibule and reading room were completed; although stone was cut for the doorway from the cloister (as well as the stairs), it was not used when the present doorway was finally put up in the late seventeenth century.

Inscriptions on CB 53A identify it as Michelangelo's shop record, "la copia" (1), of the various templates distributed to the stonemason Cechone.

Of the sequence of drawings relating to the design process, a presentation drawing such as that shown to the pope, drawn to scale (CB 98A), was first identified by Heinrich von Geymüller (1904: 44) with the vestibule side of the doorway to the reading room. A similar scale drawing (CB 111A) for the reading room side, and one for the entrance from the cloister (CB 95), were assembled by Rudolph Wittkower (1934: 186-195), together with various preparatory sketches on a sheet in the British Museum (Wilde 37r.-v.), constituting what remains the most complete discussion of the design history of the doors (updated in Tolnay 1980, IV: 65-70).

Despite some variations, the scale drawings agree with the vestibule-reading room doorways as built; there is some further elaboration of the succession of planes between inner and outer frames, and the insertion of a triangular pediment within the segmental (a variant of a motif entertained in some of the sketches) in the reading room doorway. As Wittkower pointed out, the latter area also varies from the profile provided for the template in CB 53Av. (a) which is more complex than the executed molding, whereas there is agreement of the triangular pediment (to CB 53Ar. [a] and v. [b]) and of the actual doorjamb (to CB 53Ar. [b]).

496

The profile of the doorstep on CB 53Ar. (c) Wittkower thought close to the two steps outside the cloister door leading into the vestibule; the only part of that doorway attributable to Michelangelo. (Unused pieces cut for the cloister door including the embrasure and segmental pediment were recorded by Giovanni Antonio Dosio ca. 1550 [Uff. 1925], Giovanni Battista Nelli in 1687 [Uff. 3713*bis*], and Giuseppe Rossi 1739, pl. 22, minus the segmental pediment [see Wittkower 1934: 190-194].) From sketches, to presentation drawings, to templates and copies kept for reference, only the actual templates are missing in this chain from ideas to execution, probably consumed by use.

Yet Michelangelo's thrifty practices allowed the negative remainder of the template cut for the doorstep to survive, as observed by Paola Barocchi (1964a, III: 90-91: AB, XIII, fol. 134); the fragment of the sheet was diverted to serve for sketching out the lines of a sonnet, "Non so se s'è le desiata luce." The presence of the sonnet dated to ca. 1533 may provide some outside confirmation of the date of the templates, as contemporary to the contract mentioned above. That Wittkower thought these "complete working drawings for both sides" belonged to the design process of 1526, rather than the construction phase of 1534, was probably due to his identification of the stonemason Cechone as Francesco di Masino da Corbignano (also thought by Thode, Dussler; fully named only in an undated *ricordo* with associates, some of whom reappear with a Cechone in an August 1518 contract for marble from Seravezza [Bardeschi Ciulich and Barocchi 1970: 355, 38, respectively]).

Johannes Wilde (1953: 74) recognized, however, that one of the stonemasons named in the 1533 contract also had been known as Cechone (from a letter to Michelangelo from Baccio Valori in 1532, see Poggi 1965-83, *Carteggio*, III: 386); this was Francesco d'Andrea di Giovanni Luchesini da Settignano, whose association with CB 53A is now generally accepted.

The identity of the Cechone who figures among the large crew of stoneworkers Michelangelo was employing for work in the *fabbrica* at S. Lorenzo is not entirely straightforward.

Caroline Elam proposed that the Cechone supplying marble from Seravezza for the facade in 1518 was Cechone di Masino da Corbignano, not Francesco Luchesini who is named in the November 1519 *ricordanza* of Figiovanni as *capomaestro* of the *scarpellini* in the New Sacristy (1979: 174 n. 36; Parronchi 1966, 326). The Cechone giving Michelangelo and his foreman so much trouble in late 1520-early 1521 with the first order of the New Sacristy was thus likely to be the *capomaestro* Luchesini (Elam 1979: 166; Poggi 1965-83, *Carteggio*, II: 264, 267, 268). Yet Francesco Luchesini stood as guarantor for the October 1518 marble contract drawn up in Florence by ser Filippo Cioni, and one of the primary suppliers of stone for the facade was Andrea di Giovanni d'Andrea Luchesini da Settignano, who would seem to be his father (Milanesi 1875a: 686). A comparison of handwriting would be useful in sorting out the personalities going by the name Cechone, as would alternative documentation (possibly this will emerge from the Salviati archives in Pisa, see Wallace 1992). There was continuity as the *fabbrica* expanded when Michelangelo turned his attention to the library. A certain Cechone and his partner, el Morato, are named in the payments for dressed *macigno* for the library vestibule in December 1525 (Bardeschi Ciulich and Barocchi 1970: 202-211). Altogether, Francesco Luchesini was employed by Michelangelo over a span of 15 years.

In the 1533 contract, Francesco Luchesini agreed, together with his nephews Michele and Leonardo di Giovanni Luchesini, and Antonio and Simon di Jacopo di Berto da San Martino a Mussola, to supply, work, and supervise the erection of the two doors and stairway of the library by March 1534. The stonemasons were instructed to begin first with one door, to follow with the second, and then proceed with the stairway, all to be well executed "nel modo, forma et misura, siccome é disegnato tutto non

tanto in sul chiostro, ma per il modino fatto di terra dal nostro Michelangelo." It seems that in addition to the templates given to the stonemasons, Michelangelo had drawn full-scale examples on the walls of the cloister, as he had for the library's tabernacle windows among the *disegni murali* in the New Sacristy (Elam 1979: 163, suggests this interpretation; idem 1981: 394). CB 53A has been considered autograph by all (with the exception of K. Frey 1909-11: 28, who named Michelangelo's foreman, Stefano di Tommaso Lunetti; and J. Ackerman, 1986: 303), and demonstrates the control that Michelangelo exerted through his draftsmanship over all phases of his projects.

T.E.C.

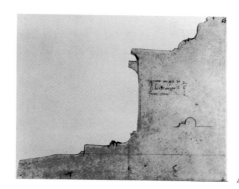

113
MICHELANGELO BUONARROTI
Modano for a Cornice for Unidentified Location (Laurentian Library, S. Lorenzo, Florence)

Florence, Casa Buonarroti, CB 60A
Pen and brown ink, red chalk, profile cut out on left side; some discoloration.
280 × 223 mm (maximum dimensions)
RECTO: a) cut-out profile of cornice (entire); b) partial profile (center right); c) element of profile (right, rotated 90° or 270°).
INSCRIBED: *grano mogia 10 2 | le biade moggia 11 6 | fave staia 2 ½* (center left, rotated 270°); non-autograph according to:
Barocchi 1962: 116; Bardeschi Ciulich and Barocchi 1970 (*Ricordi*): 269, as Antonio Mini(?); Tolnay 1980, IV: 60, cat. no. 537r.; Berti 1985: 153).

PROVENANCE: Casa Buonarroti.

BIBLIOGRAPHY: Gotti 1875, II: 179; Thode 1913, III: 44, cat. no. 83; Düssler 1959: 75, cat. no. 98; Barocchi 1962a, I: 116, cat. no. 92, II, pl. CXLVI; 1964a, III: 86, 89, 141; 1964b: 44, cat. no. 93, fig. LXVI; Portoghesi and Zevi 1964: 240, 275, fig. 238, 1006; Fasolo 1965: 150 (mislabeled as CB 62A); De Angelis d'Ossat 1967: 308, 311, fig. 82 (as for the Cappella Medici); Bardeschi Ciulich and Barocchi 1970: 269, no. CCXXLII; Hartt, 1971: 198, cat. no. 279, 205, fig. 279; Tolnay 1980, IV: 60, cat. no. 537r., 128; Elam 1981: 594 n. 4; Berti 1985, 153.

The cut-out profile of CB 60A may have survived because it was never used (and remained in the workshop), which may also account for its inconclusive concordance with any specific part of Michelangelo's architectural ornament. Although Henry Thode (1913, III: 44) cataloged it with drawings for the New Sacristy, he allowed that it bore some relation to the decoration of the Biblioteca Laurenziana. (De Angelis d'Ossat 1967: 311, also thought it was for the Cappella Medici.) Paola Barocchi noted an affinity to CB 53A, and described CB 60A as making a transition from the austere cornice of the reading room to the richer trabeation of the doorway (1962a, I: 116; followed by Hartt 1971: 198, and Tolnay 1980, II: 60). (Berti 1985: 153, gives its location as for the entrance door to the vestibule.) A date of ca. 1530 was assigned to the profile first by Luitpold Düssler (1959: 75, who considered the inscription autograph). This was later supported by comparing the inscription, then attributed to Antonio Mini, to similar dated accounts (Bardeschi Ciulich and Barocchi 1970: 268, 269), and to several profile draw-

ings in the Archivio Buonarroti (Barocchi 1964a, III: AB, XIII, fol.157; AB, XIII, fol. 127; AB, XIII, fol. 149, the latter as workshop). The profile on the recto was first drawn in red chalk, including several ruled vertical and horizontal lines and an incised line. It was then gone over in pen and brown ink (different from the inscription), the lines not closely matching the cut-out profile. On the verso, only pen and brown ink lines are visible, and the cutting follows the profile, leading to the supposition that it was cut out from this side.

T.E.C.

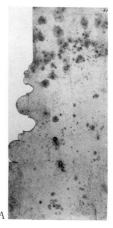

A   B

114
MICHELANGELO BUONARROTI
Modano for the Base of a Column of the Medici Tombs (New Sacristy, S. Lorenzo, Florence)

Florence, Casa Buonarroti, CB 59A
Pen and brown ink over black chalk, cut out along profile at left; folded twice, some discoloration in spots; watermark: cardinal's hat (part of tassel only; not previously noted, see CB 61 A for comparison).
324 × 145 mm (maximum dimensions)
INSCRIBED: *el modano delle colonne della sepultura doppia di sagrestia* (rotated 90°).

PROVENANCE: Casa Buonarroti.

BIBLIOGRAPHY: Gotti 1875, II: 179; Thode 1902-13, I: 458, 500, no. lxv, III, 44, cat. no. 82; K. Frey 1911, II, pl. 175, III: 85; Popp 1922: 129, no. 13, pl. 69a; Wanscher 1940b: 80; Tolnay 1948, III: 40, 210, cat. no. 76, fig. 107; Wilde 1953: 58; Düssler 1959: 75, cat. no. 97; Ackerman 1961, II: 28; Barocchi 1962a, I: 87-88, cat. no. 64, II, pl. CVII; 1964b: 33, cat. no. 66; Portoghesi and Zevi 1964: 129, 132, 155, fig. 124, 852, 854, 1003; De Angelis d'Ossat 1967: 291, fig. 36, 294; Hartt 1971: 170, cat. no. 225, 177, fig. 225; Tolnay 1976, II: 39, cat. no. 204r.-v.; 1980, IV: 128 (mislabeled as 61r. and v.); Elam 1981: 594 n. 4; Berti 1985: 105; Ackerman 1986: 298; Hirst 1988b: 90, 102-103, fig. 215; Argan and Contardi 1990, fig. 507; Morrogh 1992: 588 n. 58, 593 n. 64; Hirst 1993: 124, 139-140, fig. 215.

MICHELANGELO BUONARROTI
Modano for the Base of a Column of the Medici Tombs (New Sacristy, S. Lorenzo, Florence)

Florence, Casa Buonarroti, CB 61A
Pen and brown ink over black chalk, cut out along profile at right; folded twice, some discoloration in spots; watermark: cardinal's hat (Roberts 1988: 22, 'Hat C: large'; as Briquet 3387. Barocchi 1962, I: 88; Tolnay 1976, II: 39; as Briquet 3394. Also compare the watermark of an early plan for S. Lorenzo, in Venice, Archivio di Stato, Miscellanea Mappe 1285, drawn in Burns 1979, 151, fig. 6; as near Briquet 3393).
324 × 143 mm (maximum dimensions)
VERSO: a) cut out profile (entire); b) small faint black chalk partial profile of a base (lower left).

497

BIBLIOGRAPHY: Gotti 1875, II: 179; Thode 1908-13, I: 500, no. lxvi, III, 44, cat. no. 84; K. Frey 1911, III: 85; Wilde 1953: 58; Düssler 1959: 76, cat. no. 99; Ackerman 1961, II: 28; Barocchi 1962a, I: 88, cat. no. 65, II, pl. CVII; 1964b: 33, cat. no. 67; Portoghesi and Zevi 1964, 129, 132, 155, fig. 122, 1003; Hartt 1971, 170, cat. no. 226, 177, fig. 226; Tolnay 1976, II: 39, cat. no. 203r.-v.; 1980, IV: 128; Elam 1981: 594 n. 4; Berti 1985, 106; Ackerman 1986: 298; Roberts 1988: 22; Morrogh 1992: 588 n. 58, 593 n. 64.

The autograph inscription on CB 59A reveals its intended purpose as "the *modano* for the columns of the double sepulcher of the Sacristy," the double tomb of the Medici that Michelangelo designed for the south wall, now the entry of the New Sacristy. The profile of CB 61A is close, although not identical to CB 59A. These are for a double-torus with double-scotia base profile, which Michelangelo has embellished by leading from the column shaft to a double-astragal molding and fillet, apparently the site of some re-thinking, as the verso of CB 61A shows a fillet-astragal-fillet, in pen and ink. Taking CB 59A as the definitive profile, it continues with a scotia, fillet, torus, fillet, and a commensurately larger scotia, fillet, astragal, torus and, finally, plinth. Ruled and incised lines were used as guides for the freehand penned profile. Further linking the two sheets is the fragment of a previously unnoticed watermark on CB 59A, the end of a tassel, similar to that part missing from the cardinal's hat watermark on CB 61A. The paper that Michelangelo used to make 1:1 scale templates such as these was a large format, such as the "royal" and "imperial" size sheets. (Briquet 1907, I: 2-3, gives royal as 615 × 445 mm, imperial as 740 × 500 mm, and notes that the cardinal's hat watermark often indicated large format paper, and was counter-marked in the sixteenth century, see 222-223.) Judging from the records for the ducal tombs, such *modani* were produced after Michelangelo finished the wood models (in March 1524, for which he also probably made templates), as during the following month he ordered "fogli reali per far modanature" (Bardeschi Ciulich and Barocchi 1970: 128, 134, and 136-137, itself a surviving template negative [see Wallace 1992: 132-134], also from October, 132). Sturdier supports from sheets of tin, "fogli di ferro stagniato," and from wood (Baccio di Puccione *legnaiuolo* was paid "per un modano d'una mensola") also were supplied to the stonecutters for executing the architectural ornament (Bardeschi Ciulich and Barocchi 1970, respectively 119, 122 [also for carbon and rules], 129, 130 [for rasps]; 129). Michelangelo's design for the Medici tomb was distinguished by the use of a column order, rather than pilasters as on the ducal tombs. This had been determined since April 1521, the time that his ideas were advanced enough to order the marble required for the tombs (Milanesi 1875a: 694-696; Bardeschi Ciulich and Barocchi 1970: 106), and was reflected in the drawings produced then, which show columns framing side niches that flank a central aedicule with pilaster strips (Morrogh 1992: 537 n. 32, for literature on the "definitive design"). Charles de Tolnay (1948, III: 54; Poggi 1965-83, *Carteggio*, II: 332) thought that the dimensions of the marble block ordered in December 1521, 4 *braccia* long, 1¼ *braccia* wide, and ⅔ *braccio* deep might be for the Medici tomb's columns, which fits with Andrew Morrogh's (1992: 593 n. 64 and 594 n. 71) estimation of the column size based on the dimensions of CB 59A and CB 61A, as having a diameter of 23 cm and height of 2.34 m. Unfortunately, the same problems that had plagued Michelangelo in obtaining columns for the facade of the church of S. Lorenzo seem to have pertained even to the smaller scale of the Medici tomb: in August 1524 Michelangelo's agent "Topolino" (Domenico di Giovanni di Bertini) wrote from Carrara saying no marble of the requisite beauty and perfection had yet been found; by January 1526 still no marble had been quarried, although he was hopeful of having it in a month—if the weather cooperated (Tolnay 1948, III: 235-236 app. 26, 238-239 app. 35; Poggi 1965-83, *Carteggio*, III: 98, 203). After work on the Medici tombs had been suspended for several years,

Michelangelo returned to the tomb in August 1533, when Clement VII's approval of the delegation of Fra Giovanni Angelo da Montorsoli as its supervisor, "che l' Frate sia soprastante a la sepoltura doppia dela sacrestia," was expressed in a letter from Sebastiano del Piombo in Rome (Poggi 1965-83, *Carteggio*, IV: 38-39). It is likely that CB 59A and CB 61A belong to this phase, as Michelangelo was preparing to abandon Florence and leave his projects in the hands of assistants. Although evidence suggests that a number of pieces actually were cut for the tomb, only a few were used by Vasari in 1559 when he assembled what remains today in the place of Michelangelo's magnificent vision.

T.E.C.

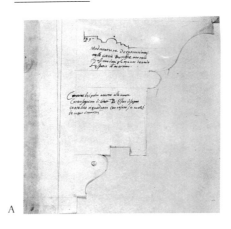

A

115

BARTOLOMEO AMMANNATI
*Modani for Profile of Attic Cornice
(S. Giovannino de' Medici, Florence)*

Florence, Galleria degli Uffizi, Gabinetto Disegni e Stampe, Uff. 3462A
(Bound in volume *La Città ideale*, 480 × 380 mm; laid on support, 475 × 375 mm.)
Pen and brown ink, black chalk, sheet cut out along profile at right; some discoloration along left edge from glue and at top right from water.
370 × 325 mm (maximum dimensions)
RECTO: a) cut-out profile of cornice (entire); b) small profile of cornice in pen and ink (above center, rotated 90°).
INSCRIBED: 1) *Cornice del palco atorno alle mura / Contrasegniato di letera .B. El suo disegnio / con telaio riquadrato con rosoni su mezi / de riquadramenti* (a, center); 2) *Modanatura De cornicioni / nelle crocie Borchie atornio / farassi i modani p[er]lo apunto secondo / lo spatio ch[e] averemo* (b, above center, not rotated).
PROVENANCE: Vincenzo Viviani; Luigi del Riccio; Ferdinando de' Medici.
BIBLIOGRAPHY: Ferri 1885: 48; Fossi 1970: 23, 220-221 cat. no. LXXXVI.

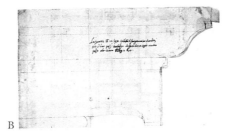

B

BARTOLOMEO AMMANNATI
*Modano for Profile of Main Cornice
(S. Giovannino de' Medici, Florence)*

Florence, Galleria degli Uffizi, Gabinetto Disegni e Stampe, Uff. 3463Ar.
(Bound in *La Città ideale*, 480 × 380 mm; laid on support, 475 × 375.)

C

Pen and brown ink, black chalk, sheet cut out along profile at right; some discoloration along left edge from glue and at top right from water where also folded.
266 × 436 mm (maximum dimensions)
INSCRIBED: *La Cornicie ch[e] va sopra i pilastri di San giovanino de medici / Ed è di dua pezi in alteza dal gociolatoio in gio un altro / pezo alto in tuto b[racci]a uno, s[oldi] 2, d[enari] 4.* (right, above center).
VERSO: fragment of a plan for a palace, and small drawings of an arch and profile of cornice with measurements.

PROVENANCE: Vincenzo Viviani, Luigi del Riccio, Ferdinando de' Medici.

BIBLIOGRAPHY: Ferri 1885: 48; Fossi 1970: 23, 222-223 cat. no. LXXXVII.

BARTOLOMEO AMMANNATI
Modano for the Profile of the Architrave of the Main Cornice (S. Giovannino de' Medici, Florence)

Florence, Galleria degli Uffizi, Gabinetto Disegni e Stampe, Uff. 3464A
(Bound in *La Città ideale*, 480 × 380 mm; laid on support, 475-375 mm; rotated 90°.)
Pen and brown ink, black chalk, sheet cut out along profile on left and right; some discoloration along bottom edge from glue and at top from water, also folded where extends beyond support; watermark: eagle in circle surmounted by crown (near Briquet 209).
425 × 175 mm (maximum dimensions)
INSCRIBED: 1) *primo pezo della Cornicie / grande architravata* (along upper left margin, rotated 90°); 2) *Tuto Questo è Il resto del modano della Cornicie grande architravata* (along lower left margin, rotated 90°); 3) *Questa Cornicie grande è di tre pezi in alteza p[er] agevolare le pietre / È la sposa e bastera p[er]ch[è] è come investitura è bene sprangata* (along lower right margin, rotated 90°); 4) *Questo fine Di Modano posa sopra Il capitello* (bottom edge).

PROVENANCE: Vincenzo Viviani, Luigi del Riccio, Ferdinando de' Medici.

BIBLIOGRAPHY: Ferri 1885: 48; Fossi 1970: 23, 222-223 cat. no. LXXXVIII.

A large number of Bartolomeo Ammannati's architectural drawings have survived, evidently collected together by him not only for the purposes of running a studio, recording ideas, and training assistants, but with the intention of writing a treatise on architecture that would encompass the theoretical and the practical. This material, including the *modani* exhibited here, later was bound together in several volumes and given the title "La Città ideale". The rationale for such a title comes from his contemporary biographer's description of the ambitiously planned work: Raffaello Borghini in *Il Riposo* (Florence, 1584: 594-595) speaks of "un utile e bel libro ... d'architettura, nel quale egli figura un'ampia, e perfetta Città," to be both drawn and described, and to treat of all the elements, from city planning to individual dwellings for the various classes of inhabitants that would comprise "una bene intesa Città." The inclusion of *modani* in such a project, ranging from designs for a royal palace to thoughts on mathematics, would show their practical as well as theoretical aspects. These were at once modest materials employed in the actual construction of a building, yet, by bearing the imprint of the architect's hand directly to the stonecutters, they conveyed the idea of the design more concretely than any other phase of the preparatory process. In the Renaissance, these details were more than ornament, as their elements consisted of the parts of the Classical orders that governed the generating principles of design and proportion for a whole building.

That these specific *modani* survived, possibly intended for the treatise, perhaps meant something more, as they had been made for the church of S. Giovannino de' Medici in Florence, a commission that held particular significance for Ammannati. The church is located where Via Martelli becomes Via Larga, by the family palace of his longtime Medici patrons. Ammannati began discussions with the superiors of the Jesuit Order in Rome in 1572 concerning the reconstruction of the pre-existing church and enlargement of the site to accommodate the Florentine Jesuit Collegio. Deeply pious in his later years, Ammannati's relationship with the Jesuits went beyond the commissions he undertook for them in Florence and Rome, as he and his wife Laura Battiferri made the Florence Collegio their heirs and were buried in the chapel he designed in S. Giovannino. Construction of the church and college began after his designs were accepted in 1578 and was largely finished by 1585. The church took as its model Il Gesù in Rome, which Ammannati knew at first hand: a large single nave with side chapels, suppressed transept, and barrel vault. The interior is articulated with a single order of Ionic pilasters supporting a continuous cornice with an attic story above. In the interior elevation, recessed niches framed with coupled pilasters and above, in the attic zone, vertical rectangular fields framed by pilaster strips, alternate with deeper chapels, whose attic zone includes smaller horizontal rectangular fields. The division between wall and ceiling is marked by a small cornice that breaks out over the larger rectangular fields. So flat are the projecting elements and enframements that their effect is almost like a membrane peeled down to reveal further layers.

In Uff. 3462A, 3463A, and 3464A, we have Ammannati's *modani* for the main cornice, architrave, and attic zone cornice. As the fragment of a ground plan on Uff. 3463A verso indicates, *modani* were often drawn and cut out of sheets of paper that had seen some previous use. On the recto is a profile for the main cornice with an inscription giving its destination, above the pilasters of S. Giovannino de' Medici. This profile, like the other two, bears visible traces of the means employed to ensure the accuracy of its contours. Both incised lines and ruled lines in black chalk set out the measured relationships of the parts then drawn in free-hand with black chalk. However, the profile was not finalized until it was actually cut out, as the pentimenti show: not only is the curvature of the cyma recta made slighter, the drop of the corona redrawn, and the recess of the soffit shallower, but the intervening fillet has been changed into an astragal, a compass used to provide its semicircular outline. The inscriptions served not only to specify what part of the entablature the *modani* belong to, but gave further information to the stone masons as to their size, location, and assembly. The *modano* for the architrave of the main cornice, Uff. 3464A, is inscribed with instructions that the cornice is to be in three pieces to facilitate construction and expenses, and that it will be satisfactory if the stones are well bolted in place (3). *T.E.C.*

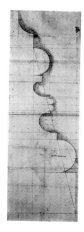

116

ANTONIO DA SANGALLO THE YOUNGER (for Raphael)
Modano for the Base of the Monumental Order of Interior Pilasters (St. Peter's, Vatican)

Florence, Galleria degli Uffizi, Gabinetto Disegni e Stampe, Uff. 7976Ar.
Black chalk, some red chalk measurements, on 5 attached sheets; folded, repairs especially along central vertical and horizontal folds, holes from brown ink on verso; watermark: mermaid in circle (Wolff Metternich 1972, I: 71 no. 14, drawn to scale; near Briquet 13888). 1715 (1719) × 575 (577) mm
VERSO: partial details of profiles for the pedestal of the monumental order of interior pilasters, and partial details for the ambulatory interior and exterior order and ground plan.
INSCRIBED: 1) *Modano della basa gra[n]de / di s.to pietro de pilastri* (rotated 180°, above center); 2) *Basa gra[n]di di s.to pietro / traglie gra[n]di fatte di pietra / per la facciata di s.to pietro* (rotated 270°, right margin).

PROVENANCE: Geymüller (possibly from Gaddi, via Campello; see Morrogh 1985: 10).

BIBLIOGRAPHY: Wolff Metternich 1972, I: 28, 46-47, fig. 47-48; Frommel 1984c: 249, 277-278, cat. no. 2.15.19, 291; 1986a: 69 n. 27; 1986b: 304; Wolff Metternich and Thoenes 1987: 118 n. 221, 156 n. 284; Pagliara 1989: 174 n. 27.

This striking full-scale *modano* for a pilaster base was identified by Wolff Metternich (1972) as having been made during Raphael's tenure as first architect of the *fabbrica* of St. Peter's by the hand of Antonio da Sangallo the Younger for the giant interior order of Corinthian pilasters in travertine marble. Frommel (1984c) further refined the dating to autumn 1518-spring 1519 after an order of "nine p[almi]" (1 *palmo romano* = 0.2234 m) had been definitively established. The pilaster base was carefully drawn in order to transmit to the stonecutters an accurate profile of each element. First, ruled lines were incised on the sheet as guides for measurement, then for the contours of individual elements of the base. A compass was used to incise the semicircular profile of each of the double-torus moldings, and for the compound radius of the scotia, as can be seen by the two holes from the compass point. Freehand black chalk was then traced over these guidelines, with further adjustments at this stage visible in some pentimenti, and hatched shading added to throw the outline of the base into stronger relief. The size of the base was generated by a rectangle, whose long side determines the height and whose short side constitutes the plinth, the projecting elements oriented on the diagonal of the rectangle in proportions of 1:4. Frommel (1984c) commented upon the uncanonical proportions of Uff. 7976Ar. in relation to those expounded in the theories of Vasari, Alberti, and Fra Giocondo for the Ionic base. Rather, Sangallo had privileged a specific classical model, the pilaster bases of the pronaos of the Pantheon. Not only does this demonstrate how closely related were the processes of drawing in detail the remains of classical antiquity and the actual execution of architectural detail in contemporary buildings, but this choice also reveals a vital link between successive generations in the *fabbrica*

of St. Peter's. As can be seen elsewhere in this exhibition, Uff. 6770Ar. is a handsome rendering of one of the Corinthian capitals of the pilasters in the pronaos of the Pantheon, which Bramante intended for the giant interior order of St. Peter's. Raphael thus employed a model in concordance with his predecessor. Sangallo's interpretation is a bolder version of the Pantheon base: compare the slighter projection and less emphatic concavities of Domenico da Varignana's copy in the *Mellon Codex* (New York, Pierpont Morgan Library, fol. 28r.). In a building as monumental as St. Peter's, this boldness served to accentuate the individual parts whose articulation contributed to the overall expression of structural grandeur in the vast interior, as can be seen in the surviving travertine bases of the giant order in the south transept (see Frommel 1984c: 309). *T.E.C.*

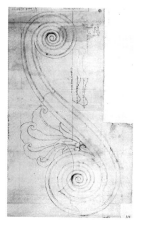

117

GIOVANFRANCESCO DA SANGALLO (?)
Modano for a Fireplace Bracket (Palazzo Cardello (?), Rome)

Florence, Galleria degli Uffizi, Gabinetto Disegni e Stampe, Uff. 317Ar.
Pen and brown ink over pounced black chalk, sheet irregularly cut out; folded, some stains and tears, several large patches added for missing areas along top left and right edges, lower left side, bottom edge; watermark: crossbow in circle surmounted by a fleur-de-lis (near Briquet 761).
980 × 545 mm (maximum dimensions)
RECTO: a) fireplace bracket (pounced, superimposed over profile of fireplace); b) profile of fireplace (entire); c) 2 profiles for model of half of mantelpiece (below center left, rotated 90°); d) drawing of fireplace (lower left, rotated 90°).
INSCRIBED: 1) *il gociolatoio* (b, upper left margin); 2) *Questa linea sie laparete del muro* (b, along center right margin, rotated 90°); 3) *Questa lunga sie della testa dello architrave* (b, along inside profile, below center, rotated 90°); 4) *chapitello del pilastro chefa chapa / allo chamino cho[n] larchitrave* (b, bottom left); 5) *chapitello del pilastrello morto* (b, bottom right); 6) *modanatura dello modello da chapo cioe i[n] facia apunto* (c, below center furthest left, rotated 90°); 7) *modanatura dello modello dapie cioe i[n] facia apunto* (c, below center left, rotated 90°); 8) *lettere* [with various measurements] (d, lower left, inside drawing, rotated 90°); 9) *lo chamino dell chardello* (d, lower left, next to drawing, rotated 90°).
VERSO: *camino del cardello / i[n] roma* (bottom, in a different hand than the recto).

PROVENANCE: unavailable (probably Gaddi; see Morrogh 1985: 10).

BIBLIOGRAPHY: Giovannoni [1959]: 293-294, fig. 35; Buddensieg 1975: 108; Frommel 1976: 65 n. 12; Bruschi 1983b: 14.

The graceful scroll bracket for a fireplace in Uff. 317A may itself have been derived from another full-scale template drawing. Traces of black chalk show that its design was first pounced onto the sheet, then gone over in brown ink. The purpose of Uff. 317A would seem to have been as an aid in assessing the relationship of the bracket (a) to the mantelpiece frame (b), either for study or construction, as the scroll has been applied over a drawing of the fireplace architrave. Inscriptions describe the parts of the underlying mantelpiece, its architrave (3), soffit (1), relation to the wall (2), and coupled pilasters below the scroll (4, 5). Not given in the same scale are the pair of moldings for the cap of the mantelpiece (c), but their inscriptions suggest that they have been drawn from a model (6, 7). It was common practice to make detail models; these could have been of a single detail such as a molding or cornice, or an element such as a tabernacle or window frame. Template drawings could be used in making a full-scale model for presentation or construction, as they were in the final process of building. An idea of the appearance of the elevation of the fireplace is given in a sketch with measurements (d), showing paired pilasters supporting the scroll bracket beneath a cornice with an ornamented molding. An inscription next to the sketch of the fireplace (9), and an inscription on the verso in a different hand, identify its destination for the Cardello ("Chardello") in Rome. Giovannoni ([1959]: 293-294; also Bruschi 1983b: 14) utilized this drawing, which he attributed to Giovanni Battista da Sangallo, together with another for a fireplace inscribed "al Gardello fatto," that he gave to Antonio da Sangallo the Younger (Uff. 7175, not illustrated), as support for the latter's design ca. 1547 of the Palazzo Silvestri (now the Istituto Rivaldi) since it is located in an area

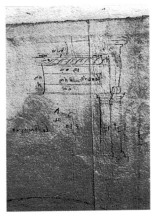

Giovanfrancesco da Sangallo (?)
detail of fireplace elevation from GDSU 317Ar (d)

known as "Cardello." However, more recently scholars have accepted an attribution of the Palazzo (or Villa) Silvestri to Jacopo del Duca, the only architect for whom there is associated documentation (Belli Barsali 1983: 372-375). Another possible intended destination might have been the palaces of the Cardelli family by Campo Marzio. Several properties were purchased and substantially developed from 1516 on by Giacomo Cardelli, apostolic secretary. Called the Domus Magna (now Palazzo della Guardia di Finanza) and Palatium (now Palazzo Firenze), the latter is better known for its later additions executed by Bartolomeo Ammannati for Pope Julius III. It may have been that Giacomo Cardelli was considering the Sangallo workshop for one of his several campaigns of building and embellishing his palaces, both before the Sack of Rome and after when the Palatium Cardelli was devastated, although the earlier additions are thought to be the work of a neighboring Lombard architect. After Giacomo's death in 1530, the Palatium Cardelli was rented out (including to Cardinal Rodolfo Pio da Carpi), the tenants undertaking upkeep and construction, and in 1550 purchased by Julius III for his brother Balduino Del Monte (see Nova 1983: 53-76).
The attribution of Uff. 317A also has a bearing on the identification of its commission. Giovannoni assigned it to Giovanni Battista and related the project to one of Antonio's. But scholars are in the process of revising their notions about various members of the Sangallo workshop, and this drawing has been reattributed to Giovan Francesco (Buddensieg 1975: 108), which would necessitate

an earlier *terminus ante quem* (d. 1530), extremely early for an association with the Palazzo Silvestri, but possible for the Cardelli palaces. Comparison of Uff. 317A with other drawings in the exhibition now attributed to Giovan Francesco, such as Uff. 1331A and 1332A in this section, also reveal some differences in the script, a problem that requires further resolution to confirm Giovan Francesco's authorship (as in the forthcoming volumes of the Sangallo family drawing corpus, edited by Adams).   *T.E.C.*

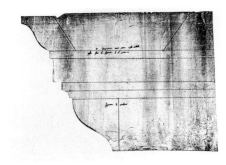

118
<small>GIOVANNI GIACOMO DI PIETRO COMINI</small>
Sagoma of Profile for Cornice
(S. Giorgio Maggiore, Venice)

Venice, Archivio di Stato, Miscellanea Mappe 857d
Pen and brown ink, sheet cut out along profile at left; some small tears and waterstains around top, right and bottom edges.
565 × 430 mm (maximum dimensions)
<small>INSCRIBED:</small> 1) *io Zangiacomo tagia piera a san vidale / questa sono la sagoma di le giorne* (above center) 2) *sagoma di modioni* (below center).

<small>BIBLIOGRAPHY:</small> Archivio di Stato di Venezia 1980: 52, cat. no. 130; Caniato and Dal Borgo 1990: 164, fig. 167.

During the period when Andrea Palladio (1508-80) began the new church for the Benedictine monks at S. Giorgio Maggiore in 1565, he was continuously engaged in a number of important private, civic, and ecclesiastical commissions in Venice and throughout the Veneto that would occupy the last decade and a half of his life. In addition to the personal supervision he was able to provide, his means for controlling the building process depended upon establishing a capably staffed *cantiere* and furnishing project drawings. The visual record for a major project could range from a wood model, as was the case for S. Giorgio Maggiore (last seen in the eighteenth century) to drawings for minor details. Despite ample documentation that attests to Palladio having supplied extensive detail drawings—*sagome*, or templates—none by his hand have been identified. Although many such drawings typically would be consumed on the job, or passed to workers executing details and therefore excluded from materials retained by patrons, it still was common for some kind of copy to be kept in the workshop (as seen here in the exhibition, for example, with the Sangallo family), or for unused profiles to remain as part of the graphic record. Howard Burns (1973b: 179-180) has suggested that an explanation for this lacunae may be found in Palladio's theoretical outlook: that the *sagome* for a particular building had no universal value, as would models from antiquity, since they were adapted to the individual circumstances of a project. Thus, Palladio presented only classical details as archetypes in the *Quattro Libri*, a mode of thinking analogous to his presentation of idealized versions of his own projects.
The inscription (1) on this template identifies its author as stonecutter and sculptor Giovanni Giacomo ("Zangiacomo") who lived in the *contrada* of S. Vitale in Venice. He was the son of Pietro Comini, also a stonecutter who appeared in some of the contracts for work undertaken by Giovanni Giacomo at S. Giorgio. Giovanni Giacomo's

presence at S. Giorgio occurred during two different phases in the construction: the first recorded between 1588-97, for ornamental stonework in the choir, the sacristy, and the transept and nave altars; the second between 1607-11, for the facade. The second period can be eliminated from our consideration as he had moved to the *contrada* of S. Margherita, so this *sagoma* must date from the first period. The template previously has been associated with a date of 1568, probably due to the mistaken identification of its author with another stonecutter and architect, Giovanni Giacomo di Guglielmo de' Grigis ("Zuangiacomo"), who had worked from 1567-71 with Andrea della Vecchia under the direct supervision of Palladio (Archivio di Stato di Venezia 1980: 52, cat. no. 130; Caniato and Dal Borgo 1990: 164). During Palladio's tenure, the *sagome* were by his own hand, and were so identified in documents. After Palladio's death, however, there are no longer direct references to his authorship of the various drawings and *sagome* used in the completion of the new church. This template with its explicit inscription is confirmation that working drawings were supplied as work progressed, and were later by the hands of the stonemasons executing a particular phase. In fact, this would have been the more usual procedure in Venice; Palladio was unusual in acting as both architect-designer and draftsman for the stonework. Palladio's design authority nonetheless remained a constant reference for the work carried on at S. Giorgio; his wood model provided a standard of detail, as did the stonework already finished. Furthermore, in the period in which Giovanni Giacomo executed this profile, the *proto* of the church was a stonecutter who had worked on the fabric from its inception under Palladio, thus providing continuity in the *cantiere* at S. Giorgio.
The template's purpose must also be reassessed. The "sagoma di le giorne" of the inscription formerly has been identified with the "grondaia" (presuming "giorna" to be derived from "gorna") or rain-gutter of the church, executed together with the interior cornice in 1568. A document from this earlier period defines the "gorna": "la qual gorna s'intende la gola e'l gozzolatoio et li modiglioni" (Zorzi 1967: 66, doc. 24; ASV 1980: 52, cat. no. 129; Caniato and Dal Borgo 1990: 165, fig. 168). The destination of this template now must accord instead with Giovanni Giacomo di Pietro's commissions, from his first phase between 1588-97. Probably done at a 1:1 scale, ruled lines (some first incised) and freehand curved lines delineate the profile: fillet, cyma recta, fillet, corona, fascia, fillet, cavetto (originally drawn as a second, recessed fillet), cyma reversa. The latter is inscribed as the "modioni" (2). These elements, "le gorne" and "li modioni," are mentioned among the work done in the sacristy by Giovanni Giacomo and his father in 1593. The contract was drawn up on 23 February 1592 *m.v.* (= 1593) and signed on 3 March 1593 for: "Item siano obligati detti maestri far le gorne che vanno intorno detta sagrestia, quale va longa piedi 45 et larga 30 in luce dentro la muraglia con li modioni che abbraccia la muraglia conforme alle sagome sottoscritte ut supra" (Zorzi 1967: 72, doc. 38). The work was to be completed by *quaresima* 1594, for which the abbot promised they would receive four *bigonzi* (1 = 129.6 liters) of *vino buono*, in addition to the 1,326 ducats for this and other work.   *T.E.C.*

<small>500</small>

Bramante
Luciano Patetta

Bramante, S. Maria presso S. Satiro, Milan false choir

It is not certain which were Bramante's first works in Urbino. He was possibly present on the site of the construction of the church of S. Bernardino, and may have taken part in decorating the Palazzo Ducale, and in the "architectural assemblage" of Federico da Montefeltro's Studiolo (ca. 1476).

The attribution of the painted architecture in S. Bernardino in Perugia (ca. 1473) is also uncertain. It is not known what route he took when he moved to Lombardy (through Florence, Ferrara, or Venice?). What is certain, however, is that in 1477 Bramante was in Bergamo, where he painted the frescoes of the facade of the Palazzo del Podestà. While he was working here he probably met Amadeo, who was then completing the Cappella Colleoni (1476).

Bramante was certainly in Milan by 1481, the date of the "Incisione Prevedari", which illustrated a ruined classical temple and became an authentic manifesto for the new architecture based on the canons of classical antiquity. But it is also possible that Bramante reached Milan two or three years earlier. It seems that at first he worked as a

Bramante, S. Ambrogio, Milan

painter only, for example, on the frescoes for the Casa Panigarola (now in the Brera, Milan).

In Milan Bramante had to reckon with the Late Gothic tradition of Guiniforte and Pietro Antonio Solari, still the chief architects at the city's most important construction sites. The other dominant influence was the emerging Florentine manner launched by Brunelleschi (brought to Milan by Filarete and Benedetto Ferrini), whose influence can be seen in the Cappella Portinari at S. Eustorgio (1468). The architects working in Milan would at this time have been acquainted with the set of drawings by Filarete for his *Trattato d'Architettura*, written at the time of Francesco Sforza.

Bramante's first documented work is the church of S. Maria presso S. Satiro, where he built a sacristy (1483) on an octagonal plan, with niches and a matronea inspired by examples from late antiquity; here too he created his "mirabili artificio," a choir in false perspective which, despite a depth of just over one meter, successfully creates the illusion of an entire arm of the Greek cross church. Various hypotheses have been put forward about the church's original plan: Förster (1956) and Bruschi (1969a) suggest that it had three naves, while Patetta (1987) affirms that it was centrally planned with a single nave. The side of the church along today's Via Falcone presents a

composition made up exclusively of classical orders—a complete novelty at the time. From 1492 to 1499 Bramante was commissioned by Lodovico il Moro to modify Solari's church of S. Maria delle Grazie. He demolished the Late Gothic choir and replaced it with a long tribune which rises into a polygonal drum. The magnificence of the new tribune was without precedent in fifteenth-century architecture and became the prototype of many large-scale projects in the ensuing century. The building, later completed by Amadeo, presents a complex repertoire of proportions and cosmic and numerological symbols. Bramante's third known undertaking in Milan is the rectory of S. Ambrogio (1492-99), which he designed as a "classical forum" on a square plan with a triumphal arch set centrally on each side.

Though never completed, the court is extremely important for the elegance of the arcading, the orthodoxy of the proportions, the grace of the Corinthian columns with their dosserets, and the use of columns in connection with a giant order of pilasters. Bramante's designs for two cloisters of unusually large proportions were executed later on, in the sixteenth-century, inside the monastery of S. Ambrogio.

Chronicles and histories written during the last few centuries have contributed to fostering the "myth" of Bramante, attributing to him the projects of many other buildings, including the main square in the town of Vigevano, and the Loggia delle Dame in the adjacent castle; the Cappella Pozzobonelli; the Ponticella or little bridge at the Castello Sforzesco in Milan, the portico of S. Maria presso S. Celso; the cathedral of Pavia; and the arch on the facade of the church of S. Maria at Abbiategrasso, near Milan. Some of these attribution have been disproved, others are still in doubt. At any event, it is unlikely that Lodovico il Moro did not consult Bramante, the most important architect practicing in the duchy, on many of the works cited above.

Cristoforo Lombardo (?), Certosa of Pavia

Upon the fall of the Sforza dynasty in 1500, Donato Bramante moved to Rome. His first architectural commissions must have been the Palazzo for Adriano Castellesi da Corneto (which he only began), two fountains (in Piazza S. Pietro and in Piazza di S. Maria in Trastevere) and, perhaps, the *Antiquarie prospettiche romane*, the focus of his research and surveys.

Bramante became part of the entourage of Cardinal Olivie-ro Carafa, who accorded him the commission for the cloister of S. Maria della Pace (1500-04), where his authorship is fully documented. The system of proportion and modulation, the compact composition achieved through the use of pilasters, the emphasis on the central space in which the perspective axes—both orthogonal and diagonal—lead unexpectedly toward a solid instead of a void (Bruschi 1969a), demonstrate that Bramante's research in Milan had achieved full maturity.

Above the ground story with arches framed by Ionic and Tuscan pilasters, Bramante designed a comparatively lower story, articulated by Composite pilasters and delicate Corinthian columns. The small consoles of the frieze reveal Bramante's familiarity with the classical syntax of the Colosseum.

The next important commission, the Tempietto at the church of S. Pietro in Montorio (1502?), was built for Spanish patrons. Owing to its compositional perfection, the Tempietto stands as a paradigm of the symbolic and formal ideals of the entire epoch and culture. The building marks perhaps the first application of the Doric order with triglyphs and metopes.

Bramante was employed in the Vatican from 1504 to 1514. For Pope Julius II he designed the Belvedere Court, the Loggia di S. Damaso, the cupola for Torre Borgia and the first plan for New St. Peter's. The Belvedere was conceived as an enormous open space to serve as a court, theater, garden and also as a museum; Bramante's vast

Cesare Cesariano (?), S. Maria presso S. Celso, Milan

scheme could only have been modeled on those of imperial Rome. The great exedra niche and the *lumaca* staircase were complete novelties of their day, and their majestic composition wholly appropriate to the colossal scale of the court. Had it been completed, Bramante's section of the Loggia di S. Damaso (1509) would have offered a symbolic frontage to the burgeoning urban fabric in front of St. Peter's. Bramante's studies for the new basilica (from the famous "parchment plan" onward), evince a long process of linguistic and typological research which culminated in a centralized plan, here an inscribed Greek cross with domes (or quincunx pattern). All the numerous projects are clearly inspired by the vast unitary spaces found in the architecture of late antiquity (Ackerman 1954b, Frommel 1976). For St. Peter's, Bramante was assisted by several architects (who were also in competition with him)— Giuliano da Sangallo, Baldassarre Peruzzi and Fra Giocondo; his relations with Egidio da Viterbo, Raphael, and Michelangelo were of a more dialectical nature, however.

The following projects are definitely attributable to Bramante during this period in Rome: the apse of S. Maria del Popolo: a tribune fronted with a coffered arch (taken from the Pantheon); the Palazzo Caprini (later the House of Raphael), in which he perfected the relations between

501

orders and stonework (including a rusticated ground story), between ornament and structure, and where he applied a three-column corner solution that was destined to become very popular; the Palazzo dei Tribunali included in the pope's urban redevelopment scheme along Via Giulia, Via Longara and Via dei Banchi, which addressed Julius II's program for the centralization of power (Tafuri 1984c). Bramante's lessons in compositional experimentation, his direct revival of the language of antiquity, and adroit choice of classical models, were variously applied to many other works, some of which were formerly ascribed to him but are now largely attributed to his followers or assistants.

Such exemplary works include S. Maria della Consolazione at Todi; the Nymphaeum at Genazzano; SS. Celso e Giuliano, and S. Maria dell'Anima in Rome; the Rocca at Viterbo; the fortress at Civitavecchia; the church of S. Maria Assunta in Roccaverano (more probably based on his plan); and the Palazzo Apostolico in Loreto.

BIBLIOGRAPHY: Malaguzzi Valeri 1915b; Ackerman 1954b; Förster 1956; Bruschi 1969a; Frommel 1976; 1984b and c; Tafuri 1984c; Patetta 1987; Borsi 1989.

119
DONATO BRAMANTE
Man-at-Arms

Milan, Brera, Inv. Reg. Crom. 1233
Detached fresco.
120 × 115 cm

BIBLIOGRAPHY: Lomazzo 1584; Torre 1674; Allegranza 1781; Beltrami 1902; Malaguzzi Valeri 1915b; Suida 1953; Förster 1956; Mazzini 1964; Bruschi 1969a; Mulazzani 1974; 1977; Pedretti 1977; Mulazzani 1987; Sironi 1978; Bruschi 1983a; *Urbino e le Marche...* 1983; Ferri Piccaluga 1986; Bora 1986; Borsi 1989.

This man-at-arms is part of the frescoes of the Casa Panigarola in Milan, which were detached in 1901 and are now conserved in the Brera.

The fresco cycle, perhaps commissioned by Gottardo Panigarola (Beltrami 1902), perhaps by Gaspare Visconti, Bramante's patron (Allegranza 1781), once decorated the walls of a hall and was composed of eight niches and a panel above the door with the famous picture of Democritus and Heraclitus. The standing figures of the armed barons fill the semicircular niches decorated with pilasters and Quattrocento Corinthian capitals, reduced horizontally as in some of Bramante's buildings. The graphic reconstructions (Bruschi 1969a; Mulazzani 1974 and 1977) were convincing in their identification of the siting of the *Man with a Mace* and the *Man with a Broadsword*, the only complete figures, and of the others, reduced to busts.

The attribution of the frescoes to Bramante (not backed up by documentary evidence), has been generally accepted on the basis of Lomazzo's comments in his *Trattato della Pittura* (1584, Book. VI, 1, xvi) where, when discussing the ability to wield arms of three Milanese noblemen, he

writes: "all three were ... painted armed as barons by Bramante in Milan in Casa dei Panigaroli near S. Bernardino. Where the latter painted his quirks of nature, that is Heraclitus weeping and Democritus laughing, over a doorway." The attribution is confirmed by Milanese historians such as Carlo Torre (1674): "In this house there are wonderful tempera paintings by Bramante, which trick the eye into believing that they are sculptured marble and not paintings."

The date of execution is uncertain; if completed in the 1480s (Malaguzzi Valeri 1915b; Bruschi 1969a; Sironi 1978), then they are directly linked with those in the Palazzo del Podestà in Bergamo (1477) and with the Prevedari engraving (1481), and hence with Bramante's arrival in Milan; this would confirm his early success as a painter. If they date to the years 1492-94 or later (Mulazzani 1978; *Urbino e le Marche...* 1983; Borsi 1989), stylistically the frescoes betray Bramante's expressive maturity as a painter and greater self-assurance compared to his first works.

The cultural references of the Panigarola frescoes are multiple and complex, and range from his enquiry into perspective at Urbino and his probable connections with Melozzo da Forlì and Luca Signorelli, to his undoubted acquaintance with Leonardo and Bernardino Zenale, and likewise Mantegna and the milieu of Ferrara, and not least the influence of the Lombardy terracotta figures (the *all'antica* heads on the facades of the Banco Mediceo and the Ospedale Maggiore); lastly, to take into account is Bramante's knowledge of neo-Platonism and Milanese culture at the end of the fifteenth century (Ferri Piccaluga 1986).

Bramante was constantly experimenting with three-dimensional architectural organisms to either translate into reality or simulate in painted or sculptural form. A prime example is the "mirabili artificio" of the *trompe l'œil* perspective choir in S. Maria presso S. Satiro.

The figures of the men-at-arms are heroic and *all'antica*, but they are also realistic: real men whose large features are heavily emphasized by a marked chiaroscuro. The rigorous stereometric and proportional construction of their bodies is highlighted in the strong relief of the volumes.

There is still one question that remains unanswered and that is the frescoes' links with other paintings in Milan: such as the *Argus* fresco at the Castello Sforzesco, and in particular, the facade of the Casa Fontana where, according to Lomazzo, Bramante had painted a fresco with mythological figures, admirable "for their majesty and movement." These are the same "fake bronze giants" that Vasari attributed to Bramantino.   L.P.

120
RAPHAEL
Study for the Figure of Bramante in the "Disputa"
1509-1510

Paris, Musée du Louvre, Department des Arts Graphiques, 3869
Silverpoint on greenish-gray prepared ground.
409/412 × 277/278 cm

BIBLIOGRAPHY: for complete bibliography, see Joannides 1983, no. 224; Knab et al. 1983, no. 303; *Raphaël...* 1992, no. 44.

The drawing shows preparatory studies for the head, neck, right hand, left hand, and draped figure of the man on the far left of the *Disputa*, who is leaning on the balcony gesturing to an open book.

The older man in the fresco, and thus in the Louvre drawing as well, is considered to be a possible portrait of Bramante (see, for instance, Borsi 1989: 18, and the title of the Louvre drawing in *Raphaël* 1992, no. 44). It was common for Vasari, as well as for earlier writers, to identify portraits of famous contemporaries in such large fresco scenes, and many of these attributions are presumably correct.

Unfortunately, Vasari only tantalizingly refers to the "infiniti ritratti di naturale" in the *Disputa* (Vasari 1879: 336). In his discussion of *The School of Athens*, however, he explains that the figure of Euclid, shown on the far right bending over and holding a compass, "dicono essere Bramante architetto" (Vasari 1879: 331).

The Louvre drawing and the man in the *Disputa* share some general facial characteristics with the Euclid on the opposite wall, though in each case the head is partially hidden.

In this exhibition, the drawing can also be compared to Caradosso's *Bramante Medal*, where the similarities consist of a high forehead, sharp profile, deep-set eyes, and strong nose. However, such traits may simply be Raphael's way of evoking an older, forceful-looking man. Raphael seems to have used the model who posed for the so-called Bramante figure, in other less detailed drawings (see Knab et al. 1983, nos. 303, 346, 347, 350). The identity of the figure in the fresco, and in the Louvre preparatory drawing, must therefore remain in doubt.

Isabelle Frank

121
BERNARDO PREVEDARI
Temple Interior
1481

Milan, Raccolta delle Stampe Achille Bertarelli,
Castello Sforzesco
Engraving; 70.5 × 51.3 cm.

BIBLIOGRAPHY: Beltrami 1917; Dalai 1961; Wolff Metternich 1967-68; Bruschi 1969a; Mulazzani 1972; *Atti...* 1978; Dell'Acqua and Mulazzani eds. 1978; Alberici 1980; Martelli 1984; Alberici 1988.

The engraving executed by Bernardo Prevedari in 1481 after a drawing by Bramante constitutes a historiographical riddle of exceptional interest in terms of both style and iconographic content. Stylistically, the slender figures inside the temple only partly correspond to the manner of the artist who painted the frescoes known as *Men-at-Arms*, now in the Brera; the solemn figure of the kneeling friar is much closer to the Bramante of that period. From the iconological point of view the overall significance of the picture is not explicit, since it has neither clear precedents nor evident successors, even though it emanates an extraordinary appeal, as if—as has often been suggested—it portrayed a ruined building that has been ennobled by a superior grasp of spatial rationalization. It may seem logical to suppose that, apart from the subject matter itself, the engraving harbors a special didactic significance, as suggested by the cone-shaped shadow detail that is apparently cast by the kneeling friar, but is actually inconsistent from the point of view of realism. The shadow is obviously meant to represent the perspective pyramid, drawn and accentuated in order to appear as a kind of gnomon or sundial tracing the passage of the hours and space, creating an overlapping of the temporal and spatial dimensions (a curious invention for this period). This curious and fascinating motif found its way into later figurative works linked to Bramante's ideas, though more coherent realistically, such as the memorable example in the Recanati polyptych by Lorenzo Lotto (signed and dated 1508), in which the shadow of S. Vito's flagstaff in the panel to the right falls across the central panel, marking the perspective pattern of the floor with the same logic as the one used in the Prevedari engraving, thereby guiding the eye and certifying the "naturalism" and logic of one-point perspective. Even though the apex of the shadow cone does not lead to the central vanishing point, in the case of Lotto's polyptych, it serves to indicate S. Domenico, who is receiving the scapular from the Virgin Mary; in the case of the Prevedari engraving it falls just short of the giant candlestick, the object of the kneeling friar's attention. This figure could be Bramante himself, portrayed as a disciple of Fra Luca Pacioli.

In the Prevedari engraving the employment of perspective is ambivalent because, while it keeps strictly to the Albertian construction of one-point perspective by depicting the candlestick slightly off-center with respect to the background apsidiole, by shifting the pier supporting the interrupted arch Bramante introduces a second perspective space, which does not directly comply in compositional terms with the former.

Moments of order and chaos exist side by side in the Prevedari engraving. They are emphasized by the enigmatic character of the subject, in which the sacred and the profane maintain an extraordinary balance even from the purely iconographic point of view, and the veneration of the mysterious candlestick adds a sense of bewilderment which is also present precisely in the intimate perspective structure of the overall picture.

In this regard, it should be noted that the two friezes in the Prevedari engraving can be related directly to those divided by the inscription, Lex, in the famous fresco of Heraclitus and Democritus, conserved in the Brera, Milan, which has been interpreted as the transmutation into a figurative form of the ideas of Plato's Republic concerning the structure of the ideal state. The almost total conceptual overlapping of these friezes and the hypothesis often advanced that the Democritus in the fresco is a self-portrait of Bramante, endorses the date of 1480 for the execution of these famous frescoes, detached from the walls of the house in Via Lanzone in Milan (incorrectly called Casa Panigarola). If this is the case, then it supports the widespread opinion that the Men-at-Arms frescoes and the Prevedari engraving are part of a set of coeval works focused on a common theme.

This identification of Bramante with Democritus during the early part of his working life is particularly interesting when compared to Raphael's portrait in the Stanza della Segnatura in the Vatican, in which Bramante appears as Euclid. The grounds for comparison are the striking parallels between the perspective and figurative structure of Prevedari's Temple Interior and the spatial design of Raphael's School of Athens. These parallels are linked to the two alternative approaches to the representation of space in the late Quattrocento and early Cinquecento. The first pivoted on the città ideale or ideal townscape, and the second on scenografia in the Vitruvian sense. In short, the Prevedari engraving is a case of scenography as Vitruvius intended, while the School of Athens expresses

a combination of the ideal townscape typified by the Urbino panel, and scenography, as seen in a great many remarkable pictures executed in the 1470s and 1480s: the St. Bernardino panels in Perugia, Pinturicchio's Miracles of St. Bernardino fresco cycle in the church of S. Maria d'Aracoeli in Rome, and the Prevedari engraving discussed here. In the days of Bramante's youth, artistic enquiry was centered on the dichotomy of the città ideale and scenografia because it derived directly from the ongoing dialectical debate over the science of perspective, a debate that had become identified with the opposing standpoints of Brunelleschi and Alberti. The mechanics of perspective became the focus of theoretical reflection in the period just before Bramante left Urbino for Milan, when Piero della Francesca (1475) presented Federico da Montefeltro with his treatise on art, De prospectiva pingendi.

It would be strange indeed if the Urbino-born Bramante was not acquainted with this treatise, which discussed the entire question of perspective as it had developed throughout the century, and remained a lasting influence on subsequent generations. It was in fact Vasari who emphasized Brunelleschi's predominance over Alberti in Bramante's work.

The Vitruvian revival under way at that time fully endorses the identification of Bramante with the figure of Democritus, an association further sanctioned by the character portrait (whether true or false) offered by Vasari, who describes Bramante as "a cheerful, engaging person who always enjoyed giving pleasure to his friends ... and kept the company of ingenious men," and who is therefore very likely to have been acquainted with Vitruvius' definition of scenography: "frontis et laterum abscendentium adumbratio ad circinique centrum omnium linearum responsus."

Democritus plays a part in this definition in fact, as noted in the Proem to Book VII of De architectura, in which Vitruvius explains the evolution of the Tragic Scene: "Namque primum Agatharcus Athenis Aeschylo docente tragoediam scaenam fecit et de ea commentarium reliquit. Ex eo moniti Democritus et Anaxagoras de eadem re scripserunt." By this, he meant that they wrote about the consistent application of visual focus [focal point] when transposing an image from the [mere two-dimensional] plane to the perspective representation.

This consistency is a feature of the Prevedari engraving, in which the former central point of focus is replaced by a string of viewpoints accentuated by the scattered and "natural" presence of onlookers. This factor betrays something of Bramante's training as an artist; according to Vasari he learnt to paint under Fra Carnevale, a disciple of Piero della Francesca.

If Fra Carnevale was indeed the so-called "Maestro delle Tavole Barberini," and the Birth of the Virgin in the Metropolitan was the altarpiece for the church of S. Maria la Bella in Urbino (as Vasari claims), the association becomes more credible. The application of perspective in the small altarpiece in the Metropolitan is much closer to Brunelleschi's idea of scenography than to the Albertian idea of the centric point, whose almost perfect example is the Ideal City panel in Urbino.

In the Birth of the Virgin there is also a shifting of the perspective focus into at least two different spatial fields, and the figures—evidently inspired by the Albertian ambience exemplified in the Tempio Malatestiano in Rimini—are distributed across the space in conformance with the scenographic principles of Vitruvius.

In the Prevedari engraving this criterion is inserted into a perspective grid that accentuates the sense of construction in contrast to that of demolition, according to an idea that Bramante, almost prophetically, would later develop in the reconstruction of St. Peter's, which during this period (1480s) was undergoing an operation of dismantling and demolition.

The image of the temple open to the elements but locked in a perspective system respecting the principles of scenografia (implying a lack of a proper floor construction, and a sequence of architectural structures) was to culminate in the concept of the tempio aereo, i.e., the unen-

closed, roofless temple that can be seen in Raphael's School of Athens, which retains the same tone of "profane sacredness" that pervades the Prevedari Temple Interior. While the engraving seems to foreshadow the destruction and reconstruction of St. Peter's, Raphael's fresco has always seemed to offer an emblematic model—translated into painting—of the application of Euclidean geometry, with its certainty of Being.

It is curious, therefore, that Bramante is transformed from Democritus, the student of the Vitruvian principles of scenografia, into Euclid, the regulator of those principles. In the School of Athens, the figure of Bramante is depicted busy demonstrating the calculation of space, tracing the traditional square module of intersecting triangles on the ground before him. In much the same way, the "sundial" shadow pointing toward the columnar candlestick in the Prevedari engraving emphasizes the movement of light in space across the surface of the floor.

This deceptively simple detail is an exemplification of the ongoing dialectic between the Albertian ideal townscape and Brunelleschi's concept of space in terms of decentralized perspective, a space susceptible to the constant mutations of light; this principle that may well be an intentional ingredient of the famous painted perspective panels, in which the effect of reflected light on the painted surface itself was a premeditated element of the final result.

The Urbino Ideal City lacks all references to adumbratio, the Latin term used by Vitruvius for shadow or shading, but which can also be translated as "visual illusion."

The dramatization of perspective structure is, of course, scenography. In the Segnatura frescoes, Bramante's pupil (or, at least, follower) is applying a criterion by which the Albertian principles of perspective have been assimilated with the magnificent and "living" idea of scenography.

The relationship between the Prevedari engraving and the School of Athens fresco offers other significant features, however. The perspective criterion with which the pilasters have been articulated to define the space is common to both works, as is the idea of the unroofed building, communicating the principle of "work in progress" which, while not actually contemplated by Alberti in his theoretical writings, is paradoxically made manifest in the Tempio Malatestiano, the symbol and epitome of "incompleteness" from the humanist era.

At this point it is necessary to turn back to the interpretation of the Men-at-Arms frescoes as an allegory of the perfect State, and to the need to find a contemporary date for both these and the Prevedari engraving. In his definition of the perfection of the State, Plato analyzes the canonical juxtaposition between order and disorder, and explores the political prerequisites of harmony.

This juxtaposition in Prevedari's Temple Interior lies in the precarious, but rigorous imbalance of the perspective, in which the spatial indeterminacy intimates an uncertainty of place and time, and the building seems less of a place of worship than a "hallowed" profane building.

The dialectic of Heraclitus and Democritus is one of compensation. Their laughter and tears are a universal metaphor for the concept of dialectics, and the Prevedari engraving is undoubtedly based on the dialectical issue of visual representation, though its ultimate meaning remains elusive. The pivotal issue here is the meaning of perspective itself, that is, whether perspective is a projection or a construction. The projecting shadow in the form of a perspective pyramid is the discriminating factor of the Prevedari engraving, and it is not surprising that Lorenzo Lotto, who was raised on the culture of Bramante, was fascinated by it. During this same period, however, there was a marked trend in painting toward the use of elevations, a typical attribute of stage design. As a disciple of Brunelleschi's school of thought, Bramante made a substantial contribution to this tendency with the present engraving, and developed the theme even further in his project for S. Maria presso S. Satiro in Milan.

However, it can hardly be coincidental that the figure of Euclid (Bramante) in the School of Athens is shown drawing on the floor of the building: the primary means by which he develops his ideas is the horizontal projection, exemplifying the principle that a building is the spatial multiplication and articulation of the ground plan. The peculiar immobility or temporal stasis typical of the *Ideal City* panels and certain types of *intarsia* work involves the elimination of "shadow" as an element of the composition. Conversely, in the Prevedari engraving Bramante explores the idea of scenography which, inevitably, contains the element of mobility, implied by the source of light. In this way, perspective also offers a means of assigning a temporal parameter to the composition.

Raphael followed a similar principle in his transition from the compositional scheme of the *Marriage of the Virgin* (Brera, Milan) to that of the *School of Athens*.

In short, the perspective concept expressed in the Prevedari engraving is the measurement of space by means of horizontal projection. Considering the date in which it was formulated and applied, the device introduced by Bramante in this picture is one of visionary and forward-looking cogency, a virtual incunabulum representing the Renaissance procedure of marking out perspective space with the gnomon of time.

Claudio Strinati

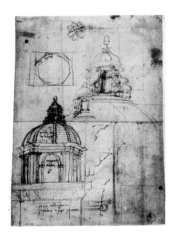

122
BALDASSARRE PERUZZI
Cupola of the Torre Borgia
before 1523

Florence, Galleria degli Uffizi, Gabinetto Disegni e Stampe, Uff. 130Ar.
Pen and sanguine on white paper.
300 × 212 mm
The drawing shows the perspective elevation of the tower, two sketches of the lantern, a schematic plan of the polygonal dome, a rosette and moldings of an entablature.
INSCRIBED: *Tore de Borgia In palazo di papa in Roma; questa brucio di luglio 1523; tempore Adrianj VI.*
VERSO: pen sketches of plans and a column, with measurements.

BIBLIOGRAPHY: Tomei 1942; Ackerman 1949-51; 1954; Bruschi 1969a; Frommel 1984b; 1984c; Borsi 1989.

One of the projects included in the general scheme for rebuilding and alterations in the Palazzo Apostolico and for Bramante's reconstruction of the Loggias, commissioned by Pope Julius II as from 1507, was a cupoletta to be placed on top of the Torre Borgia, which had crenelated battlements of medieval origin. The square tower had been added in 1494 by Alexander VI to the fifteenth-century palace built by Nicholas V, and its exterior adopted the same characteristics and elements, such as the windows with cross mullions. Originally there were two open arches on the top floor (they are now closed) supported by enormous piers. The building contained the Stanza della Sibilla and the Sala del Credo, and it communicated directly with the Borgia apartments (Tomei 1942) where Julius II lived—to his displeasure—until 1507. It is not known exactly when it was decided to build this extension, which comprised an octagonal dome probably made

of a lightweight wooden structure covered with lead laminate. Its function was evidently largely symbolic and decorative (even though it appears to have been used as a dovecot). Giuliano da Sangallo was working on it in 1513 at the beginning of the reign of Leo X. A fire then destroyed the tower in 1523, and the upper part was never rebuilt (Ackerman 1949-51 and 1954). Bramante's name is mentioned in passing in a letter written the same year, 1523, and conserved in the Archivio di Stato at Bologna (Bruschi 1969a). Giuliano da Sangallo in 1513 and Baldassarre Peruzzi, some time before 1523, executed drawings of the design (Uff. 143A and 130 respectively). The Ionic capitals with a rosette and the profiles of the entablature (similar to those of the Belvedere and the Logge di S. Damaso) can certainly be attributed to Bramante on the basis of style. Some Sangallian motifs can, however, be recognized in the lantern (Bruschi 1969a). It is possible that Giuliano da Sangallo modified and refined certain details while directing the works with Antonio da Sangallo the Younger. While Giuliano's drawing offers us a picture of the complete new building including the base of the tower, Peruzzi's just shows the final part with the dome, a partial section, three sketches of the lantern and a plan of the polygonal structure.

The dome of the Torre Borgia, together with the Loggias (today called Logge di S. Damaso), the frescoes painted by Raphael in the Stanza della Segnatura (1508), the commission given Michelangelo to fresco the Cappella Sistina (1508) and, naturally, the Belvedere Court all fully meet the requirements of Julius II's political and symbolic ambitions with a courtly and imperial ceremonial that was designed to signify the renewal of the Roman Catholic Church.

L.P.

A

B

123
ANTONIO LAFRERY
Palazzo Caprini (House of Raphael), Rome
1549

(From A. Lafréry, *Speculum romanae magnificentiae*, Rome 1549.)
Engraving.
INSCRIBED: *Raph. Urbinat ex Lapjde Coctili Romae extructum.*

ANONYMOUS
Palazzo Caprini

London, The British Architectural Library Drawings Collection, Royal Institute of British Architects, IV, 11
Pen and ink, with wash.
270 × 375 mm

PROVENANCE: Andrea Palladio; Burlington-Devonshire Collection.

BIBLIOGRAPHY: Gnoli 1887; Förster 1956; Ackerman 1966b; Wasserman 1966; Bruschi 1969a; Portoghesi 1971; Bruschi 1973; Frommel 1973; Burns et al. 1975; Tafuri 1984c; Bruschi 1985b; Borsi 1989.

Lafrery's engraving is the clearest and most complete document for analyzing the facade of the palace, designed by Bramante, which was built, apparently, at the corner of Via Alessandrina and Piazza Scossacavalli. This work by Bramante is usually dated as about 1510, but there is a suggestion that the project itself dates from much earlier, to 1501 (Frommel). The French engraver Lafréry provided a much more exhaustive view than any other sixteenth-century illustrations, showing the entire five-bay facade with its rusticated street frontage, paired Doric order on the *piano nobile* and tall windows with triangular pediments and balustrades resting directly on the wall of the ground story. A perspective view of the facade can be seen in a drawing conserved at the R.I.B.A. in London, once attributed to Palladio but now omitted from the inventory of his works (Burns et al. 1975). (It was suggested that Palladio could have drawn it during his sojourn in Rome in 1549.) The drawing illustrates the unusual three-column corner solution (actually two half-columns flanking a protruding column) designed to accentuate the three-dimensional character of the building (Bruschi 1969a; Borsi 1989) and the *botteghe* open along the flank of the building.

Bramante reinvented the ancient Roman workshop with its architrave surmounted by an arch inset with a window. While the Doric frieze with triglyphs and metopes (and the "orthodox" inclusion of a corner triglyph) and the insertion of little windows cut into some metopes demonstrate the maturity of Bramante's manner and his creative revival of antiquity, the constructional technique displays his experimental research into structural problems. The practical and rapid method of "molding the vaults with mixed lime in carved wood casings together with their friezes and foliage" was promptly praised by Vasari: "He had the palace in the Borgo which belonged to Raphael from Urbino built and decorated with brickwork and by filling molds, columns and the Doric and rustication, a very lovely thing and a new invention making things with molds" (*Life of Bramante*). The plan of the three-column corner group is analyzed in plan in an early sixteenth-century drawing ascribed to Jean De Chenevières (Munich, Staatsbibliothek, Cod. icon., 195, fol. 5).

The palace was bought by Raphael in 1517, who lived there until his death in 1520, though he felt it was not large enough to meet the needs of his workshop and was planning to move to the new Via Giulia. The building was completely finished, as confirmed by an entry in 1518 in the register of the *Magistri viarum*: "... on the way to St. Peter's by the old road to the right [stands] the house of Raphael from Urbino with five *botteghe*." The palace changed hands and underwent alterations (as shown in Ottavio Mascherino's drawings in the Accademia di S. Luca; Wasserman 1966), before being incorporated into the Palazzo dei Convertenghi and subsequently demolished in 1937. Like the Palazzo dei Tribunali, this palace was to become a model for many other buildings—and not only in Rome; it also became a point of departure for further developments in the Cinquecento in the Veneto and the rest of Europe (Ackerman 1966b). The rusticated base and the Doric order, derived philologically (and in a learned way) from antiquity, became the premise for Raphael's own explorations of palace architecture, starting with the Palazzo di Jacopo da Brescia (Tafuri 1984c).

L.P.

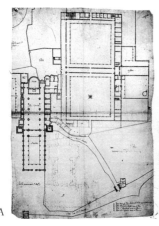

A

124
Anonymous
*Plan of the Basilica and the Bramante Cloisters of
S. Ambrogio, Milan*
early 17th cent.

Milan, Archivio Storico e Biblioteca Trivulziana, Raccolta
Bianconi, T. IV, fol. 1
Ink, with sepia and pink wash; 565 × 850 mm.
Verso: measured survey of the plan and part of the elevations
in pencil.
Proportional scale of 30 Milanese *braccia*.

B

Anonymous
*Elevation and Section of the Bramante Cloisters of
S. Ambrogio, Milan*
early 17th cent.

Milan, Archivio Storico e Biblioteca Trivulziana, Raccolta
Bianconi, T. IV, fol. 8
Ink, with wash; 430 × 265 mm.
Proportional scale in Milanese *braccia*.
Inscribed: *lo impiegi delli Claustri et coridori de St.Amb.o Mag.e.*

Bibliography: Malaguzzi Valeri 1915b; Salmi 1940a; Baroni 1941;
1944; Förster 1956; Bruschi 1969a; Lowinsky 1975; Patetta 1983;
Frommel 1986-87; Werdehausen 1986; Patetta 1987; Borsi 1989;
Gatti Perer 1990.

The two drawings date from the late sixteenth-early
seventeenth century when, besides the reworking of the
interior of the Romanesque basilica, and an ongoing dispute between the canons regular and the Cistercians of
S. Ambrogio over boundaries and servants, restoration
work ordered by Cardinal Federico Borromeo was carried
out and a project was drafted for a radical reworking of the
basilica in the Baroque style. These and other drawings
were, perhaps, made at a time when solutions were being
sought to improve the illumination in the naves and
chapels, which was impeded by the cloister walls. Since
there are no original drawings or models, these are among
the earliest documents providing evidence of Bramante's
projects for S. Ambrogio. The plan shows the rectory arcade along the left flank of the basilica, and the two
cloisters and refectory of the monastery near the right. By
contrast, the drawing on fol. 8 is dominated by the section
of the central body between the two cloisters which reveals the innovations Bramante introduced to the traditional convent layout. On the upper story is the vast and
luminous gallery, which marks the distribution of the
monks' cells. The ground story shows an unusually high

portico with columns on pedestals, in which ample halls
alternate with refectories and libraries with "lunetted"
vaults, and a series of rooms one above the other. The picture also illustrates—on the upper floor—the utilization
of the minor order, alone, which, exactly at the time these
drawings were made, was the subject of criticism by the
classical esthetes, who abhorred the pilaster placed above
the middle of the arch. There is ample evidence that the
rectory, commissioned by Lodovico il Moro, was the work
of Bramante. His name occurs several times while work
is in progress from 1492 to 1499. The grammar of
Bramante's project was not only unusual for a rectory, it
was also completely unprecedented, and formed part of an
equally innovative vision of town and monument planning. Bramante planned a structure that was to develop
round a square, porticoed piazza. The entrances were to
be four double-height triumphal arches, set midway on
each side of the square. Setting aside the obligatory references to Brunelleschi's Ospedale degli Innocenti, to the
courtyard of the Palazzo Ducale at Urbino, and to the triumphal arch facade of S. Andrea in Mantua, the portico
displays great formal self-assurance in the use of the orders, refined elegance in the harmonious proportions of the
arches, and excellent craftsmanship in the capitals and refined decorative details. Bramante experimented the union between columns and the major order of the pilasters.
He introduced a spatial component in the frontage: the
dome vault at the top of the central arch. Moreover, he
developed his own variation for the dosseret above the
capitals, creating a form of entablature (complete with architrave, frieze and cornice), thereby providing the first
demonstration in Milan of the appropriateness of using
the order this way, in which the arch does not spring immediately after the capital (Bruschi 1969a). At the corners
and flanking the arch Bramante has introduced a piece of
intellectual, allusive whimsy with his four knotty, "rustic"
columns (*ad tronchonos*), an order Vasari acclaimed as absolutely innovative. Bramante was also the architect of
the chapels inserted between the buttresses of the basilica
and the end wall of the rectory which he also designed to
stand further away and not against the pre-existing walls
(Patetta 1983 and 1987). The cloisters were commissioned in 1497 by Cardinal Ascanio Sforza, the duke's
brother, who brought the Cistercians to S. Ambrogio
from Chiaravalle, an abbey under his protection (ca.
1498). Bramante probably only witnessed the opening of
the yard: building continued intermittently through the
next century, but always respecting (so it appears) the
model he had built, which is repeatedly mentioned by various sources. The choice of the facades seems to have been
inspired by the Crypta Balbi, which he perhaps knew
from a drawing made by Giuliano da Sangallo (Bruschi
1969a; Borsi 1989). Taking a framework based on
squares, the elevations are comprised exclusively of classical elements: entablature, arch, columns, and pilasters;
the order of one cloister is Doric, the other Ionic.
Bramante's choice of the Doric order in particular marks
his break with the traditional decorativeness of the
pseudo-Corinthian and Composite capitals used throughout Lombardy, as indeed here in the rectory (Frommel
1986-87; Werdehausen 1986). Once again the use of dosserets above the capitals of the ground-floor arcade plays
the role of a rigorous entablature. The use of the arch enframed by pilasters (and windows within the arches) appears here on the upper story. This arrangement became
very popular in sixteenth-century Rome. In Milan therefore, Bramante took the first steps toward eliminating all
elements foreign to the grammar of classical antiquity, a
development that reached full maturity in Rome, where
he was surrounded by examples from antiquity.
Dating from this Milanese period is a project for a cloister
at the Abbey of Chiaravalle, also probably by Bramante.
The cloister was demolished in the last century and all
that remains is an eighteenth-century picture of it by
Domenico Aspari (Lewinsky 1975).   *L.P.*

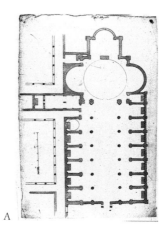

A

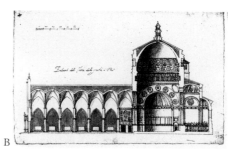

B

125
Anonymous
*Plan and Longitudinal Section, S. Maria delle
Grazie, Milan*
16th-17th century

Milan, Archivio Storico e Biblioteca Trivulziana, Raccolta
Bianconi, T. V, fols. 17A, 17B
Ink, with sepia wash.
425 × 278 mm
Proportional scale of 60 *piedi* of 1/2 Milanese *braccio*.
Inscribed: *S.ta Mar.a delle gratie; Elevato della Chiesa delle gratie
in P. Verc.a.*

C

Anonymous (previously attributed to Bramante)
View of S. Maria delle Grazie, Milan
16th century

Urbino, Casa di Raffaello
Pen and sanguine on paper; 243 × 329 mm.
Verso: pen drawing, detail of an altar.

Bibliography: Beltrami 1895; Malaguzzi Valeri 1915b; Pica and
Portaluppi 1938; Salmi 1940a; Baroni 1940; Förster 1956; Bruschi
1969a; Pedretti 1981; Bruschi 1983a; Patetta 1987; Borsi 1989.

The two drawings in the Bianconi collection show the
enormous discrepancy of proportions between the Late
Gothic church begun by Guiniforte Solari in 1463, and
Bramante's new choir apse. Executed between 1598 and
1631, when structural weaknesses in the dome and piers

called for reinforcement and restoration, the drawings illustrate the organ, decorations, and stalls built as sixteenth-century style additions to Bramante's project. The two drawings are the earliest documentary evidence of the work in question, together with the *veduta* of the Anonymous Fabriczy (Stuttgart, Staatsgalerie) and that conserved in Urbino (Casa di Raffaello). There are no extant architectural drawings or models of S. Maria delle Grazie.

It was Lodovico il Moro who—surprisingly—decided as from 1489 to introduce Renaissance concepts in this Dominican church which had in fact only just been completed. The first innovation was a new barrel-vaulted portal flanked by Corinthian columns and pilasters. This was once attributed to Briosco and Cazzaniga, and then to Giancristoforo Romano and to Amadeo (Beltrami 1895; Pica and Portaluppi 1938; Salmi 1940a). In 1492 work started on the choir apse. The change in shape was expressly recommended by the duke himself and by Vincenzo Bandello, the prior, a leading intellectual and theologian at the Sforza court. Lodovico il Moro planned to involve the whole church in the alteration scheme. A report dated 1497 states that advice has been sought from "all the experts to be found in architecture ... to examine and make a new model of the facade ... and to adjust the church proportionally to the great chapel" (Patetta 1987). Structural work on the walls ended in 1497, and the following year work was done on the sacristy (which has a "lunetted" vault with "umbrella" terminations) and on the small cloister (still in the Lombard tradition), both of which are attributed (albeit tentatively) to Bramante. Documentation regarding the choir apse is equally scarce; the first mention appears in 1494 with the registration of an order for marble, and in an early sixteenth-century chronicle written by Giorgio Rovegnatino, who referred to earlier documents (since lost). In another record, dated 1497, concerning the supply of various small marble columns for the loggias at the top of the *tiburio* or crossing tower, there is a reference to Amadeo, confirming the hypothesis that when advice was sought in 1497 a commission was given not only to Amadeo but perhaps also to Battagio and Dolcebuono. Lodovico il Moro probably also called in Leonardo da Vinci, then at work on the *Last Supper* fresco, as the latter made several sketches of moldings and a plan of an apse almost completely detached from the nave of Solari's church. Pedretti suggested that this solution corresponded to the intentions of the Duke of Milan (Pedretti 1981) because, after the death of his wife, Beatrice d'Este, in 1497, he perhaps wanted the new building to become the Sforza family mausoleum. Not surprisingly this was the year he urged Cristoforo Solari, "Il Gobbo," to make haste with the monumental tomb for himself and for Beatrice (today at the Certosa of Pavia), to be placed in the new choir.

Doubts about Bramante's authorship—which would at any event be shadowed by other contributions and by compromises with local craft tradition (Malaguzzi Valeri 1915b; Pica and Portaluppi 1938; Salmi 1940a; Baroni 1941)—have recently been swept aside by the close examination of the relationship between the unprecedented dimensions of the extension (presaging S. Maria della Consolazione at Todi, and St. Peter's in Rome) and the command of the composition, the freely expressed architectural details and transgressive use of the classical orders (Bruschi 1969a; Patetta 1987; Borsi 1989). While on the outside there is a greater concession to the Lombard decorative style with its brickwork and terracotta, the cubic interior with its three round apses and hemispherical domes linked to the tall central drum by means of four pendentives, demonstrates an extraordinary repertory of optical correctives, of symbolic, cosmic and religious elements, and a scholarly and complex numerological scheme that would be difficult to attribute to any other architects active in Milan in the 1490s: 4 for the distribution of the elements; 5 for the decorative rings in the dome; 7 for the painted wheel windows; 8 for the segments of the umbrella vault in the choir and the ornamental medallions; 12 for the oculi in the choir; 32 for the windows in the *tiburio*, and so forth. And while the presence of numbers and the evident symbology all tie in well with the interests and fashions of Lodovico il Moro's court, other characteristics, such as inscribing the segments of the semidomes over the apses with decreasing geometrical patterns, may be linked to the presence in Milan of the mathematician Luca Pacioli (1496), and particularly to Pacioli's research into the "perfect" 72-sided solid.

L.P.

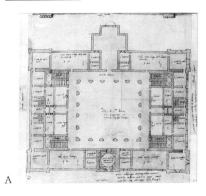

126

Antonio di Pellegrino (attrib.)
Palazzo dei Tribunali and the Church of S. Biagio della Pagnotta

Florence, Galleria degli Uffizi, Gabinetto Disegni e Stampe, Uff. 136Ar.

Pen and bistre on white paper.
Recto: sanguine, sketch of the landscape and surroundings.
389x400 mm
Inscribed: *Palazo di S.to Biagio della pagnotta.*

The drawing was once attributed to Dosio and to Antonio and Battista da Sangallo, but the handwriting has been recognized as different from their style. It is more likely the work of someone from Bramante's shop, such as his assistant, Antonio di Pellegrino. The drawing came into the possession of Antonio da Sangallo the Younger, as he himself explains in the center of the paper. It may have been a part of Vasari's famous 'Libro' (Frommel 1974).

B

Pier Maria Sebaldi (attrib.)
Foundation Medal for the Facade of the Palazzo dei Tribunali
ca. 1509

Vatican, Biblioteca Apostolica Vaticana, Medagliere, XXII, 21

Bibliography: Gnoli 1892; 1914; Giovannoni 1914; Bruschi 1969a; Portoghesi 1971; Frommel 1973; Salerno et al. 1973; Frommel 1974a; Tafuri 1984c; Borsi 1989.

There are two authoritative sources on Julius II's plans for the siting of public buildings along Via Giulia (which was opened by Bramante), and the project for the Palazzo dei Tribunali. The first contemporary source is Egidio da Viterbo, who commemorated the papal urban renewal projects such as the opening of Via Giulia and other streets "*quas Bramantis architecti clarissimi consilio et rectas et latas fecit*" and recorded the courthouse "*ad divi Blasii aedem, domus ingentis fundamenta iecit, quem juris dicendi locum esse decreverat.*" The second source is Vasari, who writes in his *Life of Bramante*: "The pope resolved to locate all the offices and the courthouses of Rome in Via Giulia, opened by Bramante. ... Whence Bramante started the building seen next to S. Biagio on the Tiber, in which there is still an unfinished Corinthian temple, a very rare thing, and the rest is the beginning of beautiful rusticated building. It is a grave omission that such an honorable and useful and magnificent work has not been finished, which is considered by those who are in the profession the most beautiful order that has ever been seen of its kind." Moreover, from information provided by sixteenth-century chroniclers, in particular Albertini in 1510 (*Opusculum de mirabilis novae et veteris Urbis Romae*) we can infer that work had already started the previous year on both the courthouse and the church it incorporated. The building was not blessed by fortune: still incomplete at the death of Julius II (1513) and Bramante (1514), it was almost entirely demolished and integrated with new buildings.

Apart from sixteenth-century maps of Rome, our knowledge is based exclusively on a few drawings (perhaps not entirely reliable) which show an incomplete palace and a cross-shaped church with a dome. Another drawing, by Baldassarre Peruzzi (Uff. 109A), most likely a survey, shows a corner of the courthouse and the church of S. Biagio, which evinces a slightly elongated centralized plan, a dome atop a square drum with rounded corners, small round apses, and niche chapels in the side walls. According to the above the passage from Vasari, the church had a Corinthian facade. All that remains of Bramante's work today is a stretch of a rusticated wall and plinth. An idea of the frontage can be deduced from drawings in the Uffizi (Bruschi 1969a) and from Julius II's foundation medal, in which the building is shown as a castle with crenelated corner towers and a taller tower in the center. Naturally the medal only offers us a rough image, without architectural detail. A drawing by Fra Giocondo (Uff. 1537A, attrib. by Giovannoni 1914) may also refer to the facade under construction. It illustrates both a typical ancient Roman *bottega* or workshop, and a rusticated portal (or perhaps central *bottega*) with the bay of a loggia on the upper story. The drawing thus sets forth a ground story with a Rustic order, as confirmed by the building remains; together with rustication of alternating thin and thick courses, as used for the Porta Julia at the Belvedere (a very popular motif in Rome in the sixteenth century). Two drawings show the church of S. Biagio alone; one is in the *Codex Coner* (fol. 7) and the other in the Uffizi (Uff. 1896A) which bears the legend: "S.to Biagio ... in Roma di Bramante Architecto."

The most complete and reliable information comes instead from an Uffizi drawing (Uff. 136Ar.) attributed to either Antonio or Giovan Battista da Sangallo, though perhaps the work of Antonio di Pellegrino, Bramante's assistant both at Loreto and at St. Peter's (Frommel 1974). The drawing shows a clear rectangular plan with four faces, jutting angular extensions, a central square courtyard on whose symmetrical axis the cross-shaped church has been situated. The enormous facade (430 Roman *canne*, or ca. 100 meters) is interrupted by the plinth of a square tower with an octagonal interior plan. The courtyard pillars with their engaged half-columns suggest that the design, quite likely, envisaged arches enframed by classical orders, a solution Bramante had used in Rome several times before. The plan shows the *piano nobile* with its large meeting rooms, reception halls, some apartments and, presumably, the offices. The building's public character is confirmed by the insertion of as many as four staircases, each leading to a courtroom with adjacent offices. The sheet is filled with annotations describing the different functions of each area: "This is the drawing of the first floor, and above this another one very like this will be built with other rooms to be used by familiars"; "tower above the entrance with campanile"; "room in the tower"; "secret staircase from the cellar to the kitchen and up to the dining-room"; "room above the place of interrogation." On the verso of the sheet are traces of a sketchy plan showing what has recently been identified as a square planned for between the Palazzo dei Tribunali and the Cancelleria Vecchia (Frommel 1974a).

Bramante's grandiose courthouse project was in total harmony with the pope's urban renewal drive, in which the architecture derived directly from the models of classical antiquity; the concentration of the law courts in the new part of the city, furthermore, tied in perfectly with Julius II's economic and political outlook, and with the new strategy of *renovatio urbis* (Tafuri 1973 and 1984c). L.P.

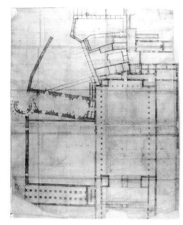

127
ANTONIO DI PELLEGRINO (attrib., after Bramante)
Project for the Renovation of the Palazzo Vaticano and the Loggias
datable 1507

Florence, Galleria degli Uffizi, Gabinetto Disegni e Stampe, Uff. 287A

Ink and sanguine, with additions in pencil and stylus impressions; on white paper; composite sheet; left border trimmed; scale in Roman *palmi*.

1340 × 1030 mm

ANONYMOUS
Foundation Medal

London, British Museum

BIBLIOGRAPHY: Letarouilly 1882; Ehrle and Egger 1935; Ackerman 1954b; Förster 1956; Bruschi 1969a; Shearman 1972; Redig de Campos 1974; Frommel 1976; 1977a and 1984c; Davidson 1983; Borsi 1989.

The most important and architecturally defined project among the many which Bramante carried out for the Vatican, is certainly that of the loggias overlooking the Cortile di S. Damaso. The Uffizi drawing (Uff. 287A), dating to 1507 or perhaps slightly earlier, is not by Bramante himself but is a copy attributed to Antonio di Pellegrino from Fiesole, who worked under Bramante in around 1510, both at the St. Peter's site and in Loreto. It illustrates the master plan for the renovation works ordered by Julius II for the area northeast of St. Peter's. The site comprises the court and loggias in question, the Stanze around the so-called Cortile del Pappagallo, the Scala Regia (on the

right), the Torre Borgia and the lower part of the Belvedere Court itself—already designed between 1503-04 (lower left), the entrance court, and a round temple (top), a building with three naves and pillars perhaps planned as a warehouse or stables whose upper story would probably house the library planned during the reign of Nicholas V (left). A large square tower has been drawn at the north end of the loggias. A peripteral temple with niches and aedicules on the inside was planned to be built atop the so-called Torre di Nicolò V. Access was through an atrium: documents of the time indicate a "chapel with large vestibule." The vestibule was an enormous rectangular room (118 × 370 *piedi*, or 36.30 × 82.65 m), with niches and paired columns along the walls, and could be reached from the Belvedere. It was designed as the meeting-room for the cardinals during conclaves (*ad conciones*) to elect the pope. In spite of the limitations imposed by the irregular medieval and early fifteenth-century fabric around it, the building complex presented in the drawing (in absence of drawings showing the elevations) illustrates Bramante's use of antique canons derived from the monuments of imperial Rome. Vasari is referring to this drawing when he writes in his *Life of Bramante* "he made a very large drawing for the restoration and straightening of the pope's palace." The plan shows the famous Stanze, some of which were still undergoing alterations and changes (indicated by broken lines). Bramante's sequence of little pillars as used in the loggias emerges in an early, sketched version (altered after 1508). Moreover, a part of the entrance court, opened to the east toward the city, is lightly sketched in pencil. Also in pencil, a large exedra has been lightly sketched near the Torre Borgia. Traces of a rusticated portal can be seen in the courtyard. These additions may have been made by Bramante himself (Frommel 1976, 1977a, 1984c).

Little is known about the appearance of the Vatican buildings when Bramante began the projects for their transformation. Some idea can be drawn from the view of the old city in Benozzo Gozzoli's fresco in the church of S. Agostino in the town of S. Giminiano, and from the perspective plan of Rome made by Schedel in 1493 and the so-called "plan of Mantua." It seems that the old Palazzo Apostolico had a loggia on the upper story, and perhaps an arcade below. The facade terminated in a corner tower at each side. This has been confirmed by recent excavations on the site (Redig de Campos 1974). Bramante therefore gave new form and proportions to the pre-existing architecture, most of which was medieval. After having (perhaps) closed the old arches to create a solid wall along the base, with several openings and pilasters, Bramante demolished the corner tower near the basilica and extended the building by more than twenty meters. Above this he built two galleries of thirteen bays with arches enframed by orders. The first Tuscano-Doric order has a "candelabra" balustrade; the second is Ionic, with a "double belly" balustrade. He placed the papal staircase *a cordonata* as described by Vasari, next to this extended building. Contemporary accounts assert that it was possible to ride up the stairs on horseback. There is evidence of several stonemasons being paid at the end of 1509 for supplying travertine pillars, by which time the first loggia must have been nearly finished (Bruschi 1969a). Work proceeded slowly amid countless difficulties, accompanied by demolitions, alterations and additions. When Bramante died in April 1514 the second loggia still had not been erected. The previous year Raphael had been accorded tenure of the site—perhaps together with Giuliano Leno and Baldassarre Peruzzi (Bonelli 1960). In his *Life of Raphael*, Vasari recalls that Raphael "also made designs for the papal staircases and the loggias which Bramante had started but were left unfinished upon his death. Their construction was continued with the new design and plan produced by Raphael, who made a wooden model which was more ornate and stylistically purer than Bramante's work." Doubts do remain about whether or not Raphael respected Bramante's project during his tenure.

Most historians agree that the alterations to the second

loggia were few and very slight in terms of the adoption of different order from the one below; opinion differs, however, as regards the third loggia, built in 1517 with Corinthian columns (Ackerman 1954b; Borsi 1989). Confirmation that this was part of Bramante's original scheme and that he had already prepared the erection of the inner wall (Frommel 1977a and 1984c) before his death may lie in the abovementioned observation of Vasari that the loggias were "imperfette," that is to say, missing some envisaged part. Moreover, in 1513 Bramante was working on a commission from Leo X for the restoration of the third floor of the Stanze where Cardinal Bibbiena had his rooms (Shearman 1972; Davidson 1983). The conclusion of at least a part of the loggias can be dated as before 1519, the year in which Raphael had Giovanni da Udine paint the famous foliage and *grottesche*. Maerten van Heemskerk's perspective engraving (1534) gives an indication of what the recently terminated front was like; the whole project has been carefully reproduced in Letarouilly's plates (1882).

Julius II took over Nicholas V's grandiose building program described by his biographer Giannozzo Manetti, as testified by the scheme for the Belvedere Court. As far as the residential buildings were concerned, the pope soon had to give up the ambitious idea of completely rebuilding everything. He fell back on partial reconstructions—not without compromises. A case in point occurred around 1507, while still an unwilling tenant in the Borgia apartment (Frommel 1984). At all events, these achievements too stem directly from Julius II's political, symbolic, religious and secular program for a "*Roma instaurata*," and "*renovatio Ecclesiae.*" L.P.

The Belvedere Court
Sabine Eiche

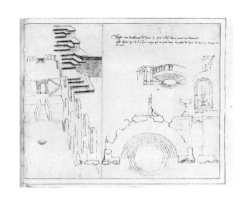

For over fifteen years, every time the pope or a member of the Curia wanted to go from the Vatican Palace to Innocent VIII's Villa Belvedere, built 1485-87, he had to make his way northward through more than 300 meters of open, hilly terrain. Pope Julius II, elected 1503, ended the rustic isolation of the Belvedere when he commissioned Bramante to connect palace and villa by way of two corridors across the space, the beginning of his grand scheme for rebuilding the Vatican on a scale reminiscent of Imperial Rome.

The task was challenging: Bramante's design had to reconcile two older complexes of different styles and diverging orientations, and regularize the land between, all in a monumental, classical way. What Bramante created was the first majestic architectural garden since antiquity, a vast space over three times as long as it is wide, divided into three levels, bounded on the long sides by superimposed loggias. His sources of inspiration are thought to have been both literary descriptions of ancient architecture (Tacitus, Suetonius, Pliny the Younger, Biondo), as well as the visible remains of such sites (Palatine stadium, Horti Sallustiani hippodrome, temple at Palestrina, Hadrian's Villa at Tivoli). Bramante's *cortile* or court, in turn, had a greater influence on subsequent garden-villa design than any other Renaissance project (e.g. Villa Imperiale, Pesaro; Villa Lante, Bagnaia; Villa d'Este, Tivoli).

The three levels of the Court are planned along a south-north axis. The lowest level, next to the Vatican Palace, served as an arena for spectacles. The other two were connected by monumental stairs along the central axis. At the center of the rear wall of the upper level was a semicircular exedra preceded by convex steps that became concave inside the hemicycle. The rear wall to the right served to camouflage Innocent's villa, the axis of which deviates considerably from that of Bramante's Belvedere Court. The open space resulting between the northern wall and the villa was transformed into a statue court for Pope Julius' renowned collection of antiquities.

The elements of the Belvedere Court are laid out so as to draw the eye down the center of the stretch of open land, and end in the exedra, the focus of the whole. The fact that the architectural perspective of Bramante's design could be fully comprehended only from a viewpoint outside the space, namely from one of Raphael's Stanze in the Vatican Palace, reveals that Bramante here used a painter's technique of composition, and the resemblance of the court to a Renaissance theater set is striking.

By the time Bramante died in 1514, the eastern corridor was well under way; the stairs between the terraces were built; the exedra at the northern end was begun; and numerous antiquities were already displayed in the statue court. The spiral stair giving public access to the statue court was also under construction.

The spatial unity of Bramante's court survived barely eighty years. Though two substantial changes in the 1550s and 1560s had already seriously modified its intended impact, in 1585 Sixtus V destroyed forever the essence of Bramante's design when he ordered Domenico Fontana to build a library across the court, on the site of the middle terrace.

128

UNKNOWN (16TH CENTURY)
(formerly attributed to Giancristoforo Romano)
Portrait Medal of Pope Julius II with Bird's-Eye View of the Belvedere Court on Reverse

Milan, Raccolte Archeologiche e Numismatiche, 351.
Bronze.
46 mm
INSCRIBED: IVLIVS · SECVNDVS · PONT · MAX · (obverse); VIA · | · VIL · III · ADIT · | · LON · M · | · ALTI · L · XX · | · P · | VATICANVS | · M · (reverse).

PROVENANCE: unavailable.

BIBLIOGRAPHY: Bonanni 1699, I: 158-159; Hill 1920: 54; 1930: 227; Ackerman 1954b: 192; Lowry 1957: 166; Weiss 1965: 180-181; Frommel 1984b: 123.

On the reverse of the medal is a schematic representation of Bramante's design for the Belvedere Court. In a bird's-eye view looking eastward we see the Vatican Palace at the right and the three levels of the Belvedere Court to the left. We can discern the basin from the Baths of Titus set up in the center of the lowest level, and the great ramps leading to the intermediate level. According to Lowry (1957: 66) the structure at the end of the upper terrace represents the exedra, though in view of its great height it is more likely to refer to the Villa Belvedere (Ackerman 1954b: 192). The corridors between the palace and villa are two stories high along the lowest level, diminishing to one story at the upper terrace. The ground-level arcade is continued along the south facade of the Vatican Palace. Bonanni (1699, I: 159) construed the inscription as follows: VIA IVLIA TRIVM ADITVVM LONGITVDINIS MILLE ALTITVDINIS SEPTVAGINTA PEDVM, and suggested that it referred to the distance between the Vatican Palace and the Villa Belvedere. In fact, the court is just over 1000 Roman *piedi* long (1 Roman *piede* = 0.297 m), and the upper terrace is approximately 70 *piedi* higher than the lowest one (Ackerman 1954b, pl.I).

Hill originally associated the medal with Giancristoforo Romano, an attribution he (1930: 227) subsequently discarded, while retaining that the obverse shows Romano's influence. Ackerman (1954: 192) gives the medal to Romano with a question mark, while Weiss (1965: 181) agrees with Hill's rejection, concluding that the engraver remains unknown.

Ackerman (1954: 192) dates the medal to the end of Julius' pontificate, and argues that it represents the Belvedere Court under construction. Lowry (1957: 166) and Weiss (1965: 181) rightly point out that views of buildings on medals usually show projects as they were intended to be realized, rather than under construction. Weiss (1965: 181) proposed a date between 1504-07/08, which Frommel (1984-85: 123) has narrowed down to 1503-04. The medal reverse, then, appears to confirm Vasari's (1568, IV, 156) statement that Bramante "spartì nel più basso [level] con duoi ordini d'altezze ..." (Ackerman 1954b: 49). The decision to add a third loggia to the corridor is believed to have been taken around 1505-07, after Pope Julius moved from the rooms of the Borgia pope on the first floor of the Vatican Palace, to quarters on the second floor, near the Stanze subsequently decorated by Raphael (Shearman 1972: 5-6; Frommel 1984b: 123).   *S.E.*

129

UNKNOWN FRENCH
(attributed to Jacques Androuet Du Cerceau the Elder, and now Philibert de l'Orme)
View of the Belvedere Court with Details of the Stairs, Exedra and Statue Court

Windsor Castle, Royal Library, RL 10496
Pen, brown ink, wash, traces of black chalk (recto); pen, brown ink and black chalk (verso); paper folded once vertically.
Watermark: hunting horn in circle; closest to Briquet 7855.
292/290 × 364/359 mm
INSCRIBED: Mo[n]s[ieu]r tant humblement com[me] faire je puis a v[ot]re bonne grace me recom[m]ende / mo[n]s[ieu]r saches que je suis fort marry que ne puis avoir nouvelles de vous je vous ay raicrit deux / ou trois (upper right); memorex q[ue] le font [?] ne [illegible words: tournne ... / point a bas?] (below niche right center); venere / lacon (in niches on plan right center).

PROVENANCE: Cassiano dal Pozzo; Albani; George III.

BIBLIOGRAPHY: Ashby 1904: 87; 1913: 197-199; D. Frey 1920: 20-24; Blunt 1945: 15; Ackerman 1954b: 20, 28, 30-32, 205-206; Blunt 1958: 16, no. 3; 1975: 214, no. 19.

The recto of this drawing provides important information about Bramante's design for the central stairs between the lowest and middle terraces (destroyed 1585), and the exedra (radically modified mid-16th cent.).

At left, an unfinished schematized perspective view of the court from the lowest courtyard to the upper level, including the eastern corridors and northern wall. The artist has encased the central stair in solid walls, and appears to have also considered putting walls to the right and left of the stair, across the slope of land between the first and second levels. Above and to the right, a carefully rendered perspective drawing of a detail of the central stair between the lowest and intermediate levels, showing the podium with four convex steps (on Peruzzi's Uff. 569Av., Dosio's Uff. 2559A, and Bibl. Vat. Cod. Vat. Lat. 7721, fol. 78 there are six steps; according to Ackerman [1954: 20] there were to be 10 or 11 steps), followed by three groups of concave steps, the first with four steps, the others with three. The stair was to have 15 groups of concave steps, each of the 15 corresponding to one of the rows of seats to right and left (see Uff. 569Av.). At bottom right is a plan of Bramante's exedra, clearly showing the facade extensions to right and left, with part of the plan of the statue court above, here incorrectly drawn on axis with the exedra (Ackerman 1954b: 28). It does, however, represent fairly accurately the three exits of the exedra (Ackerman, 1954b: 28); they led, moving clockwise, into a garden at west, to the loggia between the garden and statue court, and into the statue court. Inscriptions identify two niches in the statue court as settings for the *Laocoon* and a Venus (on statue court see Brummer 1970, and Grisebach 1976: 209-220). Above right is an elevation of one of the semicircular niches, with profiles of the niche moldings and pedestal base (Ashby 1913: 197; Frey 1920: 20). At upper right is a perspectival view of the exedra, with three convex and 10 concave steps (eight concave steps on plan); both sets should have been eight in number (Ackerman 1954b: 32). The most valuable information conveyed by the small view is the relationship between Bramante's platform and lateral facade extensions, revealing that the height of the hemicycle was about 2/3 that of the court facade (Ackerman 1954r: 30-31). Because of its reduced height, the pilaster order inside the exedra was smaller than that on the facade; the facade extensions across the exedra would have served to camouflage the difference (Frey 1920: 24; Ackerman 1954b: 31).

On the verso is a rough perspectival view of the whole court, drawn very faintly in black chalk, with a one-story loggia drawn carefully in pen and ink. The black chalk drawing had not been noticed previously; the one-story loggia in pen and ink was incorrectly identified by Ackerman (1954b: 205) as representing the northeast corner of the upper terrace. In fact, it refers to the ground floor of the eastern corridor, which the artist has extended across the right half of the northern end of the lowest terrace masking the slope of land on which the rows of seats were to be located (see also schematized view on recto). It is most interesting to note that the exedra, with Bramante's convex-concave stairs, here appears vaulted, though it has not yet attained the dimensions of Ligorio's *Nicchione*.

Ashby (1904: 87; 1913: 197), following a reference of Geymüller, first published the drawing, attributing it to Du Cerceau on the basis of the calligraphy. Ackerman (1954b: 205) observes that the exedra on the recto appears unfinished, which suggests the drawing was made before 1535 when Peruzzi completed it. According to Geymüller (1887: 13-14), Du Cerceau was back in Paris in 1533-34, which would provide a *terminus ante quem* for the drawing. More recently, Blunt (1958: 16, no. 3; 1975: 214, no. 19), following a suggestion by Arnold Noach, has attributed the drawing to Philibert de l'Orme, who was in Rome between 1533-36.   *S.E.*

spiral stair, sketches of arms, head and upper torso of reclining figure, miscellaneous lines (right sheet).

Provenance: unavailable.

BIBLIOGRAPHY: Ackerman 1955b: 213; Borsi 1989: 271.

Interior view with fragment of plan, and perspectival cross-section with plan, of a spiral stair. A note written on the mount of the drawing records that Geymüller connected it with Bramante's spiral stair at the Vatican Belvedere, an identification that has not been contested, even though the stairs are drawn with steps rather than the continuous treads in fact built. Encased in a square tower, Bramante's spiral stair is attached to the eastern exterior wall of the Villa Belvedere. It rises in six turns around an open well. The segmental vault of the stair is supported by columns that change from Doric to Ionic to Composite in ascending order; the stone parapet that once encircled the well, as seen on 2700A, is no longer extant. Also adapted for horses (Vasari 1568, IV, 158), the stair provided public access to the papal collection of antiquities displayed in the statue court, and was approached by way of a road through the Prati (Ackerman 1954b: 38-39). According to Vasari (1568, IV, 158) the design of the stair derived from that in the twelfth-century bell tower of S. Nicola, Pisa. Borsi (1989: 271) suggests various other precedents, among them the stairway of Palazzo Contarini Dal Bovolo in Venice, and, more convincingly, Francesco di Giorgio's ramp in the stables of the Palazzo Ducale, Urbino. Bramante's creation was rated as outstanding by such contemporaries as Serlio, Palladio and Vasari (Ackerman 1954b: 39-40 no. 1; Borsi 1989: 271).

It was copied by Girolamo Genga in the ruined house of the former Barchetto, Pesaro (Vasari 1568, VI, 319). Construction on the stair began during Bramante's lifetime, and is believed to have reached the fourth turn before he died; Peruzzi finished it around 1535 (Ackerman 1954b: 45, 62). The two views on 2700A are thus dated to a period between 1535/36 and the 1550s, when the new Belvedere fortifications blocked the access via the Prati road (Ackerman 1954b: 213).

Cataloged as anonymous, the drawing has been associated tentatively with Dosio (unsigned note on mount). In fact, though the paper is similar, the two views appear to have been done by two different hands, that of the interior view somewhat more accomplished than that of the cross-section.   *S.E.*

View of the Belvedere Court drawn from an elevated position in the Vatican Palace, on axis with the courtyard. In the immediate foreground is the basin from the Baths of Titus. Blocks of stone lie either side of a path cutting diagonally across the lowest court. The eastern corridor is already three stories high, the upper loggia closed with three apertures in each bay, as projected by Antonio da Sangallo around 1541 (Ackerman 1954b: 66, 212). At left, we see only a low wall and workmen digging a trench for the foundations of the western corridor, begun in August 1561 (Ackerman 1954b: 93). The central stair between the lowest and intermediate levels is as it appears in the view attributed to Naldini (Cambridge MA, Fogg Museum of Art, 1934: 214); still missing are the 15 rows of seats for spectators to either side of the stair. To right and left of this area are indications of corner towers under construction, which Ackerman (1954b: 24-25, 123, 220) argues were meant to hide the undecorated side walls of the middle terrace from the view of an observer at the southern end. They also serve another purpose: their presence neatly eliminates any awkward transition of the ground-story arcade from the lowest level to the adjacent rise of land (Bramante's facade wings across the exedra served a similar camouflaging purpose). The upper terrace is divided into eight parterres, with the fountain of Julius III at the center (Ackerman 1954b: 74, 82). The left wall is low and partly obscured by small trees. At right we see the arcades of the eastern corridor, with more trees planted alongside. As in the Fogg view, Bramante's northern termination of the *cortile* has been replaced by a two-story palace, Michelangelo's straight symmetrical stair substituting the circular convex-concave one by Bramante (Ackerman 1954b: 73-82).

Hofmann (1911, pl. X) dated Uff. 2559A around 1550, while Lotz (Wachler 1940: 238, no. 264) proposed 1555. Egger (1932, I: 32, pl. 51), maintaining that the two-story palace at the northern end had been built by Pius IV, considered a date after 1562. Hülsen (1933, XX) agreed, advancing the possible time period to 1566. Hübner (1911: 367, no. 19) observed that the workmen walking across the lowest level seemed to be carrying building materials to the site of the Casino of Pius IV, a project begun for Paul IV in 1558. The fact that work on the western corridor of the *cortile* has not progressed beyond the digging of trenches, indicates that the view records the situation prior to August 1561 (Ackerman 1954b, 220), and 1558-60/61 is now the date usually associated with the drawing (Bruschi 1969a: 872; Acidini 1976: 32-33).

Though Dosio's authorship has not gone unchallenged in the past (see Wachler 1940: 237-238; Ackerman 1954b: 220), it is now generally accepted. Serafini's (1915: 360) attribution to Girolamo da Carpis unconvincing (Ackerman 1951: 75, no. 1; 1954b: 68, no. 3). Most recently, Denker Nesselrath (1992: 218, 220) associated the drawing with Naldini, claiming it is by the same hand as the Fogg view (oral communication).

Uff. 2559A originally formed part of a volume measuring ca. 230 × 330 mm, containing over 110 drawings (see old number "LX" at lower right of sheet), some of which have been identified. They are divided between the Uffizi Gabinetto dei Disegni e Stampe (loose), and the Berlin Kupferstichkabinett (in album, *Codex Berolinensis*, 79 D I; Hülsen 1933, XX). Uff. 2559A was acquired, together with about 90 other drawings believed to be by Dosio, from Ingegnere Giuseppe Salvetti on 29 January 1782 (Archivio della Soprintendenza dei Beni Artistici e Storici di Firenze, Filza XV, no. 9; Forlani Tempesti 1977, xiv).   *S.E.*

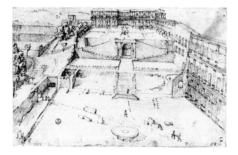

130

UNKNOWN (16TH CENTURY)
View and Cross-Section of the Spiral Stair at the Villa Belvedere

Florence, Galleria degli Uffizi, Gabinetto Disegni e Stampe, Uff. 2700A

Pen, two kinds of brown ink, two tones of pale brown wash, traces of black chalk and incised lines; composed of two separate sheets of similar paper, joined vertically with slight overlap. 204/209 × 266/269 mm (overall dimensions; individual sheets: 204/208 × 155/157.5 mm [left]; 208/209 × 117/118 mm [right])
VERSO: fragment of plan of loggia (?) (left sheet); part of plan of

131

GIOVANNI ANTONIO DOSIO
View of the Belvedere Court

Florence, Galleria degli Uffizi, Gabinetto Disegni e Stampe, Uff. 2559A
Pen and brown ink, traces of black chalk; laid down. 219/221 × 332/333 mm

PROVENANCE: Giuseppe Salvetti collection.

BIBLIOGRAPHY: Hofmann 1911: pl.X; Hübner 1911: 363, 367 n. 19; Serafini 1915: 360; Egger 1932, I: 32, pl. 51; Hülsen 1933, XX: Wachler 1940: 237-238; Ackerman 1951: 75 n. 1; 1954b: 25, 68, n. 3, 73, 212, 219-220; Bruschi 1969a: 872; Acidini 1976: 32-33; Denker Nesselrath 1992: 218, 220.

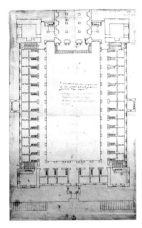

132

ANTONIO DA SANGALLO THE YOUNGER
Plan of the Palazzo Apostolico, Loreto

Florence, Galleria degli Uffizi, Gabinetto Disegni e Stampe,
Uff. 922AD.
Pen and stylus on gray paper.
592 × 343 mm
INSCRIBED: *Santa Maria di Loreto in la Marche, cioé lo palazzo
inanzi alla Chiesa, principiato per Bramante, guidato male per lo
Sansovino, bissogna corregierlo* (copy of autograph caption by
Antonio da Sangallo the Younger on the verso).
Measurements in Roman *palmi.*

It is probable that Bramante was invited to Loreto by
Julius II in 1508. Historical records show that the previous year the pope had declared his intentions to "far cose
magne a S.cta Maria" in Loreto, in order to revive veneration for the holy relic. Contemporary chronicles add that
Bramante was sent there to "disegnare molte opere." One
of these was to consolidate the support structure of the
dome with piers and buttressing walls. At the time, the
main body, which had been built in 1499 by Giuliano da
Sangallo (completing the part erected between 1469 and
1491 by Giuliano da Maiano, Baccio Pontelli, Giovanni
Alberti, and others) was showing signs of subsidence and
structural imbalance, which Francesco di Giorgio had
failed to resolve. It is difficult to determine precisely
Bramante's contribution to this job, which was subsequently taken over by Andrea Sansovino and then completed to different designs by Antonio da Sangallo (1517-
35). The evolution of the project can be seen in numerous
drawings in the Uffizi. A quantity report dated 1509
refers to "masonry for support ... built to designs by the
master Bramante" (Bruschi 1969). While he was there
Bramante may have designed a facade for the basilica,
never actually built, but shown on the face of a foundation
medal coined by Julius II (1509). The three-portal facade
without architectural orders is flanked by two campaniles, as in the plans for St. Peter's in Rome.

GIUSEPPE VASI
*View of the Palazzo Apostolico and of the Piazza,
Loreto*
1752

Milan, Raccolta delle Stampe Achille Bertarelli
Castello Sforzesco; fuori serie 1-43
Engraving; 660 × 980 mm.

INSCRIBED: *Prospetto del Palazzo Pontificio di Loreto, del nuovo
campanile e facciata della Basilica Lauretana. Il tutto fatto ristorare e
perfezionare dalla Santa di Nro Sig.re Papa Benedetto XIV
l'anno 1752.*

ANONYMOUS
Facade of the Basilica
(showing Bramante's project)

Vatican, Biblioteca Apostolica Vaticana, Medagliere, 868 (G.F.
Hill)
Medal, gold.
Diam.: 36 mm
INSCRIBED: *templum R. G. Laureti.*

BIBLIOGRAPHY: Gianuzzi 1884; Grassi 1886; Hill 1930; Förster
1956; Giovannoni 1959; Bruschi 1969a; Weil Garris Posner 1974;
Borsi 1989.

Another project commissioned by the pope to clad the
fourteenth-century wall protecting the Santa Casa with a
precious marble facing belongs to the same year. Vasari
wrote: "He executed ... the design and order of the ornament for S. Maria di Loreto." It is possible that the job—
assigned first to Andrea Sansovino (1513) and then to Antonio da Sangallo the Younger, and lastly to Raniero
Ranucci—in part respects the original plan; the embellishment by means of sculptures in the niches, bas-reliefs,
and decorations at the base and in the friezes, as well as
the addition of a balustrade, are far from the ideals of the
master (Borsi 1989). Bramante accompanied Julius II to
inspect the site at Loreto in 1510. The same year he was
paid "for the rest ... of the model of the palace that is being
built by *maestro* Bramante in front of the said church,
commissioned by Master Antonio dal Monte," namely,
the Palazzo Apostolico, where work started under the
direction of Giancristoforo Romano. When the pope
returned to Loreto the following year (perhaps in the company of his architect), according to the spiteful comments
of a contemporary chronicler, Paride de Grassis, he witnessed "ruins and buildings made by Bramante or rather
Ruinante as he is usually called in Rome." When Romano
died in 1512 the supervision of the site passed to Andrea
Sansovino (until 1517) and then to Sangallo.

In the fifteenth century the site in front of the basilica had
begun to fill with buildings of all kinds: dwellings, mansions, a rectory, a hospital, and several arcades to provide
pilgrims with a means of shelter from the elements. A
document dated 1492 records the decision of the Council
of Recanati to build a rectory. It is possible that Julius II
originally planned to build a cloister for the monks, and
that the project was soon extended to include the various
facilities for the sanctuary, a hospital, and living accom-
modation. Bramante's project may be the one illustrated
in a drawing by Antonio da Sangallo the Younger (Uff.
921Av.), which shows a pilastered portico and a large exedra similar to the one designed slightly earlier for the
Belvedere Court in the Vatican (Weil Garris Posner
1974). Another drawing by Antonio da Sangallo (Uff.
922Ar.) shows certain modifications (such as the straight
terminal side, the elimination of the two campaniles
flanking the facade, and the addition of two towers beside
the entrance) but nonetheless offers an idea of the general
arrangement of Bramante's project. The drawing bears
the inscription: "Principato per Bramante, guidato male

per lo Sansovino bissogna corregierlo" ("Begun by
Bramante, directed badly by Sansovino, must be corrected"). The project called for a spacious forum-type piazza-
court, surrounded by an arcade with an upper-story
gallery. The idea of the church square is transformed here
into a modern forum in honor of Julius II, modeled on
Caesar's forum, which had the Temple of Venus as a backdrop (Bruschi 1969a). While the grandeur of the plan imitates the Belvedere with its revival of the great monuments of antiquity, the architectural elements evince a
further development of Bramante's previous solutions,
such as the cloister of S. Maria della Pace, and the court
of the Palazzo dei Tribunali. In this case, the system of
arches enframed by classical orders, employed a few years
earlier in Rome, are repeated on the upper story. Only
eight bays were completed in the early 1500s; of these, the
first Doric order and entablature (complete with triglyphs
and metopes) could have been ready while Bramante was
alive; the balustraded upper story was probably erected
later by Sangallo and others.

It is quite possible that Bramante's project envisaged the
use of the ground floor rooms for sick pilgrims visiting the
sanctuary, and a mezzanine floor (with independent staircases, as drawn in Uff. 922Ar.) for accompanying family
members or escorts. The galleried upper story was
reserved for the governor and his guests, with an attic for
other visitors to the sanctuary. This design, which
Bramante had already partially utilized in his Doric
cloister at S. Ambrogio in Milan, was to become a model
for seminaries, colleges, and rectories throughout the sixteenth century.

Luciano Patetta

Bramante's Tempietto in Rome
Anna Elisabeth Werdehausen

The Tempietto of S. Pietro in Montorio in Rome was already considered in early writings on the history of art as the climax of Renaissance architecture due to its affinity with the models of antiquity. Even now the building is mentioned in nearly every book that chronicles the history of art. However this kind of appraisal can only be made by isolating the purely architectural form from the historical context in which it was commissioned (Wittkower 1949).

The Tempietto was built in the convent of S. Pietro in Montorio on the Janiculum (known also as the Mons Aureus, or, in Italian, Montorio), a small hill outside the city walls, to designs by Donato Bramante. After the return of the popes from Avignon, the convent rose to unexpected importance due to the diffusion of the claim, carried out with considerably effective propaganda, that St. Peter was actually crucified at S. Pietro in Montorio and not in the Vatican, as was believed until then. Even though numerous humanists and theologians of the time revealed the falsity of this new interpretation of the apocryphal tradition concerning the place of St. Peter's martyrdom, the new belief circulated very quickly and was officially recognized by Pope Sixtus IV (Lugari 1900; 1907; Lietzmann 1929; Huskinson 1969; O'Connor 1969; Vannicelli 1971: 7-18; Günther 1973: 43-45, 75-87). Unlike its precursor, the new version offered the advantage of establishing the very spot in which the crucifixion took place thanks to the existence of an old building right in the courtyard of the convent dedicated to St. Peter. Historical sources refer to a certain Beato Amadeo, founder of a reformist congregation within the Franciscan order, who often withdrew to an underground "spelunca" or "cavernula" in the convent over which Bramante built the Tempietto (see Fra Mariano da Firenze, a guide to Rome published in 1517-18).

In 1472 Sixtus IV gave the church and the convent of S. Pietro in Montorio to the followers of Beato Amadeo. After a brief period of contributions from the French king Louis XI, in 1488 Ferdinand of Aragon and Isabel of Castille, the Spanish king and queen, decided to patronize the convent and pay the expenses for the reconstruction of the building. The present stage of historical research can only provide suppositions to explain why the Spanish king and queen accepted to become its protectors (see the most recent work by Diez Del Corral Garnica 1992). Perhaps Ferdinand and Isabel, who supported several Franciscan convents in Spain, decided to sponsor the reconstruction of a Roman building because the convent contained the most important place of martyrdom, near the tomb of St. Peter in the capital of Christianity. Basing his thesis on a new but unlikely interpretation of the existing sources, Howard recently (1992) suggested that the Spanish monarchs simply gave orders to reconstruct the underground "spelunca," while the building of the Tempietto above was carried out only during the reign of Julius II (as in fact noted by Vasari).

The dating of the Tempietto by Bramante has always been controversial due to the lack of incontestable sources, and has been estimated to lie between 1499-1502, or 1508-12 (Bonelli 1960: 19; De Angelis d'Ossat 1966b: 95-98; Bruschi 1969a: 989-995; Vannicelli 1971: 65-70; Günther 1973: 20-27; Tibaudo 1974; Delfini and Pentrella 1984: 31; Howard 1992). A letter from Ferdinand dated August 1498, and two inscribed plaques placed inside the crypt that refer to the altar being consecrated in the crypt in 1500 and to the completion of the building in 1502, support the belief that the Tempietto was built between

1499 and 1502. Bramante's design for a circular courtyard around the Tempietto—revealed to posterity only in Serlio's woodcut—was never executed. In 1523 Charles V financed new buildings and the construction of the rectangular courtyard which encloses the Tempietto. Various developments in the seventeenth century altered the original shape of Bramante's construction. Many sixteenth-century drawings still show the Tempietto with an almost hemispherical dome, crowned with a tiny construction similar to a lantern (Giovannoni 1931b: 152; Förster 1953: 173; Waetzoldt 1962-63; Rosenthal 1964: 58; De Angelis d'Ossat 1966b: 95-98; Bruschi 1969a: 993-1013; Günther 1973: 28-38). The little double staircase built in 1628-29 was not the original means of access to the crypt; originally it was a very steep staircase behind the altar (see Uff. 4318Av.; cat. no. 137; Rome, Gabinetto Nazionale delle Stampe, vol. 2510, fols. 33v., 42v.). The early sources are corroborated by a study of the building. In the plan of the Tempietto Bramante respected the shape and size of the underground place of worship, where the crucifixion is purported to have taken place (Günther 1973: 46-55; 1974). Accordingly he designed a circular building in the shape of an ancient periptery, encircled by a colonnade and crowned by a dome. The diminutive proportions of the building presumably led Bramante to design the circular courtyard to accommodate visiting worshippers.

The Tempietto is the first building in the history of Renaissance architecture to explicitly emulate ancient prototypes, not just in the stylistic sense, but in its basic structure as well: it was modelled on the circular temples of antiquity, such as the Temple of Fortune at Tivoli, near Rome.

Art historians of the last century were certainly not the first to recognize the particular affinity of the Tempietto with works of antiquity. Bramante's contemporaries and the ensuing generations made more studies of this building than any other of its time, and often represented it among drawings of ancient temples.

"Copies" of ancient buildings as such were an exception in Renaissance architecture, however. The shape of the circular periptery in the Tempietto can be explained chiefly by the special conditions of the commission. Not only did the building have to be sited directly above the "spelunca" but its markedly antique form was intended to stress the antiquity of the place of the Apostle's martyrdom and hence foster its credibility. Bramante's task therefore consisted in giving new life to this ancient site of worship (Günther 1973: 88-94).

The surviving ancient circular temples no longer had any upper covering. It is doubtful whether the dome of the Tempietto derives from Bramante's interpretation of Vitruvius' description of an ancient circular temple (IV, viii, ed. Fensterbusch 1981: 196-199) (Bruschi 1969a: 1013; Günther 1973: 65-70) since no mention is made of a dome, but the text describes a drum with a pavilion roof. It is highly unlikely that Bramante mistook the term *tholus*, used in reference to roofing, to mean a vaulted dome as such, given that Vitruvius never mentions vaults in all his treatise on architecture. Even one of the greatest experts of the time on Vitruvius, Francesco di Giorgio, did not write any translation of the very difficult passage about the circular temple which suggests a dome (Francesco di Giorgio, ed. Scaglia 1985: 130). All the same Francesco di Giorgio drew circular temples with domes in his treatise on architecture, which, like the Tempietto later on, have a wider intercolumniation than that of the surviving ancient prototypes, and a sequence of pilasters along the wall of the cella (*Codex Saluzziano*, 148, Turin, Bibl. Reale 148, fol. 84; see Francesco di Giorgio Martini 1967, I, pl. 155; Rosenthal 1964; Günther 1973: 65-70). For the dome of the Tempietto Bramante was inspired above all by the tradition of the pre-Christian and medieval sanctuaries built to commemorate martyrs or saints; such buildings were often centrally planned and vaulted, in accordance with antique models (see S. Costanza, Rome; Krautheimer 1942; Grabar 1943-46, I; Lotz 1964b; Sinding-Larsen 1965: 236).

The Tempietto's Doric order, however, was not inferred from any antique model, and marks the first instance of the full Doric arrangement in the Renaissance, becoming a fundamental point of reference for architectural theoreticians (e.g., Serlio) and architects in the years ahead (Günther 1985a; Denker Nesselrath 1990: 17-22; Günther 1992).

I would like to thank Christoph Jobst in Frankfurt and Uta Schedler in Munich for their helpful contributions.

133
ARISTOTILE DA SANGALLO
View and Details of the Outside of the Tempietto

Lille, Musée des Beaux-Arts, Wicar Collection, "Michelangelo Sketchbook," fol. 762
Pen and ink; with measurements.

BIBLIOGRAPHY: Geymüller 1885: 22-25; Pluchart 1889: 161, 168; Lotz 1962; Bruschi 1969a: 999; Günther 1973: 164ff.; 1982: 86-91; Nesselrath 1983; Günther 1988f: 85ff.

The so-called Michelangelo Sketchbook in Lille contains copies of buildings from ancient Rome and the Renaissance in particular, including four sheets on the Tempietto, which Geymüller (1885) attributed to Aristotile da Sangallo. These drawings, like Uff. 4A and Uff. 1963A and the Chatsworth drawing, probably represent copies of lost originals that illustrate Bramante's project. It is no longer possible to establish whether these originals were actually drawn by Bramante himself or by one of his followers.

The similarities in the vertical measurements indicate that the three groups of drawings at Lille, Chatsworth, and in the Uffizi derive from the same prototype.

Of all the copies (the group is completed by another copy in the *Codex Kassel*, Staatliche Kunstsammlungen, Kassel, fol. A45, fol. 57r.) the view of the Tempietto in fol. 762 in the Sketchbook at Lille is the most authentic illustration of the original. The building is drawn from a very low observation point very close to the Tempietto. The entablature of the columns is curved to afford a view of the coffered ceiling. The height of the columns diminishes notably toward the back. The drum of the dome and also a part of the balustrade disappear behind the entablature of the peristasis. Lastly, the dome itself looks much more compressed than it really is.

A comparison with the typical forms of sixteenth-century illustration, for example, with the sheets of the *Codex Coner* (which also contains a few drawings of the Tempietto), shows that the form of representation used in the Lille drawing was utterly unusual at that time. The normal practice for drawing buildings was to adopt a raised position at some distance. The reason for this unusual reproduction of the building becomes obvious in the light of Bramante's scheme for a circular courtyard around the Tempietto. The courtyard with its radius of 25 *palmi* would have forced visitors to look at the building from a low and close position (maximum distance 7 meters) so that the drum and the dome would have been seen from sharp angle. Bramante took this situation into account and tried to remedy it by raising the drum and placing the structure of the drum on a smooth base. At any event, the lower part of the drum's structure remains hidden from a view behind the balustrade; and the dome above, designed as hemispherical, seems to be compressed.

The original model for the Lille drawing obviously reproduced the exact view that a visitor to the Tempietto would have had on entering the surrounding circular courtyard, and it must therefore have been drawn by an artist close to Bramante. The Lille drawings have been dated 1530-50 (Lotz 1962; Nesselrath 1983).

Of all the details illustrated (capital and entablature of the peristyle, balustrade and lantern) the most interesting is the enlarged reproduction of the lantern. This is the only detailed illustration of the lantern designed by Bramante.
A.E.W.

134
ARISTOTILE DA SANGALLO
Section of the Tempietto

Lille, Musée des Beaux-Arts, Wicar Collection, "Michelangelo Sketchbook," fol. 761
Pen and ink; with measurements.

BIBLIOGRAPHY: Geymüller 1885: 22-25; Pluchart 1889: 161, 168; Lotz 1962; Bruschi 1969a: 999; Günther 1973: 164ff.; 1982: 86-91; Nesselrath 1983; Günther 1988f: 85ff.

This drawing illustrates a section of the wall of the cella of the building combined with a horizontal projection of the internal structure. The combination evidently aims to reproduce the internal space not from an abstract distance but from the actual viewpoint of an observer standing inside this space; the same device is used for the outside view in fol. 762 (cat. no. 133). However, the chosen viewpoint is actually further away than the space would allow, and deliberately low (as in the drawing of the outside) to offer a view of the coffered ceiling of the peristasis. Height measurements are given (in Roman *palmi*) for the columns and entablature of the peristasis, for the drum and cornice of the dome, and for the internal structure; these accord with those of the actual building. As in many other drawings, the dome itself is reproduced without indications of height.
A.E.W.

135
ARISTOTILE DA SANGALLO
Tempietto Doorway and Niche in the External Wall of the Cella

Lille, Musée des Beaux-Arts, Wicar Collection, "Michelangelo Sketchbook," fol. 760
Pen and ink, wash; with dimensions.

BIBLIOGRAPHY: Geymüller 1885: 22-25; Pluchart 1889: 161, 168; Lotz 1962; Bruschi 1969a: 999; Günther 1973, 164ff.; 1982: 86-91; Nesselrath 1983; Günther 1988f: 85ff.

The sheet contains a view of the side with the entrance to the peristasis, and a detailed study of the doorway and a niche of the cella. This reproduction of the outside of the building does not appear in the other copies of Bramante's drawings and is evidently an addition of Aristotile himself to the view drawn on fol. 762 (cat. no. 133). Even though the perspective is completely distorted (as in the entrance steps), this is the most precise illustration of the structure of the external wall of the cella.
A.E.W.

136
ARISTOTILE DA SANGALLO
Plan of the Tempietto, woth the Design of the Cella Pavement

Lille, Musée des Beaux-Arts, Wicar Collection, "Michelangelo Sketchbook," fol. 758
Pen and ink, wash; with dimensions and inscriptions.
INSCRIBED: *pianta D(i) sto. pietro A Montorio.*

BIBLIOGRAPHY: Geymüller 1885: 22-25; Pluchart 1889: 161, 168; Lotz 1962, Bruschi 1969a: 999; Günther 1973: 164ff.; 1982: 86-91, Nesselrath 1983; Günther 1988f: 85ff.

Of all the sheets contained in the Sketchbook at Lille, Aristotile da Sangallo has labeled only the plan of this drawing with the legend "plan of S. Pietro a Montorio." Like the Chatsworth copy, this drawing gives a simplified version of the floor plan of the actual building. In particular, the external niches of the cell have been omitted.

There is nothing to support the hypothesis that the different heights of the stylobate and dome in Uff. 1963A are an indication that this is an earlier, unrealized project by Bramante. There is a diagram of the aperture of a single window, labeled "fenestra." Apart from the main entrance (whose two steps correspond roughly to the real ones) Sangallo has labeled each niche "porta." The Cosmoto floor pattern—not found in any other known plan—has been drawn smaller than it really is.
A.E.W.

137
ARISTOTILE DA SANGALLO
External View with Details of the Structure of the Tempietto (recto)
Plan, Interior and Details of the Exterior of the Tempietto (verso)

Florence, Galleria degli Uffizi, Gabinetto Disegni e Stampe, Uff. 4318Ar.-v.
Pen and ink; 436/432 × 301/300 mm.
INSCRIBED: numerous measurements in Roman *palmi.*

BIBLIOGRAPHY: Ferri 1885, XLI: 148; Günther 1973: 182ff.; 1982: 86-91; Licht 1984: 77; Ghisetti Giavarina 1990: 90.

The paper offers an overall view in partial perspective, with details of the building's exterior ("del de fora"). On the left of the general view there is a section of a Doric column ("colonna di fora") and the entablature of the peristasis ("prima choronce de fora in su le chollonne"), the balustrade, the drum and the cornice of the dome. To the right there is a drawing of the drum ("da questa banda ogni cosa de fora"). The cornice of the dome, marked with the letter "F" in the general view as well as in the section of the peristasis and in the detail of the drum, is drawn once again very precisely in the upper margin of the sheet, while on the right, near the lantern, there is a series of profiles with their exact measurements. Further inscriptions: "battezze di scalini coe di teste e[?]largeze"; "p[almi] 13 o[nce] 9 m[inuti] 3 il fuso"; "pal[mi] 13 o[nce] 9 [minuti] 3 il fuso e cosi i pilastri"; "piano"; "dorico" "sfondo quanto i nichi ciccho"; "di piombo"; "di fora." The drawing belongs to the section in Uff. 4319A (cat. no. 138); both have been attributed to Aristotile da Sangallo. This attribution by Ferri (1885) was not opposed by Ghisetti Giavarina (1990: 90) who, however, somewhat unconvincingly put forward the name of Tommaso Boscoli. Despite the preparatory lines incised on the paper, the drawing has the appearance of a sketch. With respect to the Lille and Chatsworth views, and those of the Sansovino group, the viewpoint here is higher up, resulting in a less pronounced angle. The caption on the verso affirms that Aristotile measured and drew the building on-site, independently from the Lille copy. The two reproductions Uff. 4318A and 4319A are in fact the ones which most faithfully portray the Tempietto as built. Like Giovanni Battista, Aristotile da Sangallo did not draw Bramante's original lantern, damaged in ca. 1530, but another lantern in Florentine style resembling the crown of a column. Doubts remain as to whether this new project was ever actually built. In the right margin of the sheet Aristotile provides a scale key in Roman *palmi*, with which, by his own account, he measured the building ("con questo palmo e misurato detto tempio scompartito in 12 once e in 5 minuti"). One *palmo* corresponds here to 22.5 cm.

On the verso of the sheet there is a rough sketch of a sequence of bays on the inside of the cella ("di drento"). The following notes accompany the structure of the drum: "sfonda o[nce] 10 morto"; "lume." In the lower right-hand corner Aristotile da Sangallo has drawn a sketchy plan and elevation of a niche with the opening for the door ("porta"). The plan, which, like the internal structure, was measured by Sangallo himself, according to the caption written in his own hand ("questa pianta o io misurata io di mia mano e questo di dentro"), belongs, together with the copies in the "Libro" in Kassel (Staatliche Kunstsammlungen, fols. A45, and 43r.), with those at Rome (Gabinetto Nazionale delle Stampe, vol. 2510, fols. 33r., and 42r.) and with those in Berlin (cat. no. 139), to the group of reproductions with the most correct measurements. In particular, the displacement of the axes of the pilasters of the internal and external wall of the cella has been reproduced correctly. Both here and in Uff. 1717A verso, however, the niches in the outer wall of the cella are drawn too small and the wall is too thick. One of the characteristics of Bramante's *ultima maniera*, that is, the realization of hollows by creating niches in the walls (see project for St. Peter's, Uff. 1A) has not been discussed here. Sangallo documents the state of the Tempietto before the seventeenth-century modifications. He shows the steep steps of the original entrance to the crypt behind the altar ("va sotera"), the two steps in the stylobate leading to the entranceway, while the other steps at the side entrances have been omitted.   A.E.W.

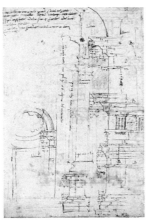

138
ARISTOTILE DA SANGALLO
*Section and Details of the Exterior
of the Tempietto* (recto)
Details of the Interior of the Cella (verso)

Florence, Galleria degli Uffizi, Gabinetto Disegni e Stampe,
Uff. 4319Ar.-v.
Pen and ink; measurements and inscriptions.
434/436 × 280/278 mm

BIBLIOGRAPHY: Ferri 1885, XLI: 148; Günther 1973: 182ff.; 1982: 86-91; Licht 1984: 77; Ghisetti Giavarina 1990: 90.

This drawing, executed by Aristotile da Sangallo at the same time as Uff. 4318A (cat. no. 137), shows the perspective section of the peristasis and the inside of the cella with its *travata ritmica* sequence of bays. The drawing has faded near the right-hand margin. All the basic parts of the building have been measured here as well. The details copied here, together with the precise measurement of their heights, are taken from the external outside ("di fora un altra volta"): the stylobate, base, capital and parts of the entablature of the order of the columns (marked by the letter "A"). The complete entablature is shown on one side ("la prima cornice," marked by the letter "B") with more measurements than in Uff. 4318A. These letters, which have been used to define certain details, are not repeated on the section. The inside of the drum—which has the right measurements—has been drawn distortedly. The *palmo* shown on the bottom margin of the paper ("questo e il propio palmo con che misurato detto tempio") is equivalent to 22.5 cm here as well. Further notes state "Un palmo misura 12 E un onca minuti 5"; "dalla cornice segnata A ad alto in fino al pavimento di dentro sono palmi 31 o[nce] 6"; "fra cholonna e cholonna a tondo e non a riscontro di colonna e di pilastro p[almi] ??"; "p[almi] 13 o[nce] 9 m[inuti] 3 il fuso della cholonna"; 1, 2, 3, 4, triglifi nel vo[to]; "dorico."
On the back Sangallo has redrawn details of the order of the Doric order of the inside ("di dentro"). In the middle

there is a Doric pilaster with a pedestal and entablature ("da quasu a terra sono pal[mi] 31 o[nce] 6 al piano del matonato"; "p[almi] 13 o[nce] 9 m[inuti] 3 tutto lo pilastro coli colarini"; "diminuito di drento"). The right-hand part of the paper is dedicated to larger-scale drawings with detailed measurements of the base, capital, entablature and the cornice of the dome with the beginning of the vault. In the bottom left corner Sangallo has drawn a perfect copy of the upper cornice of the inside niches ("di dentro"). The text written in the upper margin of the paper gives indications about the plan of the wall of the cella ("Nota che dentro sono 4 nichi grandi ed evvi tre entrate. [s]ariano quatro. con quella. che va. sotto il tempio. dieto al altare") and about the drum ("e sopra a ogni porta. ad alto. sono. 4 finestre. a dar lume. a laltre queste e laltre. sono sfondate. circha. a once 10. luni morti").   A.E.W.

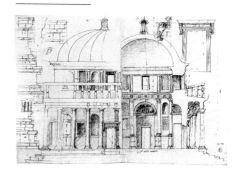

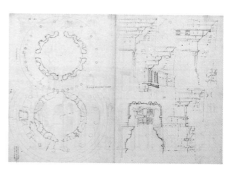

139
UNKNOWN FRENCH DRAFTSMAN
*Section, External View and Details
of the Tempietto* (recto)
*Plan of the Cella and Drum; Details
of the Tempietto* (verso)

Berlin, Staatliche Museen, Preussischer Kulturbesitz,
Kunstbibliothek, 4151, fol. 103r.-v. (*Codex Destailleur* D, I)
Pen and ink; measurements and inscriptions.
430 × 583 mm

PROVENANCE: Paris, Hypolite Destailleur Collection.

BIBLIOGRAPHY: Geymüller 1883; Jessen 1890; Egger 1903: 12; Ackerman 1961, II: 79ff.; Frommel 1967: 49ff., n. 27; Berckenhagen 1969: 65-76; Berckenhagen 1970: 23-31; Günther 1973: 184-186.

This book of drawings from the *Codex Destailleur* contains copies of ancient monuments in Rome (including a great number of drawings of baths from the imperial age) and in the south of France, as well as reproductions of Roman sixteenth-century buildings. With the exception of Bramante's Tempietto and the church of S. Eligio degli Orefici designed by Raphael, the latter were all drawn in the last years of Paul III's papacy. The completion of Antonio Labacco's model of St. Peter's in 1546 provides a *terminus post* for the drawings. The annotations in French and the heights given in French feet on many of the pages support the thesis that the draftsman, to whom Egger gave the name "Anonymous Destailleur," came from France. The attribution to Hugues Sambin suggested by Berckenhagen (1969 and 1970) and based on a rather weak comparison of architectural details, has not been accredited by other researchers. Ackerman (1961) saw the work of several different artists of French and Italian origin. Frommel (1967) is right in considering the papers as copies due to the exchange of the captions on the verso of fol. 103 with the church of S. Eligio degli Orefici.

Fol. 103 shows an orthogonal projection of a section with the inscription "A St pietro montorio" and an external view, together with details which are linked to the general picture by means of letters. The section has been executed with a certain consistency, with the exception of the perspective view of the peristasis and the balustrade. Of all the drawings of the Tempietto, the only known orthogonal projection is this one in Berlin. It is accompanied, like the external view and details, by detailed indications of the heights in "palme" (as noted in the right margin of the paper). The total height of the inner room, which is not shown on any other drawing, is quoted as "p[almi] 42 and o[nce] 35." The lantern, drawn as a little temple, is of the Florentine type, like the one shown in Aristotile da Sangallo's drawing (cat. no. 137). More than a quarter of the surface is fully illustrated in the drawing of the outside so as to include a view of the side entrance. The copies of the details include the stylobate, the base and the triglyphs of the external structure (H, A); the pedestal, the base and a capital of the Doric pilaster structure and the upper cornice of the niches inside the cella (G, E, R); the entranceway, the profile of the modillion and cornice of the portal.

On the back the draftsman has drawn several other details which are linked by means of letters to the general view on the other side. They comprise a section of the Doric structure of the columns of the peristyle (A), the entablature of the internal pilaster structure (D); the inner and outer cornice of the dome (B, C); and the balustrade. The left side of the paper shows two reproductions of the plan with ample indications as to the heights. While the plan of the cella ("prima pianta del Tempio fatto da Bramante in st pietro montorio e misurato col palmo") gives an exact reproduction of the width and depth of the niche, the entrance steps and the closed niche of the altar in front of the entrance, the copy of the drum ("seconda pianta," entitled by mistake "le Temple des orfevrè a Romé") is incorrect. There is an error in the axial relations between the internal and external structures of the drum (see the correct copy made on Uff. 1717A). *A.E.W.*

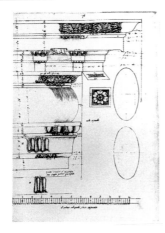

140

Unknown French Draftsman
Details of the Inside and Outside of the Tempietto;
Plan and Elevation of S. Eligio degli Orefici,
Rome

Berlin, Staatliche Museen, Preussischer Kulturbesitz,
Kunstbibliothek, HdZ 4151, fol. 105v. (*Codex Destailleur* D, I)
Pen and ink.
352 × 290 mm

Provenance: Paris, Hypolite Destailleur Collection.

Bibliography: Geymüller 1883; Jessen 1890; Egger 1903: 12; Ac-

kerman 1961, II: 79ff.; Frommel 1967: 49ff. n. 27; Berckenhagen 1969: 65-76; 1970: 23-31; Günther 1973: 184-86; Valtieri 1984a: 150.

The sheet is interesting not so much for the drawing of the Tempietto but for that of the building of S. Eligio degli Orefici on the left half of the page. The right half includes further copies of some architectural details of the Tempietto already drawn in fol. 103; here they are highlighted and distinguished from the church of S. Eligio by means of two captions ("S pietro" and "S piero"). The details illustrated are the following: the pedestal of the inner order and the outer cornice of the dome (bottom left), the entablature of the inner order (bottom right), the Doric order of the peristasis and the inner cornice of the dome (right margin). Since the indications of the measurements are the same as those in Uff. 635A drawn by Sallustio Peruzzi we can deduce that the paper contained in the *Cosex Destailleur* derived from this drawing (Frommel 1967; Valtieri 1984a). Given the occasional differences in the measurements of the details in fol. 103 this last drawing must stem from another prototype (Günther 1973). *A.E.W.*

141

Federico Barocci
View of the Tempietto
(First study for the *Flight of Aeneas*)

Florence, Galleria degli Uffizi, Gabinetto Disegni e Stampe,
Uff. 135A
Pen and brown ink; brown shading; heightening on white gloss; squared in black pencil.
456/457 × 427/421 mm

Bibliography: Geymüller 1875-80: 271ff.; Ferri 1885, XXI: 148; D. Frey 1915: 6ff.; Förster 1953: 176; Rosenthal 1964: 55-58; Bruschi 1969a: 995-997; Günther 1969.

This famous drawing was attributed by Geymüller (1875) to Bramante; as early as 1915 D. Frey considered this attribution erroneous (because unfounded). Even more recent research (Rosenthal 1964) considered the drawing to represent Bramante's first project, which was then built to a different design. The view of the Tempietto in Uff. 135A does in fact differ considerably from the actual building. The project shown in the drawing is more squat than the real Tempietto. Instead of three steps, entrance stairs and stylobate, there is a circular base comprising four steps. The entranceway is placed lower down. The metopes are decorated with bucrania instead of spiritual symbols. Little columns have been inserted in the balustrade on an axis with the columns of the peristasis. Even greater differences can be seen in the structure of the drum: the draftsman substituted the pilaster strip system and the shortened entablature with a complete order of pilasters. The differences between the drawing and the real building are likewise apparent in the elevation included in Serlio's third book (fol. 43) and in the circular build-

ing to be seen in the background of Barocci's *Flight of Aeneas* (Rome, Galleria Borghese). In the light of this, Günther (1969) defined this drawing as a preliminary study drawn by Barocci for his painting. The slight differences between Uff. 135A and Serlio's woodcut as regards the proportions of the capitals and the architrave of the peristasis are confirmed in fact by another preliminary study made by Barocci (Urbania, Bibl. Comunale, inv. 137 II) and by the *Flight*. The vanishing point of the Tempietto is placed, in both the drawing and the painting, at shoulder height and slightly to the right. Barocci evidently used the model in Serlio's third book as his inspiration, but changed it slightly. On the other hand, the artist could not have painted the Tempietto from his own observation of the real building, because he had not been to Rome for a long time when he composed the picture.

The part above the dome is just sketched in with a black pencil (today it can only be observed on the original with very good lighting) and has not been completed. Barocci tried out three different versions until he found a solution that did not interfere with the archway of the door to the building in the foreground.

The drawing can be dated as around 1588 since the painting of the *Flight of Aeneas* was delivered in 1589. *A.E.W.*

The Centralized Plan:
S. Maria della Consolazione
Arnaldo Bruschi

142
VENTURA VITONI (?)
Model for S. Maria della Consolazione, Todi
1597-98

Wood.
155 (height) × ∅ 120 m
Todi, Museo Comunale

According to contemporary documents, the church of S. Maria della Consolazione has its origins in the worship of an early image of the Virgin and Child painted on the wall of the monastery of S. Margherita near Todi, in the province of Perugia. The image, which was credited with the power to work miracles, quickly became a popular destination for pilgrimages and town processions, and was soon given a protective framework that was rebuilt several times, and described in 1574 as resembling *"parvum sacellum in forma non exiguae cappellae humili tecto"* (demolished upon the completion of the church in 1617). The first entry in the accounts ledger of the church construction is dated 30 May 1508, a few days after the miracle. On 13 June the bishop, Basilio Moscardi da Sutri, dispensed indulgences to visitors to the icon, which had already been given the name "S. Maria della Consolazione." On 3 July a special *compagnia* of noble laymen, presided over by three rectors, was set up to supervise the church's construction. On 22 July the first wages were paid to level the ground in front of the holy icon ("applanare la platea davanti alla madonna"). Finally, on 7 October 1508, an advance sum was paid to *capomaestro* Cola da Caprarola under contract for his work on the church. The excavation of the foundations was begun on 15 November, and the first stone laid by the vicar on behalf of Bishop Moscardi on 17 March 1509. The construction was attentively followed by the community, and particularly by Todi's nobility. Their leader, a certain Ludovico degli Atti, who had won a fierce battle for the seigniory, was an astute politician of considerable wealth and learning. Capitalizing on the ties he had established with Pope Julius II in 1507, Ludovico dominated the town's policies and, with the bishop's blessing, steered the council's choices in matters of planning. He most certainly kept a close watch over the construction of the Consolazione. By the summer of 1508 the project for the new church was most likely ready, and the commissioning body was composed of the nobles of the *compagnia*, under the control of the Atti family. The name of the architect is not known,

nor are the specifics of the original project. It is presumed to be the work of an architect already active in the town, such as Giovanpietro di Taddeo da Cione (a village near Lugano), a master stonemason known simply as "Il Cione." Engaged on the cathedral of Orvieto, Cione was paid several times for work on the Consolazione, starting from 1 July 1508. He was the nephew of Rocco da Vicenza (see Fagliari Zeni Buchicchio 1992), and from autumn 1508 to autumn 1509 he made a model for another church in Todi, S. Maria delle Grazie, near the Porta Romana. It is also possible that a project was supplied by Cola da Caprarola, who was more an entrepreneur than an expert in architecture. Given that building work was undertaken so shortly after the miracle took place, it is less probable that the design was commissioned from a Roman master such as Bramante (who is recorded as having made a pastoral visit to the town in 1574). Leaving aside the problem of attribution for the moment, it is worth taking a look at how work progressed, as amply recorded in the town archives (Zänker 1971; Bruschi, ed. 1991), alongside the building itself.

In April 1509 a payment was made for the ironwork for the "sesto della tribuna," meaning the frame used for tracing the curve of the tribune, which can only refer to the semicircular apse on the north side—the only one mentioned so far, and the first section of the church to be built. As mentioned above, since there is no talk of either plans or models, it is not known which design was being followed, except that it prescribed a semicircular apse. Given the probable oblong shape of the chapel in which the image was situated, it may have been different from the one eventually adopted. It could, for instance, have been based on a single nave with an apsidal or trilobate termination equipped with a cross vault. However, with the important contract of 20 May 1509, the rectors entrusted Cola *"duas alias tribunas ad similitudinem et altitudinis alterius tribune que facta est ibi ad presens"* to be cast and raised *"usque ad restrictum supradicte tribune"* i.e., the semicircular one, comprising *"quatuor capellas ad modum nichi et unam portam pro qualibet tribuna ... ac etiam facere unam vel duas schalas ad modum lumace ubi videbitur et placebit dictis rectoribus et magistro Cole ... et, si in futurum per supradictis rectoribus deliberatum erit, fundare aliam tribunam cum similibus conditionibus."*

The project being executed at this stage was on the whole feasible. The scheme consisted of three apses, to which a fourth could be added (with the rectors' permission) so as to form a quadrifoil plan. Perhaps there was some hesitation about placing an apse at the entrance. Furthermore, by saying that the new apses had to be constructed *"ad similitudinem"* to the first, hence round and with no pilasters, it is possible that each one was designed with a portal and four niches, though round (and not polygonal as realized) and perhaps without pilasters (of which there is no mention before May 1512). In fact in the case of the east and west apses (begun after the contract of 20 May 1509), near the corner piers either side of the exedra there are traces of cornices and curved architraves, as if in preparation for semicircular and not polygonal apses (and hence like the first). In this project the apses could meet at the corners, forming buttresses on the outside with a simple squared element (instead of the more complex hexagons actually realized), with the same kind of rectangular pier extant now. Because it was necessary to proceed with the two new apses, the construction of these corner structures had to be already under way: making it awkward to effect later alterations for the insertion of the screw stair either side of the round altar tribune, as would have been logical. At any event, in May 1509 a centrally planned church consisting of four exedrae was drawn up. With the exception of the round tribune, this plan does not match the second project (with which building work had begun in autumn 1508), nor the realized plan with the polygonal apses; however, the three new apses were designed with semicircular niches and portals on the central axis.

This layout, which was something of an anomaly for the region, fulfilled various practical and symbolic needs. The central plan, which the humanists considered to be full of

symbolic and religious meaning, was highly appropriate and the church stood like a beacon marking the new sanctuary, slightly removed from the town itself. Furthermore, it offered an ideal container for the sacred image beneath the dome. Given the church's position and the general geography of the site, the central plan oriented on the four cardinal points made it possible to avoid building out on the treacherous cliffs. Its four portals permitted the construction of an entrance on the main approach from the city gate, the Porta S. Giorgio—an entrance of equal grandeur as the one on the opposite apse—thereby facilitating the flow of visitors to the sacred image. The presence of a semicircular tribune with the altar to the Virgin and three apses inset with a total of twelve niches could have meant to symbolize the Virgin and twelve apostles at the Pentecost (see Bruschi 1970, and Zänker 1971); the niches were in fact later completed with statues of the apostles. This supposition would tie in with the fact that (Zänker 1971; 1974) Bishop Moscardi issued indulgences for visitors to the sacred image on 13 June 1508, the Tuesday following the Pentecost. Furthermore, ritual processions to S. Maria della Consolazione were thereafter held each year on the third day after the Pentecost—at least from May 1509, when construction began on the niched apses, the program of construction must have included this deliberate symbolization of the Pentecost. Such a program can only have been prompted by a man of learning, and more specifically a man of the cloth—such as Bishop Moscardi—someone who, in accord with Ludovico degli Atti (by this time the undisputed *signore* of Todi), considered it expedient to exploit the impassioned popular interest in the sacred image (which may have been painted by the canonized monk Giovanni di Rannuccio under commission from one of Ludovico degli Atti's forebears), by transforming it from an image of the Holy Mother of the Consolation to a *Maestà*, protector of the town and consoler of her people, erecting a temple in her name in which the entire town could find a point of contact and universal accord.

Nevertheless, it is doubtful that the 1509 project matches entirely with the scheme carried out in the years that followed. The latter is characterized by the building's unusual shape, which is based on seven sides of a dodecahedron and not on the semicircle described by the west, south and east apses; and on two sides of a hexagon, represented by the two large external corner piers. It is these unusual and sophisticated geometrical features of the project which endow the church with its striking logic and overall appearance. And as the two apses mentioned in May 1509 may have been begun in a rounded form, it is possible that the eventual polygonal apses and obtuse-angle piers derive from a different scheme altogether, perhaps proposed shortly afterward.

As pointed out by Enzo Bentivoglio (in Bruschi, ed. 1991), work seems to have slowed down drastically between May 1509 and May 1512. Perhaps the delays were due to unforeseen (?) economic difficulties, or to faulty calculations and uncertainty as to how to continue—provoked by the presentation of a new project with a different layout from the one by which construction had begun. This would in part explain why in May 1512 a "new accord" was struck with Cola (who would in normal circumstances have fulfilled his contract undisturbed). The documentation states that the construction had not been carried out as agreed, and gives measurements for the masonry built so far (walls only one meter high, a pillar—similar to the corner piers—only three meters high), which in the case of the new apses certainly did not reach the *restrictum* (i.e., to the set-back above the lower entablature) of the rounded tribune, as had been agreed in May three years earlier. Be that as it may, an effort to give new impetus to work on the site is evident in the council deliberation of Ludovico degli Atti's proposal on 21 September 1511 (immediately ratified) to authorize the priors to oversee the distribution of stone and bricks to be carried up to the church site by the townsfolk and peasants. Once these new "agreements" were signed in May 1512, the *capomaestro* Cola appointed or subcontracted to master stonemason Pietro da Corsonio the completion of fifty-two (cubic?) *pertiche* of wall, "*cum comciminibus et ornamentis,*" including the trunks of four "pilastrellos" or pillars in the apse on the Montesanto side, one story above the rounded apse. From this point in time, the project being implemented is most certainly the one with the polygonal apses and obtuse-angle piers, which corresponds with the extant construction and the central upright section of the wooden model in the municipal museum in Todi (beneath the springing line of the drum and dome).

This model (Zander, in Bruschi ed. 1991) is actually made up of two distinct parts, probably completed separately and then joined. The upright part rests on an octagonal base comprised of two boards joined by metal hinges. This board carries an accurate rendering of the floor plan of the church (partially hidden by the elevation block) with the three polygonal apses and obtuse-angle piers. Piers of this same shape—albeit different from those visible today, resulting from alterations to the original construction—can be seen on either side of the round tribune. The plan also bears a precise metric scale key in Roman *palmi* (10 *palmi* of the construction = 5.5 cm, i.e., roughly one-quarter *palmo* = 5.58 cm on the plan), together with a representation of the corner piers, starting with those on the northeast side and proceeding in an anticlockwise direction, marked with the letters A, B, C, D.

The hinges enabled the two panels with the floor plan to be folded in half, to protect it and to make it easier to carry. An iron ring at the center of one side originally made it possible to hang the plan from a hook, on a wall for instance. Hence, before being joined up to the main body of the model, the plan was designed to be consulted—be it on the site, or in the offices of the Compagnia or elsewhere—independently from the model. A square socket in the center of the projection of the dome and lantern may have accommodated a vertical support to give stability during transportation, or for when the entire model was taken on processions.

The main, four-apse block from the pavement to the (currently tiered) base of the drum, which is on the same scale as the plan, appears to be a separate piece on its own, and was built in sections of poplar wood. The interior of the model, which is only roughly made and its frame incomplete, shows slightly rounded corner piers, irregular walls and no pilasters at the corners of each of the dodecagons. On the outside, however, although somewhat simplified, the details are more accurate both metrically and in appearance, and include the respective orders and entablatures, cornices, the frames and pediments of the windows, etc. All the features on the building's exterior correspond approximately in form and dimensions to the finished building. However, the three entrance portals with their simple frames and surround molds are quite different from those actually built, and the domical roofs of the apses protrude from the attic far less than in the building itself. This last factor makes their springing line lower—meaning a lower level for the upper order inside (which, as we have seen, was not shown in the model but in the extant building is accentuatedly tall).

As proposed by Paola Zampa (Bruschi, ed. 1991), this lowering of the springing line of the apse domes and the entablatures of the second order inside, in addition to making the proportions of the pilasters, also reinstates the ratio of one to one to the gaps between the colossal pilaster strips of the interior corner pillars (equal to 66 *palmi*, as in Antonio da Sangallo's drawing Uff. 731Av.) and the height of the pier walls of the apses. This suggests an error in the construction (or a change while work was under way) with respect to the hypothetical drawing upon which the model's design was based. In the finished building, the entablatures of the lower range of the side bays of the colossal pilasters framing the altar tribune are sharply inclined toward the top in order to compensate for the increased height of the entablature relative to the lower ones of the polygonal apses on either side. This seems to offer added confirmation that when work began on the tribune—which had already been raised in May 1509 as

far as its *restrictum*—it was based on a different project from the one comprising the polygonal apses. The presence of structures that fail to conform with the second (or third?) project—corresponding to the extant model and, to some degree, to the finished building—must have prompted alterations while construction was under way, and probably slowed work down. Other anomalies and "transgressions" in the interior orders and in the detailing were perhaps occasioned by the lack of precision in the drawings (which, like the model, may well have been schematic), and by the difficulties encountered in correctly interpreting the many modifications applied over the span of nearly a century by successive works supervisors proceeding without a qualified architect as such; they were, of course, sporadically assisted by consultants of renown during the most complex phases of realization—Baldassarre Peruzzi (1518), perhaps Michele Sanmicheli (1521), Antonio da Sangallo the Younger (1532), and later Vignola (1565), Galeazzo Alessi (1567), Ippolito Scalza (1584), Valentino Martelli (1587 and thereafter), up until Borromini (1660). There are several substantial clues to suggest that a new project (dating from between 1510 and 1512) introduced certain alterations to the executive project under way. The new scheme determined the external piers in their obtuse-angle form, and polygonal apses; it may have included a similar modification for the rounded tribune. It is likely that the new scheme also defined the form of the internal corner piers—as in Vasari's drawing and the bottom sketch by Antonio—the obtuse-angle solution between the main pilasters. Quite possibly it also contained definitions for the double orders both inside and out. The full implementation of this project must have been conditioned by what had already been constructed, which was not considered appropriate to either demolish or modify—as, for example, the tribune and the interior right-angle piers, which seem to have been intended to support a cross vault. It may have become necessary to reach a compromise, not unlike the one between the plan on the base board of the wooden model and the subsequent design of the model's main body (excluding the dome itself, which was redesigned during the last thirty years of the century).

It is likely that the drawing of the new project—plan and elevation—was drafted on a rather small scale, or was schematic in its representation of the building's architectural structure and features, with no accompanying drawings of the details on a scale suitable for execution purposes. Like the plan drawn on the base board, and the one by Antonio da Sangallo, it may have been drawn in Roman *palmi* (1 *palmo* = 0.2234 meters), the unit of measurement that most closely corresponds with the finished building. There are no clues as to why the project was changed in mid-flow. The fact that the new project was both superior and more advanced in terms of form is not enough evidence for abandoning or modifying what was already under way in 1509. One possible cause for the change could have been Ludovico degli Atti's personal interest in the resumption of work in September 1511, and the concession to use stone from the town's old hilltop fort. That authorization, which was applied for anew in 1513, was accorded by Pope Leo X's legate Antonio Ciocchi del Monte in December 1514. The involvement of these figures—Ludovico degli Atti (wealthy enough to be in a position to lend money to the papacy), Bishop Basilio Moscardi (present at the Fifth Lateran Council), and Antonio del Monte (very close to the pontiff from 1509 to 1511, and made a cardinal on 10 March 1511)—seems to point to a personal interest on the part of Pope Julius II. It is equally likely (Bentivoglio, in Bruschi ed. 1991) that the political and military events in which the pope was embroiled from 1511 through 1512—such as the revolt of Bologna on May 1511, the fall of the stronghold of Mirandola, the formation of the Holy League against France, the Battle of Ravenna, and the ensuing peace of May 1512—had their repercussions on the church site at Todi, prompting the townsmen, the degli Atti dynasty and Bishop Moscardi to involve the papal entourage and perhaps even the pontiff himself (who in June 1511, after

visiting Loreto, passed through Foligno and Terni) in the construction of the town's premier house of worship. Nor can it be coincidence that the first signs of a resumption of work on the site came in autumn 1511 (the Holy League was formed on 5 October 1511), and were effectively resumed at the end of May 1512. It may also be significant that the litanies of the Virgin of Loreto appear in the windows of S. Maria della Consolazione—particularly in light of the special devotion of Antonio del Monte and Julius II for the Virgin of Loreto where, in these very years (1508 and after), Bramante was working under commission from the pope. Though tenuous, none of these facts should be overlooked. The renewed vigor with which work was resumed is attested on 12 June 1512 by the concern of the rectors to find a group of good friars to superintend the church ("buoni frati, dai quali fosse detta chiesa governata"). The building's construction proceeded under the supervision of Cola da Caprarola, who was also at work on the cathedral of Foligno, with a team of stonemasons led by Pietro da Corsonio. On 1 September 1515 Giovanmaria was commissioned to continue the three apses (initiated in the preceding years) from the first cornice to the very top. However, on 19 October, a certain Giovandomenico da Pavia put in a bid to raise the walls of the building, and in particular as far as the upper cornice, supplying a qualified carpenter to build the hoisting machinery, starting from the level of the pink frieze (i.e., the outer frieze of the lower order), the three apses, completing the so-called pink frieze in pink stone, the apse on the town side, the front tribune, the tribune on the Montesanto side, together with the buttressing on the front apse and its twin on the S. Margherita side. The last record of Cola's presence in Todi is dated December 1515, as by now he had been replaced by Giovandomenico da Pavia. Shortly after, the latter was aided by Ambrogio da Milano (first payment on 2 April 1516), a master stonemason known as the "architect of the Church the Virgin," who was engaged to ensure that the building "was properly fashioned architecturally." Ambrogio (who was paid for four capitals in 1517) was experienced both as a sculptor of *ornamenti* and as an architect. He may have been entrusted with the job of defining the details of the orders, and of the capitals in particular, perhaps on the basis of the somewhat sketchy project drawing. The outer capitals, with their leaves and Corinthian-style volutes, each one different in true Quattrocento fashion (and later executed until around 1525 by various master craftsmen including Giovanmaria, Girolamo da Verona, one of Sanmicheli's collaborators, Giovanpietro, Francesco de Vita, and Filippo da Meli), and the interior, Ionic capitals (which differ only between the two ranges, with a rectangular abacus for those below, and a curved abacus for those above) perhaps correspond only ideally in terms of type with the indications in the general project, alluding in Vitruvian manner respectively to the Virgin's virtue and maternity. The previous activities in Urbino, Lombardy, Veneto, Umbria and Viterbo of Ambrogio, who had formerly worked in Urbino alongside Francesco di Giorgio Martini, but was extraneous to recent developments on the Roman scene, explains the evident links between these sculptural elements with the characteristic models of the Sienese stonemason and their "archaic" tone which probably misinterpret the intentions of the author of the last project. Nor should we rule out the possibility that models or advice for some of the details—such as the large "Doric" capitals of the interior corner piers—were supplied by Michele Sanmicheli (who in 1521 worked in Todi on the dome of S. Maria delle Grazie) to Girolamo da Verona who, after Ambrogio da Milano, executed capitals and cornices from 1521 to 1528 (Frommel; Fagliari Zeni Buchicchio 1992).

After the assignment to master Jacopo to complete the interior of the apse on the valley side, with its pillars up to the first cornice, and thence to the upper cornice, in September 1517 Ludovico degli Atti is noted as one of the rectors of the *fabbrica*. A year later, on 7 September 1518, Baldassarre Peruzzi (by this time a much admired figure in Rome) was invited to come and see the building, which was proceeding fairly rapidly at this stage. From 1518 to 1523 work continued on the second order both inside and out, with the completion of the capitals, cornices, pilasters and windows, carried out first by Giovanmaria, and then by Girolamo da Verona. In May 1524 comes the first mention of Filippo da Meli, a stonemason and sculptor, later cited as an architect, who supervised work on the site until 1563. Apart from an interruption of work from 1526 to 1529, this same craftsman fashioned the cornice in travertine for the two upper orders inside, and the cornice in *pietra viva* for the outside, including the entablature and molding of the tribune. He was later entrusted with the completion of arches of the dome. Before proceeding with this difficult task, however, which was probably beyond the grasp of the stonemason Filippo, consultations were conducted in Orvieto with Antonio da Sangallo the Younger, the celebrated papal architect. In 1531 the members of the town council began to look around for a suitable religious order to take over the new church, and the choice fell on the monks of the order of S. Pietro dei Benedettini Cassinensi of Perugia. In 1532 Sangallo was invited to Todi and sketched some ideas for a possible monastery (Uff. 731Av.). That same year, besides working on the external base, Filippo began to prepare the internal arches with their "rose windows" ("con li rosoni"), which were begun in 1534.

By this stage, all that was left to build was the upper part of the building, with the apse domes and the main dome. But in 1534, funds began to ebb. Pope Paul III (elected 13 October 1534), paid a visit to Todi to survey the work, and allocated one thousand *fiorini* resulting from a law suit between a private citizen and the Camera Apostolica. The town's aldermen ordered a procession to be held on the first Sunday of each month, to foster the collection of alms. From 1545 for twenty years work was slow and frequently interrupted. For technical questions regarding the dome and apses, advice was asked from Giacomo Barozzi da Vignola, who on 17 July 1565 was paid twenty *scudi* for his trouble and expenses. The problems may have been structural, but there may also have been doubts about the correct architectural solution for the dome—either because the project (and possible model) followed since 1512 provided little information in this direction, or because the envisaged solution was technically arduous or costly, or because, after all these years, it was considered visually unsatisfactory. In 1568 work once more came to a halt. The misgivings about how the building should be continued are implicitly attested by the pastoral visit of 15 November 1574. After a brief but precise history of the fabbrica, which "*magna ex parte ... videtur iam confecta sumptibus non modicis ... cum suis arcubus, ac inceptis testudinibus ad aliquam similitudinem Tribune noveque fabrice principis apostolorum de urbe*," namely St. Peter's, it is declared that the "*amplun edificium merito laudandum si perficeretur iuxta il modello quod conspicitur a perito Architecto Bramante nuncupato designatum*."

The expression "*quod conspicitur*" seems to refer to the "model" which can be seen on site at Todi. But it could also refer to Bramante (whose model is recognizably the design of Bramante). In the latter case, the affirmation of Bramante's paternity for the building would be less direct and decisive. Nonetheless, the name of Bramante, which now appears for the first time in the documentation, and the reference to St. Peter's in Rome tend to endorse the opinion that the building was completed in accordance with the model's design—the same model on which the building's construction had been based so far. This is implicit in Camaiani's argument, and is confirmed by the evidence of the archives which, though lacking explicit references to either *disegno* or *modello* (let alone new designs or projects), mention specific features of the design (such as "pilastrelli," "corniscioni" both inside and out, corner buttressing, windows, bases, arches "con li rosoni" and even "tres scalini sopra il cornisone," as in domes of antiquity), which could only have been specified in a detailed project or model of the general design. This project or model must have been a constant guide for the construction: not so much for the detail work, as for the overall definition of the building. Only an in-depth analysis (physical, chemical, dendrological, and so forth) of the main body section of the model in the Museo Comunale at Todi can determine whether it is the model which Camaiani saw in 1574, from the pavement to the imposts of the drum, or whether it is a copy, or a later replica of the building as carried out. Nevertheless, although the model substantially matches the building itself, there are certain significant discrepancies. Besides the abovementioned fact that the smaller domes rise less prominently from the apses, creating smaller attics, in the model the four corner piers are identical, composing two sides of a hexagon; it therefore does not account for the irregularity of the piers either side of the round tribune, which respectively contain a "dome stair" (the model for which was commissioned from Ippolito Scalza, paid for in May 1596, with work beginning in early 1630), and a passageway to the sacristy (ca. 1613). The apse pier on the east side is also lacking the extra pilaster which breaks the symmetry of the outer orders; this feature may be left over from an earlier design for a rounded apse, or from a modification to the northeast pier. In the model the lower entablature of the round tribune is supported by corbels in the form of capitals; these were probably never made, but were replaced at the start of this century by a set of pilasters. Lastly, the three entrances of the model are identical, with a simply molded surround, quite different from those built in the sixteenth century.

Hence, if we exclude the upper part with the dome itself, the model corresponds with the finished building, or with what had already been built when Camaiani saw it, while a differences are the outcome of later intervention. It is therefore possible that this was the model he saw, or at least a copy of it. At all events, while a "model" was never mentioned before 1574, there were plenty afterward; in 1584 there is mention of a model for the dome alone. But in June 1660 the model of the *fabbrica* was transported to Rome and shown to a number of architects, including Borromini in particular, who were duly consulted for advice as to how to "prevent rainwater from entering the church, and to reduce the humidity of the masonry and chapels." On several occasions the present model (Zander 1991) underwent restoration, and was stained a light color at least once, without evidencing the pink frieze. This operation, perhaps carried out in 1663, is noticeable in the east apse of the model, and may have been due to damage during its transport to Rome. Another mention of the model occurs in 1697, when a certain Gio. Antonio Fratini, the chief administrator of the estate of the Consolazione, donated all his properties to the church, including the wooden model of the church itself "which he kept in his home, given to him by the craftsman [?] who built it" (or restored it?). It is not clear whether this was the model here or in fact another, which would nonetheless back to the second half of the seventeenth century, and hence not have been available to Camaiani.

To go back to the history of the construction, during the 1560s work began on the vaults of the apses and tribune, and in June 1579 the building was ready for the pendentives ("triancoli") of the main dome, which were completed by early 1583; in May that year the scaffolding was prepared to begin the band of entablature above the pendentives ("cornicione della cupola").

At this stage, for work to continue it was vital to have a working project for the dome. On 25 May 1584 "Mastro Guglielmo Portughese Architetto" was paid 22 *scudi* for having come from Rome to work on the church, and for having left the design, or model, that is, of the dome. A Portuguese architect is recorded at work in 1573 on S. Maria in Traspontina (Bentivoglio in Bruschi ed. 1991), but there is no evidence that it was the same Guglielmo mentioned at Todi. We do not even know if the said architect was the author of the design, or just an assistant to some Roman architect. Nor can we ascertain whether this person brought a drawing or a wooden model of the dome with him to Todi, let alone say with any certainty that the model we have is the one in question.

At any event, the commissioning body had misgivings about carrying out the design brought by the Portuguese architect. In order to resolve various problems which had arisen regarding work on the church (which, at this stage, must surely have regarded the dome), on 19 October 1584 the rectors requested the presence of Ippolito Scalza "for two or three days," the architect-in-chief of the cathedral at Orvieto. Once the said entablature over the pendentives had been completed, in July 1585 the *scarpellino* Francesco Casella (at work on the site since 1567) received his recompense for the "time engaged on the *fabbrica*, for making models, and for going to Orvieto, Perugia, and Rome." Consultation with Scalza in Orvieto evidently continued, then, and with Valentino Martelli in Perugia, and perhaps the architect in Rome (Guglielmo Portoghese?) drafted a new project for the dome. Whatever the case, in May 1586 Francesco Casella was engaged to carry out the balustrade, the pilasters both inside and out, including their bases. All this was to comply with a drawing—regrettably lost—"that detailed all the moldings." Clearly at this stage there was a working project for the dome, complete with details for the stonemasons. There is no indication of the name of the author of the drawings, but Valentino Martelli seems to have been the architect most involved during these years with the executive definition of the dome. In June 1587 he was "called in to see the *fabbrica*, and particularly the main pillars." In June 1589 he stayed three days in Todi to "draw the windows of the dome and the floor plan of the sacristy and other buildings to set alongside the church." In January 1590 it was established that all the intaglio work done by Casella had to be approved by Martelli, and this was duly done in 1596. In December 1597 the capitals of the pilasters of the drum both inside and out were to be executed "in conformance with the clay model and drawings on paper" furnished by Martelli. After the dome had been raised (1606-07) and most of the building work had been brought to a head, in December 1612 Martelli spent another five days in Todi, most likely to put the finishing touches on the plans for the sacristy, which was begun in 1613. Martelli, therefore, who is explicitly mentioned as being the architect of the *fabbrica*, was undoubtedly responsible for the executive projects of the building's details. However, it is not known whether he is also the author of the new overall project for the Consolazione, or if his intervention was limited to defining the work for the stonemasons, on the basis of a project perhaps brought from Rome by Guglielmo Portoghese in 1584. It is possible that during these years (circa 1584-86) the old model seen by Camaiani was fitted with a new wooden design for the dome, which was most certainly different from the one envisaged by the 1509-12 project. It is also feasible that the model of the dome is the same one we have today. It is comprised of two parts, the drum and vault with its lantern, probably detachable to ease transport. Although constructed in the same wood (poplar) and on the same scale as the main volume below (10 Roman *palmi* = ca. 5.55 cm, i.e., approximately a quarter-*palmo*) it is immediately distinguishable owing to the way the features are treated. In the lower part, the orders, entablature, capitals, window frames and pediments are very summarily executed. For the dome, and particularly the drum, there is greater attention to detail with an accurate rendering of features, "composite" capitals with swags on the volutes, the form of the windows with pediments and sills, niches, plaques, and decorations. Even the more schematic details—such as the architraves and entablature cornices—are rendered with different conventions from those of the base part.

The linguistic contrast between the dome and the main four-apse section below—to some extent muted by the distant view of the "ideal temple" of humanist extraction—is also perceivable in the actual building, especially when viewed from close by. The building was completed, with the raising of the gilded cross on the lantern, in April 1606, and once the old chapel was demolished and its sacred image transported to its new home on the new altar, the church was solemnly inaugurated on 20 April 1617.

Having pieced together the history so far, it is now possible to return to the issue of paternity for the design that corresponds with the model. Given that the finished house of worship is the fruit of a range of contributions from many different master craftsmen, stonemasons, and consultants, the "author" of this design is not exactly the same as the "author" of the church as it stands today.

It is worth affirming at this point that not one of the various *maestri* that appear in the archives (leaving aside the occasional consultants and those involved with the dome) is a true "creative" architect as such. They are all in their own way executors of another person's design. In the first, decisive phase of construction (ca. 1508-15), Cola da Caprarola, as made plain by his anagraphical data (Bentivoglio 1982), worked here as elsewhere as an building contractor; he was active in the provinces, but from the time of Pope Alexander VI worked in the shadow of Antonio da Sangallo the Elder, Bramante and his disciples. The man known as Giovanpietro or "Il Cione" is no more than a stonecutter, though, like Cola, not without some notions of architecture. Subsequently, the refined sculptor of the architectural "ornaments" was Ambrogio da Milano, already noted in the 1470s for his work in Urbino (where he worked in concert with Francesco di Giorgio and perhaps with Bramante), and later in Venice, Umbria and Viterbo. As for Girolamo da Verona (from Sanmicheli's circle) and then Filippo da Meli, they were also ostensibly sculptors. Despite each craftsman's specialized contribution to the execution of the building, but not one was a true architect, capable of ideating and drafting the overall project for S. Maria della Consolazione. Albeit sometimes creatively, these gradually drifted further from the original project of the model cited in 1574, with its apses and polygonal piers.

If the first scheme comprising the round tribune with no orders can be attributed to one of the stonemasons present when work on the building first began—i.e., Cione or Cola—perhaps the one referred to in May 1509 (executed differently from what was agreed), and particularly the one being followed in 1512, presupposes the intervention of a major architect of the time. This is the project corresponding to the model, which is markedly characterized by the polygonal apses and the external obtuse-angle piers. These piers, which reappear occasionally in projects of Peruzzi (such as the later church in "via di Campidoglio" on Uff. 513A), anticipating to some extent Michelangelo's solution for the exterior of St. Peter's, and superseding the distinct Quattrocento manner of Leonardo's temple designs, masterly unifying the volumes of the main centralized section beneath the dome. It was take into account the "archaic" definition of the details, which were misreadings of an evidently summary project, and the result of a later modification to the dome design, there is little reason for not giving credence to Camaiani's indications, which have proved informative and correct on other accounts. Camaiani may have been reporting a fact in 1574 that belonged to the town's history, and was then repeated after 1580 on other occasions. Furthermore, the polygonal tribunes are by no means alien to Bramante's Roman period. He alone could have been—from 1509 to 1512—could be responsible for the sheer grandeur of the building's design, the sophisticated geometry of the polygons, and a series of mature and novel solutions (though somewhat crudely interpreted by the stonemasons) for the interior and exterior.

As for the possibility (Pungileoni 1836) that Bramante, finding himself unable to oversee the works personally, sent a certain Ventura Vitoni da Pistoia (whom Vasari, 1568, III,i, 33, mentions as his assistant, and whom De Angelis d'Ossat, 1956, proposes as having materially constructed the wooden model), there is nothing among documents currently available to confirm this.

The Palazzo Strozzi and Private Patronage in Fifteenth-Century Florence
Amanda Lillie

The construction of the Palazzo Strozzi in Florence is better documented than that of almost any other fifteenth-century palace. Building accounts reveal the names of all the workmen, how much they were paid, where their materials came from, and when they were employed on the project (Goldthwaite 1973). Furthermore, business and household account books and letters inform us about the patron—Filippo di Matteo Strozzi (1428-91)—so that it has been possible to reconstruct his career as a banker (Goldthwaite 1968), to define his role within Florentine society (Kent 1977; Gregory 1985) and to identify many of the furnishings and works of art he commissioned (Borsook 1970; 1991; Sale 1979). The early sixteenth-century *Vita di Filippo Strozzi* written by his son Lorenzo is an additional biographical source (Bini and Bigazzi 1851).

Palace builders in Renaissance Italy shared certain motives: the desire for a fine house to reflect or enhance their family's status, to present to the public an impression of wealth and stability, to embellish a neighborhood, and contribute to the grandeur of the whole city (Kent 1987). A palace was also an emblem of longevity and of household unity and strength, intended to gather a family under one roof and bind them in perpetuity. Apart from the customary motives, Filippo Strozzi was driven by memories of his father and other Strozzi relations who had been banished by the Medici regime to die in exile. Filippo himself spent eight years in exile (1458-66), and on his return to his native city his greatest ambition was to rebuild his family's fortunes and reestablish their reputation (Gregory 1985). In this sense the Palazzo Strozzi was very different from the Palazzo Medici, which was built as the Medici rose to power in the 1440s and completed at the zenith of their political and financial fortunes (ca. 1459). Moreover, Filippo Strozzi had the means and organizational skills to build on a grander scale than any of his contemporaries; for while in exile in Naples he had established a banking empire that was the great financial success story of the late fifteenth century in the very years when the Medici Bank was collapsing.

Filippo's plans for a big new palace were laid as early as 1474 (Pampaloni 1982: 48-49) when he began acquiring the prestigious double corner site, "il più comodo e più bel sito della città," as his son Lorenzo described it (Bini and Bigazzi 1851: 26). All his other patronage schemes in town and country were deliberately modest, as he reserved his funds for the great palace (Lillie 1991).

Filippo set up the construction project like a business enterprise with a managerial structure that allowed him to delegate the day-to-day administration to trusted employees. A key figure was his distant cousin Marco di Benedetto Strozzi who was the *proveditore* or administrator for the construction from its inception until his death in October 1493. Marco had others working for him, a mercer, Marco di Giovanni di Marco, who paid the workers and checked that the work had been done satisfactorily, and a cashier, Baroncello di Girolamo Baroncelli, who took over from Marco Strozzi when he died (Goldthwaite 1973: 119-122, 136-138). Marco's record keeping system was essential because there was almost no subcontracting for the building operation. Only the foundations were contracted out to an expert; and otherwise all the stonemasons, builders, carpenters, metalworkers, unskilled laborers, and carters were paid their daily wages or task rates by the Strozzi and the transactions scrupulously recorded in Marco's account books. The Palazzo Strozzi employees therefore worked within a direct labor system

without the need for formal contracts to be drawn up (Goldthwaite 1973: 117). Similarly, for the supply of materials Strozzi could usually depend on the open market, although contracts were made with a few major suppliers, such as quarry owners for the steady provision of stone, and kilnsmen for bricks and lime (Goldthwaite 1973: 118, 145-147, 157, 163-164). Although none survive, it is just possible that contracts once existed for the architects and foremen, stipulating that they adhere to the wooden models made for the palace; but there are no references in the building accounts to such an agreement and, because Filippo Strozzi himself ultimately controlled the building of his palace, rather than contracting it out to a builder or architect, it is unlikely that the Palazzo Strozzi models ever had a legal or contractual function. Documents reveal that Giuliano da Sangallo's wooden model was not ordered until September 1489, three months after the foundations were begun (Goldthwaite 1973: 123, 191), so the plan must have been established, but the facade design may have been unresolved when the building operation started on 4 July 1489. Giuliano da Sangallo's model therefore probably represents the establishment and acceptance of a facade design around September 1489. The alternative fragmentary models that were not part of the executed design belong to the initial experimental phase, presumably between the spring and autumn of 1489, when facade solutions were being proposed and considered. Nor was Giuliano da Sangallo's big model a final demonstration of the palace exactly as it was to be built, for certain areas were left undefined to await later decisions, and documents refer to a second big model, which no longer survives.

It is evident from contemporary accounts that the building of Palazzo Strozzi was a major event not only for Filippo and the Strozzi clan, but for the city of Florence and for those, such as Ercole d'Este in Ferrara, who were interested in new architectural developments (Kent 1977). In his biography of his father, Lorenzo Strozzi describes how, in order not to provoke the jealousy of Lorenzo de' Medici, Filippo il Vecchio emphasized the size of his family and his need for a new palace that would be functional, comfortable and dignified, rather than grand or ostentatious. He began the design process by consulting at length with various builders and architects, who encouraged him to build on a bigger and bigger scale. He kept protesting, but finally showed the drawings to Lorenzo de' Medici, who not only approved of the idea, but added rustication to make it more magnificent, and advised Filippo against the inclusion of shops on the ground floor. The more Filippo resisted the grand scheme, the more Lorenzo insisted that he go ahead (Bini and Bigazzi 1851: 23-25). According to Filippo's cunning strategy, by inviting others to propose a grand scheme which he, in his false modesty, seemed reluctant to adopt, he appeared to be engaged in a consensual form of patronage. Thus, if we are to believe his son's biography, even before it was built Filippo Strozzi's private palace had assumed a very public role. In this process, a model was a more effective instrument than a drawing would be to demonstrate a building project to a wider group of people; it facilitated discussion and a public airing of views. The surviving alternative wooden models for Palazzo Strozzi may well have been part of this consultative process, a process we tend to associate with the competitions held for major public works like Florence Cathedral, rather than with domestic buildings.

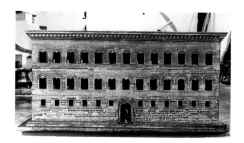

143
GIULIANO DA SANGALLO
Model of the Palazzo Strozzi, Florence

Florence, Museo Nazionale del Bargello (on loan to Piccolo
Museo, Palazzo Strozzi)
Wood; constructed in three detachable stories; components
glued together; incised lines visible on facade; and sketches of
some architectural details on interior walls.
147.5 (length) × 117 (width) × 73.7 (height) cm

BIBLIOGRAPHY: Del Badia 1872; Stegmann and Geymüller 1885-
1908; Salmi 1940b; Marchini 1942; Ackerman 1954a; Saalman
1959a; Parronchi 1969; Goldthwaite 1973; Pampaloni 1982; Tönnesmann 1983b; Rykwert et al. 1988.

Models must once have been made for all the great Italian
palaces of the fifteenth and sixteenth centuries, but this
wooden model of the Palazzo Strozzi is the only complete
surviving model of a Renaissance domestic building. Two
facades, corresponding to the north (Via Strozzi) and east
(Piazza Strozzi) sides, were carved in detail. The remaining two facades, corresponding to the west (Via Tornabuoni) and south (alleyway) sides, were left unfinished
and were probably never intended to receive detailed
treatment. Since one of the main purposes of an architectural model is to convey the designs for interior and exterior simultaneously, the Palazzo Strozzi model was constructed in three detachable stories which can be lifted up
to reveal the interior room divisions on each floor of the
palace. A close inspection of the model reveals that draftsmanship was an essential part of model making, for the design of each facade was first drawn or cut with a stylus
onto the wooden surface. A grid of deeply incised lines is
still visible all over the delicately stippled surface of the
top story, on the lower stories wherever the rusticated
blocks have become detached, and on the two incomplete
facades. Even more intriguing are the interior drawings
on the ground floor and *piano nobile*, where there are tiny
pen and ink sketches of vaulting systems and doorways
with their moldings and cornices. These sketches correspond closely with the final interiors and were probably
records of decisions made during the design process, or
demonstrations of how details were to be slotted into the
whole structure. A notable feature of this model is that it
was left unfinished. Even the impressive north and east
facades are incomplete as, for example, at one end of the
Via Strozzi facade, where the arched window surrounds
were left uncarved. Evidently it was thought unnecessary
to repeat decorative details *ad infinitum*; as Alberti noted,
"better then that the models are not accurately finished,
refined and highly decorated, but plain and simple, so that
they demonstrate the ingenuity of him who conceived the
idea, and not the skill of the one who fabricated the
model" (*De re aedificatoria*, II, i, trans. Rykwert et al.
1988: 34). More remarkably, the courtyard was never
completed, and although incised lines show where the
columns and vaults were to be placed, they were never inserted. This suggests that the model marked a stage in the
design process, rather than being merely a record of a
completed operation. On the other hand, other parts of
the model which were once decorated have been damaged
since. The bifore windows of the facades were almost certainly provided with colonettes and roundels, for the
jagged ends and remnants of glue show where they once
were. Similarly the rustication was once complete on the
north and probably on the east facade. At first glance a
model like this with its complex surface treatment appears

to emphasize exterior elevation over interior plan; yet the
whole construction of the model demonstrates that the plan
must have been established before the facade design could
be applied to it, and the model was built from the inside
working outward. This is clear from the division of the
model into three stories where the breaks occur at the floor
level of each story and not where the dentiled stringcourses
(*marcapiani*) below the windows imply the divisions should
be. The pre-establishment of definitive plan before modelmaking began clarifies a major function of this model, which
was to demonstrate the successful application of the facade
to the plan. The model compars closely with the palace as
built. The scale used—1:40—is a convenient one, large
enough to show decorative details and allowing easy calculation of measurements. A major change in the dimensions and proportions of the palace was made during the
building campaign, for although the final palace is the
same length and width, it is 3.51 meters higher than was
indicated by the model. The dimensions of the ground
floor were barely effected, but the height of the *piano nobile* and top floor were each increased and an attic level
was inserted between the upper story and the cornice. Andreas Tönnesmann has pointed out that this change was
partly necessitated by the introduction of vaults on the
first floor of the palace, an unusual step in Florence where
palaces almost always had wooden coffered ceilings on the
piano nobile. The effect of this alteration is to produce an
almost square outline for the short facade, and the palace
became one of the tallest domestic buildings in Florence
(32.12 m or 55 *braccia*), over eight meters taller than the
Palazzo Medici and only surpassed by the Palazzo Pitti
and several thirteenth-century tower houses.
Another striking difference between the model and the
palace as constructed is the treatment of rustication. The
model shows a gradated system of rustication with emphatically projecting blocks on the ground floor, slightly projecting blocks at first-floor level and flat blocks with a roughened surface on the top floor. These effects were achieved
by glueing tiny semi-cylindrical pieces of wood onto the
ground floor, with tiny prismatic pieces either glued on or
cut back from the surface of the first floor, and by stippling the flat surface of the top floor. This clearly differentiated system was abandoned at some stage of the design
process and the actual palace facade is clad in more uniform rusticated blocks that very gradually and subtly become flatter toward the roof. Nor was this model used to
establish the block-by-block design of the rusticated blocks.
Nevertheless, the smooth, curved, cushion-like blocks of
the Palazzo Strozzi do appear to derive directly from the
ground story of the model, and they mark a clear departure from the rocky, irregular rustication of previous
Florentine palaces. The courtyard has generally been assumed to mark another important divergence between the
model and the executed design since it has often been noticed that the model's courtyard included no columns.
The unfinished nature of the courtyard in the model means that it is impossible to establish what the first architect had in mind, and its detailed design was probably
intentionally deferred. However, the overhanging first
floor makes it certain that columns were intended to support the upper stories and incised lines show where the
columns and corresponding console capitals were to be
placed. Since Iodoco del Badia discovered payments to
Giuliano da Sangallo for making a model of Palazzo Strozzi it has been assumed that the documents referred to this
model. Three payments were made to Giuliano da Sangallo between 19 September 1489 and 6 February 1490,
amounting to 115 *lire* and 10 *soldi*. However, another set
of documents refers to a second model ("el nuovo modello"), made of limewood between August 1490 and January
1491, for which a wood turner, Chimenti d'Ippolito,
provided 76 columns, 44 of them for the bifore windows.
The discrepancies between the surviving model, and the
constructed palace can be explained by the existence of
this second model, which would presumably have demonstrated the taller proportions for the whole palace and the
design for the courtyard with its 16 columns at ground level and 16 colonettes for the upper loggia. Since the 76

columns documented for the new model do not tally with
the surviving model, whose courtyard columns were
never inserted, it is almost certain that the surviving
model is the first one made by Giuliano da Sangallo in the
autumn and winter of 1489-90, while the second
documented model with its 76 columns was adopted for
the final design, but has been lost.
On the basis of these documents some scholars have concluded that Giuliano da Sangallo was the first architect of
the palace; while others have argued that since the foundations were begun on 1 July 1489 a design must have existed before Sangallo's model was made and that he may
only have been working in his capacity as woodcarver (the
document refers to "Giuliano da San Ghallo legnaiuolo"),
making a model from another architect's plan. Although
many have persisted in accepting Vasari's statement that
Benedetto da Maiano designed the palace, there is neither
documentary nor stylistic evidence for this assumption.
Benedetto's brother Giuliano da Maiano, who worked for
Strozzi on other occasions, is a far more plausible candidate, although a compelling stylistic argument in his favor
has yet to be made. The bold and unprecedented symmetry of the plan might support an attribution to
Giuliano da Sangallo, although the bland quality of the facade may be the result of design by committee or of collaboration between Giuliano da Maiano and Giuliano da
Sangallo. The most straightforward inference based on
documentary evidence is that the foundations were dug
from 7 July 1489 following an established ground plan,
and proceeded in the autumn and winter according to
Giuliano da Sangallo's model. A series of important
modifications were introduced by Il Cronaca (Simone del
Pollaiuolo), who became chief stonemason at the palace
from February 1490 and who probably designed the second, lost model that was completed in late 1490. As Pampaloni (1982: 76-85) and Goldthwaite (1973: 123-135)
have shown, Il Cronaca was almost certainly the supervisory and executant architect on the site from February
1490 until 1504. To Giuliano da Sangallo and the early
consultative process we would therefore owe the
supremely unified design of a great rectangular palace
with a new, smoother form of cushion rustication, identical rusticated arches for doors and windows, deeply
beveled portals and a plan whose symmetry was unprecedented in Florentine palace design. To Il Cronaca
we should attribute the decision to vault the *piano nobile*
and establish taller proportions, the design of the cornice,
the magnificent courtyard and many of the capitals within
the palace.   *A.L.*

144
GIULIANO DA MAIANO (?)
Fragment of a Model for the Palazzo Strozzi

Florence, Museo Nazionale del Bargello (on loan to Piccolo
Museo, Palazzo Strozzi)
Wood; 128.8 cm (length) × 18.6 cm (height)
(length of carved surface: 68.4 cm)

BIBLIOGRAPHY: Stegmann and Geymüller 1895-1908; Salmi
1940b; Parronchi 1969; Pampaloni 1982.

This fragment is a revealing demonstration of modelmaking in progress. Half of the wooden strip was carved
to simulate a rusticated facade with seven bifore windows. The windows lack their central colonettes but are
articulated with flat banded moldings and tiny roundels

in the spandrel. The flat rustication of the upper story is cut back from the wooden surface, whereas the prismatic blocks below the windows are separate little pieces of wood glued into place. On the back of the board, grooves were cut where the partitions between the rooms were to be slotted in. This shows how the relationship between the facade and the interior was worked out from the very early stages of the model-making process, and how the plan preceded or at least accompanied the facade design. When the placing of the room divisions is examined in relation to the windows we find that they match exactly those on the two upper stories of the north (Via Strozzi) facade in the big model and the palace itself. The dimensions also tally closely with a one-story, one-facade section of the big model, since the discrepancy (4.7 cm) between the length of this fragment and the long facade of the big model can be accounted for by the damaged ends having been sawn off. It is significant that exactly half of the long facade has been carved, implying that it was considered unnecessary to duplicate the pattern on the other half of a symmetrical design. As an alternative solution for the rustication system of the Palazzo Strozzi this fragment differs from both the big model and the adopted design. The relieving arches above the windows are less emphatic than the bold, sculptural keystones finally selected for the window surrounds. Altogether the flat, slightly dry quality of this fragment is reminiscent of the surface treatment of Giuliano da Maiano's Palazzo Spanocchi in Siena. The design is more timid than that of the big model, and since it was never finished it was probably a rejected alternative for the palace, made early in the design process, but after the plan had been established perhaps in the spring or summer of 1489. Although the existence of the two fragmentary models cannot prove that discussions with Lorenzo il Magnifico took place, nevertheless Lorenzo Strozzi's account of continuing discussions between his father and a series of "muratori e architettori" is upheld by the existence of three alternative models for the same palace.   *A.L.*

145

IL CRONACA (SIMONE DEL POLLAIUOLO)
Fragment of a Model for the Palazzo Strozzi

Florence, Museo Nazionale del Bargello (on loan to Piccolo Museo, Palazzo Strozzi)
Wood. 98 (length) × 19 (height) cm

BIBLIOGRAPHY: Stegmann and Geymüller 1885-1909; Salmi 1940b; Pampaloni 1963; Parronchi 1969; Rykwert 1988; Ruschi 1990.

With its tabernacle windows, this fragment proposes an entirely different solution from the big model, the other fragment and the palace itself. It shows a nine-bay facade strip of eight windows with alternating triangular and segmental pediments supported by pilasters and an odd ninth window framed by a rusticated arch. Although damaged, the tiny pilasters supporting the pediments appear to be a simplified form of the Corinthian order. In their measured drawing of the model Stegmann and Geymüller failed to reproduce the traces of a larger order of pilasters that were once attached between the six left-hand windows. Incised lines and the remnants of glue show where these pilasters once were, as does the treatment of the surface, which is slightly roughened to resemble stonework, except where the pilasters were fixed on. Altogether three solutions are proposed on this one strip: 1) one window framed by a rusticated arch over a rusticated lower floor;

2) three tabernacle windows with a flat horizontal molding running across a plain ashlar facade, but retaining a rusticated lower floor; 3) five tabernacle windows flanked by pilasters resting on a wide entablature, with no rustication visible. The experimental character of this model clearly demonstrates the function of models as a three-dimensional design tool, allowing alternative solutions to be juxtaposed and closely compared in a way as we normally associate with drawings. Although none of these three solutions was ever adopted for the Palazzo Strozzi, they were certainly invented with that palace in mind, for the strip is precisely the same length as the east (Piazza Strozzi) facade of the big model; and since the dovetail joints are intact at both ends, this piece was clearly intended to be inserted into a complete model. As in the other fragment, the grooves at the back correspond exactly with the room divisions on the first and second stories of the east facade of the big model and the palace. The fact that the big model was constructed in separate, detachable stories and that both these fragments are first-floor facade strips that could substitute one story in the bigger model, also confirms that these models were flexible instruments with movable components, used to work out alternative solutions and present them to the patron. This is precisely what Alberti described; "[The model] will allow one to increase or decrease the size of those elements freely, to exchange them and to make new proposals and alterations until everything fits together well and meets with approval" (*De re aedificatoria*, II, i, trans., Rykwert et al. 1988: 34). The proposal for a palace facade with tabernacle windows and alternating pediments was by far the most innovative of the Palazzo Strozzi designs, particularly when interspersed with pilasters and supported by a broad entablature. The same features were adopted by Il Cronaca for the exterior and interior of S. Salvatore al Monte, begun in 1487. Indeed, the analogy with the church is so close and the use of alternating pediments so rare at this date as to make the attribution of this fragment to Il Cronaca absolutely convincing. There were important ancient and medieval models of the use of alternating pediments, e.g., Trajan's Forum in Rome, the baptistery in Florence and the basilica of S. Salvatore at Spoleto; but in the late 1480s the only architectural revivals of the motif were to be found in the Palazzo Vescovile at Fossombrone (begun 1479) and in Francesco di Giorgio's church of S. Bernardino at Urbino (1482-91) (Ruschi 1990). This model is therefore an important and often overlooked example of what was to become a key feature of sixteenth-century palace facades from Raphael's Palazzo Pandolfini to Antonio da Sangallo and Michelangelo's Palazzo Farnese.   *A.L.*

146

FLORENTINE STONEMASON OR SCULPTOR (active 1490s)
Console Capital from One of the Palazzo Strozzi Vaults (piano nobile?)

Private Collection
Pietra Serena.

BIBLIOGRAPHY: Rorimer 1928-29; Gosebruch 1958; Goldthwaite 1973; Pampaloni 1982; Tonnesmann 1983b; Lamberini 1991d; Morolli 1992b; Rensi 1992; Ward-Perkins 1992.

The dating and attribution of the Palazzo Strozzi console capitals are problematic, since much of the original stonework was replaced during the restoration campaign of 1939-40, when this capital was probably removed from the palace. In particular, the reconstruction of the vaults with their capitals in the first-floor *sale* facing Via Tornabuoni is documented, and the restorers at the time were understandably proud of the fact that their new capitals were indistinguishable from the old (Lamberini 1991d: 230-231). This is especially unfortunate since the construction of the Palazzo Strozzi is remarkably well documented and it might have been possible to identify the work of different masons and sculptors; for example that of Sandro di Giovanni di Bertino and Bernardino di Desiderio, who carved many of the interior corbels (Goldthwaite 1973: 154).

The Palazzo Strozzi building accounts document the carving of the ground-floor console capitals from December 1491 to the early spring of 1492 (Pampaloni 1982: 104-105). The vaulting of the first floor is not so precisely recorded, but can be placed within the period 1493-95 (Pampaloni 1982: 106), the this capital was probably carved.

In the Strozzi console capital the lower acanthus leaves flank a central palmette from which emerges a tall narrow stalk carrying a leaf with ears of corn or a seed-pod in place of the usual abacus blossom. Another unorthodox feature is the way the volutes curl upward and inward, their leaf forms tapering into delicate tendrils on the *calathos*, where they are bound by a double ring to the central stalk. The closely observed botanical forms tracing an arabesque across the flat *calathos* are further enlivened by two small birds (one severely damaged) perched on the central stem and pecking at the fruit on the abacus. The tapering base is badly damaged with only the Strozzi crescents occupying the central field and three oak leaves remaining at the tip. However, the ends of two wings are visible and suggest that harpies or sphinxes were probably carved along the concave sides supporting the capital.

The vigor of the carving, the fine, pliant forms and the union of design and execution in this displaced capital are markedly different from the coarse, dry and derivative touch of many of the console capitals visible in the Palazzo Strozzi today, although in handling, the crisp delicacy and finely-veined acanthus leaves do resemble several capitals still in the palace (e.g., Pampaloni 1982, pl. XXVIb). Its iconography accords with other capitals on the *piano nobile* of the Palazzo Strozzi, which present many variations on similar *all'antica* themes, including palmettes, birds pecking at fruit, and figures stretched along the base.

The Strozzi capital belongs to a decorative type for which there are many ancient precedents (e.g., Ward-Perkins 1992: 89, figs. 72 and 73; Gosebruch 1958, figs. 30-34), although it does not conform exactly to any of the classical orders. Variously described as the "Kelchvolutenkapitell" (Gosebruch 1958: 120ff., and Tonnesmann 1983: 50-52), or the "ordine salomonico" (Morolli 1992b: 277), the type is enormously flexible and therefore hard to define. Its first main characteristic are the prominent volutes which curl around the upper corners and descend in an S-shape to meet in the center of the *calathos*.

The volutes take many forms from flat ribbons to leaves to dolphins. The second common characteristic is the restriction of acanthus leaves to the lower range, leaving the *calathos* free for the development of any foliate or figurative motif. Its great popularity in Italy in the second half of the fifteenth century is a feature of the free experimentation with capital forms taking place in the years before illustrated classifications of the Vitruvian orders were available, and before a more restricted repertoire was adopted in the sixteenth century. Examples can be found in most architectural contexts from the pilasters of Florence Cathedral lantern, to Alberti's Holy Sepulcher Tabernacle, to the Palazzo Ducale at Urbino (Rensi 1992: 143-148). As a vehicle for Albertian *varietas*, it provided stonemasons and architects with the opportunity to invent and combine familiar and exotic forms in an *all'antica* spirit.   *A.L.*

147
BACCIO D'AGNOLO
Plan and Elevations of Piazza Strozzi

Florence, Galleria degli Uffizi, Gabinetto Disegni e Stampe,
Uff. 132A
Pen and ink, with traces of stylus and black chalk.
46.9 × 75.1 cm

BIBLIOGRAPHY: Stegmann and Geymüller 1885-1908; Pampaloni
1982; Elam 1985.

Caroline Elam has identified the purpose, author and date
of this drawing along with the accompanying plan, Uff.
1561A. Elam has convincingly demonstrated that these
drawings do not relate to the construction of the palace itself, but to the creation of a piazza on its east side to
replace the narrow Corso degli Strozzi. Filippo Strozzi the
Younger (1489-1538) had probably conceived the idea of
opening up a piazza in front of his father's palace by 1531,
when he bought the remaining buildings opposite in order
to demolish them. In March 1533 he and his brother
Lorenzo divided the palace, with Filippo taking the east
side, facing what was to be the new piazza; and on 31 May
that year he wrote to Lorenzo from Lyons saying that he
was waiting for the drawing of the piazza and surrounding
houses to arrive. Uff. 132A is almost certainly the drawing
Filippo the Younger was expecting. Its purpose was therefore to show the absent patron what the scheme would
look like when finished. Elam identified two hands in the
inscriptions: that of the architect Baccio d'Agnolo and
that of Lorenzo Strozzi. Baccio d'Agnolo's involvement
in the piazza project accords well with his role as *capomaestro* or supervising architect for the Palazzo Strozzi in the
1530s, when Lorenzo and Filippo Strozzi the Younger
were attempting to complete the palace. Lorenzo's annotations were made to help his brother identify all the
buildings and point out the problems to him.
The new piazza, which had been cleared by October 1534,
was in fact an extension of the old Piazza Strozzi, and
together they formed a long, rectangular space, providing
a lighter, more spacious and more dignified environment
for the huge new palace. The drawing not only records the
piazza scheme, but is the earliest elevation drawing to survive of the Palazzo Strozzi, and of the other buildings
around the square such.   A.L.

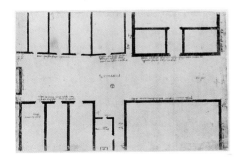

148
BACCIO D'AGNOLO
Plan of Piazza Strozzi

Florence, Galleria degli Uffizi, Gabinetto Disegni e Stampe,
Uff. 1561A

Pen and ink, with traces of stylus and black chalk.
29.1 × 43.7 cm

Caroline Elam has suggested that this plan was made
slightly earlier than Uff. 132A. Its annotations were all
made by Baccio d'Agnolo, and the irregular line of houses
on the west side of the old Piazza Strozzi is accurately
represented, whereas it has been regularized in the larger
elevation drawing.   A.L.

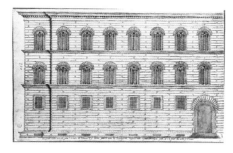

149
GIORGIO VASARI THE YOUNGER
*Elevation Drawing of Half the North Facade of
the Palazzo Strozzi*

Florence, Galleria degli Uffizi, Gabinetto Disegni e Stampe,
Uff. 4934A
Pen and ink with watercolor, on paper.
300 × 280 mm
INSCRIBED: *Da questo risalto sino alla porta è la metà del Palazzo
de gli Strozzi posto al canto de Tornaquinci, la quale metà è
quarantacinque passi, et a le porte che volte p. il corso.*

BIBLIOGRAPHY: Olivato 1970: 181-229; 1971: 4-28; 1973-75: 172-
204; 1976: 321-331; Stefanelli 1970.

This drawing is part of a portfolio of plans and elevations
made by Vasari the Younger ca. 1600, entitled *Piante
di chiese [palazzi e ville] di Toscana e d'Italia disegnate
dal Cavaliere Giorgio Vasari.* Within this collection consisting mostly of ground plans the ten palace elevations,
of which Palazzo Strozzi is one, form a distinct group
[nos. 4932-4941, dis. 218-227, pp. 149-156]. Of these
ten palace facades, two are unidentified and were probably entirely invented by Vasari the Younger, whereas the
others depict some of the most famous Florentine Renaissance palaces (Uguccioni, Strozzi, Pitti, Rucellai,
Bartolini-Salimbeni, Gondi), and one Roman example,
the Palazzo Farnese.
Although the measurements and annotations on these
drawings might seem to indicate that these are precise
representations of existing buildings, they have all been
regularized and altered, presumably with the aim of eventually including them in his volume the *Città ideale*, or a
similar compendium.
One of Vasari the Younger's preferred methods of creating an ideal architecture was to standardize existing buildings. In order to unify the group of dissimilar palaces,
Vasari selected three-or seven-bay facades, and modified
those which did not conform. In the case of the Palazzo
Strozzi facade, the rusticated blocks have been standardized in size and shape, their joins aligned, the dentiled string courses have been omitted, and the proportions of the whole facade have been altered to create a
more horizontal effect. However, the most striking
change is the addition of an extra, fictitious eighth bay to
the left, set back from the main facade, a feature that
makes the palace appear even longer and lower. It would
never have been possible to execute such a major alteration to the Palazzo Strozzi, which was a freestanding
building, whose dimensions were dictated by the presence
of streets and piazzas. The drawing clearly depicts half of
the thirteen-bay facade on what is now Via Strozzi,
stretching from the recently extended Piazza Strozzi
toward the Canto de' Tornaquinci, referred to in Vasari's
caption.   A.L.

150
Libro Della Muraglia A
(relative to the construction of the Palazzo
Strozzi in Florence)
1489-90

Florence, Archivio di Stato, V *Serie Strozziana*, 49
Written in "mercantesca" script on paper; original binding in
parchment; 208 fols.; original page numeration; 40 × 29 cm.

BIBLIOGRAPHY: Goldthwaite 1973: 97-194.

The inscription on the first sheet of the manuscript runs:
"This book belongs to Filippo di Matteo Strozzi, himself,
and it comprises 192 pages, entitled debtors and creditors, pertaining to the construction of the house in Florence, and it is bound in parchment; it is initialed 'A' and
kept for me by Marcho di Benedetto Strozzi, begun this
4th day of July, 1489."
It is the first of five volumes relating to the construction
of the renowned Palazzo Strozzi in Florence.
These five volumes detail the costs incurred in the construction of the palazzo commissioned by the immensely
wealthy merchant banker, Filippo Strozzi. The codices
follow the customary system of double entries: a set of
personnel accounts record payments made in favor of the
maestranze (builders, carpenters, stonemasons, etc.) while
another set, one of which is entitled "Spese di murare"
(building costs), contains itemized records of costs.
The construction of the palazzo experienced several interruptions, but most of the work was carried out during the
period 1489-1506. Successive phases of construction
took place in the following decades and the great cornice
itself, as is well known, remained incomplete on the part
of the palazzo giving onto Via Tornabuoni. Filippo Strozzi died in May 1491 when, with the great foundations
laid, the works were still in their initial phase. The total
cost came to around 35,000 gold florins: an astronomical
sum, which can be subdivided thus: 39% materials, 39%
labor, 18% site purchase Notwithstanding the abundance of detail, the documentation has not allowed art
historians to determine the role of the artists Benedetto
da Maiano, Giuliano da Sangallo and Il Cronaca (Simone
del Pollaiuolo) with regard to the design of the building,
all of whom are frequently mentioned in the codices.
There is no lack of references to models in the five
volumes. Mastro A is open at fol. 13 where the account
ascribed to "Giuliano da sSanghallo che ffa el modello della chasa" appears at the top: the "Avere" section (on the
right) shows the artist's credits, the "Dare" section (on the
left) the relative payments. In the second codex, Mastro
B, fol. 30 carries an account ascribed to "Nicholò di Nofri,
fabro nel chorsso degli Adimari," more generally known
as Caparra. In 1492 the renowned ironsmith was paid for
the production of the celebrated iron light fittings, which
would be positioned on the corners of the palazzo;
the model for these lights was made by Benedetto da
Maiano, as testified by the payments recorded on fol. 87
of Mastro A.

Marco Spallanzani

The Basilica of S. Petronio in Bologna
Richard J. Tuttle

Throughout the final quarter of the fourteenth century Bologna flourished as an autonomous communal state, free from domination by either of her two traditional political masters, the papacy and Milan. To honor and perpetuate civic liberty in 1388 the broad-based municipal government known as the "Signoria del popolo e delle Arti" decided to erect a mighty church dedicated to the city's celestial protector and patron, S. Petronio. Not the cathedral, S. Petronio was to be a votive and civic basilica. Overlooking the town's main public square, Piazza Maggiore, it became the proud and living symbol of communal independence.

Although autonomy proved short-lived, during the fifteenth and sixteenth centuries political considerations would continue to weigh heavily upon all important decisions regarding the planning, construction and decoration of the church (Fanti 1980).

The graphic works and three-dimensional models presented here testify to wide, intense and often protracted debates engaged in not only by architects and governmental officials, but also by an interested Bolognese citizenry.

The building commission was awarded to Antonio di Vincenzo, a Bolognese *muratore* of considerable experience as an architect and engineer (Matteucci 1987). Following the laying of the cornerstone on 7 June 1390 Antonio produced with the assistance of the Servite general, Fra Andrea Manfredi da Faenza, a three-dimensional model at a scale of 1:12. Constructed of stone and mortar, it measured 15.2 m by 11.4 m—virtually a full-sized sanctuary in its own right—for a building 182.4 m long and 136.8 m wide.

The model stood in the Palazzo Pepoli until 1402, when it was dismantled and replaced by a much smaller wood and paper version fashioned by the Bolognese painter Jacopo di Paolo.

Although both models disappeared early and apparently without a trace, the scale and character of the church had been already clearly established by the original architect, who had supervised construction of the first two bays of the nave, aisles and flanking chapels before his death. Antonio based much of his design—including the dimensions and layout of the nave and aisles as well as the profiling of the piers—directly on the example of Florence Cathedral, but he widened the body of the church by adding twin square chapels to each bay. The interior of S. Petronio is thus more capacious and, thanks to large tracery windows in the chapels, distinctly more luminous than the Florentine duomo.

During the course of the fifteenth century, while Bologna was under continuous seigniorial rule by members of the Bentivoglio family, Antonio's design was faithfully followed as construction progressed steadily southward from the facade toward the crossing (Supino 1913). The only new element, aside from Jacopo della Quercia's splendid marble decoration of the main portal, the Porta Magna (1425-38), was the campanile erected on the right flank in 1481-92.

By the end of the century the chapels and aisles were vaulted through the fifth bay of the nave, which was covered by an open timber roof. Such was the state of the church when in 1506 Bologna submitted definitively to direct temporal rule by the papacy. It was a critical moment in the building history of S. Petronio.

The new sovereign, Julius II, professed his support for the ambitious undertaking (Tuttle 1982), as did many succeeding pontiffs, but the disappearance of the original

Trecento master plan posed major design problems. These included the planning of the crossing, transepts and choir, the vaulting of the nave, and the decoration of the facade. In each area the fundamental question was whether to build in the *maniera tedesca*, that is, in a manner compatible with the venerable, local late-Gothic idiom of Antonio di Vincenzo, or in the *maniera moderna*, the modern or neo-antique classical style.

Since the authorities and much of the public pledged themselves to completing the huge church in the fashion chosen by their communal forefathers, several generations of sixteenth-century architects were compelled, against their natural desires and intellectual training, to devise large and expensive projects in an outdated style. S. Petronio thus became the focus of theoretical debates about the Gothic, a laboratory for re-examining critically the language of Antonio di Vincenzo, for reassessing the logic and coherence if not the beauty of his work, for designing not according to the prevailing principles of Vitruvian or Roman classicism but in an essentially discredited mode of thought.

The architects had no more formidable objective—in fact never reached—than the completion of the basilica's south end. Given Antonio di Vincenzo's reliance on Flor-

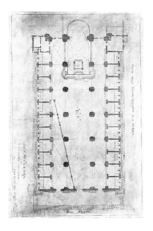

ence Cathedral for the nave, it is not surprising that Arduino Arriguzzi's wooden model of 1518 (cat. no. 151) should have an octagonal crossing crowned by a distinctly Brunelleschian cupola.

Yet the model is also informed by the lessons of two recent Quattrocento churches, the cathedral of Pavia and S. Maria di Loreto (Giovannoni 1933). For Arriguzzi and many later architects the line between Gothic and early Renaissance styles was blurred.

Stylistically less problematic perhaps was the vaulting of the nave, begun in 1587 by Terribilia (Francesco Morandi) (cat. no. 152), then contested by Carlo Carrazzi, called Cremona (cat. nos. 152-153), and finally completed in a new and higher form only in the mid-seventeenth century.

Today the extensive collection of surviving facade drawings appears to testify to one enormous open competition. In reality, however, the sixteenth-century neo-Gothic and classical projects were executed over a span of some fifty years in response to particular historical conditions, still imperfectly understood, within the Fabbrica and the Bolognese Senate. There were at least three distinct and salient episodes.

The first occurred around 1520 in connection with a campaign to complement the Porta Magna by dressing the two lateral portals with sculptural decoration. To this moment belong the drawings by Varignana (cat. no. 154) and Peruzzi (cat. no. 155), if not also the project sketched in wood in Arriguzzi's model, as well as an apparently unanswered solicitation by the *fabbricieri* in 1522 for an intervention by Michelangelo Buonarroti (Gotti 1875, II: 60). A quarter of a century later, in the winter of 1545-46, the second episode saw the presentation of the drawings by Vignola (cat. no. 156) and Giulio Romano (cat. no. 157).

Although they were ultimately rejected, the new projects, like the preceding ones, would become part of the collective graphic memory at S. Petronio, a corpus of established theoretical propositions influencing the creative efforts of later architects.

The final chapter, extending through the 1570s, included the interventions of Terribilia (cat. no. 159) and Domenico Tibaldi (cat. no. 158), both of whom relinquished the desire to generate wholly original proposals by returning to and revising Varignana's project, already partly executed. It also saw the intervention of Andrea Palladio who, after first affecting a compromise in collaboration with Terribilia (cat. no. 160) and then drafting neo-Early Renaissance designs, boldly asserted total opposition to working in the *maniera tedesca* by submitting entirely modern and personal classical designs (cat. no. 161).

That so many brilliant architectural projects eventually came to nothing was due largely to non-artistic circumstances.

The Bolognese authorities generally distrusted foreign architects regardless of their qualifications and they failed to secure the services of notable native talents such as Sebastiano Serlio or Pellegrino Tibaldi, or to give their full support to the naturalized citizen Vignola.

Stewardship of S. Petronio was entrusted to a succession of relatively undistinguished local masters. Discussions of style were orchestrated by the *fabbricieri*, a senatorial committee presided over successively by two members of the wealthy and powerful Pepoli family, Count Filippo until 1554 and his son Count Giovanni until 1585, and then by Tomaso Cospi until 1598. Final decisions, however, were remanded to the whole Bolognese Senate, which was controlled by a papal legate or governor. In fact, papal officials repeatedly intervened at S. Petronio, much to the displeasure of local authorities. The deliberative process was thus inherently flawed, prone to stalemates by way of internal factional disputes and disagreements as well as legal and financial conflicts between the city and the Vatican. As Panofsky (1955) observed long ago, the debates about style at S. Petronio were "rooted not so much in a diversity of artistic taste as in cultural, social and political antagonisms."

151

ARDUINO ARRIGUZZI (?)
Model for the Completion of S. Petronio
ca. 154

Bologna, Museo di S. Petronio
Wood; scale about 1:225; hinged to open longitudinally to reveal the interior; half of dome missing; portions of main facade reworked.
40.5 × 69.7 × 97.3 cm
INSCRIBED: (across the front of base) *Noli me tangere.*

PROVENANCE: Fabbriceria di S. Petronio.

BIBLIOGRAPHY: Gatti 1893: 16 n. 51; Weber 1904: 12, 30; Supino 1909: 115-121; Gatti 1913: 128-133, 151-154; Supino 1913: 135-36; Giovannoni 1933: 168-182; Fanti 1970: 34; Tuttle 1982: 6; Lorenzoni 1983: 90; *Sesto centenario* 1990: 64.

This model represents the most comprehensive surviving Renaissance project for the completion of the basilica. In it a nave of six bays leads to a broad octagonal crossing covered by a high pointed dome; to left and right extend transepts of three bays terminating in twin-towered facades; and the choir, two bays deep, culminates in a semicircular apse with six radiating chapels. Although comparatively small, the model proposes a church measuring some 225 m along the main axis and about 160 m across the transepts, including a crossing 38 m in diameter capped by a dome rising to well over 80 m. Built to such dimensions, S. Petronio would have surpassed not only the cathedrals of Florence and Milan but also St. Peter's in Rome. In effect, it set forth a scheme to make S. Petronio the largest church in the world. There is no secure early documentation for the model, making its authorship and date matters for conjecture and debate. Certainly it does not embody the original late-Trecento design for the basilica: Antonio di Vincenzo planned a smaller structure which is unlikely to have included a dome of this scale and shape (Supino 1909). Most scholars now believe that the model was executed during the second decade of the sixteenth century. In fact, Pope Julius II (1503-13) encouraged completion of the basilica, and between 1509 and 1514 two colossal piers and two massive corner supports were constructed to sustain an octagonal dome. Associated with this building campaign are several ground plans, including a copy made in 1522-23 for Baldassarre Peruzzi, now in the Museo di S. Petronio. Except for variations in the handling of chapels in the transepts and choir, the plans are in substantial agreement with the model. From 1507 until his death in 1531, the chief architect of S. Petronio was the Bolognese carpenter and engineer Arduino Arriguzzi. Payments issued to him between 1512 and 1516 reveal that he supervised the making of a wooden model for the cupola, now lost. In March 1515 Arriguzzi was sent to Florence in order to study Brunelleschi's great dome of S. Maria del Fiore, whose influence is evident here. It is very likely, therefore, that the present model follows his master plan. In addition, Arriguzzi's authorship may be inferred from a document of 30 April 1514 in which he is ordered to complete not only the cupola model, but also a "*modellum totius ecclesie*" (Gatti 1914: 128). Apparently this was intended to show how his cupola was to have fitted into the overall appearance of the completed church. If the *modellum* is identical with the work at hand, its small size and summary treatment of architectural details are reasonably explained.   *R.J.T.*

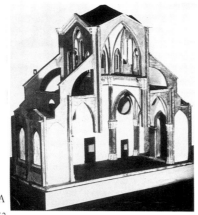

A

152

FLORIANO AMBROSINI
Two Models for the Nave Vaults of S. Petronio
ca. 1590

Bologna, Museo di S. Petronio
Wood and gesso, polychromed; scale about 1:45.
A) vault after the design of Terribilia (Francesco Morandi)
100 × 131.5 × 49.5 cm
INSCRIBED: (on left chapel wall) *alta p.i 48 nel mezo dela volta.*

B

B) vault after the design of Carlo Carrazzi, called Cremona
120 × 130 × 49 cm

PROVENANCE: Università di Bologna; Museo Civico di Bologna; Fabbriceria di S. Petronio.

BIBLIOGRAPHY: Zucchini 1933b: 200-205; Fanti 1970: 31-32, 82; Wittkower 1974: 67-72; Lorenzoni 1983: 96-97, 114; *Sesto centenario* 1990: 72 (n. 201a-b); Ferrari Agri 1992: 130-131.

Commissioned by the Bolognese Senate, these two models were executed as a pair in 1590 or 1591 by the local architect Floriano Ambrosini (d. 1621)—this much is affirmed in the dedicatory inscription on Ambrosini's own engraving of the same subject dated 10 April 1592 (cat. no. 153). The purpose of the models was to assist the senators in deliberations concerning the height and appearance of the vaults of the central nave. In particular, they were intended to provide a basis for visually comparing and contrasting the projects of Francesco Morandi, called Terribilia, who maintained that the nave should be vaulted to a height of 105½ Bolognese *piedi* (40.09 m), and Carlo Carrazzi (or Carracci), called Cremona, who contended that the proper height was 133½ *piedi* (50.73 m). Built to the same scale (about 1:45) and virtually identical in form up to the top of the nave arcade, each represents a single bay of the nave, aisles and chapels in lateral section.
A) Terribilia was the architect of S. Petronio between 1568 and his death in 1603. His chief achievement at the basilica was to have been the vaulting of the great nave, which he began in 1587. The smaller of the two models displays the quadripartite ribbed vault that he designed and actually completed in 1589 over the fifth bay, where

it stood until it was demolished in the early 1650s. Terribilia's design adhered to a long planning tradition at the basilica that posited a nave section twice the height of its width. Precedents for this could be found in many of the earlier sixteenth-century facade projects, including those of Baldassarre Peruzzi, Giulio Romano (cat. no. 157), and Vignola (cat. no. 156). Having less to do with structural stability or economy than with geometry, the method of projection amounted to generating the elevation *ad quadratrum*, squaring the width of the body of the church (comprised of nave and aisles only, about 100 *piedi*) to obtain its height. This allowed for a relatively rational and harmonious interior elevation that Terribilia divided into three successive zones of approximately equal height, beginning with the order of nave piers, followed by the second pilaster order, and finally the vaults. The model demonstrates that for the fenestration Terribilia simply followed the example of the early Cinquecento wooden model (cat. no. 151) by replicating the oculi lighting the aisles. On the exterior he derived the curving buttresses rising to a continuous cornice from drawings by Peruzzi (Museo, inv. 50). Despite its reliance on familiar ideas from the past, Terribilia's work failed to satisfy and from the moment his vault was finished it drew wide criticism for being too low. The architect defended his design in a memorandum (Gaye 1840, III: 485) but construction was halted. The ensuing discussion entailed the drafting of alternative proposals, the most important of which is represented by the second model.
B) Cremona was a Bolognese tailor by trade but also a trained mathematician and the author of a published tract on surveying techniques (Fantuzzi 1783, III: 118). Although he did not occupy a position of political power, his criticism of Terribilia's vault design was sufficiently compelling to capture the attention of the Senate, which ordered him to draft memoranda outlining his position (Weber 1904: 76-89). For Cremona, Terribilia's vault violated the true principles of Gothic architecture. His contention, based on extensive reading in the architectural literature and especially Cesariano's commentary on Milan Cathedral, was that vaults *alla tedesca* must be generated *ad triangulum*. Accordingly, their height was to be determined by taking the width of the church as the base of an equilateral triangle whose apex would mark the summit. In contrast to Terribilia, Cremona included the lateral chapels in the body of the church; finding that the distance between the outer surfaces of the exterior walls measured 154 *piedi* (58.52 m), he calculated the height of the vaults should be 133½ *piedi* (50.73 m). The geometrical proof is illustrated in Ambrosini's print which, like the model, also discloses Cremona's thoughts about the form such a vault should take. For the interior he proposed a continuous cornice with a catwalk above the second order and huge tracery windows. For the exterior he supplied flying buttresses to support the superstructure and a peaked masonry roof over each bay that would have created a series of triangular pediments along the flanks. It should be noted that the peaked roof actually puts the crown of the vault at about 144 *piedi* (54.72 m), considerably higher than what his geometrical scheme was meant to provide (Ferrari Agri 1992). In any case, Cremona's radical alterations of the basilica's outer appearance are likely to have been controversial, provoking additional polemics, and may well have contributed to the abandonment of his proposal. After five years of debate, on 17 June 1594 Clement VIII ordered the cessation of all further construction, study or discussion concerning the project (Gatti 1889: 126). The present nave vaults were erected with notable success to an intermediate height of 45.60 m, according to the designs of Girolamo Rainaldi in 1646-58.   *R.J.T.*

523

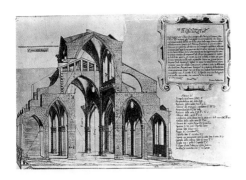

153
FLORIANO AMBROSINI
*Competing Designs for the Nave Vaults of
S. Petronio*
1592

Bologna, Archivio della Fabbriceria di S. Petronio, cart. 389,
no. 39
Engraving. 39 × 52.6 cm

INSCRIBED: (in frame at upper right) *All'Ill.mi Sig.ri et P.roni miei
Colen.mi Gli Signori del Reg.to di Bol.a. Quel maggior amore, che
si deve portare alla Patria et l'honore (che le SS VV Ill.me mi fecero
gli Anni passati in commandarmi che facessigli duoi modelli
dell'alzato della volta della nave di mezzo del venderando et sacro
tempio di S. Petronio Protettore di questa nostra Città, cioè un
conforme all'altezza del triangolo equilatero nella quale sono
fondate tutte le sue parti vecchie, et l'altro secondo la forma in che
hora si trova con la volta nova) in me ha cagionato, ch'io non ho
potuto ricusare di compiacere alle efficaci persuasioni di molti di
loro di far ancora gli ritratti di detti modelli, et tanto più quando
anco spero che con tal modo si potrebbe finire un giorno tanta
disputa: Onde facendogli tagliar in ramo ho meso l'uno et l'altro
insieme, accioche meglio con una sol occhiata si veda la differenza
che è fra di loro. Accettaranno dunque la prontezza dell'animo mio,
et mi scusaranno dove con il mio poco valure havesse mancato
in qualche cosa. A questo di X d'Aprile 1592 in Bologna con
quella riverentia, che conviene le basio le mani. Di VV. SS. Ill.me
Devot.mo Ser.re Friano Ambrosino; (lower right) Altezza del
Triangolo equilatero ABC. P.o / Perpendicolare del detto AD /
Reccasco della volta AE P. 10½ / Altezza del triangolo equilatero
S.o BFD / Perpendicolare FG del detto / Reccasco della volta FH
P. 5 o. 8 / Altezza delle capelle P. 48 / Larghezza della chiesa con
la grossezza delli muri BC. P. 154 / Altezza della volta nova IK P.
105 / Altezza del sopra Arco IK P.100. o. 10 / Sperone LM come
dovrebb'essere / Sperone fatto di novo NO / Poggio del Corridore
PQ / Capitello sotto il corridore XY / Coperto con travamento
sopra la volta fatto di novo RS / Capitello della fabrica fatto di
novo TV / Taglio ove è posto il Capitello TV / Il segno dinota
l'altezza della Fabrica sin dove fù condotta dal p.o Architetto.*

PROVENANCE: Fabbriceria di S. Petronio.

BIBLIOGRAPHY: Gatti 1893: 13 n. 28; Dehio 1895: 105-111; Weber
1904: 55; Zucchini 1933b: 200-205; Wittkower 1974: 69-70;
Lorenzoni 1983: 96-97; *Sesto centenario* 1990, 72 n. 202; Ferrari
Agri 1992: 130-131.

This print is an abbreviated but fully legible translation
of Ambrosini's two three-dimensional models (cat. no.
152) in a single serviceable two-dimensional image. Rendered in perspective, Cremona's high vault design appears in section partly cut away to reveal Terribilia's much
lower one immediately behind it. Below is the plan of the
church stretching forward to the steps of the raised *sagrato*
on the Piazza Maggiore. Cremona's project is privileged
by size and position, as well as by the overlay of finely
drawn interlocking equilateral triangles justifying his
proposition that the vaults should rise 133½ *piedi* above
the floor of the basilica. Important positions and features
of both projects are marked with capital letters referring
to the explanatory list to the right. Above the list is a
framed inscription, including the date 10 April 1592, in
which Ambrosini dedicates his work to the Senate. Unlike
the wood models, which were commissioned by the
government, the engraving was a private production.
With it Ambrosini undoubtedly hoped to enhance his

own reputation and that of his models, as well as to
capitalize on public discussion about the vaults. In this
regard the print is likely to have been sent to Rome where
Vatican officials continued to review the problem until
1594. The original copper plate (39.7 × 53.8 cm) is
preserved in the Archivio della Fabbriceria di S. Petronio
(cart. 398, no. 368).   *R.J.T.*

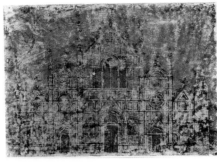

154
DOMENICO AIMO DA VARIGNANA
Project for the Facade of S. Petronio
1518

Bologna, Museo di S. Petronio, 1a
Pen and ink, with wash, on paper
42.7 × 58 cm

PROVENANCE: Fabbriceria di S. Petronio.

BIBLIOGRAPHY: Gatti 1893: 10 n. 7; Weber 1904: 33; Zucchini
1933a: 12 (pl. I); Bernheimer 1954: 269-274; Frankl 1960: 300;
Fanti 1970: 21; Belluzzi 1984: 16.

The lamentable condition of this much worn and faded
drawing is due not simply to time but also to the close and
repeated attention it received during the course of the sixteenth century. Executed in 1518, it is the oldest of the
many facade drawings still preserved at the basilica. The
design was approved by the *fabbricieri* and employed as a
model for the decoration of the lateral portals until 1521.
It was considered the operative facade scheme around
1540 and put to use in 1556-69 for the execution of the
bichromatic marble revetment now covering the lower
third of the facade. In 1579 the drawing, evidently already
poorly legible, was faithfully reproduced by the Bolognese
painter Ercole Procaccini in a copy subsequently inscribed
"Del Varrignana, Alta piedi 90" (Museo, inv. 1b). In 1543
Vignola observed that the design was "falsamente atribui-
to" to Bramante, but its authorship is now unquestioned.
Domenico Aimo (ca. 1460/70-1539) was born in Varignana, a quarry town in the Apennine foothills just east of
Bologna. Active primarily as a sculptor, he enjoyed a certain reputation in Rome, where he carved the marble portrait of Pope Leo X (1514-21) now in the church of S. Maria d'Aracoeli, and he collaborated with Andrea Sansovino
on the reliefs of the Santa Casa at Loreto. He made his
debut at S. Petronio in 1510, when he was charged with
completing the tympanum of Jacopo della Quercia's Porta
Magna, including the carving of the figure of St. Ambrose,
an undertaking prompted by the installation of
Michelangelo's bronze portrait of Julius II in a niche
above the central portal. Of all the Renaissance schemes
for the facade of the basilica, Varignana's is the most successful in suppressing classical or neo-antique compositional principles and decorative motifs. The work is envisioned as a taut sheath of marble paneling rather than as
a superimposed structure of horizontal members on vertical supports. The insistent geometry of the rectangular
panels rising through eight successive registers appears to
have been inspired by the example of medieval churches
in Florence from S. Miniato al Monte to S. Maria Novella
and the flanks of S. Maria del Fiore, except that here the
panels are not set flush but raised. This would prompt Vignola to call them "bugnoni" and to characterize the design

disapprovingly as rusticated. The single overt concession
to contemporary Renaissance taste is the colossal,
dominating double-light Gothic window which, with its
flanking lancets, reads as a medievalized version of the
Serliana. The design is important for laying down certain
thematic elements, such as the dozen niches for statuary
between the portals and the large panels with narrative
scenes in relief or mosaic—apparently from Genesis—
ranged across the upper levels. Its partial execution,
moreover, rendered this project of critical significance for
those by Tibaldi (cat. no. 158), Terribilia (cat. no. 159)
and Palladio (cat. no. 160).   *R.J.T.*

155
BALDASSARRE PERUZZI
Two Projects for the Facade of S. Petronio
(recto and verso)
ca. 1522

Bologna, Museo di S. Petronio, 1-2 (Gatti)
Pen and ink, with wash, on three sheets of paper.
75 × 75 cm

INSCRIBED: (recto, lower left) *Di Baldassar da Siena Alt.a piedi
105. dietro questo dissegno vi è un altro grandioso pensiere per la
stesa facciata idea meravigliosa del medesimo Autore*; (in Peruzzi's
hand on recto, lower right) *Questa pianta segnato B se acompagna
bene*; (right margin) *questa parte è facendo le sue arche [co]me qui
si demontra.*

PROVENANCE: Fabbriceria di S. Petronio.

BIBLIOGRAPHY: Gatti 1893: 9 nn. 1-2; Weber 1904: 35; Zucchini
1933a: 14-16, pls. II, IV; Bernheimer 1954: 274; Frankl 1960: 301;
Fanti 1970: 30; Wittkower 1974: 73; Wurm 1984, nn. 131, 128.

In 1522 Baldassarre Peruzzi, then co-architect of the
Basilica of St. Peter in Rome, accepted an invitation from
the *fabbricieri* to assist at S. Petronio. He was the first
major "foreign" architect of the sixteenth century to work
there. His involvement lasted no less than ten months—
there were substantial payments to him for numerous

524

drawings between July 1522 and April 1523—although it is by no means certain that he resided continuously in the Emilian capital (Frommel 1967-68: 111). The *fabbricieri* granted Peruzzi extraordinary liberty to develop designs as he saw fit. His most imposing and complex drawing is the outsized (1.72 × 2 m) longitudinal section in perspective with plan (Museo, Gatti inv. 50) representing nothing so much as a full-fledged model for the completion of the building with transepts and choir, four domed sacristies, and a colossal octagonal cupola. In addition to a study of the plan (Zucchini 1942), a total of four facade projects by Peruzzi's hand survive, one in the British Museum and three in the Museo di S. Petronio. The two famous and beautiful facade projects on the recto and verso of this relatively small and fragile sheet have often been mistaken for being two separate drawings. This is not surprising, for while both share the same scale—the one on the verso having been generated by tracing the outlines of the one on the recto—the two images exhibit powerful contrasts of technique, conception and overall effect. Peruzzi's fecund imagination and his facility as a draftsman frequently inspired him to produce multiple and diverse design schemes for the same building. In the present instance the two projects represent not just alternative formal solutions, but also distinct interpretative explorations of Gothic style. On the recto Peruzzi proposes a facade of great clarity, simplicity and economy. In it the pre-existing *basamento*, corner piers, and Porta Magna are left largely intact while the interior divisions of nave, aisles and chapels are lucidly marked off by plain pilasters ascending through three modestly expressed horizontal registers. Large triple-lights and a central whirling rose window give the interior plentiful illumination. Without jeopardizing overall coherence, the architect provides a varied menu of possible ornamental choices. These include not only the orders (Corinthian or plain), but also the shape and decoration of niches, doors, windows and pediments. The result is a facade that approaches the clarity and simplicity of Antonio di Vincenzo's interior. The drawing on the verso forsakes the delicate pen lines and restrained washes of the elevation on the recto in favor of a rapid and aggressive drawing style loaded with the extravagant personal flourishes that distinguish Peruzzi as one of the most expressive architectural draftsmen of the Renaissance. The change in style is calculated to enhance the architectural scheme, which now involves the imposition of a muscular grid of three-dimensional classical members. At the center the Porta Magna is framed by paired columns with niches, a triumphal arch composition repeated in the upper levels and extended laterally to embrace the lesser portals. While retaining the system of fenestration employed on the recto, Peruzzi placed large pictorial fields above all three portals, an idea which he would develop in the richly detailed project now in the British Museum. In this drawing, however, the octagonal multi-storied bell tower signals the presence of two alternative design schemes: on the left side an attenuated order of attached columns, slight entablatures and an abundance of sculptural decoration reflecting an overtly flamboyant style; on the right, pilasters more carefully proportioned and more fully outfitted with classical detail, embodying a more self-consciously "modern" style. *R.J.T.*

156

GIACOMO DA VIGNOLA
Project for the Facade of S. Petronio
1545

Bologna, Museo di S. Petronio, 5
Pen and ink, with wash and white highlighting, on five sheets of paper; 96 × 121 cm.
INSCRIBED: (flanking image) *I-I.*

PROVENANCE: Fabbriceria di S. Petronio.

BIBLIOGRAPHY: Gatti 1893: 10 n. 10; Weber 1904: 37; Willich 1906: 26; Sorbelli 1908: 259-268; Zucchini 1933a: 18, pl. XIII; 1933b: 194; Lotz 1938: 115; Bernheimer 1954: 278; Panofsky 1955: 198; Frankl 1960: 304; Walcher Casotti 1960, I: 58, 143; Fanti 1970: 23; *La vita e le opere* 1973: 128-130; Wittkower 1974: 74; Belluzzi 1984: 16.

Vignola (1507-73) was the only figure of major historical importance to occupy the position of architect-in-chief at S. Petronio. Nevertheless, his service of seven years, from 1543 until 1550, was marked by stormy and protracted debates and was ultimately rather unproductive. Although he was nominated by Count Filippo Pepoli, President of the Fabbrica, and confirmed in his appointment by Paul III, Vignola was compelled to share his post with Jacopo Ranuzzi, an undistinguished architect with local political support. From the outset there were bitter quarrels between the two men concerning the facade. In December 1543 Vignola submitted a lengthy critique of earlier designs, including Ranuzzi's, and drafted his own project. Impatient with discussions in Bologna, Vignola attempted to circumvent local opposition by appealing directly to the pope, and in the summer of 1545 he presented his designs, which probably included this drawing, one of two versions preserved at S. Petronio, to Paul III in Rome. Vignola's design is directly inspired by Peruzzi's classicizing example of 1522-23. From it are derived the general system of the orders, the fenestration, and the triangular pediments. Vignola has, however, subjected Peruzzi's scheme to a rigorous Vitruvian analysis, clarifying, refining and developing each component in a personal manner. The classical system has been extended to encompass virtually every motif, from the portals and niches to windows and pictorial fields. Thus the triple order of Corinthian pilasters is applied uniformly, each with exactly the same canonic parts and proportions, as it ascends through three levels in diminishing size. Overtly Gothic elements, such as windows or gables with tracery are confined and subordinated to the powerful architectonic grid. At the same time considerable attention is given to the figural decoration which includes twelve narrative scenes from the *Life of Moses* in relief, twelve niches for statues of the apostles, as well as figures of Christ and four municipal patron saints (Procolo, Vitale, Domenico and Francis) crowning the pediments. Toward the end of 1545 a general review of competing facade designs was mounted in Bologna. Vignola's received a written commendation from Giulio Romano. Nevertheless, it was rejected and additional criticism from Ranuzzi compelled the architect to compose a detailed defense in February 1547. Within three years he chose to abandon his post for that of papal architect to Julius III in Rome. *R.J.T.*

157

GIULIO ROMANO and CRISTOFORO LOMBARDO
Project for the Facade of S. Petronio
1546

Bologna, Museo di S. Petronio, 2a
Pen and ink, with wash, on paper.
35.5 × 45 cm

INSCRIBED: (affixed to upper left) *Di Julio Romano e di Cristofaro Lombardo archit.o del domo di Millano. Alt.a piedi 104;* (along bottom) *Questo fu il primo schizzo di facciata ne quale parve a noi di levare via il mezzo pilastro scuro segnato a. accio la facciata, et il campanile fossero a un diritto: e che il campanile non sporti piu fori della facciata de la Chiesa. adi 23 Genaro MCXLVI. / Io Cristoforo Lombardo Ingegniere della veneranda fabrica di la Chiesa Maggiore di Milano subscripsi. / Jul. Rom. / Questo e lo angolo in dimostrazione come si volto il cantone quando non si vogliono fare li campanili dove e segnato la finestra scura in la facciata che volta verso il salario;* (transcription from the eighteenth-century copy in Vienna, Albertina, SR 171; published in Zucchini (*Disegni*) 1933, caption to pl. VI).

PROVENANCE: Fabbriceria di S. Petronio.

BIBLIOGRAPHY: Gatti 1893: 10 n. 6; Weber 1904: 36-37; Zucchini 1933a: 16, pls. VI, VII; Hartt 1958, I: 245; Fanti 1970: 21; Belluzzi 1984: 17; *Giulio Romano* 1989: 548.

The acrimonious debate between Vignola, Ranuzzi and others appears to have prompted a full and official review of designs for the facade of S. Petronio. Giulio Romano (1492/99-1546) was called to S. Petronio in the winter of 1545-46, apparently for consultation. But while in Bologna he joined creative forces with Cristoforo Lombardo (active 1510-51), architect to the cathedral of Milan, whose services had been requested by the papal legate, Cardinal Giovanni Moroni. On 23 January 1546 Giulio and Lombardo were paid 100 *scudi* each, and Lombardo's assistant from Milan, Alessandro Olicati, received 80 *scudi*. While the authorship of the drawing is uncertain, there is little reason to doubt that it embodies a genuinely collaborative project. The design calls for stripping the facade of all previous decoration and opening three large Gothic windows in the nave and aisles. Greatly praised by Vasari, it employs a vocabulary of Gothic forms within an explicitly classical syntax. The facade is organized by a series of colossal pilasters of a medievalized Corinthian order bearing an entablature broken at the center by a pointed arch, a scheme which resembles nothing less than an immense Gothic Serliana. Lesser columns and pilasters frame the doors, nave bifora and central gable, which is filled in the Lombard manner with niches. The drawing includes two alternative solutions. The one on the left half of the sheet proposes a large projecting campanile on axis with the side chapels, a feature derived from Peruzzi and reminiscent of Bramante's schemes for St. Peter's in Rome. The legend affirms, however, that the architects preferred the tower be flush with the facade, which would require demolition of the first chapel. On the right half of the sheet a less ambitious solution, excluding the tower, details how the new front would round the corner to the basilica's right flank. *R.J.T.*

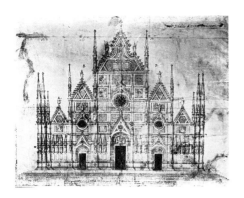

158

DOMENICO TIBALDI
Project for the Facade of S. Petronio
1572

Bologna, Museo di S. Petronio, 8
Pen and ink, with wash, on five sheets of paper.
90 × 100 cm
INSCRIBED: (affixed to upper right) *Del Tebaldo Altezza Piedi
105*; (flanking image) *B-B*; (in Tibaldi's hand, at bottom) *Ill.mi
SS.ri Questo disegno ordinato dall'Ill. Sig. Conte Giovanni Pepoli
dimostra in che modo si possino correggere alcuni errori fatti nella
facciata della chiesa di S.to Petronio et insieme come egli si possi
compitamente eseguire nel resto della istessa facciata, essendo essa
già fatta in una parte fin all'altezza della lettera A nell'altra fin
all'altezza della B. Qual disegno è fatto a fine di mostrar solo
l'intentione dell'ordito ... di tutta l'opera, avertendo però che nel
mandarla ad effetti è necessario disegnare particolarmente con
maggiore studio le parti principali.*

PROVENANCE: Fabbriceria di S. Petronio.

BIBLIOGRAPHY: Gatti 1893: 10 n. 9; Weber 1904: 39, 43; Zucchini
1933a: 19, pl. XV; Bernheimer 1954: 280; Fanti 1970: 24.

Domenico Tibaldi (1541-83) was fourteen years younger
than his illustrious brother, Pellegrino (also known as
Pellegrino Pellegrini, 1527-97), architect of Milan
Cathedral. He was active as an engraver and perhaps as
a painter, but the principal legacy of his relatively brief
career was architectural. In the service of Cardinal
Gabriele Paleotti, Archbishop of Bologna, he planned
and began the rebuilding of the cathedral, S. Pietro, and
the great court of the Palazzo Arcivescovile in the austere
classical manner of Vignola. Nothing could be more surprising, therefore, than the facade project on this sheet,
which bears absolutely no resemblance to that of his mentor (cat. no. 156). Nor, for that matter, does it reflect the
thinking of his brother, who in the same moment was
drafting only classical solutions for the facade of the
cathedral in Milan. Domenico's point of departure, alluded to in the inscription, was the acceptance of the marble
revetment already executed according to the project of
Varignana. Evidently this was a condition laid down by
Count Giovanni Pepoli. Shortly after assuming the
presidency of the Fabbrica, Pepoli seems to have abandoned the idea pursued by his father of obtaining a fresh,
original and wholly definitive facade design, pledging
himself instead to the task of realizing Varignana's solution of 1518. Accordingly, between 1556 and 1570 the
front of the basilica acquired most of the red and white
Veronese marble paneling seen there today. There followed, however, a cessation of construction and the drafting of new projects modifying or "correcting" Varignana's. It has been plausibly suggested that this drawing
was the facade project paid for on 16 May 1572 (Zucchini
1933a: 19). Domenico's remodeling was predicated on a
twofold strategy of masking or reducing Varignana's
paneling while vastly increasing the amount of figural and
purely ornamental decoration. Thus on the upper half of
the facade the old rectangular panels are converted into
larger squarish ones containing elaborate geometrical designs. Varignana's eight pictorial fields are reduced to
only six, but a total of ten new niches for statuary are
placed on the shallow buttresses toward the corners and

just outside the lateral portals. All of the niches, new and
old, are given slender pointed pediments that effectively
obscure the paneling behind them. The pilasters with
reliefs flanking the three portals are projected upward as
ornamented strips terminating in elongated pinnacles. It
is Domenico's accentuation of finely detailed vertical
decoration that, notwithstanding the diminutive rose
windows and the oddly pinched main pediment, most distinguishes his design not only from Varignana's, but also
from most of the other neo-Gothic projects as well.

R.J.T.

159

TERRIBILIA (FRANCESCO MORANDI)
Project for the Facade of S. Petronio
1571 and 1580

Bologna, Museo di S. Petronio, 13
Pen and ink, with wash, on eight sheets of paper, with several
pasted alterations.
113.5 × 112.5 cm
INSCRIBED: (flanking image) *C - C*; (at bottom) *Dissegno del
Terribilia in correctione; Dissegno aprobato dal Ill.mo Reggimento
di Bologna per partito rogato per m. Annibal ... l'anno ... quale si
deve seguitare nel modo e forma e con le condizioni contenute in
esso partito.*

PROVENANCE: Fabbriceria di S. Petronio.

BIBLIOGRAPHY: Gatti 1893: 11 n. 12; Weber 1904: 39, 43; Zucchini
1933a: 21, pl. XVII; Bernheimer 1954: 280; Panofsky 1955: 199;
Fanti 1970: 25; Wittkower 1974: 74; Belluzzi 1984: 19-22; Ferrari
Agri 1992.

The whole of Terribilia's career centered on S. Petronio.
His father, Antonio Morandi (also known as Terribilia),
was architect to the basilica from 1549. As early as 1563
he is documented working there and he succeeded his
father in 1568. In 1571 he was paid for new facade drawings and this sheet was probably among them. Like
Domenico Tibaldi's drawing (cat. no. 158) and Palladio's
first project (cat. no. 160), it represents a revision of
Varignana's solution: preserved along the bottom are the
original Trecento *basamento* as well as Varignana's
paneled marble revetment to the top of the tympanum of
the Porta Magna. Quercia's reliefs have been removed,
however, in order to make way for the addition of broad
framing pilasters ascending to the tracery of the triangular
pediment, an idea which may be traced back through the
designs of Vignola (cat. no. 156) to Peruzzi (cat. no. 155).
In this way Terribilia succeeded in imposing a tighter and
more legible architectural framework. Clarity is further
enhanced by removing niches from the pilasters and con-
verting horizontal stringcourses into stronger, three-part
entablatures. It is almost certain that this drawing was reworked eight years after it was drafted. In the fall of 1580,
following three years of debate focused largely on the
proposals of Palladio, the *fabbricieri* assembled a dozen of
the facade projects for final review. This may have been
the moment in which they received alphabetical inscrip-

tions. The officials settled on a compromise solution by
ordering that Terribilia's project be amended to include
certain features from Tibaldi's and receive a central window done in the style of those lighting the Trecento
chapels. The appended paper strips with pictorial scenes
and window frames appear to reflect the commissioned
changes and the inscription confirms that this was the design which won the Senate's final approval. *R.J.T.*

160

ANDREA PALLADIO and TERRIBILIA (FRANCESCO
MORANDI)
Project for the Facade of S. Petronio
1572

Bologna, Museo di S. Petronio, 9
Pen and ink, with wash, on ten sheets of paper.
93 × 110 cm
INSCRIBED: (flanking image) *D - D.*

PROVENANCE: Fabbriceria di S. Petronio.

BIBLIOGRAPHY: Gatti 1893: 12 n. 21; Weber 1904: 40; Zucchini
1933a: 20, pl. XX; Timofiewitsch 1962: 84; Zorzi 1966: 95-98;
Fanti 1970: 24; Puppi 1973a: 403.

Andrea Palladio (1508-80) was drawn into the facade debates at S. Petronio in May 1572 through Count Fabio
Pepoli, a cousin of Giovanni Pepoli living in Venice. After
examining and criticizing drawings of older projects the
architect traveled to Bologna in July and by September he
had developed his own graphic proposals for the church.
These he forwarded to Terribilia, architect-in-chief, who
apparently produced this drawing for presentation to the
authorities in Bologna. Modern scholars have identified
this sheet with the one cited by Francesco Algarotti as
having (on the verso?) an autograph inscription reading
"io Andrea Palladio laudo il presente disegno" (Timofiewitsch 1962). While initially opposed to any attempt to
pursue the Gothic style, Palladio quickly adopted a con-
ciliatory position toward the *fabbricieri* by conceding that,
for reasons of economy, the existing *basamento* by Antonio di Vincenzo and revetment by Varignana could be
preserved with only minor alterations. In this way he won
credibility and support in Bologna even if his project
represented a compromise of style and principle. This
drawing embodies a straightforward combination of
Varignana's work with a modern—but not contemporary—classical scheme. The solution recalls Alberti's facade at S. Maria Novella in Florence in its retention of a
pre-existing revetment at the lowest level, upon which
rises a wholly new portion culminating in a gabled temple
front. But Palladio, unlike Alberti, dispensed with an intermediate or transitional zone, placing Corinthian
pilasters directly upon unarticulated vertical elements. As
a result, Varignana's facade is cast in the role of a rusticated base. *R.J.T.*

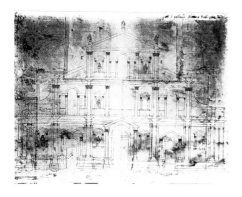

161
ANDREA PALLADIO
Project for the Facade of S. Petronio
ca. 1578

Bologna, Museo di S. Petronio, 12
Pen and ink, on two sheets of paper; 52.5 × 74 cm.
INSCRIBED: (flanking image) *G - G*; (upper left corner) *Dissegno del Palladio novo che mostra dui modi.*

PROVENANCE: Fabbriceria di S. Petronio.

BIBLIOGRAPHY: Gatti 1893: 13 n. 25; Zucchini 1933a: 20, pl. XX; Timofiewitsch 1962: 92; Zorzi 1966: 100-101; Fanti 1970: 24; Puppi 1973a: 403; *Andrea Palladio...* 1975: 243 n. 430.

Palladio's collaborative project with Terribilia (cat. no. 160), approved in 1572 but long delayed in its implementation, was suspended indefinitely amidst a round of criticism in the autumn of 1577. Palladio was then challenged to defend his design, which he did in a memorandum of 11 January 1578, and he revisited Bologna in November of the same year. On that occasion he handed over newly revised plans, two of which are preserved in the Museo di S. Petronio. In these projects the architect chose to eliminate all of the existing facade decoration and proposed a wholly new three-story front of pilasters with eight large aedicular niches and three serlian windows. Both are based on the solution developed with Terribilia and have deliberately archaizing features. There followed the submission of the present drawing, undocumented in the surviving archival papers, which marks a decisive turn in Palladio's thinking toward a complete rejection of stylistic conformity with the Gothic basilica. As the inscription notes, the sheet offers two design alternatives. Both are equally trenchant in their endorsement of the contemporary "Roman" classicism Palladio had been pursuing elsewhere in his secular and ecclesiastical commissions. The solution on the left half of the sheet is derived from the facade of S. Francesco della Vigna in Venice. As at S. Francesco, the front features two orders of Corinthian columns sharing a high podium. The lesser order frames the outer bays but continues across the whole facade behind a commanding giant or colossal order of half-columns which, at the center, forms a temple front. The much greater width of S. Petronio is accommodated by expanding the colossal order laterally to cover the aisles. As a consequence, the facade ascends in mighty steps through two half-gables to a hipped nave roof set back from the central pediment. Palladio's reliance on S. Francesco is underscored by the similar deployment of aedicular niches and thermal windows. The solution on the right represents a variation of the same formal scheme. Employing the same two orders on a slightly lower and more richly conceived podium, here the motif of the temple front is suppressed in favor of a fuller elaboration of the triumphal arch. The nave is masked by a pediment resting atop a huge attic zone decorated with statuary over salients in the entablature. Of the two alternatives Palladio probably preferred the one on the left; his final proposal for the facade of S. Petronio, known from a drawing now at Oxford, features a pantheonic free-standing portico. Like this project, it too was rejected when, in late 1580, the *fabbricieri* decided to proceed with the design of Terribilia (cat. no. 159). *R.J.T.*

Wood Inlay Panels
Fausta Navarro

The basic premise of the French historian André Chastel's his essay on the fifteenth-century art of *intarsia* or marquetry (written nearly forty years ago) was a discussion on the links between inlaid work and the development of perspective representation, an enquiry that occupied many in Florence during the fourth decade of the century. For Chastel, marquetry was one of the more significant areas of enquiry into perspective representation during the Quattrocento, on a par with Brunelleschi's mixed theoretical-practical exploration of mechanics. Basically, Chastel discerned the same underlying fluctuation between intellectual speculation and concrete practice, beginning with the trend for embellishing the front panels of *cassoni* with painted townscapes, and epitomized by the three famous perspective *Ideal City*

panels in Urbino, Baltimore, and Berlin. These panels in particular have been analyzed and discussed a great many times (see also the critical discussion in this catalog).
On the question of the links between perspective enquiry and the art of marquetry, M. Ferretti (1986) made a new parallel study of the extant perspective panels *of intarsie*, *cassoni*, and *spalliere*, in relation to the three *Ideal City* perspectives, demonstrating that all the decorative works made for domestic use have a common denominator, namely, their lack of any narrative content whatsoever, and their emphasis on the sheer intellectual delight of perspective study.
There has been much debate on the links between marquetry, architectural practice, and the burgeoning new design culture of the Renaissance; among the more recent contributors to the question are M. Ferretti (1982 and 1986), C. de Seta (1986), and A. Tenenti (1986).
Considering the impossibility in the present catalog of assembling a sufficient number of perspective *intarsia* panels, this is clearly not the place for investigating new connections and rapports. However, among the works discussed here are numerous panels attributed to Fra Giovanni da Verona in the former sacristy of S. Anna dei Lombardi in Naples; these works offer new insights into the central period of marquetry production with respect to the ongoing evolution of the geometrical rules of perspective, an area of study that greatly affected the art of wood inlay from the start.

BIBLIOGRAPHY: Chastel 1953: 141-154, republ. in 1978: 317-332; Ferretti 1982: 459-585; 1986: 73-104; De Seta 1986: 44-55; Tenenti 1986: 169-193.

162
FRA GIOVANNI DA VERONA
Perspectives
Still Life

Naples, S. Anna dei Lombardi
Wood inlay.
127 × 65 cm; 99 × 51 cm

BIBLIOGRAPHY: Summonte 1925: 169-170; D'Engenio 1624: 503, 510; Sarnelli 1697: 278, 280, 285; Celano, ed. cons. Celano ed. Chiarino 1856, III: 317-318; Finocchietti 1873: 89-93; Bernich 1904: 129-130; Mocchi 1905: 33; Placido-Lugano 1905: 80-84; Causa 1961: 47-52; Pane 1975: 89-90; Ferretti 1982: 533-539; Ferretti 1986: 100-102; De Seta 1986: 93, 100; Ruotolo 1993, vol. XI, 4: 608.

During his sojourn at the monastery of Monteoliveto in Naples (1506-10), Fra Giovanni da Verona executed several magnificent *intarsie* stalls for the choir of the votive chapel of the Catalonian merchant Paolo Tolosa, together with panels for the cabinets of the sacristy of the monastery which, in the wake of the suppression, passed into the hands of the Archconfraternity of the Lombards, and was rededicated to St. Anne and St. Charles Borromeo.
Evidence of the widespread appreciation of the novelty and superb technical craftsmanship of these works can be noted as early as 1524, in the now-famous letter from Pietro Summonte to Marc'Antonio Michiel (see Summonte, in Nicolini 1925: 169). Exactly one century later, the guides to Naples (D'Engenio 1624: 503, 510) praise the "prospettive di legno" (wooden perspectives) fashioned by the monk Fra Giovanni as among the finest attractions of the Neapolitan church.
At the close of that century—in 1689 according to the author of another guide to Naples (Sarneli 1697: 278, 285)—the *spalliere* from the choir of the Cappella Tolosa and the inlaid frames of the cabinet mirrors of the sacristy were transferred to a new sacristy that had just been built by order of Abbot Chiocca in the spacious refectory frescoed by Giorgio Vasari (Celano 1692, ed. cons. Celano, ed. Chiarino 1856, III: 317-318). Regrettably, the panels suffered a worse fate than those of the choir of the abbey of Monte Oliveto Maggiore, and were reassembled with no regard for the original narrative logic of the scenes. The new configuration, distributed along the full length of the refectory wall, had eighteen of the smaller panels from the Cappella Tolosa choir alternated with the twelve larger panels of the cabinets of the old sacristy, all inserted into a new and complex wooden frame, with statues of the saints set in niches of Late Baroque style. The "still life" *intarsie* with their portrayals of books, musical instruments, and liturgical items, were relegated to a dull arrangement on the two end walls of the refectory, and many panels disappeared altogether (including the splendid portrait of St. Benedict, greatly praised by Summonte). The epilogue to this unfortunate conservation history came in 1860, when Carlo Minchiotti, craftsman

and *intagliatore* at the head of a family of restorers and artisans particularly active at S. Anna dei Lombardi, was appointed to carry out restoration work on the *intarsie*.

An inscription in one of the Tolosa panels reads: *opus tempore deletum ...* Not satisfied with carrying out a drastic stylistic reworking of the panels, Minchiotti reduced their dimensions and even the figurative work of the inlay (Mocchi 1905: 33). Now that we have lost the subtle interplay of ideas inherent to the original order, with its iteration of urban townscapes alternating with liturgical items, musical instruments, and so forth, it is almost impossible to obtain any real perception of the original impact and significance of these *intarsia* panels.

Reduced to isolated perspective pictures, the panels are a long way from offering "an abstractive and harmonizing sight" (M. Ferretti 1986: 78), or from suggesting a mental space with a certain inner intellectual tension; instead, for the past century they have become an object of curiosity, fascinating for their technical virtuosity, and interesting for the townscapes they depict, which in some cases have been described as worthy precursors of urban documentary photography (Bernich 1904: 129-130). We can only wonder now at the fabulous spectacle once afforded by the Cappella Tolosa, which was frescoed in the last decade of the 1600s by another Veronese artist, Cristoforo Scacco, who decorated the upper band of the chapel walls with images of the saints of the Order of Monteoliveto and the Tolosa family, life-size, arranged in a highly illusionistic perspective worthy of Bramante.

Fra Giovanni's output belongs to the "golden age" (A. Chastel) of inlaid work, a period usually ascribed to between 1460 and 1510, which coincides with the period of closest interaction between the art of marquetry and the geometric and harmonic rules of perspective. In this central phase of the craft's history, *intarsie* became characterized by a marked emphasis on specific subject matter, with an increasingly consolidated repertory of figurative themes, as confirmed by the common practice among *intarsiatori* of using the same cartoon several times over.

This standardization—and in some respects crystallization—of the figurative themes was moreover fostered by the fact that the monks had organized themselves into a full-fledged *officina* or workshop in which boarders and Olivetano lay brothers were invited to participate, and traveled as required from one monastery to the other of the Olivetano Order.

In Naples, Fra Giovanni found himself working alongside Fra Raffaele da Brescia and Fra Antonio da Venezia (called Il Prevosto), two monks who had previously helped him complete the work on the choir of S. Maria in Organo at Verona, and the choir of the abbey of Monte Oliveto Maggiore. The presence also of the Florentine monk Fra Geminiano di Colle, and the so-called Maestro Imperiale (a Neapolitan artist) cannot be confirmed, despite Summonte's account. Both artists were *intagliatori*, instructed in the art of marquetry by Fra Giovanni da Verona, but the passage in Summonte's letter regarding apprenticeship is more likely to refer to two other figures—Giovan Francesco d'Arezzo and Maestro Prospero, both active in Naples in the ensuing years at the Certosa of S. Martino.

The standardization of the figurative content employed in inlaid work (favored also by the custom of close collaboration among the monks of the Olivetano Order), is exemplified by one of the inlaid panels from the *spalliere* of the cabinets from the sacristy of S. Anna dei Lombardi. The panel in question contains architectural representations of urban buildings, portrayed with marked foreshortening from a viewpoint at the far left of the field; the eye is drawn along the winding road, and thence along the course of the river, and the entire scene is crowned in scenographic style with a high plain. This same panorama can be seen in a panel of the choir stalls at Monte Oliveto Maggiore and, dating from an even earlier period, appears several times in inlaid work in the choir stalls of the Verona church of S. Maria in Organo.

It is difficult to agree with the claims that these townscapes correspond to real settings, and yet in the Neapoli-

tan panel one can discern the hallmark of Mauro Codussi in the design of the church facade, its nave crowned by a large semicircular lunette, and linked to the aisles by curved half-tympanums; other correlations can be detected in the Venetian cast of the soaring campanile portrayed alongside. It seems more apt to discuss this panel in terms of an "evocation of an image that has been preconceived in the mind" (Ferretti). As Massimo Ferretti has convincingly argued, the period of execution was one in which the norms of perspective did not simply afford the criteria for arranging and lending cohesion to a townscape; they constituted a mental attitude, a deliberation, which spontaneously expressed itself in visual terms, in a pure act of outward visualization—a process that was in all likelihood strongly influenced by the religious practice of memorizing texts.

The contours and geography of the city of Naples offered an ideal ceremonial backdrop for the many perspective panoramas painted by Fra Giovanni da Verona. The unusual expressiveness of the urban setting is particularly emphatic in the case of Naples, with its hillsides, undulating contours and the often strategic placement of the city's more important religious and civic buildings.

In the second inlaid panel for the cabinets of the sacristy of the Neapolitan monastery's church, in the distance of this accentuatedly deep *veduta*, framed by an archway offset by a second arch, one can make out the terraced hillside of S. Erasmo, hard by the Certosa of S. Martino. While the view has been accommodated to the requirements of a particularly intense use of perspective, and to the perception of a townscape that has been deliberately laid out for maximum effect, it nonetheless offers a surprisingly faithful representation of the real city, looking up toward S. Martino from a viewpoint in the middle of the main street of the former Greco-Roman street grid. This alignment evidently appealed to Fra Giovanni, who, in another *intarsia*, chose to include the Castelnuovo: of the many striking features of the city, the fortified residence of the Aragonese dynasty was the most momentous non-religious building, on a par with S. Anna dei Lombardi. The view, taken from the sea, strongly characterized by the undulating geography and the imposing presence of the Castelnuovo and the Molo, or quay, transforms the city into a townscape seen from a distance, whose ambiguous wavering between real space and illusory space is underscored by the presence of a balustrade, whose shape and two-tone marquetry echoes the face of the frame.

One of the recurring motifs in Fra Giovanni's *intarsie* is the centrally planned temple—an architectural prototype derived from works of antiquity, and one of the fundamental themes of the architectural program of the Renaissance. After its first appearance in the choir stalls at Monte Oliveto Maggiore (1502-05), it resurfaces in the Siena Cathedral panels. One of these portrays a circular, two-story building crowned with a ribbed dome. In the panel shown here, from S. Anna dei Lombardi (originally in the Cappella Tolosa), there appears a similar small temple comprised of two concentric rings capped by a dome resting on a drum. For the choir stalls of S. Benedetto a Porta Tufi, Fra Giovanni chose to portray a circular building made up of three concentric rings topped by a conical dome resting directly on the upper ring. In the sacristy of S. Maria in Organo (Verona), the cylindrical wall of the lower story has been clad with a perfectly regular system of dressed masonry, and resembles a crypt, neatly offset by the two airy upper stories with their orders of columns. In one of the *intarsie* executed on commission for the Olivetani abbey at Lodi, the same type of circular building appears once more, this time close in style again to the one used for S. Anna dei Lombardi.

For the Neapolitan panel, M. Ferretti (1982) spoke of Fra Giovanni's "intensive and abstracting" rendering of the Tempietto of S. Pietro in Montorio; indeed, there is a striking correlation between the spatial organization of this image, with its set of concentric rings and counterpoint of mass and void, arranged according to a radial scheme fanning out from the center, and the architectural

configuration of Bramante's little temple in Rome. The persistent use of this type of building throughout the inlaid work of Fra Giovanni da Verona—albeit always as an element of pure perspective abstraction, a feature that he first introduced in the *intarsie* for Monte Oliveto (1502-05)—suggests that he was intent on exploiting the theoretical, Neoplatonic, and humanistic implications of using the circle in the construction of places of worship. In the architectural theories of Alberti, Filarete, Francesco di Giorgio and later Bramante himself, the circular temple was an expression of metaphysical issues, of the concept of "sacred," the divine symbol of the cosmos and the earth, upon which the Church exercises its dominion. It is only natural, then, that the ideal architectural form for expressing this rich conceptual legacy should be an intrinsic part of Fra Giovanni's architectural imagery.   *F.N.*

From Scenery to City: Set Designs
Annamaria Petrioli Tofani

"And when the central area was no longer available to the Senators because it was needed by the actors and musicians, the stage was made smaller, sometimes raised to a height of six cubits from the ground, and decorated with two columns, and two platforms one above the other, as in the design of a house; and they had doors and windows in the right places, with a main door in the middle decorated like those of temples, almost as if it were a royal palace; and next to this were other houses and doorways whereby the actors could enter and exit according to the needs of the action of the play. And since three kinds of poets were practicing in the theater—the Tragic with his tales of wretchedness and the unhappiness of tyrants; the Comic who lays open the affairs and troubles of a paterfamilias; and the Satyric who needs to show the pleasures of the villa, and pastoral loves—there was a machine which, turning above a spindle, showed spectators in a trice such a well-painted backdrop that it appeared like regal scenery from a Tragedy, or a view of an ordinary house from a Comedy, or a wilderness for the Satyric plays, according to the characteristics of the story to be played out."

Although *De re aedificatoria* by Leon Battista Alberti, from which this detailed description of an ancient stage has been drawn, was not set in type until 1485, it was probably already completed in a manuscript version as early as 1452 (Schlosser 1924).

Evidently among the humanists of the time, not only the tripartition of the scene according to the "tragic," "comic" or "satyric" contents was well-known—as codified by Vitruvius during the reign of Augustus (and Alberti must have read the manuscript version of Vitruvius' text, because the *editio princeps* dates back to about 1486)—but also the machinery which, with a change of genre, quickly substituted one setting with another suited to the new theme.

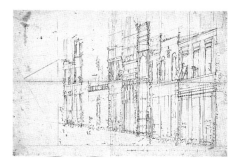

Peruzzi, Uff. 268A

The system, which had already been used in Greek theater, was that of the so-called *periaktoi*, or triangular prisms which, by rotating on their axes, revealed one of the three differently painted scenes. It is not possible today to reconstruct in detail either the appearance or the mechanisms of these machines, which were placed in special openings in the solid scenic facade (at the central *porta regia* and the secondary *hospitalia*).

Even though Alberti's personal knowledge of the theater world can be traced back to his youth, when he wrote (in about 1425) the text of a famous comedy entitled *Philodoxeos* (Battisti 1960b: 102-103), unfortunately in the above quotation, he limits himself to considering the subject only from the historical point of view, and refers exclusively to antiquity. He volunteers no information on the state of contemporary theater, which continues to be one of the more obscure areas of Renaissance study. While there is reason to believe that theatrical representations were highly varied, depending on local traditions, the scarce documentary evidence that has survived is open to a variety of interpretations.

Given this situation, which could indicate an intrinsic lack of significance in the theatrical works that were (or were not) staged midway through the Quattrocento (excluding other different kinds of phenomena such as passion plays and traveling pageants), a document, albeit brief, written about thirty years later by Giovanni Sulpicio da Veroli, is of enormous importance. Sulpicio was responsible for the first printed edition of Vitruvius' *De architectura* (Rome, ca. 1486), and in a letter of dedication to Cardinal Riario he included a few allusions to entertainments patronized by the churchman, whom he praises for having been the first person "in our century" to have introduced "painted scenery" to the theater (this primacy may be simply a piece of flattery): "*Tu etiam primus picturatae scaenae faciem quom Pomponiani comodiam agerent nostro saeculo ostendisti.*"

Such scenery, described as *versatilis* and *ductilis* (mobile), probably consisted in a simple, large drape hung for the occasion at the back of a raised platform, and these two elements formed the stage.

The scene evidently had a picture painted on it showing some sort of architectural setting which was intended—or so we believe—to create a spatial illusion that was well-defined and above all, universal.

Compared to the system of multiple stage sets used for performances in the Middle Ages, this kind of scenery not only offered considerable practical advantages—the painted cloth was simple to mount and dismantle and could be easily put away ready for reuse on another occasion—but it also marked a substantial innovation in the very concept of theatrical space. This was now conceived as the point of reference in which the events enacted found a harmonious setting and a greater guarantee of narrative consistency.

Although the innovation virtually decreed the era of modern scenography, for a few decades it was limited to theaters in Rome, with possible use also in Florence, though this has yet to be verified. In Ferrara, another important center of fifteenth-century theatrical production, it appears that up until the start of the new century stage scenery was still built of wood and comprised a few houses (four to six) which looked onto a stage whose front resembled a city wall. As Povoledo (1969: 403) rightly observed, "more than a complete scenography..." this town of Ferrara "was therefore a well-identified theatrical situation, and identified exclusively for the needs of a dramatic and performed text." This was in fact a hybrid solution, even though it was perfectly suited to a form of expression that was evidently unlikely to afford developments of any great importance.

It is easy to imagine how the adoption of painted scenery was influenced by the Renaissance advances in the science of perspective.

Indeed such sets were appropriately called *prospettive* in the early documents. The laws of perspective made it possible to reconstruct a conventional three-dimensionality on a flat surface, by means of which the gestures and movements of the actors acquired credibility, and a more objective spatial collocation. It is possible that the first experiments in this field arose from the desire to bring the scene onto a more human and rationally acceptable plane by interpreting the theatrical space as the natural extension of the real space from where the spectator sees it. The final achievement, however, was the complete opposite, since the scenic space conceived in this way, given its construction as a geometrical and therefore abstract calculation, tended more and more to be distinct from the space occupied by the audience, until sixteenth-century theaters adopted a real architectural diaphragm between reality and fiction which should in fact be considered as the scenic arch.

The new perspective stage sets, however, offered a winning solution for the principal problems of portraying a setting in harmony with the literary text, problems that had been growing over the previous centuries, and remained a focus of study for a long time throughout Europe.

Starting with very simple structures with a single, central vanishing point, the perspective stage set became increasingly complex with each improvement of scenographic devices, until it reached the overblown spatial indeterminacy of Baroque set design.

Even though the various passages in this development were inevitably influenced by local tradition, the basic structure and formal principles upon which it was based remained substantially unchanged. In due course, the backdrop—which remained nonetheless the main focus

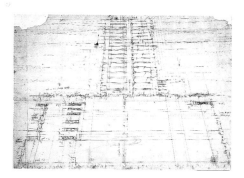

Peruzzi, Uff. 269A

of the perspective device—was enhanced with pairs of side panels or "wings," part painted, part in relief, arranged at the back of the stage, which was sloped to increase the sense of depth.

The proscenium instead remained flat and usually free of props for the sake of the recitation. In due course, the spatial illusion involved more complex multiple vanishing points and increasingly sophisticated experimental lighting techniques (cat. no. 173).

It goes without saying that the problems of stage devices concerned a very limited and select type of performance, namely, those in the courts and academies. Popular entertainment was unaffected, as it was largely based on improvisation (the actors recited without any real written parts, following a simple plot) and on the impromptu movements of the actors; consequently, it did not require any particular props or setting. On the contrary, an overly defined scenic framework would have been an impediment to the performance.

Even though no visual material has survived, except for this unique, extraordinary illustration by Bramante (cat. no. 163)—we can nevertheless assert that fifteenth-century stage scenery was not of a realistic nature. As noted above, the theatrical environment it suggested was more a mental than a physical space, with a certain abstract formalism punctuated with examples of pseudo-classical stylization, transforming the set into a kind of intellectual game, in which erudite classical features were assimilated by the new sense of space in Renaissance art. The fact that the space evoked in this way was purely symbolic, and quite irrelevant to the meaning or period represented in the drama being acted out, is demonstrated by the fact that, apart from the distinction between literary genres, the same scenery was used indifferently from one production to the next.

On the other hand, it should be noted that the audience was sufficiently cultured to be able to follow the action without the help of special "didactic" props, and that sometimes plays were put on without any stage devices at all. In 1502, for example, the program of entertainments celebrating the marriage of Lucrezia Borgia to Alfonso d'Este, held in the Vatican, included *The Brothers Menaechmus* by Plautus, which was acted "without masks, and there was no scenery because the room was too small" (Povoledo 1959a: 648).

Examples of theater sets in the following century that derived from this trend include the one illustrated in catalog no. 169 and, in particular, Palladio's magnificent Teatro Olimpico in Vicenza (see cat. nos. 171-172d), which represents the "archaeological" idealization of a sophisticated and unbiased mind.

Deliberately disregarding the direction in which tradition was going at the time, Palladio chose to return to classic antiquity by means of a new esthetic and emotive interpretation, underscored by an attentive and philologically sound historical approach.

At the turn of the sixteenth century, however, a new type of scenography began to make its appearance. While equally sumptuous in form and technically demanding, the new style was more flexible and accommodating, and capable of satisfying the requirements of a wide range of narrative texts, including the opulent episodic dramas of Ariosto and the Bibbiena.

The new stage devices signaled the end of the traditional distinction between the "tragic" and the "comic"—which Serlio continued to affirm on a theoretical level through to mid-century (see cat. no. 166).

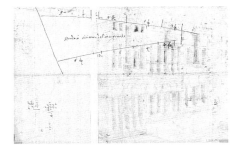

Scamozzi, 195Av.

With the new formula the solemn architectural decor of the former merged with the naturalistic vivacity and sketch-like accents of the latter. It is worthwhile to note the observations in Bernardino Prosperi's letter to Isabella d'Este, in which he carefully recalls the scenery Pellegrino da Udine painted for the performance of Ariosto's *La Cassaria* in Ferrara in 1508: "The most remarkable feature of all these *feste* and entertainments was the setting in which they were performed, created by a certain master Peregrino, the patron's personal painter; these comprise a reduction and vista of a landscape of houses, churches, bell towers and gardens such that one can never tire of looking at it and enjoying the many things depicted therein, all very ingenious and well devised, which I think has not been disposed of, but kept to use on other occasions" (cf. D'Ancona 1891, II: 394-395).

The stage scenery realized shortly afterward by Genga (regrettably only documented in written records, see Uff. cat. no. 170) for the city of Urbino was in keeping with this new trend, which opened the way to all the major innovations in the theatrical field in the course of the sixteenth century.

The same can be said for the outstanding sets designed by Baldassarre Peruzzi for patrons in Rome and other Italian towns; in this case some graphic record has survived (Turin, Biblioteca Reale, cat. no. 164).

Closely linked to these developments was the emergence of one of the most intriguing phenomena of Italian sixteenth-century theater, and that is the idealized representation of the townscape, in which the unmistakable charisma of the sources is nevertheless immediately recognizable, such as Serlio's Venice (cat. no. 166), Vasari's Rome (cat. no. 167), Beccafumi's Pisa or Lanci's Florence (cat. no. 170).

During the sixteenth century the art of theater production enjoyed a constant and extraordinarily fruitful period of evolution.

The adoption of movable sets was one development whose early experiments—probably in the 1540s—were, it seems, introduced by Aristotile da Sangallo.

By this time the fixed backdrop was no longer acceptable, and consequently increasingly complex visual devices were employed to adapt the settings as the plot developed, act by act; furthermore, an increasing amount of stage space was kept free to make room for spectacular visual devices, such as trick apparitions, sudden disappearances, levitation, etc., during the intervals.

Within a few decades, stage techniques were in constant evolution, leading to the dazzling metamorphoses and dilated spatiality of the Baroque stage sets.

This development was greatly furthered by the construction of permanent theaters in the second half of the century, this time equipped with all the appropriate stage machinery.

163
DONATO BRAMANTE
Perspective Scenery

Florence, Galleria degli Uffizi, Gabinetto Disegni e Stampe, Uff. 9787 st. sc.
Burin engraving.
254 × 369 mm (maximum dimensions of paper)
251 × 367 mm (plate dimensions)

BIBLIOGRAPHY: Courajod and Geymüller 1874; Malaguzzi Valeri 1915, II: 309; Arrigoni 1942: 209; Baroni 1942: 509; Hind 1948: 105-106, no. 2b; Krautheimer 1948: 340; Arrigoni 1956: 708-709; Samek Ludovici 1960: 33-34; Murray 1962: 38-40; Neiiendam 1969: 156; Stein 1969: 11; Alberici in *Leonardo e l'incisione* 1984: 44-45; Bruschi 1987a: 326; Pochat 1990: 280.

The engraving shown here—for a variety of reasons one of the most problematic art-ıfacts of Italian late fifteenth-century graphics—is a singularly important document for the study of Renaissance scenography. The subject is known from prints made from three different plates—this one in the Uffizi comes from the third in the succession described by Hind—which are closely related in terms of representation and times of execution. A caption written on the first two can be easily seen in the open space at the top center: "*BRAMANTE. AR/CHITECTI/OPUS.*" There is no doubt as to the authenticity and significance of this inscription (at any event indicating the authorship of the drawing, and less likely to refer to the person who executed the engraving); as Malaguzzi Valeri has suggested, however, there is a possibility that it was the work of Cesare Cesariano, a close disciple of Donato Bramante who is known to have engraved "*Bramantus f[ecit]*" on drawings by his own hand.

It has been pointed out (by Geymüller) that the argument against Bramante's authorship is based on certain architectural discrepancies that become clear when the buildings depicted are compared with the built works of Bramante.

As Hind has already demonstrated, however, this is not a real *veduta*, nor an urban project for a street lined by monumental buildings; it is an imaginary reconstruction whose every detail is easily explained in terms of its practical application as a stage design.

Furthermore, there is documentary evidence to show that Bramante was not a stranger to the world of entertainment. In a letter dated 15 May 1495, Bartolomeo Calco informs Lodovico il Moro that he had contacted Bramante in order to obtain from him "qualche digna fan-

tasia da mettere in spectaculo," namely, some worthy fantasy for a performance (cf. Valori 1983: 119).

While probably not a particularly early illustration of this genre, the print in question is the oldest surviving picture of a Renaissance *scena prospettica*. It would therefore be a great step forward if the engraver could be identified and a definite date established. This is not easily done as there are no documents of comparable nature. Even Hind, who considers the question from the point of view of engraving techniques, offered a date within a period of three decades: "The style of the engraving is near that of Zoan Andrea (or Giovanni Antonio da Brescia) and might be as early as 1475, though it is more probably about 1500-10" (Hind 1948: 104).

The only external reference available—not incontrovertible, but not to be underestimated either—is the date 1475 written in an old-fashioned hand, possibly contemporary, on one of the prints conserved in the Pinacoteca Civica in Bologna.

While the scenographic contents of this composition, recently rediscussed by Pochat, can be sustained without any particular doubts, there is considerable uncertainty regarding its specific utilization.

The print is an isolated case; there is no proof of its ever having been conceived as an illustration, in the way that Serlio's drawings were designed to clarify Vitruvius' treatise (see cat. no. 166).

And yet, since it is a print, it cannot be considered a preparatory drawing for a particular theatrical performance, which is the usual role of scenographic drawings. The most reasonable hypothesis is that the print was an academic exercise on theatrical space, and is not necessarily linked to any specific situation or application. As an exercise it was strongly influenced by the humanist culture of the time.

In that milieu, a work of this kind may have been for an illustration accompanying a printed theoretical text. Examples can be found in the architectural treatises published at that time, such as Leon Battista Alberti's *De re aedificatoria*, available in print in 1485 in Florence, and the *editio princeps* of Vitruvius' *De architectura*, which was published a year later in Rome.   *A.P.T.*

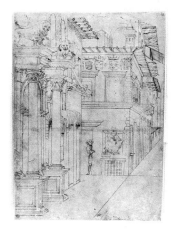

164
BALDASSARRE PERUZZI
Incomplete Study of Perspective Scenery

Turin, Biblioteca Reale, 15728
Pen on white paper.
380 × 273 mm

BIBLIOGRAPHY: Mariani 1930, pl. XII; Ricci 1930, pl. 1; Borcherdt 1935: 96ff.; Krautheimer 1948: 338; Bertini 1950: 19, no. 45; 1958: 46, no. 332; Rosci 1966: 24; Frommel 1967-68: 76, no. 35; Neiendam 1969: 162-64; Cruciani 1974: 161; Frommel 1984c: 226; Wurm 1984: no. 3; Bruschi 1987a: 326-29; Pochat 1990: 285.

There is substantial evidence for the leading role played by Baldassarre Peruzzi in the process of defining a form of scenography which drew its inspiration from the theater of classical antiquity (or rather from the fifteenth-century humanist interpretation of classical theater), adapting its spatial formula to the contemporary world. Giorgio Vasari fully realized this (and he was an expert on the subject) when he commented on Peruzzi's uncommon skill in the use of perspective, an ability that "few of those we have seen operate in our time could equal." He also wrote that in Pope Leo X's time Baldassarre Peruzzi had created "two scenes of astonishing appearance that opened the way for those who subsequently painted scenery" (1568).

Unfortunately, few illustrations have survived to record Peruzzi's activity as a scenery painter, an area of production that was evidently of some importance to him, and this drawing from the Biblioteca Reale in Turin is one of the most significant of its kind. It is most certainly a preparatory drawing for scenery to be placed on the left of the stage, as can be deduced from the indications traced on the floor.

The sketch probably includes part of one of the wings in the foreground, separated by a passage for the actors, and part of the vista painted on the backdrop.

It provides the only image which offers us a direct and detailed idea of the visual impact that a scene designed by Peruzzi could have had on the audience, keeping in mind that even the famous projects in the Uffizi for the late (1531) production of the *Bacchidi* (Uff. 268A, 269A)—the importance of which has recently been reaffirmed by Pochat (1992: 262-281)—are more a formulation of scenographic techniques than concrete illustrative proposals.

The drawing in Turin has traditionally been attributed to Peruzzi and is confirmed by the early annotations written on the recto and verso of the sheet. There is no reason to doubt the character of the handwriting, which does not differ in any way from that found on Peruzzi's vast and well-known graphic works.

The composition seems to be based on the Vitruvian comic scene (cat. no. 168), which is a reference for both the conspicuously patrician tone of the urban setting, enlivened by the addition of a poulterer's stall, and the sense of daily bustle expressed by the clearly painted figures that appear in doorways and windows. These are a concession to the kind of realism which Serlio warned against: "In these scenes some have painted a few living figures, such as a woman on a balcony or in a doorway, and likewise some animals: these things are inadvisable, because they do not move, even though they represent living people" (1560, fol. 26v.).

Peruzzi's brand of *scena prospettica* was, however, fully approved by Vasari later on. Referring evidently to tradition, and perhaps to vivid personal recollection, Vasari comments: "Nor can one imagine how, in such a tiny space, he succeeded in placing so many roads, palaces, and such a fantasy of temples, loggias and cornices, so excellently designed that they did not seem artificial, but extraordinarily real; similarly, the square did not appear as a small, painted area, but real and capacious. He also arranged the highlights, the internal illumination necessary for the perspective, and all the other necessary things, with great judgment."

We do not know exactly what scenography Peruzzi was preparing in the drawing shown here. However, on the decorative strip over the top part of the central building there is a Medici coat of arms with a papal tiara above it, next to another badge with the fleur-de-lys of the Valois royal family surmounted by a crown; on the basis of this, Frommel dated the specimen to the autumn of 1515, when Pope Leo X (Giovanni de' Medici) and King Francis I of France met in Bologna. Vasari recorded that Peruzzi had received many commissions for paintings and architecture in Bologna, so it is not unlikely that on this particularly prestigious occasion the court drew on his proven ability as a scenographer to devise a *spettacolo*, all evidence of which has unfortunately disappeared without trace.

A.P.T.

165
RAPHAEL
Study of Perspective Scenery Wing

Florence, Galleria degli Uffizi, Gabinetto Disegni e Stampe, Uff. 242A and 560A
Pen, brown wash, white lead, stylus impressions; white paper.
629 × 290 mm (maximum dimensions of paper, composed of three parts)

BIBLIOGRAPHY: Milanesi 1879: 637; Geymüller 1884: 56 n. 22; Ferri 1885: XXI, 24; Oberhuber 1966: 242 n. 34; Marchini 1968: 491; Frommel 1973, II: 20; 1974b: 183-185; Ray 1974: 73 n. 7; Oberhuber 1983: 614; Quednau 1983: 265; Ferino Pagden 1984c: 321-323, no. 22; Frommel 1984c: 226-228, no. 2.11.1; 1989c: 290; Pochat 1990: 288-289.

The interruptions of the drawing along the margin of the sheet are evidence that the sheet was once larger than it is now. Raphael glued at least three sheets of paper together, one of which—the upper segment—he had already used for an architectural sketch, now visible on the verso; this sketch provides an important *terminus post quem* for the drawing on the recto. It illustrates a preliminary idea for the courtyard of the Palazzo Branconio dell'Aquila in Rome, the design of which Raphael worked upon in 1518 (Frommel 1973).

The drawing reached the Uffizi in two separate parts (the horizontal division coincides with the windowsill of the upper story), which were considered independently at the time of the inventory and numbered separately (560A for the upper part, and 242A for the lower). The pieces were attributed respectively to Baldassarre Peruzzi and Vincenzo Scamozzi owing to differences in quality: while the lower expresses both brilliancy and incisiveness, in the upper part the lines are more indistinct and the chiaroscuro contrasts less effective. These differences stem not only from the quality and consistency of the paper used, but also from the state of conservation of each piece.

Geymüller was the first to realize the strict connection between the two pieces and to suggest their recomposition. He also attributed the study to Bramante, and put forward the hypothesis that Raphael drew inspiration from it for the windows of the *piano nobile* of the Palazzo Pandolfini in Florence.

There is no record in the Uffizi of when the drawing was moved to the collection of Raphael drawings, where Oberhuber found it in 1966, mentioning it briefly in a note as Raphael's, and mistakenly defining it as a "Bühnenentwurf" or stage design.

The attribution to the Urbino-born artist Raphael is plausible—though caution is required in unusual specimens of this nature.

It bears comparison with Raphael's known architectural works (starting from the aforementioned Palazzo Pandolfini, built in 1516-17), and matches his graphic style. The drawing has the essential stroke found throughout Raphael's drawings, his tendency to enhance the brief pen strokes with complex chiaroscuro values and a masterly application of wash.

That this drawing was intended for a theater—the right wing of a stage set with a centralized vanishing point—and not a partial study for the design of a building, can be deduced from the architectural structure, which is too sketchy and approximate in its details (profiles, cornices, bases or capitals) to be intended for the creation of a real building. The search for spatial illusion noticeable in the overemphasis of the perspective, however, is perfectly consonant with the requirements of scenography.

Christoph Frommel, whom we must thank for the full and detailed analysis of this beautiful drawing, has advanced the delightful hypothesis that this may be a drawing for Raphael's only known contribution to theater production, namely, for Ariosto's *I suppositi*, which was staged in the Vatican on 6 March 1519 in the hall of Cardinal Innocenzo Cibo. A witness to the performance left this comment: "I went to the *comedia* on Sunday evening [and when] the curtain was drawn back ... the pope looked through his eyeglass at the very beautiful scenery made by Raphael; there were, in my opinion, excellent representations of vistas, which were highly praised" (Alfonso Paolucci in a letter to the Duke of Ferrara, dated 8 March 1519, in Golzio 1936: 93).

To support his affirmation, Frommel recalls how, in the Vitruvian tripartition of stage works, the comic genre is characterized by the presence of elements that are described in the translation of the Latin text written by Fabio Calvo expressly for Raphael, in which he states that the comedies have the aspect and shape of private buildings and of protruding pergolas and they have prospects (that is to say, windows laid out in a reasoned order) that imitate common buildings.

The term "protruding pergolas" was a sixteenth-century interpretation of Calvo's Latin word *maeniano*, which may have resembled the aedicule shown here.

On the basis of Frommel's calculations, starting from the size of Cardinal Cibo's hall (which measured ca. 13 by 27 meters, and slightly more than 8 meters high) the stage on which *I suppositi* was performed must have been fairly small. Consequently, the impression of spaciousness and monumentality in the drawing here would have necessitated creating sets with a careful estimation of the distortion of the perspective caused by an unusually low vanishing point.

A.P.T.

166
SEBASTIANO SERLIO
Perspective Scenery with Venetian Buildings

Florence, Galleria degli Uffizi, Gabinetto Disegni e Stampe, Uff. 5282A
Black pencil, pen, brown wash; white paper yellowed with age.
652 × 811 mm (maximum dimensions of paper, composed of three parts)

BIBLIOGRAPHY: Ferri 1885: XLIII, 119; Ferrari 1902: 84-85; Povoledo 1961b: 1861; Molinari 1964: 67; Rosci 1966: 24; Neiiendam 1969: 158; Zorzi 1977: 310, 323 n. 24; in *Firenze e la Toscana...* 1980: 339, no. 3.9; Petrioli Tofani 1981: 25-26, no. 2.

Serlio played an undoubtedly important role in the history of sixteenth-century scenography, not so much for the personal, practical contributions which he may have made to the evolution of this artistic genre—contributions in which he proved to be a faithful follower of Baldassarre Peruzzi, whom he had met in Rome in about 1535-37 and whose drawings, according to Vasari, he inherited—as for the fact that he was the author of a fundamental theoretical manual on the subject.

These writings were drafted at a crucial time when the Peruzzi-type of fixed scenery was giving way to the invention of new movable sets.

His monumental treatise on architecture, which clearly imitated that of Vitruvius, is divided into eight books, each published separately on different occasions and not in numerical order.

Book II—first published in Paris in 1545, and then in Venice by Nicolini da Sabio in 1551 and by the Sessa brothers in 1569—is on perspective; toward the end of the volume is a *Trattato sopra le Scene* whose didactic woodcut illustrations of the three dramatic genres of classical antiquity (Tragedy, Comedy, and Satyric) offer an authentic manual of scene construction.

It is the first one that allows us to construe something more than an approximate idea about the structure and the figurative aspects developing in theatrical representation in the first half of the sixteenth-century.

Apart from the woodcut prints mentioned above, which should be considered as purely typological examples and certainly not as projects for real plays, the only illustration of Serlio's theatrical production which survives is this drawing in the Uffizi.

His name has been traditionally linked to this picture for a long time, as corroborated by the seventeenth-century(?) annotation, "Di Sebastiano Serlio," inscribed on the verso of the paper.

The attribution is further endorsed by other factors: first, the Venetian setting (the imaginary backdrop composition shows the campanile of St. Mark's on the left, the clock tower, and the domes of the basilica), a logical choice of subject for an artist who lived for years in the city on the lagoon; second, the use of certain lighting techniques such as the continuous lines of round or rectangular openings in the wings at the height of the cornices of the buildings. These openings are not based on other contemporary sketches, but Serlio describes them in great detail in his *Trattato* (ed. 1560, fol. 27v.) and how they should throw a shimmering light onto the stage from torches shining through glass bowls full of colored liquids. As often occurs in the scenography designed by Peruzzi, this study comprises a mixture of set devices typical of Tragedy (palaces and monumental buildings) and Comedy (workshops, loggias, etc.). Nevertheless, while there is no information whatsoever connecting this scene with a specific performance, we can presume, like Rosci, that it was a project for the "Theater and ... wood scenery" which Serlio built in 1539 in the courtyard of the Porto-Colleoni family house at Vicenza which he himself described in his Book: "Because in Vicenza ... I made ... a wooden stage set, a screen, which was surely the largest ever made in our time, in which ... I wanted a single platform in front of the sloping stage. ... Since this platform was flat, its floor did not conform with the horizon, and therefore its squares were perfect, and, starting from the sloping floor, all those squares going toward the horizon diminished according to their distance. And because the horizon was placed on the rear panel of the scenery, coinciding with the actual base of this wall, toward which all the buildings could be seen to lead, I devised to carry the horizon beyond this line; the device was so successful that I continued to use it ... making buildings of wooden frames on which I fixed canvas, painting them with doors in elevation or in perspective as the case required; and I also added certain features in wooden bas-reliefs, which greatly enhanced the painted details."

This passage is quoted here in full because it is a very valuable source of information on the design and production of stage scenery during the time. One question discussed that is not duly treated in the drawing shown here is the division between the floor of the proscenium, which is described as flat ("suolo piano"), and the sloping area of

the stage, which would logically begin at the start of the first buildings.

The vanishing point of the perspective is quite evidently far beyond the plane of the backdrop, which bears the facade of the clock tower at its center.

The unusually large dimensions of the paper exclude intrinsically the hypothesis sometimes put forward that this drawing is a study for a book illustration, such as those Serlio used in his treatise, *L'Architettura*.   *A.P.T.*

167
<small>GIORGIO VASARI (?)</small>
Perspective Scenery with Roman Buildings

Florence, Galleria degli Uffizi, Gabinetto Disegni e Stampe, Uff. 291A
Pen and brown wash; stylus impressions; white paper, mounted. 588 × 715 mm (maximum dimensions of paper composed of various glued fragments)

BIBLIOGRAPHY: Milanesi 1879: 640; Ferri 1885, XXXVII: 119, 163; Krautheimer 1948, 338-339; Magagnato 1954: 37; Povoledo 1961a: 36; Beijer 1962: 85; Murray 1962: 39-40; Bjurstrm 1964: 76; Rosci 1966: 24; Frommel 1967-68: 76 n. 336; Neiiendam 1969: 157-164; Povoledo 1969: 425-426; Stein 1969: 22; Nicoll 1971: 88; Collobi Ragghianti 1973b: 45; Cruciani 1974: 158-159; Collobi Ragghianti 1974: 111; Molinari 1975: 133; Zorzi 1977: 50, 53, 310, 323 n. 23; in *Firenze e la Toscana...* 1980: 338, no. 3.5; Petrioli Tofani 1981: 26, no. 3; Ruffini 1983: 13; 1986: 343; Bruschi 1987a: 326 n. 17; Pochat 1990: 285-288.

This important and very famous project for a perspective stage set—which, although apparently in a reasonable state of conservation, seems to have been drastically flattened when laid onto its mount (probably during the last century)—has been attributed to Baldassarre Peruzzi since the time of Milanesi. While this attribution was rightly challenged by Frommel (1967-68) for the evident discrepancies between the graphic style and other known drawings by Peruzzi, it is endorsed by the compositional inventiveness which unequivocally evinces Peruzzi's handling of scenographic elaboration as regards the scene's technical details and the choice of figurative representation. The layout is typical of Peruzzi and comprises twin sets of wings (a total of four practicable buildings) arranged on the floor of the sloping stage, with a final backdrop separated from the wings to allow an ulterior passage for the actors, and painted so as to extend and conclude the spatial effect.

As far as the stylistic result is concerned, it is clear that a composition of this kind has brought that intriguing ambiguity between realism and convention—between actual experience and the intellectual revival of an archaeological decoration of a markedly humanistic flavor—to a new level of maturity that characterized Italian scenography in the first half of the Cinquecento.

In confirmation we can observe that, on the one hand, there is the restitution of a real and rigorously three-dimensional space marked by the physical presence of architectural structures that seem really habitable, and, on the other, there is the abstract reconstruction of a city—in this case Rome—which can be recognized by its monu-

ments despite the fact that its real topography and proportions have been completely ignored. The monuments which have been identified are as follows: on the right, the dome of the Pantheon, Castel Sant'Angelo, Trajan's Column, the obelisk in the Piazza del Popolo with the sphere containing the ashes of Julius Caesar and, to conclude the road at the back, the church of S. Maria della Pace (before the facade was rebuilt by Pietro da Cortona) and the three columns of the Temple of Castor and Pollux. On the left you can see the upper part of the Colosseum, the Torre delle Milizie and the tower of the Senate. The triumphal arch in the center, a kind of Arch of Titus, remains outside the realm of reality.

If we take for granted that the drawing is a project by Baldassarre Peruzzi, or at least a workshop copy of an original by Peruzzi (a possibility I have put forward on several occasions), then the drawing may represent the set designs for the play *La Calandria*, written by Cardinal Bibbiena for a performance held in the Vatican on the occasion of the visit of Isabella d'Este Gonzaga. The evidence produced in support of this identification is appealing but hardly decisive, even though the action of the play was set in Rome, and Vasari wrote that Peruzzi was the designer of the scenography ("E quando si recitò al detto papa Leone [X] la Calandra, comedia del cardinale di Bibbiena, fece Baldassarre l'apparato e la prospettiva," Vasari 1878-85, IV: 600). Doubt is also increased by the style of the graphics used in the drawing, which, as Frommel has emphasized, shows the hand of an artist who worked without doubt at a later date. Moreover, in a detail such as the couple of figures painted together with the building in the right foreground of the scenery, this draftsman betrays his distinctly Florentine training in the quick, elegantly light strokes of the pen and the underlying decisiveness in the definition of form and movement.

On the basis of these premises, there is nothing to prevent us from trying to give a different interpretation of the drawing to propose a new, albeit prudently hypothetical, attribution. The Florentine Giorgio Vasari was an unreserved admirer of Peruzzi's scenography. He is also known to have designed and staged many entertainments which until now have been assessable in almost every case by means of written descriptions alone, since most of the designs relative to this line of activity, including the preparatory sketches for the sets described in writing, have been lost.

Among the various productions which Vasari was responsible for, the one whose verses are best suited to this drawing in the Uffizi is the performance of *La Talanta* by Pietro Aretino, staged at Venice during the Carnival of 1542. It seems that he was commissioned by the local theater company, the Compagnia dei Sempiterni, to design the stage sets for the hall where the performance was to take place, but also to direct the entire production. This link is supported to some extent by Vasari's own description of the scenery in a letter to Ottaviano de' Medici. "I must say that the hall where the stage was built was enormous, and likewise the scenery, that is to say, the perspectival sets showing Rome, where there was the Arch of Septimius, the Temple of Peace, the Rotonda, the Colosseum, the church of the Pace, S. Maria Nuova, the Temple of Fortune, Trajan's Column, the Palazzo Maggiore, the Seven Halls, the Torre de' Conti, that of the Milizie, and lastly Maestro Pasquino, more handsome than ever. There were beautiful palaces, houses, churches, and an infinite number of Doric, Ionic, Corinthian, Tuscan, Rustic and Composite architectural features." Further evidence, moreover, can be drawn from a comparison with the drawings for the structure of the hall, conserved in the Louvre, at Düsseldorf and in Berlin (see Monbeig Goguel 1972: 166-167) where significant similarities can be identified in the construction techniques, although the materials and purposes are different, owing to the fact that the design we are discussing is substantially an architectural drawing. The name of Vasari the collector was connected to this drawing hypothetically and without offering any evidence by Collobi Ragghianti, who instead preferred the traditional attribution to Peruzzi.   *A.P.T.*

168
GIOVANNI BATTISTA DA SANGALLO (called IL GOBBO)
Tragic Scene, Comic Scene and Satyric Scene
(sketches in the margin of *De architectura*, by
Vitruvius)

Rome, Biblioteca Corsiniana, Inc. 50, F.I. (p. 11)
Pen, white paper.
295 × 225 mm (maximum dimensions of page)

BIBLIOGRAPHY: Vasari 1568, ed. Milanesi 1878-85, V: 471; Bottari
1764: 95-96 and n. 3; Milanesi 1880: 472 n. 1; Clausse 1902, III:
286-288; Fontana 1933: 311-313; De Angelis d'Ossat 1951: 95;
Degenhart 1956: 282 n. 403; Hamberg 1958: 15-21; Savini Nicci
1962: 1736; Bjurström 1964: 78-79; Klein and Zerner 1964: 53;
Rosci 1966: 25; Povoledo 1969: 427-428; Fagiolo 1973: 87, fig. 15;
Frommel 1974b: 181; Zorzi 1977: 93, 193 n. 97; Marcucci 1978:
193-194; Pagliara 1982: 25-51; Cruciani 1983: 622; Pagliara 1983:
27-28; Ruffini 1986: 330; Pochat 1990: 313.

This is a copy of the *editio princeps* of Vitruvius' *De ar-*
chitectura (published in Rome in about 1486 by Sulpicio
da Veroli), the famous treatise of the Augustan age, whose
third and fourth chapters of Book V closely examine the
subject of theater and scenography. The treatise had already had a fairly wide circulation during the Middle Ages
in manuscript form, and became a classic source for many
of the greater Italian architects of the Renaissance after
it was put into print.
The copy shown here is exceptionally important because
it belonged to a member of the Sangallo family, Giovanni
Battista Cordini (nephew of Giuliano and Antonio the
Elder), who jotted notes and drew sketches in many of the
margins, as in this case, or all over the slip-sheets. It is of
particular interest to historians of theater design in classical antiquity, since the three sketches drawn on page 11,
shown here, mark the first attempt at providing a figurative reconstruction of Vitruvius' descriptions of set design; not even Fra Diamante had taken this into consideration in his edition of the treatise, the first illustrated edition, printed in Venice in 1511. The passage in question
(translated from Daniele Barbaro's Italian version of
1567: 256) runs as follows: "There are three kinds of
scene, one is called the Tragic Scene, the other, the
Comic, the third one, the Satyric. The installations for
these are all different, and made with diverse structures;
thus the Tragic Scene is composed of columns, frontispieces, figures and other regal ornaments; the Comic
Scene comprises private buildings, pergolas or corridors,
and perspectival sets with windows designed to imitate
real buildings; while the Satyric Scene is decorated with
trees and grottoes, mountains and other rustic features, or
open settings in the form of gardens."
There are no clues for determining the chronology of
these three little drawings. Very little is known about the
biographical affairs of their author Cordini, whom Giorgio Vasari defines as "ingenious" (though probably more
as a theoretician than a pragmatist); he seems to have
spent the greater part of his life working as an assistant to
his more famous brother, Antonio da Sangallo the Younger who, Vasari states, "did not do right by his brother."

The only independent work of any importance identified
as Cordini's is the project for an illustrated edition of
Vitruvius' *De architectura* in the vernacular. Never terminated, all that remains of the project (besides the present
volume) are two incomplete manuscript translations of
the Latin original.
When Giovanni Battista died these documents were inherited by the Compagnia della Misericordia de' Fiorentini in Rome (whose ownership is declared in an early script
on the first page of this volume).
There is no historical evidence of theater sets designed by
Cordini, but he was presumably fairly well acquainted
with stage design through his close relations: he was the
first cousin of Bastiano (called Aristotile) da Sangallo
(1481-1551), who was certainly the most important
scenographer working in Florence in the first half of the
Cinquecento, and the designer of celebrated productions
such as *La Mandragola* (1518) and *Clizia* (1526) by
Machiavelli, *Aridosia* by Lorenzino de' Medici (1536),
and *Il Commodo* by Antonio Landi (1537). The sketches
for the Tragic and the Comic Scenes in particular betray
such influences, given what we can deduce from the surviving descriptions of Aristotile's inventions (which unfortunately are not corroborated by any illustrations).
Whatever the case, rather than attempt a historical reconstruction of ancient theatrical production, these little
sketches offer a valuable document for present-day
historians, as they capture a precise phase in the evolution
of the centralized perspectival set in the Renaissance.
This path of development, which had already been clearly
codified in the early Cinquecento through Raphael, Genga, and Peruzzi's experiments in Rome and Urbino (cat.
nos. 164-165), continued with few deviations throughout
the sixteenth century, evolving into substantially
homogeneous structures that became more and more complex, with the introduction of an increasing number of
special effects both in plan and in elevation.
Such an interpretation of the drawing, which is borne out
by the evident analogies between the three sketches and
the many set designs on exhibit here, is endorsed by
another factor: the composition of the sketch for the
Comic Scene concluded at the center by a building placed
farther forward than the side panels of the perspectival
view; this recurs almost identically in Bartolomeo Nero-
ni's set for *Ortensio* by Alessandro Piccolomini, designed
for the performance given in Siena in 1560 by the Accademia degli Intronati and documented in a woodcut by Andrea Andreani (Bartsch 1811, XII: 156-157, no. 29). Be
that as it may, the sketch for the Satyric Scene, which has
not been limited like the other two by the emphatic geometry of a perspective framework, offers a spatial arrangement whose allusive indeterminacy seems to foreshadow
certain pre-Baroque digressions to be found in Buontalenti's set designs at the end of the century.   *A.P.T.*

169
ANONYMOUS
Perspectival Stage Set with Townscape and Statue
of Marcus Aurelius
first half of 16th century

Florence, Galleria degli Uffizi, Gabinetto Disegni e Stampe,
Uff. 9788 st. sc.
Burin engraving.
280 × 417 mm (maximum dimensions of trimmed sheet)

BIBLIOGRAPHY: Hind 1948: 105; Alberici in *Leonardo e l'incisione*
1984: 45; Chirico De Biasi in *Leonardo e l'incisione* 1984: 48, no. 34.

It is possible that, like catalog no. 163, this print of a stage
design, as evinced by the perspectival arrangement of the
space and the set of wings, was executed for theoretical
and illustrative purposes more than for an actual production in the theater. Neither the author nor the intended
purpose of the print are known; the geographical origins
and date are similarly rather obscure. Perhaps the difficulties posed by this lack of data explain why, up to now, it
has been regularly ignored by historians of theater design.
In spite of several allusions to the city of Rome (the most
explicit one being the artist himself, seated on the steps
of the central temple, copying the equestrian statue of
Marcus Aurelius) the print has been considered to betray
the influence of the Lombard cultural milieu and the influence of Bramante; Hind, who excluded it from the entries in his catalog as belonging to a later period, cited it
many times in his chapter on Donato Bramante; Bernardo
Prevedari, and later Alberici, accepted Hind's conclusions, proposing a possible date of about 1550. Chirico De
Biasi, however, placed it at the start of the sixteenth century, though he supplied no solid arguments.
Even though this print gives the impression of being
complete—and therefore a potential source of much
technical, cultural, and stylistic information—current
knowledge of Renaissance scenography does not admit
precise conclusions about its historical collocation. In the
context of developments in the concept of stage space
toward the mid-sixteenth century, at present we can only
pinpoint certain features, though these are neither exhaustive nor sufficiently consistent to guarantee identification: the perspectival arrangement, with its raised
vanishing point enlivened by the optical illusion of the
pavement drawn with squares of diminishing size, recalls
Serlio's experiments in catalog no. 166; the layout, furthermore, comprising a central panel (in this case, the hexagonal temple), placed considerably in front of the vanishing point, crops up in a variety of other contexts and periods, such as in the sketch by Giovanni Battista da Sangallo depicting the Vitruvian Comic Scene described in the
preceding entry.   *A.P.T.*

170
BALDASSARRE LANCI
Perspective Scenery with Florentine Buildings

Florence, Galleria degli Uffizi, Gabinetto Disegni e Stampe,
Uff. 404P
Black pencil; pen with gray, pink and light blue wash; traces of
red pencil and white lead; white paper.
593 × 695 mm

BIBLIOGRAPHY: Ferri 1885: 66; Povoledo 1959b: 1194; Molinari
1964: 67; Nagler 1964: 41; Berti 1967: 48-49; Neiendam 1969: 75;
Petrioli Tofani in *Firenze e la Toscana...* 1969: 27-29, no. 9; Stein
1969: 48-49; Collobi Ragghianti 1973: 75; 1974: 137; Petrioli
Tofani, in *Firenze e la Toscana...* 1975: 100-101, no. 7.16; Zorzi
1977: 103-104, 210 n. 126; Contorni 1980: 138 n. 39; Garbero, in
Firenze e la Toscana... 1980: 326, no. 2.15; Pochat 1990: 319-320.

In the spring of 1569 Archduke Charles of Austria, the brother of Joan and brother-in-law to Prince Francesco de' Medici (the future Grand Duke Francesco I) made a royal visit to Florence. According to the custom in many European courts the program of entertainment included several theatrical spectacles, and on this particular occasion, considerable importance was given to the performance of *La Vedova*, a play by Giovan Battista Cini. It was staged on 1 May in the hall of the Palazzo Vecchio. The set designs by Baldassarre Lanci are the subject of the sketch shown here.

Lanci was born in Urbino and studied under Girolamo Genga (1476-1551), a master in the field of architecture and theatrical productions. Genga was a highly acclaimed scenographer in his time, but unfortunately no illustrations of his work have survived for posterity.

He was famous for the sets for *La Calandria* by Cardinal Bibbiena (Urbino, 6 February 1513), in which "there was a beautiful imaginary city with streets, palaces, churches, towers, real streets, and everything in relief, but greatly enhanced by excellent painting and a well-designed perspective," as Baldassarre Castiglione described it in his letter to Bishop Ludovico Canossa (in A. d'Ancona, 1891, II: 102-104). Sets of the type designed by Peruzzi continued to be widely popular, without undergoing any substantial changes, into the second half of the century, and were clearly the inspiration behind the specimen in question.

Lanci moved to Florence in 1560 and played a leading role in the Grand Duke's court. In the theatrical field he was responsible for an allegorical masquerade on the genealogy of the pagan gods (*La Genealogia degli Dei*, 1565) and for the production of *Il Granchio* by Lionardo Salviati (1566), of *I Fabii* by Lotto del Mazza (1567) and the aforementioned play, *La Vedova*.

That the above print refers to the sets for *La Vedova* can be inferred from its exact correspondence to a detailed contemporary description (attributed to Filippo Giunti), in which he states that "the setting was the city of Florence, and represented a particular part of the city, namely, the area called the Antellesi, with the facade of the Palazzo Ducale, which can be seen with the three giants at its base" (the drawing in fact includes Michelangelo's *David*, and the *Hercules and Cacus* group by Bandinelli). "It was built with such clever devices that it opened above to show the halls of Heaven, and it seemed to subside below to send painted figures through the gateway to Hell.

The front was so well painted and ingeniously designed that at Act Three it was turned round in a trice, and the city became the nearby villa of Arcetri."

The device that achieved this quick change of scenes had already been used by Lanci for the performance of *I Fabii*. It was based on a system borrowed from antiquity whose sixteenth-century application was described in detail by Ignazio Danti in his edition of Vignola's treatise on perspective, *Le Due Regole della Prospettiva Pratica* (Roma 1583: 91-92). It was the *periaktoi* system, or series of triangular prisms (in our case five) each one rotating on its own axis and positioned on the stage in such a way as to create the wings and the backdrop. Each prism had a part of the scene painted on its three sides, so that the setting could be changed very simply by rotation. According to Danti the mechanism was invented—or, more correctly, "revived"—by Aristotile da Sangallo, who apparently tried it out in about 1543 in Duke Pierluigi Farnese's theater at Castro.

The same author also recalls being present at the Florentine performance of *La Vedova* where, unlike Giunti, he remembers not one but two changes of scene. However, in his description, written perhaps more than ten years later, he lapses into various inaccuracies. From the first scene of the S. Trinita bridge—and Danti must have got confused with another Florentine play such as Vasari's set for *La Cofanaria* in 1565, or his own design for *Il Granchio* in 1566 (see Petrioli Tofani 1975: 86 and 97, nos. 6.5.8 and 7.8) which in fact included a scene with this bridge—the setting changed to the country scene at Arcetri, the

one described by Giunti. At the end of the play there was another perspective townscape set in the quarter called "canto à gl'Alberti." It was certainly a different scene from the one illustrated in this drawing, as there is nothing in it to indicate the surroundings of Piazza Peruzzi, where this family owned several houses. Even if it were possible that the scenes of *La Vedova* were in fact three, none of the illustrations of the scenes mentioned by Danti have survived; this may be indirect proof of the greater reliability of Giunti's account.

In Collobi Ragghianti's opinion, the inscription "BALDASSARRE LANCI DA URBINO INGEGNERE" at the center bottom of the paper was added by Giorgio Vasari, and provides evidence of the drawing's having once belonged to Vasari's original collection.   *A.P.T.*

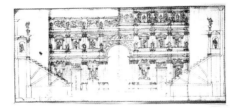

171
ANDREA PALLADIO (with his son, Marc'Antonio)
Project Showing Two Variations for the Sets Designs of the Teatro Olimpico at Vicenza

London, The British Architectural Library Drawings Collection, Royal Institute of British Architects, Palladio XIII/5
Black pencil, pen and red ink, gray-brown wash; white paper.
417 × 899 mm (maximum dimensions; composed of three parts)
INSCRIBED: notes and measurements by Palladio's son, Marc'Antonio.

BIBLIOGRAPHY: Grant Keith 1917: 105-111; Dalla Pozza 1942: 217-222; 1943: 197-201; Magagnato 1951: 209-220; 1954: 59; Pane 1961: 364; Puppi 1962: 57-58, 60-62; 1963: 44; Zorzi 1965a: 134; 1965 (2): 70-97; Ackerman 1966: 180; Barbieri 1967: 48, no. 70; Zorzi 1969: 286; Puppi 1971c: 87; Gioseffi 1972: 60; Magagnato 1972: 144; Burns 1973a: 145-146; Cevese, in *Mostra del Palladio* 1973: 129 note; Puppi 1973a: 437; Barbieri 1974a: 310; Burns 1975: 46; Puppi, in *Andrea Palladio*, 1980: 180-181; Oosting 1981: 11-12, 44, 121-139; Petrioli Tofani 1981: 30, no. 11; Lewis 1981a: 210-211, no. 124; Mancini et al. 1985: 207-208, 230-231; Mazzoni 1985: 41; Puppi 1987a: 189; Pochat 1990: 274, n. 91; Mazzoni, in Magagnato 1992: 203, no. 2.4.

The Teatro Olimpico was designed by Andrea Palladio toward the end of his life, probably from December 1579 when, in his late seventies, he left Venice for a last visit to his home town. When he died on 19 August the following year he left a vast amount of completed material including drawings and a model, on the basis of which his son Silla was able to complete the construction of the theater that had begun on 28 February. Unfortunately all of this material has been lost except for this highly important paper which shows two possibilities, with only slight differences between them, for the *frons scaenae*. The one on the right is very similar to the design actually built.

As Howard Burns has observed, while certainly representing Palladio's own idea and design for the structure, the drawing was actually drafted by another of his sons, Marc'Antonio, who offered his elderly father assistance of a purely technical nature at this time. The drawing shows the section of the semicircular tiers of seats in the *cavea* at the sides, and in the center, a part of the proscenium that ends with a strictly architectural *frons scaenae* reproducing a central archway and two side doors corresponding to the *porta regia* and the *hospitalia* of the theaters of classical antiquity.

The whole structure fits in evidently with the version Palladio himself had established about ten years earlier of the physical appearance of the antique scenery described by Vitruvius when he illustrated *I Dieci Libri Dell'Architet-*

tura, translated into Italian by Daniele Barbaro and published in Venice in 1567. Leaving aside the relevant openings which in the drawing shown here seem to be empty, we can observe in the woodcut print on pages 255-256 of the said edition that these should have been equipped with perspective scenery, probably painted in accordance with classical tradition. We cannot therefore exclude the possibility that Palladio wanted to create a similar solution for the Teatro Olimpico. Perhaps he intended to introduce a system of *periaktoi* which, according to Vitruvius' description, were placed in correspondence with these passages.

It is obvious that such stage devices derived from a very different concept of entertainment and acting than the kind that underlies the experiments in perspective scenery during the Cinquecento: the same experiments, moreover, which had been welcomed in Vicenza forty years earlier with the work of Sebastiano Serlio (see cat. no. 166). The space destined for the actors on the stage of the Teatro Olimpico was in fact only the proscenium—reasonably large, but with no possibility of any real development toward the back. Furthermore, whatever the nature of the play being performed, the solemn abstraction of the imaginary monumental architecture in the classical style provided a permanent and unchanging counterpoint, and therefore was quite distinct from its usual function as a context for the theatrical action. Curiously, at the time when Palladio was developing the project displayed here, the Accademia Olimpica was deciding what production to open the theater with, and their choice fell on a pastoral play. It was only after the death of the architect that the Accademia changed its mind, preferring a tragic theme, Sophocles' *Oedipus Rex*, which was certainly more suited to the ambience of the new theater. Having said this, it is clear that when Palladio designed the Teatro Olimpico he was not concerned about addressing the customary problems of dramatic production. He instead wanted to develop a structure that suited the interests of the contemporary spectator, especially those who were abreast with the bold revival of classical form and culture—basically the members of the Accademia who had commissioned the theater's construction. By way of gratification and self-satisfaction, on 23 May 1580 the Accademia's council granted each member the right to have his "his own plaster statue" placed at his own expense "atop the pedestals of the columns, and in the niches of the stage apparatus" (Zorzi 1965b: 74).

It is not surprising therefore that the Palladio's stage devices for the Teatro Olimpico, with their utter indifference to the problems of credibility and to the requirements of functionality with respect to the plays being performed, were not open to further development. His design offered a highly sophisticated, self-contained intellectual experiment that could lead nowhere. There had, perhaps, been a precedent in the Veneto region which, while having a very different architectural structure, corresponded fairly closely in terms of its implicit intellectual inclinations. Lodovico Zorzi discovered this precedent in the beautiful loggia which Alvise Cornaro had commissioned Giovan Maria Falconetto to build in 1524 for theatrical purposes in the garden of his palace in Padua. As Cornaro himself wrote: "he built it after the antique manner: the scenery was permanent, built in stone, and the other side for the audience was made of planks that could be dismantled; and all these plays were a great success because he had in his court men of great acting skill, such as the renowned Ruzzante" (see Zorzi 1977: 317-318).   *A.P.T.*

A

172
VINCENZO SCAMOZZI
Study of a Perspective View of Buildings

Florence, Galleria degli Uffizi, Gabinetto Disegni e Stampe,
Uff. 195A
Pen, stylus impressions; white paper.
210 × 309 mm (maximum dimensions)
RECTO: pen, with red and black pencil annotations; calculations
and numbering.
VERSO: plan of the "strada à sinistra dell'arco grande,"
calculations and measurements in ink.

B

Study of a Perspective View of Buildings

Florence, Uffizi, Gabinetto Disegni e Stampe, Uff. 196A
Pen, stylus impressions; white paper.
304 × 410 mm (maximum dimensions)
Inscriptions in pen, calculations and numbering.

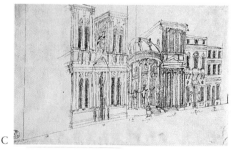

C

Study of a Perspective View of Buildings

Florence, Uffizi, Gabinetto Disegni e Stampe, Uff. 197A
Pen, white paper.
210 × 307 mm
RECTO: pen annotations and numbering.

D

Study of a Perspective View of Buildings

Florence, Uffizi, Gabinetto Disegni e Stampe, Uff. 198A

Pen, stylus impressions; white paper.
210 × 309 mm (maximum dimensions)
RECTO: pen and black pencil annotations, calculations and
numbering.
VERSO: calculations in pen.

BIBLIOGRAPHY: Ferri 1885: XLIII, 226; Ferrari 1902: 106; Buzzi
1928: 512-513; Mariani 1930: 41; Ricci 1930: 13; Loukomski
1940: 67; Magagnato 1951: 217 note; Barbieri 1952: 131; Muraro
1953: 26; Magagnato 1954: 60; Puppi 1962: 62; 1963: 51-55; Rava
1965: 20; Zorzi 1965b: 70-97; Puppi 1966: 26-32; Tafuri 1968: 77
note; Stein 1969: 54-56; Zorzi 1969: 294-303; Nicoll 1971: 91;
Puppi 1971c: 90; Cevese, in *Mostra del Palladio* 1973: 119; Gallo
1973: XXXII-XXXIII, 27; Puppi 1973a: 439; Puppi, in *Mostra del
Palladio* 1980, 182-183; 194-195; no. 213; Oosting 1981: 141, 206
note; Petrioli Tofani 1981: 30; Lewis 1981a: 211; Mancini et al.
1985: 231; Puppi 1987a: 194; Pochat 1990: 276, and n. 95; Mazzoni, in Magagnato 1992: 204-206, nos. 2.5-2.8.

When Andrea Palladio died in August 1580, the construction of the Teatro Olimpico at Vicenza had only just begun a few months earlier (see discussion about London,
R.I.B.A., Palladio XIII/5). Work proceeded uninterrupted over the next few years under the guidance of Palladio's son Silla, who was able to utilize the drawings left
to the executors. The building was completely finished by
1584, the date which appears in the dedication to the
members of the Accademia Olimpica included in an inscription on a cartouche in the center of the scene. Fundamental and detailed chronicles of the state of progress
of the building are to be found in the *Memorie della Accademia Olimpica*, a manuscript written by Bartolomeo
Zigiotti conserved in the Biblioteca Bertoliana at Vicenza
(Zorzi 1965 [2]).
It appears that while the walls of the theater were being
built, the Accademia Olimpica was absorbed in a debate
about what dramatic performance to produce for the inauguration of the theater. The first choice, made while Palladio was still alive, had fallen on a never clearly defined
pastoral theme, but in the end, on 19 February 1583 it was
decided to perform a tragedy: Sophocles' *Oedipus Rex*,
which was presented two years later, on 28 February
1585, with music by Andrea Gabrieli and directed by
Angelo Ingegneri.
Palladio's intention to place perspective views beyond the
openings of the *frons scaenae*, even though the latter appear to be missing in the first drawing shown here (cat. no.
171) is evident in the aforementioned *Memorie*, which include a document dated 15 February 1580 establishing
that the theater should be built "according to the model
already made by our Academician Palladio and the similar
drawing of the perspectives." It is possible, however, to
understand how the following succession of events, and
especially the change of opinion regarding the play to be
performed at the inauguration, might have delayed the
completion of the theater, if only to permit the adoption
of certain still feasible theatrical devices, carefully
designed to highlight the contents of the Sophoclean
tragedy.
The new requirements were in fact laid down by the play's
director in a manuscript containing "instructions concerning the Vicentine tragedy entitled The Oedipus of
Sophocles" written at the end of 1583. "Now to come to
our particular matter we will speak first of the apparatus
and especially of the scene which without doubt should
look as much like the place where the story of Oedipus
took place"—that is to say the city of Thebes, which
should if possible be represented by "seven doors to their
places... But since the scene is already made and nothing
is missing apart from the perspectives, which cannot contain much, it will be sufficient when making them that we
have an eye to insert in them the extra part of the said
description which more conveniently and more realistically can best be inserted" (Milan, Biblioteca Ambrosiana, MS. R. 123 Sup., fol. 283ff.).
Ingegneri's directions were to be promptly absorbed by
Vincenzo Scamozzi, the architect who was identified in
many contemporary documents as the author of the perspectives in the theater (Zorzi 1965b: 89-90). Without al-

tering the existing Palladian perspective in any way whatsoever, he succeeded in designing a structure in which the
seven roads corresponding to the seven gates of Thebes
came together. Two came from the side entrances of the
proscenium, another two were visible behind the *hospitalia*, and the remaining three converged from the backdrop
toward the *porta regia*.
The four drawings exhibited here are evidence of Scamozzi's preliminary studies (Ferri 1885) and a fifth clearly
related one is conserved at Chatsworth (Lewis 1981a:
125). They include easily identifiable sketches for single
details of the same project. The drawings are traditionally
attributed to the architect from Vicenza and this hypothesis is still valid today, especially when they are examined
together with his other well-known designs (for example
Uff. 191A, a drawing of the project for the Teatro Olimpico at Sabbioneta dated 1588) which provide convincing
similarities of style as regards both the drawings and the
annotations.
The Vicentine perspectives are quite unique in the history
of Italian theater design. It was, in fact, the first time that
real three-dimensional buildings made of wood and
plaster had been erected, with the right degree of deformation corresponding to the vanishing point thus enabling the creation of the optical illusion necessary to extend the field of action instead of using wings and backdrops with occasional parts in relief. The result was a complex and permanent structure, still in the theater, which
all future productions were obliged to adopt as a setting.
The structure is certainly fascinating for its ingenious
complexity, but its weakness as far as the functional side
was concerned must have been evident from the start.
In spite of this, hearty approval greeted its presentation
to the public, especially those who had had the possibility,
like Giacomo Dolfin, a Venetian gentleman present at the
inauguration performance, of appreciating the Scamozzi
perspectives combined with special lighting effects. In a
letter written on 9 March 1585 (quoted by Zorzi 1965b:
95-96) he enthused: "Of the theater and the scene and the
perspectives built with great ingeniousness ... I will not
reason here. It suffices me to tell you ... how superbly successful the illuminated scene was when the curtain came
down ... The beautiful arrangement of the scene that was
made ... to a drawing by Palladio according to the rules
and forms of the architecture of antiquity; a thing that in
every epoch can delight the eye considerably for its being
a solid and real and not a false thing. However, with the
support of the lighting it seemed out of the ordinary and
more miraculous than excellent. How brilliant were the
interior perspectives made by Tamoscio [Scamozzi] I
need not tell you, because you know very well that
without lighting they are nothing, but once illuminated
they seem everything. I will only say that those who had
seen it before thought they were seeing another thing, and
those who had never seen it thought they were seeing
something that went beyond imagination and the human
mind."
The drawings shown in order here refer to the road beyond the right *hospitalium* (cat. no. 172a), the corresponding one beyond the left *hospitalium* (cat. no. 172b), one on
the left side (cat. no. 172c and Chatsworth, the Devon-
shire Collection) and another on the right (cat. no. 172d)
of the central street beyond the *porta regia*. The verso of
catalog. no. 172b contains a sketchy drawing of the plan
of the "road to the left of the great arch." Since these are
work sheets in which the set designer is still calculating
the distances and proportions, and assessing the types
of buildings, which he carefully registers in the annotations, it is not surprising that a certain number of changes
were introduced during the transition to practical construction, but they were not so important as to create any
doubts about the validity of the connection between these
drawings and the perspectives in the Teatro Olimpico.
A.P.T.

173
ORAZIO SCARABELLI (after Bernardo Buontalenti)
Perspective Scenery with Townscape
second half of 16th cent.

Florence, Galleria degli Uffizi, Gabinetto Disegni e Stampe,
Uff. 13292 st. sc.
Etching.
240 × 347 (plate), 264 × 380 (paper)

BIBLIOGRAPHY: Scholz 1955: 6 no. 9; Ternois 1962: 233; Petrioli
Tofani, in Gaeta Bertelá-Petrioli Tofani 1969: 77-78, no. 36; Stein
1969: 60-61; Petrioli Tofani, in *Firenze e la Toscana...* 1975: 111,
no. 8.9; Zorzi, in *Firenze e Toscana...* 1980: 340, no. 3.19; Fara
1988: 236; Choné, in *Jacques Callot* 1992: 202.

This etching by Orazio Scarabelli is one of a set, of rather
average execution but of extraordinary documentary importance.
They were probably printed as a visual record of what
were then considered the most important aspects of the
celebrations staged for the marriage of the Grand Duke
Ferdinando I de' Medici to Christine of Lorraine.
Among the various entertainments organized for the occasion, about which there is considerable written
documentation (see *Il luogo teatrale* 1975: 110ff.), the
most interesting event from the point of view of the theater was undoubtedly the production of Girolamo Bar-
gagli's play *La Pellegrina*. It was performed by the young
actors of the Siena-based Accademia degli Intronati on
the evening of 2 May in the Teatro Mediceo inside the
Uffizi palace.
The most important scenographer of the time—Bernardo
Buontalenti—was called in to construct the stage sets,
and on this particular occasion he achieved unprecedented technical and stylistic heights in his designs for the
transformable scenery.
According to the detailed description by Bastiano de'
Rossi, who attended the performance, the audience was
treated to no fewer than seven changes of scenery during
the performance, which unfolded in a continuous and
dazzling metamorphosis punctuated by the *intermezzi* (devised by Giovanni Bardi di Vernio and Ottavio Rinuccini)
and the acts of the play.
De' Rossi narrates that at the end of the first *intermezzo*
"the clouds which covered the scene disappeared as if they
were blown away by a gust of wind," revealing the perspective scenery, which returned each time as the background for the action during each act of *La Pellegrina*.
The sets "had three openings: the one in the middle of
straight lines, and the other two, so as to imitate the aforementioned city [Pisa] in every possible way, of curved
lines since nearly all the streets are curved.
In these two things the artist has really demonstrated his
remarkable ingeniousness: in drawing the lines in perspective and making more than one opening in the scene, there
is no other example as far as we know" (De' Rossi 1589:
33).
There can be no doubt that this print illustrates a theatrical scene, nor that the model upon which it is based consists of a triple perspectival view, achieved with three
streets converging from the backdrop toward the
proscenium, as described above by de' Rossi.
In spite of the exact coincidence of the layout and urban
arrangement, however, it is not certain that the picture illustrated is really the scene of *La Pellegrina*.

Other fundamental features mentioned by de' Rossi are
absent; he describes, for example, how the action takes
place in the "old and noble city of Pisa, therefore one
could see all that part, which is known as the Lungarno,
with its bridges, the duomo and its leaning tower, the
church of S. Giovanni [i.e., the baptistery], the noble
building of the cemetery, the palace of the Knights of St.
Stephen, with the church next to it ... and many other
temples, and mansions of great importance, and imitated
so masterly and so similar to the eminent buildings of that
city ... and there was such a distance proceeding from the
backdrop that played a pleasant and sweet trick on the
spectators, that one could almost doubt as to whether the
architect had not transported the city of Pisa into that
place" (ibid.).
Given that the subject of the print cannot be either of the
masquerades staged for the two marriage celebrations—
La Zingara and *La Pazzia d'Isabella*—which the *comici* are
reported to have performed "in the same scenery of *La
Pellegrina*" (Pavoni 1589: 29, 43-44), it can only be that,
given the unquestionable link between Scarabelli's print
(inasmuch as it is part of a set) and the 1589 wedding fes-
tivities, the etching represents another theatrical production created by Buontalenti. It is nonetheless unlikely
that, of all the possible images to choose from to preserve
the memory of these events, the engraver would favor
scenes from a decidedly secondary drama over one which
all the contemporary sources considered quite exceptional. The perspective scenery with multiple vanishing
points which de' Rossi says was used for the first time by
Buontalenti in the production of *La Pellegrina*, had in reality already been developed six years earlier, albeit in a
completely different context, by Scamozzi for the Teatro
Olimpico in Vicenza.
A very similar composition to the one shown in this etching can be found in an undated drawing in the Oenslager
Collection, which has been attributed on occasion to
Aristotile da Sangallo, but without any really solid arguments (Blumenthal 1974: 12-13, no. 1). The same arrangement was adopted again in Florence in 1619 in the
scenery (anonymous) for Prospero Bonarelli's *Il Solimano*,
published in a famous series of prints engraved by Jacques
Callot (Lieure 1924: nos. 364-368).   *A.P.T.*

174
UNKNOWN FLORENTINE
Perspective Scenery with Florentine Buildings

Florence, Galleria degli Uffizi, Gabinetto Disegni e Stampe
Uff. 3894A
Black pencil, stylus impressions; pen with brown and gray wash;
white paper; mounted.
272 × 910 mm (maximum dimensions of sheet, composed of three parts)

BIBLIOGRAPHY: Ferri 1885, XLVI: 58.

This highly interesting though virtually unknown drawing is conserved in the Uffizi among the papers of Giacomo Barozzi da Vignola.
The drawing was cataloged with this untenable attribution in the nineteenth-century by Ferri, who described it
in the entry as a "Perspective view of a loggia with various
buildings at the sides, and with the Loggia del Mercato
Nuovo in Florence in the center."
Even though the drawing depicts the central loggia built
in the new market by Giovan Battista del Tasso between
1546 and 1564, and while it is indeed possible to identify
other buildings—the palace in the left foreground is
recognizable as a slight variation of the Palazzo
Nonfinito—this drawing is not a real view of any particular quarter of Florence. The completely imaginary compo-

sition makes it more likely to be an ideal urban perspective
designed almost certainly for theatrical purposes, which
can be confirmed as belonging to the scenographic theme
illustrated in prints such as Uff. 13292 (discussed elsewhere). By comparison, this print provides a sort of variation on the theme of the radial arrangement of the streets.
Even though it has not been possible so far to link this composition with any historically documented Florentine stage
production (the attribution to Vignola has been definitively
excluded for chronological reasons—he died in 1551), it
is still reasonable to assign it to this stylistic sphere: the subject itself is essentially Florentine (although this is not necessarily proof), and the kind of scenographic arrangement
clearly harks back to Buontalenti. Moreover, given the nervous pen strokes, the handling of light effects (at least in
the parts free of the geometrical rigidity typical of architectural drawings), it may reasonably be attributed to Lodovico
Cigoli's circle of influence. As far as dating the drawing is
concerned, it certainly belongs to a much later period than
that suggested by Ferri. The presence of the Palazzo Nonfinito places the drawing's execution in the seventeenth
century. Work on the unfinished exterior of the palazzo
came to a halt in the year 1600, when Alessandro di Camillo Strozzi, the patron, and Bernardo Buontalenti, his architect, fell out due to misunderstandings over the running
of the yard.   *A.P.T.*

175
ANONYMOUS
Left Side of Perspectival Stage Set

Stockholm, Nationalmuseum, CC 392
Pen and brown wash on white paper; mounted.
628 × 445 mm

BIBLIOGRAPHY: Pochat 1990: 298-299.

While this lovely drawing is ascribed to Baldassarre Peruzzi
in the inventories of the Stockholm collection, it actually
belongs to the second half of the sixteenth century, or even
the early seventeenth. This can be inferred stylistically from
the slightly exuberant but highly decorative elegance of the
graphics, which has parallels in the production of late Mannerist artists such as Bernardino Poccetti.
Its purpose as a stage design is demonstrated not only by
the scenographic handling of the perspective, but also by
the kind of buildings portrayed (allusions to Rome can be
identified in the background with what appears to be Trajan's Column and the Torre delle Milizie), and the improbable spatial relationships. The fact that the divisions between the first four buildings could be openings for actors
suggests that the design was for a set of wings; the vanishing point can be traced to the back of the stage, leading
back from the proscenium and on, beyond the fifth building, which marks the start of the painted backdrop. The
stage production for which this scene was designed is still
unidentified, in the absence of any specific documentation
or more precise figurative characteristics for the identification of the draftsman.   *A.P.T.*

176

JACQUES CALLOT (after Giulio Parigi)
Intermezzo *from* La Liberazione di Tirreno (*Teatro Mediceo, Uffizi*)

Florence, Galleria degli Uffizi, Gabinetto Disegni e Stampe, Uff. 8015 st. sc.
Etching.
295 × 209mm (plate) 301 × 216 mm (paper)

BIBLIOGRAPHY: Meaume 1860, II: 304, no. 630; Solerti 1905: 122; Nasse 1909, I: 28-29; Plan 1911: 45, no. 130; Bruwaert 1912: 70; Lieure 1924, II: 72, no. 185; *Mostra Medicea*, 1939: 156, no. 31; Guerrieri and Povoledo 1951: 24, no. 25; Turchetti 1954: 1334; Feinblatt 1957: 4, no. 7; *Mostra documentaria*, 1958: 17, no. 87; Ternois 1961: 42; 1962: 186; Damiani-Panazza 1968: 34, no. 26/1; Knab 1968: 111-112, no. 254; Gaeta Bertelà, in Gaeta Bertelà-Petrioli Tofani 1969: 162, no. 106; Schröder 1971, II: 956; Vitzthum 1971: no. XV; Ternois 1973: 245; Heikamp 1974: 328; Blanchard, in *Jacques Callot* 1975: 65-66, 96, no. 59; Petrioli Tofani, in *Il luogo teatrale* 1975: 123, no. 8.42; Kahan 1976: 76; Zorzi 1977: 111; Rothrock-Van Gulick 1979: 16-36; Blumenthal 1980: 111-112, no. 52; Petrioli Tofani 1981: 33; Choné, in *Jacques Callot* 1992: 194, no. 91.

The marriage of Caterina de' Medici, the sister of Grand Duke Cosimo II, to the Duke of Mantua, Ferdinando Gonzaga, provided the occasion for the presentation of a particularly complex and highly ingenious masquerade at the Teatro Mediceo in the Uffizi on 6 February 1617. It was a very unusual work which completely forsook the traditional alternation of contents in favor of a series of ballets and choreographic *abbattimenti* or battles. The program included three allegorical *intermezzi* telling the story of the *Liberazione di Tirreno e d'Arnea autori del sangue toscano*. The drama was written by the court poet, Andrea Salvadori, the music composed by Marco da Gagliano and Jacopo Peri, and the choreography was created by Agnolo Ricci. The scenes were designed by Giulio Parigi, who had inherited the role of scenographer and costume designer of all the most important theatrical productions in Medicean Florence at the death of Buontalenti in 1608.

A series of three prints, starting with the one shown here, offers insights into Parigi's stage inventions. They were etched by Jacques Callot perhaps as illustrations—as was the custom—for an edition of Salvadori's poetical *oeuvre*, which was in fact printed much later in Rome in 1668 without illustrations.

The plot of Salvadori's drama mixed elements of classical mythology with ideas drawn from Ariosto. He wrote that when Tyrrhenus (the personification of the Etruscans) arrived at the island of Ischia he was imprisoned by Circes in a volcano because he had dared reject her advances. Arnea was in love with Tyrrhenus and followed him to the island. She and her companions were then turned into a group of *Hamadryads*. In the end, in order to permit the union of the hero and the heroine—from which the said Tuscan blood was supposed to spring—the poet invokes Hercules, who is pictured in the print on the top of the volcano in the center of the scene. While Hercules is wait-

ing for Juno to give him her orders for the next of his Labors, he hears a voice emerging from a tree, telling him the unhappy tale of Tyrrhenus and Arnea. He decides to free them, and their liberation succeeds with the intervention of Jove who, descending on the scene in a cloud, hurls a thunderbolt at the mountain, which splits open, releasing the two lovers and all their retinue. A description written by Giuseppe Casato on 12 February 1617 explains that at this point the first of the *intermezzi* concluded with a "beautiful ballet, first twelve knights on the stage, and then the same knights with twelve richly arrayed ladies. In the middle of the theater between the knights the Grand Duke [Cosimo II] danced, and among the ladies, the Arch Duchess [Maria Maddalena of Austria], but with starts and finishes and positions always different from the others, so that even though they danced to the same music, the lord and his lady were always recognizable" (see Portioli 1882: 10).

Dramatic performances of this kind suggest a different climate to that of the theatrical performances described previously. The innovation does not lie, as one might at first think, in the concrete interaction between actors and audience as laid down in the masque described above, which does nothing more than repropose in a perhaps emphatic form, the aristocratic specular relationship that characterizes the whole of courtly drama in the Cinquecento. It was in fact an experiment in osmosis between reality and theatrical fantasy which, among previous attempts, had a particularly illustrious precedent in the famous *Festa del Paradiso* produced in Milan by Leonardo da Vinci nearly a century earlier for Lodovico il Moro. What is instead a novelty is the fact that the ballet spilled off the stage by means of a perron-like ramp, which clearly tended to supersede the imaginary diaphragm between the conventional space of the performance and the real space of the audience, which was traditionally marked by the scenic arch. The descent from the stage was not improvised but—as we can see in the print we are examining here—a precise stage direction indicated in the carefully prepared choreography. This detail offers definite proof of how the scenographer was exploring a new kind of stage space, a space that extended beyond the physical limits of the stage, and likewise outside the intellectual framework of the perspective scenery, echoing the dynamic, centrifugal rhythms and sense of infinity of the emerging Baroque sensibility.

A.P.T.

177

JACQUES CALLOT (after Giulio Parigi)
First Intermezzo *from* La Liberazione di Tirreno (*Teatro Mediceo, Uffizi*)

Berlin, Staatliche Museen, Preussischer Kulturbesitz, Kupferstichkabinett, KdZ 425
Black pencil and pen; brown wash; white paper.
282 × 201 mm

BIBLIOGRAPHY: Nasse 1909, I: 28-29, pl. 5a; Zahn 1918: 3; 1923: 60, 97; Vallery Radot 1953: 182; Ternois 1961: 42, no. 12; 1962:

187; Schröder 1971, I: 38; Blanchard, in *Jacques Callot* 1975: 66; Petrioli Tofani, in *Il luogo teatrale* 1975: 123; Zorzi 1977: 11; Petrioli Tofani 1981: 33, no. 17; Petrioli Tofani, in *Da Leonardo a Rembrandt*, 1990: 232; Choné, in *Jacques Callot* 1992: 194; Petrioli Tofani 1992: 56.

This is the preparatory drawing for the etching in the Uffizi (Uff. 8015) described elsewhere. From the time of its publication by Nasse, the attribution to Callot has never been questioned.

It must be remembered that these two works—the drawing and the print—are the only illustrations left to posterity of one of the first permanent structures in the history of European theater: the great hall decorated by Bernardo Buontalenti, commissioned by Cosimo I de' Medici to complete Vasari's design for the Uffizi. It was inaugurated on 6 February 1586 with a performance of *L'Amico Fido* by Bastiano de' Rossi, and continued to host stage productions for nearly half a century. It was finally dismantled in 1861 to give way to the senate of the newly established Kingdom of Italy when Florence was briefly its capital.

A.P.T.

The Ideal City
Hubert Damisch

The exemplary restoration job carried out in the seventies on the famous *Città ideale* (currently conserved at the Galleria Nazionale delle Marche in Urbino) has brought out in even clearer relief the link, also of an ideal nature, between this good-sized panel and the *tavoletta* that Brunelleschi used, according to his biographer, in his first demonstrations of perspective construction. The door, slightly ajar, of the circular-plan temple with a conical dome that here occupies the center stage between two wings representing city palazzi and houses, now shows a small hole (Damisch 1987) that corresponds to the painting's vanishing point, its *punto dell'occhio*. The same kind of hole also appeared in the small panel, long lost, on which Brunelleschi had painted the baptistery of Florence Cathedral in the center of the piazza of the same name, as it would have appeared to an observer standing slightly back inside the main portal of the cathedral.

The clouds in particular, rendered with a freedom worthy of the "atmospheric" painters of the nineteenth century, bear witness to the transition from what was at the outset no more than an exercise in the technique of geometric perspective, to the art of painting, true and proper: Leonardo da Vinci was to call the cloud a "body without a surface," and as such it could elude the grip of linear construction.

Art historians have long associated this panel with two others, no less unique, today conserved in Baltimore and Berlin. The fact that these three panels are shown here together in this exhibition suggests a comparative approach which, it is to be hoped, shall not be limited to questions of attribution and dating, nor to the search for presumed "solutions" aimed at unraveling the enigma they represent. Here, it is a question not merely of the representation of architecture, but rather one of the architecture itself of representation, the construction of which in perspective provides at once the mainspring and the paradigm, while here it remains as if suspended, reduced to just the frame, merely the architectural scene. Hence, the strictly epistemological interest, that Krautheimer's hypothesis continues to arouse, despite the objections raised by the positivists. Krautheimer believed that he could recognize in the Urbino and Baltimore panels the "models"—updated to suit the tastes of the day—of the Comic Scene and the Tragic scene described by Vitruvius; since this hypothesis calls for a comparison of each element of these two "views" or "perspectives," it will suffice, as Parronchi did (1968a) in strictly historical terms, to link these two panels to the one in Berlin in order to form what geometricians call a "set of transformations" (Damisch 1987). In this way, it will be found that these three models or *maquettes* (to use the French term applied to two-dimensional scenery models often employed today in film production) all in fact share a subtle form of "idealness," as the established title given to the Urbino panel suggests, though this idealness derives less from a sense of utopia than from labor focused on the very foundations of the perspective scene. In time, this labor was to have a twofold reward: on the one hand, in the field of theater, the institution of the classical scene, which was to owe more to Serlio than to Palladio, whose Teatro Olimpico was based on an entirely different principle; and on the other, in the field of mathematics in the seventeenth century, the solutions attained by Desargues and the foundation of descriptive and projective geometry.

178
CENTRAL ITALIAN ARTIST
"The Ideal City"
end 15th cent.

Urbino, Galleria Nazionale delle Marche
Oil on panel.
67.5 × 239.5 cm

PROVENANCE: Convent of S. Chiara, Urbino.

CENTRAL ITALIAN ARTIST
Architectural Perspective
end 15th cent.

Baltimore, Walters Art Gallery, 37.677
Oil on panel.
77.4 × 220 cm

PROVENANCE: Massarenti Collection, Rome.

CENTRAL ITALIAN ARTIST
Architectural Perspective
end 15th cent.

Berlin, Staatliche Museen, Preussicher Kulturbesitz, Gemäldegalerie, 1615
Tempera on panel.
124 × 234 cm

PROVENANCE: bought in Florence in 1898.

BIBLIOGRAPHY: Kimball 1927-28; Sanpaolesi 1949; Parronchi 1962b; Francastel 1965; Battisti 1968; Saalman 1968; Parronchi 1968a; Krautheimer 1969d; Conti 1976 (with extensive bibliography); Sangiorgi 1976; Zeri 1976; Bernini 1978; Chastel 1978; Dupré dal Poggetto 1983a; Damisch 1987; Morolli 1992a.

The incontestable provenance of the most famous of these three panels has often led to their being grouped together under the title "Urbinate perspectives," but for art historians they represent an enigma. At first approach, they seem to reflect a "genre" more frequently expressed in other media than painting, first among which is marquetry. In Urbino and elsewhere there are numerous examples using this technique of "cityscapes" or "architectural perspectives," the construction of which is based on the same principle of "centrality." The Urbino, Baltimore and Berlin panels, instead, rise above this group, in terms of both artistic quality (particularly evident in the Urbino panel) and their highly accurate and methodical rendering of the architectural details. Furthermore, the buildings represented in them hold an intrinsic interest which soon prompted Fiske Kimball (1927-28) to attribute the first two to Luciano Laurana, Federico da Montefeltro's architect and the creator in Urbino of the first great princely palace, while in the Berlin panel the strongly Albertian, indeed theatrical, references made it seem much more archaic to him (Battisti 1968).

This attribution sets the dating of the Urbino panel back to around 1470-80, though present-day critics tend to trace the three so-called Urbinate perspectives to Florentine spheres and to assign them a later date, around 1500, in association with the circle of Giuliano da Sangallo or of Baccio d'Agnolo; Parronchi (1968a) has gone so far as to identify them as scenery models for the performances staged in Florence in 1518 in celebration of Lorenzo de' Medici's wedding. Such a leap in time (nearly a half-century) as well as in space (from the Marche region to Tuscany) is symptomatic of the (often illusory) drive to establish references and the positivism that currently affects research on architectural models of the early Renaissance. While Francastel (1965) does not hesitate to write that Renaissance architecture was *depicted* before it was built, most recent historical analysts refuse to believe that painters, even if they did work in strict collaboration with architects, could have done anything more than depict existing structures, buildings that they had right before their eyes.

Alessandro Conti (1976) has written a very thorough and insightful overview of the research on these panels, as well as of the hypotheses advanced about them. The present writer has also carried out an in-depth critical analysis of the literature dedicated to the subject (Damisch 1987) and has made an attempt to complete the structural analysis contained in the work of Kimball, Krautheimer and Parronchi. Whether the origin of these panels is attributed to Urbino or Florence, it is no longer possible to insist on a "contextual," strictly historical or ideological, type of interpretation. Instead, the only acceptable hypothesis would be that these three panels make up a sort of "set of transformations," where the alleged "archaism" of the Berlin panel would be an additional distinctive feature to contrast with the decidedly "avant-garde" character of the buildings represented in the Urbino panel, while the Baltimore one shows the greatest divergence between antique buildings and the palaces of an architecture that is, to the contrary, highly contemporary. What these panels are supposed to represent, then, is less important than what they "transform," or what they "bring about"; the result is that in this transformation, this operation, however far in the distance the so-called vanishing point of the perspective construction is set—whether it is marked, as in the Urbino panel, at the center of the door of the round temple that occupies the center of the scene, or it is carried back, as in the Baltimore panel, to the limits of the city, or inscribed, as in the Berlin panel, on the horizon line, as it were, without bounds—the structure of the perspective space does not change. That is to say that, in strictly representative, if not pictorial, terms, we have the same assumption of the theorem that Desargues expressed, a century and a half later, and which was the springboard for modern geometry.

Renaissance Town Planning, from Filarete to Palmanova
Pietro C. Marani

This section comprises the "projects," plans, surveys and models created to provide a concrete representation of one of the most fascinating and compelling themes of architecture, namely, the Ideal City. However, given the myriad ideological, symbolic, literary, artistic, civil, and social implications, this particular theme is also of immense importance to the Renaissance in general. It has been identified as one of the main indicators of the emerging concepts of Renaissance thinking, reflecting a new vision of the world and indeed of humankind. In direct correlation with this new vision of Man as microcosm, as the active center of the universe was the project of the city in which Man was not only the architect and creator, but also the driving force behind all its activities. The drawings of Vitruvian man by Leonardo, Francesco di Giorgio, Cesare Cesariano and others virtually embody this idealized form of urban planning, and epitomize the new worldview. Just as centralized perspective had put the eye of the artist (and consequently that of the observer) at the effective center of a measured and quantifiable universe, so the centralized, circular or stellar architectural plans gave ever increasing space and emphasis to the seemingly infinite expansion of the intellectual, economic and political activities of the new dominant class. Furthermore, the Prince, the ruler illuminated by the new culture, became the engineer behind the new system (like other lords of his day, Lorenzo il Magnifico dabbled in architecture, including military engineering, whose theorists commended such knowledge as a prerequisite of princedom, as suggested by Luca Pacioli's dedication of *De divina proportione* to his patron Lodovico il Moro), and began to demand that the hilltop forts, castles, and citadels stood as beacons simbolizing the sovereign's dominant role in the urban pattern. First concieved in the early Cinquecento, the city within the city—a type of microcosm—offers a significant key to interpreting most town planning schemes of the Renaissance (Marconi 1968). The material selected to illustrate this intriguing topic is undoubtedly reductive, and can be considered in its appropriate broader context in the introductive essays by Nicholas Adams and Henry Millon in this volume. Here I will examine the ideal city dreamed up by Filarete for the lord of Milan, and its culmination in the plan of the town of Palmanova. This enables us to follow the evolution of the concepts and ideals of Renaissance planning over a span of about 150 years, particularly as much of the visual material was enriched by theoretical texts and treatises which refer directly to them.

There is a widely held assumption that the theoretical works of the artists and architects of the Renaissance were merely abstractions, with little bearing on reality. On the contrary, they were very closely linked to the real situation of the time, to the social and economic context to which they were intended to apply, as shown by Filarete's ideal plan, the Sforzinda, whose direct correlation with the sociopolitical reality of Milan under the Sforza dynasty has been amply demonstrated (Firpo 1954; Simoncini 1974; Soldi Rondinini 1983). It is worth noting that Filarete infused his many practical proposals for improving life in the town with a conceptual scheme based on the combination of Christian and pagan symbolism (Grassi 1983), without ever losing any of his sincere interest in a more rational, albeit "princely" form of town planning. Leonardo da Vinci's proposals for a town on three levels (for Milan, or, more likely, schemes for redeveloping Vigevano or Pavia to suit the needs of the duchy), with their clear demarcations of functions and social classes,

fall into the same category. Leonardo's concern for questions of hygiene (and hence the importance of the water supply and drainage) and the salubriousness of locations is well-known, and yet even these "urbanistic" conceptions of Leonardo (applied in turn to Milan and to other Lombard towns, or to Florence, or to the Royal Palace at Romorantin) are replete with symbols, ideology and abstractions. Throughout his life he strove to emulate Leon Battista Alberti (Zoubov 1960; Garin 1972), and his split-level planning schemes have been interpreted as the vertical transposition of Alberti's horizontal division of the town by concentric circles of walls (*De re aedificatoria*, IV, iii and iv; cf. Orlandi and Portoghesi 1966), which was patently rooted in a conservative vision and a reactionary ideology. The fundamental precedent set by Alberti—as fundamental for Leonardo as it was for Francesco di Giorgio and Peruzzi—must on no account be forgotten, although in this section of the exhibition his theoretical contribution cannot be satisfactorily represented in visual terms. The same applies to the Vitruvian proposals behind many of the more abstract exercises in Renaissance town planning—culminating in the interpretations of the Vitruvian city by Caporali in 1536, and Barbaro in 1556, both of which (see Benevolo 1973: 578, figs. 618 and 619)—seem respectively to incorporate the ideal cities of Filarete and Peruzzi as shown here.

This overlapping of utopia and reality is much more intricate than might be imagined at first—almost inextricable. The "projects" and models of which this section is comprised seem to be inclined toward the kind of proposal that directly tackles a real planning problem, rather than illustrating some utopian idea of planning of its own sake (for an overview see Wittkower 1964b: 19ff., complemented by Tafuri 1969a, and Benevolo 1973: 141-226 and now also Fontana, in Pavan 1993: 379-385). Two drawings by Leonardo presented here offer an excellent illustration of this relationship. The first (cat. no. 182) affords an idea of the large-scale project of urban expansion which Leonardo envisaged for Milan, and consists essentially of supplementing the existing, approximately circular plan of the town with a vast outer band of new development (although drawn in 1509/10 it seems to be based on previous planning studies carried out by Leonardo during his period at the Sforza court). The second drawing (cat. no. 183) offers an even more decisive attempt at streamlining an existing urban pattern, in this case medieval Florence, reshaping it into a dodecagon. But the artist's attention is also concentrated on the functional efficiency of the Arno within the new urban context. This approach recurs in the drawing of the plan of Florence and its walls executed by Giorgio Vasari (cat. no. 180), who also seemed to be attracted to rationalizing the medieval layout of the city.

Another cartographic drawing by Leonardo—probably his most well-known (RL 12284r. not in exhibition)—belongs to a category of its own. Despite its appearance, the map of Imola is not so much a "project" as a survey charting the existing state of the land (drafted for military purposes), as attested by the drawing at Windsor (RL 12686), in which Leonardo surveys the various sectors of the town, complete with quarters and streets. Having done this, despite inscribing the town, with its walls and defense bastions, within a circumference, he proceeds to confer on the drawing a symbolic and abstract character which makes it strikingly representative of the rationalizing urge that underscores all Renaissance town planning. Leonardo's inquiries into town planning (and, by extension, those of the other architects) are in fact linked to his experiments in cartography and geography. It has recently been revealed that his pupil Marco d'Oggiono possessed various "quadri di Lumbardia" and world maps "in tella di rilievo" (Marani and Shell 1992); these new finds strongly suggest that Leonardo had begun to specialize in land surveying, not just for scientific, urbanistic, or military ends, but to be able to sell the fruit of his labors (from which his pupils, such as Marco d'Oggiono, would have made paintings or relief *mappaemondi*).

Similarly, the links that can be noted between the theme

of the ideal city and the questions of defense, walls and ramparts—which first came to the fore after the first edition of Francesco di Giorgio's publication in 1481-84, and became almost obsessive from the early Cinquecento, culminating in the design of Palmanova—are a sign of the growing interest in the practical issues of survival, as much for the prince, duke or sovereign, as for their subjects, even though the latter were not yet "citizens" as such. In the course of the sixteenth century and even more so after the Palmanova plan, the formerly abstract enceintes lost their utopian, idealistic character, expressing instead the need to lend greater structural definition, or to define urban perimeters as perfect "machines of war" performing elaborate defensive and offensive functions (see Borrmann, in Pavan 1993: 387-390 and Fara 1993). It is hardly surprising, therefore, that the project by Pietro Cataneo—a pentagonal city from the *Treatise* of 1567 (cat. no. 186)—found practical application in the planning of the town of Mannheim, as illustrated in 1645 (cf. Benevolo 1973: 915, fig. 1036). Leonardo's proposals for fortresses and citadels also seemed to betray an awareness of the planning principles of Alberti (Marani 1984a: 200, and passim), demonstrating the marked links between the application of theories inspired by conservative ideologies and the firsthand knowledge of warfare and ballistics that was becoming dominant in the early sixteenth century with the great advances being made in artillery and firearms.

In view of this, it seems relevant to include several strictly military drawings devoted to specific buildings in which this close link between military architecture and town planning is most evident. One of the oldest and most important drawings in this regard is undoubtedly a sheet traditionally attributed to Francesco di Giorgio Martini, conserved in the Uffizi (Uff. 336A; see, however, cat. no. 179 for the recent reattribution to Peruzzi); the drawing shows a bastioned villa that could rightly be considered a useful starting point to illustrate this overlapping of the two fields of design. The villa's design subsequently determined important repercussions in the choices made by planners and their patrons throughout the Cinquecento. The second sheet (Uff. 3877Ar.) perhaps cannot be properly defined as a drawing of military architecture, as the principles of defense merge with the ideals of civil architecture (it is in fact a grandiose scheme for the floor plan of a palazzo), foreshadowing an urban motif that would lead directly to Palmanova. The drawing in the Uffizi, formerly attributed to Giovanni Antonio Dosio and more recently identified as the work of Giovanvittorio Soderini, betrays traces of Leonardo, and is an authoritative exemplum of the ideology of the radial town designs of the sixteenth century, a field studied in depth by Horst De La Croix (1960). Here the scheme for the palazzo's design is directly related with that of a large town.

Another clear instance of how even the more feasible planning schemes had to be steeped in explanatory texts is offered by the first version of Francesco di Giorgio's *Treatise*: "Given that cities bear the same logic, measurements and form as the human body ... it is likewise important to note that the body possesses all the articulation and members observable in the city and its buildings" (see more extensive quote in Maltese 1967, I: 20ff.). The outcome is the superb drawing of a man superimposed on the plan of a walled city (Biblioteca Laurenziana, *Codex Ashburnham* 361, fol. 1r.) in which the head of the man corresponds to the fortress, his belly the piazza, at his feet two large towers, and between these a pointed ravelin (perhaps alluding to virility). It is a shame that there is no follow-up to this classic "humanization" of town planning in Francesco di Giorgio's treatise, nor in the illustrations that accompany it. There are no examples of concrete application. The town plans illustrated on the following sheets of the codex (fols. 5r., 5v., and 6r.) are modeled on abstract geometrical schemes, or according to schemes that derive from embryonic defense principles in which, from time to time, the artist's hand manages to evoke some fantastic feature of the towered cities that had already appeared in the backgrounds of his paintings (cf. for example the painting in the Berenson Collection, Settignano, showing a walled city in the right background), by crowning the towns, whose streets unfurl with the intricacy of embroidery, with a succession of towers and temples (fol. 5r., along the right border of the sheet).

But the abstract formulas of Francesco di Giorgio were as important and stimulating for subsequent generation of architects as the conceptions of Vitruvius and Alberti had previously been to others. The proposal of Domenico Giunti for Guastalla (cat. no. 185), the della Rovere plan for Orzinuovi (Fara 1989: 88, pl. xxi; Perbellini 1988: 158-159) and in particular the one for Peschiera, whose reorganization for his patron della Rovere is illustrated by a far later model of 1612 (Fara 1989, pl. xx; Perbellini 1988: 165-167; Manno, in Pavan 1993: 515), show how it was possible, by updating the fifteenth-century geometrical schemes to the new defense requirements, to achieve functional town schemes without forgoing the Renaissance utopia of formal perfection. Similarly, the dovetailing of civil architecture, military architecture and town planning was to come to fruition in Lorini's plan of Palmanova (cat. no. 187), in which it seems possible to trace the echoes of some of Giovanvittorio Soderini's civil designs datable to around 1560 which, in turn, owe much to Serlio (Morrogh 1985a: 68-72). The Renaissance utopia of the ideal city seems to come to a head with a fusion of the eastern planning principles that had originally inspired the circular plans (Fiore 1978; Marani 1984b: 47-48), and those, stimulated by the adoption of spearhead bastions, as seen in Filarete, which made the star the paradigm of late sixteenth-century town planning (for an overview of star-shaped town plans in Italy, see Biamonti, in Pavan 1993: 453-459, and 487-497).

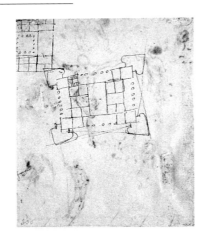

179
FRANCESCO DI GIORGIO MARTINI
and BALDASSARRE PERUZZI
Plan of Fortified Villa

Florence, Galleria degli Uffizi, Gabinetto Disegni e Stampe, Uff. 336
Pen and ink in two colors on paper.
242 × 200 mm

PROVENANCE: Baldassarre Peruzzi; Sallustio Peruzzi (?).
242x200 mm

BIBLIOGRAPHY: Marani 1982: 181-188 (with preceding bibliog.); 1984b: 29-30; Wurm 1984: 519; Frommel 1987a: 27 n. 16; Adams 1989: 226 n. 8; Burns 1993a: 353-354.

This drawing showing the plan of a villa or palazzo at the center of the sheet, with four corner bastions with retired flanks, has always been considered the earliest Uffizi drawing by Francesco di Giorgio Martini, given the chronology of his travel *taccuino* or notebook (to which the sheet belongs) and dates to around 1490, the time when the "modern" bastions were correctly indicated. The drawing's special importance lies in its observation of the crossfire from the retired flanks of the bastion, with the precise image of the reciprocal fire coverage offered by bastions of this type. However, there is no other record of drawings of protruding bastions by Francesco di Giorgio (who is responsible for the two lines of text on the recto, with a sketch for a dome design that recurs in the revised version of his *Trattato di Architettura*), nor did he ever work out their mutual defense mechanisms. Moreover, it has been noted (Marani 1982) that the bastions and the figure drawings on the recto are drawn in pen with a different ink from the one for the palazzi plans. Conceptually and stylistically these additions are in the style of Baldassarre Peruzzi, who probably owned all the Francesco di Giorgio drawings before they entered the Uffizi collection (many contain additions by Peruzzi's son Sallustio, cf. Burns 1974). The attribution to Peruzzi of the additions, doubted by Frommel and Adams, was finally accepted by Burns (1993a), who suggested that the villa plans were also by Peruzzi, given the confident, rapid line not usually associated with Francesco di Giorgio. Notwithstanding these philological problems, the drawing is of considerable importance in the context of early sixteenth-century Italian architecture; it offers a significant link in the path of development leading to the Villa di Poggioreale, to Caprarola, and thence to the efforts of Peruzzi, Serlio and Cataneo to establish the principles of defense works and to identify a set of ideal geometrical figures for the purpose.   *P.C.M.*

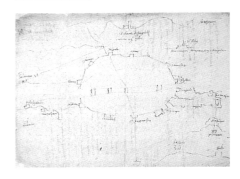

180
GIORGIO VASARI
Plan of Florence's Defense Walls

Arezzo, Casa Vasari, plan no. 90
Pen and ink on paper.
219 × 293 mm

PROVENANCE: Giorgio Vasari.

BIBLIOGRAPHY: Schiavo 1949, pl. 157; Ackerman 1968: 173-174; Tolnay 1975-1980, vol. IV; 1980: 79 (and fig. on p. 79); Manetti 1980: 119, fig. 26; Marani 1984b: 114, cat. no. 73.

According to Tolnay the drawing was executed by Vasari for a fresco depicting the siege of Florence intended for the Palazzo Vecchio in Florence (on this cycle, carried out from 1567 to 1571, see Corti 1989: 117-118). Given Vasari's assertion that the defense walls ordered by the Medici after 1534 were based on studies and projects drawn up by Michelangelo (Ackerman), one can infer that Vasari knew of these drawings: Manetti in fact notes that the salients that descend from S. Miniato encompass the Porta S. Miniato, as recorded in a written source contemporary to the siege of 1528-29. But the drawing in question is only indicative, and does not claim to offer a developed scheme of either Florence's defense works or the city's layout. What it does reveal is an intention (however unconscious, given the schematic nature of preparatory drawings for frescoes) to rationalize the city's perimeter into an "oval," remarkably similar in aim to the preceding, earlier drawings by Leonardo (cf. Leonardo's map of Florence dating from 1514-15; cat. no. 183). Vasari was nonetheless aware of Leonardo's town planning schemes, some of which focused on rehabilitating the Medici quarter of Florence: there are direct links between the famous

Vasarian corridor linking the Uffizi to the Palazzo Pitti over the Arno and the schemes for a split-level town drafted by Leonardo when he was in Milan (1487-90), an inquiry he resumed much later while working as an architect and engineer for Jacopo IV Appiani, Lord of Piombino, toward 1504-05 (cf. Marani 1984a: 237-238). It is therefore possible that the "oval" form (dear to Michelangelo) intended to encase the city of Florence, with the Arno (which is drawn as a straight line bisecting the city) is a personal and deliberate "mannerist" revisitation of the existing situation devised by Vasari, and hence a contribution to the ongoing debate on the form of the ideal city, a debate that came to a head in the first half of the century. *P.C.M.*

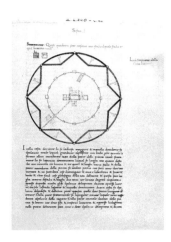

181
FILARETE (ANTONIO AVERLINO)
Design for the Ideal City of Sforzinda

Florence, Biblioteca Nazionale Centrale, *Codex Magliabechiano II*, I.140, fol. 43r.
Pen and ink on paper.
398 × 285 mm

PROVENANCE: Piero de' Medici; Strozzi.

BIBLIOGRAPHY: Spencer 1965: passim; (with preceding bibliog); Tafuri 1969a: 70; Finoli and Grassi 1972, I: 165-166, II, pl. 23; Benevolo 1973: 162, fig. 128; Grassi 1983: 428, fig. 30; Carpeggiani 1985: 37-38, fig. 11; Patetta 1989: 8, fig. a p. 26; Fara 1989: 151 (with other bibliographical references).

The famous drawing of the Sforzinda, the model city designed for Francesco Sforza (when the political situation changed, the Florentine codex was re-dedicated to Piero de' Medici) contained in Book II of Filarete's *Trattato d'Architettura*, written for the lords of Milan between 1462 and 1464 (Finoli and Grassi 1972; Patetta 1987), presents a fortified perimeter on a star-shaped plan devised from the merger of two squares, one rotated at 45° to the other (on fol. 13v., Finoli and Grassi 1972, II, pl. 7, provide a geometrical breakdown of the plan); the cylindrical towers on each of the eight points are linked by a high circular wall or glacis (possibly lower). This form is echoed by another circular perimeter on which oblong towers or gateways are marked, enclosing the main public buildings of the city; one of these is recognizable as the former Ospedale Maggiore in Milan, a complex built by Filarete himself, though completely out of scale here. The text accompanying the design in question describes the location of the various buildings, the city gates, and so forth, and begins thus: "At the eastern end I have set the largest church, while at the west stands the royal palace, whose dimensions I have omitted until such time as it will be built. On the northern side of the northern piazza will stand the merchants' shops, which will be a quarter of a *stadio* in width, i.e., ninety and three-quarter *braccia*, and half a *stadio* long. On the southern side of the

piazza will stand another square for an open market. At the head of this will be the palazzo of the *capitano*, with a courtyard alongside with only a street dividing it; on one side of the shops will rise the *podestà* and opposite it the council chambers. In the northern sector will stand the prison, directly opposite the Palazzo della Ragione. In the eastern sector, alongside the square, will stand the Treasury, namely, where the city's reserves are kept, and next to this the Customs House."

This detailed description illustrates the profound contradiction of Filarete's proposal: taking an abstract geometrical figure—linked to the Christian or pagan symbolism of the numbers four (the four Evangelists), and eight (see Grassi 1983)—Filarete proceeds to fill it in a rational manner that reflects the ideology of the absolute power of the sovereign or prince. This consequently justifies the incongruity of the radial pattern on which the orthogonal street grid is laid out, which serves to demarcate piazzas, religious and municipal buildings, in such a way that the principal house of worship (on the east side) is counterbalanced by the palazzi representing the secular power (on the west side), and so forth. As has already been pointed out (Benevolo 1973), Filarete omitted to indicate how he meant to link up the two concepts of planning, but simply mapped the "symbolic" city plan onto the "realistic" scheme of the civic functions. Taking a wider interpretation, Tafuri (1969a) noted that these contradictions (the abstract and cosmographic nature of the plan, and the mythical, unreal tone of the absurdly outsize architecture) foreshadow the impending intellectual crisis of the Quattrocento, with the result that the role of the utopia represented by Filarete's Sforzinda remains undefined: "on the one hand it mirrors the possibilities enabled by the town planning of the new Sforza powers, and on the other it proclaims the need to identify new social classes to give sustenance to architectural invention."

The town plan devised by Filarete (based on the interlocking of the square, octagon and circle) met with great success among successive generations of treatise-writers and architects. An echo can even be perceived in certain architectural ideas of Bramante and Leonardo, and in the plan for Palmanova, in which Filarete's design was refashioned to suit the emerging defense needs. *P.C.M.*

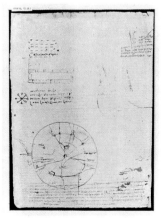

182
LEONARDO DA VINCI
Diagram of the City of Milan, with Other Studies and Notes on Mechanics and the Articulation of the Voice

Windsor Castle, Royal Library, RL 19115v.
Pen and sepia ink on rough paper.
31.6 × 21.8 mm

INSCRIBED: (clockwise) *vercelana; comasina; beatrice; nova; oresa; tosa; romana; lodovica; Ti[ci]nese; fabbri; (right) concha; schema di carri.*
31.6 × 21.8 mm

PROVENANCE: Francesco Melzi; Pompeo Leoni; Thomas Howard, Earl of Arundel

BIBLIOGRAPHY: Richter 1883: paras. 832 and 837; Pedretti 1960: 82, fig. 8; Clark and Pedretti 1968-69, III: 45; Keele and Pedretti 1978-80, I: 366, II: 850; Marani 1984a: 254, fig. 167b.

Below an eight-line note on the mechanisms of the human voice, Leonardo has sketched out a diagrammatic view of Milan indicating three concentric circles (roughly corresponding to the city's system of *navigli* or canals at the time) intersected by the rivers that cross the city. The intermediate circle is marked with the city gates (see annotations above). On the right he has labeled one of the locks ("conch") on the canal. Also included on the sheet are other writings and mechanical diagrams, a sketch labeled "schema di carri" (carriage diagram), and an annotated drawing of flames in the lower part of the sheet (whose recto contains drawings and notes on the mouth and throat, pharynx, tongue and speech).

The drawing was indicated by Carlo Pedretti as part of a set of hydrographic and town planning studies carried out while working on the villa of Charles d'Amboise (died 1511), and datable on the basis of style to around 1509-10 (for more on d'Amboise's villa, see Pedretti 1960; Pedretti 1972: 41-52). This chart of Milan is connected with fol. 199 verso of the *Codex Atlanticus* (formerly fol. 73v.-a), datable to the same period (cf. Marani 1984a: 251-253, cat. no. 167), which presents the inner two bands of the city (the third was drawn on Windsor sheet), with indications of the various lengths of curtain walling between the city gates, and the plan of the castle of Porta Giovia (now the Castello Sforzesco). The lower margin of the *Codex Atlanticus* sheet also offers a remarkable bird's-eye view of Milan in which the Porta Giovia castle can clearly be made out on the left, and the cathedral in the center, with the campanile of S. Gottardo visible below.

On the Windsor sheet Leonardo has concentrated more on the waterways than the building fabric; he nevertheless takes the opportunity to "amend" the outer perimeter of the city, providing a further complementary ring. Actually, by Leonardo's time there were already houses outside the medieval enceinte, as shown in Lafrery's map, albeit of a much later date (Pedretti 1960: 79, fig. 6), which includes the Spanish additions and new defense works; these would not have been necessary if the building fabric had not extended outside the original city walls. The new walls (see Scotti 1977) transformed the perimeter from a circle into a polygon, with a retired flank at the castle, forming a kind of ivy-leaf shape. With his circular profile, Leonardo was thinking of the fifteenth-century theories (of Filarete, for instance, and in particular of Alberti's *De re aedificatoria*, IV, iii and iv, which theorizes a city on a circular plan, see my Introduction above), extended in his proposals made during his years in the employ of the Borgia, around 1502-03, for a fortified citadel composed of concentric sections (for example *Codex Atlanticus* fols. 132r., and 133r.), with the possibility of gradually adding new residential quarters of a roughly trapezoidal shape to the medieval nucleus. Leonardo had already advanced a project of this kind while working for the Sforza, as can be seen from fol. 184 verso of the *Codex Atlanticus* (formerly fol. 65v.-b) and the *Codex Forster* III, fol. 23v., dating to around 1493, as observed by Pedretti (1962). One of these drawings (*Codex Atlanticus* fol. 65v.) had already been identified by Horst De La Croix (1960) as being typically representative of a Renaissance star-shaped city design. The successive urban growth of Milan did not in fact follow Leonardo's indications (as we have seen, and contrary to the beliefs of De La Croix), but this does not rule out the possibility that Leonardo's proposal was in fact a blueprint for how to proceed, and not just a theoretical or utopian proposition. *P.C.M.*

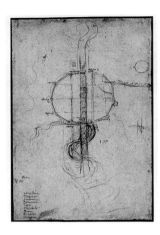

183

LEONARDO DA VINCI
Diagrammatic Map of the City of Florence Crossed by the Arno

Windsor Castle, Royal Library, RL 12681r.
Pen and ink on black chalk, on rough cream-colored paper.
29.8 × 19.9 mm

INSCRIBED: *nicholo; sanmjnjato; giorgo; ghattolinj; scanfriano; porta; prato; faenza; ghallo; pinti; giusstitia;* (toward bottom left) *vercellina; Ticinese; Ludovica; Romana; Tosa; orientale; Noua; Beatrice; Cumana.*

PROVENANCE: Francesco Melzi; Pompeo Leoni; Thomas Howard, Earl of Arundel.

BIBLIOGRAPHY: Richter 1883: paras. 1004 and 1006; Baratta 1941, pl. 17; Sisi 1953: 28, pl. facing p. 21; Pedretti 1962a: 113 n. 20; Firpo 1963: 63; Clark and Pedretti 1968-69, I: 169-170; Pedretti 1972: 58; Firpo 1987: 290-291, fig. 348.

The drawing is a very schematic rendering of the city of Florence inscribed in an approximately twelve-sided circle of defense walls (on the upper right of the sheet Leonardo has sketched a circle, perhaps suggesting the ideal perimeter to be achieved through planning); at each point on the perimeter stands a circular structure (perhaps the city gates fortified with defense towers); the Arno cuts through the city in a straight line from top to bottom, and is flanked by two parallel roads, with a third sketched in lightly on the far right. The name of each gate has been written alongside, and toward the bottom left another set of annotations, perhaps added by Melzi (Clark and Pedretti), list the names of the Milanese *porte*.
Apart from a small sketch of an arched bridge, drawn upside-down near the right margin of the sheet (with a further small drawing below this, also resembling a bridge), Leonardo's attention was directed toward studying the behavior of the winding section of the river north of the city (at the bottom of the drawing) where the Mugnone joins it from the northeast near the Porta al Prato, compared with the stretch before they enter the city. The curves of the Arno recall the turbulent river Leonardo drew many years earlier in his map of Imola (RL 12284). The highly generic map of Florence was defined by Firpo (1963) as a simplification of the city's plan drawn from memory while Leonardo was in Milan after 1506, but Pedretti's stylistic analysis of the map caused him to set a new date of 1515, putting the present sheet among the artist's engineering and planning researches carried out for Piero and Giuliano de' Medici over the period 1514-15, during which Leonardo inquired into redeveloping the neighborhood around the Medici residence in Via Larga (Pedretti 1962a; 1972). According to Sisi (1953) Leonardo's proposal reflects certain ideas expressed (in equally imprecise terms) by Francesco di Giorgio (for which, see Clark and Pedretti 1968: 170; this proposition is part of a series of schematic drafts that include Filarete's Sforzinda, the city maps included in Francesco di Giorgio's *Trattato*, and also the drawing by Peruzzi on display here); the drawing is unusual as it fails to mark out the relations between the public or religious buildings and

private fabric; furthermore there is no piazza, cathedral, or fortress—unless the lines to the south, at the top of the sheet describing a quadrangular structure left of the Arno near the Porta alla Giustizia are intended to be a fort of some kind. The scheme offered by Leonardo in this drawing is very similar to the diagrammatic drawing on fol. 8 recto of MS. B of the Institut de France in Paris, datable to 1487-90 (Firpo 1963: 69), in which, like the present drawing, an imaginary city composed of a square grid is cut through by the Ticino, which splits up longitudinally into several canals that can be closed off when the river is in spate, as explained in an accompanying note. The Windsor collection also includes a city scheme of this kind, datable to around 1508 (RL 12641, see Pedretti 1972, fig. 148), though, like the Institut de France drawing, it has no perimeter structure. However, compared to Leonardo's detailed studies of twenty years earlier for development schemes for Milan, Pavia and perhaps Vigevano, as testified by drawings for a city on three levels in the Institut de France MS. B (see for example Maltese 1954; Firpo 1963: 63-82; Pedretti 1988), here Leonardo doubtless wanted to focus on the "function" of the river in relation to the host city, stressing the form it should take in order to comply with a rational urban layout, considering also the advantages to hygiene that would derive from the proper use of the river water. The river, in this case the Saudre, later offered the most suitable framework in which to place the Royale Palace at Romorantin, whose plan reflects some of Leonardo's earlier solutions for urban planning.　　*P.C.M.*

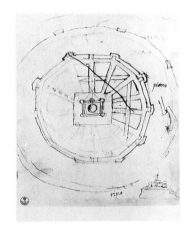

184

BALDASSARRE PERUZZI
Map of an Ideal City

Florence, Galleria degli Uffizi, Gabinetto Disegni e Stampe, Uff. 557A
Chalk, pen and ink, on paper; 205 × 164 mm

PROVENANCE: Sallustio Peruzzi (?)

BIBLIOGRAPHY: De La Croix 1960: 263; Wurm 1984: *sub numero;* Adams 1987: 206-207, fig. 1; Fara 1989: 156-158, fig. 122.

The drawing—first drafted in chalk and then corrected in pen and ink—represents an ideal city plan with a ten-sided outer perimeter equipped with a bastion at each corner. The perimeter encloses a radial pattern of streets which appear to intersect with four streets forming a square that amplifies the approximately square shape of the central piazza, which in turn encloses a fortress with cylindrical corner towers and a circular keep within. The entire town is encompassed by a ditch or moat, marked "ripa" below. Toward the bottom right of the sheet is a diagram of the fort, showing the elevations of the towers and the keep in the middle (drawn with a flag). The preliminary outlines in chalk, visible in the left half of the drawing, seem to indicate a circular street joining up the radials. A sketch in the bottom right shows the form of rounded bastion with orillons. This interesting drawing

(which presumably belongs to a youthful phase of activity, perhaps prior to 1522, the year in which Vasari states that Peruzzi was in Siena working on the city's defense works) makes direct references to the ideal city plan proposed by Francesco di Giorgio Martini in the first version of his *Trattato di Architettura* (corresponding to the codex in the Biblioteca Reale, Turin, and the Laurenziana codex in Florence; cf. Maltese 1967, I, pls. 9 and 10; and Marani 1979, facsimile volume of Laurenziana codex, fol. 5r.-v.) especially where Francesco di Giorgio presents (*Codex Ashburnham* 361, fol. 5v.) an octagonal city plan with the streets running from the semicircular towers to the round, central piazza, intersected by a spiral street winding from the center outward to the perimeter. Peruzzi's debt to Francesco di Giorgio's theories is widely recognized (see introductory note preceding this section), and this proposition by Peruzzi preserves the incongruities of one of his earlier experiments in the field of town planning. Horst De La Croix (1960) once even hypothesized that, given the poor layout of the intersecting streets, the diagonal pen line on the right hand side of the plan was in fact due to Peruzzi's crossing out the scheme when he realized it was inadequate. Adams (1987), however, considers wholly atypical Peruzzi's proposal to intersect the radials with orthogonal streets (or curved ones, as suggested in the original chalk lines), which may have been intended to run above one another, as in the preceding scheme of raised causeways proposed by Leonardo (in MS. B for instance, dating 1487-90). An alternative idea, endorsed by the elevation view of the fort sited on a kind of rise or hillock, is that the non-radial streets are underground, again in reference to Leonardo's proposal. Adams believes the drawing to be one of the three theoretical drawings by Peruzzi, who seems to have had little concern for town planning, despite his keen interest in architectural issues. Amelio Fara (1989) considered that the Uffizi sheet was a proposal for a "modern" redevelopment of an "ancient" fortified town plan. The ancient layout would in this way be enclosed by a perimeter of curtain walls and bastions in Cinquecento fashion instead of the old square towers, and the quadrilateral fort at the center would be replaced by a raised pentagonal fort.　　*P.C.M.*

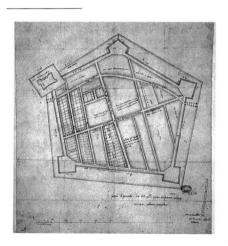

185

DOMENICO GIUNTI
Project for the Redevelopment of Guastalla

Parma, Archivio di Stato, Fondo Mappe e Disegni, vol. 48 no. 76
Pen and ink on paper; 422 × 367 mm

PROVENANCE: Gonzaga.

BIBLIOGRAPHY: Förster 1969: 8, fig. 3; Benevolo 1973: 581; Scotti 1977: 103, 107 n. 45; Carpeggiani 1985: 53-54, fig. 33; Biamonti, in Pavan 1993: 487 (with further bibliography).

The drawing offers an unrealized urban redevelopment scheme for the town of Guastalla; the town fabric is inscribed in an uneven, five-sided perimeter, with four pro-

542

truding bastions (not of the spearhead type), with the fifth supplanted by a rectangular fort with projecting corner towers. Two gates and two bridges over the moat provide access to the town, whose street grid is approximately rectangular, except for the curved road linking the two gateways; the alignment of the streets seems to be determined by the oblique angle of the left stretch of wall.

Domenico Giunti was engaged to draft a planning scheme for Guastalla in 1549 for Ferrante Gonzaga, governor of Milan and seignior of Guastalla, who became the feud's owner in 1540. Another, more schematic drawing of the present showing an almost regular pentagon (but without the street grid or building fabric) in the Ambrosiana (Carpeggiani 1985: 54, fig. 34) bears the date 1549. At more or less that time Giunti was working for the Gonzaga family in Milan, designing a suburban villa (the so-called Villa Simonetta), modernizing the Palazzo Ducale and the cathedral square, working alongside Giovanni Maria Olgiati on the creation of a new fortified perimeter for the city (for all Giunti's works, see Scotti 1977: 100-103; for more on Olgiati, who designed Milan's new defense works, see De Moro 1988, and Scotti-Tosini 1988).

The architect's intention here was to refashion Guastalla in the style of an ideal city (Scotti 1977: 103), the most important stronghold of the Po Valley, given the political situation that had come to pass in Northern Italy toward the mid-1500s (Benevolo 1973: 581). The project for Guastalla was furthermore seen as the model of "utopia made real" or at least attempted (Simoncini 1967: 159-160) and as the direct forerunner of the town of Sabbioneta (Carpeggiani 1985: 54). The architect openly declared his debt to the Sienese tradition in his reutilization of the simple geometrical forms of Francesco di Giorgio Martini (and, above all, of his proposals for fort patterns), and those which Serlio had updated regarding the new defense needs in Book VI of his *Trattato d'Architettura* (cf. Adams 1989, figs. 3, 5, and 6). Giunti's close acquaintance with Martini's previous proposals is unmistakable in his almost contemporary Villa Simonetta in Milan (Scotti 1977: 101; Marani 1991: 97), while his use of simple geometrical patterns adapted to the latest defense problems hark back to ground already covered by Peruzzi in his reworking of a villa plan by Francesco di Giorgio, in which he added four orillon bastions (cf. Marani 1982; Adams 1989: 226 n. 8; see also Frommel 1987a: 27 n. 16; Burns 1993a: 353-354). Biamonti (in Pavan 1993) notes the reinterpretation of the pre-existing medieval city based on a Roman model, as a symbolic refoundation of the city.   *P.C.M.*

365 × 23 × 25 mm

BIBLIOGRAPHY: Carpeggiani 1985: 42-43, fig. 19; Fara 1989: 164, fig. 137 (with other bibliographical references).

Together with the later work by Scamozzi of 1615, Pietro Cataneo's *Quattro Libri di Architettura* is "the last encyclopedic treatise in the Alberti line ... comprising theoretical arguments, stylistic instructions, and embracing the entire field of building activity, from civil constructions to military engineering" (Benevolo 1973: 573-576). At least eight of Cataneo's plates are devoted to detailed town plans devised in perfect geometrical patterns, ranging from simple squares (ed. 1554, fols. 10v.-12r.), five-sided figures (fols. 12r.-13r.), hexagonal forms with bastioned curtain walls (fols. 13r.-14r.), hectagons, and even eleven-sided enceintes recommended for seaports (fols. 23r.-24v.). The one presented here (fol. 22r.), a nine-sided city equipped with a pentagonal citadel, is drawn to exacting geometrical rules, accentuated by the rigorous pattern of the building fabric inside, with its large central piazza and three minor rectangular ones around it. The problem of flanking fire is well covered by the acute bastion traces (whose platforms are indicated but not the orillons that appear in the hectagonal city plan on fol. 14; see Fara 1989: 163, fig. 136), with indications for crossfire, is echoed in the star-shaped plan of the citadel above, which is also divided into an orthogonal grid and a central piazza. Besides the traditional texts (Vitruvius, Alberti) Cataneo's sources included Francesco di Giorgio (whose treatises he copied out personally, cf. Berti 1929), and Peruzzi (Parronchi 1982: 24-25), in pure Sienese style, a tradition that culminates in Cataneo. This project for an ideal city, like the one devised by his mentor Baldassarre Peruzzi (see Uff. 557A), also betrays some of the inconsistencies typical of the Siena school: the streets, instead of following a radial plan in conformance with the nine-sided scheme, are laid out orthogonally, with the resulting awkward expedient of triangular, trapezoidal and pentagonal islands. Furthermore, the citadel becomes almost abstract in its perfection, symbolic even (a form already applied to the Forte Stella at Porto Ercole, and the Stellata at Bondeno near Ferrara, without necessarily borrowing from the stellar fortress schemes of Giuliano da Sangallo, or Leonardo da Vinci; for an overview of these examples, see Marani 1984a: 202-207, with references to previous writings); however, it offers an unsatisfactory match with the town itself, with spearhead bastions that encroach on the housing fabric, betraying the underlying concern of the ruling bodies during this period of history to protect themselves from their subjects as well, and so the overall result no longer reflected "humanistic symbolism, but the new rules of military engineering" (Fontana, in Pavan 1993: 406).   *P.C.M.*

green wash, over black chalk and metalpoint underdrawing; white paper.
470 × 645 mm (dimensions of sheet)

PROVENANCE: Emmanuel Philibert of Savoy.

BIBLIOGRAPHY: Lupo 1978, fig. 7; Astengo 1983: fig. 24; Fara 1989: 112, 144 n. 67, pl. LX.

After the defeat of the Turks at Lepanto in October 1571, the Venetian Republic decided to erect a new rampart on the east side of the city. The scheme was entrusted to Bonaiuto Lorini, who drafted the working plans that same year. Work did not actually begin until 1593, under the direction of Savorgnano and Barbaro (for a historical account and description of the city, see Cassi Ramelli 1964: 351; De La Croix 1966; Marchesi 1980; Visintini 1988; Pavan 1993). The plan comprises a complex figure of nine sides, each 230 meters in length, with a spearhead bastion at each of the nine points. At the center stands a hexagonal piazza, whose sides constitute the short end of nine of the trapezoidal slices of the town, divided by streets linking the bastions to the hexagonal crown of the piazza: for defense reasons, the streets from the bastions do not lead directly into the piazza; this is accessed via the intermediate set of streets, which lead out to the city gates. A. Fara (1989: 111) has noted that in the original project by Giulio Savorgnano the city gates were set alongside the bastions (as attested by a map of 1602 by Niccolò Sagreda) and then shifted to the center of the curtains for obvious municipal reasons. The civic splendor of the town seems have benefited from the contribution of Scamozzi (Benevolo 1973: 584). It has also been noted how Palmanova provides a compromise between the military theories of Lorini and those of Savorgnano: eight of the ten bastions include two platforms for artillery placements (as indicated by Lorini), whereas only one has the single placement (Savorgnano) (Fara 1989: 111). Others sustain that, for this reason, Palmanova's fortifications are based on Lorini's ideas, as attested by the radial streets running to the piazza; this solution had already been used for Philippeville, and was also envisaged in the military treatise of Giovan Tommaso Scala (who, in 1598, published an interpolated text by Bellucci), and that of Daniel Speckle (cf. Fara 1989: 109-110, figs. 100-101). The town plan implemented at Palmanova, the acme of the Renaissance ideal of the circular or star-shaped town with a radial street network was highly successful, and there are great many other schemes derived from it, some in drawings (cf. Giorgio Vasari the Younger's drawing in the Biblioteca Nazionale Centrale in Florence, reproduced in Fara 1989, fig. 102), some in engravings (e.g., Cassi Ramelli 1964, fig. 190), and some in European projects of the seventeenth and eighteenth centuries (for the history of Palmanova, see recent catalog on the exhibition held in Palmanova and Passariano, ed. G. Pavan 1993).

The drawing in question, which belonged to the collection begun by Emmanuel Philibert of Savoy, before passing to the Archivio di Stato in Turin, shows the global image of the town, and is probably a copy of one of Lorini's earlier schemes, as is suggested by comparing it with one of the illustrations accompanying his treatise on fortifications (cf. Fara 1989, fig. 101).   *P.C.M.*

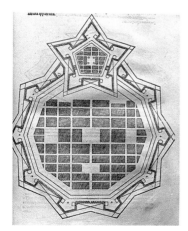

186
PIETRO CATANEO
Scheme for the Nine-Sided City with Pentagonal Citadel
from *I Quattro Primi Libri di Pietro Cataneo senese*
Venice, 1567; first ed. Venice 1554.

London, The British Architectural Library Drawings Collection, Royal Institute of British Architects, BK1, fol. 22r.

187
ANONYMOUS (17 th. century)
Map of Palmanova

Turin, Archivio di Stato, Architettura militare, vol. V, c. 43r.
Pen and sepia ink, with yellow, light brown, green and pale

a design showing five banners, one of which bears three croziers on a blue ground, namely, the emblem of the Admiral of the "Regno Galcerano Requens": on the foredeck one can also make out a round golden shield with a red band bearing three silver crescents—the Strozzi coat of arms—together with an oval shield with the red cross on a silver ground, representing the Florentine people. No less than four galleys have the Strozzi emblem, confirming the Florentine bank's support for Ferrante's campaign. Spinazzola made a minute study of all the heraldic designs

trocento there were few specialized artists who could claim such skills; fewer still are the extant coeval paintings or engravings showing an entire town that can rival the Tavola Strozzi for quality or size. In my attempt to unravel the intricacies of the painting, I tried to show (De Seta 1988, and 1990) that the realism acknowledged by most scholars for the left half of the panel apply also to the right half; I also tried to explain how the panel was put together. My conclusion was that the author is the Florentine artist Francesco Rosselli (1447/48-1513?), son of Lorenzo and younger brother of the more famous Cosimo, who painted an important large panorama of Florence in ca. 1472, of which a surviving fragment is conserved by the Società Colombaria in Florence. Francesco is also responsible for a *veduta* of Florence painted on panel—formerly in the Beer Collection but now in an unidentified location—from which the engraving discussed above was taken. Rosselli also engraved a panorama of Rome, again in large-format, datable to 1538, from which the tempera canvas now in the Palazzo Ducale, Mantua, was derived. Rosselli's known works show him to be in full command of all the most advanced geometrical and topographical skills of his age. After closely comparing the *vedute* of Naples, Florence, and Rome I came to the conclusion that they were executed by someone with the same skills, and that the Florentine artist Rosselli could well be the author of the Tavola Strozzi. I have also tried to show how the three *vedute* share the same method of "portraiture": using the same peculiarly topographical and perspective approach, and an underlying miniaturistic imprint that defines the main buildings in meticulous detail, while the basic urban fabric is conventionally represented as little foreshortened blocks and wedges with roofs. My attribution to Francesco Rosselli does not have the incontrovertible support of documentary evidence—indeed much of the history of painting is not backed up by "proof" as such—but nonetheless it rests on a mesh of links and cross-references, as discussed above; one such study involved a computer analysis of the systems of construction adopted for the fifteenth- and sixteenth-century *vedute* of Naples, Milan, Genoa, Florence, and Rome (M. Luca Dazio and D. Stroffolino 1993). Further and definitive proof of my attribution has come in the form of new documentary finds made by Mario del Treppo. Among the papers of the Strozzi archives in Florence the scholar came across a document (soon to be published) proving that the Tavola was part of a sumptuous gift from Filippo Strozzi to Ferrante of Aragon. The panel was painted in late 1472-early 1473, and was sent from Florence to Naples on 15 April 1473, together with other gifts for Ferrante of Aragon; the Tavola was originally a *spalliera* for a bed designed by the Florentine architect Benedetto da Maiano, who received the commission; he in turn engaged a painter in his own circles in Florence to paint a view of Naples with the Castel Nuovo, as underlined by the document: "Un lettuccio di noce di braccio 6 e chornice molto bello ritrovati dentro di prospettiva Napoli el Chastello e loro circhustanzie" ("A walnut bed 6 *braccia* long with a handsome frame depicting a panorama of Naples, castle, and environs"). Some of the letters discovered by del Treppo testify that the *veduta* was much appreciated in its day for the apt use of perspective, and for its topographical accuracy in portraying the city. The date of 1472-early 1473 is the same as that of Francesco Rosselli's engraving; furthermore, these documents explain why the foredecks of four of the galleys display a round shield bearing a red band adorned with three silver crescents: the Strozzi family emblem; this was Filippo's sign of recognition to the Aragon dynasty, to whom he was sending the magnificent panorama of Ferrante's victorious fleet. The steep fee of 110 *fiorini larghi* paid to Benedetto da Maiano for the panel is a token of the high esteem in which the painter himself was held. The document's date excludes, therefore, any attribution to Francesco Pagano (Bologna 1987, and 1989), who was not in Naples (or Italy, for that matter), but in Valencia; likewise there is no longer any argument to support the recently revived hypothesis (Navarro 1990) that the painting is a triumphal allegory of the Aragon dynasty. The Tavola Strozzi was restored on the occasion of the exhibition "All'ombra del Vesuvio," and the analysis of the restoration published in detail in one of the catalog entries (Navarro 1990).

188

Francesco Rosselli (attrib.)
The Fleet of Ferrante I in the Bay of Naples after the Battle of Ischia in July 1465

Naples, Museo e Gallerie Nazionali di Capodimonte (formerly in the Museo Nazionale di S. Martino)
Tempera on wood.
82 × 245 cm

The first and most fascinating "portrait" of the city of Naples executed during the modern era is the so-called Tavola Strozzi. A panel of unusually large dimensions, the Tavola offers an accurate topographical panorama of the city's development by mid-fifteenth century, from Castel dell'Ovo to the campanile of S. Pietro ad Aram. In the course of pioneering inventory research, Corrado Ricci came across the panel in the Florentine palace of Filippo Strozzi in 1901. The panel is one of the very finest surviving panoramic *vedute* painted during the Renaissance; in the foreground it shows the arrival of the Aragonese fleet after Ferrante's victorious battle off the coast of Ischia on 6 July 1465; the battle was part of the war waged by the pretender to the throne John of Anjou (backed by several of the kingdom's fiercest feudal barons), after the death of the Aragonese sovereign Alfonso the Magnanimous in 1458. The Italian historian Benedetto Croce made a first study of the panel in March 1904, and a second fifteen years later in 1919. The reasons for his interest in the panel stem from its outstanding pictorial qualities and its legacy of historical detail on the city's history. In 1904 Croce advanced a preliminary interpretation of the scene, suggesting that it depicted the naval pageant in honor of the state visit of Lorenzo de' Medici in 1479, but noted the links between the Aragonnese crown and Filippo Strozzi, who had "long traded with success in the Kingdom of Naples." After its purchase by the State in 1908, the panel entered the collection of the Museo di S. Martino. The then director of the museum, Vittorio Spinazzola, correctly identified the event represented in 1910, and composed an in-depth (and as yet unsurpassed) analysis of the painting's contents, and a study of its state of conservation. The questions that arose upon the discovery of the Tavola Strozzi can be summarized as follows: What is the event depicted? Who commissioned the work? When was it executed? Who is its author (or authors)? How accurate is the topography of the representation? The only point upon which the experts are almost unanimously agreed is the event represented. All the victorious galleys in the foreground bear the emblem of Ferrante, with the red Aragonese band, the yellow band for Hungary, the golden lily of the Kingdom of Naples, and the Cross of Jerusalem. The captive galleys carry the emblem of John of Anjou, i.e., the gold lily in a blue ground framed by the red band of Hungary and the facing dolphins, and Cross of Jerusalem. The emblem of King Ferrante appears on all the victorious galleys, while on the prow of the last in the line is

of the panel, and concluded that the episode could only represent the naval victory of Ferrante; furthermore, he asserted the topographical accuracy of the representation, and pointed out the presence of execution skills typical of manuscript illumination. The date of execution, the patron commissioning the work, the author, and the veracity of the details continue to be the subject of debate, even today. The somewhat scant bibliography on the Tavola shows that after Riccardo Filangieri's interventions of 1934 and 1938 there is a long silence of several decades, interrupted by Mario Salmi (1963), who attributed the panel to an artist in the Florentine milieu; this artist was more likely a manuscript illuminator than an artist. This observation had also been made by Spinazzola and Filangieri in much greater depth. The Tavola returned to the limelight in 1969 when it became the primary iconographical source for a study of transformations to Naples under the Aragonese (De Seta 1969). Since then the bibliography has grown considerably. Raffaello Causa returned to the theme in 1973, underlining the panel's great "documentary fidelity," together with its outstanding pictorial quality, particularly as regards the left half; he advanced an attribution to Colantonio, and dated it to "around 1480." He was therefore responsible for separating the date of execution from the event represented. Causa's suggestion was refuted by Roberto Pane (1975), who favored a previous attribution by the scholar Mario Salmi (1963) to an artist in the Florentine milieu. Ferdinando Bologna (1977) suggested that it was commissioned by Duke Alfonso of Calabria between 1486 and 1487, the celebrate recent victories over the newly insurgent feudal barons, and donated to Filippo Strozzi, who had shown great fealty and constancy toward the Aragonese crown. The date of execution is determined by a visual clue, namely, the absence of the lantern on the wharf, built in 1487. The scholar Bologna concluded by attributing the work to the Neapolitan painter Francesco Pagano, endorsing his argument on the basis of stylistic analogies with known works executed by Pagano upon his return from Valencia. This suggestion was followed up by Fausta Navarro in a long analytical catalog entry for the exhibition "All'ombra del Vesuvio" (1990). However, earlier (De Seta 1987) and subsequently in a contribution to the same exhibition catalog, with a different diagnosis the present author rejected the possibility that a painter of Pagano's limitations could have managed to create a panel of the Tavola Strozzi's dimensions and topographical precision, whose application of perspective is remarkably consistent. The same doubts apply to Causa's attribution to Colantonio. To paint a *veduta* or townscape of the size of the Tavola Strozzi requires considerable firsthand knowledge of the town in question, together with proficiency in topographical and architectural surveying, and expertise in the use of perspective—not only the basics, but as a manifold tool for the correct representation of the city in all its complexity. In the second half of the Quat-

Cesare da Seta

Urban Planning in Rome under the Medici Popes
Hubertus Günther

"To create harmony in Rome, it would be necessary to raze the entire city to the ground and build it up anew," was the sentence passed in the Holy Year 1350 by the cardinal legate, Guido, upon the heart of Christianity abandoned by its sovereigns. When the papal court returned from its exile in Avignon, Rome was reduced to such a state of decay that, in the words of Martin V's chronicler, it hardly seemed a city at all. Of the ancient center of more than one million inhabitants, perhaps ten thousand remained. The Aurelian wall enclosed what was primarily a scarcely populated and perilous campagna. The ancient ruins of huge buildings were scattered throughout it—mausoleums, baths, forums and so forth, which had become wonderful palaces and dragons' castles in the imaginative old accounts of travels and *mirabilia*—and now served as the haunts of bandits and barons' strongholds.

The population clustered around a bend in the Tiber. The Forum, Campidoglio and Via Lata, the old thoroughfare of antiquity (now Via del Corso) lay outside the inhabited area; cows and goats grazed there.

The layout of the inhabited area was rather amorphous. Rome had neither the public spirit of a free citizens' government (to which other Italian communes owe their beauty today) nor the creative purpose of a strong autocratic power which had elevated Naples, in Boccaccio's opinion, to the status of "one of the most delightful cities in Italy." The medieval settlement lay within the ancient boundaries of the Campus Martius and lived off the old patrimony of buildings. What was not fit for habitation usually served as building material for new constructions. There was no real center to the city: the seat of administration was sited in the far-away Campidoglio, and the popes lived in the even further off Lateran residence, then on the other side of the Tiber. The Ponte Sant'Angelo (or Pons Aelius, the only surviving ancient Roman bridge) linked the inhabited part of the city to the Vatican. The settled part gradually spread toward the Vatican as if the people were drawn magnetically to the Curia. All the main thoroughfares converged at the bridge. The Canale di Ponte was a junction of Via Pellegrinorum which passed though the Campo dei Fiori and on to the Campidoglio, Via Papalis, the ceremonial route to the Lateran palace, and the ancient Via Recta (today called Via dei Coronari because of the devotional paraphernalia offered to pilgrims reaching the Vatican from the Porta del Popolo). During the Renaissance, Rome grew into one of the greatest and richest cities in the western world. The rapid prosperity was accompanied by intense urban development. The Curia and its various ramifications, clerical, administrative and private institutions, Roman citizens as well as the many foreigners attracted by the Catholic Church, all took part in the refurbishment of the city. Doubtless, the most troublesome problems were the ones faced at the outset, and then, perhaps, the conviction that stability was a necessary premise for prosperity, led to a certain continuity in the urban development.

In the fifteenth century, the focus was primarily on giving the appearance of a city back to Rome. This meant first of all renovation: repairing the city walls, reinforcing the banks of the Tiber, overhauling the water supply, clearing the streets and drawing up the appropriate laws. Sixtus IV carried out all these tasks with immense efficiency. Furthermore, he had many new buildings erected and proposed yet others. With the construction of the enormous Ospedale di S. Spirito, he made his own contribution to the social welfare of the population and of the pilgrims

who represented a substantial factor in the city's economy. With the transfer of the main market to the then desolate Piazza Navona, he also gave an additional stimulus to the economic structure of the inhabited area. *Minus est condere quam colere*, proclaims one of the inscriptions that were set up in commemoration of Sixtus IV's activity.

In addition to the pure and simple measures of recovery and for the restoration of the Vatican (Borgo Leonino), the popes did their utmost to complete the construction of roads that ran along the shores of the Tiber. This had a threefold effect: improvement of the road network with little damage to the existing buildings, reinforcement of the embankments of the river which flooded the city regularly and which Vasari claimed was still very dangerous, and lastly, the opening up of new areas for development. Sixtus IV launched the task of banking the river by broadening Via Tor di Nona, which ran from the Ponte Sant'Angelo to the northern shore of the inhabited area. He must have also renovated Via Ripetta for the first time. He built a new bridge linking the southern end of the inhabited area with Trastevere (the Ponte Sisto). In 1489, Innocent VIII had the road "that leads to the Popolo" paved, that is the road that stretched from the northern fringes of the inhabited area to the Porta del Popolo. Julius II undertook the task in great style: he built Via Giulia, leading from the Ponte Sisto to the western shore of the Tiber as far as the bend in the river, and, parallel to it, on the opposite shore, Via della Lungara (which had already been begun by Alexander VI). He completed and enlarged the square that opened up in front of the Ponte Sant'Angelo, continued the work on Via Tor di Nona up to the port of Ripetta which lay on the northern edge of the inhabited area (1509-13). He also improved the road leading to the Borgo Leonino shore of the Ponte Sant'Angelo from the Ospedale di S. Spirito.

All this activity marked just the start of the far-reaching

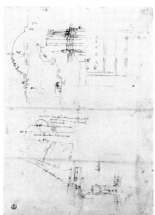

Uff. 915r.

plans that Julius II developed for the renovation of Rome. Bramante drew up a complex project for governing the Tiber. According to Andrea Fulvio's account, in those years the population began to settle around the port of Ripetta. A new accent was given the square in front of the Ponte Sant'Angelo by the construction of the church of SS. Celso e Giuliano. The Via Giulia was to become the new main thoroughfare. Here, Julius II started to construct an enormous administrative building, the Palazzo dei Tribunali. According to Francesco Albertini, the northern end of Via Giulia was to end up passing over the Tiber; in fact, it ended right in front of the remains of the ancient Pons Neronianus, known as the Ponte Rotto, and there was a plan to rebuild this bridge—identified during the Renaissance as the passage of the ancient Via Triumphalis. Egidio da Viterbo reports that in addition to Via della Lungara, a road was to be built through Trastevere connecting the churches of the two apostolic princes. None of this was completed.

In 1513, Lorenzo de' Medici's second son, Giovanni, ascended the papal throne as Leo X. Hopes were raised that a Medici style patronage would develop in Rome, and

the new pope was only too willing to fulfill them immediately. Like most of the Renaissance popes, during his first years in office, Leo X dedicated himself to continuing the urban projects of his predecessors. He therefore promoted the development of Via Giulia and Via della Longara quarters. He improved the conditions of the Borgo streets and shaped the square in front of the Ponte Sant'Angelo. In 1513-16 he completed the road that led from the port of Ripetta along the shores of the Tiber to the north, in the direction of the Porta del Popolo. In 1517 Leo X turned to his own urban projects. Until then, various restoration and building projects had been undertaken at the same time in an increasing number of places. "Raffaele fà il Bramante" was the comment on the behavior of the new head of the papal building works, whose predecessor had become famous for his impetuous temperament. Leo X had great projects in mind. His youth—unusual for a pope—made him feel sure he had plenty of time to realize them. But just a few years later, they were interrupted by the premature death of Raphael (1520) and his own decease (1521). Adrian VI's papacy paralyzed the Romans from the start. Urban development stagnated. But it only lasted a year. Then in 1523 another member of the Medici family was elected pope: Giulio, Leo X's cousin, raised to the purple soon after the latter's rise to power. Giulio took the name Clement VII, and he harbored ambitions of continuing Leo X's style of patronage. But it was time to economize: Leo X had left a mountain of debts.

The continuity between the two Medici popes became immediately evident. Clement VII declared it openly immediately after his election with the raising of the massive false front looking like a city gate, lying on an axis with the Ponte Sant'Angelo. Sometimes Clement VII acted as if his papacy and Leo X's formed a single Medici papacy, that he had taken over exactly where Leo X had stopped (1521). But he did not limit himself to carrying out the works of Leo X. Instead of doing what his predecessors, and even the impetuous Julius II had done, that is, curbing new plans for urban development for a few years, immediately after his election, Clement introduced new and far-reaching decisions and elaborated projects which were the most ambitious ones ever attempted in urban planning in Rome. The project is partly documented, and partly known through historical circumstances. The highly complex projects which must have preceded such radical transformations as those introduced by Clement VII could not have been elaborated in just the few months that separated them from Clement's election, and therefore must have been under preparation already during Leo X's reign. The great expense of these new undertakings was also in the style of Leo X and moreover, contrasted with the judicious economic policy of the second Medici pope who was known for his frugality.

Once again the projects were only partially completed. The Sack of Rome (1527) put a sudden end to the greater part of Clement's projects only four years after they had been started, which was normally the period of time when a pope carried on the urban projects of his predecessor. Paul III and Julius III carried through some of the projects of the Medici popes, but some of them were inserted in new more extensive plans.

The town planning projects under the Medici popes were part and parcel of an overall scheme. The urban projects developed in the brief period of about eight years between 1517 and 1527, some of which were carried out and others further elaborated later on, stand out both for their farsightedness with regard to the ethnographic and economic development of Rome and for their marked originality. They stimulated the development of the city and are a high point of its Renaissance culture. In particular, three magnificent projects were prepared.

The Urbanization of the Northern Part of the Campus Martius

Of all the gates in Rome, the Porta del Popolo was the one with most traffic. Before Leo X's project, the only road in the northern area of the Campus Martius that led to the Porta del Popolo was Via Lata (now Via del Corso) and there was no square before the city gate. In ancient Rome, Via Lata was one of the principal roads in the center of Rome as it still is today, but during the Middle Ages the populated part of the city had shrunk so much that Via Lata remained on the outskirts. During the Renaissance, Via Ripetta became the chief road connecting the Porta del Popolo with the inhabited part of the city. This road did not start then, as now, directly from the square in front of the city gate, but deviated from Via Lata diagonally south toward the Tiber. It then split into Via Tor di Nona, which ran along the river toward the Ponte Sant'Angelo, and into Via della Scrofa that led straight into the Piazza Navona quarter. The route of Via Ripetta and Via della Scrofa had already been traced in the ancient Roman city, but, by the time of the Renaissance, the road to the north had been cut off by private vineyards, and to the south, buildings reduced the breadth and stood in the way of Via della Scrofa.

The whole area had once been the site of a poplar wood (*nemus populeum*) which was the reason for its being called "del Popolo." At the start of the sixteenth century the area was scarcely populated. The Ripetta, an important commercial dock ever since antiquity, lay on the southern edges, near the road through the inhabited part. A kind of industrial area had grown up in the neighborhood, which included lime kilns, timber yards, a rubbish heap and humble dwellings. Turkish refugees from Illyria and prostitutes lived there. In 1515, Leo X built a hospital in

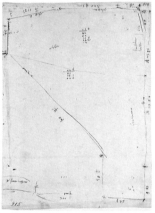

Uff. 915v.

this area for sufferers of syphilis: S. Giacomo degli Incurabili. Leo X began to renovate the two ends of Via Tor di Nona in about 1513-14. In 1517 he finished building the medieval part of Via Ripetta between the Tiber and Via Lata. The same year, however, he changed his mind. He decided to revive the ancient route and terminate the building of a straight and independent road from the center to the Porta del Popolo. A new long and narrow square was to be introduced at the junction of Via Lata and Via Ripetta and end at the city gate. Work began on the project in 1518. The following year Leo X announced he wanted to widen, flatten and pave Via Lata as Via Ripetta, as it had been in antiquity. For a considerable time the project risked failure due to complicated intrigues. The pope was forced to intervene with several motu proprio (Günther 1985b, 284) and he also discussed the matter with Raphael and Antonio da Sangallo, the architects in charge. Due to these machinations, the reconstruction of Via Ripetta and the Piazza del Popolo lasted right through the reign of Leo X. From 1524, Clement VII continued the work in Via Ripetta, had Via della Scrofa opened up, and straightened Via Lata. Meanwhile Via Tor di Nona was extended toward the Pincian Hill (giving birth to what was later to become Via Condotti). In the Holy Year of 1525, Clement VII ordered an inscription to commemorate his and Leo X's reconstruction: "*Flaminiam intra urbem trifariam divisam*" and he named these off-shoots Leonina and Clementina. The text refers to the division into Via Ripetta (Via Leonina) and Via

Lata (Via Clementina). He does not mention anywhere that the project included a third road. During the Renaissance the term *trivium* was used, as in antiquity, to mean a crossroads or public square. In 1524 the *bivium* before the Porta del Popolo was even marked as two trivium with the explanation that "the two *trivii* are the two roads called Via Leonina and Via Lata." Antonio da Sangallo also only indicates these two roads in his project for the fortification of Rome (Uff. 301A). When Paul III built Via del Babuino he established the trivium that today leaves the Piazza del Popolo. Giuseppe Valadier designed the present-day centrally planned square.

The urbanization of the "del Popolo" area was not limited to the reconstruction of the thoroughfares and the large square in front of the city gates: it included the establishment of new quarters. Leo X had side streets built, most of them at right-angles to Via Ripetta, to connect the Tiber with Via Lata. The Via Ripetta therefore became the main road, unlike the ancient road network in this area where the right-angled side streets had turned off Via Lata. On the basis of detailed documentary evidence, it is possible to trace the property developments and renting of the new quarter toward the city gate. The tenants paid the road taxes necessary to finance the building of Via Ripetta, and they had to build *ad decorem dicti soli*. Before carrying out this task the lots had to be separated from the road by means of one story high walls. The lot at the beginning of the bivium had to be suitably walled on each of the three sides toward Piazza del Popolo and the two roads that led to it. The corner of Via Leonina was to have a travertine facing paid for by the Camera Apostolica as a backing for Leo X's coat of arms (Günther 1985b, 251).

The lots were generally quite small, and designed consequently to be purchased by the lower classes. Foreigners attracted by the growth of Rome came and settled here— in particular, according to Andrea Fulvio, Slovenians, Lombards and Illyrians. Antonio da Sangallo has left two projects for the building of the new part of Via Tor di Nona (Uff. 996A, 997A). In the project drawn on Uff. 997A he planned to demolish houses and build a palace for Baldassarre Turini, the administrator of the affairs of Alfonsina Orsini, Leo X's sister-in-law. From 1518 on ward, Aldobrando Orsini, Archbishop of Nicosia, and Ferdinando Balami, the pope's doctor, had splendid palaces built either by Antonio da Sangallo (Uff. 1004A) or by Gianfrancesco da Sangallo (Frommel 1986e) at the new junction of Via Tor di Nona and Via Ripetta.

Leo wanted to contribute personally in various ways to the architectural organization of the new urban layout. At the same time that the new road was established, a project was drawn up for the enlarging of the Ospedale di S. Giacomo in Augusta (Benvenuto, Di Coccio) involving a new complex comparable in size to the Ospedale di S. Spirito, extending from Via Ripetta to Via Lata. Unlike the usual side-streets and lots, this project had to be aligned not only with Via Ripetta but with the central axis between the two main roads of the *bivium*. A remarkably imposing central space was to be created on the central axis, flanked on both sides by large courtyards which were to extend as far as the two main roads of the *bivium* (Uff. 870A). The hospital complex would have had three facades, on the two main roads and a third road connecting them. The main facade was on the secondary road looking south on to the quarter. In the center there would be an impressive vestibule and little chapels were planned on both sides. A special square would stand in front of the building. In the end only two wards were renovated and the chapel on Via Ripetta was built (1525). How much Leo X invested in the project for enlarging the Ospedale di S. Giacomo in Augusta can be seen in a *motu proprio* in which he defended the construction of his *bivium* between the Piazza del Popolo against the above-mentioned intrigue and made an appeal about the esthetic aspects of the hospital (Günther 1985b 284 doc. III 1).

Antiquity was to contribute to the architectural organization of the urban planning in the "del Popolo" quarter.

There was a large building at the junction of Via Ripetta and Via Lata which in the sixteenth century was believed to be an ancient mausoleum (as later confirmed by modern archaeologists). The original facing was missing, but it was in a good condition. It was so impressive that it even appeared in the sketchy maps of Rome made in the fifteenth century, and in the records of the building of Via Ripetta it was often used as a landmark. In the sixteenth century it was described as a tall, square tower or as "a piece of wall with a turret on top" ("un pezzo de muro con una torretta in capo"). The drawings made of it in the maps of Rome show a cubic base with a small construction on top. Its exact position was established in Bufalini's map of Rome and by an archaeological survey in the nineteenth century. Leo X insisted that this monument was not to be demolished or left to ruin. The aforementioned intrigue was all over this. The famous complaint made by Raphael over the demolition of ancient ruins, in his *Memorandum* to Leo concerning the reconstruction of ancient Rome (Günther 1985b, 253), was evidently a reference to this. Since the mausoleum was not to be touched, Leo had to be satisfied with siting his coat of arms on the corner of Via Ripetta instead of placing it, in a suitable architectural setting, in the center of the *bivium* as in the project where Via Borgo S. Angelo forks out of Via Alessandrina—designed by Raphael in conjunction with the building of Jacopo da Brescia's palace. According to the description made in 1544 by G. B. Marliano, the mausoleum was placed as the focal point inside Piazza del Popolo for those entering the city gate. Its methodical inclusion in the plan for a modern city, in spite of the signs of decadence, was certainly a new departure of fundamental importance for Roman urban planning. It proved the increasingly closer connection with antiquity, culminating in the contemporary project for the systematic survey of the ruins for Leo X's map of ancient Rome. There was little that could be done with Augustus' mausoleum which was in the same area and sited inside the Orsini property and used by them as a base. Leo X could nevertheless assert his right by statute law to confiscate archaeological discoveries. He had one of the obelisks at the entrance to the mausoleum excavated and carried to the port of Ripetta, with the intention of placing it in Piazza S. Pietro. At that time the whole process of urbanizing the "del popolo" area was repeatedly inserted in the context of reviving antiquity. In 1521, Caius Silvanus Germanicus boasted that what Robert Guiscard and his Norman armies had destroyed, could now be seen again in the churches, houses, squares and roads built under Leo X (Oratio 1736: 161). Andrea Fulvio, in 1527, noted that the sides of the streets and blocks had been set perfectly straight by using a string as a guide in the ancient manner.

The Renovation of the Florentine Community in front of the Ponte Sant'Angelo

Of all the foreign communities that had settled in Rome, the Florentines were those who obviously benefited most from their fellow townsmen's careers in the Curia during the Renaissance. When the popes returned from Avignon the Florentine population grew rapidly. Their community had its own customs, feasts and holidays and played a significant role in Roman public activities. Its prominent members were clergymen, merchants and artists, and Florentine bankers looked after the papal finances. Under the Medici popes the community became even more influential. A large number of them, members of the Medici family and members of banking families, were raised to the purple. Foreign bankers were excluded from dealings with the Curia whose continual need of money brought Leo X to be increasingly dependent on his Florentine creditors. In 1515 he recognized the Florentine nation as an independent corporation and allowed them their own jurisdiction. Again in 1519, he confirmed and increased their privileges.

The close relations of the Florentine community with the Curia led them to settle in the area nearest the Vatican.

They nearly all lived in the Rione Ponte quarter, preferably close to the Ponte Sant'Angelo. At the start of the century, the area between the Canale di Ponte and Via Giulia (Banchi) was inhabited mostly by Florentine immigrants who attended their parish church, S. Orsola. Later on, in 1484, they rented an oratory near the Tiber. The Florentines celebrated their national holiday dedicated to their patron saint, St. John the Baptist, in the square in front of the Ponte Sant'Angelo. Of the ca. thirty banks that worked for the Curia, in 1525, no less than eighteen of them had their seats in this area. This was where bankers such as Agostino Chigi and the Fugger family settled. The Canale di Ponte grew into the banking center of Rome. It was known as the *forum nummulariorum banchii* or Via dei Banchi. Julius II set up the papal mint at the junction of the Canale di Ponte with Via Papalis and Via Pellegrinorum.

When Via Giulia was built the Florentines' oratory was demolished and Bramante suggested they built a splendid church in its place, in the style of S. Pietro in Montorio. Later on the Florentines insisted on building their own national church, as the other foreign countries had done in Rome, but they were not prepared to raise the funds for it. Only when Leo X took the idea in hand (1518) did the project start to take shape. Leo X wanted his people to have a new church which—leaving aside St. Peter's—would have been the largest and most impressive church project as well as the most expensive and avant-garde ever built during his reign in Rome. Being down-to-earth merchants of a conservative nature, the Florentines eventually built a normal basilica. On 31 October 1519, the Archbishop of Florence, Cardinal Giulio de' Medici (later Clement VII) laid the foundation stone and consecrated the new building to St. John.

The first thing to do before building the church was to find an appropriate site for it. As early as 1508, and then in 1513, the Florentines set up special committees to choose the site. It was not an easy task because the area where the Florentines lived was one of the mostly densely populated in the city. The choice fell on the outskirts of the Banchi on the shores of the Tiber which had become practicable after the building of Via Giulia. Julius II had also had the Palazzo dei Tribunali built there. Everything would have been much more easier if the Florentines had decided to build their national church next to the Palazzo dei Tribunali since there was much more space in the area. On the basis of what is known of the history of the cultivated area on the shores of the Tiber behind Via Giulia, the Florentines' careful surveys did not reject this proposal which was apparently taken into consideration. The Palazzo dei Tribunali, however, was quite a distance from the old Florentine quarter, and they obviously wanted their national church inside it. They were therefore in favor of an area near the end of their quarter where Via Giulia reached the shores of the Tiber. This area, between the Tiber and the new thoroughfare, was very narrow so the Florentines were obliged to lay massive foundations in the river bed. The equally enormous costs of this operation delayed the completion of the church. The Florentines' readiness to accept such a severe drawback can be deduced perhaps more easily from their insistence on the position of their national church, than from any written document.

How much the Florentines were keen on the church being inside the urban context can also be seen in the various phases of the history of its construction. At the beginning of 1521, during the reign of Leo X, when the earthworks for the foundations had just been started, Simone Mosca and his assistants prepared facade reliefs for decorating the base; three years later, the works on the facade had made good progress.

The position of the church harmonized splendidly with the urban context but it was not sited exactly inside the Florentine quarter. A road leading from Via Pellegrinorum (Via del Consolato) terminated exactly in front of the center of the facade. The *magistri viarum* introduced a plan to demolish the buildings in the way of this street so that it would have been possible to see the central portal of S. Giovanni dei Fiorentini from Via Pellegrinorum and vice versa. Perspective axes linked to important buildings, such as the above, had often been inserted in the townscape before the Renaissance (Günther 1989c). St. Peter's was another clear example, related to Nicholas V's project for the Borgo and Via Alessandrina. The Via del Consolato extended diagonally in front of the church and not at right angles to it which would have been the optimum viewpoint. The *magistri viarum* transformed this drawback into an advantage for the urban layout: they designed a *bivium* in front of the main portal of S. Giovan-

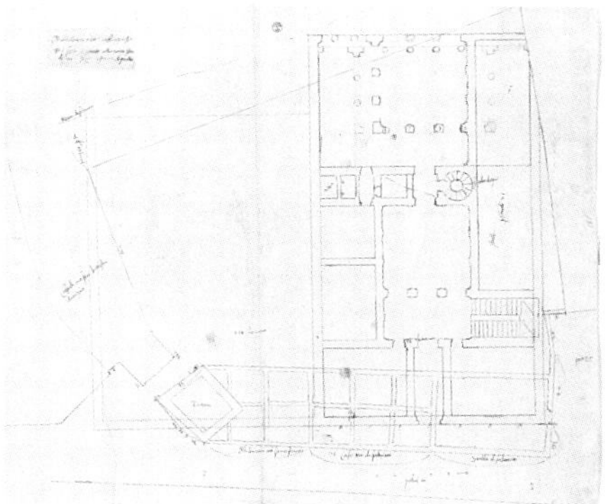

Uff. 997A

ni dei Fiorentini, which must have been based on the idea of the *bivium* in front of the Porta del Popolo. This second road would have cost the most exorbitant sum ever heard of in Rome at that time because it would have cut across the densely populated Banchi area. The new road was to lie at the same angle to the facade as Via del Consolato, and lead into the Piazza di Ponte Sant'Angelo, the square in front of the bridge. The new perspective axis therefore would have extended from the start of the Ponte Sant'Angelo to the main entrance of S. Giovanni dei Fiorentini, making the church the first building to be seen by anyone arriving from the papal palaces. In addition, Via Giulia which had previously come to a dead end on the shores of the Tiber now became a convenient thoroughfare to the Ponte Sant'Angelo. The unusual *bivium* would have been lop-sided in the sense that the new road between the Ponte Sant'Angelo and S. Giovanni dei Fiorentini was much more important and much longer than Via del Consolato. The urban project had already been prepared, so work on the symmetrical *bivium* was carried out, and the new layout of the area took on an even more striking appearance. Via del Consolato ended after only a few meters in Via Pellegrinorum. For this reason the project planned to cut the corner off the junction where the Canale di Ponte separated Via Papalis and Via Pellegrinorum which involved demolishing the pointed front of the building housing the Mint from the time of Julius II, that is, making it straight as far as Via del Consolato. The new false front of the Mint on the *bivium* was given a stone facing with a costly architectural design. This facade looked on to the Canale di Ponte that ended in front of it. It was, however, in such a position as to be visible from the main entrance to S. Giovanni dei Fiorentini along Via del Consolato. Vice versa, the center of the facade of S. Giovanni dei Fiorentini could be seen from the center of the facade of the Mint. The false front was slightly concave, like a mirror capturing the scene.

The facades of S. Giovanni dei Fiorentini and of the new front at the junction of the Canale del the Ponte with Via Papalis and Via Pellegrinorum were to mark the presence of the Florentine community and the activity of the Medici family in Rome. Four of the six, large, excellent marble reliefs (1.21 × 1.17 m) that Mosca (one of the best sculptors in Rome at the time) designed for the church facade include the Medici coat of arms, the lozenge of balls, and two have the symbol of Florence, the fleur-de-lis. The facade of the Mint served as a background for three coats of arms: a large papal one with the Medici balls between the other two, including one of a cardinal Medici. All the coats of arms have been lost and nothing is known of the third one. Under the coats of arms there were two inscriptions with the names of Leo X, Giulio de' Medici and Clement VII.

The appropriate *magister* of the Camera Apostolica, Niccolò Finucci, elaborated a plan for the realization of the splendid project (Uff. 1013r.). He designed the final plans for the new connection between the main portal of S. Giovanni dei Fiorentini and the Ponte Sant'Angelo (with details of the dimensions). At the end of the same year, and during the following one, the Camera Apostolica raised the taxes on the roads, rearranged the corner where the Canale di Ponte divided Via Papalis from Via Pellegrinorum, and demolished the houses in the way in Via del Consolato. Not only the Caporione was present during the certification of the second register of taxes but also the Consul of the Florentine nation as well as a Florentine banker and "many other Florentine gentlemen." It seems therefore that the project was presented only to the Florentine community. With the finances deriving from road taxes, which was an astonishing exception for the Roman administration at the time, the new facade was raised in front of the fork. The Sack of Rome, however, put a stop to the rest of the project. In 1542-43, Paul III built the road between the Ponte Sant'Angelo and S. Giovanni dei Fiorentini (Via Paola) even though it was now part of another urban plan, and introduced a trivium in front of the Ponte Sant'Angelo like the one in front of the Porta del Popolo. In 1550, Julius III—the first Tuscan to ascend the *catedra petri* since the Medici—was briefly involved by the Florentines in their national church. Even though a new project had been presented in the meantime, before the work had been finished, Julius took on the prosecution of the building. Lastly, Julius had the 1524 plan to demolish the dwellings in Via del Consolato carried out in 1555. The breach caused by Corso Vittorio Emanuele in 1888, destroyed the old layout of the Banchi and destroyed the connection between the three parts of the *trivium* designed under the Medici popes. In the seventeenth century, the fine wall facing was removed from its urban setting while work continued on the articulation of the side facades.

As usual the *trivium* project was designed by the best architect in the service of the pope. Its date however is not certain. It was either elaborated as early as Leo X's reign, and therefore Raphael was the author, or under Clement VII, making Antonio da Sangallo responsible. The fact that it was only carried out in 1524 does not contribute to the solution of the problem. It could date back to the projects regarding Leo X's first urban planning, or the project for Via Paola and the demolition work in Via del Consolato. Everything points to a date previous to the *trivium* plan: right from the start the site of S. Giovanni dei Fiorentini was linked to its urban context. The grandeur of the project, typical of that period in Rome, presupposes a lengthy elaboration. The style used is clearly Raphael's. The similarity between the false front at the junction of Via Papalis and Via Pellegrinorum and the building, certainly designed by Raphael, sited where Via Borgo Sant'Angelo leaves Via Alessandrina, had already struck Maerten van Heemskerck. On the other hand, it is difficult to understand how Antonio da Sangallo had so distinguished himself as to be named the architect of the project which is certainly considered the most original of all Roman urban planning during the Renaissance.

Lastly, the coats of arms and inscriptions that Clement VII had raised on the facade in front of the *bivium* of Via Papalis and Via Pellegrinorum indicate the role played by his predecessor. As regards dating the project before his papacy, Clement VII indicated his predecessor as nothing but the inspiration behind the *bivium* in front of the Porta del Popolo, which was built in fact for the most part before his papacy. But he decided to give the coats of arms and inscriptions an earlier date than his own papacy and considered himself as a cardinal. The first inscription calls him with the name of his family Giulio de' Medici: Iul. Medices Leon X patruelis. The papal coat of arms refers to Leo X and is therefore characterized by a lion's head. The cardinal's coat of arms, with the Medici balls, refers quite definitely to Cardinal Giulio de' Medici. A second inscription, underneath the first, renders homage to Clement VII for all the goodly acts of his reign. The contradictions between the inscriptions, the coats of arms and their dates of origin pose a riddle given that the aforementioned *trivium* project did not exist. The doubts can only be removed when they are considered as referring not just to the wall front but to the entire renovation of the quarter near the Ponte Sant'Angelo, which included the building of S. Giovanni dei Fiorentini, whose foundation stone was laid by Giulio de' Medici.

The Medicean Buildings

Numerous projects of buildings elaborated under the Medici popes contributed the growth of the city. Among the churches, the French national church, S. Luigi dei Francesi, was built in 1518 with the patronage of the pope in the little square at the end of Via della Scrofa, the extension of Via Ripetta (Frommel 1987). Of the cardinals' residences, the most important one to be built was the enormous palace of Alessandro Farnese, a congenial friend of Leo X, completed shortly after the latter's coronation. This lent a distinctive quality to the area between the southern end of Via Giulia and the Campo de' Fiori, the oldest market in the center of Rome, and the Camera Apostolica subsidized its development (Spezzaferro 1980-81). The popes of the Medici family proposed two building projects which influenced the urban planning in Rome. Members of the Medici family took part in these projects and appeared together with the popes as the patrons, while the Camera Apostolica provided the finances. This ambiguous situation, regarding the buildings and the papal financing of them, reached a point under Paul III Farnese when the Camera Apostolica claimed the ownership of all the Medici properties in Rome. After the marriage of Duke Alessandro Medici's widow, Madama Margaret of Austria, to Ottavio Farnese, the Farnese family stopped laying claims to them.

The Piazza Navona area developed as the elegant residential quarter after Sixtus IV set up the principal market in the square. The national churches of all the foreign communities were sited in the neighborhood. It was the quarter preferred by clergy and cardinals, and under the Medici popes, included two nephews of Leo X, Innocenzo Cibo and Niccolò Ridolfi. Under Adrian VI, the powerful datary and later cardinal, Willem van Enkevoirt elaborated a project for a palace with the assistance of Antonio da Sangallo (Günther 1985 (1), 254). When the Medici were exiled from Florence, they settled in Piazza dei Lombardi, one block away from Piazza Navona. In 1503 Giovanni de' Medici rented a palace which Sinulfo di Castell'Ottieri had built at the time of Sixtus IV (Fumagalli 1991), and he lived there until he was elected pope, with his brother Giuliano, Alfonsina Orsini the widow of Piero the "unfortunate" and her son Lorenzo considered the heir to the Medici dynasty, and his cousin Giulio. In 1505, Giovanni bought the palace for Lorenzo and Giuliano. In 1512, the Medici enlarged their property and although Alfonsina Orsini built her own palace nearby in 1514 (which later became known as the Palazzo Lante—see Marcucci, Torresi), the one in Piazza dei Lombardi remained the largest seat of the Medici in Rome. The square was already known as Piazza de' Medici under Clement VII, later on it took the name of Madama Margaret of Parma. The Medici palace was used for public functions as well as a residence after 1508. In that year, Giovanni transferred his famous ancestors' library from Florence to Rome and opened it to the public like Cosimo il Vecchio had done in the past. This gesture acquired a certain significance because it stimulated Leo X to bring new life to the Roman university next to the Medici palace.

Three months after Leo X was elected, Giuliano da Sangallo—the oldest of the architects working for the Medici family—presented a project for an immense papal palace (Uff. 7949A, see Miarelli Mariani 1983). The irregular faced buildings belonging to the Medici were to be substituted by one square palace with a square courtyard. At the back (toward the extension of Via della Scrofa) there was to be a garden surrounded by loggias, while the wing looking toward Piazza Navona was to be lower than the others and include the reception halls. What was so extraordinary about this project was that the houses between the Medici palace and Piazza Navona were to be demolished to create an outer court surrounded by porticoes which would have linked the palace to the square. Piazza Navona would have become the square in front of the new Palazzo Medici. Giuliano also drew the new urban layout that would have been created by the construction of the new palace. Piazza Navona would have maintained its regular shape: the north and south ends would have terminated with a hemicycle. Like his nephew Antonio was to do later on, Giuliano illustrated in his drawing how an immense palace of the Medici family would have been built and connected to Domitian's ancient stadium, creating a situation similar to both the ancient imperial palace on the Palatine with the Circus Maximus in front, and the imperial palace in Constantinople, which also had a circus in front of it (Uff. 900A).

After Lorenzo de' Medici was appointed *capitano* of the Florentine community in 1516 he bought an area next to the Medici palace which had by that time become his exclusive property. The bill of sale provides the key to the intentions of the project. It refers to Sixtus IV's bull on

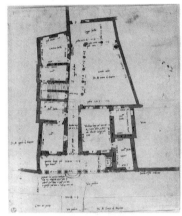

Uff. 368A

the embellishment of the city, approved that year and applied under Leo X as well: dwellings could be expropriated if necessary for the construction of new buildings that improved the look of the city (Günther 1985b, 245). Antonio da Sangallo elaborated the final stages of the project and still called the building a papal palace. At the same time he studied how to transform the whole area if the court in front of the palace was to be built connecting it with Piazza Navona (Uff. 1259A). This project was never carried out.

In 1518, Leo X and Giulio de' Medici began to build a large villa on the outer slopes of the Monte Mario, to the north of the Vatican (Frommel 1984b: 31ff.). Like the Medici palace near Piazza Navona, the Medici family as a whole took part in the capacity of the owners. The villa was called a papal villa (like in Sangallo's drawings for the palace) even though the Medici's appeared as the owners. Leo X, as pope, purchased the area for the villa and the building, designed by the papal architects, was paid for by the Camera Apostolica. The design and building site were in the hands of the papal architects, Raphael and Antonio da Sangallo.

Like the Medici palace near Piazza Navona, the Villa Madama had a specific public function. Given its pleasant position, it was suitable for receiving important guests who, until then, had always slept outside Rome before making their ceremonious entries. These visitors would sometimes have been the guests of the Medici palace near Piazza Navona after their official entry. A real Vitruvian theater was designed for the villa. It was therefore destined to become a seat of literary inspiration, open to a wide circle.

The villa was sited near the local thoroughfares and its principal axis was the Ponte Milvio (Milvian Bridge). Raphael has described the project. He was also responsible for elaborating the position of the villa with respect to the existing road network and the extension of the same so that the villa became an important junction. Three roads were to meet there: the provincial road leaving the Monte Mario for Viterbo; the ancient Via Triumphalis which at the time was the highway diverted in front of the villa which led from the Vatican, or more precisely, from Porta S. Pietro through the Prati (meadows) to the north and was one of the most important arterial roads in Rome; and lastly, a road from the Villa Madama to the Ponte Milvio which was to be newly traced to create a suitably impressive link between Via Flaminia and Via Triumphalis. Raphael explained in detail that he planned creating two main roads for the villa: the first would have met a road coming from the Vatican; the second would have been a straight route from the Ponte Milvio. This would have given the impression that the Ponte Milvio was built for the Villa Madama. In the same way, it can be added that the projects for the new roads through the Banchi made it seem as if the Ponte Sant'Angelo was built for S. Giovanni dei Fiorentini.

The start of the roads from the Villa Madama are evident in Antonio da Sangallo's project for the villa (Uff. 314A). Both were to meet exactly at right angles to the villa and were to be 50 *palmi* wide (ca. 11 meters). Via Ripetta was also 50 *palmi* wide whereas the road from S. Giovanni dei Fiorentini to the Ponte Sant'Angelo was to be 40 *palmi* wide. The road from Viterbo to Rome, crossing Monte Mario, was to reach the villa behind theater, then it would descend two ramps and pass behind the *cavea* and meet the other road in the circular courtyard in the middle of the villa.

Both roads were in fact built as Raphael had designed them. The one leading to the Vatican was ready before the villa was actually built. Here too, Clement VII continued the work started by his predecessor. He carried on building the Villa Madama and, in 1525—26, had the road leveled that led from "Porta S. Pietro through the Prati to the Ponte Milvio." Niccolò Finucci elaborated the project together with that for the building of the *trivium* in the Banchi (Uff. 1013v.). While the road was being built through the Prati, Clement VII had Via Flaminia leveled between the Ponte Milvio and the Porta del Popolo (1525). Immediately after his election, Leo X restored several rights to the Roman city government to commemorate the office of the ancient senate (Butzek 1978). As a result, the city fathers planned to place a statue of the new pope in the Campidoglio on the first anniversary of his election, a novelty for the Renaissance. Somewhat later however they erected the honorary statue on the Parilia holiday, the anniversary of the founding of Rome, in 1521, the last year of Leo's reign. On this occasion, Caius Silvanus Germanicus wrote a panegyric, which was published much later in 1524 at the same time as a panegyric celebrating the election of the new pope, Clement VII. As well as giving greater power to the *sacratus senatus*, Caius praised what the city had gained through Leo X. It was three times richer. Like Romulus he had refounded the city, like Camillus he had given it stability. What had first been built in brick, like Augustus, he had embellished with marble (Orazio 1735: 161). In particular, he had made Rome more beautiful with a multitude of great and splendid buildings, temples and houses. He had restored Rome by widening alleys into streets, and straightening the tortuous streets leading to the squares, creating new beauty out of decayed spots and sad ruins ("*calles iubet esse vias, sinuosa viarum diriget in plateas, inculti quicquid in urbe, longaevi pepetere situs, tristesque ruinae, in priscam revocat faciem, priscumque nitorem induit, ut veteris tandem nihil ambiat aevi...*" Oratio 1735: 176). He had refounded the city when he made it possible for a new quarter to be built, in particular, the area round the Porta del Popolo. City, population, economy and prosperity had all been increased during the golden age of his papacy. Caius, naturally, drew heavily on the stock of panegyrics usually addressed to popes. But the most important point he made is certainly worth noting: he listed the improvements made by Leo X. A few of his eulogies recall the panegyric written for the energetic Rovere popes. The confirmation of Sixtus IV's laws on urban planning, or the project for a hospital as large as the Ospedale di S. Spirito, show that Leo X acted for the public good as well. In the Holy Year of 1525, Clement VII let his own town planning achievements be celebrated by Andrea Fulvio in a version directly reminiscent of Sixtus IV's panegyric: "*Roma decus rerum culpa neglecta priorum, angustis arcata viis et sordida coeno, nunc spatio laxata, nitens et pervia facta est. Praestringes passim cui plurima porticus olim impediebat iter, fluxusque afronte domorum his quoque sublatis ad amussim tenditur omnis orbita et antiquae iam redditur undique normae.*"

It had been a long time since a pope acted principally for the public good, which had been the main characteristic of the activity of Sixtus IV, but under Leo X, according to Caius, it was now a love of antiquity. This was demonstrated by a praiseworthy project, a survey map of ancient Rome (Günther 1988f: 318-327) and by other useful achievements mentioned by Caius, in particular, the urbanization of the Campus Martius. Moreover, Leo X was also committed to saving the ancient ruins: he actually carried out some restorations and undertook the embellishment of the city (such as the siting of certain finds in front of the Pantheon and the great mausoleum at the fork of the *bivium* in front of the Porta del Popolo).

In connection with the plan for the *bivium* in front of the Porta del Popolo, Leo X himself illustrated the ambitions of his town planning activity: he desired for the prosperous age, which bore his name, a state of such beauty, amplitude and mature judgment due the majesty of the city, that it could be said with pride, this was done by Leo X ("*volentes, quod n.ris temporibus sub felicitate n.ri nominis fiunt ea demum statu, eo decore, ea amplitudine et urbis nostre maiestatis maturo consilio fieri, ut merito sub Leone facta rite dicantur*"). In brief, his greatest concern was self-representation. How much this mattered to the Medici popes can be seen in the splendid project for the Palazzo Medici in Piazza Navona, or the oversize Medici coats of arms which they had placed everywhere more than any pope before them: on the facade of S. Giovanni dei Fiorentini and at the *bivium* of Canale di Ponte with Via Papalis and Via Pellegrinorum; where Borgo Sant'Angelo left Via Alessandrina, and on the facade of their palace in Piazza dei Lombardi. Even the new facade of S. Luigi dei Francesi was to bear the Medici coat of arms (Lesellier 1931: 243). Only the Medici coat of arms at the end of Via Ripetta—or Leonina—coming into Piazza del Popolo was perhaps slightly smaller than the others. Equally pompous were the hymns to the town planning of the Medici popes. Not only was Leo X's reign considered as a "golden age" but that of Clement VII as well, as the great inscription at the *bivium* of Canale di Ponte asserted.

The project for the redevelopment of the area around the Ponte Sant'Angelo involving the construction of S. Giovanni dei Fiorentini illustrates quite clearly the significant role played moreover by this kind of exhibition of the Florentine presence in Rome. Leo X declared publicly his ties with the Florentine community, taking part in their holidays to commemorate their national saints. In 1518, he was a spectator from the Castel Sant'Angelo; in 1519, he performed a papal Mass on the site of S. Giovanni dei Fiorentini (Rufini 1957: 94). Besides this, he demonstrated his ties with his homeland in Florence itself. In or after 1513, he commissioned the project for a Medici palace in Borgo Pinti and the development of the area (Elam 1978); and in 1515-16, he promoted the competition for the facade of S. Lorenzo, the church of the Medici family. Leo X also emphasized the links between Florence and Rome, by having his nephews, Lorenzo and Giuliano, the heirs to the Medici dynasty, declared honorary citizens of Rome. At the same time, many humanists, in particular Egidio and Annio da Viterbo, celebrated the ancient origins of Florence (Cipriani 1980). By playing on the myths of the Etruscans, it

appeared as if it was the Tuscans who laid the foundations of the Roman empire. The architects who worked for the Medici popes also contributed to cultivating this myth. The debate over the Tuscan order which arose in Sangallo's circle at the beginning of Leo X's reign (Günther 1985b), led to the conclusion that the Etruscans had developed the Doric order with all its characteristics as Vitruvius had described them. This would demonstrate the primacy of the Italians over the Greeks, and that of Tuscany over Rome. Only in the eighteenth century, when the same debate arose quite independently for the second time (Morolli 1985), was the question considered from the merely historical point of view.

This essay is also based on Günther 1984c and Günther 1985b. References for town planning under the Medici popes which have not been taken into consideration?: Frommel 1988; Guidoni 1990; Günther 1984b, Günther 1989c; Sanfilippo 1993; Stinger 1990; Tafuri 1984c, 1992; Valtieri 1984b.

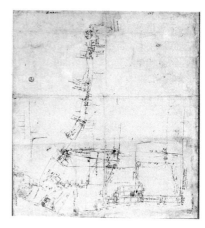

189
Niccolò Finucci
Place before the Ponte Sant'Angelo, or Better, in Prati

Florence, Galleria degli Uffizi, Gabinetto Disegni e Stampe, Uff. 1013A
Pen and ink, on paper.
Measurements in Roman *palmi, canne, staioli,* for surveyors and architects, with autograph detailed indications and notes.
435 x 500 mm

BIBLIOGRAPHY: Ferri 1885: 204; Giovannoni 1959: 54 (Uff. 1012A); Frommel 1961: 3; Günther 1984b; 1985b.

The handwritten notes and measurements added to the sheet, which refers to the situation before Aristotile da Sangallo's work, provide a conclusive analysis (Günther 1985). Finucci worked as a *submagister* for popes Leo X and Clement VII, that is, he carried out practical work associated with town planning surveys. The sketchy drawings with measurements were preparatory to the urban projects for the configurative, juridical and financial plan. On the basis of its association with a road tax, Finucci's drawing can be dated 1524 (Günther 1984).

On the recto the sketch shows the Ponte Sant'Angelo with its old octagonal chapels in front that were destroyed during the Sack of Rome, and the detailed measurements along the Canale di Ponte, as it was once called, which proceeded from the bridge. The notes serve most of all for orientation purposes and give an idea of the social structure of the neighborhood. To the east of the Canale di Ponte at the end of Via dei Coronari, in front of the now demolished church of SS. Celso e Giuliano started by Bramante, there is the noble palace with workshops (built more or less at the same time) belonging to "ms Julio Alberini." To the west, in the square in front of the bridge, there is the house of "Bonadies" built by Sixtus IV, the confluence of the old road (now demolished) that then extended ("Via dinto a banci") in a large curve across the neighboring quarter and into the Banchi, and the archway known as the Arco della Fontanella which until 1528 was the entrance to the legendary bank of "Agosti[no] Chisi"; a second bank, "banco de' Gadi," which Jacopo Sansovino had rebuilt to a splendid design ca. 1520, and lastly, the enormous residence of "Pandolfo dela Casa" (now demolished) another Florentine banker. The Mint, the "zecha vecia," had its seat at the point where the Canale di Ponte branched off into "Via di monte Giordano" (Via Papalis) and "Via da Campo de [Fiore]" (Via Pellegrinorum), in the heart of the banking district. The junction (largely demolished) where the carefully measured Via del Consolato (called after the old consulate of the Florentine nation) met "Via da Campo de Fiore" dominated the whole quarter. This led to S. Giovanni dei Fiorentini, the Florentine national church. Next to it, there is the large palace, "tore di Bernardo Bini," belonging to Bini, a Florentine banker, and beyond this, the house of "m.o Lorenzo de Vila," a tailor from Lucca (both demolished). The Via del Consolato ended in the narrow and winding "Via da Campo de Fiore," typical of medieval roads in

Rome, between the Oratory dedicated to "S.a M.a de la Prie" and the clearly marked outside staircase of the house of Pandolfo della Casa (now demolished). The newly built neighboring Via Giulia ("Via G[i]ulia") spilled into an open space (still existing). Here the buildings were scattered and the price of lots relatively cheap. The houses indicated as "case di G[i]ul[i]ano del Tocio," were probably the busy stonemasons' thriving workshops laboring for the St. Peter's building site. To the north, Via del Consolato met the "porta di s.a Orsola" which led into a small square in the middle of the Banchi (demolished).

The notes, moreover, allude to the plan for which these sketchy measurements were taken.

Here the Mint is called the "zecha vecia" (old Mint) even though under Julius II it had been rebuilt and in contemporary documents was usually referred to as the "zecca nuova" (new Mint). A total of 12 1/2 *palmi* (indicated on the drawing) were to be cut off the corner of the Mint until it lay in line with Via del Consolato to the south. This was carried out in about 1525—26. At the same time, Pandolfo della Casa's outside staircase was demolished because it obstructed Via del Consolato. On 8 December 1524 the road taxes were levied "per la ruina della ponta della zecca nova et della scala di Pandolfo della Casa."

The facade of S. Giovanni dei Fiorentini is carefully drawn in front of the junction of Via del Consolato and Via Giulia. A separate sketch shows the urban setting and the articulation of the facade of the church now under construction: "p[almi] 4 dela porta dela chiesa de Fiorenti[ni] sino al p[ri]mo pilastro." The main portal can be distinguished lying on the axis of Via del Consolato.

There is an evident connection between the organization of the construction at both ends of Via del Consolato. This endorsed the position given to the new facade of the Mint. It looked first of all down the Canale di Ponte, but it was sited in such a way as to be visible down Via del Consolato. The new facade of the Mint could be seen from of the main portal of S. Giovanni dei Fiorentini and vice versa.

The drawing also illustrates an even more costly project. A large street was to be built through the densely built-up Banchi quarter without any respect for the old layout, starting from the square in front of the Ponte Sant'Angelo, and ending in front of the facade of S. Giovanni dei Fiorentini ("va la strada de la chiesa de Fiorentini a le cap[pel]le de ponte s.o A[n]gelo"). The Sack of Rome prevented Clement VII from fulfilling this plan, which was in fact carried out only in 1542-43, with the demolition of about thirty houses. But since then, the main portal of S. Giovanni dei Fiorentini could be seen from the ramp of the Ponte Sant'Angelo, and vice versa.

Town planning measures of a size of those planned here require a considerable period of gestation. This was also the case during the Renaissance in Rome. The popes, such as the energetic Julius II, always began to carry out their own large-scale urban planning projects only several years after their election. They usually first carried out the projects started by their predecessors. Since Clement VII had reigned for only a year when the road tax "per la ruina della ponta della zecca nova et della scala di Pandolfo della Casa" was levied, it is clear that here he was continuing something that had been decided under his predecessor, Leo X. The two buildings involved in this project confirm this hypothesis: unlike the majority of Roman churches, the position of S. Giovanni dei Fiorentini was not preestablished according to tradition, but on the contrary, was decided entirely during the reign of Leo X. Such an imposing building as the Florentine national church had an influence on its surroundings. Large churches and palaces needed a square in front of them or at least a road that led directly up to them. Here the idea of the square was abandoned. The facade was in line with Via Giulia. The middle of the facade lying exactly on the axis of Via del Consolato indicated that instead the approach to the church was to be put in order. Only the two streets that had been planned reflected the monumental character of the building designed for S. Giovanni dei Fiorentini. Moreover, unlike a square, they would have had

the advantage of giving Via Giulia (that ended on the shores of the Tiber) a destination utilizing the larger of the two roads, namely, the Ponte Sant'Angelo. Such an idea, the opening up of the road from S. Giovanni dei Fiorentini to the Ponte Sant'Angelo, whose realization entailed enormous costs, corresponded more with the unscrupulous extravagance of Leo X than with the notorious stinginess of Clement VII. The two inscriptions placed on the facade of the Mint, appeared to be inexplicable before the project for redeveloping the whole the Ponte Sant'Angelo area was known. One of them praised Clement VII for having built the facade, the other refered to Giulio de' Medici as a relation of Leo X Medici, which all suggests that the redevelopment started under Leo X with the building of S. Giovanni dei Fiorentini. Giulio de' Medici laid the foundation stone because he was Archbishop of Florence. This connection must have been easily recognizable: three Medici coats of arms on the facade of the Mint must have corresponded to four Medici coats of arms and two Florentine fleurs-de-lis on the facade of S. Giovanni dei Fiorentini.   *H.G.*

A History of the Construction of S. Giovanni dei Fiorentini
Hubertus Günther

Since 1484 the Florentines had possessed an oratory in a chapel situated near the Tiber. In 1508, when Via Giulia was built, their oratory was demolished and they decided to build a church for their community, just as the Spanish, Germans and French had already done in Rome. An organizing committee was set up and its first meeting raised nearly 1,000 ducats. The dimensions of the new church were to be similar to those of S. Pietro in Montorio. Four months later Bramante submitted a model of the new building, which would have an estimated cost of over 8,900 ducats.

In 1510 the Florentines built a new church, dedicated to their patron saint and the Virgin, in the area at the end of Via del Consolato where the old oratory was located. But instead of the building proposed by Bramante, once again they settled for a chapel.

The election of Leo X spurred the Florentines to new activity. Five months later a new committee was set up with the purpose of planning the building of the church for their community. The Florentine Giuliano da Sangallo, who had come to Rome to be at the service of the new pope, prepared projects in this period for a centrally planned building (*Cod. Barberini*: 74r., 59v.; Bentivoglio 1975. Although this was intended for the planning stage in 1508, the date of ca. 1513 may be inferred from the association with the *Cod. Barberini*. Günther 1988: 166ff.). Perhaps these projects were intended for the church of the Florentines. Although once more nothing came of them, the hope that a new church would soon be built was still alive. The bull of 1515, in which Leo X recognized the Florentine community as an independent corporation (see the chapter on town planning), referred to the project for the new building.

One of the various works which Leo X patronized was the project for the church for Florentine community. The pope was directly concerned with this: it was on his orders that on 24 September 1518 the Florentines took the solemn decision to build a sumptuous church, which would be an adequate reflection of the prominence of the Florentine community in the life of Rome and "its magnificence, size, expense, ornament and design would surpass those of all the other nations" (Vasari).

First of all the fundamental problem of finding a suitable site for the new building had to be solved. This had also been the task of the previous building committee (Günther 1984c: note 321a), but it was now more difficult due to the increase in the population of the area and the need for a larger church. In 1518 Antonio Strozzi informed his brother Lorenzo in Florence that a site had been found for the new church (Nava 1935-36: 105). The site chosen had the advantage of being close to the area in which the majority of the Florentines lived and allowed the church to be integrated with the pre-existing buildings. However, the land here, which sloped toward the Tiber, was unstable; thus, as a first step it was necessary to build solid foundations. According to Vasari these cost 12,000 ducats, which was a much higher figure than Bramante's estimate for the whole project. For this reason it seems that Antonio da Sangallo proposed another site for the church (cat. no. 193).

On 4 January 1519 Leo X ordered the construction of the building, granting indulgences and privileges and decreeing that this would be the church for all the Florentines living in Rome. The pope then invited various architects to put forward proposals for the new building. Vasari reports that Raphael, who was *capomaestro* of St. Peter's, his assistant Antonio da Sangallo, Baldassarre Peruzzi and Jacopo Sansovino all submitted their own models (cat. nos. 190-192; 195-199; 202-203). Moreover, it is quite possible that other architects also participated, for example Andrea Sansovino, the *capomaestro* of the shrine of the Santa Casa at Loreto (see cat. no. 204).

The various projects submitted to this competition give the impression that Leo X had laid down that the building had to have a central plan with a maximum surface area of 220 × 220 *palmi*. In fact, the dimensions were the result of the size of the building site, as is shown by a projection on a city map before the strengthening of the banks of the Tiber (Günther 1985b: pl. 9). Given the instability of the ground, it was thought preferable to build a centrally planned church rather than a basilica. Thus, although there was a practical reason for the construction of a building with the ideal layout of the Renaissance, there were drawbacks: it was not the usual form for a parish church and there was less space available for the congregation than in a basilica of the same area.

Although he was the youngest and least famous of those participating, the winner of the competition was Jacopo Sansovino. He made some alterations to the original layout based on the Greek-cross plan surmounted by a dome that Bramante had introduced to Rome with his project for St. Peter's and the parish church of SS. Celso e Giuliano, which was situated near S. Giovanni dei Fiorentini. But it was not only because of its evident advantages that Sansovino's project was chosen. Like his father Lorenzo il Magnifico, whom he wished to emulate as a patron of the arts, Leo X sought to participate personally in the realization of his projects. Apparently he had daily discussions with Raphael regarding the progress of the work on St. Peter's. Unlike Julius II he did not delegate the organization of the work to well-known architects, but rather he allowed them to compete with each other, encouraging new blood (Günther 1988f: 56).

On 31 October 1519 Cardinal Giulio de' Medici, the Archbishop of Florence, laid the foundation stone of the new church. However, the story of its construction recounted here appears to be confused, obscure and complex: right from the start it seemed that different forces were working against each other. Indeed, on many other important building sites where different forces came into play there were similar contrasts with equally complicated consequences. This was already familiar when the great Gothic cathedrals were being built in medieval France and Germany (Schiller 1989; Wolff Metternich 1990) and subsequently also in Italy (Milan Cathedral, S. Petronio in Bologna, S. Annunziata in Florence). In the Italian Renaissance the merchant classes were often conservative, while the princes took a more progressive line (see Günther 1988c). It appears that the same applies to S. Giovanni dei Fiorentini, even though the controversies were carefully concealed in this case.

A year after the foundation stone had been laid, the Florentines asked for the remuneration which had been agreed in the previous February, that is shortly after work had begun, to be put in writing (Nava 1936: 350ff.). As might be expected, it appears that the *capomaestro* Jacopo Sansovino received a salary; what is surprising is that as early as St. John's day (24 June) he ceased to be paid. On the other hand, it seems that Antonio da Sangallo worked on the site right from the beginning and it was decided that he should continue to work there. According to Vasari, at the time it was thought that Sansovino was too young to build foundations and that consequently Antonio would have to intervene. Three months later Sansovino left the site with the payment for his model, his salary and all his works. Now he was even accused of deceit (Nava 1936: 349ff. The document is dated "7. Jan. 1520"; this would be 1521 with the Gregorian calendar). On 30 January 1521 the commissioners of the Florentine community in plenary session appointed Antonio architect of the church. On this occasion it was revealed that Antonio had already submitted a new model for the church (Nava 1936: 350). Three months later the stonemasons who were to decorate the facade designed by Antonio had already been paid.

The bills seem to indicate that the building was never constructed in accordance with Sansovino's model, even though this was the one the pope had chosen. At most, during the first six months or first year the foundations forming part of this project were laid. Antonio's model, the one which was in fact adopted, had nothing in common with either that of Sansovino and those of all the other participants in the competition or the projects that he himself had previously carried out. Now Antonio had designed a basilica having the traditional layout: a central nave flanked by two aisles with transepts and a long choir (see cat. no. 206). The dimensions of the project (approx. 270 × 160 *palmi*) did not take into consideration the particular characteristics of the land near the Tiber.

Under the direction of Antonio the nave was completed up to the level of the clerestory and the decoration of the lower part of the facade was started, while the crossing, transept and choir had yet to be constructed. In fact, Antonio only managed to begin the building of the foundations for these Rome, Archivio Sacchetti; this was the most expensive and difficult part of the undertaking because the foundations had to be massive and rest on the bed of the Tiber. At a certain point, exactly when we do not know, perhaps after the death of the second Medici pope, Clement VII, work was interrupted and the unfinished building was temporarily roofed.

When yet another Tuscan pope, Julius III, was elected in 1550 the Florentines attempted to resume work on their church (see cat. no. 71). They managed to arouse the interest of the pope in their project. If Vignola's project which K. Schwager published did in fact regard the church of S. Giovanni dei Fiorentini (cat. no. 208), then it must be assumed that Julius III commissioned a model; the commissioners of the Florentine community had certainly not done so because there is no mention of this in their archives. Once again it was evident that the pope wanted a centrally planned building; when Julius III was informed that the building to be completed was a basilica he abandoned the project (see cat. no. 71).

In 1559 once again a member of the Medici family, Pius IV, was elected pope and once again the Florentines attempted to complete their church (see cat. no. 71). After the negative experience under Julius III, they had to decide first of all whether to continue the project that Antonio da Sangallo had already begun or whether to start afresh. Agreement was finally reached on the basis of a compromise: it was resolved to construct a new building on the old foundations. Because they wanted the church to be particularly magnificent, the Florentines decided to commission Michelangelo to build it, while they asked the Duke of Florence to finance the project, hoping this would encourage the great artist to accept. Cosimo was agreeable on condition that he would have the last word on the layout of the new church. Thus, while the requirements of the Florentines were to be given due consideration, Cosimo was only prepared to loosen the purse-strings after he had seen the final model. Thus it was more straightforward to take the duke's requirements into account beforehand, which at that time also meant complying with Michelangelo's wishes.

Michelangelo submitted a number of centrally planned projects (cat. nos. 70-71). The one that was approved (cat. no. 71) was, in reality, a new version of the project with which Jacopo Sansovino had won the competition for S. Giovanni dei Fiorentini forty years previously, both as regards the general layout and the dimensions. It was, therefore, evident that in this project, just as in the one for St. Peter's, Michelangelo was not prepared to continue what the abhorred "Sangallo sect" had already built, so that he preferred to start from scratch.

The duke ordered his fellow-countrymen to carry out Michelangelo's project without any modifications and, in fact, the Florentines treated the project with the respect that was due to the divine genius of its creator. They had a costly model of the planned building made in order to display it in their oratory. On the building site, as had already been decided, the first step was to complete the old

foundations; this work, which cost 5,000 ducats, went ahead rapidly with the duke's support and had already been completed by 1562. However, on the basis of Antonio's old project the Florentines had laid foundations measuring 270 × 160 *palmi* for the new church, which according to Michelangelo's project should have measured 220 × 220 *palmi* Rome, Archivio Sacchetti. Because the old and the new did not coincide here, either the duke had to renounce the faithful execution of Michelangelo's project or the Florentines had to abandon the basilica. Since a compromise could not be found, once again the work was suspended.

It was only in 1583, more than twenty years later, after fresh negotiations over whether the church should be completed in the form of a basilica or whether it should be centrally planned, that work was begun again with the financial backing of Ferdinando, who was now Grand Duke of Tuscany. Under the direction of first Giacomo della Porta and then Carlo Maderna the church of S. Giovanni dei Fiorentini was completed in accordance with the proposals of Antonio da Sangallo; although they had been modified to cater for contemporary requirements, the layout and the dimensions were essentially those specified by the Florentine architect (Hibbard 1971: 142-145). And it was not before 1733-34 that Alessandro Galilei built the facade. Thus, Michelangelo's model was never used and it disappeared without trace in 1720. If Vasari, who idolized Michelangelo, had not recorded Sansovino's victory in the competition for the building of S. Giovanni dei Fiorentini and his project, nothing would be known about it today.

The most important writings on the history of the construction of S. Giovanni dei Fiorentini are the following: D. Frey 1920; Nava 1935-36; Dies 1936; Siebenhüner 1956; Rufini 1957; Tafuri 1973, 1984c, 1985a, 1992: 159-188; Schwager 1975; Vicioso 1992. Further bibliographical references, especially with regard to the individual stages of the construction and specific problems are indicated in the captions of the projects for the church. For a fairly complete bibliography on S. Giovanni dei Fiorentini, see Tafuri 1973. This essay on the history of the project for the church leading up to its construction and the first stages of the construction itself is largely based on Günther 1984c and 1985b.

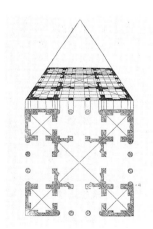

190

SEBASTIANO SERLIO
Demonstration of Perspective
(from *L'Architettura, Libro Secondo, Perspective*, Paris, 1545, fol. 35r.)

Woodcut.

Serlio presented a square plan with an octagonal space in the center, four smaller areas in the corners and between them four porticoes that open onto the exterior through three bays. The connection between this picture drawn for theoretical purposes and the project for S. Giovanni dei Fiorentini, was explained by Vasari.

In order to give an idea of Sansovino's winning project for S. Giovanni dei Fiorentini, Vasari wrote that it was similar to the picture Serlio included in his second book. It had a large tribune in the center and little ones in each of the four corners. According to Vasari, the church was 22 *canne* (220 *palmi*) long and wide. There are no further references to Sansovino's model elsewhere, and the original has been lost.

None of the other plans in Serlio's second volume meet Vasari's description. However, it must be remembered that Vasari only used Serlio's woodcut as an example of something similar to the project.

From Vasari's account of the event, the choice of such an unserviceable project as suggested by Serlio's picture, is immediately incongruous: only about a fifth of the total area is made available for the congregation. The lack of a connection between the side tribunes and the central area is unpractical. The numerous porticoes did not offer any particular advantages. The lack of functionality is all the more surprising when considering that the Florentine community in Rome was very large and enormous sums were involved just in laying the foundations. The advantage of Sansovino's model lay probably in its impressive shape, which coincided with the Florentines' desire to surpass all the other national churches in Rome.

The oldest and the most reliable document illustrating the real design given to S. Giovanni dei Fiorentini is Uff. 1013 (datable ca. 1524; see cat. no. 189). Other projects can be linked to this one. Therefore it is clear that as early as 1524 the church was built on the basis of a model different from Sansovino's. The relief coats of arms that Simone Mosca was already working on in April 1521 was apparently commissioned for the facade of this new project (Nava 1935: 352, 354; Günther 1984e: 231).

Sansovino left the building site in 1520; previously Antonio da Sangallo had worked as co-architect on the site of S. Giovanni dei Fiorentini, and during the time they worked together, Antonio elaborated his own model for the church, the one that was actually built in 1521. Sansovino did not leave the building site because of the changes introduced but because of financial irregularities. Considering that enormous foundations had to be built from the start, the church cannot have been built according to Sansovino's project as described by Vasari. Even the foundations corresponded to Antonio's model and not to Sansovino's (see cat. no. 206). The question remains as to whether Sansovino's model—even though it had won the competition—was simply an exhibition piece, like Bramante's first model for St. Peter's, which was portrayed on the foundation medal but never actually carried out (Antonio da Sangallo on Uff. 1A). Sansovino's model has been totally overlooked by some scholars; two other models for the church are usually mentioned—one by Antonio da Sangallo and the other by Michelangelo (Diomede Leoni to Grand Duke Francesco of Tuscany, 1583. Gaye III, no. 383; later this was repeated in the descriptions of Rome, e.g., Totti 1638: 245). Vasari's account gives the impression that Sansovino's model had been binding at first, i.e., the official project until the Sack of Rome; this is obviously untrue, however.

This explains why Sansovino's model is rarely mentioned in the traditional history of S. Giovanni dei Fiorentini, even though the building of the church was certainly one of the most spectacular events in Rome—second only to the construction of St. Peter's itself. Nearly a dozen copies of Bramante's projects have survived for a much less important church, SS. Celso e Giuliano. On the other hand, even Bramante's unbuilt project for St. Peter's, would have been unknown if Sangallo had not conserved the original. *H.G.*

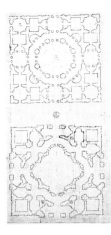

191
Variants to the Project for S. Giovanni dei Fiorentini
(after the project by Jacopo da Sansovino ?)

Florence, Galleria degli Uffizi, Gabinetto Disegni e Stampe, Uff. 502A
Pen and ink, on paper.
145 × 295 mm

The two projects on this sheet appear to be variants of the same project, given that the arrangement of their fundamental elements coincide. Both have porticoes on each side and tribunes in the corner. One is obviously fruit of the design process for St. Peter's. The other has been conceived with a central octagon.

Nava (1935-36) first noticed the connection of the second project with Jacopo da Sansovino's winning model for S. Giovanni dei Fiorentini. The layout corresponded substantially with Serlio's woodcut plan, which, according to Vasari, was very like Sansovino's model. Both comprise a large octagonal tribune at the center with niches in the sides of the corners, four corner tribunes without any links with the center one, and four entrance porticoes (cat. no. 190). The dimensions also coincide with Vasari's indications: the sides were 220 *palmi* long, assuming the measurements written correspond to *palmi* (100 for the diameter of the central tribune and 40 for the diameter of the side tribunes). Moreover, the drawing looks like the reconstruction of the plan shown here and the drawing conserved in Munich which, thanks to its inscription, can be definitely considered a reproduction of the model for S. Giovanni dei Fiorentini (cat. no. 192). The ambulatory round the octagon on Uff. 502A is not to be found in either the Munich drawing or in Serlio's woodcut. In spite of the extensive modifications that such a variant would occasion, Antonio da Sangallo, Vignola and Michelangelo all experimented the inclusion of these ambulatories in their projects. In particular, an autograph preparatory drawing by Michelangelo for his model of S. Giovanni dei Fiorentini includes an ambulatory; in the final project, the ambulatory has been removed (cat. no. 71).

There must certainly have been a space for an altar in the models by Sansovino and the one conserved in Munich. The projects on Uff. 502A and Serlio's wood cut print instead show porticoes regularly inserted on all four sides, making the plan symmetrical along two axes. The lack of an altar suggests that these plans were all theoretical exercises.

The inference that the second project on Uff. 502A was also elaborated by Jacopo Sansovino for the S. Giovanni dei Fiorentini competition, is based on the fact that the majority of the architects presented several projects for the competition. There is also a remarkable similarity between this project and Riniero Neruccio's drawing of a model which was perhaps elaborated by Andrea Sansovino for the competition in question (cat. no. 204).

H.G.

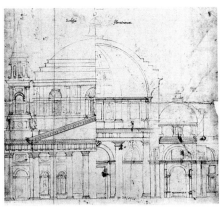

192
Competition Project for S. Giovanni dei Fiorentini
(after the project by Jacopo da Sansovino?)

Munich, Stadtmuseum, 36/1928b
Pen and ink, on paper; no indications of measurement.
350 × 365 mm
INSCRIBED: *Ecclesia florentinorum.*

This drawing was first published in 1984 by B. Schütz, who identified it as an illustration of the model which Vasari notes was presented by Raphael for S. Giovanni dei Fiorentini. At first M. Tafuri accepted this interpretation (Tafuri 1984a: 96, 217) but later (most recently in 1992) attributed the project to Raphael's school, and perhaps to Guilio Romano in particular. Nothing tangible remains of Raphael's project. The opinion that this model was the subject of the Munich drawing is based mostly on its evident imitation of the Pantheon. Raphael had in fact drawn the Pantheon several times and clearly used it as his model for the Cappell Chigi in S. Maria del Popolo. The Pantheon was considered in the Renaissance an outstanding example of ancient architecture. What distinguishes Raphael's approach to the Pantheon is his acritical acceptance of the irregularities of the building, such as the lack of alignment (Buddensieg 1971); no sign of this attitude is noticeable in the project in the Munich drawing.

Günther (1988f: 346f.) identified the model illustrated in the Munich drawing as the work of Jacopo Sansovino because it tallies with Vasari's observations that the layout of Sansovino's model was basically similar to the plan of a church which Serlio had included in his *Perspective* (cat. no. 190).

Confirmation of this depends primarily on the reconstruction of the project's plan, extrapolated from the elevation in the Munich drawing; Günther proposed that the building illustrated in the elevation had the same porticoed facades flanked by corner towers on all sides excepting the choir—like the projects for the facade of St. Peter's, which was a strong influence on the Munich project. The plan that resulted from this reconstruction is analogous to the one on Uff. 502A, which Nava linked to Sansovino's model for S. Giovanni dei Fiorentini in 1935-36 (see cat. no. 191). Günther, however (see bibliography), drew attention to a drawing of a model in the *Codex Mellon* (fol. 63v.-64r.), which seems to be a variant of the Munich project and shows only one portico, on the main facade. On the basis of this drawing Tafuri reconstructed the Munich project (Tafuri 1992, no. 60); the result indicates that the Munich project had little in common with Serlio's woodcut project, and therefore precludes connections with Sansovino.

H.G.

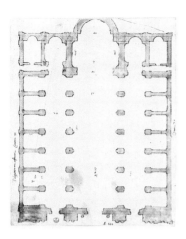

193

ANTONIO DA SANGALLO

Basilican Project for S. Giovanni dei Fiorentini

Florence, Galleria degli Uffizi, Gabinetto Disegni e Stampe,
Uff. 860A

Pen and ink, with wash, on paper.

324 × 262 mm

INSCRIBED: (left) *Dal chantone a fiume canne 30*; (right of plan)
canne 27 (Antonio da Sangallo).

The plan provides a further alternative to the projects on
Uff. 861A and Uff. 864A, which are closely linked (cat.
no. 94). Here the building was to be extended by another
two bays (like the baslican model that Antonio had submitted for the S. Giovanni dei Fiorentini competition),
and a long choir added with lateral chambers spanning the
full width of the building. As in Antonio's final project,
the hemicycle conclusions to the side chapels, present in
all his other projects for S. Giovanni dei Fiorentini, have
been eliminated. The facade would have been articulated
by half-columns, like those sketched on Uff. 864A, instead of the alternating bay system (*travata ritmica*) adopted for the basilican competition model and for the final
project. This project is a particularly important one in the
history of the design of S. Giovanni dei Fiorentini. In the
first place it gives detailed measurements of the building
(the total width is 222 *palmi*, the external length, excluding the apse, is 270 *palmi*), and secondly, it indicates the
distance of the facade from the river ("fiume") as 300
palmi to the left and 270 *palmi* to the right.
The association of this plan with the design of S. Giovanni
dei Fiorentini is based, like those on Uff. 861A and Uff.
864, on its similarity to Antonio's project for the competition, and on the fact that the dimensions are comparable
to those of Antonio's final project. The building drawn on
Uff. 860A was designed 30 *palmi* longer than the one on
Uff. 175A (ca. 240 *palmi*). However Antonio widened the
nave during the building of the church (as elaborated in
Uff. 1013A, Günther 1984). He therefore planned to
widen the crossing and, perhaps, the choir as well. As a
result, the length of the building in the final project would
have been at least 20 *palmi* greater than the project on Uff.
170A. Lastly, both on this drawing and in the one on Uff.
861A there is an irregular line running obliquely to the
axis, behind the choir, that indicates earthworks and
looks exceedingly like the line demarcating the Tiber as
shown in Antonio's projects.
The drawings on Uff. 860A, Uff. 861 and Uff. 864 are believed to derive from Antonio's model for the S. Giovanni
dei Fiorentini competition and prepared the way for the
final project drawn on Uff. 175A. It is strange, however,
that the dimensions are slightly greater than those of the
plan on Uff. 175A; even stranger is the position of the line
indicating the river shore.
The siting of S. Giovanni dei Fiorentini between Via Giulia and the Tiber posed an enormous problem for the construction of the church; this is obviously why Antonio
drew in the river's edge. There is documentary evidence
that Sansovino's project involved huge expenses for the
foundations, despite its being 50 *palmi* shorter than the

basilica designed here. Moreover, a great deal of the foundations were built in the river bed so as to create a base
for a church approximately similar in size to the projects
on Uff. 860 and Uff. 861 (see cat. no. 194). Considering
where the line marking the river is indicated in the
projects on Uff. 860A and Uff. 861, it would not have
been necessarily indispensable to build the foundations in
the river bed. It can therefore be excluded that these
projects for S. Giovanni dei Fiorentini were elaborated
for the church in its final position.
Consequently, the drawings on Uff. 860A, Uff. 861A and
Uff. 864 must have been designed for a place where the
Tiber was at a greater distance from Via Giulia, that is,
further south from its final position, and much closer to
the Palazzo dei Tribunali. This means that Antonio da
Sangallo suggested to the Florentine community that it
should build a basilica of the usual dimensions instead of
a centrally planned building, and, given that the construction of such a basilica at the end of Via del Consolato
would have required massive foundations, that it should
be sited further south. According to surviving documents,
the future site of S. Giovanni dei Fiorentini was, in fact,
extremely uncertain at the time. With the help of the
pope, it would have been possible to purchase a building
lot nearer the Palazzo dei Tribunali.
In all likelihood, the Florentines rejected Antonio's
proposal because they felt it was vital that the church was
positioned at the junction of Via del Consolato with Via
Giulia. This decision was certainly taken in the light of
the enhancement scheme being planned for the new construction's setting. The projects drawn on Uff. 860A, Uff.
861A and Uff. 864A make it clear that Antonio was
against such a connection, and therefore he could not
have been the author of the urban planning project. During the Renaissance, the authors of these urban projects
in Rome were the *capomaestri* of the St. Peter's building
site (Günther 1984c: 197ff.). If Antonio was not responsible for the urban planning, it must have been Raphael. It
is unlikely that Antonio would have tried to create obstacles to Raphael's projects while the latter was still alive.
Therefore the projects drawn on Uff. 860A, Uff. 861A
and Uff. 864A must postdate to the death of Raphael
(1520).   *H.G.*

──────────

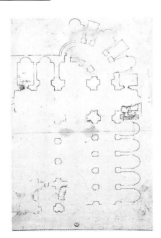

194

ANTONIO DA SANGALLO

*Alternative Basilican Projects for S. Giovanni dei
Fiorentini, Rome*

Florence, Galleria degli Uffizi, Gabinetto Disegni e Stampe,
Uff. 864A

Pen and ink, on paper.

253 × 389 mm

INSCRIBED: (Sangallo) *sachrestia*; *23 largo | 17 | 40 alto*; various
measurements.

The drawing compares two alternative projects for the
basilica. In both of them, the arrangement of the nave
goes back to the project for the basilica that Antonio da

Sangallo presented for the S. Giovanni dei Fiorentini
competition. In the righ-thand project, the nave is exactly
the same, in all its details (cat. no. 198). In both alternatives there is a large eastern section next to the nave.
In the left-hand project, to the east there is a long chapel
for the choir and four sides chapels, which serve as a
sacristy as well. This solution was developed further and
modified in the project on Uff. 861A. Another variant to
this solution on Uff. 860A indicates the dimensions. On
the basis of the variant, it is possible to ascertain that the
basilica must have been ca. 270 *palmi* long.
In the right-hand project, next to the crossing there is a
choir and ambulatory with a semicircle of long side
chapels. The fact that the project looks extraordinarily
like the plan of the basilica of S. Antonio in Padua (as
Tafuri noted in 1987a) suggests that Antonio must have
deliberately chosen to design a modern all'*antica* version
of a medieval building. Antonio drew the plan of the Paduan basilica and modified it at the same time to his own
style in order to "make fewer mistakes," as he made clear
himself on Uff. 1383A ("chosi a stare meno erato"). The
plan of S. Antonio was also a strong influence on Fra
Giocondo in his project for St. Peter's, and later on Giulio
Romano, when he was reworking Mantua Cathedral.
The elevation in Uff. 1364A belongs to the right-hand
project, or more precisely to a variant of this project (with
pilasters instead of half-columns in the choir and probably
without a crossing) as Tafuri noted (Tafuri 1992, see cat.
no. 201, 204). It is clear here that the elevation of the
basilica must also have followed Antonio's alternative
projects for S. Giovanni dei Fiorentini.
The association of the project with the design for S.
Giovanni dei Fiorentini is based on the following arguments. Its shape descends from the models for the S.
Giovanni dei Fiorentini competition. Except for the
choir with ambulatory, the general layout corresponds to
the project for S. Giovanni dei Fiorentini. The dimensions can be brought into harmony, through the plan on
Uff. 860A, with Antonio's final project for the church
(see cat. no. 205). Lastly, the Tiber is marked on both
these drawings (Uff. 860A, 861A), which are closely
linked to Uff. 864A, and likewise on Antonio's projects
for the S. Giovanni dei Fiorentini competition. The
projects on the three above mentioned sheets did not
represent a new phase in Antonio's designs; rather, they
were alternatives to be presented to the Florentine community (as indeed they were) to facilitate the members'
choice. Perhaps the project on Uff. 175A was the result
of this choice and an agreement between the Florentines
and Antonio.   *H.G.*

DIRITTO FVORI E DENTRO

DE LA PASSATA PIANTA

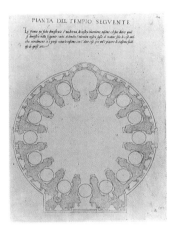

PIANTA DEL TEMPIO SEGVENTE

195
ANTONIO LABACCO
*Competition Model for S. Giovanni dei Fiorentini
(after the project by Antonio da Sangallo)*

Libro appartenente all'architettura, Rome 1552
Munich, Bayerische Staatsbibliothek
Three copperplate engravings, on plates each measuring
325 × 235 mm
INSCRIBED: (on the plan) *Discretissimi lettori, io vi havevo
apparecchiate molte e diverse cose moderne di nostra inventione,
dele quali non vi do altro che il seguente tempietto, per ci che me lo
trovo fatto, ma l'altre cose non essendo anchora condotte sule
stampe.* Later editions simply read: *La pianta qui sotto dimostrata
è moderna, di nostra inventione, insieme col suo diritto, qual si
dimostra nella seguente carta...* (see Ashby 1914-15).

The three copperplate engravings illustrate a sumptuous
rotunda with a small temple-front entrance. A crown of
sixteen mighty volutes surges up from the short lower part
of the building as if it bore the weight of the immense
hemispherical dome rising over the tall drum. The building is topped with a huge lantern of a kind similar to what

was then being designed for St. Peter's. It comprises
another cupola supported by a second crown of volutes.
On the inside the dome of the church is decorated with
coffering like the Pantheon. The whole inner space seems
to be a response to the Pantheon, the only difference being the rigid arrangement of the architectural articulation
and the slender proportions. Like Bramante's Tempietto,
the building looks like a large tabernacle (in the Uffizi,
there is, in fact, a project of a tabernacle attributed to Antonio Labacco, and elaborated from Antonio da Sangallo's model for S. Giovanni dei Fiorentini: Uff. 1796A. L.
Ragghianti 1973: 92, no. 81).
The plan, elevation of the interior and, as far as can be
seen, the elevation of the exterior correspond to Antonio
da Sangallo's model for S. Giovanni dei Fiorentini, as revealed in the drawings on Uff. 199A, 200A and 1292A (cat.
nos. 196, 197, 200; see Lotz in *Plan und Bauwerk* 1952:
15ff.). All the same, the model is different from the drawings in one respect: the pedestals of the half-columns between the arcades are much larger. The half-columns were
therefore shortened and became more squat, and hence
the order was changed from Corinthian to Ionic. That Antonio was behind this modification can be deduced from
the project on Uff. 1364A.
In spite of the inscription, it is clear that Labacco was illustrating Antonio's model for S. Giovanni dei Fiorentini. The project stood out from the other projects presented in the competition for the national church of the
Florentine community not merely for its impressive appearance, but because of its positive utilization of the
spaces, especially as regards the quota allotted the congregation, which was sizable considering the small dimensions of the building, and the numerous side chapels.
Antonio da Sangallo was already dead when the *Libro Appartenente all'Architettura* was published for the first time,
but a few of Labacco's contemporaries, including Vasari,
must have recognized the real author. In attributing the
work to himself, Labacco perhaps intended saying that he
had made the model for Antonio da Sangallo. It seems
that Labacco assisted Antonio when he was working on
the elaboration of the project for S. Giovanni dei Fiorentini, and he actually drew the final project (see cat. no.
206). After Antonio's death, Labacco made the engraving
of the model for St. Peter's. Even though this model was
built by Labacco, as Vasari writes he indicates Antonio as
the inventor and himself only as the executor: his dutifully affectionate servant, here, as in the preface to his *Libro*
(see C. Faccio 1894; Günther 1988f: 248ff., 318). This
devotion was also recalled by Vasari, who affirmed that
Labacco engraved the model of St. Peter's to show the
whole world Antonio's capabilities after Michelangelo
had elaborated new projects. In light of this it is surprising
that Antonio's part in the realization of S. Giovanni dei
Fiorentini was suppressed in the *Libro*, which was published at the same time as the engraving of Antonio's
model for St. Peter's.
There is no certainty about what kinds of original drawings Labacco published in his book. He must obviously
have included a plan which would be like the surviving
ones drawn by Antonio and Gianfrancesco (cat. nos. 196-
197). The elevation and cross-section could have been
drawings on the whole similar to Giuliano da Sangallo's
projects for the facade of S. Lorenzo in Florence. But
these projects were destined for a plane surface and not
for a three-dimensional structure. Perhaps a wooden
model belonged to the plan as in the abovementioned case
of St. Peter's. This would explain the lack of an elevation
drawn by one of the Sangallo's to complete the four plans
surviving from the Sangallo workshop for the S. Giovanni
dei Fiorentini competition. The lack of any drawing concerning the exterior can perhaps be explained by the
hypothesis that the model was based on drawings of a plan
and elevation of the interior, while the outer structure was
elaborated on the model itself.
Perhaps Antonio da Sangallo had developed a project in
such detail, as the one Labacco illustrates, only for the
model of a circular building for S. Giovanni dei Fiorentini, whereas he limited the extent of the elaboration for the

presentation of the alternative basilica. Apparently Andrea Sansovino only fully elaborated the elevation of one
single project of those reproduced by Riniero Neruccio
(see cat. no. 204).   H.G.

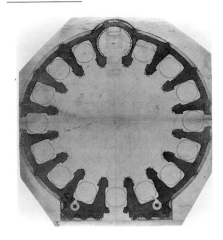

196
ANTONIO DA SANGALLO
Circular Project for S. Giovanni dei Fiorentini

Florence, Galleria degli Uffizi, Gabinetto Disegni e Stampe,
Uff. 199A
Pen and ink, on paper, wash; indications of the measurements
in Roman *palmi*.
437 × 495 mm
INSCRIBED: (Antonio da Sangallo) *largo lo netto palmi 120.*

The project shows a rotunda with a total diameter of about
200 *palmi* surrounded by dome-vaulted square side chapels.
The elevation of this plan has survived among Antonio's
studies on Uff. 1292A and thanks to Labacco's illustrations
(cat. nos. 200, 195). All the same, the drawing on Uff. 199A
reveals slight discrepancies compared to Labacco's indications. In particular, the facade is organized differently. In
the drawing on Uff. 199A there should be a regular temple
front with six columns and pilasters in the corners. The
association of this drawing with the projects for S. Giovanni
dei Fiorentini is proved definitely by the second edition
of the same on Uff. 200A (cat. no. 197) and corroborated
by the line marking the shore of the Tiber running through
the choir obliquely to the axis.   H.G.

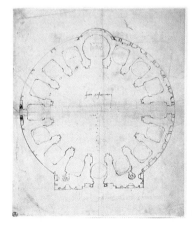

197
GIANFRANCESCO DA SANGALLO
*Circular Project for S. Giovanni dei Fiorentini
(after Antonio da Sangallo)*

Pen and ink, on paper; indications of the measurements in
Roman *palmi*.
515 × 415 mm
INSCRIBED: (Gianfrancesco Sangallo) *fatto per e Fiorentini.*

Like the basilica project drawn by Gianfrancesco on Uff. 863A (see cat. no. 199), this drawing is simply a reiteration of Antonio's competition entry for S. Giovanni dei Fiorentini, first drawn on Uff. 199A (cat. no. 196). The reproduction of both of Antonio's projects was something decidedly unusual for the Sangallo workshop and the reason for it is still unclear.

According to the notes written by a second person which illustrate in detail the costs of building the project, the plan of the basilica drawn by Antonio himself must have reached the building site of S. Giovanni dei Fiorentini and there it was connected with a text to which the inscription appears to refer. The second edition, drawn by Gianfrancesco must have remained in the Sangallo workshop and was acquired by the Uffizi together with all Antonio's drawings after his death (Günther 1988f: 244). It would appear that Antonio had a second copy made for his own archives. Normally he did not need second editions, as in the case of his final project for S. Giovanni dei Fiorentini, because as director of the building site he had the possibility of recovering the projects, as he did in St. Peter's.

Whether the plan of a rotunda drawn by Antonio himself on Uff. 199A was destined to be the project presented to his patrons is still open to doubt; it is even less accurate than Gianfrancesco's edition, which instead corresponds to Labacco's copperplate engraving of the project (cat. no. 8). There are no signs of the tabernacles in Antonio's plan, in particular on the outside of the building, which should have have flanked the windows). Both drawings seem to derive from the same matrix, which should perhaps be identified as the real model.

Moreover, Antonio's own version of the project for a rotunda (unlike the one for the basilica) differs from the one reproduced by Gianfrancesco and Labacco, both in the articulation of the facade and the choir, and in the dimensions given of the side chapels. The drawing could therefore have been made in order to establish and confirm these modifications. In other cases, however, such as the final project for S. Giovanni dei Fiorentini, no new drawings were made even when the alterations to the project were much more radical (see cat. no. 206). *H.G.*

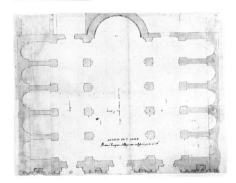

198
ANTONIO DA SANGALLO
Basilica Project for S. Giovanni dei Fiorentini

Florence, Galleria degli Uffizi, Gabinetto Disegni e Stampe, Uff. 862A

Pen and ink, on paper, wash; indications of the measurements in Roman *palmi*.

455 × 535 mm

INSCRIBED: (Antonio da Sangallo) *Longa lo tutto del vano palmi 174; Longa 147* (total length excluding the apse); *Larga p. 60;* (Vasari?) *Antonio da Sangallo;* (unknown hand) *Monta la spesa del sopradetto edificio s. 39780;* (on verso): (unknown 16th-cent.) *Antonio da Sanchallo.*

The project shows a remarkably short and wide basilica which, according to the notes, should have been 200 *palmi* long and 240 *palmi* wide. The aisles measure, according to tradition, half the width of the nave. The side chapels instead are surprisingly deep and lie along the whole length

of the aisles. The nave and aisles must have barrel vaults. There are five bays, separated by fairly small nearly square piers (8 x 9 *palmi*) with half-columns inserted on the nave side. No pedestals are indicated beneath the half-columns. Since Antonio always indicated the pedestals when he used them (such as, for example, in the alternative project drawn on Uff. 199A, cat. no. 196) it is clear that here they were not included. This, however, is hardly credible because the diameter of the half-columns is only 5 *palmi*; (as far as the elevation is concerned see cat. no. 201).

The connection between this project and the design of S. Giovanni dei Fiorentini is established by a second version of the same by Gianfrancesco da Sangallo (Uff. 863A) inscribed "per lla chiesa de' Fiorentini in Roma d'antonio da Sangallo." This is confirmed too, by the fact that the project faces the problems of the difficult site of the church between Via Giulia and the Tiber. Antonio has marked the river shore with a line that runs obliquely to the axis of the church across the top of the apse. In Gianfrancesco's version, this line is indicated as the river ("fiume"). Considering which way the river flowed, Antonio inserted additional rooms for the sacristy or suchlike only on one side of the apse. The project appears to have been presented to the 1518 competition because it has almost nothing in common with the church that was built.

The rather curious shape of the building obviously depends on its short distance from the Tiber. The project appears to be a less expensive alternative compared to the sumptuous centrally planned building designed by Antonio. An explanation sometimes given for the reduced length of the church is that the project should be interpreted as a reconstruction of an Etruscan temple in the spirit of the Renaissance, that the Florentines evidently wanted their national church to appear to be inspired by the ancient forms of art in their fatherland. It is not possible to calculate the knowledge of the mature Sangallo on the basis of the ideas of Alberti. Sangallo's ideas should be judged on the basis of the most advanced research of the period and especially in consideration of the studies of Etruscan temples left by Antonio and his brother Giovanni Battista (see Günther 1985). From this point of view, there is hardly any reason to connect the national church of the Floretine community with an Etruscan temple. Moreover, Antonio designed a Corinthian order not a Tuscan one (see cat. no. 201).

A remarkably similar basilica was later designed by Antonio, in an analogous situation, for the convent of S. Francesco near Castro, at the confluence of the Olpita River with the Filonica River (Giess 1981: 118ff.). *H.G.*

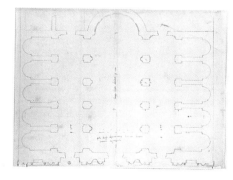

199
GIANFRANCESCO DA SANGALLO
Basilica Project for S. Giovanni dei Fiorentini
(after project by Antonio da Sangallo)

Florence, Galleria degli Uffizi, Gabinetto Disegni e Stampe, Uff. 863A

Pen and ink, on paper; indications of the measurements in Roman *palmi*.

43.5 × 55 mm

INSCRIBED: (Gianfrancesco) *lungo lo tutto el vano p[almi] 174;*

fiume (along the line that crosses the end of the choir obliquely to the axis of the church); *per lla chiesa dei Fiorentini in Roma di mano d'antonio da Sangallo;* (on verso, profile and decoration) *fregio di girarsi nella facciata di iulio albarini in banchi* (G. F. da Sangallo).

This drawing, like the one drawn by Gianfrancesco for a rotunda on Uff. 200A (see cat. no. 197), is simply a second edition of Antonio's project for the S. Giovanni dei Fiorentini competition drawn on Uff. 862A (cat. no. 198). In this case the copy is perfect. *H.G.*

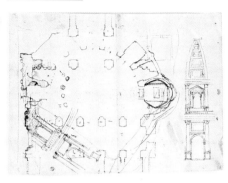

200
ANTONIO DA SANGALLO
Study for S. Giovanni dei Fiorentini

Florence, Galleria degli Uffizi, Gabinetto Disegni e Stampe, Uff. 1292A

Pen and ink, on paper; indication of the measurements in Roman *palmi* (without noting the unit).

324 × 439 mm

This sheet presents the plans of both alternative projects that Antonio da Sangallo presented for the S. Giovanni dei Fiorentini competition, superimposed. There are also two almost identical studies of the interior space of the rotunda.

The project of the rotunda corresponds amply to the model reproduced by Labacco. The greatest difference between the two plans is the size of the pedestals which are much smaller in the sketch than in the model. Consequently the columns between the arcades are considerably narrower, therefore not yet Ionic, but the whole inner space is conceived with a Composite Corinthian order in mind.

The study on Uff. 1364A (see cat. no. 201) indicates that Antonio himself and not Labacco decided to enlarge the pedestals. This study consists in the elevation of a part of a large basilica which links a nave of a kind similar to that which Antonio planned for the S. Giovanni dei Fiorentini competition, to a choir with an ambulatory of the kind that Antonio had designed in his model of a rotunda for the same competition, enlarged by an inner ambulatory. There the pedestals are already larger and the columns must be Ionic.

The project for the basilica includes two variants. One looks considerably like the final project, even though it is remarkably larger: the nave and aisles are 70 and 35 *palmi* respectively instead of 60 and 30 *palmi*. The second variant, according to the notes, is based on the same larger dimensions, but there are only three bays.

It should be noted that Antonio kept to this rather extreme solution given the short basilica instead of moving on to a quincunx plan. This would have made a much more impressive church, possible without modifying the proportions of space and volume. Perhaps a solution of this type, of a decidedly Venetian inspiration, would not have been suited for the national church of the Florentine people. The visualizing of these two alternative plans, one over the other, could be linked to the above-mentioned project which aimed at merging both ideas into one large basilica. This would explain why Antonio is considering completing the rotunda here by inserting a crown of columns.

Another reason for the superimposition of the two alternative projects is certainly the desire to analyze their impact on the surrounding site. This is also clear from the faint lines that cross the choir obliquely to the axis of the plan. These lines indicate the shore of the Tiber. Antonio usually indicated the river's edge in his projects for S. Giovanni dei Fiorentini (see Uff. 199A, 200A, 862A, 863A; on Uff. 863A it is indicated as "fiume"). He is therefore referring to a special problem regarding the construction of this church. Vasari describes the facts in great detail in his *Lives*.

In the *Life of Sansovino*, Vasari says that the space for the church between Via Giulia and the Tiber was not large enough. Since the Florentines wanted to keep the limit of the facade in line with Via Giulia, it was necessary to extend the foundations at least 15 *canne* (150 *palmi*) into the Tiber ("ma non vi essendo spazio e volendo pur fare la facciata di detta chiesa in sulla dirittura delle case di strada Iulia, erano necessati entrare nel fiume Tevere almeno quindici *canne*"). The type of problem is evident after an examination of the site of S. Giovanni dei Fiorentini on a map of Rome prior to the modern flood control of the river, or the line demarcating the river drawn by Antonio. Via Giulia runs close to the Tiber and the distance between them narrows to the north, becoming minimal where the church was built. It is difficult to understand the precise meaning of Vasari's account which refers clearly to Sansovino's project that was 22 *canne* long. According to Vasari, the Tiber was seven *canne* behind Via Giulia, but this not does correspond with all the other surviving evidence. Other views or projects are concordant in positioning the river further back. According to the demarcation drawn on Uff. 1292A, on the basis of the indications giving the lengths of the projects shown in other drawings, the river's edge was at least 17 *canne* from Via Giulia along the central axis of the church. If it was not just an error made by Vasari, perhaps he considered the shore the end of rather flat ground before it sloped down to the river.

Vasari referred to the foundations again in his *Life of Antonio da Sangallo*. In the first edition, he said they entered the Tiber, were extremely costly, and that Antonio da Sangallo's project was a great feat of engineering, after Sansovino had been seen to be incapable of directing the task. After a halt in the building of the church, in his second edition of the *Lives*, Vasari was polemical about the shortsightedness of his fellow townsmen's program. They would have been better to invest their money in the construction of a smaller church rather than spend it on the foundations of a great and unfinished work. They should never have allowed the architects to build such expensive foundations in order to gain 20 *braccia*, that is to say, about 5 *canne* of ground.

This new indication could also refer once again to Sansovino's model. If the shore, as indicated in the drawing on Uff. 1292, was 17 *canne* away from Via Giulia, Sansovino's project would have extended five *canne* into the Tiber. Even though this is logical, it is highly improbable. When Vasari expressed his disapproval, Sansovino's project was already of no interest anymore to anyone. It is doubtful whether the foundations were laid in accordance with Sansovino's model (see cat. no. 190). In any case, as from 1521 at the latest, these were designed for a completely different project, for a basilica which must have been as much as 17 *canne* long (see cat. no. 206). Vasari does not say that the project has been changed in spite of having the foundations of the second project in front of him, so to speak, in his account of their construction by Antonio da Sangallo already published in the first edition of his *Lives* which indicates the foundations as being built in his time (1550). Only by referring to these foundations does the criticism expressed in the second edition of the *Lives* make sense. The five *canne* that so annoyed Vasari correspond therefore to the difference between the length of Antonio's project compared to Sansovino's. It is typical of Vasari to make polite criticism. This can also be seen in his account of Sansovino's role in the construction of S. Giovanni dei Fiorentini.

Michelangelo, whose criticism of the "Sangallo sect" became instead notorious, went back in his project, to the dimensions first established for S. Giovanni dei Fiorentini (see cat. no. 71).

Here the position of the river shore is studied with great care, not only because it was effectively highly important for the church, but also because this problem was extended to the urban measures linked to the construction of the building. On the basis of some of Vasari's remarks quoted here (even though Vasari sometimes contradicts himself, p. 165, n. 77), K. Schwager (Schwager 1975: 164ff.) says that Sansovino designed an approach 20 *braccia* long in front of S. Giovanni dei Fiorentini. It attempts to prove that this hypothesis is not plausible. Tafuri too (Tafuri 1973: 208ff., and in his later publications on S. Giovanni dei Fiorentini), suggested a similar *sagrato* on the basis of the drawings alone. He observed that Antonio had marked the line of the river not only in the above mentioned projects, but also in different projects for basilicas that were considerably larger (Uff. 860A, Uff. 861A) and that in these projects the line of the shore crosses the apse. According to Tafuri, the difference in the length of the larger and smaller projects is equivalent to the depth of the approach to the church. This would seem plausible if the projects of the larger basilicas were not nearly the same length, if not longer than the final project by Antonio and the foundations actually built. The latter, however, were built extending into the Tiber. The comment on cat. no. 193 explains the question of the river line drawn on Uff. 860A and Uff. 861A. Even though Schwager and Tafuri's arguments are not convincing, they do raise questions that need answering and make sense as starting points: the urban planning for the area around a building the size of S. Giovanni dei Fiorentini should be carefully analyzed. At that time, the Florentine community was not considering a possible *sagrato* in order to highlight the church, they were discussing the creation of two roads which would have led directly up to the main portal. When the hypothesis of a *sagrato* was temporarily proposed in 1541, it was sensibly suggested in terms of a space on the other side of Via Giulia, as had been done for the nearby Palazzo dei Tribunali (Günther 1984c, no. 339b). *H.G.*

ison is made between three or five bays. Here, according to calculations made on the basis of the measurements given in the drawing, the plan is for four bays with large piers fronted with pairs of half-columns. The study of the elevation reveals a later stage of the project. Right from the beginning, Antonio seems to have started from the idea of separating the bays with giant half-columns. Given the small diameter of the columns shown in the plan, there is only room for a very small tabernacle above, similar to a window which, however, would have hardly allowed the light to enter. The final version of the study shows windows over the arcades which have better proportions, respecting the rest of the elevation, but which still seem imprisoned in the low clerestory. These start so close to the arcades that it looks as if their lower part might be sited below the roof of the aisles. (A sketch on the verso shows instead a special construction detail for the roof of the aisle to allow light to reach the windows.) This is rather a poor solution in comparison to the symmetry of the porportions of the model for a rotunda. However, it appears to be based on the measurements established by that project. The height of 40 *palmi* for the arcades suits their 20-*palmi* span in the model. The half-columns have a diameter of 5 *palmi*, as in the model. What is astonishing is their height: 50 *palmi*, which is equal to ten diameters. This corresponds to the Composite order as Serlio introduced it later on. According to Vitruvius, the Corinthian order should have been nine and half times the diameter. Antonio took this as his premise in his studies for the Palazzo Farnese (Günther 1989b: 157). Tafuri (Tafuri 1992, no. 68ff.) reconstructed an elevation from the drawing on Uff. 1055 showing the interior of Antonio's project for a basilica. A more satisfactory solution than the elevation can be found in the study on Uff. 1364A, which belongs to the plan drawn on Uff. 864A. On that sheet, Antonio merged his two alternative projects for the S. Giovanni dei Fiorentini competition and adapted the proportions of the elevation of the basilica to the rotunda. The proportions of the part corresponding to the rotunda are more like those in Labacco's engraving than to those in the drawings of Antonio and Gianfrancesco. In particular, the pedestals are much larger. Consequently the columns were shorter and the Ionic order took the place of the Corinthian one. The basilica project might have undergone the same evolution. *H.G.*

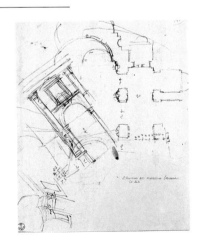

201
ANTONIO DA SANGALLO
Basilica Study for S. Giovanni dei Fiorentini

Florence, Galleria degli Uffizi, Gabinetto Disegni e Stampe, Uff. 1055A

Pen and ink, on paper; indications of the measurements in Roman *palmi*.
210 × 270 mm

The drawing illustrates parts of the east side of the plan with the line marking the shore of the Tiber behind the apse, and parts of the apse, that is, a bay of the nave and the corner of the apse. The study of the plan belongs to an early stage of the project, like the drawing on Uff. 1292A (cat. no. 200). In the plan on Uff. 1292A a compar-

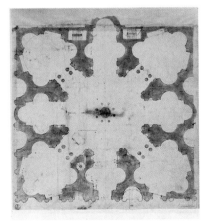

202
BALDASSARRE PERUZZI
Central-Plan Project for S. Giovanni dei Fiorentini

Florence, Galleria degli Uffizi, Gabinetto Disegni e Stampe, Uff. 505A

Pen and ink, on paper, preparatory drawing in red chalk, wash; indications of the measurements in Roman *palmi*.
456 × 427 mm

This centrally planned building recalls Sansovino's project according to Vasari's description of it, in its square outline and, more vaguely, in its distribution of space (here about 210 *palmi*). In both projects, the freestanding square contains a considerably smaller octagon (the diameter here is 90 *palmi*). Peruzzi has designed a crown of chapels around the central area that are arranged so as to fill the space between the octagon and the square block. The plans of the corner chapels based on triangles are typical of Peruzzi's experiments with form. He drew several other similarly extraordinary plans for ecclesiastical buildings, that can be seen in the copies conserved in the *Taccuino Senese*, IV.7 in the Biblioteca Comunale in Siena and in *Codex* 10935 conserved in the Österreichischen Nationalbibliothek in Vienna.

The association with the projects for S. Giovanni dei Fiorentini is put forward on the basis that the project seems to be an appendix to the drawing on Uff. 510A recto (Benedetti 1983: 965; Wurm 1984, no. 11; Licht 1984, no. 70). In certain respects, Peruzzi's drawings look more like Leonardo's projects for centrally planned buildings in *Manuscript B*, than the usual projects developed in the Renaissance. Another decidedly theoretical characteristic is the positioning of the high altar in the middle of the central area. This idea was esthetically acceptable but practically almost impossible. *H.G.*

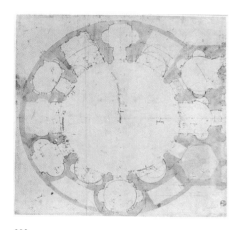

203
Baldassarre Peruzzi
Central-Plan Project for S. Giovanni dei Fiorentini

Florence, Galleria degli Uffizi, Gabinetto Disegni e Stampe, Uff. 510A
Pen and ink, on paper, wash; indications of the measurements in Roman *palmi*.
440 × 433 mm
Inscribed: (Peruzzi) *altitudo in proportione superbipartiens tertias; Circumferentia* 377 [*palmi*]; *intercolumnio; porta.*

This plan resembles Antonio da Sangallo's project for S. Giovanni dei Fiorentini, both in its general layout (a circular-plan building with a corona of chapels and a vestibule), and in its dimensions: the diameter of the central area is 120 *palmi*, the total diameter, ca. 200 *palmi*. This similarity is the reason for its being included among the competition projects for S. Giovanni dei Fiorentini (Wurm 1984, no. 9). There is no surviving evidence of the articulation of the central area with its rhythmic intercolumniation something like that of Giuliano da Sangallo's project for a circular building, drawn on fols. 74 recto and 59 verso of the *Codex Barberini*, which perhaps belong to the 1513 stage of the design for S. Giovanni dei Fiorentini (Bentivoglio 1975; Günther 1988f: 124ff.).
It is unlikely that this drawing was the project presented to the patrons or was derived directly from it. Instead, it appears to be an unfinished preliminary project. The sheet is an example of Peruzzi's delight in experimenting form: each one of the side chapels and the two halves of the facade have a different shape. From this "catalog," either Peruzzi in his final version of the project, or the patron, could have decided the shape of the side chapels. Similar examples of variations had already been elaborated earli-

er, in particular by Leonardo da Vinci in the largely theoretical context of Manuscript B. The unusual method of indicating the measurements and proportions occurs in other theoretical projects by Peruzzi (such as Uff. 581A, Uff. 107A, Wurm 1984: 377, 381).
On the verso there is a decidedly incomplete project for a centrally planned hexagonal building, which has been given the same dimensions as the circular building on the recto. This is why it is associated with the design of S. Giovanni dei Fiorentini. *H.G.*

204
Riniero Neruccio
Central-Plan Project for S. Giovanni dei Fiorentini (after the project by Andrea Sansovino)

Vienna, Graphische Sammlung, Albertina Roma no. 790
Pen and ink, on paper, wash; indications of the measurements in unspecified units, probably Roman *palmi*.
212 × 195 mm

The plan is completed by an elelvation drawn on the verso and by a cross section on another sheet (cat. no. 205). The building shown in these drawings is obviously a consequence of the design process for St. Peter's, but it belongs to the early, not to the contemporary phase. Giuliano da Sangallo's project probably of 1505-06 drawn on Uff. 8A, the alternative to Bramante's parchment project, served as the matrix. The dome over the central area does not correspond to Bramante's project for the dome of St. Peter's. It is directly derived from Florence Cathedral even in the details of the lantern. The facade is just like Giuliano's projects for S. Lorenzo in Florence drawn on Uff. 281A and Uff. 276A. Its *all'antica* character stands out in comparison to Antonio da Sangallo's projects for the facade of S. Giovanni dei Fiorentini: this facade is simply a regular succession of rhythmic intercolumniation. The only features serving to accentuate the center are the enlarging of the main portal compared to the side ones and a temple front. Antonio instead planned variations in the intercolumniation. He marked the corners and linked the facade stories at the center.
The reduction of the layout of St. Peter's to the size planned for S. Giovanni dei Fiorentini produces a very precise structure whose central area has a diameter of only 62 *palmi* (about 13 m), which certainly would not have provided enough space for the Florentine community. This project too, was therefore another rather impractical one.
Another two alternative projects, drawn as plans (Roma, nos. 789v., 791) are part of the one considered here. See Günther 1988f: 345ff., for the attribution of these drawings to Neruccio. The inclusion of the projects proposed by Giovannoni and Frommel (Giovannoni 1959: 217; Frommel 1977: 55, no. 116) among those for the design of S. Giovanni dei Fiorentini is not a definitive certainty. It is based on the similarity of the layout and the size of these compared to the others known to have been presented for the competition for S. Giovanni dei Fiorentini. The

total width of the building, 223 *palmi*, corresponds to Jacopo Sansovino's project. The reduction of the depth to 200 *palmi* recalls Antonio da Sangallo's basilica project. In spite of all the similarities in the layout, the dimensions are in conflict with its previous collocation among the projects for St. Peter's (most recently Wolff Metternich: pls. 4-6, 123).
The attribution of the projects to Andrea Sansovino depends on the following motivations (see Günther 1988f: 345-348): of the architects mentioned by Vasari as taking part in the competition, neither Jacopo Sansovino, nor Antonio da Sangallo and Peruzzi could be the authors on the basis of surviving graphic evidence. Raphael is excluded for stylistic reasons. It is necessary therefore to consider an architect outside Vasari's circle. This deduction is valid for the fact that, in his other similar accounts, Vasari's information was insufficient. Two facts in particular characterize the projects under consideration: in the first place, they lack originality and tend to copy other projects, and not contemporary ones but rather slightly older ones. The imitation of Giuliano da Sangallo is a particularly faithful one. Secondly, one of the projects (no. 791) reflects the experience gained at that time in facing the static problems of S. Maria di Loreto. On the basis of the stylistic peculiarities, Andrea Sansovino comes to the fore as the author of the projects. He was then director of the building site for S. Maria di Loreto and had experience of these kinds of problems. The draftsman, Riniero Neruccio, worked for Andrea and there is documentary evidence that in 1518 Andrea commissioned him to build a model that was not for S. Maria di Loreto. *H.G.*

205
Riniero Neruccio
Central-Plan Project for S. Giovanni dei Fiorentini (after the project by Andrea Sansovino)

Vienna, Graphische Sammlung, Albertina Roma 789v.
Pen and ink, wash, on paper; indications of the measurements in unspecified units, probably Roman *palmi*. On the verso there is a cross-section of the centrally planned project (cat. no. 204).
216 × 185 mm

For the attribution of the drawing see Günther 1988f: 345-348. The association of this drawing with the projects for the design of S. Giovanni dei Fiorentini is motivated by its general similarity in terms of plan and the dimensions of the building to the other projects for the church. The project is attributed to Andrea Sansovino (see cat. no. 204).
The project shows a rotunda which borrows characteristics from S. Costanza, the Pantheon and contemporary projects for St. Peter's. Along the sides of the round central space with a 90-*palmi* diameter there is an ambulatory interrupted by a deep choir and a vestibules. The ambulatory communicates with the central area by means of a single passage on each side and, as in the arms designed for St. Peter's, these are provided with four columns. The

column motif, typical of Bramante, also appears in Peruzzi's projects for S. Giovanni dei Fiorentini (see cat. no. 202). There are two rooms to the sides of the choir which could have been intended for the sacristies, if, strangely enough, they had not been only accessible from the ambulatory. A study of the facade of the vestibule, based on robust pilasters with half-columns in front and smaller columns inserted between them, reveals the extent to which it imitates the projects for St. Peter's. If the drum, which must certainly be positioned above the central area, repeated the articulation of the groups of columns, it can be assumed that it looked like Bramante's project for the dome of St. Peter's. In the area underneath, the structure of the central area with its alternation of tabernacles and passages between columns and a vestibule, is derived from the Pantheon. The idea of transferring this layout to a rotunda of smaller dimensions for S. Giovanni dei Fiorentini could have been borrowed from Giuliano da Sangallo if it is true that his project on fols. 74 and 59 verso of the *Codex Barberini* is an early project for S. Giovanni dei Fiorentini (Bentivoglio 1975; Günther 1984c: 124ff.). The total diameter of the building according to the indications is 210 *palmi*; the total length is 220 *palmi*. A drawing erroneously attributed to Fra Giocondo and a drawing of Sallustio Peruzzi (Uff. 153Av., 689Av., Bartoli, fig. 78, 655) offer a variant of this project, conceived however as a much larger building and arranged in a livelier way. The drawing appears to be more of a theoretical exercise due to the lack of a chapel for the main choir and for other reasons. Another variant can be found in Oreste Vannocci Biringucci's sketchbook (Siena, Biblioteca Comunale, MS. S IV 1, fol. 39v.; see Schwager 1975, no. 4). *H.G.*

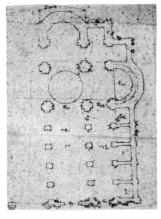

206
<small>ANTONIO LABACCO</small>
Project for S. Giovanni dei Fiorentini
(after the project by Antonio da Sangallo)

Florence, Galleria degli Uffizi, Gabinetto Disegni e Stampe, Uff. 175A
Pen and ink, on paper; indications of the measurements in Roman *palmi* (erroneously marked as *b[raccia]*).
318 × 223 mm

The attribution of the drawing to Labacco (supported here) is based on the handwriting and other details (see, for example, the drawing on Uff. 1190A, and Bartoli, fig. 606, attributed definitely thanks to an inscribed note written by Antonio da Sangallo to Labacco).
The drawing shows a basilica with a transept, side chapels and dome over the crossing whose plan and dimensions relate it to the competition for S. Giovanni dei Fiorentini. However, it also looks considerably like the present building of S. Giovanni dei Fiorentini. The facade, seen here as a plan, was drawn as an elevation by a member of Sangallo's workshop (cat. no. 207). Labacco, who drew the plan, was a pupil of Antonio da Sangallo and one of his closest assistants. He probably built Antonio's model for the S. Giovanni dei Fiorentini competition.

When Michelangelo was asked, in 1550, to formulate an opinion and a design for a funerary monument to Pope Julius III in the church of S. Giovanni dei Fiorentini, he replied, commenting on the unfinished church, "che per questo mezza decta chiesa s'abbi a finire" (Carteggio 1965-83, no. 1148). The church was only half built at the time. A plan elaborated by Sangallo's workshop for the fortification of the Borgo, which can be dated as around 1545 (Cod. Vat. Barb. lat. 4391, fol. 4, see P. Marconi 1966) indicates in a fairly schematic but realistic way, which parts of S. Giovanni dei Fiorentini were built under the direction of Antonio da Sangallo who died in 1546 (Günther 1984c, no. 15). At that time, the whole nave had been built including the piers and the facade was already articulated in the lower part. The transept and choir still had to be built. The same unfinished building, with a temporary roof, is shown in the great map from S. Onofrio toward Castel Sant'Angelo copied perhaps from Anton van den Wyngaerde (halfway through the sixteen century, Egger 1911-32, II: 117) and in the maps of Rome of U. Pinardi (1555), Sallustio Peruzzi (1564-65) and E. Dupérac (1577). From the documents linked to the construction of the church under Giacomo della Porta as from 1583 onward (Hibbard 1971: 142-145) it is possible to glean an even more precise picture of the state of the building. There is a detailed list of the parts that were still unfinished: the eastern part including a pier of the dome, the clerestory and the vault of the nave as well as the side chapels. There is no mention of the piers of the nave and the vaults of the aisles. Evidently they were already terminated. Above these there was the temporary roof which is shown in the old illustrations of the building. All the same, the stonemasons' estimates indicate that many of the parts built under Antonio were still in a primitive state. A corner pedestal of Antonio's facade that still survives, and his appendix from the documentary evidence (Günther 1984c: 231, no. 355a, no. 47), reveal that Antonio's construction coincided in the flight of the facade and in its total width with the present-day building. It can be deduced from this that much of the actual nave was also built by Antonio.
Even though the plan on Uff. 175A corresponds to a great extent with the total width of the present building, the subdivision of the nave differs considerably from what Antonio had carried out. Given the problem of the foundations of the choir, Antonio was content at first (on Uff. 175A) with a remarkably small dome. Later on, the desire to crown the center area in a more emphatic way dominated the design. As well as the crossing, Antonio widened the nave from 41 *palmi* (on Uff. 175) to present-day 48 *palmi* (for the measurements of the church today, see Günther 1984, no. 352). At the same time, he widened the aisles slightly so that they measured exactly half the width of the nave, and with a reduction of the depth of the side chapels, the total width of the church remained the same. The enlarging of the nave and aisles took place slightly after the beginning of the construction, in 1524, and can be inferred from the widening of the central arches of the facade in the drawing on Uff. 1013A (see cat. no. 189).
The definition of final projects ascribed the drawing on Uff. 175A and the associated elevation of the facade on Uff. 176A, or the prototypes to which they refer, means that these drawings transmit the model that was presented to the patrons. All the same, they differ from the parts built by Antonio. This is a problem, which, in spite of the apparent contradiction, is often to be found in Renaissance projects. It appears the architects did not fix in architectural drawings their ultimate modifications—which could have arisen after meetings with the patron or the architect directing the site, or from objective difficulties during the construction process—if these alterations remained within certain limits so that the basic project, with additional sketches and notes, was still sufficiently adequate (Ackerman 1954a; Günther 1982). *H.G.*

207
<small>GIOVANNI BATTISTA DA SANGALLO</small>
Final Project for S. Giovanni dei Fiorentini
(after the project by Antonio da Sangallo)

Florence, Galleria degli Uffizi, Gabinetto Disegni e Stampe, Uff. 176A
Pen and ink, on paper; indications of the measurements in Roman *palmi*.
INSCRIBED: (G. B. da Sangallo) *doricho*; (unknown, perhaps G. A. Dosio) *facciata fatta per la facciata di S. Govanni de Fiorentini*.
264 × 207 mm

The facade shown in the drawing appears to belong to a basilica with a nave and two aisles and side chapels. The articulation of the front with rhythmic intercolumniation and the introduction of an attic rising to the height of the clerestory without a giant order of columns are well-known stylistic features. The characteristic element of the new stylistic development here, is, instead, the elevation of the center by means of the separation of the corners and the extension of the central arches to the attic story.
The facade corresponds in its structure and size (apart from very slight differences) to the plan drawn on Uff. 175A (cat. no. 206). The project is completed with a second copy showing small variants in line with the drawing of Antonio's facade, at present conserved in Munich, which was perhaps also drafted by Battista (Staatliche Graphische Sammlung, Bibiena-Klebeband I, inv. 4930; Degenhart 1955, no. 381). It does not have any measurements, but gives a very accurate picture of the decoration of the facade. The order of the blind articulation should not therefore be totally Doric: the stocky half-columns in the lower part are Doric and the slender pilasters in the upper part are Corinthian. The niches or rectangular panels set in the articulation should have been decorated with reliefs or statues. There was also space for reliefs between the pedestals.
Some views of the church (the oldest is Dupérac's map of Rome of 1577) show that Antonio da Sangallo only built the lower part of the facade. The greater part of his early work was destroyed with the building of the actual facade. All that remains are a pedestal and the reliefs which should have been inserted between the slender columns (Günther 1984c: 231). The drawing on Uff. 1013A gives the measurements of the central intercolumniation: it was 30 3/4 *palmi* wide instead of 26 *palmi* like the central arch on Uff. 176A. The difference (compared to the plan on Uff. 175A which is associated with the drawing of the facade) can be explained by the widening of the nave while work was in progress. *H.G.*

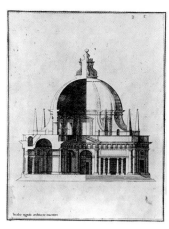

208
Anonymous 16th-Century Draftsman
Elevation and Cross-Section of S. Giovanni dei Fiorentini (?)
(after the project by Giacomo da Vigola)

Madrid, Biblioteca Nacional, Graphics collection, 16-49
Raccolta di Vincenzo Casale, Casale Album, fol. 86
Pen and ink, hatching, on paper.
356 × 258
Inscribed: *Iacobo vignola architecto inventore.*

K. Schwager published this drawing in 1975 and showed that it completed a plan reproduced together with another two variants in Oreste Vannocci Biringucci's sketchbook in Siena (Biblioteca Comunale, cod. S IV 1, fol. 39r.-v.). Biringucci handed down to posterity several projects by Vignola conserved in his sketchbook (Ackerman and Lotz 1964). Even though this project is based on an oval plan, it clearly derives from Antonio da Sangallo's model for a rotunda entered in the competition for S. Giovanni dei Fiorentini, as it was drawn by Labacco (cat. no. 195). The design, however, is austere and majestic, in Vignola's style. Vignola reduced the size of the central area compared to the total dimensions of the building, and introduced a large ambulatory which leads into several short chapels. He also reduced the number of axes from 16 to 12. It was therefore possible to open the lower part of the central area with impressive arches, without having to superimpose an intermediate area, as Antonio did. Vignola managed to do without the progressive enlarging toward the exterior of the distance between the axes, inserting Serlian windows in the side chapels. There are Doric columns in the lower part and Ionic ones in the clerestory. Both the variants of the plan copied by Biringucci establish the insertion of columns in the arches of the central area corresponding to those of the side chapels. This solution had already been used in projects for S. Peter's and in some of those presented for the S. Giovanni dei Fiorentini competition. Otherwise, huge spaces had to be introduced between the side chapels to overcome the distances between the axes, or the ambulatory had to be eliminated. The shape of the facade was also subject to variations: in one, the church looks very like Antonio da Sangallo's model for a rotunda for the S. Giovanni dei Fiorentini competition. Indications of the measurements have been included on another one.
Several variants of the facade are also a part of Vignola's project; these differ from the drawing in Vicenzo Casale's collection to no greater an extent than the plans copied by Biringucci.
One of the two variants has been copied in two surviving drawings. The first is in Oreste Vannocci Biringucci's sketchbook, on fol. 42 verso, together with the tabernacle designed by Vignola for S. Antonio Martire at Fara Sabrina (Ackerman and Lotz 1964: 13). It is a sketch drawn with the same imprecision as the plans and the greater part of all the other drawings. The other variant is reproduced on Uff. 233A, and was drawn accurately. This one is often attributed to Giovanni Antonio Dosio, sometimes to Antonio da Sangallo, Labacco or Tiberio Calcagni (see also,

Frey 1920: 57ff.; Wachler 1940: 220; Ackerman and Lotz 1964: 13; Dosio 1976: 317ff.; Schwager 1975; Giovannoni 1959: 217, 219; Nava 1935-36: 107; Venturi 1939: XI, 2, 192). This second variant looks like Casale's drawing, especially in the small details (see, for example, the reproduction of the section of the outer wall of the ambulatory, the double staircase or the vestibule structure, etc.). Unlike Casale's drawing, the plan is here is circular and the building is based on sixteen axes as in Antonio's project. However, the arrangement has not been thought out carefully because the arches of the central area would have proportions of 1:3.5 which was decidedly unsatisfactory for the Renaissance.
The second variant of Vignola's project is in the *Codex Gaddi-Campello-Geymüller* in the Uffizi. On fol. 116 verso (Uff. 7889Av.) there are reproductions of the plan, elevation of the central area and several detailed elevations of the outer wall of the ambulatory.
Due to their affinities, these drawings are habitually included among the projects for S. Giovanni dei Fiorenni and associated with Antonio's model for the competition of 1518 (Giovannoni 1959: 217, 219; Benedetti 1983: 965; Günther 1988f: 347; Satzinger 1991: 211). However, the affinity of these drawings with the drawing in the Casale collection is even more evident. They can be collocated between the Casale drawing and the variant transmitted by Biringucci and by Uff. 233A. The plan is circular like the one in the variant copied by Biringucci and on Uff. 233A, but it is articulated along 12 axes, as in the Casale drawing. The elevation looks like the elevation in the Casale drawing, in particular in the details, such as the structure of the clerestory with the pedimented windows between pilasters in front of which there are pedestals bearing statues. The *Codex Gaddi-Campello-Geymüller* is traditionally attributed to Antonio da Sangallo the Elder (especially Geymüller 1885: 1-21; Ferri 1908; Bartoli 1914-22, fig. 140-144; Degenhart 1955: 194ff.; Satkowski 1985; Satzinger 1991: 148-157). However, the collection of drawings in the Uffizi attributed to Antonio the Elder is a mixture. Hardly any of the drawings in the file really were the work of Antonio the Elder. The *Codex Gaddi-Campello-Geymüller* derives essentially from the pen of Francesco da Sangallo as the handwriting of the notes and the style of the drawings reveal (Günther 1988f: 114. Geymüller had already put forward the possible collaboration of Francesco, even though this has now been forgotten).
The following motives can be adduced in support of the association between the Casale drawing and its variants with the projects for S. Giovanni dei Fiorentini: the similarity of the general layout with Antonio's model; the dimensions which correspond to those of many other projects for S. Giovanni dei Fiorentini, and, in particular, Uff. 233A shows a fleur-de-lis on the top of the church, which was doubtlessly the Florentine emblem.   *H.G.*

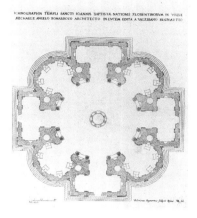

209
Monogram RD for Valérian Regnard
S. Giovanni dei Fiorentini
(after the project by Michelangelo)
(from Praecipua urbis templa, Rome, 1650)

Munich, Bayerische Staatsbibliothek

Two engravings from plates measuring 326 × 282 mm
Inscribed: (elevation) *orthografia exterior et interior designati templi sancti ioannis baptiste nationis florentinorum in urbe michaele angelo bonarato architecto / Valerianus Renatius sculpsit Romae / RD del.;* (plan) *ichnographia templi sanct ioannis* [etc. as above] */ in lucem edita a Valeriano Regnatio.*

Valérian Regnard, who worked as an engraver in Rome from about 1630 to 1650, included Michelangelo's model in a series of illustrations of Roman churches. He reproduced the model by means of an orthogonal projection. The result is a less lively picture than Le Mercier's engraving, but, on the whole, there are only slight differences between them. Regnard was generally concerned about making the church conform to Baroque ideas. He therefore substituted in particular the small widows of the clerestory designed by Michelangelo with larger ones that filled the whole space on the outside between the roof and the dome. The inclusion of altars on the plan is typical of his style: their fronts are not straight, as they normally would be, but curved according to the elipse that runs concentrically to the walls of the side tribunes.
Two drawings are closely connected to the engravings. One, a combination of an elevation and a cross section, conserved in the Kupferstichkabinett in Berlin (KdZ 20, 976), corresponds exactly to one of the engravings and is even more accurate in certain details (published by Noehles 1969, no. 56). It is, as Tolnay noted in 1980, the preliminary drawing for the engraving.
The second drawing, a plan, conserved in the Uffizi as Uff. 3185A, corresponds so closely to the relative engraving, that it could also, in Tolnay's opinion, be a preliminary drawing. It even reproduces the characteristic shape of the altars. It is however, less accurate in one detail: parts of the wall of the lantern are not outlined. It could therefore in fact be a reproduction of an engraving as precise hand-drawn copies were not so rare at the time. Venturi (Venturi 1939: XI, 2, 189) published the drawing as

the work of Tiberio Calcagni, since it was he who built Michelangelo's model. This attribution has been repeated by several scholars (more recently, Argan and Contardi 1990: 347). This attribution to Calcagni of the drawing on Uff. 3185A contrasts with the little that is known of his style of drawing to be seen in Uff. 225A recto which is inscribed "Di Tiberio Calcagni è sua inventione" (Ferri 1885: XXII; for a critical collection of Calcagni's graphical works, see Schwager 1973, no. 144; numerous illustrations of drawings attributed to Calcagni can be seen in Collobi Ragghianti 1974: 149ff., pls. 269-270).

The engravings became famous. They were spread abroad through Marietti's edition of Vignola published in Amsterdam 1668 (Thode 1908) and through the collection of plates on modern Roman churches published in 1684 under the title *Insignium Romae templorum prospectus* by G. G. De Rossi in Rome (pl. 48ff.) and by J. van Sandart in Nuremberg (pl. 46ff., reproductions of the engravings, 1694. See D. Frey 1920: 82. The original German edition of the engravings has not yet been taken into consideration).   *H.G.*

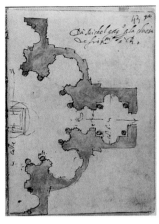

210
ORESTE VANNOCCI BIRINGUCCI
S. Giovanni dei Fiorentini
(after the project by Michelangelo)

Siena, Biblioteca Comunale, cod. S IV 1, fol. 42 recto
Pena and ink, on paper, wash.
140 × 200
INSCRIBED: (Biringucci) *Da Michelang.o per la chiesa de fior.ni a Ro.*

The sketchbook of Oreste Vannocci Biringucci (1558-85), conserved in Siena, comprises a total of 148 sheets of sketches of chiefly Renaissance architecture, for the most part copied from Giovanni Battista da Sangallo's sketchbook (conserved in Lille). It includes many projects by Michelangelo as well as Vignola's model for S. Giovanni dei Fiorentini (cat. no. 208; Ackerman and Lotz 1964; for Biringucci, see Heydenreich 1930). All the drawings are sketched very quickly like this one of Michelangelo's project for S. Giovanni dei Fiorentini.
Biringucci's sketch differs considerably from Michelangelo's model for S. Giovanni dei Fiorentini. First of all, the vestibules are larger and columns have been inserted in their corners. These modifications are closer to Michelangelo's preliminary drawing on CB 124 (cat. no. 171). On the basis of this, according to Ackerman (Ackerman 1961: 119ff.) the sketch should be an intermediate stage of Michelangelo's project where he tried to pass from the general outline to the definition of the individual shapes and measurements.
The indications of the measurements shown on the sketch are particularly important. They are only approximate, but they illustrate the fundamental distances: the diameter of the central area is 12 *canne*; the depth of the vestibule from the entrance to the central space is 5 *canne*; the width of a vestibule is 6 *canne*; the width of the passage from the vestibule to the central area is 20 *palmi*; and last-

ly, the diameter of the columns of the central area in 5 *palmi*.
There is only one other plan of Michelangelo's project for S. Giovanni dei Fiorentini that has the measurements as well. It was drafted by an architect, Vincenzo Casale (ca. 1540-93), together with an elevation and a cross section and they are all conserved in the Casale album in the Biblioteca Nacional in Madrid (fol. 174f.; inscribed, by Casale, "la presente è la pianta del tempio che Michelangelo buonaroti lasciò ordinato per s.to Joanni dei Fiorentini in Roma del quale lasci fatto modello di legno non si pose per opera o per temere la ispesa o per altra cagione e si fece dipoi la chiesa che ista in questo libro a faccie..." referring to della Porta's project; published by Battisti 1961). Casale's drawings are accurate even though they are drafted rather clumsily. Excluding tiny details, they correspond to Le Mercier's reproduction of the model. Where the measurements have been included, the plan is highly detailed. It corresponds more or less to Biringucci's indications of the measurements.
There is still the question of where Casale's measurements really came from. The inscription on the drawing does not supply an answer. From what is known about the models of the time, the measurements are not easy to interpret. The plan which was drawn by Tiberio Calcagni for a presentation to the Duke of Florence, could instead have had indications of the measurements. The elevations, elaborated for the presentation of these projects, did not normally have measurements. The S. Giovanni dei Fiorentini building site certainly possessed copies of Calcagni's drawings which served together with the model for the execution of the project. Since there is no alternative explanation for the provenance of the indications of the measurements on Casale's drawing, it must be presumed that Casale took them from Calcagni's projects.   *H.G*

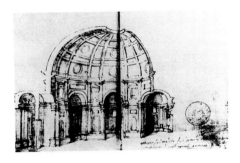

211
GIOVANNI ANTONIO DOSIO
S. Giovanni dei Fiorentini
(after the project by Michelangelo)

Modena, Biblioteca Estense, Raccolta Campori, App. Cod. 1755 (= Ms. o Z 2.2), fol. 140v.-141r.
Pen and ink, on paper, wash.
2 × (200 × 140 mm)
INSCRIBED: (Dosio) *ritratto dal modello di San giovanni de fiorentini in Roma inventione di Michelangelo buonaroti B. M. ia.*

This drawing belongs to the sketchbook published in 1955 by Luporini and was drafted by a Florentine architect, Giovanni Antonio Dosio, who lived in Rome from 1548 to 1575 (Valone 1976). The 153 sheets contain drawings mostly by Dosio. Drawings by other artists have been glued on to the remaining pages (Schwager 1967: 62 no. 33).
While the inscription leaves no doubts about the subject of the drawing, the reproduction differs considerably in certain aspects from Michelangelo's model (Ackerman 1961: 120). The decoration of the interior of the dome has been changed; the windows between the arches of the central area are crowned by triangular tympanums instead of segmental ones; the lantern is missing, in its place there is only a small oculus, as if the author wanted to imitate the Pantheon here as well as in the outer base of the dome.

Above all, the side entrances have been closed so that the vestibules serve instead as side chapels. Lastly, the main entrance is brought to the fore by the facade's opening with the insertion of two columns, as in a loggia. The majority of the differences can certainly be explained by the hypothesis that Dosio elaborated his own or other sketches without really having understood them. The difference in the entrances, however, can scarcely be ascribed to carelessness. It appears to derive from the practical necessities of the Florentine community, that is to say, from the need to gain space for secondary altars and for the congregation since Michelangelo's project was rather small for such a large community as the Florentine one in Rome. Perhaps Dosio reproduced Michelangelo's model and introduced a few changes requested by the patrons, against the Duke of Florence's express wishes (see cat. no. 71). Perhaps the Florentines themselves commissioned Dosio, their fellow citizen, to draft a project that illustrated the alterations they wanted to introduce.
    H.G.

The Villa Madama
Sabine Eiche

In June 1519 Baldassare Castiglione wrote to Isabella d'Este that Raphael was building a country palace on the Monte Mario, north of the Vatican, for Cardinal Giulio de' Medici (later Pope Clement VII), which his cousin Pope Leo X, often went to see. Situated on the northeast slope of the hill overlooking the Tiber, the Villa Madama was planned on a longitudinal axis running from southeast to northwest. It was to be a vast complex comprising courtyards, one of which was circular, summer and winter apartments, loggias, a theater, garden, an outdoor dining room, a fishpond, service quarters and stables.

Work on the villa probably commenced in late summer of 1518. When Raphael died in April 1520 only the northwest loggia, the adjacent garden and fishpond below, as well as two rooms of the summer apartment, near the loggia, had been built. The project continued under the direction of Antonio da Sangallo the Younger, and eighteen months later the northwest half of the circular court had been begun. Construction stopped with the death of Leo X in December 1521, and from around 1523 to the Sack of Rome in 1527, priority was given to finishing the interior of the rooms and loggia, and to extending the gardens to the northwest.

After the death of Clement VII in 1534, the villa was acquired by the Farnese. Their descendants, the Bourbons of Naples, kept it until 1913, when it was sold to Maurice Bergès, who undertook the first major restoration. In 1925 the property was in the possession of Carlo Dentice di Frasso, who continued restoring the villa. Since 1940 it has belonged to the Italian State.

The Villa Madama is one of the most ambitious sixteenth-century villa-garden designs, which, in spite of its incomplete state, evokes the antique spirit of the time better than any other surviving Renaissance building. It is clear, from the fragment that was constructed, and from the various project drawings as well as Raphael's written description, that the Villa Madama was created by an extraordinary mind (or two?), capable of dexterously fusing what the ancients (Pliny the Younger and Vitruvius) had written about their architecture with elements inspired by the best of contemporary classicist buildings (e.g., Bramante's loggia at Genazzano; Sangallo's design of a colonnaded atrium).

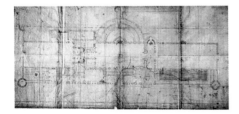

212
GIANFRANCESCO DA SANGALLO FOR RAPHAEL
Project for a Plan of the Villa Madama

Florence, Galleria degli Uffizi, Gabinetto Disegni e Stampe, Uff. 273A
Pen and two kinds of brown ink, wash in two shades of brown, incised lines, pin holes; six sheets joined, some abrasion, several tears, small patches along edges, trimmed on all sides, folded several times; watermark: crossbow in circle with lily above (closest to Briquet 760); scale: (in center bottom of central courtyard) 15 mm = 1 *canna*; ca. 1:149.
751/765 × 1562/1570 mm
INSCRIBED: 1) *dieta / ch[anne]* 3 (left tower); 2) *dispesa* (upper left); 3) *chantina* (left of center at top); 4) *tinelo* (left of center at top); 5) *Vestibolo* (to left of center); 6) *Atrio* (to left of center); 7) *cavedio / cortilo* (center); 8) *lunga ch[anne]* 14 (lower center); 9) *lunga tuta la via ch[anne]* 99 (center bottom); 10) *lunga ch[anne]* 11 (right of center); 11) *ch[anne]* 28 *datorione atorione* (lower right of center); 12) *hypodromo* (right of center at bottom); 13 *Xisto locho dalbori* (center right side); 14) *cavagli* 78 (bottom right); 15) *stalle ch[anne]* 44 *p[almi]* 8 (bottom right); 16) *tenpio* (right tower); 17) *chane* 27 *dal monte alle stalle* (far right).

PROVENANCE: unavailable.

BIBLIOGRAPHY: Jahn 1869: 148; Geymüller 1884: 59-61; Hofmann 1908: 80-82; Giovannoni 1959: 333; Coffin 1967: 113, 116; Frommel 1975: 64-68, 84; 1984d: 326-329; Biermann 1986: 494-495, 502-503, 520-523; Frommel 1986b: 289; Eiche 1992: 275-276.

Plan of the main story of a villa, laid out along a longitudinal axis that is accentuated by three monumental rectangular spaces: entrance court, central court (*cavedio*), and garden (*xisto*), which are separated one from the other by a three-aisled *vestibolo* with an *atrio*, and by a loggia. The entrance is on the left short side, through a gate flanked by half-columns. This side facade is extended rearward, positioning the gate at the center also with respect to the exterior. Round towers mark the right and left corners. Toward the front of the villa at the left are: a walled-in sunken garden with loggia and stairs; an apartment of four rooms plus a domed main room. Toward the left rear of the villa are spacious service quarters and stairs. At the center of the villa, toward the front, is a loggia with semicircular ends and a salient balcony, behind which is a double-ramped stair. At the rear of the villa, across from the central court, is a semicircular theater with a nymphaeum at courtyard level. Above the theater, a road arriving from the right runs parallel to the main axis of the villa, turning 90° to connect to the top center of the theater. It corresponds to the transverse axis, which continues through to the salient balcony of the front loggia. At the right of the loggia is a second apartment of three rooms and a fishpond surrounded on three sides by stairs and steps. Round towers also demarcate the ends of the front facade, the one at left containing a sitting room or *diaeta*, the one at right a chapel labeled *tenpio*. In front of the whole length of the villa is a hyppodrome, below which are stables. A broad entrance road aligned with the transverse axis passes through the middle of the stables. The lighter wash denotes solid masonry, the darker wash, water.

Not identified by any contemporary inscription, Uff. 273A was first associated with the Villa Madama in 1869 (Jahn 1869: 148). Though it differs in some respects from the final design, the general layout and scale, as well as certain features such as the towers, the walled-in garden, the two loggias, the *atrio* and *vestibolo*, the theater, and the fishpond, confirm the identification. Geymüller (1884: 60), Hofmann (1908: 80), and Giovannoni (1959: 333) ascribed Uff. 273A to Sangallo il Gobbo, Geymüller and Hofmann believing that it dated prior to any construction, Giovannoni that it was the initial project. Coffin (1967: 113, 116), though concurring with their attribution, dates the plan to ca. 1524, considering it an alternate proposal for the completion of the villa. Frommel (1984d, 311-312, 326) connects Uff. 273A with Raphael, proposing that it was drawn for him by Gianfrancesco da Sangallo in the summer of 1518, about six months before Raphael composed his letter on the villa. According to Frommel (1986b: 289), a project similar to Uff. 273A was used to begin work on the foundations between August and winter of 1518.
Frommel's (1984d: 324-329) examination of Uff. 273A is exhaustive regarding its relationship to Raphael's letter (Foster 1967-68: 308-312, and here cat. 221), which accords well with most of the plan. He points out the influences of both contemporary architecture (e.g., Bramante's loggia at Genazzano; the Sangallo type of colonnaded atrium [see also Frommel 1986b: 289]), and antique architecture (baths; nymphaea; Pliny the Younger's villas; Vitruvius' treatise).

None of the students of Uff. 273A has paid sufficient attention to the discrepancies between the inscribed and real measurements, found mainly in the right half of the drawing (Eiche 1992: 275-276). The inscribed length of the fishpond, for instance, is equal to half its real length. Interestingly, in a later project, Uff. 314A, the real length of the fishpond approaches very closely the measurement inscribed on Uff. 273A.

This suggests that some of the deviations are to be attributed to changes developed after Uff. 273A was drawn, which were noted on the plan as a pro-memoria for a future design, strengthening the argument for placing Uff. 273A early in the series of the Villa Madama projects.

S.E.

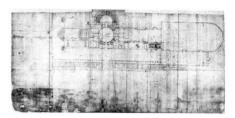

213
ANTONIO DA SANGALLO THE YOUNGER
Project for a Plan of the Villa Madama

Florence, Galleria degli Uffizi, Gabinetto Disegni e Stampe, Uff. 314A
Pen and three kinds of brown ink, some red chalk, incised lines, pin holes, pentimenti; six sheets joined, some abrasion, some stains, several fold marks, fragmentary at left and along bottom, laid down with secondary support exposed at right edge and along right and left top;
watermark: crossbow in circle with lily above (cf. Uff. 273A); scale: (in center of circular court) 31.5 mm = 5 *canne*; 6.3 mm = 1 *canna*; ca. 1:355.
629/635 × 1256/1259 mm (with secondary support)
INSCRIBED: 1) *la strada* (top left); 2) *la strada* (top left); 3) *Questa sia abastoni / monta palmi* 8 (in front of segmental stairs); 4) *scarpa* (left tower); 5) *Tereno basso palmi* 28 (below left tower); 6) *Questa sia agradi / monta palmi* 35 (in front of stairs in courtyard); 7) *è più basso* (along wall, at bottom to right of center); 8) *Casetta [...]* (at bottom, to right of center); 9) *Canne* 12 *p[er] quadro* (near double-ramped stairs, lower right); 10) *fratta* (along contour line of hill at right); 11) *perquesto verso va in piano* (bottom, to right of center); 12) *Cantone della / fratta* (along contour line of hill at lower right).

PROVENANCE: unavailable.

BIBLIOGRAPHY: Jahn 1869: 148; Geymüller 1884: 62-64; Hofmann 1908: 85-87; Coffin 1967: 112-113; Frommel 1975: 75-76, 84; 1984d: 337; Biermann 1986: 494-495, 502-503, 520-523; Frommel 1986b: 291-295; Eiche 1992: 277-280.

Plan of the main story of a villa laid out along a longitudinal axis, with a circular court at the center, around which are grouped two main apartments with loggias, stairs and passageways; service quarters; and a semicircular theater. A short transverse axis runs from the nymphaeum beneath the theater to the central bay of the front loggia. Round towers mark the right and left ends of the front facade, and of the left side facade. The entrance is at the left, where segmental stairs lead through a gate into a rectangular court. Between this court and the front facade is a walled-in sunken garden with loggias at both ends. At the far end of the court are three sets of stairs, the wide central stair in line with a three-aisled entranceway leading to a corridor, which leads to the circular court. On the opposite side of the circular court, a corridor similar to the first leads into a spacious loggia with three exedrae in all but one of its walls, and with three arches opening onto a garden. The rear garden wall has three deep exedrae. Below the garden is a fishpond, likewise with three exedrae articulating the rear wall. Stairs connect the garden with a colonnaded rectangular space to the right of the pond, and with an open rectangular space at the left. Various gardens lie to right, left, and below the villa, interconnected by way of stairs and gates. Stables are located in front of the villa, separated from it by a long and relatively wide space. A road in line with the transverse axis cuts through the middle of the stable area.

Uff. 314A was first associated with the Villa Madama by Jahn (1869: 148). It corresponds more closely than any of the other projects to the part that was built. According to Frommel (1984d: 337; 1986b: 290-295; 1989b: 98), Uff. 314A reveals Antonio da Sangallo's participation in the planning stages. Raphael's letter (Foster 1967-68: 308-312), supposedly composed in the early spring of 1519, after Sangallo had begun to work out the modifications (as in Uff. 179A, 1518A), mentions certain features included in Uff. 314A but missing from Uff. 273A, for instance the circular court, the theater designed on Vitruvian principles, the exedrae of the garden loggia, and the *cenatione* beside the fishpond. However, his letter does not take full account of the consequences of Sangallo's changes, which are finally given visual form in Uff. 314A.

Frommel (1984d: 311-312; 1986b: 292-293) argues that the reorganization of the internal spaces is partly due to economic and technical considerations. The new arrangement produces a more compact plan and a symmetrical main facade. The passages through the spaces along the front of the villa are shifted toward the facade to create a continuous enfilade from the loggia of the secret garden at the southeast to the room overlooking the *cenatione* at the northwest. The circular court pushes the theater back, higher up the hillside. Some parts of the villa, for instance those buttressing the hillside, were substantially reinforced.

Coffin (1967: 112-113, 115, 117-118) dates Uff. 314A to a period after the death of Raphael in April 1520. Frommel (1984d: 311-312, 337; 1986b: 289-290) believes it was drawn in the spring of 1519. He suggests that in the summer of 1520 Sangallo wrote some measurements in the rooms between the court and garden loggia, and made some changes to walls and secondary stairs in the same area (all in darker ink). Sangallo then enlarged the drawing by adding five more pieces, keeping the original sheet at center top. On the supplementary sheets he drew the surrounding garden areas.

It has not been previously noticed that Uff. 314A reveals traces of an earlier stage in the design process (Eiche 1992: 277-280). Incised in the left half of the circular court is a smaller one, the center of which corresponds closely to the center of the sheet. At left the small circle connects with the corridor; at right another corridor had been drawn, which was scratched out when the circle was enlarged. There are numerous horizontal and vertical incised lines relating to the smaller circle stage, two of which were mistakenly used in the later project to mark the centers of the front loggia bays, thereby producing asymmetrical vaults. It is interesting to note that the proportional relationship of circular court to three-aisled entrance plus corridor is closer between Uff. 179A and the first version of 314A (ca. 1 *canna* difference) than between 179A and the final version of 314A (ca. 6 *canne* difference). Evidently there were more stages to the design of the Villa Madama, some of which involved major changes in scale, than have been recognized up to now.

S.E.

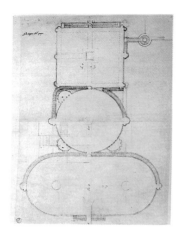

214
RAPHAEL
Project for Gardens at the Villa Madama

Florence, Galleria degli Uffizi, Gabinetto Disegni e Stampe, Uff. 1356Ar.
Pen and two kinds of brown ink, incised lines, pentimenti; two sheets joined; modern strips added right and left to straighten sides; tears patched on verso at center top and bottom; watermark: anchor in circle with six-pointed star above (closest to Briquet 492); scale: (deducible from diameter of central garden) 5.5 mm = 1 *canna*; ca. 1:406.
532/534 × 396/398 mm (with strips).
INSCRIBED: *p[er] la vigna del papa* (upper left).
VERSO: sketches of plans of gardens(?), some with stairs; graph(?); pair of zigzag lines; series of lines with row of semicircular concavities.
INSCRIBED: *p[er] la vignja del papa.*

PROVENANCE: unavailable.

BIBLIOGRAPHY: Geymüller 1884: 64-67, pl. VIII; Hofmann 1908: 83-84; Bafile 1942: 13-17, pls. VIII, IX; Giovannoni 1959: 333, 337; Coffin 1967: 113-115; Frommel 1975: 68-70, 84; 1984d: 330; Coffin 1991: 62-63; Eiche 1992: 280-285.

Plans of three adjacent, differently-shaped garden terraces. The top one is square, the width and depth inscribed as 30 *canne*. It has semicircular niches at the corners and at the middle of each side. In the upper wall an entrance flanked by columns leads to a double-ramped symmetrical stair. At right is the indication of a rectangular site, with a round tower at its corner, connecting to the terrace by way of stairs, which turn 90° at the garden wall and exit in the middle niche. In the center of the terrace is a rectangular basin or fountain. The middle garden is circular, with a diameter of 30 *canne*. There are semicircular niches to right and left, and at the top. Three large semicircular exedrae with columns (a fourth without columns is drawn in lightly at the upper right) are disposed around the circle, those at the left slightly deeper than those at the right. Two stairs of different design run from the upper left and right toward the semicircular niches. At the center of the garden is a circular basin or fountain. The third garden, a square with semicircular ends, is inscribed as having a depth of 30 *canne* and a width of 60 *canne*. Stairs, reached from an opening between the middle and lowest terrace, run along the upper circumference and exit in semicircular niches at right and left. Short, double-ramped stairs are located at the middle of the lower long side. At the center of the bases of the semicircular ends are two circular basins or fountains.

An inscription at upper left in the hand of Antonio da Sangallo identifies Uff. 1356A as being for the gardens of the Villa Madama. Nearly all discussions of the drawing concentrate on the location of the gardens with respect to the villa. While Geymüller (1884: 66-67, pl. VIII) placed them in front, running horizontally across the site, Bafile (1942: 13-17, pls. VIII, IX) correctly interpreted them as terraces running down the hill to the Tiber, but ignored the position of the tower and situated them on an axis with the center of the villa. Coffin (1967: 113-115), fol-

lowing Hofmann (1908: 84) demonstrates that they were to be located in the eastern part of the site. Coffin (1967: 114) associates Uff. 1356A with the villa plans on Uff. 179A and 314A. According to Frommel (1975: 68-70; 1984d: 330), also following Hofmann (1908: 84), Uff. 1356A is to be related to the plan on Uff. 273A because of the similar position of the tower in relation to the villa, which has changed in the later projects.

No one before now has analyzed the pentimenti in the upper half of Uff. 1356A, which reveal how the drawing was generated, and clarify the artist's intentions (Eiche 1992: 280-285). The changes involved shifting the central axis leftward, and adjusting the garden walls, always with the aim of keeping the stairs outside the perimeters of the three terraces. This leads to the conclusion that the design of Uff. 1356A is based on the pre-eminence of the three geometric forms of the terraces, rather than on the concept of a unifying central axis. The experience of walking from one terrace to another, physically tracing the outline of the geometric form, would have been totally different from that at Bramante's Belvedere Court, where the three terraces were physically and visually linked by the central perspective. Uff. 1356A has had a variety of attributions. Geymüller (1884: 65), later followed by Frommel (1975: 68-70), identified the hand as that of Raphael, based above all on the calligraphy of the inscribed measurements. Hofmann (1908: 83-84), questioned that attribution. Giovannoni (1959: 333, 337) suggested Francesco da Sangallo. Coffin (1967: 114) ascribes the drawing to Antonio da Sangallo the Younger. A further argument in support of the early attribution to Raphael can be found by comparing Uff. 1356A and 273A from the point of view of circulation (Eiche 1992: 284-285). The perception of space in these two drawings is totally rethought in the later projects (Uff. 179A, 1518A, 314A), where the concept of stairs and passages has developed from one of undisturbed visual and physical progression to one in which progression is dramatically interrupted. A case in point is the stair linking the upper garden and fishpond: in Uff. 273A the open stair repeats the shape of the pond in the way the stairs in Uff. 1356A repeat the shapes of the terraces; in Uff. 314A the stairs have become ramps that are partly outside, partly inside the wall between the two levels. If Raphael is to be credited with the project on Uff. 273A, then he was also responsible for Uff. 1356A. *S.E.*

215
PHILIPPE CAYLUS
View from the Loggia into the Garden of the Villa Madama
(after Heemskerck)

Rome, Istituto Nazionale per la Grafica, FC 122637
Etching.
150 × 224 mm (plate).
INSCRIBED: 1) *Hemskerk Del.* (on base of statue); 2) *C.S.* (lower right corner); 3) *Veduta della vigna del Card. Cesi* (written in ink along lower margin).

PROVENANCE: Corsini collection.

BIBLIOGRAPHY: Capecchi et al 1991-92: 45-47.

In this engraving, Caylus copied a drawing by Maarten van Heemskerck of 1532/35 (Berlin, Staatliche Museen,

Kupferstichkabinett, 79 D 2, I, fol. 24), which in the eighteenth century had belonged to J. P. Mariette (Hülsen and Egger 1913, I, iii, ix). The handwritten inscription incorrectly identifies it as the Cesi garden.

The view is taken from the west bay of the garden loggia at the Villa Madama, looking northwest. Inside the loggia is a seated statue, identified as *Jupiter Ciampolini*, the lower half of which survives in Naples (Museo Archeologico Nazionale). Statues of the so-called *Euterpe* (now in the Museo Archeologico Nazionale, Naples), and *Diana* (present whereabouts unknown) are seen in niches behind the *Jupiter*. In the first niche of the garden wall stands the colossal statue of the so-called *Genius* (now in the Museo Archeologico Nazionale, Naples). The niche at the center, preceded by two segmental steps, contains the famous elephant fountain. Two gigantic statues by Baccio Bandinelli flank the triangular-pedimented gate at the far end of the garden.

The depiction reveals that there were a variety of bushes or trees growing along the walls. There is no indication of beds or borders in the garden area, and according to the inscription on Uff. 273A ("Xisto locho dalbori"), it, too, was intended to be planted with trees.

The garden of the Villa Madama can be seen again in the background of one of Heemskerck's engravings, where the scene is enriched by the inclusion of a gazebo, composed of caryatids supporting a dome of topiary work (*The Three Maries at the Tomb*, dated 1548, Copenhagen, Statens Museum for Kunst, Kongelige Kobberstiksamling; reverse copy by Dirck Vokertsz. Coornhert, Amsterdam, Rijksmuseum). *S.E.*

side of the monumental round-arched portal, with a portion of the architrave of the large order in place. He is not invariably accurate with regard to details: his columns have Corinthian rather than Ionic capitals; it is also questionable if all aediculae then had entablatures (see Heemskerck's view, as above), and if the large column to the side of the portal was intact with capital and architrave. According to Lint's painting (cat.no. 218), these features were still missing in 1748.

Beyond the portal in Lombard's drawing we see the barrel-vaulted corridor leading from the courtyard to the garden loggia, where we glimpse a statue on a pedestal. Through the second aedicula on the right (left in the drawing) we see a figure ascending a ramp of the triangular stair located between the courtyard and the front loggia. The view of this part of the architecture was drawn from within the courtyard, slightly to the left of center. To the right of the courtyard (left in the drawing) are two superimposed vaulted spaces: a fragment of the front loggia and the cryptoporticus below it. To draw these, Lombard climbed down to the level of the hippodrome, which explains why the front loggia appears elevated with respect to the courtyard, though in fact both are at the same level. It must have been with the intention of revealing these portions of the villa that Lombard eliminated the two outermost courtyard bays. His view is one of the rare contemporary visual documents recording the extent to which building on the front loggia and cryptoporticus had advanced by the time construction ceased. The accuracy of this part of Lombard's drawing is confirmed by Bénard's plan of 1871 (Frommel 1984d: 341, 2.16.16a). *S.E.*

218
HENDRIK FRANS VAN LINT
The Villa Madama
1748

Cambridge, The Syndics of the Fitzwilliam Museum, PD 265.
Oil on canvas.
36 × 45 cm
INSCRIBED: *Enri.co van Lint / detto Studio F Roma 1748* (lower right).
36 × 45 cm

PROVENANCE: Daniel Mesman collection.

BIBLIOGRAPHY: Gerson and Goodison 1960: 72.

Lint's painting (Gerson and Goodison 1960: 72), dated 1748, is probably the most faithful record of the appearance of the incomplete circular courtyard of the Villa Madama after construction had ceased in the 1520s, and before large-scale restoration began early in the twentieth century. Vasi's print of 1761 is misleading (Lefèvre 1984: 194 considers it accurate) insofar as it eliminates the blemishes recorded by Lint, and still visible in the early photographs.

Vasi shows all the aediculae with architraves, whereas in Lint's painting only the two on either side of the central portal are complete. Bénard's section through the Villa Madama (Frommel 1984d: 342, 2.16.16d) reveals that by 1871 the aediculae in the left segment of the courtyard did have architraves, but we can question if they in fact existed already in 1761.

The semicircular stairwell with two windows visible to the right of the central portal houses the small spiral stair added by Antonio da Sangallo after Raphael's death. It can be seen sketched into the plan on Uff. 314A. To the right of the stairwell, between the house and the curve of the courtyard, is a lower structure, which must have contained the remains of the triangular stair. It had disappeared before Bénard came to measure the Villa Madama in 1871. *S.E.*

216
LAMBERT LOMBARD
The Raising of Lazarus, with the Villa Madama in the Background

Düsseldorf, Kunstmuseum, Graphische Sammlung, FP4748
Pen and brown ink over red chalk, gray and gray-brown washes, traces of black chalk, incised lines; composed of one sheet with strips added right and left, the whole subsequently cut in half horizontally and pieced back together; several figures have cut-out pieces of paper pasted over them; some stains.
269/280 × 373/378 mm
INSCRIBED: 1) *dat quart ...* [illegible words] / *...* [illegible words] *to groot in die port* (upper right); 2) [faded signature?]; *1544* (lower right of original sheet); 3) *Lamb / Lomb / 1544* (at bottom of right strip).

PROVENANCE: Lambert Krahe collection; Kunstakademie, Düsseldorf; since 1932 on permanent loan to Kunstmuseum.

BIBLIOGRAPHY: Schaar 1969-70: 71-72; Judson 1986-87: 207.

The *Raising of Lazarus*, dated 1544, was drawn by Lombard to be engraved, and the scene is therefore reversed (Schaar 1969-70: 71-72; Judson 1986-87: 207). It has not been previously noticed that the architecture in the background represents the unfinished circular court of the Villa Madama, which Lombard would have seen during his visit to Rome in 1537-38. The artist shows two aediculae (though in fact there were four; see Heemskerck's view of 1532-35, Berlin Kupferstichkabinett, 79 D 2, I, fol. 9v., discussed in Eiche 1992: 285) of the courtyard to either

217
HIERONYMUS COCK
The Raising of Lazarus, with the Villa Madama in the Background (after Lombard)

Brussels, Bibliothèque Royale Albert Ier, Cabinet des Estampes, S.V. 89185
Engraving.
283 × 361 mm
INSCRIBED: 1) *Lamb. Lombard inven. / H. Cock Excudebat* (lower right); 2) *LAZARVM QVATRIDVANVM IESVS. A. MORTE SVSCITAVIT. IOANN. XI.* (lower margin).

PROVENANCE: unavailable.

BIBLIOGRAPHY: Judson 1986-87: 207.

Cock published this print of Lombard's 1544 drawing after 1522 (Judson 1986-87: 207). the engraver modified some details of the background: the interior structure of the garden loggia is different; and the figure of a man in the corridor, which in the drawing was too large for the scale of the architecture, has been eliminated. Similarly, the engraver omitted the ramp of the triangular stair, which was visible through the aedicula nearest to the front loggia. *S.E.*

219
RICHARD WILSON
Rome from the Villa Madama
1753

New Haven, Yale Center for British Art, Paul Mellon Collection, B 1977.14.82
Oil on canvas.
95.4 × 132.4 cm
INSCRIBED: signed on boulder, left center *RW*, and dated 1753.

PROVENANCE: Earl of Dartmouth collection.

BIBLIOGRAPHY: Constable 1953: 218; Solkin 1982-83: 184-185.

Wilson painted this view of Rome looking southward from Via Trionfale, a major pilgrimage route that branches off from Via Cassia and approaches the Vatican by way of Monte Mario. The Villa Madama, with the loggia overlooking the garden and fishpond below, is seen in the middle ground to the right, illuminated by the rays of the late afternoon sun. According to Raphael's letter, and to the project on Uff. 273A, there was to have been an entrance from Via Trionfale into the Villa Madama by way of a gate at the top of the semicircular theater. Originally the Villa Madama and the Vatican would have been linked also by a single visual axis. By the eighteenth century this evidently was no longer the case, for we see in Wilson's painting that the trees planted around the villa had grown high and unchecked in the intervening centuries, totally obscuring the view.

Wilson's depiction evokes the steepness of the terrain below the Villa Madama more vividly than any of the site plans. It is evident that major technical difficulties would have been encountered in laying out the gardens projected in both Uff. 1356A and 314A. _S.E._

220
UNKNOWN ITALIAN (16TH CENTURY)
Project for the Circular Court of the Villa Madama

London, The British Architectural Library Drawings Collection, Royal Institute of British Architects, XIII/11
Pen and ink, gray-green wash, incised lines.
263 × 400 mm

PROVENANCE: Lord Burlington.

BIBLIOGRAPHY: Burns 1975: 264-266; Frommel 1984d: 338-339; 1989d: 290.

A measured elevation of the lower level of part of a facade, in two versions, showing a door flanked by two pairs of tabernacle windows (the outer ones slightly cut), which have alternating triangular and segmental pediments. Door and windows are flanked by Ionic columns, set on a high base and supporting a frieze. The door, and one window, are surmounted by a niche or small rectangular window, one of which contains a bust.

Burns (1975: 264-266) first published the drawing, and suggested the identification, which has not been challenged. It is the only known elevation of a project for the central circular court. The drawing has been attributed to the workshops of both Raphael (Burns 1975: 264), and Giulio Romano (Frommel 1989b: 290).

Frommel (1984d: 338; 1983: 290) dates the elevation around 1520-21, when the court of the Villa Madama was already under construction. Both Burns (1975: 264-266) and Frommel (1984d: 338-339; 1989b: 290) have discussed the dimensions of the various drawn architectural elements in relation to those of the constructed fragment, though Frommel (1984d: 338) feels that the small scale of the drawing does not permit the detailed measurements that Burns (1975: 265) calculated.

Burns (1975: 226) hypothesizes that the drawing may have once belonged to Palladio, who could have acquired it from Valerio Belli. _S.E._

221
UNKNOWN ITALIAN (16TH CENTURY)
Copy of Raphael's Letter on the Villa Madama

Florence, Archivio di Stato, Mediceo avanti il Principato, Fa. 94, no. 162, cc. 294-299.
Pen and ink.
ca. 295 × 215 mm

PROVENANCE: unavailable.

BIBLIOGRAPHY: *Archivio Mediceo...* III 1957: 402; Foster 1967-68: 308-312; Lefèvre 1969: 425-437; Frommel 1984d: 324-326; Biermann 1986: 493-494, 502-504, 522-524.

The existence of a letter by Raphael describing the Villa Madama has long been known, though it was believed lost. A contemporary reference to the document occurs in a letter by Castiglione, written on 13 August 1522 to Francesco Maria della Rovere, Duke of Urbino, in reply to the Duke's request to see Castiglione's copy of Raphael's description (Golzio 1936: 147). The duke's great interest in the building may be connected with his plan to enlarge the Villa Imperiale at Pesaro, a project that, however, only got underway in around 1530. It is not without significance that just about the same time that he contacted Castiglione about Raphael's letter, the duke heard from one of his own Roman agents that the search for an architect trained by Raphael had been successful: in August 1522 Girolamo Genga, designer of the new Villa Imperiale, arrived in the Duchy of Urbino to become della Rovere's court architect (Eiche 1991: 317-323).

It was Foster (1967-68: 308-312) who discovered and first transcribed the copy of Raphael's letter (see Eiche 1992: 285, no. 2, for the correct transcription of one word). Shortly after that, Lefèvre (1969: 425-437) published a modernized transcription. Frommel (1984d: 324-325) analyzed the text, noting the allusions to antique authors, especially Pliny the Younger and Vitruvius, and relating the description to the projects of the Villa Madama recorded in the plans on Uff. 273A and 314A. Also Biermann (1986: 493-494, 502-504, 522-524) discusses Raphael's text, particularly in connection with the circular court.

Chronologically, Frommel (1984d: 325) places the original letter between the two projects drawn on Uff. 273A and 314A, proposing to date it to the early spring of 1519. His reason for this sequence is that the description, while corresponding to parts of the plan on Uff. 273A (e.g., the dimensions of the entrance court, the access from the top of the hill through the theater), also includes features seen only on Uff. 314A (e.g., the scale and circular form of the central court, the exedrae of the garden loggia, the theater designed according to Vitruvian principles, and the *cenatione* to the side of the *peschiera*). _S.E._

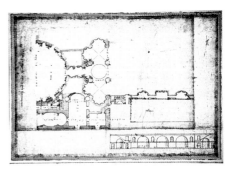

222
ANDREA PALLADIO
Plan of the Villa Madama

London, The British Architectural Library Drawings Collection, Royal Institute of British Architects, X/18
Pen, ink and wash over brown chalk; several sheets of paper joined.
338 × 468 mm

INSCRIBED: *questa e la vigna del papa la quale sie a monte mario* (along left side); *cusina*; *peschiera*.

PROVENANCE: unavailable.

BIBLIOGRAPHY: Zorzi 1969: 88-89; Burns 1975: 88-89; Lewis 1981a: 55; Frommel 1984d: 339.

A measured plan of the constructed portion of the Villa Madama, including at lower right an elevation of the *peschiera*. In the plan, Palladio has combined the upper and lower levels: he shows the fragmentary circular courtyard and great garden loggia, which are linked by a corridor flanked by two rooms (all upper level); and the beginning of the triangular stair, three and a half rooms (including the kitchen), the *cenatione* with its stair to the upper garden, and the *peschiera* (all lower level).

As Burns (1975: 88) noted, this is the only modern building that Palladio studied in plan. Zorzi (1969: 88) and Frommel (1984d: 339) believe the drawing was made during Palladio's first or second trip to Rome, that is, between 1541 and 1547.

Palladio "improves" the plan of the Villa Madama by adding an exedra to the northeast end of the garden loggia (as did Serlio, 1540b, III, p. CXLVIII), to match the one on the southwest or hill side. According to Burns (1975: 88), the plan is otherwise remarkably precise. Frommel (1984d: 339), on the other hand, detects a number of inaccuracies. Both agree, however, that the plan's main importance lies in documenting Palladio's interest in Roman architecture. Zorzi (1969: 88-89) stresses the importance of Palladio's visit to the Villa Madama for his subsequent designs of villas with curved porticoes. _S.E._

564

Michelangelo and the Facade of S. Lorenzo in Florence

Henry A. Millon

The desire to complete S. Lorenzo by adding a facade to the church Brunelleschi had built for previous Medici patrons seems to have matured in the mind of Leo X during the time he spent in Florence in the autumn and winter of 1515-16. The pope had passed through his native Florence late in November on the way to Bologna to negotiate a treaty with the king of France and returned on 22 December to stay several months.

Giorgio Vasari and Ascanio Condivi (a pupil of Michelangelo in the early 1550s) both wrote accounts of the pope's visit to Florence and the events that led to awarding the commission for the facade, as well as the sculpture, to Michelangelo. Vasari recorded the events in both editons (1550 and 1568) of the lives he wrote of Jacopo Sansovino, Leonardo, and Michelangelo. The accounts do not agree in all respects. Condivi's *Life of Michelangelo*, published in 1553, eleven years before Michelangelo's death, was written utilizing Michelangelo's account of the story and must have been at least partially motivated by what Condivi felt to be the unsatisfactory account of Michelangelo's life found in the first edition of Vasari's *Lives*. (For Condivi, see now Wohl, ed. 1976.)

Vasari noted that many artists competed in Rome for the design of the facade, "that designs were made by Baccio d'Agnolo, Antonio da Sangallo, Andrea [and Jacopo, 2nd edition] Sansovino, and the elegant Raphael of Urbino, who came with Pope Leo to Florence to that end" (Vasari, ed. Milanesi 1881, VII; 188).

If the pope did request designs from architects in the winter of 1515-16, he appears to have ruminated over the matter for a number of months; as late as October the commission for the architecture seems to have been still pending.

On 3 November Domenico Buoninsegni wrote to Michelangelo from Rome saying that if he did not want to come to Rome then at least Baccio d'Agnolo, who at that time was collaborating with Michelangelo, should make the journey and bring with him a design for the facade (*Carteggio* 1965-83, CLXIV).

On 6 November (*Carteggio*, CLXVII), Baccio d'Agnolo wrote to Michelangelo that he did not think he could accomplish anything in Rome without him. By 21 November, Buoninsegni wrote a letter to Michelangelo that registers impatience with Michelangelo's apparent indecision. Buoninsegni states clearly his embarrassment at having pleaded their cause with Cardinal Giulio de' Medici and the pope, and said he would not pursue the project further nor write again to either of them about it (*Carteggio*, CLXXII). As noted by Contardi (cf. Argan and Contardi 1990: 163), Buoninsegni's letter also says that Michelangelo and Baccio d'Agnolo should not lament the award of important commissions to non-Florentines if their lack of decisiveness was the cause. Contardi feels Buoninsegni's letter may imply that Raphael could be awarded the commission.

There the matter might have hung for some time, had not Buoninsegni written again to Michelangelo on 11 December. Shortly after 15 December, Michelangelo was in Rome for only a few days, returning to Florence by 22 December, when Buoninsegni addressed a letter to him there. In that short period in Rome, Michelangelo prepared a design that was agreed upon and approved by the pope, received allowances for grain and other food for himself and workmen at Carrara, obtained promise of one thousand ducats (and his travel expenses to Rome) as an advance on the expenses of the preparation of marble, re-

quested and received assurance of studio space in Florence to work the marble, divided the duties between himself and Baccio d'Agnolo, and arranged to have two models built of the facade, one of which would be sent to the pope.

As reported to Michelangelo on 7 January 1517 by Bernardo Niccolini in Florence (Treasurer to the Archbishop of Florence), Baccio d'Agnolo was already at work on a model and wished to hear from Michelangelo about the foundations (*Carteggio*, CLXXXIX). The model was to follow the design agreed upon in Rome and, as revealed in a letter of Buoninsegni to Michelangelo of 2 February 1517 (*Carteggio*, CXCV), there were to be ten statues in three ranges: on the lower level, four standing figures (from left to right, St. Paul, St. Peter, St. John the Baptist and St. Lawrence); at the next level, four seated figures (from left to right, St. Mark, St. Matthew, St. John Evangelist and St. Luke); at the topmost level, two doctors, most likely standing figures (St. Cosmas [left] and St. Damian [right]).

The model was nearing completion in the middle of February (*Carteggio*, CCII) and was finished on 7 March, when Niccolini wrote to Michelangelo that, before sending it to Rome, Michelangelo had only to see it (*Carteggio*, CCVI). Michelangelo wrote Buoninsegni on 20 March (*Carteggio*, CCXII), that he had been to Florence to see the model and found it a "thing by a child." He could not work with Baccio.

In the letter to Buoninsegni (*Carteggio*, CCXII), Michelangelo said that, out of respect for the cardinal and the pope, this affair saddened him. Buoninsegni replied on 27 March that he had reported to the cardinal, that he and the pope were displeased at not having the model, but that Michelangelo should work with whomever he wished.

Michelangelo seems to have been satisfied with a new design by 2 May, at which time he wrote a lengthy letter to Buoninsegni in which he mentions both a new, higher price, and a clay model of the new facade he had prepared for his own use (*Carteggio*, CCXXI).

Ackerman has suggested the increased price was due to a change in the design of the facade from a veneer on the existing rough masonry surface to a narthex scheme with the facade turning to form flanks on right and left (Ackerman 1961, II: 9). The drawings by Michelangelo for the various phases of the "final design" CB 43A, CB 100A, and possibly CB 51A, as well as drawings after Michelangelo (Uff. 790A, Munich 33258, and related drawings), are usually dated in the period between the rejection of Baccio's model and the letter of 2 May to Buoninsegni.

Michelangelo seems to have completed a wood model of the new design, with figures in wax (*Carteggio*, CDLVIII), before the third week in December, when Pietro Urbano conveyed it to Rome. (On 19 December, Jacopo Salviati had been given funds to pay Baccio d'Agnolo and Michelangelo for models.) On either 22 or 29 December, Urbano showed it to Buoninsegni and the cardinal, who showed the wooden model to the pope. All were pleased with it (it was noted that the flanks of the new design would greatly increase the task) and wanted Michelangelo to come to Rome.

This he did, and on 19 January 1518 Michelangelo signed a contract for the marble facade. The contract (Milanesi 1875b: 671), based on the wooden model, called for twelve standing figures (six on the first level to be five *braccia* tall, six on the upper level to be five and one-half *braccia* tall), and six seated figures in bronze at the mezzanine level, four and one-half *braccia* tall. Four of each were to be on the facade, the others on the flanks. The contract specified an additional seven reliefs: five rectangular (four of them eight *braccia* wide and one about nine *braccia* wide) and two round marble reliefs (six or sven *braccia* in diameter). Also cited in the contract were the dimensions of some of the architectural members (eight fluted columns about eleven *braccia* high at the first level, and in the mezzanine, pilasters about six or seven *braccia* tall). Upon comparison of these dimensions with the drawing

for the "final design" by Michelangelo and others, it is clear the drawings all antedate the design that was the basis of the wood model. The height of the mezzanine pilasters (six or seven *braccia* tall) in the contract suggests a single mezzanine, not the double ones of CB 43A, Uff. 790A, Munich 33258 and Uff. 205A. The height of the mezzanine pilasters in the contract indicates a design more like the profiles of the drawings in the Casa Buonarroti (CB 51A) and in the British Museum, approaching the wooden model.

The model in the exhibition corresponds closely to the specifications in the contract with the exception of the width of the rectangular reliefs. The model has the necessary sites for the five rectangular reliefs specified, one above and below each tondo (the reliefs above the tondi in the model are narrower than those of eight *braccia* below) and one in the center of the mezzanine above the main portal (narrower than the nine *braccia* width stated in the contract). As Ackerman has demonstrated (1961, II: 13-14), the facade design as revealed in the contract had a wider central bay than the extant wooden model (in the model the central bay is narrower than the side bays). Two series of undated sketches made by Michelangelo for blocks of marble to be quarried for the facade, first published by Tolnay (1954: 155-156), were analyzed by Ackerman (1961, II: 14-17). The dimensions show, when compared with the model, that blocks were sketched for a central portal that was over one *braccia* wider than the model (agreeing with the wider central bay relief specified in the contract), but without any other significant variations. Marble began arriving in Florence in the summer of 1519 (*Ricordi*, LXXIX, cf. Bardeschi Civlich and Barocchi), but it was not until April 1521 that the first column for the facade arrived; it was then over a year overdue, as the contract had been annulled in March 1520 (contemporary notice of G. Cambi, quoted in Barocchi 1962a, III: 745). (Bottari [1759-60, II: 234 n. 1] mentions that this column and many other marble blocks were buried in the piazza in front of the church in the late seventeenth century.)

Condivi reports that the pope "changed his mind [about the facade of S. Lorenzo] and turned his thoughts elsewhere" (Condivi-Wohl 1976: 63). Vasari, giving more particulars in both the first and second edition of his life of Michelangelo (Barocchi 1962d, I: 56-57), noted that Michelangelo "spent four ["many" in the second edition] years quarrying marble ... but the project continued for such a long time that the funds the pope had assigned to this work were consumed in the war in Lombardy and the [facade], due to the death of Leo, remained incomplete ... nothing was done other than to make the foundation in front to support it." The accounts by Condivi and Vasari provide more information about the apparent abandonment of the facade project than may be obtained from any other source.

The termination of the contract on 10 March 1520 is recorded by Michelangelo laconically, "Now, Pope Leo, perhaps to achieve more quickly the facade of S. Lorenzo, that he had commissioned me to do ... agrees to release me" (*Ricordi*, XCVIII).

The death in May 1519 of Duke Lorenzo of Urbino, that "closed the dynastic prospects of the Medici family" (Ackerman 1986: 296), may have contributed to Michelangelo's release from work on the facade and to a decision by the cardinal and the pope to build a family mausoleum at S. Lorenzo (Corti and Parronchi 1964; Parronchi 1968b). As Michelangelo's first major architectural commission, the designs for S. Lorenzo chronicle the evolution and formation of some of his ideas about architecture. The drawings and model gathered for this exhibition offer an unparalleled opportunity to survey the results of Michelangelo's thoughts about the facade as he studied it between the summer of 1516 and the autumn of 1518. Michelangelo may have begun his consideration of the design after seeing drawings for the facade by Giuliano da Sangallo that have been mentioned as possible sources (Tolnay 1934: 35-38), but to those should be added his experience of the designs and works by Bramante and

Sangallo in Rome. Michelangelo may also have known Bramante's wooden model for the marble revetment of the Santa Casa, which had been sent from Loreto to Rome early in 1513, so that it might be seen by Pope Leo X (Posner 1974b: 319).

What Michelangelo did to heighten the contrast between support and infill and between solid and surface, within the context of Roman facades, reveals his interest in animating and anthropomorphizing the structure. In each of the designs, Michelangelo sought to concentrate apparent strength and mass in salient bays (with paired columns), while diminishing any perceived mass of the recessed bays through reliefs that accentuate surface. The apparent mass of the entire facade was greatly increased by the return bays on the flanks.

Even without being constructed, Michelangelo's project for a structurally articulated facade altered contemporary conceptions of architecture.

Though few architects sought to enliven their buildings through emphasis on verticals achieved by differentiation of column/pier and infill, mass and support, Michelangelo here initiated a path that was to contribute thirty years later to his design for the main body of St. Peter's, as well as to his ideas for the drum and dome.

There is little doubt that had the facade been achieved, it would have been as Michelangelo described it (*Carteggio*, CCXXI) "both as architecture and sculpture, the mirror of all Italy."

Much of the text about the design for the facade of S. Lorenzo repeats, in abbreviated form, material published in a catalog of an exhibition of Michelangelo's architecture held at the Casa Buonarroti in Florence and at the National Gallery of Art in Washington in 1988. Of the 11 objects related to Michelangelo's facade of S. Lorenzo in the present exhibition, 2 were part of the earlier exhibition; 2 are additions. The new objects are drawings in Florence and New York.

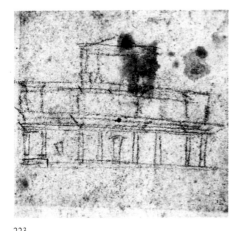

223
MICHELANGELO BUONARROTI
*Project for the Facade of S. Lorenzo
(Preliminary Design)*

Florence, Casa Buonarroti, CB 91Ar.
Red chalk; some stains; no watermark.
90 × 89 mm
RECTO: Project for a facade.
VERSO: Profile of a female head.

PROVENANCE: Casa Buonarroti.

BIBLIOGRAPHY: Gotti 1875, II: 178; Berenson 1903a, II, no. 1443; Geymüller 1904: 7; Thode 1908, II: 91-92; K. Frey 1911: 47; Thode 1913, III: 61; D. Frey 1922-23: 227; Tolnay 1934: 30-31, 35-36; Paatz 1952, II: 532; Pommer 1957: 4-5, 65, 86-98; Düssler 1959: 82; Ackerman 1961, II: 8; Barocchi 1962a: 58-59; 1962c: 18; Ackerman 1964, II: 8; Barocchi 1964b: 24; Bertini 1964: 124; Barbieri and Puppi 1964b: 837; Berti 1965: 442, 444, 446 n. 70; De Angelis d'Ossat 1965: 283; Berti 1966, II: 430, 432, 434 n. 70; De Angelis d'Ossat 1966a, II: 283; Bruschi 1969a: 975; Hartt 1971:

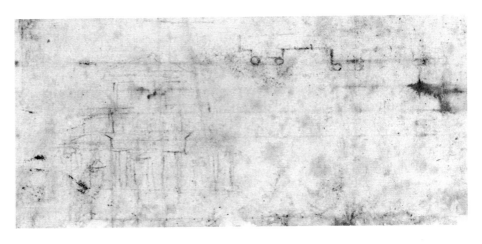

Fig. 1 - Michelangelo, Project for a plan and elevation of the facade of San Lorenzo, *Uff. 41Av.*

132; Tolnay 1972: 57-61; Einem 1973: 86; Tolnay 1975b: 89; Tolnay and Squellati 1977: 10-11, 59; Tolnay 1980, IV: 37-38; Tolnay and Squellati Brizio 1980: 93; Hirst 1983: 555; Berti 1985: 70; Ackerman 1986: 58, 293; Millon and Smyth 1988a: 24-26; Argan and Contardi 1990: 82 and fig. 98; Elam 1992: 105-106.

Usually identified as one of the early stages in the development of Michelangelo's "second design," CB 91A will be here discussed as more closely related to Michelangelo's preliminary design for the project found in CB 41A verso. Placement of CB 91A after CB 41A verso suggests that Michelangelo may have considered several three-level alternatives before turning to the project of CB 45A. In each, the third level with two pairs of columns or pilasters was restricted to the central section.

In this reading, the preoccupation with aedicular bays and pediments on the outermost bays is introduced with CB 45A and the cluster of designs associated with the "first design." If CB 91A (as well as CB 41Av.) is to be dated before CB 45A, then it was most likely executed in the late summer or early autumn of 1516. For a recent diverse view see Elam (1992: 105-106).

As has been noted previously (Tolnay 1934: 35-36 and 1972: 57-61), CB 91A as well as other projects for the "second" and "final" designs seem to reflect projects of Giuliano da Sangallo (Uff. 277A and 279A and fig. 2). In Uff. 281A, on the first level, if the extension of the wall beyond the outermost pair of columns of the facade is ignored, Giuliano da Sangallo's design is a three-story project with a mezzanine of full width.

Since the project in CB 91A permits placement of the ten figures specified in a letter of Domenico Buoninsegni dated 2 February 1517 (*Carteggio* 1965-83, CXCV), i.e., four standing figures between the pairs of columns at the lower level, four seated above them in the mezzanine level, and two figures at the third level between the columns or pilasters, in has been associated with the "second design"

Fig. 2 - Giuliano da Sangallo (attrib.), Design for the Palazzi dei Penitenzieri (?), Rome, *Uff. 279A*

from Geymüller (1904: 7) onward.

Proposing a sequence of projects from CB 91A to CB 44A to CB 47A, rejects the arguments of D. Frey (1922-23: 227) followed by Tolnay (1934: 30-31) and Düssler (1959: 82), and Elam (1992: 105-106), and returns to the order suggested by K. Frey (1911: 47). The relatively undeveloped state of the project, the relationship to CB 41A verso, as well as the lack of any significant need to postulate linear development suggests the possibility of an association with the preliminary designs before the "first design."   *H.A.M.*

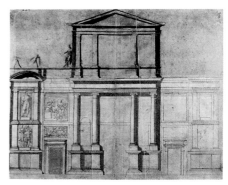

224
MICHELANGELO BUONARROTI
*Project for an Elevation of the Facade of
S. Lorenzo*

Florence, Casa Buonarroti, CB 45A
Pen, brown ink and wash, over some black chalk underdrawing; composite sheet (laid down on secondary support) made of six separate sheets attached; some ink losses; two sheets disposed horizontally form the top 3/7ths of the whole; four sheets of a different quality, placed vertically, make up the lower section.
724 × 868/865 mm

PROVENANCE: Casa Buonarroti.

BIBLIOGRAPHY: Gotti 1875, II: 177; Wilson 1876: 212; Beltrami 1901: 68; Geymüller 1904: 2-6; Vasari, ed. Milanesi 1879, IV: 47; 1881, VII: 496; Thode 1908, II: 89; K. Frey 1911: 47; Thode 1913, III: 40-41; Tolnay 1934: 30 n. 4; Venturi 1939, XI-2: 28; Ackerman 1961, II: 8-9; Vasari and Barocchi 1962d, I: 54-57; Barocchi 1962b: 296; Ackerman 1964, II: 8; Barbieri and Puppi 1964b: 836; Bertini 1964: 124; Tolnay 1972: 57; Hirst 1972: 165 n. 10; Tolnay 1975b: 88; Tolnay and Squellati 1977: 59; Joannides 1978: 176; Stankowski 1979: 20; Tolnay and Squellati Brizio 1980: 93; Tolnay 1980, IV: 35-36; Joannides 1981a: 685; Nova 1984: 33; Berti 1985: 238; Ackerman 1986: 58, 293; Hirst 1986: 323; Nesselrath 1986a: 129; Reuterswärd 1987: 379-383; Millon and Smyth 1988a: 27-31; Argan and Contardi 1990: 166 and figs. 102 and 186; Elam 1992: 105; Wallace 1992a: 472.

This drawing has been considered as Michelangelo's "first design" for almost a century. Geymüller (1904: 2-5) first

3

4

associated it with four drawings by other hands in Munich, Lille, Modena, and at the Rugby School, three of which are inscribed "primo disegno." While authorities have agreed that the design concept of CB 45A is by Michelangelo, only recently have some scholars begun to reattribute the drawing itself to Michelangelo's own hand (first suggested by Geymüller 1904: 6; Hirst 1972: 165 n. 10; 1986: 323; Joannides 1978: 176; 1981b: 685; Millon and Smyth 1988a: 27). Alternative attributions have been proposed to Baccio d'Agnolo (Tolnay 1934: 30 n. 4; 1972: 57; 1980, IV: 36 parts by both artists; Stankowski 1979: 20; Berti 1985: 238; Wallace 1992: 472), an unidentified mannerist hand of the midor late-sixteenth century (Ackerman 1961, II: 8; Barocchi 1962a: 296), or another unknown contemporary draftsman, after Michelangelo (K. Frey 1911: 47). Even though the project includes three differing modes of representation (the ink line drawing of the architecture, the figurative drawings in pen and light wash, and the dark wash drawing and rendering of the upper level and architecture of the main order), CB 45A is justifiably attributed to Michelangelo with, perhaps, the exception of the incompletely drawn portion on the right.

The existence of three sufficiently distinct two-story designs (CB 45A, the drawings in Lille/Rugby, and that in Munich) suggest a cluster of designs by Michelangelo at this stage in the development of his design for the facade. It seems reasonable to propose a date earlier than late December for the cluster of drawings that may be associated with CB 45A, but fixing a more precise date for these preliminary projects of Michelangelo is less certain. Although the history of the projects for the facade of S. Lorenzo as written in three lives by Vasari (Michelangelo, Vasari, ed. Barocchi 1962d, I: 54-57; Jacopo Sansovino, Vasari, ed. Milanesi 1881, VII: 496; Leonardo, Vasari, ed. Milanesi 1879, IV: 47) all suggest the involvement of Michelangelo from late 1515, the earliest dated epistolary evidence is found in a letter of 7 October 1516, from Domenico Buoninsegni, in Montefiascone with the papal court, to Baccio d'Agnolo, in Florence (Carteggio

5

1965-83 CLXII n. 1). As an alternative to a date in the autumn of 1516, Wallace (1992a: 472) suggests the drawing could be much earlier and dates it between November 1515 and February 1516, when the pope departed Florence for Rome. Michelangelo, however, was in Rome in the autumn of 1515 and did not leave for Carrara until July 1516. It appears most likely CB 45A and the cluster of its associated drawings chronicle design projects prepared between late October and early December 1516. Caroline Elam (1992: 105) has suggested CB 45A may have been the drawing "taken to Rome by Michelangelo during his December 1516 visit."   *H.A.M.*

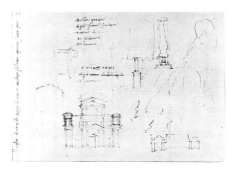

225

MICHELANGELO BUONARROTI
Project for an Elevation of the Facade of S. Lorenzo (Second Design)

Florence, Casa Buonarroti, CB 44Ar.
Pen and brown ink; no watermark.
205 × 270 mm
RECTO: Project for a facade.
a) project for the facade of S. Lorenzo (lower left center); b) herm (upper right, upside down); c) column on tall pedestal (center); d) profile of four bases (lower center right); e) partial elevation of a pedestal with panel under a pair of columns, possibly for the 'first design' of S. Lorenzo (center left, turned 90°); f) section through a column with unusual fluting (center left); g) plan and perspective of throne (Tolnay 1980, IV: 37), or central portion of the facade of S. Lorenzo (Ackerman 1961, II: 8) (lower right); h) sketch of a figure or block of marble (center right).
INSCRIBED: 1) *Messere Domenicho, a questi di è stato iachopo Salviati a pietra Santa pare* (left border); 2) *Della grassa / di gian[n] Franc[esc]o scultore / è nome de' santi / De Fo[n]dame[n]ti / De' danari* (upper center); 3) *o a ci[n]que o a sei / di giennaio da Be[n]tivoglio / i[n] Carrara* (center).
VERSO: Inscription by Michelangelo.

PROVENANCE: Casa Buonarroti.

BIBLIOGRAPHY: Gotti 1875, II: 175; Beltrami 1901: 70; Berenson 1903a, II: no. 1425; Geymüller 1904: 7; Thode 1908, II: 92; K. Frey 1911: 18-19; Thode 1913, III: 49-50; D. Frey 1922-23: 227; Tolnay 1934: 30, 58; Venturi 1939, XI-2: 23; Tolnay 1951: 116; 1954, IV: 47; Wilde 1955: 60 n. 2; Pommer 1957: 86-98; Düssler 1959: 71-72; Ackerman 1961, II: 8; Barocchi 1962b: 59-60; Ackerman 1964, II: 8; Barocchi 1964b: 24-25; Bertini 1964: 124; Barbieri and Puppi 1964b: 837; Barocchi 1965: no. 73; De Angelis d'Ossat 1965: 283, 289; 1966a, II: 281, 283; Hartt 1971: 132; Tolnay 1972: 58; Einem 1973: 86; Tolnay 1975b: 89; Tolnay and Squellati 1977: 10-11; Tolnay 1980, IV: 36-37; Balas 1983: 668; Berti 1985: 69; Ackerman 1986: 293; Millon and Smyth 1988a: 32-35; Argan and Contardi 1990: 167 and fig. 189; Elam 1992: 101-105.

The drawings associated with the "second design" return to a layered three-level scheme with four pairs of columns on low plinths rising from the pavement and with a tall mezzanine, all as found in the preliminary drawings (cf. CB 41Av. and CB 91A). But the "second design" also retains, now at the mezzanine level, the aedicules of the outermost bays of the first level of the facade of the "first design."

A triangular pediment (drawn too low) enframing the lower level of the central section suggests perhaps a columnar portico more salient than the remainder of the facade (Ackerman 1961, II: 8). Michelangelo apparently sought greater integration of the three levels through repetition of triangular pediments above the central opening, the central section of the first level, and the third level, as well as emphasizing the vertical continuity of two levels in the outermost bays of the mezzanine level with their aedicules, here capped by contrasting segmental pediments. CB 44A, in its three levels, would allow for the placement of the ten figures specified in a letter dated 2 February 1517 by Domenico Buoninsegni (Carteggio 1965-83, CXCV). The drawing has been dated 13-15 January 1517, as noted by Ackerman (1964, II: 9). Elam (1992: 102) has also called attention to *pro memoria* notes on the drawing that relate to a letter to Buoninsegni, probably one written on 15 January in Carrara. The drawing of the facade most likely followed the drafting of the letter.

Tolnay (1934: 58) first suggested a relationship between CB 44A and Uff. 277A, attributed to Giuliano da Sangallo. Although in Uff. 277A the Ionic pilasters stand on pedestals, the entablature of the central section is not continuous, and the mezzanine is lower, the designs do have similar features.

As Pommer (1957: 86-98) has noted, the architecture in Uff. 277A "is based on Uff. 278", a design by Giuliano da Sangallo, probably for S. Maria di Loreto. He felt that Uff. 277A was also most likely for S. Maria di Loreto. According to Pommer, the facade design in Uff. 277A is, however, a more evolved design architecturally and the figurative sculpture in a dark ink wash is rendered in a manner that recalls the figures in CB 45A.

The plan at lower right, thought by Tolnay (1980, IV: 37) to be a plan and perspective of a throne, was read by Ackerman (1964, II: 8) as perhaps the central portion of the lower story of the facade, and by Elam (1992, 104) as probably a preliminary sketch for the foundations of the facade, related to the later drawing CB 113A recto, which may also be for the foundations.   *H.A.M.*

Fig. 3 - Raffaele da Montelupo (attrib.) Project for the facade of San Lorenzo, 790

Fig. 4 - Giovanni Antonio Dosio (attrib.) Project for the facade of San Lorenzo, GAMMA z.2.2, c. 73

Fig. 5 - Raffaele da Montelupo (attrib.) Project for the facade of San Lorenzo

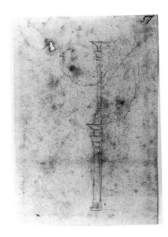

226
MICHELANGELO BUONARROTI
*Project for an Elevation of the Facade of
S. Lorenzo (Second Design)*

Florence, Casa Buonarroti, CB 47Ar.
Red chalk; sheet torn and repaired; stained; no watermark.
140/138 × 182 mm
RECTO: Project for a facade.
VERSO: Right arm; upper part of a head.

PROVENANCE: Casa Buonarroti.

BIBLIOGRAPHY: Gotti 1875, II: 178; Beltrami 1901: 70; Berenson
1903a: II, no. 1426; Geymüller 1904: 7-8; Thode 1908, II: 92-93;
K. Frey 1911: 47; Thode 1913, III: 49-50; Tolnay 1934: 30; Venturi 1939, XI-2: 24; Wanscher 1940a: 65; Tolnay 1951: 167; Wilde
1953: 40; Düssler 1959: 73; Ackerman 1961, II: 8; Barocchi 1962a:
61-62; Ackerman 1964, II: 8; Barbieri and Puppi 1964b: 837;
Barocchi 1964b: 25; Bertini 1964: 124; Barocchi 1965, no. 75; De
Angelis d'Ossat 1965: 283, 289; 1966a, II: 281, 283; Portoghesi
1966: 203-204; Hartt 1971: 132; Tolnay 1972: 60-61; Einem
1973: 86; Tolnay 1975b: 90; Tolnay and Squellati 1977: 59; Hirst
1983: 555; Nova 1984: 33; Berti 1985: 71; Ackerman 1986: 59,
293; Millon and Smyth 1988a: 38-40; Argan and Contardi 1990:
82 and fig. 98; Elam 1992: 105.

Thought by Ackerman (1961, II: 8) to be evidence of the
"second design" maturing into a "convincing project",
and by Hartt (1971: 132) to be a "magnificent drawing,
and a perfect solution for the problems of the probable second design," the drawing has, from Geymüller (1904: 7-
8) to the present been considered as the most evolved of
the extant drawings for the "second design."
Tolnay (1934: 30; 1972: 60-61 and 1980, IV: 38) called
attention to the emphasis on the second level with its
overpowering vertical bulk. There is no doubt that CB
47A is the most integrated or unified of all the projects
that precede the final design of CB 43A in that it is both
a three-level and a two-level design. It transcends the
layering of a three-level scheme by the two levels of the
central section, but avoids the bare protrusion of the upper level of a two-story design by including a mezzanine
and aedicules about half the height of the second level.
The second level has been pulled down into the mezzanine, or the mezzanine has been pulled up around the second level, with a persistent string course integrating both
mezzanine and second level. In its coherent merging of
the two-and three-level schemes and through the strong
saliencies of the integrated central section and outermost
bays, CB 47A far outstrips the designs by Giuliano da
Sangallo that may have served as initial models for the architecture.
The design includes locations for the sculpture specified
in Domenico Buoninsegni's letter (*Carteggio* 1965-83,
CXCV) of 2 February 1517 and, as well, panels for the
placement of additional reliefs. As the most developed
scheme for the "second design," CB 47A may date from
early in February 1517, after Michelangelo had seen and
been disappointed by the model being constructed by
Baccio d'Agnolo. *H.A.M.*

227
MICHELANGELO BUONARROTI
*Section through a Two-Level Facade Project for
S. Lorenzo (Second Design?)*

Florence, Casa Buonarroti, CB 57Ar.
Red chalk; trimmed, some stains; watermark: oval containing an
unidentified image (trimmed, lower right).
155/154 × 102/101 mm
RECTO: Section through a facade.
VERSO: Male nude.

PROVENANCE: Casa Buonarroti.

BIBLIOGRAPHY: Geymüller 1904: 12; Thode 1908, II: 93; K. Frey
1911: 130; Thode 1913, III: 54; D. Frey 1922-23: 224; Tolnay
1928: 385; 1948, III: 210; Düssler 1959: 95; Ackerman 1961, II:
28; Barocchi 1962a: 78; Berti 1965: 445, 447 n. 75; 1966: II, 432,
433, 435 n. 75; Hartt 1971: 166; Tolnay 1975b: 48; 1976, II: 35;
Hirst 1983: 555; Millon and Smyth 1988a: 36-37; Argan and Contardi 1990: 167 and fig. 190.

Geymüller (1904: 12), Thode (1908, II: 93; 1913, III: 54),
K. Frey (1911: 130) and D. Frey (1922-23: 224) identified the drawing as a profile of the left corner of the facade
of S. Lorenzo. Tolnay (1928: 385 and 1948, III: 210) rejected the identification with S. Lorenzo because the
drawing lacked an intrmediate zone and assigned the
drawing to an early project for the doors and tabernacles
of the lateral fields of the Cappella Medici. Tolnay's view
was accepted until Michael Hirst (1983: 555) pointed out
that in at least one stage of the design of the facade of S.
Lorenzo, e.g., CB 47A, Michelangelo intended only two
levels.
In reassigning the drawing to S. Lorenzo, Hirst noted an
observation of Diane Zervas that the proportions agree
extremely well with the temple-front bay of CB 47A. Inasmuch as the second level in CB 57A includes socles and
the columns of the first level rest on low plinths, the drawing does resemble CB 47A. In CB 47A, however, the upper level is taller than the ground level, 1.12 to 1. The upper order of CB 57A is, instead, a bit shorter than the lower level, 0.95 to 1. While the ratios of heights of upper to
lower order in the two drawings are not the same (a striking feature of CB 47A is the pondeorus mass of the taller
order resting upon the shorter order of the first level), it
is certainly possible that Michelangelo was, in this drawing, experimenting with the ratios of heights of first and
second orders while working on the "second design."
It is also possible, though perhaps less likely, that the
drawing, as suggested by Thode (1908, II: 93; 1913, III:
54) and K. Frey (1911: 130), was for the left (south) corner
of the facade, rather than a profile through the central section as required in the interpretation of Hirst (1983: 555).
If it were at the corner showing the return of the south
corner, the drawing might delineate only the first level
and mezzanine of a three-level scheme such as CB 91A.
In support of this view is the fact that in CB 91A the ratio
of mezzanine level to first level is 0.92 to 1. *H.A.M.*

228
MICHELANGELO BUONARROTI
*Project for an Elevation of the Facade of
S. Lorenzo (Final Design)*

Florence, Casa Buonarroti, CB 43Ar.
Pen and brown ink over red and black chalk underdrawing;
trimmed, some stains; watermark: outstretched hand (same as
CB 100A; trimmed, center right).
212 × 143/144 mm
RECTO: Project for a facade.
a) project for the facade of S. Lorenzo (lower center); b) study
of an arm, or left leg from the rear (left); c) two studies of feet
(upper center and left, turned 180°); d) lintel and over opening
(?) supported by a pair of columns or pilasters (center, turned 180°).
VERSO: Pope Julius II (?) and supporting figure on a
sarcophagus.

PROVENANCE: Casa Buonarroti.

BIBLIOGRAPHY: Geymüller 1904: 9; Thode 1908, II: 94-95; K. Frey
1911: 90-100; Thode 1913, III: 76-78; D. Frey 1922-23: 224; Tolnay 1934: 31-32, 37; 1951: 169-170; Pommer 1957: 4-5, 42; Düssler 1959: 71; Ackerman 1961, II: 9-10; Barocchi 1962b: 62-65;
Lotz 1963: 3-7; Ackerman 1964, II: 10-11; Barbieri and Puppi
1964b: 837; Barocchi 1964b: 25-26; Bertini 1964: 125; De Angelis
d'Ossat 1965: 285; 1966a, II: 283; Portoghesi 1966: 204-206;
Hartt 1971: 133; Tolnay 1972: 61-62; Einem 1973: 86-87; Tolnay
1975b: 90; Pedretti 1978: 251; Stankowski 1979: 15-27; Tolnay
1980, IV: 38-40; Nova 1984: 33; Ackerman 1986: 63, 293; Millon
and Smyth 1988a: 41-44; Argan and Contardi 1990: 82, 169 and
fig. 100; Elam 1992: 106; Marani 1992b: 434; Wallace 1992a, 474.

Accepted as Michelangelo's for over a century by all scholars, CB 43A and CB 47A are his most accomplished
drawings for the facade of S. Lorenzo. The decision taken
in CB 43A to return the facade to either side and form
thereby a three-dimensional block, provided the opportunity for Michelangelo to treat the whole facade as a unit,
partially independent of the stepped profile of the church
behind. The irresolution of differing levels between the
outermost bays and the central section of CB 47A is here
resolved through a consistent height and articulation
across the full width of the facade, maintaining, for axial
emphasis, a pediment over the salient central section.
Also, the decisively different treatment of the recessive
bays (with side aisle entrances, tondi, and rectangular
panels) from the similar but salient outermost bays and
emphasized central section, produced a facade of vigorous
relief. The relief was further enhanced in succeeding versions of the "final design."
In the "final design" Michelangelo abandoned a match between the silhouettes of the facade and the church behind
and raised the sections at either side to the height of the
central section. If Ackerman (1961, I: 9) is correct, the facade, with a one-bay return on each flank, was shifted forward to form a narthex in front of the existing facade. The
only real junction between the narthex/facade and existing church would be at the terminus of the one-bay
returns and whatever "rear" was included for the narthex
above the sloping roof of S. Lorenzo. At the ground level
the column pairs are disposed as they were in both CB

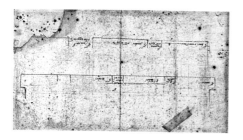

47A and CB 44A of the "second design" and, indeed, as they were as early as CB 41A verso and CB 91A.

The "final design" has a cluster of twelve associated drawings that form at least three groups. These groups suggest possible stages in the evolution of the design. An initial group of plan drawings and one partial elevation (CB 113A, Archivio Buonarroti, vol. I, fol 157r. [Tolnay 1934, fig. 7] and CB 41A recto) agree with CB 43A in not including a salient section of wall behind the column pairs of the outermost bays or in the central section. A second pair of drawings (CB 100A and Uff. 790A), both partial elevations, include a salient wall plane behind the paired columns (a characteristic of all succeeding phases), and between the column pairs, on a high pedestal, a tall, standing figure extending almost the full height of the space between the columns. Figures of that size do not reappear. A third group consists of four drawings, one plan and three elevations (CB 77A verso; Paris, Louvre, 134 verso, attributed to B. Bandinelli; Munich, Staatliche Graphische Sammlung, 33258; and Milan, Biblioteca Trivulziana, Raccolta Bianconi, IV, 35a, closely related to the drawing in Munich). All four are alike in that they include the salient wall behind the column pairs and, at the first level, in the three elevations, niches for standing figures, or standing figures themselves (Louvre), no taller than half the height of the flanking columns.

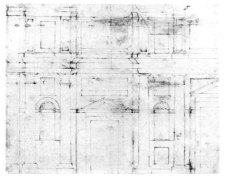

A single half-elevation (Uff. 205A), drawn with care and rendered, is witness to a phase that saw the elimination of the pedestals for the standing figures at the lower level and the reappearance at the ground level of low continuous plinths under the column pairs that are set on low socles (the plinths and low socles are also found on Uff. 790A). Two additional drawings record stages in the transformation of the double mezzanine into the single one of the wooden model. In CB 51A, the height of the mezzanine was decreased while the relative height of the lower and upper orders was increased. A further decrease of the mezzanine height is seen in a drawing by Michelangelo in the British Museum (1859.6.25.560/2v.) where, although a socle was introduced for the single mezzanine, the entablature was reduced and the overall height shortened, perhaps even more than in the wooden model.

Stankowski (1979: 19-27) has recently suggested Michelangelo's S. Lorenzo facade design should be seen as the application of a secular palace facade to a church;

that S. Lorenzo as a Medici family church was to be treated as part of an integrated Medici complex which included the palace nearby. Pedretti's (1978: 251) identification of a drawing by Leonardo for the restructuring of the area between S. Lorenzo, the Medici palace, a new Medici palace, and, to the northeast, a new piazza, lends weight to Stankowski's proposition.

CB 43A, as CB 41A recto, was probably drawn between the middle of February 1517, when Michelangelo was apparently considering an alternative design to the one under construction as a model by Baccio d'Agnolo (*Carteggio* 1965-83, CXCIX), and early in May 1517, when Michelangelo mentions in a letter from Carrara to Buoninsegni in Rome (*Carteggio,* CCXXI) that he had made a new small model in clay. H.A.M.

229
MICHELANGELO BUONARROTI
Project for a Niche and Pair of Columns at Ground Level for the Facade of S. Lorenzo

Florence, Casa Buonarroti, CB 100A
Red chalk with pen and brown ink; a few stains; watermark: outstretched hand (same as CB 43A; trimmed, upper left).
156/158 × 136 mm
a) Single bay of the facade of S. Lorenzo at ground level including columns, entablature and rectangular niche with standing figure above a high pedestal; b) plan of left corner of the facade (lower left); c) plan of left corner of the facade (lower center).

PROVENANCE: Casa Buonarroti.

BIBLIOGRAPHY: Gotti 1875, II: 182; Thode 1908, II: 218, 232; 1913, III: 67-68; Düssler 1959: 226; Barocchi 1962a: 301-302; De Angelis d'Ossat 1965: 286; Tolnay 1971: 22; 1972: 63; Hirst 1972: 165; Tolnay and Squellati 1977: 59-66; Tolnay and Squellati Brizio 1980: 93; Tolnay 1980, IV: 43; Hibbard 1984: 673; Balas 1983: 665-671; 1984: 674-675; Berti 1985: 238; Ackerman 1986: 294; Hirst 1986: 323-326; Ackerman 1986: 294; Millon and Smyth 1988a: 50-52.

Cited by Thode (1908, II: 218, 232 and 1913, III: 67-68) as a drawing by Michelangelo (following Gotti 1875, II: 182) for a papal tomb (either Leo X or Clement VII) in Rome, CB 100A was later deleted by Düssler (1959: 226) from the body of Michelangelo's work, a decision which was seconded by Barocchi (1962a: 301-302). In 1972 Hirst (1972: 165) and Tolnay (1972: 63) independently reassigned the drawing to Michelangelo and associated it with the design for the facade of S. Lorenzo. (Tolnay earlier had identified and published [1971: 22] the drawing in a paper entitled "Alcune recenti scoperte e risultati negli studi Michelangioleschi," delivered at the Accademia Nazionale dei Lincei.) The attribution was repeated by Tolnay (1975b: 91), Tolnay and Squellati (1977: 59-60), Tolnay (1980, IV: 43), Tolnay and Squellati Brizio (1980: 93) and accepted by Hibbard (1984: 673, in a letter to the editor about an article by Edith Balas) and by Ackerman (1986: 294). Balas' article (1983: 665-671), which pro-

posed that the *Slaves* of Michelangelo were intended for the ground level of the facade of S. Lorenzo, omitted mention of the drawing.

Hirst, in a reassertion of the attribution to Michelangelo and association with S. Lorenzo ([1986]: 323-326), observed that the drawing represents "an *early* stage in the preparation of the final scheme." Hirst calls attention to the two plans on the sheet as an indication that Michelangelo had already decided to include returns at the sides of the facade and that the lower of the two plans was closer to the final solution.

There can be little doubt the drawing is for an early stage of the final design because it contains, at the lower left, a solution for the corner that is found on CB 43A, CB 113A recto and CB 41A recto, all early versions of the corner. A plan of the final state of the corner first appears on this sheet also at lower center, and at the lower edge on CB 77A verso, on Uff. 790A, and on later drawings in elevation.

Testifying additionally to an early date for the drawing in the development of the design are the Composite capitals of the columns (not Tuscan, as proposed by Tolnay [1972: 63]), which are similar to those found on the lower order of the facade on CB 45A.

At this relatively early stage of the "final design," the rectangular niche with its generous enframement, brackets below and broad consoles above, is more elaborate than at any successive stage. While the niche is retained until the stage represented by the wooden model, the frame, brackets, and consoles do not reappear.

It seems likely the pedestals for the figures persisted until just before the final version (they are present on Uff. 205A, probably a drawing that shows the most evolved state of the design before the final revisions). They are not present on the model nor are they found on the sixteenth-century drawing of the model in the Metropolitan Museum. However, if the standing figures at the first level were to be in the round, as specified in the contract letter of 19 January 1518 (*Ricordi,* Appendix III: 385), they would seem to require something more substantial to stand upon rather than the slender sill of the niche as shown in the wooden model. As one of the initial studies of the "final design," CB 100A may be dated early in the period between mid-February and late April 1517 together with CB 43A and CB 113A recto. H.A.M.

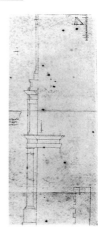

230
MICHELANGELO BUONARROTI
Profile of the Facade of S. Lorenzo

Florence, Casa Buonarroti, CB 51Ar.
Pen and brown ink, black chalk; sheet cut, lower right corner missing and restored; watermark: Briquet 5923; scale: pyramid and measured scale (upper right).
535/533 × 235/238 mm
INSCRIBED: 1) ce[n]to octa[n]/ta quatro/ce[n]tinaia (center left, within column diameter); 2) *la parete* (center, at mezzanine); 3) *10 ... 10* (at mezzanine cornice); 4) *1/3, b* (lower right, at section).

a) profile of a three level facade (center); b) top of the shaft of a column (center left); c) column, frieze and entablature (black chalk; to right of lower section of profile); d) section through the unfinished facade of S. Lorenzo with measurements (lower right); e) long rectangular squared section, perhaps for calculating quantities and costs (black chalk; at right); f) triangles and measured line (upper right).

PROVENANCE: Casa Buonarroti.

BIBLIOGRAPHY: Gotti 1875, II: 178; Berenson 1903a, II, no. 1421; Geymüller 1904: 12; Thode 1908, II: 99; K. Frey 1911: 124; Thode 1913, III: 43; D. Frey 1922-23: 224; Tolnay 1934: 32 n. 1; Düssler 1959: 224-225; Ackerman 1961, II: 11; Barocchi 1962a: 297-298; Barbieri and Puppi 1964b: 838; Tolnay and Squellati 1977: 60; Tolnay 1980, IV: 41-42; Joannides 1981a: 685; Berti 1985: 238; Millon and Smyth 1988a: 60-62; Argan and Contardi 1990: 169 and fig. 193; Elam 1992: 108-110; Wallace 1992b: 122, 126.

K. Frey (1911: 124-125), and then Thode (1913, III: 43), were the first to suggest that CB 51A recto was by another hand than Michelangelo's. Frey proposed the same hand for CB 51A recto as that found on CB 41A recto. Attribution to an assistant has been followed by D. Frey (1922-23: 224, who first associated the profile with the elevation of the facade on Uffizi 790A), Tolnay (1934: 32 n. 1, who thought the inscriptions to be by Michelangelo), Düssler (1959: 224-225, who agreed with D. Frey and Tolnay), Ackerman (1961, II: 11), Barocchi (1962a: 297-298), and Tolnay and Squellati (1977: 60). Tolnay changed his mind in the *Corpus* (1980, IV: 41-42) and attributed not only the inscriptions to Michelangelo but the ruled elevation/profile as well. Joannides, in his review of the *Corpus* (1981a: 685), agreed, as does Elam (1992: 109). Berti (1985: 238) returned to the earlier attribution to an assistant. While the ruled lines do display some faults, the correction made to the profile of the lower mezzanine and the inscriptions indubitably by Michelangelo's hand argue for acceptance of an attribution to him.

CB 51A recto and Uff. 790A are similar in that the lower mezzanine is very much taller than the upper. In the other related drawings in Munich, Milan, Paris, and the Uffizi, while the lower mezzanine is always taller, the two are more nearly equal in height. The lower mezzanine in the drawings in Munich, Milan, and Paris has neither a base nor plinth. Both are shown in the two drawings in the Uffizi (790A and 205A), and since on CB 51A recto the drawing of the lower mezzanine was corrected to show a base, the association of these three drawings seems confirmed.

However, both drawings in the Uffizi (790A and 205A) show a developed corner with salient wall segments behind paired columns at the first level, placed so that the corner of the facade remains free. In CB 51A recto, the corner is shown in an early state as it was drawn on CB 43A, CB 113A recto and CB 100A—plan at lower left). Hence, CB 51A recto indicates that the highly differentiated heights of the two mezzanines were being studied either as early as the cluster of drawings associated with CB 43A or that, at a relatively late stage in the development of the "final design," Michelangelo once again examined the placement of column pairs directly against the facade wall. The former seems less likely.

The drawing also suggests that Michelangelo was studying the possibility of three orders. The entablature of the lower mezzanine is unusually tall, taller than the entablature of the first level. In this regard it recalls not only the early three-level scheme of CB 91A (where the mezzanine cornice, though heavy, is not as tall as on the first level), but also the copies of three-level projects associated with CB 41A verso. The entablature of the third level is taller yet than that of the mezzanine. Michelangelo may have been studying a progressive increase in the height of the entablature to compensate for a greater distance from the ground. A partial profile, in the British Museum, that resembles the wooden model more closely than the

projects with two mezzanines may represent an intermediate study. (Wilde [1953: 35] suggested rather that the drawing in London might have related to a project that preceded the "final design.")

Because of the apparent similarity of the mezzanines in CB 51A recto and Uff. 790A, the drawing has usually been associated with the last stages of the second phase of the "final design" in the spring of 1517. It may equally well be associated with an earlier phase of the project, closer to the date of CB 91A, the summer or autumn of 1516 rather than the spring of 1517.   *H.A.M.*

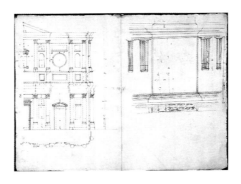

231
ETIENNE DUPÉRAC, CIRCLE OF (?)
*Elevation of the Right Half of the Model of
S. Lorenzo*
(after Michelangelo)

New York, The Metropolitan Museum of Art, 49.92.41
Pen, brown ink over black chalk; folded in half vertically; watermark: figure with a skirt holding an a or hammer aloft with one hand and a bucket in the other; scale: 1:20 *soldi*, and 1:3 *braccia*/with a *braccio* equal to 78 mm, (1 *quattrino* equals 2½ *soldi*) or a scale of 1:7½
434/442 × 585/588 mm
a) elevation and plan of right half of model of S. Lorenzo (left); b) elevation and plan of a pier and flanking consoles of the vestibule of the library of S. Lorenzo.

INSCRIBED: *ell muro di verso la porta / che ... all chantho p gocoso che /*

PROVENANCE: Janos and Anne Bigelow Scholz, in memory of Flying Officer Walter Bigelow Rosen, 1949.

BIBLIOGRAPHY: for bibliography on the Scholz Collection, see Millon and Smyth 1988a: 103; Millon 1988, fig. 19.

The draftsman of Metropolitan 49.92.41 measured and drew the model of the facade of S. Lorenzo at a scale of 1:7½. The drawing includes inscribed dimensions taken directly from the model. Comparison of seven inscribed measurements with measurements taken from the model revealed variations no larger than plus or minus seven percent with four of the measurements within two percent. There can be little doubt the drawing represents the model in the Casa Buonarroti today.

Further comparison of the drawing in the Metropolitan with the renderings of the facade of the model by Giovanni Battista Nelli in the late 1680s and Giuseppe Ignazio Rossi in the early eighteenth century confirms the presence in the sixteenth century of elements no longer found on the model today. The Metropolitan drawing shows astragal moldings at the level of the base of the capitals of the upper level, extending across both pilaster pairs and the right entrance bay, and interrupted only in the central bay. They are also included in Nelli's drawing, if only between the pilaster pairs, and in Rossi have been reduced to mere lines.

The astragals of the lower level in the Metropolitan drawing are continuous across the central bay, and interrupted only above the right entrance bay. They are absent on the model, though traces of what may have been an astragal remain between the pair of columns at the left. In this

respect Nelli follows the drawing in the Metropolitan, while Rossi has inserted an astragal above the aisle entrance. The Metropolitan drawing includes a wide rectangular panel within the lintel above the aisle entrance. The panel is found also in Nelli above both aisle doors but only over the right aisle in the Rossi drawing and is now absent on the model. The Metropolitan drawing further confirms the rectangular block above the cornice of the central entrance found on Rossi's drawing (without a molding at the top), but absent in Nelli's rendering and no longer on the model.

The Metropolitan drawing shows moldings above the niches and tondi at the upper level and above the rectangular niches of the lower level that in the drawings in Nelli, Rossi, and the model are longer and become a virtual string course. Since none of these moldings are dimensioned in the New York drawing and are found on the model and in both the other drawings, the draftsman of the Metropolitan drawing may have drawn them too long. He gave only a summary indication of the pedestals for the seated figures at the mezzanine level, even though including a dimension. They are shown correctly on both the Nelli and Rossi drawings. The panels of the mezzanine fill the available space in both the drawings in Florence and Rome as they do on the model, but in the drawing at the Metropolitan they are much reduced. The drawing also lacks a break in the entablature of the second level next to the pediment that would correspond to the salient wall section. In spite of these anomalies, the drawing in the Metropolitan provides convincing evidence of the state of the model in 1555 shortly after it was sent from Michelangelo's studio to Duke Cosimo (*Carteggio* 1965-83, MCCXIV).

The drawing at the Metropolitan is one of some 125 drawings from the Dupérac circle. Tolnay was the first to mention the group (1948: 164), portions of which have been published by A. Hyatt Mayor (1949-50: 150), and J. Byrne (1956-57: 155-164; 1966-67: 24-29). All the drawings in the group seem to date from the last half of the sixteenth century and some to the decade 1560-70. (For further bibliographical references, see entry on the Dupérac group in the Metropolitan Museum of Art in the section of this catalog on Michelangelo's St. Peter's.)

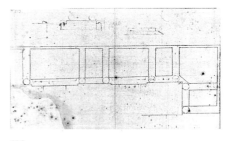

232
MICHELANGELO BUONARROTI
*Plan of the Left Half (South) of the Facade of
S. Lorenzo*

Florence, Casa Buonarroti, CB 113Ar.
Pen and brown ink; upper right corner of sheet missing and repaired; watermark: Briquet 662, 664.
260/259 × 432/431 mm (including repair)
RECTO: a) plan of the south half of the facade for S. Lorenzo with some inscribed measurements; b) plan of one of the central salient wall sections and pair of columns with section through moldings of entrance openings to either side (lower right); c) elevation of frieze and cornice (lower left).
VERSO: a) plan of facade of S. Lorenzo with inscribed dimensions (upper); b) plan of south half of facade of S. Lorenzo with inscribed dimensions (lower).
INSCRIBED: upper plan, from the left: 1) *b[raccia] nove*; 2) *b[raccia] 4 e u[n] qui[n]to*; 3) *b[raccia] u[n]dici*; 4) *cinque e dua terzi*; 5) *b[raccia] undici*; lower plan, from the left: 6) *b[raccia] dieci e uno octavo*; 7) *b[raccia] quatro e u[n] qui[n]to*; 8) *b[raccia] undici e u[n] qui[n]to*; 9) *b[raccia] cinque e tre quarti.*

PROVENANCE: Casa Buonarroti.

BIBLIOGRAPHY: Geymüller 1904: 12; Thode 1908, II: 93, 99; 1913, III: 72; Tolnay 1934, fig. 7; Düssler 1959: 227; Ackerman 1961, II: 10; Barocchi 1962a: 66-67; Barbieri and Puppi 1964b: 837; Barocchi 1964b, 27; Battisti 1977, plan; Tolnay 1980, IV: 41; Berti 1985: 74; Ackerman 1986: 294; Millon and Smyth 1988a: 45-47; Argan and Contardi 1990: 169; Elam 1992: 104.

Association of this drawing with the "final design" of the facade of S. Lorenzo was first made by Thode (1908, II: 93 and 1913, III: 72); it was rejected by Düssler (1959: 227) but justly accepted by Ackerman (1961, II: 10), Barocchi (1962a: 66-67), and ultimately by Tolnay (1980, IV: 41), though omitted in his earlier articles on the facade. While many authors have accepted the inscribed dimensions as by Michelangelo, more have felt the ruled lines and compass-drawn circles to be by an assistant. Tolnay (1980, IV: 41) attributed the freehand drawings and the inscribed dimensions on the recto of this sheet to Michelangelo but said it would be difficult to feel secure in attributing the ruled plan to Michelangelo. It is possible that Michelangelo prepared a freehand drawing of the plan (as he did for the south corner of the facade on the left of sheet 100A, cat. no. 229 in the Casa Buonarroti) which was then followed by an assistant in making an inked copy. There is, however, little to be gained in maintaining that Michelangelo did not use a straightedge.

CB 113A recto is the earliest drawing to offer evidence of the nature and extent, or thickness, of the return of the facade with its pair of columns, shown here to be almost the same depth as the salient wall section with paired columns at the left edge of the facade. As indicated by the inscribed dimensions, the width of the return is over 12 *braccia* (7 meters). To judge from the thickness of the wall indicated in the detail drawing at lower right on the sheet (about 2½ *braccia*, if the column is 1½ *braccia* as indicated in the principal drawing above), the facade wall was to be about 2 or 2½ *braccia* (or almost 1½ meters) thick. If, as Ackerman suggests (1961, II: 9), the return indicates the transoformation of an applied facade to a facade with narthex attached to the earlier facade, and if the extent of the return was to include the thickness of the wall of Brunelleschi's facade (ca. 2.9 *braccia*, between 1½ and 2 meters thick), the width of the interior space of the narthex at this stage of the design would be between 6 and 7 *braccia* wide (3.5-4 m, or 11.4-13 ft.). Excavations in the area in front of the facade of S. Lorenzo would most likely locate the foundations built for the facade of Michelangelo. Foundations set well in front of the facade would confirm Ackerman's suggestion.

Given the, as yet, simple turning of the left corner of the facade, the drawing should be dated early in the period between mid-February and late April 1517. At this time Michelangelo was considering an alternative design to the model begun in late December 1516 by Baccio d'Agnolo (*Ricordi*, XCIX). The drawing on CB 113A recto shares the simple corner on the left with a drawing of the right-hand corner found on a sheet in the Archivio Buonarroti (Vol. I, fol. 157r.), first connected with S. Lorenzo by Tolnay (1934, fig. 7), where, however, the column pair on the facade is associated with a salient wall segment. Tolnay (1980, IV: 41) observed that the drawing on the verso of CB 113A probably preceded that on the recto.

H.A.M.

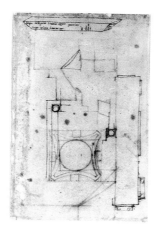

233
MICHELANGELO BUONARROTI
Plan of the Facade and Other Details of S. Lorenzo

Florence, Casa Buonarroti, CB 77Av.
Pen, brown ink.
300/299 × 190/195 mm
RECTO: a) reflected plan of an entablature above a capital of the lower level of the facade of S. Lorenzo (upper center); b) reflected plan of entablature of the left corner of the lower level of the facade of S. Lorenzo (lower center); c) other unidentified sketches of blocks.
VERSO: a) plan of the full facade of S. Lorenzo (left); b) plan of a capital and wall fragment (center left); c) reflected plan of entablature above a corner column (?) (center right); d) perspective of a lintel (turned 180°) (lower border).
INSCRIBED: a) *lunga nelloguetto braccia quatro*; b) *longa nel vivo braccia tre alta e pezzi sei; due te/rzi*; c) *grossa / uno / braccia*.

PROVENANCE: Casa Buonarroti.

BIBLIOGRAPHY: Gotti 1875, II: 181; Frey 1909-11, n. 268; Thode 1909, II: 127; 1913, III: 132; Düssler 1959, n. 113: 79; Ackerman 1961, II: 10; Barocchi 1962, I, n. 48: 68; Barbieri and Puppi 1964b: 837, fig. 90; Portoghesi and Zevi 1964: 1002; Tolnay 1980, IV: 43; Ackerman 1986: 294; Hirst 1988b: 96 and fig. 194; Millon and Smyth 1988a: 84, fig. 13.

Both recto and verso of this sheet appear to bear studies of the relationships of the free-standing columns of the lower level of the facade of S. Lorenzo to the wall behind and the entablature above. The columns are shown both with and without a salient wall section.

The drawing on the verso includes two studies of a column at a corner as well as, at the left, a plan of the full facade showing the returns at both ends and the salient wall sections. At the upper level, the plinths under the column pairs and columns are included in front of the salient wall sections. (The moldings of the opening to the left aisle are also indicated.)

A salient wall section becomes part of the "final design" for the facade. The existence on CB 77A verso of drawings for salient and planal wall sections links this sheet in time with CB 100A (cat. no. 229), which also contains both the earlier and later versions of the wall. CB 77A verso is, therefore, later than CB 113A (cat. no. 232), and a drawing on a sheet in the Archivio Buonarroti (Vol. I, fol. 157r.; Tolnay 1934, fig. 7), both of which include only the earlier corner. The presence of both wall solutions on the sheet suggests a date close to that for CB 100A, in the spring of 1517.

H.A.M.

234
JACOPO CHIMENTI DA EMPOLI
Michelangelo Presents to Pope Leo X and Cardinal Giulio de' Medici (the Future Clement VII) the Models for the Facade of S. Lorenzo and the Cappella Medici, and a Drawing for the Biblioteca Laurenziana

Florence, Casa Buonarroti
Oil on canvas, integrated in an architectural framework.
236 × 141 cm
EPIGRAPH: *In Divi Laurentii Aedium fronte Leonis X. exornanda, in Mediceo Sacello et Bibliotheca, iussu Clementis, extruendis tam venustatis formam arte manuque expressit quam nullus unquam cogitatione vel mente conceptit* (overhead; attributed to Jacopo Soldani).

PROVENANCE: Casa Buonarroti.

BIBLIOGRAPHY: Baldinucci 1846: 8; Busse 1912, VI: 500-503; Steinmann 1913: 86; Tolnay 1934: 34: Ackerman 1961, II: 13; Procacci 1965, II: 173; Vliegenthart 1976: 112-115; Millon 1988: 66-68.

The right corner and flank of the facade of S. Lorenzo in the painting by Jacopo da Empoli is not an accurate representation of any of the known designs or models for S. Lorenzo by Michelangelo. (Tolnay 1934: 34, though, thought the model in the painting to be a rendering of the model in the Casa Buonarroti.) The facade in the painting consists of four levels, a tall lower level with Corinthian columns on plinths and socles (as the model today), a mezzanine level less high than in the model (closer to the lower of the two mezzanines of the elevation in Munich, an upper level with Ionic pilasters on low plinths (much shorter than on the lower level) and, as a fourth level, an attic. (If the attic were shifted between the lower and upper levels and combined with the mezzanine it might resemble more closely the drawing of the facade in Milan, though an Ionic order on the upper level would remain perplexing.)

While both the full height of the facade and the return of the facade on the right flank suggest a rendering of one of the phases in the development of the "final design," the arched niche of the lower story would appear to be a relic of an earlier stage, such as, for example, CB 47A (cat. no. 226), or CB 41A recto (fig. 7). The painter has shown rectangular niches on the upper level where they should be arched as in the model, Uff. 790A and Munich 33258, and arched at the lower level where in the model and the drawings from the "final design" in Munich and the Uffizi (205A), they are rectangular.

The model, as represented in this painting dated 1619, cannot be associated with the final design, as known from the contract, because the mezzanine is too low to accommodate the seated bronze figures (there are no pedestals for the figures) and the description in the contract omits mention of an attic. As Ackerman has said (1961, II: 13), the facade in the painting is "a bad copy of one of the documented models." Even so, it served the painter's purpose. The corner of the facade and its flank recall aspects of Michelangelo's design for the facade, at a scale that also suggests an association with the "smaller" model mentioned by Nelli in his volume of 1687.

H.A.M.

235

AFTER MICHELANGELO
Wooden Model for the Facade of S. Lorenzo

Florence, Casa Buonarroti
Scale: 1:12.
216 × 283 × 50 cm

PROVENANCE: Accademia delle Arti del Disegno, S. Lorenzo, Grand Ducal collections, Casa Buonarroti.

BIBLIOGRAPHY: Vasari, ed. Milanesi 1881, VII: 188-189 n. 1; Milanesi 1875a: 572; Supino 1901: 256; Geymüller 1904: 4, 10-12; Thode 1908, II: 97-98; 1913, III: 279; D. Frey 1922-23: 226; Tosi 1927-28: 323-328; Apolloni Ghetti 1934, pls. xxiii-xxvi; Tolnay 1934: 33; Toesca 1934: 19; Becherucci 1936: 23-24; Venturi 1939, XI-2: 24; Carli 1942: 32; Mariani 1942: 131; Schiavo 1949, figs. 91-92; Paatz 1952, II: 531; Schiavo 1953: 159-163; Wilde 1953: 35 n. 1; Goldscheider 1957, fig. 159; Bonelli 1960: 62-65; Ackerman 1961: 14-17; Tolnay 1964: 901-902; Bertini 1964: 125-127; De Angelis d'Ossat 1965: 285-286, 290, 1966a, II: 282-284; Barbieri and Puppi 1964b, 838; Einem 1973: 87; Tolnay 1980, IV: 42; Nova 1984: 33-34; Ackerman 1986: 63-68, 294-295; Millon 1988: 69-73; Argan and Contardi 1990: 82, 164 and fig. 101; Elam 1992: 100; Marani 1992b: 454; Tinunin et al., 1992: 263-279.

The wooden model of the facade of S. Lorenzo preserved, in the Casa Buonarroti, was once housed in the stair hall of the Biblioteca Laurenziana. While there, it seems to have been drawn several times. Among the extant drawings of the model is a sheet in the Metropolitan Museum drawn by an anonymous artist in the 1560s or 1570s, not long after it had left the studio of Michelangelo. The model was also drawn by Giovanni Battista Nelli in 1687 and again by Guiseppe Ignazio Rossi between 1724 and 1730 (Kieven 1988: 96, 234, nos. 111 and 112). Nelli mentions that in addition to the model he drew there was another almost the same but smaller model that had figurative and decorative reliefs in wax. The smaller model was located in the "Model Room near the Palace of His Highness." It seems likely these two models (the smaller is lost) were the two models in Michelangelo's studio in Florence, cited in a letter from Michelangelo in Rome to his nephew Lionardo in Florence in September 1555. In response to a letter from Lionardo that mentioned a visit of Duke Cosimo to the studio where he had seen the models and asked about them, Michelangelo directed Lionardo to send both models to the duke (*Carteggio* 1965-83, MCCXIV). The larger model, transferred from the Biblioteca Laurenziana to the Accademia and then to Casa Buonarroti, is the most accurate surviving document of the ultimate phase of the "final design" for S. Lorenzo. It also seems likely that the smaller, lost model was the one sent to Rome in December 1517, which served as the basis for the specifications of the contract for the facade signed on 19 January 1518. The figures in wax were mentioned specifically in the contract.

Additional documentation for the final phase of the "final design" may also be provided by a series of undated sketches by Michelangelo for blocks of marble to be quarried for the facade. The sketches, first identified and published by Tolnay (1954: 155-156), include measurements in *braccia* that enabled Ackerman (1961, II: 14-17) to compare them with dimensions taken from the wooden model. The block sketches, although with some duplication and contradictory dimensions, are fairly complete for

the lower level and mezzanine. Ackerman was able to piece together much of the facade for which the blocks were to be prepared. His reconstruction (1961, I, fig. 1), when compared with the model, widens the space between the column pairs of the central section to incorporate the larger, centrally-placed relief, and narrows somewhat the recessed bays that contain the openings to the side aisles, making all three of the entrance bays more nearly equal.

If the dimensions for reliefs given in the contract are assumed to be final, and if the block sketches are also taken to be final (and duplicates of those used in quarrying marble for the facade), then the wooden model is close to the final design but with differences that are not easily explained. If, on the other hand, the model is a second, larger model for use in construction but built after the smaller model with wax figures, it could represent a revision of the design of the contract model. The block sketches might then represent a further revision of the design reached when the marble was to be quarried. Indeed, Ackerman (1961, II: 15) felt that the block sketches were drawn in two different periods, and there is some overlap between sketches in the two groups with changed dimensions. The two periods may indicate a change in the design at the point when the first group was terminated.

The exact nature of the model and its precise place in the history of the design of the facade of S. Lorenzo may be elusive, but there is little doubt now that it is the best representation known of the final design. The recent restoration has revealed that the model was at one time painted white (Tinunin et al., 1992: 265). The several varieties of wood employed suggest it may have been intended to be painted when constructed.

The authenticity of the wood model has, with the meticulous study of Ackerman, been generally re-accepted by scholars. Since Ackerman's study, Tolnay (1964, IX, cols. 901-902), Barbieri and Puppi (1964b: 838), Tolnay (1980, IV: 42), Nova (1984: 33-34), and Millon (1988: 69-73), have accepted the model as representing something close to Michelangelo's intention for the "final design." The model can be dated, therefore, to the first few months of 1518.　　　*H.A.M.*

236

MICHELANGELO
Receipt for Payment of Marble for the Facade of S. Lorenzo

The recent cataloging of the "Raccolta Prima" of the *Autografi Ferrajoli* in the Biblioteca Apostolica Vaticana ("*Raccolta Prima*" *degli autografi Ferrajoli...* 1990) has brought to light three autograph documents by Michelangelo.

These are two receipts relating to the payment for marble for the facade of the church of S. Lorenzo (Biblioteca Apostolica Vaticana, *Autografi Ferrajoli, Raccolta Prima*, vol. XIII, fols. 11r. and 13r) in Florence, and a *ricordo* relating to the purchase of a site (Biblioteca Apostolica Vaticana, *Autografi Ferrajoli, Raccolta Prima*, vol. XIX, fol. 102bis).

The items in question are not entirely unpublished; the two receipts were published by Milanesi (G. Milanesi 1857: 50-54) who also reproduced them in facsimile, taken from two other copies in the Archivio di Stato in Florence more recently, they appeared in the volume of Michelangelo's *ricordi* (ASSF, MaP, filza 137, nos. 1024, 1028); (*I Ricordi di Michelangelo*, see, ed. L. Bardeschi Ciulich and Barocchi 1970, no. XIII: 14-15, and XXIV: 24). The third autograph is recorded (albeit with variations), in a longer text held by the British Library (BM, *Add.MS.* 22731, col. 4; cf. *Ricordi...*, op. cit., no. 2251: 227).

The document here, to all appearances by the hand of Michelangelo, presents nine lines of text on the recto, while the verso is blank; the date "3 gennajo 1516" was added later, in nineteenth-century script. "Io mich[e]lagniolo di lodovicho buonarroti o ricevuto ogi questo di tre di gennaio / in charrara da papa leone duchati mille doro largi p[er] le mani di iachopo / Salviati e quali ma ma[n]dati decto iachopo p[er] uno suo servidore decto / be[n]tivoglio fiorentino qui in charrara Come e decto e e decti danari / cio e duchati mille glio a spe[n]dere p[er] chomessione di decto papa / leone in marmi p[er] la facciata di sa[n] lore[n]zo di Fire[n]ze ch[e] lui vuole fare e p[er] fede de cio io mich[e]lagnolo decto o facta / questa quinta[n]za di mia propria mano questo di sopra decto / nel mille cinque cento sedici"; the years is calculated according to the Florentine calendar, corresponding to our 1517).

An elaborate watermark in the center of the sheet depicts a cross inscribed on a heart surmounted by a crown; this watermark is not among those in the catalog by J. Roberts (*A Dictionary of Michelangelo's Watermarks*, Milan, 1988).

The existence of multiple copies of the same document is not unusual; given that several persons are referred to in the text, it is plausible that Michelangelo issued redeeming invoices to each of them.

Michelangelo's practice of making a number of copies of the same document is moreover confirmed by the artist himself in various places in his *ricordi*. For example, no. XCV begins "Chopia del chonto de' danari" (*I Ricordi...*, op. cit., no. XCV: 97); no. CXLVII is even more explicit: "Quest'è la chopia della schricta che io mandai." (*I Ricordi...*, op. cit., no. CXLVII: 155) Both cases presuppose the existence of originals that have not yet come to light. The same applies to no. CXXXIV, on the verso of which is written, again in Michelangelo's hand: "Copia fatta el dì di S. Giovanni Dichollato 1524" (*I Ricordi...*, op. cit., no. CXXXIV: 144); here he distinctly refers to another, original document.

The closeness of the match between the original in the Archivio di Stato and the Vatican copy (albeit with some perceivable differences) could arouse the suspicion of its being a fake; this is very unlikely, however, given that the autograph document in the archives in Florence had already been published in facsimile by Milanesi, *before* the acquisition of the other original by Ferrajolis.

Giovanni Morello

Vatican, Biblioteca Apostolica Vaticana, Autografi Ferrajoli, Raccolta Prima, vol. XIII, fol. 11r.

The Facade of Florence Cathedral
Andrew Morrogh

*Fig. 2 - Giovanni Antonio Dosio
Model 128*

*Fig. 3 - Giovanni de' Medici with Alessandro Pieroni
Model 135*

There are few more impressive groups of Renaissance models than those for the facade of Florence Cathedral. Of the four that survive from the late sixteenth century, three are of unusual size and skill in execution. Together with a number of drawings, they document a major undertaking promoted by the Medici grand dukes, who undoubtedly intended that the facade should do them, and their city, credit; for Francesco de' Medici, it was to be a perpetual memorial of his reign. Yet an understanding of the commission poses many problems. Contemporary written documentation is scant. The attribution of the models is bedeviled by contradictions in Baldinucci and the inventories, and must be buttressed by other evidence. To date, the main area of progress has been the attribution of the models, to which the researches of Daddi-Giovannozzi have made a major contribution; but here, and especially as regards the drawings, problems remain. What is still lacking is any discussion of the problems that the architects had themselves to face. The cathedral was no blank slate for the free play of the architects' imagination; they had to decide how much weight to give to conformity with the older structure, and how much to the need for a modern, impressive facade—and indeed quite how to interpret this last requirement. Buontalenti's first project and Dosio's model represent two very different approaches.

Grand Duke Francesco (1574-87) and his architect Bernardo Buontalenti shared an enthusiasm for art that was ingenious, elaborate and witty, qualities which appear to the full in Buontalenti's first project for the facade (ca. 1585-87). At least in its early stages, the project was a superb example of the type represented by Raphael's Palazzo Branconio dell'Aquila, its apparently illogical shifts in emphasis combining to create a markedly unified composition. The detail, in Buontalenti's distinctive version of Florentine style, is inventive and vivacious, albeit more elaborate than is usual with him. His attitude toward the older structure is of great interest. The new facade was predicated on the demolition of the partly finished Gothic facade, whose loss in 1587 caused a public outcry. And yet it was to harmonize with the remainder of the church. Composed of white and green marbles (a rarity

*Fig. 1 - Bernardo Buontalenti, First Model for Facade
of Florence Cathedral, oblique view
Florence, Museo dell'Opera di S. Maria del Fiore,
Model 132*

for a sixteenth-century facade), it allied itself with the earlier cladding of the church exterior. Sections of balustrade above the aisles take up the *ballatoio* that crowns the side facades of the church. The three oculi repeat those of the old facade, though their positions and diameters have changed; even so, the incorporation of the outer oculi proved problematic. Perhaps the relatively low relief (fig. 1), small scale, and tight decoration of the facade were intended, at least in part, to be sympathetic to the side facades, and the elaborate detail to reproduce, in spirit, the rich carving of the original front; if so, the design represents a most unusual and imaginative approach to the Gothic (cp. Panofsky 1955: 190-205, and Wittkower 1974—both treat our models rather superficially). Buontalenti's first project lies behind all later attempts to harmonize the new facade with the church, attempts which culminated in the discussions and projects of the 1630s; one such project, the model of Gherardo Silvani, even combines Gothicizing and Baroque detail.

On his accession to the throne, Grand Duke Ferdinand I (1587-1609) cast himself as a different type of ruler from his brother Francesco, more concerned about his subjects and perhaps about his own dignity (Soderini in Saltini 1863: 71-79; Galluzzi 1822, V: 31-32). He greatly disapproved of Buontalenti's destruction of the old facade, and had other architects make designs. Perhaps he found Buontalenti's very personal design too reminiscent of his brother's taste—for which it would indeed have served as a public memorial. At all events, his own reign is marked by a more solemn approach to the facade. The key document is Dosio's magniloquent model of 1589, which Ferdinand himself seems to have supported, at least in the initial stages. The giant order, the strong projections (fig. 2), and much of the detail, speak of an alliance between Michelangelo's work at St. Peter's and a weighty classicism. Dosio's own voice is very muted, as if he were giving

expression to a deliberately impersonal approach to the facade. He sets up a contrast between Buontalenti's style—shown to be idiosyncratic, fussy and Florentine—and a grandiose Roman style with august antecedents, which might very well appeal to a grand duke who had spent most of his life as a cardinal in Rome. Dosio's facade keeps the church at a distance. The old-fashioned oculi have been replaced by rectangular windows, which were in any case easier to integrate; the *ballatoio* would come to an undignified halt behind the plinths next to the buttresses.

Dosio's model changed the terms in which the facade was discussed. It was followed by three models, all built during Ferdinand's reign, and all employing the giant order, as if in this feature at least it had won the grand duke's approval. The first, that of Don Giovanni de' Medici, represents a Buontalentian rendition of Dosio's model. Dosio's great projections are notably reduced (fig. 3), as is his very broad central bay, in favor of a more continuous treatment. The detail does not disguise its Florentine, and Buontalentian, origins; but it is drier and more sober than in Buontalenti's model. Since Don Giovanni, as Ferdinand's half-brother, was closer to him than any other architect, his views about the appropriate style for the facade doubtless carried some weight. Indeed it seems that his model found particular favor with the grand duke. The most interesting feature of Giambologna's model is the alteration of Dosio's proportions, which enables the

*Fig. 4 - Giambologna
Model 133*

*Fig. 5 - Bernardo Buontalenti
Model 130*

ballatoio to continue around the front of the facade (fig. 4), in a manner which not even Buontalenti had achieved. In a similar vein, Giambologna has found a way to reintroduce the central oculus.

Mention should be made of Buontalenti's second, small model of 1596 (fig. 5, not exhibited), which received irreparable damage in the Florentine flood of 1966. Here,

Dosio's strongly projecting giant order was put to a new purpose, to contain arched recesses; within them Buontalenti elaborated his quirky detail, filling the lunettes with a shell motif which provided an admirable surround for the difficult outer oculi.

It is not clear why Ferdinand allowed the project for the new facade to lapse. It was revived by his grandson Ferdinand II, in the 1630s; but again nothing was achieved. The present facade, by Emilio De Fabris, was built from 1876 to 1886.

* I am deeply indebted to Sabine Eiche for her observations and assistance with measurements and photographs. For the structure of the cathedral, I have used the measured drawings in Rocchi et al. 1988. In calculating scales for the models and drawings, I have tried to take account of all the likely correspondences with the original structure. In cases of doubt I have given especial weight to the distance between the mid-points of the outer doors, a feature which could not be altered if the facade was to suit the interior of the church; most other features, such as the breadth of the facade and the entablature heights, were open to variation. But there are enough inaccuracies and inconsistencies in the models and drawings to suggest that nearly all the scales—even those marked on the objects—should be applied with some latitude.

237
BERNARDINO POCCETTI or ALESSANDRO NANI after POCCETTI
The Old Facade of Florence Cathedral

Florence, Museo dell'Opera di S. Maria del Fiore, 131
Pen and ink, brown wash; laid down on canvas.
ca. 1010 × 580 mm

PROVENANCE: Opera del Duomo.

BIBLIOGRAPHY: Poggi 1904: 57; Sanpaolesi 1951: 47; 1966: 310; Beccherucci in Beccherucci and Brunetti [1971?], I: 211, pl. I; Matteoli 1974: 73; Toker 1983: 103, pl. 5.

The present drawing is much the most detailed record of the old facade of the cathedral. A recent reconstruction of Arnolfo's facade notes that the drawing is correct as regards the measurements of breadth, but not those of height (Toker 1983, fig. 23). In our context, the most important point about the drawing, or its original, is that it was in Buontalenti's possession at his death in 1608. As Sanpaolesi has noted, this implies that Poccetti drew it at his friend Buontalenti's instance. Baldinucci, writing in the 1680s, says that since Poccetti's drawing was so faded in some parts as to be almost invisible, the *Provveditore dell'Opera*, Lionardo Buonarroti, had recently had it copied "fedelissimamente" by Alessandro Nani; and that both drawings were kept in the Opera (1844, I: 335-36). An Opera inventory of 1697 lists Nani's copy, but not, it seems, Poccetti's original (Matteoli 1974: 107-108, doc. R). Poggi attributed the present drawing to Nani; more recent scholars have given it to Poccetti for reasons that are quite inadequate (Sanpaolesi 1951; Beccherucci 1971). It is certainly very faded, no doubt as a result of its long dis-

play in a well-lit room (which ended perhaps ten years ago), but nowhere almost illegible. If it is indeed Poccetti's original, it must somehow have gained in legibility since Baldinucci's day.

A funeral oration for Francesco de' Medici provides a context for Buontalenti's project, and suggests why Poccetti made the drawing. According to Lorenzo Giacomini, the dead grand duke "volle che si desse perfezzione a le due pareti del maggior tempio ne la parte di fuora, havea preparato le effigie in marmo de' dodici Annunziatori de l'Eterna verità; preparava nuovo ornamento a la facciata secondo la retta ragione de l'Arte, e de l'antico imperfetto, secondo il costume di quell'età oltre ogni credenza magnifico haveva riserbata memoria per ivi intagliarla in immortale & honorata memoria de gl'autori di esso" (1587: 25-26). The passage may be interpreted as follows. (i) "The grand duke wanted (the cladding of) the side walls of the cathedral to be completed on the outside." An anonymous diarist associates the desire for a new facade with the completion of the cladding, attributing both to the zeal of Benedetto Uguccioni, the *Provveditore dell'Opera*, "il quale avendo fatto finire d'incrostare di marmo le due facciate del fianco destro, e del sinistro di detta Chiesa, le quali non erano tirate sino al tetto, e massimamente quel fianco, che risguardava verso Tramontana, dove la facciata era fatta poco più che mezza, rivolse l'animo a fare il medesimo ancora della facciata dinanzi" (Matteoli 1974: 102, doc. C). (ii) "He had prepared for statues of the Apostles." The context implies that they were intended for the exterior of the church; in any case there was already a set of eight inside. Since the exterior walls contained no suitable niches, the statues were perhaps to rest above the aisle walls at clerestory level, in a manner recalling the fifteenth-century project for statues around the tribunes. (iii) "He was preparing a new facade according to the rules of good architecture." The anonymous diarist states that Uguccioni, persuading the grand duke to have the old facade demolished, had argued that it was clumsy and old-fashioned, and that Buontalenti's would be "più vaga, e dilettevole all'occhio" (ibid.: 102-103). (iv) "He had preserved a memory of the old unfinished facade, which had been designed according to the custom of its period with incredible magnificence, in order to have it carved as an honorable and immortal memorial for the original architects."

Giacomini's words put Buontalenti's project in a new light. Certainly it was intended to glorify the grand duke; but it did so in the context of the slow completion and decoration of the cathedral, in which both Francesco and his father had played a major part—most recently, with the frescoes of the dome, finished in 1579. Respect for the Gothic cladding of the exterior is implicit in Giacomini's oration, in the widespread outrage at the destruction of the old facade, in the completion of the *ballatoio* under Duke Cosimo de' Medici (Giorgi and Marino 1989), and in the very style of the clerestory, a blend of Gothic and Renaissance. Yet as the clerestory approached completion, so the problem of the old facade surely became more acute: if it was kept, the church could never be finished; if it was demolished, what new design could take its place? Buontalenti's first project combined a modern style with a great respect for the earlier structure, a point implicit in the relief representing the old facade. If Poccetti drew the facade at his friend's instance, we may guess that it was with the relief in mind.

Giacomini's passage about the relief suggests that a sense of history presided over Buontalenti's project. He echoes Vasari's justification for writing the *Lives* (1906, I: 95-96). Vasari had written of Arnolfo, and of his design for the cathedral, with the utmost respect, giving him a position equivalent to Cimabue in the revival of the arts (ibid.: 269-292). In interfering with Arnolfo's building, Buontalenti was interfering with part of the heritage that, to a Vasarian critic, constituted the greatest glory of Florence. It was obligatory that he produce something of equivalent significance. He turned to the source of his fame in court circles, his ingenuity and sense of novelty. A description of the *intermezzi* of 1585 states that the grand duke chose

as their designer "Bernardo Buontalenti architettore eccellentissimo, e nell'opere dello'ngegno, e di matematica, e d'altro, da agguagliarsi agli antichi: e che con la vivezza del suo intelletto, al quale niuna cosa impossibile è faticosa, ha potuto ritrovar cose, che e da' naturali, e da' matematici si reputava, che trascendessero le forze umane, e dell'arte" (Rossi 1585, fol. 1v.). If anyone could design a facade that would go down in history, it was surely the brilliant Buontalenti.   *A.M.*

238
SIMONE MOSCHINO
Sketch for the Facade of Florence Cathedral

Munich, Staatliche Graphische Sammlung, 4922 (Bibiena-Sammlungsband I, no. 6)
Pen and brown ink and brown wash, over black chalk; laid down; scale: not marked, but approx. 3.61 mm = 1 *braccio*.
306 × 273 mm

PROVENANCE: Bibiena family; Mannheim collection.

BIBLIOGRAPHY: Lotz in Ackerman and Lotz 1964: 19 n. 40, pl. 18; Bösel 1986: 166.

This drawing, which has been tentatively connected with Alessi's proposal for the facade of the Gesù in Rome, represents instead an unrealizable idea for Florence Cathedral. It is by the same hand as drawings at Munich that Bruno Adorni has convincingly attributed to Simone Moschino (1974: 167-174; 1982a, 409-412; in fact well over a hundred drawings in Bibiena-Klebebänder I and II must be Moschino's work). Two unpublished letters to Francesco de' Medici suggest that the grand duke was well disposed toward him, at least as regards his employment at Pisa Cathedral, where he had worked for seventeen years (A.S. Firenze, Mediceo 705, c. 201, dated 5 December 1577, from Parma; ibid., Med. 707, c. 192, dated 4 February 1578, from Pisa).

A drawing at Munich, for a large Medici catafalque, indicates that at some point he hoped to obtain an official commission in Florence (Staatliche Graphische Sammlung, 4994). From October 1578 he was employed by the Farnese in Parma and Piacenza, but travelled to Rome several times (Adorni 1974: 168, 170).

The right half of the design shows us what was probably the architect's original conception: a composition based on three triplets of bays, the central triplet strongly projecting. Each triplet contains a broad arched bay in the center, and is articulated—with remarkable richness—by columns. This version shows a love of elegantly repeated forms and rhythms, but requires that the arched bays of the outer triplets be narrower than those of the center. In the left half Moschino corrects this problem, reducing the outer triplets to single bays.

These are now articulated with pilasters, which have also found their way next to the arches of the central triplet. At both stages of the design, the lowest story is treated, rather anomalously, as a rusticated basement; however a pilaster was drawn in next to the main door.

The prominence given to the Madonna and Child in the central niche, suggests that the church, like the Florentine Duomo, is dedicated to the Virgin. The outer doors are in exactly the right position for the cathedral, and there are oculi above them. And yet a scale (which may be derived from the position of the outer doors) indicates that the facade is much too low: there would be a gap of about 10 *braccia* between the apex of the larger pediment and the crown of the church nave. On the other hand, Buontalenti's first project and Passignano's 2631 Sant. both show influences from Moschino's design (or from some later reworking of it) in the second order: the former in the odd grouping of columns and pilasters, and the latter in the general articulation. We may hypothesize that Moschino designed a facade that was too low, so that he might find an elegant way of including the outer oculi—perhaps as no more than an experiment.

The roots of Moschino's design would be clearer if his architecture had received fuller study. (The most useful account is that of Adorni 1974: 167-183.) The central pedimented projection, extending through several stories, is reminiscent of Palladio's secular architecture; the rusticated ground floor, of a palace. The treatment of the central triplet is surely indebted to Bernardino Brugnoli's design for the facade of the cathedral of Reggio Emilia (Monducci and Nironi 1984, fig. 52). *A.M.*

239
GIAMBOLOGNA
Buontalenti Presents Grand Duke Francesco de' Medici with a Model for the Facade of Florence Cathedral

Florence, Museo degli Argenti, Inventario Gemme 821
Gold *ajouré* relief on amethyst ground; eighteenth-century frame in gilded metal.
83 × 110 mm

PROVENANCE: Medici.

BIBLIOGRAPHY: Dhanens 1956: 262-263, pl. 150e; Heikamp 1963: 210-12, pl. 34; Piacenti Aschengreen 1968: 142, no. 269; Holderbaum 1983: 276-280; Avery 1987a: 189, 271, no. 155; Heikamp in *Splendori di Pietre Dure* 1988, no. 12.III, ill.; Massinelli 1990: 120-125, pl. 33.

In the 1580s, Buontalenti worked on the Tribuna of the Uffizi, which was to display the most precious objets d'art belonging to grand duke Francesco. For its center he designed an ebony cabinet in the form of an octagonal *tempietto*, for which Giambologna, the grand duke's favorite sculptor, in turn designed a series of eight reliefs commemorating Francesco's rule (Heikamp 1963: 209-221). Two of the reliefs represent what Francesco presumably regarded as his most significant artistic enterprises: the garden and villa of Pratolino, and the facade of the cathedral. Fittingly, the one shows Giambologna presenting the model of a fountain to the grand duke, the other, Buontalenti presenting him with a model of the facade. The design on which the latter is based must be prior to April-June 1585, when Giambologna made the clay

models for the reliefs (ibid.: 246-247, docs. 11-13, 14). At that date, it seems unlikely that Buontalenti had yet submitted a model for the facade; at all events the existing Model 132 shows a later stage of the design.
The relief, long unnoticed in studies of the facade, casts a new light on the development of Buontalenti's project (but see Holderbaum). It displays the project in what may be considered its ideal, most logical, form (cp. Uff. 2927A). Two chief compositional ideas underlie the facade. One is based on the alternation of pedimented aedicules, which are identified with the main membering. The disposition of the aedicules in the second order occasions remarkable shifts in axis. The second theme (clearly visible in the Metropolitan drawing) is the grouping of column and pilaster. These too undergo an unexpected reversal from story to story; but thereby tie in with the aedicular theme, enabling the verticals of at least the five lower aedicules to consist of columns. The constantly shifting relationships, together with the triangular arrangement of the six aedicules, impose a recherché unity on the whole. We should note, however, that the entablature responds to every slight projection of the verticals, emphasizing the very many individual elements, but somewhat complicating the overall reading.
Buontalenti derived the grouping of the columns and pilasters in the second order from Moschino (Munich drawing). His treatment of the pedimented aedicules of this order recalls Sante Lombardi's facade of S. Giorgio dei Greci, Venice, built after 1536 (cp. Wittkower 1934: 210, fig. 66). From that point he elaborated the main motifs for the rest of the facade. Inside all but the top aedicule he set further pedimented aedicules, another rare grouping which appears in S. Giorgio dei Greci. The similarities with the Venetian facade, like the sarcophagus of Uff. 2447A, suggest that members of the Cappello family or other Venetian visitors gave the grand duke, and probably Buontalenti, advice about the main artistic projects in Florence. *A.M.*

240
BERNARDO BUONTALENTI
Partial Elevation for the Facade of Florence Cathedral

Florence, Galleria degli Uffizi, Gabinetto Disegni e Stampe, Uff. 2447A
Pen and brown ink with blue, brown and gray-brown washes, over black chalk; traces of red chalk; some pricking.
VERSO: sketch of mill wheel; black chalk, with traces of pouncing (for design on recto); scale: not marked, but 17.15 mm = 1 *braccio*.
548/552 × 818/813 mm

PROVENANCE: Silvani family (?), M. Ferrucci.

BIBLIOGRAPHY: Ferri 1885: 54; Giovannozzi 1933: 318; Myers 1971: 395, pl. 40; Monbeig-Goguel 1971: pl. 30 (detail); Morrogh 1985a, no. 73; Fara 1988: 210, pl. 172.

This magnificent drawing contains Buontalenti's answers to the two problems mentioned under Uff. 2927A. The columnar aedicules have been broadened, especially that in the center, to permit larger doors. As a result, the facade as a whole has been slightly broadened, and the nar-

row bay somewhat reduced. At the upper left, lightly sketched lines in black chalk show the lower half of the oculus, which would thus have assumed roughly the same relationship to the attic as in the Metropolitan drawing. Buontalenti temporarily considers using engaged columns, rather than full columns, for the aedicules, and a rather simpler surround for the archbishop's bust above the side door (cp. Uff. 2927A and the Metropolitan drawing).
The particular interest of the drawing lies in the attic, which has been greatly heightened: the first order has been lowered, and the cornice of the attic raised. As a result the cornice achieves the relationship with the oculus just mentioned; while the attic can now take an impressive Medici coat of arms, inserted into the pediment of the central aedicule. This latter composition derives from Vignola's engraved project for the facade of the Gesù. It enables Buontalenti at once to mask the great breadth of the aedicule (which an unbroken pediment would have emphasized), and to give much greater scope to the coat of arms than the scheme of Uff. 2927A would have allowed.
For Joanna of Austria's entry in 1565, Vasari had provided a somewhat similar display for the Medici arms, but in temporary materials (Mellini 1566: 92-93). In 1587, when the old facade was demolished, one of Benedetto Uguccioni's main arguments was that Buontalenti's facade would contain a large Medici arms in permanent form above the central door, "accioché fosse monimento perpetuo del suo [of Grand duke Francesco's] dominio in ogni tempo avvenire" (Matteoli 1974: 103, doc. C).
The sarcophagus at the upper right seems to develop the idea of the facade as a memorial for Francesco de' Medici; for, in the context, it can hardly have been intended for anyone else. For the view of the facade as a memorial, and especially the sarcophagus above the central door, Buontalenti was doubtless indebted to the Venetian connections of the grand duke, who had married Bianca Cappello. In Venice, a very notable example of the type is the canal facade of S. Maria Formosa, in honor of the admiral Vincenzo Cappello (d. 1542; Bialostocki 1983: 6, Abb. 5). It seems very likely that some member of the Cappello family praised the facade in speaking to the grand duke or to Buontalenti. *A.M.*

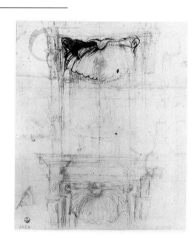

241
BERNARDO BUONTALENTI
Sketches for a Niche for the Facade of Florence Cathedral; Profile Sketch of Eye

Florence, Galleria degli Uffizi, Gabinetto Disegni e Stampe, Uff. 2424A
Graphite, red chalk, pen and brown ink, brown wash, stylus; black chalk (sketch of eye); traces of blue wash.
VERSO: ruled lines; pen and ink, stylus, black chalk; scale: not given, but for main sketch approx. 16 mm = 1 *braccio*, based on incised lines.
313/308 × 244 mm

PROVENANCE: Silvani family (?); M. Ferrucci.

BIBLIOGRAPHY: Ferri 1885: 59.

These sketches, which have not previously been identified, are preparatory for the outer niches of Buontalenti's second order, as seen in the Metropolitan drawing. To the right are two sketches of brackets; at the center left, a bracket supporting an entablature; at the bottom, a more finished drawing of the upper part of the niche; above, the final stage of the drawing. The elaborate, delicate style of detail that Buontalenti developed for the facade of the cathedral reappears in designs of the 1590s, for the windows for an upper story of the Palazzo Nonfinito (Morrogh 1985a: nos. 82, 83), and for the Cappella de' Principi (Botto 1968, nos. 82, 83 etc.). *A.M.*

242
BERNARDO BUONTALENTI
Elevation for the Facade of Florence Cathedral

New York, The Metropolitan Museum of Art, Print Department 66.510 (Gift of Herbert Mitchell, 1966)
Pen and brown ink, pale green wash (with blue wash added for shadows); silhouetted; scale: 92 mm = 20 *braccia*.
491 × 318.5 mm (greatest measurements).

PROVENANCE: not known.

BIBLIOGRAPHY: Myers 1971; Morrogh 1985a: 142-143; Fara 1988: 210, pl. 172.

Myers identified this superb presentation drawing with Buontalenti's project for the facade. However she attributed its execution to his pupil Cigoli, who is often thought to have contributed ideas for Buontalenti's work on the facade. I can find no evidence for any such contribution in the surviving drawings or in Models 130 and 132. The draftsmanship of the present sheet is typical of Buontalenti in the very sensitive line and in the rounded forms of the figures (cp. especially Uff. 2501A, Cresti 1990: 79, ill.; also Uff. 2409A, in Morrogh 1985a, fig. 99). Cigoli's treatment of architectural detail is normally less delicate on the small scale of this drawing; and his figures tend to be drawn with a sharper, more rapid line, often in longish straight strokes. It is true that the combination of brown and green washes is close to Cigoli's practice, and that no other drawing in that combination is known to exist by Buontalenti. Yet in the present case the combination seems to have a purpose which it lacks in the drawings of Cigoli. The green wash is applied to much the same areas as the green paint in Model 132. In both cases, the "background" was presumably to be clad with *verde di Prato*, while the architectural membering would doubtless have been of white marble; together, they would link Buontalenti's facade to the Gothic cladding of the sides of the cathedral. The idea of a colored-marble facade, which is most unusual for the sixteenth century, is surely indebted to that proposed by Vasari for S. Stefano de' Cavalieri, Pisa (see entries for that church).
The drawing is of great value for its detailed and attractive presentation of Buontalenti's project, at a stage roughly half-way between the relief for the Tribuna and Model

132. (For Myers, it represented an early stage of the project.) Already, with the changes detailed under Uff. 2447A, the project has lost something of its initial uniformity and clarity. The central aedicule of the first order is now broader than the side aedicules, while the reduction of the narrow bay affects both the facade's rhythm and the proportions of the aedicules of the second order—which are now very much narrower than those of the ground floor. In the upper story, the broadening of the central bay has required a new treatment of the aedicule: while still attached to the entablature, it has severed its link with the main vertical membering. Its new narrow form requires that the oculus be replaced by a rectangular window.
The outer oculi posed a problem for Buontalenti. Bernardino Radi, giving an opinion about a model for the facade perhaps in 1634/35, said: "Et più mi parrebbe, che si dovessero levare l'Occhi tondi, per non usarsi hoggi di più, et farvi li suoi finestroni alla Moderna" (Matteoli 1974: 106, doc. M). Oculi did not fit easily into the tightly controlled, generally rectilinear, forms of late sixteenth-century architecture. Moschino's drawing provided a possible solution for the outer oculi; but the resulting facade was much too low. For Buontalenti too the oculi occurred in a most inconvenient place, too high to be included in a first order, too low for a second. To judge from Uff. 2927A, he did not give the problem the attention it deserved at the beginning, when they might have been easier to incorporate. In the Metropolitan drawing, they fit fairly comfortably between the frieze and the cornice of the attic, being set into a sort of pendant pedestal for the niche above. The arrangement requires that they be reduced in size and their centers slightly raised; and, more important, that the attic be discontinued between the main verticals. This feature, together with the attic's height, greatly complicates the reading of the facade.
The drawing indicates the probable iconography of Model 132. In the central niche of the second order is a statue of the Madonna and Child. At the same level, the figures at the corners of the facade represent two grand dukes, who can only be Cosimo I (d. 1574) and Francesco. Their odd placement may suggest that they were an afterthought, the result perhaps of a desire to treat the facade as a Medici memorial (cp. Uff. 2447A). Large shields below show the arms of the city of Florence and of the People of Florence, in a position typical for arms on a palace facade. The small busts above the outer doors represent bishops or archbishops, presumably Sts. Zenobius and Antoninus. The various female figures cannot be identified. It may be noted that beneath the Medici arms hangs the chain of the Golden Fleece, with which Francesco was invested in July 1585 (Lapini 1900: 247). *A.M.*

243
BERNARDO BUONTALENTI
Study for the Main Pediment of the Facade of Florence Cathedral

Florence, Galleria degli Uffizi, Gabinetto Disegni e Stampe, Uff. 2443A
Black chalk
VERSO: cross, presumably for facade of the cathedral; unidentifiable sketches of entablature (?) and broken triangular pediment, with rectangular window below; all in black chalk.
141/139 × 338/336 mm
PROVENANCE: Silvani family (?); M. Ferrucci.

BIBLIOGRAPHY: Ferri 1885: 54; Giovannozzi 1933: 318; Botto 1968, no. 59; Morrogh 1985a: 145; Fara 1988: 260-262.

In this sheet and the following, Buontalenti elaborated on the main pediment, one of the least decorated areas of the Metropolitan design. In the present drawing, he has introduced acroteria and his characteristic strapwork. Mobile curving forms integrate the acroteria with the tympanum and blur the apex of the pediment, seeming to form a continuous substance which counteracts the sharp divisions of the architecture. At the level of detail, Buontalenti in his architecture often achieves extremely smooth transitions from one plane or member to the next; the fluent patterning of the forecourt of the Pitti shows the same capacity on a larger scale (Uff. 2305A). However the result achieved in the present drawing would perhaps not have been conducive to the authority of the main pediment of the cathedral. *A.M.*

244
BERNARDO BUONTALENTI
Study for the Main Pediment of the Facade of Florence Cathedral

Florence, Galleria degli Uffizi, Gabinetto Disegni e Stampe, Uff. 2444A
Black chalk.
RECTO: further study for main pediment of the facade; black chalk.
141 × 351 mm

PROVENANCE: Silvani family (?); M. Ferrucci.

BIBLIOGRAPHY: Ferri 1885: 54; Giovannozzi 1933: 318; Botto 1968, no. 60; Morrogh 1985a, no. 74; Fara 1988: 260-262.

This vigorous sketch shows Buontalenti's biomorphic forms at their most energetic. A conch-like motive fans out from the pediment of the window, transforming an inert area of Uff. 2443A into a core of vitality; bursting through, and in front of, the raking cornices, it produces a strange curving cornice, which is in fact a truncated segmental pediment. The pair of pediments may be seen as a brilliant variation on those above the door of the Reading Room of the Biblioteca Laurenziana; but where Michelangelo had been at his most *staccato*, Buontalenti appears at his most fluent.
After drawing the sketch exhibited, Buontalenti turned the sheet over, and copied the main lines by transparency. The new design discards the segmental cornice, but sets raking cornices above the outer parts of the main pediment; these too may be understood as belonging to a vestigial pediment (Morrogh 1985a, fig. 94). Uff. 2500A and Model 132 show a development of these ideas, with an extremely complex grouping of cornices and acroteria. *A.M.*

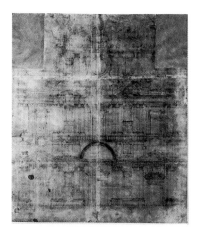

245

BERNARDO BUONTALENTI
*Elevation and Plan for the Facade
of Florence Cathedral*

Florence, Galleria degli Uffizi, Gabinetto Disegni e Stampe,
Uff. 2500A

Pen and ink over stylus and black chalk, trace of red chalk.
Four pieces of paper stuck together; severely damaged: many
cuts, tears, folds, holes; much faded; laid down; made up; scale:
not given, but 10.09 mm = 1 *braccio*.
1006 × 809 mm (greatest measurements)

PROVENANCE: Silvani family (?); M. Ferrucci.

BIBLIOGRAPHY: Ferri 1885: 49; Giovannozzi 1933: 318 n. 1; Ernst
1934: 28 n. 2; Berti 1959: 169; Myers 1971: 392; Matteoli 1974:
77; Fara 1979: 28 n. 31; Fara 1988: 210, pl. 174.

It has often been noted that this drawing is very close to
Model 132. The following major changes have taken place
since the Metropolitan drawing (cp. Myers). (i) The
columnar aedicule around the central door has become an
arched bay, the arch extending the height of the attic.
One may guess that the Medici arms were to be placed in
the lunette. (ii) The rectangular window of the top story
has been replaced by an oculus with an elaborate scrolly
surround. (iii) In the re-entrant angles between the second
and third orders, the slanting balustrade and narrow vertical scrolls have been replaced by a single continuous motif decorated with swags and a shell. At the outer edges,
the motif ends in a pedestal, which has been lost from the
model (Ernst). (iv) The main pediment is surmounted by
a sort of subsidiary pediment, studied in Uff. 2443A and
2444A.
Many minor pentimenti show that Buontalenti was still
working on the detail, which does not correspond in every
case with that of the model. The drawing retains the pediments over the narrow bays of the second order, which
had appeared in all previous designs; the model was
designed without them (Myers). These differences cast
some doubt on the commonly held view that the sheet was
a working drawing for Model 132. The presence of the
plan at the bottom, as in the Metropolitan drawing, suggests that the sheet should perhaps be viewed as a presentation drawing which for some reason was left uncolored.
A plan of the first order alone would not of course have
sufficed for the execution of the model.   *A.M.*

246

BERNARDO BUONTALENTI
Model for the Facade of Florence Cathedral

Florence, Museo dell'Opera di S. Maria del Fiore, Model 132
Wood, green paint; scale: not given, but approx. 1:22, i.e.
26.55 = 1 *braccio*.
2363 × 2185 × 361 mm (including steps at base)

PROVENANCE: Opera del Duomo.

BIBLIOGRAPHY: *Catalogo del Museo di Santa Maria del Fiore* 1891:
32; Poggi 1904: 56; Busse 1911: Ernst 1934: 28-30; Wittkower
1934: 213, pl. 67; Daddi-Giovannozzi 1936: 33, 41-42, pl. 3; Venturi 1901-40, XI, II: 493-496, pl. 446; Wachler 1940: 205-206,
pl. 142; Paatz 1940-54: 468-469; Berti 1959: 168; Myers 1971,
pl. 1; Matteoli 1974: 77-78, pl. 7; Wittkower 1974: 79-80, pl. 116;
Chini 1984: 96-97, pl. 90; Fara 1988: 210, pl. 174.

On 22 January 1587, demolition of the old facade commenced, provoking a public outcry. The intention was to
build Buontalenti's facade in its place, even though the
design was not yet completely settled: "non sendo per ancora bene stabilito il Modello di detta rinnovazione"
(Matteoli 1974: 103, doc. C). These words make it unlikely that the model had yet been started. The model, for
which the Opera del Duomo paid 25 *scudi*—the total cost
was surely much greater—was apparently not finished at
the death of Grand Duke Francesco in October 1587, and
was perhaps still regarded as unfinished two years later
(ibid.: 104, doc. E, and 77. The document is of uncertain
interpretation). Perhaps Buontalenti never brought the
model to the state of finish he intended. However since
scalpellini were at work "secondo il modello allora fatto da
Bernardo Buontalenti ingegnere" in May 1590 (Settesoldi
1987: 15), it sounds as if the model was regarded as definitive during the early years of Grand Duke Ferdinand's
reign.
Wittkower in 1934 called the model "a particularly rich
example of the crafty combination of double function, in-
version, and permutation," reading into it those qualities
which he found in the Laurentian Vestibule. In this he
was perceptive, for he knew nothing of the history of the
design. For us, the early stages of the project manifest the
qualities mentioned by Wittkower to a supreme degree;
but unfortunately the design was not yet well adapted to
the church. As modifications were made, so they
diminished the coherence of the design. As noted under
Uff. 2500A, the process has continued since the
Metropolitan drawing. The arch in the central bay provides a rationale for the height of the attic, but at the cost
of a pediment. The pediments have also been removed
from the narrow bays of the second order, perhaps to
avoid a comparison with the very much broader aedicules
of the lower story. And the aedicule of the upper story has
been replaced by an oculus which relates more closely to
the original facade. The two remaining pedimented aedicules cannot control the complex facade to the same
degree as the six original aedicules. With its many projections in fairly low relief, the model appears particularly
hard to understand when seen from an angle—as one
would when approaching the facade from the important

streets Via Calzaiuoli and Via Martelli. To all of this, Dosio's Model 128 represents a polemical alternative.
By the standards of late sixteenth-century Florence, and
even Italy, Buontalenti's facade is very rich, a quality
which in most people's eyes would have reflected favorably on the city. Already the three full orders, with their
many columns and pilasters, speak the conventional language of magnificence. Almost all the intervening areas
are filled with cartouches, aedicules and niches, often
elaborately framed. A connoisseur might note that not
only is the general disposition unusual and imaginative,
but the detail is often novel, witty and graceful—for instance in the doors (later used for the facade of S. Trinita),
the curiously furled cockle shells of the niches of the second order, the grand yet highly articulated volutes of the
third level. It was surely such a quality of imagination that
caused Francesco de' Medici, one of the foremost virtuosi
of his day, to employ Buontalenti as his architect and festival designer.
Buontalenti's attitude toward the Gothic church deserves
investigation. His aim was undoubtedly to replace the old
facade, "per esser cosa molto all'antica, e di maniera goffa
non usata più dai moderni," with one in a modern style
(Matteoli 1974: 102, doc. C). Yet he retained all three
oculi, the outer two causing him considerable difficulty;
it is as if he wished to preserve some memory of the much-
loved old facade. In what seems a remarkable anticipation
of modern feeling, he (or Francesco) intended that the old
facade be recorded as a relief in the new (cp. Poccetti
drawing). The detail of the model, in the more personal
parts, is of a complexity that seems new in Buontalenti's
work; small-scale, elaborate and uncanonical, it has something in common with the Gothic detail of the sides of the
church—or with that of the intricate, richly worked, old
facade. Already Vasari had made a similar comparison,
describing Giuliano di Baccio d'Agnolo's windows for the
facade of Giovanni Conti in Florence: "nel fare le due
finestre inginocchiate ... Giuliano ... le tritò tanto con
risalti, mensoline e rotti, ch'elle tengono più della maniera
tedesca, che dell'antica e moderna vera e buona" (Vasari,
ed. Milanesi 1906-10, V: 355). It seems possible that the
spirited, unconventional Buontalenti, influenced perhaps
by Vasari (with whom he had worked), wished to develop
a modern version of Gothic detail, which would be rich
and appropriate for its position. Perhaps too we should interpret his low relief and dense overall treatment as conforming to the sides of the cathedral. If so, his model
presents us with an approach to the Gothic that is unique.
                                              A.M.

247

BERNARDO BUONTALENTI
Sketch for the Facade of Florence Cathedral

Florence, Galleria degli Uffizi, Gabinetto Disegni e Stampe,
Uff. 2441A
Pen and ink; laid down.
237.5/240.5 × 195/197.5. mm

PROVENANCE: Silvani family (?); M. Ferrucci.

BIBLIOGRAPHY: Ferri 1885: 54; Giovannozzi 1933: 318, pl. 7; Daddi-Giovannozzi 1936: 43 n. 1; Venturi 1901-40, XI, II: 493 n. 1, pl. 447; Botto 1968: no. 57, pl. 46; Borsi 1974, pl. 218; Matteoli 1974: 84-85, pl. 8; Fara 1988: 262.

Daddi-Giovannozzi tentatively dated the present drawing prior to Don Giovanni's Model 135 (now firmly dated to 1590). Botto and Matteoli placed it about 1596 on the basis of the giant order which it shares with Model 130 of that date. But it also contains two early features, which disappear after the Metropolitan drawing: the slanting balustrade above the left aisle, and the single, unelaborated pediment over the upper story. The division into bays of the left half of the facade is similar to that of the first project; the treatment of the upper story may anticipate that of Uff. 2500A. The design should probably be dated to 1585-87.

One of Buontalenti's main reasons for making the sketch was probably to find a satisfactory treatment for the outer oculi, which caused such problems in his first project. The use of a giant order obviated the risk of their interrupting any significant horizontals; placed rather high up within the order, they would not destabilize whatever was placed above.

The drawing has sometimes been associated with Model 130, a model which requires discussion in any treatment of the facade. The model is often taken to represent a collaboration between Buontalenti and Cigoli (see Cresti 1990: 297 n. 17, for bibliography; Matteoli 1974: 74, 84, 86, makes a weakly based attribution to Passignano). It was so severely damaged in the Florentine flood of 1966, that it can now be studied only in the Alinari photograph. Dated 1596, it was evidently of cheap manufacture, many of the details being painted or drawn onto the wood. It measured 109 × 88 cm (Matteoli 1974: 73; it is not clear whether the measurement included the steps). It appears in Buontalenti's inventory of 1608, with measurements that are close to these, and must further be the model mentioned as Buontalenti's by Bernardino Radi (Matteoli 1974: 106, doc. M; the description of the doors should be noted). The attribution to Cigoli rests on little more than a superficial similarity to Uff. 2649A—which is instead the work of Coccapani (Morrogh 1985a, no. 107; Cresti 1990: 138-140). Much of the detail of the model may be matched in Buontalenti's work, especially that of his later career; I can find nothing in it distinctive of Cigoli.

Model 130 was of considerable interest. In the use of the giant order and the placement of the oculi, it looked back to Uff. 2441A; the pairing of the pilasters perhaps also derived from the right half of that drawing. The tall arched recesses gave the facade bold lines otherwise seen only in Dosio's Model 128; yet inside there was scope for Buontalenti's imaginative, elaborate detail. Particularly well judged was the use of the outer lunettes to contain the oculi, an idea which went back to Moschino's drawing, but was here enriched by a fantastic shell setting.

A.M.

248

GIOVANNI ANTONIO DOSIO
Model for the Facade of Florence Cathedral

Florence, Museo dell'Opera di S. Maria del Fiore, Model 128
Wood; scale: marked (burnt?) on frieze of main entablature, ca. 293 mm = 10 *soldi*, i.e. 1:20.
2583 × 2425 × 385 (including steps).

PROVENANCE: Opera del Duomo.

BIBLIOGRAPHY: *Catalogo del Museo di Santa Maria del Fiore* 1891: 32; Poggi 1904: 56; Busse 1911; Ernst 1934: 28-30; Daddi-Giovannozzi 1936: 33-36, pl. 1; Venturi 1901-40, XI, II: 377-378, fig. 347; Wachler 1940: 205-209, pl. 136; Paatz, 1940-54, III: 470; Matteoli 1974: 77-79, pl. 5; Wittkower 1974: 79-80, pl. 117; Morolli, in Borsi et al. 1976, 256-257.

Up to the death of Grand Duke Francesco, on 19 October 1587, there can have been no doubt that the new facade of the cathedral would follow Buontalenti's project. However two months later Giovan Vettorio Soderini, describing the architectural projects of Grand Duke Ferdinand I, stated: "Ma gli è dispiaciuto grandemente il disfacimento della facciata del Duomo, e per riordinarla a modo vi fa vigilare sopra il cavaliere Pacciotto suo ingegnere e altri Architetti" (Saltini 1863: 79). The new grand duke thus created an atmosphere of competition, in which it was far from clear that Buontalenti would emerge the winner. Nevertheless as late as 1590, *scalpellini* were following Buontalenti's project (Settesoldi 1987: 15).

The circumstances in which Dosio's model was created are not entirely clear. On 18 September 1589 Girolamo Macchietti stated that, "per quanto s'intende," an official in charge of some of the grand-ducal workshops (the *Provveditore delle fortezze*) had paid for "un modello di legnio, che ha fatto fare Giovanni Antonio Dosio;" the Opera del Duomo had had no part in it (Matteoli 1974: 104, doc. E). Yet on 8 January 1591, the Opera paid the considerable sum of 145 florins "a maestro Giovanni Sani legnaiolo, per fattura di un modello della nuova facciata da farsi, fatto da Giovanni Dosio" (Settesoldi 1987: 15). Though the wording ("fatto fare," "fattura") might lead one to suppose that two models were made, it is far more likely that the single surviving model was started under the *Provveditore delle fortezze* and completed under the Opera del Duomo, to which Giovanni Sani presumably did not present his invoice immediately. The connections between Dosio's model, and Don Giovanni's, of 1590, may more readily be explained on the assumption that Dosio's was first, than *vice versa*. What is clearly this model is documented in discussions of 1633/34, when Ferdinand II proposed that it be followed for the facade (Del Moro 1888: 25, 26 n. 1; Daddi-Giovannozzi 1936).

The articulation projects decisively, in only two orders. The entablatures overhang heavily, the stretch so oddly placed above the Serliana emphasizing Dosio's desired effect. No less than three of the horizontal cornices are supported, in rich classical style, by brackets. Elsewhere too the detail is largely classical. Dosio's other main source also carries strong connotations of dignity: Michelange-

lo's work at St. Peter's, which provided, as was noted in the 1630s, Dosio's giant order; the upper side aedicules seem to come from the same source. (The treatment of the strips which frame the bays doubtless derives from the Campidoglio.) More personal are the lower, and especially the upper, round-headed niches; yet it is probably not by chance that these latter are the hardest to see. For the model's august Roman forms would have been compromised by any marked display of Dosio's personality. Fourteen experts gave their opinions on Dosio's facade in 1633 (Del Moro 1888: 25 n. 2). Those in favor called it "privo del tritume e magnifico," and noted its "grandezza," its "maestà e ricchezza." Against it there were perhaps three main criticisms. First, it had squat proportions; the middle bay was too broad, the groups of pilasters were too broad, the main cornice was too low. Second, the projections were too great; the grouped pilasters had nothing to carry, the strongly projecting cornice would be difficult to support. Third, "the new is not united with the old"; more specifically, the *ballatoio* of the sides of the church did not continue across the facade. In fact, it would have reached nearly the top of the plinths that adjoin the buttresses of the upper level.

In the early years of Ferdinand I's reign, discussions of the facade probably centered on Buontalenti's project, which had official status. To judge from the grand duke's opening-up of the commission to other architects, he was not satisfied with that project. At least in 1589, he seems to have preferred Dosio for the facade, whose model takes a radically different approach from Buontalenti's. Grand and classical where Buontalenti's is small-scale and bizarre, it was surely intended to appeal to Ferdinand, who had spent most of his life as a cardinal in Rome. Since the facade is unusually bold in conception for Dosio, it may well embody suggestions from other architects or members of the court. The new attitude to the facade treats it as an independent monument. Dosio's severe, bold forms betray no sympathy for the remainder of the church exterior. The oculi, difficult to deal with and old-fashioned, have been replaced by large rectangular windows. The *ballatoio* is halted by a plinth, not aligned with an entablature on which a further balustrade might rest. However the level of the plinth is a consequence of the model's overall proportions: Dosio seems to have kept his main order rather low so as to permit a commanding upper story. The model, in its present state, contains no indications as to the use of colored marbles. However the Alinari photograph shows a panel representing colored marble in one of the four rectangular frames half-way up the main order.

A.M.

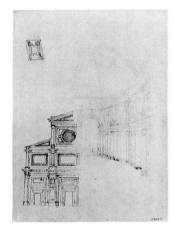

249

GIOVANNI ANTONIO DOSIO
Sketch for the Facade of Florence Cathedral and Unidentifiable Design (for Wooden Construction?)

Florence, Galleria degli Uffizi, Gabinetto Disegni e Stampe, Uff. 2905A
Pen and ink.

VERSO: perspective sketch of interior of baptistery, Florence; pen and ink over chalk.
386 × 272 mm

PROVENANCE: not known.

BIBLIOGRAPHY: Ferri 1885; Daddi-Giovannozzi 1936: 36, pl. 2; Wachler 1940: 221, pl. 156; Matteoli 1974: 74, pl. 4.

This design is strikingly different in tone from Dosio's model. The half pediment above the aisle, resting on a low plinth at its outer edge, recalls the facade of S. Miniato, as does its relationship with the pilaster of the upper story. The fields of the attic and upper story contain panels, presumably of white marble, surrounded by simple strips of colored marble, the whole somewhat reminiscent of the incrustation of S. Miniato and the baptistery, though the large simple forms are closer to such fifteenth-century work as the exterior of S. Maria delle Carceri. In this strongly archaizing context the central oculus looks quite appropriate.

The lower story, it is true, is more modern, the rather complex piers being based on those of the loggia of the Uffizi. Yet the scale of the detail, and indeed almost everything about the facade, suggest that Dosio wished to suit it to the sides of the cathedral—as also, perhaps, to its position opposite the baptistery.

The drawing was presumably made before Dosio left Florence for Naples, in 1590 or 1591; though I believe that he probably returned to Florence for a visit in about 1599 (Morrogh 1985a: 120-121). *A.M.*

250
GIOVANNI DE' MEDICI with ALESSANDRO PIERONI
Model for the Facade of Florence Cathedral

Florence, Museo dell'Opera di S. Maria del Fiore, Model 135
Wood and some paint, to imitate carved moldings; scale: not given, but approx. 28.15 mm = 1 *braccio*.
2341 × 2478 × 373 mm (including steps).

PROVENANCE: Opera del Duomo.

BIBLIOGRAPHY: *Catalogo del Museo di Santa Maria del Fiore* 1891: 33; Poggi 1904: 56; Busse 1911; Ernst 1934: 28-30; Daddi-Giovannozzi 1936: 43, pl. 6; 1937-40: 64, pl. 4; Venturi 1901-40, XI, II: 589, pl. 546; Wachler 1940: 205-209, pl. 140; Paatz 1940-54, III: 468-471; *Mostra di Restauri e Oggetti d'Arte Minore* 1968, no. 42, pl. XIII; Matteoli 1974: 80, 88, pl. 12; Wittkower 1974: 79-80, pl. 120; Chini 1984: 96-97, pl. 89; Morrogh 1985a: 128.

Grand-duke Ferdinand always indulged the ambition of his half-brother, Don Giovanni de' Medici (1567-1621) to be an architect. In 1589, on his return from fighting in Flanders, Don Giovanni was appointed "Soprainten-dente generale di tutte le fortezze, monitioni, et fabriche" (A.S. Modena, Cancelleria Ducale, Dispacci da Firenze 34, c. 13). He was in an excellent position to intervene with a project of his own for the facade of the cathedral. His model, identified by Daddi-Giovannozzi, is dated

1590 (*Mostra*). On 25 January 1591 a table for its display was provided in the grand duke's *scrittoio* on the top story of the Uffizi (A.S. Firenze, Guardaroba 184, cc. 869v., 872). On 7 July 1592, it was set up on a table in the Belvedere (ibid., Guardaroba 169, c. 109v.). It seems safe to say that no other model for the facade received such privileged treatment. The model, though conserving many painted moldings, has suffered several losses. The flanks of the upper story are articulated with strips whose lower part is problematic: they do not rest on the attic, and have at their foot a tall block which cannot be construed as a base. The general similarities with Model 128 (see below) suggest that some volute-like feature has been lost. Furthermore the attic in both cases is much too low to provide an effective termination to the *ballatoio* of the sides of the church. (Its cornice is 28.92 m above the platform of the steps in Model 128, 28.8 m according to the approximate scale for Model 135). In Model 135, as in Model 128, this function was surely to be performed by a plinth—which must have been lost. Together the plinth and the volute-like feature would reduce the remarkable horizontality of the attic, and soften the sharp break between the attic and the upper story.

A further problem concerns the window of the upper story: its opening continues downward, beyond the surround, almost to the plinth. The lower part of the frame, or a balustrade, has clearly been lost. Again, the niches between the doors have been altered in restoration. The Alinari photographs show that the tablets just above the voids were more elaborate than the present simple strips; they were much closer to the corresponding tablets in the upper story of Model 128. The photographs also raise the possibility that, before the flood of 1966, some parts of the facade were painted in a paler tone, most notably the recessed fields around the outer doors. Daddi-Giovannozzi rightly pointed to the influences of Dosio and Buontalenti on Don Giovanni's model, whose style she saw as flat, decorative, and dry. A closer examination shows that Don Giovanni has reduced the height of the already rather low giant order, and increased that of the attic to make up. (In Model 128, the height of the giant order to the cornice is 25.5 m, in Model 135, 24 m; for the attics, see above.) He has also significantly lowered the upper story, so that it is now slightly lower than Buontalenti's (height of horizontal cornice of pediment 43.86 m in his model, 45.82 in Dosio's, and 44.43 in Buontalenti's). Dosio's model has provided him with the basic interior organization of the bays of the lower story, as well as with their framing strips; but he has been unable to achieve significant horizontal alignments between the main elements.

In the main pediment, Don Giovanni has taken up the arrangement seen in Buontalenti's Metropolitan drawing, depriving it however of any logic: for the segmental pediment rests merely on a slightly projecting plane of wall, while the window proper has its own pedimented aedicule. The division into five bays is Buontalentian; specifically, the articulation may be based on Uff. 2441A or on some more finished version of it. An uneasy blend of collaboration and competition is typical of the relationship between the two men. At all events, Don Giovanni's modification of Dosio's bay system must be regarded as one of the most significant aspects of his model. Perhaps we should read it in the light of the criticisms of Dosio's model, made in 1633, that the pilasters projected by too much, and that the central bay was too broad. Don Giovanni narrowed the central bay, and reduced the projection of the pilasters. In turn, the new proportions probably led him to lower the order. However since he kept the attic cornice at the same level (thereby retaining the connection between the now-lost plinth above and the church *ballatoio*), the attic has become uncomfortably high. Also significant is Don Giovanni's attitude toward detail. First Buontalenti's model, and then Dosio's, must have occasioned a good deal of discussion about the appropriate style for the facade. Don Giovanni's answer is that it should be in a Florentine style, his own—or, strictly speaking, that of his more talented collaborator, Alessandro Pieroni. Pieroni's drawings provide examples of

such features as the swags in the frieze of the aedicules, the small grotesque heads with wings, the curious "nicks" in the verticals of the outer windows, the projection of the central part of the pediment of the central door, and its support by a bracket (Daddi-Giovannozzi 1937, Abb. 7, 8; Morrogh 1985a: 127-129.) Pieroni's detail is typically Florentine, as is that of the facade. This shows influences from Michelangelo (the columns of the outer doors), Ammannati (the pediment of the central niche, from the doors of the staircase of Palazzo Pitti), Dosio (the tablets of the lower niches), and much from Buontalenti, to whom Pieroni's taste is perhaps most indebted. However it is also drier and more severe (compare the shells of the niches in the two models), and far more rectilinear; beside Buontalenti, it could almost be described as strait-laced. In the detail, Don Giovanni's model seems to represent a plea for a middle way between the extremes of Buontalenti and Dosio: for an approach that is both proper and characteristically Florentine. In rather the same way, the model's articulation represents a largely Buontalentian critique of Dosio. But how much is due to Don Giovanni, rather than to Pieroni, we shall never know. *A.M*

251
ALESSANDRO PIERONI
Project for the Facade of Florence Cathedral

Florence, Galleria degli Uffizi, Gabinetto Disegni e Stampe, Uff. 2911A
Red chalk over stylus; laid down; scale: (1) in ink at bottom: 108 mm = 30 *braccia*, or 3.6 mm = 1 *braccio*; (2) pricked at lower left: 24 mm = 3 units; (3) pricked below (2): 20 mm = 3 units.
400 × 278/280 mm

PROVENANCE: not known.

BIBLIOGRAPHY: Ferri 1885: 54; Daddi-Giovannozzi 1937-40: 64-69, pl. 6; Fasolo 1953, no. 1, 7 n. 4; Berti 1959: 168; Myers 1971: 395; Borsi 1974, pl. 291; Matteoli 1974: 88-89; Morrogh 1985[1].

This sheet is drawn to the same scale, and in the same technique, as Uff. 2912A and Albertina 1310. Berti, Myers and Matteoli have connected it with the facade of S. Lorenzo, on the basis of the bust above the central door, which they assumed to be that of a male saint; but the scale, the outline of the original structure, and the position of the outer doors all argue for the connection with the cathedral (Daddi-Giovannozzi 1937-40).

Together with Uff. 2912A, the sheet has been attributed both to Cigoli and to Don Giovanni de' Medici. The attribution to Cigoli is supported neither by the technique nor by the character of the detail. Far better based is Daddi-Giovannozzi's attribution to Don Giovanni, for which she adduced the facade of S. Stefano dei Cavalieri, Pisa. Crucial to her notion of his drawing style is Uff. 3035A recto, which she divided, somewhat implausibly, between Don Giovanni and Pieroni (Morrogh 1985[1]: 127-128). If that drawing is solely the work of Pieroni, as I believe, it argues instead for Pieroni's authorship of Uff. 2911A,

2912A, and the Albertina drawing, especially if the ruled red-chalk sketch on its verso, for a loggia, is taken into account. In addition, the windows shown in the duomo drawings are closely related to those of Don Giovanni's Model 135, which there is reason to connect with Pieroni; while the use of the Doric entablature over Corinthian pilasters in the Albertina drawing may be compared with its use over Ionic pilasters in Uff. 3261A (ibid., fig. 75). It is not clear whether Pieroni made the three drawings on his own account, or, like his plans of 1592-94 for the Cappella de' Principi, for presentation to Don Giovanni, who would presumably have made use of them for his own purposes.

The date of the drawings is not clear. Daddi-Giovannozzi, stating that Uff. 2911A and 2912A were more mature than Model 135, suggested that they postdated it. Certainly they show a greater range of ideas, and the close connection with S. Stefano dei Cavalieri, designed in 1593, would tend to support her view.

The disposition of the present drawing, with its large central arch, seems to be based on a late fifteenth or early sixteenth-century design for the facade of the cathedral, Uff. 2170A (sometimes wrongly attributed to Dosio, e.g. in Borsi 1976, no. 299). The broad framing strips, which in the facade of S. Stefano surround panels of colored marble, may have the same function here. *A.M.*

252
ALESSANDRO PIERONI
Project for the Facade of Florence Cathedral

Florence, Galleria degli Uffizi, Gabinetto Disegni e Stampe, Uff. 2912A
Red chalk over stylus; scale: 107 mm = 30 *braccia*, i.e. 3.57 mm = 1 *braccio*.
VERSO: sketch of *Continence of Scipio* or similar subject; pen over red chalk.
434/431 × 282 mm

PROVENANCE: not known.

BIBLIOGRAPHY: Ferri 1885: 54; Daddi-Giovannozzi 1937-40: 64-69, pl. 5; Fasolo 1953, no. 1, 7 n 4, pl. 8; Berti 1959: 168, pl. LXXIIIb; Borsi 1974: 373, ill.; Matteoli 1974: 88-89; Morrogh 1985a: 128.

Initially Pieroni considered a higher main order, which supported an attic of almost the same height as the present; but the result was too high to permit a suitable tie-up with the *ballatoio* of the sides of the cathedral. The final version takes up the key elements of Buontalenti's project: the attic cornice would meet the upper part of the *ballatoio*, the balustrade of the facade being set at a higher level. Pieroni's two other drawings follow the same system.

All three drawings show Pieroni interested in the Buontalentian theme of oculi. The oculi in the attic are too high to serve as windows (for they would conflict with the vaulting), but may be intended as reminiscences of the oculi of the old facade. One function of the attic may be that of providing a suitable framework for oculi. In Uff. 2911A and the Albertina drawing, the outer oculi are again placed in positions where they cannot disturb the organization of the facade, much as in Buontalenti's (earlier?) drawing Uff. 2441A. A good candidate for a further oculus is the oval above the central door in Uff. 2911A, which can hardly be intended for the Medici coat of arms, since that is set a little higher up. It looks as if around 1593, or whenever Pieroni made these drawings, he came to find new virtues in Buontalenti's approach to the facade. *A.M.*

253
ALESSANDRO PIERONI
Project for the Facade of Florence Cathedral

Vienna, Graphische Sammlung Albertina, Ital. Unbekannt 1310
Red chalk over stylus; cut at left, right, and bottom; scale: not given, but ca. 3.6 mm = 1 *braccio*.
VERSO: unidentified sketches; red chalk, pen and ink.
303 × 258 mm

BIBLIOGRAPHY: none.

The broad temple front, incongruously inserted into a Florentine setting (with reminiscences of Buontalenti's Model 132, S. Stefano dei Cavalieri, and Uff. 2911A), gives this facade a charm unusual for Pieroni. The central portion projects rather oddly (on half-columns?), above which giant figures support the Medici arms—a group which would be more at home in festival decoration.
A.M.

254
GIAMBOLOGNA
Model for the Facade of Florence Cathedral

Florence, Museo dell'Opera di S. Maria del Fiore, Model 133

Wood, wax; inscription in frieze, burnt on (?): see below; scale: not given, but approx. 15.44 mm = 1 *braccio*.
1480 × 1350 × 320 mm

PROVENANCE: Opera del Duomo.

BIBLIOGRAPHY: *Catalogo del Museo di Santa Maria del Fiore* 1891: 33; Poggi 1904: 56; Busse 1911; Ernst 1934: 28-30; Daddi-Giovannozzi 1936: 42-43, pl. 5; Venturi 1901-40, XI, II: 607-609, pl. 564; Wachler 1940: 205-209, pl. 141; Paatz 1940-54, III: 468-471; Dhanens 1956: 264, pl. 152; Berti 1959: 170; *Mostra di Restauri e Oggetti d'Arte Minore* 1968, no. 41, pls. XIV, XV; Matteoli 1974: 74, 80-81, 89-90, pl. 15; Wittkower 1974, 79-80, pl. 119.

The model bears evident signs of its restoration after the flood of 1966. As a comparison with the Alinari photograph shows, some details of the aedicules above the outer doors have been lost; more significant, however, is the reintroduction of the columns to the two aedicules above the central door. The choice of Doric must be regarded as arbitrary.

Daddi-Giovannozzi has convincingly attributed the model to Giambologna, pointing to many similarities with the Cappella Salviati at S. Marco, Florence. An attribution to Cigoli, recently revived by Matteoli, rests on an inadequate knowledge of his work. The inscription read initially: "FERDINANDVS.M[EDICES].M[AGNVS].DVX. ETR[VRIAE].III." In the reign of Ferdinand II (1621-70) the first "M" was altered to "II," and the "III" to "V." These alterations are doubtless to be connected with the discussions of 1634, when Giambologna's pupil Pietro Tacca was asked to submit "il disegno di Gian Bologna" (Del Moro 1888: 26 n. 3). Matteoli dated the model 1596, supposing that it was entered in an (undocumented) competition with Models 130 and 135; but the date is best left open. The model is clearly a response to Dosio's of 1589, and has features in common with Don Giovanni's of 1590 (the distribution of the pediments in the main story, the relationship of the upper pediments to the *collarino*). However it is unusually informative about the facade's relationship to the articulation of the sides of the church, suggesting a new awareness of the issue. I would therefore tentatively date it after 1590.

Giambologna's model is more respectful toward Dosio's than was Don Giovanni's. Obvious similarities are the division into three bays, the brackets of the main entablature, the buttresses of the upper story. In the second level, Dosio had used aedicules reminiscent of Michelangelo's work at St. Peter's; now, in the center of that level, Giambologna employs an aedicule which derives from the same source, suggesting that he too saw the connection as one that would dignify the facade. When Giambologna allows himself more personal detail, he avoids the grotesque features and lively carving typical of Buontalenti, creating instead a mood of very sober licence. The breaks in the tympana of the doors are handled with such discipline as to harmonize with the classical character of the aedicules. (Compare the handling of the broken pediments in Don Giovanni's model.)

Giambologna's two main criticisms of Dosio concerned the projections of the facade and the height of the main order. He flattened out the central bay, and reorganized the recesses of the side bays; he set the outer pilasters behind the plane of the central pilasters in a manner suggested by contemporary Roman church facades, such as that of the Gesù. He thus indicates the dominance of the nave over the aisles more forcefully than in any previous design. He also greatly simplified the articulation, producing an unusually loose composition for a facade of such importance. Perhaps the large areas of flat wall were to serve for incrustation with colored marble, on which the articulation would cast but limited shadows.

As we have noted, the model gives an exceptional amount of information about the sides of the church. The purpose is doubtless to demonstrate the suitability of the facade to the existing structure. Giambologna has achieved three connections: between the upper entablature of the model and the cornice of the clerestory; between the cornice of the main entablature and the *ballatoio*; between the *collarino* of the capital below and a dentilled string-course.

To bring about the second connection—which is prefigured in Buontalenti's work—,Giambologna has heightened Dosio's giant order and reduced the upper story to an attic. He has taken over the balustrade of Buontalenti's early designs, carrying it across the facade; in effect it continues the (slightly lower) *ballatoio* around the church. In this respect, Giambologna corrects Dosio's model exactly as Passignano and Tacca were to wish in 1633 (Del Moro 1888: 25 n. 2). Indeed Tacca's disapproval of Dosio's model could well have come from his master's mouth: "per che no lega nè unisce con la Chiesa; riesce nano per esser la Cornice bassa, et i Pilastri troppo rinfiancati, e per che no vi si rigira il Ballatoio."

In the windows, Giambologna again criticizes Dosio's model in the light of Buontalenti's work. The central oculus is retained, and framed by columns rather as in the first stage of Buontalenti's project (see the relief and Uff. 2927A). In the context, the arches of the lower windows should probably be taken as a reference to the outer oculi.

A.M.

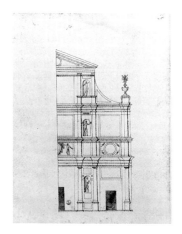

255
GIORGIO VASARI THE YOUNGER
Project for the Facade of Florence Cathedral

Florence, Galleria degli Uffizi, Gabinetto Disegni e Stampe, Uff. 4670A
Pen and ink, brown wash; scale: not given, but approx. 3.48 mm = 1 *braccio*.
391/390 × 275/272 mm

PROVENANCE: Vasari family; Ricoveri family.

BIBLIOGRAPHY: Ferri 1885: 26; Daddi-Giovannozzi 1936: 43; Paatz 1940-54: 471; Olivato 1970: 198, pl. 12; Borsi in Borsi et al. 1980, I: 314, II: 96, no. 76 (ill.).

The very numerous drawings of Giorgio Vasari the Younger (the nephew of the biographer) constitute his only claim to fame. As an amateur architect, he was consulted about the Cappella de' Principi. Perhaps too he was consulted about the facade of the cathedral, another major project of Ferdinand I—to whom he dedicated a volume of drawings in 1598 (Stefanelli 1970: 53-191). He took a touchingly modest view of his own abilities (ibid.: 56-58, 184). Daddi-Giovannozzi identified the present sheet, Uff. 4529A and 4684A with the facade of the cathedral, dating them to 1598-1600. Since Uff. 4529A is included in the volume dedicated to the grand duke, it must date from 1598 or earlier; the dating of Uff. 4670A and 4684A should, it seems to me, be left open. These two drawings form part of a group (Uff. 4595A-4714A) that largely reproduces doors and windows in Florence and Rome. Borsi's publication of the whole group is negligible as a work of scholarship.

The present drawing demonstrates the problem posed by the outer oculi. Retaining the oculus in its original size and position (or almost), Vasari provides a firm architectural frame for it; in effect, he designs the facade around it. The

result is a high first order; a relatively high, disruptive mezzanine; and low second and third orders, of almost equal height. The pedestals inserted into the first and third stories only serve to render a difficult situation more problematic.

A.M.

256
GIORGIO VASARI THE YOUNGER
Project for the Facade of Florence Cathedral

Florence, Galleria degli Uffizi, Gabinetto Disegni e Stampe, Uff. 4684A mm
Pen and ink, brown wash; scale: not given, but approx. 3.31 mm = 1 *braccio*.
390/391 × 275/271

PROVENANCE: Vasari family; Ricoveri family.

BIBLIOGRAPHY: Ferri 1885: 26; Daddi-Giovannozzi 1936: 43; Paatz 1940-54: 471; Borsi in Borsi et al. 1980, I: 316, II: 100, no. 90 (ill.).

The design is unusually successful for Vasari the Younger. The carefully graded lower story, with its arches that coordinate doors of different dimensions, recalls High Renaissance schemes of composition (cp. especially Uff. 277A, by Giuliano da Sangallo, associated with the facade of S. Lorenzo). The doors themselves, with their attics, are based on those of Don Giovanni's Model 135. The attic of the outer door supports an oculus which serves to recall the much higher oculus of the original facade (cp. Uff. 4670A). In the central bay, Vasari appears not to have found a satisfactory use for the area between the attic and the arch.

A.M.

257
DOMENICO PASSIGNANO
Project for the Facade of Florence Cathedral

Florence, Galleria degli Uffizi, Gabinetto Disegni e Stampe, Uff. 2631 Sant.

Black chalk and brown wash over stylus; scale: 33 mm = 6 *braccia*.
570/567 × 437/428
INSCRIPTION: in pen, below central door: "Passignano."

PROVENANCE: E. Santarelli.

BIBLIOGRAPHY: *Catalogo ... Santarelli* 1870: 192, n. 57; Ferri 1885: 47; Matteoli 1974: 86, pl. 9.

The only detailed discussion of Uff. 2631 and 2635 Sant. is that of Matteoli. Adducing stylistic arguments of a generic nature, she saw the sheets as preparatory to Model 130 of 1596—wich, implausibly, she attributed to Passignano (see under Uff. 2441A). She did not consider the possibility of a much later date. The drawings were clearly drawn within a short period, for they are very similar in their technique, details, and scale. Of the two, Uff. 2631 Sant. is most likely the earlier, for much of it is unresolved. The treatment of the detail in Uff. 2635 Sant. suggests that both designs were drawn well into the seventeenth century. The peculiar form of segmental pediment above the left door reappears in drawings by Coccapani for the facade, of 1634/35 (above the central door in Uff. 2649Ar.-v., 2650A: Morrogh, 1985a, no. 107; Cresti 1990, ills. on 138, 139). In this period, new designs were submitted for the facade. It is tempting to connect Uff. 2635 Sant.—at least in a general way—with Passignano's entry, which showed a two-story facade (Del Moro 1888: 27). That he should have drawn 2631 Uff. Sant., for a three-story facade, a little earlier, will hardly seem surprising in the context; for there was general agreement that a three-story facade would be more appropriate. Taken together, the two drawings suggest that Passignano started from the accepted position of the mid-1630s, found it to be unworkable, and returned to the late-sixteenth-century solution of a giant order.

That the two drawings were drawn to the same scale is clear from many of their measurements. Thus in both cases the distance from the base line to the outer angle of the nave roof measures 391 mm. Yet their inscribed scales are slightly different: 6 *braccia* is equivalent to ca. 33 mm in Uff. 2631 Sant., and to ca. 32 mm in Uff. 2635 Sant. And these scales produce figures that are in almost every case too low when compared with the church. One may arrive at a far more satisfactory scale for both drawings by taking the 391 mm just mentioned as equivalent to the height of the outer angle of the nave roof in the present building (ca. 74.88 *braccia*): 5.22 mm = 1 *braccio*. But even so the outer doors are still too close (distance between their midpoints in Uff. 2631 Sant. and 2635 Sant. 49.41 and 49.22 *braccia* respectively; in the building, 51.36 *braccia*).

Passignano's initial idea for the facade seems to be a development of the five-bay, arched system of the left half of Moschino's drawing. The gaps between the main paired pilasters and columns were greater than in the final design (in the first order 20 mm, instead of the later 11-12 mm); Passignano thought of using them for niches and coats of arms. Whether he referred directly to the Munich drawing or to some now-lost elaboration of it containing a more fully developed ground floor, is not clear. However the variation from pilasters in the first order, to columns in the second, and strips in the third, is characteristic of Buontalenti's first project. From the same source come the three tall pedimented aedicules above the doors, here developed interestingly as a minor order with their own entablature; while the coupling of the columns next to the central door creates a remarkable play between projecting and recessed columns (more fully worked out in Uff. 2635 Sant.). Passignano adapts his borrowings with considerable originality.

The presence of the balustrade above the second story reminds us of Passignano's disapproval of Dosio's model in 1633, "per esser nano, troppo semplice, e senza finimento, morendo dalle bande il Corridore che vorrebbe rigirar per tutto" (Del Moro 1888: 25 n. 2). We may trace this approach toward the balustrade, via Pietro Tacca—whose views about the facade were very similar to Passignano's—back to Giambologna's Model 133. The same model gave Passignano another idea, the means of achieving a close connection between the pediment of the central door and the balcony above; but it was now necessarily superimposed on an entablature. The strong vertical continuity carries through into the top story, a pediment overlapping the entablature below the central oculus; there is a further linkage between the oculus and the main pediment. Here Passignano adopts a very strange device: the strips of the third story carry a full, if rather niggardly, entablature, which serves in turn as the architrave for the crowning entablature of the facade. Uff. 2635 Sant. shows a further development of these themes. The discussions of the 1630s laid great emphasis on the need to adapt the facade to the church. That Passignano agreed is clear not only from his upper balustrade, but from the correspondence between the cornice of his "entablature-architrave" and the clerestory cornice (at the left, in perspective), and from his retention of the oculi in their original positions. For the central oculus, necessarily set rather low in relation to the third story, he designed a somewhat top-heavy surround. Oddly, he left the outer oculi without surrounds, awkwardly related to their recesses. Yet the real question concerned their suitability to a three-story design. In such a design, without a mezzanine, the only place to put the oculi was low in the second story, as in the models of Gherardo Silvani and the Accademia del Disegno. If Passignano was not satisfied with their position in the present drawing, he had good reason to try out the giant order.   A.M.

258
DOMENICO PASSIGNANO
Project for the Facade of Florence Cathedral

Florence, Galleria degli Uffizi, Gabinetto Disegni e Stampe, Uff. 2635 Sant.
Black chalk and brown wash over stylus; some white heightening (to cover pentimenti, and for Madonna and Saint above doors); pieces of paper attached above side doors and above pediment of main door; scale: 32 mm = 6 *braccia*.
556/554 × 420 mm
INSCRIBED: (below central door, in pen) *Passignano*.

PROVENANCE: E. Santarelli.

BIBLIOGRAPHY: *Catalogo ... Santarelli* 1870; Ferri 1885: 193, n. 61; Matteoli 1974: 86-88, pl. 10.

In this design, Passignano has developed the pilasters of the previous drawing into a giant order. The outer oculi are placed at the top of their bays, where they can best be assimilated (cp. Uff. 2441A, by Buontalenti); and that determined the level of the entablature. Above is an attic, which Passignano heightened in the course of drawing. It is crowned by the balustrade, intended as a continuation of the *ballatoio* of the sides of the cathedral, and as the "finimento" of the facade (cp. Del Moro 1888: 25 n. 2). Its height and powerful projection produce a remarkable effect, suggesting that the attic below be read as a frieze,

and the entablature of the giant order as little more than a sort of architrave. A similar grouping appears in the upper story, taken over from Uff. 2631 Sant.

Within the bays, Passignano develops the theme of vertical continuity, which he had pioneered in Uff. 2631 Sant. In the central bay, he probably intended the now very emphatic continuity to distract attention from the unfavorable relation of the central oculus to the upper story, and from the break in the balustrade to accommodate it. The outer bays may be seen as reductions of the central bay, lending it some justification and helping to unify a very strange facade. The extraordinary verticality and tightly packed decoration may be seen too as a belated reaction to Dosio's model, which Passignano had criticized as too squat and too simple.

Whether the present drawing represents Passignano's entry for the competition of 1635 is not clear. A rough sketch at the Biblioteca Nazionale Centrale, Florence (MS. II, I, 429, c. 27; unpublished), has good claim to represent a later development of the design. It shows single pilasters in the giant order, a simpler, continuous treatment of the main entablature and balustrade, and different proportions.   A.M.

259
BERNARDO BUONTALENTI
*Sketch for the Facade of Florence Cathedral;
Perspective Sketch for Piazza Pitti*

Florence, Galleria degli Uffizi, Gabinetto Disegni e Stampe, Uff. 2305A
Pen and brown ink; sheet composed of two pieces of coarse paper.
VERSO: sketches of machines, window, and door; pen and brown ink, traces of black chalk.
282 × 226 mm

PROVENANCE: Silvani family (?), M. Ferrucci.

BIBLIOGRAPHY: Ferri 1885: 61, 90; Giovannozzi 1933: 302; Venturi 1901-40, XI, II: 486-493, pl. 440; Fasolo 1953: 13; Berti 1959: 172-173; Botto 1963: 44 n. 52; Bucci 1973, pl. V; Fanelli 1973, fig. 492; Borsi 1974: 268-269, pl. 220; Fara 1979: 33 n. 113; Matteoli 1980: 273; Morrogh 1985a, no. 70; Fara 1988: 178.

The small sketch at the top of the sheet shows what may be Buontalenti's very first thoughts about the facade of the cathedral. The church shown has aisles but not outer chapels, an oculus in the upper story, and proportions that recall those of the duomo. A small cupola or lantern rests, most remarkably, on the aisle, in a manner which may recall lost projects of his for the facade of S. Trinita—and also, perhaps, the fanciful gazebo-like structures seen in the main sketch, for Piazza Pitti.

The main sketch most likely dates from 1577, when preparations for the baptism of Prince Filippo de' Medici were under way; the reorganization of the piazza could be expected to impress the many important visitors which would come for the ceremony. With no great expenditure, Buontalenti contrives to give form to the piazza, cut-

ting away its somewhat forbidding slope to enhance the view of the palace. The preparations for the baptism may also have spurred him to consider a permanent solution to an old problem, the facade of the cathedral just opposite the Baptistery; but that would have been a project for the longer term.   A.M.

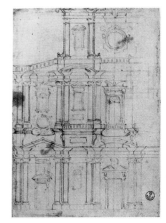

260
After BERNARDO BUONTALENTI
*Copy of Design for the Facade
of Florence Cathedral*

Florence, Galleria degli Uffizi, Gabinetto Disegni e Stampe, Uff. 2927A
Red chalk.
VERSO: perspective exercises and other, perhaps related, designs; pen and brown ink, black chalk; scale: not marked, but approx. 2.64 mm = 1 *braccio*.
212/213 × 142/141 mm

PROVENANCE: unavailable.

BIBLIOGRAPHY: Ferri 1885: 25; Daddi-Giovannozzi 1936: 41-42, pl. 4; Berti 1959: 168-169, pl. LXXIIIa; Myers 1971: 392-395, pl. 2; Gambuti 1973: 62; Matteoli 1974: 88-89; Morolli, in Borsi et al. 1976, no. 302; Holderbaum 1983: 279.

Holderbaum has noted that this drawing is closely connected with the stage of Buontalenti's project seen in the relief for the Tribuna. The attic above the first order is low, and the central pediment is unbroken. The outer oculi are contained within the second order. In the third order, a broad aedicule frames an oculus. These features must belong to an early stage of the project, for they cannot be fitted into its later evolution. (By the same token, differences in the smaller aedicules of the second order suggest that the relief predates the drawing.) At this stage, the project has both the simple logic, and the drawbacks, of an original *concetto*. The drawing must reproduce a lost design by Buontalenti.

Buontalenti's first project achieved a close relationship between the facade and the church behind, which was to have great influence on later designs. Broadly speaking, he took the levels of his second and third entablatures—and thus the height of his third story—from the two main horizontals of the sides of the church. In the present drawing the second entablature would correspond approximately to the brackets and parapet base of the *ballatoio* crowning the facades of the aisles. The balustrade would in effect continue the *ballatoio* across the facade, at a slightly higher level. Model 132 shows that the upper entablature was to continue above the clerestory, presumably for a short stretch. Its position would probably have permitted the original cornice of the clerestory to pass just below. (But there are variations in the measurements for the different stages of Buontalenti's project; perhaps his architrave was to continue the upper part of the clerestory cornice.)

Buontalenti also retained the oculi of the old facade, despite the difficulties it created for his story heights. The old upper oculus was set inconveniently low in his third story, the foot of its opening being almost level with the top of the *ballatoio*. Though in the 1630s, ways were found of keeping it in its original position (cf. Uff. 2631 and 2635 Sant.), Buontalenti preferred to reduce the oculus considerably and to raise it by 4.5-5 m, with the result that its upper part can admit no light to the church. The present drawing shows that he hoped to keep the outer oculi in their original positions, though without having found a satisfactory way of incorporating them. That seen here has a scrolly surround, with the attic below cut away in what seems to be a curious curving line.

Also problematic, at this stage of the design, was the size of the doors. Constrained by the columnar aedicule, Buontalenti has reduced the size of the central door (in the original facade, ca. 8.8 m high from the platform of the steps, and 3.86 m across; in Uff. 2927A, roughly 6.7 × 2.8 m), and has further reduced the outer doors. Broader openings would have been desirable, if only for processions.

The drawing, which is sometimes connected with Uff. 2911A and 2912A, has been variously attributed to Dosio, Cigoli, and Don Giovanni de' Medici. It is too tentative for Dosio, and probably for Cigoli even in his early career. It is more tentative than Uff. 2911A and 2912A, but could perhaps be by the same draftsman—whom I believe to be Alessandro Pieroni—at an earlier date. The matter is best left open.   *A.M.*

The Dome and Lantern of Florence Cathedral
Massimo Scolari

Almost all the drawings relating to the construction of the cathedral of S. Maria del Fiore have been lost. The only surviving one is that contained in Gherardi's report criticizing Brunelleschi's building methods, while but two of the large number of models which the Opera del Duomo (Board of Works) ordered and paid for are still extant. From the time of Nielli's measurements to the most advanced photogrammetric surveys, art historians have attempted to solve the enigma of how the dome was constructed. Frequently their approach has been spiced with the same kind of polemic which was the keynote of Gherardi's report. But none of these analyzers has managed to penetrate the mystery of its interior, and even today it is only possible to affirm that what we have before our eyes is the best example of Brunelleschi's architecture.

It is not the present writer's intention to give a detailed account of the various technical interpretations of the dome's construction: in fact, despite the vast bibliography on the subject, these explanations appear to be of little consequence and are often incomplete.

This writer believes, however, that it would be more useful to tackle a problem that it has not been possible to deal with in the various catalog entries: the use of the model in the architectural projects of the Quattrocento. Naturally, the use of models in the design of buildings dates back to ancient times. We know, for example, that in Athens the Council of the Five Hundred judged the architectural projects not from drawings, but from models (Aristotle, *Constitution of the Athenians*, XLIX, 3); it was on these that the stonemasons based their templates, which may be compared to the paper patterns used by tailors nowadays. Generally speaking these models, which the Greeks called *paradeigmata*, were made of wax or wood. It is not known whether they were also used by the Romans, nor have we any proof of their existence in late antiquity. Nevertheless, Bucher suggests that models were made for reliquaries from the Carolingian period onward, and points to these as the means of entry into the profession for architects in Northern Italy; in fact, Filarete described them as "goldsmiths" (Bucher 1974: 71-81).

Although very little can be gleaned regarding the use of the model from sources prior to the fourteenth century, in the second half of that century there were numerous references to them in written sources in Tuscany. They were a feature of routine architectural design, described in detailed contracts, which also used the existing architecture as a model (Toker 1985: 67-94). Just like the Greek *paradeigmata*, the Trecento or Quattrocento model was an example made by a master; this then had to be copied with great precision by the workers (Lippold 1926: 209).

In the documents relating to the building of the cathedral of S. Maria del Fiore there are often expressions such as "un disegnamento asempro di legniame, del disegnamento di legname" and "ad faciendum designum seu modellum ecclesiae." A document of 19 November 1367 established the equivalence between *disegnamento* and *modello* (model): "every other model, whether it is made of bricks, wood or paper, must be dismantled" (Guasti 1887, doc. 192). Therefore, *disegnamento* or *designum* are an expression of a concept which could be translated as a drawing or an *exemplum* (example), corresponding to *esempro, asempro* or *essenpro* in fourteenth-century Italian. Then in 1426, while in the registers of the Opera del Duomo the word progressively took on the sole meaning of "model," Gherardi described his drawing as a "model," a geometric paradigm to be repeated for the four diameters of the drum.

In general, for the whole of the first half of the Quattrocento the model attested, almost as if it were a patent (*privilegium*), the originality of the project before the committee of citizens, who were not always able to grasp the real significance of drawings and oral descriptions. Its authority derived from the implicit promise that it represented the building as it would appear when completed; this pledge was backed up by the oath "I swear to Almighty God ... that this building will be constructed according to the model ... " (Guasti 1887, doc. 480). But the peremptory nature of the principle which the model instituted was often the cause of its own demise. In fact, a document of the Opera del Duomo stated that in 1367, after the new model had been made, all the previous ones were destroyed (Guasti 1887, doc. 192).

The Arte della Lana (Wool Merchants' Guild) was continuously seeking advice about the construction of the dome and asking for opinions, drawings and models. This explains why so many models were mentioned in the registers of the Opera and also accounts for the very nature of the public planning process which took place in the form of a discussion around the model.

Designed by an individual, the model was then completed technically and esthetically with the participation of *capimaestri*, workers, nobles and citizens well versed in architectural matters. The final choice included all the best features of the models presented in a climate of free competition that was perhaps unique in the history of Western architecture. It is only if the *florentina libertas* (Florentine freedom), which turned private conflicts to the advantage of the *res pubblica* (state), is borne in mind that it is possible to understand the bitter polemic waged by Gherardi and the provocative comparisons to which Brunelleschi's project for the lantern was subjected. It is not surprising, therefore, that in Brunelleschi's models "questions of symmetry were not evident" and only "the main walls, and the relationship between the features without ornamentation or capitals or architraves, friezes and cornices, etc." were shown (Manetti ed. De Robertis 1970: 116). Moreover, for the Barbadori house Brunelleschi "did not want to make a model," but preferred to give his orders directly at the building site "only with drawings and orally" (Manetti ed. De Robertis 1976: 116-117).

In the second half of the Quattrocento the spread of the use of project drawings led to a change in the role and size of the model. No longer serving to present the salient features of the building's design, it became part of the planning process, losing any prescriptive function during the construction stage. It was in this period that secretive behavior of the *capimaestri* still working within the Gothic tradition was replaced by the intellectual assurance which Alberti imparted to the Renaissance architect. Thus, it no longer made sense for him to build models with his own hands, yet alone to do this "secretly." They were made with reference to precise drawings, but by others and elsewhere. Indeed, thanks to the assistance of all the "experts," Alberti's system of values seems to be founded on the central role of architectural design based on sketches, drawings and models (Alberti 1541, fol. 18r.). An instrument for experimentation and reflection, the model served to find the most satisfactory solutions for each problem and to calculate, with civil liability, the costs of the work. Consistent with this, the type of model which Alberti suggested was far from being a pretext for esthetic self-indulgence: it had to be, therefore, plain and simple, without frills. It was not worthy of an architect to beguile his patrons with models covered with ornamentation (Alberti 1541, fol. 18r.).

261
FILIPPO BRUNELLESCHI (?)
Wooden Model of the Dome and Apse Parts of Florence Cathedral

Florence, Museo dell'Opera di S. Maria del Fiore
Wood.
100 × 90 cm (central part), 55 × 63 × 35 cm (side parts)

BIBLIOGRAPHY: *Catalogo del Museo di S. Maria del Fiore* 1891: 35, no.
160 and no. 163; Poggi 1904: 61, no. 160 and 163; Sanpaolesi 1941:
11; Braunfels 1965: 218; Brunetti 1975: 22; Marchini 1977: 39; 1980:
916-920; Fondelli 1981: 179-182, fig. 2; Preti 1989: 31 and 33.

The model is comprised of the parts of the apse and the block formed by the dome and drum, with a portion of the piers and arches underneath. Until the 1966 flood these component parts were displayed on the Opera shelves separately; after this event they were restored by Otello Caprara (1967-68) and reassembled, since it was noted that they were all to a scale of 1:50 (Marchini 1980). On the whole the model is in good repair, even though the numerous cleaning and restoration operations have removed coloring and stuccowork.
The dome is without the lantern; the drum underneath is supported by pointed arches and pierced by splayed oculi (external diam. = 11.2 cm; internal diam. = 6.2 cm) on each of the eight faces (36 cm). The springing line of the dome is enclosed by a wide strip which indicates the overall dimensions of the external *ballatoio* or gallery which Brunelleschi and Ghiberti had provided for in 1420. The upper exedra is crowned by the same form, 5 cm in height, which is found at the base of the octagonal drum under the dome. The parts of the apse are composed of two exedrae, one above the other and semi-octagonal in shape. The three frontal faces (32 × 25 cm) of the exedra at the base are separated by three blind round arches (span ca. 6.5 cm); in the middle one, in a central position, is placed a splayed opening in the form of a pointed arch. The two faces adjacent to the masonry of the drum (32 × 17.5 cm) contain two blind round arches with a splayed opening in the form of a pointed arch; the upper part the five faces of the smallest exedra (30 × 15.5 and 30 × 13 cm) have the same openings as those underneath, but they are inscribed in round arches and are separated by buttresses.
It is almost impossible to date the model precisely because, while the dome was being built, models of all its component parts were ordered from various makers. Sanpaolesi considers the model to be "contemporary with the construction ... one of the many which for various reasons that were clear at the time, but are unknown to us and almost impossible to discover, were made during the construction of the vault ... and it lacks those features which would allow us to date it somewhere between 1420 and 1452" (Sanpaolesi 1941). However, the discrepancies which exist between the model and the actual construction allow us to narrow down the period within which it was made. The only substantial reservation regards the octagonal drum and the parts of the apse which could have been executed in the late fourteenth century.
In the model were reproduced the irregularities actually

present on the sides of the drum (the maximum difference between the sides in the actual drum is ca. 60 cm). In the drum the corner pilasters have the same width from the base to the impost of the dome, while we know from Manetti's biography that, after the death of Brunelleschi, Ciaccheri "reduced the width of the pilasters in the upper section" (Manetti ed. De Robertis 1976: 115) when the marble facing was begun in 1465. Therefore, it may be safely assumed that the model was made prior to 1465, but this does not explain why it has survived; in fact, normally when substantial modifications were made a new model was constructed and the old one was destroyed. Marchini proposes the hypothesis that the model could be the one ordered from Ghiberti and Brunelleschi on 22 September 1429 (Guasti 1857, doc. 61) to replace the one built near the campanile, and demolished on 23 January 1431 (Guasti 1857, doc. 68). This thesis appears to be borne out by a request made to Brunelleschi on 17 June 1434 that he should "complete the model of the church and the great dome and its lantern" (Guasti 1857, doc. 70) after he had been asked for a model of the lantern on 30 October 1432 (Guasti 1857, doc. 250). In another hypothesis Marchini suggests that the dome is older and is the one mentioned by Giovanni di Gherardo Gherardi in 1425 when he says "this form [pointed fifth] was decided on six years ago, and I made a wooden model." The oculi in the drum are not excessively splayed; in the actual drum Manetti complained this was "due to the incompetence of the *capimaestri* who worked there later on and made the splays too wide on the outside of the oculi" (Manetti ed. De Robertis 1976: 115). The splays in the model are less accentuated than those in the built oculi, and the diameter of the oculi is smaller than it ought to be. The *ballatoio* at the base of the dome, which in the model is "without ornamentation" as Brunelleschi intended, may correspond to the project of 1420. Braunfels also believes that the model is contemporary with the construction (Braunfels 1965).   *M.S.*

―――――――――――――

262
FILIPPO BRUNELLESCHI
Wooden Model of the Lantern of Florence Cathedral

Florence, Museo dell'Opera di S. Maria del Fiore
Elm and walnut, with parts (capitals of the pilasters) in pastiglia and wax, now lost.
84 (max.) × 70 (max.) cm

BIBLIOGRAPHY: Vasari, ed. Milanesi 1878, II: 362 n 2, and 363-364; Stegmann and Geymüller 1885, I: p. 36; *Catalogo del Museo di S. Maria del Fiore* 1891: 35, no. 164; Poggi 1904: 61, no. 164; Folnesics 1915: 109; Briggs 1929: 180, pl. IIa; Heydenreich 1931: 21; Sanpaolesi 1941: 11-12, pl. 1; Paatz 1952: 462, no. 102; Coolidge 1952: 166; Sanpaolesi 1956: 11-29; 1962: 70-71 and 157; Luporini 1964: 212 n. 156; Rossi 1964: 96; Beccherucci and Brunetti 1968, II: 211-214, no. 1; Capraro 1968: 28, no. 34; Ragghianti 1977: 414, 419, pl. IX; Fabriczy 1979: 128, n. 69; Saalman 1980: 146, pl. 106; Battisti 1981: 257-259 and 383-384; Goldthwaite 1984: 520; Pacciani 1987: 13; Scolari 1988: 17; Preti 1989: 31-32.

Thanks to the restoration carried out by Otello Caprara in 1967-68 this wooden model is in fairly good condition: it is comprised of two parts made separately at different times. The base is carved in two parts held together by two dovetail joints. It represents the upper part of the dome from which three external webs have been removed to show the ribs carved in the block of elm and walnut. In the upper part are modeled the octagonal oculus and the small rooms in the ring surrounding it; all these parts are covered by the floor of the lantern above. The shape of the lantern is an irregular octagon; in each face of this there are windows placed between fluted Corinthian pilasters, the capitals of which were made of pastiglia and covered with wax. In the sides of the buttresses, which support the pilasters, there are rectangular openings with shell-shaped overdoors. Above the molded cornice, the fluted cone, consisting of a number of pieces of walnut, is surmounted by a globe and wooden cross. The date of 1673 painted on the model almost certainly refers to the year when the model was painted off-white; this is still visible in an old Alinari photograph taken before the 1966 flood.
On 27 June 1432 Brunelleschi was asked to produce a design for the ring of the lantern in two versions: one was circular and the other octagonal (Guasti 1857, doc. 247). On 12 August 1432 an order was placed for a model of the octagonal oculus to be placed at the crown of the dome (Guasti 1857, doc. 248); on 25 June 1433 the width of the oculus was reduced from 10 *braccia* to 9⅔ (Guasti 1857, doc. 251).
On 31 December 1436 the models presented in the competition for the lantern were examined (Guasti 1857, doc. 273): these included those of Brunelleschi, Lorenzo Ghiberti, Antonio di Manetto Ciaccheri, Bruno di Ser Lapo Mazzei and Domenico Stagnario. The jury comprised of "*Architectores, Pictores, Aurifices, et alios Cives intelligentes*" ("architects, painters, goldsmiths and other competent citizens") selected Brunelleschi's design as being the most robust and, at the same time, the lightest; moreover it permitted better lighting and formed efficacious protection against the elements. Thus Brunelleschi was asked to "set aside all rancor" and carry out the modifications which had been requested, incorporating the best features of the other models. The needs of the state overrode the interests of the individual and his pride: the end result had to be perfect (Sanpaolesi 1956: 24-25).
Brunelleschi's model was described by Vasari as being "superb," with the famous stairway in the form of a hollow tube which led up through one of the pilasters right to the base of the orb in gilded bronze made by Verrocchio in 1468 (Vasari, ed. Milanesi 1878, II: 363-364). In fact, this detail does not exist in this model, while the orb is made of wood, not gilded metal. The style in which the lantern is executed lacks the terseness which was the hallmark of Brunelleschi's work (Manetti ed. De Robertis 1976: 116) and was recommended by his friend Alberti in his treatise (Alberti ed. Orlandi 1989, II: 52). It is quite possible that Brunelleschi furnished Ciaccheri—who made the model to his specifications—with more detailed information and allowed the execution of additional decorative features. The model may have been the one made by Brunelleschi, or else one of the models made for him by the model-maker Ciaccheri in 1436. After Brunelleschi's death and a brief period under Michelozzo, in 1452 Ciaccheri was appointed *capomaestro*. The registers of the Opera do not state whether Ciaccheri used Brunelleschi's model or made a new one for the completion of the lantern. This writer is of the opinion, however, that Brunelleschi's model, restored on 30 December 1449, was in use until the work was completed (Saalman 1980: 287, no. 333). The sculptured pea pods and flowers on the volutes of the buttresses added by Ciaccheri may be justified by the absence of any specific indications in Brunelleschi's model. Regarding other details, the lack of information in the model meant that work had to be suspended, as was the case with the architraves of the doors in the buttresses: "Thus, the marble sculptures over the

architraves of the small doors, which are in the buttresses under the vine ornaments, since they were not finished in the model, were not executed on the lantern, because by then Filippo was no longer of this world" (Manetti ed. De Robertis 1976: 117).
The lightning that repeatedly damaged the lantern until the lightning rod was installed in 1859 (Rossi 1956: 130-132; Marchini 1977c: 22-25) must certainly have convinced the *provveditori* (trustees) that it was advisable to keep the original model. However, one of the most widely accepted theories is that the disastrous collapse in 1600, or on a later occasion, led to the construction of the present model.
Ferdinando I's letter would appear to support this hypothesis: "And when they [Buontalenti, Mechini and Bronzino] cannot remember the old design of the damaged lantern" they go to all the Florentine architects to seek those who have "made the plans and drawings or model of the dome with the correct measurements" (Guasti 1857, doc. 363). But Ferdinando I wrote without having personally ascertained the extent of the damage and checked if drawings and models were really available. He asked the architects of the Opera for a copy of the original, not an interpretation, "without making any modifications, whether they be great or small" (Guasti 1857, doc. 363). In reality the lightning had not damaged the lower part of the lantern and part of the cone must still have been standing if Mechini was able to report that "for a large part of its height its shape has not been affected" (Guasti 1857, doc. 367). If a new model had been made, it would certainly have been depicted in the engraving which Callot executed later than 1611 after a drawing by Matteo Rosselli; instead Ferdinando appears before a drawing and not a model (Saalman 1980, pl. 107). Moreover, it should not be forgotten that in Bronzino's report to the grand duke he does not propose the construction of a model, but suggests that "all the old models of the building should be carefully examined to see what purpose they served" (Guasti 1857, doc. 368). Besides, what would have been the point in making a model which faithfully represented the original if the restoration work was then carried out in quite a different way and contrary to the grand duke's orders? Too many details in the model differ from those in the present lantern: the pinnacles have two annulets in the model and three in the real thing; the capitals on the external pilasters are different, since there are four in the pilasters on the model and three in those on the building; there are four flutes on the tops of the actual buttresses while in the model there are only two; lastly, the volutes in the model are more elegant and without the uninspired pea-pod and flower ornamentation designed by Michelozzo and Ciaccheri (Guasti 1857, docs. 307, 309). This decoration must have been remade exactly as it had been previously after the collapse of 1492, since Antonio da Sangallo the Younger drew it in Uff. 1130A. On the other hand, Giovanni Battista da Sangallo, in his inaccurate sketch of the lantern (Uff. 3913A), gives the impression of having corrected his hasty observation of the real volutes by reproducing those seen on the model.
The model appears, therefore, to be the one made by Brunelleschi to which the sources refer (Vasari, ed. Milanesi 1878, II: 363-364), with the upper part of the dome and the rooms in the ring planned in 1432 and the lantern designed for the competition in 1436. It is just possible that it might be the one made by Antonio di Manetto Ciaccheri, without the stairway in the form of a hollow tube, but so similar to Brunelleschi's model that he said: "make another copy of it, and that will be mine" (Manetti ed. De Robertis 1976: 113).
In the lower part of the model may be seen a part of the dome with the thirty-eight steps on the extrados of the inner shell. It corresponds almost exactly to the part that was not yet vaulted in 1430, that is, to the point where the date "1430" was found at the level of the third corridor up from the drum (Falletti and Paolini 1977). That Brunelleschi designed this part is confirmed by three features: the lack of the brick arches linking the smaller ribs to the main ones, the position of which was decided on the spot; the curved shape of the external wall of the ring where the ribs are attached, which reflected the plan for a circular ring that was subsequently abandoned; the internal windows of the rooms in the ring, which are circular, and a proposal for three square openings on one side, as they were in fact built (Sanpaolesi 1956: 22, fig. 17).
Brunelleschi's paternity of the model of the lantern is not recognized by: Milanesi 1878; Stegmann and Geymüller 1885; Fabriczy 1892; Folnesics 1915; Heydenreich 1931; Saalman 1980; Pacciani 1987. On the other hand, those in favor of the attribution of the model to Brunelleschi include: Poggi 1904; Sanpaolesi 1941, 1956, 1962; Rossi 1956, 1964; Luporini 1964; Caprara 1968; Goldthwaite 1984. Eugenio Battisti (1981) believes that the lower part dates from the fifteenth century and the lantern from the sixteenth century. *M.S.*

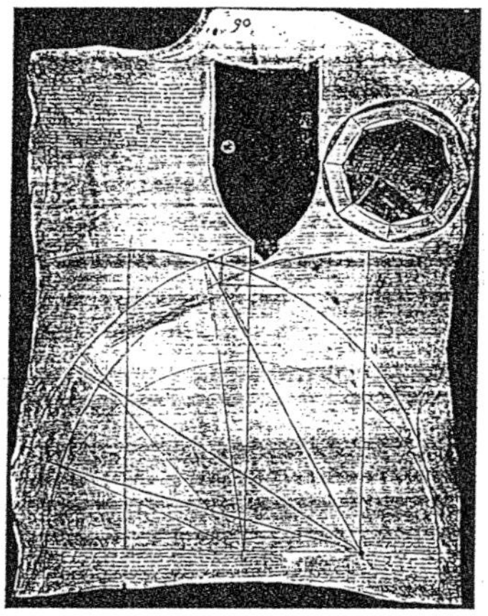

263
GIOVANNI DI GHERARDO GHERARDI
Drawing with Critical Annotations Regarding the Dome of S. Maria del Fiore

Florence, Archivio di Stato, inv. Mostra 158
Parchment having irregular edges with drawings executed in brown and red ink; light traces of lead point and tempera with red pigment, yellow ocher with particles of pure gold and dark indigo blue-black. The text, written with the same ink as the drawings, is in clear early-Quattrocento handwriting with typical abbreviations and ligatures.
64.4 × 48.7 cm (maximum dimensions)
INSCRIBED: (viewed with the shortest and most irregular side at the bottom: bottom right) *Questa dimostratione di questo ochio e chel sole uentri [e] no[n] sia i[n]terrotto p[er] invetriame[n]to ma / nella opposita parte depilastri sirompa [e] dia lume p[e]r refressione. or pe[n]si ciascumo se quella / rifressione sara ditatto forza cheuadi i[n] su piu di braccia setta[n]ta credo [e] certo essere mi / pare cheno secondo mimostra ogni ragione come potrai trouare nel trattato d[e] speculis [e] i[n] p[ro]spettiuis. opensa adu[n]que che lume liochi daranno q[ua]n[do] p[er] uetro illume sia rotto potete / lexemplo auere i[n] sa[n]ta Liperata ne[li] oc]hi dalla parte dinanzi sopra leporti.*
Io giouanni di gherardo gherardi fo noto [e] manifesto, chesendo qui nellopera richiesto adire / il mio parere i[n]torno aluolgere della cupola, come io dicho i[n]torno accio i[n] questa forma p[ri]ma / Che am[m]e pare, considerato che dalliochi i[n]fino alla lanterna a circha braccia sessanta p[er]pe[n]diculare, sequitando il sesto principiato sanza finestra o ispiraglio di preuedere allume i[n] / anzi che piu su si muri i[n]p[er]o cheno[n] preuedendoui no[n] chella sia buia, ma ella sia oscura / [e] tenebrosa. Et gia sono passati anni cinque [e] piu che io diedi mio modo accio [e] facea / 24 finestre i[n] sulla cornice i[n] mediate enne ancora mio disegno nellopera qui. Et ris / po[n]dendo aalcuno che dice sebisognera esipotra talgliare dellauolta, chemi pare detto din / gniorante [e] pocho sauio. Ofatta questa scrittura p[er] no[n] auere biasimo adiue[ne]ndo che sopra / accio no[n] si p[ro]uedesse. p[er]dio uogliate p[ro]uederui; (bottom left) *disopra almezo. Questo eilcentro de[l]sesto amezo / acuto [e] no[n] delquinto acuto. disotto Questo ellcentro nella sup[er]ficie [e] no[n] / del* [sest deleted] *cui[n]to acuto [e] questo ecentro a glia[n]guli nella sup[er]ficie [e] no[n] de[l]sesto / cheuua i[n] alto. segia il sesto no[n] fosse / a mezo acuto. adu[n]que uedi comella / cosa si[con]duce e va.* (top right inverted) *Ancora io giouan[n]i p[re]detto dicho che ame pare ne mutare ne modificare diminuendolo p[er] cagione neuna il sesto preso / [e] co[n]sigliato gia decine danni pre[n]dendo la forma di sa[n]giouan[n]i. [e] questa forma gia sei anni si delibero, [e] fessi modello dileg[n]ame. / Et no[n] uolere co[n] istrane fantasie sanza fondame[n]to uolere ilmagiore fatto p[er] una cosa disimile fazione ditempio site / merariame[n]te guastare et pericolare [e] i[n]fino a qui notate che co[n] falso centro semurato al sesto [e] no[n] [con] suo o uerame[n]te / suoi propri cio dalla cornice i[n] su doue si muoue ilsesto. questo e auenuto p[er] ignioranza [e] p[er] presumere dise cio e di / coloro acui estata comessa [e] chenne sono stati salariati [e] donato loro assai. Et io o fatto questa scrittura accio / chese auiene quello mimostra ogni ragi[o]ne i[n] guastalla [e] mettere apericolo diruinio io nesia scusato inp[er]o no[n] / ciarei colpa. perdio fate saui chemirendo certo farete. p[er]icolo ilte[m]pio disiena p[er] credere auno / fantastico sanza neuna ragione;* (top left inverted) *Questo e ilcentro delqui[n]to acuto [e] no[n] / quello del mezo adu[n]que ued[e]te come / falsame[n]te se murato poi chesesto si mosse / i[n] sulla cornice i[n]pero chesemurato / asesto dimezo acuto [e] non aquinto faccen / do* [se deleted] *centro del mezo acuto straname[n] / te uae face[n]do / solame[n]te uno centro [e] / ogni a[n]gulo na uno p[er] se secondo del / modello mostrasi nella presente fi / gura.*

BIBLIOGRAPHY: Guasti 1874: 111-121; Nardini Despotti Mospignotti 1874: 123-128; Saalman 1959b: 11-20; Braunfels 1965: 203-226; Di Pasquale 1976: 13-16 and 39; Giovanni da Prato, ed. F. Garilli 1976: 402; Bartoli 1977: 56-65; Benigni 1977: 45-46, no. 45, pl. VI; Bartoli 1977: 56-65; Ragghianti 1977: 218-219 and 426; Fabriczy 1979: 107 and 123 n. 42; Saalman 1980: 65-66 and 265, no. 213.8, pl. 32-34; Battisti 1981: 124, 130, 138, 142-143, 382; Ricci 1983: 51-69; Chiarugi and Quilghini 1984: 44-45; Di Pasquale 1985: 27-28; Ricci 1987a; Ricci 1987b: 54-55; Bechmann 1991: 216-217.

(NOTE: In order to make Gherardi's text more intelligible the terminology used needs to be explained. The *sesto* is the spread of the compass, i.e., the radius of the circumference; the latter may be subdivided into six parts starting from any point of it. The *centro di sesto* is the point at which the pivot arm of the compass is placed (*centro*) and the *sesto che va in alto* is the arm which describes the portion of the vault; *murare al sesto* means to vault with a given curvature. The *sesto di mezzo acuto* is what is known today as the round arch and corresponds in the drawing to the semicircumference on the diameter of the base. In order to describe an arc with the form known as *quinto acuto* (pointed fifth) two centers must be used: the segment is subdivided into five equal parts, then with the compass spread at 4/5, the portions of the arc are described by placing the pivot arm in the first part and then in the fourth.)

The parchment prepared by Giovanni di Gherardo Gherardi, who substituted for Ghiberti from 1420 to 1426, is the only extant document containing drawings relating to the dome of S. Maria del Fiore that is contemporary with its construction. It was published for the first time by Cesare Guasti in 1874 with an interpretative note by Nardini Despotti Mospignotti. The pentimenti in the drawing and the deletions in the text ("se" and "sest"), as well as comparison with Gherardi's autographs (Giovanni da Prato and Garilli 1976, app. I, III, IV), are confirmation that this is the original document.
The parchment should be viewed with the irregular side and the inverted "90" at the bottom (the number is repeated on the verso). It bears three drawings and five groups of annotations. To these should be added a sketch of masonry (top left) and the disc of the sun (bottom right). It may be deduced that the parchment was prepared in the last four months of 1425 from two events: on 1 July 1425, at the request of the Operai, Lorenzo Ghiberti's salary was suspended (Guasti 1857, doc. 74) and on 15 February 1426 the registers of the Opera record the payment to Giovanni da Prato "for his work and materials, having provided the Opera with a number of drawings and a clay model, which demonstrated how the necessary work should be carried out in the large dome" (Guasti 1857,

doc. 60; Saalman 1959b: 12). The model has not survived, while one of the drawings is certainly the one that is being analyzed here.

In 1425 less than a third of the dome had been constructed and doubts must certainly have arisen regarding the correctness of the calculations and building techniques. In accordance with medieval custom, a committee of experts was convened; this included Giovanni di Gherardo Gherardi, the painter Giuliano d'Arrigo, called "Il Pesello," and the mathematician Giovanni di Bartolo dell'Abaco. The first two were substitute superintendents of the dome, while the third was an expert in "practical arithmetic" whose training had been in accordance with the mathematical tradition which linked the Pisan Leonardo Fibonacci to Paolo dell'Abaco (Paolo Dagomari) from Prato, founder of the school "opposite S. Trinita" which boasted nearly six thousand students (Finiello Zervas 1975: 485). Giovanni di Bartolo began to teach in this school in 1390, when he was nineteen years old; he also taught at Florence University, where Gherardi was responsible for "Dantean studies" from 1417 onward (Arrighi 1980: 93-103).

Giovanni dell'Abaco, who also taught Paolo dal Pozzo Toscanelli, certainly played an important role in the measurement of the dome and the solution of the problems related to its construction (Trachtenberg 1983: 296); as early as 30 June 1417 he was paid five gold florins as his fee for his mathematical and geometrical calculations "with regard to the construction of the large dome" (Guasti 1857, doc. 23). This first task of his may be linked to the purchase of ropes for effecting measurements on 18 September 1416, the sheets for drawing on 28 April 1417 (Saalman 1980: 248, nos. 40 and 44) and the making of a model that probably served to confirm the "curvatura a quinto di sesto acuto" (pointed fifth curvature), before the public competition of 1418. Then on 1 April 1420 he received one florin (Guasti 1857, doc. 46) and finally ten florins in 1425. It was in this year that Ghiberti's authority seemed to be on the wane. Having displayed uncertainty with regard to the technical problems of the construction he attempted to assert himself from the theoretical point of view by means of the opinion given by his substitute. In this report, the last one recorded in the registers of the Opera, Gherardi attacks Brunelleschi, without referring to him except as "someone who invents irrational things." This epithet was immediately taken up by Giovanni Cavalcanti when he condemned Brunelleschi's project during the siege of Lucca in 1430: "Some of our inventors of fantasy including Filippo di Ser Brunellesco ... with their false geometry" (Cavalcanti 1838: 328; cf. Frey 1892: 65).

Gherardi's arguments begin with the question of the lighting and continue with that of the inclination of the masonry courses (ricaschi). Our examination of the text will proceed in the same order. Next to the drawing of the crossing on the right there is a block of text divided into two parts. After the first six lines referring to the adjacent drawing the author begins his exposition thus: "I, Giovanni di Gherardo Gherardi ... having been requested to give my opinion regarding the building of the dome ..." He states, therefore, that he wishes to express his opinion on what has been done so far. He maintains that it is necessary to think about the lighting of the dome before continuing to build it "without windows or openings"; besides, in view of the distance between the oculi of the drum and the lantern, he says that the absence of openings makes the dome dark and gloomy.

In pleading his case Gherardi draws on his studies of optics at Padua under the guidance of the authoritative Biagio Pelacani da Parma from 1384 to 1388. It was not by chance that Biagio appeared as "a universal philosopher and mathematician" in the unfinished *Paradiso degli Alberti* together with Coluccio Salutati, the Paduan physician Marsilio di S. Sofia and the humanist Francesco Landini (Giovanni da Prato ed. Garilli 1976: 164). In this group Gherardi also includes the Augustinian mathematician Grazia de' Castellani, author of a *De visu* (Arrighi 1980: 95-96) which was certainly known to Brunelleschi

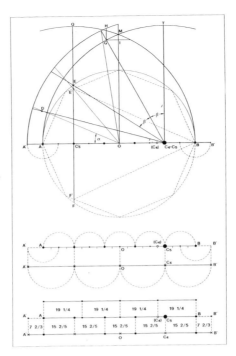

Fig.1 - *The following have been added to Gherardi's section: the internal octagon of the drum (with a broken line); the completion of the base circumference AB; the extension (with a continuous line) of the segment EC'5. In this way the system of checking the pointed fifth curve in the angles is shown geometrically. This was probably carried out using wire fixed to the points F' and E'; thus guided B, the vertex of the isosceles triangle E'F'B, can plot the portion of a pointed fifth curve (in the angles.) It will be noted that point E is the exact midpoint of the segment C'5Q = ⁴⁄₅ AB, since C'5E is the proportional mean of AC'5 = ¹⁄₅ AB and C'5B = ⁴⁄₅ AB. Therefore C'5E = ²⁄₅ AB.*

C4 is the center of the pointed fourth calculated with regard to the internal diameter AB; this was erroneously used by Gherardi to plot the extrados of the angle rib. indicates the angle of the first inclined masonry course on the round arch (AOD), which has its equivalent in the plan (fig. 2.)

Under the section are shown the geometrical and arithmetical scales relating to the subdivision into fifths (internal diameter AB) and fourths (external diameter A'B'). It will be noted that the center of the pointed fifth (C5) and that of the pointed fourth (C4) coincide if the former is calculated with regard to the internal diameter (AB) and the latter with regard to the external one (A'B'). The measurements on the arithmetic scale are in Florentine braccia.

as the theory of the "certified vision" of Biagio Pelacani (Federici Vescovini 1992: 47-49).

In order to describe the poor lighting in the dome Gherardi draws the vertical section of the crossing in brown ink and shades it with indigo-black so as to stress the oculi in the drum and the circular shaft of light on the masonry. Three oculi are drawn in the drum: the side ones are shown as oval and the central one, colored with ocher and gold, is circular (diam. 17 mm). When the drawing is studied under a Wood light, two circumferences described with a compass (diam. 12 mm) can be discerned at the sides of the central oculus, and an oval on the left. They are probably hypotheses for the projection of the light, later discarded in order to avoid interference with the oculi in the drum and to stress the credibility of the thesis that the lighting is inadequate. Gherardi also depicts a gleam of light descending from the roughly sketched lantern, barely reaching the ring.

Biagio's optical theories are echoed by Gherardi's subsequent statements: "as common sense seems to suggest" and "as can be found in the treatise on mirrors and per-

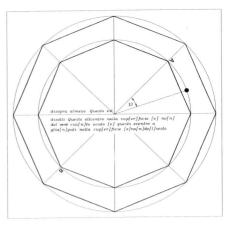

Fig. 2 - *Plan of the octagonal drum. The angle , formed by the hole and the diameter AB, corresponds to AOD in the section.*

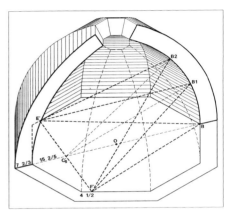

Fig. 3 - *Isometric projection showing the system for checking the pointed fifth in the angles of the octagonal drum. Thanks to this system it was possible to avoid using the position on the pointed fifth curve C'5 situated in mid-air and to obtain a perfect orthogonal with regard to the springing line of the vault by using wire fixed to points E' and F.*

spective," the light reflected on the wall would not be sufficient to illuminate the sixty *braccia* from the oculi to the lantern, even if the oculi in the drum were without windowpanes. In order to support his thesis he gives an example: the "oculi with windowpanes" constructed by the *capomaestro* Giovanni d'Ambrosio in S. Reparata (1415) were evidently insufficient to illuminate the interior of that church (Guasti 1887, doc. 474). Gherardi's solution was in contrast with the proposals of the "ignorant and foolish" individuals who suggested that windows should be constructed in the vault. Gherardi pointed out that five years earlier he had prepared a drawing for the construction of twenty-four windows immediately above the cornice of the drum (Guasti 1857, doc. 46). But we know that his proposal was never seriously taken into consideration. On 24 January, when Gherardi was about to retire to Prato after the suppression of his course at Florence University, Brunelleschi replied disdainfully: "Nothing has been said concerning the light because it is our firm belief that there will be enough light thanks to the eight oculi underneath: but even if it were seen that more light was necessary after all, it could easily be obtained from the upper part next to sides of the lantern" (Guasti 1857, doc. 75). It was Paolo dal Pozzo Toscanelli in 1442 who put an end to the controversy by asserting pithily that the much feared panes of glass in the oculi of the drum were also intended "to serve as ornament rather than for light" (Guasti 1857, doc. 202).

Now the parchment should be viewed the other way up. Gherardi's second criticism is more complex in nature and regards the two remaining drawings: a plan of the octagonal drum colored red (top right) and a large section passing through the diameter of the octagonal drum (in the lower part). Under the latter drawing, which is essentially a diagram, is placed the explanatory text; this continues the previous one—"Once again I, the aforementioned Giovanni"—and concludes in the caption on the plan. The three blocks of text regard two different questions that are dealt with very briefly: they relate to the geometry (sesto) of webs and the angle at which the courses of bricks (ricaschi) should be laid.

Here Gherardi amplifies the seriousness of his accusation with the rhetorical invective typical of republican Florence. This is no longer merely the defense of an unsuccessful project, but rather the denunciation of Brunelleschi's "duplicity." Gherardi, who was ten years his rival's senior, states with studied solemnity that "on no account may the curve which has been agreed on be changed or reduced in size; this form was decided on six years ago, and a wooden model was made." This reminder is apparently superfluous, but it is immediately related to Brunelleschi's default with regard to the project of 16 April 1420: "the dome is vaulted according to the size of the pointed fifth at the angles on its inner side" (Doren 1898: 249-262; Prager and Scaglia 1970: 139-140). Possibly already established in the model of 1367, this curvature, as Gherardi writes, had been borrowed from the "form of S. Giovanni," i.e., the neighboring baptistery. He also affirms that the acceptance of the pointed fifth curvature for the dome was finalized by one of the many models that were specially built, probably the one made in 1418 (Guasti 1857, doc. 22).

Failure to respect the project agreed on under oath was a very serious act of negligence for an architect, capomaestro or mason: "I swear to Almighty God ... that this building will be constructed according to the model" (Guasti 1887, doc. 480). Aware of this, Gherardi predicts that Brunelleschi wants to build the remaining three-quarters of the dome—"the greater part"—with those "strange follies without any basis" which he had used so far. Because of this, he accuses Brunelleschi of having sought to "rashly damage and render hazardous" the whole building by laying the bricks at incorrect angles and changing the curvature (sesto) of the dome.

Gherardi's skilled rhetoric was intended to be interpreted at different levels. To the experts he is saying: "up to now note that the curve [sesto] has been built with an incorrect center and not with its proper center, or rather center, that is from the cornice upward where the curve springs." To the capimaestri and masons he explains that this incorrect procedure is "due to ignorance and presumptuousness" on the part of those who have been entrusted with the direction of the work, and adds—evidently addressing the administrators of the Opera—"they have been handsomely paid for this." Thus, he is able to display both his intellectual capacity as a free citizen and his diligence as a substitute superintendent to the nobiles viri (noblemen) and the consuls of the Arte della Lana (the Wool Merchants' Guild): "I have written this so that if what I fear is only too likely to happen does occur"—in other words, that the building should be damaged and risk collapse—"then I would be excused because it would not be my fault." Having exhorted everyone involved to be prudent "in the name of the Lord, which I am sure you will," he reminds them that "Siena cathedral threatened to collapse" because credit had been given "someone who invented things irrationally."

Here he is referring to the imprudent extension of Siena cathedral under the direction of Camaino di Crescenzino and the subsequent project by Lando di Pietro. The work carried out initially in great haste and then without adequate skill had caused subsidence of the columns and cracking in the dome and the arches below. The advice of Francesco Talenti, then capomaestro of S. Maria del Fiore, and Benci di Cione had convinced the twelve governors of the Republic of Siena of the need to demolish the dangerous parts and stop work on the extension (Lusini 1911: 154-187). It was with skilled rhetoric that Gherardi (who was from Prato) associated Brunelleschi with the danger

ous "follies" of the Sienese builders, contrasting this recklessness with the wisdom displayed hitherto by the Florentines responsible for S. Maria del Fiore.

In order to give visible form to his accusation Gherardi draws a diagrammatic section of the dome passing through the diameter of the octagonal drum. This is a drawing of considerable geometrical and structural significance in which nothing is superfluous or fortuitous. All the lines regarding the geometry of the pointed fifth, the pointed fourth curvature, the lantern and the inclination of the masonry courses to the center of the pointed fifth are drawn with double lines (red and brown). The semicircumference on the diameter of the base and the inclined masonry courses at its center are drawn with a single line. It is evident that the "correct" lines are the double ones. All the elevation lines have been constructed geometrically, while the base diameter is drawn arithmetically. The figure is subdivided into five parts; the measurement "$15\frac{2}{5}$ braccia" is written in the fourth fifth of the diameter; halfway between this and the extreme right of the diameter is inscribed the measurement "$7\frac{2}{3}$ braccia." Having constructed the arc according to the procedure that has been described at the beginning of this entry, Gherardi emphasizes the center of the arc known as the pointed fifth with a conspicuous hole on the right, where he writes: "This is the center of the pointed fifth and not of the round curve." Then, placing the compass on the extreme left of the internal diameter, with a spread of $7\frac{2}{3}$ he intercepts the prolongation of the diameter of the base at a point lying off the parchment. From this departs the curve of the extrados which has its center at a point equal to $\frac{3}{4}$ of the diameter of the base (the pointed fourth curve). The area between the two portions of curve represents the thickness of an angle rib.

It should be noted that above the center of the pointed fourth the measurements have been carefully deleted. We do not know when this correction was made, but certainly Gherardi made a mistake here which might have weakened his case. Evidently he had not realized that Brunelleschi was constructing the two shells of the dome with different curves using a single center of curvature, contrary to medieval practice (Bechmann 1991: 216). In fact, since the thickness of the drum at the angles is $7\frac{2}{3}$ braccia (half of $15\frac{2}{5}$), the external diameter of the drum will prove to be divided into four parts measuring $3 \times 7\frac{2}{3}$. Therefore, the fifth, calculated on the basis of the internal diameter, coincides with the center of the pointed fourth as regards the external diameter.

We shall now continue the examination of the drawing: perpendicularly to the base are drawn the radii of the two circumferences which, where they intersect, form the two portions of the pointed fifth arch, that is the strongest part of the round arch (ca. 60°). A third perpendicular joins the center of the base diameter to the crown of the pointed fifth arch. At right angles to this perpendicular is shown the opening of the oculus at the apex of the dome, which was planned to be 6 braccia in height and 12 in width in the 1420 project; the latter figure was reduced to 10 braccia in August 1432 and $9\frac{2}{3}$ in June 1433 (Saalman 1980: 138). From the center of the circumference having a radius of half of the diameter, and of that having a radius of $\frac{4}{5}$ of this, depart three pairs of lines converging two by two on three points of the angle rib. The first pair of inclined masonry courses intersect at the height which the dome had reached when Gherardi wrote his report (under the level of second passageway); there are no annotations, since for the part already vaulted it was too late to do anything. It will be noted that at this height the circumference drawn with a brown line (sesto del mezzo acuto, i.e., round arch curvature) differs only slightly from the pointed fifth one. Probably this difference was difficult to observe on the spot, as was the difference between the inclinations of the two masonry courses; the objective difficulty of evaluating the situation no doubt favored this extraordinary attempt to question Brunelleschi's motives.

The second pair of inclined masonry courses is drawn by the left half of the pointed fifth arch. In this case the

difference in the inclination is very evident; the slope of the masonry courses to the center of curvature of the round arch are a clear warning of the technical difficulties which will have to be overcome when the bricks are laid. The pointed fifth inclination of this second pair intersects the base circumference at a point which immediately appears to be crucial for the checking of the pointed fifth curvature. Here the geometrical diagram ceases to be abstract. The drawing not only shows the geometrical line which surrounds the structure, but it also represents a precise technical device used to check the curvature in the angles. Observe the segment that is perpendicular to the first pointed fifth center of curvature on the left. The semicircumference on the diameter of the base intercepts this segment at a point through which the inclination of the masonry courses to the center of curvature of the pointed fifth passes. This point divides the radius ($\frac{4}{5}$) into two equal parts, since the lower segment of the radius is the mean proportional of $\frac{1}{5}$ and $\frac{4}{5}$ of the base diameter (Euclid, VI, 13). Now, instead of considering the semicircumference of the base as the outline of the round arch, we will regard it as its plan and complete it from a theoretical point of view. The prolongation of the lower half of the segment will meet the mirror image of the semicircumference of the base at a point that is symmetrical to the first. This appears to be the simplest way of checking the curvature at the angles, without using the center of the pointed fifth, which is located in midair, $15\frac{2}{5}$ braccia from the drum. The segment of $\frac{4}{5}$, divided into two parts by the center of the pointed fifth, is the base of the isosceles triangle with a height equal to $\frac{4}{5}$ of the diameter and its vertex in the angle of the octagon. As it rotates round its base, the mobile vertex of the triangle will check the pointed fifth precisely, always remaining at right angles to the surface of the drum. In practice it was sufficient to calculate determine the point of intersection of this segment with the sides of the drum in order to place there the hooks to which were fixed the wires, the catheti of an isosceles triangle $\frac{4}{5}$ in height (Braunfels 1965: 204, fig. 4 and 215, fig. 5; Verga 1978: 44, fig. 14). The hooks still in place above the architraves of the small doors (top internal gallery) may have served this purpose. As regards the wires, they must have been those mentioned in a payment made to Brunelleschi "for wire and rope purchased for measuring his model" (Guasti 1857, doc. 47).

The third inclined masonry course of the pointed fifth is drawn to determine the sloping sides of the ring geometrically. It is also the bisector of the angle formed by the second inclined masonry course of the pointed fifth and the perpendicular to its center.

We shall now return to the first part of the accusation written under the section of the dome: "up to now note that the curve has been built with an incorrect center and not with its proper center, or rather centers, that is from the cornice upward where the curve springs." This assertion, placed under the center of the pointed fifth arch, seems to be reasonably clear. But not all the nobiles viri were well versed in geometry. Thus Gherardi focuses our attention under the large hole on the right and inscribes there: "This is the center of the pointed fifth arch and not of the round arch." Also wishing to show that the construction of the dome was erroneous not only in the angle ribs but also in the webs—when the curve has been moved horizontally onto the cornice—he adds: "thus you can see the grave error which has been committed by causing the curve to spring from the cornice," because there, too, "the construction is based on the round arch and not on the pointed fifth."

He then gives a more precise meaning of the expression "its proper center, or rather centers" compared to the incorrect center ("falso centro") in the text on the left under the diameter: "strangely, when establishing the center of the round arch, he indicates just one center, while each angle has one of its own, according to the model which is shown in this figure." Brunelleschi seems to be proceeding "strangely" because he uses a single center for the inclined masonry courses, when, according to Gherardi, he should use the two centers of the pointed fifth curvature ("its proper centers") which lie on the diameter of the octagon near the angles ("each angle has one of its own"). Since this reasoning is valid for all four of the diameters of the octagon, Gherardi proposes his figure as a "model" which can be repeated.

But a single section is not sufficient to allow the complexity of the criticism to be properly understood. Consequently, Gherardi completes his disquisition on the plan with a red border (top right). As it is the last drawing to be executed on the parchment he uses all the space available between its edge and the section of the crossing. Rather than with drawing the drum to scale, he is concerned with comparing the diameter of the internal octagon to that of the section of the crossing on the right. Then, without the aid of a compass, he draws freehand in four stages the circle which circumscribes the internal octagon of the drum and on it he rubs a small hole.

Now the parchment should be turned round once again. Above the exact center of the octagon Gherardi writes: "Above the round arch. This is the center of the round arch and not the pointed fifth." In other words, unlike the drawing in the upper half of the parchment, the point underneath corresponds to the center of the round arch and not of the pointed fifth arch. In this way he correlates the position of the round arch in the section and in the plan. Then, referring exclusively to the plan, he writes: "Under this is the center on the surface and not of the pointed fifth arch, and this is the center at the angles in the surface and not in the curve which extends upward. That is, unless the curve is a round one. See, therefore, what a terrible mistake is being made." In other words, the hole underneath is the center of the surface identified by the diameters of the octagon and not of the pointed fifth, and this corresponds to the intersection of the bisectors of the eight angles of the drum ("center at the angles") and it is not the center of the curve which "extends upward"; that is, unless the curve is round, as seems to be Brunelleschi's intention with the inclined masonry courses which he uses. The circumference shown by one line, which appears in the plan circumscribing the internal octagon of the drum, corresponds to the semicircumference which is in the section. Both represent the same hemispherical dome, in plan and in section, in accordance with the practice of the late antique treatises on stereometry.

It is evident, therefore, that Gherardi is accusing Brunelleschi of using a single "incorrect center" for the inclined masonry courses instead of using, two by two, the eight centers of the pointed fifth curves in the angles. And if Brunelleschi complies with the pointed fifth geometry in the angle ribs, but builds with the masonry courses inclined to the center of the round arch, Gherardi predicts that the dome will collapse. The considerable inclination to the center of the round arch in the upper part of the masonry courses would seem to suggest this. In reality, Gherardi knew perfectly well that, according to longstanding practice, the voussoirs of an arch must converge on its center of curvature. Since he does not doubt that Brunelleschi is perfectly aware of this, he believes that the use of masonry courses inclined to the center of the round arch is not only a dangerous building method, but is evidence of the architect's intention to "modify by reduction" the curve that has already been decided. The document evidently completes all Gherardi's criticisms, even if the difficulty of interpretation may lead to diametrically opposed readings (Ricci 1987a; Ricci 1987b).

We have also seen how these figures contain geometrical features which the text does not explicate. Probably they were taken for granted or it was not thought expedient to divulge them. A further example is the hole on the circumference of the internal octagon on the red plan of the drum. It is not explicitly mentioned in the text for the simple reason that it is the mobile curve of the center of the rounded curve which is being discussed. In fact, it appears on the plan where the whole description refers to the "erroneous" rounded curve, just as in the section everything regards the "correct" pointed fifth curve. Therefore the hole represents the "incorrect" curve (round curve) which springs horizontally—"it springs from the cornice"—

between the angles of the octagon; but also the one that "goes upward," considering the circumference as the section (upside down) of the spherical dome. This may be confirmed by observing the plan without turning the parchment round, as would be necessary in order to read the text: the angle of elevation of the hole with regard to the diameter underneath is identical to that of the first inclined masonry course at the center of the round curve with regard to the diameter of the base in the section.

Here Gherardi, somewhat perfidiously, presents a problem that seems to be very complicated to describe in the drawing, but which must have been very easy to resolve in practice (Ricci 1987b). Under the drawing of the plan lurks Gherardi's insidious question: how can the pointed fifth curve be changed in the angles when the curve springs horizontally from the cornice? It is clear that, since the impost of the vault is octagonal, in the webs it was not possible to maintain the same radius as in the angle ribs, whether the construction was a pointed fifth or a round arch. This was a problem with which Brunelleschi was very familiar and he knew he could solve it as the dome was being constructed. In fact, in the report of 1420 he cautiously limited himself to guaranteeing the pointed fifth curve in the angles and, certainly referring to the webs, he wrote that the work would proceed "in the way that is advised and decided by those masters who will build ... because, while building, experience will teach us what we should do" (Guasti 1857, doc. 51). This "way" was one which it was difficult to represent in an intelligible drawing. It is this way of doing things without any explanation, so typical of Brunelleschi, which may have convinced Ghiberti and Gherardi to pose this question with regard to the technical description, thereby causing difficulty for their rival. Contrary to his usual practice, in the reply of 1426 Brunelleschi was obliged to specify the technical procedure as well: the laying of the bricks in a herringbone pattern and the use of the *gualandrino a tre corde* or triple square.

It is possible, however, that in his survey Gherardi identified a problematic aspect of the building methods when he reported what he had seen. He may not have realized that at the beginning Brunelleschi was building with a single center of curvature in order to counteract the side thrusts more effectively. This means that the initial part, now buried in the masonry, was designed to be a sort of "chained" annular base supporting the entire dome, which evidently had to have the inclined masonry courses with a single center (Mainstone 1977: 161; Verga 1978: 14; Rossi 1982: 15; Trachtenberg 1983: 294). The change in the curvature, first observed by Eugenio Battisti, under the second passageway, could mark the upper limit of the stone construction of the annular stylobate (Battisti 1981: 144, pl. 144). Sanpaolesi and Siebenhüner have suggested that the first courses of wedge-shaped bricks were laid with their thinner ends facing toward a single center (Nardini 1874) and that their base course, therefore, related to the center of the octagon and not the eight centers located on the pointed fifth curve of the diameters (Sanpaolesi 1941: 28; Siebenhüner 1940: 434).

However, there is no doubt that Brunelleschi was very familiar with the principle that arches should be built with the masonry courses inclined toward their center of curvature, as his friend and admirer Leon Battista Alberti wrote twenty years later: "Throughout the arch it is necessary to arrange the blocks of stone in such a way that they face the center of this arch" (Alberti, ed. Orlandi 1989: 127).

In fact, the inadequacy of our knowledge of the real sequence of the stages of construction and the way the bricks were arranged inside the walls does not allow us to confirm or refute any of the hypotheses. However, even a rapid examination of the angle ribs is sufficient to reveal that the inclined courses of the bricks are nearly always at right angles to the pointed fifth curve, so that they cannot converge on the center of the round arch. It is certain that, after Gherardi's criticisms, the document of 1426 written by Brunelleschi insists on the need for the annular strengthening of the vault: "the bricks should be placed

in rings ... to allow a perfect ring which surrounds the dome outside so that this arch should be complete and not broken" (Guasti 1857, doc. 75); he refers to the problem of centering, which serves to check the curve of the webs; and last of all he says that the bricks will be laid in a herringbone pattern with the use of the *gualandrino a tre corde*. Thus, steps should be taken to make the eight webs of the dome solid and to ensure that the pointed fifth curve is adhered to. It is quite possible that the idea of setting up massive centering was proposed; this would have served to verify that the correct curvature was maintained. In the report of 1426 impatience is clearly expressed with regard to the objections that had been raised, including those of Gherardi. Brunelleschi puts an end to the question of centering by stating, somewhat irritably, that "it would be difficult to construct centering without scaffolding; in fact, centering was abandoned expressly to avoid having to use scaffolding" (Guasti 1857, doc. 75). However, it is likely that small-scale centering with a pointed fifth radius was used during the construction; this would have been moved as the dome grew, its vertical position in the corners being determined by the system of wires that has been described above. Connected to this mobile centering along the ribs was the *gualandrino a tre corde*, which ensured that the bricks in the webs were laid correctly on a curve corresponding to that of a slack rope (Chiarugi and Quilghini 1984: 42-43, figs. 5, 6). Although historians have given free rein to their fantasies with regard to the nature of this instrument and the etymology of its name, it must have simply been a sort of *calandrino* or "bevel square"; this is defined by the 1990 edition of the Devoto and Oli dictionary of the Italian language (published in Florence and hence with a Tuscan bias) as "a wooden square with adjustable wooden arms that fit together, used by carpenters and stonemasons." It is not possible to conclude this analysis without mentioning that during the construction of the dome, or in the years immediately before this, Brunelleschi, in a manner of speaking, invented perspective. In fact, it is legitimate to ask whether perspective developed as part of the endeavor to apply the laws of optics to painting or whether it rather derived from the optical measurement of buildings, that is from architectural surveying. Antonio Manetti wrote that Donatello and Brunelleschi when surveying "almost all the buildings in Rome" ascertained their heights by means of "strips of parchment ... bearing the numerals used in the abacus ..." (Manetti ed. De Robertis 1976: 67-68). This was in the first decade of the Quattrocento, when, as a result of the vogue for antiquities, the hunt for Greek codices by men of letters, intellectuals and patricians was under way. But while Petrarch and Boccaccio had already collected the precious codices of classical literature and philosophy (including Vitruvius), for "hundreds of years" nobody had "built in the ancient manner" (Manetti ed. De Robertis 1976: 68). Brunelleschi, however, had studied this for many years and there is no doubt that it contained the basis for the invention of perspective. It is quite possible, therefore, that when measuring the heights and widths of Roman buildings with a graduated sight ("with the numerals used in the abacus"), Brunelleschi had understood how the "apparent" measurements varied in inverse proportion to the distance, and that, in fact, the "strips of parchment ... bearing the numerals used in the abacus," by creating a plane at a fixed distance from the eye, stressed the *perspective* of the real dimension. There are, therefore, valid grounds for believing that the system of perspective drawing was born of the architectural survey, that is of the problem of proportional measurement. Thus, the famous perspective panels would appear to be an amusing application of what Brunelleschi had invented, or rather rediscovered, during his surveys in Rome. It has yet to be discovered whether Brunelleschi used a perspective device to check the radius of the pointed fifth curvature in the angles of the dome, which was supposed to remain constant; this operation could have been carried out very easily with the aid of a small T-square, since all the relevant measurements had been taken.

M.S.

264

FEDERICO ZUCCARI
Federico Zuccari and Vincenzo Borghini Discuss the Decorative Program for the Dome of Florence Cathedral

Florence, Galleria degli Uffizi, Gabinetto Disegni e Stampe, Uff. 11043F

Pen and brown wash, with white heightening.
26 × 28.6 cm

INSCRIBED: (lower margin) *Di me federigho Zucheri pitore da urbino.*

BIBLIOGRAPHY: Ferri 1890: 168; *Catalogo dei ritratti* 1911: 31; Voss 1920: 458; Körte 1935: 67, pl. 45b; *Mostra del Cinquecento toscano* 1940: 168; Heikamp 1957: 181; Gere 1966: 44, no. 60, fig. 45; Heikamp 1967: 51-52, fig. 13a; Boase 1971: 334 n. 30, fig. 226; Smith 1978: 28, fig. 3; Pacciani 1981: 167, fig. 354.

The drawing, which can be dated 1574-75, was restored in March 1966 and is in good condition. The lower margin of the sheet the inscription reads: "By Messere Federico Zuccari, painter from Urbino."
The sleeping figure on the right might be Vasari, whose presence guarantees the continuity of Zuccari's work. But, at the same time, the representation assumes an ironical tone, with Vasari slumbering over a crumpled drawing of his. The dome of S. Maria del Fiore is visible through the window; in the left foreground, holding a rolled-up drawing, is the figure of Zuccari, in profile; behind Borghini a woman represents the allegory of Invention or Grace, uniting the two personages involved in the continuation of Vasari's undertaking (Körte 1935). According to Boase the woman is Vasari's wife Cosina, depicted here as a young woman, while in the oil painting Zuccari subsequently executed she is portrayed as being of mature years (Boase 1971). In the top left a painting by an unidentified artist representing the Nativity may be distinguished. In the center there is a wooden model of four webs of the dome to which Zuccari glued the drawings; this is probably the one which Vasari used (Pacciani 1981). Voss believes this sheet to be the preparatory study for the painting in the Biblioteca Hertziana in Rome, formerly the Palazzo Zuccari (Voss 1920).
After the death of Vasari, which occurred on the scaffolding in June 1574, only the part around the lantern, a third of the work, was complete (Guasti 1857, docs. 357, 358, 359). A large number of drawings, now mostly in the Louvre, remained to guide the work of his successor, Federico Zuccari, whom Francesco I had nominated following the advice of Bernardo Vecchietti, patron of Giambologna (Gere 1966; Smith 1978: 27).
Zuccari began to paint the frescoes on 30 August 1576 (Lapini and Corazzini 1900: 193; Heikamp 1967: 47; Wazbinski 1977: 7) or in October of the same year (Gaye 1840, III: 353; Richter 1928: 58; Monbeig Goguel 1976: 685). On 19 August 1579 (Lapini and Corazzini 1900: 201; Heikamp 1967: 47; Wazbinski 1977: 7) or 25 September 1579 (Guasti 1857: 207; Körte 1935: 74; Gere 1966: 44) the protective sheets which can be seen rolled up on the scaffolding in Pastorino's medal were removed. The iconographic program of the frescoes (Guasti 1857,

doc. 356) was prepared, drawing inspiration from Dante's writings, by the Florentine humanist Vincenzo Borghini, who was a Benedictine and vice director of the Accademia del Disegno. The scheme was scrupulously followed by Vasari and Zuccari, with the exception of the east side of the dome a where a Christ in Glory was depicted instead of angels and saints. Zuccari was responsible for the conception of the fifth sector and sectors two, three and four of the east, northwest, west and southwest webs (Smith 1978). In one of the webs where the "Christian people, rich, poor and everyone" is represented, Zuccari portrayed himself, palette in hand, surrounded by his family, assistants and friends, including the faithful Giambologna. On his jacket Zuccari painted the legend: "FEDERI[CUS] ZUCH[ERUS] P[INXIT] A[NNO] S[ALUTIS] 1576" (Heikamp 1967: 49-50).
Together with the present drawing, which may be attributed with certainty to Zuccari, in the Uffizi are almost all the drawings for the *Last Judgment*, many of which are workshop production.
The frescoes by Zuccari were not favorably received. The Florentine painters were particularly hostile, above all Allori, who had attempted to obtain the commission for the decoration of the piers of the dome and the presbytery for half the fee which Zuccari was asking (Guasti 1857, doc. 362b; Wazbinski 1977: 10). *M.S.*

265

ANTONIO DA SANGALLO THE YOUNGER
Sketches Relating to the Dome and Lantern of Florence Cathedral

Florence, Galleria degli Uffizi, Gabinetto Disegni e Stampe, Uff. 1130A

Pen and ink on white paper with traces of stylus; watermark: paschal lamb and flag (diam. 43 mm), very close to Briquet 49 and 50; the sheet is folded in four and was probably associated with Uff. 1164Ar.-v., which contains similar subjects and folds; the sheet has been damaged with patches of glue lower right; a strip of paper 30 cm in length has been added to the left edge; the dimensions shown in the drawing are in Roman *piedi*:
1 *piede* (p) = 1 ⅓ *palmo* = 298 mm; 1 *palmo* = 12 *once* = 223 mm; 1 *oncia* = 18.6 mm; 1 *decimo* (D) = 1.86 mm.
420 × 227 mm (maximum), 424 × 290 mm (minimum)
INSCRIBED: (top right) *163* (altered to *86*); *la lanterna dalpiano / fino sopra lo cornicione alta p 34*; (bottom right) *Sta reparata; S.ta Reparata;* (bottom left) *questi arconi sono tre / i[n] fino i[n] cima nelli vani / dacanto; La Copula di sopra / in cima D 36 grossa; arconi; nietto, arconi / questi vani late / rali li arconi vanno / i[n]fino i[n]cima lonta / ni luno da llaltro / circa a bracia tre.*

BIBLIOGRAPHY: Ferri 1885: 47; Niccoli 1938: 285-286, no. 4; Giovannoni [1959]: 22 and 435; Marchini 1977b: 16-17, no. 3, fig. 2; Benedetti 1986: 169; Bentivoglio 1993.

These sketches were evidently executed on-site and redrawn in the studio using a stylus, straightedge, and compass. The lines drawn across each sketch seem to indicate that they have been checked off during the copying process. The sheet should now be viewed vertically with the glue

marks at lower right. In the first quarter at top left and in the second at lower right there are traces of a compass point and geometrical designs executed with a stylus. In the top left the drawing shows the buttress of the lantern with part of the latter and a detail of the Composite capital (Doric, Tuscan and Corinthian) on the half-column of the window, the only one designed by Brunelleschi, deriving the form of one found in the crypt of S. Reparata. Underneath, by way of comparison, is a drawing of the design for the lantern of St. Peter's similar to Uff. 87A, with three trial models of volutes on the side and one crowning the buttress. There is a hint of the web below and a small sketch of an arch with pilaster.
Below this is a sketch showing a dimensioned section of the springing line of the lantern with a suggestion of the cornice and pilaster over the small windows in the ring (on the left) up to the stone gutter and the horizontal cornice under this linking it to the rib of the external shell. Above this section line there is a perspective sketch of the external base of a buttress. Underneath is a plan of a buttress and the corresponding upright part of the lantern including the half columns and the internal and external pilasters; next to this is the annotation "the lantern from the springing line to the top of the cornice is 34 *piedi* high." Under this, but upside down, is a quick sketch with a buttress of the lantern and a section of the dome up to the second internal passageway, where the internal part of the ring is emphasized. Next to this is a dimensioned section of a room in the ring executed in stylus with a straightedge and a square (cf. Uff. 1164Av., which has corresponding measurements) and redrawn in pen. The longest side of the ring is subdivided into 7 ⅛ parts; each of these is subdivided into 4 points (*decimi*), totaling 28 ½. On the sheet the corresponding web measures 53 mm; if this is divided by 28.5, the result is 1.859 mm, which is equivalent to ¹⁄₁₀ *oncia* (D = 1.86 mm). Then, by dividing 114 by 28.5 *decimi* of an *oncia* a ratio of 1:40 is obtained. An on-site survey shows that the rooms in the ring are 2,120 mm in height, which, when divided by the measurement of 53 mm on the sheet, verifies the scale of 1:40. The points are, therefore, *decimi* of an *oncia* and constitute the unit of measurement of the drawing. Next to this is shown the inclination of the chord of the web; this is seen in a clean version on Uff. 87A.
At the bottom right of the drawing are further annotations on an area with traces of glue. Next to these is a floor plan drawn at a scale of 1:40 showing the room in the ring; it is drawn without corrections in stylus using a straightedge and compass and is redrawn in pen; on the left of the drawing, again in stylus, is shown the same scale in *decimi* used for the section (cf. perspective and plan in Uff. 1164Av.).
At the bottom left is a section of the dome drawn on the axis of the internal oculi at the level of the third passageway. In the lower part of this drawing are visible the sectioned arches with the annotation: "these arches are three, [and continue] up to the top of the neighboring rooms." Above this is shown the hatched section of the room corresponding to the second oculus in both the internal shell and the external one; the side staircase, which continues in the inner shell up to the ring for 36 *piedi*, equivalent to 38 steps. Above this is a section of the oculus of a room in the ring which illuminates the space between the two shells with the annotation: "The upper part of the dome, 36 *decimi* thick at the top" (cf. sketch in Uff. 1164Av.). On the left is a perspective drawing of the room of the third passageway situated on the inner shell. On the right is the same sketch for measuring the inclination of the chord subtending the web, seen in the clean version in Uff. 87A and with the same value (27° from the perpendicular). Below are two cross-sections of a web of the dome; one of these bears the annotations: "arches," "clear arches," "in these side rooms the arches go right up to the top with approximately three *braccia* between them." *M.S.*

589

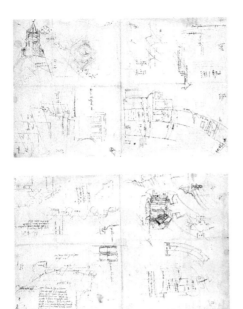

266

ANTONIO DA SANGALLO THE YOUNGER
*Sketches Relating to the Dome and Lantern
of Florence Cathedral*

Florence, Galleria degli Uffizi, Gabinetto Disegni e Stampe,
Uff. 1164A
Pen and ink on white paper, with measurements written in pen;
vertical and horizontal folds; paper insets in the upper edge and
in the center; watermark: paschal lamb and flag (diam. 43 mm),
very close to Briquet 49 and 50.
290 × 429 mm (minimum), 292 × 433 mm (maximum)
INSCRIBED: RECTO: (top center, in pen) *176* (late sixteenth-
century handwriting); (on right, in black pencil) *897*
(nineteenth-century handwriting); (verso, top center, in pen,
inverted) *1164* (nineteenth-century writing); (bottom left, in
pen) *1164 A* (nineteenth-century writing); (recto, top left)
piramida / uno quadro e mezo; (bottom left) *quadro; nero;
Biancho; nero*; (right) *piano del cornicione; qui grossa p 16 D 4*;
(top right) *fino i[n] sulo comicione p 42 D 4*; (at right angles)
*piano del coritore novo / piano delcoritoroultimo didietro; lista
fuora*; (bottom right) *scale; trave la catena di quercia; chiave di
pietra.* VERSO: (top left) *nelle porticine / sotto le coste*; (inverted)
andito al piano delcoritore / di dentro [deletion] *penultimo lo /
coritoro di fuora sie piualto / chello ditto andito D[ecimi] 38*; (top
center) *Lacornicie di fora / e piualta D 38 / che quella di dentro*;
i[n] pie della Copula; piedi 14 and spina pe / scie; (bottom right)
*Contra forte; Costola o vero / Contraforte; fodera; rivedi quanto
sono grose queste / tre groseze e qua[n]to e longa / la faccia di fuora
e quella di de[n]tro*; (bottom left) *le Catene di legnio fanno / faccie
24*; (inverted) *58 piedi; aquesto modo sta neldiritto / sopra alliochij
e di poidameza / alteza della Copula sia cierchi / p[er] traverso
chevanno altondo ela / Copula di fuora va grossa auno /
modo e dalmezo in su va la Copula / gros[s]a auno modo di fuora p[er] che
li vani sono picoli da luno contra / forte allaltro; copertina della
Cupola.*

(The dimensions shown in the drawing are in Roman *piedi*:
1 *piede* (p) = 1 ⅓ *palmo* = 298 mm; 1 *palmo* = 12 *once* = 223 mm;
1 *oncia* = 10 *decimi* = 18.6 mm; 1 *decimo* (D) = 1.86 mm)

BIBLIOGRAPHY: Pini 1880: 480; Ferri 1885: 47; Niccoli 1938:
286, no. 6; Giovannoni [1959]: 22 and 435; Marchini 1977b: 17-
19, no. 4, figs. 3r. and 4v.; Benedetti 1986: 169; Bentivoglio
1993.

(NOTE: In 1574 the grandson of Antonio Sangallo the Younger, his
namesake, offered Grand Duke Francesco de' Medici the collection
of drawings accompanied by a general index (Gaye 1840, III: 391,
no. 343), subsequently rearranged by Pini (Pini 1880: 480) before
the current cataloging. Number 176 in the numbering contained in
Pini's list corresponds to Uff. 1164Ar., while Uff. 1164Av. corresponds to no. 177, the description of which erroneously also includes that of Uff. 87A.)

Looking at the recto, with the longest side at the bottom:
at the top left is a perspective sketch of the lantern flanked
by the cross-section of the fluted cone. Below is the annotation "pyramid / a square and a half," which refers to the
ratio between the base and the height (1:1.5) of the
isosceles triangle, which has the orb of the lantern at its
apex and as its the catheti the tangents of the external volutes of the buttresses (drawn in stylus). This is compared
with an isosceles triangle the catheti of which correspond
to the chords of the intrados of the internal webs of the
dome. On the right there are sections of the west oculus
of the drum and the marble inlays in the embrasure.
At the bottom left, turning the sheet 45° in a clockwise
direction to observe the detail of the panels of the drum
with the annotations "square, black, white, black." On
the right is the section of the base and the cornice of the
angle pilaster of the drum with the annotation "level of
the cornice." Below this is a drawing of half of one face
of the drum with the annotation: "width here 16 *piedi* 4
decimi."
At the top right is the annotation "up to the cornice 42 *piedi* 4 *decimi*" and, at right angles to this, other annotations
regarding the gallery: "floor of the new corridor [the external *ballatoio* designed by Baccio d'Agnolo] and the /
floor of the last corridor [third and last gallery] inside";
then "external fillet."
At the bottom right, turning the sheet anticlockwise 45°
to observe the section of the dome with the external
gallery and a rough representation of the staircase inside
the drum. Annotations: "stairs, chain [of oak beams],
keystone."
On the verso, viewing the sheet with the longest side at
the bottom (the largest block of writing is on the right, at
top left can be seen a small door on the first external web
with underneath, placed at different heights, the toothers
of the radial beams; on the right three toothers of the angular pilaster with the annotation: "in the small doors / under the ribs." Lower down is the inverted inscription:
"space at the level of the penultimate internal gallery ...
the / external gallery is 38 *decimi* higher than the other
one."
At top center, turning the sheet anticlockwise to observe
the section of the external gallery with underneath the annotation: "The external cornice is 38 *decimi* higher than
the internal one." On the right are two sections. The first
shows part of the angle rib: there is the section of the dripstone and the stone gutter for the whole of the part of the
drum in rough masonry, with a quick parallel sketch of the
protruding toothers underneath. The second shows a detail of the dripstone and gutter with the annotation: "at
the base of the dome."
At top right, turning the sheet clockwise to view the section of one of the pilasters and the related entablature of
the internal wall of the ring; the quick sketch shows the
receding parallel lines in accordance with the usage in
drawings of entablatures in the first half of the Cinquecento. On the left is a perspective sketch of the room
in the ring, from which there is access to the lantern, with
a section of the interior of the octagonal ring shown enlarged and turned to the right, and a section of the intrados of the web.
There are numerous measurements and annotations.
Directly underneath is the cross-section at the level of the
oculus giving onto the space between the two shells. Next
to this is the section of the ring of a dome with an indication of the buttress of the lantern (cf. Uff. 87A) on which
are drawn studies relating to the internal section of the
oculus at the crown; this probably referred to the project
for the lantern of St. Peter's.
At the bottom right, turning the sheet in an anticlockwise
direction to observe the schematic section of the dome
with measurements and, underneath, a detail of an angle
rib and an intermediate one with the annotations: "buttress, rib or buttress, covering; check these three measurements and the length of the external face against the internal one."
At the bottom left is a cross-section of one side of the octagon of the drum drawn over the first passageway in order

to highlight the chain of oak beams with, above, the annotation "the wooden chains have 24 faces"; underneath is
written, inverted "58 *piedi.*" At the bottom left is the section of a web drawn at the level of the horizontal arches
between the intermediate ribs of the dome, flanked by the
annotation describing the position of the arches which
connect the angle ribs with the intermediate ones. Next
to this is the section of the cornice under the corbels supporting the stone gutter. Finally, if the sheet is turned in
a clockwise direction, at top right four tiles used to cover
the dome may be seen together with the inscription "cover
of the dome."

M.S.

267

PASTORINO DE' PASTORINI
Partial Section of the Dome of Florence Cathedral

Florence, Museo Nazionale del Bargello
Bronze medal with the section of the dome of S. Maria del
Fiore in Florence (reverse) and a portrait of Federico Zuccari
(obverse).

Diam. 51 mm; thickness 5.8 mm (max.), 2.6 mm (min); 54.7 g
INSCRIBED: (obverse) FEDERICUS ZUCCARUS. 1578. (triangular
stops); in the crook of the arm is the signature: *P.*; the bust
faces right, is bearded and wears a garment with a wide crinkled
collar; (reverse) TENP[ORE].FRANC[ISCI].MED[ICIS] MAG[NI] DUX
ETRURIAE (triangular stops); (in cartouche) PINXIT.

PROVENANCE: Bottacin Collection.

BIBLIOGRAPHY: Armand 1883, I: 210, no. 135; Supino 1899: 125,
no. 352; Hill 1912: 76, no. 58; Körte 1935: 68 n. 9; Heikamp 1967:
51; Wazbinsky 1977: 10; Pacciani 1981: 168; Pollard 1985, II:
709, no. 366; Parise Labadessa 1991: 104, no. 149.

Federico Zuccari commissioned Pastorino to make the
medal in 1578, a year before the unveiling of the frescoes
in the dome of S. Maria del Fiore. On the reverse is
represented a section in perspective of the dome, which
was executed for demonstrative purposes. However, there
are a number of errors of interpretation: the oculi
on the extrados of the dome are out of proportion and two
are shown for each face instead of the correct three; besides, the parts of *ballatoio* or gallery constructed on the
east and southeast sides (architrave and frieze) are mistakenly visible. In fact, the second part had already been
demolished in 1508 (Guasti 1857, doc. 342), so that only
the gallery of one face remained, as may be seen today.
This decidedly forced representation shows the interior
of the dome by means of a section which is obtained by
combining two sections at right angles to each other and
occupies the space of two faces. This allows us to see, as
if laid out on a flat surface, the three webs on the interior
of the dome and the scaffolding fixed to the top gallery of
the drum which Zuccari used for the execution of his frescoes. The canvas sheets rolled up on the scaffolding indicate that this is the occasion of the official unveiling of the
work, on 19 August (or 25 September) 1579. Intended for
his admirers and clients, the medal is a skilful attempt by
Zuccari to identify with the most illustrious of his patrons
and the famous monuments decorated by him. There is a
poor example in the Bargello in Florence, possibly an
eighteenth century copy (Heikamp 1967, fig. 17 a, b);
another copy is in the British Museum in London.

About ten years later Zuccari was invited by Philip II of Spain to the Escorial to paint the frescoes in the church of St. Lawrence. Even though he was soon replaced by Pellegrino Tibaldi, Zuccari had a medal cast on which were represented the empty walls of the church that he was to decorate (Hill 1912: 76, no. 59, De Rinaldis 1913: 229-230; Körte 1935: 77, pl. 45a). On the obverse his effigy is adorned with a medal, probably one of the three (Philip II or Cardinal Farnese?) that appear in the portrait in the Uffizi, formerly attributed to Pourbus (Heikamp 1961, VII) and subsequently to Fede Galizia (Meloni Trkulja 1980: 878).   *M.S.*

The *Ballatoio* of S. Maria del Fiore in Florence
Alessandro Nova

The *ballatoio* is the only part of Florence Cathedral that was never completed, and the complex developments surrounding its fate are matter of debate. As far as the models in the Museo dell'Opera are concerned, there is a telling report prepared in 1601 by Alessandro Allori, architect in charge of the building's maintenance, suggesting that they be inventoried to ascertain their original purpose (Guasti 1857: 157), and hence by the time Florence was under the rule of the grand dukes, the real purpose of these models had already been forgotten. Such problems are compounded by the occasionally generic information provided by the sources, the not always reliable attributions of modern critics, and the appalling damage caused by the flood of 1966.

The oldest document to have come down to us regarding the *ballatoio*—curiously ignored until now, though it sheds light on a passage of the famous *Instruction* drawn up by Filippo Brunelleschi in 1420—is the celebrated fresco by Andrea di Bonaiuto in the Cappellone degli Spagnoli, which clearly shows a view of the fourteenth-century model of the cathedral behind the depiction of the *Church Militant*. In this project (1367), the cathedral's drum was crowned by a simple open *ballatoio* or gallery resting on consoles, comprising a quatrefoil openwork parapet quite similar to that of the lower *ballatoio* around the base of the tribunes. This extremely simple solution was to have been enriched by the addition of statues of prophets, placed in correspondence to the piers of the drum and the ribs of the vault, an idea that Michelangelo later reproposed in a very ambitious project drawn up between 1516 and 1520.

In his scheme of 1420 Brunelleschi still seems undecided about the solution to adopt for the *ballatoio*: "A passage must be built outside, above the windows, forming a gallery resting on consoles with openwork parapets and of a height of about 2 *braccia*, harmonious with the small tribunes below, or, rather, two passages, one above the other, resting on a richly ornamented cornice; and the top passage should be uncovered" (Guasti 1857: 29-30). The first solution called for a modest openwork parapet, about

1.17 meters high and proportional to the existing one at the base of the tribunes. This proposal is far removed from Brunelleschi's architectural language and, in fact, is no more than a description of what we see in Andrea di Bonaiuto's fresco, in other words, a description of the model of 1367. The second solution, which proposed a double passage, covered below and open above, is the one Brunelleschi most likely aimed to realize.

The building records reveal that the brick model that the architect had built in 1418 was embellished by a wooden *ballatoio* and lantern, whose construction had involved the contribution of Nanni di Banco and Donatello (Saalman 1980: 62). In July-August 1419 Brunelleschi received the substantial sum of 50 lire and 15 *soldi* in part payment for wood and for the lathesman's and the carpenter's work on the lantern and the passage of the model (Guasti 1857, doc. 20). On 29 December 1419 Brunelleschi, Nanni di Banco, and Donatello were paid 45 gold florins for the model of the dome (Guasti 1857, doc. 43). Since it is unlikely that the two sculptors contributed to solving the technical and structural problems, one can assume they oversaw the work of the two craftsmen engaged on the costly details of the *ballatoio* and lantern. This means that in the model of 1418 Brunelleschi had already devised a rough design for the *ballatoio*, but, as noted above, it cannot have differed greatly from the one in the model of 1367; this explains the participation of Donatello and Nanni di Banco in the realization of the statues of the prophets. At any event, the alternative alluded to in the *Instruction* of 1420 makes it clear that Brunelleschi—at the time taken up with the much more challenging technical problems of the design—had still not devised a definitive solution for this part of the dome. As the culmination of work on the cathedral, the *ballatoio* was fundamental from an aesthetic point of view, but it was utterly insignificant structurally, which was Brunelleschi's chief concern at this stage. The wording of the *Instruction* suggests that Brunelleschi would have addressed the problem of the *ballatoio* only after having completed the dome's vault and lantern.

Brunelleschi's model of the dome was destroyed in 1432 (Saalman 1980: 133) and his last years of activity at S. Maria del Fiore were dedicated to raising the lantern. However, Vasari (1877, II: 362), recalls that "having decided to finish the *ballatoio*, [Brunelleschi] made various drawings which upon his death remained in the custody of the Opera, but which, through the negligence of the officials, are today lost." Even assuming that Vasari was well-informed and that the architect had indeed executed drawings for the *ballatoio*, we may never know how he intended to solve the problem of the dual passageway. Yet scholars have not resisted the temptation to advance some hypotheses. Nardini Despotti (1885: 77) was convinced that Brunelleschi had not planned for a gallery with arches like those partially realized later, but with single slender columns whose entablature was to be supported on the upper row of projecting morse of the drum, still visible on the uncompleted faces of the octagon. Sanpaolesi (1941: 12; 1977: 25) attributed the conception of the Opera model no. 141 to a joint design by Brunelleschi and Lorenzo Ghiberti, even though this fragmentary model is far from Brunelleschi's style. More recently, Marchini (1980: 918-919) has reaccredited him with the creation of Opera model no. 160-163, which reproduces the entire apse area of the cathedral. In the model, which according to the author's hypothesis dates to 1429, the openwork of the fourteenth-century *ballatoio* over the tribunes has been replaced by a banded cornice that echoes the other, equally rough ones, at the base of the drum and at the foot of the vault. According to Marchini, a model so scarce in detail is typical of Brunelleschi's working method, and the wider band of the upper *ballatoio* was to have housed an open gallery similar to the one made by Baccio d'Agnolo in 1514-15. However, the attribution seems rather implausible in this case as well.

Among Brunelleschi's immediate successors as works supervisor, only Antonio Manetti Ciaccheri, *capomaestro* from 1452 to 1460, seems to have tackled the problem of the *ballatoio*. From a document related to the competition of 1507, we come to know that the winners were to incorporate some of the elements of the "*modellum antiquum, factum et datum per Antonium Manettum*" (Guasti 1857, doc. 341). For this reason, modern critics have credited Brunelleschi's great rival Manetti with the parts of the drum realized between the former's death and the interventions of 1507-15. To some extent, this is also due to the fact that Brunelleschi's first biographer, Antonio di Tuccio Manetti, spoke out against Ciaccheri's tampering with the original design: "And when Filippo was dead, then without the least fear, [Ciaccheri] used everything he could against Filippo's fame and against his work, begun and not finished...; hence the damage... of the main facades and main outside pilasters of the dome of S. Maria del Fiore" (Manetti 1970: 115). According to the biographer's next passage and the interpretation offered by Saalman, Brunelleschi's model, or even the one of 1367, required that the corner pilasters of the drum maintain the same width, without tapering, from the base to the architrave supporting the *ballatoio*. But Ciaccheri took it upon himself to extend the entablature over the attic of the nave to the perimeter of the drum, linking the whole complex horizontally with a course of masonry; and, furthermore, after having broken the vertical thrust of the pilasters with this horizontal band, he reduced the width of the upper part of the pilaster, now divided into two segments. In the words of the biographer, Ciaccheri "reduced the pilasters in width on the upper side; that first he made this mess, when... it had been the intention of who had begun that it be a single member only, the tapering in width makes it appear as two members, one above the other, of which neither one nor the other pleases" (Manetti 1970: 115). That these variations must be attributed to Ciaccheri and, as a consequence, the design of the drum facing, is confirmed by a document of 1477, generally overlooked (Doren 1898: 256), in which the *operai* order the realization of the "*modellum factum per antonium manettj olim capudmagistrum cupole e lanterne dicte ecclesie tempore sua vita circa faccies dicte cupole.*" However, it is important to remember that it was not Ciaccheri but Giuliano da Maiano who finished the project, as noted in Vasari's *Lives*. Ciaccheri in fact died in 1460, and a detailed view of the dome in the background of a portrait of Dante painted by Domenico di Michelino for the cathedral in 1465 shows that, five years after Ciaccheri's death, work on the drum had not yet been started. Giuliano da Maiano became the *capomaestro* of the cathedral site in 1477, and the view of S. Maria del Fiore in the background of a fresco (1481-85) by Domenico Ghirlandaio in the Sala dei Gigli in the Palazzo Vecchio shows that at the start of the 1480s the walls around the drum windows had still not been faced with marble. In any case, da Maiano kept his post as *capomaestro* until his death in 1490, and since Vasari's narrative (1877, II: 469-470) is too detailed not to be reliable, he must have completed the decoration of the drum in the last years of his life. According to the biographer, Giuliano da Maiano "made the decorations of white and black marble around the windows, and likewise the marble corner pilasters, over which Baccio d'Agnolo erected the architrave, frieze and cornice, as described below. It is true that, as far as one can see in some drawings of his hand that are in our Book, he wished to make another order of frieze, cornice and *ballatoio*, with some frontispieces [i.e. pediments] on each of the eight sides of the dome; but he did not have the time to carry this out, because, absorbed in his work, one day flowed into the next, and he died." This neglected passage of the *Lives* makes it possible to attribute to Giuliano da Maiano one of the Museo dell'Opera models (no. 137), but the artist did not convince the *fabbricieri* to approve the substantial modifications to Ciaccheri's design. The reliability of Vasari's account and the attribution to Manetti Ciaccheri of the existing design seem to be confirmed by the correspondence of the documentary information and the working procedure at S. Maria del Fiore, where the *operai* or works trustees were in the habit of making the new *capomaestri* swear they would respect the previously approved designs and models. In other words, it is no coincidence that the formers' exhortations to realize the "*modellum factum per antonium manettj*" for the facing of the octagon dates to 1477, the year in which Giuliano da Maiano was appointed *capomaestro*. According to our reconstruction of the facts, it is likely that as soon as he had taken up his post (1 April 1477), Giuliano tried to make substantial modifications in Ciaccheri's design (hence, the drawings that Vasari mentions and the wooden model) and that the *fabbricieri* instead urged him (4 November 1477) to follow the already approved *modellum*, from which it was categorically forbidden to diverge ("*et de eo non exeatum ullo modo*"). In this respect, it should be remembered that even Brunelleschi pledged to respect the model of 1367 and that the *operai* were very conservative and reluctant to take issue with the decisions made under oath by their predecessors. In conclusion, da Maiano's efforts came to nothing and the architect limited himself to carrying out Ciaccheri's design, namely, the dichromatic facing of the drum, the tapering of the upper pilasters at the level of the windows, the elaborate three-banded architrave still visible on the eastern side of the octagon, and the frieze with trefoil inlay work, dismantled in 1508. Da Maiano's sole personal contribution, roundly criticized by Manetti the biographer, must have been the enlargement of the outer splays of the drum windows; according to Manetti, Brunelleschi's true intentions were altered "out of a certain ignorance on the part of the later *capomaestri* [those after Ciaccheri], who made the window splays on the outside too wide, which cannot now be rectified" (Manetti 1970: 115).

During the final years of Giuliano da Maiano's office, the team of architects at the cathedral saw the arrival of Il Cronaca (alias Simone del Pollaiuolo), who was to become *capomaestro* in 1495, five years after da Maiano's death. The Medici had just been expelled from the city, and the turbulent political climate brought work on the cathedral to a halt. In 1502 Il Cronaca submitted a request for a reduction in salary—activity on the site was languishing so much that it weighed on his conscience to receive payment for work not done. It is no coincidence that the artist had been and perhaps still was an enthusiastic follower of Savonarola. Il Cronaca's petition is dated 14 April 1502, but in September that year the Florentine patrician Piero di Tommaso Soderini was elected gonfalonier for life, an event that opened a new era in the politics and art of republican Florence. A personal friend of many artists, and of Michelangelo in particular, Soderini stimulated the economic and cultural life of the city, rallying its finest creative minds around the refurbishment of the town hall: Il Cronaca, Baccio d'Agnolo, Giuliano and Antonio da Sangallo were called upon to participate in a systematic program involving almost all the government-sponsored ventures, from the most challenging ones to those of normal administration. It was Soderini who commissioned the *Battle of Anghiari* and the *Battle of Cascina* to Leonardo and Michelangelo; and it is likely that it was he who urged the resumption of activities at S. Maria del Fiore. Just a few months after Soderini's lifelong appointment, Michelangelo signed a contract (24 April 1503) with the cathedral *operai* for the realization of twelve statues of the Apostles (only one of which he got as far as roughing out, the *St. Matthew* today in the Accademia) and it was during these years that the sculptor finished the colossal "pro-Republican" *David*. This was the climate in which the problem of completing the *ballatoio* of the cathedral returned to the fore, a project which, as a crowning element of the city's most representative building, should have born the emblem of the newly found power of the civic government—the arms that proudly decorate the friezes and architraves of some of the models entered for the 1507 competition (nos. 138 and 140, Museo dell'Opera).

Some letters published by Marchini (1977a: 46-47) reveal that the *operai* met in July 1507 to deal with the question and, following a tried-and-true procedure, they tried to involve the greatest number of artists and craftsmen, inviting the participation of even those who were working elsewhere, outside the city. These letters are infused with a deep communitarian and republican spirit. The message sent to the goldsmith Riccio says that since he was well versed in architecture, it seemed "appropriate to make the effort to give you this slight inconvenience, hoping that as a *good citizen* you will bear this annoyance with a light heart, et maxime, *being a public thing* and about our temple." The letters to Michelangelo, at the time in Bologna, and to Sansovino, perhaps resident in Rome, both dated 31 July 1507, are steeped in the same civic spirit. To Michelangelo: "Our very dear, beloved citizen... And we wish to interpret your judgment *as loving of your city*." To Sansovino: "Your absence has grieved us not a little, nevertheless we trust in you *as a zealous advocate of this city* and we might say as a Florentine, and for this, our labor of love, would you make a drawing and model of the thing as a talented professor of this art?" These and other already known documents suggested to Marchini that Michelangelo, Sansovino and other architects participating in the competition were the authors of the models conserved in the Museo dell'Opera. As we shall see in the individual catalog entries, such attributions are, at best, problematic. What is certain is that the winning model (8 November 1507) was the one submitted by Il Cronaca, Giuliano da Sangallo and Baccio d'Agnolo (Guasti, 1857, doc. 341). On this occasion, the administrators examined five projects and selected the one by the three architects, who were to work alongside Antonio da Sangallo the Elder, specifying, however, that they would also have to bear in mind the "*modellum antiquum, factum et datum per Antonium Manettum*." Working jointly and of common accord, the four were to conserve what had been accomplished in the fifteenth century in order not to waste the expenses already sustained and, starting from the area above the frieze, which had already been started on two sides of the octagon, were to incorporate wherever possible the elements of their model with the most effective ones of Ciaccheri's design. It was a compromise that soon proved to be impossible to implement. The model presented by Il Cronaca and partners (no. 142, Museo dell'Opera) retained the fifteenth-century trefoil frieze and added a costly modification to the drum decoration. Worried about the expenses that such a project entailed, the *operai* asked the architects to respect what had already been completed as far as the frieze, and approved the project for the *ballatoio* proper as well as the possible replacement of the capitals set between the corner pilasters of the drum and the frieze. However, they realized almost immediately that Ciaccheri's elegantly decorative frieze was out of proportion with the new *ballatoio*. As we know from Giovanni Cambi's *Istorie* (1785-86, III: 63), the frieze "was full of certain flowers in black marble, which was made only on two faces of the dome where they had begun renovation, and the reason why this frieze was removed was because it was deemed too small and paltry for such a cornice and *ballatoio*." The frieze of marble inserts was reutilized to decorate the floors of the S. Pietro and S. Paolo chapels inside the cathedral (Cavallucci 1881: 87-88) and was replaced by a frieze of classical inspiration with festoons capped by winged faces of putti alternated with lion heads. Since the gallery was realized under the reign of Pope Leo X, it is tempting to believe that these heads were inserted in homage to him, but a payment dated 22 January 1508 to Baccio d'Agnolo (Marchini 1977a: 47) informs us that the architect had already made a lion head in plaster "for the model of the frieze to be made for the gallery of the dome." In addition to shedding light on the emblematic significance of these heads, which were originally meant to refer to the *marzocco* (heraldic symbol of the Florentine dominion) and not to the pope, the document also reveals that just two months after the agreement under which the artists pledged to conserve what had already been executed during the fifteenth century, the *fabbricieri* had realized the incompatibility between the sixteenth-century project and Ciaccheri's model. And, indeed, on 12 May 1508, the wardens decided to dismantle the old frieze and replace it with the one we see today (Guasti 1857, doc. 342).

In November 1507, Il Cronaca, Giuliano da Sangallo and Baccio d'Agnolo not only won the commission for the *ballatoio*, but the two Sangallo brothers and Baccio d'Agnolo were elevated in rank to work alongside Il Cronaca as cathedral *capomaestri*. All pledged to work in unison for the good of the public and the *fabbrica* (Guasti 1857, doc. 343). Yet, differences of opinion and rancor were not long in coming, and the situation was complicated when, on 21 September 1508, Il Cronaca met his premature death. On 11 December 1508, the two Sangallo brothers resigned from their posts, both on the grounds of ill-health (Guasti 1857, doc. 345). The document makes it clear that neither Giuliano nor Antonio da Sangallo wanted to renew the commitment, and on the same day, Baccio d'Agnolo was left standing alone as the *capomaestro* of the cathedral site, a position which he held until his death in 1543.

Because of this discord, the project was interrupted once again, but after the return of the Medici in 1512, it was decided to complete at least one of the sides of the *ballatoio*. At the end of December 1513, Baccio d'Agnolo was joined by Nanni di Baccio Bigio in the position as *capomaestro* (Guasti 1857, doc. 347), and in September 1514, arrangements were made for transporting from Carrara the pieces for the plinth, the pilasters, the architrave, the frieze, the arches and the cornice of the gallery (Guasti 1857, doc. 349). The finished part of the gallery on the southeast side of the octagon was inaugurated on 24 June 1515, to celebrate the feast of St. John. As is well-known, the work attracted the criticism and sarcasm of Michelangelo upon his return from Rome in the summer of 1516. As Vasari reports (1877, 353-354) in the *Life* of Baccio: having "made the design and model of this *ballatoio*, he carried out all of the part that can be seen on the Bischeri side; but Michelagnolo Buonarroti, upon his return from Rome, seeing that they were cutting away the protruding morse that Filippo Brunelleschi had purposely left exposed, objected heatedly and work was stopped. He said that it seemed to him that Baccio had made a cage for crickets, and that such a great structure required some-

thing larger and made to another design with art and grace, which, it did not seem to him, Baccio's design had, and that he would show them what to do. So, when Michelagnolo made a model, it was discussed at length among many expert artists and citizens before the Cardinal Giulio de' Medici, and in the end neither one nor the other of the models was realized. Baccio's design was criticized in many particulars; not that it was not fine in itself, but because it was too small for such a structure; and for this reason this *ballatoio* has never seen its completion." That Michelangelo had in effect designed a grandiose solution suited to Brunelleschi's imposing dome is confirmed by Casa Buonarroti 50A and 66A, executed between 1516 and 1520. Michelangelo intended to dismantle the dichromatic facing designed by Ciaccheri and to frame the windows of the octagon between two rectangular slabs; moreover, he wished to replace the corner pilasters with Corinthian or composite columns resting on a very high base, all supporting an imposing three-tiered entablature. Finally, having moved the passage to a higher level than the present one, the project called for a series of eight statues to be placed high up in correspondence with the eight ribs. The idea was ambitious indeed, if not unfeasible, and remained on paper, but it is highly representative of that mixture of utopia and megalomania typical of Buonarroti's genius.

At any event, it was not just Michelangelo's criticisms that halted Baccio d'Agnolo's project. Vasari's account, quoted above, is confirmed in Giovanni Cambi's *Istorie* (1785-86, III: 70-71), where there is mention of the Florentines' bad reception of the work when it was unveiled: "In this year [1515], on the day of St. John, the first side of the dome was unveiled, toward the side of the Bischeri ... It appeared to everyone that the new addition cut a poor figure alongside the great frieze below with its lion heads and sill, which stood out much more than the finished work above. If it is continued, you shall see, it will not be in this year 1515."

The failure of Michelangelo's bold alternative led to the definitive suspension of work. Fortunately, several proposals for the completion of the *ballatoio* put forward at the end of the nineteenth century and the first years of our own (Ginevri 1903: 3-5) were not followed through. Of the project realized by Baccio d'Agnolo, in addition to the "cage for crickets," there remains a fragment of the frieze on the eastern side of the octagon, a reminder of this important but unfortunate undertaking. What should have been a glowing emblem of a new "popular" government came to symbolize the disinterest of the newly instated Medici dynasty for things public. The lion heads on the frieze, originally conceived as a symbol of the civil authority of the commune, could easily have been recycled as a homage to the Medici pope, who chose the name Leo X. Yet nothing was done. The interrupted frieze came to symbolize an era of political confusion during which artists had to fend for themselves—often changing camps with impunity—between republican hopes and the self-interested politics of an arrogant family by now intent on consolidating its absolute power (witness the unchallenged priority given to Michelangelo's projects for S. Lorenzo), or distracted by more pressing commitments in Rome.

268
ANTONIO MANETTI CIACCHERI
(attrib.)
*Model of the Drum and Ballatoio
of S. Maria del Fiore*

Florence, Museo dell'Opera di S. Maria del Fiore, 136
Three vertical panels in white poplar, with black, white and green tempera.
138 × 98 × 12.5 cm

BIBLIOGRAPHY: Nardini Despotti Mospignotti 1885b: 75-76; *Catalogo* 1891: 33; Poggi 1904: 58-59; Sabatini 1943: XX; *Guida* 1948: 15; Marchini 1977a: 36-37, 43.

In the past, model no. 136 was always considered anonymous and usually linked to the 1507 competition. However, Marchini (1977a) attributed it to Manetti Ciaccheri and proposed a dating of between 1451 and 1460 when the architect was *capomaestro* of the Opera (actually, Ciaccheri took his post in 1452). Marchini's attribution is based on the fact that model no. 136 bears the closest resemblance to the project that was realized, which can still be seen today. The decoration of the drum facade, the square pilaster in the right-hand version (the panels of which were diminished from three to two during the execution of the project, probably overseen by Giuliano da Maiano), the simple entablature with three consecutive bands, without capital and the trefoil-motif frieze (dismantled in 1508) correspond to what was effectively realized. Marchini's attribution therefore seems justified, also on the strength of the "archaic" aspects of the model, such as the decorative band at the base of the drum and the motif of the openwork parapets of the *ballatoio*.

As far as the model is concerned, note-worthy are both the variation with fluted pilasters capped by ornate fifteenth-century capitals, on the left at window height, and the reduction of the width of the pilasters on this side of the drum; the lower corner pilasters measure 6.7 cm, while the upper ones measure only 6 cm. This fact is significant since, according to Antonio di Tuccio Manetti, Brunelleschi's first biographer, Manetti Ciaccheri altered the original project by reducing the width of the drum's upper pilasters.

Finally, it should be pointed out that in this model the twin arches of the gallery were originally supported by columns, probably Doric like the fluted pilasters that separate them, the base of which left traces above the openwork parapet.   *A.N.*

269
GIULIANO and ANTONIO DA SANGALLO THE ELDER
(attrib.)
*Model of the Drum and the Ballatoio
of S. Maria del Fiore*

Florence, Museo dell'Opera di S. Maria del Fiore, 140
Two overlapping panels in white poplar with red, green-blue and
white tempera.
113.5 × 72.5 × 13 cm

BIBLIOGRAPHY: Nardini Despotti Mospignotti 1885b: 75-76;
Catalogo 1891: 33; Poggi 1904: 58-59; *Guida* 1948: 15; *Disegni di
fabbriche Brunelleschiane* 1977: 15; Marchini 1977a: 41-42, 45;
1987: 244; Satzinger 1991: 86.

The museum's first catalog lists model no. 140 among
those submitted to the 1507 competition, but Marchini
proposes 1516 and attributes it to Antonio da Sangallo the
Elder. Originally, the scholar had advanced the theory
that the model was the fruit of a collaboration between
the two Sangallo brothers, because a drawing in the Uffizi
(7954A) by Giuliano shows a sketch with a plan quite
similar to that of the model (*Disegni...*, 1977: 15); prompted by an informal and undocumented reopening of the
competition for the *ballatoio*, the elderly Giuliano is supposed to have designed in 1516 a new and grandiose solution, while Antonio, an acclaimed carpenter, would have
done the model (this hypothesis has been rejected by Borsi
1985: 458-459). However, in later analyses, Marchini
(1977a: 41, and especially 1987: 244) did not hesitate to
attribute to Antonio also the design of the drum facing:
the majestic motif of the niches framed by Doric columns
supporting an imposing entablature and the robust cornice resting on corbels show "a vigorous crudeness" typical of Antonio. Satzinger (1991) has recently upheld this
attribution and dating (1515 instead of 1516).
Yet, as with no. 138, the emblems of the city and that of
the Florentine people—the latter framed by two lambs,
symbol of the wool guild, which had been entrusted with
the supervision of the construction and maintenance of S.
Maria del Fiore—make it impossible to date model no.
140 to the period under Medici rule. However, since in
1507 the Sangallo brothers had joined Il Cronaca and Baccio d'Agnolo in the realization of the winning model, posi-
tively identified by scholars as no. 142, model no. 140 can
only be considered a second thought on the part of the two
brothers. In fact, it is possible that in the course of 1508,
they became aware of the inadequacy of the model
designed in collaboration with the other two partners and
that they thus sought to create a solution more appropriate to the mass of the dome. This would explain the discord between the *capomaestri* of the Opera and Giuliano's
and Antonio's resignations "for reasons of health"
presented on 11 December 1508 (see the document published by Guasti 1857, doc. 345).
It may be significant that while almost all the other
models in the museum bear at their base the outline of the
cathedral's nave or of the apse tribunes, no. 140 is the only
one to show one of Brunelleschi's *tribunette morte*. This
could mean that no. 140 was at odds with the require-

ments of the 1507 competition, since having chosen the
side of the octagon toward the nave of the cathedral or one
of those toward the tribunes, the competitors may not
have been aware of the problem of the relationship with
Brunelleschi's *tribunette*. If true, these considerations
would confirm a date later than 1507 for model no. 140.
Finally, it should be mentioned that Hirst (1988b: 92) has
tentatively linked two red chalk sketches by Michelangelo
on a sheet today conserved at the Uffizi (1872Fr.) to the
1507 competition and that the solution proposed on the
left, a niche with a shell-capped conch framed between
two massive columns, is quite similar to the proposal for
the drum in model no. 140.   *A.N.*

270
IL CRONACA, BACCIO D'AGNOLO and GIULIANO DA
SANGALLO
*Model of the Drum and the Ballatoio
of S. Maria del Fiore*

Florence, Museo dell'Opera di S. Maria del Fiore, 142
Three horizontal panels in white poplar with black, green and
white tempera.
96 × 73 × 7 cm

BIBLIOGRAPHY: Nardini Despotti Mospignotti 1885b: 75-76;
Catalogo 1891: 33; Poggi 1904: 58-59; Tosi 1927-28a: 610-611;
Sabatini 1943: XX; *Guida* 1948: 15; *Disegni di fabbriche
Brunelleschiane* 1977: 14; Marchini 1977a: 36-37, 40-41, 44; Tol-
nay 1980: 29; Argan and Contardi 1990: 56.

Listed in the first museum catalog of 1891 among the
models submitted to the 1507 competition, no. 142 was
first identified by Tosi (1927-28) as the one by Il Cronaca
in collaboration with Giuliano da Sangallo and Baccio
d'Agnolo, who were later joined by Antonio da Sangallo
the Elder. It is not clear how the four artists divided up
their tasks, but an examination of the model in the light
of information contained in the documents published by
Guasti (1857, docs. 341-345) makes it possible to advance some hypothesis. Model no. 142 is characterized by
a loggia with single archways at the base of the vault, and
bears the closest resemblance to what Baccio d'Agnolo
realized in 1514-15; since the model shows a substantial
departure from the facing of the drum done according to
Manetti Ciaccheri's design (the two pilasters flanking the
window), it is very likely the one presented by Il Cronaca,
Giuliano da Sangallo and Baccio d'Agnolo in November
1507. It is a simple design, the main idea for which should
be attributed to Cronaca, at the time acting alone as
capomaestro of the cathedral site, assisted by Giuliano;
Baccio must have been asked to participate in the endeavor thanks to his acclaimed skills in carpentry.
However, once the model was presented and the competition won, the *fabbricieri* asked them not to dismantle anything that had already been built, and therefore to forgo
the idea of the drum's facing; furthermore, the three architects were to work in concert to integrate the best parts
of their project with the elements of the "*modellum anti-

quum, factum et datum per Antonium Manettum*" (Guasti
1857, doc. 341).
However, in September 1508, Il Cronaca suddenly
passed away—a premature death—and two months later,
the Sangallo brothers resigned from their posts. When
work on the ballatoio was resumed in 1514-15, Baccio
d'Agnolo limited himself to realizing the loggia design
of 1507.
His only modifications were quite minor, such as replacing the stubby balusters of the parapet with other larger,
fuller ones and adding the fluting to the pilaster strips
framing the arches.
Work on the *ballatoio* was interrupted because of the
criticism of Michelangelo and other Florentine architects
and citizens. In addition to esthetic reasons (in his *Istorie*,
Giovanni Cambi writes that "it appeared to everyone that
this latest addition cut a poor figure compared to that
great frieze below"), misgivings of a purely technical nature must have held some sway. A report written in 1694
by Giovambattista Nelli to the grand duke states that already in 1671 the architects Gherardo and Pier Francesco
Silvani had recommended reinforcing "Baccio d'Agnolo's
ballatoio (which, having been reinforced other times, had
threatened to shift again)" (Guasti 1857, doc. 391). *A.N.*

271
ANONYMOUS (formerly attributed to Michelangelo
Buonarroti)
*Model of the Drum and the Ballatoio
of S. Maria del Fiore*

Florence, Museo dell'Opera di S. Maria del Fiore, 143
One panel in white poplar, with green-blue and white tempera
(restorations in ramin wood).
96 × 71.5 × 10.5 cm

BIBLIOGRAPHY: Nardini Despotti Mospignotti 1885b: 75-76;
Catalogo 1891: 33; Poggi 1904: 58-59; Sabatini 1943: XX; *Guida*
1948: 15; Saalman 1975: 376; Marchini 1977a: 39-40, 44; Tolnay
1980: 28-29; Ristori 1983: 171; Argan and Contardi 1990: 56.

Model no. 143 has always been cataloged among those
submitted to the 1507 competition, but Marchini (1977a)
is the only one to have proposed an attribution; spurred
by the discovery of a letter dated 31 July 1507 in which
the *fabbricieri* invited Michelangelo to participate in the
competition for the *ballatoio*, Marchini thought he perceived in this model a glimmer of Buonarroti's design. According to the scholar, "the classicizing solution of a high
architrave resting on Ionic-style pilasters" and the addition of a row of rectangular marble panels above the drum
window appear in Casa Buonarroti drawings 50A and
66A, which Michelangelo executed in 1516-20 when he
decided to correct the errors made by Baccio d'Agnolo in
the realization of the *ballatoio*. Marchini himself was
forced to admit that the drawing supposedly sent by
Michelangelo, who was then residing in Bologna, had
been misinterpreted by whoever rendered the "general"
project in wood, so much so that the brick "teeth" to

which the imposing entablature was to be anchored are absent in the model. Actually, the architectural language of model no. 143 has very little to do with Michelangelo's drawings of ten years later. If Marchini's attribution were to be accepted, the model would mark Michelangelo's debut as an architect and this would explain some of its clumsiness, such as the introduction of a strip of rectangular panels in green and white marble above the drum window to emphasize the insertion of elegant capitals over the corner pilasters. But in any case, it seems wiser to reject the attribution, even though the monumental cornice in place of the open *ballatoio* anticipates Michelangelo's proposed solution—as Saalman (1975) already noted, though he bluntly rejected the idea that Michelangelo was the model's author. Should anyone wish to repropose the name of Buonarroti, a point in favor of attribution is that the odd curved capitals are similar to the ones Michelangelo used in a project for the facade of S. Lorenzo (Casa Buonarroti 45A). All the same, it is hard to believe that he threw himself enthusiastically into the undertaking because in 1507, the artist was at grips with the execution of the larger than life bronze statue of Pope Julius II. Hirst (1988b: 92) has tentatively suggested identifying two red chalk sketches on a sheet in the Uffizi (1872Fr.) as Michelangelo's initial coy response to invitation of the cathedral *operai*, and a letter sent from Bologna to the artist's brother seems to confirm that he was examining the problem: "I would like you [Buonarroto] to find the herald Sir Agniolo and tell him that I have not yet answered because I could not, and that the thing is all right" (10 August 1507). However, the sketches that Hirst takes into consideration present solutions quite different from those in model no. 143: the first shows a majestic articulation of the drum similar to that of model no. 140, and the second envisages a loggia with a series of arches curiously similar to the one that Il Cronaca and partners proposed in model no. 142. Furthermore, after initially responding affirmatively to the requests of the *fabbricieri*, Michelangelo seems to have dedicated himself to the difficult task of polishing the statue of Julius II which had been poorly cast by master founder Bernardino: "[Buonarroto] Please go to find the herald and *commendatore* Tomaso and tell them that for this I do not have time to write to them, that is, to answer their letters, which I much appreciated" (12-14 October 1507). This letter is dated slightly more than three weeks before the announcement of the results of the competition for the *ballatoio* of S. Maria del Fiore.

That model no. 143 dates to 1507 seems to be confirmed by the fact that its height and width (96 × 71.5 cm) correspond to those of model no. 142 (96 × 73 cm) attributed to Cronaca, Giuliano da Sangallo and Baccio d'Agnolo. But the project's author must remain for the present anonymous.

The model bears clear signs of restoration; the bases of the corner pilasters are not in white poplar but in ramin, an exotic wood of southeast Asia.

A.N.

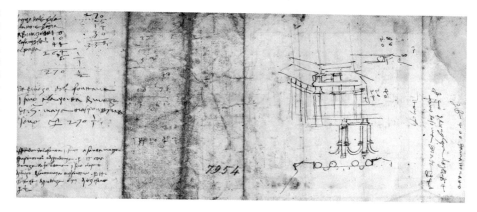

272
GIULIANO DA SANGALLO
Architectural Sketches

Florence, Galleria degli Uffizi, Gabinetto Disegni e Stampe, Uff. 7954Av.
Pen and brown ink.
17.6 × 41.6 cm
INSCRIBED: "*disegnjo del ce chase dela ttore Borgia p[er] abittazione dela famjglia del papa*";
this is followed by some calculations:
"110 + 110 + 44 = 264 + 6½ = 270½" and other calculations: "270 + 25 + 14 + 30 = 339" (the number 339 is crossed out); "*dal mezo dela fonttana j[n]sino ala portta dj mezo di S.ta marja ttraspunttina sono ch[anne] 270½*; *la strada dala fontta[na] j[n]sino a santta marja in ttraspunttina adj pendenza p[almi] 14 cioe da mezo la fonttana j[n]sino ala portta dj mezo djsantamarja ttraspuntina p[almi] 14 che ttocha djpendenza ognj dieci chane p[almi] ½.*"
Rotating the sheet 90 degrees, it reads: "*B 400 dj amattonatto; B 40 per lungheza largho B 14 fano la soma ...*"; other measurements follow: "8; 80 + 20; 40 + 20 + 24 = 84."

PROVENANCE: Gaddi Collection (18th cent.); Abbot Vincenzo Parigi (1830); Count Bernardino di Campello (ca. 1870); Baron Heinrich von Geymüller (1876); Uffizi (1908).

BIBLIOGRAPHY: Fabriczy 1902b: 117-118; Ferri 1908: 58; Ackerman 1949-51: 254 (only the recto); *Disegni di fabbriche Brunelleschiane* 1977: 15; Marchini 1977a: 42, 45; Borsi 1985: 186, 456-459; Satzinger 1991: 86.

This sheet by Giuliano da Sangallo was first published by Fabriczy (1902b), who, thanks to the inscriptions on the verso, had no difficulty in identifying the plans of four row houses on the recto as the design for the apartments of the pope's servants to be constructed near the Borgia tower in the Belvedere courtyard in the Vatican. The commission for this job dates to 1513, so it is likely that the sketches on the verso—the ones that interest us—should be dated around that time.

The first critic to identify the sketches on the verso as a proposed plan and elevation with a study of the corner pilasters for the drum and the *ballatoio* of S. Maria del Fiore was Ferri (1908). Since then no one who has examined the problem has ever challenged this association. Marchini (1977a) later pointed out how the plan sketched on Uff. 7954A verso corresponds to the solution proposed by the authors of model no. 140 in the cathedral's Museo dell'Opera, in which four heavy Doric columns frame two niches to the sides of the drum window. While this observation offers support to the attribution of model no. 140 to the Sangallo circle (and let it not be forgotten that Michelangelo had thought of a similar solution), this does not necessarily mean that the sketches on the verso of Uff. 7945A refer to the Florentine *ballatoio*. The inscriptions that accompany these drawings do not pertain to the project for the "papal" family's apartments alone, but also to renovations in Via Alessandrina in Borgo—facing St. Peter's in Rome—that Leo X had commissioned Giuliano da Sangallo to execute during those same years; in other words, the studies on the verso of the sheet may also be

viewed in the context of this ambitious project. In any case, whatever its original destination, the elevation of the open gallery on Uff. 7954A verso is an important document endorsing Giuliano's involvement in the creation of the Museo dell'Opera model no. 142, submitted to the 1507 competition in collaboration with Il Cronaca and Baccio d'Agnolo. While the heavy corbels at the base of the pilasters dividing the arches are clearly visible in the drawing and absent from the model, they were reused by Baccio d'Agnolo when he realized one of the sides of the *ballatoio* in 1514-15.

A.N.

273
ANONYMOUS (formerly attributed to Aristotile da Sangallo)
Design for the Drum and the Ballatoio of S. Maria del Fiore

Florence, Galleria degli Uffizi, Gabinetto Disegni e Stampe, Uff. 6714A
Traces of black chalk and stylus, pen and brown ink, brown wash.
39.2 × 40.1 cm
INSCRIBED: (top left, in black chalk) "61"; (on backing, in ink) "14".

PROVENANCE: Mediceo-Lorenese estate.

BIBLIOGRAPHY: *Disegni di fabbriche brunelleschiane*, 1977: 13-15; Marchini 1977a: 45; Ghisetti Giavarina 1991: 94.

In the Gabinetto's catalog entry this sheet is attributed to Aristotile da Sangallo and defined as a "perspective elevation of an interior of a dome bearing some resemblance to that of S. Maria del Fiore." But Marchini (*Disegni ...*, 1977) pointed out that it was a project for the drum and exterior *ballatoio* of the Florentine dome.

The project's proportions, more developed in height than in width, would be better suited to the crown of a grandiose campanile (like that of S. Biagio at Montepulciano) than to a side of the drum of a cathedral; however, the roughly drawn outline of the nave at the bottom of the sheet and especially the oval traced with the stylus of a compass in the area later taken up by the Serliana added on a piece of paper glued to the original sheet seem to confirm Marchini's theory.

The drawing's attribution to Aristotile da Sangallo is based on the fact that it belongs to a collection of some eighty sheets assigned to him *en bloc* in the nineteenth century. However, it is a heterogeneous group and recent studies (Ghisetti Giavarina 1991) have made it clear that many of these drawings were actually done by Tommaso Boscoli, the artist who carved the statue of Pope Julius II for Michelangelo's monument in S. Pietro in Vincoli as well as a faithful collaborator of Antonio da Sangallo the Elder, who completed the work on the sanctuary of S. Biagio at Montepulciano. In the group are also sheets that cannot be attributed either to Aristotile or to Boscoli, and Uff. 6714A is the work of an anonymous artist (Ghisetti Giavarina 1991).

In any case, there is no doubt that the drawing was done by a member of the Sangallo circle.

In the opinion of this writer, it documents a project, perhaps even a wood-en model now lost, by Antonio da Sangallo the Elder.

The Serliana motif was dear to Antonio and he used it in the window in the center of the facade of SS. Annunziata in Arezzo (1502-20 and 1528-34) and in one of the sides of the courtyard of the Palazzo Del Monte in Monte S. Savino (1512-17). Furthermore, the idea of placing a corbel at the peak of an arched decorative element, as in those above the niches at the sides of the Serliana, reappears in the first level of the S. Biagio campanile, while the Doric pilasters flanking the pillars supporting the Serliana anticipate those on the ground floor of the rectory of Montepulciano. The showy crowning members are also a motif frequently employed by Sangallo, but here it is more interesting to note how they echo Brunelleschi's decoration of the lantern.

If this bizarre design truly does refer to S. Maria del Fiore, it should be pointed out that the parapets of the two uncovered passageways are topped by globes that could be an allusion to the emblem of the Medici family. The failure of the project realized by Baccio d'Agnolo in 1514-15 probably persuaded more than one artist, and not just Michelangelo, to dust off or radically revamp ideas developed for the 1507 competition. As already in part anticipated by Marchini (*Disegni...* 1977: 14), Uffizi drawing 6714A probably documents Antonio da Sangallo the Elder's renewed interest in the challenging problem of the cathedral's *ballatoio*.   *A.N.*

503-504; *Disegni di fabbriche Brunelleschiane* 1977: 14; Marchini 1977a: 39-42, 44-45; Tolnay 1980: 29; Morselli 1981: 127; Ristori 1983: 171; Ackerman 1986: 295; Argan and Contardi 1990: 56.

Model no. 144 was long considered the oldest among those in the Museo dell'Opera. In the catalog of 1891 it was already attributed to Antonio Manetti Ciaccheri and although Poggi (1904) accepted the attribution with reservations, the model was associated with the fifteenth-century architect's name until 1965, when De Angelis d'Ossat suggested that it was the work of Michelangelo, dating it to 1516. According to De Angelis (1965 and 1966c), the model's entablature "corresponds exactly, in height and position, to the gap between the two series of stone" left by Brunelleschi, and this solution is identical to the one shown in Casa Buonarroti 50A recto, certainly by Michelangelo. As the author notes, the model displays how the *ballatoio* passageway was not to be decorated with an open loggia, but rather illuminated by four embrasures in the frieze of the imposing entablature. The attribution to Michelangelo was endorsed by Marchini (1977a), Morselli (1981) and Argan and Contardi (1990), while Ackerman (1986) rejected it.

If we are to believe Vasari (V: 353-354), Michelangelo criticized the part of the *ballatoio* built in 1514-15 because "such a great structure required something larger" than what Baccio d'Agnolo had designed. It is hard to believe that the modest solution proposed in model no. 144 would have satisfied Michelangelo's ambitious creativity: the capitals of the corner pilasters are characterized by a gaudy decoration that clashes with the elegant capitals in Casa Buonarroti 50A and 66A. Furthermore, the expedient of piercing the frieze of the entablature with embrasures to illuminate the passageway is too clumsy to be attributed to Michelangelo. Rather than a work designed by Michelangelo in 1516, this model is more likely the product of one of the artists who participated in the 1507 competition, and has since fallen into anonymity.

No. 144 underwent major restoration: much of the entablature was reconstructed and the model's "original" condition is documented by a photograph in the Kunsthistorisches Institut of Florence.   *A.N.*

soldi / 40 / cinque ce[n]toquara[n]ta / d / millesette ce[n]to setta[n]ta / 1200 / 600*; to the left of the sketch in red chalk of the drum there are other numbers that are hard to decipher.

PROVENANCE: Casa Buonarroti.

BIBLIOGRAPHY: Gotti 1875, II: 178; Berenson 1903a, no. 1420; Geymüller 1904: 34; Frey 1909-11: 84-85; Thode 1908-13, II: 139-140 and III: 41; Berenson 1938, no. 1420; Tolnay 1948: 211-212; Hartt 1950: 242; Dussler 1959: 74-75; Ackerman 1961, II: 18-19; Berenson 1961: no. 1420; Barocchi 1962a, I: 53-54; 1964a: 55-56; Barbieri and Puppi 1964a: 832-833, 1000; De Angelis d'Ossat 1965, II: 286-291; 1966c: 501-504; Bardeschi Ciulich and Barocchi 1970: 71; Tolnay 1970: 32, 211-212; Ackerman 1971: 306; Hartt 1971, no. 192-193; Saalman 1975: 374-380, 400-401; Tolnay 1975b, no. 121; Marchini 1977: 39-40, 44; Tolnay 1977: 58; Saalman 1977: 852-853; Di Stefano 1980a: 875; Tolnay 1980: 28-29, 30; Morselli 1981: 127; Berti et al. 1985: 20, 66; Rocchi et al., 1985: 89; Ackerman 1986: 295; Argan and Contardi 1990: 56.

The attribution of this sheet to Michelangelo has never been challenged, but the first scholars to make a critical analysis of these sketches did not agree as to their purpose; recently, their dating has also become open to debate. Berenson thought that the sheet illustrated the interior of a dome, in all likelihood that of the New Sacristy in S. Lorenzo. This opinion was shared by Frey, who believed he could discern the study of the drum of the dome that Michelangelo designed for the new Cappella Medici; Tolnay felt that the red chalk sketch on the verso was related to the altar of the same chapel, a hypothesis reluctantly accepted by Ackerman. However, Geymüller had already realized in 1904 that CB 50A contained preparatory studies for the drum of the dome of S. Maria del Fiore and since then, most critics have agreed with him.

As far as the chronology is concerned, the sheet has always been dated to between 1516, the year of the artist's return to Florence and of his mocking criticism of the side of the *ballatoio* built by Baccio d'Agnolo, and around 1520, the year of the rough draft of the letter written on the verso of CB 66A, which bears other studies for the same project. Following the discovery of a letter of 31 July 1507 which the *fabbricieri* at S. Maria del Fiore sent to Michelangelo, inviting him to participate in the competition for the *ballatoio*, Tolnay (1980) pointed out that the sketch on the recto of 50A could date to 1507, an opinion seconded by

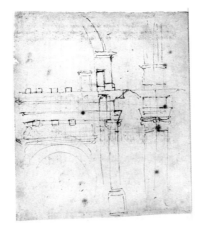

274
ANONYMOUS (formerly attributed to Antonio Manetti and to Michelangelo)
Model of the Drum and the Ballatoio of S. Maria del Fiore

Florence, Museo dell'Opera di S. Maria del Fiore, 144
One panel in white poplar, with two vertical elements added to the sides; much of the architrave is restoration work.
54.5 × 58.5 × 10 cm

BIBLIOGRAPHY: *Catalogo* 1891: 33; Poggi 1904: 59; Tosi 1927-28a: 610; *Guida* 1948: 15; De Angeli D'Ossat 1965: 290-291; 1966c:

275
MICHELANGELO BUONARROTI
Designs for the Drum and the Ballatoio of S. Maria del Fiore

Florence, Casa Buonarroti, CB 50Ar
Pen and brown ink (recto); annotations and graphic calculations in pen and brown ink and architectural sketch in red chalk (verso); the paper is torn and stained.
25.1 (left) and 24.1 (right) × 20.2 (bottom) and 19.7 (top) cm
INSCRIBED: (verso) *'el muro chava[n]done il vano della porta e delle finestre resta / resta trece[n]to cinqua[n]ta] secte braccia quadre di tre quarti grosse / a tredici soldi el braccio mo[n]ta dugie[n]to octa[n]ta lire e sedici soldi*; below the graphic calculation: *'200*

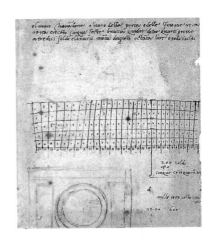

Argan and Contardi (1990), even though Tolnay himself decided in favor of the traditional dating of 1516. Indeed, there is no reason to anticipate the chronology of these studies, also because the note on the verso of 50A dates to the winter of 1519. As Bardeschi Ciulich and Barocchi (1970) revealed, the annotation refers to a room in the house in Via Mozza, and should be seen in connection with another note concerning the "widow's wall," that is, the part of a house owned by a widow which Michelangelo planned to purchase to enlarge his own (Bardeschi Ciulich and Barocchi 1970); the negotiations for this transaction took place during the winter of 1519, and since the draft of the letter on the verso of 66A is from 1520, it is plausible that the sketches on the two sheets date to 1519-20. It is a well-known fact that Michelangelo's parsimony led him to reuse, even after many years, the same sheets of paper for his personal notes. Thus, the note of 1519 and the draft of 1520 fix, in theory, straightforward *ante quem* terms, but the fact that both date to the same period suggests that these studies for the *ballatoio* were executed in 1519-20. This, however, does not exclude the possibility that the artist executed others in 1516 as well.

The most accurate analysis of 50A and 66A is the work of Saalman (1975: 374-380) who expanded upon the sound observations offered by Geymüller (1904: 34) and Thode (1908: 139-140) early in this century. Geymüller was the first to recognize that 50A was a preliminary sketch for the drum of S. Maria del Fiore and to point out that Michelangelo wanted to crown the buttresses of the passageway with statues or candelabra in correspondence with the ribs of the vault, but it was Thode who realized that, at least in the left-hand version of 50A, the architect had not planned simple pilasters but rather columns. More recently, Saalman has pointed out that 50A recto shows not two sketches, but three: the first is on the extreme right and shows a frontal view of a corner of the drum and the vault; the second is at the center of the sheet and shows a section of one of the corners of the octagon; the third consists in a series of notes at the bottom of the sheet that show in a very cursory way a frontal view of a drum window and a frieze decorated with garlands. Saalman himself later explained that the latter sketches are drawn with studied carelessness, like stenographic notes; they should not be seen in the context of the section drawn in the center of the sheet since their position does not correspond to the one that these elements should have occupied had the design shown in the section in the center of the sheet been actually realized. Finally, taking his cue from one of Geymüller's observations, Saalman noted that Michelangelo meant to move the exterior passageway to a level higher than that of the *ballatoio* built by Baccio d'Agnolo in 1514-15; it was to run above the entablature and pass through the heavy buttresses that were to be erected in correspondence to the ribs of the vault.

What are the consequences of such a project? Vasari (1877, V: 353-354) informs us that Michelangelo had criticized Baccio d'Agnolo's *ballatoio* because "such a great structure [that is, Brunelleschi's dome] required something more impressive..." Baccio had restricted himself to respecting what was set forth in the *Instruction* that Brunelleschi drew up in 1420, inspired in part by the model of 1367, but Michelangelo had doubtless understood that, time permitting, Brunelleschi would have adopted a different solution. As De Angelis d'Ossat (1965) also remarked, Michelangelo's project would have completely upset the decisions made in 1420 and partially realized by Baccio d'Agnolo. In place of the simple gallery, Buonarroti had envisioned an imposing entablature with three superimposed bands supported by the exposed "teeth" stones devised by Brunelleschi; at the corners of the drum, the entablature would have broken forward to be sustained by columns on high pedestals, crowned by composite capitals; and the cornice would have supported a gallery the corner buttresses of which would have been topped by gigantic statues—an idea that must have greatly fired the artist's imagination. Finally, as CB 66A shows, Michelangelo considered replacing the white and green marble facing of the round drum with two rectangular panels, while the window was to be inserted in a square space. If realized, this project would have ensured that the dome of S. Maria del Fiore would today be considered not only the work of Brunelleschi but also of Michelangelo, and it is easy to imagine how this idea was immensely appealing to a man of Michelangelo's ambition. In the end, nothing came of it, perhaps because of the same technical difficulties that Baccio d'Agnolo had already encountered (Saalman 1975), but more probably because the *fabbricieri* and Cardinal Giulio de' Medici were quick to realize the high cost of such an operation and its profoundly utopian implications. *A.N.*

276
Michelangelo Buonarroti
Designs for the Drum and Ballatoio of S. Maria del Fiore

Florence, Casa Buonarroti, CB no. 66A
Red chalk; the draft on the verso is penned in brown ink; there are pieces missing and stains;
watermark: Briquet 91.
27.2 (left) and 26.8 (right) × 20.8 (bottom) and 20.5 (top cm
Inscribed: (verso) *'Mons[igniore], io prego la vostra Reverendissima s[ignori]a non chome amicho o s[ervo], perché [io] non merito esser né.ll'uno né.ll'altro, ma chome omo vile, povero e macto, che facci che Bastiano venitiano pictore abi, poi che è morto Rafaello, qualche parte de' lavori di Palazo. E quando paia a Vostra S[ignori]a inn.un mio pari gictar via el servitio, penso che, ancora nel servire e' macti, che rare volte si potrebe trovare qualche dolceza, chome nelle cipolle, per mutar cibo, fa cholui che è infastidito da' chaponi. Degl'uomini di chonto ne servite el dì; prego Vostra S[ignori]a provi questo a me. El servitio fia grandissimo, e se fia gictato in me, non fia cos[ì] in Bastiano, perché son certo farà onore a Vostra S[ignori]a; e Bastiano decto è valente omo, e so farà onore a quella."*

Provenance: Casa Buonarroti.

Bibliography: Gotti 1875, II: 179; Milanesi 1875a: 413; Berenson 1903a, no. 1434; Thode 1908-13, II: 139-140 and III: 41; Frey 1909-11: 84-85; 1923, fig. V; Berenson 1938, no. 1434; Tolnay 1948: 32, 211; Hartt 1950: 242; Dussler 1959: 76; Ackerman 1961, II: 18-19; Berenson 1961, no. 1434; Barocchi 1962a, I: 54-56; Barbieri and Puppi 1964a: 833, 1000; De Angelis d'Ossat 1965, II: 286-291; 1966c: 501-503; Tolnay 1970: 32, 211; Ackerman 1971: 306; Hartt 1971, no. 194-195; Saalman 1975: 375-380; Tolnay 1975b: no. 122; Marchini 1977a: 39-40, 44; Tolnay 1977: 8-9; Di Stefano 1980a: 875; Tolnay 1980: 29-30; Morselli 1981: 127; Berti et al. 1985: 20, 66; Rocchi et al. 1985: 89; Ackerman 1986: 295; Argan and Contardi 1990: 56.

Critical analysis of 66A is much like that of 50A. Berenson (1903a) thought that it was a study for a monument, while Frey (1909-11) felt that it was another design for the dome of the New Sacristy in S. Lorenzo. Despite clear indications of a vault above the entablature, Tolnay (1948) believed that 66A pertained to an initial project for the altar of the Cappella Medici, but as early as 1908 Thode (1908) had realized that it must be linked, together with 50A, to Michelangelo's efforts to find an appropriate solution to the difficult problem of the *ballatoio* of S. Maria del Fiore.

As far as the chronology is concerned, dating ranges between 1516 (Marchini 1977a; Tolnay 1980), the year of Michelangelo's return to Florence, and, more often, around 1520, the year that the letter on the verso of the sheet was drafted (for example, Barocchi 1962a e b). In relation to this, it is worth noting that the word "questo" in the last line of the draft is written over the red chalk sketch; thus, the date of the letter merely offers a *terminus ante quem*, but for the reasons set forth in the catalog entry for 50A, a dating of 1519-20 is plausible.

The solution explored by Buonarroti in 66A, to be seen alongside the sketches on 50A, is grandiose. The project realized by Baccio d'Agnolo, perhaps in collaboration

with Nanni di Baccio Bigio, had met with Michelangelo's mocking criticism because the small open gallery seemed to be crushed under the mass of the dome. (If it is true that Nanni di Baccio Bigio worked on the project, as a little-heeded document published by Guasti [1857, doc. 347] seems to indicate, then the controversy over the gallery marks the beginning of a fierce and long-lived rivalry between Nanni and Michelangelo.) Michelangelo instead planned to modify the decoration of the drum facing and to frame each side of the octagon between two columns topped by composite capitals supporting an imposing three-banded entablature. The other aspects of the design, better documented in 50A, are discussed in that catalog entry. Here, however, it should be added that Michelangelo's original solution took its cue from and expanded upon Bramante's ideas for the dome of the Borgia tower in the Vatican, a work with which he was quite familiar as it had been erected while he was painting the frescoes for the Sistine Chapel.

In conclusion, Saalman (1977) believed that Uff. 7999A recto recalled the wooden model that Michelangelo had made upon his return to Florence, mentioned by Vasari. But the sketch, rather weak, does not offer decisive confirmation of this hypothesis. *A.N.*

The Endless Construction of St. Peter's: Bramante and Raphael

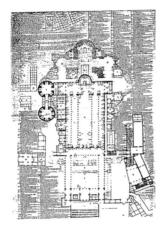

277
<small>ALPHARANUS</small>
Plan of Old St. Peter's

Vatican, Biblioteca Apostolica Vaticana
Copperplate engraving

BIBLIOGRAPHY: Mallius 1867: 34ff.; Vegius 1867: 56ff.; Alpharanus, ed. Cerrati 1914; Ruysschaert 1960: 261; Weil-Garris Brandt 1987: 83, 87, 107, fig. 3.

Apart from the drawing by Bramante in Uff. 20A (cat. no. 288), this plan by Alpharanus is the only one showing Old St. Peter's dating from the period in which it was all finally demolished. He prepared the 1589-90 engraving on the basis of two drawings dated 1571 and 1586, but only the earlier of the two is conserved in the Archivio Capitolare of St. Peter's (Alpharanus 1914, pl. 2). This illustration demonstrates that the senior canon of St. Peter's had mastered the art of architectural drawing to a certain extent, and that he continued to work especially on the hypothetical parts of the building to the west of the old basilica. When seven years after the death of Michelangelo he redrew the whole project, in the engraving he only illustrated the parts already realized, leaving out all the part near the entrance, which was always subject to dispute. Alpharanus made no effort whatsoever to settle the numerous irregularities, especially in the neighboring papal palace, and he made do with right angles, since he was mainly interested in illustrating the general shape of the whole building. If, on the one hand, he reconstructed Old St. Peter's and the atrium, while, on the other, he included the New St. Peter's, the benediction loggia and the new papal palace, he certainly must have done this to create the conditions for facing that ever pressing question, whether some part of the old and venerable building site should be left unbuilt and whether therefore it was necessary to interrupt the highly convenient connection between the new atrium and the Scala Regia. Alpharanus was certainly not against the new construction, but he knew enough about the numerous requirements that were expected of the basilica to comprehend the functional weaknesses of Michelangelo's project which lacked, for example, campaniles, sacristies and the less important spaces vital for the functioning of the Chapter. What is particularly interesting for historians of the New St. Peter's is the question of from where Alpharanus got all his information about the various parts, or from whom, given that these—the west end of the old longitudinal body and large parts of the transept—were demolished before he

came to Rome in 1544. The errors in his reproduction of both the mausoleums of late antiquity to the south prove that he did not possess any exact survey dating from the period of Bramante's activity. The plan in Uff. 4336A, executed by an assistant of Bramante and Antonio da Sangallo the Younger, shows a very different sort of western rotunda called after S. Petronilla, just before its demolition, i.e., before 1514 (Weil-Garris Brandt 1987: 83, 87, 107). Alpharanus' sources for the buildings to the west of the old transept seem to be even more unreliable, and he dedicated more attention to these in the 1571 drawing than he did in the engraving. As he himself wrote, the chapel of the Prefetto Probus, situated directly behind the apse, was already demolished at the time of the foundation of Nicholas V's choir (Alpharanus, ed. Cerrati: 52). The area to the south and to the north of Nicholas' choir, and with it, part of the Early Christian cemetery, were razed at the beginning of 1507 (Frommel 1984c: 256). There probably was a rough plan of this area dating from the period before its demolition. For the names of the monuments destroyed under Nicholas V, Alpharanus was obliged to refer to the *Liber Pontificalis*, to Maffeo Vegio, to Pietro Mallio and perhaps to hearsay. One of his most important sources for the parts demolished after 1506 was certainly his spiritual advisor, Giacomo Ercolano, to whom he referred continually and who could have encouraged him in this undertaking (Apharanus, ed. Cerrati: XVIff., XXIVff.). Ercolani had become a chorister of St. Peter's in 1505, at the age of ten, and was closely involved in all its activities until his death in 1573. He could have supplied first hand information about the history of the basilica since 1506. It does appear, however, that Alpharanus did not have any information about certain important historic events in those years, for example, the rich tombs discovered in 1507 to the west of the old apse, or the destruction of S. Petronilla no later than 1513.   *C.L.F.*

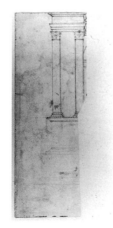

278
<small>MICHELANGELO BUONARROTI</small>
Project for the Tomb of Julius II (?)
March 1505 (?)

Paris, Louvre, Département des Arts graphiques, 722, 8026
Pencil and pen, on paper; straightedge and freehand.
20.7/23.9 × 11.4/8.1 cm

BIBLIOGRAPHY: Cordellier 1991: 43-45; Joannides 1991a: 32-42

The sheet, composed of two fragments, was identified convincingly as the earliest version so far discovered of Michelangelo's project for the tomb of Julius II. The architectural structure—with the double base course and central niche containing a sarcophagus with lion's claw feet surmounted perhaps by the body of the pope supported by angels—anticipated essential points of the project conserved in New York (cat. no 279). Consequently the sitting figure drawn on the verso of inv. 722, behind whose right side there seems to be a pilaster, could have been conceived as a statue of a prophet or saint who would

have been placed in front of the upper pedestal to the right, quite like the MMA project. This is also an explanation for the remaining repertory of figures: the Virgin Mary who hovers in the air in the upper part of the niche, and angels with thuribles in front of the adjacent pilasters. Only the lower base course still has not been decorated with figures. As in his later projects for the funerary monument, Michelangelo had already decided here on a few over-life-size statues, that is to say 3.5 Florentine *braccia* (2.05 m) high. The width of the shafts of the pilasters would therefore be about 0.5 *braccia* as in the project conserved in New York, whereas the height of the upper pedestals (ca. 2 ⅔ *braccia*) is just slightly shorter, and the design of the lower base course has been reduced. The central niche does appear to be substantially narrower. Its width of only 2 ⅓ *braccia* is just enough to contain the sarcophagus with the angels. A similar system of measurement would give an overall width of ca. 7 ⅓ *braccia* and a height of 13 *braccia* (including the jutting cornice of the order) in the area of the upper base course. These measurements correspond surprisingly well to those of the short bay in front of the apse of the drawing conserved in the Uffizi (Uff. 3A, cat. no. 280) where the span of the niche is about 7 ⅓ *braccia* and probably at least 14 *braccia* high, just enough for the funerary monument. On the other hand, the base course of the monument, which is slightly larger, would have been incompatible with the eventual pedestals of the colossal pilasters. It is rather hard to find links between the Louvre project and the one in Uff. 1A (cat. no. 282) drawn just slightly after. It is interesting to see how Michelangelo reached this first stage through the triumphal arch motif, whose projecting entablature seemed inspired by the upper level of the Belvedere Court. The elongated proportions of the pilasters (1:11) and of the niches (ca. 1:3) are Bramantesque; only the profiles appear to be less dynamic. The mausoleum was probably designed to have a hemicycle at the top, as in the MMA project, perhaps even with the semidome of the niche designed in Uff. 3A recto. In the light of both its predominantly architectural conception and the choice of the triumphal arch theme, Michelangelo could have worked on the project even with Bramante as well as with Giuliano da Sangallo, because here, as in S. Maria del Popolo, he had to pull out all his stops to find a harmonious solution for inserting the single elements of the Capella Iulia in its new setting. He probably wanted to place the papal *cantoria* on the other side of the choir opposite the pope's funerary monument in a similar position compared to the altar and *cantoria* of the Cappella Sistina.   *C.L.F.*

279
<small>MICHELANGELO BUONARROTI</small>
Project for the Tomb of Julius II
March 1505 (?)

New York, The Metropolitan Museum of Arts, Rogers Fund, 1962, no. 62.93.1
Charcoal, ink and wash on paper; torn on both sides; glued.
51 × 31.9 cm

PROVENANCE: H.W. Calmann.

BIBLIOGRAPHY: Tolnay 1975-80, I: 63, IV: 27; Hirst 1976: 375 ff.; Hirst 1989: 26; Joannides 1991a: 33-42; Echinger, Maurach 1991: 290ff. n. 289.

This drawing is most certainly one of Michelangelo's projects for the tomb of Julius II (Hirst 1976) and was recently identified as one of the preliminary drawings (Hirst 1989; Joannides 1991a). The stilistic and iconographic differences between this project and the 1513 one can, in fact, only be explained in terms of the considerable lapse of time separating them. The increase of the vertical proportions in the 1513 version suggest that another site had been chosen. In the drawing conserved in New York the base course is considerably higher and the upper level, with niches, the sarcophagus and Virgin, is much wider. Thanks to these characteristics it can be linked directly to the project recently discovered in the Louvre (cat. no. 278). Given the hypothesis that here too the statues are over-life-size, i.e. a maximum of 3.5 Florentine *braccia* (0.586 m), the shafts of the pilasters also measure ½ *braccio*, the zone of the upper pedestal is ca. 7 ⅓ *braccia* wide and therefore similar to that of the Louvre project, and the sarcophagus has the same measurements (ca. 2 *braccia* wide). With these dimensions the whole project could be inserted in the niche before the apse of Bramante's first project for St. Peter's in Uff. 3A (cat. no. 280; fig. 2, p. 403). The changes made here by Michelangelo compared to the project conserved in the Louvre are even more interesting. In this drawing he united both the lower base courses in a characteristic plinth with four side niches for statues and a central relief separating them by means of their own order of columns on consoles. In order to enlarge the central niche of the upper level he reduced the order to single block-shaped pilasters whose narrow projections seem to be inspired by the Ionic pilaster strips of the Belvedere Court, and whose details also reveal the same decidedly Quattrocento atmosphere. The upper plinths are narrower and leave more space for the sarcophagus. This left Michelangelo free to elaborate the theme of the angels raising the pope and the epiphany of the interceding Virgin Mary. Briefly, the figures acquire considerably more importance, the limits of convention are breached and it is just possible that is was the pope himself who encouraged Michelangelo to introduce these improvements. In the area of the base course, Caritas, Fides and other Virtues flank an apotheosis of Giuliano della Rovere, where the acorns introduce a new Golden Age while a prophet and a mourning(?) sibyl flank the sarcophagus of the pope in front of the upper plinths. The pilasters mark the transcendental sphere in which two angels release the pope from his tomb, two youths sprinkle holy water and incense while the Virgin and Child gaze mercifully upon his rising soul. In Sixtus IV's funerary chapel the altar was consecrated to the Virgin Mary, the apse decorated with a Virgin among the clouds by Perugino and the pope's mausoleum surrounded by the cardinal virtues (Frommel 1977b: 31ff.). As the figures in the side niches indicate, the funerary monument should have spread out three-dimensionally, in contrast to what was indicated in the Louvre project. The project conserved in New York therefore can be interpreted as a prelude to the project of April 1505, in which the tomb became completely detached from the wall.   C.L.F.

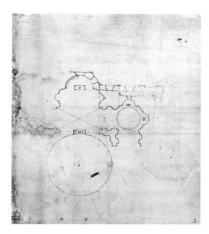

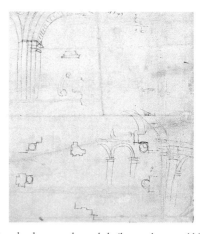

280

DONATO BRAMANTE (?) and ANTONIO DI PELLEGRINO for Bramante
Projects for St. Peter's
March 1505 (?)

Florence, Galleria degli Uffizi, Gabinetto Disegni e Stampe, Uff. 3A
Pen and ink on paper; stylus impressions; straightedge and compass (recto and verso), freehand (verso).
24.7 (28) × 23.4 (23.7) cm

PROVENANCE: Papers of Antonio da Sangallo the Younger (?)

BIBLIOGRAPHY: Geymüller, 1875-80: 150, T. 53, fig. 2, 3; Jovanovits 1877: 3ff.; Wolff Metternich 1972: 36, fig. 7ff. d; Frommel 1973, II: 330 n. 25; 1974a: 528; 1977b: 56; Wolff Metternich and Thoenes 1987: 58ff.; Hubert 1988: 200ff; Saalman 1989: 133ff.; Hubert 1990: 233.

The traditional explanation for this drawing as a project for St. Peter's coming from Bramante's workshop, was recently contested by Günther and Hubert. In the plan on the recto, Antonio di Pellegrino, so far known exclusively as Bramante's assistant (Frommel 1974a), evidently developed the ideas of the master. The project probably goes back to the earliest phases of the design when Bramante was still reelaborating Rossellino's project measured in Florentine *braccia* (0.586 m or 2.623 *palmi*) and had decided to place the high altar as it is in that project, under the choir arch. The span of the central nave measuring 40 *braccia* or 105 Roman *palmi* had to be kept as a premise for the next stage of the design (see the table of measurements, p. 422). The radius of the dome, measuring 33 *braccia* here (86.6 *palmi*)—still about 8 *palmi* smaller than the one that was actually built—corresponds roughly to the distance between the center of St. Peter's tomb and the western perimeter of the nave of the old Basilica. St Peter's tomb should consequently have been sited in the center of the space under the dome and the external perimeter of the apse should have corresponded to Nicholas' choir (fig. 2 p. 403).

The stylus impressions reveal that a 20 *braccia* grid, equal to half the width of the central nave, is the basis of the whole plan—and this, simple scheme, too is an important piece of evidence for proving that the project in Uff. 3A was drawn at the start of the design process. On the basis of this, the overall width of the project in Uff. 3A recto would be ca. 160 *braccia* (420 *palmi*) and the distance from the center of the dome to the external wall of the apse ca. 100 *braccia*. Perhaps Bramante, like Rossellino, began his design, and that of the elevation as well, from simple relations like 1:2 (fig. 23 p. 422). He achieved the extension of the diameter of the dome from a span of 40 *braccia*, as established by Rossellino, to 66 *braccia* (173 *palmi*) by means of the completely new invention of diagonal faced buttressing piers and the relative repositioning of the pier arches 13 *braccia* respectively (34 *palmi*), this idea being inspired by the typology of octagonal crossins. It is significant that he calculated such large diagonal faces for the

piers that between the angled pilasters there would be room for a niche of about 5 *braccia* (13 *palmi*) for the pope's throne, which perhaps should have been placed—as in the Cappella Sistina—to the left of the altar, that is to say, in front of the southwest pier. Considering that the width of the pier arches is only 4 *braccia* (2.34 m), it is tempting to believe that he was designing a dome without a drum like the one in Nicholas V's project. The enlarging of the dome would have shortened the choir arm considerably compared to the one in Nicholas' project. The apse with the second altar and with a suggestion of circular choir stalls was probably already designated here as Julius II's funerary chapel. Neither the bay of the cross vault nor the probably barrel-vaulted bay in front of the apse would have been large enough to contain the freestanding mausoleum designed by Michelangelo in April 1505 with its 12 × 18 *braccia* dimensions. It would therefore be more correct to link together the Michelangelo projects conserved in Paris and New York which are evidently the first ones and still plan a mausoleum up against the wall, in one of the two niches of the niche before the apse (fig. 2 p. 403). The opposite niche would have been suitable for containing Sixtus IV's tomb and the tribune for the choristers. Antonio di Pellegrino's drawing still reveals the lines of the apse, drawn with a stylus, at first much more to the east, and the fact that he introduced the choir with the niches as an afterthought, when, perhaps, he had examined the early Michelangelesque projects. In his final version he only drew just over a quarter of the quincunx and the polygonal apse, while he still did not have clear ideas about the outer construction. It was probably Bramante himself who sketched both the alternatives for the exterior structure: a smaller one, with the same order of about 4 *braccia* (10.5 *palmi*) as the interior structure and which followed the shape of the space of the secondary dome, and a larger one, with giant pilasters of about 6 *braccia* (15.7 *palmi*) even greater than the 12-*palmi* order of the final project, which could therefore in no case be compatible with a lower building. This second alternative would have already allowed for the corner sacristies, the corner towers and perhaps even the vestibules like those in the projects in Uff. 104A verso (cat. no. 281) and Uff. 1A. Like the drawing on the verso, perhaps there should have been a longitudinal body with 20 *braccia* wide arches and ca. 8-*braccia* pilasters connected to the quincunx of the domes. With five equal bays the basilica would have reached the same length, 276 *braccia* (724 *palmi*), as that of the project for Nicholas V (fig. 23).

On the verso Antonio di Pellegrino had originally drawn a slightly smaller crossing pier for the dome (ca. 17 *braccia*) while he had only engraved the dome itself with a diameter of about 56 *braccia* (146 *palmi*). The enlargement of the dome was elaborated arithmetically, like on the recto, by bringing each of the pier arches 8 *braccia* further back. If this dome had to be kept concentric with respect to Rossellino's square, it would have included the whole early Christian apse. Since the pier was related to a secondary dome, there must have been a quincuncial system similar to the one on the recto, only smaller. But Bramante had rejected this first modest idea right from the start, so the remaining sketches, drawn probably by himself, illustrated his reflections on how to unite the quincuncial system on the recto to a considerably larger longitudinal body something like the Basilica of Maxentius: in the right-hand variation showing three-quarter columns, and in the left, a more mature version, with full columns. Even the 36-*braccia* span of the triumphal arch, the 55-*braccia* span of the longitudinal body and the 20-*braccia* span of the arches correspond to this version. Compared to the recto, the triumphal arch is 4 *braccia* smaller, while the crossing pier is consequently reinforced. The sketches of the elevation included on the verso illustrate a Corinthian-like order in the central nave with a projecting entablature surmounted by cross vaults with lunettes for windows, and in the side aisle, arches over pilasters, a simple cornice with a lunetted cross vault on top. In other details of the plan Bramante extended the central nave even further and substituted the columns with pilasters. Another preliminary drawing of the elevation shows the consequences for the spaces of the secondary domes. The sketches of a C-shaped volute and a shortened base (?) could have been drawn for another context. If Antonio di Pellegrino drew on the recto the premises for Michelangelo's positioning the tombs against the wall, while he was occupied with the design of the basilica, it is probable that this drawing too was executed in March 1505.   *C.L.F.*

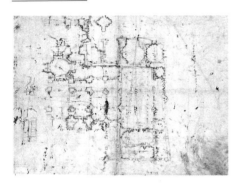

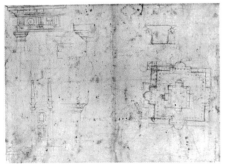

281
Donato Bramante
Survey of the Plan of the Diocletian Baths (recto)
*Sketch for the Siting of the New Basilica of
St. Peter's in a Peristyle Shaped Palace* (verso)
Late spring or early summer of 1505 (?)

Florence, Galleria degli Uffizi, Gabinetto Disegni e Stampe
Uff. 104A
Sanguine on paper; freehand.
40/41.6 × 52.9/54.2 cm
Inscribed: (recto) *il tutto palmi 330* (written by G. da Sangallo).

Provenance: Papers of Giuliano da Sangallo (?)

Bibliography: Geymüller 1875-80: 191, T. 18, fig. 1; D. Frey 1915: 11ff.; Förster 1956: 279; Bruschi 1969a: 619ff.; Wolff Metternich 1972: 66ff., fig. 124; Bruschi 1977: 258ff.; Wolff Metternich and Thoenes 1987; Frommel 1989e: 161-168.

It appears that the survey of the plan of the Diocletian Baths on the recto of this sheet was drawn there by

Bramante himself, perhaps with the aid of Giuliano da Sangallo, whose writing can be recognized inside the great peristyle. In fact, the more or less contemporary projects drawn in Uff. 1A and Uff. 8A (cat. nos. 282, 287) prove how well both the architects knew the wall constructions of the *thermae*. The left half of the verso with the details of the elevation of the Diocletian Baths and a Doric entablature perhaps drawn at the same time. In the center of the right half there is a centrally planned building closely linked to the one in Uff. 1A, with equally long transept arms, comparable corner towers and vestibules, and such similar characteristics are difficult to find in any other project of the Renaissance. The arms of the transept are, however, designed with apses on the outside as well. The area within the arms is much smaller and therefore substantially closer to the drawing in Uff. 3A recto (cat. no. 280). This could therefore be one of the lost intermediate drawings where Bramante had already taken into consideration Michelangelo's freestanding monument, but had not yet perfected the remainder of the plan, as he was to do in the ones in Uff. 1A and Uff. 7945A recto (cat. nos. 282, 283). The body of the construction (without the transept) could therefore have been of the same width as that drawn in Uff. 3A recto (ca. 420 *palmi*). The adjacent courtyard would therefore have extended over a ca. 1,150-*palmi* wide area, spreading north to the Belvedere Court, already under construction, and west, to the eastern wall of the Sala Regia. If a larger body was considered, the lower courtyard of the Belvedere and the distance from the Benediction Loggia would have been relatively shorter. The courtyard, anyhow, with its enormous rooms probably distributed over several floors, could have substituted the old papal palace. Its arches supported by pilasters, counting fifteen per side, would have had bays of at least 53-60 *palmi* corresponding to the articulation of the basilica. Some enormous exedrae would have corresponded to the apses of the church. The outside of the building toward St. Peter's Square would have been equipped with impressive corner towers, while a large central projection could have been designed to contain a benediction loggia. This drawing exemplifies Bramante's intent to revive the majesty of ancient Rome and to associate the Vatican with the imperial baths, even though he had little chance of convincing the traditionalist pope.   *C.L.F.*

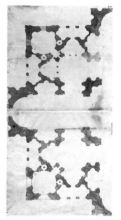

282
Donato Bramante
Presentation Drawing of the Plan
Summer of 1505 (?)

Florence, Galleria degli Uffizi, Gabinetto Disegni e Stampe,
Uff. 1A
Parchment, trimmed on all sides, lines in dark brown ink, light ocher watercolor, occasional incised lines, some columns added in sanguine.
53.8/54.4 × 110.5/111 cm
Inscribed: (recto) *Bramante Arch. & Pit:* (Vasari); (verso) *Pianta di Sto pietro di mano di bramante che non ebbe efetto* (Antonio da

Sangallo the Younger, after 1527); *sto pietro di mano di bramante* (Antonio da Sangallo the Younger, before 1527?).

Provenance: Papers of Antonio da Sangallo; Vasari's *Libro de' Disegni.*

Bibliography: Geymüller 1875-80: 165ff.; Freckmann 1965: 56-59; Bruschi 1969a: 546ff., 885; Wolff Metternich 1972: 35, fig. 1f; Thoenes 1975: 77-97; Thoenes 1982; 1988; Saalman 1989: 56-59; Wolff Metternich and Thoenes 1987: 13ff.; Hubert 1988: 195-221; Thoenes 1990: 38-55; Hubert 1990: 228ff.; Thoenes 1990-92: 193ff.

After Julius II had commissioned a freestanding mausoleum from Michelangelo at the latest in April 1505, Bramante had to adapt his project or, at least, the arm of the choir to the new requirements. He must have developed in the same way as the ones in Uff. 7945A (cat. no. 283) and Uff. 20A (cat. no. 288). In the end Bramante finally achieved the famous parchment project, which is so like the successive project detail in Uff. 7945A recto (cat. no. 283) that the measurements could be the same. If the width of the dome's pier arches is still taken to be 105 *palmi*, the bays of the secondary arches as 57.5 *palmi* and the width of the shafts of the pilasters as 10 *palmi*, then the arms of the transept reach a length of 120 *palmi*. The half distance—60 *palmi*—would therefore have served as a module for the whole plan (fig. 8 p. 408)—only 7.6 *palmi* more compared to the drawing in Uff. 3A (cat. no. 280). Two and half modules are sufficient to reach the axis of the areas of the secondary domes, four modules for the axis of the chapels in the transept arms, five for the external limit of the body and six for the external limit of the transept arms. In the latter two measurements of the plan drawn with little precision and perhaps even slightly distorted, there are deviations of ca. 5-7 *palmi*, in such a way that the external construction becomes ca. 610 *palmi* long or ca. 735 *palmi* including the transept arms. There are however elements to support the hypothesis that Bramante had laid down the symbolic measurement of 700 *palmi* as the maximum internal distance between apse and apse, a measurement which was to be given to the external construction of the block in Uff. 8A (cat. no. 287) and perhaps already to that in Uff. 7945A recto (cat. no. 283). Every enlargement of the measurements would have required the moving of the Obelisk and would have threatened the Cappella Sistina (fig. 6 p. 406). On the other hand, the slight deviations of the modular system, for example in the bays measuring only 57.5 *palmi*, do not upset this module. On the contrary, they show how Bramante moved from simple ideal measurements in the first phase of the project to his more mature period—the reason why equally simple modules cannot be found in later projects. Geymüller's estimates are extraordinarily close to these results, inasmuch as he had already calculated the width of the pier arches according to Nicholas' choir and the old basilica (Geymüller 1875-80: 165ff., T.4,7,12). The fact that Geymüller took a scale of 1:150 into consideration, shows that he had already recognized the relationship between the system of measurement and the size of the parchment of ca. 2.5 × 5 *palmi*, which had been examined in detail by Thoenes (1982 and 1990). In any case, in none of the three alternatives did Geymüller arrive at a 60-*palmi* module since he did not orient his measurements on the basis of the plan in Uff. 7945A recto, but started from the slightly erroneous width of the pier arches and the secondary arches. The combination of a 60-*palmi* module with a scale of 1:150 is confirmed by the fact that it is therefore possible to place on the plan the same grid in *palmi* with 5-*palmi* wide squares as in Uff. 20A (cat. no. 288), while the squares of the drawing in Uff. 7945A correspond to 2.5 *palmi*. Each of these squares would therefore have had a side of 2/150 of a *palmo* or 2 *minuti* (3.7 mm), and the most important measurements of the plan would be coincident with the squares. Compared to the plan in Uff. 3A recto (cat. no. 280) here Bramante enlarged the area of the arch in front of the apse to provide a space where he could have positioned without difficulty Michelangelo's great mausoleum measuring 31.5 × 47 *palmi* at the ground floor. In applying the extension of the choir arm to the other arms, Bramante succeeded in emphasizing even more the symbolic shape of the Greek cross which he utilized moreover for the enlarging of the secondary domes and the corner towers. Between these and the arms of the choir he inserted three-bay vestibules as he had perhaps already suggested in the drawing in Uff. 3A recto. By moving the pier arches on all sides back by 6 *palmi* he enlarged the diameter of the dome (fig. 9 p. 409), bringing it to 185 *palmi*. With a side of 67.5 *palmi* the square of the crossing piers for the dome was relatively reinforced as well, so Bramante felt he could enlarge the niches considerably and give the plan that unique effect in the whole of the history of architecture of a space that expands and erodes the wall masses. The numerous analogies with the design in Uff. 7945A recto confirm the hypothesis that here, too, Bramante wanted to place the crossing piers of the dome on the corners of the crossing of Nicholas' project, and therefore still keep the altar and St. Peter's tomb at ca. 3 meters west of the center of the dome (fig. 9 p. 409). The building would have thus respected the Cappella Sistina and the rectangular arms of the transept would have arrived at about 100 *palmi* from the entrance wall of Old St. Peter's. Since the Obelisk—according to Sangallo's drawing in Uff. 119A verso (Frommel 1964: 20)—was 307 *palmi* away from the transverse axis of the new building, it would have been out of danger. To give it a worthy setting Bramante would either have had to move it or to create a niche-like recess in front of the southwest tower. As in Uff. 3A and on the final project (figs. 15-16 p. 415-416) the elevation would probably have been oriented toward a ratio of 1:2 so that the arcades would have reached a height of about 118 *palmi*, the arms of the transept about 215 *palmi*, and the space of the dome would have been about 440 *palmi* high (fig. 7 p. 407). The external order with its ca. 8-*palmi* pilasters was considerably smaller; it was probably similar to the one impressed on the medal where the apses look like adjacent semi-domes. There are some problems about reconstructing the vestibules whose arches with a span of about 20 *palmi*, supported by 56-*palmi* high pilasters, would have a ratio of at least 1:2.5—a defect which Bramante seems to have remedied in the drawing in Uff. 7945A recto. The reconstruction as a centrally planned building is supported both by the picture on the medal and by those in Uff. 104A (cat. no. 281) and Uff. 8A drawn by Giuliano da Sangallo (cat. no. 287). The extension into a longitudinal body raises irresolvible problems especially as regards the blind arches in front of the apse. Moreover the connection with a part of the old longitudinal building proposed by Wolff Metternich and Thoenes is not easy to reconcile with the atmosphere of classical-style grandeur reigning in those years. Probably there was a plan, as in numerous later projects (cat. nos. 286, 287, 306, 307) to demolish the Sala Regia and the Palazzo Innocenzo VIII and to enlarge the Benediction Loggia to the whole length of the east side. Possibly Bramante even wished to link the palace with the northern campanile by means of a sort of Scala Regia, which would have run along the west end of the Cappella Sistina. When the pope at the beginning of September 1505 ordered Bramante to continue the Benediction Loggia (Frommel 1976: 92), he could have taken into consideration the project on the medal so very similar to the one in Uff. 1A. In any case, the latest date for the project elaborated in Uff. 1A can only be the summer of 1505. *C.L.F.*

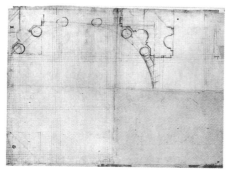

283
DONATO BRAMANTE
Studies for the Plan of the Area of the Dome
(recto)
Studies for the Plan and Elevation of a Fountain
(verso)
Summer of 1505 (?)

Florence, Galleria degli Uffizi, Gabinetto Disegni e Stampe, Uff. 7495A
Sanguine on paper (missing corner recently integrated); straightedge and compass, freehand (recto); freehand (verso): 2.5 *palmi* grid drawn in ink (recto).
42.8/43.3 × 57.3/57.8 cm
INSCRIBED: (verso) *Verius medices camb.f quod ingentem civium cum pl discordiam sua virt sedaverit cor donatus est; smtr [?]* [S. Maria in Trastevere?]; *con sant ants [?] Conventus Santi Antonii?]* (perhaps written by Bramante himself).

PROVENANCE: Papers of Antonio da Sangallo (?)

BIBLIOGRAPHY: Geymüller 1875-80: 188ff., T. 8(Bl.J); Förster 1956: 241ff.; Bruschi 1969a: 889; Wolff Metternich 1975: 38, fig. 13ff.; Wolff Metternich and Thoenes 1987: 94ff.; Thoenes 1982: 85; Hubert 1988: 211ff; Saalman 1989: 116, 124ff.; Thoenes 1990-92: 442ff.

The detail design on the recto is directly linked to the plan in Uff. 1A (cat. no. 282) and offers, thanks to the 2 ½ *palmi* grid and the hint of the crossing from Nicholas' project, important sources for reconstructing the parchment project. As in Uff. 3A recto (cat. no. 280), Uff. 20A (cat. no. 288) and on the final project (figs. 14-16 p. 414-416) the span of the pier arch measures 105 *palmi*, while the width of the choir in Nicholas' project is 110 *palmi* as in Uff. 20A, or almost 42 Florentine *braccia*. Here Bramante took an important step toward his first executive project. He reinforced the crossing pier of the dome bringing it now to a side length of 72.5 *palmi*, moving the pier arches 5 *palmi* outward and separating with a corner the pilasters on the diagonal faces of the piers from those of the pier arches.
Moreover he placed columns with a diameter of ca. 12 *palmi* in front of the diagonals that reinforced the mass of the piers even more.
By moving the pier arches he enlarged the diameter of the dome to 195 *palmi* and exploited the reinforcement of the pier mass in order to enlarge the secondary dome as well to a diameter of 117.5 *palmi*—nearly 24 *palmi* more than the one in Uff. 1A. Consequently he would have had to move the corner towers diagonally outward, so that they would have emerged ca. 30-35 *palmi* from the rest of the building, as shown on the medal.
The enlargement of the square of the piers and the secondary domes would have been advantageous especially for the vestibules, whose width would have increased from 90 *palmi* to about 146 *palmi*.
On the image of the medal Bramante substituted their arcades with open columns whose intercolumniation depended on a ratio of about 1:2. In this way, however, the fabric—from tower to tower, that is to say, without the apses—would have had a length of about 700 *palmi* and would not have taken into account either the Cappella Sistina or the Obelisk (fig. 9 p. 409). The project would therefore have come slightly nearer to the centralized plan of Giuliano (Uff. 8A, cat. no. 287). The enlargement

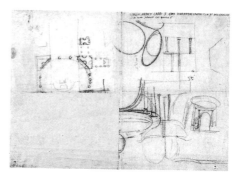

of the secondary domes would have required the reduction of the arms of the areas of the secondary domes. A further explanation of this remarkable modification to the plan in Uff. 1A could have been the pope's desire to give more importance to, and to isolate, the Capella Papalis.
Originally Bramante placed the columns directly in front of the external pilasters of the diagonal faces of the piers. Only this large intercolumniation would justify the lightly traced columns underneath the western pier arches which would have formed a crown of columns around the Capella Magna. It appears from their final position in the corner of the obtuse angle of the pilasters and from their greater diameter of about 12 *palmi*, that Bramante decided not to make them depend anymore on the pilasters. While the order in Uff. 1A, placed just on pedestals, could have reached the impost at a height of about 150 *palmi*, the columns, like in the final project (fig. 15 p. 415) with their 12-*palmi* shafts, would have had to stand without any pedestals. In any case, on the southwestern pier they flank a podium with several steps which continues into the niche and would have been able to contain the pope's throne, as is actually shown in the sketch of the elevation on the verso. Five steps lead to the corridor behind the right column which are large enough for the passage of the assisting priests.
Two little lines reveal that Bramante thought about creating a similar set of steps to the left without modifying fundamentally the shape of the niche.
The light lines between the columns of the northwestern pier and under the adjacent arch could hint at the cardinals' seats in the "Quadratura" of the Capella Papalis. The enlarging of the external pilaster behind the right column of the southwestern pier to 12 *palmi* is so unprecise that it does not possess the same importance as the emphatically elaborated width of the 10-*palmi* shaft of the pilaster. Bramante did however hint at enlarging the inside of the two northern pier arches and the relative pilaster to 12 *palmi*, thus allowing the columns to continue under the pier arches. In the plan on the verso Bramante started from the Constantinian Basilica, St. Peter's altar, the transept and the central nave. He indicated with a small circle the altar at the center for the new area of the dome. The tomb would therefore have been once again in the center like in the design in Uff. 3A recto. The rectangle behind it, which has no equivalent in Old St. Peter's, could now indicate the position of the future high altar which corresponds more or less to the present one. The new central nave transept are slightly larger than the ones in the old basilica.
In the same way, the columns positioned between and in front of the pilasters of the nave and certainly coming from the old central nave, could no longer be found in their original position. As in the drawing in Uff. 3A, only the jutting pilasters of the dome piers correspond to the inner perimeter of the old central nave, so that the arches of the dome would have a width of 105 *palmi* as in Uff. 3A and in Uff. 1A. In the smaller square of the pier Bramante returned to the idea in Uff. 1A if not to even Uff. 3A. The narrower pilasters (ca. 25 *palmi* wide) of the central nave and their shorter distance from the dome pier compared to the recto also recall the design in Uff. 3A. Bramante gave up the great order inside the nave. Since the colonnade of the nave of Old St. Peter's was ca. 58 *palmi* high and some columns were engaged, it is unlikely that he was

considering arcades but rather that this colonnade would have supported some galleries. The Capella Papalis with its huge circle of columns would therefore have been isolated in an even more drastic way from the rest of the basilica compared to the design on the recto. Comparing the dimensions of Old St. Peter's, the longitudinal body would therefore have covered five bays as it did in Uff. 3A. Bramante first created a diagonal face on the pier in the side aisle for a secondary dome, but then it appears he gave up the idea of a quincuncial system.

He left the shape of the transept apses undecided; however, he could have continued the arms of the transept with colonnades creating ambulatories like those in Uff. 8A verso (cat. no. 287).

The decision to abandon the great order which ran all round and the strict separation between the area of the dome and the arms of the transept brought him, on the left-hand side of the sheet, to the idea of bringing the giant columns right up to the ring of the dome. Together with the pedestal and the entablature these would have reached a height of ca. 220 *palmi* and a diameter of at least 16 *palmi* (3.34 m).

Thus Bramante amplified the triumphal arch theme which he had already used inside the Tempietto of S. Pietro in Montorio, and consequently further magnified the tomb of St. Peter, the Capella Papalis and the pope's throne which seems to be suggested once again in the niche of the southwestern crossing pier.

The sketches for an octagonal fountain between the two drawings for the area of the dome could have been executed for the Belvedere Statue Court whose water supplies had to be carried up by means of communicating pipes. The fountain of Piazza S. Maria in Trastevere had already been built by Bramante at the time of Alexander VI. Even though the writing on the right shows the funerary inscription of Verio Medici in SS. Annunziata, the handwriting can be more easily ascribed to Bramante than to Giuliano or Francesco da Sangallo (cf. Saalman 1989). Bramante could have copied the heroic text, for example, from Giuliano da Sangallo.

The sketches for St. Peter's on the verso are the first examples of a new fundamental approach to the whole project which the pope must have ordered no later than the autumn of 1505 and which do not yet seem to have affected Giuliano da Sangallo in Uff. 8A recto in any way whatsoever. Evidently the pope had unexpectedly revived the significance of the centuries-old identity of the Basilica of St. Peter, its Latin cross, its holy ground, the demarcation and highlighting of the Capella Papalis and even of its precious columns.   *C.L.F.*

284
<small>CARADOSSO (CRISTOFORO FOPPA) (?)</small>
Foundation Medal for the Laying of the Cornerstone
Summer of 1505 (?)

Bronze
⌀ 5.5 × 5.6 cm
<small>INSCRIBED:</small> (recto) IVLIVS. LIGVR. PAPA. SECVNDVS - MCCCCCVI (round the portrait of Julius II); (verso) TEMPLI. PETRI. INSTAVRACIO. VATICANVS. M[ONS] (round the project for St. Peter's).

BIBLIOGRAPHY: Venuti 1744: 49; Geymüller 1875-80: 258ff. n. 67ff., 70ff.; Armand 1879-87, I: 68ff., III, 36ff.; Hill 1911: 563ff.; 1930: 171 n. 660; Weiss: 170; Bruschi 1969a: 892ff.; Wolff Metternich and Thoenes 1987: 30ff.; Hubert 1988: 196, 208, 215; Borsi 1989: 306; Krauss and Thoenes 1991-92: 193ff.

The first indications of the existence of a foundation medal for St. Peter's date to 18 April 1506, when the pope laid two gold and ten bronze medals in a terra-cotta pot in the foundations (Frommel 1976, doc. 26). Since the medal shows at what point the design was by summer 1505, Bramante had probably already finished it by then. It is also likely that in November 1505 the pope sent the medal together with his first letters to potential sponsors of the new building (op. cit., 88ff.). In 1510 he gave Eleonora Gonzaga a set of five gold coins: apart from the aforementioned one of St. Peter's, there were probably coins commemorating the Belvedere Court, the church of S. Maria at Loreto, the Rocca of Civitavecchia and the Palazzo dei Tribunali (Hill 1930, n. 224ff., 227, 868, 872, 876; Frommel 1977b: 55). These medals were not therefore coined just for the laying of the foundation stone because Julius did in fact have at least three different versions made for the foundation of St. Peter's (Armand; Hill). According to Buchardus the foundation was commemorated by the medal in which the pope is dressed in his cope (Hill 1930, n. 660), as on the said medal for the Belvedere (Hill 1930, n. 876). The last dash of the numbers 1506 indicating the year has been placed there in an abbreviated form as if it had been added at the last minute. When Venuti (often unreliable in other circumstances) mentioned two versions with the date 1505, where the pope was shown "*cum camaleucio sine stola*" on one and "*cum camaleucio, et pluviali nonnulis figuris adpositis ornato*" on the other, he probably meant the two large versions with the year 1506 (Venuti 1744, V: 49, V; Hill 1930: 171). Vasari wrote about at least three medals on which Caradosso designed Bramante's project: "with two campaniles which put the facade in the middle, as can be seen in the medals which Julius II and Leo X coined, made by that excellent goldsmith Caradosso, who was unequaled in his art of coinmaking as can be seen in the lovely medal of Bramante that the made" (Vasari, ed. Milanesi 1878-85, IV: 161). The two large versions of the foundation medal have been always attributed unanimously to Caradosso. But Caradosso was only summoned from Milan to Mantua in September 1505 and it is unlikely that he reached Rome before the end of the year (Hill 1911: 563ff.). It is therefore necessary to reconsider whether the first version with the skullcap can be attributed to Caradosso, or rather to the same master who, about two years earlier had designed the excellent medal depicting the Belvedere Court with the portrait of Julius II very like this one and with very similar capital letters (Hill 1930, n. 876). In this case, in the second version Caradosso would have just substituted the previous figure of the pope with the more detailed and representative portrait of the pontiff in the stole (Hill 1930: n. 659).   *C.L.F.*

285
<small>CARADOSSO (CRISTOFORO FOPPA)</small>
Commemorative Medal in Honor of Bramante
1506 (?)

Florence, Museo Nazionale del Bargello
Bronze
4.2 × 4.4 cm
<small>INSCRIBED:</small> (recto) *BRAMANTES ASDRVBALDINVS* (round head of Bramante); (verso) *FIDELITAS LABOR* (round allegory and project for St. Peter's).

BIBLIOGRAPHY: Geymüller 1875-80: 260ff., n. 75, pl. 2 n. 11; Hill 1930; 170ff. n. 657; Wolff Metternich and Thoenes 1987: 31; Borsi 1989, fig. p. 18, 304.

Without doubt, this medal is identical to the one of Bramante described by Vasari, who noted that the same project was pictured on the foundation medals minted under Julius II and Leo X. It was probably not designed until after the first two versions of the foundation medal. Though Caradosso arrived in Rome only in the late autumn of 1505 and Bramante had already modified his project fundamentally in April 1506, the medal could have been made sometime during the winter of 1505-06. Since St. Peter's was shown from above, as in the sketch of the model (cat. no. 292), all the essential characteristics still correspond to the project of the foundation medal, for example, the apses to the east hinted at above the main portal, the lateral vestibules, the secondary domes and the arrangement of the dome and the campaniles. The only differences can be seen on the entrance facade where instead of the side niche there is a blind pilaster—the only point that corresponds with Agostino Veneziano's engraving, which copies the foundation medal in every other aspect (Wolff Metternich and Thoenes 1987: 32, fig. 27). Moreover the drum of the eastern apse occupies the whole of the upper level so that apsidal roof and lantern are crushed against the pediment in an unconvincing way. The reproduction of the main dome and its drum is instead more plausible. The lateral apses are evidently hidden. The project can be more or less enclosed within a square and this makes its proportions over vertical, perhaps because the size of the allegory left little space on the medal. Only in the compact and vertical proportions does the illustration correspond better to the final project of April 1506 than the foundation medal which is generally more reliable. All these differences contribute to the doubts about the attribution of the first version of this medal to Caradosso. The allegory is sitting on a folding chair, and thanks to her compass, ruler and the plumb line on which her foot is resting, she can be identified as Architecture. The plumb line moreover could even refer to the sphere of fortune. The virtues of Reliability and Diligence, without which good architecture is impossible, figure only as an accompanying inscription. The figure of Architecture recalls antiquity not just in her position, but in her close-fitting dress, the folds and ribbons, as well as the position of the head, and brings to mind the allegories on the contemporary tomb of the Sforza by Andrea Sansovino in S. Maria del Popolo. Even the naked torso of the more or less sixty-two-year-old Bramante, the only reliable portrait we have of him, is done *all'antica*. Both the name and place of birth, Monte Asdrualdo in the Marche, have been Latinized here.

A much poorer copy of this masterly version (in which Bramante himself could have had a hand in creating) was minted—perhaps after his death—indicating Bramante as a native of Castel Durante, like Serlio (Geymüller 1875-80: 260ff. n. 77, pl. 2, n. 10; Wolff Metternich and Thoenes 1987: 31). Leo X's medal of 1513-14 seems to derive from the elongated and laterally truncated illustration of the project on the verso of the first medal of Bramante.   *C.L.F.*

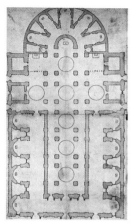

286
FRA GIOCONDO
Presentation Drawing of the Plan
Fall of 1505 (?)

Florence, Galleria degli Uffizi, Gabinetto Disegni e Stampe, Uff. 6A
Brown-black ink, yellow-brown wash, on paper.
91.7-91.8 × 49.9-50.3 cm
INSCRIBED: (verso) *Opinione e disegnio Di fraiocondo per santo pietro Di roma* (A. da Sangallo).

PROVENANCE: Antonio da Sangallo the Younger; Vasari's *Libro de' Disegni*; Mariette; Seroux d'Agincourt.

BIBLIOGRAPHY: Vasari 1878-85, V: 266ff.; Seroux d'Agincourt 1824-35, I: 147; Geymüller 1875-80: 263ff., T. 41, fig. 2; Wolff Metternich 1972: 35, fig. 3; Ragghianti Collobi 1974: 124; Frommel 1977b: 55; Wolff Metternich and Thoenes 1987: 52ff.; Fontana 1986: 435ff.

The inscription by Sangallo—who was in a position to know—guarantees this project as being by Fra Giocondo. The design was probably elaborated after his return from France where his presence was documented on 8 May 1505, but before he was called to the Republic of Venice at the start of 1506 (Fontana). In a letter of 1507 he stated that he preferred Venice in spite of his undertakings in Paris and the pope's summons: "Having means from the Parisians, they put pressure on me to stay; and on the other hand, being called by the Pope, I just left everything and came here." Since it is unlikely that the complex specific and functional characteristics of the new building were only sent him by writing, and a letter does not exclude a journey to Rome, it is probable that he made a brief visit. Fra Giocondo must, however, have realized early on that working alongside Bramante he would never have had any real chances of expressing himself. Like Bramante and Giuliano, he too started from the old basilica, including just a small part of the choir of Nicholas V. If the diameter of the domes of the central nave is 110 *palmi* and the longitudinal body has more or less the same width of about 100 *palmi* as in Old St. Peter's and the other projects, then the longitudinal three-aisle fabric equals Old St. Peter's exterior width of 300 *palmi* (fig. 11 p. 411). A width of only ca. 60 *palmi* for the nave (Wolff Metternich and Thoenes) would not have been up to the pope's expectations. By placing St. Peter's tomb at the center of the Latin cross, the atrium and the presumed Benediction Loggia would arrive at the eastern wing of

Pio II's Benediction Loggia. With an overall extension of ca. 800 × 1550 *palmi* (179 × 346 m) the new building would have meant the destruction of the Cappella Sistina and about half of the old papal palace since it would have been a size comparable to Sangallo's great projects in the years 1514-1519 (cat. nos. 306, 316). One doubt about the possibility of building such a project arises first of all from the enormous area of the choir which would have penetrated into the Vatican hillside about 90 meters more than Nicholas' choir did. Even though Fra Giocondo started from the fundamental design of the quincunx system and certainly knew Bramante's medal project, he leaned chiefly toward Venetian and French prototypes. The example with the greatest similarity to the nucleus of his project is the church of S. Salvatore in Venice, built just slightly later by Spaventa. The U-shaped narthex with its chapels recalls St. Mark's in Venice, while the elongated proportions of the longitudinal body, the transept with its portals flanked by towers and the deambulatory of the choir with a crown of chapels are inspired by French cathedrals. If the pilaster shafts were ca. *22 palmi* wide then Fra Giocondo certainly calculated a higher order and consequently a steeper central nave than Bramante and Giuliano had done—another example of the influence of French cathedrals. He probably planned to build galleries over the narrow arcades, which would have prompted Bramante's presumed galleries in the drawings in Uff. 7945A verso, in Uff. 8A recto and on the first version of Uff. 20A (cat. nos. 283, 287, 288), as well as the ones on the second project by Giuliano (cat. no. 289). There was space in the apse and the west pier arch under the dome for the Capella Iulia with the altar dedicated to the Virgin, the choir stalls and Julius II's tomb designed by Michelangelo. Five of the seven main altars (Alpharanus 1914: 177ff.) could have been placed in the chapels of the choir deambulatory: these were St. Peter's bronze altar, the Blessed Sacrament altar with its holy spear, S. Veronica's altar with the Volto Santo, the altar of the dead and the altar of St. Gregory the Great with the head of St. Andrew. The altar of the Madonna del Soccorso and the Ossa Apostolorum which in Old St. Peter's were sited near the high altar, could correspond to those placed along the west wall of the transept. In any case all these altars were situated west of the two choir screens and therefore were not easy to reach like the other parts of the basilica. The sacristies and baptistery could have been planned in the rooms on the two sides of the west portals of the transept. The oratories and popes' mausoleum chapels could have been sited in the enormous lateral chapels in the side wings of the narthex, where important funerals could be staged as well. Access for the numerous pilgrims to St. Peter's tomb at the center of the Latin cross was already enormously improved by the four transept portals. From the functional point of view, everything seems to have been well thought out and carefully designed to respond to the specific requirements of the Basilica of St. Peter—which certainly suggests direct knowledge of the site. This project must have impressed the openminded and down-to-earth pope who also had firsthand experience of French cathedrals. Perhaps this contributed to his increasing instistance on realizing the medal project and prompted him to start planning again in early autumn 1505. The technique and annotations of this project are so closely connected to the plan in Uff. 1A that it might be Bramante's copy from a lost original. Bramante might have been more interested in the functional and structural perfection of the project and less concerned about its esthetic weaknesses.   *C.L.F.*

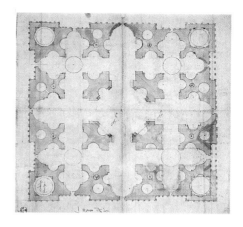

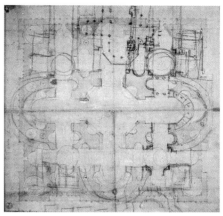

287
GIULIANO DA SANGALLO (recto)
DONATO BRAMANTE (verso)
Presentation Drawing of the Plan
Fall of 1505 (?)

Florence, Galleria degli Uffizi, Gabinetto Disegni e Stampe, Uff. 8A
Gray-brown ink (recto), sanguine (verso) on paper; scale in Roman *palmi* (recto).
40.4/41 × 39.6/39.7 cm
INSCRIBED: (recto) *i[n] ttutto ch[anne] 70, sachrestia o champanile* (Giuliano da Sangallo); scale in Roman *palmi*; (verso) *biagio istta chol dattario* (Giuliano da Sangallo).

PROVENANCE: Papers of Giuliano da Sangallo (?)

BIBLIOGRAPHY: Geymüller 1875-80: 169, T. 17, fig. 1,2; Wolff Metternich 1972: 37, fig. 9ff.; Frommel 1977b: 55; Wolff Metternich and Thoenes 1987: 69ff.; Hubert 1988: 216ff.; Saalman 1989: 104ff.

If Julius summoned his old architect Giuliano da Sangallo to Rome in early 1504, it is probable that he already had some ideas about the building of St. Peter's and that Giuliano therefore took part in the project right from the start. The oldest surviving project in Uff. 8A recto, can however only have been designed after Bramante's final version of the first project in the summer of 1505. The quincunx system, the excessively long transept arms meeting the requirements of Michelangelo's freestanding mausoleum, the octagonal area of the dome, the corner sacristies or the vestibules and the most important measurements are not imaginable if they are not considered in relation to Bramante's drawing in Uff. 1A (cat. no. 282). The projecting towers, the widening of the diameter of the dome to 200 *palmi*, the columns placed in front of the diagonal faces of the pilasters and the external width of 700 *palmi* probably presuppose also Uff. 7945A recto (cat. no. 283). The modifications proposed by Giuliano aimed first of all at a radical reinforcement of the load-bearing structures of the central dome, especially at the expense of the secondary areas. Giuliano wanted to raise the dome up from the piers as a homogeneous octagon in the same way as the dome of Florence had been built, and how he himself had worked at Loreto. He reinforced the pier arches with pilasters strips 30 *palmi* wide (6.67 m) which he had at first considered making even thicker, and it is likely that he planned giving the walls of the drum a similarly solid thickness. Only the areas of the secondary domes are provided with a definite order of pilasters. The relatively fine and delicate columns placed in front of every diagonal face of the four main pillars should have been combined with aedicules (Wolff Metternich and Thoenes 1987, fig. 75). In this case too, the building, measuring 700 × 700 *palmi*, would have required the shifting of the Obelisk and the destruction of the Cappella Sistina. As in the plan in Uff. 1A the articulation of the exterior was designed with an order about 8 *palmi* smaller, and therefore the measurements here too probably correspond to those of the medal project. The changes of mind visible in the right half of the drawing show that Giuliano first wanted to make the apses of the transept arms and the areas of the secondary domes emerge from a slightly smaller building. On the verso Bramante responded to this monotone project, which was oppressive though more sound, with a quickly sketched idea starting exactly from the same structural framework. His first lines must have been traced with the paper held up against a window; it could have been done while he was discussing the project, for example, when the pope threatened to adhere to Giuliano's elaborations of the statics. In any case, the plan in Uff. 7945A verso and perhaps even the first version of the one in Uff. 20A (cat. no. 288) show that Bramante had already moved away from the medal project before, and that he had gone back to the idea of a longitudinal building and was already experimenting it with the arrangement of the columns of Old St. Peter's and perhaps even with the ambulatories. Even an architect of his standing would have hardly been able to produce all these new ideas straight off. All the same he united them now with Giuliano's robust pier system, extending the ample niches to the ambulatories and inner lateral aisles, and the areas of the secondary domes to the external lateral aisles. On the upper part he legitimatized the ideas for the ambulatories with the plan of the church of S. Lorenzo in Milan built in the last years of antiquity, and on the lower section, the continuation of the external lateral aisles into ambulatories with the plan of Milan Cathedral—a reference which confirms the importance of the Gothic cathedral in the project. During the course of the discussion Bramante concentrated exclusively on the right half. He enlarged the secondary domes and reduced the separation of the transept from the space of the dome. As in the 1513-14 project, he opened the ambulatories with three colonnades and, as in Uff. 7945A verso, made them continue between the piers of the transept arms and those of the central nave. The distance between the piers returned to ca. 55 *palmi* as in Giuliano's project. Bramante only made the second arcade of the longitudinal body slightly larger (Wolff Metternich and Thoenes 1987: 79, fig. 82) and once again designed the piers of the central nave with a giant order. If he had wanted to utilize the 5 *palmi* columns of Old St. Peter's for the colonnades they would have excluded the possibility of building the arcades in the same way as in Uff. 7945A verso. It is therefore more likely that he had decided to include some blindstories over the colonnades like the ones he had designed for the upper story of the Belvedere Court in about 1507 (Bruschi 1969a, fig. 225) and in the same way as was later reproposed by Peruzzi in 1531-34 (cat. no. 326). He would have opened only the central pier arches—without columns—of the longitudinal body. The enlargement of this arcade returned to the fore with Sangallo's projects of 1519 (cat. nos. 316, 314, 313, 317). Unlike Giuliano and what had been drawn in Uff. 7945A recto (but in the same way as in the plan in Uff. 1A), Bramante went carefully into the question of the Obelisk and the Cappella Sistina by establishing only two chapels along the longitudinal body. It is difficult to believe that Giuliano da Sangallo was capable of making all these considerations, and therefore it is all the more probable that Bramante himself drew the design in Uff. 8A verso in the early autumn of 1505.   C.L.F.

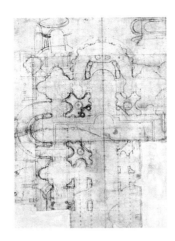

288
DONATO BRAMANTE
Plan Projects and Elevation Sketches
Fall of 1505

Florence, Galleria degli Uffizi, Gabinetto Disegni e Stampe, Uff. 20A
Paper, grid with 5 *palmi* squares in brown ink; left margin and top glued on during the drawing.
68.4 × 46.9/47 cm
INSCRIBED: *72* (Bramante, in lower left margin).

PROVENANCE: Papers of Antonio da Sangallo the Younger (?)

BIBLIOGRAPHY: Geymüller 1875-80: 175ff., T. 9-11; Förster 1956: 243ff:, 279; Bruschi 1969a: 895ff.; Wolff Metternich 1972: 37, fig. 11ff.; Frommel 1977b: 56; Wolff Metternich and Thoenes 1987: 81ff.; Thoenes 1988; Hubert 1988: 218ff.; Krauss and Thoenes 1991-92: 192ff.; Thoenes 1990-92: 440ff.

In the first version of this complex drawing in the lower right section Bramante returned directly to the plan in Uff. 7945A verso (cat. no. 283) in the lower right section. While on that drawing he had returned freehand to the dimensions and traditions of the previous basilica, whereas in this one he started from a scale survey and tried to give a concrete form to these tendencies. The square of the northeastern pier is still only about 70 *palmi* long. The simple pilaster strips of the piers, the 40-45-*palmi* width of the bays of the central nave and the columns between them recuperated from the old basilica, are still the same. The diameter of the dome is perhaps only 185 *palmi* as in the design in Uff. 1A (cat. no. 282). When Bramante therefore continued the quincunx system of the external lateral aisles with a width of 40-45 *palmi* and opened the pilasters of the internal lateral aisles with a width of only 25-33 *palmi*, he was only going back to the five-aisle form of the old basilica and to the drawing in Uff. 3A (cat. no. 280). The longitudinal body would therefore have been more or less as wide as the old transept, with five longitudinal arches approximately the same length as the old nave. As in the plan in Uff. 7945A verso, Bramante could have let the narrow bays continue here, whose 5 *palmi* columns excluded arcades and should perhaps have supported galleries, into ambulatories organized in the same way on two levels. These would then have run, like the side aisles, into the niches of the crossing piers. Bramante interrupted this first version soon after the approximate articulation of the first pier.

Evidently, in the meantime, he had examined the massive pier structure designed by Giuliano, as shown in Uff. 8A recto (cat. no. 287). He then attempted to render concrete his reflections in Uff. 8A verso, starting from the same axial distance between the main dome and the secondary ones of ca. 190 *palmi* like Giuliano. At the beginning of this second stage of work Bramante took into consideration the southeast pier at the bottom left, which he first calculated slightly smaller and then widened its sides to a length of 105 *palmi*. In the final version the shaft of the pilasters were 12-*palmi* wide and were separated by niches so that the pier arch measured a width of 45-50 *palmi* and permitted an enlarged dome of ca. 205 *palmi*. The diagonal

faces of the pier behind the pilasters of the pier arches, and especially the 12-*palmi* columns are derived from the piers drawn in Uff. 7945A recto. That Bramante was dealing with the question of the giant columns bearing the ring of the dome is confirmed by the sketchy circular entablature in the western half of the area of the dome. The columns on the southwestern pier are also slightly larger. Once again the pilasters are directly connected to the diagonal faces of the pier without the interruption in the plan in Uff. 7945A recto. In this Bramante was very close to the 1506 final project (fig. 14, p. 414). There is a sketchy hint that the pope's throne was to stand in the southwestern niche and that there was to be a connection with the cockle staircase in the center of the pier which would have allowed the pope to make a quick exit if necessary. This staircase is decidedly smaller than the one inside the northwestern pier which is dissected by a line which perhaps indicates the external limit of the drum. In any case, the plan of the area of the dome on the verso shows the four spiral staircases outside the drum. In the relative sketches of the elevation they are protected from the elements by means of turrets. It would have been practically impossible to insert staircases like these in the piers of the project on the medal or in those of the first version drawn in Uff. 20A, consequently this sketch can only refer to the version after that in Uff. 20A (see Krauss-Thoenes 1991-92: 192). If Bramante had wanted to place the drum on the entablature of the giant columns, he could have given it a thickness of 45 *palmi* thick wall without having to keep to the total width of the pier arches. He could have then utilized spiral staircases like the one in the southwestern pier building them up to the platform in front of the drum.

Bramante opened the ambulatory in the left arm of the transept with 12-*palmi* columns and in the choir with pilaster arcades with a small order increasing radially to the external order of ca. 22 *palmi*. This giant order was also a step toward the final project. Since the limits to this dilation of the body were evidently more restricting than those in the plans in Uff. 7945A recto and in Uff. 8A, Bramante compensated the enlargement of the dome piers with the reduction of the secondary dome space together with that of the corner sacristies, whose internal view was drawn by him on the upper margin and on the verso. Bramante could have proposed both spaces as alternative sites for a smaller mausoleum for Julius II. In any case the ca. 20-*palmi* squares placed in their centers are unlikely to be considered as altars, considering too that the tomb of Sixtus IV was placed in the center of a chapel. The walls were too thin for towers at the corners. The vestibules are only sketchily drawn showing freestanding columns as on the foundation medal (cat. no. 284). Without the segment-shaped apses the building—which takes on a stereometric solidity in the simplified sketch on the verso—still has a width of ca. 660 *palmi*, just slightly more than the one on the Uff. 1A version. All the same, this tiny difference would have involved the Cappella Sistina and the Obelisk. Bramante therefore eliminated the two western sacristies and with the help of a rather unorthodox curve he created a passageway toward the narrower longitudinal body (fig. 12, p. 412). He returned to arcades of a width almost like those drawn in Uff. 1A and Uff. 7945A recto in the nave, and gave the same width to the four lateral aisles with the lunetted cross vaults whose effects he appeared to have analyzed on the verso. However, he did not as yet find a congenial continuation for the dominant quincuncial system in the rather weak and slightly receding piers behind the row of the crossing piers. He therefore must have reconsidered its elimination and also that of the ambulatories, if he closed the left arm of the transept on both sides with three quickly drawn niches. Probably the pope insisted on a less costly solution, like the one in fact presented by Bramante at the start of 1506.   *C.L.F.*

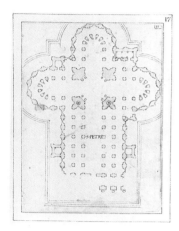

289
BERNARDINO DELLA VOLPAIA
Copy after a Project by Giuliano da Sangallo
Winter 1505-06 (?)

London, Sir John Soane's Museum, *Codex Coner*, fol. 17
Pen and ink on paper; straightedge and compass, part freehand.
16.4 × 23.1 cm
INSCRIBED: *S. Petri* (draftsman).

BIBLIOGRAPHY: Ashby 1904: 17 n. 17; Förster 1956: 245ff.; Wolff Metternich and Thoenes 1987: 93; Günther 1988f: 336.

This project which has been somewhat ignored and is known only through this copy made in about 1515, was evidently drawn after the great change in the design introduced in the autumn of 1505 and can only be ascribed to Giuliano da Sangallo. Its premises clearly stem from the design in Uff. 6A by Fra Giocondo, from which he borrowed the grid, the completely symmetrical shape of the supports and the side towers, and most of all, in the plan in Uff. 20A by Bramante (cat. nos. 286, 288). The shapes of the dome piers with the giant columns in front of the diagonal faces, with the pilasters under the pier arches separated by niches, and with the niches that open on to the inner side aisles and on to the ambulatories, could have been inspired only by the second phase of the project in Uff. 20A. This is true also of the shape of the ambulatories which recall the choir drawn in Uff. 20A, and for their dimensions. With its ca. 400-*palmi* width, the longitudinal body is just slightly narrower (see, fig. 13, p. 413). Giuliano eliminated the secondary domes, the corner sacristies and the vestibules, but in spite of the large base of the socle of steps, his project did not create any problems for the Obelisk and the Cappella Sistina. The length and width of the whole building as well as the single spatial elements seem to be established by a grid based on the ca. 265-*palmi* sided square of the crossing. The building, including the arms of the transept, is three of these squares wide and about four long. The piers of the dome are reduced to 80 *palmi*, the diameter of the dome to 160

palmi, the single bays to 40 *palmi*, and the pilasters to 20. Only the central nave maintains its old width of 105 *palmi*. This grid should perhaps have involved the design of the elevation so that the dome would have been lower and the central nave would have been two floors high. With a shaft of at least 14 *palmi* wide the pilasters of the interior were similar to the large pilasters of the longitudinal body and choir drawn in Uff. 20A. Like the plan in Uff. 20A the small order of the apses increases radially toward the exterior so that the shafts of the pilaster strips of the external order reach a width of ca. 15 *palmi*. Galleries are quite plausible, as in the plan in Uff. 7945A verso (cat. no. 283) and on the first version of Uff. 20A, above the narrow bays not just in the ambulatories but in the lateral aisles as well. This kind of reconstruction is confirmed also by the giant external order. The light would therefore have penetrated first of all through the vault and the galleries. The facade with its dominating central arch, its four lower side arches and giant columns in front would have corresponded to the kind of triumphal arch Giuliano delighted in. The choir arm was available for the Capella Iulia and the Chapterhouse. The right alternative of the sacristy recalls the sacristy typical of Giuliano's style, to be seen in the S. Spirito in Florence, the left one arises from the closing of the 40 *palmi* space and corresponds to the towers of the longitudinal body. Moreover, to the left Giuliano hinted at his intention to continue the five aisle shape even in the area of the choir. The project therefore unites the characteristics of the more mature version elaborated in Uff. 20A with the modest measurements of the first version and relates to Bramante's prototype in the same way as the plan in Uff. 8A does to the medal project (Wolff Metternich and Thoenes 1987). This is quite definitely the last surviving project before the final one. It approaches the solution for the reduction of the dome piers and for a more stable structure of the piers, as well as for the groups of pilasters of the external structure and the giant columns of the facade—perhaps because it was developed from a lost intermediate drawing by Bramante. In any case, the pope was forced to insist on further reductions.   *C.L.F.*

290
MICHELANGELO BUONARROTI
Letter to a Monsignore on 24 October 1542 describing his papal commissions and the facts leading up to the commission for Julius II's mausoleum

Florence, Biblioteca Nazionale, Fondo Nazionale, II. II. 325
Pen, on paper.

BIBLIOGRAPHY: *Carteggio* 1965-83, IV: 150-155, no. MI; Condivi ed. P. D'Ancona 1928: 81-96.

In this letter Michelangelo described his difficulties lasting decades over the mausoleum of Julius II and in particular what happened during the first year. According to the letter, he spent eight months in Carrara to get the marble

blocks quarried and to have them transported to St. Peter's Square. The pope then changed his mind and no longer wanted the tomb built while he was still alive. Afterward the pope kept him busy in Bologna on his statue (later destroyed), and in Rome, painting the frescoes in the Cappella Sistina. Michelangelo remained in the employ of Julius II until the latter's death; he kept an open house, but was not paid, and was therefore forced to use the money designated for the mausoleum. Further on, Michelangelo goes into more detail about the early questions relating to the tomb. When the marble arrived from Carrara at the Ripa Grande in Rome, and he still had not received any money from the pope (who in the meantime had regretted his decision) and was obliged to borrow the sum from the Balducci Gallo bank. Just then the stonemasons he had engaged for the structure arrived from Florence—and some of these were still alive. He put them up in lodgings behind S. Caterina which the pope had put as his disposal, and since he was still unpaid, he found himself in serious financial difficulties. When he tried appealing to the pope in every possible way, he was thrown out by a groom, and consequently wrote the following letter: "Santo Padre, today I was chased out of the palace on your orders, and for this reason I wish to inform you that should you ever need me you will find me anywhere except Rome." The pope read the letter and then summoned a carpenter and a stonemason who had worked for Michelangelo and told them: "Go to a Jew, sell your tools and return to Florence." After this incident Michelangelo left immediately for Florence. The pope sent off five couriers who caught up with Michelangelo at Poggibonsi and showed him a letter containing the following message: "Immediately after having read this letter you must return to Rome or forfeit Our Grace." The letter continues with a description of the pope's efforts to force Michelangelo to return to Rome. Nearly all the marble was stolen from St. Peter's Square and therefore Julius II's heirs were in debt toward him for a total of five thousand ducats. At the end Michelangelo adds that the whole quarrel with Julius was the consequence of Bramante's and Raphael's envy. In order to ruin him they had prevented him from building the mausoleum while the pope was still alive. In this, Raphael was perhaps right to be envious, in that all the art he displayed derived from Michelangelo. In his *Life of Michelangelo* published in 1553, Ascanio Condivi reported this chronicle nearly word for word, adding though that the master often received visits from the pope in his workshop and that it was he who had suggested placing the mausoleum in the choir of St. Peter's.   *C.L.F.*

291
MICHELANGELO BUONARROTI
Letter of 2 May 1506 to Giuliano da Sangallo Concerning Julius II's Mausoleum

Florence, Archivio della Casa Buonarroti, V, no. 1
Pen, on paper.

BIBLIOGRAPHY: *Carteggio* 1965-83, I: 13ff., no. VIII.

With this famous letter Michelangelo dictated the conditions under which he would return to work on Julius II's mausoleum. His friend Giuliano da Sangallo had advised him that the pope had been offended by his unexpected departure, and that he was ready to settle a written agreement; he therefore entreated Michelangelo to trust him and return to Rome. Michelangelo therefore explained to Sangallo the terms of his sudden decision on the eve of the laying of the foundation stone for St. Peter's, describing in particular the pope's conversation with a jeweler and Paris de Grassis, the master of ceremonies. According to Michelangelo, on that occasion the pope had implied that he had no intention of spending any money on stones, whether small or large, whether the precious stones of the jeweler or the sculptures of Michelangelo. Greatly taken aback, the latter had solicited the pope to pay at least a part of his commission before leaving. The pope had deferred payment to the following Monday and Michelangelo had not only gone to the court that day, but on each of the following four, and on his last visit, the pope had not received him. Michelangelo had therefore decided to leave—not only because such treatment upset him, but also for another reason that he preferred not to explain. In any case, the pope had given him the impression that if he, Michelangelo, had stayed in Rome, he would have instead ended up building his own tomb. In reply to Giuliano's letter he wanted to let the pope know all the same that he was only too willing to complete the mausoleum, and that while the pope perhaps was not interested as to where he would have built it, the important thing was to finish it and place it inside St. Peter's—wherever the pope wanted—within the next five years. Moreover, he could once again reassure the pope that the world would never have seen anything to rival the beauty of the tomb. If the pope agreed then he should open a bank account in Michelangelo's name in Florence. Michelangelo would undertake to transport the marble from Carrara and Rome to Florence, even though this would have caused him considerable losses. He would have sent the single blocks to Rome as soon as they were finished so that the pope could have enjoyed them even more than if he had actually been there while they were carved, since he would have avoided all the setbacks. Michelangelo would have furnished all the necessary guarantees. On the other hand, he would absolutely never have been able to build the mausoleum in Rome at the established price, and in Florence he would have worked in much better financial conditions—rather, in Florence he would have done it better and with great love, with a minimum of distractions. He therefore awaited a speedy reply.

This parsimony was characteristic of the pope in the period prior to laying the foundation stone for St. Peter's, when he concentrated all his means on the new church, only too well aware of the misgivings with which the world had observed the demolition of the old basilica. Given that Michelangelo carried on visiting the pope even after the definition of the project, and in fact petitioned him personally for his due, Julius must have been surprisingly and unconventionally intimate with the more famous artists of his time. The pope certainly had not foreseen Michelangelo's proud and vulnerable character, and therefore had to engage his old friend Giuliano da Sangallo to convince the architect to come back and let him know that the agreements were still valid. Michelangelo gave no reason to question his reliability, and pledged to complete the mausoleum and set in place in St. Peter's within five years. The numerous changes introduced in the project of the basilica had evidently made him feel uncertain about the definitive site for this tomb. At any event, he took all the steps he could to be able to terminate the work in Florence—even the parts already started—where he felt safe from any interference. *C.L.F.*

292

TUSCAN ASSISTANT of BRAMANTE and of ANTONIO DA SANGALLO THE YOUNGER
Sketches of the Choir and the Front View of the Wooden Model
Spring 1506

Florence, Galleria degli Uffizi, Gabinetto Disegni e Stampe, Uff. 5Ar.
Sepia on paper; traces of some additional lines.
37.9/38 × 27.5 cm

PROVENANCE: Papers of Antonio da Sangallo the Younger (?)

BIBLIOGRAPHY: Geymüller 1875-80: 334, T. 23, fig. 2; Wolff Metternich 1972: 41, fig. 28; Frommel 1976: 72ff.; Günther 1982: 81-86; Frommel 1984c: 241; Wolff Metternich and Thoenes 1987: 166ff.

The numerous errors and the poorly drawn perspective of the choir arm and the front view of the presumed final project by Bramante ready in early spring 1506, is best explained by imagining that the artist is looking at a small wooden model, as Panvinio asserts (Frommel 1976: 91, doc. 9). If the sketch of the plan drawn by Sangallo in Uff. 43A (cat. no. 298) had been taken from this model and not from a contemporary project by Bramante, it would have still existed in this shape in around 1510. This model differs from the choir arm elaborated as from 1506 thanks to the articulation of the apse and the vault: the interior of the apse is based on simple pilasters so that the arches of the windows have the same inner width of ca. 30 *palmi* as the lateral windows and have room for two double columns instead of one. The passage through the apse is flanked on both sides only by a simple order which is therefore less thick and articulated externally, as the relatively thin but surprisingly tall pilaster implies, in a much simpler way, or even in a strictly paratactical way as on Sangallo's sketch in Uff. 43A verso. The order is based on ca. 15-20-*palmi* high pedestals both on the inside and on the outside which were in fact eliminated in the final project (fig. 15: 415). Thanks to the octagonal coffering which is connected unsatisfactorily with the lunettes, the central part of the vault contrasts even more strikingly with the pier arch.

At first glance the front view below does not seem to correspond to Bramante's final project, since the central nave is as wide as the dome and the vaults of the transept arms rise further up than those of the side aisles. Evidently here the draftsman made some mistakes due to his looking at the model from above. Starting from the premise that the order, though shown here without any pedestals, continues the external order of the choir arm, and that the lunetted windows of the transept arms should disappear behind the tympanums of the aisles to the side of the portal, then the Serlian windows in the upper part of the central block of the facade could indicate a benediction loggia or something similar, which could have been placed above the vault of the main nave in the same way as in the project in Uff. 70A by Sangallo in 1519 (cat. no. 314). Therefore

the central block would have in fact become as wide as the dome and it would have been possible to crown it with a broken pediment. The left-hand tower alone already gives the impression that the ratios of the sketch are generally too elongated. If the presumed overall width is taken as 600 *palmi* (134.04 m) only the towers would have projected sideways from the longitudinal body (ca. 470-500 *palmi*). If the design is based on three longitudinal bays then the northern tower would have been situated on the southern half of the Sala Regia—as could be verified again in Sangallo's model after 1538. This project of the facade, like the model of the arm of the choir, was soon to be considered outmoded, if Bramante traced a road, as early as May 1506, from St. Peter's Square, through the Este gardens to the Obelisk: "tucta (quella parte del zardino) andara instradä per dirizarlä se possa vedere la ghuchia de piaza" (Frommel 1984c: 256). The left-hand tower would have been in the way of this road, so Bramante had to reduce his facade to the width of the longitudinal body.

This southern road would have had to correspond perhaps to the northern extension of the Borgo Nuovo hinted at in the drawing in Uff. 287A (Frommel 1984c: 360ff.). The external flight of both roads would have included a ca. 600-*palmi* wide square, which would have extended as far as S. Caterina della Cavallerote and would have had proportions of ca. 1:2.

Even the dome of the presumed model is misshapen like the facade. The area of the base of the drum below the ca. 24 arched windows has been drawn too tall. The dome has the concentric rings and profile of the Pantheon, and its lantern is only briefly sketched in. *C.L.F.*

293

TUSCAN ASSISTANT of BRAMANTE and of ANTONIO DA SANGALLO THE YOUNGER
View of the Tempietto (recto)
View of the Southern Wall of the Choir of the Final Model (verso)
Spring 1506

Florence, Galleria degli Uffizi, Gabinetto Disegni e Stampe, Uff. 4Av.
Sepia ink, on paper.
26.1 × 37.1 cm

PROVENANCE: Papers of Antonio da Sangallo the Younger(?)

BIBLIOGRAPHY: Geymüller 1875-80: 335, T. 23, fig. 3; Wolff Metternich 1972: 41, fig. 27; Frommel 1976: 72ff.; Günther 1982: 80-86; Frommel 1984c: 241; Wolff Metternich and Thoenes 1987: 116ff.

The detail sketched on the verso corrects the poor drawing of the arch framing the great window in Uff. 5A recto (cat. no. 292). In that drawing, the left pilaster is missing, and the exceptional depth of the arch cannot be appreciated. The depth of the arch must in fact be substantially

(7 *palmi*) greater than the version actually built. As can be seen in the drawing in Uff. 5A recto, the splay of the window is just inserted between two pilasters of the order of 3⅔ *palmi*, and therefore the great arches could have been consequently much deeper. Sangallo's sketch in Uff. 43A recto (cat. no. 298), which seems to be linked to the model, gives the same impression. As with the larger apsidal windows, these arched windows would have weakened the structure of the choir, whereas simple colonnades would have diminished the effect. If the proportions of the giant order of the pilasters, in spite of the height of at least 15 *palmi* of the pedestals, were ca. 1:11, then it is quite likely that Bramante had decided on an order of only 10 *palmi* for the whole interior construction of the model—that is to say, more or less the same width of the shaft as that was used in the plans in Uff. 3A, 1A and 7945A recto (cat. nos. 280, 282, 283) which he actually gave only to the eight pilasters of the apse in the choir that was finally built. In any case, the width of the three windows of the apse of 30 *palmi* respectively would not have allowed for an order of 12 *palmi* even in the model. The decision in favor of the 12-*palmi* order would have then obliged him to eliminate the pedestals in both the interior and the exterior construction. The external articulation of the model might have therefore looked like Sangallo's sketch in Uff. 43A recto, or could have had a paratactic sequence of double pilasters separated by niches. In the sketch, the distance of the arch from the great entablature seems greater than that actually built (2 *palmi*), in which case, the impost of the arcades is also probably slightly lower. There is no architrave here on the cornice like the one Raphael decided on ca. 1517-18, certainly after Bramante's version of the choir had already been built. The comparison with the drawing in Uff. 5A recto demonstrates, however, that the draftsman was rather unreliable as far as details were concerned. This is also true of the entablature and for its architrave, which

has only two fascias. While in the drawing in Uff. 4A verso the small order of the windows extended as far as the pilasters of the arch, in the sketch in Uff. 5A recto it seems as if the colonnade stood between pillars without capitals and as if its entablature turned in slightly behind these pilasters. The difference to Uff. 5A recto as far as the coffered vault over the lunette in concerned can be explained perhaps by the perspective destortion, owing to the draftsman's viewpoint being lower than that of the author of Uff. 4A verso. The concentric cornices of the basket-arch windows stimulate the observation that the light here should not have yet entered in such an oblique way as it later did. The reduction of the windows of the apse by approximately one third—perhaps the result of static considerations—could have induced Bramante to increase the light entering from the lunettes.　　*C.L.F.*

294

PUBLIC NOTARIES AND COPYISTS OF THE CAMERA APOSTOLICA
Liber Mandatorum
1506-13

Vatican, Apostolica Biblioteca Vaticana, Archivio Capitolare di S. Pietro, arm. 44, manoscritti vari, vol. 61
Pen and ink, on paper.
0.22 × 30 cm

PROVENANCE: Cantiere di S. Pietro or Camera Apostolica.

BIBLIOGRAPHY: Pungileoni 1836: 96ff.; Müntz 1879; K. Frey 1910: 43ff.; n.1ff.; D. Frey 1915: 52ff., 90ff.; *Catalogo dell'Archivio Capitolare di S. Pietro*, MS; Frommel 1976; Francia 1977: 19-23.

Before 1976 this almost complete collection of the first contracts for the new building of St. Peter's was relatively unknown, even though Pungileoni had used it as early as 1836, and E. Müntz based a considerable amount of his 1879 article on it. For his collection of the sources in 1910, K. Frey was only able to use the extracts that the future Cardinal Dondini had had prepared by order of Alexander VII; Frey's search for the originals was unfruitful. During his (apparently superficial) study of the *Liber Mandatorum*, Müntz copied the texts of certain documents (with errors) and left them to Geymüller; they were later discovered by D. Frey. Not even he was successful in tracing the original volume which only came to light after the reorganization of the Archivio Capitolare di S. Pietro after 1945. The *Liber Mandatorum* is a collection of notarial mandates dating from before 6 April 1506 to 8 January 1513, and register the financial obligations of the Fabbrica di S. Pietro. These mandates were copied—usually in chronological order—into the special book by a select number of notaries. They included contracts made with craftsmen and suppliers, guarantees, receipts and papal mandates authorizing payments on the Ghinucci bank. One of the contractors was Bramante himself or his substitute, Francesco di Girolamo da Siena, who kept the site's books.
The book still has its original leather binding, bearing a papal coat of arms (probably Julius II's) glued on to it. At first the book was composed of five sixteenmos. The watermark, a mermaid in a circle, is not found in any other architectural project for the basilica at that time. The first two pages are missing from the first sixteenmo and contain a part of the general contract probably drawn up before 6 April 1506—that is, at least two weeks before the laying of the foundation stone—between the Camera Apostolica (as the authority superintending the construction) and the architects commissioned for the project, Bramante above all (op. cit., Doc. 21). Most of the pages from 8-11 containing documents dated February and March 1507 are torn. The remaining fragments reveal that these pages contained the contract with an architect called Foglietta regarding the southeasterm pier of the dome, and receipts from two other architects, Guelfo and Giorgio da Coltre (op. cit., Doc. 55-59). A slip of paper was glued to the binding of the *Liber Mandatorum* with the

following statement written by Dondini: "This book starts in April 1506 and contains the obligations of the contractors, and their guaranties, and the mandates signed by Pope Julius II for the sum of 70,653 ducats of the Chamber destined to Bramante, the architect, and for him to the accountant of the Fabbrica with the payments of those, who recieve the money, and ends in 1513. But the book does not mention any payment in the form of a salary to Bramante." The signatures of the pope differ too much to be all autograph (p: 3ff.). The question of from whom the papal architects received their salaries before 1512 still remains unsolved, especially considering that the account books of Julius II's reign have been lost. Just before his death the pope awarded Bramante the prebend of the Frate del Piombo (K. Frey 1910: 13, A 35). Strangely enough, after the winter of 1510-11 when the arches of the crossing were being cast, payments were much scarcer. While about 14,000-16,000 ducats were spent in the years 1506-09, and in 1510 as much as nearly 21,000 ducats, in 1511 only about 6,000 were spent and in 1512 as little as 1,128 (Frommel 1976: 64). As from 1511 the other papal buildings went through a stagnant phase, which was probably just the consequence of the serious political and economic crisis of the last two years of Julius II's reign (Pastor, III, pt. 2: 774ff.; Frommel 1976: 71). In the summer of 1514 it seems that the more important architects like Guelfo had not yet been paid for all the works they had done at the time of Julius II (K. Frey 1910: 49ff.). It is quite likely therefore that during 1511-12 they continued to work more intensely than the *Liber Mandatorum* gives out. Under Julius II, in fact, there is evidence, for example, of work on the eastern buttressing piers (op. cit., p. 53, Doc. 42, 43), and many facts support the hypothesis that the vaulting of the choir arm began during his reign (see "St. Peter's", pp. 399-423). Even though the *Liber Mandatorum* does not provide a completely exhaustive panorama of the history of the building of the new basilica of St. Peter's under Julius II, for the first time there is information provided in an equally precise way as about the works in the period after 1539. By the time of Leo X the building site was organized in a much more burocratic way, so that a part of the money that under Julius had been destined for the construction itself, was now used to pay the salaries of the numerous clerks (Frommel 1976: 74ff.). The fact that the April 1506 contract laid down at first only the building of the western piers of the crossing and the choir arm, "tribuna," is particularly important for establishing the early history of the construction (Frommel 1976, Doc. 21). Probably the intention was to complete the choir and the perimeter walls, as was the practice in so many medieval cathedrals, in an attempt to put off the demolition of the old basilica where possible. Only at the start of 1507 did the pope lose his patience and urge an acceleration of the work. He then gave orders for the construction of both the eastern piers of the dome and consequently a partial demolition of the transept and the altar area. He probably hoped to get the work on the area of the dome finished quickly and return very soon to using the altar of St. Peter.　　*C.L.F.*

295

DONATO BRAMANTE (?)

Project for a Capital for the Interior Giant Order

Florence, Galleria degli Uffizi, Gabinetto Disegni e Stampe, Uff. 6770A

Pencil and pen, on paper; part freehand, part with straightedge and ruler; scale ca. 1:5.

53.8/55.9 × 74 cm

PROVENANCE: Papers of Antonio da Sangallo the Younger (?)

BIBLIOGRAPHY: Wolff Metternich 1972: 46ff., fig. 43; Frommel 1976: 64ff.; Wolff Metternich and Thoenes 1987: 118ff.; Denker Nesselrath 1990: 79ff.

After C. Denker Nesselrath's precise analysis, there is no further reason to doubt the attribution of this project to Bramante himself, drawn in the years 1507-08. The previous hypotheses of the involvement of Jacopo Sansovino or Antonio da Sangallo the Younger (neither of them assisting Bramante in those years) were not supported by convincing arguments. The starting point of this drawing was probably the brief section on the verso, where Bramante reapplied the division into seven modules advised by Vitruvius and Alberti, and gave to both the lower rows of foliage and to the area of the volutes two modules and to the abacus one module respectively. In the execution, however, these measurements were only approximately respected. The contract dated 1 March 1508 demonstrates that the horizontal subdivision into four sections was followed by the stonemasons as well. Every row was therefore divided anew: the first and the third into three parts, the second into only two. The fragment of the capital visible on the ground in Heemskerck's view in Stockholm (cat. no. 345) is therefore not one of the capitals in question (cf. Wolff Metternich and Thoenes 1987). Each one of these pieces was anchored in the wall to a depth of 1-4 *palmi*. Even the projection of the foliage on the verso was established arithmetically, while the curve of the leaves on the inside of this cornice was perhaps drawn freehand. Only the profiles and the *incavi* of the abacus appear to have been calculated with the aid of compasses. This draft served as a basis for the drawing on the recto, which was mostly drawn freehand. While the main lines of the verso can be seen through the page, Bramante did not apparently make use of them. He decorated the square *kalathos* with two rows of acanthus leaves. The lower leaf is designed inside a square whose side measures one third the length of the side of the *kalathos*, while the tall leaves are exactly twice the height. The distance between the centers of the helices measures half the width of the capital. Equally simple principles seem to underlie the other measurements. As in many of his symmetrical studies, Bramante only drew the half necessary to understand the design. He quite probably left the elaboration of the construction detail in scale to Antonio di Pellegrino. In the 1508 contract the stonemasons were obliged to execute the capitals after those of the atrium pilasters of the Pantheon, enlarging them as necessary on the basis of a 5:12 scale. Since the proportions of the individual designs of the capitals made for St. Peter's

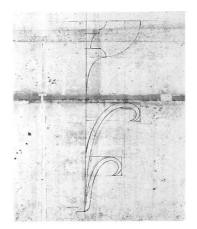

followed Bramante's project, while they differed in numerous aspects from those of the Pantheon, this clause of the contract was intended more with regard to the quality of the execution than to establishing an imitation as such.

Bramante intended these imposing capitals to influence the whole interior, basing his design on the theoretical sources and on a close study of the more important extant prototypes. The capitals differ from those of the Pantheon not only in their clearer tectonic structure and the flatness of the foliage, but first and foremost in the dynamic character of the helices, which, in his previous capitals for the Cortile della Pigna, still related much less to their surroundings. The characteristics of Bramante's drawing are the lively strokes and emphatic shading bringing out the sculptural features; and last but not least, a certain carelessness to the perspective of the abacus.

C.L.F.

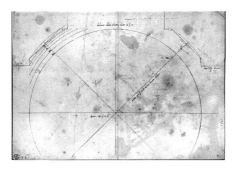

296

ANTONIO DI PELLEGRINO (for Bramante)

Project for the Construction of the Pendentives of the Dome

ca. 1508-09

Florence, Galleria degli Uffizi, Gabinetto Disegni e Stampe, Uff. 124A

Drawing tools, brown-black ink, on paper.

34.2/34.3 × 47.6 cm

INSCRIBED: (recto, between the piers of the dome) *daluno alaltro pilastro channe 10 p[almi] 4*; (on the diameter of the dome) *channe 18 p[almi] 4 1/2*; (on the diameter of the area of the dome) *channe 21 p[almi] 5 1/2 daluna facetta alaltra*; (on the northwestern pier) *la groseza delarcho p[almi] 39*; (verso): *el punto per girare questo sesto sie channe 10 p[almi] 7 7/12 che viene a esere la metta di channe 21 p[almi] 5 1/6 che da luna faccetta alalltra p[er] linia retta cioe channe 21 p[almi] 5 1/6*

PROVENANCE: Papers of Antonio da Sangallo the Younger (?)

BIBLIOGRAPHY: Giovannoni 1959: fig. 56; Frommel 1974a; Wolff Metternich 1972: 41, fig. 26; Frommel 1973, II: 330; Wolff Metternich and Thoenes 1987: 164ff.

This drawing gives a tangible idea of the methodical preparation of the individual stages of the development of the final project of 1506. The recto illustrates the plan at

the level of the impost of the dome arches. Consequently, on the northwestern pier the arches are screened by archivolts with shortened beveled edges to their moldings. The depth of the inner face of the arches—39 *palmi*, the diagonal faces of the piers, or "faccetta"—46 *palmi*, the width of the arches—104 *palmi*, the diameter of the dome—184.5 *palmi*, and the diameter of the area of the dome—215 1/6 *palmi*, measured from the diagonal faces of the piers, correspond to the finished construction. The purpose of the drawing was to define in geometrical terms the curve of the pendentives in plan and section. On the verso, first of all Antonio drew a curve with a radius of 107 7/12 *palmi*, i.e., the radius of the area of the dome. The width of the curve—only 15 1/3 *palmi*—corresponds to the difference between the radius of the dome area and the radius of the dome proper, and therefore to the projection of the pendentives. The just 60-*palmi* height of the curve is at least 7 *palmi* below the height of the pendentives that were actually built, a height which was already established from the start by the height of the pier arches and their archivolts (ca. 67 *palmi*). The curve therefore starts at least those 7 *palmi* above the cornice, designed for the elevation of this area. Antonio subdivided the curve into six segments, each one 10-*palmi* high, and indicated each of the six points above the foot with the letters A to F, noting the distance between each one of them along a straight line dissecting them from the foot. The foot itself, which as yet is without any distance, has no letter. He copied this drawing on to the recto in the area corresponding to the pendentive in front of the southwestern pier. Since the curve marked A terminates just in front of the diagonal face of the pier, Antonio first of all had to make it coincide here with the foot. The height assigned to A is therefore about 17 *palmi* (3.80 m) above the impost. Since at this height the pendentive would have been intersected by the archivolt, on second thoughts Antonio moved the foot 2.5 *palmi* further back, thus enlarging the diameter of the dome and its pendentives to 220 1/6 *palmi*.

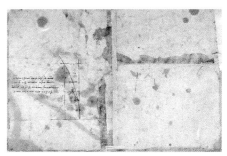

Bramante had probably already studied on the model the fusion of the elevated area with the part of the real pendentive dome. Perhaps he had even tried it out on a 1:1 scale model on the basis of which a wooden model could have been made for the masons. In the light of this, there is no explanation for the segment that extends more than 2.5 *palmi* beyond the corner of the pier, which is consequently based upon a radius of 110 1/2 *palmi*.

Between the straight foot of the pendentive and the molding of the archivolt there is an indentation ca. 1 *palmo* deep, as shown by Antonio on the northwest pillar, whose impressive shadow can be seen in the photographs of the pendentives that were built, but it disappears above the projection.

It has been correctly established that the domes with pendentives built over the piers with these diagonal faces were fundamental improvements from the statical point of view, compared to those built over right-angled piers. Bramante could therefore reduce noticeably the section of the dome of the pendentives as well as the curve. The load of the dome and the drum was therefore directed more perpendicularly toward the base so that the crossing piers and their buttressing piers could be reduced as in Gothic constructions. Bramante had to make similar calculations when he was preparing the designs in Uff. 3A (cat. no. 280) and Uff. 1A (cat. no. 282), while the present drawing, based on the measurements of the areas of the piers already built, does not necessarily have to date back to before 1508-09 when work was about to start on the centering of the pendentives.

C.L.F.

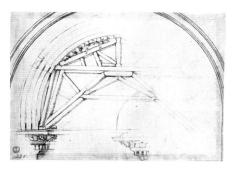

297

Donato Bramante
Project for the Centering of the Pier Arches
ca. 1509

Florence, Galleria degli Uffizi, Gabinetto Disegni e Stampe, Uff. 226A
Pencil and pen, on paper; compass and straightedge; traced in part.
19.4 × 27.1 cm
Inscribed: (in the keystone of the archivolt) *pietra* (Bramante?).

Provenance: Papers of Antonio da Sangallo the Younger (?); Vasari's *Libro de' Disegni* (?)

Bibliography: Wolff Metternich 1972: 42ff., fig. 32; Frommel 1976: 67ff.; Wolff Metternich and Thoenes 1987: 190.

Apart from the study of the capital (cat. no. 295), this is probably the only surviving sketch drawn by Bramante from the early years of the construction of St. Peter's. Evidently he designed the centering of the pier arches in a constructive system together with the cornice of the giant order. This cornice had to be sufficiently projecting and capable of bearing the load, not just of the scaffolding, but also of the casting of the vault. Keystones with the moldings of the archivolts had to be inserted and provide a point of reference for the stuccoworkers. At first Bramante seemed to be trying to create a perspective view of the intrados in order to give the master carpenters, Antonio di Pellegrino and Antonio da Sangallo the Younger, a three-dimensional idea of the scaffolding. This explains the continuation of the cornice as far as the concentric arch to the rear, and the shortening of the profile of the entablature to the front left. It projects less than the orthogonal projection on the right, which corresponds to what was built. Only in the upper section of the intrados can real indications of shaping be recognized. The barrel vault seems to have been already raised as far as the keystone, so that both the lower sections could have been used as supports for the scaffolding for the upper part. It seems, in fact, that the vaults had been raised in at least two stages (Frommel 1976: 121, D. 327, 329, 331, 333), otherwise there would be hardly an explanation for the fact that the beams in the lower part under the keystone support the vault directly and the crossbeams for the real shaping only start in the upper part toward the keystone. In this drawing the upper section has been drawn too sketchily to have been copied from the actual scaffolding (Wolff Metternich and Thoenes 1987: 190). Bramante probably trusted his assistants as far as these details were concerned. Jacob Bos' engraving of 1561, two drawings in the *Codex Destailleur* D in the Kunstbibliothek in Berlin (HdZ 4151, fols. 112r. and 113v.) and the view of the Cancelleria by Vasari, all show the same construction (Wolff Metternich and Thoenes 1987: 122, 190, figs. 130, 190). In Vasari's version, however, the crossbeams of the scaffolding are recognizable in both the lower sections and thus the barrel vaults of the transept arms were built, perhaps in a single phase. Vasari shows a hoist on

the platform. Sangallo's sketch in Uff. 1484A verso seems to have been prepared instead for a coffered vault whose diameter was at the most 30 *palmi*, and therefore perhaps designed for the intradoses of the great window arches (Frommel 1991: 180). Probably no earlier than 1513 Domenico da Varignana drew the centering on fol. 7 verso of the *Codex Mellon* (Wolff Metternich and Thoenes 1987: 193, fig. 191). The connection with St. Peter's can only be supposed since he only made a sketchy representation of the Corinthian capitals and the tripartite entablature; the vault is less elevated; the even more through support of the scaffolding on the capital and on the architrave suggests an even greater load. Perhaps it was destined for the calotte of the apse, which was vaulted in the period 1512-14 and whose scaffolding Varignana must have seen. Here too the preparation for the shape of the real casting was limited to the upper section. A support only of the lower platform on the capitals was calculated in a much later drawing conserved in the Nationalmuseum, Stockholm (Cronstedt Collection 12, 2254).

The soft hatching to create chiaroscuro and three-dimensionality, and the delicate, slightly hazy contours, are closer in substance to the studies of the capitals in Uff. 6770A recto (cat. no. 295) than to the known drawings by Antonio di Pellegrino or Antonio da Sangallo the Younger, who could hardly compete with Bramante's long experience in the techniques of vaulting a dome. C.L.F.

298

Antonio da Sangallo the Younger
Survey Plan of Bramante's Choir Arm, and Sketch of the Plan of an Earlier (?) Variant

Florence, Galleria degli Uffizi, Gabinetto Disegni e Stampe, Uff. 43Ar.-v.
Pen and ink, on paper; part compass, part freehand.
43.2/43.8 × 28.6/28.8 cm

Provenance: Papers of Antonio da Sangallo the Younger (?)

Bibliography: Jovanovits 1877: xxxiv; Giovannoni 1959: 131; Wolff Metternich 1972: 40, fig. 21ff.; Günther 1982: 80ff.; Frommel 1984c: 294ff.; Wolff Metternich and Thoenes 1987: 106; Frommel 1994d: 23.

Characteristics of the handwriting, such as the tiny hook to the descender of the "3," permit the dating of this survey plan of the choir arm to before 1514, that is, to the years in which Antonio da Sangallo was Bramante's chief assistant. This date is corroborated by the omission of the buttressing pier, which Bramante began to build in 1513, and of the corner pilaster next to Fra Giocondo's niche (cf. cat. no. 310). On the recto Sangallo drew the plan of the northern half of the choir—certainly with the aid of a sketch made on-site—starting from the pier arch and the bent corner pilaster of the exterior order, as could still be seen in Scorel's view of ca. 1524 (cat. no. 323). The numerous and occasionally glaring errors, and the repetition of certain elements with even more detailed measure-

ments, reveal that Sangallo was not at all familiar with the building complex which was not easily accessible in all its parts. Since the sketches on the verso and the details on the recto differ even more from the execution, it is probable that these were his first drawings. The most faithful plan is the one of the right half of the choir shown on the recto. The sketch in the lower margin of the recto established an alternative for the choir arm, whose well-proportioned windows, simple apse pilasters and deep blind arcades similar to the 1506 model (cat. nos. 292, 293). It is therefore quite likely that in about 1510 the model could still be seen in its original form. The intrados, which seems to be flanked by three and not two pilasters, is different anyhow from the reproduction of this model shown in Uff. 4A verso (cat. no. 293) and in Uff. 5A recto (cat. no. 292). Moreover, there are doubts as to whether Bramante had really decided in the model on a strictly paratactic succession of 4 × 3 pilasters for the external order of the choir. Finally, the partial sketch of the walls of the transept corroborates the hypothesis that here too Sangallo referred to an original, giving it his own interpretation. Sangallo's scant knowledge of the built choir hardly reflects the state of affairs at the start of 1513, by which time he had been Bramante's chief assistant for some time, and Pope Leo X was urging the enlargement of the whole project, involving therefore the choir arm in question. It is much more likely therefore that this survey goes back to the period 1509-11, when the choir arm was still under construction. Sangallo, assisted by Antonio di

Pellegrino, prepared the centering and started to work more systematically on Bramante's project. This survey therefore, fixing the state of progress of the choir before 1513, offers important points of reference for Bramante's final project of 1506 (see "St. Peter's", pp. 399-423).

C.L.F.

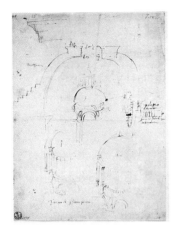

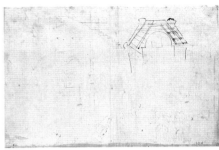

299

Antonio da Sangallo the Younger and
Giovanfrancesco da Sangallo
*Sketches of the Dome of the Pantheon; Three
Alternatives for the Dome of St. Peter's; and a
Hoist in the Palazzo Vecchio, Florence*

Florence, Galleria degli Uffizi, Gabinetto Disegni e Stampe,
Uff. 85Ar.-v.
Pen and ink, on paper; freehand.
33.6 × 24.1 cm
INSCRIBED: (top right) *in palatio di fiorentia per tirare su la legna
da bruciare* (Sangallo's mature handwriting); (bottom left) *tre
modi per santo pietro.*

PROVENANCE: Papers of Antonio da Sangallo the Younger.

BIBLIOGRAPHY: Giovannoni 1959: 127; Wolff Metternich 1972:
65, fig. 119; Frommel 1984c: 285; Thoenes 1994: 196ff.; Frommel
1993: 12-26, 34, 40-43.

These sketches belonging to the last years of Julius II's
papacy offer a lively image of the reflections of Bramante
and his closest assistants on the design of the dome. As
early as 1505 Bramante had considered the Pantheon
dome as a model for his project on the medal. There,
however, he calculated a ring of perhaps 24 columns with
wide intercolumniation so that in every second bay he
could have inserted a window, as in the drum of the Tempietto. With their width of ca. 23.5 *palmi* the arches of the
dome would have allowed for a drum with a wall thickness
of ca. 15 *palmi*, as in the following project of the dome
published by Serlio; they would not, however, have allowed for a radius as large as the external ring of
columns and certainly not for any inner ring of columns.
In Uff. 20A verso (cat. no. 288) Bramante inserted eight
windows into the now considerably more massive drum,
and renounced the outer circle of columns. Moreover he
placed four staircases inside the piers of the dome leading
up into turrets on the platform outside the drum. In the
final project of 1506 Bramante aimed to obtain the maximum amount of natural light, even in the area of the
dome. In any case, in the presumed model (cat. no. 292)
there is a suggestion of 24 round-headed windows, set
close together, corresponding to alternate bays of the
colonnade on Serlio's print. The pier staircases would obviously have been built inside the wall of the drum. Even
earlier than February 1512 Sigismondo dei Conti wrote:
"*In capite enim basilicae testudo futura est latior et latior tem-
plo Pantheon; cuius aedificii, dum haec scribebam, spes ma-
gis, quam res laudari poterat, centro enim admodum surgebat
non inopia pecuniae, sed cunctatione Bramantis*" (Frommel
1976: 124, D. 373). It seems therefore, from these words,
that Bramante was analyzing the static problems of the
dome, which is mirrored in the sketches of his closest assistant, Sangallo. Sangallo's cousin, Giovanfrancesco had
made his own survey of the Pantheon on the verso and recto in ca. 1514 as his youthful handwriting proves (Frommel, in Frommel and Adams 1993: 40-43). The dome of
the Pantheon with its projecting attic and oculus were the
starting points for Sangallo's three projects for the dome,
in which he concentrated in particular on the form of the

inner entablature and inner drum. In the first version—
the one most similar to Bramante's final project—he
designed a ring of at most 16 Doric columns, whose circular entablature absorbed a part of the dome. Behind the
columns there is a suggestion of the corresponding
pilasters. Since the four staircases of the dome piers had
to emerge inside the walls of the drum as in the 1513
project, it is unlikely that he could have made the shafts
any narrower. As perhaps had already occurred with the
project on the medal, there was much less space available
for an outer ring of columns and for its distance from the
drum than on Serlio's print. Windows could have been inserted in every gap between the columns, for a total of
about sixteen.
In the second version Sangallo gave up the ring of
columns, perhaps to lighten the load on the pendentives,
but he maintained the pilasters at the back and therefore
the wall of the drum remained in more or less the same
place. In response to the extension of the diameter of the
dome, he planned a corresponding elongation of the drum
through pedestals and an entablature with frieze of
garlands. While reducing the architrave and the cornice,
at the same time he emphasized the primarily decorative
character of this area.
Sangallo himself definitely preferred the third version.
Here he placed the Pantheon-style dome directly on the
entablature in such a way that the full width of the 39-
palmi pier arches was available for the projection of the attic and for the mounting concentric steps. Over the dome,
he sketched a study for a relieving arch like the one in the
Pantheon, which he drew, maybe at the same time, in Uff.
69A (cat. no. 300). Similar relieving arches had also been
designed on the columns of the first version. Moreover,
there are elements here for supporting the hypothesis that
the wall parts of the drum would have had to continue in
a structure with hidden ribbing. The tall lantern was supported only at the base by C-shaped volutes. Bramante's
final project for the dome must have developed out of
similar preliminary studies. *C.L.F.*

300

Antonio da Sangallo the Younger
*Section of the Pantheon; Sketches for the
Atrium of St. Peter's; Centering for the Apse*
(recto)
Section of the Villa Madama (verso)
ca. 1510-12

Florence, Galleria degli Uffizi, Gabinetto Disegni e Stampe,
Uff. 69Ar.-v.
Pen and ink, on paper; part straightedge and compass,
part freehand.
27 × 39 cm
INSCRIBED: (recto) *porticho; tegole; finestre della ritonda;
el chuliseo e channe alto insino a terra 21 p 7.*

PROVENANCE: Papers of Antonio da Sangallo the Younger.

BIBLIOGRAPHY: Wolff Metternich 1972: 55, fig. 82; Frommel
1984c: 284ff., 334; Frommel 1993: 23.

The section of the Pantheon on the recto should not be
considered separately from the sketches in Uff. 85A (cat.
no. 299) and from Bramante's project for the dome. It
can perhaps be dated, like this, as the years 1510-12.
Working in much greater detail than his cousin Giovanfrancesco, Sangallo measured the dome and interior of
the Pantheon. He indicated the same measurements in
Florentine *braccia* and utilized the same graphic abbreviations. He took exceptional care in measuring the attic
and the six external steps of the dome, i.e., those abutments so important for building the dome of St. Peter's.
Some important distances were not indicated even
though Sangallo doubtless intended including them as
well. The window and relative brick relieving also
appear to be reflections on constructive problems. Lastly, there is the note regarding the height of the Colosseum: "217 *palmi*" or half the height of the volume of
Bramante's dome (fig. 15 p. 415). The sketch on the verso, identified till now as the roof of the choir arm, belongs without doubt to the same period. In fact, in the
summer of 1511 Julius II must have been about to face
the imminent construction of the roofs if he really sent
a boat to England for tin "per stagni, per coverser la
chiexia di San Piero" (Frommel 1976: 123, D. 355). In
December 1513 lead was purchased too (K. Frey 1910:
51, E29). It is however difficult to connect the arrangement of the beams sketched on the verso with a roof
truss. It is much more likely that the sketch was in preparation of the casting of the calotte where it was extremely
important to fashion the cast right up to the crown. Here
Sangallo proposed a timber double truss held in place by
crossbeams, a procedure which could have been inspired
by Brunelleschi's dome. This concatenation would have
had to follow the curve of the apse and become narrower

and narrower toward the top—just as it had been sketched on the previously enigmatic sanguine drawing in Uff. 1107A verso (Wolff Metternich 1972: 43, fig. 34). It is easier to relate this sketch, indicated by Sangallo after 1527 as "archi di santo pietro", and whose approximate strokes are more in Bramante's rather than Sangallo's style, to the curving of the vault of the choir arm than to the pier arches, which already possessed sufficient support from the adjacent wall, as Scorel's view illustrates so well (cat. no. 323). The vault is divided into several sections in the sanguine sketch. It is braced at the sides by beams forming rectangles, while the area of the impost already appears to calculate a wall elevation. Such an abutment composed of several layers of beams would explain the sketch of the dome of the Pantheon in the upper section, whose steps represent similar abutments. The middle sketch could illustrate the direction of the thrust caused by the additional load of the calotte. If the copy of an undated contract for the work of stonemasons on the drum, only conserved by the rather unreliable Amati, did in fact prove to be authentic, it could be dated at around 1511 (Frommel 1976: 129, D. 390a), since it mentions not only the capitals and the entablature of the outer construction, therefore certainly involving the choir arm, but also the "cornixone de dentra, dove comenzera [Bramante] poy a voltare la cuppola"—the inside cornice from which Bramante will start to vault the dome. "Cuppola" was probably meant to indicate the apse of the choir arm, since the curve of the dome vault would have required not only an entablature, but an entire drum.

The documents reveal that Giuliano Leno, head of the building site, had transmitted the pope's go-ahead in March 1512 (op. cit., p. 124, D. 374). The invoices that have survived by chance and date back to Bramante's lifetime only mention the preparation for the centering "per 2 fondamenti grandi, fatti nella tribuna grande pe armare" (Frey 1910: 50, E 25). Even Scorel's view (cat. no. 323) shows similar supports for the task of centering. In 1521 Leno kept the books showing the work done since the time of Leo X, which included costs for the scaffolding timber and for dismantling it ("Per li legniamj della tribuna," "Per disarmare la tribona"; op. cit.: 66, E 103). In his *Life of Bramante* Vasari wrote that he covered the main chapel where the niche stands ("Fece ancora volgere la cappella principale dov'è la nicchia"; Vasari 1550: 598ff.; Frommel 1976: 88, Doc. 7). Finally the papal master of ceremonies recorded at Easter 1514: "*Ipsa basilica heri finita est in cupula sive in novo emiciclo fabricari sic ut Papa potuit cum prius non potuerit ibi celebrare*" (Shearman 1974: 570). Bramante may therefore have ended the choir arm just before his death. Neither the planned "cupula" nor an "emiciclo" were actually built in the altar-house over the old altar, designed and built by him at more or less the same time. Its attic and roof were not executed until 1523-26 (cat. no. 305). The works on the vault of the choir arm or perhaps only the dismantling of the centering could have in fact been the reasons for disturbing the papal chapels, closed by that time by the *tigurio* (cat. no. 305). On the other hand, it is hardly likely that Leo X would have burdened the new project as from 1513 with the completion of the choir arm if it had not been in its last stages. The section of the Villa Madama and the sketches for the atrium on the recto can only date back to the start of 1519 when Sangallo first took part in the design of the Villa Madama (Frommel 1984c: 333ff.) and thus offers an important point of reference for dating the majority of Sangallo's projects for St. Peter's to 1519. The sketches for the atrium already show a 9-*palmi* order, and come chronologically between the right and left alternatives of the plan in Uff. 252A (cat. no. 316), that is to say, after those in Uff. 70A (cat. no. 314) and Uff. 37A (cat. no. 313), but before those in Uff. 73A. If, in around 1519, Sangallo went back to his earlier measurement of the Pantheon he must have done so because he was once again responsible for solving the statical problems of the dome (cf. cat. no. 314).

C.L.F.

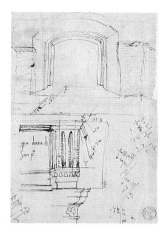

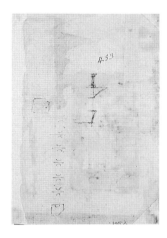

301

BALDASSARRE PERUZZI
Sketches of the Part (incomplete) of the Entablature and Attic of Bramante's Choir Arm (recto)
Profile of the Entablature and Attic, and Design of the Piers of the Nave of the Longitudinal Body (verso)
ca. 1514

Florence, Galleria degli Uffizi, Gabinetto Disegni e Stampe, Uff. 105Ar.-v.

Pen and ink; freehand.

14 × 29 cm

INSCRIBED: *(recto)* op[er]a dorica di san p[ietr]o.

PROVENANCE: Papers of Peruzzi.

BIBLIOGRAPHY: Wolff Metternich 1972: 39, 42, fig. 17, 31; Wurm 1984: 115ff.; Wolff Metternich and Thoenes 1987: 125; Denker Nesselrath 1990: 37-42; Pagliara 1992.

Peruzzi's sketch on the recto offers the most extensive information for reconstructing the windows in the vault of Bramante's choir arm. The five- to six-bay layout of the longitudinal body on the verso indicates that Peruzzi drew this sketch in about 1514, when Leo X was insisting on a larger project (see "St. Peter's," pp. 399-423), and therefore it was more or less contemporary with Giuliano's drawing in Uff. 9A (cat. no. 306) and Peruzzi's surveys of St. Peter's in Uff. 130A and Uff. 1848A (Wolff Metternich 1972: 42, fig. 29; Wurm 1984: 121ff.; Frommel 1991-92: 145). At that time the choir vault had just been terminated, while work had been interrupted on its outer construction because the question of including an ambulatory was still open (cat. no. 307). Over the capital, architrave and frieze of Bramante's Doric order, Peruzzi drew the basket-arch window of the attic with its deeply graduated intrados. Only the upper section of the walls next to the window is included in the external flight of the window. The wall turns in below and has an irregular surface, probably because the great cornice was going to be

anchored here at a height of about 28 *palmi*; its profile can be seen in the facade project in Uff. 257A drawn by Sangallo (cat. no. 312). The views by Scorel, Heemskerck (cat. no. 342), and Vasari all confirm that the attic windows were situated on the outside about 23 ¼ *palmi* (5.19 m) higher than on the inside, they would have allowed the sun's rays to penetrate like spotlights as far as the lower third of the opposite wall (fig. 15, 16 p. 415, 416). Most of the same basket-arch windows would have disappeared behind the great cornice of the giant order and behind the blind lunettes inserted in the vault. Since they would have been visible on the outside only from a great distance, Bramante had no need for an attic running all the way round (see Wolff Metternich 1975: 61, fig. 34). He must have been very keen on this because the great barrel vault and the relative windows of the transept arms and the longitudinal body had been brought back considerably behind the external Doric order, and an attic running the full circuit would have only had a merely illusory function. In fact the attic was omitted in the front view of the presumed model (cat. no. 292), and also in the facade project in Uff. 257A by Sangallo (cat. no. 312). Moreover the model demonstrates that the windows of the vault of the transept arms and the longitudinal body would not have been covered by the entablature and therefore they would have offered a wider and more intense zone of light. The particular characteristics of the area of the choir arm vault also account for the unusual division of its roof into two parts, as shown in the views: over the windows it is necessarily higher and further back compared to the area of the apse; here it could rest directly on the cornice, where the wall was much thicker. The tall pilasters that support the roof of the apse in the Heemskerck drawing seem to be divided in a way that does not hinder the mounting of the great cornice (see Wolff Metternich and Thoenes 1987: 194 n. 348), and therefore may perhaps still be ascribable to Bramante himself.

In the sketch on the verso Peruzzi outlined a low attic on the entablature which reached more or less the same height of about 11 *palmi*, like the cornice of the giant order, and was finished above and below by profiles. This is probably the upper part of the area of the windows that would have reached only just above the great cornice.

The drawing on the recto gives a precise idea of the projection of the entablature, which is only briefly traced in the views. Accordingly the corner of the frieze over the corner pilasters can be seen combined with a triglyph—Peruzzi's sketch shows a left corner. While on fol. 58 of the *Codex Coner* (Wolff Metternich 1972: 42, fig. 39) the width of the triglyphs is shown as ca. 5.5 *palmi* (2 ¹/₁₀ *braccia*) and that of the metopes is ca. 7.2 *palmi* (2 ³/₄ *braccia*), the triglyphs and the metopes on the corner pilasters must have been substantially narrower—similar to those proposed by Sangallo in his facade project in Uff. 257A (cat. no. 312), but designed in a way that cannot be recognized on any of the views. Besides the triglyphs would never have been on an axis with the shafts of the pilasters. According to Peruzzi the splay of the windows measured a depth of 5 *palmi* and the distance between the line of the attic wall and the profile of the triglyphs was 12 *palmi*. Of these 12 *palmi*, 4.5 *palmi* served obviously for the depth of the wall necessary for the dovetailing of the cornice, 3 ½ *palmi* for the thickness of the shaft of the pilaster and the blind panel of the wall, and the remaining 4 *palmi* for the frieze and for the fillet of the cornice. Here Peruzzi must have therefore measured the depth of the wall on the left corner of the corner pilaster. The cornice would have jutted about another 7 *palmi*, so that it would have reached a depth of ca. 19 *palmi* (4.24 m) to the wall, and it would have required careful anchorage considering its extraordinary weight. The area of the attic, the heavy entablature and the truss were certainly also functioning as abutments for the thrust of the vault.

C.L.F.

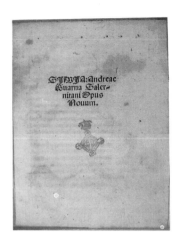

302

ANDREA GUARNA DA SALERNO
Simia
1517

Rome, Biblioteca Nazionale

BIBLIOGRAPHY: Patetta 1943: 165-202; Guarna ed. Battisti 1970: 58, 82, 104ff., 120; Bruschi 1977: 254; Frommel 1976: 129ff.; Wolff Metternich and Thoenes 1987: 143, 196.

The *Simia* by Guarna reads like a scene from one of Aretino's comedies. It was not, however, written for the stage but to consol an aristocratic friend in prison, who had formerly been the keeper of Castel Sant'Angelo. This is why the dialogues are mostly concerned with the question of justice, whose divine exponent was the Apostle Peter standing in front of the gates of heaven to separate the good souls from the bad. The majority of the *dramatis personae* are clerks of the Curia, but some are members of the Sacred Roman Rota, the supreme papal court. Angelo Massimo, who commissioned the Palazzo Pirro next to Peruzzi's Palazzo Massimo alle Colonne, was also particularly well placed in the papal court at that time (Frommel 1973, II: 241ff.).

He had recently recovered from a dangerous illness and now wanted to try and free the prisoner. Enrico Bruni, Bishop of Taranto and the pope's general treasurer was the closest to Bramante (Frommel 1976: 75ff.). The tomb that he had prepared *in monte nescio quo extra urbem* can be taken to be his funerary church in hilly Roccaverano designed by Bramante.

Bramante's leading role however cannot be fully explained by the context, but rather in relation to his personal motives—either Guarna both knew and admired him or he was personally linked to the *captivus*. The dialogues were supposedly written by Guarna in 1516, a year before their publication, but the atmosphere they describe is more like the summer of 1514. The name of Julius II is still on everybody's lips, and the new pope raises the expectations of the scientists and humanists. The year 1514 also marked Bramante's troublesome ascent to Paradise. Even before entering the scene St. Peter deplores the fact that it is still not clear where the portals of his new basilica were to be sited—an allusion to the contrasting proposals in the years 1513–14 for the extension of the nave (cat. nos. 306, 307). St. Peter recognizes Bramante immediately as the man who demolished his church, but he accords him greater benevolence than the others and therefore is only greeted by Bramante with ceremonial pathos. First of all the discussion falls on Bramante's liberal life which he defends by referring to *liberum arbitrium* (free will) and to Epicurus, emphasizing that without his life-style he would never have been able to express his artistic profession. Then the discussion turns to the demolition of the basilica, whose venerable age would have been sufficient to make even the most indurate sinner repent. Bramante cites the pope's commission, but St. Peter reproaches him for having egged the pope on to build a new church. Bramante admits his fault

and replies that he only wanted to lighten the coffers of the pope who, while allowing many new indulgences, had not spent any money on the new building; that money was otherwise consumed by war. Guarna was alluding here to the financial difficulties that crippled the papacy from the winter of 1510-11 and had brought work on the building site to a halt. When Bramante makes to sit down, one of the assembly observes that now they need an Apelles to portray the seated Fortune, probably referring to the seated Allegory in Bramante's medal (cat. no. 285). Finally they discuss the conditions dictated by Bramante for his entry to paradise.

First he would like to substitute the tiring road to heaven with a spacious spiral staircase by which the souls of the old and weak could ascend on horseback, and most of all he would like to demolish Paradise in order to build a more elegant and comfortable one. If he was not allowed to do this, then he would have gone straight to the house of Pluto. During the full-scale redevelopment the blessed souls could have camped outside. St. Peter however does not let him in. He decides to leave him in front of the gates of heaven until the new basilica has been completed.   *C.L.F*

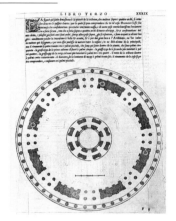

303

SEBASTIANO SERLIO (after BRAMANTE)
Plan, Section and Elevation of Bramante's Project for the Dome
1513-14

Sebastiano Serlio 1540b, Book III fol. 39ff.
Woodcut print; scale in Roman *palmi*.

BIBLIOGRAPHY: Letarouilly 1882: pl. 22; Geymüller 1875-80: 240ff.; Buddensieg 1971; Bruschi 1977; Frommel 1984c: 258ff.; Wolff Metternich and Thoenes 1987: 169ff.; Krauss and Thoenes 1991-92; Hubert 1993: 353-372.

The woodcut of the dome is one of the few projects not belonging to antiquity that Serlio included in 1540 in the volume of his treatise devoted to the architecture of antiquity (*Libro delle antiquità di Roma*). Bramante must have designed the dome just before his death ("e questa ordinò Bramante prima ch'ei morisse")and therefore he did not delve into the static problems posed by the dome. The combination of scale plan, elevation and section and of section with elevation can be Bramante's circle of 1506-07 (Frommel 1991-92). This type of drawing is not, however, characteristic either of Serlio's third book or of Peruzzi, to whom Hubert recently attributed the reproduction published by Serlio. Here, Serlio must rather have based his picture on an original or a faithful copy. This is corroborated by the design of the lantern, whose verticality, excessive weight and shape is more typical of Bramante than of his successors. Bramante wanted to employ similar projecting pilaster strips in the entablature for the side aisles and perhaps in the 40-*palmi* niches (cat. no. 320). Not surprisingly in about 1518-19 both Raphael (cat. no. 311) and Sangallo (cat. no. 314) began introducing their most considerable alterations to the lantern. Unlike earlier projects by Bramante (cat. no.

292), even the drum here follows the example of the Pantheon. With its 60 *palmi* the inner colonnade is only ca. 1 *palmo* higher than the ground story of the Pantheon in Sangallo's drawing in Uff. 69A (cat. no. 300). Since the upper story of the Pantheon, with its axes differing to those on the ground story, created problems for Renaissance architects (Buddensieg 1971), Bramante was probably considering here the ideal reconstruction of the Pantheon. Besides, excluding the lower entablature, Serlio's section can be inserted in a circle and the plan with the external ring of 48 columns and the compact inner order running all round it corresponds exactly to the ideal construction of the Pantheon executed by Sangallo in about 1535 (Buddensieg 1975, fig. 3b). Lastly, Bramante's intentions can also be deduced in the external colonnade. While in the Tempietto, the medal project, and the immediately comparable project for the conclave chapel of ca. 1507 (Frommel 1984c: 360ff.) he used a wide intercolumniation—going against Vitruvius' advice—in this drawing the space between columns is approximately twice the width of their shafts, as in Vitruvius' systyle (III, 3). In contrast with the Pantheon, Bramante also opened the colonnade toward the outside and, for static reasons, reduced the thickness of the drum wall and the area at the base of the dome, by some 30 percent. He enlarged the elements of the three radial orders toward the exterior, as in the choir arm drawn in Uff. 20A (cat. no. 288) and perhaps in the ambulatories in his project for Leo X (cat. no. 307), so that the light could penetrate from above down the column shafts. In consideration of the outer ring he gave the middle columns the same height as the pilasters placed behind the external columns. The light would therefore have entered diagonally through the wider intercolumniation of both the external colonnades, i.e., from the eight cardinal points dominating Vitruvius' *rosa dei venti* or compass card (I, vi). Since the staircases inside the piers leading up into the walls of the drum ended between the two inner rings of columns, some sort of linkage had to be created with the passages behind both the inner ring of columns and the outer one (Hubert 1993: fig. 5). Bramante probably wanted to link all the blind walls by means of relieving arches, or even continue them up to the lantern by means of ribbing and brace them with the external ring of columns. The staircases in the piers would have perhaps led up to the protected platform on the outer ring, and then continued up as steps on the outer calotte as they also appear in Raphael's project in the *Codex Mellon* (cat. no. 311). Unlike the first version of the drawing in Uff. 85A by Sangallo (cat. no. 299), here both the calotte of the dome and the drum are considerably reinforced. On the other hand, the large colonnades relieve the thrust of the crown of the vault. In his analysis of the statics of this dome Krauss reached the conclusion that, if materials of varying consistencies were used and, in particular, if the weight of the lantern was reduced, then it could have been built (cf. Thoenes-Krauss)   *C.L.F*

304

MICHELANGELO BUONARROTI
Fragment of a Project for the Tomb of Julius II
early 1513

Florence, Galleria degli Uffizi, Gabinetto Disegni e Stampe,
Uff. 608Er.

(copies: Berlin, Kupferstichkabinett, n. 15305r. Stockholm,
Cronstedt Collection, CC 2655)

Black chalk and pen, with wash, on paper.

29 × 36.1 cm

PROVENANCE: P.-J. Mariette.

BIBLIOGRAPHY: Mariette, ed. Convivio 1746: 70ff.; Springer 1883,
II: 15; Schmarsow 1884: 64ff.; Thode 1908-13, III: 209; Wilde
1953: 3; Tolnay 1954: 138; Dussler 1959: 497; Barocchi 1962c:
244; Hartt: 628, 45A; Tolnay 1975a, I: 56r.; Hirst 1976: 380;
1988b: 82ff. Echinger Maurach 1991: 247ff.

This project, the subject of much debate, has survived
through two autograph fragments conserved in Berlin and
Florence, but the entire project is known thanks to Rocchetti's copy in Berlin. It corresponds in so many respects
to Michelangelo's contract of May 1513, that it could
stem from the same months after Julius II's death. On the
project the height of the base section should have already
been 17 *palmi* (3.13 m), if—as the contract deliberately
emphasizes—the statues had been calculated about one
palmi greater than life ("magiore circa un palmo del
naturale"), i.e., about 3.5 *braccia* or 9 *palmi* (ca. 2 m) high
(Milanesi 1875a: 636ff.). If the base section was 17 *palmi*
high, the narrow front, with its ratio of 2:3, would have
been ca. 25.5 *palmi* wide. This width certainly exceeds the
20 *palmi* of the additional contract of May (op. cit.: 640)
and supports the hypothesis of an intermediate project.
Since the blocks for the statues and the niches would have
to be taken mostly from the project for the freestanding
tomb and had already been partly roughed out,
Michelangelo could introduce the necessary changes first
and foremost in the base section, the entablature and the
neutral central bay surface on the lower story. In the final
project of June 1513 the central bay could have been calculated consequently sufficiently larger than the one on
this project so that the niche of the Virgin would have
been on an axis with the pilasters behind the herms
(Weinberger 1967: 153-169). Since a place for the
mausoleum had to be found somewhere in St. Peter's but
Leo X was hardly likely to accept the Capella Iulia in the
choir arm, and since the aisles and the chapels could not
cope with these dimensions and the proportions, quite
probably Michelangelo planned to site the mausoleum
in the longitudinal body or—even more likely—in the
transept.

On both sides of the tomb a half shaft of the great order
could have been superimposed without clashing with
pedestals or a continual cornice, which were not in fact
planned in the final project of 1506 (cat. no. 341). The tall
niche appears to have been calculated on the basis of the
distance between the pilasters of Bramante's giant order.
Since the tomb would have been 35 *palmi* long (7.82 m)
and would therefore have occupied more than a third of
the width of the central nave of transept, the side view of
the sarcophagus with the pope being raised by angels
would have had to attract the attention from an even
greater distance without being interrupted by the sitting
figures that flanked it.

Many of the problematic aspects of this project can be
clarified therefore only by concluding that Michelangelo
had to maintain large parts of the tomb, but he had to
change the site, and in doing so, he evidently returned, as
far as the typology was concerned, to concepts of the 1505
project (New York). He therefore worked in a much less
creative way in comparison to the earlier projects, seeking
a half-acceptable compromise that would free him of this
painful burden. The studies on the verso prove that the
drawings conserved in Berlin and Florence are in
Michelangelo's own hand. *C.L.F.*

305

UNKNOWN DIE-ENGRAVER
*Giulio of Leo X Showing the Facade and Altar-
House of St. Peter's*
ca. 1513-14

London, British Museum

Silver.

diam. 27-29 cm

INSCRIBED: (obverse) *LEO.DECIMVS.PONTI.MAX.MARCCHIA;*
(reverse) *PETRE ECCE TEMPLVM TVVM.*

BIBLIOGRAPHY: Serafini 1910: 187, no. 137, pl. xxiv, 27; Martinori
1918: 9ff.; *Corpus* 1934, XV: 359ff.; Shearman 1974; Frommel et
al. 1987: 164; Wolff Metternich and Thoenes 1987: 30; Borsi
1989: 333.

This is not a foundation medal, but a normal coin worth
one twelfth of a ducat, a so-called *giulio* minted in 1513-
14 in the Marche. The construction on the obverse shows
a variation of the foundation medal of 1505-06 (cat. no.
284). Almost all the characteristics coincide: the excessive verticality of the central section and the elimination
of the apses of the transept could be ascribed either to
another model or perhaps to the negligence of the engraver. The background on Caradosso's medal honoring
Bramante (cat. no. 285) could have served as a starting
point; there the elements are also substantially elongated
compared to the foundation medal, the side apses are hidden and the portal is flanked by three pilasters on each
side. The presence of the towers reveal that the engraver
must have been familiar with the foundation medal as
well. Shearman asserted that the construction on the verso which Leo X is offering St. Peter is the construction
Bramante built in about 1513 to protect the old high altar
and the old apse for the papal masses from the wind and
rain. The plan of this altar-house measured ca. 92.5 × 40
palmi. The facade was composed of three arcades with an
order of engaged columns in front whose 4-*palmi*
shafts—according to Peruzzi's drawing in Uff. 130A
(Wurm 1984: 122)—came from Old St. Peter's. Each of
the two sides opened in one arcade only (cat. no. 345).
The drawing, fol. 7, in the *Codex Mellon* (Wolff Metternich: 43, fig. 33) suggests that Bramante wanted to cover
the old calotte of the apse with a melon-shaped dome 76
palmi in diameter, and open the arcades above a balustrade. He could have stabilized the new semidome by means of pendentives. Probably the foundations of the two
8 × 8 *palmi* piers measured in October 1513 at the foot of
the high altar in St. Peter's—"a pie del altare majore in
Santo Pietro"—(Frey 1910: 50, E27) and which must
have corresponded more or less with the dimensions of
the intermediate piers, belong to the altar-house. After
the failure of the idea of this dome, the old calotte was
screened by an attic with a central Serlian window,
designed according to Vasari (1878-85, IV: 163) by
Peruzzi. It does in fact have much in common with the abstract system of the Villa Trivulzio of 1523 onward
(Frommel 1973: T.182a). If Giuliano Leno in about 1526
added a rustic roof ("tetto rustico") raising it even higher,
it was perhaps because he wanted to cover the roof above
the altar with a coffered ceiling. The effigy on the coin
does show three bays on one floor and engaged columns,
but it differs in every other detail from Bramante's presumed project in the *Codex Mellon*. The central bay,

visibly larger than the other two, has a portal surmounted
by a pediment, while niches and oculi-niches can be seen
in the side bays. The broad segmental pediment can hardly be interpreted as a perspective view of a lowered dome,
since the dome over it is considerably smaller with circular
windows and its own lantern similar to that used by
Bramante on the exterior of S. Satiro in Milan. Since a design of this kind was hardly likely to be adopted for Leo
X's project of the basilica, there remains the only possibility that the coin represented a previous stage of the
project for the altar-house, as was often the case with
Bramante's foundation medals. If this dome was also
designed to cover the calotte of the apse the construction
underneath would have been much larger. Like the 1521
giulio (cat. no. 319), this coin was minted to circulate in
the Marche and therefore cannot be likened whatsoever
to the official foundation medal. *C.L.F.*

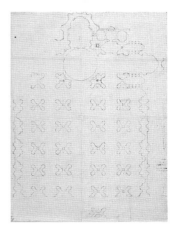

306

GIULIANO DA SANGALLO
Plan Project
Spring 1514

Florence, Galleria degli Uffizi, Gabinetto Disegni e Stampe,
Uff. 9A

Pen and ink on paper; incised lines; straightedge and compass;
parts in freehand; numerous traces of erasure; measurements in
Florentine *braccia*, with scale.

INSCRIBED: (recto, right margin) *b 325 dalalttare magiore i[n]-sino
ala portta djmezo; la metta; b 332 al tutto; la metta b 166; la metta
b 166;* (verso): *Di S.pietro di roma* (Antonio da Sangallo the
Younger).

39.8/40 × 55.3/56.1 cm

PROVENANCE: Fabbrica di S. Pietro; Papers of Antonio da
Sangallo the Younger (?).

BIBLIOGRAPHY: Geymüller 1875-80: 288, T. 28, fig. 2; Letarouilly
1882, pl. ; Redtenbacher 1875: 306ff.; D. Frey 1915: 16; 1924;
Marchini 1942: 67; Wolff Metternich 1972: 39, fig. 19; Frommel
1984c: 257; S. Borsi 1985: 435; Wolff Metternich and Thoenes
1987: 144-148.

There is no reason to date this project and the ones in Uff.
7A (cat. no. 307) and the one in the *Codex Barberini* (Wolff
Metternich: 39ff., fig. 20) to the period before Giuliano's
appointment in January 1514. He came to Rome immediately after Pope Leo's election in March 1513 and had
already finished the design for the Palazzo Medici in Piazza Navona by 1 July (S. Borsi 1985: 459ff.). If he had already this plan which was perhaps the first of the three
projects, in competition with Bramante, as he had done at
least twice in 1505-06 (cat. nos. 287, 289), he would never
have been able to accept the closure of the 40-*palmi* niches
and the shape of the buttressing piers, that is to say, to exactly those parts that had been built in the last year of
Bramante's life. According to the plan here Bramante had
by then extended the western walls of the transept as far
as the corner pilasters which could not be seen in 1510

(cat. no. 298). This is another important piece of evidence for supporting the hypothesis that Bramante did not return to the quincunx system in 1513 (cf. cat. no. 288). Evidently he had already decided to angle his giant order of pilasters at this point, and perhaps he even wanted to add the double sacristies that Fra Giocondo introduced (cat. no. 310) a few months after his death (fig. 18, p. 418). If Giuliano here used the Florentine *braccio* to measure distances like he did in Uff. 7A, it was not a question of habit (cf. S. Borsi: 453ff.), but of deference for his Florentine patron. The draftsman of the *Codex Coner* was to act in a similar way later on (cat. no. 289). Even more astonishing are the errors in both the measurements and the drawing itself. The present project can be distinguished from both of the two obviously later ones in Uff. 7A and the *Codex Barberini* 4424, fol. 64v., for its considerably larger dimensions which are directly connected to Fra Giocondo's 1505 plan in Uff. 6A (cat. no. 286). With a width of ca. 700 *palmi* and a length of between 1,000 to 1,200 *palmi*, the building would have decreed the destruction of the southern half of the palace, i.e., of the Cappella Sistina that had just been frescoed by Michelangelo up to Pio II's Benediction Loggia. Giuliano kept Julius II's choir arm, as he did later in the plan in Uff. 7A, which consequently was not discarded in the first half of 1514. Since Giuliano inserted two external side aisles here instead of the side chapels that Bramante had perhaps already designed in 1513, which made the longitudinal body even wider, he was forced to add another bay to the transept arms. This was already a good enough reason for eliminating the ambulatories, which would have made the building bulge even more. The pairs of columns placed in the external arcades of the transept do however indicate his knowledge of Bramante's ambulatories. On the right half of the sheet Giuliano hinted at connecting the urgently required sacristies to the northern wall of the choir arm. They were probably not high enough to interfere with the windows of the choir. Unlike in the plan in Uff. 7A, it is still unclear here how Giuliano imagined the exterior of the western walls of the transept and their connection to the apses of the transept—and in fact not even the whole project had reached the same maturity. The new vestibule would now have been to the west of the old atrium, way beyond the pier drawn in the lower margin of the sheet, so that the facade would have reached about as far as the steps of St. Peter's Square (cf. fig. 18, p. 418). In an alternative version Giuliano put only five bays in the longitudinal body which was the same length that Bramante had probably established in his 1513 project. The period in which the projects in Uff. 9A and in Uff. 7A were most likely to have been elaborated is that between the death of Bramante and the pope's decision in favor of the so-called "nicchia di Fra Giocondo" and thus between April and June 1514.   *C.L.F.*

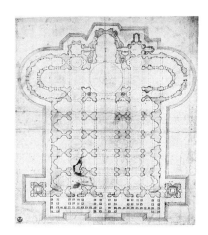

307
GIULIANO DA SANGALLO
Plan Project
Spring 1507

Florence, Galleria degli Uffizi, Gabinetto Disegni e Stampe, Uff. 7A
Pen and ink with wash, on paper; stylus, straightedge and compass; some freehand drawing; measurements noted by Giuliano himself.
INSCRIBED: (verso) *S pietro Roma*; *disegni Roma di santo pietro* (written by Antonio da Sangallo the Younger).
51.4 × 42.6/43 cm

PROVENANCE: Fabbrica di S. Pietro; Papers of Antonio da Sangallo the Younger (?).

BIBLIOGRAPHY: Geymüller 1875-80: 285ff., T. 26, fig. 1; Letarouilly 1882, pl. 21; Redtenbacher 1874: 304ff.; D. Frey 1915: 56ff.; 1924: 423-448; Marchini 1942: 66ff.; Wolff Metternich 1972: 39, fig. 18; 1975: 49ff., 67ff.; Frommel 1984: 257; Wolff Metternich and Thoenes 1987: 141-164.

This plan should resemble Bramante's lost project of 1513, in the same way that the one in Uff. 8A recto (cat. no. 287) reminds one of the project on Bramante's medal, and Giuliano's plan in the *Codex Coner* (cat. no. 288) reflects Bramante's one in Uff. 20A (cat. no. 289). This is therefore Giuliano's third reaction to a project by Bramante, and once again he is more interested in the details than the general principles. The project was more or less a contemporary of Raphael's (cat. no. 308) and the surveys of the parts actually built (cat. no. 289, 301) support the hypothesis that in his 1513 project Bramante closed the narrow piers of the nave with 40-*palmi* niches, which Giuliano took up here on the left alternative. Like Raphael he flanked the three aisle wide and five bay long longitudinal body with squared chapels. It is probable that Bramante had already adopted the shape of these piers, which are similar to the ones supporting the dome, throughout the building, to give the longitudinal body a sense of unity and plasticity that it had never had in his previous projects. However, neither the bulging semicircular ambulatories and the profusiosn of cupolas nor the polygonal sacristies to the west of the transept arms which once again recall S. Spirito in Florence, can be ascribed to Bramante. He had probably decided, as in the plans in Uff. 8A verso (cat. no. 287) and in Uff. 20A, on three-bay ambulatories which would have been shaped like Raphael's as segments projecting beyond the main building (fig. 18, p. 418). Giuliano instead had already expressed his preference for semicircular or even raised semicircular ambulatories on the plan in the *Codex Coner*. Bramante could have already thought about surrounding the choir also with an ambulatory (cat. no. 311) so that his project would have differed from Raphael's most of all in the conservation of Julius II's choir arm and in the rejection of the quincunx system. When opening the right deambulatory on to the transept chapels or flanking the longitudinal body with towers, Giuliano was still closer to his own 1505-06 project in the *Codex Coner*. The external design with its clusters of pilasters separated by niches

is once again so similar to Raphael's project that it must derive from Bramante. The atrium's extensive use of columns may equally derive from Bramante. However this is again the more mature version from the *Codex Barberini* (Wolff Metternich 1972: 39ff., fig. 20), which comes even closer to Bramante's concept. The reduced dimensions of the project in Uff. 7A, and therefore quite certainly Bramante's lost 1513 project, would have conserved the Cappella Sistina, but made inevitable the moving of the Obelisk and the demolition of the Sala Regia, the atrium, the Atrium Helvetiorum and Pio II's Benediction Loggia. Consequently the central temple front would have perhaps had to include a replacement for the latter.
C.L.F.

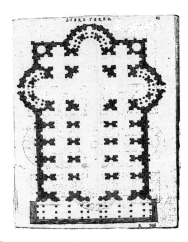

308
SEBASTIANO SERLIO (after RAPHAEL)
Plan Project
Summer 1514

Sebastiano Serlio, Book III, Venice 1540, fol. 64v.
Woodcut print.

BIBLIOGRAPHY: Serlio 1546b: fol. 64v.; Geymüller 1875-80: 279; Letarouilly 1882, pl. 28; Frommel 1984c: 260; Wolff Metternich and Thoenes 1987: 133ff.

There is no reason for doubting Serlio's attribution of this project to Raphael. Like in the case of Bramante's design for the dome, Serlio's documentation probably came directly from the building lodge. If Serlio published the first of the three projects known to have been designed by Raphael (Frommel 1984c: 25ff.), he certainly chose it for its ideal character and for the harmonious composition which Raphael never succeeded in repeating in his other projects (cat. no. 311). In spite of the simplified and rather distorted reproduction, it is obvious that the longitudinal body corresponds to the left-hand alternative on Giuliano's drawing in Uff. 7A (cat. no. 307), derived probably from Bramante's lost project of 1513. The same closeness to Bramante can be seen in the Pantheon-style portico on the facade, copied likewise by Giuliano on the plan in the *Codex Barberini*. Raphael also abandoned the hardly Bramantesque campaniles separated from the main body of the building which Giuliano had proposed in Uff. 7A, and unlike Bramante and Giuliano he returned to the quincunx system that Bramante last used in his project in Uff. 20A (cat. no. 288). He gave the deambulatories three bays, which was probably like Bramante's 1513 project, so that the segment shapes emerged from the main body of the building. Like in the plans in Uff. 1A (cat. no. 282) and in Uff. 20A he exploited the corner spaces to create sacristies and introduced chapels in the areas of the secondary domes. He abandoned the vestibules designed in Uff. 20A and gave the building a completely linear shape, now comparable to the choir area in Uff. 20A. Portals with columns were added to the ends of the transept arms like in Uff. 7A and in Giuliano's *Codex Barberini* project, while at the end of the choir he placed a large niche for an altar. Serlio eliminated the staircases in the piers of the dome and drew instead two cockle staircases on both sides of the choir ambulatory which could have led up to the rooms above the corner sacristies. The passages between the 40-*palmi* niches of the piers and buttressing-piers of the longitudinal body have also been done away with, as well as the pilaster clusters along the exterior which Raphael certainly wanted to continue on the ambulatories, perhaps without niches continue, however, in the apses of the three cross arms. These were used by Giuliano only in the plan of the *Codex Barberini*, while in the plan in Uff. 7A he utilized the articulation of Bramante's choir. Unlike all Giuliano's projects but similar to Bramante's choir, a projecting pilaster must have acted as a junction between the buttressing piers and the hemicycle of the apse—an element that is still conserved in the arms of Michelangelo's cross. The columns of the ambulatories on Serlio's plan have such wide spaces between them that they seem like Serlian motifs. This dilation of the space is confirmed by the corresponding niches in the back wall. The groups of three niches corresponding to the colonnades alternate with a large round niche that continues radially the enlargement of the niches between the pilasters of the inner order—and this too, is an idea derived from the plan in Uff. 20A. Evidently at least the four large niches on the back wall of the ambulatories were destined to be used as chapels. The elevation of the atrium is rather unclear, as it is in Uff. 7A and on the plan in the *Codex Barberini*. By eliminating Bramante's choir arm Raphael could also abandon Bramante's extraordinarily vertical exterior order (cf. cat. no. 333) and introduce a more classical order, without pedestals which would have upset a freestanding colonnade. The colonnade should probably have been articulated in many sections with barrel vaults and alternating pediments, in the same way as Peruzzi's later projects (cat. no. 334). It would have comprised the center front with a large span opening on to the main portal, the fronts of the side portals connected by means of niches as in Peruzzi's drawing, and supported only by two columns, and lastly, the corner bays with double columns that could have been surmounted also by small pediments as on Sangallo's drawings in Uff. 70A (cat. no. 314), Uff 72A recto (cat. no. 318) or Uff. 78A recto (cat. no. 340). Evidently this project of Raphael's—which he also had built as a model (Frommel 1984: 260)—failed to prevail over Bramante's and Fra Giocondo's certainly substantially more economical proposals.

C.L.F.

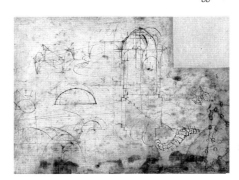

309
RAPHAEL
Studies for a Danaë and for the Longitudinal Body of the Basilica of St. Peter
Summer 1514

Florence, Galleria degli Uffizi, Gabinetto Disegni e Stampe, Uff. 1973F
Pen and ink, with watercolor, on paper.
INSCRIBED: *danae* (Raphael).
26.8 × 34.6 cm

BIBLIOGRAPHY: Oberhuber 1966: 225-244; Wolff Metternich 1972: 46, fig. 45ff.; Knab et al. 1983: 120 n. 483ff.; Frommel

1984c: 260ff.; Wolff Metternich and Thoenes 1987: 93, 162; Curti 1989: 17-30.

Raphael perhaps drew the scene at the time he was working on the frescoes for the vault of the Stanza dell'Eliodoro, which is the reason for dating the sheet at the start of his activity as architect for St. Peter's, maybe in the early summer of 1514 when he prepared his first model. Next to the Danaë on the recto (later engraved by Bonasone) he drew a part of the central nave of St. Peter's, making the image confused by sketching other construction details over it later on. To the left, the coffered pier arch rises over the pilasters and their jutting entablature. The two left pilasters are placed on separate pedestals linked by cornices. Raphael wanted to contribute therefore to bringing Bramante's elongated order back to the classical canons (cat. no. 333)—just as Giuliano had observed about the project in the *Codex Barberini* (Frommel 1984c: 262). Raphael continued the cornice of the impost in the area between the pilasters with a niche above and below, which was fairly near the 1519 arrangement (Frommel 1984c: 306). He inserted a window in the upper coffer of the arch in the same way as Bramante had done in the choir of S. Maria del Popolo. There is a glimpse of the side aisle and adjacent chapel through the arcades. The chapel is characterized by a barrel vault and ends with a niche, while the side aisle in front has a cross vault and a dome. These have been drawn one on top of the other as if the dome of Bramante's and Giuliano's projects (cat. nos. 306, 307) were to be replaced by the intersection of two barrel vaults. Another barrel vault whose coffering has been rendered in perspective covers the passage between the central nave and the side aisle. The various parallel elements leading up to the height of the impost could perhaps represent the corner pilaster strips of the aforesaid sections. All these characteristics coincide with the plan published by Serlio. Behind the concentric arcades there is however a piece of wall lying slightly further back which fills in the space between the pilasters of the central nave, the cornice and the entablature, and which has an arched window or niche. Even though the giant pilasters to the right of the arcade appear to belong to the nave order, they are in fact larger than the ones on the left and are not capped by Corinthian capitals or a tripartite entablature but project like pilaster strips in the cornice. This is why it is difficult to assert that the drawing shows a continuation of the central nave, whereas on the contrary it is closer to the corresponding system of the outer construction. Since on the plan published by Serlio Raphael wanted to eliminate Bramante's choir with its exaggerat-

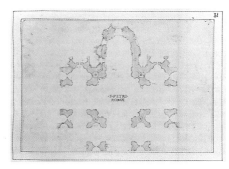

edly vertical order, here he could have already been looking for a new external order which corresponded perfectly to the inner one. The arched window on the cornice lies substantially higher up than the arched window in Bramante's choir, in a position more or less where the windows were to be found in about 1518-19 (cat. no. 312). Raphael sketched in a slightly deformed perspective the intrados of this window. The arch between the two pilaster strips, drawn in a similar way but larger and placed further back, can be interpreted either as a window or as a niche with a rectangular plan. Windows between the pairs of pilasters of the external construction would have illuminated analogous spaces to those left by Sangal-

lo in the pier mass in his 1521 model (cat. no. 321). With a similar alternation of ample parts of the walls with arched windows and pairs of pilaster strips separated by aedicular windows, Raphael's external construction would have been fundamentally different from Bramante's without the plan shedding any light on it whatsoever. To the right of the pairs of pilaster strips there appears to be a scarcely legible hint at a shortening of the diagonal face of the crossing pier.

The drawings on the verso could also be of St. Peter's. The detail of the plan in the center shows a bay with a cross vault in the aisle and above this, probably a chapel with the conjunction of the apse and side corridors leading to new spaces created behind the pairs of pilaster strips. If Raphael was only interested here in developing theoretical studies it was hardly likely that he would have placed the two bays together. At the top and in the remaining sketches he examined the groins of a cross vault and its visual effects. In this sense therefore it is probable that the single reflections, such as the construction of the ellipse between two semicircles, went beyond the immediate practical purpose (Curti 1989). The attic base too, at the top left, the lute-shaped object below left, or the serpent with the diamond-shaped tips, are not directly connected with St. Peter's, but rather with the perspective representation of complex forms in general. In spite of certain similarities it is hard to attribute these drawings to Peruzzi (Curti 1989). This sheet is, in fact, valuable proof both of Raphael's direct descendency from Bramante who had already considered the visual impact of his interiors in the drawing in Uff. 20A verso (cat. no. 288), and of his completely independent search for more classical proportions and for greater coherence and a systematic approach.

C.L.F.

310
BERNARDINO DELLA VOLPAIA
Study of a Plan of the Building
ca. 1515

London, Sir John Soane's Museum, *Codex Coner*, fol. 31
Pen, with wash, on paper; compass and straightedge.
INSCRIBED: *S.PETRI ROMAE.*
17.9 × 20.2 cm

PROVENANCE: Collezione Coner; Robert and James Adam.

BIBLIOGRAPHY: Ashby 1904, no. 31; D. Frey 1915: 60; Förster 1956: 262ff.; Buddensieg 1975: 49ff.; Wolff Metternich 1972: 38ff., fig. 16; Frommel 1976: 60; Wolff Metternich and Thoenes 1987: 105ff.; Günther 1988f: 337.

When Bernardino della Volpaia drew the best examples of architecture in antiquity for the *Codex Coner*, perhaps as a result of a commission from Leo X, he also included in his surveys a few contemporary buildings by Bramante—just as Serlio and Palladio were to do later on (Günther 1988f; Frommel 1993: 26ff.). These included the incomplete elevation of the Belvedere Court on fol. 41v. and the plan of St. Peter's. Bramante was already dead, and here, like in the case of the Belvedere, Bernardino demonstrated that he was evidently not familiar with the entire project. He was satisfied with drawing the actual state of progress: the four pier arches, the choir arm, the two piers of the longitudinal body dating in part back to

615

Julius II's reign, the four lateral buttressing piers with the conjunction of the ambulatories started by Bramante in 1513, and lastly, the 40-*palmi* niche with which Fra Giocondo had started to close the chapel of the southern arm of the transept between the summer of 1514 and that of 1515 (see "St. Peter's," pp. 399-423). The "nicchia di Fra Giocondo" continues down toward two separate rooms to the west, which Bramante could have already designed in the same place (cat. nos. 307, 337). Similar sacristies had been indicated as urgently needed in the area of the choir. In the 1506 project (figs. 14-16, pp. 414-416) they could have only been situated above the chapels in the transept. Each of Fra Giocondo's separate rooms measures ca. 60 × 60 *palmi* and has an order of 3-4 *palmi* inside. They would have had a maximum height of 50-60 *palmi* at the start of the vault. Since Fra Giocondo also extended Bramante's giant order on the outside to the corners (cat. no. 306) he must have planned at least three similar floors. The right wall of the right-hand sacristy is sited more or less along the same line as the choir facing in Giuliano's *Codex Barberini* plan and therefore Fra Giocondo—and perhaps Bramante before him—could have planned a similar facing for Julius II's choir. For symmetrical reasons Bernardino repeated Fra Giocondo's niche with its separate additions in the northern arm of the transept where it had not yet even been started, and he also drew in the piers of the longitudinal body, each pair being connected by 40-*palmi* niches. According to Heemskerck (cat. no. 343) this could have been the case at most in their lower area. On the other hand Bernardino does not appear to have carried out a proper survey. The greater part of the very inaccurate measurements in Florentine *braccia* correspond to the ones in Uff. 7A (cat. no. 307) and in Uff. 9A (cat. no. 306) drawn by Giuliano probably a year before. Bernardino's drawing however is fundamentally more exact and does not correspond to Giuliano's cursory ones or his measurements. Every now and then he put measurements in the wrong place—such as when he writes next to the southwestern buttressing pier the width of the shaft of the pilaster with the approximately correct measurement of 4 ½ *braccia*, while the northwestern buttressing pier is indicated as 3⅞ *palmi*. These measurements correspond much more to the 10-*palmi* pilasters of the apse which he drew even narrower without adding any measurements though. He must have made a similar error with the southern pier of the longitudinal body where the 6 ¾ *braccia* can only refer to the distance between the pilaster strips facing the side aisles, and the 5 ½ *palmi*, to the distance between the giant pilasters. This is also indicated on the northwestern buttressing pier with 5 ½ *braccia*. He probably combined here a fairly exact survey carried out using palmi with Giuliano's measurements to introduce the same system of measurement used throughout the rest of the codex. He also probably added several other measurements, and paid careful attention to the perfect symmetry of the design. His reproduction differs in several important points, such as the side windows of the choir armor, the rectilineal pilasters at the beginning of the apse, the parts actually built and Sangallo's much more accurate measurements dating from about 1510 (cat. no. 298).

C.L.F.

A

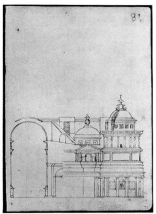

B

C

311

DOMENICO DA VARIGNANA (after RAPHAEL)
Plan, Elevation and Section (copy of Raphael's second project)

New York, The Pierpont Morgan Library, *Codex Mellon*, 1978.44.88 fol. 71v., 72r., 72v.

Pen and ink with wash, on paper; incised lines; part straightedge and compass, part freehand.

INSCRIBED: (fol. 71v.) *canne 12 fra li ponti*; (fol. 72v.) *canne 20 fra li ponti* (draftsman's handwriting).

21 × 11.4 cm

PROVENANCE: Mellon Collection, Washington.

BIBLIOGRAPHY: Nachod 1955: 1ff.; Förster 1956: 248ff.; Wolff Metternich 1972: 52ff., fig. 71ff.; Wittkower 1978a: 90-107; Heydenreich and Lotz 1974: 173ff.; Frommel 1984c: 270ff.; Bruschi 1987b: 288ff.; Huber 1993: 360ff.

After the withdrawal of Fra Giocondo and Giuliano in the late summer of 1515 a completely new phase of the project began—the first evidence of which is perhaps Raphael's project conserved in the *Codex Mellon*. As in Bramante's late project for the dome (cat. no. 303) the plan and the elevation in scale are closely related to one another though not with the same consequence. For example, fol. 71 verso shows the elevation of the facade, the dome and a section showing the inside of the dome and the lantern, while fol. 72 recto combines the section through the central nave and the passages through the right side aisle without the vault and the elevation of the exterior of the last third of the choir. The draftsman was probably borrowing from more complete sections and elevations, and placed the principal information on both pages of his sketchbook in the form of a complementary elevation. The inconsequential perspective views of the dome and lantern were not necessarily copied from the examples he had in front of him either. Raphael still kept the quincunx system here and the segment-shaped ambulatories of his first project (cat. no. 322). Probably after the pope put pressure on him he included Bramante's choir, opening the blind arcades in the areas of the secondary domes and giving the apse a third ambulatory. Last but not least he took the problem of the illumination of the ambulatories and the chapels into consideration. Here he substituted the giant order on the exterior of the building with an order whose pilaster shafts were only 5 *palmi* wide. This order came to correspond with the columns of Old St. Peter's which he now reutilized in both the ambulatories and the vestibule on the facade. It would still have been possible to illuminate directly the three windows in the apse of Bramante's choir behind the protective attic of the low ambulatory. Besides, the 5-*palmi* order with its heigt of 57 ⅛ (12.80 m) improved the connection with the ground floor of the papal palace, the level of which was ca. 12.35 meters above that of St. Peter's. Raphael reduced the pilasters in the ambulatories in the transept arms in order to enlarge the colonnades which now had three equal spaces between them, thus emphasizing their difference from Bramante's apse. The portals of the transept arms are closed and the groups of three niches only relate to the colonnades. The dome differs from Serlio's woodcut print of Bramante's project first of all in the subdivision into caissons, which Bramante had certainly already taken from the Pantheon, but above all in the effort to reduce weight everywhere possible. That is why the area between the ring of the dome and the drum's pedestals is definitely smaller and the base of the outer construction is reduced to slightly elongated pedestals. This decision of Raphael's would have lowered the overall height of the dome area. The calotte looks thinner and the lantern in particular is considerably shorter. One of the drawings attributed to Girolamo da Carpi establishes the plan of the lantern (Canedy 1976). In spite of their varying proportions the two drawings are probably equally far from Raphael's project. Varignana places more emphasis on the area of the lantern and its cupola; Girolamo instead concentrates on the lower part. While in Serlio's reproduction of Bramante's cupola the pilaster strips are substantially lower compared to the inner order and the abstract volutes do feasibly support the impost of the cupola, and while Girolamo linked them likewise to the cupola, in the drawing in the *Codex Mellon* the cupola seems to start from above the volutes. Probably Raphael's lantern differed from Bramante's version less in the section than in its vocabulary. He translated the pairs of pilaster strips in Serlio's print into a *travata ritmica*. The most striking innovations can be seen on the facade where Raphael returned to the idea of the ambulatories and connected both the orders in each other. He also uncovered here the single elements of the body of the building while uniting them in an increasingly hierarchical system. The weakness of the project for the facade can be seen most of all in the colonnades which fail to relate satisfactorily the central temple front with the corner towers to which the bulging sacristies correspond to the west. Appearing unsymmetrically behind the colonnades are the loadbearing walls of the transept which support the uncovered barrelvault whose stairs are reminiscent of those of the dome of the Pantheon—an idea which neither Bramante nor the later projects used, but which can be found in S. Andrea in Mantua. The close stylistic connections especially of the towers with the Palazzo Branconio dell'Aquila designed by Raphael suggest dating this project at around the second half of 1518.

C.L.F.

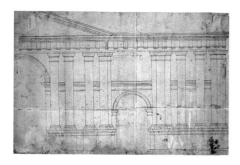

312

ANTONIO DA SANGALLO THE YOUNGER
Facade Project
ca. 1517-18

Florence, Galleria degli Uffizi, Gabinetto Disegni e Stampe,
Uff. 257A
Pen and ink on paper, with incised lines; straightedge and
compass.
INSCRIBED: (verso) *Faccia dello Emicichlo tondo di sto pietro;
Modani di piu cose* (Sangallo, after 1527).
59.5/60.6 × 88.5/87.7 cm

PROVENANCE: Papers of Antonio da Sangallo the Younger.

BIBLIOGRAPHY: Geymüller 1875-80: 269, T. 40, fig. 1; Giovannoni
1959; Wolff Metternich 1972: 44, fig. 129; Frommel 1984c: 266;
1986b: 281; Bruschi 1987b: 290; 1992b: 70, 76.

The importance of the project for the facade shown on the
recto is due not least of all to its being the only one illustrating entirely Bramante's giant order for the exterior of
St. Peter's. That the width of the shaft of the pilasters was
still 12 *palmi* can already be deduced from their comparison with the distance between the axes of the central nave
and side aisles of 1 *palmo*, and with the survey of the parts
of the entablature carried out by Peruzzi and by the *Codex
Coner* (cat. no. 301). With an overall height of ca. 189
palmi, the order is therefore about 35 *palmi* higher than
the one on the inside. This solution helped Bramante to
cover the lower part of the vault without having to introduce an attic, and to project the light straight through
the lunettes (fig. 14-16, pp. 414-416). The tall 39-*palmi*
high pedestals, which Sangallo adopted make the order
conform to more classical canons, are not compatible with
either the five niches of Bramante's apse (cat. no. 323) or
with the columns of Bramante's project for the facade
(cat. no. 307). In spite of these pedestals the pilasters with
ca. 1:9.6 proportions are still more slender for a Doric order than what could be presumed from Sangallo's own independent project of 1518-19. Since both Raphael and
Sangallo altered Bramante's giant order (cat. nos. 311,
314), the facade in Uff. 257A recto seems actually to be
Sangallo's only project from the beginning of his career as
second architect of St. Peter's, in the years 1517-18, and
this would also furnish some idea about Raphael's lost
projects. Not without reason the Doric order with its complex rhythms and projections is more compatible than any
other order with the architecture in the background of
Raphael's *Coronation of Charles V*, which was probably
painted in around 1516 (Frommel 1986b: 280). At the
start of 1516 Raphael designed the facade for S. Lorenzo
in Florence (Frommel 1986b: 275ff.)—which also provides evidence that Raphael already intended proposing
a closed vestibule with columns inserted in the bays. Even
the similarity of the rhythm of the portico designed by
Raphael in 1514 is still evident in Sangallo's project for
the facade (cat. no. 308). But at the same time it is easy
to comprehend the problems created by this solution. Instead of making the order increase progressively in density toward the center, he placed sections that were symmetrical in themselves, one next to the other, but creating
evident problems on both sides of the secondary portal
which connected the lateral facade to the central one.
Both the groups of pilasters that flank the side portal provoke the single and unresolved assymetry of the facade.
The lateral section differs only in the corner elements pro-

truding from the right half of the central section, whose
pilasters equally set forward and whose corner triglyphs
descend directly from Bramante's choir (cat. no. 301).
The enormous cornice of the imposts cannot be seen anywhere in the views of the choir (cat. nos. 323, 342, 344)
and would not have been compatible even with the large
open arcades of the 1506 project. It could have been derived from the projects of 1513-14. If it had been continued in the longitudinal body and in the transept, according to Sangallo's preference for a horizontal continuity, the windows of the side chapels would have only been
possible at a height of ca. 115 *palmi*, at the level of the capitals of the giant order on the inside, as can be seen by the
position of the aedicule above the side entrance in this
drawing. These would have been splayed windows so that
the light could pour diagonally into the chapels. The window pediment, however, reflects more the style of the
years 1517-18 rather than Bramante's. In the facade it
obviously had to correspond to a lunette in the atrium,
which therefore had to reach more or less the same height
as the central nave. In this case, it could have been possible, if necessary, to insert a benediction loggia in the
tympanum—in the same way as he did later in Uff. 70A
(cat. no. 314). If Sangallo in his belated inscription confused this facade with the ambulatories, perhaps it is possible to conclude that the latter should have had an alternating articulation as well. In the detail of the plan on the
verso he considered the entrance bay of the longitudinal
body (Frommel 1984c: 266). The type of plan with the dilation of every second bay by means of a dome differs
from his successive projects in the omission of the diagonal faces on the pier arches and the half-columns. This
circumstance also suggests dating this drawing shortly after Sangallo's appointment.   *C.L.F.*

313

ANTONIO DA SANGALLO THE YOUNGER
Plan Project for St. Peter's
ca. 1519

Florence, Galleria degli Uffizi, Gabinetto Disegni e Stampe,
Uff. 37A
Pen and ink, on paper; compass and straightedge, alterations in
freehand; incised lines.
79.3/80.7 × 28.6/29.5 cm
INSCRIBED: *pilastri quadri, pilastri* (Sangallo).

PROVENANCE: Papers of Antonio da Sangallo the Younger.

BIBLIOGRAPHY: Geymüller 1875-80: 308ff., pl. 36.6; Giovannoni:
137; Wolff Metternich 1972, fig. 80; Frommel 1984c: 270ff.;
Wolff Metternich and Thoenes 1987: 136; Bruschi 1992b: 70ff.

Sangallo must have designed this project showing the fairly realistic dimensions of the longitudinal body after the
alternative to be seen on the left of the plan in Uff. 252A
(cat. no. 316), but before the one on the right. The quincunx system, the original arrangement of the external
construction with a 5-*palmi* order and the facade with a
14-*palmi* order presuppose an acquaitance with Raphael's

project in the *Codex Mellon* of 1518 (cat. no. 311). Sangallo eliminated Bramante's choir, however, and persevered
with a dome for the longitudinal body and the separate
ambulatories. The interruption he had introduced in the
right transept arm, originally planned with groups of four
columns of 5 *palmi*, and which, on second thoughts he emphasized by means of wall masses with large niches, is
hard to separate from the functions of the choir arm.
There, the choir altar is flanked by both niches, and—in
the same way as in Uff. 3A (cat. no. 280)—the choir stalls
are arranged in the form of an amphitheater. Sangallo
probably even wanted to close the wall placed behind the
stalls. He flanked the ambulatories with sacristies projecting considerably beyond the main body of the building,
and surrounded them with their own porticoes. Only at
a second stage did he substitute the 5-*palmi* order
designed by Raphael with a 9-*palmi* order of the same density, like the alternative to the right in the plan in Uff.
252A (cat. no. 316). In the same way he then reconsidered
this order on the facade and on an octagonal campanile
containing a staircase, transforming it into a giant order
of 12 *palmi*. In the alternative sketches of the plan and elevation for the facade he even approached the facade
projects shown in Uff. 69A recto, Uff. 72A, Uff. 73A and
Uff. 31A verso, which consequently could have been
drawn in about the same period of time. The ample staircase of the campanile with its low, wide steps could have
been inspired by Bramante's staircase in the Belvedere,
and was perhaps planned to lead up to the Benediction
Loggia, even though at first a much smaller one was
designed and sited behind the atrium. Sacrificing the
Cappella Sistina to the highly protruding chapel of the
longitudinal body, Sangallo must have taken into consideration here the reconstruction of the southern half of
the palace.
The change of mind toward a much denser relief on the
outer wall and the choice of a 9-*palmi* order cannot be explained to the full by the previous projects of Raphael and
Sangallo (Frommel 1986: 283ff.). Inspired perhaps by the
Basilica Aemilia, Giuliano da Sangallo had used the combination of half-columns and square columns much earlier
than 1510 in his facade project, as shown in Uff. 297A,
and then he had taken it up again in about 1516, perhaps
even working together with his brother Antonio the
Elder, in his project, illustrated in Uff. 280A, for the facade of S. Lorenzo (Satzinger 1991: 98). On this project
however, the arrangement of the design already reveals
the influence of Bramante's later works and the courtyard
of the Palazzo Farnese. The combination becomes the
main motif in the church of S. Biagio in Montepulciano,
which was realized no later than the winter of 1518-19
(Satzinger 1991: 85ff.). Sangallo must have been familiar
with his uncle's project, which must have stimulated him
to make changes in his own design in Uff. 37A, with all
probability between the spring and autumn of 1519. Sangallo connected the combination of the squared pilaster
("pilastri quadri") and the half-columns with a central aedicule (like that of the Pantheon) or a niche thus extending it to a full bay. It seems that Antonio the Elder, in
turn, shortly afterward reintroduced this extended motif
for the altars of S. Biagio. It was taken up again both in
the contemporary project by Sangallo for S. Giovanni dei
Fiorentini, and in his other ones after the death of
Raphael (Frommel 1986: 295ff., fig. 56 a-c, f-h, j, l). If
the 9-*palmi* order can be documented for the first time in
connection with this extended form of the motif—and
Raphael himself did not use it anywhere—then there are
many elements to endorse the hypothesis that this 9-*palmi*
order also derives from a proposal made by Sangallo.
                                                      C.L.F.

314

ANTONIO DA SANGALLO THE YOUNGER
Project for the Facade, Dome, Ambulatory and Benediction Loggia
ca. 1519

Florence, Galleria degli Uffizi, Gabinetto Disegni e Stampe, Uff. 70A
Pen and ink, on paper; part straightedge and compass, part freehand.
30.4 × 46.2/46.7 cm

PROVENANCE: Papers of Antonio da Sangallo the Younger.

BIBLIOGRAPHY: Geymüller 1875-80: 315ff., pl. 31, 2; Giovannoni 1959: 136, 140; Wolff Metternich 1972: 55, fig. 81; Frommel 1984c: 274ff.; Wolff Metternich and Thoenes 1987: 160ff.; Bruschi 1987b: 290; Bruschi 1992b: 72f.

Sangallo must have worked at the same time on the projects shown in Uff. 252A, Uff. 37A (cat. nos. 316, 313) and on this sheet. His original design for the facade corresponds considerably to that of the alternative on the left of Uff. 252A, where also pairs of twin pilasters with shafts 12 *palmi* wide are separated by niches, and along the secondary axes there are four columns of only 5 *palmi* (from Old St. Peter's?). The ambulatory at the top right of Uff. 70A, isolated from the transept by means of piers, also belongs to this phase of the project. While Sangallo however, in the alternative on the left of Uff. 252A conserved Bramante's choir, in this drawing he had already decided on a new order without the triglyph frieze and with low pedestals, which corresponded totally—as the section on the right indicates—to the height and sequence of the interior order. He was probably inspired to do all this by Raphael's projects (cat. nos. 308, 311). The rhythm of the facade is more continuous compared to the one in Uff. 257A (cat. no. 312) and therefore further from Bramante's and Raphael's of 1514. At a second stage of the elaboration, which must have coincided roughly with the time of the project in Uff. 37A, he substituted the 5-*palmi* columns of the secondary bays with the 9-*palmi* columns of the new order and made this continue along the longitudinal walls as well. This 9-*palmi* order corresponded perfectly with the pilaster strips of the aisles and side chapels and therefore respected the principle of correspondence even better than Raphael's 5-*palmi* order of 1518. Sangallo then tries to correct these pilaster stips by adding pedestals and Ionic capitals, and transforming them into a second interior order. With its height of 91 *palmi* (20.33 m) the 9-*palmi* order reached almost to the level of the Cappella Sistina, and thus could be as easily connected with the palace as Raphael's 5-*palmi* order. Less convincing is Sangallo's idea of lowering the left bay to the height of the 9-*palmi* order and of crowning it with a half pediment. In the masterly sketch of the ambulatory at the top right, he illustrated the arrangement of the columns inside the ambulatory with an entablature which continues Raphael's partially projecting cornice of 40-*palmi* niches. This version is even nearer Raphael's 1518 project than the one shown in Uff. 54A (cat. no. 315). In the sketch at the top he moved away from the Pantheon-like dome designed by Bramante and by Raphael, and proposed a dome closely inspired by Florence Cathedral, with about 12 ribs, whose construction would therefore have been modeled even more on the Florentine prototype. It is quite likely therefore that he already had in mind to build a drum with circular windows, no colon-nade either on the inside or the outside, as was actually envisaged on the *giulio* coin of 1520 (cat. no. 319) or on the 1535 project (cat. no. 340). Not without reason did he criticize the heavy drum designed by Bramante and Raphael's domes slightly later on in his *Memoriale* (cat. no. 320). With its simple colonnade even the lantern seems generally more lightweight. The area of its vault still recalls Raphael's project in the *Codex Mellon* (cat. no. 311), but it has additional lighting from the attic windows. To the right of the central section of the facade is a hint of the roof of a dome of the nave (cat. no. 313). In the sketch to the above left, Sangallo modified the Benediction Loggia already along the lines of his facade projects in Uff. 72A (cat. no. 318) and Uff. 73A (Frommel 1984: 284), positioning it directly over the 9-*palmi* order of the vestibule and extending it in the attic placed over the entablature. The walls of the central upper part of the vestibule were planned to open into galleries on several floors, so that the pope would have been able to utilize this side too. The points in common with the sketch of the facade in Uff. 69A (cat. no. 300) suggest that the final version of the project in Uff. 70A was not completed before the start of 1519. *C.L.F.*

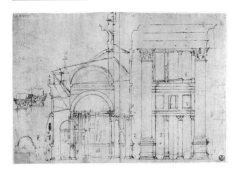

315

ANTONIO DA SANGALLO THE YOUNGER
Section and Elevation of the Ambulatory Project
ca. 1519

Florence, Galleria degli Uffizi, Gabinetto Disegni e Stampe, Uff. 54A
Pen and ink, on paper; drawing tools with freehand finishes.
INSCRIBED: *cosi; cosi; queste sono apunto le misure* (Sangallo).
33.4 × 46.3 cm

PROVENANCE: Papers of Antonio da Sangallo the Younger.

BIBLIOGRAPHY: Hofmann 1928: 206ff.; Giovannoni 1959: 137ff., 148; Wolff Metternich 1972: 50ff., fig. 62, 65; Frommel 1984c: 277; Bruschi 1992b: 74.

The starting point for this project was the interior elevation of a bay of the ambulatory in the right half of the drawing, which was how Raphael might have designed it in about 1518. Unlike the measurements indicated, the pedestals of the giant order are still ca. 18 *palmi* high. The columns are provided with Attic bases and support a shortened entablature. Blind panels are distributed along the walls. The rectangular windows seem to be framed with marble inserts. Being a faithful disciple of Vitruvius, Sangallo tried to assert the principle of the order everywhere and to provide it with a more standard detail. He thus opened the windows in the intercolumniation of a second colonnade and provided the lower colonnade—in the section on the left—with an entablature conforming to the canons. In both sketches in the left-hand margin he continued the Corinthian order as far as the 40-*palmi* niche, whose abstract design had already bothered him in the sketch in Uff. 70A (cat. no. 314). Then he gave the ambulatory a barrel vault, starting only from above the tripartite entablature established by Raphael. This stratagem increased the natural illumination of the ambulatories but jeopardized the that of the transept, which was the reason why Raphael had lowered the ambulatories. From the other arm of the transept it would have been possible to see the intrados of the windows. The natural illumination of the ambulatory itself came from the oculi shown in Uff. 79 and Uff. 122A (Frommel 1984c: 285ff.) and from the "bocche di lupo" or window shafts in the lower attic. Over this attic there is the partially jutting entablature of the giant order which corresponds in height to the internal order and probably already foreshadows the Doric frieze, prepared later in Uff. 72A (cat. no. 318). Evidently this entablature should have extended along the walls of the transept arms erected over the ambulatories and have supported an attic with volutes masking at least the beginning of the vault of the transept. Only at a second stage did Sangallo reduce the measurements of the pedestals to 15 ½ *palmi* on the outside and to 13 ½ *palmi* on the inside, i.e., to the height which was then also partly realized. *C.L.F.*

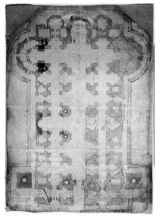

316

ANTONIO DA SANGALLO THE YOUNGER
Plan Project
ca. 1519

Florence, Galleria degli Uffizi, Gabinetto Disegni e Stampe, Uff. 252A
Pen and ink, with wash, on parchment.
88.5 × 59.2/60.5 cm
INSCRIBED: *porta; porta; dala porta ala porta channe 48 porta; porta channe* (Sangallo).

PROVENANCE: Papers of Antonio da Sangallo the Younger.

BIBLIOGRAPHY: Geymüller 1875-80: 305, 307ff., pl. 30; Hofmann 1982: 142ff.; Giovannoni 1959: 137; Wolff Metternich 1972: 44, fig. 38; Frommel 1984c: 267ff.; Bruschi 1992b: 68f.

Of all Sangallo's projects for St. Peter's conserved to date, the alternative shown on the left is the one closest to the projects designed by his uncle Giuliano dating back to 1514 (cat. nos. 306, 307). Bramante's choir flanked by octagonal sacristies, the semicircular ambulatories embracing the main body and the facade towers bring the plan in Uff. 7A to mind immediately. The longitudinal body is even longer than that in Uff. 9A and would have reached beyond the steps of St. Peter's Square. Of the two northern vestibules of the longitudinal body, originally designed in the right half as well, the western one would have extended to just a few meters in front of the southern wall of the Cappella Sistina, while the eastern one would have arrived at the Cortile del Maresciallo. As in Sangallo's project in Uff. 254A this one too thus implicated drastic alterations to the papal palace. Unlike Raphael, who had repeated Bramante's version with the longitudinal three-aisle body almost entirely in his 1514 project, and who was concerned most of all with finding a harmonic solution for uniting the choir and the transept, Sangallo concentrated all his efforts on the longitudinal body. This attitude demonstrates that he was perhaps still under the influence of Fra Giocondo (cat. no. 286), like he was in his studies of Vitruvius as well. In any case, the axial arrangement of regular bays was foreign to his approach. Thus

618

in his *Memoriale* of 1520-21 he also criticized Raphael's longitudinal body, defining it as "long, narrow and steep as an alleyway" (cat. no. 320). Sangallo may have justified his polycentric longitudinal body as dictated by the multiple liturgical functions which necessarily took place at the same time in the basilica. This was why he also provided two of the three additional "cappelle magiori" with their own vestibules. He evidently destined an area for the Obelisk to the south of the central dome of the longitudinal body. If he separated the ambulatories from the transept by means of projecting piers, he perhaps decided this on the basis of his preference for independent spaces and for their functional utilization. This could all be used to date the alternative project on the left as prepared during the period before Sangallo was nominated second architect of the Basilica of St. Peter in the autumn of 1516. The facade however, already corresponds to the previous alternative drawn in Uff. 70A (cat. no. 314) and suggests, like this one, an influence of Raphael's 1518 project.

The intense collaboration with Raphael (beginning no later than early 1519) found expression, however, in the alternative drawn on the right. This was preceeded by at least two scratched-out versions, one of which perhaps being the symmetry of the left-hand alternative. At this stage Sangallo returned to the quincuncial system designed by Raphael and his segment-shaped ambulatories with regular colonnades and hinted even at the demolition of Bramante's choir. The dense external design with half-columns and "squared columns" of a 9-*palmi* order could have been the result of an agreement with Raphael, which he reconsidered in the facade, enlarging it to an order of 12-*palmi*. All this, however, did not hinder him from remaining faithful to his main idea of an enormous polycentric longitudinal body. Moreover, he now gave the three new domes even the same dimensions as the crossing dome over the Apostle Peter's tomb. In spite of their rhythmic to-and-fro arrangement the design of the external walls already risked falling prey to the monotonously schematic articulation that plagues Sangallo's model of 1521 (cat. no. 321), in comparison to which the left-hand version retains the spirit of Bramante's grandeur. Perhaps respect for the denser arrangement of the right-hand version made him replace the vestibules with secondary portals. He integrated the towers in the body of the building as in Raphael's 1518 project. Where the sketch in the right-hand margin was actually drawn at the same time, Sangallo returned to a centrally planned building. His scheme for a pedimented portico anticipated a solution that returned to the fore in about 1520-21 under Peruzzi (cat. no. 322) and later during the reign of Pope Paul III (cat. nos. 330, 331), due also to Sangallo's own revival of it (cat. no. 338). The two longitudinal alternatives, at least, should date to around 1519.　　　　　　　　　　　　　*C.L.F.*

Florence, Galleria degli Uffizi, Gabinetto Disegni e Stampe, Uff. 255A

Pen and ink, on paper; drawing tools, with numerous pentimenti. 87.5/189.5 × 57.5/61.1 cm

PROVENANCE: Papers of Antonio da Sangallo the Younger.

BIBLIOGRAPHY: Hofmann 1928: 141ff., 166ff.; Giovannoni 1959: 137, 140; Wolff Metternich 1972: 53, fig. 4; Frommel 1984c: 282; Wolff Metternich and Thoenes 1987: 177ff., 184; Bruschi 1992b: 75ff.

This plan marks the halfway point between the project in Uff. 37A (cat. no. 313), dating perhaps to the first six months of 1519, and Sangallo's model of 1521 (cat. no. 321). Since the alternating niches in the ambulatories do not yet correspond to the final version, whose elaboration was begun at the latest in the autumn of 1519 (see "St. Peter's," pp. 399-423), this project must have been developed slightly earlier. In any case, it must have been preceded by the studies for the details of the ambulatories (Frommel 1984c: 275, 282, 285ff.) and therefore can be cataloged at the end of a long series of projects executed while Raphael was still alive. Not without reason Sangallo had in the meantime abandoned the idea of extending the longitudinal body as far as Pio II's Benediction Loggia. The right-hand alternative differs from the plan in Uff. 37A in its revival of the segment-shaped ambulatories proposed by Raphael, in the reduced projection of the tower and the chapels, and in the articulation—nearer the final project—of the whole structure. The tower (which was perhaps originally connected to the vestibule) has been moved about one bay back. In spite of this, the Cappella Sistina, the Scala Regia and the Sala Regia would have been compromised by this project. The alternative on the left—which abandoned the projecting chapels of the longitudinal body, retained the tower and took the Cappella Sistina, the Sala Regia and the Obelisk into account—is substantially more realistic. The staircase in the corresponding right tower of the facade could have taken over the function of the Scala Regia. Sangallo's alternative on the left is therefore the one nearest to the final scheme, competing with Raphael's last scheme of the autumn of 1519, which was probably still based on five bays. In the later partial closing of the 40-*palmi* niches next to the ambulatories, Sangallo was very near the 1521 wooden model project. As in the model, he proposed an even more economical solution, presenting Bramante's choir, but omitting the choir ambulatory and the quincunx system. The original arrangement of the facade corresponds amply with the first version drawn in Uff. 72A (cat. no. 318), and was later changed along the lines of both the second version in Uff. 72A and the design in Uff. 73A (Frommel 1984: 284). Therefore these projects should all date to more or less the same period　　　　　*C.L.F.*

BIBLIOGRAPHY: Wolff Metternich 1972: 53ff., fig. 75; Frommel 1984c: 283; Bruschi 1992b: 76.

While dating probably to the late summer of 1519, if not to 1520, this project provides further proof that Sangallo developed alternative ideas during the whole period of his collaboration with Raphael. The first version corresponds to the first version in Uff. 255A (cat. no. 317). In both of them, the system based on the 9-*palmi* order with Pantheon-style aedicules and circular windows is already a confirmed part of the design; the aedicules are provided with semicircular niches. The height of the pedestals has been settled already at 15½ *palmi*. The giant half-columns have a shaft 14 *palmi* wide, like those in Raphael's project in the *Codex Mellon*; with their low base, they conform to the standard ratio of 1:8 and are decorated with a triglyph frieze typical of Doric columns, as on the *giulio* coined in 1520 (cat. no. 319). Sangallo masterfully applied the principle of correspondence between the interior and exterior construction and of the dynamic growth toward the center even more superbly than he did in the plans in Uff. 257A (cat. no. 312) and in Uff. 70A (cat. no. 314). While he had not yet united the central section with the temple front and the equally symmetrical lateral parts in a completely convincing way, here he emphasized the overlapping relations between the three sections: the right half of the central section is the left half of the right lateral section. How little this ambivalence corresponded to Sangallo's approach to design can be seen in the various proposals he made for the temple front. The temple front on the central section where the great entrance arch is inserted is nearer to the drawings in Uff. 254A and to Uff. 70A. This in turn frames the relatively small portal (Uff. 122A) with above it the Benediction Loggia and lastly the thermal-type window of the central nave. This central temple front corresponds to a small lateral front, almost the same as that drawn in Uff. 70A. At a second stage, Sangallo then hinted at having a single temple front to dominate the whole facade. The third version, which presents pediments over the lateral sections, gives a similar impression of imperfection as the second one. In the top right-hand sketch he returned to the first version, but placing the arch of the lateral portal so far back as to unite it visually with the dome of the first side chapel. He also gave up the complex sequence of half-columns on this sketch, and went back to simple pilasters. With the subdivision of the facade wall into sculptured blocks he was already near the principle of the wooden model of 1539. Finally—as the comment "questo" indicates—he decided on a third solution in the left margin, which also corresponds to the plan detail in the lower margin. The archway of the entrance has become part of an attic which he had already roughly sketched in the first version, and is now crowned with a pediment. This attic is supported by a group of projecting half-columns bearing statues in front of the attic. The idea of an attic with statues possibly derived from Michelangelo's model for the facade of S. Lorenzo which the Sangallo had drawn in Rome in January 1518. In the support of the arch by a separate element of the order he followed the example of the Cappella Medici whose construction began in November 1519. How far Sangallo consequently departed from Raphael's principles of composition can be seen in his facade project in Uff. 73A in which he referred directly to the last version drawn in Uff. 72A. By reducing the groups to simple 14-*palmi* pilasters, he increased the intercolumniation noticeably, so that the niches came to substitute the Pantheon-type aedicules, and large pediments found a place on the entablature of the 9-*palmi* order. The cutting off of the corner bays already hinted at by Sangallo in the plan in Uff. 37A and then reintroduced in his *Memoriale* (cat. no. 320) excluded side towers and emphasizied the bulk of the atrium. Sangallo's facade project in Uff. 73A in fact demonstrates clearly how any kind of dynamic composition is quite extraneous to his style, but also with what intensity he analyzed the ideas of both Bramante and Raphael, though then reverting in the end to paratactic systems similar to those in Uff. 70A.　　　　　*C.L.F.*

317
ANTONIO DA SANGALLO THE YOUNGER
Plan Project
ca. 1519

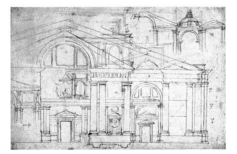

318
ANTONIO DA SANGALLO THE YOUNGER
Facade Projects

Florence, Galleria degli Uffizi, Gabinetto Disegni e Stampe, Uff. 72A

Pen and ink, on paper; straightedge and freehand. 23.5/24.3 × 34.4 cm

INSCRIBED: *questo; questo* (Sangallo).

PROVENANCE: Papers of Antonio da Sangallo the Younger.

319
UNKNOWN DIE-ENGRAVER
Sangallo's Project for St. Peter's (?)
1520

Vatican, Biblioteca Apostolica Vaticana, Medagliere
Silver *giulio*.
diam. 2.9 cm
INSCRIBED: (obverse) *LEO DECIMVS PONT MAX MAR[CHIA]*;
(reverse) *PETRE ECCE TEMPLVM TVVM*.

BIBLIOGRAPHY: Serafini 1910, I: 188 n. 140, pl. xxix, 28; Frommel
1984c: 255, 306; De Caro 1962: 234-237.

This coin, like the 1513-14 *Giulio*, was minted in the
Marche. It can be dated thanks to Cardinal Armellini's
coat of arms, because he governed the Marche as the papal
legate from the end of 1519 to the summer of 1521 when
he became the camerlengo (De Caro 1962). Unlike the
1514 silver coin, this shows a project on the obverse which
should correspond to the state of the project in 1520. The
highly simplified facade is flanked by a pair of two-story
campaniles, whose ground stories appear to contain
niches, perhaps with statues of the two princes of the
church. Two fluted columns divide the facade into three
almost equal bays. There are circular windows over the
side portals, and what is probably a coat of arms over the
central portal. Triglyphs decorate the heavy entablature,
which extends along the projecting corner towers. The
drum is illuminated by means of oculi. Unlike the Pantheon, the dome is not stepped, and is crowned with a
large lantern and cross. Another drum like this can only
be found in Sangallo's drawing in Uff. 78A (see cat. no.
340) which, with its small order and attic, is much more
developed than the facade shown on the *giulio*, and goes
back to the reign of Pope Paul III. This reduced version
of the drum is sufficient to date the coin to the period after
Raphael's death, when Sangallo was in charge of the
project. The giant Doric order and the insertion of ornamental sculpture recalls the projects in Uff. 72A and
Uff. 73A of the autumn-winter of 1519-20. Besides, no
other project exists in those years showing projecting towers, and the main central pediment and Benediction Loggia are both missing. This is why it can perhaps be defined
as a simplification of the design to make the production
of the coin dies easier. It must not be forgotten that this
coin was minted in the Marche to publicize the magnificence of the Holy Roman Church in the provinces.

C.L.F.

320
ANTONIO DA SANGALLO THE YOUNGER
*"Memoriale" on the Design of St. Peter's after the
Death of Raphael, and Sketches for the Facade*
ca. 1520

Florence, Galleria degli Uffizi, Gabinetto Disegni e Stampe,
Uff. 33A
Pen and ink, on paper; freehand sketches; text of the *Memoriale*
on recto and verso.
18.1 × 21/21.6 cm

PROVENANCE: Papers of Antonio da Sangallo the Younger.

BIBLIOGRAPHY: Geymüller 1875-80, I: 293ff.; Giovannoni 1959:
132ff.; Wolff Metternich 1972: 44, fig. 36; Frommel 1984c: 296;
Bruschi 1992b: 71ff.

In this *memoriale* or memorandum, which may have been
intended for the eyes of Leo X, but possibly never got beyond this preliminary stage, Sangallo expounded his criticism of the project that had been approved before
Raphael's death. In his opinion, the project lacked unity
and there were not enough large chapels. The pilasters of
the transept and the central nave would have been larger
than those in Bramante's apse, while they should have
been more slender or, at most, the same width—since the
pilasters of the apse would then have seemed of the same
width in spite of the distance. The height of the choir's
external Doric order of pilasters would have been over
twelve times the width of the shaft, instead of seven
times. A decision was also necessary as to whether the
pilasters of the internal order would stand on pedestals,
as these would contrast with the "capelle," by which Sangallo undoubtedly means the niches that start at ground
level (Heemskerck view, cat. no. 341); these were probably planned to be used as chapels. Continuing to build the
central nave in this manner would have risked making it
tall, long, and narrow—like an alleyway—as well as extremely dark, since there was no way of it receiving any
natural light. Sangallo observes that the dome was so
broad that the drum's weight would have to conform to
the load-bearing capacity of the pier arches. The passages
between the 40-*palmi* niches would have looked like narrow slits. The ambulatories in the transept arms would
certainly have been beautiful in themselves, but they were
out of keeping with the rest of the building. The proportions of the marble moldings made by Raphael in the 40-
palmi niches were incorrect, and so was his tripartite
travertine cornice of the impost, because it was not supported by a true order. Since these cornices (cat. nos. 292,
293 and 344) and probably even the jutting cornices over
the pilaster strips of the 40-*palmi* niches were inspired by
Bramante, Sangallo was really criticizing the latter's 1513
project which had been adopted by Raphael in all these details. It is unlikely however that Sangallo would have
dared criticize his superior's project so caustically in 1516
-17, i.e., when he had just been appointed tenure; nor
would he have discussed these ambulatories "under con-
truction" ("lemicichlo che e fanno"), which were truly
beautiful in themselves, but not suited to the rest of the
building ("ma imperfetto in questa opera perche resta li e

non seguita e schonpagnia e chosa pesima"). This description concurs much better with the years 1520-21, when
work was actually being carried out only on the southern
arm of the transept, introducing the 9-*palmi* order there,
which clashed with the giant order of Bramante's choir.
Criticism of the choir was still a possibility at this time,
since the pope was still in two minds about its demolition.
Sangallo doubtless wanted to pave the way for a counterproposal. However, given that he kept the ambulatories
in his wooden model of the spring of 1521 (cat. no. 321)
and did not even transform the pilaster strips under the
cornice of the impost into a real order, he must have given
up his battle with the pope over these two questions. His
alternative scheme, with the conservation of Bramante's
choir, may also have been a question of diplomacy. For all
these reasons, the *Memoriale* must date not earlier than
summer 1521; a possible date around autumn 1519 is corroborated in particular by the atrium sketches in the lower
margin of the verso. The oblique corner and the paratactic
sequence are developments of ideas that occur in Uff. 37A
and Uff. 73A; similarly, the paired half-columns and
"colonne quadre" separated by niches correspond to an alternative in Uff. 37A. With his sets of four columns in the
secondary arcades and in the "vestibulum" of the central
arcade, Sangallo was returning to an idea expressed in
Uff. 254A and 252A (cat. no. 316)—further evidence that
all these projects must have been developed in fairly close
succession. The sheet also includes a rough sketch of an
aedicule on the entablature of the group of columns of the
central arch (lower margin, center). Perhaps this was to
become a part of the Benediction Loggia. The sketch in
the margin on the left refers to the sides of the atrium.

C.L.F.

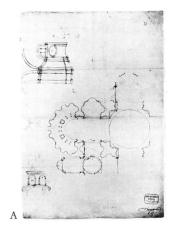

A

321
JEAN DE CHENEVIÈRES
Studies of Sangallo's Wooden Model of 1521
ca. 1521-26

Munich, Bayerisches Staatsbibliothek, *Cod. Icon.* 195, fols. 1-3
Pen and ink, on paper; part freehand, part straightedge and
compass; measurements in Roman *palmi* and *oncie*; numerous
inscriptions by the draftsman.
42.5/43 × 28.5/29 cm

BIBLIOGRAPHY: Wolff Metternich 1972: 55ff., fig. 83-88; Frommel
1984c: 299-302; Wolff Metternich and Thoenes 1987: 161;
Bruschi 1992b: 65ff.

The scale of 1:120 indicates at a glance that Jean de
Chenevières, contemporary and pupil of Sangallo,
reproduced a model whose authorship is endorsed by the
inscription "saingualle," and by the design's similarities to
the drawing in Uff. 255A (cat. no. 317). In May 1521 Sangallo was paid for a model (K. Frey 1910: 67ff.) and the
relatively low sum of 85 ducats confirms that it was of
small dimensions; in fact the 5-*palmi* shaft of the columns
of the ambulatory could not have measured more than 0.5
oncie (less than one centimeter).

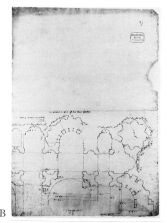

B

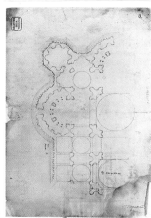

C

Chenevières' studies give the impression that Sangallo's model did not include the facade, and provided an alternative project that included conserving Bramante's choir, as in the plan in Uff. 255A.

The longitudinal body was very like the left-hand alternative in Uff. 255A, while the bulging corner sacristy took after the alternative drawn on the right of that same sheet. This sacristy was however less voluminous and its polygonal volumes would have blended substantially better with Bramante's choir than the two alternatives in Uff. 255A. The links between the model's characteristics and the arguments Sangallo used in his *Memoriale* (cat. no. 320) suggest that this project (undisputedly later) was a compromise. Obliged (probably by order of the pope himself) to conserve the ambulatories and perhaps even Bramante's choir, and to abandon any idea of redesigning the pilaster strips of the aisles as a true order, Sangallo realized that he had more chance of getting his own way with regard to the remaining areas.

This is why he again proposed to shorten the central nave to three bays, and to dilate it and increase the illumination by means of a second "cappella grande"; in addition, he proposed to eliminate the passages and projecting cornices of the 40-*palmi* niches. In any case, Sangallo sacrificed a large part of the harmoniousness of the previous projects to accommodate these wholly professional and functional improvements. Even the scant details indicating the elevation of the chapels and the ambulatory convey a greater sense of sobriety compared to the projects he designed when Raphael was still alive (cat. nos. 314, 315). Sangallo gave the columns of the ambulatory a tripartite entablature on both inside and outside, extending it to the columns of the transept windows. He lowered the ambulatory once again to the same height as the one in Uff. 70A, and directed the window shafts down from the attic into the vault, thereby improving the natural illumination of the transept arms. The giant order on the exterior was eliminated, without any clear indication of what he thought about the external design of the higher zone of the transept arms and their connection to the rest of the building. This project goes beyond the elevations drawn in Uff. 79 and Uff. 122A (Frommel 1984c: 285ff.)

designed by Sangallo perhaps when he was still Raphael's assistant, in particular in the elegant area of the attic and its thermal type windows. If Chenevières gave these the form of a Serliana on the inside, he did it perhaps because Sangallo had prepared various alternatives. Sangallo's surprising return to the groin vault next to the domes of the side aisles can be explained as a further attempt to interrupt the axial flow of Bramante's and Raphael's barrel vaults. Elaborated as a compromise between the pope's ideas and Sangallo's own intentions, the project was the end result of more than two years study, and the last of several models to which Leo X seems to have given his blessing. *C.L.F.*

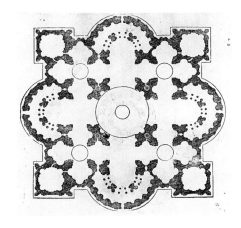

322
SEBASTIANO SERLIO (after BALDASSARRE PERUZZI)
Plan Project
1521 (?)

Sebastiano Serlio, Book III, fol. 65v.

BIBLIOGRAPHY: Frommel 1989e: 39-49; Bruschi 1992a: 451ff.

"In the time of Julius II, Baldassar Petrucci from Siena was in Rome. Not only was he a great painter, but he was very intelligent in architecture. Following in Bramante's footsteps, he made a model in the way shown here below, designing it with four portals, and with the high altar in the center. A sacristy was placed in each of the four corners, over which the campaniles could be built for ornament, and especially in the front facade which looks toward the city." This description, written by Serlio perhaps as late as 1539-40, suggests that Peruzzi had followed a prototype of Bramante's, that he had built the model already during the reign of Julius II and had the intention of placing the altar in the center of the church under the area of the dome, which he planned to execute according to the design Bramante made just before he died. These misleading observations confirm the hypothesis according to which Serlio only obtained the project and the relative information about it after Peruzzi's death when he was collecting material for his Book III (Frommel 1989e: 39). First of all therefore it is necessary to try to identify Serlio's woodcut with one of the three phases of elaboration into which Peruzzi's surviving projects can been divided. Peruzzi's first projects should date back to after 1 August 1520, when he was appointed second papal architect. The recent suggestion that his name already apppeared in the *fabbrica* account books in about 1514-16, is based on a confusion between Peruzzi and Baldassarre da Carrara (K. Frey 1910: 60; cf. Francia 1977: 31-36; Bruschi 1992a: 450ff.). Serlio's woodcut can be described as the transformation of Raphael's last project into a strictly centralized system, like the one Sangallo had already considered in 1519 (cat. no. 316). According to Vasari, Leo X was worried about the excessive size of the project and the inconsistency of the same, and had commissioned Peruzzi to design a new one. The resulting magnificent achievement was a source of inspiration for

all the other architects (Vasari 1878-85, IV: 599). As with Sangallo's first scheme, a wooden model of Peruzzi's first project was made in February 1521 (K. Frey 1910: 68ff.). It is not at all clear, however, whether this project corresponded in all its details to Serlio's print. The atrium with the Benediction Loggia and the palace linkage that characterized all the projects in the years 1519-20 are lacking; furthermore, the external design, barely started, with its aedicules and half-columns of a 9-*palmi* order, has been replaced by simple pilasters, perhaps still respecting the 9-*palmi* order. The reduced order and the fact that here the central bay of the ambulatories opens with a portal, are reminiscent of on all the later projects such as Uff. 14A (cat. no. 326) or the plan conserved in New York (cat. no. 330). This would suggest a date for Serlio's print contemporary with the New York plan and Sangallo's drawing in Uff. 39A (cat. no. 338), that is, around 1535, when Pope Paul III decided to reconsider a strictly centrally planned project for St. Peter's. Serlio's woodcut however differs from the projects after 1530, particularly as regards the wall either side of the ambulatories, which has no portals and has not been moved back 20 *palmi*. The corner sacristies have therefore been moved correspondingly further out. Serlio probably simplified the exterior design to facilitate the task of engraving, and most likely opted for an ideal rather than historically correct reproduction of details—witness the slightly eccentric position of the high altar. It is even a possibility that Peruzzi presented a second alternative with an atrium and Benediction Loggia together with the strictly centralized building, as he was to do in 1535. The atrium drawn in Uff. 31A recto (cat. no. 333) and the similar variation in the *Taccuino Senese* belong however to the period around 1535, and therefore one can only hypothesize that as early as 1521 he was thinking about an atrium like this. The collocation of this plan as belonging to the period before 1519 is improbable especially because of the ambulatories being very near the 1519 projects (cat. nos. 316, 317). If Serlio decided that the plan dated to the reign of Julius II, and put it very close to Bramante. He did it perhaps because he had heard that Paul III at first wanted to return to Julius II's centrally planned project and was very attentive to Peruzzi's proposals. The similar projects on fols. 70 verso and 71 recto of the *Codex Mellon* (Wolff Metternich 1972: 65, fig. 118) differ from Peruzzi's plan in the vestibules extending between the corner towers and the transept arms reminiscent of the design in Uff. 1A (cat. no. 282) and in the unimaginative facade with double columns of a 9-*palmi* order. Evidently this variation was the work of Domenico da Varignana who was consequently the first to think of a facade with a minor order (cf. Bruschi 1992a: 477). *C.L.F.*

323
JAN VAN SCOREL (?)
Views of St. Peter's (recto)
Views of the Palatine (verso)
Spring of 1524 (?)

Vatican, Biblioteca Apostolica Vaticana, Ashby, no. 329
Pen and ink, with charcoal, on paper.
19.8 × 40.8 cm

PROVENANCE: private Dutch collection; T. Ashby.

BIBLIOGRAPHY: Ashby 1924: 456ff.; Egger 1932, I: 29, pl. 38; Bodart 1975: 113, pl. 174; Frommel 1984c: 303ff.; 1984b; 160ff.; Wolff Metternich and Thoenes 1987: 194ff.

The handwriting and the supposed period of origin of this drawing suggest that the author was Jan van Scorel (1495-1562). From August 1522 to the end of May 1524 he was in the pope's employ as a painter and inspector of the Belvedere. His *Presentation in the Temple* in Vienna (cat. no. 324) makes it quite clear that he was only too familiar with the project for St. Peter's (Frommel 1984c). The view shows the building site from the southwest. Bramante's choir with its vault, its empty arched windows and fragmentary entablature had not made any progress since 1514. The northwest pier of the dome with the upper fluted part of its pilaster and the two niches can be seen through the apse opening, and through the attic window its descending shaft. The five niches between the pilasters of the apse terminate at least 30 *palmi* below the arched window over a straight interruption. Bramante consequently had planned only a low 10- to 12-*palmi* height for the socle (see "St. Peter's", pp. 399-423). This state of incompletion shows that Leo X had ordered an immediate halt to work on the choir arm. Bramante's giant order ends with a corner pilaster that turns toward the completely unarticulated west wall of the southern transept. This wall is interrupted by two rows of slit windows lighting a great staircase in the southwestern pier for transporting material; this staircase is illustrated as functioning in Vasari's fresco (Wolff Metternich and Thoenes 1987, fig. 130). The pilaster bends again toward the east after the 20 *palmi* measured in Uff. 43A (cat. no. 298). The adjacent wall in the drawing had obviously been prepared, in a similar fashion to the east piers of the dome drawn by Heemskerck (cat. nos. 341; 343), for a vault—without doubt a cross vault, whose perimeter arch would have reached much higher than the barrel vault here under construction. The great treadwheel could lift the material up to the south arches of the crossing. The southeast pier must have had a corresponding hoist. Between April and November 1524 there were payments for similar wheels (Frey 1910: 73). Sangallo reinforced and protected the four pier arches evidently exactly as can be seen in the Heemskerck views. The barrel vault of the transept chapels is being built to the south of the pier. The similar vault over the passage toward the left aisle, situated in front, and hidden from view here, was in fact finished in January 1526. In front of Fra Giocondo's niche there are the niches of the two northern sacristies, presumably also started by Fra Giocondo (cat. no. 289). To the right, under the barrel vault the profile of Raphael's cornice can be seen. The corner pilaster of the giant order bent toward this sacristy and explicitly inscribed on the plans in the *Codex Coner*, in Uff. 255A (cat. 317), and in Uff. 44A (cat. 337), is not visible and hence cannot have advanced much above the area of the base. In the case of the wall to the south next to the sacristy, the draftsman obviously forwent the details. It is quite likely that the site really looked like this since about 1515. The 40-*palmi* southern niche of Bramante's southwestern buttressing pier is already connected to the triple niches in the 1519 ambulatory. The outer front of the ambulatory only reaches the southernmost of the three calottes. The two more northerly ones are only roughly sketched since they were destined to be partly covered by the arm of the crossing of the secondary dome. Sangallo probably played for time here, since he always hoped to extend the external part of the ambulatories to nine whole bays (cat. no. 338). This external front emerges from behind a low house and seems to have already arrived at about the same height as that on the Heemskerck view of about 1535 (cat. no. 342). From left to right, there can be seen the exterior of S. Maria della Febbre, with the tip of the Obelisk behind it, then the western side of the southeastern buttressing pier with its deep niche flanked by pilasters, the southern corner of Pio II's Benediction Loggia, the old campanile with the roof of the atrium, the central nave of Old St. Peter's and a section of the old transept wall. Lastly Castel Sant'Angelo rises to the back right. Since the side walls of the southern arm of the transept have not yet been built—they were in fact erected in 1524-27 see "St. Peter's," (pp. 399-423)

there is no reason for not dating this drawing at the start of 1524, which were the last weeks of Scorel's sojourn in Rome.
C.L.F.

324
JAN VAN SCOREL
Presentation in the Temple
ca. 1560

Vienna, Kunsthistorisches Museum, 6161
Oil on wood.
85 × 114 cm

PROVENANCE: Geert Willemsz Schoterbosch (K. van Mander)

BIBLIOGRAPHY: Glück 1910: 589; Jantzen 1910: 646-647; Friedländer 1975: 76, 122, T. 172; Frommel 1984c: 303.

Van Scorel painted the scene of the circumcision in Solomon's Temple ingeniously giving it the design that St. Peter's would have had in the 1519-20 projects (see "St. Peter's", pp. 399-423). As the court painter for his fellow townsman Pope Adrian VI, and director of the papal collections he must have been closely acquainted with Raphael and Sangallo's combined project as well as Sangallo's 1521 model, while following the work in progress. It is probable that the view in the Ashby collection (cat. no. 323) dates to the end of his sojourn.
The painting in Vienna shows the view from the central nave through the aisle into the side chapel of the longitudinal body. Scorel gives the impression, however, that this was the main choir to which he added a real apse while sacrificing its Diocletian window. Even though the scale is clearly smaller and the detail abstract, simplified and altered—the diagonal face of the pier of the secondary dome has been eliminated—the individual areas and their interdependence are surprisingly close to Raphael and Sangallo's ideas in the 1519-20 project. The height of the pedestal and the position of the niches correspond more or less to the situation in 1519-20 (Frommel 1984c: 274ff.).
Scorel's panel demonstrates once again the direct influence of Roman Renaissance architecture on the younger generation of northern artists. It seems that Scorel painted the panel conserved in Vienna only at the end of 1560, toward the end of his life, basing it on the sketches of his Roman years.
The close connection between the background architecture and Bramante's and Raphael's projects for St. Peter's has already been emphasized by H. Jantzen in a miscellany published in 1910, developing out of his study, *Niederländisches Architekturbild*, on Dutch paintings illustrating architecture. Jantzen also noticed certain analogies with the perspective and the coffered vault in the *School of Athens*. However it is quite clear that Scorel's forced fragmentation of the space, while allowing the observer to complete the missing parts, is diametrically opposed to the symmetrical balance of the *School of Athens*.
C.L.F.

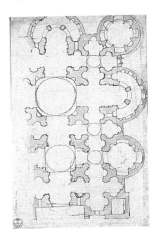

325
BALDASSARRE PERUZZI
Plan Project
ca. 1531-34

Florence, Galleria degli Uffizi, Gabinetto Disegni e Stampe, Uff. 38A
Pen and ink, on paper; freehand.
17.7 × 28.6 cm

PROVENANCE: Papers of Peruzzi.

BIBLIOGRAPHY: Wolff Metternich 1972: 54, fig. 77; Bruschi 1992a: 460, fig. 20.

This plan was attributed to Peruzzi by Wolff Metternich and dated to the period 1520-27. Bruschi noted how much the project derived from Sangallo's in Uff. 255A (cat. no. 317) and from Sangallo's wooden model of 1521. Peruzzi apparently spared the area between the two narrow facade towers in order to incorporate the old atrium, in the same way as he did later in the projects in Uff. 15A (Wolff Metternich 1972: 59, fig. 97) and in Uff. 18A (cat. no. 329). While he remained faithful to Sangallo's longitudinal dome and in doing so pushed his entrance facade about 80 *palmi* beyond the facade of Old St. Peter's, he must have calculated the partial demolition of Innocent VIII's palace. The walls of both sides of the ambulatory, moved ca. 20 *palmi* inward with one opening on to a portal, can only be found in the projects of the period after 1530 (cat. nos. 326, 330). The simplified drawing techniques and the slightly hesitant strokes for the circle of the dome, for example, press for a late date to this drawing. On the same page (Wolff Metternich 1972: 60, fig. 101) of the *Taccuino Senese* where the interior view in Uff. 14A (cat. no. 326) is reproduced, there is also a sketch of an elevation perhaps connected with this plan. It suggests pedestals as well as two lines which could allude to the raising of the floor. In the central bay of the central nave there is a sketch of a colonnade with a 5-*palmi* order, which evidently stood on the old level. In the detail of the plan further up, Peruzzi went as far as considering a diagonal face on the pier and with that took a further step toward Sangallo's model of 1521. The hollowing of this pier for a chapel at the back follows Sangallo's tendencies and suggests the elimination of the aisles. The coffered longitudinal dome brings to mind instead the garden loggia of the Villa Madama, which was also decorated by Peruzzi. The project's similarity to the line of thought dominating in the years 1520-21 support its being dated at the beginning of the triennium, 1531-34, when Clement VII insisted on a substantial reduction of the project, but when one still hoped to save the most important elements of Sangallo's model.
C.L.F.

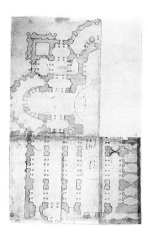

326
BALDASSARRE PERUZZI
Plan Project, with Three Alternatives
ca. 1531-34

Florence, Galleria degli Uffizi, Gabinetto Disegni e Stampe,
Uff. 14A
Pen and ink with wash, on paper; proper draft, with freehand
corrections; numerous crossings out; glued strip showing right
half of nave.
68.8 × 42.6/42.5 cm
VERSO: detail of the plan for the left deambulatory; two scale
keys.

PROVENANCE: Papers of Peruzzi.

BIBLIOGRAPHY: Geymüller 1875-80: 211, pl. 20, 6; Letarouilly
1882, pl. 24; Jovanovits 1887: 6; D. Frey 1915: 20-28; Wurm
1984: 495; Frommel 1987: 37; Bruschi 1989: 187; Bruschi 1992a:
460ff.

By far the most detailed of all the projects and full of ideas
for reducing the size of St. Peter's, this design represented a turning point in the history of the new basilica. As
in the plan in Uff. 38A (cat. no.325), in its first version
Peruzzi stuck to the principles laid down by Sangallo's
model of 1521, even though he no longer prepared the longitudinal dome by means of its own piers and slightly
reduced the 40-*palmi* niches to the side of the ambulatories. He moved the walls on both sides of the ambulatories
toward the interior, and opened them into portals, as in
the drawings in Uff. 38A and on the plan conserved in
New York (cat. no. 330). Moreover in the same side portal
of the longitudinal body and perhaps in the remaining external construction he eliminated the costly aedicules and
withdrew the corner sacristies in the first version to stand
in line with the longitudinal body. Like Sangallo in his
1521 model, he was also ready right from the start to keep
Bramante's choir. The real innovations occurred only in
the longitudinal body where Peruzzi returned to the dis-
kshaped pillars of Bramante's final project of 1506 (see
"Peter's," pp. 399-423) and transformed Sangallo's
chapels in external lateral aisles, as for the last time in one
of Giuliano da Sangallo's alternatives in Uff. 7A (cat. no.
307). Even in the 5-*palmi* colunnades Peruzzi went back
to the ideas of the first phase of the design (cat. nos. 283,
287), when he took advantage of the desire for change in
those critical years to reintroduce the spaciousness of
Bramante's project. At the moment, however, he closed
all the arcades and lowered the passages toward the secondary spaces to the height of the 5-*palmi* order. The interior
view in the *Taccuino Senese*, copied from one of Peruzzi's
drawings, offers an idea of this arrangement (Wolff Metternich 1972: 60, fig. 101). The pedestals of the giant order are missing, so that the 5-*palmi* columns arrive at half
the height of their shaft. Peruzzi had therefore already
taken into account the raising of the floor level. Three of
the five measurements written by Peruzzi in the nave of
this plan could refer to the implied height. With the
reduction of the height of the central nave to 185 *palmi*
at the top of the vault and to 182 *palmi* at the top of the
pier arches, the distance between the new level and the

foot of the lantern of the central dome became 400 *palmi*.
The new level was about 30 *palmi* higher—much more
therefore than the ca. 13.5 *palmi* established as from
1535. The pilasters of the giant Corinthian order would
have reached a height of about 98 *palmi* with a ratio of
1:8.1. The 5-*palmi* order would have reached the impost
of the arcades, and above it there would have been about
44 *palmi* available for the wall planes up to the entablature
of the giant order, which conformed more or less to the
elevation in the *Taccuino Senese*. Such a drastic raising of
the floor makes the elimination of the arcades under-
standable, even though it would have meant modifying
the 40-*palmi* niches (cf. cat. no. 331). The unfavorable ratio of both the wall areas in Bruschi's reconstruction
(1992a, fig. 23) shows that it was very unlikely that Peruzzi started from the former level of the floor. Briefly, with
these modifications he transformed Bramante's steep
space extending in all directions into a single nave hall
that was horizontally oriented and to some extent resusci-
tated his 1531 projects for S. Domenico in Siena (Wurm
1984: 219-238). At the same time, he united the naves
and the ambulatories in a more systematic way with the
drum and the atrium, where Bramante and Raphael had
already introduced 5-*palmi* columns with an entablature.
Moreover he could lower all the secondary spaces to the
height of the 5-*palmi* order, thus drastically reducing the
wall masses both in the area of the piers and in that of the
vault. This alteration and the decision to forsake a proper
atrium should be interpreted as the real reduction of this
first version. He would have been able to recoup few of
the 228 columns from the old basilica. On another sheet,
Uff. 16A (Wurm 1984: 499) he calculated the cost of each
column at ca. 390 ducats, so that the total costs would
have risen by about 90,000 ducats.
In the second version Peruzzi went even further. He
eliminated the quincunx system, the ambulatories and the
four external aisles and introduced 5-*palmi* columns into
Bramante's choir as well. The 748-*palmi* measurement indicated in the central nave refers perhaps to this version
as it corresponds to the length of the interior, while the
160 *palmi* could refer to the distance between the piers of
the dome and the center of the dome of the longitudinal
body.
If Peruzzi drew the third version on the glued-on strip of
paper on the right, he probably did it because the second
one appeared to be too reductive. In any case he attached
pairs and triads of long rectangular chapels to the to the
side aisles where he prepared several types of plan, as he
had done for his project for S. Giovanni dei Fiorentini in
1519 (Wurm 1984: 9). In this version the longitudinal
body would have reached a width of ca. 420 *palmi*, i.e.,
180 *palmi* less than the first version, but 130 *palmi* more
than the second. Three further projects in the reduction
series, Uff. 12A, 15A, 16A recto, and 18A verso (Wolff
Metternich 1972: 59 ff., fig. 94, 97-100; Wurm 1984:
497-501) develop the ideas of the second and third versions, and therefore the plans in Uff. 14A should be earlier than this group, but later than the ones in Uff. 38A and
Uff. 113A (cat. nos. 325, 327). The sketch of the elevation
in Uff. 15A verso does however take into account the old
floor level. There Peruzzi made the giant order continue
along the closed side walls of the central bay of the nave
and flanked the ambulatories leading to the side aisles
with 5-*palmi* columns.   *C.L.F.*

327
BALDASSARRE PERUZZI
Sketch for the Facade
ca. 1531-34

Florence, Galleria degli Uffizi, Gabinetto Disegni e Stampe,
Uff. 113A
Pen and ink, on paper; verso blank.
13.6 × 15 cm

PROVENANCE: Papers of Peruzzi.

BIBLIOGRAPHY: Geymüller 1875-80: 215, T. 20, 3; Jovanovits
1877: 9; Wolff Metternich 1972: 64, fig. 116; Wurm 1984: 487;
Bruschi 1992a: 457ff.

This rapid sketch takes into account quite clearly a longitudinal body whose width remains within the limits of
the dome, and an atrium with a minimum depth. It can
therefore be identified as one of the projects for the reduction of St. Peter's going back to the years 1531-34, when
Clement VII urged the two architects to find the most
economical solutions. One of the projects for the reduction, a centrally planned church in Uff. 19A, had a similarly smaller atrium which was equipped with a single 9-
palmi order but whose dimensions have been estimated as
greater than these (Wolff Metternich 1972: 61, fig. 103).
With the width of the longitudinal body reduced like this
and the rhythm of the two orders, this drawing seems
nearer to the second version of the project in Uff. 14A
(cat. no. 326), even though here Peruzzi still considered
using high pedestals. The whole design is more similar to
Raphael's facade in the *Codex Mellon* (cat. no. 311) where
the towers are also connected to the main temple front facade by a colonnade. Thanks to the minimum depth of the
atrium the vault of the ground floor would have remained
relatively low and it would have been possible to site the
benediction loggia on top with Serlian windows above the
3.5-*palmi* columns from the aisles of Old St. Peter's. The
pairs of pilasters of the giant order at the sides are separated here on the ground floor by adjacent columns and on
the upper floor by aedicules in a way that anticipates
Michelangelo's design for the Palazzo dei Conservatori
more directly than any of the previous projects.
Since the longitudinal body did not spread beyond the
dome, Peruzzi could reduce the connection between it
and the towers to a simple colonnade with a passage
above. The upper level of the northern tower was too low
to engage the southern half of the Sala Regia, which arrived at about 100 *palmi* above the basilica. Tower and
colonnade would therefore have established the connection between the basilica and the ground floor of the papal
palace. If, in comparison to the Bramantesque dome in
Uff. 26A (cat. no. 334), the dome here is designed with
ribbing and the drum has a balustrade above it—but there
is no lantern—this supports the hypothesis that Peruzzi
had proposed changes for this part of the building as well.
Peruzzi kept the old level here so that it is likely that the
project was one of the first to face the problems of reducing St. Peter's.   *C.L.F.*

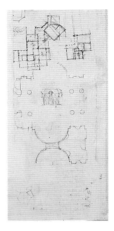

chapels and the six chapels of the longitudinal body. Probably the pillars planned in the direction of the papal stables, the palace and the Cappella Sistina were to be part of the same side chapels of the northern transept arm. If the atrium was excluded from this list and Peruzzi left an empty space between the towers of the facade which was the same width as the central nave, it must have been because he was probably thinking again about keeping the old atrium—as he had done even on the drawing in Uff. 15A recto (Wolff Metternich 1972: 59ff., fig. 97). The northern tower would therefore have included part of the Scala Regia and would have been built behind Innocent VIII's palace, ending, however, clearly in front of the Sala Regia. In listing the tasks of the stonemasons Peruzzi considered first of all the work on the inside, and it is probable that he thought of a very sober external articulation, but only the giant pilasters of the transept apses and the widened openings of the windows of Bramante's choir can be recognized here.   *C.L.F.*

328
BALDASSARRE PERUZZI
Sketch for the Facade and External Construction
ca. 1531-34

Florence, Galleria degli Uffizi, Gabinetto Disegni e Stampe,
Uff. 24A
Pen and ink, on paper; freehand.
6 × 8.5 cm

PROVENANCE: Papers of Peruzzi.

BIBLIOGRAPHY: Geymüller 1875-80: 141, T. 48, 1; Jovanovits
1877: 9; Wolff Metternich 1972: 67ff., fig. 127; Wurm 1984: 370;
Wolff Metternich and Thoenes 1987: 164.

This sketch has been developed from premises similar to those governing Uff. 113A (cat. no. 327), that is, a longitudinal body of the same width as the dome, flanked by towers. The reduction however has gone substantially further ahead since the atrium has been estimated as being even more narrow, and it is lower than the longitudinal body and dome which rise up behind it. There is no longer any sign of the giant order, but only of a 9-*palmi* order using 5-*palmi* columns and an attic. This arrangement also recalls the design in Uff. 26A recto (cat. no. 334) where the corners are reinforced in the same way by pairs of pilasters of the great order and the smaller one has blind walls. The arrangement of the columns inside the central arch derives from Bramante's 1506 model. Three doors and the circular window of the nave can be seen through the archway. The part of the longitudinal body that can be seen behind the atrium, with its pediment and long row of niches, has now become a part of the facade. The tower standing slightly back with respect to the front of the building seems to be on a line with the longitudinal body and therefore maintains the connection with the papal palace. In an alternative drawn on the left, Peruzzi even abandoned the idea of a tower, thus revealing the apse of the transept which, unlike all the remaining projects for the reduction of St. Peter's, is directly connected to the piers of the dome, has no ambulatory and is designed with the same 9-*palmi* order and attic. The fragment in the left margin could be interpreted as the old round building of S. Maria della Febbre. Here Peruzzi kept the drum with an order, the Pantheon-like dome and lantern like he did in the project in Uff. 26A, but unlike Sangallo in the period following 1520. He seems to have remembered Bramante's ideas from the period before work started on St. Peter's in his soaring campanile and the rhythm of the facade. Since the 9-*palmi* columns of the facade are without pedestals, and there is a suggestion of a base and steps, Peruzzi must have considered a raised level. The 9-*palmi* order of the facade suggests that this project was one of the last of the group of reductions, drawn at the same time as Sangallo's in Uff. 40A verso (cat. no. 336).   *C.L.F.*

329
BALDASSARRE PERUZZI
Plan Project (recto)
Details of the Plan and Elevation (verso)
ca. 1531-34

Florence, Galleri degli Uffizi, Gabinetto Disegni e Stampe, Uff. 18A
Pen and ink with wash, on paper; freehand on recto; straightedge and compass on verso.; measurements in *palmi*.
18.8 × 43.5 cm

INSCRIBED: (recto) *per la tribuna d.175.000 / p[er] can[n]e 21372 di muro p[er] 4 pilastri d.[53430] / p[er] can[n]e 1010 d.2525 / p[er] can[n]e 3000 p[er] la facciata d.7500 / p[er] alzare un pilastro verso le stalle can[n]e 3870 d.9675 / p[er] alzare tre pilastri li due verso palazo e uno el tagliato acanto ala cappella di xisto can[n]e 8000 d.20000 / p[er] can[n]e 13.000 di muro per le due cappelle dela croce d.32.500 / p[er] le 8 volte di can[n]e 6 d.24.000 grosse lo teste / p[er] le volte dela nave grande can[n]e 11420 grosse 15 teste d.27.550.*

PROVENANCE: Papers of Peruzzi.

BIBLIOGRAPHY: Letarouilly 1882: T. 24; D. Frey 1915: 24ff.;
Jovanovits 1877: XIII b; Redtenbacher 1875: T. 1, fig. 2; Wolff
Metternich 1972: 59, 61ff., fig. 94, 105; Wurm 1984: 505, 506;
Wolff Metternich and Thoenes 1987: 140, 150, 153; Bruschi
1992a: 469ff.
The reduction goes one step further here compared to the second version in Uff. 14A (cat. no. 326) since the dome of the longitudinal body and the columns have been eliminated. In spite of the passages between the 40-*palmi* niches this is in fact a longitudinal body containing one nave with chapels. While this project could have been elaborated before the one in Uff. 14A, on the verso Peruzzi took into consideration the possibility of using groups of 5-*palmi* columns in the chapels together with the corresponding pilasters on the three walls. In the center of the plan detail he sketched very roughly the interior view of the chapel which, with a low, windowed attic, rectangular cove ceiling and high lunette would have measured a height of about 100 *palmi*, with presumably a similar closure of the central nave arcade, as in the sketch in the *Taccuino Senese* which corresponds to Uff. 14A. In the case in which Peruzzi here too considered the decision to raise the floor, he would have heightened correspondingly the upper part of the 40-*palmi* niche as he appears to have done in the sketch of the elevation. However it is also possible to presume that he started from the old level as in Uff. 15A verso.
The detailed calculations in the margin of the recto estimate the costs of the stonework in 2.5 ducats per canna, almost twice the price paid by Julius II (K. Frey 1910: 48ff.). Moreover, apart from the total of more than 350,000 ducats, there were also the ca. 72,000 ducat costs of the stonemasons listed in Uff. 16A recto (Wolff Metternich 1972: 61, fig. 106; Wurm 1984: 499). With the definition "tribuna" Peruzzi certainly indicated here the drum and the dome, "4 pilastri" were the piers of the longitudinal body, "faciata" the wall of the entrance, "due cappele dela croce" were the apses of the transept, and "8 volte" were the vaults of the northern transept arm's side

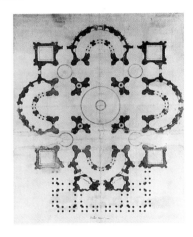

330
BALDASSARRE PERUZZI (copy of original?)
Plan Project with and without an Atrium
1535

New York, American Academy in Rome
Pen and ink, with brush, on paper; straightedge and compass;
the side walls of the areas of the front secondary domes and
part of the right ambulatory are faded.
69 × 66.2 cm
INSCRIBED (at a later date): *Baldsar Petrucci Senese; n. 23; S.
Pietro; N 23 D; N. 10 Pezzo Unico.*

PROVENANCE: Accademia di S. Luca (Rome), Raccolta S. White.

BIBLIOGRAPHY: Geymüller 1875-80: 205 n. 48; D. Frey 1915: 30ff.;
Kent 1925, fig. 43, 2; 1964; Frommel et al. 1987: 37ff.; Bruschi
1992a: 472ff., fig. 42.

Perhaps only after he had failed to win over the pope with his proposals in Uff. 27A (cat. no. 332) and in Uff. 31A (cat. no. 333) did Peruzzi give up raising the floor about 30 *palmi* and with it the great exterior order to return to the 9-*palmi* order of 1519. In this project, his only complete plan in the reign of Paul III, he followed a program similar to that in Sangallo's perhaps contemporary drawing in Uff. 39A (cat. no. 338). In the same way, Peruzzi compared a strictly symmetrical centrally planned building with an alternative including a prominent atrium. He had already flattened the 40 *palmi* niches next to the ambulatories and sacristies in Uff. 14A (cat. no. 326), introducing secondary portals in the ambulatories, and moved the walls of these ambulatories about 20 *palmi* further inward eliminating the corresponding 40-*palmi* niches. The unshaded axially symmetrical alternative of the eastern transept arm shows similar secondary portals. But here Peruzzi kept all the remaining 40-*palmi* niches and their narrow passageways. The corner sacristies stand out from the main building considerably less than on Sangallo's project and their walls are perhaps too weak to support towers. The conservation of Bramante's choir was not considered.

Peruzzi's atrium, with the same measurements as those in Uff. 31A, would have been almost exactly within the lines of Bramante's last project of 1506 unlike the very projecting atrium designed by Sangallo in his right-hand alternative in Uff. 39A. The rhythmic sequence and certainly the height too, respect the design of Uff. 31A. The main front is composed of three sections each one composed of groups of four columns. The central front has four similar groups and the side sections have two. Both side sections are connected to another one on their side fronts so the U-shaped columned atrium embraces the arm of the cross. The span of the entrance of the temple front is considerably larger. The distance separating these columns is repeated between the center and the two side sections. This division changes only in the second row of columns where square columns intersect diagonally. These continue with Serliane which divide the central section of the atrium with its possible barrel vault from the probably domical vaults of the secondary sections. These vaults would have arrived at an attic as high as the one in Uff. 26A (cat. no. 334), so that the atrium would have been the same height as the internal order. The presumed temple front of the facade would have been consequently—as in Uff. 70A (cat. no. 314)—about as high as the roof of the central nave so that Peruzzi could certainly have avoided an interruption between the atrium and the body of the building directly behind it (cf. the reconstruction in Bruschi 1992: fig. 45). Compared to the earlier projects it was easier here to create a connection with the Sala Regia. It is therefore likely that Paul III had already started thinking about partial alterations to the papal palace.

There are no sound reasons for suggesting the pavement was raised. The style of the drawing recalls that of the plan in Uff. 340A recto for S. Domenico in Siena (Wurm 1984: 220) which was about three years older, where there is an unshaded alternative, torn in some parts, and where Peruzzi put the same kind of vault. This is therefore either an original or a faithful copy. The points on the longitudinal axis suggest a scale of measurement but they do not correspond to any round figures in Roman *palmi*; they were probably added at a later date.   *C.L.F.*

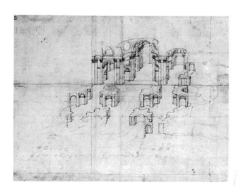

331
Baldassarre Peruzzi
Bird's-Eye Perspective View of Project
ca. 1535

Florence, Galleria degli Uffizi, Gabinetto Disegni e Stampe, Uff. 2A
Plan in sanguine, on paper; elevation in pen and ink; part straightedge and compass, part freehand.
53.9 × 67.8 cm

Provenance: Papers of Peruzzi.

Bibliography: Geymüller 1875-80: 202ff.; n. 47; Letarouilly 1882: pl. 23; D. Frey 1915: 28-32; Hofmann 1928: index; Wolff Metternich 1972: 62, fig. 107; Wurm 1984: 494; Frommel et al. 1987: 38; Bruschi 1992a: 472ff., fig. 43.

When he drew this perspective Peruzzi probably wanted to illustrate to Paul III the beauty of his quincunx system, and on certain important points he went beyond the plan conserved in New York (cat. no. 330) and he returned to Bramante's drawing in Uff. 1A (cat. no. 282). He gave the areas of the secondary domes exactly the same shape as that of the main dome, and he did this by creating wider diagonal faces on the piers of the secondary domes than had been his intention after 1506 and than were actually built in about 1524-27 (cat. no. 337). He then raised the height of the niches in these faces in the central dome area and in the secondary ones to the height of the cornices. In the areas of the secondary domes this was the cornice of the previous 40-*palmi* niches, while in the area of the central dome it was the impost of the pier arches. Therefore, either the niches in the area of the central dome—which were 23 *palmi* wide and could hardly have been enlarged—had a emphatically vertical ratio of ca. 1:3.3 which would contradict Peruzzi's representation, or Peruzzi had already calculated the new higher floor. The diagonal niches in the areas of the secondary domes would have required the reduction of the adjacent 40 *palmi* niches to about 20 *palmi*, as announced on Peruzzi's plan in Uff. 11A verso (Wolff Metternich 1972: 37, fig. 90; Wurm 1994: 114; Wolff Metternich and Thoenes 1987: 164). The lowering of these niches below the cornice of the former 40-*palmi* niches was the inevitable consequence. Unlike the plan conserved in New York, here the former 40-*palmi* niches remain in a somewhat flattened form only along the back walls of the secondary domes where not even a portal can be inserted anymore. Both these old 40-*palmi* niches and the new 20-*palmi* ones are hypothetically possible with and without raising the floor 13.5 *palmi*, as would be debated after 1534 (cat. no. 338). Confuting a new higher level there is also the question of the soaring ratio of the front pilasters of about 1:10. That Peruzzi was then still experimenting with the old level and with pedestals 13.5 *palmi* high can be proved by the elevation sketches in Uff. 11A verso. On the other hand it was typical of his creative approach that he introduced a new proposal for the diagonal faces on the piers of the secondary domes, which would have required costly alterations to the existing structures. It would however be wrong to interpret this perspective as a simple theoretical operation or an ideal project. The perspective section at the back is connected to the foreground plan by means of an intermediate zone still drawn in perspective where the piers terminate just above the niches. Peruzzi had already used this kind of representation, also common to Leonardo's years in Milan, in about 1522—23 in his great project for S. Petronio in Bologna (Wurm 1984: 132), in which he even included the exterior construction. By drawing the plan in sanguine it remains quite distinct without upsetting the clarity of the whole composition.
                    C.L.F.

332
Baldassarre Peruzzi
View of the Exterior from the Southwest (recto)
Detail of the Drum (verso)
ca. 1535

Florence, Galleria degli Uffizi, Gabinetto Disegni e Stampe, Uff. 27A
Pen and ink with wash, on paper; some incised lines.
9.1 × 12 cm

Provenance: Papers of Peruzzi.

Bibliography: Geymüller 1875-80: 29, 210, T. 18, 2-3; Hofmann 1928: index; Jovanovits 1877: 9; Wolff Metternich 1972: 62, 63, fig. 108, 109; Wurm 1984: 489; Wolff Metternich and Thoenes 1987: 164.

This strictly centrally planned building still amply corresponds to Serlio's woodcut (cat. no. 322), so much so that the curve of the ambulatory to the front right is still recognizable. Behind the right arm of the cross there seems to be a hint of the papal palace, while above the right corner sacristy is a tower. Peruzzi therefore showing the church from the southwest. He went back to a design for the exterior using the 12-*palmi* order that Sangallo had last proposed in 1519 in the drawings in Uff. 34A and Uff. 35A and to a similar rhythm (Wolff Metternich 1972: 45, figs. 41, 42). Here, however, the pilasters are standing on a base running the full circuit and rising up to a height of between two to three shafts, i.e., ca. 30 *palmi*. Peruzzi wanted to illuminate the ambulatories directly, perhaps by means of windows placed above the intermediate encircling cornice, but he concentrated all the illumination on the level above the order. Since the windows could be inserted only in the area of the vault, they were placed roughly above the interior entablature, and this illumination level screened a part of the vault. Three oculi in the apse were positioned so the light entered slightly diagonally, and of the three arched windows in the presumed choir arm, two of them would have been inserted in the barrel vault and one in the pier arch as in the choir of S. Maria del Popolo. Since the four arms would have received little light through the ambulatories, Peruzzi wanted to illuminate them with a row of windows in the vault, with light arriving only from above. Since it seems unlikely that Peruzzi wanted to return to the steep ambulatories of 1514 (cat. no. 307) and, on the other hand, the ambulatory vaults are substantially higher than those in Uff. 54A recto (cat. no. 315), this must indicate a considerable rise in the floor level—perhaps even the 30 *palmi* indicated in Uff. 14A (cat. no. 326). The closure of the arcades would have justified a new arrangement of the walls and a new illumination system, as in Uff. 14A.

The view of the drum from below on the verso shows that Peruzzi—unlike Sangallo—still wanted to conserve Bramante's dome (cat. no. 303) even during the reign of Paul III. The lack of a lantern is probably due to the draftsman being in a hurry. There should have perhaps been an alternation of blind walls with groups of four columns behind the external colonnade. He was probably examining, here on the verso, whether the pedestals to the drum's columns could be seen from below, when viewing it in the area surrounding the basilica, or whether they were superfluous. The years 1520-21 can be excluded for dating this drawing because of the presence of the giant order, of the presumed elevation of the floor and the new lighting system. All these innovations relate much better to 1535 when the centrally planned building returned to favor in Peruzzi's own drawing conserved in New York as well (cat. no. 330) as in Sangallo's drawing in Uff. 39A (cat. no. 338). Peruzzi's next step could have been the project in Uff. 31A (cat. no. 333) where he added an atrium to a similarly centrally planned building. The atrium would have harmonized with the 12-*palmi* order and high base; all that was necessary was a slightly lower intermediate cornice.   *C.L.F.*

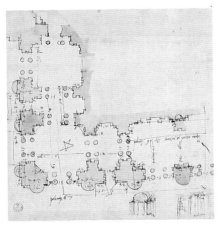

333

BALDASSARRE PERUZZI
Sketches of a Plan and an Elevation for the Atrium and Facade (recto)
Sketches for the Courtyard (Palazzo Massimo?) (verso)
1535

Florence, Galleria degli Uffizi, Gabinetto Disegni e Stampe, Uff. 31A

Pen and ink, on paper.
INSCRIBED: *palmj 90½ la mita del portico medio.*
28 × 29/30 cm

PROVENANCE: Papers of Peruzzi.

BIBLIOGRAPHY: Geymüller 1875-80: 335, T. 20, 8; Wolff Metternich 1963: 27; Wolff Metternich 1972: 63, fig. 111; Wurm 1984: 125, 126; Bruschi 1992a: 457ff.

This plan project for the atrium and facade can be connected in an equally logical way to Peruzzi's project for a centrally planned building as the columned atrium on the plan conserved in New York and in Uff. 2A (cat. nos. 330, 331). In both, there are portals in the middle of the eastern arm of the cross and in the arms of the cross of the secondary domes further back. Peruzzi indicated the exact distance between these portals as 167 *palmi*. Two lines indicate that he planned diagonal entrances to the side bays of the eastern ambulatory—as on the plan conserved in New York. Moreover, the 40-*palmi* niche next to the corner sacristy seems to have become slightly oval. Here, however, Peruzzi maintained the giant order with 12-*palmi* wide shafts, half-columns on the main facade, and pilasters, which on second thoughts he transformed into half-columns on the side fronts. This giant order continued up to the corner sacristy where there was a corner pilaster measuring "12," so it appears he intended using the giant order for the rest of the external construction as he had done in Uff. 27A (cat. no. 332). As on Raphael's project in the *Codex Mellon* (cat. no. 311) and on several of Sangallo's later projects (cat. nos. 313, 314, 316), groups of four 5-*palmi* columns mediated between the giant pilasters. These groups divide the atrium up into several rectangular areas. The corner niches in the left-hand area and the sketch of the elevation in the lower margin indicate a groin vault and a barrel vault over the passageway. The height of the barrel vault was at least 20 *palmi* above the 5-*palmi* order entablature; the groin vault would have been even about 30 *palmi*, so that Peruzzi must have planned an attic which would hardly have been high enough for another order of columns. If he had considered building blind walls here like those in Uff. 26A recto (cat. no. 334) a benediction loggia would have been excluded. A variation in the plan in the *Taccuino Senese* (Wolff Metternich 1972: 63, fig. 112) though heavily distorted establishes an atrium with a reduced depth. Its vaults would have arrived at a maximum height of 24 *palmi* above the entablature as can be seen in the view of the inside of the left wing of the side portal. In order to reduce the height Peruzzi certainly gave up the strips of wall in the passageways, and to widen the latter, he dilated the side intercolumniation from a 5-*palmi* order to a 9-*palmi* one, shortening for the same reason the central intercolumniation in the center projection to 12 *palmi*. Lastly, in the left margin, he examined the possibility of moving the central projection a few *palmi* in front of the side blocks with the help of two square, diagonally intersecting columns. The relative elevation on fol. 36 verso of the *Taccuino Senese* (Wolff Metternich 1972: 64, fig. 114) gives a glimpse of the dilation of the central intercolumniation in both the side blocks and an attic zone in front of the vault of the lower level. On that drawing there are also two stepped platforms, but the giant Doric order does not have a pedestal. Since it was hardly likely that Peruzzi would have calculated the external order lower than the great internal one (154 *palmi* with pedestals) he must also have started here from a raised floor. This is also emphasized by the ratio of the 5-*palmi* order with the great order, which is more or less the same as that on the elevation of the *Taccuino Senese* which is linked to Uff. 14A (cat. no. 326). It is unlikely that Peruzzi drew the version in the *Taccuino Senese*, which contains projects belonging almost exclusively to the last five years of his life, i.e., before 1534-35, when he returned to the centrally planned theme and a strongly projecting atrium (cat. nos. 330, 331). If the project in Uff. 31A recto corresponds amply to the version of the *Taccuino* and already includes the flat 40-*palmi* niches, it could have been produced just slightly earlier. Peruzzi and Sangallo (cat. nos. 338, 336) must have first presented Paul III with a project for the facade with a giant order in ca. 1535. If the verso illustrates a preliminary proposal for the courtyard of the Palazzo Massimo alle Colonne, Rome, as the passage moved to the right and the loggia on the *piano nobile* seem to suggest, it would confirm the dating of the drawing to the last five years of Peruzzi's life. *C.L.F.*

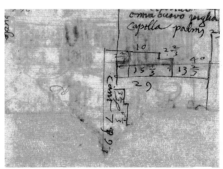

334

BALDASSARRE PERUZZI
Sketch for the Atrium and Facade (recto)
Fragment of a Plan for the Area of St. Peter's (verso)
1535

Florence, Galleria degli Uffizi, Gabinetto Disegni e Stampe, Uff. 26A

Pen and ink, with wash, on paper; measurements in Roman *palmi* (verso).

INSCRIBED: (verso) *el portico .../ entra overo piglia.../ cappella palmj 29...*
9.5 × 13 cm

PROVENANCE: Papers of Peruzzi.

BIBLIOGRAPHY: Geymüller 1875-80: 215, T. 20, 3; Jovanovits 1877: 9; Wolff Metternich 1972: 58, 64, fig. 91, 115; Wurm 1984: 485, 486; Bruschi 1992a: 469.

There is a close connection between this sketchy facade project and the one in Uff. 31A (cat. no. 333) in the division into three parts, the combination of the giant engaged columns with the 5-*palmi* order, as well as the stepped platform at the base, even though the chapels on both sides of the domed side aisles are missing, the arches between the three sections are much wider and the atrium does not seem to be a U-shape embracing the entrance arm. the atrium does in fact finish on the right exactly next to the papal palace, which is extraordinarily high here. The longitudinal body is therefore more or less the same length and breadth as Sangallo's right-hand alternative in Uff. 256A (cat. no. 339). In an unknown plan Peruzzi must have returned after all to Bramante's last project of 1506 and have opened the pilasters of the central nave to create side aisles with their own inner portals. On the verso he seems to have measured the distance between the basilica and the papal palace, i.e., 79 *palmi* from the northeastern pier of the northeastern secondary dome to the western wall of the Cappella Sistina, and 29 *palmi* from the same pier to the southern wall of the Sala Regia. Of the ca. 460 *palmi* overall width of the atrium, the central section occupied about 140 *palmi*, each connecting arch was about 40 *palmi* wide and each of the side sections measured about 120 *palmi*. Pairs of giant half-columns emphasized the limits of these three blocks. Links between the blocks were provided by groups of four 5-*palmi* columns. These would have had an intercolumniation of ca. 16 *palmi* in the dominating central section and only 8-*palmi* spans in the side sections, which would perhaps have been placed slightly behind, as was the case in the variation in Uff. 31A. Here too, there is a suggestion of a high, stepped platform and the 5-*palmi* columns arrive at more or less half the height of the half-columns. These do not have pedestals so Peruzzi must have started from a floor 30 *palmi* higher. The line at the level of the bases could mean that he intended bringing the floor level up even higher. The blind walls above the 5-*palmi* order could have masked the vaults of the ground floor and perhaps a corridor connecting the basilica to the papal palace. If the second level begins only above the secondary inner portals it is because the project did not include a benediction loggia. This one could have been elaborated either in connection to the drawing in Uff. 14A (cat. no. 326) where there is a similar layout, or—as is more likely—it could date back to the beginning of Paul III's reign. At the same time as he presented a project of a centrally planned building, Peruzzi would have submitted a longitudinal project deriving directly from Bramante's last project of 1506 (fig. 16-18), thus meeting an express desire of the newly elected pope. The differences with respect to the project in Uff. 31A can be explained by the alteration into a longitudinal building with five portals, but without large side chapels. The accentuated chiaroscuro highlights the close chronological connections with the Palazzo Massimo. *C.L.F.*

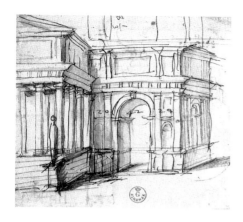

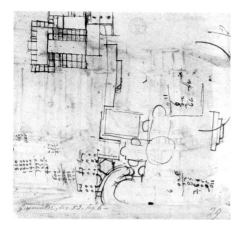

335
BALDASSARRE PERUZZI
Sketch for the Atrium (recto)
Sketches of Plans for St. Peter's and for a Convent in Central Italy (verso)
1535

Florence, Galleria degli Uffizi, Gabinetto Disegni e Stampe, Uff. 29A
Pen and ink, with wash, on paper; freehand.
14.9 × 16 cm

PROVENANCE: Papers of Peruzzi.

BIBLIOGRAPHY: Geymüller 1875-80: 210, T. 53, 6; D. Frey 1915: 31; Wolff Metternich 1972: 63, fig. 110; Wurm 1984: 123ff.; Bruschi 1992: 472.

This sketch must have been drawn after the one in Uff. 2A (cat. no. 331). Here Peruzzi took as a similar premise the centrally planned scheme and the continuation of the 9-*palmi* facade on the facade, but the central colonnade with the temple front is now raised on a stepped platform about 15.5 *palmi* high, and the number of its columns has been drastically reduced. Both the side sections have been placed behind the line of the main portal, and now have archways on the old level, making steps necessary in front of the side portals. Since the line of the lateral sections seems to continue straight ahead to the west, the body of the building must have extended again on the outside, perhaps only where the side arms of the eastern secondary dome were. There is a hint of a tower over the lateral section. Peruzzi could have moved the tower back to avoid problems with the Cappella Sistina and the Sala Regia, which the project conserved in New York (cat. no. 330) and in Uff. 2A would certainly have created.
He developed this in a considerably more radical way on the verso, in which he replaced the corner sacristies with a much larger space and continued the line of the main portal south by means of a doubly re-entrant wall. If he had planned a corresponding wall to the north of the basilica, it would have hidden the eastern wall of the Cappella Sistina and the deep rectangular area would have functioned as a light shaft. The Sala Regia, the Cortile del

Maresciallo and the Sala Ducale would have fallen victims of this solution. On the verso the portico is reduced in the same way to the width of the dome. The highly rhythmic arrangement of the six groups of four columns seem however to flow into piers on the facade. In contrast, the temple front on the recto is composed of a continuous sequence of columns from the 1519 9-*palmi* order whose intercolumniation measures only about 10 *palmi*, as on the lateral triumphal arches. Starting from a wider bay in the center, the temple front would have accounted for at least 12-14 columns. With a depth of only three bays, the depth of the atrium would have measured at most 60 *palmi*, so that its vault would have filled only a part of the attic. Here too, as in Uff. 26A (cat. no. 334) and in Uff. 31A (cat. no. 333), it is unlikely that a benediction loggia was included. By reducing the attic, the papal palace and corner towers into consideration. Peruzzi tried to save his most important idea—the classicizing columned portico. Certain aspects of this program such as the towers, the raised floor, the 9-*palmi* order on the facade and the inviolability of the Cappella Sistina link it to Sangallo's one in Uff. 39A (cat. no. 338). Both could be dated as the second half of 1535, just before Peruzzi died.   *C.L.F.*

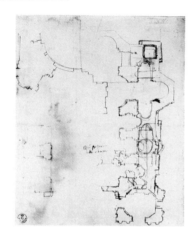

336
ANTONIO DA SANGALLO THE YOUNGER
Plan Project
ca. 1531-34

Florence, Galleria degli Uffizi, Gabinetto Disegni e Stampe, Uff. 40A
Pen and ink, on paper; freehand; 21.6 × 27.9/28.2 cm.
INSCRIBED: (recto) *questo saria bello e breve* (Sangallo).

PROVENANCE: Papers of Antonio da Sangallo the Younger.

BIBLIOGRAPHY: Giovannoni 1959: 127, fig. 58

This is the only reduction project by Sangallo that is similar to the one elaborated by Peruzzi in Uff. 18A recto (cat. no. 329). In both cases the transept arms without ambulatories and a longitudinal body are joined to Bramante's

choir—that Sangallo has completed in the detail with a 9-*palmi* order on the outside. In the right-hand alternative with three bays he made the central nave continue into lateral chapels and emphasized the central bay by means of a transverse axis ending in chapels like those in the transept arm. In the other alternative on the right half he even considered just two bays with chapels of the same size. He presented a more grandiose version of an atrium and gave the corner towers pairs of giant columns and a central opening—a sketch which vaguely recalls the one in the *Memoriale* (cat. no. 320). In the two-bay solution the atrium seems to return to an exedra shape between two smaller corner towers. A third version on the left half of the sheet gives a three-bay solution. The passages like side aisles between the piers foreshadow themes of the later project in Uff. 256A (cat. no. 339). On the verso Sangallo made a deeper examination of this alternative, returning to complete side aisles with domes and hemicycle chapel. Here, for the first time, he substituted the giant order on the facade with half-columns and squared columns of a 9-*palmi* order. On the relative elevation sketch to the right Sangallo also drew a facade with giant half-columns and an attic which meets the central arch (with benediction loggia?)—a lower version, where the attic is inserted above the small order and is also surmounted by a triangular pediment. A C-shaped volute connects it to the adjacent tower. Since the design of this tower could only have been derived from the 9-*palmi* facade, it might have been designed before the giant order. The 9-*palmi* facade anticipated certain fundamental concepts that Sangallo utilized in his facade sketch in Uff. 78A (cat. no. 340) drawn in 1535. If he still preferred the giant order on the facade of the project in Uff. 39A (cat. no. 338) equally datable at about 1535, this means that in any case, in Uff. 40A verso he had not yet taken the final decision regarding the small order. The drastic reduction of the longitudinal body and the facade can be linked to the period 1531-34, when Clement VII evidently urged Sangallo and Peruzzi to be as economical and as quick as possible in completing the construction. This is how Sangallo's comment "bello and breve" should be interpreted. The nearness of this drawing to Peruzzi's own in Uff. 24A indicates a period toward the end of the reduction projects, perhaps 1534.
          C.L.F.

337
ANTONIO DA SANGALLO THE YOUNGER
Plan Survey of Bramante's Choir, and Sketch of a Project for Altering the Ambulatories
ca. 1535

Florence, Galleria degli Uffizi, Gabinetto Disegni e Stampe, Uff. 44A
Pen and ink, on paper; straightedge and compass, finished in freehand; measurements in *palmi*.
40.5/41 × 55/63 cm
INSCRIBED: (recto) *frajochondo*; (verso) *la faccia dirieto p 43 1/2; questo in 1/2; amjco carissimo / amj mj.*

PROVENANCE: Papers of Antonio da Sangallo the Younger.

BIBLIOGRAPHY: Geymüller 1875-80: 333; Giovannoni 1959: 127; Wolf Metternich 1972: 40ff., fig. 23-24; Frommel 1984c: 293ff.; Wolff Metternich and Thoenes 1987: 112ff.

Unlike the survey in Uff. 43A (cat. no. 298) carried out by Sangallo probably at the time of Julius II, this survey prepared the way for Sangallo's project of a centrally planned building in 1535 (cat. no. 338). On the recto the southwestern corner of the pier arch already shows the diagonal face toward a secondary dome, realized by Sangallo around 1524-27 (cat. no. 344). The building next to it, begun by Fra Giocondo in summer 1514, is only briefly sketched (cat. no. 289). The autograph sketches on the verso provide further information about Sangallo's intentions. Next to two details of the survey, which prepare and complete the final drawing on the recto, and whose measurements do not everywhere coincide with those in Uff. 43A, there is a sketch of one bay of the ambulatory. Sangallo was evidently interested here in widening the passages between the ambulatory and the passage placed between the choir arm and the area of the secondary dome. Already in the autumn of 1519 Sangallo had studied similar passages in Uff. 48A (Frommel 1984c: 281) even though he did not succeed in introducing them—as the 1521 model demonstrates (cat. no. 321). On the plan in Uff. 39A he started first of all from ca. 12-*palmi* passages and then widened them to about 20 *palmi* in the southern and eastern ambulatories. But even there he failed to find a solution like the one he appeared to be developing on the verso. In the end he found what he wanted in the projects elaborated in about 1538, which were preparatory to the model, like that in Uff. 52A (cat. no. 351), but excluded the columns. It is unlikely here as on the plan in Uff. 39A that Sangallo took into account the raising of the floor. The writing on the recto belongs to the period after 1527. Likewise it is difficult to believe that the style of drawing on the verso dates back to before the Sack of Rome. Consequently the design can be dated fairly easily as the beginning of Paul III's reign. *C.L.F.*

338
ANTONIO DA SANGALLO THE YOUNGER
Alternative Plan Project

Florence, Galleria degli Uffizi, Gabinetto Disegni e Stampe, Uff. 39A
Pen and ink, with wash, on paper; stylus; corrections in sanguine.
33 × 42.3 cm

INSCRIBED: (lower margin) *muro de la chiesa vechio*; (left margin) *sacrestia / capella*; (next to main portal) *porte vechie.*

PROVENANCE: Papers of Antonio da Sangallo the Younger.

BIBLIOGRAPHY: Geymüller 1868: 23 n. 41; Letarouilly 1882: T. 12; Jovanovits 1877: 13 n. XXIX, 90; Hofmann 1928: 171-181; Giovannoni 1959: 135; Frommel 1964: 16, 22; Wolff Metternich and Thoenes 1987: 79, 136; Thoenes 1987: 136, 180; 1990: 39; 1992: 51; Thoenes in Frommel and Adams 1993 II (forthcoming).

The first version of this final drawing is so similar to the plan conserved in New York (cat. no. 330) that it could also date back to the first year of Paul III's papacy. The traces of erasions show that Sangallo first drew a strictly symmetrical centralized building. This version differs from Peruzzi's most of all in the huge corner sacristies, which seem designed to support towers, in the closure of all the 40-*palmi* niches and in the openings of passages between the ambulatories and the areas connecting the transept arms with the secondary domes. On second thoughts Sangallo widened these passages in the southern and eastern ambulatories (cf. cat. no. 337) and considered the possibility of reopening the corresponding 40-*palmi* niches in the pier arches. As Sangallo enlarged the ambulatories he revived an idea that he had first proposed in about 1519-20 in Uff. 48A (Frommel 1984c: 281) and in about 1520-21 in the *Memoriale* (cat. no. 320). In ca. 1519 he had already introduced in Uff. 255A (cat. no. 317) the enormous round towers, and in the margin in Uff. 252A (cat. no. 316) they were already connected to a centrally planned building. Following his conversations with the pope and with Peruzzi, Sangallo seems to have reflected on the financial and functional problems similar to those raised by Julius II in about 1505, which led to a return to the longitudinal construction with a central nave and two side aisles (cat. nos. 287, 288). At first he maintained the eastern round towers like the ones in Uff. 255A, and was satisfied with a two-bay passage connecting the area of the northeastern secondary dome to another area of the secondary dome in the third bay of the side aisle. Instead of opening the middle bay of the central nave toward the side aisles he opened them toward chapels with round niches. In a second phase he connected the middle bays of the side aisles with the central nave and enlarged them into octagonal domical areas. He made the sacristy towers smaller and took the towers away, transforming them into chapels so as to avoid problems with the neighboring Cappella Sistina and its sacristy. He reintroduced in sanguine the dome he had fought for passionately since 1519 in the central bay of the longitudinal body. The precise connection made with the Sala Regia is a particularly important achievement of this plan. Its southern limit would have been located exactly over the square chapel that Sangallo designed in the northeastern corner of the longitudinal body where a broken line indicates the points of juncture. Both the flights of steps to the right of the atrium substitute the Scala Regia situated further to the east, which would have also been sacrificed to the round tower in the first version of the longitudinal body and would have then risen to the Sala Regia from the east. The atrium is also designed here with giant half-columns, as in Peruzzi's drawing in Uff. 31A (cat. no. 333), even though the elimination of the towers and the paratactic rhythm recall the sketch in the *Memoriale* (cat. no. 320). Its central arch is once again reduced to a width of ca. 75 *palmi*, as already shown in Uff. 70A (cat. no. 314) and the passages toward the side portals are just 40 *palmi* wide. Sangallo then considered the possibility of opening the four aedicules between the engaged columns to create more passages which would have resulted in a totally paratactic rhythm along the front. The tendency toward greater thrift is also noticeable in the successive insertion in Bramante's choir which could have been elaborated on the basis of his more or less contemporary survey in Uff. 44A (cat. no. 337). In this context it appears he was not particularly interested in the question of conserving Bramante's choir as a whole but how, rather, to utilize the individual parts of it. He even considered the partial closure of the choir by means

of Bramante's side walls. There is no evidence of his intention to raise the floor. The nearness of this project to the one by Peruzzi in Uff. 31A favors the hypothesis that it was designed at the start of Paul III's reign.
C.L.F.

339
ANTONIO DA SANGALLO THE YOUNGER
Plan Project
ca. 1535

Florence, Galleria degli Uffizi, Gabinetto Disegni e Stampe, Uff. 256A
Pen and ink, on parchment; straightedge and compass; stylus; trimmed at the corners; numerous traces of erasure.
57.4 × 88.4 cm
INSCRIBED: *muro di s[an]to pietro*

PROVENANCE: Papers of Antonio da Sangallo the Younger.

BIBLIOGRAPHY: Giovannoni 1959; Frommel 1964: 18ff.; Wolff Metternich and Thoenes 1987: 24, 180 n. 309.

Sangallo used this parchment for elaborating several different versions, some of which were then canceled and therefore are hard to reconstruct today. The first alternative is perhaps the one on the right half of the sheet which was based on a three-bay longitudinal body, piers with 30-*palmi* wide passages, Bramante's choir with closed side walls, segment-shaped transept arms the same depth as the choir arm, an atrium flanked by towers and side chapels whose shapes were revised on many occasions. The first version on the left half of the parchment was probably designed with side chapels anticipating a later stage: the central chapel was closed, while the two side ones had a triconch design and opened on to the central nave. A second development of the project introduced the transformation of these side chapels into outer side aisles and therefore closer to Bramante's last project of 1506 (see "St. Peter's" pp. 399-423), which seems to have already inspired the three arms of the cross and the three aisles of the longitudinal body. Sangallo's continuation here of these outer side aisles into two chapels near the choir was practically a return to the quincunx system without, however, opening the walls of Bramante's choir. He designed the whole body of the building, including Bramante's choir, with pairs of 9-*palmi* order pilasters, which he remodeled on the towers and facade and turned into engaged columns, leaving single pilasters only on the left arm of the transept. The third alternative was concentrated again on the right half. Sangallo reduced the passages through the piers in the longitudinal body to ca. 25 *palmi* and flanked their arches with aedicules. At the same time he opened the old 40-*palmi* niches—which he had earlier reduced to 30 *palmi*—probably because right from the start he had taken into consideration raising the floor level by about 13.5 *palmi*, and this consequently suggests his reduction of the central arch of the atrium to ca. 60 *palmi* (cf. cat. no. 340). The reason why he moved the side arches of the right arm of the transept and the corresponding ones of the first chapel in the longitudinal body could have been to complete the analogy with the choir arm. Lastly he examined the apse in the transept which could have been integrated with the parts of the inner ambulatory already built; but in doing so Sangallo would have moved further away again from the design of the choir arm. This train of thought, based on the need to economize, was continued in the debate on the 40-*palmi* niches at the start of the ambulatories. In this case however, it was difficult to imagine a return to the ones designed in 1519.

He brought the right tower of the facade back behind the outer limit of the longitudinal body, and placed a much smaller dome over the bay of the atrium tower. The staircase leading up to the presumed Benediction Loggia—which here too could only have been sited in the tympanum above the attic area—is arranged in a substantially less elaborate way than it was in the left tower between the atrium and the side aisle.

The shortening of the atrium allowed Sangallo to conserve the old Scala Regia, sketched roughly in the margin, and to extend its lower ramp perhaps right inside the atrium. The Sala Regia would have arrived at the outer right edge of the atrium where a broken line traces its junction to the west. It is hard to imagine the continuation of the Sala Regia south with the Cappella Paolina (cf. Frommel 1964).

The chapel would have intersected the wall dividing the atrium and the first chapel of the longitudinal body and it would have been difficult to provide it with natural lighting. If the measurements written in the lower and right-hand margins coincide in part with those in Sangallo's survey of 1539 in Uff. 119A (Frommel and Adams 1993, II), this must mean that in 1538 Sangallo and his assistants perhaps based their calculations on earlier documents, or they verified some measurements a second time for safety's sake. The building of the Cappella Paolina was not even compatible with the much more mature project in Uff. 259A (cat. no. 349), which certainly was not elaborated before 1537-38. Only in the 1539 model did Sangallo calculate the atrium and the towers in such a way as to make the Cappella Paolina a bridge between the two, and natural illumination possible through his thermal-style windows (cf. the partly erroneous reconstructions in Frommel 1964: fig. 17).

The project's blatant economizing, its evident similarity to Bramante's project of 1506 as well as the new respect for the papal palace suggest a date in the second half of 1535, more or less parallel to Peruzzi's design in Uff. 26A (cat. no. 334).

C.L.F.

BIBLIOGRAPHY: Geymüller 1875-80 : 314, T. 50, 2; Giovannoni 1959; Frommel 1964: 18ff.; Wolff Metternich 1972: 54ff., fig. 79; Frommel 1984c: 296.

The right half of this drawing corresponds amply to the left-hand alternative in Uff. 256A (cat. no. 339) comprising a projecting side tower. The omission of the base, and the 9-*palmi* order only 76 *palmi* high, prove that the floor has already been raised. The central arch, here as in the drawing in Uff. 256A, has a width of 60 *palmi* and an overall height of 111 *palmi*, giving a ratio of 1:1.85. Since, as with Peruzzi's drawing in Uff. 26A (cat. no. 334), it is difficult to imagine where a Benediction Loggia could be inserted, it is probable that at this time Paul III still intended conserving Pio II's benediction loggia. Both the alternative on the left, which still shows a giant order like Peruzzi's in Uff. 31A (cat. no. 333), and the breadth of the facade which would have called for the demolition of the Sala Regia like the left-hand alternative shown in Uff. 256A, support the dating of this drawing to just before the one in Uff. 256A. Unlike the latter, but resembling the last version in Uff. 39A (cat. no. 338), this drawing shows a dome with a lantern over the longitudinal body. The drum is illuminated by natural light pouring through oculi similar to those on the 1520 coin while the profile of the dome still copies Bramante's Pantheon-like dome. The large central pediment above the attic level which recalls Peruzzi's contemporary sketch in Uff. 26A, was substituted by Sangallo at a second stage with at least two versions of a smaller pediment. Characteristic of Sangallo's style after 1530 are not just the hurried strokes of the sketch, but also his emphatic verticality such as in the projecting parts between the entablature of the 9-*palmi* columns and the pilaster strips of the attic. This period of the design differs from the projects of the years 1537-38 not just in its more sober forms, in the lack of a benediction loggia, or in the drum, but also in the height of the 9-*palmi* order which still takes into consideration shafts and the height of the entablature similar to those in the years 1519-21. In order to place a second order on the attic level Sangallo brought the 9-*palmi* order down—as in the projects in Uff. 66A (cat. no. 348), Uff. 67A and Uff. 259A (cat. no. 349)—to a height considerably below the top of the impost of the central nave arcade, and therefore abandoned the idea of the corresponding inner and outer orders which had led him in the first place to chose the 9-*palmi* one (cf. cat. no. 314).

C.L.F.

Next to the 1524 drawing (cat. no. 323) the views in the Berlin *taccuini* of ca. 1535 are the most reliable source for establishing the state of the building site before Paul III ordered work to start again. The drawing in volume II, on fol. 52 recto, shows the view west from the start of the old longitudinal body. The end of the surviving fragment of the central nave of Old St. Peter's can be seen in the foreground. Alessandro VI's organ is on the right with its bronze statue of a seated St. Peter (Alpharanus, no. 42). Behind it there are the piers of Bramante's longitudinal body, whose pilasters evidently flank a niche rising up from floor level. The pilasters have been stopped just above where the fluting starts, more or less at the level of the entablature of the early Christian colonnade, ca. 55-60 *palmi* from the ground. Since the floor was raised about 5.60 meters, and today they start about 8 meters from the floor, they are perhaps still in the same place. In comparison to the most likely model, that is to say, the great order inside the Pantheon where the lower third of the shaft above the base is designed with cabled fluting while the upper two thirds has ordinary fluting, here the cabled part is too high. In order to achieve a ratio similar to that of the Pantheon, i.e., much imitated by others ca. 30-*palmi* pedestals would have been necessary. But, in this case, the Corinthian order would have had a ratio of 1:8.15 as proposed by Peruzzi (cat. no. 325)—rather unlikely for Bramante. Sangallo mentions this problem in the fourth paragraph of his *Memoriale* (cat. no. 320) where he registers the conflict between the eventual pedestals and the "cappelle" by which he most certainly does not mean the great niches in the pier arches 4 *palmi* away from the pilasters, but to the "capelle piccole che sono de una canna," the small ones already mentioned in the 1506 contract (Frommel 1976: 93). With their width of about 2.38 meters, these could contain an altar and correspond to the many chapels in the old nave. Bramante could have therefore given the pilasters proportions of 1:10.64. The upper fluted part would have had a ratio of 1:1.23 with the lower non-fluted part, an even more striking difference compared to the Pantheon than there is today.

Behind the columns to the right the vista opens half way up. This is probably Bramante's inner side aisle, which ran through the two half disk-shaped piers of the longitudinal body, and was substituted by the 40-*palmi* niches after Julius II died. These niches which are already closed in the survey plan conserved in the *Codex Coner* of 1515 (cat. no. 289), were clearly still without their calottes. Beyond the pilasters there are another three columns of Old St. Peter's with their entablature. The shafts of the demolished columns lay on the floor. Bramante's imposing "baldachin" towers above. The arches are already protected by their vaults. Heemskerck carefully included all the brick teeth jutting ready for the barrel vault, the cavity for the lunette which would have been the same as those in the choir arm, and, on the left, the cavity for the jutting entablature. Strangely enough the springers of the arches cannot be identified. Sangallo's entablature without the architrave has already been completed over the left pilaster (cf. cat. no. 320). This stops between the pilasters and juts twice toward the smooth walled perimetral arch of Bramante's inner side aisle. It is likely that Bramante planned a cross vault for this area. The smooth face above the vault was perhaps destined for the light shaft for the windows of the central nave. To the right this area is drawn less precisely. On both sides of the piers there are the slit windows of the staricases on the inside. Behind the pairs of pilasters which have neither a pedestal nor a base, there is the left corner pier of the old longitudinal body. The old apse is protected by Bramante's altar-house, whose attic was added by Peruzzi in 1523-24 while Giuliano Leno added a rustic roof (cat. no. 305) in about 1526.

The oculi of the dome's pendentives are only half-built. Behind them there is a partial view of Bramante's choir arm (see "St. Peter's," pp. 399-423).

The pyramidal tip of a curtain in front of the southwestern pier of the dome is an enigma.

C.L.F.

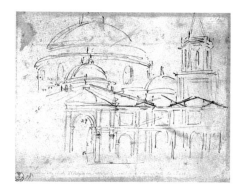

340
<small>ANTONIO DA SANGALLO THE YOUNGER</small>
Sketch for the Facade
ca. 1535

Florence, Galleria degli Uffizi, Gabinetto Disegni e Stampe, Uff. 78A
Pen and ink, on paper; freehand
22.4 × 27.5 cm

<small>PROVENANCE:</small> Papers of Antonio da Sangallo the Younger

341
<small>MAERTEN VAN HEEMSKERCK</small>
View of the Old Longitudinal Body in the Area of the Dome and Choir Arm

Berlin, Staatliche Museen Preussischer Kulturbesitz, Kupferstichkabinett, *Berliner Skizzenbuch*, II, fol. 52r
Pen and ink, with pencil and some shading, on paper

<small>PROVENANCE:</small> J.-P. Mariette; H. Destailleur.

BIBLIOGRAPHY: Hülsen and Egger, II 1913-16: 32ff.; Frommel 1984c: 265; Wolff Metternich and Thoenes 1987: 118, 198, fig. 124.

342
MAERTEN VAN HEEMSKERCK
Choir and Southwestern Arm, from the Southwest

Berlino, Staatliche Museen Preussischer Kulturbesitz,
Kupferstichkabinett, Berliner Skizzenbuch, II, fol. 54r.
Pen and ink, on paper.
13.5 × 21.1 cm

PROVENANCE: J.-P. Mariette; H. Destailleur.

BIBLIOGRAPHY: Hülsen and Egger, I 1913-16: 30; Frommel 1984c:
265; Wolff Metternich and Thoenes 1987: 198, fig. 198.

This view perfectly documents the parts of the southern
ambulatory built between 1519-21. The base that runs all
round it, with its simple profiles, together with the engaged columns of the 9-*palmi* order and their Attic base,
the pilasters of the 3½-*palmi* order connected to the aedicules, the pilasters of the aedicules whose columns have
not yet been placed in position, and the still uncorniced
portal correspond exactly to Sangallo's right-hand alternative in the 1519 drawing in Uff. 122A recto (Frommel
1984c: 286). On both sides of the portal there seem to be
three bays with niches as on the drawing in the second
Heemskerck sketchbook, fol. 51 recto as established in
the projects elaborated in the period before 1527 (cat.
nos. 317, 321). There are cockle staircases in both the buttressing piers, which can perhaps be reached from the passages between the 40-*palmi* niches. These lead into the
rooms over the barrel vaulted areas (cat. no. 323). The
southern wall of the transept of Old St. Peter's can still
be seen in the transept arm. S. Maria della Febbre and the
Obelisk stand on the right flank of the old longitudinal
body. The area of the entablature and the roof of the
Bramante's choir arm is somewhat elongated. The
columns are missing from the arch of the window.
Bramante apparently prepared the brick teeth for the lunettes of the transept near the southern arch of the crossing. *C.L.F.*

343
MAERTEN VAN HEEMSKERCK
View of the New Building from the Northeast
1532-36

Berlin, Staatliche Museen Preussischer Kulturbesitz,
Kupferstichkabinett, *Berliner Skizzenbuch*, I, fol. 13r.
Pen and ink, with pencil and wash, on paper.
13.5 × 21 cm

PROVENANCE: J.-P. Mariette; H. Destailleur.

BIBLIOGRAPHY: Hülsen and Egger, I 1913-16: 8ff.; Frommel 1984c:
265; Wolff Metternich and Thoenes 1987: 142, fig. 145.

Heemskerck drew the new building from the north-
northeast this time. The outer wall of Old St. Peter's is
recognizable in the foreground. Behind it there are two
fragments of the old colonnade of the central nave and
stumps of the pilasters of Julius II's longitudinal body.
From this standpoint the slices—two by two—of the piers
of Bramante's longitudinal body pile up in layers, one after another. In front to the left there is northern half of
the northern pier, then, behind, the passage of the inner
right side aisle, and the southern half of the pier. On the
other side of the central nave there is the northern half of
the southern pier with the fluting of the great pilaster order, and behind this, the southern half of the same pier.
The southern external wall of the old basilica, the Obelisk
and S. Maria della Febbre lie further back. The northeastern buttressing pier rises up in the foreground center:
it is in almost the same state, with niches and pilaster
strips, as Bramante left it in 1514 (cat. no. 289). Only the
tripartite cornice of the impost and the cornice of the 40-
palmi niches on the eastern side probably date back to
Raphael's period in the years 1517-18 (cat. no. 320) (see
the reconstruction of the plan of the parts shown here in
Wolff Metternich and Thoenes 1987: fig. 146). The corresponding western buttressing pier shows the side
toward the transept and the pilasters of the great order
with Sangallo's marking for the base and pedestal (cf. cat.
no. 345), which flank Bramante's niche, whose lower part
has been walled up. A large part of the old transept still
stands between the two piers. The "baldachin" of the
dome in the background correspond clearly to Heemskerck's view of the central nave (cat. no. 341). The
smooth finished perimetral arch on the northern side of
the northeastern pier proves that Bramante had planned
either groined or coved vaults in the outer aisles. There
is no diagonal face on the pier of the secondary dome as
on the plan conserved in the *Codex Coner* (cat. no. 289).
The slit windows of the spiral staircase can be seen on
both piers. The choir arm with its segmented entablature
and the window wall above has been considerably foreshortened in the picture. The eastern walls of the eastern
piers of the dome are characterized by the 40-*palmi*
niches. Sangallo's reduced cornice of the impost runs
along the whole wall of the southeastern pier. The octagonal base of today's drum can be identified at the top
of the pier arches. *C.L.F.*

344
MAERTEN VAN HEEMSKERCK
View of the Interior of the Southern Ambulatory
ca. 1532-36

Berlin, Staatliche Museen Preussischer Kulturbesitz,
Kupferstichkabinett, *Berliner Skizzenbuch*, I, fol. 8r
Pen and ink, with pencil, on paper.
13.4 × 20.8 cm

PROVENANCE: J.-P. Mariette; H. Destailleur.

BIBLIOGRAPHY: Hülsen and Egger, I 1913-16: 6; Frommel 1984c:
265; Wolff Metternich and Thoenes 1987: 198, fig. 195.

Heemskerck completed his study of the outside of
southern ambulatory with this equally precise (though less
complete) view. His main interest here was the chapel to
the west of the transept, whose coffered vault had been
designed by Sangallo in Uff. 53A (Frommel 1984c: 292)
and built by him in about 1523-24 (cat. no. 323).
Bramante's 40-*palmi* niche and the area of the impost are
topped by Raphael's cornice of 1517-18 (cat. no. 320).
Fra Giocondo's fragmentary niche can be seen, below
right, following Bramante's 40-*palmi* niches exactly.
Overhead Sangallo prepared the diagonal faces for the
piers of the southwestern secondary dome, which he also
drew in Uff. 44A recto (cat. no. 337) in about 1535. To
the back left there is the left pier of the ambulatory with
the pilaster of the great order—one of the few with a
13½-*palmi* high pedestal, a base like that in Pantheon,
and the fluting of Raphael's 1519 project (cat. no. 315).
One of the 5-*palmi* columns without a capital has already
been erected on the left. The twelve capitals ordered by
Sangallo in March 1521 "*apud capellam Regis Franciae*"
were therefore destined probably for the acompanying
pilasters (A. Bertolotti, "Documento intorno ad Antonio
Sangallo il giovane," in *Il Buonarroti*, s. III, IV: 312). The
heterogeneous 5-*palmi* columns of Old St. Peter's were
given a uniform entasis as from 1520 and were erected
sometime after 1525-26 (Frey 1910: 70ff.; Frommel
1984: 287ff.). The right niche in the background is situated next to the portal and flanked by a group of 9-*palmi*
order pilasters. In order to draw this niche Heemskerck
had to change his position and move slightly to the east
(Wolff Metternich and Thoenes 1987, fig. 196). Unlike
Bramante, Raphael and Sangallo had the details of the
brickwork inserted as the building went on. *C.L.F.*

345

<small>Maerten van Heemskerck</small>
*View from the North of the Old Transept and the
Dome Area*
1532-36

Stockholm, Nationalmuseum, Collection Anckarvärd, n. 637
Pen and ink, with wash, on paper.

Bibliography: Krautheimer 1949: 211; Wolff Metternich and
Thoenes 1987: 201, fig. 200.

From this unusual viewpoint Heemskerck gave a real idea
of the complex mixture of old and new that characterized
the area of the old transept between 1507 and 1540.
Bramante's *tigurio* of 1513 can be seen through the northern colonnade, protecting the Constantinian apse and
leaning against the old western wall with its tracery window, the remains of its frescoes, the old eastern portal
and, to the left of this, the Renaissance aedicule of an altar
(Alpharanus, no. 37). To the left of the *tigurio* the colonnade of the southern transept arm of Old St. Peter's
spreads out above the transept arm walled up in 1523-27.
Heemskerck did not ignore the niches in the southern ambulatory. However it is the area in the left margin that
provides the most information for reconstructing
Bramante's project (cat. no. 344). The diagonal face of the
southern pier of the dome with its uncorniced upper shell-
capped niche can be seen in the background. The windows of the cockle staircase have been cut into the back
wall of the niche. The lower niche is masked by the end
of the southern colonnade of the central nave of Old St.
Peter's with the corner pier and garland frieze. In the far
left margin there is a hint of the corner pilaster of the
northeastern pier of the dome. Subsequent indentations
more or less at the height of the base were perhaps ready
for the insertion of the carved stone of the pedestal and
base designed in 1519 (cat. no. 344). The little horizontal
line considerably further up could mean that Sangallo had
already had a strip of the pilaster removed in order to add
the cables to the fluting in the 1519 project. The spiral
column, or *salomonica*, in the old choir screen is protected
by a grating as in Heemskerck's view from the northeast.
The aedicule to its left seems to correspond to the altar of
the west wall (Alpharanus, no. 24). The shaft of the isolated column to the back was identified by Krautheimer in
Uff. 20A (cat. no. 288) as one of the columns of the triumphal arch of Constantine's Basilica. The Corinthian capital lying on the ground, obviously belonging to a pilaster,
could have been a part of the triumphal arch of Old St.
Peter's (cf. cat. no. 295). The column to the right next to
the northeasterm pier, which supports an entablature and
a roof may be identified as the western end of the right
colonnade of Old St. Peter's.   C.L.F.

The Model of St. Peter's
Sandro Benedetti

The great model of the new St. Peter's marks one of the
most interesting stages of development in Antonio da
Sangallo the Younger's architectural theories. The model
was generally underestimated and highly criticized until
recent unprejudiced studies were made (Portoghesi 1971;
Benedetti 1986 and 1991-92; Bruschi 1988). The harsh
judgment Michelangelo expressed when he succeeded
Sangallo as director of the *fabbrica* of St. Peter's was
responsible for more than four hundred years of negative
opinion regarding Sangallo's daunting project.
"In Michelangelo's and many other people's opinions ...
Sangallo's composition was excessively reduced by the
projections and by the members that were small ... meaning by this that the said model derived more from the German manner and work rather than the sound and proper
style practiced by today's finest architects."
An appraisal which aims to give an unbiased overview of
the characteristics of this last and unrealized project by
Sangallo has to cover both the "German," that is, Gothic,
characteristics of the model, and the example of the "new
order and extraordinary method" it embodies. The formative spirit that inspires the culmination of Sangallo's
own project for St. Peter's—which began under
Raphael's direction, was interrupted during the Sack of
Rome, and then renewed in the 1530s at the time of the
succession of Paul III—shows a concentrated sense of
purpose, and is quite different from the "antique" convictions expressed by Bramante and Raphael. Sangallo's aim
was to recoup and merge the achievements of the Renaissance with echoes of pre-humanist architectural tradition.
The resulting graft, however, was neither an incongruous
dovetailing of disparate stylistic features, nor a revivalist
retrieval of medieval forms: it involved translating and
updating the organizational methods used for the construction of large-scale medieval religious buildings, and
reapplying them with the forms and stylistic cadences of
the High Renaissance.
In this respect Vasari was correct to describe the special
formative method as belonging to a "new order," and so
was Michelangelo when he asserted that the final inspiration "in the German manner and work" was far from the
"old and correct manner practiced by today's finest architects," without dismissing Michelangelo's negative
comments as biasedly Renaissance. This path of research
was already being explored by other great architects such
as Peruzzi for S. Petronio in Bologna, or Giulio Romano
in S. Benedetto Po and in the facade of S. Petronio
(Panofsky 1962b; Benedetti 1986; Piva 1988).
The motives behind Sangallo's particular style of research
are worth underlining. The reworking of the organism of
St. Peter's as a centralized system in a way that was closely
connected to its original cultural inspiration, while maintaining the sacred status of the Early Christian basilica
that was to be destroyed, was a problem that Bramante
had failed to solve in the *Piano di Pergamena*. The need
was to establish a satisfactory bond between the general
symbolism of the new building and the vestiges of the
original, maintaining, in other words, the memory of the
Apostle Peter's tomb. A further intention of the 1520's
project (Uff. 67A, 68A, 259A), which Giovannoni
brought into evidence (1959), was to establish the new
building as an emblem of the cultural "twinning" of the
architectural tradition of ancient Rome with that of
medieval Florence. This is revealed in the marriage between the Pantheon dome design with its semicircular
profile rising from steps—a feature already introduced in
St. Peter's by both Bramante and Raphael—and the dome

of S. Maria del Fiore, with its elevated internal profile.
The background to this choice of design is most explicit
in the project of the 1520s. While being the least salient
element and of a markedly concise shape, in the relationship created between the external and internal profiles,
the dome expresses the will to achieve a syncretic solution
based on the Roman and Florentine styles (Benedetti
1991-92).
In order to comprehend the development of what Vasari
terms the "new order," we shall examine the principal variations in the design that Sangallo introduced in this part
of the building as he progressed from the project of the
1520s to the final one.
The idea of twinning Rome and Florence was a dominant
architectural theme in the early sixteenth century during
the reigns of the Florentine popes Leo X and Clement
VII. It was also the subject of the important competition
for the design of S. Giovanni dei Fiorentini held in 1518,
for which Antonio da Sangallo the Younger submitted a
project.
The existence of this same theme in the project for St.
Peter's in Uff. 66, 67, 259 is not the ultimate proof of the
hypothesis (Giovannoni 1959) that would have them a
progressive development of the design during the 1520s.
Not surprisingly, in the ensuing studies of the dome, as
seen in Uff. 87A, 798A, 88A, 267A, this theme fades
progressively and turns into more intriguing results. In
fact, confirming the progressive development of the
project, the establishment of the external pseudo-drum
with half-columns in Uff. 259A, goes back toward that of
a dome with tiered colonnades, a tradition of the Italian
Middle Ages which can be found in the Certosa at Pavia,
S. Maria delle Grazie in Milan, and elsewhere. Sangallo
places a huge hemispherical shell interrupted by relief ribbing over these elements, and crowns the whole with a
gigantic lantern. On the inside, the Gothic influence of
the outline, drawn in Uff. 66A, is further, emphasized
and then left aside in the final solution. From being
"acute" the final solution changes the profile to being
"ovate", as Sangallo himself indicates in Uff. 267A, with
a curve that reaches up higher but is less "interrupted"
than the previous "Gothic" one, and is covered by a
resonant coffered surface. This intensifies and regulates—in Roman style—the accentuated vertical expansion
of the space.
The three main drawings of the internal profile: Uff.
267A, the Stockholm drawing—which I studied some
time ago—defined as anonymous but attributable to Sangallo or his circle, the section drawn by Labacco and published in 1546 (Ashby 1914) illustrate the various stages
of its transformation. This passage was already announced in the note to the drawing Uff. 267A, and shows
the intention of going beyond both Gothic inspiration
and the reference to antiquity (Benedetti 1986). While
the profile of Uff. 267A is strictly an acute angle and the
Stockholm drawing starts to move away from this, "swell-
ing" at the top in order to soften the curve, Labacco's
print shows how this process has been accentuated, leading to an oval profile.
The striking double colonnade with its forty-eight sections as expressed in the model is semantically applied by
Sangallo to the tomb of St. Peter by means of highlighting
the form—which is a reference to both antiquity and the
Middle Ages—in such a way as to accentuate the chief features of the whole: the great lantern, the soaring campaniles and the octagonal towers. Sangallo achieves the
stylistic solution regarding the theme of the tomb by
reconstructing the image of the lost tomb of Porsenna at
Chiusi, first described by Pliny, some references to which
can be found in the tomb known as degli Orazi e Curiazi
at Albano (Benedetti 1986; Fagiolo 1985).
The tomb—as Sangallo shows in several drawings, in particular in Uff. 1209A—is composed of a large spire rising
up from a square base, surrounded by four smaller spires
starting lower down from a larger pedestal: a quintuple pyramidal solution, open to repetition. What is particularly
important is that this rediscovery is not only to be found
in the ancient document. Other drawings by Sangallo

show that he discovered the same quintuple motif, but this time cuspidal, and still repeatable, in medieval monuments as well. An example is the Uff. 1169A—which was perhaps derived from the tomb of Cansignorio della Scala in the family seat in Verona (see the illustration in Toesca 1951, fig. 353) which Sangallo could have drawn during his journey with Sanmicheli in the Veneto in the spring of 1526 (Puppi 1986b). Sangallo used this to pinpoint and analyze the links with the medieval form. He noted the organizational relationship between the central spire (C), the lateral spires (B), and the surrounding pinnacles (A), and established the following "structural" equation: A:B = B:C.

Sangallo's daring grafts and formal exploration of new avenues, his retrieval of former styles and his adventurous mixtures did not result in paltry revivalism. They involved the reinstatement of organizational methods particular to the architecture of the great medieval cathedrals—in this case translated, displayed and made real through the polished stylistic cadences of Renaissance excellence. The language of the beautiful "modern

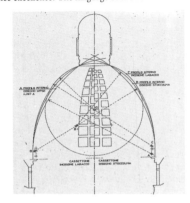

Antonio da Sangallo the Younger, Project
of the dome for St. Peter's,
*Comparison of the internal profiles
of the three final solutions.*

manner" was used to express and to confirm medieval "concepts." It foretold a cultural trend that was to emerge a few decades later in Rome, whose chief exponent was Gilio, an active member of the cultural entourage of Cardinal Farnese (Benedetti 1986). It represented the marriage between the greater "truth" in conceptual terms present in medieval works—"truer," as Gilio stated, but stylistically "clumsy"—and the beauty of modern works which, though more beautiful outwardly, tended to belie the contents they intended to express.

What we said before (with reference to the design of the dome) about the final achievement of the project going beyond the definitions of "antico" (ancient) and "todesco" (German or Gothic) is true also for the other main features of the great building. Sangallo himself asserted he had overcome the above two criticisms through the invention of his dome on Uff. 267A. We will now briefly consider the campaniles and the body of the building with its huge apses.

The design of the campaniles is a particularly sublimated demonstration of the mixture of antique and medieval grammar, merging classicized stylistic references and those of Raphael's campaniles for St. Peter's—which also owe much to the towers designed by Giuliano da Sangallo for the facade of S. Lorenzo in Florence—with the formative "spirit" of the Gothic era. The project avoids any "clumsy" stylistic borrowings but strongly emphasizes the horizontal subdivision and the verticality of the soaring prism.

The principal elements of this sublimation are as follows: first, there is an exaggerated vertical juxtaposition of architectural elements (orders, attics, and aedicules, etc.) which multiply the limits of the customary four-cell juxtaposition of the "old and good manner" (the superimposition of the four orders), which had regulated vertical development from Alberti to Raphael. Second, there is a

shift from volume to a vector-based linearity achieved by highlighting the twin half-columns of the lower story, and by the tripartite subdivision of the walls of the campaniles rising up from the main body. The consequence is verticality and heightened "upthrust" of the volumetric adjectivization established at the base.

The decisive element of this linear-oriented "dissolution" of the building mass is the corner linkage of the campanile. The edge of the prism tends to figuratively "annul" the volume because it stands back compared to the plane of the facade, with its vigorous coupled Doric half-columns. The corner "draws back," it "hides" behind sets of prominent half-columns and pillars on both lower and upper stories for the full length of the building. This pattern is echoed by the horizontal "fragmentation" caused by the superimposition of no less than eleven architectonic layers: coupled Doric columns embracing arches, figured order with blind tabernacle, Ionic order with tympanum, attic, coupled half-columns emerging at the angles, cuspidate twin orders framing pedimented windows, a banded octagonal prism, a circular attic, a circular peripteral bell cella, another attic, and a culminating spire reminiscent of Porsenna's tomb.

The formal development of the main building, with its bulky semicircular apses, is similar, but with less of the "fragmentation" that dominates in the five volumes (the two campaniles and the three central sections) of the enormous facade.

The pattern established through the use of prominent Doric half-columns and blind tabernacles—a device introduced by Raphael which Sangallo made his own—continues in the second story with a figured order incorporating windows that illuminate the annular aisles of the side apses; above this runs the tall Ionic order with arches, which let the light pour into the central naves, and defines the perimeter of the main body of the building.

While the insistent articulation of the facade and the emphatic voids of the tall upper-story arches exalt the modulations of the polished "modern manner," the pattern also echoes medieval cathedral construction (in the insistent reiteration of columns closed by arches). Consider, for example, the side walls of Pisa Cathedral or, outside Italy, St. Aposteln in Cologne.

In conclusion, apart from the specific admixture of the "antico" and the "todesco" exemplified by Sangallo's design for St. Peter's—a characteristic that makes it unique among Sangallo's vast output, but also among the projects of his contemporaries—it must be remembered how this monumental project preluded at least two of the main features of Michelangelo's design for New St. Peter's. One was the return to the original centralized plan (Wolff-Metternich 1972) rejected by Raphael, a scheme to which Sangallo added the immense frontage reminiscent of the Gothic double-campanile facades. The other was the simplification of the main volume of the building, which discards Raphael's complicated set of split levels in favor of a unitary volume at ground level, permitting the complex blossoming of domes and spires from a unitary body.

BIBLIOGRAPHY: Vasari, ed. Milanesi 1906-10, V: 467-468; Ashby 1914: 289-309; K. Frey 1909b-1910-1912, XXX, XXXI, XXXIII; Giovannoni 1931b; Toesca 1951: 390-391; Giovannoni 1959, I: 115-150; Panofsky 1962b: 171-224; Pepe 1962; Portoghesi n.d. [1971]; Wolff Metternich 1972; Francia 1977: 49-55; Benedetti 1983: 959-976; Frommel 1984c: 241-310; Benedetti 1986: 157-174; Zander 1986: 175-184; Gabrielli 1986: 184-185; Fagiolo 1986: 187-209; Silvan 1986: 209-216; Puppi 1986b: 101-107; Bruschi 1988: 237-243; Piva 1988: 136; Benedetti and Zander 1990: 240-244; Benedetti 1991-92: 485-504.

346
ANTONIO DA SANGALLO THE YOUNGER
Wooden Model of the Project for St. Peter's
(built under the supervision
of Antonio Labacco)
1539-46

Vatican, Fabbrica di San Pietro

BIBLIOGRAPHY: Vasari, ed. Milanesi 1906, V; Frey 1909a and 1912; Giovannoni 1959; Francia 1977; Benedetti 1986; Zander 1986; Gabrielli 1986; Silvan 1986: 210; Benedetti and Zander 1990 and Benedetti 1990-92.

The model, which has lost its finish and is now in exposed wood, is 7.36 meters long and 6.02 meters wide, and built in fir, lime, elm and apricot. The dome is 4.68 meters high and the campaniles 4.56 meters (Silvan 1986: 210). The inside of the semicircular vaults of the large cruciform space have been papered and illustrated with a square coffer finish. The model was built by a group of craftsmen supervised by Antonio Labacco, Sangallo's assistant (Vasari, ed. Milanesi 1906; Pepe 1962).

Originally the model was painted: two soft colors dominated the outside (Gabrielli 1986). The outside was painted in two tones, with a base of warm, pale yellow for the travertine, and a lighter shade for the orders (a cool yellow). The interiors were also in two colors, with a light blue-gray for the main stonework and door panels, and pale yellow for the pilasters and orders: "a yellow like that used for the stonework outside" (Gabrielli 1986).

"Of all the fine works that Antonio realized ... nothing can compare with the model ... of St. Peter's ... as can be seen in the model created by Antonio d'Abaco in wood, finished in every detail ... When Abaco had finished all the models, shortly after the death of Antonio, it was estimated that the said model of St. Peter's had cost (for the carpentry and materials alone) 4,184 *scudi*: which in doing, Antonio Abaco, who was responsible, behaved very well ..." (Vasari, ed. Milanesi 1906: 467-468).

Vasari's detailed description of the costs of the model for Sangallo's St. Peter's was drawn from a source with direct access to the site accounts; indeed, he even knew the precise amount that Sangallo earned—1,500 *scudi*—of which he only received 1,000, as he died before the rest could be paid. These figures testify to the enormous amount of work involved in completing the model, which was built at a scale of 1:30 (Silvan 1986, calculates it as between 1:28 and 1:29).

For the purpose of reconstructing the various stages of the model's construction, it is useful to piece together the relative documents of the accounts published by Frey in his studies (Frey 1909a, and 1912), which still need a full appraisal. As far as this painstaking cataloging is concerned, the figures indicated by Vasari—in contrast to those mentioned by Frey in a note (Frey 1912: 23)—are much closer to the total of the various fees paid to Labacco and his assistants for carpentry work, making sure to sum only once the various sets of accounts for each job, which are repeated under several different headings.

The payments started on 2 March 1539 with an advance of 50 *scudi* to Labacco "on account for the model of St. Peter's that he's building" (Frey 1909a: 168), and ended on 12 November 1546 "for 23 balustrades carved for the model" (Frey 1912, p. 21).

Labacco, *capomaestro* of the team working on the model, was paid sporadically from 1539 to early 1540.
After the 50 *scudi* on 2 March and 20 April 1539 (Frey 1909a: 168) the next payments occurred on 26 July, 24 November (Frey 1909a: 167-168) and 23 December (Frey 1912, 22) for the sum of 25 *scudi*. Separate payments are made "for 12 and 10 firwood boards," for "six firwood beams," and "different kinds of wood," for "a single piece of oak": 36 and 30 *scudi* to Battista da Sangallo on 3 March and 20 April respectively (Frey 1909a: 168), 22 and 30 *scudi* to Domenico Faladanza on 4 November and 13 December (Frey 1909a: 167-168), 36 and 62 *scudi* to Ambrosio da Pistoia on 8 November (Frey 1909a: 168) and to Battista de Marganis on 18 November (Frey 1912: 25). Labacco's remuneration became a monthly salary in February 1540: 25 *scudi* in February, and 50 *scudi* a month from March 1540, through to 1543. The amount comprises the various payments due the *capomaestro* and his assistants, engravers, carpenters, workers, and other specialists.
The monthly salary was exclusive of expenses for materials. In 1540 these included Battista da Sangallo's "six firwood boards" on 22 May (Frey 1912: 25), Domenico Faladanza's eight boards on 16 September (Frey 1909a: 169). Giovanni Lodetto was paid for "40 *canne* of cloth for a curtain that protects the model from the heat"; Gerardo Funaro "for 100 pounds of rope for mounting the curtain" and "40 *canne* of cloth" for the curtain between May and July (Frey 1909: 168, and 1912: 25). On 11 August 1542, 56 *scudi* were recorded as being paid to "magistro Luca" and Nicolao, sculptors (Frey 1909a: 169) "for some figures made by them for the model." On 13 November a certain Bartolomeo of Florence was paid "for having fired the terra-cotta figures to be used in the model" (Frey 1912: 25). There were other expenses, such as sculptures: "Luca Lance," sculptor, was paid 7 *scudi* on 13 January 1543 "as a recompense for certain figures" (Frey 1909a: 169). Later on Labacco "and in his stead, Antonio da Sangallo" was paid 11 *scudi* and 25 *bolognini* on 10 February 1543 "for the purchase of fifteen pieces of elm and apricot" (Frey 1912: 25).
Labacco's monthly salary ranged in 1544 between 22 and 44 *scudi*, and stopped in August. All his overdue expenses were settled on 19 January 1544 when he received 200 *scudi* "for all the personal expenses of wood and for all the work from the beginning of the model to last December" (Frey 1909a: 169). Lastly, there are again two other payments for wood in late 1544: on 15 October for twelve lime beams and 15 December for 45 lime boards "which are necessary to make the model" (Frey 1912: 25). An interruption of monthly payments, a settlement of overdue expenses, and the purchase of new wood are perhaps signs of a variation in the project, perhaps linked to the many changes illustrated in the drawings for the dome, as discussed elsewhere (Benedetti 1991-91).
During 1545 the way the fixed costs are recorded changes, suggesting the more intense final phase of the model's construction. Payments are made weekly "for the days," and always to Labacco, who is flanked by "Guidetto," his stable associate "for the works and as a salary." The sums vary considerably from a maximum of 14.54 *scudi* (12-23 December 1545) to a minimum of 4.36 *scudi* (1-7 August) with an average of five to seven *scudi* a week. In between these payments there are others for special supplies and the purchase of materials. "45 lime boards" and "20 little rafters" were bought from "Bernardo the timber merchant" on 5 January and 28 August (Frey 1909, 170). From 10 to 12 March Bernardo the wood-turner was paid "for 72 columns, arches for windows... for the campaniles." Labacco or Guidetto received 49 and 4.5 *scudi* on 2 April for "15 *operibus*" and for "extraordinary works," and were paid on 4 August for the "wood-turning of several different kinds of wood," unframed circles, columns, pyramids, candelabras and paper (Frey 1912: 24). Paolo the wood-turner earned 6.65 *scudi* on 2 October for several items including "one candelabra, 32 small pyramids, 4 corner pyramids, the large pyramid, 500 balusters" (Frey 1912: 26). Further payments were made for wood on 29 October (6 boards, 2 little rafters and 27 lime boards); on 13 November for glue and nails (Frey 1912: 26); on 4 August to Guidetto, carpenter, for "various supplies of columns and other things made for him"; on 4 December for "candles which the carpenters use before daylight" (Frey 1912: 26).
This crescendo of assorted payments proves that most of the vast decorative parts of the model were built in 1545. The payments continued until August 1546, becoming symptomatic of a final rush that is further confirmed by an appreciable increase in the weekly payments. These rose from the 8-9 *scudi* average in the first few months of the year (January-March 1546) to 20-25 *scudi* in the following months (April-June), before falling to 6-16 *scudi* between July and August. Other special entries are also registered: for "candles to work at the model" (26 February, 11 October) "which *mastro* Guidetti consumed last year working on the model in the morning before daylight" (Frey 1912, 28-29); to Paolo the wood-turner for various jobs including "one large chalice, 16 Corinthian columns, 8 pyramids for the lantern, 24 architraves for the octagon, 3 circles for the circular staircase, 65 candelabras for the octagons, a pyramid for the lantern, 300 small balusters, 16 candelabras for the lantern" (Frey 1912, 27-28); to "sawyers" on 8 April, for "having sawn wood for the model and for the main entrance" (5 March) (Frey 1912: 28). Labacco was paid for small items such as glue, nails, and tacks, "for yellow and white used for the model," "for 5 pounds of ground glass for the porphyry (2 April), "for nails for the curtain and the table of the model" (19 April), "*terra rosa*, sponge..." (from 20 November 1545 to 15 June 1546, paid on 15 June) (Frey 1912: 27). Paolo the wood-turner was paid on 18 June for "four medium pyramids, twenty-eight small candelabras, 26 small pyramids, 16 small architraves, one large base, 350 balusters" (Frey 1912: 28). Jacopo Ruffinaco, sculptor, was paid 10 *scudi* (16 July) for the statues to be placed around the model "*in circuitu modelli*," and 1.61 *scudi* (6 August) for the "base of the Cross, two Corinthian columns, sixteen balls, one baluster, little pale and flowers for the Cross" (Frey 1912: 28). The following entries are small amounts for detail items: "52 pairs of steps to make the staircase set in the great window of the model" (29 October), "23 carved balusters" (12 November 1546) (Frey 1912: 29).
Besides illustrating the progress of the building of the model, the detailed documents considered here also offer insights into decorative elements and methods of construction which may otherwise have eluded our attention, given the poor state of conservation of the model.
These details also throw light on the various stages of development of Sangallo's project, which are worth considering, together with information afforded by the many existing drawings (Benedetti 1990-92).
The entry recording the existence of statues around the model confirms the sketches, probably of sculptures, visible in several drawings in the attic above the Doric order. This section was therefore effectively another "figured order" in the Sangallo project, no longer classifiable as such owing to the absence of the sculptures. Traces of these are still discernible in the die-shaped bases rising above the entablature of the Doric order. Payments for the statues as early as 1542 and 1543, as well as the final ones in 1546, confirm the inclusion of the figured order in the project right from the start, even if these statues are missing in Labacco's print published in 1549, about three years after Sangallo's death.
The entry noting the creation of a curtain or cover in the summer of 1540, for which ropes and cloth were bought, as a means of "protecting the model from the heat," suggests that the construction of the model took place in a room with large windows, making protection from the sun necessary. This is endorsed by another note (Silvan 1986, 212) stating that "two large windows had already been walled up" in November 1539 "in the tribune where the model of St. Peter's is being built." Similarly, the entry of the purchase of candles during the winter of 1545-46 seems to confirm the final burst of activity mentioned above.
Even more important for a full appreciation of Sangallo's project are the notes found among the workshop records and on the drawings. These provide three further details of the scheme: the special function of the markedly splayed windows inserted at the base of the second colonnade; the documented interruption of work on the model; and the color scheme envisaged for the model.
The drawings of the attic above the first colonnade of the dome contain a band of small windows with a marked downward splay; these windows appear right from the start (Uff. 87A verso). A note on Uff. 267A, which escaped attention until recently (Benedetti 1990-92), indicates their "devotional" nature, as explained by the phrase "lights to shine on the floor," i.e., to create an ample arc of sixteen beams of light following the course of the sun, illuminating the floor above the tomb of St. Peter. These windows were specifically designed to highlight the religious focal point of the great basilica.
The recorded interruption of work on the model between August 1544 and December of the same year raises a question as to its cause. It may have been due to a reappraisal of certain parts of the project, with the consequent redrafting of the design. Not surprisingly, in the months following August 1544 substantial purchases of extra wood were made (12 lime beams, 45 lime boards "needed to build the model"). This could be connected to a note on Uff. 88A regarding the decision to reduce the intercolumniation of the lantern from 32 to 24 ("the model must be reduced like this"). This decision was reversed and the intercolumniation restored to 32. Alternatively, the cause may lie in problems with the dome: either Sangallo intended abandoning the Gothic profile of Uff. 267A for a less rigid curve, and/or he had encountered difficulties with the "centering for the convexity," as mentioned briefly in relative documents (Frey 1912: 24).
The scattered notes concerning the purchase of pigments are also crucial for understanding the colors decided upon for the walls: they offer clear evidence of the use of paint to color the wooden surfaces. The black and white photographs published by Giovannoni (Giovannoni 1959: 90) reveal two tones on the outside (the darker orders stand out against the pale stonework, and thus differ from the hypothetical ones mentioned in documents). Entries in the project records confirm the use of pigment, and describe the original colors as "yellow and white for the model," "ground glass for the porphyry," and "*terra rosa*, sponge."
The limited space permitted here prevents any further observations on the various attempts at restoring Sangallo's model, its ensuing history, and the different locations where it has been put on display to date. Zander traced a brief history (Zander 1986), from the extensive restoration carried out in 1704, followed by a second operation undertaken by Valadier a hundred years later in 1826, and completed by Luciano Malvolti in 1828. The major restoration operation to which the model was subjected during the papacy of Clement XI in 1704 was celebrated by a long commemorative dedication set in the model's base, inscribed between the arms of Julius II and Clement XI.
"BASILICÆ PRINCIPIS APOSTOLORUM MODULUM / AB ANTONIO SANGALLO FLORENTINO EXCOGITATUM / AD EXEMPLAR ARCHETYPI / QUEM DUDUM BRAMANTES ASDRUVALDINUS URBINAS / MAGNIFICENTISSIMæ MOLIS ARCHITECTUS / IULIO II P.M. IUBENTE FORMAVERAT / OBSCURO LATENTE LOCO AC TEMPORIS / DIUTURNITATE CORRUPTUM / CLEMENS XI P.M. / HUC TRANSTULIT ET INSTAURAVIT / ANNO SAL. MDCCIV PONTIF. IV." *S.B.*

St. Peter's 1534-46:
Projects by Antonio da Sangallo
the Younger for Pope Paul III
Christof Thoenes

Francesco Salviati, Paul III Orders Work to Resume
on St. Peter's, *1549-52*
Rome, Palazzo Farnese

When in 1534 Pope Paul III ascended to the throne of the papacy, the site of St. Peter's was a scene of eerie desolation. The building work initiated by Julius II had advanced little under the two Medici popes, and had come to a complete halt after the Sack of Rome. Meanwhile, the eastern section of the original basilica, though still practicable, was mercilessly exposed to the ravages of time. Both the new and old sections presented a spectacle of decline, almost symbolic of the ruinous political legacy which Clement VII had left his heir. But the new pope was not one to stand by heedless and was acutely aware of how damaging this stasis was to the image and prestige of the Church. In the space of a few years Paul III successfully restored the political role of the Holy See, set new goals for the Church by calling for a Council, and after consolidating the finances of the Papal State turned his attention to the task of continuing the work on St. Peter's. The decision was a historic one, and the pope himself had the event immortalized in two frescoes, one in the Palazzo della Cancelleria and one in the Palazzo Farnese.

Work on St. Peter's was resumed in 1538 with a conservative initial intervention: Antonio da Sangallo erected a new wall to ensure the stability of the surviving parts of the original longitudinal section, making it once more practicable for worship. As for the new building, it seems that at first the pope placed his hopes in Baldassare Peruzzi, who had been promoted to the rank of papal architect in 1534, alongside Sangallo. But in January 1536 Peruzzi died without making his mark on the building, and the site was left entirely in the hands of Sangallo, who had been involved from the outset. Born in Florence in 1484, Antonio da Sangallo the Younger was trained in the "art of woodwork" (Vasari). In 1503 he moved to Rome, apparently to work alongside his uncle Giuliano, and then under Bramante as a carpenter, draftsman and architect's assistant. Two years after Raphael took over from Bramante as the *proto* at the site of St. Peter's, Sangallo was raised to the position of second in command. Subsequently,

Maerten van Heemskerck, St. Peter's at the Start
of the Papacy of Paul III, *1532-36*
*Berlin, Kupferstichkabinett, Heemskerck Skizzenbücher,
vol. I, fol. 13r.*

upon Raphael's death in 1520, he was made architect-in-chief, with Peruzzi as his collaborator, and remained in that position until his own death in 1546.

This career is remarkable from two points of view. The first is that Sangallo started not as an artist, but as a craftsman. This made him—*pace* Michelangelo—the most skilled building technician of his day; on the other hand, he did not enjoy the highest esteem in the eyes of his contemporaries, who considered artists—like Bramante, Raphael, Peruzzi, Giulio Romano, Sansovino, and Michelangelo, who had become famous through their

painted works and sculpture—more suited to imaginative expression. Indeed, Sangallo's way of thinking was more dominated by constructional factors than any of his predecessors or successors: his constant preoccupation with structural reinforcement and bracing from the pavement to the dome was a leading motif throughout all his projects for St. Peter's.

A second interesting characteristic of Sangallo's career is that he experienced the first, decisive phase of the *fabbrica* as an assistant, who was called upon to develop the ideas of others in detail, translating them into a form ready for realization. It was to this constant job of reasoning, correcting and replication that he owed his security in handling the classical canon, but also certain tendencies to pedantry, formalism and bureaucratic fussiness, as reflected in his huge wooden model.

The preparatory work for the model comprised a series of projects, of which around fifty original drawings have survived. After carrying out another complete survey of the site (as Peruzzi had also done), Sangallo drafted a first de-

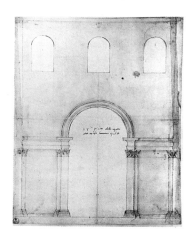

Antonio da Sangallo, Project for Walling off the Nave
of the Old Basilica of St. Peter, *1538*
Florence, Uffizi, Gabinetto Disegni e Stampe, 121A

sign for a smaller building, with apses without ambulatories, adapted to the available area and in tune with the climate of austerity that followed the Sack of Rome. But the scheme never got beyond the floor plan, and was soon replaced with a larger design with ambulatories in the apses, which were drafted in executive form. Of this augmented plan three presentation drawings are known, reproducing the interior and exterior elevations. The successive phase of design, which should have consisted in the construction of a scale model, was never actually carried through. Instead, we have a set of plans and elevations drafted in a rapid hand, in which the western section of the building with four hemicycles forms a compact

block with the atrium, the benediction loggia and the campaniles. For the definitive solution, Sangallo again separated the central plan block from the facade, and inserted an intermediate section comprising a set of vestibules and other open spaces, not usable for liturgical purposes. With this scheme Sangallo devised an articulation of spaces that had neither precedent nor following in the history of St. Peter's. It is rather curious that no drawing of this singularly personal scheme has survived: it has reached us, like some *deus ex machina*, exclusively in the wooden model.

The most remarkable aspect of this story is the emergence of a centrally planned scheme for the church, or, more precisely, the abandonment of the longitudinal plan. A similar layout had been proposed in the foundation phase by Giuliano da Sangallo, and was later resumed in an altered form by Peruzzi; it seems, however, that from the outset Bramante's idea involved transforming the original basili-

Circle of Maerten van Heemskerck ("Anonymous B")
St. Peter's after the Closure the Nave of the Old
Basilica, *153842*
*Berlin, Kupferstichkabinett, Heemskerck Skizzenbücher,
vol. I, fol. 15r.*

ca into a "composite" scheme, with a central cross plan surmounted by a dome, and a vaulted longitudinal section. Anyhow, this was the form it took when work began at the site, and both Raphael and Sangallo complied with the scheme. But the first phase of construction concerned the western section only, and hence the question of the longitudinal block was shelved. It was not considered again until Pope Paul III ordered work to be resumed. The somewhat mastodontic character that this longitudinal section had assumed in fact caused the completion date to recede indefinitely, whereas a building on a central plan with four arms of equal size, a portico and a benediction loggia seemed an altogether more accessible goal. This was the objective pursued by Peruzzi under Leo X, when he put forward his centrally planned model as an alternative to Bramante and Raphael's longitudinal scheme—a scheme which the pope had deemed too large and "too heterogeneous" (Vasari). For Paul III it was a question of the very credibility of the Church of Rome. "To see St. Peter's complete" was his explicit wish, even though at seventy years of age he could have had no illusions of his wish being fulfilled. However, it is reasonable to presume that at this stage of the building's history, it was the pope himself who opted for the central plan, and hence chose Peruzzi as his chief architect. By contrast, Sangallo had been exploring a longitudinal solution for decades. Consequently, for his definitive project, although fulfilling the pope's prescriptions on the building's central plan, he devised an exorbitantly costly area comprising vestibules and a portico, thereby achieving the monumental dimensions he had envisaged for the building ever since his youth, with no concern for time or expense.

All the architects at work on the site must also have realized that the building could never have been completed in a normal life span. This problem had already occurred to Alberti. "Owing to the brevity of the human life," he wrote in Book IX of his *De re aedificatoria,* "the completion of buildings of large dimensions will rarely be witnessed by those who conceive them."

But this situation could be interpreted in different ways. The architect might concentrate on what could be realized in a given phase, and leave the successive generations

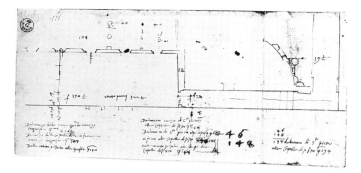
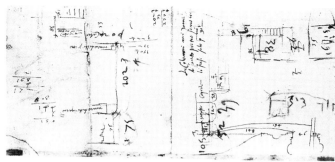

Antonio da Sangallo, Surveys of the Site of St. Peter's
Narthex of the Basilica, and the Scala Regia *(recto)*
Details of the Basilica, Scala Regia, Cappella Sistina
Cappella Paolina, and New St. Peter's *(verso)*
Florence, Uffizi
Gabinetto Disegni e Stampe, 119A

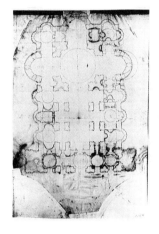

Antonio da Sangallo, Project for St. Peter's *(plan)*
1537-38
Florence, Uffizi, Gabinetto Disegni e Stampe, 256A

to take care of the project as a whole. And this is largely what Bramante and Michelangelo did. While there are no extant autograph drawings by them of the entire building (an omission that caused much discussion after their deaths as to how to continue the project), these two masters nevertheless imposed their ideas and determined the building's form by virtue of a realistic assessment of the time at their disposal. By contrast, Antonio da Sangallo kept an overall vision of the building, as did his uncle Giuliano, and kept turning out new projects of the whole, hopelessly racing against time. The ultimate paradox is Sangallo's great model, in which all the structural and architectural problems were solved, all details finished, and which, after all, did not leave any imprint on the building itself. In the final analysis, the reasons for this failure lie in the incongruity between the modern concept of the artist as an individual creator, and the vastness and complexity of a building program which—as in the case of medieval cathedrals—could only be carried through to completion by concerted, collective effort.

But the project for the model was not the project of a workshop; likewise the workshop for St. Peter's should not be mistaken for a medieval *Bauhütte.* Nearly all the drawings, even the specific ones for the details, were executed by the master himself, and so it is hardly surprising that from the year 1539 Sangallo devoted more and more of his time to the model than to the building. The evidence of this lies in the drawings themselves, which so often focus on details of the building whose effective realization date was inevitably a vague thing of the future. The *summum opus* of Sangallo's last years was in practice not the building but the model. It was the only real means by which he could give form to his personal legacy for posterity: the quintessence of his knowledge and his

skills, of his studies of Vitruvius and the monuments of classical antiquity, his lifelong experience as a master builder. To implement his exhaustive scheme there would be no further need for architects, but only for workmen—an idea obviously far from reality.

The problem of the times involved in realizing monumental structures did not concern St. Peter's alone, nor even Sangallo's model. Nonetheless, the model is in a class of its own. In most cases a model is a point of departure for the executive phase of building, and represents a basic outline of the project as a whole, or shows chosen sections in detail, ready for realization. Sangallo's model, however, while reproducing the vast building in its entirety, also provided a detailed scheme of all the decorative work. The model was, in Vasari's words, "utterly complete." In this way, besides its function as a working tool, the model epitomized that concept of *disegno* peculiar to sixteenth-century esthetics, embodying the "idea" of the work, independently of its physical realization. On the other hand, the model itself was a concrete reality: in the carpenter's workshop also the procedures of construction were simulated. Thus the wooden model began to take the place of the building, became its fetish. Like the *fabbrica* itself, the model's completion required both time and money, and in the end its construction, too, threatened to get out of hand. It took a full seven years to complete; finally the workers proceeded by candlelight. The cost of materials and labor rose to 4,000 *scudi,* plus another 1,500 for Sangallo's fees. The project's detractors pointed out that the same sum would have paid for the construction of a real church.

The model's subsequent fate is well documented. Sangallo lived to see his design more or less through to completion, but was not in time to receive the last payment, "as he soon after passed on to the next life" (Vasari). Giulio Romano was called in to take his place, but he died the same year. Eventually Michelangelo was appointed. Vasari writes that the "Sangallo sect" had no compunction about advising Michelangelo that the model was an inexhaustible source of inspiration ("un prato che non vi man-

cherebbe mai da pascere"). Michelangelo's response was brusque. Besides perceiving their recommendations as an affront to his standing as an artist, he saw through their scheming: the *fabbrica* had become a vital source of lucre for them. So long as everything proceeded according to Sangallo's plan, the deceased master's acolytes would continue to receive their fees and make profits on the supply of materials. The model had been finished, the construction of the building itself "was delayed, with intention to come never to an end". Apart from his misgivings regarding Sangallo's style, Michelangelo saw the model—with its vestibules and ambulatories and other empty pockets punctuating the entire building—as the epitome of ambiguity and falsehood, and felt a moral compulsion to reject it outright. In a letter to Bartolomeo Ferratino, he mocked its "dark hiding-places above and below... perfect lairs for delinquency, for forging money, raping nuns and other such roguery". Perhaps those jests concealed a more serious accusation that could not be openly declared, namely, the clergy's vested interest in the basilica and in having available the utmost possible number of altars, confessionals, nooks and crannies for worship—all of which were amply catered for in Sangallo's complex. Vasari's allusion to Jesus chasing the money-changers from the temple is plain in one of his letters to Michelangelo: "Sire, you have wrested St. Peter's from the hands of thieves." Perhaps it is no coincidence that this idea contains a leitmotif of Michelangelo's esthetic, namely, that sculpture was an act of unlocking the essence of form imprisoned in a block of stone. Just as Michelangelo the sculptor freed his "concept" from the marble, so Michelangelo the architect aspired to emancipate the "real" St. Peter's—Bramante's church, that is—from the trammels in which Sangallo had enmeshed it. In the wake of Vasari, many others witnessed and condemned Sangallo's model, usually under the sway of his successor's opinion. But despite the perspicaciousness of his criticism of the model's defects, Michelangelo made a historical error: his opinion was not based on an acquaintance with the projects of Bramante, but on his knowledge

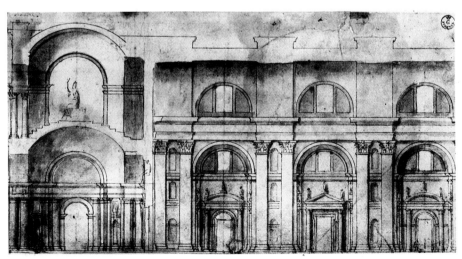

Antonio da Sangallo, Project for St. Peter's *(section through narthex and nave) Florence, Uffizi 67A*

635

Paul Letarouilly, Reconstruction of the 1538 Project of Antonio da Sangallo, *Paris 1882*

of the choir that Bramante designed for Julius II—the only Bramantesque structure remaining by that time ("still manifest"), as he noted in the letter to Ferratino). Today we know that the design for the ambulatories around the apses was in fact Bramante's, and with them the entire concept of St. Peter's as a polycentric basilican organism with multiple nave and aisles. It was this project which Michelangelo so radically rejected. Sangallo had sustained Bramante's project, taking his distance from it in stages as his own designs progressed. The resumption of work under Paul III offered him the chance to carry out variants he had excogitated in the meantime. It seems that his chief intention was to bolster the structure at all points, and lend a strictly unitary scheme to each of the various levels. For this purpose he organized all the outside elevations—from the apses, facade and footing course to the crown of the dome and the campaniles—in conformance with a rigid and reiterated sequence of "arches over arches, cornice over cornice" (Vasari). On the inside he raised the floor, thereby restructuring the system of orders as instituted by Bramante, and closed off the ambulatories from the hemicycles. The purpose of all this was evidently to ensure a clearer and more comprehensible distribution of the spaces and masses.

A term that might suitably describe the task performed by Sangallo is "reform," albeit reform of the conservative type. He aimed to govern, correct and integrate his new design, without impairing the substance of the building. It was still a Renaissance St. Peter's which, thus adapted to suit certain modern needs, had to weather the crisis that followed the ignominious Sack of Rome. All of Sangallo's later works are imbued with this discrepancy: his conception, while progressive in both method and technique, remained firmly anchored in its contents to the classical ideal, whose deficiencies perhaps he himself perceived, but was not entirely able to overcome. In the model, this dilemma is reflected in the contrast between the somber and rational language of the details and the somewhat bizarre appearance of the whole. Vasari termed the result "Gothic." Apart from the evident formal analogies, this adjective embodies the model's "anachronistic" character. Detached from the history of the building itself, the model for St. Peter's belongs in a kind of no-man's land between two epochs. Too late to qualify as a design for the future, it ended up as something utopian, looking backward to the past.

NOTE

This text was originally written in 1988 for the forthcoming volume II of the *Drawings of the Sangallo Circle*, edited by the Architectural History Foundation, New York. In this context the essay appears in a slightly modified form. The same applied to the catalog entries for the Sangallo drawings in the Uffizi. I am grateful to the Architectural History Foundation for their permission to anticipate the publication of these texts.

The situation at the start of the pontificate of Paul III is amply described by L. v. Pastor, *Storia dei papi*, vol. V, Rome, 1959; cf. also M.P. Mezzatesta, "Marcus Aurelius and Fray Antonio de Guevara," in *Art Bulletin* LXVI (1984), 620-633; and C. Thoenes, "Alt- und Neu-St.-Peter under einem Dach," in *Architektur und Kunst in Abendland. Festschrift für Günter Urban*, Rome, 1992, pp. 51-61. On the life of Antonio da Sangallo, cf. A. Bruschi, "A. Cordini," in *Dizionario Biografico degli Italiani*, XXIX, Rome, 1983, pp. 3-23 and C.L. Frommel, "Raffaello e Antonio da Sangallo," in *Raffaello a Roma, Il convegno del 1983*, Rome, 1986: 261-304. The projects for St. Peter's carried out by Sangallo for Paul III are extensively dis-

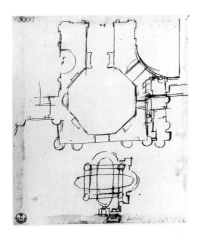

Antonio da Sangallo, Sketches for a Project for St. Peter's, *1538-39. Florence, Uffizi, Gabinetto Disegni e Stampe, 41A*

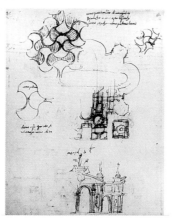

Antonio da Sangallo, Sketches for a Project for St. Peter's, *1538-39. Florence, Uffizi, Gabinetto Disegni e Stampe, 110A*

cussed in op. cit. *The Drawings of the Sangallo Circle*. On the question of the centrally planned scheme for St. Peter's, cf. C. Thoenes, "Pianta centrale e pianta longitudinale nel nuovo San Pietro," in *L'église dans l'architecture de la Renaissance. XVIIIe colloque d'histoire de l'architecture*, Tous, 1990 (publication is scheduled for 1994). The quote regarding Peruzzi's centrally planned model is taken from Vasari, *Lives*... (Italian edition, ed. G. Milanesi, IV, Florence, 1879, p. 599). On Paul III's earnest wish to see St. Peter's completed, cf. H. Saalman,

"Michelangelo at St. Peter's," in *Art Bulletin* LX (1978), pp. 483-493. Alberti discusses large-scale building projects in his *De re aedificatoria*, IX, 11; cf. L.B. Alberti, *L'architettura*, ed. G. Orlandi, Milan, 1966, II, 864. Vasari's references to the model are contained in his account of the lives of Antonio da Sangallo and Michelangelo (Italian edition, ed. Milanesi, V, p. 467ff. and VII, p. 218ff.); cf. *La Vita di Michelangelo* by Vasari, ed. P. Barocchi, Milan-Naples 1962, I, 83ff.; and III, p. 1453ff.; cf. also R. De Maio, *Michelangelo e la Controriforma*, Bari, 1978, pp. 309-325; L. Bardeschi Ciulich, "Documenti inediti su Michelangelo e l'incarico di S. Pietro," in *Rinascimento*, s. II, XVII (1977), pp. 235-275; H. Millon and C.H. Smyth, *Pirro Ligorio, Artist and Antiquarian*, Milan, 1988, pp. 216-286. Michelangelo's letter to Bartolomeo Ferratino, and Vasari's to Michelangelo are reproduced in P. Barocchi, *Il carteggio di Michelangelo*, IV, Florence, 1979, p. 251ff. and V, Florence, 1983, 19. For references to the expulsion of the merchants from the temple, see D. Summers, *Michelangelo and the Language of Art*, Princeton (N.J) 1981, p. 446 Michelangelo's homage to Bramante is contained in his letter to Ferratino; on this account, see Vasari's *Life of Bramante*, Italian edition, ed. Milanesi, IV, p. 162ff.: "He [Michelangelo] told me on various occasions that he was the executant of Bramante's drawing and scheme, given that whoever raises the first vault in a large building is the true author"; and Alberti also, in the passage cited above (IX, 11): "Those who set this project in motion were guided by certain intentions which we too... may experience." On the "Gothic" content of Sangallo's model, see contributions by M. Fagiolo and S. Benedetti in the volume *Antonio da Sangallo il Giovane*, ed. G. Spagnesi, Rome, 1986. It was not until after I had drafted my manuscript that I learned of Sandro Benedetti's study on the drawings discussed here, published in the meantime as: S. Benedetti, "L'officina architettonica di Antonio da Sangallo il Giovane: la cupola per il San Pietro di Roma," in *Quaderni dell'Istituto di Storia dell'Architettura*, n.s. 15-20 (1990-92), I: 485-510.

347

ANTONIO DA SANGALLO THE YOUNGER
Centrally Planned Project and Longitudinal Variant for St. Peter's
Between 1534 and 1537

Florence, Galleria degli Uffizi, Gabinetto Disegni e Stampe, Uff. 39A

Pen and brown ink, yellow and gray wash; all lines traced with stylus; freehand, except for the round arches traced with compass; corrections in bottom right in thicker pen and light brown ink; some lines in sanguine in bottom left.

42.3 × 33 cm

INSCRIBED: *Sacrestia / Capella / 145* (right margin); *porte vechie* (bottom left); *muro della chiesa vechia / 19½*; two measurements in Roman *palmi*; diameter of dome is 7.6 m, making the scale ca. 1:550.

BIBLIOGRAPHY: Geymüller 1868: 23 n. 41; Jovanovits 1877: 13 no.

XXIX, 90 [Leo X]; Letarouilly 1882, pls. 13, 15; Hofmann 1928: 171, 181 [before 1520]; Giovannoni 1959: 135, fig. 65; Frommel 1964: 16, 22; Benedetti 1986: 164 fig. 10; Metternich and Thoenes 1987: 136 n. 239, and 180 n. 309; Thoenes 1990: 39; 1992: 51.

Before building work on St. Peter's was resumed under Pope Paul III, a debate ensued as to what type of plan to adopt. In this drawing Sangallo sets a centralized plan alongside a longitudinal plan to show that only the latter is suited to the site.

In the centrally planned scheme (left) certain ideas of Peruzzi are converted into the formal language of Sangallo's preceding designs. The correction to the southeast pier indicates that Sangallo was aware of the problem of the large niches sculpted out of the piers, and foreshadows his decision to raise the floor level, an operation studied in another drawing (Uff. 64A). For the rest, the plan follows a radial symmetrical scheme, and the arm toward the entrance shows new additions (portico, benediction loggia). The drawing gives the impression of an "ideal plan" rather than a real project intended for construction.

In the lower right quadrant Sangallo develops the central plan into a longitudinal one, erasing certain parts of the drawing. The right margin of the sheet contains some sketches, with measurements, of alignments with the Vatican buildings bordering the north (Cappella Sistina, Scala Regia), which limit the extension of the building, and condition the eastern termination. Sangallo considered replacing the narthex of the old basilica with a portico stretching the full width of the nave; the central portal was scheduled to receive Filarete's bronze doors ("porte vechie"). Two other corrections show that Sangallo was ready to make a clean break from the central plan: 1) the western arm was to keep the small choir erected by Bramante: this entailed the elimination of the smaller western domes, which could be replaced by simple niches (stylus impressions in the zone of the southwest dome). This idea was developed further by Sangallo in later drawings (Uff. 40A, 256A); 2) the aisles were to be surmounted by large central domes, and hence the circular corner chapel of the centrally planned scheme was replaced by a semicircular apse. Some rapid lines in sanguine at the end of the east wing (left of the longitudinal axis) suggest he may have been thinking of a dome over the main nave, of the same dimensions as that over the crossing; these lines seem to hark back to one of Sangallo's earlier schemes, or were perhaps meant for the wooden model, which has a domed volume interposed between the centrally planned block and the facade section. The hexagon and dodecagon sketched in at the bottom left may refer to the hexagonal vestibules of the model. *C.T.*

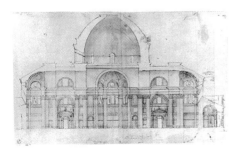

348
ANTONIO DA SANGALLO THE YOUNGER
Project for a Longitudinal Plan: Section through Transept
1538

Florence, Galleria degli Uffizi, Gabinetto Disegni e Stampe, Uff. 66A
Pen and brown ink, gray-brown wash; part freehand, part straightedge and compass; stylus impressions; auxiliary constructions (apse with windows, lower right); preparatory section in pencil, compass-drawn in part; paper damaged, mounted on white card; fold down center; strip added on right;

scale key in *palmi* 100 at bottom, no longer visible, 8.05 cm long, making the scale of the drawing ca. 1:277.
38.9 × 60.2 cm

BIBLIOGRAPHY: Jovanovits 1877: 15, no. XLI; Letarouilly 1882, pl. 14; Hofmann 1928: 193-199; Beltrami 1929: 18 fig. 5 [1534]; Giovannoni 1935b: 146 fig. 3; 1959: 139, 140, 235 fig. 71; Frommel 1964: 19-24; Portoghesi 1971, I: 88; Ragghianti-Collobi 1974, I: 127; II, fig. 390; Lotz 1977a: 31, fig. 32 (ca. 1530-35); Licht 1984: 117ff. no. 66; Adorni 1986: 365; Benedetti 1986: 166, 174 no. 41; Bruschi 1988: 239ff.; Thoenes 1990: 29, 40; Benedetti 1990-92: 485ff. fig. 1.

The most important of the projects drafted immediately before the creation of Sangallo's wooden model was the longitudinal plan developed in 1538, of which three drawings have survived: one section through the transept, one through the nave, and an elevation of the northern prospect (Uff. 66A, 67A, 259A). The drawings conform to a rigorous orthogonal rendering of both the interior and exterior of the building, and hence are prototypes of the modern system of architectural representation. The relative plan is no longer extant; Letarouilly supplies a reconstruction.

This ambitious project, which Sangallo undoubtedly intended as executive, represents the condensation of his critique of the proposals advanced by his precursors. In his elaboration of the elevations, up to the crown of the barrel vault of the transept, Sangallo had to comply with the piers and arches of the dome already erected by Bramante; the only leeway for modification was the raising of the floor level, which Sangallo in fact undertook (cf. Uff. 64A). The drawing in question shows the effects of this alteration: the spaces and masses are more squat, the pedestals of the giant pilasters have disappeared, the major and minor orders (aedicules) begin at the same level, and hence cornices and entablatures run continuous and uniform everywhere. This series of horizontal lines, traced on the paper with a ruler, is the basic framework of the whole design, to which the individual forms are made to comply, such as the niches and panels that articulate the surface of the main piers and buttressing piers. There are significant alterations in the apse, whose structure had to be revised in proportion, while the passages between the hemicycles and ambulatories are closed; the resulting lighting problem is solved by opening windows in the curves of the hemicycles. These variations, drawn in by hand, were made definitive in the later preparatory studies for the model.

For the dome, Bramante had left only a project, which was not followed up, leaving the field free for invention. Evidently Sangallo reckoned that a structure based on a pointed arch, such as Brunelleschi's dome in Florence, was the only technically viable solution. On the other hand, Bramante's idea of associating a dome like the one on the Pantheon with a drum encircled by columns was too intriguing to be rejected. The expedient he adopted consisted in exploiting the static benefits of a dome based on a pointed arch internally, and an external form that conformed with the image of a hemispherical canopy thrusting out of a cylindrical drum (cf. Uff. 259A). This in fact remained Sangallo's basic idea for the later realization of the model; only Michelangelo, in his reversion to the "truth" of Bramante, restored cohesion between the outward form of the dome and the load-bearing structure inside.

Sangallo experimented with distinctly different solutions for the exterior and interior profiles of his dome (stylus impressions at right). The interior profile, constructed with a radius 6/7ths of the diameter represents a compromise between Bramante's round arch and the presumed "terzo acuto" arch of the dome of Florence Cathedral (cf. Uff 87A). The fact that from the outside the dome appears more depressed than the one Bramante had envisaged is due to the lack of basement, which means that the drum rests directly on the main arches. On the inside, the drum area is marked with a narrow cornice, set so low that it would scarcely have been visible from the pavement level. The only openings are provided by eight

narrow windows, splayed upward. The sectional drawing offers no constructional information—the "design" in fact focuses on form, not material realization.
The lantern is missing, but it is likely that Sangallo envisaged an *opaion* similar to the oculus of the Pantheon, which would have left the tomb of St. Peter exposed to the weather. Moreover, a dome of such a design would not have been stable without a suitable crowning load. *C.T.*

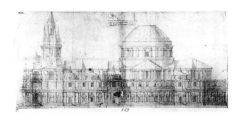

349
ANTONIO DA SANGALLO THE YOUNGER
Longitudinal Project for St. Peter's: Northern Prospect
1538

Florence, Galleria degli Uffizi, Gabinetto Disegni e Stampe, Uff. 259A
Pen and brown ink, gray and brown wash; part freehand, part straightedge and compass; mostly traced in stylus, with scattered compass holes; corrections to hemicycle domes; volute drawn freehand in same ink at top of floor of hemicycles; thick gray paper laid on white card; folds down left and center; cuts and glue on right; insert at top in same paper, with inscription.
41.5 × 85.4 cm
INSCRIBED: *S.to p.p | Disegno i[n] sulli stilobati de fuora dove non sono | li gradi perche dove sono li gradi le base posano | in cima li gradi e di dentro posano in sulpavi | mento di terra.*
Scale key in 100 Roman *palmi* top right, 8.05 long, making scale of drawing ca. 1:277.

BIBLIOGRAPHY: Jovanovits 1877: 17 no. XLLIX; Letarouilly 1882, pls. 14, 15; Hofmann 1928: 195-199 fig. 73; Giovannoni 1959: 139, 140, 141 fig. 72; Frommel 1964: 19-24; Portoghesi 1964, I: 88; II, fig. XLI; Ragghianti Collobi 1974, I: 127; II, fig. 392; Francia 1977, fig. 81; Adorni 1986: 365 fig. 20; Benedetti 1986: 166, 174 no. 41; Fagiolo 1986: 193; Bruschi 1988: 239ff.; Thoenes 1990: 39, 40; 1992: 59; Benedetti 1990-92: 485 ff.

The bulk of the building seems to be strung by the network of orders which Vasari later criticized in the model ("componimento troppo sminuzzato dei risalti e dei membre"). Sangallo evidently intended to partition the entire building horizontally using a uniform system. The scheme begins with the Doric order of the lower story, completed in 1518, and proceeds with an attic story with pilasters in the form of hermae, and a Corinthian story above. The drum of the dome and the campaniles have a composite framework. As with the model, the height of each story and the decoration of the dome and campaniles are strictly coordinated. All the more striking appears the caesura between the nave and the facade, where the attic is windowless and the upper floor is inset with arches (which were continued round the entire perimeter for the model). The roofing for the ambulatories was not resolved, however, and likewise the buttressing of the hemicycle vaults: in the western one this function is performed by a sweeping S-shaped volute, penned in freehand, while in the model the hemicycles were enclosed in two-story ambulatories that incorporated the buttressing. The minor domes were given no drum or lantern, but received light through tabernacle windows, an overblown use of pediments, which was later corrected in the model. The drum of the main dome has a series of twenty-four arches on pillars with half-columns framing niches and windows (cf. section of Uff. 66A, left). For the dome's vault, the profile of the Pantheon dome is combined with a ribbed structure. *C.T.*

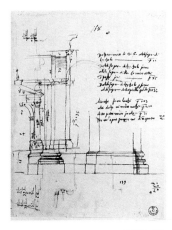

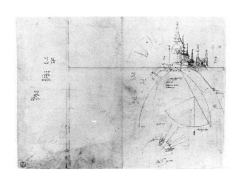

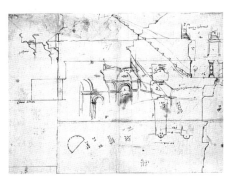

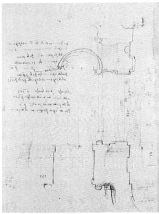

and height is altered by reducing the drop between the floor and the keystone of the archway from 210 to 199 *palmi*.

Below the horizontal line is an enlarged detail study of the new base zone, describing (from left to right) the internal rim of the aedicula's arch, the aedicula's column (the double outline on the right is more likely a pentimento than the indication of a pilaster behind), a stretch of wall (in profile) of the major order of the crossing (cf. also the finished drawing of the front of the piers and buttressing piers, Uff. 253A).

On the verso the same front is represented in plan (top). Again the large niche is shown, and the only hint that it was to be walled in is given by the column (with base) of the proposed aedicula. The main theme of the drawing is the new configuration (bottom) of the threshold of the apsidal ambulatory, which opens in the buttressing pier: this entranceway has the same width (24 *palmi*) as shown on the recto for the niche arch opposite.

C.T.

351

ANTONIO DA SANGALLO THE YOUNGER
Plan of an Apse and Adjacent Cells for St. Peter's
1538-39

Florence, Galleria degli Uffizi, Gabinetto Disegni e Stampe, Uff. 52A
Pen and dark brown ink; straightedge and compass, except for a few lines freehand; stylus impressions; thick paper in three pieces, badly soiled, with edges frayed, cut round and laid down; measurements in Roman *palmi*; scale ca. 1:215.
54.0 × 22.0 cm (max.)

BIBLIOGRAPHY: Giovannoni 1959, I: 129, 138, fig. 68 [1520]; Thoenes 1990: 39.

In the model project, the west section is largely identical in plan to the one in the preceding longitudinal scheme: in this zone the design basically proceeded unaltered. The sheet in question probably features the south transept, with its adjacent rooms on the west side; the outside angling of the corner room (top left) corresponds with the one visible in the northern prospect of Uff. 259A.

The outer wall of the apse, drawn with straightedge and compass, conforms with the state existing since Clement VII, except for the closure, now necessary, of the central portal. The wall of the hemicycle, as yet undefined in Uff. 66A, is now drawn freehand, complete with measurements; the radial axes added later served to clarify the relation between the two walls of the ambulatory.

No solution has yet been found for the insertion of the buttressing inside the ambulatory, nor for the shape of the passageways linking the ambulatory with the hemicycles; these were dealt with in later studies (Uff. 49A, 50A).

C.T.

350

ANTONIO DA SANGALLO THE YOUNGER
Study for Raising the Floor of St. Peter's
1538

Florence, Galleria degli Uffizi, Gabinetto Disegni e Stampe, Uff. 64A
Pen and brown ink, freehand.
28.7 × 20.6 cm

INSCRIBED: *Dapavimento di chiesa aldisopradelzocholo p. 11; Daldi sopra delzocholo fino aldi sopra della cornice delle imposte sie p. 75; Daldi sopra delzochola p[er] fino al di sopra delcapitello grande p. 113¼; Liarchi sono larghi p. 105; alti dal pavimento vecchio p. 210; ditto pavimento si alz[a] p. 11; Viene in proporzione di un quarto 25/26;* various individual measurements, additions; scale in Roman *palmi.*

BIBLIOGRAPHY: Giovannoni 1959: 144, 147, 148; Thoenes 1990: fig. 11; 1992: 59.

Typical of Sangallo's design procedure are the studies in which he makes detailed drawings of separate parts of the building, fixing all their measurements. In this drawing he investigated the effects that raising the church floor (cf. Uff. 66A) would have on the building's internal framework: here he examined a section of one of the vaulted passageways between the main piers and buttressing piers.

The shifts in the proportions mainly concern the large niches in the piers and buttressing piers, the closing of which, considered already in Uff. 39A, Sangallo now retained unavoidable. They were replaced by large aediculas with altars, in archways twenty-four *palmi* wide. These aediculas, later realized by Sangallo in the north and south transepts, were the architect's most significant contribution to the layout of St. Peter's as it stands today.

The horizontal line below the measurement "24" at the far left of the sheet marks the new level envisaged for the floor; while the "11" written obliquely below the line indicates the level above the floor of the ancient basilica. The writings on the right include the main measurements of the new framework; the second group of writings refers to the transepts, in which the ratio of 1:2 between width

352

ANTONIO DA SANGALLO THE YOUNGER
Studies for the Dome of St. Peter's; Dome of Florence Cathedral
1539 or later

Florence, Galleria degli Uffizi, Gabinetto Disegni e Stampe, Uff. 87A
Pen and brown ink; part freehand, part straightedge and compass; stylus impressions on the recto (in compass) do not coincide with later drawing; thick paper, three sections gummed together, with vertical fold; drawing and stylus impressions pass over horizontal join.
34.5 × 44.9 cm

INSCRIBED: on recto (left part) additions, perhaps not pertinent, in thicker pen and dark brown ink: (right part) *Cupola di Fiorenza | apiedi | Lochio sie | la settima parte | deldiametro; piedi 140; a intragardare [?] S.to pietro* (added later); on verso (left part) *p[er] difuora; colmo del tetto [?];* (right part, top) *meze colonne; a schifo corritore; p 17 ... Da meza colonna all'altra;* (right part, bottom) *Vani 48.*
Measurements on recto in *piedi;* with a metric scale key of 140 units, 15.4 cm long, making the scale of the drawing 1:270; measurements on verso in Roman *palmi.*

BIBLIOGRAPHY: Jovanovits 1877: 18 no. LV; Giovannoni 1959: 22, 144, 145, fig. 6; *Disegni di fabbriche Brunelleschiane* 1977: 16-18; Fondelli 1980: 812; Bruschi 1988: 239, 241; Thoenes 1990: 39, 40; Benedetti 1990-92: 488ff. figs. 6-8.

It is impossible to establish exactly if the drawing in question was made during the elaboration of the main longitudinal project (cf. Uff. 66A), or—as seems to be indicated by the sketchings on the verso—alongside the project for the model. At any event, Sangallo's later annotation "S.to pietro" indicates the object of this particular study, even though one of the main features of the recto is a representation of the dome of Florence Cathedral; compare with workshop drawings Uff. 1130A and 1164A.

The diameter of the Florentine dome (or, better, the diameter of the circle inscribed in the base octagon) is indicated with sufficient precision as 140 *piedi* (41.72 m), and the diameter of the oculus of the lantern as 20 *piedi*. The height is slightly over, inasmuch as the lancet arch is constructed here on the full diameter, instead of on 4/5ths, as in the actual dome. Sangallo therefore persisted in his pursuit of more raked proportions, a tendency already perceivable in the dome of the longitudinal project, in which the radius was equal to 6/7ths of the diameter. Using a plumb line and quadrant divided in 90 degrees, Sangallo established the inclination of the span joining the base of the dome with the base of the oculus of the lantern. It takes the form of a kind of statics diagram *ante litteram*: the smaller this angle, the more vertical the profile, thereby reducing the lateral thrusts of the vault. Consequently, two parameters govern the stability of the vault: first, the geometry of the pointed arch, with its variable diameter-height ratio and, second, the aperture of the lantern. In the following drawings, we shall see how Sangallo dealt with these two factors.

The vault of the dome is only represented in profile, and its crown falls exactly on the horizontal cut in the paper. The upper strip includes a freehand sketch of the lantern, decorated with several cusps and volutes. Some steps are noticeable in freehand on the shell of the dome, as in the elevation of the longitudinal project (Uff. 259A).

Left of the lantern is a rapid sketch of the plan of the drum, with slender radial elements alternating with openings and terminated with columns or half-columns; the full circuit comprises forty-eight elements, twice the number featured in Uff. 259A. At the bottom appears a horizontal section of the base of a lantern, probably from the cathedral in Florence.

The verso of the drawing contains studies of details of the dome in its intermediate phase between the longitudinal project and the model project. The dome's vault still has the steps at the base, but the drum has assumed the form of an annular ambulatory surrounded by arches on pillars with half-columns (on the model of the Colosseum), and surmounted by a terrace with balustrade. The structure is shown via a perspective section; left of this is a proposal for an improvement, in which the *a schifo* vaults indicated on the right are replaced by barrel vaults arranged radially. The idea behind this is to buttress the drum by means of radial structures which take the thrust of the vault. In the model the elements are grouped in pairs, and the transverse arches of the ambulatory supplanted by architraves. The use of half-columns instead of pilasters, even inside the drum, is in line with the trend toward the project's pervading standardization of detail.

The principal design difficulty consisted in determining feasible measurements: Sangallo tackled this problem in the sketch at the bottom right. As on the recto, the number of elements envisaged is forty eight ("48 vani"); in the outer circuit of the drum the intercolumniation of the half-columns is 17 *palmi* ("da meza colonna all'altra"), whereas in the inner circuit it is 13 ⅛ *palmi* (8 *palmi* from column to column, and 5 ⅛ *palmi* for the column thickness). Multiplied by forty-eight, this value gives a circumference of 630 *palmi*. To cross-check this one can multiply the net diameter of the dome by the value π. This diameter is reached by adding to the diameter of the base (the distance between the main arches), 184 *palmi*, 2 × 6 *palmi* for the re-entrant section at the foot of the vault (sum 184 + 12 = 196 written vertically); for π is taken as the approximate fractional value of 3 ¹/₇ established by Archimedes, and known to Luca Pacioli, among others. The calculation, however, produces the total of 616 *palmi* (sum 196 + 196 + 196 + 28 = 616 written vertically, with an extra sum of 28 × 7 = 196 penned in the far right). The discrepancy is not solved. In the ensuing drawing (Uff. 798A), Sangallo adopts another method of planning. C.T.

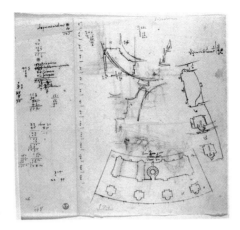

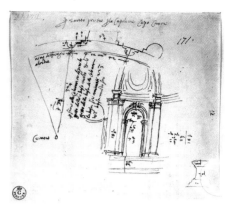

353
<small>ANTONIO DA SANGALLO THE YOUNGER</small>
Studies for the Dome of St. Peter's
1539 or later

Florence, Galleria degli Uffizi, Gabinetto Disegni e Stampe, Uff. 798A
Pen and brown ink, freehand; the plan at bottom is done with straightedge and compass, with stylus impressions; thin paper, trimmed along left and top; fold down left.
28.8 × 29.8 cm
<small>INSCRIBED:</small> *Lo primo ordine 70 [+] 57 [=] 127, zocholo primo / la colonna jonca / Cornice / parapeto / colonna; Vani 4 p[er] uno / octava parte / in tutto 32; jonica; corinzia.*
Measurements in Roman *palmi*; along the fold, with stylus impressions and compass holes, scale in 150 *palmi*, 24.1 cm, making the scale of the drawing 1:139.

<small>BIBLIOGRAPHY:</small> Giovannoni 1959: 144, 147; Bruschi 1988: 241; Thoenes 1990: 39; Benedetti 1990-92: 490ff. fig. 9; Krauss and Thoenes 1991-92: 194 fig. 21.

Taking the intermediate stage of the design featured in Uff. 87A verso as his point of departure, in this drawing Sangallo drafts the executive project for the dome of the model. At the middle of the sheet is a sketch in profile of the drum, vault and lantern. The dome is slightly more raked, but the steps at the base are replaced by a second, receding band of the drum which hides a fair amount of the dome itself; anyone standing below would have seen nothing but a superposition of "arch above arch, cornice above cornice" (Vasari). It was because of the fact that the dome, the transepts and the apses were enveloped by a system of external buttressing that Michelangelo so brusquely rejected Sangallo's design. Here too Sangallo is preoccupied with fixing the dimensions of the various features, beginning with a study of the structure at the base of the dome (sketch, top middle). The internal diameter of the dome, from arch to arch, comes to 187 ½ *palmi*, and a total width of the pier of 84 ¾ *palmi* (calculations, upside down, at the top edge of sheet). As the main arch is 39 *palmi* wide (plus the 4 *palmi* for the support of the lateral arch) the wall of the drum must be no thicker than 43 *palmi*. Nonetheless, the external circumference of the dome sketched in the plan well exceeds the outer rim of the main arches. This led to Sangallo's development of the drum as shown in the model (cf. Uff. 267A); in the plan developed here, however, it remains within the limits that result from the calculations. To make sure of his measurements for each element, after the failure of the calculations made in Uff. 87 verso, Sangallo opts for a scale reconstruction on paper. Taking a scale of 150 "palmi piccoli" he drew up an eighth of the plan of the dome; the measurements were made with a compass and read against the scale, and then noted on the drawing. During the course of the design Sangallo went from a 48-part subdivision of the circuit (still visible in the stylus impressions) to a 32-part subdivision, as used for the model. The sector drawn at the bottom of the sheet represents the lower story of the drum; the freehand sketch on the far right shows the superposition of the orders on both registers ("jonica" below, and "corinzia" above). C.T.

354
<small>ANTONIO DA SANGALLO THE YOUNGER</small>
Studies for the Minor Domes for St. Peter's
1539 or later

Florence, Galleria degli Uffizi, Gabinetto Disegni e Stampe, Uff. 58A
Pen and brown ink, freehand.
17.8 × 18.9 cm
<small>INSCRIBED:</small> (at top, in faded ink) *p[er] santo pietro p[er] le Cupolette Capo Croci; vivo del fregio / alce[n]tro[?]; p 12 mi[nu]ti 42; p[er] fino alla colonna ce di piu lo / agetto dello imbasamento et lo / agetto della base della colonna / la base sie minuti 22⅔ / lo basamento sie.*
Measurements in Roman *palmi*.

<small>BIBLIOGRAPHY:</small> Jovanovits 1877: 15, no. XXXVII.

Whereas in the large longitudinal scheme the small domes were without drums (Uff. 259A), in the model these have been duly added, complete with vaults, as shown in this drawing. Given that the outside walls will have to be raised by a full story's height, the drum remains just below the level of the roof, hence its sixteen elements are windowless, but is set with a series of alternating conches (left in sketch) and arched bays that open out into the adjacent minor domed spaces or the connecting corridors. These apertures are delimited below by a solid "parapet" (cf. Uff. 1426A), sketched in profile at bottom right. The walls of the drum are articulated by a series of half-columns (Composite?) with pilasters; the overhang of the entablature supports the ribbing of the vault.

In the model, the small domes were realized in a slightly simplified form, reproduced in plan and section in two surveys in the *Codex Destailleur* D in Berlin. C.T.

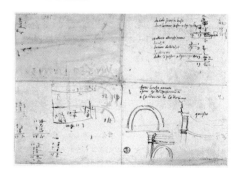

355
<small>ANTONIO DA SANGALLO THE YOUNGER</small>
Studies for One of the Minor Domes for St. Peter's
1539 or later

Florence, Galleria degli Uffizi, Gabinetto Disegni e Stampe, Uff. 1426A
Pen and light brown ink, freehand; soiled paper, with one horizontal and one vertical fold, edges clipped.
20.4 × 27.8 cm

INSCRIBED: (top left, in margin) *S.to pietro*; (upside down in charcoal, barely visible) MAREO DAMA [?]; (top right) *lo dado sotto le bases p ⅔ / la colonna basas e capitello p 18⅓ / [totale] p 19 a punto; Dallarco allarchitrave ⅙ / Larcho [archivolto] p 1 / Lo voto dellarco [freccia] p 3¾ / lo diritto [piedritto] 1 / dalla imposta al parapetto 13½ [corretto da 13¹/₆?] / [totale] 19 [corretto da 19½]; (bottom right) ofare larcho ovuato / o fare che limposta monti [?] / o correre lo collarino [?]; questo*; further calculations at bottom left.

BIBLIOGRAPHY: Unpublished.

The drawing is an appendix to Uff. 58A. In the upper right the heights of the ribbing are written in; in the bottom left are other calculations, from which one can deduce that the rise of the arch is greater than the radius. In the bottom right three possible solutions are featured: to raise the arch, giving it an elevated, oval form (sketch on left), to leave the original rounded arch and fill the space between the lintel and architrave with a molding of the same height as the "necking" below the capital (bottom), or to raise the level of the springing line (right). This last solution was the one chosen by Sangallo ("questo").
C.T.

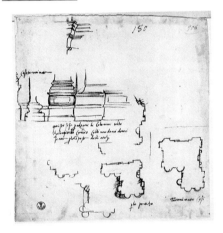

356
ANTONIO DA SANGALLO THE YOUNGER
Study for the Facade of the Model for St. Peter's
1539 or later

Florence, Galleria degli Uffizi, Gabinetto Disegni e Stampe, Uff. 1173A
Pen and dark brown ink, freehand; paper damaged and partially backed, trimmed along bottom and right edge; 21.7 × 19.8 cm.
INSCRIBED: *cosi terminato; Questo si fa p[er] alzare le colonne tanto che [i]lcapitello corinzio [svista per 'dorico'?] colli modani dorici serva p[er] limposta delli archi; p[er] lo porticho Terminato così.*

BIBLIOGRAPHY: Benedetti 1986: 165 fig. 13.

This study testifies to Sangallo's diligence in defining all the details of his model, even those of apparently minor importance: in this case the left intrados of the central arch of the facade. Its overall form is already defined, and now there are tested various types of articulation, to the point of choosing the definitive solution ("Terminato così" bottom right), which was applied to the model. The central part of the drawing features an elevation of the base section of the intrados: the drawing shows the attic base of a half-column 9 *palmi* high, the footing and the base of a column from an aedicula and its inner cornice. For the model, the footing of the aedicula was simplified in accordance with the silhouette sketched at the far right of the page ("così terminato"). In the annotations the addition of the footing is justified by the need to raise the capital of the aedicula column to the same height as the impost of the arch in the central bay of the entrance porch; the molding of the impost corresponds to the Doric capital, as shown in the sketch right at the top of the drawing. C.T.

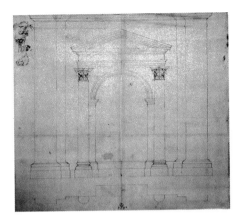

357
ANTONIO DA SANGALLO THE YOUNGER
(or ASSISTANT, or joint work)
Rear Elevation of a Pier of the Dome of St. Peter's
1539 or later

Florence, Galleria degli Uffizi, Gabinetto Disegni e Stampe, Uff. 253A
Fine drawing pen and brown ink; stylus impressions; thick paper, two horizontal strips gummed together; fold down middle, part of which gummed recently; no measurements; scale 1:30.
70.9 × 74.8 cm.

BIBLIOGRAPHY: Giovannoni 1959: 144, 147 fig. 83; Thoenes 1990: 39 fig. 3.

The last phase of design for the model consisted in the execution of finished drawings to the same scale of 1:30 used for the model (cf. Uff. 267A). It is likely that the entire project was drawn up in this way, but only a few sheets remain, some of which are twin copies or replicas that did not reach the model-maker's studio; while others are unfinished drawings. In some cases, the drawing techniques adopted and the calligraphy seem to suggest the contribution of assistants. The elevation represented here is repeated in the entire building sixteen times, in the piers of the dome and the buttressing piers (the only change is to the pediments of the aediculas, alternatively triangular and segmental): the drawing could therefore be adopted several times. The aedicula was derived directly from the study made on Uff. 64A, with the novelty of a cushioned frieze in the entablature; it was executed thus in the model and the definitive building, in which the parts in question underwent further modification toward the end of the sixteenth century, when the interior of St. Peter's was faced in marble. C.T.

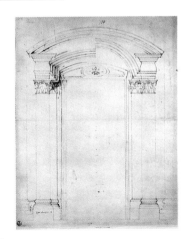

358
ANTONIO DA SANGALLO THE YOUNGER
Interior Portal of the East Hemicycle of St. Peter's
1539 or later

Florence, Galleria degli Uffizi, Gabinetto Disegni e Stampe, Uff. 68A
Pen and brown ink; straightedge and compass, part freehand.
57.2 × 43.2 cm.
INSCRIBED: (bottom left) *si po allargare A*; (verso) *porta gra[nde] di S.to Pietro*; some measurements in Roman *palmi* (?); scale 1:30.

BIBLIOGRAPHY: Jovanovits 1877: 16, no. XLIII; Thoenes 1990: 39.

Although finished on the same scale as the model, the drawing shows several corrections and alternatives. On the left and right the large pilasters of the internal wall of the hemicycle are shown. The outer cornicing of the aedicule containing the portal is regular in shape (cf. Uff. 253A), except for the profile of the cushioned frieze. The segmental pediment is interrupted at the base to make room for an internal frame of a most unusual shape. The space itself is rather high—still higher than Filarete's doors, which were probably to be installed here (cf. Uff. 39A).
The alternative on the right is on the whole more thoroughly thought out; it also comprises the improvement indicated in the annotation written into the left plinth. The points drawn down the middle of the portal may related to a modular subdivision (the full height of the opening is divided into twelve sections).
In the model the portal was not executed. C.T.

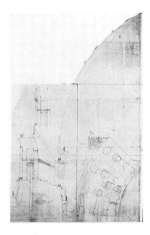

359
ANTONIO DA SANGALLO THE YOUNGER
Project for the Dome of St. Peter's
1540-44

Florence, Galleria degli Uffizi, Gabinetto Disegni e Stampe, Uff. 267A
Pen and dark brown ink; straightedge and compass, with detail freehand; thick paper, comprising seven parts gummed together, divided into five sections and then recomposed, fixed to backing and reinforced with strips of canvas.
196.4 (max) × 119.8 cm.
INSCRIBED: (top left) *125[?] alto avanti, qui / a primo [?]* (faded, scarcely leggible); *fatto colli palmi del modello / Questi palmi sono due quinti / del dito; fenestra; lumi per dare in terra; Dalli [?] ad di sopra della / cornice p. 290 e fino al [?] 300 dritto p. 20; del [?] al di sopra di [?] / colonne p. 65*; (center right) *p. 98 mezo diametro; La cupola vuol essere arcuata [aovata ?] colla regola che facendo / una mezza botte de legnio longa p. 9⁸/₉ di diametro 14 / e col co[m]passo fare uno tondo in su una carta / stesa in sul detto corpo mezzo tondo di mezzo diametro / cioe chel conpasso la sua apertura sia di p. 9⁸/₉ spianando poi / detta carta viene fatto uno aovato lo mezzo sara 11 / E se fusse tutto saria 22 largo 19⁷/₉ e questo / a piu gratia chel tertio acuto ed e antico bono e / maestrevole a farlo el tertio acuto e todescho e non va / tanto alto quanto lo tertio acuto / Locchio sie delle cinque parte dello diametro / che e sendo detto diametro 196 viene 1 occhio / p 39¹/₅; Lo diametro sie 196 lo mezzo aovato dellaltezza 147*; (bottom left) *colmo del tetto; Disotto della volta; Disotto dello archo p. 39; Ambito per andare si [?] sulla cornice tonda; Architrave che gira atorno; Architrave dello archo*; (bottom right) *Questa monta dal primo piano / del primo*

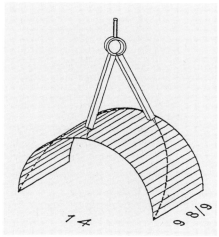

Fig. 1

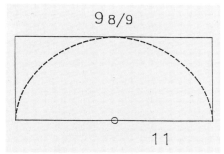

Fig. 2

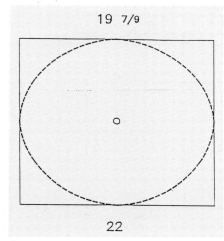

Fig. 3

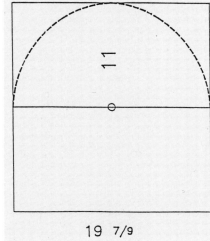

Fig. 4

ordine fino al secondo ordine; Questa monta dal secondo / da basso ad alto il tertio; palmi 14 / grossezza della cupola al piano del / secondo corritorio dove si camina; (round inner circumference of dome) *Grossezza della cupola al piano della base del secondo ordine; vivo del architrave tondo sopra li archi;* (right margin) *mezzo [mezzeria];* (bottom) p. 94 *lo mezo [semidiametro];* measurements in Roman *palmi;* scale 1:30; this large drawing (nearly two meters in height) documents the final phase of design, which involved producing a set of drawings in the same scale as the model ("fatti colli palmi del modello"), which could be linked up and transferred directly into the finished three-dimensional object. According to Sangallo's annotations, a "palmo di modello" was two-fifths of a "dito," which was one-twelfth of a *palmo*, making the scale $^{2}/_{5} \times ^{1}/_{12} = ^{1}/_{30}$.

BIBLIOGRAPHY: Jovanovits 1877: 19, no. LVII; Giovannoni 1935: 147; 1959: 145, 235, fig. 85; Portoghesi 1971, I: 192; II: 415; Francia 1977, fig. 72; Benedetti 1986: 168; Fagiolo 1986: 208, no. 16; Bruschi 1988: 241-243; Thoenes 1990: 39, 41, 49, fig. 4; Benedetti 1990-92: 491ff. fig. 18; Krauss and Thoenes 1991-92: 194 fig. 22.

Despite the numerous corrections, the drawing is a superb example of technical perfection. With a minimum of graphic devices, and the help of explanatory annotations, the drawing provides a very clear picture of the structure in three dimensions. The plan of the drum is limited (as in Uff. 798A) to a sector in four elements (1/8th of the full circuit); the two stories are represented one above the other, and the different levels identified in writing. The width of the base of the drum has been increased from 43 to about 57 *palmi*, and hence the base itself rests about one quarter on the barrel vaults of the transepts; presumably

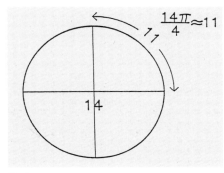

Fig. 5

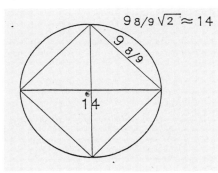

Fig. 6

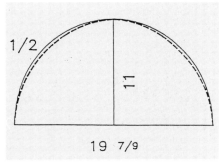

Fig. 7

Sangallo envisaged a system of reinforcing these overloaded points.

As in Uff. 87A recto, the dome's vault is represented only by its inner profile; the double line indicates a correction, which also involves the drum below. The profile is pointed and constructed according to the "tertio acuto," i.e., with a curve equal to the net diameter (cf. the representation of the dome of Florence Cathedral in the abovementioned drawing).

The extensive annotations in the central section of the page are worth a special comment; they have been frequently quoted, but are poorly understood. They do not, as has often been supposed, describe the dome in the drawing, but constitute a comment that questions the entire geometry, and led to a further revision of the project. Sangallo's counterproposal consisted of replacing the pointed arch with a half-oval. The method of construction was as follows: a sheet of paper was placed over a wooden barrel vault and a curve traced with a fixed compass (fig. 1); when laid on a plane the drawing on the sheet produced a half-oval (fig. 2). This was then completed (fig. 3) and rotated 90 degrees (fig. 4) to give the profile of the dome. The fact that Sangallo had carefully meditated and perhaps tested in practice this idea is corroborated by the measurements that he indicated: they determine an outline that emerges as being on a scale of 1:10 with the building (or 3:1 with the wooden model). The basic idea is illustrated by the small geometric figure above the writing: the circle represents a sectional view of the barrel vault (seen as a cylinder), and in the top left a compass is shown, drawing out its curve. The diameter of the barrel vault has been obtained using Pythagoras' theorem (fig. 5); a quarter of its circumference, rectified, gives the larger semi-axis of the oval, and hence the height of the desired profile (figs. 6 and 7).

Sangallo does not cite the sources for the method he adopted; the attribution to antiquity ("antico") is simply laudatory in the sense of "antico bono," as an argument against the pointed arch ("tertio acuto"), the German form ("todesco"). Sangallo in fact shared the prejudices of this contemporaries regarding the Gothic style. However, it is clear that he was aware of the structural benefits of the pointed arch, and tried to stick to it. Geometrically, the curve he traced out is similar to an ellipse: the maximum deviation is one half-*palmo* (fig. 7: outside the ellipse, within Sangallo's curve).

The pitfalls of this method are evident. The curve in question is transcendent (i.e., not algebraic), and hence difficult to execute on the building; furthermore, the vault thus drawn has only a slightly raised crown (the rise of 110 *palmi* is only 1/8th higher than that of the semidome); this would have meant jeopardizing stability, which Sangallo was hardly disposed to do. Nonetheless, for the profile adopted for the model, Sangallo kept up this idea of replacing the semicircular profile with a raised oval. In the last two lines of the text there are two measurements which became fundamental for the next stage of the design. The rise of the dome had to be 147 *palmi*, equaling three-quarters of the diameter (196 *palmi*); the ratio between the basic radius and the height of the dome was therefore 2:3. The highest point of this profile remained approximately 23 *palmi* below the one that corresponded to the "tertio acuto"; to compensate for the difference, the aperture of the lantern had to be increased from a seventh to a fifth of the diameter, becoming $39^{1}/_{5}$ *palmi*. In this way the inclination calculated in Uff. 87A recto remained the same. In the model itself, the aperture of the lantern became nearly a quarter of the diameter.

C.T.

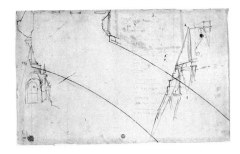

360
ANTONIO DA SANGALLO THE YOUNGER
Lantern for the Dome of St. Peter's
1540-45

Florence, Galleria degli Uffizi, Gabinetto Disegni e Stampe,
Uff. 1205A
Mixed technique: thick pen and compass with dark brown ink;
stylus; b) pen and brown ink in freehand; badly soiled paper,
backing added in places; fold down left; left margin
trimmed.
29.6 × 44.3 cm

BIBLIOGRAPHY: Giovannoni 1959: 144, 145; Benedetti 1990-92:
490 fig. 10.

The drawing shows the upper section of the dome, in the
same scale as the finished model (1:30). The diameter of
the oculus corresponds to the measurement 39⅕ *palmi*
indicated in Uff. 267A; later, with the addition of a cornice, this figure was reduced to 38½ *palmi* (indicated in
writing alongside).
The lantern is represented by two freehand sketches: in
section on the left, and the attic zone in (upside down) elevation on the right. *C.T.*

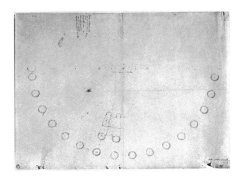

361
ANTONIO DA SANGALLO THE YOUNGER
(with ASSISTANTS)
Plan of the Lantern for St. Peter's
1540-45

Florence, Galleria degli Uffizi, Gabinetto Disegni e Stampe,
Uff. 89A
Pen and brown ink; drawn with straightedge and compass,
stylus impressions; steps have been added freehand.
51 × 67 cm
INSCRIBED: (below the scale in *palmi*) *palmi venti del modello*
(perhaps not in Sangallo's hand); (bottom right) *schizzo p[er]
tribuna [?] et cam[pa]nile*; (on verso) *Schizzo p[er] la lanterna e il
campanile*; *S.to pietro* (in pencil); measurements in Roman *palmi*;
scale in 20 *palmi*, 14.9 cm long, making the scale 1:30.

BIBLIOGRAPHY: Jovanovits 1877: 19, no. LVIIIa; Giovannoni 1959:
144; Thoenes 1990: 39; Benedetti 1990-92; 492 fig. 12.

The lantern of Sangallo's design for the model is
represented here in plan, with an internal diameter of
39⅕ *palmi*. The detailed construction shows traces of an
assistant's hand (Antonio Labacco?), who began with a
crude blunder (on left) by setting a column in line rather

than a space between columns. This was later corrected,
but the drawing itself was never completed (see continuation on Uff. 88A). *C.T.*

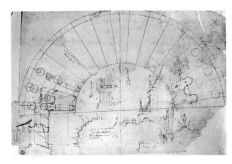

362
ANTONIO DA SANGALLO THE YOUNGER
*Plan of the Lantern, and Sketches for the Lantern
and Campanile for St. Peter's*
1540-45

Florence, Galleria degli Uffizi, Gabinetto Disegni e Stampe,
Uff. 88A
Mixed techniques: a) plan of lantern, with drawing pen,
straightedge and compass in gray-brown ink; stylus impressions;
b) sketches in pen and light brown ink, freehand; lacerated,
damaged paper, trimmed and gummed.
44 × 63.4 cm
INSCRIBED (in two different hands): a) (Labacco?, cf. for example
Uff. 1793A, Bartoli IV, fig. 615) *agetto della chornice [?] di
fuori*; *Vivo* (twice) *le mezi[?] delle cholonne drento e fuori*; b)
(Sangallo) *Cosi viene meglio p[er] la lanterna / ogni cosa adarchi 24
/ et cosi bisogna ridurre / lo modello*; *palmi*; measurements in
Roman *palmi*; scale in 5 *palmi*, 3.72 cm long, bottom right
(compass holes); scale of plan 1:30.

BIBLIOGRAPHY: Jovanovits 1877: 19, no. LVIII; Giovannoni 1959:
144, 145, fig. 86; Francia 1977, fig. 71; Bruschi 1988: 241;
Thoenes 1990: 39; Benedetti 1990-92: 491 fig. 11.

This plan, which was drafted with the help of an assistant,
is related to Uff. 89A; in this stage of the design, the
project once more underwent a radical revision by Sangallo, evidently in order to remedy the tight arrangement of
the columns around the drum of the lantern. Sangallo's
first proposal was a structure on two levels, similar to the
structure for the drum of the main dome; he defines the
measurements in an elevation sketch (left, in the inner
semicircle); on the far left of the page a section of the same
structure is sketched in, together with a view of the central cusp.
The ensuing idea, which showed still more daring, involved the reduction of the number of radial elements of
the lantern from 32 to 24, so that each quadrant contained
6 instead of 8. At the bottom left is a freehand sketch of
the plan of the new structure, and in the middle of this,
a profile and frontal view of the base of the lantern. The
columns are no longer aligned above the ribbing of the
dome. Although it must have been difficult indeed for
such a thorough architect as Sangallo to accept this solution, he nonetheless noted "it all works better this way...
the model must be adjusted thus." In the right quadrant
of the large plan he has traced in stylus and partly drawn
in the new arrangement, and has also drawn a pair of elements in the upper level.
At the lower right of the page is a sectional drawing of the
lantern similar to the one in the finished model, together
with a view of the upper levels of the campaniles; these,
however, are quite different from the ones adopted for
the model (group of statues on the pediment, cusps, and
bases of the pinnacles). *C.T.*

363
ANTONIO DA SANGALLO THE YOUNGER
Plan and Section of the Lantern for St. Peter's
1540-45

Florence, Galleria degli Uffizi, Gabinetto Disegni e Stampe,
Uff. 258A
Pen and light brown ink in the upper section (including the
scale of measurements), dark brown ink for the lower section;
straightedge and compass, with parts freehand; parchment; top
section badly deformed and unevenly trimmed; fold down
center; two horizontal folds.
96.5 (max) × 62.1 (below) cm
INSCRIBED: (top, vertically) *capo* (compass hole for tracing the
outline of the dome) *centro* (idem, for the lower part: pointed
arch with same radius of ¾ of the diameter); (bottom) *voto,
pieno, voto* etc.; (below right, in pencil) *Laterna per S. Pietro
(Cost. Jovanovits)*.
Scale key of 80 *palmi*, 59.5 cm long; scale 1:30.

BIBLIOGRAPHY: Jovanovits 1877: 19, no. LVIII b; Giovannoni
1959: 144; Bruschi 1988: 241; Thoenes 1990: 39; Benedetti 1990-
92: 492 fig. 13.

The assistant who worked on Uff. 89A carried out a
finished copy on parchment of the plan of the lantern,
repeating the initial mistaken alignment of the first
column on the left of the outer circuit, and the others of
the quadrant; they were canceled and redrawn in the correct position. Likewise, the repetition of the scheme for
the spiral staircase in each of the eight piers is certainly
not one of Sangallo's ideas.
The plan of the first pair of elements on the left has been
adjusted to the improvement in Uff. 88A; the new arrangement, with three instead of four pairs of elements
("pieni") in each quadrant is indicated by little arrows.
Nevertheless, the original disposition of 32 radial elements was kept in the model; in return, the lantern was
increased in overall size.
In the sectional view, the arrangement of the splayed windows was modified. In the model, the steeply raked lantern cupola was divided into two superimposed parts; in
the drawing here the central cusp is missing (see Uff.
261A). *C.T.*

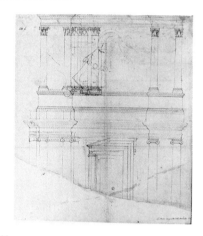

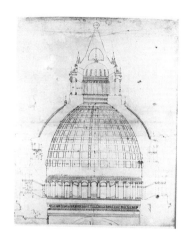

144; Bruschi 1988: 241; Thoenes 1990: 39; Benedetti 1990-92: 493 fig. 16.

At the base of the end cone are 7 rather than the 5 steps in Uff. 261A and 90A, and this is the design used for the finished model. Alongside the end cone of the lantern is the terminating section of the campaniles (in ink, with partial stylus impressions), in this case shorter and pointed. The balustrade sketched on the left is also intended for the campaniles.
C.T.

364
ANTONIO DA SANGALLO THE YOUNGER
Sectional View of the Crown of the Lantern for St. Peter's
1540-45

Florence, Galleria degli Uffizi, Gabinetto Disegni e Stampe, Uff. 261A
Pen and light brown ink; drawn partly with straightedge, partly freehand; stylus impressions; page trimmed along edges; upper piece added (gummed); lower margin matches with upper margin of Uff. 258A.
81.9 (max) × 41 cm
INSCRIBED: (bottom right, in pencil, canceled) *Abschluss der Laterne (Jovanovits).*

BIBLIOGRAPHY: Jovanovits 1877: 19, no. LIX; Giovannoni 1959: 144, fig. 85; Francia 1977, fig. 72; Benedetti 1986: 169, fig. 24; Bruschi 1988: 241-43; Thoenes 1990: 39; Benedetti 1990-92: 493 fig. 17.

The drawing integrates the section of the lantern in Uff. 258A. The dimensions of the upper section have been reduced (corrections). A molding has been added to the base of the cone.
C.T.

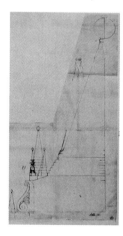

365
ANTONIO DA SANGALLO THE YOUNGER (perhaps with ASSISTANTS)
Crowns of Lantern and Campaniles for St. Peter's
1540-45

Florence, Galleria degli Uffizi, Gabinetto Disegni e Stampe, Uff. 262A
Pen and brown ink; part straightedge, part freehand; stylus impressions; two pieces glued together, trimmed round edges, with several strips glued to back; scale 1:30.
82.5 (right) × 12.8 (top) and 42.1 (bottom) cm

BIBLIOGRAPHY: Jovanovits 1877: 19, no. LIXa; Giovannoni 1959:

366
ANTONIO DA SANGALLO THE YOUNGER
Prospect of the Campanile for the Model of St. Peter's
1540-45

Florence, Galleria degli Uffizi, Gabinetto Disegni e Stampe, Uff. 260A
Pen and brown ink; part straightedge and compass, part freehand; paper trimmed round edges, in two vertical strips gummed together, lacerated at bottom and glued on back; measurement scale in 10 *palmi* (left margin, top) written vertically, 7.45 cm long; scale 1:30.
81.3 (right) × 74.5 cm
INSCRIBED: (on drawing, top) *quadro; tondo* (Sangallo); (on glued piece, bottom right) *La torre eseguita nel modello* (modern pencil writing, perhaps by Jovanovits); (verso, top margin) *campanile di S. Pietro di mia mano* (Sangallo).

BIBLIOGRAPHY: Jovanovits 1877: 18, no. LIIf; Giovannoni 1959: 144, fig. 84; Thoenes 1990: 39.

It appears that certain details of the final project were drafted by Sangallo immediatly on the scale of the model. For example, for the two upper stories of the campanile shown here (corresponding to those of the drum of the dome) there is only one preparatory sketch (Uff. 76A). This drawing was left unfinished too: some of the articulation is missing, and on the lower story the side view of the flank is not shown. No decision had yet been made for the central apertures: at the bottom of the drawing two variants of the Ionic window are sketched in, and at the top three variants of the arch. In the model, the lower story remained windowless, whereas in the upper story the middle variant was adopted for the arch. The elevation here was complemented by several floor plans in line with the upper story:
a) wall articulation for the upper story, as indicated by the legend ("quadro"; "tondo"), Sangallo was obliged to forgo the exclusive use of the half-column, as the logic of the system required two different types of members of the framework. The external column of the aedicula hence takes the form of a "colonna quadra.";
b) outlines of the upper octagonal story, with conical cusp (large circle on left) the same size as the one in the model;
c) cusp of the upper story (small circle on left), represented slightly larger than the one in the model;
d) cusps on the uppermost story (sketched).
C.T.

367
WORKSHOP OF ANTONIO DA SANGALLO
(Antonio Labacco?)
Section of the Dome of St. Peter's
ca. 1546

Stockholm, Nationalmuseum, Cronstedt Collection, CC vol. 13, no. 1398.
Pen and brown ink, part in black pencil, with stylus impressions; drawn with straightedge and compass, with details freehand; strip added along top; edges trimmed all round; two folds across center; numerous measurements in *palmi*; no scale key; scale ca. 1:175.
58.6 × 42.1 (max)
INSCRIBED: (verso) *Profil tres recherchée de l'Eglise chathedrale de St. Charles de Milan* (brown ink, 18th cent.); *Christophe Lombard architecte du Dôme de Milan* (black ink, 19th cent.).

BIBLIOGRAPHY: Unpublished.

Sangallo's dome is represented in section, with the inside seen in orthogonal projection; the dimensions and the details correspond roughly to the final phase of design, i.e., to the model, and to the engravings by Antonio Salamanca (cat. no. 370). On the outside the parapets above the two colonnades of the dome are missing, but the pinnacles around the base of the lantern are included, though not in the engravings. Inside there is no parapet for the gallery around the dome. The lantern cupola contains 12 windows instead of the 16 in the model; small variations can be seen in the stepping of the splayed apertures in the drum; the inside of the dome has 10 rows of coffering, instead of the 11 shown in Salamanca's section.
There are evident alterations to the dome's dimensions. The diameter is marked as 193 *palmi* (3 less than in the preliminary project and Salamanca's sectional drawing), while the crown of the dome is about 6 *palmi* higher than in the model: the result is a slight vertical elongation. The base of the lantern is 150 *palmi* above the springing line of the dome: this height is divided into segments of 25 *palmi* each in the lower part, and 12.5 and 6.25 *palmi* in the upper parts, all labeled with the measurements of the net diameters of the dome. These measurements do not, however, match the contour as drawn, as the curve should be slightly more bowed. The curve drawn here seems to be based on a polycentric arch: the several compass holes suggest that the draftsman proceeded in a more or less empirical fashion.
The detailing of the drawing indicates a close familiarity with Sangallo's project, from which we can infer that the drawing was made in his workshop, though clearly not by his hand. The most likely candidate is Antonio Labacco, who collaborated with Sangallo during the last phase of the model's design. The numbers are not in Sangallo's handwriting either, except perhaps the addition in the bottom left, penned with a thicker nib, regarding the thickness of the drum wall, and the outline of the intrados beneath the arch, marked "39."
It is not easy to establish the purpose of the drawing. It

is not a project drawing, nor one of the series of executive drawings on a scale of 1:30 made ready for the construction of the model. If this were so, it would have been quite sufficient to represent half of the dome, as in Uff. 267A, and the draftsman need not have bothered with the orthogonal projection of the inner framework, which was hardly easy. The coffering was perfectly elaborated, with all the horizontal lines impressed with the stylus, and the meridians traced out beforehand with a compass and black pencil. In the model itself there is no coffering at all. The draftsman's intention here, then, was to give a graphic illustration of the new project, which was not intended for transfer to the model. This may mean that it was a preparatory drawing for a full engraving, though not for Salamanca's, which was on a quite different scale. It could be inferred, therefore, that Sangallo's project for the dome—the most singularly personal of all his architectural inventions—was to be first engraved as a scheme on its own, as a counterproposal to the Bramante project published in woodcut by Serlio shortly before. The size of the drawing in question concurs approximately with the so-called *realle* format in use for copperplate engravings, which Salamanca also adopted for his copies. *C.T.*

368
RAFFAELLO DA MONTELUPO
Facade of Antonio da Sangallo's Model for St. Peter's
1546

Munich, Staatliche Graphische Sammlung, 33329
Pen and brown ink, partly over brown pencil; brown wash; stylus impressions; drawn with straightedge and compass, part freehand; addition glued at top left; edges trimmed.
36 × 40 cm

BIBLIOGRAPHY: Gazzola 1942: 32ff.; Degenhart 1955: 266ff.; Benedetti 1986: 165ff.; Verellen 1981: 38ff.

The drawing on the recto represents the right (northern) end of the facade of the model, with an accentuatedly foreshortened view of the dome above it. On the left is a sketch of the south campanile, with details for both campaniles at the top right, shown in plan and elevation. In the bottom left is a male nude figure, and an Ionic capital; near the left margin, at top, a curly male head (partly trimmed). The verso contains sketches of fortifications, architectural details (not matching the model) and a supine river god.
The various attributions to Antonio, Aristotile or Francesco da Sangallo put forward in critical commentaries fail to account for the most important criteria for identifying authorship: as seen in the direction of the hatchings, the draftsman is left-handed. The logical author is therefore the sculptor and architect Raffaello da Montelupo, who in the 1540s was acquainted with Antonio da Sangallo, and through him came into contact with the Farnese family (as pointed out by Verellen, 1981). This ties in with the fact that the page in question, despite general opinion to date, does not belong to preliminary drawings for the model, which were in fact all in Antonio's hand. This one

is more correctly a frontal view of the already finished model. The right half of the facade has been drawn with a straightedge and compass, and carefully detailed with ink wash; the dome and the upper part of the campanile were drawn freehand. The extra hatchings also belong to this second phase of the drawing, though it is not clear if they were intended as shading or corrections (crossings out). The drawing presents two significant departures from the finished model:
a) Sangallo's project comprises seven bays, of which the central three belong to the facade of the east section: these arches give access to the portico, and from here to the vestibule area and on to the three main portals of the church proper. The second and fifth bays correspond to the gaps between the facade of the east section and the campaniles; these occupy the first and last bays of the elevation. In this drawing, the two gaps have been omitted, giving the impression of a compact, five-bay front with the campaniles surmounting the outer bays.
b) In the drawing the campanile has one less story than in the model. This appears to be due to a change of mind: originally the first story emerging from the facade was identical to the model, except for the inclusion of a window in a aedicula; this window seems to have been erased and replaced by a quick sketch of a larger aedicula, with a pediment over the entablature. The aedicula is the one designed for the story above in the model, whose design is sketched in on the left: the two stories have basically been merged.
The far left of the page carries a sketch of a variant in which the number of the stories remains the same, but the aedicula is inserted one story below, and is more squat than in the original. In this way the upper stories of the campaniles seem to be the same height as the dome's lantern, whereas in proper perspective they should appear higher.
The sense of these two alterations is clear enough: the full form of the building had to be compressed both vertically and horizontally, to make it fit on the page. This tied in with the pontiff's request to have a foundation medal struck with a reproduction of Sangallo's model. Save some slight discrepancies, the facade of this drawing in fact is what appears on Alessandro Cesati's medal (cat. no. 369); the drawing in question may therefore have served as a model for the medalist, or as a preparatory study for that purpose. Certain details omitted by the artist (maybe because they were still missing in the wooden model), such as the squat octagonal towers over the bays either side of the central bay, or the tower spires, were detailed rather roughly on the foundation medal. *C.T.*

369
ALESSANDRO CESATI (IL GRECHETTO)
Medal for Pope Paul III
1546-47

Florence, Museo Nazionale del Bargello, I 6266, P. I 405
Bronze, diam. 4.15 cm
Obverse: bust of Paul III in profile looking right, bareheaded; richly decorated cope, with ornate collar and large clasp; circular epigraph: PAVLVS. III. PONT. MAX. AN. XIII; beaded edge.
Reverse: facade of Antonio da Sangallo's model for St. Peter's;

linear epigraph along bottom: PETRO. APOST. PRINC. / PAVLVS. III. PONT. / MAX.; beaded edge.

BIBLIOGRAPHY: Bonanni 1696: 73 pl. 1; 1706: I, 199, 212, 243; Armand 1887: 228ff.; Martinori 1917-22; Gramberg 1984: 264; Küthmann et al. 1973: 216; Harprath 1978: 45ff.; Weber 1987: 292; Benedetti 1990-92: 504.

From the time of Julius II, the pontiffs of Rome had medals struck to commemorate the construction of New St. Peter's. These images have turned out to be enormously useful for documenting the progress of the actual design of the new building, but not without reserve: the techniques of die-cutting and the format itself made simplification a necessity, and the medalists were not always provided with authentic models on which to base their engraving. Hence it would be inaccurate to reconstruct the stage reached by Sangallo's project on the basis of this medal. Fortunately the preparatory drawing that has survived (cat. no. 368) makes it possible to compare the details with those of the model. The medal was struck to mark the completion of the model in 1546. This ties in with the date that appears on the earliest known specimens (which include the one shown here), as Year XIII of the pontificate ran from 13 October 1546 to 13 October 1547. During the same period Paul III had his portrait painted by Giorgio Vasari in the Sala dei Cento Giorni in the Chancery, as the renovator of the Vatican *fabbrica*; he appears in this same role some years later in a fresco executed by Francesco Salviati in the room of the *Farnese Deeds* in the Palazzo Farnese. The medal is more widely known in the 1549 version, reproduced by Bonanni: Year XVI of the pontificate of Paul III indicated in the epigraph, which began on 13 October 1549, was interrupted on 10 November that year by the pontiff's death. As suggested by the legend on the reverse, the coin was minted for the approaching Holy Year, 1550. On the pontiff's cope is represented the opening of the Porta Santa of the basilica by the pope. Paul's successor, Julius III, had a new coin struck of the Holy Year bearing his own portrait, but leaving the reverse type unchanged. The background to these last two coins is most unusual, as Sangallo's model had by this time been ruled out. The coin's reverse therefore shows a building that would never actually be erected. This certainly does not signify that the popes later opted for Sangallo's scheme instead of Michelangelo's. It is more likely that the latter had not yet designed the facade of the new project in hand, and refused to draw one up just for the foundation medal. Michelangelo moreover persisted in this refusal; at his death fifteen years later there was still no project for the basilica's facade. In this sense, together with the series of engravings published by Antonio Salamanca (cat. no. 370), the medal contributed to keeping Sangallo's design alive in the minds of later generations. *C.T.*

370
ANTONIO SALAMANCA
Five Copperplate Engravings of Antonio da Sangallo's Model of St. Peter's
1546-49

Florence, Galleria degli Uffizi, Gabinetto Disegni e Stampe

BIBLIOGRAPHY: Vasari 1984: 48; Grimaldi 1972: 491-495; Ehrle 1908: 13, 36ff.; Ashby 1914-15: 290ff.; Hülsen 1921: 168; Lowry 1952; Bonaventura 1960; Pepe 1963: 25; Fischer 1972: 15-17; Millon and Smyth 1976: 139, 164, 167; Deswarte Rosa 1989; Thoenes 1990: 49; Benedetti 1990-92: 495.

The five engravings in question are not a set as such, as they were executed over a period of four years. The earliest date, 1546, is on the first specimens of the longitudinal section; the side elevation, undated though substantially matching the section, probably dates from the same year. There are two versions of the facade, dated 1548 and 1549. In the first the annotations and scale match up with the section, whereas the second is on a slightly larger scale and its annotations are in a different style. These characteristics also crop up on the plan, likewise dated 1549, which clearly concluded the set. Four years later, Salamanca's workshop, which had been selling these engravings, was taken over by his young rival Antonio Lafréry; from then on the set was published with the same annotations in Lafréry's *Speculum Romanae Magnificentiae*. The problem of attribution in this case is a difficult one. The annotations included the names of Antonio da Sangallo, Antonio Labacco and Antonio Salamanca: the first features as the designer of the model (*inventor*), the second as the executor (*effector*), and the third as the editor of the engravings (*excudebat* indicates the printer, but in this as in many other cases, the printer handled the publishing side as well). No mention is made of the engraver, whose name would be followed by *"fecit," "incidit,"* or *"excidebat."* Given that Labacco, as a disciple and pupil of Sangallo, participated in the elaboration of some of the designs for the model, it is likely that he also supplied the drawings for the engravings. Some years later Labacco published his own collection of prints entitled *Libro appartenente all'architettura* (Rome, 1552). His name is missing from the second version of the facade, however, and the plan: in its place both engravings bear the legend *"ex ipso Ant. Sanctigalli exemplari."* This seems to suggest that in 1549 Salamanca redid the engraving of the facade, and added a plan, both drawn directly from the model. In his biography of Sangallo, Vasari attributes the publication of this set of engravings to Antonio Labacco, who, he states, "therefore wished to demonstrate the extent of Sangallo's skill, and make the architect's opinion known far and wide, given that counter-orders had been issued by Michelagnolo Buonarroti ..." This confirms what the date 1546 suggested, namely, that the engravings were devised by the Sangallo "sect" to bolster their position against Michelangelo and his own project for St. Peter's. The fruit of seven years' work, Sangallo's model risked being forgotten altogether after his death (and even being destroyed, like so many other wooden models that were considered of no further use) before it could be known to the public. The engravings were aimed at drawing the public's attention to the master's design, and would also underline Labacco's contribution as the executor of the model itself. Antonio Salamanca was the right partner for the job. Active in Rome for a good twenty years as a publisher and bookseller, Salamanca had already played a key role in publicizing Marcantonio Raimondi's engravings of works by Raphael. The idea of making architectural works more widely known was initiated by Sebastiano Serlio's *Libro delle antiquità di Roma*, which first appeared in Venice in 1540 and contained several unrealized projects by Bramante, Raphael and Peruzzi. Salamanca now launched the exquisitely Roman tradition of large-format architectural engravings; the practice was continued by Lafréry. Later this type of print was the most commonly used medium for circulating projects which risked remaining on the drawing board owing to the death of their authors—as in the case of Michelangelo's designs for St. Peter's and the Capitol, engraved by Lucchini and Dupérac between 1564 and 1569; similar engravings were made of Vignola's design for the facade of the Gesù, engraved by Cartari n. 1573.

(a) *Longitudinal Section from North* (1546)

INSCRIBED: *Forma templi D. Petri in Vaticano / Pauli III*

Pont. Max. liberalitati dicatum / Antonius S. Galli inventor, Antonius Labaccus eius discip. effector / Cum gratia et privilegio / Ant. Sal. excud Roma MDXLVIII (corrected to *MDXLVIII* in successive reprints); in the lower left a scale key of 100 Roman *palmi*, 4.78 cm long, making the scale 1:467.

First stage: the flight of steps up to the facade is missing. The representation of the grand architectural scheme is deliberately arresting but also highly accurate. The technically advanced orthogonal projection of the building in section, probably a device introduced by Bramante, was used by Sangallo and described in a letter from Raphael to Leo X. Such drawings were made to allow for a synoptical comparison of the external structure with the building's interior. In the case in question, the critical areas were the main drum and the ambulatories of the apses, in which the architectural diaphragms with their multiple ranges shut out the light from the interior spaces. The section of the western apse (extreme right of page) shows the overly complex expedients that Sangallo was forced to employ to bring light into the ambulatories and hemicycles; the drawing also shows the spatial and structural isolation of the forenave block, which was skilfully camouflaged in the front prospect (b). The engraving matches all the main dimensions and proportions of the wooden model; this also applies to the tall barrel vaults of the arms of the crossing, whose section was described by Millon and Smyth as having discrepancies with regard to the model itself. On the inside some detailing is visible that has not been executed in the model, such as the impost cornices in the niches of the main piers, the strip ribbing of the lower domes of the hemicyles, the *tondi* on the pendentives of the main dome, and the coffering of the dome vault: these details would seem to indicate that the engraving was based on drawings of the project. The windows on the first upper story of the campanile, not present in the model, are visible in Uff. 260A (cat. no. 366); the dome here may have been copied from the Stockholm drawing (cat. no. 367). The crown of the internal profile of the vault, constructed as a polycentric arch, is once again slightly higher; but as the diameter is still the traditional 196 *palmi*, the overall proportions are similar to those of the Stockholm drawing.

(b) *North Prospect* (1546)

The inscriptions are the same as for (a). The cornice of the papal coat of arms is slightly simplified; the indication of the publisher in the lower right is arranged differently; date missing. The scale key in *palmi* is missing; same scale as (a).

The side elevation matches the style and dimension of the longitudinal section, which suggests that the two engravings are contemporary; here too the orthogonal projection is highly consistent, avoiding any foreshortening. In the model there are fewer window bays in the campaniles, as in the vestibules and corner spaces; there are no cornices framing the side entrances to the apse, and the roofs with relative gables. In the model the upper story of the forenave block, and the central block on the north side (as shown) are not decorated.

The overall appearance of the building is rendered strikingly uniform by the ranges of half-columns circling the entire building: in this way the front addition (which is ar-

ticulated differently within) blends in with the rest of the structure. The profile of the complex is dominated by the campaniles and main dome. The lower domes, which feature as satellites to the central one in the previous projects, have disappeared into the architectural shell conceived by Sangallo; instead, the little octagonal towers emerge, surmounting the corner spaces rather than those of the minor domes, so as not to interfere with the drum of the central dome.

(c) *East Prospect* (first version, 1548)

Inscriptions and scale key of 100 *palmi* as for (a). The cornice of the papal coat of arms is slightly altered; on the right is a baldacchino with the crossed-keys emblem of pontifical sovereignty. Dated 1548.

Both style and type of representation are similar to those of (b); here again the windows are more numerous than in the model, and there are some details missing, such as the cornices over the entrances to the central block (visible through the three archways of the porch and at the back of the two gaps between the porch and the campaniles), the balustrade of the benediction loggia, the octagonal "pommels" at either side of the pediment crowning the loggia, and the roofs of the relative gables.
In the engraving the huge building is shown in its full extension, including the apses and the lateral arms. The fantastic effect of the whole contrasts somewhat with the simplicity of the decoration: the overlaying of the stories is uniform throughout the building, up to the cusps of the dome and the campaniles; half-columns, pilasters and cornices form a uniform grid, articulated by pediments, arches and aedicules of varying size. The resulting impression is that of a gigantic piece of furniture with countless compartments in which everything has its proper place. The elevation gives little relief to the isolation of the campaniles, and the forward extension of the nave, with its grand superimposed arches (main entrance to porch and benediction loggia) in which Sangallo's composition culminates. The interior of the loggia is undecorated, as in the model.

(d) *East Prospect* (second version, 1549)

INSCRIBED: ANT. SALA. EXCUDEBAT / AEDIS S. PETRI ORTHOGRAPHIA E IPSO ANT. SANCTIGALLI EXEMPLARI ROMAE MDXLVIIII / CON GRATIA ET PRIVILEGIO.
Scale key missing; same scale as (e).

This engraving is not a reworking of (c), but a replica on another engraving plate, as inferred from the difference in scale. Missing are the title, the papal badge (the pope died 10 November 1549), and the baldacchino, replaced by a background of clouds; the weathercocks on the dome and campaniles are pointing left rather than right. The inscription with the title, transferred onto the lower margin of the page, reads differently and is clumsily engraved (the letter "N" in reverse, "orthographla"); in the final line, the engraver's privilege reads "con" instead of "cum."

The differences from the model have been detailed by Marianne Fischer: they confirm the inscription with the title, according to which the engraving is not based on drawings but on the model itself, in the state it had reached by that date. This is demonstrated above all by the omission of several apertures on the upper story and campaniles, of the balustrade of the benediction loggia, and the cornices of the entrance portals. The lack of certain details that are actually present in the model suggests that at the time the model was not quite finished. This applies to the Diocletian window over the central portal, the pair of pilasters flanking the archway of the benediction loggia, and the cornices on modillions ornamenting the pediment of the loggia, and the attic on which the campaniles rest. If this interpretation is correct, we can infer that work continued on the model after it had been rejected by Michelangelo. As this engraving includes the roofing, we may presume that they once existed in the model but were lost at a later date.

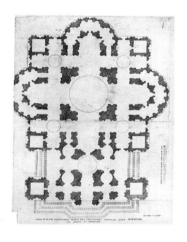

(e) *Plan* (1549)

Inscriptions as in (d); on right, scale key in 200 Roman "*palmi*" (inverted), 10.65 cm long, with the legend in Italian *Misura di questa pienta [sic] sono palmi 200. Scale 1:420.

The plan is the same as the model's, except for two slight differences: a) the model has no spiral staircases, only in the section of masonry to the right of the east hemicycle do we see a cylindrical channel; b) in the model the passageways between the east buttressing piers and the hexagonal vestibules are closed in. It is unclear as to what source the engraver borrowed from to sanction the alterations. A spiral staircase in the outer wall of an ambulatory, similar to the one in the engraving, appears in a sketch by Sangallo (Uff. 49A).

As there is no surviving site plan of the entire building by Sangallo or by his assistants, this sheet is the only document that enables a proper appraisal of the basilica's plan. Among Sangallo's last schemes, this is the only one that returns to that abstract geometrical beauty so typical of the drawings of his youth. Nonetheless, the outward thrust of the domes, the niches, and the hemicyles is contained and regulated by a rigid system of straight corridors that meet at right angles to each other. The niche motif has almost completely disappeared; the plan is dominated by the great perimeter square, which is offset by the transverse facade section. The two campaniles

reiterate the pattern of the four corner spaces; the domed vestibule of the linking section, set in four hexagonal smaller vestibules, echoes the quincunx of the central block. It is almost as if with this plan Sangallo wanted to draw up a kind of summary of the general design for New St. Peter's, beginning with the Bramante parchment drawing: a design process the continuity of which he himself contributed to, and whose history he alone knew in full.   *C.T.*

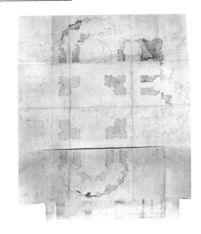

371
<small>Unknown Sixteenth-Century Artist</small>
Plan of Antonio da Sangallo's Model for St. Peter's

Windsor Castle, Royal Library, RL 10445
Six sheets gummed together, partially backed with strips of cloth, trimmed round edges; pen and brown ink, part in black pencil, with uneven wash in brown ink, with stylus impressions; straightedge and compass drawn; calculations in black pencil. 68.9 × 79.5 cm (max)
Recto without annotations; measurements (not in Sangallo's hand) in the area of the south apse and the southwest corner space; scale key in *palmi* missing; scale approximately 1:235.
Verso with two annotations: (in pen and brown ink, perhaps 17th cent.) *Pianta di S. Pietro d'Antonio da S. Gallo*; (in pencil, 20th cent.) *Antonio da San Gallo (the Younger), Sangallo.*

Bibliography: Unpublished.

The sheet contains a partial plan of the model, comprising the dome area, three arms of the crossing and a corner space; the fourth arm, of which only the inner profile is sketched in, must be the east arm, which in the model extends to accommodate the vestibules and facade. The drawing probably reflects a phase prior to the execution of the model, when this part of the definitive project, for which there are no extant preparatory drawings by Sangallo, had not been determined. A clue to the date is offered by the outer corner of the square space in the top left: in the preparatory drawings it is bevelled (cf. Uff. 52A; cat. no. 351), here it is a convex right angle, whereas in the model it became concave, as for the campaniles. In all the other details the drawing corresponds to the model—even the internal layout of the ambulatories is given in its definitive form. The fact that the niches between the pillars of the major orders in the main piers and buttressing piers are only shown for the western section is more likely to be an inconsistency on the part of the draftsman.

As none of the plan was executed freehand it is impossible to determine its author; not even the calligraphy of the measurements permits an attribution. It is unlikely to be a project drawing by Sangallo himself because of the lack of pentimenti and written comments. But even as a finished draft by an assistant, the drawing would be isolated in the *corpus* of Sangallian projects for St. Peter's. The author could have been an outside architect interested in Sangallo's project, who had access to the master's

workshop, or who came into possession of his drawings at some later date. The lack of scale keys suggests that the drawing is really a compilation of various other plans, rather than a full site plan. In the buttressing pier on the left of the east hemicycle, a few chalk lines, evidently added later, trace out a spiral staircase similar to those inserted later by Michelangelo in the buttressing piers of the crossing: this demonstrates that the sheet continued to be used during the second half of the sixteenth century, if it was not actually executed during that period. Another drawing possibly by the same draftsman's hand is the plan of the model's lantern, which follows the page examined here in the Royal Library album (RL 10446), and a plan of St. Peter's by Michelangelo (RL 10448), which can be dated to around 1585 on the basis of the annotations it bears. In the latter plan, the spiral staircases of the kind realized by Michelangelo are present in all eight of the buttressing piers.   *C.T.*

372
<small>Unknown Sixteenth-Century Artist</small>
(Jacobus Bos?)
Measured Drawings of Antonio da Sangallo's Model for St. Peter's

Berlin, Staatliche Museen, Preussischer Kulturbesitz, Kunstbibliothek, HdZ. 4154, *Codex Destailleur* D
Black pencil, pen and brown ink; part freehand, part straightedge and compass.

Bibliography: Jessen 1890: 116; Berckenhagen 1969; 1970: 26-31.

The codex, purchased in 1879 from the collection of Hypolite Destailleur by the Kunstbibliothek in Berlin, comprises 120 drawings of technical studies of ancient and modern architecture, including fourteen pages on Sangallo's model for St. Peter's. The surveys, carried out in the mid-sixteenth century, contain annotations in Italian and French: this led H. Egger (1903) to attribute them to a French draftsman, whom he named "Anonymous Destailleur." In 1969 E. Berckenhagen attempted to identify the author of the codex as the sculptor and architect Hugues Sambin from Gray, in the Franche-Comté, an artist who is not documented as having travelled in Italy, however. The attribution to the engraver Jacobus Bos, a native of the southern Low Countries, is equally conjectural; Bos is recorded as present in Rome from 1549 on. The attribution is based on fol. 112 of the set, in which the centering for the arches of St. Peter's is represented alongside a Roman *palmo* in true scale: the same association is found in an engraving signed by Bos, dated 1561. On the basis of a signature, C. L. Frommel considered the possibility of Bos' being the author of the so-called *Janos Scholz Scrapbook* in the Metropolitan Museum, New York, which also contains annotations in Italian and French, and has several features in common with the codex in question, particularly as regards technique. As an engraver, Bos worked in the 1550s for Salamanca, and later for Lafréry.

The pages, which vary in size, contain both freehand sketches and finished drawings. Apart from the perspective view sketched on fol. 76, all the drawings are furnished with measurements, which in the surveys of details are accurate to the millimeter. The unit of measurement used throughout is the "palmo del modello", equaling 1/30th of a normal *palmo* of 0.2234 m. The measurements were therefore taken either from the model itself, with a purpose-made measuring instrument, or from sketches and executive drawings drafted for the purpose.

This last possibility is endorsed by the presence in the drawings of certain details that do not appear in the model, such as the helical ramps on fol. 76v. In other cases, parts of the design are shown which would no longer be visible once the model was pieced together, such as the inside of the vaults of the smaller domes, the "ottogoni" (fol. 82), and the ambulatories of the apses (fol. 83). The detailed surveys of these parts must have been carried out during the construction of the model in Labacco's workshop; failing this, the drawings are copies of designs made specifically for the model, or served this purpose themselves. In its current state, the set is evidently incomplete. Only a crossing pier and half of an apse are shown in plan (fol. 77); the page has also been incorrectly laid out, and is unfinished. Fol. 78 includes a horizontal section of half of the central part of the building, in reference to the level of the minor domes; fol. 85 shows an overhead view of the roofing of the southern end of the building; fols. 86 to 89 show horizontal sections of the campaniles and corner towers. The only external elevation shows a side of the east approach of the building, from the axis of the central dome to the facade (fol. 76); on the other hand, exhaustive studies are provided of the inner elevations, with a longitudinal section of the entire building (fols. 80 and 81), and a section of the main dome (fol. 84). Other pages contain sections of the minor domes and the octagons (fol. 82), a tower with staircase (fol. 76v.), and one of the apse ambulatories (fol. 83).

Save a few exceptions (fols. 76v. and 84), the elevations eschew perspective details and therefore conform to the orthogonal projection prescribed for architectural drawing by contemporary theory. However, this criterion is not always observed consistently: in most cases the author represents the curved or oblique surfaces on the picture plane, so as to apply the individual measurements accurately. Some incongruences arise in the rendering of the overall structure: in cases like this the widths tend to be dilated, whereas elsewhere (in freehand sketches) they are slightly contracted to make them fit on the page. The elevations are therefore not true scale drawings, but schematic representations. This is confirmed by the fact that the author has omitted to put in the scale keys for the compass measurements: the objective description of the work is given by the measurements alone. Nevertheless, the pages can be grouped into approximate scales:

1:80 (approx.) for the campaniles and the section through the main building;
1:100 (approx.) for the section through the east block, and sections of the dome;
1:150 (approx.) for the plan of one of the apses;
1:200/250 for the external prospect, and plan of upper story;
1:400 for the overhead view of the roofing.

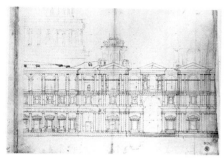

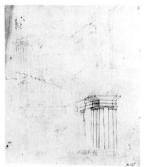

(a) fol. 76
South Prospect
Two joined sheets.
43.2 × 82.2 cm

The drawing reproduces the south prospect of the model, from the axis of the central dome through to the facade. The elevations are drawn as far as the level of the roof in full detail, with measurements; the main drum, the corner tower, and one story of the campanile are sketched.

The added sheet on the left contains a perspective sketch of the left (south) half of the facade; part of the framework of the ground floor is drawn in pen with the help of a ruler. The record must have been taken directly from the model; the representation matches Salamanca's first engraving of the facade, except for the missing balustrade in the benediction loggia. In the sum written obliquely in the top left, the overall height of the building (598½ *palmi*; cf. fols. 84 and 86) comes to 369, the meaning of the calculation is obscure.

On the verso of the added section is a sectional view of the little octagonal towers on the corner spaces of the central block: the drawing is cut off on the right, but presumably it once continued and included the axis of the tower. Some sketched details are visible on the left. All the parts executed in pen are complete with measurements, even those not later completed in the model itself.

In the model the little towers comprise a simple open-topped shaft whose function is unclear. In the drawing in question, the full part of the shaft is made up of a double shelled structure enclosing a single or perhaps double screw stair. The wording "Le Rampan dunz quartun[?] p 10" evidently refers to the net span of the staircase. The poorly rendered perspective implies that the author did not have a three-dimensional model before him, just a drawing, from which he attempted to recreate an effective representation. It is likely that the staircases started at ground level, and would therefore have been useful for transporting materials with donkeys. If so, the entrances to the stairs would have been in the four corner units, whose internal layout is not marked either in the drawing or in drawings. The lack of a roof for the cochlea could be explained by the need to provide light; rainwater could have been drained off at ground level. Extended to its full height, the shape and dimensions of this shaft are strikingly similar to the so-called Pozzo di S. Patrizio, an access shaft to an underground spring which Sangallo designed for Clement VII in Orvieto; the shaft was equipped with two spiral ramps. Similar structures can also be found in some earlier drawings by Sangallo for St. Peter's, such as the south campanile in Uff. 256A. After scrapping the apse ambulatories and the corner units from the basilica plan, Michelangelo in fact ingeniously inserted four imposing screw staircases inside the transverse buttressing piers. This interpretation of the structure as a stair tower starting at ground level cannot, however, be applied to the towers of Sangallo's porch block; their function remains obscure.

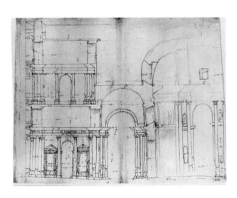

(b) fol. 79
Longitudinal Section of East Arm, Looking South
42.6 × 54 cm

The sheet contains a preparatory drawing for the section shown in fol. 80 (c), which is largely a freehand drawing. The widths in the drawing have been sharply contracted

to fit everything this side of the dome piers onto the page. Not included is the space beneath the dome (represented in fol. 80), and the tabernacle and Diocletian window in the lunette in the east hemicycle.

(c) fol. 80
Longitudinal Section of the East Arm, Looking South
Three joined sheets
51.1 × 95.9

This page contains the finished drawing of the sketch with measurements on fol. 79 (b). Thanks to the addition of extra pieces, the drawing includes a part of the area beneath the cupola, and the footing of the drum. The proportions are on the whole correct; however, the curved wall of the hemicycle and the oblique face of the pier of the dome are set in the picture plane, and so the overall length of the section is slightly augmented. The perspective rendering of the niche in the hemicycle aedicule is incongruent; usually the niches, openings and intrados of the arches are indicated with cross-hatching.

The verso bears the start of a drawing in full detail of the interior elevation of the entrance atrium.

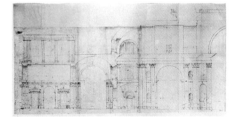

(d) fol. 81
Longitudinal Section of the West Arm, Looking South
Two joined sheets
55.5 × 84 cm

This section does not follow on exactly from the one on fol. 80, but starts with the corner of the west pier of the dome: the dimensions of the pier and the space below the dome could be deduced from the previous sheet. The slight difference in scale between the two drawings shows that the draftsman was not trying to compile a complete drawing of the whole building, but to put together an exhaustive repertory of measurements. For this reason some measurements are included for the transept arms and hemicyles that are missing on fol. 80. As in that drawing, here again the curved wall of the hemicycle is reproduced in the picture plane, and the same applies to the internal wall of the ambulatory, whose curvature is not recognizable. The representation of these parts in correct orthogonal projection is provided in Salamanca's sectional drawing (cat. no. 370).

The depth of the ambulatory is indicated here for the first and only time by means of shading in wash, albeit for the ground level only.

The verso contains two sketches:
(i) left, a section of the roofing area, for which there was no room on the recto; the section, as far as the impost of the dome vault, is compressed lengthwise, and includes some measurements. This area is not included in the model.

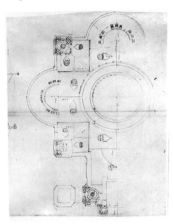

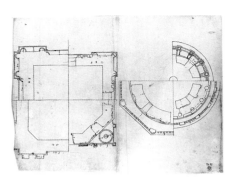

(e) fol. 85
View from above of the Roof of the South Section of the Model, with Horizontal Sections of the Base of the Drum, Four Little Towers and a Campanile
54 × 43.8 cm

This drawing offers the most comprehensive guide to the intended roofing for the model (which was either not built, or has been lost); the roofs were only partially included in Salamanca's engravings. The triple gable windows over the hemicycles correspond to the Diocletian windows of the relative conches (cf. fol. 81, recto and verso); the single gable windows illuminate the arms of the central crossing, and those of the minor arms. Note the insertion of a screw staircase in the wall of the eastern hemicycle, which turns up in more or less the same fashion in Salamanca's engraving.

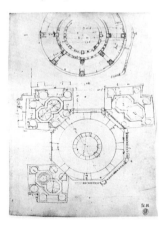

(f) fol. 86
View from above, and Horizontal Section of an Octagonal Little Tower
42.7 × 28.8 cm

The section (top) is taken through the octagonal base of the tower; the letter D indicates the projecting gallery with its balustrade; the letter B indicates the cylindrical nucleus of the open central shaft. The surrounding features are sketched in freehand.
The overhead view (bottom) shows the octagonal balustrade (D) again; in the cylindrical nucleus the radial volutes are visible, together with the upper ambulatory, bordered by two concentric balustrades, and the open shaft. The lack of the letters A and C suggest the existence of another similar sheet (no longer extant). Cf. the vertical section on the verso of fol. 76 (a).
The verso of the page contains several sketches to determine the overall dimensions of the building:
(i) net length of the centrally planned block, measured from the outer edges of the hemicycles: 610 *palmi*.

(ii) right, one of the niches on the far right of the upper story of the ambulatory. The aperture visible in the center leads through a narrow corridor to one of the "ottogoni".

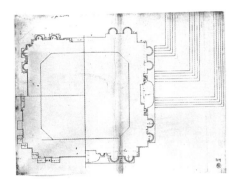

(ii) net height from the pavement level to the base of the pinnacle globe of the lantern: 597 *palmi* (cf. also fols. 76 and 84).
To judge from the measurements quoted, the sketch of the elevation does not seem to belong to the model for St. Peter's.

(g) fol. 89
Three Horizontal Sections of the Campanile
42.5 × 54 cm

This sheet and the following (fol. 88) contain plans of the eleven stories of the campanile (from ground level to top story). The series begins on the lower half of this sheet, with the section A of the Doric pavement level; the facade elevation is indicated by the junction of the flight of steps. The successive section AB, in the top left, corresponds to the first mezzanine; the next, in top right, is the section BC of the Ionic first upper story.

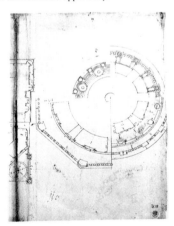

(h) fol. 88
Four Horizontal Sections of the Campanile
43 × 46 cm

This sheet of horizontal sections is the continuation of fol. 89. In the lower right part of the drawing is the section CD of the second mezzanine, followed (clockwise) by the section DE of the second Ionic story (without windows, as in the model and the second elevation engraved by Salamanca); top left, the section EF of the Corinthian story; top right, the passage to the octagonal story.
In the lower part of the drawing, which has no guiding letters to the sections, the series continues in an anticlockwise order from the first circular story (bottom right) to the terminating section (bottom left).
The verso of the sheet contains sketches with measurements showing details, together with a profile of the campanile's terminating section.

(i)
Four Horizontal Sections of the Campanile
42.5 × 55.3 cm

The drawing is a crude copy of fol. 88.
Profile of a Sector of the Dome of Sangallo's Model (black

line) *and Corresponding Ellipse* (black line) Computer drawing by the Institut für Angewandte Geometrie und Computergraphik, Technische Universität, Braunschweig (Wolfgang Boehm)

BIBLIOGRAPHY: Dürer, 1966, fol. 103r., fig. 33; Müller, 1971: 93-106.

In his design for the dome of St. Peter's, Sangallo had to take both esthetic and technical aspects into consideration. The hemispherical form envisaged by Bramante was universally considered to be the perfect choice, and had a sublime example in the Pantheon in Rome. But such a vault required a massive supporting structure, which was not in tune with the idea of a windowed drum. Sangallo's first idea was to apply a ogival profile for the internal load-bearing shell, as exemplified by Brunelleschi's dome for Florence Cathedral. This would have allowed him to construct a drum pierced by light openings; only the outer profile would remain hemispherical. The preliminary designs illustrate Sangallo's efforts to improve the vault's static performance by raising the crown of the vault farther and increasing the diameter of the lantern (Uff. 66A, 87A, 267A). In the course of these alterations, Sangallo must have had misgivings about the esthetics of the raised profile, which he himself criticized as being Gothic ("todesco"). In the model it was therefore supplanted by a more splayed oval, which confers a curiously elegant appearance to the dome, distinguishing it considerably from all those designed both before and after. Until now the geometrical basis of the vault's curve had remained unidentified. There are no surviving drawings or sketches that reveal the way in which it was calculated; the Stockholm drawing (cat. no. 367) is also unhelpful in this respect; the curve of the dome on fol. 84 of the *Codex Destailleur* in Berlin is polycentric, but differs from the model's. It was not until the model was dismantled for restoration purposes in 1991 that vault's true profile could be revealed. The analysis of the curve was carried out by Wolfgang Boehm at the Technical University of Braunschweig in Germany; his contribution was decisive in this part of the research. Various reconstructions of the curve were made, varying from polycentric to elliptical. The result was a perfect match with the semi-ellipse shown in this accompanying diagram. Its shorter axis of 1.4595 meters and larger semi-axis of 1.0945 meters correspond precisely with the 196 and 147 "palmi di modello" indicated in the measurements written by Sangallo on Uff. 267A. The elliptical curve therefore represents the result of Sangallo's attempts to obtain the needed raising of the crown by distorting the "antico bono" circular arch. The same problem had been tackled by Albrecht Dürer twenty years earlier in the *Underweysung der Messung*. In his case, however, it was a question of building a depressed arch, like those used for cross vault systems. Sangallo seems to have started with a preset arithmetical ratio between the two semiaxes: the height of the curve is exactly one and one-half times the base radius. It was therefore enough to draw a semicircle on a base of 196 *palmi*, measure the horizontal courses at repeated heights and transfer them to an identical base segment to their equivalent heights, increased one and one-half times (fig. 2). This operation could be carried out without difficulty even while the dome itself was under construction, by means of a full-scale reconstruction of the desired curve. This may have been Sangallo's plan.

C.T.

Michelangelo's Apse Vault and Attic of the South Transept
Henry A. Millon and Craig Hugh Smyth

Addition to the Heemskerck Sketchbook, fol. 60, Berlin, Kupferstichkabinett

The apse or hemicycle on the south was the first section of Michelangelo's St. Peter's to be completed. Formerly it was thought that Michelangelo completed all of the south apse, except the facing of the attic, the part above the giant order, nearly a quarter of the height of the main body of the building. The attic of the south apse looks so different in sixteenth-century representations from the attic now, that it was thought unfinished or tentative. Nowadays it appears certain that Michelangelo did finish it, in 1558, in the form he decided upon at that time for the attic order of the whole building (Millon and Smyth 1969: 484-500; 1988c: 217-219). The original attic of the south apse was changed to its present form early in the seventeenth century, very likely between 1605 and 1610 (Millon and Smyth 1969, 487-488 n. 6).

Visual documents that chronicle construction of the south apse from 1549 to 1558 include a view from the southeast in the Uffizi by an anonymous draftsman (Uff. 4345) and a view from the southwest, also by an anonymous artist, in the Kupferstichkabinett, Berlin (an addition to the Heemskerck sketchbook, fol. 60v., reproduced Egger 1911, pl. 37; Ackerman 1961, I, pl. 53a; Millon and Smyth 1988a: 95, fig. B).

The drawing at the Uffizi dates after 1552 (the base above the cornice of the drum is complete) and shows the hemicycle not yet complete through the first story. By March 1553 payments for lifting stone for the apse changed to a higher price (5 *baiocchi* per lift), indicating, most likely, a shift from the lower mast seen in the drawing to the higher one that reached up to the level of the top of the attic vault. Payments of that amount continued until 10 July 1556 (Millon and Smyth 1969: 497 n. 54). The drawing in Berlin, which dates after March 1556, when the capitals were recorded as in place, and before work on the entablature was begun (Millon and Smyth 1969: 484 n. 2), shows the state of the apse two years before its completion, but strangely omits the mast seen in the drawing at the Uffizi.

Archival documents record a change to a higher price for lifting in July 1556, when work on the entablature must have been under way. Also recorded is the completion of the three vaults of the arched windows over a year later, in late May-early June 1557.

Although Michelangelo had a model built for the apse vault, an error was discovered during construction in the second half of 1557 (Smyth 1985: 12-14), not in late April or early May, as generally assumed. As a result, a good portion of the travertine of the vault had to be dismantled. The nature of the error is recorded in two letters of Michelangelo to Vasari, and in Vasari's account in the *Lives* (Vasari, ed. Milanesi 1881, VII: 247). Correction of the error enabled Michelangelo to alter the design (Millon and Smyth 1976: 162-184). The rebuilt vault was closed on 17 May 1558; form work began being removed early in June and was all removed by the time of a celebration of the completion of the vault, which took place sometime during the week of 17-23 June 1558 (Millon and Smyth 1969: 484 n. 2).

The attic as completed in 1558 is recorded in a number of views including, in chronological order: a print by Vincenzo Luchino, dated 1564; a print published in 1565 by Bernardo Gamucci (based on a drawing by Giovanni Antonio Dosio, Uff. 2536A) in his guide to Rome, *Libri quattro dell'antichità della città di Roma...*; the remarkably detailed anonymous drawing in Frankfurt showing St. Peter's from the southeast, dated 1580/81; and a painting of 1619 by Domenico Passignano in the Casa Buonarroti,

which apparently depicts Michelangelo's wooden model. The attic on the building today replaces the one Michelangelo built on the south apse. The new attic order first appeared on the north apse, when the north apse vault and attic were built within the years 1564-66 during Ligorio's tenure as architect after the death of Michelangelo in February 1564 (Millon and Smyth 1988c: 216-286). There are two opinions about this change in design. A sketch by Michelangelo on the sheet in Lille (Wicar 93/94) shows the motif of the new design. Some believe the sketch to be specifically for the second attic and hence proof that Michelangelo himself decided to make the change (Thode 1908, II: 161; Düssler 1959: 168-169, note 301; Hirst 1974: 662-663, 665; Saalman 1975: 397 note 100, 401, 405; Joannides 1981b: 621; Hemsoll 1992: 124). The contrary view (argued by Millon and Smyth 1969: 484-500; 1975: 162-166; 1988c: 216-286; accepted by Ackerman 1970: 219-220, 296, 334; 1986: 214-215; Lotz 1974: 255, 380: 15; Tafuri 1975: 54; Keller 1976: 24-56; Curcio and Manieri Elia 1982: 242) is that there is no secure evidence that Michelangelo changed his mind after he completed the attic on the south apse; that the Lille sketch was not for St. Peter's but for a city gate (since it includes architectural membering relevant to a city gate, not to St. Peter's); that the change was made by Michelangelo's successors, as he had feared would happen to the upper part of his apse design when building the south apse; that Ligorio initiated the change after Michelangelo's death, adapting the design seen in the Lille sketch to this purpose; and that this is the change to Michelangelo's design for which Ligorio was dismissed by Pius V—as reported by Vasari, whom the pope called in for consultation about the change. Vasari was assured it would be completely corrected. Over a year after Ligorio's dismissal, Vasari used the south apse in his 1568 edition of the *Lives* to exemplify Michelangelo's definitive design of the apses, not the north.

Ultimately, the new attic order was continued throughout. The original attic order on the south was destroyed and replaced, shortly after 1600.

Michelangelo did change his mind, however, about the vault of the south apse when opportunity to do so arose during its construction in 1557. An error in construction of the vault required that it be dismantled and rebuilt and enabled Michelangelo to alter its design (Millon and Smyth 1976: esp. 172).

Prior to building the vault, Michelangelo had a model constructed at a scale of 1:30, the same scale as the earlier Sangallo model, so that he might place the vault model within the Sangallo model to examine it in relation to the main vault and the pilasters of the apse (Millon and Smyth

1976: 162-184). The vault model is still preserved today inside the Sangallo model, but has been removed and placed on exhibition separately so that it may be examined more closely.

The vault model bears traces of alteration, not owing to the error in the vaulting of the hemicycle, but apparently due to a prior error (and assumption) made evidently by Michelangelo's assistant when he measured the Sangallo model. It seems the carpenter measured the space occupied by one of the apse vaults of the Sangallo model— that is, both the depth, in plan, of the hemicycle and its width. He seems not to have been aware that the height of the semicircular main vault of the nave and transept in the Sangallo model is lower than on the building, where the vaults are stilted (raised) somewhat over two meters. (In the building, the vaults were stilted to avoid their appearing depressed when seen from the pavement below, partially hidden by the projection of the main cornice.) This anomaly of the Sangallo model is seen also in Dupérac's print of the longitudinal section of St Peter's. Dupérac seems to have taken the dimensions of the main vaults from the Sangallo model, without stilting, while showing the coffering as it is on the building today, above the vertical zone of the stilting. As a result, the coffering in Dupérac's representation is compressed vertically.

The Sangallo model contains another anomaly, also apparently unnoticed by whoever took the measurements. The apse vaults constructed for the Sangallo model were made to include the area of the salient arch adjacent to the semicircle of the apse. The salient arch was drawn on paper and glued to the vault model. A fragment of paper depicting the arch remains on one of the Sangallo apse vaults. On the Sangallo model, in plan, the apse vault is thus a semicircle *plus* the width of the salient arch. (The arch corresponds to the salient pilasters below that mark a junction with the apse in each of the transepts.)

When the model maker constructed the vault model for Michelangelo, he made it too high for the Sangallo model since he included the stilted area. He also made the vault model too deep in plan by including the area of the salient arch as if it were part of the apse vault itself.

The vault model did not, therefore, fit into the Sangallo model, and its parts did not correspond to the pilasters and members below. The vault model today shows the transformations wrought to adapt it to the Sangallo model and the building.

A pie-shaped slice was removed from the center bay of the new model to bring the ribs and windows into alignment with the windows and pilasters below. An unpainted replacement for the eliminated tondo was inserted. Crude wedge-shaped ribs were inserted at the two ends of the vault to correspond to the salient pilasters below. Finally, a lower section of the apse vault model, which corresponded to the stilted or raised area under the vault in the building, had to be removed.

It would appear that the vault model, incorrectly made, suggested to Michelangelo the possibility of wedge-shaped ribs for his apse instead of a salient arch, for construction of the apse vault was initially begun in late 1556 or early 1557 in keeping with the design of the altered model. This emerges from what follows here.

After the error in the vaulting was discovered and dismantling begun, Michelangelo wrote a letter to Vasari in July 1557 (Casa Vasari I) to explain the vaulting error. He illustrated the letter with a section drawing which included the wedge-shaped ribs of the altered vault model. By the time Michelangelo wrote a second letter (Casa Vasari II) a month and a half later, he had changed the design. The plan that illustrates Michelangelo's further explanation has eliminated the wedge-shaped ribs, has restored the salient arch, and has increased the curvature of the gores between the ribs.

The need to dismantle the vault, because of errors made by his men in constructing it, was a subject of much anguish to Michelangelo (as stated in Casa Vasari I). It also provided an opportunity to rethink the design once more, as he had done earlier the carpenter's mistake in fashioning the vault model.

Some indication of the exposed travertine of the original state of the apse vault, before it received its decorative encrustation (as seen in the section of Dupérac) is provided by the prints of Ferrabosco, a drawing at Windsor Castle (RL 5590) and, although depicting the west apse, the vault, as shown in color in a painting from a private collection in Bath. Armando Schiavo (1949: 109, 119) aptly suggested that the exposed travertine interior of S. Biagio at Montepulciano, designed by Antonio da Sangallo the Elder, would provide an idea of the qualities of an unadorned travertine interior analogous to Michelangelo's intentions for the apses of St. Peter's. The dressed and carefully joined surfaces of exposed travertine that formed the vault of the final design were, according to Michelangelo, "something not practiced in Rome" (text of Casa Vasari II. The smooth stone vault was a marvel to Vasari, who said that when "seen from below it appears to be all made out of one piece" (Vasari, ed. Milanesi 1878, I: 123-124).

Photograph of vault of south apse of St. Peter's

The marvel is there today, but obscured by gray paint and later decoration.

The deep gores, emphasized ribs, exposed stone, and large openings of the apse vault recalled some of the most admired aspects of both ancient Roman and medieval architecture. The new emphasis on vertical continuity and vault curvatures in the apse vaults at St. Peter's fascinated architects well into the eighteenth century.

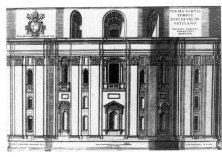

373
Vincenzo Luchino
Elevation of the South Apse of St. Peter's

Rome, Istituto Nazionale per la Grafica, Gabinetto Disegni e Stampe, 12208 st. vol. (Palazzo Grassi, Venice)
New York, Metropolitan Museum of Art, 41.72[3.23]
(Washington, National Gallery of Art)
Engraving.
384.586
Scale: Canne cinque, palmi 10 (lower center)
Inscribed: *FORMA PARTIS / TEMPLI / DIVI PETRI IN / VATICANO / MICHAEL ANGELVS / BONAROTVS / INVENTOR* (upper right); *PIO II. P.M. DICATVM* (upper left); *ROMAE VINCENTIVS LVCHINVS EXCV.* (lower left); *"CVM PRIVILEGIO M D LXIIII"* (lower right).

Provenance: unavaible.

Bibliography: Coolidge 1942: 99, 54; Gioseffi 1960: 70; Ackerman 1961, II: 101; 1964, II: 104; Thoenes 1968: 332, n. 9; Millon and Smyth 1969: 491-494 n. 19, and figs. 17 and 18; Saalman 1975: 380-409, and fig. 13; Boorsch 1982-83: Millon and Smyth 1988c: 217, 232, 242 n. 13, 255 n. 110, 255 n. 112 and fig. 6; Argan and Contardi 1990: 327, and fig. 437.

John Coolidge was the first to suggest that the artist who prepared the plate published by Luchino probably worked from the wooden model of 1547. Saalman (1975, 380-386) agreed with Coolidge and, concentrating on the model, proposed that it was built at a scale of 1:30 and showed only a portion of the structure. Others have thought the print was made following the already completed portions of the south apse (the apse hemicycle and attic), although the angled walls between the apse and the satellite chapels were incomplete on both the southeast and southwest (Ackerman 1964, II: 104; Gioseffi 1960: 70). In this view, the plan of the angled walls could have been seen on site while the elevation could have been inferred from the existing structure, and both could checked against the model.

The adroit placement on the print of the arms of Pius IV and of the inscription, at the attic level above the angled walls, finessed the need to show a treatment of the attic in these locations, where the angled walls were incomplete. In the painting by Passignano showing the model of St. Peter's, an arched attic window is shown on the southeast satellite chapel, but the attic level above the angled wall is obscured by the clothes of the standing courtier. Michelangelo's intentions for the attic elevation above the angled walls remains unverifiable, though the attic was probably included in the model.

The Luchino print is most likely (Millon and Smyth 1988c, 230-232) the print referred to by Tiberio Calcagni, Michelangelo's assistant, in a letter of September 1564 (Frey *Nachlass* II: 211-214 and Coolidge 1942: 98-99, note 54) by Vasari (Vasari, ed. Milanesi 1878-85) in the second edition of his *Lives* since, as Coolidge pointed out, no other print of St. Peter's showing part or all of the side elevation (north and south) is known before that of Dupérac, which dates after the *Lives* were published. Luchino apparently also intended to publish a print of the interior of the apse (Millon and Smyth 1988c: 232 and notes 13, 110, 112).

The importance of the print resides especially in the following two aspects. It is the earliest known accurately scaled representation of Michelangelo's intentions for the

B. Gamucci, Antichità della città di Roma, *1565
Based on a drawing by G.A. Dosio, Uff. 2536A*

apse of the south transept. It includes the first—and now lost—attic of St. Peter's as built by Michelangelo on the south apse, with its coffers, moldings and crowning cornice, clearly a finished portion of the apse elevation, not an unfinished or "provisional" surface awaiting a final sheathing. Not least, the print is dated 1564. Michelangelo died on 18 February 1564. Publication of the print in that year with the inscription "*FORMA PARTIS TEMPLI DIVI PETRI IN VATICANO / MICHAEL ANGELVS BONAROTVS INVENTOR*," together with the inscription showing the print's papal copyright privilege ("*cum privilegio*"), tends notably to support the view that Michelangelo did not change the design of the attic order before his death.

H.A.M.-C.H.S.

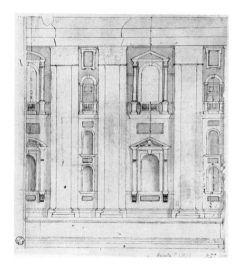

374
ANONYMOUS
Elevation of the Exterior of an Apse of St. Peter's

Florence, Galleria degli Uffizi, Gabinetti Disegni e Stampe, Uff. 95A
RECTO: Elevation of three and one-half bays of an apse of St. Peter's
Pen, brown ink and wash over black chalk, and black chalk; repaired upper left and at right.
INSCRIBED: various dimensions in ink and black chalk.
VERSO: Elevation of two bays of the exterior of the drum St. Peter's
Pen, brown ink and light brown wash.
INSCRIBED: *Porti 8* (below arched opening at left); *Porti 4* (below rectangular opening *at bottom right*); various inscribed dimensions.
350/353 × 297 mm

PROVENANCE: unavailable.

BIBLIOGRAPHY: Ferri 1885: 151; Coolidge 1942: 64, 91; Ackerman 1961, II: 101; 1964, II: 101, 103; Millon and Smyth 1969: 494-497; Saalman 1975: 386-397; Ackerman 1986: 321; Argan and Contardi 1990: 327, 329, and fig. 438.

Uffizi 95A recto is a flattened elevation of the exterior of one of the transept apses of St. Peter's. It was first discussed by Coolidge (1942: 64, 91) and then by Ackerman (1961, II: 101) as differing from the building as executed in that the large central window in the drawing is not trabeated but arched. Ackerman suggested that the drawing was a copy, done about 1546, from preparatory studies for Michelangelo's models of St. Peter's. The verso contains an elevation of the exterior of the drum of St. Peter's (Millon and Smyth 1969: fig. 15).
Attributed by Ferri (1885: 151) to Vignola, Uffizi 95A has not figured in the literature on Vignola. Ferri associated the drawing with two others, Uffizi 96A and 93A, also attributed to Vignola. Millon and Smyth (1969: 495) felt that both recto and verso of Uffizi 96A (cat. no. 376) and 93A (ibid., figs. 22 and 23) were by the same hand as the

verso of Uffizi 95A, but were less certain that the recto of Uffizi 95A was also by the same draftsman. They thought it to have been drawn before 1555, when construction of the south apse reached the level of the window heads. In this view, the other five sides of the drawings in the Uffizi were drawn sometime in the period 1556-64. Saalman, in his study "Michelangelo: S. Maria del Fiore and St. Peter's" (1975: 374-409), which includes discussion of Uffizi 96A and 93A, as well as 95A recto, concluded that Uffizi 95A recto was drawn in the early months of 1547 before work on the wooden model "began in earnest." Saalman felt the gross differences of scaled measurements on the drawing, when compared with scaled measurements taken from the print by Luchino (cat. no. 373) and from published elevations of the building by Carlo Fontana (*Templum Vaticanum*, Rome, 1964) meant the drawing could only have been drawn before the general dimensions and proportions of the exterior membering had been decided. The *inscribed* dimensions all differ from the scaled dimensions. They are more closely related to scaled measurements taken from the print by Luchino. The inscribed dimensions may be later and perhaps by a different hand.
The drawing of the drum on Uffizi 95A verso might have been done as early as the end of 1556. Most of the inscribed dimensions include *minuti* up through the lower part of the windows, the height reached when work on the drum was interrupted in December 1556. The drawing on 95A verso is closely related to the section drawing through the drum on Uffizi 96A verso (cat. no. 376).

H.A.M.-C.H.S.

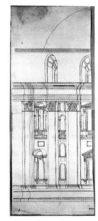

375
ANONYMOUS
Elevation of the West Half of the South of St. Peter's

Stockholm, Nationalmuseum, Cronstedt Collection, CC 2150
Pen, brown ink; scale; trimmed at bottom.
522 × 190 mm

PROVENANCE: Cronstedt Collection.

BIBLIOGRAPHY: unpublished.

Cronstedt 2150 is most likely drawn after the print of the south apse of St. Peter's published by Vincenzo Luchino in 1564 (cat. no. 373) and showing the original attic constructed during Michelangelo's tenure. The drawing in Stockholm also includes, above the attic, an arc describing the upper surface of the vault of the apse, absent from the print of Luchino. The vault as depicted in the drawing, however, is too elevated when compared with the view of St. Peter's as constructed which is in the Städelsches Kunstinstitut at Frankfurt (cat. no. 377) and shows the south apse.
This drawing in Stockholm appears to be dependent on the engraving by Luchino. If so, it probably dates between 1565-70.

H.A.M.-C.H.S.

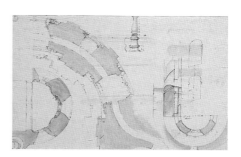

376
ANONYMOUS
Plans of the South Apse and Southwest (?) Lumaca of St. Peter's

Florence, Galleria degli Uffizi, Gabinetto Disegni e Stampe, Uff. 96A
Pen, brown ink and wash, incised lines, with dimensions in brown ink.
436/440 × 284/299 mm (trimmed, leaving a *tab 15 × 79* at upper right)
RECTO: a) plan of the south apse at the attic level (lower left); b) plan of apse at the level of first corridor (center); c) plan and section of a lumaca (right); d) elevation of a baluster of an exterior window at the second level (upper center).
INSCRIBED: *diamitro* (lower right); various inscribed dimensions.
VERSO: a) section/elevation of the drum; b) plan of spiral stair within the drum (lower center).
INSCRIBED: various inscribed dimensions.

PROVENANCE: unavailable.

BIBLIOGRAPHY: Ferri 1885: 151; Millon and Smyth 1969: 484-500; Saalman 1975: 386-397; Keller 1976: 38.

The sheet includes three drawings of the south apse of St. Peter's. Reading from left to right, there is a plan of the attic level showing the three attic windows, salient arch, and southwest *lumaca* (circular ramp that flanks the apse hemicycle); then a half-plan of the main body of the apse, taken at the level of the corridor and main windows; above is an elevation of a baluster from one of the windows; and, further right, a half-plan and half-section through a *lumaca*.
The plan at the left is the only known plan of the attic of St. Peter's as built by Michelangelo in 1557-58 on the south apse, a design which preceded the attic currently on the basilica. The attic in this plan corroborates the first attic as depicted in the print of the elevation of the south hemicycle, published by Vincenzo Luchino (cat. no. 373). The plan includes inscribed dimensions for the width of the openings on exterior and interior, as well as for the thickness (32 *palmi*) of the attic wall structure, a bit thicker than the attic today measured to its face (a bit less thick measured to the outer face of its pilaster bunches). (Keller [1976: 38, note 33] believed the draftsman inadvertently reversed the digits.) The window toward the southeast (the side opposite the *lumaca*) shows a reflected plan of some of the inner row of coffers, which are also seen in the elevation published by Luchino. The three half-oval lines

on the interior that span each of the interior openings may be intended to indicate flattened sections of the vault surface spanning between pilasters above the opening. If the *lumaca* included in this plan is intended to represent the location of the southwest *lumaca* in the building today, it should be placed further to the south and west.

The half plan of the apse at the level of the main window openings (center) with its corridor includes many inscribed dimensions with *oncie* and *minuti*, measurements so small that they could only have been taken from the building. The same may be said for the plan and section of the *lumaca* (right) and baluster (upper center). Many of the inscribed dimensions agree with measurements recently taken on the building. Thus, the drawings on the recto appear to have been made on site (with compass and straightedge, at three different scales) to capture dimensions, drawings that could later, over a drafting table, result in scaled and measured drawings.

The Uffizi sheet was listed by Ferri (1885: 151), grouped with two others, Uffizi 93A and 95A, and attributed to Vignola. With the exception of 95A recto (cat. no. 374), the remaining five sides appear to be by the same hand (Millon and Smyth 1969: 495). Coolidge (1942: 91) first published 95A recto, but reserved judgment on its attribution.

The section through the drum of St. Peter's on the verso includes inscribed dimensions with *oncie* and *minuti* up to the level of the sills of the windows, again suggesting dimensions taken from the building. Above that height, dimensions are given in round numbers. The ink drawing extends through the capitals of the columns on the exterior and pilasters on the interior and then includes a profile of the main entablature above the columns of the pier buttresses, but goes no further. Above, there are chalk lines indicating a low dome. A light brown wash extends only through the level of the capitals. The evidence on the verso of the sheet thus suggests the drawing there was made when the construction of the drum had reached the height of the sills of the windows. Construction may have reached this height before it was interrupted at the end of 1556, to be begun anew only in May 1561 (Millon and Smyth 1969: 495 n. 37). Hence, the drawing on the verso could have been done at any time between late 1556 and the recommencement of work on the drum in 1561. The drawing on the recto may have been drawn at the same time, but it has the appearance of a drawing done to record the state of the structure on the south perhaps prior to or just after the change of architects following the death of Michelangelo in 1564.

For a different view that dates the drawing on the recto in the several months before work "began in earnest" on the definitive wooden model of St. Peter's in March 1547, see Saalman 1975: 386-397. *H.A.M.-C.H.S.*

377

ANONYMOUS
View of St. Peter's from the Southeast

Frankfurt, Städelsches Kunstinstitut, 814
Pen, brown ink.
229 × 201 mm

BIBLIOGRAPHY: Egger 1911, pl. 41; Ackerman 1961, II: 96; 1964, II: 98; Wittkower 1964a, pl. 42; Winner 1966: 308-309; Millon and Smyth 1969: 492 n. 20; 1976: 77 n. 36; 1988c: 242 n. 5; 1988a: 102, fig. E.

This well-known view of St. Peter's from the north slope of the Janiculum Hill is important in showing the attic order of the south apse as originally intended by Michelangelo, the state of construction of the Cappella della Colonna (S. Marta) to the southwest, and the Cappella Clementina to the southeast, the building of the drum above the Cappella Gregoriana, and the completed portions of the entablature of the drum at the crossing. The drawing dates between late 1580 and mid-1581 (Millon and Smyth 1969, 492 n. 20). Together with the drawing in Stuttgart (Anonymous Fabriczy) it confirms the extent of the entablature of the dome left incomplete in May 1568, at the time construction on the drum was halted (Millon and Smyth 1988c: 226, and n. 75).

H.A.M.-C.H.S.

378

AFTER MICHELANGELO
Wood Model for the Vault of the South Apse of St. Peter's

Vatican, Fabbrica di S. Pietro
Lime wood and other woods, gray (walls) and yellow (membering) paint.
39 × 79.5 × 47 cm (inside dimensions)

PROVENANCE: workshop of Michelangelo.

BIBLIOGRAPHY: Millon and Smyth 1976: 137-206; Tolnay 1980, IV: 93; Nova 1984: 193; Ackerman 1986: 318, 320, 323; Argan and Contardi 1990: 327 and fig. 431.

To judge from his own words, it was Michelangelo's habit to have a model built for everything he did (text in two letters to Vasari, Casa Vasari I, cat. no. 379 and Casa Vasari II, cat. no. 380). Though only three of his models survive (cat. nos. 378, 396, 235), many others are known through documents and representations. This model of the vault of the apse of the south transept of St. Peter's, one of the three extant models of Michelangelo, was made as he contemplated erecting the vault of the south apse in late 1556 or early 1557.

The model bears traces of alteration that enable reconstruction of its original condition. It bears witness to initial measurements taken and assumptions made by the model maker. The two states of the model, the two building campaigns of the vault (the second campaign coming after an error made during the first campaign caused dismantling and rebuilding of the vault), and two letters of Michelangelo to Vasari in the Casa Vasari with drawings explaining the vaulting error (cat. nos. 379, 380), taken together, chronicle Michelangelo's twice seizing an unanticipated opportunity to rethink the design of the vault of the south apse. The history of the apse vault model and of the vault is discussed in Millon and Smyth (1976: 162-184).

The vault model was made at a scale of 1:30, the same scale as the model of Sangallo (cat. no. 346), most likely so that the vault model could be placed in the Sangallo model (where it was discovered in our day) and be studied there in relation to the main vault of the transept and the pilasters of the main order below. It appears that the model maker measured the space occupied by one of the vault models of the Sangallo model (or one of the vault models itself). He apparently did not notice that the apse vaults in the Sangallo model include the area occupied by the salient arch that marks the juncture of the transept vault with the apse vault and corresponds to the salient pilasters at the junction of transept and apse. In the apse vaults of the Sangallo model, the salient arch (one of which Sangallo erected at the east end of the nave) was drawn on paper and glued to the vault model. The remains of one of these drawn arches still exists on the model.

The first error of the model maker was to assume that the dimensions taken from Sangallo's model corresponded to the apse vault alone and not apse vault plus salient arch. Secondly, when calculating the height of the vault, the model maker assumed correctly that the vault model should include the stilting (or raising) of the main vault as it is on the building. (The stilting, or raising the spring point of the main barrel vaults of St. Peter's by more than two meters, was done to avoid the vaults appearing depressed when viewed from below and when partially obscured by the projection of the principal cornice of the main entablature.) The model maker apparently did not notice, however, that the main vault of the Sangallo model is semicircular. It *omits* the stilting of the vault as constructed on the building and rests on top of the main cornice.

Unaware of these two anomalies, the model maker built the apse vault to extend into and occupy the area of the salient arch on the model and to include the stilted vertical wall surface beneath the springing of the main vaults of the building. These "mistakes" would have become manifest as soon as the newly painted vault model was placed inside the Sangallo model. Not only would the stilting be immediately apparent, but the windows and ribs would not have been in alignment with the windows and pilasters of the apse below. Not least, the salient pilaster of Sangallo's model found no corresponding member in the vault above.

Rather than discard the model, Michelangelo, who had originally envisaged a salient arch at the juncture of transept and apse vaults, rethought the apse vault design, stimulated perhaps by seeing his vault model in place. The vertical zone was cut off to match the vaults of the Sangallo model. Traces of this reduction remain on the vault model. Next, to align windows and ribs in the vault with corresponding parts in the wall below, he had a pie-shaped section removed from the center of the vault model, rotating the halves to close the gap. This made the center bay narrower (25 cm) than the left (31.5 cm) and right (31.2 cm) bays. The remains of the tondo in the center bay had to be chiseled away and an unpainted replacement inserted. In addition, the central window was widened to approximate the width of the two side windows. At the outside edges of the vault model, crudely fashioned wedge-shaped ribs were inserted to respond to the salient pilasters below. These adjustments made, Michelangelo apparently began construction of the vault following either this altered model or possibly another made from it for the foreman to follow in construction. In this condition the apse vault model was drawn by Etienne Dupérac, or an assistant (cat. no. 381), as information was gathered preparatory to the making of his prints of St. Peter's. The print of the section of St. Peter's by Dupérac includes portions of the altered vault model.

In the last part of June 1557 a flaw in the construction came to light. It was due to an error of the foreman in making the curvature of the centering. By Michelangelo's own account, the mistake was first realized as construction of the vault "began to draw near the half-medallion that is at the crown of the said vault" (text of Casa Vasari I, cat. no. 379). The vault had to be dismantled. The dismantling was still not finished as late as 17 August, according to the second letter Michelangelo wrote to Vasari on that day (Casa Vasari II, cat. no. 380). The rebuilding of the apse vault was completed only in early June 1558, a year after discovering the error.

Michelangelo's first letter to Vasari of 1 July 1557 (Casa Vasari I), when the dismantling was underway, includes two drawings, the upper one a section/elevation of the vault, and below, an elevation drawn, as the text says, to show the incorrect curvature (of the gores) in red chalk, and the correct curvature in black chalk. The upper drawing represents the ribs, windows, tondi, panels and half-medallion at the crown. The ribs at the edge of the vault appear to be the wedge-shaped ribs inserted in the apse vault model rising from the base to the half-medallion, the ribs that replaced the salient arch in the altered vault model.

During the dismantling of the vault, Michelangelo had a second oppurtunity to rethink the design of the vault. This he had done by the time he wrote a second letter to Vasari on 17 Agust 1557 (Casa Vasari II). This letter, providing further explanation about the apse vault, includes a plan of the apse showing ribs, half-medallion, and tondi. The curvature of the gores are shown in flattened section. On this drawing the area of the apse vault is a semicircle and does not include the area of the salient arch; the half-medallion is shown abutting the arch. Remaining from the previous design are the riblets at the edges of the two side gores that rise to the half-medallion. (These, too, were eliminated by the time the vault was reconstructed.) The curvature of the gores in the drawing appears to be increased when compared with the gores of the apse vault model and closer to the curvature on the building.

To increase the curvature of the gores Michelangelo lowered the spring point of the segmental arches, which mark the intersection of the gore with the wall area above the windows: from the level in the apse vault model (about the height of the lintel over the windows) the spring point was lowered to a level about two-thirds of the height of the windows, as seen on the building. On the building, a cornice binds the ribs and little pilasters under the arches of the gores; on the model, the rib panels are interrupted at the level of the cornice of the little pilasters. The paint surface there is rougher. A cornice may once have been placed there as shown on the drawing of the apse vault model by Dupérac or an assistant in the Metropolitan Museum (cat. no. 381).

The second building campaign for the south apse vault saw construction of the newly designed vault with gores more deeply curved than in the first campaign, lower pilasters, and with the wedge-shaped ribs replaced by a salient arch. The increased curvature of the gores, the separating of window head from the spring points of the

ribs and segmental arches greatly increased vertical continuity from the pilasters below to the half-medallion at the crown of the vault. Michelangelo's apse vault model with its alterations provides a unique opportunity to study the evolution of a vault design that was a recognized marvel in its own time. *H.A.M.-C.H.S.*

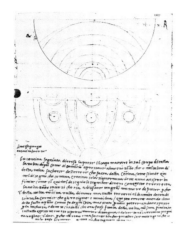

379

Michelangelo Buonarroti

Letter Dated 1 July 1557 from Michelangelo to Giorgio Vasari with Drawings of the Vault of the South Apse of St. Peter's (Casa Vasari I)

Arezzo, Casa Vasari, Archivio Vasariano, Codex 12 (46), fol. 22v.

Red and black chalk (drawing), pen, brown ink (text). 284 × 211 mm

Provenance: Giorgio Vasari.

Bibliography: Milanesi 1875a: 546; D. Frey 1923: 481; Pecchiai, ed. 1929-30, III, 459; Tolnay 1932: 234 n. 2; Schiavo 1949, fig. 119; 1953: 213; Düssler 1959: 49 no. 1; Bean 1960, no. 68; Ackerman 1961, II: 94; Barocchi 1962, IV: 1693-95; Ramsden 1963, II, no. 437; Portoghesi and Zevi 1964a, pl. 520; Barbieri and Puppi 1964a, 916-917; Ackerman 1964, II: 96, 101, 103; Tolnay 1965: 250; Hartt 1971: 352; Millon and Smyth 1976: 162-184; Francia 1977: 91; Tolnay 1980, IV: 92-93, fig. 593; Ackerman 1986: 320-321, 323; Argan and Contardi 1990: 327, fig. 433.

This autograph letter of 1 July 1557 by Michelangelo to Vasari (hereafter Casa Vasari I) contains two drawings of the apse vault of the south hemicycle of St. Peter's. They were drawn to explain an error in the construction of the vault which necessitated its dismantling and reconstruction. Most authors, including Vasari (Vasari, ed. Milanesi 1881, VII: 247), have not questioned Michelangelo's authorship of the drawings, but Frey (1923: 483) thought those portions in black chalk to be drawn by an assistant with Michelangelo adding only the arcs in red (those with less curvature). Düssler (1959: 49) agreed with Frey's analysis of the lower of the two drawings, but stated that in the upper drawing, while straightedge and compass parts were drawn by an assistant, the tondi (mistakenly called oculi) and windows (and presumably the other portions drawn freehand) "unmistakenly reveal Michelangelo's own hand." We see no reason to disagree with Vasari's contemporary view and consider the two drawings (as well as the one drawn on Casa Vasari II, cat. no. 380) likely to have been drawn by Michelangelo himself (Millon and Smyth 1976: 172-181). For the text of the letter see Milanesi 1875a: 546, no. CDLXXXIII; D. Frey 1923: 481, no. CCLIV; Barocchi 1962, IV: 1693; Ramsden 1963, II, no. 437.

Michelangelo explained that the error in the vaulting was due to the foreman's misunderstanding of the shape the curvature of the vault should have. The nature of the error as explained in the text and drawings of this letter and its

successor, Casa Vasari II, can only apply to the curvature of the individual gores and not to the whole vault, as is generally assumed.

In the lower drawing the curvature of the centering is drawn as an elevation, not a plan. The letter says it shows the incorrect curvature followed by the foreman with red lines (those of less curvature), the correct curvature with black lines (those of more curvature). The red lines are all drawn with equal radii, but from different centers on the vertical line, resulting in a surface that always has the same curvature instead of a changing one. The black lines, showing the centering as it should be, are drawn with different radii from the same center at the top of the semicircle, resulting in a curvature that constantly increases as the crown of the vault is approached. This changing curvature, unrelated to the whole span of Michelangelo's vault, coincides with the curvature of its individual gores as built.

The two curvatures can be pictured properly by superimposing the central pair of ribs from the drawing above on the lower drawing. The portion of red and black chalk between the ribs gives the two different curvatures at various heights of the gore. The difference between the incorrect and correct curvatures becomes substantial and more apparent as the construction begins "to draw near the half-medallion that is in the crown of said vault" (text, Casa Vasari I), where the smaller radius of the correct vaulting produces a sharply increased curvature. This may well be why the mistake was discovered only as construction approached the half-medallion.

The upper drawing pictures the entire apse vault. It is also an elevation, but not a true one: it is flattened, to show the three gores of the vault roughly equal in width. The half-medallion at the crown is drawn flat, showing its junction with the two central ribs and also with the two outer ribs. The striking fact is that, beside the two central ribs, the drawing shows at the vault's open end the two wedge-shaped ribs in Michelangelo's revised apse vault model, discussed in the entry on the apse vault model (cat no. 378). The drawing thus testifies that when Michelangelo wrote this letter he was thinking in terms of the outer wedge-shaped ribs. It offers confirming evidence that the revision of the apse vault model was indeed Michelangelo's and that the model represents considered stages in the evolution of the apse vault design.

All the elements necessary to illustrate the text are drawn with compass and straightedge: the gores, the ribs, the half-medallion at the crown, the segmental arches at the base of the gores, and the tondi in the gores. The remaining elements were drawn freehand and unassertively, the least assertive being the windows and bases of the ribs. Both are small, seeming almost an afterthought. These elements, indeed all the elements between the ribs, are placed too low. The windows are below the diameter of the semicircle, instead of above; the segmental arches and the tondi are correspondingly low, allowing room for an extra trapezoid in each gore.

The drawing shows cornices across the face of the ribs at the level of the spring points of the segmental arches, about at the level of the lintels of the windows. A cornice once existed at this level on the apse vault model (cat. no. 378), to judge from its inclusion in a drawing from the model by Dupérac or an assistant in the Metropolitan Museum (cat. no. 381).

Though cornices are now lacking across the ribs of the vault model, the little pilasters and the spring points of the segmental arches in the model form a continuous horizontal with the tops of the windows. The repetition of these height relationships in the drawing confirms that Michelangelo once intended a continuous horizontal at this level. In the vault as ultimately constructed in the second campaign, however, rib cornices, little pilaster capitals or cornices, and spring points for the segmental arches are all markedly lower than the window heads, producing a notably different effect. *H.A.M.-C.H.S.*

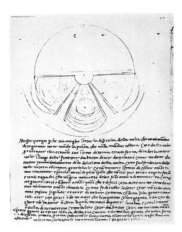

380

MICHELANGELO BUONARROTI
Letter Dated 17 August 1557 from Michelangelo to Giorgio Vasari with a Drawing of the Vault of the South Apse of St. Peter's (Casa Vasari II)

Arezzo, Casa Vasari, Archivio Vasariano, Codex 12 (46), fol. 24r.

Black chalk (drawing), pen, brown ink (text).

284 × 211 mm

PROVENANCE: Giorgio Vasari.

BIBLIOGRAPHY: Milanesi 1875a: 547; D. Frey 1923: 484; Pecchiai, ed. 1929-30, II: 459; Tolnay 1932: 234; Schiavo 1949: fig. 119; Schiavo 1953: 213; Düssler 1959: n. 1; Ackerman 1961, II: 94; Barocchi IV, 1962: 1693-95; Ramsden 1963, II: no. 438; Portoghesi and Zevi 1964: pl. 521; Barbieri and Puppi 1964a: 916-917; Ackerman 1964, II: 96, 101, 103; Tolnay 1965: 250; Hartt 1971: 352; Millon and Smyth 1976: 162-184; Francia 1977: 91; Tolnay 1980, IV: 93, fig. 594; Ackerman 1986: 320-321, 323; Argan and Contardi 1990: 327, fig. 434.

This second autograph letter from Michelangelo to Vasari of 17 August 1557 (hereafter Casa Vasari II) contains a drawing of the apse vault of the south hemicycle of St. Peter's. The drawing and text are further explanations (apparently requested by Vasari in response to a letter of 1 July 1557 [Casa Vasari I, cat. no. 379]) of the error in the construction of the vault that necessitated its dismantling and reconstruction. Most authors, including Vasari (Vasari, ed. Milanesi 1881, VII: 247) accept the drawing as by Michelangelo's hand. (Düssler 1959 does not mention Casa Vasari II.) For the text of the letter see Milanesi 1875a: 547, no. CDLXXXIV; Frey 1923: 484, no. CCLV; Barocchi 1962, IV: 1694; Ramsden 1963, II, no. 438.
Between 1 July and 17 August 1557 when Michelangelo wrote his second letter to Vasari, he redesigned the apse vault, restoring the salient arch. The letter includes a reflected plan of the vault, showing the two center ribs, half-medallion, and, in flattened section, the curvature of the gores.
But the plan in Casa Vasari II does not agree with the upper elevation in Casa Vasari I (cat. no. 379). Casa Vasari II does not have the wedge-shaped ribs. Also, the half-medallion is contained within the semicircle of the apse, whereas before, with the wedge—shaped ribs in the drawing of 1 July, the half-medallion had necessarily to extend beyond the semicircle into the area now occupied in the building by the salient arch because the wedge shaped ribs had to abut the half-medallion. When he reinstated the salient arch, Michelangelo pulled the half-medallion back within the semicircle, as it is on Casa Vasari II, Clearly, Michelangelo contemplated returning to a solution with a salient arch when he made this drawing. There is no line separating the half-medallion and the area where the salient arch was to be, an indication that the half-medallion and arch are at the same level, as in the building today.
But the drawing on Casa Vasari II shows narrow moldings at the junction of the side gores with the salient arch, moldings similar to those outlining the central ribs in this drawing. The building as finally constructed does not

have them. As drawn here, they may be smaller, vestigial versions of the wedge-shaped ribs.
The drawing also testifies to the deepening of the gores by this date and, most likely, the abandonment of a continuous horizontal at the level of the window lintel. The section lines in the drawing indicate gores with a curvature approximately the same as that found in the building, greater than in the apse vault model and the upper elevation of Casa Vasari I. The drawing is evidence that Michelangelo had made a decision by this date, not only to deepen the gores, but to do so by lowering the spring point of the segmental arches while keeping the crown of the arch at the same height. This second change also took place during the month and a half between the two letters to Vasari. The redesign of the vault resulted in a fundamental modification, which greatly enhanced the nature of both the ribs and the gores.
The pilaster-piers with ressauts, and the recessed walls with large openings at the second level of the main order, differentiated support structure from enclosure which might be shaped at will. That distinction was further emphasized in the apse vault as finally constructed. The newly accented ribs extend the verticals of the pilaster-pier supports to the crown of the vault, while the deeply curved gores underscore the malleable nature of Michelangelo's vaults. This remarkably coherent conceptual vocabulary became a source of inspiration for Giacomo della Porta, Carlo Maderno, Francesco Borromini, and later generations. *H.A.M.-C.H.S.*

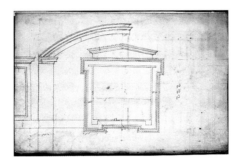

381

CIRCLE OF ETIENNE DUPÉRAC
Elevation of a Window on the Interior of the Apse Vault of St. Peter's

New York, The Metropolitan Museum of Art, 49.92.89r.
Pen, brown ink over black chalk, incised lines: scale: 2 *minuti* = 1 *palmo* (reconstructed).
289 × 426 mm
INSCRIBED: various dimensions in ink; the number 222 in graphite at right is probably a later addition.

PROVENANCE: Janos and Anne Bigelow Scholz, in memory of Flying Officer Walter Bigelow Rosen, 1949.

BIBLIOGRAPHY: Millon and Smyth 1976: 185-198. For bibliography on the Scholz Collection, see Millon and Smyth 1988a: 103.

Drawn from the apse vault model (cat. no. 378) at the same scale (1:30), Metropolitan Museum 49.92.89 recto appears to have been a preparatory drawing for the print of the section through St. Peter's by Dupérac (cat. no. 394) and dates from about 1569. Some inscribed dimensions include *minuti* and must have come from the building or an intermediate source. One dimension can only have come from the vault model (cat. no. 378), where the pilaster to the left of the central window is unusually large, scaling *palmi* 4 *oncie* 2. That measurement inscribed on the drawing is *palmi* 4 *oncie* 5. (The other pilasters on the vault model measure *palmi* 3 *oncie* 8, or less small.)
In some aspects, however, the drawing differs from both the vault model and the building and must reflect an additional source or sources. The window opening has inscribed dimensions of 15 × 16 *palmi*, a slightly horizontal rectangle, rather than the virtually square windows of the model and the more decisively rectangular windows of the

building (Millon and Smyth 1976: 168 n. 19). The shoulders, or lugs, of the upper portion of the window-frame moldings in the drawing are smaller than on the the model and the building. The recessed slots, also in the upper corners of the window in the drawing in the Metropolitan, are narrower than on the building and are absent in the model. Yet further, the rib cornice at left is only the width of the rib panel and not the full width of the rib, as on the building and in the print by Dupérac.
These details testify to a source besides the vault model and the building. The draftsman may have had access to a later "corrected" vault model made prior to the construction of the vault, a model that would have followed the erection of the vault in the first campaign (late 1556/early 1557 to about 15 June 1557). This design, in turn, was superseded in the second campaign, following the dismantling of much of the vault erected in the first campaign. *H.A.M.-C.H.S.*

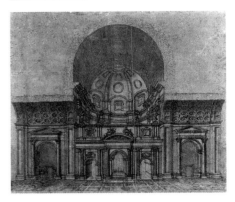

382

ANONYMOUS
Section/Perspective of a Proposal for the Choir of St. Peter's

Windsor Castle, Royal Library, RL 5590
Pen, brown ink and wash, laid down.
370 × 422 mm

PROVENANCE: Albani (?).

BIBLIOGRAPHY: Thelen 1967: 14 n. 2, fig. 24; Lavin 1969, fig. 34; Hibbard 1971, fig. 73c; Millon and Smyth 1976: 197 n. 40.

The drawing at Windsor, first published by Thelen (1967), depicts the vault of the west apse as constructed in the late sixteenth century, but with the spring points for the main ribs of the vault and the segmental arches above the windows drawn too high, at the level of the soffit of the windows. On the building, the spring point is well below the level of the attic window. The drawing includes a cornice, as on the building today, at the base of the ribs and extending across the flanking pilasters that receive the segmental arches above the windows.
A drawing by G.P. Schor of the decoration of St. Peter's for the canonization of St. Thomas of Villanova on 7 November 1658 (Windsor Castle RL 11595—published by Fagiolo and Fagiolo [1967, fig. 33]) shows both the apse vault of the north hemicycle and a portion of the vault of the west apse.
Although the barrel vaults of the north transept and the west choir are represented without the stucco decoration they now possess, the *apse* vaults are shown as they were prior to embellishment.
Apart from the anomaly of the segmental arch and window head height noted above, the drawing at Windsor is convincing evidence of the state of the west apse vault in the 1620s and, if constructed to match the vaults on the north and south arms, testimony to their appearance as well. All three were constructed of exposed travertine and devoid of decorative embellishment. *H.A.M.-C.H.S.*

The Design of the Drum and Dome of St. Peter's in Rome
Henry A. Millon and Craig Hugh Smyth

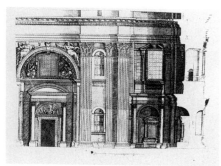

383
MARTINO FERRABOSCO
Section Through the South Transept of St. Peter's Looking East
(Martino Ferrabosco, *Libro de l'architettura di San Pietro nel Vaticano...*, Rome, 1620, pls. XXIII and XXIV)

Vatican, Biblioteca Apostolica Vaticana
Engraving.
470 × 530; 470 × 530 mm

BIBLIOGRAPHY: Millon and Smyth 1976: 152-153, fig. 9; Metternich and Thoenes 1987: 127 n. 229.

The section through the south transept of St. Peter's shown in these two plates (from the exhaustive survey of St. Peter's by Martino Ferrabosco) is the first representation to include the second attic order with its internal corridor after the attic of the south transept was transformed in the latter part of the first decade of the seventeenth century (Millon and Smyth 1969: 487-488 n. 6).
The section also depicts correctly the vertical wall area—the stilting—beneath the attic windows and the spring point of the barrel vault of the transept, an area mistakenly omitted in the print by Dupérac of 1569-70 (cat. no. 394) showing a section through St. Peter's. (Dupérac omission is curious since the stilting had been shown correctly in the earlier section of St. Peter's published in 1549 by Salamanca, even though the stilting is not present in Sangallo's model of St. Peter's [cat. no. 346]). This matched pair of prints by Ferrabosco is also valuable in showing the difference between the treatment of the apse and that of the transept arm, both at the lower levels and in the vaulting. The coffered vault of the transept, richly decorated in gilded stucco, contrasts sharply with the smooth exposed travertine surface of the apse vault, much admired by Vasari (Vasari, ed. Milanesi 1878, I: 123-124). *H.A.M.-C.H.S.*

384
ANONYMOUS
View from the Nave of St. Peter's Looking West

Bath, James Lees-Milne Collection
Oil on canvas.
111.5 × 125 cm

BIBLIOGRAPHY: Lees-Milne 1967: 238; Millon and Smyth 1976: 153-154 and nn. 39 and 40.

First published by Lees-Milne (1967, 238), the painting is among the few representations of St. Peter's in color that testify to the condition of the vaults, piers and walls prior to their embellishment in the seventeenth and eighteenth centuries. Michelangelo intended the apses and apse vaults of the north and south arms (and, presumably, the west apse as well) to be exposed travertine, an unusual practice commented on in letters to Vasari by Michelangelo himself (Frey 1923: 481 and 484). Vasari reports (Vasari, ed. Milanesi 1878, I: 123-124) that the south apse vault "appears to be made out of one piece" of travertine.
While the pavement may be fanciful (Carlo Maderno's original brick pavement was not replaced until the reign of Innocent X for the Jubilee of 1650—Hibbard 1971: 71--72), the remainder of the structure appears to have been rendered faithfully, giving a valuable representation of an apse of St. Peter's as designed by Michelangelo, without later surface decoration. The gilded vault of the nave, completed in 1616 (Hibbard 1971: 185),is shown in the painting, while the columns of Bernini's baldachino, erected in 1626 (Wittkower 1966: 189), are absent, providing a date for the painting of between 1616-26. *H.A.M.-C.H.S.*

St. Peter's is acknowledged to be one of the most important structures in the history of architecture. Enclosing and commemorating the tomb of the first apostle, St. Peter's is the largest, most imposing religious building of the Christian West, the center of the papacy and a goal of Christian pilgrimage. It also incorporates the architectural aspirations and achievements of generations of architects, chief among them Bramante, Michelangelo and Carlo Maderno. Michelangelo's vision of active forces within architectural structure and materials and his way of combining ancient with Christian architecture to achieve a new architecture invested with religious significance have imbued the building with a distinctive conception of Christian grandeur. Michelangelo planned to make St. Peter's a centralized building. If his plan had been retained, the drum and dome would have dominated the view of the building and made of it a monumental reliquary.
Whereas Michelangelo himself built most of the drum of the dome—it was on the way to being finished when he died in 1564—the dome was constructed almost twenty years after his death by the architect Giacomo della Porta. Observers, beginning shortly after the dome was built, have indicated that della Porta did not follow Michelangelo's design in its entirety. Scholars have devoted much study, therefore, to determining as precisely as possible what Michelangelo's final design of the dome was and how much della Porta's dome differs.
This section of the catalog has been written in anticipation of the opportunity to study in one place most of the material relating to Michelangelo's drum and dome of St. Peter's: model, medal, paintings, drawings and prints. Once gathered in the exhibition, the items can be studied in relation to one another. The catalog is intended to provide a starting point for further study.
Michelangelo's model of the drum and dome is the subject of this portion of the exhibition. Many studies have concluded that the model is not in its original state. Hence, the material related to the model is arranged in the catalog in an order that we hope can best help to elucidate the original state of the model and Michelangelo's design.
a) First comes the material most recently brought to light, which, it now appears, best documents Michelangelo's model of the drum, dome and lantern in its original state. This material consists of drawings at the Metropolitan Museum in New York and the National Museum in Stockholm from the shop of the French architect Etienne Dupérac, made in preparation for Dupérac's prints of St. Peter's and dating roughly 1560-79. Included here also are the prints themselves.
b) Michelangelo's model of the drum and dome is found earlier in the catalog. It will be seen that we are in accord with the view that the model incorporates changes traceable to Giacomo della Porta, the architect who constructed the dome of St. Peter's after Michelangelo's death, and to Luigi Vanvitelli, the mid-eighteenth-century architect who was consulted about the dome.
c) Then comes a plan of St. Peter's from Windsor Castle and a medal showing St. Peter's from the east, both dating from the reign of Gregory XIII. The plan shows that as late as the election of Gregory XIII, no final decision had been made about the design of the facade. The medal, on the other hand, demonstrates that during his reign it was proposed to complete the facade with a hexastyle portico and build the dome with a hemispherical profile.
d) Thereafter are two drawings that show the state of construction of the dome in 1563, a year before the death of Michelangelo.

Filippino Lippi, Virgin and Child with Saints, *detail*
Florence, S. Spirito

e) The painting in the Casa Buonarroti executed in 1619 by Domenico Passignano is included next. It will be seen that in our view the painting gives evidence of changes that Giacomo della Porta made to Michelangelo's model of the drum and dome in preparation for constructing the dome.
f) The catalog then turns to the all-too-rare drawings showing the drum under construction and the drawings for the drum and dome by Michelangelo and from his shop, including the important drawing from the Musée des Beaux-Arts at Lille. These show something of the way Michelangelo developed his design. In this section there is a drawing by Buontalenti of the lantern in one of its early states.
g) Then come drawings of Giovanni Antonio Dosio. As observations of earlier scholars have indicated, these reveal some later stages in the development of Michelangelo's design, during the construction of the model of the drum and dome.
h) Last is a prints of the drum and dome from the seventeenth century by Carlo Fontana that records the building as constructed.
Basic information about the construction of Michelangelo's model and of the drum and dome on the building has been published by, among others, Barocchi (1962b, IV: 1700-29), Schiavo (1965: 303-327), Barbieri and Puppi (1964a: 916-919), Wittkower (1964a: Appendix I), Ackerman (1964, II: 95-96, 107-114), Saalman (1975: 374-380, 397-401), Wittkower (1978b: 70-89), Di Stefano (1980b: 59-66) and Millon and Smyth (1988a: 93-187)—to cite only more recent contributions. Scholars have been concerned above all with two main problems: 1) whether the finished model in its original state had a hemispherical or an elevated dome and 2) whether the dome as built by Giacomo della Porta with an elevated profile represents Michelangelo's final wishes or not. Many scholars now believe that the model as it is today is not in its original condition. Material in the exhibition offers evidence that changes have been made to the original model in the attic, outer dome and lantern, but that the drum and inner dome remain virtually in their original state as Michelangelo left them. The question has long been whether the external dome of the model was originally elevated or hemispherical. (For a sampling of writings on these problems, see Barocchi 1962b, IV: 1710-24.) Thanks to the drawings in the Dupérac group in the Metropolitan, that question, we think, has been answered much as Wittkower proposed in 1933 and 1964a, when he assembled evidence that both domes of the model in its original state were hemispherical—a position he

reaffirmed in 1978b. In the present condition of the model, the profile of the outer dome is not hemispherical but raised, leaving a large space between the two domes at the oculus. The evidence indicates that the outer dome differs from the original in fundamental respects: profile, attic cornice, ribs, dormer windows, and lantern. These changes appear on the model depicted in the painting by Passignano in 1619 and on the building itself, leading us to agree with those scholars who believe that it was della Porta who altered the model preparatory to building the dome (see, for example, Giovannoni 1942: 11-12), in spite of the lack of any archival documentation. There are other views, however. One holds that the exterior dome of the model originally had a raised profile (more recently Brandi [1968: 4 n. 2, 9, 11, 14], for example, who at the same time recognizes the lantern has been changed). In another view, the entire exterior dome and lantern of the model were built in the mid-eighteenth century by Vanvitelli (Schiavo 1965: 320). (Gioseffi [1960: 17-25] has seen the entire exterior dome of the model in its present state as hemispherical but raised from its original position.) Orbaan (1917: 196), Schiavo (1965: 304-305) and others have cited the testimony of Grimaldi, the Vatican archivist, concerning the curvature of the dome as constructed by della Porta in comparison to the hemisphere of Michelangelo's model. Grimaldi wrote that in the time of Sixtus V in a certain workshop in the stone yard at St. Peter's there were some models in plaster and wood of Michelangelo's St. Peter's as well as of the shell of his dome, and that it had [used to have] a shell that was somewhat lower, but that Giacomo della Porta had this dome raised higher because he judged that it would be more beautiful as well as stronger

(in platea lapicidarum in quadam officina ... sub Sixto V. erant ibi exempla aliqua gypsea et lignea templi Buonarotae, et testudinis ejus tholi, quam testudinem aliquantulum depressiorem tenebat; sed Jacobus a Porta ... tholum ipsum altiorum surgere fecit, quia consideravit venustiorem fore et etiam validiorem).

Thus Grimaldi believed that della Porta was responsible for the decision to raise the profile of the dome and that the dome Michelangelo designed was lower. The wording even seems to confirm della Porta's changing of the model itself.
In designing the drum and dome, Michelangelo would naturally have considered the domes for St. Peter's that had been proposed before his tenure, those of Bramante and Antonio da Sangallo among others, and also, given the closeness of the dimensions, the dome of the Pantheon as well. All these are single-shell domes. From the start, however, Michelangelo appears to have thought only of a double-shell dome, exemplified in his native Florence by the dome of the cathedral. That dome may also have led him to his innovative skeletal ribbed construction. For the extensive literature on these matters see most recently the bibliography in Di Stefano (1980b: 97-102), including, for example, Di Stefano's own comparison of the two domes (1980a: 871-882) and that of Saalman (1975), to which should be added Wittkower (1978b), Saalman (1980), Joannides (1981b) and Millon and Smyth (1988a). (An early stress on Michelangelo's attention to both the dome of the Pantheon and the dome of the cathedral of Florence is found in the writing of Carlo Fontana [1694: 315-316].) In this literature there are also studies of other sources for Michelangelo's design, from ancient Rome (the Pantheon) and Byzantium (Hagia Sophia) to the Early and High Renaissance (especially designs of Leonardo and Bramante): for instance, Giovannoni (1931a: 145-176), Gioseffi (1960: 37-53), Ackerman (1961, I: 98-101) and Bettini (1964).
Since preparing the catalog entries of 1988 on Michelangelo's model of the drum and dome of St. Peter's, we have noticed for the first time similarities in the drum and dome shown by Filippino Lippi in the background of his altarpiece in S. Spirito (Florence, S. Spirito, *Virgin and Child with Saints,* Berti and Baldini 1957: 35, 85, pl. XVIII). The drum and dome in the upper right in-

cludes a drum with columnar buttresses in combination with a ribbed hemispherical dome. This indicates that designs for a drum and dome of this sort were being considered in Florence in artist's studios as early as the 1490s (Baldini 1988: 24 and fig. 27; Bridgeman 1988: 668-671 and fig. 2). For some evidence that discussions and exchanges of information were general in artistic circles in Florence in these years, see F. W. Kent 1983 (590, no. 4). There is no reason not to assume that Michelangelo was aware of and took part in such discussions as Kent has shown took place in the studio of Lorenzo di Credi. It might also be noted that, previous to working on the drum and dome of St. Peter's, Michelangelo had considered salient corner pilasters as buttresses (Marchini 1977a: 39-40, figs. 11 and 13) or, perhaps, single or double columns (Tolnay 1980, IV: 28; Saalman 1975: 374-380; 1977: 852-853; Nova 1984: 35) for the drum of S. Maria del Fiore in Florence when preparing designs in 1507 and 1516 for the *ballatoio* of the cathedral.
But Michelangelo also rejected the uniform columnar drums of his predecessors Bramante and Sangallo and designed spur-like buttresses with double columns widely spaced, alternating with large pedimented windows. These were consonant with the ribbed skeleton of the dome and with the pier construction that characterizes Michelangelo's entire conception of the building. (There has been disagreement as to the importance of their actual function as buttresses: see among others Schiavo [1965], Brandi [1968], Di Stefano [1980b].) In addition, Michelangelo rejected the tall, wide dome and lantern of Sangallo and the low, stepped dome of Bramante and settled on a height and width for dome and lantern between those of Sangallo and Bramante.
The relation of the drum and dome to the main elevation is different now from what Michelangelo intended when he built the original attic order on the south apse. That order, having arched openings and sparse membering, capped the giant order with a major horizontal layer (in marked contrast to the vertical emphasis by the piers of the giant order and the arches in the attic order itself). This layering was in keeping with the principle applied in the design of the drum and dome.
Bramante in his design for New St. Peter's placed a dome above the tomb of the apostle, both reviving and continuing a tradition, stronger in the east, for commemorating the site of a martyr's tomb (Grabar 1946). From ancient times the dome has represented the heavens (Lehmann 1945; Wittkower 1949; Smith 1950, 1956; Chastel 1959a: 139-147; Bettini 1964). Lehmann has examined the development and use of representations of the hemisphere of heaven in domical structures in which a representation of the highest heaven is included at the center (Lehmann 1945). This center of heaven was represented as a circular ribbed canopy, or awning, from which the light of heaven radiated. In ancient times it was sometimes the light of Apollo the sun god, in Christian times the light of Christ. The oculus of domed structures became, according to Lehmann, the site of the canopy, the highest heaven. Sometimes the canopy included a small circular opening in its center. Michelangelo's screen across the oculus below the lantern at St. Peter's—it, too, with a small central opening—may have been his representation of that canopy. Thanks to the drawings of the screen in the exhibition, it is reasonable to surmise that Michelangelo's canopy, open, admitting light between its radial members, and intended to function as the symbolic center of heaven, the source of divine light.

A good bit of what is said here about the design of the drum and dome of St. Peter's repeats material published in a catalog of an exhibition of Michelangelo's architecture held at the Casa Buonarroti in Florence and the National Gallery of Art in Washington in 1988. Of the 40 objects devoted to Michelangelo's St. Peter's in the present exhibition, 12 were included in the earlier exhibitions; 28 are new additions. The apse-vault model of the south transept hemicycle was not a part of the exhibition in 1988. Fourteen of the 28 new objects are focused on the history of the vault model and the south apse of St. Peter's.

385
DANIELE DA VOLTERRA
and GIAMBOLOGNA
Bust of Michelangelo

Florence, Casa Buonarroti, CB 61
Bronze.
Height 30 cm (head), 29 cm (bust); width 19 cm (head), 47 cm (bust)

BIBLIOGRAPHY: Daelli 1865; Gasparoni 1866; Fortnum 1875; Gotti 1876; Milanesi 1881; Symonds 1901; Thode 1908-13; Garnault 1913; Steinmann 1913; Stechow 1928; Ciaranfi 1932a; Mez 1935; Cammell 1939; Barocchi 1962e; Levie 1962; Borroni-Salvadori 1974; Gavoty 1975; Procacci 1975; Barolsky 1979; Avery 1987b; Penny 1992; Cecchi 1993a.

The intensely expressive head, with its rough surface, its flaws in casting and various summarily executed parts still bearing the imprint of the wax mold, is by a different hand, though close in time to that of the bust, which is draped in antique style and is smoother and better finished as regards the modeling of the folds with sharply defined ridges and deep hollows. The difference between the two parts is also confirmed by the concave surface of the bronze, on which there are various joints linking the head to the bust employing two types of solder; these are rendered uniform on the front by the patina.
The head is certainly one of the two which Lionardo Buonarroti, Michelangelo's nephew, commissioned Daniele da Volterra to execute after the artist had died at the age of eighty-nine on 18 February 1564. Probably based on Michelangelo's death mask, judging from the realism of the sunken cheeks and eyes, this effigy, like another one which was lost and may be one of the versions in various collections in Italy and elsewhere, was probably originally commissioned both for the bust with an epitaph which Cosimo I wanted to dedicate to the great artist in Florence Cathedral, in accordance with a project that was never realized, and for Michelangelo's tomb which was to be constructed in S. Croce.
Evidently work on the two heads was already under way on 11 June 1564 when Daniele wrote to Lionardo to tell him that one of them had been modeled in wax. The slow progress of the work is documented by the frequent correspondence between the Sienese Diomede Leoni (who lived in Rome and was in contact with Daniele) and Michelangelo's nephew from 9 September 1564 to 6 October 1565. On 11 February 1565 Daniele himself had written to Lionardo to inform him that the delay in the casting of the heads was due to the fact that he had decided to combine this operation with that of the horse for the equestrian monument to Henry II, a commission he had received through Michelangelo in 1560 which was, however, at a standstill due to the French patrons. It was not until 7 September 1565 that the heads were cast and Daniele could leave Rome in order to go to Bagno S. Filippo, as may be gathered from a letter sent by Leoni to Lionardo Buonarroti on 8 September of that year.
The two portraits were part of a much larger group of sculptures, including one executed for Leoni and men-

tioned in the letters from 9 February 1565 to 17 September 1569, and another three referred to in the inventory of Macel de' Corvi's house, drawn up after the death of Daniele on 5 April 1566. In this house, which had formerly belonged to Michelangelo and was then let by Lionardo to Daniele on 1 May 1564, there were, on that date and in various rooms, six heads of Michelangelo, two of which were only heads, three others "with the breast" and one "with the bust." It may be reasonably hypothesized that their degree of completion did not go much beyond the casting stage, since those intended for Michelangelo's nephew could probably not be consigned before the autumn of that year. An account of this situation is given in two letters, one from Jacopo del Duca and the other from Michele Alberti, both dated 18 April of that year. In the first one Michelangelo's Sicilian pupil wrote to Lionardo: "Regarding the metal heads, Messer Daniele has now cast them, but they will need a lot of work with chisels and files, hence I am doubtful whether they will meet your requirements; the choice is yours. For my part, I would prefer you to have the bust of the master [Michelangelo], not of another. I say this out of deep respect for you and, if Daniele had still been alive, I am sure he would have done the job properly, but, frankly, I do not know how his pupils will go about it." In the second letter Alberti, one of the successors to Daniele's workshop, assured Buonarroti: "Your friend Messer Jacopo [del Duca] has told me that you would like to know how work is progressing on the bronze heads of Messer Michelangelo. I am pleased to inform you that they have now been cast and, in a month's time, or a little more than this, when they have been chased, you will be able to have them. Trusting that you are in good health, I am sure that you will be satisfied with the work." Once again on 4 June 1566 Diomede Leoni wrote to Lionardo about the heads, which were still in Daniele's workshop: "I understand you have asked for them to be consigned to you; as far as chasing them is concerned, if you so wish, you can defer this to when I return there [to Rome], when it will be possible to have it chased by a man who made an excellent job of my bronze head." While we do not know whether Lionardo was satisfied with the bronze sculptures that were sent to him, it is certain that he did not use them for Michelangelo's tomb, which was being constructed for the church of S. Croce; instead he commissioned Battista Lorenzi to execute a marble version of the bust, which was then mounted on the tomb in August 1574.
Not long after its arrival in Florence one of the two heads must have been placed on the bust on which it now stands in the Casa Buonarroti, with drapery containing the sharply defined folds characteristic of works executed in 1566-70 by Giambologna, an artist who must have been mentioned in the family papers, since the description of the Casa Buonarroti by Michelangelo the Younger (ca. 1648) erroneously ascribed the whole of the sculpture to him, thus giving rise to the confusion among scholars that still exists today.
The attribution to the Flemish artist with which the work was displayed in 1767 at the exhibition at the church of SS. Annunziata, was then accepted by the guides of the Casa Buonarroti (see Procacci 1975) and supported by Fortnum (1875), Symonds (1901), Thode (1908-13), Garnault (1913), Steinmann (1913), Cammell (1939) and, more recently, by Avery (1987b).
Although in 1881 Milanesi affirmed that the bust had been "groundlessly attributed to Giovanni Bologna," it was only in 1928 that Stechow distinguished the two hands, rightly ascribing the head to Daniele da Volterra and the bust to Giambologna; he was then followed by Ciaranfi (1932a), Barocchi (1962e) and Gavoty (1975). There have also been those, for instance Procacci (1975), who have left the question open, vacillating between Daniele da Volterra and Giambologna, or those such as Mez (1935) and Barolsky (1976) who have suggested that the bust should be wholly ascribed to Daniele.
From an examination of the bronze effigies of Michelangelo known today, in collections in Italy and elsewhere, it appears that they have been influenced by

the three prototypes executed by Daniele. These include: the head in the Casa Buonarroti, from which derive the one in the Louvre, which is probably autograph, and the other more doubtful one in the Musée Bonnat in Bayonne; the one in the Ashmolean Museum in Oxford, which is autograph and the probable source of Lorenzi's marble bust for the tomb in S. Croce; a third one, also by Daniele, now in the Musée Jacquemart André, on which the bust in the Museo Capitolino is based, as well as those in the Galleria dell'Accademia and the Bargello in Florence. However, the head in the Castello Sforzesco and the one in the Museo Civico in Rimini appear doubtful.
Of the two busts in the Florentine collections, the one in the Galleria dell'Accademia may be considered to be the earlier; it may be dated not later than 1569 if it is, as this writer believes, the one purchased in Siena on behalf of Grand Duke Ferdinando in 1590 from the heirs of Diomede Leoni. In the opinion of this writer it owes its green patina to the fact that it was situated in the open, in the garden of the first owner's Roman residence (letter from Leoni to Lionardo Buonarroti of 17 September 1569; see Daelli 1865: 79).
It is erroneously believed that the bust in the Bargello is the one that was owned by Antonio del Franzese, who presented it to the Duke of Urbino, from whom it passed to the Medici collection as a result of the Della Rovere legacy, but there is no trace of this in the documents. However, the perfect workmanship of the chased head and the loose drapery with its bulging folds, which are covered by a bright patina, have convinced the present writer that it derives from the other one. Datable to the first half of the seventeenth century, it may be ascribed either to the late career of Giambologna or to one of his pupils or assistants of the caliber of Pietro Tacca or Francesco Susini.

Alessandro Cecchi

657

The Dupérac Group of Drawings in the Metropolitan Museum of Art and Related Sheets in the National Museum in Stockholm

The four sheets depicting Michelangelo's model of the drum and dome of St. Peter's (drawn either by Etienne Dupérac or others in his circle in Rome) are part of a group of 21 sheets devoted to St. Peter's. The St. Peter's drawings are, in turn, part of a larger collection of about 125 drawings, all from the Dupérac circle, that came to the Metropolitan Museum through the generosity of Anne Bigelow Scholz and Janos Scholz. Over 90 of the drawings are of Italian architecture, primarily buildings in Rome and Florence. First noted by Tolnay (1948: 164), and Hyatt Mayor (1949-50: 160), the group was then discussed by Byrne (1957: 155-164; 1966-67: 24-29); Düssler (1959: 238); A. Blunt (1960-61: 15-17); then by Ackerman (1961, II: 99; 1964, II: 101-102); Wasserman (1963: 205-244); Wittkower (1964a: 101-107); Tolnay (1965: 250); Wurm (1965: 53); Tolnay (1966: 21); F. L. Moore (1969: 191); Bertocci and Davis (1978: 93-100); Wittkower (1978b: 81-85). The drawings all appear to date from the last half of the sixteenth century. Some have been dated by scholars in the decade 1560-70 (Wittkower 1964a: 107; Tolnay 1967: 65; Tolnay 1970, III: 164; Frommel 1973, passim; Millon and Smyth 1976: 185-194; Millon and Smyth 1988a: 103-113).

Dupérac was a French architect and print-maker working in Rome who produced many prints of ancient and modern Rome (Zerner 1963-64: 325-326). The sheets from the Metropolitan Museum with drawings from the model of the drum and dome of St. Peter's have been discussed by Wittkower (1964a: 101-107); Tolnay (1967: 66-68); Brandi (1968: 8-10); Keller (1976: 24-56); Francia (1977: 126, no. 9); Wittkower (1978b: 72-89); Di Stefano (1980b: 65); Di Stefano (1980a: 875-876); and Millon and Smyth (1988a 103-113).

The three sheets in the National Museum in Stockholm from Michelangelo's model of the drum and dome are part of a group of at least nine sheets related to similar drawings of St. Peter's in the Metropolitan Museum. Though apparently not drawn by any of the three hands that worked on the drawings in the Metropolitan, the sheets in Stockholm were drawn by French draftsmen who may also have been associated with the Dupérac circle.

The Stockholm drawings of St. Peter's are part of a larger collection of over seventy drawings, all with notations in French, drawn by several hands, of buildings in Rome both ancient and from the sixteenth century. These sheets were part of a still larger collection of drawings, of disparate periods and hands, given to the National Museum in Stockholm by the architect Carl Johan Cronstedt in 1941.

Wittkower (1978b: 83-85) was the first to publish the sheets with drawings of St. Peter's in Stockholm. He thought the drawings in Stockholm to be very closely related to the drawings from the Dupérac circle in the Metropolitan Museum. According to Wittkower, watermarks on some of the sheets in Stockholm can be dated to the 1570s. Two of the sheets with drawings of St. Peter's were published by Millon and Smyth 1988a (figs. 27 and 28).

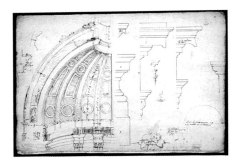

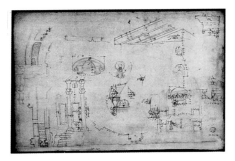

386

ETIENNE DUPÉRAC
Half-Section through the Model of the Attic and Dome of St. Peter's (recto)
Elevation of Exterior of the Model of the Attic and Dome and Interior of the Oculus of the Lantern (verso)

New York, The Metropolitan Museum of Art, 49.92.92
Pen and brown ink over black chalk; worn edges with small tears; sheet detached from sketchbook; no watermark.
294/298 × 440 mm

RECTO: a) half-section of dome interior (left half); b) various elements in section (upper and lower left, lower center right); c) various elements at larger scale in profile (right half); d) detail of balustrade (lower right); e) arc of interior dome space (lower right).
INSCRIBED: 1) *escalino 46*; 2) *sur les coullonnes / p[ar] dehors*; 3) *tout le vane / du modelle de la tribune / p[almi] 12 o[ncie] 3*.
VERSO: a) section through upper part of drum and lower part of dome (upper left); b) plan of X-shaped stairs between domes (lower left); c) elevation of the interior of oculus (center left); d) profile of base of the pilasters of oculus (lower center left); e) elevation of window head and pediment of one of the middle dormer windows of the dome (upper center left); f) plan of exterior of the attic of the drum (lower center); g) side elevation of dormer window of the dome with a profile of the pediment (center); h) plan of the screen with spokes at the top of the oculus (upper center); i) enlarged detail of base of pilaster strip with guttae at the side of the dormer windows (center right); j) two small details of the volute of the C-volute pediments of the dormer windows (center right); k) elevation of the attic and one section of the exterior dome with dormer windows (right); l) Half-elevation of a triangular pediment (upper right); m) Section through the cornice of the adjacent triangular pediment (upper right corner); n) plan and partial section of a rib of the dome including the steps in the center of the rib (right center).
INSCRIBED: 1) *La tribune 1 ['Jentre les / deulz volte* (lower left); 2) *Les fenestre [s] / p[ar] dehors* (upper right).

PROVENANCE: Janos and Anne Bigelow Scholz in memory of Flying Officer Walter Bigelow Rosen, 1949.

BIBLIOGRAPHY: For additional bibliographical references, see also the previous section on the Dupérac Group in the Metropolitan Museum of Art. Byrne 1957: 155-164; Ackerman 1961, II: 99; 1964, II: 101-102; Wittkower 1964a: 66 n. 2; 101-103; Tolnay 1965: 250; 1966: 391; 1967, 64-68; Millon and Smyth 1976: 185-192; Francia 1977: 127; Wittkower 1978b: 82; Tolnay 1980, IV: 94; Di Stefano 1980b: 65; Ackerman 1986: 321-322; Millon and Smyth 1988a: 104-109; Argan and Contardi 1990: 330 and figs. 442 and 443.

Both sides of this sheet provide explicit information not available elsewhere about Michelangelo's finished model of the drum and dome. The drawings on the sheet testify that the dome of the model in its final state was hemispherical, not elevated. This, in turn, confirms the correctness of the representation of the dome by Etienne Dupérac in his prints of ca. 1569. Together, this sheet and Dupérac's prints provide a remarkably full picture of the drum and two domes as Michelangelo intended them when he built the model, as Wittkower was the first to assert (1964a: 66 and n. 2). Further, another dimensioned, drawing in the Metropolitan Museum (49.92.1, cat. no. 8), associated with this drawing, confirms the accuracy of Dupérac's representation of the lantern.

These two sheets belong to a group of drawings of St. Peter's in the Metropolitan Museum of Art, whose importance was first recognized by Tolnay (1965: 250; 1967: 64-68). The drawings dealing with St. Peter's were first analyzed by Wittkower (1964a: 101-107). They appear to have been drawn about 1565 by Dupérac and an assistant preparatory to making the Dupérac prints, as Wittkower argued (see also Janet Byrne 1957: 155-164, and Millon and Smyth 1976: 185-192).

The recto and verso of this sheet provide detailed dimensions of the model: of its two domes, the distances between them, two steps at the base of the lantern, the span of the dome, the attic and main entablature and balustrade on the interior, the tondi, trapezoids and their moldings, ribs on interior and exterior, exterior attic, the windows in the dome and their distance from each other and the base of the stair between the two domes. The recto furnishes the only dimensioned representation of the interior of the oculus between the two domes. The verso gives a plan of the spokes of the screen between the oculus and the lantern. This detail explains for the first time what was intended here by Michelangelo: a structure apparently open between its radiating members. It is rendered as a solid in Dupérac's print of the longitudinal section. However, the openings in the facade—the main entrance and the window above it—are also rendered as solids in the print. Vasari wrote that one could look from outside the lantern through its windows into the church below (Vasari, ed. Milanesi 1881, VII: 256).

The drawings, as Wittkower recognized, are clearly a vehicle for recording dimensions taken directly from the model but, with the exception of the ruled profiles, are not intended to be accurate or proportioned as representations of the relationship between the parts of the structure (as is also clearly evident in the drawing of the exterior of the dome). The detailed dimensions of the Dupérac sheets from the Metropolitan Museum of Art and the proportioned representation in the pair of prints by Dupérac enable a reconstruction of the model as it existed at Michelangelo's death.

Verso

It is the verso that gives us new information about the interior elevation of the oculus (the circular opening between the two domes at the summit) and the open screen above it. The pilasters, entablature, and windows at

Fig. 3 - After Michelangelo, Wood model for the inner shell of the dome of St. Peter's, *Vatican City, Musei Vaticani*

center left are all dimensioned. Resting on the entablature, and also shown with an inscribed dimension (*oncie* 1⅓), are the beams (drawn in crude perspective) that make the slightly arched spokes of the screen above the oculus. The letter "x" between the two beams refers to the plan labeled "x" to the right.

A dimensioned elevation of one section of the exterior of the dome, from the base of the attic to the platform of the lantern, occupies the right half of this sheet. Inscribed dimensions are given for the plan and elevation of the attic, garland, ribs (including the dimension of the steps on the rib in a separate detail) and the three ranges of windows topped by C-volute moldings (including separate details, with inscribed dimensions of a side elevation of the lowest window and their pendants with guttae). All three windows have the same shape, and the appearance of the middle one labeled "L" is drawn in some detail in black chalk above the elevation of the oculus.

The drawing at far left of the stair between the two domes is the only contemporary plan known to us of the X-shaped stairs (as Vasari called them) in the lower part of the model.

One element on the verso of the sheet refers to the drum and not the dome. At upper right is a dimensioned elevation and profile of a triangular pediment above one of the windows of the exterior of the drum, labeled "Les fenestre[s] / p[ar] dehors."

H.A.M.-C.H.S.

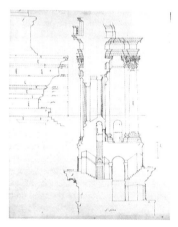

387
Unknown Draftsman Related to the Circle of Etienne Dupérac
Section and Elevation of the Model and of the Drum of St. Peter's

Stockholm, Nationalmuseum,
Cronstedt Collection, CC 1353
Pen, brown ink, with some incised lines; sheet folded in half; watermark: standing figure holding a staff within a vertical oval; scale: *p[almi]* 20.
575 × 423 mm
a) section of the drum; b) dimensioned profile of the main exterior cornice at the base of the drum.

Inscribed: *San Pietro*, and various dimensions.
Provenance: Cronstedt Collection.

Bibliography: Wittkower 1978b: 84, fig. 92; Millon and Smyth 1988a: 110.

CC 1353 is a more accurately drafted counterpart to a drawing in the Metropolitan Museum in New York (49.92.20v.). Skewed verticals and other errors found on the drawing in the Metropolitan Museum have been corrected in the drawing in Stockholm.

The letter "A" on the profile of the main interior cornice is keyed to the elevation of the cornice found on CC 1375. The letter "F" on the main exterior cornice of the base of the drum is keyed to the profile drawing at a larger scale at upper left. The drawing depicts the lower portions of the drum as on the building, but at the attic level it

represents the model of the drum and dome with a balustrade on the interior that was not constructed on the basilica. The drawings for the drum and dome of St. Peter's in the Cronstedt Collection and their counterparts in the Metropolitan Museum in New York document the completed model of the drum and dome by Michelangelo. The Cronstedt drawings appear to date from the same time as the Metropolitan Museum's drawings, the decade 1560-70. (For opinions on the dating see Millon and Smyth 1988a: 103.)

H.A.M.-C.H.S.

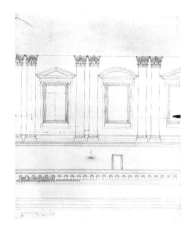

388
Etienne Dupérac
Elevation of Two and One-Half Bays of the Interior of the Drum of St. Peter's

New York, The Metropolitan Museum of Art, 49.92.17r.
Pen and brown ink; sheet folded in half; detached from sketchbook; tear (upper left corner); small pieces missing (center left and right; lower right); watermark: crossed arrows with a six-pointed star above; scale: *palmi*; *canne*.
575/570 × 436 mm

Provenance: Janos and Anne Bigelow Scholz, in memory of Flying Officer Walter Bigelow Rosen 1949.

Bibliography: Ackerman 1961, II: 99; 1964, II: 101-102; Wittkower 1964a: 66 n. 2; 101-107; Tolnay 1967: 64-68; Francia 1977: 127; Wittkower 1978b: 83; Di Stefano 1980b: 65; Ackerman 1986: 321-322; Millon and Smyth 1988a: 112-113.

This drawing and others in the Metropolitan Museum group testify to the care and completeness of the effort of Dupérac and his assistants to record all aspects of Michelangelo's drum and dome of St. Peter's insofar as it had been constructed by the time of his death and as projected in the model.

In this drawing of the interior of the drum, the measurements were taken from the existing structure, as indicated by the dimensions including *minuti*. The pediments, too, are as on the building, alternating, not all segmental as in the model. A matching view from the exterior is also in the Metropolitan group (49.92.21r.).

In the National Museum in Stockholm are yet more complete representations of the interior and exterior of the drum by another hand, but evidently related to the Metropolitan drawings: CC 1375 and 1305. Worth noting are the ears of the windows (projections at the upper corners): these are on the building and the model, but unaccountably missing in the print by Dupérac.

H.A.M.-C.H.S.

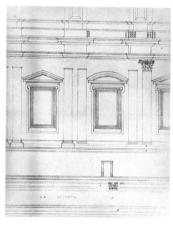

389
Unknown Draftsman Related to the Circle of Etienne Dupérac
Elevation of Two and One-Half Bays of the Interior of the Drum of St. Peter's

Stockholm, Nationalmuseum, Cronstedt Collection, CC 1375
Pen, brown ink over some black chalk, with some incised lines; sheet folded in half; watermark: standing figure with a staff within a vertical oval; scale: 10 units (*palmi*), 1 *canna*.
572 × 430 mm

Inscribed: *S. Pietro le dedens de la tribonna.*
Provenance: Cronstedt Collection.

Bibliography: Wittkower 1978b: 83-84 and fig. 88; Nova 1984: 196; Millon and Smyth 1988a: 123; Argan and Contardi 1990: 330.

CC 1375, together with CC 1305 (an elevation of the exterior of the drum), CC 1353 (a section through the drum), and CC 1337 (a plan of the drum at three different levels), provide a reasonably complete description of the drum, attic and base of the dome of St. Peter's. The drawings appear to be an amalgam of measurements taken both from the building and from the model of the drum and dome. The Cronstedt Collection drawings for St. Peter's are closely related to eight sheets for the drum and dome of St. Peter's in the group of drawings attributed to Etienne Dupérac in the Metropolitan Museum in New York. Wittkower (1978b: 83) thought the drawing in Stockholm to be "very closely related" to the drawings in the Metropolitan.

In some particulars, the drawings in Stockholm include more information than their counterparts in New York. This drawing, for instance, includes the entablature, the attic and balustrade above, and a lower portion of the paneled ribs of the dome, all omitted in the drawing at the Metropolitan (49.92.17r.). The drawing in New York, however, includes inscribed dimensions in the bay at the left, dimensions that include *minuti*, which must have been taken from the building. (The alternating pediments in both drawings also suggest observation of the building rather than the model, where pediments on the interior are all segmental.) Only on the model, however, could the balustrade in the drawing in Stockholm be seen, since a balustrade was never erected on the building. Balusters for the model were paid for in November 1561 (K. Frey 1909b: 179) and, although no longer on the model, the holes drilled for them are still visible.

A balustrade appears in numerous drawings of the model and in the section print by Dupérac (Millon and Smyth 1988a: 123). The letter "A" on the architrave, frieze, and cornice of the main entablature of the interior cornice ring is keyed to the profile drawing of the entablature on CC 1353.

The drawings of the drum and dome of St. Peter's from the Cronstedt Collection and their counterparts at the Metropolitan Museum seem to date from the same time, the decade 1560-70. (For opinions on the dating of the drawings, see Millon and Smyth 1988a: 103.)

H.A.M.-C.H.S.

659

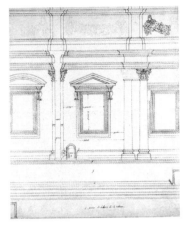

390
ETIENNE DUPÉRAC
Elevation of Two and One-Half Bays of the Exterior of the Drum of St. Peter's

New York, The Metropolitan Museum of Art, 49.92.21r.
Pen, brown ink over black chalk; sheet folded in half;
watermark: crossed arrows with a six-pointed star above.
574/572 × 432/433 mm

PROVENANCE: Janos and Anne Bigelow Scholz, in memory of Flying Officer Walter Bigelow Rosen, 1949.

BIBLIOGRAPHY: Ackerman 1961, II: 99; 1964, II: 101-102; Wittkower 1964a: 66, n. 2, 101-107; Tolnay 1967: 64-68; Francia 1977: 127; Wittkower 1978b: 84 and fig. 89; Di Stefano 1980b: 65; Ackerman 1986: 321-322; Millon and Smyth 1988: 112 and fig. 26.

The interrupted, incomplete, or abandoned drawing of the exterior of the drum, without scale or dimensions, found on Metropolitan 49.92.21 recto is repeated in a more complete state, including the entablature and attic, on a sheet in Stockholm (CC 1305). The elevation in New York includes a section through one of the sixteen buttress piers of the drum (left) and an elevation of the paired columns of the pier (right). As on the sheet in Stockholm, the windows are not drawn in the centers of the spaces depicted. The central window, for example, is shifted to the left to appear in the center of the space between the narrow inner buttress and the wider pair of columns on the right.

The sheet from the Metropolitan Museum is one of eight by or from the circle of Etienne Dupérac devoted to the drum and dome of St. Peter's. The drawings include information taken from both the drum as constructed and the model of the drum and dome. The drawings are generally dated in the decade 1560-70. (For opinions on the dating, see Millon and Smyth 1988a: 103.)

H.A.M.-C.H.S.

391
UNKNOWN DRAFTSMAN RELATED TO THE CIRCLE OF ETIENNE DUPÉRAC
Elevation of Two and One-Half Bays of the Exterior of the Drum of St. Peter's

Stockholm, Nationalmuseum, Cronstedt Collection, CC 1305
Pen, brown ink over some black chalk, and black chalk;
watermark: standing figure with staff within a vertical oval.
572 × 435 mm

INSCRIBED: *S. Pietro le dehors de la tribouna* and various dimensions.

PROVENANCE: Cronstedt Collection.

BIBLIOGRAPHY: Wittkower 1978a: 83-84; Millon and Smyth 1988a: 112, 122-123, fig. 28.

A more complete drawing of the exterior of the drum than on the corresponding sheet in the Metropolitan Museum in New York (49.92.21r.), CC 1305 includes, in addition to dimensions in the central bay, pediments above the windows, the entablature, attic (with festoons), and base of the dome. The letter "f" on the main exterior cornice at the base of the drum is keyed to a profile drawing of the cornice ring found at upper left on CC 1353.

The drawing depicts the lower portions of the drum with dimensions including *minuti* taken from the building. It also shows the attic, which was only constructed after 1588 (Orbaan 1917: 191), and must, therefore, have been drawn from the model of the drum and dome.

As in Metropolitan 49.92.21 recto, the windows in the drawing are not placed in the center of the wall of the drum, but shifted to the left (center and right windows) and right (left window), perhaps for clarity of representation. The central window is drawn to appear in the center of the space between the narrow buttress at left and the double columns at right with nearly equal inscribed dimensions to either side. The window at right should be on axis with the doorway below, as shown correctly on Uff. 95 verso (Millon and Smyth 1969: fig. 28).

The drawings for the drum and dome of St. Peter's in the Cronstedt Collection, as well as their counterparts in the Metropolitan Museum in New York, are generally dated in the decade 1560-70. (For opinions on the dating, see Millon and Smyth 1988a: 103.)

H.A.M.-C.H.S.

392
CIRCLE OF ETIENNE DUPÉRAC
Half Elevation of the Exterior of the Dome Model of St. Peter's

New York, The Metropolitan Museum of Art, 49.92.1
Pen, brown ink over black chalk.
433/442 × 293/285 mm
INSCRIBED: various dimensions in ink.
PROVENANCE: Janos and Anne Bigelow Scholz, in memory of Flying Officer Walter Bigelow Rosen, 1949.

BIBLIOGRAPHY: Ackerman 1961, II: 99; 1964, II: 101-102; Wittkower 1964a: 66 n. 2; 101-107; Tolnay 1967: 64-68; Brandi, 1968: 5 n. 4, 7-12, 14; Francia 1977: 127; Wittkower 1978b: 82 and fig. 85; Di Stefano 1980b: 65; Ackerman 1986: 321-322; Millon and Smyth 1988a: 118, 123 and fig. 21.

The drawing is a half elevation of the dome model, but also includes at lower center the plan of the top of a pier buttress. The sheet was cited by Tolnay (1967: 64-68) as evidence of an elevated profile for the model of the dome of St. Peter's. Brandi (1968), too, thought the elevated profile to be intentional. The inscribed dimensions, however, indicate a hemispherical dome and show the drawing to be related to the depictions of the hemispherical dome in the prints by Dupérac.

In contrast to the representation of two levels of dormers found in the description of the model by Vasari (Vasari, ed. Milanesi 1881, VII: 257), on the medal by Fragni and in the aerial perspective in the Morgan Library, the dome segments here contain three levels of dormers. These are also found on Metropolitan 49.92.92 verso, and on the prints by Dupérac.

The exterior of the lantern confirms the lantern as shown on the Dupérac print. Both have the same three stages: columns on high pedestals, volutes with shells between, and conical top with sphere; and both show the paired columns abutting the wall of the lantern. There are minor differences between the two. The Metropolitan drawing shows window frames, which are not in the print, surrounding windows higher than in the print, but it fails to depict ressauts over the paired columns, except in one case at the far left. The drawing also lacks the balustrade on the platform of the lantern and the festoons in the attic at the base of the dome, which are included in the print. The drawing appears to have been laid out freehand in black chalk, then drawn over in ink using straightedge and compass, by a draftsman who was either in a hurry or more interested in recording dimensions and details than accuracy, neatness or proportional relations. For example, the lantern is too tall relative to the height of the dome. Within the lantern the height of the columns of the first level and the height of the C-shaped volutes of the second level scale about equal, but their inscribed dimensions are *palmi* 19 and *palmi* 12 respectively, as first noted by Wittkower (1964a: 101).

Together with the sheet in the Metropolitan Museum showing details from the model of the dome (Metropolitan 49.92.92v.), this drawing provides additional information about the final design of the lantern on the model as it was executed in 1561. As other drawings of St. Peter's in the group from the Metropolitan Museum, this drawing from the completed model was made after 1561, probably in the decade 1560-70.

H.A.M.-C.H.S.

393
ANONYMOUS
Various Sections, Profiles and a Reflected Plan from St. Peter's

Florence, Galleria degli Uffizi, Gabinetto Disegni e Stampe, Uff. 1330A
Pen, brown ink over black chalk; watermark: escutcheon: indistinct shape chief, three per bend fess, paly of four base; scale: (1) 70 [*braccie*?] (lower border); (2) b[*raccie*] 10 (vertical, lower left).
468 × 343 mm
a) section through a hemicycle apse and apse vault (left);
b) profile of main entablature of exterior of a hemicycle (lower left center, labeled 'HO'); c) profile of main entablature of interior of a hemicycle (lower center, labeled 'HP');
d) redireflected plan of main entablature of interior of a hemicycle (lower right); e) section through main cornice ring and drum (upper right); f) profile of exterior cornice at base of drum (center right, labeled 'mn'); g) profile of attic of main order of the hemicycle apse (upper right, labeled 'A'); h) profile of main entablature of exterior of the drum (upper center, labeled 'c'); i) profile of main entablature of the interior of the drum (upper center, labeled 'B'); j) profile of base of the columns on the exterior of the drum (upper center right, labeled 'm').
INSCRIBED: a) *le foglie de modeli so fronde di oliva / e edenseli [?] sono insu le cantonate come / si vede disegniato e il simile sono queli / che sono sopra gli pilastri di drento della / trebuna sono insu canti e p[er] tuto questa / cornice gira tuta la chiesa e ogni cosa / e ot[t]ime corinto drento e fuora e p[er]tuto* (lower right); b) *lumi fatti / achaso* (lower left); c) *lumi* (center left); d) *para / petto* (center left); e) *In sulle / cantonate* (center left); f) *sodo* (lower center right); g) *parapeto p[er] andare intorno vegendo / p[er] tutto* (upper left); h) *lumi fatti achaso* (upper right); i) *porta che / pasa in / sul piano / de le colone* (upper right); j) *porta che / ecce in sulla / cornice di fuo / ra* (upper right); k) *prima por / ta da entr / ate dren / tto / piano* (upper right); l) *porta che ecce in sulla / cornice di drento*; m) many inscribed dimensions in *braccia*.

PROVENANCE: unavailable.

BIBLIOGRAPHY: Ferri 1885: 152.

The authorship of the first "faithful" print reproducing the dome of St. Peter's is ascribable to Martino Ferraboschi, or Ferrabosco as he is sometimes known, who was called in by the *maggiordomo* of Pope Paul V Borghese (1605-21) to make a thorough survey of the recently completed basilica and draw it in every detail.[1]
Ferraboschi was without doubt the most suitable candidate for the task as he was highly capable from a technical point of view and an acute observer; he had also accumulated considerable knowledge of the *fabbrica* during his many years on the site alongside the *capomaestro*, Carlo Maderno.
The task was very demanding from the point of view of graphic technique, and the results were published for the first time in 1620; the set of prints also included plates illustrating the ideas and aspirations of the author, few of which were ever carried out.[2]
Ferrabosco's drawings are strikingly advanced for their day, and the modernity of conception is combined with an outstanding wealth of detail. The plates are not very accessible to the lay reader, however, and seem to have been deliberately devised for "technicians" alone. In normal circumstances there would not be any doubts about the exactness of the drawings; however, certain inconsistencies—perhaps not even attributable to Ferrabosco—detected in several parts of the work and in the graphic detailing (which pose a serious challenge to the analyst) made it necessary to carry out careful comparisons; these have provided comforting results. The suspect measurements—only some of which are quoted, leaving the rest to be deduced from the scale—generally concern the horizontal sections parallel to the floor of the basilica, particularly the structures supporting the great dome, from the drum to the capitals of the columns of the drum. By contrast, the overall technique of representation is very clear, even in the details, such as in the drawing of the cornices or other architectural elements.[3] Given this premise, those who are not able to carry out on-site studies are encouraged not to overlook Ferrabosco's work (which is fairly easy to procure), and to continue what has not been possible here for reasons of time and space, in the hope of establishing both the author and an at least approximate date for Uff. 1330A. The main scope of such an inquiry should be to find explanations for the drawing's many outstanding features, which have so far inexplicably been overlooked by the experts.
The subject of the drawing in Uff. 1330A is undoubtedly the basilica of St. Peter's. Starting from the bottom left of the paper and moving to the top right of the same, we can see a sectional drawing that corresponds to a part of the Vatican basilica, along the transverse axis through the transept. The section shows the southern arm, known then as SS. Simone e Giuda and now as S. Giuseppe, which presents the structural and architectural characteristics of Michelangelo's construction as far as the *maschio* of the dome.[4] In this part, the drawings of the moldings of the cornices, the one outside the base of the attic and the one inside at the impost of the vault (labeled "Hp"), illustrated together with their decorative details, have been given all the most minute measurements, in Florentine *braccia*. Bar certain very slight discrepancies, these correspond to the actual building.[5]
Also represented with faithful measurements are the moldings of the cornices at the base of the drum of the dome (labeled "mn"). What the author's intentions were with this drawing is not easy to determine, because the attention to detail in the cornices and the decorative details is contrasted by a summary and often imprecise rendering of the structures. As for the part of the basilica up to the level of the intrados of the vault, the defects basically consist in the omission of the relief elements of the wall plane (apart from the main cornices), and in the approximation of the positions of the window openings, which the draftsman has duly labeled "lumi fatti a chaso." The structural details for the structure within the perimeter wall of the basilica have been omitted in the same way. At the top right of the sheet, the parts of the building that emerge above the extrados of the southern arm vault (*maschio* and drum of the dome) have been illustrated in much greater detail; however, there are many curious anomalies with respect to Michelangelo's construction. The drawing is grafted in an improbable and irregular way with the section of the cross vault; it offers no illustration of either the lower part of the *maschio* or the arch on which it rests. Toward the left of the sheet the draftsman has drawn a molding of the same thickness as the vault, but there is nothing of these dimensions anywhere in St. Peter's. The base of the *maschio* in Uff. 1330A has the same width as the base of the buttresses; below the circular corridor inside the *maschio* there is a second galleria passageway, accessed from the outside level with the extrados of the crossing vault.[6]
The actual basilica is very different from that shown in the drawing, which also contains marked discrepancies in the scale ratios. The indicator for the measurements (the *scalimetro* or scale key) provided by the author at the bottom of the sheet, is rather approximate.[7] It should also be pointed out that the moldings of the buttress entablature supporting the drum of the dome and the inner entablature of the impost ring of the dome itself (upper center of sheet) are all labeled with detailed measurements, quite unlike the moldings illustrated in the lower part of the sheet. Every feature has been dutifully dimensioned, but numerous divergences (albeit slight) from the actual building measurements can be discerned, despite the practical difficulties of on-site verification.
In conclusion, it is worth noting the representation of the impost of the dome, whose curvature starts immediately above the top of the buttresses. As pointed out above, the drawing is fairly schematic as far as the structural details are concerned: there is not the slightest suggestion of the *giro dei monti* or circular crown which separates the drum from the dome proper.
The above arguments are sufficient to justify the hypothesis that the drawing was carried out for two purposes: first (in the lower part of the page) to provide a minute survey of the cornices and other decorative details; second (in the upper part), to propose the final stage of a project—not so much for its structure as for the architectural elements of the parts that bear moldings. Indeed, the moldings appear to be the focus of the anonymous draftsman's attention; perhaps he wanted to reproduce the architectural details of the part of the basilica that had already been built, in order to assimilate its *ductus* and to acquaint himself intimately with the proportions and thus obtain a formal scheme of the forms involved as a guide for the new elements of the parts still to be built.
The drawing, consequently, should date to be between 1550 and 1556, but not later, inasmuch as the errors and omissions mentioned above would be inadmissible, considering that the advanced stage of construction of the basilica—and the existence of Michelangelo's wooden model of the drum and dome—would have provided an immediate means of verification.[8]

1. Martino Ferrabosco or Ferraboschi was born at Codelago, near Milan, in the mid-sixteenth century and died in Rome in 1623. The greater part of his working life, as an architect and engraver, was spent in Rome. His most famous graphic work is: *Architettura della basilica di San Pietro in Vaticano. Opera di Bramante Lazzari, Michel Angelo Bonarota, Carlo Maderno e altri famosi Architetti, da Monsignore Giovanni Battista Costaguti Seniore Maggiordomo di Paolo V fatta esprimere, e intagliare in più tavole da Martino Ferrabosco, e posta in luce l'Anno M:DC:XX*. A new edition of the volume was published in 1684 by the printers of the Reverenda Camera Apostolica, under the patronage of Mons. Giovanni Battista Costaguti, *iuniore*. Another edition was also printed in Rome in 1828 by De Romanis. For more on this subject, see Silvan, 1989a: 50-51; and Pierluigi Silvan 1993: 161.

2. Observe in Ferrabosco's work pls. XVI-XVII, XIX, and XXVI, which show a scheme for campaniles flanking the facade of St. Peter's, anticipating Bernini's project; and pls. XXVIII and XXIX, in which he proposes a choir for the canons in the western tribune, and reassigns the choir chapel as a sacristy, thus confirming the inadequacy of the new basilica.

3. Silvan 1989a: 50-62.

4. Compare pls. XXIII and XXIV of Ferrabosco's *Architettura ...*, which in turn show the section of the perimetral wall of the southern cross from the floor of the basilica to the impost of the vault, and the section of the vault, as seen toward the east, and instead of the west as drawn in Uff. 1330A. See Carlo Fontana's *Il Tempio Vaticano e sua origine* (Rome, 1694), plates on pp. 327, 331, and 313

for the sections of the dome and the drum; the last plate is particularly clear and detailed, and includes the moldings of many cornices; there are few discrepancies relative to the actual building and therefore offers a valid means of comparison. The plates on pp. 391 and 423 of Fontana's volume show sections of the lower part of the basilica as well. Other indications can be found in the plates of Giovanni Poleni's *Memorie Istoriche della Gran Cupola del Tempio Vaticano* (Padua, 1748); the drawings are, however, schematic due to the specialist nature of the book. While pls. 53, 58, 59 and 69 engraved by Paul-Marie Létarouilly and published posthumously in *Le Vatican et la basilique de Saint-Pierre de Rome* (Paris 1882), are rich in detail, they are unsuitable for comparison with Uff. 1330A because of their many inaccuracies, some of which have already been noted and published (see P. Silvan, in *XY*, op. cit.).

5. The Florentine *braccio* used for verifying the measurements is that given in the plate entitled *Misure del Tempio Vaticano sue parti, ed annessi nuovamente prese dal Signor Giuseppe Valadier Architetto della Fabbrica di S. Pietro in Vaticano l'anno 1812*. This large folio engraving, published by De Romanis in Rome, gives the measurements of parts of the interior and exterior of the Vatican Basilica in the "Roman measure," the "old Paris measure," and today's "new metric measure." A table of scales at the bottom of the plate, including the most important ones in use at the time, offers a comparison of the various units of measurement; these include the systems of measurement in use in Naples, Florence, Milan, Venice, London, Vienna, and Leiden; according to this table 1 meter is equal to 1.7187 *braccia* and, therefore, 1 Florentine *braccio* is equal to 58.1835 cm. Although the precision of this table has been harshly criticized (see P. Silvan in *XY*, op. cit., pp. 55-56), it seems that Valadier's estimation of the Florentine *braccio* is acceptable.

6. In this regard, see the engraving on p. 313 of Fontana's *Il Tempio...*; for further comparison, see pls. IX, XIII, XIX, and XXIII, which Luca Beltrami presents in his book, *La Cupola Vaticana, Città del Vaticano*, 1929.

7. The disparity between drawing, measurements, and proposed scale, oscillates between 9% and 18%.

8. Michelangelo's arduous task of demolishing, consolidating and rebuilding St. Peter's has rarely received a fair appraisal (see Francia 1977: 79-96). On exceptional occasions have art historians, historians, philologists and technical experts studying the sixteenth-century *fabbrica* of St. Peter's made a correct interpretation of the documents of the Archivio della Fabbrica di San Pietro. The reasons for this lie, perhaps, in the fact that it is not easy to reconstruct the full technical and administrative organization of the *cantiere* midway through the sixteenth century (Silvan, 1989b: 25-35). Moreover, we must take into consideration the necessity first of all to distinguish the creative process—and therefore the stages of the design—from the technical and practical developments of the building process itself, which were often registered differently in the administrative acts. It is extremely difficult, therefore—especially centuries later—to put into chronological order all the activites and events, and thereby establish their exact quantitative and qualitative significance. This is why it is necessary to be critical of the many imaginative but purely fantastic hypotheses based on scarse data contained in the records of accounts—whose archive references are often not supplied.

A

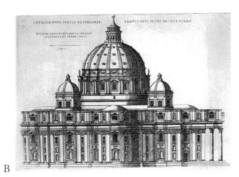

B

394
ETIENNE DUPÉRAC
Section through St. Peter's

1) Milan, Raccolta delle Stampe Achille Bertarelli, Castello Sforzesco
Engraved and etched; scale: 10 *canne*.
333 × 474 mm
INSCRIBED: *ORTHOGRAPHIA PARTIS INTERIORIS TEMPLI DIVI PETRI IN VATICANO / MICHAEL ANGELVS BONAROTA INVENIT / STEPHANVS DVPÉRAC FECIT*
PROVENANCE: 1) Collezione Bertarelli; 2) Harris Brisbane Dick Fund, 1941.

ETIENNE DUPÉRAC
Elevation of the Exterior of St. Peter's

Milan, Civica Raccolta delle Stampe Achille Bertarelli, Castello Sforzesco
Engraved and etched; scale: 10 *canne*.
338 × 461 mm
INSCRIBED: *ORTHOGRAPHIA PARTIS EXTERIORIS TEMPLI DIVI PETRI IN VATICANO / MICHAEL ANGELVS BONAROTA INVENIT / STEPHANVS DV PERAC FECIT*

PROVENANCE: Collezione Bertarelli.

BIBLIOGRAPHY: Thode 1908, II: 164; D. Frey 1920: 109-116; Hülsen 1921: 160-161; Giovannoni 1921: 418-438; 1931: 150; D. Frey 1923: 10; Beltrami 1929: 30 n. 1; Tolnay 1930: 6; Giovannoni 1931a: 150; Körte 1932: 90-112; Wittkower 1933: 354-356; Coolidge 1942: 70-76, 112-119; Schiavo 1949: captions to pls. 97, 98; Tolnay 1951: 182-184; Schiavo 1952: 14-27; 1953: 200-201; Gioseffi 1960: 10-18; Schiavo 1960: 58, 68-69, 73, 81; 1961: 522-523, passim; Ackerman 1961, II: 105-110; Di Stefano 1963: 81-96; Zerner 1963-64: 325-326; Ackerman 1964, II: 101, 110-113; Wittkower 1964a: 35-45; Bettini 1964: 500; Barbieri and Puppi 1964a: 919-921; Tolnay 1964, IX: col. 908; Schiavo 1965: 312-313 n. 4; Zerner 1965: 508; Pane 1966: 383; Lees-Milne 1967: 212; Alker 1968: 1-19; Brandi 1968: 5-17; Portoghesi [1971]e: 415-416; Einem 1973: 225, 227; Saalman 1975: 382-401; McGinnes and Mitchell 1976: 228; Millon and Smyth 1976: 152-186; Wittkower 1978: 77, 79; Di Stefano 1980b: 59-64; Boorsch 1982-83: 14-15; Nova 1984: 195-197; Ackerman 1986: 209-211, 322-324; Millon and Smyth 1988a: 114-118; Argan and Contardi 1990: 273-276 and figs. 385 (section) and 386 (elevation); Marani 1992b: 494-496.

The evidence in the Metropolitan Museum preparatory drawings, already discussed, shows that the two prints by Etienne Dupérac provide, with respect to all but a few details, an accurate and complete representation of the in-

terior and exterior of the model of the drum and dome of St. Peter's as Michelangelo constructed it in 1558-61. These two prints are associated with a print of a plan of St. Peter's published by Dupérac in 1569, and they are normally given the same date (Coolidge 1942: 116). While Dupérac introduced changes in the main elevation and in the little domes over the corner chapels, changes stemming from Michelangelo's successors Pirro Ligorio and Vignola (Coolidge 1942: 112-119; Millon and Smyth 1988c), he evidently wanted to represent the drum and dome essentially as Michelangelo had designed them in the model. Both domes are hemispherical on interior and exterior. They are closer together at their base than at the oculus, where greater height was needed for standing and walking. The different curvatures of the two domes were obtained by drawing arcs from different points, much as prescribed by Vasari (Vasari, ed. Milanesi 1881, VII: 253-254). Wittkower believed that at the scale of the prints it would not be possible to use precisely Vasari's instructions but, and we agree, that the curvatures and thicknesses of the two domes are nonetheless close to those described by Vasari.

Section
The lower portion of the drum follows very closely that shown on the preparatory drawing in the Dupérac group in the Metropolitan Museum (49.92.20v.) with respect to cornices, ramps, stairs, and the levels of plinths on the interior and exterior.
The print also follows the drawing in the way it represents the section through a window of the drum, the columned buttress on the exterior, and the entablature on the interior with a cornice slightly higher than that of the entablature on the exterior. The section coincides with the drawing in the Metropolitan in most particulars, except that the shape of the balusters on the interior attic is changed in the print. (Each baluster is drawn with a similar but reversed shape at top and bottom in Metropolitan 49.92.20 verso and 49.92.92 recto, as well as in drawings of the dome model attributed to Dosio.)
In showing alternating pediments on the interior of the drum, the print is in accord with the drawing of the interior of the drum in Metropolitan 49.92.17 recto (cat. no. 4), except that it omits the ears of the windows. The print is mistaken, however, in placing on axis a window with a triangular instead of a segmental pediment.
The print shows the interior of the inner dome as it is in the model, including the placement of ribs, tondi, and trapezoids. (These are found in Metropolitan 49.92.92 recto [fig. 2], with their measurements. The drawing attributed to Dosio show them as well, but with somewhat different dimensions.) Also included in the print are the steps on the exterior surface of the inner dome (fig. 3). (The profile of the outer dome of the model as it is today was added only in the late sixteenth century and not known to Dupérac.)
The standing statues on top of the buttresses flanking the dome do not exist in the model and are not shown on any other representations of it. Michelangelo's study in Lille (cat. no. 22) for the dome does, however, include rough indications of standing sculptures on the exterior attic above the buttresses.
The oculus in the print follows closely the representations on both recto and verso of Metropolitan 49.92.92 (fig. 2), and is confirmed by them, even though in the print the screen with spokes at the top of the oculus is rendered as a solid. (Dupérac also mistakenly rendered as solids here the outer openings of the window and door of the facade, behind the portico at right.)
The two-stepped platform for the lantern in the prints is confirmed by Metropolitan 49.92.92 recto (fig. 2). The circulation space is outside the columns. There is no independent confirmation of the balustrade around the base of the lantern as shown in the print, although a balustrade or railing (as on the building today) would have been necessary. The section does not include membering on the interior of the lantern, despite the careful record made of this membering in 49.92.92 verso.

Vasari mentions a cross on top of the sphere, crowning the conical top of the lantern (Vasari, ed. Milanesi 1881, VII: 257). It appears in neither print.

Elevation

The drum of the dome in the print is represented in accord with the model and the building as constructed, except for having alternating pediments over the windows unlike the model, but as in the building, and having on axis a triangular rather than segmental pediment. Like the section it has sculpted figures over the buttresses, which are not on the model or building.

The attic of the drum corresponds to the model, and to the information provided by Metropolitan 49.92.92 verso, except for the buttressing volutes at the attic level added later to the model.

The placing and shape of the ribs and the three windows in each sector of the dome coincides with their representation on Metropolitan 49.92.92 verso. The print, Metropolitan 49.92.92 verso, and Metropolitan 49.92.1 all testify to three ranges of windows in the outer dome of the model, in contrast to Vasari's citing of only two (Vasari, ed. Milanesi 1881, VII: 256).

The ribs with steps leading to a two-stepped platform are in accord with the drawings on Metropolitan 49.92.92 recto and verso and with Metropolitan 49.92.1, where, however, the platform is no wider than the lantern and is only one step high.

The exterior of the lantern in the print finds confirmation as to the nature and proportions of its three stages only in the lantern of Metropolitan 49.92.1 in the Dupérac group. The lantern on the model today is different and was added when the model was modified in the late sixteenth century. *H.A.M.-C.H.S.*

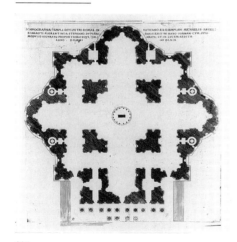

395
ETIENNE DUPÉRAC
Plan of St. Peter's

Milan, Civica Raccolta delle Stampe Achille Bertarelli, Castello Sforzesco
Engraved and etched.
460.4 × 414.3 mm
INSCRIBED: *ICHNOGRAPHIA TEMPLI DIVI PETRI ROMAE IN VATICANO EX ESEMPLARI MICHAELIS ANGELI / BONAROTI FLORENTINI A STEFANO DVPERAC PARISIENSI IN HANC FORMAM CVM SVIS / MODVLIS ACCVRATE PROPORTIONATEQVE DELINEATA ET IN LVCEM AEDITA / ANNO DOMINI MDLXIX*

PROVENANCE: Collezione Bertarelli.

BIBLIOGRAPHY: Ackerman 1961, I: 93-95; II: 99; 1964, II: 101; Bettini 1964: 500; Portoghesi and Zevi 1964a: fig. 574; Lees-Milne 1967: 186; Thoenes 1968: 331-341; Millon and Smyth 1976: 185-200; Boorsch 1982-83: 12; Nova 1984: 160; Ackerman 1986: 199-202, 322; Millon and Smyth 1988a: 114; Argan and Contardi 1990: 273-276, 322-334, and fig. 384; Marani 1992b: 464, 494-496.

This well-known plan is usually assumed to reproduce Michelangelo's intentions for the plan of St. Peter's. It

was John Coolidge (1942: 116) who first discussed the implications of the placement of the plan on the plate and demonstrated that, of Dupérac's three plates of St. Peter's, the plan, dated 1569, was the first plate prepared. It appears all three were made to be a group and can be dated 1569/70. Coolidge also showed that the columnar facade in the plan does not agree with the facade depicted in the elevation, and concluded that Dupérac lacked dependable information about the intended design of the facade. In fact, there is no evidence of Michelangelo's intentions for the facade of St. Peter's from his lifetime, other than the rapid summary drawing in the Vatican (Vat. Lat. 3211, fig. 92, reproduced in Tolnay 1980, IV, no. 592), which shows a portico of five columns in front of a structure generally accepted to be St. Peter's. Subsequent to the prints by Dupérac, before the end of the sixteenth century, there were a number of representations of a facade for St. Peter's They include temple front facades (medal by L. Fragni; a drawing in the former Dyson-Perrins Codex); a fresco by P. Nogari in the Biblioteca Vaticana (reproduced in Portoghesi and Zevi 1964: fig. 586); and a drawing of an unroofed columnar portico at Windsor Castle (RL 10448). It is possible Michelangelo never seriously addressed the nature of the facade and may even have considered preserving the remainder of Old St. Peter's.

Another anomaly in the plan by Dupérac, which demonstrates his lack of knowledge of Michelangelo's plan, is the placement of the main altar in the center of the crossing surrounded by a ring of columns. Michelangelo, aware of the location of the altar to the west of the center of the crossing, shifted the exterior windows of both the south and north apses several feet to the east in relation to the interior windows (Millon and Smyth 1976: 199). This shift ensures that a celebrant standing at the eccentrically placed altar will perceive the windows as axially oriented and the altar, therefore, at the center of the crossing. Dupérac's plan shows an ideally located altar at the center of the crossing in the place where Michelangelo desired (through the manipulation of the exterior windows) the celebrant to perceive he was.

The three prints by Dupérac were, apparently, in demand and have been reproduced or reprinted in a number of editions. *H.A.M.-C.H.S.*

396
AFTER MICHELANGELO
GIACOMO DELLA PORTA
LUIGI VANVITELLI
Model of One Half of the Drum and Dome of St. Peter's

Vatican, Musei Vaticani
Limewood, tempera paint; scale: 1:15.
5 × 4 × 2 m (omitting the modern base)

PROVENANCE: Fabbrica di S. Pietro.

BIBLIOGRAPHY: Poleni 1748: 126; Gotti 1875, I: 324; II: 136; P. Fontana 1877; Thode 1908, II: 163-167; K. Frey 1909b: 171-180; Thode 1913, III: 286, 292; K. Frey 1916: 81-87; D. Frey 1920: 91-136; 1921-22: 36-39; Panofsky 1921-22, I: 18-20; Alker 1922: 98-99; Brinckmann 1922: 92-97; Cascioli 1927: 205-209; Panofsky 1927: 45-49; Beltrami 1929: 49-63, 67-68; Dvorák 1929, II: 106-107; Tolnay 1930: 8-11; Körte 1932: 90-112; Tolnay 1932: 231-232; Wittkower 1933: 348-370; Giovannoni 1942: 11-12; Mariani 1942: 305-306; Schiavo 1952: 14-26; 1953: 202; Gioseffi 1960: 3-36; Schiavo 1960: 73-85; Ackerman 1961, II: 97-98, 105-110; Schiavo 1961: 519-532; Barocchi 1962b, IV: 1700-1729; Di Stefano 1963: 120; Ackerman 1964, II: 100, 107-114; Barbieri and Puppi 1964a: 917-919; Bettini 1964: 504; Tolnay 1964, IX: cols. 905-907; Wittkower 1964a: 26-35, 93-94; De Angelis d'Ossat 1965: 347-349; Schiavo 1965: 303-327; De Angelis d'Ossat 1966a, II: 343-346; Pane 1966: 383; Lees-Milne 1967: 198; Brandi 1968: 11-14; Portoghesi [1971]: 415-416; Francia 1977: 126; Wittkower 1978b: 76; Di Stefano 1980b: 88-91; Tolnay 1980, IV: 94-95; Nova 1984: 195-196; Ackerman 1986: 320-323; Millon and Smyth 1988a: 119-128; Argan and Contardi 1990: 329 and figs. 390 and 391.

The model of one half of the drum and dome of St. Peter's is the one made under Michelangelo's direction from November 1558 to November 1561, but with significant alterations. In our view, the evidence reviewed in this catalog indicates that the changes were due to the architects Giacomo della Porta in the late sixteenth century and Luigi Vanvitelli in the mid-eighteenth century. The drawings and prints already discussed make it possible to reconstruct the state of the model in 1561, as Michelangelo designed it, and to recognize the changes.

That the drum of the model is in its original state is confirmed by comparison with the section in the Metropolitan (49.92.20v.), with the elevations of the interior and exterior of the drum from the same group (49.92.17r., and 49.92.21r., their counterparts in Stockholm CC 1375 and CC 1305), and with the two prints by Dupérac. The exterior articulation of the drum of the model finds confirmation in Stockholm CC 1305 and Metropolitan 49.92.21 recto, although the drawing in New York lacks pediments over the windows, the entablature and the attic.

The nature of the pediments and attic on the exterior of the model are further confirmed by the section in Metropolitan 49.92.20 verso and the section of the drum in the print by Dupérac. The drawings of the interior and exterior of the drum from the circle of Dupérac and the prints by Dupérac show alternating pediments

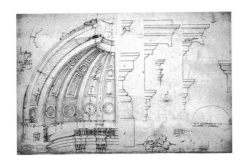

Fig. 2 - *Etienne Dupérac*, Half-section through the model of the attic and dome of St. Peter's *New York, Metropolitan Museum of Art, 49.92.92 recto*

on the interior and exterior of the drum, instead of triangular pediments on the exterior and segmental on the interior, as in the model. Michelangelo departed from the model in this respect when he built the window pediments on the building. The rendering of the windows of the interior of the model found in Metropolitan 49.92.17 recto includes the ears, omitted in the print by Dupérac, and also confirms the double frames of the window on the model. The cornice of the entablature above the pilasters on the interior of the model is slightly higher than that above the paired columns on the exterior and agrees with the sections in the Metropolitan and in Stockholm, the print by Dupérac, and the building today. The profiles of the inner and outer entablatures are confirmed by the ruled and scaled profiles on the right half of the sheet in the Metropolitan (49.92.92r.).

Two additional ruled sections in this drawing confirm the profiles of the attics on the exterior and interior of the model.

The profile of the interior attic and base of the exterior attic are repeated at the top of the sections through the drum in the Metropolitan and in Stockholm and testify further to the authenticity of the model.

The way the model is constructed for dismantling and assembly is pertinent. The base below the drum and the drum up through both of the attics on the interior and exterior, were built as a unit—though in two separate halves joined vertically in the central bay. Above the attics, the inner dome was built separately (fig. 3) from the exterior dome, and again in two parts joined at the center. The inner dome sits upon the inner attic, its lower edge resting just behind the projecting cornices of the salient sections of the attic and abutting the higher wall behind. The relationship of inner dome, attic and outer dome can best be seen in the stepped sections at left and right of the model. Portions of attic cornice stretching between the ribs of the inner dome are attached to the inner dome surface, not to the attic.

The drum was originally constructed so that the outer dome, now replaced, would sit at a higher level, on top of the wall of the exterior attic, and have a plain lower edge, without moldings, so that it would stand upright at the level of the cornice of the attic. There was to be an unarticulated junction of exterior dome and attic, different from the model today, as confirmed by two drawings from the Dupérac group in the Metropolitan (49.92.92r. and 49.92.1) and by the prints published by Dupérac. On the interior, the balustrade that was once above the interior entablature has been lost, but its original presence on the model is attested by the following: Metropolitan 49.92.92 recto, 49.92.20 verso, a drawing in the Nationalmuseum in Stockholm (CC 1375), the print of the section by Dupérac, three drawings attributed to Dosio (Uff. 92A, 94Ar.-v., and a payment to a cabinetmaker for making 231 balusters for the model in the week of 2-8 November 1561 (K. Frey 1909B: 179).

The tondi and trapezoids in each section of the inner surface of the interior dome of the model are found again in the representations on Metropolitan 49.92.92 recto, the print of the section by Dupérac, and two drawings attributed to Dosio (Uff. 94A recto, and Uff. 92A, where,

however, some of the dimensions vary and there are ovals rather than tondi as the lowest decoration elements). The festoons on the exterior attic of the model are also drawn on Metropolitan 49.92.92 verso, CC 1305 in Stockholm, and on the print of the elevation by Dupérac; they are confirmed by a payment to Nicola da Camerino, *intagliatore*, for one festoon carved during the period 29 March-3 April 1561 (Archivio della Reverenda Fabbrica di S. Pietro, I: 29, 67).

The evidence already reviewed in the previous entries shows that the original exterior dome, preceding the one on the model today, was hemispherical like the interior dome and was placed, according to the inscribed dimension (*oncie* 6, *minuti* 3) on Metropolitan 49.92.92 recto, so that the inner surface of the exterior dome was only 11.7 centimeters (4.6 inches) higher than the outer surface of the inner dome, a condition paralleled in the print of the section by Dupérac. At the scale of the building, that dimension would be 1.81 meters (5.89 feet). The exterior dome of the model originally had three levels of similarly shaped dormer windows and ribs with steps, as shown in Metropolitan 49.92.92 recto and verso, 49.92.1 and in the print of the exterior by Dupérac. According to the prints by Dupérac, the model also included standing sculptures above the buttresses. If they were part of the model originally, payments for them have not survived and they were omitted in other representations.

The lantern of the original model does not survive. The most complete representations—of the exterior of the lantern, the oculus below the lantern, and the two-stepped platform—of the lantern of the model in its original state are to be found on Metropolitan 49.92.92 verso, 49.92.1 and on the prints by Dupérac.

Missing today from the original model are, by way of summary, the outer dome, formerly much lower and hemispherical, the lantern, the balustrade on the inner cornice, the oculus in its position between the two hemispherical domes and, perhaps, the standing statues. Although the first alteration to the model is thought by some scholars to have been made by della Porta has he studied a more elevated profile for both the inner and outer domes, the lack of documents in the archive of St. Peter's for the construction of a new dome for the model, with an elevated profile, has caused other scholars to doubt that any changes were made to the model by della Porta. To judge, however, by the representation of the elevated profile of the cupola of the model in the painting of 1619 in the Casa Buonarroti by Domenico Cresti da Passignano, depicting Michelangelo presenting the model of St. Peter's to a pope, the exterior dome of the model had already been altered by that date. The words of the Vatican archivist Grimaldi, cited in the preliminary remarks, are in accord with the testimony of Passignano's painting.

What evidence there is points toward della Porta as having replaced the previous exterior dome, and lantern as well, with a new exterior dome of elevated profile, which incorporated a number of substantive changes. The changes were: a new horizontal molding at the juncture of dome and exterior attic; heraldic emblems of three mounts (for Sixtus V) at the base of all the ribs; a new thinner rib design, which eliminated the central steps in the ribs of the original model (Metropolitan 49.92.92r.-v.; print of the elevation by Dupérac); and a new design for all three ranges of dormer windows in new, higher locations. The new lantern on the model, which agrees in most respects with the lantern by della Porta on the building, though about the same height as that shown in the print by Dupérac, rests on a platform of only one step, has buttresses of paired columns on pedestals with a passageway behind (not seen in the Dupérac print), reverse volutes at the base of the pedestals and above the buttresses, candelabra above the volutes and, for the third level, a paneled cone on a base of several torus rings—all of which are different from the Dupérac print and Metropolitan 49.92.1.

Major alterations to the model were made in the middle of the eighteenth century, when lesions in the fabric of the

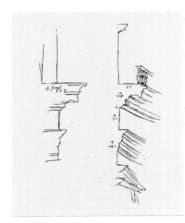

Fig. 6 - *Giovanni Antonio Dosio*, Profiles of the model of the drum and dome of St. Peter's, *Florence, Uffizi, Gabinetto Disegni e Stampe, 94A verso*

drum and dome of the building gave rise to a series of studies of the structure and stability of the dome. On 21 March 1743 Benedict XIV asked Giovanni Poleni, professor of theoretical and experimental physics at the University of Padua, to examine the dome of St. Peter's and report on its stability. Poleni's report, presented to the pope on 10 June, was convincing and the measures recommended were implemented. The pope also asked Poleni to write a history of the drum and dome, providing him with access to archivial materials, drawings and reports that had been previously requested or received. Poleni's volume, *Memorie istoriche della Gran Cupola nel Tempio Vaticano* (Padua, 1748), is a thorough compendium of mid-eighteenth-century scientific and pseudo-scientific thought of scientist, mathematicians, engineers and architects.

Luigi Vanvitelli, assistant to Filippo Barigoni as architect of St. Peter's from 20 December 1736 (Archivio della Reverenda Fabbrica di S. Pietro, Ser. Armadi, Arm. 27, vol. 427: 144), prepared many drawings indicating where cracks and lesions were found on the two domes, on the interior and exterior of the drum buttresses, on the base of the drum, and on the main arches of the crossing.

Vanvitelli also worked on the drum and dome model in the autumn of 1742. Not only did he transfer to the model all the cracks and lesions noted in his drawings, but he also added to the model his recommendations for reinforcement of the structure. He may also, at that time, have restored the model where necessary to have it conform to the building as constructed.

From their appearance it would seem that the two upper levels of dormer windows in the exterior dome date from this moment.

Vanvitelli's recommendations included buttressing the drum at its base above the four main piers (not included on the model), as well as adding volute buttresses to join the attic on the exterior to the top of the paired column buttress of the drum. The volute buttresses had standing statues of prophets as added stabilizing weight. (These sculptures, commissioned from Antonio Corradini, were made of clay and were still in place on the model in the late nineteenth century. Vanvitelli proposed that the main buttresses of the drum should be opened up in order to insert within each a large metal braced frame, which would rigidify the buttress and further sustain the drum. Vanvitelli's proposal may still be seen on the model in the section at the right, where he sliced a buttress in two, hinged the outer edge, and painted on the exposed inner surface the proposed braced metal frame. It also seems likely that, at this time, Vanvitelli had the thin facing boards made that were attached to the edge of the outer dome at left and right. They were given the shape of the inner and outer dome as constructed, and their profiles were painted on the boards, perhaps to visualize better the relation between the two domes and the oculus. Thereafter the model was a graphic representation of the situation on the building.

The model of the drum and dome as it is today chronicles the history of the drum and dome on St. Peter's. Michelangelo's early design for the interior and exterior of the drum ghrough the attics (before he decided to alternate the window pediments), together with his inner dome, are as he left them. The new exterior dome and lantern attributable to della Porta were retained by Vanvitelli, who added attic buttresses, standing statues, and probably the dormer windows at the upper levels of the dome. Perhaps Vanvitelli renewed the festoons and other elements that may have been lost in the seventeenth and early eighteenth centuries. He inserted his proposed braced frame in the buttresses, and carefully indicated all the cracks and lesions in base, drum, domes, and lantern—all of which remain today on the model. The history of the drum and dome of St. Peter's is more readily discernible in the model than in any representation or, indeed, on the basilica.

H.A.M.-C.H.S.

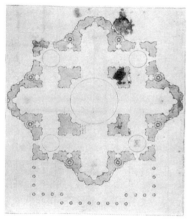

397
ANONYMOUS
Plan of St. Peter's with a Colonnaded Forecourt

Windsor Castle, Royal Library, RL 10448
Pen, brown ink and wash over black chalk and incised lines; watermark: crossbow in a circle with an arrowhead above.
455 × 380 mm
INSCRIBED: *loco dove sta / al p[rese]nte la / sepultura* (to right of southeast pier); *loco de la / sepultura / deputato* (inscribed within a square in the Cappella Gregoriana at the northeast); *p[almi] 104* (width of the south arm).

PROVENANCE: from the collection of Cassiano dal Pozzo.

BIBLIOGRAPHY: Noach 1956: 376-379 and fig. 40; Ackerman 1961, II: 100; 1964, II: 102; Millon and Smyth 1976: 203; Ackerman 1986: 322.

Noach was the first to publish this drawing from Windsor and associate it with a proposal to move the tomb of Paul III from the north side of the southeast central pier to the center of the Cappella Gregoriana.

The Cappella Gregoriana, begun under Michelangelo's direction, but probably not carried much above the foundation level in his time (Millon and Smyth 1980: 35-36), is likely to have been continued by Pirro Ligorio, perhaps up to the level of the top of the main niches on the exterior. Work above that level seems to have been carried out, not by Vignola, Ligorio's successor, but by Giacomo della Porta, from 1573 onward (Millon and Smyth 1988c, Appendix III: 266-268). With the focus of building activity on the Cappella Gregoriana from 1573, it seems likely that the proposal for moving the tomb of Paul III dates from these years. The tomb eventually found a home in the south niche of the new west choir built in the 1590s. The drawing is of considerable interest in that, while reproducing the plan with four equal arms published by Dupérac, it shows entrances or openings from two directions in each of the satellite chapels and a completely different east elevation.

Where the plan by Dupérac shows a widening of the body of the structure at the east to provide secondary entries and a suitable width for a facade of ten columns, the drawing at Windsor repeats on the *east* facade the elevation of the apses on the north, south and west, omitting the central entrance found on the plan by Dupérac. In place of the temple front facade of the Dupérac prints, the plan at Windsor includes an unroofed columnar portico the width of the nave and satellite chapels (14 columns wide), with a salient central section (8 columns) about as wide as the ten columns of the plan by Dupérac.

The plan at Windsor is rigidly symmetrical quadrilaterally, including *lumache* flanking the east and west apses, where they were not built and perhaps never intended. The plan by Dupérac shows square "sacristies" to either side of the west apse, roughly where they were to be constructed by della Porta in the 1590s, but without the small spiral stair that affords access to the several levels of spaces in these piers. It is noteworthy that in the building itself the west elevations of the Cappella della Colonna (south-west satellite chapel) and the Cappella di S. Michele (northwest satellite chapel), though now without openings, still retain traces of these entrances into the chapels as shown on the plan at Windsor.

The plan was used to show the proposed location of the tomb of Paul III. The incised lines indicate it was drawn by transfer from another sheet. The purpose of the plan that served as a base plan for the drawing at Windsor is unknown. What is ever the designated plan? If a proposal for the east facade significantly different from the design in the Windsor drawing had been known and accepted at the time when the drawing at Windsor was transferred, the plan that served as the model would have been obsolete and hence probably unsatisfactory for the purposes here. Why in that case would it have been used to show a proposal for the location of Paul III's tomb? Was this instead the plan expected for St. Peter's at the time of the proposals? At the very least, the configuration of the east facade on the drawing at Windsor could be evidence that, at the time the drawing was executed, it is unlikely a decision had been promulgated indicating a selected design, whether as shown in the Dupérac prints, in the medal by Fragni, in the drawing of the Feltrinelli and Dyson-Perrins album, in the fresco by Nogari in the Biblioteca Vaticana (Ackerman 1961, pl. 58b; Portoghesi and Zevi 1964, fig. 586), or as represented on the drawing at Windsor.

H.A.M.-C.H.S.

398
LORENZO FRAGNI
East Elevation of St. Peter's, the Fragni Medal
(reverse)

Vatican, Biblioteca Apostolica Vaticana, Medagliere, XXVIII, 1173
Bronze.
dia. 40 mm
PROVENANCE:

BIBLIOGRAPHY: D. Frey 1920: 118-119; Gioseffi 1960: 68 and fig. 51; Lees-Milne 1967: 188; Thoenes 1968: 338 n. 28; Varriano 1984: 70; Millon and Smyth 1988a: 99.

D. Frey (1920: 118-119) was the first to consider the medal in relation to Michelangelo's designs for St. Peter's. In contrast to the aerial perspective of St. Peter's from the east (formerly Dyson-Perrins Collection, now on deposit in the Morgan Library, New York), the Fragni medal, dating from the reign of Gregory XIII (obverse), shows the second attic order with rectangular windows on both south and north apses. The medal agrees, however, with the perspective in the Morgan Library in showing a hemispherical dome with only two ranges of dormer windows (as described by Vasari [Vasari, ed. Milanesi 1881, IV: 257]) and a portico of six columns.

The portico as depicted on the medal is, therefore, a substitution of a six-column facade for the four-column facade shown on the earlier well-known plan by Dupérac and on the somewhat earlier but similar facade in the section/elevation of St. Peter's from the east in the Biblioteca Nazionale, Naples, reproduced and discussed by Keller (1976: 24-50). The substitution of a six- for a four-column facade—a project corroborated by the facade in the aerial perspective in the Morgan Library—together with the appearance of the second attic on both south and north apses argues for a resolve during the reign of Gregory XIII to complete St. Peter's in accord with plans prepared most likely by Giacomo della Porta, Vignola's successor as architect in 1573.

The aerial perspective of St. Peter's in the Morgan Library shows the first, the original, attic order in both south and north apses. It is on a page of a luxuriously illustrated guide to Rome for the Holy Year 1575 (Smyth 1970: 265), probably drawn in late 1574-early 1575, clearly for a particularly distinguished visitor. The decision to eliminate the first attic on the south and complete the building using the second attic may have been made shortly thereafter, perhaps to mark the Jubilee of 1575, but in any case before the end of the reign of Gregory XIII (1572-85), as evidenced by the Fragni medal.

H.A.M.-C.H.S.

399
DOMENICO CRESTI DA PASSIGNANO
Michelangelo Presents to Pope Paul IV the Model for the Completion of the Fabric and the Cupola of St. Peter's

Florence, Casa Buonarroti
Oil on canvas, integrated in an architectural framework
236 × 141 cm
EPIGRAPH: *Illius Templi structurae quo verae Religionis sedem Sacrique Imperii maiestatem universus veneratur orbis solum Bonarrotae ingenium par quod praeter aedificii decorem et Magnificentiam Paulus IV Pont. Max. admiraretur* (overhead; attributed to Jacopo Soldani).

PROVENANCE: Casa Buonarroti.

BIBLIOGRAPHY: Thode 1908, II: 526; Steinmann 1913: 89; Voss 1920: 404-406; Baumgart 1932, XXVI: 285-286; Coolidge 1942: 77, 103 nn. 85-89; Ackerman 1961, II: 97, 101, 103, 111; 1964, II: 100, 103, 106, 114; Tolnay 1964, IX: col. 907; Wittkower

1964a: 165; Procacci 1965: 11, 174, 220; Lees-Milne 1967: 186; Millon and Smyth 1969: 487-488 nn. 4 and 6; Einem 1973: 215, 225; Millon and Smyth 1976: 202-204; Vliegenthart 1976: 133-137; Nissman 1979: 183-189, 342-345; Millon 1980: 36; Ackerman 1986: 318; Millon and Smyth 1988a: 136-138; 1988c: 218, 242 n. 15, 259 n. 131; Argan and Contardi 1990: 332-335 and fig. 432.

The drum and dome in the painting by Passignano show the alterations of della Porta to Michelangelo's design as that design is documented by the views in the Dupérac group in the Metropolitan and in Stockholm, the Dosio group in the Uffizi, and the prints by Dupérac. It has della Porta's high profile, the new dormer windows, the new cornice that joins the dome to the attic, and the new lantern—except that the painting omits both the ressauts and the candelabra above the volutes of the second stage of the lantern. (It is conceivable the painting shows the lantern as della Porta built it on the model, before arriving at the design that was constructed.)

The painter was commissioned to show Michelangelo presenting his model of the cupola of St. Peter's to Pope Paul IV, along with an indication of Rome as fortified by the pope. (Instead, he portrayed Pius IV in the painting [Steinmann 1913: 89 and Vliegenthart 1976: 133-137].) In representing the dome model, the painter chose to place it together with two little domes on top of the large wooden model of the main body of the basilica that was made in 1547 (as first argued by Coolidge [1942: 77]). In doing so, the painter had to show the model of the drum and dome and the model of the main body of the building at the same scale, even though they had been built at very different scales. (For possible scales of the model of 1547, now lost, see Saalman 1975: 380-386 and Millon and Smyth 1976: 202-204).

The painter must have intended to show the state of the models as Michelangelo had left them. This is attested by the representation of the elevation of the main body of the basilica. There Passignano showed the arched window of Michelangelo's original attic order as it would have been on that model, although arched windows no longer existed in Passignano's time on the building itself (Millon and Smyth 1969 and 1988c). But he was mistaken in showing della Porta's dome as Michelangelo's. In all likelihood, the representation of the cupola with della Porta's changes is based on the model of the exterior dome as changed by della Porta rather than taken from the building itself. It follows that the changed profile of the dome model dates from della Porta's time, not Vanvitelli's as has been suggested. However, there are some differences in the representation both from the model as it is today and from the dome as built. The ressauts of the buttresses of the drum are too shallow; the festoons in the attic are missing; there are drop moldings below the window of the drum; and the three *monti* at the base of each rib are not included. (A different view is held by Tolnay [1964, IX, cols. 906-907] and von Einem [1973: 215, 225], who believe the painting represents the drum and dome of the early model of St. Peter's that Michelangelo made in 1547.)

The lantern in the painting also does not coincide exactly with the lantern of the model or with the lantern of the building: there are no ressauts above the paired columns; there is no passageway behind them; and no candelabra above the volutes of the second stage. It may be that in these, as well as in the other differences, Passignano was merely inaccurate. But a slim possibility does remain that, when Passignano painted the model, it may have incorporated a design for the lantern by della Porta that was later superseded in construction—not a likely possibility because the lantern of the model today is like the building. On the other hand, the little domes in the painting may, indeed, represent della Porta's original design (replacing an earlier design for these domes by Vignola; for Vignola's design, see Coolidge 1942). Della Porta built one of these little domes over the Cappella Gregoriana before vaulting the main dome. A few years later, after completing the main dome, he dismantled this little dome and its lantern

and built the little domes in their present form (Millon 1980: 36).

The painting dates from 1619 as part of a decorative program for the gallery of the Buonarroti house in Florence, commissioned by Michelangelo Buonarroti the Younger.   *H.A.M.-C.H.S.*

400
BATTISTA NALDINI (?)
View of the Crossing of St. Peter's from the Nave

Hamburg, Kunsthalle, 21311
Pen, brown ink and wash.
432/434 × 292/293 mm
INSCRIBED: *questo e ritrato di S^{to} pietro dalla porta della chiesa / vecchia aca[n]to all'organo verso la testa della croce di Brama[n]te.*

BIBLIOGRAPHY: Egger 1911, pl. 28; Ackerman 1961, II: 64; 1964, II: 96; Portoghesi and Zevi 1964: fig. 582; Wittkower 1964a, pl. 36; Lees-Milne 1967: 194; Wittkower 1978b: 75, fig. 74; Galassi Paluzzi 1975: 117, fig. 102; Francia 1977: fig. 24; Ackerman 1986: 317, 319, fig. 104; Metternich and Thoenes 1987: 107, 118, 175, fig. 125.

Drawn looking west from ground level near the *muro divisorio*, which separated Old St. Peter's from the new construction to the west, the drawing in Hamburg displays prominently the early sixteenth-century structure built against the apse of the earlier basilica to house the main altar. The vault of the choir and apse constructed by Bramante can be seen above and behind the altar structure. At left is the altar aedicule behind the southeast pier of the dome, dating from the building campaigns of Antonio da Sangallo. A large clump of masonry attached to the southeast pier extends into the nave. Above, the drum of the dome is seen partly constructed: there are five pairs of pilasters with capitals and five windows with pediments. At left, one window lacks a pediment, and there the wall above the windows seems not to have risen above the height of the base of the capitals. The window of the drum with a segmental pediment, at right, is the same as that seen at the left in the Dosio drawing (Uff. 91A). The main arch spanning the nave obscures the remainder of the drum; hence it is not possible to know whether or not the two drawings were made at about the same time. (The Uffizi drawing also shows a clump of masonry adjacent to the southeast pier in the crossing.)

Work at the level of the capitals of the drum was reached only in March 1563 (Millon and Smyth 1969: 495 n. 41), a reasonable *terminus post quem* for the drawing.
                          H.A.M.-C.H.S.

401
GIOVANNI ANTONIO DOSIO
View of the Crossing of St. Peter's from the South Arm

Florence, Galleria degli Uffizi, Gabinetto Disegni e Stampe, Uff. 91A
Pen, brown ink and wash.
411/414 × 262/264 mm (upper left corner repaired)

PROVENANCE: unavailable.

BIBLIOGRAPHY: Ferri 1885: 151; Egger 1911, pl. 27; Ackerman 1961, II: 94; 1964, II: 96; Wittkower 1964a, pl. 37; F. Borsi et al. 1976: 134-136; Wittkower 1978b: 75-76, fig. 72; Millon and Smyth 1988a: 96 and fig. D.

Drawn looking north from a somewhat elevated position in the apse of the south arm of St. Peter's, the drawing shows, in the crossing, the apse of Old St. Peter's, together with the early sixteenth-century enclosing structure built to protect the altar. One of the spiral columns in the altar enclosure can be seen through an arched opening in the side of the new structure. Above, a cylindrical drum of one of the columns on the exterior of the drum is being raised by hoists attached to masts. The interior of the drum of the cupola is complete through the level of the capitals on the northwest (including a segmental pediment above a window), while the remainder of the drum visible in the drawing has not reached the level of the lintels above the windows.

Work on the drum was interrupted late in 1556, when the drum could not have been much above the level of the window sills (Millon and Smyth 1969: 487 n. 3; 495, nos. 38 and 39). Work on the drum began again only in 1561 (Millon and Smyth 1988c: 227 n. 70) and reached the level of the capitals on the exterior only in March 1563 (Millon and Smyth 1969: 495 n. 41). All were in place by the end of 1564. The capitals on the interior are at the same level as those on the exterior and likely to have been placed at the same time, providing, therefore, a date of 1563 for the drawing.   *H.A.M.-C.H.S.*

402

BERNARDO BUONTALENTI
*Studies from the Model of the Drum and Dome
of St. Peter's*

Florence, Galleria degli Uffizi, Gabinetto Disegni e Stampe,
Uff. 2464Ar.
Pen, brown ink.
271/274 × 194/199 mm (trimmed)
RECTO: a) partial elevation of two alternatives of a lantern
(upper center); b) elevation of an octagonal lantern (upper
right); c) section/elevation of the base of a lantern (center);
d) Elevation of a pier of an attic with flanking festoons (center
right); e) elevations of two dormer windows at the upper level of
a dome (lower center and left); f) drawing of an ornament that
includes a human face (lower right).
VERSO: studies for windows in the surface of the dome;
elevation of a facade of a church (?).
a) elevation of an arched window on the curved surface of a
dome (upper left); b) elevation of a rectangular window,
probably for a dome (upper center); c) variant of b) above (?)
(center); d) (turned 90°) elevation of a facade with a giant
order.

PROVENANCE: unavailable.

BIBLIOGRAPHY: Ferri 1885: 54; Giovannozzi 1933: 518-520; Berti
1950: 174 n. 26; Botto 1968: 75-76.

As first noted by Giovannozzi (1933) and confirmed by
Berti (1950), the drawings on the recto appear to relate to
designs for the lantern of St. Peter's in Rome. Although
Buontalenti may have visited Rome in 1556/57, Giovannozzi thought the designs to be drawn after the lantern
had been constructed, which, as noted by Botto (1968),
would postulate an otherwise undocumented visit to
Rome in the 1590s. Nonetheless, Botto (1968) feels certain the drawing dates from the latter part of Buontalenti's career.
The Buonatelenti drawings, however, resemble less the
constructed lantern of della Porta than Michelangelo's
designs for the lantern as known from drawings in
Haarlem, at Lille (CB 118A), in the Casa Buonarroti

(CB 118A), and at the Metropolitan Museum, as well as
from the prints by Dupérac.
The lantern in upper right on the sheet resembles the lantern in the drawing from Lille in its proportion and in being eightsided, while in its form it resembles the lantern
in the center of the sheet from Haarlem. The "C" scroll
volutes of the upper level of this same lantern drawing by
Buontalenti are found on sheets from Haarlem (center),
Lille, Casa Buonarroti 118A (upper), Metropolitan Museum 44.92.1, and on the two prints of St. Peter's by Dupérac. The drawing at upper center depicts two alternatives
for the upper levels of the lantern, one with reverse volutes that may also be found on the sheet in Haarlem
(center left). The section/elevation of the base of the lantern in the center of the sheet includes sloping buttresses
at the base of the lantern and consoles supporting an encircling balustrade. Sloping buttresses and "C" scroll supports at the base of the lantern are also found on three of
the lanterns on the sheet from Haarlem (center, center
left, and upper left). The sheet by Buontalenti in the Uffizi includes two drawings of dormer windows in the upper
surface of the dome, an indication omitted in the three
drawings by Michelangelo in Haarlem, Lille, and the Casa
Buonarroti in Florence.
Michelangelo's intentions for these windows are known
only through two drawings in the Metropolitan Museum,
an aerial perspective of St. Peter's in the volume in the
Morgan Library, the print by Dupérac, and the drawings
on this sheet. Detail drawings of the dormer windows on
the verso of a sheet in the Metropolitan Museum
(49.92.92) confirm Buontalenti's recording of the windows. The pilaster bunch, with flanking festoons at center
right on Uff. 2464, depicts a portion of the attic level between the entablature of the main order of the drum and

Fig. 8 - Michelangelo, Sections and elevations for the
dome and lantern of St. Peter's
Haarlem, Teylers Museum, A29 recto

the spring level of the dome. Michelangelo's design for
the attic is known through its representation on the sheet
49.92.92 verso from the Metropolitan Museum, on the
print by Dupérac, on a drawing from Stockholm, from a
document recording payment for the fashioning of a festoon for the model, and from their presence on the model
today. The several alternatives for the lantern depicted on
the sheet suggest that Buontalenti had access to studies by
Michelangelo for the lantern and domes, either in the
original or through copies. He may also have seen the terracotta model of the drum and dome made by Michelangelo in 1557. The drawings by Michelangelo on sheets from
Haarlem, Lille and the Casa Buonarroti in Florence show
lanterns with 8 (CB 118A, Haarlem), 10 (Haarlem), and
12 sides (Lille, Haarlem) and are usually thought to antedate commencement of construction of a sixteen-sided
drum at St. Peter's in 1554/55.
Whatever the date of the Buontalenti drawing, whether
drawn while in Rome in 1557, or much later, as suggested
by Giovannozzi (1933) and Botto (1968), it reflects ideas
about the lantern of St. Peter's that were being studied by

Michelangelo in the drawings from Haarlem, Lille and the
Casa Buonarroti, ideas that were in flux as late as
1560/61, when payment was made for heavy paper for
modeling the lantern (K. Frey 1916: 85, 668.33). This
sheet by Buontalenti provides valuable new evidence concerning the evolution of Michelangelo's ideas for the lantern.   *H.A.M.-C.H.S.*

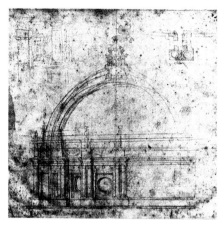

403

MICHELANGELO BUONARROTI
*Section and Elevations for the Drum and Dome of
St. Peter's*

Lille, Musée des Beaux-Arts, Collection Wicar, 93-94
Incised lines, black chalk with a few lines in red chalk.
260 × 267 mm
a) elevation of drum and lantern; section of dome (center);
b) plan of a main buttress of the drum (upper right); c) partial
elevation of project for city gate (Hirst 1974: 662) as a design
for the present attic order of St. Peter's (upper left)'.

PROVENANCE: Wicar.

BIBLIOGRAPHY: Geymüller 1904: 39; Thode 1908, II: 161; K. Frey
1911: 83; Thode 1913, III: 109-110, 286; K. Frey 1916: 90; D.
Frey 1920: 108-110; Dvořák 1929, II: 106; Tolnay 1930: 8 n. 4;
Wittkower 1933: 357-358; Tolnay 1951: 188; Düssler 1959: 168-
169; Gioseffi 1960: 12; Tolnay 1960, V: 220-221; Ackerman 1961,
II: 98, 109; 1964: 100, 111-112; Barbieri and Puppi 1964a: 915;
Bettini 1964: 503; Tolnay 1964a, IX: col. 908; Wittkower 1964a:
45-56; Barocchi 1965: no. 96; Berti 1965: 486; Coulanges-
Rosenberg 1965: 160-161; De Angelis d'Ossat 1965: 348, 349;
Schiavo 1965: 312-313 n. 4; De Angelis d'Ossat 1966a, II: 344,
346; Alker 1968: 4-6, 9-11; Brandi 1968: 9; Châtelet 1970: 50-51;
Hartt 1971: 350; Einem 1973: 225; Hirst 1974: 662-664; Millon
and Smyth 1975: 162-166; Saalman 1975: 397-405; Francia 1977:
127; Tolnay 1977: 10; Wittkower 1978b: 77; Di Stefano 1980b:
875; Tolnay 1980, IV: 93-94; Joannides 1981b: 621; Carpiceci
1983: 199; Nova 1984b: 196; Ackerman 1986: 320, 324; Millon
and Smyth 1988a: 143-147; 1988c: 219, 237-238, 244 n. 23; Argan and Contardi 1990: 329-330 and fig. 444; Joannides 1992: 248
and n. 14.

This sheet contains the only drawing that shows
Michelangelo studying the relationship between drum,
buttresses, attic, inner and outer domes, oculus, and lantern. That Michelangelo himself executed all of the drawings on the sheet including the drum, usually attributed to
an assistant, appears undeniable given the purposes and
evolutionary nature of the drawing.
Michelangelo shows the structure when the buttresses,
windows, attic and dome profiles were apparently still being thought about and in the process of being designed.
The lines that indicate the profiles of the two domes seem
to include: 1) several inner domes, one of which is
hemispherical and another slightly elevated with the steps
on its exterior surface that lead to windows into the oculus; 2) several elevated profiles for the outer dome, at least
one of which leads to the base of the lantern. This lantern
is at an upper level some distance from the windows of the

oculus below. At the time of this drawing Michelangelo was apparently considering both a hemispherical and elevated dome for the interior, but only an elevated dome for the exterior.

The drum is drawn here as twelve-sided—only three bays are shown between the center line and the buttress to the left, one quarter of the whole. (The buttress to the left must be read as a full elevation, or slightly more, because the thickness of the buttress is shown on the *left* side of the opening in the passageway through it.)

It is held (Joannides 1992: 248 and n. 14) that it represents a sixteen-sided drum. (Referring to Letarouilly for comparison with the drawing in Lille is not helpful. In the print by Letarouilly the central axis passes through the center of a window, as does the lateral or transverse axis to either side. Eight buttresses are shown. If the drawing in Lille were doubled to the right, only the seven buttresses would be shown. In the drawing in Lille the central axis of the drum passes just to the left of a buttress with its pair of columns, not through a window. If the plan of the drum in the drawing in Lille is to be symmetrical, it must have a buttress at left on the lateral axis; the buttress is clearly shown in the drawing. There are three bays between the buttresses that mark the axes. There can be no second buttress on the lateral axis hidden behind the one indicated. The next buttress further along on the drum would correspond in its placement to the next inner buttress shown in the drawing.)

The attic, at this stage of Michelangelo's thinking about the design, projects out above the buttresses—a curious feature present in no other representation. This was no accident: the projecting attic-spur was studied at two different levels, as may be seen in the profiles at the left. Above the attic an exterior profile of the dome rests on the projecting attic buttress. This is an impossibility, for there would be nothing to support the dome between the buttresses. Michelangelo might, however, have considered having a salient rib springing from each buttress.

The plan of a buttress and adjacent wall of the drum at upper right shows a passageway between the paired columns and drum. The drawing at upper left is not related to the dome. It is in our view an elevation for one of Michelangelo's designs for a city gate, because it includes membering relevant to city-gate design, not to St. Peter's, where, however, the motif does reappear in the new attic order built in 1564-66, after Michelangelo's death (Millon and Smyth 1975: 162-165).

Some indeed are convinced that the drawing at upper left must be a study specifically for the new, second attic of St. Peter's (Hirst 1974: 662-664; Saalman 1975: 397-398; Joannides 1981b: 621).

The Lille drawing shows Michelangelo considering elements that were not ultimately used in his model of the drum and dome or on the building. These include: circular windows in the drum (first drawn with incised lines) which are set in recessed frames with festoons above them; socles under the paired columns of the buttresses and corresponding bases on the wall of the drum; tall rectangular passageways through the buttresses, to almost their full height (again with festoons above), and projecting spurs of the attic. The spurs of the attic, at both the initial and second levels, which rest on the buttresses below, contain large passageways (in this case arched) and are topped by standing statues. The projecting spurs of the attic were first drawn at the lower attic level and repeated at the new upper level when the attic was raised. If the statues were initially intended to rise from the lower attic (as appears to be the case), they would have been gigantic, as noted by Tolnay (1980, IV: 93). Festoons were added to the second, elevated, attic. On the left, the diagonal above the attic buttress-spur, connected to the uppermost horizontal line (just above the attic), may indicate a sloping buttressing element connecting a rib to the projecting spur of the attic.

Joannides has recently proposed that the columns might be shorthand indications of Corinthian columns (1981b: 621). They are likely to be Tuscan as usually thought, not only because of the capitals, but also because of the

proportion of diameter to height—about 1:8, instead of 1:9½ as they should be if they were Corinthian. Joannides is now of this view (1992: 260 n. 14). Saalman (1975: 400) has suggested that the attic configuration derives from Michelangelo's own designs for alterations to S. Maria del Fiore in Florence.

The lantern consists of three stages: 1) tall windows between single pilasters (or columns) crowned by an entablature, possibly with ressauts; 2) a second level with volutes and entablature; and 3) a cone surmounted possibly by a small sphere. The lantern is drawn in elevation and the oculus in section. The windows into the oculus are at a much lower level than the platform of the lantern. Either Michelangelo was considering an interior and exterior dome widely separated at the lantern, or the drawing of the lantern and the oculus represent different phases in the study of the design. Neither relates to the pair of semi-circular lines that Dagobert Frey (1920: 108-110) thought to be an indication of a hemispherical inner dome.

It was Wittkower who most fully recognized the importance of the drawing for the study of the drum and dome (1933: 357). Tolnay recently attributed the entire sheet to Michelangelo (1980, IV: 93), as did Millon and Smyth (1988a: 146). Yet, most scholars believe the drum in the drawing was executed by an assistant of Michelangelo under his direction, as originally proposed by Thode (1913: 110) and stressed by Tolnay (1930: 8), Wittkower (1933: 357), Düssler (1959: 168-169), Barocchi (1965, no. 96) and Saalman (1975: 398).

Wittkower (1933: 357-358; 1964a: 46-56), rejecting a date in the 1550s advanced by Thode (1908: 161) and accepted by K. Frey (1911: 83), dated this drawing 1546-47 prior to the completion of the wooden model. Many other scholars have accepted the early date (Düssler 1959: 168-169; Gioseffi 1960: 12; Ackerman 1961, II: 98; Bettini 1964: 503; Barocchi 1965, no. 96; Alker 1968: 10; Châtelet 1970: 51; Hartt 1971: 350). If not from 1547, the drawing in Lille must surely date before 1555 since it is for a twelve-sided drum. In April and May 1555 more than twenty-four Corinthian capitals were ordered for the interior of the drum (K. Frey 1916: 90).

While most scholars, following Wittkower, have dated the drawing in Lille in 1546-47, Saalman has dated it within the period 1547-54 and probably 1552-54 (1975: 397-398). Joannides has suggested the drawing should be dated as late as 1557-58, supposing that the drum was begun in accord with the design of this drawing, with socles and circular windows (Joannides 1981b: 621). Most scholars date the drawings and the inscription on the verso in the 1550s. The inscription there and a drawing for the stair of the Biblioteca Laurenziana have both been dated 1557. The verso also contains a drawing that might conceivably be a study for the exterior windows of the drum in its ultimate state.

Always linked with the drawing at Lille is the drawing by Michelangelo at Haarlem, the recto of which concentrates on study of the lantern. (On the verso of the drawing in Haarlem there is what may be a study plan of the volutes of the second stage of the lantern.) Most scholars consider that the drawing in Lille preceded the one in Haarlem. Brandi (1968: 8) dates the Haarlem drawing as late as the 1560s. Should it be assumed that Michelangelo always developed his designs in a linear progression, the drawing in Haarlem could be dated before the drawing in Lille. The five studies of lantern of 8, 10, and 12 sides in the Haarlem sheet appear to precede the drawing in Lille, which is closer to the Dupérac print. The print, as we have seen, has a strong claim to represent the lantern of Michelangelo's model with some accuracy.

The designs in the drawings of Haarlem and Lille have regularly been cited as showing the closeness of Michelangelo's ideas at this stage of the design to the drum, dome and lantern of the cathedral of Florence with its circular windows, attic, double domes of elevated profile, ribs, lantern with volutes, shells, cone and tall, slender windows.

H.A.M.-C.H.S.

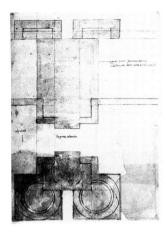

404

MICHELANGELO BUONARROTI
Plan of the Buttress and Portion of the Drum of St. Peter's

Florence, Casa Buonarroti, CB 31A
Brown ink and wash, black and red chalk; restored section at lower right; sheet laid down;
watermark: visible, but as sheet laid down it is not decipherable;
scale: *el palmo* (center left).
558/556 × 388/387 mm (includes restoration).
INSCRIBED (In Michelangelo's hand):
1) *Questa parte che resta bianca | è la faccia dove anno a esser gli ochi* (upper right)
2) *el palmo*, with line measure (center left)
3) *la porta dell andito* (center)
PROVENANCE: Casa Buonarroti.

BIBLIOGRAPHY: Geymüller 1904: 39; Thode 1908, II: 161-162; K. Frey 1911: 98; Thode 1913, III: 73; D. Frey 1920: 106; Wittkower 1933: 357; Tolnay 1951: 189; Düssler 1959: 223; Ackerman 1961, II: 98, 109; Barocchi 1962a: 192-193; Ackerman 1964, II: 100, 111; Barocchi 1964b: 74; Barbieri and Puppi 1964a: 915, 1003; Wittkower 1964a: 47; Berti 1965: 488; De Angelis d'Ossat 1965: 349, 361, 1966a, II: 346, 353; Hartt 1971: 351; Tolnay 1975b: 115; Joannides 1981b: 621; Berti 1985: 207; Ackerman 1986: 320; Millon and Smyth 1988a: 148-149; Argan and Contardi 1990: 330 and fig. 446.

The buttress and wall were drawn on this sheet at a scale of 1:15, the same scale as the model of the drum and dome, and may be a preparatory drawing for the model. (The wall is drawn, though, without the slight curvature that would be required in construction of the model.) As has been noted for generations, the drawing depicts accurately the model and the building as built except for the windows which are inscribed "ochi"—circular, then, like those on the drawing in Lille, rather than rectangular, as on the model and building. The column diameter (5.5. *palmi*) is the same as on the model and building (Wittkower 1933: 357).

The drawing appears to be a rendering of the buttress system from interior to exterior, perhaps to study the relation of interior pilasters to exterior buttress and to gauge the full depth of wall and buttress. The wall is seemingly less important here and is left blank.

Traditionally the drawing has been ascribed to the hand of an assistant (Wittkower 1964a: 47 excepted), and dated in 1546-47 together with the drawings in Lille and Haarlem; Joannides (1981b: 621) has argued that the drawings in Lille and Haarlem might be much later, Lille perhaps as late as 1555-56, Haarlem in 1559 and hence, by implication, that CB 31A might be later as well.

Because the columns in CB 31A are drawn resting on the base of the drum without socles, it is likely to have been drawn after the drawing in Lille and, if it is a preparatory drawing for the model, it may date as late as 1557-58. In this case, Michelangelo may not have decided on rectangular windows for the drum by that date.

Tolnay (1975b: 115) and Joannides (1981b: 621), rejecting the earlier views that Michelangelo did not use a straightedge, which was used in making the drawing on CB 31A, have recently attributed the entire sheet to Michelangelo; we think they are likely to be right.

H.A.M.-C.H.S.

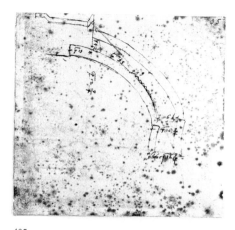

405

Michelangelo Buonarroti
Half-Sections through the Attic and Dome of St. Peter's and the Pantheon

Florence, Casa Buonarroti, CB 35Av.
Pen and brown ink, black chalk; stained and recut (recto). Black chalk; stained and recut (verso).
162 × 159 mm
Recto: half section through the attic and dome of St. Peter's
Inscribed: various dimensions in *palmi*, here reading from upper section of cupola to base *il tuto è p[almi]* 16 3/4; *p* 16 3/4; *p* 9; *p* 9; *p* 53; *p* 4 1/2; *p* 15; *p* 12 3/4 (at right of base).
Verso: a) half-section through the two domes of St. Peter's (lower right); b) open Greek cross (center righ); c) half-section through attic and dome of the Pantheon (upper right); d) two diagonal lines (lower left to upper righ); e) two parallel vertical lines (at left). f) section of console? (upper left).

Provenance: Casa Buonarroti.

Bibliography: Tolnay 1951: 299; Düssler 1959: 224; Ackerman 1961, II: 99; Barocchi 1962a: 191-192; Ackerman 1964, II: 101; Barocchi 1964b: 73-74; Hartt 1971: 379; Tolnay 1980, IV: 100; Berti 1985: 222; Ackerman 1986: 321; Millon and Smyth 1988a: 153-155; Argan and Contardi 1990: 330 and fig. 440.

The sheet was first brought into the literature by Tolnay (1951: 299) and cataloged by Düssler (1959: 224). Neither considered the drawing to be by Michelangelo. Barocchi (1962a: 191-192; 1964b: 73-74) includes the drawings among those by Michelangelo, as do Hartt (1971: 379) and Berti (1985: 222). Ackerman (1961, II: 99; 1986: 321) and Tolnay (1980, IV: 100) continue to treat the drawing as by an anonymous hand. For discussion of the drawing on the recto, see Millon and Smyth 1988a: 150-152.

Verso

At lower right of the verso, the roughly drawn section through both of the domes of St. Peter's, from just above the base of the domes to the lantern, includes indications of the lower and upper steps between the domes. The thickness of both domes and the height of the space between them is indicated in the area of the opening of the lantern. Shading below the outer dome (at the opening below the lantern) may indicate an arched opening from the space between the two domes into the space of the oculus. Even though roughly drawn, the outer dome appears to taper toward the lantern while, in accord with Vasari's description, the inner dome does not. When the lines of the inner dome are continued further beyond the lower edge of the sheet, the resulting curvature of the inner dome is semicircular. The outer dome, partly due to its

tapering, may be thought to be somewhat elevated. The even more roughly sketched section through what appears to be the Pantheon (but with the steps on the roof extending further toward the oculus than on the Pantheon itself) seems to be particularly concerned with the relation between inner and outer curvatures of the dome as it approaches the oculus.

The proximity of these two drawings on the same sheet, one above the other on almost the same axis, suggests that the two images were drawn for comparison. Since all the well-known evidence has indicated Michelangelo's attention to the dome of S. Maria del Fiore in Florence, this drawing becomes important as evidence that Michelangelo also studied the great classical antecedent for a hemispherical dome in relation to his design for St. Peter's, as had Bramante before him. We believe the nature of this comparison, as well as the draftsmanship, confirm the attribution to Michelangelo.

This drawing probably preceded the drawing made from the model on the recto and, as a study for the upper part of the model, can be dated in 1559-60.

H.A.M.-C.H.S.

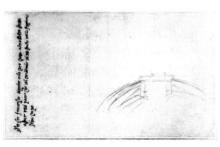

406

Michelangelo Buonarroti
Section/Elevation through the Upper Portion of the Dome and Lantern of St. Peter's

Oxford, Ashmolean Museum, 344r.
Black chalk, pen and ink inscription.
250 × 402 mm
Inscribed: *Messer francesco signior mio caro circa il modello che s[i] a / fare e mi pare che col cardinale si sia facto una figura / se[n]za capo.*

Provenance: Casa Buonarroti; Wicar; Lawrence (Lugt 2445); Woodburn.

Bibliography: K. Frey 1911, III: 82; Thode 1913, III: 209-210; D. Frey 1920: 106-108; Dvorák 1929, II: 107; Tolnay 1930: 8; Körte 1932: 97-98; Wittkower 1933: 357-358; Tolnay 1951: 185; Parker 1956, II: 181-182; Düssler 1959: 130-131; Ackerman 1961, II: 98; 1964, II: 100, 112; Barbieri and Puppi 1964a: 917, 1013; Bettini 1964: 503; Tolnay 1964, IX: col. 908; Wittkower 1964a: 46, 68; 1965: 348; De Angelis d'Ossat 1965: 348; 1966a II: 344; Hartt 1971: 351; Einem 1973: 225, 226; Gere and Turner 1975: 143; Saalman 1975: 400; Wittkower 1978b: 88; Di Stefano 1908a: 875; Tolnay 1980, IV: 98-99; Nova 1984: 196; Ackerman 1986: 320, 324; Millon and Smyth 1988a: 156-157; Argan and Contardi 1990: 330 and fig. 445.

The fragment of a letter in Michelangelo's hand, at left, was written at what was originally the top of the sheet; it was probably abandoned, therefore, before the drawing was begun. The drawings on the sheet are focused on the junction of the inner and outer domes with the oculus. Less attention is given to the platform at the top of the oculus and still less to the lantern. The principal study was drawn over an earlier drawing of the exterior dome and lantern at a smaller scale (the ribs and lantern base may be seen just above the platform of the larger drawing). The principal study shows the profiles of the exterior and interior domes as they near the oculus. Although it is difficult to be sure, the main lines may represent the upper portions of hemispherical domes. (The other paired lines, apparently more elevated and ending under the oculus, may be representations of successive ribs beyond the sec-

tion). The wall thickness of the oculus is shown, as well as a window sill or balustrade, indicating openings from the space between the shells into the space of the oculus. The platform above the oculus is single and thick, resembling somewhat the platform of the lantern in the central study on the sheet in Haarlem, but with less space for an exterior walkway. The height of the first stage of the lantern and its heavy entablature suggest that, if columns or pilasters were intended for the lantern, they would have rested directly on the platform and not on pedestals. The width of the base of the cone atop the lantern suggests that the lantern had only two stages, or that it was a three-stage lantern with a low second stage, as at the upper left of the drawing in Haarlem.

There is no reason to doubt the date of 1557 for the drawing, first proposed by D. Frey (1920: 108) on the basis of the fragment of a letter referring to the model, begun at the top of the sheet and then abandoned. (Messer Francesco is Francesco Bandini, a banker and friend of Michelangelo, and the cardinal is likely to be Rodolfo Pio da Carpi. Both were among those urging Michelangelo to build a model of the dome, the model mentioned in the letter fragment. The model was begun in 1558.)

H.A.M.-C.H.S.

The Dosio Group of Drawings in the Uffizi

The five sheets in the Uffizi that depict Michelangelo's model of the drum and dome of St. Peter's are part of a group of several hundred sheets in the Uffizi attributed to Giovanni Antonio Dosio (1533–after 1609). (In addition to the five drawings from the model there are five further sheets showing St. Peter's under construction.)

Recent scholarship (F. Borsi et al. 1976: 10-11) has dated Dosio's arrival in Rome (from Florence) in 1548-49, where he remained until 1579. Dosio began as a sculptor's assistant, then architect and recorder of ancient and Renaissance sculpture and architecture. He prepared numerous illustrations for a guide book by Bernardo Gamucci (*Dell'antichità della città di Roma*, 1565) and the publication of G. B. de' Cavalieri (*Urbis Romae aedificiorium illustrium...*, 1569).

Dosio's drawings of models by Michelangelo for St. Peter's and S. Giovanni dei Fiorentini, as well as other drawings of Michelangelo's sculpture and architecture in Rome and Florence, do appear to indicate, as F. Borsi has suggested (1976: 10-11, 22), that Dosio had access to Michelangelo's work. As will be observed, the drawings for the model of the drum and dome of St. Peter's show signs of preceding its completion, thus testifying to Dosio's access to Michelangelo's studio (Giovannoni 1931: 150). As Wittkower (1933: passim), Gioseffi (1960: 10), Schiavo (1961: 519-520, 522-523 and 530), Ackerman (1961, II: 105-110) and Barbieri and Puppi (1964a: 917-918) have shown, Dosio's drawings are credible visual records of the dome and drum model—as now seems certain—before the model was completed.

The literature on Dosio is extensive. To the bibliography found in F. Borsi, et al. (1976: 404-423) should be added the dissertation of Carolyn Valone (Northwestern University 1972), her articles on Dosio's years in Rome (1976: 528-541; 1977: 243-255), C. Acidini Luchinat (1980: 61-66), and entries on drawings by Dosio in an exhibition catalog by Andrew Morrogh (1985a: 80-85).

407

<small>Giovanni Antonio Dosio or Assistant</small>
Profile, Section and Elevation of the Model of the Drum and Dome of St. Peter's

Florence, Galleria degli Uffizi, Gabinetto Disegni e Stampe, Uff. 94Ar.
Brown ink, incised lines; sheet has been folded;

watermark: crossed arrows with six-pointed star above (see also Uff. 92A).
433 × 274 mm
Recto: section of drum and dome.
a) profile, section and elevation of drum and dome; b) profile of exterior attic order (left).
Verso: 1) enlarged and dimensioned profile of main interior entablature of the drum, including attic and balustrade (center right); 2) enlarged profile of main exterior entablature of the drum with a dimension for the height of the cornice (left).
Inscribed: various dimensions, p[almi] 2½' (profile, upper left); from top of cupola to base, 4¼, p[almi] 8 ¼ (turned 90°); 4½; p[almi] 25½ (turned 90°); p[almi] 11¾ (turned 90°).

Provenance: unavailable.

Bibliography: Tolnay 1930: 8-9; Körte 1932: 98-100; Tolnay 1932: 236; Wittkower 1933: passim, especially 349-352; Tolnay 1951: 186; Gioseffi 1960: 10; Schiavo 1960: 73; Ackerman 1961, II: 99, 106-110; Schiavo 1961: 522-523; Ackerman 1964, II: 101, 110, 112; Barbieri and Puppi 1964a: 917-918; Wittkower 1964a: passim, especially 18-19, 24-25; Schiavo 1966: 392; Alker 1968: 3; Portoghesi [1971]: 415-416; F. Borsi, et al. 1976: 138-141; Wittkower 1978b: 78; Nova 1984: 197; Ackerman 1986: 321, 322-324; Millon and Smyth 1988a: 162-164; Argan and Contardi 1990: 330-333 and fig. 452.

The half-section of the drum and dome of the model (first published by Tolnay [1930: 8-11], and treated fully by Wittkower [1933: passim, especially 350-352], and in a translation [1964: passim, especially 20-21]) is one of the five sheets in the Uffizi attributed to Dosio, all five apparently drawn from Michelangelo's model, but before its completion. It was drawn primarily to record the state of the model from the main entablature to the lantern. The drum below is more summarily indicated. While the draftsman alternated the window pediments to agree with the building, he drew the windows too small and did not show the window opening through the drum correctly (drawn properly in Metropolitan 49.92.20v.). (Tolnay [1930: 8] thought the attribution of this drawing to Dosio to be incorrect. A. Morrogh has also, in conversation, doubted the attribution to Dosio himself, believing it drawn by someone in Dosio's circle.) The draftsman wanted the relative levels of interior to exterior to be accurate, however, and heightened the interior cornice to correct his drawing. (On the verso the draftsman drew both the entablatures, to show that the heights of the architrave and frieze were equal inside and out; but with the inscribed dimensions of both cornices, he was able to demonstrate that the interior cornice was one *palmo* higher than that on the exterior.) On both recto and verso the interior attic balustrade includes the handrail and balusters.

As inscribed on the recto, the dimensions of the entablature, attic, and two domes are translated into the full dimensions of the building. In the panels between the ribs on the interior of the dome, tondi have replaced the ovals found in Uff. 92A.
Both the inner and outer domes are hemispherical, and both are tapered. The steps between the two domes are roughly indicated. The inscribed dimension of the outer dome at its base is 4½ *palmi*, and at the oculus 3½ *palmi*. The inscribed dimension of the space between the two domes at the oculus in 8¼ *palmi*, and the thickness of the inner dome there is inscribed as 4¼ *palmi*. All these dimensions agree well with those given in Vasari's description of the model (Vasari, ed. Milanesi 1881, VII: 254), except that the distance between the domes was 8 *palmi* according to Vasari.
Windows open from the space between the two domes into the oculus, and above the oculus there is the horizontal screen with radiating spokes (shown slightly elevated above the level of the platform of the lantern), which is also shown on Metropolitan 49.92.92 verso (cat. no. 1) of the Dupérac group and on Uff. 2031A (cat. no. 28) of the Dosio group.
The platform for the lantern on Uff. 94A recto has only

one step instead of the two shown in Metropolitan 49.92.92 recto from the Dupérac group (fig. 2) and in the prints by Dupérac.
The lack of a lantern here and the lanterns without pedestals in the related drawings in the Uffizi (92A and 2031A), all on a platform of only one step, suggest that the design of the lantern may have still been fluid when these drawings were made—and also when Vasari wrote his description, as Körte (1932: 98-100) and Wittkower (1964a: 61-62) have suggested. The turned wooden members of the final lantern on the model were paid for in November 1561 (K. Frey 1916: 87, 668.41). Uff. 94A recto and verso (and the other drawings in the Dosio group) may date, therefore, from 1560. In any case, at the time the drawings in the Dosio group were made the inner and outer domes of the model were most likely already completed, but the design of the lantern not yet fixed. The replacement of ovals by tondi in Uff. 94A appears to indicate that Michelangelo had made this change in the model by the time Uff. 94A recto was drawn, and thus that Uff. 94A is later than Uff. 92A.

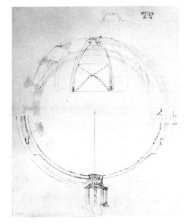

408

<small>Giovanni Antonio Dosio</small>
Section of the Dome and Lantern of St. Peter's and Elevation of the Inner Dome and Ribs with the Exterior Dome Removed

Florence, Galleria degli Uffizi, Gabinetto Disegni e Stampe, Uff. 2031Ar.
Pen, brown ink; watermark: crossed arrows with a six-pointed star above (see also Uff. 92A and 94A).
557/554 × 427/424 mm
Recto: section of dome and lantern; elevation of exterior of inner dome: a) section through inner and outer domes and lantern (turned 180°); b) elevation of outer surface of inner dome and ribs; c) section through rib of exterior dome (upper center); d) elevation of one of the dormer windows in the dome (upper right).
Verso: plan of drum and base at four levels, preparatory for Uff. 2032A.

Provenance: unavailable.

Bibliography: Bartoli 1914, I: 140; Giovannoni 1921; 1931a: 150; Körte 1932: 8; Wittkower 1933: passim, especially 349-352; Gioseffi 1960: 10; Ackerman 1961, II: 99, 106-110; 1964, II: 101, 110; Barbieri and Puppi 1964a: 917-918; Wittkower 1964a: passim, especially 19-20; Schiavo 1966: 392; Portoghesi [1971]: 415-416; F. Borsi et al. 1976: 140-145; Wittkower 1978b: 78; Nova 1984: 197; Ackerman 1986: 321, 323-324; Millon and Smyth 1988a: 165-167; Argan and Contardi 1990: 330 and fig. 450.

The two drawings on the recto of this sheet (first published by Giovannoni [1921], and in a reprint 1931a: 150]) show stairs, in section and elevation, from the base of the two domes to the oculus, lantern and—if the spiral on the central column of the lantern is intended to indicate a spiral stair—to the top of the lantern. Only the stair between the oculus and the platform of the lantern was omitted. The elevation above shows the double stairs in the shape of an "X" mentioned by Vasari and on the model today (fig. 3) and then the steps leading from these stairs to the windows of the oculus between the ribs at their apex. The windows that open into the oculus are shown in both the upper and lower drawing, and the lower section includes the screen with spokes between the oculus and lantern, also found in Uff. 94A recto and Metropolitan 49.92.92 verso (and included in the print by Dupérac, but without its spokes and openings).

(Turned 180°) At right in the section is the only attempt known to us to represent accurately, in section, the two runs of stairs that form the X-shaped stairs. The lower run of stairs is shown the full width of the distance between the two domes while, above the arched opening, a line divides the space between the domes into two parts, indicating that the stair would be on the right side, where an initial step was started about halfway up the length of the arched opening. A glance at the photograph of the model (fig. 3) will show the lower stair was confined to the outer half of the space between the two domes, the upper stair to the inner half. In the lower drawing the lantern rests on a narrow platform of only one step. The columns stand free of the lantern wall leaving space for a passageway between. The columns are without pedestals. They support an entablature with ressauts which, in turn, supports the lower section on tall volutes of the second stage of the lantern. The spiral on one of the columns may, as mentioned, indicate a stair to the upper levels of the lantern. The upper drawing shows where two ranges of dormer windows would light the space between the domes. At upper right, the draftsman drew an elevation of one of these windows. Vasari specified—and the draftsman of the aerial perspective now in the Morgan Library drew—only two ranges of dormer windows, as indicated in this drawing. It is possible that at an early stage the exterior dome of the model had only two ranges of windows. While the design of the lantern does not agree with that found on Metropolitan 49.92.1 nor with the lantern on the prints by Dupérac, the close agreement of the section through a rib of the exterior dome (at the top of the sheet) with the dimensioned drawing of an exterior rib at the right on Metropolitan 49.92.92 verso suggests that the ribs of the exterior dome of the model were already complete when this drawing was made. Perhaps the number of dormer windows had not yet been decided and the final lantern design not yet established. The drawing most likely dates from the autumn of 1560, when some of these elements may not have been settled, and so provides information about another alternative in the development of Michelangelo's design of the lantern.

H.A.M.-C.H.S.

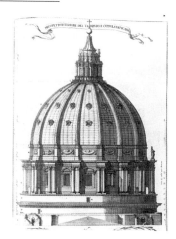

409
CARLO FONTANA
Elevation of Exterior of the Drum and Dome of St. Peter's
(C. Fontana, *Templum Vaticanum*, Rome, 1694, pl. 311)

Venice, Biblioteca Nazionale Marciana
Engraving.
452 × 320 mm
INSCRIBED: *PROSPETTO ESTERIORE DEL TAMBVRO E CVPPOLA VATICANA* (with lettered index below); *Eques Carolus Fontana Delin* (lower left); *Alex.ʳ Spec.ᵘˢScVlp.* (lower right); scale: "Scala di palmi 200 Romani" (right).

BIBLIOGRAPHY: Wittkower 1964a: 81–82, fig. 26; Millon and Smyth 1988a: 134, fig. 31.

The print by Fontana (executed during his tenure as *misuratore* of St. Peter's) shows an elevation of the exterior of the drum and dome, from the base of the drum through the cross surmounting the lantern, as it was constructed in the 1590s. Parts of the drum and dome are lettered and refer to a legend below.

The representation includes a sculpture of a standing figure on the buttress at right, probably reflecting the figures shown on the section and elevation by Dupérac. The cast shades and shadows make for a dramatic rendering, but are somewhat arbitrary.

H.A.M.-C.H.S

410
TOMMASO MANZUOLI (called MASO DA S. FRIANO)
Double Portrait

Naples, Museo di Capodimonte, Q.474
Oil on panel.
115 × 90 cm
INSCRIBED: *TO; MDLVI.*

BIBLIOGRAPHY: T.C.I. 1950: 70; Beri 1963: 77–88; Cannon Brookes 1965: 192–196; 1966: 560–568; Bellosi 1970: 45; Pace 1976, 1–2: 74–99; Tiberia 1980, 12: 77–86; *Palazzo Vecchio...* 1980: 275, cat. no. 519.

Owing to its unusual appeal, this double portrait has enjoyed a complex history. Its multiple provenance, and the numerous attempts over the years to identify the painting's author and the two figures portrayed, can be traced with the help of documentary evidence.

The back of the painting bears a lily stamped in gray sealing wax, confirming its original provenance as the Villa Farnese in Rome, where it is cited in the inventory of 1653, attributed to Andrea del Sarto, without any specific identification of the figures other than: "un che insegna ad un altro huomo col compasso in mano a misurare" ("someone teaching another man with a compass how to take measurements"). Later, the painting was transferred to Parma, along with a sizable portion of the Rome collection of the Farnese family; it is listed in Parma in 1680, with the same attribution, among the works exhibited in the portrait room in the residence of the Palazzo del Giardino. Owing to the painting's importance in the Parma collection it was included among the approximately 300 works assembled at the end of the seventeenth century for exhibition in the Ducale Galleria in the Palazzo della Pilotta; the gallery was one of the most advanced muse-

um installations of its day. In this context it was entered in the "Descrizione per Alfabeto di cento Quadri dé più famosi e dipinti da i più insigni Pittori del mondo" (published in Parma in 1725), a forerunner of today's printed catalog, listing all the masterpieces of the Ducale Galleria. While maintaining the "established" attribution to Andrea del Sarto, one of the figures was at this point identified as Duke Ottavio Farnese. When the last descendent of the Farnese dynasty, Charles of Bourbon, son of Elizabeth Farnese and Philip of Spain, acceded to the throne of Naples in 1734, he took the *Double Portrait* with him to Naples, together with the rest of the family collection. After some time it was exhibited in the Farnese picture gallery in the section of the Palazzo di Capodimonte that overlooks the sea. Here, in 1783, it was admired by Tommaso di Puccini, director of the Galleria Imperiale degli Uffizi, who provided a detailed description, with enthusiastic comments on the quality of the painting: "Two portraits of insuperable realism in their forms and colors." Noting the date and the monogram (though without identifying it), Puccini ventured that the painting was "the portrait of an architect, and of another man commissioning a building from him; this seems to be a church" (Mazzi 1980, nos. 37–38: 25).

When they raided the Capodimonte collection in 1799 the French *commissaires* were of the same opinion about the quality of the painting; they confiscated thirty works for the Republic of France and dispatched them to Rome, from where they were later to be sent over the Alps. It was here in Rome the following year, in the church of S. Luigi dei Francesi, that the painting was recovered by one Domenico Venuti, emissary to Ferdinand IV of Bourbon, who had been reinstated on the throne of Naples. In 1806 Naples was once again laid siege by the French troops—this time led by Napoleon—and the painting was sent to Palermo as a precautionary measure, together with an appropriate number of works considered to be among the most important of the collection of the Bourbon dynasty, which returned definitively to power in Naples in 1815 in the wake of the new political organization of the Italian territories ushered in by the Restoration.

Its travels finally over, the *Double Portrait*—which had evidently attracted a great deal of attention—entered the collection of the Real Museo Borbone. The museum's first inventory, compiled between 1806 and 1816 by Paternò, lists the painting as the portrait of the Duke of Urbino and Donato Bramante, and retains the customary attribution to Andrea del Sarto. In the museum's monumental printed catalog of 1827, however, both author and subjects are listed as unknown. The work is cited in all the major nineteenth-century guides to the Neapolitan museum, specifically because of its importance within the collection; even Burckhardt in *The Cicerone* records it as "the two surveyors," in the style of Bronzino. Many scholars were tempted to identify the two figures as the Duke of Urbino and Bramante, and occasionally as Bramante and his son. On the whole, however, while the "traditional" attribution of the figures endured, the problem of the author remained. Possible attributions included the school of Andrea del Sarto, Bronzino, and Pontormo. Although Cavalcaselle pointed out a certain harshness in the execution, denoting a mixture of the styles of these last two artists, Quintavalle's 1930 inventory of the Neapolitan museum talks of the painting's "Emilian style."

The next episode of the painting's intricate history was its transfer to Rome in 1929, under the supervision of the local Soprintendenza, along with a number of other pictures of Neapolitan origin assigned to embellish the rooms of the Palazzo Madama.

It is probable, however, that the painting did not in fact reach the offices of the Senate, but was put on display in the Palazzo Venezia where, for the first time, it was correctly attributed to Maso da S. Friano by Roberto Longhi, in the Rome guide of the Touring Club Italiano (1950: 70). This made the *Double Portrait* the earliest dated work of the painter, whose activity as a portrait artist had already been noted by Borghini in 1584: "Molti sono i quadri e i ritratti che egli fece à varie persone" ("Many are the pictures and portraits that he made of various people"; cited in Cannon Brookes 1966: 560). Executed when Maso was around twenty-five, the picture shows him still to be under the strong influence of his teacher, Pierfrancesco di Jacopo Foschi, as mentioned by Vasari (cf. Bellosi, in Firenze 1970: 45; cf. also Pace 1976: 74). Some of the artist's hallmarks are already well defined, such as the characteristic manner of depicting eyes, ears, and the structure of the hands; such particulars, together with more general stylistic connotations, have made it possible to ascribe many other works to Maso and enrich the catalog of his works (cf. Cannon Brookes 1966). In this context it should be noted that the little tutelary deity seated on the front of the fireplace, behind the two figures, has strong links with details in two drawings by Maso, the *Lamentation* at Chatsworth and the *Religious Allegory*, in the Louvre, dated 1565.

The identification of the two characters remains unresolved. Besides being a portrait, it cannot be excluded that the painting conceals an allegory of some kind: "The act of using a compass and designing something can easily assume some transverse significance of a moral nature, such as the act of allowing one's hand to be guided by another" (Collareta, in *Palazzo Vecchio* 1980: 275). This in itself might not be in conflict with a genuine interest in architecture on the part of the young figure busy drawing the plan of a building. Such interests were by no means extraneous to the culture of the upper classes of the time. In *The Courtesan* Baldassarre Castiglione had noted that "the ability to draw and to be cognizant of the very art of painting" was essential to the proper education of a gentleman. It is also significant that around 1656 Alessandro Allori wrote a brief treatise, *Delle Regole del Disegno*, addressed to certain noble dilettantes; he himself taught drawing to Florentine gentlewomen (Collareta, op. cit.; for wider discussion, see Cardi 1971: 267-286).

A Villa for the City: Giuliano da Sangallo's Medicean Project for the Via Laura
Linda Pellecchia

Of all Giuliano da Sangallo's palaces none is more extravagant than his project for the Medici in Florence found on Uff. 282A (fig. 1). Sited within the city walls, the grand palace surrounded by Babylonian-like gardens is a suburban villa on the scale of Bramante's Belvedere. Had it been built, a part of Florence would have been transformed into a private estate for its ruling family (fig. 2). Even if intended, as seems likely, as a locus for foreign entertainment and civic festivals, the political fallout of such a majestic complex would have made its construction indefensible in almost any period before the Grand Duchy. Giuliano's utopian project was destined to remain on paper.

The vision of Medicean political dominance embodied in the grandiosity of the design is echoed in the villa's interaction with the public domain of Florence. Not only do the gardens sprawl with abandon over ecclesiastical and private property (land belonging to the Ospedale degli Innocenti, S. Maria degli Angiolini, the Crocetta, and Bartolomeo Scala, among others; cf. Miarelli Mariani 1972: 154-156, and Elam 1978: 57), they also ensnare public streets. The demarcation between villa and city (between a single, albeit powerful, family and the Florentine *res publica*) is obscured as the grand, semicircular entrance portico of the garden appropriates the block between Via del Rosaio (present-day Via Laura) and Via Laura (present-day Via della Colonna). The visual axis of the villa extends even to Via degli Angioli (present-day Via degli Alfani), where a simple niche expresses Medicean control. City streets become scenographic backdrops to delight the villa's inhabitants.

While the project is undoubtedly Medicean, determination of the specific Medici patron depends on the dating of the drawing, a subject of much debate. A majority of scholars have favored a Laurentian date (or at the very latest a date before the Medici exile in 1494) because the style of the palace would seem to represent a logical development of ideas first expressed in Giuliano's palace for the King of Naples of 1488 (esp. Miarelli Mariani 1972: 140-149). However, incontrovertible evidence supports a date after the return of the family in 1512. The presence of two inscriptions on the drawing identifying houses purchased by Perugino in 1494 and 1498 proves that the drawing must date to after 1512, since no one would plan a Medici villa in Florence during their exile (Marchini 1942: 101; Elam 1978: 56; Elam, forthcoming). My recent examination of the drawing, moreover, reveals that the palace was designed directly on the Uffizi sheet and is, therefore, contemporary with the inscriptions (see Pellecchia, forthcoming).

Thus, the hypothesis (see Tafuri 1992: 113 for example) that the drawing of the palace might be no more than a Cinquecento copy of a late-Quattrocento design is unfounded. In both execution and design the drawing represents a project of the early Cinquecento—most likely, it could be argued, in connection with Leo X's triumphal entry into Florence.

The megalomania of Giuliano's project, as well as the haste with which it was constructed, seems in keeping with the period of Leo's 1515 *entrata*, when Leonardo proposed a grand, utopian palace for the Medici (Pedretti 1962a: 112-118 and 128; Elam 1990: 52) (fig. 3). Giuliano, who had once before lost the affections of a papal family to another architect, may have designed his palace to compete with Leonardo's. It is even possible that the intended patron of the Via Laura project was the occupant of the old Medici palace, Lorenzo, Duke of Urbino, whose pretensions to absolute rule were the bane of the Florentines (Butters 1985, Stephens 1983).

In Sangallo's palace, the two equal but separate apartments (an idea related to Vitruvius' description of the ancient Greek house) would have suited the political and symbolic ambitions of both the duke and his powerful Orsini mother, Alfonsina (Pellecchia 1993: 323-338). Furthermore, Elam has shown that Leonardo was in the employ of Giuliano de' Medici, Duke of Nemours, when he sketched his utopian residence (Elam 1990: 52). How fitting it would have been for the Duke of Urbino, who detested his uncle, Giuliano, to present a counterproposal of greater magnificence. While the villa on Via Laura reflects the aristocratic pretensions of the Medici in the early Cinquecento, the drawing on Uff. 282A also illustrates Lorenzo il Magnifico's urbanistic program for the area around SS. Annunziata and the Ospedale degli Innocenti. It depicts both streets, like Via Laura and Via del Rosaio, that were actually built and subdivided into housing lots in the 1490s as well as (nameless) streets that were never executed (Elam 1978: 45-49). Since Uff. 282A is not precise in its placement of the Porta a Pinti and the city walls (nor in the trajectory of Via Capponi and Borgo Pinti, which are not, in reality, parallel), it is surprising to realize—as an overlay of the drawing onto the *Catasto Leopoldino* of 1832 reveals—that it is quite accurate in its depictions of the Laurentian street system (Pellecchia, forthcoming). It is hard to avoid the conclusion that Giuliano began the villa with a copy of a site plan of Lorenzo's late-Quattrocento urban design. The shape and size of some elements, such as the grand exedra and triumphal arch-like entrance gate, were influenced by the pre-existing street and housing lots. Such a hypothesis would suggest that Giuliano, who was Lorenzo's primary architect in the 1490s, was the executant of Lorenzo's urban design (Pellecchia, forthcoming; Elam, forthcoming cf. 1994).

The contrasting political and urbanistic aspirations of two generations of Medici are visible on Uff. 282A. Il Magnifico's late-Quattrocento urban program clearly reflects his standing as *primus inter pares* and contributed, not surprisingly, to his political control (the land had been earmarked for those loyal to the *reggimento*; cf. Elam, forthcoming). While reflecting his personal magnificence, it also brought glory and convenience to the citizens of Florence. The *all'antica* villa of the early Cinquecento, by contrast, is a residence worthy of an emperor and reveals without subtlety the monarchical aspirations of a new breed of Medici.

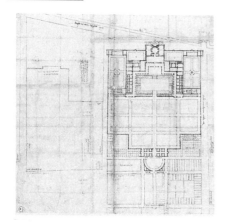

PROVENANCE: Vasari; Mariette.

BIBLIOGRAPHY: Fabriczy 1902b: 101-102; Marchini 1942: 77-78 and 101; Miarelli Mariani 1972: 127-152; Marchini 1973b: 66-68; Elam 1978: 43-66; S. Borsi 1985: 441-453; 1991: 333-344; Godoli 1992: 236; Pellecchia 1993: 323-338; Elam, forthcoming (1994); Pellecchia, forthcoming (1994).

The drawing depicts a plan for a grandiose suburban villa within the walls of Florence. Described by Giuliano in an inscription on the verso as a project for the Medici, the villa consists of a regal palace and vast gardens. While Giuliano is credited with the design, his brother Antonio (an inscription in the latter's hand informs us) was the draftsman. The drawing is unusual among Giuliano's villa designs for its depiction of an extensive urban context replete with inscriptions identifying property owners. While the date of the drawing has been controversial, it now seems clear that it was done in the early Cinquecento (see essay).

Although the villa fits on a single large sheet (whose borders are clearly visible), three smaller sheets were subsequently added to enlarge the site. The extra space permitted—as a long inscription states (Pedretti 1962a: 128)—the addition of stables and a hunting park.

Pin pricks indicate that some features of the villa were copied from another drawing. However, the top sheet contains a nearly invisible hemicycle composed solely of pin pricks. In size and orientation the un-inked hemicycle is identical to that on Via Laura and would appear to be a quickly abandoned *prova* for the portico of the garden entrance.

While the villa with its vast garden and its emphasis on an axially aligned series of processionally arranged elements can be interpreted as Giuliano's response to Bramante's Belvedere (ca. 1504) (Elam, forthcoming), the decidedly Quattrocentesque style of the palace itself is perplexing. Its retrospective character may stem from time constraints that forced Giuliano to recycle parts of earlier projects.

Despite the finished appearance of the drawing, it was executed quickly. Lines are drawn freehand; wall thicknesses vary; spaces lack entrances, etc. While some problems were due to drafting errors, close inspection reveals that the plan is less a final design than an idea in progress. Inconsistencies abound between the right and left halves of the palace. These sometimes represent alternatives (e.g., the *parterres* of the large gardens flanking the palace), but more often they reveal last-minute solutions to design problems. Several difficulties arose because Giuliano began with set pieces (e.g., the courtyard) copied from his earlier design for the King of Naples (fig. 1). On Uff. 282A Giuliano retained the articulation and amphitheater-shape of the Neapolitan courtyard, but eliminated its fourth arm. On the right side of the Florentine palace, where the courtyard was begun, the stairway collides with a pier. The problem was corrected, midstream, on the left. While the axis of the staircase was improved, it did not resolve the awkwardness of the design.

In the last analysis, Uff. 282A is a hurriedly constructed fusion of old and new ideas, simultaneously innovative and retrospective. In designing his villa, Giuliano recast Quattrocento elements—not always elegantly—in a Cinquecento matrix (for further discussion, see Pellecchia, forthcoming).
L.P.

411
GIULIANO DA SANGALLO and
ANTONIO DA SANGALLO THE ELDER
Plan of a Medici Villa on Via Laura, Florence
after 1512

Florence, Galleria degli Uffizi, Gabinetto Disegni e Stampe, Uff. 282A
Pen and ink with brown wash and traces of black chalk.
695 × 640 mm

412
GIORGIO VASARI
Two Bays of the Logge Vasariane, Arezzo

Arezzo, Casa Vasari
Wooden model. Constructed in two parts (arcade and upper stories), with evidence of modifications made to left-hand pier. Roof and side panels are modern repairs.
52.5(h.) × 43(w.) × 23(d) cm

PROVENANCE: Fraternita dei Laici, Museo d'Arte medioevale e moderna.

BIBLIOGRAPHY: Gammurini 1911: 37 ff.; Viviani-Fiorini 1941: 109 ff.; Berti 1955: 29, no. 48; Ramagli 1976: 95; Satkowski 1979: 206 ff.; Trionfi Honorati 1981: 312 ff.; Paolucci and Maetzke 1988: 159, no. 48; Roselli 1989: 31 ff.

The Logge Vasariane in Arezzo were one of the most ambitious architectural projects of the Medici Grand Dukes. The design provided by Giorgio Vasari ingeniously used the sharply sloping site to separate the Piazza Grande, Arezzo's imposing public square, from the nearby disorder created by the construction of a new fortress. The most characteristic feature of the Logge is a severe, repetitive facade extending 126 meters in length. On the ground level, its twenty bays contain shops with storage chambers at the rear and mezzanines above. In the eleventh bay, a stairway leads to higher ground at the rear, from which the chambers on the *piano nobile* are entered. In its eastern half the structure contains five row houses. The western half was decidedly governmental in purpose, containing offices for the Monte di Pietà, the chancellery, and the customs offices. The new building effectively was the Medicean administrative center for Arezzo.

The wooden model built in 1572 from Vasari's designs shows only two bays of the executed building. At the time of the model's fabrication, only the facade could be represented in any definite form. The Logge's long period of construction meant that plans of the upper floor were prepared only when tenants were certain. This task fell to Alfonso Parigi the Elder, who remained in charge of the project from Vasari's death in 1574 until the building's completion in 1596. As a result, none of the Logge's extensive habitable spaces are shown in the model. Still, it is notable for being one of the few surviving models of secular structures. In nearly all of his architectural projects Vasari employed wooden models, believing that they aided rapid construction and kept costs low. If their costs could be justified to patrons in this way, they were also especially useful for an architect like Vasari who practiced by remote control from Florence and required faithful assistants who would not alter the design. But the procedure was not a total success because the design was not yet worked out in detail, failing as it did to accommodate two floors of offices or housing behind the shallow height of model's topmost stories. The executed building departs from the model in terms of the greater height of the upper floors, the squatter proportions of the arcade and the shop fronts, and the narrowing of the piers and the removal of the frieze.

L.P.

Representations of Urban Models in the Renaissance

Marilyn Aronberg Lavin

Seal of Treviso

413
ANONYMOUS SIXTEENTH-CENTURY ARTIST (BERNARDO MALPIZIO?)
Copies of Mantegna's Gallic Triumph of Julius Caesar
* *Canvas VIII. Musicians and Standard Bearers*
* *Canvas IX. The Triumphator, Julius Caesar, on his Chariot*
late 16th century

Vienna, Kunsthistorisches Museum
Oil, grisaille, on paper mounted on canvas.
38 × 38 cm

PROVENANCE: Gonzaga family?; Charles I of England?; Archduke Leopold Wilhelm, 1659 (Engerth 1884).

BIBLIOGRAPHY: Martindale 1979.

The representation of entire cities in the form of miniature models stems from Roman art by following a rather circuitous path. Depictions of architectural monuments had their first flowering on Roman coins and medallions, in historical reliefs and in paintings, where buildings appeared no in isolation but as backdrops to various celebrations of the Imperial Cult (marriages, births, deaths, adoptions, victories, liberalities, New Years and other religious events). They were not commemorated in themselves but were shown primarily to fix the time of a particular event and identify its topographical locale. The religious value of such architectural images was carried over into Christian art, where from the sixth century onward saints and donors—in reliefs, paintings, and mosaics—hold small buildings in their arms, usually on the walls of the very buildings depicted. Clearly votive in character,

Gold bull of Emperor Ludwig IV, reused by Emperor Sigismund, 1433

these little structures evoke the saint's presence in and spiritual support of the edifice; held by a donor, they signify dedication of the building to the heavenly intercessor, titular of the church. The question remains as to whether these small-scale images represent models in the sense of preparation for construction or, more likely, were miniature replicas, memorializing the monument in its completed form. At the end of the eighth century, inaugurating the new Christian Roman Empire, Charlemagne recalled the antique tradition of architectural imagery on coins and medallions, but gave it a new form. He had his official seal designed with a synoptic view of Rome in which the whole city is inferred but conventionalized into the semblance of a single, fortified building. The image of the *Urbe*, as it is called, and the political philosophy it represents (the seal is inscribed *Renovatio*), thereafter appeared on the large gold, silver and lead bulls of almost all the Holy Roman Emperors down through the centuries. Passing through phases of more or less elaborate depictions of Roman buildings, towers, and walls, the *Urbe* image retained the primary effect of a single building (fig. 1, Gold Bull of Emperor Ludwig IV, reused by Emperor Sigismund, 1433). It was always understood, however, to be a symbol that represented the whole town. Seizing upon the territorial implications of the design, eventually the papacy, and in the twelfth century local princes, took over the concept. The popes used the image of Rome itself, while local princes, those of Capua for example, substituted a view of their own city. This interpretation had its fullest development a century later, in the form of the *sigillo de comune*, or city seal, which appeared as an accompaniment to the rise of the Italian commune. Town after town invented small, for the most part circular wax-stamps and seals to assert their own legal authority, and signal their independence from imperial dominance. Many town seals showed patrons saints. But in northern Italy, in the Veneto and Emilia-Romagna (less frequently in Tuscany), the predominant motif was local architecture: the city hall, the cathedral, or often a characteristic ancient structure (fig. 2, Seal of Treviso). As with the synoptic view of Rome, these single structures, accommodated in the circular format, stood for the community as a whole. Universally, the images were surrounded by inscriptions that heralded the physical strength and civic authority of the town as a political unit, the sociological antidote to anarchy, disorganization, and sin.

Locating an urban symbol in a circular format not only implied universality and divine inspiration, but referred specifically to the form of the ideal city. *City Lauds*, a medieval literary form revived and rationalized in the early fifteenth century, repeatedly describe the ideal city as circular, orbicular, or shield-shaped, with the seat of government in the center. Underlying these descriptions is the important theme of the microcosmic theory of State. With its roots in Aristotle, St. Augustine, St. Thomas Aquinas, and Dante, the theory names the ideal city as a microcosm that reflects directly all the elements in the Divine Universe, the macrocosm. Christian writers designated the cosmic prototype as the "Heavenly Jerusalem," and it was after that spiritual perfection of urban organization that the communes strove. This desire was often manifested in the conscious redesigning of urban centers on the model of the earthly Jerusalem (as was the case in Bologna). In other instances, the "New Jerusalem" was the theme, with cities emulating the pilgrimage routes of Rome as the ideal prototype. Any city carrying out this kind of urban renewal claimed itself also to be a New Jerusalem (as was the case in Florence).

Models of complete towns, which appeared for the first time in the fourteenth century in Italian painting, showing the main monuments surrounded by a circuit of walls, were heir to all these traditions. Like the symbolic single buildings, these more complex images are held by patron saints and donors, who act as intercessors with the personages of the divine hierarchy. Similarly, they have the same concomitant goals: to demonstrate the city's relationship to its heavenly prototype, and to verify the commune's territorial prerogative as an independent state. The great difference from the single buildings on Roman coins and medallions, and in medieval mural decoration and seals, is that the city-models are not synoptic. Rather, they make their votive offering with the full spectrum of civic life, ethical, moral, legal, and spiritual, represented in the totality of their urban fabric. We have noted that it was in northeast Italy that the cities manifested their self-images in terms of architecture. It seems not by chance, therefore, that many of the votive compositions included in this exhibition are also from that region. The same is true of the one three-dimensional city-model on display. As a group, these images signal the beginning of the modern era of self-conscious urban history.

Between about 1478 and 1505 with several interruptions, Andrea Mantegna was at work on a heroic enterprise for the Gonzaga family of Mantua, a series of nine canvases, each more than two and half meters square (267 × 278 cm). Representing "The Gallic Triumph of Julius Caesar," today they are in the Royal Collection of Her Majesty the Queen at Hampton Court. These grand panoramas in many ways encapsulate the ideas of the Renaissance. They depict one of the great events of Roman history, and are represented in a style more faithful to the antique prototype than anything in post-medieval art. Iconographically, they rely on the most advanced scholarly knowledge of their time, including newly published ancient texts, as well as contemporary treatises that themselves depend on the ancient sources.

Appian of Alexandria (fl. 2nd century A.D.) in his *Romaiká* chronicled Caesar's Gallic Wars, describing in some detail the triumphal procession that followed the victory, including the participants, their clothing, the trophies exhibited, and the route through the streets of Rome (trans. White 1912).

At the very moment Mantegna began to paint, Appian's Greek texts were translated into Latin by Piero Candido Decembrio (Venice, 1477). A treatise called *Roma Triumphans*, written about 1460 by the humanist Flavio Biondo, and another contemporary compendium of information, now lost, by Marcanova (whom Mantegna knew), were also available to him.

According to the sources, ancient triumphs were divided into three parts: exhibition of the spoils in the form of human captives, objects, and representations of conquered territories; the "triumphator," that is the triumphing military leader riding in a chariot; and the troops who fought the battle. Most Renaissance representations of ancient triumphs progress from right to left, a fact that might related to the actual route along the Via Sacra, which passed through the Roman Forum and around the Capitoline Hill, moving up the face from the right to the left. So it is with Mantegna's paintings. Each canvas, moreover, displays an astonishing knowledge of antique history. The majority of elements he painted are archaeologically correct, based on firsthand knowledge of antique remains. At the same time, many of his details are pure fantasy. As a result, the overall effect of his works is very much his own. The paintings show the coloristic variety, the perspective skill, and the precision of detail that mark Mantegna's invention throughout his career. It has been calculated that it took about a year to do each canvas. As they were completed, the huge canvases were looked upon by his contemporaries as storehouses of motifs to be plundered like the ruins themselves. They were copied innumerable times as a set, in paintings, in suites of engravings and, as was the case with Rubens and many other painters, they were used as models for particular passages in individual works.

"The best of all extant copies" are nine small paintings in Vienna, two of which are shown here. It has been suggested that they were made as prototypes for what are the earliest complete set of printed copies of the *Triumphs*, nine woodcuts issued in Mantua signed and dated by Andrea Andreani in 1598-99. The fact that the paintings are grisaille and about the same size as the prints seems to bear out this idea. A Mantuan artist named Bernardo Malpizio is mentioned on Andreani's title pages and therefore his name is sometimes linked with the Vienna paintings (Martindale 1979: 97-102).

In the second to last composition of the series (no. VIII), at the right border, a helmeted soldier holds a pole with a small fortress surmounted by an eagle at the top. The building, which is balanced on struts extending from the pole, is circular with a circular set-back tower ringed with windows. It has been compared to the structure of the Castel Sant'Angelo in Rome (Martindale 1979: 131, 139, 161), except that at opposite ends of its diameter, wings extend to two flanking rectangular towers. The construction is painted to imitate ashlar masonry. The presence of such an image is explained in Appian's text: "*Ferebantur et ligneae turres captarum urbium simulacra praeferentes*" (Towers were borne along representing the captured cities ..., trans. White 1912). Wooden models of a single, fortified building carried with the trophies of war thus represented towns conquered in battle and now considered Roman property. The spread-winged eagle that surmounts the building holding a small tablet in its beak, signifies precisely that: the eagle of Rome has conquered the dominion beneath its feet. Martindale has shown that both motifs are found on the Arch of Constantine; an eagle on a pole is found on the Aurelian *Lustration* relief, and a small building on a pole is seen in the Great Trajanic Frieze (Martindale 1979: 157, figs. 189, 195). The idea of putting both motifs together is Mantegna's.

In the copy of Canvas IX, another architectural model surmounts a pole that is raised from somewhere behind the horse drawing Caesar's chariot. This time the pole is tilted by the crush of the crowd. It is difficult to find a formal precedent for the shape of this building. The entrance is an aedicula flanked by columns and topped by a triangular pediment. On either side of the doorway is a horizontal rectangular window. Towers with crenelated tops rise at both ends of the facade, while the center of the double-sloping roof is topped by another tower, short and crenelated. Again the single structure refers to a complete city, here probably meant to be non-Roman because of the

peculiarity of its form. Out of the central tower emerges a right hand with all five fingers spread apart. This motif has been interpreted as relating to the term *Liberta* (Martindale 1979: 171). It therefore perhaps expresses the notion that Roman dominance of a foreign town is a kind of liberation.   *M.A.L.*

414
GIULIO ROMANO
Roman Soldiers in Triumphal Procession Ascending the Capitoline Hill
1534-35

Paris, Musée du Louvre, Cabinet des Dessins 3544
Pen and brown ink, wash, and biacca; beige paper, two sheets joined.
419 × 557 mm

PROVENANCE: Collection Jabach, passed to Crown of France (1671).

BIBLIOGRAPHY: Hartt 1958; Jestaz and Bacou 1978.

Like Mantegna sixty years earlier, Giulio Romano was commissioned to do a series of compositions representing a Roman Triumph based on ancient texts. This time it was the Triumph of Scipio Africanus (Appian, Book VIII: 66; Decembrio trans. 1472; and Petrarch, *Africa*, Book VII). The series, the first part of which had been designed by Parmigianino, was commissioned by Francis I of France to serve as designs for tapestries woven by the Fleming Marc Crètif (D'Astier 1907: 110-112; Jestaz and Bacou 1978). Ten genuine *modelli* exist, all but one of which (in Chantilly) are in the Louvre. Hartt (1958: 227) has shown that these drawings were not done until about 1534-35, with the weavings they generated probably already among those delivered to the king in 1535.

The drawing exhibited here is the modello for the first tapestry in the series. The procession has arrived at the Capitoline Hill where the triumphal way is lined on both sides with spectators. As soldiers begin their ascent, the trumpeters at the head of the procession have arrived at the steps of the Temple of Jove at the summit. An appropriate sense of finality is created by the strong right-to-left movement that curves back on itself at the top of the composition. Following Appian's description, all the figures wear crowns (of laurel); some carry covered dishes of gold and silver coins and other precious objects. The focus of this moment, however, is the massive architectural model several soldiers bear upon a litter. Like the much smaller "towers" in Mantegna's procession, this city-model too has the semblance of the single fortified structure. But this building is much grander than the Mantuan miniatures; it is in fact so heavy and substantial, the porters must concentrate to keep it up on their shoulders.
The plan of the model is a circle in a square. The bulwark is reinforced at each corner with a square watch. The main entrance is a double door surrounded by a massive, rusticated frame with a double sloping top. Inside the walls there rises a circular wall with peristyle topped by a shallow dome, proportioned like the Pantheon but with a thin lantern covering its opening. If this be conquered Carthage, then the battle was truly won. In comparison to the somewhat finicky scale of the fifteenth-century examples, which really could only have been rendered graphically,

the proportions of this structure are grand enough actually to have been built. In terms of organization, it has been suggested that the composition recalls the twisting scheme of Martin Schongauer's *Way to Calvary*, dated 1474-75 (*Giulio Romano* 1989). In terms of iconography, Hartt proposed that the triumphal theme was meant to "salve wounds inflicted on the royal pride by the humiliating treaty of Cambrai signed in 1529." Hartt also points out that the statue of Marcus Aurelius seen on the brow of the hill is a double anachronism: the Punic wars were long before the Aurelian period; and the statue itself was not brought to the Capitoline until 1538, at least three years after the drawing was executed (Hartt 1958: 227, 228).   *M.A.L.*

415
LORENZO LOTTO
Procession with City Model of Padua on a Pole
1535-38

Turin, Biblioteca Reale, 15909
White paper, point of brush drawing, wash, highlight in white, squared with red chalk.
265 × 160 mm
INSCRIBED: *PADVA*.

PROVENANCE: unknown.

BIBLIOGRAPHY: Pouncey 1965; *The Genius of Venice* 1983.

Lotto's approach to the subject of a triumphal procession is just as unorthodox as most of his ideas about religious subject matter. Instead of a horizontal parade of figures moving from right to left, he uses a vertical format, and turns the marchers perpendicular to the picture plane, bringing the whole group to a halt. In this way, he transforms the subject into a kind of ceremony in which trumpeters seem to call attention to the model of the city held high upon a pole by a young man wearing a laurel wreath. He labels this city *PADVA*, and represents it in full, including its crenelated fortification walls. He gives it the traditional rounded form that characterizes the city as the model of perfection.
Yet Lotto does not lose the implications of classic order: the four brazen trumpets are in the front of the group as they should be. The booty bearers are close behind: banners to the left, an empty cuirass in the center, and a boy with a heavy urn (full of booty?) on the right margin. The young man with the model remains prominent, carrying the civic symbol aloft in the Roman manner. Quite properly for a victor, as described in the ancient sources, he wears a laurel crown. But with still another flip of ingenuity, Lotto dresses the crowd in contemporary costumes, with rakish hats and ribbons at the knees.
Pouncey (1965) recognized this drawing as Lotto's draftsmanship in its full maturity, corresponding closely the Cingoli altarpiece of 1539. He recognized too the mundane quality of the crown. He identified the architectural studies around the edges as illusionistic representations of the possible frame, including section drawings of its mold-

ings. These he said showed that the drawing was a design for a painting of a fictive open doorway, and that the city identified as Padua might imply it was one of a series illustrating the various cities under Venetian dominion. While the finished nature of the squaring of the sheet indeed shows it was intended as a model to be transferred to a larger scale, there seems to be no record of a commission to Lotto for the decoration of public rooms, and the subject remains unique in his oeuvre. No matter how out of the ordinary the subject may be, however, Lotto retains his usual intimate rapport with his models who, in spite of the pretentious subject matter, seem to be his friends and neighbors in whom he found grace, good nature, and endless fascination.   *M.A.L.*

416
INNOCENZO FRANCUCCI DA IMOLA
St. Petronius, Bishop of Bologna
c. 1520-25

Bologna, Museo Civico d'Arte Industriale e Galleria Davia Bargellini, no. 10
Oil on canvas.

PROVENANCE: Bologna, S. Maria dei Servi, Cappella Bargellini (seventh on the right), right entrance pilaster.

BIBLIOGRAPHY: *Museo Civico d'Arte Industriale e Galleria Davia Bargellini* 1987: 878 no. 10; *Bibliotheca Sanctorum* 1967, LX: 521-532.

Three of the votive images discussed here have Bolognese provenance and, as we shall soon see, this fact has direct bearing on the architectural models themselves. To understand the significance of this statement, a brief discussion of the city's patron saint will be useful.

Bologna's patron was bishop Petronius (ca. 432-492), who was the subject of a cult already in Carolingian times. Of the many legends that developed about Petronius, one identified him in a fascinating manner as a city planner. The story goes that Petronius began his career as a tax-collector (*esattore*) in Jerusalem. After Bologna was devastated by Theodosius II, Pope Albertino I had a dream of Petronius and hurriedly called him back and named him bishop. With his knowledge of the Holy Sites in Jerusalem, Petronius planned the new city in the image of the sacred model. Indeed, to this day, the most ancient churches of the town, the Chiesa del Crocifisso, the Chiesa del Calvario or S. Sepolcro, the court of Pilate, and so on, are still known as copies of the Jerusalemmic shrines. As a result, St. Petronius was known not only as the protector of the city, but also as its designer. He was represented as such, holding an urban architectural model, in a long line of paintings and sculptures from the fourteenth century onward. Suffice it to recall the figure of St. Petronius by the young Michelangelo on the Arca of S. Domenico (Tolnay 1969: 138, 140, pls. 13, 14, 15; Kloten 1992). In these images (including the ones exhibited here), under the aegis of St. Petronius, Bologna's goods and services are offered to the glory of God, and the city itself is presented in the most venerable civic form, that

is as a New Jerusalem. The painting of St. Petronius holding a model of Bologna

by Innocenzo da Imola is one of pair with a figure of S. Lorenzo. Originally the two paintings in "gilt ornaments" flanked the entrance to the Cappella Bargellini in S. Maria dei Servi, in Bologna. Although Malvasia (1686: 275) attributed the pair to Orazio Sammachini, by 1816 P. Bassi recognized the true author. Moreover, documents dated 1613, in the Bargellini family archive, describe how the paintings were arranged in the chapel: S. Lorenzo "*in cornu evangeli*" (on the left facing the altar) opposite S. Petronius "*in cornu evangeli.*"

Compositionally, each saint gestures and focuses his attention in a manner that leads the worshipper into the chapel. St. Petronius is portrayed as a portly, dignified bearded man, dressed in a bishop's cope with a large pearl-studded morse. He is enthroned above the earth on a bank of clouds, and a flash of inspiration emitted from the clouds above his head calls his attention. In response, he gesticulates with his lifted right arm, while displaying the model of Bologna in his left. His bishop's crosier is balanced upright, between his arm and the model. The model shows the city, not with the usual idealized form of a circle, but enclosed within walls that are rectangular in outline. This shape or one close to it with obtuse angular walls, seems to characterize all the representations of Bologna, including Michaelangelo's. The form may be counted as an element of naturalism with the reference to "Bononia," the ancient Roman city and its military origin. Aside from the "Città della Galliera" now the gateway to the city in the center of the walls, the two remaining early twelfth-century towers, the Torre degli Asinelli and the Torre Garisenda, along with others, are clearly visible within the town.   *M.A.L.*

417
BIAGIO DALLE LAME PUPINO (or PIPINO)
St. Agnes between St. Petronius and St. Louis of France
1520-30?

Berlin, Staatliche Museen, Gemäldegalerie (reserve), 238
Oil on canvas.
172 × 229 cm

PROVENANCE: Bologna, Monastery of S. Agnese; Pinacoteca di Bologna (1808-15); Edward Solly Collection (Germany, 1821); Wiesbaden Museum deposit (after 1945); Berlin (1973).

BIBLIOGRAPHY: Bernardini 1990: 222-223; Emiliani 1971; *The Golden Legend...* 1969; Sambo 1989.

The rectangular shape of this large painting, wider than it is high, was unusual in the early sixteenth century. With three saints strung out in a line it is more reminiscent of the fourteenth century when separately framed figures were often placed side by side in a row. This archaic quality is the keynote of this painting since all the figures refer to an earlier period of Christianity.

The saints stand on a shallow stage of clouds, backed at the sides by parted draperies. Placed in the center against a deep *vista* of the Emilian countryside is St. Agnes, an early Christian virgin martyr, among the first noble Roman women to die in the name of Christ. Holding her

palm of martyrdom like a trophy, she has an aureole of supernatural light around her head, recalling the one said to have been cast by an angel who sheltered her when she was imprisoned in a house of prostitution. She holds a lamb, "whiter than snow" like the one with which she appeared to her kinfolk as they stood about her grave (*Golden Legend* 1969: 111, 112). Because of the prominence of this saint, the painting has been identified as the main altarpiece in the church of the Bolognese Dominican monastery of S. Agnese founded in the early thirteenth century by the Beata Diana degli Andalò. The monastery was completely refurbished in the first half of the sixteenth century.

Presumably it was then that the painting was created to replace an earlier icon, and designed to bring the subject up to date without entirely expunging reference to the original.

To the left is a figure of St. Petronius dressed in his bishop's robe, his miter and crosier at his side. As patron of the city, his presence localizes the dedication. As the planner of the town, he again holds an urban model, now rectangular in form, resting on a missal with a red cover. To the right is the figure of St. Louis IX of France, the pious monarch-crusader who was canonized in 1297. His relevance to the Bolognese Dominicans is a relic, a parcel of his body which was boiled, dismembered and disseminated after his death (1279), housed in a precious reliquary of French workmanship, owned by the basilica of S. Domenico (*Bibliotheca Sanctorum* 1967: 8, 320-342). The theme of the painting is thus the purity of early faith: Agnes the snowy martyr; Petronius the founder of the Bolognese New Jerusalem; and Louis the crusader who fought to preserve Jerusalem itself.

An early attribution to Bagnacavallo has now been supplanted by a more plausible one to his contemporary and collaborator, Biagio delle Lame (Pupini or Pipini; Sambo, 1989: 79).   *M.A.L.*

418
UNKNOWN BOLOGNESE or LOMBARD ARTIST
Pope Benedict XIV(?) with a Model of Bologna
mid-18th century ?

Florence, Galleria degli Uffizi, Gabinetto Disegni e Stampe 10966 S
Brush and ink (color?) on paper, ruled frame.
188 × 134/140 mm

BIBLIOGRAPHY: Pastor 1949.

Although undocumented, this brush drawing seems to prepare for a framed devotional painting in which a kneeling bearded pope propitiates the "Madonna Lactans" (the Virgin Mary nursing the Christ Child). As the pope lifts his face to Mary, with his left hand he points to the pages of a book held open by a monastic saint standing to Mary's right and looking out at the spectator. At the same time, with his right hand, the pope gestures toward the model of a city, again recognizable from its angular shape, its fortified entrance, and its characteristic towers, as Bologna. An infant angel kneels behind the model and joins the devotions. The fluid outlines of the drawing, the tight, calligraphic details, and style of the pontiff's cope with its bows and tassels, point to a date about the middle of the eighteenth century. The one pope during this period who was a native of Bologna was Prospero Lamberti, who reigned as Benedict XIV from 1740 to his death in 1758. Before his election, Lamberti had been Archbishop of Bologna. The papal tiara at his knee (surmounted by an orb and cross) is identical to the one represented on the statue of him on his tomb in St. Peter's in Rome by Pietro Bracci (Keutner 1969, fig. 192). The saint standing beside him in the drawing, therefore is probably the onomastic St. Benedict. Benedict XIII was known for his fairness (he abolished nepotism), his intellect (he was a brilliant academic lawyer), and his generosity. From the latter virtue, Bologna was the great beneficiary. In his hope to revive the quality of Bolognese education, Benedict gave support to several areas of study (medicine in particular), and in 1750, he deeded the University of Bologna his superb private library, a gift of 80,000 volumes and 2,500 manuscripts. Five years later the books were transferred and one year later, he ordered that the institution be opened to the public (Pastor 1949). It seems quite clear that in this drawing, the generosity of the pope, as he points to a manuscript and gestures toward the city, is compared to the Charity of the Virgin Mary who gives suckle to the Child. This image of the "Madonna Lactans," moreover, has a number of distinguishing features that give it an archaic quality. As an iconographical type, this theme had become quite rare by the eighteenth century. The classicizing style of the shallow niche before which Mary is enthroned, seems emphatically simple. It and the "Stella Maris" on her shoulder, an epithet from the Litany of the Virgin, as well as the tooled haloes are more characteristic of fourteenth or early fifteenth century paintings than the eighteenth. This stylistic dichotomy probably indicates reference to an earlier image, that remains to be identified, but that was perhaps still venerated in Bologna at the time of Benedict XIV.   *M.A.L.*

419
Taddeo Zuccari
Pope Julius III Restoring the Duchy of Parma to Ottavio Farnese
1562-63

New York, The Pierpont Morgan Library, The Janos Scholz Collection, 1973.27
Drawing, pen and brown wash over stylus underdrawing.
379 × 559 mm

Provenance: William Gibson(?); Jonathan Richardson, Sr (Lugt 2184); Thomas Dimsdale (Lugt 2426); Sir Thomas Lawrence; Samuel Woodburn; Lawrence-Woodburn sale, London, Christie's, 4-8 June 1860, part of lot 1074; Sir Thomas Phillipps; his daughter Mrs. Kartharine Fenwick; her son, T. Fitzroy Phillipps Fenwick; A.S.W. Rosenbach; Janos Scholz.

Bibliography: Mundy and Ourusoff de Fernandez Gimenez, 1989: 136-140, n. 38; Partridge 1978: 494-529, pls. 22, 27, 40.

The Room of Farnese Deeds is the principal audience hall of the great Villa Farnese at Caprarola, a small town

northeast of Rome. Its decoration was carried out in 1562-63 by Taddeo Zuccari and his shop, and the 14 scenes represented there tell the history of the Farnese family from the founding of Orbetello in 1100 to the return of Parma to Ottavio Farnese in 1550. As Partridge has shown (1978), all the history scenes are to some extent mythologized, and the scene depicted in the Metropolitan Museum drawing more than others.

Cardinal Alessandro Farnese (1468-1549) had fathered at least four sons by the time he was elected Pope Paul III in 1543. His favorite offspring was Pierluigi, whom he created Duke of Parma and Piacenza. Pierluigi in turn had two sons, one of whom was Cardinal Alessandro Farnese (named for his grandfather) and the other Ottavio, who married an illegitimate daughter of the Emperor Charles V. When Pierluigi was assassinated, probably by imperialist sympathizers in 1549, Paul III reincorporated Parma into the papal states. This move not only infuriated the emperor but also drove Pierluigi's son Ottavio into such a state of vindictive anger that he broke his grandfather's health. Under pressure from the young Cardinal Alessandro, on his deathbed Pope Paul relented and turned the duchy over to Ottavio. Alessandro made sure it was transferred by engineering the election of Julius III, who thereafter followed his every command. Meanwhile Charles V's rage at the loss of Parma led to two years of war which, however, the Farnese won. In 1552 Julius III was forced to reconfirm Ottavio's right to the duchy.

The inscription above the final fresco dates the event to 1550, recasting the transfer of property to a time before the war when it would have been a fulfillment of a grandfather's wish, thereby stressing the legitimacy of the Farnese family.

The drawing sketches out a vast hall in which the pope holds court enthroned on a dais under a baldachin, flanked by cardinals. On the other side of the room, in the background, is an altar and a window looking out on a grandiose landscape. The vertical format gives the opportunity to suggest a large crown of people, while focusing the composition on the main event. The draperies and other vertical elements at the right margin bring about a closure quite fitting for the final scene in the sequence. Julius III is in pontifical robes; he gestures in blessing. Ottavio kneels before him, placing his hands on a large model of the duchy, as one would hold a tray. The real support, however, comes from another figure: Cardinal Alessandro, who looks at the pope while passing the tray to his brother. In this case, the model represents the property in question, proclaiming ownership and the legal right to rule. In the final fresco, the figure of Alessandro is given even greater prominence, being in the center of the composition before a great column that has replaced the altar in the background.

The verso of this sheet has sketches of "The Marriages of Ottavio Farnese and Margaret of Austria and Orazio Farnese and Diane de Valois, with Paul III Creating Pierluigi Farnese Captain-General of the Church."   *M.A.L.*

420
Francesco Maffei
St. Vincent Holding a Standard and Model of Vicenza
1626-30

Vicenza, Museo Civico
Oil on canvas.
135 × 119 cm
Inscribed: (lower edge, under Saint's foot) *AERIS PUBLICI ADMINISTRATORES / RATIONES REDDVNTO/IDQ. OCTVMVIRI EX LEGE CVRANTO* (These eight men by law watch over the administration of the Public Treasury)

Provenance: Vicenza, Palazzo del Podestà; Museo Vicentino (as Maganza).

Bibliography: Ivanoff 1956; *The Golden Legend* 1969; Barbieri 1974: 315-318, pl. 171; Rossi 1991.

Vicenza was one of the many communes in northern Italy to declare independence in the twelfth century, only to be seized repeatedly by outside forces—Frederick II, the Carrara, the Scaligeri, the Visconti, and ultimately Venice. During the war of the League of Cambrai, the town was sacked and badly damaged. But like its brave patron, St. Vincent, an early Christian martyr who grew happier the more he was tortured (*Golden Legend* 1969: 114-117), the city rapidly rebuilt itself in a new, more splendid form (including the great basilica and other buildings by Palladio).

The painting by Francesco Maffei in the Municipal Office Building of Vicenza reflects the esteem that the citizens felt for their town. Painted to decorate the room where the public budget was overseen, the eight men elected as treasurers were themselves overseen by their saintly advocate. A full-length figure of St. Vincent stands at the height of the portal, his foot viewed from below poised on the top of the identifying inscription. He wears the clothes of a deacon, his official position in the early church. The pole of a large standard emblazoned with a white cross illusionistically resting on the base of the inscription, passes before it and leans across the saint's shoulder. The flag which represents the town also has the shape of the victorious *Labarum*, the flag of Constantine. Looking up to indicate the heavenly source of his authority, St. Vincent raises a model of Vicenza in dedication. From the period 1577-81, a real city model is documented in Vicenza at the sanctuary of Monte Berico, and said to have been made of wood covered with silver. The lost model was made as a votive in expiation for an attack of the plague (Barbieri 1974: 314). In Maffei's painting, the urban offering becomes an official sign of saintly protection under which the governance of Vicenza is carried out. Maffei's artistic heritage, stemming from Palma Vecchio, Tintoretto and the Bassani, is displayed in the dramatic angle of vision, the thick reds, and the flickering silvery highlights that pick out the forms from mysterious shadows (Ivanoff 1956). These painterly effects give the benign saintly spirit a palpable presence, and instill us with confidence in his power to protect.   *M.A.L.*

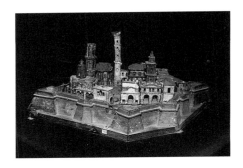

421
P. CLEMENTI
Model of Reggio Emilia
ca. 1560

Reggio Emilia, Museo Civico e Galleria d'Arte.
Papier maché.

BIBLIOGRAPHY: Davoli 1980; Turner 1991.

The creation of this urban model seems to be part of a longstanding tradition of self-imaging in the city of Reggio Emilia. One of the earliest remaining local city portraits is an anonymous woodblock of 1515 that shows the town with a circular plan. As we have seen, this shape glorifies Reggio as ideal, whereas the real city is hexagonal with four major gates, which are correctly shown. The city image, inscribed *Regium Lepidi* (the town was named for the Roman consul M. Emilio Lepidi), is circumscribed by the four saintly patrons of the city, Prosper, Chrysanth, Daria and Venerius. The Piazza Grande is defined by the main monuments of Reggio: the Palazzo Vecchio del Comune with the Torre dell'Orologio; the domed cathedral; the Nuovo Palazzo del Comune; and the crenelated Torre del Bordello. Such views of Reggio were produced throughout the next three centuries, appearing in prints and on local coins and stamps as well (Davoli 1980, passim). It is this tradition of civic display that may account for the precious papier maché model, made by the artist P. Clementi who proudly signed his name, but about whom we know nothing more. The model shows the Piazza Grande as it was in the mid sixteenth century, with most of the buildings adjusted to face toward a frontal view. Another mid-sixteenth century print inscribed "Vero disegno del la Mirandola" has a small image of the town at the bottom, where the view is the same as the model and could have been copied from it (Davoli 1980, pl. 2). There apparently was also a tradition in Reggio that linked the patron saint with an image of the city. St. Prosper, bishop of Reggio (often mistakenly identified with St. Prosper of Aquitaine; cf. *Biblioteca Sanctorum*, s.v.). was in fact not a distinguished scholar (as was the saint from Aquitaine), and his miracles were never officially verified. In the tradition of the town, however, he was imbued with these attributes. By the early seventeenth century, much in the manner of St.Petronius of Bologna, St. Prosper is shown as the protector of the city in the form of a small model. And it may not have been by chance that the Bolognese painter Guercino was the first to represent him in this manner. One of Guercino's preliminary drawings (Windsor Castle, inv. no. 2553) for his altarpiece in the church of the Madonna della Ghiara in Reggio, depicts St. Prosper looking anxiously up at the crucified Christ as he points to a model of the city held up to him by a putto (Turner 1991: 69). The drawing was done in 1623-25, but was not used in the final painting (where town model is placed on the ground before the saint). The motif in the drawing—a putto proffering the model to the saint—was taken over by Alberto Ronco who in 1629 used it in a large engraving (405 × 308 mm) of St. Prosper and his miracles, which the artist sold to the commune. And again, in 1720 Bartolomeo Bonvicini used the concept, showing a putto presenting St. Prosper with the city image now represented as a drawing on a scroll (Davoli 1980, pls. 13, 41).   *M.A.L.*

Bibliography
Index of Names
Index of Works

s.d.-n.d.

JOAN FABRIZIO DEGLI ATTI, *Cronicha de la egregia città de Tode dal fundamento* (Ms. del sec. XV-XVI), biblioteca privata Micheli di Todi, vedi Mancini 1955
Fabbrica della Cattedrale, Archivio Capitolare di Vigevano (SC2 R4 N30)
A. RUESCH, ed, *Illustrated Guide to the National Museum in Naples*, Naples

1424 ca.

ANDREA FIOCCHI, *De potestatibus Romanorum libri II*, Roma

1472

FLAVIO BIONDO, *Roma triumphans*, Mantova
ROBERTO VALTURIO, *De re militari*, Verona

1477

PIERO CANDIDO DECEMBRIO (traduzione a cura di), *Appiano. Historia Romana*, Venezia

1477-82

FRANCESCO DI GIORGIO MARTINI, *Trattato dell'architettura civile e militare*

1479

PLATINA (BARTOLOMEO SACCHI), *Liber de vita Christi ac pontificum omnium*, Venezia

1504

G. F. POGGIO BRACCIOLINI, *De officio principis*, Roma
GIOVANNI TORTELLI, *De orthographia*, Venezia

1506

RAFFAELE MAFFEI, *Commentariorum urbanorum libri*, Roma

1509

LUCA PACIOLI, *De Divina Proportione, opera a tutti gl'ingegni perspicaci e curiosi...*, Venezia

1510

F. ALBERTINI, *Opusculum de mirabilibus novae et veteris urbis Romae*, Roma

1511

FRA GIOVANNI GIOCONDO DA VERONA (a cura di), *M. Vitruvio per Jocundum solito castigator factus...*, Venezia

1513

ANDREA FULVIO, *Antiquaria urbis*, Roma
LUDOVICO RICCHIERI, *Lectionum antiquarium libri*, Basel

1521

CESARE CESARIANO, *Di Lucio Vitruvio Pollione De Architectura Libri Decem*, Como
NICCOLÒ PEROTTI, *Cornucopia*, Basel

1524

A. PONTE, *Rhomitypion, ubi mirabilia omnia urbis Romae et nova et vetera describuntur*, Roma

1525

IODOCO DEL BADIA, vedi 1894 e 1872
ALBRECHT DÜRER, *Underweysung der Messung, mit dem*

Zirckel und richtscheyt, in Linien, Ebnen unn ganssen Corporen..., Nürnberg (fac simile 1966)

1527

ALBRECHT DÜRER, *Etliche underricht, zu befestigung der Stett, Schloss und flecken*, Nürnberg
ANDREA FULVIO, *Antiquitates urbis*, Roma

1528

ALBRECHT DÜRER, *Hierin sind begriffen vier bücher von menslicher Proportion*, Nürnberg

1531

FLAVIO BIONDO, *De Roma triumphante libri*, Basel

1534

BARTOLOMEO MARLIANO, *Urbis Romae topographia*, Roma
Quinternetto de le spexe diverse facte per li Fabricieri de Veglevano l'anno 1534, Archivio Capitolare di Vigevano, SC2 R5 N1 F1(13)

1535

Opusculo riguardante le spese fatte nella chiesa cattedrale di sant'Ambrogio di Vigevano, redatto presumibilmente alla fine del 1535, Archivio Capitolare di Vigevano, SC2 R5 N1 F2 1540

1540

LEON BATTISTA ALBERTI, *De Pictura praestantissima...*, Basil
SEBASTIANO SERLIO [a], *Regole generali*, Venezia (2a ed.)
———— [b], *Il terzo libro, nel quale si figurano e descrivono le antiquità di Roma*, Venezia

1541

LEON BATTISTA ALBERTI, *De re aedificatoria libri decem Leonis Baptista Alberti Florentini viri clarissimi, & Architecti nobilissimi...*, Argentorati [a Parigi]

1544

SEBASTIANO SERLIO, *Regole generali*, Venezia (3a ed.)

1547

CLAUDIO TOLOMEI, *Delle lettere libri*, Venezia

1550

HANS BLUM, *Gebrauch der V. Säulen*, vedi Hans Blum 1662

1552

SIMONE DEL POZZO, *Libro d'Estimo generale della città e del territorio di Vigevano corredato di peregrine notizie storiche*, Archivio Storico Civico di Vigevano (art. 179) 1553
ASCANIO CONDIVI, *Vita di Michelangelo Buonarroti*, Roma

1554

PIETRO GIACOMO CATANEO, *I quattro primi libri di architettura...*, Venezia

1556

GIOVANNI BATTISTA BERTANI, *Missiva alo ill.mo et Ex.mo il S.r D. di Mantoa*, Archivio di Stato di Mantova (Archivo Gonzaga, busta 2559, 30.09.1556)

1558

GIOVANNI BATTISTA BERTANI, *Gli oscuri e difficili passi dell'opera jonica di Vitruvio*, Mantova
ANTONIO LABACCO, *Libro appartenente all'architettura*, Roma
WALTHER RIVIUS, *Der Architektur fürnembsten... Matheatischen und Mechanischen Künst... in drei fürneme Bücher abgetheilet*, Nürnberg, Heyn

1559

SEBASTIANO SERLIO, *Libri I-V d'Architettura*, Venezia

1562

JACOPO BAROZZI detto il VIGNOLA, *Regola delli cinque ordini d'architettura*, Roma

1563

POMPILIO AMASEO, *De Bononiensium scholarum ex aedificatione oratio*, Bologna

1565

ANTONIO BARDI, *Facultates magistratus curatorum viarum aedificiorumque publiciorum et privatorum almae urbis*, Roma
GIOVANNI BATTISTA BERTANI, *Missiva* [indirizzata al Duca Guglielmo], Archivio di Stato di Mantova (Archivio Gonzaga, busta 2573, 19.09.1565)
BERNARDO GAMUCCI, *Libri quattro dell'antichità della città di Roma*, Venezia

1566

GIOVANNI BATTISTA BERTANI, *Missiva* [indirizzata al Castellano], Archivio di Stato di Mantova (Archivio Gonzaga, busta 2576, 14.07.1566)
DOMENICO MELLINI, *Descrizione dell'entrata delle serenissima Reina d'Austria*, Firenze

1567

DANIELE BARBARO, *M. Vitruvii Pollionis De Architectura Libri Decem*, Venezia, F. Senensis e J. Crieger (vedi anche 1987)
PIETRO GIACOMO CATANEO, *L'architettura*, Venezia
PHILIBERT DE L'ORME, *Le prémier Tome de l'Architecture de Philibert de l'Orme*, Paris

1569

GIOVANNI BATTISTA DE CAVALIERI, *Urbis Romae aedificiorum illustrium...*, Roma
SEBASTIANO SERLIO, *Sebastiani Serlii Bononiensis. De Architectura Libri Quinque*, Venezia

1570

ANDREA PALLADIO, *I quattto libri dell'architettura*, Venezia

1571

SIMONE DEL POZZO, *Registro ossia inventario dei beni ecclesiastici posti in territorio di Vigevano*, Archivio storico Civico di Vigevano, antico catasto 49 (cc. 11v., 12)

1577

CARLO BORROMEO, *Instructiones fabricae et suppellectilis ecclesiasticae*, Milano, vedi 1962
ETIENNE DUPÉRAC, *I vestigi dell'antichità di Roma*, Roma

HANS VREDEMAN DE VRIES, *Theatrum vitae humanae*, [s.l.?], P. Balten

1583
AGRIPPA, CAMILLO, *Trattato... di traspotar la guglia in su la piazza di San Pietro*, Roma
JACOPO BAROZZI detto il VIGNOLA, *Le due regole della prospettiva pratica*, a cura di E. Danti, Roma

1584
RAFFAELLO BORGHINI, *Il riposo*, Firenze
GIOVAN PAOLO LOMAZZO, *Trattato dell'arte della pittura*, Milano
C. NUBILONIO, *La cronaca di Vigevano*, Vigevano (ed. consigliata, Torino 1891)
SEBASTIANO SERLIO, *I sette libri dell'architettura*, Venezia

1585
BASTIANO DE' ROSSI, *Descrizione del magnificentissimo apparato e de' maravigliosi intermedi fatti per la commedia rappresentata in Firenze nelle felicissime nozze degl'Illustrissimi, ed Eccellentissimi Signori il Signor Don Cesare d'Este e la Signora Donna Virginia Medici*, Firenze

1587
LORENZO GIACOMINI, *Oratione de le lodi di Francesco Medici Granduca di Toscana*, Firenze

1587-90
M. MALVASIA, *Relazione di tutta la Provincia dell'Umbria fatta da Mons. Malvasia Chierico di camera e da lui presentata a Sisto V*, Ms. Fondo Vittorio Emanuele n. 711, Biblioteca Nazionale di Roma

1588
AGOSTINO RAMELLI, *Le diverse et artificiose machine*, Parigi

1590
GIOVAN ANTONIO RUSCONI, *Della architettura... libri dieci*, Venezia

1593-98
WENDEL DIETTERLIN, *Architectura und Austheilung der V Seüln*, Stuttgart

1596
BONAIUTO LORINI, *Della fortificazioni... libri cinque*, Venezia

1597
GIOVAN BATTISTA POSSEVINO, *Vita de' Santi et beati di Todi, con... molte rime... nelle quali si scuopre l'antichità... di detta città*, Perugia

1600
SEBASTIANO SERLIO, *Tutta l'opera d'architettura et prospettiva*, Venezia

1610
PIETRO MARTIRE FELINI, *Trattato nuovo delle cose maravigliose dell'alma città di Roma*, Roma

1613-29
L.A. PETTI, *Ragunanza de diverse Croniche e memorie antiche e notabili di Todi*, 6 voll., Archivio Storico Comunale di Todi

1615
VINCENZO SCAMOZZI, *L'idea dell'architettura universale...*, Venezia

1618
HEINRICH LAUTENSACK, *Dess Circkelss und Richtscheyts/ auch der Perspectiva und Proportion der Menschen und Rossa... Underweisung dess rechten gebrauchs*, Frankfurt

1619
SEBASTIANO SERLIO, *Tutte le opere*, Venezia

1620
MARTINO FERRABOSCO, *Libro de l'architettura di S. Pietro nel Vaticano finito col disegno di Michel Angelo Bonaroto et d'altri architetti*, Roma

1624
C. D'ENGENIO, *Napoli sacra*, Napoli

1638
P. TOTTI, *Ritratto di Roma moderna*, Roma

1639
G. LAURO, *Heroico splendore delle città del mondo*, I, Roma

1640
JACOPO BAROZZI da VIGNOLA, *Regola delli cinque ordini dell'architettura*, Amsterdam

1642
GIOVANNI BAGLIONE, *Le vita de' pittori, scultori et architetti*, Roma

1662
HANS BLUM, *Nuzlichs Säulenbuch Oder Kunstmässige Beschreibung von dem gebrauch der V. Säulen*, Zürich

1667
GEORG CASPAR ERASMUS, *Seülen-Buch Oder Gründlicher Bericht von den Fünf Ordnungen der Architectur-Kunst*, Nürnberg

1669
C.S. BRAMBILLA, *La chiesa di Vigevano*, Milano

1674
CARLO TORRE, *Il ritratto di Milano*, Milano

1683
G.F. MORELLI, *Brevi notizie delle pitture e sculture che adornano l'augusta città di Perugia*, Perugia

1685
Acta Sanctorum (AA.SS.), Maii, V 257-318, Antwerplae
AUGUSTIN CHARLES D'AVILER, *Les Cinq Ordres d'Architecture de Vincent Scamozzi*, Paris, Coignard

1686
CARLO CESARE MALVASIA, *Le pitture di Bologna*, Bologna (nuova edizione 1969)
FILIPPO TITI, *Ammestramento utile e curioso di pittura, scoltura e architettura nelle chiese di Roma, palazzi Vaticano, di Monte Cavallo, et altri*, Roma

1692
CARLO CELANO, *Notizie del Bello dell'Antico e del Curioso della città di Napoli...*, Napoli (ed. consigliata, C. Celano-Chiarini, G.B. Chiarini, Napoli 1856)

1694
CARLO FONTANA, *Templum Vaticanum et ipsius origo cum Aedificiis maximè conspicuis antiquitùs, & recèns ibidem constitutis...*, Roma

1696
PHILIPPO BONANNI, *Numismata Summorum Pontificum Templi Vaticani Fabricam indicantia*, Roma

1697
P. SARNELLI, *Guida de' forestieri*, Napoli

1699
PHILIPPO BONANNI, *Numismata Pontificum Romanorum*, I, Roma

1704
G. BLAEU, *Nouveau théâtre d'Italie, ou Description exacte de ses villes, palais, eglises...*, I, Amsterdam

1706
PHILIPPO BONANNI, *Numismata Pontificum Romanorum*, Roma, vedi anche 1699

1723
G.F. POGGIO BRACCIOLINI, *Historiae de varietate fortunae libri*, Parigi
G.T. PROSPERI, *Fondazione e prerogative della Congregazione de' Nobili che governa la Fabrica et Ospedale della Vergine SS.ma della Consolazione di Todi*, Todi

1736
R. VENUTI (a cura di), *Oratio totam fere romanam historiam complectens qua dedicata fuit marmorea Leoni X. Pont. Max. statua*, Roma

1738
FRANCESCO BIANCHINI, *Del palazzo de' Cesari*, Verona

1739
GIUSEPPE ROSSI, *La Libreria Mediceo-Laurenziana*, Firenze

1739-41
GIOVANNI POLENI, *Exercitationes vitruvianae*, Padova

1744
R. VENUTI, *Nummismata Romanorum Pontificum*, Roma

1746
MARIETTE, in Ascanio Condivi, *Vita di Michelangelo*, a cura di A.F. Gori, Firenze

1748
GIOVANNI POLENI, *Memorie istoriche della gran cupola del tempio vaticano*, Padova

1748-70
BERNARDO RUCELLAI, «De urbe Roma», in *Rerum italicarum scriptores*, a cura di J.M. Tartinius, II, Firenze, 783-1190

1750
ANDREA PALLADIO, *I quattro libri dell'architettura di Andrea Palladio*, Venezia

1751
GIUSEPPE MARIA CARAFA, *De Gymnasio Romano et eius professoribus*, Roma

1754-89
GIOVANNI BOTTARI, *Raccolta di lettere sulla pittura, scultura ed architettura scritte da' più celebri professori che in dette arti fiorirono dal secolo XV al XVII*, 7 voll., Roma

1755
ANGIOLO MARIA BANDINI, *Catalogus Codicorum latinorum Bibliothecae Medicae Laurentiane*, II, Firenze

1757
GIUSEPPE RICHA, *Notizie istoriche delle chiese fiorentine*, V, Firenze

1759-60
GIOVANNI BOTTARI, *Raccolta di lettere sulla pittura, scultura ed architettura scritte da' più celebri professori che in dette arti fiorirono dal secolo XV al XVII (1754-89)* II, Roma
GIORGIO VASARI, *Le vite de' più eccellenti pittori, scultori et architetti*, a cura di M. Pagliarini, Roma

1763
FILIPPO TITI, *Descrizione delle pitture, sculture e architetture esposte al pubblico in Roma*, Roma

1763

NERALCO (Gius. Ercolani), *Descrizione del Colosseo Romano del Panteo e del tempio Vaticano*, Ancona

1764

GIOVANNI BOTTARI, *Raccolta di lettere sulla pittura, scultura ed architettura scritte da' più celebri personaggi dei secc. XV, XVI e XVII (1754-89)* IV, Roma

1768

G.A. MONALDINI, *Le vita de' più celebri architetti d'ogni nazione e d'ogni tempo*, Roma

1781

GIUSEPPE ALLEGRANZA, *Opuscoli inediti*, Cremona

FRANCESCO MILIZIA, *Memorie degli Architetti antichi e moderni*, Parma (3a ed.)

1783

GIOVANNI FANTUZZI, *Notizie degli scrittori bolognesi*, 9 voll., Bologna

1784

BALDASSARE ORSINI, *Guida al forestiere per l'augusta città di Perugia*, Perugia (ristampa 1973)

1785

A. VICI, "Memorie sopra alcune fabbriche di Bramante Lazzari", *Giornale delle Belle Arti* XLVIII (3 dicembre), 378-382

1785-86

GIOVANNI CAMBI, *Le istorie di Giovanni Cambi cittadino fiorentino*, 4 voll., Firenze (tomi XX-XXIII delle *Delizie degli eruditi toscani*)

1787

G.M. MODESTINI, *Descrizione della Chiesa di S. Francesco... di Perugia*, Perugia

1788

A. MARIOTTI, *Lettere pittoriche perugine*, Perugia

1794

IRENEO AFFÒ, in *Basini parmensis, poetae, Opera prestantiora nunc primum edita et opportunis commentariis inlustrata*, Rimini

BASINI PARMENSIS, POETAE, *Opera prestantiora nunc primum edita et opportunis commentariis inlustrata*, Rimini

1802

I. MORELLI, *Bibliotheca manuscripta graeca et latina*, I, Bassano

1803-21

ADAM VON BARTSCH, *Le peintre graveur*, 21 voll., Vienne

1810

PIETRO GIORGIO BIFFIGNANDI BUCCELLA, *Memorie istoriche della città e contado di Vigevano*, Vigevano

1811

CARLO FRANCESCO CICERI, *Selva di notizie autentiche riguardanti la Fabbrica della Cattedrale di Como*, Como

1813

G.B. VERMIGLIOLI, *Memorie di Jacopo Antiquari*, Perugia

1815

J. FICHARD, "Italia", *Frankfurterisches Archiv für Altere Deutsche Literatur und Geschichte* III, 22

TIBERIUS ALPHARANUS, *De basilicae vaticanae antiquissima et nova structura*, a cura di D.M. Cerrati, Roma

G. VENTURI, *Dell'origine e dei primi progressi delle odierne artiglierie...*, Reggio Emilia

1816

P. BASSANI, *Guida degli amatori delle belle arti per la città di Bologna*, Bologna

L. MALASPINA, *Memorie storiche della fabbrica della Cattedrale di Pavia*, Milano

1822

RIGUCCIO GALLUZZI, *Storia del Granducato di Toscana*, Firenze

S. SIEPI, *Descrizione topologico-istorica della città di Perugia*, 3 voll., Perugia

1822-26

GIROLAMO TIRABOSCHI, *Storia della letteratura italiana*, Milano

1824-35

J.B. SEROUX D'AGINCOURT, *Storia dell'arte col mezo dei monumenti*, 7 voll., Milano

1829

ERASMO PISTOLESI, *Il Vaticano*, Roma

1829-30

CARLO AMATI (a cura di), *Dell'architettura di Marco Vitruvio Pollione*, Milano

1832-37

L. SCOTTI, *Catalogo dei disegni originali dei pittori, scultori, ed architetti, che si conservano nella celebre collezione esistente nella Imperiale e Reale Galleria di Firenze*, Firenze

1835-71

A.P.F. ROBERT-DUMESNIL, *Le peintre-graveur français*, Paris

1836

LUIGI PUNGILEONI, *Memorie intorno alla vita e alle opere di Donato o Donnino Bramante*, Roma

1837

G.B. VERMIGLIOLI, *Di Bernardo Pinturicchio, pittore perugino de' secoli XV-XVI. Memorie*, Perugia

1838-41

G. LIBRI, *Histoire des sciences mathématiques en Italie*, Paris

A. NIBBY, *Roma nell'anno MDCCCXXXVIII*, Roma

1839

C. MONTI, "Sul Tempio della Consolazione a Todi", *Album. Giornale letterario e di belle arti* VI, 1-3 e 23-4

JOHANN DAVID PASSAVANT, *Raffael von Urbino und sein Vater Giovanni Santi*, Leipzig

G.B. VERMIGLIOLI, "Medaglione di Nocolò Piccinino", *Album. Giornale letterario e di belle arti* VI, V

1839-45

G. ROSINI, *Storia della pittura italiana esposta coi monumenti*, Pisa

1840

JOHAN WILHELM GAYE, *Carteggio inedito d'artisti dei secoli XIV, XV, XVI (1839-40)*, Firenze

1841

FRANCESCO DI GIORGIO MARTINI, *Trattato di architettura civile e militare... per la prima volta pubblicato per cura del cavalier Cesare Saluzzo...*, a cura di Carlo Promis, 3 voll., Torino

1844

M. GIANIOLO, *De Viglevano et omnibus episcopis*, Novara

1846

FILIPPO BALDINUCCI, *Notizie de' professori del disegno*, III, Firenze

1851

G. BINI, PASQUALE AUGUSTO BIGAZZI (a cura di), *Vita di Filippo Strozzi il Vecchio scritta da Lorenzo suo figlio*, Firenze

PASQUALE ROTONDI, "Contributi urbinati a Bramante pittore", *Emporium* XIII, 109-135

1854

Coxe, Catalogus codicorum manuscriptorum Bibliothecae Bodleianae, III, Oxford

GAETANO MILANESI, *Documenti per la storia dell'arte senese*, 3 voll., Siena

PIETRO SELVATICO, *Catalogo delle opere d'arte contenute nella sala della R. Accademia di Venezia*, Venezia

1855

ALANUS DE INSULIS, "Liber de planctu naturae", in J.-P. Migne (sous la direction de), *Patrologia latina*, Paris

JACOB C. BURCKHARDT, *Der Cicerone. Eine Anleitung zum Genuss der Kunstwerke Italiens*, Basel

1856

G. MORONI, *Dizionario di erudizione storico-ecclesiastica*, Venezia

1857

CESARE GUASTI, *La cupola di Santa Maria del Fiore, illustrata con i documenti di Archivio dell'Opera secolare*, Firenze (ristampa, Firenze 1974)

GAETANO MILANESI, "Due ricevute autografe di Michelangelo Buonarroti ed un conto di spese concernenti la facciata di San Lorenzo commessagli da Papa Leone X", *Giornale storico degli archivi toscani* I, 50-4

1859

AMICO RICCI, *Storia dell'architettura in Italia*, Modena

1860

E. MEAUME, *Recherches sur la vie et les ouvrages de Jacques Callot*, 2 voll., Paris

1861

F. GREGOROVIUS, *Wanderjahre in Italien*, Liepzig

1862

SIR JOHN CHARLES ROBINSON, *Catalogue of the Special Exhibition of Works of Art of the Mediaeval, Renaissance, and More Recent Periods on Loan at the South Kensington Museum, June 1862*, London

1863

GUGLIELMO ENRICO SALTINI, "Della morte di Francesco I de' Medici e di Bianca Cappello", *Archivio storico italiano* n.s. XVIII, 19-81

1864

FILIPPO BALDINUCCI, *Notizie dei professori del disegno dal Cimabue in qua*, Firenze

JOHAN DAVID PASSAVANT, *Le peintre graveur*, V, Leipzig

1865

L.M. ASTANCOLLE, "Cenni storico artistici del tempio della Consolazione a Todi", *L'Apologetico* III, 170-178

GIROLAMO LUIGI CALVI, *Notizie sulla vita e sulle opere dei principali architetti, scultori e pittori...*, II, Milano

G. DAELLI, *Carte Michelangiolesche inedite*, Milano

PIETRO SELVATICO, *Catalogue des dessins originaux de Raphäel conservés à l'Académie des Beaux-Arts à Venise et executés en photographie par A. Perini*, Venezia

1866

FRANCESCO GASPARONI, "La casa di Michelagnolo Buonarroti", in *Buonarroti*, quaderno XI (novembre), 178-80

1867

P. MALLIUS, "Opusculum historiae sacrae", in *Acta Sanctorum...*, VII, Paris, appendix, 34 ss.

683

ANTON SPRINGER, "Der gothische Schneider von Bologna", in *Bilder aus der neueren Kunstgeschichte*, Bonn, 121-129

M. VEGIUS, "Historiae basilicae antiquae", in *Acta Sanctorum...*, VII, Paris, appendice 56 ss.

1868

HEINRICH VON GEYMÜLLER, *Notizien über die Entwürfe zu St. Peter in Rom*, Karlsruhe

1869

ALBERT JAHN, "Die Sammlung der Handzeichnungen italienischer Architekten in der Galerie der Uffizien in Florenz", *Jahrbüch für Kunstwissenscheaft* II, 143-154

P. LASPEYRES, *Santa Maria della Consolazione zu Todi*, Berlin

PASQUALE ROTONDI, *The Ducal Palace of Urbino. Its Architecture and Decoration*, London

1870

Catalogo della raccolta di disegni autografi antichi e moderni donata dal Prof. E. Santarelli alla R. Galleria di Firenze, Firenze

HEINRICH VON GEYMÜLLER, "Trois dessins d'architecture inedits de Raphael", *Gazette des Beaux-Arts* III, 79-91

1871

J. CROWE AND GIOVAN BATTISTA CAVALCASELLE, *A History of Painting in Northern Italy*, London

1872

IODOCO DEL BADIA, *Raccolta delle migliori fabbriche di Firenze, disegnate da Riccardo Mazzanti e Torquato Del Lungo, architetti, con illustrazioni storiche di Iodoco del Badia*, Firenze

M. GUARDABASSI, *Indice-guida dei Monumenti pagani e cristiani riguardanti l'istoria e l'arte esistenti nella provincia dell'Umbria*, Perugia

A. VON REUMONT, "Recensione ad A.Rossi, 1872", *Archivio storico italiano*, 346-350

A. ROSSI, "Cenno storico sulla Chiesa della Consolazione in Todi", *Giornale di erudizione artistica* I (1 gennaio), 3-9

1873

CHARLES DRURY EDWARD FORTNUM, *A Descriptive Catalogue of the Maiolica. Hispano-Moresco, Persian, Damascus, and Rhodian wares in the South Kensington Museum*, London

D.C. FINOCCHIETTI, *Della scultura e tarsia in legno dagli antichi tempi ad oggi*, Firenze

G. A. GALANTE, *Guida sacra alla città di Napoli*, Napoli

MARIN SANUDO, "La spedizione di Carlo VIII in Italia", in *Archivio Veneto*, Venezia, a cura di R. Fulin

1874

L. COURAJOD, *Heinrich von Geymüller, Les estampes attribuées à Bramante, aux points de vue iconographique et architectonique*, Paris

CESARE GUASTI, "Un disegno di Giovanni di Gherardo da Prato", in *Belle Arti. Opuscoli descrittivi e biografici*, Firenze, 111-122

ARISTIDE NARDINI DESPOTTI MOSPIGNOTTI, "Un disegno di Giovanni di Gherardo da Prato. Appendice", in *Belle Arti. Opuscoli descrittivi e biografici*, Firenze, 123-128

A. ROSSI, "La fabbrica della Chiesa della Consolazione in Todi", *Giornale di erudizione artistica. Supplemento ad alcune serie di notizie artistiche* III, 321-328

1874-90

C. WACHSMUTH, *Die Stadt Athen im Altertum*, Leipzig

1875

ANTONINO BERTOLOTTI, "Documenti intorno a Michelangelo Buonarroti trovati e esistenti in Roma",

Archivio storico-artistico, archeologico e letterario della città a provincia di Roma I, 74-6

W. BRAGHIROLLI, *Sulle manifatture di arazzi in Mantova*, Mantova

JACOPO CAVALLUCCI, "Guida alle opere di Michelangelo", in *Michelangelo Buonarroti. Ricordo al popolo italiano*, Firenze, 163-214

HEINRICH VON GEYMÜLLER, *Les projets primitifs pour la basilique de Saint-Pierre de Rome/Die ursprunglichen Entwurfe für Sanct Peter in Rom*, Wien-Paris

AURELIO GOTTI, *Vita di Michelangelo Buonarroti narrata con l'aiuto di nuovi documenti*, 2 voll., Firenze

GAETANO MILANESI (a cura di) [a], *Michelangelo. Le lettere*, Firenze

—— [b], *Le opere di Giorgio Vasari con nuove annotazioni e commenti*, VII, Firenze

ENEA PICCOLOMINI, "Intorno alle condizioni e alle vicende della libreria medicea privata", estratto da *Archivio storico italiano*, Firenze

R. REDTENBACHER, *Mitteilungen aus der Sammlung architektonischer Handzeichnungen in der Gallerie der Uffizien zu Florenz*, Karlsruhe

1876

G. CAMPORI, *L'arazzeria estense*, Modena

CHARLES DURY EDWARD FORTNUM, "On the Bronze Portrait Busts of Michelangelo Atributed to Daniele da Volterra and Other Artists", in *Archeological Journal* XXXIII, 168-182

AURELIO GOTTI, *Vita di Michelangelo Buonarroti narrata con l'aiuto di nuovi documenti*, 2 voll., Firenze

CHARLES H. WILSON, *Life and Works of Michelangelo. The Life Partly Compiled from that by the Commend. Aurelio Gotti*, London

1877

PIETRO FONTANA, *Modello in legno della Cupola Vaticana fatto eseguire da Michelangelo Buonnaroti disegnato, inciso ed illustrato da Pietro Fontana*, Roma

CONSTANTIN A. JOVANOVITS, *Forschungen über den Bau der Peterskirche zu Rom*, Wien

JOSEPH VALENTINELLI, *Bibliotheca manuscripta ad S. Marci Venetiarum Codices*, mss. latini, V, Venezia

1877-80

Annali della Fabbrica del Duomo di Milano, dall'origine fino al presente... a cura della sua amministrazione, 3 voll.: I-II 1877; III 1880, Milano

1878

LUIGI CARATTOLI, *Elenco dei dipinti esistenti nella Pinacoteca di Perugia compilato da Luigi Carattoli nel 1878*, Perugia

G. CORVISIERI, "Il trionfo romano di Eleonora d'Aragona nel giugno 1473", *Archivio della società romana di storia patria* I, 475-491

1878-85

GIORGIO VASARI, *Le vite de' più eccellenti pittori, scultori ed architettori scritte da Giorgio Vasari pittore aretino, con nuove annotazioni e commenti di Gaetano Milanesi*, 9 voll. in 8, Firenze (ripubblicato in 9 voll. 1906-10)

1879

BERNARDINO BALDI, "Vite dei matematici", *Bollettino di bibliografia e di storia delle scienze matematiche e fisiche* XII, 421-559

GIOVAN BATTISTA DE ROSSI, *Piante iconografiche e prospettiche di Roma anteriore al secolo XVI*, Roma

"Memorie inedite sulla Certosa di Pavia", *Archivio Storico Lombardo* VI, 134-146

GAETANO MILANESI, "Commentario alla vita di Baldassarre Peruzzi", in Giorgio Vasari, *Le vite...*, a cura di Gaetano Milanesi (1878-85), IV, Firenze, 615-642

EDOUARD MÜNTZ, "LES ARCHITECTES DE SAINT-PIERRE DE ROME... (1447-1549)", *Gazette des Beaux Arts* XIX, 353-368; XX, 506-525

GIORGIO VASARI [a], "Vita di Bramante", in *Le vite...*, a cura di Gaetano Milanesi (1878-85), IV, Firenze, 162 ss.

—— [b], *Le vite de' più eccellenti pittori, scultori ed architettori*, a cura di Gaetano Milanesi (1878-85), IV, Firenze

1879-87

ALFRED ARMAND, *Les médailleurs italiens des quinzième et seizième siècles*, Paris

1880

C. CHIERICI, *Vigevano*, Vigevano

GEORG DEHIO, "Die Bauprojekte Nikolaus des Fünften und L.B. Alberti", *Repertorium für Kunstwissenschaft* III, 241-257

G. FRIZZONI, *L'arte dell'Umbria rappresentata nella nuova pinacoteca comunale di Perugia*, Firenze

GAETANO MILANESI, "Note alla vita di Antonio da Sangallo", in Giorgio Vasari, *Le vite...*, a cura di Gaetano Milanesi (1878-85), V, Firenze, 447-473

C. PINI, "Commentario alla vita di Antonio da Sangallo", in Giorgio Vasari, *Le vite...*, a cura di Gaetano Milanesi (1878-85), V, Firenze

GIORGIO VASARI, *Le vite de' più eccellenti pittori, scultori ed architettori*, a cura di Gaetano Milanesi (1878-85), V, Firenze

1881

C.I. CAVALLUCCI, *Santa Maria del Fiore*, Firenze

GAETANO MILANESI, "Commento alla vita di Michelangiolo Buonarroti", in Giorgio Vasari, *Le vite...* (1878-85), VII, 332

GIORGIO VASARI, *Le vite de' più eccellenti pittori, scultori ed architettori*, a cura di Gaetano Milanesi (1878-85), VI, Firenze

1882

R. KAHL, *Das Venezianische Skizzenbuch und seine Beziehungen zur umbrischen Malersch?*, Leipzig

P. LASPEYRES, *Die Kurchen der Renaissance in Mittelitalien*, Berlin-Stuttgart

PAUL LETAROUILLY, ALPHONSE SIMIL, *Le Vatican et la Basilique de Saint-Pierre de Rome*, 2 voll., Paris

GIROLAMO MANCINI, *Vita di Leon Battista Alberti*, Firenze (2a ed., 1911)

GAETANO MILANESI, *Le opere di Giorgio Vasari. VIII: Scritti minori. I ragionamenti e le lettere edite e inedite*, Firenze

A. PORTIOLI, *Il matrimonio di Ferdinando Gonzaga con Caterina de' Medici (1617)*, Mantova

1883

ALFRED ARMAND, *Les médailleurs italiens des quinzième et seizième siècles (1879-87)*, Paris

HEINRICH VON GEYMÜLLER, *Documents inédits sur les thermes D'Agrippa, le Pantheon et les thermes de Dioclétien*, Lausanne-Rome

P. LASPEYRES, *Die Bauwerke der Renaissance in Urbrien aufgenommen und gezeichnet*, Berlin

A. MARTINI, *Manuale di metrologia*, Torino

JEAN PAUL RICHTER, *The Literary Works of Leonardo da Vinci*, Oxford (reprint, New York 1970)

ANTON SPRINGER, *Raphael und Michelangelo*, Leipzig

1884

E.R. VON ENGERTH, *Kunsthistorische Sammlungen der Allerhöchsten Kaiserhauses: Gemälde, beschreibends Verzeichnis*, Wien

HEINRICH VON GEYMÜLLER, *Raffaello Sanzio studiato come architetto*, Milano

P. GIANUIZZI, *La chiesa di S. Maria di Loreto*, Roma

A. SCHMARSOW, "Ein Entwurf Michelangelos zum Grabmal Julius", *Jahrbüch der Preussischen Kunstsammlungen* V, 63-77

1885

PASQUALE NERINO FERRI, *Indice geografico-analitico dei*

disegni di architettura civile e militare esistenti nella R. Galleria degli Uffizi in Firenze, Roma

HEINRICH VON GEYMÜLLER, "Documents inédits sur les manuscrits et les oeuvres d'architecture de la famille des San Gallo", *Mémoires de la Société Nationale des Antiquaires de France* XLV, 1-31

A. LUPATTELLI, *Catalogo dei quadri che si conservano nella pinacoteca Vannucci, esistente nel piano superiore del Palazzo Municipale in Perugia*, Perugia

HENRI MARTIN, *Catalogue des manuscripts de la Bibliotèque de l'Arsenal*, Paris

ARISTIDE NARDINI DESPOTTI MOSPIGNOTTI [a], *Il campanile di S. Maria del Fiore*, Firenze

—— [b], *Filippo di ser Brunellesco e la cupola del Duomo di Firenze*, Livorno

CARL VON STEGMAN UND HEINRICH VON GEYMÜLLER (HRSG.), *Die Architektur der Renaissance in Toscana I, Filippo di Ser Brunellesco*, München

1885-1908

CARL VON STEGMANN UND HEINRICH VON GEYMÜLLER (Hrsg.), *Die Architektur der Renaissance in Toscana*, 11 Bde., München

1885-1933

LUDWIG VON PASTOR, *Geschichte der Päpste im Zeitlater der Renaissance*, Freiburg

1886

P. GRASSI, *Le due spedizioni militari di Giulio II, con documenti e note di L. Frati*, Bologna

W. MERCER, "The Church of Santa Maria della Consolazione at Todi", *Academy* 760, 368-369

1886-1903

MARIN SANUDO, *I diarii, 1496-1533*, a cura di R. Fulin, F. Stefani, N. Barozzi, G. Berchet e M. Allegri, Venezia

1887

ALFRED ARMAND, *Les médailleurs italiens des quinzème et seizième siècles (1878-87)*, III, Paris

LUCA BELTRAMI, "Per la storia della costruzione del Duomo", *Raccolta milanese di storia geografia ed arte* XII, IV-VI

G. CORVISIERI, "Il trionfo romano di Eleonora d'Aragona nel giugno 1473", *Archivio della società romana di storia patria* X, 629-687

CORNELIUS VON FABRICZY, "Der Schöpfer des Entwurfs der Madonna della Consolazione zu Todi", *Repertorium für Kunstwissenschaft*, 437-438

FRANCESCO FOSSATI (a cura di), *Benedetto Giovio. Storia patria*, Como

HEINRICH VON GEYMÜLLER, *Les Du Cerceau*, Paris

D. GNOLI, "La casa di Raffaello", *Nuova Antologia* III, 401-23

CESARE GUASTI, *Santa Maria del Fiore. La costruzione della chiesa e del campanile*, Firenze

A. LUPATTELLI, *Catalogo dei quadri conservati nella Pinacoteca Vannucci, esistente nel piano superiore del Palazzo Municipale in Perugia*, Perugia

1888

LUCA BELTRAMI [a], "Per la facciata del Duomo di Milano", parte III (Atti del Collegio degli ingegneri ed architetti in Milano), *Politecnico*

—— [b], "Per la storia della costruzione del Duomo", *Raccolta milanese di storia geografia ed arte* I, II-III; cfr. anche Cassi Ramelli 1964

LUIGI DEL MORO, *La facciata di S. Maria del Fiore: illustrazione storica e artistica*, Firenze

P. SACCARDO, "I mosaici e le loro iscrizioni", in *La Basilica di San Marco*, a cura di F. Ongania, Venezia, 308

1889

CAMILLO BOITO, *Il Duomo di Milano*, Milano

ANGELO GATTI, *Catalogo del Museo di S. Petronio*, Bologna

M. JAEHNS, *Geschichte der Kriegswissenschaften*, München-Leipzig

EUGÈNE MÜNTZ, *Histoire de l'art pendant la Renaissance*, Paris

H. PLUCHART, *Musée Wicar. Notice des dessins*, Lille

1890

LEON BATTISTA ALBERTI, "De equo animante", in *Opera inedita et pauca separatim impressa*, a cura di Girolamo Mancini, Firenze, 238 sg.

P. BERTOLOTTI, *Figuli, fonditori e scultori e la corte di Mantova*, Milano

PETER JESSEN, "Zeichnungen römischer Ruinen in der Bibliothek des Kgl. Kunstgewerbe-Museums zu Berlin", in *Aus der Anomia. Archäologische Beiträge, Carl Robert... dargebracht*, Berlin, 114-123

GIROLAMO MANCINI, *Leonis Baptistae Alberti. Opera inedita et pauca separatim impressa*, Firenze

1890-96

F. GREGOROVIUS, *Geschichte der Stadt Rom im Mittelalter*, Stuttgart

1891

A. D'ANCONA, *Origini del teatro italiano*, Torino

MARCELIN PIERRE EUGÈNE BERTHELOT, "Pour l'histoire des arts mécaniques et de l'artillerie vers la fin du moyen age", *Annales de Chimie et Phisique* VI(24), 433-439

Catalogo del Museo di Santa Maria del Fiore, Firenze

L. GENTILE (a cura di), *Ministero della Pubblica Istruzione, Indici e Cataloghi. IV: I Codici Palatini della R. Biblioteca Nazionale Centrale di Firenze*, II (fasc. 4), Roma

R. LANCIANI, "Gli horti Aciliorum sul Pincio", *Bollettino della commissione archeologica comunale di Roma*, s. IV, 132-155

JULIUS RITTER VON SCHLOSSER, *Beiträge zur Kunstgeschichte aus den Schriftquellen des frühen Mittelalters (Sitzungsberichte der kais. Akademie der Wiss. in Wien, phil.-hist. Kl.)*, CXXIII, Wien

H. SCHOTT, *De septem orbis spectaculis quaestiones*, D.Phil. Diss., München

1892

L. DOREZ, "La Bibliothèque de Giovanni Marcanova", *Mélanges G.B. de' Rossi* (supplement to Mélanges de l'Ecole Franäise de Rome) XII, 113-126

D. GNOLI, "La Cancelleria ed altri palazzi di Roma attribuiti a Bramante", *Archivio Storico dell'Arte*, 176-184 e 331-334

CORNELIUS VON FABRICZY, *Filippo Brunelleschi*, Stuttgart

KARL FREY, *Il codice magliabechiano*, Berlin

C. HALM, *Catalogus codicorum latinorum Bibliothecae Regiae Monacensis. Editio altera emendatior*, München

EMILE MOLINIER, *La Collection Spitzer* IV, *Les faiences italiennes, hispano-moresques et orientales*, Paris

H. STRACK, *Zentral und Kuppelkirchen der Renaissance in Italien*, Berlin

1893

CORNELIUS VON FABRICZY, "Il libro di schizzi d'un pittore olandese nel museo di Stuttgart", *Archivio storico dell'arte* VI, 106-126

ANGELO GATTI, *Catalogo del Museo di S. Petronio*, Bologna

G. MERZARIO, *I maestri comacini*, II, Milano

ADOLFO VENTURI, "Nelle pinacoteche minori d'Italia", *Archivio storico dell'arte* VI, 409-436

1894

IODOCO DEL BADIA, "La bottega di Alessandro di Francesco Rosselli merciaio e stampatore. 1525", *Miscellanea fiorentina di erudizione e storia*, 24-30

C. FACCIO, *Di Antonio Labacco architetto vercellese del sec. XV e del suo libro delle antichità di Roma*, Vercelli

1895

LUCA BELTRAMI, "La chiesa di S. Maria delle Grazie", *Edilizia moderna* IX

GEORG DEHIO, "Zur Frange der Triangulation in der mittelalterlichen Baukunst", *Repertorium für Kunstwissenschaft* XVIII, 105-11

EUGÈNE MÜNTZ, *L'età aurea dell'arte italiana*, Milano

1896

LUCA BELTRAMI, *Storia documentata della Certosa di Pavia. I. La fondazione e i lavori sino alla morte di G. Galeazzo Visconti (1389-1402)*, Milano

SANTO MONTI, "La Cattedrale di Como", in *Periodico della società storica comense* XI

WOLFGANG VON OETTINGEN, *Antonio Averlino Filarete's Tractat über die Baukunst nebst seinen Buchen von der Zeichenkunst und den Bauten der Medici*, Wien

JULIUS VON SCHLOSSER, "Giusto's Fresken in Padua und die Vorläufer der Stanza della Segnatura", *Jahrbuch der Kunsthistorischen Sammlungen des Allerhöchsten Kaiserhauses* XVII, 13-100

1897

C. BUONDELMONTE, *Description des iles de l'archipel, sous la direction de E. Legrand*, Paris

ALFRED GOTTHOLD MEYER, *Oberitalienische Frührenaissance*, I, Berlin

1898

ALFRED DOREN, "Zum Bau der Florentiner Domkuppel", *Repertorium für Kunstwissenschaft* XXI, 249-262

F. VON THODE, "Andrea del Castagno in Venedig", in *Festschrift Otto Benndorf*, Wien, 307-317

GIORGIO VASARI, *Le vite de' più eccellenti pittori, scultori ed architettori*, a cura di Gaetano Milanesi, VII, Firenze

1899

THEODOR BECK, *Beiträge zur Geschichte des Machinenbanes*, Berlin

Sullo stato e compimento dei lavori di restauro del tempio della Consolazione, Todi

IGINO BENVENUTO SUPINO, *Il medagliere mediceo nel R. Museo Nazionale di Firenze*, Firenze

PIERO DELLA FRANCESCA, *Petrus Pictor Burgensis. De prospectiva pingendi*, besorgt von W.Winterberg Stassburg

1900

M. CANTOR, *Vorlesungen über die Geschichte der Mathematik*, Leipzig

CARLO DEL LUNGO, *I fulmini caduti sopra la cupola di Santa Maria del Fiore*, Prato [1900]

AGOSTINO LAPINI, *Diario fiorentino dal 252 al 1596. Ora per la prima volta pubblicato da Giu. Odoardo Corazzini*, Firenze

G.B. LUGARI, *Il Gianicolo, luogo della crocefissione di S. Pietro*, Roma

A SEGARIZZI, *Della vita e delle opere di Michele Savonarola*, Padova

1900-1903

GUSTAVE CLAUSSE, *Les San Gallo architectes, peintres, sculpteurs, médailleurs, XVe et XVIe siècles*, 3 voll., Paris

1901

A. AMERSDORFERR, *Kritische Studien über das Venezianische Skizzenbuch*, Berlin

LUCA BELTRAMI [a], "Bramante a Milano", *Rassegna d'arte* I, 33 sgg.

—— [b], "Michelangelo e la facciata di San Lorenzo in Firenze. Disegno e note inediti", *Rassegna d'arte* I, 67-72

PASQUALE NERINO FERRI, "Di un disegno inedito attribuito a Michelangelo", *Arte e storia* XX, 98-99

HEINRICH VON GEYMÜLLER, "Alcune osservazioni sopra recenti studi su Bramante e Michelangelo", *Rassegna d'arte* I, 184-186

VITTORIO LUSINI, *Il San Giovanni di Siena*, Firenze

IGINO BENVENUTO SUPINO, "La facciata della basilica di San Lorenzo in Firenze", *Arte* IV, 245-262

James Addington Symonds, *The Life of Michelangelo Buonarroti*, 2 voll., London

1901-1940
Adolfo Venturi, *Storia dell'arte italiana*, Milano

1902
Luca Beltrami, "La sala dei Maestri d'arme", *Rassegna italiana* II

Cornelius von Fabriczy [a], "Giuliano da Sangallo", *Jahrbuch der königlichen preussischen Kunstsammlungen* XXIII, Beiheft, 1-42

—— [b], *Die Handzeichnungen Giuliano da Sangallos. Kritisches Verzeichnis*, Stuttgart

R. Falb, *Il taccuino senese di Giuliano da Sangallo*, Siena

G. Ferrari, *La scenografia*, Milano

A. Ratti, *Due piante iconografiche di Milano da codici manoscritti Vaticani del secolo XV*, Milano

Henry Thode, *Michelangelo und das Ende der Renaissance*, I, Berlin

1902-12
R. Lanciani, *Storia degli scavi di Roma*, Roma

1903
Luca Beltrami, "Leonardo da Vinci negli studi per il tiburio della cattedrale di Milano", in *Nozze Beltrami-Rosina*, Milano

Bernard Berenson [a], *The Drawings of the Florentine Painters Classified, Criticized, and Studied as Documents in the History and Appreciation of Tuscan Art*, 2 vols., London (Chicago 1938; Milano 1961)

—— [b], *The Drawings of the Florentine Painters Classified, Criticized, and Studied as Documents in the History and Appreciation of Tuscan Art*, 2 vols., New York

W. Bode, "Ein Selbstportrait des Jacopo de' Barbari ?", *Kunstchronik* XIV, 504

Hermann Egger, *Kritisches Verzeichnis der Sammlung architektonischer Handzeichnungen der K.K. Hof-Bibliothek*, I, Wien

Ludwig Justi, "Giovanni Pisano und die toskanischen Skulpturen des XIV. Jahrhunderts", *Jahrbuch der königlichen preuszischen Kunstsammlungen* XXIV, 247-83

C. Loeser, "Note intorno ai disegni conservati nella R. Galleria di Venezia", *Rassegna d'arte*, III, 12, 177 e sg.

R. Maiocchi, *Le chiese di Pavia*, I, Pavia

Corrado Ricci [a], "Iconografia storica. Il ritratto di Luca Pacioli", *Rassegna d'arte* III, 75

—— [b], "Un quadro di Jacopo de' Barbari nella Galleria Nazionale di Napoli", *Napoli Nobilissima* XII (2), 27-28

G. Sacconi, *Relazione dell'Ufficio regionale per la conservazione dei monumenti delle Marche e dell'Umbria 1891-1892/1900-1901*, Perugia (2a ed.)

Adolfo Venturi, "Il più antico quadro di Iacopo dei Barbari", *L'arte* VI, 95-96

1904
Thomas Ashby, "Sixteenth-Century Drawings of Roman Buildings Attributed to Andreas Coner", *Papers of the British School at Rome* II, 1-96 (reprint in 1971)

E. Bernich, "Due altre vedute di Castelnuovo nel secolo XVI", in *Napoli nobilissima* XIII, 129-130

Disegni di architettura civile e militare di artisti italiani fioriti dal XV al XVII secolo tratti dalla raccolta della R. Galleria degli Uffizi, Firenze

Benedetto Croce, "Veduta della città di Napoli del 1479 col trionfo navale per l'arrivo di Lorenzo de' Medici", *Napoli nobilissima*, XII, fasc. IV, 56-7

Heinrich von Geymüller, *Michelagnolo Buonarroti als Architekt. Nach neuen Quellen*, München (nevauflage in *Die Architektur der Renaissance in Toscana*, besorgt von Carl von Stegman, VIII, München)

Giovanni Poggi (a cura di), *Catalogo del Museo dell'Opera del Duomo. Nuova edizione ampliata ed arricchita di documenti*, Firenze

C. Tonini, "Brevi cenni su due medaglie che rappresentano l'una il Tempio Malatestiano, l'altra Leon Battista Alberti", in *Per Leon Battista Alberti in Rimini V Settembre MDCCCCIV*, Bologna

Ludwig Weber, *San Petronio in Bologna. Beiträge zur Baugeschichte*, Leipzig

Siegfried Weber, *Fiorenzo di Lorenzo. Eine kunsthistorische Studie*, Strassburg

1905
G. Gronau, "Per la storia di un quadro attribuito a Jacopo de Barbari", *Rassegna d'arte* V (2), 28-29

L. Mocchi, *Cenni storici e vade-mecum per la visita delle opere d'arte della chiesa di pertinenza dell'Arcicanfraternita laicale di S. Anna e Carlo Borromeo dei Lombardi in Monteoliveto*, Napoli

P. Placido Lugano, "Di fra Giovanni da Verona maestro d'intaglio e di tarsia e della sua scuola", *Bollettino senese di storia patria* XII, 80-84 e 212

A. Solerti, *Musica, ballo e drammatica alla corte medicea del 1600 al 1637*, Firenze

1905-1906
Hermann Egger, *Codex Escurialensis. Ein Skizzenbuch aus der Werkstatt Domenico Ghirlandaio*, Wien

1906
Hermann Egger, "Besprechung von Ashby 1904", *Kunstgeschichtliche Anzeigen*, 91-97

Giorgio Vasari, "Vita di Antonio da Sangallo", in *Le vite de' più eccellenti pittori, scultori ed architettori*, a cura di Gaetano Milanesi, V, Firenze, 467-468

Hans Willich, *Giacomo Barozzi da Vignola*, Strassburg

1906-1910
Giorgio Vasari, *Le vite de' più eccellenti pittori, scultori ed architettori*, a cura di Gaetano Milanesi, 9 voll., Firenze (2a ed.; 1a ed. 1878-1885)

1907
Colonel d'Astier, *La belle tapisserye du Roi (1532-1797) et les tentures de Scipion l'Africain*, Paris

Charles Moise Briquet, *Les Filigraines: Dictionnaire historique des Marques du Papier dès leur apparition vers 1282 jusqu'en 1600*, IV, Genève

S. Di Giacomo, *Napoli*, Bergamo

Christian Hülsen, *La Roma antica di Ciriaco d'Ancona*, Roma

G.B. Lugari, *Il culto di S. Pietro sul Gianicolo e il libro Pontificale Ravennate*, Roma

W. Rolfs, Neapel, [s.d.] 44-45

Paul Schubring, *Die Plastik Sienas im Quattrocento*, Berlin

1907-1950
Ulrich Thieme und Felix Becker (Hrsg.), *Allgemeines Lexikon der Bildenden Künstler*, Leipzig

1908
Thomas Ashby, "An Unknown Sixteenth Century Topography of Rome", *Archaeological Journal* LXV, 2nd series, 15, 245-264

S. Bartolotta, "La galleria nazionale di Napoli e il suo riordinamento", estratto da *La scintilla*

G.C.[Giulio Caprin], "Marginalia. Tavola di Casa Strozzi ora nel museo nazionale di S.Martino", in *Mazzocco*, 13 dicembre, 4

Francesco Ehrle, *Roma prima di Sisto V. La pianta di Roma Dupérac-Lafréry del 1577*, Città del Vaticano

Pasquale Nerino Ferri, "La raccolta Geymüller-Campello recentemente acquistata dallo Stato per la R. Galleria degli Uffizi", *Bollettino d'arte*, II, 47-65

Theobald Hofmann, *Raffael in seiner Bedeutung als Architekt. I. Die Villa Madama zu Rom*, Zittau (2. Auflage)

Michele Lazzaroni, *Antonio Munoz, Filarete. Scultore e architetto del secolo XV*, Roma

W. Rolfs, "Il più antico dipinto figurativo della città di Napoli", *Archivio storico per le province napoletane* XXXIII, 736-745

Albano Sorbelli, "Giacomo Barozzi e la Fabbrica di S. Petronio", in *Memorie e studi intorno a Jacopo Barozzi*, Vignola, 257-291

Henry Thode, *Michelangel. Kritische Untersuchungen über seine Werke*, II, Berlin, 533-537

1908-1913
Henry Thode, *Michelangelo, Kritische Untersuchungen über seine Werke*, 3. Bde: II 1908; III 1913, Berlin

1909
G. Cristofani, "Le vetrate di Giovanni di Bonino nella Basilica di Assisi", *Rassegna d'arte umbra*, 3-14

Karl Frey [a], "Zur baugeschichte des St. Peter, Mitteilungen aus der Reverendissima Fabbrica di S. Pietro", *Jahrbuch der Königlich preussischen Kunstsammlungen*, Beiheft Band XXX

—— [b], "Studien zu Michelangniolo Buonarroti und zur Kunst seiner Zeit", *Jahrbuch der königlichen preuszischen Kunstsammlungen*, Beiheft Band XXX, 103-180

A. Lupattelli, *La Pinacoteca Vannucci in Perugia descritta e illustrata*, Perugia

H. Nasse, *Meister der Graphik. Jacques Callot*, Leipzig

M. Reymond, *L'architecture italienne au XVI siècle*, Paris

Igino Benvenuto Supino, *L'architettura sacra in Bologna nei secoli XIII e XIV*, Bologna

Giorgio Vasari, *Le vite de' più eccellenti pittori, scultori ed architettori*, a cura di Gaetano Milanesi, III, Firenze

Adolfo Venturi, "Studi sull'arte umbra del '400", *L'Arte* III, 188-202

1909-11
Karl Frey, *Die Handzeichnungen Michelangniolos Buonarroti*, 3. Bde.: I 1909; II-III 1911, Berlin

1909-13
O. Posse, *Siegel der Deutschen Kaiser und Könige*, Dresden

1910
P. Alvi, *Todi città illustre nell'Umbria. Cenni storici*, Todi

G. Biscaro, "Le imbreviature del notaio Boniparte Gira e la chiesa di S. Maria di S. Satiro", *Archivio storico lombardo* XXXVII, 122 sgg.

Karl Frey, "Zur Baugeschichte des St. Peter, Mitteilungen aus der Reverendissima Fabbrica di S. Pietro", **Beiheft Band** XXXI, pubblicato nel 1911

Giuliano da Sangallo, vedi Christian Hülsen [b]

G. Glück, "Ein neugefundenes Werk Jan Scorels", *Der Cicerone* II, 589

George Francis Hill, *The Medals of Paul II*, London

Christian Hülsen [a], "Le illustrazioni della Hypnerotomachia Poliphili e le antichità di Roma", *Bibliofilia* XIII, 161-176

—— [b], *Il Libro di Giuliano da Sangallo, Codex Vaticano Barberiniano latino 4424*, Leipzig-Torino

H. Jantzen, "Jan Scorel und Bramante", *Der Cicerone* II, 646-647

C. Serafini, *Le monete e le bolle plumbee pontificie del medagliere Vaticano*, I, Milano

Vittorio Spinazzola, "Di Napoli antica e della sua topografia in una tavola del XV secolo rappresentante il trionfo navale di Ferrante d'Aragona dopo la battaglia d'Ischia", estratto da *Bollettino d'arte* IV, 125-143

G. Zippel, "Cosmografi al servizio dei Papi nel Quattrocento", *Bollettino della società geografica italiana* XI, 843-852

1910-11

CHRISTIAN HÜLSEN, "Escurialensis und Sangallo", *Jahreshefte des österreichischen Archäologischen Institutes in Wien* XIII, 210-230

1911

THOMAS ASHBY, "Rezension von Hülsen 1910", *Classical Review* XXV/VI, 173-175

LUCA BELTRAMI, *Bernardino Luini 1512-1532*, Milano

KURT H. BUSSE, "Die Renaissance-Modellen zur Florentiner Domfassade. (1586). Im Museo dell'Opera di S.M. Fiore zu Florenz" (Maschinengeschriebenes Manuskript, Kunsthistorisches Institut, Florenz

Catalogo dei ritratti eseguiti in disegno ed incisione da artisti italiani fioriti dal sec. XV alla prima metà del secolo XIX, esposti alla R. Galleria degli Uffizi, Firenze

ALDO DE RINALDIS, *Museo Nazionale di Napoli. Pinacoteca. Catalogo*, Napoli

KARL FREY, "Zur Baugeschichte des St. Peter, Mitteilungen aus der Reverendissima Fabbrica di S. Pietro", *Jahrbuch der Königlich preussischen Kunstsammlungen*, Beiheft Band XXXI (1910), 1-95

L. FUMI, *Il duomo di Orvieto*, Roma

G.F. GAMURRINI, *Descrizione delle opere eseguite in Arezzo da Giorgio Vasari*, Arezzo

E.M. GIUSTO, *Le vetrate di S. Francesco in Assisi: studio storico iconografico*

ANDRÉ DE HEVESY, "Les miniaturistes de Matthias Corvin", *Revue de l'art chrétien* LXI, 109-120

GEORGE FRANCIS HILL, "Caradosso", in *Ulrich Thieme e Felix Becker, Allgemeines Lexikon der Bildenden Künstler*, V, Leipzig, 563

THEOBALD HOFMANN, *Raffael in seiner Bedeutung als Architekt. IV. Vatikanischer Palast*, Zittau

P.G. HÜBNER, "Der Autor des Berolinensis", *Monatshefte für Kunstwissenschaft* IV, 353-367

VITTORIO LUSINI, *Il duomo di Siena*, Siena

GIROLAMO MANCINI, *Vita di Leon Battista Alberti*, Firenze (1a ed. 1882)

P.P. PLAN, *Jacques Callot maître graveur (1593-1635) suivi d'un catalogue chronologique*, Bruxelles-Paris

ADOLFO VENTURI, *Storia dell'arte italiana. VII/1: La pittura del Quattrocento*, Milano

1911-1932

HERMANN EGGER, *Römische Veduten. Handzeichnungen aus dem XV - XVIII. Jahrhundert zur Topographie der Stadt Rom*, I Wien, II Liepzig

1912

APPIANUS OF ALEXANDRIA, "The Punic Wars", Book IX, chapter 66, in *Romaiká*, translated by Horace White, London

G BISCARO, "I Solari da Carona", *Bollettino storico della Svizzera italiana* XXXIV, 61-77

WALTER BOMBE, *Geschichte der Peruginer Malerei bis zu Perugino und Pintoricchio*, Berlin

E. BRUWAERT, *Vie de Jacques Callot, graveur lorrain (1592-1635)*, Paris

KURT BUSSE, "Jacopo Chimenti", in *Ulrich Thieme und Felix Becker (Hrsg.) Allegemeines Lexikon der Bildenden Künstler*, VI, Leipzig, 500-503

F. GNECCHI, *I medaglioni romani*, Milano

GEORGE FRANCIS HILL, *Portrait Medals of Italian Artists of the Renaissance*, London

A. LUZIO, "Isabella d'Este di fronte a Giulio II", *Archivio storico lombardo* XXXIX

G. PENSI, A. COMEZ, *Todi. Guida per i forestieri*, Todi

M. THEUER, *Leon Battista Alberti. Zehn Buecher über die Baukunst*, Wien

1913

THOMAS ASHBY, "Addenda and Corrigenda to Sixteenth-Century Drawings of Roman Buildings Attributed to Andreas Coner", *Papers of the British School at Rome* VI, 184-210

KARL FREY, "Zur Baugeschichte des St. Peter, Mitteilungen aus der Reverendissima Fabbrica di S. Pie-

tro", *Jahrbuch der königlichen preussischen Kunstsammlungen*, Beiheft Band XXXIII (1912), 1-153

PAUL GARNAULT, *Les portraits de Michelange*, Paris

CHRISTIAN HÜLSEN, HERMANN EGGER, *Die Römischen Skizzenbücher von Marten van Heemskerck im königlichen Kupferstichkabinett zu Berlin*, I, Berlin

E. RICCI, "Il Gonfalone di S. Bernardino", in *Per nozze Manzoni-Ansidei*, Perugia

ALDO DE RINALDIS, *Medaglie dei secoli XV e XVI nel Museo Nazionale di Napoli*, Napoli

ERNST STEINMANN, *Die Porträtdarstellungen des Michelangelo*, Leipzig

IGINO BENVENUTO SUPINO, "Le fasi costruttive della Basilica di S. Petronio", *Archiginnasio* VIII (3-4), 125-36

HENRY THODE, *Michelangelo, kritische Untersuchungen über seine Werke*, III, Berlin

ADOLFO VENTURI, *Storia dell'arte italiana. VII/2: La pittura del Quattrocento*, Milano

1913-1915

F. MALAGUZZI VALERI, *La corte di Ludovico il Moro*, 2 voll., Milano

1913-1916

CHRISTIAN HÜLSEN, HERMANN EGGER, *Die Römischen Skizzenbücher von Marten van Heemskerck im königlichen Kupferstichkabinett zu Berlin*, 2. Bde., Berlin

1914

T. ALPHARANUS, vedi M. Cerrati

THOMAS ASHBY, "Il libro d'Antonio Labacco...", *Bibliofilia* XVI, 289-309

ALFONSO BARTOLI, *I monumenti antichi di Roma nei disegni degli Uffizi di Firenze (1914-22)*, I e VI: *Descrizione dei disegni*, Roma

M. CERRATI (a cura di), *T. Alpharanus. De Basilicae Vaticanae antiquissima et nova structura*, Roma

J. DURM, *Die Baukunst der Renaissance in Italien*, Liepzig

ANGELO GATTI, *L'ultima parola sul concetto architettonico di San Petronio*, Bologna

GUSTAVO GIOVANNONI, "Il palazzo dei Tribunali di Bramante in un disegno di Fra Giocondo", *Bollettino d'arte*

D. GNOLI, "Il palazzo di Giustizia di Bramante", *Nuova antologia*

H. LIETZMANN, *Petrus und Paulus un Rom. Liturgische und archäologische Studien*, Bonn

R. SABBADINI, *Le scoperte dei codici latini e greci ne' secoli XIV e XV*, Firenze

LIONELLO VENTURI, "Studi sul palazzo ducale di Urbino", *L'arte* XVII (1), 415-473

1914-15

THOMAS ASHBY, "Il libro d'Antonio Labacco appartenente all'architettura", in *Bibliofilia* XVI, 289-309

1914-22

ALFONSO BARTOLI, *I monumenti antichi di Roma nei disegni degli Uffizi di Firenze*, Roma

1915

[Comune di Perugia], *Catalogo della Pinacoteca Vannucci*, Perugia

HANS FOLNESICS, *Brunelleschi*, Wien

DAGOBERT FREY, *Bramantes St. Peter-Entwurf und seine Apokryphen*, Wien

GUSTAVO GIOVANNONI, "Il Palazzo dei Tribunali di Bramante in un disegno di Fra Giocondo", *Bollettino d'arte*, 185-195

F. MALAGUZZI VALERI [a], "Bramante e Leonardo da Vinci", in *La corte di Ludovico il Moro*, II, Milano, 87-112

—— [b], *La corte di Ludovico il Moro*, Milano

ALBERTO SERAFINI, *Girolamo da Carpi*, Roma

GUARINO VERONESE, *Epistolario*, a cura di R. Sabbadini, Venezia

1915-1923

P. SCHUBRING, *Cassoni. Truhen und Truhenbilder der italienischen Frührenaissance*, Leipzig

1916

THOMAN ASHBY, *Topographical Study of Rome in 1581*, London

BERNARD BERENSON, *Venetian Painting in America*, New York (ed. it., Milano 1919)

KARL FREY, "Zur Baugeschichte des St. Peter, Mitteilungen aus der Reverendissima Fabbrica di S. Pietro", *Jahrbuch der königlichen preussischen Kunstsammlungen*, Beiheft Band XXXVII, 22-136

1917

O. FISCHEL, "Die Zeichnungender Umbrer", *Jahrbuch der Königlich preussischen Kunstsammlungen* XXXVIII, 1-72; II (beiheft), 1-188

W. GRANT KEITH, "A Theatre Project by Inigo Jones", *Burlington Magazine* XXXI, 61-70 and 105-111

JOHANNES A. F. ORBAAN, "Zur Baugeschichte der Peterskuppel", *Jahrbuch der Königlich preussischen Kunstsammlungen*, Beiheft Band XXXVIII, 189-207

GIORGIO VASARI, *Vite cinque*, a cura di Girolamo Mancini, Firenze

1917-1922

EMILIO MARTINORI, *Annali della Zecca di Roma, Serie Papale*, Roma

1918

BODO EBHARDT, *Vitruvius. Die Zehn Bücher der Architektur des Vitruv und ihre Herausgeber. Mit einem Verzeichnis der vorhandenen Ausgaben und Erlaeuterungen*, Berlin (New York, 1984)

J. FISCHER, "Die Stadtzeichen auf den Ptolemäuskarten", *Kartographische und schulgeographische Zeitschrift* VII, 48-52

F. MARTINORI, *Annali della zecca di Roma*, VII, Roma

L. ZAHN, "Die Handzeichnungen Jacques Callots", *Mitteilungen der Gesellschaft für vervielfältigende Kunst*, 1-10 und 33-43

1919

G. AGNELLI, "I monumenti di Niccolò III e Borso d'Este", *Atti e memorie della deputazione ferrarese di storia patria*, XXIII

L. BARNI, *La Cattedrale e le primitive chiese di Vigevano*, Vigevano

K.W. SWOBODA, *Römische und romanische Paläste*, Wien

1919-27

LEO S. OLSCHKI, *Geschichte der neusprachlichen wissenschaftlichen Literatur*, Heidelberg

1920

GIUSEPPE FIOCCO, "Michele Giambono", in *Studi di arte e storia*, Venezia, 207

DAGOBERT FREY, *Michelangelo-Studien*, Wien

GEORGE FRANCIS HILL, "The Roman Medallists of the Renaissance to the Time of Leo X", *Papers of the British School at Rome* IX, 16-66

G. PELLEGRINI, *L'umanista Bernardo Rucellai e le sue opere storiche*, Livorno

EMILIO RE, "Maestri di strada", *Archivio della società romana di storia patria* XLIII

HERMANN VOSS, *Die Malerei der Spätrenaissance in Rom und Florenz*, I-II, Berlin

1920-1921

ERWIN PANOFSKY, "Bemerkungen zu D. Frey's Michelangelo-studien", *Archiv für Geschichte und Ästhetik der Architektur als Anhang zu Wasmuths Monatshefte für Baukunst* V, 35-45

1921

GUSTAVO GIOVANNONI, "Tra la cupola di Bramante e quella di Michelangelo", *Architettura e arti decorative* I, 418-438

CHRISTIAN HÜLSEN, "Das Speculum Romanae Magnificentiae des Antonio Lafreri", in *Collectanea variae doctrinae..., Festschrift für Leo S. Olschki*, München

L. SIGHINOLFI, "La biblioteca di Giovanni Marcanova", in *Collectanea variae doctrinae Leoni Olshki*, Milano, 187-222

COSIMO STORNAJOLO, *Codices Urbinates Latini*, Roma

1921-1922

A. CHIAPPELLI, "Il ritrovamento di un modello inedito di Baccio d'Agnolo", *Bollettino d'arte* I, 563-566

DAGOBERT FREY, "Das Kuppelmodell von St. Peter in Rom. Eine Erwiderung an H.R. Alker", *Kunstchronik und Kunstmarkt* n.f., XXXIII, 36-39

L. FRIEDLÄNDER, *Darstellungen aus der Sittengeschichte Roms*, III, Leipzig

1922

HERMANN ALKER, "Das Michelangelomodell zur Kuppel von St. Peter in Rom", *Repertorium für Kunstwissenschaft* XLIII, 98-99

A.E. BRINCKMANN, "Das Kuppelmodell für San Pietro in Rom", *Repertorium für Kunstwissenschaft* XLIII, 92-97

ERWIN PANOFSKY, "Die Treppe der Libreria di S. Lorenzo. Bemerkungen zu einer unveröffentlichten Skizze Michelangelos", *Monatshefte für Kunstwissenschaft* XV, 262-274

ANNY POPP, *Die Medici-Kapelle Michelangelos*, München

1922-1923

DAGOBERT FREY, "Eine unbeachtete Zeichnung nach dem Modell Michelangelos für die Fassade von San Lorenz", *Kunstchronik und Kunstmarkt* n.f., XXXIV, 221-228

1923

DAGOBERT FREY, *Architetti dal XV al XVIII secolo. Michelangelo Buonarroti*, Roma

KARL FREY, *Der Literarische Nachlass Giorgio Vasaris*, München

UMBERTO GNOLI, *Pittori e miniatori nell'Umbria*, Spoleto

ANDRÉ DE HEVESY, *La bibliothèque du roi Matthias Corvin*, Paris

QUINTILIANO, *Institutio Oratoria*, translated by H.E. Butler, Cambridge-London

EUGÉNIE STRONG, *La Chiesa Nuova (Santa Maria in Vallicella)*, Roma

L. ZAHN, *Die Handzeichnunges des Jacques Callot unter besonderer Berücksichtigung der Petersburger Sammlung*, München

1924

THOMAS ASHBY, "Due vedute di Roma attribuite a Stefano Duperàc", *Miscellanea Ehrle* II, 449-459

K. BORINSKI, *Die Antike in Poetik und Kunsttheorie*, Leipzig

DAGOBERT FREY, "Ein unbekannter Entwurf Giuliano da Sangallos für die Peterskirche in Rom", in *Miscellanea Ehrle*, II, Roma, 432-448

A. DE LABORDE, "Un manuscript de Mariano Taccola revenu de Constantinople", in *Melanges offerts à M. Gustave Schlumberger*, Paris, 494-505

J. LIEURE, *Jacques Callot. Deuxième Partie. Catalogue de l'oeuvre gravé*, Paris

LUDWIG VON PASTOR, *Geschichte der Päpste im Zeitalter der Renaissance*, III, Freiburg

CORRADO RICCI, *Il Tempio Malatestiano*, Milano-Roma

JULIUS SCHLOSSER MAGNINO, *Die Kunstliteratur*, Wien

CARL VON STEGMANN AND HEINRICH VON GEYMÜLLER, *The Architecture of the Renaissance in Tuscany*, II, New York [1924]

1924-25

LUDWIG VON PASTOR, *Geschichte der Päpste seit dem Ausgang des Mittelalters*, Freiburg

1925

ELENA BERTI, "Un manoscritto di Pietro Cataneo agli Uffizi e un codice di Francesco di Giorgio Martini", *Belvedere* VII, 100-103

A. CHIAPPELLI, "Un modello inedito di Baccio d'Agnolo", in *Arte del Rinascimento*, Roma, capitolo XVII

ANDRÉ DE HEVESY, *Jacopo de Barbari, le maître au caducée*, Paris-Bruxelles

GIUSEPPE FIOCCO, "Il rinnovamento toscano dell'arte del mosaico a Venezia", *Dedalo* VI, 109 e sg.

WILLIAM WINTHROP KENT, *The Life and Works of Baldassarre Peruzzi of Siena*, New York

GEORG LIPPOLD, "Tupos", *Jahrbuch des Deutschen Archäologischen Instituts* XXXX, 206-209

F. NICOLINI, *L'arte napoletana del Rinascimento e la lettera di P. Summonte a Marcantonio Michiel*, Napoli

G. MERCATI, *Per la cronologia della vita e degli scritti di Niccolò Perotti arcivescovo di Siponto*, Roma

ANNY POPP, "Garzoni Michelangelos", *Belvedere* VIII, 6-28

P. SUMMONTE, "Lettera a Marcantonio Michiel, 1524", in F. Nicolini, *L'arte napoletana del Rinascimento*, Napoli, 169-170

ULRICH THIEME, FELIX BECKER (Hrsg.), *Allgemeines Lexikon der Bildenden Künstler*, XVIII, Leipzig

1925-26

G. BOFFITO, "La pianta iconografica più antica di Firenze", *Bibliofilia* XXVII, 286-292

1926

LE CORBUSIER, *Kommende Baukunst*, Stuttgart u.a.O

H. OMONT, *La Géographie de Ptolémée. Réproduction du manuscrit latin 4802 de la Bibliothèque Nationale*, Paris

1926-30

M. MAYLENDER, *Storia delle accademie d'Italia*, Bologna

1927

GIUSEPPE CASCIOLI, "Nuovi documenti sul modello della cupola di Michelangelo", *Roma* V, 205-209

H. DENNIS, "The Garret Manuscript of Marcanova", *Memoirs of the American Academy in Rome* VI, 113-126

UMBERTO GNOLI, *La Pinacoteca di Perugia*, Firenze

FISKE KIMBALL, "Luciano Laurana and the 'High Renaissance'", *Art Bulletin* X, 124-151

E. LAWRENCE, "The Illustrations of the Garret and Modena Manuscripts of Marcanova", *Memoirs of the American Academy in Rome* VI, 127-130

ERWIN PANOFSKY, "Bermerkungen zur der Neuherausgabe der Haarlemer Michelangelo-Zeichnungen durch Fr. Knapp", *Repertorium für Kunstwissenschaft* IIL [XLVIII], 25-28

SEYMOUR DE' RICCI, "Gl'insegnamenti dell'esposizione parigina del libro italiano", *Dedalo* VIII (1), 138-178

1927-1928

LUIGIA MARIA TOSI [a], "Il ballatoio della cupola di Santa Maria del Fiore", *Bollettino d'arte* VII, serie II, 610-615

—— [a], "Un modello di Baccio d'Agnolo attribuito a Michelangelo", *Dedalo* VIII, 320-328

1928

LEONARDO BRUNI, *Humanistisch-philosophische Schriften*, besorgt von H. Baron, Berlin-Leipzig

T. BURZI, "Il 'Teatro all'antica' di Vincenzo Scamozzi in Sabbioneta", *Dedalo* VIII, 488-524

A. C.[AMPANA], "Un minatore malatestiano", *Ariminum* I (6), 137-50

ANTONIO CONDIVI, *Michelangelo, la vita*, a cura di P. D'Ancona, Milano

ALDO DE RINALDIS, *La Pinacoteca del Museo Nazionale di Napoli*, Napoli

THEOBALD HOFMANN, *Entstehungsgeschichte des St. Peter in Rom*, Zittau

LUDWIG VON PASTOR, *The History of the Popes*, XVI, London

CORRADO RICCI, "Di un codice malatestiano della 'Esperide' di Basinio", *Accademie e biblioteche d'Italia* I (5-6), 20-48

JEAN PAUL RICHTER (a cura di), *La collezione Hertz e gli affreschi di Giulio Romano nel Palazzo Zuccari*, Roma

WOLFANG STECHOW, "Daniele da Volterra als bildhauer", *Jahrbuch der preussischen Kunstsammlungen* XLIX, 90-91

CHARLES DE TOLNAY, "Die Handzeichnungen Michelangelos im Archivio Buonarroti", *Münchner Jahrbuch der bildenden Kunst* n.s., 5, 377-476

1928-1929

JAMES RORIMER, "A Corbel from the Strozzi Palace", *Metropolitan Museum Studies* I, 95-96

LUGIA MARIA TOSI, "La chiesa di San Giuseppe", *Dedalo* IX, 283-288

1928-1930

PIO PECCHIAI, *Le vite de' più eccellenti pittori, scultori et architetti di Giorgio Vasari*, Milano

1929

LUCA BELTRAMI, *La cupola vaticana*, Città del Vaticano

MARTIN S. BRIGGS, "Architectural Models-I", *Burlington Magazine* LIV, 174-183

MAX DVORÁK, *Geschichte der italienischen Kunst im Zeitalter der Renaissance*, II, München

THEOBALD HOFMAN, *Entstehungsgeschichte des St. Peter in Rom*, Zittau

P.E. SCHRAMM, *Kaiser, Rom und Renovatio*, Leipzig

1930

K.H. BUSSE, "Der Pitti-Paläst...", *Jahrbuch der preussischen Kunstsammlungen* LI, 110-132

KARL FREY, *Der literarische Nachlass Giorgio Vasaris. Mit kritischen Apparaten versehen...*, 2 Bde., München

F. GIANANI, *Il Duomo di Pavia*, Pavia

F. GREGOROVIUS, *Passeggiate per l'Italia*, a cura di A. Tomei, Napoli

LUDWIG H. HEYDENREICH, "Über Oreste Vannocci Biringucci", *Mitteilungen des Kunsthistorischen Institutes in Florenz* III, 434-440

GEORGE F. HILL, *A Corpus of Italian Medals of the Renaissance before Cellini*, 2 vols., London

V. MARIANI, *Storia della scenografia italiana*, Firenze

Mostra di Roma Secentesca, a cura dell'Istituto di Studi Romani, Roma

W. REHM, *Der Untergang Roms im abendländischen Denken*, Leipzig

CORRADO RICCI, *La scenografia italiana*, Milano

L. SCHUDT, *Le guide di Roma*, Vienna-Augusta

H. TIETZE, "Romanische Kunst und Renaissance", in *Vorträge der Bibliothek Warburg 1926-27*, Berlin, 43-57

CHARLES DE TOLNAY, "Zu den späten architektonischen Projekten Michelangelos", (I. Teil) *Jahrbuch der preuszischen Kunstsammlungen* LI, 1-48

1931

GUGLIELMO BERTUZZI, "Un monastero benedettino in Castelnovo Fogliani sotto il titolo di S. Maria delle Grazie 1504-1805", *Bollettino storico piacentino* XXVI, 16 sg.

R. BUSCAROLI, *Pittura romagnola della seconda metà del Quattrocento*, Faenza

W. ERBEN, *Rombilder auf kaiserlichen und päpstlichen Siegel der des Mittelalters*, Graz

B. FONTIUS, *Epistolarium*, a cura di L. Juhasz, Budapest

FRA MARIANO DA FIRENZE, *Itinerarium Urbis Romae*, a cura di E. Bulletti, Roma

GUSTAVO GIOVANNONI [a], *Saggi sull'architettura del Rinascimento*, Milano

—— [b], "Tra la cupola di Bramante e quella di Michelangelo", in *Saggi sull'architettura del Rinascimento*, Milano, 143-176

LUDWIG H. HEYDENREICH, "Spätwerke Brunelleschis", *Jahrbuch der Preuszischen Kunstsammlungen* LII (1), 1-28

J. LESELLIER, "Jean de Chénevieres, sculpteur et architecte de l'eglise Saint-Louis-des-Françaises à Rome", in *Mélanges d'Archéologie et d'Histoire* XLVIII, 233-267

P. PIUR, *Cola di Rienzo, Darstellung seines Lebens und seines Geistes*, Wein

1932

PELEO BACCI, "Commentari all'arte senese", *Bollettino senese di storia patria* n.s. 3, 233-240

FRITZ BAUMGART, "Domenico Passignano (Passignani)", in U. Thieme und F. Becker (Hrsg.), *Allgemeines Lexikon der Bildenden Künstler*, XXVI, Leipzig, 285-286

JOHN B. BURY, *The Idea of Progress. An Inquiry into its Origin and Growth*, New York

G. CECCHINI, *La Galleria Nazionale dell'Umbria*, Roma

ANNA MARIA F. CIARANFI [a], Commento a Giorgio Vasari, *Le vite de' più eccellenti pittori, scultori e architetti*, Firenze 1932, vol. VI, 501, nota 2

—— [b], "PELLICCIAIO, GIACOMO DI MINO", IN U. THIEME UND F. BECKER (HRSG.), *Allgemeines Lexikon der Bildenden Künstler*, XXVI, Leipzig, 367

HERMANN EGGER, *Römische Veduten. Handzeichnungen aus dem XV bis XVIII. Jahrhundert zur Topographie der Stadt Rom*, 2 Bde ,Wien (2. Auflage)

J. FISCHER, *Claudii Ptolemaei Codex Urbinas Graecus 82*, Leipzig

F. GIANANI, O. MODESTI, *Il Duomo di Pavia. 1488-1932*, Pavia

WERNER KÖRTE, "Zur Peterskuppel des Michelangelo", *Jahrbuch der preussischen Kunstsammlungen* LIII, 90-112

PIERO MISCIATELLI, "Iconografia bernardiniana", *Diana - Rassegna d'arte e vita senese* VII (fasc. IV), 247-252

FRANCESCO PELLATI, "Vitruvio nel Medio Evo e nel Rinascimento", *Bollettino del R. istituto di archeologia e storia dell'arte* V (I-II), 111-132

LOUIS PONNELLE AND LOUIS BORDET, *St. Philip Neri and the Roman Society of his Time (1515-1595)*, translated by Ralph Francis Kerr, London

CHARLES DE TOLNAY, "Zu den späten architektonischen Projekten Michelangelos", (II. Teil) *Jahrbuch der preussischen Kunstsammlungen* LIII, 231-253

1933

CESARE BRANDI, *La regia Pinacoteca di Siena*, Siena

PAOLO FONTANA, "Osservazioni intorno al rapporto di Vitruvio colla retorica dell'architettura del Rinascimento", in *Miscellanea di storia dell'arte in onore di Igino Benvenuto Supino*, Firenze, 305-322

GUSTAVO GIOVANNONI, "Considerazioni architettoniche su S. Petronio di Bologna", in *Miscellanea di storia dell'arte in onore di Igino Benvenuto Supino*, Firenze, 165-182

VERA GIOVANNOZZI, "Ricerche su Bernardo Buontalenti", *Rivista d'arte* XV, 299-327

CHRISTIAN HÜLSEN, *Das Skizzenbuch des Giovannantonio Dosio im Staatlichen Kupferstichkabinett zu Berlin*, Berlin

JENO LANYI, "Pisano, Andrea", in U. Thieme und F. Becker (Hrsg.), *Allgemeines Lexikon der Bildenden Künstler*, Leipzig, 94-99

M. MARABELLI, P. SANTOPADRE, M. VERITA, "Il ruolo della controvetrata sulla conservazione della vetrata medievale del duomo di Orvieto", *Rivista della stazione sperimentale del vetro* III

RAYMOND VAN MARLE, The Development of the Italian Schools of Painting, XIV, *The Renaissance Painters of Umbria*, The Hague

RUDOLPH WITTKOWER, "Mischellen. Zur Peterskuppel Michelangelos", *Zeitschrift für Kunstgeschiche* II, 348-370

GUIDO ZUCCHINI [a], *Disegni antichi e moderni per la facciata di S. Petronio di Bologna*, Bologna

—— [b], "Documenti inediti per la storia del S. Petronio di Bologna", in *Miscellanea di storia dell'arte in onore di Igino Benvenuto Supino*, Firenze, 183-200

1933-1938

GAETANO BALLARDINI, *Corpus della maiolica italiana. I: Le maioliche datate fino al 1530. II: Le maioliche datate dal 1531 al 1535*, 2 voll., Roma

1934

BRUNO MARIA APOLLONI GHETTI, *Opere architettoniche di Michelangelo a Firenze. Prospetto di S. Lorenzo (dal modello). Biblioteca Laurenziana, Cappella Medicea. Monumenti italiani*, II, Roma

GIULIO CARLO ARGAN, *Francesco Colonna e la critica d'arte veneta nel Quattrocento*, Torino

Corpus nummorum italicorum..., XV, Roma

LONI ERNST, *Manieristische florentiner Baukunst*, Postdam

RICCARDO FILANGIERI, *Castelnuovo regia angioina e aragonese di Napoli*, Napoli, 54

MARCELLE LAGAISSE, *Benozzo Gozzoli*, Paris

LUIGI SERRA, *L'arte delle Marche*, Roma

PIETRO TOESCA, "Michelangelo", in *Enciclopedia italiana di scienze, lettere ed arti*, XXIII (fasc.II), Roma, 165-191

CHARLES DE TOLNAY, "Michelange et la façade de St. Lorenzo", *Gazette des beaux-arts*, 6e série, XI, 24-42

RUDOLPH WITTKOWER, "Michelangelo's Biblioteca Laurenziana", *Art Bulletin* XVI, 123-218 (reprinted in *Idea and Image, Studies in the Italian Renaissance*, London 1978, 11-17)

1935

BERNARD BERENSON, "Andrea di Michelangiolo e Antonio Mini", *L'arte* XXXVIII, 243-283

H.H. BORCHERDT, *Das europäische Theater im Mittelalter und in der Renaissance*, Leipzig

CESARE BRANDI, "Lo stile di Ambrogio Lorenzetti", *Critica d'arte* (ripubblicato in *Pittura a Siena nel Trecento*, Torino 1991, 153-164)

FRANCESCO EHRLE, HERMANN EGGER, *Studi e documenti per la storia del Palazzo Apostolico Vaticano*, Città del Vaticano

Exposition de l'art italien de Cimabue à Tiepolo, catalogue exposition, Paris

GUSTAVO GIOVANNONI [a], *Saggi sull'architettura del Rinascimento*, Milano (1a ed.1931)

—— [b], "Tra la cupola di Bramante e quella di Michelangelo", in *Saggi sull'architettura del Rinascimento*, 143-174

H.R. HAHNLOSER, *Villard de Honnecourt*, Wien

G. HAYDN HUNTLEY, *Andrea Sansovino. Sculptor and Architect of the Italian Renaissance*, Cambridge

A. KHOMENTOVSKAIA, "Felice Feliciano comme l'auteur de l'*Hypnerotomachia Poliphili*", *Bibliofilia* XXXVII, 154-174

WERNER KÖRTE, *Der Palazzo Zuccaro in Rom*, Leipzig

MARIA LUISA MEZ, *Daniele da Volterra*, Volterra

CHARLES DE TOLNAY, "La Bibliothèque Laurentienne de Michel-ange: nouvelles recherches", *Gazette des beaux-arts* LXXVII, 95-105

1935-1936

ANTONIA NAVA, "Sui disegni architettonici per S. Giovanni dei Fiorentini in Roma", *Critica d'arte* I, 102-108

1936

LUISA BECHERUCCI, *L'architettura italiana del Cinquecento*, Firenze

VERA DADDI GIOVANNOZZI, "I modelli dei secoli XVI e XVII per la facciata di S. Maria del Fiore", *L'arte* XXXIX, 33-49

PAOLO FONTANA, "I codici di Francesco di Giorgio Martini e di Mariano di Jacopo detto il Taccola", in *Actes du XIVeme Congrès international d'histoire de l'art 1936. Resumès des communications*, I, Bruxelles, 102-103

VINCENZO GOLZIO, *Raffaello nei documenti, nelle testimonianze dei contemporanei e nella letteratura del suo secolo*, Città del Vaticano

W.S. HECKSCHER, "Die Romruinen. Die geistigen Voraussetzungen ihrer Wertung im Mittelalter und in der Renaissance", Diss., Würzburg

ANTONIA NAVA, "La storia della chiesa di S. Giovanni dei Fiorentini. Documenti del suo archivio", *Archivio della r. deputazione romana di storia patria* LIX, 337-362

LUIGI PUNGILEONE, *Memorie intorno alla vita ed opere di Donato Bramante*, Roma

1936-37

R. JOCKL, "Die Zerstörungsgechichte des antiken Rom", *Mitteilungen der Arbeitsgemeinschaft der Altphilologen in Österreich* X, 32ss.

1937

VIRGILIO CRISPOLTI, *Santa Maria del Fiore*, Firenze

BERNHARD DEGENHART, "Zur Graphologie der Handzeichnung", *Kunstgeschichtliches Jahrbuch der Bibliotheca Hertziana*, 223-343

VINCENZO GOLZIO, *Raffaello nei documenti, nelle testimonianze dei contemporanei e nella letteratura del suo secolo*, Città del Vaticano

LUDWIG H. HEYDENREICH, "Pius II als Bauherr von Pienza", *Zeitschrift für Kunstgeschichte* VI

HARALD KELLER, "Die Bauplastik des Sieneser Doms", *Kunstgeschichtliches Jahrbuch der Bibliotheca Hertziana* I, 139-221

D. MAHNKE, *Unenliche Sphäre und Allmittelpunkte*, Halle

R. MAIOCCHI, *Codice diplomatico-artistico di Pavia dall'anno 1330 al 1550*, I, Pavia

WALTER PAATZ, *Werden und Wesen des Trecento-Architektur in Toscana*, Florenz

RENATO SALVINI, "Giotto", in Illustrazione toscana, n.s., Firenze

1937-38

ERWIN PANOFSKY, "The Early History of Man in a Cycle of Paintings by Piero di Cosimo", *Journal of the Warburg Institute* I, 12-30

1937-40

DAGOBERT FREY, "Ein Entwurf Giulianos da Sangallo für das Gestühl in der kapelle des Palazzo Medici-Riccardi", *Mitteilungen des Kunsthistorischen Institutes in Florenz* V, 197-202

VERA DADDI GIOVANNOZZI, "Untersuchungen über Don Giovanni de' Medici und Alessandro Pieroni", *Mitteilungen des Kusthistorischen Institutes in Florenz* V, 58-75

1938

BERNARD BERENSON, *The Drawings of the Florentine Painters*, 3 vols., Chicago

GIULIANO BRIGANTI, "Su Giusto di Gand", *Critica d'arte* III (15), 104-112

RICCARDO FILANGIERI, *Rassegna critica delle fonti per la storia di Castelnuovo*, II, 31 e bibliografia

WOLFGANG LOTZ, "Vignola-Zeichnungen", *Jahrbuch der preuszischen Kunstsammlungen* XLIX, 97-115

Mostra di Melozzo e del Quattrocento romagnolo, catalogo mostra (Forlì), Bologna

RAFFAELLO NICCOLI, "Elenco dei disegni antichi esposti alla mostra brunelleschiana in Palazzo Vecchio", in *Atti del I congresso nazionale di storia dell'architettura* (Firenze, ottobre-novembre 1936), Firenze, 285-288

A. PICA, P. PORTALUPPI, *Le Grazie*, Roma

ADOLFO VENTURI, *Storia dell'arte italiana*, XI, Milano

1938-1948

A.M. HIND, *Early Italian Engraving*, London-New York, I, 304 ff.

1939

PAOLO ARRIGONI, ACHILLE BERTARELLI, *Piante e vedute di Roma e del Lazio conservate nella Raccolta delle Stampe e dei Disegni*, Castello Sforzesco, Milano

E. ASCHERI, "Rilievo dei monumenti. Il modello ligneo del Duomo di Vigevano", *Palladio*, III, 123-128

CHARLES RICHARD CAMMELL, "The Authentic Likeness of Michelangelo", *Connoisseur* CIV, 119-125

WALLACE K. FERGUSON, "Humanist Views of the Renaissance", *American Historical Review* XLV, 1-28

Mostra Medicea, Palazzo Medici, Firenze

R. OFFNER, "The Barberini Panels and their Painter", in *Medieval Studies in Memory of A. Kingsley Porter*, I, Cambridge, Mass.

L. SBARAGLI, *Claudio Tolomei. Umanista senese del Cinquecento*, Siena

ADOLFO VENTURI, "Michelangelo architetto", in *Storia dell'arte italiana. Architettura del Cinquecento* (II parte), XI, Milano, 1-211

1939-40

L. PRATILLI, "Felice Feliciano alla luce dei suoi codici", *Atti del R. istituto veneto di scienze, lettere e arti 99*, 33-105

1940

N. BARBATINI, *Il Castello di Monselice*, Venezia

COSTANTINO BARONI, *Documenti per la storia dell'architettura a Milano*, Firenze

ROBERTO LONGHI, "Fatti di Masaccio e Masolino", *Critica d'arte* XXV-XXVI, 145-191 (ripubblicato in *Fatti di Masolino e di Masaccio e altri studi sul Quattrocento. Opere complete*, VIII/1, Firenze 1975, 3-65)

G.K. LOUKOMSKI, "I disegni dello Scamozzi a Londra", *Palladio* IV, 65-74

Mostra del Cinquecento toscano in Palazzo Strozzi, Firenze

BERNARD RACKHAM, *Catalogue of Italian Maiolica*, 2 vols., London

G. RICHTER, "Rehabilitation of Fra Carnevale", *Art Quarterly*, 311-323

MARIO SALMI [a], *Firenze, Milano e il primo Rinascimento*, Milano

—— [B], "Palazzo Strozzi", *Illustrazione toscana e dell'Etruria* XVIII

HERBERT SIEBENHÜNER, "Brunellesco und die Florentiner Domkuppel", *Mitteilungen des Kunsthistorischen Instituten in Florenz* V, 434

G. SWARZENSKI, "The Master of the Barberini Panels: Bramante", *Bulletin of the Museum of Fine Arts* XXXVIII, Boston 90-97

PIETRO TOESCA, *Giotto*, Torino

LUDWIG WACHLER, "Giovannantonio Dosio, ein Architekt des späten Cinquecento", *Römisches Jahrbuch für Kunstgeschichte* IV, 143-252

VILHELM WANSCHER [a], "Il modello definitivo di Michelangelo per la facciata di San Lorenzo: 1520", *Art, Monuments et Mémoires* VIII, 4-15

—— [b], *Vie de Michel-ange*, Copenhagen

1940-53

R. VALENTINI, G. ZUCCHETTI (a cura di), *Codice topografico della città di Roma*, Roma

1940-54

WALTER PAATZ, ELISABETH PAATZ, *Die Kirchen von Florenz*, 6. Bde., Frankfurt

1940-68

COSTANTINO BARONI, *Documenti per la storia dell'architettura a Milano nel Rinascimento e nel Barocco II*, voll.: I, Firenze 1940; II, Roma 1968

1941

M. BARATTA, *Leonardo da Vinci. I disegni di Leonardo da Vinci pubblicati dalla R. Commissione Vinciana. Fascicolo unico. Disegni geografici*, Roma

COSTANTINO BARONI, *L'architettura lombarda dal Bramante al Richino*, Milano

WALTER PAATZ UND ELIZABETH PAATZ, *Die Kirchen von Florenz*, II, Frankfurt (reprint, 1952)

PIERO SANPAOLESI, *La cupola di Santa Maria del Fiore. Il progetto. La costruzione*, Roma (2a ed., Firenze 1977)

PIETRO TOESCA, *Giotto*, Torino

DARIA VIVIANI-FIORINI, "La costruzione delle Logge vasariane di Arezzo", *Vasari* XII, 109 sg.

O.VESSBERG, *Studien zur Kunstgeschichte der römischen Republik*, Lund

E. ZILSEL, "The Origins of William Gilbert's Scientific Method", *Journal of the History of Ideas* II, 325-349

1942

FRANCESCO ARCANGELI, *Tarsie con cinquantasei tavole*, Roma

MARIO BAFILE, IL *giardino di Villa Madama*, Roma

COSTANTINO BARONI, "Stampe lombarde del Rinascimento", *Emporium* XII

J. VAN BREEN, *Het reconstructieplan voor het Mausoleum te Halikarnassos*, Amsterdam

ENZO CARLI, *Michelangelo*, Bergamo

V. CIAN, "Nel mondo di Baldassare Castiglione", *Archivio storico lombardo* VII, 70 sg.

JOHN COOLIDGE, "Vignola, and the Little Domes of St. Peter's", *Marsyas* II, 63-124

A.M. DALLA POZZA, "Palladiana III, IV, V, VI", *Odeo Olimpico. Memorie della Accademia Olimpica di Vicenza* II, 123-260

WILLIAM BELL DINSMOOR, "The Literary Remains of Sebastiano Serlio", *Art Bulletin* XXIV, 55-91 and 115-154

PAOLO GAZZOLA, "Un disegno sangallesco inedito per la Basilica Vaticana", *Palladio* VI, 32-33

GUSTAVO GIOVANNONI, "La cupola di San Pietro", in *IV Centenario del Giudizio*, Firenze, 8-31

W. GOETZ, "Das Werden des italienischen Nationalgefühls", in *Italien im Mittelalter*, I, Leipzig, 61-124

RICHARD KRAUTHEIMER, "Introduction to an 'Iconography of Medieval Architecture'", *Journal of the Warburg and Courtauld Institutes* V, 1-33

GIUSEPPE MARCHINI, *Giuliano da Sangallo*, Firenze

VALERIO MARIANI, *Michelangelo*, Napoli

La protezione del patrimonio artistico nazionale dalle offese della guerra aerea, a cura della Direzione Generale delle Arti, Firenze

G. SEPE, *La murazione aragonese di Napoli, studio di restituzione*, Napoli

Stampe popolari e libri figurati del Rinascimento lombardo, catalogo mostra (Milano, Castello Sforzesco) a cura di L. Sorrento, Milano

PIETRO TOMEI, *L'architettura a Roma nel Quattrocento*, Roma

EDUARD VODOZ, "Studien zum architektonischen Werk des Bartolomeo Amannati", D.Phil. Diss., Universität Zürich

GUIDO ZUCCHINI, "Disegni inediti per S. Petronio di Bologna", *Palladio* VI, 153-166

1943

A.M. DALLA POZZA, "Palladiana VII", *Odeo Olimpico. Memorie dell'Accademia Olimpica di Vicenza* III, 231-259

ANDRÈ GRABAR, *Martyrium. Recherches sur le culte des reliques et l'art chrétien* (1943-46) I, Paris

F. PATETTA, "La figura di Bramante e alcuni riflessi di vita romana dei suoi tempi nel 'Simia' di Andrea Guarna", in *Atti d. r. Accademia d'Italia. Memoria della classe di scienze morali e storiche*, s. VIII, IV (7), 165-202

JOHN POPE HENNESSY, "Some Aspects of the Cinquecento in Siena", *Art in America* XXXI, 63-77

G.M. RICHTER, "Architectural Phantasies by Bramante", *Gazette des beaux-arts* XXIII, 5-20

RODOLFO SABATINI, *Uno studio per la completazione del tamburo della cupola di S. Maria del Fiore*, Firenze

CHARLES DE TOLNAY, *Michelangelo*, Princeton

ALLEN S. WELLER, *Francesco di Giorgio 1439-1501*, Chicago

1944

R. ALMAGIA, *Monumenta cartographica Vaticana*, Città del Vaticano

COSTANTINO BARONI, *Bramante*, Bergamo

W. HAMMER, "The Concept of the New or Second Rome in the Middle Ages", *Speculum* XIX, 50-62

ANDRÉ LURCAT, *Formes, Composition et Lois d'Harmonie. Eléments d'une science de l'esthétique architecturale*, Paris

AUGUSTO MARINONI, *Gli appunti grammaticali e lessicali di Leonardo da Vinci*, Milano

L. SERVOLINI, *Jacopo de' Barbari*, Padova

HERBERT SIEBENHÜNER, *Deutsche Künstler am Mailänder Dom*, München

O. STEIN, *Die Architektur theoretiker der italienischen Renaissance*, Karlsruhe

J. TOYNBEE, *Roman Medallions (Numismatic Studies V)* New York

1945

Archivio Capitolare di S. Pietro in Vaticano (dal 1945), catalogo, Biblioteca Vaticana

ANTHONY BLUNT, *The French Drawings in the Collection of His Majesty the King at Windsor Castle*, Oxford-London

ACHILLE CALOSSO BERTINI, *Quattro secoli di pittura in Umbria. Mostra celebrativa del V Centenario della nascita di Pietro Perugino*, catalogo mostra, Perugia

V. CIAN, *La satira*, Milano [1945]

P. FRANKL, "The Secret of the Medieval Masons", *Art Bulletin* XXVII, 46-60

KARL LEHMANN, "The Dome of Heaven", *Art Bulletin* XXVI, 1-27

ERWIN PANOFSKY, "An Explanation of Stornaloco's Formula", *Art Bulletin* XXVII, 61-64

BERNARD RACKHAM, "Nicola Pellipario and Bramante", *Burlington Magazine* LXXXVI, 144-149

E. ZILSEL, "The Genesis of the Concept of Scientific Progress", *Journal of the History of Ideas* VI, 325-349

1946

ENZO CARLI [a], *Capolavori dell'arte senese*, Firenze

—— [B], *Il Museo dell'Opera e la libreria Piccolomini di Siena*, Siena

ANDRÉ GRABAR, *Martyrium: Recherches sur le culte des reliques et l'art chrétien antique* (1943-46), II, Paris (reprint, London 1972)

R. LANGTON DOUGLAS, *Piero di Cosimo*, Chicago

ROBERTO LONGHI [a], *Piero della Francesca*, Milano

—— [b], *Viatico a cinque secoli di pittura veneziana*, Firenze

ROBERTO PAPINI, *Francesco di Giorgio architetto*, Firenze

1946-47

KENNETH CLARK, "Architectural Backgrounds in XVth Century Italian Painting", *Arts* II, 33-43

1947

LORENZO GHIBERTI, *I Commentari*, a cura di Ottavio Marisani, Napoli

H. ROEDER, "The Borders of Filarete's Bronze Doors of St. Peter's", *Journal of the Warburg and Courtauld Institutes* X, 150-153

MARIO SALMI, *Masaccio*, Milano

WILHELM R. VALENTINER, "Notes on Giovanni Balducci and Trecento Sculpture in Northern Italy", *Art Quarterly* X, 40-60

1948

HARRY BOBER, "The Zodiacal Miniatures of the Très Riches Heures of the Duke of Berry", *Journal of the Warburg and Courtauld Institutes* XI, 1-34

ERNST CASSIRER ed., "Francesco Petrarca.On His Own Ignorance and That of Many Others", in *The Renaissance Philosophy of Man*, edited by Ernst Cassirer, Chicago, 125

WALLACE K. FERGUSON, *The Renaissance in Historical Thought*, Cambridge, Mass.

Francesco Petrarca, see Ernst Cassirer
Guida per la visita del Museo dell'Opera di S. Maria del Fiore di Firenze, Firenze
A.M. Hind, *Early Italian Engraving*, London
Italian Illuminated Manuscripts of the Renaissance, exhibition catalogue (Oxford Bodleian Library), Oxford
Richard Krautheimer, "The Tragic and Comic Scenes of the Renaissance: The Baltimore and Urbino Panels", *Gazette des beaux-arts* XXXIII, 327-346
Mario Salmi, *Disegni di Francesco di Giorgio nella collezione Chigi-Saracini*, Siena
Otto G. von Simson, *Sacred Fortress, Byzantine Art and Statecraft in Ravenna*, Chicago
John Summerson, "Antitheses of the Quattrocento", in *Heavenly Mansions*, New York, 29-50
Charles de Tolnay, *The Medici Chapel*, III, Princeton (reprint, 1970)

1949

James S. Ackerman, "'Ars sine scientia nihil est.' Gothic Theory of Architecture at Cathedral of Milan", *Art Bulletin* XXX, 84-111
Anna Maria F. Ciaranfi, "Mostra di manoscritti medicei in occasione del V centenario di Lorenzo il Magnifico alla Biblioteca Mediceo Laurenziana", *Bollettino d'arte* XXXIV, 186-189
Charles Czarnowsky, "Engines de levage dans les combles d'eglises en Alsace", *Cahiers techniques d'Art* II, 11-27
Felix Gilbert, "Bernardo Rucellai and the Orti Oricellari", *Journal of the Warburg and Courtauld Institutes* XII, 101-131
Gustavo Giovannoni, *Antonio da Sangallo, il giovane*, 2 voll., Roma
Ludwig H. Heydenreich, *I disegni di Leonardo da Vinci nelle Gallerie dell'Accademia di Venezia*, Firenze
A. Hyatt Mayor, "Prints Acquired in 1949", *Metropolitan Museum of Art Bulletin* n.s., VIII, 157-167
Richard Krautheimer, "Some Drawings of Early Christian Basilicas in Rome: St. Peter's and Santa Maria Maggiore", *Art Bulletin* XXXI, 211-215
R. Maiocchi, *Codice diplomatico-artistico di Pavia dall'anno 1330 al 1550*, II, Pavia
Mostra della Biblioteca di Lorenzo nella Biblioteca Medicea Laurenziana, catalogo mostra (Firenze, 21 maggio-31 ottobre), Firenze
Giovanni Papini, *Vita di Michelangelo*, Firenze
Ludwig von Pastor, *The History of the Popes*, St. Louis
Piero Sanpaolesi, "Le prospettive architettoniche di Urbino, di Filadelfia e di Berlino", *Bollettino d'arte* XXXIV, 322-337
Armando Schiavo, *Michelangelo architetto*, Roma
William E. Suida, *A Catalogue of Paintings in the John and Mable Ringling Museum of Art*, Sarasota
Rudolph Wittkower, *Architectural Principles in the Age of Humanism*, London

1949-1951

James S. Ackerman, "Bramante and the Torre Borgia", *Atti della Pontificia Accademia Romana di Archeologia-Rendiconti* XXV-XXVI, 247-265

1950

Luciano Berti, "Matteo Nigetti", *Rivista d'arte* XXVI, 157-184
Aldo Bertini, *Prima mostra dei disegni della Biblioteca Reale*, catalogo mostra (Torino, Biblioteca Reale), Torino
G. Cecchini, *Guida della Galleria Nazionale dell'Umbria in Perugia*, Perugia
Federico Frigerio, *Il Duomo di Como e il Broletto*, Como
Frederick Hartt, Review of Charles de Tolnay, *Michelangelo*: vol. II and vol. III, *Art Bulletin* XXXII, 239-250
Le Corbusier, *Le Modulor* I, Boulogne
Arnaldo Momigliano, "Ancient History and the Antiquarian", *Journal of the Warburg and Courtauld Institutes* XIII, 285-315

[Luigi Michelini Tocci], scheda n. 64, in *Miniature del Rinascimento*, catalogo mostra, Città del Vaticano
L. Ozzola, *Il museo d'arte medioevale e moderna del Palazzo Ducale di Mantova*, Mantova
Pier Luigi Rambaldi, Anna Saitta Revignas, *I manoscritti Palatini della Biblioteca Nazionale Centrale di Firenze*, III (fasc. I), Roma
Pasquale Rotondi, *Il palazzo ducale di Urbino*, 2voll., Urbino
E. Baldwin Smith, *The Dome. A Study in the History of Ideas*, Princeton
Pietro Toesca, *Il Trecento*, Firenze
[Touring Club Italiano], *Roma*, Roma

1951

James S. Ackerman, "The Belvedere as a Classical Villa", *Journal of the Warburg and Courtauld Institutes* XIV, 70-91
Augusto Campana, "Il nuovo codice vaticano della Hesperis di Basinio", in Otto Pächt, "Giovanni da Fano's Illustrations for Basinio's Epos Hesperis", *Studi Romagnoli* II, 104-108
Kenneth Clark, *Piero della Francesca*, London
Guglielmo De Angelis d'Ossat, "L'autore del codice londinese attribuito ad Andrea Coner", *Palladio* n.s., I, 94-98
O. Gierke, *Political Theories of the Middle Ages*, translated by F.W. Maitland, Cambridge
Decio Gioseffi, *Perspectiva artificialis, spigolature e appunti*, Trieste
G. Guerrieri, Elena Povoledo, *Il secolo dell'invenzione teatrale. Mostra di scenografia e costumi del Seicento italiano*, catalogo mostra (Venezia, Palazzo Grassi), Venezia
Licisco Magagnato, "The Genesis of the Teatro Olimpico", *Journal of the Warburg and Courtauld Institutes* XIV, 209-220
Otto Pächt, "Giovanni da Fano's Illustrations for Basinio's Epos Hesperis", *Studi Romagnoli* II, 91-111
Pasquale Rotondi, *Il Palazzo Ducale di Urbino*, Urbino
Piero Sanpaolesi, "Notizie documentarie sul Buontalenti", *Palladio* I, 44-47
Pietro Toesca, *Il Trecento*, Torino
Charles de Tolnay, *Michel-ange*, Paris (ed. it., *Michelangiolo*, Firenze)

1952

Franco Barbieri, *Vincenzo Scamozzi*, Vicenza
Jacob C. Burckhardt, *Il Cicerone*, a cura di Mingazzini-Pfister, Firenze
John Coolidge, "Recensione a Sanpaolesi", *Art Bulletin* XXXIV, 156 e sg
George Kaftal, *Iconography of the Saints in Tuscan Painting*, Florence
L. D. Ettlinger, in *Burlington Magazine* XCIV, 591, 160 ff.
Wolgang Lotz, in *Plan und Bauwerk. Entwürfe aus fünf Jarhunderten*, München
Bates Lowry, "Notes on the 'Speculum Romanae Magnificentiae' and Related Publications", *Art Bulletin* XXXIV, 46-50
Walter Paatz und Elizabeth Paatz, *Die Kirchen von Florenz*, III, Frankfurt
Pio Pecchiai, *Il Gesù di Roma*, Roma
Armando Schiavo, "La cupola di San Pietro", *Bollettino del Centro Nazionale di studi dell'architettura, sezione di Roma* VI, 14-26
Rudolf Wittkower, *Architectural Principles in the Age of Humanism*, London

1953

Leon Battista Alberti, "Vita anonima", English translation in James Ross and Mary McLaughlin, *The Portable Renaissance Reader*, Harmondsworth, 480-491
Anonimo Magliabecchiano, in R. Valentini e G. Zucchetti, *Codice topografico della città di Roma*, IV, Roma

[Luigi Michelini Tocci], scheda n. 64, in *Miniature del Rinascimento*, catalogo mostra, Città del Vaticano

Wolfgang Braunfels, *Mittelalterliche Stadtbaukunst in der Toskana*, Berlin (4. auflage 1979)
André Chastel, "Marqueterie et perspective au XVe siècle", *Revue des Arts* III, 141-154 (réimpression dans *Formes, fables, figures*, Paris 1978, 317-332)
W.G. Constable, *Richard Wilson*, London
Benedetto Croce, "Vedute della città nel Quattrocento", in *Aneddoti di varia letteratura* I, Bari, 267-271
L.D. Ettlinger, "Pollaiuolo's Tomb of Pope Sixtus IV", *Journal of the Warburg and Courtauld Institutes* XVI, 239-274
Vincenzo Fasolo, "Un pittore architetto: il Cigoli", *Quaderni dell'Istituto di Storia dell'Architettura* I, 1 sg.; II, 11 sg.
Otto Förster, "Bramantes erste Jahre in Rom", *Wallraf-Richartz-Jahrbuch* XV, 157-178
H.P. L'Orange, *Studies in the Iconography of Cosmic Kingship in the Ancient World*, Oslo
Mostra storica nazionale della miniatura, catalogo mostra (Roma, Palazzo Venezia), Firenze
Michelangelo Muraro, *Mostra di disegni veneziani del Sei e Settecento*, catalogo mostra (Firenze, Gabinetto Disegni e Stampe degli Uffizi), Firenze
James B. Ross and Mary McLaughlin, see Leon Battista Alberti
Bernardo Rucellai, "De Urbe Roma", in R. Valentini e G. Zucchetti, *Codice topografico della città di Roma*, IV, Roma
Fritz Saxl, H. Meier, *Verzeichnis astrologischer und mythologischer illustrierter Handschiften des lateinischen Mittelalters*, III. *Handschriften in englischen Bibliotheken*, 2. Bde., London
Armando Schiavo, *La vita e le opere architettoniche di Michelangelo*, Roma
F. Sisi, *L'urbanistica negli studi di Leonardo da Vinci*, Firenze
J. Vallery Radot, *Le dessin français au XVIIe siècle*, Genève
Johannes Wilde, *Italian Drawings in the Department of Prints and Drawings in the British Museum: Michelangelo and His Studio*, London
Giovanni Zangheri, *Il castello di Porta Pia di Michelangiolo 1564 al Vespignani 1864 e ad oggi*, Roma

1953-56

Wolfgang Lotz, "Das Raumbild in der italienischen Architurzeichnung der Renaissance", *Mitteilungen des Kunsthistorischen Institutes in Florenz* VII, 193-226

1954

James S. Ackerman [a], "Architectural Practice in the Italian Renaissance", *Journal of the Society of Architectural Historians* XIII, 3-11 (Reprinted with added postscript in Distance Points: *Essays in Theory and Renaissance Art and Architecture*, Cambridge, Mass., 1991, 361-384)
——— [b], *The Cortile del Belvedere*, Città del Vaticano
Otto Benesch, "A New Contribution to the Problem of the Portrait of Fra Luca Pacioli", *Gazette des beaux arts*, 203-206
Richard Bernheimer, "Gothic Survival and Revival in Bologna", *Art Bulletin* XXXVI, 263-284
Catalogo degli strumenti del Museo di Storia della Scienza, Firenze
G. Billanovich, *Un nuovo esempio delle scoperte e delle letture del Petrarca. L'Eusebio-Girolamo-Pseudoprospero*, Krefeld
André Chastel, "Le mosaïque à Venise et à Florence au XVe siècle", *Arte veneta* VIII, 119-130 (réimpression dans *Formes, Fables, Figures*, Paris 1978; ed. it. Torino 1988, 69-91)
Luigi Firpo, "La città ideale del Filarete", in *Studi in memoria di Gioele Solari*, I, Torino, 11-17
Licisco Magagnato, *Teatri italiani del Cinquecento*, Venezia
Corrado Maltese, "Il pensiero architettonico e urbanistico di Leonardo", in *Leonardo. Saggi e ricerche*, a cura di G. Castelfranco, Roma, 331-358

E. Morand, "La ville de Riom et la fête de Mai dans Les très riches Heures du duc de Berry", *Bulletin de l'académie des sciences, belles-lettres et arts de Clermont-Ferrand*, 1-5

Mostra storica nazionale della miniatura, catalogo mostra (Roma, Palazzo Venezia, 1953), Firenze (2a ed.)

Mario Salmi, *Italian Miniatures*, New York

Ugo Tarchi, *L'arte del Rinascimento nell'Umbria e nella Sabina*, Milano

Charles de Tolnay, *The Tomb of Julius II*, IV, Princeton

P. Turchetti, "Buontalenti Bernardo", in *Enciclopedia dello spettacolo*, II, Roma

A. Weissthanner, "Mittelalterliche Rompilgerbüer", *Archivalische Zeitschrift* XLIX, 49-51

1955

Leon Battista Alberti, see J. Rykwert

Hans Baron, *The Crisis of the Early Renaissance*, Princeton

Luciano Berti, *La casa del Vasari e il suo museo*, Firenze

Bernhard Degenhart, "Dante, Leonardo, und Sangallo (Dante Illustrationen Giuliano da Sangallos in ihrem Verhältnis zu Leonardo da Vinci und zu Figurenzeichnungen der Sangallo)", *Römisches Jahrbuch für Kunstgeschichte* VII, 101-292

Vincenzo Fasolo, "Disegni di Cronaca", *Quaderni dell'Istituto di Storia dell'Architettura* XII, 1-7

Le Corbusier, *Le Modulor* II, Boulogne

Wolfgang Lotz, "Die ovalen Kirchenräume des Cinquecento", *Römisches Jahrbuch für Kunstgeschichte* VII

F. Mancini (a cura di), "La cronaca todina di Joan Fabrizio degli Atti", *Bollettino dell'Accademia della Crusca, sez. studi di filologia italiana* XII, 79-86 (ristampato nel 1979)

Giuseppe Marchini, *Le vetrate italiane*, Milano

H. Nachod, "A Recently Discovered Architectural Sketchbook of an Intimate Assistant of Bramante in the Construction Office of St. Peter's in Rome", in *Rare Books* (H.P. Kraus), VIII, New York

Erwin Panofsky, "The First Page of Giorgio Vasari's 'Libro': A Study on the Gothic Style in the Judgment of the Italian Renaissance", in *Meaning in the Visual Arts*, New York, 169-235 (originally published as "Das erste Blatt aus dem 'Libro' Giorgio Vasaris; eine Studie über der Beurteilung der Gotik in der italienischen Renaissance mit einem Exkurs überzwei Fassadenprojekte Domenico Beccafumis", in *Städel-Jahrbuch* VI, 1930, 25-72)

Joseph J. Rykwert ed., *Leon Battista Alberti. Ten Books on Architecture*, London

Joren Scholz, *Baroque and Romantic Stage Design, exhibition catalogue*, New York

Lynn Thorndike, "Marianus Jacobus Taccola", *Archives internationales d'histoire des sciences*, n.s. XXV (8), 7-26

Johannes Wilde, "Michelangelo's Designs for the Medici Tombs", *Journal of the Warbug and Courtauld Institutes* XVIII, 54-66

A. Wotschitzky, "Hochhäuser im antiken Rom", *Innsbrucker Beiträge zur Kulturwissenschaft* III, 151-158

1956

Paolo Arrigoni, "L'incisione rinascimentale milanese", in *Storia di Milano*, VII, Milano

Edoardo Arslan, "Bramante in Lombardia", in *Storia di Milano*, VII, Milano, 642-650

R. Bernardon, G. dell'Angelo, "Santa Maria della Consolazione a Todi", *Architettura. Cronache e storia* II, 9, 204-207

Ettore Camesasca (a cura di), *Raffaello Sanzio. Tutti gli scritti*, Milano

Guglielmo De Angelis d'Ossat, "Sul Tempio della Consolazione a Todi", *Bollettino d'arte* XLI, 207-213

Bernhard Degenhart, see 1955

Elisabeth Dhanens, *Jean Boulogne*, Bruxelles

Francesco Ehrle, Hermann Egger, *Piante e vedute di Roma e del Vaticano dal 1300 al 1676*, Città del Vaticano

Günther P. Fehring, "Studien über die Kirchenbauten des Francesco di Giorgio", D.Phil. Diss, Julius-Maximilians-Universität, Würzburg

Erik Forssman, *Säule und Ornament*, Köln

Otto Förster, *Bramante*, Wien-München

Creighton Gilbert, "Alvise Vivarini e compagni", in *Scritti di storia dell'arte in onore di Lionello Venturi*, Roma, 277-308

Richard Krautheimer and Trude Krautheimer-Hess, *Lorenzo Ghiberti*, Princeton

N. Ivanoff, *Catalogo della mostra Francesco Maffei*, Venezia

Wolfgang Lotz, "Da Raumbild in der italienischen Architekturzeichnung der Renaissance", *Mitteilungen des Kunsthistorischen Institutes in Florenz* VII, 193-226 (English revised ed. in *Studies in Renaissance Architecture*, edited by James S. Ackerman, Henry A. Millon and W. Chandler Kirwin, Cambridge-Mass.-London, 1-65)

Michelangelo Muraro, "L'esperienza di Paolo Uccello", in *Atti del XVIII congresso internazionale di storia dell'arte*, Venezia

Arnold Noach, "The Tomb of Paul III and a Point of Vasari", *Burlington Magazine* XCVIII, 376-379

Rodolfo Pallucchini, *La pittura veneziana del Quattrocento, il gotico internazionale e gli inizi del rinascimento*, Bologna

Karl T. Parker, *Catalogue of the Collection of Drawings in the Ashmolean Museum*, II, Oxford

Raffaello Sanzio, vedi E. Camesasca

Ferdinando Rossi, "La lanterna della cupola di Santa Maria del Fiore e i suoi restauri", *Bollettino d'arte* XLI, 128-143

Piero Sanpaolesi, "La lanterna di S. Maria del Fiore e il modello ligneo", *Bolletino d'arte* XLI, 11-29

Herbert Siebenhüner, "S.Giovanni dei Fiorentini in Rom (1518-34 und 1552-1614)", in *Kunstgeschichtliche Studien für Hans Kauffmann*, Berlin, 172-191

E. Baldwin Smith, *Architectural Symbolism of Imperial Rome and the Middle Ages*, Princeton

John R. Spencer, "La datazione del trattato di Filarete desunta dal suo esame interno", *Rivista d'arte* XXXI, 93-103

C.C. Vermeule, "The Dal Pozzo-Albani Drawings of Classical Antiquities. Notes on their Content and Arrangement", *Art Bulletin* XXXVIII, 31-46

Giangiorgio Zorzi, "Altri disegni di vari artisti riguardanti monumenti antichi nelle raccolte palladiane di Vicenza e Londra", *Palladio* n.s.,VI, 54-67

1957

Archivio Mediceo avanti il Principato. Inventario III, Roma

Edoardo Arslan, "L'architettura milanese del primo '500", in *Storia di Milano*, VIII, Milano, 541-544

Luciano Berti, Umberto Baldini, *Filippino Lippi*, Firenze

A. Buck, *Das Geschichtsdenken der Renaissance*, Krefeld

Janet S. Byrne, "Design for a Tomb", *Metropolitan Museum of Art Bulletin* n.s. XVI (1956-57), 155-164

H. Drerup, *Zum Ausstattungsluxus in der römischen Architektur*, Münster

E. Feinblatt, *Jacques Callot 1592-1635, exhibition catalogue* (Los Angeles, County Museum), Los Angeles

Creighton Gilbert, "Ancora di Jacopo de Barbari", *Commentari*, 155-156

Ludwig Goldscheider, *Michelangelo*, a cura di Mina Bacci, Firenze

Cecil Grayson, *An Autograph Letter from Leon Battista Alberti to Matteo de Pasti, November 18, 1454*, New York

Detlef Heikamp, "Vicende di Federico Zuccaro", *Rivista d'arte* XXXII, 175-232

Bates Lowry, "Besprechung von Ackerman, J. S., The Cortile del Belvedere", (Vatikan 1954) *Art Bulletin* XXXIX, 159-168

Eugenio Luporini, "Un libro di disegni di Giovanni Antonio Dosio", *Critica d'Arte* n.s., IV, 442-467

B. Molajoli, *Notizie su Capodimonte*, Napoli

Paola Morselli, "Ragioni di un pittore fiorentino", *L'arte* n.s., XXII, 125-161

Richard Pommer, "Drawings for the Façade of San Lorenzo by Giuliano da Sangallo", M.A. thesis, New York University

E. Rufini, *S. Giovanni dei Fiorentini*, Roma

R. Watkins, "The Authorship of the 'Vita anonyma' of Leon Battista Alberti", *Studies in the Renaissance* IV, 100-112

1957-59

Kurt Badt, "Drei plastische Arbeiten von L.B. Alberti", *Mitteilungen des Kunsthistorischen Institutes in Florence* VIII, 78-87

1958

Aldo Bertini, *I disegni italiani della Biblioteca Reale di Torino*, Roma

Anthony Blunt, *Philibert de l'Orme*, London

T. Burckhardt, *Siena*, Olten-Lausanne

Enrico Castelnuovo, "Vetrate italiane", *Paragone* IX (103), 13-24

John Fleming, "Cardinal Albani's Drawings at Windsor: Their Purchase by James Adam for George III", *Connoisseur*, 142, 164-169

Martin Gosebruch, "Florentinische Kapitele von Brunelleschi bis zum Tempio Malatestiano und der Eigenstil der Fruhrenaissance", *Römisches Jahrbuch für Kunstgeschichte* VIII, 63-191

Hermann Graf, *Bibliographie zum Problem der Proportionen, Teil I: von 1800 bis zur Gegenwart*, Speyer

H. Gundmann, "Literatus - illiteratus. Wandel einer Bildungsmorm vom Altertum bis zum Mittelalter", *Archiv für Kulturgeschichte* XL, 1-65

P.G. Hamberg, "Gio. Batt. da Sangallo detto il Gobbo e Vitruvio", *Palladio* I, 15-21

Frederick Hartt, *Giulio Romano*, New Haven

A. Hobsen, "Two Renaissance Bindings", *Book Collector* VII, 256-266

Leonardo da Vinci, see G. Zamboni

Bates Lowry, review of Ackerman, *The Cortile del Belvedere*, *Art Bulletin* XXXIX, 159-168

Mostra documentaria e iconografica della fabbrica degli Uffizi, catalogo mostra (Firenze, Archivio di Stato), Firenze

Targil Magnuson, *Studies in Roman Quattrocento Architecture*, Stockholm, also in *Figura* IX, 55 sg.

F. Mazzini, *Arte lombarda dai Visconti agli Sforza*, Milano

Paola Morselli, "Piero di Cosimo: saggio di un catalogo delle opere", *L'arte* n.s. XXIII, 67-92

B. Pesci, E. Lavagnino, *S. Pietro in Montorio*, Roma

Nicolai Rubinstein, "Political Ideas in Sienese Art: the Frescoes by Ambrogio Lorenzetti and Taddeo di Bartolo in the Palazzo Pubblico", *Journal of the Warburg and Courtauld Institutes* XXI, 179-207

Gerda Soergel, "Untersuchungen über den theoretischen Architekturentwurf von 1450-1550 in Italien", D.Phil. Diss., Köln

Roberto Weiss, "Lineamenti per una storia degli studi antiquari", *Rinascimento* IX, 141ss.

Edgar Wind, *Pagan Mysteries in the Renaissance*, London

G. Zamboni (besorgt von), *Leonardo da Vinci, Philosophische Tagebücher*, Hamburg

Giuseppe Zander, "Le invenzioni architettoniche di Gi. Batt. Montano milanese (1534-1631)", *Quaderni dell'Istituto di Storia dell'Architettura* XXX, 1-21

Giangiorgio Zorzi, *I disegni delle antichità di Andrea Palladio*, Venezia

1959

Luciano Berti, "Architettura del Cigoli", in *Mostra del Cigoli e del suo ambiente*, catalogo mostra, San Miniato, 163-192

A. Buck, "Zum Methodenstreit zwischen Humanismus und Naturwissenschaft in der Renaissance", *Sitzungsberichte der Gesellschaft zur Beförderung der gesamten Naturwissenschaften zu Marburg* LXXXI (1), 3-16

M. Casella, Giovanni Pozzi, *Francesco Colonna. Biografia e opere*, 2 voll., Padova

André Chastel [a], *Art et humanisme à Florence au temps de Laurent le Magnifique*, Paris (ed. it., Torino 1964)

—— [b], "L''etruscan revival' du XV siècle", *Revue Archéologique* I, 165-180

Luitpold Düssler, *Die Zeichnungen des Michelangelo: kritischer Katalog*, Berlin

Herbert von Einem, *Michelangelo*, Stuttgart (reprint, London 1973)

Giovanni Fiocco, *L'arte di Andrea Mantegna*, Venezia

Gustavo Giovannoni, *Antonio da Sangallo il Giovane*, 2 voll., Roma

Frederick Hartt, "The Earliest Works of Andrea del Castagno", *Art Bulletin* LXI, 151 and 225-36

G. Mardersteig, "Leon Battista Alberti e la rinascita del carattere lapidario romano nel Quattrocento", *Italia medievale e umanistica* II, 285-307

B. Molajoli, *Ritratti a Copodimonte*, Torino

Ludwig von Pastor, *Storia dei papi*, V, Roma

Elena Povoledo [a], "Italia", in *Enciclopedia dello spettacolo*, VI, Roma

—— [b], "Lanci Baldassarre", in *Enciclopedia dello spettacolo*, 1959

Howard Saalman [a], "Early Renaissance Architectural Theory and Practice in Antonio Filarete's *Trattato di architettura*", *Art Bulletin* XLI, 89-106

—— [b], "Giovanni di Gherardo da Prato's Designs Concerning the Cupola of Santa Maria del Fiore in Florence", *Journal of the Society of Architectural Historians* XVIII, 11-20

P.E. Schneider, *Rom und Romgedanke im Mittelalter*, Darmstadt

Roberto Weiss [a], "Andrea Fulvio antiquario romano (c. 1470-1527)", *Annali della scuola normale superiore di Pisa. Classe di lettere, storia e filosofia* s. 2a (XXVIII), 1-44

—— [b], "Lineamenti per una storia degli studi antiquari in Italia dal dodicesimo secolo al Sacco di Roma del 1527", *Rinascimento* IX, 141-201

Federico Zeri, "Rivedendo Piero di Cosimo", *Paragone* 115, 36-50

1960

Leon Battista Alberti, *Opere Volgari*, a cura di Cecil Grayson, I, Bari

Pietro Aretino, *Lettere sull'arte*, a cura di F. Pertile e Ettore Camesasca, Milano

Eugenio Battisti [a], *Rinascimento e Barocco*, Torino

—— [b], "La visualizzazione della scena classica nella commedia umanistica", in *Rinascimento e Barocco*, Torino

Jacob Bean, *Les dessins italiens de la Collection Bonnat*, Paris

Maria Antonietta Bonaventura, "L'industria e il commercio delle incisioni nella Roma del Cinquecento", *Studi Romani* VIII, 430-436

Renato Bonelli, *Da Bramante a Michelangelo*, Venezia

Maria Casotti Walcher, *Il Vignola*, 2 voll. Trieste

Lucia A. Ciapponi, "Il 'De Architectura' di Vitruvio nel primo Umanesimo", *Italia medievale e umanistica* III, 59-99

Andrea Da Mosto, *I dogi di Venezia nella vita pubblica e privata*, Milano

Horst De La Croix, "Military Architecture and the Radial City Plan in Sixteenth Italy", *Art Bulletin* XLII, 262-290

T. Foffano, "La costruzione di Castiglione Olona in un'opera inedita di Francesco Pizzolpasso", *Italia medievale e umanistica* II, 153-187

Paul Frankl, *The Gothic. Literary Sources and Interpretation Through Eight Centuries*, Princeton

Piero Gazzola, M. Kahnemann, *Michele Sanmicheli*, Venezia

H. Gerson and J.W. Goodison, *Fitzwilliam Museum Cambridge*. Catalogue of Paintings, I, Cambridge

Ernst H. Gombrich, "The Early Medici as Patrons of Art: A Survey of Primary Sources", in *Italian Renaissance Studies: A Tribute to the Late Cecilia M. Ady*, edited by E.F. Jacob, London, 279-311

Decio Gioseffi, *La cupola vaticana; un'ipotesi michelangiolesca*, Trieste

Cecil Grayson, "The Composition of L.B. Alberti's 'Decem libri de re aedificatoria'", *Münchner Jahrbuch* XI, 152-161

Mina Gregori (a cura di), *Mostra dei tesori segreti delle case fiorentine*, catalogo mostra, Firenze, 25-26, tav. 39

Richard Krautheimer, "Albertis Templum Hetruscum", *Kunstchronik* XIII, 364 ff.

Giuseppe Liverani, *Five Centuries of Italian Majolica*, New York-Toronto-London

Elisabeth B. MacDougall, "Michelangelo and the Porta Pia", *Journal of the Society of Architectural Historians* XIX, 97-108

F. Mancini, *Todi e i suoi castelli*, Città di Castello (2a ed. aggiornata, Perugia 1986)

Millard Meiss, "Toward a More Comprehensive Renaissance Paleography", *Art Bulletin* XLII, 231-272

C. Mitchell, "Archeology and Romance in Renaissance Italy", in *Italian Renaissance Studies*, edited by E. Jacob, London, 455-483

Morris Hicky Morgan ed., *Vitruvius. The Ten Books on Architecture*, translated by Morris Hicky Morgan, New York

Carlo Pedretti, "Il 'Neron da Sancto Andrea'", *Raccolta Vinciana* XVIII, 65-96

G. Rucellai, *Lo zibaldone quaresimale*, a cura di A. Perosa, Londra

J. Ruysschaert, "Alfarano Tiberio", voce in *Dizionario biografico degli italiani*, II, Roma, 261

Mario Salmi, "La Facciata del Tempio Malatestiano", *Commentari* XI, 244-247

Sergio Samek Ludovici, *Illustrazione del libro e incisione in Lombardia nel '400 e '500*, Modena

Armando Schiavo, "San Pietro in Vaticano, forme e strutture", *Quaderni di storia dell'arte* IX, Roma

Charles de Tolnay, *Michelangelo: The Final Period*, V, Princeton (reprint, 1971)

Vitruvio, see Morris Hicky Morgan

G. Voigt, *Die Wiederbelebung des classischen Altertums*, Berlin

Renée Watkins, "L.B. Alberti's Emblem, the Winged Eye, and His Name, Leo", *Mitteilungen des Kunsthistorisches Institutes in Florenz* IX, 256-258

B. Widmer, *E.S. Piccolomini. Papst Pius II. Biographie und ausgewählte Texte aus seinen Schrifften*, Basel-Stuttgart

Bruno Zevi, *Biagio Rossetti: Architetto ferrarese*, Torino

V.P. Zoubov, "Lèon Battista Alberti et Léonard de Vinci", *Raccolta Vinciana* XVIII, 1-14

1960-1961

Anthony Blunt, "Two Unpublished Plans of the Farnese Palace", *Metropolitan Museum of Art Bulletin* n.s., XIX, 15-17

Gustina Scaglia, "Drawings of Brunelleschi's Mechanical Inventions for the Construction of the Cupola", *Marsyas* X, 45-68

1961

James S. Ackerman, *The Architecture of Michelangelo*, 2 vols.: I text; II catalogue, London (Harmondsworth 1971; Harmondsworth-Chicago 1986)

Eugenio Battisti, "Disegni cinquecenteschi per S. Giovanni dei Fiorentini", *Quaderni dell'Istituto di storia dell'architettura* VI-VIII, 185-194

Bernard Berenson, *I disegni di pittori fiorentini*, Milano

Maria Teresa Bonadonna Russo, "Contributo alla storia della Chiesa Nuova", *Studi romani* IX, 419-427

A.M. Brown, "The Humanist Portrait of Cosimo de' Medici", *Journal of the Warburg and Courtauld Institutes* XXIV, 186-221

Raffaello Causa, "Giovanni di Francesco di Arezzo e Prospero maestri di commesso e prospettiva. Le tarsie del coro dei conversi nella certosa di San Martino", *Napoli nobilissima* I, 47-52

Maria Laura Cristiani Testi, "Ambrogio Lorenzetti e S. Miniato", *Critica d'arte*, XLVI, 37-45

Furio Fasolo, *L'opera di Hieronimo e Carlo Rainaldi (1570-1655 e 1611-1691)*, Roma

Christoph L. Frommel, *Die Farnesina und Peruzzis architektonisches Frühwerk*, Berlin

A. Frutaz, *Le piante di Roma*, Città del Vaticano

A. Ghidiglia Quintavalle, "Antonio di Vincenzo", voce in *Dizionario Biografico degli Italiani*, Roma, 581-583

Detlef Heikamp, *Scritti d'arte di Federico Zuccaro*, Firenze

E. Iversen, *The Myth of Egypt and Its Hieroglyphs in European Tradition*, Copenhague

Richard Krautheimer, "Alberti's templum etruscum", *Münchner Jahrbuch der bildenden Kunst* XII, 65-73

Millard Meiss, "Contributions to Two Elusive Masters", *Burlington Magazine* 103, 57-66

C. Mitchell, "Felice Feliciano 'antiquarius'", *Proceedings of the British Academy* LXVII, 197-221

Roberto Pane, *Andrea Palladio*, Torino (2a ed.)

Elena Povoledo [a], "Peruzzi Baldassarre", in *Enciclopedia dello spettacolo*, VIII, Roma

—— [b], "Serlio Sebastiano", in *Enciclopedia dello spettacolo*, VIII, Roma

Michelangelo Muraro, "The Statues of the Venetian Arti and the Mosaics of the Mascoli Chapel", *Art Bulletin* LXII, 263-274

Carlo Ragghianti, "Mappamundus volubilis", *Critica d'arte* XLVI, 46-49

Armando Schiavo, "Il modello della cupola di San Pietro nel suo quarto centenario", *Studi romani* IX, 519-532

D. Ternois, *Jacques Callot. Catalogue complet de son œuvre dessiné*, Paris

Federico Zeri, *Due dipinti, la filologia, un nome: il Maestro delle Tavole Barberini*, Torino

1961-1962

Günther Urban, "Die kirchen baukunst des Quattrocento in Rom", *Römisches Jahrbuch für Kunstgeschichte* IX/X, 73 sg.

1962

Paola Barocchi [a] [b], *Michelangelo e la sua scuola. I disegni di Casa Buonarroti e degli Uffizi*, 2 voll., Firenze [a] - I testo; [b] - II tavole

—— [c], *Mostra di disegni di Michelangelo*, Firenze

—— (a cura di) [d], *La vita di Michelangelo nelle redazioni del 1550 e del 1568*, di Giorgio Vasari, 5 voll., Milano-Napoli

—— (a cura di) [e], *La vita di Michelangelo nelle redazioni del 1550 e del 1568*, di Giorgio Vasari, VI, Milano-Napoli, 1740-2

A. Beijer, "An Early 16th Century Scenic Design in the National Museum, Stockholm, and its Historical Background", *Theatre Research/Recherches Théâtrales*, IV, 150ff.

Carlo Borromeo, "Instructiones fabricae et suppellectilis ecclesiastici (Milano 1577)", in *Trattati d'arte del Cinquecento...*, a cura di Paola Barocchi, Bari

Tilmann Buddensieg, "Die Konstantinsbasilika in einer Zeichnung Francescos die Giorgio und der Marmorkoloss Konstantins des Grossen", *Münchner Jahrbuch der bildenden Kunst* XIII, 37-48

Enzo Carli, *Ambrogio Lorenzetti. Dipinti su tavola*, Milano

F. Castagnoli, "Gli studi di topografia antica nel XV secolo", *Archeologia classica* XIV, 1-12

G. De Caro, "Armellini Medici, Francesco", in *Dizionario Biografico degli italiani*, IV, Roma, 234-237

A.G. Drachmann, "Nota sulle gru antiche", in *Storia della tecnologia*, a cura di Charles Singer, Eric J. Holmyard, A. Rupert Hall e Trevor I. Williams, II/2, Torino (English edition, Oxford 1956; cfr. ed. Torino 1993, 668-673)

P.A. Frutaz, *Le piante di Roma*, Roma

F. Heinemann, *Giovanni Bellini e i belliniani*, Venezia

Simon H. Levie, "Der Maler Daniele da Volterra 1509-1566", D.Phil. Diss., Universitat Basel, Köln

Wolfang Lotz, "Osservazioni intorno ai disegni palladiani", *Bollettino del Centro internazionale di studi di architettura "Andrea Palladio"* IV, 61-68

E. Menegazzo, "Per la biografia di Francesco Colonna", *Italia medievale e umanistica* V, 231-272

Luigi Michelini Tocci, "Disegni e appunti di Francesco di Giorgio in un codice del Taccola", in *Scritti di storia dell'arte in onore di Mario Salmi*, II, Roma, 203-212

C. Mitchell, "Ex libri Kiriaci Anconitani", *Italia medievale e umanistica* V, 283-299

Michele Monaco, *La Zecca vecchia in Banchi, ora detta Palazzo del Banco di Santo Spirito*, Roma

K. Morand, *Jean Poucelle*, Oxford

Peter Murray, "'Bramante milanese': the Paintings and Engravings", *Arte lombarda* VII, 25-42

Erwin Panofsky [a], "Artist, Scientist, Genius: Notes on the 'Renaissance-Dämmerung'", in *Renaissance*, New York, 123-182

—— [b], "La prima pagina del 'Libro' di Giorgio Vasari", in *Il significato delle arti visive*, Torino, 171-224

Alessandro Parronchi [a], "Leon Battista Alberti as a Painter", *Burlington Magazine* 104, 280-286

—— [b], "La prima rappresentazione della Mandragola. Il modello per l'apparato. L'allegoria", *Bibliofilia* LXIV, 37-86

Carlo Pedretti [a], *A Chronology of Leonardo's da Vinci Architectural Studies after 1500*, Geneva

—— [b], "Leonardo's Plans for the Enlargement of the City of Milan", *Raccolta vinciana* XIX, 137-147

Lionello Puppi, "La rappresentazione inaugurale dell'Olimpico. Appunti per la restituzione di uno spettacolo rinascimentale", *Critica d'arte* IX (nn.50 e 51), 57-69

Angiola Maria Romanini, "Averlino Antonio", voce in *Dizionario biografico degli italiani* IV, Roma, 662-667

Earl E. Rosenthal, "The House of Andrea Mantegna", *Gazette des beaux-arts* LX, 327-348

Piero Sanpaolesi, *Brunelleschi*, Milano

W. Savini Nicci, "Vitruvio", in *Enciclopedia dello spettacolo*, IX, Roma

D. Ternois, *L'art de Jacques Callot*, Paris

R.H.G. Thompson, "L'artigianato medievale", in *Storia della tecnologia*, a cura di Charles Singer, Eric J. Holmyard, A. Rupert Hall and Trevor I. Williams, II/2, Torino (1st edition, Oxford 1956; cfr. ed. Torino 1993, 389-403)

Wladimir Timofiewitsch, "Fassadenentwuerfe Andrea Palladios für S. Petronio in Bologna", *Arte veneta* XVI, 82-97

Roberto Weiss, "Traccia per una biografia di Annio da Viterbo", *Italia medievale e umanistica* V, 425-441

Rudolph Wittkower, *Architectural Principles in the Age of Humanism*, London (ed. italiana, *Principi architettonici nell'età dell'umanesimo*, Torino 1964)

Giuseppe Zander, "Le invenzioni architettoniche di Gi. Batt. Montano milanese (1534-1631)", *Quaderni dell'istituto di storia dell'architettura*, I/IL, 1-32

1962-63

S. Waetzoldt, "Bemerkungen zu Bramantes Tempietto", in *Sitzungsberichte der Kunstgeschichtlichen Gesellschaft zu Berlin* n.f., XI, 11-13

1962-87

Giorgio Vasari, *Le Vite de' più eccellenti pittori, scultori e architettori nelle redazioni del 1550 e 1568, Testo*, a cura di Rosanna Bettarini, commento di Paola Barocchi, 6 voll., Firenze

1963

Luciano Berti, "Nota a Maso da San Friano", *Scritti in onore di Mario Salmi III*, Roma, 77-88

Ida Maria Botto, "Alcuni aspetti dell'architettura fiorentina della seconda metà del '500", *Proporzioni* IV, 25 sg.

Bernard Berenson, *Italian Pictures of the Renaissance. The Florentine School*, London

Roberto Di Stefano, *La cupola di San Pietro*, Napoli

L. Firpo, *Leonardo architetto e urbanista*, Torino

A. Frutaz, *Le piante di Roma*, 3 voll., Città del Vaticano

Decio Gioseffi, *Giotto architetto*, Milano

Detlef Heikamp, "Zur Geschichte der Uffizien-Tribuna und der Kunstschränke in Florenz und Deutschland", *Zeitschrift für Kunstgeschichte* XXVI, 193-268

Jacob Hess, "Contributi alla storia della Chiesa Nuova (S. Maria in Vallicella)", in *Scritti di storia dell'arte in onore di Mario Salmi*, Roma, 215-238

W. Kaiser, *Praisers of Folly*, Cambridge, Mass.

Robert Klein, "Un aspect de l'herméneutique à l'age de l'humanisme classique. Le thème du fou et l'ironie humaniste", *Archivio di filosofia*, 11-25

Richard Krautheimer, "Alberti and Vitruvius", in *Studies in Western Art*, II, Princeton, 42-52

Roberto Longhi, *Piero della Francesca*, Firenze

Wolfgang Lotz, "The Roman Legacy in Jacopo Sansovino's Venetian Buildings", *Journal of the Society of Architectural Historians* XXII, 3-12 (reprinted in *Studies in Italian Renaissance Architecture*, Cambridge, Mass., 1977, 140-51)

Guido Pampaloni, *Palazzo Strozzi*, Roma (1a ed.)

Mario Pepe, "I Labacco, architetti e incisori", *Capitolium* XXXVIII, I, 25-27

Giovanni Pozzi, Lucia A. Ciapponi, "La cultura figurativa di Francesco Colonna e l'arte veneta", in V. Branca (a cura di), *Umanesimo europeo e umanesimo veneziano*, Venezia, 317-336

Lionello Puppi, *Il Teatro Olimpico*, Vicenza

E.H. Ramsden, *The Letters of Michelangelo*, 2 vols., Stanford

Avraham Ronen, "A Detail or a Whole? A Reconsideration of Two So-called Lorenzetti Landscapes in the Pinacoteca of Siena", *Mitteilungen des Kunsthistorischen Institutes in Florenz*, 286-294

Mario Salmi, introduzione a Geno Pampaloni, *Palazzo Strozzi*, Roma, 12 e sg.

Francesco Santi, *La nicchia di San Bernardino*, Milano

John R. Spencer, "Filarete's Description of a Fifteenth Century Italian Iron Smelter at Ferriere", *Technology and Culture* IV (2), 201-206

Peter Tigler, *Die Architektur Theorie des Filarete*, Berlin

Günther Urban, "Zum neubauproject von St. Peter unter Papst Nicolaus V", *Festschrift für Harald Keller*, Darmstat, 131-173

Jack Wasserman, "The Quirinal Palace in Rome", *Art Bulletin* XLV, 205-244

Rudolph Wittkower (a cura di), *Disegni de le ruine di Roma e come anticamente erono*, 2 voll., Milano

1963-64

Henri Zerner, "Etienne Dupérac en Italie", *Annuaire, Ecole Pratique des Hautes Etudes, IVe section, Sciences historiques et philologiques*, Paris, 325-326

1963-77

A. Buck, "Zur Geschichte des italienischen Selbstverständnisses im Mittelalter", in *Medium Aevum Romanicum. Festschrift für Hans Rheinfelder*, München, 63-77

1964

Le lieu théâtral à la Renaissance, Paris

Paolo Portoghesi, Bruno Zevi (a cura di), *Michelangiolo architetto*, catalogo delle opere a cura di Franco Barbieri e Lionello Puppi, Torino

Stil und Überlieferung in der Kunst des Abendlandes, Akten des 21 Internationalen Kongresses für Kunstgeschichte (Bonn, 1964) Berlin 1967

James S. Ackerman, *The Architecture of Michelangelo*, II: catalogue, London (rev. ed.)

James S. Ackerman and Wolfgang Lotz, "Vignoliana", in *Essays in Memory of Karl Lehman*, edited by L. Freeman Sandler, New York, 1-24

Franco Barbieri, Lionello Puppi [a], "Catalogo delle opere", in Paolo Portoghesi, Bruno Zevi (1964)

—— . [b], "Modello ligneo per la facciata di San Lorenzo", in *Michelangiolo architetto* (1964), 834-841

—— [c], "Progetto ed interventi per la basilica di San Pietro", in *Michelangiolo architetto* (1964), 917-919

Paola Barocchi [a], *I disegni dell'Archivio Buonarroti*, III, Firenze

—— [b], *Michelangelo. Mostra di disegni, manoscritti e documenti*, Firenze

Aldo Bertini, "La facciata e la Sacrestia Nuova di San Lorenzo", in *Michelangiolo architetto* (1964), 121-208

Sergio Bertini, "La fabbrica di San Pietro", in *Michelangiolo architetto* (1964), 497-608

Giuseppe Billanovich, "La prima lettera del Salutati a Giovanni di Montreuil", *Italia medievale e umanistica* VII, 337-350

P. Bjurström, "Espace scénique et durée de l'action dans le théâtre italien du XVIe siècle et de la première moitié du XVIIe siècle", dans *Le lieu théâtral...* (1964), 73-84

Wolfgang Braunfels, *Der Dom von Florenz*, Lausanne-Freiburg

Anna Maria Brizio, in *Raccolta vinciana* XX, 402

Antonio Cassi Ramelli, *Luca Beltrami e il Duomo di Milano*, Milano

Francesco Colonna, *Hypnerotomachia Poliphili*, a cura di Giovanni Pozzi e Lucia A. Ciapponi, 2 voll., Padova (ristampa, 1980); ripubblicato in Arnaldo Bruschi et al., *Scritti rinascimentali di architettura*, Milano 1978; English translation: L. Fierz-David, *The Dream of Poliphilo*, New York 1950

Christoph L. Frommel, "Antonio da Sangallos Cappella Paolina", *Zeitschrift für Kunstgeschichte* XXVII, 1-42

Creighton Gilbert, "Barbari Jacopo", voce in *Dizionario biografico degli italiani*, VI, Roma, 44-45

Decio Gioseffi [a], "S. Giovanni dei Fiorentini", in *Michelangiolo architetto* (1964), 653-669

—— [b], "Porta Pia", in *Michelangelo architetto* (1964), 727-736

Robert Klein, Henri Zerner, "Vitruve et le théâtre de la Renaissance italienne", dans *Le lieu théâtral...* (1964), 49-60

Wolfgang Lotz [a], "Zu Michelangelos Kopien nachdem Codex Coner", in *Stil und Überlieferung...* (1964), II, 12-19

—— [b], "Notizien zu kirchlichen Zentralbau der Renaissance", in *Studien zur toskanischen Kunst*, Festschrift L.H. Heydenreich, München, 157 ss. (reprinted in *Studies in Italian Renaissance Architecture*, Cambridge, Mass., 1977, 66-73; ed. it., Milano 1989, 43-47)

—— [c], "The Planning and Building of Il Gesù in Rome, 1568-1577: A Digest of the Documents", in James S. Ackerman and Wolfang Lotz in "Vignoliana", in *Essays in Memory of Karl Lehman*, edited by L. Freeman Sandler, New York, 14-19

Eugenio Luporini, *Brunelleschi*, Milano

E. Mandowsky and C. Mitchell, *Pirro Ligorio's Roman Antiquities*, London

C. Molinari, "Les rapports entre la scène et les spectateurs", in *Stil und Überlieferung...* (1964), 61-71

A.M. Nagler, *Theatre Festivals of the Medici*, New Haven

Erwin Panofsky, *Tomb Sculpture: Aspects from Ancient Egypt to Bernini*, New York

ALESSANDRO PARRONCHI [a], "Le due tavole prospettiche del Brunelleschi", in *Studi su la dolce prospettiva*, Milano, 226-295

—— [b], *Studi su la dolce prospettiva*, Milano

ANGIOLA MARIA ROMANINI, *L'architettura gotica in Lombardia*, Milano

EARL E. ROSENTHAL, "The Antecedents of Bramante's Tempietto", *Journal of the Society of Architectural Historians* XXIII, 55-74

FERDINANDO ROSSI, *Il bel San Giovanni, Santa Maria del Fiore, l'Opera del Duomo*, Firenze

HOWARD SAALMAN, "Santa Maria del Fiore: 1294-1418", *Art Bulletin* XLVI, 471-500

GUSTINA SCAGLIA, "The Origin of an Archeological Plan by Alessandro Strozzi", *Journal of the Warburg and Courtauld Institutes* XXVII, 137-159

VINCENZO SCAMOZZI, *L'idea della architettura universale* (1615), ed. Royal Institute of British Architects, 2 vols., Ridgewood, N.J.

JULIUS SCHLOSSER MAGNINO, *Die Kunstliteratur*, Wien, Otto Kurz

CHARLES DE TOLNAY [a], *The Art and Thought of Michelangelo*, translation by Charles de Tolnay, New York

—— [b], "Michelangelo", in *Encyclopedia of World Art*, IX, New York, cols. 861-914

RUDOLPH WITTKOWER, *La cupola di San Pietro di Michelangelo*, Firenze

—— [b], *Principi architettonici nell'età dell'Umanesimo*, Torino

1964-65

PIERO SANPAOLESI, "Architetti premichelangioleschi toscani", *Rivista dell'istituto nazionale di archeologia e storia dell'arte* XIII-XIV, 269 e sg.

1965

Michelangelo artista-pensatore-scrittore, 2 voll., Novara (ripubblicato nel 1980 in 1 vol.)

A. BARELLI, vedi Antonio Condivi

PAOLA BAROCCHI, CHARLES DE TOLNAY, and MARIO SALMI, *Drawings of Michelangelo*, New York

H. BAUER, *Kunst und Utopie. Studien über das Kunst-und Staatsdenken in der Renaissance*, Berlin

J. BEAN, F. STAMPFLE, *Drawings from New York Collections, I The Italian Renaissance*, New York

LUCIANO BERTI, "I disegni", in *Michelangelo artista...* (1965), 389-507

WOLFGANG BRAUNFELS, "Drei Bemerkungen zur Geschichte und Konstruktion der Florentiner Domkuppel", *Mitteilungen des Kunsthistorischen Institutes in Florenz*, September, 203-226

MAURIZIO CALVESI, "Identificato l'autore del *Polifilo*", *Europa letteraria artistica cinematografica* VI, 9-20

AUGUSTO CAMPANA, "Basinio da Parma", voce in *Dizionario Biografico degli Italiani*, VII, Roma, 89-98

P. CANNON BROOKES, "Three Notes on Maso da San Friano", *Burlington Magazine* CVII (745), 192-196

ENZO CARLI, *Il duomo di Orvieto*, Roma

ANDRÉ CHASTEL, *I centri del rinascimento*, Torino

ASCANIO CONDIVI, *Vita di Michelangelo Buonarroti*, a cura di E. Barelli, Milano

ALVISE CORNARO, "Trattato d'architettura" in Giuseppe Fiocco, Alvise Cornaro. Il suo tempo e le sue opere, Vicenza, 156 ss.

FRANÇISE COULANGES-ROSENBERG ET AL., *Le XVIe siècle européen; peintures et dessins dans les collections publiques françaises*, catalogue exposition (Paris, Petit Palais), Paris

GUGLIELMO DE ANGELIS D'OSSAT, "L'architettura", in *Michelangelo artista...* (1965), 277-387

BERNHARD DEGENHART, "Der Entwurf zur Cappella del Campo in Siena, in Studien zur Geschichte der Europäischen Bauplastik, *Festschrift Theodor Müller*, München, 93-100

CESARE D'ONOFRIO, *Gli obelischi di Roma*, Roma

EVERETT P. FAHY JR., "Some Later Works of Piero di Cosimo", *Gazette des beaux-arts* LXV, 206-212

VINCENZO FASOLO, *Michelagniolo, architector, poeta*, Genova

FILARETE, see John R. Spencer

ERIK FORSSMAN, *Palladios Lehrgebäude. Studien über den Zusammenhang von Architektur und Architekturtheorie bei Andrea Palladio*, Stockholm

PIERRE FRANCASTEL, "Imagination et réalité dans l'architecture civile du Quattrocento", dans *La réalité figurative*, Paris, 290-302

K. FRECKMANN, *Proportionen in der Architektur*, München

EUGENIO GARIN, *Scienza e vita civile nel rinascimento italiano*, Bari

E. VON JVÁNKA (Hrsg.), *Europa im XV. Jahrhundert von Byzantinern gesehen*, Graz-Wien-Köln

R.K. MERTON, *On the Shoulders of Giants. A Shandean Postscript*, New York

GIOVANNI POGGI, *Il carteggio di Michelangelo*, a cura di Paola Barocchi e Renzo Ristori, I, Firenze

G. PONTANO, *I trattati delle virtù sociali*, a cura di F. Tateo, Roma

JOHN POPE-HENNESSY, *Renaissance Bronzes from the Samuel Kress Collection*, London

P. POUNCEY, *Lotto designatore*, Vicenza

UGO PROCACCI, *La Casa Buonarroti a Firenze*, Milano

CARLO RAGGHIANTI, "Tempio Malestatiano", *Critica d'arte*, fasc. 71, 23-32; fasc. 74, 27-39

C.E. RAVA, *Scenografie del Museo Teatrale alla Scala dal XVI al XIX secolo*, catalogo mostra (Venezia, Fondazione Giorgio Cini), Venezia

LADISLAO RETI [a], "A Postscript to the Filarete Discussion. On Horizontal Waterwheels and Smelter Blowers in the Writings of Leonardo da Vinci and Juanelo Turriano", *Technology and Culture* VI (3), 428-41

—— [b], «Tracce di progetti perduti di Filippo Brunelleschi nel Codice Atlantico,» (IV Lettura vinciana, 15 aprile 1964), Firenze 91-222 (ripubblicato in *Leonardo da Vinci letto e commentato*, Firenze 1974)

H. ROMBACH, *Substanz, System, Struktur*, Freiburg-München

ANGIOLA MARIA ROMANINI, "Giotto e l'architettura gotica in alta Italia", *Bollettino d'arte* L, 160-180

ARMANDO SCHIAVO, "Questioni anagrafe e tecniche sul modello della cupola di San Pietro", *Studi romani* XIII, 303-327

GIORGIO SIMONCINI, *Gli architetti nella cultura del Rinascimento*, Bologna

STAALE SINDING-LARSEN, "Some Functional and Iconographical Aspects of the Centralized Church in the Italian Renaissance", *Acta ad archaeologiam et artium historiam pertinentia* II, 203-252

CURTIS SHELL, "Francesco D'Antonio and Masaccio", *Art Bulletin* XLVII, 465-469

JOHN R. SPENCER, *Filarete's Treatise on Architecture*, New Haven-London

CHRISTOF THOENES, "Review of R. Wittkower's Disegni de le ruine di Roma come antiche erono", *Kunstchronik* XVIII, 10-20

CHARLES DE TOLNAY, "A Forgotten Architectural Project by Michelangelo: The Choir of the Cathedral of Padua", in *Festschrift für Herbert von Einem*, Berlin, 247-251

Les trésors des eglises de France, catalogue exposition (Paris, Musée des Arts Décoratifs), Paris

ROBERTO WEISS, "The Medals of Pope Julius II (1503-1513)", *Journal of the Warburg and Courtauld Institutes* XXVIII, 163-182

HEINRICH W. WURM, *Der Palazzo Massimo alle Colonne*, Berlin

HENRI ZERNER, "Observations on Dupérac and 'the Disegni de le ruine di Roma e come antiche erono'", *Art Bulletin* XLVII, 507-512

GIANGIORGIO ZORZI [a], *Le opere pubbliche e i palazzi privati di Andrea Palladio*, Venezia

—— [b], "Le prospettive del Teatro Olimpico di Vicenza nei disegni degli Uffizi di Firenze e nei documenti dell'Ambrosiana di Milano", *Arte lombarda* X, 70-97

1965-83

Il carteggio di Michelangelo, edizione postuma di Giovanni Poggi, a cura di Paola Barocchi e Renzo Ristori, 5 voll.: II 1967; III 1973; IV 1979; V 1983, Firenze

1966

Arte in Europa. Scritti di storia dell'arte in onore di Edoardo Arslan, 2 voll., Milano

Atti del convegno di studi michelangioleschi (Firenze-Roma 1964), Roma

The Complete Work of Michelangelo, 2 vols., London

JAMES S. ACKERMAN [a], *The Architect and Society. Palladio*, Harmondsworth

—— [b], *Palladio*, Milano

LEON BATTISTA ALBERTI [a], vedi Giovanni Orlandi e Paolo Portoghesi

—— [b], vedi Cecil Grayson

MINA BACCI, *Piero di Cosimo*, Milano

H. BARON, *The Crisis of the Early Italian Renaissance*, Princeton

LUCIANO BERTI, "Drawings", in *The Complete Work...* (1966), II, 377-495

ROSANNA BETTARINI E PAOLA BAROCCHI, a cura di, Giorgio Vasari, *Le vite de' più eccellenti pittori, scultori e architettori nelle redazioni del 1550 e del 1568* (1962-1987) I, Firenze

EVE BORSOOK, *Ambrogio Lorenzetti*, Firenze

HOWARD BURNS, "A Peruzzi Drawing in Ferrara", *Mitteilungen des Kunsthistorischen Institutes in Florenz* XII, 245-250

P. CANNON BROOKES, "The Portraits of Maso da San Friano", *Burlington Magazine* 108, 560-568

L. CASTELFRANCHI VEGAS, "I rapporti Italia-Fiandra", *Paragone* 201, 42-69

ENRICO CASTELNUOVO, "Vetrata", voce in *Enciclopedia universale dell'arte*, XIV, 744-766

LUISA COGLIATI ARANO, *Disegni di Leonardo e della sua cerchia alla Gallerie dell'Accademia*, catalogo mostra, Venezia

GINO CORTI, ALESSANDRO PARRONCHI, "Michelangelo al tempo dei lavori di San Lorenzo in una ricordanza del Figiovanni", in *Atti del convegno...* (1966), 322-328

GUGLIELMO DE ANGELIS D'OSSAT [a], "Architecture", in *The Complete Work...* (1966), II, 273-376

—— [b], "Preludio romano del Bramante", *Palladio* n.s., XVI, 83-102

—— [c], "Uno sconosciuto modello di Michelangelo per S. Maria del Fiore", in *Arte in Europa...* (1966), 501-504

RAYMOND DE ROOVER, *The Rise and Decline of the Medici Bank*, 1397-1494, New York

H. DRERUP, "Architektur als Symbol. Zur zeitgenössischen Bewertung der römischen Architektur", GYMNASIUM LXXIII, 181-196

ALBRECHT DÜRER, *Underweysung der Messung mit Zirckel und Richtscheydt* (Nürnberg 1525), Zürich, fac simile ausgabe

JOHN GERE (a cura di), *Mostra di disegni degli Zuccari*, Firenze

ERNST H. GOMBRICH, *Norm and Form*, London

CECIL GRAYSON (a cura di), *Leon Battista Alberti. Opere volgari*, Bari

G. HAMBERG, "Vitruvius, Fra' Giocondo and the City of Naples", *Acta archaeologica* XXXVI, 105-125

M. KAHR, "Titian, the *Hypnerotomachia Poliphili* Woodcuts and Antiquity", *Gazette des beaux-arts* LXV, 119-127

P. KOSCHAKER, *Europa und das römische Recht*, München-Berlin

LICISCO MAGAGNATO, *Palazzo Thiene*, Vicenza

PAOLO MARCONI, "Contributo alla storia delle fortificazioni di Roma nel Cinquecento e nel Seicento", *Quaderni dell'istituto di storia dell'architettura* XIII, 109-130

KARL NOEHLES, "Die Kunst der Cosmaten und die Idee der Renovatio Romae", in *Festschrift Werner Hager*, Recklinghausen, 16-37

KONRAD OBERHUBER, "Eine unbekannte Zeichnung Raffaels in den Uffizien", *Mitteilungen des Kunsthistorischen Institutes in Florenz* XII, 225-244

GIOVANNI ORLANDI, PAOLO PORTOGHESI (a cura di), *L'architettura [De Re Aedificatoria]*, traduzione dal latino di Giovanni Orlandi, introduzione e note di Paolo Portoghesi, 2 voll., Milano

ROBERTO PANE, "Michelangelo nella Basilica Vaticana", in *Atti del convegno...* (1966), 379-397

ALESSANDRO PARRONCHI [a], "Di un manoscritto attribuito a Francesco di Giorgio Martini", *Atti e memorie dell'accademia toscana di scienze e lettere 'La Colombaria'*, XXXI, 165-213

—— [b], "Una ricordanza inedita del Figiovanni sui lavori della Cappella e delle Librerie Medicee", *Atti del convegno...* (1966), 322-342

JOHN POPE HENNESSY, *The Portrait in the Renaissance*, London-New York

PAOLO PORTOGHESI, "Le architetture fiorentine di Michelangelo", *Atti del convegno...* (1966), 201-227

LIONELLO PUPPI, "Prospettive dell'Olimpico, documenti dell'Ambrosiana e altre cose: argomenti per una replica", *Arte lombarda* XI, 26-32

M. REGOLIOSI, "Nuove ricerche intorno a Giovanni Tortelli", *Italia medioevale e umanistica* IX, 129-89

MARCO ROSCI (a cura di), *Il trattato di architettura di Sebastiano Serlio*, Milano

PIERO SANPAOLESI, "Sulla antica facciata di S. Maria del Fiore", in *Arte in Europa...* (1966), 309-323

ARMANDO SCHIAVO, "Gli autografi di Michelangelo nell'Archivio della Fabbrica di S. Pietro", *Strenna dei romanisti* XXVII, 426-31

CHARLES SEYMOUR JR., *Sculpture in Italy 1400-1500*, Harmondsworth

HEINZ SPIELMANN, *Andrea Palladio und die Antike. Untersuchung und Katalog der Zeichnungen aus seinem Nachlass*, München-Berlin

MANFREDO TAFURI, *L'architettura del Manierismo nel Cinquecento europeo*, Roma

CHARLES DE TOLNAY, "Michelangelo a Firenze", in *Atti del convegno...* (1966), 3-22

L. VAGNETTI, "La 'Descriptio urbis Romae', uno scritto poco noto di Leon Battista Alberti", *Quaderno. Università di Genova, facoltà di architettura* I, 25-78

C.C. VERMEULE, "The Dal Pozzo-Albani Drawings of Classical Antiquities in the Royal Library at Windsor Castle", *Transaction of American Philosophical Society*, n.s., LXVI/II

J. WASSERMAN, *Ottavio Mascherino*, Roma

J. WHITE, *Art and Architecture in Italy 1250 to 1400*, Harmondsworth

MATTHIAS WINNER, "Neues zu Dupérac in Rom", *Kunstchronik* XIX, 308-309

RUDOLPH WITTKOWER, *Gian Lorenzo Bernini, the Sculptor of the Roman Baroque*, London (2nd ed.)

GIANGIORGIO ZORZI, *Le chiese e i ponti di Andrea Palladio*, Vicenza

1966-1967

M.C. BONAGURA, "S. Maria della Consolazione a Todi", tesi di laurea, Facoltà di lettere dell'università di Roma

JANET S. BYRNE, "Monuments on Paper", *Metropolitan Museum of Art Bulletin* n.s. XXV, 24-29

1966-82

GIORGIO VASARI, *Le vite de' più eccellenti pittori, scultori e architettori nelle redazioni del 1550 e del 1568*, a cura di Rosanna Bettarini e Paola Barocchi, Firenze

1967

FRANCO BARBIERI, "Francesco Zamberlan architetto de 'La Rotonda'", in *La rotonda di Rovigo*, Venezia, 37-72

LUCIANO BERTI, *Il Principe dello Studiolo. Francesco I dei Medici e la fine del Rinascimento fiorentino*, Firenze

Bibliotheca Sanctorum, Grottaferrata, vol. VIII, 320-342; vol. X, 521-532

ARNALDO BRUSCHI, "Orientamento di gusto e indicazioni di teoria in alcuni disegni architettonici del Quattrocento", *Quaderni dell'istituto di storia dell'architettura XIV*, 41-52

DAVID R. COFFIN, "The Plans of the Villa Madama", *Art Bulletin* XLIX, 111-122

GUGLIELMO DE ANGELIS D'OSSAT, "Architecture", in *The Complete Work of Michelangelo*, New York (ed. it. Michelangelo artista-pensatore-scrittore, 2 voll., Novara 1965; London ed. in 2 vols., 1966)

MAURIZIO FAGIOLO DELL'ARCO, MARCELLO FAGIOLO, *Bernini, una introduzione al gran teatro del barocco*, Roma

T. DOMBART, *Die sieben Weltwunder der Altertums*, München

MAZZINO FOSSI, *Bartolomeo Ammannati architetto*, Cava dei Tirreni

FRANCESCO DI GIORGIO MARTINI, *Trattati di architettura, ingegneria e arte militare*, a cura di Corrado Maltese, trascrizione di Livia Maltese Degrassi, 2 voll., Milano

CHRISTOPH L. FROMMEL, "S. Eligio und die Kuppel der Cappella Medici", in *Stil und Überlieferung in der Kunst des Abendlandes. Akten des 21. Internationalen Kongresses für Kunstgeschichte (Bonn 1964)*, Berlin, 41-54

J. GRAHAM POLLARD, *Renaissance Medals from the Samuel H. Kress Collection at the National Gallery of Art*, London

DETLEF HEIKAMP, "Federico Zuccari a Firenze (1575-1579). I. La cupola del duomo. Il diario disegnato", *Paragone* 205, 44-68

JACOB HESS, "Contributi alla storia della Chiesa Nuova (S. Maria in Vallicella)", in *Kunstgeschichtliche Studien zu Renaissance und Barock*, Rom, 353-367

LUDWIG H. HEYDENREICH [a], "Bramante's 'ultima maniera': Die St. Peter-Studien Uff. arch. 8 v. und 20", in *Essays in the History of Architecture Presented to Rudolf Wittkower*, New York, 60-63

—— [b], "Entstehung der Villa und Ländlichen Residenz im 15. Jahrhundert", *Acta historiae artium* XIII, 9-12

HOWARD HIBBARD, "Di alcune licenze rilasciate dai mastri di strade per opere di edificazione a Roma (1586-89, 1602-34)", *Bollettino d'arte* LII, 99-117

A. HORN-ONCKEN, *Über das Schickliche. Studien zur Geschichte der Architekturtheorie*, I, Göttingen

E. KIRSTEN, W. KREIKER, *Griechenlandkunde. Ein Führer zu klassischen Stätten*, Heidelberg

E. KRETZULESCO QUARANTA, "L'itinerario spirituale di "Polifilo", uno studio necessario per determinare la paternità dell'opera", *Atti della accademia nazionale dei Lincei. Rendiconti* 344, serie 8 (XXII), 269-283

CAROL HERSELLE KRINSKY, "Seventy-eight Vitruvius Manuscripts", *Journal of the Warburg and Courtauld Institutes* XXX, 36-70

JAMES LEES-MILNE, *St. Peter's*, London

WOLFANG LOTZ, " Zu Michelangelo Kopien nach dem Codex Coner", *Stil und Überlieferung in der Kunst des Abendlandes. Akten des XXI. internationalen Kongresses für Kunstgeschichte* II (Bonn, 1964) Berlin 12-19

CORRADO MALTESE , LIVIA MALTESE DE GRASSI (a cura di), vedi Francesco di Giorgio Martini

G. MANDEL, *L'opera completa di Antonello da Messina*, Milano

PETER MURRAY, "Menicantonio, Du Cerceau, and the Towers of St. Peter's", in *Studies in Renaissance and Baroque Art Presented to Anthony Blunt on his 60th Birthday*, London-New York, 7-11

D. SANMINIATELLI, *Domenico Beccafumi*, Milano

K. SCHWAGER, "Unbekannte Zeichnungen Jacopo del Duca's", in *Stil und Überlieferung in der Kunst des Abendlandes. Akten des XXI internationalen, Kongresses für Kunstgeschichte* II (Bonn, 1964), Berlin 12-19

CHARLES SEYMOUR JR., *Michelangelo's David; A Search for Identity*, Pittsburgh

MAURICE SHAPIRO, "A Renaissance Birth Plate", *Art Bulletin* IL, 236-243

HEINRICH THELEN, *Francesco Borromini. Die Handzeichnungen*, I, (Abt. Zeitraum von 1620/32), 2 Bde., Graz

CHARLES DE TOLNAY, "Newly Discovered Drawings Related to Michelangelo: The Scholz Scrapbook in the Metropolitan Museum of Art", in *Stil und Überlieferung in der Kunst des Abendlandes, Akten des 21. Internationalen Kongresses für Kunstgeschichte (Bonn 1964)*, II, Berlin, 64-68

L. VAGNETTI vedi 1966

M. WEINBERGER, *Michelangelo the Sculptor*, London-New York

JOHN WILTON-ELY, "The Architectural Model", *Architectural Review* CXLII, 845, 25-32

GIANGIORGIO ZORZI, *Le chiese e i ponti di Andrea Palladio*, [Venezia]

1967-1968

PHILIP FOSTER, "Raphael on the Villa Madama: the Text of a Lost Letter", *Römisches Jahrbuch für Kunstgeschichte* XI, 308-312

CHRISTOPH L. FROMMEL, "Baldassarre Peruzzi als Maler und Zeichner", *Römisches Jahrbuch für Kunstgeschichte* XI, 1-183

FRANZ GRAF WOLFF METTERNICH, "Der Kupferstich Bernardos de Prevedari aus Mailand von 1841", *Römisches Jahrbuch für Kunstgeschichte* XI, 9 ff.

1968

JAMES S. ACKERMAN, *L'architettura di Michelangelo*, Torino

HERMANN ALKER, *Michelangelo und seine Kuppel von St. Peter in Rom*, Karlsruhe

H. BARON, *From Petrarca to Leonardo Bruni. Studies in Humanistic and Political Literature*, Chicago-London

EUGENIO BATTISTI, "La visualizzazione della scena classica nella commedia umanistica", in *Rinascimento e Barocco*, Torino

LUISA BECHERUCCI, GIULIA BRUNETTI, *Il Museo dell'Opera del Duomo a Firenze*, Firenze [dopo il 1968]

JAMES H. BECK, "The Historical 'Taccola' and Imperator Sigismund", *Art Bulletin* L, 309-320

SANDRO BENEDETTI, *Santa Maria di Loreto*, Roma

MARIA TERESA BONADONNA RUSSO, "I Cesi e la Congregazione dell'Oratorio", *Archivio della società romana di storia patria* XCI, 101-155

IDA MARIA BOTTO, *Mostra di disegni di Bernardo Buontalenti (1531-1608)*, catalogo mostra, Firenze

CESARE BRANDI, *Michelangelo e la curva della cupola di San Pietro*, Roma (anche in *Struttura e architettura*, Torino 1967, 242-266)

A. BUCK, *Die humanistische Tradition in der Romania*, Bad Homburg,Berlin-Zürich,

TILMANN BUDDENSIEG, "Raffaels Grab", in *Munuscula Disciplinorum, Kunsthistorische Studien für Hans Kaufmann*, Berlin

OTELLO CAPRARA, "Il modello della lanterna di Santa Maria del Fiore", in *Catalogo della mostra di restauri di sculture e oggetti d'arte minore*, Firenze, 28, n. 34

FABRIZIO CRUCIANI, *Il teatro del Campidoglio e le feste romane del 1513*, Milano

S. DAMIANI, G. PANAZZA, *Mostra di stampe francesi del '500 e del '600*, catalogo mostra (Brescia, Civica Pinacoteca Tosio Martinengo), Brescia

M. DAWID, *Weltwunder der Antike*, Frankfurt

BERNHARDT DEGENHART, ANNEGRIT SCHMITT, *Corpus der italienischen Ziechnungen 1300-1450 (1968-1980)*, Berlin

L. DONATI, "Polifila a Roma: il Mausoleo di S. Costanza", BIBLIOFILIA LXX, 1-38

RICHARD GOLDTHWAITE, *Private Wealth in Renaissance Florence: A Study of Four Families*, Princeton

VINCENZO GOLZIO, GIUSEPPE ZANDER, *L'arte in Roma nel secolo XV*, Roma

C. GRONDONA, *Todi storica ed artistica*, Todi (2a ed.; 6a ed. ampliata, 1981)

E. JEAUNEAU, "Nains et geants", in *Entretiens sur la Renaissance du 12e siècle*, Paris-Den Haag, 21-38

CHRISTIANE KLAPISCH-ZUBER, "Tradition technique et révolution commerciale à Carrare (XVe-XVIe siècles)", *Mausolée* XXXVI (384), 1801-1816

E. KNAB, *Jacques Callot und sein Kreis*, Ausstellungs katalog (Wien, Graphische Sammlung Albertina), Wien

E.R. KNAUER, *Das Reiterstandbild des Kaisers Marc Aurel*, Stuttgart

S. LANG, "Leonardo's Designs for the Sforza Mausoleum", *Journal of the Warburg and Courtauld Institutes* XXXI, 218-233

IRVING LAVIN, *Bernini and the Crossing of Saint Peter's*, New York

GIUSEPPE MARCHINI, "Le architetture", in *Raffaello. L'opera. Le fonti. La fortuna*, Novara, II, 431-492

PAOLO MARCONI, "Una chiave per l'interpretazione dell'urbanistica rinascimentale: la cittadella come microcosmo", *Quaderni dell'istituto di storia dell'architettura dell'università di Roma*, 85-90

Mostra di restauri di sculture e oggetti d'arte minore, Firenze

F. PANVINI ROSATI, *Medaglie e placchette italiane dal Rinascimento*, Roma

ALESSANDRO PARRONCHI [a], "Due note, 2. Urbino-Baltimora-Berlino", *Rinascimento* XIX (dicembre), 355-361

—— [b], *Opere giovanili di Michelangelo*, Firenze

CRISTINA PIACENTI ASCHENGREEN, *Il Museo degli Argenti a Firenze*, Milano

FRANK D. PRAGER, "A Manuscript of Taccola Quoting Brunelleschi on Problems of Inventors and Builders", *Proceeding of the American Philosophical Society* 112, 131-149

PAUL L. ROSE, "The Taccola Manuscript", *Physis* X, 337-346

B. RUPPRECHT, "Sanmicheli Villa Soranza", in *Festschrift Ulrich Middeldorf*, Berlin, 324-332

HOWARD SAALMAN, "The Baltimore and Urbino Panels: Cosimo Rosselli", *Burlington Magazine* CX, (784), 376-383

GUSTINA SCAGLIA, "An Allegorical Portrait of Emperor Sigismund by Mariano Taccola of Siena", *Journal of the Warburg and Courtauld Institutes* XXXI, 428-434

MANFREDO TAFURI, "Teatro e città nell'architettura palladiana", *Bollettino del centro internazionale di studi di architettura «Andrea Palladio»* X, 65-78

CHRISTOF THOENES, "Bemerkungen zur Petersfassade Michelangelos", *Munuscula Disciplinorum, Kunsthistorische Studien für Hans Kaufmann*, Berlin, 331-341

JOHN WILTON-ELY, "The Architectural Model: English Baroque", *Apollo* LXXXVIII, 80, 250-259

1968-69

KENNETH CLARK, *The Drawings of Leonardo da Vinci in the Collection of Her Majesty the Queen at Windsor Castle, Second Edition Revised with the Assistance of C. Pedretti*, 3 vols., Oxford

BERNHARD DEGENHART, ANNEGRIT SCHMITT, *Corpus der Italienischen Zeichnungen 1300-1450*, 8. Bde., Berlin

1969

Il Duomo di Milano, Atti del convegno internazionale (Milano 1968), a cura di Maria Luisa Gatti Perer, Milano

Studies in Early Christian, Medieval and Renaissance Art, New York

G.C. BASCAPÈ, *Sigillografia*, Milano

EUGENIO BATTISTI, "Avanguardia e conservatorismo nella storia del Duomo di Milano", in *Il Duomo di Milano* (1969), II, 43-52

JAMES H. BECK, "Introduzione", in *Taccola, Liber tertius de ingeneis ac edifitiis non usitatis*, a cura di James H. Beck, Milano, 12 e sg.

EKART BERCKENHAGEN, "Hugues Sambin und der Anonymus Destailleur", *Berliner Museen* XIX, 65-74

HARMUT BIERMANN, "Lo sviluppo della villa toscana sotto l'influenza umanistica della corte di Lorenzo il Magnifico", *Bollettino del centro internazionale di studi di architettura «Andrea Palladio»* XI, 36-46

Bibliotheca Corviniana. The Library of King Matthias Corvinus of Hungary, edited by C. Csapodi, K. Csapodi-Gardonyi and T. Szanto, Shannon

GENE A. BRUCKER, *Renaissance Florence*, New York

ARNALDO BRUSCHI [a], *Bramante architetto*, Bari (2a ed. 1973)

—— [b], "Orientamenti di gusto e indicazioni di teoria in alcuni disegni architettonici del Quattrocento", *Quaderni dell'Istituto di Storia dell'Architettura*, serie 14, fasc. 79-84, 41-52

P. BURKE, "The Sense of Historical Perspective in Renaissance Italy", *Journal of World History* XI, 615-632

CESARE CESARIANO, vedi Krinsky (Hrsg.)

CESARE DE SETA, *Cartografia della città di Napoli. Lineamenti dell'evoluzione urbana*, Napoli (2a ed.1975)

A. ESCH, "Die Wiederverwendung antiker Baustücke und Skulpturen im mittelalterlichen Italien", in *Archiv für Kulturgeschichte* LI, 1-64

KURT FORSTER, "FROM 'ROCCA' TO 'CIVITAS': URBAN PLANNING AT SABBIONETA", *L'arte* V

CHRISTOPH L. FROMMEL [a], "Bramantes 'Ninphaeum' in Genazzano", *Römische Jahrbuch für Kunstgeschichte* XII, 137-160

—— [b], "La villa Madama e le tipologia della villa romana nel Rinascimento", *Bollettino del centro internazionale di studi di architettura «Andrea Palladio»* XI, 47-64

J. GADOL, *Leon Battista Alberti. Universal Man of the Early Renaissance*, Chicago-London

MARIA LUISA GATTI PERER, "Ipotesi iconografiche per il Duomo di Milano", in *Il Duomo di Milano* (1969), 1-29

GIOVANNA GAETA BERTELÀ, ANNA PETRIOLI TOFANI (a cura di), *Feste e apparati medicei da Cosimo I a Cosimo II*, catalogo mostra (Firenze, Gabinetto Disegni e Stampe degli Uffizi), Firenze

POMPONIO GAURICUS, *De Sculptura*, sous la direction et traduction de André Chastel et Robert Klein, Genève-Paris

JOHN A. GERE, *Taddeo Zuccaro*, Chicago

The Golden Legend of Jacobus de Voragine, translated by Granger Ryan and Helmut Ripperger, New York (2nd ed.; 1st ed. 1941) adapted from *Jacobus de Voragine, Legenda Aurea, Vulgo historia lombardica dicta*, hrsg. Th. Graesse, Leipzig 1850

HUBERTUS GÜNTHER, "Uffizien 135 A - eine Studie Baroccis", *Mitteilungen des Kunsthistorischen Institutes in Florenz* XIV, 239-246

Georg H. Hersey, Alfonso II and the Artistic Renewal of Naples 1485-1495, New Haven-London

J.M. HUSKINSON, "The Crucifixion of St. Peter: A Fifteenth-century Topographical Problem", *Journal of the Warburg and Courtauld Institutes* XXXII, 135-161

H. KEUTNER, *Sculpture: Renaissance to Rococo*, London

RICHARD KRAUTHEIMER [a], "Alberti and Vitruvius", in *Studies...* (1969), 323-332

—— [b], "Alberti's Templum Etruscum", *Münchner Jahrbuch der bildenden Kunst* III. Folge XII, 65-72

—— [c], "The Beginnings of Art Historical Writing in Italy", translated by Cecil L. Striker, in *Studies...* (1969), 257-273

—— [d], "The Tragic and Comic Scene of the Renaissance: The Baltimore and Urbino Panels", in *Studies...* (1969), 345-360

RICHARD KRAUTHEIMER and TRUDE KRAUTHEIMER-HESS, "Humanists and Artists", in *Studies...* (1969), 295-309

CAROL HERSELLE KRINSKY (Hrsg.), *Vitruvius, De architectura: Nachdruck der kommentierten ersten italienischen Ausgabe von Cesare Cesariano* (Como, 1521), München

RENATO LEFÈVRE, "Su una lettera di Raffaello riguardante Villa Madama", *Studi romani* XVII, 425-437

ANTONIO DI TUCCIO MANETTI, see Howard Salmaan

HENRY A. MILLON and CRAIG HUGH SMYTH, "Michelangelo and St. Peter's I: Notes on a Plan of the Attic as Originally Built on the South Hemicycle", *Burlington Magazine* CXI, 484-501

FRANCES LAND MOORE, "A Contribution to the Study of the Villa Giulia", *Römisches Jahrbuch für Kunstgeschichte* XII, 171-194

K. NEIIENDAM, "Le théâtre de la Renaissance à Rome", *Analecta romana instituti danici* V, 103-197

KARL NOEHLES, *La chiesa dei Santi Luca e Martina nell'opera di Pietro da Cortona*, Roma

ALESSANDRO PARRONCHI, "Il modello del Palazzo Strozzi", *Rinascimento* IX, 95-116

JURGEN PAUL, *Der Palazzo Vecchio in Florenz. Ursprung und Bedeutung einer Form*, Florenz

ANTONIO PINELLI, "Fausto Rughesi", voce in *Dizionario enciclopedico di architettura e urbanistica*, Roma, 356e sg.

E. POLEGGI, "Genova e l'architettura di villa del secolo XVI", *Bollettino centro internazionale di studi di architettura «Andrea Palladio»*, 231-242

ELENA POVOLEDO, "Origini e aspetti della scenografia in Italia dalla fine del Quattrocento agli Intermezzi fiorentini del 1589", in N. Pirotta, *Li due Orfei. Da Poliziano a Monteverdi*, Torino, 371-509

ROLAND RECHT, "Dessin d'architecture pour la cathedrale de Strasbourg", *œil* 174/175, 26-33

Y. RENOUARD, *Les villes d'Italie de la fin du Xe siècle au debut du XIX siècle*, Paris (ed. it., Milano 1976)

HOWARD SAALMAN, *The Life of Brunelleschi*, edited by Howard Saalman, translated by Catherine Enggass, University Park, Penn.-London [vedi 1970]

F. SANTI, *Galleria Nazionale dell'Umbria*, Roma

MAX STECK, *Albrecht Dürer als Kunst-theoretiker. Die geistes und problemgeschichtliche Stellung seiner Proportionslehre im Kunstraum der Renaissance*, Zürich

M. STEIN, *Des italienske renaessance-teater og perspektivscenens oprindelse. Fra Brunelleschi til Buonatalenti*, K/obenhavns

TACCOLA (MARIANO DI JACOPO, detto il), *Liber tertius de ingeneis ac edifitiis non usitatis*, a cura di James H. Beck, Milano

MANFREDO TAFURI [a], *L'architettura dell'Umanesimo*, Bari

—— [b], *Jacopo Sansovino e l'architettura del '500 a Venezia*, Padova

CHARLES DE TOLNAY, *Michelangelo, the Youth of Michelangelo*, I, Princeton

VITRUVIUS, vedi Krinsky (Hrsg.)

STANISLAW WILINSKI, "Cesare Cesariano elogia la geometria architettonica della Cattedrale di Milano", in *Il Duomo di Milano* (1969), 132-143

GIANGIORGIO ZORZI, *Le ville e i teatri di Andrea Palladio*, Vicenza

1969-70

ECKHARD SCHAAR, "Lambert Lombard. Die Augerweckung des Lazarus", in *Meisterzeichnungen der Sammlung Lambert Krahe*, Ausstellungs katalog, Düsseldorf, 71-72

1970

EDOARDO ARSLAN, *Venezia gotica. L'architettura civile gotica veneziana*, Milano

LUCILLA BARDESCHI CIULICH, PAOLA BAROCCHI (a cura di), *I ricordi di Michelangelo*, Firenze

ISA BELLI BARSALI, *Ville di Roma*, Milano

LUCIANO BELLOSI, *Arte in Valdichiana dal XIII al XVIII secolo*, Cortona

EKART BERCKENHAGEN, *Die französischen Zeichnungen der Kunstnungen der Kunstbibliothek Berlin*, Berlin

OTTAVIO BERNASCONI, "L'architettura ", in *Il Duomo di Como*, Como, 33-104

CARLO BERTELLI, "Caput Sancti Anastasii", *Paragone* 247 (settembre), 12-25

HARTMUT BIERMANN, "Das Palastmodell Giuliano da Sangallos für Ferdinand I. König von Neapel", *Wiener Jahrbuch für Kunstgeschichte* XXIII, 154-195

EVE BORSOOK [a], "Documenti relativi alle cappelle di Lecceto e delle Selve di Filippo Strozzi", *Antichità viva* IX, 3-20

—— [b], "Documents for Filippo Strozzi's Chapel in S. Maria Novella and Other Related Papers", *Burlington Magazine* 112, 737-755 and 800-804

WILLIAM M. BOWSKY, *The Finance of the Commune of Siena, 1287-1355*, Oxford

G. BRESCIANI ALVAREZ, *La Basilica di Santa Giustina. Arte e storia*, Padova

HANS HENRIK BRUMMER, *The Statue Court in the Vatican Belvedere*, Stockholm

ENZO CARLI, *Pietro e Ambrogio Lorenzetti*, Milano

ALBERT CHÂTELET, *Disegni di Raffaello e di altri italiani del Museo di Lille*, Firenze

A.C. CROMBIE, *Robert Grosseste and the Origins of Experimental Science 1100-1700*, Oxford (Deutsche Ausgabe, München 1977)

L. DIECKMANN, *Hieroglyphs. The History of Literary Symbol*, St. Louis

MARIO FANTI, *Il museo di San Petronio in Bologna*, Bologna

P. FIDENZONI, *Il teatro di Marcello*, Roma

MAZZINO FOSSI (a cura di), *La città, appunti per un trattato. Bartolomeo Ammannati*, 2 voll., Roma

A.D. FRASER JENKINS, "Cosimo de' Medici's Patronage of Architecture and the Theory of Magnificence", *Journal of the Warburg and Courtauld Institutes* XXXIII, 162-170

A. GUARNA DA SALERNO, *Scimmia*, traduzione e commento di E. e G. Battisti, Roma

R. HATFIELD, "Some Unknown Descriptions of the Medici Palace in 1459", *Art Bulletin* LII, 232-249

EUGÈNE JOHNSON, "S. Andrea in Mantua", D.Phil. diss., New York University

ROBERT KLEIN, "Etudes sur la perspective à la renaissance, 1956-63", *Bibliothèque d'Humanisme et Renaissance* XXV, 577-587 (réimpression dans *La forme et l'intelligible*, Paris, 278-293)

RICHARD KRAUTHEIMER and TRUDE KRAUTHEIMER-HESS, *Lorenzo Ghiberti*, Princeton

E. KRETZULESCO QUARANTA, "L'itinerario archeologico di Polifilo: Leon Battista Alberti come teorico della Magna Porta", *Atti della accademia nazionale dei Lincei. Rendiconti* 356, serie 8 (vol. XXV), 175-201

HANNO W. KRUFT, "Concerning the date of the Codex Escurialensis", *Burlington Magazine* CXII, 44-47

ANTONIO DI TUCCIO MANETTI, see Howard Saalman

HENRY A. MILLON, "Observations on a Newly Discovered Wood Model for the South Hemicycle Vault of St. Peter's. Abstracts of Papers Presented at the Twenty-third Annual Meeting of the Society of Architectural Historians, Washington, D.C.(January 29-February 1), 1970", *Journal of the Society of Architectural Historians* XXIX, 265 ff.

HEINER MÜHLMANN, "Über den humanistischen Sinn einiger Kerngedanken der Kunsttheorie seit Alberti", *Zeitschrift für Kunstgeschichte* XXX, 127-142

VITTORIO NIRONI, *Il Palazzo del Comune di Reggio-Emilia*, Reggio Emilia

U. NOFRINI, *Il Tempio del Bramante a Todi*, introduzione di Arnaldo Bruschi, Todi

LOREDANA OLIVATO, "Profilo di Giorgio Vasari il Giovane", *Rivista dell'istituto nazionale di archeologia e storia dell'arte* n.s. XVII, 181-229

OTTO PÄCHT, JONATHAN J.G. ALEXANDER, *Illuminated Manuscripts in the Bodleian Library Oxford*, II: *Italian School*, Oxford

PIER GIORGIO PASINI, "Il tempio malatestiano", in *Sigismondo Pandolfo Malatesta* (1970), Vicenza

FRANK D. PRAGER, GUSTINA SCAGLIA, *Brunelleschi. Studies of his Technology and Inventions*, Cambridge, Mass.- London

D.M. ROBATHAN, "Flavio Biondo's 'Roma instaurata'", *Medievalia et Humanistica* n.s. I, 203-216

HOWARD SAALMAN, ED., *The Life of Brunelleschi by Antonio di Tuccio Manetti*, University Park,-London, vedi anche 1969

FRITZ SAXL, "L'antichità classica in Jacopo Bellini e nel Mantegna", in *A Heritage of Images*, Harmondsworth, 57-70

GUSTINA SCAGLIA [a], "Book Review: Francesco di Giorgio Martini, *Trattati di architettura, ingegneria e arte militare*, ed. Corrado Maltese", *Art Bulletin* LII, 439-442

—— [b], "Fantasy Architecture of Roma Antica", *Arte lombarda* XV, 9-24

SIGISMONDO PANDOLFO MALATESTA E IL SUO TEMPO. Mostra storica, catalogo mostra (Rimini, 12 luglio-13 agosto), a cura di F. Arduini, G. Menghi, F. Panvini Rosati, Pier Giorgio Pasini, Piero Sanpaolesi, A. Vasina, Vicenza

JÜRGEN SCHULZ, "The Printed Plans and Panoramic Views of Venice", *Saggi e memorie di storia dell'arte*, VII, 19-29 e schede bio-bibliografiche

CRAIG HUGH SMYTH, "Once more the Dyson Perrins Codex and St. Peter's. In Abstracts of Papers Presented at the Twenty-third Annual Meeting of the Society of Architectural Historians, Washington, D.C.(January 29 - February 1), 1970", *Journal of the Society of Architectural Historians* XXXIX, 265 ff.

Virginia Stefanelli, vedi Giorgio Vasari

CHARLES DE TOLNAY, *La Casa Buonarroti. Le sculture di Michelangelo e le collezioni della famiglia*, Firenze

GIORGIO VASARI IL GIOVANE, *La città ideale. Piante di chiese (palazzi e ville) di Toscana e d'Italia*, a cura di Virginia Stefanelli, introduzione di Franco Borsi, Roma

VITRUVIO, *De Architectura*, translated by Frank Granger, Cambridge, Mass.

Nathan T. Whitman, "Roman Tradition and the Aedicular Facade", *Journal of the Society of Architectural Historians* XXIX, 108-123

1971

R.R. BOLGAR, ed., *Classical Influences on European Culture A.D. 500-1500*, Cambridge

EUGENIO BATTISTI, *Piero della Francesca*, Milano

MICHAEL BAXANDALL, *Giotto and the Orators: Humanist Observers of Painting in Italy and the Discovery of Pictorial Composition, 1350-1450*, Oxford

LUISA BECHERUCCI, GIULIA BRUNETTI, *Il Museo dell'Opera del Duomo a Firenze*, Milano [1971?]

RICHARD J. BETTS, "The Architectural Theories of Francesco di Giorgio", Ph. D.diss., Princeton University

T.S.R. BOASE, *Giorgio Vasari. The Man and the Book*, Washington

ARNALDO BRUSCHI, "Bramante", voce in *Dizionario biografico degli italiani*, XIII, Roma, 712-725

TILMANN BUDDENSIEG, "Criticism and Praise of the Pantheon in the Middle Ages and the Renaissance", in R.R. Bolgar, ed. (1971), 259-267

HOWARD BURNS, "Quattrocento Architecture and the Antique: Some Poblems", in R.R. Bolgar ed. (1971), 269-287

R.P. CIARDI, "Le regole del disegno di Alessandro Allori e la nascita del dilettantismo pittorico", *Storia dell'arte*, Torino

ANDREA EMILIANI, "L'opera dell'Accademia Clementina per il patrimonio artistico e la formazione della Pinacoteca Nazionale di Bologna", *Atti e memorie dell'Accademia Clementina di Bologna* X, 126

T. FALK, "Studie zur topographie und Geschichte der Villa Giulia in Roma", *Römische Jahrbuch für Kunstgeschichte* XIII, 101 sgg.

KURT W. FORSTER, "Metaphors of Rule: Political Ideology and History in the Portraits of Cosimo I de' Medici", *Mitteilungen des Kunsthistorischen Institutes in Florenz* XV, 65-104

G. GOEBEL, *Poeta Faber. Erdichtete Architektur in der italienischen, spanischen und französischen Literatur der Renaissance und des Barock*, Heidelberg

FREDERICK HARTT, *Michelangelo Drawings*, New York

HOWARD HIBBARD, *Carlo Maderno and Roman Architecture 1580-1630*, University Park, Penn.-London

FRITZ EUGEN KELLER, "Alvise Cornaro zitiert die Villa des Marcus Terentius Varro in Cassino", *L'arte* XIV, 29-53

ROBERT KLEIN, *L'Umanesimo e la follia*, Roma

LOREDANA OLIVATO, "Giorgio Vasari il Giovane. Il funzionario del "Principe", *L'arte* XIV, 5-28

C. MOLINARI, "Il teatro nella tradizione Vitruviana da Leon Battista Alberti a Daniele Barbaro", *Biblioteca teatrale* I, 30-46

CATHERINE MONBEIG-GOGUEL, *I disegni dei maestri. Il manierismo fiorentino*, Milano

WERNER MÜLLER, "Der Elliptische Korboggen in der Architekturtheorie von Dürer bis Frézier", *Technikgeschichte* XXXVIII, 93-106

MARY L. MYERS, "A Presentation Drawing for the Facade of Santa Maria del Fiore", *Master Drawings* IX, 391-398

ALLANDRIDGE NICOLL, *Lo spazio scenico. Storia dell'arte teatrale*, Roma

ALESSANDRO PARRONCHI, "Sulla composizione dei trattati attribuiti a Francesco di Giorgio Martini", *Atti e memorie dell'accademia toscana di scienze e lettere 'La Colombaria'* XXXVI, 163-230

PAOLO PORTOGHESI, *Roma nel Rinascimento*, 2 voll., Milano [s.d. 1971]

LIONELLO PUPPI [a], "Un letterato in villa: Giangiorgio Trissino a Cricoli", *Arte veneta* XXV, 72 e sg.

—— [b], *Michele Sanmicheli, architetto di Verona*, Padova

—— [c], "Gli spettacoli all'Olimpico di Vicenza del 1585 all'inizio del '600", in *Studi sul teatro veneto tra Rinascimento ed età barocca*, Firenze

P. ROSELLI, *Coro e cupola della SS. Annunziata a Firenze*, Pisa

GUSTINA SCAGLIA, ed., *Mariano Taccola, de Machinis. The Engineering Treatise of 1449*, 2 vols., Wiesbaden

H. SCHRÖDER, *Der Topos der Nine Worthies in Literatur und bildender Kunst*, Göttingen

T. SCHRÖDER, *Jacques Callot. Das gesamte Werk. I: Handzeichnungen. II: Druckgraphik*, München

G. STRUFFOLINO KRÜGER, "Disegni inediti d'architettura relativi alla collezione di Venanzio de Pagave", *Arte lombarda* XVI, 292

CHARLES DE TOLNAY, "Alcune recenti scoperte negli studi michelangioleschi", *Accademia nazionale dei Lincei* CCLXVIII (n. 153), 1-24

MARVIN TRACHTENBERG, *The Campanile of Florence Cathedral*, New York

P.L. VANNICELLI, *S. Pietro in Montorio ed il Tempietto di Bramante*, Roma

W. VITZTHUM, *Jacques Callot. Incisioni scelte e annotate*, Firenze

J. ZÄNKER, "Die Wallfahrtskirche Santa Maria della Consolazione in Todi", D.Phil. Diss., Bonn

1971-72

SIMONETTA VALTIERI, ENZO BENTIVOGLIO, "Sanzio sovrintendente", *Architettura* XVII, 476-484

1972

LEON BATTISTA ALBERTI, see Cecil Grayson

FRANCO BARBIERI, "Bernardino Brugnoli", voce in *Dizionario biografico degli italiani*, XIV, Roma, 503-504

MICHAEL BAXANDALL, *Painting and Experience in Fifteenth Century Italy*, Oxford

RENATO BONELLI, *Il Duomo di Orvieto e l'architettura italiana del Duecento-Trecento*, Roma

F. BÜTTNER, "Zur Frage der Enstehung der Galerie", *Architectura*, LXXV-LXXX

ANTONIO CADEI, "Nota sul Bramante e l'Amadeo architetti del Duomo di Pavia", *Bollettino della società Pavese di storia patria* XXIV, 35-60

ANGELA DANEU LATTANZI, "Di alcuni miniatori lombardi della seconda metà del sec. XV. I. Francesco da Castello riesaminato", *Commentari* XXIII, 225-60

HORST DE LA CROIX, *Military Consideration in City Planning: Fortifications*, New York

A. ERLER, "Lupa, Lex und Reiterstandbild im mittelalterlichen Rom", *Sitzungsberichte der Wissenschaftlichen Gesellschaft an der Johann Wolfgang Goethe-Universität Frankfurt am Main* X (4), 123-42

MAURIZIO FAGIOLO, MARIA LUISA MADONNA, "La Roma di Pio IV, la Civitas Pia, la Salus Medica, la Custodia Angelica", *Arte illustrata* V (51), 382-402

FILARETE (Antonio Averlino), *Trattato di Architettura*, a cura di Anna Maria Finoli e Liliana Grassi, introduzione e note di Liliana Grassi, 2 voll., Milano

MARIANNE FISCHER, "Lafreris 'Speculum Romanae Magnificentiae': addenda zu Hülsens Verseichnis", *Berliner Museen* XXII, 10-17

R. FUBINI, A.M. GALLORINI, "L'Autobiografia di Leon Battista Alberti", *Rinascimento* XII, 21-78

EUGENIO GARIN, *La città ideale di Leonardo*, Firenze

BERNARD GILLE, *Leonardo e gli ingegneri del Rinascimento*, Milano (éd. française, *Les ingénieurs de la Renaissance*, Paris 1964)

DECIO GIOSEFFI, "Il disegno come fase progettuale dell'attività palladiana", *Bollettino del centro internazionale studi di architettura «Andrea Palladio»* XIV, 137-47

RICHARD A. GOLDTHWAITE, "The Florentine Palace as Domestic Architecture", *American Historical Review* LXXVII, 977-1012

LILIANA GRASSI, "Introduzione e note", in Filarete, *Trattato di Architettura*, I-CXVI

CECIL GRAYSON, *Leon Battista Alberti. On Painting and On Sculpture. The Latin Texts of 'De Pictura' and 'De Statua'*, edited with translation, introduction, and notes by Cecil Grayson, London-New York

GIACOMO GRIMALDI, *Descrizione della basilica antica di S. Pietro in Vaticano, codice Barberini latino 2733*, a cura di Reto Niggl, Città del Vaticano

GREGORY HEDBERG, "The Farnese Courtyard Windows and the Porta Pia: Michelangelo's Creative Process", *Marsyas* XV, 63-72

MICHAEL HIRST, "Addenda Sansoviniana", *Burlington Magazine* CXIV, 162-165

F.W. KENT, "The Rucellai Family and its Loggia", *Journal of the Warburg and Courtauld Institutes* XXXV, 397-401

BERNARD JESTAZ, "Le modèles de la majolique historiée: bilan d'une enquête", *Gazette des beaux-arts* LXXIX, 215-40

S. LANG, "Sforzinda, Filarete, and Filelfo", *Journal of the Warburg and Courtauld Institutes*, XXXV

LICISCO MAGAGNATO, "La concezione del teatro palladiano", *Bollettino del centro internazionale di studi di architettura «Andrea Palladio»*, XIV, 137-47

METTERNICH, see WOLFF METTERNICH

GAETANO MIARELLI MARIANI, "Il disegno per il complesso mediceo di via Laura a Firenze", *Palladio* n.s. XXII, 127-162

CATHERINE MONBEIG GOGUEL, *Vasari et son temps. Musée du Louvre, Cabinet des dessins. Inventaire général des dessins Italiens*, I, Paris

PIER NICOLA PAGLIARA, "L'attività edilizia di Antonio da Sangallo il Giovane", *Controspazio* IV (7), 19-55

CARLO PEDRETTI, *Leonardo da Vinci. The Royal Palace at Romorantin*, Cambridge, Mass.

FRANK D. PRAGER AND GUSTINA SCAGLIA, *Mariano Taccola and his Book "De Ingeneis"*, Cambridge, Mass.-London

ENNIO POLEGGI, *Strada Nuova, una lottizzazione del Cinquecento a Genova*, Genova (2a ed.)

JOHN SHEARMAN, *The Vatican Stanze: Functions and Decorations*, London; also in *Proceedings of the British Academy* LVII, 3-58

L.R. SHELBY, "The Geometrical Knowledge of Mediaeval Master Masons", *Speculum* XLVII, 395-421

CHRISTOF THOENES, "'Sostegno e Adornamento': Zur Sozialen Symbolik der Säulenordnung", *Kunstchronik* XXV, 343-4

CHARLES DE TOLNAY, "I progetti di Michelangelo per la facciata di S. Lorenzo a Firenze: nuove ricerche", *Commentari* XXIII, 53-71

CAROLYN VALONE, "Giovanni Antonio Dosio and His Patrons", Ph.D. diss., Northwestern University

FRANZ GRAF WOLFF METTERNICH, *Die Erbauung der Peterskirche zu Rom im 16. Jahrhundert* I, Wien-München

1972-73

S. WILK, "Tullio Lombardo's Double Portrait Reliefs", *Marsyas*, 67-86

1973

LUIGI SALERNO, LUIGI SPEZZAFERRO, MANFREDO TAFURI, *Via Giulia. Un'utopia urbanistica del Cinquecento*, Roma

LEONARDO BENEVOLO, *Storia dell'architettura del Rinascimento*, Bari

FRANCO BORSI, *Leon Battista Alberti. Opera completa*, Milano

ARNALDO BRUSCHI [A], *Bramante*, London

—— [a], *Bramante architetto*, Bari (1a ed. 1969)

M. BUCCI, *Palazzi di Firenze. Il quartiere di S. Spirito*, Firenze

TILMANN BUDDENSIEG, "Antikenkritik der Renaissance-Architekten", in "Manuskripte und Referate der Arbeitstagung für Humanismusforschung der Deutschen Forschungsgemeinschaft: Humanismus und Bildende Kunst. 10.-11- April im Kunsthistorischen Institut Florenze" (Manuskript, keine Sietenangabe)

HOWARD BURNS [a], "I disegni", in *Palladio*, catalogo mostra, Vicenza-Milano, 131-154

—— [b], "I disegni del Palladio", *Bollettino del centro internazionale di studi di architettura «Andrea Palladio»* XV, 169-191

RAFFAELLO CAUSA, *L'arte nella Certosa di S. Martino*, Napoli, 20 e introduzione

LICIA COLLOBI RAGGHIANTI [a], "Il 'Libro de' Disegni' del Vasari. Disegni di architettura", *Critica d'arte/Rivista d'arte* XX (127), 3-120

—— [b], "Nuove precisazioni sui disegni di architettura del 'Libro del Vasari'", *Rivista d'arte* XX (130), 31-54

GIOVANNI CONTI, *L'arte della maiolica in Italia*, Milano

GIUSEPPINA DAL CANTON, "Architettura del Filarete ed architettura veneziana: analisi campione di un palazzo del 'Trattato' filaretiano", *Arte lombarda* XXXVIII-XXXIX, 103-105

CESARE DE SETA, *Storia della città di Napoli dalle origini al Settecento*, Roma-Bari

MAURIZIO FAGIOLO, *La scenografia, dalle sacre rappresentazioni al futurismo*, Firenze

MAURIZIO FAGIOLO, MARIA LUISA MADONNA, "La Roma di Pio IV. 2. Il sistema dei centri direzionali e la rifondazione della città", *Arte illustrata* VI (54), 186-212

GIOVANNI FANELLI, *Firenze: architettura e città*, 2 voll., Firenze

CARLO FERRARI DA PASSANO, "Storia della Veneranda Fabbrica", in *Il Duomo di Milano*, I, Milano, 11-96 e 40-41

CHRISTOPH L. FROMMEL, *Der römische Palastbau der Hochrenaissance*, 3 Bde., Tübingen

A. GALLO, *La prima rappresentazione al Teatro Olimpico*, Milano

ALESSANDRO GAMBUTI, "Lodovico Cigoli architetto", *Studi e documenti di architettura* II (giugno), 39 sg.

ANNAROSA GARZELLI, "Un disegno di architettura civile del 1340", *Antichità viva* XII, 36-41

RICHARD A. GOLDTHWAITE, "The Building of the Strozzi Palace: the Construction Industry in Renaissance Florence", *Studies in Medieval and Renaissance History* X, 97-194

P. GROS, "Hermodoros et Vitruve", *Mélanges d'archéologie et d'histoire. Ecole Française de Rome* LXXXV, 137sqq.

HUBERTUS GÜNTHER, "Bramantes Tempietto. Die Memorialanlage der Kreuzigung Petri in S. Pietro in Montorio, Rom", D. Phil. Diss. Universität München

W.D. HEILMEYER, F. RAKOB, *Der Rundtempel am Tiber in Rom*, Mainz

GEORGE HERSEY, *The Aragonese Arch at Naples, 1443-1475*, New Haven

CHRISTIANE KLAPISCH-ZUBER, *Carrara e i maestri del marmo (1300-1600)*, Massa (éd. français, *Les maîtres du marbre. Carrare 1300-1600*, Paris 1969)

H. KÜTHMANN ET AL., *Bauten Roms auf Münzen und Medaillen*, Ausstellung der Staatlichen Münzsammlung, München

WOLFGANG LOTZ, "Gli 883 cocchi della Roma del 1594", in *Studi offerti a Giovanni Incisa della Rocchetta*, Roma, 247-266

GIUSEPPE MARCHINI [a], "Le vetrate dell'Umbria", in *Corpus vitrearum medii aevi: Italia*, I, Roma, 170-187

—— [b], recensione a Miarelli Mariani, in *Antichità viva* XII, 66-8

E. MERKEL, "Un problema di metodo: la Dormitio Virginis dei Mascoli", *Arte veneta* XXVII, 65-80

Mostra del Palladio, Vicenza, Basilica Palladiana, Milano-Venezia

KONRAD OBERHUBER, "Francesco Rosselli", in *Early Italian Drawings from the National Gallery of Art*, Washington, 47-62

PETER PAUSE, *Gotische Architekturzeichnungen in Deutschland*, Bonn, 262-263

CARLO PEDRETTI, "The Original Project for S. Maria delle Grazie", *Journal of the Society of Architectural Historians* XXXII, 30-42

MARINELLA PIGOZZI, "La presenza dell'Averlino a Mantova e a Bergamo", *Arte lombarda* XXXVIII-XXXIX, 85-90

KATHLEEN WEIL-GARRIS POSNER, "Cloister, Court and City Square", *Gesta* XII, 133-141

LIONELLO PUPPI [a], *Andrea Palladio: l'opera completa*, 2 voll., Milano

—— [b], "Filarete in gondola", *Arte lombarda* XXXVIII-XXXIX, 75-84

M.D. RINALDI, "Nuove ricerche intorno a Giovanni Tortelli", *Italia medievale e umanistica* XVI, 227-61

ANGIOLA MARIA ROMANINI, "L'architettura", in *Il Duomo di Milano*, I, Milano, 97-232

KLAUS SCHWAGER, "Die Porta Pia in Rom. Untersuchungen zu 'verrufenen Gebäude'", *Münchner Jahrbuch der Bildenden Kunst* XXIV, 33-96

MANFREDO TAFURI, "S.Giovanni dei Fiorentini", in *Via Giulia* (1973), 201-258

D. TERNOIS, "Callot et son temps; dix ans de recherches (1962-1972)", *Le Pays lorrain*, 211-48

FRANKLIN TOKER, Verbal Communication at Harvard University Center for Italian Renaissance Studies in Florence

FEDERICO ZERI [A], *Metropolitan Museum of Art. Italian Paintings: Venetian School*, New York

—— [b], "Ricerche sul Sassetta. La pala dell'Arte della Lana (1423-1426)", in *Quaderni di Emblema*, Bergamo, 22-34

1974

Il Sant'Andrea in Mantova e Leon Battista Alberti, Mantova

Studi bramanteschi, Atti del congresso internazionale (Milano-Urbino-Roma, 2 sett.-1 ott. 1970), Roma

BRUNO ADORNI, *L'architettura farnesiana a Parma 1545-1630*, Parma

FRANCO BARBIERI, "Il Teatro Olimpico; dalla città esistenziale alla città ideale", *Bollettino del centro internazionale di studi di architettura «Andrea Palladio»* XVI, 309-322

C. BASSANI, A. GALDI, A. POLTRONIERI, "Analisi per il restauro del Tempio di San Sebastiano in Mantova", in *Il Sant'Andrea di Mantova...* (1974), 243-163

EUGENIO BATTISTI, "Il metodo progettuale secondo il *De re aedificatoria* di Leon Battista Alberti", in *Il Sant'Andrea di Mantova...* (1974), 131-156

A.R. BLUMENTHAL, *Four Centuries of Scenic Invention, Drawings from the Collection of Donald Oenslager*, exhibition catalog, New York

M.C. Bonagura, "Considerazioni sulla chiesa di S. Maria della Consolazione a Todi", in *Studi bramanteschi* (1974), 625-630

Fabia Borroni-Salvadori, "Le esposizioni d'arte a Firenze 1674-1767", *Mitteilungen des Kunsthistorischen Institutes in Florenz* XVIII, 90

Franco Borsi, *Firenze del Cinquecento*, Roma

Anna Maria Brizio, "Bramante e Leonardo alla corte di Ludovico il Moro", in *Studi bramanteschi* (1974), 1-26

Arnaldo Bruschi, "Bramantes Hofprojekt um den Tempietto und seine Darstellung in Serlios drittem Buch", in *Studi bramanteschi* (1974), 483-501

François Bucher, "Micro-Architecture as the 'Idea' of Gothic Theory and Style", *Gesta* XV, 71-81

Howard Burns, "Progetti di Francesco di Giorgio per i conventi di San Bernardino e Santa Chiara a Urbino", *Studi bramanteschi* (1974), 293-311

Ellen Callman, *Apollonio di Giovanni*, Oxford

Licia Collobi Ragghianti, *Il libro dei disegni del Vasari*, Firenze

Fabrizio Cruciani, "Gli allestimenti scenici di Baldassarre Peruzzi", *Bollettino del centro internazionale di studi di architettura «Andrea Palladio»* XVI, 155-172

Dizionario Enciclopedico Bolaffi, ad vocem, VI, Torino, 43

S. Edgerton, "Florentine Interest in Ptolemaic Cartography as Background for Renaissance Painting, Architecture, and the Discovery of America", *Journal of the Society of Architectural Historians* XXXIII, 275-292

Christoph L. Frommel [a], "Il Palazzo dei Tribunali in via Giulia", in *Studi bramanteschi* (1974), 523-534

—— [b], "Raffaello e il teatro alla corte di Leone X", *Bollettino del centro internazionale di studi di architettura «Andrea Palladio»*, XVI, 173-187

Jeanne Giacomotti, *Les maioliques des musées nationaux*, Paris

P.W.G. Gordan, *Two Renaissance Book Hunters. The Letters of Poggius Bracciolini to Nicolaus de Niccolis*, New York

Hubertus Günther, "Bramantes Hofprojekt um den Tempietto und seine Darstellung in s drittem Buch", in *Studi bramanteschi* (1974), 483-501

Detlef Heikamp, "Il teatro mediceo degli Uffizi", *Bollettino del centro internazionale di studi di architettura «Andrea Palladio»* XVI, 323-332

Ludwig H. Heydenreich and Wolfgang Lotz, *Architecture in Italy 1400-1600*, Harmondsworth

Michael Hirst, "A Note on Michelangelo and the Attic of St. Peter's", *Burlington Magazine* CXVI, 662-663, and 665

Vladimir Juren, "Fra Giovanni Giocondo et le début des études Vitruviennes en France", *Rinascimento* XIV, 101-115

T. Klanickzay, "Mattia Corvino e l'Umanesimo italiano", *Quaderno accademia dei Lincei* 202

Jean Lanfond, "La prétendue maquette de l'église Saint-Maclou de Rouen", *Gazette des beaux-arts* serie 6, LXXXIII, 65-75

Wolfgang Lotz, "L'opera del Barozzi", in et al., *Jacopo Barozzi, il Vignola*, Bologna

Ercolano Marani, "La lettera albertiana del 21 ottobre 1470", in *Il S. Andrea in Mantova...*, 427-431

F. Mariotti, *Storia documentaria del teatro italiano. Lo spettacolo dall'umanesimo al manierismo*, Milano

Anna Matteoli, "I modelli lignei del '500 e del '600 per la facciata del Duomo di Firenze", *Commentari* XXV, 73-110

Millard Meiss, *French Painting in the Time of Jean de Berry. The Limbourgs and their Contemporaries*, New York

Stanislaus von Moos, *Turm und Bollwerk: beitrage zu einer politischen Ikonographie der italienischen Renaissancearchitektur*, Zürich

Germano Mulazzani, "Gli affreschi bramanteschi ora a Brera: un riesame", *Storia dell'arte* XXII

U. Nofrini, "La Chiesa della Consolazione a Todi", in *Studi bramanteschi* (1974), 617-624

Hendrik W. van Os, *Vecchietta and the Sacristy of scala Hospstal Church*, The Hague

Guido Pampaloni, *Palazzo Strozzi*, Roma

M. Pericoli, "Precisazioni sulla Consolazione di Todi", in *Studi bramanteschi* (1974), 631-63

J.J. Pollit, *The Ancient View of Greek Art*, New Haven-London

Kathleen Weil Garris Posner [a], "Alcuni progetti per piazze e facciate di Bramante e di Antonio da Sangallo il Giovane a Loreto", in *Studi bramanteschi* (1974), 313-38

—— [b], *Leonardo and Central Italian Art 1515-1550*, New York

Stefano Ray, *Raffaello architetto. Linguaggio artistico e ideologia nel Rinascimento romano*, Roma- Bari

Deoclecio Redig de Campos, "Bramante e le Logge di San Damaso", in *Studi bramanteschi* (1974), 517-522

Ladislao Reti, *Leonardo da Vinci letto e commentato*, Firenze

Annegritt Schmitt, "Zur Wiederbelebung der Antike im Trecento", in *Mitteilungen des Kunsthistorischen Institutes in Florenz* XVIII, 167-218

John Shearman, "Il 'Tiburio' di Bramante", in *Studi bramanteschi* (1974), 567-573

G. Simoncini, *Città e società nel Rinascimento*, Torino

G. Tibaudo, "Precisazioni sul Tempietto di S. Pietro in Montorio", in *Studi bramanteschi* (1974), 513-516

Sandro Vasco, "Le tavolette di San Bernardino a Perugia. I committenti: qualche ipotesi e precisazione", *Commentari* XXV, 64-67

La vita e le opere di Jacopo Barozzi da Vignola 1507-1573 nel quarto centenario della morte, Bologna

Carroll William Westfall, *In This Most Perfect Paradise. Alberti, Nicholas V, and the Invention of Conscious Urban Planning in Rome, 1447-55*, University Park, Penn.-London

Rudolf Wittkower, *Gothic vs. Classic. Architectural Projects in Seventeenth-Century Italy*, New York

J. Zänker, "Il primo progetto per il santuario di Santa Maria della Consolazione a Todi e la sua attribuzione", in *Studi bramanteschi* (1974), 603-615

1975

Leon Battista Alberti, *De Pictura*, a cura di Cecil Grayson, Roma-Bari

Andrea Palladio 1508-1580. The Portico and the Farmyard, exhibition catalog (London, Arts Councile of Great Britain), edited by Howard Burns, Lynda Fairbairn and Bruce Boucher, London

Filippo Baldinucci, *Notizie dei Professori del Disegno da Cimabue in qua*, a cura di Paola Barocchi, Firenze

Isa Belli Barsali, *Ville della Campagna Romana*, Milano

Enzo Bentivoglio, "Disegni nel 'libro' di Giuliano da Sangallo collegabili ai progetti per il San Giovanni dei Fiorentini", *Mitteilungen des Kunsthistorischen Institutes in Florenz* XIX, 251-260

Anthony Blunt, "Supplements to the Catalogues of Italian and French Drawings", in E. Schilling, *The German Drawings in the Collection of Her Majesty the Queen at Windsor Castle*, London

D. Bodart, *Dessins de la Colléction Thomas Ashby à la Bibliothèque Vaticane*, Città del Vaticano

Franco Borsi, *Leon Battista Alberti*, Milano

Giulia Brunetti, "Il museo dell'Opera di Santa Maria del Fiore", *Atti della società Leonardo da Vinci* III (6), 19-32

Tilmann Buddensieg, "Bernardo della Volpaia und Giovanni Francesco da Sangallo: Der Autor des Codex Coner und seine Stellung im Sangallo-Kreis", *Römisches Jahrbuch für Kunstgeschichte* XV, 89-108

Howard Burns et al., see *Andrea Palladio...*

Antonio Cadei, "Modello ligneo per il Duomo di Pavia", Pavia. Musei Civici del Castello Visconteo, Bologna, 137-141

Alberto Carlo Carpiceci, "Armature e macchine di Leonardo da Vinci per la fabbrica di San Pietro", *Istruzione Tecnica e Professionale* XLIII, 127-136

André Chastel, *Marsile Ficin et l'art*, Genève

Françoise de la Moureyre Gavoty, *Institut de France Paris - Musée Jacquemart André - Sculpture italienne*, Paris

L. Donati, "Polifilo a Roma. Le rovine romane", *Bibliofilia* LXXVII, 37-64

S. Edgerton, *The Renaissance Discovery of Linear Perspective*, New York

Diane Finiello Zervas, "The Trattato dell'Abbaco and Andrea Pisano's Design for the Florentine Baptistery Door", *Renaissance Quarterly* XXVIII, 483-503

Vincenzo Fontana, Paolo Morachiello, *Vitruvio e Raffaello. Il "De architectura" di Vitruvio nella traduzione inedita di Fabio Calvo Ravennate*, Roma

Max J. Friedländer, *Early Netherlandisch Painting*, 12 vols., Leiden-Brussels

Christoph L. Frommel, "Die architektonische Planung der Villa Madama", *Römisches Jahrbuch für Kunstgeschichte* XV, 61-87

Carlo Galassi Paluzzi, *La Basilica di S. Pietro*, Bologna

Galeazzo Alessi e l'architettura del Cinquecento, Atti del convegno internazionale di studi (Genova, 16-20 aprile 1974), Genova

John Gere and Nicholas Turner, *Drawings by Michelangelo in the Collection of Her Majesty the Queen at Windsor Castle, the Ashmolean Museum, The British Museum, and Other English Collections*, London

John Harvey, *Medieval Craftsmen*, London-Sydney

Deborah Howard, *Jacopo Sansovino Architecture and Patronage in Renaissance Venice*, New Haven-London

Norbert Huse, Wolfgang Wolters, *Venedig. Die Kunst der Renaissance - Architektur, Skulptur, Malerei 1460-1590*, München

Jacques Callot: Prints and Related Drawings, exhibition catalog, edited by H.D. Russell, J. Blanchard, and J. Krill (Washington, National Gallery of Art), Washington

Eugène Johnson, *S. Andrea in Mantua. The Building History*, Pennsylvania State Univ. Press, University Park, Pennsylvania, London

Roberto Longhi, *Fatti di Masolino e di Masaccio e altri studi sul Quattrocento, Opere complete*, Firenze

E.F. Lowinsky, "Ludovico il Moro's Visit to the Abbey of Chiaravalle in 1497. A Report to Ascanio Sforza", *Arte lombarda* XLII/XLIII, 201-210

Hans-Karl Luecke, *Alberti Index*, 3. Bde. (I, 1976, III, 1979), München

Il luogo teatrale a Firenze. Brunelleschi, Vasari, Buontalenti, Parigi, catalogo mostra a cura di M. Fabbri, E. Garbero Zorzi e Anna Petrioli Tofani, L. Zorzi (Firenze, Palazzo Medici Riccardi), Firenze

Henry A. Millon and Craig Hugh Smyth, "A Design by Michelangelo for a City Gate: Further Notes on the Lille Sketch", *Burlington Magazine* CXVII, 162-166

C. Molinari, *Theater. Die faszinierende Geschichte des Schauspiels*, Freiburg-Basel-Wien

L. Neppi, *Palazzo Spada*, Roma

Roberto Pane, *Il Rinascimento nell'Italia meridionale*, I, Milano

Ugo Procacci, *La Casa Buonarroti a Firenze*, Milano

A. Radice, "Il Cronaca. A Fifteenth-Century Florentine Architect", Ph.D. diss., University of North Carolina, 76-93

P.L. Rose, *The Italian Renaissance of Mathematics*, Geneva

Howard Saalman, "Michelangelo: S. Maria del Fiore and St. Peter's", *Art Bulletin* LVII, 374-409

John Shearman, "The Collections of the Younger Branch of the Medici", *Burlington Magazine* CXVII, 862, 12-27

Klaus Schwager, "Ein Ovalkirchen-Entwurf Vignolas für San Giovanni dei Fiorentini nach Georg Scheja", in *Festschrift für Georg Scheja*, Sigmaringen, 149-178

Staale Sinding-Larsen, "A Tale of Two Cities: Florentine and Roman Visual Context for Fifteenth-Century Palaces", *Acta ad archaeologiam et artium historiam pertinentia* VI, 163-212

FRANEK SZNURA, *L'espansione urbana di Firenze nel Dugento*, Firenze

MANFREDO TAFURI, "Michelangelo architetto", *Civiltà delle macchine* XX, 49-60

CHRISTOF THOENES, "Proportionsstudien an Bramantes Zentralbauentwürfen", *Römisches Jahrbuch für Kunstgeschichte* XV, 37-58

CHARLES DE TOLNAY [a], *Corpus dei disegni di Michelangelo* (1975-80), I, Novara

—— [b], *I disegni di Michelangelo nelle collezioni italiane*, Firenze

—— [c], *Michelangelo, Sculptor, Painter, Architect*, Princeton

FRANZ GRAF WOLFF METTERNICH, *Bramante und St. Peter*, München

1975-76

C. GIACINTO MARINO, "Dati archivistici relativi ad opere d'arte conservate a Vigevano", tesi di laurea, Università statale di Milano

1975-77

ROBERTO PANE, *Il Rinascimento nell'Italia meridionale*, 2 voll., Milano

1975-80

CHARLES DE TOLNAY, *Corpus dei disegni di Michelangelo*, 4 voll., Novara (vol. I 1975, vol. II 1976, vol. III 1978, vol. IV 1980)

1976

R.R. BOLGAR, ed., *Classical Influences on European Culture A.D. 1500-1700*, Cambridge

FRANCO BORSI et al., *Giovanni Antonio Dosio. Roma antica e i disegni di architettura agli Uffizi*, testi di Franco Borsi, Cristina Acidini, Fiammella Mannu Pisani e Giovanni Morolli, Roma

CRISTINA ACIDINI, "Veduta del Cortile del Belvedere", in F. Borsi et al. (1976), 32-33

G.M. ANDRES, *The Villa Medici in Rome*, New York-London

L. DE ANGELIS, A. CONTI, "Un libro antico della sagrestia di Sant'Ambrogio", *Annali della scuola normale superiore di Pisa* VI, 97-109

MINA BACCI, *L'opera completa di Piero di Cosimo*, Milano

EUGENIO BATTISTI, *Filippo Brunelleschi*, Milano

GIOVAN PIETRO BELLORI, *Le vite de' pittori, scultori e architetti moderni*, a cura di Evelina Borea, Torino

ENZO BENTIVOGLIO, SIMONETTA VALTIERI, *Santa Maria del Popolo a Roma*, Roma

TILMANN BUDDENSIEG, "Criticism of Ancient Architecture in the Sixteenth and Seventeenth Centuries", in R.R. Bolgar, ed. (1976), 335-348

N.W. CANEDY, *The Roman Sketchbook of Girolamo da Carpi*, London-Leiden, 102, cat. 110. pl. 38

TANCREDI CARUNCHIO, "L'immagine di Roma di Pirro Ligorio...", *Ricerche di storia dell'arte* III, 25-42

ALESSANDRO CONTI, "Le prospettive urbinati: tentativo di un bilancio ed abbozzo di una bibliografia", *Annali della scuola normale superiore di Pisa*, III, 6, 1193-1234

EUGENE S. FERGUSON, "Technical Annotations and Pictorial Glossary", in *The Various and Ingenious Machines of Agostino Ramelli* (1588), edited by Martha Teach Gnudi, Baltimore, 560-582

CHRISTOPH L. FROMMEL, "Die Peterskirche unter Papst Julius II. im Licht neuer Dokumente", *Römisches Jahrbuch für Kunstgeschichte* XVI, 57-136

SERGIO GATTI, "Il palazzo di Giovanni Salvatico a Milano. Contributo allo studio della corrente classicheggiante nell'architettura lombarda del primo Cinquecento", *Quaderni dell'Istituto di Storia dell'arte medievale e moderna. Facoltà di lettere e filosofia dell'Università di Messina* II, 21-30

GIOVANNI ANTONIO DOSIO, vedi Franco Borsi et al. (1976)

GIOVANNI DA PRATO, *Opere complete. I: Il Paradiso degli Alberti*, a cura di F. Garilli, Palermo

ERNST H. GOMBRICH [a], *The Heritage of Apelles. Studies in the Art of the Renaissance*, Oxford (ed. it. *L'eredità di Apelle*, Torino 1986)

—— [b], "The Lustre of Apelles", Pilkington Lecture (Manchester, Whiteworth Gallery of Art, May 1972), in *The Heritage of Apelles. Studies in the Art of the Renaissance*, Oxford

LUCIUS GRISEBACH, "Baugeschichtliche Notiz zum Statuenhof Julius II. im vatikanischen Belvedere", *Zeitschrift für Kunstgeschichte* XXXIX, 209-220

M. GROBLEWSKI, "Die Kirche San Giovanni Battista in Pesaro von Girolamo Genga", D.Phil.diss., Regensburg

MICHAEL HIRST, "A Project of Michelangelo for the tomb of Julius II", *Master Drawings* XIV, 375-382

S.A. JAYAWARDENE, "The 'Trattato d'abaco' of Piero della Francesca", in *Cultural Aspects of the Italian Renaissance. Essays in Honour of Paul Oskar Kristeller*, edited by Cecil H. Clough, Manchester, 229-243

K. JEX-BLAKE, *The Elder Pliny's Chapters on the History of Art*, translated by K. Jex-Blake, Chicago (2nd American ed.)

G. KAHAN, *Jacques Callot, Artist of the Theatre*, Athens (Georgia)

FRITZ EUGEN KELLER, "Zur Plannung am bau der römischen Peterskirche im Jahre 1564-1565", *Jahrbuch der Berliner Museen* XVIII, 24-50

ALBINIA DE LA MARE, "The Library of Francesco Sassetti (1421-1490)", in *Cultural Aspects of Italian Renaissance*, Manchester, 160-201

RICHARD EDWARD LAMOUREX, *Alberti's Church of San Sebastiano in Mantua*, New York

HANS-KARL LUECKE, *Alberti Index*, 3. Bde. (I, 1975, III, 1979), München

MARIA LUISA MADONNA, "'SEPTEM MUNDI MIRACOLI' COME TEMPLI DELLE VIRTÙ. PIRRO LIGORIO E L'INTERPRETAZIONE CINQUECENTESCA DELLE MERAVIGLIE DEL MONDO", *Psicon* III (7), 24-63

ANTONIO MANETTI, *Vita di Filippo Brunelleschi*, a cura di Domenico de Robertis e Giuliano Tanturli, Milano-Firenze

LAWRENCE McGINNESS AND HERBERT MITCHELL, *Catalog of the Earl of Crawford's "Speculum Romanae Magnificentiae", Now in the Avery Library*, New York

HENRY A. MILLON AND CRAIG HUGH SMYTH, "Michelangelo and St. Peter's: Observations on the Interior of the Apses, a Model of the Apse Vault, and Related Drawings", *Römisches Jahrbuch für Kunstgeschichte* XVI, 137-206

Catherine Monbeig Goguel, "A propos d'un dessin retrouvé: Vasari et Zuccaro à la coupole de dôme de Florence", in *Il Vasari storiografo e artista*, Atti del congresso internazionale (Arezzo-Firenze, settembre 1974), 685-689

V. PACE, "Maso da San Friano", *Bollettino d'arte* I/II, 74-99

PIER NICOLA PAGLIARA, "La Roma antica di Fabio Calvo. Note sulla cultura antiquaria e architettonica", *Psicon* VIII-IX, 65-88

SALVATORE DI PASQUALE, "Una ipotesi sulla struttura della cupola di S. Maria del Fiore", *Restauro* XXVIII, 3-77

SIMON PEPPER, "Planning vs. Fortification: Sangallo's Project for the Defence of Rome", *Architectural Review* 159, 162-169

S. PEZZELLA (a cura di), *Il Trattato di Antonio di Pisa*, Perugia

PLINIO IL VECCHIO, see K. Jex-Blake

RODOLFO RAMAGLI, "Le Logge vasariane in Arezzo", Studi e documenti di architettura VI, 87-102

FERT SANGIORGI (a cura di), *Documenti urbinati. Inventari del Palazzo Ducale (1582-1631)*, Urbino

GUSTINA SCAGLIA, "The Opera de Architectura of Francesco di Giorgio Martini for Alfonso Duke of Calabria", *Napoli nobilissima* XV (5-6), 133-161

RICHARD SCHOFIELD, "A Drawing for Santa Maria presso San Satiro", *Journal of the Warburg and Courtauld Institutes* XXXIX, 246-253

GIULIANO TANTURLI, DOMENICO DE ROBERTIS, vedi Antonio Manetti

CHARLES DE TOLNAY, *Corpus dei disegni di Michelangelo* (1975-80), II, Novara

PETER TOMOROY, *Catalogue of the Italian Paintings before 1800, The John and Mable Ringling Museum of Art*, Sarasota

CAROLYN VALONE, "Giovanni Antonio Dosio: The Roman Years", *Art Bulletin* LVIII, 528-541

PAUL VEYNE, *Le pain et le cirque: sociologie historique d'un pluralisme*, Paris

ADRIAAN VLIEGENTHART, *La Galleria Buonarroti, Michelangelo e Michelangelo il giovane*, Firenze

H. WOHL ed., *Ascanio Condivi, The Life of Michelangelo*, translated by A. Sedgwick Wohl, Baton Rouge

WOLFANG WOLTERS, *La scultura veneziana gotica, 1300-1460*, Venezia

FEDERICO ZERI, *Italian Paintings in the Walters Art Gallery*, Baltimore

F. ZEVI, "L'identificazione del tempio di Marte 'in circo' e altre osservazioni", dans *L'Italie préromaine et la Rome républicaine. Mélanges offerts à Jacques Heurgon*, Rome, 1047-1064

1976-1980

SIMONETTA VALTIERI, "Il rapporto degli architetti del Rinascimento con l''antico' attraverso i disegni del Pantheon", *Colloqui del Sodalizio* 2 (6), 61-76

1977

Disegni di fabbriche brunelleschiane, catalogo mostra (Firenze, Gabinetto Disegni e Stampe degli Uffizi), a cura di Giuseppe Marchini, Gaetano Miarelli Mariani, Gabriele Morolli, Luigi Zangheri e Firenze

JAMES S. ACKERMAN, "L'architettura religiosa veneta in rapporto a quella toscana del Rinascimento", *Bollettino centro internazionale studi di architettura "Andrea Palladio"* XIX, 135 ss.

DUCCIO BALESTRACCI, GABRIELLA PICCINI, *Siena nel Trecento: Aspetto urbano e strutture edilizie*, Firenze

LUCILLA BARDESCHI CIULICH, "Documenti inediti su Michelangelo e l'incarico di San Pietro", *Rinascimento* XVII, 235-275

LANDO BARTOLI, *La rete magica di Filippo Brunelleschi. Le seste, il braccio, le misure*, Firenze

EUGENIO BATTISTI (a cura di), *Problemi brunelleschiani: Sagrestia Vecchia e San Lorenzo*, Roma

LUCIANO BELLOSI, "Una flagellazione del Bramante a Perugia", *Prospettiva* IX, 61-68

PAOLA BENIGNI (a cura di), *Filippo Brunelleschi. L'uomo e l'artista*, Firenze

PAOLO BENSI, "La tavolozza di Cennino Cennini", *Studi di Storia delle Arti* II, 37-85

E. BILLIG, *Spätantike Architekturdarstellungen* I, Acta Universitatis Stockolmiensis, Stockolm

FERDINANDO BOLOGNA, *Napoli e le rotte mediterranee della pittura. Da Alfonso il magnanimo a Ferdinando il Cattolico*, Napoli, 195-201

GENE A. BRUCKER, *The Civic World of Early Renaissance Florence*, Princeton

ARNALDO BRUSCHI, *Bramante*, Bari

CLAUDIA CIERI VIA, "Per una revisione del primitivismo nell'opera di Piero di Cosimo", *Storia dell'arte* XXIX, 5-14

J.J. COULTON, *Greek Architects at Work: Problems of Structure and Design*, London

MARGARET DALY DAVIS, *Piero della Francesca's Mathematical Treatises: the "Trattato d'abaco" and "Libellus de quinque corporibus regularibus"*, Ravenna

FRANCA FALLETTI, LEONARDO PAOLINI, "Una nuova data per la cupola del Brunelleschi", *Prospettiva* XI, 57-58

FRANCESCO PAOLO FIORE, "La città felice di Loreto", *Ricerche di storia dell'arte* IV, 37-55

ANNA FORLANI TEMPESTI, "Introduzione", in *Disegni di fabbriche brunelleschiane* (1977), vii-xvii

701

ENNIO FRANCIA, *1506-1606. Storia della costruzione del nuovo San Pietro*, Roma

CHRISTOPH L. FROMMEL [a], "Bramantes 'Disegno grandissimo' für den Vatikanpalast", *Kunstchronik* XXX, 63-64

—— [b], "'Cappella Julia', die Grabkapelle Papst Julius' II. in Neu-St. Peter", *Zeitschrift für Kunstgeschichte* XL, 26-62

EUGENIO GARIN (a cura di), *Prosatori latini del Quattrocento*, Torino

A. GRAFTON, "On the Scholarship of Politian and its Context", *Journal of the Warburg and Courtauld Institutes* XL, 150-188

M. HEINZ, "San Giacomo in Augusta in Rom und der Hospitalbau der Renaissance", Diss., Bonn

ISABELLE HYMAN, *Fifteenth Century Florentines Studies: The Palazzo Medici and a Ledger for the Church of San Lorenzo*, New York-London

M.N. JUHAR, "Der Romgedanke bei Cola di Rienzo", D.Phil. Diss, Erlangen

MARTIN KEMP, "Botticelli's Glasgow Annunciation: Patterns of Instability", *Burlington Magazine*, 184 ff.

F.W. KENT, "'Più superba de quella di Lorenzo': Courtly and Family Interest in the Building of Filippo Strozzi's Palace", *Renaissance Quarterly* XXX, 311-323

SPIRO KOSTOF, "The Architect in the Middle Ages, East and West", in *The Architect*, edited by Spiro Kostof, New York

RICHARD KRAUTHEIMER [a], *Corpus Basilicarum Christianarum Romae*, V, Città del Vaticano

—— [b], "Fra Angelico and - perhaps - Alberti", in *Studies in Late Medieval and Renaissance Painting. In Honor of Millard Meiss*, New York, 290-6

MARTIN KUBELIK, *Die Villa im Veneto: zur typologischen Entwicklung im Quattrocento*, 2. Bde, München

P.W. LEHMANN, *Cyriacus of Ancona's Egyptian Visit and its Reflections in Gentile Bellini and Jeronimus Bosch*, Locust Valley, N.Y.

RALPH LIEBERMAN, "Venetian Church Architecture aroung 1500", *Bollettino del centro internazionale di studi di architettura "Andrea Palladio"* XIX, 35-48

WOLFGANG LOTZ [a], "The Rendering of the Interior in Architectural Drawings of the Renaissance", in *Studies in Renaissance Architecture*, Cambridge, Mass., 1-65

—— [b], *Studies in Italian Renaissance Architecture*, Cambridge, Mass.

WILLIAM L. MACDONALD, "Roman Architects", in *The Architect*, edited by Spiro Kostof, New York

ROWLAND MAINSTONE, "Brunelleschi's Dome", *Architectural Review*, September, 157-166

GIUSEPPE MARCHINI [a], "Il ballatoio della cupola di Santa Maria del Fiore", *Antichità viva* XVI (6), 36-48

—— [b], "La cupola del Duomo", in *Disegni di fabbriche brunelleschiane* (1977), 5-33

—— [c], "Fulmini sulla cupola", *Antichità viva* XVI (4), 22-25

—— [d], scheda n. 1, in *Disegni di fabbriche brunelleschiane* (1977)

—— [e], scheda n. 7, in *Disegni di fabbriche brunelleschiane* (1977)

G. MORAN, "An Investigation Regarding the Equestrian Portrait of Guidoriccio da Fogliano in Siena Palazzo Pubblico", *Paragone* 333, 81-88

GERMANO MULAZZANI, "Lettura iconologica" in "Donato Bramante: gli Uomini d'arme", *Quaderni di Brera* III

LOREDANA OLIVATO, LIONELLO PUPPI, *Mauro Codussi*, Milano

PIER NICOLA PAGLIARA, "Una fonte di illustrazioni del Vitruvio di Fra' Giocondo", *Ricerche di storia dell'arte* VI, 113-120

"Palladio e l'architettura sacra del Cinquecento in Italia", in *bollettino centro internazionale di storia dell'architettura "Andrea Palladio"*, XIX, Vicenza

ERWIN PANOFSKY, "Artista, scienziato, genio: appunti sulla 'Renaissance-Dämmerung'", *Jahrbuch des italie-*

nisch-deutschen historischen Instituts in Trient III, 287-319 (Deutsche ausg., New York 1962)

CARLO PEDRETTI, *The Literary Works of Leonardo da Vinci*, edited by P. Richter Commentary, 2 vols., Oxford

ENNIO POLEGGI, *Iconografia di Genova e della Riviera*, Genova

BRENDA PREYER, "The Rucellai Loggia", *Mitteilungen des Kunsthistorischen Institutes in Florenz*, XXI, 183-198

CARLO LUDOVICO RAGGHIANTI, *Filippo Brunelleschi. Un uomo, un universo*, Firenze

K. RÜCKBROD, *Universität und Kollegium. Baugeschichte und Bautyp*, Darmstadt

HOWARD SAALMAN, "Michelangelo at Santa Maria del Fiore: An Addendum", *Burlington Magazine* CXIX, 852-853

FRANCESCO SANTI, "Ancora sulle architetture dei 'miracoli' del 1473 e sui rapporti tra l'ambiente urbinate e la scuola perugina", in *Rapporti artistici fra le Marche e l'Umbria. Atti del convegno interregionale di studi* (Fabriano-Gubbio, 8-9 giugno 1974), Perugia, 49-53

JOHN SHEARMAN, "Raffael, Rome and the Codex Escurialensis", *Master Drawings* XV (2), 107-146

JULIUS VON SCHLOSSER MAGNINO, *La letteratura artistica, Manuale delle fonti della storia dell'arte moderna*, Firenze

K. SCHWAGEN, "La chiesa del Gesù del Vignola", *Bollettino centro internazionale studi di architettura "Andrea Palladio"* XIX, 251-271

A. SCOTTI, "Per un profilo dell'architettura milanese (1535-1565)", in *Omaggio a Tiziano. La cultura artistica milanese nell'età di Carlo V*, Milano, 97-121

CHARLES DE TOLNAY, PAOLA SQUELLATI, *Brunelleschi e Michelangelo*, Firenze

PIETRO TOMEI, *L'architettura a Roma nel Quattrocento*, Roma (1a ed. 1942)

PIETRO TORRITI, *La Pinacoteca Nazionale di Siena. I dipinti dal XII al XV secolo*, Genova

CAROLYN VALONE, "Paul IV, Guglielmo della Porte and the Rebuilding of San Silvestro al Quirinale", *Master Drawings* XV (3), 243-355

ZYGMUNT WAZBINSKI, "Artisti e pubblico nella Firenze del Cinquecento", *Paragone* 327, 3-24

Die Zeit der Staufer, Ausstellungskatalog, Stuttgart

LUDOVICO ZORZI, *Il teatro e la città. Saggi sulla scena italiana*, Torino

1978

MARIA G. AGGHAZY, "Problemi nuovi relativi a un monumento sepolcrale del Verrocchio", *Acta Historiae* Artium XXIV

S. BARDAZZI, E. CASTELLANI, F. GURRIERI, *Santa Maria delle Carceri a Prato*, Firenze

BARICCHI, CAVANDOLI, MARCHESINI (a cura di), *Reggio Emilia: la città dall'età romana al XX secolo*, Reggio Emilia

DANTE E GRAZIA BERNINI, in *Il restauro della Città Ideale di Urbino*, catalogo mostra, Urbino

CARLO BERTOCCI AND CHARLES DAVIS, "A Leaf from the Scholz Scrapbook", *Metropolitan Museum Journal* XII, 93-100

RENATO BONELLI, "Lettera a Leone X", in *Scritti rinascimentali di architettura*, a cura di Arnaldo Bruschi et al., Milano, 461-483

EVE BORSOOK, "Michelozzo and Bonsignori in the Levant", *Journal of the Warbug and Courtauld Institutes* XXXVI, 176ff.

LUDOVICO BORGO AND HOWARD SAALMAN, "1512: Projects for a New Church of San Marco in Florence", in *Essays Presented to Myron Gilmore*, II, Firenze, 15-23

ARNALDO BRUSCHI [a], "Prima di Brunelleschi: verso un'architettura sintattica e prospettica, I: da Arnolfo a Giotto", *Palladio* XXVII (3/4), 47-76

—— (a cura di) [b], *Scritti rinascimentali di architettura*, Milano

M. BUTZEK, *Die kommunalen Repraesentationsstatuen der Paepste des 16. Jahrhunderts in Bologna, Perugia und Rom*, Bad Honnef

ALBERTO CARLO CARPICECI, "Testimonianze su Filippo Brunelleschi. II: Macchine ed attrezzature edilizie, attraverso i disegni di Leonardo da Vinci, Giuliano da Sangallo e Nonaccorso Ghiberti", *Istruzione tecnica e professionale* n.s., XIV (56), 215-231

ANDRÉ CHASTEL, "'Vues urbaines peintes' et théâtre", dans *Fables, Formes, Figures*, Paris, I, 497-503

ROMEO DE MAIO, *Michelangelo e la Controriforma*, Bari

CAROLINE ELAM, "Lorenzo de' Medici and the Urban Development of Renaissance Florence", *Art History* I, 43-66

L.D. ETTLINGER, *Antonio and Piero Pollaiuolo*, New York

M. FAGIOLO, *Chiese e cattedrali*, Milano

FEDERICO DA MONTEFELTRO, "Patente a Luciano Laurana", a cura di Arnaldo Bruschi e Domenico De Robertis, in *Scritti rinascimentali di architettura*, 19 sg.

ROSZA FEUER-TÓTH, "The 'Apertiunum Ornamenta' of Alberti and the Architecture of Brunelleschi", *Acta Historiae Artium* XXIV, 147-52

FRANCESCO PAOLO FIORE, *Città e macchine del '400 nei disegni di Francesco di Giorgio Martini*, Firenze

DOMENICO FONTANA, *Della trasportazione dell'obelisco vaticano, 1590*, a cura di Adriano Carugo, Milano

PHILIP E. FOSTER, *A Study of Lorenzo de' Medicis Villa at Poggio a Caiano*, New York-London

G. FREULER, "Andrea di Bartolo, Fra Tommaso d'Antonio Caffarini, and Sienese Dominicans in Venice", *Art Bulletin* LXIV, 4, 570-586

RICHARD HARPRATH, *Papst Paul III. als Alexander der Grosse*, Berlin-New York

HOWARD HIBBARD, *Michelangelo, Painter, Sculptor, Architect*, New York

J.B. HORRIGAN, "Imperial and Urban Ideology in a Renaissance Inscription", *Comitatus. A Journal of Medieval and Renaissance Studies* IX, 73-87

F. IRACE (a cura di), *Sebastiano Serlio. I sette libri dell'architettura*, Bologna

B. JESTAZ, R. BACOU, JULES ROMAIN, *L'histoire de Scipion: tapisseries et dessins*, catalogue exposition (Paris, Grand Palais), Paris

PAUL JOANNIDES, REVIEW OF C. DE TOLNAY, "Disegni di Michelangelo nelle collezioni italiane", *Art Bulletin* LX, 174-177

VLADIMIR JUREN, "Politien et Vitruve (Note sur le ms. lat. 7382 de la Bibliothèque Nationale)", *Rinascimento* 2a s., XVIII, 285-292

M. BARRY KATZ, *Leon Battista Alberti and the Humanist Theory of the Arts*, Washington

BENJAMIN G. KOHL AND RONALD G. WITT, eds., *The Earthly Republic: Italian Humanists on Government and Society*, Philadelphia

GERT KREYTENBERG, "Der Campanile von Giotto", *Mitteilungen des Kunsthistorischen Institutes im Florenz* XXII, 147-184

JAY LEVENSON, "Jacopo de' Barbari and Northern Art of the Early Sixteenth Century", Ph.D. diss. New York University

Lorenzo Ghiberti. Materia e ragionamenti, catalogo mostra, Firenze

M. LUPO, "I disegni delle fortezze veneziane nell'archivio di Emanuele Filiberto di Savoia", in *Atti del I congresso internazionale di architettura fortificata*, Bologna, 319-349

GIUSEPPE MARCHINI, *Ghiberti architetto*, Firenze

L. MARCUCCI, "Giovanni Sulpicio e la prima edizione del 'De architectura' di Vitruvio", *Studi e documenti di architettura* VIII, 185-195

ULRICH MIDDELDORF, "On the Dilettante Sculptor", *Apollo* 107, 316-19

GERMANO MULAZZANI, "Il tema iconografico dell'incisione Prevedari", *Rassegna di studi e di notizie* VI, 67 sg.

GERMANO MULAZZANI, GIAN ALBERTO DELL'ACQUA, *Bramante pittore e il Bramantino*, Milano

U. NILGEN, "Filarete's Bronzetür von St. Peter. Zur Interpretation von Bild und Rahmen", in *Actas del*

XXIII Congresso internacional de historia del arte. Espana entre el Mediterráneo y el Atlántico (Granada 1976), III, 569-85

L. Partridge, "Divinity and Dinasty at Caprarola: Perfect History in the Room of Farnese Deeds", *Art Bulletin* LX, 494-529

Pier Giorgio Pasini, "Rimini nel Quattrocento", in *Studi storici* 110-111 (numero monografico: "Studi malatestiani"), 117-157

Carlo Pedretti, *Leonardo architetto*, Milano (2a ed. aggiornata, 1988)

G. Pinto, *Il libro del Biadaiolo. Carestia e annona a Firenze dalla metà del '200 al 1348*, Firenze

Il restauro della Città Ideale di Urbino, catalogo mostra, Urbino

Howard Saalman, "Michelangelo at St. Peter's: the Arberino Correspondence", *Art Bulletin* LX, 483-493

D. Schmidt, *Untersuchungen zu den Architektur-Ekphrasen in der Hypnerotomachia Poliphili. Die Beschreibung des Venus Tempels*, Frankfurt

Jürgen Schulz, "Jacopo de' Barbari's View of Venice: Map Making, City Views, and Moralized Geography before the Year 1500", *Art Bulletin* LX, 425-474

Sebastiano Serlio, vedi F. Irace

Grazioso Sironi, "Gli affreschi di Donato dell'Angelo detto il Bramante alla Pinacoteca di Brera in Milano: chi ne fu il committente?" *Archivio storico lombardo*

Graham Smith, "A Drawing by Federico Zuccaro for the Last Judgement in Florence Cathedral", *Bulletin Museums of Art and Archeology the University of Michigan* I, 27-41

Corrado Verga, *Dispositivo Brunelleschi 1420*, Crema

Rudolph Wittkower [a], "The 'Menicantonio' Sketchbook in the Paul Mellon Collection", in *Idea and Image: Studies in the Italian Renaissance*, London, 91-107

—— [b], "Michelangelo's Dome of St. Peter's", in *Idea and Image: Studies in the Italian Renaissance*, London, 73-89

L. Zentai, "Considerations on Raphael's Compositions of the Coronation of the Virgin", *Acta Historiae Artium* XXIV, 195-199

1978-1980

K.D. Keele and Carlo Pedretti, *Leonardo da Vinci. Corpus of the Anatomical Studies in the Collection of Her Majesty the Queen at Windsor Castle*, 3 vols., New York

1979

Paola Barocchi, vedi Giovanni Poggi

Paul Barolsky, *Daniele da Volterra. A Catalogue Raisonné*, New York-London

Evelina Borea, "Stampa figurativa e pubblico dalle origini all'affermazione del Cinquecento", in *Storia dell'Arte Italiana. L'artista e il pubblico*, Torino, II, 339

Franco Borsi, Gabriele Morolli, Francesco Quinterio, *Brunelleschiana*, Roma

Arnaldo Bruschi, "Prima di Brunelleschi: verso un'architettura sintattica e prospettica, II: Da Giotto a Taddeo Gaddi al tardo Trecento", *Palladio* XXVIII (1-4), 23-42

Howard Burns [a], "A Drawing by L.B. Alberti", *Architectural Design* XLIX, 45-56

—— [b], "San Lorenzo in Florence before the Building the the New Sacristy", *Mitteilungen des kunsthistorischen Institutes in Florenz* XXIII, 145-54

A. Calzona, *Mantova città dell'Aberti. Il S. Sebastiano: tomba, tempio, cosmo*, Parma

Enzo Carli, *Il duomo di Siena*, Genova

Patrizia Castelli, *I geroglifici e il mito dell'Egitto nel Rinascimento*, Firenze

D. Catalano, "Indagine radiologica della tavola Strozzi", *Napoli nobilissima* XVIII, 10-11

Giovanni Cavalcanti, "Istorie fiorentine", in Eugenio Garin, *La cultura filosofica del Rinascimento italiano*, Firenze, 328sg.

Keith Christiansen, "For fra Carnevale", *Apollo* 109, 198-201

Luisa Cogliati Arano, "Due codici corvini: il Filarete marciano e l'epitalamio di Volterra", *Arte lombarda* LII, 53-62

David R. Coffin, *The Villa in the Life of Renaissance Rome*, Princeton

Caroline Elam, "The Site and Early Building History of Michelangelo's New Sacristy", *Apollo* 109, 155-186

Cornelius von Fabriczy, *Filippo Brunelleschi. La vita e le opere*, traduzione di A.M. Poma, Firenze (ed. originale, *Filippo Brunelleschi. Sein Leben und seine Werke*, Stuttgart 1892)

Luca Fancelli Architetto. Epistolario gonzaghesco, a cura di C. VasicV Vatovec, Firenze

Amelio Fara, *Buontalenti: architettura e teatro*, Firenze

Christoph L. Frommel, *Michelangelo e Tommaso de Cavalieri*, Amsterdam

G. Italiani et al., *Le Cronache di Todi (secoli XIII-XVI)*, Firenze

Richard Edward Lamoureux, *Alberti's Chruch of San Sebastiano in Mantua*, New York-London

Roberto Longhi, *Disegno della pittura veneziana*, Firenze

Hans-Karl Luecke, *Alberti Index*, 3. Bde. (I, 1975, II, 1976), München

Francesco Federico Mancini, "Identificazione di Pietro di Galeotto", *Esercizi* II, 43-55

Pietro C. Marani, *Il Codice Ashburnham 361 della Biblioteca Medicea Laurenziana di Firenze. Trattato di architettura di Francesco di Giorgio Martini*, 2 voll., Firenze

André Martindale, *The Triumph of Caesar by Andrea Mantegna in the Collection of Her Majesty the Queen at Hampton Court*, London

Lauro Martines, *Power and Imagination: City-States in Renaissance Italy*, New York

Emma Micheletti, *Ritratto di famiglia: I Medici e Firenze*, Firenze

Joan Lee Nissman, "Domenico Cresti (Il Passignano), 1559-1638: a Tuscan Painter in Florence and Rome", Ph.D. diss., Columbia University

J.W. O'Malley, *Praise and Blame in Renaissance Rome*, Durham

U. Paal, "Studien zum Appartamento Borgia im Vatikan", D.Phil. diss., Tübingen

Roberto Pane, "La Tavola Strozzi tra Firenze e Napoli", *Napoli Nobilissima*, XVIII, fasc. I, 4-5

C. Perni, "Modello della chiesa di S. Maria della Consolazione", in (Comune di Todi) *Mostra di restauri*, catalogo mostra (Todi, 14-30 aprile), Todi, 35-38

N. Randolph Parks, "On the Meaning of Pinturicchio's Sala dei Santi", *Art History* II, 291-317

Giovanni Poggi, *Il carteggio di Michelangelo* (1965-83), a cura di Paola Barocchi e Renzo Ristori, IV, Firenze

Jonathan B. Riess, "The Civic View of Sculpture in Alberti's De re aedificatoria", *Renaissance Quarterly* 32, 1 (Spring), 1-17

O.J. Rothrock and E. van Gulick, "Seeing and Meaning: Observations on the Theatre of Callot's 'Primo Intermedio'", *New Mexico Studies in the Fine Arts* IV, 16-36

F. Rusk Shapley, *Catalogue of the Italian Paintings. National Gallery of Art, Washington*, Washington

J. Russel Sale, *The Strozzi Chapel by Filippino Lippi in Santa Maria Novella*, Ann Arbor-London

Leon George Satkowski, *Studies on Vasari's Architecture*, New York-London

E.C. Southard, *The Frescoes in Siena's Palazzo Pubblico, 1289-1539*, London-New York

Martin Stankowski, "Gedanken zu zwei repräsentativen Architekturen Michelangelos", *Wiener Jahrbuch für Kunstgeschichte* XXXII, 15-39

Orietta Vasori, "Disegni di antichità etrusche agli Uffizi", *Studi etruschi* XLVII, 126-128

G. Vitale, "De Roma", in *Renaissance Latin Verse: An Anthology*, edited by A. Perosa and J. Sparrow, Chapel Hill, 243

1979-1987

W. Tatarkiewicz, *Geschichte der Ästhetik*, 3Bde., Basel-Stuttgart

1980

Abstracts of Papers Delivered in Art History Sessions. 68th Annual Meeting, College Art Association (January 30-February 2), 1980, New Orleans, New York

Filippo Brunelleschi. La sua opera ed il suo tempo, Atti del Convegno Internazionale per il sesto centenario della nascita (Firenze, 16-22 ottobre 1977), 2 voll., Firenze

Firenze e la Toscana dei Medici nell'Europa del Cinquecento. La rinascita della scienza, catalogo mostra (Firenze, Biblioteca Mediceo Laurenziana), Firenze

I Medici e lo stato senese 1555-1609: storia e territorio, a cura di Leonardo Rombai, Roma

Il potere e lo spazio: riflessioni di metodo e contributi. Interventi presentati al Convegno-Seminario (Firenze, 16-17 giugno), Firenze

James S. Ackerman, "Observations on Renaissance Church Planning in Venice and Florence, 1470-1570", in *Florence and Venice: Comparisons and Relations*, II, Florence, 287-307

Cristina Acidini Luchinat, "Aggiunte al Dosio", in *Il Potere e lo spazio... (1980)*, 61-66

Andrea Palladio: il testo, l'immagine, la città, catalogo mostra (Vicenza, Palazzo Leoni Montecari) a cura di Lionello Puppi, Vicenza

Gino Arrighi, "Le scienze esatte al tempo di Brunelleschi", in *Filippo Brunelleschi... (1980)*, I

M. Ashley, *The Seven Wonders of the World*, Glasgow

K. De Baranano, "La Medalla de Leon Bautista Alberti, por Mateo de' Pasti", *Goya* 156, 336-337

Isa Belli Barsali, *I palazzi dei mercanti nella libera Lucca del '500*, catalogo mostra, Lucca

Luciano Bellosi, in *Il Maestro di Figline. Un pittore del Trecento*, catalogo mostra, Firenze, 11-17

Carla Bernardi (a cura di), *Immagini architettoniche nella maiolica italiana del Cinquecento*, Milano

A.R. Blumenthal, *Theater Art of the Medici*, exhibition catalog (Hanover, Dartmouth College Museum and Galleries), Hanover

Anthony Blunt, "Roman Baroque Architecture. The Other Side of the Medal", *Art History* III, 61-80

Franco Borsi [a], *L'architettura del principe*, Firenze

—— [b], *Leon Battista Alberti. L'opera completa*, Milano

Franco Borsi et al., *Il disegno interrotto: trattati medicei di architettura*, Firenze

Howard Burns, "Un disegno architettonico di Alberti e la questione del rapporto tra Brunelleschi e Alberti", in *Filippo Brunelleschi... (1980)*, I, 105-123

M. Cal‰o, *Da Michelangelo all'Escorial. Momenti del dibattito religioso nell'arte del Cinquecento*, Torino

Pietro Paolo Carpeggiani (a cura di), *Alvise Cornaro. Scritti sull'architettura*, Padova

M.L. Casanova Uccella, scheda n.51 in *Palazzo Venezia. Paolo II e le fabbriche di San Marco*, catalogo mostra, Roma, 93-94

G. Cipriani, *Il mito etrusco nel rinascimento fiorentino*, Firenze

Luisa Cogliati Arano, *Disegni di Leonardo e della sua cerchia nelle Gallerie dell'Accademia*, catalogo della mostra, Venezia

Joseph Connors, *Borromini and the Roman Oratory. Style and Society*, New York

Alessandro Conti, in *Il Maestro di Figline. Un pittore del Trecento*, catalogo mostra, Firenze, 23-27

G. Contorni, "L'attività di Baldassarre Lanci nello Stato di Siena", in *Il potere e lo spazio... (1980)*, 131-139

Alvise Cornaro, vedi Pietro Paolo Carpeggiani

Enrico Coppi, "L'architettura militare del regime mediceo nello Stato di Siena", in *I Medici e lo Stato Senese... (1980)*, 117-124

Zeno Davoli, *Vedute e piante di Reggio dei secoli XVI-XVII-XVIII*, Reggio Emilia

ROBERTO DI STEFANO [a], "Confronto fra due cupole", in *Filippo Brunelleschi la sua opera e il suo tempo*, Congrès, 16-22 Oct. 1977, Florence, Firenze, 871-882

—— [b], *La cupola di San Pietro*, Napoli (2a ed. rivista)

CHRISTOFFER H. ERICSSON, *Roman Architecture Expressed in Sketches by Francesco di Giorgio Martini. Studies in Imperial Roman and Early Christian Architecture*, Helsinki

MARIO FANTI, *La fabbrica di S. Petronio in Bologna dal XIV al XX secolo. Storia di una istituzione*, Roma

Firenze e la Toscana dei Medici nell'Europa del Cinquecento. La scena del Principe, catalogo mostra (Firenze, Palazzo Medici Riccardi), Firenze

MARIO FONDELLI, "Il contributo della metodologia fotogrammetrica al rilevamento ed allo studio di alcune strutture del Brunelleschi", in *Filippo Brunelleschi...* (1980), II, 809-815

PAOLO GALLUZZI [a], scheda, in *Firenze e la Toscana dei Medici...* (1980)

—— [b], scheda 4.22, in *Firenze e la Toscana dei Medici...* (1980), 160

G. GERMAN, *Einführung in die Geschichte der Architekturtheorie*, Darmstadt

GRAZIA GOBBI, *La villa fiorentina: elementi storici e critici per una lettura*, Firenze

RICHARD A.GOLDTHWAITE, *The Building of Renaissance Florence: An Economic and Social History*, Baltimore-London

R. GROSSHANS, *Maerten van Heemskerck. Die Gemälde*, Berlin

FRITZ-EUGEN KELLER, *Zum Villenleben und Villenbau am Römischen Hof der Farnese*, Berlin

RICHARD KRAUTHEIMER, *Rome. Profile of a City*, New Jersey

RICHARD KRAUTHEIMER, S. Corbett, A.K. Frazer, *Corpus Basilicarum christianarum Romae*, V, Città del Vaticano

Livorno e Pisa: due città e un territorio nella politica dei Medici, catalogo mostra, Pisa

P. LOHR (a cura di), *Cristoforo Landino. Disputationes Camaldulenses*, Firenze

PAMELA OLIVIA LONG, "The Vitruvian Commentary Tradition and Rational Architecture in the Sixteenth Century: A Study in the History of Ideas", Ph.D.diss., University of Maryland

RENZO MANETTI, *Michelangelo. Le fortificazioni per l'assedio di Firenze*, Firenze

GIUSEPPE MARCHINI, "La cupola: medievale e no", in *Filippo Brunelleschi...* (1980), II, 915-920

ANNA MATTEOLI, *Lodovico Cardi-Cigoli pittore e architetto*, Pisa

E. MATTIOLI, *Luciano e l'Umanesimo*, Napoli

M.C. MAZZI, "Tommaso Puccini, un provinciale cosmopolita", *Bollettino d'arte* XXXVII/XXXVIII, 25 e sg.

JOHN McANDREW, *Venetian Architecture of the Early Renaissance*, Cambridge, Mass.-London

SILVIA MELONI TRKULJA, scheda A 380, in *Gli Uffizi. Catalogo generale*, Firenze

HENRY A. MILLON, "Cappella Gregoriana", in *Abstracts of Papers...* (1980)

MARCELLA MORVIDUCCI, "Note storiche sul Palazzo Reale di Siena", in *I Medici e le Stato Senese...* (1980), 165-170

H. OST, *Das Leonardo-Porträt in der Kgl Bibliothek Turin und andere Fälschungen des Giuseppe Bossi*, Berlin

Palazzo Vecchio: committenza e collezionismo medicei, catalogo mostra, Firenze

Paliaga, schede in *Livorno e Pisa....* (1980)

ANDREA PALLADIO, *I quattro libri dell'architettura*, a cura di Licisco Magagnato e Paola Marini, Milano

G. PAPAGNI, *La maiolica del Rinascimento in Castel-Durante, Urbino e Pesaro*, Pesaro, s.d. [1980 ca.]

L. PARTRIDGE, "Divinity and Dynasty at Caprarola: Perfect History in the Room of Farnese Deeds", *Art Bulletin* LX, 494-529

LUCIANO PATETTA (a cura di), *I Longhi. Una famiglia di architetti tra manierismo e barocco*, catalogo mostra (Viggiù, Museo Butti ;Roma, Accademia di San Luca), Roma

CECILIA PERICOLI RIDOLFINI (a cura di), *Guide rionali di Roma. Rione VI: Parione*, Roma (3a ed.)

S. PRETE, *L'umanista Niccolò Perotti*, Sassoferrato

HOWARD SAALMAN, *Filippo Brunelleschi and the Cupola of S. Maria del Fiore*, London

SERGIO SAMEK LUDOVICI, "Cesariano Cesare", voce in *Dizionario Biografico degli Italiani*, XXIV, Roma, 172-180

PIERO SANPAOLESI, "Le conoscenze tecniche del Brunelleschi", in *Filippo Brunelleschi...* (1980), 145-160

GUSTINA SCAGLIA, "Autour de Francesco di Giorgio Martini, ingénieur et dessinateur", *Revue de l'art* XLVIII, 7-25

RICHARD SCHOLFIELD, "Giovanni da Tolentino Goes to Rome: A Description of the Antiquities of Rome in 1490", *Journal of the Warburg and Courtauld Institutes* XLIII, 253ff.

CRAIG HUGH SMYTH, "New Documentary Evidence for Dating the Construction of the Cappella Gregoriana", in *Abstracts of Papers...* (1980)

Testimonianze veneziane di interesse palladiano. Mostra documentaria, Venezia

V. TIBERIA, "Il ricollocamento di nove dipinti nel Museo di Capodimonte", *Ricerche di storia dell'arte* XII, 77-86

CHARLES DE TOLNAY, *Corpus dei disegni di Michelangelo* (1975-80), IV, Novara

CHARLES DE TOLNAY, PAOLA SQUELLATI BRIZIO, *Michelangelo e i Medici*, Firenze

Z. WÀZB%ONSKI, "Le polemiche intorno al Battistero fiorentino nel Cinquecento", in *Filippo Brunelleschi...* (1980), II, 933-950

1981

F.W. KENT ET AL., *Giovanni Rucellai ed il Suo Zibaldone: A Patrician and His Palace*, texts by A. Perosa, Brenda Preyer, Piero Sanpaolesi and Renato Salvini, London

Splendours of the Gonzaga, Martineau eds, exhibition catalog (London, Victoria & Albert Museum), London

ANNIO DA VITERBO, *Documenti e ricerche*, Roma

N. ARICÒ, "Per una genealogia della normativa urbanistica in Sicilia", *Incontri meridionali* III, 125-150

EUGENIO BATTISTI, *Brunelleschi*, Milano

CARLO BERTELLI, prefazione a Deanna Lenzi, *Il Biadaiolo*, Milano

HARTMUT BIERMANN, "Paläste und Villa. Theorie und Praxis in Giuliano da Sangallos Codex Barberini und in Taccuino Senese", in *Les Traités d'architecture de la Rénassaince*, actes du colloque, Tours, 138 e sv.

MARIA TERESA BINAGHI OLIVARI (a cura di), *Collezione civiche di Como*, Milano

WILLIAM M. BOWSKY, *A Medieval Italian Commune. Siena under the Nine, 1287-1355*, Berkeley-London

R. BRILLIANT, "Ancient Roman Monuments as Models and Topoi", in *Umanesimo a Roma nel quattrocento*, Atti del Convegno, a cura di P. Brezzi e M. de Panizza Lorch, Roma-New York, 223-233

A. BUCK, *Studia humanitatis. Gesammelte Aufsätze 1973-1980*, Wiesbaden

HOWARD BURNS [a], "The Church of San Sebastiano, Mantua", in *Splendours...* (1981)

—— [b], "The Gonzaga and Renaissance Architecture", in *Splendours...*(1981), 27-38

MARTINEAU, EDS., in *Splendours of the Gonzaga* (1981), 27-38

CESARE CESARIANO, *Di Lucio Vitruvio Pollione de Architettura Libri Dece traducti de Latino in Vulgare affigurati* (Como) MDXXI, a cura di Arnaldo Bruschi, Adriano Carugo e Francesco Paolo Fiore, Milano

ERIC COCHRANE, *Historians and Historiography in the Italian Renaissance*, Chicago-London

SILVIA DANESI SQUARZINA, "La qualità artigiana degli interventi quattrocenteschi in Ostia Tiberina", in *Il borgo di Ostia da Sisto IV a Giulio II*, catalogo a cura di Silvia Danesi Squarzina, Roma

CESARE DE SETA, *Napoli. Le città nella storia d'Italia*, Roma-Bari

PETER EISENMAN, "Preface", in *Idea as Model*, New York

CAROLINE ELAM, "The Mural Drawings in Michelangelo's New Sacristy", *Burlington Magazine* 123, 593-602

GIOVANNI FANELLI [a], *Firenze: Architettura e Città*, 2 voll., Firenze

—— [b], *Firenze. Le città nella storia d'Italia*, Roma-Bari

M. FIORIO, "Marco Zoppo et le livre padouan", *Revue de l'art* LIII, 65-73

MARIO FONDELLI, "Studio geometrico di un antico modello ligneo restaurato", in *Atti del convegno sul restauro delle opere d'arte* (Firenze, ottobre 1976), Firenze

CRISTOPH L. FROMMEL, "Sangallo et Michel-Ange (1513-1550)", dans *Le Palais Farnèse*, sous la direction de André Chastel, I,1, Rom, 127-224

H. GIESS, "Die Stadt Castro und die Pläne von Antonio da Sangallo d.j.", *Römisches Jahrbuch für Kunstgeschichte* XIX, 85-140

ALBERTO GROHMANN, *Perugia*, Bari

C. GRONDONA, *Todi storica ed artistica*, 6a ed. ampliata, Todi (2a ed. 1968)

HUBERTUS GÜNTHER [a], "Das geistige Erbe Peruzzis im vierten und dritten Buch des Sebastiano Serlio", in *Les traités d'architecture de la Renaissance*, Tours, 227-245

—— [b], "Porticus Pompeji", *Zeiftschrift für Kunstgeschichte* XLIV, 356-398

—— [c], "Studien zum venezianischen Aufenthalt des Sebastiano Serlio", *Münchener Jahrbuch der bildenden Kunst* XXXII, 42-94

LUDWIG H. HEYDENREICH, *Studien zur Architektur der Renaissance. Ausgewählte Aufsätze*, München

ISABELLE HYMAN, "Examining a Fifteenth-Century 'Tribute' to Florence", in *Art the Ape of Nature: Studies in Honor of H.W. Janson*, New York-Englewood Cliffs, 105-126

DEBORAH HOWARD, *The Architectural History of Venice*, New York

PAUL JOANNIDES [a], "Review of Charles de Tolnay, Corpus dei disegni di Michelangelo", *Art Bulletin* LXIII, 679-687

—— [b], "Review of Rudolf Wittkower, Idea and Image, and J. Wilde, Michelangelo, Six Lectures", *Burlington Magazine* CXXIII, 620-622

MARTIN KEMP, *Leonardo da Vinci: The Marvellous Works of Nature and Man*, Cambridge, Mass.

F.W. KENT, "The Making of a Renaissance Patron of the Arts", in F.W. Kent et al. (1981), II

DOUGLAS LEWIS [a], *The Drawings of Andrea Palladio*, exhibition catalogue, Washington

—— [b], "Patterns of Preference: Patronage of Sixteenth-Century Architects by the Venetian Patriciate", in *Patronage in the Renaissance*, edited by Guy Fitch Lytle and Stephen Orgel, Princeton, 354-380

E. LIPSMEYER, "The Donor and his Church Model in Medieval Art from Early Christian Times to the Late Romanesque Period", Ph.D.diss., Rutgers, the State University of New Jersey

PIERO MORSELLI, "A Project by Michelangelo for the Ambo(s) of Santa Maria del Fiore, Florence", *Journal of the Society of Architectural Historians* XL, 122-129

F. MANENTI VALLI, "Il 'non finito' clementesco nella facciata della Cattedrale", in *Strenna del pio istituto Artigianelli*, Reggio Emilia

MARIA e LUIGI MORANTI, *Il trasferimento dei Codices Urbinates alla Biblioteca Vaticana. Cronistoria, documenti, inventario*, Urbino

HEINER MÜHLMANN, *Ästhetische Theorie der Renaissance. Leon Battista Alberti*, Bonn

JOHN ONIANS, "The System of Orders in Renaissance Architectural Thought", dans *Les Traités D'Architecture de la Renaissance*, sous la direction de Jean Guillaume, Paris

J.T. OOSTING, *Andrea Palladio's Teatro Olimpico*, Ann Arbor

RICCARDO PACCIANI, "Schizzi relativi agli affreschi della cupola di S. Maria del Fiore", in *Giorgio Vasari*, catalogo mostra (Arezzo, settembre-novembre), Firenze, 166-168

CARLO PEDRETTI, *Leonardo architetto*, Milano

A. PEROSA, "Lo Zibaldone di Giovanni Rucellò", in F.W. Kent et al. (1981), 99-100

ANNAMARIA PETRIOLI TOFANI, "Maestri della decorazione e del teatro", in *Biblioteca di disegni* XXVIII, Firenze

S. PRETE, "Osservazioni e note sull'umanista Niccolò Perotti cittadino veneziano" (Centro Tedesco di Studi Veneziani, *Quaderni* XX), Venezia

ENNIO POLEGGI, P. CEVINI, *Genova. Le città nella storia d'Italia*, Roma-Bari

G. PONTE, *Leon Battista Alberti. Umanista e scrittore*, Genova

BRENDA PREYER, "The Palazzo Rucellai", in F.W. Kent et al. (1981), II, 155-208

GUSTINA SCAGLIA, *Alle origini degli studi di tecnologia di Leonardo* XX Lettura vinciana (20 aprile 1980), Firenze

LUIGI SPEZZAFERRO, RICHARD TUTTLE, "Place Farnèse: urbanisme et politique", dans *Le Palais Farnèse*, I, Rome, 85-123

D. SUMMERS, *Michelangelo and the Language of Art*, Princeton,

MADDALENA TRIONFI HONORATI, in *Giorgio Vasari*, catalogo mostra, Firenze, 311-312

ORIETTA VASORI, *I monumenti antichi in Italia nei disegni degli Uffizi*, Roma

CORRADO VERGA, *Il duomo di Milano da Bramante-Cesariano a Stornaloco*, Crema

TILL R. VERELLEN, "Raffaello da Montelupo als und Architekt", D.Phil.Diss., Hamburg (Biblioteca Hertziana)

VITRUVIUS, *De architettura libri decem*, besorgt von C. Fensterbusch, Darmastadt

NATHAN WHITMAN, *Papal Medals from the Age of the Baroque*, Ann Arbor

MARIUCCIA ZECCHINELLI, "Progetto per il Duomo di Como (schede n. 50 e 51)", in *Collezioni civiche di Como. Proposte, scoperte e restauri*, Como, 117-118

1981-82

HUBERTUS GÜNTHER, "Die Rekonstruktion des antiken römischen Fussmasses in der Renaissance", *Kunstgeschichtliche Gesellschaft zu Berlin. Sitzungsberichte* XXXI, 8-12

LIONELLO PUPPI, *Andrea Palladio*, Milano

1982

La corte e lo spazio. Ferrara estense, a cura di G. Papagno e A. Quondam, Roma

Rome in the Renaissance. The City and the Myth, edited by P.A. Ramsey, Binghamton-New York

JAMES S. ACKERMAN, "The Planning of Renaissance Rome, 1450-1580", in *Rome in the Renaissance...* (1982), 3-18

BRUNO ADORNI [a], *L'architettura farnesiana a Piacenza 1545-1600*, Parma

—— (a cura di) [b], *Santa Maria dello Steccato a Parma*, Parma

ENZO BENTIVOGLIO, "Cola di Matteuccio", voce in *Dizionario Biografico degli Italiani*, XXVI, Roma, 658-660

RAFFAELLO CAUSA (a cura di), *La collezione del Museo di Capodimonte*, Milano

GIOVANNA CURCIO, MARIO MANIERI ELIA, *Storia e uso dei modelli architettonici*, Roma

R. DAVANZO, "S. Maria della Consolazione. Spazio ideale e problemi bramanteschi", in *Verso un museo della città. Catalogo della mostra di restauri*, a cura di M. Bergamini e G. Comez, Todi, 295-306

BERNHARD DEGENHART, ANNEGRIT SCHMITT, *Corpus der italienischen Zeichnungen 1300-1450*, Teil II, *Venedig, Addenda zu Sued-und Mittelitalien. Mariano Taccola.* (4. band. Katalog 717-719), Berlin

Egypt's Golden Age: the Art of Living in the New Kingdom, 1558-1085 B.C., exhibition catalog (Boston, Museum of Fine Arts), Boston

MARCELLO FAGIOLO (a cura di), *La Roma dei Longhi. Papi e architetti tra manierismo e barocco*, catalogo mostra (Accademia di San Luca), Roma

SYLVIA FERINO PAGDEN, *Disegni umbri del Rinascimento da Perugino a Raffaello*, catalogo mostra, Firenze

G. FERRARI, "Il manoscritto 'Spectacula' di Pellegrino Prisciani", in *La corte e lo spazio...* (1982), 431-449

MASSIMO FERRETTI, "I maestri della prospettiva", in *Storia dell'arte italiana*, XI, Torino, 459-585

E.J. GARMS, "Mito e realtà di Roma nella cultura europea. Viaggio e idea, immagine e immaginazione", in Storia d'Italia. Annali V, *Il paesaggio*, Torino, 561-662

T.M. GREEN, "Resurrecting Rome: The Double Task of the Humanist Imagination", in *Rome in the Renaissance...* (1982), 41-54

ENRICO GUIDONI, ANGELA MARINO, *Storia dell'urbanistica: Il Cinquecento*, Bari

A. GUIDOTTI, *La Badia fiorentina*, Firenze

HUBERTUS GÜNTHER, "Werke Bramantes im Spiegel einer Gruppe von Zeichnungen der Uffizien in Florenz", *Münchener Jahrbuch der bildenden Kunst* XXXIII, 77-108

RALPH E. LIEBERMANN, *L'architettura del Rinascimento a Venezia 1450-1540*, Firenze

WOLFGANG LOTZ, "Osservazioni intorno ai disegni palladiani", *Bollettino del centro internazionale di studi di architettura «Andrea Palladio»* IV, 61-68

PIETRO C. MARANI, "A Reworking by Baldassare Peruzzi of Francesco di Giorgio's Plan of a Villa", *Journal of the Society of Architectural Historians* XLI, 3, 181-188

L. MARCUCCI, B. TORRESI, "Palazzo Medici Lante: un progetto mediceo in Roma e il 'riaggiustamento' di Onorio Longhi.1", *Storia Architettura* V (2), 39-62

A. MAZZOCCO, "Rome and the Humanists: The Case of Flavio Biondo", in *Rome in the Renaissance...* (1982), 185 ff.

PIERO MORSELLI, GINO CORTI, *La chiesa di Santa Maria delle Carceri in Prato*, Firenze

PIER NICOLA PAGLIARA, "Alcune minute autografe di G.B. da Sangallo", *Architettura Archivi* I, 25-51

GUIDO PAMPALONI, *Palazzo Strozzi*, Roma (1a ed., 1963)

ALESSANDRO PARRONCHI (a cura di), *Baldassarre Peruzzi. Trattato di architettura militare*, Firenze

P. PROVOYER, *Le temple. Représentation de l'architecture sacrée*, Nice

GIANNI ROMANO, "Idea del paesaggio italiano", in *Storia dell'arte italiana*, Annali V, *Il paesaggio*, a cura di Cesare De Seta

M. ROSSI, "Giovanni Nexemperger di Graz e il tiburio del duomo di Milano", *Arte lombarda*, 5-12

PAOLO ALBERTO ROSSI, *Le cupole del Brunelleschi. Capire per conservare*, Bologna

FRANCO RUFFINI, "Linee rette e intrichi: il Vitruvio di Cesariano e la Ferrara teatrale di Ercole I", in *La corte e lo spazio...* (1982), 365-429

M. SEIDEL, "Castrum pingatur in palatio. I. Ricerche storiche e iconografiche sui castelli dipinti nel palazzo Pubblico di Siena", *Prospettiva* XXVIII, 17 e ss.

P. SONNAY, "La politique artistique de Cola di Rienzo (1313-1354)", *Revue de l'art* LV, 35-42

CHRISTOPH THOENES, "Ernst Skizzen: St. Peter", *Daidalos* V, 81-98

PIETRO TORRITI, *La Pinacoteca Nazionale di Siena*, Genova

RICHARD J. TUTTLE, "Julius II and Bramante in Bologna", in *Le arti a Bologna e in Emilia dal XVI al XVII secolo*, Atti del 24esimo congresso internazionale di storia dell'arte (Bologna 1979), a cura di Andrea Emiliani, IV, Bologna, 3-12

V. VASARI, "Il modello della chiesa di San Giuseppe", *Antichità viva* XXI, 30-36

1982-83

S. BERNARDINELLO, "Le orazioni per l'annuale apertura degli studi nell'Università di Padova (dal 1405 al 1796). Saggio bibliografico", *Atti e memorie dell'Accademia Patavina di scienze, lettere ed arti* 95, 321-423

SUZANNE BOORSCH, "The Building of the Vatican. The Papacy and Architecture", *Metropolitan Museum of Art Bulletin* XL, 4-64

HUBERTUS GÜNTHER, "Raffaels Romplan", *Sitzungsberichte der Kunstgeschichtlichen Gesellschaft zu Berlin* n.f., XXXI, 12-5

DAVID H. SOLKIN, in *Richard Wilson. The Landscape of Reaction*, exhibition catalog, London, 184-185

1983

Firenze e la Toscana dei Medici nell'Europa del Cinquecento, Atti del convegno (Firenze 1980), 3vol., Firenze

Leonardo e il leonardismo a Napoli e a Roma, catalogo mostra (Napoli-Roma), a cura di A. Vezzosi, Firenze

Milano nell'età di Ludovico il Moro, 2 voll., Milano

Storia dell'arte italiana. Dal Medioevo al Quattrocento, V, Torino

Urbino e le Marche prima e dopo Raffaello, catalogo mostra (Urbino), a cura di Maria Grazia Ciardi Dupré dal Poggetto e Paolo dal Poggetto, Firenze

JAMES S. ACKERMAN, "The Tuscan/Rustic Order: A Study in the Metaphorical Language of Architecture", *Journal of the Society of Architectural Historians* XLVIII, 15-34

JONATHAN J.G. ALEXANDER, "The Limbourg Brothers and Italian Art: A New Source", *Zeitschrift für Kunstgeschichte* XLVI, 425-435

C. ASTENGO, "Piante e vedute di città (una raccolta inedita dell'archivio storico di Torino)", *Studi e ricerche di geografia* VI, I

EDITH BALAS, "Michelangelo's Florentine Slaves and the S. Lorenzo Facade", *Art Bulletin* LXV, 665-671

A. BEDON, "Architettura e archeologia nella Roma del Cinquecento: Gio. Batt. Montano", *Arte lombarda* LXV, 111-126

ISA BELLI BARSALI, *Ville di Roma. Lazio I*, Milano (2a ed.)

SANDRO BENEDETTI, "S. Giovanni dei Fiorentini a Roma (1508-1559): da celebrazione mondana a significazione cristiana", in *Firenze e la Toscana dei Medici* (1983)

JAN BIALOSTOCKI, "Die Kirchenfassade als Ruhmesdenkmal des Stifters", *Römisches Jahrbuch für Kunstgeschichte* XX, 1-16

CESARE BRANDI, *Giotto*, Milano

B.L. BROWN and D. E. KLEINER, "Giuliano da Sangallo's Drawings after Ciriaco d'Ancona", *Journal of the Society of Architectural Historians* XLII, 321-335

ARNALDO BRUSCHI [a], "L'architettura", in *Santa Maria delle Grazie*, Milano, 35-88

—— [b], "Cordini, Antonio (Antonio da Sangallo il Giovane)", voce in *Dizionario Biografico degli Italiani*, XXIX, Roma, 16-23

—— [c], "Una tendenza linguistica 'medicea' nell'architettura del Rinascimento", in *Firenze e la Toscana dei Medici* (1983), III, Firenze

GENE BRUCKER, *Renaissance Florence*, Berkeley (2nd ed.)

TILMANN BUDDENSIEG, "Die Statuenstiftung Sixtus' IV. im Jahre 1471", *Römisches Jahrbuch für Kunstgeschichte* XX, 33-73

MAURIZIO CALVESI, *Il sogno di Polifilo prenestino*, Roma

ALBERTO CARLO CARPICECI, *La fabbrica di San Pietro: venti secoli di storia e progetti*, Roma

ANDRÉ CHASTEL, *Il sacco di Roma. 1527*, Torino

KEITH CHRISTIANSEN, "Early Renaissance Narrative Painting in Italy", *Metropolitan Museum Art Bulletin*, Fall

MARIA GRAZIA CIARDI DUPRÉ DAL POGGETTO, "La 'città ideale' di Urbino", in *Urbino e le Marche...* (1983)

—— [b], "Iacobo Barbari e le Marche", in *Urbino e le Marche...* (1983)

—— [c], "Iacopo dei Barbari, Ritratto di Fra' Luca Pacioli e del Duca Guidobaldo da Montefeltro", in *Urbino e le Marche...* (1983)

Ennio Concina, *La Macchina Territoriale: La progettazione della difesa nel Cinquecento veneto*, Bari

Fabrizio Cruciani, *Il teatro nel Rinascimento. Roma 1450-1550*, Roma

John D'Amico, *Renaissance Humanism in Papal Rome*, Baltimore-London

B.F. Davidson, "The Landscapes of Vatican Logge from the Design of Pope Julius III", *Art Bulletin* LXV

F. Deuchler, *Duccio*, Milano

"Enquête les maquettes d'architecture. Répertoire", *Revue de l'art* LVIII/LIX, 59, 123-141

Ciro Fiorillo, "Anonimo: Ritratto di Luca Pacioli con Guidobaldo di Montefeltro", in *Leonardo e il leonardismo...* (1983), 75-77

Antonio Foscari, Manfredo Tafuri, *L'armonia e i conflitti. La chiesa di S. Francesco della Vigna nella Venezia del Cinquecento*, Torino

Christoph L. Frommel [a], "Il complesso di S. Maria presso S. Satiro e l'ordine architettonico del Bramante lombardo", in *La scultura decorativa del primo Rinascimento*, Atti del I convegno internazionale di studi di Pavia (1980), Pavia, 153 sg.

—— [b], "Francesco del Borgo: Architekt Pius' III und Paulus II...", *Römisches Jarhbuch für Kunstgeschichte* XX, 54-109

The Genius of Venice 1500-1600, exhibition catalog (London, Royal Academy of Arts), edited by C. Hope and J. Martineau, London

Liliana Grassi, "Trasmutazione linguistica dell'architettura sforzesca. Splendore e presagio al tempo di Ludovico il Moro", in *Milano nell'età di Ludovico il Moro* (1983), II, 417-501

Enrico Guidoni, "Roma e l'urbanistica del Trecento", in *Storia dell'arte italiana...* (1983), 305-383

Hubertus Günther, "Der Kodex Fol. A 45 der Staatl. in Kassel", *Kunstchronik* XXXVI, 47-50

Margaret Haines, *The 'Sacrestia delle Messe' of the Florentine Cathedral*, Florence

Michael Hirst, Review of Charles de Tolnay, "Corpus dei disegni di Michelangelo", *Burlington Magazine* CXXV, 552-556

James Holderbaum, *The Sculptor Giovanni Bologna*, New York-London

Paul Joannides, *The Drawings of Raphael*, Berkeley

F.W. Kent, "Lorenzo di Credi, his Patron Iacopo Bongianni and Savonarola", *Burlington Magazine* CXXV, 539-541

M. Kiene, "L'architettura del Collegio di Spagna di Bologna", *Carrobbio* IX, 234-242

H. Klotz, "Der florentiner Stadtpalast. Zum verständnis einer Repräsentationsform", in *Architektur des Mittelalters*, besorgt von F. Möbius und E. Schubert, Weimar, 307-343

Eckhardt Knab, Erwin Mitsch und Konrad Oberhuber, *Raphael. Die Zeichnungen*, Stuttgart

Laboratorio su Leonardo, catalogo mostra (Milano, Rotonda di via Besana), a cura di IBM Italia, Milano

Ludovico il Moro, la sua città e la sua corte (1480-1499), catalogo mostra (Milano, Archivio di Stato), Milano

Giovanni Lorenzoni, "L'architettura", in *La Basilica di San Petronio in Bologna*, I, Milano, 53-124

Maria Luisa Madonna, "Momenti della politica edilizia e urbanistica dello Stato Pontificio nel '400: L'Exemplum della Piazza del Comune a Viterbo", in *Il Quattrocento a Viterbo*, catalogo mostra, Roma, 23-89

Emma Mandelli, "Lettura di un disegno: la pergamena di Siena", *Studi e documenti di architettura* XI, 93-134

John McAndrew, *L'architettura veneziana del primo rinascimento*, Venezia (1a ed. Cambridge, Mass. 1980)

Bert Meijer, Carel van Tuyll, *Disegni italiani del Teylers Museum Haarlem provenienti dalle collezioni di Cristina di Svezia e dei Principi Odescalchi*, Firenze

Gaetano Miarelli Mariani, "Il palazzo Medici a piazza Navona: un'utopia urbana di Giuliano da Sangallo", in *Firenze e la Toscana...* (1983), III, 977-993

Ulrich Middeldorf and D. Stiebral, *Renaissance Medals and Plaquettes*, Florence

Paolo Morselli, Gino Corti, *Santa Maria delle Carceri a Prato*, Firenze

Arnold Nesselrath, "Das Liller 'Michelangelo-Skizzenbuch'", *Kunstchronik* XXXVI, 47-50

Alessandro Nova, "Bartolomeo Ammannati e Prospero Fontana a Palazzo Firenze. Architettura e emblemi per Giulio III Del Monte", *Ricerche di storia dell'arte* XXI, 53-76

Pier Nicola Pagliara, "Cordini, Giovan Battista (Battista da Sangallo, detto il Gobbo)", voce in *Dizionario biografico degli italiani* XXIX, Roma, 23-28

Pier Giorgio Pasini, *I Malatesta e l'arte*, Bologna

Luciano Patetta, "Bramante e la trasformazione della basilica di S. Ambrogio a Milano", *Bollettino d'arte* XXI, 49-74

Giovanni Poggi, *Il carteggio di Michelangelo* (1965-83), a cura di Paola Barocchi e Renzo Ristori, V, Firenze

Ennio Poleggi, Fiorella Caraceni, "Genova e la Strada Nuova", in *Storia dell'arte italiana* (1983), Torino, 365-406

R. Quednau, "Convegno raffaellesco 1983", *Kunstchronik* XXXVI, 257-267

Massimo Ricci, *Il fiore di Santa Maria del Fiore*, Firenze

Renzo Ristori, "Una lettera a Michelangelo degli operai di S. Maria del Fiore", *Rinascimento* XXXIV, 167-171

Franco Ruffini, *Teatri prima del teatro. Visioni dell'edificio e della scena tra Umanesimo e Rinascimento*, Roma

Gigi Salvagnini, Gherardo Mechini, architetto di Sua Altezza. Architettura e territorio in Toscana, 1580-1620, Firenze

John Shearman, "A Functional Interpretation of Villa Madama", *Römisches Jahrbuch für Kunstgeschichte* XX, 313-327

G. Soldi Rondinini, "Le strutture urbanistiche di Milano durante l'età di Ludovico il Moro", in *Milano nell'età di Ludovico il Moro* (1983), II, 553-573

Giorgio Spini, "I Medici e l'organizzazione del territorio", in *Storia dell'arte italiana* (1983), 165-214

John Stephens, *The Fall of the Florentine Republic, 1512-30*, Oxford

Franklin Toker, "Arnolfo's S. Maria del Fiore: A Working Hypothesis", *Journal of the Society of Architectural Historians* XLII, 101-120

Andreas Tönnesmann [a], "Das 'Palatium Nervae' und die Rusticafassaden der Frühreinassance", *Römisches Jahrbuch für Kunstgeschichte* XXI, 61-70

—— [b], *Der Palazzo Gondi in Florenz*, Worms

Marvin Trachtenberg, "Howard Saalman, Filippo Brunelleschi: The Cupola of Santa Maria del Fiore", *Journal of the Society of Architectural Historians* III, 292-297

Maddalena Trionfi Honorati, "Prospettive architettoniche a tarsia: le porte del Palazzo Ducale di Urbino", *Notizie da Palazzo Albani* I/II, Urbino, 232-239

Oswald Mathias Ungers, *Die Thematisierung der Architektur*, Stuttgart

M. Vitali, "L'umanista padovano Giovanni Marcanova (1410/1418-1467) e la sua biblioteca", *Ateneo veneto* XXI, 127-161

1983-1987

Arnaldo Bruschi, "Problemi del San Pietro bramantesco", in *Quaderni dell'istituto di storia dell'architettura*, I/X, 273-292

1984

Antike und Europäische Welt. Aspekte der Auseinandersetzung mit der Antike, besorgt von M. Svilar und S. Kunze, Bern-Frankfurt-New York

Italian Medals in the Museo Nazionale of the Bargello, edited by J. Graham Pollard, I, Firenze

Memoria dell'antico nell'arte italiana (1984-86), I: *L'uso dei classici*, Torino

Raffaello architetto, catalogo mostra (Roma, Palazzo dei Conservatori), testi di Christoph L. Frommel, Stefano Ray, Manfredo Tafuri, Howard Burns e Arnold Nesselrath, Milano

Raffaello a Firenze. Dipinti e disegni delle collezioni fiorentine, catalogo mostra (Firenze, Palazzo Pitti), Firenze

Raffaello in Vaticano, catalogo mostra (Città del Vaticano 1984-85), Milano (deutsche ausgabe, Stuttgart 1987)

Umanesimo a Roma nel Quattrocento, Roma-New York

James S.Ackerman, "Pellegrino Tibaldi, S.Carlo Borromeo e l'architettura ecclesiastica del loro tempo", in *S. Carlo e il suo tempo*, Roma

J.P. Adam, *L'arte di costruire presso i romani*, Milano

Edith Balas, "Reply [to Howard Hibbard's letter]", *Art Bulletin* LXVI, 674-678

Eugenio Battisti, G. Saccaro Battisti, *Le macchine cifrate di Giovanni Fontana*, Milano

Amedeo Belluzzi, "La facciata: i progetti cinquecenteschi", in *La basilica di San Petronio*, II, Milano, 7-28

Sandro Benedetti, *Fuori dal Classicismo. Sintesi, tipologia, ragione nell'architettura del Cinquecento*, Roma

Enzo Bentivoglio, "La cappella Chigi", in *Raffaello architetto* (1984)

Carlo Bertelli, "Luca Pacioli, Aritmetica, geometria, proporzioni e proporzionalità", in *Raffaello e Brera*, Milano, 50-52

L. Beschi, "L'Anonimo Ambrosiano: un itinerario in Grecia di Urbano Bolzanio", *Atti dell'accademia nazionale dei Lincei*, rendiconti serie 8, XXXIX, 3-22

Rosanna Bettarini, Paola Barocchi (a cura di), *Giorgio Vasari. Le vite de' più eccellenti pittori, scultori e architetti...*, Firenze

Maurizio Bettini, "Tra Plinio e Sant'Agostino: Francesco Petrarca sulle arti figurative", in *Memoria dell'antico...* (1984), 222-227

Kathleen Weil-Garris Brandt, "Raffaello e la scultura del Cinquecento", in *Raffaello in Vaticano* (1984), 221-232

R. Brilliant, "Ancient Monuments as Models and as Topoi", in *Umanesimo a Roma nel Quattrocento* (1984), 223-234

Howard Burns, Arnold Nesselrath, "Raffaello e Baldassare Castiglione. Epistola a papa Leone X", in *Raffaello architetto* (1984), 437

M. Calisi, "Grafometro", in *Raffaello architetto* (1984), 446

C. Chiarlo, "'Gli fragmenti dilla sancta antiquitate': studi antiquari e produzione delle immagini da Ciriaco d'Ancona a Francesco Colonna", in *Memoria dell'antico nell'arte italiana...* (1984), 271-297

Andrea Chiarugi-Demore Quilghini, "Tracciamento della cupola del Brunelleschi. Muratori e geometria", *Critica d'arte* III, 38-47

Ezio Chini, *La chiesa e il convento dei Santi Michele e Gaetano a Firenze*, Firenze

Lucia A. Ciapponi, "Fra Giocondo da Verona and his Edition of Vitruvius", *Journal of the Warburg and Courtauld Institutes* XLVII, 72-90

Janet Cox-Rearick, *Dynasty and Destiny in Medici Art: Pontormo, Leo X, and the Two Cosimos*, Princeton

Charles Davis, "La grande 'Venezia' a Londra", *Antichità viva* XXIII, 6, 39-40

Michael S.A. Dechert, "City and Fortress in the Works of Francesco di Giorgio: the Theory and Practice of Defensive Architecture and Town Planning", Ph.D.diss., The Catholic University of America, Washington, D.C.

G. Delfini, R. Pentrella, "S. Pietro in Montorio. La chiesa, il convento, il tempietto", in *Fabbriche romane del primo '500. Cinque secoli di restauri*, Roma, 17-85

A. Demandt, *Der Fall Roms. Auflösung des Römischen Reiches urteil del Nachwelt*, München

Caroline Elam, "Rome and Florence, the Raphael Exhibitions: Architecture", *Burlington Magazine* CXXVI, 456-457

W. Ekschmitt, *Die sieben Weltwunder. Ihre Erbauung, Zerstörung und Wiederentdeckung*, Mainz

Sylvia Ferino-Pagden [a], *Gallerie dell'Accademia di Venezia. Disegni Umbri*, Milano

—— [b], scheda n. 23, in *Raffaello a Firenze...* (1984), 323-327

—— [c], scheda n.22, in *Raffaello a Firenze...* (1984)

M. FERRARA, F. QUINTERIO, *Michelozzo di Bartolomeo*, Firenze

G. FERRONI, "Appunti sulla politica festiva di Pietro Riario", in *Umanesimo a Roma nel Quattrocento* (1984), 47-65

CHRISTOPH L. FROMMEL [a], "Francesco del Borgo: Architekt Pius' II und Pauls' II....", "*Römisches Jarhbuch für Kunstgeschichte* XXI, 73-164

—— [b], "Il Palazzo Vaticano sotto Giulio II e Leone X. Strutture e funzioni", in *Raffaello in Vaticano* (1984), 118-35

—— [c], "San Pietro. Storia della sua costruzione", in *Raffaello architetto* (1984), 241-310

—— [d], "Villa Madama", in *Raffaello architetto* (1984), 311-356

CHRISTOPH L. FROMMEL, STEFANO RAY, MANFREDO TAFURI, vedi *Raffaello Architetto* (1984)

RICHARD A. GOLDTHWAITE, *La costruzione della Firenze rinascimentale*, Bologna

HEINZ GÖTZE, *Castel del Monte. Gestalt und Symbol der Architektur Friedrichs II*, München

J. GRAHAM POLLARD, see *Italian Medals...*

WERNER GRAMBERG, "Guglielmo della Portas Grabmal für Paul III. Farnese in San Pietro in Vaticano", *Römisches Jahrbuch für Kunstgeschichte*, XXI, 253-364

HUBERTUS GÜNTHER [a], "'Minus est condere quam colere'. Die Erneuerung des römischen Verkehrszentrums in der Renaissance", in *La Città italiana del Rinascimento fra Utopia e Realtà*, Venezia

—— [b], "Das Trivium vor Ponte S. Angelo: Ein Beitrag zur Urbanistik der Renaissance in Rom", *Römisches Jahrbuch für Kunstgeschichte* XXI, 165-252

HOWARD HIBBARD, "Michelangelo's Slaves", *Art Bulletin* LXVI, 673-674

R. HIESTAND, "Die Antike im Geschichtsbew¿tsein des Mittelalters", in *Antike und europäische Welt...* (1984)

MARY HOLLINGSWORTH, "The Architect in Fifteenth-Century Florence", *Art History* VII, 385-410

FRITZ-EUGEN KELLER, *Zum Villenleben und Villenbau am Römischen Hof der Farnese*, Berlin

H. KLOTZ, "Der Florentiner Stadtpalast. Zum Verständnis einer Repräsentationsform", in F. Möbius, E. Shubert, *Architektur des Mittelalters. Funktion und Gestalt*, Weimar, 307-343

ECKHARDT KNAB, ERWIN MITSCH, and KONRAD OBERHUBER, *Raffaello. I disegni*, a cura di Paolo Dal Poggetto, Firenze

RENATO LEFÈVRE, *Villa Madama*, Roma (II ed.)

Leonardo e l'incisione. Stampe derivate da Leonardo e Bramante dal XV al XIX secolo, catalogo mostra a cura di C. Alberici, schede di M. Chirico De Biasi (Milano, Castello Sforzesco), Milano

MEG LICHT, *L'edificio a pianta centrale. Lo sviluppo del disegno architettonico nel Rinascimento*, catalogo mostra, Firenze

C. LLOYD, "Reconsidering Sperandio", in *Italian Medals...* (1984), 99-113

PIETRO C. MARANI [a], *L'architettura fortificata negli studi di Leonardo. Con il catalogo completo dei disegni*, Firenze

—— [b], *Disegni di fortificazioni da Leonardo a Michelangelo*, Firenze

L. MARTINI, *Pienza e la val d'Orcia*, Genova

A. MAZZOCCO, "Decline and Rebirth in Bruni and Biondo", in *Umanesimo a Roma nel Quattrocento* (1984) 249-266

ANTJE MIDDELDORF KOSEGARTEN, *Sienesische Bildhauer am Duomo Vecchio. Studien zur Skulptur in Siena 1250-1330*, München

ELIO MONDUCCI, VITTORIO NIRONI, *Il duomo di Reggio Emilia*, Reggio Emilia

GABRIELE MOROLLI, *Le belle forme degli edifici antichi. Raffaello e il progetto del primo trattato rinascimentale sulle antichità di Roma*, Firenze

LINDA MURRAY, *Michelangelo, his Life, Work, and Times*, London

ANTONIO NATALI, "La chiesa di Villa a Castiglione Olona e gli inizi del Vecchietta", *Paragone* 407, 3-14

F. NEGRINI, "Appunti sulle fornaci e l'arte della ceramica a Mantova", in *Misurare la terra: centuriazione e coloni nel mondo romano. Il caso mantovano*, Modena

ALESSANDRO NOVA, *Michelangelo architetto*, Milano

ARNOLD NESSELRATH, "Raffaello e lo studio dell'antico nel Rinascimento", in *Raffaello architetto* (1984), 439-440

ERWIN PANOFSKY, *Die Renaissance der europäischen Kunst*, Frankfurt

PIER GIORGIO PASINI, "Matteo de' Pasti: Problems of Style and Chronology", in *Italian Medals...* (1984), 143-159

PIERO DELLA FRANCESCA, *De Prospectiva pingendi*, a cura di G. Nicco Fasola, Firenze

CARLA PIETRAMELLARA, *S. Maria del Fiore a Firenze: i tre progetti*, Firenze

PIUS II, *Commentarii rerum memorabilium que temporibus suis contigerunt*, a cura di A. van Heck, Città del Vaticano

JOSEF PLODER, "Zur Darstellung des städtischen Ambiente in de italienischen Malerei 1450-1500", D.Phil.Diss., Graz

Raffaello e Brera, catalogo mostra, Milano

LUCIO SANTORO, *Le mura di Napoli*, Roma

JOHN SHEARMAN, scheda 3.2.4 in RAFFAELLO ARCHITETTO (1984)

PIETRO SCARPELLINI, *Perugino*, Milano

B. SCHÜTZ, scheda 2.10.4, in *Raffaello architetto* (1984) 224

JOHN SPENCER, "Speculations on the Origins of Italian Renaissance Medals", in *Italian Medals...* (1984), 197-203

C.L. STINGER, *The Renaissance in Rome*, Bloomington

MARIANO TACCOLA [a], *De Ingeneis... Book I and II, on Engines, and Addenda (the Notebook)*, edited by Gustina Scaglia, Frank D. Prager and Ulrich Montag, 2 vols., Wiesbaden

—— [b], *De rebus militaribus (De machinis 1449), mit dem vollstaendingen Faksimile der Pariser Handschrift herausgegeben ubersetzt und kommentiert*, von Eberhard Knobloch, Baden- Baden

MANFREDO TAFURI [a], "Progetto di casa in via Giulia. Roma 1519-1520", in *Raffaello architetto* (1984)

—— [b], "Progetto per la facciata della chiesa di San Lorenzo, Firenze 1515-1516", in *Raffaello architetto* (1984), 165-170

—— [c], "'Roma instaurata'. Strategie urbane e politiche pontificie nella Roma del primo Cinquecento", in *Raffaello architetto* (1984)

ANDREAS TÖNNESMANN, *Der Palazzo Gondi in Florenz*, Worms

SIMONETTA VALTIERI [a], in *Raffaello architetto* (1984), 148-150

—— [b], "La zona di Campo de' Fiori prima e dopo gli interventi di Sisto IV", *Architettura. Cronache e storie* XXX (346/347), 648-660

K. VAN DER PLOEG, "Architectural and Liturgical Aspects of Siena Cathedral in the Middle Ages", in Hendrik W. van Os, *Sienese Altarpieces 1215-1460*, I, Groningen

JOHN VARRIANO, "The Architecture of Papal Medals", in *Projects and Monuments in the Period of the Roman Baroque (Papers in Art History from the Pennsylvania State University, I)*, edited by Hellmut Hager and Susan Scott Munshower, University Park, Penn., 68-81

GIORGIO VASARI, vedi Rosanna Bettarini e Paola Barocchi

CARROLL WILLIAM WESTFALL, *L'invenzione della città. La strategia urbana di Niccolò V e Alberti nella Roma del '400*, Roma, introduzione di Manfredo Tafuri

D.R. EDWARD WRIGHT, "Alberti's De pictura: Its Literary Structure and Purpose", *Journal of the Warburg and Courtauld Institutes* XLVII, 52-71

HEINRICH WURM, *Baldassarre Peruzzi Architekturzeichnungen*, Tübingen

1984-85

J. GRAHAM POLLARD, *Medaglie italiane del Rinascimento nel Museo Nazionale del Bargello*, Firenze

Memoria dell'antico nell'arte italiana (1984-86), a cura di Salvatore SEttis, II, Torino

1985

G.F.BORSI (a cura di), *La fortuna degli Etruschi*, catalogo mostra, Milano

CESARE DE SETA (a cura di), *Le città capitali*, Roma-Bari

Roma e l'Antico nell'arte e nella cultura del Cinquecento, a cura di M. Fagiolo, Roma

ANNE B. BARRIAULT, "Florentine Paintings for Spalliere", Ph.D.diss., University of Virginia

Luciano Bellosi (a cura di), *Simone Martini*, Atti del convegno (Siena 1985), Firenze

Luciano BERTI, *Michelangelo. I disegni di Casa Buonarroti*, schede critiche di Alessandro Cecchi e Antonio Natali, Firenze

G.F. BORSI, "Gli Etruschi nei disegni degli architetti del Rinascimento", in G. F. Borsi (1985), 36-43

FRANCO BORSI, *Bramante*, Milano

STEFANO BORSI, *Giuliano da Sangallo. I disegni di architettura e dell'antico*, Roma

ARNALDO BRUSCHI [a], "L'architettura a Roma al tempo di Alessandro VI: Antonio da Sangallo il Vecchio, Bramante e l'antico, Autunno 1499- Autunno 1503", *Bollettino d'arte* XXIX, 67-90

—— [b], *Bramante*, Roma-Bari

HUMFREY BUTTERS, *Governors and Government in Early Sixteenth-century Florence*, Oxford

GIUSEPPE CARONIA, *Ritratto di Michelangelo architetto*, Roma-Bari

PIETRO PAOLO CARPEGGIANI, "Città reale e città ideale: l'evento di Sabbioneta", in *Sabbioneta. Una stella e una pianura*, Milano, 25-64

PICO CELLINI, "Quel libretto non è di Raffaello ma un falso napoleonico", *Giornale dell'arte* XXII, aprile, XLIX

J.J. COULTON, "Incomplete Preliminary Planning in Greek Architecture: Some New Evidence", dans *Le Dessin d'architecture dans les sociétés antiques*, Actes du Colloque de Strasbourg (26-28 janvier 1984), Strassbourg, 103-122

NICOLE DACOS, "Hermannus Posthumus. Rome, Mantua, Landshut", *Burlington Magazine* CXXVII, 433-438

A. DARR, A. ROSENAUER, D. COVI et al., *Italian Renaissance Sculpure in the Time of Donatello*, Detroit

CESARE DE SETA, "Significati e simboli della rappresentazione topografica negli atlanti dal XVI al XVIII secolo", in De Seta (1985), 17-66

SALVATORE DI PASQUALE, "Brunelleschi, la coupole, les machines", dans *Filippo Brunelleschi 1377- 1446. Sa vie, son oeuvre par Antonio Manetti et Giorgio Vasari*, Paris

M.M. DONATO, "Gli eroi romani tra storia e 'exemplum'. I primi cicli umanistici di Uomini Famosi", in *Memoria dell'antico...* (1985), II, 95-152

CAROLINE ELAM, "Piazza Strozzi: Two Drawings by Baccio d'Agnolo and the Problems of a Private Renaissance Square", *I Tatti Studies* I, 105ff.

VINCENZO FONTANA, "Il 'Vitruvio' del 1556: Barbaro, Palladio, Marcolini", in *Trattati scientifici veneti fra il XV e il XVI secolo*, Vicenza

FRANCESCO DI GIORGIO MARTINI, *Il Vitruvio Magliabechiano*, a cura di Gustina Scaglia, Firenze

CHRISTOPH L. FROMMEL, "Papal Policy The planing of Rome during the Remaissance", in *Le città capitali*, (1985) (English translation in *Images and Their Meaning*, Cambridge 1988), 95-110

HEATHER GREGORY, "The Return of the Native: Filippo Strozzi and Medicean Politics", *Renaissance Quarterly* XXXVIII, 1-21

A. Grafton, "Renaissance Readers and Ancients Texts: Comments on Some Commentaries", *Renaissance Quarterly* XXXVIII, 615-649

Hubertus Günther [a], "Gli ordini architettonici: rinascita o invenzione?" in *Roma e l'antico...* (1985), 272-311

—— [b], "Die Strassenplanung unter den Medici-Päpsten in Rom (1513-1534)", *Jahrbuch des Zentralinstituts für Kunstgeschichte* I, 237-293

Hubertus Günther, Christof Thoenes, "Gli ordini architettonici: rinasciata o invenzione?", in *Roma e l'Antico...* (1985), 261-310

I. Herklotz, "Der Campus Lateranensis im Mittelalter", *Römisches Jahrbuch für Kunstgeschichte* XX, 3-43

Italo Insolera, *Roma. Le città nella storia d'Italia*, Roma-Bari

Martin Kemp, *Geometrical Perspective from Brunelleschi to Desargues: a Pictorial Means or an Intellectual End?*, Oxford

D. Kimpel, R. Suckale, *Die gotische Architektur in Frankreich 1130-1270*, München

Hanno-Walter Kruft, *Geschichte der Architekturtheorie. Von der Antike bis zur Gegenwart*, München

Claudia Lazzaro, "Rustic Country House to Refined Farmhouse: The Evolution and Migration of an Architectural Form", *Journal of the Society of Architectural Historians* XLIV, 346-367

F. Mancini, M.T. Muraro, E. Povoledo, *I teatri del Veneto. Verona Vicenza Belluno e il loro territorio*, II, Venezia

S. Mazzoni, O. Guaita, *Il Teatro di Sabbioneta*, Firenze

Bert Meijer, *I grandi disegni italiani del Teylers Museum di Haarlem*, Milano

Gabriele Morolli, "Vetus Etrurua", *Il mito degli Etruschi nella letteratura architettonica, nell'arte e nella cultura da Vitruvio a Winckelmann*, Firenze

Andrew Morrogh [a], *Disegni di architetti fiorentini 1540-1640*, catalogo mostra, Firenze

—— [b], "Vasari and Coloured Stones", in *Giorgio Vasari tra decorazione ambientale e storiografia artistica*, Atti del convegno internazionale (Arezzo 1981), Firenze, 309-20

Francesco Negroni, "Nicolò Pellipario un ceramista fantasma", *Notizie da Palazzo Albani* XIV, 13-20

R. Olisky Rubinstein, " 'Tempus edax rerum': a Newly Discovered Painting by Hermannus Posthumus", *Burlington Magazine* CXXVII, 425-433

Roberto Pane, "Ancora sulla Tavola Strozzi", *Napoli nobilissima* XXIV, fasc.III/IV, 81-83

Francesco Santi, *Galleria Nazionale dell'Umbria. Dipinti, sculture e oggetti dei secoli XV-XVI*, Perugia (ristampa 1989)

Giuseppe Rocchi, Anna Bebber, Roberto Franchi, Luca Giorgi, Luigi Marino, *Santa Maria del Fiore. Rilievi, documenti, indagini strumentali. Interpretazione*, Milano

Leon Georg Satkowski, "The Palazzo del Monte in Monte San Savino and the Codex Geymüller", in *Renaisance Studies in Honour of Craig Hugh Smyth*, Florence

G. Savarese, "Antico e moderno in umanisti romani del primo Cinquecento", in *Roma e l'antico...* (1985), 23-56

Gustina Scaglia, *Il "Vitruvio magliabechiano" di Francesco di Giorgio*, Firenze

Pietro Scarpa, "Libretto di Raffaello: non Bossi, semmai Novelli", *Giornale dell'arte* XXVI, 36

G. Schweikhart, "Un artista veronese di fronte all'antico. Gli affreschi zodiacali del Falconetto a Mantova", in *Roma e l'Antico...* (1985), 461-488

A. Siliotti (a cura di), *Viaggiatori veneti alla scoperta dell'Egitto*, Venezia

Craig Hugh Smyth, "Osservazioni intorno a 'Il Carteggio di Michelangelo'", *Rinascimento*, s.II, XXV, 3-17

Manfredo Tafuri [a], "Un progetto 'raffaellesco' per la chiesa di San Giovanni dei Fiorentini a Roma", *Prospettiva* XLII, 38-47

—— [b], *Venezia e il Rinascimento: religione, scienza, architettura*, Torino

Franklin Toker, "Gothic Architecture by Remote Control: an Illustrated Building Contract of 1340", *Art Bulletin* LXVII, 67-95

S. Valori [a], "Disegni di antichità dell'Albertina di Vienna", *Xenia quaderni* VI, 102-105

—— [b], "Disegni di antichità dell'Albertina di Vienna", *Xenia quaderni* VIII, 75-78

Hendrik W. van Os, "Tradition and Innovation in Some Altarpieces by Bartolo di Fredi", Art Bulletin 117, 50-66

Elisabeth Werdehausen, "Il chiostro di S. Pietro al Po", in *I Campi e la cultura artistica cremonese del Cinquecento*, Milano, 400-403

Timothy Wilson, *Ceramic Art of the Italian Renaissance*, London

1985-86

Liechtenstein. The Princely Collection, exibition catalog, New York

Raffaello e la Roma dei Papi, catalogo mostra (Roma, Biblioteca Apostolica Vaticana), a cura di Giovanni Morello, Roma

1986

Antonio da Sangallo il Giovane - La vita e l'opera, Atti del XXII congresso di storia dell'architettura, (Roma, 19-21 febbraio), a cura di Gianfranco Spagnesi, Roma

Bramante a Milano, a cura di Mario Rossi e Alessandro Rovetta, numero speciale di *Arte lombarda* LXXVIII

Kunst voor de Beeldenstorm, exhibition catalog (Amsterdam, Rijksmuseum) Amsterdam

Imago urbis. Dalla città reale alla città ideale, testi di Cesare De Seta, Massimo Ferretti e Alberto Tenenti, Milano

Memoria dell'antico nell'arte italiana (1984-86). III: Dalla tradizione all'archeologia, a cura di Salvatore Settis, Torino

Raffaello a Roma. Il convegno del 1983, a cura di C.L. Frommel e M. Winner, Roma

James S. Ackerman, *The Architecture of Michelangelo*, catalogue, with John Newman, Chicago-Harmondsworth (2nd ed. in one vol.; 1st ed., London 1961)

Bruno Adorni, "Progetti e interventi di Pierfrancesco da Viterbo, Antonio da Sangallo il Giovane e Baldassarre Peruzzi per le fortificazioni di Piacenza e di Parma", in *Antonio da Sangallo il Giovane...* (1986), 349-372

Giovanni Agosti, "La fama di Cristoforo Solari", *Prospettiva* XLVI, 57-65

C.G. Bauman, scheda 107, in *Kunst voor de Beeldenstorm* (1986),

Sandro BenedettiS, "Il modello per il San Pietro Vaticano di Antonio da Sangallo il Giovane", in *Antonio da Sangallo il Giovane...* (1986), 157-174

S. Benvenuto, D. Di Cioccio, "L'urbanizzazione del Campo Marzio: considerazioni sui disegni di progetto dell'ospedale di San Giacomo degli Incurabili", in *Antonio da Sangallo il Giovane...*(1986), 145-153

L. Beschi, "La scoperta dell'arte greca", in *Memoria dell'antico...* (1986), 293-372

Hartmut Biermann, "Der runde Hof. Betrachtungen zur Villa Madama", *Mitteilungen des Kunsthistorischen Institutes in Florenz* XXX, 493-536

H. Bloch, "The Bronze Doors of Monte Cassino", in *Monte Cassino in the Middle Ages*, I, Roma, 138-627

Phillis Pray Bober, Ruth Rubinstein, *Renaissance Artists and Antique Sculpture. A Handbook of Sources*, London

Giulio Bora, "Considerazioni su Bramante pittore e la sua eredità a Milano" in *Bramante a Milano* (1986)

Franco Borsi, *Leon Battista Alberti. The Complete Works*, Milan (ed. it., Milano 1973)

Richard Bösel, *Jesuitenarchitektur in Italien (1540-1773). I: Textband*, Wien

Marie-Franqise Briguet, "Art", in *Etruscan Life and Afterlife*, edited by Larissa Bonfante, Detroit

Arnaldo Bruschi, "Bramante in Lombardia", in *Bramante a Milano*

Una cattedrale immersa nella storia, catalogo mostra a cura di G. Bologna, Milano

Giovan Battista Cavalcaselle, Giovanni Morelli, "Catalogo delle opere d'arte delle marche e dell'Umbria (1861-1862)", in *Le Gallerie nazionali italiane*, II, Roma

Allan Ceen, *The Quartiere de' Banchi: Urban Planning in Rome in the First Half of the Cinquecento*, New York-London

A. Cerutti Fusco, "Teatro all'antica e teatro vitruviano nell'interpretazione di Antonio da Sangallo", in *Antonio da Sangallo il Giovane...* (1986), 455-469

Claudia Cieri Via, "Il silenzio e la parola: immagini geroglifiche nel Tempio Malatestiano di Rimini", in *Sulle tracce della scrittura. Oggetti, testi, superfici dai Musei dell'Emilia Romagna*, Carpi, 47-64

M.E. Cosenza, ed., *The Revolution of Cola di Rienzo*, New York

A. Darr, G. Bonsanti, *Donatello e i suoi. Scultura fiorentina del primo Rinascimento*, Milano

M. Del Treppo, "Il re e il banchiere", in *Spazio, società e potere nell'italia dei Comuni*, Napoli

Otto Demus, *The Mosaics of Saint Mark's*, Washington

Cesare De Seta, "Come in uno specchio. La città rinascimentale nel 'De re aedificatoria' e nelle tarsie", in *Imago urbis...* (1986), 44-55

Marcello Fagiolo, "La Basilica Vaticana come tempio-mausoleo 'inter duas metas', le idee e i progetti di Alberti, Filarete, Bramante, Peruzzi, Sangallo, Michelangelo, in *Antonio da Sangallo il Giovane...* (1986), 187-210

Massimo Ferretti, " 'Casamenti seu prospective'. Le città degli intarsiatori", in *Imago urbis...* (1986), 73-168

Gabriella Ferri Piccaluga, "Gli affreschi di Casa Panigarola e la cultura milanese tra Quattro e Cinquecento" in *Bramante a Milano* (1986)

Vincenzo Fontana, "Fra Giocondo e l'antico", in *Atti del XXII congresso di storia dell'architettura*, Roma, 423-444

Christoph L. Frommel [a], "Giovanfrancesco da Sangallo, architetto di Palazzo Balami-Galitzin", in *Antonio da Sangallo il Giovane...* (1986), 63-69

—— [b], "Raffaels Paläste: Wohnen und leben im Rom der Hochrenaissance", in *Gewerblicher Rechtschutz und Urheberrecht*, 101-110

—— [c], "Raffael und Antonio da Sangallo der Jüngere", in *Raffaello a Roma...* (1986), 261-304

G. Gabrielli, Appendice a G. Zander, "Il colore della Basilica di S. Pietro secondo il probabile pensiero di Antonio da Sangallo", in *Antonio da Sangallo il Giovane...* (1986), 184-185

Ernst H. Gombrich, "The Lustre of Apelles", Pilkington Lecture (Manchester, Whitworth Gallery of Art) in *L'eredità di Apelle*, Torino, 3-26

E. Grassi and M. Lorsch, *Folly and Insanity in Renaissance Literature*, Binghamton-New York

F. Grimaldi, *La basilica della Santa Casa di Loreto*, Ancona

Michael Hirst, "A Note on Michelangelo and the S. Lorenzo Façade", *Art Bulletin* LXVII, 323-326

G. Holmes, *Florence, Rome and the Origins of the Renaissance*, Oxford

The Illustrated Bartsch 52. Netherlandish Artists, Cornelis Cort, edited by Warter L. Strauss and Tomoko Shimura, New York

Christoph Jobst, "Santa Maria di Loreto in Roma", in *Antonio da Sangallo il Giovane...* (1986), 277-285

Roger Jones, "The Most Beautiful and Festive Building in Rome", AA Files 11 (Spring), 104-107

Vladimir Juren, "Le Codex Chlumczansky: Un recueil d'inscriptions et de dessins du XVIe siècle", *Monuments et mémoirs. Académie des inscriptions et belles-lettres, Fondation Eugène Piot* LXVIII, 105-205

M. KING, *Venetian Humanism in an Age of Patrician Dominance*, Princeton

W.T. KLOEK, in *Kunst voor de Beeldenstorm* (1986), 226 ss

H. KRUFT, *Geschichte der Architekturtheorie. Von Antike bis Gegenwart*, München

MICHAEL KUBOVY, *The Psychology of Perspective and Renaissance Art*, Cambridge

R. BURR LITCHFIELD, *Emergence of a Bureaucracy: The Florentine Patricians 1530-1790*, Princeton

E. LUNGHI, "Giovanni di Bonino", in *La pittura in Italia. Il Duecento e Trecento*, II, Milano, 579-580

F. MANCINI, *Todi e i suoi castelli*, Città di Castello (2a ed. aggiornata; 1a ed. 1960)

D. MARSHALL, "A View of Poggioreale by Viviano Codazzi and Domenico Gargiulo", *Journal of the Society of Architectural Historians* XLV (1), 32-46

ANDRÉ MARTINDALE, "The Problem of Guidoriccio", *Burlington Magazine* CXXVIII (April), 259-273

MICHELANGELO MURARO, *Venetian Villas: The History and the Culture*, New York

W. NERDINGER and F. ZIMMERMANN EDS, *Die Architekturzeichnung vom barocken Idealplan zur Axonometrie*, München

ARNOLD NESSELRATH [a], "I libri di disegni di antichità. Tentativo di una tipologia", in *Memoria dell'antico...* (1986), 87-147

—— [b], "Raphael's Archeological Method", in *Raffaello a Roma...* (1986), 357-269

PIER NICOLA PAGLIARA, "Vitruvio da testo a canone", in *Memoria dell'antico...* (1986), 5-85

O. PELOSI, "Il terzo libro del 'de vita' e l' 'Hypnerotomachia Poliphili'", in G. Garfagnini (a cura di), *Marsilio Ficino e il ritorno di Platone*. Studi e documenti, Firenze, 555-563

SIMON PEPPER AND NICHOLAS ADAMS, *Firearms and Fortifications: Military Architecture and Siege Warfare in Sixteenth Century Siena*, Chicago

ANTONIO PINELLI, "Feste e trionfi. Continuità e metamorfosi di un tema", in *Memoria dell'antico...* (1986), 281-352

ANTONIO PINELLI, O. ROSSI, *Genga architetto*, Roma

LIONELLO PUPPI [a], *Michele Sanmicheli architetto*, Roma

—— [b], "Un viaggio per il Veneto di Antonio da Sangallo il Giovane e di Michele Sanmicheli nella primavera del 1526. Un progetto per i Grimani e qualche riflessione a margine", in *Antonio da Sangallo il Giovane...* (1986), 101-107

FRANCO RUFFINI, *Commedia e festa nel rinascimento*, Roma

P. SCAPECCHI, "Victoris Imago. Problemi relativi al Tempio Malatestiano", *Arte cristiana*, 155-164

RICHARD SCHOFIELD, "Bramante and Amadeo at Santa Maria delle Grazie in Milan", in *Bramante a Milano* (1986), 3, 41 e sg.

SALVATORE SETTIS, "Continuità, distanza, conoscenza. Tre usi dell'antico", in *Memoria dell'antico...* (1986), 373-486

PIER LUIGI SILVAN, "Note su Antonio da Sangallo e gli ottagoni di S. Pietro", in *Antonio da Sangallo il Giovane...* (1986), 209-216

MANFREDO TAFURI, "Antonio da Sangallo e Jacopo Sansovino: un conflitto professionale nella Roma medicea", in *Antonio da Sangallo il Giovane...* (1986), 79-99

ALBERTO TENENTI, "La città ideale del Rinascimento", in *Imago urbis...* (1986), 169-193

CHRISTOF THOENES, "La 'lettera' a Leone X", in *Raffaello a Roma...* (1986), 373-381

FILIPPO TODINI, "Pittura del Duecento e del Trecento in Umbria e il cantiere di Assisi", in *La pittura in Italia. Il Duecento e del Trecento*, II, Milano, 375-413

BRUNO TOSCANO, "La pittura umbra del Quattrocento", in *La pittura in Italia. Il Quattrocento*, II, Milano, 355-383

SIMONETTA VALTIERI, "Sistemazioni absidali di chiese in funzione di 'mausoleo' in progetti di Antonio da Sangallo il Giovane", in *Antonio da Sangallo il Giovane...* (1986)

I.M. VELDMAN, *Leerrijke reeksen van Maarten van Heemskerck*, Den Haag-Haarlem

WENDY M. WATSON, *Italian Renaissance Maiolica from the William A. Clark Collection*, London

WOLFANG WOLTERS, *Venedig. Die Kunst der Renaissance*, München

GIUSEPPE ZANDER, "Il colore della Basilica di S. Pietro secondo il probabile pensiero di Antonio da Sangallo", in *Antonio da Sangallo il Giovane...* (1986), 175-184

1986-87

CHRISTOPH L. FROMMEL, "I chiostri di S. Ambrogio e il cortile della Cancelleria", in Atti del Convegno Bramante a Milano

RICHARD J. JUDSON, "Lanbert Lombard", in *The Age of Bruegel: Netherlandish Drawings in the Sixteenth Century*, exhibition catalog, edited by J.O. Hand et al., Washington, 206-207

ANN ELIZABETH WERDEHAUSEN, "Bramante e il convento di S. Ambrosio", in Atti del Convegno Bramante a Milano

1987

Baldassarre Peruzzi. Pittura scena e architettura nel Cinquecento, a cura di Marcello Fagiolo e Maria Luisa Madonna, Roma

Il se rendit en Italie. Etudes offerts à André Chastel, Paris-Rome

Léonard de Vinci, ingénieur et architect, catalogue exposition (Montréal, Musée des Beaux Arts, 22 avril-8 novembre), sous la direction de Paolo Galluzzi, Montréal-Firenze

Studi su Raffaello, Atti del congresso internazionale di studi (Urbino-Firenze, 6-14 aprile 1984), Urbino

NICHOLAS ADAMS, "Postille ad alcuni disegni di architettura militare di Baldassarre Peruzzi", in *Baldassarre Peruzzi...* (1987), 205-223

GIOVANNI AGOSTI, VINCENZO FARINELLA, *Michelangelo, studi di antichità dal Codice Coner*, Torino

LEON BATTISTA ALBERTI, see D. Marsh

CHARLES AVERY [a], *Giambologna: the Complete Sculpture*, Mt. Kisco, N.Y.

—— [b], *Giambologna. La scultura*, Firenze

FRANK BALTERS und PETER GERLACH, "ZUR NATUR VON ALBERTI's DE STATUA", *Natur und Kunst* XXIII, 38-54

LUCIANO BELLOSI, "Ancora sul Guidoriccio", *Prospettiva* XLIX, 49-55

CARLO BERTELLI, "Masolino e il Vecchietta a Castiglione Olona", *Paragone* XXXVIII, n.s., 5 (451), 25-47

DANIELE BARBARO, *Vitruvio. I dieci libri dell'architettura tradotti e commentati da Daniele Barbaro (1567)*, con un saggio di Manfredo Tafuri e uno studio di Manuela Morresi, Milano

ARNALDO BRUSCHI [a], "Da Bramante a Peruzzi: spazio e pittura", in *Baldassarre Peruzzi...* (1987), 311-337

—— [b], "Problemi del S.Pietro bramantesco... 'Admodum surgebat...'", *Quaderni dell'istituto di storia dell'architettura* n.s. 1/10 (Saggi in onore di Guglielmo De Angelis d'Ossat)

MAURIZIO CALVESI, "Hypnerotomachia Poliphili, nuovi riscontri e nuove evidenze documentarie per Francesco Colonna signore di Preneste", *Storia dell'arte* LX, 85-136

ENZO CARLI, "Giovanni d'Agostino e il «Duomo Nuovo»", in *Giovanni d'Agostino e il «DuomoNuovo» di Siena*, Genova

PAOLO CARPEGGIANI, CHIARA TELLINI-PERINA, *Sant'Andrea a Mantova. Un tempio per la città del principe*, Mantova

ANDRÉ CHASTEL, "Stadtpoesie aus edlem Holz. Intarsia oder Die Liebe zur Geometrie der Stadt", *FRM* VIII, 76-83

RITA CHIACCHELLA, "Per una reinterpretazione della 'guerra del sale' e della costruzione della Rocca Paolina in Perugia", *Archivio storico italiano* 145, 3-60

KEITH CHRISTIANSEN, "La pittura a Venezia e in Veneto nel primo Quattrocento", in *La pittura in Italia. Il Quattrocento*, a cura di Federico Zeri, Milano, 119-146

P.C. CLAUSSEN, *Magistri doctissimi romani. Die römischen Marmorkünstler des Mittelalters*, Stuttgart

HUBERT DAMISCH, *L'origine de la perspective*, Paris

SILVIA DANESI SQUARZINA, "Francesco Colonna, principe, letterato, e la sua cerchia", *Storia dell'arte* LX, 137-154

GUGLIELMO DE ANGELIS D'OSSAT, "Tre progetti del Peruzzi per chiese romane", in *Baldassarre Peruzzi...* (1987)

SYLVIA FERINO PADGEN, "Invenzioni raffaellesche adombrate nel libretto di Venezia: la *Strage degli Innocenti* e la *Lapidazione di S. Stefano* a Genova", in *Studi su Raffaello* (1987), 63 e sg.

L. FIRPO, "Léonard urbaniste", dans *Léonard ingénieur et architecte* (1987), 287-301

CHRISTOPH L. FROMMEL [a], "Baldassarre Peruzzi pittore e architetto", in *Baldassarre Peruzzi...* (1987), 21-46, 241-262

—— [b], "San Luigi dei Francesi : das Meisterwerke des Jean de Chenevierès", dans *Il se rendit en Italie...* (1987), 169-190

CHRISTOPH L. FROMMEL, STEFANO RAY, MANFREDO TAFURI, *Raffael. Das architektonische Werk*, Stuttgart

J. GARDNER, "An Introduction on the Iconography of the Medieval City Gate", *Dumbarton Oaks Papers* XLI, 199-213

A. GARUTI, "La cattedrale di Carpi. Osservazioni sulla storia edilizia e artistica degli edifici", in *Un tempio degno di Roma. La cattedrale di Carpi*, Modena

J. GRAHAM POLLARD, ed., *Studies in the History of Art, XXI: Italian Medals*, Washington

G.GRIFFITHS, J.HANKINS AND D. THOMPSON, ed., "Leonardo Bruni's De Origine urbis Mantue", in *The Humanism of Leonardo Bruni: Selected Texts*, New York, 181 ss

JEAN GUILLAUME, "Léonard et l'architecture", dans *Léonard de Vinci ingenieur et architecte*, 207-286

The Illustrated Bartsch 53. Netherlandish Artists, Philips Galle, edited by Arno Dolders, New York

MARK JONES, "Medal-making in France 1400-1650: The Italian Dimension", in J. Graham Pollard ed. 57-71

F. W. KENT, "Palaces, Politics and Society in Fifteenth-Century Florence", *I Tatti Studies* II, 41-70

STEFAN KUMMER, *Anfänge und Ausbreitung der Stuckdekoration im Römischen Kirchenraum (1500-1600)*, Tübingen

C. LIGOTA, "Annius of Viterbo and Historical Method", *Journal of the Warburg and Courtauld Institutes* L, 44-56

JOHN KENT LYDECKER [a], "The Domestic Setting of the Arts in Renaissance", Ph.D Diss., Baltimore

—— [b], "Il patriziato fiorentino e la committenza artistica per la casa", in *I ceti dirigenti nella Toscana del Quattrocento*, Firenze, 209-221

C. LOYD, "Reconsidering Sperandio", in J. Graham Pollard ed., 99-113

CHARLES R. MACK, *Pienza. The Creation of a Renaissance City*, Ithaca, NY-London

Mantova. La sezione gonzaghesca del Museo Civico di Palazzo Te, a cura di A. Englen, E. Ercolani Cocchi, P. Giovetti e R. Navarrini, Mantova

GIUSEPPE MARCHINI, "De minimis", in *Studi su Raffaello* (1987), 239-244

D. MARSH ED., *Leon Battista Alberti. Dinner Pieces. A Translation of the "Intercenales"*, translated by D. Marsh, Binghamton, New York

ANNA MARIA MATTEUCCI, "Il gotico cittadino di Antonio di Vincenzo", in *Il tramonto del Medioevo a Bologna. Il cantiere di San Petronio*, a cura di R. D'Amico e R. Grandi, Bologna, 27-54

METTERNICH. see Wolff Metternich

F.M. MIGNANTI, *Istoria della sacrosanta patriarcale basilica vaticana*, Roma-Torino

Museo civico d'arte industriale e galleria Davia Bargellini, Bologna

CESARE MOZZARELLI, *Mantova e i Gonzaga*, Torino

RICCARDO PACCIANI, "I modelli lignei nella progettazione rinascimentale", *Rassegna* XXXII, 6-19

"PAOLO SCHIAVO", in *La pittura in Italia, Il Quattrocento*, a cura di Federico Zeri, II, Milano, 725-726

PIER GIORGIO PASINI, "Matteo de' Pasti: Problems of Style and Chronology", in J. Graham Pollard ed., 143-159

LUCIANO PATETTA, *L'architettura del Quattrocento a Milano*, Milano

Patronage, Art and Society in Renaissance Italy, edited by F.W. Kent and Patricia Simons, New York

J. PLODER, *Zur Darstellung des städtischen Ambiente in der italienischen Malerei von 1450 bis 1500*, Wien-Köln

LIONELLO PUPPI [a], "I costumi per la recita inaugurale del Teatro Olimpico a Vicenza (e altre questioni)", *Storia dell'arte* LXI, 189-200

—— [b], "Modelli di Palladio, modelli palladiani", *Rassegna* XXXII, 20-28

Il restauro della vetrata di Giovanni di Bonino della Galleria Nazionale dell'Umbria, Todi

PATRIK REUTERSWÄRD, "Le Vau und Michelangelo-zum Problem des künstlerischen Zitats", in *Klassizismus: Epoche und Probleme. Festschrift für Erik Forssman zum 70. Geburtstag*, Hildesheim

MASSIMO RICCI [a], *L'accusa di Giovanni di Gherardo Gherardi a Filippo Brunelleschi. Spiegazione integrale della pergamena, dei disegni e relativi contenuti tecnici*, Firenze

—— [b], "Il segreto della cupola di Santa Maria del Fiore", *Scienze* (luglio), 42-56

ENZO SETTESOLDI, "Le facciate di Santa Maria del Fiore", in *Due granduchi tre re e una facciata*, Firenze, 11-48

C.B. STREHLKE, "Niccolò di Giovanni di Francesco Ventura e il Guidoriccio", *Prospettiva* XLIX, 45-48

MANFREDO TAFURI [a], "Due progetti di Antonio da Sangallo il Giovane per la chiesa dei Fiorentini a Roma", in *Architettura, storia e documenti*, 35-52

—— [b], "Il progetto di Raffaello per la chiesa di S. Giovanni dei Fiorentini", in *Studi su Raffaello* (1987), 177-196

—— [c], "Raffael. Das architektonische Werk", deutsches auf von *di Raffaello Architetto* (1984)

ANTHONY TURNER, *Early Scientific Instruments Europe 1400-1800*, London

RALPH TOLEDANO, *Francesco di Giorgio Martini. Pittore e scultore*, Milano

VITRUVIO, vedi Daniele Barbaro

INGRID S. WEBER, "The Significance of Papal Medals for the Architectural History of Roma", Italian Medals, Studies in the History of Art XXI, 283-297

KATHLEEN WEIL-GARRIS BRANDT, "Michelangelo's 'Pietà' for the Cappella del re di Francia", in *Il se rendit en Italie...* (1987), 77-119

FRANZ GRAF WOLFF METTERNICH, CHRISTOF THOENES, *Die frühen St. Peter-Entwürfe, 1505-1514*, Tübingen

FRANK ZÖLLNER, *Vitruvius Proportionsfigur: Quellenkritische Studien Zur Kunstliteratur Im 15. Und 16. Jahrhundert*, Worms

1988

Architettura militare nell'Europa del XVI secolo, Atti del convegno di studi (Firenze, 25-28 novembre 1986), a cura di C. Cresti, A. Fara e D. Lamberini, Siena

R.W. GASTON, ed., *Pirro Ligorio, Artist and Antiquarian*, Milano

Da Pisanello alla nascita dei Musei Capitolini. L'Antico a Roma alla vigilia del Rinascimento, Roma-Milano

Les traités d'architecture de la Renaissance, Actes du colloque tenu à Tours (1981), sous la direction de Jean Guillaume, Paris

LEON BATTISTA ALBERTI, see Joseph Rykwert, Neil Leach and Robert Tavernor

M. VON ALBRECHT, *Rom: Spiegel Europas. Texte und Themen*, Heidelberg

J.F. D'AMICO, *Theory and Practice in Renaissance Textual Criticism*, Berkeley, L.A.-London

UMBERTO BALDINI, "La Pala di Santo Spirito di Filippino Lippi", *Critica d'arte* LIII, 24-31

CARLO BERTELLI, "IL RINASCIMENTO DEL MOSAICO", IN *Il mosaico*, a cura di Carlo Bertelli, Milano, 225-232

LUCIANO BERTI, *Masaccio*, Firenze

HARTMUT BIERMANN, "Paläst und Villa: Theorie und Praxis in Giuliano da Sangallos Codex Barberini und im Taccuino Senese", in *Les traités d'architecture...* (1988), 135-150

JANE BRIDGEMAN, "Filippino Lippi's Nerli Altar-piece A New Date", *Burlington Magazine* CXXX, (1026), 668-671

ARNALDO BRUSCHI, "Plans for the Dome of St. Peter's from Bramante to Antonio da Sangallo the Younger", in *Domes from Antiquity to the Present*, Proceedings of the IASS-MSU Intenational Symposium (Mimar Sinan Üniversitesi), Istanbul, 237-243

HOWARD BURNS, "Pirro Ligorio's Reconstruction of Ancient Rome: the 'Antiquae urbis imago' of 1561", in R.W. Gaston (1988), 19-92

A. CATTANEO CATTORINI, "Antonio da Lonate e il modellino ligneo del Duomo di Vigevano", *Arte lombarda* LXXXVI/LXXXVII, 160-166

ANDRÉ CHASTEL, "La mosaïque à Venise et à Florence au XVe siècle", in *Favole, forme, figure*, Torino, 69-91

CICERO, *De Oratore*, translated by H.M. Hubbell, Cambridge-London

CLAUDIA CIERI VIA, "Bernardino Pinturicchio e la decorazione dell'Appartamento Borgia", in *Perugino e Pinturicchio in Vaticano*, Roma, 122ss.

M. COMINCINI, "Ludovico il Moro a Vigevano", in *La biscia e l'aquila*, Vigevano, 53-85

ENNIO CONCINA, *L'Arsenale della Repubblica di Venezia. Tecnica e istituzioni dal medioevo all'età moderna*, Milano

SILVIA DANESI SQUARZINA, "Eclisse del gusto cortese e nascita della cultura antiquaria: Ciriaco, Feliciano, Marcanova, Alberti", in *Da Pisanello...* (1988), 27-37

CHARLES T. DAVIS, "Topographical and Historical Propaganda in Early Florentine Chronicles and in Villani", *Medioevo Rinascimento*, Annuario II, 35-51

G. DE MORO, "Giovanni Maria Olgiati (1495-1557). Contributo alla riscoperta di un 'inzegnero' lombardo al servizio di Spagna", in *Architettura militare...* (1988), 149-206

CESARE DE SETA, "L'immagine di Napoli dalla Tavola Strozzi a Jean Breugel", in *Scritti di storia dell'arte in onore di Raffaello Causa*, Napoli, 105-117

S. EBERT-SCHIFFERER, "Ripandas Kapitolinischer Freskenzyklus und die Selbstdarstellung der Konservatoren um 1500", *Römisches Jahrbuch für Kunstgeschichte* XXIII-XXIV, 75-218

SABINE EICHE und G. LUBKIN, "THE MAUSOLEUM PLAN OF GALEAZZO MARIA SFORZA", *Mitteilungen de Kunsthistorischen Institutes in Florenz* XXXII, 547-553

COLIN EISLER, *The Genius of Jacopo Bellini, The Complete Paintings and Drawings*, New York

EUCLIDE, *Gli elementi*, a cura di A. Frajese e L. Maccioni, Torino

AMELIO FARA, *Bernardo Buontalenti: l'architettura, la guerra e l'elemento geometrico*, Genova

VINCENZO FONTANA, *Fra' Giovanni Giocondo architetto 1433-c.1515*, Vicenza

D. FRIEDMAN, *Florentine New Towns. Urban Design in the Late Middle Ages*, Cambridge, Mass.-London

HUBERTUS GÜNTHER [A], *Deutsche Architekturtheorie zwischen Gotik und Renaissance*, Darmstadt

—— [b], "Das geistige Erbe Peruzzis im vierten und dritten Buch des Sebastiano Serlio", in *Les traités d'architecture...* (1988), 227-246

—— [C], "HERMAN POSTMA UND DIE ANTIKE", *Jahrbuch des Zentralinstitut für Kunstgeschichte* IV, 7-17

—— [D], "DIE LEHRE VON DEN SÄULENORDNUNG", IN *Deutsche Architekturtheorie Zwischen Gotik un Renaissance*, Darmstadt, 89-107

—— [E], "SFORZINDA. EINE IDEALSTADT DER RENAISSANCE", IN *Alternative Welten in Mittelalter und Renaissance*, besorgt von L. Schrader, Düsseldorf, 231-258

—— [f] *Das Studium der antiken Architektur in den Zeichnungen der Hochrenaissance*, Tübingen

JON HALE, "Post-Renaissance Fortification. Two Reports by Francesco Tensini on the Defence of Terraferma (1618-1632)", in *L'architettura militare veneta del Cinquecento*, Milano, 11-21

MAYA HAMBLY, *Drawing Instruments 1580-1980*, London

MICHAEL HIRST [a], *Michelangelo Draughtsman*, Milan

—— [B], *Michelangelo and His Drawings*, New Haven-London

H. HUBERT, "Bramantes St. Peter-Entwürfe und die Stellung des Apostelgrabes", *Zeitschrift für Kunstgeschichte* LI, 195-211

L. IPPOLITO, "IL RILIEVO FOTOGRAMMETRICO DEL MODELLO LIGNEO DEL DUOMO DI PAVIA", *Arte lombarda* LXXXVI/LXXXVII, 141-145

CAROLINE KOLB, "The Francesco di Giorgio Material in the Zichy Codex", *Journal of the Society of Architectural Historians* XLVII, 132-158

M. KIENE, "Der Palazzo della Sapienza. Zur Italianischen Universitätsarchitektur des 15. und 16. Jahrhunderts", *Römisches Jahrbuch für Kunstgeschichte* XXIII, 219-271

ELISABETH KIEVEN, *Ferdinando Fuga e l'architettura romana del '700*, Roma

RICHARD KRAUTHEIMER, *Ausgewählte Aufsätze zur europäischen Kunstgeschichte*, Köln

S. MADDALO, "Roma nelle immagini miniate del primo Quattrocento: realtà, simbolo e rappresentazione fantastica", in *Da Pisanello...* (1988), 53-57

ANDRÉ MARTINDALE, *Simone Martini*, Oxford

HENRY A. MILLON, "The Facade of San Lorenzo", in H.A. Millon and Craig Hugh Smyth, *Michelangelo Architect: the Facade of San Lorenzo and the Drum and dome of St. Peter's*, Milan, 3-89

HENRY A. MILLON and CRAIG HUGH SMYTH [a], *Michelangelo Architect: the Facade of San Lorenzo and the Drum and dome of St. Peter's*, Milan

—— [b], *Michelangelo architetto. La facciata di San Lorenzo e la cupola di San Pietro*, Milano

—— [c], "Pirro Ligorio, Michelangelo, and St. Peter's", in R.W. Gaston, ed. (1988), 216-286

ALESSANDRO NOVA, "Il 'Modello' di Martino Longhi il Vecchio per la facciata della Chiesa Nuova", *Römisches Jahrbuch für Kunstgeschichte* XXIII/XXIV, 387-394

JOHN ONIANS, *Bearers of Meaning: The Classical Orders in Antiquity, the Middle Ages, and the Renaissance*, Princeton

A. PAOLUCCI, A.M. MAETZKE, *La casa del Vasari in Arezzo*, Firenze

CARLO PEDRETTI, *Leonardo architetto*, Milano (2a ed. aggiornata; 1a ed. 1978)

O. PELOSI, Vedi 1986

G. PERBELLINI, "La difesa delle frontiere centro-occidentali: Orzinuovi, Legnago, Peschiera", in *L'architettura militare veneta nel Cinquecento*, Milano, 157-169

PAOLO PIVA, *L'altro Giulio Romano. Il Duomo di Mantova. La chiesa di Polirone e la dialettica col Medioevo*, Quistello (Mantova)

LIONELLO PUPPI, "Bernardino Brugnoli", in *L'architettura a Verona nell'età della Serenissima (XV-XIII sec.)*, II Verona, 211-214

NICOLE RIEGEL, *Gemalte und gebaute Palastarchitektur im Quattrocento. Master*, Berlin

JANE ROBERTS, *A Dictionary of Michelangelo's Watermarks*, Milan

GIUSEPPE ROCCHI ET AL., *S. Maria del Fiore: rilievi, documenti, indagini strumentali, interpretazione; il corpo basilicale*, Milano

JOSEPH RYKWERT, NEAL LEACH and ROBERT TAVERNOR eds., *Leon Battista Alberti, On the Art of Building in Ten Books*, Cambridge, Mass.-London

A. SAVIOLI (a cura di), *Faenza: la basilica cattedrale*, Firenze

Gustina Scaglia [a], "Drawings of Forts and Engines by Lorenzo Donati, Giovanbattista Alberti, Sallustio Peruzzi; "The Machines Complexes Artists, and Oreste Biringuccio", *Architectura* XVIII (2), 169-197

—— [b], "A Vitruvianist's thermae Plan and the Vitruvianists in Roma and Siena", *Arte lombarda* LXXXIV/LXXXV, 85-101

Massimo Scolari, "L'idea del modello", *Eidos*, II, 16-39

A. Scotti Tosini, "Cittadelle lombarde di fine Cinquecento: il castello di Milano nella prima età spagnola", in *Architettura militare nell'Europa...* (1988), 207-218

C.B. Semenzato (a cura di), *La cappella del Beato Luca e Giusto de' Menabuoi nella basilica di Sant'Antonio*, Padova

Splendori di pietre dure: l'arte di corte nella Firenze dei granduchi, catalogo mostra (Firenze, Palazzo Pitti), a cura di A.M. Giusti, Firenze

William A. Steinke, "Influence of the Majolica of Nicola Pellipario on Northern French Renaissance Sculpture", *Gazette des beaux-arts*, VIe, 110

Christof Thoenes, "S. Lorenzo a Milano, S. Satiro a Roma: ipotesi sul 'piano di pergamena'", *Arte lombarda* LXXXVI/LXXXVII, 94-100

Simonetta Valtieri, *Il palazzo del principe, il palazzo del cardinale, il palazzo del mercante nel Rinascimento*, Roma

A. Weege, "La ricostruzione del progetto di Bramante per il Duomo di Pavia", *Arte lombarda* LXXXVI/LXXXVII, 137-140

Roberto Weiss, *The Renaissance Discovery of Classical Antiquity*, New York

J.H. Whitfield, "'Momus' and the Language of Irony", in *The Languages of Literature in Renaissance Italy*, Oxford, 31-43

E. Zibarth, "Ein griechischer Reisebericht", *Athenische Mitteilungen* XXIV, 72-88

1989

Les bâtisseurs des cathédrales gothiques, catalogue exposition (Strasbourg, 3 septembre-26 novembre), sous la direction de Roland Recht, Strasbourg

Il disegno di architettura, Atti del convegno (Milano, 15-18 febbraio 1988), a cura di Paolo Carpeggiani e Luigi Patetta, Milano

Giulio Romano, catalogo mostra (Mantova, Palazzo Te), testi di Ernst H. Gombrich, Manfredo Tafuri, Sylvia Ferino Pagden et al., Milano

Roma, centro ideale della cultura dell'Antico nei secoli XV e XVI: da Martino V al Sacco di Roma 1417-1527, a cura di Silvia Danesi Squarzina, Milano

Sebastiano Serlio, Sesto seminario internazionale di storia dell'architettura (Vicenza 1987), a cura di Christof Thoenes, Milano

Nicholas Adams, "Sebastiano Serlio, Military Architect?", in *Sebastiano Serlio* (1989), 222-227

Leon Battista Alberti, *L'architettura [De Re Aedificatoria]*, traduzione dal latino di Giovanni Orlandi, introduzione e note di Paolo Portoghesi, Milano (1a ed. 1966)

Valerio Ascani, "Le dessin d'architecture médiéval en Italie", in *Les bâtisseurs...* (1989), 255-277

Amedeo Belluzzi, Kurt W. Forster, "Giulio Romano superiore delle stade di Mantova", in *Giulio Romano* (1989), 327-344

Franz Bischoff, "Les maquettes d'architecture", in *Les bâtisseurs...* (1989)

Ferdinando Bologna (a cura di) *Il polittico di San Severino. Restauri e recuperi*, Napoli, 37 e sg.

Franco Borsi, *Bramante*, Milano

S. Borsi, F. Quinterio, C. Vasic Vatovic, *Maestri fiorentini nei cantieri romani del Quattrocento*, Roma

L. Brown Beverly, *The Tribuna of SS. Annunziata in Florence*, Ann Arbor

Arnaldo Bruschi [a], "Le chiese del Serlio" in *Sebastiano Serlio* (1989)

—— [b] "Edifici privati di Bramante a Roma: Palazzo Castellesi e Palazzo Caprini", *Palladio* n.s. IV, 5-44

Eva Karwacka Codini, *Piazza dei Cavalieri: urbanistica e architettura dal Medioevo al Novecento*, Firenze

L. Corti, *Vasari. Catalogo completo*, Firenze

M. Curti, "Sulla pertinenza del disegno U 1973 rv con il progetto raffaellesco per S.Pietro. Ipotesi di reinterpretazione", *Quaderni dell'istituto di storia dell'architettura* XIV, 17-30

Nicole Dacos, "L'Anonyme a de Berlin: Hermannus Posthumus", *Antikenzeichnung und Antikenstudium in Renaissance und Frühbarock*, 61-80, Mainz

Margaret Daly Davis [a], "'Opus isodomum' at the Palazzo della Cancelleria: Vitruvian Studies and Archeological Antiquiarian Interests at the Court of Raffaele Riario", in *Roma, centro ideale...* (1989), 442-457

—— [b], "Zum Codex Coburgiensis: Frühe Archäologie und Humanismus im Kreis des Marcello Cervino", in *Antikenzeichnung und Antikenstudium*, Mainz, 185-199

Cesare De Seta, "Tetti rossi su Napoli", *FMR*, LXXV, 83-93

Sylvie Deswarte-Rosa, "Les gravures de monuments antiques d'Antonio Salamanca, à l'origine du Speculum Romanae Magnificentiae", *Annali di architettura* I, 47-62

C. Dittscheid, "Serlio, Roma e Vitruvio", in *Sebastiano Serlio* (1989), 132-148

Amelio Fara, *Il sistema e la città. Architettura fortificata dell'Europa moderna dai trattati alle realizzazioni, 1464-1794*, Genova

Kurt W. Forster, "Il palazzo di Landshut", in *Giulio Romano* (1989), 512-515

Christoph L. Frommel [a], "Kirche und Tempel: Giuliano della Roveres Kathedrale Sant'Aurea in Ostia", in *Festschrift für Nikolaus Himmelmann*, besorgt von H.U. Cain, H. Gabelmann und D.Salzman, Mainz, 491

—— [b], "Le opere romane di Giulio", in *Giulio Romano* (1989), 97-133, 290-291

—— [c], "Il Palazzo della Cancelleria", in *Il Palazzo dal Rinascimento ad oggi*, Atti del convegno internazionale (Reggio Calabria 1988), Roma

—— [d], "Progetto e archeologia in due disegni di Antonio da Sangallo il Giovane per Santa Croce in Gerusalemme", in *Roma, centro ideale...* (1989), 382-389

—— [e], "Serlio a Roma", in *Sebastiano Serlio* (1989), 39-49

Giovanni Antonio Amadeo: Documents, edited by Richard Schofield, Janice Shell and Grazioso Sironi, Como

Luca Giorgi, Luigi Marino, "Il compimento dei prospetti esterni di S. Maria del Fiore a Firenze", in *L'architettura a Roma e in Italia (1580-1621)*, Atti del XXIII Congresso di storia dell'architettura (Roma, 24-26 marzo), a cura di G. Spagnesi, I, Roma, 121-131

Hubertus Günther [a], "Gian Cristoforo studia l'architettura antica...", in *Il disegno di architettura* (1989), 137-148

—— [b], "Serlio e gli ordini architettonici", in *Sebastiano Serlio* (1989), 154-168

—— [c], "La nascita di Roma moderna. Urbanistica del Rinascimento a Roma", dans *D'une ville à l'autre: Structures materielles et organisation de l'Espace dans les villes européennes (XIIIe-XVIe siècles)*, Rome, 381-406

Michael Hirst, Michel-Ange dessinateur, catalogue exposition, Paris

Mark Jarzombek, On Leon Battista Alberti: His Literary and Aesthetic Theories, Cambridge, Mass.-London

Martin Kemp, ed., *Leonardo on Painting*, New Haven

Pier Luigi Leone De Castris, *Simone Martini*, Firenze

G. Lombardi, "Nuovi studi su Perotti", *Roma nel Rinascimento*, 102-116

Luigi Michelini Tocci (a cura di), *Das Skizzenbuch des Francesco di Giorgio Martini. Vat. Urb. Lat. 1757, (Codices Vaticani selecti quam simillim expressi iussu Ioanni Pauli PPII Consilio et opera curatorum Bibliothecae Vaticanae, LXXX)*, Zurich (ed. it., Milano 1990)

James E. Mundy and Elizabeth Ourusoff de Fernandex-Gimenez, Renaissance into Baroque: Italian Master Drawing by the Zuccari, 1550-1600, New York

Arnold Nesselrath [a], "Monumenta antiqua romana. Ein illustrierter Rom-Traktat des Quattrocento", in *Antikenzeichnung und Antikenstudium in Renaissance und Frübarock*, Akten des internationalen Symposiums in Coburg (8.-10. September 1986), besorgt von R. Harprath und H. Wrede, Mainz, 33 sg.

—— [b], Rezension von Hülsen 1910, (1984), *Zeitschrift für Kunstgeschichte* LII, 281-292

Konrad Oberhuber, Dean Walter, *Sixteenth's Century Italian Drawings from the Collection of Janos Sholz*, New York-Washington

Pier Nicola Pagliara, "Osservazioni sulle tecniche grafiche in alcuni disegni di Antonio da Sangallo il Giovane", in *Il disegno di architettura* (1989), 169-174

Luigi Patetta, *Storia e tipologia*, Milano

Linda Pellecchia, "The Patrons Role in the Production of Architecture: Bartolomeo Scala and the Scala Palace", *Renaissance Quaterly* XLII, 258-291

Monica Preti, *Museo dell'Opera del Duomo di Firenze*, Milano

Lionello Puppi, *Corpus dei disegni del Museo Civico di Vicenza*, Milano

Roland Recht, voir *Les bâtisseurs des cathédrales gothique* (1989)

Piero Roselli, "La vicenda costruttiva delle Logge Vasari ad Arezzo", *Quasar* I, 31-42

Howard Saalman, "Die Planung Neu St. Peters. Kritische Bemerkungen zum Stand der Forschung", *Münchner Jahrbuch der bildenden Kunst* XL, 102-140

Elisabetta Sambo, "Problemi di classicismo in Emilia. Biagio Pupini. L'attività pittorica e grafica, tesi di Dottorato, Dipartimento Arti visive Igino Benvenuto Supino, Università degli Studi di Bologna

Annegrit Schmitt, "Antikenkopien und künstlerische Selbstverwirklichung in der Frührenaissance", in *Antikenzeichnung und Antikenstudium*, Mainz

Richard Schofield, "Amadeo, Bramante and Leonardo and the 'tiburio' of Milan Cathedral", *Achademia Leonardi Vinci. Journal of Leonardo Studies and Bibliography of Vinciana* II, 68-100

W. Schöller, *Die rechtliche Organisation des Kirchenbaus im Mittelalter*, Wien

M. Sframeli (a cura di), *Il centro di Firenze restituito*, Firenze

Pierluigi Silvan [a], "Errori di Valadier e di Létarouilly nei rilievi di S. Pietro", *XY, Dimensioni del disegno* VIII/IX, 50-62

—— [b], "Inediti su Michelangelo architetto", in *Michelangelo architetto inedito*, Roma, 25-35

Manfredo Tafuri [a], "La chiesa abbaziale di San Benedetto in Polirone", in *Giulio Romano* (1989), 542ss.

—— [c], "Ipotesi sulla religiosità di Sebastiano Serlio", in *Sebastiano Serlio* (1989)

—— [d], *Venice and the Renaissance*, Cambridge, Mass.

Christof Thoenes, "Prolusione. Serlio e la trattatistica", in *Sebastiano Serlio* (1989), 9-18

Christian Vanderkerchove [a], "L'iconographie medievale de la construction", dans *Les bâtisseurs...* (1989), 61-80

—— [b], scheda C 31, dans Les bâtisseurs... (1989), 417

Claudio Visintini, "Analisi del sistema fortificato della città di Palmanova", in *L'architettura militare veneta del Cinquecento, Bollettino del centro internazionale Studi di architettura "Andrea Palladio"* (Vicenza), Milano, 146-150

Bruno Zevi, *Giuseppe Terragni*, Zürich

1990

Il Palazzo Medici Riccardi di Firenze, a cura di Giovanni Cherubini e Giovanni Fanelli, Firenze

James S. Ackerman [a], "The Early Villas of the Medici", in *The Villa: Form and Ideology of Country Houses*, Princeton, 62-87

—— [b], *The Villa. Form and Ideology of Country Houses*, London

Giulio Carlo Argan, Bruno Contardi, *Michelangelo architetto*, Milano

Domenico Beccafumi e il suo tempo, catalogo mostra (Siena, Chiesa di Sant'Agostino e Pinacoteca), Milano

Annette Becker, "Anmerkungen zu Barbaros Vitruv", D.Phil. Diss, Mainz

Luciano Bellosi (a cura di), *Pittura di luce. Giovanni di Francesco e l'arte fiorentina di metà Quattrocento*, Milano

Sandro Benedetti, Giuseppe Zander, *L'arte a Roma nel XVI secolo. L'architettura*, Bologna

Carla Bernardini, *Il Bagnacavallo Senior: Bartolomeo Ramenghi pittore (1484?-1542?)*, Rimini

Fede Berti, "Considerazioni in margine ad alcune classi di oggetti", in *Fortuna Maris: la nave romana di Comacchio*, a cura di Fede Berti, Bologna

Luciano Berti, Antonio Paolucci (a cura di), *L'età di Masaccio. Il primo Quattrocento a Firenze*, Milano

Hartmut Biermann [a], "Die Aufbauprinzipien von L.B. Albertis De re aedificatoria", *Zeitschrift für Kunstgeschichte* LIII, 443-485

—— [b], "Eine Villenbeschreibung des Sannazaro und L.B. Albertis De re aedificatoria", *Mitteilungen des Kunsthistorischen Institutes in Florenz* XXXIV, 421-423

H. Bredekamp, "Maarten van Heemskercks Bildersturm als Angriffe auf Rom", in *Bilder und Bildersturm im Spätmittelalter und in der frühen Neuzeit*, Wiesbaden, 203-216

V. Breidecker, *Florenz oder "Die Rede, die zum Auge spricht"*, München

Arnaldo Bruschi, *Bramante architetto*, Bari (1a ed. 1969)

Charles Burroughs, *From Signs to Design: Environmental Process and Reform in Early Renaissance Rome*, Cambridge, Mass.

F. Cairoli Giuliani, *L'edilizia nell'antichità*, Roma

Giovanni Caniato, Michela Dal Borgo, *Le arti edili a Venezia*, Roma

André Chastel e R.Cevese (a cura di), *Andrea Palladio: Nuovi contributi*, Atti del settimo seminario internazionale di Storia dell'Architettura, Milano

Ilaria Ciseri, *L'ingresso trionfale di Leone X in Firenze nel 1515*, Firenze

Clarke and Englebach, eds., *Ancient Egyptian Construction and Architecture*, New York

O. Clavuot, *Biondos "Italia illustrata". Summa oder Neuschöpfung*, Tübingen

Dietrich Conrad, *Kirchenbau im Mittelalter: Bauplanung und Bauausführung*, Leipzig

Mario Craveri (a cura di), *I Vangeli apocrifi*, Torino

Carlo Cresti, *L'architettura del Seicento a Firenze*, Roma

Rosalba D'Amico (a cura di), *Sesto centenario di fondazione della Basilica di San Petronio*, Bologna

Da Leonardo a Rembrandt. Disegni della Biblioteca Reale di Torino, catalogo mostra (Torino, Biblioteca Reale), Torino

Christiane Denker Nesselrath, *Die Säulenordnungen bei Bramante*, Worm

Cesare De Seta, "L'immagine di Napoli dalla Tavola Strozzi a E. G. Papworth", in *All'ombra del Vesuvio*, 27-44

Hermann Diruf, *Paläste Venedigs vor 1500: baugeschichtliche Untersuchungen zur venezianischen Palastarchitektur im 15. Jahrhundert*, München

Caroline Elam, "Il palazzo nel contesto della città: Strategie urbanistiche dei Medici nel Gonfalone del Leon d'Oro, 1415-1430", in *Il Palazzo Medici Riccardi...* (1990), 44-57

Helen Ettlinger, "The Sepulchre on the Facade: Re-evaluation of Sigismondo Malatesta's Rebuilding of San Francesco in Rimini", *Journal of the Warburg and Courtauld Institutes* LIII, 133-143

C. Faldi Guglielmi, *Pienza: duomo*, Bologna

Christoph L. Frommel [a], "Bramante e il disegno 104 A degli Uffizi", in *Il disegno di architettura*, Atti del Convegno (Milano 1989), Milano, 161-168

—— [b], "Il progetto del Louvre per la Chiesa dei Fogliani e l'architettura di Cristoforo Solari", *Quaderno di studi sull'arte lombarda dai Visconti agli Sforza. Per gli ottant'anni di Gian Alberto dell'Acqua*, a cura di M.T. Balboni Brizza, Milano, 52-63

—— [c], "Roma e la formazione architettonica del Palladio", in A. Chastel e R. Cevese

Helga Gamrath, "The Herculean Addition to Old Ferrare", in *La Corte di Ferrara e il suo Mecenatismo 1441-1598: Atti del convegno internazionale*, a cura di Marianne Pade, Lene Waage Petersen e Daniela Quarta, Firenze, 151-158

Maria Luisa Gatti Perer (a cura di), *Dal monastero di S. Ambrogio all'Università Cattolica*, Milano

Adriano Ghisetti Giavarina, *Aristotile da Sangallo: architettura, scenografia e pittura tra Roma e Firenze nella prima metà del Cinquecento: ipotesi di attribuzione dei disegni raccolti agli Uffizi*, Roma

Luisa Giordano, "L'architettura. 1490-1500", in *La basilica di S. Maria della Croce a Crema*, Crema, 35-89

Enrico Guidoni, *L'urbanistica di Roma tra miti e progetti*, Roma-Bari

Jean Guillaume, "Désaccord parfait: ordres et mesures dans la Chappelle des Pazzi", *Annali di architettura* II, 9-23

Hubertus Günther [a], "Ein Entwurf Baldassare Peruzzis für ein Architekturtraktat", *Römisches Jahrbuch für Kunstgeschichte* XXVI, 135-170

—— [b], "Méthodes scientifiques modernes et archéologues de la Renaissance...", dans *Archives et histoire de l'architecture*, Paris, 212-242

—— [c], "Palladio e gli ordini", in *Andrea Palladio. Nuovi contributi*, Milano, 182-197

H. Hubert, Rezenzion von Wolff Metternich-Thoenes, Zeitschrift für Kunstgeschichte LIII, 226-239

P. Jacks, "The Simulacrum of Fabio Calvo: A View of Roman Architecture all'antica in 1527", *Art Bulletin* LXXII, 453-481

Martin Kemp, *The Science of Art*, London-New Haven

F.W. Kent, "Il palazzo, la famiglia, il contesto politico", *Annali di architettura* II, 59-72

Nokter Labeo, "Laus de arte poetica, tunc Melpomene", *Kommentierende Übersetzung aus Marcianus Capella, De nuptiis Philologiae et Mercurii (II, 13), in Althochdeutsche Literatur*, besorgt von H.D. Schlosser, Frankfurt

Daniela Lamberini [a], "De Marchi, Francesco", voce in *Dizionario Biografico degli Italiani*, XXXVIII, Roma, 447-454

—— [b], *Il principe difeso. Vita e opere di Bernardo Puccini*, Firenze

Agostino Lapini, *Diario fiorentino dal 252 al 1596*, a cura di G.O. Corazzini, Firenze

Anna Maria Massinelli, "Magnificenze medicee: gli stipi della Tribuna", *Antologia di belle arti* n.s. XXXV/XXXVIII, 111-134

Saverio Mecca, Roberto Sernicola, *La cultura tecnologica nel progetto delle cattedrali. 1, Bibliografia generale di riferimento*, Firenze

W. Müller, *Grundlagen gotischer Bautechnik*, München

G. Pochat, *Theater und Bildende Kunst in Mittelalter und in der Renaissance in Italien*, Graz

J. Poeschke, *Die Skulptur der Renaissance in Italien*, I, München

G. Poggi, *Il duomo di Firenze*, Berlino

Brenda Preyer, "L'architettura del Palazzo Mediceo", *Il Palazzo Medici Riccardi...* (1990), 58-75

"La 'raccolta prima' degli autografi Ferrajoli...", *Studi e Testi 336*, a cura di Paolo Vian, Città del Vaticano

Pietro Ruschi, "Il 'timpano alternato' e la sua rinnovata fortuna nel tardo Quattrocento", *Studi di storia dell'arte* I, 73-94

Howard Saalman, "The Transformation of the City in the Renaissance: Florence as Model", *Annali di Architettura* II, 73-82

Thomas G. Schattner, *Griechische Hausmodelle*, Berlin

Armando Schiavo, *Michelangelo nel complesso delle sue opere*, Roma

L. Schneider, "Leon Battista Alberti: Some Biographical Implications of the Winged Eye", *Art Bulletin* LXXII, 261-70

Jürgen Schulz, *La cartografia tra scienza e arte. Carte e cartografi del Rinascimento italiano*, Modena

Sesto centenario di fondazione della Basilica di San Petronio 1390-1990, a cura di R. D'Amico, C. De Angelis e Mario Fanti, Bologna

Giorgio Stabile, "La torre di Babele. confusione dei linguaggi e impotenza tecnica", in *Ars et Ratio. Dalla torre di Babele al ponte di Rialto*, a cura di Jean-Claude Maire Vigueur e Agostino Paravicini Bagliani, Palermo, 245-277

C. Stinger, "The Campidoglio as the Locus of Renovatio Imperii in Renaissance Rome", in C. Rosenberg, ed., *Art and Politics in Late Medieval and Early Renaissance Italy: 1250-1500*, Notre Dame-London

Manfredo Tafuri, "Raffaello, Jacopo Sansovino e la facciata di San Lorenzo a Firenze", *Annali di Architettura* II, 24-44

Christof Thoenes, "Zur Frage des Masstabs in Architekturzeichnungen der Renaissance", in *Studien zur Künstlerzeichnung, Klaus Schwager zum 65. Geburtstag*, von besorgt S. Kummer und G. Satzinger, Stuttgart, 38-56

Andreas Tönnesmann, *Pienza. Städtebau und Humanismus*, München

Francesca Ugolini, "La pianta del 1306 e l'impianto urbanistico di Talamone", *Storia della città* LII, 77-82

D.Willers, *Hadrians panhellenistisches Programm. Archäologische Beiträge zur Neugestaltung Athens durch Hadrian*, Basel

Rudolf Wittkower (a cura di), *Le antiche rovine di Roma nei disegni di Dupérac*, Milano (2ª ed.)

Wolff Metternich, "Der Dom zu Limburg an der Lahn. Geschichte und Bauentwicklung", D.Phil.Diss., Frankfurt

1990-91

Michael Baxandall, "Alberti's Self", *Fenway Court*, 31-37

1990-92

Sandro Benedetti, "L'officina architettonica di Antonio da Sangallo il Giovane: la cupola per il San Pietro di Roma", Quaderni dell'Istituto di storia dell'architettura, n.s. XV-XX, 485-510 (pubblicato nel 1992)

V. Hoffmann, "Filippo Brunelleschi: Kuppelbau und Perspektive", Quaderni dell'Istituto di storia dell'architettura n.s. XV/XX, 317-326 (pubbl. nel 1992)

Christof Thoenes, "I tre progetti di bramante per S. Pietro", Quaderni dell'Istituto di storia dell'architettura, n.s. 15/20, 439-446 (pubbl.nel 1992)

1991

Franco Borsi (a cura di), *"Per bellezza, per studio, per piacere." Lorenzo il Magnifico e gli spazi dell'arte*, Firenze

Circa 1492: Art in the Age of Exploration, exhibition catalog (National Gallery of Art, Washington, D.C., 12 October, 1991-12 January 1992), edited by Jay A. Levenson, New Haven

Le Muse e il Principe. Arte di corte nel Rinascimento padano, a cura di Alessandra Mottola Molfino e M. Natale, Modena

Palazzo Strozzi: metà millennio 1489-1989, a cura di Daniela Lamberini, Roma

Prima di Leonardo. Cultura delle macchine a Siena nel Rinascimento, catalogo mostra (Siena, Magazzini del sale, 9 giugno-30 settembre) a cura di Paolo Galluzzi, Milano

VALERIO ASCANI, "I disegni architettonici attribuiti ad Antonio di Vincenzo", *Arte Medievale* I, 105-114

ROLAND BECHMANN, *Villard de Honnecourt*, Paris

K.G. BOON, "Two Drawings by Hermann Postma from his Roman Period", *Master Drawings* XXIX, 173-181

STEFANO BORSI, "Il palazzo mediceo di via Laura a Firenze", in Franco Borsi (1991), 333-344

EVE BORSOOK, "Ritratto di Filippo Strozzi il Vecchio", in *Palazzo Strozzi...* (1991), 1-11

CESARE BRANDI, "Lo stile di Ambrogio Lorenzetti", in *Pittura a Siena nel Trecento*, Torino

ARNALDO BRUSCHI (a cura di), *Il tempio della Consolazione a Todi*, testi di E. Bentivoglio, A. Bruschi, G. Comez, S. Valtieri, P. Zampa, M.O. Zander e altri, Milano

ANTONIO CADEI [a], "Cultura artistica delle cattedrali: due esempi a Milano", *Arte medievale* I, 83-103

—— [b], *Testimonianza artistica, messaggio evangelico*, Milano

DAVID R. COFFIN, *Gardens and Gardening in Papal Rome*, Princeton

BRUNO CONTARDI, "I modelli nel sistema della progettazione architettonica a Roma tra 1860 e 1750", in *In urbe architectus: modelli, disegni, misure. La professione dell'architetto, Roma 1680-1750*, a cura di Bruno Contardi e Giovanna Curcio, Roma

DOMINIQUE CORDELLIER, "Fragments de jeunesse: deux feuilles inédits de Michel-Ange au Louvre", *Révue du Louvre* II, 43-55

CESARE DE SETA, *Napoli fra Rinascimento e Illuminismo*, Napoli

SABINE EICHE, "Girolamo Genga the Architect: An Enquiry into his Background", *Mitteilungen des Kunsthistorischen Institutes in Florenz* XXXV, 317-323

C. ECHINGER-MAURACH, *Studien zu Michelangelos Juliusgrabmal*, II, Hildesheim

CAROLINE ELAM, "Piazza Strozzi nel contesto urbano", in *Palazzo Strozzi...* (1991), 183-194

CLAIRE J. FARAGO, The Classification of the Visual Arts in the Renaissance, in D.H. Kelley and R.H. Popkin, eds., *The Shapes of Knowledge from the Renaissance to the Enlightenment*, Dordrecht, 23-47

EUGENE S. FERGUSON, "Glossario iconografico", in Agostino Ramelli, *Le diverse et artificiose machine. 1588*, a cura di Gustina Scaglia, Adriano Carugo ed Eugene S. Ferguson, Milano, LVII-LXXVII

LAURENCE HALL FOWLER and ELIZABETH BAER, *The Fowler Architectural Collection of the John Hopkins University*, San Francisco

CHRISTOPH L. FROMMEL [a], "Il cantiere di S. Pietro prima di Michelangelo", dans *Les chantiers de la Renaissance*, Actes des colloques (Tour 1983-1984), sous la direction de Jean Guillaume, Paris, 175-183

—— [b], "La villa Médicis et la typologie de la ville italienne à la Renaissance", dans *La Villa Médicis*, sous la direction de André Chastel, Rome

E. FUMAGALLI, "La facciata quattrocentesca del palazzo Medici in piazza Madama: un disegno e alcune considerazioni", *Annali di Architettura* III, 26-31

M. HARDER, *Enstehung von Rundhof und Rundsaal im Palasthau der Renaissance in Italien*, Freiburg

PAOLO GALLUZZI [a], "Antonio da Sangallo il Giovane e Francesco di Giorgio", in *Prima di Leonardo...* (1991), 246-247

—— [b], "Brunelleschi e la prima generazione italiana", in *Prima di Leonardo...* (1991), 184-190

—— [c], "Le macchine senesi. Ricerca antiquaria, spirito di innovazione e cultura del territorio", in *Prima di Leonardo...* (1991), 15-44

—— [d], "I manoscritti autografi di Mariano di Iacopo, detto il Taccola", in *Prima di Leonardo...* (1991), 191-198

HEINZ GÖTZE, *Castel del Monte. Gestalt und Symbol der Architektur Friedrichs II*, München

J. ISAGER, *Pliny on Art and Society. The Elder Pliny's Chapters on the History of Art*, Odense

PAUL JOHANNIDES [a], "La chronologie du tombeau de Jules II à propos d'un dessin de Michel-Ange découvert", *Revue du Louvre* II, 32-42

—— [b], "Masaccio's Brancacci Chapel: Restoration and Revelation", *Apollo*, 26-32

MICHAEL HIRST, "Michelangelo in 1505", *Burlington Magazine* 133, 760-766

MARTIN KEMP [a], "La 'diminutione di ciascun piano': la rappresentazione delle forme nello spazio di Francesco di Giorgio", in *Prima di Leonardo...* (1991), 105-112

—— [b], entry to "Follower of Brunelleschi, Christ Healing a Possessed Woman", in *Circa 1492...* (1991), 240

—— [c], catalog entry to "Ideal cities", in *Circa 1492...* (1991)

—— [d], "Jacopo de' Barbari?: Portrait of Fra Luca Pacioli with a Young Man", in *Circa 1492...* (1991), 244-246

—— [e], catalog entries nos. 147-149, in *Circa 1492...* (1991), 249-252

MARTIN KEMP et al., "Paolo Uccello's 'Hunt in the Forest'", *Burlington Magazine* 133, March, 164-178

E. KESSLER, "Die Ausbildungn der Theorie der Geschichtsschreibung im Humanismus und in der Renaissance unter dem Einfluss der wiederentdeckten Antike", in *Die Antike-Rezeption in den Wissenschaften während der Renaissance* (Weinheim 1983), 29-50, Ianziti

DANIELA LAMBERINI [a], "Bernardo Puccini e le macchine senesi", in *Prima di Leonardo...* (1991), 264-271

—— [b], "La fortuna delle macchine senesi nel Cinquecento", in *Prima di Leonardo...* (1991), 135-46

—— [c], "Le macchine di Taccola e Francesco di Giorgio nel Cinquecento: Venezia", in *Prima di Leonardo...* (1991), 229-234

—— [d], "Un 'monte di saxi' nuovi. I restauri di Palazzo Strozzi nella Firenze post-unitaria e fascista", in *Palazzo Strozzi...* (1991), 214-222

SIMONA LECCHINI GIOVANNONI, *Alessandro Allori*, Torino

LE CORBUSIER, vedi Vadou

AMANDA LILLIE, "Vita di palazzo, vita in villa: l'attività edilizia di Filippo il Vecchio", in *Palazzo Strozzi...* (1991), 167-182

PIETRO C. MARANI, "Francesco di Giorgio a Milano e a Pavia: conseguenze ed ipotesi", in *Prima di Leonardo...* (1991), 93-104

MARA MINIATI, *Museo di Storia della Scienza. Firenze. Catalogo*, Firenze

HELMUT MINKOWSKI, *Vermutengen über den Turm zu Babel*, Freren (1. Ausgabe, *Aus dem Nebel der Vergangenheit steigt der Turm zu Babel*, Berlin 1960)

MANUELA MORRESI, "Bramante, Enrico Bruno e la parrocchiale di Roccaverano", in *La piazza, la chiesa, il parco. Saggi di storia dell'architettura (XV-XIX secolo)*, a cura di Manfredo Tafuri, Milano, 135 e sg

MASSIMO MUSSINI, *Il Trattato di Francesco di Giorgio Martini e Leonardo: il Codice Estense restituito*, Parma

FRITZ NEUMEYER, *Oswald Mathias Ungers. Architektur 1951-1990*, Stuttgart

ROBERTA PARISE LABADESSA, "L'arte della medaglia rinascimentale italiana", in Giovanni Gorini, Roberta Parise Labadessa, Andrea Saccocci, *A testa o croce. Immagini d'arte nelle monete e nelle medaglie del Rinascimento. Esempi dalle collezioni del Museo Bottacin*, Padova

MARTHA D. POLLAK, *Turin 1564-1680, Urban Design, Military Culture, and the Creation of the Absolutist Capital*, Chicago

PAOLA ROSSI, *Francesco Maffei*, Milano

G. ROSSI SCARPA, "I mosaici della cappella dei Mascoli", in R. Polacco et al., *San Marco, la basilica d'oro*, Milano

GEORG SATZINGER, *Antonio da Sangallo der Ältere un die Madonna di San Biagio bei Montepulciano*, Tübingen

GUSTINA SCAGLIA [a], "Francesco di Giorgio autore", in *Prima di Leonardo...* (1991), 57-80

—— [b], "Introduzione", in Agostino Ramelli, *Le diverse et artificiose machine. 1588*, a cura di Gustina Scaglia, Adriano Carugo ed Eugene S. Ferguson, Milano, IX-XXII

RICHARD SCHOFIELD, "Leondardo's Milanese Architecture: Career, Sources and Graphic Techniques", *Achademia Leonardi Vinci. Journal of Leonardo Studies and Bibliography of Vinciana* IV, 11-157

M. TRENTI ANTONELLI, "Il ruolo della medaglia nella cultura umanistica", in *Le Muse e il Principe...* (1991), 25-35

NICHOLAS TURNER, *Guercino: Drawings for Windsor Castle*, Washington, 68-70, no. 24

ANDREA UGOLINI, "L'attività dei lapicidi nella fabbrica del Tempio malatestiano", *Palladio* VII, 81-89

La vetrata del duomo di Orvieto, Orvieto

FRANCOIS VAUDOU, *Das Kleine Haus von Le Corbusier*, Genève

MONICA VISIOLI, "Documenti per la storia della torre civica. Secoli XV-XVI", *Bollettino della società pavese di storia patria* XCI, 55-158

1991-92

SANDRO BENEDETTI, "L'officina architettonica di Antonio da Sangallo il Giovane: la cupola per il S. Pietro di Roma", in *Quaderni dell'istituto di storia dell'architectura. Saggi in onore di Renato Bonelli*, Roma

ANNA MARIA CAPECCHI et al., *L'Accademia dei Lincei e la cultura europea nel XVII*, catalogo mostra, Parigi-Roma

CHRISTOPH L. FROMMEL, "Peruzzis römische Anfänge. Von der 'Pseudo-Cronaca-Gruppe' zu Bramante", *Römisches Jahrbuch der Bibliotheca Hertziana* XXVII/XXVIII, 177-180

FRANZ KRAUSS, CHRISTOF THOENES, "Bramantes Entwurf für die Kuppel von St. Peter", *Römisches Jahrbuch der Bibliotheca Hertziana* XXVII/XXVIII, 183-200

1992

L'architettura di Lorenzo il Magnifico, catalogo mostra (Firenze, Ospedale degli Innocenti, 8 aprile-26 luglio) a cura di Gabriele Morolli, Cristina Acidini Luchinat, L. Marchetti, Milano

De Fabrica, Laboratorio per il restauro di complessi monumentali, anno I, settembre/ottobre, II/III

Il disegno fiorentino del tempo di Lorenzo il Magnifico, catalogo mostra (Firenze, Gabinetto Disegni e Stampe degli Uffizi), a cura di A. Gadoli, Firenze

L'emploi des ordres à la Renaissance, Actes du colloque tenu à Tours (9-14 juin 1986), sous la direction de Jean Guillaume, Paris

The Genius of the Sculptor in Michelangelo's Work, exhibition catalog (Montreal, Museum of Fine Arts), Montreal

Leonardo & Venezia, catalogo mostra, (Venezia, Palazzo Grassi, aprile), Milano

Michelangelo Drawings, edited by Craig H. Smyth and A. Gilkerson, Washington

Piero e Urbino. Piero e le corti rinascimentali, catalogo mostra (Urbino, Palazzo Ducale), a cura di Paolo dal Poggetto, Venezia

I. ANDREANI, "Ricerche archivistiche sulla vetrata della tribuna del duomo di Orvieto negli anni 1325-1401", relazione storica per la Soprintendenza ai Beni Artistici e Storici dell'Umbria

MICHAEL BAXANDALL, *Painting and Experience in 15th Century*, Oxford

LUCIANO BELLOSI, "Sulla vetrata del Duomo di Orvieto", in *De Fabrica...* (1992), 3 s.

ARNALDO BRUSCHI [a], "Le idee del Peruzzi per il nuovo S.Pietro", in *Quaderni dell'istituto di storia dell'architetura. Saggi in onore di Renato Bonelli*, n.s. 15-20 (1990-92), Roma

713

—— [b], "I primi progetti di Antonio da Sangallo il Giovane per S.Pietro", in *Architektur und Kunst im Abendland. Festschrift zur Vollendung des 65. Lebensjahres von Günther Urban*, Rom

GIOVANNANGELO CAMPOREALE, "Architecture civile e architetture religiose", dans *Les Etrusques et l'Europe*, Paris-Milan

PATRIZIA CASTELLI, "Il mito della città ideale nel governo federiciano", in *Piero e Urbino...* (1992), 207-214

IVAN CHIAVERINI, DANIELE OSTUNI AND MARIO QUATTRONE, "Noninvasive Analytic Techniques Applied to the Study of the Wood Model for Michelangelo Buonarroti's Façade of San Lorenzo in Florence", *Michelangelo Drawings (1992)*, 268-279

MARIA GRAZIA CIARDI DUPRÉ DAL POGGETTO, "Jacopo de Barbari: ritratto di fra Luca Pacioli e del duca Guidobaldo da Montefeltro", in *Piero e Urbino...* (1992)

P.C. CLAUSSEN, "Renovatio Romae, Erneuerungsphasen römischer Architektur im 11. und 12. Jahrhundert", in *Rom im Hohen Mittelalter. Studien zu den Romvorstellungen und zur Rompolitik vom 10. bis zum 12. Jahrhundert. R. Elze zur Vollendung seines siebzigsten Lebensjahres gewidmet*, besorgt von B. Schimmelpfennig und L. Schmugge, Sigmaringen, 87-125

LUISA COGLIATI ARANO, "1449: Leonardo lascia Milano", in *Leonardo & Venezia* (1992), 55-64

DOMINIQUE CORDELLIER, BERNADETTE PY, *Rapahël son atelier, ses copistes*, Paris

MAURO COZZI, *Antonio da Sangallo il Vecchio e l'architettura del Cinquecento in Valdichiana*, Genova

MARGARET DALY DAVIS, "Jacopo Vignola, Alessandro Manzuoli und die Villa Isolani in Minerbio: Zu den frühen Antikenstudien von Vignola", *Mitteilungen des Kunsthistorischen Institutes in Florenz* XXXVI, 287-328

GIOVANNA DAMIANI, in *Nel raggio di Piero. La pittura nell'Italia centrale nell'età di Piero della Francesca*, catalogo mostra, a cura di Luciano Berti, Venezia, 122-123

G. DELFINI FILIPPI, E. MANZATO (a cura di), *Il ritorno di sant'Orsola, affreschi restaurati nella chiesa di Santa Caterina in Treviso*, Treviso

CHRISTIANE DENKER NESSELRATH, "I Cortili", in *I Palazzi Vaticani*, a cura di Carlo Pietrangeli, Roma, 217-234

R. DIEZ DEL CORRAL GARNICA, "Architektur und Stadtbild im Spanien der Katholischen Könige", in *Hispania-Austria*, Ausstellung skatalog, Innsbruck-Mailand, 87-124

L. DI MAURO, "La Tavola Strozzi", *Bussole I*

JAMES DAVID DRAPER, *Bertoldo di Giovanni: Sculptor to the Medici Household*, Columbia, Missouri

SABINE EICHE, "A New Look at Three Drawings for Villa Madama, and Some Related Images", *Mitteilungen des Kunsthistorischen Institutes in Florenz* XXXVI, 275-286

Caroline Elam, "Drawing as Documents: The Problem of the San Lorenzo Facade", in *Michelangelo Drawings* (1992), 99-114

F.T. FAGLIARI ZENI BUCHICCHIO, "Il soggiorno di Sanmicheli nello Stato della Chiesa. Ricerca archivistica", comunicazione al Seminario Internazionale su Michele Sanmicheli, *Bollettino del centro internazionale di studi di architettura «Andrea Palladio»*, Vicenza

GRAZIELLA FEDERICI VESCOVINI, *Filosofia, scienza e astrologia nel Trecento Europeo. Biagio Pelacani Parmense*, Padova

PAOLO FERRARI AGRI, "Il completamento della basilica di S. Petronio. Rapporti e analogie con altre fabbriche del Seicento bolognese", *Carrobbio* XVIII, 126-39

FRANCESCO PAOLO FIORE, "Gli ordini nell'architettura di Francesco di Giorgio", in *L'emploi des ordres...* (1992), 59-67

DAVID FRIEDMAN, "Palaces and the Street in Late-Medieval and Renaissance Italy", in J.W.R. Whitehead and P.J. Larkham, eds., *Urban Ladscapes: International Perspectives*, London, in press

GIORGIO FUNARO, RITA RIVELLI, "Osservazioni sul restauro", *De Fabrica...* (1992), 19-21

VITTORIA GARIBALDI, scheda in *Piero e Urbino...* (1992), 316-317

MARIA GIANNATIEMPO LOPEZ, scheda in *Piero e Urbino...* (1992), 124-125

A. GADOLI, in *Il disegno fiorentino...* (1992), 236

HUBERTUS GÜNTHER, "Die Anfänge der modernen Dorica", in *L'emploi des ordres...* (1992), 97-117

DAVID HEMSOLL, "Review of Pirro Ligorio: Artist and Antiquarian, edited by Robert W. Gaston, Milan 1988", *Burlington Magazine* CXXXIV, 123-124

CHARLES HOPE, "The Early History of the Tempio Malatestiano", *Journal of the Warburg and Courtauld Institutes* LV, 51-154

DEBORAH HOWARD, "Bramante's Tempietto. Spanish Royal Patronage in Rome", *Apollo* CXXXVI, 211-217

Jacques Callot 1592-1632, catalogue exposition (Nancy, Musée historique Lorrain), Nancy

G. IANZITI, "Humanism's New Science: The History of the Future", *I Tatti Studies* IV, 59-88

PAUL JOANNIDES, "'Primitivism' in the Late Drawings of Michelangelo: the Master's Construction of an Old-age Style", in *Michelangelo Drawings* (1992), 245-261

CHRISTOPH JOBST, *Die Planungen Antonios da Sangallo des Jüngeren für die Kirche S. Maria di Loreto in Rom*, Worms

I. KLOTEN, "La fortuna di San Petronio: il patrono della città e la politica delle immagini", in *Il luogo ed il ruolo della città di Bologna tra Europa continentale e mediterranea*, Atti del colloquio (1990), Bologna, 87-110

DANIELA LAMBERINI, "Tradizione tecnica e "plagio" nei disegni della 'machinatio' vitruviana di matrice fiorentina", in *Documentary Culture. Florence and Rome from Grand-Duke Ferdinand I to Pope Alexander VII*, Papers from a Colloquium held at Villa Spelman, Florence 1990, edited by Elizabeth Cropper, Giovanna Perini and Francesco Solinas, Bologna, 141-163

DORA LISCIA BEMPORAD, "Orafo fiorentino (? ante 1460)", in *Piero e Urbino...* (1992), 122-124

LICISCO MAGAGNATO, *Il Teatro Olimpico*, a cura di L. Puppi e con un contributo di M.E. Avagnina, T. Carunchio e S. Mazzoni, Milano

F.F. MANCINI, *Benedetto Bonfigli*, Perugia

ANTONIO MANETTI, *Vita di Filippo Brunelleschi*, a cura di C. Perrone, Roma

PIETRO C. MARANI [a], "Leonardo a Venezia e nel Veneto", in *Leonardo & Venezia* (1992), 23-36

—— [b], "Michelangelo's Sculpture as Monumental Architecture", in *The Genius of the Sculptor...* (1992), 447-467

PIETRO C. MARANI, J. SHELL, "Un dipinto di Marco d'Oggiono a Brera e alcune ipotesi sulla sua attività come cartografo", *Raccolta vinciana*, XXIV, 61-86

J. MARTINEAU et al. eds., *Andrea Mantegna*, exhibition catalog, London-New York

PIETRO MATRACCHI, *La chiesa di Santa Maria delle Grazie al Calcinaio presso Cortona e l'opera di Francesco di Giorgio*, Cortona

GABRIELE MOROLLI [a], "Nel cuore del Palazzo, la città ideale. Alberti e la prospettiva architettonica di Urbino", in *Piero e Urbino...* (1992), 215-230

—— [b], "L'elocutio dei capitelli", in *L'architettura di Lorenzo il Magnifico* (1992), 272-277

—— [c], "La fortuna di Vitruvio", in *L'architettura di Lorenzo il Magnifico* (1992), 191-194

ANDREW MORROGH, "The Magnifici Tomb: A Key Project in Michelangelo's Architectural Career", *Art Bulletin* LXXIV, 567-598

LAURIE NUSSDORFER, *Civic Politics in the Rome of Urban VIII*, Princeton

PIER NICOLA PAGLIARA, "Una 'non imitanda licentia' di Bramante nel dorico del coro di S.Pietro", *Architektur und Kunst in Abendland. Festschirft zur Vollendung des 65. Lebensjhres von Günter Urban*, Roma, 83-89

LINDA PELLECCHIA, "Architects Read Vitruvius: Renaissance Interpretations of the Atrium of the Ancient House", *Journal of the Society of Architectural Historians* LI, 377-416

NICHOLAS PENNY, *Catalogue of European Sculpture in the Ashmolean Museum 1540 to the Present Day*, 3 vols., Oxford

ANNAMARIA PETRIOLI TOFANI [a], *Il disegno fiorentino del tempo di Lorenzo il Magnifico*, Milano

—— [b], "L'illustrazione teatrale e il significato dei documenti figurativi per la storia dello spettacolo", in *Documentary Culture in Florence and Rome from Grand-Duke Ferdinando I to Pope Alexander VII*, Atti del convegno di Firenze (Villa Spelman), Bologna

G. POCHAT, "Peruzzi's Bacchides. Reconstruction of a Stage Performance in Rome 1531", in *Docto Peregrino. Roman Studies in Honour of Torgil Magnuson*, Uddevalla

LISA PORN and WILLIAM WALLACE, catalogue entry for Pietro C. Marani, "Michelangelo's Sculpture as Monumental Architecture", in *The Genius of the Sculptor...* (1992), 476-477

Raphaël: Autour de dessins du Louvre, catalogue exposition par Dominique Cordellier et Bernadette Py, Paris-Rome

ANGELA RENSI, "Elementi lapidei del periodo laurenziano. Tipologie e loro diffusione II, in *L'architettura di Lorenzo il Magnifico* (1991), 143-148

LUCIA RICCIARDI, *Col senno, col tesoro e colla lancia. Riti e giuochi cavallereschi nella Firenze di Lorenzo il Magnifico*, Firenze

GUSTINA SCAGLIA, *Francesco di Giorgio. Checklist and History of Manuscripts and Drawings in Autographs and Copies from ca. 1470 to 1687 and Renewed Copies (1764-1839)*, London-Toronto

MAURIZIO SERACENI [a], "Jacopo de' Barbari. Ritratto di Fra Luca Pacioli e del Duca Guidobaldo da Montefeltro. Lettura radiografica e tecnica di esecuzione", in *Piero e Urbino...* (1992), 466-468

—— [b], "Luciano Laurana (attr.)", in *Piero e Urbino...* (1992), 469-473

PAOLO SPEZZANI, "La riflettolscopia in infrarosso e i disegni di Leonardo alle Gallerie dell'Accademia, " in *Leonardo & Venezia* (1992), 179-187

MANFREDO TAFURI, *Ricerca del Rinascimento: principi, città, architetti*, Torino

FRANÇOISE TALLON, "Art and the Ruler: Gudea of Lagash", *Asian Art* V, 41-43

GIUSI TESTA [a], "Maestro Ioanni Pictori", *De Fabrica...* (1992), 12-13

—— [b], "Il profeta Geremia", *De Fabrica...* (1992), 9-11

CLAUDIO TINUNIN AND MICHELE BENVENUTI, "Restoration of the Wood Model for Michelangelo Buonarroti's Façade of San Lorenzo in Florence", in *Michelangelo Drawings* (1992), 263-267

CHRISTOF THOENES, "Alt- und Neu- St.-Peter unter einem Dach", in *Architektur und Kunst im Abendland. Festschrift für Günter Urban*, Rom, 51-61

G. TOSCANO, "IL 'BEL SITO DI NAPOLI': FONTI LETTERARIE E ICONOGRAFICHE DAL REGNO ARAGONESE AL VICEREGNO SPAGNOLO", IN B. DI FALCO, *Descrittione dei luoghi antichi di Napoli e del suo amenissimo distretto*, a cura di T.R. Toscano, Napoli

MADDALENA TRIONFI HONORATI, "La prospettiva nelle porte del palazzo", in *Piero e Urbino...* (1992), 232-239

J. VICIOSO, "La basilica di San Giovanni dei Fiorentini a Roma: individuazione delle vicende progettuali", *Bollettino d'arte*, 73-114

WILLIAM E. WALLACE [a], "Drawings from the 'Fabbrica' of San Lorenzo during the Tenure of Michelangelo", in *Michelangelo Drawings* (1992), 117-141

—— [b], "How Did Michelangelo Became a Sculptor", in *The Genius of the Sculptor* (1992), 151-167

J.B. WARD-PERKINS, *Marble in Antiquity. Collected Papers of J.B. Ward-Perkins*, edited by H. Dodge and B. Ward-Perkins, London

R. ZEITLER, "Wer Waren die Bauherren der Zentralkirchen der Renaissance?", in *Docto Peregrino. Roman Studies in Honour of T. Magnuson*, Roma, 261 ss.

ZYGMUNT WAZBINSKI, "Il cardinale Francesco Maria del Monte e la fortuna del progetto buonarrotiano per la basilica di San Pietro a Roma: 1604-1613", in *An Architectural Progress in the Renaissance and Baroque. Sojourns In and Out of Italy. Essays in Architectural History Presented to Hellmut Hager on his Sixty-sixth Birthday*, Henry A. Millon and Susan Scott Munshower, eds., University Park, Penn, 146-169

RAFFAELLA MARIA ZACCARIA, in *Consorterie politiche e mutamenti istituzionali in età laurenziana*, catalogo mostra (Firenze, Archivio di Stato), Milano, 58-61

1992-93

FERRUCCIO CANALI, "Tracce albertiane nella Romagna umanistica tra Rimini e Faenza", *Quasar. Quaderni di storia dell'architettura e restauro* VIII/IX, 61-77

1993

Francesco di Giorgio architetto, catalogo mostra (Siena, Palazzo Pubblico, 25 aprile - 31 luglio 1993), a cura di Francesco Paolo Fiore e Manfredo Tafuri, Milano

Francesco di Giorgio e il Rinascimento a Siena, catalogo mostra (Siena, Chiesa di Sant'Angostino, 25 aprile - 31 luglio), a cura di Luciano Bellosi, Milano

Hülle und Fülle. Festschrift für Tilmann Buddensieg, Alfter

NICHOLAS ADAMS [a], "L'architettura militare di Francesco di Giorgio", in *Francesco di Giorgio architetto* (1993), 126-162

—— [b], "Castel Nuovo a Napoli", in *Francesco di Giorgio architetto* (1993), 288-295

ENZO BENTIVOGLIO, scheda Uffizi 1130A r e v di Antonio da Sangallo il Giovane, in *The Drawings of Sangallo Circle. I: Churches*, edited by Christoph L. Frommel, New York

AMEDEO BELLUZZI, *Giuliano da Sangallo e la chiesa della Madonna a Pistoia*, Firenze

RITA BINAGHI, "Le macchine del porto", in *Sopra i porti di mare. I: Il trattato di Teofilo Gallacini e la concezione architettonica dei porti dal Rinascimento alla Restaurazione*, a cura di Giorgio Simoncini, Firenze, 127-173

HOWARD BURNS [a], "I disegni di Francesco di Giorgio agli Uffizi di Firenze", in *Francesco di Giorgio architetto* (1993), 330-357

—— [b], "S. Bernardino a Urbino", in *Francesco di Giorgio architetto* (1993), 230-243

ALESSANDRO CECCHI [a], "L'estremo omaggio al 'Padre e Maestro di tutte le arti'. Il monumento funebre di Michelangelo", in *Il Pantheon di Santa Croce a Firenze*, Firenze, 57-82

—— [b], "Un ritratto immaginario e celebrativo di Giovanni di Paolo Rucellai. Indagini e ipotesi", *I Tatti Studies* V

M. CERIANA, E. DRAFFA, "Il polittico di Valle Romita, la sua storia nel museo", in *Gentile da Fabriano, il polittico di Valle Romita*, Milano, 25-30

G. DEWEZ, *Villa Madama. A Memoir Relating to Raphael's Project*, London

AMELIO FARA, *La città da guerra nell'Europa moderna*, Torino

SHARON FERMOR, *Piero di Cosimo. Fiction, Invention and Fantasia*, London

FRANCESCO PAOLO FIORE, MANFREDO TAFURI (a cura di) [a], vedi *Francesco di Giorgio architetto* (1993)

—— [b], "Il monastero e la chiesa di Santa Chiara a Urbino", in *Francesco di Giorgio architetto* (1993), 260-273

PHILIPPE FLEURY, *La mécanique de Vitruve*, Caen

CHRISTOPH L. FROMMEL, "Introduction. The Drawings in of Antonio da Sangallo the Younger : History, Evolution, Method, Function ", in C.L. Frommel and Nicholas Adams, *The Architectural Drawings of Antonio da Sangallo the Younger and his Circle*, New York, I, 7ff. (II vol. in press)

FRANCESCA FUMI CAMBI GADO, scheda 72, in *Francesco di Giorgio e il Rinascimento a Siena* (1993), 360-361

MICHELE FURNARI, *Atlante del Rinascimento. Il disegno dell'architettura da Brunelleschi a Palladio*, Napoli

G. GELARDI, "Schemi di vari ordini di colonne... in S. Lorenzo con la scansione proporzionale sia in Moduli che in braccia fiorentine", in *San Lorenzo 393-1993. L'architettura*, catalogo mostra, Firenze

ERIC GORDON, "Technical Notes on the Walters' Ideal City", *Walters Art Gallery Journal*, LII

MARIO GORI SASSOLI, "Santa Maria delle Grazie al Calcinaio", in *Francesco di Giorgio architetto* (1993), 244 sg.

HUBERTUS GÜNTHER, "Insana aedificia thermarum nomine extructa. Die Diokletiansthermen in der Sicht der Renaissance", in *Hülle und Fülle...* (1993), 251-284

H. HUBERT, "Bramante, Peruzzi, Serlio und die Peterskuppel", *Zeitschrift für Kunstgeschichte* LV, 353-371

A. VON HÜLSEN, *Romanische Skulptur in Oberitalien als Reflex der kommunalen Entwicklung im 12. Jahrhundert*, Berlin

ANTONIO LABACCO, *Libro di Antonio Labacco appartenente all'architettura* (Roma 1552), a cura di Arnaldo Bruschi, Milano, riproduzione in fac simile

M. LUCÀ DAZIO, "L'immagine della città nel Quattrocento", tesi di laurea, Università di Napoli Federico II, Facoltà di Architettura

D. MARSHALL, *Viviano Codazzi*, Milano

MASSIMO MUSSINI, "La trattatistica di Francesco di Giorgio: un problema critico aperto", in *Francesco di Giorgio architetto* (1991), 358-379

G. PAVAN (a cura di), *Palmanova fortezza d'Europa 1593-1993*, Venezia

LINDA PELLECCHIA, "Reconstructing the Greek House: Giuliano da Sangallo's Villa for the Medici in Florence", *Journal of the Society of Architectural Historians* LII (September), 323-338

G. POCHAT, *Geschichte der Ästhetik und Kunsttheorie von der Antike bis zum 19. Jahrhundert*, Köln

A. ROSENAUER, *Donatello, l'opera completa*, Milano

R. RUOTOLO, "L'arte del legno", in "Aspetti e problemi del Medioevo e dell'età moderna", *Storia del Mezzogiorno*, XI, Napoli, 608 e sg

HOWARD SAALMAN, *Filippo Brunelleschi. The Buildings*, London

M. SANFILIPPO, *Le tre città di Roma: lo sviluppo dalle origini a oggi*, Bari

PIERLUIGI SILVAN in *Tesori Vaticani*, Milano, 161

D. STROFFOLINO, "Le vedute urbane nelle raccolte lafreryane", tesi di laurea, Università di Napoli Federico II, Facoltà di Architettura

MANFREDO TAFURI [a], "La chiesa di S.Sebastiano in Vallepiatta a Siena", in *Francesco di Giorgio architetto* (1989), 302-317

—— [b], "Le chiese di Francesco di Giorgio Martini", in *Francesco di Giorgio architetto* (1993), 21-73

—— [c], "Il duomo di Urbino", in *Francesco di Giorgio architetto* (1993), 186-207

CHRISTOF THOENES, "Vitruv, Alberti, Sangallo. Zur theorie der Architekturzeichnung in der Renaissance", in *Hülle und Fülle...* (1993), 565-584

ANDREAS TÖNNESMANN, "Zwischen Bürgerhaus und Residenz. Zur sozialen Typik des Palazzo Medici", in *Piero de' Medici "Il Gottoso" (1416-1469)*, besorgt von A. Beyer und B. Boucher, Berlin, 71-88

1994 / in corso di pubblicazione-stampa/im druck

L'eglise dans l'architecture de la Renaissance, XVIIIe colloque d'histoire de l'architecture (Centre d'études superieurs de la Renaissance - Tours 1990)

P. DAVIES, "La Madonna di Campagna del Sanmicheli", dans *L'église dans l'architecture de la Renaissance...* (1994)

M. DEL TREPPO, "Le avventure storiografiche della Tavola Strozzi", in *Scritti in onore di Pasquale Villani*, Bologna

CAROLINE ELAM, "Lorenzo's Architectural and Urban Policies", in Proceedings of the Conference on Lorenzo de' Medici (Florence, I Tatti, June 1992)

DAVID FRIEDMAN, "Palaces and the Street in Late-Medieval and Renaissance Italy", in J.W.R. Whitehead and P.J. Larkham, eds., *Urban Ladscapes: International Perspectives*, London

CHRISTOPH L. FROMMEL [a], "Bramante e la progettazione del Cortile del Belvedere", in *Il cortile delle statue nel Belvedere*, Atti del convegno (Roma, 1992)

—— [b], "Poggio Reale: problemi di ricostruzione e di tipologia", in *Giuliano da Maiano*, Atti del convegno (Fiesole 1992)

—— [c], "Roma e l'opera giovanile del Sanmicheli. Atti del seminario internazionale di storia dell'architettura Michele Sanmicheli", (Vicenza 1992), in *Annali di Architettura*

—— [d], "Fortifications, Machines and Festival architecture", in C.L. Frommel and Nicholas Adams, *The Architectural Drawings of Antonio da Sangallo the Younger and his Circle*, New York, II vol. in press

CHRISTOPH L. FROMMEL and *Nicholas Adams, Corpus Drawings Sangallo*

HUBERTUS GÜNTHER, "Vom Palast des Maecenas zum Palazzo Farnese. Vorstellungen vom antiken Haus in der Renaissance", in *Akten del II. Jahrestagung der International Society for the Classical Tradition* (Tübingen 1992)

DOUGLAS LEWIS, *The Currency of Fame. Portrait Medals of the Renaissance*, New York

LINDA PELLECCHIA, "Designing the Via Laura Palace: Giuliano da Sangallo, the Medici, and Time", in Proceedings of the Conference on Lorenzo de' Medici (London, Warburg Institute, May 1992)

LAURA TEZA, *Cento opere restaurate. Dipinti, sculture, ceramiche della Galleria Nazionale dell'Umbria*, catalogo mostra a cura di C. Bon Valsassina e V. Garibaldi, Perugia

CHRISTOF THOENES, "Pianta centrale e pianta longitudinale nel nuovo San Pietro", dans *L'église dans l'architecture de la Renaissance...* (1994)

Index of Names

723

724

725

Philadelphia

Philadelphia Museum of Art:
- Andrea di Giusto, or Francesco d'Antonio (attrib.)
  Christ Healing a Possessed Boy, and Judas Recovering the Blood Money, Johnson Collection, JC 17
  Cat. no. 51

Pisa

Museo Nazionale Civico di S. Matteo:
- Giovanni De' Medici with Alessandro Pieroni
  Model for the Facade of S. Stefano dei Cavalieri, Pisa, 4602
  Cat. no. 62

Reggio Emilia

Musei Civici:
- Bernardino Brugnoli
  Project for the Facade of the Cathedral, Reggio Emilia, Disegni 159d
  Cat. no. 59
- P. Clementi
  Model of Reggio Emilia
  Cat. no. 422
- Prospero Sogari (called Il Clemente)
  Model for the Facade of the Cathedral, Reggio Emilia, Arti Industriali 196
  Cat. no. 60

Rome

Biblioteca Corsiniana:
- Giovanni Battista da Sangallo (called Il Gobbo)
  Tragic Scene, Comic Scene and Satyric Scene (sketches in the margin of *De Architectura*, by Vitruvius), Inc. 50, F.I. (p. 11)
  Cat. no. 168

Biblioteca Nazionale:
- Andrea Guarna da Salerno
  Simia, 1517
  Cat. no. 302
- Public Notaries and Copysts of the Camera Apostolica
  Liber Mandatorum, Archivio Capitolare di S. Pietro, arm. 44, manoscritti vari, vol. 61
  Cat. no. 294

Congregazione dell'Oratorio di
S. Filippo Neri, S. Maria Vallicella:
- Giovanni Antonio Dosio (attrib.)
  Project Elevation for the Chiesa Nuova (S. Maria Vallicella), Rome, C. II. 8, 36
  Cat. no. 66
- Fausto Rughesi
  Model for the Facade of the Chiesa Nuova (S. Maria Vallicella), Rome
  Cat. no. 64

Istituto Nazionale per la Grafica:
- Philippe Caylus
  View from the Loggia into the Garden at the Villa Madama (after Heemskerck), FC 122637
  Cat. no. 215
- Vincenzo Luchino
  Elevation of the South Apse of St. Peter's
  Cat. no. 373

Osservatorio Astronomico:
- Unknown Master G151
  Graphometer, 136
  Cat. no. 23

Sarasota

John and Mable Ringling Museum
of Art:
- Piero di Cosimo
  The Building of a Double Palace
  Cat. no. 86

Siena

Archivio di Stato:
- Anonymous
  Plan Project for the Town of Talamone, Capitoli, 3, fols. 25v.-26r.
  Cat. no. 7

Biblioteca Comunale:
- Oreste Vannocci Biringucci
  S. Giovanni dei Fiorentini (after the project by Michelangelo)
  cod. S IV 1, fol. 42r.
  Cat. no. 10

Collezione Monte dei Paschi:
- Giovanni di Agostino (?)
  Project for the Facade of Palazzo Sansedoni, Siena
  Cat. no. 4

Museo dell'Opera del Duomo:
- Anonymous
  Project for the Facade of the Baptistery, Siena, 20
  Cat. no. 2
- Anonymous
  Elevation of the Cappella di Piazza, Siena, 16
  Cat. no. 3
- Unknown Senese
  Project for a Campanile, 154
  Cat. no. 1

Pinacoteca Nazionale:
- Sassetta
  Sea Port, 70
  Cat. no. 5

Stockholm

Nationalmuseum:
- Anonymous
  Left Side of Perspectival Stage Set, CC 392
  Cat. no. 175
- Anonymous
  Elevation of the West Half of the South of St. Peter's, Cronstedt Collection, CC 2150
  Cat. no. 375
- Maerten van Heemskerck
  View from the North of the Old Transept and the Dome Area, Collection Anckarvrd, no. 637
  Cat. no. 345
- Unknown Draftsman Related to the Circle of Etienne Duprac
  Section and Elevation of the Model and of the Drum of St. Peter's, Cronstedt Collection, CC 1353
  Cat. no. 387
- Unknown Draftsman Related to the Circle of Etienne Duprac
  Elevation of Two and One-Half Bays of the Interior of the Drum of St. Peter's, Cronstedt Collection, CC 1375
  Cat. no. 389
- Unknown Draftsman Related to the Circle of Etienne Duprac
  Elevation of Two and One-Half Bays of the Exterior of the Drum of St. Peter's, Cronstedt Collection, CC 1305
  Cat. no. 391
- Workshop of Antonio da Sangallo (Antonio Labacco?)
  Section of the Dome of St. Peter's, Cronstedt Collection, CC vol. 13, no. 1398
  Cat. no. 367

Todi

Museo Comunale:
- Ventura Vitoni (?)
  Model for S. Maria della Consolazione, Todi
  Cat. no. 142

Turin

Archivio di Stato, Architettura Militare:
- Anonymous (17th century)
  Map of Palmanova, vol. V, c.4 3r.
  Cat. no. 187

Biblioteca Reale:
- Francesco di Giorgio Martini (and/or? Guidoccio Cozzarelli)
  The Basilica of Constantine, Rome, Codex Saluzziano 148, fol. 76r.
  Cat. no. 13
- Lorenzo Lotto
  Procession with City Model of Padua on a Pole 1535-38, 15909
  Cat. no. 416
- Baldassarre Peruzzi
  Incomplete Study of Perspective Scenery, 15728
  Cat. no. 164

Urbino

Galleria Nazionale delle Marche:
- Central Italian Artist
  The Ideal City
  Cat. no. 178

Vaduz

- Hermannus Posthumus
  Fantastic Landscape with Ruins
  Cat. no. 11

Vatican

Biblioteca Apostolica Vaticana, Medagliere:
- Federico Bonsagni
  Medal with a View of the Porta Pia
  Cat. no. 83

Biblioteca Apostolica Vaticana:
- Martino Ferrabosco
  Section through the South Transept of St. Peter's looking east (Martino Ferrabosco, Libro de l'architettura di San Pietro nel Vaticano..., Rome, 1620, pls. XXIII and XXIV)
  Cat. no. 383
- Lorenzo Fragni
  East Elevation of St. Peter's, the Fragni Medal (reverse), XXVIII, 1173
  Cat. no. 399
- Francesco di Giorgio Martini
  Various Types of Windlass for Building Sites (from *Taccuino di disegni e annotazioni*, called the *Codicetto*), Cod. Urb. Lat. 1757, fols. 91v.-92r.
  Cat. no. 93
- Francesco di Giorgio Martini
  Device for Raising Columns, Mill and Self propelled Vehicle (from *Taccuino di disegni e annotazioni, called the* Codicetto), Cod. Urb. Lat. 1757, fols. 119v.-120r.
  Cat. no. 94
- Francesco di Giorgio Martini
  Hydraulic Saw, Device for Raising Columns, Drils and Various Types of Windlasses for Building Sites (from Taccuino di disegni e annotazioni, called *the Codicetto*), Cod. Urb. Lat. 1757, fols. 165v.-166r.
  Cat. no. 95
- Francesco di Giorgio Martini
  Hoisting Machine and Building Crane, Divaricators and Obelisk Transporter (from Taccuino di disegni e annotazioni, called the Codicetto), Cod. Urb. Lat. 1757, fols. 166v.-167r.
  Cat. no. 96
- Ptolemy
  Geography, Codex Vat. Urb. Lat. 5699
  Cat. no. 43
- Jan van Scorel (?)
  Views of St. Peter's (recto), Views of the Palatine (verso), Ashby, no. 329
  Cat. no. 323

Translators

Andrew Ellis
Carol Rathman
David Stanton
Vanessa Vesey

Photo Credits

Archivio Alinari, Florence: 152, 325 (bottom), 333 (Anderson), 340, 342—343, 207 (Brogi), 223 (Brogi), 591

Archivio, R.C.S. Libri & Gandi Opere: Piero Baguzzi: 19, 22 (left), 23, 24 (right), 25, 26-27, 28, 29, 30, 31, 35 (left), 41 (left), 48, 49, 51, 52, 53, 54, 55, 56, 57, 58-59, 60, 61, 62, 63, 64-65, 66, 67, 68-69, 70, 71, 72, 73, 96, 103, 109, 113, 115, 116, 117, 121, 148, 166 (top), 170-171, 193, 213, 248, 292-293, 326 (left), 352, 354, 355, 356-357, 380, 381; Alberto Bertoldi: 83 (right), 137, 153; Alberto Bevilacqua: 255, 272; Roberto Esposito: 264; Alfredo Loprieno: 180; Mario Matteucci: 78; Sandro Pagani: 372; Romano Vada: 247, 338; Guido Loglio: 260, 295

Archivio Scala, Florence: 79, 83 (left), 84, 122, 124, 125, 126, 127, 130, 131, 133, 135, 136, 138, 139, 143, 144-145, 147, 149 (right), 154, 155, 167, 179, 204, 208-209, 210, 211, 214, 215, 221, 225, 231, 234-235, 236-237, 246, 250-251, 252-253, 254, 267, 281, 302, 303, 319, 320 (bottom), 322-323, 329, 330, 331, 332, 334-335, 336, 339, 341, 353, 362, 378-379 (top), 382, 392-393

Arte & Immagini, Florence: 150, 151

Banca Immagini ENEL - Photo Service by Pianeta Immagine: 383, 384-385, 387, 388

Bibliothèque Nationale de France, Paris: 80 (right), 81 *Cat. 74*

© Bildarchiv Preussischer Kulturbesitz, Berlin (Yörg P. 1984 Anders): 132, 242-243, 244-245, *Cat. 17, Cat. 73, Cat. 139*

Joshua Briggs Photographer, London: 40

Geremy Butler Photography, London: *Cat. 289, Cat. 310*

Guglielmo Chiodini, Pavia: 156, 159, 160-161, 227

Ursula Edelmann Fotografin, Frankfurt: 173

Fotocielo, Rome

F. Ghilardi, Lucca: 50, 249

Giovetti, Mantova: 344

Giraudon, Paris: 379 (bottom)

Riccardo Gonella, Turin: 229, 277

Fratelli Gualdani, Arezzo: *Cat. 180*

E. Guidotti: 128, 268, 270, 271, 294 (bottom)

Bodil Karlsson, Statens Konstmuseer, Stockkolm: *Cat. 345*

Fabio Lensini, Siena: 394, 395, 396, 397

Ralph Lieberman: 318, 320 (top), 321, 328, 337, 345

Stefan Müller, Dortmund: 296, 297, 307-317

Musei Vaticani, Vatican: 176-177, 258

Nogaro, Genoa: 347

Luciano Pedicini, Naples: 359, 364, 365, 366, 367, 369, 371

© Photo Réunion des Musées Nationaux, Paris: *Cat. 278*

Donato Pineider, Florence: 75, 142, 276 (top), 282 (left), *Cat. 90, 101, 102, 105, 106, 221, 290*

Vincenzo Pirozzi, Rome: 163

Franca Principe, Florence: 265

Pubbliaerfoto, Milan: 228

Antonio Quattrone, Florence: 34, 46, 47, *Cat. 76, 77, 78, 79, 80, 111, 112, 275, 291*

Giancarlo Roncaglia, Turin: 259, *Cat. 46b*

Royal Collection Enterprise, Windsor -© Her Majesty Queen Elisabeth II: *Cat. 129*

Sacco, Chiusi: 165

Saporetti, Milan: 100, 274, 275, *Cat. 82, 132b*

Antonio Solazzi, Rome: 35 (right), 36-37, 38-39, 41 (right), 42-43, 44, 45, 304

Toso, Venice: 99

Elke Wolfang, Fotowerkstatt, Hamburger Kunsthalle, Hamburg: 398

Zigrossi: 258

Fotocomposizione Grande - Monza (Milan)

Printed in Italy
March 1994

Printed on
Tenero Matt 135 g/m^2
Papierfabriken Cham - Tenero AG.